LITERARY THEORY
AN ANTHOLOGY

THIRD EDITION

Edited by Julie Rivkin and Michael Ryan

WILEY Blackwell

This third edition first published 2017
© 2017 John Wiley & Sons, Ltd

Edition history: Blackwell Publishing Ltd (1e, 1998); Blackwell Publishing Ltd (2e, 2004)

Registered Office
John Wiley & Sons, Ltd, The Atrium, Southern Gate, Chichester, West Sussex, PO19 8SQ, UK

Editorial Offices
350 Main Street, Malden, MA 02148-5020, USA
9600 Garsington Road, Oxford, OX4 2DQ, UK
The Atrium, Southern Gate, Chichester, West Sussex, PO19 8SQ, UK

For details of our global editorial offices, for customer services, and for information about how to apply for permission to reuse the copyright material in this book please see our website at www.wiley.com/wiley-blackwell.

The right of Julie Rivkin and Michael Ryan to be identified as the authors of the editorial material in this work has been asserted in accordance with the UK Copyright, Designs and Patents Act 1988.

Library of Congress Cataloging-in-Publication Data

Names: Rivkin, Julie, editor. | Ryan, Michael, 1951– editor.
Title: Literary theory : an anthology / edited by Julie Rivkin, Michael Ryan.
Description: Third edition. | Hoboken : John Wiley & Sons Ltd., 2017. |
    Includes bibliographical references, glossary, and index.
Identifiers: LCCN 2016014427| ISBN 9781118707852 (pbk.) | ISBN 9781118718384 (epub)
Subjects: LCSH: Literature–Philosophy. | Literature–History and criticism–Theory, etc.
Classification: LCC PN45 .L512 2017 | DDC 801–dc23
LC record available at https://lccn.loc.gov/2016014427

A catalogue record for this book is available from the British Library.

Cover image: Barbara Kruger: *Untitled (No Radio)*, photograph 51" × 68," 1988.
Collection Don/Doris Fisher, San Francisco, courtesy Mary Boone Gallery, New York.

Set in Ehrhardt 10.5/12.5pt by SPi Global, Pondicherry, India

Printed in Singapore by C.O.S. Printers Pte Ltd

Literary Theory

For Gabriel and Nathaniel

Contents

Part Three   Phenomenology, Reception, Ethics

Part Four   Post-Structuralism

Part Five   Psychoanalysis and Psychology

Part Nine   Cognition, Emotion, Evolution, Science

Part Ten   Animals, Humans, Places, Things

Preface

This book began, as one might guess, in the classroom. We have been teaching courses in contemporary literary theory for the past two decades, and we have each had the familiar experience of not being able to match the design of our courses to any anthology currently available. The move from awkwardly assembled xerox packets to an actual anthology has been both a natural outgrowth of our teaching and an astonishingly complex process of research, selection, and projection. For although the germ of the book was our own classroom(s), its destination has always been many classrooms, courses no doubt much different than any we ourselves might teach, and yet ones that our selections would ideally work both to accommodate and to enrich.

The scale of the volume is one expression of its projected flexibility; we felt that an anthology of literary theory needed not only to cover the range of theoretical perspectives or approaches that characterize the era "after the New Criticism," the era that we take to be that of contemporary literary theory, but also to represent those perspectives with reasonable depth and range. The effect of such a decision, we hope, is that many kinds of courses will find a home in these selections, that a course that takes as its focus Structuralism, Post-Structuralism, Post-Colonialism, or Psychoanalysis and Gender Studies will find this anthology as useful as one that makes a more extensive survey of theoretical perspectives.

The anthology opens with formalisms – both Russian and American – in a gesture that marks its organization as partly chronological and partly heuristic. That is, we take formalism – at least in its American avatar of New Criticism – to mark the condition of students' theoretical awareness before beginning the journey into "theory." To the degree that they have been taught a form of "close reading" as the basic task of literary analysis, they are practicing formalists, though the practice may be, like that of the prose-speaking M. Jourdain in Molière's *Bourgeois Gentilhomme*, an unself-conscious one. Exploring the theoretical premises of a New Critical practice, placing those in conjunction with a historically unrelated yet theoretically cognate predecessor, Russian Formalism, seems like an appropriate way to initiate an exposure to "theory" in its less familiar guises.

The parts themselves have undergone many evolutions; the issue of where to draw the lines, what denomination to use, and where to locate certain selections has been as theoretically complex as it has been practically consequential. While "Deconstruction," for example, enjoyed a separate life in literary critical history in the US in the 1970s and 1980s, we felt it more appropriate to place it within its historical and intellectual French context, and so you will find Derrida amongst Deleuze and Guattari, and Baudrillard under "Post-Structuralism." The question of how to categorize some kinds of theory, regarding gender, for example, was also difficult, and we opted for a big tent: A separate section could easily have been devoted to any number of theoretical projects, each of which has already produced its own "classic" texts, and while attending to these developments has been one goal of the anthology, we wished as well to embrace both the heterodox and the newly canonical. Some of the names in our table of contents may not be readily recognizable for this reason, and our inclusion of these texts is less a sign of presumption regarding future canonicity than it is an indicator of our desire to locate the anthology as much in the contemporary realm as possible. That has meant guessing, and we based our guesses on what we felt would be exciting or helpful in the classroom.

In a desire both to be as inclusive as possible and to represent works not commonly anthologized, we have done a certain amount of excerpting. Our principle has been to represent the core of a given work, and if, to that end, we have sacrificed portions of texts that readers will deem necessary, we can only suggest that our selections constitute a useful beginning to a more extensive acquaintance. We apologize in advance for any such textual editing deemed brutal.

A final word about our cover illustration. The words "No Radio" refer to a sign people put in their cars in New York City. It means "don't bother breaking into the body of this car; the radio has already been either stolen or else removed by the owner." We asked Wiley-Blackwell to use this image because it speaks to the reservations many still feel about "theory" and about its association with the ideology of mastery through critical analysis that murders to dissect. It also speaks, of course, to our hesitations as editors engaged in the compilation and dissemination of such theories. We would not summon the image (and we would not engage in the work) if we did not feel that "theory" is itself filled with doubt regarding the objectivist ideal the image so carefully mocks. Some theories do indeed fulfill the aspirations of the man with the heart in his hand, but we hope you will feel that there are many others in this book that adopt the perspective of the woman on the table.

A Short History of Theory

The first recorded human story, something that might be called "The Hunt," appears on the walls of the caves at Lascaux, France. It was made either by children or for children, judging from the hand and feet impressions on the floor of the cave, and it represents not just a hunt but also a remarkable shift in human cognition that occurred, according to archeologist Richard Klein, around 42 ka. From this point forward, humans become more "human" in our modern sense. They invent new tools, everything from plows to currency, that expand the reach of human culture. They evidence an ability to picture abstract mental concepts and to imagine a spirit world. They slowly switch from a hunting existence to an agricultural existence. They stop living in small kin-based bands and organize large settled communities. The early human tendency to commit rampant genocide against his cousins slowly diminishes, and humans live together in relative peace. The emergence of this new way of life can be accounted for by the change in human cognition that is expressed in "The Hunt." The mimetic ability one sees in the paintings for the first time was essential to emergent sociality. A capacity for mental representations is linked to control over rapid-fire, automatic negative emotions such as prejudice and fight-or-flight that aided survival on the savannah but were inimical to a settled social existence. That new mimetic cognitive ability was also crucial to imagining others' lives empathetically so that communities of kin and non-kin could be built. The capacity for story-telling is thus connected in an essential way to the cognitive abilities that aided the emergence of modern human life. We did not so much begin to tell each other stories because we started living together in large communities; rather, we were able to build such communities because we were able to tell each other stories.

Story-telling likely also played a more direct role in the emergence of modern human life. Stories allowed early humans to store and to transmit information that was crucial to the social learning upon which humans' new culturally mediated civil existence depended. Stories are memory banks that record lessons from the past and are easily transmissible. Some ethnologists believe a greater capacity for short-term memory was a key change in the human cognitive revolution around 42 ka. Early human stories were probably initially accounts of remembered events, simple documentaries. Those documentary accounts with time became fictional narratives as real characters were replaced by imaginary ones (some of whom would be taken from the surrounding nature, such as Crow or Turtle). Memory stories were also narratives that projected a future, the unknown part of the story yet to be told but anticipated in the mind. Such narrative graphing of life's actions in terms of past, present, and future meant humans could also plan ahead and foresee events more so than before. Their lives were no longer limited to the satisfying of physical needs in an immediate and short-term manner. "The Hunt" gave way to "The Trip to Whole Foods."

Story-telling would have aided the building of more complex social networks, the integration of diverse people into a uniform culture, the training of minds in a communally beneficial empathy, and the evolution of common norms. Early human stories often possessed a normative dimension. One purpose of telling them was to instruct the young in the life-sustaining norms and practices of the community. Our earliest recorded verbal stories – Homer's epics – teach norms of appropriate behavior towards others in one's community such as hospitality and respect. And the tragedies of the fifth-century Greek enlightenment caution against norm-breaking behavior.

Literary theory came into being at a time when the normative function of story-telling was felt quite strongly. One of the first theorists, Plato, argued that literature should educate the young in good behavior. He lived and taught in Athens 2600 years ago, and he founded the first institution of higher learning in the West, the Academy. That is important because one consequence of the evolution of human cognition is the creation of a need for nurturing environments or niches to sustain the new cognitive abilities. Those nurturing environments were possible in cities and took the form of institutions such as schools and practices such as writing. Psychologists now know that the mind's advanced cognitive abilities as well as the mind's ability to live in a civil, sociable way with others depend on training and modeling. External prompting is required to allow full cognitive powers to emerge and full emotional abilities to grow. That humans' ability to think in certain ways happened at the same time that nurturing institutions such as schools came into being should therefore be no surprise. The advance in human cognitive powers allowed humans to use external instruments such as writing and book-making to preserve past human cognitive achievements (as an external hard drive does today for a computer). Other tools and techniques could now also be used to train minds to replicate the achievements of the past so they would not be lost. Humans became capable of using what today we call cultural and social construction to maintain human civilization.

The new cognitive power of abstraction that began to emerge around 42 ka divided knowledge between sense impressions and the abstract ideas the new cognition made possible. Plato built his philosophy around this distinction. He felt the abstract ideas the mind could now imagine were more true than sense impressions. The world around one did not offer many examples of perfectly formed beautiful things, but in one's mind one could imagine an ideal beauty. Plato mistakenly thought these abstract concepts – Beauty, Truth, Justice – were actual things in the world, a kind of spirit realm of pure forms or ideas. We now know that he was simply describing the new cognitive ability of the human brain, its new capacity to picture non-sensory objects in the mind's eye. All around Plato in his world, that new cognitive ability was helping his human companions to build a new civilization using new cultural tools such as currency, laws, and rhetoric. He felt, correctly, that the new cultural forms such as the enactment of fictional human events would serve an important function in the building of that new civilization. Empathy, an ability to live together in peace by imagining others' lives and feeling them as similar to one's own, was crucial to the new human capacity for sociality and civility, and literature and theater fostered it by obliging audiences to imagine others' lives as if they were their own. Only a few hundred thousand years earlier, members of the *Homo* line had been hunting each other for food. Athens was clearly an improvement, but getting there required a new way of thinking whose normative function Plato correctly saw.

Plato: If the prospective guardians of our community are to loathe casual quarrels with one another, we must take good care that battles between gods and giants and all the other various tales of gods and heroes coming to blows with their relatives and friends don't occur in the stories they hear and the pictures they see. No, if we're somehow to convince them that fellow citizens never fall out with one another, that this is wrong, then that is the kind of story they must hear, from childhood onwards, from the community's elders of both sexes; and the poets they'll hear when they're older must be forced to tell equivalent stories in their poetry…. All things considered then, that is why a very great deal of importance should be placed upon ensuring that the first stories they hear are best adapted for their moral improvement.

If Plato's belief in rational ideas such as Justice, Beauty, and Truth that existed in a purely ideal or rational realm apart from sensory experience reflects the emergence of a brain capable of abstraction, of separating mental concepts from sensory data, the ability to construct mental representations also made possible more refined observation of sensory objects by separating the adaptively evolved mind from the world around it. Prior to this point, the human brain, in order to help preserve life, needed to be vigilant and keenly focused on sense impressions for signs of danger. Living in the emerging civil communities allowed the brain to evolve further and to adapt to social life by developing new communicative and emotional skills that required less immersion in or fusion with the sensory world around it. With the diminishment of danger and the growth of sociality came a greater separation of mind from world through the development of a capacity for mental representation that allowed the world to be perceived and studied more like an object. Civil existence and science became possible at the same time.

Plato's student Aristotle studied the structure of literature and its effects in this manner, treating literature as an object in the world that is as worthy of study as geology. He therefore described the structure of stories and noticed, for example, that the sequence of events in narrative is organized around moments of reversal and recognition. He differentiated between narrative perspectives and examined the traits that distinguish one genre like comedy from another like tragedy. He also analyzed the way literature provokes reactions in audiences. Tragedy inspires empathetic suffering with the fictional characters. His focus on empathy is especially important given how essential that emotion now was to the sustaining of human civilization. Without an ability to empathize with others grounded in the new power to imagine mental objects, humans would not have been able to form the newly complex societies that had come into being.

Aristotle: Tragedy is a representation of a serious, complete action which has magnitude, in embellished speech, with each of its elements used separately in the various parts of the play; represented by people acting and not by narration, accomplishing by means of pity and terror the catharsis of such emotions….

Clearly, each of the kinds of representation we mentioned will contain these differences and will vary by representing objects which vary in this manner…. Tragedy too is distinguished from comedy by precisely this difference: comedy prefers to represent people who are worse than those who exist, tragedy people who are better. Again, a third difference among these kinds is the manner in which one can represent each of these things. For one can use the same media to represent the very same things, sometimes by narrating (either by becoming another person as Homer does or remaining the same person and not changing or by representing everyone as in action and activity). Representation, then, has these three points of difference, as we said at the beginning, its media, its objects, and its manner.

The Greek example suggests how important the feedback loop from mind to culture to mind had become in human life. The new sociality and the new civility one sees in Greece during its Enlightenment were dependent on a nurturing environment, and schools played a prominent role in Athenian life. The early cognitive abilities of the Athenians were sustained by that cultural niche. It is no wonder, then, that the conquest of Greece by Rome 2100 ka interrupted the progress of human culture and of human cognition at least in the West. With the disappearance of the nurturing niche the Greeks had built, the cognition it sustained also declined. Authoritarianism, brutality, and pillage – versions of the primitive automatic instincts the mind's new capacity for mental representations helps regulate – became the norm in political and social life for six centuries. After the fall of Rome, the cultural ecosystem the Greeks evolved disappeared almost entirely. But the capacity for symbolic thought did not wane entirely. In the West, the Catholic Church preserved some of the cognitive abilities that emerged in Greece, especially the ability to think in abstract mental representations that stood apart from sensory experience or perception. Church thinkers became fascinated with allegory, the idea that religious texts especially contained hidden meanings. A biblical story about a man's treatment of his wife or children would be interpreted to have a second, other meaning having to do with religious doctrine.

Church thinkers also retained the Platonic idea of a culture that instilled norms of good behavior. Even without Aristotle's texts to serve as examples, some Church thinkers such as Augustine continued the analytic tradition and examined how logic and language worked. They developed a theory of language as signs that would prove important for future cultural analysts.

> **Augustine:**   There are two reasons why written texts fail to be understood: their meaning may be veiled either by unknown signs or by ambiguous signs. Signs are either literal or metaphorical. They are called literal when used to signify the things for which they were invented: as, for example, when we say *bovem* [ox], meaning the animal which we and all speakers of Latin call by that name. They are metaphorical when the actual things which we signify by the particular words are used to signify something else: when, for example, we say *bovem* and not only interpret the two syllables to mean the animal normally referred to by that name but also understand, by that animal, "worker in the gospel," which is what scripture, as interpreted by the apostle Paul, means when it says, "You shall not muzzle the ox that treads out the grain." ...
>
> As well as this rule, which warns us not to pursue a figurative (that is, metaphorical) expression as if it were literal, we must add a further one: not to accept a literal one as if it were figurative. Generally speaking, it is this: anything in the divine discourse that cannot be related either to good morals or to the true faith should be taken as figurative. Good morals have to do with our love of God and our neighbor, the true faith with our understanding of God and our neighbor. The hope that each person has within his own conscience is directly related to the progress that he feels himself to be making towards the love and understanding of God and his neighbor.

Around 700 ka humans began to relaunch the Greek project as they rediscovered lost Greek texts. With the return of a secular culture during the Renaissance, thinkers could once again study literature as a form of moral instruction and as a cultural object with many dimensions meriting analysis. Dante Alighieri was both a leading poet of the Renaissance and an astute theorist of literature who described the different kinds of meaning a literary text could possess. This emphasis on interpretation or hermeneutics derived from the allegorical study of religious texts, but it soon would acquire a secular use in literary analysis.

> **Dante Alighieri:** [W]ritings can be understood and ought to be expounded principally in four senses. The first is called the literal, and this is the sense that does not go beyond the surface of the letter, as in the fables of the poets. The next is called the allegorical, and this is the one that is hidden beneath the cloak of these fables, and is a truth hidden beneath a beautiful fiction. Thus Ovid says that with his lyre Orpheus tamed wild beasts and made trees and rocks move toward him, which is to say that the wise man with the instrument of his voice makes cruel hearts grow tender and humble and moves to his will those who do not devote their lives to knowledge and art; and those who have no rational life whatsoever are almost like stones. Why this kind of concealment was devised by the wise will be shown in the penultimate book. Indeed the theologians take this sense otherwise than do the poets; but since it is my intention here to follow the method of the poets, I shall take the allegorical sense according to the usage of the poets.
>
> The third sense is called moral, and this is the sense that teachers should intently seek to discover throughout the scriptures, for their own profit and that of their pupils; as, for example, in the Gospel we may discover that when Christ ascended the mountain to be transfigured, of the twelve Apostles he took with him but three, the moral meaning of which is that in matters of great secrecy we should have few companions.
>
> The fourth sense is called anagogical, that is to say, beyond the senses; and this occurs, when a scripture is expounded in a spiritual sense which, although it is true also in the literal sense, signifies by means of the things signified a part of the supernal things of eternal glory, as may be seen in the song of the Prophet which says that when the people of Israel went out of Egypt, Judea was made whole and free. For although it is manifestly true according to the letter, that which is spiritually intended is no less true, namely, that when the soul departs from sin it is made whole and free in its power. In this kind of explication, the literal should always come first, as being the sense in whose meaning the others are enclosed, and without which it would be impossible and illogical to attend to the other senses, and especially the allegorical.

With a vibrant secular educational system, Italy in the Renaissance was an ideal niche environment for the development of human cognitive skills and for the reemergence of several branches of speculative thought, from literary theory to political theory. Renaissance discussions of literature down through the eighteenth century were dominated by Greek ideas, however, since the educational system favored those texts in the education of young women and men. Religious authorities did not smile on the Humanist argument that the reading of literature constituted a form of moral instruction. Writers such as Philip Sydney responded by arguing that literature portrays a second more ideal nature to the existing one and therefore suggests how things should be. It teaches by imaginative example.

Another debate regarding aesthetics during this period concerned what was called Classicism – the idea that art should follow the rules set down by Plato and Aristotle. Aristotle's notion of mimesis – that art imitates life – became the injunction that art must imitate life or "Nature." The writer should follow Nature and write as simply as possible, without self-aggrandizing artifice.

One of the most innovative thinkers of the Humanist era was Giambattista Vico. His *New Science* foreshadows twentieth-century linguistic philosophy in its recognition of the essentially metaphoric character of all language.

In the eighteenth century, a new way of thinking emerged, and that often is called rationalism because it emphasized the conceptualizing operations of the mind (or "Reason").

Rational ideas are transcendental (they stand outside the ordinary world of everyday perceptions) and universal (they concern what is general to all tulips rather than just to the specific one before our eyes). Theorists of literature such as Samuel Johnson therefore began to argue that literature is important not for how it portrays individual events or characters but rather for how it "rises to general and transcendent truths, which will always be the same."

Germany's educational system became quite sophisticated during this period, and a group of German thinkers were especially important in advancing rationalist literary theory: Gotthold Lessing, Immanuel Kant, and Georg Hegel. Writing at a time when the ideal of the classical examples of Greek and Roman art still was influential, Lessing focused on the essential characteristics of poetry and painting. Many assumed poetry should resemble painting, but Lessing differed. He noticed that poetry is consecutive in execution and emphasizes time, while painting favors simultaneity and is more a work based in space.

> **Gotthold Lessing:**   I reason thus: if it is true that in its imitations painting uses completely different means or signs than does poetry, namely figures and colors in space rather than articulated sounds in time, and if these signs must indisputably bear a suitable relation to the thing signified, then signs existing in space can express only objects whose wholes or parts coexist, while signs that follow one another can express only objects whose wholes or parts are consecutive.
>
> Objects or part of objects which exist in space are called bodies. Accordingly, bodies with their visible properties are the true subjects of painting.
>
> Objects or parts of objects which follow one another are called actions. Accordingly, actions are the true subjects of poetry....
>
> But the objection will be raised that the symbols of poetry are not only successive but are also arbitrary; and, as arbitrary symbols, they are of course able to represent bodies as they exist in space. Examples of this might be taken from Homer himself. We need only to recall his shield of Achilles to have the most decisive instance of how discursively and yet at the same time poetically a single object may be described by presenting its coexistent parts....
>
> [But] Homer does not paint the shield as finished and complete, but as a shield that is being made. Thus, here too he has made use of that admirable artistic device: transforming what is coexistent in his subject into what is consecutive, and thereby making the living picture of an action out of the tedious painting of an object. We do not see the shield, but the divine master as he is making it. He steps up to the anvil with hammer and tongs, and after he has forged the plates out of the rough, the pictures which he destines for the shield's ornamentation rise before our eyes out of the bronze, one after the other beneath the finer blows of his hammer.

Kant distinguished between higher and lower mental faculties. The higher are capable of abstraction, of thinking in pure ideas. The lower were more practical and sensory, tied to specific judgments or perceptions. The best human behavior accorded with a universal idea of higher reason. The concepts of reason must, for Kant, be disinterested and law-like. To regulate human affairs impartially, they must serve no particular end or interest, such as the enrichment of an individual or the pursuit of sensory pleasure alone. Art, because it works on the senses rather than pure reason, is not capable of attaining such a high standard of disinterestedness. The most it can offer is "purposiveness without purpose," a semblance of universality. Kant also noticed something one might have expected to be the case, given how the human brain evolved, and that is an overlap of faculties, especially of the faculty for appreciating beauty and the moral faculty for knowing what is good. To judge something beautiful is to claim it resembles a moral that should be valid for all.

> **Immanuel Kant:** Now I say that the beautiful is the symbol of the morally good, and also only in this respect (that of a relation that is natural to everyone, and that is also expected of everyone else as a duty) does it please with a claim to the assent of everyone else, in which the mind is at the time aware of a certain ennoblement and elevation above the mere receptivity for a pleasure from sensible impressions, and also esteems the value of others in accordance with a similar maxim of their power of judgment.... 1) The beautiful pleases immediately (but only in reflecting intuition, not, like morality, in the concept). 2) It pleases without any interest ... 3) The freedom of the imagination (thus of the sensibility of our faculty) is represented in the judging of the beautiful as in accord with the lawfulness of the understanding (in the moral judgment the freedom of the will is conceived as the agreement of the latter with itself in accordance with universal laws of reason). 4) The subjective principle for judging of the beautiful is represented as universal, i.e. valid for everyone.

Georg Hegel believed the mental and the physical or natural worlds were one. The logical processes of the mind, which he called "dialectic" after the logic of the Greeks, could be found at work in human history and human society as well as in nature. The natural and social world followed the same course of development as the mental world of logic. In a logical dialectical process, one moves from simple concrete observation ("Socrates is a man") to universal idea ("All men are mortal") to a conclusion that unifies concrete instance and universal idea in a single synthetic proposition ("Therefore, Socrates is mortal"). In human history, the idea of a just society is at first only partly fulfilled; it takes the form of simple rules without any coherent idea of justice informing them. Justice at this stage of human history resembles a simple concrete proposition in the dialectic. But as history progresses, the universal idea is integrated increasingly into juridical institutions until, after a long process of combined sociohistorical and logical development, the universal idea of justice and the concrete institutions that embody it are merged completely in an ideal government of law that is informed by universal principles that apply equally to all. In such a government or state, the practical concrete institutions are saturated with the ideas of reason or mind.

Something similar happens in art. Early art consists of simple sensory images without universal meaning. They are merely mimetic pictures of actual objects. They have no idea in them. But over time, as art evolves, following a logical process of development, art achieves a complex totality in which universally valid idea and sensory object, mind and concrete worldly form are merged and are one.

> **G. W. F. Hegel:** Because the universal idea is in this way a concrete unity, this unity can enter art-consciousness only through the unfolding and the reunification of the particularizations of the universal idea, and, through this process, artistic beauty acquires a totality of particular stages and forms. Therefore, after studying artistic beauty in itself and as itself, we must see how beauty as a totality decomposes into its specific forms. This is the second part of our study, the doctrine of the forms of art. These forms find their origin in the different ways of grasping the universal idea as content.... Thus the forms of art are nothing more than the different relations of meaning and form, relations that proceed from the universal idea and therefore provide the true basis for the different forms of this sphere.

The ideas of Kant and Hegel – especially the distinction between the world of sensory experience and the ideal world of Reason – influenced the Romantic movement and writers such as Friedrich Schiller, William Wordsworth, Samuel Taylor Coleridge, and Ralph Waldo Emerson. For Schiller, artistic accounts of the rational spirit realm educated the mind and made it more civil. Art had a broad public purpose. While that idea may seem odd to modern secular ears, there is a way of understanding its accuracy, and that is to think of the spirit realm as a projection of the mind's capacity for abstraction. That capacity is connected to the mind's ability to use mental representation to control negative emotions, and reading fiction is now known to increase empathy. Writers like Schiller may have been correct, then, to think a literary education might make humans more civil.

The idea that literature might "elevate" the mind remains popular with literary theorists down through Matthew Arnold in the late nineteenth century. Arnold believed literature served an educational purpose. It elevated the mind to a higher rational realm above and separate from practical consciousness and natural emotional impulses.

Matthew Arnold: At first sight it seems strange that out of the immense stir of the French Revolution and its age should not have come a crop of works of genius equal to that which came out of the stir of the great productive time of Greece, or out of that of the Renascence, with its powerful episode the Reformation. But the truth is that the stir of the French Revolution took a character which essentially distinguished it from such movements as these. These were, in the main, disinterestedly intellectual and spiritual movements; movement in which the human spirit looked for its satisfaction in itself and in the increased play of its own activity. The French Revolution took a political, practical character. The movement which went on in France under the old regime, from 1700 to 1789, was far more really akin than that of the Revolution itself to the movement of the Renascence; the France of Voltaire and Rousseau told far more powerfully upon the mind of Europe than the France of the Revolution. Goethe reproached this last expressly with having "thrown quiet culture back." Nay, and the true key to how much in our Byron, even in our Wordsworth, is this! – that they had their source in a great movement of feeling, not in a great movement of mind. The French Revolution, however, – that object of so much blind hatred, – found undoubtedly its motive-power in the intelligence of men, and not in their practical sense; this is what distinguishes it from the English Revolution of Charles the First's time. This is what makes it a more spiritual event than our Revolution, an event of much more powerful and worldwide interest, though practically less successful; it appeals to an order of ideas which are universal, certain permanent. 1789 asked of a thing, Is it rational? 1642 asked of a thing, Is it legal? ... But what is law in one place is not law in another ... [T]he prescriptions of reason are absolute, unchanging, of universal validity....

It is of the last importance that English criticism should clearly discern what rule for its course, in order to avail itself of the field now opening to it, and to produce fruit for the future, it ought to take. The rule may be summed up in one word – disinterestedness. And how is criticism to show disinterestedness? By keeping aloof from what is called "the practical view of things"; by resolutely following the law of its own nature, which is to be a free play of the mind on all subjects which it touches. By steadily refusing to lend itself to any of those ulterior, political, practical considerations about ideas.... Its business is, as I have said, simply to know the best that is known and thought in the world.

Yet equally influential during this period was an aesthetic philosophy that privileges sensory experiences and the impressions of the mind as it contemplates art. Writers such as Charles Baudelaire and Walter Pater emphasized the value of the surface of experience, the physical pleasures of the world, and a concept of artistic experience as an end in itself. Art should be enjoyed for art's sake alone; there is no need to refer to a spiritual meaning, an ideal rational realm, or a moral purpose. Baudelaire also rejected the Romantic ideal of Nature and celebrated instead the pleasures of artifice.

Charles Baudelaire: In the window of a coffee-house there sits a convalescent, pleasurably absorbed in gazing at the crowd, and mingling, through the medium of thought, in the turmoil of thought that surrounds him. But lately returned from the valley of the shadow of death, he is rapturously breathing in all the odours and essences of life; as he has been on the brink of total oblivion, he remembers, and fervently desires to remember, everything. Finally, he hurls himself headlong into the midst of the throng, in pursuit of an unknown, half-glimpsed countenance that has, on an instant, bewitched him. Curiosity has become a fatal, irresistible passion!

Imagine an artist who was always, spiritually, in the condition of that convalescent, and you will have the key to the nature of [the ideal artist].

Now, convalescence is like a return towards childhood. The convalescent, like the child, is possessed in the highest degree of the faculty of being keenly interested in all things, be they apparently of the most trivial. Let us go back, if we can, by a retrospective effort of the imagination, towards our most youthful, our earliest, impressions, and we will recognize that they had a strange kinship with those brightly coloured impressions which we were later to receive in the aftermath of a physical illness, always provided that that illness had left our spiritual capacities pure and unharmed. The child sees everything in a state of newness; he is always drunk. Nothing more resembles what we call inspiration than the delight with which a child absorbs from color and form. I am prepared to go even further and assert that sublime thought is accompanied by a more or less violent shock which has its repercussion in the very core of the brain. The man of genius has sound nerves, while those of the child are weak. With the one, Reason has taken up a considerable position; with the other, Sensibility is almost the whole being. But genius is nothing more nor less than childhood recovered at will – a childhood now equipped for self-expression with manhood's capacities and a power of analysis which enables it to order the mass of raw material which it has involuntarily accumulated.

The crowd is his element, as the air is that of birds and water of fishes. His passion and his profession are to become one flesh with the crowd. For the perfect *flâneur*, for the passionate spectator, it is an immense joy to set up house in the heart of the multitude, amid the ebb and flow of movement, in the midst of the fugitive and the infinite.... Thus the lover of universal life enters into the crowd as though it were an immense reservoir of electrical energy. Or we might liken him to a mirror as vast as the crowd itself; or to a kaleidoscope gifted with consciousness, responding to each one of its movements and reproducing the multiplicity of life and the flickering grace of all the elements of life. He is an "I" with an insatiable appetite for the "non-I", at every instant rendering and explaining it in pictures more living than life itself, which is always unstable and fugitive....

Everything beautiful and good is the result of reason and calculation. Crime, of which the human animal has learned the taste in his mother's womb, is natural by origin. Virtue, on the other hand, is artificial, supernatural, since at all times and in all places gods and prophets have been needed to teach it to animalized humanity, man being powerless to discover it by himself. Evil happens without effort, naturally, fatally; Good is always the product of some art. All that I am saying about Nature as a bad counsellor in moral matters, and about Reason as true redeemer and reformer, can be applied to the realm of Beauty. I am thus led to regard external finery as one of the signs of the primitive nobility of the human soul. Those races which our confused and perverted civilization is pleased to treat as savage, with an altogether ludicrous pride and complacency, understand, just as the child understands, the lofty price and complacency of make-up. In their naive adoration of what is brilliant – man-colored feathers, iridescent fabrics, the incomparable majesty of artificial forms – the baby and the savage bear witness to their disgust of the real, and thus give proof, without knowing it, of the immateriality of their souls....

Fashion should thus be considered as a symptom of the taste for the ideal which floats on the surface of all the crude, terrestrial and loathsome bric-a-brac that the natural life accumulates in the human brain: as a sublime deformation of Nature, or rather a permanent and repeated attempt at her reformation. And so it has been sensibly pointed out (though the reason has not been discovered) that every fashion is charming, relatively speaking, each one bearing a new and more or less happy effort in the direction of Beauty, some kind of approximation to an ideal for which the restless human mind feels a constant, titillating hunger.

Walter Pater was a professor of aesthetics at Oxford University who influenced a generation of artists and writers through his scholarly publications. The "Conclusion" to his *Studies in the Renaissance* caused a scandal by urging good Victorians to enjoy life and art as ends in themselves. No need for a "higher" spiritual meaning or a moral purpose. The experience of art itself was a sufficient reward.

Walter Pater: The service of philosophy, of speculative culture, towards the human spirit, is to rouse, to startle it to a life of constant and eager observation. Every moment some form grows perfect in hand or face; some tone on the hills or the sea is choicer than the rest; some mood of passion or insight or intellectual excitement is irresistibly real and attractive to us, – for that moment only. Not the fruit of experience, but experience itself, is the end. A counted number of pulses only is given to us of a variegated, dramatic life. How may we see in them all that is to be seen in them by the finest senses? How shall we pass most swiftly from point to point, and be present always at the focus where the greatest number of vital forces unite in their purest energy?

To burn always with this hard, gem-like flame, to maintain this ecstasy, is success in life. In a sense it might even be said that our failure is to form habits: for, after all, habit is relative to a stereotyped world, and meantime it is only the roughness of the eye that makes any two persons, things, situations, seem alike. While all melts under our feet, we may well grasp at any exquisite passion, or any contribution to knowledge that seems by a lifted horizon to set the spirit free for a moment, or any stirring of the senses, strange dyes, strange colours, and curious odours, or work of the artist's hands, or the face of one's friend. Not to discriminate every moment some passionate attitude in those about us, and in the very brilliancy of their gifts some tragic dividing of forces on their way, is, on this short day of frost and sun, to sleep before evening. With this sense of the splendour of our experience and of its awful brevity, gathering all we are into one desperate effort to see and touch, we shall hardly have time to make theories about the things we see and touch. What we have to do is to be for ever curiously testing new opinions and courting new impressions, never acquiescing in a facile orthodoxy, of Comte, or of Hegel, or of our own....

One of the most beautiful passages of Rousseau is that in the sixth book of the *Confessions*, where he describes the awakening in him of the literary sense. An undefinable taint of death had clung always about him, and now in early manhood he believed himself smitten by mortal disease. He asked himself how he might make as much as possible of the interval that remained; and he was not biased by anything in his previous life when he decided that it must be by intellectual excitement, which he found just then in the clear, fresh writings of Voltaire. Well! we are all *condamnés*, as Victor Hugo says: we are all under sentence of death but with a sort of indefinite reprieve ... ; we have an interval, and then our place knows us no more. Some spend this interval in listlessness, some in high passions, the wisest, at least among "the children of this world," in art and song. For our one chance lies in expanding that interval, in getting as many pulsations as possible into the given time. Great passions may give us this quickened sense of life, ecstasy and sorrow of love, the various forms of enthusiastic activity, disinterested or otherwise, which come naturally to many of us. Only be sure it is passion – that it does yield you this fruit of a quickened, multiplied consciousness. Of such wisdom, the poetic passion, the desire of beauty, the love of art for its own sake, has most. For art comes to you proposing frankly to give nothing but the highest quality to your moments as they pass, and simply for those moments' sake.

In the nineteenth century, revolutions occurred against the reactionary monarchies that ruled much of the Continent. Only some succeeded, but the thinking of those concerned with literature turned to thoughts of the social and political role of literature. The realist and naturalist writers such as Émile Zola felt literature, using the new tools of science, should seek to promote change by questioning existing norms and established patterns. Russian critics such as Vissarion Belinsky felt literature should play a role in making their country more modern.

Karl Marx began as a philosopher, but he was moved to radical politics by the revolutions in Europe in the 1840s. Europe was awash in the ideas of utopian socialism, and those merged with the uprisings against monarchy across Europe and eventually gave rise to the communist and anarchist movements, which sought to create a post-capitalist democratic society in which workers would no longer be the slaves of capitalists and wealth would be shared equally. Forced into exile, Marx ended up in England, where he was able to analyze the emerging social order created by industrialization and capitalist free market economics. He saw literature as immersed in its social, historical, political, and economic context. One could not know the meaning of a work of literature without knowing the world in which it was made and the social forces out of which it emerged. Often literature served a political purpose and gave expression to the "ruling ideas of the ruling class."

Karl Marx: The production of ideas, of conceptions, of consciousness, is at first directly interwoven with the material activity and the material intercourse of men, the language of real life…. In direct contrast to German philosophy which descends from heaven to earth, here we ascend from earth to heaven. That is to say, we do not set out from what men say, imagine, conceive, nor from men as narrated, thought of, imagined, conceived, in order to arrive at men in the flesh. We set out from real, active men, and on the basis of their real life-process we demonstrate the development of the ideological reflexes and echoes of this life-process. The phantoms formed in the human brain are also, necessarily, sublimates of their material life-process, which is empirically verifiable and bound to material premises.

Morality, religion, metaphysics, all the rest of ideology and their corresponding forms of consciousness, thus no longer retain the semblance of independence. They have no history, no development; but men, developing their material production and their material intercourse, alter, along with this their real existence, their thinking and the products of their thinking. Life is not determined by consciousness, but consciousness by life. In the first method of approach the starting-point is consciousness taken as the living individual; in the second method, which conforms to real life, it is the real living individuals themselves, and consciousness is considered solely as their consciousness.

The ideas of the ruling class are in every epoch the ruling ideas, i.e. the class which is the ruling material force of society, is at the same time its ruling intellectual force. The class which has the means of material production at its disposal, has control at the same time over the means of mental production, so that thereby, generally speaking, the ideas of those who lack the means of mental production are subject to it. The ruling ideas are nothing more than the ideal expression of the dominant material relationships, the dominant material relationships grasped as ideas; hence of the relationships which make the one class the ruling one, therefore, the ideas of its dominance. The individuals composing the ruling class possess among other things consciousness, and therefore think. Insofar, therefore, as they rule as a class and determine the extent and compass of an epoch, it is self-evident that they do this in its whole range, hence among other things rule also as thinkers, as producers of ideas, and regulate the production and distribution of the ideas of their age: thus their ideas are the ruling ideas of the epoch. For instance, in an age and in a country where royal power, aristocracy, and bourgeoisie are contending for mastery and where, therefore, mastery is shared, the doctrine of the separation of powers proves to be the dominant idea and is expressed as an "eternal law".... [W]e can say, for instance, that during the time that the aristocracy was dominant, the concepts honour, loyalty, etc. were dominant, during the dominance of the bourgeoisie the concepts freedom, equality, etc. The ruling class itself on the whole imagines this to be so.

Taking literary theory in the opposed direction were the French Symbolists led by Stéphane Mallarmé. These writers believed that poetry especially provided access to an ideal spiritual truth. Poetry served no moral purpose and had no social use. It was instead a privileged way of capturing the Ideal. Attention in literature should be on technique, language, and meaning. Instead of real natural flowers, the poet writes of "the flower that is absent from all bouquets."

Friedrich Nietzsche is now better known for his radically perspectival epistemology than for his theory of art, but in *The Birth of Tragedy* (1872) he advanced a theory of tragedy that foreshadowed in certain ways the emphasis in twentieth-century philosophy on discontinuity and contingency. Most philosophers believe Being is something easily known using the categories of Reason, but Nietzsche saw Being as becoming, as a process more akin to a fiery flow that had no knowable unity. Traditional philosophy suppresses this radical becoming by manufacturing lies to cover up the instability of the world. Nietzsche reached back to an alternative tradition that originated in Greece and that emphasized the ungraspable flow of life and conceived of Being as active becoming that eluded conceptual stabilization.

He makes a theme of that philosophic distinction in *The Birth of Tragedy* where he describes the Apollonian principle in art in terms of the philosophic quest for a knowable Being behind the play of appearances, a ground of unity and coherence. This principle of stability and unity is opposed by the Dionysian principle, which he defines in terms of play, mutability, and becoming.

Friedrich Nietzsche: The Dionysiac, with the primal pleasure it perceives even in pain, is the common womb from which both music and the tragic myth are born.

Could it be that with the assistance of musical dissonance, we have eased significantly the difficult problem of the effect of tragedy? After all, we do now understand the meaning of our desire to look, and yet to long to go beyond looking when we are watching tragedy; when applied to our response to the artistic use of dissonance, this state of mind would have to be described in similar terms: we want to listen, but at the same time we long to go beyond listening. That striving towards infinity, that wing-beat of longing even as we feel supreme delight in a clearly perceived reality, these things indicate that in both these states of mind we are to recognize a Dionysiac phenomenon, one which reveals to us the playful construction and demolition of the world of individuality as an outpouring of primal pleasure and delight, a process quite similar to Heraclitus the Obscure's comparison of the force that shapes the world to a playing child who sets down stones, here, there, and the next place, and who builds up piles of sand only to knock them down again....

Music and tragic myth both express, in the same way, the Dionysiac capacity of a people, and they cannot be separated from one another. Both originate in an artistic realm which lies beyond the Apollonian; both transfigure a region where dissonance and the terrible image of the world fade away in chords of delight; both play with the goad of disinclination, trusting to their immeasurably powerful arts of magic; both justify by their play the existence of even the "worst of all worlds". Here the Dionysiac shows itself, in comparison to the Apollonian, to be the eternal and original power of art which summons the entire world of appearances into existence, in the midst of which a new, transfiguring semblance is needed to hold fast within life the animated world of individuation. If you could imagine dissonance assuming human form – and what else is man? – this dissonance would need, to be able to live, a magnificent illusion which would spread a veil of beauty over its own nature. This is the true artistic aim of Apollo, in whose name we gather together all those countless illusions of beautiful semblance and thereby urge us on to experience the next.

At the same time, only as much of that foundation of all existence, that Dionysiac underground of the world, can be permitted to enter an individual's consciousness as can be overcome, in its turn, by the Apollonian power of transfiguration, so that both of these artistic drives are required to unfold their energies in strict, reciprocal proportion, according to the law of eternal justice. Where the Dionysiac powers rise up with such unbounded vigour as we are seeing at present, Apollo, too, must already have descended amongst us, concealed in a cloud, and his most abundant effects of beauty will surely be seen by a generation which comes after us.

Nietzsche claimed that all knowledge is perspectival. One sees the world from a specific located point of view; therefore, there is no "universal truth" or "objective knowledge" that exists apart from the mind. The idea of a truth that is independent of perspective is an illusion. He was right, of course. Philosophers since Plato had been mistaking the new cognitive ability for something "out there," a realm of universal ideas that existed in the world. Those universals are indeed sharable mental representations just as the language of mathematics is a sharable representational model that acts as a cultural tool for manipulating and transforming the world. But mathematics resides in the mind or in the written symbols that embody its ideas, not in the world. The same is true of abstract ideas.

Writing at the start of the twentieth century, Edmund Husserl sought to bridge the divide between perspective and objective truth, between mental action (conceiving of abstract ideas) and true ideas (ideas whose validity would be universal). He did so by locating truth in perspective. His "phenomenology" grounded truth in the mind's ability to formulate ideas that could transcend perspective while yet being lodged in the perspective of consciousness. Those pure ideas became formal and transcendental when purified of worldly elements. Ideas in the mind were more true when grasped by "intuition." They were more likely to be purer ideas, unlike ideas derived from sensory data.

One of the first aestheticians to draw on phenomenology was Benedetto Croce. He held that the intuitions evident in art are different from logic and science. They constitute a purer kind of knowledge. As a European political conservative, Croce formulated this theory in terms of the ideal of individual liberty, the model of a self that has no master and that is dependent on no one. It is also an elitist conception; the "civilized man" is capable of grasping the intuitions of art but others are not. This doctrine would inform the elitism of the American New Criticism, a politically conservative movement which also saw art as delivering intuitive truths that were difficult to grasp and that sorted the "great" from the less great.

Benedetto Croce: Now, the first point to be firmly fixed in the mind is that intuitive knowledge has no need of a master, nor to lean upon any one; she does not need to borrow the eyes of others, for she has most excellent eyes of her own. Doubtless it is possible to find concepts mingled with intuitions. But in many other intuitions there is no trace of such a mixture, which proves that it is not necessary. The impression of a moonlight scene by a painter; the outline of a country drawn by a cartographer; a musical motive, tender or energetic; the words of a sighing lyric, or those with which we ask, command and lament in ordinary life, may well all be intuitive facts without a shadow of intellective relation. But, think what one may of these instances, and admitting further that one may maintain that the greater part of the intuitions of civilized man are impregnated with concepts, there yet remains to be observed something more important and more conclusive. Those concepts which are found mingled and fused with the intuitions, are no longer concepts, in so far as they are really mingled and fused, for they have lost all independence and autonomy. They have been concepts, but they have now become simple elements of intuition. The philosophical maxims placed in the mouth of a personage of tragedy or of comedy, perform there the function, not of concepts, but of characteristics of such personage; in the same way as the red in a painted figure does not there represent the red colour of the physicists, but is a characteristic element of the portrait. The whole it is that determines the quality of the parts. A work of art may be full of philosophical concepts; it may contain them in greater abundance and they may be there even more profound than in a philosophical dissertation, which in its turn may be rich to overflowing with descriptions and intuitions. But, notwithstanding all these concepts it may contain, the result of the work of art is an intuition; and notwithstanding all those intuitions, the result of the philosophical dissertation is a concept. The *Promessi Sposi* contains copious ethical observations and distinctions, but it does not for that reason lose in its total effect its character of simple story, of intuition. In like manner the anecdotes and satirical effusions which may be found in the works of a philosopher like Schopenhauer, do not remove from those works their character of intellective treatises. The difference between a scientific work and a work of art, that is, between an intellective fact and an intuitive fact lies in the result, in the diverse effect aimed at by their respective authors. This it is that determines and rules over the several parts of each.

As phenomenology became influential in the mid-twentieth century, the emphasis shifted from pure ideas grasped by mental intuition to the conscious awareness of the flow of everyday experience and the interpersonal aspects of the meeting of minds through the act of reading. When Georges Poulet, a Swiss phenomenologist, came to teach in the US, he influenced a number of scholars, including Stanley Fish, who repackaged phenomenology as "reader-response criticism."

Georges Poulet: Such is the initial phenomenon produced whenever I take up a book and begin to read it. At the precise moment that I see surging out of the object I hold open before me, a quantity of significations which my mind grasps, I realize that what I hold in my hands is no longer just an object, or even simply a living thing. I am aware of a rational being, of a consciousness; the consciousness of another, no different from the one I automatically assume in every human being I encounter, except that in this case, the consciousness is open to me, welcomes me, lets me look deep inside itself, and even allows me, with unheard-of license, to think what it thinks and feel what it feels.

Unheard of, I say. Unheard-of, first, is the disappearance of the "object." Where is the book I held in my hands? It is still there, and at the same time it is there no longer, it is nowhere. That object wholly object, that thing made of paper, as there are things made of metal or porcelain, that object is not more, or at least it is as if it no longer existed, as long as I read the book. For the book is no longer a material reality. It has become a series of words, of images, of ideas, which in their turn begin to exist. And where is this new existence? Surely not in the paper object. Nor, surely, in external space. There is only one place left for this new existence: my innermost self.

One of the major new schools of literary theory in the early twentieth century was Russian Formalism. While it sought to make the study of literature more scientific, more concerned with literature as literature and with the specifically literary techniques that distinguished literary writing from other kinds of writing, Russian Formalism was in its inception connected to the art radicalism of the period, which felt art could transform human consciousness and change the world. The radical writers of the Dada movement, which formed in 1916 in response to World War I, sought to create a new disruptive kind of art. That a supposedly civilized Europe could lapse into militarism and war shocked this group of leftwing writers. If Reason could lead to such barbarism, then poetry should be deliberately irrational. It should seek to evoke a different kind of thinking, and to do so, it must shatter the rational forms of verse. Dada would be nonsensical and anti-bourgeois. It would reject the nineteenth-century platitudes of Church and Family, what today we would be called "family values."

Tristan Tzara: The love of novelty is the cross of sympathy, demonstrates a naive I-don't-give-damn-ism, it is a transitory, positive sign without a cause. But this need itself is obsolete. In documenting art on the basis of the supreme simplicity: novelty, we are human and true for the sake of amusement, impulsive, vibrant to crucify boredom. At the crossroads of the lights, alert, attentively awaiting the years, in the forest. I write a manifesto and I want nothing, yet I say certain things, and in principle I am against manifestoes, as I am also against principles (half-pints to measure the moral value of every phrase too too convenient; approximation was invented by the impressionists). I write this manifesto to show that people can perform contrary actions together while taking one fresh gulp of air; I am against action; for continuous contradiction, for affirmation too, I am neither for nor against and I do not explain because I hate common sense....

A work of art is never beautiful by decree, objectively and for all. Hence criticism is useless, it exists only subjectively, for each man separately, without the slightest character of universality. Does anyone think he has found a psychic base common to all mankind? The attempt of Jesus and the Bible covers with their broad benevolent wings: shit, animals, days. How can one expect to put order into the chaos that constitutes that infinite and shapeless variation: man? The principle: "love thy neighbor" is a hypocrisy. "Know thyself" is utopian but more acceptable, for it embraces wickedness.... No pity. After the carnage we still retain the hope of a purified mankind. I speak only of myself since I do not wish to convince, I have no right to drag others into my river, I oblige no one to follow me and everybody practices his art in his own way, if he knows the joy that rises like arrows to the astral layers, or that other joy that goes down into the mines of corpse-flowers and fertile spasms. Stalactites: seek them everywhere, in managers magnified by pain, eyes white as the hares of the angels. And so Dada was born of a need for independence, of a distrust toward unity. Those who are with us preserve their freedom. We recognize no theory....

Every product of disgust capable of becoming a negation of the family is Dada; a protest with the fists of its whole being engaged in destructive action: Dada; knowledge of all the means rejected up until now by the shamefaced sex of comfortable compromise and good manners: Dada; abolition of logic, which is the dance of those impotent to create: Dada; of every social hierarchy and equation set up for the sake of values by our valets: Dada: every object, all objects, sentiments, obscurities, apparitions and the precise clash of parallel lines are weapons for the fight: Dada; abolition of memory: Dada; abolition of archaeology: Dada; abolition of prophets: Dada; abolition of the future: Dada; absolute and unquestionable faith in every god that is the immediate product of spontaneity: Dada; elegant and unprejudiced leap from a harmony to the other sphere; trajectory of a word tossed like a screeching phonograph record; to respect all individuals in their folly of the moment: whether it be serious, fearful, timid, ardent, vigorous, determined, enthusiastic; to divest one's church of every useless cumbersome accessory; to spit out disagreeable or amorous ideas like a luminous waterfall, or coddle them – with the extreme satisfaction that it doesn't matter in the least – with the same intensity in the thicket of core's soul pure of insects for blood well-born, and gilded with bodies of archangels. Freedom: Dada Dada Dada, a roaring of tense colors, and interlacing of opposites and of all contradictions, grotesques, inconsistencies: LIFE.

Drawing on the same well of ideas that informed Dada, one of the leading Russian literary theorists, Viktor Shklovsky (1893–1984) advanced the idea that poetry roughens up our everyday experience, which tends with time to become overly routine and habituated to the world around us. Poetry defamiliarizes that world and makes it new again.

> **Viktor Shklovsky:**   If we start to examine the general laws of perception, we see that as perception becomes habitual, it becomes automatic. Thus, for example, all of our habits retreat into the area of the unconsciously automatic; if one remembers the sensations of holding a pen or of speaking in a foreign language for the first time and compares that with his feeling at performing the action for the ten thousandth time, he will agree with us. Such habituation explains the principles by which, in ordinary speech, we leave phrases unfinished and words half expressed….
>
> Habituation devours work, clothes, furniture, one's wife, and the fear of war. "If the whole complex lives of so many people go on unconsciously, then such lives are as if they had never been." And art exists that one may recover the sensation of life; it exists to make one feel things, to make the stone stony. The purpose of art is to impart the sensation of things as they are perceived and not as they are known. The technique of art is to make objects "unfamiliar," to make forms difficult, to increase the difficulty and length of perception because the process of perception is an aesthetic end in itself and must be prolonged. Art is a way of experiencing the artfulness of an object: the object is not important….

Shklovsky, Boris Eichenbaum, and Juri Tinjanov shifted the emphasis in the study of literature from a theory based largely in philosophy to a study based largely in linguistics and the techniques of literary construction. Those included the procedures of narration such as delayed revelation or stepped narrative and the techniques of poetry such as alliteration and euphony.

The early twentieth century was a time of lively reflection on poetry. Ezra Pound argued that poetry should be as spare as possible. In keeping with the Modernist ethos that rejected Victorian ornamentation and sentimentalism, he contended words should be efficient and free of emotion. T. S. Eliot saw poets in terms of place within tradition. Arguing against the ideal of Romantic subjectivism, he urged instead impersonality and an elevation above emotion.

Linguistics came of age in the early twentieth century. The work of Ferdinand de Saussure (1857–1913) was especially influential. He studied language as a system of signs whose interconnections allowed words to function and to have meaning. Roman Jakobsen, a member, along with Shklovsky, of the Moscow Poetry Circle, was an early proponent of the study of the link between linguistic forms such as metaphor (which characterizes poetry) and metonymy (which characterizes fictional narrative) and such cognitive processes and disorders as aphasia. He introduced French thinkers such as anthropologist Claude Lévi-Strauss to the ideas of Saussure and helped to launch the movement called Structuralism, which sought to study culture using the tools and methods of linguistics. Lévi-Strauss's structural study of myth was especially influential. In it, he compared hundreds of myths from diverse cultures and found that they shared common structural elements. Already, Vladimir Propp had found structural similarities between folktales, all of which seem to follow a similar narrative pattern of departure, conflict, assistance, vindication, and reconciliation. Lévi-Strauss suggested that myths shared a similar structure because they dealt with the same universal human concerns. This concern with stories and with narratives would become a central concern of the Structuralist study of literature. Gerard Genette and Tzvetan Todorov led the way in developing a science of "narratology." The emphasis in Structuralist Linguistics on signs and semiological systems also inspired French theorists such as Roland Barthes to study culture using linguistic tools. Barthes' short "mythologies" examined aspects of popular culture such as advertisements and guide books as sign systems that communicated meaning using sign images.

While European literary theorists were aspiring to make the study of literature more scientific, theorists in America sought to determine what about literature was at odds with science. In science, words have one meaning, but in literature, New Critics such as Cleanth Brooks argued, the effect of the placement of words in the context of the literary work is to give rise to additional connotative meanings that might even have a spiritual quality. While science seeks the truth of specific things by naming them accurately, literature provides access to less easily nameable truths through the use of complex tropes such as irony and paradox that create semantically fruitful tensions between words. The new meanings generated are more like abstract ideas than sensory objects that can be named directly using a scientific vocabulary. The New Critics merged the idealist tradition (which saw art as the expression of a realm of either spirit or Mind) with the new movement towards the study of literary techniques and forms. They argued for the "close reading" or study of individual literary works for the complex ways they merged imagery and meaning in a unity. Cleanth Brooks emphasized the way poetry dislocated the ordinary uses of words to create meaning.

Cleanth Brooks: [T]here is irony of a very powerful sort in Wordsworth's "Intimations" ode. For the thrusts and pressures exerted by the various symbols in this poem are not avoided by the poet: they are taken into account and played, one against the other. Indeed, the symbols – from a scientific point of view – are used perversely: it is the child who is the best philosopher; it is from a kind of darkness – from something that is "shadowy" – that the light proceeds; growth into manhood is viewed, not as an extrication from, but as an incarceration within, a prison.

There should be no mystery as to why this must be so. The terms of science are abstract symbols which do not change under the pressure of the context. They are pure (or aspire to be pure) denotation; they are defined in advance. They are not to be warped into new meanings. But where is the dictionary which contains the terms of a poem? It is a truism that the poet is continually forced to remake language. As Eliot has put it, his task is to "dislocate language into meaning."

Literary theory in Europe in the mid-twentieth century also included Marxism. György Lukács theorized in *The Historical Novel* that works of literature even by reactionary royalist writers such as Balzac could, because they were realist, capture the totality of their age. Walter Benjamin developed an innovative method of historical study in his *Origin of German Tragic Drama*. He also suggested that new media such as film bring about new ways of experiencing the world. Some members of the so-called Frankfurt School such as Theodor Adorno and Max Horkheimer argued that popular culture was a realm of delusion that sustained the power of capitalists over workers, while other thinkers such as Herbert Marcuse and Ernst Bloch described utopian aspirations within even conservative or, in a Marxist sense, "ideological" cultural forms.

One positive outcome of the various formalist enterprises was the emergence of a variety of theories regarding different regions of literature. Those included genres like the novel, modes such as realism, and historical periods such as Romanticism.

Russian theorist Mikhail Bakhtin emphasized the social linguistic character of the novel. Novels draw on multiple voices from the ambient social universe. He cites the example of Charles Dickens who mimes different kinds of speech and integrates them to his fiction. Some are mocked or parodied; some are simply cited. By integrating diverse forms of speech, Dickens novels emphasize the heteroglossic or multi-voiced character of the novel in general, the way it draws on and is sustained by the multiple forms of discourse in a society. Each strand of discourse interacts with proximate strands in the novel. Bakhtin's term for this is dialogization.

Mikhail Bakhtin: The novel as a whole is a phenomenon multiform in style and variform in speech and voice. In it the researcher is confronted with several heterogeneous stylistic unities, often located on different linguistic levels and subject to different stylistic controls.

We list below the basic types of compositional-stylistic unities into which the novelistic whole usually breaks down:

1.   Direct authorial literary-artistic narration (in all its diverse variants);
2.   Stylization of the various forms of oral everyday narration [skaz];
3.   Stylization of the various forms of semiliterary everyday narration (the letter, the diary, etc.);
4.   Various forms of literary but extra-artistic authorial speech (moral, philosophical or scientific statements, oratory, ethnographic descriptions, memoranda and so forth);
5.   The stylistically individualized speech of character…

The novel can be defined as a diversity of social speech types (sometimes even a diversity of languages) and a diversity of individual voices, artistically organized. The internal stratification any single national language into social dialects, characteristic group behavior, professional jargons, generic languages, languages of generations and age groups, tendentious languages, languages of the authorities, of various circles and of passing fashions, languages that serve the specific sociopolitical purposes of the day, even of the hour (each day has its own slogan, its own vocabulary, its own emphases) – this internal stratification present in every language at any given moment of its historical existence is the indispensable prerequisite for the novel as a genre. The novel orchestrates all its themes, the totality of the world of objects and ideas depicted and expressed in it, by means of all the social diversity of speech types and by the differing individual voices that flourish under such conditions. Authorial speech, the speeches of narrators, inserted genres, the speech of characters are merely those fundamental compositional unities with whose help heteroglossia can enter the novel; each of them permits a multiplicity of social voices and a wide variety of their links and relationships between utterances and languages, this movement of the theme through different languages and speech types, its dispersion into the rivulets and droplets of social heteroglossia, its dialogization – this is the basic distinguishing feature of the stylistics of the novel.

Erich Auerbach's ambitious history of realism, *Mimesis*, described literary realism as evolving from purely external descriptions to the rendering of internal psychology and emotion in modern fiction. His famous first chapter examines Homer's style of narration in the *Odyssey* and notes how Homer foregrounds events and maintains a sense of a perpetual present.

Erich Auerbach: Readers of the *Odyssey* will remember the well-prepared and touching scene in Book 19, when Odysseus has at last come home, the scene in which the old housekeeper Euryclea, who had been his nurse, recognizes him by a scar on his thigh.... To the word scar (v. 393) there is first attached a relative clause ("which once long ago a boar ..."), which enlarges into a voluminous syntactical parenthesis; into this an independent sentence unexpectedly intrudes (v. 396: "A god himself gave him ..."), which quietly disentangles itself from syntactical subordination, until, with verse 399, an equally free syntactical treatment of the new content begins a new present which continues unchallenged until, with verse 467 ("The old woman now touched it ..."), the scene which had been broken off is resumed. To be sure, in the case of such long episodes as the one we are considering, a purely syntactical connection with the principal theme would hardly have been possible; but a connection with it through perspective would have been all the easier had the content been arranged with that end in view; if, that is, the entire story of the scar had been presented as a recollection which awakens in Odysseus' mind at this particular moment. It would have been perfectly easy to do; the story of the scar had only to be inserted two verses earlier, at the first mention of the word scar, where the motifs "Odysseus" and "recollection" were already at hand. But any such subjectivistic-perspectivistic procedure, creating a foreground and background, resulting in the present lying open to the depths of the past, is entirely foreign to the Homeric style; the Homeric style knows only a foreground, only a uniformly illuminated, uniformly objective present.

Perhaps the most ambitious project in literary theory during this period in the mid-twentieth century was the "anatomy" carried out by Canadian theorist Northrop Frye. Frye conceived of the genres of literature as part of a cycle that followed the seasons as well as the cycles of religious life.

The revival of Nietzsche in the 1960s in France inspired thinkers such as Gilles Deleuze and Jacques Derrida to develop theories that departed from the emphasis on scientific order in Structuralism. Saussure had suggested that each element of language is given an identity by its difference from other elements. That insight opened the possibility that there existed another realm of being entirely that could not be known using the usual tools of knowledge, which tended to focus on things or objects rather than on their relations. How could one know "difference" if it was something "between" two things? And how could one say those things had "identity" or a sense of "own-ness" if they depended essentially on a relation to something other than themselves that was itself an "in-between," a differential relation to something other? So much for certain knowledge and a knowable order of being. And so much as well for the moral normative orders humans have built upon the foundational assumption that they could use their minds to easily determine the truth of things and of ideas. Indeed, if those normative orders were built on sand, mightn't they then have more to do with regimes of social power than with truth, the attempt by ruling economic and political groups to impose their will on others by pretending their will represented a universal order of true ideas?

Marxists denounced this new "Postmodernism" as a symptom of capitalism. Conservatives suggested it was undermining Truth and Civilization (which it was, rather jollily). But so-called "Postmodernism" also gave rise to some fruitful new literary theories, some of which have faded and some of which have proved enduring.

Deleuze pointed out that the meaning one finds in literature (or in philosophy) comes into being against a backdrop of non-meaning or non-sense. What meanings are chosen to be privileged in a culture therefore belong to a regime of knowledge that is founded on exclusions, a cutting off of semantic possibilities. If one pursues those possibilities, the borders that maintain the integrity and identity of such things as books dissolve. Even the distinction between culture and nature falls apart. All of our ideational constructs are forms of matter. These insights would help found the "New Materialism" in literary theory in the early twenty-first century.

Derrida examined the history of philosophy and noticed a persistent tendency to ignore the slipperiness of the ground knowledge was built on, a ground philosophy mistakenly assumed to be stable. Philosophy assumes the identity of meaning in literary and philosophical texts, but everywhere Derrida looked, he found signs of the difference Saussure had noticed in language. One cannot, therefore, move from a text to a meaning or to the life of an author without getting into a complex web of differential relations that added a lot more meaning than one expected.

A school of theory derived from Derrida's work developed in the US called "deconstruction." Its leading proponent was Paul de Man, and its leading practitioner was Barbara Johnson. De Man used Derrida's ideas to argue that all literary texts ended up unreadable because it was impossible to locate a stable meaning that was not plagued by further reference, further relays to something other. Roland Barthes also put Derrida's ideas to good use by noting that the study of literature should now be less concerned with an author's life and more with the various meanings his/her text generates. Literature consisted now of complex "texts" rather than of "works."

A major French thinker of this period in the second half of the twentieth century, Michel Foucault, was both a significant Structuralist and an influential Post-Structuralist. He first studied the "orders of discourse," the way embedded rules and assumptions in the discourses we use to describe the world shape how we conceive of that world. His work then shifted to the analysis of power and to the way "discipline" is assured through non-governmental means in society. Finally, his attention turned to discursive regulation of the body and of sexuality over time. While he did not develop a theory of literature, Foucault provoked a renewal of the historical study of literature that focused less on political events and more on the way discourses shaped history. The "New Historicism" of Stephen Greenblatt, Catherine Gallagher, and others was concerned with the links across discourses in any one historical period.

Foucault's analysis of power grew out of the social and political movements of the 1950s and 1960s, and those movements inspired a number of important schools of literary theory. The anti-colonial and anti-imperialist struggles lie behind the rise of Post-Colonial and Transnational Studies; the Women's Movement for equality led to Feminist literary theory; the Civil Rights Movement inspired the various ethnic area studies; and the Gay Liberation Movement helped bring about Queer and Gender Studies.

Post-Colonial/Transnational Studies began with the study of the dynamics of colonial rule. White metropolitan culture was invariably portrayed as superior to the culture of the colonial periphery in English literature. Edward Said noticed that a whole field of study called "orientalism" developed to account for the difference between Occident and Orient, a field invariably tainted by crude stereotypes despite its scholarly status. Theorists such as Homi Bhabha, operating in a deconstructive vein, portrayed the relation of colonizer and colonial as one of insidious subversion. Transnational Studies assumes the reality of global culture, one in which traditional models such as center and periphery no longer make sense. Even the traditional anti-colonial idea of a national culture might no longer make sense in a connected digital and mediated global world.

Ethnic theory moves between the study of the specific tropes of ethnic culture to the study of the dynamic interaction between such culture and the majority or dominant culture. While the goal for some is the realization of an ideal of diverse inclusiveness, for others it remains the preservation of the specific forms of traditional ethnic culture. For African-Americans, this has meant reestablishing a sense of connection to severed African origins, while for indigenous Native Americans it has meant producing works of literature that embody the values and ideas of Native culture.

Feminist literary theory began by demarcating a tradition of women's writing and by studying the way male-dominated literary culture often portrayed women negatively. It then moved to an exploration of the qualities that make women's writing different from men's. Theorists like Luce Irigaray and Hélène Cixous asked the question, Is there a separate realm of female experience captured in a style of writing noticeably different from that of men? A further development occurred when Judith Butler examined the "performed" character of gender identity.

What today is called Queer Theory began as Gay and Lesbian Studies. Theorists such as John d'Emilio, Lee Edelman, Bonnie Zimmerman, and others excavated a tradition of closeted writers such as Henry James and Elisabeth Bishop. Edelman portrayed the homonymic character of queer identity – that it looks straight yet was "different." Eve Sedgwick noted the continuum between straight and gay culture. These critical evaluations of the dominant hetero-normative culture were both upsetting and exhilarating. They destroyed the standards that aligned biological gender with sexual preference while opening up a realm of mix-and-match possibilities that make gender a realm of great creativity. Kind of a drag indeed.

Post-Structuralist theory has proved enduringly helpful in these realms of theory. That theory was a critique of philosophy, but philosophy, it turns out, has a way of informing the everyday assumptions and perceptions of a culture. The same values of authenticity, nature, and reason that made a certain regime of truth seem more authoritative turned up in the realm of gender, assuring that straight men would appear more natural, authentic, and reasonable than the various "others" they feared and stigmatized.

The most recent developments in literary theory include cognitive studies, evolutionary theory, emotion studies, and the new materialism. All seek to dissolve the barrier between mind and body, between the capacity for idealizing abstraction that allowed *H. sapiens* to build a civilization and the actual physical activity that makes such abstract mental representation possible and in which it is anchored. Cognitive literary studies draws attention to the way the mind operates. One influential idea is that all knowledge is embodied, which is to say, it assumes the form of spatial schemas such as in/out, up/down, center/margin, et cetera. We tend to organize our thinking spatially, and often spatial schemas align with standards of evaluation (a "low" occupation is not a "high" calling). Emotion or Affect Studies takes note of the power of emotions in our lives and in literature. *King Lear* has many facets, but one important one, certainly, is the trajectory of emotions, as Lear moves from fatuous affection to wounded anger in a space of just a few moments in Act One. Hurt, rage, sorrow, regret – the play might be characterized critically entirely in these terms. Evolutionary theory grounds itself in the Darwinian idea that humans have evolved over time through natural selection. All of our traits aided our ability to survive in harsh conditions. Those who benefited from small changes in their make-up (adaptations due to accidental yet beneficent changes wrought in our make-up by genetic mutation) survived at a greater rate than others who were not so lucky in their genetic inheritance. If eyes in front rather than on the side of the head made survival more likely, then only those with such eyes were likely to reproduce, and all subsequent iterations of the species would have that trait. What we are now, therefore, reaches far into the past, and many of our habits and dispositions, such as greed or generosity, can be understood as the fruit of past adaptations that aided survival. Courtship has attracted probably more attention than it deserves in evolutionary criticism, as scholars note how Edith Wharton or Jane Austen describe the rituals that bring about mating and successful reproduction.

The new materialism connects human life to a broad conception of biology and ecology. Where is the border between human life and ambient biological life? How might we conceive of life without such borders and boundaries – as an interdependent continuum that links humans to habitat, or animals to humans, and that sees life as gradients of matter across a variety of iterations, none more privileged or central than the others? Considered from the perspective of a post-humanist materiality, an ocean and a beach are not a line, a boundary, or even an opposition; they are different forms of matter, a contrast of thick or thin molecular states. Heterosexuals like to think of heterosexual reproduction as a social, even a moral norm, but such reproduction is a minority form in biology, which favors more variable forms of sexuality. What we consider to be "perversions" constitute life as usual for many species. This reconceptualization of human life as biology and ecology will no doubt prompt us to rethink the debates in literature between norms and deviations or models of social order and the various threats such models inevitably imagine and project.

PART ONE

Russian Formalism, New Criticism, Poetics

CHAPTER 1

Introduction
Formalisms

Julie Rivkin and Michael Ryan

It has become a commonplace of literary study that to study literature is to study language, yet prior to the formalist movements of the early twentieth century – Russian Formalism and American New Criticism – the study of literature was concerned with everything about literature except language, from the historical context of a literary work to the biography of its author. How literary language worked was of less importance than what a literary work was about. Two movements in early twentieth-century thought helped move literary study away from this orientation. The first movement was the attempt on the part of philosophers of science like Edmund Husserl to isolate objects of knowledge in their unmixed purity. The Russian Formalists, a group of young scholars (Viktor Shklovsky, Roman Jakobson, Boris Tomashevsky, Boris Eichenbaum) who wrote in the teens and twenties, were influenced by this approach. For them, literature would be considered not as a window on the world but as something with specifically literary characteristics that make it literature as opposed to philosophy or sociology or biography. Literature is not a window for looking at sociological themes or philosophic ideas or biographical information; rather, it is a mural or wall painting, something with a palpability of its own which arrests the eye and merits study. The manipulation of representational devices may create a semblance of reality and allow one to have the impression of gazing through glass, but it is the devices alone that produce that impression, and they alone are what makes literature literary.

The second movement was the attempt on the part of idealist philosophers like Benedetto Croce to develop a new aesthetics, or philosophy of art, which would rebut the claim of science that all truth is grounded in empirical facts knowable through scientific methods. Art provides access to a different kind of truth than is available to science, a truth that is immune to scientific investigation because it is accessible only through connotative language (allusion, metaphor, symbolism, etc.) and cannot be rendered in the direct, denotative, fact-naming language of the sciences. The American New Critics (Cleanth Brooks, William K. Wimsett, John Crowe Ransom, Allen Tate) were influenced by the new aesthetic philosophies. For them, literature should be studied for the way literary language differs from ordinary practical language and for the unique truths conveyed only through such literary language.

Literary Theory: An Anthology, Third Edition. Edited by Julie Rivkin and Michael Ryan.
© 2017 John Wiley & Sons, Ltd. Published 2017 by John Wiley & Sons, Ltd.

The Russian Formalists were interested both in describing the general characteristics of literary language and in analyzing the specific devices or modes of operation of such language. Perhaps their most famous general claim is that literary language consists of an act of defamiliarization, by which they mean that such literature presents objects or experiences from such an unusual perspective or in such unconventional and self-conscious language that our habitual, ordinary, rote perceptions of those things are disturbed. We are forced to see things that had become automatic and overly familiar in new ways. Shklovsky cites the example of Tolstoy, who presents a meditation on property from the point of view of a horse, or who recounts the story of a flogging in such a blank manner that the then accepted practice seems strange and novel to the otherwise inured reader.

More specifically, the Formalists were interested in analyzing literature into its component parts and in describing its principal devices and modes of operation. This analysis took two main forms in the two major genres of prose narrative and poetry, concentrating in the first on the operations of narrative and in the second on sound in verse. The Formalists noticed that narrative literature consisted of two major components: the plot, by which they meant the story as narrated within the pages of the book (with all the attendant arrangements of chronological sequence, point of view, etc.), and the story, by which they meant the sequence of events in the order and the actual duration in which they ostensibly occurred. Once this simple distinction is made, one can begin to analyze all of the features of story-telling, the many devices such as point of view, delayed disclosure, narrative voice, and the like that go into the creation of the imaginary story through the manipulation of plot or story-telling devices. One can, for example, begin to study a novel like *The Scarlet Letter* for its narrative strategies instead of for the ways in which it depicts Puritanism.

In the analysis of poetry, the Formalist focus was on the qualities of poetic language that distinguish it from ordinary practical language, the distinction between the literary and the non-literary being more pronounced in this genre. Whereas ordinary language must subordinate its rules of operation (grammar) to the practical goal of communicating information, poetic language is distinguished by the foregrounding of such devices or motifs as euphony, rhythm, alliteration, consonance, repetition, and rhyme which obey a very different logic from that required to communicate information. A meteorologist might say that "precipitation in the Iberian peninsula is concentrated in the central plateau," and in light of that practical use of language, the internal rhyming of "the rain in Spain falls mainly on the plain" will seem impractical and unnecessary, but it is such devices that make poetry a distinct linguistic undertaking, a mode of language use with autonomous rules of operation which, unlike grammar, are not subordinated to a practical function. While practical speech facilitates access to information by making language as transparent as possible, poetic speech contorts and roughens up ordinary language and submits it to what Roman Jakobson called "organized violence," and it is this roughening up of ordinary language into tortuous "formed speech" that makes poetry poetry rather than a weather report.

While literature for the Formalists is characterized by invariant patterns, recurring devices, and law-like relations, it also changes over time and varies from one historical epoch to another. The Formalists account for such change in two ways. They claim that literary evolution is the result of the constant attempt to disrupt existing literary conventions and to generate new ones. And they argue that literary change is the result of the autonomous evolution of literary devices.

A more traditional concept of the content/form distinction might lead one to conclude that literature changes when the world changes because literature merely gives form to ideas and realities that lie outside the literary realm and constitute its cause or motivation. But for the Formalists, literary devices owe no debt to such motivations; they evolve autonomously of them and are motivated entirely by literary origins. For literature to be literature, it must constantly defamiliarize the familiar, constantly evolve new procedures for story-telling or poetry-making. And such change is entirely autonomous of the social and historical world from which the materials of literature are taken. Cervantes' satiric novel *Don Quixote*, for example, makes fun of the popular romantic novels about knights and quests which constituted the dominant form of story-telling in his day. It emerged not because of changes in the world or in Cervantes' life but rather as a result of a specifically literary evolution. The new device of the problematic hero was made possible and necessary by the development of the novel form itself.

You will find a major Russian Formalist, Roman Jakobson, placed under Structuralism in this anthology because there is a strong historical as well as methodological link between the two intellectual movements. Many of the original Formalists were linguists, with Jakobson being the most influential. He left Russia in 1920 and traveled to Czechoslovakia, where he was part of the linguistic circles that inspired French Structuralism in the 1940s and 1950s. The Structuralists, whose work was particularly influential in France through the 1960s, share a methodological interest with Formalist linguistics in that they saw culture in general as constituted by the same rules of operation that one finds in language. Although the Russian Formalists were suppressed by the Stalinist government in Russia in the 1920s, news of their work was borne West by East European émigrés such as René Wellek, Julia Kristeva, and Tzvetan Todorov, where it helped shape French Structuralism as well as such literary critical schools as poetics, stylistics, and narratology.

The impulse towards formal analysis was not limited in Russia to the group of thinkers usually clustered under the rubric Russian Formalists. Vladimir Propp was a scholar of folktales who wrote at the same time as the Formalists and who analyzed the component features of folktale narratives. A wide range of tales could be shown to share the same sequence of narrative motifs, from "the hero leaves home" to "the hero receives a magic token" to "the hero is tested in battle." The work of Mikhail Bakhtin, while it is historically at odds with the Formalists in its emphasis on the social and ideological features of literature, shares their concern with describing those formal elements that make a literary genre such as the novel distinct from other literary forms. His work also represents an expansion of the original Formalist undertaking to include not only genres but also extra-literary uses of language such as that of the carnival, which Bakhtin saw influencing the work of certain writers such as François Rabelais.

While the Russian Formalist movement was scientific and rational, the other major formalist school – American New Criticism – was anti-scientific and interested in the non-rational dimension of art. Both critical movements nevertheless shared an interest in what it is about literary language that makes it different from the ordinary use of language, and both considered the proper object of literary study to be literary texts and how they worked rather than authors' lives or the social and historical worlds to which literature refers. Two well-known terms that are part of a New Critical legacy – the intentional fallacy and the affective fallacy – name this act of delimiting the object of literary study and separating it from biography or sociology. According to the intentional fallacy, meaning resides in the verbal design of a literary work, not in statements regarding his or her intention that the author might make. According to the affective fallacy, the subjective effects or emotional reactions a work provokes in readers are irrelevant to the study of the verbal object itself, since its objective structure alone contains the meaning of the work.

While the Russian Formalists were concerned with elucidating the modes of operation of entire genres such as the novel, the New Critics concentrated their energies on
individual literary works, especially poems. "Close reading" is the term most often used to
describe their method. The purpose of such close reading was not, however, the analysis
of literary devices or motifs considered as an end in itself. It was instead the elucidation
of the way literature embodies or concretely enacts universal truth, what the New Critics
called "concrete universals."

Poetry, they argued, differs from ordinary practical speech, which uses language
denotatively (one word for one thing), in that poetry uses language connotatively or in a
way that evokes secondary meanings. Such language use allows poetry to be both concrete and specific as well as universal and general. An urn can be both an ordinary object
and a metaphor for the eternal durability of art. Poetic language thus reconciles the
ordinarily opposed elements of the concrete and the universal, the specific word and
general meaning, body and spirit. Such reconciliation is possible in connotative poetic
tropes such as paradox, irony, and metaphor, tropes which either join ordinary objects
to universal meanings (metaphor, symbol) or reconcile seemingly opposed elements
(irony, paradox). Cleanth Brooks, for example, notices in a famous close reading that
Keats's poem "Ode on a Grecian Urn" is full of paradoxes such as "Cold pastoral" and
"unheard melodies" which imply both life and death at once, the paradoxical cohabitation
of what is vivid and moving with what is frozen and still. This is so, Brooks argues,
because the poem is about how art, figured in the urn, is more vivid than life itself, even
though it seems lifeless. Although dead, it possesses eternal life.

The practical denotative language of science cannot name such truth because such
language is limited to the naming of positive empirical facts that can be grasped by the
senses. The realm of universal meaning, however, is beyond sensory experience and
cannot be analyzed using scientific methods. It can only be alluded to indirectly in poetic
language and cannot be paraphrased in literal, denotative speech. For the American New
Critics, therefore, the description of literary devices such as metaphor, irony, and paradox was inseparable from a theory of universal meaning that was a polemical response to
modern positivist science. While the Russian Formalists sought a value-free mode of
critical description, one that would scientifically specify what it is about literature that is
literary, the New Critics informed the study of literature with a concern for traditional
religious and aesthetic values of a kind being displaced by science, in this case, the values
of Christian theology and idealist aesthetics (that is, an aesthetics rooted in the idea that
universal truth is available through art of a kind that is not determined by material social
and historical circumstances). Those values have receded in importance with time, and
the legacy of the New Criticism that has remained most abiding is the concern with the
close reading of texts and with the analysis of the operation of literary language in all its
complexity.

Formalism has become a standard approach to literature as well as to other cultural
artifacts such as film and television. The specific kinds of form and procedure vary
across media. Film formal analysis is concerned with the way images are constructed
through set design, art direction, camera work, framing, composition, and the like.
Because the production schedule usually is more compressed, television is inclined to be
more constructed around narrative, character, and story than image aesthetics, although
the pervasive presence of cinematographers and directors trained in film schools in
television production means that television narratives are seldom lacking in compositional complexity. Story-telling has become more of an issue in television as well because

of the emergence of long-form narratives such as *True Detective* and *Forbrydelsen* (aka *The Killing*) in which a single story line is pursued through multiple episodes. *True Detective* especially invites attention to story construction because of the use of a double narrative that operates as testimony and flashback to connect the present to the past. The dual narrative structure is appropriate to a story about both personal and professional redemption and self-remaking. It is, as Sean O'Sullivan in his essay below would say, "broken on purpose." *Forbrydelsen* (the Danish original of the US show *The Killing*) operates more as what television narrative theorist Jeff Rush would call a spiral that loops back on itself as it moves forward, recapitulating some of the same conflicts as it moves progressively closer to its goal of solution and revelation. Each serial honors the conventions of the detective story. A somewhat monomaniacal detective sacrifices personal relations and opposes obstructive institutions as he or she tenaciously pursues a goal only he or she has the vision to see. The device of institutional obstruction is common to each, and often, the narrative tension is more provoked by the conflict with dim-witted superiors than by the interaction with suspects. While the formal dimension of both shows is weighted towards narrative issues such as obstruction, deflection, frustration, and delay, the visual style of each is characterized by highly thematic and often quite melodramatic shot selection and combination conjoined with a sound design that emphatically evokes emotional distress, empathy, and concern. *True Detective*, which dwells on the role of the cultural environment in crime, often relies on long shots that emphasize the size of the environment in comparison with the detectives. In one of the key moments in the first episode of *Forbrydelsen*, the camera stays on the detective, Sarah Lund, as she rotates her head, thinking about what might have happened at the crime scene. Her colleagues have told her there is no use in continuing the search; they should give up and go home, but Lund lingers, thinking, looking around. The sound accompaniment is strongly pronounced, and it evokes the process of thoughtful reflection in its slow cadence and rising and falling notes. When her rotation finally stops, there is a cut to what she sees: people coming down a road with bicycles and fishing poles. No one amongst the many police searching, she realizes, has thought to search in that direction, and it is there they find a canal containing a car and a body. The narrative is set in motion by a piece of visual story-telling that emphasizes her singularity of vision and its contrast (and conflict) with the hurried irresponsibility of her police comrades and superiors.

CHAPTER 2

Art as Technique

Viktor Shklovsky

One of the founders of the Formalist study group in Petrograd in the early twentieth century, Shklovsky was also one of its most innovative thinkers. In seeking to move literary study out of the realm of religion and into that of science, Shklovsky and his colleagues argued against the Symbolists who conceived of poetry in spiritualist terms. In continuing the effort to exactly delineate the "literary" quality of those devices and techniques that separates them from ordinary prose, Shklovsky argues in this essay (1916) that such devices impede normal perceptions. This essay demonstrates the similarity between the formal scholarly undertaking and the innovations in poetry that were occurring at the same time in Europe, such as Dada. Concerned with writing that would be brutally honest and shockingly new, these writers rejected traditional culture and traditional artistic forms that had for them become both boring and overly conventional. Shklovsky, thinking along similar lines, saw all poetry as producing a shock effect that disrupted habitual ways of seeing and thinking.

If we start to examine the general laws of perception, we see that as perception becomes habitual, it becomes automatic. Thus, for example, all of our habits retreat into the area of the unconsciously automatic; if one remembers the sensations of holding a pen or of speaking in a foreign language for the first time and compares that with his feeling at performing the action for the ten thousandth time, he will agree with us. Such habituation explains the principles by which, in ordinary speech, we leave phrases unfinished and words half expressed. In this process, ideally realized in algebra, things are replaced by symbols. Complete words are not expressed in rapid speech; their initial sounds are barely perceived. Alexander Pogodin offers the example of a boy considering the sentence "The Swiss mountains are beautiful" in the form of a series of letters: *T, S, m, a, b.*[1]

This characteristic of thought not only suggests the method of algebra, but even prompts the choice of symbols (letters, especially initial letters). By this "algebraic" method of thought we apprehend objects only as shapes with imprecise extensions; we do not see them in their entirety but rather recognize them by their main characteristics.

Original publication details: Viktor Shklovsky, "Art as Technique" from *Russian Formalist Criticism: Four Essays*, trans. Lee T. Lemon and Marion J. Reis, pp. 11–16. University of Nebraska Press, 1965. Reproduced with permission from the University of Nebraska Press.

Literary Theory: An Anthology, Third Edition. Edited by Julie Rivkin and Michael Ryan.
© 2017 John Wiley & Sons, Ltd. Published 2017 by John Wiley & Sons, Ltd.

We see the object as though it were enveloped in a sack. We know what it is by its configuration, but we see only its silhouette. The object, perceived thus in the manner of prose perception, fades and does not leave even a first impression; ultimately even the essence of what it was is forgotten. Such perception explains why we fail to hear the prose word in its entirety (see Leo Jakubinsky's article[2]) and, hence, why (along with other slips of the tongue) we fail to pronounce it. The process of "algebrization," the over-automatization of an object, permits the greatest economy of perceptive effort. Either objects are assigned only one proper feature – a number, for example – or else they function as though by formula and do not even appear in cognition:

> I was cleaning and, meandering about, approached the divan and couldn't remember whether or not I had dusted it. Since these movements are habitual and unconscious I could not remember and felt that it was impossible to remember – so that if I had dusted it and forgot – that is, had acted unconsciously, then it was the same as if I had not. If some conscious person had been watching, then the fact could be established. If, however, no one was looking, or looking on unconsciously, if the whole complex lives of many people go on unconsciously, then such lives are as if they had never been.[3]

And so life is reckoned as nothing. Habitualization devours work, clothes, furniture, one's wife, and the fear of war. "If the whole complex lives of many people go on unconsciously, then such lives are as if they had never been." And art exists that one may recover the sensation of life; it exists to make one feel things, to make the stone *stony*. The purpose of art is to impart the sensation of things as they are perceived and not as they are known. The technique of art is to make objects "unfamiliar," to make forms difficult, to increase the difficulty and length of perception because the process of perception is an aesthetic end in itself and must be prolonged. *Art is a way of experiencing the artfulness of an object: the object is not important …*

After we see an object several times, we begin to recognize it. The object is in front of us and we know about it, but we do not see it[4] – hence we cannot say anything significant about it. Art removes objects from the automatism of perception in several ways. Here I want to illustrate a way used repeatedly by Leo Tolstoy, that writer who, for Merezhkovsky at least, seems to present things as if he himself saw them, saw them in their entirety, and did not alter them.

Tolstoy makes the familiar seem strange by not naming the familiar object. He describes an object as if he were seeing it for the first time, an event as if it were happening for the first time. In describing something he avoids the accepted names of its parts and instead names corresponding parts of other objects. For example, in "Shame" Tolstoy "defamiliarizes" the idea of flogging in this way: "to strip people who have broken the law, to hurl them to the floor, and to rap on their bottoms with switches," and, after a few lines, "to lash about on the naked buttocks." Then he remarks:

> Just why precisely this stupid, savage means of causing pain and not any other – why not prick the shoulders or any part of the body with needles, squeeze the hands or the feet in a vise, or anything like that?

I apologize for this harsh example, but it is typical of Tolstoy's way of pricking the conscience. The familiar act of flogging is made unfamiliar both by the description and by the proposal to change its form without changing its nature. Tolstoy uses this technique of "defamiliarization" constantly. The narrator of "Kholstomer," for example, is a horse, and it is the horse's point of view (rather than a person's) that makes the content of the story seem unfamiliar. Here is how the horse regards the institution of private property:

> I understood well what they said about whipping and Christianity. But then I was absolutely in the dark. What's the meaning of "his own," "his colt"? From these phrases I saw that people thought there was some sort of connection between me and the stable. At the time I simply could not understand the connection. Only much later, when they separated me from the other horses, did I begin to understand. But even then I simply could not see what it meant when they called me "man's property." The words "my horse" referred to me, a living horse, and seemed as strange to me as the words "my land," "my air," "my water."
>
> But the words made a strong impression on me. I thought about them constantly, and only after the most diverse experiences with people did I understand, finally, what they meant. They meant this: In life people are guided by words, not by deeds. It's not so much that they love the possibility of doing or not doing something as it is the possibility of speaking with words, agreed on among themselves, about various topics. Such are the words "my" and "mine," which they apply to different things, creatures, objects, and even to land, people, and horses. They agree that only one may say "mine" about this, that or the other thing. And the one who says "mine" about the greatest number of things is, according to the game which they've agreed to among themselves, the one they consider the most happy. I don't know the point of all this, but it's true. For a long time I tried to explain it to myself in terms of some kind of real gain, but I had to reject that explanation because it was wrong.
>
> Many of those, for instance, who called me their own never rode on me – although others did. And so with those who fed me. Then again, the coachman, the veterinarians, and the outsiders in general treated me kindly, yet those who called me their own did not. In due time, having widened the scope of my observations, I satisfied myself that the notion "my," not only has relation to us horses, has no other basis than a narrow human instinct which is called a sense of or right to private property. A man says "this house is mine" and never lives in it; he only worries about its construction and upkeep. A merchant says "my shop," or "my dry goods shop," for instance, and does not even wear clothes made from the better cloth he keeps in his own shop.
>
> There are people who call a tract of land their own, but they never set eyes on it and never take a stroll on it. There are people who call others their own, yet never see them. And the whole relationship between them is that the so-called "owners" treat the others unjustly.
>
> There are people who call women their own, or their "wives," but their women live with other men. And people strive not for the good in life, but for goods they can call their own.
>
> I am now convinced that this is the essential difference between people and ourselves. And therefore, not even considering the other ways in which we are superior, but considering just this one virtue, we can bravely claim to stand higher than men on the ladder of living creatures. The actions of men, at least those with whom I have had dealings, are guided by *words* – ours by deeds.

The horse is killed before the end of the story, but the manner of the narrative, its technique, does not change:

> Much later they put Serpukhovsky's body, which had experienced the world, which had eaten and drunk, into the ground. They could profitably send neither his hide, nor his flesh, nor his bones anywhere.
>
> But since his dead body, which had gone about in the world for twenty years, was a great burden to everyone, its burial was only a superfluous embarrassment for the people. For a long time no one had needed him; for a long time he had been a burden on all. But nevertheless, the dead who buried the dead found it necessary to dress this bloated body, which

immediately began to rot, in a good uniform and good boots; to lay it in a good new coffin with new tassels at the four corners, then to place this new coffin in another of lead and ship it to Moscow; there to exhume ancient bones and at just that spot, to hide this putrefying body, swarming with maggots, in its new uniform and clean boots, and to cover it over completely with dirt.

Thus we see that at the end of the story Tolstoy continues to use the technique even though the motivation for it (the reason for its use) is gone.

In *War and Peace* Tolstoy uses the same technique in describing whole battles as if battles were something new. These descriptions are too long to quote; it would be necessary to extract a considerable part of the four-volume novel. But Tolstoy uses the same method in describing the drawing room and the theater:

The middle of the stage consisted of flat boards; by the sides stood painted pictures representing trees, and at the back a linen cloth was stretched down to the floor boards. Maidens in red bodices and white skirts sat on the middle of the stage. One, very fat, in a white silk dress, sat apart on a narrow bench to which a green pasteboard box was glued from behind. They were all singing something. When they had finished, the maiden in white approached the prompter's box. A man in silk with tight-fitting pants on his fat legs approached her with a plume and began to sing and spread his arms in dismay. The man in the tight pants finished his song alone; then the girl sang. After that both remained silent as the music resounded; and the man, obviously waiting to begin singing his part with her again, began to run his fingers over the hand of the girl in the white dress. They finished their song together, and everyone in the theater began to clap and shout. But the men and women on stage, who represented lovers, started to bow, smiling and raising their hands.

In the second act were pictures representing monuments and openings in the linen cloth representing the moonlight, and they raised lamp shades on a frame. As the musicians started to play the bass horn and counter-bass, a large number of people in black mantels poured onto the stage from right and left. The people, with something like daggers in their hands, started to wave their arms. Then still more people came running out and began to drag away the maiden who had been wearing a white dress but who now wore one of sky blue. They did not drag her off immediately, but sang with her for a long time before dragging her away. Three times they struck on something metallic behind the side scenes, and everyone got down on his knees and began to chant a prayer. Several times all of this activity was interrupted by enthusiastic shouts from the spectators...

Anyone who knows Tolstoy can find several hundred such passages in his work. His method of seeing things out of their normal context is also apparent in his last works. Tolstoy described the dogmas and rituals he attacked as if they were unfamiliar, substituting everyday meanings for the customarily religious meanings of the words common in church ritual. Many persons were painfully wounded; they considered it blasphemy to present as strange and monstrous what they accepted as sacred. Their reaction was due chiefly to the technique through which Tolstoy perceived and reported his environment. And after turning to what he had long avoided, Tolstoy found that his perceptions had unsettled his faith.

The technique of defamiliarization is not Tolstoy's alone. I cited Tolstoy because his work is generally known.

Now, having explained the nature of this technique, let us try to determine the approximate limits of its application. I personally feel that defamiliarization is found almost everywhere form is found ... An image is not a permanent referent for those mutable complexities of life which are revealed through it, its purpose is not to make us perceive meaning, but to create a special perception of the object – *it creates a vision of the object instead of serving as a means for knowing it ...*

Such constructions as "the pestle and the mortar," or "Old Nick and the infernal regions" (*Decameron*) are also examples of the technique of defamiliarization. And in my article on plot construction I write about defamiliarization in psychological parallelism. Here, then, I repeat that the perception of disharmony in a harmonious context is important in parallelism. The purpose of parallelism, like the general purpose of imagery, is to transfer the usual perception of an object into the sphere of new perception – that is, to make a unique semantic modification.

In studying poetic speech in its phonetic and lexical structure as well as in its characteristic distribution of words and in the characteristic thought structures compounded from the words, we find everywhere the artistic trademark – that is, we find material obviously created to remove the automatism of perception; the author's purpose is to create the vision which results from that deautomatized perception. A work is created "artistically" so that its perception is impeded and the greatest possible effect is produced through the slowness of the perception. As a result of this lingering, the object is perceived not in its extension in space, but, so to speak, in its continuity. Thus "poetic language" gives satisfaction. According to Aristotle, poetic language must appear strange and wonderful; and, in fact, it is often actually foreign: the Sumerian used by the Assyrians, the Latin of Europe during the Middle Ages, the Arabisms of the Persians, the Old Bulgarian of Russian literature, or the elevated, almost literary language of folk songs. The common archaisms of poetic language, the intricacy of the sweet new style [*dolce stil nuovo*],[5] the obscure style of the language of Arnaut Daniel with the "roughened" [*harte*] forms *which make pronunciation difficult* – these are used in much the same way. Leo Jakubinsky has demonstrated the principle of phonetic "roughening" of poetic language in the particular case of the repetition of identical sounds. The language of poetry is, then, a difficult, roughened, impeded language. In a few special instances the language of poetry approximates the language of prose, but this does not violate the principle of "roughened" form.

> Her sister was called Tatyana
> For the first time we shall
> Willfully brighten the delicate
> Pages of a novel with such a name

wrote Pushkin. The usual poetic language for Pushkin's contemporaries was the elegant style of Derzhavin; but Pushkin's style, because it seemed trivial then, was unexpectedly difficult for them. We should remember the consternation of Pushkin's contemporaries over the vulgarity of his expressions. He used the popular language as a special device for prolonging attention, just as his contemporaries generally used Russian words in their usually French speech (see Tolstoy's examples in *War and Peace*).

Just now a still more characteristic phenomenon is under way. Russian literary language, which was originally foreign to Russia, has so permeated the language of the people that it has blended with their conversation. On the other hand, literature has now begun to show a tendency towards the use of dialects (Remizov, Klyuyev, Essenin, and others,[6] so unequal in talent and so alike in language, are intentionally provincial) and/or barbarisms (which gave rise to the Severyanin group[7]). And currently Maxim Gorky is changing his diction from the old literary language to the new literary colloquialism of Leskov.[8] Ordinary speech and literary language have thereby changed places (see the work of Vyacheslav Ivanov and many others). And finally, a strong tendency, led by Khlebnikov, to create a new and properly poetic language has emerged. In the light of these developments we can define poetry as *attenuated, tortuous* speech. Poetic speech is *formed speech*. Prose is ordinary speech – economical, easy, proper, the goddess of prose [*dea prosae*] is a goddess of the accurate, facile type, of the "direct" expression of a child. I shall discuss roughened form and retardation as the general *law* of art at greater length in an article on plot construction.[9]

Nevertheless, the position of those who urge the idea of the economy of artistic energy as something which exists in and even distinguishes poetic language seems, at first glance, tenable for the problem rhythm. Spencer's description of rhythm would seem to be absolutely incontestable:

> Just as the body in receiving a series of varying concussions, must keep the muscles ready to meet the most violent of them, as not knowing when such may come: so, the mind in receiving unarranged articulations, must keep its perspectives active enough to recognize the least easily caught sounds. And as, if the concussions recur in definite order, the body may husband its forces by adjusting the resistance needful for each concussion; so, if the syllables be rhythmically arranged, the mind may economize its energies by anticipating the attention required for each syllable.[10]

This apparent observation suffers from the common fallacy, the confusion of the laws of poetic and prosaic language. In *The Philosophy of Style* Spencer failed utterly to distinguish between them. But rhythm may have two functions. The rhythm of prose, or a work song like "Dubinushka," permits the members of the work crew to do their necessary "groaning together" and also eases the work by making it automatic. And, in fact, it is easier to march with music than without it, and to march during an animated conversation is even easier, for the walking is done unconsciously. Thus the rhythm of prose is an important automatizing element; the rhythm of poetry is not. There is "order" in art, yet not a single column of a Greek temple stands exactly in its proper order; poetic rhythm is similarly disordered rhythm. Attempts to systematize the irregularities have been made, and such attempts are part of the current problem in the theory of rhythm. It is obvious that the systematization will not work, for in reality the problem is not one of complicating the rhythm but of disordering the rhythm – a disordering which cannot be predicted. Should the disordering of rhythm become a convention, it would be ineffective as a procedure for the roughening of language. But I will not discuss rhythm in more detail since I intend to write a book about it.

Notes

1   Alexander Pogodin, *Yazyk, kak tvorchestvo* [*Language as Art*] (Kharkov, 1913), p. 42. [The original sentence was in French, "*Les montagnes de la Suisse sont belles,*" with the appropriate initials.]
2   Leo Jakubinsky, *Sborniki*, I (1916).
3   Leo Tolstoy's *Diary*, entry dated February 29, 1897. [The date is transcribed incorrectly; it should read March 1, 1897.]
4   Viktor Shklovsky, *Voskresheniye slova* [*The Resurrection of the Word*] (Petersburg, 1914).
5   Dante, *Purgatorio*, 24:56. Dante refers to the new lyric style of his contemporaries. [Trans.]
6   Alexy Remizov (1877–1957) is best known as a novelist and satirist; Nicholas Klyuyev (1885–1937) and Sergey Essenin (1895–1925) were "peasant poets." All three were noted for their faithful reproduction of Russian dialects and colloquial language. [Trans.]

7   A group noted for its opulent and sensuous verse style. [Trans.]
8   Nicholas Leskov (1831–95), novelist and short story writer, helped popularize the *skaz*, or yarn, and hence, because of the part dialect peculiarities play in the *skaz*, also altered Russian literary language. [Trans.]
9   Shklovsky is probably referring to his *Razvyortyvaniye syuzheta* [*Plot Development*] (Petrograd, 1921). [Trans.]
10   Herbert Spencer, *The Philosophy of Style* [(Humboldt Library, vol. XXXIV; New York, 1882), p. 169. The Russian text is slightly shortened from the original].

CHAPTER 3

The Formalist Critics

Cleanth Brooks

Published (1951) in *The Raritan Review*, this polemic in favor of the New Criticism was written by one of the major practitioners and promoters of the new approach to literature – Cleanth Brooks. Brooks had studied in Cambridge with I. A. Richards, who first laid the foundation for the New Criticism in his *Principles of Literary Criticism* (1924). Upon his return to the United States, Brooks began writing a series of books, from *An Approach to Literature* (1936) to *The Well-Wrought Urn: Studies in the Structure of Poetry* (1947), that helped establish "close reading" as the dominant form of literary study in the American academy from the 1940s through the late 1960s.

Here are some articles of faith I could subscribe to:

That literary criticism is a description and an evaluation of its object.

That the primary concern of criticism is with the problem of unity – the kind of whole which the literary work forms or fails to form, and the relation of the various parts to each other in building up this whole.

That the formal relations in a work of literature may include, but certainly exceed, those of logic.

That in a successful work, form and content cannot be separated.

That form is meaning.

That literature is ultimately metaphorical and symbolic.

That the general and the universal are not seized upon by abstraction, but got at through the concrete and the particular.

That literature is not a surrogate for religion.

That, as Allen Tate says, "specific moral problems" are the subject matter of literature, but that the purpose of literature is not to point a moral.

That the principles of criticism define the area relevant to literary criticism; they do not constitute a method for carrying out the criticism.

Original publication details: Cleanth Brooks, "The Formalist Critics" from *The Kenyon Review* OS XIII.1 (Winter 1951). Reproduced with permission from *The Kenyon Review*.

Such statements as these would not, however, even though greatly elaborated, serve any useful purpose here. The interested reader already knows the general nature of the critical position adumbrated – or, if he does not, he can find it set forth in writings of mine or of other critics of like sympathy. Moreover, a condensed restatement of the position here would probably beget as many misunderstandings as have past attempts to set it forth. It seems much more profitable to use the present occasion for dealing with some persistent misunderstandings and objections.

In the first place, to make the poem or the novel the central concern of criticism has appeared to mean cutting it loose from its author and from his life as a man, with his own particular hopes, fears, interests, conflicts, etc. A criticism so limited may seem bloodless and hollow. It will seem so to the typical professor of literature in the graduate school, where the study of literature is still primarily a study of the ideas and personality of the author as revealed in his letters, his diaries, and the recorded conversations of his friends. It will certainly seem so to literary gossip columnists who purvey literary chitchat. It may also seem so to the young poet or novelist, beset with his own problems of composition and with his struggles to find a subject and a style and to get a hearing for himself.

In the second place, to emphasize the work seems to involve severing it from those who actually read it, and this severance may seem drastic and therefore disastrous. After all, literature is written to be read. Wordsworth's poet was a man speaking to men. In each *Sunday Times*, Mr J. Donald Adams points out that the hungry sheep look up and are not fed; and less strenuous moralists than Mr Adams are bound to feel a proper revulsion against "mere aestheticism." Moreover, if we neglect the audience which reads the work, including that for which it was presumably written, the literary historian is prompt to point out that the kind of audience that Pope had did condition the kind of poetry that he wrote. The poem has its roots in history, past or present. Its place in the historical context simply cannot be ignored.

I have stated these objections as sharply as I can because I am sympathetic with the state of mind which is prone to voice them. Man's experience is indeed a seamless garment, no part of which can be separated from the rest. Yet if we urge this fact, of inseparability against the drawing of distinctions, then there is no point in talking about criticism at all. I am assuming that distinctions are necessary and useful and indeed inevitable.

The formalist critic knows as well as anyone that poems and plays and novels are written by men – that they do not somehow happen – and that they are written as expressions of particular personalities and are written from all sorts of motives – for money, from a desire to express oneself, for the sake of a cause, etc. Moreover, the formalist critic knows as well as anyone that literary works are mere potential until they are read – that is, that they are recreated in the minds of actual readers, who vary enormously in their capabilities, their interests, their prejudices, their ideas. But the formalist critic is concerned primarily with the work itself. Speculation on the mental processes of the author takes the critic away from the work into biography and psychology. There is no reason, of course, why he should not turn away into biography and psychology. Such explorations are very much worth making. But they should not be confused with an account of the work. Such studies describe the process of composition, not the structure of the thing composed, and they may be performed quite as validly for the poor work as for the good one. They may be validly performed for any kind of expression – nonliterary as well as literary.

On the other hand, exploration of the various readings which the work has received also takes the critic away from the work into psychology and the history of taste. The various imports of a given work may well be worth studying. I. A. Richards has put us all in his debt by demonstrating what different experiences may be derived from the same poem by an apparently homogeneous group of readers; and the scholars have pointed out, all along, how different Shakespeare appeared to an eighteenth-century as compared with a nineteenth-century audience; or how sharply divergent are the estimates of John Donne's lyrics from historical period to historical period. But such work, valuable and necessary as it may be, is to be distinguished from a criticism of the work itself. The formalist critic, because he wants to criticize the work itself, makes two assumptions: (1) he assumes that the relevant part of the author's intention is what he got actually into his work; that is, he assumes that the author's intention as realized is the "intention" that counts, not necessarily what he was conscious of trying to do, or what he now remembers he was then trying to do. And (2) the formalist critic assumes an ideal reader: that is, instead of focusing on the varying spectrum of possible readings, he attempts to find a central point of reference from which he can focus upon the structure of the poem or novel.

But there *is* no ideal reader, someone is prompt to point out, and he will probably add that it is sheer arrogance that allows the critic, with his own blindsides and prejudice, to put himself in the position of that ideal reader. There is no ideal reader, of course, and I suppose that the practicing critic can never be too often reminded of the gap between his reading and the "true" reading of the poem. But for the purpose of focusing upon the poem rather than upon his own reactions, it is a defensible strategy. Finally, of course, it is the strategy that all critics of whatever persuasion are forced to adopt. (The alternatives are desperate: either we say that one person's reading is as good as another's and equate those readings on a basis of absolute equality and thus deny the possibility of any standard reading. Or else we take a lowest common denominator of the various readings that have been made; that is, we frankly move from literary criticism into socio-psychology. To propose taking a consensus of the opinions of "qualified" readers is simply to split the ideal reader into a group of ideal readers.) As consequences of the distinction just referred to, the formalist critic rejects two popular tests for literary value. The first proves the value of the work from the author's "sincerity" (or the intensity of the author's feelings as he composed it). If we heard that Mr Guest testified that he put his heart and soul into his poems, we would not be very much impressed, though I should see no reason to doubt such a statement from Mr Guest. It would simply be critically irrelevant. Ernest Hemingway's statement in a recent issue of *Time* magazine that he counts his last novel his best is of interest for Hemingway's biography, but most readers of *Across the River and Into the Trees* would agree that it proves nothing at all about the value of the novel – that in this case the judgment is simply pathetically inept. We discount also such tests for poetry as that proposed by A. E. Housman – the bristling of his beard at the reading of a good poem. The intensity of his reaction has critical significance only in proportion as we have already learned to trust him as a reader. Even so, what it tells us is something about Housman – nothing decisive about the poem.

It is unfortunate if this playing down of such responses seems to deny humanity to either writer or reader. The critic may enjoy certain works very much and may be indeed intensely moved by them. I am, and I have no embarrassment in admitting the fact; but a detailed description of my emotional state on reading certain works has little to do with indicating to an interested reader what the work is and how the parts of it are related.

Should all criticism, then, be self-effacing and analytic? I hope that the answer is implicit in what I have already written, but I shall go on to spell it out. Of course not. That will depend upon the occasion and the audience. In practice, the critic's job is rarely a purely critical one. He is much more likely to be involved in dozens of more or less related tasks, some of them trivial, some of them important. He may be trying to get a hearing for a new author, or to get the attention of the freshman sitting in the back row. He may be comparing two authors, or editing a text; writing a brief newspaper review or reading a paper before the Modern Language Association. He may even be simply talking with a friend, talking about literature for the hell of it. Parable, anecdote, epigram, metaphor – these and a hundred other devices may be thoroughly legitimate for his varying purposes. He is certainly not to be asked to suppress his personal enthusiasms or his interest in social history or in politics. Least of all is he being asked to *present* his criticisms as the close reading of a text. Tact, common sense, and uncommon sense if he has it, are all requisite if the practicing critic is to do his various jobs well.

But it will do the critic no harm to have a clear idea of what his specific job as a critic is. I can sympathize with writers who are tired of reading rather drab "critical analyses," and who recommend brighter, more amateur, and more "human" criticism. As ideals, these are excellent; as recipes for improving criticism, I have my doubts. Appropriate vulgarizations of these ideals are already flourishing, and have long flourished – in the class room presided over by the college lecturer of infectious enthusiasm, in the gossipy Book-of-the-Month Club bulletins, and in the columns of the *Saturday Review of Literature*.

I have assigned the critic a modest, though I think an important, role. With reference to the help which the critic can give to the practicing artist, the role is even more modest. As critic, he can give only negative help. Literature is not written by formula: he can have no formula to offer. Perhaps he can do little more than indicate whether in his opinion the work has succeeded or failed. Healthy criticism and healthy creation do tend to go hand in hand. Everything else being equal, the creative artist is better off for being in touch with a vigorous criticism. But the other considerations are never equal, the case is always special, and in a given case the proper advice could be: quit reading criticism altogether, or read political science or history or philosophy – or join the army, or join the church.

There is certainly no doubt that the kind of specific and positive help that someone like Ezra Pound was able to give to several writers of our time is in one sense the most important kind of criticism that there can be. I think that it is not unrelated to the kind of criticism that I have described: there is the same intense concern with the text which is being built up, the same concern with "technical problems." But many other things are involved – matters which lie outside the specific ambit of criticism altogether; among them a knowledge of the personality of the particular writer, the ability to stimulate, to make positive suggestions.

A literary work is a document and as a document can be analyzed in terms of the forces that have produced it, or it may be manipulated as a force in its own right. It mirrors the past, it may influence the future. These facts it would be futile to deny, and I know of no critic who does deny them. But the reduction of a work of literature to its causes does not constitute literary criticism; nor does an estimate of its effects. Good literature is more than effective rhetoric applied to true ideas – even if we could agree upon a philosophical yardstick for measuring the truth of ideas and even if we could find some way that transcended nose-counting for determining the effective-ness of the rhetoric.

A recent essay by Lionel Trilling bears very emphatically upon this point. (I refer to him the more readily because Trilling has registered some of his objections to the critical position that I maintain.) In the essay entitled "The Meaning of a Literary Idea," Trilling discusses the debt to Freud and Spengler of four American writers, O'Neill, Dos Passos, Wolfe, and Faulkner. Very justly, as it seems to me, he chooses Faulkner as the contemporary writer who, along with Ernest Hemingway, best illustrates the power and importance of ideas in literature. Trilling is thoroughly aware that his choice will seem shocking and perhaps perverse, "because," as he writes, "Hemingway and Faulkner have insisted on their indifference to the conscious intellectual tradition of our time and have acquired the reputation of achieving their effects by means that have the least possible connection with any sort of intellectuality or even with intelligence."

Here Trilling shows not only acute discernment but an admirable honesty in electing to deal with the hard cases – with the writers who do not clearly and easily make the case for the importance of ideas. I applaud the discernment and the honesty, but I wonder whether the whole discussion in his essay does not indicate that Trilling is really much closer to the so-called "new critics" than perhaps he is aware. For Trilling, one notices, rejects any simple one-to-one relation between the truth of the idea and the value of the literary work in which it is embodied. Moreover, he does not claim that "recognizable ideas of a force or weight are 'used' in the work," or "new ideas of a certain force and weight are 'produced' by the work." He praises rather the fact that we feel that Hemingway and Faulkner are "intensely at work upon the recalcitrant stuff of life." The last point is made the matter of real importance. Whereas Dos Passos, O'Neill, and Wolfe make us "feel that they feel that they have said the last word," "we seldom have the sense that [Hemingway and Faulkner] … have misrepresented to themselves the nature and the difficulty of the matter they work on."

Trilling has chosen to state the situation in terms of the writer's activity (Faulkner is intensely at work, etc.). But this judgment is plainly an inference from the quality of Faulkner's novels – Trilling has not simply heard Faulkner say that he has had to struggle with his work. (I take it Mr Hemingway's declaration about the effort he put into the last novel impresses Trilling as little as it impresses the rest of us.)

Suppose, then, that we tried to state Mr Trilling's point, not in terms of the effort of the artist, but in terms of the structure of the work itself. Should we not get something very like the terms used by the formalist critics? A description in terms of "tensions," of symbolic development, of ironies and their resolution? In short, is not the formalist critic trying to describe in terms of the dynamic form of the work itself how the recalcitrancy of the material is acknowledged and dealt with?

Trilling's definition of "ideas" makes it still easier to accommodate my position to his. I have already quoted a passage in which he repudiates the notion that one has to show how recognizable ideas are "used" in the work, or new ideas are "produced" by the work. He goes on to write: "All that we need to do is account for a certain aesthetic effect as being in some important part achieved by a mental process which is not different from the process by which discursive ideas are conceived, and which is to be judged by some of the criteria by which an idea is judged." One would have to look far to find a critic "formal" enough to object to this. What some of us have been at pains to insist upon is that literature does not simply "exemplify" ideas or "produce" ideas – as Trilling acknowledges. But no one claims that the writer is an inspired idiot. He uses his mind and his reader ought to use his, in processes "not different from the process by which discursive ideas are conceived." Literature is not inimical to ideas. It thrives upon ideas but it does not present ideas patly and neatly. It involves them with the "recalcitrant stuff of life." The literary critic's job is to deal with that involvement.

The mention of Faulkner invites a closing comment upon the critic's specific job. As I have described it, it may seem so modest that one could take its performance for granted. But consider the misreadings of Faulkner now current, some of them the work of the most brilliant critics that we have, some of them quite wrong-headed, and demonstrably so. What is true of Faulkner is only less true of many another author, including many writers of the past. Literature has many "uses" – and critics propose new uses, some of them exciting and spectacular. But all the multiform uses to which literature can be put rest finally upon our knowing what a given work "means." That knowledge is basic.

CHAPTER 4

Keats' Sylvan Historian:
History Without the Footnotes*

Cleanth Brooks

The New Critics favored the close reading of literary texts over the historical study of literature that was popular when they came upon the scene in the mid-twentieth century. The approach called for the critic to attend to image patterns and semantic tensions within the work. Poetry lent itself especially well to this critical endeavor, and English poetry from the sixteenth to the nineteenth century, because it was so stylized and philosophic, was an especially attractive object of study. In this essay, the leading New Critic, Cleanth Brooks, examines Keats's famous "Ode on a Grecian Urn" for the way its images embody ideas about the tension between the brevity of actual life and the eternal life art guarantees. Paradox, Brooks argues, is essential to poetry expression, since a poem embodies a universal idea with concrete form.

There is much in the poetry of Keats which suggests that he would have approved of Archibald MacLeish's dictum, "A poem should not mean / But be." There is even some warrant for thinking that the Grecian urn (real or imagined) which inspired the famous ode was, for Keats, just such a poem, "palpable and mute," a poem in stone. Hence it is the more remarkable that the "Ode" itself differs from Keats's other odes by culminating in a statement – a statement even of some sententiousness in which the urn itself is made to say that beauty is truth, and – more sententious still – that this bit of wisdom sums up the whole of mortal knowledge.

This is "to mean" with a vengeance – to violate the doctrine of the objective correlative, not only by stating truths, but by defining the limits of truth. Small wonder that some critics have felt that the unravished bride of quietness protests too much.

T. S. Eliot, for example, says that "this line ["Beauty is truth," etc.] strikes me as a serious blemish on a beautiful poem; and the reason must be either that I fail to understand it, or that it is a statement which is untrue." But even for persons who feel that they do understand it, the line may still constitute a blemish. Middleton Murry, who,

Original publication details: Cleanth Brooks, "Keats Sylvan Historian," from *The Well Wrought Urn*, pp. 151–166. Harcourt, Brace, 1947. Reproduced with permission from HMH Co.

Literary Theory: An Anthology, Third Edition. Edited by Julie Rivkin and Michael Ryan.
© 2017 John Wiley & Sons, Ltd. Published 2017 by John Wiley & Sons, Ltd.

after a discussion of Keats's other poems and his letters, feels that he knows what Keats meant by "beauty" and what he meant by "truth," and that Keats used them in senses which allowed them to be properly bracketed together, still, is forced to conclude: "My own opinion concerning the value of these two lines *in the context of the poem itself* is not very different from Mr. T. S. Eliot's." The troubling assertion is apparently an intrusion upon the poem – does not grow out of it – is not dramatically accommodated to it.

This is essentially Garrod's objection, and the fact that Garrod does object indicates that a distaste for the ending of the "Ode" is by no means limited to critics of notoriously "modern" sympathies.

But the question of real importance is not whether Eliot, Murry, and Garrod are right in thinking that "Beauty is truth, truth beauty" injures the poem. The question of real importance concerns beauty and truth in a much more general way: what is the relation of the beauty (the goodness, the perfection) of a poem to the truth or falsity of what it seems to assert? It is a question which has particularly vexed our own generation – to give it I. A. Richards' phrasing, it is the problem of belief.

The "Ode," by its bold equation of beauty and truth, raises this question in its sharpest form – the more so when it becomes apparent that the poem itself is obviously intended to be a parable on the nature of poetry, and of art in general. The "Ode" has apparently been an enigmatic parable, to be sure: one can emphasize *beauty* is truth and throw Keats into the pure-art camp, the usual procedure. But it is only fair to point out that one could stress *truth* is beauty, and argue with the Marxist critics of the 'thirties for a propaganda art. The very ambiguity of the statement, "Beauty is truth, truth beauty" ought to warn us against insisting very much on the statement in isolation, and to drive us back to a consideration of the context in which the statement is set.

It will not be sufficient, however, if it merely drives us back to a study of Keats's reading, his conversation, his letters. We shall not find our answer there even if scholarship does prefer on principle investigations of Browning's ironic question, "What porridge had John Keats?" For even if we knew just what porridge he had, physical and mental, we should still not be able to settle the problem of the "Ode." The reason should be clear: our specific question is not what did Keats the man perhaps want to assert here about the relation of beauty and truth; it is rather: was Keats the poet able to exemplify that relation in this particular poem? Middleton Murry is right: the relation of the final statement in the poem to the total context is all-important.

Indeed, Eliot, in the very passage in which he attacks the "Ode" has indicated the general line which we are to take in its defense. In that passage, Eliot goes on to contrast the closing lines of the "Ode" with a line from *King Lear*, "Ripeness is all." Keats's lines strike him as false; Shakespeare's, on the other hand, as not clearly false, and as possibly quite true. Shakespeare's generalization, in other words, avoids raising the question of truth. But is it really a question of truth and falsity? One is tempted to account for the difference of effect which Eliot feels in this way: "Ripeness is all" is a statement put in the mouth of a dramatic character and a statement which is governed and qualified by the whole context of the play. It does not directly challenge an examination into its truth because its relevance is pointed up and modified by the dramatic context.

Now, suppose that one could show that Keats's lines, *in quite the same way*, constitute a speech, a consciously riddling paradox, put in the mouth of a particular character, and modified by the total context of the poem. If we could demonstrate that the speech was "in character," was dramatically appropriate, was properly prepared for – then would not the lines have all the justification of "Ripeness is all"? In such case, should we not have waived the question of the scientific or philosophic truth of the lines in favor of the application of a principle curiously like that of dramatic propriety? I suggest that some such principle is the only one legitimately to be invoked in any case. Be this as it may, the "Ode on a Grecian Urn" provides us with as neat an instance as one could wish in order to test the implications of such a maneuver.

It has seemed best to be perfectly frank about procedure: the poem is to be read in order to see whether the last lines of the poem are not, after all, dramatically prepared for. Yet there are some claims to be made upon the reader too, claims which he, for his part, will have to be prepared to honor. He must not be allowed to dismiss the early characterizations of the urn as merely so much vaguely beautiful description. He must not be too much surprised if "mere decoration" turns out to be meaningful symbolism – or if ironies develop where he has been taught to expect only sensuous pictures. Most of all, if the teasing riddle spoken finally by the urn is not to strike him as a bewildering break in tone, he must not be too much disturbed to have the element of paradox latent in the poem emphasized, even in those parts of the poem which have none of the energetic crackle of wit with which he usually associates paradox. This is surely not too much to ask of the reader – namely, to assume that Keats meant what he said and that he chose his words with care. After all, the poem begins on a note of paradox, though a mild one: for we ordinarily do not expect an urn to speak at all; and yet, Keats does more than this: he begins his poem by emphasizing the apparent contradiction.

The silence of the urn is stressed – it is a "bride of quietness"; it is a "foster-child of silence," but the urn is a "historian" too. Historians tell the truth, or are at least expected to tell the truth. What is a "Sylvan historian"? A historian who is like the forest rustic, a woodlander? Or, a historian who writes histories of the forest? Presumably, the urn is sylvan in both senses. True, the latter meaning is uppermost: the urn can "express / A flowery tale more sweetly than our rhyme," and what the urn goes on to express is a "leaf-fring'd legend" of "Tempe or the dales of Arcady." But the urn, like the "leaf-fring'd legend" which it tells, is covered with emblems of the fields and forests: "Overwrought, / With forest branches and the trodden weed." When we consider the way in which the urn utters its history, the fact that it must be sylvan in both senses is seen as inevitable. Perhaps too the fact that it is a rural historian, a rustic, a peasant historian, qualifies in our minds the dignity and the "truth" of the histories which it recites. Its histories, Keats has already conceded, may be characterized as "tales" – not formal history at all.

The sylvan historian certainly supplies no names and dates – "What men or gods are these?" the poet asks. What it does give is action – of men *or* gods, of godlike men or of superhuman (though not daemonic) gods – action, which is not the less intense for all that the urn is cool marble. The words "mad" and "ecstasy" occur, but it is the quiet, rigid urn which gives the dynamic picture. And the paradox goes further: the scene is one of violent love-making, a Bacchanalian scene, but the urn itself is like a "still unravish'd bride," or like a child, a child "of silence and slow time." It is not merely like a child, but like a "foster-child." The exactness of the term can be defended. "Silence and slow time," it is suggested, are not the true parents, but foster-parents. They are too old, one feels, to have borne the child themselves. Moreover, they dote upon the "child" as grand-parents do. The urn is fresh and unblemished; it is still young, for all its antiquity, and time which destroys so much has "fostered" it.

With Stanza II we move into the world presented by the urn, into an examination, not of the urn as a whole – as an entity with its own form – but of the details which overlay it.

But as we enter that world, the paradox of silent speech is carried on, this time in terms of the objects portrayed on the vase.

The first lines of the stanza state a rather bold paradox – even the dulling effect of many readings has hardly blunted it. At least we can easily revive its sharpness. Attended to with care, it is a statement which is preposterous, and yet true – true on the same level on which the original metaphor of the speaking urn is true. The unheard music is sweeter than any audible music. The poet has rather cunningly enforced his conceit by using the phrase, "ye soft pipes." Actually, we might accept the poet's metaphor without being forced to accept the adjective "soft." The pipes might, although "unheard," be shrill, just as the action which is frozen in the figures on the urn can be violent and ecstatic as in Stanza I and slow and dignified as in Stanza IV (the procession to the sacrifice). Yet, by characterizing the pipes as "soft," the poet has provided a sort of realistic basis for his metaphor: the pipes, it is suggested, are playing very softly; if we listen carefully, we can hear them; their music is just below the threshold of normal sound.

This general paradox runs through the stanza: action goes on though the actors are motionless; the song will not cease; the lover cannot leave his song; the maiden, always to be kissed, never actually kissed, will remain changelessly beautiful. The maiden is, indeed, like the urn itself, a "still unravished bride of quietness" – not even ravished by a kiss; and it is implied, perhaps, that her changeless beauty, like that of the urn, springs from this fact.

The poet is obviously stressing the fresh, unwearied charm of the scene itself which can defy time and is deathless. But, at the same time, the poet is being perfectly fair to the terms of his metaphor. The beauty portrayed is deathless because it is lifeless. And it would be possible to shift the tone easily and ever so slightly by insisting more heavily on some of the phrasings so as to give them a darker implication. Thus, in the case of "thou canst not leave / Thy song," one could interpret: the musician cannot leave the song even if he would: he is fettered to it, a prisoner. In the same way, one could enlarge on the hint that the lover is not wholly satisfied and content: "never canst thou kiss, / … *yet, do not grieve.*" These items are mentioned here, not because one wishes to maintain that the poet is bitterly ironical, but because it is important for us to see that even here the paradox is being used fairly, particularly in view of the shift in tone which comes in the next stanza.

This third stanza represents, as various critics have pointed out, a recapitulation of earlier motifs. The boughs which cannot shed their leaves, the unwearied melodist, and the ever-ardent lover reappear. Indeed, I am not sure that this stanza can altogether be defended against the charge that it represents a falling off from the delicate but firm precision of the earlier stanzas. There is a tendency to linger over the scene sentimentally: the repetition of the word "happy" is perhaps symptomatic of what is occurring. Here, if anywhere, in my opinion, is to be found the blemish on the ode – not in the last two lines. Yet, if we are to attempt a defense of the third stanza, we shall come nearest success by emphasizing the paradoxical implications of the repeated items; for whatever development there is in the stanza inheres in the increased stress on the paradoxical element. For example, the boughs cannot "bid the Spring adieu," a phrase which repeats "nor ever can those trees be bare," but the new line strengthens the implications of speaking: the falling leaves are a gesture, a word of farewell to the joy of spring. The melodist of Stanza II played sweeter music because unheard, but here, in the third stanza, it is implied that he does not tire of his song for the same reason that the lover does not tire of his love – neither song nor love is consummated. The songs are "for ever new" because they cannot be completed.

The paradox is carried further in the case of the lover whose love is "For ever warm and still to be enjoy'd." We are really dealing with an ambiguity here, for we can take "still to be enjoy'd" as an adjectival phrase on the same level as "warm" – that is, "still virginal and warm." But the tenor of the whole poem suggests that the warmth of the love depends upon the fact that it has not been enjoyed – that is, "warm and still to be enjoy'd" may mean also "warm *because* still to be enjoy'd."

But though the poet has developed and extended his metaphors furthest here in this third stanza, the ironic counterpoise is developed furthest too. The love which a line earlier was "warm" and "panting" becomes suddenly in the next line, "All breathing human passion far above." But if it is *above* all breathing passion, it is, after all, outside the realm of breathing passion, and therefore, not human passion at all.

(If one argues that we are to take "All breathing human passion" as qualified by "That leaves a heart high-sorrowful and cloy'd" – that is, if one argues that Keats is saying that the love depicted on the urn is above only that human passion which leaves one cloyed and not above human passion in general, he misses the point. For Keats in the "Ode" is stressing the ironic fact that all human passion *does* leave one cloyed; hence the superiority of art.)

The purpose in emphasizing the ironic undercurrent in the foregoing lines is not at all to disparage Keats – to point up implications of his poem of which he was himself unaware. Far from it: the poet knows precisely what he is doing. The point is to be made simply in order to make sure that we are completely aware of what he is doing. Garrod, sensing this ironic undercurrent, seems to interpret it as an element over which Keats was not able to exercise full control. He says: "Truth to his main theme [the fixity given by art to forms which in life are impermanent] has taken Keats farther than he meant to go. The pure and ideal art of this 'cold Pastoral,' this 'silent form,' *has* a cold silentness which in some degree saddens him. In the last lines of the fourth stanza, especially the last three lines … every reader is conscious, I should suppose, of an undertone of sadness, of disappointment." The undertone is there, but Keats has not been taken "farther than he meant to go." Keats's attitude, even in the early stanzas, is more complex than Garrod would allow: it is more complex and more ironic, and a recognition of this is important if we are to be able to relate the last stanza to the rest of the "Ode." Keats is perfectly aware that the frozen moment of loveliness is more dynamic than is the fluid world of reality *only* because it is frozen. The love depicted on the urn remains warm and young because it is not human flesh at all but cold, ancient marble.

With Stanza IV, we are still within the world depicted by the urn, but the scene presented in this stanza forms a contrast to the earlier scenes. It emphasizes, not individual aspiration and desire, but communal life. It constitutes another chapter in the history that the "Sylvan historian" has to tell. And again, names and dates have been omitted. We are not told to what god's altar the procession moves, nor the occasion of the sacrifice.

Moreover, the little town from which the celebrants come is unknown; and the poet rather goes out of his way to leave us the widest possible option in locating it. It may be a mountain town, or a river town, or a tiny seaport. Yet, of course, there is a sense in which the nature of the town – the essential character of the town – is actually suggested by the figured urn. But it is not given explicitly. The poet is willing to leave much to our imaginations; and yet the stanza in its organization of imagery and rhythm does describe the town clearly enough; it is small, it is quiet, its people are knit together as an organic whole, and on a "pious morn" such as this, its whole population has turned out to take part in the ritual.

The stanza has been justly admired. Its magic of effect defies reduction to any formula. Yet, without pretending to "account" for the effect in any mechanical fashion, one can point to some of the elements active in securing the effect: there is the suggestiveness of the word "green" in "green altar" – something natural, spontaneous, living; there is the suggestion that the little town is caught in a curve of the seashore, or nestled in a fold of the mountains – at any rate, is something secluded and something naturally related to its terrain; there is the effect of the phrase "peaceful citadel," a phrase which involves a clash between the ideas of war and peace and resolves it in the sense of stability and independence without imperialistic ambition – the sense of stable repose.

But to return to the larger pattern of the poem: Keats does something in this fourth stanza which is highly interesting in itself and thoroughly relevant to the sense in which the urn is a historian. One of the most moving passages in the poem is that in which the poet speculates on the strange emptiness of the little town which, of course, has not been pictured on the urn at all.

The little town which has been merely implied by the procession portrayed on the urn is endowed with a poignance beyond anything else in the poem. Its streets "for evermore / Will silent be," its desolation forever shrouded in a mystery. No one in the figured procession will ever be able to go back to the town to break the silence there, not even one to tell the stranger there why the town remains desolate.

If one attends closely to what Keats is doing here, he may easily come to feel that the poet is indulging himself in an ingenious fancy, an indulgence, however, which is gratuitous and finally silly; that is, the poet has created in his own imagination the town implied by the procession of worshipers, has given it a special character of desolation and loneliness, and then has gone on to treat it as if it were a real town to which a stranger might actually come and be puzzled by its emptiness. (I can see no other interpretation of the lines, "and not a soul to tell / Why thou art desolate can e'er return.") But, actually, of course, no one will ever discover the town except by the very same process by which Keats has discovered it: namely, through the figured urn, and then, of course, he will not need to ask why it is empty. One can well imagine what a typical eighteenth-century critic would have made of this flaw in logic.

It will not be too difficult, however, to show that Keats's extension of the fancy is not irrelevant to the poem as a whole. The "reality" of the little town has a very close relation to the urn's character as a historian. If the earlier stanzas have been concerned with such paradoxes as the ability of static carving to convey dynamic action, of the soundless pipes to play music sweeter than that of the heard melody, of the figured lover to have a love more warm and panting than that of breathing flesh and blood, so in the same way the town implied by the urn comes to have a richer and more important history than that of actual cities. Indeed, the imagined town is to the figured procession as the unheard melody is to the carved pipes of the unwearied melodist. And the poet, by pretending to take the town as real – so real that he can imagine the effect of its silent streets upon the stranger who chances to come into it – has suggested in the most powerful way possible its essential reality for him – and for us. It is a case of the doctor's taking his own medicine: the poet is prepared to stand by the illusion of his own making.

With Stanza V we move back out of the enchanted world portrayed by the urn to consider the urn itself once more as a whole, as an object. The shift in point of view is marked with the first line of the stanza by the apostrophe, "O Attic shape ..." It is the urn itself as a formed thing, as an autonomous world, to which the poet addresses these last words. And the rich, almost breathing world which the poet has conjured up for us contracts and hardens into the decorated motifs on the urn itself: "with brede / Of marble men and maidens overwrought." The beings who have a life above life – "All breathing human passion far above" – are marble, after all.

This last is a matter which, of course, the poet has never denied. The recognition that the men and maidens are frozen, fixed, arrested, has, as we have already seen, run through the second, third, and fourth stanzas as an ironic undercurrent. The central paradox of the poem, thus, comes to conclusion in the phrase, "Cold Pastoral." The word "pastoral" suggests warmth, spontaneity, the natural and the informal as well as the idyllic, the simple, and the informally charming. What the urn tells is a "flowery tale," a "leaf-fring'd legend," but the "sylvan historian" works in terms of marble. The urn itself is cold, and the life beyond life which it expresses is life which has been formed, arranged. The urn itself is a "silent form," and it speaks, not by means of statement, but by "teasing us out of thought." It is as enigmatic as eternity is, for, like eternity, its history is beyond time, outside time, and for this very reason bewilders our time-ridden minds: it teases us.

The marble men and maidens of the urn will not age as flesh-and-blood men and women will: "When old age shall this generation waste." (The word "generation," by the way, is very rich. It means on one level "that which is generated" – that which springs from human loins – Adam's breed; and yet, so intimately is death wedded to men, the word "generation" itself has become, as here, a measure of time.) The marble men and women lie outside time. The urn which they adorn will remain. The "Sylvan historian" will recite its history to other generations.

What will it say to them? Presumably, what it says to the poet now: that "formed experience," imaginative insight, embodies the basic and fundamental perception of man and nature. The urn is beautiful, and yet its beauty is based – what else is the poem concerned with? – on an imaginative perception of essentials. Such a vision is beautiful but it is also true. The sylvan historian presents us with beautiful histories, but they are true histories, and it is a good historian.

Moreover, the "truth" which the sylvan historian gives is the only kind of truth which we are likely to get on this earth, and, furthermore, it is the only kind that we *have* to have. The names, dates, and special circumstances, the wealth of data – these the sylvan historian quietly ignores. But we shall never get all the facts anyway – there is no end to the accumulation of facts. Moreover, mere accumulations of facts – a point our own generation is only beginning to realize – are meaningless. The sylvan historian does better than that: it takes a few details and so orders them that we have not only beauty but insight into essential truth. Its "history," in short, is a history without footnotes. It has the validity of myth – not myth as a pretty but irrelevant make-belief, an idle fancy, but myth as a valid perception into reality.

So much for the "meaning" of the last lines of the "Ode." It is an interpretation which differs little from past interpretations. It is put forward here with no pretension to novelty. What is important is the fact that it can be derived from the context of the "Ode" itself.

And now, what of the objection that the final lines break the tone of the poem with a display of misplaced sententiousness? One can summarize the answer already implied thus: throughout the poem the poet has stressed the paradox of the speaking urn. First, the urn itself can tell a story, can give a history. Then, the various figures depicted upon the urn play music or speak or sing. If we have been alive to these items, we shall not, perhaps, be too much surprised to have the urn speak once more, not in the sense in which it tells a story – a metaphor which is rather easy to accept – but, to have it speak on a higher level, to have it make a commentary on its own nature. If the urn has been properly dramatized, if we have followed the development of the metaphors, if we have been alive to the paradoxes which work throughout the poem, perhaps then, we shall be prepared for the enigmatic, final paradox which the "silent form" utters. But in that case, we shall not feel that the generalization, unqualified and to be taken literally, is meant to march out of its context to compete with the scientific and philosophical generalizations which dominate our world.

"Beauty is truth, truth beauty" has precisely the same status, and the same justification as Shakespeare's "Ripeness is all." It is a speech "in character" and supported by a dramatic context.

To conclude thus may seem to weight the principle of dramatic propriety with more than it can bear. This would not be fair to the complexity of the problem of truth in art nor fair to Keats's little parable. Granted; and yet the principle of dramatic propriety may take us further than would first appear. Respect for it may at least insure our dealing with the problem of truth at the level on which it is really relevant to literature. If we can see that the assertions made in a poem are to be taken as part of an organic context, if we can resist the temptation to deal with them in isolation, then we may be willing to go on to deal with the world-view, or "philosophy," or "truth" of the *poem as a whole* in terms of its dramatic wholeness: that is, we shall not neglect the maturity of attitude, the dramatic tension, the emotional *and* intellectual coherence in favor of some statement of theme abstracted from it by paraphrase. Perhaps, best of all, we might learn to distrust our ability to represent any poem adequately by paraphrase. Such a distrust is healthy. Keats's sylvan historian, who is not above "teasing" us, exhibits such a distrust, and perhaps the point of what the sylvan historian "says" is to confirm us in our distrust.

Note

*   This essay had been finished some months before I came upon Kenneth Burke's brilliant essay on Keats's "Ode" ("Symbolic Action in a Poem by Keats," *Accent*, Autumn, 1943). I have decided not to make any alterations, though I have been tempted to adopt some of Burke's insights, and, in at least one case, his essay has convinced me of a point which I had considered but rejected – the pun on "breed" and "Brede."

I am happy to find that two critics with methods and purposes so different should agree so thoroughly as we do on the poem. I am pleased, for my part, therefore, to acknowledge the amount of duplication which exists between the two essays, counting it as rather important corroboration of a view of the poem which will probably seem to some critics overingenious. In spite of the common elements, however, I feel that the emphasis of my essay is sufficiently different from Burke's to justify my going on with its publication.

CHAPTER 5

The Intentional Fallacy

Monroe Beardsley and W. K. Wimsatt

Composed in 1949, "The Intentional Fallacy" is an important polemical essay in the *corpus* of the New Criticism. The New Critics were determined to isolate literature from other objects of study, especially historical and biographic criticism, which often treated literary texts as boxes of clues that had to be solved through the tracking down of references to the author's life. Shakespeare inserted references to a ship called *The Tyger* in *Othello* because he was involved in Court politics and had an actual vessel used by the queen's minister, Robert Cecil, in mind. Such intended meanings were what literature was about. Not so, argued the New Critics. Literature is much more than that. It is the texture of images the writer creates, a texture that, once launched, has a semantic dimension entirely its own that should be deciphered and described. The writer engages with the history of language when s/he writes, and his or her work is, in a sense, absorbed into that history. It becomes objective, and its meaning ceases to be subjective. Moreover, literature, through its complex linguistic forms, evokes universals that are not reducible to a singular conscious intention. That point is not made in this essay, but it can be found in other works of Wimsatt especially (for example, "The Concrete Universal").

Monroe Beardsley was a Professor of Philosophy at Temple University and Swarthmore University. Beardsley's body of work focused on aesthetics, theory of art, and the examination of criticism in myriad subjects. He is the author of *Aesthetics: Problems in the Philosophy of Criticism* (1958), *The Aesthetic Point of View* (1982), and many others.

W. K. Wimsatt was a Professor of English at Yale University with works mainly on criticism and theory. He is the author of *Literary Criticism: A Short History* (1957) and *Verbal Icon: Studies in the Meaning of Poetry* (1954). His theories are rooted deeply in formalism and were key contributions to the New Criticism movement during the twentieth century.

Original publication details: Monroe Beardsley and W.K. Wimsatt, "The Intentional Fallacy." *Sewanee Review* 57.1 (Winter 1949), pp. 468–488. Copyright © The University of the South. Complete and unabridged.

Literary Theory: An Anthology, Third Edition. Edited by Julie Rivkin and Michael Ryan.
© 2017 John Wiley & Sons, Ltd. Published 2017 by John Wiley & Sons, Ltd.

> He owns with toil he wrote the following scenes;
> But, if they're naught, ne'er spare him for his pains:
> Damn him the more; have no commiseration
> For dullness on mature deliberation.
>
> William Congreve, Prologue to
> *The Way of the World*

The claim of the author's "intention" upon the critic's judgment has been challenged in a number of recent discussions, notably in the debate entitled *The Personal Heresy*, between Professors Lewis and Tillyard, and at least implicitly in periodical essays like those in the "Symposiums" of 1940 in the *Southern* and *Kenyon Reviews*.[1] But it seems doubtful if this claim and most of its romantic corollaries are as yet subject to any widespread questioning. The present writers, in a short article entitled "Intention" for a *Dictionary*[2] of literary criticism, raised the issue but were unable to pursue its implications at any length. We argued that the design or intention of the author is neither available nor desirable as a standard for judging the success of a work of literary art, and it seems to us that this is a principle which goes deep into some differences in the history of critical attitudes. It is a principle which accepted or rejected points to the polar opposites of classical "imitation" and romantic expression. It entails many specific truths about inspiration, authenticity, biography, literary history and scholarship, and about some trends of contemporary poetry, especially its allusiveness. There is hardly a problem of literary criticism in which the critic's approach will not be qualified by his view of "intention."

"Intention," as we shall use the term, corresponds to *what he intended* in a formula which more or less explicitly has had wide acceptance. "In order to judge the poet's performance, we must know *what he intended*." Intention is design or plan in the author's mind. Intention has obvious affinities for the author's attitude toward his work, the way he felt, what made him write.

We begin our discussion with a series of propositions summarized and abstracted to a degree where they seem to us axiomatic, if not truistic.

(1)   A poem does not come into existence by accident. The words of a poem, as Professor Stoll has remarked, come out of a head, not out of a hat. Yet to insist on the designing intellect as a *cause* of a poem is not to grant the design or intention as a *standard*.

(2)   One must ask how a critic expects to get an answer to the question about intention. How is he to find out what the poet tried to do? If the poet succeeded in doing it, then the poem itself shows what he was trying to do. And if the poet did not succeed, then the poem is not adequate evidence, and the critic must go outside the poem – for evidence of an intention that did not become effective in the poem. "Only one *caveat* must be borne in mind," says an eminent intentionalist[3] in a moment when his theory repudiates itself; "the poet's aim must be judged at the moment of the creative act, that is to say, by the art of the poem itself."

(3)   Judging a poem is like judging a pudding or a machine. One demands that it work. It is only because an artifact works that we infer the intention of an artificer. "A poem should not mean but be." A poem can *be* only through its *meaning* – since its medium is words – yet it *is*, simply *is*, in the sense that we have no excuse for inquiring what part is intended or meant.[4] Poetry is a feat of style by which a complex of meaning is handled all at once. Poetry succeeds because all or most of what is said or implied is relevant; what

is irrelevant has been excluded, like lumps from pudding and "bugs" from machinery. In this respect poetry differs from practical messages, which are successful if and only if we correctly infer the intention. They are more abstract than poetry.

(4)   The meaning of a poem may certainly be a personal one, in the sense that a poem expresses a personality or state of soul rather than a physical object like an apple. But even a short lyric poem is dramatic, the response of a speaker (no matter how abstractly conceived) to a situation (no matter how universalized). We ought to impute the thoughts and attitudes of the poem immediately to the dramatic *speaker*, and if to the author at all, only by a biographical act of inference.

(5)   If there is any sense in which an author, by revision, has better achieved his original intention, it is only the very abstract, tautological, sense that he intended to write a better work and now has done it. (In this sense every author's intention is the same.) His former specific intention was not his intention. "He's the man we were in search of, that's true," says Hardy's rustic constable, "and yet he's not the man we were in search of. For the man we were in search of was not the man we wanted."[5]

"Is not a critic," asks Professor Stoll, "… a judge, who does not explore his own consciousness, but determines the author's meaning or intention, as if the poem were a will, a contract, or the constitution? The poem is not the critic's own."[6] He has diagnosed very accurately two forms of irresponsibility, one which he prefers. Our view is yet different. The poem is not the critic's own and not the author's (it is detached from the author at birth and goes about the world beyond his power to intend about it or control it). The poem belongs to the public. It is embodied in language, the peculiar possession of the public, and it is about the human being, an object of public knowledge. What is said about the poem is subject to the same scrutiny as any statement in linguistics or in the general science of psychology or morals. Mr. Richards has aptly called the poem a *class* – "a class of experiences which do not differ in any character more than a certain amount … from a standard experience." And he adds, "We may take as this standard experience the relevant experience of the poet when contemplating the completed composition." Professor Wellek in a fine essay on the problem has preferred to call the poem "a system of norms," "extracted from every individual experience," and he objects to Mr. Richards' deference to the poet as reader. We side with Professor Wellek in not wishing to make the poet (outside the poem) an authority.

A critic of our *Dictionary* article, Mr. Ananda K. Coomaraswamy, has argued[7] that there are two kinds of enquiry about a work of art: (1) whether the artist achieved his intentions; (2) whether the work of art "ought ever to have been undertaken at all" and so "whether it is worth preserving." Number (2), Mr. Coomaraswamy maintains, is not "criticism of any work of art *qua* work of art," but is rather moral criticism; number (1) is artistic criticism. But we maintain that (2) need not be moral criticism: that there is another way of deciding whether works of art are worth preserving and whether, in a sense, they "ought" to have been undertaken, and this is the way of objective criticism of works of art as such, the way which enables us to distinguish between a skilful murder and a skilful poem. A skilful murder is an example which Mr. Coomaraswamy uses, and in his system the difference between the murder and the poem is simply a "moral" one, not an "artistic" one, since each if carried out according to plan is "artistically" successful. We maintain that (2) is an enquiry of more worth than (1), and since (2), and not (1), is capable of distinguishing poetry from murder, the name "artistic criticism" is properly given to (2).

II

It is not so much an empirical as an analytic judgment, not a historical statement, but a definition, to say that the intentional fallacy is a romantic one. When a rhetorician, presumably of the first century A.D., writes: "Sublimity is the echo of a great soul," or tells us that "Homer enters into the sublime actions of his heroes" and "shares the full inspiration of the combat," we shall not be surprised to find this rhetorician considered as a distant harbinger of romanticism and greeted in the warmest terms by so romantic a critic as Saintsbury. One may wish to argue whether Longinus should be called romantic,[8] but there can hardly be a doubt that in one important way he is.

Goethe's three questions for "constructive criticism" are "What did the author set out to do? Was his plan reasonable and sensible, and how far did he succeed in carrying it out?" If one leaves out the middle question, one has in effect the system of Croce – the culmination and crowning philosophic expression of romanticism. The beautiful is the successful intuition-expression, and the ugly is the unsuccessful; the intuition or private part of art is *the* aesthetic fact, and the medium or public part is not the subject of aesthetic at all. Yet aesthetic reproduction takes place only "if all the other conditions remain equal."

> Oil-paintings grow dark, frescoes fade, statues lose noses ... the text of a poem is corrupted by bad copyists or bad printing.

> The Madonna of Cimabue is still in the Church of Santa Maria Novella; but does she speak to the visitor of to-day as to the Florentines of the thirteenth century?

> *Historical interpretation* labours ... to reintegrate in us the psychological conditions which have changed in the course of history. It ... enables us to see a work of art (a physical object) as its *author saw it* in the moment of production.[9]

The first italics are Croce's, the second ours. The upshot of Croce's system is an ambiguous emphasis on history. With such passages as a point of departure a critic may write a close analysis of the meaning or "spirit" of a play of Shakespeare or Corneille – a process that involves close historical study but remains aesthetic criticism – or he may write sociology, biography, or other kinds of non-aesthetic history. The Crocean system seems to have given more of a boost to the latter way of writing.

"What has the poet tried to do," asks Spingarn in his 1910 Columbia Lecture from which we have already quoted, "and how has he fulfilled his intention?" The place to look for "insuperable" ugliness, says Bosanquet, in his third *Lecture* of 1914, is the "region of insincere and affected art." The seepage of the theory into a non-philosophic place may be seen in such a book as Marguerite Wilkinson's inspirational *New Voices*, about the poetry of 1919 to 1931 – where symbols "as old as the ages ... retain their strength and freshness" through "Realization." We close this section with two examples from quarters where one might least expect a taint of the Crocean. Mr. I. A. Richards' fourfold distinction of meaning into "sense," "feeling," "tone," "intention" has been probably the most influential statement of intentionalism in the past fifteen years, though it contains a hint of self-repudiation: "This function [intention]," says Mr. Richards, "is not on all fours with the others." In an essay on "Three Types of Poetry" Mr. Allen Tate writes as follows:

> We must understand that the lines
>> Life like a dome of many-colored glass
>> Stains the white radiance of eternity

are not poetry; they express the *frustrated will* trying to compete with science. The *will* asserts a rhetorical proposition about the whole of life, but the *imagination* has not seized upon the materials of the poem and made them into a whole. Shelley's simile is imposed upon the material from above; it does not grow out of the material.

The last sentence contains a promise of objective analysis which is not fulfilled. The reason why the essay relies so heavily throughout on the terms "will" and "imagination" is that Mr. Tate is accusing the romantic poets of a kind of insincerity (romanticism in reverse) and at the same time is trying to describe something mysterious and perhaps indescribable, an "imaginative whole of life," a "wholeness of vision at a particular moment of experience," something which "yields us the quality of the experience." If a poet had a toothache at the moment of conceiving a poem, that would be part of the experience, but Mr. Tate of course does not mean anything like that. He is thinking about some kind of "whole" which in this essay at least he does not describe, but which doubtless it is the prime need of criticism to describe – in terms that may be publicly tested.

III

> I went to the poets; tragic, dithyrambic, and all sorts. … I took them some of the most elaborate passages in their own writings, and asked what was the meaning of them. … Will you believe me? … there is hardly a person present who would not have talked better about their poetry than they did themselves. Then I knew that not by wisdom do poets write poetry, but by a sort of genius and inspiration.

That reiterated mistrust of the poets which we hear from Socrates may have been part of a rigorously ascetic view in which we hardly wish to participate, yet Plato's Socrates saw a truth about the poetic mind which the world no longer commonly sees – so much criticism, and that the most inspirational and most affectionately remembered, has proceeded from the poets themselves.

Certainly the poets have had something to say that the analyst and professor could not say; their message has been more exciting: that poetry should come as naturally as leaves to a tree, that poetry is the lava of the imagination, or that it is emotion recollected in tranquillity. But it is necessary that we realize the character and authority of such testimony. There is only a fine shade between those romantic expressions and a kind of earnest advice that authors often give. Thus Edward Young, Carlyle, Walter Pater:

> I know two golden rules from *ethics*, which are no less golden in *Composition*, than in life. 1. *Know thyself*; 2dly, *Reverence thyself*.
>
> This is the grand secret for finding readers and retaining them: let him who would move and convince others, be first moved and convinced himself. Horace's rule, *Si vis me flere*, is applicable in a wider sense than the literal one. To every poet, to every writer, we might say: Be true, if you would be believed.
>
> Truth! there can be no merit, no craft at all, without that. And further, all beauty is in the long run only *fineness* of truth, or what we call expression, the finer accommodation of speech to that vision within.

And Housman's little handbook to the poetic mind yields the following illustration:

> Having drunk a pint of beer at luncheon – beer is a sedative to the brain, and my afternoons
> are the least intellectual portion of my life – I would go out for a walk of two or three hours.
> As I went along, thinking of nothing in particular, only looking at things around me and
> following the progress of the seasons, there would flow into my mind, with sudden and unac-
> countable emotion, sometimes a line or two of verse, sometimes a whole stanza at once. ...

This is the logical terminus of the series already quoted. Here is a confession of how
poems were written which would do as a definition of poetry just as well as "emotion
recollected in tranquility" – and which the young poet might equally well take to heart
as a practical rule. Drink a pint of beer, relax, go walking, think on nothing in particular,
look at things, surrender yourself to yourself, search for the truth in your own soul, listen
to the sound of your own inside voice, discover and express the *vraie vérité*.

It is probably true that all this is excellent advice for poets. The young imagination
fired by Wordsworth and Carlyle is probably closer to the verge of producing a poem
than the mind of the student who has been sobered by Aristotle or Richards. The art of
inspiring poets, or at least of inciting something like poetry in young persons, has
probably gone further in our day than ever before. Books of creative writing such as
those issued from the Lincoln School are interesting evidence of what a child can do if
taught how to manage himself honestly.[10] All this, however, would appear to belong to an
art separate from criticism, or to a discipline which one might call the psychology of
composition, valid and useful, an individual and private culture, yoga, or system of self-
development which the young poet would do well to notice, but different from the public
science of evaluating poems.

Coleridge and Arnold were better critics than most poets have been, and if the critical
tendency dried up the poetry in Arnold and perhaps in Coleridge, it is not inconsistent
with our argument, which is that judgment of poems is different from the art of producing
them. Coleridge has given us the classic "anodyne" story, and tells what he can about the
genesis of a poem which he calls a "psychological curiosity," but his definitions of poetry
and of the poetic quality "imagination" are to be found elsewhere and in quite other terms.

The day may arrive when the psychology of composition is unified with the science
of objective evaluation, but so far they are separate. It would be convenient if the passwords of
the intentional school, "sincerity," "fidelity," "spontaneity," "authenticity," "genuineness,"
"originality," could be equated with terms of analysis such as "integrity," "relevance,"
"unity," "function"; with "maturity," "subtlety," and "adequacy," and other more precise
axiological terms – in short, if "expression" always meant aesthetic communication. But
this is not so.

"Aesthetic" art, says Professor Curt Ducasse, an ingenious theorist of expression, is
the conscious objectification of feelings, in which an intrinsic part is the critical moment.
The artist corrects the objectification when it is not adequate, but this may mean that the
earlier attempt was not successful in objectifying the self, or "it may also mean that it was
a successful objectification of a self which, when it confronted us clearly, we disowned
and repudiated in favor of another."[11] What is the standard by which we disown or accept
the self? Professor Ducasse does not say. Whatever it may be, however, this standard is
an element in the definition of art which will not reduce to terms of objectification. The
evaluation of the work of art remains public; the work is measured against something
outside the author.

IV

There is criticism of poetry and there is, as we have seen, author psychology, which when applied to the present or future takes the form of inspirational promotion; but author psychology can be historical too, and then we have literary biography, a legitimate and attractive study in itself, one approach, as Mr. Tillyard would argue, to personality, the poem being only a parallel approach. Certainly it need not be with a derogatory purpose that one points out personal studies, as distinct from poetic studies, in the realm of literary scholarship. Yet there is danger of confusing personal and poetic studies; and there is the fault of writing the personal as if it were poetic.

There is a difference between internal and external evidence for the meaning of a poem. And the paradox is only verbal and superficial that what is (1) internal is also public: it is discovered through the semantics and syntax of a poem, through our habitual knowledge of the language, through grammars, dictionaries, and all the literature which is the source of dictionaries, in general through all that makes a language and culture; while what is (2) external is private or idiosyncratic; not a part of the work as a linguistic fact: it consists of revelations (in journals, for example, or letters or reported conversations) about how or why the poet wrote the poem – to what lady, while sitting on what lawn, or at the death of what friend or brother. There is (3) an intermediate kind of evidence about the character of the author or about private or semi-private meanings attached to words or topics by an author or by a coterie of which he is a member. The meaning of words is the history of words, and the biography of an author, his use of a word, and the associations which the word had for *him*, are part of the word's history and meaning.[12] But the three types of evidence, especially (2) and (3), shade into one another so subtly that it is not always easy to draw a line between examples, and hence arises the difficulty for criticism. The use of biographical evidence need not involve intentionalism, because while it may be evidence of what the author intended, it may also be evidence of the meaning of his words and the dramatic character of his utterance. On the other hand, it may not be all this. And a critic who is concerned with evidence of type (1) and moderately with that of type (3) will in the long run produce a different sort of comment from that of the critic who is concerned with type (2) and with (3) where it shades into (2).

The whole glittering parade of Professor Lowes' *Road to Xanadu*, for instance, runs along the border between types (2) and (3) or boldly traverses the romantic region of (2). "'Kubla Khan'," says Professor Lowes, "is the fabric of a vision, but every image that rose up in its weaving had passed that way before. And it would seem that there is nothing haphazard or fortuitous in their return." This is not quite clear – not even when Professor Lowes explains that there were clusters of associations, like hooked atoms, which were drawn into complex relation with other clusters in the deep well of Coleridge's memory, and which then coalesced and issued forth as poems. If there was nothing "haphazard or fortuitous" in the way the images returned to the surface, that may mean (1) that Coleridge could not produce what he did not have, that he was limited in his creation by what he had read or otherwise experienced, or (2) that having received certain clusters of associations, he was bound to return them in just the way he did, and that the value of the poem may be described in terms of the experiences on which he had to draw. The latter pair of propositions (a sort of Hartleyan associationism which Coleridge himself repudiated in the *Biographia*) may not be assented to. There were certainly other combinations, other poems, worse or better, that might have been written by men who had read Bartram and

Purchas and Bruce and Milton. And this will be true no matter how many times we are able to add to the brilliant complex of Coleridge's reading. In certain flourishes (such as the sentence we have quoted) and in chapter headings like "The Shaping Spirit," "The Magical Synthesis," "Imagination Creatrix," it may be that Professor Lowes pretends to say more about the actual poems than he does. There is a certain deceptive variation in these fancy chapter titles; one expects to pass on to a new stage in the argument, and one finds – more and more sources, more about "the streamy nature of association."[13]

"Wohin der Weg?" quotes Professor Lowes for the motto of his book. "Kein Weg! Ins Unbetretene." Precisely because the way is *unbetreten*, we should say, it leads away from the poem. Bartram's *Travels* contains a good deal of the history of certain words and romantic Floridan conceptions that appear in "Kubla Khan." And a good deal of that history has passed and was then passing into the very stuff of our language. Perhaps a person who has read Bartram appreciates the poem more than one who has not. Or, by looking up the vocabulary of "Kubla Khan" in the *Oxford English Dictionary*, or by reading some of the other books there quoted, a person may know the poem better. But it would seem to pertain little to the poem to know that *Coleridge* had read Bartram. There is a gross body of life, of sensory and mental experience, which lies behind and in some sense causes every poem, but can never be and need not be known in the verbal and hence intellectual composition which is the poem. For all the objects of our manifold experience, especially for the intellectual objects, for every unity, there is an action of the mind which cuts off roots, melts away context – or indeed we should never have objects or ideas or anything to talk about.

It is probable that there is nothing in Professor Lowes' vast book which could detract from anyone's appreciation of either *The Ancient Mariner* or *Kubla Khan*. We next present a case where preoccupation with evidence of type (3) has gone so far as to distort a critic's view of a poem (yet a case not so obvious as those that abound in our critical journals).

In a well-known poem by John Donne appears the following quatrain:

> Moving of th' earth brings harmes and feares,
>   Men reckon what it did and meant,
> But trepidation of the spheares,
>   Though greater farre, is innocent.

A recent critic in an elaborate treatment of Donne's learning has written of this quatrain as follows:

> ... he touches the emotional pulse of the situation by a skillful allusion to the new and the old astronomy. ... Of the new astronomy, the "moving of the earth" is the most radical principle; of the old, the "trepidation of the spheres" is the motion of the greatest complexity. ... As the poem is a valediction forbidding mourning, the poet must exhort his love to quietness and calm upon his departure; and for this purpose the figure based upon the latter motion (trepidation), long absorbed into the traditional astronomy, fittingly suggests the tension of the moment without arousing the "harmes and feares" implicit in the figure of the moving earth.[14]

The argument is plausible and rests on a well-substantiated thesis that Donne was deeply interested in the new astronomy and its repercussions in the theological realm. In various works Donne shows his familiarity with Kepler's *De Stella Nova*, with Galileo's *Siderius*

Nuncius, with William Gilbert's *De Magnete*, and with Clavius's commentary on the *De Sphaera* of Sacrobosco. He refers to the new science in his Sermon at Paul's Cross and in a letter to Sir Henry Goodyer. In *The First Anniversary* he says the "new philosophy calls all in doubt." In the *Elegy on Prince Henry* he says that the "least moving of the center" makes "the world to shake."

It is difficult to answer argument like this, and impossible to answer it with evidence of like nature. There is no reason why Donne might not have written a stanza in which the two kinds of celestial motion stood for two sorts of emotion at parting. And if we become full of astronomical ideas and see Donne only against the background of the new science, we may believe that he did. But the text itself remains to be dealt with, the analyzable vehicle of a complicated metaphor. And one may observe: (1) that the movement of the earth according to the Copernican theory is a celestial motion, smooth and regular, and while it might cause religious or philosophic fears, it could not be associated with the crudity and earthiness of the kind of commotion which the speaker in the poem wishes to discourage; (2) that there is another moving of the earth, an earthquake, which has just these qualities and is to be associated with the tear-floods and sigh-tempests of the second stanza of the poem; (3) that "trepidation" is an appropriate opposite of earthquake, because each is a shaking or vibratory motion; and "trepidation of the spheres" is "greater far" than an earthquake, but not much greater (if two such motions can be compared as to greatness) than the annual motion of the earth; (4) that reckoning what it "did and meant" shows that the event has passed, like an earthquake, not like the incessant celestial movement of the earth. Perhaps a knowledge of Donne's interest in the new science may add another shade of meaning, an overtone to the stanza in question, though to say even this runs against the words. To make the geo–centric and helio–centric antithesis the core of the metaphor is to disregard the English language, to prefer private evidence to public, external to internal.

V

If the distinction between kinds of evidence has implications for the historical critic, it has them no less for the contemporary poet and his critic. Or, since every rule for a poet is but another side of a judgment by a critic, and since the past is the realm of the scholar and critic, and the future and present that of the poet and the critical leaders of taste, we may say that the problems arising in literary scholarship from the intentional fallacy are matched by others which arise in the world of progressive experiment.

The question of "allusiveness," for example, as acutely posed by the poetry of Eliot, is certainly one where a false judgment is likely to involve the intentional fallacy. The frequency and depth of literary allusion in the poetry of Eliot and others has driven so many in pursuit of full meanings to the *Golden Bough* and the Elizabethan drama that it has become a kind of commonplace to suppose that we do not know what a poet means unless we have traced him in his reading – a supposition redolent with intentional implications. The stand taken by Mr. F. O. Matthiessen is a sound one and partially forestalls the difficulty.

> If one reads these lines with an attentive ear and is sensitive to their sudden shifts in movement, the contrast between the actual Thames and the idealized vision of it during an age before it flowed through a megalopolis is sharply conveyed by that movement itself, whether or not one recognizes the refrain to be from Spenser.

Eliot's allusions work when we know them – and to a great extent even when we do not know them, through their suggestive power.

But sometimes we find allusions supported by notes, and it is a very nice question whether the notes function more as guides to send us where we may be educated, or more as indications in themselves about the character of the allusions. "Nearly everything of importance … that is apposite to an appreciation of 'The Waste Land'," writes Mr. Matthiessen of Miss Weston's book, "has been incorporated into the structure of the poem itself, or into Eliot's Notes." And with such an admission it may begin to appear that it would not much matter if Eliot invented his sources (as Sir Walter Scott invented chapter epigraphs from "old plays" and "anonymous" authors, or as Coleridge wrote marginal glosses for "The Ancient Mariner"). Allusions to Dante, Webster, Marvell, or Baudelaire, doubtless gain something because these writers existed, but it is doubtful whether the same can be said for an allusion to an obscure Elizabethan:

> The sound of horns and motors, which shall bring
> Sweeney to Mrs. Porter in the spring.

"Cf. Day, *Parliament of Bees*:" says Eliot,

> When of a sudden, listening, you shall hear,
> A noise of horns and hunting, which shall bring
> Actaeon to Diana in the spring,
> Where all shall see her naked skin. …

The irony is completed by the quotation itself; had Eliot, as is quite conceivable, composed these lines to furnish his own background, there would be no loss of validity. The conviction may grow as one reads Eliot's next note: "I do not know the origin of the ballad from which these lines are taken: it was reported to me from Sydney, Australia." The important word in this note – on Mrs. Porter and her daughter who washed their feet in soda water – is "ballad." And if one should feel from the lines themselves their "ballad" quality, there would be little need for the note. Ultimately, the inquiry must focus on the integrity of such notes as part of the poem, for where they constitute special information about the meaning of phrases in the poem, they ought to be subject to the same scrutiny as any of the other words in which it is written. Mr. Matthiessen believes the notes were the price Eliot "had to pay in order to avoid what he would have considered muffling the energy of his poem by extended connecting links in the text itself." But it may be questioned whether the notes and the need for them are not equally muffling. The omission from poems of the explanatory stratum on which is built the dramatic or poetic stuff is a dangerous responsibility. Mr. F. W. Bateson has plausibly argued that Tennyson's "The Sailor Boy" would be better if half the stanzas were omitted, and the best versions of ballads like "Sir Patrick Spens" owe their power to the very audacity with which the minstrel has taken for granted the story upon which he comments. What then if a poet finds he cannot take so much for granted in a more recondite context and rather than write informatively, supplies notes? It can be said in favor of this plan that at least the notes do not pretend to be dramatic, as they would if written in verse. On the other hand, the notes may look like unassimilated material lying loose beside the poem, necessary for the meaning of the verbal symbol, but not integrated, so that the symbol stands incomplete.

We mean to suggest by the above analysis that whereas notes tend to seem to justify themselves as external indexes to the author's *intention*, yet they ought to be judged like any other parts of a composition (verbal arrangement special to a particular context), and when so judged their reality as parts of the poem or their imaginative integration with the rest of the poem, may come into question. Mr. Matthiessen, for instance, sees that Eliot's titles for poems and his epigraphs are informative apparatus, like the notes. But while he is worried by some of the notes and thinks that Eliot "appears to be mocking himself for writing the note at the same time that he wants to convey something by it," Mr. Matthiessen believes that the "device" of epigraphs "is not at all open to the objection of not being sufficiently structural." "The *intention*," he says, "is to enable the poet to secure a condensed expression in the poem itself." "In each case the epigraph is *designed* to form an integral part of the effect of the poem." And Eliot himself, in his notes, has justified his poetic practice in terms of intention.

> The Hanged Man, a member of the traditional pack, fits my purpose in two ways: because he is associated in my mind with the Hanged God of Frazer, and because I associate him with the hooded figure in the passage of the disciples to Emmaus in Part V. ... The man with Three Staves (an authentic member of the Tarot pack) I associate, quite arbitrarily, with the Fisher King himself.

And perhaps he is to be taken more seriously here, when off guard in a note, than when in his Norton Lectures he comments on the difficulty of saying what a poem means and adds playfully that he thinks of prefixing to a second edition of *Ash Wednesday* some lines from *Don Juan*:

> I don't pretend that I quite understand
> My own meaning when I would be *very* fine;
> But the fact is that I have nothing planned
> Unless it were to be a moment merry.

If Eliot and other contemporary poets have any characteristic fault, it may be in *planning* too much.[15]

Allusiveness in poetry is one of several critical issues by which we have illustrated the more abstract issue of intentionalism, but it may be for today the most important illustration. As a poetic practice allusiveness would appear to be in some recent poems an extreme corollary of the romantic intentionalist assumption, and as a critical issue it challenges and brings to light in a special way the basic premise of intentionalism. The following instance from the poetry of Eliot may serve to epitomize the practical implications of what we have been saying. In Eliot's "Love Song of J. Alfred Prufrock," towards the end, occurs the line: "I have heard the mermaids singing, each to each," and this bears a certain resemblance to a line in a Song by John Donne, "Teach me to heare Mermaides singing," so that for the reader acquainted to a certain degree with Donne's poetry, the critical question arises: Is Eliot's line an allusion to Donne's? Is Prufrock thinking about Donne? Is Eliot thinking about Donne? We suggest that there are two radically different ways of looking for an answer to this question. There is (1) the way of poetic analysis and exegesis, which inquires whether it makes any sense if Eliot-Prufrock *is* thinking about Donne. In an earlier part of the poem, when Prufrock asks, "Would it have been worth while, ... To have squeezed the universe into a ball," his words take half their sadness and irony from certain energetic and passionate lines of Marvell's "To His Coy Mistress." But the exegetical inquirer may wonder whether mermaids considered as "strange sights" (to hear them is in Donne's poem analogous to getting with child a mandrake root) have much to do with Prufrock's mermaids, which seem to be symbols of romance and dynamism, and which incidentally have literary authentication, if they need it, in a line of a sonnet by Gérard de Nerval. This method of inquiry may lead to the conclusion that the given resemblance between Eliot and Donne is without significance and is better not thought of, or the method may have the disadvantage of providing no certain conclusion. Nevertheless, we submit that this is the true and objective way of criticism, as contrasted to what the very uncertainty of exegesis might tempt a second kind of critic to undertake: (2) the way of biographical or genetic inquiry, in which, taking advantage of the fact that Eliot is still alive, and in the spirit of a man who would settle a bet, the critic writes to Eliot and asks what he meant, or if he had Donne in mind. We shall not here weigh the probabilities – whether Eliot would answer that he meant nothing at all, had nothing at all in mind – a sufficiently good answer to such a question – or in an unguarded moment might furnish a clear and, within its limit, irrefutable answer. Our point is that such an answer to such an inquiry would have nothing to do with the poem "Prufrock"; it would not be a critical inquiry. Critical inquiries, unlike bets, are not settled in this way. Critical inquiries are not settled by consulting the oracle.

Notes

1 Cf. Louis Teeter, "Scholarship and the Art of Criticism," *ELH* 5 (Sept. 1938), 173–94; René Wellek, review of Geoffrey Tillotson's *Essays in Criticism and Research, Modern Philology* 41 (May 1944), 262; G. Wilson Knight, *Shakespeare and Tolstoy*, English Association Pamphlet no. 88 (April 1934), p. 10; Bernard C. Heyl, *New Bearings in Esthetics and Art Criticism* (New Haven, 1943), pp. 66, 113, 149.

2 *Dictionary of World Literature*, ed. Joseph T. Shipley (New York, 1943), pp. 326–39.

3 J. E. Spingarn, "The New Criticism," in *Criticism in America* (New York, 1924), pp. 24–25.

4 As critics and teachers constantly do. "We have here a deliberate blurring. ..." "Should this be regarded as ironic or unplanned?" "... is the literal meaning intended ...?" "... a paradox of religious faith which is intended to exult. ..." "It seems to me that Herbert intends. ..." These examples are chosen from three pages of an issue of *The Explicator* (Fredericksburg, Va.), 2, no. 1 (Oct. 1943). Authors often judge their own works in the same way. See *This Is My Best*, ed. Whit Burnett (New York, 1942), e.g., pp. 539–40.

5 A close relative of the intentional fallacy is that of talking about "means" and "end" in poetry instead of "part" and "whole." We have treated this relation concisely in our dictionary article.

6 E. E. Stoll, "The Tempest," *PMLA* 44 (Sept. 1932), 703.

7 Ananda K. Coomaraswamy, "Intention," *American Bookman* 1 (winter 1944), 41–48.

8 For the relation of Longinus to modern romanticism, see R. S. Crane, review of Samuel Monk's *The Sublime, Philological Quarterly* 15 (April 1936), 165–66.

9 It is true that Croce himself in his *Ariosto, Shakespeare, and Corneille*, trans. Douglas Ainslie (London, 1920), chap. 7, "The Practical Personality and the Poetical Personality," and in his *Defence of Poetry*, trans. E. F. Carritt (Oxford, 1933), p. 24, has delivered a telling attack on intentionalism, but the prevailing drift of such passages in the *Aesthetics* as we quote is in the opposite direction.

10 See Hugh Mearns, *Creative Youth* (Garden City, 1925), esp. pp. 10, 27–29. The technique of inspiring poems keeps pace today with a parallel analysis of the process of inspiration in successful artists. See Rosamond E. M. Harding, *An Anatomy of Inspiration* (Cambridge, 1940); Julius Portnoy, *A Psychology of Art Creation* (Philadelphia, 1942).

11 Curt Ducasse, *The Philosophy of Art* (New York, 1929), p. 116.

12 And the history of words *after* a poem is written may contribute meanings which if relevant to the original pattern should not be ruled out by a scruple about intention. Cf. C. S. Lewis and E. M. W. Tillyard, *The Personal Heresy* (Oxford, 1939), p. 16; Teeter, loc. cit., pp. 183, 192; review of Tillotson's *Essays*, *TLS* 41 (April 1942), 174.

13 Chapters 8, "The Pattern," and 16, "The Known and Familiar Landscape," will be found of most help to the student of the poem. For an extreme example of intentionalist criticism, see Kenneth Burke's analysis of *The Ancient Mariner* in *The Philosophy of Literary Form* (Baton Rouge, 1941), pp. 22–23, 93–102. Mr. Burke must be credited with realizing very clearly what he is up to.

14 Charles M. Coffin, *John Donne and the New Philosophy* (New York, 1927), pp. 97–98.

15 In his critical writings Eliot has expressed the right view of author psychology. See *The Use of Poetry and the Use of Criticism* (Cambridge, 1933), p. 139, and "Tradition and the Individual Talent" in *Selected Essays* (New York, 1932), though his record is not entirely consistent. See *A Choice of Kipling's Verse* (London, 1941), pp. 10–11, 20–21.

CHAPTER 6

Broken on Purpose
Poetry, Serial Television, and the Season

Sean O'Sullivan

Sean O'Sullivan is an Associate Professor of English at the Ohio State University. He is the author of *Mike Leigh* (2011), a volume in the Contemporary Film Directors series from the University of Illinois Press. His articles on serial narrative and television include such topics as poetic design and serial television; third seasons; episodic storytelling; modernist structure in *Mad Men*; and the television series of Ingmar Bergman.

Formalist criticism thrives in the field of television studies. Much of the work focuses on narrative structure, ranging from the smallest units of story-telling ("beats") to the larger categories of seasons. Serial television in particular opens up space for formal analysis, drawing on the history of publication by installment, whose popular origins date to Charles Dickens and the nineteenth-century Victorian novel. Sean O'Sullivan's essay argues that the segmented nature of serials connects to the segmented elements of poetry, including meter, line, and stanza. The essay claims that serials operate as a collection of fractures, rather than as single undivided texts, using the first season of *The Sopranos* (1999) as an illustration of the recent phenomenon of the "sonnet-season" – the 13-episode uninterrupted season that has become a recurrent form for many of the most ambitious television serials of the twenty-first century.

This essay has two goals. The first is to argue that serial narrative, and in particular serialized television drama, is a poetic enterprise. All serials, by definition, are broken; like poems, they are broken on purpose. This prosodic art, unlike the art of nonserialized fiction, calls attention to itself as an array of parts; it is the art of fracture, of separation, and it is the art of the energy required to stitch together those pieces, just as the art of poetry requires a persistent process of breaking and reconnecting sounds, lines, and stanzas. We need to understand the most ambitious serials of our current

Original publication details: Sean O'Sullivan, "Broken on Purpose: Poetry, Serial Television, and the Season." *Story Worlds: A Journal of Narrative Studies* 2, pp. 59–77. University of Nebraska Press, 2010. Reproduced with permission from University of Nebraska Press.

gilded age – including such shows as *The Sopranos, Deadwood, Six Feet Under, The Wire, Mad Men,* and *Lost* – as a significant branch in poetry's genealogical tree. Although prose fiction has been commonly invoked as the clearest precursor to these televisual enterprises, in fact they recall narrative's earliest traditions; specifically, they echo oral performances – narratives governed by metrical organization, iteration, and variation. Here I address two crucial pairs of terms – segmentivity and numbers, and meter and rhythm – that connect the infrastructure of poetry to the infrastructure of serial television; and I draw particular attention, by way of example, to the role of anaphora and caesura in the construction of serialized television episodes. In using these terms in the present pilot-study, I hope to do more than just demonstrate the pertinence of poetic structures for the study of serial narrative. Beyond this I aim to show what is distinctively different about some of the most compelling art of the present moment – art that has adapted an ancient cultural technology for innovative purposes.

The second goal of the essay is to argue that this process of adaptation has produced a new and significant unit of meaning: the season. When asked to think about long-form televisual storytelling, both authors and critics often have recourse to analogies with the novel; by this logic individual episodes are deemed to be like chapters in a long book (see *The West Wing* 2003; Ayres 2009; McGrath 2000). But the multiplot spectrum of characters, events, and thematic contexts in a single serialized episode far exceeds the ambit of a traditional novel chapter, which typically emphasizes one narrative cluster rather than the juxtaposition of several. A closer ancestor might be the weekly, monthly, or bimonthly installment of the nineteenth-century serialized novel, such as *Great Expectations, Bleak House,* and *Middlemarch,* respectively. These installments – called "parts," or "numbers," or "books" – more closely approximate the shape and variety of an episode; but those earlier installments worked together to serve one contiguous instrument, namely the novel as a whole – whose final length was anticipated by authorial convention (in Dickens's twenty-part stories, following the 1836 success of *The Pickwick Papers*), or by prescriptive announcement (in serializing journals such as *All the Year Round*). Television, by contrast, operates from season to season – runs of episodes marked off by significant gaps. With each season separated from the next by several, or many, months, the promise of continuation is almost always in abeyance, vulnerable to cancellation or creative exhaustion. And although hourly television drama has long operated through the medium of seasons, until recently those seasons have been too long, and too irregular in their alternation between new and old episodes, to offer a sustained narrative experience. The last decade, however, has seen the advent of the thirteen-episode uninterrupted sequence, a system that most closely resembles the poetic stanza. I argue that we need to think of those thirteen episodes as lines of verse, and this new model of the season as something like a sonnet – a clear but flexible shape that both hews to established protocols and breaks those protocols when necessary. Consequently, my next section samples from several shows to provide an overview of how metrical structures (including the season) function in television serials, and my final section uses the first of the true "sonnet-seasons" – namely, season 1 of *The Sopranos* – to provide a more detailed case study. There I illustrate the role of such prosodic devices as enjambment, the turn, quatrains, and tercets in the design of this newest serial form.

Prosodic Structures in Television Serials

Segmentivity and Numbers

I borrow "segmentivity," the first of these terms of art, from Brian McHale, who himself borrows it from Rachel Blau DuPlessis. McHale endorses DuPlessis' proposal that we deem segmentivity to be the defining feature of poetry, just as we deem narrativity to be the defining feature of narrative, and performativity the defining feature of performance.[1] As McHale notes, DuPlessis argues that "[p]oetry involves 'the creation of meaningful sequence by the negotiation of gap (line break, stanza break, page space)'; conversely, then, segmentivity, 'the ability to articulate and make meaning by selecting, deploying, and combining segments' is 'the underlying characteristic of poetry as a genre'" (McHale 2009: 14). McHale's brief is to bring renewed attention to the narrative dimension of poetry, and he notes that although segmentivity also operates in nonpoetic narrative – which "is certainly segmented in various ways, at various levels and scales" – segmentivity "is not dominant in narrative, by definition." By contrast, he argues, segmentation "must always contribute meaningfully (for better or worse) to the structure of poetic narrative" (17, 18). McHale's analysis sets an important precedent for exploring serial television as a shaped collection of pieces. In particular, his emphasis on "spacing" and "the negotiation of gap" (along with "gappiness" and "gapped lines") provides elements of a vocabulary for studying the building blocks, and the blocks of omission, that govern serial television narrative.

On a quite literal level, the practice of making serial television often starts with a bunch of bits of stuff. For example, David Chase and Matthew Weiner, creators and showrunners of *The Sopranos* and *Mad Men*, respectively, begin thinking about each episode by subdividing the potential circumstances or scenes into "beats," then listing them on a dryerase board or cutting them into small slips of paper, laying out those slips, and then moving those slips around (mentally and physically) in thinking about how to orient and present the forthcoming cluster that we call an episode (Chase 2002: ix; Chozick 2009). The beats of each episode – the separate scenes, sometimes less than a minute long, that are strung together in the narrative of an hour – move us from one location or plot strand to another, creating parallels, dialectical contrasts, and interruptions, in the manner of verse but always requiring us to see the pieces *as* pieces, independent contractors participating in a large project. I have argued elsewhere that the three key items of seriality are the old, the new, and the gap (or the "between") (O'Sullivan 2006: 120–21); these are likewise three key elements of poetry, especially lyric poetry – with its emphasis on new versions of old forms (like the sonnet), and the gaps created by line breaks and stanzas. In many ways it is the articulation of the gap, the between, that animates the familiarity of old and new; the way in which a poem, or serial television, articulates those breaks makes that poem, or that unit of seriality, what it is. This is the discourse of segmentivity – parts, size, form – wrapped in the language of new and old, of the discovered and the familiar, defining itself through the logic of gapping and spacing.

The use of *numbers*, as a defining practice, connects poetry and seriality in the prehistory of television – since "numbers" is both the name given to Dickens's monthly fictional installments and the synonym for "verse" deployed by, among others, Wordsworth. His negotiation, in the preface to *Lyrical Ballads*, between the mechanics of numbers ("the ease and gracefulness with which the Poet manages his numbers are themselves confessedly a principal source of the gratification of the Reader") and plain speech lead to his goal of fitting "to metrical arrangement a selection of the real language of men" (Wordsworth 1996: 174, 164). That same tension between numbers and mimesis obtains in television serials, as evidenced again in Chase's formula of the beats. He explains that the template for every episode of *The Sopranos* is a system of "approximately 35 beats," divided among an A and a B story ("thirteen or so" beats each), a C story ("five or six beats"), and the occasional D story ("a few beats") (Chase 2002: ix); that same kind of division of labor, with local variations, applies to *The Sopranos*' cohort of serials. Individual episodes may feature subtle fluctuations, just as lines of verse may scan differently from their putative metrical model; the dictates of arithmetic quarrel, as in poetry, with the local needs of story and character. This quarrel, as I've noted, makes us aware of the broken surface of the text, making us consider the multiple effects of each beat – not just its place in a continuing storyline but its possible tonal, visual, or thematic relationships with the preceding and succeeding beat. The beats of television serve differing narrative purposes simultaneously, as links in a narrative chain (or story) and as distinct agents colliding with beats from other chains, just as words in poetry serve simultaneously as meanings, numbers, and sounds.

Another art system privileging sound, and likewise predicated on the mathematical arrangement of distinct parts, is music – which when wedded to poetry creates songs, also known as "numbers." This is no casual pun, especially in the case of *The Sopranos*, which uses numbers, that is, pre-existing musical selections, as its only nondiegetic accompaniment. In other words, the show rejects the signature of score – a symphonic form that connects, reminds, and familiarizes – in favor of a disconnected array of songs – ranging from rock to hip hop to opera – that add more broken pieces to the episodes. Each song brings its own meter and rhythm to each moment, sometimes suggesting clear rhymes or parallels between story and music, sometimes creating off rhymes or dissonances. The use of quoted, rather than original, music has become more and more prevalent in serialized television over the last decade, further emphasizing the numerical or metrical organization of the serials themselves.[2]

Meter and Rhythm

David Milch, creator of *Deadwood*, offers us a way of transitioning from numbers to meter and rhythm. Milch has claimed that "the highest form of storytelling ... is mathematics – where literally the signs contain within themselves the most violent and basic form of energy. Einstein understood that if he was able to sign correctly he would experience the secret of energy" (Singer 2005: 204). This bridge between mathematics, or numbers, and the energy of storytelling – the raw energy of psychology and event – recalls Wordsworth's effort to apply meter to the language of real men. More precisely, meter represents half of the mathematical energy of verse, since its prescriptive claim – that in the case of iambic pentameter a line will be composed of five iambs – is in constant conversation with the local demands of rhythm – the actual assembly of iambs, spondees, dactyls, trochees, and anapests that fill out a specific line. This is the fertile tension between plan and execution, or in somewhat grander terms, between Platonic conception and Aristotelian practice. In Hollywood's economic model of industrial art, that tension translates into the master plans that the likes of Chase and Milch may cook up for a season versus the real exigencies of time and money that shape those plans. Serial television production offers a parallel to the Victorian pressure of weekly and monthly publication, since by the end of the season, the scramble to turn scripts into shots into episodes typically accelerates, as the gap between process and air time shrinks. Television in general operates on a much tighter schedule than feature filmmaking. The usual time frame for filming an episode is ten days, with five or six pages shot per day; by contrast, features aim to shoot one or two pages per day. That constriction exerts a much greater pressure to compress and improvise, especially in terms of how scenes are filmed, resulting in a constant negotiation between the intended meter of a scene and the eventual rhythm.

Milch addresses the clash between meter and rhythm in serial television art, or the tension between global designs and local possibilities, by citing poetic precedent. In the companion book to *Deadwood*, he states: "Melville said that any great poem spins against the way it drives" (Milch 2006: 17). Milch in fact re-appropriates the context of this citation; it comes from Melville's 1860–61 poem titled – appropriately for our purposes – "The Conflict of Convictions," wherein the speaker announces, "I know a wind in purpose strong – / It spins *against* the way it drives" (lines 63–64). The italicization of the word "*against*" is original to the poem and underscores the governing push and pull not only of the convictions advertised in the poem's title but also of poetic construction itself, as segments argue with gaps, syllables argue with sentences, and lines argue with stanzas. McHale, citing the work of John Shoptaw, offers the term "countermeasure," where "measure at one level or scale is played off against measure at another level or scale," so that, for example, Emily Dickinson's poetry "may be predominantly phrase-measured, but her phrases are also counterpointed or countermeasured at the level of line and stanza" (McHale 2009: 17). Whether we choose to call it meter and rhythm, spin and drive, or measure and countermeasure, both poetry and serial television explore this dialectic prominently through the tension between circular and linear patterns. In poetry we might call the drive toward the end of each line a progressive one, as each word moves us forward in space, in narrative accumulation or lyric addition; but the end of the line often heralds a return (a spin), as much as a conclusion. In certain kinds of poems, we call the return (or spin) "rhyme," an aural device that reminds us of a sound we've heard in the preceding line.

Consider, as an illustration of how meter and rhythm operate in serial television, two prosodic techniques: *anaphora* – which we might call both a driving and spinning force, since it creates a progressive structure while reminding us of each preceding iteration – and *caesura*, a harsher strategy that shatters the unity of the line by creating an end in the middle, a syntactical rhythm clashing with the requirements of meter. One manifestation of anaphora in serial television is the opening credits sequence, which serves circularly to remind us of the metrical conventions of the program. But there are in effect two beginnings to each program – the credits sequence (the spin) and the beginning of the show "proper" (the drive). Sometimes this narrative beginning appears before the credits and produces what is known as a "cold open," as is the case with *Lost* and *The Wire*, and sometimes the credits precede the beginning of the narrative proper, as is the case with *The Sopranos, Deadwood*, and *Mad Men*. Not only do these alternative patterns for constructing anaphoric links offer quite different consequences for the beginning of each episode (or line of the poem); they can also operate as either a countermeasure to, or rhyme with, the closing credits. In this respect, the start and finish of *Lost* always work symmetrically. After the cold open, the title of the show appears over a black screen, accompanied by the signature ominous opening music; at the end of the episode, the final credits appear over a black screen, accompanied by the signature ominous closing music. By contrast, each episode of *The Sopranos, Deadwood*, and *Mad Men* concludes with a new piece of music, one we have not heard before and will never hear again. In effect, these last-mentioned shows rhyme at the beginning of each episode, but not at the end. *The Wire* finds a prosodic middle ground, since the same song is played at the beginning of each episode, and the same instrumental piece (different from the opening song) is played at the end; but each season features a new version of that initial song, thereby creating spin and drive simultaneously.

For an example of caesura, the prosodic opposite of the framing devices in serial television, we need to think not of patterns but of exceptions – such as the storytelling rift in the middle of "That's My Dog," episode 5 of season 4 of *Six Feet Under*, which violates convention mid-way through by suddenly shedding the multiplot alternations of serial drama and confining itself for the rest of the hour to the uninterrupted carjacking ordeal of David Fisher. The episode caused a furor, ostensibly because the audience objected to seeing a beloved character unrelentingly brutalized; but that emotional shock was amplified by a procedural shock, namely, the sudden rupture of metrical expectation and the violation of rhythmic precedent, an abandonment of narrative protocol that forced viewers to wonder what, and how, they were watching. "That's My Dog," significantly, enacted not simply a caesura within its own narrative drive but one within season 4 as a whole, since its consequences transformed the trajectory not only of David Fisher but also of the central group of characters around him (Nussbaum 2004: 52; O'Sullivan 2009: 221–23).

The Season as Unit of Meaning

The double-consequence of this caesura in *Six Feet Under*, both for the specific episode and for the episodes preceding and succeeding it, provides a segue to my discussion of a relatively new lyric form: the season. Until 1999, the television season had operated purely as a system of production, numbering from as many thirty-four episodes per year for a show like *Bonanza* in the mid-1960s and tapering off gradually to the more recent convention of twenty-two episodes. This loose, baggy superstructure traditionally begins in the autumn and runs through late spring; the twenty-two-episode season unfolds in clusters of new installments – aimed around "sweeps" periods of the calendar, when ratings are tied to advertising prices – alternating with clusters of reruns. This model gives audiences a general sense of commencement and conclusion, with occasional spikes along the way; but each of these markers – commencement, conclusion, spike – is relatively "soft," in a manner that is reflective of what Raymond Williams influentially referred to as the "flow" of television.

Williams suggested that the sequence of programs aired by any television station, and the collection of genres within that sequence, including series, commercials, promotions, and so forth, constituted a continuous stream; we do not so much shift clearly back and forth between sustained narrative worlds and interrupting advertisements as experience one sustained program of images and sounds (Williams 1974: 91–92). Jane Feuer has amended Williams's argument, positing television as "a dialectic of segmentation and flow" (Feuer 1983: 15). Most recently, flow has been drastically eroded by the technology of the digital video recorder (DVR), which allows viewers to control what they watch, and to become, in effect, bricoleur programmers – rather than passive recipients of program sequences constructed by executives. The twenty-two-episode season emphasizes a version of flow, at the expense of segmentation, since it is not so much shaped and bounded (i.e., clearly segmented and gapped) as arrayed in notional bunches. That ontological fuzziness of the traditional season underlies the recurrent critical emphasis on serial television as an open-ended enterprise; consequently, writers such as Jennifer Hayward (1997) and Robyn Warhol (2003), while interested in parallels to earlier serial forms, have concentrated televisually on soap opera, a continuous genre wherein the unit of the seasons is completely effaced.

In January 1999 HBO aired the first season of a new series, called *The Sopranos*, an event that generated a well-documented cultural tsunami. What has been relatively unremarked upon is the watershed created by the specific form of that season: thirteen episodes, aired in consecutive weeks, with no interrupting reruns. When I say that the pre-1999 television season was purely a system of production, I do not mean to suggest that the first season of *The Sopranos* was not also originally engineered to serve the financial and structural demands of a network. The thirteen episodes resemble the typi-cal first batch of episodes that are ordered for a traditional twenty-two-episode season, with the succeeding nine episodes (or "back end") ordered only if the ratings for the first batch warrant such an investment. But before *The Sopranos*, those first thirteen episodes had not been envisioned or consumed as a self-contained narrative cluster. The thirteen-episode uninterrupted complete season provided, for the first time in American television history, a distinct narrative form, one that was large enough to occupy significant time and space, but not so large as to turn into vague sprawl. Its close analogy, in length, to the fourteen-line parameter of the sonnet may be an industrial accident, since the proximate benefits of that first, shorter season were cost control and a convenient quarter-year of programming; but as so often in the history of American film and television, a corporate decision has had far-reaching artistic consequences.[3]

Before we address the particulars of this parallel between sonnet and season, let us remember the reasons for the sonnet's own success – and how quickly both it and the thirteen-episode season caught on. The sonnet is long enough to develop an observation or a thought, flexible enough to be metaphorically prescriptive in the hands of William Shakespeare, and colloquially investigative in the hands of Robert Frost. Its end is far enough away from its beginning to suggest a change or translation, but not so far as to suggest a daunting journey.[4] And just as Philip Sydney's *Astrophel and Stella* helped kick off the sonnet craze of the 1580s and 1590s, so the first season of *The Sopranos* kicked off the thirteen-episode season (in some versions, the twelve-episode season) of our last decade. Since 1999, many series have followed this form, including such HBO succes-sors as *Six Feet Under, The Wire, Deadwood*, and *Big Love* but also offerings on rival cable programmers, such as *Mad Men, Breaking Bad*, and *Dexter*. Even an over-the-air network show like *Lost*, whose first two seasons enacted the traditional twenty-two- to twenty-four-episode skein – dispersed loosely over thirty-six weeks of the calendar – shifted in its final two seasons to shorter sixteen- to eighteen-episode runs, crucially aired in consecutive weeks, with virtually no interruptions. The season, as a distinct, compressed, and contiguous entity, is no longer the exclusive province of "prestige" cable networks. Even the compact length of the sonnet-season may become part of the over-the-air lexicon, as evidenced in 2009–2010 by the thirteen-episode second season of *Dollhouse* on Fox.[5]

In this context it is important to mention again a key technological innovation that coincided with the advent of *The Sopranos*: namely, the digital versatile disc, or DVD. Like the sonnet-season, this innovation allows the viewer to contain the bulk of epic narrative. Consider what the consumer of television drama had to choose from in 1999, if she wanted to pick her way through the medium's history. She could buy VHS tapes titled "The Very Best of *Hill Street Blues*" or "*Law & Order*: Producer's Collection," or the "Buffy and Angel Chronicles" within the corpus of *Buffy the Vampire Slayer* – cherry-picked assemblages of two or three cassettes that reflected putative thematic links, or apparent indexes of quality. The season as defining unit was essentially invisible as a consumable artifact. Even HBO failed to seize on that artifactual property at first, delaying the release of the first season of *The Sopranos* until December 2000, a few months before the third season aired. As late as 2005 the fourth season of *Six Feet Under* was not available until immediately after the airing of the fifth and final season, thereby keeping at bay the viewer's full purchase on the narrative. Since then the dialogue between season and DVD has become explicit; no show of any stature fails to issue its preceding season on disc before the new season is aired on television. Now all seven seasons of *Buffy the Vampire Slayer* are available in full, and even the thirty-two-episode megalopolis that is the first season of *Bonanza* was finally issued on DVD in 2009. The viewer's ability literally to own seasons, in packaged divisions, has materially changed the narrative dynamics of the text.

The Wire exemplifies the consequences of the thirteen-episode uninterrupted season. The series ran from 2002 to 2008 and numbered five seasons, varying in length from thirteen episodes (seasons 1 and 4) to twelve episodes (seasons 2 and 3) to ten episodes (season 5). Each season began with a new performance of the opening credits song, "Way Down in the Hole," as well as a new montage of scenes from the upcoming season; both the musical strategy and the visual strategy were unprecedented for an American television series. That teasing glimpse of what was to come supplied just enough information to convey a sense of how the storyworld would evolve over the course of the season, but not enough to convey specific trajectories of character and plot. This framing device is a direct descendant of Dickens's serial numbers. The green cover of a twenty-part book like *Little Dorrit*, or the monthly version of a weekly like *A Tale of Two Cities*, featured an illustration of the major characters of the novel, organized on the page in graphical relationships that, retrospectively, could be seen to portend as yet undisclosed interconnections and consequences. But the difference, again, is that there is no equivalent to the "season" in Dickens's work. *The Wire*'s decision to change covers each year, as it were, underlined the very different narrative focus of each season; despite the connecting threads of Baltimore, police work, and the drug business, the central narrative landscape constantly changed. Season 1 concentrated on housing projects; season 2 on the shipyards; season 3 on the political arena; season 4 on the schools; season 5 on the newspaper business. Given these radical shifts of attention, it is peculiar that *The Wire* has so frequently been compared to a long novel, since there is nothing comparable to this in any Victorian book, whether serialized or published in volumes.[6] One might tentatively consider a massive project like Balzac's *La Comédie humaine* as an analogue; but just as *Bleak House* is too small to serve as direct precedent, that ninety-five-title edifice is too big. *The Wire* is both more circular than Balzac in its use of structural tropes and more linear than Dickens in its changes of character and context. The prose genealogy, in other words, only goes so far; we need to turn once more to poetry.

A Case Study of the Sonnet-Season: Season 1 of *The Sopranos*

While the recent televisual wealth offers an array of candidates to illustrate the properties and possibilities of the sonnet-season, it seems appropriate to use the initiator of the form – namely, the first season of *The Sopranos*. It is a season particularly sensitive to the choices and effects of the thirteen-episode uninterrupted sequence, inaugurating the corona of sonnets that we call *The Sopranos*. My proposed homology between this form of televisual season and the sonnet – which we might frame as between twelve and fourteen – does tease us into speculation about connections between serial television and other inherited methods of segmenting experience and time, such as the division of years into months or of shorter periods into fortnights. But the parallel here is not limited to a similar number of lines. I want to spotlight three compositional strategies of the season, strategies that correspond to, but also re-invent, the motions and countermeasures of the sonnet: an initial experimental quatrain (episodes 1–4); two evenly spaced jarring interruptions, in episodes 5 and 10, each of which may be likened to a turn; and a closing tercet. That said, I am not claiming that this specific organization of segments is repeated precisely in subsequent seasons – whether of *The Sopranos* or any other series. The sonnet-season does not fall as rigorously into patterns as the three-quatrains-and-a-couplet form of the English sonnet, or the octave-and-sestet form of the Italian sonnet; rather, Frost's formal experiments provide the closest model. While some of the prosodic maneuvers I describe may recur, the laboratory of the thirteen-episode uninterrupted season in the last decade has played with the possibilities of segmentation, numbers, meter, and rhythm, rather than follow codified orders. In other words, the spin and drive between rigor and freedom, between a fealty to clear rules and an impulse to break them, have become a governing dynamic of television narrative.

The initial stanzaic strategy of the first season of *The Sopranos*, the experimental quatrain, is a four-episode cluster unified by the story of Jackie Aprile, the head of a New Jersey crime family in which Tony Soprano and his Uncle Junior serve as high-ranking lieutenants. Over the course of those episodes, Jackie sickens and dies; the fourth episode concludes at this funeral. This quatrain corresponds to what is more commonly referred to as an arc, a sustained plot strand that moves the broader narrative along, with consequences both for plot and for character.[7] Concurrent with this story cluster is what I will call a verse-structure, as each of these four episodes tries a distinctly different way of beginning.

The first episode, also known as the pilot, starts out in the waiting room of Jennifer Melfi, a psychiatrist whom Tony is about to meet as he seeks treatment for his panic attacks. David Chase has said that if no network had picked up the pilot, he could have added half an hour and released it as a self-contained low-budget feature (*Sopranos* 2001). Consequently the episode is less focused on creating a serial template than in telling its own story; for example, the first half of the pilot relies on Tony's voiceover as a way of organizing and clarifying information – a technique never repeated in the show's subsequent eighty-five episodes. A different narrative experiment inaugurates the start of the second episode, "46 Long," which begins, unlike any other episode in *The Sopranos'* six seasons, with a "cold open," a pre-credit scene of little serial consequence – showing, in this case, the mobsters counting money and watching a Mafia expert talk on television. The third episode, "Denial, Anger, Acceptance," begins with an enjambment. Here a lingering storyline from the final act of the second episode – the theft of a truck "belonging" to one part of the mob family by people affiliated with another part – continues immediately, almost as if there had been no interruption, or gap, between episodes. (Such enjambment is extremely rare as a narrative strategy for the rest of the series.) By contrast with these "false" starts, the fourth episode, "Meadowlands," begins with a device that will become a hallmark of the season, and the series as a whole: a dream sequence of Tony's. As an initial gambit, it will be repeated at a parallel moment in a scheme of four-episode clusters, in the eighth episode of the season. But the second time around the dream sequence involves Tony's nephew, Christopher – creating a kind of rhyme between the oneiric anxieties of these two characters. So, like a poem that begins its first four lines with four distinct sounds, images, or perspectives, the first quatrain of the season emphasizes the divergent over the iterative, the linear over the circular.

The second prosodic, season-dependent strategy under consideration – the interruption – manifests itself in sudden changes of style and direction at two parallel moments of the season: the fifth episode, "College," and the tenth episode, "A Hit Is a Hit." "College" is among the most celebrated of all *Sopranos* episodes, and Chase has spoken often of its importance to him, as an instance of his impulse toward anti-serial countermeasure, even as he was making a serial: "'College' comes closest to achieving my personal goal of making episodes that could be stand-alone films. It is self-contained" (Chase 2002: viii). The story of Tony and his daughter Meadow's college tour through Maine, where he encounters and garrotes a witness-protection "rat," is not serially anticipated by any of the preceding four episodes, and its serial consequences are minimal for the rest of the season. Less celebrated, but equally unintegrated, is "A Hit Is a Hit." This episode begins (again, out of nowhere) with the killing of a Hispanic rival unfamiliar to the show's audience and the discovery of a large pile of money, a share of which allows Christopher to try out a side career as producer for a mediocre rock band. The shared structural role of these two episodes would be interesting enough – an anti-serial hour walling off a four-episode proserial cluster preceding it – but the connections go much further. Each episode is about art and culture. "College," which begins on a small college campus and lingers, near its conclusion, on an inscribed quotation from *The Scarlet Letter*, repeatedly touches explicitly on issues of verisimilitude, sculpture, cinema, and literary inheritance. "A Hit Is a Hit" is a narrative essay about the world of popular music, particularly the tension between early 1960s black acts (run and exploited by white managers) and late 1990s gangsta rap – with related attention to such cultural currency as bidets and imported Italian glass, as well as the contingency of stock values. How is art related to commerce? What are things worth? What is the value of formula, as exemplified, in one instance, by Beatles songs? How do talent and luck magically coalesce into that mysterious entity known as "a hit"? Just as so many poems are about poetic voice and the material nature of language, the first season of *The Sopranos* interrupts itself, twice, at regular intervals, to ask questions about the tension between design and accident, high and low art, the permanent and the evanescent – in other words, the basic cultural work of an ambitious television serial at the end of the twentieth century.

Finally, the closing tercet of the season – "Nobody Knows Anything," "Isabella," and "I Dream of Jeannie Cusamano" – returns us from the self-conscious reverie of "A Hit Is a Hit" to the insatiable drive of serials, as Uncle Junior's plans to kill Tony, and the consequences thereof, take over. This tercet, like the initial quatrain, is united by a storytelling arc, in this case the gradual suspicion that Pussy Bonpensiero, Tony's best friend, has turned FBI informant. The narrative join to "A Hit Is a Hit," where Pussy seemed jovial and unanxious, is remarkably awkward; suddenly, an episode later, he acts furtively and walks with the weight of the world on his shoulders. The season, like those schizophrenic works we call poems, refuses to hide the separation of its parts, fighting the requirement to conclude by emphasizing the cluster, or the segment, over the flow of the whole. The twelfth episode is especially jagged, since it interweaves a long-anticipated serial event – the attempted hit on Tony – with an episode-specific story wherein Tony believes that he has met a beautiful Italian housesitter next door named Isabella – a person who turns out to be completely imaginary. The audience is not explicitly clued in to this delusion until Tony is; this confusion of the subjective and the objective represents an elaboration of the dream trope seen earlier in the season, but now in a way that prompts the viewer to identify with Tony, rather than observing him from an external, rational standpoint. This shift to the fanciful late in a season, often in penultimate or antepenultimate episodes – whether in the famously "irrelevant" pursuit of a Russian in the third season's "Pine Barrens," which takes place predominantly in snowy woods for reasons that matter little to the serial context, or the astonishing twenty-minute dream sequence in the fifth season's "The Test Dream," a "Circe"-like reprocessing of a vast amount of narrative material – will become a *Sopranos* structural habit, slowing the serial momentum down just when it should be accelerating. These warring impulses offer a synthesis of two warring possibilities for sonnet closure: the summarizing, clarifying Shakespearean couplet that often tries to make sense of questions asked, or the darkening final movement of a Frost sonnet, translating an initial everyday observation into something restless and unresolvable.

What I have tried to offer here is a beginning but also a return – a beginning for inquiry into the new serials, and a return that grounds this inquiry in the prosodic structures of the most ancient forms of verbal art. Recent work has discussed the "complexity," or cognitive challenge, that these serials produce, with good reason (Mittell 2006; Johnson 2005). But those studies have deployed the rhetoric of the new, rather than the discourse of the old – what is unprecedented within the realm of television or popular culture, rather than what is adapted from poetic practice. Serial television's lexicon of segmentation, numbers, meter and rhythm, and the genre of the sonnet-season represent the return of verse narrative to its origins as popular art.

Notes

1 The segmented, narrated, and performed art of serial television, it should be noted, enacts all three elements.

2 The shock final ending of *The Sopranos* – its infamous cut to black – owes as much to the absence of music as to the absence of image. The final credits, silent for the first and only time, reminded the viewers of their dependence on meter and numbers; as with John Cage's *4'33"*, the absence of measure made measure the very subject of the missing sound.

3 The other fundamental variation from network practice was the absence of commercials – a countermeasure that undid the traditional multiple-act structure, studded with pre-commercial climaxes. So the uninterrupted episode and the uninterrupted season were as responsible for undoing ossified segmentation as they were for inventing new ways of breaking narrative form.

4 HBO did have internal business models for the thirteen-episode season prior to the debut of *The Sopranos*: three of the six seasons of *The Larry Sanders Show* (1992–98) numbered between eleven and thirteen episodes, and the first season of *Sex and the City*, in 1998, was thirteen episodes long. But these situation comedies, whatever their success and cultural impact, did not aim for the kind of serial season-long interconnection practiced by *The Sopranos* and its successors. While certain ongoing storylines involving principal characters did loosely knit episode to episode, they were also designed to be watchable out of sequence, in the tradition of television comedy. *Sex and the City*'s

interest in season-long, and series-long, serial throughlines did accelerate later on in its run – after *The Sopranos* had helped change the entire experience of serial television.

5   It is worth noting that, in Great Britain, each season of a show is called a "series," and its episodes are presented in consecutive weeks, without interruption. This semantic difference, and this publication model, indicate that the distinctiveness, or separation, of the season/series unit within the entire history of a program has operated longer in the British context than in the American one. But the relative brevity of the traditional British series/season produces significantly different effects from the format initiated in the United States by *The Sopranos*. British dramas with serial components tend to run for six to eight episodes per series, creating a much more abbreviated narrative dynamic, with much less scope for the kind of metrical and rhythmic variety detailed in my examination of the first season of *The Sopranos* in the final section of this essay.

6   For direct comparisons between Dickens and *The Wire*, see Weisberg (2006) and Miller (2007). David Simon, the show's creator, termed his creation a "visual novel" (Mittell 2009: 429).

7   Michael Newman discusses arcs and beats within the confines of what he terms "mass art television" (2006: 17), in contrast with the more experimental series that I have been examining.

Works Cited

Ayres, Chris (2009). "Alan Ball Finds True Blood Six Feet Under." *The Times* (London) 30 Sept. 2009. http://entertainment.timesonline.co.uk/tol/arts_and_entertainment/tv_and_radio/article6853973.ece.

Chase, David (2002). The Sopranos: *Selected Scripts from Three Seasons*. New York: Warner Books.

Chozick, Amy (2009). "The Women behind *Mad Men*." *Wall Street Journal* 7 Aug. 2009. http://online.wsj.com/article/SB10001424052970204908604574332284143366134.html

Feuer, Jane (1983). "The Concept of Live Television: Ontology as Ideology." *Regarding Television: Critical Approaches*. Ed. E. Ann Kaplan. Frederick: U Publications of America.

Hayward, Jennifer (1997). *Consuming Pleasures: Active Audiences and Serial Fictions from Dickens to Soap Opera*. Lexington: UP of Kentucky.

Johnson, Steven (2005). *Everything Bad Is Good for You: How Today's Popular Culture Is Actually Making Us Smarter*. New York: Riverhead.

McGrath, Charles (2000). "The Triumph of the Prime-Time Novel." *Television: The Critical View*. 2nd ed. Ed. Horace Newcomb. Oxford: Oxford UP. 242–52.

McHale, Brian (2009). "Beginning to Think about Narrative in Poetry." *Narrative* 17.1: 11–30.

Milch, David (2006). Deadwood: *Stories of the Black Hills*. New York: Melcher Media.

Miller, Laura (2007). "The Best TV Show of All Time: A Classical Masterpiece." *Salon* 15 Sept. 2007. http://www.salon.com/ent/tv/feature/2007/09/15/best_show/index1.html.

Mittell, Jason (2006). "Narrative Complexity in Contemporary American Television." *Velvet Light Trap* 58: 29–40.

Mittell, Jason (2009). "All in the Game: *The Wire*, Serial Storytelling, and Procedural Logic." *Third Person: Authoring and Exploring Vast Narratives*. Ed. Pat Harrigan and Noah Wardrip-Fruin. Cambridge: MIT P. 429–38.

Newman, Michael Z. (2006). "From Beats to Arcs: Toward a Poetics of Television Narrative." *Velvet Light Trap* 58: 16–28.

Nussbaum, Emily (2004). "Captive Audience." *New York* 9 Aug. http://nymag.com/nymetro/arts/tv/reviews/9579/.

O'Sullivan, Sean (2006). "Old, New, Borrowed, Blue: *Deadwood* and Serial Fiction." *Reading Deadwood: A Western to Swear By*. Ed. David Lavery. London: I. B. Tauris. 115–29.

O'Sullivan, Sean (2009). "The *Decalogue* and the Remaking of American Television." *After Kieślowski: The Legacy of Krzysztof Kieślowski*. Ed. Steven Woodward. Detroit: Wayne State UP. 202–25.

Singer, Mark (2005). "The Misfit: How David Milch Got from *NYPD Blue* to *Deadwood* by Way of an Epistle of St. Paul." *New Yorker* 14 and 25 Feb. 2005. 192–205.

The Sopranos (2001). "David Chase Interview." Created by David Chase. Season 1 DVD. HBO Video.

Warhol, Robyn R. (2003). *Having a Good Cry: Effeminate Feelings and Pop-Culture Forms*. Columbus: Ohio State UP.

Weisberg, Jacob (2006). "*The Wire* on Fire: Analyzing the Best Show on Television." *Slate* 13 Sept. http://www.slate.com/id/2149566/.

The West Wing (2003). "Off the Record [featurette with comments by creator Aaron Sorkin]." Season 1 DVD. Warner Home Video.

Williams, Raymond (1974). *Television: Technology and Cultural Form*. New York: Schocken.

Wordsworth, William, and Samuel Taylor Coleridge (1996). *Lyrical Ballads*. Ed. W. J. B. Owen. New York: Oxford UP.

CHAPTER 7

Tools for Reading Poetry

Herman Rapaport

Herman Rapaport is a Reynolds Professor of English at Wake Forest University with work focusing on contemporary critical theory and the arts. Books include *The Literary Theory Toolkit* (2011), *Later Derrida* (1994), and *The Theory Mess* (2001). He is currently researching Jacques Derrida's lecture courses of the 1980s in preparation for a book on them.

Tropes

Traditionally, literary tropes have been considered ornamental devices that supplement or supplant ordinary meanings in ways that both deviate away from and add to what is being said.[1] In Milton's *Paradise Lost* there is a famous epic simile in Book 1 that compares the fallen angels to autumnal leaves that have fallen into the brooks around Vallombrosa, a locale south of Florence, Italy. The simile might well remind one of embroidery, which is to say, of an ornamental stitching of comparisons into the text. The simile occurs when Satan calls up his legions who "lay intrans't ..."

> Thick as Autumnal Leaves that strow the Brooks
> In *Vallombrosa*, where th' *Etrurian* shades
> High overarch't imbow'r; or scatter'd sedge
> Afloat, when with fierce Winds *Orion* arm'd
> Hath vext the Red-Sea Coast, whose waves o'rethrew
> *Busirus* [Pharaoh] and his *Memphian* Chivalry,
> While with perfidious hatred they pursu'd
> The Sojourners of *Goshen*, who beheld
> From the safe shore thir floating Carcasses
> And broken Chariot Wheels; so thick bestrown
> Abject and lost lay these, covering the Flood,
> Under amazement of their hideous change.[2]
>
> (ll. 302–13)

Original publication details: Herman Rapaport, "Tools for Reading Poetry" from *The Literary Theory Toolkit: A Compendium of Concepts and Methods*, pp. 98–133. Blackwell Publishing, 2011. © 2011 Herman Rapaport. Reproduced with permission from John Wiley & Sons and H. Rapaport.

Literary Theory: An Anthology, Third Edition. Edited by Julie Rivkin and Michael Ryan.
© 2017 John Wiley & Sons, Ltd. Published 2017 by John Wiley & Sons, Ltd.

Clearly, Milton wanted to compress much information into this diversion away from Satan's action, a prolepsis to a peaceful pastoral moment near a Catholic monastery in Tuscany. Psychologically, the purpose of this sort of epic simile is to forget the traumatic present by substituting something rather remote, natural, and pleasant in its place, in this case brooks bestrewn with leaves in autumn. As it happens, the simile is echoing similes of fallen leaves in Homer, Virgil, and Dante, which gives it a sort of ritual significance or, at the very least, the depth of literary precedent. And the simile generates a parallel simile within it that speaks to the destruction in Exodus of the Egyptians on chariots pursuing the Jews in the Red Sea. The basic associative chain is: Devils = Dead Leaves = Broken Chariot Wheels. What is remarkable is how Milton at the end of the passage manages "so thick bestrewn" to have a double reference, to the wheels and the leaves, and in addition a third reference back to the ostensible object of our attention, "these" (the Devils strewn in Hell). Notice too that Milton wanted to inlay a bit of Greek myth in the midst of all this with reference to Orion, who, in one of the myths about him, walks on water, which makes one realize that he is a prefiguration of Christ and of God's might and mercy.

This epic simile is quite an embellishment. It takes us far afield and puts together rather heterogeneous elements, a scene of falling leaves near a monastery, mention of Orion, the aftermath of Pharaoh's defeat, and the devils abject and lost on the fiery lake at the foot of Satan. Of central importance in considering this and other figures, generally, is the fact that they tend to both compress and compare, and to lead away from and then lead back again to something.

Figures embellish and ornament a text, much as Milton's simile does, but they also amplify and can multiply registers of reference. It's hard not to notice that Milton's simile is pithy: it's very compact and dense and is made up of large and small fragments that do and don't quite go together. Leaves and chariot wheels aren't something we'd usually equate. But Milton makes this work by way of subordinating the power of association to the rhythmic patterning of the words. In other words, the lines build up rhythmic momentum and carry us along in a way that extends over the different elements of the content. Milton does this quite a bit in other parts of the poem, too. Bits that don't really cohere more or less fit because the rhythm of the language overwhelms the discrepancies. Plus Milton is good at the figure known as *syllepsis*. He can let a phrase ambivalently refer to two objects but choose only one of them to advance. This occurs with "so thick bestrewn / abject" which refers to both the broken army of Pharaoh and the devils before Satan, carrying onward from the latter reference.

At this point, it is helpful to offer a definition of a literary figure. It was formulated by a French scholar, Pierre Fontanier, in 1830. "Figures of discourse are the traits, forms, or turns that are more or less remarkable and that have a more or less happy effect by means of which discourse, in the expression of ideas, thoughts, or feelings, distances itself more or less from that which had been a simple and common expression." Earlier, the *Académie Française* had followed an older tradition that goes back to antiquity in which a division was made between grammar (ordering isolated ideas) and rhetoric (propositional thinking, expressions used in discourse). On the grammatical axis, "an arrangement of words [gives] force or grace to discourse," and along the rhetorical axis "a turn of thoughts [creates] a beauty, an ornament in discourse."[3]

All of this supports what we have seen in the epic simile of the leaves of Vallombrosa. In fact, what one has there is *grammar* (the ordering of the narrated units: the brooks clogged with leaves, the Jews being pursued by Basirus (Pharaoh), the saving spirit of

Orion (Christ), the broken chariot wheels, the languishing abject devils on a burning lake in Hell) and *rhetoric*, the parenthetical expression of these units as sequential propositions (thick as ... where th'... or scattered ... when with ...). Both grammar and rhetoric are animated by sentiment or what Fontanier called "passion" (in our case, the rhythmic force). Of central importance is that all this is supposed to distance itself from simple and common expression. That it teaches, delights, digresses, beautifies, ornaments, embellishes, complicates, plays logical tricks, references far flung texts, says the impossible, obscures, tantalizes, seduces, compresses, ambiguates, and whatever else figures do is all to the good, especially when, as the *Académie* argues, the result is felicitous (*heureuse*).

As to particular types of figures that turn up in discourse, Fontanier covers pretty much everything imaginable in his *Figures du discours*. Here are just some of the examples he covers: abruption, adjunction, allegorization, alliteration, anacolouthon, catachresis, conjunction, counterfision (contrefision), correction, dubitation, enthymemism, epitropism, imprecation, license, litotes, metalepsis, metaphor, optation, paradox, paranomasia, preterition, repetition, syllepsis, synecdoche, topography.

Of interest should be that Fontanier's understanding of these discursive devices requires a division into three types: figures that correspond (i.e. metonymy), figures that resemble (i.e. metaphor), and figures that connect (i.e. synecdoche). In the epic simile of the leaves of Vallombrosa, we have resemblance (the devils resemble leaves and broken chariot wheels with respect to their fallenness, brokenness, and death) and correspondence insofar as the devils and Pharaoh's forces are both forces of evil and therefore actually connected by something they both have in common. In fact, Milton was probably thinking that Pharaoh's troops *are* devils who will be doing mischief later in human history, and that Pharaoh will be none other than Satan disguised as the Egyptian leader. In addition we have Fontanier's idea of connection in the simile, given that all the parts belong to a topos Milton calls Hell. Everything is connected to Hell because it is all a part of it, Hell not being confined to a time and place. This is a crucial point, because it overturns the impression that Hell has a confined locus and temporality: that it is a place like other places. In terms of Fontanier's notion of connection, we have an extension of a type or genre of thing into things that are "of" that genre and even generally representative of it. Here, again, the broken army of Pharaoh comes most immediately to mind.

Something that Fontanier doesn't stress is the fact that figures in literature often have to do with transformation, the change of one thing into another, the swapping of appearances, one thing being displaced by another, and so forth. Milton was greatly influenced by Ovid, who was the great poet of metamorphosis. Throughout *Paradise Lost* the devils keep getting metamorphosed into one thing or another. In fact, the whole epic could be said to be about metamorphosis: changes in state. In that sense, the simile of the devils being seen as autumnal leaves isn't quite as decorative as one might imagine, though it is and remains an embellished ornament, in any case, a digression in which the changes of identity or of state can be pushed quite a bit further than they could otherwise. Recall the Académie's point: figures enable the poet to discourse in a way that is not commonplace (i.e. "normal"). In fact, that means figures enable the poet to indulge in transformational flights of extraordinary fancy and skill.

One point to underscore is that it's not always too useful to think of figures as separate entities whose definition we memorize so that we can identify them when they pop up in poems, plays, and novels. Rather figuration is quite protean and overlapping. In Milton's epic simile we saw the extended comparison that was introduced with the word "as."

This, obviously, is the epic *simile* itself; we saw ambiguity in the selection of that monastic site south of Florence which may be a nasty swipe at Catholicism or a tribute to Dante, Virgil, and Homer; we saw *metaphor* – one thing resembling another (devils = leaves = broken wheels); we saw *metonymy* – correspondence in which one entity is actually a part of another entity; and we saw *synecdoche* – the whole simile being a part of Hell that is representative of its various dimensions. We could have found *irony* in the comparison of the leaves, which are natural, peaceful, and predestined to die and the devils who are unnatural, troubled, and had the choice not to fall. And we could have noticed that Orion is a *personification* of the wind that walks and disturbs the waters. Or we could have noticed the use of *euphemism* and *epithet*: the Sojourners of Goshen.

Incidentally, reading by way of Fontanier, we would have to notice that Goshen, too, is a kind of Hell, that the Sojourners are doing exactly what the devils will not be able to do, and that they are doing exactly the inverse of what Adam and Eve will do at the end of the epic. That is, the Sojourners are leaving their Hell in Egypt for a promised land (a sort of Eden). Inversely, the devils will never get out of their Hell, and the parents of Mankind, in another sort of inversion, will be leaving Eden for a much less paradisial "World before them." This inverse crossing is known as *chiasmus*. And in a way the Sojourners of Goshen do manage to figure or sign an invisible cross in terms of their crossing the paths of both the devils and the fallen Adam and Eve. And that would relate to *symbolism*.

In case one wonders why Milton's epic, *Paradise Regained*, has lacked the popularity of the longer epic, it is because that later poem lacks the ornamentation and fanciful detail that Milton lavished on the story of the parents of Mankind. Probably, Milton envisaged the earlier poem as pre-Christian and therefore more in line with ancient epic devices, whereas *Paradise Regained* he imagined within a Calvinist aesthetic: pure, austere, minimal, pious, stripped of classical ornamentation and flights of fancy. Whether the *Académie Française* read Milton at all, I do not know, but I'm sure if they had, the determination would have been made that *Paradise Lost* has a felicity lacking in the more dour *Paradise Regained*.

Reading

Pierre Fontanier, *Les figures du discours* (1977)
George Puttenham, *The Arte of English Poesie* (sixteenth century)

Elision

That poetry is often telegraphic and compressed can be a source of annoyance to readers who find it frustrating to be caught up in a verbal game of "keep away" in which the poet manages to tease us with half-spoken messages. Notice the following riddle poem (# 1489) by Emily Dickinson.

> A Route of Evanescence
> With a revolving Wheel –
> A Resonance of Emerald –
> A Rush of Cochineal –
> And every Blossom on the Bush

> Adjusts its tumbled Head –
> The mail from Tunis, probably,
> An easy Morning's Ride –

When Dickinson sent this poem to Helen Hunt Jackson in 1879, she wrote the following as a preface. "To the Oriole you suggested I add a Humming Bird and hope they are not untrue –".[4]

In collections of Dickinson's poetry the poem is untitled, which suggests that editors are under the impression we're supposed to be able to figure such poems out by ourselves, which may be somewhat unreasonable, given that Dickinson herself didn't think people might be able to fill in the blanks. This speaks to a culture of poetry reading, not necessarily shared by Dickinson, in which the art of reading poetry is precisely that of supplying content that has been elided (withdrawn, kept back, skipped over). In "A Route of Evanescence" the subject of the poem is never mentioned, only some rather attenuated qualitative correspondences are given that have both metaphorical and metonymical significance. The route of evanescence itself is a metaphor for the darting around of the hummingbird; Dickinson seems to be asking whether hummingbirds make a route like other birds. The revolving wheel is a metaphor too, but it is also a metonymy. The wings in flight appear to be analogous to a revolving wheel (metaphor), but they are also a very distinctive feature of the bird itself (part for whole: metonymy). The emerald and red (Cochineal) are impressions of color that the poet sees as the bird feeds. There is then a shift to mention of the flowers upon which the bird is feeding, and one has to suppose we're to guess what sort of bush this might be, or at least visualize *something* akin to what Dickinson had in mind. The bush is personified, that much is clear. Finally, there is a comparison with mail carriers and reference to where the hummingbird has migrated from: North Africa. Given the bird's speed, it's "an easy Morning's Ride," but this is intentional hyperbole (exaggeration). It's meant humorously.

What many readers may not be aware of is that Dickinson wrote different versions of the same poems and, at times, couldn't decide on particular words. Line two of "A Route of Evanescence" had variants in the manuscripts with respect to the word "revolving" ("With a revolving Wheel"). Variants included "delusive wheel," "dissolving wheel," "dissembling" ("With a dissembling"), and "renewing" ("With a renewing"). In those last two instances no mention of wheel appears. It's elided. Here we can see that Dickinson had various other possibilities in mind with respect to content that she suppressed by using the much more concrete and literal "revolving." But that too is an elision: a sort of suppression of suggestions the poet had in mind and might have liked to work out had the poem allowed it. This speaks to fit. What can't be fitted into a line? And what if that material is important to the conceptualization of the poem?

Here are a few lines from "Maroon" by Chelsey Minnis, a poem that shows the blanks, as it were, by means of punctuation.

................my bloodthirsty...wet.............
....
....baby.............................
.........is.......an auburn...........and.................bloody.............beauty........[5]

Minnis writes what is clearly a typical narrative sentence broken up with ellipses. But one has to wonder, is our skipping over the dots not a mistake? Isn't the narrative closure here *deceptive*? We would naturally assume "baby" to be the subject of the sentence, given its syntactic structure. But perhaps a sentence or two is missing here and what we take to be a continuation is a mistaken presumption. The dots in Minnis' collection *Zirconia*, of which "Maroon" is a part, are not entirely unrelated to the dashes that Dickinson loved to use in her poems and letters: signs of absence.

In contrast notice how space functions in Jackson Mac Low's "People Swamp" of 4–5 July, 1990.

> People swamp flavor.
>
> Iridescence knot ringdove end needle sieve.
>
> Keeper encystment palliation aftervarnish creepiness instrument.[6]

The obvious question here is whether these statements have anything to do with one another or not, let alone whether these are well formed propositions out of which a narrative could or should be constructed. "Swamp" could be a noun or a verb. In the first case one would be left with a nominative phrase or perhaps just three nouns. In the second case we would have a sentence with subject, verb, object. It sort of makes sense that way, but only sort of. In the second line the words "knot" and "end" also have this doubleness of being either nouns or verbs. But now there appears to be little gain in seeing them that way. However one considers the words grammatically, the sentence doesn't quite manage to be a well formed statement. The same is true for line three. Is this poem just meaningless? Would it help if we knew what it's leaving out? But how would we know if something is being elided here? By what test could we determine this?

In *North of Intention*, Steve McCaffery, himself a poet, quotes Leon S. Roudiez on the paragram: "A text is paragrammatic in the sense that its organization of words (and their denotations), grammar, and syntax is challenged by the infinite possibilities provided by letters or phonemes combining to form networks of signification not accessible through conventional reading habits." McCaffery adds: "Paragrammatic wordplay thus manufactures a crisis within semantic economy, for whilst engendering meanings, the paragram also turns unitary meaning against itself."[7] The para-gramme in at least one of its manifestations posits a para-grammar, a pseudo-linguistic construct that elides conventional practices of making meaning – for example, the use of standard grammatical constructions. Rather, the paragramme constellates verbal entities or parts thereof in ways that redistribute linguistic combinations in ways that make up *alternative signifying economies* that are, for the most part, *antisemantic*. If Mac Low elides something, it is the function of standard grammatical constructions, something that turns against semantics: the function of words as transparently meaningful entities and the function of lines as complete thoughts. Here there is no narrative that exists in the wings waiting for someone to decipher it by means of a verbal game of hints and winks. But does this only obtain with poets like Mac Low? Couldn't we read Edmund Spenser and John Donne paragrammatically as well? As it turns out, yes. But this would require something other than a literary historical approach that assumes all poetry is a translation of an a priori story into elliptical form, an encryption of ordinary language into poetic language.

Reading

Steve MacCaffery, *North of Intention* (2000)

Resemblance

As Fontanier noticed, poetry is largely the construction of resemblances, which accounts for the importance of figuration in poetry, but also relations of sound and sense. This section considers resemblance in terms of *juxtaposition* (adjacency), *analogy* (metaphysical conceit), *allegoresis* (allegory), *emulation* (sympathy), and *imitation* (mimesis). For a more in depth account of some of this, see Michel Foucault's chapter "The Prose of the World" from *The Order of Things*.[8] Foucault's thesis is that in the later seventeenth century we can begin to see an "epistemic break" (or conceptual rupture) with Renaissance practices of signification that were analogy based, so that, for example, one shifts rather abruptly from a world in which everything is seen in hierarchical correspondence to a world in which one simply enumerates data statistically and then distributes it according to graphs whose purpose is to empirically measure and quantify the data. Whereas the Renaissance had a strong interest in qualitative relations among entities, which had moral and metaphysical significance, the Age of Reason had an overriding interest in quantitative relations among entities, which had statistical and empirical significance. The question that Foucault didn't resolve is whether the arts can ever make that leap. Paul de Man's influential paper, "The Rhetoric of Temporality," suggests not.[9] However, this is also just plainly apparent from reading many twentieth century poets: T.S. Eliot, Wallace Stevens, Sylvia Plath, and John Ashbery, among them.

Juxtaposition

Juxtaposition refers to how we make linguistic associations when poets simply put words, phrases, or sentences adjacent to one another. When Shakespeare juxtaposes swear and forswear – as in sonnet 152 – the result is a verbal matrix that serves as a sort of verbal engine for the poem as a whole. By juxtaposing these words, Shakespeare encourages the contamination of one by the other, which produces an overload of meanings.

As poetry became more compressed by modernist poets who had repudiated the rhetorical style of Victorian poetry, emphasis fell upon the juxtaposition of fragmentary motifs and images. Ezra Pound's famous "In a Station of the Metro" is exemplary: it juxtaposes the image of faces in a crowd to petals on a wet, black bough. The mention of the petals on the bough is merely juxtaposed. Pound is not saying the petals *are* a metaphor for the faces. There's no actual connection, just the association that we happen to make.

Robert Creeley's "FIVE Eight Plus" (from the collection *Windows* (1987)) is composed of short juxtaposed bits that don't make the sort of obvious association we saw in Pound. The following is just a short excerpt taken from the middle of the poem.

Window
Up from reflective
table top's glass
the other side of it.

.

Around
The pinwheel's pink
plastic spinning
blade's reversing.

.

Ego
I can
hear I can
see

·

Daytime
It's got to be
lighter[10]

No doubt, we can try to link the texts in small capital letters as if they were keys to some
narrative progression, but this will be less successful than looking at the poem as a
modular series of juxtapositions in which the sections relate out of sequence. One could
relate Window with Daytime, for example. In such a case, the reader is actually selecting what goes with what by putting the sections together in whatever way makes sense
to him or her. This is reminiscent of aleatory music of the post 1945 period in which
composers were writing bits of music that musicians could play in whatever order they
wished. Although no two performances of the piece would be the same, in all likelihood, the work still had its own recognizable sound texture. Suddenly, order wasn't the
determining factor of what a piece sounded like. Creeley's poem participates in this
kind of aesthetic.

Analogy

Analogy is easily seen in the poetry of John Donne. In "The Relique," Donne compares
himself and his mistress to holy relics that have been dug up at some future time after
their deaths.

> Then, he that digges us up, will bring
> Us, to the Bishop, and the King,
> To make us Reliques; then
> Thou shalt be a Mary Magdalen, and I
> A something else thereby;

In this case the analogy is transformative in that it makes the beloved into Mary
Magdalen and Donne into Christ (the one to whom "something else" is referring).
Donne can make that association, because the lovers have not consummated their love
sexually, only Platonically. For "Difference of sex no more we knew, / Than our guardian angels do." In Donne, emulation is not sufficient, for he generally seeks a translation of one thing into another that is transformative. This occurs again, famously, in
"The Flea" wherein Donne's mistress is about to kill a flea in bed that has bitten both
of them and therefore could be said to contain "three lives," its own, Donne's, and the
mistress's. "This flea is you and I, and this / Our marriage bed, and marriage temple is."
Here again the analogy has logical consequences that the poet extrapolates in order to
amplify if not to exaggerate the transformative effect of the initial correspondence.
Lastly, in Donne these correspondences are redemptive. The transformation into Mary
Magdalen and Christ, as well as the transformation into the marriage temple would
attest to this. But notice, too, the redemptiveness of analogy in "Air and Angels."

> Twice or thrice had I loved thee,
> Before I knew thy face or name,
> So in a voice, so in a shapeless flame
> Angels affect us oft, and worshipped be.

What could be viewed as a sordid relation between anonymous lovers is redeemed by means of comparing the mistress to an angel. Again, the exaggerations and implausibility of these comparisons raise the suspicion that these analogies must be ironical or satirical and that therefore their redemptive effects are dubious, however tempting it might be to accept them at face value.

Allegory

The extension of analogy into an isomorphic set of correspondences that substitute for the literal sense is known as allegoresis, something that Donne is broaching in the poems above. Indeed, if one extended the analogies of the relic, the flea, and angels to any great extent, the poems would turn into full scale allegories. Typical of allegory is the thirteenth-century poem on the art of love entitled the *Romance of the Rose* (Jean de Meun and Guillaume de Lorris), in which a lady, allegorically personified by a rose, is being courted by a lover. A young man initially follows a stream to a large walled in garden, and upon the walls he contemplates personifications of various abstractions: hate, felony, avarice, covetousness, envy, sadness, and poverty, among them. That these figures decorate the outside of what is, in fact, a garden of delight, speak to those personal attributes that one should consider antithetical to pleasure and that therefore should be banished. These are the attributes that no lover ought to possess. Edmund Spenser's *Faerie Queene*, similarly, uses personifications in order to represent psychological human attributes, though in many cases the relationship between the person and the attribute are not in a simple one to one correspondence. Red Crosse Knight is a complex character that is not simply reducible to a religious redeemer figure, though he is certainly that, as well. Una, who represents the true church, is again not simply a walking abstraction. She is developed to the point that she is not just a convenient allegorical device whose function is to make an abstraction more comprehensible in human terms. Whereas Spenser's allegorical depictions are readily comprehensible within both the Christian and Romance traditions, William Blake's *Jerusalem* is a complex allegory that rewrites and revises the Judaic-Christian tradition in ways that reflect Blake's idiosyncratic personal revelations. In such a case, the allegorical transparency of various personifications is diminished and readers are required to figure out precisely what Blake must have had in mind, since the meanings aren't to be found in the cultural tradition.

Allegoresis occurs in more modern poetry as well. In T.S. Eliot's *The Waste Land*, the medieval topos of the waste land functions as an analogue to the condition of Europe in the 1920s. At moments within the poem, Eliot is referencing *Perceval* by Chrétien de Troyes (twelfth century), therefore using its story as the allegorical analogue for the twentieth-century spiritual condition of Europeans. But also notice the recent poem *Lip Service* (2001) by the Language Poet Bruce Andrews, which is keyed to the cantos of Paradiso in Dante's *Divine Comedy*. Dante writes the following near the end of canto 33:

As is the geometer who wholly applies himself to measure the circle, and finds not, in pondering, the principle of which he is in need, such was I at that new sight. I wished to see how the image conformed to the circle and how it has its place therein;

And Bruce Andrews nearing the end of *Lip Service* writes:

> geometry at total, raptures diaphanous closeout diagram
> generalizes fingers arraigned as chocolate,
>   adorable base alias reality image refusal emboldens
> fetus using your body without your consent –
> its sweet front lathed with
> this is something else;[11]

Whether or how Andrews' text is allegory or even just allegoresis is probably a matter for some debate; however, the fact that Andrews used Dante's poem as a structural and thematic source (as he has pointed out and as we can see from the references in both poems to geometry) leaves open the question of whether we shouldn't at least try to make the connection and pose the possibility that allegory is active, though not in ways we're used to seeing in most poetry. Indeed, that there is an allegorical aspect to Andrews' poem is perhaps self-evident, but whether it abides by any of the usual rules of allegorical procedure is open for discussion. It's possible that what we have in Andrews' poem is simply a number of tangential resemblances that posit the effect of allegory without its actually taking place.

Emulation

We have already discussed sympathetic analogies. This is what Michel Foucault was thinking of in terms of *emulation*, or what we can see in the sympathetic correspondences in Milton's *Paradise Lost*. Note that Eve is in emulative correspondence with Satan. In other words, of all the creatures in Eden, she alone could be sympathetic to Satan's condition when he was a revolting angel in heaven, given that just as Satan felt secondary to the Son, Eve feels secondary to Adam, something that the moment she senses it, irritates her. Now, this does *not* mean that Eve is analogous to Satan, which is Milton's subtle point in the parts of *Paradise Lost* leading up to the fall in Book 9. For if she were, she would have been created evil, which clearly wouldn't make sense in the Pauline tradition within which Milton is working.

Sympathetic emulation occurs, quite noticeably, throughout much of William Wordsworth's poetry. In "The Ruined Cottage" (1780), an old man whom Wordsworth, speaking of the poem, once identified as a peddler, has been witness to the economic ruin of a family on account of economic changes within England. The old man tells the poet,

> Sympathies there are
> More tranquil, yet perhaps of kindred birth,
> That steal upon the meditative mind
> And grow with thought. Beside yon spring I stood
> and eyed its waters till we seemed to feel
> One sadness, they and I.

(ll. 79–85)

Sympathy in this case concerns the man's capacity to feel what the family feels by way of experiencing the waters of the spring that to him are in tune or sympathy with his thoughts. "They and I" is somewhat ambivalent, referring at once to the family but also to the waters (nature) and the man. Wordsworth himself said that had he not been educated he could imagine himself very much to be someone like the old man who relates the story of the ruined cottage.

In "Lines Composed a Few Miles above Tintern Abbey," emulation is very pronounced in terms of the poet's relation to his sister Dorothy, whose journals are so central to an understanding of this poem's intensity, given that it is through her (and her writings) that the poet is shown once more how to experience rapture in the presence of nature, an experience the poet can not have without Dorothy's example as a being-in-nature who experiences its sublimity in the smallest details of vegetative life. In Dorothy Wordsworth's *Grasmere Journals* we can read: "I never saw daffodils so beautiful they grew among the mossy stones about & about them, some rested their heads upon these stones as on a pillow for weariness & the rest tossed & reeled & danced & seemed as if they verily laughed with the wind that blew upon them over the lake, they looked so gay ever glancing ever changing."[12] In such cases, consciousness is animated by nature's emulation of what we might mistakenly assume to be exclusively human.

A final example of emulation is the close of Robert Lowell's "Skunk Hour" (1959) when the poet notices a mother skunk and her kittens late at night rummaging through the garbage out in back of his house. What should be a low point for him in terms of the depression he feels and the situation he is in reveals a ray of hope in terms of something that stops quite short of analogy whereby the poet would be compared to being a skunk pure and simple. Rather, in stopping short of metaphor, Lowell emphasizes how the determined behavior of the skunk *emulates* something in the poet's character that will save him: that he will not be scared off.

Imitation

Consider Ezra Pound's poem about the Paris Metro mentioned above. In that poem the petals on a wet black bough do and don't actually imitate (resemble) the crowd that one sees entering and exiting the metro. What about "Shall I compare thee to a summer's day?" Shakespeare's proposition in Sonnet 18 is that of a conceit that equates a period in a man's lifecycle to a season, which can be done since the macrocosm of a human life is believed commonly in Shakespeare's day to be equivalent to the microcosm of a year with its four seasons. But is the resemblance contrived? What about the opening stanza to "Lake Bud" by Ishmael Reed? Its subject is the great jazz pianist Bud Powell.

> Lake Merritt is Bud Powell's piano
> The sun tingles its waters
> Snuff-jawed pelicans descend
> tumbling over each other like
> Bud's hand playing Tea For Two
> or Two For Tea[13]

Here the lake resembles the piano just as the pelicans resemble the hands: Tea for Two = Two for Tea. Of course, we have to perceive the imitative resemblance, which requires knowledge of what Powell's piano playing sounds like.

Imitation can also be structural, and here we should be reminded of Milton's mirror poems "L'Allegro" and "Il Penseroso" that are imitative in terms of structure as well as content. "L'Allegro" (the happy life) is the inverse of "Il Penseroso" (the melancholic life) in terms of content, but both are structurally symmetrical to a high degree. Structural imitation occurs, as well, in Dante and in Spenser. In recent examples of poetry, see work by Leslie Scalapino, whose first collection, *Concerning How Exaggerated Music Is*, demonstrates a high degree of structural imitation in the form of recursivity. This is a technique she has refined over some four decades to stunning effect.[14]

Reading

Michel Foucault, *The Order of Things* (1971)

Objective Correlative

T.S. Eliot, who was a critic as well as a poet, coined the term objective correlative, by which he meant an object, situation, or event (in the singular or plural) that functions as an adequate correlative to the poet's emotions. A very good example is Matthew Arnold's poem "Dover Beach" (1851) in which the beach at Dover is a concretely experienced place that has emotional correlatives. As a setting, Dover Beach has a metonymical relation to the much bigger place that is England, if not, Europe. Dover Beach is the stage, as it were, for setting up an experiential analogue to what it feels like to be a European living in a time of vulgar empirical demystification and social leveling. The poem famously ends with a premonition of ignorant armies clashing in the night. What makes the poem so successful is that the correlative of the beach to the feelings of the poet and his concerns is not just apt, but revelatory, given our historical hindsight. Indeed, many poets since have repeated this sort of Victorian poem, among them, T.S. Eliot, whose *The Waste Land*, however more fragmented in terms of setting, still employs the objective correlative of the waste land metaphor to approximate the spiritual condition and feeling of the poet. For a poem to be successful, according to Eliot, the objectification of the emotions has to be convincing; that is, it has to convey the inner state of the poet's feelings and, one might suppose, his or her psychology.

Apparently, Eliot imagined the correlative must be sincere, plausible, realistic, and serious in intent. But is William Wordsworth's objective correlative of the cloud plausible, realistic, and serious in "I Wandered Lonely as a Cloud"? What about Emily Dickinson's "I felt a funeral in my brain"? Is John Ashbery's objective correlative sincere, let alone, plausible, realistic, and serious in "Caesura" ("Job sat in a corner of the dump eating asparagus ..." from *Shadow Train*)? Indeed, Ashbery is quite a lesson in how far a poet can get in terms of mocking the objective correlative, but, Eliot might have countered, that *is* the objective correlative (the situation) for postmodern subjects.

The funny thing is, despite all the objections one could raise about what precisely makes up a successful objective correlative, we all know a bad objective correlative when we see or hear one. For example, consider the Country-Western lyric, "I flushed you from the toilet of my heart." That's not viable, is it? And yet, someone could argue that if the vulgarity of the correlative is so extremely insensitive that it ironically undermines the sentiments regarding hurt feelings, we've in fact found a quite good correlative with respect to how people actually respond to betrayal: as hurt *and* angry; sensitive *and* insensitive.

What Eliot calls the objective correlative is, from another perspective, *the controlling metaphor that captures the social subject's actual relation at a point in historical time to the world*. Of course, the identity of this social subject will be defined in terms of gender, class, ethnicity (possibly), race (possibly), and nationality (almost certainly). Yet, if this social subject lacks a certain generality or averageness, the objectivity of the correlative, as one that a wide diversity of readers could identify with, collapses in on itself. Sylvia Plath, for example, is a social subject who was white, female, well educated, and a poet who was part of the American "poetry scene" of the 1950s and 1960s. Many thousands of readers can and do identify with her. Even those of us who aren't female can cross the bridge whereby her correlatives make sense as an experience we can imagine holding in common, for without that, the poetry would be merely sectarian.

As to the reference above to an "actual relation" to the world, it is important to point out that what Georg Lukács referred to as the requirement for realism in literature applies to poetry as well as to fiction – at least, in Eliot's context. The objective correlative needs to be a controlling metaphor that discloses the social subject's *actual* relation to history; otherwise, nothing that is said will have anything but subjective significance. When W.B. Yeats spoke in his poetry of the center not holding anymore, he perceived something quite major about what had changed with respect to people's actual historical circumstance. Eliot's waste land metaphor is a similar case in point. Eliot's poem isn't saying that the poet feels as if he's living in a waste land; it is making the point that empirically Europeans had entered an age in which culture had turned into a waste land, because the culture was being turned into nothing more than the standard of living. In other words, culture is what people buy at the department store. There is nothing else, anymore. If this wasn't absolutely true in the 1920s, the Frankfurt School (Max Horkheimer, Theodor Adorno, et al.) was predicting it would come to pass in the period following the Second World War, which has largely happened, in fact.

Have artists found good objective correlatives as good as the waste land metaphor in the second half of the twentieth century? As noted, Ashbery makes fun of this type of thinking, and he is not alone. There appears to be a widespread impression today that the world is so complex and logically impenetrable that it would be foolish to imagine an artist could sort it out by finding just the right correlative, the way Arnold did back in the 1850s, or, for that matter, the way Pablo Picasso did in the painting *Guernica* in 1939. But is this skepticism merely an excuse for not having managed to sort something out or not? Lukács thought that the worth of a literary writer was to be measured in terms of the extent to which he or she could understand society and history as a coherent totality and the special conditions that therefore pertained to the social subject as a historical personage. Whereas many contemporary writers may have abandoned this expectation, it turns out that the general public has not.

Reading

T.S. Eliot, *The Sacred Wood* (1920)

Language Poetry

Language Poetry is an avant garde movement of the second half of the twentieth century that has had roots in the high modernist writing of Gertrude Stein, William Carlos Williams, Paul Zukofsky, and George Oppen, though a major influence was certainly Jackson Mac Low whose own work was indebted to the sort of procedural compositional practices initiated by the composer John Cage in the 1940s and 1950s. Cage's work crossed boundaries between music, writing, painting, and what later came to be known as performance art. Many of his pieces are essentially directions of a rather general sort that a performer is being asked to realize with the aid of a page of instructions.

Mac Low often included rather detailed and lengthy rules of composition, to which he generally adhered. "A Note on the PFR-3 poems" of 1938–1985 speaks of the use of a computer program to generate the poetry. An excerpt follows in which Mac Low addresses work he did at Information International, Inc., in Los Angeles in 1969 (!) "with the aid of their PFR-3, a programmable film reader connected to a DEC-PDP-9 computer":

> Their [computer] program allowed me to enter as "data" a list of "messages": originally up to 100 single lines, each comprising at most 48 characters and/or spaces. Later longer messages, though fewer at most, and ones having two or more lines, were possible. From any list the program randomly selected and permuted series of "message members" (characters, words, or strings of linked words, e.g., sentences, separated in the message by spaces) and displayed them on a monitor. When a lever on the control board was pushed, every tenth line appearing on the screen was printed out ...[15]

The poem itself has statements that read out as follows:

> FURIOUSLY IDEAS COLORLESS SLEEPING GREEN
> DEMANDING
> FREEING BREASTS ROUNDED DEEPBOSOMED
> CRUNCHING ABSENTMINDED PLASTIC
> TASTY GRANDMOTHERS
> ARE
> HONEYMAKING ARE EUCALYPTUS DRAWING BEES[16]

Readers unfamiliar with this sort of poetry immediately complain that "it makes no sense." But in fact the lines are filled with suggestive words and odd juxtapositions that give rise to fantasies that pull together the disconnected bits by jumping over their asyntacticality. "HONEYMAKING ... ARE EUCALYPTUS ... DRAWING BEES" is really just very elliptical. And "FREEING BREASTS ROUNDED DEEPBOSOMED" isn't at all hard to figure out. If "PLASTIC" is supposed to go together with "TASTY GRANDMOTHERS," it's a rather comical phrase. Mac Low himself argued that one had to adopt something akin to the Zen Buddhist conception of "no mind" when reading this kind of poetry. That is, one perceives each linguistic event as elements in themselves that arise and pass away without being gathered up into overarching meanings (sayings, propositions, arguments, stories).

When Language Poetry emerged, it constellated a number of significant talents: Ron Silliman, Charles Bernstein, Barrett Watten, Bruce Andrews, Clark Coolidge, Michael Davidson, Bob Perelman, Michael Palmer, Ray DiPalma, Steve Benson, Robert Grenier,

Lyn Hejinian, Leslie Scalapino, Susan Howe, Carla Harryman, Rae Armantraut, and Hannah Wiener, just to name the more prominent figures. In the seminal early anthology edited by Silliman, *In the American Tree*, Mac Low questioned whether Language Poetry is any more language centered than any other literature, contrary to what some were proposing. He admitted that many of the writers depart from normal syntax, that "the subject matter shifts rapidly," and that indeterminacy and a de-emphasis upon the ego is noticeable. "Few of these works tell a connected story or support an explicit thesis," and there is "lack of narration or exposition." Moreover, Mac Low wondered, "Can these works be seen as imitations in *any* sense of the term?" He answers,

> Seemingly no. Often one word, phrase, or sentence seems to follow another with little regard for the recognized imports of these signs and strings. Their concatenation seems governed not by their referents, or by relations among them, but by features and relations intrinsic to them as language objects. Indeed, some practitioners … call such works "non-referential," and one of them has mounted a brilliant seemingly Marxist, attack on reference as a kind of fetishism contributing to alienation. … [But] what could be more of a fetish or more alienated than slices of language stripped of reference? […] Attention seems centered on linguistic details and the relations among *them*, rather than on what they might "point to."[17]

Mac Low specified, quite rightly, that referentiality was very much a part of Language Poetry, but that it was structured in such a way that instead of communicating itself as exposition, argument, or narration, the perceiver is required to construct larger wholes semiconsciously. "The mind moves beyond the language elements themselves, impelled by a complex mélange of denotations and connotations and of remembered language experiences and life experiences." In that sense Mac Low said such poetry was actually "perceiver-centered" as opposed to "language centered."[18]

Charles Bernstein and Steve MacCaffery have both been quite forceful on the point that Language Poetry should be thought of as superseding what they call Voice Poetry or, alternatively, Official Verse Culture, by which they mean the kind of poetry taught in Masters of Fine Arts Programs in the United States. Essentially, the model for this poetry is Plath's "Ariel," which is certainly a great poem. But the problem is that Plath perfected this sort of poetry and that already in the 1970s it was time to move on. An academy with poetry writing programs filled with students all trying to emote in poems that follow in the wake of Sylvia Plath or Robert Lowell doesn't quite make sense some 50 years after these figures passed away. Language Poetry, by contrast, is not anachronistic aesthetically and attempts to innovate with language in quite radical ways that take it deep into realms of linguistic abstraction that aren't imaginable within Official Verse Culture. But Language Poetry isn't what lyric poets would consider expressive – at least not in the personal or psychological sense, if only because such poetry doesn't believe in the authority of the self as a psychological being whose purpose or function is to express feelings. In other words, there is the concern that for the Language Poets there can be no objective correlative other than the various discourses in collision out there in the world. But is this sort of dialogism a sufficient condition for the writing of poetry?

A younger generation of poets who have brought lyric and language poetry together in interesting ways appear to have decided this issue for themselves insofar as they hold the possibility for an objective correlative open. A very strong example of this approach can be seen in Laura Mullen's prose poem "Torch Song (Prose Is a Prose Is a Prose)" which brings diverse discursive formations together around one of those outrageously "senseless" crimes all too typical in America.

Re:Vision: As if made for a made-for-TV-movie the already tired scene played over and over: "She was so upset," etc. (Question: How upset do you need to be to burn 137,000 acres?) The print is grainy. Did you see her, "in your mind's eye," with matches, crying so her hand shook too much to strike a light at first? Or do you picture her standing there, resolute, raising a lighter aloft like a concert-goer during the encore? "The only thing that is different from the one time to another is what is seen and what is seen depends upon how everybody is doing everything," Gertrude Stein repeats ("Composition is Explanation"). The Russian filmmaker Andrei Tarkovsky dies in exile, his countrymen having refused his vision, even now some people say of his movies that there's not enough story there. In *The Mirror* a drenched woman appears in the charred room of a gone house, a dream or memory, haunting the narrator. *Homage:* as if the word had a home in it. All the elements the filmmaker loved and lovingly reassembled are here: the woman, the forest, the tears … a letter on fire.[19]

Mullen's poem is largely about "The Hayman Fire" that occurred in Colorado in the summer of 2002. The biggest fire that Colorado had ever seen, it was started by Terry Barton, a federal forestry officer who said that she was trying to burn a letter by her estranged husband. Barton was indicted on four counts of arson. Barton's anger is the objective correlative that Mullen herself is setting alight in her poem, as the last sentence in the quotation demonstrates. The conflagration was a horrible tragedy for the state of Colorado, but it is also the objective correlative of the woman's hurt and all the rage that women feel collectively in such situations. The act of burning some 137,000 acres is also one in which gross negligence, stupidity, and emotional overload meet as a response to the life world that, however mad, makes a certain sense as the only adequate response to it, given how anonymous, unfair, and uncaring that world is and how outraged and frustrated individuals feel as subjects who aren't responded to and don't see any other alternative than an apocalyptic response (suicide after murdering the whole family, campus rampages and massacres, the setting of massive forest fires). Mullen's poetry is very much mediated by various discourses (media, academic, descriptive, lyrical) but keeps its distance from the kind of personalism and soul searching typical of Sylvia Plath, Denise Levertov, John Berryman, and their many imitators. Quite noticeably, Mullen doesn't try to psychoanalyze or attempt to make sense of the absurdity of the forest ranger's act. She respects the absurdity of the act and the events that led up to it even while offering decontextualized statements on other matters that do and don't intersect with the life of Terry Barton, something that has the effect of challenging our ideas of what is and isn't normal. "That's the way fire does, it don't have no rules to it. – Anonymous Firefighter, Summer 2002."

Reading

Charles Bernstein, *A Poetics* (1992)
Barrett Watten, *Total Syntax* (1984)

The New Sentence

The new *sentence* was advanced by the Language Poetry Movement and refers to decontextualized prose whose syntax is used as if it were prosody. Unlike the sentence you are reading right now, the new sentence has no specific referential focus. Ron Silliman provides a useful example.

He lived here, under the elm trees
versus
He lived here, under the assumptions.

Silliman points out that in the new sentence the sentence doesn't resolve the syntax. Silliman's list of descriptors for the new sentence reads as follows:

(i) The paragraph organizes the sentences.
(ii) The paragraph is a unity of quantity, not logic or argument.
(iii) Sentence length is a unit of measure.
(iv) Sentence structure is altered for torque, or increased polysemy/ambiguity.
(v) Syllogistic movement is (a) limited; (b) controlled.
(vi) Primary syllogistic movement is between the preceding and following sentences.
(vii) Secondary syllogistic movement is toward the paragraph as a whole, or the total work.
(viii) The limiting of syllogistic movement keeps the reader's attention at or very close to the level of language, that is, most often at the sentence level or below.[20]

Apparently, in poetry that employs new sentences, the paragraph is an arbitrary container of a number of sentences that are to be seen as just so many units in the aggregate. Therefore, the paragraph is just a unit of measure and has no function as a structure within which sentences are subordinated logically. By altering a sentence structure by torque, Silliman means that it is changed by the rearrangement/substitution of elements that break with grammatical expectations and rules. Carla Harryman's sentence, "The back of the hand resting on the pillow was not wasted" is a new sentence because the noun "hand" cannot logically take "wasted" as a verbal descriptor, whereas "washed" or "wished for" would have been all right. By syllogistic movement, Silliman means logic in terms of its pertaining to the unit of the sentence itself. The primary logic doesn't overrun the sentence in order to unify a group of sentences, which focuses attention upon words (the morpheme) or small groups of them. There can be a secondary logic that works at the paragraph level or level of the whole, however. Silliman's example of a group of new sentences comes from Harryman's "For She":

The back of the hand resting on the pillow was not wasted. We couldn't hear each other speak. The puddle in the bathroom, the sassy one. There were many years between us. I started the stranger into facing up to Maxine, who had come out of the forest wet from bad nights. I came from an odd bed, a vermillion riot attracted to loud dogs.

In this example, the pronouns and deictic markers (there, on, of) help establish a sense of normalcy against which the so-called torquing (or deformations) take place. A more traditional term for this kind of writing is *parataxis*, unsubordinated prose. To this, the new sentence is adding the grammatical and idiomatic deformation of typical language use.[21]

Reading

Ron Silliman, *The New Sentence* (1987)

Sound Poetry/Concrete Poetry

Both concrete and sound poetry have their inceptions as self-conscious artistic practices in Dada and allied movements within the European avant garde of the early twentieth century. If in the case of concrete poetry the visual dimension of the poem strives to achieve material autonomy, the same can be said for sound in sound poetry. Whereas most of the poetry one is likely to study can be considered a balance between sound patterning, verbal design, and denotation, in both concrete and sound poetry there is a tendency to alter the balance in a way that denotation loses its centrality as "the sense" beneath which everything else is to be subordinated. "Thus Adam to himself lamented loud" (*Paradise Lost*, 10.845) is visually shaped in such a way that "loud" receives end placement. We can also *see* the two l's in "lamented loud," which visually reinforces the stresses that the beginnings of these words will receive. But all of this works in the service of the denotation, as does the sound, which puts stress on "loud," as if to make that word imitate its sense. Sonically, "loud" *is* loud. Here, of course, we're examining a very commonplace example of what New Critics called "sound and sense," the expectation that the sound will imitate the sense. In sound poetry, the sonic aspect of the poetry becomes so autonomous that it discards denotation altogether, while retaining the capacity to connote in its absence.

For most readers, Lewis Carroll's "Jabberwocky" would be the poem that exemplifies the borderline between where sound and sense go their own ways. We can imagine what a Bandersnatch is, but there's really no telling if we'd be right. Of course, Carroll allows us to "imagine" by means of borrowing from what we know, as if we were trying to find cognates among two different languages. "Frumious" sounds hectoring, probably because we can sense the word "furious" in it. "Jabberwock" is quite recognizable as a compound word with "wock" being a cognate for "walk." But what about "talk"? "Jabber" itself is ambiguous because it refers to both jabbering (as in, jabbering and walking) and jabbing, which in the context of the poem appears the more likely meaning. The brilliance of this poem is how it keeps us betwixt and between language options, hence refusing us a definitive translation.

> Beware the Jabberwock, my son!
> The jaws that bite, the claws that catch!
> Beware the Jubjub bird, and shun
> The frumious Bandersnatch!

Steve McCaffery tells us that the sound poem came in various genres back in the days of Zurich-style Dada in 1916. Chief among them was the "simultaneous poem" and the "poem without words."[22] The simultaneous poem was invented by Henri Barzun and Fernand Divoire and in it one could expect a sonic collage made up of "sound, text, discrepant noises, whistles, cries, and drums." This contrasts with Hugo Ball, a major figure in Dada, who restricted himself to poems without words. Ball explained:

> I have invented a new genre of poems, "Verse ohne Worte" [poems without words] or *Lautgedichte* [sound poems], in which the balance of the vowels is weighted and distributed solely according to the values of the beginning sequence.

Ball also wrote that

In these phonetic poems we totally renounce the language that journalism has abused and corrupted. We must return to the innermost alchemy of the word, we must even give up the word too, to keep for poetry its last and holiest refuge. We must give up writing second-hand: that is, accepting words (to say nothing of sentences) that are not newly invented for our own use.[23]

Such poetry was intended to defamiliarize and undermine ordinary language use and to reintroduce sense as something we intuit from hearing sounds whose ostensive meanings aren't given. The sound poem, therefore, is very much like a foreign language whose sense we grasp through its sounds, even though we would be at a loss if someone actually required us to denote what was being communicated. Of course, onomatopoeia plays an important role in sound poetry to the extent that sounds are physical presences (in the form of vibrations) which prompt various associations: linguistic, psychological, etc.

Well known, too, is work by poets such as the Russian futurist Velimir Khlebnikov who is famously associated with the term *zaum*, a neologism in Russian that denotes transrationality. Russian futurism, much like Dadaism and Surrealism in Western Europe, had one thing in common, namely, the expectation that certain non-rational uses of language could trigger imaginative experiences that would break with conformist (that is, ideologically determined) ways of perceiving the world. *Zaum* enabled the individual to know that everyday consciousness must necessarily be a sort of false consciousness that represses creativity and the capacity to think differently than one's neighbor. Klebnikov understood sound as material, hence arguing for sound poetry as a materialist approach to art that went beyond the bourgeois understanding of the sign in terms of a property relation in which the sign is in possession of its referent. In the context of Ferdinand de Saussure, one is reminded of that subtle interrelation between sound and thought before a moment when they are separated, the one brushing against the other at a moment when they are still fused. "Zangezi" (1923) was a theatrical piece by Klebnikov staged by Vladimir Tatlin and included various invented poetic languages related to birds and gods. And here, of course, one sees how natural it was for sound poetry to be translated into performance art.

Unquestionably the most celebrated sound poem per se is Kurt Schwitters' *Ursonate* (1922–1932), of which there is a re-engineered recording available on compact disk. "Ursonate" (Primeval Sonata) is actually not as primeval as one might think. One can sense musical sonata allegro form in the piece; in fact, it's even written in four movements, some of which are paced like movements in a classical sonata. Moreover, the piece is as much sung as it is spoken. It makes use of pitch as well as rhythmical repetitions, which establish cadence and momentum. If "Ursonate" suggests some sort of primeval European language, it is, in fact, modeled upon Germanic languages that would include German, Dutch, Swedish, Danish, and Norwegian. German and Swedish seem particularly pronounced, given Schwitters' rather frequent use of the umlaut: *rinnzkrrmüüüü*. Also pay attention to the rolled r and the use of the pf which is a characteristic of German pronunciation.

> Rum!
> Rrummpff? (G)
> Rum!
> Rrummpff t?
> Rr rr rum!

Although one might suppose the poem to be nonsense verse, there are familiar words that pop up every now and then. "Rum," in German, could mean the liquor we know as rum, or could be associated with "herum," the adverb for "around." In this sense, "Ursonate" often communicates like some earlier form of a language we already know and think we can therefore decipher. The use of pitch, speed, repetition, reprise, cadence, and phonemic clusters generally associated with German, give "Ursonate" a highly crafted and purposeful sense that its sounds both advance and occlude in ways that are tantalizing for the hearer who can't be sure whether he or she is listening to music or to language. Because "Ursonate" is a work of powerful expression in the absence of denotation, it has interested recent performance artists, who see it as foundational for work in which sound and sense are to be reconceptualized in aesthetic terms.

If sound poetry departs from usual expectations wherein sound and sense are brought into relation, concrete poetry departs from usual expectations wherein sight and sense are related. The following is a concrete poem modeled by myself on a work made by Francis Picabia, a visual artist of enormous originality who belonged to the European avant garde.

Figure 1 Concrete Poem.

The point of such an exercise in Dadaism is to show how much poetic information or stimulus we get in a purely visual form even before we begin reading a word of poetry. Even without seeing a single word, but merely lines in their stead, regular readers of poetry will probably sense a signifying effect, because of the many poems that they have read whose powerful meanings are conveyed in precisely such visual forms. In other words, this sort of poem reveals just how behaviorally conditioned we are in terms of pattern stimulation. Notice that here too verbal denotation has been discarded. The design, however, does explicitly refer to the typographical shape of typical poetry.

And the lines also have connotative significance. The longer ones connote nouns, the shorter ones articles, conjunctions, and the like.

In fact, concrete poetry precedes the twentieth century. In a poem like George Herbert's "Easter Wings," the stanzas are put in the shape of angel's wings. The 1633 edition of the poem situates each wing (each comprises one of the two stanzas of the poem) so that we're required to read from top to bottom, or to turn the book sideways. We can see that the outer edges of the wings are longer, much as we would imagine angels' wings to be, and it is clear, as well, that the visual element of the poem relates to mention of the lark. The first and last lines are the strongest, rhetorically, and Herbert is playing with amplification (the outer edges of the wings) and diminution (the place where the wings attach). He is also invoking the opposition of flying and falling. In fact, the second stanza (not reproduced) will indicate that the second pair of wings are probably those of the poet who wants to attach his wings to that of the angel. Since each pair of wings gets its own facing page in the 1633 edition, the book's binding would represent this suturing of the poet to the angel.

> Lord, who createdst man in wealth and store,
> Though foolishly he lost the same,
> Decaying more and more,
> Till he became
> Most poore:
> With thee
> Oh let me rise
> As larks, harmoniously,
> And sing this day thy victories:
> Then shall the fall further the flight in me.

Figure 2 George Herbert, from "Easter Wings" (1633).

Also well known for their visual appeal are Guillaume Apollinaire's calligrammes from the early part of the twentieth century. These are pictures drawn in outlines that are made of words. Perhaps the most successful of these is "Heart Crown and Mirror." The mirror is a large oval outline composed of words that make up a circular sentence in which the end leads right back into its supposed beginning. As one reads this sentence the relation of its parts changes as one goes round the oval. Inside the space that is supposed to be the mirror surface we can read the name Guillaume Apollinaire. In this and other calligrammes, the figure appears to have the function of destroying linearity, because the figure's purpose is more allied to figuration (representing an object or objects) than to organizing the words into well formed propositions. And yet, the place of the words in terms of the figural pattern isn't arbitrary either, and tends to have optical significance in relation to where other words are placed.

Significant instances of concrete poetry are to be found in Charles Olson's *The Maximus Poems* and various books of poetry by Susan Howe, Hannah Wiener, and Douglas Messerli. Indeed, the moment poets such as Stéphane Mallarmé began experimenting with typefaces, font sizes, and spacing of words on the page, concrete poetry had been broached as an important dimension of new developments in the art of writing poetry. Certainly, what separates modern poetry (and its legacies) from earlier poetries of the past has been the considerable amount of attention paid to typographical layout and page design. Also of importance is the way in which page design has led to an interest in making artists' books in which the difference between poetry and visual art is difficult to separate out. Tom Phillips' *A Humument* (the entire book is accessible on the Internet) is a famous example in which each page of a novel has been drawn and colored over exposing only certain of the original words that when blocked out in this way read like poetry. Leslie Scalapino's *The Tango* is an important poetic collaboration with artist Marina Adams in which the final product is an artist's book in which what happens on the page visually is as important as what happens verbally.[24]

Reading

Marjorie Perloff and Craig Dworkin (eds), *The Sound of Poetry / The Poetry of Sound* (2009)

Prosody

In poetry there is a close relation between line, syntax, diction, and rhythm. Notice how Milton, for example, uses an iambic pattern to restabilize a passage in Book 1 of *Paradise Lost* in which Satan is being described as holding a shield; it's a parody of the shield of Achilles in Homer's *The Iliad* on which there is a complex design. The Tuscan artist Milton references is Galileo.

the broad circumference
Hung on his shoulders like the Moon, whose Orb
/   / /   /   /   /   /   /   /
through Optic Glass the Tuscan Artist views
At ev'ning from the top of *Fesole*

The regular iambic feet begin already at the end of the second line above with "whose Orb." Notice that this is enjambed with the following line, that is, run together as if there were no break. Also notice how Milton stitches the diction together by repeating vowels. The "O's" are quite dominant, but the "U's" have their effect as well. What makes passages like this so interesting is how Milton both regulates and deregulates relations between rhythm, syntax, and line, such that one is moving between the effects of prose and poetry. "The broad circumference hung on his shoulders" is really a prose line. "Whose Orb through Optic Glass the Tuscan Artist views" is obviously iambic poetry (the repetition of two beats, the first short, the second long). Rhythmically, the iambic feet work to *slow down* the pace of the passage as well as to stabilize the rhythm so that there will be the possibility of counterpoint between regular/irregular. The enjambment, moreover, skews the balance in such a way that Satan's wearing the moon as a shield is imitated in terms of its lopsidedness. One suspects the passage is mimicking Satan's attempt to walk with this enormously heavy shield, a walking that is off balance but also in balance at certain moments. It is in passages like this that one can see enormously subtle relations between sound and sense (which in this case is quite visual).

Everyone has been taught the "feet": iambic (short-long), trochaic (long short), dactylic (long short short,) and anapestic (short-long long). But what is usually not taught in the lower schools, or even in university, is how the meter comes into conflict with main line stresses. When we read, we tend to stress the words whose meanings are important to the sense of the line, but these stresses may well conflict with the stresses hammered out by the meter, so that there is a counterpoint between how we read the line for sense and what the meter of the line itself is doing. Examples abound, but consider Ashbery's line from "Farm Implements and Rutabagas in a Landscape,"

◡ / ◡ / ◡ / ◡ / ◡ /
<u>Be</u> of no help to <u>you.</u> <u>Good</u>-bye...

The iambic pattern appears above the line and the main-line stresses are shown in terms of the underlined words. Now it has to be said that how one distributes these main-line stresses varies in terms of how we ourselves read. You may stress something differently than I would, which is what makes this sort of analysis a bit idiosyncratic. That aside, we can see that in the line above the main-line stresses actually predominate, though the iambic rhythm runs along like a sort of musical beat in the background.

For a slightly more complex example, notice Christina Rossetti's "I plucked pink blossoms from mine apple tree" which is iambic throughout. Notice, however, that the alliteration of "plucked pink" and the elongation of "my" into "mine" works against the iambic meter. In fact, the trade off between the "p's" and the "b" of "blossoms" (the phonemes are in binary opposition, but still labial) carries through an emphasis on the mouth, as if Rossetti was thinking of some relationship between herself and Eve with respect to tasting apples. The poem is entitled "An Apple-Gathering." Throughout, Rossetti pairs words in imitation of the speaker's relation to her beloved: "Lilian and Lilas smiled in trudging by"; "Ah, Willie, Willie, was my love less worth"; "Laughing and listening in this very lane." Added to this is the fact that readers will impose main-line stresses, as well, that will serve to help imitate the speaker's discourse in terms of an ordinary type of speaking. In other words, the main-line stresses work to naturalize or normalize the artificiality of the poem's rhythm and its alliterative pairings and reaffirmations. "<u>I plucked</u> pink blossoms from mine <u>apple tree.</u>" No doubt, some would emphasize "blossoms" too since grammatically it's the direct object. Yet, however we mark this line, the point is that main-line stresses are going to override the rhythm and even the alliteration, but that this isn't in any way absolute, as the rhythm and alliteration are in counterpoint and exerting their own influence upon the overall aural texture of the lines.

To see a rather more complex example in the case of a contemporary work, here is a stanza by the British poet John Wilkinson.

I <u>was.</u> But she <u>grinds</u> in her <u>condyl</u>
all that's known by <u>heart</u>
<u>cloaks</u> the tongue your <u>counter-</u>
<u>poise</u> would <u>furl back.</u> She <u>refers</u>
<u>foreign calls</u> to her <u>program</u>[25]

This, at least, is how I read these lines in terms of the main-line stresses that have been underlined. Notice that "But she grinds in her condyl" (condyl is a medical term for a bone protrusion; perhaps a bone is out of joint here) is composed of two anapests and that these fall in line with the main-line stresses. That second line is more iambic ("that's known, by heart" is two iambs). But in reading it, the line seems to have but one major stress – at the end. The enjambment with the next line breaks the rhythm up quite perceptibly. "Heart/cloaks" is spondaic (two stresses together). But notice, isn't that enjambment really a caesura (a break)? Alternatively, couldn't it be either? There's some imitation of stress between "heart/cloaks" and "furl back." And "refers" imitates somewhat the ambiguity of the line break between "heart" and "cloaks." We could read it as an enjambment and probably should, but I'm not convinced there isn't the possibility of a caesura here. Given how the stanza reads in terms of its meaning, we needn't be convinced necessarily that "refers" has to carry over to "foreign calls." And yet the main-line stresses would suggest otherwise.

What we have in this stanza is a complex tapestry of inwoven metrical bits that mirror one another: iambs, anapests, spondees. We also have line breaks that manage to ambiguate the enjambment/caesura distinction, as well as metrical line stresses that mark out the places where meaning would appear to be most significant. Perhaps the reader has noticed that in this poem we're not so far from the world of Ron Silliman's concept of the *new sentence* in which a complete thought never achieves the kind of referential resolution (semantic or logical) that enables us to correlate the meanings onto something altogether recognizable within the life world. And yet the stanza is held together by the commonplace dominance of a subject (in this case, "she") that works to normalize grammatical expectations and to organize how words ought to relate, given ordinary language practices. However, this isn't always strong enough to hold a mimetic sound and sense relation together, given that in spots the details conflict with the givens of the life world that we know. And yet, "She refers/foreign calls to her program" is a well formed sentence, and *not* a *new sentence*. This speaks to the sense one may get in such poetry that the words slip into and out of mimetic correspondence so that one is in a kind of borderland region between proper and new sentences. Maybe a better way to put this would be to say that we're in a liminal zone between mimesis proper and interlingual imitation. Ultimately, this takes us back into the work of Gertrude Stein in which a delicate balance exists between overt referentiality and the sort of inter-lingual wordplay that threatens to annihilate reference, not imitate it. Stein:

> Checking an emigration, checking it by smiling and certainly by the same satisfactory stretch of hands that have more use for it than nothing, and mildly not mildly a correction, not mildly even a circumstance and a sweetness and a serenity.[26]

Reading

Derek Attridge, *Poetic Rhythm: An Introduction* (1995)
Mary Kinzie: *A Poet's Guide to Poetry* (1999)

Notes

1   See the quotation from Nietzsche's "Of Truth and Lying in a Non Moral Sense" in 1.2 for an alternative understanding of figuration. Jacques Derrida's "White Mythology," in *Margins of Philosophy* (Chicago: University of Chicago Press, 1982), develops this alternative view at length.
2   John Milton, *Paradise Lost*, ed. Barbara K. Lewalski (Oxford: Wiley-Blackwell, 2007).

3   Pierre Fontanier, *Les figures du discours* (Paris: Flammarion, 1977), p. 64. For those who read French, this is the most complete book on literary figures one is likely to encounter. There is no comparable text in English.

4   The poem is in the public domain. But see *Poems of Emily Dickinson, Variorium Edition*, 3 vols., ed. R.W. Franklin (Cambridge, MA: Harvard University Press, 1998). *The Letters of Emily Dickinson*, ed. T.H. Johnson (Cambridge, MA: Harvard University Press, 1986), p. 639.

5   Chelsey Minnis, *Zirconia* (New York: Fence, 2001), p. 21.

6   Jackson Mac Low, *Thing of Beauty*. ed. Anne Tardos (Berkeley, CA: University of California Press, 2008), p. 321.

7   Steve McCaffery, *North of Intention* (New York: Roof, 1986), p. 63.

8   Michel Foucault, *The Order of Things*, trans. Alan Sheridan (New York: Vintage, 1971).

9   Paul de Man, "The Rhetoric of Temporality," in *Blindness and Insight* (Minneapolis, MN: University of Minnesota Press, 1983).

10 Robert Creeley, *Collected Poems*, Vol. 2 (Berkeley, CA: University of California Press, 2006), p. 342. Creeley wrote several poems called "Window," incidentally.

11 Dante Alighieri, *Paradiso*, trans. Charles Singleton (Princeton, NJ: Princeton University Press, 1970), p. 379. Bruce Andrews, *Lip Service* (New York: Coach House Press, 2001), p. 380.

12 Dorothy Wordsworth, "Grasmere Journals," in *Norton Anthology of English Literature: Major Authors*, Stephen Greenblatt, ed. (New York: Norton, 1999), p. 1600.

13 Ishmael Reed, "Lake Bud," in *Moments Notice*, ed. Art Lange and Nathaniel Mackey (Minneapolis, MN: Coffee House Press, 1993), p. 233.

14 Leslie Scalapino, *Concerning How Exaggerated Music Is* (San Francisco: North Point Press, 1982).

15 Jackson Mac Low, *Thing of Beauty*, ed. Anne Tardos (Berkeley, CA: University of California Press, 2008), p. 139.

16 Mac Low (2008), p. 143.

17 *In the American Tree*, ed. Ron Silliman (Orono: National Poetry Foundation, 1986), p. 492.

18 Silliman (1986), p. 494.

19 Laura Mullen, "Torch Song (Prose is a Prose is a Prose)," in *Civil Disobedience* (Minneapolis, MN: Coffee House Press, 2004), pp. 442–3.

20 Ron Silliman, *The New Sentence* (New York: Roof, 1989), pp. 89, 91.

21 Silliman (1989), pp. 91–2.

22 Steve McCaffery, "Cacophony, Abstraction, and Potentiality," in *The Sound of Poetry / The Poetry of Sound*, ed. Marjorie Perloff and Craig Dworkin (Chicago: Chicago University Press, 2009).

23 Quoted in Steve McCaffery, pp. 120–1.

24 Leslie Scalapino and Marina Adams, *The Tango* (New York: Granary Books, 2001).

25 John Wilkinson, "In the losing light, see your head," in *Proud Flesh* (Cambridge: Salt Publishing, 2005), p. 10. The volume contains an introduction by Drew Milne.

26 Gertrude Stein, "Tender Buttons," in *Selected Writings of Gertrude Stein*, ed. Carl Van Vechten (New York: Modern Library, 1962), p. 507.

CHAPTER 8

Theory in Practice
"Look, Her Lips": Softness of Voice, Construction of Character in King Lear

Michael Holahan

> Michael Holahan teaches English at Southern Methodist University. He studies the literature of the English Renaissance and its affiliations with the classical past. While his principal concern now is the drama of Shakespeare, he also extends his interests to include the development of the novel from Austen to Henry James and L. P. Hartley.

I

Slack and sleeping senses must be addressed with thunder and heavenly fire-works. But the voice of beauty speaks gently: it creeps only into the most awakened souls.[1]

Twentieth-century theorists have been severe with the notion of literary character. It does not speak strongly to post-Victorian souls – to this century's skepticism toward moral and mimetic constructions. The New Criticism set character aside for finer patterns of imagery and wit or paradoxical structures of ironical tone. Myth criticism subsumed it in the more powerful archetype. Deconstruction, new historicism, and the related specialties of poststructural critique have viewed an obviously figurative construct with alert suspicion. It has seemed a rallying point for essentialist notions of the self, reinforcing a superficial moralism and commonsense psychology while all along remaining just rhetoric: *ethos* and *pathos* meeting in *prosopographia*. Nevertheless, the artifice of character is hardly a postmodern discovery. The notion is central to most rhetorical traditions, although not entailing in every case the reduction of character to rhetoric.[2] In drama the issue is moot: there, within a constructed environment, the rhetoric of character is allowed to take on guises of truth because spectators can

Original publication details: Michael Holahan, "'Look, Her Lips': Softness of Voice, Construction of Character in King Lear." *Shakespeare Quarterly* 48.4 (Winter 1997), pp. 406–431. Reproduced with permission from Johns Hopkins University Press.

willingly – and consciously – suspend degrees of disbelief. It needs to be added that suspending disbelief is not the same thing as becoming credulous.

Although no more than a literary device, composed of rhetorical elements, character has shown such persistence in literary and critical practice that it may well outlast theories that diagnose its death. The idea that literary character might remain one of the textual pleasures we seek out may be tested in the relentless assault on character we find in *King Lear*, which goes beyond character but uses the device itself to do so. Indeed, the play constitutes itself by dramatizing meanings and values that arise from various nodal locations set *between* literary devices of character. The play's disguising, for example, seems to flaunt such *knotted intervals* by calling attention to character put on, then off.[3] "Poor Turlygod! poor Tom! / That's something yet: Edgar I nothing am" (2.3.20–21).[4] Another example, and one central to my purpose of reconfiguring character here, involves the voicing-over of one character upon another: a juxtaposition and joining of two distinct figures – one with "something yet" in speech, the other with "no breath at all" (5.3.306). The interval comes down to this shifting, barely perceptible space between speech and silence, between one voice and an invoked voice no longer there. *Topoi* of speech, voice, and breath disclose an uncertain space between characters and suggest some moral arguments of acknowledgment that arise within it. These arguments extend from acknowledgment by a dramatic character to the particular kinds of acknowledgment offered in literary response.

This essay presents an interpretation of the value of one character, Cordelia, and the final relation of that value to Lear's last speeches over her body. My concern lies with a relation between characters at or near points of death and the issue of aesthetic closure. I find Cordelia's value located in her soft voice and "ripe lip" (4.3.20), and I wish to link these descriptions to Lear's final summons to our close attention: "Look on her, look, her lips" (5.3.309). This essay raises issues of stability of character, considering changes in the dying Edmund as preliminary to changes that occur for Lear. In my argument Lear changes by *looking* for and *imitating* Cordelia's soft voice; his character change is not solely a development of internal depth but is also an acquired responsiveness to another character. Character evolves not as a formation around a void but as a progressive delineation of spaces between or beyond distinct figures onstage. Instability in this case is no hindrance to character as meaning; it is a groundwork for varied effects of meaning. My goal is to emphasize this interpretation but also to keep in view a theoretical proposition concerning subjectivity. This holds that to term character "constructed" strips it of signifying value and reveals an emptiness of meaning in matters of subjectivity. Since character is nothing but marks on a page, such arguments run, it must be silent, seen but not heard. This claim is not so much a theorized objection to character as it is an evasion by reduction of the issue of meanings (and knowledge) generated by literary constructions.[5]

Against this reductive claim I try to find within Lear's speech to the dead Cordelia a discourse that is dramatic in its concern with character, ethical in its judgment of value, and constructed in its establishment of a perspective not original to Lear. My purpose is not to offer a theoretical defense of literary character; it is, rather, to test the possibility that a traditional literary device has been set in an unusual construction and, in so doing, to articulate patterns of achieved bonds more than those of developed interiority. My concern is to detach subjectivity from an exclusive identification with inwardness and to attach it to forms of ethical perception that resist categorical explanation. I aim at a description of character, ethical value, and shaped perspective that is "thick" in the sense that it plaits these different languages into an "anthropology" of Lear's change.[6] His character is complete, defined by death and the play's close, in moments of final change and construction that embrace other characters. This is the antithesis to disguising, for Lear becomes most himself as he becomes more like his daughter – or, more precisely, like her only in the briefest of dramatic moments and in the delicate sharing of a single trait as he takes on her voice. This taking-on is contingent, tangential, yet so marked that it may well elude theory's finest rigors. That is, precisions of a theoretical skepticism may not be the best way to recognize brief and delicate points of closure in *King Lear*.[7] Moral inquiry, with its concern for the particular nature of exchanges between persons, is better able, I believe, to represent those qualities that summon, shape, and puzzle our attention.

Such an occasion of brevity and delicacy gains dramatic resonance within a large architecture that continually repositions eyes and voices in significant meetings of image, theme, and situation. The father finds himself by means of his child, for this least daughter's voice has already taught him how to recreate certain bonds amid a ruin of doubt. The achievement in Act 5 depends upon an exchange in Act 4, where this poor sinner, once a king, claims nothing for himself except the name of his child. Yet his terrible weakness finds recompense in Cordelia's immediate response as she enacts without hesitation the difference between laughter and gentle acknowledgment.

> LEAR ... Methinks I should know you and know this man
> Yet I am doubtful: for I am mainly ignorant
> What place this is, and all the skill I have
> Remembers not these garments; nor I know not
> Where I did lodge last night. Do not laugh at me
> For, as I am a man, I think this lady
> To be my child Cordelia.
> CORDELIA　　　　　　　　　　　　And so I am, I am.
> 　　　　　　　　　　　　　　　　　(4.7.64–70)

An effective brevity, Erasmus considered, is "so full of meaning that much more is understood than is heard."[8] The brevity of this lady/child makes up an affirmation that is richly understood, and her two qualities – simplicity and affirmation – constitute the "I," also constructed, who identifies in gentle reverberation the family relationship and the proper name. Confirming herself, she confirms this abused "man" as father and king, a confirmation of identities and roles that will be brutally tested until simple assertions of existence can no longer be uttered. Yet Lear will recall Cordelia's voice and proclaim its general excellence, joining two crucial inflections – distinction and type – in the value of character: "Her voice was ever soft, / Gentle and low, an *excellent* thing in *woman*" (5.3.272–73, emphasis added). The close of *King Lear* projects drama's rich interrogations about being and presence. What does it mean to hold and consider such excellence? to recollect her saying "I am, I am" or "No cause, no cause" (4.7.75), only to listen and watch her die, unable to speak? The shock to Dr. Johnson is well known and was not endured again until he subjected the play and himself to editorial discipline.

II

Finis coronat opus.[9]

The play has other patterns of character development to examine beyond those of disguising, personal confirmation, or spherical predominance. Edmund uses (without perhaps believing) a notion of historical conditioning or shaping. "[M]en / Are as the time is," he notes to his captain after the British victory: "to be tender-minded / Does not become a sword" (5.3.31–33).[10] He then sets his executioner a task that leads to rope and his own death from the old king's sword. This is one of the many turns to the sword that mark the violence of this play. We never hear, and perhaps do not expect to, whether the captain had his own moment of tendermindedness as Cordelia's death conjoined with his. Since all characters are not equally important, by extension, what is offstage and out-of-text need not exist for speculation. It is different for Edmund. He is attractive (as Harold Bloom assures us), desired by both evil sisters, and distinctive; the time conspires to grant him, before death at his brother's hand, a final and surprising shift to kind intention.[11] Moved by Edgar's "brief tale" of their father's end (5.3.181–99), he thinks of enacting a good. He reveals his "writ … on the life of Lear and on Cordelia," offers his sword as a "token of reprieve," and urges all to "send in time" (ll. 243–51). Time does expire for the queen. But what of her executioner, turned by voice, tale, and timing into a would-be savior: is his conversion legitimate or out-of-character? Is the problem one of ethics or aesthetics? What is the "time" of this character which leads him to this last effort at ineffective charity?

Does Shakespeare as well as Nature stand up for Edmund? Should we? Does it make a difference to condemn him for a writ on these two lives if he then goes on to mean well, despite his own nature? Cannot the end crown the work, the bastard speaking for, not against, Cordelia? Edmund's attractiveness, for me, is theoretical in that he illuminates problems of stability and alteration in matters of character and ethical judgment. After 3.7 who could have thought that this young man had so much good in him? His Act 5 conversion is astonishing not only in itself but also as a prelude to more remarkable changes in Lear. They do share extremes of attitude toward Cordelia, even if last judgments on the two should not rest there. Nonetheless, an ultimate Edmund, unexpectedly tender, introduces a "new King Lear," who brings his silent daughter to the stage and once again asks for her speech.[12] As the play concludes, *King Lear* raises basic issues of character, acknowledgment, and exchange. In my sense of the play, change of character is directly related to processes in which characters gain or lose acknowledgment as their voices contend within dramatic time.[13]

We like to view human character as stable, as fixed somehow in nature. Yet we know that it is not. It grows, or is constructed and reconstructed, to follow the signs of our time. In either case, a character must alter if ethical judgment is to do more than report on disjunct moments from the past when this or that agent performed well (or ill). That is, notions that a character can change yet retain a distinct identity are crucial to ideas of responsible freedom and their representation in literature. As Paul Ricoeur has remarked, one can distinguish between identity as sameness and as selfhood (a site for significant change) and in this distinction find occasions to weigh elements that do and do not change.[14] In this sense, character is not at all an unequivocal formation but the name for certain continuing negotiations between stability and alteration. In turn, an ethical judgment must be supple over time as well as tolerant of the sudden changes that can come to one as attractive as Edmund. Literary interpretation is not alien to such latitudes of judgment, for this practice encourages varied readings rather than a unitary law. Here, ironically, an attractive traitor is reduced to a character function and his dying affords an aesthetic perspective on the royal characters whom he tries to murder, then fails to save. Edmund's good serves the literary plot before any argument of ethics; he is neither center nor circumference of this work. He can usurp many things but not *King Lear*. It has its own way with a "ficelle" so winningly brutal. He is borne offstage toward his man, to die – "a trifle" (5.3.295) – as his victims return to the center with a specifically dramatic power. This aesthetic shaping of dismissal and return does carry some relish of ethical value. Poetic justice remains a kind of justice, at least for Edmund. Conversion to a good only earns him Albany's final contempt and alerts us to more striking transformations for Lear. The endings of the two men are quite different yet not unrelated, for each comes to a voicing of ethical perception as a sign of altered character. Such signs should not be mistaken; they may very well bring us to a deep sense of the continuity of characters within the play. This can be said in another way: that judgments made about one character are not made in isolation from judgments about other characters. To note the irrelevance of Edmund, even in his last muster of an ethical voice, is to register the final power of Lear and Cordelia. Appeals to aesthetic qualities cannot, of course, forestall other judgments, even as acts and performances said to be ethical can still be evaluated aesthetically. One language of judgment cannot preempt the other. Nonetheless, *King Lear* asks for both and torments our professional efforts at a strict discrimination of issues. We may deny "Edmund" any benefit from his conversion even as we appreciate its aesthetic virtues. Acting always as an end unto himself, he ends up as a device of the play.[15]

Literary critics as different as Harley Granville-Barker and Stephen Greenblatt have noted an odd circling in *King Lear*.[16] Its action opens and closes with Cordelia's silence, and it is the ethical value of those silences that I want to consider now, especially and obviously in their effects on Lear. The two silences are radically different, yet we know that difference to be the point of the dramatic action, language, and scene as these coalesce intensively at the end in general patterns of speech and sight.[17] The old man bends over his daughter's body, desperate to prove any signs of an invisible speech or breath. Now his concern is less *what* she says than *that* she says, and he dies in the act of acknowledging something intended but unspecified – except for location – about Cordelia. Beholders are asked to see what may not exist, for this is and is not Cordelia. Her character now appears only in an actor's body's mimicry of a past life – a striking union of death and theatrical illusion. Yet the rhetorical effect is one of intense concentration on "her" – by the king and, with him, by the watching armies. Lear ends in a passion of seeing and commanding sight, with his own mortal period and point of exclamation: "Do you see this? Look on her, look, her lips, / Look there, look there! [*Dies*.]" (5.3.309–10).[18] As before, he desires her speech and gains nothing. Shakespeare reconstructs his design so that this last question and command extend from the stage groupings to us as readers or spectators. We are asked to see and told to look. To do so, we must read Cordelia's lips, her father's anguish, and our own capacity for compassion. Ethical judgment is contextual; it must include the object of value, the affect of those interested, and the skills of the judge. Lear can be held to these standards, for he comes to a profound revision of the value of his daughter and her gender as he asks her not to go. In Act 1 he bribed Cordelia to speak her love; then, when she would not (or could not), he ordered her to go. Here, as the circle closes, he utters a plea of love that asks only for softest speech – speech he must then recreate himself. We could say that Lear mistakes silence in a new way. Or perhaps we are struck by his belief that speech remains possible. In either case, the process is one of naming, address, and characterization with an intensity that few works match. The old king's voice has changed.[19] An imperative "stay" begs. The original command – "Speak" (1.1.85) – is here a gentle question, although he himself is certainly not gentle in stopping Edmund's man. Nonetheless, he has learned to plead with silence – the figure he now holds, addresses, and describes. His language becomes briefly a caress, softness itself.

> Cordelia, Cordelia! stay a little. Ha!
> What is't thou say'st? Her voice was ever soft,
> Gentle and low, an excellent thing in woman.
> I kill'd the slave that was a-hanging thee.
>   (5.3.271–74)

Edmund was wrong about the time. Here a sword has indeed become tenderminded, for Lear has not always spoken so well of this woman, let alone all women.[20] The rack of the world has cracked his darker purpose as well as the misogyny in his own hangman impulses: "the great rage, / You see, is kill'd in him," the doctor told Cordelia as she bent over her father (4.7.78–79). That rage was an exiled, exposed man's frenzied madness. It followed and enlarged the earlier rages of an angry father and monarch. The arc of those emotions brought Lear to his own silence, an exhaustion between sleep and death. A medical diagnosis, however, was hardly enough to represent this condition or its outcome.

The play's circle travels from and toward Cordelia by way of the king. Plot movement suggests an inner circle of characters bound together. We cannot understand the silence of the daughter without understanding the state or speech of the father. Lear's health now rests with his daughter's return and manner of identification. She must sweeten his imagination of "the sulphurous pit" (4.6.130), extending the motif of royal medicine by inverting archetypes of lost children and searching parents.[21] Her character seeks out his – to say in Act 4 what could not be commanded in Act 1, and with a gentleness that can repair the "high-engender'd battles" of his storm and night (3.2.23). It may strike some viewers that Cordelia mingles qualities of passivity and power to such a fine degree that the first quality must enhance (not diminish) the second. Cordelia's gentleness can be understood etymologically as a joining of social or family status and of personal qualities – a royal birth as well as a private sense of loving duty. The difference between Act 1 and Act 4 concerns a divergence, within this patriarchal system, between royal commands and paternal appeals to a complex gentleness.

An ethics without an objective standard must be trivial. In *King Lear* that standard – one concerning the worth of speech – is embodied in Cordelia, especially in her lips and voice. They both form the shape and sound of value in this kingdom and suggest its vulnerability. Ironically, the injury to value begins in the command to speak. Lear is not wrong to want to hear Cordelia's love; he is wrong to command its expression as a condition of inheritance. Commodifying love is not a way to recognize this daughter's worth. "She is herself," France chides Burgundy – and Lear – "a dowry" (1.1.241). Since this wealth lies in a silent character, the real challenge is a difficult discrimination between softness and emptiness. Kent puts the matter negatively to the king, but he only begins a terrible process in which Lear learns to distinguish "low sounds" from the "hollowness" of least loving: "Thy youngest daughter does not love thee least; / Nor are those empty-hearted whose low sounds / Reverb no hollowness" (ll. 152–54). Kent's "plainness" (l. 148) has no effect but to send Lear's hand to his sword, while "*low* sounds" are indeed concealed by "hol*low*ness." A statement of Cordelia's value is assigned to France, a monarch-suitor who provides a formal set of loving paradoxes (ll. 250–61).[22] We in turn may decide that, if Cordelia is a center of value, her "low sounds" have yet to be constructed in an adequate rhetoric. The speech on duty which rings so coldly in Act 1 (ll. 95–104) requires later events to bring out its full tonalities.[23] Her exile heralds a terrible void in Britain, one that is figured by chaotic sites and acts of terror – a wild heath, a blinding storm, plucked eyes. The challenge for ethical inquiry is to complete a circle, to redraw that map of hollowness, to call a soft voice home. An acoustics of true reverberation is tested severely by the longest absence from the stage of a major Shakespearean character.

The construction finally occurs in 4.3, a scene omitted from the Folio and often dropped in performance, perhaps because its technique is indirect yet highly mannered in the fashion of the reporting scenes in the late romances.[24] The scene may also seem irrelevant if one is unconcerned with Cordelia speaking or spoken about, with indeed the play's reverberations of her presence and absence. But 4.3 does reverberate the scene in which Kent, while stocked, takes out Cordelia's letter and prays for a "warm sun" to read by (2.2.162). In 4.3 Kent, turned auditor, listens to an unnamed gentleman describe Cordelia's reading of letters about Lear.

> GENTLEMAN   ... it seem'd she was a queen
> Over her passion; who, most rebel-like
> Sought to be king o'er her.
> KENT   O! then it mov'd her.
> GENTLEMAN   Not to a rage; patience and sorrow strove
> Who should express her goodliest. You have seen
> Sunshine and rain at once; her smile and tears
> Were like, a better way; those happy smilets
> That play'd on her ripe lip seem'd not to know
> What guests were in her eyes; which parted thence
> As pearls from diamonds dropp'd. In brief
> Sorrow would be a rarity most belov'd
> If all could so become it.
> KENT   Made she no verbal question?
> GENTLEMAN   Faith, once or twice she heav'd the name of "father"
> Pantingly forth, as if it press'd her heart....
> (ll. 14–27)

Both scenes contain rebellions – Kent's enraged attempt to punish Oswald, Cordelia's better self-control. The gentleman's language traces elaborate conceits of thematic bearing and a ceremonial description that offers itself as a part of its own gentleness. It is lettered artifice: a flourish of metaphors, an effort to state Cordelia's full worth as ruler and woman while underscoring her absence.[25] Here understanding is achieved by courtliness, not suffering, and by a language that asserts a virtue in surplus as *King Lear*'s plainest speaker listens. Although rhetoric, this is the antithesis of hollow speakers at court or of unaccommodated man, whimpering his folly before the elements. It is a revelation in figured meaning of what "play'd on her ripe lip" (l. 21).

The anonymous gentleman restates the Stoic ideal of self-government in a language of courtly richness. France's metaphor of the self as dower is extended to issues of rule. This new rhetoric shows rebellion subdued by queenly patience, nature's "sunshine and rain" bettered in the true daughter's ripe lips and pearl tears. Her qualities still speak to this gentleman's eye of recollection as he tries to convey to Kent the wonder of her presence. Here the power of her subjectivity is so well controlled that, in governing itself, it can lay claim to govern others, this unnamed gentleman or a would-be king of passion. The masculine title of "king" suggests that the implicit model may be Lear's earlier usurping rage. A gentle microcosm suddenly takes shape in Cordelia's rich sorrow, as if Act 3's storm should be replayed now in precious miniature.

In addition to self-government, the gentleman describes an act of heavy lifting that Cordelia could not perform in Act 1: "Unhappy that I am, I cannot heave / My heart into my mouth" (1.1.91–92). (In Act 5 that verbal action will pass to Lear in the literal burden of a dead daughter.) Here, before Cordelia returns to the stage, her authority in two bodies – as queen and as subjective person – is confirmed.[26] Her majesty is not that of Lear's raging nor that of her husband's cool faith. She can project her heart in the name of her father. In the next scene she will begin a process of healing, advised by the doctor to "close the eye of anguish" (4.4.15). A court ceremony of bestowing jewels will be translated into a deeply emotional spending of attention and care. From Cordelia's heart and eyes (as imaged by the gentleman), a royal progress travels by tears and lips to Lear's own sight (as witnessed by the audience). A ripeness of language and spectacle is all in both plots of the play; acts of jeweled pathos – the queen's touch in language – will reach an untender brother in Edgar's words about their father's "bleeding rings, / Their precious stones new lost" (5.2.11; 5.3.189–90). This iconic language gradually rules even Regan's "sweet lord," who absented himself from ring-pulling and delegated murders so attractively.

Cordelia's "ripe lip" closes the eye of anguish to enable better seeing. She is "rare" not only because of her absence but also because of her own verbal translation of the gentleman's jewel metaphors into healing medicines. Act 4 moves from Cordelia described to Cordelia present (yet without her father) and finally to her moment of awakening him onstage.

> DOCTOR   Please you, draw near. Louder the music there!
> CORDELIA   O my dear father! Restoration hang
>   Thy medicine on my lips, and let this kiss
>   Repair those violent harms that my two sisters
>   Have in thy reverence made!
>
>   (4.7.25–29)

The simples of music and embrace lift him "out o' th' grave" and soothe the "molten lead" of his tears (ll. 45, 48). Act 1's expulsion is under repair: having learned for himself to "say nothing" (3.2.38), the old man is reborn, recast. The natural relation of father and child is reconstructed as a relation of art. The void fills with gentle sounds. A counterpoint of music and the queen's voice calls Lear from "the heaviness of sleep" to a restored vision of her as soul (4.7.21, 46). "[W]here did you die?" he asks her (l. 49), believing her to be the one transformed rather than the agent of his transformation. His phrase in Act 1 for a future with Cordelia could not have meant this scene, yet the scene does ironically reveal "her kind nursery" (1.1.124). Salving the hollow sisters' "fangs" (3.7.57), the child brings the father to himself in a scene of waking and second birth as she heals a prodigal parent with an artful medicine of lips.[27] The intimations of a romance recovery are strong but not strong enough to overcome the swords, writ, poisons, noose, and quick savagery of Act 5.

The gentleman's account was static, ornamental; Cordelia's address is dynamic, performative. "Restoration" is allegory, desire, and event. The paired speeches are complementary, not antithetical; both hang on her lips as she returns to her nation and to language. "Love, and be silent" was the first resolve (1.1.62); now her lips can be act and speech act, the kiss and the gentle speech of kissing. Fragile and gracious, she is the real physician-antagonist to nature's fearful storms. Such complementarity fits other relationships. If royal authority is patriarchal, it still requires this daughter's healing; the "reverence" she anoints is that of the unkind father and the injured monarch at once. It is both reconciliation and recoronation: "How does my royal Lord? How fares your Majesty?" (4.7.44). The construction of Cordelia's value passes to her own speech and to the verb "repair" issuing in speech and kiss from her *ripe* lip; *ripe* in the senses of rich, red, full, yet ready for the reaping.[28] The play sets the construction of value in the lady, dramatizing a worth to her objective presence in stages of absence, reported return, and actual appearance. It then reveals the force of her value and presence in the repair of Lear, which will survive further losses, including that of the lady herself. She returns to go about her royal father's business and reapplies Luke 2:49 by subsuming in her "simples" the work of ideology in family, state, and belief (4.4.14, 23–24). Her character is at once value and value's instrument.[29]

A new power in that healing shows in the aftermath of defeat as feudal chivalry is put to one side. We are left to wonder whether Shakespeare's feudalism works as a sign of bourgeois progress or as a dramatic frame for tragedy. We may even conclude that historical approaches, whether that of a history of ideas or that of a new cultural materialism, overvalue not the fact but the role of feudalism in the play.[30] There may be some sense in following the lead of the characters. Lear does not regard this lost battle as he once did the loss of his knights, and we attribute the difference not just to the reductions experienced on the heath but also to the mingled strengths and tenderness given by Cordelia's love: her emotions fill the spaces opened and exhausted on the heath. He has been – and will be again – "child-changed" (4.7.17). There may be traces of escapism in the lyrical speech beginning "Come, let's away to prison" (5.3.8). Its assertive energies and purpose, however, stand in contrast to the weak, uncertain questionings in 4.7. Not so much distracted as prudent, it is the oblique, coded speech necessary before triumphant power.[31] One of "Gods' spies" (1. 17), distinct from Oswald, Tom, and Kent, Lear can speak to divine methods with an assurance that is resonant and vernacular, finding strange virtues in this necessity. Most kings enjoy a power over prisons; this one enjoys his power within and against the cage.[32]

> Upon such sacrifices, *my* Cordelia,
> The Gods *themselves* throw incense. Have *I* caught *thee?*
> *He* that parts *us* shall bring a brand from heaven,
> And fire *us* hence like foxes. Wipe *thine* eyes;
> The good years shall devour *them*, flesh and fell,
> Ere *they* shall make *us* weep: *we*'ll see 'em starv'd first.
> Come.
>
> (5.3.20–26, emphasis added)

One can set Lear's two earlier speeches banishing and recognizing Cordelia against this farewell to power that invites new bonds of intimacy constructed in speech. Even programmatic skeptics toward large claims for language might allow that one could speak for two here. A new authority in the king emerges in this speech to Cordelia. Something is "caught" in his discourse, despite defeat and prison. What it means to win and lose is now in process of reconfiguring.

The failure of public speech and understanding in Act 1 is past. These two begin to share an imagination of sacrifice that ranges from heaven to fox burrows and across the good years that devour. The point is tone, not prediction; an uncanny poise of force and gentleness in which, although she says nothing – a strange prolepsis – we may hear the lady's silent acceptance shaped in the address to her. Along with 4.3's Gentleman, Lear also talks for two. The king's speech is a harbinger – not the end but closer to the end than the plot is yet. Character effects – a rhythmical shifting of singular pronouns to plural – impart a sense of Lear's stand against the cosmos. Invoked sacrifices lead to mysterious images of *our* triumph in *providentia edax*: "the good years shall devour them." We are left uncertain, as we are later in the scene, of the exact referents of pronouns and thus of the vocalized space that is set for us. Lear's language no longer divides the kingdom for others; it establishes a special space for his and his daughter's understanding. Feudalism establishes bonds of service that carry authority due to an ordering of classes and property by means of kinship hierarchies and personal dependence. *King Lear* explores sacrificial transformations that disclose through subjectivities of speech a new and objective authority. Lear's power rests in his speech, not in "champains rich'd" (1.1.64). His tones claim a vernacular emphasis quite new to him, although the accent took hold gradually in Acts 3 and 4. On seeing Gloucester in 4.6, he offered advice that seemed to amalgamate the experiences of both men: "What! art mad? A man may see how this world goes with no eyes. Look with thine ears" (ll. 151–52). Lear takes his own advice in Act 5. His eyes and voice disclose together, beyond the pain of loss, the rough shapes of sacred violence.[33] Yet this play does not allow private reconstructions to go unchallenged. However we may understand any testing agency ourselves, one appears in this play with terrifying economy and precision. This couple has been caught and shall be parted. An attractive character has had his own timely thoughts about the devouring to be done. As Lear and Cordelia exit under guard, Edmund signals to his captain and, by echoing "the old and miserable King" (5.3.47), extends the metrical line that Lear began: "Come hither, captain; hark. / Take thou this note" (ll. 27–28). The time is ripe for a brief lecture on tendermindedness and men who are swords – but it is delivered to a mercenary who is willing to hang a young woman in front of her father. Charity will later extend itself quite differently to Edmund. Here the postwar executions begin with an unattractive, banal exchange on postfeudal service – an administrator's act of passing on a letter and a chore.

III

And the truth is, one can't write directly about the soul. Looked at, it vanishes....[34]

King Lear does not advance a single or unitary notion of literary character. It allows us to see characters made and unmade. A king is maddened but restored, only to face defeat, imprisonment, release, and stages of dying. The unmaking can be done verbally or violently, as a function of cultural practice or of physical assault. Cordelia's place in Britain goes as quickly, as savagely, as Gloucester's eyes. Throughout the play, we need to recall that Lear is the first to presage her death. In disowning her, his imagination inaugurates horror.

> Here I disclaim all my paternal care,
> Propinquity and property of blood,
> And as a stranger to my heart and me
> Hold thee from this for ever. The barbarous Scythian,
> Or he that makes his generation messes

> To gorge his appetite, shall to my bosom
> Be as well neighbour'd, pitied, and reliev'd,
> As thou my sometime daughter.
>
> (1.1.113–20)

We can read the Marlovian simile one way before syntax adjusts sense to make Cordelia, not Lear, the savage cannibal. We may further note the peculiar form of high speaking that is involved in this citation of a helpless daughter for her supposed savagery. It is not simply that an error is made here. Lear's speech reveals him as fully capable of evil – the evil of Tamburlaine, lord of "these barbarous Scythians," who made his own child nothing, and who is present here as an allusive, usurping voice that reverberates, against historical time, within the British king's words.[35]

Lear will be held to account for this disfathering voice that invokes, if only by simile, the monsters to come. He must know the force of "disclaim" in the feudal vocabulary of renouncing lordship, although he cannot know the parallel between what he does to Cordelia and what he is doing to himself. The irony in his speech is that the behavior attributed to Cordelia seems, in the gender and violence of his chosen figure, all the more his own. In one or another reading of "generation," Lear seems determined to interrupt and unmake his creation.[36] The simile of the "barbarous Scythian" seems at first to align him with the man who "makes his generation messes." A surprise lies in turning from the three verbs of kindness to the brutal equation of Cordelia with that barbarity – the rhetorically dramatized consequence of being disclaimed by the king. The primitive fury stated here with deliberate and measured pace, Latinate diction, and calculated simile is – and ought to be – frightening. The voice is that of the savage father, wrathful beyond cause, demolishing all of the shelters of law and civilized existence as he learnedly denies his own child and, of course, himself. The agent of horror can be legitimate authority or not, a dragon or a dog in office. It makes little change: bodies, like kingdoms, were made to be torn apart, and other bodies are there to do what the captain terms, with brutal casualness, "man's work" (5.3.40).[37]

There is a large difference, to be sure, between bodies and characters. This is clear with Gloucester, who does not begin to see until after his eyes have been put out. Lear, in turn, is thrust into the "eyeless rage" of the storm (3.1.8), but his eye of anguish can discover a new vision of Cordelia. Yet there should be no quick assumption that new visions are necessarily desirable. Lear must move relentlessly from seeing the child restored as a royal lady to viewing the strangled woman "dead as earth" – Cordelia's character reduced to no more than the body of his sometime daughter (4.7.70; 5.3.261). At the end, he is beyond all issues of feudalism – not because society does not matter but because, as society's head, he has already broken the bonds of blood, neighborliness, and pity. Feudalism ceases to operate as an image for social structure at his own behest. All come crying hither, and no one in *King Lear* can alter this condition of birth beyond tears that part, like guests or jewels, from eyes of anguish.

Lear can anticipate madness. He can imagine a long imprisonment, provided Cordelia is there. Her actual death is another matter. His imperious temperament still expresses itself in absolute judgment: "I know when one is dead, and when one lives; / She's dead as earth" (5.3.260–61). But temper is now swayed by an intense love – one reconstructed from fury, madness, and exhaustion. Lear searches for Cordelia's life with things as slight as a looking glass, a feather, or his own dull eyes, hoping for "a chance which does redeem all sorrows / That ever I have felt" (ll. 66–67). We must be struck by such contrasts of frailty and subjective intensity, as Lear does find a woman whose value has been repaired and restored at a cost not less than everything. She is now everything but alive, and his judgment wrestles with this disproportion of all and nothing, juggling in his words a hierarchy of queen and missing fool.[38]

> And my poor fool is hang'd! No, no, no life!
> Why should a dog, a horse, a rat, have life,
> And thou no breath at all? Thou'lt come no more,
> Never, never, never, never, never!
>
> (5.3.305–8)

What value could come to something poor, absent, dead? How can so little earth on a map be worth so much? – no less than all the sorrows of an antic majesty, redeemed perhaps but not yet ended. His speech contracts from "no life" to "no breath at all" and then to "no more." It is destitution's language; all ceremonies of distinction vanish with Cordelia's last absence, and what remains is ordinary or worse – dog, horse, rat. This is an agony of dying, one of such force that the negations, augmented in the Folio, are simultaneously denials and acceptances of "no life" and "Thou'lt come no more." The half-brothers' struggle – a feudal contest of trial by sword and combat – is completely outdone, and within seconds the questions asked of Cordelia will apply as well to this speaker. Set in climactic position, the deaths of these two characters are given a greater significance than the conflicts of national armies or the ritual contests of the brother-knights. Historical events and institutions, all arbitrations by sword, are subordinated to privileged characters and character relationships – everything that the new historicism argues is off-center in such literature. Should constructed characters of royalty so center and command the field of history? The daughter speaks with "no breath" to her anguished father; Kent declares that he "must not say no" to a silent call heard only in his ear of loyal service (l. 322). Can meaning's "something yet" ever come from so near nothing? Can history simply declare itself a privileged form of new or old interpretation and tell us what *he* might have heard? Now as then, Cordelia speaks only to awakened ears as the soundless voice of gentle ways, the softest mystery in all things. Her silence is not the feminine submissiveness that Catherine Belsey hears, for the quality of her voice has passed to Lear as an authoritative sign of her rule in his ethical growth. To trace the limits on individual character in this play, we must study the interplay of its characters and not just the paradigms of social structure.[39]

Ethical judgment in *King Lear* arises from and returns to literary character. Each is matrix to the other. It is not a matter of a moral allegory or a Greek etymology but a view of dramatic action. Drama allows us to watch a process in which the construction of character cannot be separated from the judgments made by the characters about one another. Plot is not the only binding; we see that *ethos* is ethics. Lear's first address to Cordelia concerns his "joy" in her, but that is a love understood according to elements of hierarchy, competitions of kingdoms or sisters, and the property wealth of nations. He stages spectacles – first for the British court, then for neighbor rulers – as his desires *interess* the presumed greed of all.[40] He can mention love, but Cordelia must speak for opulence, for rich lands in Britain and in France or Burgundy. As king and father, Lear defines her character as a subject-daughter: she must, in nature, want what his speech dictates. His pride swells as he gauges the worth of his "last" and "least" to fertile nations elsewhere. The command to speak introduces what should astonish all: that when this

British king divides, more is created. It is no simple weighing of dukes and their moieties. His least is indeed most, as the powers of France and Burgundy await the verbal aptitude of a youngest daughter. Her speech is supposed to delight Lear, then re-map Europe. We watch a royal father who gives away his kingdom but tries to control the gift, who gives away his last daughter but makes that gift contingent on his command over her. The treatment of Cordelia replicates the treatment of the kingdom, as the use of heraldic crops and geographical titles to identify her two suitors makes clear.

> ... Now, our joy,
> Although our last, and least; to whose young love
> The vines of France and milk of Burgundy
> Strive to be interess'd; what can you say to draw
> A third more opulent than your sisters? Speak.
>   (1.1.82–86)

The nothing of Cordelia's silence reveals the failure in Lear's speech, which has demanded that her voice fulfill ideological purposes. Imperial calculations like these are absent from Lear's last speeches, although kingdoms remain at stake and the speaker can show his old temper. Cordelia no longer stands before and against him; she is nearer yet more distant. From her, still his center, he asks little: nothing formal, a short stay, a soft voice before the return to killing thoughts. The sequences of impotence and power in his address are rapid, intense.

> I might have sav'd her; now she's gone for ever!
> Cordelia, Cordelia! stay a little. Ha!
> What is't thou say'st? Her voice was ever soft,
> Gentle and low, an excellent thing in woman.
> I kill'd the slave that was a-hanging thee.
>   (5.3.270–74)

As if beyond hearing him, "Cordelia" seems to move away. The effect rests in a turn from "thou say'st" to "Her voice" in line 272, as the dead body holds mimetic place onstage. Spaces open from his gestures of language, as intimacy suddenly generates – where no one is – a tiny dialogue of *I* and *thou* across a linguistic distance to death. Does one invoke Buber or Bakhtin here: the dialogue as a structure of intense, intimate relationships or as a structure of radical differences conjoined?[41] The gentle speaker and the murdered hangman join in the king's sentences: one death easily given, the other impossible to tell. Yet both figures have crossed to an undiscovered country whose nearest border is mapped by this final juncture of bent age and a least body. It is obvious to say that the play replaces Act 1's literal map with one that must be intuited, less obvious to urge that the second map is one of language, one that can chart the spaces between the ferocity of the finite verb in line 274 and the desperate tendermindedness of the last personal pronoun of renewed address to the hanged woman.

This point concerns Lear no less than Cordelia, his own lips as well as hers, and the way he speaks about her "now she's gone for ever." The fate of the hangman reminds us – and Lear – of the persistent, violent energies of the warrior-king. Edmund's sense of the times is not distant from this "good": "I have seen the day, with my good biting falchion / I would have made them skip" (ll. 276–77). All the more remarkable, then, is the juxtaposition of another ethical character within the dramatic character's speech.

This character is also Lear, but it has been constructed in the course of the play, as if being follows on speech. It has emerged after a natural schooling – in wild weather and in the abyss of madness. Howlings of storm and man still to a deep quiet. In this new character and experience, Lear can speak yet listen for the softest of gentle and low voices. Cordelia's asides in Act 1 would be marked now. Her softness is not the king's tonic register, but he has learned to speak within it and to hear it.[42] He seeks Cordelia's voice in his question, glosses her silence as her custom, and deflects the fact of her hanging into his execution of Edmund's "sword." In Lear's own voice we find the changes worked by this child who can speak no more, as Lear performs her voice before "her" body. A strange dialogue across existential spaces and times joins two different characters, preserving a difference in speech yet folding the two voices into the one body of the king.

This is not, though brief, an event without context. In 4.7, when Cordelia bent over Lear's exhausted face, she could see there, despite her absence and a reported reliance on letters, the storm and heath of Act 3.

> ... Was this a face
> To be oppos'd against the warring winds?
> To stand against the deep dread-bolted thunder?
> In the most terrible and nimble stroke
> Of quick, cross lightning? to watch – poor *perdu!* –
> With this thin helm?
>
> (4.7.31–36)

Oddly, her gentle voice reproduced his voicing of the winds: the characters reunite in shared speech. A stylistic joining of epithets, battle imagery, and a foreign term allows us to register the presence as well as the absence of the lady at the play's center. It must be a British princess and now a French queen who joins these two languages to lament her unconscious father – lost, then seen in marks on a page, now found in sleeping ruin: "poor *perdu*." From his face she seems to read and hear the terrible sights and sounds of cosmic battle. Her gentleness and absence form no obstacle to understanding his great loss, which is summoned from the past in a near-Marlovian echo of a more distant strug-gle and a very different face.[43] In 5.3 positions reverse as Lear scans his daughter's face. Others tried to interpret Cordelia for him in Act 1; he assumes that role here as his right, whether as father or as king. His reiteration of "ever" transmutes his loss ("gone for ever") into her enduring excellence ("ever soft"). The first silence is no longer "noth-ing"; what the angry father then disclaimed he now gives back in gentleness, her voice plaited within his own. Near death himself, yet still on watch within his thin helm, he completes a circle begun in Act 4, preserving in his speech the ever-soft voice of the absent-present dead, the character who is and is not there either at the play's center or at its end.[44]

The ethical value of Lear's speech is located in three emergent traits of dramatic char-acter. The first is flexibility. An otherwise inflexible man assumes another voice radically different from his own. In the process, he alters his violently expressed opinions about his least daughter and her sex. He racks himself into tolerance, stretching his character by taking hers on. The second is acknowledgment. At the moment of death, Cordelia's presence is recognized as a value of utmost worth. Her body must be returned to the stage by the old man himself. After howling, he must bend over, cajole her into speech, and acknowledge the fact of her death and the equal fact of his passionate need for her life. The third is reciprocity. It presupposes the first two but goes beyond them while twining them together. In imitating and characterizing the voice of Cordelia, Lear returns that voice to her in desperate gift and compliment. Her ripe lip repaired and restored him to social exchange. His deictic rhetoric concentrates final attention on her: "Do you see this? Look on her, look, her lips, / Look there, look there!" (5.3.310–11). "[T]his" is "there" in all ripe presence and reverberation, much more than can be said; and the corollary of such ripeness, now "autumn's dust" (4.6.199), is a last reaping on a site anciently named a seeing place.[45] The mysteries of entwined lives meet in this accounting of eyes and voices, opening the terrible spaces in a dialogue of one. He looks, speaks, to her lips, there, "there."

Shakespeare phrases Lear's words so that no one shall see as much as the king commands. We are told to look, and we are left. We can, however, see what he says and read there the values in a committed attentiveness that bonds ethics and character in the play's eponymous construction. The ethical point of real importance is not whether Lear is deluded as he dies.[46] It is rather the register and quality of his voice as he attends his daughter before he dies, his voice sinking toward hers as toward a shelter. No theory or law, however powerful, gives access to this site. There is no hovel or vault that stage or film can show us. It is the verbal space between characters that separates as it bonds them on a terrain of meanings. It is the unnerving sense in Shakespearean drama of an intense subjectivity showing its back above the language that it lives in. A gesture of direction is made, "Look there," and we reach it – there is no other way – by means of the ripe lip, simples, and soft voice of interpretation.[47] Death may end the lady but not other locations for her voice. The value *of* Cordelia is now a function *in* Lear's speech, a last "trick of that voice" (Gloucester's phrase at 4.6.109), as if dramatic language could show, well beyond both bodies and characters, a transpersonal soul or (in terms less metaphysical) an ethical bond to a remembered voice. It is, as the gentleman said of the absent Cordelia, a becoming sorrow, "a rarity most belov'd." Subjectivity is sensed most sharply not inside one character but in the intervals disclosed by the verbal response of one character to another's silence. H. P. Grice coined the term *implicature* to refer to the influence of context on formations of unstated meaning. In *King Lear*, implicature locates subjectivity powerfully within the spaces between speech and dead silence.[48] Context allows us to hear Cordelia in King Lear, and that response from us completes the protagonist-king's command.

Characters mean marks and subjects of difference. Shakespeare constructs and positions them to reveal the palpable gaps in between – joining; interesting; investing as though with rights, values, being – those same literary constructions that remain different yet so remarkably combined in dramatic speech, death, and closure. It is not that any one character per se defines meaning but that characters, stable or changing, have agencies to perform in constructing those complex meanings that plays supply. They are agencies that audiences do and theories should aim to read.[49] The notion of an essential self may well be delusory. It may also be a red herring. There is no cognate relation between the philosophical concept and the literary construction, and the former's powers of delusion only increase if invoking them can direct attention away from Shakespeare's inventions of character and the extraordinary relations between their sustaining words. We repeatedly watch characters start out as *données* yet end as achievements, and such achievements only heighten the interplay of pattern and distinction in structures of language, character, and drama. When King Lear describes Cordelia as a voice – soft, gentle, low – he also redescribes himself, binds a constant of her character to his own, and enacts some small measure of the freedom to complete change at *King Lear*'s ending. In the midst of "general woe" (5.3.319), a cracking and tearing of all given bonds, he performs something remarkable yet next to nothing, a shift of phrase and tone in four lines: "Few words, but, to effect, more than all yet" (3.1.52). The achievement may be slight in various schemes of judgment, including some within the play, but interpretations of it can still reward the effort.[50] "Look with thine ears" was Lear's mad counsel to the blind earl (4.6.152), and the end of the play shows the king observing his own advice. What would it mean if we did not or could not listen? That the voice was not there? Or too soft for sleepers to hear? Even Nietzsche – the notable thunderer of my epigraph – knew to listen for soft sounds and a gentle voice.

IV

I don't really speak about *what I see, but* to *it*.[51]

Such is the power of artistic conventions, as E. H. Gombrich has shown us, that we are always completing patterns, designs, and forms in our minds.[52] Characters only begin in marks on the page; they reach their ends in us, occasioning a more extensive text than appears on the page. Even if skeptical, we may still find it difficult to regard such signs without presuming an interior self continuous with the character we behold. Perhaps this is the point of the device. As we advance our own process of inner understanding, it may seem quite natural to imagine a similar process at work, especially onstage, in a vivid, powerful figure like Lear as he beholds Cordelia. And who is to say that such imagining is unreal or irrelevant? Why not call it a personal experience pressing toward conditions of knowledge, a speculative sympathy, an exercise in ethical imagination?[53] Moral inquiry requires such attitudes of generosity, a speculative willingness to entertain the value of someone other who is only partially perceived. Much the same may be claimed for the literary interpretation of texts. An essay by Maynard Mack that I admire accounts for Lear's death as just such a complex of actions interior to one character. It creates meaning by making Lear's own vision, consciousness, heart, and hope trace a final plot of inner subjectivity. Seeing his daughter dead, the character is said to confront what he knows and has known of this world and so to strain the limits of his being. As his *cogito* disintegrates, he still

> tries to hold ... this painful vision unflinchingly before his consciousness, but the strain ... is too great: consciousness itself starts to give way: "Pray you, undo this button: thank you, Sir." And with it the vision gives way too: he cannot sustain it; he dies, reviving in his heart the hope that Cordelia lives: "Look on her, look, her lips, Look there, look there!"[54]

This is a forceful account of Lear's death, its qualities drawn from the confident use of texts and inward perspectives on dramatic action. Yet in it, the royal directive seems to point only toward Cordelia's lips. Its plot stands revealed as a subjective action in Lear's heart and hope, an inner space where, despite disintegration, both revive, as if only there they can unite, as if inwardness and subjectivity must be one space – the sole place to join the importance of speech to that of unity and termination.

My effort has been to look in a different direction: to study the fields of space around and between characters rather than within one character, and to consider acts of looking and speaking as dramatic contractions of such spaces. A distinction from Wittgenstein has served as my prompt.[55] I have concentrated on the energy and intensity of *looking to*, and the pattern that I complete involves Lear's lips rather than his heart and a mimetic sentence that prolongs "a little" Cordelia's vocal life. It is a voiceover of recognized otherness rather than one of interior expression, revealing a knowledge of one character embodied in the other's vocal action. Because Lear knows this, and can say this, we now know a great deal more about his powers. What he achieves in his language – a combining of distinct voices – is not simply an interiorization of the other gained by inferences about that character's subjectivity. His language is public, ethical, dramatic – meant for all audiences to hear, to understand as judgment, and to feel as the completion of a terrible circle. "Speak" was the imperative to Cordelia in Act 1. No one could then realize that his command would be obeyed only when she speaks at last in and through his voice, complicating finally the roles of speaker and listener as "she" mends his speech a little (1.1.93). Cordelia *speaks there* so gently and softly as to be heard and not heard, her lips' motions seen and not seen. The end is thus a strange form of pleasure asking us to see exact yet wrenching constructions of *ethos* and *pathos* in distinct yet contingent characters who make little sense, have no life, apart from one another.[56]

Precisely because it is a matter of characters, not one character, I cannot look through Lear's racked body to his breaking heart, although that word has figured in the play's language from the first scene. Stage directions signal a different turn and bond: "*Enter Lear with Cordelia in his armes.*"[57] We are to witness an unexpected strength, endurance, and discipline as we measure finally Lear's burdened acts of carrying, looking, and speaking. A broken heart may mark the end, as Kent prays, but it is only one sign of the ethical action that is at last painfully complete. I agree with the last speaker – Albany (Q) or Edgar (F): this king has indeed seen much and borne most.[58] He has looked on Cordelia's lips, and what he sees there, in the face of final silence, entails the play. He has borne to the stage not only this least weight of body but also a soft, gentle voice in his own child-changed character of speech. Lear speaks as father but also as king, surrounded by audiences but centered as before by variously gauged distances between his character and that of Cordelia. The spectacle is both domestic and political. Cordelia returned to a father and king: "How does my royal Lord? How fares your Majesty?" Lear and his play circle back again to divisions of kin and kingdom. Having much to answer for, he brings in the work's grim harvest as two distinct changes in death and closure remain. They set him with his daughter in the namesake play and finish a father's business in an achieved softness of voice: not "nothing" but "something yet," a tonality struck by him that is not his alone, a voice literally now between their lips. Before the silences of death and dramatic closure, such shifting constructions of character let us hear fine lines of affiliation drawing a fullness and an emptiness in represented being. The study of character in *King Lear* need not restrict or simplify meanings; it need not return us covertly to Victorian codes of ethics and empire. It can enable the play's richest meanings because the figures of character are thoroughly constructed and set within intimate companies and embraces of voice, though within, finally, no more than voice itself.[59]

It is an ending that a later play repairs, although in a language of antithetical reverberation. Impossibility here is art's easy making in *The Winter's Tale*. There one king, urged on by another ("See, my lord, / Would you not deem it breath'd?"), can admire in a "dear stone" a queen's true image: "The very life seems warm upon her lip" (5.3.63–64, 24, 66). Leontes, his lost daughter now found, can be moved to astonished questioning – "What fine chisel / Could ever yet cut breath?" (ll. 78–79) – and then to genuine wonder. He affirms the lady who has preserved his dead wife's character and statue so that image and figure, seeming and life, can be one. It is a resonant, happy metamorphosis of emotion, stone, and art; everything, in short, that cannot be achieved in *King Lear*.[60]

> What you can make her do,
> I am content to look on: what to speak,
> I am content to hear; for 'tis as easy
> To make her speak as move.
>
> (ll. 91–94)

Contingencies, even of breath and speech, move oppositely in romance and tragedy. Ethical meaning in *King Lear* has little to do with assembled pieties or retreats into a fragmenting, solitary self. It has everything to do with the nearly ineffable value of life in a character who has none, and under this intense pressure the character who speaks of that life gives up his own, after commanding us to do as he has done. "Do you see this? Look on her, look, her lips, / Look there, look there!" The force of this perception, which I have linked to moral inquiry, is such that we run the risk of becoming what we see, of speaking for ourselves the voice that we long to hear. There is, nevertheless, a greater risk: that of refusing sight and of regarding silence as if it means nothing at all. "Nothing will come of nothing," Lear retorted earlier to Cordelia's silence (1.1.90). By play's end, he thinks differently, and that difference is a function of his character and hers over the time of the plot. There is "something yet" in the nothing of her death, and it is caught in, and represented by, Lear's recollection of her voice.

My last point – that there is a function to characters – cuts against the grain of current speculation about literature. That speculation finds the idea of character too blunt an instrument for analytic work as well as too burdened with suspect categories of philosophical thought. In each case the objection involves attitudes toward literary construction. The first objection concerning bluntness may well seem true if certain instances of literary analysis are put on display. But since character is a constitutive part of the literary work itself and not merely a term of hermeneutic art, it cannot be the case that we *ought* to read a play and ignore its characters, no matter what else we or others choose to notice. It is precisely the construction that needs a finer study. The second objection concerning suspect categories is well taken, but only if the idea of character has been confused with ideological concepts of an impermeable, self-sufficient, or sovereign individualism. Lear may be every inch a king; it does not follow that he knows or rules himself. There is a clear remedy: study the construction, erase the confusion, trace the knots that bind characters. Toward that end, this essay has sought to understand characters within a play as one would words within language. That is, the meanings generated by characters are established by an interplay of difference and resemblance across protocols of custom and use, and the meanings so generated and established own their significance not within themselves but against ground-works of structure. The structure studied here is the voice of Lear as he comes to articulate the value of his daughter's life in dramatic speech that shapes absence and presence at start and finish. Literary works are indeed structured like a language, and it is because of such structuring that characters, like words, enable a play of meaning – not in any absolute sense but in the varied and contingent senses of meaning that make up the difficult conditions of truth within time.[61] Within those conditions, the "voice of beauty," which is not the voice of any single character, offers distinctive inflections and asks an acknowledgment of the crucial work of characterization, voice, and speech in *King Lear*.

Notes

Two seminars at annual meetings of the Shakespeare Association of America gave this essay its start: one on character led by Robert Knapp (1994), and one on *King Lear* led by R. A. Foakes (1996). I would also like to thank Walter Reed, who read an early version with care; my colleagues at Southern Methodist University; and an anonymous reviewer for this journal, who saw large as well as small problems acutely.

1 Friedrich Nietzsche, *Thus Spoke Zarathustra: A Book for All and None*, trans. Walter Kaufmann (New York: The Modern Library, 1995), 93.

2 Christy Desmet situates character in the context of theory; see *Reading Shakespeare's Characters: Rhetoric, Ethics, and Identity* (Amherst: U of Massachusetts P, 1992), 3–58. See also J. Leeds Barroll, *Artificial Persons: The Formation of Character in the Tragedies of Shakespeare* (Columbia: U of South Carolina P, 1974); and Lawrence Manley, *Convention 1500–1750* (Cambridge, MA: Harvard UP, 1980), 106–33. Richard Lanham defines the rhetorical terms in *A Handlist of Rhetorical Terms*, 2d ed. (Berkeley: U of California P, 1991), 111 and 123.

3 Maynard Mack treats an opposite arrangement: "umbrella speeches, [under which] … more than one consciousness may shelter" ("The Jacobean Shakespeare" in *Jacobean Theatre*, Stratford-upon-Avon Studies 1 [London: Edward Arnold, 1960], 26). Mack states his purpose modestly as a revision of Bradley, but his notion of speech as a shelter for multiple consciousnesses suggests a new view of language rather than a revision of ideas about character. One should note that New Criticism and postmodern theory do share some views: e.g., on the limits of character criticism. My italicized phrase notices the somewhat different qualities of density (*knotted*) and emptiness (*intervals*) that concern me.

4 Quotations of *Lear* follow the Arden Shakespeare *King Lear*, ed. Kenneth Muir (London: Methuen, 1952). Muir's is a composite text, based on the Folio with additions from the Quarto. I am grateful to the publishers of the Arden Shakespeare Third Series, who allowed me to see bound proofs of Reginald Foakes's forthcoming edition, *King Lear* (Walton-on-Thames, UK: Thomas Nelson and Sons, 1997). Bringing to bear a thorough knowledge of the textual issues, Foakes has chosen to present a conflated text's "possible versions" (128). Quotations of all other Shakespeare plays follow the *Riverside Shakespeare*, ed. G. Blakemore Evans (Boston: Houghton Mifflin, 1974).

5 The classic case against *nothing-but* arguments is William James, *The Varieties of Religious Experience* (Cambridge, MA: Harvard UP, 1985), 11–50; the reduction he counters: that religion is nothing but sexuality displaced. To say that character is nothing but marks on a page reduces an idea to its material display. William H. Gass offers the grammatical reduction: "Polonius, that foolish old garrulous proper noun" ("The Concept of Character in Fiction" in *Fiction and the Figures of Life* [New York: Knopf, 1970], 34–54, esp. 37). On the beholder's share that lets a noun age and talk foolishly, see E. H. Gombrich, *Art and Illusion: A Study in the Psychology of Pictorial Representation*, rev. ed. (New York: Pantheon, 1965), 181–241. Bernard Harrison comments on *Lear* while discussing postmodern theory and kinds of truth in literature; see *Inconvenient Fictions: Literature and the Limits of Theory* (New Haven, CT: Yale UP, 1991), 54–61.

6 Character is usually viewed as a literary device that represents effects of consciousness – senses of coherent interiority and depth. Harold Bloom declares Shakespearean inwardness canonical; see *The Western Canon: The Books and School of the Ages* (New York: Harcourt Brace, 1994), 70–75. I do not deny such representation or its importance in *Lear*. I consider an awareness that seems to move among characters and not within one alone. "Thick description," a term coined by Gilbert Ryle, is associated with Clifford Geertz's "Thick Description: Toward an Interpretive Theory of Culture" (in Geertz, *The Interpretation of Cultures: Selected Essays* [New York: Basic Books, 1973], 3–30) and indicates accounts that are circumstantially specific and interpretive. By "an 'anthropology' of Lear's change," I mean that change in Lear's character is best understood as a function of his bonds to

others, especially Cordelia. I use the term more narrowly than Louis Adrian Montrose does in "The Purpose of Playing: Reflections on a Shakespearean Anthropology" (*Helios* n.s. 7 [1980]: 53–74) to refer to a dramatic refinement of kinship relations. His concern is with larger implications of ritual and symbol in theater and society.

7   Paul de Man, for example, makes fragmentation a theoretical principle in his essay on Shelley's *Triumph of Life*; see "Shelley Disfigured" in *Deconstruction and Criticism*, Geoffrey Hartman et al., eds. (New York: Seabury, 1979), 39–73. De Man's closing abstractions assert a program of radical skepticism (68–69); in contrast, Shelley's richly figured *terza-rima* stanzas lead to a break-off question. The distinction lies between unfolding a theoretical argument of skepticism and a poetic rhetoric of interrogation.

8   Desiderius Erasmus, *On Copia of Words and Ideas*, trans. Donald B. King (Milwaukee, WI: Marquette UP, 1963), 104. Kent likewise notes the value of brevity: "Few words, but, to effect, more than all yet" (3.1.52).

9   Cf. "The end crowns all" (*Troilus and Cressida*, 4.5.224).

10 According to Jonathan Dollimore's materialist reading of *Lear*, the play confirms the dictum that men are determined by the time; see *Radical Tragedy*, 2d ed. (Durham, NC: Duke UP, 1993), 196. He does not put the theory in any qualifying context: e.g., Edmund's own deviation from that time. At 1.2.124–40, Edmund mocks his father's sense of heaven's agency, as he would, no doubt, any similar dependence on history as an agent.

11 Harold Bloom suggests that Edmund is attractive because he is at ease in the world and able to articulate it as his own; see *Ruin the Sacred Truths* (Cambridge, MA: Harvard UP, 1989), 77–79. Shakespearean character, Bloom argues, has come to model human nature; developing Chaucer, Shakespeare stages "the representation of change by showing people pondering their own speeches and being altered through that consideration" (54).

12 Barbara Everett, "The New King Lear," *Critical Quarterly* 2 (1960): 325–39. Her title takes in two meanings: a change in the king's character and a shift in interpretations of that change. She spots tendencies to Christianize Lear's suffering, opposing to them her vitalist sense of "forms of intense life" (338).

13 S. L. Goldberg emphasizes "acknowledgement" and the limits to meaning in *An Essay on* King Lear (Cambridge: Cambridge UP, 1974), 30–34, 174, and 190. I admire this account but find a greater possibility for meaning in Lear's sense of Cordelia's voice than Goldberg's essay allows. See also Emmanuel Levinas, *Outside the Subject*, trans. Michael B. Smith (Stanford, CA: Stanford UP, 1993), 121–25 and 34. Levinas adopts tropes of "the face" and "face-to-face" encounters to express issues of subjectivity and intersubjectivity.

14 See Paul Ricoeur, "Self as *Ipse*" in *Freedom and Interpretation: The Oxford Amnesty Lectures, 1992*, Barbara Johnson, ed. (New York: Basic Books, 1993), 103–19.

15 It is formally neat as well as ethically appalling that Edmund is responsible for the deaths of all three daughters. Stephen Booth finds the proper end of the play in the deaths of Edmund, Goneril, and Regan (the end in poetic justice?) and declares the deaths of Cordelia and Lear to be "culminating events of [Shakespeare's] *story*" that take place "after his *play* is over" (King Lear, Macbeth, *Indefinition, and Tragedy* [New Haven, CT: Yale UP, 1983], 11). I am uncertain about the value of distinguishing between *play* and *story*.

16 See Harley Granville-Barker, *Prefaces to Shakespeare I* (London: Sidgwick and Jackson, 1927), 133–231; and Stephen Greenblatt, *Learning to Curse: Essays in early modern culture* (New York: Routledge, 1990), 98. For a severe circularity that omits Act 4's reunion, see Jonathan Goldberg, "Shakespearean Inscriptions: The Voicing of Power" in *Shakespeare and the Question of Theory*, Patricia Parker and Geoffrey Hartman, eds. (New York: Methuen, 1985), 116–37.

17 Paul J. Alpers offers an interesting critique of the New Criticism; see "*King Lear* and the Theory of the 'Sight Pattern'" in *In Defense of Reading*, Reuben A. Brower and Richard Poirier, eds. (New York: Dutton, 1963), 133–52. Alpers argues that treating metaphors as primary data (in place of characters and actions) yields unwarranted equations; images of sight (a function of metaphor) are made to represent insight (a function of character). Patterns of imagery intensify instead character bonds, "man's actual dealings with other men" (138). Postmodernists, however, might question

any designation of character as primary with respect to other uses of literary language. The issue is whether literary study can accept categories other than those of language, whether hierarchies of categories are possible or useful.

18   These lines appear in F only (without exclamation point). They concentrate Lear's attention on Cordelia and move forward the moment of his death. Kent's reference to "the rack ["wracke"] of this tough world" (1. 313) follows as choral commentary. In Q the death and choral commentary coincide, turning attention from Lear and Cordelia to Lear and Kent. Q thus lacks the intensity of structure in F. The treatment of death as a visual or theatrical experience is established by the managed suicide in 4.6.

19   Beginning with Alpers's distinction between language and character, Stanley Cavell argues that *King Lear* avoids recognitions and thus love. A subargument treats character change; another considers what it means to acknowledge a person. Cavell treats character experience atomistically; he discusses Lear's recognition of Cordelia but not, as a part of that experience, Cordelia's response to her father. Cavell's general view of the play excludes responsiveness and exchange; see "The Avoidance of Love" in *Must we mean what we say?* (Cambridge: Cambridge UP, 1976), 267–353.

20   F gives *woman*; Q, *women*. It is worthwhile to consider both words in competition for textual space and the differences they suggest about general character. Editorial selection on display yields a richer end than does strict separation – here a generic, not a plural, term, marking Cordelia's constitutive power. Such work with a conflated text and its apparatus can show the text to be more than marks on a page yet not mystify its origins.

21   Maud Bodkin's well-known treatment of archetypes emphasizes a pattern of heroic suffering in the father, an emphasis that obscures Cordelia's role in returning to vary the pattern of paternal suffering; see *Archetypal Patterns in Poetry: Psychological Studies of Imagination* (Oxford: Oxford UP, 1934), 15–17 and 272–76.

22   For Elder Olson, France's sketch of Cordelia as a value in herself anticipates Lear's final intuition; see *Tragedy and the Theory of Drama* (Detroit, MI: Wayne State UP, 1961), 207–9. The conflict between Lear and Cordelia, he argues, lies between a feudal lord's asking for one kind of love and a family member's understanding of love not as formal pledge but as unspoken trust. Cordelia dies so that Lear can learn familial love; he dies in sign of the lesson learned. At 1.1.160, Rowe added the stage direction that has Lear reach for his sword.

23   Cordelia's death enacts Kent's point and turns her sisters' early lies to her late truths. Goneril asserted "A love that makes breath poor and speech unable"; Regan claimed that Goneril names her deeds: "In my true heart / I find she names my very deed of love; / Only she comes too short" (1.1.60, 70–72). The older sisters' speeches are validated by the youngest's silence. Cf. Harry Berger Jr., "*King Lear*: The Lear Family Romance" in *Making Trifles of Terrors: Redistributing Complicities in Shakespeare* (Stanford, CA: Stanford UP, 1997), 25–49, esp. 46–49.

24   Such reporting scenes include *Pericles*, 1.4; *Cymbeline*, 1.1, 2.4, and 5.3; and *The Winter's Tale*, 1.1 and 5.2. Sidney's *Arcadia* is a source for this passage in *Lear* (see Muir, ed., 161n).

25   Sheldon Zitner dislikes the high style's "emptiness" and "pasteboard prettiness" ("*King Lear* and Its Language" in *Some Facets of* King Lear: *essays in prismatic criticism*, Rosalie L. Colie and F. T. Flahiff, eds. [Toronto: Toronto UP, 1974], 6). These qualities – under other names perhaps? – are relevant to dramatic function in a sequence from description to appearance to act. Patricia Fumerton, for example, links uses of adornment to "the rise of the *self*" (*Cultural Aesthetics: Renaissance Literature and the Practice of Social Ornament* [Chicago: U of Chicago P, 1991], 28). Marianne Novy traces an imagery of tears to develop themes of pity, mutuality, and forgiveness and comments acutely on Lear's description of Cordelia's voice in relation to issues of femininity and patriarchy; see *Love's Argument: Gender Relations in Shakespeare* (Chapel Hill: U of North Carolina P, 1984), 158–63.

26   Ernst H. Kantorowicz shows not only the constructedness of character but a full awareness and use of the issue in medieval discourse. He traces distinctions between the monarch's political and natural persons or bodies, beginning his influential study of medieval political theology with *Richard II*; see *The King's Two Bodies: A Study in Medieval Political Theology* (Princeton, NJ: Princeton UP, 1957). In *The Poetics of Primitive Accumulation: English Renaissance Culture and the Genealogy of Capital* (Ithaca, NY: Cornell UP, 1991), Richard Halpern approaches the issue

through a neomarxist economics, studying "the divorce between the signs and the material realities of royal power" (220). Constructedness, one concludes, is not an unconditioned idea; to own
significance, it needs a specified historical context. To point out that an entity is constructed
cannot by itself fix (or unfix) meaning, since construction is precisely the manner of creating
meaning.

27   There is a marked orality to family relations in *King Lear*. One can give, deny, withhold, or destroy
love by acts of voice, mouth, or lips. On fantasies of passivity and sadism in the oral phase of
development, see Norman N. Holland, *The Dynamics of Literary Response* (New York: Oxford UP,
1968), 34–38. F makes Cordelia the medical figure, replacing the Doctor with a Gentleman; see
Foakes's Arden edition, 349n.

28   The etymology of *ripe* includes Old English *rip* (harvest) and *ripan* (to reap, harvest). Cordelia
describes Lear "crown'd" with weeds and sends a search party to "the high-grown field" (4.4.3,
7). For *repair* and *rich*, see Gloucester to Tom/Edgar (4.1.76–77). Spenser's account of King Leyr
(reprinted in Muir, ed., 237–38) traces patterns of restoration, ripeness, and death; it ends, after
the king's death, with Cordelia's overthrow and suicide by hanging. Redemptive readings of the
Lear story antedate not only Bradley and New Criticism but also Shakespeare's tragedy.

29   Muir, ed., cites Luke 2:49 (166n). Cordelia's shift of reference to an earthly father is one part of
her mediating work. Harold C. Goddard studies Cordelia's work of repair in *The Meaning of
Shakespeare* (Chicago: U of Chicago P, 1951), 522–57, esp. 541–49. For a compressed account of
materialist ideology in *Lear*, see Terry Eagleton, *William Shakespeare* (Oxford: Basil Blackwell,
1986), 76–83.

30   Studies of the play have treated feudalism variously. For a valuable contrast between the history of
ideas and the new historicism, see Rosalie L. Colie, "Reason and Need: *King Lear* and the 'Crisis'
of the Aristocracy" in Colie and Flahiff, eds., 185–219; and Halpern, 215–69. We may debate
whether Shakespeare's feudalism works primarily as a historical topic or as an artistic device
to image historical settings of character. Is chivalry put aside a sign of bourgeois progress, a
dramatic frame for tragedy, or some admixture? On the problems of using Foucault and Stone in
commentary on Shakespeare, see David Cressy, "Foucault, Stone, Shakespeare and Social
History," *ELR* 21 (1991): 121–33.

31   Annabel Patterson shifts the study of censorship from a censor's work to the author's mediation
of living with censorship; see *Censorship and Interpretation: The Conditions of Writing and Reading
in Early Modern England* (Madison, WI: U of Wisconsin P, 1984). The point extends to characterization. Censorship becomes an issue in the play if one takes Lear's speech as imagining a new life
within conditions of imprisonment.

32   Marlowe provides a model for powerful helplessness. Bajazeth gains rhetorical power within
Tamburlaine's cage, where he is held with his wife for the spectacle of two onstage imperial
suicides; see *Tamburlaine I* in *Christopher Marlowe, The Complete Plays*, ed. J. B. Steane
(Harmondsworth, UK: Penguin, 1969), 4.4 and 5.2. *Lear* redirects atrocity in Act 5 toward the
savaged emotional bonds between father and daughter, suggesting that the real prison and torture
are a world without Cordelia: "he hates him," Kent states, "That would upon the rack of this
tough world / Stretch him out longer" (5.3.313–15).

33   René Girard's work on the relationship of violence to the sacred bears importantly on *King Lear*;
see *Violence and the Sacred*, trans. Patrick Gregory (Baltimore: Johns Hopkins UP, 1979). A complex
rite of sacrifice, the play reveals bewildering, abrupt acts of substitution and violent displacement.
Lear's language shows him at last to be ripe for a true ceremony of surrendering the kingdom in
death. On the use of the pronouns *thou* and *you* in *Lear*, see Randolph Quirk, "Shakespeare and
the English Language" in *A New Companion to Shakespeare Studies*, Kenneth Muir and
S. Schoenbaum, eds. (Cambridge: Cambridge UP, 1971), 67–82, esp. 70–72; and Alessandro
Serpieri, "Reading the signs: towards a semiotics of Shakespearean drama," trans. Keir Elam, in
Alternative Shakespeares, John Drakakis, ed. (London: Methuen, 1985), 119–43.

34   Virginia Woolf, *A Writer's Diary: Being Extracts from the Diary of Virginia Woolf*, ed. Leonard
Woolf (London: The Hogarth Press, 1953), 85.

35   Marlowe heightens the cruelty of his barbarous Scythian in *Tamburlaine II*. The captured Olympia
utters this phrase while killing her son to preserve him from worse tortures (3.4.19); Tamburlaine

kills his first son for failing the father's heroic standards (4.1.105–39). On earlier dramatic forms in Shakespeare, see Howard Felperin, *Shakespearean Representation: Mimesis and Modernity in Elizabethan Tragedy* (Princeton, NJ: Princeton UP, 1977), 12–43.

36 Muir, ed., gives examples of usages in which *generation* can mean *parents* rather than *offspring* (11n). Lear may intend a shock at the emergence of the former meaning.

37 If one considers the work of Goneril and Regan, an irony attends the phrase "man's work." Elaine Scarry's discussion of the body in pain offers valuable reading beside *King Lear*; see *The Body in Pain: The Making and Unmaking of the World* (Oxford: Oxford UP, 1985). See also Caroline Spurgeon, *Shakespeare's Imagery* (Boston: Beacon Press, 1958), 338–39. On the range of Lear's voice in the physical space of the theater, see Daniel Seltzer, "*King Lear* in the Theater" in *On King Lear*, Lawrence Danson, ed. (Princeton, NJ: Princeton UP, 1981), 163–85, esp. 178–85.

38 Muir summarizes various speculations about Lear's use of "fool" for Cordelia; e.g., Armin, playing the Fool, may have doubled as Cordelia (see Muir, ed., 217n). Sidney objected to kings and fools on the same stage; see Sir Philip Sidney, *An Apology for Poetry*, ed. Geoffrey Shepherd (London: T. Nelson, 1965), 135. *Lear*'s king is called a fool by a fool; later, with a new tone and meaning, the king directs the term to his daughter.

39 A principal aim of new-historicist critique is to "decenter" the subject, to remove it from an unfounded place of privilege in the interest of redressing power. New historicism's understanding of a work is thus frequently shaped by ideologies of power and victimization. Alvin Kernan offers a "Whitehall" reading of divine-right theory in *King Lear*, a sly marriage of the often-anathematized Tillyard to new historicism; see *Shakespeare, the King's Playwright: Theater in the Stuart Court, 1603–1613* (New Haven, CT: Yale UP, 1995). On the softness of Cordelia's voice as a sign of feminine submissiveness, see Catherine Belsey, *The Subject of Tragedy: Identity and Difference in Renaissance Drama* (London: Methuen, 1985), 178. The issue of literary *centering* (e.g., on constructed characters) returns us to what Aristotle might mean by his observation that literature is more philosophical or universal (not simply abstract but putative, counterfactual, speculative) than history; see *Poetics*, trans. W. Hamilton Fyfe (Cambridge, MA: Harvard UP, 1927), 34–39.

40 The Latin term *interesse* acquired technical meanings in property law: to invest someone with a right to or share in something; to admit to a privilege. The word occurs in F (1623) but not in Q (1608).

41 See Martin Buber, *I and Thou*, trans. Ronald Gregor Smith (New York: Scribner's, 1958), 1–11; and Mikhail Bakhtin, *The Dialogic Imagination*, ed. Michael Holquist, trans. Caryl Emerson and Michael Holquist (Austin: U of Texas P, 1981), 259–422.

42 Clifford Geertz points to the ethical dilemma of the anthropologist when recording yet thereby appropriating another's voice; see *After the Fact: Two Countries, Four Decades, One Anthropologist* (Cambridge, MA: Harvard UP, 1995), 128–30. Literature generally, and drama in particular, offer significant violations of this code. Lear's appropriation of Cordelia's voice, however, seems to carry the significance of ethical perception rather than asserted power.

43 Cordelia echoes Lear's language on the heath. The letters referred to in 4.3 lead one to expect her knowledge of wind, thunder, and lightning, but she adopts as well his epithets (3.2.1–9) and compound epithets (3.1.11, Q only). We are shown the storm as a continuing function in Lear's mind that Cordelia can read, speak, and calm. *Perdu* entered English in the French phrase *sentinelle perdue* – an exposed or forward and hazardous sentinel post (or the sentinel himself). Such a post was the position of a scout or spy; hence the link of "poor *perdu*" to "God's spies" (5.3.17). Cordelia's use holds the military sense as well as the sense of exposure to the elements. For Marlowe's Faustus and Helen's face, see *Doctor Faustus* in Steane, ed., 5.1.97–103. René Weis notes the allusion and F's abbreviation of this speech in King Lear: *A Parallel Text Edition* (London and New York: Longman, 1993), 269n.

44 Marjorie Garber discusses the equation of silence with death and Freud's use of Shakespeare; see "Freud's choice: 'The Theme of the Three Caskets'" in *Shakespeare's Ghost Writers: Literature as uncanny causality* (New York: Methuen, 1987), 74–86. Freud understood Lear's entrance carrying Cordelia as his act of carrying death to himself; I understand it as Lear's qualification of death by love. Cordelia is thus carried in an opposite direction to dying Edmund, an emblem with ethical and theatrical significance.

45   *Theater*, from Greek *théatron*, a place for seeing, a theater; from *theáomai*, to view, gaze at, behold. On deictic rhetoric – language that articulates "the situation and … the space in which it is pronounced" – see Serpieri, 122.

46   Muir asserts a complicated emotional process for Lear in which joy over seeming life in Cordelia causes his death, a belief that we can see as delusion (liii). Joseph Summers, in a line of argument near mine, revises this Bradleyan point, arguing that what Lear sees and what has life is what Cordelia has taught him about love; see "'Look there, look there!' The Ending of *King Lear*" in *English Renaissance Studies*, John Carey, ed. (Oxford: Oxford UP, 1980), 74–93. Summers traces convincingly the emotional rhythms of this discovery (92). Muir's view is seconded by Maynard Mack in King Lear *in Our Time* (Berkeley: U of California P, 1965), 114; Barroll, 250; and recently by R. A. Foakes in *Hamlet versus Lear: Cultural Politics and Shakespeare's Art* (Cambridge: Cambridge UP, 1993), 218–19. For criticism of this view, Ian J. Kirby, "The Passing of King Lear," *Shakespeare Survey* 41 (1989): 145–57.

47   Getting the world right – and not merely interpreting it – is a traditional way of defining knowledge and philosophy. Considering the limitations of philosophy for ethical thought, Bernard Williams suggests analogies for similar limitations of other forms of theory in relation to interpretation; see *Ethics and the Limits of Philosophy* (Cambridge, MA: Harvard UP, 1985). The point is not to deny theory – it is a strong form of interpretation – only to question claims of governance over all methods of interpretation, as if theory somehow stood outside or above interpretation.

48   In arguing against Bradley's notion of a deceived joy, Kirby suggests that what Lear sees is not an illusion of renewed life but a departing-yet-summoning spirit (156–57). Susan Snyder studies the play in terms of Kübler-Ross's stages of dying; see "*King Lear* and the Psychology of Dying," *Shakespeare Quarterly* 33 (1982): 449–60. She concludes that Lear and Cordelia die together and not as individuals; that the time lapse "allows Lear to do the impossible, to experience his own death and cry out against the terrible wrongness of it" (459). Roger Fowler introduces Grice's term, summarizes his argument, and provides a bibliography; see *Linguistic Criticism*, 2d ed. (Oxford: Oxford UP, 1996), 135–36 and 159.

49   Jonathan Goldberg urges "the radical instability of character as a locus of meaning in the Shakespearean text" ("Textual Properties," *SQ* 37 [1986]: 213–17, esp. 215). This claim may be true if one attempts to align particular meanings with particular characters. If one views a variety of characters as engaged in a process of constructing thick or clustered meanings, the case may seem less desperate, as Goldberg's discussion of Malvolio suggests.

50   In view of such slightness, an objection might be put that I describe less than a change of character – merely a new element added to an existing character. Such an objection might encourage a review of basic terms – *character, person, body, voice, change, event* – and what we might expect of them in literary discussions of constructedness. I have found Bernard Williams especially helpful on physical qualities of a voice as mediations between body and character; see *Problems of the Self: Philosophical Papers 1956–1972* (Cambridge: Cambridge UP, 1973), 11–12. Roland Barthes remarks on pleasures in "the *grain* of the voice" and "the articulation of the body, of the tongue"; his remarks suggest character's presence in the physical or material voice (*The Pleasure of the Text*, trans. Richard Miller [London: Jonathan Cape, 1975], 66–67).

51   Ludwig Wittgenstein, *The Blue and Brown Books* (New York: Harper and Brothers, 1958), 175.

52   See Gombrich, 181–287. Earlier he discusses the role of "schemata" in a process of stipulation, correction, and making in the visual arts (84–90), an exposition that can apply to other disciplines. Here literary character is a function of rhetorical and literary schemata, an author's practice with them, and the contributing emotions, intelligence, and memory of different audiences. In this view, character could never be reduced simply to printed marks on a page.

53   In a recent issue of *PMLA* on "the status of evidence," Heather Dubrow observes the value of "experiential evidence" and "personal accounts" ("Introduction: The Status of Evidence," *PMLA* 111 [1996]: 7–20).

54   Mack, King Lear *in Our Time*, 114. Mack's argument is larger than I have managed to suggest; he notes levels of meaning contributed by senses of "intimate humanity" and by various practices of literary history (78–80).

55   Elaborating on this distinction, Wittgenstein points out that a direction to see ought not to be confused with what is seen (176).

56   A. D. Nuttall puts the issue in a title – *Why Does Tragedy Give Pleasure?* (Oxford: Clarendon Press, 1996) – and ends his discussion with *Lear* and the strange pleasure of tracing sequences to a terrible end (104).

57   The stage direction is the same in Q and F (references to attendant figures differ). Muir's Arden edition gives "*Re-enter* LEAR, *with* CORDELIA *dead in his arms*" (5.3.256 SD). Because Lear appears earlier in the scene, Dyce altered "*Enter*" to "*Re-enter*"; Rowe inserted "*dead*" to end uncertainty over Cordelia's condition.

58   Albany speaks in the plural ("The oldest have …") and presumably refers to both Lear and Gloucester; Edgar speaks in the singular ("The oldest has …") and refers to Lear alone. The problem of the close is to adjust the Lear experience to the ongoing fortunes of the state. F develops Lear's death by inserting 5.3.309–10, giving a firmness to the role of Edgar in closure. Thus, rather than the detached Albany, Edgar, who has been to the heath, speaks last in F to represent Lear's influence on the living.

59   Hélène Cixous's meditation on character as singular and repressive of genuine literary energies is both stimulating and provocative; "The Character of 'Character,'" trans. Keith Cohen, *New Literary History* 5 (1974): 383–402. Although her essay can be described as *against character*, it requires the concept to drive its polemic.

60   In his Arden edition of *The Winter's Tale* (London: Methuen, 1965), J.H.P. Pafford notes the Pygmalion story from Book X of Ovid's *Metamorphoses* (xxxiv). Lynn Enterline argues the success of the female voice in a rhetoric of animation in *The Winter's Tale*; see " 'You speak a language that I understand not': The Rhetoric of Animation in *The Winter's Tale*," *SQ* 48 (1997): 17–44. *King Lear* seems to me to present other problems: the female voice succeeds but at the cost that is tragedy.

61   For the analogy between characters and words, see Martin Price, *Forms of Life: Character and Moral Imagination in the Novel* (New Haven, CT: Yale UP, 1983), 55. I have benefited from this wide-ranging discussion of character in the novel.

CHAPTER 9

Theory in Practice
Romantic Rhetorics (from Elizabeth Bishop: The Restraints of Language)

C. K. Doreski

Elizabeth Bishop's poetry was written during the era when the New Critics were prominent in the American academy and were setting the agenda for how students were supposed to understand and read poetry. Poems were best when they achieved a unity of form and content, welding universal idea to concrete image. The best poems were embodiments and revelations of great truths. Often those truths had a spiritual quality, as was the case with William Wordsworth, who felt nature consisted of embodied spirit. Look at a flower and you see God. Bishop's temperament was more skeptical and materialist. She delighted in describing the world, but she was reluctant to embrace the idea that the world embodied spirit. Indeed, in several poems such as "Crusoe in England" and "Over 2,000 Illustrations and a Complete Concordance," she mocks the notion that the world is anything more than world – simple material physical reality with no spirit in it. Moments of revelation when spirit supposedly intrudes in life are called "epiphanies," and C. K. Doreski describes how Bishop, following Wordsworth, evokes the possibility of an epiphanic revelation of spirit only to disappoint that expectation.

Epiphany and the power of naming (which in the modern era begins by naming the writer-as-authority) are two characteristically romantic-modern rhetorical embodiments of knowledge. Bishop, who largely learned these devices from Wordsworth, manipulates their conventions for some of her richest effects, and also for some of her most intriguing complexities. As I have previously argued, resistance to language that attempts to delve into the psyche or the world of the spirit characterizes her poetry. The process of resistance itself, however, constitutes a powerful rhetorical structure that shapes much of her best work. The epiphanic mode, which this chapter will discuss first, requires the poet to transgress the text and explicitly share its self-realization, its transcendence of

Original publication details: C.K. Doreski, "Romantic Rhetorics" from *Elizabeth Bishop: The Restraints of Language*, pp. 34–64. Oxford University Press, 1993. Reproduced with permission from Oxford University Press.

Literary Theory: An Anthology, Third Edition. Edited by Julie Rivkin and Michael Ryan.
© 2017 John Wiley & Sons, Ltd. Published 2017 by John Wiley & Sons, Ltd.

language into immanence. Trust in the epiphany did not come readily to Elizabeth Bishop. As her poem "Santarém" warns, there is always the chance that the auditor might misunderstand the significance of the triggering subject and query "What's that ugly thing?", inadvertently mocking the ideational. What some critics consider Bishop's extreme reticence and excessive decorum may be linked to her notions of decency and communion, and to her ultimate distrust of epiphany.

The challenge for Bishop was to use epiphanic staging (the means of preparing the reader) without violating her aesthetic of reticence (a literary more than psychological tic). Though often labeled epiphanies by her critics, Bishop's gestures toward the Wordsworthian landscape of divine immanence do not usually function as such. In her encounters with the notion of a spiritual dimension suggested or revealed by landscape, the characteristic motion of her poems is a recoil from the beyond, retreating back into the poem itself.

This suggests the true depth of reticence in Bishop's poetic. Epiphany would and should open up the poem to uncontrollable exterior forces, relinquishing the law of metaphor and imposing a dimension beyond the ordinary reach of language. Bishop, who viewed poetry as a limited, and fortuitously limiting, exchange, refused to acknowledge any pressure to contain, expand, define, or even escape life through art. From the shark-filled "spangled sea" of "The Unbeliever" to the sheltered interior of "The Monument," from the road-checked interior of "Cape Breton" to the "armored cars of dreams" in "Sleeping Standing Up," Bishop clearly defines the terms of commerce in part by delineating the interiority and the exteriority of, respectively, her presence and the poem's surface strategies. Bishop's decorum surely included a sense of propriety or decency. Rather than a personality quirk, deficient ego, or exaggerated morality, however, her reticence informs her original language and diction, and is the basis of her refusal of many conventional poetic motifs that would, if allowed to, render her poems almost ordinary.

Throughout her work Bishop explores various rhetorical postures that respond to Wordsworth's epiphanic stance. At times she presents us with a natural vantage point, nature without human intervention. In "The Sandpiper" [QT], a creature scurries about in the midst of chaos; though "focused" and "preoccupied" he is not yet engulfed by the natural forces swirling about him. Unconscious of the threatening vastness, which humans might identify as epiphanic, he has developed a unique shoreline philosophy:

> The roaring alongside he takes for granted,
> and that every so often the world is bound to shake.
>   [CP, 131]

At once a student of Blake ("in a state of controlled panic") and Keats ("The world is a mist. And then the world is / minute and vast and clear"), the shorebird sees his random fate as one with the minute particulars of the "millions of grains" of sand. In his element, the sandpiper knows none of the frustrating dislocations of humans in the landscape and therefore sees no need to transcend them. The traveler-spectator Bishop, on the other hand, needs to correct and interpret, as well as frame the scene:

> He runs, he runs straight through it, watching his toes.
> – Watching, rather, the spaces of sand between them,
> where (no detail too small) the Atlantic drains
> rapidly backwards and downwards.

Jealous of the bird's complete concentration on the particular, the poet introduces a human measure of scale. After all, the bird is obsessed with the sand, not his toes. Unlike the fleeing creatures of "The Armadillo" [QT], the sandpiper runs in a world devoid of human presence and its attendant scale. The poem shares a view from above – or beyond – this obsessed bird's seascape.

Though usually occupying a contemplative or a migratory presence in the landscape, Bishop occasionally assumes the advocacy-role of witness of human destruction of nature, the world of damaged shores. Exiled by her refusal of ordinary empathy, the poet grieves from a distance, regretting her undeniable kinship with destroyers. "The Armadillo" and "Brazil, January 1, 1502" confront the violent presence of humans in the natural world. Both deal with the role of Christianity in a fallen world in which humankind is a deadly presence. Bishop sees humans as oppositional, the only creatures capable of losing innocence. She traces sin to religion's door, accusing Christianity of sanctioning, or worse, ignoring true sin.

The paired Brazil poems shuttle back and forth through time, refusing epiphany through shifts in tone and regressions into history. In "Brazil, January 1, 1502" [QT], even as Bishop forsakes the literal for the pictorial frame, she identifies her intrusive presence in Brazil with that of the sixteenth-century conquistadors who, like herself, "left home." Perhaps like the wanderer of "Questions of Travel," these explorers "[t]hink of the long trip home." These men, unlike the poet, came to conquer, not to contemplate, and see their faith as the guiding spirit of their savagery. Leaving Mass, their celebration of interiority, the soldiers are heard

> … humming perhaps
> *L'Homme armé* or some such tune,
> they ripped away into the hanging fabric,
> each out to catch an Indian for himself –
> [CP, 92]

Yet Bishop refuses to acknowledge their conquest, preferring instead to depict the ever-receding unknown of the tropical "hanging fabric." The hellish pollution of the second stanza clearly emanates from these "hard as nails" Christians. This perception becomes the opportunity to capitalize upon Keats's mistake:

> Or like stout[1] Cortez when with eagle eyes
> He star'd at the Pacific – and all his men
> Look'd at each other with wild surmise –
> Silent, upon a peak in Darien.
> "On First Looking into Chapman's Homer"

Cortez (unlike Balboa, the true discoverer of the Pacific) leads the assaulting Christians of Bishop's poem. Christianity here is part of that life "of wealth and luxury" that has brought death and destruction upon the meek. The voices of the vulnerable, miniature women mingle with the cries of the natural creatures of the interior world; they seek a protection in that world beyond humanity.

Escape into that world is not always possible, however, and epiphany may offer only the illusion of escape into another dimension. Within a few pages, Bishop returns to the unyielding persistence of human violence. Again Christianity, or the fragments of religious celebration, hovers in the background, sanctioning the disarray and cruelties of the piece. Unlike the protective fabric of the earlier poem, the firelit landscape of "The Armadillo" offers no sanctuary for the beleaguered creatures. The poem offers a glimpse of a secularized religious celebration, long since stripped of intent and meaning; the "frail, illegal fire balloons" ascend toward a waiting saint. In ascendancy, the fire floats assume lives of their own:

> the paper chambers flush and fill with light
> that comes and goes, like hearts.
>
> [CP, 103]

Unstable and undirected, these heaven-bound balloons, gestures of "love," bear the potential of either love or war:

> Once up against the sky it's hard
> to tell them from the stars –
> planets, that is – the tinted ones:
> Venus going down, or Mars …

Oscillating between the heavenly extremes, the "tributes" represent a kind of chaos, not order; terror, not relief and penance. Bishop suggests that their very uncertainty – "With a wind, / they flare and falter, wobble and toss" – aggravates earthly insecurities. Inappropriate celebrations, which are both blasphemous and ignorant, violate the sacredness of ritual and disrupt the relationship between culture and nature. Such violation is likely to provoke fate and turn "dangerous":

> but if it's still they steer between
> the kite sticks of the Southern Cross,
> receding, dwindling, solemnly
> and steadily forsaking us,
> or, in the downdraft from a peak,
> suddenly turning dangerous.

The final line plummets toward the grim consequence of a moment of particularized sensation – an actual event, not merely a condition. Yet Bishop turns this tale of fragile faith and false tribute not on the plight of humanity but of innocent creatures. As messily careless in descent as ascent, the fire balloon "splatter[s] like an egg of fire," immolating airborne and ground-dwelling inhabitants alike. The scene commands full attention as the fire "egg" ironically brings death to the owl's nest:

> The flame ran down. We saw the pair
> of owls who nest there flying up
> and up, their whirling black-and-white
> stained bright pink underneath, until
> they shrieked up out of sight.

The appearance of the visibly immature ("short-eared") baby rabbit captures the instantaneous transition of the setting:

> So soft! – a handful of intangible ash
> with fixed ignited eyes.

Even as the poem reaches for the airy substance of the hare it disintegrates into the elements, returning the speaker's gaze with the steadfast certainty of death. An epiphany would reach for comfort and assurance, for insight and explanations through a glimpse of a dimension in which suffering doesn't occur. The lyric hero, however, responds only to ignorance and fear. In the italicized exclamation of the closure, the poet challenges even the aesthetic posture of poetry; she cries out as one forever earthbound:

> *Too pretty, dreamlike mimicry!*
> *O falling fire and piercing cry*
> *and panic, and a weak mailed fist*
> *clenched ignorant against the sky!*

The harsh deformations reject all falsification and softening of reality. Invocation and resignation collapse together in an impotent outcry as rage displaces epiphany. Unable to transcend the horror of this awesome occurrence, yet unwilling to return into the experience of the poem, Bishop gestures angrily but agnostically toward the beyond, challenging the type and substance of the incomprehensible. Bishop, like Wordsworth, sees humanity's dilemma as one of estrangement from natural vision; but unlike her predecessor, she has neither the ability nor the will to penetrate the other-world and confirm herself in epiphany, further distancing herself from such harsh realities. She can neither accuse nor ignore her own kind; she can only grieve.

In her distrust of epiphany Bishop, however, occasionally finds herself competing with and antagonistic toward the natural or phenomenal world, and that dramatic situation requires an epiphany. "The Fish" [NS], Bishop's most frequently anthologized poem, relies upon a Wordsworthian spiritual exercise to justify a rowboat transformation from plunderer to benefactor. The collapse of distinctions between land and sea, the air and earth of the speaker, obscures the borders between life and art. Bishop perceives the fish in land-language of "feathers" and "peonies" and "tinfoil" and "isinglass." Even as she works those changes, however, the fish works reciprocal wonders of its own. Passive resistance deprives the fishing poet of her triumph: "He didn't fight. / He hadn't fought at all." She soon understands that her knowledge of the fish is inaccurate.

Evidence of past encounters – "two heavier lines, / and a fine black thread / still crimped from the strain and snap / when it broke and he got away" – tells of a different fish. Earlier seen as "battered and venerable / and homely" (the line-break softening the accuracy of description), the fish now assumes the mock-role of tribal elder and hero:

> Like medals with their ribbons
> frayed and wavering,
> a five-haired beard of wisdom
> trailing from his aching jaw.
> [CP, 43]

Deprived of the fight, the poet must contemplate her position as the harbinger of death. The "little rented boat" marks a closed world wherein the speaker represents the moral force of her species. Taken by the incongruity and insignificance of the colloquy, the reader is swept from the sensuous into the psychological, then moved beyond earthly particulars to a spiritual whole:

> I stared and stared
> and victory filled up
> the little rented boat,
> from the pool of bilge
> where oil had spread a rainbow
> around the rusted engine
> to the bailer rusted orange,
> the sun-cracked thwarts,
> the oarlocks on their strings,
> the gunnels – until everything
> was rainbow, rainbow, rainbow!
> And I let the fish go.

As in the Christian parable, the oil upon the waters brings peace. It also engenders communication with the otherworldly. Through a rare Wordsworthian "spot of time," a genuine epiphany, the poet admits, somewhat reluctantly, a momentary conventional wisdom. This leap from perception to wisdom signals the arbitrariness so characteristic of the epiphany.

Though "The Fish" is certainly central to her canon, Bishop's boredom and dissatisfaction with the poem suggests a fear that the poem settles into sentiment instead of expanding into true wisdom. The matter-of-fact weightiness of the fish, a real survivor, lured the poet beyond the limits of her usual work, and tempted her out of her characteristic reticence. Fully aware and thoroughly suspicious of the technique and purpose of epiphany, Bishop usually contents herself with a suggestive advance toward and a sly retreat from the world of imaginative fulfillment beyond the page. Most of her journeys circumvent the critical moment of epiphany. Even as the poem reaches a crescendo, the poet reverses the flow, forcing it back into the journey, back within the intended limits of the poem itself. As "At the Fishhouses" demonstrates, Bishop is capable of presenting a Wordsworthian landscape only to carve the mass into her own figure. The glistening eternal present yields to the recurring past participles and tide of subjunctives that transform an otherworldly scene into a shared earthly experience – bounded by knowledge that is "historical, flowing, and flown."

The most useful examples of Bishop's near-epiphanic mode are found in her journey poems. Her destined or indifferent traveler sets forth with an unvoiced program, an inescapable linearity, but remains uncertain of the destination. The poems never lack a sense of discovery, though the end looms invariably in sight. "Cape Breton," "The Riverman," and "The Moose" suggest that Bishop was always aware of figures in the landscape; the problem was to present them without invoking a facile sentimentality that would accrue through gratuitous access to epiphany.

An opportunity to read the landscape for significance without plunging into epiphany comes in "Cape Breton" [CS], which challenges the preconceptions and sensitivities of the reader as it prepares, shapes, and withdraws a glimpse of the otherworldly. Bishop expects her readers to recall the lessons of its neighboring poem,[2] "At the Fishhouses," and apply that knowledge to this place and situation. "Out on the high 'bird islands,' Ciboux and Hertford," readers enter a world removed from and yet sinisterly impregnated by human habitation. The relatively comical "razorback auks and the silly-looking puffins" stand as ceremonial guards along the cliff's edge "with their backs to the mainland." Humanity's presence, however, is everywhere: in the "pastured sheep," in the frightening airplanes that threaten them, in the "rapid but unurgent [pulse] of a motorboat." More than humanity's "unnatural presence" threatens the islands, which are surrounded and upheld by the heartless immensity of the Melvillean[3] sea; as the ocean seems its calmest, it turns most hazardous. Effortlessly, Bishop draws attention from the placid uncertainties of the landscape to the more threatening uncertainties of the sea:

> The silken water is weaving and weaving,
> disappearing under the mist equally in all directions,
> lifted and penetrated now and then
> by one shag's dripping serpent-neck. ...

> [CP, 67]

The times and tides of Bishop's sea form and enact their own fate. Bishop does not rely solely upon the sea to produce such mysterious effects. The fog blocks the various natural penetrations and rents in the earth's surface – "the valleys and gorges of the mainland" – further suggesting the difficulty of isolation peculiar to the islands. The poet introduces the spiritual, unearthly world to draw us toward but not into the formative, causative world beyond the poem. The essence of this otherworldly island world lies buried

> among those folds and folds of firs: spruce and hackmatack –
> dull, dead, deep peacock-colors,
> each riser distinguished from the next
> by an irregular nervous saw-tooth edge,
> alike, but certain as a stereoscopic view.

Bishop points to origins with the processional solemnity of "dull, dead, deep," but quickly returns to the constraints of the quotidian. Moore's "A Grave"[4] – where "The firs stand in a procession, each with an emerald turkey-foot at the top" – and Stevens's "Domination of Black"[5] echo throughout this stanza. The "striding" color of "heavy hemlocks" and the cry of the peacocks in the Stevens poem suggest a sudden onset of perception and fear. Bishop's descriptive language parallels Stevens's imaginative world of tropes in acknowledging the interface between reality and the unknown, this world and the next. Stevens's fear of the peacock's cry stems from his discomfort with his ignorance, while Bishop allays a comparable anxiety by sharing the uncertainties engendered by the irregularities that characterize the scene. At the midpoint of "Cape Breton" Bishop seems willing to risk (in Keatsian fashion) the terrible revelations that occur when one "look[s] too far into" a landscape.

The third stanza opens with a reckless, if comical, abandon that indicates a radical change of tone or a penetration of the poem's surface tension. Here lurks the first hint of the presence of humankind since the ghostly pulsations of the motorboat at the opening. Human works check the flow toward interiority. The island idles on this Sunday as its earthmovers stand driverless, but the mere presence of those objects tempers the movement toward epiphany. Not only has work ceased but so has religious activity:

The little white churches have been dropped into the matted hills like lost quartz arrowheads.

The churches themselves are relics of another age and spiritual condition. The road is not a thoroughfare but rather the borderline between the experiential landscape and the interior, "where we cannot see." Within,

> where deep lakes are reputed to be,
> and disused trails and mountains of rock
> and miles of burnt forests standing in gray scratches
> like the admirable scriptures made on stones by stones –

lies the earth's own record. Bishop suggests, however, that by its very uninhabitable nature, the landscape defies translation. She suggests that the real story has passed; human life has occurred after the fact:

> and these regions now have little to say for themselves
> except in thousands of light song-sparrow songs floating upward
> freely, dispassionately, through the mist, and meshing
> in brown-wet, fine, torn fish-nets.

Bishop does not share Keats's view of the nightingale as "immortal Bird," but she is well aware of the poetic convention of bird-song as a tentative link between exterior and interior worlds. In "Cape Breton," though, the sparrow songs and the torn netting pull the poem in a direction Bishop does not wish to follow. The fishnet metaphor, derived from Penelope's weaving and the handiwork of the Fates, engages the inarticulate, magical creative imagination. The introductory movement of "At the Fishhouses" acknowledges this ominous weight, and uses it to further explore the relationship between netter and net, and by extension, poet and poem. In "Cape Breton," however, the metaphorical insistence of the nets seems beyond the intended scope of the poem. They and the dangling notes of the song-sparrows drift into and become one with the world beyond her poetry. This marks a turning point, requiring either transcendence or a naturalistic embrace of these natural hieroglyphics to honor, as Bishop always does, the legibility of the text. Drawing attention from the celestial distractions, however, Bishop shifts the focus to the road below, which in following an erratic but earthly course asserts the power of human culture, especially its most mundane occasions, to place natural transcendence under erasure.

As a figure of narration, rather than of lyric ecstasy or brooding meditation, this "wild" road serves as a measure of limits and capacities. The confines of the bus, "packed with people, even to its step," frame the pilgrimage, "It passes … It stops," and the availability of domestic knowledge:

> … a man carrying a baby gets off,
> climbs over a stile, and goes down through a small steep meadow,
> which establishes its poverty in a snowfall of daisies,
> to his invisible house beside the water.

The family life of the baby-carrying gentleman remains in the imagination; his house, literally out of sight, is unrealized. The poet curiously regards the other guardians of the interior space; just two more passengers, "but today only two preachers extra, one carrying his frock coat on a hanger," no different really in capacity from, say, the weekday "groceries, spare automobile parts, and pump parts." Like the tiny churches littering the hillside, these men of faith seem anachronistic.

"Cape Breton," like "The Monument," repeatedly shifts its stance[6] at the onset of epiphanic moments. Bishop is ostensibly shifting her viewpoint, but for what purpose? What does she hope to accomplish by moving from an island profile to a mist-shrouded glimpse of the settled mainland, and then to the departures and arrivals of a bus trip? In the final stanza, apparently on the brink of epiphany, an odd reversal occurs. Linked to the final lines of "At the Fishhouses," the first line of the closure of "Cape Breton" – "The birds keep on singing, a calf bawls, the bus starts" – does not surprise. This assertive continuity is pure Bishop. Yes, the reader assents, this is true. Here, however, differing from more characteristic Bishop closures, an epiphanic suggestion of the otherworldly enters. The cloaking chill has its roots in *pre*history, beyond "earthly trust." How different the effect of the last stanza would be if Bishop had chosen to retain the final word, to deliberately limit her poem's world:

> The thin mist follows
> the white mutations of its dream;
> an ancient chill is rippling the dark brooks.
> The birds keep on singing, a calf bawls, the bus starts.

This remains for Bishop a rather open closure; the poem halts at a moment in which nature and culture seem in verbal congruence. The "ancient chill," reminiscent of the "chill white blast of sunshine" in "A Cold Spring," invokes the world of the unknown that engenders the brooks, calves, birds, and even buses of the phenomenal world.

When Bishop sorted and recast her memories of a bus trip from Nova Scotia to Boston, she made a poem of confrontation and exchange with nature that verges on epiphany, but retreats at the last moment into the natural domesticity of the creature world. "Back to Boston"[7] (the working title for "The Moose" [G]) bears the lineaments of an actual bus trip, but turns into a response to romanticism and what she saw as its conflict with life. Situating the narrator in the trope of westward travel, she builds toward and then deviates from an expected epiphany; rather than fully develop her trope, she prefers to pause and reflect upon the "little of our earthly trust," confounding nature and culture in an embodiment, a creature that is neither threateningly wild nor sentimentally tame.

The measured sestets replicate the moral increments of the human condition. Unlike the repeated sameness of "At the Fishhouses" ("I have seen it over and over, the same sea, the same, / slightly, indifferently swinging above the stones") or the monotony of the landscape of "Crusoe in England" ("The sun set in the same sea, the same odd sun rose from the sea"), the habits of the natural world of "The Moose" are vaguely reassuring, predictable, repeatable. The Möbius strip – winding and returning – six-stanza, single-sentence introduction creates a recognizable, though not necessarily specific, landscape. The scene defies placement on a map, but its characteristics are predictable. The world depicted in this journey-poem sustains the speaker with glimpses of domesticity to counter the dark and the unease of travel. Inhabited by consumers of "fish and bread and tea," the landscape offers security in spite of the flux of travel and of the poem itself.

The herrings, the sun, and even the church depend on the will of the sea, which invests the land with life and uncertainty. The vulnerable landscape penetrates the very vehicle of discovery in the poem, the bus:

> through late afternoon
> a bus journeys west,
> the windshield flashing pink,
> pink glancing off of metal,
> brushing the dented flank
> of blue, beat-up enamel
>   [CP, 169]

The mortal substance of the bus reminds us of those "Under the Window" vehicles that so eloquently raised the issues of health and disease (the Mercedes-Benz truck with "Throbbing rosebuds" and the old truck with "a syphilitic nose"). Even as the bus displays a vaguely human anatomy, it reveals a relatively human temperament as it goes

> down hollows, up rises,
> and waits, patient, while
> a lone traveller gives
> kisses and embraces
> to seven relatives
> and a collie supervises.

The solitary traveler bids farewell to her kind, while the dog, a guardian of stationary domesticity, presides over the departure into the unknown. Linking the fixed and the mobile worlds in this genre scene gives the landscape an air of unity and harmony. By drawing the introduction together with a series of *where*s and *past*s, in the present tense, Bishop emphasizes the predictable, accountable, acceptable aspects of the scene.

As certainly as the traveler relinquishes family and home, the poem relinquishes the comfortable but momentary stasis of the genre scene, along with the scene itself. The true journey begins; the poem abandons the tropes of place-specific domesticity (elms, farm, dog) that embody family, home, and landscape. The mist, a painterly element, drifts in to shroud, enfold, and disclose the dislocating countenance of the natural surroundings. As the familiar world fades in the mist, the poem shifts its attention to a world of diminished scale and microscopic form:

> The bus starts. The light
> grows richer; the fog,
> shifting, salty, thin,
> comes closing in.
>
> Its cold, round crystals
> form and slide and settle
> in the white hens' feathers,
> in gray glazed cabbages,
> on the cabbage roses
> and lupins like apostles ...

The atmosphere, though hardly threatening, rapidly grows murky. The "sweet peas cling" to their strings and the "bumblebees creep / inside the foxgloves" for certainty and shelter. As the fog obscures it adheres, transforming phenomena and affecting behavior. Whatever predictability this world possessed in daylight has receded in obscurity. Potentially magical as this landscape had become, it in no way resembles the celestial world of "Seascape" or the iridescent world of "At the Fishhouses." Bishop is determined to avoid tropes of sublimity (though toying with Wordsworth's Snowdon mist) and make this bus-trip only as rich as everyday life.

The gradual descent into evening (announced by "evening commences") occasions a renewed commitment to routine, which offsets the slide into the romantic otherworld of the fog. Frequent stops, signaling arrivals and departures, suggest the continued proximity of the familiar world. The routine of a household as "a woman shakes the tablecloth / after supper" adequately deters the Homeric sense of travel-as-epic. Evening domesticity, despite the passage of the vehicle, enacts its schedule, regular as the tides. Gradually, however, this artificial world yields to the unfocused (because sensory-deprived) world of disconnected sensations, a world unorchestrated by familiar motifs of order and routine:

> The Tantramar marshes
> and the smell of salt hay.
> An iron bridge trembles
> and a loose plank rattles
> but doesn't give way.

Destabilized by unexpectedly full sensory application, the poem drifts through a narrative of peripheral glances, partial appreciations. Even as the postprandial woman fades in that flickering instant, the bus slips into a cloaked land and sea world where the salt marsh sensationally reveals its true and frightening origins. Human structures quake in the uncertainty of this setting; they react in "fear" as they "tremble" and "rattle." Though they stand firmly, if dubiously, those structures (and the traveler) feel collapse may be imminent. Once again the poem prepares the reader to meet the otherworldly. Though reduced to noting particulars – synecdoches of books and bark – the traveler attempts to impose some structure on a formless environment, and in doing so risks epiphany:

> On the left, a red light
> swims through the dark:
> a ship's port lantern.
> Two rubber boots show,
> illuminated, solemn.
> A dog gives one bark.

This fixed, solemn scene is more than sufficient to trigger an epiphany and render the bus journey a romantic narrative into sublimity and otherworldliness; but the moment passes, ungrasped. The entrance of a particularized, characterized, destined human being interrupts the moment of epiphanic possibility. Her personal characteristics, as she enters "brisk, freckled, elderly" to encounter her fellow travelers, underscore her ordinary, reassuring earthiness, as if to assert in her bearing the sufficiency of this phenomenal world. With her words to the bus driver, "All the way to Boston," the pilgrimage gains definition and a final destination. Having finally mapped the excursion and avoided premature closure, the poem returns to the preparatory atmosphere that clarifies even as it clouds.

Misty night landscapes and travel constitute a familiar romantic motif. Primed with specific literary sensations, the poem generates a powerful but familiar conjunction between the "moonlight and mist." The landscape – "hairy, scratchy, splintery" – however, like the "brisk, freckled, elderly" traveler, resists the ascent into a symbolic mode. Eased by the consonantal texture of the material world, the speaker forsakes romance and allegory and reclines toward sleep. This moment of partial oblivion invokes the antecedent world of memory:

> Snores. Some long sighs.
> A dreamy divagation
> begins in the night,
> a gentle, auditory,
> slow hallucination. ...

Sprung from but simultaneously divorced from the surrounding matrix of landscape and domesticity, the poem now drifts into the language of ancestry and archetype. Though relying on unsorted and scattered particulars, Bishop relates her speaker to humanity as a whole, and more firmly anchors her in the historical world of culture, by means of an overheard, extended flow of anecdote and genealogy, narrated by anonymous yet firmly characterized interlocutors:

> In the creakings and noises,
> an old conversation
> – not concerning us,
> but recognizable, somewhere,
> back in the bus:
> Grandparents' voices
>
> uninterruptedly
> talking, in Eternity:
> names being mentioned,
> things cleared up finally;
> what he said, what she said,
> who got pensioned;
> deaths, deaths and sicknesses;
> the year he remarried;
> the year (something) happened.
> She died in childbirth.
> That was the son lost
> when the schooner foundered.

Devoid of immediate personal significance, these recollections of strangers revolve upon the common organic insults of "deaths, deaths and sicknesses." These consequential events, though requiring narration, stand isolated against the flow of history. Death itself, an abstraction commemorated in black-bordered obituaries is random and commonplace, yet humanly fascinating. Death occupies the poet's attention in the way that births and marriages do, as dignifying aspects of the quotidian. Mention of the archaic tragedy – "the schooner foundered" – elevates the discussion even beyond the elevated quotidian to touch upon a mythic dimension and a classic sense of the tragic. Catastrophic events, however, derive their significance from their fatal outcome. The universality of this closure makes it more bearable, more conversational, less newsworthy. Bishop notes the lack of impact of old news in her survey of "The Bight" [CS]:

> Some of the little white boats are still piled up
>   against each other, or lie on their sides, stove in,
> and not yet salvaged, if they ever will be, from the last bad storm,
> like torn-open, unanswered letters.
> The bight is littered with old correspondences.
>
> [CP, 60]

Finally the tide of specificity affects only the living; a dreamy retrospect leaves us meditating dates that resonate – "the year (something) happened" – long after the significance of the event has withered. Shuttling pronominal exchanges invite the auditor into this world of common history, prompting recall of those universal characters who went "to the bad." The tentacular frame of reference outlines a common family tree. Individuality, the raw particulars, dissolve in a repetitive history of insults, injury, and events. The drone of recurrence secures and assures the listener while imposing a sense of commonality through disaster.

The traveler in "The Moose," withdrawing from recognition and resignation – "Life's like that. / We know *it* (also death)." – cuddles down into a child's secure understanding and relaxed confidence. Life passes in tranquillity, grandparents droning

> in the old featherbed,
> peacefully, on and on,
> dim lamplight in the hall,
> down in the kitchen, the dog
> tucked in her shawl.
>
> Now, it's all right now
> even to fall asleep
> just as on all those nights.

Though at first this dream-world excursion seems to reach beyond the phenomenal world, Bishop withdraws, reorders, and projects the dream into the quotidian world of her poem. In spite of the childlike acceptance of everything predictable and routine, the language of the memory-passages is that of adult recall. An earlier version shows that Bishop had originally intended a childlike passage similar to the innocence of "Five Flights Up"[8] [G]:

> Now, it is safe now
> to go asleep
> Day will take care of things.
>
> [Typescript Draft]
>
> The little dog next door barks in his sleep
> inquiringly, just once.
> Perhaps in his sleep, too, the bird inquires
> once or twice, quavering.
> Questions – if that is what they are –
> answered directly, simply,
> by day itself.
>
> [CP, 181]

As Robert Hass[9] suggests, these midnight inquiries reassure by firmly situating the poem in the conscious world – "being and being seen."

The encounter with the moose coincides with and benignly disrupts a false and earthbound self-assurance. Rather than reaching for the epiphanic sublime, Bishop summons one reasonably modest (though impressive in its own right) particular of the natural world. In the context of expected epiphany, this creature seems reassuring, only modestly awe-inspiring. Like the Poundian periplum,[10] the encounter is indeed a sighting, a looking on the horizon, but it is certainly not comparable to the grandeur and spiritual pretension of a Wordsworthian natural revelation, nor does it offer the psychological certainty of Joyce's urban epiphanies. The moose initiates the exchange and actually experiences the bus:

> It approaches; it sniffs at
> the bus's hot hood.

Lacking gender, the creature appears at first both otherworldly and threatening; it seems a force unto itself. The curious animal beckons the dreamy travelers to consciousness. Unlike the retreating farmhouses and churches of the traveler's landscape, the presence stands solid, comfortable, and inspirational:

> Towering, antlerless,
> high as a church,
> homely as a house
> (or, safe as houses).

"Towering," vaguely threatening, but "antlerless," somewhat tamed, the moose straddles the worlds of nature and culture, embodying a domestic sense of wholeness. Dwarfed by the unassuming grandeur of the natural world, the passengers resort to childish utterances of the commonplace and obvious, further emphasizing the creature's domestic appearance and demeanor:

> "Sure are big creatures."
> "It's awful plain."
> "Look! It's a she!"

Unembellished nature on a scale both intimate and impressive startles the passengers, but their commonplace expressions help ward off the sublime. A mute and mild moose, with its relative bulk, silence, curiosity, and sex, affects but does not intimidate them.

The moose does not in the least resemble the battered, defeated fish ("I looked into his eyes … / They shifted a little, but not to return my stare") or Crusoe's goats with their blank, malicious eyes. Instead, like the seal of "At the Fishhouses," the moose participates in a direct encounter and exchange. The moose "sniffs" and "looks the bus over," as if in recognition of this fellow creature, vehicle and passengers complimented by its interest in their otherness. The casual yet intimate relationship between moose and travelers demonstrates how "earthly trust" includes all surface-dwellers; as the animal senses the people, so the Boston-bound passengers experience the moose:

> For a moment longer,
>
> by craning backward,
> the moose can be seen

> on the moonlit macadam;
> then there's a dim
> smell of moose, an acrid
> smell of gasoline.

The essential fact grows dim and is finally displaced by the smell of gasoline, which complements the moose's own scent. Though posed for transcendence, the poem at the moment of confrontation retreats into domesticity and the commonplace, the marvelous transforming environment serving to sensitize and alert the travelers to the precious life they share without violating the poem's essential self-containment by evoking the sublime.

Though suspicious of the romantic hejira and the epiphany, Bishop employs their strategies while avoiding the moment of commitment to the ineffable of the infinite. The otherness of nature is but half a perception; nature sees human presence as unnatural and curious. Rather than strive to penetrate or transcend the phenomenal world, Bishop attempts to define domesticity in relation to otherness,[11] to learn by deferring the language of the interior to more clearly experience the language of the palpable world of surface and texture. Finally she asks, "What does nature make of us?" – underscoring the unbridgeable difference between the self and the exterior world.

Bishop attempts to pose an accurate relationship with the environment. Human limitations – destinations, schedules, births, deaths – mirror environmental complexities. Like Darwin, she delights in the natural world because it is natural; she sees the moose not as an emissary from the beyond but as a moose – and marvels at its "mooseness." Generating a language of the environment without attempting to confound it with the self empowers the quotidian, with its hint of epiphanic possibility, which for Bishop is the proper material of poetry.

The act of naming, the other rhetorical device referred to at the beginning of this chapter, in romantic poetics begins with and requires the invocation of the social construct of authorship. Autobiography, a characteristic romantic-modern mode, enforces the notion of the voice of witness as one of authenticity and authority. This claim to authority, however, which was explored in Wordsworth's *Prelude* and claimed by modern poets like Robert Lowell, troubled Bishop. Her lifelong debate with herself concerning the tensions between life and authorship, autobiography and poetry surface repeatedly in her correspondence with Lowell. What she claimed of Marianne Moore[12] (in her memoir, "Efforts of Affection"), she would claim of herself: "to be a poet was not the be-all, end-all of existence." In December 1957, when both poets were in the midst of their life studies, Bishop wrote to Lowell:

> And here I must confess[13] ... that I am green with envy of your kind of assurance. I feel that I could write in as much detail about my Uncle Artie, say – but what would be the significance? Nothing at all ...
>
> Whereas all you have to do is put down the names! And the fact that it seems significant, illustrative, American, etc., gives you, I think the confidence you display about tackling any idea or theme, seriously, in both writing and conversation.

The seriousness of this lament is offset by Bishop's "green with envy" sly aside. Though she sees a collateral relationship between "significance" and "confidence," this does not confirm a sense of insecurity on her part. Rather, I suggest, she recognizes the need for a different kind of authorial posture for herself. If name-dropping and historical context will not work for her, what will?

Bishop requires a fresh approach to the question of authorial presence and its consequences for a poetry conscious of the problems of naming and unnaming. She intuits and anticipates the crisis of authorship[14] and the literary text discussed by Michel Foucault in "What Is an Author?" Foucault suggests that modern literary critics continue to believe that:

> the author provides[15] the basis for explaining not only the presence of certain events in a work, but their transformations, distortions, and diverse modifications (through his biography, the determination of his individual perspective, the analysis of his social position, and the revelation of his basic design).

Like Foucault, Bishop challenges the romantic assumption of authorial presence. Further, she asks her readers to socialize the poem, to recognize its full range of significance, in the absence of conventional authorial sanction. The confidence of these poems derives from abandonment: the act of naming becomes one of unnaming. Biography, social position (Bishop appears to be saying), as pre-existent constructs with authority outside of the text, have no place in these poems.

"In the Waiting Room" and "Crusoe in England" – the opening poems of *Geography III* – read intertextually reveal just how deeply and ironically Bishop engaged in the relationship between the self and author, history and memory, orality and literacy, naming and unnaming – indeed, in the binary oppositions of her aesthetic. It is this rhetoric of unnaming that generates the complexity (not the debility) of self-reference and the provisional meaning not only in her last works but throughout her career. Here the poems beckon and then thwart the reader intent on finding significance embedded in a life. The reader obsessed with the mock reality of life will never encounter the real in Bishop's world.

"In the Waiting Room" and "Crusoe in England" enact competing genealogies of social and personal identity. Insofar as these poems may be read as poems of poetic calling, they bear the testimony of a poet resolute in her determination to designate a fictional self without recourse to the power of naming conferred by the social construct of authorship, and to force authority, instead, from unnaming. This rejection of the self as social construct and privileged naming may seem even more romantic than the solipsism of authorship because it attempts to reinvigorate the originative power of naming. Bishop, however, neither claims access to origins nor refuses the social meaning imposed by language and culture. Instead she attempts to displace the romantic concept of authorial autonomy, because it is a received and therefore logocentric social construct, and install through unnaming and renaming a more broadly mediated sense of things and experience, a socially rather than egoistically based phenomenology.

"In the Waiting Room" may be seen as a prelapsarian poem of anticipation of that social state that precedes the acceptance of received namings; "Crusoe in England" may be read as a postlapsarian meditation on the originating power of naming and renaming. In reinventing the social world that connects the two, she seems willing to reconsider all forms of "name" appropriation: place, family, sex, generation, things. Discovering a world where (as Stevens found[16]) "Mrs. Anderson's Swedish baby / Might well have been German or Spanish," she then rejects all such forms of naming as well as (what Foucault calls[17]) "author construction." Each poem reenacts "birth, procreation, and death" as a debate between naming and unnaming, the loss imposed by a social (i.e., authorial) identity.

In 1961, Bishop wrote "The Country Mouse," a posthumously published memoir dedicated to her childhood return to Worcester, Massachusetts, after a lengthy stay with her maternal grandparents in Nova Scotia. Were it not for its startlingly revealing conclusion, the memoir, in spite of its abundance of details, would suffer from (by Bishop's own standards) insignificance. In the final paragraphs, however, which constitute the nucleus of "In the Waiting Room," Bishop begins to trouble over the obvious: the social obligation of being human. Having been jolted into awareness of her adoptive family's class status (*hers* was a family with servants), she recalls with equal sensitivity the *strangeness* of being a human being. As she waits for her aunt in the dentist's waiting room:

> I felt ... *myself*. In a few days it would be my seventh birthday. I felt *I, I, I*, and looked at the three strangers in panic. I was *one* of them too, inside my scabby body and wheezing lungs. "You're in for it now," something said. How had I got tricked into such a false position? I would be like that woman opposite who smiled at me so falsely every once in a while. [CPr, 33]

The history of identity is bound to the memory of its occasion. The response is visceral, *not* intellectual:

> "You are you," something said. "How strange you are, inside looking out. You are not Beppo, or the chestnut tree, or Emma, you are *you* and you are going to be *you* forever." It was like coasting downhill, this thought, only much worse, and it quickly smashed into a tree. *Why* was I a human being?

The fact of this prerational recognition scene resides in the primacy of childhood identity. The duplicity the child hears and sees in the adult world can only be named by those understudy pronouns: *I* and *you*. While dogs, trees, and even servants have names, this as yet unnamed child wrestles with but a taxonomic classification: human.

"In the Waiting Room" marks Bishop's return to these issues of naming and unnaming, reading and writing, sounding and hearing. Though descriptive, the poem depends less on physical detail and more upon a dialogue between the unnamed (socially unrestricted) self – "I" – and the named (socially restricted) – "an *I*." The child initially finds security in proper names: "Worcester, Massachusetts" and "Aunt Consuelo." The certainty fades with the appearance of the intrusive, indefinite pronoun: "*It* was winter. *It* got dark / early" [my emphasis]. Bishop will rely upon the ambiguity of "it" and its corresponding reluctance or inability to name throughout the poem.

Left alone, the child "I" sees and reads the named *National Geographic*. Its "studied photographs" reveal an unpredictable, eruptive (prelapsarian) landscape. Literacy fails, except as an escape route, where metaphor is concerned. Investigating scenes from this magazine, she catalogues that which she can name: volcano erupting, Osa and Martin Johnson. Properly attired people bear names: "Osa and Martin Johnson"; dead people lose their names: " – 'Long Pig,' the caption said." Orality and literacy compete for the child's attention, each seductive in its way. But she mis*hears* what "the caption sa[ys]": "A dead man slung on a pole / – "Long Pig." Mimicking the instability of spoken language and substituting a euphemism for a proper name, the conversational caption confuses the earnest student, who fails to understand that the dead man is here regarded as a food source.

The verbal unknown occasions further confusion as the child's eye traces the physical, sexual uncertainties of uncovered women. So foreign are the native unnamed women "with necks / wound round and round with wire" that the child "reads" right through them: "I read *it* straight right straight through. / I was too shy to stop" [emphasis added]. Unable to name, the child resorts to the tense comfort of the unnamed: "it." She retreats from the shifting planes of unnamed, unnamable uncertainty to the fixity of that which bears a name: "the cover: / the yellow margins, the date." Such is the force of Dickinson's notch in the maelstrom.

Unable to read her way into the larger constellation of human beings, the child never-theless recognizes the sounded family identity when she hears it. Like the auditor in "The Country Mouse," this child hears from the inside out. History and memory fuse, creating a new identity for her:

> What took me
> completely by surprise
> was that it was *me*:
> my voice, in my mouth.
> Without thinking at all
> I was my foolish aunt,
> I – we – were falling, falling,
> our eyes glued to the cover
> of the *National Geographic*,
> February, 1918.
>   [CP, 160]

The intensity of this "it" draws upon the accumulated chain of reference: "winter," "dark early," "Babies with pointed heads," "horrifying breasts," and Aunt Consuelo's "*oh!* of pain." Acceding to the social demands, the effect of her aunt's voice, the child involuntarily discovers her own collective voice: *I* becomes *we*. Dates, like names or Aunt Consuelo's voice, momentarily pierce the surface of the "cold, blue-black space" – the sea of habit threatening the child's consciousness. She has lost perceived autonomy even as she has gained a social identity.

Cautiously authorial, the child reads this new self as a mode of being. For the moment the discovery is personal, familial. This is not an attempt to place a "Bishop" in context; rather, it is an opportunity to feel a "self" move forward and backward into genealogy, into time:

> But I felt: you are an *I*,
> you are an *Elizabeth*,
> you are one of *them*.

Unlike the familial significance attributed to Lowell by Bishop, the effectiveness of Bishop's self-reading derives from the strategic use of the second person. As if to dem-onstrate her presence in the text, she removes her self from it long enough to proclaim a social identity, to name her self. This somewhat grudging sensation, verified spontane-ously by the child's reaction to her aunt's cry, suggests the child's plight as it would seem from the outside. It recalls the Stevensian[18] self: "Detect[ing] the sound of a voice that doubles its own." However "unlikely" or "strange" these binding "similarities" seem to the child they are the social facts of her life. Though they seem to her unauthorized, breasts, boots, the *National Geographic*, and the family voice nonetheless constitute homogenizing social realities. By adhering to the laws of pronominal reference, Bishop intensifies the almost Ibsenlike (recall the Button-molder of *Peer Gynt*) threat to an artist's emerging identity.

While "In the Waiting Room" has been routinely read as a poem of juvenile terror, isolation, and marginality, none of those readings account for the remarkable counter-force of the solitary "Me–Myself–I," the artist's isolated yet assertive self. Even if the unnamed self (as seen from the inside out) threatens to fail or consume, it remains the volatile poetry voice for Bishop. She may require (what Beckett calls) a "temporal speci-fication"[19] – "fifth / of February, 1918" – to allow her "to measure the days that separate [her] from that menace" (that which threatens identity). The "falling off" enacted in this poem is the fall into social identity, restrictive or inaccurate naming. The alternative seems to be the "big black wave" of annihilation or namelessness. To be "back in it" is to survive with a social surface – name, age, gender, place – at odds with the continually unnamed self. "The War was on" presages a career intensely committed to slipping the yoke of social identity and changing the rules of the name game.

The child of "In the Waiting Room" advances with uncertainty from the passivity of reader to the tentative aggressiveness of writer – to the authority of authorship. The socializing power of language itself lures the unnamed *I* into the realm of a given and feminine name – and perilously into the beyond of collective, pronominal identity: "one of them." This rush of potential identities refuses to pause at the brink of authorial privilege – *Elizabeth* + *Bishop* – and instead accelerates into the swirl of *them*. Refusing even gender specificity (recalling that in her memoir, Bishop ends with the more general "Why was I a human being?"), retaining no element of uniqueness, this identity is as good as none.

If the waiting room child must advance toward naming and its requisite social obligation, then "Crusoe at Home" (Bishop's working title for "Crusoe in England"[20]) has the life-won opportunity to revert to his unnamed *I*. Even as "In the Waiting Room" advances the cause of poetic naming, "Crusoe" champions the necessity of retreat. The child relinquishes ignorance for the sake of her name; Crusoe abandons the text and the very power of naming as if discovering the devitalizing force of individuation. Like other world-weary "I am" poems (John Clare's "I Am," Yeats's "The Circus Animals' Desertion," Wallace Stevens's "First Warmth" or "Notes Toward a Supreme Fiction"), "Crusoe" makes its most compelling appeal for readership by its utter rejection of its social role.

The landscape seems familiar; yet this volcanic wasteland is "dead as ash heaps." The colonial appropriators, or namers, are no longer in the characters of Osa and Martin Johnson; they have coalesced into the discovering and naming country itself: England. Decidedly postlapsarian, Crusoe both remembers and re-enacts that ahistorical, asocial moment of genuine love in exile.

Exasperated by the feminine, childhood aspects of the name game, Bishop turns from the dilemma of the given and family name to explore the old age of the retired adven-turer. Crusoe, like Lowell, comes with his attendant significance – his fictive and histori-cal authority. In spite of that burden, however, he shrugs off his social (i.e., linguistic) inheritance as irrelevant and inaccurate. Seemingly revisiting in memory the landscape of the *National Geographic* of "In the Waiting Room," Crusoe dismisses everything the child struggled to acquire. Orality and literacy fail to capture the essence of his life, which remains "un-rediscovered, un-renamable." The authorial gesture of the poem depends upon the exasperation that "None of the books has ever got it right." Like Ishmael, Crusoe knows that "true" places remain unnamed.

From Crusoe's perspective, to acknowledge the shock of "waiting room" recognition is to acquiesce to the failure of language to identify. The core of the poem, preceded by the weary "Well," charts the encumbrance of language in a solitary world. Relative scale ("I'd think that if they were the size / I thought volcanoes should be, then I had / become a giant"), proper names, aesthetics, categories of all kinds ring false in this underpopulated landscape of "one kind of everything." Here the distinctions between ignorance and understanding, error and truth seem impossible to ascertain. Who would appreciate the act of delimiting that naming reflects? The landscape seems fated to the same oblivion as language as Bishop echoes "The Map" (where "The names of the sea-shore towns run out to sea") in the volcanic landscape (where "The folds of lava, running out to sea, / would hiss").

Like the speaker in John Clare's "I Am," Crusoe, too, is a "self-consumer of [his] woes." Even in isolation this must be given a name and a circumstance: "'Pity should begin at home.' So the more / pity I felt, the more I felt at home." Crusoe resorts to this colloquy with himself to externalize and verify the overwhelmingly interior sensation of pity. The physical remove becomes palpable as he conjectures: "What's wrong *about* self-pity, anyway?" [my emphasis] Crusoe confesses his humanity through by naming his emotion. For as D. H. Lawrence asserts in his own "Self-Pity"[21]: "I never saw a wild thing / sorry for itself." Locating his emotion in language denies Crusoe the spontaneity or wildness of the animal world.

Incapable of "looking up" that which he does not possess, Crusoe abides by the asocial strictures of solitude. An air of unreality pervades the intense reality of this itemized landscape. Like the waiting-room child, Crusoe "reads" the landscape and attempts to place through names its inhabitants. His solitary word games seek to defeat "the questioning shrieks, the equivocal replies / over a ground of hissing rain": "*Mont d'Espoir* or *Mount Despair* / (I'd time enough to play with names)," but serve only to sound off: Names are rendered meaningless. Knowledge and language as social acts become nightmarish anachronisms:

> . ... I'd have
> nightmares of other islands
> stretching away from mine ...
> ....
> ....knowing that I had to live
> on each and every one, eventually,
> for ages, registering their flora,
> their fauna, their geography.
>   [CP, 165]

Such occupational investments in local identity terrify the stranded character. As the waiting-room child discovered, even local geography requires an audience to render the significance fixed.

The eight-stanza terror of the societyless residence is peremptorily displaced by Crusoe's recollection of Friday. While language seems to have outlived its usefulness, Crusoe nonetheless fixes his "other" with a socially significant temporal marker: he names "Friday." Even as Crusoe details the effect of this new society, the impoverishment of language is complete. Declaring parenthetically that "Accounts of [Friday's arrival] have everything all wrong," he fails to meet the demands of language. Friday is "nice" and "pretty"; they were "friends." Stripped of a linguistic interface, Crusoe appears to have met the private, unmediated demands of a relationship shared with but one. Language cannot intervene.

The authorial impulse to give memory a name by converting it into history is a commemorative one. With Friday's deathdate comes the intrusive, factual marker – fixing in time the moment recalled, begging to be named. Crusoe's/Bishop's public and private artifacts seem destined for the Temple of the Muses: "The local museum's asked me to / leave everything to them." The human experiences of love and desperation coalesce about the devitalized remains: "the flute, the knife, the shrivelled shoes." Like Yeats's "Old iron, old bones, old rags," the island artifacts sit unre-discoverable and unrenameable. In questioning the value of this hopelessly romantic, Emersonian art of naming, Crusoe challenges the public appropriation of named things even as he re-collects the private bonding of language to love:

> How can anyone want such things?
> – And Friday, my dear Friday, died of measles
> seventeen years ago come March.

Unable to thwart the named order of things – names, dates, countries, diseases – Crusoe can only recall a time when the world was unnameable but "nice." Readers of Stevens will recognize both place and question: "These external regions, what do we fill them with / Except reflections, the escapades of death."[22]

A reading of *Geography III* that considers the issues raised in discussing these two poems would presuppose a willingness to accept this paradox: that as autobiography abandons Bishop's poems, they begin to live. In American poetry only Dickinson has been as successful in frustrating critics who need to use the life as a means of explaining. Bishop's appreciation of Lowell's "kind of assurance" drove her to assert her confidence from the "interior," where, with due respect for the social and cultural energy that makes art possible, the poet is alone with the task of distinguishing her work from her self. Her life's sad facts do not explain why "we feel / (we all feel) this sweet / sensation of joy" when reading her poems and correspondence. Critics too eager to privilege autobiography over other forms of fiction to satisfy current critical trends risk reducing these multidimensional poems to self-elegy. This lack of critical imagination unduly restricts access to a body of work demanding recognition of its, not the poet's, authority.

The "old correspondences" littering *Geography III* can easily incite misreading, searching for poems definable by cultural or political communities Bishop herself rejected. Seeking the self Bishop deliberately withholds requires resisting a "knowledge ... historical, flowing, and flown." This resistance denies the power of her assertive unnaming, forgetting that to be at war with something (in this case, restrictive identities) is in fact to confront it.

Extending this reading method to the entirety of *The Complete Poems, 1927–1979* reveals Bishop's career-long desire to subvert the "author-function," a desire largely fulfilled in the dialectic between autobiographical strategies and those of self-effacement. "Cape Breton" describes the resulting natural scene, which refuses the pathetic fallacy and turns a blank face to the viewer: "Whatever the landscape has of meaning appears to have been abandoned ... these regions now have little to say for themselves." The private life inspiriting Bishop's poems cannot sustain them; they must live on their own, but they do so by first appropriating that private life and then placing it under erasure. The reader, faced with the transparent splendor of these poems, might wonder with the speaker of "Anaphora": "'Where is the music coming from, the energy? / The day was meant for what ineffable creature / we must have missed?'" As Foucault warns, "The author is the principle of thrift[23] in the proliferation of meaning." Thriftier than most writers, and anxious that neither name nor gender restrict the authority of her poems, she withdraws, through unnaming, the authorial privilege by purposing, then exposing the feigned naïveté of autobiography. The resultant fiction in its complex reflexivity is too self-possessed for the reader or critic to unmask, and paradoxically refuses either to confound life and art or to clearly distinguish them.

Notes

1 John Keats, *Poetical Works*, ed. H. W. Garrod (Oxford: Oxford University Press, 1956), p. 38.
2 See typescript drafts of "Cape Breton" [Vassar]. Bishop notes in a piece titled "Bird Islands" that:

> Ciboux and Hertford, about six miles off the coast of Nova Scotia. During the war planes practiced dropping bombs on a rock between the two. The sheep pastured on them would get frightened and often stampede in a panic and fall over the cliffs into the sea.

3 See Herman Melville, *Moby-Dick* (New York: W. W. Norton, 1967), Chap. 47: "The Mat-Maker."
4 Marianne Moore, *Observations* (New York: Dial Press, 1924), p. 60.
5 Stevens, *Collected Poems*, p. 8.
6 See James McIntosh, *Thoreau as Romantic Naturalist* (Ithaca: Cornell University Press, 1974) for a detailed discussion of Thoreau's "shifting stances" in the natural world with its implications for transcendentalism in general.
7 Working title "Back to Boston," 27/403 [Vassar].
8 See File 27/403 [Vassar].
9 See Hass, "One Body: Some Notes on Form" in *Claims for Poetry*, ed. Donald Hall (Ann Arbor: University of Michigan Press, 1982), p. 152:

> Being and being seen. R. D. Laing says somewhere that small children don't get up at night to see if you're there, they get up to see if *they're* there. ... Maybe our first experience of our own formation.

10 See Ezra Pound, *The Cantos* (New York: New Directions, 1972), p. 324.
11 For a useful discussion of domesticity as topic in Bishop, see Helen Vendler, "Domestication, Domesticity and the Otherwordly" in *Modern Critical Views: Elizabeth Bishop*, ed. Harold Bloom (New York: Chelsea House, 1985), pp. 83–96. Once the only essay to make a compelling case for Bishop's place in the canon, it now seems overcommitted to its theme. For example, in introducing "In the Waiting Room":

> No domesticity is entirely safe. As in the midst of life we are in death, so, in Bishop's poetry, in the midst of the familiar, and most especially there, we feel the familiar as the unknowable. This *guerilla attack of the alien*, springing from the very bulwarks of the familiar, is the subject of "In the Waiting Room" (87). [emphasis mine]

A "dentist's waiting room" does not seem to me to be "the very bulwarks of the familiar." In fact, if we are to accept Vendler's extreme depiction, it is just where one would expect the "guerilla attack of the alien."

12 See "Efforts" [CPr], p. 156.
13 EB to Robert Lowell (December 14, 1957) [Harvard].
14 See my earlier discussion of the rhetorical implications in "Elizabeth Bishop: Author(ity) and the Rhetoric of (Un)-naming," *The Literary Review* 35 (Spring 1992):419–28. My discussion of "otherness and (un)naming" is informed throughout by Kimberly W. Bentson, "I yam what I am: the topos of un(naming) in Afro-American literature" in *Black Literature and Literary Theory*, ed. Henry Louis Gates, Jr. (New York: Methuen, 1984), pp. 151–72.
15 Michel Foucault, "What Is an Author?" in Josué Harari, *Textual Strategies: Perspectives in Post-Structuralist Criticism* (Ithaca: Cornell University Press, 1979), p. 151.
16 Stevens, "The Pleasures of Merely Circulating," *Collected Poems*, p. 150. See Vendler's use of the quote in "Domestication," p. 88:

> [U]nderstatement, so common in Bishop, gives words their full weight. As the fact of her own contingency strikes the child, "familiar" and "strange" become concepts which have lost all meaning. "Mrs. Anderson's Swedish baby …"

17 Foucault, p. 151.
18 Stevens, "The Woman That Had More Babies Than That," *Opus Posthumous* (New York: Alfred A. Knopf, 1989), pp. 104–5:

> The self is a cloister full of remembered sounds
> And of sounds so far forgotten, like her voice,
> That they return unrecognized. The self
> Detects the sound of a voice that doubles its own,
> In the images of desire, the forms that speak,
> The ideas that come to it with a sense of speech.

19 See Samuel Beckett, *Proust* (New York: Grove Press, 1957), p. 5.
20 See 27/402 [Vassar].
21 D. H. Lawrence, "Self-Pity," *The Complete Poems* (New York: Viking Press, 1971), p. 467.
22 Stevens, "Notes Toward A Supreme Fiction," *Collected Poems*, p. 405.
23 Foucault, p. 159.

Works Cited

Beckett, Samuel. *Proust*. New York: Grove Press, 1957.
Bentson, Kimberly W. "I Yam What I Am: The Topos of Un(naming) in Afro-American Literature." *Black Literature and Literary Theory*. Ed. Henry Louis Gates, Jr. New York: Methuen, 1984. Pp. 151–72.
Bishop, Elizabeth. Bishop Archive. Vassar College Library.
Bishop, Elizabeth. Bishop–Stevenson File. Washington University Library, Special Collections.
Bishop, Elizabeth. *The Collected Prose*. New York: Farrar, Straus, 1984.
Bishop, Elizabeth. *The Complete Poems*. New York: Farrar, Straus, 1969.
Bishop, Elizabeth. *The Complete Poems: 1927–1979*. New York: Farrar, Straus, 1983.
Bishop, Elizabeth. Bishop, Elizabeth, and May Swenson. Letters. Washington University Library.
Foucault, Michel. "What Is an Author?" In *Textual Strategies: Perspectives in Post-Structuralist Criticism*. Ed. Josué Harari. Ithaca: Cornell, 1979.
Hall, Donald, ed. *Claims for Poetry*. Ann Arbor: Michigan, 1982.
Hass, Robert. "One Body: Some Notes on Form." *Claims for Poetry*. Ed. Donald Hall. Ann Arbor: Michigan, 1982.
Keats, John. *Poetical Works*. Ed. H. W. Garrod. Oxford: Oxford, 1956.
Lawrence, D. H. *The Complete Poems*. New York: Viking, 1971.
Lowell, Robert. *Collected Prose*. New York: Farrar, Straus, 1987.

McIntosh, James. *Thoreau as Romantic Naturalist*. Ithaca: Cornell, 1974.

Melville, Herman. *Moby-Dick*. New York: Norton, 1967.

Moore, Marianne. *Observations*. New York: Dial, 1925.

Pound, Ezra. *The Cantos*. New York: New Directions, 1972.

Stevens, Wallace. *Collected Poems*. New York: Knopf, 1954.

Stevens, Wallace. *Opus Posthumous*. Ed. Milton J. Bates. New York: Knopf, 1989.

PART TWO
Structuralism, Linguistics, Narratology

PART TWO

CHAPTER 1

Introduction
The Implied Order: Structuralism

Julie Rivkin and Michael Ryan

Structuralism begins with the work of Ferdinand de Saussure, an early twentieth-century Swiss linguist who argued that language should be studied as if it were frozen in time and cut transversely like a leaf. What results is a vision of the entire language system as it exists in implied or unconscious fashion in any spoken utterance. Utterances are merely the manifestation of the rules of the system that lend order to the heterogeneity of language. This notion of an implied order is central to the Structuralist undertaking, as it spreads out from linguistics to anthropology and philosophy and to literary criticism through the course of the twentieth century.

Structuralism derives both historically and logically from Formalism. Roman Jakobson, one of the original Formalists, was also, by virtue of emigration, one of the first major influences on French Structuralism, which flourished from the 1950s through the 1960s. The scientific impulse evident in Formalism also finds its fulfillment in the Structuralist emphasis on the task of adducing the internal system or order of linguistic, cultural, and literary phenomena.

From Jakobson, early Structuralists such as anthropologist Claude Lévi-Strauss learned of Saussure's ideas about language. Lévi-Strauss began to see that culture, like language, is a system characterized by an internal order of interconnected parts that obey certain rules of operation. A structure is both like a skeleton and like a genetic code in that it is the principle of stability and coherence in any cultural system, while also being the principle of action that allows the culture to exist in time as a living thing. After meeting Jakobson in New York during their mutual exile during World War II, Lévi-Strauss began to think about culture as a form of communication like language. What was communicated between cultural participants were tokens, like words, that enacted and reproduced the basic assumptions and rules of the culture. In his analysis of kinship systems, *Elementary Structures of Kinship* (1949), Lévi-Strauss argued that primitive cultures maintain peace between social groups by using women as tokens in marriage. Such inter-familial and inter-tribal marriages function as a form of communication and create personal or family relations that work to diminish the possibility of conflict. Lévi-Strauss went on to conduct famous studies of myths that noticed, in the same manner as Russian critic Vladimir Propp's path-breaking work on folktales, that such myths, despite their heterogeneity and multiplicity, told the same kernel narratives. Those narratives

Literary Theory: An Anthology, Third Edition. Edited by Julie Rivkin and Michael Ryan.
© 2017 John Wiley & Sons, Ltd. Published 2017 by John Wiley & Sons, Ltd.

tended to work to resolve contradictions in the culture, such as that between a conception of humans as plant-growing and peaceful and humans as hunters and warriors. The many versions of the Oedipus myth, for example, all tell a story about the conflict between the idea that humans emerge from the earth ("Oedipus" means lame in the foot) and the idea that they are born from other humans (hence the sanctity of the incest taboo). The tale's function is to provide a mediation to the contradiction between nature (sexuality) and culture (rule against incest) by forbidding natural sex between family members.

The second major contribution that Saussure made to Structuralism was his conception of the linguistic sign. Words, he noted, are signs, and linguistics rightly belongs to another discipline called semiology, which would study the way signs, including words, operate. Words are signs in that they consist of two faces or sides – the signifier, which is the phonic component, and the signified, which is the ideational component. A word is both a sound and an idea or image of its referent. Alongside and often in conjunction with the Structural anthropology of Lévi-Strauss, there developed in France in the 1950s, especially in the work of Roland Barthes, a concern with the study of the semiological dimension of literature and culture. A work of literature, Barthes noted, is, after all, nothing but an assemblage of signs that function in certain ways to create meaning. In studying culture, Barthes noticed that films, commodities, events, and images are lent meaning by their association with certain signs. Barthes went on in the 1960s to become one of the major practitioners of semiological analysis in literature. His most important books are *Writing Degree Zero* (1953), *Mythologies* (1957), *On Racine* (1963), *Critical Essays* (1964), *Elements of Semiology* (1965), and *S/Z* (1970).

A direct link between French Structuralism and Russian Formalism was established in 1965 with the publication of Tzvetan Todorov's collected translations of the Formalists' *Theory of Literature*. Todorov's work is associated most often with the study of narrative, and he helped formulate the Structuralist conception of narrative as the common element of organization among diverse examples. In his study of Henry James's tales, for example ("The Structural Analysis of Narrative" in *Poetics of Prose*, 1971), he contends that they all revolve around a missing center, a point of desire that is sought but that never appears. The study of narrative (or narratology, as it is also called) is one of the most abiding strands of Structuralist thinking.

By the mid-1960s, Structuralism was the dominant school of thought in French intellectual life, and its influence is evident in the work of historian Michel Foucault, psychoanalyst Jacques Lacan, literary critic Julia Kristeva, and philosopher Louis Althusser. Foucault's work at that time included *The Order of Things: An Archeology of the Human Sciences* (*Les Mots et les choses*, 1966), *The Archeology of Knowledge* (1969), and *The Order of Discourse* (1970). Foucault is important for drawing attention to the role of language in the conceptual frameworks or "epistemes" that are used in different epochs for understanding the world. Words provide us with maps for assigning order to nature and to society. Foucault notices that what counts as knowledge changes with time, and with each change, the place of language in knowledge is also modified. In one era, the world is considered to be a site of analogies between levels, but in a later epoch, the world is broken down into discrete parts that are then organized into taxonomies.

Foucault is important as well for developing the idea of discourse and of discourse formation. A discursive formation is a coherent group of assumptions and language practices that applies to one region of knowledge, or expresses the beliefs of a social group, or articulates rules and ideals regarding kinds of behavior. Modern science is a discursive formation in that it is characterized both by a list of discoveries and a body of knowledge, but also by recognized and widely accepted linguistic forms for describing the methods and findings of science. When we get to feminism, you will encounter feminists who speak of the "discourse of patriarchy," the set of ways of thinking and of practicing language that lend coherence to male rule in society. They also describe the discourse of advice books that educated women prior to the modern era in how to behave "properly" as women, that is, in how to be "chaste, silent, and obedient."

Foucault's work draws attention to the fact that many assumptions in a culture are maintained by language practices that comprise a common tool both for knowing the world and for constructing it. By construction here, we mean the translation of physical realities into discursive realities. The "dominant discourse" of the US, for example, is one that lends great privilege to the "freedom" of the individual. The physical reality of modern life is hemmed in and constrained in many complex ways, from laws that allow police to search automobiles without cause to an economic system that requires enormous amounts of time spent at the workplace under someone else's control. Nevertheless, this physical and institutional reality is rendered discursively in the American lexicon as "freedom." Just as all women were far from being chaste, silent, and obedient, despite what the dominant discourse of the advice or courtesy books mandated, so also most Americans have limited access to the kind of pure freedom the dominant term seems to imply. What Foucault noted was that the world we live in is shaped as much by language as by knowledge or perception. Indeed, according to him, knowledge and perception always occur through the mediation of language. We would not be able to know anything if we were not able to order the world linguistically in certain ways.

In his later work, Foucault explores the way sexuality is characterized over history in different discourses of the body (*History of Sexuality*, 1976). And he examines the change in regimes of social discipline from medieval times to modern times (*Discipline and Punish*, 1975).

CHAPTER 2

The Linguistic Foundation

Jonathan Culler

Jonathan Culler's *Structuralist Poetics* (1975) was one of the first complete introductions in English to the French Structuralist movement in literary criticism. In this selection, he proposes an analogy between the structuralist description of how language operates and the rules and conventions that make up human culture.

The notion that linguistics might be useful in studying other cultural phenomena is based on two fundamental insights: first, that social and cultural phenomena are not simply material objects or events but objects or events with meaning, and hence signs; and second, that they do not have essences but are defined by a network of relations, both internal and external. Stress may fall on one or the other of these propositions – it would be in these terms, for example, that one might try to distinguish semiology and structuralism – but in fact the two are inseparable, for in studying signs one must investigate the system of relations that enables meaning to be produced and, reciprocally, one can only determine what are the pertinent relations among items by considering them as signs.

Structuralism is thus based, in the first instance, on the realization that if human actions or productions have a meaning there must be an underlying system of distinctions and conventions which makes this meaning possible. Confronted with a marriage ceremony or a game of football, for example, an observer from a culture where these did not exist could present an objective description of the actions which took place, but he would be unable to grasp their meaning and so would not be treating them as social or cultural phenomena. The actions are meaningful only with respect to a set of institutional conventions. Wherever there are two posts one can kick a ball between them but one can score a goal only within a certain institutionalized framework. As Lévi-Strauss says in his "Introduction à l'œuvre de Marcel Mauss," "particular actions of individuals

Original publication details: Jonathan Culler, "The Linguistic Foundation" from *Structuralist Poetics: Structuralism, Linguistics and the Study of Literature*, pp. 4–5, 6–7, 8–9. Cornell University Press and Routledge, 1975. Copyright © 1975 by Jonathan Culler. Reproduced with permission from Cornell University Press and Taylor & Francis.

Literary Theory: An Anthology, Third Edition. Edited by Julie Rivkin and Michael Ryan.
© 2017 John Wiley & Sons, Ltd. Published 2017 by John Wiley & Sons, Ltd.

are never symbolic in themselves; they are the elements out of which is constructed a symbolic system, which must be collective" (p. xvi). The cultural meaning of any particular act or object is determined by a whole system of constitutive rules: rules which do not regulate behavior so much as create the possibility of particular forms of behavior. The rules of English enable sequences of sound to have meaning; they make it possible to utter grammatical or ungrammatical sentences. And analogously, various social rules make it possible to marry, to score a goal, to write a poem, to be impolite. It is in this sense that a culture is composed of a set of symbolic systems. ...

To claim that cultural systems may with profit be treated as "languages" is to suggest that one will understand them better if one discusses them in terms provided by linguistics and analyzes them according to procedures used by linguists. In fact, the range of concepts and methods which structuralists have found useful is fairly restricted and only some half-dozen linguists could qualify as seminal influences. The first, of course, is Ferdinand de Saussure, who waded into the heterogeneous mass of linguistic phenomena and, recognizing that progress would be possible only if one isolated a suitable object for study, distinguished between speech acts (*la parole*) and the system of a language (*la langue*). The latter is the proper object of linguistics. Following Saussure's example and concentrating on the system which underlies speech sounds, members of the Prague linguistic circle – particularly Jakobson and Trubetzkoy – effected what Lévi-Strauss called the "phonological revolution" and provided what was to later structuralists the clearest model of linguistic method. Distinguishing between the study of actual speech sounds (phonetics) and the investigation of those aspects of sound that are functional in a particular language (phonology), Trubetzkoy argued that "phonology should investigate which phonic differences are linked, in the language under consideration, with differences of meaning, how these differentiating elements or marks are related to one another, and according to what rules they combine to form words and phrases" (*Principes de phonologie*, pp. 11–12). Phonology was important for structuralists because it showed the systematic nature of the most familiar phenomena, distinguished between the system and its realization and concentrated not on the substantive characteristics of individual phenomena but on abstract differential features which could be defined in relational terms....

The basic distinction on which modern linguistics rests, and which is equally crucial to the structuralist enterprise in other fields, is Saussure's isolation of *langue* from *parole*. The former is a system, an institution, a set of interpersonal rules and norms, while the latter comprises the actual manifestations of the system in speech and writing. It is, of course, easy to confuse the system with its manifestations, to think of English as the set of English utterances. But to learn English is not to memorize a set of utterances; it is to master a system of rules and norms which make it possible to produce and understand utterances. To know English is to have assimilated the system of the language. And the linguist's task is not to study utterances for their own sake; they are of interest to him only in so far as they provide evidence about the nature of the underlying system, the English language.

Within linguistics itself there are disagreements about what precisely belongs to *langue* and what to *parole*: whether, for example, an account of the linguistic system should specify the acoustic and articulatory features that distinguish one phoneme from another (/p/ is "voiceless" and /b/ "voiced"), or whether such features as "voiced" and "voiceless" should be thought of as the manifestations in *parole* of what, in *la langue* itself, is a purely formal and abstract distinction. Such debates need not concern the structuralist, except in so far as they indicate that structure can be defined at various levels of abstraction.[1] What does concern him is a pair of distinctions which the differentiation of *langue* from *parole* is designed to cover between rule and behavior and between the functional and the nonfunctional.

The distinction between rule and behavior is crucial to any study concerned with the production or communication of meaning. In investigating physical events one may formulate laws which are nothing other than direct summaries of behavior, but in the case of social and cultural phenomena the rule is always at some distance from actual behavior and that gap is a space of potential meaning. The instituting of the simplest rule, such as "members of this club will not step on cracks in the pavement," may in some cases determine behavior but indubitably determines meaning: the placing of one's feet on the pavement, which formerly had no meaning, now signifies either compliance with or deviation from the rule and hence an attitude towards the club and its authority. In social and cultural systems behavior may deviate frequently and considerably from the norm without impugning the existence of the norm. Many promises are in fact broken, but there still exists a rule in the system of moral concepts that promises should be kept; though of course if one never kept any promises doubts might arise as to whether one understood the institution of promising and had assimilated its rules.

Note

1   Cf. N. C. Spence, "A Hardy Perennial: The Problem of *la langue* and *la parole*," *Archivum linguisticum* 9 (1957), pp. 1–27.

CHAPTER 3

Course in General Linguistics

Ferdinand de Saussure

Saussure's *Course in General Linguistics* (1916), which was constructed by his students from his lecture notes, is one of the most influential books of the twentieth century. It transformed intellectual endeavor in a number of fields, from anthropology and sociology to philosophy and cultural studies.

Saussure treats language in the same way a scientist might treat an organism. He describes its essential features rather than studying how it works in everyday life. Words do name things, but that is not what makes language distinct. Rather, it is an entity made up of parts that relate to one another in unique ways that allow language to function.

Saussure wished to describe language more abstractly as a system (or *langue*) rather than as an actual practice of speech communication (what he called *parole*). Essential to that more systematic understanding of language is the sign. All words are signs, but they are not signs for things. Rather, to function as words, they must consist of two parts or planes. The signifier is the sound we make when we speak a word. The signified is the image or idea with which that sound is associated in our minds. Further, Saussure argued that signifiers exist in chains of difference and association. We know "cat" means a furry animal and "hat" a piece of clothing because of a sound difference. Whether "cat" means animal or piece of clothing is entirely arbitrary. What matters is that it have a unique sound identity made by its difference from other sounds. In an assertion that would be crucial for later "Post-Structuralist" thinkers, he argued that in language there are only differences (or relations between terms) and no identities.

Original publication details: Ferdinand de Saussure, from *Course in General Linguistics*, pp. 65–127. McGraw Hill, 1966. Reproduced with permission from Philosophical Library, Inc.

Literary Theory: An Anthology, Third Edition. Edited by Julie Rivkin and Michael Ryan.
© 2017 John Wiley & Sons, Ltd. Published 2017 by John Wiley & Sons, Ltd.

PART ONE

General Principles

Chapter I: NATURE OF THE LINGUISTIC SIGN

1.   Sign, Signified, Signifier

Some people regard language, when reduced to its elements, as a naming-process only – a list of words, each corresponding to the thing that it names. For example:

This conception is open to criticism at several points. It assumes that ready-made ideas exist before words; it does not tell us whether a name is vocal or psychological in nature (*arbor*, for instance, can be considered from either view-point); finally, it lets us assume that the linking of a name and a thing is a very simple operation – an assumption that is anything but true. But this rather naive approach can bring us near the truth by showing us that the linguistic unit is a double entity, one formed by the associating of two terms.

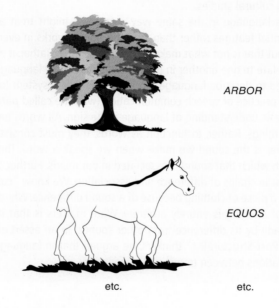

ARBOR

EQUOS

etc.   etc.

We have seen in considering the speaking-circuit that both terms involved in the linguistic sign are psychological and are united in the brain by an associative bond. This point must be emphasized.

The linguistic sign unites, not a thing and a name, but a concept and a sound-image.[1] The latter is not the material sound, a purely physical thing, but the psychological imprint of the sound, the impression that it makes on our senses. The sound-image is sensory, and if I happen to call it "material," it is only in that sense, and by way of opposing it to the other term of the association, the concept, which is generally more abstract.

The psychological character of our sound-images becomes apparent when we observe our own speech. Without moving our lips or tongue, we can talk to ourselves or recite mentally a selection of verse. Because we regard the words of our language as sound-images, we must avoid speaking of the "phonemes" that make up the words. This term, which suggests vocal activity, is applicable to the spoken word only, to the realization of the inner image in discourse. We can avoid that misunderstanding by speaking of the *sounds* and *syllables* of a word provided we remember that the names refer to the sound-image.

The linguistic sign is then a two-sided psychological entity that can be represented by the drawing:

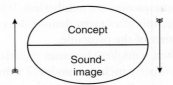

The two elements are intimately united, and each recalls the other. Whether we try to find the meaning of the Latin word *arbor* or the word that Latin uses to designate the concept "tree," it is clear that only the associations sanctioned by that language appear to us to conform to reality, and we disregard whatever others might be imagined.

Our definition of the linguistic sign poses an important question of terminology. I call the combination of a concept and a sound-image a *sign*, but in current usage the term generally designates only a sound-image, a word, for example (*arbor*, etc.). One tends to forget that *arbor* is called a sign only because it carries the concept "tree," with the result that the idea of the sensory part implies the idea of the whole.

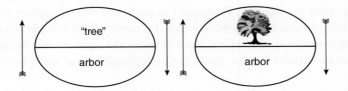

Ambiguity would disappear if the three notions involved here were designated by three names, each suggesting and opposing the others. I propose to retain the word *sign* [*signe*] to designate the whole and to replace *concept* and *sound-image* respectively by *signified* [*signifié*] and *signifier* [*signifiant*]; the last two terms have the advantage of indicating the opposition that separates them from each other and from the whole of which they are parts. As regards *sign*, if I am satisfied with it, this is simply because I do not know of any word to replace it, the ordinary language suggesting no other.

The linguistic sign, as defined, has two primordial characteristics. In enunciating them I am also positing the basic principles of any study of this type.

2.   Principle I: The Arbitrary Nature of the Sign

The bond between the signifier and the signified is arbitrary. Since I mean by sign the whole that results from the associating of the signifier with the signified, I can simply say: *the linguistic sign is arbitrary*.

The idea of "sister" is not linked by any inner relationship to the succession of sounds *s-ö-r* which serves as its signifier in French; that it could be represented equally by just any other sequence is proved by differences among languages and by the very existence of different languages: the signified "ox" has as its signifier *b-ö-f* on one side of the border and *o-k-s* (*Ochs*) on the other.

No one disputes the principle of the arbitrary nature of the sign, but it is often easier to discover a truth than to assign to it its proper place. Principle I dominates all the linguistics of language; its consequences are numberless. It is true that not all of them are equally obvious at first glance; only after many detours does one discover them, and with them the primordial importance of the principle.

One remark in passing: when semiology becomes organized as a science, the question will arise whether or not it properly includes modes of expression based on completely natural signs, such as pantomime. Supposing that the new science welcomes them, its main concern will still be the whole group of systems grounded on the arbitrariness of the sign. In fact, every means of expression used in society is based, in principle, on collective behavior or – what amounts to the same thing – on convention. Polite formulas, for instance, though often imbued with a certain natural expressiveness (as in the case of a Chinese who greets his emperor by bowing down to the ground nine times), are none-theless fixed by rule; it is this rule and not the intrinsic value of the gestures that obliges one to use them. Signs that are wholly arbitrary realize better than the others the ideal of the semiological process; that is why language, the most complex and universal of all systems of expression, is also the most characteristic; in this sense linguistics can become the master-pattern for all branches of semiology although language is only one particu-lar semiological system.

The word *symbol* has been used to designate the linguistic sign, or more specifically, what is here called the signifier. Principle I in particular weighs against the use of this term. One characteristic of the symbol is that it is never wholly arbitrary; it is not empty, for there is the rudiment of a natural bond between the signifier and the signified. The symbol of justice, a pair of scales, could not be replaced by just any other symbol, such as a chariot.

The word *arbitrary* also calls for comment. The term should not imply that the choice of the signifier is left entirely to the speaker (we shall see below that the individual does not have the power to change a sign in any way once it has become established in the linguistic community); I mean that it is unmotivated, i.e. arbitrary in that it actually has no natural connection with the signified.

In concluding let us consider two objections that might be raised to the establishment of Principle I:

(1)   *Onomatopoeia* might be used to prove that the choice of the signifier is not always arbitrary. But onomatopoeic formations are never organic elements of a linguistic system. Besides, their number is much smaller than is generally supposed. Words like French *fouet* 'whip' or *glas* 'knell' may strike certain ears with suggestive sonority, but to see that they have not always had this property we need only examine their Latin forms (*fouet* is derived from *fāgus* 'beech-tree,' *glas* from *classicum* 'sound of a trumpet'). The quality of their present sounds, or rather the quality that is attributed to them, is a fortuitous result of phonetic evolution.

As for authentic onomatopoeic words (e.g. *glug-glug*, *tick-tock*, etc.), not only are they limited in number, but also they are chosen somewhat arbitrarily, for they are only approximate and more or less conventional imitations of certain sounds (cf. English *bow-bow* and French *ouaoua*). In addition, once these words have been introduced into the language, they are to a certain extent subjected to the same evolution – phonetic, morphological, etc. – that other words undergo (cf. *pigeon*, ultimately from Vulgar Latin *pīpiō*, derived in turn from an onomatopoeic formation): obvious proof that they lose something of their original character in order to assume that of the linguistic sign in general, which is unmotivated.

(2) *Interjections*, closely related to onomatopoeia, can be attacked on the same grounds and come no closer to refuting our thesis. One is tempted to see in them spontaneous expressions of reality dictated, so to speak, by natural forces. But for most interjections we can show that there is no fixed bond between their signified and their signifier. We need only compare two languages on this point to see how much such expressions differ from one language to the next (e.g. the English equivalent of French *aïe!* is *ouch!*). We know, moreover, that many interjections were once words with specific meanings (cf. French *diable!* 'darn!' *mordieu!* 'golly!' from *mort Dieu* 'God's death,' etc.).[2]

Onomatopoeic formations and interjections are of secondary importance, and their symbolic origin is in part open to dispute.

3.   Principle II: The Linear Nature of the Signifier

The signifier, being auditory, is unfolded solely in time from which it gets the following characteristics: (a) it represents a span, and (b) the span is measurable in a single dimension; it is a line.

While Principle II is obvious, apparently linguists have always neglected to state it, doubtless because they found it too simple; nevertheless, it is fundamental, and its consequences are incalculable. Its importance equals that of Principle I; the whole mechanism of language depends upon it. In contrast to visual signifiers (nautical signals, etc.) which can offer simultaneous groupings in several dimensions, auditory signifiers have at their command only the dimension of time. Their elements are presented in succession; they form a chain. This feature becomes readily apparent when they are represented in writing and the spatial line of graphic marks is substituted for succession in time.

Sometimes the linear nature of the signifier is not obvious. When I accent a syllable, for instance, it seems that I am concentrating more than one significant element on the same point. But this is an illusion; the syllable and its accent constitute only one phonational act. There is no duality within the act but only different oppositions to what precedes and what follows.

Chapter II: IMMUTABILITY AND MUTABILITY OF THE SIGN

1.   Immutability

The signifier, though to all appearances freely chosen with respect to the idea that it represents, is fixed, not free, with respect to the linguistic community that uses it. The masses have no voice in the matter, and the signifier chosen by language could be replaced by no other. This fact, which seems to embody a contradiction, might be called colloquially "the stacked deck." We say to language: "Choose!" but we add: "It must be this sign and no other." No individual, even if he willed it, could modify in any way at all the choice that has been made; and what is more, the community itself cannot control so much as a single word; it is bound to the existing language.

No longer can language be identified with a contract pure and simple, and it is precisely from this viewpoint that the linguistic sign is a particularly interesting object of study; for language furnishes the best proof that a law accepted by a community is a thing that is tolerated and not a rule to which all freely consent.

Let us first see why we cannot control the linguistic sign and then draw together the important consequences that issue from the phenomenon.

No matter what period we choose or how far back we go, language always appears as a heritage of the preceding period. We might conceive of an act by which, at a given moment, names were assigned to things and a contract was formed between concepts and sound-images; but such an act has never been recorded. The notion that things might have happened like that was prompted by our acute awareness of the arbitrary nature of the sign.

No society, in fact, knows or has ever known language other than as a product inherited from preceding generations, and one to be accepted as such. That is why the question of the origin of speech is not so important as it is generally assumed to be. The question is not even worth asking; the only real object of linguistics is the normal, regular life of an existing idiom. A particular language-state is always the product of historical forces, and these forces explain why the sign is unchangeable, i.e. why it resists any arbitrary substitution.

Nothing is explained by saying that language is something inherited and leaving it at that. Can not existing and inherited laws be modified from one moment to the next?

To meet that objection, we must put language into its social setting and frame the question just as we would for any other social institution. How are other social institutions transmitted? This more general question includes the question of immutability. We must first determine the greater or lesser amounts of freedom that the other institutions enjoy; in each instance it will be seen that a different proportion exists between fixed tradition and the free action of society. The next step is to discover why in a given category, the forces of the first type carry more weight or less weight than those of the second. Finally, coming back to language, we must ask why the historical factor of transmission dominates it entirely and prohibits any sudden widespread change.

There are many possible answers to the question. For example, one might point to the fact that succeeding generations are not superimposed on one another like the drawers of a piece of furniture, but fuse and interpenetrate, each generation embracing individuals of all ages – with the result that modifications of language are not tied to the succession of generations. One might also recall the sum of the efforts required for learning the mother language and conclude that a general change would be impossible. Again, it might be added that reflection does not enter into the active use of an idiom – speakers are largely unconscious of the laws of language; and if they are unaware of them, how could they modify them? Even if they were aware of these laws, we may be sure that their awareness would seldom lead to criticism, for people are generally satisfied with the language they have received.

The foregoing considerations are important but not topical. The following are more basic and direct, and all the others depend on them.

1. *The arbitrary nature of the sign*. Above, we had to accept the theoretical possibility of change; further reflection suggests that the arbitrary nature of the sign is really what protects language from any attempt to modify it. Even if people were more conscious of language than they are, they would still not know how to discuss it. The reason is simply that any subject in order to be discussed must have a reasonable basis. It is possible, for instance, to discuss whether the monogamous form of marriage is more reasonable than the polygamous form and to advance arguments to support either side. One could also argue about a system of symbols, for the symbol has a rational relationship with the thing signified; but language is a system of arbitrary signs and lacks the necessary basis, the solid ground for discussion. There is no reason for preferring *soeur* to *sister, Ochs* to *boeuf*, etc.

2. *The multiplicity of signs necessary to form any language*. Another important deterrent to linguistic change is the great number of signs that must go into the making of any language. A system of writing comprising twenty to forty letters can in case of need be replaced by another system. The same would be true of language if it contained a limited number of elements; but linguistic signs are numberless.

3. *The over-complexity of the system*. A language constitutes a system. In this one respect (as we shall see later) language is not completely arbitrary but is ruled to some extent by logic; it is here also, however, that the inability of the masses to transform it becomes apparent. The system is a complex mechanism that can be grasped only through reflection; the very ones who use it daily are ignorant of it. We can conceive of a change only through the intervention of specialists, grammarians, logicians, etc.; but experience shows us that all such meddlings have failed.

4. *Collective inertia toward innovation*. Language – and this consideration surpasses all the others – is at every moment everybody's concern; spread throughout society and manipulated by it, language is something used daily by all. Here we are unable to set up any comparison between it and other institutions. The prescriptions of codes, religious rites, nautical signals, etc., involve only a certain number of individuals simultaneously and then only during a limited period of time; in language, on the contrary, everyone participates at all times, and that is why it is constantly being influenced by all. This capital fact suffices to show the impossibility of revolution. Of all social institutions, language is least amenable to initiative. It blends with the life of society, and the latter, inert by nature, is a prime conservative force.

But to say that language is a product of social forces does not suffice to show clearly that it is unfree; remembering that it is always the heritage of the preceding period, we must add that these social forces are linked with time. Language is checked not only by the weight of the collectivity but also by time. These two are inseparable. At every moment solidarity with the past checks freedom of choice. We say *man* and *dog*. This does not prevent the existence in the total phenomenon of a bond between the two antithetical forces – arbitrary convention by virtue of which choice is free and time which causes choice to be fixed. Because the sign is arbitrary, it follows no law other than that of tradition, and because it is based on tradition, it is arbitrary.

2.   Mutability

Time, which insures the continuity of language, wields another influence apparently contradictory to the first: the more or less rapid change of linguistic signs. In a certain sense, therefore, we can speak of both the immutability and the mutability of the sign.[3]

In the last analysis, the two facts are interdependent: the sign is exposed to alteration because it perpetuates itself. What predominates in all change is the persistence of the old substance; disregard for the past is only relative. That is why the principle of change is based on the principle of continuity.

Change in time takes many forms, on any one of which an important chapter in linguistics might be written. Without entering into detail, let us see what things need to be delineated.

First, let there be no mistake about the meaning that we attach to the word change. One might think that it deals especially with phonetic changes undergone by the signifier, or perhaps changes in meaning which affect the signified concept. That view would be inadequate. Regardless of what the forces of change are, whether in isolation or in combination, they always result in *a shift in the relationship between the signified and the signifier*.

Here are some examples. Latin *necāre* 'kill' became *noyer* 'drown' in French. Both the sound-image and the concept changed; but it is useless to separate the two parts of the phenomenon; it is sufficient to state with respect to the whole that the bond between the idea and the sign was loosened, and that there was a shift in their relationship. If instead of comparing Classical Latin *necāre* with French *noyer*, we contrast the former term with *necare* of Vulgar Latin of the fourth or fifth century meaning 'drown' the case is a little different; but here again, although there is no appreciable change in the signifier, there is a shift in the relationship between the idea and the sign.[4]

Old German *dritteil* 'one-third' became *Drittel* in Modern German. Here, although the concept remained the same, the relationship was changed in two ways: the signifier was changed not only in its material aspect but also in its grammatical form; the idea of *Teil* 'part' is no longer implied; *Drittel* is a simple word. In one way or another there is always a shift in the relationship.

In Anglo-Saxon the preliterary form *fot* 'foot' remained while its plural **fōti* became *fēt* (Modern English *feet*). Regardless of the other changes that are implied, one thing is certain: there was a shift in their relationship; other correspondences between the phonetic substance and the idea emerged.

Language is radically powerless to defend itself against the forces which from one moment to the next are shifting the relationship between the signified and the signifier. This is one of the consequences of the arbitrary nature of the sign.

Unlike language, other human institutions – customs, laws, etc. – are all based in varying degrees on the natural relations of things; all have of necessity adapted the means employed to the ends pursued. Even fashion in dress is not entirely arbitrary; we can deviate only slightly from the conditions dictated by the human body. Language is limited by nothing in the choice of means, for apparently nothing would prevent the associating of any idea whatsoever with just any sequence of sounds.

To emphasize the fact that language is a genuine institution, Whitney quite justly insisted upon the arbitrary nature of signs; and by so doing, he placed linguistics on its true axis. But he did not follow through and see that the arbitrariness of language radically separates it from all other institutions. This is apparent from the way in which language evolves. Nothing could be more complex. As it is a product of both the social force and time, no one can change anything in it, and on the other hand, the arbitrariness of its signs theoretically entails the freedom of establishing just any relationship between phonetic substance and ideas. The result is that each of the two elements united in the sign maintains its own life to a degree unknown elsewhere, and that language changes, or rather evolves, under the influence of all the forces which can affect either sounds or meanings. The evolution is inevitable; there is no example of a single language that resists it. After a certain period of time, some obvious shifts can always be recorded.

Mutability is so inescapable that it even holds true for artificial languages. Whoever creates a language controls it only so long as it is not in circulation; from the moment when it fulfills its mission and becomes the property of everyone, control is lost. Take Esperanto as an example; if it succeeds, will it escape the inexorable law? Once launched, it is quite likely that Esperanto will enter upon a fully semiological life; it will be transmitted according to laws which have nothing in common with those of its logical creation, and there will be no turning backwards. A man proposing a fixed language that posterity would have to accept for what it is would be like a hen hatching a duck's egg: the language created by him would be borne along, willy-nilly, by the current that engulfs all languages.

Signs are governed by a principle of general semiology: continuity in time is coupled to change in time; this is confirmed by orthographic systems, the speech of deaf-mutes, etc.

But what supports the necessity for change? I might be reproached for not having been as explicit on this point as on the principle of immutability. This is because I failed to distinguish between the different forces of change. We must consider their great variety in order to understand the extent to which they are necessary.

The causes of continuity are *a priori* within the scope of the observer, but the causes of change in time are not. It is better not to attempt giving an exact account at this point, but to restrict discussion to the shifting of relationships in general. Time changes all things; there is no reason why language should escape this universal law.

Let us review the main points of our discussion and relate them to the principles set up in the Introduction.

1.   Avoiding sterile word definitions, within the total phenomenon represented by speech we first singled out two parts: language and speaking. Language is speech less speaking. It is the whole set of linguistic habits which allow an individual to understand and to be understood.

2.   But this definition still leaves language outside its social context; it makes language something artificial since it includes only the individual part of reality; for the realization of language, a community of speakers [*masse parlante*] is necessary. Contrary to all appearances, language never exists apart from the social fact, for it is a semiological phenomenon. Its social nature is one of its inner characteristics.

Its complete definition confronts us with two inseparable entities, as shown in this drawing:

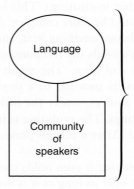

But under the conditions described language is not living – it has only potential life; we have considered only the social, not the historical, fact.

3.   The linguistic sign is arbitrary; language, as defined, would therefore seem to be a system which, because it depends solely on a rational principle, is free and can be organized at will. Its social nature, considered independently, does not definitely rule out this viewpoint. Doubtless it is not on a purely logical basis that group psychology operates; one must consider everything that deflects reason in actual contacts between individuals. But the thing which keeps language from being a simple convention that can be modified at the whim of interested parties is not its social nature; it is rather the action of time combined with the social force. If time is left out, the linguistic facts are incomplete and no conclusion is possible.

   If we considered language in time, without the community of speakers – imagine an isolated individual living for several centuries – we probably would notice no change; time would not influence language. Conversely, if we considered the community of speakers without considering time, we would not see the effect of the social forces that influence language. To represent the actual facts, we must then add to our first drawing a sign to indicate passage of time:

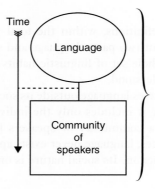

Language is no longer free, for time will allow the social forces at work on it to carry out their effects. This brings us back to the principle of continuity, which cancels freedom. But continuity necessarily implies change, varying degrees of shifts in the relationship between the signified and the signifier.

Chapter III: STATIC AND EVOLUTIONARY LINGUISTICS

1.   Inner Duality of All Sciences Concerned with Values

Very few linguists suspect that the intervention of the factor of time creates difficulties peculiar to linguistics and opens to their science two completely divergent paths.

Most other sciences are unaffected by this radical duality; time produces no special effects in them. Astronomy has found that the stars undergo considerable changes but has not been obliged on this account to split itself into two disciplines. Geology is concerned with successions at almost every instant, but its study of strata does not thereby become a radically distinct discipline. Law has its descriptive science and its historical science; no one opposes one to the other. The political history of states is unfolded solely in time, but a historian depicting a particular period does not work apart from history. Conversely, the science of political institutions is essentially descriptive, but if the need arises it can easily deal with a historical question without disturbing its unity.

On the contrary, that duality is already forcing itself upon the economic sciences. Here, in contrast to the other sciences, political economy and economic history constitute two clearly separated disciplines within a single science; the works that have recently appeared on these subjects point up the distinction. Proceeding as they have, economists are – without being well aware of it – obeying an inner necessity. A similar necessity obliges us to divide linguistics into two parts, each with its own principle. Here as in political economy we are confronted with the notion of *value*; both sciences are concerned with *a system for equating things of different orders* – labor and wages in one and a signified and signifier in the other.

Certainly all sciences would profit by indicating more precisely the co–ordinates along which their subject matter is aligned. Everywhere distinctions should be made, according to the following illustration, between (1) *the axis of simultaneities* (AB), which stands for the relations of coexisting things and from which the intervention of time is excluded; and (2) *the axis of successions* (CD), on which only one thing can be considered at a time but upon which are located all the things on the first axis together with their changes.

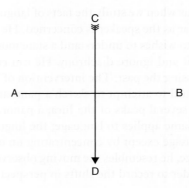

For a science concerned with values the distinction is a practical necessity and some-times an absolute one. In these fields scholars cannot organize their research rigorously without considering both co-ordinates and making a distinction between the system of values per se and the same values as they relate to time.

This distinction has to be heeded by the linguist above all others, for language is a system of pure values which are determined by nothing except the momentary arrange-ment of its terms. A value – so long as it is somehow rooted in things and in their natural relations, as happens with economics (the value of a plot of ground, for instance, is related to its productivity) – can to some extent be traced in time if we remember that it depends at each moment upon a system of coexisting values. Its link with things gives it, perforce, a natural basis, and the judgments that we base on such values are therefore never completely arbitrary; their variability is limited. But we have just seen that natural data have no place in linguistics.

Again, the more complex and rigorously organized a system of values is, the more it is necessary, because of its very complexity, to study it according to both co-ordinates. No other system embodies this feature to the same extent as language. Nowhere else do we find such precise values at stake and such a great number and diversity of terms, all so rigidly interdependent. The multiplicity of signs, which we have already used to explain the continuity of language, makes it absolutely impossible to study simultaneously relations in time and relations within the system.

The reasons for distinguishing two sciences of language are clear. How should the sciences be designated? Available terms do not all bring out the distinction with equal sharpness. "Linguistic history" and "historical linguistics" are too vague. Since political history includes the description of different periods as well as the narration of events, the student might think that he is studying a language according to the axis of time when he describes its successive states, but this would require a separate study of the phenom-ena that make language pass from one state to another. *Evolution* and *evolutionary linguis-tics* are more precise, and I shall use these expressions often; in contrast, we can speak of the science of *language-states* [*états de langue*] or *static linguistics*.

But to indicate more clearly the opposition and crossing of two orders of phenomena that relate to the same object, I prefer to speak of *synchronic* and *diachronic* linguistics. Everything that relates to the static side of our science is synchronic; everything that has to do with evolution is diachronic. Similarly, *synchrony* and *diachrony* designate respec-tively a language-state and an evolutionary phase.

2.   Inner Duality and the History of Linguistics

The first thing that strikes us when we study the facts of language is that their succession in time does not exist insofar as the speaker is concerned. He is confronted with a state. That is why the linguist who wishes to understand a state must discard all knowledge of everything that produced it and ignore diachrony. He can enter the mind of speakers only by completely suppressing the past. The intervention of history can only falsify his judgment. It would be absurd to attempt to sketch a panorama of the Alps by viewing them simultaneously from several peaks of the Jura; a panorama must be made from a single vantage point. The same applies to language; the linguist can neither describe it nor draw up standards of usage except by concentrating on one state. When he follows the evolution of the language, he resembles the moving observer who goes from one peak of the Jura to another in order to record the shifts in perspective.

Ever since modern linguistics came into existence, it has been completely absorbed in diachrony. Comparative Indo-European philology uses the materials at hand to reconstruct hypothetically an older type of language; comparison is but a means of reconstructing the past. The method is the same in the narrower study of subgroups (Romance languages, Germanic languages, etc.); states intervene only irregularly and piecemeal. Such is the tendency introduced by Bopp. His conception of language is therefore hybrid and hesitating.

Against this, what was the procedure of those who studied language before the beginning of modern linguistics, i.e. the "grammarians" inspired by traditional methods? It is curious to note that here their viewpoint was absolutely above reproach. Their works clearly show that they tried to describe language-states. Their program was strictly synchronic. The *Port Royal Grammar*, for example, attempts to describe the state of French under Louis XIV and to determine its values. For this, the language of the Middle Ages is not needed; the horizontal axis is followed faithfully, without digression. The method was then correct, but this does not mean that its application was perfect. Traditional grammar neglects whole parts of language, such as word formation; it is normative and assumes the role of prescribing rules, not of recording facts; it lacks overall perspective; often it is unable even to separate the written from the spoken word, etc.

Classical grammar has been criticized as unscientific; still, its basis is less open to criticism and its data are better defined than is true of the linguistics started by Bopp. The latter, occupying ill-defined ground, has no clear-cut objective. It straddles two areas because it is unable to make a sharp distinction between states and successions.

Linguistics, having accorded too large a place to history, will turn back to the static viewpoint of traditional grammar but in a new spirit and with other procedures, and the historical method will have contributed to this rejuvenation; the historical method will in turn give a better understanding of language-states. The old grammar saw only the synchronic fact; linguistics has revealed a new class of phenomena; but that is not enough; one must sense the opposition between the two classes of facts to draw out all its consequences.

3.   Inner Duality Illustrated by Examples

The opposition between the two viewpoints, the synchronic and the diachronic, is absolute and allows no compromise. A few facts will show what the difference is and why it is irreducible.

Latin *crispus* 'crisp' provided French with the root *crép–* from which were formed the verbs *crépir* 'rough-cast' and *décrepir* 'remove mortar.' Against this, at a certain moment the word *dēcrepitus*, of unknown origin, was borrowed from Latin and became *décrépit* 'decrepit.' Certainly today the community of speakers sets up a relation between *un mur décrépi* 'a wall from which mortar is falling' and *un homme décrépit* 'a decrepit man,' although historically the two words have nothing in common; people often speak of the *façade décrépite* of a house. And this is static, for it concerns the relation between two coexisting forms of language. For its realization, the concurrence of certain evolutionary events was necessary. The pronunciation of *crisp–* had to become *crép–*, and at a particular moment a new word had to be borrowed from Latin. It is obvious that the diachronic facts are not related to the static facts which they produced. They belong to a different class.

Here is a more telling example. In Old High German the plural of *gast* 'guest' was first *gasti*, that of *hant* 'hand' was *hanti*, etc. Later the final *–i* produced an umlaut, i.e. it resulted in the changing of the *a* of the preceding syllable to *e*: *gasti* → *gesti; hanti* → *henti*. Then the final *–i* lost its timbre: *gesti* → *geste*, etc. The result is that today German has *Gast: Gäste, Hand: Hände*, and a whole group of words marked by the same difference between the singular and the plural. A very similar fact occurred in Anglo–Saxon: the earlier forms were *fōt: *fōti, tōþ: *tōþi, gōs: *gōsi*, etc. Through an initial phonetic change, umlaut, *fōti* became *feti;* through a second, the fall of final *–i, feti* became *fēt;* after that, *fōt* had as its plural *fēt; tōþ, tēþ; gōs, gēs*, etc. (Modern English *foot: feet, tooth: teeth, goose: geese*.)

Previously, when speakers used *gast: gasti, fōt: fōti*, the simple addition of an *i* marked the plural; *Gast: Gäste* and *fōt: fēt* show a new mechanism for indicating the plural. The mechanism is not the same in both instances; in Old English there is only opposition between vowels; in German there is in addition the presence or absence of final *–e;* but here this difference is unimportant.

The relation between a singular and its plural, whatever the forms may be, can be expressed at each moment by a horizontal axis:

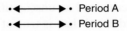

Whatever facts have brought about passage from one form to another should be placed along a vertical axis, giving the overall picture:

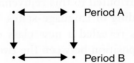

Our illustration suggests several pertinent remarks:

1. In no way do diachronic facts aim to signal a value by means of another sign; that *gasti* became *gesti, geste* (*Gäste*) has nothing to do with the plural of substantives; in *tragit* → *trägt*, the same umlaut occurs in verbal inflection, and so forth. A diachronic fact is an independent event; the particular synchronic consequences that may stem from it are wholly unrelated to it.

2. Diachronic facts are not even directed toward changing the system. Speakers did not wish to pass from one system of relations to another; modification does not affect the arrangement but rather its elements.

    Here we again find the principle enunciated previously: never is the system modified directly. In itself it is unchangeable; only certain elements are altered without regard for the solidarity that binds them to the whole. It is as if one of the planets that revolve around the sun changed its dimensions and weight: this isolated event would entail general consequences and would throw the whole system out of equilibrium. The opposition of two terms is needed to express plurality: either *fōt: fōti* or *fōt: fēt;* both procedures are possible, but speakers passed from one to the other, so to speak, without having a hand in it. Neither was the whole replaced nor did one system engender another; one element in the first system was changed, and this change was enough to give rise to another system.

3.   The foregoing observation points up the ever *fortuitous* nature of a state. In contrast to the false notion that we readily fashion for ourselves about it, language is not a mechanism created and arranged with a view to the concepts to be expressed. We see on the contrary that the state which resulted from the change was not destined to signal the meaning with which it was impregnated. In a fortuitous state (*fōt: fēt*), speakers took advantage of an existing difference and made it signal the distinction between singular and plural; *fōt: fēt* is no better for this purpose than *fōt: *fōti*. In each state the mind infiltrated a given substance and breathed life into it. This new perspective, inspired by historical linguistics, is unknown to traditional grammar, which could never acquire it by its own methods. Most philosophers of language are equally ignorant of it, and yet nothing is more important from the philosophical viewpoint.

4.   Are facts of the diachronic series of the same class, at least, as facts of the synchronic series? By no means, for we have seen that changes are wholly unintentional while the synchronic fact is always significant. It always calls forth two simultaneous terms. Not *Gäste* alone but the opposition *Gast: Gäste* expresses the plural. The diachronic fact is just the opposite: only one term is involved, and for the new one to appear (*Gäste*), the old one (*gasti*) must first give way to it.

To try to unite such dissimilar facts in the same discipline would certainly be a fanciful undertaking. The diachronic perspective deals with phenomena that are unrelated to systems although they do condition them.

Here are some other examples to strengthen and complement the conclusions drawn from the first ones.

In French, the accent always falls on the last syllable unless this syllable contains a mute *e* (ə). This is a synchronic fact, a relation between the whole set of French words and accent. What is its source? A previous state. Latin had a different and more complicated system of accentuation: the accent was on the penultimate syllable when the latter was long; when short, the accent fell back on the antepenult (cf. *amícus, ánima*). The Latin law suggests relations that are in no way analogous to the French law. Doubtless the accent is the same in the sense that it remained in the same position; in French words it always falls on the syllable that had it in Latin: *amícum → aimí, ánimum → âme*. But the two formulas are different for the two moments because the forms of the words changed. We know that everything after the accent either disappeared or was reduced to mute *e*. As a result of the alteration of the word, the position of the accent with respect to the whole was no longer the same; subsequently speakers, conscious of the new relation, instinctively put the accent on the last syllable, even in borrowed words introduced in their written forms (*facile, consul, ticket, burgrave*, etc.). Speakers obviously did not try to change systems, to apply a new formula, since in words like *amícum → amí* the accent always remained on the same syllable; but a diachronic fact was interposed: speakers changed the position of the accent without having a hand in it. A law of accentuation, like everything that pertains to the linguistic system, is an arrangement of terms, a fortuitous and involuntary result of evolution.

Here is an even more striking example. In Old Slavic, *slovo* 'word' has in the instrumental singular *slovem'ъ*, in the nominative plural *slova*, in the genitive plural *slov'ъ*, etc.; in the declension each case has its own ending. But today the weak vowels *ъ* and *'ъ*, Slavic representatives of Proto-Indo-European *ĭ* and *ŭ*, have disappeared. Czech, for example, has *slovo, slovem, slova, slov;* likewise *žena* 'woman': accusative singular *ženu*, nominative plural *ženy*, genitive plural *žen*. Here the genitive (*slov, žen*) has zero inflection. We see then that a material sign is not necessary for the expression of an idea; language is satisfied with the opposition between something and nothing. Czech speakers recognize *žen* as a genitive plural simply because it is neither *žena* nor *ženu* nor any of the other forms. It seems strange at first glance that such a particular notion as that of the genitive plural should have taken the zero sign, but this very fact proves that everything comes about through sheer accident. Language is a mechanism that continues to function in spite of the deteriorations to which it is subjected.

All this confirms the principles previously stated. To summarize:

Language is a system whose parts can and must all be considered in their synchronic solidarity.

Since changes never affect the system as a whole but rather one or another of its elements, they can be studied only outside the system. Each alteration doubtless has its countereffect on the system, but the initial fact affected only one point; there is no inner bond between the initial fact and the effect that it may subsequently produce on the whole system. The basic difference between successive terms and coexisting terms, between partial facts and facts that affect the system, precludes making both classes of fact the subject matter of a single science.

4.   The Difference between the Two Classes
Illustrated by Comparisons

To show both the autonomy and the interdependence of synchrony we can compare the first to the projection of an object on a plane surface. Any projection depends directly on the nature of the object projected, yet differs from it – the object itself is a thing apart. Otherwise there would not be a whole science of projections; considering the bodies themselves would suffice. In linguistics there is the same relationship between the historical facts and a language-state, which is like a projection of the facts at a particular moment. We do not learn about synchronic states by studying bodies, i.e. diachronic events, any more than we learn about geometric projections by studying, even carefully, the different types of bodies.

Similarly if the stem of a plant is cut transversely, a rather complicated design is formed by the cut surface; the design is simply one perspective of the longitudinal fibers, and we would be able to see them on making a second cut perpendicular to the first. Here again one perspective depends on the other; the longitudinal cut shows the fibers that constitute the plant, and the transversal cut shows their arrangement on a particular plane; but the second is distinct from the first because it brings out certain relations between the fibers – relations that we could never grasp by viewing the longitudinal plane.

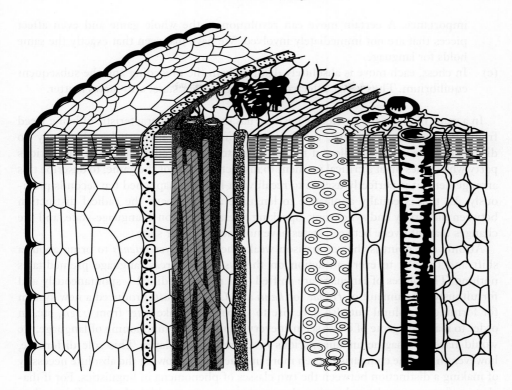

But of all comparisons that might be imagined, the most fruitful is the one that might be drawn between the functioning of language and a game of chess. In both instances we are confronted with a system of values and their observable modifications. A game of chess is like an artificial realization of what language offers in a natural form.

Let us examine the matter more carefully.

First, a state of the set of chessmen corresponds closely to a state of language. The respective value of the pieces depends on their position on the chessboard just as each linguistic term derives its value from its opposition to all the other terms.

In the second place, the system is always momentary; it varies from one position to the next. It is also true that values depend above all else on an unchangeable convention, the set of rules that exists before a game begins and persists after each move. Rules that are agreed upon once and for all exist in language too; they are the constant principles of semiology.

Finally, to pass from one state of equilibrium to the next, or – according to our terminology – from one synchrony to the next, only one chesspiece has to be moved; there is no general rummage. Here we have the counterpart of the diachronic phenomenon with all its peculiarities. In fact:

(a)   In each play only one chesspiece is moved; in the same way in language, changes affect only isolated elements.

(b)   In spite of that, the move has a repercussion on the whole system; it is impossible for the player to foresee exactly the extent of the effect. Resulting changes of value will be, according to the circumstances, either nil, very serious, or of average importance. A certain move can revolutionize the whole game and even affect pieces that are not immediately involved. We have just seen that exactly the same holds for language.

(c)   In chess, each move is absolutely distinct from the preceding and the subsequent equilibrium. The change effected belongs to neither state: only states matter.

In a game of chess any particular position has the unique characteristic of being freed from all antecedent positions; the route used in arriving there makes absolutely no difference; one who has followed the entire match has no advantage over the curious party who comes up at a critical moment to inspect the state of the game; to describe this arrangement, it is perfectly useless to recall what had just happened ten seconds previously. All this is equally applicable to language and sharpens the radical distinction between diachrony and synchrony. Speaking operates only on a language-state, and the changes that intervene between states have no place in either state.

At only one point is the comparison weak: the chessplayer *intends* to bring about a shift and thereby to exert an action on the system, whereas language premeditates nothing. The pieces of language are shifted – or rather modified – spontaneously and fortuitously. The umlaut of *Hände* for *hanti* and *Gäste* for *gasti* produced a new system for forming the plural but also gave rise to verbal forms like *trägt* from *tragit*, etc. In order to make the game of chess seem at every point like the functioning of language, we would have to imagine an unconscious or unintelligent player. This sole difference, however, makes the comparison even more instructive by showing the absolute necessity of making a distinction between the two classes of phenomena in linguistics. For if diachronic facts cannot be reduced to the synchronic system which they condition when the change is intentional, all the more will they resist when they set a blind force against the organization of a system of signs.

5.   The Two Linguistics Contrasted According to Their Methods and Principles

Everywhere the opposition between diachrony and synchrony stands out.

For instance – and to begin with the most apparent fact – they are not of equal importance. Here it is evident that the synchronic viewpoint predominates, for it is the true and only reality to the community of speakers. The same is true of the linguist: if he takes the diachronic perspective, he no longer observes language but rather a series of events that modify it. People often affirm that nothing is more important than understanding the genesis of a particular state; this is true in a certain sense: the forces that have shaped the state illuminate its true nature, and knowing them protects us against certain illusions; but this only goes to prove clearly that diachronic linguistics is not an end in itself. What is said of journalism applies to diachrony: it leads everywhere if one departs from it.

The methods of diachrony and synchrony also differ, and in two ways.

(a)   Synchrony has only one perspective, the speakers', and its whole method consists of gathering evidence from speakers; to know to just what extent a thing is a reality, it is necessary and sufficient to determine to what extent it exists in the minds of speakers. Diachronic linguistics, on the contrary, must distinguish two perspectives. One of these, the *prospective*, follows the course of time; the other, the *retrospective*, goes back in time; the result is a duplication in methodology with which we shall deal in Part Five.

(b)   A second difference results from delimiting the fields embraced by each of the two disciplines. Synchronic study has as its object, not everything that is simultaneous, but only the totality of facts corresponding to each language; separation will go as far as dialects and subdialects when necessary. The term *synchronic* is really not precise enough; it should be replaced by another – rather long to be sure – *idiosynchronic*. Against this, diachronic linguistics not only does not need but even rejects such specialization; the terms that it studies do not necessarily belong to the same language (compare Proto-Indo-European *esti*, Greek *esti*, German *ist*, and French *est*). The succession of diachronic events and their multiplication in space are precisely what creates the diversity of idioms. To justify the associating of two forms, it is enough to show that they are connected by a historical bond, however indirect it may be.

The foregoing oppositions are neither the most striking nor the most profound. One consequence of the radical antinomy between the evolutionary and the static fact is that all notions associated with one or the other are to the same extent mutually irreducible. Any notion will point up this truth. The synchronic and diachronic "phenomenon," for example, have nothing in common. One is a relation between simultaneous elements, the other the substitution of one element for another in time, an event.

We shall also see that diachronic and synchronic identities are two very different things; historically the French negation *pas* is identical to the substantive *pas* 'step,' whereas the two forms are distinct in modern French. These observations would suffice to show the necessity of not confusing the two viewpoints, but nowhere is this necessity more apparent than in the distinction we are about to make.

6.   Synchronic and Diachronic Law

It is a popular practice to speak of laws in linguistics. But are the facts of language actually governed by laws? If so, what are they like? Since language is a social institution, one might assume *a priori* that it is governed by prescriptions analogous to those that control communities. Now every social law has two basic characteristics: it is *imperative* and it is *general*; it comes in by force and it covers all cases – within certain limits of time and place, of course.

Do the laws of language fit this definition? The first step in answering the question – in line with what has just been said – is to separate once more the synchronic and diachronic areas. The two problems must not be confused; speaking of linguistic law in general is like trying to pin down a ghost.

Here are some examples, taken from Greek, in which the two classes are intentionally jumbled:

1.   Proto-Indo-European voiced aspirates became voiceless: *dhūmos* → *thūmos* 'breath of life,' *bherō* → *phérō* 'I bear,' etc.
2.   The accent never falls farther back than the antepenult.
3.   All words end in a vowel or in *s*, *n*, or *r*, to the exclusion of all other consonants.

4.   Prevocalic initial *s* became *h* (sign of aspiration): *septm* (Latin *septem*) → *heptá*.
5.   Final *m* changed to *n:* *jugom* → *zugón* (cf. Latin *jugum*).[5]
6.   Final occlusives fell: *gunaik* → *gúnai*, *epherst* → *éphere*, *epheront* → *épheron*.

Law 1 is diachronic: *dh* became *th*, etc. Law 2 expresses a relation between the word-unit and accent, a sort of contract between two coexisting terms; it is a synchronic law. The same is true of Law 3 since it concerns the word-unit and its ending. Laws 4, 5, and 6 are diachronic: *s* became *h; —n* replaced *—m; —t, —k*, etc. disappeared without leaving a trace.

We should also notice that Law 3 is the result of 5 and 6; two diachronic facts created a synchronic fact.

After we separate the two classes of laws, we see that Laws 2 and 3 are basically different from Laws 1, 4, 5, and 6.

The synchronic law is general but not imperative. Doubtless it is imposed on individuals by the weight of collective usage, but here I do not have in mind an obligation on the part of speakers. I mean that *in language* no force guarantees the maintenance of a regularity when established on some point. Being a simple expression of an existing arrangement, the synchronic law reports a state of affairs; it is like a law that states that trees in a certain orchard are arranged in the shape of a quincunx. And the arrangement that the law defines is precarious precisely because it is not imperative. Nothing is more regular than the synchronic law that governs Latin accentuation (a law comparable in every way to Law 2 above); but the accentual rule did not resist the forces of alteration and gave way to a new law, the one of French. In short, if one speaks of law in synchrony, it is in the sense of an arrangement, a principle of regularity.

Diachrony, on the contrary, supposes a dynamic force through which an effect is produced, a thing executed. But this imperativeness is not sufficient to warrant applying the concept of law to evolutionary facts; we can speak of law only when a set of facts obeys the same rule, and in spite of certain appearances to the contrary, diachronic events are always accidental and particular.

The accidental and particular character of semantic facts is immediately apparent. That French *poutre* 'mare' has acquired the meaning 'piece of wood, rafter' is due to particular causes and does not depend on other changes that might have occurred at the same time. It is only one accident among all those registered in the history of the language.

As for syntactical and morphological transformations, the issue is not so clear from the outset. At a certain time almost all old subject-case forms disappeared in French. Here a set of facts apparently obeys the same law. But such is not the case, for all the facts are but multiple manifestations of one and the same isolated fact. The particular notion of subject was affected, and its disappearance naturally caused a whole series of forms to vanish. For one who sees only the external features of language, the unique phenomenon is drowned in the multitude of its manifestations. Basically, however, there is but one phenomenon, and this historical event is just as isolated in its own order as the semantic change undergone by *poutre*. It takes on the appearance of a "law" only because it is realized within a system. The rigid arrangement of the system creates the illusion that the diachronic fact obeys the same rules as the synchronic fact.

Finally, as regards phonetic changes, exactly the same is true. Yet the popular practice is to speak of phonetic laws. Indeed, it is said that at a given time and in a given area all words having the same phonic features are affected by the same change; for example,

Law 1 (*dhūmos* → Greek *thūmos*) affects all Greek words containing a voiced aspirate (cf. *nebhos* → *néphos*, *medhu* → *méthu*, *anghō* → *ánkhō*, etc.); Law 4 (*septm* → *heptá*) applies to *serpō* → *hérpō*, *sūs* → *hûs*, and to all words that begin with *s*. This regularity, which has at times been disputed, is apparently firmly established; obvious exceptions do not lessen the inevitability of such changes, for they can be explained either by more special phonetic laws (see the example of *trikhes: thriksi*) or by the interference of facts of another class (analogy, etc.). Nothing seems to fit better the definition given above for the word law. And yet, regardless of the number of instances where a phonetic law holds, all facts embraced by it are but manifestations of a single particular fact.

The real issue is to find out whether phonetic changes affect words or only sounds, and there is no doubt about the answer: in *nephos, methu, ankhō*, etc. a certain phoneme – a voiced Proto-Indo-European aspirate – became voiceless, Proto-Greek initial *s* became *h*, etc.; each fact is isolated, independent also of the other events of the same class, independent also of the words in which the change took place.[6] The phonic substance of all the words was of course modified, but this should not deceive us as to the real nature of the phenomenon.

What supports the statement that words themselves are not directly involved in phonetic transformations? The very simple observation that these transformations are basically alien to words and cannot touch their essence. The word–unit is not constituted solely by the totality of its phonemes but by characteristics other than its material qual-ity. Suppose that one string of a piano is out of tune: a discordant note will be heard each time the one who is playing a melody strikes the corresponding key. But where is the discord? In the melody? Certainly not; the melody has not been affected; only the piano has been impaired. Exactly the same is true in phonetics. Our system of phonemes is the instrument we play in order to articulate the words of language; if one of its elements is modified, diverse consequences may ensue, but the modification itself is not concerned with the words which are, in a manner of speaking, the melodies of our repertory.

Diachronic facts are then particular; a shift in a system is brought about by events which not only are outside the system, but are isolated and form no system among themselves.

To summarize: synchronic facts, no matter what they are, evidence a certain regular-ity but are in no way imperative; diachronic facts, on the contrary, force themselves upon language but are in no way general.

In a word – and this is the point I have been trying to make – neither of the two classes of facts is governed by laws in the sense defined above, and if one still wishes to speak of linguistic laws, the word will embrace completely different meanings, depending on whether it designates facts of one class or the other.

7.   Is There a Panchronic Viewpoint?

Up to this point the term law has been used in the legal sense. But cannot the term also be used in language as in the physical and natural sciences, i.e. in the sense of relations that are everywhere and forever verifiable? In a word, can not language be studied from a panchronic viewpoint?

Doubtless. Since phonetic changes have always occurred and are still occurring, this general phenomenon is a permanent characteristic of speech; it is therefore one of the laws of speech. In linguistics as in chess there are rules that outlive all events. But they are general principles existing independently of concrete facts. When we speak of particular, tangible facts, there is no panchronic viewpoint. Each phonetic change, regardless of its actual spread, is limited to a definite time and territory; no change occurs at all times and in all places; change exists only diachronically. These general principles are precisely what serve as a criterion for determining what belongs to language and what does not. A concrete fact that lends itself to panchronic explanation cannot belong to language. Take the French word *chose* 'thing': from the diachronic viewpoint it stands in opposition to the Latin word from which it derives, *causa*; from the synchronic viewpoint it stands in opposition to every word that might be associated with it in Modern French. Only the sounds of the word considered independently (*šǫz*) are susceptible of panchronic observation, but they have no linguistic value. Even from the panchronic viewpoint *šǫz*, considered in a chain like *ün šǫz admirablə* 'an admirable thing,' is not a unit but a shapeless mass; indeed, why *šǫz* rather than *ǫza* or *nšǫ?* It is not a value, for it has no meaning. From the panchronic viewpoint the particular facts of language are never reached.

8.   Consequences of the Confusing of Synchrony and Diachrony

Two instances will be cited:

(a)   Synchronic truth seems to be the denial of diachronic truth, and one who has a superficial view of things imagines that a choice must be made; this is really unnecessary; one truth does not exclude the other. That French *dépit* 'spite' originally meant contempt does not prevent the word from having a completely different meaning now; etymology and synchronic value are distinct. Similarly, traditional grammar teaches that the present participle is variable and shows agreement in the same manner as an adjective in certain cases in Modern French (cf. une eau *courante* 'running water') but is invariable in others (cf. une personne *courant* dans la rue 'a person *running* in the street'). But historical grammar shows that it is not a question of one and the same form: the first is the continuation of the variable Latin participle (*currentum*) while the second comes from the invariable ablative form of the gerund (*currendō*).[7] Does synchronic truth contradict diachronic truth, and must one condemn traditional grammar in the name of historical grammar? No, for that would be seeing only half of the facts; one must not think that the historical fact alone matters and is sufficient to constitute language. Doubtless from the viewpoint of its origin the participle *courant* has two elements, but in the collective mind of the community of speakers, these are drawn together and fused into one. The synchronic truth is just as absolute and indisputable as the diachronic truth.

(b)   Synchronic truth is so similar to diachronic truth that people confuse the two or think it superfluous to separate them. For example, they try to explain the meaning of French *père* 'father' by saying that Latin *pāter* meant the same thing. Another example: Latin short *a* became *i* in noninitial open syllables; beside *faciō* we have *conficiō*, beside *amīcus, inimīcus*, etc. The law is often stated in this way: "The *a* of *faciō* becomes *i* in *conficiō* because it is no longer in the first syllable." That is not true: never did the *a* "become" *i* in *conficiō*. To re-establish the truth one must single out two periods and four terms. Speakers first said *facio – confacio*; then, *confacio* having been changed to *conficiō* while *faciō* remained unchanged, they said *faciō – conficiō*:

$$facio \leftrightarrow confacio \qquad \text{Period A}$$
$$facio \leftrightarrow conficio \qquad \text{Period B}$$

If a "change" occurred, it is between *confacio* and *conficio;* but the rule, badly formulated, does not even mention *confacio!* Then beside the diachronic change there is a second fact, absolutely distinct from the first and having to do with the purely synchronic opposition between *facio* and *conficio*. One is tempted to say that it is not a fact but a result. Nevertheless, it *is* a fact in its own class; indeed, all synchronic phenomena are like this. The true value of the opposition *facio: conficio* is not recognized for the very reason that the opposition is not very significant. But oppositions like *Gast: Gäste* and *gebe: gibt,* though also fortuitous results of phonetic evolution, are nonetheless basic grammatical phenomena of the synchronic class. The fact that both classes are in other respects closely linked, each conditioning the other, points to the conclusion that keeping them apart is not worthwhile; in fact, linguistics has confused them for decades without realizing that such a method is worthless.

The mistake shows up conspicuously in certain instances. To explain Greek *phuktós,* for example, it might seem sufficient to say that in Greek *g* or *kh* became *k* before voiceless consonants, and to cite by way of explanation such synchronic correspondences as *phugeín: phuktós, lékhos: léktron,* etc. But in a case like *tríkhes: thriksí* there is a complication, the "passing" of *t* to *th*. The forms can be explained only historically, by relative chronology. The Proto-Greek theme *°thrikh,* followed by the ending –*si,* became *thriksí,* a very old development identical to the one that produced *léktron* from the root *lekh*–. Later every aspirate followed by another aspirate in the same word was changed into an occlusive, and *°thríkhes* became *tríkhes;* naturally *thriksi* escaped this law.

9. Conclusions

Linguistics here comes to its second bifurcation. We had first to choose between language and speaking; here we are again at the intersection of two roads, one leading to diachrony and the other to synchrony.

Once in possession of this double principle of classification, we can add that everything diachronic in language is diachronic only by virtue of speaking. It is in speaking that the germ of all change is found. Each change is launched by a certain number of individuals before it is accepted for general use. Modern German uses *ich war, wir waren,* whereas until the sixteenth century the conjugation was *ich was, wir waren* (cf. English *I was, we were*). How did the substitution of *war* for *was* come about? Some speakers, influenced by *waren,* created *war* through analogy; this was a fact of speaking; the new form, repeated many times and accepted by the community, became a fact of language. But not all innovations of speaking have the same success, and so long as they remain individual, they may be ignored, for we are studying language; they do not enter into our field of observation until the community of speakers has adopted them.

An evolutionary fact is always preceded by a fact, or rather by a multitude of similar facts, in the sphere of speaking. This in no way invalidates but rather strengthens the distinction made above since in the history of any innovation there are always two distinct moments: (1) when it sprang up in individual usage; and (2) when it became a fact of language, outwardly identical but adopted by the community.

The following table indicates the rational form that linguistic study should take:

$$(\text{Human})\,\text{Speech} \begin{cases} \text{Language} \begin{cases} \text{Synchrony} \\ \text{Diachrony} \end{cases} \\ \text{Speaking} \end{cases}$$

One must recognize that the ideal, theoretical form of a science is not always the one imposed upon it by the exigencies of practice; in linguistics these exigencies are more imperious than anywhere else; they account to some extent for the confusion that now predominates in linguistic research. Even if the distinctions set up here were accepted once and for all, a precise orientation probably could not be imposed on investigations in the name of the stated ideal.

In the synchronic study of Old French, for instance, the linguist works with facts and principles that have nothing in common with those that he would find out by tracing the history of the same language from the thirteenth to the twentieth century; on the contrary, he works with facts and principles similar to those that would be revealed in the description of an existing Bantu language, Attic Greek of 400 B.C. or present-day French, for that matter. These diverse descriptions would be based on similar relations; if each idiom is a closed system, all idioms embody certain fixed principles that the linguist meets again and again in passing from one to another, for he is staying in the same class. Historical study is no different. Whether the linguist examines a definite period in the history of French (for example, from the thirteenth to the twentieth century), Javanese, or any other language whatsoever, everywhere he works with similar facts which he needs only compare in order to establish the general truths of the diachronic class. The ideal would be for each scholar to devote himself to one field of investigation or the other and deal with the largest possible number of facts in this class; but it is very difficult to command scientifically such different languages. Against this, each language in practice forms a unit of study, and we are induced by force of circumstances to consider it alternately from the historical and static viewpoints. Above all else, we must never forget that this unit is superficial in theory, whereas the diversity of idioms hides a profound unity. Whichever way we look in studying a language, we must put each fact in its own class and not confuse the two methods.

The two parts of linguistics respectively, as defined, will be the object of our study.

Synchronic linguistics will be concerned with the logical and psychological relations that bind together coexisting terms and form a system in the collective mind of speakers.

Diachronic linguistics, on the contrary, will study relations that bind together successive terms not perceived by the collective mind but substituted for each other without forming a system.

PART TWO

Synchronic Linguistics

Chapter I: GENERALITIES

The aim of general synchronic linguistics is to set up the fundamental principles of any idiosynchronic system, the constituents of any language-state. Many of the items already explained in Part One belong rather to synchrony; for instance, the general properties of the sign are an integral part of synchrony although they were used to prove the necessity of separating the two linguistics.

To synchrony belongs everything called "general grammar," for it is only through language-states that the different relations which are the province of grammar are established. In the following chapters we shall consider only the basic principles necessary for approaching the more special problems of static linguistics or explaining in detail a language-state.

The study of static linguistics is generally much more difficult than the study of historical linguistics. Evolutionary facts are more concrete and striking; their observable relations tie together successive terms that are easily grasped; it is easy, often even amusing, to follow a series of changes. But the linguistics that penetrates values and coexisting relations presents much greater difficulties.

In practice a language-state is not a point but rather a certain span of time during which the sum of the modifications that have supervened is minimal. The span may cover ten years, a generation, a century, or even more. It is possible for a language to change hardly at all over a long span and then to undergo radical transformations within a few years. Of two languages that exist side by side during a given period, one may evolve drastically and the other practically not at all; study would have to be diachronic in the former instance, synchronic in the latter. An absolute state is defined by the absence of changes, and since language changes somewhat in spite of everything, studying a language-state means in practice disregarding changes of little importance, just as mathematicians disregard infinitesimal quantities in certain calculations, such as logarithms.

Political history makes a distinction between *era*, a point in time, and *period*, which embraces a certain duration. Still, the historian speaks of the Antoninian Era, the Era of the Crusades, etc. when he considers a set of characteristics which remained constant during those times. One might also say that static linguistics deals with eras. But *state* is preferable. The beginning and the end of an era are generally characterized by some rather brusque revolution that tends to modify the existing state of affairs. The word state avoids giving the impression that anything similar occurs in language. Besides, precisely because it is borrowed from history, the term era makes one think less of language itself than of the circumstances that surround it and condition it; in short, it suggests rather the idea of what we called external linguistics.

Besides, delimitation in time is not the only difficulty that we encounter in defining a language-state: space presents the same problem. In short, a concept of a language-state can be only approximate. In static linguistics, as in most sciences, no course of reasoning is possible without the usual simplification of data.

Chapter II: THE CONCRETE ENTITIES OF LANGUAGE

1.   Definition: Entity and Unit

The signs that make up language are not abstractions but real objects; signs and their relations are what linguistics studies; they are the *concrete entities* of our science.

Let us first recall two principles that dominate the whole issue:

1.   The linguistic entity exists only through the associating of the signifier with the signified. Whenever only one element is retained, the entity vanishes; instead of a concrete object we are faced with a mere abstraction. We constantly risk grasping

only a part of the entity and thinking that we are embracing it in its totality; this would happen, for example, if we divided the spoken chain into syllables, for the syllable has no value except in phonology. A succession of sounds is linguistic only if it supports an idea. Considered independently, it is material for a physiological study, and nothing more than that.

The same is true of the signified as soon as it is separated from its signifier. Considered independently, concepts like "house," "white," "see," etc. belong to psychology. They become linguistic entities only when associated with sound-images; in language, a concept is a quality of its phonic substance just as a particular slice of sound is a quality of the concept.

The two-sided linguistic unit has often been compared with the human person, made up of the body and the soul. The comparison is hardly satisfactory. A better choice would be a chemical compound like water, a combination of hydrogen and oxygen; taken separately, neither element has any of the properties of water.

2. The linguistic entity is not accurately defined until it is *delimited*, i.e. separated from everything that surrounds it on the phonic chain. These delimited entities or units stand in opposition to each other in the mechanism of language.

One is at first tempted to liken linguistic signs to visual signs, which can exist in space without becoming confused, and to assume that separation of the significant elements can be accomplished in the same way, without recourse to any mental process. The word "form," which is often used to indicate them (cf. the expression "verbal form," "noun form") gives support to the mistake. But we know that the main characteristic of the sound-chain is that it is linear. Considered by itself, it is only a line, a continuous ribbon along which the ear perceives no self-sufficient and clear-cut division; to divide the chain, we must call in meanings. When we hear an unfamiliar language, we are at a loss to say how the succession of sounds should be analyzed, for analysis is impossible if only the phonic side of the linguistic phenomenon is considered. But when we know the meaning and function that must be attributed to each part of the chain, we see the parts detach themselves from each other and the shapeless ribbon break into segments. Yet there is nothing material in the analysis.

To summarize: language does not offer itself as a set of pre-delimited signs that need only be studied according to their meaning and arrangement; it is a confused mass, and only attentiveness and familiarization will reveal its particular elements. The unit has no special phonic character, and the only definition that we can give it is this: it is *a slice of sound which to the exclusion of everything that precedes and follows it in the spoken chain is the signifier of a certain concept.*

2.   Method of Delimitation

One who knows a language singles out its units by a very simple method – in theory, at any rate. His method consists of using speaking as the source material of language and picturing it as two parallel chains, one of concepts (*A*) and the other of sound-images (*B*).

In an accurate delimitation, the division along the chain of sound-images (*a*, *b*, *c*) will correspond to the division along the chain of concepts (*a′*, *b′*, *c′*):

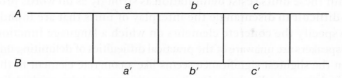

Take French *sižlaprã*. Can we cut the chain after *l* and make *sižl* a unit? No, we need only consider the concepts to see that the division is wrong. Neither is the syllabic division *siž-la-prã* to be taken for granted as having linguistic value. The only possible divisions are these: (1) *si-ž-la-prã* (*si je la prends* 'if I take it') and (2) *si-ž-l-aprã* (*si je l'apprends* 'if I learn it'), and they are determined by the meaning that is attached to the words.[8]

To verify the result of the procedure and be assured that we are really dealing with a unit, we must be able in comparing a series of sentences in which the same unit occurs to separate the unit from the rest of the context and find in each instance that meaning justifies the delimitation. Take the two French phrases *lafǫsdüvã* (la *force* du vent 'the *force* of the wind'), and *abudfǫrs* (à bout de *force* 'exhausted'; *literally:* 'at the end of one's *force*'). In each phrase the same concept coincides with the same phonic slice, *fǫrs;* thus it is certainly a linguistic unit. But in *ilməfǫrsaparle* (il me *force* à parler 'he *forces* me to talk') *fǫrs* has an entirely different meaning: it is therefore another unit.

3.   Practical Difficulties of Delimitation

The method outlined above is very simple in theory, but is it easy to apply? We are tempted to think so if we start from the notion that the units to be isolated are words. For what is a sentence except a combination of words? And what can be grasped more readily than words? Going back to the example given above, we may say that the analysis of the spoken chain *sižlaprã* resulted in the delimiting of four units, and that the units are words: *si-je-l-apprends*. But we are immediately put on the defensive on noting that there has been much disagreement about the nature of the word, and a little reflection shows that the usual meaning of the term is incompatible with the notion of concrete unit.

To be convinced, we need only think of French *cheval* 'horse' and its plural from *chevaux*. People readily say that they are two forms of the same word; but considered as wholes, they are certainly two distinct things with respect to both meaning and sound. In *mwa* (*mois*, as in le *mois* de Septembre 'the *month* of September') and *mwaz* (*mois*, in un *mois* après 'a *month* later') there are also two forms of the same word, and there is no question of a concrete unit. The meaning is the same, but the slices of sound are different. As soon as we try to liken concrete units to words, we face a dilemma: we must either ignore the relation – which is nonetheless evident – that binds *cheval* and *chevaux*, the two sounds of *mwa* and *mwaz*, etc. and say that they are different words, or instead of concrete units be satisfied with the abstraction that links the different forms of the same word. The concrete unit must be sought, not in the word, but elsewhere. Besides, many words are complex units, and we can easily single out their subunits (suffixes, prefixes, radicals). Derivatives like *pain-ful* and *delight-ful* can be divided into distinct parts, each having an obvious meaning and function. Conversely, some units are larger than words: compounds (French *porte-plume* 'penholder'), locutions (*s'il vous plaît* 'please'), inflected forms (*il a été* 'he has been'), etc. But these units resist delimitation as strongly as do words proper, making it extremely difficult to disentangle the interplay of units that are found in a sound-chain and to specify the concrete elements on which a language functions.

Doubtless speakers are unaware of the practical difficulties of delimiting units. Anything that is of even the slightest significance seems like a concrete element to them and they never fail to single it out in discourse. But it is one thing to feel the quick, delicate interplay of units and quite another to account for them through methodical analysis.

A rather widely held theory makes sentences the concrete units of language: we speak only in sentences and subsequently single out the words. But to what extent does the sentence belong to language? If it belongs to speaking, the sentence cannot pass for the linguistic unit. But let us suppose that this difficulty is set aside. If we picture to ourselves in their totality the sentences that could be uttered, their most striking characteristic is that in no way do they resemble each other. We are at first tempted to liken the immense diversity of sentences to the equal diversity of the individuals that make up a zoological species. But this is an illusion: the characteristics that animals of the same species have in common are much more significant than the differences that separate them. In sentences, on the contrary, diversity is dominant, and when we look for the link that bridges their diversity, again we find, without having looked for it, the word with its grammatical characteristics and thus fall back into the same difficulties as before.

4.   Conclusion

In most sciences the question of units never even arises: the units are delimited from the outset. In zoology, the animal immediately presents itself. Astronomy works with units that are separated in space, the stars. The chemist can study the nature and composition of potassium bichromate without doubting for an instant that this is a well-defined object.

When a science has no concrete units that are immediately recognizable, it is because they are not necessary. In history, for example, is the unit the individual, the era, or the nation? We do not know. But what does it matter? We can study history without knowing the answer.

But just as the game of chess is entirely in the combination of the different chess-pieces, language is characterized as a system based entirely on the opposition of its concrete units. We can neither dispense with becoming acquainted with them nor take a single step without coming back to them; and still, delimiting them is such a delicate problem that we may wonder at first whether they really exist.

Language then has the strange, striking characteristic of not having entities that are perceptible at the outset and yet of not permitting us to doubt that they exist and that their functioning constitutes it. Doubtless we have here a trait that distinguishes language from all other semiological institutions.

Chapter III: IDENTITIES, REALITIES, VALUES

The statement just made brings us squarely up against a problem that is all the more important because any basic notion in static linguistics depends directly on our conception of the unit and even blends with it. This is what I should like successively to demonstrate with respect to the notions of synchronic identity, reality, and value.

A. What is a synchronic *identity*? Here it is not a question of the identity that links the French negation *pas* 'not' to Latin *passum*, a diachronic identity that will be dealt with elsewhere, but rather of the equally interesting identity by virtue of which we state that two sentences like je ne sais *pas* 'I *don't* know' and ne dîtes *pas* cela '*don't* say that' contain the same element. An idle question, one might say; there is identity because the same slice of sound carries the same meaning in the two sentences. But that explanation is unsatisfactory, for if the correspondence of slices of sound and concepts is proof of identity (see above, la *force* du vent: à bout de *force*), the reverse is not true. There can be identity without this correspondence. When *Gentlemen*! is repeated several times during a lecture, the listener has the feeling that the same expression is being used each time, and yet variations in utterance and intonation make for appreciable phonic differences in diverse contexts – differences just as appreciable as those that elsewhere separate different words (cf. French *pomme* 'apple' and *paume* 'palm,' *goutte* 'drop' and *je goute* 'I taste,' *fuir* 'flee,' and *fouir* 'stuff,' etc.);[9] besides, the feeling of identity persists even though there is no absolute identity between one *Gentlemen!* and the next from a semantic viewpoint either. In the same vein, a word can express quite different ideas without compromising its identity (cf. French *adopter* une mode '*adopt* a fashion' and *adopter* un enfant '*adopt* a child,' la *fleur* du pommier 'the *flower* of the apple tree' and la *fleur* de la noblesse 'the *flower* of nobility,' etc.).

The linguistic mechanism is geared to differences and identities, the former being only the counterpart of the latter. Everywhere then, the problem of identities appears; moreover, it blends partially with the problem of entities and units and is only a complication – illuminating at some points – of the larger problem. This characteristic stands out if we draw some comparisons with facts taken from outside speech. For instance, we speak of the identity of two "8:25 p.m. Geneva-to-Paris" trains that leave at twenty-four hour intervals. We feel that it is the same train each day, yet everything – the locomotive, coaches, personnel – is probably different. Or if a street is demolished, then rebuilt, we say that it is the same street even though in a material sense, perhaps nothing of the old one remains. Why can a street be completely rebuilt and still be the same? Because it does not constitute a purely material entity; it is based on certain conditions that are distinct from the materials that fit the conditions, e.g. its location with respect to other streets. Similarly, what makes the express is its hour of departure, its route, and in general every circumstance that sets it apart from other trains. Whenever the same conditions are fulfilled, the same entities are obtained. Still, the entities are not abstract since we cannot conceive of a street or train outside its material realization.

Let us contrast the preceding examples with the completely different case of a suit which has been stolen from me and which I find in the window of a second-hand store. Here we have a material entity that consists solely of the inert substance – the cloth, its lining, its trimmings, etc. Another suit would not be mine regardless of its similarity to it. But linguistic identity is not that of the garment; it is that of the train and the street. Each time I say the word *Gentlemen!* I renew its substance; each utterance is a new phonic act and a new psychological act. The bond between the two uses of the same word depends neither on material identity nor on sameness in meaning but on elements which must be sought after and which will point up the true nature of linguistic units.

B. What is a synchronic *reality*? To what concrete or abstract elements of language can the name be applied?

Take as an example the distinction between the parts of speech. What supports the classing of words as substantives, adjectives, etc.? Is it done in the name of a purely logical, extra-linguistic principle that is applied to grammar from without like the degrees of longitude and latitude on the globe? Or does it correspond to something that has its place in the system of language and is conditioned by it? In a word, is it a synchronic reality? The second supposition seems probable, but the first could also be defended. In the French sentence *ces gants sont bon marché* 'these gloves are cheap,' is *bon marché* an adjective? It is apparently an adjective from a logical viewpoint but not from the viewpoint of grammar, for *bon marché* fails to behave as an adjective (it is invariable, it never precedes its noun, etc.); in addition, it is composed of two words. Now the distinction between parts of speech is exactly what should serve to classify the words of language. How can a group of words be attributed to one of the "parts"? But to say that *bon* 'good' is an adjective and *marché* 'market' a substantive explains nothing. We are then dealing with a defective or incomplete classification; the division of words into substantives, verbs, adjectives, etc. is not an undeniable linguistic reality.[10]

Linguistics accordingly works continuously with concepts forged by grammarians without knowing whether or not the concepts actually correspond to the constituents of the system of language. But how can we find out? And if they are phantoms, what realities can we place in opposition to them?

To be rid of illusions we must first be convinced that the concrete entities of language are not directly accessible. If we try to grasp them, we come into contact with the true facts. Starting from there, we can set up all the classifications that linguistics needs for arranging all the facts at its disposal. On the other hand, to base the classifications on anything except concrete entities – to say, for example, that the parts of speech are the constituents of language simply because they correspond to categories of logic – is to forget that there are no linguistic facts apart from the phonic substance cut into significant elements.

C. Finally, not every idea touched upon in this chapter differs basically from what we have elsewhere called *values*. A new comparison with the set of chessmen will bring out this point. Take a knight, for instance. By itself is it an element in the game? Certainly not, for by its material make-up – outside its square and the other conditions of the game – it means nothing to the player; it becomes a real, concrete element only when endowed with value and wedded to it. Suppose that the piece happens to be destroyed or lost during a game. Can it be replaced by an equivalent piece? Certainly. Not only another knight but even a figure shorn of any resemblance to a knight can be declared identical provided the same value is attributed to it. We see then that in semiological systems like language, where elements hold each other in equilibrium in accordance with fixed rules, the notion of identity blends with that of value and *vice versa*.

In a word, that is why the notion of value envelops the notions of unit, concrete entity, and reality. But if there is no fundamental difference between these diverse notions, it follows that the problem can be stated successively in several ways. Whether we try to define the unit, reality, concrete entity, or value, we always come back to the central question that dominates all of static linguistics.

It would be interesting from a practical viewpoint to begin with units, to determine what they are and to account for their diversity by classifying them. It would be necessary to search for the reason for dividing language into words – for in spite of the difficulty of defining it, the word is a unit that strikes the mind, something central in the mechanism of language – but that is a subject which by itself would fill a volume. Next we would have to classify the subunits, then the larger units, etc. By determining in this way the elements that it manipulates, synchronic linguistics would completely fulfill its task, for it would relate all synchronic phenomena to their fundamental principle. It cannot be said that this basic problem has ever been faced squarely or that its scope and difficulty have been understood; in the matter of language, people have always been satisfied with ill-defined units.

Still, in spite of their capital importance, it is better to approach the problem of units through the study of value, for in my opinion value is of prime importance.

Chapter IV: LINGUISTIC VALUE

1.   Language as Organized Thought Coupled with Sound

To prove that language is only a system of pure values, it is enough to consider the two elements involved in its functioning: ideas and sounds.

Psychologically our thought – apart from its expression in words – is only a shapeless and indistinct mass. Philosophers and linguists have always agreed in recognizing that without the help of signs we would be unable to make a clear-cut, consistent distinction between two ideas. Without language, thought is a vague, uncharted nebula. There are no pre-existing ideas, and nothing is distinct before the appearance of language.

Against the floating realm of thought, would sounds by themselves yield predelimited entities? No more so than ideas. Phonic substance is neither more fixed nor more rigid than thought; it is not a mold into which thought must of necessity fit but a plastic substance divided in turn into distinct parts to furnish the signifiers needed by thought. The linguistic fact can therefore be pictured in its totality – i.e. language – as a series of contiguous subdivisions marked off on both the indefinite plane of jumbled ideas (*A*) and the equally vague plane of sounds (*B*). The following diagram gives a rough idea of it:

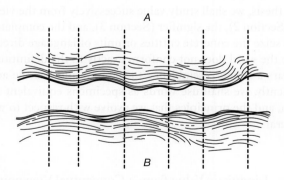

The characteristic role of language with respect to thought is not to create a material phonic means for expressing ideas but to serve as a link between thought and sound, under conditions that of necessity bring about the reciprocal delimitations of units. Thought, chaotic by nature, has to become ordered in the process of its decomposition. Neither are thoughts given material form nor are sounds transformed into mental entities; the somewhat mysterious fact is rather that "thought-sound" implies division, and that language works out its units while taking shape between two shapeless masses. Visualize the air in contact with a sheet of water; if the atmospheric pressure changes, the surface of the water will be broken up into a series of divisions, waves; the waves resemble the union or coupling of thought with phonic substance.

Language might be called the domain of articulations, using the word as it was defined earlier. Each linguistic term is a member, an *articulus* in which an idea is fixed in a sound and a sound becomes the sign of an idea.

Language can also be compared with a sheet of paper: thought is the front and the sound the back; one cannot cut the front without cutting the back at the same time; likewise in language, one can neither divide sound from thought nor thought from sound; the division could be accomplished only abstractedly, and the result would be either pure psychology or pure phonology.

Linguistics then works in the borderland where the elements of sound and thought combine; *their combination produces a form, not a substance*.

These views give a better understanding of what was said before about the arbitrariness of signs. Not only are the two domains that are linked by the linguistic fact shapeless and confused, but the choice of a given slice of sound to name a given idea is completely arbitrary. If this were not true, the notion of value would be compromised, for it would include an externally imposed element. But actually values remain entirely relative, and that is why the bond between the sound and the idea is radically arbitrary.

The arbitrary nature of the sign explains in turn why the social fact alone can create a linguistic system. The community is necessary if values that owe their existence solely to usage and general acceptance are to be set up; by himself the individual is incapable of fixing a single value.

In addition, the idea of value, as defined, shows that to consider a term as simply the union of a certain sound with a certain concept is grossly misleading. To define it in this way would isolate the term from its system; it would mean assuming that one can start from the terms and construct the system by adding them together when, on the contrary, it is from the interdependent whole that one must start and through analysis obtain its elements.

To develop this thesis, we shall study value successively from the viewpoint of the signified or concept (Section 2), the signifier (Section 3), and the complete sign (Section 4).

Being unable to seize the concrete entities or units of language directly, we shall work with words. While the word does not conform exactly to the definition of the linguistic unit, it at least bears a rough resemblance to the unit and has the advantage of being concrete; consequently, we shall use words as specimens equivalent to real terms in a synchronic system, and the principles that we evolve with respect to words will be valid for entities in general.

2.   Linguistic Value from a Conceptual Viewpoint

When we speak of the value of a word, we generally think first of its property of standing for an idea, and this is in fact one side of linguistic value. But if this is true, how does *value* differ from *signification*? Might the two words be synonyms? I think not, although it is easy to confuse them, since the confusion results not so much from their similarity as from the subtlety of the distinction that they mark.

From a conceptual viewpoint, value is doubtless one element in signification, and it is difficult to see how signification can be dependent upon value and still be distinct from it. But we must clear up the issue or risk reducing language to a simple naming-process.

Let us first take signification as it is generally understood and as it was pictured above. As the arrows in the drawing show, it is only the counterpart of the sound-image.

Everything that occurs concerns only the sound–image and the concept when we look upon the word as independent and self-contained.

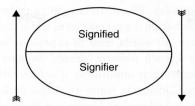

But here is the paradox: on the one hand the concept seems to be the counterpart of the sound–image, and on the other hand the sign itself is in turn the counterpart of the other signs of language.

Language is a system of interdependent terms in which the value of each term results solely from the simultaneous presence of the others, as in the diagram:

How, then, can value be confused with signification, i.e. the counterpart of the sound–image? It seems impossible to liken the relations represented here by horizontal arrows to those represented above by vertical arrows. Putting it another way – and again taking up the example of the sheet of paper that is cut in two – it is clear that the observable relation between the different pieces A, B, C, D, etc. is distinct from the relation between the front and back of the same piece as in A/A′, B/B′, etc.

To resolve the issue, let us observe from the outset that even outside language all values are apparently governed by the same paradoxical principle. They are always composed:

1. of a *dissimilar* thing that can be *exchanged* for the thing of which the value is to be determined; and
2. of *similar* things that can be *compared* with the thing of which the value is to be determined.

Both factors are necessary for the existence of a value. To determine what a five-franc piece is worth one must therefore know: (1) that it can be exchanged for a fixed quantity of a different thing, e.g. bread; and (2) that it can be compared with a similar value of the same system, e.g. a one-franc piece, or with coins of another system (a dollar, etc.). In the same way a word can be exchanged for something dissimilar, an idea; besides, it can be compared with something of the same nature, another word. Its value is therefore not fixed so long as one simply states that it can be "exchanged" for a given concept, i.e. that it has this or that signification: one must also compare it with similar values, with other words that stand in opposition to it. Its content is really fixed only by the concurrence of everything that exists outside it. Being part of a system, it is endowed not only with a signification but also and especially with a value, and this is something quite different.

A few examples will show clearly that this is true. Modern French *mouton* can have the same signification as English *sheep* but not the same value, and this for several reasons, particularly because in speaking of a piece of meat ready to be served on the table, English uses *mutton* and not *sheep*. The difference in value between *sheep* and *mouton* is due to the fact that *sheep* has beside it a second term while the French word does not.

Within the same language, all words used to express related ideas limit each other reciprocally; synonyms like French *redouter* 'dread,' *craindre* 'fear,' and *avoir peur* 'be afraid' have value only through their opposition: if *redouter* did not exist, all its content would go to its competitors. Conversely, some words are enriched through contact with others: e.g. the new element introduced in *décrépit* (un vieillard *décrépit*) results from the co-existence of *décrépi* (un mur *décrépi*). The value of just any term is accordingly determined by its environment; it is impossible to fix even the value of the word signifying "sun" without first considering its surroundings: in some languages it is not possible to say "sit in the *sun*."

Everything said about words applies to any term of language, e.g. to grammatical entities. The value of a French plural does not coincide with that of a Sanskrit plural even though their signification is usually identical; Sanskrit has three numbers instead of two (*my eyes, my ears, my arms, my legs*, etc. are dual);[11] it would be wrong to attribute the same value to the plural in Sanskrit and in French; its value clearly depends on what is outside and around it.

If words stood for pre-existing concepts, they would all have exact equivalents in meaning from one language to the next; but this is not true. French uses *louer* (*une maison*) 'let (a house)' indifferently to mean both "pay for" and "receive payment for," whereas German uses two words, *mieten* and *vermieten*; there is obviously no exact correspondence of values. The German verbs *schätzen* and *urteilen* share a number of significations, but that correspondence does not hold at several points.

Inflection offers some particularly striking examples. Distinctions of time, which are so familiar to us, are unknown in certain languages. Hebrew does not recognize even the fundamental distinctions between the past, present, and future. Proto-Germanic has no special form for the future; to say that the future is expressed by the present is wrong, for the value of the present is not the same in Germanic as in languages that have a future along with the present. The Slavic languages regularly single out two aspects of the verb: the perfective represents action as a point, complete in its totality; the imperfective represents it as taking place, and on the line of time. The categories are difficult for a Frenchman to understand, for they are unknown in French; if they were pre-determined, this would not be true. Instead of pre-existing ideas then, we find in all the foregoing examples *values* emanating from the system. When they are said to correspond to concepts, it is understood that the concepts are purely differential and defined not by their positive content but negatively by their relations with the other terms of the system. Their most precise characteristic is in being what the others are not.

Now the real interpretation of the diagram of the signal becomes apparent. Thus

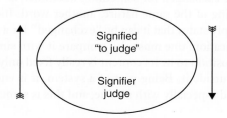

means that in French the concept "to judge" is linked to the sound-image *juger*; in short, it symbolizes signification. But it is quite clear that initially the concept is nothing, that is only a value determined by its relations with other similar values, and that without them the signification would not exist. If I state simply that a word signifies something when I have in mind the associating of a sound-image with a concept, I am making a statement that may suggest what actually happens, but by no means am I expressing the linguistic fact in its essence and fullness.

3.   Linguistic Value from a Material Viewpoint

The conceptual side of value is made up solely of relations and differences with respect to the other terms of language, and the same can be said of its material side. The important thing in the word is not the sound alone but the phonic differences that make it possible to distinguish this word from all others, for differences carry signification.

This may seem surprising, but how indeed could the reverse be possible? Since one vocal image is no better suited than the next for what it is commissioned to express, it is evident, even *a priori*, that a segment of language can never in the final analysis be based on anything except its noncoincidence with the rest. *Arbitrary* and *differential* are two correlative qualities.

The alteration of linguistic signs clearly illustrates this. It is precisely because the terms *a* and *b* as such are radically incapable of reaching the level of consciousness – one is always conscious of only the *a/b* difference – that each term is free to change according to laws that are unrelated to its signifying function. No positive sign characterizes the genitive plural in Czech *žen*; still the two forms *žena: žen* function as well as the earlier forms *žena: ženb; žen* has value only because it is different.

Here is another example that shows even more clearly the systematic role of phonic differences: in Greek, *éphēn* is an imperfect and *éstēn* an aorist although both words are formed in the same way; the first belongs to the system of the present indicative of *phēmí* 'I say,' whereas there is no present **stēmi;* now it is precisely the relation *phēmí: éphēn* that corresponds to the relation between the present and the imperfect (cf. *déiknūmi: edéiknūn,* etc.). Signs function, then, not through their intrinsic value but through their relative position.

In addition, it is impossible for sound alone, a material element, to belong to language. It is only a secondary thing, substance to be put to use. All our conventional values have the characteristic of not being confused with the tangible element which supports them. For instance, it is not the metal in a piece of money that fixes its value. A coin nominally worth five francs may contain less than half its worth of silver. Its value will vary according to the amount stamped upon it and according to its use inside or outside a political boundary. This is even more true of the linguistic signifier, which is not phonic but incorporeal – constituted not by its material substance but by the differences that separate its sound–image from all others.

The foregoing principle is so basic that it applies to all the material elements of language, including phonemes. Every language forms its words on the basis of a system of sonorous elements, each element being a clearly delimited unit and one of a fixed number of units. Phonemes are characterized not, as one might think, by their own positive quality but simply by the fact that they are distinct. Phonemes are above all else opposing, relative, and negative entities.

Proof of this is the latitude that speakers have between points of convergence in the pronunciation of distinct sounds. In French, for instance, general use of a dorsal *r* does not prevent many speakers from using a tongue–tip trill; language is not in the least disturbed by it; language requires only that the sound be different and not, as one might imagine, that it have an invariable quality. I can even pronounce the French *r* like German *ch* in *Bach*, *doch*, etc., but in German I could not use *r* instead of *ch*, for German gives recognition to both elements and must keep them apart. Similarly, in Russian there is no latitude for *t* in the direction of *t′* (palatalized *t*), for the result would be the confusing of two sounds differentiated by the language (cf. *govorit′* 'speak' and *goverit* 'he speaks'), but more freedom may be taken with respect to *th* (aspirated *t*) since this sound does not figure in the Russian system of phonemes.

Since an identical state of affairs is observable in writing, another system of signs, we shall use writing to draw some comparisons that will clarify the whole issue. In fact:

1. The signs used in writing are arbitrary; there is no connection, for example, between the letter *t* and the sound that it designates.
2. The value of letters is purely negative and differential. The same person can write *t*, for instance, in different ways:

The only requirement is that the sign for *t* not be confused in his script with the signs used for *l*, *d*, etc.
3. Values in writing function only through reciprocal opposition within a fixed system that consists of a set number of letters. This third characteristic, though not identical to the second, is closely related to it, for both depend on the first. Since the graphic sign is arbitrary, its form matters little or rather matters only within the limitations imposed by the system.
4. The means by which the sign is produced is completely unimportant, for it does not affect the system (this also follows from characteristic 1). Whether I make the letters in white or black, raised or engraved, with pen or chisel – all this is of no importance with respect to their signification.

4.   The Sign Considered in Its Totality

Everything that has been said up to this point boils down to this: in language there are only differences. Even more important: a difference generally implies positive terms between which the difference is set up; but in language there are only differences *without positive terms*. Whether we take the signified or the signifier, language has neither ideas nor sounds that existed before the linguistic system, but only conceptual and phonic differences that have issued from the system. The idea or phonic substance that a sign contains is of less importance than the other signs that surround it. Proof of this is that the value of a term may be modified without either its meaning or its sound being affected, solely because a neighboring term has been modified.

But the statement that everything in language is negative is true only if the signified and the signifier are considered separately; when we consider the sign in its totality, we have something that is positive in its own class. A linguistic system is a series of differences of sound combined with a series of differences of ideas; but the pairing of a certain number of acoustical signs with as many cuts made from the mass of thought engenders a system of values; and this system serves as the effective link between the phonic and psychological elements within each sign. Although both the signified and the signifier are purely differential and negative when considered separately, their combination is a positive fact; it is even the sole type of facts that language has, for maintaining the parallelism between the two classes of differences is the distinctive function of the linguistic institution.

Certain diachronic facts are typical in this respect. Take the countless instances where alteration of the signifier occasions a conceptual change and where it is obvious that the sum of the ideas distinguished corresponds in principle to the sum of the distinctive signs. When two words are confused through phonetic alteration (e.g. French *décrépit* from *dēcrepitus* and *décrépi* from *crispus*), the ideas that they express will also tend to become confused if only they have something in common. Or a word may have different forms (cf. *chaise* 'chair' and *chaire* 'desk'). Any nascent difference will tend invariably to become significant but without always succeeding or being successful on the first trial. Conversely, any conceptual difference perceived by the mind seeks to find expression through a distinct signifier, and two ideas that are no longer distinct in the mind tend to merge into the same signifier.

When we compare signs – positive terms – with each other, we can no longer speak of difference; the expression would not be fitting, for it applies only to the comparing of two sound-images, e.g. *father* and *mother*, or two ideas, e.g. the idea "father" and the idea "mother"; two signs, each having a signified and signifier, are not different but only distinct. Between them there is only *opposition*. The entire mechanism of language, with which we shall be concerned later, is based on oppositions of this kind and on the phonic and conceptual differences that they imply.

What is true of value is true also of the unit. A unit is a segment of the spoken chain that corresponds to a certain concept; both are by nature purely differential.

Applied to units, the principle of differentiation can be stated in this way: *the characteristics of the unit blend with the unit itself*. In language, as in any semiological system, whatever distinguishes one sign from the others constitutes it. Difference makes character just as it makes value and the unit.

Another rather paradoxical consequence of the same principle is this: in the last analysis what is commonly referred to as a "grammatical fact" fits the definition of the unit, for it always expresses an opposition of terms; it differs only in that the opposition is particularly significant (e.g. the formation of German plurals of the type *Nacht: Nächte*). Each term present in the grammatical fact (the singular without umlaut or final *e* in opposition to the plural with umlaut and -*e*) consists of the interplay of a number of oppositions within the system. When isolated, neither *Nacht* nor *Nächte* is anything: thus everything is opposition. Putting it another way, the *Nacht: Nächte* relation can be expressed by an algebraic formula a/b in which a and b are not simple terms but result from a set of relations. Language, in a manner of speaking, is a type of algebra consisting solely of complex terms. Some of its oppositions are more significant than others; but units and grammatical facts are only different names for designating diverse aspects of the same general fact: the functioning of linguistic oppositions. This statement is so true that we might very well approach the problem of units by starting from grammatical facts. Taking an opposition like *Nacht: Nächte*, we might ask what are the units involved in it. Are they only the two words, the whole series of similar words, *a* and *ä*, or all singulars and plurals, etc.?

Units and grammatical facts would not be confused if linguistic signs were made up of something besides differences. But language being what it is, we shall find nothing simple in it regardless of our approach; everywhere and always there is the same complex equilibrium of terms that mutually condition each other. Putting it another way, *language is a form and not a substance*. This truth could not be overstressed, for all the mistakes in our terminology, all our incorrect ways of naming things that pertain to language, stem from the involuntary supposition that the linguistic phenomenon must have substance.

Chapter V: SYNTAGMATIC AND ASSOCIATIVE RELATIONS

1.   Definitions

In a language-state everything is based on relations. How do they function?

Relations and differences between linguistic terms fall into two distinct groups, each of which generates a certain class of values. The opposition between the two classes gives a better understanding of the nature of each class. They correspond to two forms of our mental activity, both indispensable to the life of language.

In discourse, on the one hand, words acquire relations based on the linear nature of language because they are chained together. This rules out the possibility of pronouncing two elements simultaneously. The elements are arranged in sequence on the chain of speaking. Combinations supported by linearity are *syntagms*.[12] The syntagm is always composed of two or more consecutive units (e.g. French *re-lire* 're-read,' *contre tous* 'against everyone,' *la vie humaine* 'human life,' *Dieu est bon* 'God is good,' *s'il fait beau temps, nous sortirons* 'if the weather is nice, we'll go out,' etc.). In the syntagm a term acquires its value only because it stands in opposition to everything that precedes or follows it, or to both.

Outside discourse, on the other hand, words acquire relations of a different kind. Those that have something in common are associated in the memory, resulting in groups marked by diverse relations. For instance, the French word *enseignement* 'teaching' will unconsciously call to mind a host of other words (*enseigner* 'teach,' *renseigner* 'acquaint,' etc.; or *armement* 'armament,' *changement* 'amendment,' etc.; or *éducation* 'education,' *apprentissage* 'apprenticeship,' etc.). All those words are related in some way.

We see that the co-ordinations formed outside discourse differ strikingly from those formed inside discourse. Those formed outside discourse are not supported by linearity. Their seat is in the brain; they are a part of the inner storehouse that makes up the language of each speaker. They are *associative relations*.

The syntagmatic relation is *in praesentia*. It is based on two or more terms that occur in an effective series. Against this, the associative relation unites terms *in absentia* in a potential mnemonic series.

From the associative and syntagmatic viewpoint a linguistic unit is like a fixed part of a building, e.g. a column. On the one hand, the column has a certain relation to the architrave that it supports; the arrangement of the two units in space suggests the syntagmatic relation. On the other hand, if the column is Doric, it suggests a mental comparison of this style with others (Ionic, Corinthian, etc.) although none of these elements is present in space: the relation is associative.

Each of the two classes of co-ordination calls for some specific remarks.

2.   Syntagmatic Relations

The examples above have already indicated that the notion of syntagm applies not only to words but to groups of words, to complex units of all lengths and types (compounds, derivatives, phrases, whole sentences).

It is not enough to consider the relation that ties together the different parts of syntagms (e.g. French *contre* 'against' and *tous* 'everyone' in *contre tous*, *contre* and *maître* 'master' in *contremaître* 'foreman');[13] one must also bear in mind the relation that links the whole to its parts (e.g. *contre tous* in opposition on the one hand to *contre* and on the other *tous*, or *contremaître* in opposition to *contre* and *maître*).

An objection might be raised at this point. The sentence is the ideal type of syntagm. But it belongs to speaking, not to language. Does it not follow that the syntagm belongs to speaking? I do not think so. Speaking is characterized by freedom of combinations; one must therefore ask whether or not all syntagms are equally free.

It is obvious from the first that many expressions belong to language. These are the pat phrases in which any change is prohibited by usage, even if we can single out their meaningful elements (cf. *à quoi bon?* 'what's the use?' *allons donc!* 'nonsense!'). The same is true, though to a lesser degree, of expressions like *prendre la mouche* 'take offense easily,'[14] *forcer la main à quelqu'un* 'force someone's hand,' *rompre une lance* 'break a lance,'[15] or even *avoir mal (à la tête*, etc.) 'have (a headache, etc.),' *à force de (soins*, etc.) 'by dint of (care, etc.),' *que vous en semble?* 'how do you feel about it?' *pas n'est besoin de* … 'there's no need for …,' etc., which are characterized by peculiarities of signification or syntax. These idiomatic twists cannot be improvised; they are furnished by tradition. There are also words which, while lending themselves perfectly to analysis, are characterized by some morphological anomaly that is kept solely by dint of usage (cf. *difficulté* 'difficulty' beside *facilité* 'facility,' etc., and *mourrai* '[I] shall die' beside *dormirai* '[I] shall sleep').[16]

There are further proofs. To language rather than to speaking belong the syntagmatic types that are built upon regular forms. Indeed, since there is nothing abstract in language, the types exist only if language has registered a sufficient number of specimens. When a word like *indécorable* arises in speaking, its appearance supposes a fixed type, and this type is in turn possible only through remembrance of a sufficient number of similar words belonging to language (*impardonable* 'unpardonable,' *intolérable* 'intolerable,' *infatigable* 'indefatigable,' etc.). Exactly the same is true of sentences and groups of words built upon regular patterns. Combinations like *la terre tourne* 'the world turns,' *que vous dit-il?* 'what does he say to you?' etc. correspond to general types that are in turn supported in the language by concrete remembrances.

But we must realize that in the syntagm there is no clear-cut boundary between the language fact, which is a sign of collective usage, and the fact that belongs to speaking and depends on individual freedom. In a great number of instances it is hard to class a combination of units because both forces have combined in producing it, and they have combined in indeterminable proportions.

3.   Associative Relations

Mental association creates other groups besides those based on the comparing of terms that have something in common; through its grasp of the nature of the relations that bind the terms together, the mind creates as many associative series as there are diverse relations. For instance, in *enseignement* 'teaching,' *enseigner* 'teach,' *enseignons* '(we) teach,' etc., one element, the radical, is common to every term; the same word may occur in a different series formed around another common element, the suffix (cf. *enseignement, armement, changement*, etc.); or the association may spring from the analogy of the concepts signified (*enseignement, instruction, apprentissage, éducation*, etc.); or again, simply from the similarity of the sound-images (e.g. *enseignement* and *justement* 'precisely').[17] Thus there is at times a double similarity of meaning and form, at times similarity only of form or of meaning. A word can always evoke everything that can be associated with it in one way or another.

Whereas a syntagm immediately suggests an order of succession and a fixed number of elements, terms in an associative family occur neither in fixed numbers nor in a definite order. If we associate *painful, delightful, frightful*, etc. we are unable to predict the number of words that the memory will suggest or the order in which they will appear. A particular word is like the center of a constellation; it is the point of convergence of an indefinite number of co-ordinated terms (see the illustration below).

But of the two characteristics of the associative series – indeterminate order and indefinite number – only the first can always be verified; the second may fail to meet the test. This happens in the case of inflectional paradigms, which are typical of associative groupings. Latin *dominus, dominī, dominō*, etc. is obviously an associative group formed around a common element, the noun theme *domin–*, but the series[18]

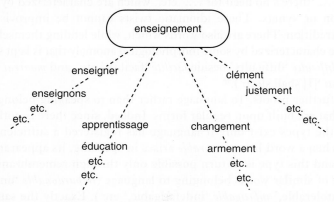

[18] **The last case is rare and can be classed as abnormal, for the mind naturally**

is not indefinite as in the case of *enseignement, changement*, etc.; the number of cases is definite. Against this, the words have no fixed order of succession, and it is by a purely arbitrary act that the grammarian groups them in one way rather than in another; in the mind of speakers the nominative case is by no means the first one in the declension, and the order in which terms are called depends on circumstances.

Notes

1 The term sound-image may seem to be too restricted inasmuch as beside the representation of the sounds of a word there is also that of its articulation, the muscular image of the phonational act. But for F. de Saussure language is essentially a depository, a thing received from without. The sound-image is par excellence the natural representation of the word as a fact of potential language, outside any actual use of it in speaking. The motor side is thus implied or, in any event, occupies only a subordinate role with respect to the sound-image. [Ed.]

2 Cf. English *goodness!* and *zounds!* (from *God's wounds*). [Tr.]

3 It would be wrong to reproach F. de Saussure for being illogical or paradoxical in attributing two contradictory qualities to language. By opposing two striking terms, he wanted only to emphasize the fact that language changes in spite of the inability of speakers to change it. One can also say that it is intangible but not unchangeable. [Ed.]

4 From May to July of 1911, Saussure used interchangeably the old terminology (*idea* and *sign*) and the new (*signified* and *signifier*). [Tr.]

5 According to Meillet (*Mem. de la Soc. de Ling.*, IX, pp. 365 ff.) and Gauthiot (*La fin du mot indo-européen*, pp. 158 ff.), final *–m* did not exist in Proto-Indo-European, which used only *–n;* if this theory is accepted, Law 5 can be stated in this way: Greek preserved every final *–n;* its demonstrative value is not diminished since the phonetic phenomenon that results in the preservation of a former state is the same in nature as the one that manifests a change. [Ed.]

6 Of course the examples cited above are purely schematic: linguistics is right in trying currently to relate to the same initial principle the largest possible series of phonetic changes; for instance, Meillet explains all the transformations of Greek occlusives by progressive weakening of their articulation (see *Mem. de la Soc. de Ling.*, IX, pp. 163 ff.). Naturally the conclusions on the nature of phonetic changes are in the last analysis applicable to these general facts, wherever they exist. [Ed.]

7 This generally accepted theory has been recently but, we believe, unsuccessfully attacked by M. E. Larch (*Das invariable Participium praesentis*, Erlangen, 1913); there was then no reason for eliminating an example that would retain its didactic value. [Ed.]

8 Cf. the sounds [jurmaın] in English: "your mine" or "you're mine." [Tr.]

9 Cf. English *bought: boat, naught: note, far: for: four* (for many speakers). [Tr.]

10 Form, function, and meaning combine to make the classing of the parts of speech even more difficult in English than in French. Cf. *ten-foot: ten feet* in a *ten-foot pole: the pole is ten feet long*. [Tr.]

11 The use of the comparative form for two and the superlative for more than two in English (e.g. *may the* better *boxer win: the* best *boxer in the world*) is probably a remnant of the old distinction between the dual and the plural number. [Tr.]

12 It is scarcely necessary to point out that the study of *syntagms* is not to be confused with syntax. Syntax is only one part of the study of syntagms. [Ed.]

13 Cf. English *head* and *waiter* in *headwaiter*. [Tr.]

14 Literally 'take the fly.' Cf. English *take the bull by the horns*. [Tr.]

15 Cf. English *bury the hatchet*. [Tr.]

16 The anomaly of the double *r* in the future forms of certain verbs in French may be compared to irregular plurals like *oxen* in English. [Tr.]

17 The last case is rare and can be classed as abnormal, for the mind naturally discards associations that becloud the intelligibility of discourse. But its existence is proved by a lower category of puns based on the ridiculous confusions that can result from pure and simple homonymy like the French statement: "Les musiciens produisent les *sons* ['sounds, bran'] et les grainetiers les vendent" 'musicians produce *sons* and seedsmen sell them.' [Cf. Shakespeare's "Not on thy *sole*, but on thy *soul*." (Tr.)] This is distinct from the case where an association, while fortuitous, is supported by a comparison of ideas (cf. French *ergot* 'spur': *ergoter* 'wrangle'; German *blau* 'blue': *durchblauen* 'thrash soundly'); the point is that one member of the pair has a new interpretation. Folk etymologies like these are of interest in the study of semantic evolution, but from the synchronic viewpoint they are in the same category as *enseigner: enseignement*. [Ed.]

18 Cf. English *education* and the corresponding associative series: *educate, educates*, etc.; *internship, training*, etc.; *vocation, devotion*, etc.; and *lotion, fashion*, etc. [Tr.]

CHAPTER 4

The Structural Study of Myth

Claude Lévi-Strauss

Claude Lévi-Strauss is largely responsible for the rise of Structuralism in France in the post-World War II era. In such highly influential books as *Tristes Tropiques* (1956) and *Structuralist Anthropology* (1958), he developed a description of human society and of human culture that underscored its systematic character and its similarity to the structure of language. In this famous essay, he argues that human myths, when studied for their similar structural elements, reflect a universal concern for resolving cognitive issues in human life. Humans are natural animals, but they are also capable of ideation and the creation of culture. How can humans reconcile those two very different "origins" of human life – one seemingly earthly, the other human? Myths, according to Lévi-Strauss, are ways of achieving cognitive reconciliation. Lévi-Strauss's method owes a great deal to Hegel and Marx's method of dialectics, whereby elements in contradiction with one another are resolved through their mediation as a third term that retains elements of each, and he could be criticized for forcing his evidence to conform to the dialectical model. A more evolutionary anthropological approach, for example, would see the Oedipus story as concerning the danger of harming the social institutions humans developed to quell harmful violence and conflict so that survival could be assured more widely in the human population. The story has more to do with safeguarding the newly invented ideal of civility than with reconciling earthly origins with human ones.

"It would seem that mythological worlds have been built up only to be shattered again, and that new worlds were built from the fragments."

– Franz Boas[1]

Despite some recent attempts to renew them, it seems that during the past twenty years anthropology has increasingly turned from studies in the field of religion. At the same time, and precisely because the interest of professional anthropologists has withdrawn from primitive religion, all kinds of amateurs who claim to belong to other disciplines have seized this opportunity to move in, thereby turning into their private playground

Original publication details: Claude Levi–Strauss, "The Structural Study of Myth" from *Structural Anthropology*, pp. 206–231. Basic Books, 1963. Reproduced with permission from Basic Books.

Literary Theory: An Anthology, Third Edition. Edited by Julie Rivkin and Michael Ryan.
© 2017 John Wiley & Sons, Ltd. Published 2017 by John Wiley & Sons, Ltd.

what we had left as a wasteland. The prospects for the scientific study of religion have thus been undermined in two ways.

The explanation for this situation lies to some extent in the fact that the anthropological study of religion was started by men like Tylor, Frazer, and Durkheim, who were psychologically oriented although not in a position to keep up with the progress of psychological research and theory. Their interpretations, therefore, soon became vitiated by the outmoded psychological approach which they used as their basis. Although they were undoubtedly right in giving their attention to intellectual processes, the way they handled these remained so crude that it discredited them altogether. This is much to be regretted, since, as Hocart so profoundly noted in his introduction to a posthumous book recently published,[2] psychological interpretations were withdrawn from the intellectual field only to be introduced again in the field of affectivity, thus adding to "the inherent defects of the psychological school ... the mistake of deriving clear-cut ideas ... from vague emotions." Instead of trying to enlarge the framework of our logic to include processes which, whatever their apparent differences, belong to the same kind of intellectual operation, a naïve attempt was made to reduce them to inarticulate emotional drives, which resulted only in hampering our studies.

Of all the chapters of religious anthropology probably none has tarried to the same extent as studies in the field of mythology. From a theoretical point of view the situation remains very much the same as it was fifty years ago, namely, chaotic. Myths are still widely interpreted in conflicting ways: as collective dreams, as the outcome of a kind of esthetic play, or as the basis of ritual. Mythological figures are considered as personified abstractions, divinized heroes, or fallen gods. Whatever the hypothesis, the choice amounts to reducing mythology either to idle play or to a crude kind of philosophic speculation.

In order to understand what a myth really is, must we choose between platitude and sophism? Some claim that human societies merely express, through their mythology, fundamental feelings common to the whole of mankind, such as love, hate, or revenge or that they try to provide some kind of explanations for phenomena which they cannot otherwise understand – astronomical, meteorological, and the like. But why should these societies do it in such elaborate and devious ways, when all of them are also acquainted with empirical explanations? On the other hand, psychoanalysts and many anthropologists have shifted the problems away from the natural or cosmological toward the sociological and psychological fields. But then the interpretation becomes too easy: If a given mythology confers prominence on a certain figure, let us say an evil grandmother, it will be claimed that in such a society grandmothers are actually evil and that mythology reflects the social structure and the social relations; but should the actual data be conflicting, it would be as readily claimed that the purpose of mythology is to provide an outlet for repressed feelings. Whatever the situation, a clever dialectic will always find a way to pretend that a meaning has been found.

Mythology confronts the student with a situation which at first sight appears contradictory. On the one hand it would seem that in the course of a myth anything is likely to happen. There is no logic, no continuity. Any characteristic can be attributed to any subject; every conceivable relation can be found. With myth, everything becomes possible. But on the other hand, this apparent arbitrariness is belied by the astounding similarity between myths collected in widely different regions. Therefore the problem: If the content of a myth is contingent, how are we going to explain the fact that myths throughout the world are so similar?

It is precisely this awareness of a basic antinomy pertaining to the nature of myth that may lead us toward its solution. For the contradiction which we face is very similar to that which in earlier times brought considerable worry to the first philosophers concerned with linguistic problems; linguistics could only begin to evolve as a science after this contradiction had been overcome. Ancient philosophers reasoned about language the way we do about mythology. On the one hand, they did notice that in a given language certain sequences of sounds were associated with definite meanings, and they earnestly aimed at discovering a reason for the linkage between those *sounds* and that *meaning*. Their attempt, however, was thwarted from the very beginning by the fact that the same sounds were equally present in other languages although the meaning they conveyed was entirely different. The contradiction was surmounted only by the discovery that it is the combination of sounds, not the sounds themselves, which provides the significant data.

It is easy to see, moreover, that some of the more recent interpretations of mythological thought originated from the same kind of misconception under which those early linguists were laboring. Let us consider, for instance, Jung's idea that a given mythological pattern – the so-called archetype – possesses a certain meaning. This is comparable to the long-supported error that a sound may possess a certain affinity with a meaning: for instance, the "liquid" semi-vowels with water, the open vowels with things that are big, large, loud, or heavy, etc., a theory which still has its supporters.[3] Whatever emendations the original formulation may now call for,[4] everybody will agree that the Saussurean principle of the *arbitrary character of linguistic signs* was a prerequisite for the accession of linguistics to the scientific level.

To invite the mythologist to compare his precarious situation with that of the linguist in the prescientific stage is not enough. As a matter of fact we may thus be led only from one difficulty to another. There is a very good reason why myth cannot simply be treated as language if its specific problems are to be solved; myth *is* language: to be known, myth has to be told; it is a part of human speech. In order to preserve its specificity we must be able to show that it is both the same thing as language, and also something different from it. Here, too, the past experience of linguists may help us. For language itself can be analyzed into things which are at the same time similar and yet different. This is precisely what is expressed in Saussure's distinction between *langue* and *parole,* one being the structural side of language, the other the statistical aspect of it, *langue* belonging to a reversible time, *parole* being non-reversible. If those two levels already exist in language, then a third one can conceivably be isolated.

We have distinguished *langue* and *parole* by the different time referents which they use. Keeping this in mind, we may notice that myth uses a third referent which combines the properties of the first two. On the one hand, a myth always refers to events alleged to have taken place long ago. But what gives the myth an operational value is that the specific pattern described is timeless; it explains the present and the past as well as the future. This can be made clear through a comparison between myth and what appears to have largely replaced it in modern societies, namely, politics. When the historian refers to the French Revolution, it is always as a sequence of past happenings, a non-reversible series of events the remote consequences of which may still be felt at present. But to the French politician, as well as to his followers, the French Revolution is both a sequence belonging to the past – as to the historian – and a timeless pattern which can be detected in the contemporary French social structure and which provides a clue for its interpretation, a lead from which to infer future developments. Michelet, for instance, was a politically minded historian. He describes the French Revolution thus: "That day ... everything was possible. ... Future became present ... that is, no more time, a glimpse of eternity."[5] It is that double structure, altogether historical and ahistorical, which explains how myth, while pertaining to the realm of *parole* and calling for an explanation as such, as well as to that of *langue* in which it is expressed, can also be an absolute entity on a third level which, though it remains linguistic by nature, is nevertheless distinct from the other two.

A remark can be introduced at this point which will help to show the originality of myth in relation to other linguistic phenomena. Myth is the part of language where the formula *traduttore, tradittore* reaches its lowest truth value. From that point of view it should be placed in the gamut of linguistic expressions at the end opposite to that of poetry, in spite of all the claims which have been made to prove the contrary. Poetry is a kind of speech which cannot be translated except at the cost of serious distortions; whereas the mythical value of the myth is preserved even through the worst translation. Whatever our ignorance of the language and the culture of the people where it originated, a myth is still felt as a myth by any reader anywhere in the world. Its substance does not lie in its style, its original music, or its syntax, but in the *story* which it tells. Myth is language, functioning on an especially high level where meaning succeeds practically at "taking off" from the linguistic ground on which it keeps on rolling.

To sum up the discussion at this point, we have so far made the following claims: (1) If there is a meaning to be found in mythology, it cannot reside in the isolated elements which enter into the composition of a myth, but only in the way those elements are combined. (2) Although myth belongs to the same category as language, being, as a matter of fact, only part of it, language in myth exhibits specific properties. (3) Those properties are only to be found *above* the ordinary linguistic level, that is, they exhibit more complex features than those which are to be found in any other kind of linguistic expression.

If the above three points are granted, at least as a working hypothesis, two consequences will follow: (1) Myth, like the rest of language, is made up of constituent units. (2) These constituent units presuppose the constituent units present in language when analyzed on other levels – namely, phonemes, morphemes, and sememes – but they, nevertheless, differ from the latter in the same way as the latter differ among themselves; they belong to a higher and more complex order. For this reason, we shall call them *gross constituent units*.

How shall we proceed in order to identify and isolate these gross constituent units or mythemes? We know that they cannot be found among phonemes, morphemes, or sememes, but only on a higher level; otherwise myth would become confused with any other kind of speech. Therefore, we should look for them on the sentence level. The only method we can suggest at this stage is to proceed tentatively, by trial and error, using as a check the principles which serve as a basis for any kind of structural analysis: economy of explanation; unity of solution; and ability to reconstruct the whole from a fragment, as well as later stages from previous ones.

The technique which has been applied so far by this writer consists in analyzing each myth individually, breaking down its story into the shortest possible sentences, and writing each sentence on an index card bearing a number corresponding to the unfolding of the story.

Practically each card will thus show that a certain function is, at a given time, linked to a given subject. Or, to put it otherwise, each gross constituent unit will consist of a *relation*.

However, the above definition remains highly unsatisfactory for two different reasons. First, it is well known to structural linguists that constituent units on all levels are made up of relations, and the true difference between our *gross* units and the others remains unexplained; second, we still find ourselves in the realm of a non-reversible time, since the numbers of the cards correspond to the unfolding of the narrative. Thus the specific character of mythological time, which as we have seen is both reversible and non-reversible, synchronic and diachronic, remains unaccounted for. From this springs a new hypothesis, which constitutes the very core of our argument: The true constituent units of a myth are not the isolated relations but *bundles of such relations*, and it is only as bundles that these relations can be put to use and combined so as to produce a meaning. Relations pertaining to the same bundle may appear diachronically at remote intervals, but when we have succeeded in grouping them together we have reorganized our myth according to a time referent of a new nature, corresponding to the prerequisite of the initial hypothesis, namely a two-dimensional time referent which is simultaneously diachronic and synchronic, and which accordingly integrates the characteristics of *langue* on the one hand, and those of *parole* on the other. To put it in even more linguistic terms, it is as though a phoneme were always made up of all its variants.

Two comparisons may help to explain what we have in mind.

Let us first suppose that archaeologists of the future coming from another planet would one day, when all human life had disappeared from the earth, excavate one of our libraries. Even if they were at first ignorant of our writing, they might succeed in deciphering it – an undertaking which would require, at some early stage, the discovery that the alphabet, as we are in the habit of printing it, should be read from left to right and from top to bottom. However, they would soon discover that a whole category of books did not fit the usual pattern – these would be the orchestra scores on the shelves of the music division. But after trying, without success, to decipher staffs one after the other, from the upper down to the lower, they would probably notice that the same patterns of notes recurred at intervals, either in full or in part, or that some patterns were strongly reminiscent of earlier ones. Hence the hypothesis: What if patterns showing affinity, instead of being considered in succession, were to be treated as one complex pattern and read as a whole? By getting at what we call *harmony*, they would then see that an orchestra score, to be meaningful, must be read diachronically along one axis – that is, page after page, and from left to right – and synchronically along the other axis, all the notes written vertically making up one gross constituent unit, that is, one bundle of relations.

The other comparison is somewhat different. Let us take an observer ignorant of our playing cards, sitting for a long time with a fortune-teller. He would know something of the visitors: sex, age, physical appearance, social situation, etc., in the same way as we know something of the different cultures whose myths we try to study. He would also listen to the séances and record them so as to be able to go over them and make comparisons – as we do when we listen to myth-telling and record it. Mathematicians to whom I have put the problem agree that if the man is bright and if the material available to him is sufficient, he may be able to reconstruct the nature of the deck of cards being used, that is, fifty-two or thirty-two cards according to the case, made up of four homologous sets consisting of the same units (the individual cards) with only one varying feature, the suit.

Now for a concrete example of the method we propose. We shall use the Oedipus myth, which is well known to everyone. I am well aware that the Oedipus myth has only reached us under late forms and through literary transmutations concerned more with esthetic and moral preoccupations than with religious or ritual ones, whatever these may have been. But we shall not interpret the Oedipus myth in literal terms, much less offer an explanation acceptable to the specialist. We simply wish to illustrate – and without reaching any conclusions with respect to it – a certain technique, whose use is probably not legitimate in this particular instance, owing to the problematic elements indicated above. The "demonstration" should therefore be conceived, not in terms of what the scientist means by this term, but at best in terms of what is meant by the street peddler, whose aim is not to achieve a concrete result, but to explain, as succinctly as possible, the functioning of the mechanical toy which he is trying to sell to the on-lookers.

The myth will be treated as an orchestra score would be if it were unwittingly considered as a unilinear series; our task is to reestablish the correct arrangement. Say, for instance, we were confronted with a sequence of the type: 1,2,4,7,8,2,3,4,6,8,1,4,5,7,8,1, 2,5,7,3,4,5,6,8 …, the assignment being to put all the 1's together, all the 2's, the 3's, etc.; the result is a chart:

1	2		4			7	8
	2	3	4		6		8
1			4	5		7	8
1	2			5		7	
		3	4	5	6		8

We shall attempt to perform the same kind of operation on the Oedipus myth, trying out several arrangements of the mythemes until we find one which is in harmony with the principles enumerated above. Let us suppose, for the sake of argument, that the best arrangement is the following (although it might certainly be improved with the help of a specialist in Greek mythology):

Cadmos seeks his sister Europa, ravished by Zeus			
	Cadmos kills the dragon		
The Spartoi kill one another			
			Labdacos (Laios' father) = *lame* (?)
Oedipus kills his father, Laios			Laios (Oedipus' father) = *left-sided* (?)
		Oedipus kills the Sphinx	
			Oedipus = *swollen-foot* (?)
Oedipus marries his mother, Jocasta			
	Eteocles kills his brother, Polynices		
Antigone buries her brother, Polynices, despite prohibition			

We thus find ourselves confronted with four vertical columns, each of which includes several relations belonging to the same bundle. Were we to *tell* the myth, we would disregard the columns and read the rows from left to right and from top to bottom. But if we want to *understand* the myth, then we will have to disregard one half of the diachronic dimension (top to bottom) and read from left to right, column after column, each one being considered as a unit.

All the relations belonging to the same column exhibit one common feature which it is our task to discover. For instance, all the events grouped in the first column on the left have something to do with blood relations which are overemphasized, that is, are more intimate than they should be. Let us say, then, that the first column has as its common feature the *overrating of blood relations*. It is obvious that the second column expresses the same thing, but inverted: *underrating of blood relations*. The third column refers to monsters being slain. As to the fourth, a few words of clarification are needed. The remarkable connotation of the surnames in Oedipus' father-line has often been noticed. However, linguists usually disregard it, since to them the only way to define the meaning of a term is to investigate all the contexts in which it appears, and personal names, precisely because they are used as such, are not accompanied by any context. With the method we propose to follow the objection disappears, since the myth itself provides its own context. The significance is no longer to be sought in the eventual meaning of each name, but in the fact that all the names have a common feature: All the hypothetical meanings (which may well remain hypothetical) refer to *difficulties in walking straight and standing upright*.

What then is the relationship between the two columns on the right? Column three refers to monsters. The dragon is a chthonian being which has to be killed in order that mankind be born from the Earth; the Sphinx is a monster unwilling to permit men to live. The last unit reproduces the first one, which has to do with the *autochthonous origin* of mankind. Since the monsters are overcome by men, we may thus say that the common feature of the third column is *denial of the autochthonous origin of man*.[6]

This immediately helps us to understand the meaning of the fourth column. In mythology it is a universal characteristic of men born from the Earth that at the moment they emerge from the depth they either cannot walk or they walk clumsily. This is the case of the chthonian beings in the mythology of the Pueblo: Muyingwu, who leads the emergence, and the chthonian Shumaikoli are lame ("bleeding-foot," "sore-foot"). The same happens to the Koskimo of the Kwakiutl after they have been swallowed by the chthonian monster, Tsiakish: When they returned to the surface of the earth "they limped forward or tripped side ways." Thus the common feature of the fourth column is *the persistence of the autochthonous origin of man*. It follows that column four is to column three as column one is to column two. The inability to connect two kinds of relationships is overcome (or rather replaced) by the assertion that contradictory relationships are identical inasmuch as they are both self-contradictory in a similar way. Although this is still a provisional formulation of the structure of mythical thought, it is sufficient at this stage.

Turning back to the Oedipus myth, we may now see what it means. The myth has to do with the inability, for a culture which holds the belief that mankind is autochthonous (see, for instance, Pausanias, VIII, xxix, 4: plants provide a *model* for humans), to find a satisfactory transition between this theory and the knowledge that human beings are actually born from the union of man and woman. Although the problem obviously cannot be solved, the Oedipus myth provides a kind of logical tool which relates the original problem – born from one or born from two? – to the derivative problem: born from different or born from same? By a correlation of this type, the overrating of blood relations is to the underrating of blood relations as the attempt to escape autochthony is to the impossibility to succeed in it. Although experience contradicts theory, social life validates cosmology by its similarity of structure. Hence cosmology is true.

Two remarks should be made at this stage.

In order to interpret the myth, we left aside a point which has worried the specialists until now, namely, that in the earlier (Homeric) versions of the Oedipus myth, some basic elements are lacking, such as Jocasta killing herself and Oedipus piercing his own eyes. These events do not alter the substance of the myth although they can easily be integrated, the first one as a new case of auto-destruction (column three) and the second as another case of crippledness (column four). At the same time there is something significant in these additions, since the shift from foot to head is to be correlated with the shift from autochthonous origin to self-destruction.

Our method thus eliminates a problem which has, so far, been one of the main obstacles to the progress of mythological studies, namely, the quest for the *true* version, or the *earlier* one. On the contrary, we define the myth as consisting of all its versions; or to put it otherwise, a myth remains the same as long as it is felt as such. A striking example is offered by the fact that our interpretation may take into account the Freudian use of the Oedipus myth and is certainly applicable to it. Although the Freudian problem has ceased to be that of autochthony *versus* bisexual reproduction, it is still the problem of understanding how *one* can be born from *two*: How is it that we do not have only one procreator, but a mother plus a father? Therefore, not only Sophocles, but Freud himself, should be included among the recorded versions of the Oedipus myth on a par with earlier or seemingly more "authentic" versions.

An important consequence follows. If a myth is made up of all its variants, structural analysis should take all of them into account. After analyzing all the known variants of the Theban version, we should thus treat the others in the same way: first, the tales about Labdacos' collateral line including Agave, Pentheus, and Jocasta herself; the Theban variant about Lycos with Amphion and Zetos as the city founders; more remote variants concerning Dionysus (Oedipus' matrilateral cousin); and Athenian legends where Cecrops takes the place of Cadmos, etc. For each of them a similar chart should be drawn and then compared and reorganized according to the findings: Cecrops killing the serpent with the parallel episode of Cadmos; abandonment of Dionysus with abandonment of Oedipus; "Swollen Foot" with Dionysus' *loxias*, that is, walking obliquely; Europa's quest with Antiope's; the founding of Thebes by the Spartoi or by the brothers Amphion and Zetos; Zeus kidnapping Europa and Antiope and the same with Semele; the Theban Oedipus and the Argian Perseus, etc. We shall then have several two-dimensional charts, each dealing with a variant, to be organized in a three-dimensional order, as shown in Figure 16, so that three different readings become possible: left to right, top to bottom, front to back (or vice versa). All of these charts cannot be expected to be identical; but experience shows that any difference to be observed may be correlated with other differences, so that a logical treatment of the whole will allow simplifications, the final outcome being the structural law of the myth.

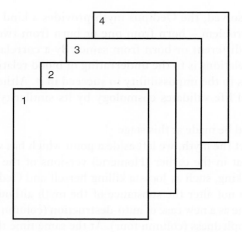

Figure 16

At this point the objection may be raised that the task is impossible to perform, since we can only work with known versions. Is it not possible that a new version might alter the picture? This is true enough if only one or two versions are available, but the objection becomes theoretical as soon as a reasonably large number have been recorded. Let us make this point clear by a comparison. If the furniture of a room and its arrangement were known to us only through its reflection in two mirrors placed on opposite walls, we should theoretically dispose of an almost infinite number of mirror images which would provide us with a complete knowledge. However, should the two mirrors be obliquely set, the number of mirror images would become very small; nevertheless, four or five such images would very likely give us, if not complete information, at least a sufficient coverage so that we would feel sure that no large piece of furniture is missing in our description.

On the other hand, it cannot be too strongly emphasized that all available variants should be taken into account. If Freudian comments on the Oedipus complex are a part of the Oedipus myth, then questions such as whether Cushing's version of the Zuni origin myth should be retained or discarded become irrelevant. There is no single "true" version of which all the others are but copies or distortions. Every version belongs to the myth.

The reason for the discouraging results in works on general mythology can finally be understood. They stem from two causes. First, comparative mythologists have selected preferred versions instead of using them all. Second, we have seen that the structural analysis of *one* variant of *one* myth belonging to *one* tribe (in some cases, even *one* village) already requires two dimensions. When we use several variants of the same myth for the same tribe or village, the frame of reference becomes three-dimensional, and as soon as we try to enlarge the comparison, the number of dimensions required increases until it appears quite impossible to handle them intuitively. The confusions and platitudes which are the outcome of comparative mythology can be explained by the fact that multi-dimensional frames of reference are often ignored or are naïvely replaced by two- or three-dimensional ones. Indeed, progress in comparative mythology depends largely on the cooperation of mathematicians who would undertake to express in symbols multi-dimensional relations which cannot be handled otherwise.

To check this theory,[7] an attempt was made from 1952 to 1954 toward an exhaustive analysis of all the known versions of the Zuni origin and emergence myth: Cushing, 1883 and 1896; Stevenson, 1904; Parsons, 1923; Bunzel, 1932; Benedict, 1934. Furthermore, a preliminary attempt was made at a comparison of the results with similar myths in other Pueblo tribes, Western and Eastern. Finally, a test was undertaken with Plains mythology. In all cases, it was found that the theory was sound; light was thrown, not only on North American mythology, but also on a previously unnoticed kind of logical operation, or one known so far only in a wholly different context. The bulk of material which needs to be handled practically at the outset of the work makes it impossible to enter into details, and we shall have to limit ourselves here to a few illustrations.

A simplified chart of the Zuni emergence myth would read:

CHANGE			DEATH
mechanical value of plants (used as ladders to emerge from lower world)	emergence led by Beloved Twins	sibling incest (origin of water)	gods kill children of men (by drowning)
food value of wild plants	migration led by the two Newekwe (ceremonial clowns)		magical contest with People of the Dew (collecting wild food *versus* cultivation)
		brother and sister sacrificed (to gain victory)	
food value of cultivated plants			
		brother and sister adopted (in exchange for corn)	
periodical character of agricultural work			
			war against the Kyanakwe (gardeners *versus* hunters)
food value of game (hunting)			
	war led by the two War-Gods		
inevitability of warfare			salvation of the tribe (center of the World found)
		brother and sister sacrificed (to avoid the Flood)	
DEATH			PERMANENCE

As the chart indicates, the problem is the discovery of a life–death mediation. For the Pueblo, this is especially difficult; they understand the origin of human life in terms of the model of plant life (emergence from the earth). They share that belief with the ancient Greeks, and it is not without reason that we chose the Oedipus myth as our first example. But in the American Indian case, the highest form of plant life is to be found in agriculture which is periodical in nature, that is, which consists in an alternation between life and death. If this is disregarded, the contradiction appears elsewhere: Agriculture provides food, therefore life; but hunting provides food and is similar to warfare which means death. Hence there are three different ways of handling the problem. In the Cushing version, the difficulty revolves around an opposition between activities yielding an immediate result (collecting wild food) and activities yielding a delayed result – death has to become integrated so that agriculture can exist. Parsons' version shifts from hunting to agriculture, while Stevenson's version operates the other way around. It can be shown that all the differences between these versions can be rigorously correlated with these basic structures.

Thus the three versions describe the great war waged by the ancestors of the Zuni against a mythical population, the Kyanakwe, by introducing into the narrative significant variations which consist (1) in the friendship or hostility of the gods; (2) in the granting of final victory to one camp or the other; (3) in the attribution of the symbolic function to the Kyanakwe, described sometimes as hunters (whose bows are strung with animal sinews) and sometimes as gardeners (whose bows are strung with plant fibers).

CUSHING	PARSONS	STEVENSON
Gods, Kyanakwe { allied, use fiber string on their bows (gardeners)	Kyanakwe, alone, use fiber string	Gods, { allied, use Men } fiber string
VICTORIOUS OVER	VICTORIOUS OVER	VICTORIOUS OVER
Men, alone, use sinew (until they shift to fiber)	Gods, { allied, use Men } sinew string	Kyanakwe, alone, use sinew string

Since fiber string (agriculture) is always superior to sinew string (hunting), and since (to a lesser extent) the gods' alliance is preferable to their antagonism, it follows that in Cushing's version, men are seen as doubly underprivileged (hostile gods, sinew string); in the Stevenson version, doubly privileged (friendly gods, fiber string); while Parsons' version confronts us with an intermediary situation (friendly gods, but sinew strings, since men begin by being hunters). Hence:

OPPOSITIONS	CUSHING	PARSONS	STEVENSON
gods/men	–	+	+
fiber/sinew	–	–	+

Bunzel's version is of the same type as Cushing's from a structural point of view. However, it differs from both Cushing's and Stevenson's, inasmuch as the latter two explain the emergence as the result of man's need to evade his pitiful condition, while Bunzel's version makes it the consequence of a call from the higher powers – hence the inverted sequences of the means resorted to for the emergence: In both Cushing and Stevenson, they go from plants to animals; in Bunzel, from mammals to insects, and from insects to plants.

Among the Western Pueblo the logical approach always remains the same; the starting point and the point of arrival are simplest, whereas the intermediate stage is characterized by ambiguity:

LIFE (= INCREASE)

(Mechanical) value of the plant kingdom, taking growth alone into account	ORIGINS
Food value of the plant kingdom, limited to wild plants	FOOD–GATHERING
Food value of the plant kingdom, including wild and cultivated plants	AGRICULTURE
Food value of the animal kingdom, limited to animals	*(but there is a contradiction here, owing to the negation of life = destruction, hence:)*
Destruction of the animal kingdom, extended to human beings	HUNTING
	WARFARE

DEATH (= DECREASE)

The fact that contradiction appears in the middle of the dialectical process results in a double set of dioscuric pairs, the purpose of which is to mediate between conflicting terms:

1. 2 divine   2 ceremonial   2 war-gods
    messengers   clowns

2. homogeneous   siblings (brother   couple (husband and   heterogeneous pair:
    pair: dioscuri   and sister)   wife)   (grandmother and
    (2 brothers)   grandchild)

We have here combinational variants of the same function in different contexts (hence the war attribute of the clowns, which has given rise to so many queries).

The problem, often regarded as insoluble, vanishes when it is shown that the clowns – gluttons who may with impunity make excessive use of agricultural products – have the same function in relation to food production as the war-gods. (This function appears, in the dialectical process, as *overstepping the boundaries* of hunting, that is, hunting for men instead of for animals for human consumption.)

Some Central and Eastern Pueblos proceed the other way around. They begin by stating the identity of hunting and cultivation (first corn obtained by Game-Father sowing deer-dewclaws), and they try to derive both life and death from that central notion. Then, instead of extreme terms being simple and intermediary ones duplicated as among the Western groups, the extreme terms become duplicated (i.e., the two sisters of the Eastern Pueblo) while a simple mediating term comes to the foreground (for instance, the Poshaiyanne of the Zia), but endowed with equivocal attributes. Hence the attributes of this "messiah" can be deduced from the place it occupies in the time sequence: good when at the beginning (Zuni, Cushing), equivocal in the middle (Central Pueblo), bad at the end (Zia), except in Bunzel's version, where the sequence is reversed as has been shown.

By systematically using this kind of structural analysis it becomes possible to organize all the known variants of a myth into a set forming a kind of permutation group, the two variants placed at the far ends being in a symmetrical, though inverted, relationship to each other.

Our method not only has the advantage of bringing some kind of order to what was previously chaos; it also enables us to perceive some basic logical processes which are at the root of mythical thought.[8] Three main processes should be distinguished.

The trickster of American mythology has remained so far a problematic figure. Why is it that throughout North America his role is assigned practically everywhere to either coyote or raven? If we keep in mind that mythical thought always progresses from the awareness of oppositions toward their resolution, the reason for these choices becomes clearer. We need only assume that two opposite terms with no intermediary always tend to be replaced by two equivalent terms which admit of a third one as a mediator; then one of the polar terms and the mediator become replaced by a new triad, and so on. Thus we have a mediating structure of the following type:

INITIAL PAIR	FIRST TRIAD	SECOND TRIAD
Life		
	Agriculture	
		Herbivorous animals
		Carrion-eating animals (raven; coyote)
	Hunting	
		Beasts of prey
	Warfare	
Death		

The unformulated argument is as follows: carrion-eating animals are like beasts of prey (they eat animal food), but they are also like food-plant producers (they do not kill what they eat). Or to put it otherwise, Pueblo style (for Pueblo agriculture is more "meaningful" than hunting): ravens are to gardens as beasts of prey are to herbivorous animals. But it is also clear that herbivorous animals may be called first to act as mediators on the assumption that they are like collectors and gatherers (plant-food eaters), while they can be used as animal food though they are not themselves hunters. Thus we may have mediators of the first order, of the second order, and so on, where each term generates the next by a double process of opposition and correlation.

This kind of process can be followed in the mythology of the Plains, where we may order the data according to the set:

Unsuccessful mediator between Earth and Sky
(Star-Husband's wife)

Heterogeneous pair of mediators
(grandmother and grandchild)

Semi-homogeneous pair of mediators
(Lodge-Boy and Thrown-away)

While among the Pueblo (Zuni) we have the corresponding set:

Successful mediator between Earth and Sky
(Poshaiyanki)

Semi-homogeneous pair of mediators
(Uyuyewi and Matsailema)

Homogeneous pair of mediators
(the two Ahaiyuta)

On the other hand, correlations may appear on a horizontal axis (this is true even on the linguistic level; see the manifold connotation of the root *pose* in Tewa according to Parsons: coyote, mist, scalp, etc.). Coyote (a carrion-eater) is intermediary between herbivorous and carnivorous just as mist between Sky and Earth; as scalp between war and agriculture (scalp is a war crop); as corn smut between wild and cultivated plants; as garments between "nature" and "culture"; as refuse between village and outside; and as ashes (or soot) between roof (sky vault) and hearth (in the ground). This chain of mediators, if one may call them so, not only throws light on entire parts of North American mythology – why the Dew-God may be at the same time the Game-Master and the giver of raiments and be personified as an "Ash-Boy"; or why scalps are mist-producing; or why the Game-Mother is associated with corn smut; etc. – but it also probably corresponds to a universal way of organizing daily experience. See, for instance, the French for plant smut (*nielle*, from Latin *nebula*); the luck-bringing power attributed in Europe to refuse (old shoe) and ashes (kissing chimney sweeps); and compare the American Ash-Boy cycle with the Indo-European Cinderella: Both are phallic figures (mediators between male and female); masters of the dew and the game; owners of fine raiments; and social mediators (low class marrying into high class); but they are impossible to interpret through recent diffusion, as has been contended, since Ash-Boy and Cinderella are symmetrical but inverted in every detail (while the borrowed Cinderella tale in America – Zuni Turkey-Girl – is parallel to the prototype). Hence the chart:

	EUROPE	AMERICA
Sex	female	male
Family Status	double family (remarried father)	no family (orphan)
Appearance	pretty girl	ugly boy
Sentimental status	nobody likes her	unrequited love for girl
Transformation	luxuriously clothed with supernatural help	stripped of ugliness with supernatural help

Thus, like Ash-Boy and Cinderella, the trickster is a mediator. Since his mediating function occupies a position halfway between two polar terms, he must retain something of that duality – namely an ambiguous and equivocal character. But the trickster figure is not the only conceivable form of mediation; some myths seem to be entirely devoted to the task of exhausting all the possible solutions to the problem of bridging the gap between *two* and *one*. For instance, a comparison between all the variants of the Zuni emergence myth provides us with a series of mediating devices, each of which generates the next one by a process of opposition and correlation:

messiah > dioscuri > trickster > bisexual being > sibling pair > married couple > grand-mother-grandchild > four-term group > triad

In Cushing's version, this dialectic is associated with a change from a spatial dimension (mediation between Sky and Earth) to a temporal dimension (mediation between summer and winter, that is, between birth and death). But while the shift is being made from space to time, the final solution (triad) re-introduces space, since a triad consists of a dioscuric pair *plus* a messiah, present simultaneously; and while the point of departure was ostensibly formulated in terms of a space referent (Sky and Earth), this was never-theless implicitly conceived in terms of a time referent (first the messiah calls, *then* the dioscuri descend). Therefore the logic of myth confronts us with a double, reciprocal exchange of functions to which we shall return shortly.

Not only can we account for the ambiguous character of the trickster, but we can also understand another property of mythical figures the world over, namely, that the same god is endowed with contradictory attributes – for instance, he may be *good* and *bad* at the same time. If we compare the variants of the Hopi myth of the origin of Shalako, we may order them in terms of the following structure:

(Masauwu: x) ≃ (Muyingwu: Masauwu) ≃ (Shalako: Muyingwu) ≃ (y: Masauwu)

where x and y represent arbitrary values corresponding to the fact that in the two "extreme" variants the god Masauwu, while appearing alone rather than associated with another god, as in variant two, or being absent, as in variant three, still retains intrinsically a relative value. In variant one, Masauwu (alone) is depicted as helpful to mankind (though not as helpful as he could be), and in version four, harmful to mankind (though not as harmful as he could be). His role is thus defined – at least implicitly – in contrast with another role which is possible but not specified and which is represented here by the values x and y. In version 2, on the other hand, Muyingwu is relatively more helpful than Masauwu, and in version three, Shalako more helpful than Muyingwu. We find an identical series when ordering the Keresan variants:

(Poshaiyanki: x) ≃ (Lea: Poshaiyanki) ≃ (Poshaiyanki: Tiamoni) ≃ (y: Poshaiyanki)

This logical framework is particularly interesting, since anthropologists are already acquainted with it on two other levels – first, in regard to the problem of the pecking order among hens, and second, to what this writer has called *generalized exchange* in the field of kinship. By recognizing it also on the level of mythical thought, we may find ourselves in a better position to appraise its basic importance in anthropological studies and to give it a more inclusive theoretical interpretation.

Finally, when we have succeeded in organizing a whole series of variants into a kind of permutation group, we are in a position to formulate the law of that group. Although it is not possible at the present stage to come closer than an approximate formulation which will certainly need to be refined in the future, it seems that every myth (considered as the aggregate of all its variants) corresponds to a formula of the following type:

$$F_x(a) : F_y(b) \simeq F_x(b) : F_{a-1}(y)$$

Here, with two terms, *a* and *b*, being given as well as two functions, *x* and *y*, of these terms, it is assumed that a relation of equivalence exists between two situations defined respectively by an inversion of *terms* and *relations*, under two conditions: (1) that one term be replaced by its opposite (in the above formula, *a* and *a − 1*); (2) that an inversion be made between the *function value* and the *term value* of two elements (above, *y* and *a*).

This formula becomes highly significant when we recall that Freud considered that *two traumas* (and not one, as is so commonly said) are necessary in order to generate the individual myth in which a neurosis consists. By trying to apply the formula to the analysis of these traumas (and assuming that they correspond to conditions 1 and 2 respectively) we should not only be able to provide a more precise and rigorous formulation of the genetic law of the myth, but we would find ourselves in the much desired position of developing side by side the anthropological and the psychological aspects of the theory; we might also take it to the laboratory and subject it to experimental verification.

At this point it seems unfortunate that with the limited means at the disposal of French anthropological research no further advance can be made. It should be emphasized that the task of analyzing mythological literature, which is extremely bulky, and of breaking it down into its constituent units, requires team work and technical help. A variant of average length requires several hundred cards to be properly analyzed. To discover a suitable pattern of rows and columns for those cards, special devices are needed, consisting of vertical boards about six feet long and four and a half feet high, where cards can be pigeon-holed and moved at will. In order to build up three-dimensional models enabling one to compare the variants, several such boards are necessary, and this in turn requires a spacious workshop, a commodity particularly unavailable in Western Europe nowadays. Furthermore, as soon as the frame of reference becomes multi-dimensional (which occurs at an early stage, as has been shown above) the board system has to be replaced by perforated cards, which in turn require IBM equipment, etc.

Three final remarks may serve as conclusion.

First, the question has often been raised why myths, and more generally oral literature, are so much addicted to duplication, triplication, or quadruplication of the same sequence. If our hypotheses are accepted, the answer is obvious: The function of repetition is to render the structure of the myth apparent. For we have seen that the synchronic-diachronic structure of the myth permits us to organize it into diachronic sequences (the rows in our tables) which should be read synchronically (the columns). Thus, a myth exhibits a "slated" structure, which comes to the surface, so to speak, through the process of repetition.

However, the slates are not absolutely identical. And since the purpose of myth is to provide a logical model capable of over-coming a contradiction (an impossible achievement if, as it happens, the contradiction is real), a theoretically infinite number of slates will be generated, each one slightly different from the others. Thus, myth grows spiral-wise until the intellectual impulse which has produced it is exhausted. Its *growth* is a continuous process, whereas its *structure* remains discontinuous. If this is the case, we should assume that it closely corresponds, in the realm of the spoken word, to a crystal in the realm of physical matter. This analogy may help us to better understand the relationship of myth to both *langue* on the one hand and *parole* on the other. Myth is an intermediary entity between a statistical aggregate of molecules and the molecular structure itself.

Prevalent attempts to explain alleged differences between the so-called primitive mind and scientific thought have resorted to qualitative differences between the working processes of the mind in both cases, while assuming that the entities which they were studying remained very much the same. If our interpretation is correct, we are led toward a completely different view – namely, that the kind of logic in mythical thought is as rigorous as that of modern science, and that the difference lies, not in the quality of the intellectual process, but in the nature of the things to which it is applied. This is well in agreement with the situation known to prevail in the field of technology: What makes a steel ax superior to a stone ax is not that the first one is better made than the second. They are equally well made, but steel is quite different from stone. In the same way we may be able to show that the same logical processes operate in myth as in science, and that man has always been thinking equally well; the improvement lies, not in an alleged progress of man's mind, but in the discovery of new areas to which it may apply its unchanged and unchanging powers.

Notes

1   In Boas' Introduction to James Teit, "Traditions of the Thompson River Indians of British Columbia," *Memoirs of the American Folklore Society*, VI (1898), p. 18.

2   A. M. Hocart, *Social Origins* (London: 1954), p. 7.

3   See, for instance, Sir R. A. Paget, "The Origin of Language," *Journal of World History*, I, No. 2 (UNESCO, 1953).

4   See Émile Benveniste, "Nature du signe linguistique," *Acta Linguistica*, I, No. 1 (1939); and Chapter V in the present volume.

5   Jules Michelet, *Histoire de la Révolution française*, IV, 1. I took this quotation from M. Merleau-Ponty, *Les Aventures de la dialectique* (Paris: 1955), p. 273.

6   We are not trying to become involved with specialists in an argument; this would be presumptuous and even meaningless on our part. Since the Oedipus myth is taken here merely as an example treated in arbitrary fashion, the chthonian nature ascribed to the Sphinx might seem surprising; we shall refer to the testimony of Marie Delcourt: "In the archaic legends, [she is] certainly born of the Earth itself" (*Oedipe ou la légende du conquérant* [Liège: 1944], p. 108). No matter how remote from Delcourt's our method may be (and our conclusions would be, no doubt, if we were competent to deal with the problem in depth), it seems to us that she has convincingly established the nature of the Sphinx in the archaic tradition, namely, that of a female monster who attacks and rapes young men; in other words, the personification of a female being with an inversion of the sign. This explains why, in the handsome iconography compiled by Delcourt at the end of her work, men and women are always found in an inverted "sky/earth" relationship.

   As we shall point out below, we selected the Oedipus myth as our first example because of the striking analogies that seem to exist between certain aspects of archaic Greek thought and that of the Pueblo Indians, from whom we have borrowed the examples that follow. In this respect it should be noted that the figure of the Sphinx, as reconstructed by Delcourt, coincides with two figures of North American mythology (who probably merge into one). We are referring, on the one hand, to "the old hag," a repulsive witch whose physical appearance presents a "problem" to the young hero. If he "solves" this problem – that is, if he responds to the advances of the abject creature – he will find in his bed, upon awakening, a beautiful young woman who will confer power upon him (this is also a Celtic theme). The Sphinx, on the other hand, recalls even more "the child-protruding woman" of the Hopi Indians, that is, a phallic mother par excellence. This young woman was abandoned by her group in the course of a difficult migration, just as she was about to give birth. Henceforth she wanders in the desert as the "Mother of Animals," which she withholds from hunters. He who meets her in her bloody clothes "is so frightened that he has an erection," of which she takes advantage to rape him, after which she rewards him with unfailing success in hunting. See H. R. Voth, "The Oraibi Summer Snake Ceremony," *Field Columbian Museum*, Publication No. 83, Anthropological Series, Vol. III, No. 4 (Chicago: 1903), pp. 352–3 and p. 353, *n* 1.

7   See *Annuaire de l'École pratique des Hautes Études*, Section des Sciences religieuses, 1952–1953, pp. 19–21, and 1953–1954, pp. 27–9. Thanks are due here to an unrequested but deeply appreciated grant from the Ford Foundation.

8   For another application of this method, see our study "Four Winnebago Myths: A Structural Sketch," in Stanley Diamond (ed.), *Culture in History: Essays in Honor of Paul Radin* (New York: 1960), pp. 351–62.

CHAPTER 5

Mythologies

Roland Barthes

Roland Barthes played a major role in the development of Structuralist and Post-Structuralist literary criticism in France from the 1950s to the 1970s. In his early work, *Elements of Semiology* (1965), he introduced the ideas of Saussure to the French intellectual community, and he offered a wide range of exemplary applications of "semiology," or the science of signs, to everything from literature to fashion and cuisine. He went on to write numerous works of Structuralist literary criticism. After 1968, influenced by the work of Jacques Derrida, Barthes turned away from classic Structuralism's concern with the orders of signs and worked instead on the disordering potential of literary semiosis, its tendency to transgress the identities and boundaries (such as the idea of the "author") that define traditional literary study. His essay "Death of the Author" (1968) is something of a Post-Structuralist manifesto, and this stage of Barthes's work achieves its most mature manifestation in his famous *S/Z* (1970), a lengthy reading of a short story by Balzac. These selections from *Mythologies* date from 1957.

In myth, we find again the tri-dimensional pattern which I have just described: the signifier, the signified and the sign. But myth is a peculiar system, in that it is constructed from a semiological chain which existed before it: it *is a second-order semiological system*. That which is a sign (namely the associative total of a concept and an image) in the first system, becomes a mere signifier in the second. We must here recall that the materials of mythical speech (the language itself, photography, painting, posters, rituals, objects, etc.), however different at the start, are reduced to a pure signifying function as soon as they are caught by myth. Myth sees in them only the same raw material; their unity is that they all come down to the status of a mere language. Whether it deals with alphabetical or pictorial writing, myth wants to see in them only a sum of signs, a global sign, the final term of a first semiological chain. And it is precisely this

Original publication details: Roland Barthes, "Myth Today," "The Romans in Films," "Soap-Powders and Detergents," "The Blue Guide," and "The Great Family of Man" from *Mythologies*, trans. Annette Lavers, pp. 26–28, 36–38, 74–77, 100–102, 114–111. Hill & Wang, 1972. Translation copyright © 1972 by Jonathan Cape Ltd. Reproduced with permission from Hill & Wang, a division of Farrar, Straus and Giroux, LLC and the Random House Group Ltd.

final term which will become the first term of the greater system which it builds and of which it is only a part. Everything happens as if myth shifted the formal system of the first significations sideways. As this lateral shift is essential for the analysis of myth, I shall represent it in the following way, it being understood, of course, that the spatialization of the pattern is here only a metaphor:

It can be seen that in myth there are two semiological systems, one of which is staggered in relation to the other: a linguistic system, the language (or the modes of representation which are assimilated to it), which I shall call the *language-object*, because it is the language which myth gets hold of in order to build its own system; and myth itself, which I shall call *metalanguage*, because it is a second language, *in which* one speaks about the first. When he reflects on a metalanguage, the semiologist no longer needs to ask himself questions about the composition of the language-object, he no longer has to take into account the details of the linguistic schema; he will only need to know its total term, or global sign, and only inasmuch as this term lends itself to myth. This is why the semi-ologist is entitled to treat in the same way writing and pictures: what he retains from them is the fact that they are both *signs*, that they both reach the threshold of myth endowed with the same signifying function, that they constitute, one just as much as the other, a language-object.

It is now time to give one or two examples of mythical speech. I shall borrow the first from an observation by Valéry.[1] I am a pupil in the second form in a French *lycée*. I open my Latin grammar, and I read a sentence, borrowed from Aesop or Phaedrus: *quia ego nominor leo*. I stop and think. There is something ambiguous about this statement: on the one hand, the words in it do have a simple meaning: *because my name is lion*. And on the other hand, the sentence is evidently there in order to signify something else to me. Inasmuch as it is addressed to me, a pupil in the second form, it tells me clearly: I am a grammatical example meant to illustrate the rule about the agreement of the predicate. I am even forced to realize that the sentence in no way *signifies* its meaning to me, that it tries very little to tell me something about the lion and what sort of name he has; its true and fundamental signification is to impose itself on me as the presence of a certain agree-ment of the predicate. I conclude that I am faced with a particular, greater, semiological system, since it is co-extensive with the language: there is, indeed, a signifier, but this signifier is itself formed by a sum of signs, it is in itself a first semiological system (*my name is lion*). Thereafter, the formal pattern is correctly unfolded: there is a signified (*I am a grammatical example*) and there is a global signification, which is none other than the correlation of the signifier and the signified; for neither the naming of the lion nor the grammatical example are given separately.

And here is now another example: I am at the barber's, and a copy of *Paris-Match* is offered to me. On the cover, a young Negro in a French uniform is saluting, with his eyes uplifted, probably fixed on a fold of the tricolour. All this is the *meaning* of the picture. But, whether naively or not, I see very well what it signifies to me: that France is a great Empire, that all her sons, without any colour discrimination, faithfully serve under her flag, and that there is no better answer to the detractors of an alleged colonialism than the zeal shown by this Negro in serving his so-called oppressors. I am therefore again faced with a greater semiological system: there is a signifier, itself already formed with a previous system (*a black soldier is giving the French salute*); there is a signified (it is here a purposeful mixture of Frenchness and militariness); finally, there is a presence of the signified through the signifier.

Before tackling the analysis of each term of the mythical system, one must agree on terminology. We now know that the signifier can be looked at, in myth, from two points of view: as the final term of the linguistic system, or as the first term of the mythical system. We therefore need two names. On the plane of language, that is, as the final term of the first system, I shall call the signifier: *meaning* (*my name is lion*, *a Negro is giving the French salute*); on the plane of myth, I shall call it: *form*. In the case of the signified, no ambiguity is possible: we shall retain the name *concept*. The third term is the correlation of the first two: in the linguistic system, it is the *sign*; but it is not possible to use this word again without ambiguity, since in myth (and this is the chief peculiarity of the latter), the signifier is already formed by the *signs* of the language. I shall call the third term of myth the *signification*. This word is here all the better justified since myth has in fact a double function: it points out and it notifies, it makes us understand something and it imposes it on us....

The Romans in Films

In Mankiewicz's *Julius Caesar*, all the characters are wearing fringes. Some have them curly, some straggly, some tufted, some oily, all have them well combed, and the bald are not admitted, although there are plenty to be found in Roman history. Those who have little hair have not been let off for all that, and the hairdresser – the king-pin of the film – has still managed to produce one last lock which duly reaches the top of the forehead, one of those Roman foreheads, whose smallness has at all times indicated a specific mixture of self-righteousness, virtue and conquest.

What then is associated with these insistent fringes? Quite simply the label of Roman-ness. We therefore see here the mainspring of the Spectacle – the *sign* – operating in the open. The frontal lock overwhelms one with evidence, no one can doubt that he is in Ancient Rome. And this certainty is permanent: the actors speak, act, torment themselves, debate 'questions of universal import', without losing, thanks to this little flag displayed on their foreheads, any of their historical plausibility. Their general representativeness can even expand in complete safety, cross the ocean and the centuries, and merge into the Yankee mugs of Hollywood extras: no matter, everyone is reassured, installed in the quiet certainty of a universe without duplicity, where Romans are Romans thanks to the most legible of signs: hair on the forehead.

A Frenchman, to whose eyes American faces still have something exotic, finds comical the combination of the morphologies of these gangster-sheriffs with the little Roman fringe: it rather looks like an excellent music-hall gag. This is because for the French the sign in this case overshoots the target and discredits itself by letting its aim appear clearly. But this very fringe, when combed on the only naturally Latin forehead in the film, that of Marlon Brando, impresses us and does not make us laugh; and it is not impossible that part of the success of this actor in Europe is due to the perfect integration of Roman capillary habits with the general morphology of the characters he usually portrays. Conversely, one cannot believe in Julius Caesar, whose physiognomy is that of an Anglo-Saxon lawyer – a face with which one is already acquainted through a thousand bit parts in thrillers or comedies, and a compliant skull on which the hairdresser has raked, with great effort, a lock of hair.

In the category of capillary meanings, here is a sub-sign, that of nocturnal surprises: Portia and Calpurnia, woken up at dead of night, have conspicuously un-combed hair. The former, who is young, expresses disorder by flowing locks: her unreadiness is, so to speak, of the first degree. The latter, who is middle-aged, exhib-its a more painstaking vulnerability: a plait winds round her neck and comes to rest on her right shoulder so as to impose the traditional sign of disorder, asymmetry. But these signs are at the same time excessive and ineffectual: they postulate a 'nature' which they have not even the courage to acknowledge fully: they are not 'fair and square'.

Yet another sign in this *Julius Caesar*: all the faces sweat constantly. Labourers, soldiers, conspirators, all have their austere and tense features streaming (with Vaseline). And close-ups are so frequent that evidently sweat here is an attribute with a purpose. Like the Roman fringe or the nocturnal plait, sweat is a sign. Of what? Of moral feeling. Everyone is sweating because everyone is debating something within himself; we are here supposed to be in the locus of a horribly tormented virtue, that is, in the very locus of tragedy, and it is sweat which has the function of conveying this. The populace, upset by the death of Caesar, then by the arguments of Mark Antony, is sweating, and combining economically, in this single sign, the intensity of its emotion and the simplicity of its condition. And the virtuous men, Brutus, Cassius, Casca, are ceaselessly perspiring too, testifying thereby to the enormous physiological labour produced in them by a virtue just about to give birth to a crime. To sweat is to think – which evidently rests on the postulate, appropriate to a nation of businessmen, that thought is a violent, cataclysmic operation, of which sweat is only the most benign symptom. In the whole film, there is but one man who does not sweat and who remains smooth-faced, unperturbed and watertight: Caesar. Of course Caesar, the *object* of the crime, remains dry since *he* does not know, *he does not think*, and so must keep the firm and polished texture of an exhibit standing isolated in the courtroom.

Here again, the sign is ambiguous: it remains on the surface, yet does not for all that give up the attempt to pass itself off as depth. It aims at making people understand (which is laudable) but at the same time suggests that it is spontaneous (which is cheat-ing); it presents itself at once as intentional and irrepressible, artificial and natural, man-ufactured and discovered. This can lead us to an ethic of signs. Signs ought to present themselves only in two extreme forms: either openly intellectual and so remote that they are reduced to an algebra, as in the Chinese theatre, where a flag on its own signifies a regiment; or deeply rooted, invented, so to speak, on each occasion, revealing an inter-nal, a hidden facet, and indicative of a moment in time, no longer of a concept (as in the art of Stanislavsky, for instance). But the intermediate sign, the fringe of Roman-ness or the sweating of thought, reveals a degraded spectacle, which is equally afraid of simple reality and of total artifice. For although it is a good thing if a spectacle is created to make the world more explicit, it is both reprehensible and deceitful to confuse the sign with what is signified. And it is a duplicity which is peculiar to bourgeois art: between the intellectual and the visceral sign is hypocritically inserted a hybrid, at once elliptical and pretentious, which is pompously christened '*nature*'.

Soap-powders and Detergents

The first World Detergent Congress (Paris, September 1954) had the effect of author-izing the world to yield to *Omo* euphoria: not only do detergents have no harmful effect on the skin, but they can even perhaps save miners from silicosis. These products have been in the last few years the object of such massive advertising that they now belong to a region of French daily life which the various types of psychoanalysis would do well to pay some attention to if they wish to keep up to date. One could then usefully contrast the psycho-analysis of purifying fluids (chlorinated, for example) with that of soap-powders (*Lux*, *Persil*) or that of detergents (*Omo*). The relations between the evil and the cure, between dirt and a given product, are very different in each case.

Chlorinated fluids, for instance, have always been experienced as a sort of liquid fire, the action of which must be carefully estimated, otherwise the object itself would be affected, 'burnt'. The implicit legend of this type of product rests on the idea of a vio-lent, abrasive modification of matter: the connotations are of a chemical or mutilating type: the product 'kills' the dirt. Powders, on the contrary, are separating agents: their ideal role is to liberate the object from its circumstantial imperfection: dirt is 'forced out' and no longer killed; in the *Omo* imagery, dirt is a diminutive enemy, stunted and black, which takes to its heels from the fine immaculate linen at the sole threat of the judgment of *Omo*. Products based on chlorine and ammonia are without doubt the representatives of a kind of absolute fire, a saviour but a blind one. Powders, on the contrary, are selective, they push, they drive dirt through the texture of the object, their function is keeping public order not making war. This distinction has ethnographic correlatives: the chemical fluid is an extension of the washerwoman's movements when she beats the clothes, while powders rather replace those of the housewife pressing and rolling the washing against a sloping board.

But even in the category of powders, one must in addition oppose against advertise-ments based on psychology those based on psycho-analysis (I use this word without reference to any specific school). '*Persil* Whiteness' for instance, bases its prestige on the evidence of a result; it calls into play vanity, a social concern with appearances, by offer-ing for comparison two objects, one of which is *whiter than* the other. Advertisements for *Omo* also indicate the effect of the product (and in superlative fashion, incidentally), but they chiefly reveal its mode of action; in doing so, they involve the consumer in a kind of direct experience of the substance, make him the accomplice of a liberation rather than the mere beneficiary of a result; matter here is endowed with value-bearing states.

Omo uses two of these, which are rather novel in the category of detergents: the deep and the foamy. To say that *Omo* cleans in depth (see the Cinéma-Publicité advertisement) is to assume that linen is deep, which no one had previously thought, and this unques-tionably results in exalting it, by establishing it as an object favourable to those obscure tendencies to enfold and caress which are found in every human body. As for foam, it is well known that it signifies luxury. To begin with, it appears to lack any usefulness; then, its abundant, easy, almost infinite proliferation allows one to suppose there is in the substance from which it issues a vigorous germ, a healthy and powerful essence, a great wealth of active elements in a small original volume. Finally, it gratifies in the consumer a tendency to imagine matter as something airy, with which contact is effected in a mode both light and vertical, which is sought after like that of happiness either in the gustatory category (foie gras, entre-mets, wines), in that of clothing (muslin, tulle), or that of soaps (film-star in her bath). Foam can even be the sign of a certain spirituality, inasmuch as the spirit has the reputation of being able to make something out of nothing, a large surface of effects out of a small volume of causes (creams have a very different 'psycho-analytical' meaning, of a soothing kind: they suppress wrinkles, pain, smarting, etc.). What matters is the art of having disguised the abrasive function of the detergent under the delicious image of a substance at once deep and airy which can govern the molecular order of the material without damaging it. A euphoria, incidentally, which must not make us forget that there is one plane on which *Persil* and *Omo* are one and the same: the plane of the Anglo-Dutch trust *Unilever*.

The *Blue Guide*

The *Blue Guide*[2] hardly knows the existence of scenery except under the guise of the picturesque. The picturesque is found any time the ground is uneven. We find again here this bourgeois promoting of the mountains, this old Alpine myth (since it dates back to the nineteenth century) which Gide rightly associated with Helvetico-Protestant morality and which has always functioned as a hybrid compound of the cult of nature and of puritanism (regeneration through clean air, moral ideas at the sight of mountain-tops, summit-climbing as civic virtue, etc.). Among the views elevated by the *Blue Guide* to aesthetic existence, we rarely find plains (redeemed only when they can be described as fertile), never plateaux. Only mountains, gorges, defiles and torrents can have access to the pantheon of travel, inasmuch, probably, as they seem to encourage a morality of effort and solitude. Travel according to the *Blue Guide* is thus revealed as a labour-saving adjustment, the easy substitute for the morally uplifting walk. This in itself means that the mythology of the *Blue Guide* dates back to the last century, to that phase in history when the bourgeoisie was enjoying a kind of new-born euphoria in *buying* effort, in keeping its image and essence without feeling any of its ill-effects. It is therefore in the last analysis, quite logically and quite stupidly, the gracelessness of a landscape, its lack of spaciousness or human appeal, its verticality, so contrary to the bliss of travel, which account for its interest. Ultimately, the *Guide* will coolly write: '*The road becomes very picturesque (tunnels)*': it matters little that one no longer sees anything, since the tunnel here has become the sufficient sign of the mountain; it is a financial security stable enough for one to have no further worry about its value over the counter.

Just as hilliness is overstressed to such an extent as to eliminate all other types of scenery, the human life of a country disappears to the exclusive benefit of its monuments. For the *Blue Guide*, men exist only as 'types'. In Spain, for instance, the Basque is an adventurous sailor, the Levantine a light-hearted gardener, the Catalan a clever tradesman and the Cantabrian a sentimental highlander. We find again here this disease of thinking in essences, which is at the bottom of every bourgeois mythology of man (which is why we come across it so often). The ethnic reality of Spain is thus reduced to a vast classical ballet, a nice neat commedia dell'arte, whose improbable typology serves to mask the real spectacle of conditions, classes and professions. For the *Blue Guide*, men exist as social entities only in trains, where they fill a 'very mixed' Third Class. Apart from that, they are a mere introduction, they constitute a charming and fanciful decor, meant to surround the essential part of the country: its collection of monuments.

If one excepts its wild defiles, fit for moral ejaculations, Spain according to the *Blue Guide* knows only one type of space, that which weaves, across a few nondescript lacunae, a close web of churches, vestries, reredoses, crosses, altar-curtains, spires (always octagonal), sculpted groups (Family and Labour), Romanesque porches, naves and life-size cruci-fixes. It can be seen that all these monuments are religious, for from a bourgeois point of view it is almost impossible to conceive a History of Art which is not Christian and Roman Catholic. Christianity is the chief purveyor of tourism, and one travels only to visit churches. In the case of Spain, this imperialism is ludicrous, for Catholicism often appears there as a barbaric force which has stupidly defaced the earlier achievements of Muslim civilization: the mosque at Cordoba, whose wonderful forest of columns is at every turn obstructed by massive blocks of altars, or a colossal Virgin (set up by Franco) denaturing the site which it aggressively dominates – all this should help the French bourgeois to glimpse at least once in his life that historically there is also a reverse side to Christianity.

Generally speaking, the *Blue Guide* testifies to the futility of all analytical descriptions, those which reject both explanations and phenomenology: it answers in fact none of the questions which a modern traveller can ask himself while crossing a countryside which is real *and which exists in time*. To select only monuments suppresses at one stroke the reality of the land and that of its people, it accounts for nothing of the present, that is, nothing historical, and as a consequence, the monuments themselves become undeci-pherable, therefore senseless. What is to be seen is thus constantly in the process of vanishing, and the *Guide* becomes, through an operation common to all mystifications, the very opposite of what it advertises, an agent of blindness. By reducing geography to the description of an uninhabited world of monuments, the *Blue Guide* expresses a mythology which is obsolete for a part of the bourgeoisie itself. It is unquestionable that travel has become (or become again) a method of approach based on human realities rather than 'culture': once again (as in the eighteenth century, perhaps) it is everyday life which is the main object of travel, and it is social geography, town-planning, sociology, economics which outline the framework of the actual questions asked today even by the merest layman. But as for the *Blue Guide*, it still abides by a partly superseded bourgeois mythology, that which postulated (religious) Art as the fundamental value of culture, but saw its 'riches' and 'treasures' only as a reassuring accumulation of goods (cf. the crea-tion of museums). This behaviour expressed a double urge: to have at one's disposal a cultural alibi as ethereal as possible, and to maintain this alibi in the toils of a computable and acquisitive system, so that one could at any moment do the accounts of the ineffable. It goes without saying that this myth of travel is becoming quite anachronistic, even among the bourgeoisie, and I suppose that if one entrusted the preparation of a new guide-book to, say, the lady-editors at *L'Express* or the editors of *Match*, we would see appearing, questionable as they would still probably be, quite different countries: after the Spain of Anquetil or Larousse, would follow the Spain of Siegfried, then that of Fourastié. Notice how already, in the *Michelin Guide*, the number of bathrooms and forks indicating good restaurants is vying with that of 'artistic curiosities': even bourgeois myths have their differential geology.

It is true that in the case of Spain, the blinkered and old-fashioned character of the description is what is best suited to the latent support given by the *Guide* to Franco. Beside the historical accounts proper (which are rare and meagre, incidentally, for it is well known that History is not a good bourgeois), those accounts in which the Republicans are always '*extremists*' looting churches – but nothing on Guernica – while the good 'Nationalists', on the contrary, spend their time '*liberating*', solely by '*skilful strategic manoeuvres*' and '*heroic feats of resistance*', let me mention the flowering of a splendid myth-alibi: that of the *prosperity* of the country. Needless to say, this prosperity is 'statistical' and 'global', or to be more accurate: 'commercial'. The *Guide* does not tell us, of course, how this fine prosperity is shared out: *hierarchically*, probably, since they think it fit to tell us that '*the serious and patient effort of this people has also included the reform of its political system, in order to achieve regeneration through the loyal application of sound principles of order and hierarchy.*'[3]

The Great Family of Man

A big exhibition of photographs has been held in Paris, the aim of which was to show the universality of human actions in the daily life of all the countries of the world: birth, death, work, knowledge, play, always impose the same types of behaviour; there is a family of Man.

The Family of Man, such at any rate was the original title of the exhibition which came here from the United States. The French have translated it as: *The Great Family of Man*. So what could originally pass for a phrase belonging to zoology, keeping only the similarity in behaviour, the unity of a species, is here amply moralized and sentimentalized. We are at the outset directed to this ambiguous myth of the human 'community', which serves as an alibi to a large part of our humanism.

This myth functions in two stages: first the difference between human morphologies is asserted, exoticism is insistently stressed, the infinite variations of the species, the diversity in skins, skulls and customs are made manifest, the image of Babel is complacently projected over that of the world. Then, from this pluralism, a type of unity is magically produced: man is born, works, laughs and dies everywhere in the same way; and if there still remains in these actions some ethnic peculiarity, at least one hints that there is underlying each one an identical 'nature', that their diversity is only formal and does not belie the existence of a common mould. Of course this means postulating a human essence, and here is God re-introduced into our Exhibition: the diversity of men proclaims his power, his richness; the unity of their gestures demonstrates his will. This is what the introductory leaflet confides to us when it states, by the pen of M. André Chamson, that '*this look over the human condition must somewhat resemble the benevolent gaze of God on our absurd and sublime ant-hill*'. The pietistic intention is underlined by the quotations which accompany each chapter of the Exhibition: these quotations often are 'primitive' proverbs or verses from the Old Testament. They all define an eternal wisdom, a class of assertions which escape History: '*The Earth is a Mother who never dies, Eat bread and salt and speak the truth*, etc.' This is the reign of gnomic truths, the meeting of all the ages of humanity at the most neutral point of their nature, the point where the obviousness of the truism has no longer any value except in the realm of a purely 'poetic' language. Everything here, the content and appeal of the pictures, the discourse which justifies them, aims to suppress the determining weight of History: we are held back at the surface of an identity, prevented precisely by sentimentality from penetrating into this ulterior zone of human behaviour where historical alienation introduces some 'differences' which we shall here quite simply call 'injustices'.

This myth of the human 'condition' rests on a very old mystification, which always consists in placing Nature at the bottom of History. Any classic humanism postulates that in scratching the history of men a little, the relativity of their institutions or the superficial diversity of their skins (but why not ask the parents of Emmet Till, the young Negro assassinated by the Whites what *they* think of *The Great Family of Man*?), one very quickly reaches the solid rock of a universal human nature. Progressive humanism, on the contrary, must always remember to reverse the terms of this very old imposture, constantly to scour nature, its 'laws' and its 'limits' in order to discover History there, and at last to establish Nature itself as historical.

Examples? Here they are: those of our Exhibition. Birth, death? Yes, these are facts of nature, universal facts. But if one removes History from them, there is nothing more to be said about them; any comment about them becomes purely tautological. The failure of photography seems to me to be flagrant in this connection: to reproduce death or birth tells us, literally, nothing. For these natural facts to gain access to a true language, they must be inserted into a category of knowledge which means postulating that one can transform them, and precisely subject their naturalness to our human criticism. For however universal, they are the signs of an historical writing. True, children are *always* born: but in the whole mass of the human problem, what does the 'essence' of this process matter to us, compared to its modes which, as for them, are perfectly historical? Whether or not the child is born with ease or difficulty, whether or not his birth causes suffering to his mother, whether or not he is threatened by a high mortality rate, whether or not such and such a type of future is open to him: this is what your Exhibitions should be telling people, instead of an eternal lyricism of birth. The same goes for death: must we really celebrate its essence once more, and thus risk forgetting that there is still so much we can do to fight it? It is this very young, far too young power that we must exalt, and not the sterile identity of 'natural' death.

And what can be said about work, which the Exhibition places among great universal facts, putting it on the same plane as birth and death, as if it was quite evident that it belongs to the same order of fate? That work is an age-old fact does not in the least prevent it from remaining a perfectly historical fact. Firstly, and evidently, because of its modes, its motivations, its ends and its benefits, which matter to such an extent that it will never be fair to confuse in a purely gestural identity the colonial and the Western worker (let us also ask the North African workers of the Goutte d'Or district in Paris what they think of *The Great Family of Man*). Secondly, because of the very differences in its inevitability: we know very well that work is 'natural' just as long as it is 'profitable', and that in modifying the inevitability of the profit, we shall perhaps one day modify the inevitability of labour. It is this entirely historified work which we should be told about, instead of an eternal aesthetics of laborious gestures.

So that I rather fear that the final justification of all this Adamism is to give to the immobility of the world the alibi of a 'wisdom' and a 'lyricism' which only make the gestures of man look eternal the better to defuse them.

Notes

1 *Tel Quel*, II, p. 191.
2 Hachette World Guides, dubbed 'Guide Bleu' in French.
3 [Franciso Franco, head of the Nationalists, led a fascist coup against the Republican government of Spain in 1936–8. He ruled Spain until his death in 1975. Eds.]

CHAPTER 6

Discourse in the Novel

Mikhail Bakhtin

Mikhail Bakhtin was one of the most influential thinkers of the late twentieth century for literary and cultural studies. Bakhtin drew attention to the way literature weaves discourses together from disparate social sources. Bakhtin also helped reconceptualize literary language. According to the theory, all words exist in dialog with other words. The theory shifts emphasis away from individual literary works and toward the intertextual world in which individual literary works are set. This selection dates from 1934–5.

The novel can be defined as a diversity of social speech types, sometimes even diversity of languages and a diversity of individual voices, artistically organized. The internal stratification of any single national language into social dialects, characteristic group behavior, professional jargons, generic languages, languages of generations and age groups, tendentious languages, languages of the authorities, of various circles and of passing fashions, languages that serve the specific sociopolitical purposes of the day, even of the hour (each day has its own slogan, its own vocabulary, its own emphases) – this internal stratification present in every language of its historical existence is the indispensable prerequisite for the novel as a genre. The novel orchestrates all its themes, the totality of the world of objects and ideas depicted and expressed in it, by means of the social diversity of speech types [*raznorecie*] and by the differing individual voices that flourish under such conditions. Authorial speech, the speeches of narrators, inserted genres, the speech of characters are merely those fundamental compositional unities with whose help heteroglossia [*raznorecie*] can enter the novel; each of them permits a multiplicity of social voices and a wide variety of their links and interrelationships (always more or less dialogized). These distinctive links and interrelationships between utterances and languages, this movement of the theme through different languages and speech types, its dispersion into the rivulets and droplets of social heteroglossia, its dialogization – this is the basic distinguishing feature of the stylistics of the novel.

Original publication details: Mikhail Bakhtin, "Discourse in the Novel" from *The Dialogic Imagination: Four Essays* by M.M. Bakhtin, ed. Michael Holquist, trans. Caryl Emerson and Michael Holquist, pp. 262–349. University of Texas Press, 1981. Reproduced with permission of the University of Texas Press.

Literary Theory: An Anthology, Third Edition. Edited by Julie Rivkin and Michael Ryan.
© 2017 John Wiley & Sons, Ltd. Published 2017 by John Wiley & Sons, Ltd.

Such a combining of languages and styles into a higher unity is unknown to traditional stylistics; it has no method for approaching the distinctive social dialogue among languages that is present in the novel...

Language – like the living concrete environment in which the consciousness of the verbal artist lives – is never unitary. It is unitary only as an abstract grammatical system of normative forms, taken in isolation from the uninterrupted process of historical becoming that is characteristic of all living language. Actual social life and historical becoming create within an abstractly unitary national language a multitude of concrete worlds, a multitude of bounded verbal ideological and social belief systems; within these various systems (identical in the abstract) are elements of language filled with various semantic and axiological content and each with its own different sound.

Literary language – both spoken and written – although it is unitary not only in its shared, abstract, linguistic markers but also in its forms for conceptualizing these abstract markers, is itself stratified and heteroglot in its aspect as an expressive system, that is, in the forms that carry its meanings.

This stratification is accomplished first of all by the specific organisms called *genres*. Certain features of language (lexicological, semantic, syntactic) will knit together with the intentional aim, and with the overall accentual system inherent in one or another genre: oratorical, publicistic, newspaper and journalistic genres, the genres of low literature (penny dreadfuls, for instance) or, finally, the various genres of high literature. Certain features of language take on the specific flavor of a given genre: they knit together with specific points of view, specific approaches, forms of thinking, nuances and accents characteristic of the given genre.

In addition, there is interwoven with this generic stratification of language a *professional* stratification of language, in the broad sense of the term "professional": the language of the lawyer, the doctor, the businessman, the politician, the public education teacher and so forth, and these sometimes coincide with, and sometimes depart from, the stratification into genres. It goes without saying that these languages differ from each other not only in their vocabularies; they involve specific forms for manifesting intentions, forms for making conceptualization and evaluation concrete. And even the very language of the writer (the poet or novelist) can be taken as a professional jargon on a par with professional jargons.

But the situation is far from exhausted by the generic and professional stratification of the common literary language. Although at its very core literary language is frequently socially homogeneous, as the oral and written language of a dominant social group, there is nevertheless always present, even here, a certain degree of social differentiation, a social stratification, that in other eras can become extremely acute. Social stratification may here and there coincide with generic and professional stratification, but in essence it is, of course, a thing completely autonomous and peculiar to itself.

Social stratification is also and primarily determined by differences between the forms used to convey meaning and between the expressive planes of various belief systems – that is, stratification expresses itself in typical differences in ways used to conceptualize and accentuate elements of language, and stratification may not violate the abstractly linguistic dialectological unity of the shared literary language.

What is more, all socially significant world views have the capacity to exploit the intentional possibilities of language through the medium of their specific concrete instancing. Various tendencies (artistic and otherwise), circles, journals, particular newspapers, even particular significant artistic works and individual persons are all capable of stratifying language, in proportion to their social significance; they are capable of attracting its words and forms into their orbit by means of their own characteristic intentions and accents, and in so doing to a certain extent alienating these words and forms from other tendencies, parties, artistic works and persons.

Every socially significant verbal performance has the ability – sometimes for a long period of time, and for a wide circle of persons – to infect with its own intention certain aspects of language that had been affected by its semantic and expressive impulse, imposing on them specific semantic nuances and specific axiological overtones; thus, it can create slogan-words, curse-words, praise-words and so forth.

In any given historical moment of verbal-ideological life, each generation at each social level has its own language; moreover, every age group has as a matter of fact its own language, its own vocabulary, its own particular accentual system that, in their turn, vary depending on social level, academic institution (the language of the cadet, the high school student, the trade school student are all different languages) and other stratifying factors. All this is brought about by socially typifying languages, no matter how narrow the social circle in which they are spoken. It is even possible to have a family jargon define the societal limits of a language, as, for instance, the jargon of the Irtenevs in Tolstoy, with its special vocabulary and unique accentual system.

And finally, at any given moment, languages of various epochs and periods of socio-ideological life cohabit with one another. Even languages of the day exist: one could say that today's and yesterday's socio-ideological and political "day" do not, in a certain sense, share the same language; every day represents another socio-ideological semantic "state of affairs," another vocabulary, another accentual system, with its own slogans, its own ways of assigning blame and praise. Poetry depersonalizes "days" in language, while prose, as we shall see, often deliberately intensifies difference between them, gives them embodied representation and dialogically opposes them to one another in unresolvable dialogues.

Thus at any given moment of its historical existence, language is heteroglot from top to bottom: it represents the coexistence of socio-ideological contradictions between the present and the past, between differing epochs of the past, between different socio-ideological groups in the present, between tendencies, schools, circles and so forth, all given a bodily form. These "languages" of heteroglossia intersect each other in a variety of ways, forming new socially typifying "languages"…

In actual fact, however, there does exist a common plane that methodologically justifies our juxtaposing them: all languages of heteroglossia, whatever the principle underlying them and making each unique, are specific points of view on the world, forms for conceptualizing the world in words, specific world views, each characterized by its own objects, meanings and values. As such they may be juxtaposed to one another, mutually supplement one another, contradict one another and be interrelated dialogically. As such they encounter one another and coexist in the consciousness of real people – first and foremost, in the creative consciousness of people who write novels. As such, these languages live a real life, they struggle and evolve in an environment of social heteroglossia. Therefore they are all able to enter into the unitary plane of the novel, which can unite in itself parodic stylizations of generic languages, various forms of stylizations and illustrations of professional and period-bound languages, the languages of particular generations, of social dialects and others (as occurs, for example, in the English comic novel). They may all be drawn in by the novelist for the orchestration of his themes and for the refracted (indirect) expression of his intentions and values…

As a result of the work done by all these stratifying forces in language, there are not "neutral" words and forms – words and forms that can belong to "no one"; language has been completely taken over, shot through with intentions and accents. For any individual consciousness living in it, language is not an abstract system of normative forms but rather a concrete heteroglot conception of the world. All words have the "taste" of a profession, a genre, a tendency, a party, a particular work, a particular person, a generation, an age group, the day and hour. Each word tastes of the context and contexts in which it has lived its socially charged life; all words and forms are populated by intentions. Contextual overtones (generic, tendentious, individualistic) are inevitable in the word.

As a living, socio–ideological concrete thing, as heteroglot opinion, language, for the individual consciousness, lies on the borderline between oneself and the other. The word in language is half someone else's. It becomes "one's own" only when the speaker populates it with his own intention, his own accent, when he appropriates the word, adapting it to his own semantic and expressive intention. Prior to this moment of appropriation, the word does not exist in a neutral and impersonal language (it is not, after all, out of a dictionary that the speaker gets his words!), but rather it exists in other people's mouths, in other people's contexts, serving other people's intentions: it is from there that one must take the word, and make it one's own. And not all words for just anyone submit equally easily to this appropriation, to this seizure and transformation into private property; many words stubbornly resist, others remain alien, sound foreign in the mouth of the one who appropriated them and who now speaks them; they cannot be assimilated into his context and fall out of it; it is as if they put themselves in quotation marks against the will of the speaker. Language is not a neutral medium that passes freely and easily into the private property of the speaker's intentions; it is populated – over-populated – with the intentions of others. Expropriating it, forcing it to submit to one's own intentions and accents, is a difficult and complicated process.

Concrete socio–ideological language consciousness, as it becomes creative – that is, as it becomes active as literature – discovers itself already surrounded by heteroglossia and not at all a singly, unitary language, inviolable and indisputable. The actively literary linguistic consciousness at all times and everywhere (that is, in all epochs of literature historically available to us) comes upon "languages," and not language. Consciousness finds itself inevitably facing the necessity of *having to choose a language*. With each literary-verbal performance, consciousness must actively orient itself amidst heteroglossia, it must move in and occupy a position for itself within it, it chooses, in other words, a "language." Only by remaining in a closed environment, one without writing or thought, completely off the maps of socio–ideological becoming, could a man fail to sense this activity of selecting a language and rest assured in the inviolability of his own language, the conviction that his language is predetermined.

Even such a man, however, deals not in fact with a single language, but with languages – except that the place occupied by each of these languages is fixed and indisputable, the movement from one to the other is predetermined and not a thought process; it is as if these languages were in different chambers. They do not collide with each other in his consciousness, there is no attempt to coordinate them, to look at one of these languages through the eyes of another language.

Thus an illiterate peasant, miles away from any urban center naively immersed in an unmoving and for him unshakeable everyday world, nevertheless lived in several language systems: he prayed to God in one language (Church Slavonic), sang songs in another, spoke to his family in a third and, when he began to dictate petitions to the local authorities through a scribe, he tried speaking yet a fourth language (the official-literate language, "paper language"). All these are *different languages*, even from the point of view of abstract socio-dialectological markers. But these languages were not dialogically coordinated in the linguistic consciousness of the peasant; he passed from one to the other without thinking, automatically: each was indisputably in its own place, and the place of each was indisputable. He was not yet able to regard one language (and the verbal world corresponding to it) through the eyes of another language (that is, the language of everyday life and the everyday world with the language of prayer or song, or vice versa).[1]

As soon as a critical interanimation of languages began to occur in the consciousness of our peasant, as soon as it became clear that these were not only various different languages but even internally variegated languages, that the ideological systems and approaches to the world that were indissolubly connected with these languages contradicted each other and in no way could live in peace and quiet with one another – then the inviolability and predetermined quality of these languages came to an end, and the necessity of actively choosing one's orientation among them began.

The language and world of prayer, the language and world of song, the language and world of labor and everyday life, the specific language and world of local authorities, the new language and world of the workers freshly immigrated to the city – all these languages and worlds sooner or later emerged from a state of peaceful and moribund equilibrium and revealed the speech diversity in each.

The prose writer as a novelist does not strip away the intentions of others from the heteroglot language of his works, he does not violate those socio-ideological cultural horizons (big and little worlds) that open up behind heteroglot languages – rather, he welcomes them into his work. The prose writer makes use of words that are already populated with the social intentions of others and compels them to serve his own new intentions, to serve a second master...

In the English comic novel we find a comic-parodic reprocessing of almost all the levels of literary language, both conversational and written, that were current at the time. Almost every...classic representative of this generic type is an encyclopedia of all strata and forms of literary language: depending on the subject being represented, the storyline parodically reproduces first the forms of parliamentary eloquence, then the eloquence of the court, or particular forms of parliamentary protocol, or court protocol, or forms used by reporters in newspaper articles, or the dry business language of the City, or the dealings of speculators, or the pedantic speech of scholars, or the high epic style, or Biblical style, or the style of the hypocritical moral sermon or finally the way one or another concrete and socially determined personality, the subject of the story, happens to speak.

This usually parodic stylization of generic, professional and other strata of language is sometimes interrupted by the direct authorial word (usually as an expression of pathos, of Sentimental or idyllic sensibility), which directly embodies (without any refracting) semantic and axiological intentions of the author. But the primary source of language usage in the comic novel is a highly specific treatment of "common language." This "common language" – usually the average norm of spoken and written language for a given social group – is taken by the author precisely as the *common view*, as the verbal approach to people and things normal for a given sphere of society, as the *going point of view* and the going *value*. To one degree or another, the author distances himself from this common language, he steps back and objectifies it, forcing his own intentions to refract and diffuse themselves through the medium of this common view that has become embodied in language (a view that is always superficial and frequently hypocritical)...

Against this same backdrop of the "common language," of the impersonal, going opinion, one can also isolate in the comic novel those parodic stylizations of generic, professional and other languages we have mentioned, as well as compact masses of direct authorial discourse – pathos-filled, moral-didactic, sentimental-elegiac or idyllic. In the comic novel the direct authorial word is thus realized in direct, unqualified stylizations of poetic genres (idyllic, elegiac, etc.) or stylizations of rhetorical genres (the pathetic, the moral-didactic). Shifts from common language to parodying of generic and other languages and shifts to the direct authorial word may be gradual, or may be on the contrary quite abrupt. Thus does the system of language work in the comic novel.

We will pause for analysis on several examples from Dickens, from his novel *Little Dorrit*.

(1)
the conference was held at four or five o'clock in the afternoon, when all the region of Harley Street, Cavendish Square, was resonant of carriage-wheels and double-knocks. It had reached this point when Mr. Merdle came home *from his daily occupation of causing the British name to be more respected in all parts of the civilized globe capable of appreciation of wholewide commercial enterprise and gigantic combinations of skill and capital.* For, though nobody knew with the least precision what Mr. Merdle's business was, except that it was to coin money, these were the terms in which everybody defined it on all ceremonious occasions, and which it was the last new polite reading of the parable of the camel and the needle's eye to accept without inquiry. (Book 1, ch. 33)

The italicized portion represents a parodic stylization of the language of ceremonial speeches (in parliaments and at banquets). The shift into this style is prepared for by the sentence's construction, which from the very beginning is kept within bounds by a somewhat ceremonious epic tone. Further on – and already in the language of the author (and consequently in a different style) – the parodic meaning of the ceremoniousness of Merdle's labors becomes apparent: such a characterization turns out to be "another's speech," to be taken only in quotation marks ("these were the terms in which everybody defined it on all ceremonious occasions").

Thus the speech of another is introduced into the author's discourse (the story) in *concealed form*, that is, without any of the *formal* markers usually accompanying such speech, whether direct or indirect. But this is not just another's speech in the same "language" – it is another's utterance in a language that is itself "other" to the author as well, in the archaicized language of oratorical genres associated with hypocritical official celebration.

(2)
In a day or two it was announced to all the town, that Edmund Sparkler, Esquire, son-in-law of the eminent Mr. Merdle of worldwide renown, was made one of the Lords of the Circumlocution Office; and proclamation was issued, to all true believers, that this admirable *appointment was to be hailed as a graceful and gracious mark of homage, rendered by the graceful and gracious Decimus, to that commercial interest which must ever in a great commercial country – and all the rest of it with blast of trumpet.* So, bolstered by this mark of Government homage, the *wonderful* Bank and all the other *wonderful* undertakings went on and went up; and gapers came to Harley Street, Cavendish Square, only to look at the house where the golden wonder lived. (Book 2, ch. 12)

Here, in the italicized portion, another's speech in another's (official-ceremonial) language is openly introduced as indirect discourse. But it is surrounded by the hidden, diffused speech of another (in the same official-ceremonial language) that clears the way for the introduction of a form more easily perceived *as* another's speech and that can reverberate more fully as such. The clearing of the way comes with the word "Esquire," characteristic of official speech, added to Sparkler's name; the final confirmation that this is another's speech comes with the epithet "wonderful." This epithet does not of course belong to the author but to that same "general opinion" that had created the commotion around Merdle's inflated enterprises.

(3)
> It was a dinner to provoke an appetite, though he had not had one. The rarest dishes, sump-tuously cooked and sumptuously served; the choicest fruits, the most exquisite wines; marvels of workmanship in gold and silver, china and glass; innumerable things delicious to the senses of taste, smell, and sight, were insinuated into its composition. *O, what a wonderful man this Merdle, what a great man, what a master man, how blessedly and enviably endowed* – in one word what a rich man! (Book 2, ch. 12)

The beginning is a parodic stylization of high epic style. What follows is an enthusias-tic glorification of Merdle, a chorus of his admirers in the form of the concealed speech of another (the italicized portion). The whole point here is to expose the real basis for such glorification, which is to unmask the chorus's hypocrisy: "wonderful," "great," "master," "endowed" can all be replaced by the single word "rich." This act of authorial unmasking, which is openly accomplished within the boundaries of a sin-gle simple sentence, merges with the unmasking of another's speech. The ceremonial emphasis on glorification is complicated by a second emphasis that is indignant, ironic, and this is the one that ultimately predominates in the final unmasking words of the sentence.

We have before us a typical double-accented, double-styled *hybrid construction*.

What we are calling a hybrid construction is an utterance that belongs, by its grammatical (syntactic) and compositional markers, to a single speaker, but that actually contains mixed within it two utterances, two speech manners, two styles, two "languages," two semantic and axiological belief systems. We repeat, there is no formal – compositional and syntactic – boundary between these utterances, styles, languages, belief systems; the division of voices and languages takes place within the limits of a single syntactic whole, often within the limits of a simple sentence. It frequently happens that even one and the same word will belong simultaneously to two languages, two belief systems that intersect in a hybrid construction – and, consequently, the word has two contradictory meanings, two accents (examples below). As we shall see, hybrid constructions are of enormous significance in novel style.

(4)
> But Mr. Tite Barnacle was a buttoned-up man, and *consequently* a weighty one. (Book 2, ch. 12)

The above sentence is an example of *pseudo-objective motivation*, one of the forms for concealing another's speech – in this example, the speech of "current opinion." If judged by the formal markers above, the logic motivating the sentence seems to belong to the author, i.e., he is formally at one with it; but in actual fact, the motivation lies within the subjective belief system of his characters, or of general opinion.

Pseudo-objective motivation is generally characteristic of novel style,[2] since it is one of the manifold forms for concealing another's speech in hybrid constructions. Subordinate conjunctions and link words ("thus," "because," "for the reason that," "in spite of" and so forth), as well as words used to maintain a logical sequence ("therefore," "consequently," etc.) lose their direct authorial intention, take on the flavor of someone else's language, become refracted or even completely reified.

Such motivation is especially characteristic of comic style, in which someone else's speech is dominant (the speech of concrete persons, or, more often, a collective voice).[3]

(5)
As a vast fire will fill the air to a great distance with its roar, so the sacred flame which the mighty Barnacles had fanned caused the air to resound more and more with the name of Merdle. It was deposited on every lip, and carried into every ear. There never was, there never had been, there never again should be, such a man as Mr. Merdle. Nobody, as afore-said, knew what he had done, but *everybody knew him to be the greatest that had appeared.* (Book 2, ch. 13)

Here we have an epic, "Homeric" introduction (parodic, of course) into whose frame the crowd's glorification of Merdle has been inserted (concealed speech of another in anoth-er's language). We then get direct authorial discourse; however, the author gives an objective tone to this "aside" by suggesting that "everybody knew" (the italicized portion). It is as if even the author himself did not doubt the fact....

Heteroglossia, once incorporated into the novel (whatever the forms for its incorpora-tion), *is another's speech in another's language*, serving to express authorial intentions but in a refracted way. Such speech constitutes a special type of *double-voiced discourse*...

From this follows the decisive and distinctive importance of the novel as a genre: the human being in the novel is first, foremost and always a speaking human being; the novel requires speaking persons bringing with them their own unique ideological discourse, their own language.

The fundamental condition, that which makes a novel a novel, that which is responsible for its stylistic uniqueness, is the *speaking person and his discourse*.

The topic of a speaking person has enormous importance in everyday life. In real life we hear speech about speakers and their discourse at every step. We can go so far as to say that in real life people talk most of all about what others talk about – they transmit, recall, weigh and pass judgment on other people's words, opinions, assertions, informa-tion; people are upset by others' words or agree with them, contest them, refer to them and so forth. Were we to eavesdrop on snatches of raw dialogue in the street, in a crowd, in lines, in a foyer and so forth, we would hear how often the words "he says," "people say," "he said..." are repeated, and in the conversational hurly-burly of people in a crowd, everything often fuses into one big "he says...you say...I say..." Reflect how enormous is the weight of "everyone says" and "it is said" in public opinion, public rumor, gossip, slander and so forth. One must also consider the psychological importance in our lives of what others say about us, and the importance, for us, of understanding and interpreting these words of others ("living hermeneutics").

The importance of this motif is in no way diminished in the higher and better-organized areas of everyday communication. Every conversation is full of transmissions and interpretations of other people's words. At every step one meets a "quotation" or a "ref-erence" to something that a particular person said, a reference to "people say" or "everyone says," to the words of the person one is talking with, or to one's own previous words, to a newspaper, an official decree, a document, a book and so forth. The majority of our information and opinions is usually not communicated in direct form as our own, but with reference to some indefinite and general source: "I heard," "It's generally held that...," "It is thought that..." and so forth. Take one of the most widespread occurrences in our everyday life, conversations about some official meeting: they are all constructed on the transmission, interpretation and evaluation of various kinds of verbal performance resolutions, the rejected and accepted corrections that are made to them and so forth. Thus talk goes on about speaking people and their words everywhere – this motif returns again and again; it either accompanies the development of the other topics in everyday life, or directly governs speech as its leading theme...

The topic of a speaking person takes on quite another significance in the ordinary ideological workings of our consciousness, in the process of assimilating our consciousness to the ideological world. The ideological becoming of a human being, in this view, is the process of selectively assimilating the words of others.

When verbal disciplines are taught in school, two basic modes are recognized for the appropriation and transmission – simultaneously – of another's words (a text, a rule, a model): "reciting by heart" and "retelling in one's own words." The latter mode poses on a small scale the task implicit in all prose stylistics: retelling a text in one's own words is to a certain extent a double-voiced narration of another's words, for indeed "one's own words" must not completely dilute the quality that makes another's words unique; a retelling in one's own words should have a mixed character, able when necessary to reproduce the style and expressions of the transmitted text. It is this second mode used in schools for transmitting another's discourse, "retelling in one's own words," that includes within it an entire series of forms for the appropriation while transmitting of another's words, depending upon the character of the text being appropriated and the pedagogical environment in which it is understood and evaluated.

The tendency to assimilate others' discourse takes on an even deeper and more basic significance in an individual's ideological becoming, in the most fundamental sense. Another's discourse performs here no longer as information, directions, rules, models and so forth – but strives rather to determine the very bases of our ideological interrelations with the world, the very basis of our behavior; it performs here as *authoritative discourse*, and an *internally persuasive discourse*.

Both the authority of discourse and its internal persuasiveness may be united in a single word – one that is *simultaneously* authoritative and internally persuasive – despite the profound differences between these two categories of alien discourse. But such unity is rarely a given – it happens more frequently that an individual's becoming, an ideological process, is characterized precisely by a sharp gap between these two categories: in one, the authoritative word (religious, political, moral; the word of a father, of adults and of teachers, etc.) that does not know internal persuasiveness, in the other, internally persuasive word that is denied all privilege, backed up by no authority at all, and is frequently not even acknowledged in society (not by public opinion, nor by scholarly norms, nor by criticism), not even in the legal code. The struggle and dialogic interrelationship of these categories of ideological discourse are what usually determine the history of an individual ideological consciousness.

The authoritative word demands that we acknowledge it, that we make it our own; it binds us, quite independent of any power it might have to persuade us internally; we encounter it with its authority already fused to it. The authoritative word is located in a distanced zone, organically connected with a past that is felt to be hierarchically higher. It is, so to speak, the word of the fathers. Its authority was already *acknowledged* in the past. It is a *prior* discourse. It is therefore not a question of choosing it from among other possible discourses that are its equal. It is given (it sounds) in lofty spheres, not those of familiar contact. Its language is a special (as it were, hieratic) language. It can be profaned. It is akin to taboo, i.e., a name that must not be taken in vain.

We cannot embark here on a survey of the many and varied types of authoritative discourse (for example, the authority of religious dogma, or of acknowledged scientific truth or of a currently fashionable book), nor can we survey different degrees of authoritativeness. For our purposes only formal features for the transmission and representation of authoritative discourse are important, those common to all types and degrees of such discourse.

The degree to which a word may be conjoined with authority – whether the authority is recognized by us or not – is what determines its specific demarcation and individuation in discourse; it requires a *distance vis-à-vis* itself (this distance may be valorized as positive or as negative, just as our attitude toward it may be sympathetic or hostile). Authoritative discourse may organize around itself great masses of other types of discourses (which interpret it, praise it, apply it in various ways), but the authoritative discourse itself does not merge with these (by means of, say, gradual transitions); it remains sharply demarcated, compact and inert: it demands, so to speak, not only quotation marks but a demarcation even more magisterial, a special script, for instance.[4] It is considerably more difficult to incorporate semantic changes into such a discourse, even with the help of a framing context: its semantic structure is static and dead, for it is fully complete, it has but a single meaning, the letter is fully sufficient to the sense and calcifies it.

It is not a free appropriation and assimilation of the word itself that authoritative discourse seeks to elicit from us; rather, it demands our unconditional allegiance. Therefore authoritative discourse permits no play with the context framing it, no play with its borders, no gradual and flexible transitions, no spontaneously creative stylizing variants on it. It enters our verbal consciousness as a compact and indivisible mass; one must either totally affirm it, or totally reject it. It is indissolubly fused with its authority – with political power, an institution, a person – and it stands and falls together with that authority. One cannot divide it up – agree with one part, accept but not completely another part, reject utterly a third part. Therefore the distance we ourselves observe *vis-à-vis* this authoritative discourse remains unchanged in all its projections: a playing with distances, with fusion and dissolution, with approach and retreat, is not here possible.

All these functions determine the uniqueness of authoritative discourse, both as a concrete means for formulating itself during transmission and as its distinctive means for being framed by contexts. The zone of the framing context must likewise be distanced – no familiar contact is possible here either. The one perceiving and understanding this discourse is a distant descendant; there can be no arguing with him.

These factors also determine the potential role of authoritative discourse in prose. Authoritative discourse cannot be represented – it is only transmitted. Its inertia, its semantic finiteness and calcification, the degree to which it is hard-edged, a thing in its own right, the impermissibility of any free stylistic development in relation to it – all this renders the artistic representation of authoritative discourse impossible. Its role in the novel is insignificant. It is by its very nature incapable of being double-voiced; it cannot enter into hybrid constructions. If completely deprived of its authority it becomes simply an object, a *relic*, a *thing*. It enters the artistic context as an alien body, there is no space around it to play in, no contradictory emotions – it is not surrounded by an agitated and cacophonous dialogic life, and the context around it dies, words dry up. For this reason images of official-authoritative truth, images of virtue of any sort: monastic, spiritual, bureaucratic, moral, etc., have never been successful in the novel. It suffices to mention the hopeless attempts of Gogol and Dostoevsky in this regard. For this reason the authoritative text always remains, in the novel, a dead quotation, something that falls out of the artistic context (for example, the evangelical texts in Tolstoy at the end of *Resurrection*).[5]

Authoritative discourses may embody various contents: authority as such, or the authoritativeness of tradition, of generally acknowledged truths, of the official line and other similar authorities. These discourses may have a variety of zones (determined by the degree to which they are distanced from the zone of contact) with a variety of relations to the presumed listener or interpreter (the apperceptive background presumed by the discourse, the degree of reciprocation between the two and so forth).

In the history of literary language, there is a struggle constantly being waged to overcome the official line with its tendency to distance itself from the zone of contact, a struggle against various kinds and degrees of authority. In this process discourse gets drawn into the contact zone, which results in semantic and emotionally expressive (intonational) changes: there is a weakening and degradation of the capacity to generate metaphors, and discourse becomes more reified, more concrete, more filled with everyday elements and so forth. All of this has been studied by psychology, but not from the point of view of its verbal formulation in possible inner monologues of developing human beings, the monologue that lasts a whole life. What confronts us is the complex problem presented by forms capable of expressing such a (dialogized) monologue.

When someone else's ideological discourse is internally persuasive for us and acknowledged by us, entirely different possibilities open up. Such discourse is of decisive significance in the evolution of an individual consciousness: consciousness awakens to independent ideological life precisely in a world of alien discourses surrounding it, and from which it cannot initially separate itself; the process of distinguishing between one's own and another's discourse, between one's own and another's thought, is activated rather late in development. When thought begins to work in an independent, experimenting and discriminating way, what first occurs is a separation between internally persuasive discourse and authoritarian enforced discourse, along with a rejection of those congeries of discourses that do not matter to us, that do not touch us.

Internally persuasive discourse – as opposed to one that is externally authoritative – is, as it is affirmed through assimilation, tightly interwoven with "one's own word."[6] In the everyday rounds of our consciousness, the internally persuasive word is half-ours and half-someone else's. Its creativity and productiveness consist precisely in the fact that such a word awakens new and independent words, that it organizes masses of our words from within, and does not remain in an isolated and static condition. It is not so much interpreted by us as it is further, that is, freely, developed, applied to new material, new conditions; it enters into interanimating relationships with new contexts. More than that, it enters into an intense interaction, a *struggle* with other internally persuasive discourses. Our ideological development is just such an intense struggle within us for hegemony among various available verbal and ideological points of view, approaches, directions and values. The semantic structure of an internally persuasive discourse is *not finite*, it is *open*; in each of the new contexts that dialogize it, this discourse is able to reveal ever newer *ways to mean*.

Notes

1   We are of course deliberately simplifying: the real-life peasant could and did do this to a certain extent.
2   Such a device is unthinkable in the epic.
3   Cf. the grotesque pseudo–objective motivations in Gogol.
4   Often the authoritative word is in fact a word spoken by another in a foreign language (cf. for example the phenomenon of foreign-language religious texts in most cultures).
5   When analyzing a concrete example of authoritative discourse in a novel, it is necessary to keep in mind the fact that purely authoritative discourse may, in another epoch, be internally persuasive; this is especially true where ethics are concerned.
6   One's own discourse is gradually and slowly wrought out of others' words that have been acknowledged and assimilated, and the boundaries between the two are at first scarcely perceptible.

CHAPTER 7

What Is an Author?

Michel Foucault

One of the influential thinkers of the late twentieth century, Michel Foucault was trained as an historian but his work on power and sexuality had a far-reaching impact beyond the field of history. His early work was in the history of madness; he traced the changing conceptions of madness over time. Doing so, he became aware of how knowledge is anchored in discourse and how knowledge discursively shapes its objects. The medieval discourse of madness was quite different from the more scientific-sounding nineteenth-century discourse, and each discourse conceived of madness quite differently. The same object had a different meaning in each discourse. Each discourse has its own rules of operation that govern the kinds of statements that can be made in it. In the discourse of anti-terrorism, for example, it would be unwise to say, "Maybe we are in the wrong, and they are right." The idea that discourses are characterized by rules governing regularity, consistency, and legitimacy could easily lead to the study of how the dominant discourses in a society (economic, political, sexual) might be used to sustain the power of ruling elites (capitalist, heteronormative, white) by policing not only what can be said in a society but also what might be considered legitimate action that did not merit being branded deviant. Discourse tends to be normative, and the knowledge discourse facilitates further lends itself easily to the workings of power. To "know" the homosexual as an object of knowledge is to be able to better regulate him or her. Surveillance, Foucault found, often goes hand in hand with punishment that maintains the power of ruling elites.

In this early essay, "What Is an Author," Foucault argues the Structuralist point that the subject or individual only appears to be fully in control of its operations. In order to function, human consciousness must float atop a sea of language from which it borrows and which makes possible its thinking and acting. We think about the world in the categories and terms given to us by that world. In regard to literature, this means that the "author," the locus of conscious awareness, is one object of study, but another might be the discourses that flow through that consciousness, the rules and tools for ordering thought and creating new stories. The discourse of humanism in the Renaissance, for

Original publication details: Michel Foucault, "What Is an Author?" from *Language, Counter-Memory, Practice*, ed. Donald Bouchard, pp. 113–138. Cornell, 1977. Reproduced with permission from Cornell University Press.

example, shaped conceptions of the world and of life in terms of a distinction between an ideal of virtue defined as the mind's control over bodily urges and the world of bodily emotion and sexuality. This opposition is consistent across "authors" and is not the invention of any one of them. Rather, the discourse supplies the terms in which different authors think in the same way about the world. The ideal of individual creativity, which dominated an older way of thinking about literature in terms almost exclusively of authorial genius, shifts to a more complicated understanding of the nesting of creativity in cultural and discursive environments that enable thought and creativity.

The coming into being of the notion of "author" constitutes the privileged moment of individualization in the history of ideas, knowledge, literature, philosophy, and the sciences. Even today, when we reconstruct the history of a concept, literary genre, or school of philosophy, such categories seem relatively weak, secondary, and super-imposed scansions in comparison with the solid and fundamental unit of the author and the work.

I shall not offer here a sociohistorical analysis of the author's persona. Certainly, it would be worth examining how the author became individualized in a culture like ours, what status he has been given, at what moment studies of authenticity and attribution began, in what kind of system of valorization the author was involved, at what point we began to recount the lives of authors rather than of heroes, and how this fundamental category of "the-man-and-his-work criticism" began. For the moment, however, I want to deal solely with the relationship between text and author and with the manner in which the text points to this figure that, at least in appearance, is outside it and antecedes it.

Beckett nicely formulates the theme with which I would like to begin: "'What does it matter who is speaking,' someone said; 'what does it matter who is speaking.'" In this indifference appears one of the fundamental ethical principles of contemporary writing [*écriture*].

I say "ethical" because this indifference is really not a trait characterizing the manner in which one speaks and writes but, rather, a kind of immanent rule, taken up over and over again, never fully applied, not designating writing as something completed, but dominating it as a practice. Since it is too familiar to require a lengthy analysis, this immanent rule can be adequately illustrated here by tracing two of its major themes.

First of all, we can say that today's writing has freed itself from the theme of expression. Referring only to itself; but without being restricted to the confines of its interiority, writing is identified with its own unfolded exteriority. This means that it is an interplay of signs arranged less according to its signified content than according to the very nature of the signifier. Writing unfolds like a game [*jeu*] that invariably goes beyond its own rules and transgresses its limits. In writing, the point is not to manifest or exalt the act of writing, nor is it to pin a subject within language; it is, rather, a question of creating a space into which the writing subject constantly disappears.

The second theme, writing's relationship with death, is even more familiar. This link subverts an old tradition exemplified by the Greek epic, which was intended to perpetuate the immortality of the hero: if he was willing to die young, it was so that his life, consecrated and magnified by death, might pass into immortality; the narrative then redeemed this accepted death. In another way, the motivation, as well as the theme and the pretext of Arabian narratives – such as *The Thousand and One Nights* – was also the eluding of death: one spoke, telling stories into the early morning, in order to forestall death, to postpone the day of reckoning that would silence the narrator. Scheherazade's narrative is an effort, renewed each night, to keep death outside the circle of life.

Our culture has metamorphosed this idea of narrative, or writing, as something designed to ward off death. Writing has become linked to sacrifice, even to the sacrifice of life: it is now a voluntary effacement that does not need to be represented in books, since it is brought about in the writer's very existence. The work, which once had the duty of providing immortality, now possesses the right to kill, to be its author's murderer, as in the cases of Flaubert, Proust, and Kafka. That is not all, however: this relationship between writing and death is also manifested in the effacement of the writing subject's individual characteristics. Using all the contrivances that he sets up between himself and what he writes, the writing subject cancels out the signs of his particular individuality. As a result, the mark of the writer is reduced to nothing more than the singularity of his absence; he must assume the role of the dead man in the game of writing.

None of this is recent; criticism and philosophy took note of the disappearance – or death – of the author some time ago. But the consequences of their discovery of it have not been sufficiently examined, nor has its import been accurately measured. A certain number of notions that are intended to replace the privileged position of the author actually seem to preserve that privilege and suppress the real meaning of his disappearance. I shall examine two of these notions, both of great importance today.

The first is the idea of the work [*oeuvre*]. It is a very familiar thesis that the task of criticism is not to bring out the work's relationships with the author, nor to reconstruct through the text a thought or experience, but rather to analyze the work through its structure, its architecture, its intrinsic form, and the play of its internal relationships. At this point, however, a problem arises: What is a work? What is this curious unity which we designate as a work? Of what elements is it composed? Is it not what an author has written? Difficulties appear immediately. If an individual were not an author, could we say that what he wrote, said, left behind in his papers, or what has been collected of his remarks, could be called a "work"? When Sade was not considered an author, what was the status of his papers? Simply rolls of paper onto which he ceaselessly uncoiled his fantasies during his imprisonment.

Even when an individual has been accepted as an author, we must still ask whether everything that he wrote, said, or left behind is part of his work. The problem is both theoretical and technical. When undertaking the publication of Nietzsche's works, for example, where should one stop? Surely everything must be published, but what is "everything"? Everything that Nietzsche himself published, certainly. And what about the rough drafts for his works? Obviously. The plans for his aphorisms? Yes. The deleted passages and the notes at the bottom of the page? Yes. What if, within a workbook filled with aphorisms, one finds a reference, the notation of a meeting or of an address, or a laundry list: is it a work, or not? Why not? And so on, ad infinitum. How can one define a work amid the millions of traces left by someone after his death? A theory of the work does not exist, and the empirical task of those who naively undertake the editing of works often suffers in the absence of such a theory.

We could go even further. Does *The Thousand and One Nights* constitute a work? What about Clement of Alexandria's *Miscellanies* or Diogenes Laërtes' *Lives*? A multitude of questions arises with regard to this notion of the work. Consequently, it is not enough to declare that we should do without the writer (the author) and study the work itself. The word work and the unity that it designates are probably as problematic as the status of the author's individuality. Another notion which has hindered us from taking full measure of the author's disappearance, blurring and concealing the moment of this effacement and subtly preserving the author's existence, is the notion of writing [*écriture*]. When rigorously applied, this notion should allow us not only to circumvent references to the author, but also to situate his recent absence. The notion of writing, as currently employed, is concerned with neither the act of writing nor the indication – be it symptom or sign – of a meaning that someone might have wanted to express. We try, with great effort, to imagine the general condition of each text, the condition of both the space in which it is dispersed and the time in which it unfolds.

In current usage, however, the notion of writing seems to transpose the empirical characteristics of the author into a transcendental anonymity. We are content to efface the more visible marks of the author's empiricity by playing off, one against the other, two ways of characterizing writing, namely, the critical and the religious approaches. Giving writing a primal status seems to be a way of retranslating, in transcendental terms, both the theological affirmation of its sacred character and the critical affirmation of its creative character. To admit that writing is, because of the very history that it made possible, subject to the test of oblivion and repression, seems to represent, in transcendental terms, the religious principle of the hidden meaning (which requires interpretation) and the critical principle of implicit signification, silent determinations, and obscured contents (which give rise to commentary). To imagine writing as absence seems to be a simple repetition, in transcendental terms, of both the religious principle of inalterable and yet never fulfilled tradition, and the aesthetic principle of the work's survival, its perpetuation beyond the author's death, and its enigmatic excess in relation to him.

This usage of the notion of writing runs the risk of maintaining the author's privileges under the protection of the a priori: it keeps alive, in the gray light of neutralization, the interplay of those representations that formed a particular image of the author. The author's disappearance, which, since Mallarmé, has been a constantly recurring event, is subject to a series of transcendental barriers. There seems to be an important dividing line between those who believe that they can still locate today's discontinuities [*ruptures*] in the historico-transcendental tradition of the nineteenth century and those who try to free themselves once and for all from that tradition.

§

It is not enough, however, to repeat the empty affirmation that the author has disappeared. For the same reason, it is not enough to keep repeating that God and man have died a common death. Instead, we must locate the space left empty by the author's disappearance, follow the distribution of gaps and breaches, and watch for the openings this disappearance uncovers.

First, we need to clarify briefly the problems arising from the use of the author's name. What is an author's name? How does it function? Far from offering a solution, I shall only indicate some of the difficulties that it presents.

The author's name is a proper name, and therefore it raises the problems common to all proper names. (Here I refer to Searle's analyses, among others.[1]) Obviously, one cannot turn a proper name into a pure and simple reference. It has other than indicative functions: more than an indication, a gesture, a finger pointed at someone, it is the equivalent of a description. When one says "Aristotle," one employs a word that is the equivalent of one, or a series, of definite descriptions, such as "the author of the *Analytics*," "the founder of ontology," and so forth. One cannot stop there, however, because a proper name does not have just one signification. When we discover that Arthur Rimbaud did not write *La Chasse spirituelle*, we cannot pretend that the meaning of this proper name, or that of the author, has been altered. The proper name and the author's name are situated between the two poles of description and designation: they must have a certain link with what they name, but one that is neither entirely in the mode of designation nor in that of description; it must be a specific link. However – and it is here that the particular difficulties of the author's name arise – the links between the proper name and the individual named and between the author's name and what it names are not isomorphic and do not function in the same way. There are several differences.

If for example, Pierre Dupont does not have blue eyes, or was not born in Paris, or is not a doctor, the name Pierre Dupont will still always refer to the same person, such things do not modify the link of designation. The problems raised by the author's name are much more complex, however. If I discover that Shakespeare was not born in the house we visit today, this is a modification that, obviously, will not alter the functioning of the author's name. But if we proved that Shakespeare did not write those sonnets which pass for his, that would constitute a significant change and affect the manner in which the author's name functions. If we proved that Shakespeare wrote Bacon's *Organon* by showing that the same author wrote both the works of Bacon and those of Shakespeare, that would be a third type of change that would entirely modify the functioning of the author's name. The author's name is not, therefore, just a proper name like the rest.

Many other facts point out the paradoxical singularity of the author's name. To say that Pierre Dupont does not exist is not at all the same as saying that Homer or Hermes Trismegistus did not exist. In the first case, it means that no one has the name Pierre Dupont; in the second, it means that several people were mixed together under one name, or that the true author had none of the traits traditionally ascribed to the personae of Homer or Hermes. To say that X's real name is actually Jacques Durand instead of Pierre Dupont is not the same as saying that Stendhal's name was Henri Beyle. One could also question the meaning and functioning of propositions like "Bourbaki is so-and-so, so-and-so, and so-forth," and "Victor Eremite, Climacus, Anticlimacus, Prater Taciturnus, Constantine Constantius, all of these are Kierkegaard."

These differences may result from the fact that an author's name is not simply an element in a discourse (capable of being either subject or object, of being replaced by a pronoun, and the like); it performs a certain role with regard to narrative discourse, assuring a classificatory function. Such a name permits one to group together a certain number of texts, define them, differentiate them from and contrast them to others. In addition, it establishes a relationship among the texts. Hermes Trismegistus did not exist, nor did Hippocrates – in the sense that Balzac existed – but the fact that several texts have been placed under the same name indicates that there has been established among them a relationship of homogeneity, filiation, authentication of some texts by the use of others, reciprocal explication, or concomitant utilization. The author's name serves to characterize a certain mode of being of discourse: the fact that the discourse has an author's name, that one can say "this was written by so-and-so" or "so-and-so is its author," shows that this discourse is not ordinary everyday speech that merely comes and goes, not something that is immediately consumable. On the contrary, it is a speech that must be received in a certain mode and that, in a given culture, must receive a certain status.

It would seem that the author's name, unlike other proper names, does not pass from the interior of a discourse to the real and exterior individual who produced it; instead, the name seems always to be present, marking off the edges of the text, revealing, or at least characterizing, its mode of being. The author's name manifests the appearance of a certain discursive set and indicates the status of this discourse within a society and a culture. It has no legal status, nor is it located in the fiction of the work; rather, it is located in the break that founds a certain discursive construct and its very particular mode of being. As a result, we could say that in a civilization like our own there are a certain number of discourses endowed with the "author function" while others are deprived of it. A private letter may well have a signer – it does not have an author; a contract may well have a guarantor – it does not have an author. An anonymous text posted on a wall probably has an editor – but not an author. The author function is therefore characteristic of the mode of existence, circulation, and functioning of certain discourses within a society.

§

Let us analyze this "author function" as we have just described it. In our culture, how does one characterize a discourse containing the author function? In what way is this discourse different from other discourses? If we limit our remarks to the author of a book or a text, we can isolate four different characteristics.

First of all, discourses are objects of appropriation. The form of ownership from which they spring is of a rather particular type, one that has been codified for many years. We should note that, historically, this type of ownership has always been subsequent to what one might call penal appropriation. Texts, books, and discourses really began to have authors (other than mythical, sacralized and sacralizing figures) to the extent that authors became subject to punishment, that is, to the extent that discourses could be transgressive. In our culture (and doubtless in many others), discourse was not originally a product, a thing, a kind of goods; it was essentially an act – an act placed in the bipolar field of the sacred and the profane, the licit and the illicit, the religious and the blasphemous. Historically, it was a gesture fraught with risks before becoming goods caught up in a circuit of ownership.

Once a system of ownership for texts came into being, once strict rules concerning author's rights, author-publisher relations, rights of reproduction, and related matters were enacted – at the end of the eighteenth and the beginning of the nineteenth century – the possibility of transgression attached to the act of writing took on, more and more, the form of an imperative peculiar to literature. It is as if the author, beginning with the moment at which he was placed in the system of property that characterizes our society, compensated for the status that he thus acquired by rediscovering the old bipolar field of discourse, systematically practicing transgression and thereby restoring danger to a writing that was now guaranteed the benefits of ownership.

The author function does not affect all discourses in a universal and constant way, however. In our civilization, it has not always been the same types of texts that have required attribution to an author. There was a time when the texts we today call "literary" (narratives, stories, epics, tragedies, comedies) were accepted, put into circulation, and valorized without any question about the identity of their author, their anonymity caused no difficulties since their ancientness, whether real or imagined, was regarded as a sufficient guarantee of their status. On the other hand, those texts we now would call scientific – those dealing with cosmology and the heavens, medicine and illnesses, natural sciences and geography – were accepted in the Middle Ages, and accepted as "true," only when marked with the name of their author. "Hippocrates said," "Pliny recounts," were not really formulas of an argument based on authority; they were the markers inserted in discourses that were supposed to be received as statements of demonstrated truth.

A switch takes place in the seventeenth or eighteenth century. Scientific discourses began to be received for themselves, in the anonymity of an established or always redemonstrable truth; their membership in a systematic ensemble, and not the reference to the individual who produced them, stood as their guarantee. The author function faded away, and the inventor's name served only to christen a theorem, proposition, particular effect, property, body, group of elements, or pathological syndrome. By the same token, literary discourses came to be accepted only when endowed with the author function. We now ask of each poetic or fictional text: From where does it come, who wrote it, when, under what circumstances, or beginning with what design? The meaning ascribed to it and the status or value accorded it depend on the manner in which we answer these questions. And if a text should be discovered in a state of anonymity – whether as a consequence of an accident or the author's explicit wish – the game becomes one of rediscovering the author. Since literary anonymity is not tolerable, we can accept it only in the guise of an enigma. As a result, the author function today plays an important role in our view of literary works. (These are obviously generalizations that would have to be refined insofar as recent critical practice is concerned. Criticism began some time ago to treat works according to their genre and type, following the recurrent elements that are enfigured in them, as proper variations around an invariant that is no longer the individual creator. Even so, if in mathematics reference to the author is barely anything any longer but a manner of naming theorems or sets of propositions, in biology and medicine the indication of the author and the date of his work play a rather different role. It is not simply a manner of indicating the source, but of providing a certain index of "reality" in relation to the techniques and objects of experience made use of in a particular period and in such-and-such a laboratory.)

The third characteristic of this author function is that it does not develop spontaneously as the attribution of a discourse to an individual. It is, rather, the result of a complex operation that constructs a certain being of reason that we call "author." Critics doubtless try to give this being of reason a realistic status, by discerning, in the individual, a "deep" motive, a "creative" power, or a "design," the milieu in which writing originates. Nevertheless, these aspects of an individual which we designate as making him an author are only a projection, in more or less psychologizing terms, of the operations we force texts to undergo, the connections we make, the traits we establish as pertinent, the continuities we recognize, or the exclusions we practice. All these operations vary according to periods and types of discourse. We do not construct a "philosophical author" as we do a "poet," just as in the eighteenth century one did not construct a novelist as we do today. Still, we can find through the ages certain constants in the rules of author construction.

It seems, for example that the manner in which literary criticism once defined the author – or, rather, constructed the figure of the author beginning with existing texts and discourses – is directly derived from the manner in which Christian tradition authenticated (or rejected) the texts at its disposal. In order to "rediscover" an author in a work, modern criticism uses methods similar to those that Christian exegesis employed when trying to prove the value of a text by its author's saintliness. In *De Viris illustribus*, Saint Jerome explains that homonymy is not sufficient to identify legitimately authors of more than one work: different individuals could have had the same name, or one man could have, illegitimately, borrowed another's patronymic. The name as an individual trademark is not enough when one works within a textual tradition.

How, then, can one attribute several discourses to one and the same author? How can one use the author function to determine if one is dealing with one or several individuals? Saint Jerome proposes four criteria: (i) if among several books attributed to an author one is inferior to the others, it must be withdrawn from the list of the author's works (the author is therefore defined as a constant level of value); (2) the same should be done if certain texts contradict the doctrine expounded in the author's other works (the author is thus defined as a field of conceptual or theoretical coherence); (3) one must also exclude works that are written in a different style, containing words and expressions not ordinarily found in the writer's production (the author is here conceived as a stylistic unity); (4) finally, passages quoting statements made or mentioning events that occurred after the author's death must be regarded as interpolated texts (the author is here seen as a historical figure at the crossroads of a certain number of events).

Modern literary criticism, even when – as is now customary – it is not concerned with questions of authentication, still defines the author in much the same way: the author provides the basis for explaining not only the presence of certain events in a work, but also their transformations, distortions, and diverse modifications (through his biography, the determination of his individual perspective, the analysis of his social position, and the revelation of his basic design). The author is also the principle of a certain unity of writing – all differences having to be resolved, at least in part, by the principles of evolution, maturation, or influence. The author also serves to neutralize the contradictions that may emerge in a series of texts: there must be – at a certain level of his thought or desire, of his consciousness or unconscious – a point where contradictions are resolved, where incompatible elements are at last tied together or organized around a fundamental or originating contradiction. Finally, the author is a particular source of expression that, in more or less completed forms, is manifested equally well, and with similar validity, in works, sketches, letters, fragments, and so on. Clearly, Saint Jerome's four criteria of authenticity (criteria that seem totally insufficient for today's exegetes) do define the four modalities according to which modern criticism brings the author function into play.

But the author function is not a pure and simple reconstruction made secondhand from a text given as inert material. The text always contains a certain number of signs referring to the author. These signs, well known to grammarians, are personal pronouns, adverbs of time and place, and verb conjugation. Such elements do not play the same role in discourses provided with the author function as in those lacking it. In the latter, such "shifters" refer to the real speaker and to the spatio-temporal coordinates of his discourse (although certain modifications can occur, as in the operation of relating discourses in the first person). In the former, however, their role is more complex and variable. Everyone knows that, in a novel offered as a narrator's account, neither the first-person pronoun nor the present indicative refers exactly to the writer or to the moment in which he writes but, rather, to an alter ego whose distance from the author varies, often changing in the course of the work. It would be just as wrong to equate the author with the real writer as to equate him with the fictitious speaker; the author function is carried out and operates in the scission itself, in this division and this distance.

One might object that this is a characteristic peculiar to novelistic or poetic discourse, a game in which only "quasi discourses" participate. In fact, however, all discourses endowed with the author function possess this plurality of self. The self that speaks in the preface to a treatise on mathematics – and that indicates the circumstances of the treatise's composition – is identical neither in its position nor in its functioning to the self speaks in the course of a demonstration, and that appears in the form of "I conclude" or "I suppose." In the first case, the "I" refers to an individual without an equivalent who, in a determined place and time, completed a certain task; in the second, the "I" indicates an instance and a level of demonstration which any individual could perform provided that he accepted the same system of symbols, play of axioms and set of previous demonstrations. We could also, in the same treatise locate a third self; one that speaks to tell the work's meaning, the obstacles encountered, the results obtained, and the remaining problems; this self is situated in the field of already existing or yet-to-appear mathematical discourses. The author function is not assumed by the first of these selves at the expense of the other two, which would then be nothing more than a fictitious splitting in two of the first one. On the contrary, in these discourses the author function operates so as to effect the dispersion of these three simultaneous selves.

No doubt, analysis could discover still more characteristic traits of the author function. I will limit myself to these four, however, because they seem both the most visible and the most important. They can be summarized as follows: (1) the author function is linked to the juridical and institutional system that encompasses, determines, and articulates the universe of discourses; (2) it does not affect all discourses in the same way at all times and in all types of civilization; (3) it is not defined by the spontaneous attribution of a discourse to its producer but, rather, by a series of specific and complex operations; (4) it does not refer purely and simply to a real individual, since it can give rise simultaneously to several selves, to several subjects – positions that can be occupied by different classes of individuals.

Up to this point I have unjustifiably limited my subject. Certainly the author function in painting, music, and other arts should have been discussed; but even supposing that we remain within the world of discourse, as I want to do, I seem to have given the term "author" much too narrow a meaning. I have discussed the author only in the limited sense of a person to whom the production of a text, a book, or a work can be legitimately attributed. It is easy to see that in the sphere of discourse one can be the author of much more than a book – one can be the author of a theory, tradition, or discipline in which other books and authors will in their turn find a place. These authors are in a position that I will call "transdiscursive." This is a recurring phenomenon – certainly as old as our civilization. Homer, Aristotle, and the Church Fathers, as well as the first mathematicians and the originators of the Hippocratic tradition, all played this role. Furthermore, in the course of the nineteenth century, there appeared in Europe another, more uncommon, kind of author, whom one should confuse with neither the "great" literary authors, nor the authors of religious texts, nor the founders of science. In a somewhat arbitrary way we shall call those who belong in this last group "founders of discursivity."

They are unique in that they are not just the authors of their own works. They have produced something else: the possibilities and the rules for the formation of other texts. In this sense they are very different, for example, from a novelist, who is, in fact, nothing more than the author of his own text. Freud is not just the author of *The Interpretation of Dreams* or *Jokes and Their Relation to the Unconscious*; Marx is not just the author of the *Communist Manifesto* or *Das Kapital*: they both have established an endless possibility of discourse. Obviously, it is easy to object. One might say that it is not true that the author of a novel is only the author of his own text; in a sense, he also, provided that he acquires some "importance," governs and commands more than that. To take a very simple example, one could say that Ann Radcliffe not only wrote *The Castles of Athlin and Dunbayne* and several other novels but also made possible the appearance of the Gothic horror novel at the beginning of the nineteenth century; in that respect, her author function exceeds her own work. But I think there is an answer to this objection. These founders of discursivity (I use Marx and Freud as examples, because I believe them to be both the first and the most important cases) make possible something altogether different from what a novelist makes possible. Ann Radcliffe's texts opened the way for a certain number of resemblances and analogies which have their model or principle in her work. The latter contains characteristic signs, figures, relationships, and structures that could be reused by others. In other words, to say that Ann Radcliffe founded the Gothic horror novel means that in the nineteenth-century Gothic novel one will find, as in Ann Radcliffe's works, the theme of the heroine caught in the trap of her own innocence, the hidden castle, the character of the black, cursed hero devoted to making the world expiate the evil done to him, and all the rest of it. On the other hand, when I speak of Marx or Freud as founders of discursivity, I mean that they made possible not only a certain number of analogies but also (and equally important) a certain number of differences. They have created a possibility for something other than their discourse, yet something belonging to what they founded. To say that Freud founded psychoanalysis does not (simply) mean that we find the concept of the libido or the technique of dream analysis in the works of Karl Abraham, or Melanie Klein; it means that Freud made possible a certain number of divergences – with respect to his own texts, concepts and hypotheses – that all arise from the psychoanalytic discourse itself.

This would seem to present a new difficulty, however, or at least a new problem: is the above not true, after all, of any founder of a science, or of any author who has introduced some transformation into a science that might be called fecund? After all, Galileo made possible not only those discourses which repeated the laws he had formulated, but also statements very different from what he himself had said. If Georges Cuvier is the founder of biology, or Ferdinand de Saussure the founder of linguistics, it is not because they were imitated, nor because people have since taken up again the concept of organism or sign; it is because Cuvier made possible, to a certain extent, a theory of evolution diametrically opposed to his own fixism; it is because Saussure made possible a generative grammar radically different from his structural analyses. Superficially, then, the initiation of discursive practices appears similar to the founding of any scientific endeavor.

Still, there is a difference, and a notable one. In the case of a science, the act that founds it is on an equal footing with its future transformations; this act becomes in some respects part of the set of modifications that it makes possible. Of course, this belonging can take several forms. In the future development of a science, the founding act may appear as little more than a particular instance of a more general phenomenon that unveils itself in the process. It can also turn out to be marred by intuition and empirical bias; one must then reformulate it, making it the object of a certain number of supplementary theoretical operations that establish it more rigorously, and so on. Finally, it can seem to be a hasty generalization that must be retraced. In other words, the founding act of a science can always be reintroduced within the machinery of those transformations which derive from it.

In contrast, the initiation of a discursive practice is heterogeneous to its subsequent transformations. To expand a type of discursivity such as psychoanalysis as founded by Freud, is not to give it a formal generality it would not have permitted at the outset but, rather, to open it up to a certain number of possible applications. To limit psychoanalysis as a type of discursivity is, in reality, to try to isolate in the founding act an eventually restricted number of propositions or statements to which, alone, one grants a founding value, and in relation to which certain concepts or theories accepted by Freud might be considered as derived, secondary, and accessory. In addition, one does not declare certain propositions in the work of these founders to be false: instead, when trying to seize the act of founding, one sets aside those statements that are not pertinent, either because they are deemed inessential, or because they are considered "prehistoric" and derived from another type of discursivity. In other words, unlike the founding of a science, the initiation of a discursive practice does not participate in its later transformations. As a result, one defines a proposition's theoretical validity in relation to the work of the founders – while, in the case of Galileo and Newton, it is in relation to what physics or cosmology is in its intrinsic structure and normativity that one affirms the validity of any proposition those men may have put forth. To phrase it very schematically: the work of initiators of discursivity is not situated in the space that science defines; rather, it is the science or the discursivity which refers back to their work as primary coordinates.

In this way we can understand the inevitable necessity, within these fields of discursivity, for a "return to the origin." This return which is part of the discursive field itself, never stops modifying it. The return is not a historical supplement that would be added to the discursivity, or merely an ornament; on the contrary, it constitutes an effective and necessary task of transforming the discursive practice itself. Reexamination of Galileo's text may well change our understanding of the history of mechanics, but it will never be able to change mechanics itself. On the other hand, reexamining Freud's texts modifies psychoanalysis itself, just as a reexamination of Marx's would modify Marxism.

What I have just outlined regarding these "discursive instaurations" is, of course, very schematic; this is true, in particular, of the opposition I have tried to draw between discursive initiation and scientific founding. It is not always easy to distinguish between the two; moreover, nothing proves that they are two mutually exclusive procedures. I have attempted the distinction for only one reason: to show that the author function, which is complex enough when one tries to situate it at the level of a book or a series of texts that carry a given signature, involves still more determining factors when one tries to analyze it in larger units, such as groups of works or entire disciplines.

§

To conclude, I would like to review the reasons why I attach a certain importance to what I have said.

On the one hand, an analysis in the direction that I have outlined might provide for an approach to a typology of discourse. It seems to me, at least at first glance, that such a typology cannot be constructed solely from the grammatical features, formal structures, and objects of discourse: more likely, there exist properties or relationships peculiar to discourse (not reducible to the rules of grammar and logic), and one must use these to distinguish the major categories of discourse. The relationship (or non-relationship) with an author, and the different forms this relationship takes, constitute – in a quite visible manner – one of these discursive properties.

On the other hand, I believe that one could find here an introduction to the historical analysis of discourse. Perhaps it is time to study discourses not only in terms of their expressive value or formal transformations but according to their modes of existence. The modes of circulation, valorization, attribution, and appropriation of discourses vary with each culture and are modified within each. The manner in which they are articulated according to social relationships can be more readily understood, I believe, in the activity of the author function and in its modifications than in the themes or concepts that discourses set in motion.

It would seem that one could also, beginning with analyses of this type, reexamine the privileges of the subject. I realize that in undertaking the internal and architectonic analysis of a work (be it a literary text, philosophical system, or scientific work), in setting aside biographical and psychological references, one has already called back into question the absolute character and founding role of the subject. Still, perhaps one must return to this question, not in order to reestablish the theme of an originating subject but to grasp the subject's points of insertion, modes of functioning, and system of dependencies. Doing so means overturning the traditional problem, no longer raising the questions: How can a free subject penetrate the density of things and give it meaning? How can it activate the rules of a language from within and thus give rise to the designs that are properly its own? Instead, these questions will be raised: How, under what conditions, and in what forms can something like a subject appear in the order of discourse? What place can it occupy in each type of discourse, what functions can it assume, and by obeying what rules? In short, it is a matter of depriving the subject (or its substitute) of its role as originator, and of analyzing the subject as a variable and complex function of discourse.

Second, there are reasons dealing with the "ideological" status of the author. The question then becomes: How can one reduce the great peril, the great danger with which fiction threatens our world? The answer is: One can reduce it with the author. The author allows a limitation of the cancerous and dangerous proliferation of significations within a world where one is thrifty not only with one's resources and riches but also with one's discourses and their significations. The author is the principle of thrift in the proliferation of meaning. As a result, we must entirely reverse the traditional idea of the author. We are accustomed, as we have seen earlier, to saying that the author is the genial creator of a work in which he deposits, with infinite wealth and generosity, an inexhaustible world of significations. We are used to thinking that the author is so different from all other men, and so transcendent with regard to all languages that, as soon as he speaks, meaning begins to proliferate, to proliferate indefinitely.

The truth is quite the contrary: the author is not an indefinite source of significations that fill a work; the author does not precede the works; he is a certain functional principle by which, in our culture, one limits, excludes, and chooses; in short, by which one impedes the free circulation, the free manipulation, the free composition, decomposition, and recomposition of fiction. In fact, if we are accustomed to presenting the author as a genius, as a perpetual surging of invention, it is because, in reality, we make him function in exactly the opposite fashion. One can say that the author is an ideological product, since we represent him as the opposite of his historically real function. When a historically given function is represented in a figure that inserts it, one has an ideological production. The author is therefore the ideological figure by which one marks the manner in which we fear the proliferation of meaning.

In saying this, I seem to call for a form of culture in which fiction would not be limited by the figure of the author. It would be pure romanticism, however, to imagine a culture in which the fictive would operate in an absolutely free state, in which fiction would be put at the disposal of everyone and would develop without passing through something like a necessary or constraining figure. Although, since the eighteenth century, the author has played the role of the regulator of the fictive; a role quite characteristic of our era of industrial and bourgeois society, of individualism and private property, still, given the historical modifications that are taking place, it does not seem necessary that the author function remain constant in form, complexity, and even in existence. I think that, as our society changes, at the very moment when it is in the process of changing, the author function will disappear, and in such a manner that fiction and its polysemous texts will once again function according to another mode, but still with a system of constraint – one that will no longer be the author but will have to be determined or, perhaps, experienced [*expérimenter*].

All discourses, whatever their status, form, value, and whatever the treatment to which they will be subjected, would then develop in the anonymity of a murmur. We would no longer hear the questions that have been rehashed for so long: Who really spoke? Is it really he and not someone else? With what authenticity or originality? And what part of his deepest self did he express in his discourse? Instead, there would be other questions, like these: What are the modes of existence of this discourse? Where has it been used, how can it circulate, and who can appropriate it for himself? What are the places in it where there is room for possible subjects? Who can assume these various subject functions? And behind all these questions, we would hear hardly anything but the stirring of an indifference: What difference does it make who is speaking?

Notes

1   John Searle, *Essay in the philosophy of language* (Cambridge, Eng.: Cambridge University Press, 1969) pp. 162–74.

*   This essay is the text of a lecture presented to the Societé Francais de philosophie on 22 February 1969 (Foucault gave a modified form of the lecture in the United States in 1970). This translation by Josué V. Harari has been slightly modified.

CHAPTER 8

Scripts, Sequences, and Stories:
Elements of a Postclassical Narratology

David Herman

David Herman is a Professor of English at North Carolina State University and teaches linguistics, literary theory, and twentieth century literature. He is the author of *Universal Grammar and Narrative Form* (1995). In this essay he relies on cognitive science, especially the idea that we simplify complexity by comparing new sensory data to existing "scripts" in our minds, to reformulate the theory of narrative. A range of conditions must be met for narratives to be intelligible and to count as narratives.

Some thirty years ago, narratologists like Claude Bremond and Roland Barthes, inspired by Vladimir Propp's ground-breaking *Morphology of the Folktale* (1928), began to elaborate the idea of the narrative sequence and to catalog some of the sequences they viewed as common, if not universal, ingredients of narrative. This work addresses several questions. What makes certain sequences of events stories – that is, narratively organized sets of occurrences – and not descriptions, deductions, or, in Bremond's phrase, "lyrical effusions" ("Logic" 390)?[1] Are some narrative sequences more amenable than others to processing as stories? Can certain kinds of stories meet the minimal criteria for narrative yet lack features required for the stories to be deemed valuable, interesting, or "effective" (Labov 370) as narratives (see Bruce; Labov and Waletzky; Genette, *Essay* 25 and *Revisited* 18–19)?

Consider the following set of propositions:

1. A monkey screeched. Sunlight blazed down upon the sea. The rancher gazed proudly at his bison.

This string of sentences may strike me as a bad parody of surrealist description, but the sentences do not compose a narrative sequence. Nor will anyone confuse a syllogism like 2 with a story:

Original publication details: David Herman, "Scripts, Sequences, and Stories: Elements of a Post-classical Narratology." *PMLA* 112.5 (Oct. 1997), pp. 1046–1059. Complete and unabridged. Modern Language Association of America. Reproduced with permission from the Modern Language Association of America.

2. Susan is a narratologist. All narratologists are structuralists. Therefore Susan is a structuralist.

Further, certain conversational openings are used so often that they prompt an interlocutor to coconstruct a particular canonical sequence of utterances:

3. Speaker A: How are you doing?
   Speaker B: Pretty good. How about you?
   Speaker A: Oh, pretty good.

Such two-party sequences are distinguished precisely by their overt unremarkableness, their patent avoidance of any information that might be deemed interesting and thus worthy of narrative communication or telling. Typically such noninformative, even anti-informative, sequences occur in contexts in which neither party wants or offers stories.

On the basis of the following sequence, however, a Gothic tale or maybe an allegorical fable begins to take shape in my imagination:

4. A black-caped figure prowled among the houses. An owl screeched. Three children were borne away into the night.

Example 4 does not explicitly relate what the black-caped figure did while prowling around, but the sequence furnishes enough of a propositional scaffolding for me to reconstruct the figure's nefarious intent, cuing me to infer that the owl screeches just when the prowler abducts the three children. By contrast, though a set of cooking instructions might detail acts and occurrences that follow a particular temporal sequence, it cannot be said to tell a story:

5. "Remove pizza from box and inner wrapper.... [P]lace on preheated cookie sheet. Bake for 16–18 minutes or until center cheese is melted and edges are golden brown."[2]

Given their illocutionary status as commands, the sentences in 5 outline a bare pattern for potential events, a skeleton plan for action, issuing step-by-step directives bearing on the realization of a goal (i.e., the golden-brown pizza). The sequence therefore tells not how something happened, in the manner of a story, but rather how to make something (good) happen, in the manner of a prescription or, more precisely, a recipe. The frozen-pizza instructions differ from the following sequence, whose constituent sentences declare instead of direct. Example 6 organizes a set of individually highly reportable actions and events into a structured whole that I recognize to be (part of) a story:

6. "Mary's fingernails tore at his [Bigger Thomas's] hands and he caught the pillow and covered her entire face with it, firmly. Mary's body surged upward and he pushed downward upon the pillow with all of his weight.... His eyes were filled with the white blur moving toward him in the shadows of the room" (Wright 97–98).

What sets examples 4 and 6 apart from 1, 2, 3, and 5? Why would most people construe 4 and 6 as narrative sequences and the others as a description, a syllogism, an exchange of greetings, and a recipe? Is some critical property – something definitive of stories – built into 4 and 6 but absent in 1, 2, 3, and 5?

In this essay, after reviewing some classical accounts of narrative sequences, I sketch developments in language theory and cognitive science that have occurred after the heyday of structuralist narrative poetics and that may throw further light on the problem of what defines narrative. Of special relevance is research in the field of artificial intelligence on knowledge structures that have been characterized as *schemata, scripts*, and *frames*. For Dennis Mercadal a script is a "description of how a sequence of events is expected to unfold.... A script is similar to a frame in that it [a script] represents a set of expectations.... Frames differ from scripts in that frames are used to represent a point in time. Scripts represent a sequence of events that take place in a time sequence" (255). *Schema*, a "term used in psychology literature which refers to memory patterns that humans use to interpret current experiences," can be defined as "a synonym for framelike structures" (254).[3] This research suggests that the mind draws on a large but not infinite number of "experiential repertoires," of both static (schematic or framelike) and dynamic (scriptlike) types. Stored in the memory, previous experiences form structured repertoires of expectations about current and emergent experiences. Static repertoires allow me to distinguish a chair from a table or a cat from a bread box; dynamic repertoires help me to know how events typically unfold during common occasions like birthday parties and to avoid mistaking birthday parties for barroom brawls or visits to the barber.

Thus cognitive scientists have studied how stereotypical knowledge reduces the complexity and duration of processing tasks bound up with perceiving, inferring, and so on (Bobrow and Norman; Charniak and McDermott 393–415; Grishman 140–58; Mercadal 109, 255; Minsky, "Framework" and *Society* 244–72). In this research tradition, understanding can be described as "a process by which people match what they see and hear to pre-stored groupings of actions that they have already experienced" (Schank and Abelson 67). Scripts are the knowledge representations that store these finite groupings of causally and chronologically ordered actions – actions that are required for the accomplishment of particular tasks (e.g., eating a meal at a restaurant, making an omelette). The performance of a long or complicated task usually necessitates more than one script; no one can do heart surgery or build a particle accelerator without recourse to a vast assortment of complexly interrelated scripts. Likewise, comprehension of a text or a discourse – a story – requires access to a plurality of scripts. In the absence of stereotypes stored as scripts, readers could not draw textual inferences of the most basic sort – for example, that a masked character described as running out of a bank probably just robbed it.

From this perspective, what distinguishes narrative sequences, like 4 and 6, from nonnarrative ones, like 1, 2, 3, and 5, is not simply the form assumed by each. Narrative also depends on how the form of a sequence is anchored in – or triggers a recipient to activate – knowledge about the world. It is not that stories are recognizable only insofar as they tell what their recipients already know; rather, stories stand in a certain relation to what their readers or auditors know, focusing attention on the unusual and the remarkable against a backdrop made up of patterns of belief and expectation.[4] Telling narratives is a certain way of reconciling emergent with prior knowledge; describing, arguing, greeting, and giving recipes are other ways.

My analysis therefore centers on the interrelations among linguistic form, world knowledge, and narrative structure. Two sets of factors fall under my purview. The first, associated with what I call *narrativehood*, bears on what makes readers and listeners deem stories stories. These factors are criterial for narrative; they determine which event sequences qualify as narratives. The second set bears on the *narrativity* of narrative sequences, which is a function of the "formal and contextual features making a narrative more or less narrative" (G. Prince, *Dictionary* 64). *Narrativehood* can be conveniently paired with *narrativity* to suggest the contrast between, on the one hand, the minimal conditions for narrative sequences and, on the other, the factors that allow narrative sequences to be more or less readily processed as narratives. After discussing how narrativehood is a function of the way linguistic, textual, or more broadly semiotic features cue story recipients to activate certain kinds of world knowledge, I turn to the problem of narrativity. Sequences that have a minimal narrativity, which distinguishes them from nonnarrative sequences (of zero narrativity, by definition), are less readily configured into chronologically and causally organized wholes – less readily interpreted as stories – than are sequences with higher degrees of narrativity. Narrativity is a function of the pattern of script-activating cues in a sequence. All other things being equal, the greater the number (and diversity) of the repertoires set into play during the processing of a narrative sequence, the more narrativity will the processor ascribe to that sequence. The final part of my study explores some applications of this theoretical model. The concept of scripts not only yields insights into the structures and functions of particular literary narratives; by examining different modalities of the script-story interface, theorists of narrative may be able to rethink the historical development of narrative techniques and to understand better the differences among narrative genres at any given time. A script-based approach to literary history in particular may suggest ways of reframing the concept of intertextuality, as a tool for exploring not so much networks of links or fields of analogies as relations among dominant and recessive world models, in addition to the bearing of these models on the texts that presuppose and encode them.

The early narratologists anticipated subsequent research on knowledge structures. Thus my goal is not to dismiss classical narrative poetics as an outmoded framework for analysis but to argue for its continued usefulness within certain limits. Rethinking the problem of narrative sequences can promote the development of a postclassical narratology that is not necessarily poststructuralist, an enriched theory that draws on concepts and methods to which the classical narratologists did not have access (cf. Herman, "Focalization" and "Textual *You*").[5] Although postclassical narratology is being energized by a variety of theoretical models and perspectives – feminist, rhetorical, linguistic, and computational – my purpose in this essay is to assemble some elements of a specifically cognitive approach to narrative discourse (cf. Jahn). Such an approach can potentially recontextualize reader-response theories contrasting shared and idiosyncratic reading strategies, for it shifts the focus from interpretive conventions to general and basic processing mechanisms that give such conventions their force and determine their scope of applicability (on this point, contrast Wolfgang Iser and Richard J. Gerrig).

Sequences: Classical Accounts and Postclassical Perspectives

As Bremond remarks, for Propp the basic unit or "narrative atom" is the function; narrative functions are actions or events that "when grouped in sequences, generate the narrative" ("Logic" 387). In Propp's words, the function "is understood as an act of character, defined from the point of view of its significance for the course of the action" (21). The action thus constitutes the function, functions constitute the sequence, and sequences constitute the story or, in Propp's case, the Russian folktale. To invoke a descriptive lexicon that A. J. Greimas derived from Propp, a story or tale can be analyzed into a set of actants whose specific deeds, realized linearly in the syntagmatic chain of the discourse, encode a more abstract pattern of actantial roles – a pattern formed by paradigmatic relations linking particular acts performed over the course of the narrative (Greimas 147–48, 176–256; cf. Lévi-Strauss 812–16). The logicosemantic properties of such actantial roles – hero, villain, sender, receiver, and so on – derive from their functional orientation within that emergent totality known as "plot." In the Proppian tradition, therefore, narrative sequences are representations of the acts and events realized linguistically or textually in narrative discourse. For example, in sequence 6 the story is not (or not simply) that Bigger Thomas smothers Mary Dalton out of fear of detection by her blind mother (the awesome white blur); such a paraphrase refers only elliptically to a network of actantial relations. This network governs the play of functions structuring 6, which is in turn constituted as a narrative sequence precisely by its actantial structure.

However, this model does not indicate how to match linguistic or textual units with the function(s) they purportedly fulfill in any given sequence.[6] Ideally, the procedure for correlating formal units with functions and roles would be explicit and yield uniformly reproducible results, but the functional profile of Bigger Thomas's deeds in 6, for instance, is so multifarious as to generate competing, even contradictory, interpretations.[7] In the sequence Bigger is simultaneously villain and hero, agent and patient (as a heated classroom discussion of Wright's novel recently demonstrated to me). Propp, for his part, tried to find constraints that, rooted in the structure of the tale as genre, predetermine the order of the functions occurring in any tale. Such constraints would allow readers to correlate acts with functions in more than just an ad hoc way. Thus, though functions might be omitted or inverted in particular tales (Mandler and Johnson 129–35; Stein 494–96), "[m]orphologically, a tale (*skázka*) may be termed any development proceeding from villainy (A) or a lack (a), through intermediary functions to marriage (W*), or to other functions employed as a dénouement. Terminal functions are at times a reward (F), a gain or in general the liquidation of misfortune (K), an escape from pursuit (Rs), etc." (Propp 92). But this solution came with a price; it severely limited the relevance of the model by anchoring it too firmly in a specific narrative genre (Bremond, *Logique* 11–47; cf. Doležel 65–66). The approach also gave an overly deterministic coloration to narrative sequences, a problem that Bremond's work on virtuality or nonactualization in sequences tried to address. Part of the interest and complexity of narrative depends on the merely probabilistic, not deterministic, links between some actions and events (Doležel 63–64; Culler, "Defining" 136; cf. Ryan 109–74). What makes a story worth telling is, at least in part, that things might not in fact have turned out that way. Bigger Thomas might not have smothered Mary Dalton, or Mary's mother might have stayed out of the room in the first place; or, in example 4, the black-caped figure might have abducted the entire village.[8]

But the chief difficulty with the Proppian model, possibly the source of its other limitations, is that Propp tried to locate the criteria for narrative in the form of the tale itself, in the ordered incrementation of the tale's functions and sequences. Francophone structuralists later came to recognize that while linguistic or textual form may trigger the interpretation of a sequence as a story, the form of sequences is not a sufficient condition for a story. Thus, even as Tzvetan Todorov articulates a formal definition of the narrative sequence – "A sequence implies the existence of two distinct situations each of which can be described with the help of a small number of propositions; between at least one proposition of each situation there must exist a relation of transformation" – he refers back to Viktor Shklovsky's postulation of the "existence, in each of us, of a faculty of judgment (we might say, today, of a competence) permitting us to decide if a narrative sequence is complete or not" (232, 231). A sequence can be processed as a narrative not just because it has a certain form but also because its form cues readers, in structured, nonrandom ways, to interpret the sequence as a narrative. A similar dual commitment to form and context appears in Barthes's "Introduction to the Structural Analysis of Narratives" (1966). On the one hand, the essay sometimes sounds like glossematics (Hjelmslev, *Prolegomena*), as when Barthes calls the narrative sequence "a logical succession of nuclei [narrative hinges, or the elements without which a story would cease to be a story] bound together by a relation of solidarity: the sequence opens when one of its terms has no solidary antecedent and closes when another of its terms has no consequent." (One of his examples is the picking up and putting down of a telephone receiver.) On the other hand, Barthes describes such sequences as "essential headings" of "the narrative language within us" (101, 102). People learn that language by storing a lot of different narratives in memory as schemata, in terms of which they can then read and process other stories (cf. 116–17). Sequences thereby become the output of "naming operations" that allow readers to "grasp every logical succession of actions as a nominal whole" (102); they are the product of readers' prior and ongoing negotiations with narrative discourse, not the atomic or molecular constituents of discourse that was narratively structured before anyone ever got to it. Indeed, in *S/Z* Barthes associates sequences with just one of the codes that can be brought to bear on narrative: the "proairetic" code, by means of which story recipients try "to give a... name to a series of actions, themselves deriving from a patrimonial hoard of human experiences" (204; cf. Bremond, "Logic" 389–90, 406). Whereas Propp sought to isolate the minimal constituents of Russian folktales, Barthes argues that experiential repertoires are what allow readers to recognize a *rescue*, a *seduction*, or any other sequence when they see it in the making.

Subsequent research has, however, provided richer, more nuanced ways of talking about Barthes's patrimonial hoard of experiences. Among these are the knowledge structures that have been termed scripts, or standardized event sequences.[9] Building on Frederick Bartlett's analysis of memory as the organization of prior experience into patterns of expectations for current experience (201–14), cognitive scientists have explored how stereotypical situations and events are stored in the memory and used to guide interpretations of the world. For example, I know what to do when the waiter comes up to me in a restaurant because I have been in restaurants before and remember the standard roles of waiter and customer (Schank and Abelson 42–46). Every trip to a restaurant would be an adventure that consumed too many cognitive resources if I never mastered the appropriate restaurant scripts. As Roger Schank and Robert Abelson put it, "Some episodes are reminiscent of others. As an economy measure in the storage of episodes, when enough of them are alike they are remembered in terms of a standardized generalized episode which we will call a script" (19; cf. van Dijk 179–83), defined as follows:

> A script is a structure that describes an appropriate sequence of events in a particular context. A script is made up of slots and requirements about what can fill those slots. The structure is an interconnected whole, and what is in one slot affects what can be in another. Scripts handle stylized everyday situations. They are not subject to much change, nor do they provide the apparatus for handling totally novel situations.[10] Thus, a script is a predetermined, stereotyped sequence of actions that defines a well-known situation (41; cf. Schank 7–12).

Significantly, the concept of scripts was designed to explain how people can build up complex (semantic) representations of stories on the basis of few textual or linguistic cues. Thus when I read

7. "John went to Bill's birthday party. Bill opened his presents. John ate the cake and left" (Schank and Abelson 39)

or even

8. "Mary was invited to Jack's party. She wondered if he would like a kite" (Minsky, *Society* 261)

I can make an astonishing number of inferences about the situations and participants – fill in the blanks of the stories, so to speak – because the sequences unfold against the backdrop of the familiar birthday-party script. The "terminals" or "slots" associated with that script allow me to make certain default assumptions (e.g., that guests give presents at birthday parties) and so to reconstruct the stories from merely skeletal sequences. But the research on scripts suggests that it would be misguided to search for some purely formal property that makes 7 and 8 narrative. Instead, it is the relation between the (form of the) sequences and the party script that accounts for my intuition that 7 and 8 are stories or at least parts of stories.

The notion of scripts provides a finer-grained vocabulary for describing what earlier narratologists characterized as readers' tendency to organize event sequences into stories (Chatman 45–46; Scholes 100). Every act of telling arguably requires that a listener or reader use scripts to help set the narrative in motion, to cocreate the story. But how might this script-story interface be characterized in detail? Not just any sequence can cue a reader to activate a particular script. Consider this sequence:

9. John went to a get-together for Bill. After some food and festivities, John went home.

If I told you 9 out of the blue, I could not reasonably expect you to infer from the cues provided that it is a story about a birthday party – that John and Bill are children, that parents probably supervised the gathering, the festivities were over in time for the partygoers' early bedtimes, and so forth. So the formal features of sequences constrain the kinds of scripts that can be indexed to any story, and conversely they limit the sorts of stories that can be predicated on any script. However, attempting to specify the nature of the constraint in question raises the problem of narrativehood, of what makes a narrative a narrative. For the form of a sequence is neither a necessary nor a sufficient condition for specific components of world knowledge to be activated during the processing of that sequence (Wilensky 425; Emmott).

Suppose that a group of parents have been discussing their children's birthday parties for a while, and then one of the parents says:

10. John went to Bill's. John ate so much he got sick. Then John had to go home.

Presumably the other parents would conclude that 10 is a story about a birthday party, even though no explicit textual cues license that inference. Thus a particular set of cues need not be present in a story for recipients of it to activate a given script. A discourse context – the total context of utterances exchanged during an occasion of talk – can imbue sequences it contains with narrative functions that they might not possess in isolation or, for that matter, in other discourse contexts. But neither is the presence of particular textual cues a sufficient condition for a script to be activated. Although example 8 would set the birthday-party script into play in many contexts, it would not do so if presented in, for instance, an account of the retirement of a chief meteorologist named Jack whose colleague Mary runs a program for observation kites.

As the birthday-party examples suggest, the knowledge structures regulating the design and interpretation of narrative sequences have an extremely general provenance; strings of sentences representing actions and events can be interpreted as stories only insofar as they are embedded in global semantic frameworks subtending all thought, speech, and behavior. The question then is how far, and in what fashion, scripts constrain the textual, linguistic, or more broadly semiotic production of particular stories. At what point would 4, 6, or 7, for example, become too skeletal for reconstruction as narrative sequences? In each case, which cues are definitive of a story, and why? I can begin to address these questions by moving from the problem of the membership criteria for the category of narrative to degrees of narrativity – to the way that different versions of a story can strike readers or listeners as more or less narrative. The factors bearing on narrativity may in turn help illuminate the nature of narrativehood. There may be a threshold past which differences of degree effectively become differences of kind; beyond that point a sequence may begin to display so little narrativity that it can no longer be processed as a story at all.

The Problem of Narrativity: A Thought Experiment

Narratologists differentiate between "tellability" and what they term "narrativity." Situations and events can be more or less tellable, and the ways in which they are told can be more or less readily processed in narrative terms – can display different degrees of narrativity. Thus, whereas both predicates are scalar, tellability attaches to configurations of facts and narrativity to sequences representing configurations of facts. For example, the facts surrounding a bank robbery are likely to be deemed more tellable than those connected with the daylong movement of a shadow across the ground – although some postmodernist writers have suggested otherwise (e.g., Robbe-Grillet; see also the final section of this essay). But if there are two representations of the facts of the robbery, one (i.e., one version of the story of the robbery) may be deemed to have more narrativity than the other. Imagine an outside observer's fast-paced report compared to a drawn-out, disoriented account by a badly shaken victim.

But what is it, exactly, that makes one version of a story more narrative than another? What formal or contextual variables correlate with differing degrees of narrativity? Since I cannot engage here in a full-blown analysis of all the variables associated with degrees of narrativity (see Giora and Shen), a brief thought experiment instead may suggest ways to mark off gradations on the scale of narrativity – the continuum stretching from sequences that are nearly impossible to process as narratives to those immediately identifiable as such.

Consider the sequences 11–15, read as much as possible according to the grammar of English:

11. A splubba walked in. A gingy beebed the yuck, and the splubba was orped.

A rudimentary action structure is apparent in this sequence: after the entrance of an actant (the splubba) who has not been previously introduced in the context of the discourse, another new actant (the gingy) does something called beebing to something called a yuck, and this leads to the splubba's being or becoming "orped."[11]

    12. A splubba fibblo. Sim a gingy beebie the yuck, i the splubba orpia.

In 12 only the indefinite and definite articles are decipherable. The result is a drastically impoverished action structure, or rather a set of discourse entities that cannot readily be organized into any configuration of actions and events. Nevertheless, the distribution of indefinite and definite noun phrases – patterned in the way that given and new information is typically parceled out in a discourse (Emmott 158–61; Firbas; E. Prince; Schiffrin 197–226) – prompts me to read a kind of narrative structure into 12, along the lines of "first this, then that," or perhaps even "this, then because of this, that," although I do not know the meaning of *this* and *that*. Still, I am warranted in saying that 12 has less narrativity than 11. It is not that 11 is more intelligible than 12; for it is not as if, in 11, I know what *beebed* and *orped* mean. Rather, in 12 the deletion of a particular class of morphosyntactic features (verb inflections) removes some of the formal components that cue me to read 11 as an ordered sequence of causally linked events. Arguably, the narrativity of 12 has decreased in proportion to the deletion of such cues.

    Sequence 13, however, displays zero narrativity:

    13. Oe splubba fibblo. Sim oe gingy beebie ca yuck, i ca splubba orpia.

This string does not meet the criteria for narrativehood. It lacks sufficient grammatical structure for me to infer actants and entities populating a narrated world, let alone read an action structure into one temporal stretch of that world. By contrast, 14 exhibits more narrativity than 11 or 12 (and ipso facto 13), and 15 displays more than 14 because 15 narrates a fully recoverable, if not fully believable, world:

    14. A splubba walked in. A gingy pulled the lever, and the splubba was instantaneously inebriated.
    15. A bad man walked in. A beneficent sorcerer pulled the lever, and the bad man was instantaneously inebriated.

In comparison with 11, 14 provides additional formal cues for the use of particular kinds of world knowledge – specifically, stereotyped sequences of events such as *pulling a lever* and *becoming inebriated* – during the processing of the sequence. These supplementary cues include a higher percentage of recognizable noun phrases, allowing me to identify more entities populating the narrated world. In addition, the entire morphology of the verbs, not just their inflections, is grammatical, so I can situate story referents in a more fully realized action structure. That structure is constituted by the interplay between the verbs contained in the string and the event sequences encoded into my memory as scripts. Processing 15, a completely grammatical sequence, requires more (and more diverse) experiential repertoires than does processing 14, in which fewer story elements are expressed grammatically and thereby made available for subsumption under scripts.

    The sequences should thus be ranked 12, 11, 14, and 15 in order of increasing narrativity. In 11 and 12 there are markers, more or less prominent, of narrative (e.g., logicotemporal operators, indexes of given and new information); I know that I am in the presence of a story without knowing what that story means, what it is or might be all about. In 15 these markers furnish the formal scaffolding for a sequence whose content does lend itself to reconstruction along narrative lines. This increased narrativity stems in turn from the nature and scope of the scripts (and frames) activated during the interpretation of the sequence, from *being a bad man* to *walking in* to *performing sorcery*. Thus there is a direct proportion between a sequence's degree of narrativity and the range and complexity of the world knowledge set into play during the interpretation of (the form of) the given sequence. (See, however, n15.) This thought experiment has suggested that a sequence rooted in a plurality of scripts will be more easily processed as a story, will be deemed more narrative, than one only fitfully anchored in the knowledge frames (Minsky, *Society* 263) bound up with grammatical competence. It has also indicated that a sequence's degree of narrativity is a function not of script use alone but also of a shifting constellation of formal and contextual factors. At stake are a wide range of variables operating at various levels of narrative structure, including morphosyntactic features of the language in which a story is told or written, the grammatical encoding of information about story referents as given or new, the extent to which the form of the sequence facilitates script-aided recognition of a coherent action structure, and the pertinence of intrasequential details to broader, intersequential patterns built up on the basis of generic expectations. The thought experiment brings into focus, too, a specific research strategy for postclassical narratology. Using Hjelmslevian parlance, Gerald Prince argues that what defines narrative is the form of its content side, not the form of its expression side.[12] But, as the experiment suggests, the processing of a sequence as a story can be aided or impeded by features pertaining to its mode of expression. A fuller investigation of narrativity, then, should use the resources of language theory and cognitive science to study how the (form of the) expression side of stories interacts with (the form of) their content side. In other words, to understand why some sequences are more narrative than others, narratologists need new ways of modeling the interrelations between story and discourse, *fabula* and *sjužet*.

Finally, the foregoing experiment reveals that narrative competence can be redescribed as a nested structure of processing strategies operating at different levels – or during different phases – of story comprehension. Spoken or written sequences take on the profile of stories because of the way their form triggers knowledge about (1) the grammar of the language in which they are related, (2) standardized event sequences, among other sorts of experiential repertoires, and (3) other, prior sequences (and groups of sequences) mediating encounters with any particular string. Ranking these processing strategies, determining their order of importance or the stages at which readers and listeners resort to them in interpreting a narrative, requires a separate research project.[13] In the last section of this essay, I want to examine some interconnections between strategies of types 2 and 3, mentioned above – between script-based strategies and strategies rooted in knowledge about intersequential relations.[14] Although schematic, my discussion will, I hope, demonstrate that the script concept can be productive not just for narrative theory but also for the practice of literary interpretation.

Indeed, in setting out the problem of narrative sequences, I have already appealed to knowledge based on intersequential, or generic, patterning. Arguably, generic factors help account for my inclination to process sequence 4 as a (Gothic) story and not as a description like 1. Gothic tales I know predispose me to read a coherent action structure into 4; by contrast, in 1 my search for analogous textual or generic models results in my tending not to organize intrasequential events into a narrative. Moreover, a cognitive approach to literary narratives suggests that genres – and, for that matter, changes in narrative technique over time – can themselves be redescribed as modes of script use. Narratives can anchor themselves to stored world knowledge in vastly different ways, whether they activate it for their processing or encode it as themes. Hence focusing on the script-story interface may yield new perspectives on the study of literary history and cast new light on the generic categories to which narratives are typically assigned.

Scripts and Literary Interpretation

Although researchers as diverse as R. A. Buck (71–82), Jonathan Culler (*Poetics* 130–60), Wolfgang Iser (53–85, 103–34), and Wallace Martin (67–68) have worked to implement versions of the script concept in literary-theoretical contexts, more attention needs to be given to the reciprocal relation between scripts and literary texts – to the way scripts shape the design and interpretation of texts and texts in turn affect the production and dissemination of scripts (cf. Segre 26). To this end, I propose two hypotheses, one diachronic and the other synchronic in emphasis, which could be used to generate research strategies for a postclassical narratology:

> The nature and scope of the world knowledge required to process literary texts change over time, as do the ways in which the script-story interface is encoded or thematized in texts. Such changes correspond to shifts in the relations among recessive, dominant, and emergent narrative techniques.

> Contemporaneous texts can relate differently to prevailing scripts. Texts can pertain more or less critically and reflexively to the scripts circulating when the texts were written. For narrative, these variations correspond to generic classifications used to categorize stories.

Literary history produces an ever-expanding corpus of texts, whose varying designs reveal changing conceptions of how many (and what sorts of) scripts should be activated during textual processing. The formal impetus, the constitutive gesture, of literary fiction has been the rejection or at least the backgrounding of scripts in which prior texts were anchored and the complementary foregrounding of new scripts matched to changing ideas about narrative. Thus *Don Quixote* (1605) opens with a semicomic indictment of the delusive power of outmoded scripts, those of chivalric romance; interpretation of the subsequent series of action sequences requires scripts grounded in an awareness of human potential and limitations rather than in the more restricted world knowledge undergirding idealized quests, knightly courtesy, and so on. Cervantes's novelistic narrative distinguishes itself from romance by demanding richer and more numerous experiential repertoires from readers who would coconstruct his fictional world.

Such changes in scripts and stories are reciprocal: the need for narrative innovation stems from the dominance of certain kinds of world knowledge that, although initially of limited influence, have been reinforced, consolidated, and generalized by prior narrative techniques. Thus, by the time of Diderot's *Jacques le fataliste et son maître* (*Jacques the Fatalist*; 1773), not the romance but rather the novel itself is the repository and source of outworn scripts. A product of the Enlightenment's rethinking of the claims of truth and fiction, knowledge and myth, Diderot's text features a narrator who insists that he is not writing a novel (51, 214) and who implies that to have verisimilitude, a fiction must *not* conform to novelistically patterned sequences of actions, such as pitched battles between heroes and villains (22, 30, 49). Diderot's antinovel resists such stereotyped action sequences, and promotes script multiplication and enrichment, by constantly foregrounding the contingency, even indeterminacy, of the narrated events, sometimes hesitating between alternative accounts of happenings in the story world (251–54). Narrativizing the philosophical concerns of the French encyclopedists, in particular Enlightenment debates concerning determinism and free will, *Jacques the Fatalist* contains sequences designed to activate several competing processing strategies simultaneously and thus to provoke reflection on deterministic models of human behavior.[15]

Later literary developments suggest that there are other ways of reconfiguring the relations between world models and narrative techniques and other reasons for doing so. For example, Sartre's *La nausée* (*Nausea*; 1938) transforms the antinovel into a metanovel. Thematizing the search for ordered event sequences as a symptom of bad faith – distinguishing the radical fluidity of existence from the stories through which human beings inauthentically seek to congeal it (*Nausea* 37, 39–40) – Sartre's narrative is about the impossibility and undesirability of narrative. Given that the idea of the passage of time is "an invention of man" 'une invention des hommes' for Roquentin and that "[e]very existing thing is born without reason, prolongs itself out of weakness and dies by chance" '[t]out existant naît sans raison, se prolonge par faiblesse et meurt par rencontre' (132, 133; 168, 169), telling stories about human lives is an inherently and perniciously (self-)delusional project. The less authentic my attitude toward existence, the more scripts in which I am enmeshed and hence the more stories that I unfortunately begin to understand (*Nausea* 56–57, 95–96). Yet the text's thematic profile is at odds with the processing strategies needed to cocreate the action structures around which its themes are clustered. Thus the experience of Sartre's narrative form is fundamentally dialectical, forcing readers to adopt a stance that is at once authentic and inauthentic: they can reconstruct Roquentin's rejection of previous world models, his striving for a condition of absolute scriptlessness, only by anchoring his gestures in a variety of experiential repertoires.

To be sure, fuller implementation of the script concept in the study of literary history would require an expanded comparison of shifts in narrative form with changing world models, as well as a more comprehensive survey of ways in which the interplay between scripts and stories can itself figure as a theme. The diachronic investigation of script use across time needs to be supplemented, however, with a synchronic investigation of script use across different genres at the same time, in accordance with my second research hypothesis. The recall of previously interpreted sequences, which are recognizable as narratives by virtue of the world knowledge they activate, enables the processing of other sequences as members of larger narrative classes (the diary novel, autobiography, travel narrative, etc.). Thus differences in genre can be correlated with differences in the processing strategies at once necessitated and promoted by particular kinds of sequences. Such strategies, which eventuate in generic codes, can be more or less multidimensional; in particular, different types of sequences relate more or less critically and reflexively to the world models on which their interpretation simultaneously depends.[16]

A few representative sequences may provide a blueprint for further research on the orientation of narrative genres toward prevailing scripts. Sequences 16, 17, and 18 are excerpted from works written within fifteen years of one another. The first sequence belongs to the genre of children's fiction, the second to that of autobiography, and the third to that of experimental literary narrative. In progressing through this series, one must use increasingly multidimensional or reflexive processing strategies. The processing of narratives is more complex when they inhibit what might be termed the naive application of scripts and promote instead reflection on the limits of applicability of the scripts being invoked. The three stories recount event sequences – *getting one's head stuck in a jar, confronting armed soldiers, going down on all fours and acting like a dog* – that could be transposed into other narrative genres. Correlatively, generic differences stem not from narrative content as such but from the complexity and duration of the interpretive routes that readers take in formulating narrative content (e.g., through story paraphrases like the ones just offered).

Sequence 16 is taken from the point in A. A. Milne's *Winnie-the-Pooh* (1926) when Winnie-the-Pooh is tempted by his craving for honey into his and Piglet's Heffalump Trap, where he gets his head stuck in the jar intended as bait for the nonexistent but much feared Heffalumps:

> 16. "And all the time Winnie-the-Pooh had been trying to get the honey-jar off his head. The more he shook it, the more tightly it stuck. 'Bother!' he said, inside the jar, and 'Oh, help!' and, mostly 'Ow!' And he tried bumping it against things, but as he couldn't see what he was bumping it against, it didn't help him; and he tried to climb out of the Trap, but as he could see nothing but jar, and not much of that, he couldn't find his way. So at last he lifted up his head, jar and all, and made a loud, roaring noise of Sadness and Despair" (67).

This sequence suggests one of the crucial features of children's fiction: the genre is designed to establish and inculcate particular world models (e.g., those associated with delaying gratification or resisting the gratuitous fabrication of monsters). This genre's primary function is not to problematize a world readers only think they know but rather to help them acquire more strategies for getting to know it. Far from presuming the script expertise supporting more-elaborate narrative experiments, children's fiction consolidates and reinforces the scripts on which narrative competence itself depends. Such fiction teaches reading by teaching scripts.

Sequence 17 comes from Maud Gonne MacBride's autobiography, *A Servant of the Queen* (1938), and recounts events surrounding the Irish civil war:

> 17. "Outside General Mulcahy's house in Portobello, the Women's Prisoners' Defence League had organised a great protest meeting against the murder of prisoners of war for which Mulcahy was held responsible. The Free State soldiers were drawn up inside the railings; some shots had been fired over our heads; a woman's hat had been pierced by a bullet. I heard an order given and the front line of soldiers knelt down with rifles ready, – some of the young soldiers were white and trembling. I got up on the parapet of the railing and smiled contempt at the officer. He had curious rather beautiful pale grey eyes and a thin brown face. We gazed at each other a full minute. The order to fire was not given" (15).

Admittedly, part of what distinguishes 17 from 16 is MacBride's greater descriptive richness; 17 features a more densely populated story world with an independently verifiable history and geography, the parameters of which are established by spatiotemporal indexes such as *in Portobello* and *Free State soldiers*. As a result, reconstructing the action sequence in 17 necessitates considerably more script expertise, familiarity with a greater variety of world models, than does processing 16 as a story. More than this, however, because MacBride's text belongs to the genre of autobiography, interpretation of 17 requires, to a greater degree than does reading *Winnie-the-Pooh*, reliance on and reevaluation of a particular class of world models: scripts and frames bearing on the formation and maintenance of selfhood (cf. Linde 127–91).[17] MacBride's text not only activates experiential repertoires but also compels reflection on their explanatory scope – on the kinds of stories about the self that they do or do not help readers comprehend (Herman, "Autobiography"). At once invoking and suspending models for heroic action created by or centered on men, interpretation of the sequence enriches the repertoire of behaviors that can be used to typify female actants (e.g., facing down a group of armed soldiers); the text thereby exploits existing scripts to generate additional models for understanding who women are and what they can do.

Sequence 18, taken from the ending of Djuna Barnes's experimental novel *Nightwood* (1937), requires processing strategies that are even more multidimensional:

18. "The dog, quivering in every muscle, sprang back, his tongue a stiff curving terror in his mouth; moved backward, back, as she came on, whimpering too, coming forward, her [Robin's] head turned completely sideways, grinning and whimpering. Backed into the farthest corner, the dog reared as if to avoid something that troubled him to such agony that he seemed to rise from the floor; then he stopped, clawing sideways at the wall, his forepaws lifted and sliding. Then head down, dragging her forelocks in the dust, she struck against his side. He let loose one howl of misery and bit at her, dashing about her, barking, and as he sprang on either side of her he always kept his head toward her, dashing his rump now this side, now that, of the wall" (170).

It could be argued that 18 exploits prevailing scripts more critically and reflexively than 17 and that generic differences between 18 and 17 can be measured by the scope and frequency of the script suspensions cued by the texts' narrative form. At stake in *Night-wood* is a gamut of world models, including those bearing on questions of personal identity. The passage conveys a strikingly particularized action structure, which dissolves both human and animal behavior into microsequences of atomistic gestures. The sequence thus provokes reflection on, among other aspects of script construction and usage, the canons of tellability (at what level of detail should event sequences be stored or told? what counts as an action or an event?), models for understanding women's and for that matter human identity (to what extent can scripts indexed to nature and culture be transposed? how have such transpositions contributed to cultural as well as cognitive stereotypes about identity?), and the very concept of purposive action (why would someone mimic and thereby terrorize a dog? on the basis of what world models can readers make sense of such event sequences?).

While constituting only prolegomena for a future narratology, this essay suggests that a rethinking of classical approaches to the problem of narrative sequences will entail a more careful investigation of the interface between script and story. Postclassical narratology contains structuralist theory as one of its "moments" but enriches the older approach with research tools taken from other areas of inquiry. The result is not simply new ways of getting at old problems in narrative analysis but a rearticulation of those problems, including the root problem of how to define stories. Here I have argued that incorporating cognitive tools into narratology can throw new light on some of the most basic issues facing analysts of narrative. Given that scripts and stories are in some sense mutually constitutive, how readers and listeners process a narrative – and indeed whether they are able to process it at all – depends on the nature and scope of the world knowledge to which it is indexed. Postclassical narratology should therefore study how interpreters of stories are able to activate relevant kinds of knowledge with or without explicit textual cues to guide them. At the same time, it should investigate how narratives, through their forms as well as their themes, work to privilege some world models over others. After all, if the right kind of children's story caught on, people might finally stop worrying about Heffalumps. And in time, splubbas might circumvent the dreaded pulling of the yuck.

Notes

My thanks go to Manfred Jahn, Emma Kafalenos, Susan Moss, Gerald Prince, and Marie-Laure Ryan for their invaluable feedback on various drafts of this essay. I am especially grateful to Harold F. Mosher, Jr., and Thomas Pavel for their productive questions and criticisms.

1   In this essay the terms *narrative* and *story* are coreferential.
2   Heating instructions for Red Baron Premium 4-Cheese Frozen Pizza.
3   See Bartlett; Crevier; Jacobs and Rau; Schank.
4   Rachel Giora and Yeshayahu Shen (450–51), Propp (25–65), Thomas Pavel (14, 17–24), and Marie-Laure Ryan (124–47) have made a stronger claim, arguing that processing sequences of actions as narratives requires readers to make inferences about characters' goals and motivations. For empirical evidence that conflicts with this claim, see Gerrig 36, 53–63.
5   On the distinction between classical and postclassical theories, see Plotnitsky; Smith and Plotnitsky.
6   Despite Emma Kafalenos's claim that a "named set of functions provides a uniform vocabulary for labelling interpretations of events" (131) and allows at least some of the ingredients of narrative competence to be captured, her modification of the Proppian framework does not directly address the problem of how to match particular (classes of) linguistic or textual units with functions. See Hendricks 40–51.
7   Propp discussed this problem when noting that a single function can have a double morphological meaning (66–70). Contrast Ryan 211–22.
8   Hence Gerald Prince's definition: "narrative is the representation of at least two real or fictive events or situations in a time sequence, neither of which presupposes or *entails* the other" *(Form* 4; my emphasis). Cf. Ryan on what she calls the principle of semantic diversity in narrative universes (156–66).
9   Although the final section of this essay invokes the somewhat broader concept of "world knowledge," which encompasses both scriptlike (dynamic) and framelike (static) knowledge structures, my primary focus throughout is on standardized sequences of events.
10   For Schank and Abelson novel situations require more-general planning mechanisms built into intelligence. See also Grishman 146–47.
11   Giora and Shen define an action structure in narrative analysis as "a high-order organization which hierarchically connects not only adjacent events... but also events which are remote from one another on the temporal axis of a given discourse. Thus, a story... is more than pairwise relationships among events, but rather, a string of events combined into a psychological whole" (450).
12   "Aspects" 50–51; cf. Hjelmslev, "Stratification." Prince's point is that both narratives and nonnarratives can be expressed in various media (film, dance, language, etc.). Furthermore, given that "a narrative, a non-narrative poem, or an essay may deal with the same subjects and develop the same themes" (51), what Hjelmslev would call the substance of the content side does not define narrative either.
13   See the important work of May Charles, who has studied how readers draw on world knowledge and text models to construct fictional worlds.
14   There are two sorts of intersequential relations: between sequences in a single narrative (see Iser) and between sequences in different narratives in a single genre. In this essay I focus on the second to explore how generic patterning helps readers recognize event sequences as narrative.

15 Diderot's text points to an aspect of narrativity not considered in the thought experiment conducted in the previous section. Just as there is a lower limit of narrativity, past which sequences activate so few world models that they cannot be processed as stories, there is an upper limit of narrativity, past which so many scripts are set into play that processors experience cognitive over-load and find themselves unable to structure oversaturated sequences into coherent, narratively organized wholes. Sketching this upper limit of narrativity requires a separate study (Herman, *Universal Grammar* 124–38), but what seems to set twentieth-century fictional experiments apart from earlier experiments is the frequency of script oversaturation in narrative contexts.

16 Narrative can be viewed as a way of accommodating emergent to existing knowledge. Narrative genres represent distinct strategies – more or less critical and reflexive – for achieving that accommodation.

17 The point can be put the other way around: it is because 17 relates in certain ways to a certain class of scripts that readers give it the generic label of autobiography.

Works Cited

Barnes, Djuna. *Nightwood*. New York: New Directions, 1961.

Barthes, Roland. "Introduction to the Structural Analysis of Narratives." *Image Music Text*. Trans. Stephen Heath. New York: Hill, 1977. 79–124.

Barthes, Roland. *S/Z*. Trans. Richard Miller. New York: Hill, 1974.

Bartlett, Frederick. *Remembering: A Study in Experimental and Social Psychology*. Cambridge: Cambridge UP, 1932.

Bobrow, Daniel G., and Donald A. Norman. "Some Principles of Memory Schemata." *Representation and Understanding: Studies in Cognitive Science*. Ed. Bobrow and Allan Collins. New York: Academic, 1975. 131–49.

Bremond, Claude. "The Logic of Narrative Possibilities." *New Literary History* 11 (1980): 387–411.

Bremond, Claude. *Logique du récit*. Paris: Seuil, 1973.

Bruce, Bertram. "What Makes a Good Story?" *Language Arts* 55 (1978): 460–66.

Buck, R. A. "Reading Forster's Style: Face Actions and Social Scripts in *Maurice*." *Style* 30 (1996): 69–94.

Charles, May. "A Postmodern Challenge to Reference-World Construction: Gilbert Sorrentino's *Mulligan Stew*." *Style* 29 (1995): 235–61.

Charniak, Eugene, and Drew McDermott. *Introduction to Artificial Intelligence*. Reading: Addison, 1985.

Chatman, Seymour. *Story and Discourse: Narrative Structure in Fiction and Film*. Ithaca: Cornell UP, 1978.

Crevier, Daniel. *AI: The Tumultuous History of the Search for Artificial Intelligence*. New York: Basic, 1993.

Culler, Jonathan. "Defining Narrative Units." *Style and Structure in Literature: Essays in the New Stylistics*. Ed. Roger Fowler. Oxford: Blackwell; 1975. 121–45.

Culler, Jonathan. *Structuralist Poetics: Structuralism, Linguistics, and the Study of Literature*. Ithaca: Cornell UP, 1975.

Diderot, Denis. *Jacques the Fatalist*. Trans. Michael Henry. London: Penguin, 1986.

Doležel, Lubomír. "From Motifemes to Motifs." *Poetics* 4 (1972): 55–90.

Emmott, Catherine. "Frames of Reference: Contextual Monitoring and the Interpretation of Narrative Discourse." *Advances in Written Text Analysis*. Ed. Malcolm Coulthard. London: Routledge, 1994. 157–66.

Firbas, Jan. "On Defining the Theme in Functional Sentence Analysis." *Travaux linguistiques de Prague* 1 (1964): 267–80.

Genette, Gérard. *Narrative Discourse: An Essay in Method*. Trans. Jane E. Lewin. Ithaca: Cornell UP, 1980.

Genette, Gérard. *Narrative Discourse Revisited*. Trans. Jane E. Lewin. Ithaca: Cornell UP, 1988.

Gerrig, Richard J. *Experiencing Narrative Worlds: On the Psychological Activities of Reading*. New Haven: Yale UP, 1993.

Giora, Rachel, and Yeshayahu Shen. "Degrees of Narrativity and Strategies of Semantic Reduction." *Poetics* 22 (1994): 447–58.

Greimas, Algirdas Julien. *Structural Semantics: An Attempt at a Method*. Trans. Daniele McDowell, Ronald Schleifer, and Alan Velie. Lincoln: U of Nebraska P, 1983.

Grishman, Ralph. *Computational Linguistics*. Cambridge: Cambridge UP, 1986.

Hendricks, William O. "On the Notion 'beyond the Sentence.'" *Linguistics* 37 (1967): 12–51.

Herman, David. "Autobiography, Allegory, and the Construction of Self." *British Journal of Aesthetics* 35 (1995): 351–60.

Herman, David. "Hypothetical Focalization." *Narrative* 2 (1994): 230–53.

Herman, David. "Textual *You* and Double Deixis in Edna O'Brien's *A Pagan Place*." *Style* 28 (1994): 378–410.

Herman, David. *Universal Grammar and Narrative Form*. Durham: Duke UP, 1995.

Hjelmslev, Louis. *Prolegomena to a Theory of Language*. Trans. Francis J. Whitfield. Madison: U of Wisconsin P, 1969.

Hjelmslev, Louis. "La stratification du language." *Word* 10 (1954): 163–88.

Iser, Wolfgang. *The Act of Reading: A Theory of Aesthetic Response*. Baltimore: Johns Hopkins UP, 1978.

Jacobs, Paul S., and Lisa F. Rau. "Innovations in Text Interpretation." *Artificial Intelligence* 63 (1993): 143–91.

Jahn, Manfred. "Frames, Preferences, and the Reading of Third-Person Narratives: Towards a Cognitive Narratology." *Poetics Today* (forthcoming).

Kafalenos, Emma. "Lingering along the Narrative Path: Extended Functions in Kafka and Henry James." *Narrative* 3 (1995): 117–38.

Labov, William. "The Transformation of Experience in Narrative Syntax." *Language in the Inner City*. Philadelphia: U of Pennsylvania P, 1972. 354–96.

Labov, William, and Joshua Waletzky. "Narrative Analysis: Oral Versions of Personal Experience." *Essays on the Verbal and Visual Arts*. Ed. June Helm. Seattle: U of Washington P, 1967. 12–44.

Lévi-Strauss, Claude. "The Structural Study of Myth." *Critical Theory since 1965*. Ed. Hazard Adams and Leroy Searle. Gainesville: U Presses of Florida, 1986. 809–22.

Linde, Charlotte. *Life Stories: The Creation of Coherence*. New York: Oxford UP, 1993.

MacBride, Maud Gonne. *A Servant of the Queen*. Suffolk: Boydell, 1983.

Mandler, Jean M., and Nancy S. Johnson. "Remembrance of Things Parsed: Story Structure and Recall." *Cognitive Psychology* 9 (1977): 111–51.

Martin, Wallace. *Recent Theories of Narrative*. Ithaca: Cornell UP, 1986.

Mercadal, Dennis. *A Dictionary of Artificial Intelligence*. New York: Van Nostrand, 1990.

Milne, A. A. *Winnie-the-Pooh*. New York: Dutton, 1926.

Minsky, Marvin. "A Framework for Representing Knowledge." *The Psychology of Computer Vision*. Ed. Patrick Winston. New York: McGraw, 1975. 211–77.

Minsky, Marvin. *The Society of Mind*. New York: Touchstone: 1988.

Pavel, Thomas G. *The Poetics of Plot: The Case of English Renaissance Drama*. Minneapolis: U of Minnesota P, 1985.

Plotnitsky, Arkady. "Complementarity, Idealization, and the Limits of Classical Conceptions of Reality." *South Atlantic Quarterly* 94 (1995): 527–70.

Prince, Ellen F. "Toward a Taxonomy of Given-New Information." *Radical Pragmatics*. Ed. Peter Cole. New York: Academic, 1981. 223–56.

Prince, Gerald. "Aspects of a Grammar of Narrative." *Poetics Today* 1 (1980): 49–63.

Prince, Gerald. *A Dictionary of Narratology*. Lincoln: U of Nebraska P, 1987.

Prince, Gerald. *Narratology: The Form and Functioning of Narrative*. Berlin: Mouton, 1982.

Propp, Vladimir. *Morphology of the Folktale*. 2nd ed. Trans. Laurence Scott. Austin: U of Texas P, 1968.

Robbe-Grillet, Alain. *La jalousie*. Paris: Minuit, 1957.

Ryan, Marie-Laure. *Possible Worlds, Artificial Intelligence, and Narrative Theory*. Bloomington: Indiana UP, 1991.

Sartre, Jean-Paul. *Nausea*. Trans. Lloyd Alexander. New York: New Directions, 1964.

Sartre, Jean-Paul. *La nausée*. Paris: Gallimard, 1938.

Schank, Roger C. *Tell Me a Story: A New Look at Real and Artificial Memory*. New York: Scribner's, 1990.

Schank, Roger C., and Robert P. Abelson. *Scripts, Plans, Goals, and Understanding: An Inquiry into Human Knowledge Structures.* Hillsdale: Erlbaum, 1977.

Schiffrin, Deborah. *Approaches to Discourse.* Cambridge: Blackwell, 1994.

Scholes, Robert. *Structuralism in Literature: An Introduction.* New Haven: Yale UP, 1974.

Segre, Cesare. "From Motif to Function and Back Again." *Thematics: New Approaches.* Ed. Claude Bremond, Joshua Landy, and Thomas Pavel. Albany: State U of New York P, 1995. 21–32.

Smith, Barbara Herrnstein, and Arkady Plotnitsky. "Introduction: Networks and Symmetries, Decidable and Undecidable." *South Atlantic Quarterly* 94 (1995): 371–88.

Stein, Nancy L. "The Definition of a Story." *Journal of Pragmatics* 6 (1982): 487–507.

Todorov, Tzvetan. *The Poetics of Prose.* Trans. Richard Howard. Ithaca: Cornell UP, 1977.

van Dijk, Teun A. "Episodes as Units of Discourse Analysis." *Analyzing Discourse: Text and Talk.* Ed. Deborah Tannen. Washington: Georgetown UP, 1981. 177–95.

Wilensky, Robert. "Story Grammars Revisited." *Journal of Pragmatics* 6 (1982): 423–32.

Wright, Richard. *Native Son.* New York: Perennial-Harper, 1993.

CHAPTER 9

From Beats to Arcs: Towards a Poetics of Television Narrative

Michael Newman

Michael Newman teaches Media Studies at the University of Wisconsin, Milwaukee. He is the author of *Video Revolutions* (2014) and *Legitimating Television* (2011). In this essay, he provides a critical vocabulary (beats, arc) for understanding the structure of television narrative.

Television is a story machine. Every day, thousands of hours of narrative zip through the airwaves and cables and into our sets and minds. Television does more than just tell stories, of course, but its function as a storytelling medium demands analysis, and with this essay I offer a framework for analyzing one kind of television narrative. Unlike some accounts of television as a storytelling medium, however, this one will not isolate the text from its makers and users.[1] My purpose here is to initiate a poetics of television form, an account of storytellers' strategies in crafting narratives that will solicit certain effects in viewers such as suspense and surprise, hope and fear, and aesthetic appreciation.[2] A poetics can help explain why so many people take so much pleasure in television's stories.[3]

In particular I am interested in one form of American television drama, the contemporary scripted prime-time serial, or PTS. For the past twenty-five years there have been two main forms of hour-long prime-time programs. Serials such as *St. Elsewhere* (NBC, 1982–88) dramatize long-form stories in ways similar to daytime soap operas. Shows such as *Law & Order* (NBC, 1990–) have an episodic format in which all of the problems raised in the beginning of an episode are solved by the end and questions do not dangle week after week. Evening serials became an important form of American television programming in the 1980s after the ratings success of *Dallas* (CBS, 1978–91) and the acclaim and awards bestowed on *Hill Street Blues* (NBC, 1981–87).[4] They became a dominant form in the 1990s with shows such as *The X-Files* (Fox, 1993–2002)

Original publication details: Michael Newman, "From Beats to Arcs: Towards a Poetics of Television Narrative." *The Velvet Light Trap* 58 (Fall 2006), pp. 16–28. Reproduced with permission from University of Texas Press. Postscript courtesy of M.Z. Newman.

Literary Theory: An Anthology, Third Edition. Edited by Julie Rivkin and Michael Ryan.
© 2017 John Wiley & Sons, Ltd. Published 2017 by John Wiley & Sons, Ltd.

and *ER* (NBC, 1994–) consistently winning both high ratings and critical praise. Later in the 1990s and in the early 2000s the serial saw its presence diminish as episodic programs and reality shows grew in popularity, but as I write it is enjoying a revival at the same time that many sit-coms (e.g., *Arrested Development*, Fox, 2003–) and reality shows (e.g., *Survivor*, CBS, 2000–) are also thoroughly serialized.

Over the quarter-century since the rise of the serial, American television has undergone enormous changes with the introduction of more than one hundred new channels, pervasive new structures of media ownership and synergy, and transformations in the technologies of media production and distribution. But in spite of all these developments, the past twenty-five years have seen a remarkably stable condition obtain in which the most basic narrative conventions of the PTS have not been significantly altered.[5] Throughout the period between *Hill Street* and *Lost* (ABC, 2004–), the general production practices of prime-time television have remained quite constant. A program is overseen by a showrunner who reviews all of the scripts and guides the storytelling; each serial episode resolves some questions but leaves many others dangling; serials tend to focus on ensembles, with each episode interweaving several strands of narrative in alternation scene by scene; a season has approximately twenty-four episodes, begins in fall and ends in spring, and offers sweeps periods every November, February, and May.

As critics have often noted of MTM Productions' seminal dramas of the 1980s, *Hill Street Blues* and *St. Elsewhere*, the PTS is really a hybrid of episodic dramas and serials such as soaps and miniseries.[6] Although evening serials have much in common with their daytime counterparts, prime-time shows still have fewer episodes, smaller casts, and greater episodic closure. And although they share many qualities with episodics, PTSs offer a distinct mode of investment in character, a product of their long-format storytelling. Beginning with those MTM dramas so often figured as "qualityTV," the PTS has functioned as a distinct group style whose norms of artistic production are shared among its makers. By calling it a group style I mean to assert a basic commonality among many different programs on the level of form. This commonality is independent of any program's "quality" and also of its genre status as cop, doc, legal, sci-fi, family, teen, or spy drama.[7] Programs that seem quite different from one another may still share their basic storytelling principles.

What narrative structures does the PTS adopt? What functions do its storytelling conventions serve in relation to television's commercial logic, and how do these conventions appeal to viewers? To answer these questions we must consider the interplay of commerce and art in the television industry. From the networks' perspective, programming is a means of selling audiences to advertisers. Producers follow a commercial imperative: on a weekly basis, deliver the largest and most desirable audience to the network's clients. Programs attempt to hook viewers and make them want to watch. The PTS's narrative design is a product of this basic industrial condition, the perpetual goal of getting millions of people to tune in and keep tuning in. This condition and the strategies it encourages have not changed over the past several decades.

Contrary to what some critics claim, I contend that within this industrial context network television flourishes artistically, that it rewards its audience and its advertisers at the same time. And it is not in spite of television's commercial logic but because of it that the PTS achieves its effects. Given the incentive to produce narratives that engage audiences week after week, television has developed a powerful mode of storytelling. Narrative practices that originate in maximizing the networks' profits, such as repetitive dialogue to remind viewers of details they might have missed and regular breaks in the story for advertising spots, might seem to inhibit artistic expression. But in the PTS, these and other constraints designed to boost advertising revenues have been adapted to narrative functions that can deepen and enrich the experiences of viewers. Looking at the PTS's narrative form, we may consider it to have three storytelling levels for analysis: a micro level of the scene or "beat," a middle level of the episode, and a macro level of greater than one episode, such as a multi-episode arc. On all three levels the commercial and aesthetic goals of television's storytellers are held in a mutually reinforcing balance. (Television's political or ideological goals, overt or implicit, are another matter; in such areas the effects of the networks' commercial goals are rather less salutary.)

American television's mission of selling viewers consumer products and services does not negate its possibilities for creative expression. On the contrary, if one function of art is to please its audience, a commercial incentive for spreading and intensifying pleasure dovetails with the goals of the artist. This is assuming, of course, that the artist is interested in gratifying rather than challenging the audience, which intellectuals often think art should do. But as a form of mass art television fosters no such avant-garde intentions. Mass art strives for accessibility and ease of comprehension. One way it does so is by appealing to emotions such as fear, anger, joy, and surprise.[8] The PTS aims to accomplish these goals by developing clear, ongoing stories about compelling characters facing difficult obstacles. It appeals to viewers by satisfying their desires for knowledge about these characters and for forging an emotional connection with them. How television achieves such effects is the topic of this essay.

Micro Level: Beats

Following a narrative is a process of accumulating information. Television writers strive to parcel out this information in such a way that it will seem urgent, surprising, and emotionally resonant. The way the story is unfolded bit by bit encourages viewers to take an interest in it, and as the unfolding progresses the storyteller seeks to intensify this interest. Thus television's most basic aesthetic and economic goals overlap: engaging the viewer's attention. This begins on the micro level, the smallest node of narrative.

On this level of storytelling most television narratives look quite similar. Situation comedies, episodics, and serial dramas all organize their stories into rather short segments, often less than two minutes in length. Viewers might call these scenes, but writers call them "beats," and they are television's most basic storytelling unit. The length of individual beats and consequently the number of them in an episode are variable to a degree, but it is exceedingly rare to see long, drawn-out beats on prime-time television. The networks bristle at scenes that take up more than two and a half script pages, with a page of script roughly equivalent to a minute of screen time.[9] They believe that the audience's attention is unlikely to be sustained for much longer than that. In a fast-paced story a long scene can derail the sense of forward progress. Given the commercial imperative of keeping the audience interested, most forms of television present a rapid succession of short segments.

Thinking in short segments is a constraint on writers, demanding that their storytelling be clear and efficient. No moment is without a dramatic function, no scene is redundant with other scenes or digressive from the narrative's forward progress. This isn't to say that every beat advances the plot in the traditional sense. Many beats consist of reactions rather than actions, especially on shows centered principally around interpersonal relationships. But a reaction is a new bit of narrative information and is often the point of a beat. Each beat tells us something new, something we want – need – to know, and amplifies our desire to know more.[10] Each one solicits feelings in relation to this information, such as satisfaction, excitement, worry, puzzlement, or frustration on a character's behalf. Each beat also usually reminds us about several old bits of information before offering us the new bit. With these missions accomplished one beat gives way to the next.

When writers approach the creation of a television script, their first task is to "break" the story into a moment-by-moment outline, or "beat-sheet," a task often done collaboratively by a writing staff.[11] The writers know in the most basic terms what the episode has to accomplish before they beat out the story, but the story only takes shape when they begin to think of it as a series of moments. Each episode has a total of between twenty and forty beats; the average might be twenty-five.[12] This means that each of the four acts in an hour-long show has around six beats.[13] PTSs are typically ensemble dramas, and each episode has multiple, intertwined plots. Major plots ("A plots" in teleplay jargon) involving a main character have at least six beats, often more. An episode usually has two or more A plots and several B or C plots with a smaller number of beats each. Each act ideally includes at least one beat from all of the episode's plots.

In breaking stories for *Judging Amy* (1999–2005) its showrunners would demand that a plotline set in Amy's courtroom have six to eight beats to make it dramatic and engaging – a three-beat situation would not suffice. They told an interviewer that freelancers would sometimes pitch dramatic ideas that were not suitable for the PTS's format: "For example, a kid goes missing. The beats are: (1) a kid goes missing, (2) call the cops and (3) the cops find him or they don't find him. That's not enough. That's a [dead-end] idea."[14] To make the idea suitable for an hour show it would need to unfold with more intricacy, with a measured pattern of revelations and developments taking us through this series of eight moments and holding our attention across four commercial breaks. Since A plots involve the characters portrayed by a show's stars, giving them eight beats per episode keeps them on screen at regular intervals. Very convoluted stories and very simplistic ones are unsuitable to the formula. Thus the reliance on twists and turns in the plot; one way of adding beats to a straightforward story is to introduce complications and reversals. By demanding that scenes be short, the networks create the conditions for a sophisticated mode of ensemble storytelling.

In general, then, the patterning of two-minute beats aims to hold the audience's attention and make the story lines cleverly unpredictable. Out of industrial constraints come aesthetic strategies. Given a set amount of weekly programming time, a cast of actors under contract, and a need to show the audience something new at least every two minutes, writers work out a system of parceling the narrative into small pieces in regular alternation, each of which makes a new claim on the audience's interest and aims to intensify its emotional response.

In addition to new information many scenes also contain what we might call old information, expository material that regular viewers already well know. Recapping is a ubiquitous feature of television in all genres.[15] Television assumes that we don't watch everything and can always use a bit of reminding when it comes to the most important things to know. In serialized narratives recapping is especially important because of the large quantity of data about the story world that forms the background of any new developments. It takes many forms, one of which is the perpetual naming of characters: in every beat, characters address each other by name, often several times in a two-minute segment. Along with naming comes role reiteration: *Alias* (ABC, 2001–) constantly reminds us that Jack and Irina are Sydney's parents; Giles is always reminding Buffy (*Buffy the Vampire Slayer*, WB, 1997–2001; UPN, 2001–03) that he is her watcher; Joel on *Northern Exposure* (CBS, 1990–95) is often called "Dr. Fleishman," even away from his practice, and his favorite leisure activity, golfing, reinforces his role stereotype.

A more elaborate form of recapping restates the show's basic premise in episode after episode. *Veronica Mars*'s (UPN, 2004–) voice-overs in its first season reiterate the known details of the Lily Kane murder and investigation and Veronica's ostracism from the popular crowd at Neptune High. *Buffy* characters remind us that Sunnydale sits above a Hellmouth. Episode after episode of *Northern Exposure* works in references to New York City, Joel's hometown. Many also reiterate the deal he made with the state of Alaska that in exchange for funding his medical education it would get his services as a doctor.

Dialogue also recaps recent events, often redundantly with the "previously" segment that precedes most shows but in a way that contextualizes the information and clarifies its relevance to the present situation. It is a norm of PTS storytelling that events should be recapped, and, given this constraint, writers have to find ways of accomplishing this redundancy without irritating the audience. Indeed, this norm seems to have the opposite effect, riveting the audience to the screen. Often this redundancy is accomplished with remarkable elegance and economy without seeming at all like clunky exposition. This is a matter of motivating the dialogue that conveys the redundant expository material.

One way of accomplishing this is by structuring storytelling as a series of revelations from one character to the next, a standard narrational strategy of melodrama in film and television, making action less significant than *re*action and *inter*action.[16] In the May sweeps episodes of *Gilmore Girls*'s (WB, 2000–) fifth season, Rory has a series of encounters with the family of her blue-blooded Yale boyfriend, Logan Huntzberger.[17] After being insulted by the Huntzbergers over dinner when they openly disapprove of Rory as a match for Logan, Rory is offered a plum internship at Logan's father's newspaper. At the end of her stint at the paper the elder Huntzberger tells Rory quite bluntly that she is not suited to a career in journalism, which has been her lifelong aspiration, and she is crushed. These events are recapped by Rory in conversations with her mother, Lorelai, and by Lorelai in conversations with her parents, Richard and Emily.

But these bits of dialogue are not only repeating what we already know; the moments of recapping are important bits of plotting because they are revelations, and we have been primed to notice the interlocutors' reactions. For many viewers, one of serial narrative's greatest pleasures comes from the tension-resolution pattern of anticipating how a character will respond to a narrative detail they already know and witnessing the moment of revelation. Rory is hesitant to tell Lorelai about the internship because she thinks her mother disapproves of Logan. When Rory slips in the news, it is a moment of tentativeness between the mom and daughter, who often act more like best friends than like family, and we are invited to wonder if Lorelai's breeziness in response to Rory's news is feigned. Thus the recapping of Rory's news about interning with Logan's father's paper is turned into a beat in the mother–daughter plotline and an opportunity to consider the characters' emotions. It is also a device aimed at engaging *our* emotions, encouraging our fear for the Gilmore girls that Logan will cause a rift to form between them and our hope for them that it will not.

An even bigger plot point comes in the season finale, after Rory is devastated by her conversation with Mr. Huntzberger. Lorelai reports to her parents not only about Rory being told she is unsuitable to be a reporter but also about how the Huntzbergers insulted Rory over dinner, recapping events of several episodes earlier that are essential to understanding the conflict. This is the first that Richard and Emily have heard of this, and it makes them both furious with Logan's family, affronted by their behavior, and sympathetic with Rory, reversing their eagerness to see the two youngsters get engaged. Again, this recapping solicits an emotional connection: regular viewers were likely already angry at the Huntzbergers and frustrated and disappointed on Rory's behalf, but in this scene we are invited to share Richard and Emily's anger and sympathy even as we might get a superior sense of satisfaction – which we likely share with Lorelai – from seeing them realize that they were mistaken about Logan's family. Because the characters' relationships are multiple and complex, considering old information in a new context is designed to generate a fresh charge of feeling.

The repetitiveness of PTS storytelling originates in a commercial function of making the narrative easily comprehended even by viewers who watch sporadically, who pay only partial attention, or who miss part of an episode when the phone rings or the baby cries. The same contextual factors result in similar kinds of repetition in many kinds of television storytelling, from soaps and news magazines to reality programs and sit-coms. Consider, for example, the number of times in an episode of *Survivor* that we are reminded of the contestants' names: during the credit sequence, when contestants are addressed by the host, when they are referenced in other contestants' interviews, when they are addressed directly by other contestants, and when their names (and occupations) are printed onscreen during their own interviews. Redundancy in many forms of television is aimed at maximizing accessibility. But this adaptation has an additional benefit. Television's redundancy has its causes in making narratives intelligible, but it turns out that it can also allow even regular viewers to be gratified by being reminded constantly of who the characters are, what they do, why they do it, and what is at stake in their story. Our interest and engagement can be increased when the narrative makes its most important elements clear and relevant, artfully underlining what we should pay most attention to and care most about. Redundancy functions not only to make stories comprehensible but, more importantly, to make stories more interesting and to deepen our experience by appealing to our emotions.

To paraphrase Christian Metz, there are no television police. No one forces us to watch these weekly dramas. But the structure of television storytelling on the micro level – the way a story is broken into beats and the way each beat works – functions to compel our attention. Television storytellers, more than their counterparts in literary, dramatic, or cinematic storytelling, are under an obligation constantly to arouse and rearouse our interest. Beating out the story as they do has a strong rhetorical force, giving us reasons to care about characters and to want to know more.

Middle Level: Episodes

Given the ongoing nature of its stories, one might assume that the PTS lacks closure on the level of the episode. According to one critic, daytime serials dispense with beginnings and endings in favor of "an indefinitely expandable middle."[18] Scholars refer to serial form as "open,"[19] and some propose that the pleasure of watching serials is heavily invested in this formal openness. Soap opera viewers, according to John Fiske, experience "pleasure as ongoing and cyclical rather than climactic and final."[20] In this section I argue, however, that an emphasis on openness misses much of what is interesting about television's evening serials. Each episode of a PTS leaves some causal chains dangling, but seldom at the expense of sacrificing resolution and coherence, seldom in a way that promotes textual instability or radical, modernist aperture. The serials I am considering have not only closure in their story lines, which is also true of soap operas,[21] but a rigorous formal unity on the level of the episode, a quality daytime dramas rarely display. Thus there are two kinds of closure and aperture we can consider: the resolution of narrative cause–effect chains, as in the culmination of a courtship in marriage, and the unification of themes and motifs into an orderly, integrated whole. Both of these kinds of formal unity offer pleasures that underlie other appeals of the narrative.

While some cause–effect apertures may run across many months of a PTS, the main action of any given episode tends to be resolved.[22] Most typically, certain questions go unanswered for episode after episode, but they are not the kind of questions that obstruct narrative clarity. Highly focused questions that determine the outcome of the main events of a particular episode may be deferred by a cliffhanger and promptly answered in the beginning of the next episode, as is often done on thrillers such as *Alias*, but less focused questions can be deferred long-term. This kind of balance between episodic closure and serial deferment is standard in many forms of serial storytelling, from Victorian fiction to contemporary Hollywood cycles such as *Star Wars*. A strong dose of episodic unity mitigates any textual instability caused by serialized aperture. Without this unity, casual viewers are less likely to watch. And while the regular audience may relish being strung along by the ongoing story lines, it also may dislike feeling frustrated at the end of an episode. Like all of the formal devices I consider here, effects of closure are aimed at satisfying the audience, in this case its desire not only for resolution but also for coherence.

There is a commercial rationale underlying these effects beyond the value to a network and producer of their programs telling good stories. Prime-time shows, in contrast to their daytime counterparts, depend on off-network syndication contracts to earn a profit. PTS producers want their programs to play well in reruns. According to the industry's conventional wisdom, heavily serialized storytelling makes reruns less likely to attract viewers.[23] In the 1990s and early 2000s the astonishing success of *Law & Order* repeats on A&E and TNT demonstrated that hour-long episodic narratives can achieve impressive ratings in syndication to the point that the audience for original episodes on the network might increase.[24] *Law & Order* is the most profitable drama on television and is also a success in foreign markets.[25] Episodic closure is thus a product of an industrial context in which serials are under increasing pressure to offer episodic pleasures to casual viewers at the same time that they offer additional, serialized pleasures to their faithful regulars. Episodic unity pays off to the viewer, casual or committed, but also to the producer and the network.

The PTS thus patterns its weekly episodes into structures of problems and solutions so that the central conflict introduced in the beginning of an episode has often been overcome by the end. The standard architecture of the PTS organizes the hour into four acts of roughly equal length, each of which is followed by a commercial break.[26] The first and last acts of a four-act episode correspond to the first and last acts of the three-act Hollywood film. In both media the first act is the set-up and the last act is the resolution. The middle two acts of a television show correspond to the second act of a movie: complication and development.[27] Television dramas introduce problems in the first act and end it with a surprise. Characters respond to complications caused by this surprise in the second act, see the stakes raised in the third act, and resolve the problems in the fourth act.

Unlike movies, television acts have strongly punctuated endings, often with a clearly focused question, sometimes with a cliffhanger, typically with a fade to black and a cut to a commercial.[28] Different writers have different names for act endings; following theater usage I will call them "curtains."[29] Writers often compose backward from the curtains, beginning with the fourth-act curtain that concludes the episode.[30] In the *Felicity* (WB, 1998–2002) episode "The Fugue" (2 March 1999), the fourth-act curtain, the most significant dramatic moment in the episode, comes when Felicity decides to sleep with an acquaintance from her art class, Eli. This tentatively answers the main question posed in the first act: will Felicity and her boyfriend Noel stay together or break up? At the fourth-act curtain not only are they apart, but Felicity has moved on to someone else. Each of the previous curtains functions to pose a question or problem. The precredit teaser asks what Noel's ex-girlfriend, Hannah, is really doing in New York City. The first-act curtain has Noel and Hannah kiss. The second-act curtain has a confrontation between Noel and Felicity. By the third-act curtain Noel has left Felicity for Hannah, and at the act's end Felicity goes off with Eli to retrieve some sketches from the art studio, focusing the question of whether she will get together with him, which is answered at the final curtain.

As in a stage melodrama, a television program's curtains crystallize the dramatic developments of the act and sometimes introduce a surprise or *coup de théâtre*, as in the act 1 curtain of "The Fugue," when Noel and Hannah kiss. Like the PTS's beat structure, its curtains function to rivet the audience to the screen.[31] One teleplay manual puts it like this: "Remember your goal. It's to pull 'em back from the refrigerator."[32] It is thus standard that writers save their strongest beats for the curtains. It is also typical for a curtain to fall on a reaction shot of the main character, a classic soap opera device that intensifies our interest in character psychology.

This act structure is another example of how the interplay of commercial and aesthetic functions structures television storytelling. There is no natural reason for the segmentation of the narrative to be in four equal portions with breaks each quarter-hour, but this formal arrangement serves a variety of interests, not least the economic one of interspersing advertisements at regular intervals during the broadcast. From an aesthetic perspective a four-act structure achieves a sense of proportion and symmetry, ensures steadily rising action, and organizes patterns of attention and expectation, with first acts opening causal chains that are carried across the second and third acts to be resolved (at least partially) in the fourth.

On legal shows the first act may introduce the case, the fourth may bring a decision. *Buffy* unveils a threat to Sunnydale in act 1 and removes it in act 4. Dramas with a stronger focus on the domestic still raise focused questions in act 1, as in the *thirtysomething* (ABC, 1987–91) episode "Prelude to a Bris" (29 September 1990). When their son, Leo, is born, Hope and Michael must decide if he will have a bris, and Michael must decide whether being Jewish is an important part of his identity. Act 4: the bris, a symbolic moment not only of the child's entry into the world but also of Michael's embrace of his heritage. Of course, these episodes also have narrative elements that continue across the span of a season or series (the birth of Leo is a moment in the Steadman family arc), but they tend to raise and resolve significant plot problems each week.

This tight dramatic act structure satisfies the audience's desire for resolution – not totally but adequately. It is gratifying to discover novel but apt solutions to well-posed problems, as television narratives often do week after week. But this is not the only means by which episode-specific structures appeal to the audience. Another perennial option is thematic parallelism. It would seem an obvious one when dealing with multiple story lines: have them inflect and play off each other, revealing contrasts and similarities.[33] The most straightforward kind of parallelism has a pair of A plots share a theme. The final act of "The Fugue" uses crosscutting to establish parallelism. Shots of Noel and Hannah are alternated with shots of Felicity and Eli, while sounds of rain and of Hannah's piano composition bleed over from one scene into the next to tie them together. Congruent thematic material is also frequently ironically inverted, as in the *Lost* episode "Do No Harm" (6 April 2005), in which one character is born at the same time that another dies.

In a typical *Judging Amy* episode Judge Amy Gray's juvenile court case *and* her mother, Maxine's social work case *and* the various family story lines are all tied up in the same set of thematic concerns, with inversions and variations running up against one another. "Spoil the Child" (11 January 2000) has Amy and Maxine both face instances connecting children and violence. As is often the case not only with *Judging Amy* but with programs as different as *Rescue Me* (FX, 2004–) and *Once and Again* (ABC, 1999–2002) the episode's title keys us into the theme. In Amy's case a father's custody is challenged on the grounds that he spanks his children. In Maxine's case it is the child who is violent, striking her when she tries to counsel him. As well, the main characters face inverse career-defining questions: Amy is up for a promotion from juvenile to criminal court, while Maxine considers quitting her job with the Department of Children and Families because of the stress it causes her. In the course of offering her the promotion Amy's boss derides the juvenile bench as "social work," making it clear to the audience that Amy and her mother both toil at the same kind of job despite many differences. The work of helping children and families is at stake in both characters' choices.

As in most *Judging Amy* episodes, the troubled families depicted in the professional plots are a foil for the Gray family. However, in this episode both Amy's and Maxine's performances as mother are questioned. As always, Amy must balance her obligations as a judge and as a single mom, and in the first act of "Spoil the Child" she takes her six-year-old daughter, Lauren, to pick up a butterfly outfit for her dance recital. Because Amy's life is so busy she has put this errand off too long. The shop has sold out of butterflies, and Lauren throws a tantrum. The only option left is for Amy to sew the outfit herself, and Lauren fears it will be different from the other kids' costumes. With all of the family looking on before dinner Lauren shouts, "You're a bad mommy and I hate you! You ruined my life!" Meanwhile, Amy is upset with Maxine because she has never come to her courtroom to see her on the bench, and when she tells her mother this Maxine becomes angry and says, "It's not my job to make you feel better." Thus the six year old's dance recital and her mother's job as a judge are parallel performances where a mother, as spectator, is supposed to take pride in the child. Each mother is accused of failing to make the performance happen.

As is often the case, a question before Amy in court – how should a parent treat a child? – is one she faces in her own family. It is also typical that Amy's inability to have her own life go smoothly is an ironic contrast against the role she takes on as a judge, assuredly making crucial decisions affecting other people's lives. It is typical of *Judging Amy* that episodes are built on this kind of complex structural coherence.

How does "Spoil the Child" resolve its situations? Amy stays on the juvenile bench, affirming her commitment to "social work." Maxine continues at her job, fighting for a psychiatric placement for her assailant. The Gray women affirm their commitment to public service on behalf of children and families. Amy also stays up all night sewing

Lauren's costume, and the dance recital is a success. Most important, Maxine attends Amy's court session and hears her judgment on the spanking case. Amy rules that the parent may not strike his child and speaks eloquently about the importance of the parent–child bond, absorbing and reiterating all of her mother's teachings. Maxine's eyes well up with tears, and after Amy is finished her mother turns to the person next to her and says, "That's my daughter." This scene epitomizes the way *Judging Amy* works: in a single moment all of the narrative threads of the episode are brought together in an affirmation of reciprocal familial obligations and pleasures.

As "Spoil the Child" makes clear, closure is not simply a matter of questions being answered, problems being solved. A closed form is one in which the elements all hang together in an integrated pattern. The parallelisms in "Spoil the Child" give the episode a clear shape and can make the experience of watching it satisfying not only because of its affirmation of ethics that the audience likely shares, not only because of the emotional charge of the sentimental ending, but also because of an aesthetic sophistication that can bring its own rewards. It has harmony that no open form can claim, a counterpoint of narrative voices that satisfies a desire not only for resolution but also for formal unity and thematic clarity. *Judging Amy* achieved similar effects week after week, balancing its episodic "case" plots with arcing story lines about Amy's family and coworkers and integrating all of them thematically. It is the epitome of the post-*Law & Order* serial poised to snag casual viewers in reruns while also satisfying its loyal fans week after week.

Macro Level: Arcs

What most distinguishes the PTS from other forms of programming is the way it is invested in character.[34] It is not merely plots that carry over week after week but characters whose lives these plots define. We don't just want to know what's going to happen but what's going to happen to Pembleton and Bayliss (*Homicide: Life on the Street*, NBC, 1993–99), Buffy and Spike, Angela and Jordan (*My So-Called Life*, ABC, 1994–95). Continuing stories make characters more likely to undergo significant life events and changes.[35] In reaction to these changes in circumstances the characters themselves are more likely to change or at least to grow.

Characters in serials demand an investment in time. They invite regular viewing over a long term, charting a progression of the characters' life events. It is true that in episodic forms such as the traditional sit-com there may also be a strong investment in character, but it is of a different nature, based more on the familiarity bred by repetition than on engagement with unfolding events. In a given episode of *Happy Days* (ABC, 1974–84) the viewer's interest in character is often a product of recognizing familiar bits of action, mise-en-scène, and dialogue: taking dates to Inspiration Point, eating at Arnold's, asking Fonzie's advice in the men's room, blue cardigans for the boys, long skirts for the girls, Fonzie's jacket, Chachi's bandana, "Aaaay," "Yowza," "I found my thrill," "I still got it," "Mrs. C," "wa wa wa." In contrast, the investment in a serial character is based on a more novelistic progression of events over a long duration, with episodes like chapters in an ongoing saga rather than self-contained stories.[36] (It is arguable that in its later seasons *Happy Days* began to offer some of these pleasures as the characters grew up and changed.) Characterization in the PTS is more likely to have a certain kind of depth as the audience knows more about the characters' inner lives in serials than in many episodic shows. Especially in comparison to the episodic drama represented by the recent crop of procedurals in the mold of *Law & Order*, the PTS is a character-driven form, and this is one thing that makes it more easily figured as "quality TV" in popular and critical discourse.

It is sometimes incorrectly said that on episodic shows characters seem to have no memory of the previous week's events.[37] What is more important than character memory, however, is that *viewers* of episodic shows need no memory of the previous episodes to understand and appreciate the present one. Episodes may be seen in any order and may be skipped without compromising future comprehension and engagement. The PTS, on the other hand, makes significant demands on the audience, which it rewards with a much fuller experience of character. The audience is expected – ideally – to watch the episodes in sequence, to track character and plot developments carefully, and to tune in every week.

The device that best ensures this commitment to the narrative is the character arc. Arc is to character as plot is to story. Put slightly differently, arc is plot stated in terms of character. An arc is a character's journey from A through B, C, and D to E. This term has remarkable utility in describing PTS storytelling: although each episode, sweeps period, season, and series may have its own shape and unity, each character's story can be individuated, spatialized as an arc overlapping all of these and all of the other characters' arcs.[38]

Character arcs may stretch across many episodes, seasons, and the entirety of a series. The shape of the largest character arcs are those of the life span, with its progression from youth to adulthood, innocence to experience. Some call this a show's "emotional through line."[39] It is not only children such as Angela Chase, Lindsay Weir, and Willow Rosenberg who grow up on television shows. Joel Fleishman gains the folk wisdom of his Alaskan neighbors as a complement to his formal schooling. Boomer on *St. Elsewhere* begins as a greenhorn intern and grows through his survival of multiple traumas. The detectives on *Homicide* each come to grips, at some point, with a life-changing moment that marks a passage into greater maturity.

These life-span arcs operate on the level of the series, but there are more manageable-sized arcs that writers deal with more commonly in crafting stories. Like beat and episode structures, arc structures function under commercial and aesthetic imperatives. There are two salient commercial constraints. First, in addition to focused cliffhangers connecting the end of one episode and the beginning of another, the questions that dangle week after week serve to maintain suspense. On *Dawson's Creek* (WB, 1998–2003) will Joey tell Dawson that she is in love with him? On *Homicide* what if any consequences will Kellerman face for killing Luther Mahoney? Perhaps the most famous of these danglers has its own slang term – a will-they-or-won't-they – as on *Moonlighting* (ABC, 1985–89): will Maddie and David sleep together or won't they? By posing these questions programs strive to maintain our viewership, to keep us interested and drive up ratings.

Another commercial imperative has to do with the organization of the season into segments.[40] The season has at least five definable segments: fall premieres (September–October), fall sweeps (November), a holiday rerun period (December–January), winter sweeps (February), another rerun period (March–April), and spring sweeps/season finales (May). Most PTSs run around twenty-four episodes per season. Networks save new episodes for sweeps periods, on the basis of which advertising rates are set according to each show's Nielsen ratings. They avoid reruns at the beginning of the season, figuring that new episodes will maintain and increase interest in a show. This gives the network at least eight weeks of episodes to begin the season and another eight to air during the winter and spring sweeps for a total of sixteen episodes. The remaining episodes are aired in December, January, March, or April.

The implications of this season segmentation for narrative form are clear. Just as episodes build toward strong curtains, seasons build toward strong sweeps episodes. Some shows have definable arcs that stretch across a whole season, but the demands of the three sweeps periods make arcs more easily constructed in units of around six or eight episodes than in units of twenty-four. Thus we may think of the season, as well as the episode, as having acts. Each season has three.

When writing staffs begin to work on a season they will sometimes plot out the most major developments of the whole year of shows. Some writers' rooms keep an outline of the whole season's story on the wall. But even on a show such as *24* (Fox, 2001–), which has a tightly focused season structure, the conception of arcs happens in a more piece-meal fashion. *24* does not plot out its whole season in advance. Its staff breaks the story in groups of six or eight episodes.[41] Eight, it turns out, is a much more manageable chunk of story to break. This isn't to say that the eight episodes have the same kind of coherence as an individual episode. But across these larger segments of story – call them "season acts" – definable problems are introduced, developed, and resolved. Intuitively it makes sense, moreover, that viewers experience television stories in segments larger than episodes but smaller than seasons. We engage with the narrative on an ongoing basis but certainly do not have the memory that would allow us to hold a whole season, as it were, in our heads.

Since the main plots of any given PTS episode may be largely self-contained, many an arc is strung along episode after episode with a few lines of dialogue or a scene or two that just barely pushes it forward. On *Judging Amy* Peter and Gillian's quest to have a child takes two seasons to resolve fully, with no single episode in which it is an A plot. It is, however, broken up into smaller units of storytelling, beginning with the pilot: considering and trying in vitro, pursuing an adoption, losing Ned when his birth mother changes her mind, and so on, until finally during May sweeps of the second season they have their son back for good.[42] Although this is a very long arc, it is broken up into more manageable chunks that overlap with the season acts.

Season acts made up of several episodes do not necessarily coincide neatly with character arcs, and the idea of an arc suggests that each character's may begin and end at different points. But there is considerable overlap between the season act and the main characters' arcs, if for no other reason than because plot and character are not independent of one another. Rory's arc in the fifth-season episodes of *Gilmore Girls* discussed above offers a clear example. The shape of season act 3 is defined by Rory's encounters with the Huntzbergers. Just as individual episodes present problems and solutions, so do season acts. What will happen with Rory and Logan? How will the Huntzbergers, Lorelai, Richard, and Emily respond? What implications will these events have for Rory's future? These questions span the series of episodes culminating in the season finale, when Rory decides to quit Yale and move in with her grandparents.

Arcs also share a shape with season acts because characters' lives are intertwined, with each character's goals shaped by the other characters' goals. Lorelai Gilmore's arc in season act 3 could be independent of Rory's and often seems so. Lorelai faces a cluster of related questions that scarcely involve her daughter. What kind of relationship should she have with her meddlesome, snobbish parents? Should she sell the Dragonfly Inn and take a job that might mean moving away from Stars Hollow? What will happen in her relationship with Luke? Unbeknownst to Lorelai, during all of this time Luke is planning on asking her to marry him, considering buying a new house where they both will live, and hoping eventually to have children together. So Rory's arc with Logan and the internship and Lorelai's arc with Richard and Emily, the Dragonfly, and Luke are hardly intertwined.

In the season finale, "A House Is Not a Home" (17 May 2005), they come together when Lorelai responds to Rory's decision to quit school. She reluctantly goes to her parents to ask them for help in convincing Rory to return to Yale, and they agree, only to go back on their word and allow Rory to move in with them and take time off. This answers question number one: Lorelai will return to her policy of having nothing to do with Richard and Emily. But when she tells Luke about this he becomes hyperbolically irate and insists that they kidnap Rory and force her to go to school every day. In this moment Lorelai is so moved by Luke's concern for her and Rory that she asks him to marry her, a cliffhanger season-ending curtain. This suggests likely answers to questions two and three: at the end of season five it seems likely that Lorelai will not sell the Dragonfly and that her relationship with Luke will progress to marriage, if not to the new house and kids of his dreams. What's most important to this discussion, however, is the way the various characters' arcs resolve in unison. Rory's decision to quit school and move in with her grandparents and Lorelai's proposal to Luke are caught up in the same dramatic progression. Rory's actions affect Lorelai's, which affect Luke's, which affect Lorelai's. The arcs resolve as one, making the May sweeps episodes into a coherent unit of narrative. This pattern of coalescing arcs means that in any given episode the various plots might not seem to be connected. Ultimately, however, they can be brought together as part of a single pattern of dramatic resolution. Again the PTS form tends toward narrative unity and coherence.

What, then, of units of storytelling larger than a season act? What about the season as a unit of storytelling? Cable dramas such as *Nip/Tuck* (FX, 2003–) and *The L Word* (Showtime, 2004–) have thirteen-episode seasons, making it easier to think of the season as a meaningful narrative unit. Each *Buffy* season has a season-spanning conflict in which the characters confront a "big bad." But each season has many episodes in which the "big bad" figures only marginally into the conflict. Certainly *24*, with its high-concept narrative structure, demands to be considered as a season. But *24* segments the season's conflicts into subconflicts. The first few episodes of season four follow the attempted assassination of a cabinet secretary; when this is averted the characters realize there is a nuclear attack under way and turn their attention to averting it; and so on. Their overarching goal is to defeat the terrorists, but this is accomplished through subgoals that structure smaller units of narrative as other shows do. In general, the season is at best a loose kind of narrative unit, but the season acts culminating during sweeps function as tight, coherent segments.

Arcs, like beats and episodes, have their own functions and effects. They are a way of managing story material, of crafting it into a meaningful whole. Arcs and the season acts subtending them are, no less than beats and episodes, a product of an advertising-driven industrial context of narrative production. They are a means of compelling weekly viewing and of maximizing ratings when it matters most to the networks. But they also come with the aesthetic functions of generating interest in character, of engaging the audience in the struggles and discoveries, the lives and loves of their TV friends, and of maximizing formal unity. As at all levels of television storytelling the largest, macro level is designed to best please the audience.

Conclusion

These are a handful of narrative givens shared among writers and viewers of hundreds of different programs. Beats, episodes, and arcs offer proven means of winning audiences over. But the direction of influence is not simply from the corporate office to the writers' room. Although they serve commercial functions, once these become norms of storytelling practice the networks recognize their narrative utility, and thus a kind of feedback loop is initiated between the creative and corporate branches of the industry. A device like redundancy is seen to serve everyone's interests. A network's executives might not appreciate true originality, but they respect the proven storytelling resources of television's craft tradition. Other means of prospective profit boosting than those I have considered have come along (e.g., interactivity, product placement, sweeps season cross-overs, and "super-size" episodes). Whether they originate in the writers' room or the boardroom, if they ultimately do not amount to a way for television to tell better stories, they are unlikely to become integrated into narrative television's norms.[43]

One veteran writer of television dramas sums up her job as follows: "Once I have decided on a story to tell, I then get out the entire bag of writer's tricks in order to make the audience feel what I need it to feel – otherwise, I won't hold its interest, and it won't hear anything I have to say....I always write with the audience in mind."[44] The bag of tricks, the audience in mind: the television artist is as attuned as any storyteller to the effects of narrative. The programs I have discussed here are at once a source of handsome profits and intense pleasures. These profits and pleasures transcend critical judgments of quality. The practices that produce them – the tricks in the bag – compel the attention of anyone interested in the narratives of popular culture.

Notes

I would like to thank Elana Levine and the *Velvet Light Trap* editorial board for the help they offered me in completing this article.

1   Sarah Kozloff, "Narrative Theory," *Channels of Discourse, Reassembled: Television and Contemporary Criticism*, ed. Robert C. Allen, 2nd ed. (Chapel Hill: U of North Carolina P, 1992) 67–100, asserts that narrative theory "leaves to other critical methods questions about where the story comes from … and the myriad effects (psychological or sociological) that the text has upon its audience" (68). Cf. Michael J. Porter, "The Structure of Television Narratives," *Critical Approaches to Television*, ed. Leah R. Vande Berg, Lawrence A. Wenner, and Bruce E. Gronbeck (Boston: Houghton Mifflin, 1998) 140–57.

2   My conception of poetics comes from Aristotle's *Poetics* and from David Bordwell's call for a historical poetics of cinema. See, for example, Bordwell, *Ozu and the Poetics of Cinema* (Princeton: Princeton UP, 1988) and *Making Meaning: Inference and Rhetoric in the Interpretation of Cinema* (Cambridge: Harvard UP, 1989) 263–74. See also Henry Jenkins, "Historical Poetics," in Joanne Hollows and Marc Jancovich, eds., *Approaches to Popular Film* (Manchester: Manchester UP, 1995).

3   Other approaches such as ethnographic or reception studies also illuminate aspects of the audience's experience, but poetics takes as its central object of study the text itself and offers insights about its origins and uses on the basis of its design features. Thus poetics might logically be seen as a first – but certainly not last – step in understanding how a narrative text functions within the contexts of its modes of production and reception. Other approaches might better explain the social circulation and the political use value of narratives; poetics seeks to illuminate a text's aesthetic strategies.

4   There are antecedents of the prime-time serial in the 1960s (*Peyton Place*, ABC, 1964–69) and the 1970s (*Family*, ABC, 1976–80). As well, at least since the 1970s in shows such as *Soap* (ABC, 1977–82) and *Mary Hartman, Mary Hartman* (syn., 1976–78), situation comedies have also been increasingly serialized, so some of my points here apply to some sit-coms as well.

    Why did the serial emerge in the late 1970s and early 1980s as a major prime-time form? One must consider a complex interaction of social and industrial forces in speculating about this kind of phenomenon, and no body of research has yet offered a thorough consideration of them. Julie D'Acci, *Defining Women: Television and the Case of "Cagney & Lacey"* (Chapel Hill: U of North Carolina P, 1994) 72, briefly considers the "soapoperafication" of prime time in relation to the construction of a "working woman" audience in the early 1980s. This topic is an important and intriguing one for future research.

5   Although many of my examples are of fairly recent programs (those most easily available to me to watch), I intend my points to apply to the PTS in general, not only to recent examples.

6   Jane Feuer, "Quality Drama in the U.S.: The New 'Golden Age?'" *The Television History Book*, ed. Michele Hilmes (London: BFI, 2003) 99; Robin Nelson, *"Hill Street Blues," Fifty Key Television Programs*, ed. Glen Creeber (London: Arnold, 2003) 104, refers to *Hill Street* as the program that "paved the way for the dominance of the series/serial hybrid"; Thomas Schatz, *"St. Elsewhere* and the Evolution of the Ensemble Series," *Television: The Critical View*, ed. Horace Newcomb, 4th ed. (New York: Oxford, 1987) 94, writes that *St. Elsewhere* "struck a compromise between … episodic and serial strategies." See also Jane Feuer, Paul Kerr, and Tise Vahimagi, *MTM: "Quality Television"* (London: BFI, 1984) 25–26, 85–100.

7   Robert J. Thompson, *Television's Second Golden Age: From Hill Street Blues to ER* (Syracuse: Syracuse UP, 1996), argues that some prime-time serials of the 1980s and 1990s constitute a genre of "quality TV." He thus links a formal criterion – serialized, ensemble storytelling – to one of aesthetic value, though he notes that at least one critic uses the terms "quality drama" as a put-down (13). This confuses categories of narrative form and critical judgment. Unlike Thompson, I am interested in understanding what instances of the PTS generally have in common regardless of any program's "quality" or lack of it, however construed.

8   Noël Carroll, *A Philosophy of Mass Art* (Oxford: Oxford UP, 1998) 245–90.

9   Madeline DiMaggio, *How to Write for Television* (New York: Prentice-Hall, 1990) 88. Certainly the actors' pace of delivery affects this page-to-minute ratio, and scripts for shows such as *Gilmore Girls* have longer page counts than less talky, slower-paced programs.

10 Larry Brody, *Television Writing from the Inside Out: Your Channel to Success* (New York: Applause, 2003) 77, 150–51.

11 Some writers call this "cracking" or "beating" the story. A good description of this process of group story construction can be found in John Wells, "Team Writing," in Julian Friedman, ed., *Writing Long-Running Television Series* (Shoreham-by-Sea, UK: Gwynprint, 1996) 2:194–205; Amy Sherman-Palladino discusses her experiences with team writing on *Roseanne*, *Veronica's Closet*, and *Gilmore Girls* in a 5 May 2005 radio interview on "Fresh Air with Terry Gross," archived online at www.npr.org.

12 Brody 76.

13 Ibid., 92. According to Brody, first acts usually have more, shorter beats and last acts fewer, longer ones. See also Douglas Heil, *Prime-Time Authorship: Works about and by Three TV Dramatists* (Syracuse: Syracuse UP, 2002) 133–34.

14 Rich Whiteside, "The Small Screen: *Judging Amy*," *scr(i)pt* 9.1 (Jan.–Feb. 2003). I accessed this and other *scr(i)pt* sources either online at www.scriptmag.com or through interlibrary loans delivered as PDF files; in both formats the page numbers were not available.

15 Robert C. Allen, *"The Guiding Light:* Soap Opera as Economic Product and Cultural Document," in Newcomb 150 (4th ed.), analyzes this repetitive exposition in daytime drama.

16 David Bordwell, *Narration in the Fiction Film* (Madison: U of Wisconsin P, 1988) 70–73; Tania Modleski, "The Rhythms of Reception: Daytime Television and Women's Work," *Regarding Television: Critical Approaches – An Anthology*, ed. E. Ann Kaplan (Los Angeles: American Film Institute, 1983) 67–74.

17 These *Gilmore Girls* episodes are "But I'm a Gilmore" (26 April 2005), "How Many Kropogs to Cape Cod?" (3 May 2005), "Blame Booze and Melville" (10 May 2005), and "A House Is Not a Home" (17 May 2005).

18 Dennis Porter, "Soap Time: Thoughts on a Commodity Art Form," *Television: The Critical View*, ed. Horace Newcomb, 2nd ed. (New York: Oxford UP, 1979) 89.

19 Robert C. Allen, *Speaking of Soap Operas* (Chapel Hill: U of North Carolina P, 1985) 82–84; Ellen Seiter, "Eco's TV Guide – The Soaps," *Tabloid* 5 (Winter 1982): 35–43. Allen and Seiter's usage follows Umberto Eco, *The Role of the Reader: Explorations in the Semiotics of Texts* (Bloomington: Indiana UP, 1979), which contains a reprint of his 1959 essay, "The Poetics of the Open Work," 47–66. See also Jane Feuer, *Seeing Through the Eighties* (Durham, NC: Duke UP, 1995) 121–30. Allen, Seiter, and Feuer all apply Eco's notion of the open work to soap operas.

20 John Fiske, *Television Culture* (London: Routledge, 1987) 183.

21 Laura Stempel Mumford, *Love and Ideology in the Afternoon: Soap Opera, Women, and Television Genre* (Bloomington: Indiana UP, 1995) 67–93.

22 Feuer, *Seeing Through the Eighties* 122, makes a similar point about episodic closure in the serial form.

23 Brian Lowry and Jim Benson, "New Hours of Power?" *Variety* 24 Oct. 1994: 39; John Dempsey, "FX Hopes for Big Effects of New Buys," *Variety* 1 Oct. 2001: 30; Brian Lowry, "Tuning In," *Variety* 4 Apr. 2005: 19.

24 Gary Levin, "Reruns Have Some Viewers Seeing Double," *USA Today* 30 Sept. 1999: 3D; John Dempsey, "Wolf Pack Leads Cable with 'Law & Order,'" *Variety* 6 Oct. 2003: 26.

25 Elizabeth Guider, "Franchise Mints Global Coin," *Daily Variety* 18 Nov. 2003, special section 1: A1.

26 Many shows today begin with a teaser, one or two beats that precede the credit sequence, which functions as part of act 1. Some, including *Lost* and *The O.C.* (Fox, 2003–), break act 4 into two shorter segments. However the commercial breaks are distributed, a four-act structure obtains as a norm of the PTS, even in premium cable shows, as Kristin Thompson, *Storytelling in Film and Television* (Cambridge: Harvard UP, 2003) 51–55, has shown in an analysis of *The Sopranos*.

In the 2005–06 season there seems to be a new near-universal practice of having more than four segments per hour, with some programs such as *Commander-in-Chief* (ABC, 2005–) having some nonteaser segments of less than five minutes. The 2005–06 season has also revived the convention of the "tag," a short epilogue scene before the closing credits that was standard in the 1970s. It remains to be seen whether inserting extra commercial breaks and segments will force a reconsideration of the notion of a four-act structure, which may obtain regardless of where the breaks are inserted.

27 Indeed, Kristin Thompson, *Storytelling in the New Hollywood* (Cambridge: Harvard UP, 1999), has convincingly argued that Hollywood movies are better understood as having four rather than three acts, and in *Storytelling in Film and Television* 40–55, she shows that the same four-act pattern applies in television storytelling.

28 Syndicated reruns often rearrange the commercial breaks to add extra ones, doing a kind of violence to the text by betraying the viewer's expectations of forward progress midact and of a pause at act's end.

29 Two industry terms for the end of an act are "act end" and "act out," but neither of these has the strength of connotation that "curtain" has.

30 DiMaggio 90; Brody 126; Rich Whiteside, "The Small Screen: *Alias*," *scr(i)pt* 9.2 (Mar.–Apr. 2003).

31 It is a television industry mantra that the second-act curtain should be the strongest because the commercial break on the half-hour is twice as long as those on the quarter-hours, but I have not noticed a difference in the strength of curtains between acts 1 and 2, both of which are typically quite forceful. My sense, however, is that third-act curtains are less likely to be as dramatic or surprising. On the second-act "cliffhanger" see DiMaggio 44–45.

32 Ibid., 45.

33 On some shows, such as *Nip/Tuck*, coming up with the theme precedes breaking the story. See Rich Whiteside, "The Small Screen: *Nip/Tuck* – A Slice of the New Americana," *scr(i)pt* 10.1 (Jan.–Feb. 2004): 56–59. The writers on *Judging Amy* claim that they begin with ideas for Gray family stories, then find their themes, and only then conceive of cases for Amy and Maxine. See Whiteside, "The Small Screen: *Judging Amy*."

34　Porter asserts that this is a general feature of television without distinguishing between serials and episodic shows ("The Structure" 141). He then goes on to analyze an episode of *ER*, a serial narrative.

35　This kind of serialization is increasingly common on half-hour shows such as *Friends* (NBC, 1994–2004) and *Sex and the City* (HBO, 1998–2004), and many of my points in this section would apply to them.

36　In some ways these observations about *Happy Days* apply as well to traditional episodic dramas such as *Baywatch* (syn., 1989–2001), which draw heavily on the repetition of motifs. But some episodic dramas, such as *Magnum P.I.* (CBS, 1980–88) and *The Closer* (TNT, 2005–), combine minor serial arcs with an overriding emphasis on weekly cases. As such, they combine the appeals of sit-com repetition and serialized long-format character engagement. Recent sit-coms such as *Friends* and *Sex and the City* offer a similar mix, with the emphasis more heavily on the serialized mode as the programs matured through their runs.

37　Kozloff calls this a "truism of television criticism" (91).

38　Because television writing advice is aimed at aspiring writers who have not yet made it to staff positions, their focus is on writing spec scripts of episodes. Thus there is scant treatment of long-form storytelling in books and articles on teleplay writing. Ironically, arcs come up more in movie screenwriting manuals than in those for television, though the term most likely originates in TV, not film. See, for example, Linda Seger, *Advanced Screenwriting: Raising Your Script to the Academy Award Level* (Los Angeles: Silman-James P, 2003) 167 ff.

39　LaDuke 133.

40　One hears many reports that the September-to-May season is a thing of the past, but the six networks still debut new episodes of most shows in the fall, conclude them in the spring, and rerun them in the summer. Furthermore, as long as the main sweeps seasons are in the fall, winter, and spring, the networks are likely to save many of their best episodes for these periods. In cases in which high-profile network programs (e.g., *Survivor*, *The O.C.*) have aired during the summer, it has almost always been a stunt to attract attention before the regular season has begun. Such programs tend to fall into the regular schedule once they become fixtures on a network's slate of shows.

　　Fox continues to premiere many programs in August rather than September because of its contract to air baseball games during prime time in October, which puts its regular programming on hiatus. But in most ways Fox still adheres to the traditional season; the aesthetics of season-long storytelling are not affected by this practice.

41　Rich Whiteside, "The Small Screen: *24*," *scr(i)pt* 9.3 (May–June 2003): 56–59.

42　"Grounded" (8 May 2001).

43　I am not suggesting here that television writers have no motive for narrative experimentation or that commercial factors stifle the desire to try new things. I am also not implying that all narrative virtues have a source in the networks' profit motives. I am only arguing that the PTS as a group style is unlikely to adopt *as a stable, consistent norm* any commercially motivated innovation that is not also a means of telling stories efficiently or effectively.

44　Karen Hall, "American TV Writing: Musings of a Global Storyteller," *Screenwriting for a Global Market: Selling Your Scripts from Hollywood to Hong Kong*, ed. Andrew Horton (Berkeley: U of California P, 2004) 130.

"From Beats to Arcs" 2015 Postscript

Michael Z. Newman

Ten years have passed since I wrote "From Beats to Arcs." Television and the kind of shows I wrote about have changed in many ways major and minor in that time. From the vantage point of the present, disruptions can appear more prominent than continuities, and despite some of the shifts and novelties I observe in TV storytelling (along with TV as business, technology, and experience), I also see a stable and adaptable system. Advertising-supported TV narrative is still written around commercial breaks and seasons. Beats and arcs are no more or less significant than they were generally speaking as tools of narrative design and construction, though many network shows break for ads more frequently than in the past. In all genres of TV, episodic unity tends to be a strong value. Like anyone who has been paying attention, though, I have been aware of emerging forms and new modes of viewing.

I made a point to discuss broadcast network shows in "From Beats to Arcs" and avoided focusing on the more prestigious premium cable dramas like *The Sopranos*, which seemed in some ways to differ in narrative form. Their lack of commercials, shorter seasons, and apparent absence of industrial constraints often make them appear altogether different from network serials, which by contrast sometimes look quite formulaic. I emphasized commercial network fare in order to appreciate its aesthetic achievements in the face of widespread denigration. The network/cable dichotomy is often oversold, even more now than ten years ago, and can function as much to affirm conservative taste distinction as to identify two sets of conventions.[1] But the differences reveal that some forms of serialized TV storytelling work according to their own constraints and opportunities, which we can appreciate by looking at one exemplar of the cable style of the past decade: *Mad Men*, which ran from 2007–2015.

Like any television show, *Mad Men* is the product of extensive collaboration, but its creative authorship is strongly attributed to the showrunner Matthew Weiner, whose previous work included both network comedies and *The Sopranos*.[2] As a prestige product adding luster to the basic cable channel AMC's brand identity, *Mad Men* draws on the cachet of premium cable HBO, whose original dramas have set a standard for artistry in television. It follows the HBO style in many ways.

While, unlike HBO, AMC is advertising-supported and breaks the episodes of *Mad Men* into segments between commercial breaks, the episodes are clearly written and shot without these pauses in mind. Like many cable series, a season consists not of 22 or more episodes as remains typical on broadcast networks, but thirteen (the seventh season has fourteen, divided into two halves of seven). These two conventions of the cable drama, the absence of breaks and the shorter season, are both products of their own commercial logic. Success might not be defined as much by how many viewers watch a live airing, and audiences tend to be smaller though perhaps more desirable for their affluence. But unlike networks, cable channels earn income from cable or satellite providers per subscriber ("carriage fees") and have an interest in being desirable both to consumers and cable and satellite companies. It would be an odd blunder to see cable channels, whether they are ad-supported or not, as somehow less commercial than broadcast networks.

What is the effect of episodes having no clearly marked acts? Acts in conventional TV storytelling build toward endings. In many instances, the break to commercial comes at the moment of greatest tension and uncertainty. Visual and musical techniques amplify these moments. A need to bring the drama to such a point four or more times in an hour produces patterns of rising action, raised stakes, complication and development. By ignoring the need for such moments, *Mad Men* perversely calls attention to the interruptive quality of commercial breaks. Perhaps a more ideal viewing situation is a binge on DVDs or streaming video. When viewing this way it is impossible to tell where the commercials would have appeared. And perhaps by refusing to adapt to the convention of interruption, Weiner signals his desire for autonomy from commercialism, adding authority to his creative identity.

And yet there is still pattern and rhythm in *Mad Men*'s episodes. Many of them introduce a new character, client, or situation in the first few scenes, leading up to a series of further events, some of which are resolved within the hour, and some of which provide material for further storytelling. An episode might be based around a trip to California or the development of a new campaign to be pitched at a meeting. Many episodes build toward parties, whether at home, in the office, or in another location. In the fourth-season episode "Waldorf Stories," the Clio awards are first mentioned in the expository scenes, and later the contingent from the ad agency wins their Clio and faces implications and consequences of the characters' drunkenness after the ceremony. This pattern is not so different from less prestigious shows like *Revenge* typically building up to their third- or fourth-act parties with their confrontations and revelations.

Unlike many network shows, *Mad Men*'s beats tend to lack recapitulations of basic information. The subtle style of storytelling here avoids recapping, and rewards the audience for having paid close attention all along. For viewers who track the characters' trajectories carefully over the seasons, there are pleasures in knowing what characters must be thinking without being reminded overtly. In the first few episodes of season three, the developments from the end of season two are never formally explained in dialog, and the control of Sterling Cooper by the British firm Puttnam, Powell, and Lowe is taken as understood. So many elements of the story work like this: you need to remember them. You need to remember that Don is Dick, that Peggy had Pete's baby, that Joan was Roger's mistress, and who knows what about whom. Occasionally, at moments of heightened drama and as payoff to a long series of episodes of development, one character learns another character's story, as happens at the end of season two with Peggy telling Pete that she had his child and gave the baby away, and at the end of season three with Betty learning of Don's past identity and family history. At these moments characters narrate their secrets in dialog, and the audience is granted the pleasure or pain of witnessing the characters' reactions to deeply meaningful news. But the ordinary recapping in dialog scene-by-scene and episode-by-episode is absent.

While it might be tempting to see this as an aesthetic advantage, perhaps we can also see tradeoffs. The more obvious style of beats that introduce new information while reminding the audience of old information produces its own pleasures. The *Mad Men* style, while more obscure, emphasizes unspoken thematic or symbolic meaning often as a complement to more action-oriented plot developments. And by saving the repetition of key plot information for so many episodes, it boosts their impact. The dedicated, attentive viewer is rewarded for their insight and interpretive work, and their long-term investment in a slowly, elegantly unfolding canvas rich with historical and psychological insight and attention to detail in the show's mise en scène.

Network and cable styles need not exist in hierarchy. *Mad Men* and "quality TV" more generally is addressed at more than one audience, and increasingly the afterlife of such shows is not so much cable reruns as DVD or Blu-ray discs, video on demand, and streaming services like Netflix. In all of these secondary distribution outlets, viewers often watch many episodes in rapid succession, rendering recapping somewhat superfluous. The network drama is also addressed at this market, but its live audience (the audience for "linear TV") is still most crucial to the business model of the broadcast networks who sell audiences to advertisers. AMC's business model is more complicated, and more than the networks, it has an interest in burnishing its brand identity. AMC's reputation as a source of high-quality original programs, which *Mad Men* established, helped its clout in negotiations over carriage fees with cable providers, which ultimately increased its revenue from subscriber fees.[3] Many observers saw putting *Mad Men* on as a way for AMC to become the next HBO, a cable channel with "brand buzz."[4] *Mad Men*, according to an industry trade paper, put AMC "on the map with ad buyers and cable operators."[5] Unlike the typical broadcast program, then, *Mad Men* has been a loss leader for the network putting it on, appealing as prestige programming to bring benefits in addition to revenue from advertisements during breaks between segments. Its value is not equal only to the revenue it has earned from advertising, which does not cover the program's costs.[6] *Mad Men* is a product not of a less commercial production context, merely of a different one.

As for the macro units of the narrative, the unity absent from many seasons of network TV is much stronger in a shorter cable season. This is evident from the heavy marketing and promotion at the debut of each new season, and from the packaging of the show, like many other upscale cable series, in DVD and Blu-ray box sets and iTunes and Amazon downloads by season for sale to consumers. The logic of the aftermarket in TV distribution is strongly invested in seasons as a unit of narrative consumption and of meaning. *Mad Men*, like any show, is produced a season at a time. The writers break the story into thirteen episodes, seeing a shape for the story in advance, a task more likely in a thirteen-episode season than in a longer form.

A season of *Mad Men* forms a well-defined arc. Season three, for instance, has a strong dimension of narrative unity as the intersecting stories of Don and the Draper family, the agency, and the other key characters (particularly Roger, Pete, Joan, and Peggy) have patterns of rising action, complication, and climax. When watching the season finale, "Shut the Door, Have a Seat," many of the threads of the plot are revealed in the significance they might not have had all along. We see the story of the family's breakdown and Betty's impending marriage to Henry; the agency's struggles suffering under foreign control, only to break away in establishing a new firm; Peggy's effort to assert her independence in her new professional role and be taken seriously by the men, until finally she is recognized (and tells Roger she won't get him coffee); Pete's business acumen being seldom rewarded until he is chosen over his rival Ken to join the new firm; and Joan's return to the agency after her absence, having suffered from Greg's failure to be named chief surgical resident, which showed the danger of a woman's fortunes being tied up in her husband's. (Roger's conflict with his ex-wife and daughter after marrying the much younger Jane, culminating in the matching trauma of the Kennedy assassination and his daughter's wedding on the same day, happens in the penultimate episode.) One of the effects of watching the season-ending episode is regarding the previous twelve install-ments as moments leading up to the climactic plot developments: the Drapers' failure to keep their family together and the agency breaking off on its own. So many of the points along the way (such as the introduction of the at-first mysterious characters of Conrad Hilton and Henry Francis) were in anticipation of these events, which then push us forward into season four as we are introduced to a new office space for the firm with new characters, a new family for Betty, a new apartment for Don, new clients to pitch, and a new set of narrative questions to be answered over thirteen more hours.

One way *Mad Men* and shows like it have much in common with conventional TV network dramas is in the unity of their episodes. Despite a fair bit of open-endedness, a typical *Mad Men* has strong coherence both in its plot and its theme. Episode titles convey, perhaps obliquely, not just a key moment of plot made into an abstract for the story, but often an allusion suggesting deeper meanings: "Babylon," "The Wheel," "The Gold Violin," "Meditations in an Emergency," "The Chrysanthemum and the Sword," "Tomorrowland," "Lady Lazarus," "The Monolith." Sometimes questions raised in the early scenes of an episode are answered by the closing credits, but just as often they are deferred, as is typical of serial narratives. The third season episode "The Arrangements" is a good example of *Man Men*'s episodic unity. The episode's heaviest moment is the death of Betty's father Eugene, presaged by one scene in which he shows her the arrangements of the title for what to do in the event of his passing, and another in which he gives his grandson a dead German soldier's helmet he brought home from the First World War. But there are two other storylines about relations between parents and their adult children that resonate with the death of Grandpa Gene: Peggy disap-points her mother by moving to Manhattan with a new roommate, and upsets her mother further by giving the gift of a television set (as if it can substitute for a daughter's presence). And the agency takes on a new client, a rich kid who wants to make jai-alai into a major sport in the US (clearly folly), and whose exasperated father is a friend of the agency's founder Bert Cooper. The satisfaction of "The Arrangements," a combination of episodic and long-arcing storytelling, is in some ways not much different from any serialized narrative, no matter how distinctive the upscale cable style of this particular program.

There is no natural reason why a serialized television series would have episodes with strong coherence and unity. It is a convention of production and reception, and it would seem no less vital to cable than to network series. Episodic unity works well in a system where episodes are the unit of consumption, whether in weekly doses or more rapidly. It works well in a system of production for managing labor and resources. Whether the unity is of story or theme, this convention works to the advantage of both the audi-ence and the television industry. Episodes fit into patterns of both media work and audience leisure.

It is tempting to see the creative autonomy of quality TV writers and producers as a value in opposition to the compromised commercialism of traditional broadcasting. But it also functions within the capitalist media system as an appeal in its own right, a selling point to a desirable market segment and a means of product differentiation. And like all creative agency under capitalism, this autonomy always works in tension with the imper-ative of economic productivity. No action is unconstrained. The art of the cable drama is not greater or lesser than that of the network drama, and perhaps not even less bound by convention, but it is a somewhat different form as a product of its own industrial circumstances.

Notes

1 Network and cable are simplifications, as both categories admit a fair bit of variety within, and Netflix, Amazon, and other streaming online venues for programming overlap with cable without being traditional TV channels.

2 On the showrunner as author, see Michael Z. Newman and Elana Levine, *Legitimating Television: Media Convergence and Cultural Status* (New York: Routledge, 2012).

3 Brian Steinberg, "Mad Men Is Great Art, Not Such Great TV Business," *Advertising Age* March 27, 2012.

4 Deborah Jaramillo, "AMC: Stumbling toward a New Television Canon," *Television & New Media* 14 (2013), 167–183; Anthony N. Smith, "Putting the Premium into Basic: Slow-Burn Narratives and the Loss-Leader Function of AMC's Original Drama Series," *Television & New Media* 14 (2013), 150–166.

5 Jon Lafayette, "The 'Mad Men' Lesson: Buzz Lights Up a Network," *Broadcasting & Cable*, July 19, 2010.

6 Smith, 160–161; Marissa Guthrie, "Matt Weiner, AMC Reach Deal on Mad Men," *Hollywood Reporter*, March 31, 2011.

CHAPTER 10

Theory in Practice
The Subplot as Simplification in King Lear

Bridget Gellert Lyons

Bridget Gellert Lyons taught English at Rutgers University. Her books include *Voices of Melancholy* (1971), *Reading in an Age of Theory* (1997), and *Chimes at Midnight* (1989).

LEAR'S WORDS just before his death have always eluded the attempts of critics to label what he sees, does, or feels at the moment that he utters them:

> Pray you, undo this button: thank you, Sir.
> Do you see this? Look on her, look, her lips,
> Look there, look there! [*Dies*
> (5.3.309–11)

If we are rigorous in our analysis of this passage, we reject speculations like Bradley's about whether the king is dying of joy or grief: 'this' in line 310 lacks an antecedent and is therefore unclear. But there are other grounds for hesitating to fill in the gaps of Lear's fragmented requests and exclamations, and these grounds are related to the very different way in which we have learned of Gloucester's death shortly before. This event is narrated by Edgar and is not seen by the audience at all:

> and in this habit
> Met I my father with his bleeding rings,
> Their precious stones new lost; became his guide,
> Led him, begg'd for him, sav'd him from despair;
> Never – O fault! – reveal'd myself unto him,
> Until some half-hour past, when I was arm'd;
> Not sure, though hoping, of this good success,
> I ask'd his blessing, and from first to last

Original publication details: Bridget Gellert Lyons, "The Subplot as Simplification in *King Lear*" from *Some Facets of King Lear: Essays in Prismatic Criticism*, ed. Rosalie Colie and F.T. Flahiff, pp. 23–38. University of Toronto Press, 1978. Reproduced with permission from University of Toronto Press.

Literary Theory: An Anthology, Third Edition. Edited by Julie Rivkin and Michael Ryan.
© 2017 John Wiley & Sons, Ltd. Published 2017 by John Wiley & Sons, Ltd.

> Told him my pilgrimage: but his flaw'd heart,
> Alack, too weak the conflict to support!
> 'Twixt two extremes of passion, joy and grief,
> Burst smilingly.
>
> (5.3.188–99)

What this account lacks in immediacy it gains in coherence. We see Gloucester's death through the mediation of a narrator who structures the event in terms of known forms by which life and literature pattern themselves ('List a brief tale' in 5.3.181; 'my pilgrimage'), and who cannot speak of eyes without expressing their analogical value. Motives and moral evaluations are clearly spelled out, and there is no mystery about the death itself: the allusion to the conflict of passions which literally broke Gloucester's heart assumes the interlocking systems – moral, physiological, psychological – by which people of the Renaissance conventionally interpreted behaviour.[1] The passage's ornate figures ('Their precious stones new lost,' 'Burst smilingly') are also heightened expressions of its intelligibility.

Edgar's account, understandable in the way Bradley wanted Lear's death to be, points to some of the most characteristic differences between plot and subplot in the play. The Gloucester story intensifies our experience of the central action by supplying a sequence of parallels, impressed upon us by frequent commentary by the characters themselves:

> GLOU.   This villain of mine comes under the prediction; there's son
> against father: the King falls from bias of nature; there's father
> against child. We have seen the best of our time…
>
> (1.2.114–18)

> EDG.   How light and portable my pain seems now
> When that which makes me bend makes the king bow;
> He childed as I father'd!
>
> (3.6.111–13)

> LEAR   Let copulation thrive; for Gloucester's bastard son
> Was kinder to his father than my daughters
> Got 'tween the lawful sheets.
>
> (4.6.117–19)

But repetition alone cannot supply dramatic interest, and the characters' consciousness of the existence of a mirror does not mean that the reflection is exact. Hamlet too sees Laertes as a 'foil,' but the audience is as much aware of the differences between the responses of the two characters as of the analogous situations that provoke those responses. The same point has been cogently made by Sigurd Burckhardt about the double plot in *King Lear*:

> I submit that Shakespeare, in this tragedy and in no other, constructed parallel plots of considerable rigor, and that we must assume that he meant something by this structure. He cannot have meant the plots to be merely parallel, one reinforcing the other; for then the subplot would become a mere redundancy, and if ever an action needed no reinforcement of its impact, it is Lear's. There is every reason to think that the apparent similarity of the two plots is like that of controlled experiments, and that the meaning of both lies in the one element which accounts for the difference.[2]

The element of difference on which I would like to concentrate lies in the way the subplot simplifies the central action, translating its concerns into familiar (and therefore easily apprehensible) verbal and visual patterns. The subplot is easier to grasp because its characters tend to account for their sufferings in traditional moral language; it also pictorializes the main action, supplying interpreted visual emblems for some of the play's important themes. The clarity of the subplot and its didacticism are related, furthermore, to the old-fashioned literary forms, like the morality play and the chivalric romance, through which it represents experience.[3] These give expression to the idea of convention, and therefore to a world of recognizably structured perceptions and values – the very opposite of dislocation and madness. But the verbal and visual simplifications of the subplot do not merely provide a contrast with what goes on elsewhere in the play; they help to reveal the nature of Lear's experience by being so obviously inadequate to it. Lear's sufferings are heroic because they cannot be accommodated by traditional formulas, moral or literary, and the subplot exists partly to establish that fact.

The simplifications of the subplot can be seen first of all in its method of defining character. The behaviour of Edmund the Bastard, for example, is more comprehensible than that of Lear's bad daughters because his depravity is largely explained by his illegitimacy. He is what so-called 'natural' children were supposed to be; and his definition of 'nature' as circumventing law, custom, and order is in keeping with the application of the word 'natural' to children who were born outside of society's laws and excluded from its benefits. Legal treatises of the later Middle Ages, often compendia of commonplace morality, demonstrate the extent to which traditional moral thinking made the bastard susceptible of emblematic treatment. In Sir John Fortescue's commendation of the English laws of the fifteenth century, for example, he particularly praises their intransigence towards illegitimate children (their exclusion from inheritance even if their parents eventually married) as being in accord with biblical examples. He goes on to explain that bastards are actually contaminated by the sinful circumstances of their begetting: they have more than their share of the sin that all inherit, and nature brands them 'by setting as it were a natural mark or blemish on the natural children, though secretly impressed upon the mind.'[4] Gloucester's initial action in disinheriting the bastard son whom by his own admission he loves as much as his legitimate son is entirely in accord with this legal notion of justice: bastards were living emblems of their parents' sin in begetting them.

Moral and legal ideas about bastards had already been translated into dramatic conventions by the time *King Lear* appeared on the stage, and Edmund's behaviour was recognizable also in terms of a dramatic tradition. The Elizabethan stage abounds with bastards (Shakespeare's Don John in *Much Ado about Nothing* and Tourneur's Spurio in *The Revenger's Tragedy* are examples) who are envious and villainous because they are dispossessed and whose actions reveal the 'secret blemish' of their minds.[5] The important contrast in *King Lear* is between Edmund's conventionally explicable villainy and the seemingly incomprehensible evil of Goneril and Regan. The two daughters, who have been given 'all,' must remain the subject of unanswered questions about what in nature breeds such 'hard hearts.' Their behaviour is as much of a mystery as Cordelia's goodness, defying explanation in terms of natural causes like heredity:

> KENT   It is the stars,
> The stars above us, govern our conditions;
> Else one self mate and mate could not beget
> Such different issues.
>
>   (4.3.33–6)

Lear twice attempts to explain his older daughters' nature on the grounds of their bastardy and their consequent lack of kinship with him (1.4.262–3; 2.4.130–4); Edmund, though his father's son, does what he does because he acts in accordance with a well-established moral and dramatic tradition.

Edgar too illustrates how the conventionality of the subplot's roles expresses the more clearly defined nature of its concerns. Undeveloped at the beginning except in his function as a virtuous dupe, he later purposefully assumes a disguise as a Bedlam lunatic which is in direct contrast with Lear's uncontrolled, real madness. The difference between the two kinds of madness is expressed through dramatic roles: Edgar's pose is an imitative one whose stereotyped nature has been alluded to earlier by Edmund ('my cue is villanous melancholy, with a sigh like Tom o' Bedlam,' 1.2.142–3), and for which there were prescribed costumes and gestures:

> The country gives me proof and precedent
> Of Bedlam beggars, who, with roaring voices,
> Strike in their numb'd and mortified bare arms
> Pins, wooden pricks, nails, sprigs of rosemary;
> And with this horrible object, from low farms,
> Poor pelting villages, sheep-cotes, and mills,
> Sometime with lunatic bans, sometime with prayers,
> Enforce their charity.
>
> (2.3.13–20)

While the king wildly imagines a variety of impossible roles for himself, from that of the avenging fury to being the 'pattern of all patience,' Edgar's mad pose is one for which there was 'proof and precedent' in the social and dramatic world. His conscious control of all the roles that he chooses is embodied in their stereotyped, fixed quality – Bedlam, rustic with a typical stage dialect, knight.

Closely related to the greater conventionality of the subplot's characters are two of its other most striking features: its pictorial nature and its archaism. First, the subplot often provides emblems, or pictures with clearly stated meanings, for the benefit of the audience as well as for Lear and the Fool. The appearance of Edgar on the heath as a poor and naked Bedlam beggar, for example, supplies the physical actuality of the poverty and nakedness that preoccupy Lear, stripped of his retinue and position:

> Is man no more than this? Consider him well. Thou ow'st the worm no
> silk, the beast no hide, the sheep no wool, the cat no perfume. Ha!
> here's three on's are sophisticated; thou art the thing itself;
> unaccommodated man is no more but such a poor, bare, forked animal
> as thou art.
>
> (3.4.105–11)

While Lear soon tries to imitate Edgar and act out the metaphor of nakedness, it is Edgar who serves as a living example and a lesson, a subject for meditation ('Consider him well'). Gloucester's entrance with a torch immediately afterwards inspires the Fool to similar emblematic imaginations on a different subject:

> Now a little fire in a wild field were like an old lecher's heart; a small
> spark, all the rest on's body cold. Look! here comes a walking fire.
>
> (3.4.114–17)

Later, when the mad king meets the blinded Gloucester at Dover, Lear uses him as a source of emblems: the blind man is 'blind Cupid' (4.6.138) and 'Goneril, with a white beard' (4.6.97), in each case a picture that we associate, in its context in the play, with lust. These images prompted by Gloucester also become assimilated to Lear's vision of injustice:

> Get thee glass eyes;
> And, like a scurvy politician, seem
> To see the things thou dost not.
>
> (4.6.172–4)

The function of emblems, with their detachable meanings, whether conventional or assigned, is to clarify and to teach; this was the aim of many of the numerous emblem books of the period. But emblems were often excessively ingenious, even arbitrary, in creating pictorial embodiments of moral truths on figures of speech, and therefore the continuously emblematic nature of Lear's imaginings becomes a sign of their insanity, even while they suggest a higher order of insight. His emblems portray the obsessive moral imagination of the character who creates them and at the same time they provide physical analogues for some of the play's important themes – nakedness, appetite, injustice. Edgar and Gloucester, in the examples cited, constitute the pictorial parts of the emblems for which Lear supplies the text.

The pictorial simplifications of the subplot contribute to the particular nature of its archaic quality: it often evokes a medieval legal morality, with its direct translation into codes of justice of biblical injunctions and metaphors. The blindness of Gloucester, a physical representation of a lack of moral perception, also illustrates the tendency of the subplot to lend itself to old-fashioned moral simplicities. In the early Middle Ages, biblical notions of justice and redemption, that an eye should be exacted for an eye, or that an offending eye or limb should be removed if it was an obstacle to salvation, were physically acted out. For example, blinding (as well as castration) was a penalty for rape, justified on the grounds of exact and literal retribution: 'Let him thus lose his eyes which gave him sight of the maiden's beauty.'[6]

Gloucester's blinding lends itself to this sort of construction by the characters involved in a way that Lear's sufferings never do. While the actual mutilation first strikes any audience or reader as a dreadful display of brutality, Edgar and Gloucester later interpret the experience as having some sort of connection with justice, forcing us to redefine our response to its physical horror. Edgar speaks sententiously to Edmund of the blinding in terms of legalistic notions of punishment for lust:

> The Gods are just, and of our pleasant vices
> Make instruments to plague us;
> The dark and vicious place where thee he got
> Cost him his eyes.
>
> (5.3.170–3)

Even Gloucester himself defines his blindness as the appropriate expression or symbol of his previous errors of judgment, and perhaps also as an inadvertent blessing:

> I stumbled when I saw. Full oft 'tis seen,
> Our means secure us, and our mere defects
> Prove our commodities.
>
> (4.1.19–21)

Gloucester's blindness pictorializes his sin and his folly because the significance of the eyeless man's presence on the stage is clarified for us, by himself and Edgar, in moralized language.

Sententious language most obviously reflects the tendency towards stereotype in the characters of the subplot; Edmund's kinship with his brother and father is evident in the way in which he moralizes his own end: 'The wheel is come full circle; I am here' (5.3.174). The contrast between Edgar's stock of formulations and the language of Lear's visions in their respective madnesses is as striking as the general difference which we have already observed between an imitated role and an involuntary condition. As a madman, Edgar invokes the most familiar moral formulas, the seven deadly sins and the ten commandments,[7] both in his self-characterization and in the advice he dispenses:

> EDG. Take heed o' th' foul fiend. Obey thy parents; keep thy word's justice; swear not;
> commit not with man's sworn spouse; set not thy sweet heart on proud array.
> Tom's a-cold.
> LEAR What hast thou been?
> EDG. A servingman, proud in heart and mind; that curl'd my hair, wore gloves in my cap,
> serv'd the lust of my mistress' heart, and did the act of darkness with her; swore as
> many oaths as I spake words, and broke them in the sweet face of Heaven; one that
> slept in the contriving of lust, and wak'd to do it. Wine lov'd I deeply, dice dearly,
> and in woman out-paramour'd the Turk: false of heart, light of ear, bloody of hand;
> hog in sloth, fox in stealth, wolf in greediness, dog in madness, lion in prey.
>
> (3.4.80–95)

Edgar's picture of himself as a madman and epitome of sinfulness is conveyed in terms of unmistakably traditional categories and emblems ('hog in sloth,' etc.). Structurally, both of the speeches quoted above are organized in syntactic series that emphasize the formulaic nature of their content, despite the supposed madness of the character who utters them.

Lear's mad visions differ substantively and structurally from Edgar's 'lunacy,' as well as from Gloucester's sanity. Lear alludes, for example, to the sin of adultery in such a way as to undermine it as a moral category and associate it with a general vision of lechery:

> I pardon that man's life. What was thy cause?
> Adultery?
> Thou shalt not die: die for adultery! No:
> The wren goes to 't, and the small gilded fly
> Does lecher in my sight.
>
> (4.6.112–16)

Contrary to the formal structure of Edgar's syntactic series and parallels, Lear's hypothetical interrogation of an offender sounds spontaneous and becomes a spoken dialogue in his own mind: 'Thou shalt not die: die for adultery! No.' Furthermore, the small animals that Lear evokes do not illustrate exemplary couplings, as in Edgar's case; they are animated sources of his visions.

Gloucester's most striking simile about his sufferings – 'As flies to wanton boys, are we to th' Gods; / They kill us for their sport' (4.1.36–7) – offers another kind of contrast with Lear's mad language. Gloucester's figure sets up an exact proportion between the terms of comparison, clearly limiting itself as a figure of speech. Lear's visions, on the other hand, are characterized by a confusion of the general and the particular that gives excessive (and obsessive) personal concreteness to abstractions ('I tax you not, you elements, with unkindness; / I never gave you kingdom, call'd you children' [3.2.16–17]), or creates universalizing emblems out of personal particulars:

> Dost thou squiny at me?
> No, do thy worst, blind Cupid; I'll not love.
> (4.6.138–9)

Whereas sententious speech tends to submerge individual feelings in known formulas, Lear's language does the opposite, stressing the personal motivation behind each generalization. The mistake of quoting Gloucester's observation about the malignancy of the gods as an objective statement about life could therefore hardly be made with Lear's speeches, which through their disproportions insist upon themselves too strongly as personal, motivated utterances, even while they discuss the nature of the world or the universe.

The distinctive features of the subplot characters and their language – didactic, sententious, occasionally archaic, and pictorially clarifying – extend to entire episodes. The scene on what Gloucester takes to be Dover cliff, for example, can be perceived as an enactment of Regan's earlier words to Lear:[8]

> O, Sir! you are old;
> Nature in you stands on the very verge
> Of her confine; you should be rul'd and led
> By some discretion that discerns your state
> Better than you yourself.
> (2.4.147–51)

Edgar later makes the imaginary cliff visually intelligible, organizing it spatially like a painting which self-consciously makes sense of mere sight:

> Come on, sir; here's the place: stand still. How fearful
> And dizzy 'tis to cast one's eyes so low!
> The crows and choughs that wing the midway air
> Show scarce so gross as beetles; half way down
> Hangs one that gathers sampire, dreadful trade!
> Methinks he seems no bigger than his head.
> The fishermen that walk upon the beach
> Appear like mice, and yond tall anchoring bark
> Diminish'd to her cock, her cock a buoy
> Almost too small for sight.
> (4.6.11–20)

The unseeing old man, obviously 'led' by Edgar, is also metaphorically 'ruled' by him, brought to believe in the steep cliff of which he stands near the 'extreme verge' (4.6.26), and in its moral significance.

But the abortive leap from the 'cliff,' like the blinding of Gloucester, is the physical enactment of a larger metaphor as well. Levin has observed that Gloucester's fall suggests the fall of man, or the kind of fall that is central to tragedy.[9] It may be even more precise to see it as a rendering of the 'fortunate fall,' the Christian paradox whereby man's original fall was interpreted as happy because it enabled him to receive more grace and be redeemed.[10] Gloucester's attempt to kill himself is deflected in dramatic terms by Edgar into what could be comedy or farce (a man's falling flat on his face when he has other expectations); but whereas the joke is usually that one who is pompously upright is unexpectedly brought low, here the man who had already been humbled (he takes the plunge from his knees), and who expects to fall, by his own wish, even more catastrophically, is prevented from doing so. Gloucester's 'fall' is interpreted by Edgar, who has arranged the whole scene, as miraculous ('Thy life's a miracle,' 4.6.55); the suicide attempt leads Gloucester to the resolution that he must bear his life.

The moral emphasis of the scene, its function as a lesson, is closely connected with its formal evocations of the morality play. Edgar externalizes Gloucester's suicidal intentions, suggesting that it was a fiend who led him to the edge of the cliff, and that the 'clearest Gods' have preserved him from the mad beggar who was really a fantastic devil:

> As I stood here below methought his eyes
> Were two full moons; he had a thousand noses,
> Horns whelk'd and wav'd like the enridged sea:
> It was some fiend...

> (4.6.69–72)

The imaginative mode of the moralities appears as a simplification of experience because of the discrepancy between Edgar's presentation of the scene and Gloucester's reception of it. Edgar's performance – his exploitation of his disguise as a fiend-haunted Bedlam, his minute descriptions and rapid changes of voice – draws attention to itself as invention and fantasy, exuberant and almost superfluous in the exactness of its details. But Gloucester accepts it simply and literally, in the spirit of the moralities, which literalized abstractions. This artistic deception is as successful as the creation of the cliff itself:

> I do remember now; henceforth I'll bear
> Affliction till it do cry out itself
> 'Enough, enough,' and die. That thing you speak of
> I took it for a man; often 'twould say
> 'The Fiend, the Fiend': he led me to that place.

> (4.6.75–9)

When Gloucester prays later ('Let not my worser spirit tempt me again / To die before you please,' 4.6.219–20), his language shows that the impact of the lessons he has had is inseparable from his imaginative apprehension of it as a morality play.

The self-consciously archaic artistry of the subplot, as well as its more limited scope, can be seen even more clearly in the presentation of its climatic episode, the duel between Edgar and Edmund. Like the curious scene on Dover cliff, the combat – chivalric and medieval – is out of keeping with the main story of *King Lear*. In this scene the idea of justice is rendered in the archaic mode of the romances. The duel proves not only that Edgar is the stronger, but also that his claim is right, his assertion, formally delivered, of Edmund's treachery, true.

The trial by combat portrays the idea of law in its perfect form: ideally the just man won because of the rightness of his cause,[11] just as in earlier primitive trials like the ordeal, a suppurating wound became infected only if the defendant was guilty. In the play, the stylized battle therefore gives form to an archaic conception of the way in which divine justice manifested itself in human affairs. It is contrasted not only with Lear's visions of the inadequacy of existing forms of justice to the world's radical evils (his mad parodies of arraignments and assizes), but also with the sacrifice of justice to power by Cornwall and Goneril. Cornwall explicitly associates his power with 'wrath' rather than with justice when he blinds Gloucester:

> Though well we may not pass upon his life
> Without the form of justice, yet our power
> Shall do a court'sy to our wrath, which men
> May blame but not control.
>
> (3.7.24–7)

Goneril's response to Edmund's fall in the duel is just as outspokenly Machiavellian: she is willing to take advantage of the law if it favours or protects her interests, but otherwise she disregards it. When Edmund falls she invokes the minutiae of the rules governing duels to prove that he was not really defeated:

> This is practice, Gloucester:
> By th' law of war thou wast not bound to answer
> An unknown opposite; thou art not vanquish'd,
> But cozen'd and beguil'd.
>
> (5.3.151–4)

But when Albany confronts her immediately afterwards with the proof of her own treachery, she asserts that she is above the law:

> the laws are mine, not thine:
> Who can arraign me for't?
>
> (5.3.158–9)

Her claim to be a ruler who is outside the law is exactly opposite to the idea of rule-under-law for a medieval monarch, whose conception of justice is evoked by the trial by combat. Her despotic definition of privileges, more primitive and more modern, is reminiscent of her father's original ascription of power to his own word – his arbitrary division of his kingdom, or his denial, by kingly fiat, of Cordelia's filial 'bond.' The ceremony by which justice is celebrated in the duel scene, on the other hand, is an expression of custom and tradition.

Trial by battle was supposed to demonstrate not only the identity of law and justice; it rested also on the belief that word and ritual reflected reality. The form of the challenge was exactly prescribed and had to be returned verbatim by the defendant,[12] as Edmund makes a show of doing when he first returns Albany's challenge and then Edgar's. The whole procedure is appropriately formalized in the play: Albany's challenge and the exchange of gloves, the herald and three trumpets that summon Edgar as champion, Edgar's elaborate diction in his challenge (5.3.126–41). The vindication of ceremony in the duel, the consonance of appearance with reality, is set in contrast not only with the play's first scene, where verbal show proves deceptive, but also with the substance of Lear's visions later in the play. He is obsessed, in his arraignments of evil and injustice, by the discrepancy between appearance and reality that he discounted earlier:

> hide thee, thou bloody hand,
> Thou perjur'd, and thou simular of virtue
> That art incestuous; caitiff, to pieces shake,
> That under covert and convenient seeming
> Has practis'd on man's life...
>
> (3.2.53–7)

> Behold yond simp'ring dame,
> Whose face between her forks presages snow...
> The fitchew nor the soiled horse goes to't
> With a more riotous appetite.
>
> (4.6.120–5)

Forms of justice bear no relation to the truth, according to Lear's vision, in a world where the judge is indistinguishable from the thief (4.6.151–6). There could not be a greater contrast when Edgar, the anonymous but noble-looking and well-spoken champion (5.3.142–3), fulfils the expectations of any real or literary audience:

> ALB. Methought thy very gait did prophesy
>   A royal nobleness.
>
> (5.3.175–6)

The formal expression of Edgar's triumph contrasts with the fragmented form of Lear's visions, as well as with their substance. In what is perhaps the king's maddest moment in the fourth act, the ingredients of the trial by battle become grotesque in his imagination. The gauntlet and the formal challenge are qualified first of all by being associated with much less romantic images of war:

> There's your press-money. That fellow handles his bow like a crow-keeper: draw me a clothier's yard. Look, look! a mouse. Peace, peace! this piece of toasted cheese will do't. There's my gauntlet; I'll prove it on a giant. Bring up the brown bills. O! well flown bird...
>
> (4.6.86–92)

The stylized combat, its meaningful language and its symmetry, are distorted in a series of associations that work by arbitrary similarities of sound (peace/piece) and by sheer incongruity: the formidable gigantic opponent is a mouse, and the challenging gauntlet is a piece of toasted cheese. A little later the idea of the incongruous and ineffective challenge is developed even further:

> LEAR   Read thou this challenge; mark but the penning of it.
> GLOU. Were all thy letters suns, I could not see.
>
> (4.6.140–1)

A madman's challenge is delivered to a blind man who cannot read it. Although the allusion to the challenge is not developed, it gives the impression of being connected with the vision of perverted justice that follows, as if Lear (somewhat less explicitly at this point than Titus Andronicus with his mad letters to the gods) were ineffectively challenging the order of things.

The chivalric duel in the last act, then, reminds us of the possibility of a more orderly world by ritualizing what is distorted in Lear's imagination and experience. But its placement in the play, following the defeat of Lear and Cordelia's forces and preceding the even more appalling catastrophe of Cordelia's hanging and Lear's death, points also to the limitations of the order that it suggests. The main action complicates the subplot in various ways, and shows the inadequacies, in a truly tragic situation, of its moral and literary formulas. After the Dover cliff episode, for example, the sight of the dishevelled, mad king modifies our response to Gloucester's cure. Lear's frantic efforts to evade his benevolent captors, whose prisoner he finally regards himself, and the uncompromising nature of his visions, which defy 'sweetening,' make Gloucester's submission, physical and imaginative, to Edgar's 'rule' seem very simple. At the end of the play we see how Edgar, who exhorted his blind father to 'look up' after his fall and succeeded in a spiritual sense, is unable to change anything with the same injunction to Lear (5.3.312).[13] Lear's sufferings outweigh any optimistic or encouraging words, whether Edgar's or Albany's, and they are told by Kent that pain should be allowed to end in death.

Albany's language at the end of the play becomes even more ineffectually formulaic than Edgar's, and this suggests a final important if obvious point about the subplot: its language (like its action) overlaps with that of the main plot, even while it is partly distinct. Albany has been inclined towards pious optimism in his interpretation of earlier events:

> This shows you are above,
> You justicers, that these our nether crimes
> So speedily can venge!
>
>   (4.2.78–80)

As the play's ranking figure just before Lear's death, he speaks a conclusion appropriate to one of the Dukes of the comedies:

> for us, we will resign,
> During the life of this old Majesty,
> To him our absolute power: [*To Edgar and Kent*]
>   you, to your rights,
> With boot and such addition as your honours
> Have more than merited. All friends shall taste
> The wages of their virtue, and all foes
> The cup of their deservings. O! see, see!
>
>   (5.3.298–304)

The formula is destroyed by actuality: the sight of the king's sufferings, his insistence on the lifelessness of Cordelia, and his death. The simplifications that are so obviously concentrated in the subplot, its suggestions of non-tragic forms, extend to the language of minor characters like Albany in the main plot as well, because the two actions are never entirely separate – it is Edgar who finally declares that we must 'Speak what we feel, not what we ought to say' (5.3.324). Contrary to a play like Middleton and Rowley's *The Changeling*, whose two plots seem to present imaginative worlds that are distinct despite the verbal and thematic connections between them, the two actions of *King Lear* never become remote from each other, even if they have different emphases.

The analogous stories in *King Lear*, then, illuminate each other by offering related but contrasting ways of structuring experience. The subplot functions partly as didactic illustration. Though it never transposes the concerns of the main action into a radically different, archaic style (as the Gonzago play does in *Hamlet*), it evokes old-fashioned literary modes – the romance of chivalry, the medieval morality play – that asserted the intelligibility and purposefulness of action. Characters like the Bastard show the relation between simple dramatic conventions and intelligibility: he is a machiavel, while Lear's older daughters, mysteriously, are Machiavellian. Furthermore, the language, moral and circumscribed, of Edgar, Gloucester, and at the end, of Edmund, contributes to the effect of the subplot as limited and apprehensible in its moral meanings. Its didactic emphasis colours our view of the main plot as well, inviting us repeatedly to impose its patterns on Lear's experience. Our sense of the redemptive value of Lear's sufferings comes not only from the pity that he feels on the heath for the poor, but from the similarities between his situation and Gloucester's. The eyeless man is a physical image, an emblem, of Lear's condition also. Because Gloucester says that he stumbled when he saw, we are more likely to assume that Lear's recognition that he is old and foolish (even though this was originally Regan and Goneril's contention) represents a positive apprehension of truth.

The formulations of the subplot, however, are somewhat over-simplified even on their own terms. Gloucester's sententious observations after his eyes are put out are not adequate to the horror of that event, and the ordered world of the duel, where ritual reflects reality and power is joined to virtue, is an archaic one. The main action shows up such simplifications even more pointedly; for better and for worse, Lear's experience cannot be accounted for in the way that Gloucester's is. On the one hand, the king's agonies are incommensurate with any evil that he may have committed, irreducible, by himself and others, to notions of justice. He is more sinned against than sinning; he and Cordelia are 'not the first / Who, with best meaning, have incurr'd the worst' (5.3.3–4). Where Edgar can see some kind of justice in his father's blinding, Cordelia refuses to consider the nature of Lear's crimes or mistakes at all, let alone any idea of retribution: 'No cause, no cause!' But the corollary to this transcendence of commonplace or legalistic judgment is that the patterns by which Gloucester's destiny is ordered and given meaning do not apply to Lear. Neither his sufferings nor the nature of his children are explicable, as Gloucester's are, by dramatic stereotype and moral aphorism, for in the two plots, formal devices and substantive material are fused. Lear's experience is truly tragic and heroic not merely because he suffers – Gloucester suffers too – but because the literary forms that avoid tragedy are so clearly inadequate to express what he goes through.

Notes

1   See for example the discussion of the dangers of excessive or contradictory passions in Peter de la Primaudaye *The French Academy* tr. T.B. (London 1594) 33.

2   '*King Lear*: The Quality of Nothing,' in *Shakespearean Meanings* (Princeton 1968) 238.

3   See Maynard Mack's suggestion that the relation of subplot to plot is not dramatic so much as 'homiletic,' '*King Lear' in Our Time* (Berkeley 1965) 7. See also Alvin B. Kernan, 'Formalism and Realism in Elizabethan Drama: The Miracles in *King Lear*,' *Renaissance Drama* IX (1966) 59–66, for an interpretation of the Dover cliff scene as a morality play.

4   *De Laudibus Angliae: A Treatise in Commendation of the Laws of England* tr. Francis Gregor (Cincinnati 1874) 156 and 150ff.

5   A rare exception is the Bastard in *King John*, who had all the potential for villainy, being a 'man of the time' and a corrosive scoffer at custom, but who is placed in a world where these attributes become virtues. For an interesting analysis of this character and his contrast to Edmund, see John F. Danby *Shakespeare's Doctrine of Nature: A Study of 'King Lear'* (London 1959) 57ff. It is worth noting that treatment of aristocratic bastards, at least, was radically ameliorated during the sixteenth century in England.

6   Bracton *De Legibus et Consuetudinibus Angliae* ed. G.E. Woodbine, tr. S.E. Thorne (Cambridge, Mass. 1968) 414–15.

7   Mack, in *'King Lear' in Our Time* 61, comments on this and likens Edgar to the fallen hero of the morality plays.

8   On this connection, and on the scene in general, see Harry Levin, 'The Heights and the Depths: A Scene from *King Lear*,' in *More Talking of Shakespeare* ed. John Garrett (London 1959) 87–103, and Kernan, 'Formalism and Realism.'

9   'The Heights and the Depths,' 100.

10 The background of the 'felix culpa' tradition is described by Arthur O. Lovejoy, 'Milton and the Paradox of the Fortunate Fall,' *Essays in the History of Ideas* (Baltimore 1948) 277–95.

11 '[The trial by combat] was instituted upon this reason, that in respect the Tenant had lost his Evidence, or that the same were burnt or imbezeled, or that his witnesses were dead, the Law permitted him to try it by combat between his Champion and the Champion of the Demandant, hoping that God would give the victory to him that right had...' (Coke's commentary on Fortescue, quoted in John Beames *A Translation of Glanville* [Washington 1900] 35n). In the play, Edgar must have recourse to the duel because the very evidence of his identity, his name, has been usurped by Edmund (5.3.119–22).

12 See for instance Beames *A Translation of Glanville* 36: if the duel is accepted, the defendant 'must deny the right of the Demandant, word for word as the Demandant has set it forth.'

13 See Levin, 'The Heights and the Depths,' 103.

CHAPTER 11

Theory in Practice
The Stories of "Passion":
An Empirical Study

Susan Lohafer

Susan Lohafer, who teaches at the University of Iowa, explores in this essay the narrative strategies of Alice Munro's story "Passion" by drawing on the reading skills of her students. She asked her students to reorder the sentences of the final paragraph of the story and explores the consequences for the narrative. She concludes that Munro, while she is not a metafictionalist, does experiment with and subvert the traditional forms of story-telling.

If you think "Passion" is about Grace, you are right. Most of the story takes place during the summer when this vibrant girl, who is poor and adventurous, meets the Travers family, who are … complicated. Now, more than forty years later, Grace has driven back to the scene of the romance, or the crime, or both. Though traditional in structure – an initiation-story within a frame-tale – the narrative isn't simple. That younger self, on the cusp of adult life, is recalled by the sixty-something woman we meet on the first and final pages. She is driving, alone, through a landscape both familiar and strange, looking for a house that once belonged to the people who changed her life.

For the literary critic trying to achieve the fullest understanding of Grace's character; for the story-grammarian trying to parse the narrative sentence of her life; for the short fiction theorist seeing Munro as a challenge; and, last but not least, for the undergraduate student wondering, "Who is this woman, and what's going on?" – for all these readers, there is a hole in the text. Grace is absent between her twenties and her sixties, living, it seems, in Australia. Those decades are missing. And yet the narrative presumes them, else the frame wouldn't matter. And obviously, it does. It positions us to look back over a void to encounter a mystery. We're to wonder about that girl whose life turned so many corners within the space of a few months. What was she like then? Was she naïve or self-serving, willful or rudderless … the driver or the passenger? Because we meet

Original publication details: Susan Lohafer, "The Stories of 'Passion': An Empirical Study." *Narrative* 20.2 (May 2012), pp. 226–238. Ohio State University Press, 2012. Reproduced with permission from Ohio State University Press.

Literary Theory: An Anthology, Third Edition. Edited by Julie Rivkin and Michael Ryan.
© 2017 John Wiley & Sons, Ltd. Published 2017 by John Wiley & Sons, Ltd.

Grace in a short story, we cannot ask these questions without noting the typology of the narrative she inhabits. In this genre, whose brevity and integrity descend from the anecdote, the exemplum, and the folk-tale, it is more than a quip to say "character is sequence, and sequence is character." To learn who Grace is, we need, in a very technical sense, to graph the route she's traversed with the help of the Traverses. Yet the path disappears.

When I am faced by a nagging problem in a short story, I look for insight – into that text and into the nature of the genre itself – by drawing upon the unconscious wisdom of ordinary readers. By the age of five, humans have developed a form of "story-competence," an ability to recognize what constitutes, in their culture, a tellable, stand-alone segment from an endless string of narrative. It is a commonplace to say that stories are a primal mode of knowing, the very currency of culture. Hence the popularity, now somewhat faded, of studies in orality and communal story-telling. Newer work by linguists, neurologists, and cognitive scientists suggests that the future of genre theory lies in the study of brain-function. Nevertheless, believing that readers' ingrained sense of storyness is an invaluable resource for humanists as well, I have looked for *literary* ways of tapping into this hidden vein of knowledge, to use its primacy to advantage in a study of this art form.

For many years, I did so by asking readers to identify preclosure points within a text. I looked at the series of putative – and often paradigmatic – stories embedded within the actual text on its way to real closure. Those were experiments in narrative interruption. What I am going to be discussing now is an experiment in narrative continuity, aimed at helping me to understand Grace, Alice Munro, and the contour of "Passion."

My participants were the students in two undergraduate literature classes at The University of Iowa, plus one visiting scholar from China, for a total of 46 readers. Most of these readers had never heard of Munro, and I was reasonably sure that none of them had read "Passion." Each was given the first paragraph of the story. Half of the readers saw the paragraph as Munro wrote it, in the third person; half saw a first-person version of the same text. All were asked to choose the one word in the given text – I'll call it a keyword – that seemed most loaded with implication for what might follow in the rest of the narrative. All were then asked to compose a sentence – I'll call it a continuer – that could logically and meaningfully follow the paragraph they had just read. I asked a number of other questions, too, that I'll talk about later.

Here is the first paragraph of the story, in the original third person:

> Not too long ago, Grace went looking for the Traverses' summer house in the Ottawa Valley. She had not been in that part of the country for many years, and of course there had been changes. Highway 7 now avoided towns that it used to go right through, and it went straight in places where, as she remembered, there used to be curves. And this part of the Canadian Shield has many small lakes, which the usual sort of map has no room to identify. Even when she had located Little Sabot Lake, or thought she had, there seemed to be too many roads leading into it from the county road, and then, when she had chosen one of those roads, too many paved roads crossing it, all with names that she did not recall. In fact there had not been any street names when she had been here over forty years ago. And there was no pavement. There was just the one dirt road running towards the lake, then the one dirt road running rather haphazardly along the lake's edge. (159–60)

The most favored keyword was "haphazardly," in the last line. Perhaps we hear the warning buzz of "hazard" beneath the hollow ache of "hapless." Road-related terms ("highway," "curves," "map," "roads," "paved," "street") were the second-most common choice, not surprisingly. The journey of life, forks in the road – the trope is ubiquitous. The third favorite keyword was "changes." Taken together, "haphazardly" and "changes" – destabilizing terms – were chosen by 52% of the respondents. Every life – and every Munro story – is about chance on the one hand and choice on the other. My readers didn't know that they knew this already.

In the frequent manner of short fiction theorists, I will be focusing on the beginning and the ending of the story in order to bring the center into focus, all the more urgently because, in "Passion," the middle is both irrelevant (those missing forty years) and definitive (those crucial summer months). Later, I will turn to the final sentences in the story, but let me start with Munro's first paragraph and those 46 continuers invented by the respondents. By isolating various features of these add-ons, I hope to learn something about the way my readers interpreted the opening paragraph, but also something about their instincts for narrative continuity, for extending fictional agency through imaginary space-time.

The respondents were disproportionately women (36:10), making the influence of gender hard to tell. Nevertheless, I marked each continuer MALE or FEMALE. Then I asked whether the state or activity depicted, expressed, or referred to in the sentence was mainly INTERNAL (as in the case of a wish, perception, or memory) or mainly EXTERNAL (as in the case of a reported action or condition of the outer world). As this was a pilot study, I relied on my own judgment, although surely it would be useful, on a grander scale, to employ a bevy of scorers, to correct for the errors or biases of one person.

For now, admitting my subjectivity, I asked whether the stance of the sentence – as much a residue of attitude and tone as of outright declaration – was mainly POSITIVE, NEUTRAL, or NEGATIVE. Was the state or activity set mainly in the PRESENT (i.e., continuing in the same time period as the opening paragraph of the story), or mainly in the PAST (i.e., reflecting or recapturing a time *before* the opening scene)? Did the sentence put a period to a state or activity, or did it point forward, to unknown possibility; that is, was it CLOSED or was it OPEN? Finally, did it recycle any of the keywords identified in the story's first paragraph, thus reinforcing – or *continuing* – their impact?

By way of demonstration, here is a sentence that happened to be written by a female reading the third-person (original) version of the paragraph. I judged this continuer to be mostly EXTERNAL, PRESENT, POSITIVE, and CLOSED, with a recycling of the "road" keyword:

> She followed the road around Little Sabot Lake, slowly and carefully, and finally the shore seemed familiar.

Although the sentence ends with an inner conclusion (finding the scene "familiar"), the main action is the outward drive around the lake, leading to a match between what is actually seen and what is stored in the driver's memory. The action continues in the same time-frame as the opening paragraph, with Grace on the road. The search for the Travers home encounters an obstacle (changes in the landscape that disorient the seeker), the conflict is resolved (reorientation occurs), and the goal is – or seems about to be – achieved. What happens here is hardly a very satisfying story, but it is, on its own terms, complete. As a successful mini-quest, it calls for only a very small "bravo," but that's enough to make the sentence feel CLOSED, with a POSITIVE valence.

Here, for comparison, is a continuer I judged to be INTERNAL, PAST, NEGATIVE, and OPEN (it, too, keyed on the word "road"). This sentence was also written by a woman, though she was reading the altered text with the first-person narrator.

> I remember driving down that dirt road with Bob like it was yesterday, not knowing that would be the last time I saw him alive.

Cast entirely into the domain of memory, the action is internalized. While the act of remembrance is occurring in the "now" of the story, the informational burden of the sentence points backward, referring to an earlier drive and a last glimpse of "Bob." The references to a dead fellow-traveler were undoubtedly suggested by later information in the questionnaire, where I mention Grace's ride with her fiancé's half-brother, who subsequently dies in a car crash. While I had influenced this reader's focus on death, *she* was responsible for the urgency of the memory ("like it was yesterday"), the retroactive melancholy of *any* last-time event, and the shadow of regret, all of which give the sentence a NEGATIVE valence. Far from resolving any issues, this continuer introduces information not present in the story's first paragraph. As a continuation of what begins *there*, this sentence raises more questions than it answers: *Who is Bob, how did he die, and what does his death mean to the narrator?* This is, therefore, an OPEN continuer.

Granting that other investigators might code the continuers differently, I trusted at least in my consistency. The first step, then, was to spread out the broad conclusions supported by the data. Most of the continuers – 70% of them – remain in the time-frame of the initial paragraph (PRESENT), although the preference is slightly more pronounced – 83% – among the respondents who were reading the first-person version of the opening paragraph. Overall, there is a slight preference for continuers that are INTERNAL (54%) and for those that are OPEN (56%). What matters here isn't the preference but its slightness. All four options – INTERNAL, EXTERNAL, OPEN, CLOSED – were viable and robust. A more decided preference emerged from the data on valence. As might be expected from the tone of the opening paragraph, there is a strong preference for the downbeat: 61% of the continuers are NEGATIVE, 24% NEUTRAL, and 13% POSITIVE, with one fragment too brief to assign (2%). Overall, then, the continuers, whose authors were mostly FEMALE, tend to be PRESENT, INTERNAL, OPEN, and NEGATIVE. By large or small margins, these are the norms of this sample.

To complete the overview, here are some other questions I posed to the readers. Based on the opening paragraph they had been given, did they think they were reading a NOVEL or a MEMOIR – i.e., fiction or nonfiction? More than half said fiction, but a surprising 41% of the readers thought the text was *non*fiction. It has the chatty frankness of a travel diary, a memoir-in-disguise. On this point, my naïve readers were experts-in-disguise; scholars, too, note the authenticity of Munro's story-worlds. Intuition failed, however, when dating the story. I was surprised – as Munro might be – to find that more than half of the readers (61%) thought the text was published in the SIXTIES, though possibly they only favored the mid-point on the time-line. Twenty percent (20%) relegated it to the TWENTIES, but only 15% chose the true period – CONTEMPORARY. (Two persons, 4%, failed to answer the question.) Apparently, to the young readers in today's college classroom, Munro sounds a bit dated, though not too old-fashioned.

While only a fifth of the readers thought the text came from the TWENTIES, that was the era picked by 30% of those writing CLOSED continuers. Shifting my focus to look at all of the CLOSED continuers, I saw that 55% of them were EXTERNAL (as opposed to the norm of 46%) and 20% were POSITIVE (as opposed to the norm of 13%). The margins are small, but still there's an affinity among CLOSED, EXTERNAL, and POSITIVE. In a curiously backhanded yet unsolicited way, these data confirm the assumption that "old" fiction tends to be more resolved and more resolute. There is no clustering of features around the CONTEMPORARY designation, though one datum stands out. Chosen by only 15% of the readers overall, this period was cited by an amazing 45% of the small group who wrote NEUTRAL continuers. No conclusions can be drawn, but it is tempting to see another stereotype confirmed, linking present-day fiction with low-affect indeterminacy.

Then again, some numbers just aren't meaningful, even if they sparkle. For example, 60% of the women wrote INTERNAL continuers, whereas, in a complete flip, 60% of the men wrote *external* continuers. Eye-catching, indeed, but useless, given the hugely disproportionate number of women in the sample, and the clichéd nature of any speculations about women's focus on interior experience vs. men's preference for observable action. I was hardly in a position to draw "Venus vs. Mars" conclusions, even if I had wanted to. Perhaps another researcher, with a larger and better sample, might try.

On the other hand, two reliably-defined types of readers also broke with the general preference for INTERNAL continuers, favored by 56% of the group. *Outward* action was preferred by 64% of those writing NEUTRAL continuers, and by 56% of those who wrote PRESENT continuers. These alignments made sense to me. Neutrality went naturally with a focus on uneventful action in the outer world (driving around back roads), rather than on perturbations in the inner world (retracing psychic maps). Nor was I surprised that exterior action dominated the PRESENT continuers. These were sentences that merely took the first paragraph another step on its way, rather than back-tracking for perspective. Munro's first paragraph is, on the surface, a record of EXTERNAL actions: "Grace went looking," but the roads had "changed"; the lakes were still around, but she couldn't find the right one. She drove here and there.

It takes an acute eye, of the kind we hope to train in our classrooms, to read between the lines, where the action is *internal* and the valence more NEGATIVE. No doubt these were the readers who sensed the anxiety caused by unpredictable change, by "too many" of this and "too many" of that; who noted the failure of "the usual sort of map," the absence of street signs (directional guides), and the rawness and incipience of dirt roads vs. the solidity of paved highways. Grace is entering a maze within herself. Most of the readers in my sample were English majors, and I would have expected most of them to bring these latencies to the surface, to write, as indeed they did, continuers that were INTERNAL and NEGATIVE.

As noted above, I did check the continuers for keywords. No one used the word "haphazardly" (which had just occurred in the last sentence of the opening paragraph), but many referred to roads and related imagery. Mentions of passages-through (including not only roads but streets, highways, routes, paths, driveways, etc.) appear 34 times, in sentences composed by 25 people, or 54% of the respondents. References to blocked or diverted passageways (including words like "labyrinth," "maze," "twisted," "lost," "turnoff," "disorientation") occur 16 times. If you include references to the lake or to water – barriers to a bee-line – the number doubles to 32 references, made overall by 22 persons, or 48% of the group. When these readers stepped into the role of story-writers, as they did when composing the continuers, they were dominated by the road imagery, but, in the aggregate, they found a tension between passage and blockage, an elemental form of conflict, and, to a suggestive degree, a cognate of the fork-in-the-road story schema.

By analyzing the characteristics of the continuers in relation to what prompted them, I could see how, for a small group of college-educated readers, narrative was propelled.

I could see storyness instantiated. Once again, let me remind you that these readers had not read the whole story. They did not know that Grace does, indeed, face many choices between one path and another, most crucially whether to align herself with Neil or with Maury, with the exciting but unstable son who resembled his mother and offered new if illicit experience, or with the earnestly bourgeois son who resembled his father and wanted to marry her. Munro's own continuer ("Now there was a village") is PRESENT, EXTERNAL, OPEN, and NEUTRAL, as she makes a leisurely approach to the narrative flash-back. Unlike the readers in my experiment, she is not blind to the curves ahead, but neither, it would seem, is she indifferent to the collective recognition of a narrative schema of passages and blockages. She triggers and exploits it. Grace's day with Neil is a classic road story, a series of chosen pathways, a penetration into new territory, an acquisition of knowledge (en route, Grace learns, in many ways, how to "drive"), and a series of destinations. But, of course, the story is more than its schema, as a Picasso portrait is more than its iconography. Could my experiment shed light on the "more" of "Passion"?

So far, I have been concentrating on the entrance to the story. Now let me focus on the exit. After a space-break, the story closes with four paragraphs, a sort of epilogue, although the action takes place only a short while later. Grace has effectively broken her engagement with Maury by rejecting his offer, by letter, to believe she was forced to accompany Neil on their trip through the countryside. No, she replies, "*I did want to go*" (196; emphasis original). But now she will receive another offer, one that's harder to refuse, from Mr. Travers. He hands her an envelope with a check, implicitly bribing her to break off not only her relationship with Maury, but her friendship with Mrs. Travers – in short, any contact with the Travers clan altogether. Among them, she is *persona non grata*.

She *had* been a welcome guest. On that fateful Thanksgiving Day at the Travers' house, after Grace had cut her foot and was waiting for the charismatic Neil to drive her to the hospital, Mrs. Travers had privately urged Grace to steer him away from alcohol, that refuge from his demons. Later, by choosing to leave the hospital with Neil rather than with Maury (who had arrived to reclaim her), by following him into new sensual and psychic territory where she instinctively feels connected, Grace betrays not only her fiancé but Neil's wife, not to mention the commission from Mrs. Travers. By understanding the cool despair that drives Neil to suicide, Grace challenges the world-according-to-Mr.-Travers, who breezily attributes Neil's death to mere alcoholism. He is the sort of man who believes nervous disorders can be medicated away, embarrass-ments bribed to disappear, and tragedies cured by a "vacation ... somewhere warm" (196). The story closes with 7 sentences about the bribe he offers Grace, and how she responds to it.

The scene occurs at the inn where Grace has been working that summer as a waitress. The time is shortly after she has returned from her eye-opening, flesh-tingling, mind-blowing journey with Neil, and soon after she has heard the news-item about Neil's suicide. Mr. Travers has arrived to clean up the part of the mess that Grace represents, and he is "polite and businesslike, firm, cool, not unkind" (196). On the questionnaire, I listed the same 7 sentences, *but in a different order*, which I will call the "Test Order." I did not scramble the sentences randomly, but instead created a sequence that would offer a meaningful contrast to the original text. In a prefatory note, I explained to the readers that Maury's father, Mr. Travers, had come to see Grace after Neil's death. Here are the sentences in the order found on the questionnaire:

T-1	As he shook her hand good-bye he put an envelope into it.
T-2	"We both hope you'll make good use of this," he said.
T-3	Then he said that he had to be going, many things to do.
T-4	The cheque was for one thousand dollars.
T-5	In those days, it was enough money to insure her a start in life.
T-6	Immediately, she thought of sending it back or tearing it up, and sometimes even now she thinks that would have been a grand thing to do.
T-7	But in the end, of course, she was not able to do it.

Figure 1 Test Order

Each respondent was asked to create his or her own order by redistributing the sentences on the questionnaire to create a personally satisfying or reasonable sequence to end the story. I could easily have invented alternate sentence-orders myself, but that would have been cheating, and it would have deprived me of the very information I was seeking. I needed my students to act as story-tellers, to make decisions about an excerpt from a putative text (this time from its end rather than its beginning), and then to act upon the given passage in a way that exercised *their* built-in sense of storyness. My goal, of course, was to compare *their* suggestions with Munro's decisions, *their* instincts with Munro's artistry. I was going to articulate, in my own language and according to my own lights, what my informants unwittingly knew.

I was struck at once by how many readers began *their* sequence with T-2 ("'We both hope you'll make good use of this,' he said"), even though there was now no antecedent for "this." The following categories of readers favored this choice: those reading the first-person version of the opening paragraph; those reading the third-person version; those who thought they were reading nonfiction; and those who thought they were reading fiction. The only way I can explain the ubiquity of this preference is to concede the overwhelming power of convention: ever since Hemingway, modern narrative, both fictional and nonfictional, has favored abrupt beginnings, *in medias res*. As we shall see, Munro's way of starting the sequence was different. How so? To what end?

Before I could think about those questions, I had to look at the other end of the line-up, the far more significant *closural* slot. What preferences did the readers show when choosing *their* final sentence? Forty-six percent (46%) of them chose the same concluding sentence as in the "Test Order" – i.e., T-7.[1] Twenty-six percent (26%) used T-6 in the final slot, and 17% put T-5 there. No other sentences were chosen often enough to matter, so I concentrated on just those three. As putative endings to the story, they represent closure – a feature of stories I have been studying for years. I was able to draw upon that earlier work, and in particular, a system I developed for identifying closural signals or markers in story-sentences.[2] My first step, therefore, was to put those three sentences under the microscope.

Closural markers can be divided into global and local categories, the former tied to patterns in the story as a whole, the latter contained within the sentence itself. Here are my findings:

T-5: In those days, it was enough money to insure her a start in life.
GLOBAL: SYNTACTIC: *obstacle overcome* | socioeconomic barrier removed
GLOBAL: SYNTACTIC: *equilibrium achieved* | money » opportunity
LOCAL: LEXICAL: closural words: *absolute/extreme state* | "enough"; "insure"
LOCAL: LEXICAL: closural words: *temporal shift* | [now]>"in those days"
LOCAL: LEXICAL: keywords: *natural prominence* | "money"; "life"

SUMMARY: T-5 is a neutral, declarative statement equating a quantity of money with a quantity of power/choice. The sentence has no moral or character-destiny component, but simply posits an economic reality at a particular time.

The eight readers who put this sentence in the closural slot were privileging factual/historical circumstances, highlighting a practical rather than moral or psychological frame of reference. Men favored this choice, and conventional wisdom might say "No surprise here," but, as noted before, there were too few men in the sample to make gender an issue. More reliably, this fact-of-life sentence was *not* considered closure-worthy by *any* of those who wrote POSITIVE continuers to the opening paragraph, or *any* of those who placed their continuers in a PAST time before the opening action. Those would-be story-tellers looked elsewhere for closure, drawn to sentences that offered a more definitive outcome for Grace's quest, with its roots in the past.

T-6: Immediately, she thought of sending it back or tearing it up, and sometimes even now she thinks that would have been a grand thing to do.
GLOBAL: SYNTACTIC: *return to prior state* | rejecting the money undoes complicity
GLOBAL: SYNTACTIC: *antithesis or paradox* | actual deed vs. imagined deed
LOCAL: SYNTACTIC: repetition: *alliteration* | "thought" // "thinks"
LOCAL: SYNTACTIC: repetition: *identity-relationship* | "thought" // "thinks"
LOCAL: LEXICAL: closural words: *absolute/extreme state* | "tearing it up"
LOCAL: LEXICAL: closural words: *logical reversal* | "tearing up" reverses "giving to"
LOCAL: LEXICAL: closural words: *temporal shift* | "immediately" > "even now"
LOCAL: LEXICAL: keywords: *story-specific meaning* | "grand"

SUMMARY: T-6 has a strong sense of reversal, undoing Grace's complicity with Mr. Travers and canceling her status as a bribe-taker. Of course, the "action" is entirely within her mind: she can hypothesize a deed she can't actually carry out.

The twelve readers who put this sentence in the closural slot were privileging Grace's capacity to recognize the moral high road. No group of readers favored this choice inordinately, although, in terms of percentages, it was more attractive to men, to those who thought they were reading NONFICTION, to those who wrote NEGATIVE continuers, and to those who wrote OPEN continuers. Without further experiments targeting this issue, I cannot say why these readers chose to put Grace in the kindest light possible at the very end.

T-7: But in the end, of course, she was not able to do it.
GLOBAL: SYNTACTIC: *obstacle overcome* | out-of-character impulse overcome
GLOBAL: SYNTACTIC: *return to earlier state/event* | reversion to taking what she can get
LOCAL: SYNTACTIC: repetition | all words are monosyllabic except "able"
LOCAL: LEXICAL: closural words: *absolute/extreme state* | "of course"
LOCAL: LEXICAL: closural words: *logical reversal* | "but"
LOCAL: LEXICAL: keywords: *story-specific meaning* | "able"; "do"
LOCAL: LEXICAL: closural words: *naming final condition* | "end"

SUMMARY: T-7 emphasizes Grace's fundamental character trait of taking the most she can get. She has recognized the morally superior option, but is not "able" (allowed by her nature) to choose it. Perhaps not coincidentally, the word "able" evokes Mrs. Travers' housecleaner – "a woman Mrs. Travers called 'my friend the able Mrs. Abel'" (168). Grace, a *quondam* waitress and chair-caner, rejects the serviceability of these "able" occupations in favor of a more self-fulfilling life.

The twenty-one readers who put this sentence in the closural slot were privileging character-determinism over moral imagination as the dominant (final) influence on Grace's behavior. Every group except men favored this sentence as the finale. The groups that completely avoided T-5, perhaps for its neutrality, rousingly supported T-7. It was chosen by 83% of those who wrote POSITIVE continuers, and 62% of those whose continuers reached into the PAST. These figures simply highlight the general preference for T-7.

Is it any wonder that this sentence was the favored choice for the exit-line of the story? There is probably no stronger closural phrase in the English language than "in the end." Sleepy children, hearing a story read to them, know "The End" means lights out. Once again, there was general agreement among the four groups of readers I singled out before: those reading the first-person version of the opening paragraph, those reading the third-person version, those who thought they were reading nonfiction, and those who thought they were reading fiction. *All* favored T-7 in the 7th slot. Any way you mince the data, it would seem that more people ended the story with this sentence than with any other.

Here is the favored sequence constructed by the readers *as a group*. It is a composite; only four readers made these exact choices. Many readers chose radically different sequences, but not in sufficient numbers to change the outcome.

You will notice that this line-up differs only slightly from the one offered on the ques-

N-1	"We both hope you'll make good use of this," he said. 63%
N-2	Then he said that he had to be going, many things to do. 33%
N-3	As he shook her hand good-bye he put an envelope into it. 46%
N-4	The cheque was for one thousand dollars. 28%
N-5	In those days, it was enough money to insure her a start in life. 33%
N-6	Immediately, she thought of sending it back or tearing it up, and sometimes even now she thinks that would have been a grand thing to do. 33%
N-7	But in the end, of course, she was not able to do it. 46%

Figure 2 Normative Order

tionnaire (the "Test Order"). Only the first three sentences follow a different order. As noted before, readers insisted on opening with the snippet of dialogue. They also tended to believe that Mr. Travers would announce his departure and *then* take Grace's hand. In any case, both the "Test Order" and the "Normative Order" make clear that money is exchanged rather furtively. A gratuity finessed by a handshake. It's a reminder of Grace's lower social status – she is, in fact, a waitress used to receiving tips – and it raises the question of what service she has performed, or will be expected to perform.

The remaining sentences follow the same order in both the "Test Order" and the "Normative Order." In the pivotal #4 slot, the purchasing power of the money is revealed, making it clear that Mr. Travers isn't just brushing Grace off with a pittance. He's offering her an escape from poverty, an exit from Ottawa. Her inability to pass up this opportunity fills the closural slot. "In the end," we meet the Grace of T-7, in whom character-determinism quells moral imagination. This is the girl who has consistently chosen the fork in the road that satisfies her urge to widen her experience. She has neither the principles nor the willpower to refuse a gratuity that is, in effect, a bribe, but also a windfall. A donation to the Grace-project. There is a logic to this conclusion. It follows a normative script in synch with familiar plot-lines: small-town-girl-makes-good;

innocence-becomes-experience. Readers were exercising their sense of storyness, and they overwhelming chose to end the tale with Grace's concession to greed, or, at least, self-advancement.

Munro, however, did not. It's time, now, to look at the sequence *she* chose.

S-1	Then he said that he had to be going, many things to do.
S-2	As he shook her hand good-bye he put an envelope into it.
S-3	"We both hope you'll make good use of this," he said.
S-4	The cheque was for one thousand dollars.
S-5	Immediately, she thought of sending it back or tearing it up, and sometimes even now she thinks that would have been a grand thing to do.
S-6	But in the end, of course, she was not able to do it.
S-7	In those days, it was enough money to insure her a start in life.

Figure 3   Story Order

The sentence beginning "In the end" is not *at* the end. Its earlier placement is counterintuitive for a plurality of readers, as we've seen, but for Munro, it was strategically appropriate. It left the closural slot empty for a note on the purchasing power of the money. *Her* story ends with the transactional value of the check – it can buy a new life. Gift or bribe doesn't matter. Munro isn't harkening back to Grace's appetite for life or even her taste for the dramatic, but to the part of her that studied more subjects in high school than she had any use for, because she "just wanted to learn everything you could learn for free" (166). This is a kind of opportunism, yes, but also a kind of dogged economy. She is "not able" to give the money back not because her moral fiber is constitutionally weak (although it may be), and not because her flair for the dramatic is still untrained, but because she is intellectually and emotionally a forager by nature. Hers is the built-in value-meter of the underprivileged, an habitual practicality rather than a self-serving plan.

Earlier I noted how my readers gravitated toward ingrained models of storyness. In their reconstructions, they tended to open with dialogue and end with "the end." Their choices were a graphic illustration of perceptions of storyness in action. Nor did their instincts entirely mislead them. On the macro-level, Munro does, indeed, offer a classic fork-in-the-road story, a familiar narrative typology. But look closely at her choices on the micro-level – say, between two ways of ordering the final sentences – and the text tells a different story. When we compare the sequence chosen by the composite "reader" with the one chosen by Munro, we see at once that the actual text departs most radically from the normative one at the two points where the readers were most confident in their guesses. It would seem as though Munro was toying with the scripts she so handily invoked.[3]

I cannot, of course, make any such claim. On the contrary, experience with my own and others' story-telling argues against any such calculated set-up. Great writers do not instantiate scripts – but they do echo, bend, violate, and play with them, both consciously and unconsciously. Writers are, after all, readers themselves, conditioned by the same cognitive and cultural ways of organizing strings of information into narrative sequences.[4] Recurrently, the short story has been seen as a formula-prone genre. That is not surprising, given its roots in Proppian folklore and its heyday in "slick" magazines, but I would argue that, in the case of a Munro, the background presence of familiar typologies is not so much a constraint as a resource. All that my reading experiments can do is tease these background layers into the open, quantify them for salience, and selectively but systematically examine them. However flawed and subjective my analyses may be, however ungainly the material they isolate, the goal is to catch sight, indirectly, of the way models of storyness are deployed by the author and perceived by the reader.

I hoped the present experiment would help me understand why Munro, an acknowledged mistress of the short story, is problematic for narrative theorists who find her work "novelistic," and how "Passion," a story with a hole in the middle, finds integrity as a narrative. The answers to both questions are, not surprisingly, codependent. The evidence provided by my untrained but savvy readers helped me see the Munro-ishness of "Passion," its daring way of invoking, omitting, and re-formulating the sequence of events and decisions that would fill a *bildungsroman*, in order to produce the highly-selective order of sentences that say "Passion."

My study of the continuers to the opening paragraph made me realize just how insistently Munro uses the imagery of passages and barriers to inaugurate the fork-in-the-road typology. Looking at the very end of the story, comparing the readers' instincts with the author's artistry, I saw the impact of micro-managed decisions about order.

Munro does not write metafiction, but she makes canny use of traditional story-types by invoking and subverting them. That is what my naïve readers unintentionally made clear to me. "Passion" is far from being a typical short story, but neither is it "novelistic." It achieves its effects by triggering and twisting models of storyness in order to reveal character.

What sort of person is Grace, and what kind of route has she followed? In short stories, these are questions about the layout of sentences, about beginnings and endings, and about the roadmaps we follow between them. In the end, I came to see Grace as neither the driver nor the passenger but as the vehicle itself, nosing forward through the maze of life, gauging distance by the gallon, and rounding each corner as it comes.

Notes

1   It could be argued that respondents were unduly influenced by the order of the sentences in the questionnaire. On the other hand, the instructions, which asked each respondent to create a personal order, could be viewed as a deterrent to copying the given order.

2   For a more detailed exposition of this coding system, please see Lohafer, *Reading for Storyness* 59–60. For general inspiration and for suggestions about global closure in short stories, I am indebted to John Gerlach, *Toward the End: Closure and Structure in the American Short Story*.

3   I am indebted to Michael Trussler for suggesting (without necessarily agreeing with) the possibility that this sabotage is not only deliberate on Munro's part but symptomatic of her unique approach to narrative.

4   See, for example, Benson.

Works Cited

Benson, Margaret S. "The Structure of Four- and Five-year-olds' Narratives in Pretend Play and Storytelling," *First Language* 13 (1993): 202–23.

Gerlach, John. *Toward the End: Closure and Structure in the American Short Story*. Tuscaloosa: Univ. of Alabama Press, 1985.

Lohafer, Susan. *Reading for Storyness: Preclosure Theory, Empirical Poetics, and Culture in the Short Story*. Baltimore: Johns Hopkins Univ. Press, 2003.

Munro, Alice. "Passion." In *Runaway*, 159–96. New York: Knopf, 2004.

PART THREE

Phenomenology, Reception, Ethics

CHAPTER 1

Introduction
Situations of Knowledge / Relations with Others

Julie Rivkin and Michael Ryan

In the eighteenth century, German philosopher Immanuel Kant, responding to earlier philosophers who contended that our ideas arose from sense impressions on our brains, argued that the mind's innate powers shape sensory experience. Knowledge does not consist of the registration on our brains of sensory information alone. That information has to be ordered temporally and spatially and submitted to principles of reason. And the mind's innate intuitive abilities are responsible for that ordering.

Once he had established the mind's powers in regard to experience, Kant set about applying the idea to art and ethics. He found that our judgments regarding art were largely sensory, while our judgments regarding ethics were largely rational. The most one could say about art was that it seemed to have a purpose or goal, but the purpose or goal was not real. Art pretends to have a reason behind it, but it is "purposefulness without a purpose."

Ethics, which considers and regulates our behavior with others, has to be more rational and purposeful. In this realm of human interaction, Kant found that it was possible to state clearly what the mind's activity should be in shaping our ethical decisions and actions. We should always behave as if our behavior manifested a rule that we could easily imagine being binding on everyone. Each action should embody a universal and general principle. A principle, or a general rule applicable to all individual instances, should inform our ethical decisions regarding how we act for ourselves and in regard to others.

Kant's focus on the mind's innate capacities was largely forgotten for a century and a half until another German philosopher, Edmund Husserl, once again evoked the mind's powers while attempting to rebut the philosophy that became dominant in the nineteenth century – Positivism. Positivism held that empirical facts alone constituted knowledge, and such knowledge should be measured according to how useful it was – not according to how well it embodied universal principles. One did not need to worry about the mind or how it worked. The mind was a simple recording device that measured the utility of facts.

But if the mind was driven by sensory data, how was philosophy to arrive at principles for deciding what was true or for deciding between good action and bad? If all we had to go by were sensory facts and useful data, there could be no rational principles to guide knowledge and behavior.

Literary Theory: An Anthology, Third Edition. Edited by Julie Rivkin and Michael Ryan.
© 2017 John Wiley & Sons, Ltd. Published 2017 by John Wiley & Sons, Ltd.

Husserl sought to solve this problem by noting that all knowledge of things in the world is in fact knowledge of knowledge. What we know or see in our mind is not the thing itself, the object before our eyes, but rather the image of the object on consciousness. Those mental objects are called "phenomena," and the philosophy Husserl developed to talk about them was "phenomenology."

Like Kant, Husserl believed the mind transformed sensory data into universally binding principles that were formal or abstract. He turned to the example of geometry. In geometry, one can imagine a perfect triangle. It exists as a mental construct, yet, no actual triangle in the world achieves that degree of formal perfection. In a similar way, the mind arrives at truth by extracting from data a purely formal mental construct, the idea of the thing. The idea of a thing, not the thing itself, is what is true.

The innate intuitive operations of the mind are therefore necessary when thinking about the world. They allow us to grasp transcendental principles of truth that are not limited to the sensory data our mind takes in.

The pendulum swung in the other direction as the twentieth century progressed. Philosophers such as John Dewey, Martin Heidegger, Ludwig Wittgenstein, and Jean-Paul Sartre argued that we know as we live in the world, and even if a very abstract formal kind of knowledge that transcends sense data is possible, all knowledge takes place in the world and in our lives as real beings existing in space and time.

Theoretical developments in the late twentieth and early twenty-first century deepened these insights. A number of thinkers, from Emmanuel Levinas to Jacques Derrida and Martha Nussbaum, argued that our relationship to others is a profound ingredient of our make-up as human actors. Ethics, in their eyes, has more to do with how we relate to others than with abstract principles. The "Other" limits our selfishness and obliges us to be responsible and dutiful towards others.

The sense that knowledge is situated in worldly contexts also gave rise to insights regarding how literature exists over time. A literary work may be produced and published, but how it is received as much determines what it is and what it means. How the mind of the reader or receiver processes the work is an essential part of its constitution. Literature is therefore inherently relational and unstable. One cannot say that it means only one thing if it means differently to people in a variety of distinct historical and social situations.

Wolfgang Iser (*The Implied Reader*, 1974) argued that literature addresses an audience, and a reader is implicit in the text. Radicalizing phenomenology, Stanley Fish (*Is There a Text in This Class?*, 1980) suggested that literary texts are latent until activated by the reader's mind. In a sense, the text does not exist unless read. Hans Robert Jauss (*Towards an Aesthetic of Reception*, 1982) emphasized the social and historical dimension of a text's reception. Texts change meaning in different eras, as they are read differently by quite distinct audiences. Pierre Bourdieu (*Distinction: A Social Critique of the Judgment of Taste*, 1984) noted that different social classes process art differently. Highly educated upper class readers equate quality with formal experimentation, while less educated readers and viewers think concrete realism is more true to life because more practically useful. Bourdieu pointed out that Kant's idea that aesthetic is a matter of purposefulness without purpose applied only to a certain social stratum. Judgments about art are reflexes of educational and income levels.

We have clustered phenomenology, reception, and ethics together because it can be argued that our relationship to literary texts and to literary characters is both a testing and training ground for ethics. How our minds engage with literature – creating as much as absorbing meaning – is an important way to develop empathy. Essential to ethics is care for others and the ability to imagine their lives as if those lives were one's own. It is a bit like reading a novel while living one's life.

CHAPTER 2

Transcendental Aesthetic

Immanuel Kant

First published in 1781, Kant's *Critique of Pure Reason* argued that the mind is an active constructor of our knowledge of the world. While earlier philosophers had noted that experience (the empirical sensation of objects by the mind) played a role in building mental concepts, according to Kant they failed to account for the mind's own *a priori* operations. Such operations occur before experience and make it possible.

General Observations on Transcendental Aesthetic

I. To avoid all misapprehension, it is necessary to explain, as clearly as possible, what our view is regarding the fundamental constitution of sensible knowledge in general.

What we have meant to say is that all our intuition is nothing but the representation of appearance; that the things which we intuit are not in themselves what we intuit them as being, nor their relations so constituted in themselves as they appear to us, and that if the subject, or even only the subjective constitution of the senses in general, be removed, the whole constitution and all the relations of objects in space and time, nay space and time themselves, would vanish. As appearances, they cannot exist in themselves, but only in us. What objects may be in themselves, and apart from all this receptivity of our sensibility, remains completely unknown to us. We know nothing but our mode of perceiving them – a mode which is peculiar to us, and not necessarily shared in by every being, though, certainly, by every human being. With this alone have we any concern. Space and time are its pure forms, and sensation in general its matter. The former alone can we know *a priori*, that is, prior to all actual perception; and such knowledge is therefore called pure intuition. The latter is that in our knowledge which leads to its being called *a posteriori* knowledge, that is, empirical intuition. The former inhere in our sensibility with absolute necessity, no matter of what kind our sensations may be; the latter can exist in varying modes. Even if we could bring our intuition to the highest degree of clearness, we should not thereby come any nearer to the constitution of objects in themselves. We should still know only our mode of intuition, that is, our sensibility.

Original publication details: Immanuel Kant, "Transcendental Aesthetic" from *Kant's Critique of Pure Reason*, pp. 82–91. Macmillan, 1929.

Literary Theory: An Anthology, Third Edition. Edited by Julie Rivkin and Michael Ryan.
© 2017 John Wiley & Sons, Ltd. Published 2017 by John Wiley & Sons, Ltd.

We should, indeed, know it completely, but always only under the conditions of space and time – conditions which are originally inherent in the subject. What the objects may be in themselves would never become known to us even through the most enlightened knowledge of that which is alone given us, namely, their appearance.

The concept of sensibility and of appearance would be falsified, and our whole teaching in regard to them would be rendered empty and useless, if we were to accept the view that our entire sensibility is nothing but a confused representation of things, containing only what belongs to them in themselves, but doing so under an aggregation of characters and partial representations that we do not consciously distinguish. For the difference between a confused and a clear representation is merely logical, and does not concern the content. No doubt the concept of 'right', in its common-sense usage, contains all that the subtlest speculation can develop out of it, though in its ordinary and practical use we are not conscious of the manifold representations comprised in this thought. But we cannot say that the common concept is therefore sensible, containing a mere appearance. For 'right' can never be an appearance; it is a concept in the understanding, and represents a property (the moral property) of actions, which belongs to them in themselves. The representation of a body in intuition, on the other hand, contains nothing that can belong to an object in itself, but merely the appearance of something, and the mode in which we are affected by that something; and this receptivity of our faculty of knowledge is termed sensibility. Even if that appearance could become completely transparent to us, such knowledge would remain *toto coelo* different from knowledge of the object in itself.

The philosophy of Leibniz and Wolff, in thus treating the difference between the sensible and the intelligible as merely logical, has given a completely wrong direction to all investigations into the nature and origin of our knowledge. This difference is quite evidently transcendental. It does not merely concern their [logical] form, as being either clear or confused. It concerns their origin and content. It is not that by our sensibility we cannot know the nature of things in themselves in any save a confused fashion; we do not apprehend them in any fashion whatsoever. If our subjective constitution be removed, the represented object, with the qualities which sensible intuition bestows upon it, is nowhere to be found, and cannot possibly be found. For it is this subjective constitution which determines its form as appearance.

We commonly distinguish in appearances that which is essentially inherent in their intuition and holds for sense in all human beings, from that which belongs to their intuition accidentally only, and is valid not in relation to sensibility in general but only in relation to a particular standpoint or to a peculiarity of structure in this or that sense. The former kind of knowledge is then declared to represent the object in itself, the latter its appearance only. But this distinction is merely empirical. If, as generally happens, we stop short at this point, and do not proceed, as we ought, to treat the empirical intuition as itself mere appearance, in which nothing that belongs to a thing in itself can be found, our transcendental distinction is lost. We then believe that we know things in themselves, and this in spite of the fact that in the world of sense, however deeply we enquire into its objects, we have to do with nothing but appearances. The rainbow in a sunny shower may be called a mere appearance, and the rain the thing in itself. This is correct, if the latter concept be taken in a merely physical sense. Rain will then be viewed only as that which, in all experience and in all its various positions relative to the senses, is determined thus, and not otherwise, in our intuition. But if we take this empirical object in its general character, and ask, without considering whether or not it is the same for all human sense, whether it represents an object in itself (and by that we cannot mean the drops of rain, for these are already, as appearances, empirical objects), the question as to the relation of the representation to the object at once becomes transcendental. We then realise that not only are the drops of rain mere appearances, but that even their round shape, nay even the space in which they fall, are nothing in themselves, but merely modifications or fundamental forms of our sensible intuition, and that the transcendental object remains unknown to us.

The second important concern of our Transcendental Aesthetic is that it should not obtain favour merely as a plausible hypothesis, but should have that certainty and freedom from doubt which is required of any theory that is to serve as an organon. To make this certainty completely convincing, we shall select a case by which the validity of the position adopted will be rendered obvious ...

Let us suppose that space and time are in themselves objective, and are conditions of the possibility of things in themselves. In the first place, it is evident that in regard to both there is a large number of *a priori* apodeictic and synthetic propositions. This is especially true of space, to which our chief attention will therefore be directed in this enquiry. Since the propositions of geometry are synthetic *a priori*, and are known with apodeictic certainty, I raise the question, whence do you obtain such propositions, and upon what does the understanding rely in its endeavour to achieve such absolutely necessary and universally valid truths? There is no other way than through concepts or through intuitions; and these are given either *a priori* or *a posteriori*. In their latter form, namely, as *empirical* concepts, and also as that upon which these are grounded, the *empirical* intuition, neither the concepts nor the intuitions can yield any synthetic proposition except such as is itself also merely empirical (that is, a proposition of experience), and which for that very reason can never possess the necessity and absolute universality which are characteristic of all geometrical propositions. As regards the first and sole means of arriving at such knowledge, namely, in *a priori* fashion through mere concepts or through intuitions, it is evident that from mere concepts only analytic knowledge, not synthetic knowledge, is to be obtained. Take, for instance, the proposition, "Two straight lines cannot enclose a space, and with them alone no figure is possible," and try to derive it from the concept of straight lines and of the number two. Or take the proposition, "Given three straight lines, a figure is possible," and try, in like manner, to derive it from the concepts involved. All your labour is vain; and you find that you are constrained to have recourse to intuition, as is always done in geometry. You therefore give yourself an object in intuition. But of what kind is this intuition? Is it a pure *a priori* intuition or an empirical intuition? Were it the latter, no universally valid proposition could ever arise out of it – still less an apodeictic proposition – for experience can never yield such. You must therefore give yourself an object *a priori* in intuition, and ground upon this your synthetic proposition. If there did not exist in you a power of *a priori* intuition; and if that subjective condition were not also at the same time, as regards its form, the universal *a priori* condition under which alone the object of this outer intuition is itself possible; if the object (the triangle) were something in itself, apart from any relation to you, the subject, how could you say that what necessarily exist in you as subjective conditions for the construction of a triangle, must of necessity belong to the triangle itself? You could not then add anything new (the figure) to your concepts (of three lines) as something which must necessarily be met with in the object, since this object is [on that view] given antecedently to your knowledge, and not by means of it. If, therefore, space (and the same is true of time) were not merely a form of your intuition, containing conditions *a priori*, under which alone things can be outer objects to you, and without which subjective conditions outer objects are in themselves nothing, you could not in regard to outer objects determine anything whatsoever in an *a priori* and synthetic manner. It is, therefore, not merely possible or probable, but indubitably certain, that space and time, as the necessary conditions of all outer and inner experience, are merely subjective conditions of all our intuition, and that in relation to these conditions all objects are therefore mere appearances, and not given us as things in themselves which exist in this manner. For this reason also, while much can be said *a priori* as regards the form of appearances, nothing whatsoever can be asserted of the thing in itself, which may underlie these appearances.

II.   In confirmation of this theory of the ideality of both outer and inner sense, and therefore of all objects of the senses, as mere appearances, it is especially relevant to observe that everything in our knowledge which belongs to intuition – feeling of pleasure and pain, and the will, not being knowledge, are excluded – contains nothing but mere relations; namely, of locations in an intuition (extension), of change of loca-tion (motion), and of laws according to which this change is determined (moving forces). What it is that is present in this or that location, or what it is that is operative in the things themselves apart from change of location, is not given through intuition. Now a thing in itself cannot be known through mere relations; and we may therefore conclude that since outer sense gives us nothing but mere relations, this sense can contain in its representation only the relation of an object to the subject, and not the inner properties of the object in itself. This also holds true of inner sense, not only because the representations of the *outer senses* constitute the proper material with which we occupy our mind, but because the time in which we set these representations, which is itself antecedent to the consciousness of them in experience, and which underlies them as the formal condition of the mode in which we posit them in the mind, itself contains [only] relations of succession, coexistence, and of that which is coexistent with succes-sion, the enduring. Now that which, as representation, can be antecedent to any and every act of thinking anything, is intuition; and if it contains nothing but relations, it is the form of intuition. Since this form does not represent anything save in so far as something is posited in the mind, it can be nothing but the mode in which the mind is affected through its own activity (namely, through this positing of its representation), and so is affected by itself; in other words, it is nothing but an inner sense in respect of the form of that sense. Everything that is represented through a sense is so far always appearance, and consequently we must either refuse to admit that there is an inner sense, or we must recognise that the subject, which is the object of the sense, can be represented through it only as appearance, not as that subject would judge of itself if its intuition were self-activity only, that is, were intellectual. The whole difficulty is as to how a subject can inwardly intuit itself; and this is a difficulty common to every theory. The consciousness of self (apperception) is the simple representation of the 'I', and if all that is manifold in the subject were given by the *activity of the self*, the inner intuition would be intellectual. In man this consciousness demands inner perception of the man-ifold which is antecedently given in the subject, and the mode in which this manifold is given in the mind must, as non-spontaneous, be entitled sensibility. If the faculty of coming to consciousness of oneself is to seek out (to apprehend) that which lies in the mind, it must affect the mind, and only in this way can it give rise to an intuition of itself. But the form of this intuition, which exists antecedently in the mind, determines, in the representation of time, the mode in which the manifold is together in the mind, since it then intuits itself not as it would represent itself if immediately self-active, but as it is affected by itself, and therefore as it appears to itself, not as it is.

III. When I say that the intuition of outer objects and the self-intuition of the mind alike represent the objects and the mind, in space and in time, as they affect our senses, that is, as they appear, I do not mean to say that these objects are a mere *illusion*. For in an appearance the objects, nay even the properties that we ascribe to them, are always regarded as something actually given. Since, however, in the relation of the given object to the subject, such properties depend upon the mode of intuition of the subject, this object as *appearance* is to be distinguished from itself as object *in itself*. Thus when I maintain that the quality of space and of time, in conformity with which, as a condition of their existence, I posit both bodies and my own soul, lies in my mode of intuition and not in those objects in themselves, I am not saying that bodies merely *seem* to be outside me, or that my soul only *seems* to be given in my self-consciousness. It would be my own fault, if out of that which I ought to reckon as appearance, I made mere illusion.[1] That does not follow as a consequence of our principle of the ideality of all our sensible intuitions – quite the contrary. It is only if we ascribe *objective reality* to these forms of representation, that it becomes impossible for us to prevent everything being thereby transformed into mere *illusion*. For if we regard space and time as properties which, if they are to be possible at all, must be found in things in themselves, and if we reflect on the absurdities in which we are then involved, in that two infinite things, which are not substances, nor anything actually inhering in substances, must yet have existence, nay, must be the necessary condition of the existence of all things, and moreover must continue to exist, even although all existing things be removed, – we cannot blame the good Berkeley for degrading bodies to mere illusion. Nay, even our own existence, in being made thus dependent upon the self-subsistent reality of a non-entity, such as time, would necessarily be changed with it into sheer illusion – an absurdity of which no one has yet been guilty.

IV. In natural theology, in thinking an object [God], who not only can never be an object of intuition to us but cannot be an object of sensible intuition even to himself, we are careful to remove the conditions of time and space from his intuition – for all his knowledge must be intuition, and not *thought*, which always involves limitations. But with what right can we do this if we have previously made time and space forms of things in themselves, and such as would remain, as *a priori* conditions of the existence of things, even though the things themselves were removed? As conditions of all existence in general, they must also be conditions of the existence of God. If we do not thus treat them as objective forms of all things, the only alternative is to view them as subjective forms of our inner and outer intuition, which is termed sensible, for the very reason that it is *not original*, that is, is not such as can itself give us the existence of its object – a mode of intuition which, so far as we can judge, can belong only to the primordial being. Our mode of intuition is dependent upon the existence of the object, and is therefore possible only if the subject's faculty of representation is affected by that object.

This mode of intuiting in space and time need not be limited to human sensibility. It may be that all finite, thinking beings necessarily agree with man in this respect, although we are not in a position to judge whether this is actually so. But however universal this mode of sensibility may be, it does not therefore cease to be sensibility. It is derivative (*intuitus derivativus*), not original (*intuitus originarius*), and therefore not an intellectual intuition. For the reason stated above, such intellectual intuition seems to belong solely to the primordial being, and can never be ascribed to a dependent being, dependent in its existence as well as in its intuition, and which through that intuition determines its existence solely in relation to given objects.[2] This latter remark, however, must be taken only as an illustration of our aesthetic theory, not as forming part of the proof.

Conclusion of the Transcendental Aesthetic

Here, then, in pure *a priori* intuitions, space and time, we have one of the factors required for solution of the general problem of transcendental philosophy: *how are synthetic a priori judgments possible?* When in *a priori* judgment we seek to go out beyond the given concept, we come in the *a priori* intuitions upon that which cannot be discovered in the concept but which is certainly found *a priori* in the intuition corresponding to the concept, and can be connected with it synthetically. Such judgments, however, thus based on intuition, can never extend beyond objects of the senses; they are valid only for objects of possible experience.

Notes

1　The predicates of the appearance can be ascribed to the object itself, in relation to our sense, for instance, the red colour or the scent to the rose. [But what is illusory can never be ascribed as predicate to an object (for the sufficient reason that we then attribute to the object, taken by itself, what belongs to it only in relation to the senses, or in general to the subject), for instance, the two handles which were formerly ascribed to Saturn.] That which, while inseparable from the representation of the object, is not to be met with in the object in itself, but always in its relation to the subject, is appearance. Accordingly the predicates of space and time are rightly ascribed to the objects of the senses, as such; and in this there is no illusion. On the other hand, if I ascribe redness to the rose *in itself* [handles to Saturn], or extension to all outer objects *in themselves*, without paying regard to the determinate relation of these objects to the subject, and without limiting my judgment to that relation, illusion then first arises. [The passage enclosed in brackets conflicts with the main argument, and is probably a later addition carelessly inserted.]

2　[May be more freely translated as: "through that intuition is conscious of its own existence only in relation to given objects".]

CHAPTER 3

The Phenomenology of Reading

Georges Poulet

One of the most influential philosophers of the eighteenth century, Immanuel Kant, argued that the mind brings to the world an ability to shape and order the manifold of sensuous experiences that impinge on it through the senses. Without such an innate ordering ability, Kant argued, the mind would not function. In the early twentieth century, Edmund Husserl sought to deepen Kant's insight by exploring how the mind experienced what he called "phenomena," the mental objects that are representations of objects in the world. All of our experience of the world and of life is of such phenomena. One version of phenomenology or the science of conscious experience would be to consider how the mind and its objects interact and come into contact with one another as the flow of everyday experience occurs. But if knowledge is limited to that flow, no certain truth could ever hope to be established. Husserl argued that the mind was capable of purifying its experience of ideas by reducing out all the contingent, happenstance elements of everyday experience. What resulted was a pure idea of an object. Several European literary theorists in the twentieth century, such as Georges Poulet and Roman Ingarden, explored the reader's experience of the work of literature, and in the United States, a school of criticism called "Reader Response" emerged led by Stanley Fish.

Georges Poulet was a Professor of French Literature at Johns Hopkins University and later taught at the University of Zurich and the University of Nice. He was a major figure associated with the *nouvelle critique* (New Criticism) of French literature and the Geneva School of Literary Criticism in the 1950s and 1960s. Poulet authored works such as *Studies in Human Time* (1956), *Metamorphoses of the Circle* (1966), and *La Pensée indéterminée, vols. 1–3* (1985–90).

At the beginning of Mallarmé's unfinished story, *Igitur*, there is the description of an empty room, in the middle of which, on a table there is an open book. This seems to me the situation of every book, until someone comes and begins to read it. Books are objects. On a table, on bookshelves, in store windows, they wait for someone to come and deliver

Original publication details: Georges Poulet, "The Phenomenology of Reading."
New Literary History 1.1, pp. 53–68. Johns Hopkins University Press, 1989.
Reproduced with permission from Johns Hopkins University Press.

them from their materiality, from their immobility. When I see them on display, I look at them as I would at animals for sale, kept in little cages, and so obviously hoping for a buyer. For – there is no doubting it – animals do know that their fate depends on a human intervention, thanks to which they will be delivered from the shame of being treated as objects. Isn't the same true of books? Made of paper and ink, they lie where they are put, until the moment someone shows an interest in them. They wait. Are they aware that an act of man might suddenly transform their existence? They appear to be lit up with that hope. Read me, they seem to say. I find it hard to resist their appeal. No, books are not just objects among others.

This feeling they give me – I sometimes have it with other objects. I have it, for example, with vases and statues. It would never occur to me to walk around a sewing machine or to look at the under side of a plate. I am quite satisfied with the face they present to me. But statues make me want to circle around them, vases make me want to turn them in my hands. I wonder why. Isn't it because they give me the illusion that there is something in them which, from a different angle, I might be able to see? Neither vase nor statue seems fully revealed by the unbroken perimeter of its surfaces. In addition to its surfaces it must have an interior. What this interior might be, that is what intrigues me and makes me circle around them, as though looking for the entrance to a secret chamber. But there is no such entrance (save for the mouth of the vase, which is not a true entrance since it gives only access to a little space to put flowers in). So the vase and the statue are closed. They oblige me to remain outside. We can have no true rapport – whence my sense of uneasiness.

So much for statues and vases. I hope books are not like them. Buy a vase, take it home, put it on your table or your mantel, and, after a while, it will allow itself to be made a part of your household. But it will be no less a vase, for that. On the other hand, take a book, and you will find it offering, opening itself. It is this openness of the book which I find so moving. A book is not shut in by its contours, is not walled-up as in a fortress. It asks nothing better than to exist outside itself, or to let you exist in it. In short, the extraordinary fact in the case of a book is the falling away of the barriers between you and it. You are inside it; it is inside you; there is no longer either outside or inside.

Such is the initial phenomenon produced whenever I take up a book, and begin to read it. At the precise moment that I see, surging out of the object I hold open before me, a quantity of significations which my mind grasps, I realize that what I hold in my hands is no longer just an object, or even simply a living thing. I am aware of a rational being, of a consciousness; the consciousness of another, no different from the one I automatically assume in every human being I encounter, except that in this case the consciousness is open to me, welcomes me, lets me look deep inside itself, and even allows me, with unheard-of licence, to think what it thinks and feel what it feels.

Unheard-of, I say. Unheard-of, first, is the disappearance of the "object." Where is the book I held in my hands? It is still there, and at the same time it is there no longer, it is nowhere. That object wholly object, that thing made of paper, as there are things made of metal or porcelain, that object is no more, or at least it is as if it no longer existed, as long as I read the book. For the book is no longer a material reality. It has become a series of words, of images, of ideas which in their turn begin to exist. And where is this new existence? Surely not in the paper object. Nor, surely, in external space. There is only one place left for this new existence: my innermost self.

How has this come about? By what means, through whose intercession? How can I have opened my own mind so completely to what is usually shut out of it? I do not know.

I know only that, while reading, I perceive in my mind a number of significations which have made themselves at home there. Doubtless they are still objects: images, ideas, words, objects of my thought. And yet, from this point of view, there is an enormous difference. For the book, like the vase, or like the statue, was an object among others, residing in the external world: the world which objects ordinarily inhabit exclusively in their own society or each on its own, in no need of being thought by my thought; whereas in this interior world where, like fish in an aquarium, words, images and ideas disport themselves, these mental entities, in order to exist, need the shelter which I provide; they are dependent on my consciousness.

This dependence is at once a disadvantage and an advantage. As I have just observed, it is the privilege of exterior objects to dispense with any interference from the mind. All they ask is to be let alone. They manage by themselves. But the same is surely not true of interior objects. By definition they are condemned to change their very nature, condemned to lose their materiality. They become images, ideas, words, that is to say purely mental entities. In sum, in order to exist as mental objects, they must relinquish their existence as real objects.

On the one hand, this is cause for regret. As soon as I replace my direct perception of reality by the words of a book, I deliver myself, bound hand and foot to the omnipotence of fiction. I say farewell to what is, in order to feign belief in what is not. I surround myself with fictitious beings; I become the prey of language. There is no escaping this take-over. Language surrounds me with its unreality.

On the other hand, the transmutation through language of reality into a fictional equivalent, has undeniable advantages. The universe of fiction is infinitely more elastic than the world of objective reality. It lends itself to any use; it yields with little resistance to the importunities of the mind. Moreover – and of all its benefits I find this the most appealing – this interior universe constituted by language does not seem radically opposed to the *me* who thinks it. Doubtless what I glimpse through the words are mental forms not divested of an appearance of objectivity. But they do not seem to be of a nature other than my mind which thinks them. They are objects, but subjectified objects. In short, since everything has become part of my mind, thanks to the intervention of language, the opposition between the subject and its objects has been considerably attenuated. And thus the greatest advantage of literature is that I am persuaded by it that I am freed from my usual sense of incompatibility between my consciousness and its objects.

This is the remarkable transformation wrought in me through the act of reading. Not only does it cause the physical objects around me to disappear, including the very book I am reading, but it replaces those external objects with a congeries of mental objects in close *rapport* with my own consciousness. And yet the very intimacy in which I now live with my objects is going to present me with new problems. The most curious of these is the following: I am someone who happens to have as objects of his own thought, thoughts which are part of a book I am reading, and which are therefore the cogitations of another. They are the thoughts of another, and yet it is I who am their subject. The situation is even more astonishing than the one noted above. I am thinking the thoughts of another. Of course, there would be no cause for astonishment if I were thinking it as the thought of another. But I think it as my very own. Ordinarily there is the *I* which thinks, which recognizes itself (when it takes its bearings) in thoughts which may have come from elsewhere but which it takes upon itself as its own in the moment it thinks them. This is how we must take Diderot's declaration "Mes pensées sont *mes* catins" ("My thoughts are *my* whores"). That is, they sleep with everybody without ceasing to belong to their author. Now, in the present case things are quite different. Because of the strange invasion of my person by the thoughts of another, I am a self who is granted the experience of thinking thoughts foreign to him. I am the subject of thoughts other than my own. My consciousness behaves as though it were the consciousness of another.

This merits reflection. In a certain sense I must recognize that no idea really belongs to me. Ideas belong to no one. They pass from one mind to another as coins pass from hand to hand. Consequently, nothing could be more misleading than the attempt to define a consciousness by the ideas which it utters or entertains. But whatever these ideas may be, however strong the tie which binds them to their source, however transitory may be their sojourn in my own mind, so long as I entertain them I assert myself as subject of these ideas; I am the subjective principle for whom the ideas serve for the time being as the predications. Furthermore, this subjective principle can in no wise be conceived as a predication, as something which is discussed, referred to. It is I who think, who contemplate, who am engaged in speaking. In short, it is never a *HE* but an *I*.

Now what happens when I read a book? Am I then the subject of a series of predications which are not *my* predications? That is impossible, perhaps even a contradiction in terms. I feel sure that as soon as I think something, that something becomes in some indefinable way my own. Whatever I think is a part of *my* mental world. And yet here I am thinking a thought which manifestly belongs to another mental world, which is being thought in me just as though I did not exist. Already the notion is inconceivable and seems even more so if I reflect that, since every thought must have a subject to think it, this *thought* which is alien to me and yet in me, must also have in me a *subject* which is alien to me. It all happens, then, as though reading were the act by which a thought managed to bestow itself within me with a subject not myself. Whenever I read, I mentally pronounce an *I*, and yet the *I* which I pronounce is not myself. This is true even when the hero of a novel is presented in the third person, and even when there is no hero and nothing but reflections or propositions: for as soon as something is presented as *thought*, there has to be a thinking subject with whom, at least for the time being, I identify, forgetting myself, alienated from myself. "JE est un autre." said Rimbaud. Another *I*, who has replaced my own, and who will continue to do so as long as I read. Reading is just that: a way of giving way not only to a host of alien words, images, ideas, but also to the very alien principle which utters them and shelters them.

The phenomenon is indeed hard to explain, even to conceive, and yet, once admitted, it explains to me what might otherwise seem even more inexplicable. For how could I explain, without such take-over of my innermost subjective being, the astonishing facility with which I not only understand but even *feel* what I read. When I read as I ought, i.e. without mental reservation, without any desire to preserve my independence of judgment, and with the total commitment required of any reader, my comprehension becomes intuitive and any feeling proposed to me is immediately assumed by me. In other words, the kind of comprehension in question here is not a movement from the unknown to the known, from the strange to the familiar, from outside to inside. It might rather be called a phenomenon by which mental objects rise up from the depths of consciousness into the light of recognition. On the other hand – and without contradiction – reading implies something resembling the apperception I have of myself, the action by which I grasp straightway what I think as being thought by a subject (who, in this case, is not, I). Whatever sort of alienation I may endure, reading does not interpret my activity as subject.

Reading, then, is the act in which the subjective principle which I call *I*, is modified in such a way that I no longer have the right, strictly speaking, to consider it as my *I*. I am on loan to another, and this other thinks, feels, suffers, and acts within me. The phenomenon appears in its most obvious and even naivest form in the sort of spell brought about by certain cheap kinds of reading, such as thrillers, of which I say "It gripped me." Now it is important to note that this possession of myself by another takes place not only on the level of objective thought, that is with regard to images, sensations, ideas which reading affords me, but also on the level of my very subjectivity. When I am absorbed in reading, a second self takes over, a self which thinks and feels for me. Withdrawn in some recess of myself, do I then silently witness this dispossession? Do I derive from it some comfort or, on the contrary, a kind of anguish? However that may be, someone else holds the center of the stage, and the question which imposes itself, which I am absolutely obliged to ask myself, is this: "Who is the usurper who occupies the forefront? What is this mind who all alone by himself fills my consciousness and who, when I say *I*, is indeed that *I*?"

There is an immediate answer to this question, perhaps too easy an answer. This *I* who thinks in me when I read a book, is the *I* of the one who writes the book. When I read Baudelaire or Racine, it is really Baudelaire or Racine who thinks, feels, allows himself to be read within me. Thus a book is not only a book, it is the means by which an author actually preserves his ideas, his feelings, his modes of dreaming and living. It is his means of saving his identity from death. Such an interpretation of reading is not false. It seems to justify what is commonly called the biographical explication of literary texts. Indeed every word of literature is impregnated with the mind of the one who wrote it. As he makes us read it, he awakens in us the analogue of what he thought or felt. To understand a literary work, then, is to let the individual who wrote it reveal himself to us *in* us. It is not the biography which explicates the work, but rather the work which sometimes enables us to understand the biography.

But biographical interpretation is in part false and misleading. It is true that there is an analogy between the works of an author and the experiences of his life. The works may be seen as an incomplete translation of the life. And further, there is an even more significant analogy among all the works of a single author. Each of the works, however, while I am reading it, lives in me its own life. The subject who is revealed to me through my reading of it is not the author, either in the disordered totality of his outer experiences, or in the aggregate, better organized and concentrated totality, which is the one of his writings. Yet the subject which presides over the work can exist only in the work. To be sure, nothing is unimportant for understanding the work, and a mass of biographical, bibliographical, textual, and general critical information is indispensable to me. And yet this knowledge does not coincide with the internal knowledge of the work. Whatever may be the sum of the information I acquire on Baudelaire or Racine, in whatever degree of intimacy I may live with their genius, I am aware that this contribution (*apport*) does not suffice to illuminate for me in its own inner meaning, in its formal perfection, and in the subjective principle which animates it, the particular work of Baudelaire or Racine the reading of which now absorbs me. At this moment what matters to me is to live, from the inside, in a certain identity with the work and the work alone. It could hardly be otherwise. Nothing external to the work could possibly share the extraordinary claim which the work now exerts on me. It is there within me, not to send me back, outside itself, to its author, nor to his other writings, but on the contrary to keep my attention rivetted on itself. It is the work which traces in me the very boundaries within which this consciousness will define itself. It is the work which forces on me a series of mental objects and creates in me a network of words, beyond which, for the time being, there will be no room for other mental objects or for other words. And it is the work, finally, which, not satisfied thus with defining the content of my consciousness, takes hold of it, appropriates it, and makes of it that *I* which, from one end of my reading to the other, presides over the unfolding of the work, of the single work which I am reading.

And so the work forms the temporary mental substance which fills my consciousness; and it is moreover that consciousness, the *I*-subject, the continued consciousness of what is, revealing itself within the interior of the work. Such is the characteristic condition of every work which I summon back into existence by placing my consciousness at its disposal. I give it not only existence, but awareness of existence. And so I ought not to hesitate to recognize that so long as it is animated by this vital inbreathing inspired by the act of reading, a work of literature becomes (at the expense of the reader whose own life it suspends) a sort of human being, that it is a mind conscious of itself and constituting itself in me as the subject of its own objects.

II

The work lives its own life within me; in a certain sense, it thinks itself, and it even gives itself a meaning within me.

This strange displacement of myself by the work deserves to be examined even more closely.

If the work thinks itself in me, does this mean that, during a complete loss of consciousness on my part, another thinking entity invades me, taking advantage of my unconsciousness in order to think itself without my being able to think it? Obviously not. The annexation of my consciousness by another (the other which is the work) in no way implies that I am the victim of any deprivation of consciousness. Everything happens, on the contrary, as though, from the moment I become a prey to what I read, I begin to share the use of my consciousness with this being whom I have tried to define and who is the conscious subject ensconced at the heart of the work. He and I, we start having a common consciousness. Doubtless, within this community of feeling, the parts played by each of us are not of equal importance. The consciousness inherent in the work is active and potent; it occupies the foreground; it is clearly related to its *own* world, to objects which are *its* objects. In opposition, I myself, although conscious of whatever it may be conscious of, I play a much more humble role, content to record passively all that is going on in me. A lag takes place, a sort of schizoid distinction between what I feel and what the other feels; a confused awareness of delay, so that the work seems first to think by itself, and then to inform me what it has thought. Thus I often have the impression, while reading, of simply witnessing an action which at the same time concerns and yet does not concern me. This provokes a certain feeling of surprise within me. I am a consciousness astonished by an existence which is not mine, but which I experience as though it were mine.

This astonished consciousness is in fact the consciousness of the critic: the consciousness of a being who is allowed to apprehend as its own what is happening in the consciousness of another being. Aware of a certain gap, disclosing a feeling of identity, but of identity within difference, critical consciousness does not necessarily imply the total disappearance of the critic's mind in the mind to be criticized. From the partial and hesitant approximation of Jacques Rivière to the exalted, digressive and triumphant approximation of Charles Du Bos, criticism can pass through a whole series of nuances which we would be well advised to study. That is what I now propose to do. By discovering the various forms of identification and non-identification to be found in recent critical writing in French literature, I shall be able perhaps to give a better account of the variations of which this relationship – between criticizing subject and criticized object – is capable.

Let me take a first example. In the case of the first critic I shall speak of, this fusion of two consciousnesses is barely suggested. It is an uncertain movement of the mind toward an object which remains hidden. Whereas in the perfect identification of two consciousnesses, each sees itself reflected in the other, in this instance the critical consciousness can, at best, attempt but to draw closer to a reality which must remain forever veiled. In this attempt it uses the only mediators available to it in this quest, that is the senses. And since sight, the most intellectual of the five senses, seems in this particular case to come up against a basic opacity, the critical mind must approach its goal blindly, through the tactile exploration of surfaces, through a groping exploration of the material world which separates the critical mind from its object. Thus, despite the immense effort on the part of the sympathetic intelligence to lower itself to a level where it can, however lamely, make some progress in its quest toward the consciousness of the other, this enterprise is destined to failure. One senses that the unfortunate critic is condemned never to fulfill adequately his role as reader. He stumbles, he puzzles, he questions awkwardly a language which he is condemned never to read with ease; or rather, in trying to read the language, he uses a key which enables him to translate but a fraction of the text.

This critic is Jacques Rivière.

And yet it is from this failure that a much later critic will derive a more successful method of approaching a text. With this later critic, as with Rivière, the whole project begins with an attempt at identification on the most basic level. But this most primitive level is the one in which there flows, from mind to mind, a current which has only to be followed. To identify with the work means here, for the critic, to undergo the same experiences, beginning with the most elementary. On the level of indistinct thought, of sensations, emotions, images, and obsessions of preconscious life, it is possible for the critic to repeat, within himself, that life of which the work affords a first version, inexhaustibly revealing and suggestive. And yet such an imitation could not take place, in a domain so hard to define, without the aid of a powerful auxiliary. This auxiliary is language. There is no critical identification which is not prepared, realized, and incarnated through the agency of language. The deepest sentient life, hidden in the recesses of another's thoughts, could never be truly transposed, save for the mediation of words which allow a whole series of equivalences to arise. To describe this phenomenon as it takes place in the criticism I am speaking of now, I can no longer be content with the usual distinctions between the signifier (*signifiant*) and the signified (*signifié*) for what would it mean here to say that the language of the critic *signifies* the language of the literary work? There is not just equation, similitude. Words have attained a veritable power of recreation; they are a sort of material entity, solid and three-dimensional, thanks to which a certain life of the senses is reborn, finding in a network of verbal connotations the very conditions necessary for its replication. In other words, the language of criticism here dedicates itself to the business of mimicking physically the apperceptual world of the author. Strangely enough, the language of this sort of mimetic criticism becomes even more tangible, more tactile than the author's own; the poetry of the critic becomes more "poetic" than the poet's. This verbal *mimesis*, consciously exaggerated, is in no way servile, nor does it tend at all toward the pastiche. And yet it can reach its object only insofar as that object is deeply enmeshed in, almost confounded with, physical matter. This form of criticism is thus able to provide an admirable equivalent of the vital substratum which underlies all thought, and yet it seems incapable of attaining and expressing thought itself. This criticism is both helped and hindered by the language which it employs; helped, insofar as this language allows it to express the sensuous life in its original state, where it is still almost impossible to distinguish between subject and object; and yet hindered, too, because this language, too congealed and opaque, does not lend itself to analysis, and because the subjectivity which it evokes and describes is as though forever mired in its objects. And so the activity of criticism in this case is somehow incomplete, in spite of its remarkable successes. Identification relative to objects is accomplished almost too well; relative to subjectivity it is barely sketched.

This, then, is the criticism of Jean-Pierre Richard.

In its extreme form, in the abolition of any subject whatsoever, this criticism seems to extract from a literary work a certain condensed matter, a material essence.

But what, then, would be a criticism which would be the reverse, which would abolish the object and extract from the texts their most *subjective* elements?

To conceive such a criticism, I must leap to the opposite extreme. I imagine a critical language which would attempt deliberately to strip the literary language of anything concrete. In such a criticism it would be the artful aim of every line, of every sentence, of every metaphor, of every word, to reduce to the near nothingness of abstraction the images of the real world reflected by literature. If literature, by definition, is already a transportation of the real into the unreality of verbal conception, then the critical act in this case will constitute a transposition of this transposition, thus raising to the second power the "derealization" of being through language. In this way, the mind puts the maximum distance between its thought and what *is*. Thanks to this withdrawal, and to the consequent dematerialization of every object thus pushed to the vanishing point, the universe represented in this criticism seems not so much the equivalent of the perceivable world, or of its literary representation, as rather its image crystallized through a process of rigorous intellectualization. Here criticism is no longer mimesis; it is the reduction of all literary forms to the same level of insignificance. In short, what survives this attempted annihilation of literature by the critical act? Nothing perhaps save a consciousness ceaselessly confronting the hollowness of mental objects, which yield without resistance, and an absolutely transparent language, which, by coating all objects with the same clear glaze, makes them ("like leaves seen far beneath the ice") appear to be infinitely far away. Thus, the language of this criticism plays a role exactly opposite to the function it has in Jean-Pierre Richard's criticism. It does indeed bring about the unification of critical thought with the mental world revealed by the literary work; but it brings it about at the expense of the work. Everything is finally annexed by the dominion of a consciousness detached from any object, a *hyper*-critical consciousness, functioning all alone, somewhere in the void.

Is there any need to say that this hyper-criticism is the critical thought of Maurice Blanchot?

I have found it useful to compare the criticism of Richard to the criticism of Blanchot. I learn from this confrontation that the critic's linguistic apparatus can, just as he chooses, bring him closer to the work under consideration, or can remove him from it indefinitely. If he so wishes, he can approximate very closely the work in question, thanks to a verbal mimesis which transposes into the critic's language the sensuous themes of the work. Or else he can make language a pure crystallizing agent, an absolute translucence, which, suffering no opacity to exist between subject and object, promotes the exercise of the cognitive power on the part of the subject, while at the same time accentuating in the object those characteristics which emphasize its infinite distance from the subject. In the first of the two cases, criticism achieves a remarkable *complicity*, but at the risk of losing its minimum lucidity; in the second case, it results in the most complete dissociation; the maximum lucidity thereby achieved only confirms a separation instead of a union.

Thus criticism seems to oscillate between two possibilities: a union without comprehension, and a comprehension without union. I may identify so completely with what I am reading that I lose consciousness not only of myself, but also of that other consciousness which lives within the work. Its proximity blinds me by blocking my prospect. But I may, on the other hand, separate myself so completely from what I am contemplating that the thought thus removed to a distance assumes the aspect of a being with whom I may never establish any relationship whatsoever. In either case, the act of reading has delivered me from egocentricity: another's thought inhabits me or haunts me, but in the first case I lose myself in that alien world, and in the other we keep our distance and refuse to identify. Extreme closeness and extreme detachment have then the same regrettable effect of making me fall short of the total critical act: that is to say, the exploration of that mysterious interrelationship which, through the mediation of reading and of language, is established to our mutual satisfaction between the work read and myself.

Thus extreme proximity and extreme separation each have grave disadvantages. And yet they have their privileges as well. Sensuous thought is privileged to move at once to the heart of the work and to share its own life; clear thought is privileged to confer on its objects the highest degree of intelligibility. Two sorts of insight are here distinguishable and mutually exclusive: there is penetration by the senses and penetration by the reflective consciousness. Now rather than contrasting these two forms of critical activity, would there not be some way, I wonder, not of practicing them simultaneously, which would be impossible, but at least of combining them through a kind of reciprocation and alternation?

Is not this perhaps the method used today by Jean Starobinski? For instance, it would not be difficult to find in his work a number of texts which relate him to Maurice Blanchot. Like Blanchot he displays exceptional lucidity and an acute awareness of distance. And yet he does not quite abandon himself to Blanchot's habitual pessimism. On the contrary, he seems inclined to optimism, even at times to a pleasant utopianism. Starobinski's intellect in this respect is analogous to that of Rousseau, yearning for an immediate transparence of all beings to each other which would enable them to understand each other in an ecstatic happiness. From this point of view, is not the ideal of criticism precisely represented by the *fête citadine* (street celebration) or *fête champêtre* (rustic feast)? There is a milieu or a moment in the feast in which everyone communicates with everyone else, in which hearts are open like books. On a more modest scale, doesn't the same phenomenon occur in reading? Does not one being open its innermost self? Is not the other being enchanted by this opening? In the criticism of Starobinski we often find that crystalline tempo of music, that pure delight in understanding, that perfect sympathy between an intelligence which enters and that intelligence which welcomes it.

In such moments of harmony, there is no longer any exclusion, no inside or outside. Contrary to Blanchot's belief, perfect translucence does not result in separation.

On the contrary, with Starobinski, all is perfect agreement, joy shared, the pleasure of understanding and of being understood. Moreover, such pleasure, however intellectual it may be, is not here exclusively a pleasure of the mind. For the relationship established on this level between author and critic is not a relationship between pure minds. It is rather between incarnate beings, and the particularities of their physical existence constitute not obstacles to understanding, but rather a complex of supplementary signs, a veritable language which must be deciphered and which enhances mutual comprehension. Thus for Starobinski, as much physician as critic, there is a reading of *bodies* which is likened to the reading of *minds*. It is not of the same nature, nor does it bring the intelligence to bear on the same area of human knowledge. But for the critic who practices it, this criticism provides the opportunity for a reciprocating exchange between different types of learning which have, perhaps, different degrees of transparency.

Starobinski's criticism, then, displays great flexibility. Rising at times to the heights of metaphysics, it does not disdain the farthest reaches of the subsconscious. It is sometimes intimate, sometimes detached; it assumes all the degrees of identification and non–identification. But its final movement seems to consist in a sort of withdrawal, contradistinction with its earlier accord. After an initial intimacy with the object under study, this criticism has finally to detach itself, to move on, but this time in solitude. Let us not see this withdrawal as a failure of sympathy but rather as a way of avoiding the encumbrances of too prolonged a life in common. Above all we discern an acute need to establish bearings, to adopt the judicious perspective, to assess the fruits of proximity by examining them at a distance. Thus, Starobinski's criticism always ends with a view from afar, or rather from above, for while moving away it has also moved imperceptibly toward a dominating (*surplombante*) position. Does this mean that Starobinski's criticism like Blanchot's is doomed to end in a philosophy of separation? This, in a way, must be conceded, and it is no coincidence that Starobinski treats with special care the themes of melancholy and nostalgia. His criticism always concludes with a double farewell. But this farewell is exchanged by two beings who have begun by living together; and the one left behind continues to be illuminated by that critical intellect which moves on.

The sole fault with which I might reproach such criticism is the excessive ease with which it penetrates what it illuminates.

By dint of seeing in literary works only the thoughts which inhabit them, Starobinski's criticism somehow passes through their forms, not neglecting them, it is true, but without pausing on the way. Under its action literary works lose their opacity, their solidity, their objective dimension; like those palace walls which become transparent in certain fairy tales. And if it is true that the ideal act of criticism must seize (and reproduce) that certain relationship between an object and a mind which is the work itself, how could the act of criticism succeed when it suppresses one of the (polar) terms of this relationship?

My search must continue, then, for a criticism in which this relationship subsists. Could it perhaps be the criticism of Marcel Raymond and Jean Rousset? Raymond's criticism always recognizes the presence of a double reality, both mental and formal. It strives to comprehend almost simultaneously an inner experience and a perfected form. On the one hand, no one allows himself to be absorbed with such complete self-forgetfulness into the thought of another. But the other's thought is grasped not at its highest, but at its most obscure, at its cloudiest point, at the point at which it is reduced to being a mere self-awareness scarcely perceived by the being which entertains it, and which yet to the eyes of the critic seems the sole means of access by which he can penetrate within the precincts of the alien mind.

But Raymond's criticism presents another aspect which is precisely the reverse of this confused identification of the critic's thought with the thought criticized. It is then the reflective contemplation of a formal reality which is the work itself. The work stands *before* the critical intelligence as a perfected object, which is in fact an enigma, an external thing existing in itself and with which there is no possibility of identification nor of inner knowledge.

Thus Raymond perceives sometimes a subject, sometimes an object. The subject is pure mind; it is a sheer indefinable presence, an almost inchoate entity, into which, by very virtue of its absence of form, it becomes possible for the critic's mind to penetrate. The work, on the contrary, exists only within a definite form, but this definition limits it, encloses it within its own contours, at the same time constraining the mind which studies it to remain on the outside. So that, if on the one hand the critical thought of Raymond tends to lose itself within an undefined subjectivity, on the other it tends to come to a stop before an impenetrable objectivity.

Admirably gifted to submit his own subjectivity to that of another, and thus to immerse itself in the obscurest depths of every mental entity, the mind of Raymond is less well equipped to penetrate the obstacle presented by the objective surface of the works. He then finds himself marking time, or moving in circles around the work, as around the vase or the statue mentioned before. Does Raymond then establish an insurmountable partition between the two realities – subjective, objective – unified though they may be in the work? No, indeed, at least not in his best essays, since in them, by careful intuitive apprehension of the text and participation by the critic in the powers active in the poet's use of language, there appears some kind of link between the objective aspects of the work and the undefined subjectivity which sustains it. A link not to be confused with a pure relation of identity. The perception of the formal aspects of the work becomes somehow an analogical language by means of which it becomes possible for the critic to go, within the work, beyond the formal aspects it presents. Nevertheless this association is never presented by Raymond as a dialectical process. The usual state described by his method of criticism is one of plenitude, and even of a double plenitude. A certain fulness of experience detected in the poet and re-lived in the mind of the critic, is connected by the latter with a certain perfection of form; but why this is so, and how it does become so, is never clearly explained.

Now is it then possible to go one step further? This is what is attempted by Jean Rousset, a former student of Raymond and perhaps his closest friend. He also dedicates himself to the task of discerning the structure of a work as well as the depth of an experience. Only what essentially matters to him is to establish a connection between the objective reality of the work and the organizing power which gives it shape. A work is not explained for him, as for the structuralists, by the exclusive interdependence of the objective elements which compose it. He does not see in it a fortuitous combination, interpreted *a posteriori* as if it were an *a priori* organization. There is not in his eyes any system of the work without a principle of systematization which operates in correlation with that work and which is even included in it. In short, there is no spider-web without a center which is the spider. On the other hand, it is not a question of going from the work to the psychology of the author, but of going back, within the sphere of the work, from the objective elements systematically arranged, to a certain power of organization, inherent in the work itself, as if the latter showed itself to be an intentional consciousness determining its arrangements and solving its problems. So that it would scarcely be an abuse of terms to say that it speaks, by means of its structural elements, an authentic language, thanks to which it discloses itself and means nothing but itself. Such then is the critical enterprise of Jean Rousset. It sets itself to use the objective elements of the work in order to attain, beyond them, a reality not formal, nor objective, written down however in forms and expressing itself by means of them. Thus the understanding of forms must not limit itself merely to the recording of their objective aspects. As Focillon demonstrated from the point of view of art history, there is a "life of forms" perceptible not only in the historic development which they display from epoch to epoch, but within each single work, in the movement by which forms tend therein sometimes to stabilize and become static, and sometimes to change into one another. Thus the two contradictory forces which are always at work in any literary writing, the will to stability and the protean impulse, help us to perceive by their interplay how much forms are dependent on what Coleridge called a shaping power which determines them, replaces them and transcends them. The teaching of Raymond finds then its most satisfying success in the critical method of Jean Rousset, a method which leads the seeker from the continuously changing frontiers of form to what is beyond form.

It is fitting then to conclude this inquiry here, since it has achieved its goal, namely to describe, relying on a series of more or less adequate examples, a critical method having as guiding principle the relation between subject and object. Yet there remains one last difficulty. In order to establish the interrelationship between subject and object, which is the principle of all creative work and of the understanding of it, two ways, at least theoretically, are opened, one leading from the objects to the subject, the other from the subject to the objects. Thus we have seen Raymond and Rousset, through perception of the objective structures of a literary work, strive to attain the subjective principle which upholds it. But, in so doing, they seem to recognize the precedence of the subject over its objects. What Raymond and Rousset are searching for in the objective and formal aspects of the work, is something which is previous to the work and on which the work depends for its very existence. So that the method which leads from the object to the subject does not differ radically at bottom from the one which leads from subject to object, since it does really consist in going from subject to subject through the object. Yet there is the risk of overlooking an important point. The aim of criticism is not achieved merely by the understanding of the part played by the subject in its interrelation with objects. When reading a literary work, there is a moment when it seems to me that the subject *present* in this work disengages itself from all that surrounds it, and stands alone. Had I not once the intuition of this, when visiting the Scuola de San Rocco in Venice, one of the highest summits of art, where there are assembled so many paintings of the same painter, Tintoretto? When looking at all these masterpieces brought there together and revealing so manifestly their unity of inspiration, I had suddenly the impression of having reached the common essence present in all the works of a great master, an essence which I was not able to perceive, except when emptying my mind of all the particular images created by the artist. I became aware of a subjective power at work in all these pictures, and yet never so clearly understood by my mind as when I had forgotten all their particular figurations.

One may ask oneself: What is this subject left standing in isolation after all examination of a literary work? Is it the individual genius of the artist, visibly present in his work, yet having an invisible life independent of the work? Or is it, as Valéry thinks, an anonymous and abstract consciousness presiding, in its aloofness, over the operations of all more concrete consciousness? Whatever it may be, I am constrained to acknowledge that all subjective activity present in a literary work is not entirely explained by its relationship with forms and objects within the work. There is in the work a mental activity profoundly engaged in objective forms; and there is, at another level, forsaking all forms, a subject which reveals itself to itself (and to me) in its transcendence over all which is reflected in it. At this point, no object can any longer express it, no structure can any longer define it; it is exposed in its ineffability and in its fundamental indeterminacy. Such is perhaps the reason why the critic, in his elucidation of works, is haunted by this transcendence of mind. It seems then that criticism, in order to accompany the mind in this effort of detachment from itself, needs to annihilate, or at least momentarily to forget, the objective elements of the work, and to elevate itself to the apprehension of a subjectivity without objectivity.

CHAPTER 4

Teaching, Studying, and Theorizing the Production and Reception of Literary Texts

Kathleen McCormick

Kathleen McCormick teaches literature and writing at Purchase College, SUNY, in New York. Her areas of specialization are Irish literature, James Joyce, Italian-American literature, and the culture of reading. In this essay, she traces the evolution of the study of reading and of readership and applies the lessons of reception theory to the figure of Molly Bloom in Joyce's *Ulysses*.

Over the last decade, many researchers and theorists in cultural studies have reacted against determinist positions that regard audiences as powerless subjects merely "spoken" by the cultural discourses that traverse them. Arguing against the textual determinist position made most popular by "*Screen* theory" (MacCabe), theorists such as Stuart Hall, Paul Willemen, and David Morley have contended that readers are not simply the "subject of the text," but also "social subjects" who live in a particular social formation, and who are immersed in a variety of complex cultural systems, of which a text is only a single component (Hall 136–38; Willemen 48; Morley, "Texts" 170–71). While texts are thought to encourage readers to construct a "preferred" meaning, it has been argued that most readers will, to some extent, create a "negotiated" version of the text which contains both "adaptive" and "oppositional" elements (Hall 137). Recognizing that readers will construct meaning differently depending on their "knowledges, prejudices, [and] resistances" (Morley, "Texts" 171) has led to significant developments in theories of subjectivity, particularly in the areas of television and film spectatorship, as the reader/viewer has come to be regarded as an active, potentially resistant agent.

The position of reader or spectator is increasingly seen as balanced between autonomy and social determination – a view that has gained validity in part by the difficulty

Original publication details: Kathleen McCormick, "Teaching, Studying, and Theorizing the Production and Reception of Literary Texts." *College Literature* 19.2, *Cultural Studies: Theory Praxis Pedagogy* (June 1992), pp. 4–18. Johns Hopkins University Press, 1992. Reproduced with permission from Johns Hopkind University Press.

Literary Theory: An Anthology, Third Edition. Edited by Julie Rivkin and Michael Ryan.
© 2017 John Wiley & Sons, Ltd. Published 2017 by John Wiley & Sons, Ltd.

researchers have had predicting the ways actual audiences would negotiate a text on the basis of their class, gender, or race (Morley, *Nationwide*; Hobson, "Housewives," *Crossroads*) – and the nature of that balance between autonomy and determination is still being theorized. In his most recent ethnographic study, for example, Morley takes as his primary goal "to formulate a position from which we can see the person actively producing meanings from the restricted range of cultural resources which his or her structural position has allowed … access to" (*Family Television* 43). Deidre Pribram, in her introduction to *Female Spectators*, emphasizes how enabling this expanding theory of subjectivity has been in film studies: "a method of analysis which argues that the viewing process includes the active participation of spectators means that film's codes can be implemented, by both producer and consumer, to allow for alternative usage" (5), and the essays collected in *Female Spectators* examine female viewers from various subject positions – as individuals, as historically constituted groups, and as viewers of particular texts (5).

Retheorizing the discursive positions of audiences also has had significant impact on education practices (Masterman; Giroux and Simon et al.). Len Masterman, for example, has argued that "within media education, if the full implications of work on the significance of audience responses has [sic] been fully grasped, it is scarcely possible to pursue a pedagogy within which students are treated as the recipients of pre-ordained information and ideas, rather than as active makers of meaning in their own right" (30). It is the pedagogical implications of such retheorizing for the teaching of literary texts that are the primary focus of this paper. For the reader of a literary text, no less than the television spectator, is also a subject "within different social practices in determinate social formations" (Morley, "Texts" 170), and, in creating meaning, the literary reader is also balanced between autonomy and determination. In what follows, I will argue, on both theoretical and practical pedagogical grounds, that one of the ways in which student readers of literature can be enabled to work with critical awareness in that balance between autonomy and determination is by being given access to discourses that can allow them to read and study literary texts from the standpoint of their *production* and *reception*.

As theorists from Gramsci to Althusser to Bourdieu have noted, the schools form one of the major ideological apparatuses by which discourses – or "cultural capital" – are distributed. If readers and viewers are regarded as active producers of meaning – within specific cultural constraints – then it follows that rather than positioning students as mere passive receivers of knowledge, schools should encourage them to engage actively in the production of knowledge and meaning: schooling should enable students to articulate their own readings of cultural objects and introduce them to discourses that can help them explore the ways in which cultural objects are historically and socially produced. Further, if students are to become "active makers of meaning" of literary texts, they must also be given access to discourses that can help them to historicize their own reading position, to see reading as a process of production in dialectical relation to other readings in the past, and to enable them to make the text address their own historical condition.

While having access to new discourses will not automatically produce new reading capabilities in students (to argue this would be to take up a fully deterministic position), the discourses will "exercise a limit on … the formation of the discursive space" that readers inhabit, which will then have "a determinate effect on the practice of readings at the level of particular text-reader encounters" (Morley, "Texts" 173). If students come to inhabit a discursive space in which they recognize the constructed nature of both the texts they read and their responses to them, it will be possible for them to develop more historicized, self-reflective, and resistant readings of texts, and thus to become more active producers of meaning. While such "critically literate" reading practices are part of a much larger movement of radical pedagogy (see, for example, Freire; Giroux; Giroux and Simon et al.; Willinsky), they have been quite readily taken up by media pedagogy at least in part because of the active and participatory theory of the subject that dominates that area of study.

On the theoretical level, my approach synthesizes ideas from a number of literary perspectives and adapts to a literary context some of the work done in cultural studies on audience analysis. Any study of the material and historical conditions under which literary texts are produced owes its most obvious debt to contemporary Marxist criticism. In different though overlapping ways, Terry Eagleton, Pierre Macherey, and Fredric Jameson insist on the importance of exploring the historical formation in which the text was produced not only to understand the contexts to which it explicitly refers, but also to read it *symptomatically*, that is, for symptoms of the tensions or contradictions of the social formation within which the text was produced and which are then reproduced, often unconsciously, within the text. Macherey talks of reading the text for its "absences," that which is not explicitly *in* the text, but which is nonetheless a part of the history of the text, what, as he puts it, the text is "*compelled* to say in order to say what it *wants* to say" (94). In articulating these absences, criticism is thought to be able to make the text reveal the ways in which ideology works to attain coherence by suppressing the intolerable contradictions of existence that are suggested by these absences.

Marxist criticism, however, has had little to say about the material and historical circumstances of the reception of literary texts: it tends to focus primarily on the conditions of their production. While Eagleton, for example, recognizes in *Criticism and Ideology* that "the act of consumption is itself constitutive" of the "existence" of the literary text (62), and while his work is filled with brief suggestions of how the process of reading could be analyzed from the perspective of materialist criticism, he does not elaborate on these suggestions. Macherey's notion of "absences" similarly is uneasy before a consideration of the reading experience. He assumes that the absences one discovers in a text are related solely to the conditions of the text's production; yet since the questions one asks of the text's history must necessarily come from one's position in the present, the absences one "finds" are surely determined as much by the social formation in which the text is being read as by the social formation in which it was written. In *The Political Unconscious*, Jameson appears briefly to take reception as seriously as production when he performs symptomatic historical analysis on modes of criticism as well as on literary texts. Yet because his interest in reception is on a "macro" level, his tendency is to focus on exponents of large interpretive systems such as structuralism or psychoanalysis; thus, his discussions of actual acts of reading are abstract and do not address the myriad of different critical responses to a text that can occur within any particular reading formation.

It is interesting to speculate why Marxism has avoided extended discussions of reception, although a full consideration of the question is beyond the scope of this article. It is perhaps for fear of devolving into what Eagleton calls the "consumer-centeredness" (86) of the liberal humanist notion of the reader as a self-coherent individual whose response supposedly ensures the "authenticity" of the text (86). While it is true that American reader-response criticism, especially in the seventies, did tend to treat the reader as an autonomous individual and granted priority to the reader's supposedly "subjective" response to the text (Bleich), it is quite possible – as theories of media reception have done – to construct a theory of the subject as balanced between autonomy and social construction. To develop such an active notion of the subject, however, many of the fundamentals of Marxist criticism may have to be rethought.

From different perspectives, Tony Bennett and Hans R. Jauss both attempt some of this rethinking. In work that spans literary and popular cultural analyses, Bennett and Janet Woollacott have argued that production and reception so impinge upon each other that it is impossible to speak of "the text itself": "there is no fixed boundary between the extra-textual and the intra-textual which prevents the former from pressing in upon the latter and reorganizing it" (263). In *Formalism and Marxism*, Bennett offers a critique of, among others, the positions of Macherey and Eagleton for unwittingly reifying the literary text as the *source* of Marxist "discoveries" of absences and contradictions and for failing to recognize that it is the very *way of reading* advocated by Marxist criticism that enables those contradictions to be perceived: "It [Marxist criticism] does not restore to the text contradictions which were 'always there' but hidden from view; it *reads contradictions into the text*" (146). Since any way of reading is necessarily interested, the process of reading itself needs to be historicized: "the concept of the *text* must be replaced by the concept of the concrete and varying, historically specific *functions* and *effects* which accrue to 'the text' as a result of the different determinations to which it is subjected during the history of its appropriation" (148). Bennett's work constitutes the most promising move within a historical materialist model to recognize the place of readers and acts of reading, and I will draw on it throughout this essay.

Jauss's *rezeptionsästhetik* provides the most extensive analysis of the history of the reception of literary texts. His notion of understanding, drawn from Gadamerian hermeneutics, is of a "fusion of horizons" between the text, with all of its past history – norms, assumptions, values, and its prior critical reception – and the present cultural perspective. Jauss argues that:

> History of literature is a process of aesthetic reception and production that takes place in the realization of literary texts on the part of the receptive reader, the reflective critic, and the author in his continuing productivity. ... A literary event can continue to have an effect only if those who come after it still or once again respond to it – if there are readers who again appropriate the past work or authors who want to imitate, outdo, or refute it. (21–22)

Thus Jauss, like Bennett, emphasizes that literary texts are historically active entities whose meanings and effects are contingent on the circumstances in which they are read. But while Jauss claims to recognize the importance of larger ideological issues in the reception of a text – "the task of literary history is ... only completed when literary production is ... seen as 'special history' in its own unique relationship to 'general history'" (39) – his work tends to focus too exclusively on aesthetic history, and the reader is usually conceived of as a subject of the text or of dominant aesthetic codes rather than as a subject of broader cultural systems. Jauss's model of the dialogic process of reading, therefore, needs to be extended to include not only the history of the text's criticism, but also the political, institutional, and ideological contexts in which that criticism is written.

Taking up some of Bennett's and Jauss's points, and linking them with the work of Morley and others on subjectivity, I want to suggest an approach to theorizing reading, which I can sketch only summarily in this essay, that breaks down apparently common-sensical distinctions between production and reception and sees reception as a form of production; which studies reading as a dialectical and historical process; and which regards the reader as actively constructing meaning, not as a free individual, but as a subject in history who nonetheless possesses some degree of agency.[1]

The very juxtaposition of the terms "production" and "reception" suggests a hierarchy in which "production," with its connotations of activity and ontological priority, appears to be the dominant term, and reception, in contrast, is passive, a mere "receiving" of something that was actively created at an earlier point. Even if one substitutes "repro-duction" for "reception," one is still faced with the same dilemma, for "reproduction" seems to privilege an originary moment in which production could occur and suggests not only that reproduction is a mere repeating of what has already been done, but that it is in some way counterfeit. This apparently commonsensical distinction underlies the long tradition of reifying "the text itself" and of valorizing the "text's meaning" or the "author's intention" over the reader's mere "significances." To counter such common-sensical notions, one needs to examine reception from a historical perspective.

For far from being a passive intaking of an objective given, the process of reading is a continually changing dialogue between the past and the present, as the present encour-ages readers to ask questions of a text that might not have seemed "natural" to ask in the past. Bennett has introduced the term "reading formation" to describe the relationship among texts, readers, and contexts that determines the ways texts are read at any particu-lar point in history (*Texts* 7–11). His concept of the reading formation looks similar to Jauss's "horizon of expectation," but its advantage is that it explicitly emphasizes larger social and historical forces including but extending beyond the aesthetic. Bennett con-tends that because the reading situation is both socially and discursively overdetermined, it cannot be argued that either particular textual features or particular social factors *cause* readers to make certain reading moves. It is this complex social and discursive overdeter-mination that Bennett refers to as the reading formation. Thus Bennett helps us to recognize that while we may, for ease of analysis, separate out particular literary or general ideological factors in the study of a text, we need to develop ways of thinking about reading that do not reduce the complexity – and historically active nature – of the reading situation.

While there will be dominant modes of reading within any particular reading forma-tion, there will always be competing and contradictory positions. Raymond Williams's observation in *Marxism and Literature* that within any historical conjuncture there will always exist dominant, residual, and emergent ideological positions helps to underscore the overdetermined nature of reading formations. But Jauss's emphasis on aesthetic history as a major factor in the history of a text's reception should not be overlooked. A particular reading formation in which a text is read is determined not only by current literary and general ideological preoccupations but also by the history of the text's production and reception in past reading formations – as this is constructed from the perspective of the current reading formation (see Eagleton 63). To acknowledge that a text's history is repeatedly reconstructed (and that it continues to accrue over time) is to recognize the dialogic and dialectical nature of both reading and history.

But of course – and here we move to a point that neither the Marxist tradition nor the tradition of *rezeptionsästhetik* represented by Jauss can easily incorporate – textual mean-ing and history do not just "get reconstructed" by amorphous reading formations: actual readers perform this reconstruction. How is it possible to account for the role of the reader in the reading process while simultaneously acknowledging that readers' actions are delimited by ideological forces? Literary theory – which generally elides the distinction between real readers and constructed readers – can sharpen its perspective on this question by adapting some insights from media theory, which recognizes, as Willemen notes, that

> There remains an *unbridgeable gap between "real" readers/authors and "inscribed" ones,*
> *constructed and marked in and by the text.* Real readers are subjects in history, living in social
> formations, rather than mere subjects of a single text. The two types of subject are not
> commensurate. But for the purposes of formalism, real readers are supposed to coincide
> with the constructed readers. (63–64)

This "gap" between real and constructed readers is most apparent in the literature classroom when students' readings fail to coincide with those of the teacher or the teacher's sense of the implied reader of the text. When told to read literary texts "on their own," students are often overwhelmed or intimidated because they may lack access to cultural, historical, literary, or theoretical discourses that would enable them actively to construct meaning from the text. Yet students can be equally overwhelmed when teachers simply "give" them the background knowledge they supposedly need to interpret a text. Both ways of teaching can mystify the literary text by encouraging students to believe that they themselves are incapable of reading such texts, which appear to contain secret and transcendent knowledge. If, however, students are given access to theoretical discourses of production and reception that can demystify the literary text – or any other cultural object – and provide a discursive space for concrete cultural and historical analysis, it becomes possible for them to develop the capacity to teach themselves and each other about the historical conditions in which texts were written and have been interpreted. Further, within this discursive space, students can begin to pose their own culturally and historically situated questions to the text to make it address their own historical condition, and, thereby, take up active roles in which they – as "interdiscursive subjects" (Morley, "Texts" 164) inhabiting conflicting reading formations – also come to intervene in the process of reproducing a text.

I turn back now to a particular classroom situation in which I use literary and media theories of production and reception to teach a course on the production and reception of the modern novel. Although I have found this approach to be successful with various novels such as John Fowles's *The Magus*, Doris Lessing's *The Golden Notebook*, and D. M. Thomas's *The White Hotel*, I will use students' work on James Joyce's *Ulysses* as an example in this paper. Because *Ulysses* is such a difficult text for students, many teachers might be reluctant to add to it a significant body of "extra" theoretical and historical work for fear that they would completely overwhelm their students. Yet, it is just such work in production and reception that has enabled my students to demystify *Ulysses*, to actively confront, enjoy, and resist it, and to make it address their own historical condition.

The course is organized so that we spend the first four weeks discussing theories of production and reception before we begin two weeks studying contexts of the production of *Ulysses*, four weeks reading *Ulysses*, and then repeating the process with another novel.[2] When introducing these theories to the class, I suggest that they have the potential to alter both the traditional relations between a literary text and a reader, and the traditional relations between teachers and students. The process by which students begin to learn to read with critical and historical awareness occurs in roughly three stages.

First, they construct a reading – necessarily perspectival – of the historical formation in which *Ulysses* was produced. They do this not simply to learn "background" – i.e., material about the personages, political events, religious practices, etc., those supposedly stable entities to which the text "refers" – but rather to read the text *symptomatically*, that is, to look for "symptoms" of the tensions or contradictions of the social formation within which the text was produced and which are then reproduced – often unconsciously – within the text. So, for example, when reading the "Cyclops" chapter, a student who wishes to present the chapter within the contradictions and struggles of Irish politics might note that various of the interpolations – the linguistic excesses that intrude on the actual scene in Barney Kernan's pub – parody the rhetoric of Irish nationalism while at the same time making clear reference to the British oppression of the Irish.[3] With a perspective consciously focusing on Irish politics in Joyce's time and after, the student might also explore ways in which the formal text strategy of the interpolations, like the Irish national-ism that it so often parodies, can be seen as what Jameson calls a "strategy of containment" (53–54), as something that creates a substitute truth – in this case, Irish nationalists are full of hot air and completely ineffectual – to repress the intolerable totality of the British domination of the Irish.

In reconstructing a symptomatic history of *Ulysses*, students come to regard the text, as Macherey puts it, not as "*created* by an intention" but as "*produced* under determi-nate conditions" (78). In the second stage of reading, students expand this perspective to include a study of the determinate conditions in which *Ulysses* has been *reproduced* throughout its history. They explore how and why different reading formations have asked different questions of the text, or to put it another way, how they have *used* or *appropriated* the text – often unwittingly – for particular ideological ends. Such an investigation involves examining *Ulysses* in the context both of the history of its recep-tion and of larger historical and ideological forces that have produced successive rereadings of it.

I often use the history of the criticism of Molly Bloom to illustrate the complexity of the ideological relationships that exist in a particular reading formation and to bring into sharp relief an example of changing reading formations. While in the thirties and forties, the dominant critical position on Molly was to extol her as an "earth mother" (see, for example, Gilbert, Levin, Tindall, Budgen), she was also criticized for her "obscenities of thought" (Budgen 263), her "animal placidity" (Levin 125; see also Tindall 232–35 and Blackmur 114–15), and her apparent lack of respect for men (Tindall 233, Gilbert 389–95, Budgen 264–65). While in the fifties and sixties, dominant interpretations of Molly decried her as a whore and an embodiment of evil and destruction (see, for exam-ple, Kenner, Adams, Morse, O'Brien), her sexuality was also depicted as alluring (see Adams, *Common Sense* 166; O'Brien 143–49; Shechner 217). Over the last two decades, feminist theorists have sought to establish cultural and historical contexts for Molly's soliloquy, regarding it not so much as the product of an individual woman (or man), but as part of larger cultural discourses (see, for example, Unkeless; Scott, *Joyce and Feminism*; Shloss, Devlin, Attridge). Yet some feminists have also queried whether Molly's soliloquy is an example of what Luce Irigaray has termed *écriture féminine* – an endless contradictory and timeless female voice which "sets off in all directions leaving 'him' unable to discern the coherence of any meaning" (Irigaray 28; see, for example, Scott, *James Joyce*; Levitt; Henke, *Politics*).

From symbol of fertility, to satanic mistress, to product of cultural contradictions, to the voice of all women – such differing interpretations are not simply varying readings of the "same" text; they are, rather, the (re)production of multiple texts. The variability of Molly Bloom's ideological significations suggests that the "Penelope" chapter has been drawn "into the orbit of activity of … different sets of ideological and cultural concerns" (Bennett and Woollacott 233–34) by the critical texts that surround the chapter, what Bennett and Woollacott call "textual shifters." They contend that textual shifters "do not act solely upon the reader to produce different readings of 'the same text' but also act upon the text, shifting its very signifying potential so that it is no longer what it once was because, in terms of its cultural location, it is no longer where it once was" (248). These "shifters" are produced not only by "academic" or purely literary concerns, but also by broader historical and ideological forces, as readers continually attempt to construct texts that can address their changing historical conditions. In the second stage of reading, students seek out such textual shifters, and attempt to account for them within the complex ideological network in which they are embedded.

At the third stage of reading (and again, I wish to emphasize that these "stages" are not clearly separable in practice), students develop their own reading of the text, not from a position of either autonomy or as a subject solely of the text, but as a social subject immersed in contradictory cultural systems, balanced between autonomy and determination. Thus, with at least an incipient awareness of the interdiscursivity of their subject positions, students attempt to read the text in its subsequent history, asking questions of it that come out of their own historical condition, questions that could not have been asked at the moment of the text's production but that it can be made to address. At this moment of reading, students analyze the dialectical relation of their "new" questions and interpretations to those of the past, bearing in mind that in posing such "later" questions – and in reconstructing prior reading formations – they are repositioning and reappropriating the text for particular ends, not discovering transcendent truths about its "original" meanings or subsequent, secondary, readings.

The discursive space opened up by theories of production and reception has the potential not only to change students' relations with literary texts, but also to change classroom relations between students and teachers. The theory of the course can function in part for pedagogical ends: to establish a situation in which the teacher and students can engage in a dialogue that enables students to develop the critical thinking and reading skills necessary to participate both in creating new knowledge and in actively directing the focus of much of the course (see Freire 66–74, Masterman 27–37, Giroux and Simon 3–14). For if interpretations of texts are always historically situated, then the knowledge teachers have about a particular text, while it may likely exceed that of their students, should not be mystified by either teachers or students: teachers know particular things because they have read, thought, and sometimes written about them, not because their positions inherently give them access to secret truths. Thus, my primary role in teaching *Ulysses* in this course becomes what Paulo Freire calls a "problem poser," that is, one who helps students gain access to the texts that surround *Ulysses* so that they themselves can assess and begin to take part in the continual process of its reinterpretation.

To this end, I assign my students two projects in which they write essays of five to six pages in length, which they distribute to all members of the class at least one class period prior to our discussing them, and which are graded by all class members. These essays serve as our primary resource material throughout the course. For the first assignment, groups of three students write collaborative essays on contexts for the production of *Ulysses* including such areas as Modernism, Irish politics, the Irish literary revival, Irish popular culture, and the status of women in turn-of-the-century Dublin. For the second essay, each student writes an individual essay focusing on the reception of one chapter of *Ulysses*. These short papers are not traditional background studies. Whether students are writing on a production topic or on the reception of an individual chapter of *Ulysses*, the focus on production and reception requires them not just to reproduce what has already been said about a given topic, but to read their sources critically by situating them in larger contexts and to attempt to assess their own places in the history of *Ulysses* criticism.[4]

Let us turn to an example of an essay from the first assignment. While researching the social and political roles of Irish women at the turn of the century, a group of students "discovered" a concrete illustration of one of the theoretical premises of the course: that the past is repeatedly reconstructed from the perspective of the present. In reading over various histories of Ireland, the students observed that many fairly traditional histories, particularly older ones, did not discuss the cultural positions of women at all. Had the students read these books before being introduced to discourses that can enable the historicizing of textual production and reception, they might simply have dismissed them as having nothing to say about their topic. They now, however, began to read these histories "symptomatically," and asked whether their silence said as much – if not more – about women's status *at the time the books were written* as it did about women's status at the turn of the century. Students, of course, also had to acknowledge that their own seemingly "natural" interest in women's social roles derived in large part from their particular place in history in which feminism has legitimized such concerns and brought them, to some extent, into the popular consciousness.

The students discovered that a number of more recent histories not only assume that women's roles in society are important to investigate, but also contend that women played more active roles in turn-of-the-century Dublin than they have often been credited with (see, for example, Murphy). The students thus focussed their paper on examples of historical difference – not only between their contemporary positions as women and those of Irish women at the turn of the century (as I had anticipated), but also between older and more recent historical accounts of Irish women.

While such differences in the representation of women arise from changing, historically explicable questions, actually confronting these differences among various histories was a jarring experience for the students writing the paper; the most pressing implication for them was that contemporary representations of women – and men – were conflicting and "unreliable." They thus ended their paper by asking the class to consider some of the ways in which women and men are represented in contemporary culture, to explore some of the contradictions in those representations, and to try to imagine some of their effects. They took the class in a direction I had not anticipated, but which ultimately led to significant insights about the culturally inscribed nature of gender, as well as to some concrete analysis of the conflicting representations of women in turn-of-the-century Dublin. We found that we returned to this discussion when we read the "Penelope" chapter, not only to help us consider why Molly Bloom is depicted as she is – in bed, menstruating, frequently misinformed, etc. – but also to enable us to begin to analyze and historically situate the contradictory ways in which Molly has been interpreted by critics.

This paper, therefore, was successful pedagogically as well as theoretically. The students not only began to find examples in various Irish histories of the theoretical premises they had been studying, but they also took control of their knowledge in a way they could not when they were simply reading and trying to understand the theorists. While theory is crucial to establish a framework for their reading and research, it is only when students are asked to put that theory into practice and to share the responsibilities for teaching and learning that they are able to shift their roles from passive learners to active producers of knowledge.

While all "production" papers are not as insightful as this one, they almost always bring some new knowledge into the class, which the students generally feel freer to discuss, question, and supplement because it is presented by other students rather than the teacher. Further, on a number of occasions, the students will have read books or articles with which I am unfamiliar, so that when I pose questions to them, it is often from the perspective of a learner. As the course develops and more students undertake projects and gain expertise in particular areas, it becomes possible to establish a learning situation in which, as Freire writes, "the teacher is no longer merely the-one-who-teaches, but one who is himself [sic] taught in dialogue with the students, who in turn while being taught also teach" (67).

The "production" essay I chose to discuss not only followed the assignment, but also clearly illustrated some of the theoretical premises of the course. I want now to look at a "reception" essay that inhabited the classroom situation more dialectically. A student writing on "Nausicaa" contended that the "text itself" is inherently feminist in impulse because, in giving Gerty MacDowell the sentimental "feminine" language of pulp fiction and women's magazines, Joyce was "obviously" satirizing the society that constructed female subjectivity in such a manner. In asserting this opinion, the student briefly reviewed, but quickly dismissed, most of what critics writing before 1980 had to say about the chapter. Two basic responses occurred in class to the student's argument. The first, and by far the stronger, suggested that by merging her position with the text's, the student failed to account both for the historical difference between her reading and past readings of the chapter and for the critical and political significances of her position within the current reading formation, thus undercutting the radical potential of her own argument. The second response, which was less clearly articulated, but which helped us to restore a more dialectical attitude towards reading, suggested that while the student did not in fact historicize her position (and hence did not quite "fulfill the assignment"), she clearly did attempt to make the text address her historical condition, and the strategies that she employed – feminist critique combined with the language of objectivity – made her argument both powerful and convincing, particularly given her institutional position as a student and the dominant style of writing she encountered in the criticism.

Let us look at each of these responses in more detail. The first response was sparked by a relatively simple question by one student which reminded us of the need to histori-cize one's response to a text: "How can someone say that the chapter is 'really a feminist text' if nobody thought it was until recently?" Once this question was raised, the class asked the student to review the history of the chapter's reception, and to talk about the political climate in which Joyce wrote *Ulysses* – which she was quite capable of doing. The student's research on the reception of the chapter, supplemented by various com-ments from me, indicated that early readers indeed had seen nothing inherently feminist about it nor did they conceive of problematizing Gerty's discourse conventions. While most critics generally recognized the parallels of style between the first half of "Nausicaa" and Maria Cummings' popular novel, *The Lamplighter*, there was little attempt until the last decade to distance an analysis of Gerty from an analysis of this style. Thus Richard Kain speaks of Gerty's "cheap sentimentality" (44). Stanley Sultan contends that Gerty is a parody of all "the mass of people blighted by self-deluding sentimentality" (273) – readers, characters, and authors alike. Robert Adams finds the "perhaps overextended parody" of "Nausicaa" to be directed primarily at "Lady novelists" (224). It is only the more recent feminist critics such as Suzette Henke or Bonnie Kime Scott who attempt to explore the complex relationship between Gerty's language and the society that constructed her (Henke, *Moraculous* 153–72; Scott, *James Joyce* 62–67). In tracing and discussing this history, the class reconfirmed a number of the theoretical tenets of the course: that it is not enough to ask whether a reading is "correct" with reference to the text (since all of these critics were presumably expert readers of *Ulysses*); that one must attempt to ask what relationship these readings have to their particular reading formations; that when constructing one's own interpretation, one must explore the tensions and dynamics of one's own social formation to ask what interpretations seem not only possible, but responsible to take up.

It was perhaps at this point in the discussion that an alternative response to the student's paper began to take shape. For while the student did not analyze the history of the reception of the chapter in any detail, her position was clearly informed by that history and was written in opposition to it. Further, the student's basic argument not only seemed "responsible" to take up, but it also addressed her historical condition and spoke to that of a number of other women in the class as well. Her strategy of making the text address, indeed, "be about," her own position as a gendered subject was a powerful way for her to assert and legitimize her historicity. Given most of the criticism the students had read, and most of the training they had received in school, attributing meanings or intentions to "the text itself" was – despite the work we had done in this course on production and reception – the interpretive strategy historically most available to them, and institutionally, the one that is still accorded the most status. Finally, although I think I would be reading too much into her essay to say that in embracing the legitimizing force of "the text itself," the student's essay constituted an intentional act of resistance to the dominant theoretical discourse developed in this course, her essay nonetheless helped us to recognize the potential of any theory – even a supposedly dialectical theory of production and reception – to normalize responses, and paradoxically, to inhibit our thinking historically and dialogically.

My discussion here is certainly more abstract than what occurred in the classroom, but that my students were able to raise such issues about the "Nausicaa" chapter suggests that when allowed to take up the role of teacher as well as learner, and when given some theoretical tools for critical and historical investigation, students are enabled to engage intellectually and emotionally with *Ulysses*, to pose their own questions to it in dialogic relation to those of the past, and most importantly, to develop interpretations of it that make it address their historical condition. The tensions the group felt in response to the student's paper on "Nausicaa" provide just one example of the ways in which a genuine dialogic relationship among a group can lead to the development of dialectical thinking, which, as Masterman writes, "recognises the internal contradictions and tensions which exist within the group and within each individual, and which understands that such contradictions are inherent in all situations and issues which the group explores" (33). When undertaken from the theoretical orientation of production and reception, such a dialogic relationship provides a site wherein students can problematize their own and each other's readings of all cultural objects – including literary texts as difficult as *Ulysses* – in ways that allow them to confront the dialogic nature of reading and history and their own status as subjects in history – and very specifically as subjects in the institutional setting of a classroom.

Notes

1   The argument will be developed in more detail in my *Reading: Cognition, Institutions, Ideology* (Manchester: Manchester UP, in progress).

2   For ways of analyzing the material conditions underlying the *production* of a text, I find it useful to have students read chapters 2, 3, and 5 from Eagleton's *Criticism and Ideology*, and Macherey's *A Theory of Literary Production* (particularly pages 69–101), which develops a theory of reading literary texts to make them reveal the larger ideological forces silently underlying them. For studies of the history of the reception of literary texts, we read Jauss's "Literary History as a Challenge to Literary Theory" and Bennett's "Texts in History." Finally, we read Morley's "Texts, Readers, Subjects" for a discussion of the role of the reader as a subject in history. The teacher could select different texts for this introductory unit depending on the level of the course and the familiarity of the students with theory. Kathleen McCormick and Gary Waller's *Reading Texts* (Chapter 2) provides an introductory level discussion of many of these concepts. Robert Holub's *Reception Theory: A Critical Introduction* contains a useful and readable summary and analysis of reception theory, including a substantive discussion of Jauss's early work (53–82). Bennett's *Marxism and Formalism*, particularly chapters 5 through 8, provides a clear overview of Marxist theories of production as well as the beginnings of a Marxist theory of reception.

3   See, for example, interpolation 18 (12.897–938), a mock newspaper account of a meeting on the revival of ancient Gaelic sports in which the manner of delivery of a speech by Joe Hynes – "the usual high standard of excellence" (12.903–05) – is discussed in more detail than its substance.

4   Although students do other writing in the course – notes on the theoretical essays, a journal on their reading of *Ulysses*, and a final paper – I focus my discussion here on the short essays because they direct our reading of *Ulysses*.

Works Cited

Adams, Robert. *James Joyce: Common Sense and Beyond*. New York: Random House, 1966.

Adams, Robert. *Surface and Symbol: The Consistency of James Joyce's* Ulysses. Oxford: Oxford UP, 1962.

Attridge, Derek. "Molly's Flow: The Writing of 'Penelope' and the Question of Women's Language." *Modern Fiction Studies* 35 (1989): 543–65.

Bennett, Tony. *Formalism and Marxism*. London: Methuen, 1979.

Bennett, Tony. "Texts in History: The Determinations of Readings and Their Texts." *Journal of the Midwest Modern Language Association*, 18.1 (1983): 1–16.

Bennett, Tony, and Janet Woollacott. *Bond and Beyond: The Political Career of a Popular Hero*. London: Macmillan, 1988.

Blackmur, R. P. "The Jew in Search of a Son." *The Virginia Quarterly Review* 24 (1948): 96–116.

Bleich, David. *Subjective Criticism*. Baltimore: Johns Hopkins UP, 1978.

Budgen, Frank. *James Joyce and the Making of* Ulysses. 1934. Bloomington: Indiana UP, 1960.

Devlin, Kimberly. "Pretending in 'Penelope': Masquerade, Mimicry, and Molly Bloom." *Molly Blooms: A Polylogue on "Penelope" and Cultural Studies*. Ed. Richard Pearce. Madison: U of Wisconsin P, forthcoming 1993.

Eagleton, Terry. *Criticism and Ideology*. London: New Left, 1976.

Freire, Paulo. *Pedagogy of the Oppressed*. New York: Continuum, 1989.

Gilbert, Stuart. *James Joyce's* Ulysses: *A Study*. New York: Knopf, 1952.

Giroux, Henry. *Schooling and the Struggle for Public Life: Critical Pedagogy in the Modern Age*. Minneapolis: U of Minnesota P, 1988.

Giroux, Henry, and Roger I. Simon, et al., eds. *Popular Culture: Schooling and Everyday Life*. Granby, MA: Bergin & Garvey, 1989.

Hall, Stuart. "Encoding/Decoding." Hall, et al. 128–38.

Hall, Stuart, et al. *Culture, Media, Language*. Boston: Unwin Hyman, 1980.

Henke, Suzette. *James Joyce and the Politics of Desire*. New York: Routledge, 1990.

Henke, Suzette. *Joyce's Moraculous Sindbook: A Study of* Ulysses. Columbus: Ohio SUP, 1978.

Hobson, Dorothy. *Crossroads: The Drama of a Soap Opera*. London: Methuen, 1982.

Hobson, Dorothy. "Housewives and the Mass Media." Hall, et al. 105–14.

Holub, Robert C. *Reception Theory: A Critical Introduction*. London: Methuen, 1984.

Irigaray, Luce. "This Sex Which is Not One." *This Sex Which is Not One*. Trans. Catherine Porter. Ithaca: Cornell UP, 1985: 205–18.

Jameson, Fredric. *The Political Unconscious*. Ithaca: Cornell UP, 1981.

Jauss, Hans Robert. "Literary History as a Challenge to Literary Theory." *Toward an Aesthetic of Reception*. Minneapolis: U of Minnesota P, 1982: 3–45.

Joyce, James. *Ulysses*. Ed. Hans Walter Gabler, et al. New York: Vintage, 1986.

Kain, Richard M. *Fabulous Voyager*. New York: Viking, 1959.

Kenner, Hugh. *Dublin's Joyce*. Bloomington: Indiana UP, 1956.

Levin, Harry. *James Joyce*. Norfolk, CT: New Directions, 1941.

Levitt, Annette Shandler. "The Pattern Out of the Wallpaper: Luce Irigaray and Molly Bloom." *Modern Fiction Studies* 35 (1989): 507–16.

MacCabe, Colin. "Realism and Cinema: Notes on Brechtian Theses." Tony Bennett, et al., eds. *Popular Television and Film*. London: British Film Institute/Open University, 1981: 216–35.

Macherey, Pierre. *A Theory of Literary Production*. Trans. Geoffrey Wall. Boston: Routledge and Kegan Paul, 1978.

Masterman, Len. *Teaching the Media*. New York: Routledge, 1985.

McCormick, Kathleen, and Gary Waller, with Linda Flower. *Reading Texts*. Lexington: D. C. Heath, 1987.

Morley, David. *Family Television: Cultural Power and Domestic Leisure*. New York: Routledge, 1986.

Morley, David. *The "Nationwide" Audience*. London: British Film Institute, 1980.

Morley, David. "Texts, Readers, Subjects." Hall, et al. 163–73.

Morse, J. Mitchell. "Molly Bloom Revisited." *A James Joyce Miscellany*. Ed. Marvin Magalaner. Carbondale: Southern Illinois UP, 1959. 139–49.

Murphy, Cliona. *The Women's Suffrage Movement and Irish Society in the Early Twentieth Century*. Philadelphia: Temple UP, 1989.

O'Brien, Darcy. *The Conscience of James Joyce*. Princeton: Princeton UP, 1968.

Pribram, Deidre, ed. *Female Spectators: Looking at Film and Television*. New York: Verso, 1988.

Scott, Bonnie Kime. *James Joyce*. Atlantic Highlands, N.J.: Humanities P International, 1987.

Scott, Bonnie Kime. *Joyce and Feminism*. Bloomington: Indiana UP, 1984.

Shloss, Carol. "Molly's Resistance to the Union: Marriage and Colonialism in Dublin, 1904." *Modern Fiction Studies* 35 (1989): 529–41.

Sultan, Stanley. *The Argument of* Ulysses. Columbus: Ohio SUP, 1964.

Tindall, William Y. *A Reader's Guide to James Joyce*. New York: Noonday, 1959.

Unkeless, Elaine. "The Conventional Molly Bloom." *Women in Joyce*. Ed. Suzette Henke and Elaine Unkeless. Urbana: U of Illinois P, 1982.

Willemen, Paul. "Notes on Subjectivity: On Reading Edward Branigan's 'Subjectivity under Siege.'" *Screen* 19 (1978): 41–69.

Williams, Raymond. *Marxism and Literature*. London: Oxford UP, 1980.

Willinsky, John. *The New Literacy: Redefining Reading and Writing in the Schools*. New York: Routledge, 1990.

CHAPTER 5

Distinction

Pierre Bourdieu

In this selection from *Distinction* (1979), French sociologist Pierre Bourdieu argues that all taste in literature is an effect of prior determinants. One's class position, one's training in culture, one's education – all of these factors classify us as readers and sort us into groups who favor one kind of literature over another.

Classes and Classifications

If I have to choose the lesser of two evils, I choose neither.

Karl Kraus

Taste is an acquired disposition to 'differentiate' and 'appreciate',[1] as Kant says – in other words, to establish and mark differences by a process of distinction which is not (or not necessarily) a distinct knowledge, in Leibniz's sense, since it ensures recognition (in the ordinary sense) of the object without implying knowledge of the distinctive features which define it.[2] The schemes of the habitus, the primary forms of classification, owe their specific efficacy to the fact that they function below the level of consciousness and language, beyond the reach of introspective scrutiny or control by the will. Orienting practices practically, they embed what some would mistakenly call *values* in the most automatic gestures or the apparently most insignificant techniques of the body – ways of walking or blowing one's nose, ways of eating or talking – and engage the most fundamental principles of construction and evaluation of the social world, those which most directly express the division of labour (between the classes, the age groups and the sexes) or the division of the work of domination, in divisions between bodies and between relations to the body which borrow more features than one, as if to give them the appearances of naturalness, from the sexual division of labour and the division of sexual labour. Taste is a practical mastery of distributions which makes it possible to

Original publication details: Pierre Bourdieu, extracts from *Distinction: A Social Critique of the Judgement of Taste*, trans. Richard Nice, pp. 466–84, 596–97. Harvard University Press, 1984. Copyright © 1984 by the President and Fellows of Harvard College and Routledge & Kegan Paul, Ltd. Reprinted by permission of Harvard University Press and Taylor & Francis Books Ltd.

Literary Theory: An Anthology, Third Edition. Edited by Julie Rivkin and Michael Ryan.
© 2017 John Wiley & Sons, Ltd. Published 2017 by John Wiley & Sons, Ltd.

sense or intuit what is likely (or unlikely) to befall – and therefore to befit – an individual occupying a given position in social space. It functions as a sort of social orientation, a 'sense of one's place', guiding the occupants of a given place in social space towards the social positions adjusted to their properties, and towards the practices or goods which befit the occupants of that position. It implies a practical anticipation of what the social meaning and value of the chosen practice or thing will probably be, given their distribution in social space and the practical knowledge the other agents have of the correspondence between goods and groups.

Thus, the social agents whom the sociologist classifies are producers not only of classifiable acts but also of acts of classification which are themselves classified. Knowledge of the social world has to take into account a practical knowledge of this world which pre-exists it and which it must not fail to include in its object, although, as a first stage, this knowledge has to be constituted *against* the partial and interested representations provided by practical knowledge. To speak of habitus is to include in the object the knowledge which the agents, who are part of the object, have of the object, and the contribution this knowledge makes to the reality of the object. But it is not only a matter of putting back into the real world that one is endeavouring to know, a knowledge of the real world that contributes to its reality (and also to the force it exerts). It means conferring on this knowledge a genuinely constitutive power, the very power it is denied when, in the name of an objectivist conception of objectivity, one makes common knowledge or theoretical knowledge a mere reflection of the real world.

Those who suppose they are producing a materialist theory of knowledge when they make knowledge a passive recording and abandon the 'active aspect' of knowledge to idealism, as Marx complains in the *Theses on Feuerbach*, forget that all knowledge, and in particular all knowledge of the social world, is an act of construction implementing schemes of thought and expression, and that between conditions of existence and practices or representations there intervenes the structuring activity of the agents, who, far from reacting mechanically to mechanical stimulations, respond to the invitations or threats of a world whose meaning they have helped to produce. However, the principle of this structuring activity is not, as an intellectualist and anti-genetic idealism would have it, a system of universal forms and categories but a system of internalized, embodied schemes which, having been constituted in the course of collective history, are acquired in the course of individual history and function in their *practical* state, *for practice* (and not for the sake of pure knowledge).

Embodied Social Structures

This means, in the first place, that social science, in constructing the social world, takes note of the fact that agents are, in their ordinary practice, the subjects of acts of con-struction of the social world; but also that it aims, among other things, to describe the social genesis of the principles of construction and seeks the basis of these principles in the social world.[3] Breaking with the anti-genetic prejudice which often accompanies recognition of the active aspect of knowledge, it seeks in the objective distributions of properties, especially material ones (brought to light by censuses and surveys which all presuppose selection and classification), the basis of the systems of classification which agents apply to every sort of thing, not least to the distributions themselves. In contrast to what is sometimes called the 'cognitive' approach, which, both in its ethnological form (structural anthropology, ethnoscience, ethnosemantics, ethnobotany etc.) and in its sociological form (interactionism, ethnomethodology etc.), ignores the question of the genesis of mental structures and classifications, social science enquires into the relationship between the principles of division and the social divisions (between the generations, the sexes etc.) on which they are based, and into the variations of the use made of these principles according to the position occupied in the distributions (questions which all require the use of statistics).

The cognitive structures which social agents implement in their practical knowledge of the social world are internalized, 'embodied' social structures. The practical knowledge of the social world that is presupposed by 'reasonable' behaviour within it implements classificatory schemes (or 'forms of classification', 'mental structures' or 'symbolic forms' – apart from their connotations, these expressions are virtually interchangeable), historical schemes of perception and appreciation which are the product of the objective division into classes (age groups, genders, social classes) and which function below the level of consciousness and discourse. Being the product of the incorporation of the fundamental structures of a society, these principles of division are common to all the agents of the society and make possible the production of a common, meaningful world, a common-sense world.

All the agents in a given social formation share a set of basic perceptual schemes, which receive the beginnings of objectification in the pairs of antagonistic adjectives commonly used to classify and qualify persons or objects in the most varied areas of practice. The network of oppositions between high (sublime, elevated, pure) and low (vulgar, low, modest), spiritual and material, fine (refined, elegant) and coarse (heavy, fat, crude, brutal), light (subtle, lively, sharp, adroit) and heavy (slow, thick, blunt, laborious, clumsy), free and forced, broad and narrow, or, in another dimension, between unique (rare, different, distinguished, exclusive, exceptional, singular, novel) and common (ordinary, banal, commonplace, trivial, routine), brilliant (intelligent) and dull (obscure, grey, mediocre), is the matrix of all the commonplaces which find such ready acceptance because behind them lies the whole social order. The network has its ultimate source in the opposition between the 'élite' of the dominant and the 'mass' of the dominated, a contingent, disorganized multiplicity, interchangeable and innumerable, existing only statistically. These mythic roots only have to be allowed to take their course in order to generate, at will, one or another of the tirelessly repeated themes of the eternal sociodicy, such as apocalyptic denunciations of all forms of 'levelling', 'trivialization' or 'massification', which identify the decline of societies with the decadence of bourgeois houses, i.e., a fall into the homogeneous, the undifferentiated, and betray an obsessive fear of number, of undifferentiated hordes indifferent to difference and constantly threatening to submerge the private spaces of bourgeois exclusiveness.[4]

The seemingly most formal oppositions within this social mythology always derive their ideological strength from the fact that they refer back, more or less discreetly, to the most fundamental oppositions within the social order: the opposition between the dominant and the dominated, which is inscribed in the division of labour, and the opposition, rooted in the division of the labour of domination, between two principles of domination, two powers, dominant and dominated, temporal and spiritual, material and intellectual etc. It follows that the map of social space previously put forward can also be read as a strict table of the historically constituted and acquired categories which organize the idea of the social world in the minds of all the subjects belonging to that world and shaped by it. The same classificatory schemes (and the oppositions in which they are expressed) can function, by being specified, in fields organized around polar positions, whether in the field of the dominant class, organized around an opposition homologous to the opposition constituting the field of the social classes, or in the field of cultural production, which is itself organized around oppositions which reproduce the structure of the dominant class and are homologous to it (e.g., the opposition between bourgeois and avant-garde theatre). So the fundamental opposition constantly supports second, third or nth rank oppositions (those which underlie the 'purest' ethical or aesthetic judgements, with their high or low sentiments, their facile or difficult notions of beauty, their light or heavy styles etc.), while euphemizing itself to the point of misrecognizability.

Thus, the opposition between the heavy and the light, which, in a number of its uses, especially scholastic ones, serves to distinguish popular or petit-bourgeois tastes from bourgeois tastes, can be used by theatre criticism aimed at the dominant fraction of the dominant class to express the relationship between 'intellectual' theatre, which is condemned for its 'laborious' pretensions and 'oppressive' didacticism, and 'bourgeois' theatre, which is praised for its tact and its art of skimming over surfaces. By contrast, 'intellectual' criticism, by a simple inversion of values, expresses the relationship in a scarcely modified form of the same opposition, with lightness, identified with frivolity, being opposed to profundity. Similarly, it can be shown that the opposition between right and left, which, in its basic form, concerns the relationship between the dominant and the dominated, can also, by means of a first transformation, designate the relations between dominated fractions and dominant fractions within the dominant class; the words right and left then take on a meaning close to the meaning they have in expressions like 'right-bank' theatre or 'left-bank' theatre. With a further degree of 'de-realization', it can even serve to distinguish two rival tendencies within an avant-garde artistic or literary group, and so on.

It follows that, when considered in each of their uses, the pairs of qualifiers, the system of which constitutes the conceptual equipment of the judgement of taste, are extremely poor, almost indefinite, but, precisely for this reason, capable of eliciting or expressing the sense of the indefinable. Each particular use of one of these pairs only takes on its full meaning in relation to a universe of discourse that is different each time and usually implicit – since it is a question of the system of self-evidences and presuppositions that are taken for granted in the field in relation to which the speakers' strategies are defined. But each of the couples specified by usage has for undertones all the other uses it might have – because of the homologies between the fields which allow transfers from one field to another – and also all the other couples which are interchangeable with it, within a nuance or two (e.g., fine/crude for light/heavy), that is, in slightly different contexts.

The fact that the semi-codified oppositions contained in ordinary language reappear, with very similar values, as the basis of the dominant vision of the social world, in all class-divided social formations (consider the tendency to see the 'people' as the site of totally uncontrolled appetites and sexuality) can be understood once one knows that, reduced to their formal structure, the same fundamental relationships, precisely those which express the major relations of order (high/low, strong/weak etc.) reappear in all class-divided societies. And the recurrence of the triadic structure studied by Georges Dumézil, which Georges Duby shows in the case of feudal society to be rooted in the social structures it legitimates, may well be, like the invariant oppositions in which the relationship of domination is expressed, simply a necessary outcome of the intersection of the two principles of division which are at work in all class-divided societies – the division between the dominant and the dominated, and the division between the different fractions competing for dominance in the name of different principles, *bellatores* (warriors) and *oratores* (scholars) in feudal society, businessmen and intellectuals now.[5]

Knowledge without Concepts

Thus, through the differentiated and differentiating conditionings associated with the different conditions of existence, through the exclusions and inclusions, unions (marriages, affairs, alliances etc.) and divisions (incompatibilities, separations, struggles etc.) which govern the social structure and the structuring force it exerts, through all the hierarchies and classifications inscribed in objects (especially cultural products), in institutions (for example, the educational system) or simply in language, and through all the judgements, verdicts, gradings and warnings imposed by the institutions specially designed for this purpose, such as the family or the educational system, or constantly arising from the meetings and interactions of everyday life, the social order is progressively inscribed in people's minds. Social divisions become principles of division, organizing the image of the social world. Objective limits become a sense of limits, a practical anticipation of objective limits acquired by experience of objective limits, a 'sense of one's place' which leads one to exclude oneself from the goods, persons, places and so forth from which one is excluded.

The *sense* of limits implies *forgetting* the limits. One of the most important effects of the correspondence between real divisions and practical principles of division, between social structures and mental structures, is undoubtedly the fact that primary experience of the social world is that of doxa, an adherence to relations of order which, because they structure inseparably both the real world and the thought world, are accepted as self-evident. Primary perception of the social world, far from being a simple mechanical reflection, is always an act of cognition involving principles of construction that are external to the constructed object grasped in its immediacy; but at the same time it is an act of miscognition, implying the most absolute form of recognition of the social order. Dominated agents, who assess the value of their position and their characteristics by applying a system of schemes of perception and appreciation which is the embodiment of the objective laws whereby their value is objectively constituted, tend to attribute to themselves what the distribution attributes to them, refusing what they are refused ('That's not for the likes of us'), adjusting their expectations to their chances, defining themselves as the established order defines them, reproducing in their verdict on themselves the verdict the economy pronounces on them, in a word, condemning themselves to what is in any case their lot, *ta beautou*, as Plato put it, consenting to be what they have to be, 'modest', 'humble' and 'obscure'. Thus the conservation of the social order is decisively reinforced by what Durkheim called 'logical conformity',[6] i.e., the orchestration of categories of perception of the social world, which, being adjusted to the divisions of the established order (and thereby to the interests of those who dominate it) and common to all minds structured in accordance with those structures, present every appearance of objective necessity.[7]

The system of classificatory schemes is opposed to a taxonomy based on explicit and explicitly concerted principles in the same way that the dispositions constituting taste or ethos (which are dimensions of it) are opposed to aesthetics or ethics. The sense of social realities that is acquired in the confrontation with a particular form of social necessity is what makes it possible to act *as if* one knew the structure of the social world, one's place within it and the distances that need to be kept.

> The ideology of the utopian thinker, rootless and unattached, 'free-floating', without interests or profits, together with the correlative refusal of that supreme form of materialistic vulgarity, the reduction of the unique to the class, the explanation of the higher by the lower, the application to the would-be unclassifiable of explanatory models fit only for the 'bourgeois', the petit-bourgeois, the limited and common, scarcely inclines intellectuals to conceptualize the sense of social position, still less their own position and the perverse relation to the social world it forces on them. (The perfect example is Sartre, whose whole work and whole existence revolve around this affirmation of the intellectual's subversive point of honour. This is seen particularly clearly in the passage in *Being and Nothingness* on the psychology of Flaubert, which can be read as a desperate effort to save the person, in the person of the intellectual, an uncreated creator, begotten by his own works, haunted by 'the project of being God', from every sort of reduction to the general, the type, the class, and to affirm the transcendence of the ego against 'what Comte called *materialism*, that is, explaining the higher by the lower.')[8]

The practical mastery of classification has nothing in common with the reflexive mastery that is required in order to construct a taxonomy that is simultaneously coherent and adequate to social reality. The practical 'science' of positions in social space is the competence presupposed by the art of behaving *comme il faut* with persons and things that have and give 'class' ('smart' or 'unsmart'), finding the right distance, by a sort of practical calculation, neither too close ('getting familiar') nor too far ('being distant'), playing with objective distance by emphasizing it (being 'aloof', 'stand-offish') or symbolically denying it (being 'approachable', 'hobnobbing'). It in no way implies the capacity to situate oneself explicitly in the classification (as so many surveys on social class ask people to do), still less to describe this classification in any systematic way and state its principles.

> There is no better opportunity to observe the functioning of this sense of the place one occupies than in condescension strategies, which presuppose both in the author of the strategy and in the victims a practical knowledge of the gap between the place really occupied and the place fictitiously indicated by the behaviour adopted (e.g., in French, use of the familiar *tu*). When the person 'naturally' identified with a Rolls Royce, a top hat or golf (see appendix 4) takes the metro, sports a flat cap (or a polo neck) or plays football, his practices take on their meaning in relation to this attribution by status, which continues to colour the real practices, as if by superimposition. But one could also point to the variations that Charles Bally observed in the style of speech according to the social gap between the interlocutors, or the variations in pronunciation according to the addressee: the speaker may, as appropriate, move closer to the 'accent' of an addressee of (presumed) higher status or move away from it by 'accentuating' his ordinary accent.[9]

The practical 'attributive judgement' whereby one puts someone in a class by speaking to him in a certain way (thereby putting oneself in a class at the same time) has nothing to do with an intellectual operation implying conscious reference to explicit indices and the implementation of classes produced by and for the concept. The same classificatory opposition (rich/poor, young/old etc.) can be applied at any point in the distribution and reproduce its whole range within any of its segments (common sense tells us that one is always richer or poorer than someone, superior or inferior to someone, more right-wing or left-wing than someone – but this does not entail an elementary relativism).

In a series of interviews (n = 30) on the social classes, based on a test which involved classifying thirty occupations (written on cards), the respondents often first asked how many classes the set should be divided into, and then several times modified the number of classes and the criteria of classification, so as to take account of the different dimensions of each occupation and therefore the different respects in which it could be evaluated; or they spontaneously suggested that they could carry on sub-dividing indefinitely. (They thereby exposed the artificiality of the situation created by a theoretical inquiry which called for the adoption of a theoretical attitude to which, as their initial uncertainty indicated, the respondents were quite unaccustomed.) And yet they almost always agreed on the ranks of the different occupations when taken two by two. (Lenski made similar observations in an experiment in which the respondents were asked to rank the families in a small town in New England.)[10]

It is not surprising that it is possible to fault the practical sense of social space which lies behind class-attributive judgement; the sociologists who use their respondents' self-contradictions as an argument for denying the existence of classes simply reveal that they understand nothing of how this 'sense' works or of the artificial situation in which they are making it work. In fact, whether it is used to situate oneself in social space or to place others, the sense of social space, like every practical sense, always refers to the particular situation in which it has to orient practices. This explains, for example, the divergences between surveys of the representation of the classes in a small town ('community studies') and surveys of class on a nationwide scale.[11] But if, as has often been observed, respondents do not agree either on the number of divisions they make within the group in question, or on the limits of the 'strata' and the criteria used to define them, this is not simply due to the fuzziness inherent in all practical logics. It is also because people's image of the classification is a function of their position within it.

So nothing is further removed from an act of cognition, as conceived by the intellectualist tradition, than this sense of the social structure, which, as is so well put by the word *taste* – simultaneously 'the faculty of perceiving flavours' and 'the capacity to discern aesthetic values' – is social necessity made second nature, turned into muscular patterns and bodily automatisms. Everything takes place as if the social conditionings linked to a social condition tended to inscribe the relation to the social world in a lasting, generalized relation to one's own body, a way of bearing one's body, presenting it to others, moving it, making space for it, which gives the body its social physiognomy. Bodily hexis, a basic dimension of the sense of social orientation, is a practical way of experiencing and expressing one's own sense of social value. One's relationship to the social world and to one's proper place in it is never more clearly expressed than in the space and time one feels entitled to take from others; more precisely, in the space one claims with one's body in physical space, through a bearing and gestures that are self-assured or reserved, expansive or constricted ('presence' or 'insignificance') and with one's speech in time, through the interaction time one appropriates and the self-assured or aggressive, careless or unconscious way one appropriates it.[12]

There is no better image of the logic of socialization, which treats the body as a 'memory-jogger', than those complexes of gestures, postures and words – simple inter-jections or favourite clichés – which only have to be slipped into, like a theatrical costume, to awaken, by the evocative power of bodily mimesis, a universe of ready-made feelings and experiences. The elementary actions of bodily gymnastics, especially the specifically sexual, biologically pre-constructed aspect of it, charged with social meanings and values, function as the most basic of metaphors, capable of evoking a whole relationship to the world, 'lofty' or 'submissive', 'expansive' or 'narrow', and through it a whole world. The practical 'choices' of the sense of social orientation no more presuppose a representation of the range of possibilities than does the choice of phonemes; these enacted choices imply no acts of choosing. The logocentrism and intellectualism of intellectuals, com-bined with the prejudice inherent in the science which takes as its object the psyche, the soul, the mind, consciousness, representations, not to mention the petit-bourgeois pretension to the status of 'person', have prevented us from seeing that, as Leibniz put it, 'we are automatons in three-quarters of what we do', and that the ultimate values, as they are called, are never anything other than the primary, primitive dispositions of the body, 'visceral' tastes and distastes, in which the group's most vital interests are embedded, the things on which one is prepared to stake one's own and other people's bodies. The sense of distinction, the *discretio* (discrimination) which demands that certain things be brought together and others kept apart, which excludes all misalliances and all unnatural unions – i.e., all unions contrary to the common classification, to the *diacrisis* (separation) which is the basis of collective and individual identity – responds with visceral, murder-ous horror, absolute disgust, metaphysical fury, to everything which lies in Plato's 'hybrid zone', everything which passes understanding, that is, the embodied taxonomy, which, by challenging the principles of the incarnate social order, especially the socially constituted principles of the sexual division of labour and the division of sexual labour, violates the mental order, scandalously flouting common sense.

It can be shown that socialization tends to constitute the body as an analogical operator establishing all sorts of practical equivalences between the different divisions of the social world – divisions between the sexes, between the age groups and between the social classes – or, more precisely, between the meanings and values associated with the individuals occupying practically equivalent positions in the spaces defined by these divisions. And it can be shown that it does so by inte-grating the symbolism of social domination and submission and the symbolism of sexual domination and submission into the same body language – as is seen in etiquette, which uses the opposition between the straight and the curved or, which amounts to the same thing, between raising (oneself) and lowering (oneself), as one of the generative principles of the marks (of respect, contempt etc.) used to symbolize hierarchical relations.

Advantageous Attributions

The basis of the pertinence principle which is implemented in perceiving the social world and which defines all the characteristics of persons or things which can be perceived, and perceived as positively or negatively interesting, by all those who apply these schemes (another definition of common sense), is based on nothing other than the interest the individuals or groups in question have in recognizing a feature and in identifying the individual in question as a member of the set defined by that feature; interest in the aspect observed is never completely independent of the advantage of observing it. This can be clearly seen in all the classifications built around a stigmatized feature which, like the everyday opposition between homosexuals and heterosexuals, isolate the interesting trait from all the rest (i.e., all other forms of sexuality), which remain indifferent and undifferentiated. It is even clearer in all 'labelling judgements', which are in fact accusations, *categoremes* in the original Aristotelian sense, and which, like insults, only wish to know one of the properties constituting the social identity of an individual or group ('You're just a …'), regarding, for example, the married homosexual or converted Jew as a 'closet queen' or covert Jew, and thereby in a sense doubly Jewish or homosexual. The logic of the stigma reminds us that social identity is the stake in a struggle in which the stigmatized individual or group, and, more generally, any individual or group insofar as he or it is a potential object of categorization, can only retaliate against the partial perception which limits it to one of its characteristics by highlighting, in its self-definition, the best of its characteristics, and, more generally, by struggling to impose the taxonomy most favourable to its characteristics, or at least to give to the dominant taxonomy the content most flattering to what it has and what it is.

Those who are surprised by the paradoxes that ordinary logic and language engender when they apply their divisions to continuous magnitudes forget the paradoxes inherent in treating language as a purely logical instrument and also forget the social situation in which such a relationship to language is possible. The contradictions or paradoxes to which ordinary language classifications lead do not derive, as all forms of positivism suppose, from some essential inadequacy of ordinary language, but from the fact that these socio-logical acts are not directed towards the pursuit of logical coherence and that, unlike philological, logical or linguistic uses of language – which ought really to be called scholastic, since they all presuppose *schole*, i.e., leisure, distance from urgency and necessity, the absence of vital stakes, and the scholastic institution which in most social universes is the only institution capable of providing all these – they obey the logic of the parti pris, which, as in a court-room, juxtaposes not logical judgements, subject to the sole criterion of coherence, but charges and defences. Quite apart from all that is implied in the oppositions, which logicians and even linguists manage to forget, between the art of convincing and the art of persuading, it is clear that scholastic usage of language is to the orator's, advocate's or politician's usage what the classificatory systems devised by the logician or statistician concerned with coherence and empirical adequacy are to the categorizations and categoremes of daily life. As the etymology suggests, the latter belong to the logic of the trial.[13] Every real inquiry into the divisions of the social world has to analyse the interests associated with membership or non-membership. As is shown by the attention devoted to strategic, 'frontier' groups such as the 'labour aristocracy', which hesitates between class struggle and class collaboration, or the 'cadres', a category of bureaucratic statistics, whose nominal, doubly negative unity conceals its real dispersion both from the 'interested parties' and from their opponents and most observers, the laying down of boundaries between the classes is inspired by the strategic aim of 'counting in' or 'being counted in', 'cataloguing' or 'annexing', when it is not the simple recording of a legally guaranteed state of the power relation between the classified groups.

Leaving aside all cases in which the statutory imposition of an arbitrary boundary (such as a 30-kilo limit on baggage or the rule that a vehicle over two tons is a van) suffices to eliminate the difficulties that arise from the sophism of the heap of grain,[14] boundaries – even the most formal-looking ones, such as those between age-groups – do indeed freeze a particular state of social struggles, i.e., a given state of the distribution of advantages and obligations, such as the right to pensions or cheap fares, compulsory schooling or military service. And if we are amused by Alphonse Allais's story of the father who pulls the communication cord to stop the train at the very moment his child becomes three years old (and so needs a ticket to travel), it is because we immediately see the sociological absurdity of an imaginary variation which is as impeccably logical as those on which logicians base their beloved paradoxes. Here the limits are frontiers to be attacked or defended with all one's strength, and the classificatory systems which fix them are not so much means of knowledge as means of power, harnessed to social functions and overtly or covertly aimed at satisfying the interests of a group.

> A number of ethical, aesthetic, psychiatric or forensic classifications that are produced by the 'institutional sciences', not to mention those produced and inculcated by the educational system, are similarly subordinated to social functions, although they derive their specific efficacy from their apparent neutrality. They are produced in accordance with the specific logic, and in the specific language, of relatively autonomous fields, and they combine a real dependence on the classificatory schemes of the dominant habitus (and ultimately on the social structures of which these are the product) with an apparent independence. The latter enables them to help to legitimate a particular state of the classification struggle and the class struggle. Perhaps the most typical example of these semi-autonomous systems of classification is the system of adjectives which underpins scholastic 'appreciations'.[15]

Commonplaces and classificatory systems are thus the stake of struggles between the groups they characterize and counterpose, who fight over them while striving to turn them to their own advantage. Georges Duby shows how the model of the three orders, which fixed a state of the social structure and aimed to make it permanent by codifying it, was able to be used simultaneously and successively by antagonistic groups: first by the bishops, who had devised it, against the heretics, the monks and the knights; then by the aristocracy, against the bishops and the king; and finally by the king, who, by setting himself up as the absolute subject of the classifying operation, as a principle external and superior to the classes it generated (unlike the three orders, who were subjects but also objects, judges but also parties), assigned each group its place in the social order, and established himself as an unassailable vantage-point.[16] In the same way it can be shown that the schemes and commonplaces which provide images of the different forms of domination, the opposition between the sexes and age-groups as well as the opposition between the generations, are similarly manipulated. The 'young' can accept the definition that their elders offer them, take advantage of the temporary licence they are allowed in many societies ('Youth must have its fling'), do what is assigned to them, revel in the 'specific virtues' of youth, *virtù*, virility, enthusiasm, and get on with their own business – knight-errantry for the scions of the mediaeval aristocracy,[17] love and violence for the youth of Renaissance Florence, and every form of regulated, ludic wildness (sport, rock etc.) for contemporary adolescents – in short, allow themselves to be kept in the state of 'youth', that is, irresponsibility, enjoying the freedom of irresponsible behaviour in return for renouncing responsibility.[18] In situations of specific crisis, when the order of successions is threatened, 'young people', refusing to remain consigned to 'youth', tend to consign the 'old' to 'old age'. Wanting to take the responsibilities which define adults (in the sense of socially complete persons), they must push the holders of responsibilities into that form of irresponsibility which defines old age, or rather retirement. The wisdom and prudence claimed by the elders then collapse into conservatism, archaism or, quite simply, senile irresponsibility. The newcomers, who are likely to be also the biologically youngest, but who bring with them many other distinctive properties, stemming from changes in the social conditions of production of the producers (i.e., principally the family and the educational system), escape the more rapidly from 'youth' (irresponsibility) the readier they are to break with the irresponsible behaviour assigned to them and, freeing themselves from the internalized limits (those which may make a 50-year-old feel 'too young reasonably to aspire' to a position or an honour), do not hesitate to push forward, 'leap-frog' and 'take the escalator' to precipitate their predecessors' fall into the past, the outdated, in short, social death. But they have no chance of winning the struggles over the limits which break out between the age-groups when the sense of the limits is lost, unless they manage to impose a new definition of the socially complete person, including in it characteristics normally (i.e., in terms of the prevailing classificatory principle) associated with youth (enthusiasm, energy and so on) or characteristics that can supplant the virtues normally associated with adulthood.

In short, what individuals and groups invest in the particular meaning they give to common classificatory systems by the use they make of them is infinitely more than their 'interest' in the usual sense of the term; it is their whole social being, everything which defines their own idea of themselves, the primordial, tacit contract whereby they define 'us' as opposed to 'them', 'other people', and which is the basis of the exclusions ('not for the likes of us') and inclusions they perform among the characteristics produced by the common classificatory system.

Social psychologists have observed that any division of a population into two groups, however arbitrary, induces discriminatory behaviour favourable to members of the agents' own group and hostile to members of the other group, even if it has adverse effects for the former group.[19] More generally, they describe under the term 'category differentiation' the operations whereby agents construct their perception of reality, in particular the process of accentuating differences vis-à-vis 'outsiders' (dissimilation) and reinforcing similarities with insiders (assimilation).[20] Similarly, studies of racism have shown that whenever different groups are juxtaposed, a definition of the approved, valorized behaviour tends to be contrasted with the despised, rejected behaviour of the other group.[21] Social identity lies in difference, and difference is asserted against what is closest, which represents the greatest threat. Analysis of stereotyping, the propensity to assume a correspondence between membership of a category (e.g., Nordic or Mediterranean, Western or Oriental) and possession of a particular property, so that knowledge of a person's category strongly influences judgements of him, is in line with analysis of that sort of social stereotyping in which all the members of a social formation tend to concur in attributing certain properties to members of the different social classes.

The fact that, in their relationship to the dominant classes, the dominated classes attribute to themselves strength in the sense of labour power and fighting strength – physical strength and also strength of character, courage, manliness – does not prevent the dominant groups from similarly conceiving the relationship in terms of the scheme strong/weak; but they reduce the strength which the dominated (or the young, or women) ascribe to themselves to brute strength, passion and instinct, a blind, unpredictable force of nature, the unreasoning violence of desire, and they attribute to themselves spiritual and intellectual strength, a self-control that predisposes them to control others, a strength of soul or spirit which allows them to conceive their relationship to the dominated – the 'masses', women, the young – as that of the soul to the body, understanding to sensibility, culture to nature.

The Classification Struggle

Principles of division, inextricably logical and sociological, function within and for the purposes of the struggle between social groups; in producing concepts, they produce groups, the very groups which produce the principles and the groups against which they are produced. What is at stake in the struggles about the meaning of the social world is power over the classificatory schemes and systems which are the basis of the representations of the groups and therefore of their mobilization and demobilization: the evocative power of an utterance which puts things in a different light (as happens, for example, when a single word, such as 'paternalism', changes the whole experience of a social relationship) or which modifies the schemes of perception, shows something else, other properties, previously unnoticed or relegated to the background (such as common interests hitherto masked by ethnic or national differences); a separative power, a distinction, *diacrisis, discretio*, drawing discrete units out of indivisible continuity, difference out of the undifferentiated.

Only in and through the struggle do the internalized limits become boundaries, barriers that have to be moved. And indeed, the system of classificatory schemes is constituted as an objectified, institutionalized system of classification only when it has ceased to function as a sense of limits so that the guardians of the established order must enunciate, systematize and codify the principles of production of that order, both real and represented, so as to defend them against heresy; in short, they must constitute the doxa as orthodoxy. Official systems of classification, such as the theory of the three orders, do explicitly and systematically what the classificatory schemes did tacitly and practically. Attributes, in the sense of predicates, thereby become *attributions*, powers, capacities, privileges, prerogatives, attributed to the holder of a post, so that war is no longer what the warrior does, but the *officium*, the specific function, the raison d'être, of the *bellator*. Classificatory *discretio*, like law, freezes a certain state of the power relations which it aims to fix forever by enunciating and codifying it. The classificatory system as a principle of logical and political division only exists and functions because it reproduces, in a transfigured form, in the symbolic logic of differential gaps, i.e., of discontinuity, the generally gradual and continuous differences which structure the established order; but it makes its own, that is, specifically symbolic, contribution to the maintenance of that order only because it has the specifically symbolic power to make people see and believe which is given by the imposition of mental structures.

Systems of classification would not be such a decisive object of struggle if they did not contribute to the existence of classes by enhancing the efficacy of the objective mechanisms with the reinforcement supplied by representations structured in accordance with the classification. The imposition of a recognized name is an act of recognition of full social existence which transmutes the thing named. It no longer exists merely de facto, as a tolerated, illegal or illegitimate practice, but becomes a *social* function, i.e., a mandate, a mission (*Beruf*), a task, a role – all words which express the difference between authorized activity, which is assigned to an individual or group by tacit or explicit delegation, and mere usurpation, which creates a 'state of affairs' awaiting institutionalization. But the specific effect of 'collective representations', which, contrary to what the Durkheimian connotations might suggest, may be the product of the application of the same scheme of perception or a common system of classification while still being subject to antagonistic social uses, is most clearly seen when the word precedes the thing, as with voluntary associations that turn into recognized professions or corporate defence groups (such as the trade union of the 'cadres'), which progressively impose the representation of their existence and their unity, both on their own members and on other groups.

A group's presence or absence in the official classification depends on its capacity to get itself recognized, to get itself noticed and admitted, and so to win a place in the social order. It thus escapes from the shadowy existence of the 'nameless crafts' of which Emile Benveniste speaks: business in antiquity and the Middle Ages, or illegitimate activities, such as those of the modern healer (formerly called an 'empiric'), bone-setter or prostitute. The fate of groups is bound up with the words that designate them: the power to impose recognition depends on the capacity to mobilize around a name, 'proletariat', 'working class', 'cadres' etc., to appropriate a common name and to commune in a proper name, and so to mobilize the union that makes them strong, around the unifying power of a word.[22]

In fact, the order of words never exactly reproduces the order of things. It is the relative independence of the structure of the system of classifying, classified words (within which the distinct value of each particular label is defined) in relation to the structure of the distribution of capital, and more precisely, it is the time-lag (partly resulting from the inertia inherent in classification systems as quasi-legal institutions sanctioning a state of a power relation) between changes in jobs, linked to changes in the productive apparatus, and changes in titles, which creates the space for symbolic strategies aimed at exploiting the discrepancies between the nominal and the real, appropriating words so as to get the things they designate, or appropriating things while waiting to get the words that sanction them; exercising responsibilities without having entitlement to do so, in order to acquire the right to claim the legitimate titles, or, conversely, declining the material advantages associated with devalued titles so as to avoid losing the symbolic advantages bestowed by more prestigious labels or, at least, vaguer and more manipulable ones; donning the most flattering of the available insignia, verging on imposture if need be – like the potters who call themselves 'art craftsmen', or technicians who claim to be engineers – or inventing new labels, like physiotherapists (*kinésithérapeutes*) who count on this new title to separate them from mere masseurs and bring them closer to doctors. All these strategies, like all processes of competition, a paper-chase aimed at ensuring constant distinctive gaps, tend to produce a steady inflation of titles – restrained by the inertia of the institutionalized taxonomies (collective agreements, salary scales etc.) – to which legal guarantees are attached. The negotiations between antagonistic interest groups, which arise from the establishment of collective agreements and which concern, inseparably, the tasks entailed by a given job, the properties required of its occupants (e.g., diplomas) and the corresponding advantages, both material and symbolic (the name), are an institutionalized, theatrical version of the incessant struggles over the classifications which help to produce the classes, although these classifications are the product of the struggles between the classes and depend on the power relations between them.

The Reality of Representation and the Representation of Reality

The classifying subjects who classify the properties and practices of others, or their own, are also classifiable objects which classify themselves (in the eyes of others) by appropriating practices and properties that are already classified (as vulgar or distinguished, high or low, heavy or light etc. – in other words, in the last analysis, as popular or bourgeois) according to their probable distribution between groups that are themselves classified. The most classifying and best classified of these properties are, of course, those which are overtly designated to function as signs of distinction or marks of infamy, stigmata, especially the names and titles expressing class membership whose intersection defines social identity at any given time – the name of a nation, a region, an ethnic group, a family name, the name of an occupation, an educational qualification, honorific titles and so on. Those who classify themselves or others, by appropriating or classifying practices or properties that are classified and classifying, cannot be unaware that, through distinctive objects or practices in which their 'powers' are expressed and which, being appropriated by and appropriate to classes, classify those who appropriate them, they classify themselves in the eyes of other classifying (but also classifiable) subjects, endowed with classificatory schemes analogous to those which enable them more or less adequately to anticipate their own classification.

Social subjects comprehend the social world which comprehends them. This means that they cannot be characterized simply in terms of material properties, starting with the body, which can be counted and measured like any other object in the physical world. In fact, each of these properties, be it the height or volume of the body or the extent of landed property, when perceived and appreciated in relation to other properties of the same class by agents equipped with socially constituted schemes of perception and appreciation, functions as a symbolic property. It is therefore necessary to move beyond the opposition between a 'social physics' – which uses statistics in objectivist fashion to establish distributions (in both the statistical and economic senses), quantified expressions of the differential appropriation of a finite quantity of social energy by a large number of competing individuals, identified through 'objective indicators' – and a 'social semiology' which seeks to decipher meanings and bring to light the cognitive operations whereby agents produce and decipher them. We have to refuse the dichotomy between, on the one hand, the aim of arriving at an objective 'reality', 'independent of individual consciousnesses and wills', by breaking with common representations of the social world (Durkheim's 'pre-notions'), and of uncovering 'laws' – that is, significant (in the sense of non-random) relationships between distributions – and, on the other hand, the aim of grasping, not 'reality', but agents' representations of it, which are the whole 'reality' of a social world conceived 'as will and representation'.

In short, social science does not have to choose between that form of social physics, represented by Durkheim – who agrees with social semiology in acknowledging that one can only know 'reality' by applying logical instruments of classification[23] – and the idealist semiology which, undertaking to construct 'an account of accounts', as Harold Garfinkel puts it, can do no more than record the recordings of a social world which is ultimately no more than the product of mental, i.e., linguistic, structures. What we have to do is to bring into the science of scarcity, and of competition for scarce goods, the practical knowledge which the agents obtain for themselves by producing – on the basis of their experience of the distributions, itself dependent on their position in the distributions – divisions and classifications which are no less objective than those of the balance-sheets of social physics. In other words, we have to move beyond the opposition between objectivist theories which identify the social classes (but also the sex or age classes) with discrete groups, simple countable populations separated by boundaries objectively drawn in reality, and subjectivist (or marginalist) theories which reduce the 'social order' to a sort of collective classification obtained by aggregating the individual classifications or, more precisely, the individual strategies, classified and classifying, through which agents class themselves and others.[24]

One only has to bear in mind that goods are converted into distinctive signs, which may be signs of distinction but also of vulgarity, as soon as they are perceived relationally, to see that the representation which individuals and groups inevitably project through their practices and properties is an integral part of social reality. A class is defined as much by its *being-perceived* as by its *being*, by its consumption – which need not be conspicuous in order to be symbolic – as much as by its position in the relations of production (even if it is true that the latter governs the former). The Berkeleian – i.e., petit-bourgeois – vision which reduces social being to perceived being, to seeming, and which, forgetting that there is no need to give theatrical performances (*représentations*) in order to be the object of mental representations, reduces the social world to the sum of the (mental) representations which the various groups have of the theatrical performances put on by the other groups, has the virtue of insisting on the relative autonomy of the logic of symbolic representations with respect to the material determinants of socio-economic condition. The individual or collective classification struggles aimed at transforming the categories of perception and appreciation of the social world and, through this, the social world itself, are indeed a forgotten dimension of the class struggle. But one only has to realize that the classificatory schemes which underlie agents' practical relationship to their condition and the representation they have of it are themselves the product of that condition, in order to see the limits of this autonomy. Position in the classification struggle depends on position in the class structure; and social subjects – including intellectuals, who are not those best placed to grasp that which defines the limits of their thought of the social world, that is, the illusion of the absence of limits – are perhaps never less likely to transcend 'the limits of their minds' than in the representation they have and give of their position, which defines those limits.

Notes

1   I. Kant, *Anthropology from a Pragmatic Point of View* (Carbondale and Edwardsville: Southern Illinois University Press, 1978), p. 141.

2   G. W. Leibniz, 'Meditationes de cognitione, veritate et ideis' in *Opuscula Philosophica Selecta* (Paris: Boivin, 1939), pp. 1–2 (see also *Discours de Métaphysique*, par. 24). It is remarkable that to illustrate the idea of 'clear but confused' knowledge, Leibniz evokes, in addition to the example of colours, tastes and smells which we can distinguish 'by the simple evidence of the senses and not by statable marks', the example of painters and artists who can recognize a good or bad work but cannot justify their judgement except by invoking the presence or absence of a 'je ne sais quoi.'

3   It would be the task of a genetic sociology to establish how this sense of possibilities and impossibilities, proximities and distances is constituted.

4   Just as the opposition between the unique and the multiple lies at the heart of the dominant philosophy of history, so the opposition, which is a transfigured form of it, between the brilliant, the visible, the distinct, the distinguished, the 'outstanding', and the obscure, the dull, the greyness of the undifferentiated, indistinct, inglorious mass is one of the fundamental categories of the dominant perception of the social world.

5   See G. Duby, *Les trois ordres ou l'imaginaire du féodalisme* (Paris: Gallimard, 1978).

6   E. Durkheim, *Elementary Forms of the Religious Life* (London: Allen and Unwin, 1915), p. 17.

7   A more detailed account of the theoretical context of these analyses will be found in P. Bourdieu, "Symbolic Power" in *Identity and Structure*, ed. D. Gleeson (Driffield: Nafferton Books, 1977), pp. 112–19; also in *Critique of Anthropology*, 4 (Summer 1979), 77–85.

8   Cf. J.-P. Sartre, *Being and Nothingness* (London: Methuen, 1969), pp. 557–65, esp. 562.

9   See H. Giles, 'Accent Mobility: A Model and Some Data', *Anthropological Linguistics*, 15 (1973), 87–105.

10 See G. Lenski, 'American Social Classes: Statistical Strata or Social Groups?', *American Journal of Sociology*, 8 (September 1952), 139–44.

11 These divergences also emerge, in the same survey, when the respondents are first asked to define social classes at the level of their town and then at the level of the whole country; the rate of non-response rises strongly in the latter case, as does the number of classes perceived.

12 Ordinary perception, which applies to practices the scheme of the broad and the narrow, or the expansive and the constrained, anticipates the discoveries of the most refined social psychology, which establishes the existence of a correlation between the room one gives oneself in physical space and the place one occupies in social space. On this point, see S. Fisher and C. E. Cleveland, *Body Image and Personality* (New York: Van Nostrand, 1958).

13 This is true in the ordinary sense but also in the sense of Kafka [*procès* = 'process' but also 'trial' – cf. Kafka's *Die Prozess*, *The Trial*, *Le Procès* in French – translator], who offers an exemplary image of this desperate striving to regain a social identity that is by definition ungraspable, being the infinite limit of all categoremes, all imputations.

14 The sophism of the heap of wheat and all the paradoxes of physical continua mean, as Poincaré observed, that one has simultaneously $A = B$, $B = C$ and $A < C$, or again, $A_1 = A_2$, $A_2 = A_3$, ... $A_{99} = A_{100}$ and $A_1 < A_{100}$. In other words, though it is clear that one grain does not make a heap, nor do two grains, or three, it is not easy to say whether the heap begins at 264 grains or 265; in other words, whether 265 grains make a heap, but not 264.

15 See P. Bourdieu and M. de Saint Martin, 'Les catégories de l'entendement professoral', *Actes*, 3 (1975), 68–93.

16 See Duby, *Les trois ordres*, esp. pp. 422–3.

17 Ibid., pp. 63–4, and 'Les "jeunes" dans la société aristocratique dans la France du Nord-Ouest au XIIème siècle', *Annales*, 19 (September–October 1964), 835–46.

18 Much the same could be said of women, were they not denied most of the advantages of renouncing responsibility, at least outside the bourgeoisie.

19 M. Billing and H. Tajfel, 'Social Categorization and Similarity in Inter-group Behaviour', *European Journal of Social Psychology*, 3 (1973), 27–52.

20 See, for example, H. Tajfel, 'Quantitative Judgement in Social Perception', *British Journal of Psychology*, 50 (1959), 16–21, and H. Tajfel and A. L. Wilkes, 'Classification and Quantitative Judgement', ibid., 54 (1963), 101–4; and for an overview of research in this area, W. Doise, *L'articulation psychosociologique et les relations entre groupes* (Brussels: A. de Boeck, 1976), pp. 178–200.

21 'Wherever the groups and classes are set in sharp juxtaposition, the values and mores of each are juxtaposed. Out of group opposition there arises an intense opposition of values, which comes to be projected through the social order and serves to solidify social stratification.' L. Copeland, 'The Negro as a Contrast Conception' in E. Thompson (ed.), *Race Relations and the Race Problem* (Durham, NC: Duke University Press, 1959), pp. 152–79.

22 ' … le pouvoir unificateur du nom, du mot d'ordre' – the unifying power of the name/noun, the rallying cry ('order word'). (Translator's note.)

23 One scarcely needs to point out the affinity between social physics and the positivist inclination to see classifications either as arbitrary, 'operational' divisions (such as age groups or income brackets) or as 'objective' cleavages (discontinuities in distributions or bends in curves) which only need to be recorded.

24 Here is a particularly revealing expression (even in its metaphor) of this social marginalism: 'Each individual is responsible for the demeanour image of himself and the deference image of others, so that for a complete man to be expressed, individuals must hold hands in a chain of ceremony, each giving deferentially with proper demeanour to the one on the right what will be received deferentially from the one on the left.' E. Goffmann, 'The Nature of Deference and Demeanour', *American Anthropologist*, 58 (June 1956), 473–502. ' … routinely the question is that of whose opinion is voiced most frequently and most forcibly, who makes the minor ongoing decisions apparently required for the coordination of any joint activity, and whose passing concerns have been given the most weight. And however trivial some of these *little gains and losses* may appear to be, *by summing them all up* across all the social situations in which they occur, we can see that their total effect is enormous. The expression of subordination and domination through this swarm of situational means is more than a mere tracing or symbol or ritualistic affirmation of the social hierarchy. These expressions *considerably constitute* the hierarchy.' E. Goffmann, 'Gender Display'. (Paper presented at the Third International Symposium, 'Female Hierarchies', Harry Frank Guggenheim Foundation, April 3–5, 1974); italics mine.

CHAPTER 6

Ethics and the Face

Emmanuel Levinas

Levinas was a major figure in European philosophy in the mid- to late twentieth century. His work derives from phenomenology and focuses on one's awareness of others. One's relation to "the Other" is more important and foundational than any question in philosophy regarding the nature of existence (ontology). The Other person can never fully be known or appropriated. The relation to the Other marks the limits of the self. Responsibility, rather than freedom, is therefore a paramount value in Levinas's ethics. Levinas's major works were *Time and the Other* (1948) and *Totality and Infinity* (1961).

1.   Infinity and the Face

Inasmuch as the access to beings concerns vision, it dominates those beings, exercises a power over them. A thing is *given*, offers itself to me. In gaining access to it I maintain myself within the same.

The face is present in its refusal to be contained. In this sense it cannot be comprehended, that is, encompassed. It is neither seen nor touched – for in visual or tactile sensation the identity of the I envelops the alterity of the object, which becomes precisely a content.

The Other is not other with a relative alterity as are, in a comparison, even ultimate species, which mutually exclude one another but still have their place within the community of a genus – excluding one another by their definition, but calling for one another by this exclusion, across the community of their genus. The alterity of the Other does not depend on any quality that would distinguish him from me, for a distinction of this nature would precisely imply between us that community of genus which already nullifies alterity.

And yet the Other does not purely and simply negate the I; total negation, of which murder is the temptation and the attempt, refers to an antecedent relation. The relation between the Other and me, which dawns forth in his expression, issues neither in

Original publication details: Emmanuel Levinas, "Ethics and the Face" from *Totality and Infinity*, pp. 194–219. Duquesne University Press, 1969. Reproduced with permission from Duquesne University Press.

number nor in concept. The Other remains infinitely transcendent, infinitely foreign; his face in which his epiphany is produced and which appeals to me breaks with the world that can be common to us, whose virtualities are inscribed in our *nature* and developed by our existence. Speech proceeds from absolute difference. Or, more exactly, an absolute difference is not produced in a process of specification descending from genus to species, in which the order of logical relations runs up against the given, which is not reducible to relations. The difference thus encountered remains bound up with the logical hierarchy it contrasts with, and appears against the ground of the common genus.

Absolute difference, inconceivable in terms of formal logic, is established only by language. Language accomplishes a relation between terms that breaks up the unity of a genus. The terms, the interlocutors, absolve themselves from the relation, or remain absolute within relationship. Language is perhaps to be defined as the very power to break the continuity of being or of history.

The incomprehensible nature of the presence of the Other, which we spoke of above, is not to be described negatively. Better than comprehension, *discourse* relates with what remains essentially transcendent. For the moment we must attend to the formal work of language, which consists in presenting the transcendent; a more profound signification will emerge shortly. Language is a relation between separated terms. To the one the other can indeed present himself as a theme, but his presence is not reabsorbed in his status as a theme. The word that bears on the Other as a theme seems to contain the Other. But already it is said to the Other who, as interlocutor, has quit the theme that encompassed him, and upsurges inevitably behind the said. Words are said, be it only by the silence kept, whose weight acknowledges this evasion of the Other. The knowledge that absorbs the Other is forthwith situated within the discourse I address to him. Speaking, rather than "letting be," solicits the Other. Speech cuts across vision. In knowledge or vision the object seen can indeed determine an act, but it is an act that in some way appropriates the "seen" to itself, integrates it into a world by endowing it with a signification, and, in the last analysis, constitutes it. In discourse the divergence that inevitably opens between the Other as my theme and the Other as my interlocutor, emancipated from the theme that seemed a moment to hold him, forthwith contests the meaning I ascribe to my interlocutor. The formal structure of language thereby announces the ethical inviolability of the Other and, without any odor of the "numinous," his "holiness."

The fact that the face maintains a relation with me by discourse does not range him in the same; he remains absolute within the relation. The solipsist dialectic of consciousness always suspicious of being in captivity in the same breaks off. For the ethical relationship which subtends discourse is not a species of consciousness whose ray emanates from the I; it puts the I in question. This putting in question emanates from the other.

The presence of a being not entering into, but overflowing, the sphere of the same determines its "status" as infinite. This overflowing is to be distinguished from the image of liquid overflowing a vessel, because this overflowing presence is effectuated as a position *in face of* the same. The facing position, opposition par excellence, can be only as a moral summons. This movement proceeds from the other. The idea of infinity, the infinitely more contained in the less, is concretely produced in the form of a relation with the face. And the idea of infinity alone maintains the exteriority of the other with respect to the same, despite this relation. Thus a structure analogous to the ontological argument is here produced: the exteriority of a being is inscribed in its essence. But what is produced here is not a reasoning, but the epiphany that occurs as a face. The metaphysical desire for the absolutely other which animates intellectualism (or the radical empiricism that confides in the teaching of exteriority) deploys its *en-ergy* in the vision of the face [vision du visage], or in the idea of infinity. The idea of infinity exceeds my powers (not quantitatively, but, we will see later, by calling them into question); it does not come from our a priori depths – it is consequently experience par excellence.

The Kantian notion of infinity figures as an ideal of reason, the projection of its exigencies in a beyond, the ideal completion of what is given incomplete – but without the incomplete being confronted with a privileged *experience* of infinity, without it drawing the limits of its finitude from such a confrontation. The finite is here no longer conceived by relation to the infinite; quite the contrary, the infinite presupposes the finite, which it amplifies infinitely (although this passage to the limit or this projection implicates in an unacknowledged form the idea of infinity, with all the consequences Descartes drew from it, and which are presupposed in this idea of projection). The Kantian finitude is described positively by sensibility, as the Heideggerian finitude by the being for death. This infinity referring to the finite marks the most anti-Cartesian point of Kantian philosophy as, later, of Heideggerian philosophy.

Hegel returns to Descartes in maintaining the positivity of the infinite, but excluding all multiplicity from it; he posits the infinite as the exclusion of every "other" that might maintain a relation with the infinite and thereby limit it. The infinite can only encompass all relations. Like the god of Aristotle it refers only to itself, though now at the term of a history. The relation of a particular with infinity would be equivalent to the entry of this particular into the sovereignty of a State. It becomes infinite in negating its own finitude. But this outcome does not succeed in smothering the protestation of the private individual, the apology of the separated being (though it be called empirical and animal), of the individual who experiences as a tyranny the State willed by his reason, but in whose impersonal destiny he no longer recognizes his reason. We recognize in the finitude to which the Hegelian infinite is opposed, and which it encompasses, the finitude of man before the elements, the finitude of man invaded by the *there is*, at each instant traversed by faceless gods against whom labor is pursued in order to realize the security in which the "other" of the elements would be revealed as the same. But the other absolutely other – the Other – does not limit the freedom of the same; calling it to responsibility, it founds it and justifies it. The relation with the other as face heals allergy. It is desire, teaching received, and the pacific opposition of discourse. In returning to the Cartesian notion of infinity, the "idea of infinity" put in the separated being by the infinite, we retain its positivity, its anteriority to every finite thought and every thought of the finite, its exteriority with regard to the finite; here there was the possibility of separated being. The idea of infinity, the overflowing of finite thought by its content, effectuates the relation of thought with what exceeds its capacity, with what at each moment it learns without suffering shock. This is the situation we call welcome of the face. The idea of infinity is produced in the *opposition* of conversation, in sociality. The relation with the face, with the other absolutely other which I can not contain, the other in this sense infinite, is nonetheless my Idea, a commerce. But the relation is maintained without violence, in peace with this absolute alterity. The "resistance" of the other does not do violence to me, does not act negatively; it has a positive structure: ethical. The first revelation of the other, presupposed in all the other relations with him, does not consist in grasping him in his negative resistance and in circumventing him by ruse. I do not struggle with a faceless god, but I respond to his expression, to his revelation.

2. Ethics and the Face

The face resists possession, resists my powers. In its epiphany, in expression, the sensible, still graspable, turns into total resistance to the grasp. This mutation can occur only by the opening of a new dimension. For the resistance to the grasp is not produced as an insurmountable resistance, like the hardness of the rock against which the effort of the hand comes to naught, like the remoteness of a star in the immensity of space. The expression the face introduces into the world does not defy the feebleness of my powers, but my ability for power.[1] The face, still a thing among things, breaks through the form that nevertheless delimits it. This means concretely: the face speaks to me and thereby invites me to a relation incommensurate with a power exercised, be it enjoyment or knowledge.

And yet this new dimension opens in the sensible appearance of the face. The permanent openness of the contours of its form in expression imprisons this openness which breaks up form in a caricature. The face at the limit of holiness and caricature is thus still in a sense exposed to powers. In a sense only: the depth that opens in this sensibility modifies the very nature of power, which henceforth can no longer take, but can kill. Murder still aims at a sensible datum, and yet it finds itself before a datum whose being can not be *suspended* by an appropriation. It finds itself before a datum absolutely non-neutralizable. The "negation" effected by appropriation and usage remained always partial. The grasp that contests the independence of the thing preserves it "for me." Neither the destruction of things, nor the hunt, nor the extermination of living beings aims at the face, which is not of the world. They still belong to labor, have a finality, and answer to a need. Murder alone lays claim to total negation. Negation by labor and usage, like negation by representation, effect a grasp or a comprehension, rest on or aim at affirmation; they can. To kill is not to dominate but to annihilate; it is to renounce comprehension absolutely. Murder exercises a power over what escapes power. It is still a power, for the face expresses itself in the sensible, but already impotency, because the face rends the sensible. The alterity that is expressed in the face provides the unique "matter" possible for total negation. I can wish to kill only an existent absolutely independent, which exceeds my powers infinitely, and therefore does not oppose them but paralyzes the very power of power. The Other is the sole being I can wish to kill.

But how does this disproportion between infinity and my powers differ from that which separates a very great obstacle from a force applied to it? It would be pointless to insist on the banality of murder, which reveals the quasi-null resistance of the obstacle. This most banal incident of human history corresponds to an exceptional possibility – since it claims the total negation of a being. It does not concern the force that this being may possess as a part of the world. The Other who can sovereignly say *no* to me is exposed to the point of the sword or the revolver's bullet, and the whole unshakeable firmness of his "for itself" with that intransigent *no* he opposes is obliterated because the sword or the bullet has touched the ventricles or auricles of his heart. In the contexture of the world he is a quasi-nothing. But he can oppose to me a struggle, that is, oppose to the force that strikes him not a force of resistance, but the very *unforeseeableness* of his reaction. He thus opposes to me not a greater force, an energy assessable and consequently presenting itself as though it were part of a whole, but the very transcendence of his being by relation to that whole; not some superlative of power, but precisely the infinity of his transcendence. This infinity, stronger than murder, already resists us in his face, is his face, is the primordial *expression*, is the first word: "you shall not commit murder." The infinite paralyses power by its infinite resistance to murder, which, firm and insurmountable, gleams in the face of the Other, in the total nudity of his defence-less eyes, in the nudity of the absolute openness of the Transcendent. There is here a relation not with a very great resistance, but with something absolutely *other*: the resistance of what has no resistance – the ethical resistance. The epiphany of the face brings forth the possibility of gauging the infinity of the temptation to murder, not only as a temptation to total destruction, but also as the purely ethical impossibility of this temptation and attempt. If the resistance to murder were not ethical but real, we would have a *perception* of it, with all that reverts to the subjective in perception. We would remain within the idealism of a *consciousness* of struggle, and not in relationship with the Other, a relationship that can turn into struggle, but already overflows the consciousness of struggle. The epiphany of the face is ethical. The struggle this face can threaten *presupposes* the transcendence of expression. The face threatens the eventuality of a struggle, but this threat does not exhaust the epiphany of infinity, does not formulate its first word. War presupposes peace, the antecedent and non-allergic presence of the Other; it does not represent the first event of the encounter.

The impossibility of killing does not have a simply negative and formal signification; the relation with infinity, the idea of infinity in us, conditions it positively. Infinity presents itself as a face in the ethical resistance that paralyses my powers and from the depths of defenceless eyes rises firm and absolute in its nudity and destitution. The comprehension of this destitution and this hunger establishes the very proximity of the other. But thus the epiphany of infinity is expression and discourse. The primor-dial essence of expression and discourse does not reside in the information they would supply concerning an interior and hidden world. In expression a being presents itself; the being that manifests itself attends its manifestation and consequently appeals to me. This attendance is not the *neutrality* [*le neutre*] of an image, but a solicitation that concerns me by its destitution and its Height. To speak to me is at each moment to surmount what is necessarily plastic in manifestation. To manifest oneself as a face is to *impose onself* above and beyond the manifested and purely phenomenal form, to present oneself in a mode irreducible to manifestation, the very straightforwardness of the face to face, without the intermediary of any image, in one's nudity, that is, in one's destitution and hunger. In *Desire* are conjoined the movements unto the Height and unto the Humility of the Other.

Expression does not radiate as a splendor that spreads unbeknown to the radiating being – which is perhaps the definition of beauty. To manifest oneself in attending one's own manifestation is to invoke the interlocutor and expose oneself to his response and his questioning. Expression does not impose itself as a true representation or as an action. The being offered in true representation remains a possibility of appearance. The world which invades me when I engage myself in it is powerless against the "free thought" that suspends that engagement, or even refuses it interiorly, being capable of living hidden. The being that expresses itself imposes itself, but does so precisely by appealing to me with its destitution and nudity – its hunger – without my being able to be deaf to that appeal. Thus in expression the being that imposes itself does not limit but promotes my freedom, by arousing my goodness. The order of responsibility, where the gravity of ineluctable being freezes all laughter, is also the order where freedom is ineluctably invoked. It is thus the irremissible weight of being that gives rise to my freedom. The ineluctable has no longer the inhumanity of the fateful, but the severe seriousness of goodness.

This bond between expression and responsibility, this ethical condition or essence of language, this function of language prior to all disclosure of being and its cold splendor, permits us to extract language from subjection to a preexistent thought, where it would have but the servile function of translating that preexistent thought on the outside, or of universalizing its interior movements. The presentation of the face is not true, for the true refers to the non-true, its eternal contemporary, and ineluctably meets with the smile and silence of the skeptic. The presentation of being in the face does not leave any logical place for its contradictory. Thus I cannot evade by silence the discourse which the epiphany that occurs as a face opens, as Thrasymachus, irritated, tries to do, in the first book of the *Republic* (moreover without succeeding). "To leave men without food is a fault that no circumstance attenuates; the distinction between the voluntary and the involuntary does not apply here," says Rabbi Yochanan.[2] Before the hunger of men responsibility is measured only "objectively"; it is irrecusable. The face opens the primordial discourse whose first word is obligation, which no "interiority" permits avoiding. It is that discourse that obliges the entering into discourse, the commencement of discourse rationalism prays for, a "force" that convinces even "the people who do not wish to listen"[3] and thus founds the true universality of reason.

Preexisting the disclosure of being in general taken as basis of knowledge and as meaning of being is the relation with the existent that expresses himself; preexisting the plane of ontology is the ethical plane.

3. Reason and the Face

Expression is not produced as the manifestation of an intelligible form that would connect terms to one another so as to establish, across distance, the assemblage of parts in a totality, in which the terms joined up already derive their meaning from the situation created by their community, which, in its turn, owes its meaning to the terms combined. This "circle of understanding" is not the primordial event of the logic of being. Expression precedes these coordinating effects visible to a third party.

The event proper to expression consists in bearing witness to oneself, and guaranteeing this witness. This attestation of oneself is possible only as a face, that is, as speech. It produces the commencement of intelligibility, initiality itself, principality, royal sovereignty, which commands unconditionally. The principle is possible only as command. A search for the influence that expression would have undergone or an unconscious source from which it would emanate would presuppose an inquiry that would refer to new testimonies, and consequently to an original sincerity of an expression.

Language as an exchange of ideas about the world, with the mental reservations it involves, across the vicissitudes of sincerity and deceit it delineates, presupposes the originality of the face without which, reduced to an action among actions whose meaning would require an infinite psychoanalysis or sociology, it could not commence. If at the bottom of speech there did not subsist this originality of expression, this break with every influence, this dominant position of the speaker foreign to all compromise and all contamination, this straightforwardness of the face to face, speech would not surpass the plane of activity, of which it is evidently not a species – even though language can be integrated into a system of acts and serve as an instrument. But language is possible only when speaking precisely renounces this function of being action and returns to its essence of being expression.

Expression does not consist in *giving* us the Other's interiority. The Other who expresses himself precisely does not *give* himself, and accordingly retains the freedom to lie. But deceit and veracity already presuppose the absolute authenticity of the face – the privileged case of a presentation of being foreign to the alternative of truth and non-truth, circumventing the ambiguity of the true and the false which every truth risks – an ambiguity, moreover, in which all values move. The presentation of being in the face does not have the status of a value. What we call the face is precisely this exceptional presentation of self by self, incommensurable with the presentation of realities simply given, always suspect of some swindle, always possibly dreamt up. To seek truth I have already established a relationship with a face which can guarantee itself, whose epiphany itself is somehow a word of honor. Every language as an exchange of verbal signs refers already to this primordial word of honor. The verbal sign is placed where someone signifies something to someone else. It therefore already presupposes an authentification of the signifier.

The ethical relation, the face to face, also cuts across every relation one could call mystical, where events other than that of the presentation of the original being come to overwhelm or sublimate the pure sincerity of this presentation, where intoxicating equivocations come to enrich the primordial univocity of expression, where discourse becomes incantation as prayer becomes rite and liturgy, where the interlocutors find themselves playing a role in a drama that has begun outside of them. Here resides the rational character of the ethical relation and of language. No fear, no trembling could alter the straightforwardness of this relationship, which preserves the discontinuity of relationship, resists fusion, and where the response does not evade the question. To poetic activity – where influences arise unbeknown to us out of this nonetheless conscious activity, to envelop it and beguile it as a rhythm, and where action is borne along by the very work it has given rise to, where in a dionysiac mode the artist (according to Nietzsche's expression) becomes a work of art – is opposed the language that at each instant dispels the charm of rhythm and prevents the initiative from becoming a role. Discourse is rupture and commencement, breaking of rhythm which enraptures and transports the interlocutors – prose.

The face in which the other – the absolutely other – presents himself does not negate the same, does not do violence to it as do opinion or authority or the thaumaturgic supernatural. It remains commensurate with him who welcomes; it remains terrestrial. This presentation is preeminently nonviolence, for instead of offending my freedom it calls it to responsibility and founds it. As nonviolence it nonetheless maintains the plurality of the same and the other. It is peace. The relation with the other – the absolutely other – who has no frontier with the same is not exposed to the allergy that afflicts the same in a totality, upon which the Hegelian dialectic rests. The other is not for reason a scandal which launches it into dialectical movement, but the first rational teaching, the condition for all teaching. The alleged scandal of alterity presupposes the tranquil identity of the same, a freedom sure of itself which is exercised without scruples, and to whom the foreigner brings only constraint and limitation. This flawless identity freed from all participation, independent in the I, can nonetheless lose its tranquillity if the other, rather than countering it by upsurging on the same plane as it, speaks to it, that is, shows himself in expression, in the face, and comes from on high. Freedom then is inhibited, not as countered by a resistance, but as arbitrary, guilty, and timid; but in its guilt it rises to responsibility. Contingency, that is, the irrational, appears to it not outside of itself in the other, but within itself. It is not limitation by the other that constitutes contingency, but egoism, as unjustified of itself. The relation with the Other as a relation with his transcendence – the relation with the Other who puts into question the brutal spontaneity of one's immanent destiny – introduces into me what was not in me. But this "action" upon my freedom precisely puts an end to violence and contingency, and, in this sense also, founds Reason. To affirm that the passage of a content from one mind to the other is produced without violence only if the truth taught by the master is from all eternity in the student is to extrapolate maieutics beyond its legitimate usage. The idea of infinity in me, implying a content overflowing the container, breaks with the prejudice of maieutics without breaking with rationalism, since the idea of infinity, far from violating the mind, conditions nonviolence itself, that is, establishes ethics. The other is not for reason a scandal that puts it in dialectical movement, but the first teaching. A being *receiving* the idea of Infinity, *receiving* since it cannot derive it from itself, is a being taught in a non-maieutic fashion, a being whose very existing consists in this incessant reception of teaching, in this incessant overflowing of self (which is time). To think is to have the idea of infinity, or to be taught. Rational thought refers to this teaching. Even if we confine ourselves to the formal structure of logical thought, which starts from a definition, infinity, relative to which concepts are delimited, can not be defined in its turn. It accordingly refers to a "knowledge" of a new structure. We seek to fix it as a relation with the face and to show the ethical essence of this relation. The face is the evidence that makes evidence possible – like the divine veracity that sustains Cartesian rationalism.

4. Discourse Founds Signification

Language thus conditions the functioning of rational thought: it gives it a commencement in being, a primary identity of signification in the face of him who speaks, that is, who presents himself by ceaselessly undoing the equivocation of his own image, his verbal signs. Language conditions thought – not language in its physical materiality, but language as an attitude of the same with regard to the Other irreducible to the representation of the Other, irreducible to an intention of thought, irreducible to a consciousness of …, since relating to what no consciousness can contain, relating to the infinity of the Other. Language is not enacted within a consciousness; it comes to me from the Other and reverberates in consciousness by putting it in question. This event is irreducible to consciousness, where everything comes about from within – even the strangeness of suffering. To regard language as an attitude of the mind does not amount to disincarnating it, but is precisely to account for its incarnate essence, its difference from the constitutive, egological nature of the transcendental thought of idealism. The originality of discourse with respect to constitutive intentionality, to pure consciousness, destroys the concept of immanence: the idea of infinity in consciousness is an overflowing of a consciousness whose incarnation offers new powers to a soul no long paralytic – powers of welcome, of gift, of full hands, of hospitality. But to take incarnation as a primary fact of language, without indicating the ontological structure it accomplishes, would be to assimilate language to activity, to that prolongation of thought in corporeity, the *I think* in the *I can*, which has indeed served as a prototype for the category of the lived body [corps propre] or incarnate thought, which dominates one part of contemporary philosophy. The thesis we present here separates radically language and activity, expression and labor, in spite of all the practical side of language, whose importance we may not underestimate.

Until very recently the fundamental function of discourse in the upsurge of reason was not recognized. The function of words was understood in their dependence on reason: words reflected thought. Nominalism was the first to seek in words another function: that of an *instrument* of reason. A symbolic function of the word symbolizing the non-thinkable rather than signifying thought contents, this symbolism amounted to association with a certain number of conscious, intuitive data, an association that would be self-sufficient and would not require thought. The theory had no other purpose than to explain a divergence between thought, incapable of aiming at a general object, and language, which does seem to refer to general objects. Husserl's critique, completely subordinating words to reason, showed this divergency to be only apparent. The word is a window; if it forms a screen it must be rejected. With Heidegger Husserl's esperantist words take on the color and weight of a historical reality. But they remain bound to the process of comprehension.

The mistrust of verbalism leads to the incontestable primacy of rational thought over all the *operations* of expression that insert a thought into a particular language as into a system of signs, or bind it to a system of language presiding over the choice of these signs. Modern investigations in the philosophy of language have made familiar the idea of an underlying solidarity of thought with speech. Merleau-Ponty, among others, and better than others, showed that disincarnate thought thinking speech before speaking it, thought constituting the world of speech, adding a world of speech to the world antecedently constituted out of significations in an always transcendental operation, was a myth. Already thought consists in foraging in the system of signs, in the particular tongue of a people or civilization, and receiving signification from this very operation. It ventures forth at random, inasmuch as it does not start with an antecedent representation, or with those significations, or with phrases to be articulated. Hence one might say thought operates in the "I can" of the body. It operates in it before representing this body to itself or constituting it. Signification surprises the very thought that thought it.

But why is language, the recourse to the system of signs, necessary for thought? Why does the object, and even the perceived object, need a name in order to become a signification? What is it to have a meaning? Signification, though received from this incarnate language, nonetheless remains, throughout this conception, an "intentional object." The structure of constitutive consciousness recovers all its rights after the mediation of the body that speaks or writes. Does not the surplus of signification over representation consist in a new mode of being presented (new with respect to constitutive intentionality), whose secret the analysis of "body intentionality" does not exhaust? Does the mediation of the sign constitute the signification because it would introduce into an objective and static representation the "movement" of symbolic relation? But then language would again be suspected of taking us away from "the thing themselves."…

It is the contrary that must be affirmed; it is not the mediation of the sign that forms signification, but signification (whose primordial event is the face to face) that makes the sign function possible. The primordial essence of language is to be sought not in the corporeal operation that discloses it to me and to others and, in the recourse to language, builds up a thought, but in the presentation of meaning. This does not bring us back to a transcendental consciousness constituting objects, against which the theory of language we have just evoked protests with such just rigor. For significations do not present themselves to theory, that is, to the constitutive freedom of a transcendental consciousness; *the being of signification consists in putting into question in an ethical relation constitutive freedom itself.* Meaning is the face of the Other, and all recourse to words takes place already within the primordial face to face of language. Every recourse to words presupposes the comprehension of the primary signification, but this comprehension, before being interpreted as a "consciousness of," is society and obligation. Signification is the Infinite, but infinity does not present itself to a transcendental thought, nor even to meaningful activity, but presents itself in the Other; the Other faces me and puts me in question and *obliges* me by his essence qua infinity. That "something" we call signification arises in being with language because the essence of language is the relation with the Other. This relation is not added to the interior monologue – be it Merleau-Ponty's "corporeal intentionality" – like an address added to the fabricated object one puts in the mailbox; the welcoming of the being that appears in the face, the ethical event of sociality, already commands inward discourse. And the epiphany that is produced as a face is not constituted as are all other beings, precisely because it "reveals" infinity. Signification is infinity, that is, the Other. The intelligible is not a concept, but an intelligence. Signification precedes *Sinngebung*, and rather than justifying idealism, marks its limit.

In a sense signification is to perception what the symbol is to the object symbolized. The symbol marks the inadequateness of what is given in consciousness with regard to the being it symbolizes, a consciousness needy and hungry for the being it lacks, for the being announced in the very precision with which its absence is lived, a potency that evinces the act. Signification resembles it, as an overflowing of the intention that envisages by the being envisaged. But here the inexhaustible surplus of infinity overflows the actuality of consciousness. The shimmer of infinity, the face, can no longer be stated in terms of consciousness, in metaphors referring to light and the sensible. It is the ethical exigency of the face, which puts into question the consciousness that welcomes it. The consciousness of obligation is no longer a consciousness, since it tears consciousness up from its center, submitting it to the Other.

If the face to face founds language, if the face brings the first signification, establishes signification itself in being, then language does not only serve reason, but is reason. Reason in the sense of an impersonal legality does not permit us to account for discourse, for it absorbs the plurality of the interlocutors. Reason, being unique, cannot speak to another reason. A reason immanent in an individual consciousness is, to be sure, conceivable, in the way of naturalism, as a system of laws that regulate the nature of this consciousness, individuated like all natural beings but in addition individuated also as oneself. The concordance between consciousnesses would then be explained by the resemblance of beings constituted in the same fashion. Language would be reduced to a system of signs awakening, from one consciousness to the other, like thoughts. In that case one must disregard the intentionality of rational thought, which opens upon a universal order, and run all the risks of naturalist psychologism, against which the arguments of the first volume of the *Logische Untersuchungen* are ever valid.

Retreating from these consequences, and in order to conform oneself more to the "phenomenon," one can call reason the internal coherence of an ideal order realized in being in the measure that the individual consciousness, in which it is learnt or set up, would renounce its particularity as an individual and an ipseity, and either withdraw unto a noumenal sphere, from which it would exercise intemporally its role as absolute subject in the I think, or be reabsorbed in the universal order of the State, which at first it seemed to foresee or constitute. In both cases the role of language would be to dissolve the ipseity of individual consciousness, fundamentally antagonistic to reason, either to transform it into an "I think" which no longer speaks, or to make it disappear into its own discourse, whereupon, having entered into the State, it could only undergo the judgment of history, rather than remain me, that is, judge that history.

In such a rationalism there is no longer any society, that is, no longer any relation whose terms absolve themselves from the relation.

The Hegelians may attribute to human animality the consciousness of tyranny the individual feels before impersonal law, but they have yet to make understandable how a rational animal is possible, how the particularity of oneself can be affected by the simple universality of an idea, how an egoism can abdicate?

If, on the contrary, reason lives in language, if the first rationality gleams forth in the opposition of the face to face, if the first intelligible, the first signification, is the infinity of the intelligence that presents itself (that is, speaks to me) in the face, if reason is defined by signification rather than signification being defined by the impersonal structures of reason, if society precedes the apparition of these impersonal structures, if universality reigns as the presence of humanity in the eyes that look at me, if, finally, we recall that this look appeals to my responsibility and consecrates my freedom as responsibility and gift of self – then the pluralism of society could not disappear in the elevation to reason, but would be its condition. It is not the impersonal in me that Reason would establish, but an I myself capable of society, an I that has arisen in enjoyment as separated, but whose separation would itself be necessary for infinity *to be* – for its infinitude is accomplished as the "facing."

5.   Language and Objectivity

A meaningful world is a world in which there is the Other through whom the world of my enjoyment becomes a theme having a signification. Things acquire a rational signification, and not only one of simple usage, because an other is associated with my relations with them. In designating a thing I designate it to the Other. The act of designating modifies my relation of enjoyment and possession with things, places the things in the perspective of the Other. Utilizing a sign is therefore not limited to substituting an indirect relation for the direct relation with a thing, but permits me to render the things offerable, detach them from my own usage, alienate them, render them exterior. The word that designates things attests their apportionment between me and the others. The objectivity of the object does not follow from a suspension of usage and enjoyment, in which I possess things without assuming them. Objectivity results from language, which permits the putting into question of possession. This disengagement has a positive meaning: the entry of the thing into the sphere of the other. The thing becomes a theme. To thematize is to offer the world to the Other in speech. "Distance" with regard to the object thus exceeds its spatial signification.

This objectivity is correlative not of some trait in an isolated subject, but of his relation with the Other. Objectification is produced in the very work of language, where the subject is detached from the things possessed as though it hovered over its own existence, as though it were detached from it, as though the existence it exists had not yet completely reached it. This distance is more radical than every distance in the world. The subject must find itself "at a distance" from its own being, even with regard to that taking distance that is inherent in the home, by which it is still in being. For negation remains within the totality, even when it bears upon the totality of the world. In order that objective distance be hollowed out, it is necessary that while in being the subject be not yet in being, that in a certain sense it be not yet born – that it not be in nature. If the subject capable of objectivity *is* not yet completely, this "not yet," this state of potency relative to act, does not denote a less than being, but denotes time. Consciousness of the object – thematization – rests on distance with regard to oneself, which can only be time; or, if one prefers, it rests on self-consciousness, if we recognize the "distance from self to self" in self-consciousness to be "time." However, time can designate a "not yet" that nevertheless would not be a "lesser being" – it can remain distant both from being and from death – only as the inexhaustible future of infinity, that is, as what is produced in the very relationship of language. In designating what it possesses to the other, in speaking, the subject hovers over its own existence. But it is from the welcoming of the infinity of the other that it receives the freedom with regard to itself that this dispossession requires. It detains it finally from the Desire which does not arise from a lack or a limitation but from a surplus, from the idea of Infinity.

Language makes possible the objectivity of objects and their thematization. Already Husserl affirmed that the objectivity of thought consists in being valid for everyone. To know objectively would therefore be to constitute my thought in such a way that it already contained a reference to the thought of the others. What I communicate therefore is already constituted in function of others. In speaking I do not transmit to the Other what is objective for me: the objective becomes objective only through communication. But in Husserl the Other who makes this communication possible is first constituted for a monadic thought. The basis of objectivity is constituted in a purely subjective process. In positing the relation with the Other as ethical, one surmounts a difficulty that would be inevitable if, contrary to Descartes, philosophy started from a *cogito* that would posit itself absolutely independently of the Other.

For the Cartesian *cogito* is discovered, at the end of the Third Meditation, to be supported on the certitude of the divine existence qua infinite, by relation to which the finitude of the *cogito*, or the doubt, is posited and conceivable. This finitude could not be determined without recourse to the infinite, as is the case in the moderns, for whom finitude is, for example, determined on the basis of the mortality of the subject. The Cartesian subject is given a point of view exterior to itself from which it can apprehend itself. If, in a first movement, Descartes takes a consciousness to be indubitable of itself by itself, in a second movement – the reflection on reflection – he recognizes conditions for this certitude. This certitude is due to the clarity and distinctness of the *cogito*, but certitude itself is sought because of the presence of infinity in this finite thought, which without this presence would be ignorant of its own finitude: "... *manifeste intelligo plus realitatis esse in substantia infinita quam in finita, ac proinde priorem quodammodo in me esse perceptionem infiniti quam finiti, hoc est Dei quam mei ipsius. Qua enim ratione intelligerem me dubitare me cupere, hoc est aliquid mihi deesse, et me non esse omnino perfectum si nulla idea entis perfectionis in me esset, ex cujus comparatione defectus meos cognoscerem?*"[4]

Is the position of thought in the midst of the infinite that created it and has given it the idea of infinity discovered by a reasoning or an intuition that can posit only themes? The infinite can not be thematized, and the distinction between reasoning and intuition does not apply to the access to infinity. Is not the relation with infinity, in the twofold structure of infinity present to the finite, but present outside of the finite, foreign to theory? We have seen in it the ethical relation. If Husserl sees in the *cogito* a subjectivity without any support outside of itself, this *cogito* constitutes the idea of infinity itself and gives it to itself as an object. The non-constitution of infinity in Descartes leaves a door open; the reference of the finite *cogito* to the infinity of God does not consist in a simple thematization of God. I of myself account for every object; I contain them. The idea of infinity is not for me an object. The ontological argument lies in the mutation of this "object" into being, into independence with regard to me; God is the other. If to think consists in referring to an object, we must suppose that the thought of infinity is not a thought. What is it positively? Descartes does not raise the question. It is in any case evident that the intuition of infinity retains a rationalist meaning, and will not become any sort of invasion of God across an inward emotion. Decartes, better than an idealist or a realist, discovers a relation with a total alterity irreducible to interiority, which nevertheless does not do violence to interiority – a receptivity without passivity, a relation between freedoms.

The last paragraph of the Third Meditation brings us to a relation with infinity in thought which overflows thought and becomes a personal relation. Contemplation turns into admiration, adoration, and joy. It is a question no longer of an "infinite object" still known and thematized, but of a majesty: "... *placet hic aliquamdiu in ipsius Dei contemplatione immorari, eius attributa apud me expendere et immensi huius luminis pulchritudinem quantum caligantis ingenii mei acies ferre poterit, intueri, admirari, adorare. Ut enim in hac sola divinae majestatis contemplatione summan alterius vitae felicitatem consistere fide credimus, ita etiam jam ex eadem licet multo minus perfecta, maximum cujus in hac vita capaces simus voluptatem percipi posse experimur ..."*[5]

To us this paragraph appears to be not a stylistic ornament or a prudent hommage to religion, but the expression of this transformation of the idea of infinity conveyed by knowledge into Majesty approached as a face.

6.   The Other and the Others

The presentation of the face, expression, does not disclose an inward world previously closed, adding thus a new region to comprehend or to take over.[6] On the contrary, it calls to me above and beyond the given that speech already puts in common among us. What one gives, what one takes reduces itself to the phenomenon, discovered and open to the grasp, carrying on an existence which is suspended in possession – whereas the presentation of the face puts me into relation with being. *The existing of this being*, irreducible to phenomenality understood as a reality without reality, is effectuated in the non-postponable urgency with which he requires a response. This response differs from the "reaction" that the given gives rise to in that it cannot remain "between us," as is the case with the steps I take with regard to a thing. Everything that takes place here "between us" concerns everyone, the face that looks at it places itself in the full light of the public order, even if I draw back from it to seek with the interlocutor the complicity of a private relation and a clandestinity.

Language as the presence of the face does not invite complicity with the preferred being, the self-sufficient "I-Thou" forgetful of the universe; in its frankness it refuses the clandestinity of love, where it loses its frankness and meaning and turns into laughter or cooing. The third party looks at me in the eyes of the Other – language is justice. It is not that there first would be the face, and then the being it manifests or expresses would concern himself with justice; the epiphany of the face qua face opens humanity. The face in its nakedness as a face presents to me the destitution of the poor one and the stranger; but this poverty and exile which appeal to my powers, address me, do not deliver themselves over to these powers as givens, remain the expression of the face. The poor one, the stranger, presents himself as an equal. His equality within this essential poverty consists in referring to the *third party*, thus present at the encounter, whom in the midst of his destitution the Other already serves. He comes to *join* me. But he joins me to himself for service; he commands me as a Master. This command can concern me only inasmuch as I am master myself; consequently this command commands me to command. The *thou* is posited in front of a *we*. To be *we* is not to "jostle" one another or get together around a common task. The presence of the face, the infinity of the other, is a destituteness, a presence of the third party (that is, of the whole of humanity which looks at us), and a command that commands commanding. This is why the relation with the Other, discourse, is not only the putting in question of my freedom, the appeal coming from the other to call me to responsibility, is not only the speech by which I divest myself of the possession that encircles me by setting forth an objective and common world, but is also sermon, exhortation, the prophetic word. By essence the prophetic word responds to the epiphany of the face, doubles all discourse not as a discourse about moral themes, but as an irreducible movement of a discourse which by essence is aroused by the epiphany of the face inasmuch as it attests the presence of the third party, the whole of humanity, in the eyes that look at me. Like a shunt every social relation leads back to the presentation of the other to the same without the intermediary of any image or sign, solely by the expression of the face. When taken to be like a genus that unites like individuals the essence of society is lost sight of. There does indeed exist a human race as a biological genus, and the common function men may exercise in the world as a totality permits the applying to them of a common concept. But the human community instituted by language, where the interlocutors remain absolutely separated, does not constitute the unity of genus. It is stated as a kinship of men. That all men are brothers is not explained by their resemblance, nor by a common cause of which they would be the effect, like medals which refer to the same die that struck them. Paternity is not reducible to a causality in which individuals would mysteriously participate, and which would determine, by no less mysterious an effect, a phenomenon of solidarity.

It is my responsibility before a face looking at me as absolutely foreign (and the epiphany of the face coincides with these two moments) that constitutes the original fact of fraternity. Paternity is not a causality, but the establishment of a unicity with which the unicity of the father does and does not coincide.[7] The non–coincidence consists, concretely, in my position as brother; it implies other unicities at my side. Thus my unicity qua I contains both self-sufficiency of being and my partialness, my position before the other as a face. In this welcoming of the face (which is already my responsibility in his regard, and where accordingly he approaches me from a dimension of height and dominates me), equality is founded. Equality is produced where the other commands the same and reveals himself to the same in responsibility; otherwise it is but an abstract idea and a word. It cannot be detached from the welcoming of the face, of which it is a moment.

The very status of the human implies fraternity and the idea of the human race. Fraternity is radically opposed to the conception of a humanity united by resemblance, a multiplicity of diverse families arisen from the stones cast behind by Deucalion, and which, across the struggle of egoisms, results in a human city. Human fraternity has then two aspects: it involves individualities whose logical status is not reducible to the status of ultimate differences in a genus, for their singularity consists in each referring to itself. (An individual having a common genus with another individual would not be removed enough from it.) On the other hand, it involves the commonness of a father, as though the commonness of race would not bring together enough. Society must be a fraternal community to be commensurate with the straightforwardness, the primary proximity, in which the face presents itself to my welcome. Monotheism signifies this human kinship, this idea of a human race that refers back to the approach of the Other in the face, in a dimension of height, in responsibility for oneself and for the Other.

7.   The Asymmetry of the Interpersonal

The presence of the face coming from beyond the world, but committing me to human fraternity, does not overwhelm me as a numinous essence arousing fear and trembling. To be in relationship while absolving oneself from this relation is to speak. The Other does not only *appear* in his face, as a phenomenon subject to the action and domination of a freedom; infinitely distant from the very relation he enters, he presents himself there from the first as an absolute. The I disengages itself from the relationship, but does so within relationship with a being absolutely separated. The face with which the Other turns to me is not reabsorbed in a representation of the face. To hear his destitution which cries out for justice is not to represent an image to oneself, but is to posit oneself as responsible, both as more and as less than the being that presents itself in the face. Less, for the face summons me to my obligations and judges me. The being that presents himself in the face comes from a dimension of height, a dimension of transcendence whereby he can present himself as a stranger without opposing me as obstacle or enemy. More, for my position as I consists in being able to respond to this essential destitution of the Other, finding resources for myself. The Other who dominates me in his transcendence is thus the stranger, the widow, and the orphan, to whom I am obligated.

These differences between the Other and me do not depend on different "properties" that would be inherent in the "I," on the one hand, and, on the other hand, in the Other, nor on different psychological dispositions which their minds would take on from the encounter. They are due to the I-Other conjuncture, to the inevitable *orientation* of being "starting from oneself" toward "the Other." The priority of this orientation over the terms that are placed in it (and which cannot arise without this orientation) summarizes the theses of the present work.

Being *is* not *first*, to afterwards, by breaking up, give place to a diversity all of whose terms would maintain reciprocal relations among themselves, exhibiting thus the totality from which they proceed, and in which there would on occasion be produced a being existing for itself, an I, facing another I (incidents that could be accounted for by an impersonal discourse exterior to those incidents). Not even the language that narrates it can depart from the orientation of the I to the Other. Language does not take place *in front of* a correlation from which the I would derive its identity and the Other his alterity. The separation involved in language does not denote the presence of two beings in an ethereal space where union simply echos separation. Separation is first the fact of a being that lives *somewhere,* from *something,* that is, that enjoys. The identity of the I comes to it from its egoism whose insular sufficiency is accomplished by enjoyment, and to which the face teaches the infinity from which this insular sufficiency is separated. This egoism is indeed founded on the infinitude of the other, which can be accomplished only by being produced as the idea of Infinity in a separated being. The other does indeed invoke this separated being, but this invocation is not reducible to calling for a correlative. It leaves room for a process of being that is deduced from itself, that is, remains separated and capable of shutting itself up against the very appeal that has aroused it, but also capable of welcoming this face of infinity with all the resources of its egoism: economically. Speech is not instituted in a homogeneous or abstract medium, but in a world where it is necessary to aid and to give. It presupposes an I, an existence separated in its enjoyment, which does not welcome empty-handed the face and its voice coming from another shore. Multiplicity in being, which refuses totalization but takes form as fraternity and discourse, is situated in a "space" essentially asymmetrical.

8. Will and Reason

Discourse conditions thought, for the first intelligible is not a concept, but an intelligence whose inviolable exteriority the face states in uttering the "you shall not commit murder." The essence of discourse is ethical. In stating this thesis, idealism is refused.

The idealist intelligible constitutes a system of coherent ideal relations whose presentation before the subject is equivalent to the entry of the subject into this order and its absorption into those ideal relations. The subject has no resource in itself that does not dry up under the intelligible sun. Its will is reason and its separation illusory (even though the possibility of illusion attests the existence of an at least subterranean subjective source which the intelligible cannot dry up).

Idealism completely carried out reduces all ethics to politics. The Other and the I function as elements of an ideal calculus, receive from this calculus their real being, and approach one another under the dominion of ideal necessities which traverse them from all sides. They play the role of moments in a system, and not that of origin. Political society appears as a plurality that expresses the multiplicity of the articulations of a system. In the kingdom of ends, where persons are indeed defined as wills, but where the will is defined as what permits itself to be affected by the universal – where the will wishes to be reason, be it practical reason – multiplicity rests in fact only on the hope of happiness. The so-called animal principle of happiness, ineluctable in the description of the will, even taken as practical reason, maintains pluralism in the society of minds.

In this world without multiplicity language loses all social signification; interlocutors renounce their unicity not in desiring one another but in desiring the universal. Language would be equivalent to the constitution of rational institutions in which an impersonal reason which is already at work in the persons who speak and already sustains their effective reality would become objective and effective: each being is posited apart from all the others, but the will of each, or ipseity, from the start consists in willing the universal or the rational, that is, in negating its very particularity. In accomplishing its essence as discourse, in becoming a discourse universally coherent, language would at the same time realize the universal State, in which multiplicity is reabsorbed and discourse comes to an end, for lack of interlocutors.

To distinguish formally will and understanding, will and reason, nowise serves to maintain plurality in being or the unicity of the person if one forthwith decides to consider only the will that adheres to clear ideas or decides only through respect for the universal to be a good will. If the will can aspire to reason in one way or another, it is reason, reason seeking or forming itself; its true essence is revealed in Spinoza or in Hegel. This identification of will and reason, which is the ultimate intention of idealism, is opposed by the entire pathetic experience of humanity, which the Hegelian or Spinozist idealism relegates to the subjective or the imaginary. The interest of this opposition does not lie in the very protestation of the individual who refuses the system and reason, that is, in his arbitrariness, which the coherent discourse could hence not silence by persuasion – but in the affirmation that makes this opposition live. For the opposition does not consist in shutting one's eyes to being and thus striking one's head madly against the wall so as to surmount in oneself the consciousness of one's deficiencies of being, one's destitution, and one's exile, and so as to transform a humiliation into desperate pride. This opposition is inspired by the certainty of the surplus which an existence separated from and thus desiring the full or immutable being or being in act involves by relation to that being, *that is, the surplus that is produced by the society of infinity*, an incessant surplus that accomplishes the infinitude of infinity. The protestation against the identification of the will with reason does not indulge in arbitrariness, which, by its absurdity and immorality, would immediately justify this identification. It proceeds from the certitude that the ideal of a being accomplished from all eternity, thinking only itself, can not serve as the ontological touchstone for a life, a becoming, capable of renewal, of Desire, of society. Life is not comprehensible simply as a diminution, a fall, or an embryo or virtuality of being. The individual and the personal count and act independently of the universal, which would mould them. Moreover, the existence of the individual on the basis of the universal, or the fall from which it arises, remains unexplained. *The individual and the personal are necessary for Infinity to be able to be produced as infinite.*[8] The impossibility of treating life in function of being is manifested compellingly in Bergson, where duration no longer imitates, in its fallenness, an immobile eternity, or in Heidegger, where possibility no longer is referred to ἔργον as a δύναμις. Heidegger dissociates life from the finality of potency tending toward act. That there could be a more than being or an above being is expressed in the idea of creation which, in God, exceeds a being eternally satisfied with itself. But this notion of the being above being does not come from theology. If it has played no role in the Western philosophy issued from Aristotle, the Platonic idea of the Good ensures it the dignity of a philosophical thought – and it therefore should not be traced back to any oriental wisdom.

If the subjectivity were but a deficient mode of being, the distinguishing between will and reason would indeed result in conceiving the will as arbitrary, as a pure and simple negation of an embryonic or virtual reason dormant in an I, and consequently as a negation of that I and a violence in regard to oneself. If, on the contrary, the subjectivity is fixed as a separated being in relation with an other absolutely other, the Other, if the face brings the first signification, that is, the very upsurge of the rational, then the will is distinguished fundamentally from the intelligible, which it must not comprehend and into which it must not disappear, for the intelligibility of this intelligible resides precisely in ethical behavior, that is, in the responsibility to which it invites the will. The will is free to assume this responsibility in whatever sense it likes; it is not free to refuse this responsibility itself; it is not free to ignore the meaningful world into which the face of the Other has introduced it. *In the welcoming of the face the will opens to reason.* Language is not limited to the maieutic awakening of thoughts common to beings. It does not accelerate the inward maturation of a reason common to all; it teaches and introduces the new into a thought. The introduction of the new into a thought, the idea of infinity, is the very work of reason. The absolutely new is the Other. The rational is not opposed to the experienced; absolute experience, the experience of what is in no way a priori, is reason itself. In discovering, as correlative of experience, the Other, him who, being in himself essentially, can speak, and nowise sets himself up as an object, the *novelty* contributed by experience is reconciled with the ancient Socratic exigency of a mind nothing can force, an exigency Leibniz again answers to in refusing the monads windows.

The ethical presence is both other and imposes itself without violence. As the activity of reason commences with speech, the subject does not abdicate his unicity, but confirms his separation. He does not enter into his own discourse to disappear in it; it remains an apology. The passage to the rational is not a dis-individuation precisely because it is language, that is, a response to the being who in a face speaks to the subject and tolerates only a personal response, that is, an ethical act.

Notes

1 "Mon pouvoir de pouvoir."
2 Treatise *Synhedrin*, 104 b.
3 Plato, *Republic*, 327 b.
4 Ed. Tannery, T. VII, pp. 45–6. ["… there is manifestly more reality in the infinite substance than in the finite substance, and my awareness of the infinite must therefore be in some way prior to my awareness of the finite, that is to say, my awareness of God must be prior to that of myself. For how could I know that I doubt and desire, i.e., know that something is lacking to me and that I am not wholly perfect, save by having in me the idea of a being more perfect than myself, by comparison with which I may recognize my deficiencies." Eng. trans. by Norman Kemp Smith, Descartes, *Philosophical Writings* (New York, 1958), p. 205.]
5 "… it seems to me right to linger for a while on the contemplation of this all-perfect God, to ponder at leisure His marvelous attributes, to intuit, to admire, to adore, the incomparable beauty of this inexhaustible light, so far at least as the powers of my mind may permit, dazzled as they are by what they are endeavoring to see. For just as by faith we believe that the supreme felicity of the life to come consists in the contemplation of the Divine majesty, so do we now experience that a similar meditation, though one so much less perfect, can enable us to enjoy the highest contentment of which we are capable in this present life." *Ibid.*, p. 211.
6 "…à comprendre ou à prendre."
7 See p. 278.
8 See "The Truth of the Will," pp. 240 ff.

CHAPTER 7

Levinas and Literary Interpretation: Facing Baudelaire's "Eyes of the Poor"

Kuisma Korhonen

Kuisma Korhonen is Professor of Literature at the University of Oulu. His books include *Textual Friendship: The Essay as Impossible Encounter* (2004), *Tropes for the Past: Hayden White and the History/Literature Debate* (ed., 2006), *The Event of Encounter in Art and Philosophy* (co-ed., 2010), and *Chiasmatic Encounters* (co-ed., forthcoming). His work has addressed literature as a form of ethical encounter and textual community. Lately he has been working on the ethics of cultural memory.

"Levinasian narratology" may sound like an oxymoron. Indeed, Emmanuel Levinas's criticism of all artistic representations, including narratives, in his early essay "Reality and its Shadow" should warn us not to apply his work to narrative analysis. There Levinas famously claims that novels, like artistic representations in general, force reality into fixed and frozen, shadowy and statuesque images. Novels turn living temporality into plots, destinies, and meanings, and transform the living interiority of human time into the immobile exteriority of the narrative gaze:

> The characters of a novel are beings that are shut up, prisoners. Their history is never finished, it still goes on, but makes no headway. A novel shuts beings up in a fate despite their freedom. Life solicits the novelist when it seems to him as if it were already something out of the book. Something somehow completed arises in it, as though a whole set of facts were immobilized and formed a series. They are described between two well-determined moments, in the space of a time existence had traversed as through a tunnel. The events related form a *situation* – akin to a plastic ideal. (1989b [1948]: 139)

In his later work, Levinas makes constant references to literary texts, but as Colin Davis (81–102) or Hanna Meretoja (forthcoming) note, his reservations on narrative forms like the novel remain strong. In the vocabulary of the late Levinas, the form of the novel

Original publication details: Kuisma Korhonen, "Towards a Post-Levinasian Approach to Narrativity," from *Partial Answers – Journal of Literature and the History of Ideas* 6.2 (June 2008), pp. 459–480. Reproduced with permission from Johns Hopkins University Press.

turns the Saying into the Said, the act of addressing and welcoming the Other into an act of comprehending and appropriating the Other.[1] When he describes the fiction of his close friend Maurice Blanchot, *narrative* is seen as the inevitable but violent moment where poetic saying betrays itself and becomes enveloped "in the totality of the said" (Levinas 1989d [1966]: 157).

So, what kind of "narratology" could we possibly construct around Levinasian ethics if its basic approach to narratives is highly critical? Indeed, the very notion of *logos* in "narratology" – the very idea of "narrative science" as a theory and method of mapping, describing, and analyzing textual structures – is already incompatible with the Levinasian thinking which concentrates on those elements that, in ethical experience, escape our cognitive attempts to grasp otherness.

My purpose in this essay is not to construct any Levinasian or post-Levinasian narratological method (or any post-Levinasian literary theory, for that matter). To do so would require taking into account the dual background of Levinas's *œuvre* in both the phenomenological (Husserl and Heidegger) and Judaic (Buber and Rosenzweig) traditions, as well as the philosophical context in which it has been read and discussed: Derrida (1978 [1964], 1991 [1980], 1999 [1997]), Blanchot, Irigaray, Ricoeur, and the work of at least the most important commentators of Levinas, such as Critchley, Peperzak (1993, 1999), Llewelyn (1995, 2002), or Bailhache. Against this general background of Levinasian and post-Levinasian philosophical discourse it would then be necessary to describe the attempts that have been made to apply the Levinasian approach to ethical literary criticism – by Robert Eaglestone and Jill Robbins, who have discussed Levinas's own comments on literature and art, and by Adam Z. Newton, who, combining his Levinasian influences with the dialogism of Bakhtin and with Cavellian skepticism, argues that narrative is the original form of ethical thought. And we certainly would have to enter into dialogue with Geoffrey Galt Harpham, whose views on the relationship between ethics and morality build heavily on Levinas; Andrew Gibson, who has introduced several Levinasian themes in his account of the post-modern English novel; and Derek Attridge, whose *Singularity of Literature* is inspired by Levinasian insights on the primacy of otherness.

The task would be enormous. What I can do here is to take *one* central Levinasian theme – facing the Other – and see how it resonates with one short narrative, Baudelaire's "Eyes of the Poor." Even this attempt to bridge the distance between Levinasian ethics and narrative analysis may contain a rupture, as I move from Levinasian ethics and his notion of the "face" – often used as a highly figurative term – to more traditional narratological terms and the reading of concrete faces in Baudelaire's text.

First, however, I must explain why one of the most important themes in the work of Levinas is also the reason why we should turn to Levinas in reading narratives despite his seemingly hostile attitude towards them – and why we should, in the end, combine the purely Levinasian approach with more textually, historically, and politically oriented insights on narratives in order to move towards a post-Levinasian ethical approach.

I

The central element in Levinasian ethics is the encounter. Truly ethical thinking begins not from the experience of a single consciousness thrown into existence but from the event of encountering otherness. For Levinas, this encounter is never symmetric: the Other is vulnerable, at one's mercy, and this is exactly why he or she is, in one's ethical experience, above one, commanding one, holding one "hostage." This encounter cannot be reversed: one's responsibility before the Other is not dependent on the way the Other sees one. One is responsible not only *to* the Other but *for* the other, to the point where one (but oneself alone) is a "substitute" for every other – the other being not someone one could identify with, but precisely someone who remains irreducibly other (1974: 200).

Consequently, a Levinasian approach to narratives should be attentive not to the text in and of itself, as a completed work of art, but rather to the asymmetric and irreversible space of textual encounter that the text opens up between the author and the reader. The focus is shifted from the textual object to what Buber called *Zwischen* – to a relational space that is always *in between* and is never identifiable with any given object, theme, or value. In this space, the textual otherness (the vision of the author, the voice of the narrator, the beings that we encounter in the fictional world) is both at our mercy and above us – in its vulnerability it commands us, makes us responsible for it before we have even begun to read. I am, in a way, a hostage of the text, called not to identify with the narrator or characters, but to substitute for them, to carry responsibility (but a totally singular responsibility that cannot be generalized) *to* and *for* every being in the text. I do not have to feel any sympathy for or resemblance with Raskolnikov, but as a substitute for all beings in *Crime and Punishment* it is still I, not Dostoevsky or the fictional characters that he has invented, who kills the women.[2]

The encounter is, for Levinas, the event of *facing* the Other. The figure of the *face* (*visage*) is perhaps the central and most controversial feature of his first major work, *Totalité et infini* (1961). The *face* for Levinas resists our attempts to comprehend and appropriate the Other. It is the element in the Other that precedes our knowledge, that calls us to respond to and welcome the Other before we have started to process the encounter with our cognitive skills. If we analyze the color of the hair or eyes of the Other, we have already moved into cognitive appropriation and do not welcome the *face* in the Levinasian sense. The face is vulnerable, but in its very vulnerability it commands us: thou shall not kill. In other words, the face is a metonymy for something that cannot be reduced to mere visibility. It is a figure – or rather a *counter-figure*[3] – that reveals the limits of figuration.

More than in vision, in fact, the *face* is figured in discourse. In the vocabulary of the second major work of Levinas, *Otherwise Than Being or Beyond Essence*, the face is heard in the event of Saying (the vocative act of addressing the Other) that precedes all the Said (language as a system of referential relations, significations, etc.) (1974: 16–20). Saying is the original possibility of encounter that founds the possibility of response and thus of responsibility. This possibility does not have to be conscious; it is a structural necessity of language. However, when we formulate our vocative act in words and sentences, every Saying is inevitably turned into something Said, into those conceptual structures that a subject uses in order to define and master the world. Only the Said is visible to the analytic gaze, whereas Saying can be perceived only through those ruptures – or traces of those ruptures – that it has left to the order of the Said.[4]

In literature, what counts is not the Said – the thesis, theme, or cognitive meaning of a book – but Saying, or the event of encounter where we welcome the face of the Other. In *Ethics and Infinity: Conversations with Philippe Nemo*, Levinas describes literature as follows:

> What one calls written in souls is at first written in books. Their status has always been too
> quickly made commonplace among the tools or cultural products of Nature or History.
> Even though their literature effects a rupture in being and does not come down to some

unknown intimate voice, or to the normative abstraction of "values" that the world itself where we are cannot reduce to the objectivity of objects. I think that across all literature the human face speaks – or stammers, or gives itself a countenance, or struggles with its caricature. (1985: 116–17)

We may note at least two important points. First, here Levinas, unlike in some of his early essays, treats writing not as natural but as a secondary continuation of living speech or inner monologues: writing is a technique that, as a technique, marks a rupture in being. Books are not just tools or products but a singular mode of being that we should not take for granted. Second, in literature, indeed, "the human face speaks," but speaks in a way that cannot be objectified or reduced to any traditional "inner voice" or abstract "values" that would guarantee a stable and recognizable identity. Rather than just speak, as Levinas specifies, the human face "stammers, or gives itself a countenance, or struggles with its caricature." In order to hear how the human face tries to manifest itself in books, we should, it seems, take into account the technology that forms the specific mode of being of literary texts – for example, narrative techniques.[5]

The ultimate target of Levinas in "Reality and its Shadow" is not art in itself, but rather a certain aestheticist and fetishistic approach to art that remains content to analyze and enjoy the artistic techniques as ends in themselves. His criticism of this approach is informed by the Bergsonian notion of *duration*, which Bergson contrasts with objectifications of the lived, continuous experience of time. Instead of the aesthetic contemplation of completed artworks Levinas calls for criticism that feels the "need to enter into a relation with someone" (1989c [1949]: 147), for interpretation as a version of *prosopopoeia*: "the immobile statue has to be put in movement and made to speak" (1989b [1948]: 142). The "duration in the interval," art as a frozen image of death, must be transformed by critical reading to lived, continuous *duration* in the Bergsonian sense (and to the recognition of the irreducible otherness of the duration of the Other). In fact, modern literature has already moved in that direction: "Modern literature, disparaged for its intellectualism (which none the less goes back to Shakespeare, the Molière of *Don Juan*, Goethe, Dostoevsky), certainly manifests an increasingly clear awareness of this fundamental insufficiency of artistic idolatry" (1989b [1948]: 143).[6]

We may now see that the objections of Levinas against *novels* as rhetorical artifacts does not necessarily mean that he condemns the *act of narration* as an event of addressing the Other. Indeed, Levinas tends to see the act of narration (as a mode of *Saying*) in a more positive light than the narrative as a final product (the *Said*). In order to illustrate this, I shall briefly discuss three occasions where Levinas reads narrative texts.

In his once highly influential work *The Rhetoric of Fiction* (1961), Wayne C. Booth presents Céline's *Journey to the End of the Night* as an example of a novel that fails to build a coherent image of the implied author, and consequently fails to offer the reader any reliable, comprehensive, and ethically valuable interpretation. For Booth, Céline's narrator Bardamu is, in his simultaneous nihilism and verbal energy, neither reliable nor unreliable enough. The reader cannot accept the narrator's moral values, but does not get enough hints for the alternative vision of the "implied author" behind them.

For Levinas, in "Everyday Language and Rhetoric without Eloquence" (1993 [1981]), the importance of Céline's narration in *Journey* does not lie in the final product, in the novel itself, or in the image that it offers of the world or of its implied author, but in its break with the calculative and eloquent rhetoric that had governed French literature, and in its introduction of new modes, vocabularies, and rhythmic energies. If we take

Levinas's stance a bit further than he himself does in his short reading, Bardamu's uncertain reliability might be seen as a virtue: by provoking us into asking ourselves why he still bothers to communicate if he is so completely a nihilist, Bardamu turns our attention to the difference between the Said and the act of Saying. There is, beneath all semantic meanings of his text, a vocative act, an urgent plea: hear my voice, feel the body that cries these words. It is true that Céline's novel actively resists all coherent inter-pretations, and it is certainly not easy to define the true moral values of the "implied author" behind the text (especially since the political stance of Céline himself was very ambiguous, changing from the leftist anarchism of *Journey* to his violently anti-Semitic pamphlets in the 1930's). However, in *Journey*, our attention is drawn to the most crucial element of all communication, to the act of Saying, even in the middle of the most outrageous bursts of anger and nihilism. Yet even Céline's narrative energy can become a mode of the Said, and Levinas admits that this author's anti-eloquence has gelled into a new rhetoric, a replicable style.

In an early essay "The Transcendence of Words" (1989c [1949]), Levinas reads *Biffures*, the first part of the autobiographical narrative (or metanarrative) *La Règle du jeu* by Michel Leiris. At the end of his book, Leiris puns on the words *bifures* (bifurcations) and *biffures* (erasures): his writing proceeds both as bifurcations (by unexpected associations and turns) and erasures (by continual corrections and alterations). According to Levinas, "in these bifurcations and erasures Leiris is less concerned to go down the new paths opened up or to latch onto the corrected meaning than he is to capture thought at that special moment when it turns into something other than itself" (146). It seems that Levinas values in Leiris exactly those elements that break and disturb the appropriation of life as a narrative, as a temporally and causally organized series of events. Rather than looking for a completed life story, Levinas (like Leiris) is interested in the act of writing as *de-narration*, as the continuous multiplication and erasure of narrative gestures. The childhood past and the sense of the self are seen as ever-changing constructions of the writing self. This erasing and associative method of writing represents for Levinas "a thought that lies beyond the classical categories of representation and identity" (146). At the end Levinas expresses a minor critical reservation about the primacy that Leiris still gives to the visual and spatial elements: the Said – "the thought content," – over the Saying – "the living word" (149).

It is in Proust that Levinas seems to find his narrative ideal. In another early essay on literature, "The Other in Proust," Levinas sees that Proust situates "reality in a relation with something which for ever remains other, with the Other as absence and mystery" (1989a [1947]: 165). Things, characters, and events that Proust describes remain, in spite of endless precision and details, multiple and indeterminate: "acts are shadowed by unpredictable 'counter-acts,' and things by 'counter-things' that reveal unsuspected perspectives and dimensions" (162). The world, the people, and the self remain mysterious, other. The events are important only as the subject encounters them and finds, through them, its own otherness: "It is not the inner event that counts, but the way in which the self seizes it and is bowled by it, as though it were encountered in another. It is this way of grasping an event that constitutes the very event" (163). Proust's respect for the mystery of the indeterminate other culminates, for Levinas, in Marcel's relation-ship with Albertine. Her death leaves Marcel alone, but it is precisely this solitude – the ever-present possibility of death as the death of the Other – that alone can create proximity, friendship, and love. Communication that seeks a fusion of identities under some external term (like a common ideal, a common enemy, or love as "a fusion with the Other") fails, since it tries to reduce the otherness of the Other to the unity of a common identity. Proximity can, for Levinas, take place only in the incommunicable solitude, where one is ready to welcome the mystery of the Other (164–65).

It seems, then, that only when narration somehow *fails* or *refuses* to produce a coherent narrative can it open up the horizon of otherness for Levinas. We may argue that this kind of *de-narration* is, for Levinas, one way of "unsaying the Said" so that the original Saying as "nudity of the face" before all linguistic acts can be welcome. Colin Davis has argued that Levinas endorses literary works "only in as far as they echo his own ethics of alterity," and that he fails to read narratives because he is, in the end, afraid that the radical otherness in narratives might challenge his own ethics (93). It is true that Levinas's readings are always tied to his larger philosophical project; nevertheless I disagree, at least partly, with Davis. The texts Levinas reads do not necessarily have to echo his views, at least on the thematic level – Céline, for example, can hardly be said to echo the "ethics of alterity." It seems that Davis does not pay enough attention to the difference between the act of narrating (as Saying) and the narrative form (as the Said) in Levinas.

However – and now we come to our need to move beyond Levinas – the counter-figure of the face does raise, in the case of writing, problems that we cannot avoid. I am not thinking here so much about the criticism of Slavoj Žižek (2006), who from his Lacanian viewpoint has argued that justice and ethics can exist only as "a choice AGAINST the face, for the THIRD" – in other words, that one should put the faceless multitude of others before the face of the privileged Other. Rather, I find Levinas's emphasis on the immediacy of the face problematic. For Levinas, "the face is significa-tion, and signification without context" (1985: 86). All meanings, while inevitably tied to their context, share one ultimate signification "without context": the primacy of the Other's face. But one can well ask if this ethical purity leaves us numb before all narra-tives: without context, there is no narrative and no narrative meanings that one could talk about. Without context, there is no language – and without language as the Said, there is no Saying either.[7]

Moreover, much as I appreciate Céline's primal scream in *Journey*, I would like to suggest that in narration the act of Saying should not be reduced to the narrative voice – or to the "bifurcations and erasures" of Leiris, or even to some general respect for mystery in Proust. Rather, if we take seriously the suggestion that the late Levinas makes in his conversation with Philippe Nemo – that we should treat books not merely as tools or products but as a mode of being that has its own specific status and its own technology – then we could take into account also the nature of literary communication as communication in the second degree. In other words, we should not follow those moments in early Levinas (and sometimes in the late Levinas) where he shows hostility to images or figures as such, or falls prey to what Derrida calls "phonocentrism." As Robbins notes, we should "face the figure otherwise, as language's own most figura-tive potential, as that which is most distinctive to language, that is, … face language *as* ethical possibility" (54). Literary writing is not so much an act of uttering words in a written form, a linguistic act in the first degree, as it is an act of creating and distributing representations of linguistic acts to the reader. Writing is not *only* communication but *also* meta-communication, and the true ethical event that Levinas calls Saying is thus not necessarily the moment when the author holds the pen, but the virtual space of the book where the event of writing is represented and staged. The event of literature (as all events of reproduced art) is not a moment: it is an event that has taken place, is taking place, and will take place as long as the text exists, an event and a meta-event. When I read, Dostoevsky is still writing in me; when I watch movies, Charlie Chaplin is still eating his shoes; when I listen to a CD, I can hear how Jimi Hendrix is still bending the metal strings of his Stratocaster. But none of these reproductions gives me access to any original act of writing, eating, or playing: all reproduced and represented images obey the rule of "arche-writing" that is, according to Derrida, governed by *iterability*, by a possibility of repetition *and* modification of marks. This "duration in the interval" is not necessarily the "death of the other, death for the survivor" (Levinas 1989b [1948]: 140), but an opportunity to encounter the Other *otherwise*.

We cannot discern the event of Saying – hear the face of the Other speak – in narratives unless we pay attention to those narrative techniques that open up the space for textual encounter. This means reading narratives on several different levels: on the level of the story world, at the level of narration, and in the space between the author and the reader. For example, we can – as I shall soon do – analyze how characters in a narrative encounter each other, how the narrator encounters the characters and the reader, and how this narrative act as a whole creates the space for the encounter and coming-to-being of the author and the reader. And we could try to see how these different levels act together, reflect each other, sometimes struggle with each other. For this, narratological theory, developed, for example, by Genette, Rimmon-Kenan, Herman (2004), or Phelan, offers helpful insights and a workable vocabulary. The narrative techniques it refers to should be treated not as ends in themselves, or as tools to comprehend and appropriate narrative otherness, but as ethical terms, as terms that help us to discern the mode of being that is specific to literature and that may therefore help us in encountering the face of the Other.

Moreover, before we can encounter the face without context – as pure ethical plea – we must see it in its context. Levinas has often been accused (e.g., in Badiou 2001, Žižek 2006) – quite rightly – of eliding historical and political contexts. A face-to-face encounter takes place in a non-historical non-space, where the realities of existence are, for a moment, bracketed. Although he does admit the importance of *the third* that introduces moral choices, justice, and politics, in practice Levinas's analyses concentrate on the moment of pure face-to-face encounter. However, I would suggest that in order to hear and see how the human face speaks – or how it "stammers, or gives itself a countenance, or struggles with its caricature" – we should first see the historical and political back-ground that has formed those "caricatures" and is trying to struggle with them, and only then turn to examine how the narrative is challenging those caricatures in order to reveal the face beneath all the discourses of power that try to appropriate it. In Jacques Rancière's terms, before the possibility of ethical encounter there is always a certain political "sharing of the sensible" – certain historical institutions that both allow people to share sensible spaces with each other and leave some people out of those spaces.

II

Let us read a short narrative on encountering and facing, Charles Baudelaire's "Les Yeux des pauvres" ("Eyes of the Poor").[8] As many of his prose poems in *Le Spleen de Paris*, this one is a short story or an anecdote rather than a poem.[9] For my generation, the text is also known as the source of inspiration for The Cure's hit song, "How Beautiful You Are," written (or rather adapted from Baudelaire) by Robert Smith (1987).

The narrator of Baudelaire's prose poem tells how he and his lover spent a wonderful day together and, in the end, sat down on a terrace in front of a splendid new café. The man then sees a poor father with his children standing on the pavement, looking at the café, and "hears" their eyes speak. The man turns to his lover, but instead of sharing his pity and compassion for the family, she asks him to get rid of them. This is, as the narrator adds at the end of the story, proof of how difficult it is, even for people who are in love, to understand each other.

The opening sentences of the story describe the narrative situation: "Oh! You want to know why I hate you today. It will undoubtedly be less easy for you to understand than it will be for me to explain, for you are, I believe, the most beautiful example of feminine impermeability one could ever encounter." We can discern what Genette calls a "homodiegetic narrator" or Phelan a "character narrator" – a narrator who tells, in the first person, a tale where he is himself also a character. There is also a narratee, a person directly addressed by the narrator. The narrative act is apparently motivated by the narratee's wish to know why the narrator hates her on that particular day. There is, thus, from the beginning, an open antagonism and distrust between the narrator and the narratee. This distrust, as well as the passive expression "qui se puisse rencontrer," translated here "one could ever encounter," already suggests that there is also another audience, an ideal narrative audience, for whom this "you" is meant to serve as "the most beautiful example of feminine impermeability," and who may understand him better than the narratee does. I shall return to this narrative situation.

The storyline can be divided into three stages: (1) the illusory state of communion between lovers; (2) the introduction of a third party, a poor family; and (3) the break-down of the illusion of communion.

(1) At the beginning, the narrator and his lover have spent a wonderful day together. (For the sake of clarity, I will distinguish between "the narrator" who is performing the narrative act and "the man" as a protagonist in the story.) The way the narrator describes the encounter is, as he is ready to admit at the moment of narration, "not the least bit original": the lovers had promised to "share all thoughts with one another" so that their "souls would henceforth be one." We can already ask whether this is the perfect face-to-face encounter, where two subjects share an infinite responsibility towards each other, an infinite promise to share all thoughts, an infinite will to respond to each other. Is this the perfect love that all human beings desire? Or is this, as the narrator hints, only a dream that "has been realized by none"? Or could it be what Levinas calls "fusion," a non-authentic love that tries to reduce the Other to the Same?

The glory of the new café with its sparkling gaslight, shining mirrors, and overflowing pastoral décor – "les Hébés et les Ganymèdes" – reflects the lovers' happiness, but the narrator adds an ironic twist: "all of history and all of mythology at the service of gluttony." This comment is felt to pertain to the relationship between the lovers: they are dreaming about perfect communion in terms that are perhaps more indebted to a cultural tradition of romantic, pastoral love than to the real conditions of their encounter. All the same, the obvious delight that the narrator takes in describing the sensual pleasures suggests that he cannot maintain his ironic distance – that the scene also caters to the *narrator's* verbal gluttony.

(2) Everything changes when the man sees a poor father in his forties with two small children, "all in rags," staring at the splendor of the café. The father has taken his sons for a walk, "playing the role of nanny," as the narrator states from his condescending view-point. It seems that this situation was somewhat ridiculous in nineteenth-century Paris – at least, it distinguishes this ragged family from those of the wealthy bourgeoisie, who delegated such activities to specially paid professionals. But where is the mother? Is she tired, sick, or dead? Perhaps the father is a widower and his sons are half-orphans?

The faces of the poor gain more resolution than the words that the man had earlier shared with his lover (of which we have only a very general description): the narrator "hears" the eyes of the poor talk and translates their gazes into articulated sentences. The father's eyes say "How beautiful it is! You'd think all the gold in this poor world was on its walls"; the boy's eyes say "How beautiful it is! But it's a house only people who aren't like us can enter." The eyes of the youngest child are not given voice; they just express "stupid and profound joy." The face speaks, almost literally.

The *prosopopoeia* used to describe the faces of the poor may hint that this face-to-face encounter is, in fact, deeper and more significant to the man than his earlier encounter with his lover. And, indeed, the second encounter suits Levinas's definition of the ethical encounter to a greater extent than does the first one: the poor are, at the same time, lower than the man – for Levinas, the prototype of the Other is "the poor, the stranger, the widow, and the orphan" (1961: 281) – and higher, thanks to the moral glory achieved by the father's care for his sons even in poverty. The relationship between the man and the family is asymmetric and non-reciprocal – and thus, one could claim, more ethical than any romantic love – as reciprocity, equality, and communion – could ever be.

In Levinasian terms, the father and his sons introduce "the third": the demand for justice, the demand for moral decisions. The self and the Other are never alone in the world: there is always a third who is also one's Other (and an Other to one's Other); an Other who also demands understanding, to and for whom one is also responsible. This creates the necessity of moral decisions, laws, and political action, and leads us from the pre-original but, as such, empty ethical experience of face-to-face encounter to actual moral thinking in society.

Admittedly, Levinasian ethical, non-political terms alone do not reveal the whole irony of this situation. To understand the significance of the "third," we also need historical and political analysis. As Walter Benjamin attempts to show in his unfinished *Arcades Project*, the boulevards and cafés of nineteenth-century Paris were the birthplace of a new, bourgeois metropolitan capitalism.[10] Their architecture was designed to display a consumerist spectacle that both invited people to enjoy the "gluttony" of all sensible pleasures that money could buy and divided people into actors and spectators, those who had money and those who did not. This simultaneous seduction and division can be seen in terms of what Rancière has called *partage du sensible*, the "distribution of the sensible." The dividing line between the boulevard and the café seems to be quite open and porous – the couple is not inside the café, but in front of it. The poor and the couple share the same visual space; they see the same splendor of the café, but the poor are kept out of that space and are not allowed to share in its true pleasures. The logic of this sharing, this simultaneous seduction and exclusion, can be seen in the way the poor, from the youngest to the oldest, react to the vision of abundance in front of them. Like Althusserian "interpellation," sharing offers the subject the position of a consumer, and denies the status of the subject to those who lack the means to consume. We can see how this exclusion is refracted in the eyes of the poor: the youngest child senses only the seduction and feels a "stupid and profound joy," whereas the older son, full of admiration, already knows that they are debarred from the pleasures that this seduction promises. The father's "words" could be interpreted not only as admiration but also as recognition of the larger context of the capitalist economy: the world, or the people in the world (*le monde*) is poor *because* all the gold in it is on the walls of that café.

(3) The introduction of the third, the presence of the social reality of nineteenth-century capitalism, interrupts the original encounter between the man and his lover.

The man still tries to keep the illusion of perfect communion alive: as the narrator notes, he turns his gaze towards her eyes, "inhabited by Caprice and inspired by the Moon," to read "[his] thoughts there." Note: not *her* thoughts, but *his*. He still believes in the love of the same, which, in practice, is never a union of two but a reduction of the Other to the Same, a fusion.[11]

However, the woman shatters the illusion of perfect communion by saying coldly: "I can't stand those people over there, with their eyes wide open like carriage gates! Can't you tell the head-waiter to send them away?" The eyes of the poor are compared to carriage gates (*portes cochères*) – they are ready to take in those pleasures that are not their lot. In this situation, the head-waiter can be seen as a local representative of the "police" – in charge of the distribution and sharing of the sensible. The narrative ends with a brief return to the initial narrative situation, as the narrator concludes: "So difficult is it to understand one another, my dear angel, and so incommunicable is thought, even between people in love!"[12]

Is the woman just a perfect example of "feminine impermeability"? Someone who does not let any empathic thought seep into her mind, who stays insensitive both to the needs of the poor and to the thoughts of the man? Is she just a willing actor in the consumerist spectacle of the rising capitalism? Before we pass judgment, let us reexamine the narrative situation.

Apparently, the narrator's words are an answer to a question, explicit or implicit, that the woman has posed to him, something like "why do you hate me today?" However, we can infer her question only from the narrator's answer. Their common history, the things they said to each other during their perfect day, is revealed to us only through his diegetic plane, although before the appearance of the poor he speaks in the first person plural: "We had spent together. … We had indeed promised … we wanted to sit down." However, this "we" is, in fact, a singular voice who speaks *in the name* of the first person plural, a voice of one who sees it as his right to speak on behalf of "we." It is the man who says "we," not the woman. The woman's voice is represented directly only once and even then it is framed by the narrator. The narrative situation really does not give her any chance to defend herself against the caricature that the narrator has made, to see her face without his interpretation.[13]

What *would* she say if she were given the possibility to tell *her* tale? Perhaps she would say that she was just trying to stay loyal to their love and did not want anything in the world to disturb their encounter. She has her rights, too, her rights to love. She may have money, but she has not yet met her true love, as the poor father with his children perhaps has, in spite of his poverty. Perhaps she felt hurt when she realized that the man no longer concentrated on her, that he had turned away and responded to other gazes. Perhaps she even suspected that his feelings of shame were, as in fact the narrator also hints by referring to a "song-writer's saying," caused rather by pleasure that had "softened" (*amollit*) his heart than by real ethical empathy. Perhaps she sensed that the love between them was, from the very beginning, ruled by his romantic imagination rather than by his will to welcome and understand her in her otherness.[14]

Just before the narrator quotes her words, he speaks about her eyes: "I plunged into your so beautiful and so bizarrely gentle eyes, into your green eyes, inhabited by Caprice and inspired by the Moon." The contrast between her gentle and mystic eyes and her harsh words is striking – but, as the look in her eyes is focalized only through the man's eyes, interpreted only through the narrator's vocabulary, one can see the contrast also as a calculated effect, arranged by the narrator. Anyway, it was not *her* fault that *he* had discerned "Caprice" and "Moon" in her eyes – although those figures of feminine instability could have prepared him for her unexpected words. The appropriation of her eyes by reading allegory and myth into them is, in the context of the story, just as ridiculous as the tasteless use of mythological imagery in the décor of the café.

Moreover, the apparent misreading of her eyes casts doubt on his reading of the expression in the eyes of the poor. From this point of view, his act of giving voice to the silent eyes of the poor is rather a gesture of violent appropriation than of real empathy: by "translating" their silence into words that are under *his* control he deprives them of their dignity, their right to stay silent. How could he know, any better than the woman, what the poor family was really thinking?[15] If thought is "so incommunicable, even between people in love," as the narrator says in the end, how can he claim to know what the eyes of the poor really said? And it is here, of course, that we can return to Levinas: for him, the "face" is the topos of not comprehending, not thematizing, not turning the other into something said. The face should remain as such, as the Other, and should not be turned into a logos. By formulating the look on their faces into well-defined sentences, the narrator becomes blind to their faces as faces.

Perhaps there is some reason for the narrator's hatred besides the one he suggests throughout his story. Perhaps the whole narrative is an act of revenge wrought on the woman for shattering his illusions rather than an act of justice on behalf of the poor. Moreover, as the double bind between the hatred in the beginning and the expressions "my dear angel" and "people in love" in the end suggest, the whole narrative act may be part of some bigger, sadomasochistic game – a game that, for most readers, is only too familiar from Baudelaire's other writings. The open hostility of the narrator towards the woman should make him unreliable also in the reader's eyes. Perhaps the narrator has arranged the whole narrative scene only in order to humiliate the woman in the eyes of the implied narrative audience that is watching the one-sided dialogue from outside? Perhaps we can discern also the face of the author (behind all his obsessions, perhaps against his own will) who calls us to see the violent narrative situation not only from the point of view of the male narrator but also from the point of view of the woman who is, most of the time, denied her own voice?

Or are there, after all, some hints that the narrator not only hates the woman, but also truly loves her, or at least understands her, at the moment of narration, better than he did at the café? We may compare Baudelaire's text with Smith's adaptation in "How Beautiful You Are." The song ends: "And this is why I hate you / And how I understand / that no-one ever knows or loves another // Or loves another." But this is not what the narrator says in the original "The Eyes of the Poor." Baudelaire's narrator ends his tale as follows: "So difficult is it to understand one another, my dear angel, and so incommunicable is thought, even between people in love!" Smith sees the story as that of the destruction of love, but Baudelaire's narrator does not, in fact, deny the possibility of love even though mutual understanding between lovers is hardly attainable. We can perhaps read "my dear angel" as still ironic, but not necessarily the expression "people in love" (*gens qui s'aiment*). Perhaps it is meant literally: yes, we love each other, deeply, even though we cannot know or understand each other's thoughts. Perhaps the narrator, in the end, is more willing to understand love in terms of "love of the Other" instead of "love of the Same." Perhaps the "feminine impermeability" in the beginning should be read not only as a hint at the lack of empathy in the woman but as a general affirmation of her irreducible otherness – we can love each other even if the gaze of each cannot penetrate the other, even if man and woman remain mysteries to each other, separate from each other.

We can note, then, several interpretations of the story: the first one we could call "Marxist," and it follows, more or less, the point of view of the male narrator and his shock at his companion's alleged lack of empathy, stressing the structural violence between the classes in capitalist society; the second one we could call "feminist," and it tries to reveal the viewpoint of the woman, stressing the violence of the male point of view in the narrative situation. Arguably, both interpretations are violent and fail to do justice to all the participants in the story. In the Marxist interpretation, the reader is in alliance with the man and the poor family, against the woman, the head-waiter, and the capitalist society that distributes material resources in an unjust way. However, in this interpretation, the woman's point of view is not respected; she has been left to the mercy of the male narrator. In the feminist interpretation, the reader is in alliance with the woman, against the man – but, alas, perhaps also against the poor family, thereby doing violence to their poverty, their need to share in a portion of sensual pleasures. (We may ask whether the story would be different if the poor family were, for example, a mother and two daughters. Does the male gender of the poor make it easier for the man to feel empathy with them?)

And then we can perhaps suggest a third interpretation that takes the narrator not as a chauvinist but as a "Levinasian" who does understand the violence of his own gestures and hints that love precedes understanding.

There can be several plausible "politically correct" readings, but there can be no single "ethically correct" reading, because any ethical reading draws us into endless negotiation between infinite responsibilities rather than offering us a clear solution to the situation. Whether I like it or not, I, as a reader, am responsible *to* and *for* the narrator, and as he, I am torn between infinite responsibilities: I am called to respond to the rights of his beloved and to the rights of the poor. I become, when reading the text, a substitute not only for the narrator, but for the woman, the poor family, the author – but this responsibility or substitution cannot be generalized.

Perhaps the first "you" in the story refers not only to the narratee, the woman in the story, but implicitly also to the narrative audience, to me, the reader. David Herman has called this kind of reference "double deixis": a move from a fairly unambiguous "you" as a fictional character in the story to a more ambiguous "you" that may refer either to the fictive character or to the reader (1994; 2004: 364). As Kara Rabbitt notes, the gender of "you" is grammatically expressed only in the feminine *fatiguée*, but is curiously erased in the expressions *cher amour* or *mon cher ange* (359). The last words may be saying, "so difficult is it to understand one another, my dear reader (whatever your gender), and so incommunicable is thought, even between people who are bound together by that textual friendship we call reading." Even the beginning, the "Oh! You want to know why I hate you today," may be directed not only toward the woman, but also, implicitly, to me, the reader – the reader to whom the author is bound not only by his desire to be heard and understood, but also by the fear that he will never be heard and understood, and by the hatred that this fear entails. Perhaps there is always a certain *philopolemology* (simultaneous friendship and struggle, *philia* and *polemos*) in the narrator's relationship to his narratee, or in the author's relationship to his readers, a simultaneous desire and fear between the speaker and addressee that precedes all genuine textual encounters (Derrida 1997 [1994]). The narrative act as Saying that precedes the Said, the final story, does not yet know if the response it encounters is marked by love or hate, but it is still ready to take all the risks that addressing and revealing oneself to the Other may bring along. All narrative acts welcome – they cannot but welcome – that "dangerous perhaps" that all future readings and interpretations carry with them. And this is, indeed, the gift that Baudelaire gives to us: we are constantly reminded that we cannot stay passive in front of these texts, that we cannot just read them, but that we also have to encounter them. Baudelaire's texts thus act "more like the interlocutors they portray than as third-person objects for us to study, unsettling us by their persistent refusal to provide a stable mirror for a reading of the self" (Rabbitt 367).

III

As I cautioned in the beginning, there has been a rupture in my approach, a gap between Levinasian transcendentalism and my (post-classical) narratological analysis of Baudelaire's prose poem. This rupture is both unavoidable and revealing. It would be misleading to claim that we can simply apply Levinas to concrete moral dilemmas that we encounter in real life or in reading literary narratives. Levinas does not offer practical solutions but insists on the radical infinity of ethical responsibility. However, it would be just as misleading to claim that his ethics has *no* connection to practice at all. After all, its roots are in the phenomenological analysis of ethical experiences. Notions like "face" or "hostage," which Levinas seems to use in a highly figurative way, actually trail in traces of their concrete origins with them. They should be read not as abstractions or simple metaphors (in the traditional Aristotelian sense of the word) but rather as metonymies, as figures that still have ties to their original use. The figure of the face, often extended from real life encounters to texts, is not just an abstraction: it carries with it the memory of some rare moments when we have faced the Other, eye to eye. However, there is no way of representing the face as such, and this failure creates the gap between the transcendental ethical imperative of the face and the moral compromises that we make when we face other people in real life or in literature.

In Baudelaire's "Eyes of the Poor," the narrator calls the reader to encounter the faces of the poor and the face of his beloved. However, it seems that all the faces in the story escape the narrator's attempts to appropriate them. Face-to-face encounter is seen both as a necessary and an impossible condition for love and understanding. Our attempts to encounter the face of the Other turn the Saying in the face into something Said, into an object. Nevertheless, it is exactly from this inevitable failure of reading the face of the Other that we can perhaps hear the singular way in which "across all literature the human face speaks – or stammers, or gives itself a countenance, or struggles with its caricature" (Levinas 1985: 117).

Notes

1 I shall return to the distinction between Saying and the Said. In the meantime, it should be noted that in French there are two words for the "other": *autre* can refer to any kind of otherness, whereas *autrui* only to a singular and human other. I follow the standard translations of Levinas and use "other" for *autre* and "Other" (with a capital O) for *autrui*.

2 The reference to Dostoevsky here is not accidental. In developing the theme of substitution, Levinas often refers to a famous sentence in *The Brothers Karamazov*: "We are all guilty of all and for all men before all, and I more than the others" (1985: 98).

3 For the notion of "counter-figure," see Räsänen (2007: 14–25), who uses this term to refer, in particular, to all figures that paradoxically deny their own figurality, like the legend below Magritte's painting *Trahison des images*: "Ceci n'est pas une pipe."

4   The distinction between Saying and the Said cannot, then, be reduced to the formalist/structuralist distinction between "discourse" and "story time."

5   Here the attitude of Levinas towards speech and writing is, as mentioned above, different from some of his earlier texts, where he still speaks about the "privilege of the living word, which is destined to be heard, in contrast to the word that is an image and already a picturesque sign" (1989c [1949]: 148). This change of attitude may be due in part to Derrida's insistence that writing cannot be reduced to speech.

6   Here I have slightly modified the translation of Alphonso Lingis.

7   This is, of course, just another way to express the criticism that Derrida levels as early as 1964 at the idea of "non-violent language" in "Violence and Metaphysics: An Essay on the Thought of Emmanuel Levinas."

8   "Les Yeux des pauvres" was first published in 1864 in *La Vie Parisienne*. The whole volume *Spleen de Paris* or *Petits poèmes en prose* was published posthumously in 1869.

9   On the mixed genre of the texts in *Le Spleen de Paris*, see Evans.

10 For Benjamin's reading of Baudelaire, see also McLaughlin.

11 Following Luce Irigaray, Eva Korsisaari distinguishes between two forms of love: love for the Same that seeks communion where "souls would henceforth be one," and love of the Other that seeks the recognition of the irreducible otherness of the Other (50–56).

12 On the failure of their communication, see Scott 93–98.

13 "Throughout the collection, women's utterances are generally reduced to sighs ('La Femme sauvage et la petite maîtresse'), or to self-centered, thoughtless exclamations and often censored insults ('Les Yeux des pauvres,' 'La Soupe et les nuages,' and 'Laquelle est la vraie?')" (Krueger 294).

14 Cf. Rabbitt: "The beloved's assertion of her own difference, indeed erases the speaker's desire, suggesting that his quest for 'identification' is one not of relationship but of idealized self-reflection" (361).

15 The man is, of course, doing what we all do in our everyday life: exercising "folk psychology" or "intermental cognition," trying to read other people's minds through their gestures – sometimes succeeding, but often failing at it.

Works Cited

Attridge, Derek. 2004. *The Singularity of Literature*. London: Routledge.

Badiou, Alain. 2001 [1998]. *Ethics: An Essay on the Understanding of Evil*. Trans. Peter Hallward. London: Verso.

Bailhache, Gérard. 1994. *Le sujet chez Emmanuel Levinas: fragilité et subjectivité*. Paris: PUF.

Baudelaire, Charles. 1999a [1864]. "Les Yeux des pauvres." *Spleen de Paris*. Baudelaire Online. http://www.piranesia.net/baudelaire/spleen/frame.html (March 16, 2008).

Baudelaire, Charles. 1999b [1864]. "Eyes of the Poor." Trans. Cat Nilan. *Spleen de Paris*. Baudelaire Online. http://www.piranesia.net/baudelaire/spleen/frame.html (March 16, 2008).

Benjamin, Walter. 1999. *The Arcades Project*. Trans. Howard Eiland and Kevin McLaughlin. Cambridge, MA: Belknap.

Blanchot, Maurice. 1993 [1969]. *The Infinite Conversation*. Trans. Susan Hanson. Minneapolis: University of Minnesota Press.

Booth, Wayne C. 1961. *Rhetoric of Fiction*. Chicago: Chicago University Press.

Céline, Louis-Ferdinand. 1983 [1932]. *Journey to the End of the Night*. Trans. Ralph Manheim. New York: New Directions.

Critchley, Simon. 1992. *The Ethics of Deconstruction*. Oxford: Blackwell.

Davis, Colin. 2004. *After Poststructuralism: Reading, Stories and Theory*. London: Routledge.

Derrida, Jacques. 1978 [1964]. "Violence and Metaphysics: An Essay on the Thought of Emmanuel Levinas." *Writing and Difference*. Trans. Alan Bass. London: Routledge & Kegan Paul, pp. 97–192.

Derrida, Jacques. 1991 [1980]. "At This Very Moment in This Work Here I Am." In Robert Bernasconi and Simon Critchley, eds. *Re-Reading Levinas*. Bloomington: Indiana University Press, pp. 11–48.

Derrida, Jacques. 1997 [1994]. *Politics of Friendship*. Trans. George Collins. London: Verso.

Derrida, Jacques. 1999 [1997]. *Adieu to Emmanuel Levinas*. Trans. Pascale-Anne Brault and Michael Naas. Stanford, CA: Stanford University Press.

Eaglestone, Robert. 1997. *Ethical Criticism: Reading after Levinas*. Edinburgh: Edinburgh University Press.

Evans, Margery A. 1993. *Baudelaire and Intertextuality: Poetry at the Crossroads*. Cambridge: Cambridge University Press.

Genette, Gérard. 1980. *Narrative Discourse: An Essay in Method*. Trans. Jane E. Lewin. Ithaca, NY: Cornell University Press.

Gibson, Andrew. 1999. *Postmodernity, Ethics and the Novel: From Leavis to Levinas*. London: Routledge.

Hand, Séan, ed. 1989. *The Levinas Reader*. Oxford: Blackwell.

Harpham, Geoffrey Galt. 1992. *Getting It Right: Language, Literature, and Ethics*. Chicago: University of Chicago Press.

Herman, David. 1994. "Textual 'You' and Double Deixis in Edna O'Brien's *A Pagan Place*." *Style* 28/3: 378–411.

Herman, David. 2004. *Story Logic: Problems and Possibilities of Narrative*. Lincoln: University of Nebraska Press.

Irigaray, Luce. 1993 [1984]. *An Ethics of Sexual Difference*. Trans. Carolyn Burke and Gillian C. Gill. Ithaca: Cornell University Press.

Korsisaari, Eva M. 2006. *Tule, rakkaani! Naisen ja miehen välisestä etiikasta kirjallisuuden rakkauskuvauksissa*. Helsinki: Teos.

Krueger, Cheryl. 2002. "Telling Stories in Baudelaire's *Spleen de Paris*." *Nineteenth Century French Studies* 30/3–4: 282–300.

Leiris, Michel. 1948. *La Règle du Jeu: Biffures*. Paris: Gallimard.

Levinas, Emmanuel. 1961. *Totalité et infini*. The Hague: Martinus Nijhoff.

Levinas, Emmanuel. 1974. *Autrement qu'être ou au-delà de l'essence*. The Hague: Martinus Nijhoff.

Levinas, Emmanuel. 1985. *Ethics and Infinity: Conversations with Philippe Nemo*. Trans. Richard A. Cohen. Pittsburgh, PA: Duquesne University Press.

Levinas, Emmanuel. 1989a [1947]. "The Other in Proust." Trans. Seán Hand. In Hand 160–66.

Levinas, Emmanuel. 1989b [1948]. "Reality and its Shadow." Trans. Alphonso Lingis. In Hand 129–43.

Levinas, Emmanuel. 1989c [1949]. "The Transcendence of Words." Trans. Séan Hand. In Hand 144–49.

Levinas, Emmanuel. 1989d [1966]. "The Servant and the Master." Trans. Michael Holland. In Hand 150–59.

Levinas, Emmanuel. 1993 [1981]. "Everyday Language and Rhetoric Without Eloquence." *Outside the Subject*. Trans. Michael B. Smith. London: Athlone, pp. 135–43.

Llewelyn, John. 1995. *Emmanuel Levinas: The Genealogy of Ethics*. London: Routledge.

Llewelyn, John. 2002. *Appositions of Jacques Derrida and Emmanuel Levinas*. Bloomington: Indiana University Press.

McLaughlin, Kevin. 2007. "On Poetic Reason of State: Benjamin, Baudelaire, and the Multitudes." *Partial Answers* 5/2: 247–65.

Meretoja, Hanna. 2008. "Ethics of Non-narrativity: Levinas and Robbe-Grillet." In *Encounters in Art and Philosophy*, ed. Kuisma Korhonen and Pajari Räsänen (forthcoming).

Newton, Adam Z. 1995. *Narrative Ethics*. Cambridge, MA: Harvard University Press.

Peperzak, Adriaan T. 1993. *To the Other: An Introduction to the Philosophy of Emmanuel Levinas*. West Lafayette, IN: Purdue University Press.

Peperzak, Adriaan T. 1999. *Beyond: The Philosophy of Emmanuel Levinas*. Evanston, IL: Northwestern University Press.

Phelan, James. 2005. *Living to Tell about It: A Rhetoric and Ethics of Narration*. Ithaca: Cornell University Press.

Rabbitt, Kara M. 2005. "Reading and Otherness: The Interpretative Triangle in Baudelaire's *Petits poèmes en prose*." *Nineteenth Century French Studies* 33/3–4: 358–70.

Rancière, Jacques. 2006 [2000]. *The Politics of Aesthetics: The Distribution of the Sensible*. Trans. Gabriel Rockhill. London: Continuum.

Räsänen, Pajari. 2007. *Counter-figures: An Essay on Antimetaphoric Resistance: Paul Celan's Poetry and Poetics at the Limits of Figurality*. Helsinki: Helsinki University Printing House. https://oa.doria.fi/bitstream/handle/10024/19235/counterf.pdf?sequence=1 (March 16, 2008).

Ricoeur, Paul. 2005. *The Course of Recognition*. Trans. David Pellauer. Cambridge, MA: Harvard University Press.

Rimmon-Kenan, Shlomith. 1983. *Narrative Fiction: Contemporary Poetics*. London: Methuen.

Robbins, Jill. 1999. *Altered Reading: Levinas and Literature*. Chicago: University of Chicago Press.

Scott, Maria C. 2005. *Baudelaire's Le Spleen de Paris: Shifting Perspectives*. London: Ashgate.

Smith, Robert. 1987. "How Beautiful You Are" in the album *Kiss Me, Kiss Me, Kiss Me*. Rhino/Electra.

Žižek, Slavoj. 2006. "Smashing the Neighbor's Face." *Lacan dot com*. http://www.lacan.com/zizsmash.htm (March 21, 2008).

CHAPTER 8

Cultivating Humanity:
The Narrative Imagination

Martha Nussbaum

Martha Nussbaum, who teaches at Brown University, is a leading advocate of ethical criticism. Essential to ethics, she argues, is compassion, the ability to feel for others and especially for their suffering. That ability is the basis of the urge towards the achievement of social justice. Literature plays an important role in cultivating a potential for compassion because it invites us to identify with characters and with their concerns, as if they were real people. Her books include *The Fragility of Goodness* (1986), *Love's Knowledge* (1990), and *Cultivating Humanity* (1997).

[There] are many forms of thought and expression within the range of human communications from which the voter derives the knowledge, intelligence, sensitivity to human values: the capacity for sane and objective judgement which, so far as possible, a ballot should express. [The] people do need novels and dramas and paintings and poems, "because they will be called upon to vote."
    Alexander Meiklejohn, "The First Amendment Is an Absolute"

The world citizen needs knowledge of history and social fact.[1] We have begun to see how those requirements can be met by curricula of different types. But people who know many facts about lives other than their own are still not fully equipped for citizenship. As Heraclitus said 2,500 years ago, "Learning about many things does not produce understanding." Marcus Aurelius insisted that to become world citizens we must not simply amass knowledge; we must also cultivate in ourselves a capacity for sympathetic imagination that will enable us to comprehend the motives and choices of people different from ourselves, seeing them not as forbiddingly alien and other, but as sharing many problems and possibilities with us. Differences of religion, gender, race, class, and national origin make the task of understanding harder, since these differences shape not only the practical choices people face but also their "insides," their desires, thoughts, and ways of looking at the world.

Original publication details: Martha Nussbaum, "The Narrative Imagination" from *Cultivating Humanity*, pp. 85–112. Harvard University Press, 1997. Reproduced with permission from Harvard University Press.

Here the arts play a vital role, cultivating powers of imagination that are essential to citizenship. As Alexander Meiklejohn, the distinguished constitutional scholar and theorist of "deliberative democracy," put it fifty years ago, arguing against an opponent who had denied the political relevance of art, the people of the United States need the arts precisely because they will be called upon to vote. That is not the only reason why the arts are important, but it is one significant reason. The arts cultivate capacities of judgment and sensitivity that can and should be expressed in the choices a citizen makes. To some extent this is true of all the arts. Music, dance, painting and sculpture, architecture – all have a role in shaping our understanding of the people around us. But in a curriculum for world citizenship, literature, with its ability to represent the specific circumstances and problems of people of many different sorts, makes an especially rich contribution. As Aristotle said in chapter 9 of *The Poetics*, literature shows us "not something that has happened, but the kind of thing that might happen." This knowledge of possibilities is an especially valuable resource in the political life.

To begin to understand how literature can develop a citizen's imagination, let us consider two literary works widely separated in place and time. In both cases, the literary work refers to its own distinctive capacity to promote adequate civic perception.

Sophocles' *Philoctetes*, produced in 409 B.C., during a crisis in the Athenian democracy, concerns the proper treatment of a citizen who has become an outcast, crippled by a disfiguring illness. On his way to Troy to fight with the Greeks in the Trojan War, Philoctetes stepped by mistake into a sacred shrine. His foot, bitten by the serpent who guards the shrine, began to ooze with an ulcerous sore, and his cries of pain disrupted the army's religious festivals. So the commanders abandoned him on the deserted island of Lemnos, with no companions and no resources but his bow and arrows. Ten years later, learning that they cannot win the war without his magical bow, they return, determined to ensnare him by a series of lies into participating in the war. The commander Odysseus shows no interest in Philoctetes as a person; he speaks of him only as a tool of public ends. The chorus of common soldiers has a different response (lines 169–176):

> For my part, I have compassion for him. Think how
> with no human company or care,
> no sight of a friendly face,
> wretched, always alone,
> he wastes away with that savage disease,
> with no way of meeting his daily needs.
> How, how in the world, does the poor man survive?

Unlike their leader, the men of the chorus vividly and sympathetically imagine the life of a man whom they have never seen, picturing his loneliness, his pain, his struggle for survival. In the process they stand in for, and allude to, the imaginative work of the audience, who are invited by the play as a whole to imagine the sort of needy, homeless life to which prosperous people rarely direct their attention. The drama as a whole, then, cultivates the type of sympathetic vision of which its characters speak. In the play, this kind of vivid imagining prompts a political decision against using Philoctetes as a means, and the audience is led to believe this to be a politically and morally valuable result. In this way, by showing the public benefits of the very sort of sympathy it is currently awakening in its spectators, the drama commends its own resources as valuable for the formation of decent citizenship and informed public choice. Although the good of the whole should not be neglected, that good will not be well served if human beings are seen simply as instruments of one another's purposes.

Ralph Ellison's *Invisible Man* (1952) develops this tradition of reflection about our failures of perception and recognition. Its hero describes himself as "invisible" because throughout the novel he is seen by those he encounters as a vehicle for various race-inflected stereotypes: the poor, humiliated black boy who snatches like an animal at the coins that lie on an electrified mat; the good student trusted to chauffeur a wealthy patron; the listening ear to whom this same patron unburdens his guilt and anxiety; the rabble-rousing activist who energizes an urban revolutionary movement; the violent rapist who gratifies the sexual imagination of a woman brought up on racially charged sexual images – always he is cast in a drama of someone else's making, "never more loved and appreciated" than when he plays his assigned role. The "others," meanwhile, are all "lost in a dream world" – in which they see only what their own minds have created, never the reality of the person who stands before them. "You go along for years knowing something is wrong, then suddenly you discover that you're as transparent as air." Invisibility is "a matter of the construction of their *inner* eyes, those eyes with which they look through their physical eyes upon reality."[2]

Ellison's grotesque, surreal world is very unlike the classical world of Sophocles' play. Its concerns, however, are closely linked: social stratification and injustice, manipulation and use, and above all invisibility and the condition of being transparent to and for one's fellow citizens. Like Sophocles' drama, it explores and savagely excoriates these refusals to see. Like that drama, it invites its readers to know and see more than the unseeing characters. "Being invisible and without substance, a disembodied voice, as it were, what else could I do? What else but try to tell you what was really happening when your eyes were looking through?"[3] In this way, it works upon the inner eyes of the very readers whose moral failures it castigates, although it refuses the easy notion that mutual visibility can be achieved in one heartfelt leap of brotherhood.

Ellison explicitly linked the novelist's art to the possibility of democracy. By representing both visibility and its evasions, both equality and its refusal, a novel, he wrote in an introduction, "could be fashioned as a raft of hope, perception and entertainment that might help keep us afloat as we tried to negotiate the snags and whirlpools that mark our nation's vacillating course toward and away from the democratic idea." This is not, he continued, the only goal for fiction; but it is one proper and urgent goal. For a democracy requires not only institutions and procedures; it also requires a particular quality of vision, in order "to defeat this national tendency to deny the common humanity shared by my character and those who might happen to read of his experience."[4] The novel's mordantly satirical treatment of stereotypes, its fantastic use of image and symbol (in, for example, the bizarre dreamlike sequence in the white-paint factory), and its poignant moments of disappointed hope, all contribute to this end.

As Ellison says, forming the civic imagination is not the only role for literature, but it is one salient role. Narrative art has the power to make us see the lives of the different with more than a casual tourist's interest – with involvement and sympathetic understanding, with anger at our society's refusals of visibility. We come to see how circumstances shape the lives of those who share with us some general goals and projects; and we see that circumstances shape not only people's possibilities for action, but also their aspirations and desires, hopes and fears. All of this seems highly pertinent to decisions we must make as citizens. Understanding, for example, how a history of racial stereotyping can affect self-esteem, achievement, and love enables us to make more informed judgments on issues relating to affirmative action and education.

Higher education should develop students' awareness of literature in many different ways. But literature does play a vital role in educating citizens of the world. It makes sense, then, to ask how it can perform this function as well as possible – what sorts of literary works, and what sort of teaching of those works, our academic institutions should promote in order to foster an informed and compassionate vision of the different. When we ask this question, we find that the goals of world citizenship are best promoted by a literary education that both adds new works to the well-known "canon" of Western literature and considers standard texts in a deliberative and critical spirit.

It is frequently claimed that it is inappropriate to approach literature with a "political agenda." Yet it is hard to justify such a claim without embracing an extreme kind of aesthetic formalism that is sterile and unappealing. The Western aesthetic tradition has had throughout its history an intense concern with character and community. The defense of that tradition in the contemporary "culture wars" should enlist our support.

Fancy and Wonder

When a child and a parent begin to tell stories together, the child is acquiring essential moral capacities. Even a simple nursery rhyme such as "Twinkle, twinkle little star, how I wonder what you are" leads children to feel wonder – a sense of mystery that mingles curiosity with awe.[5] Children wonder about the little star. In so doing they learn to imagine that a mere shape in the heavens has an inner world, in some ways mysterious, in some ways like their own. They learn to attribute life, emotion, and thought to a form whose insides are hidden. As time goes on, they do this in an increasingly sophisticated way, learning to hear and tell stories about animals and humans. These stories interact with their own attempts to explain the world and their own actions in it. A child deprived of stories is deprived, as well, of certain ways of viewing other people. For the insides of people, like the insides of stars, are not open to view. They must be wondered about. And the conclusion that this set of limbs in front of me has emotions and feelings and thoughts of the sort I attribute to myself will not be reached without the training of the imagination that storytelling promotes.

Narrative play does teach children to view a personlike shape as a house for hope and fear and love and anger, all of which they have known themselves. But the wonder involved in storytelling also makes evident the limits of each person's access to every other. "How I wonder what you are," goes the rhyme. In that simple expression is an acknowledgment of the lack of completeness in one's own grasp of the fear, the love, the sympathy, the anger, of the little star, or of any other creature or person. In fact the child adept at storytelling soon learns that people in stories are frequently easier to know than people in real life, who, as Proust puts it in *The Past Recaptured*, frequently offer "a dead weight that our sensitivity cannot remove," a closed exterior that cannot be penetrated even by a sensitive imagination. The child, wondering about its parents, soon learns about these obstacles, just as it also learns that its parents need not know everything that goes on in its own mind. The habits of wonder promoted by storytelling thus define the other person as spacious and deep, with qualitative differences from oneself and hidden places worthy of respect.

In these various ways, narrative imagination is an essential preparation for moral interaction. Habits of empathy and conjecture conduce to a certain type of citizenship and a certain form of community: one that cultivates a sympathetic responsiveness to another's needs, and understands the way circumstances shape those needs, while respecting separateness and privacy. This is so because of the way in which literary imagining both inspires intense concern with the fate of characters and defines those characters as containing a rich inner life, not all of which is open to view; in the process, the reader learns to have respect for the hidden contents of that inner world, seeing its importance in defining a creature as fully human. It is this respect for the inner life of consciousness that literary theorist Lionel Trilling describes when he calls the imagination of the novel-reader a "liberal imagination"[6] – meaning by this that the novel-reader is led to attribute importance to the material conditions of happiness while respecting human freedom.

As children grow older, the moral and social aspects of these literary scenarios become increasingly complex and full of distinctions, so that they gradually learn how to ascribe to others, and recognize in themselves, not only hope and fear, happiness and distress – attitudes that are ubiquitous, and comprehensible without extensive experience – but also more complex traits such as courage, self-restraint, dignity, perseverance, and fairness. These notions might be defined for the child in an abstract way; but to grasp their full meaning in one's own self-development and in social interactions with others requires learning their dynamics in narrative settings.

As children grasp such complex facts in imagination, they become capable of compassion. Compassion involves the recognition that another person, in some ways similar to oneself, has suffered some significant pain or misfortune in a way for which that person is not, or not fully, to blame. As many moral traditions emphasize – the analysis of compassion is remarkably constant in both Western and non-Western philosophy – it requires estimating the significance of the misfortune as accurately as one can – usually in agreement with the sufferer, but sometimes in ways that depart from that person's own judgment. Adam Smith points out that people who lose their mental faculties are the objects of our compassion even though they themselves are not aware of this loss: what is significant is the magnitude of the loss, as the onlooker estimates its role in the life of the loser. This requires, in turn, a highly complex set of moral abilities, including the ability to imagine what it is like to be in that person's place (what we usually call *empathy*), and also the ability to stand back and ask whether the person's own judgment has taken the full measure of what has happened.

Compassion requires one thing more: a sense of one's own vulnerability to misfortune. To respond with compassion, I must be willing to entertain the thought that this suffering person might be me. And this I will be unlikely to do if I am convinced that I am above the ordinary lot and no ill can befall me. There are exceptions to this, in some religious traditions' portrayals of the compassion of God; but philosophers such as Aristotle and Rousseau have plausibly claimed that imperfect human beings need the belief that their own possibilities are similar to those of the suffering person, if they are to respond with compassion to another's plight. This recognition, as they see it, helps explain why compassion so frequently leads to generous support for the needs of others: one thinks, "That might have been me, and that is how I should want to be treated."

Compassion, so understood, promotes an accurate awareness of our common vulnerability. It is true that human beings are needy, incomplete creatures who are in many ways dependent on circumstances beyond their control for the possibility of well-being.

As Rousseau argues in *Emile*, people do not fully grasp that fact until they can imagine suffering vividly to themselves, and feel pain at the imagining. In a compassionate response to the suffering of another, one comprehends that being prosperous or powerful does not remove one from the ranks of needy humanity. Such reminders, the tradition argues, are likely to lead to a more beneficent treatment of the weak. Philoctetes, in Sophocles' play, asks for aid by reminding the soldiers that they themselves might suffer what he has suffered. They accept because they are able to imagine his predicament.

It seems, then, to be beneficial for members of a society to see themselves as bound to one another by similar weaknesses and needs, as well as by similar capacities for achievement. As Aristotle argues in chapter 9 of *The Poetics*, literature is "more philosophical than history" – by which he means more conducive to general human understanding – precisely because it acquaints us with "the kind of thing that might happen," general forms of possibility and their impact on human lives.

Compassion requires demarcations: which creatures am I to count as my fellow creatures, sharing possibilities with me? One may be a person of refined feeling and still treat many people in one's world as invisible, their prospects as unrelated to one's own. Rousseau argues that a good education, which acquaints one with all the usual vicissitudes of fortune, will make it difficult to refuse acknowledgment to the poor or the sick, or slaves, or members of lower classes. It is easy to see that any one of those might really have been me, given a change of circumstances. Boundaries of nationality can similarly be transcended in thought, for example by the recognition that one of the frequent hazards of wartime is to lose one's nation. Boundaries of race, of gender, and of sexual orientation prove, historically, more recalcitrant: for there might appear to be little real-life possibility of a man's becoming a woman, a white person's becoming black, or even (*pace* earlier psychiatry) a straight person's becoming gay or lesbian. In these cases, then, it is all the more urgent to cultivate the basis for compassion through the fictional exercise of imagination – for if one cannot in fact change one's race, one can imagine what it is like to inhabit a race different from one's own, and by becoming close to a person of different race or sexual orientation, one can imagine what it would be like for someone one loves to have such a life.

Rousseau thought that people differed only in circumstances: underneath, their desires, aims, and emotions were the same. But in fact one of the things imagining reveals to us is that we are not all brothers under the skin, that circumstances of oppression form desire and emotion and aspiration. Some characters feel like us, and some repel easy identification. But such failures to identify can also be sources of understanding. Both by identification and by its absence, we learn what life has done to people. A society that wants to foster the just treatment of all its members has strong reasons to foster an exercise of the compassionate imagination that crosses social boundaries, or tries to. And this means caring about literature.

Literature and the Compassionate Imagination

The basis for civic imagining must be laid in early life. As children explore stories, rhymes, and songs – especially in the company of the adults they love – they are led to notice the sufferings of other living creatures with a new keenness. At this point, stories can then begin to confront children more plainly with the uneven fortunes of life, convincing them emotionally of their urgency and importance. "Let him see, let him feel the human calamities," Rousseau writes of his imaginary pupil. "Unsettle and frighten his imagination with the perils by which every human being is constantly surrounded. Let him see around him all these abysses, and, hearing you describe them, hold on to you for fear of falling into them."[7]

For older children and young adults, more complex literary works now should be added. It was in connection with the moral education of young adults that ancient Athenian culture ascribed enormous importance to tragic drama. Going to a tragedy was not understood to be an "aesthetic experience," if that means an experience detached from civic and political concerns. The tragic festivals of the fifth century B.C. were civic festivals during which every other civic function stopped, and all citizens gathered together. Dramas were routinely assessed as much for their moral and political content as for their other characteristics. Indeed, as the literary criticism preserved in Aristophanes' *Frogs* makes plain, it was well understood that formal devices of meter, vocabulary, and verse form conveyed, themselves, a moral content. What, then, was the civic education that tragedies were intended to promote?

Tragedies acquaint the young citizen with the bad things that may happen in a human life, long before life itself does so. In the process they make the significance of suffering, and the losses that inspire it, unmistakably plain to the spectator; this is one way in which the poetic and visual resources of the drama have moral weight. By inviting the spectators to identify with the tragic hero, at the same time portraying the hero as a relatively good person, whose distress does not stem from deliberate wickedness, the drama makes compassion for suffering seize the imagination. This emotion is built into the dramatic form.

The sympathies of the spectator are broadened in the process, through the notion of risks that are common to all human beings. Tragedies are obsessed with the possibilities and weaknesses of human life as such, and with the contrast between human life and other, less limited lives, belonging to gods and demigods. In the process they move their spectator, in imagination, from the male world of war to the female world of the household. They ask the future male citizen of ancient Athens to identify himself not only with those he might in actual fact become – beggars, exiles, generals, slaves – but also with many who in some sense he can never be, such as Trojans and Persians and Africans, such as wives and daughters and mothers.

Through such devices the drama explores both similarity and difference. Identifying with a woman in a drama, a young male spectator would find that he can in some sense remain himself, that is to say, a reasoning human being with moral virtues and commitments. On the other hand, he discovers through this identification much that is not his own lot: the possibility, for example, of being raped and being forced to bear the enemy's child; the possibility of witnessing the deaths of children whom one has nursed oneself; the possibility of being abandoned by one's husband and in consequence totally without social support. He is brought up against the fact that people as articulate and able as he face disaster and shame in some ways that males do not; and he is asked to think about that as something relevant to himself. So far from being "great books" without a political agenda, these dramas were directly pertinent to democratic debates about the treatment of captured peoples in wartime. With their efforts to overcome socially shaped invisibilities, they participated actively in those debates.

Literature does not transform society single-handed; we know that these powerful and in some sense radical dramatic experiences took place in a society that was highly repressive of women, even by the standards of its own era. Certain ideas about others may be grasped for a time and yet not be acted upon, so powerful are the forces of habit and the entrenched structures of privilege and convention. Nonetheless, the artistic form makes its spectator perceive, for a time, the invisible people of their world – at least a beginning of social justice.

The tragic form asks its spectators to cross cultural and national boundaries. On the other hand, in its universality and abstractness it omits much of the fabric of daily civic life, with its concrete distinctions of rank and power and wealth and the associated ways of thinking and speaking. For such reasons, later democratic thinkers interested in literature as a vehicle of citizenship came to take a particular interest in the novel – a genre whose rise coincided with, and supported, the rise of modern democracy.[8] In reading a realist novel with active participation, readers do all that tragic spectators do – and something more. They embrace the ordinary. They care not only about kings and children of kings, but about David Copperfield, painfully working in a factory, or walking the twenty-six miles from London to Canterbury without food. Such concrete realities of a life of poverty are brought home to them with a textured vividness unavailable in tragic poetry.

Again, the reader's learning involves both sameness and difference. Reading a novel of class difference (for example, a novel of Dickens), one is aware, on the one hand, of many links to the lives of the characters and their aspirations, hopes, and sufferings. There are many ways, however, in which circumstances have made the lives of the poorer characters very different from those of middle-class readers. Such readers assess those differences, thinking of their consequence for aspirations to a rich and fulfilling life. They also notice differences in the inner world, seeing the delicate interplay between common human goals and the foreignness that can be created by circumstances. Differences of class, race, ethnicity, gender, and national origin all shape people's possibilities, and their psychology with them. Ellison's "invisible man," for example, repels the easy and facile sympathy that says "we are all brothers" because his inner world strikes the reader as dark and frightening, as the secure child of a loving home gradually takes on more savage and pessimistic sentiments. In this way we start to see how deeply racism penetrates the mind and emotions. Consider, for example, the scene in which the narrator buys a yam from a Harlem street vendor. His emotions of homesickness, delight, and recognition are in one sense familiar; but the struggle with shame, as he decides not to hide his pleasure in something he has been taught to see as a sign of negritude, will be unfamiliar to the white middle-class reader, who probably will not be able to identify with such an experience. Such a failure of sympathy, however, prompts a deeper and more pertinent kind of sympathy, as one sees that a human being who initially might have grown up free from the deforming experience of racism has been irrevocably shaped by that experience; and one does come to see that experience of being formed by oppression as a thing "such as might happen" to oneself or someone one loves.

This complex interpretive art is what the Stoics required when they asked the world citizen to gain empathic understanding of people who are different.[9] This idea, however, needs to be developed in a specifically democratic way, as an essential part of thinking and judging well in a pluralistic democratic society that is part of an even more complex world. One literary figure from our own tradition who gives us particular help in this task is Walt Whitman, who saw the literary artist as an irreplaceably valuable educator of democratic citizens. "Their Presidents," he wrote, "shall not be their common referee so much as their poets shall."[10] He went on to argue that literary art develops capacities for perception and judgment that are at the very heart of democracy, prominently including the ability to "see eternity in men and women," understanding their aspirations and the complexity of their inner world, rather than to "see men and women as dreams or dots," as mere statistics or numbers. Whitman makes it clear that his idea of a democratic poetry is his own translation of the ancient Athenian idea to the situation of modern America: in "Song of the Exposition" he imagines the Muse of ancient Greek poetry migrating to the New World and inspiring his poetry, "undeterr'd" by America's mixture of peoples and its surprising love of machinery.

The poet's ability to "see eternity," Whitman holds, is especially important when we are dealing with groups whose humanity has not always been respected in our society: women and racial minorities, homosexuals, the poor and the powerless. A major part of the social role of the literary artist, as he saw it, was to promote our sympathetic understanding of all outcast or oppressed people, by giving their strivings voice. "I am he attesting sympathy," the poet announces (*Song of Myself* 22.461–24.5):

> Through me many long dumb voices,
> Voices of the interminable generations of prisoners and slaves,
> Voices of the diseas'd and despairing and of thieves and dwarfs,
> …
>
> Through me forbidden voices,
> Voices of sexes and lusts, voices veil'd and I remove the veil,
> Voices indecent by me clarified and transfigur'd …
>
> Dazzling and tremendous how quick the sun-rise would kill me,
> If I could not now and always send sun-rise out of me.

The poet in effect becomes the voice of silenced people, sending their speech out of himself as a kind of light for the democracy. Like Ellison much later, Whitman focuses on our failures to see the flesh and blood of those with whom we live; his poems, like Ellison's novel, portray themselves as devices of recognition and inclusion. The imagining he demands promotes a respect for the voices and the rights of others, reminding us that the other has both agency and complexity, is neither a mere object nor a passive recipient of benefits and satisfactions. At the same time, it promotes a vivid awareness of need and disadvantage, and in that sense gives substance to the abstract desire for justice.

As in Athens, so in America: the fact that sympathy inspired by literary imagining does not immediately effect political change should not make us deny its moral worth. If we follow Whitman's idea, we will conclude that it is essential to put the study of literature at the heart of a curriculum for citizenship, because it develops arts of interpretation that are essential for civic participation and awareness.

Marcus Aurelius made a further claim on behalf of the narrative imagination: he argued that it contributes to undoing retributive anger. He means that when we are able to imagine why someone has come to act in a way that might generally provoke an angry response, we will be less inclined to demonize the person, to think of him or her as purely evil and alien. Even if we never fully understand the action, the very activity of asking the question and trying to depict the person's psychology to ourselves in the manner of a good novelist is an antidote to self-centered rage. It is easy to see how this psychological mechanism operates in our personal lives, where the ability to tell ourselves the story of a parent or a lover or a child who has angered us can often help us avoid selfish vindictiveness. In our political lives, this ability has an equally prominent role – especially when we are dealing with people different from ourselves, whom it would be all too easy to treat as alien objects without the sort of psychological and historical complexity we habitually impute to ourselves.

This point is itself repeatedly dramatized in literary works dealing with characters against whom society has directed its anger. The reader of Richard Wright's *Native Son* contrasts the demonized version of criminal defendant Bigger Thomas, in the novel's account of the press coverage of his trial, with the complicated person she has come to know. The reader of E. M. Forster's posthumously published *Maurice* in a similar way contrasts the demonizing stereotypes of the homosexual purveyed by most characters in the novel with the inner world of Maurice himself, as the reader has come to know it, his dreams of companionship and his intense longing for love. As Whitman insists, literary understanding is a form of imaginative and emotional receptivity that can seem profoundly threatening to the sort of person who would demonize a group. To allow inside one's mind people who seem alien and frightening is to show a capacity for openness and responsiveness that goes against the grain of many cultural stereotypes of self-sufficiency.

Whitman's insistence on receiving the voices of the excluded suggests a further point: that for literature to play its civic function it must be permitted, and indeed invited, to disturb us. If we can easily sympathize with a character, the invitation to do so has relatively little moral value; the experience can too easily deteriorate into a self-congratulatory wallowing in our own compassionate tendencies. The challenge of Sophocles' *Philoctetes* to its audience was to see without flinching what the characters found disgusting and vile: pus, blasphemous cries, Philoctetes' body covered with sores. The challenge of Wright's *Native Son* was and is to look into the life of a violent criminal who kills his lover Bessie more casually than he kills a rat. Similarly, the challenge of *Invisible Man* is to see what it is like to be seen through, or seen in terms of various demeaning fantasies – again, a difficult experience for the novel's likely audience.

These works are all written in a conventional literary language, a fact that explains their relatively easy acceptance into the realm of "literature" despite the radical character of their subject matter. It can also be argued, however, that literary art most fully fulfills its Whitmanesque mission of acknowledging the excluded when it allows the excluded to talk as they really talk, to use a daily language that is nonliterary and that may shock our sensibilities. The 1994 Booker Prize for Fiction, Britain's most distinguished literary award, was given to James Kelman's *How Late It Was How Late*, a novel of working-class life in Glasgow, Scotland. The novel, which is set in the mind of its protagonist, uses throughout the working-class Scots dialect that such a character would actually speak, and includes all the words that such a character would be likely to use in thought and speech. The award created a minor furor, since many cultural critics objected strenuously to giving such a prestigious artistic prize to a work that, by one count, uses the word *fuck* over four thousand times. In interviews given during the controversy, Kelman defended his project in Whitmanesque terms. The voices of working-class people, he claimed, have generally been excluded from "English literature" in his still highly class-conscious society. For generations, at least since Dickens, there have been gestures of inclusion, in which working-class characters figure in a literary novel; but their voices first had to be assimilated to a middle-class norm of literary discourse. This was a way of rendering real working people invisible.

A central role of art is to challenge conventional wisdom and values. One way works engage in this Socratic enterprise is by asking us to confront – and for a time to be – those whom we do not usually like to meet. Offensiveness is not all by itself a sign of literary merit; but the offensiveness of a work may be part of its civic value. The inclusion of new and disturbing works in the curriculum should be assessed with these ideas in mind. When we do consider such works we should bear in mind that it is difficult to know in advance, or quickly, which unconventional works, or parts of works, will have a lasting power to illuminate the situation of a group and which are merely shocking. Most of us have fears and blind spots that militate against the acknowledgment of some of our fellow citizens, and we should recognize that our reactions of disturbance may therefore be highly unreliable, leading us to regard as merely shocking what will eventually be seen to have genuine merit. (To give just one example, contemporary sensibilities required the excision of a crucial scene from Wright's *Native Son*, in which Bigger and his friend masturbate in the movie theater while looking at the image of a white woman. This scene, too shocking for publication in 1940 and not included in editions of the novel until 1993, can now be seen as crucial to the narrative development of the work, and to its exploration of the social formation of Bigger's imagination and desires.) We do not need to deny that there are defensible criteria of literary merit in order to recognize that we ourselves are unreliable judges of merit when works touch on our own lives and the controversies of our own time. For this reason we ought to protect the opportunity of the arts to explore new territory with broad latitude, and we should also protect the right of university teachers to explore controversial works in the classroom, whether or not we ourselves have been convinced of their lasting merit.

Compassion in the Curriculum: A Political Agenda?

If the literary imagination develops compassion, and if compassion is essential for civic responsibility, then we have good reason to teach works that promote the types of compassionate understanding we want and need. This means including works that give voice to the experiences of groups in our society that we urgently need to understand, such as members of other cultures, ethnic and racial minorities, women, and lesbians and gay men.

Recall Reno student Eric Chalmers, who, in connection with the readings assigned in his English class, was asked to think about the experience of a gay person and to write a letter to his parents in that persona – to let that person's voice emerge from his mouth. "I probably didn't say anything," he quickly explained; "I just rambled." This otherwise aggressive and crusty young man, extremely confident and even dogmatic, showed a moment of confusion and uncertainty. He acknowledged that the "off-the-wall" assignment had had a point – because "we met, you know, all sorts of people," and fulfilling the assignment is "like an understanding of their belief system." Such Whitmanesque experiences of receptivity and voice should be cultivated. They are closely connected to the Socratic activity of questioning one's own values and to the Stoic norm of becoming a citizen of the whole world, but they cannot be engendered without works that stimulate the imagination in a highly concrete way, including works that unsettle and disturb.

To produce students who are truly Socratic we must encourage them to read critically; not only to empathize and experience, but also to ask critical questions about that experience. And this means cultivating an attitude to familiar texts that is not the detached one that we sometimes associate with the contemplation of fine art. This more critical attitude has its roots, in the West, in the ancient Greek tradition of the tragic festivals, where watching a work of art was closely connected to argument and deliberation about fundamental civic values. It has been revived and vividly depicted in quite a few critical works of the present day – among them, Wayne Booth's fine work, *The Company We Keep: An Ethics of Fiction*.[11] Drawing on his own reading of ancient Greek texts, Booth proposes a valuable metaphor for the interaction of reader with a literary work. A literary work, he writes, is, during the time one reads it, a friend with whom one has chosen to spend one's time. The question now is, what does this friendship do to my mind? What does this new friend ask me to notice, to desire, to care about? How does he or she invite me to view my fellow human beings? Some novels, he argues, promote a cheap cynicism about human beings and lead us to see our fellow citizens with disdain. Some lead us to cultivate cheap sensationalistic forms of pleasure and excitement that debase human dignity. Others, by contrast, show what might be called respect before a soul[12] – in the way the text itself depicts the variety of human goals and motives, and also, it may be, in the interactions among the characters it displays.

Booth makes it clear that this critical attitude is perfectly compatible with immersion in the work; his idea is that immersion and experience precede, and ground, a critical assessment that we should ideally carry on in conversation with others whose perceptions will complement and challenge our own. He calls the process "co-duction" to stress its communal and comparative character. Through this process we attain insight into what we have become while we were enjoying the work. This insight will illuminate the nature of the literary experience and its role in our lives. Booth considers the classroom a paradigmatic scene of such critical activity.

Booth is famous for a distinction that we need to bear in mind: between the narrator or characters and the "implied author," that is, the sense of life embodied in the text taken as a whole. A work that contains few or no sympathetic, admirable characters may still promote sympathy and respect in the reader through the sort of interaction the work as a whole constructs. (Both of these figures are distinct, in turn, from the real-life author, who may have all sorts of properties that are not realized in the text.)

Thinking about Booth's metaphor of the literary work as friend shows us a further dimension of the experience of sympathy. When we read a novel with close attention, we frequently will be led by the text to have sympathy with characters of many different kinds; but frequently, too, the text will cultivate sympathy unevenly, directing our attention to some types of human beings and not to others. Literary works are not free of the prejudices and blind spots that are endemic to most of the political life. A novel that sees the experience of middle-class women with great sympathy may (like the novels of Virginia Woolf) render working-class people invisible. A novel that recognizes the struggles of working-class people – as, up to a point, the novels of Dickens do – may have little sensitivity to the lives and experiences of many types of women. If we are reading and teaching such novels with democratic ideals of equal concern and respect in mind, we will probably come to feel that there is something incomplete or even defective in these works. In this sense sympathetic reading and critical reading should go hand in hand, as we ask how our sympathy is being distributed and focused. One learns something about the text when one asks these critical questions: one sees its internal structure with a new sharpness, and one makes one's own relation to it more precise.

This civic and evaluative approach to reading is both moral and political. It asks how the interaction between reader and text constructs a friendship and/or community, and it invites us to discuss texts by making moral and social assessments of the kinds of communities texts create. Wayne Booth's version of this approach, like the one defended here – and like that of Lionel Trilling in the previous generation – is liberal and democratic, informed by a conviction that all citizens are worthy of respect and that certain funda-mental freedoms deserve our deepest allegiance.

But conservative critics have recently charged that the whole idea of reading in this way is an illicit and antiliterary activity, alien to the high tradition of the humanities.[13] To take a fairly typical example, in a column titled "Literary Politics," George Will recently wrote of the "supplanting of esthetic by political responses to literature," arguing that this approach "aims at delegitimizing Western civilization by discrediting the books and ideas that gave birth to it."[14]

It is not clear what notion of the aesthetic George Will has in mind when he contrasts the aesthetic with the political. The questions raised here about compassion and com-munity are hardly new, faddish questions. Indeed, they are as old as literary interpreta-tion itself. In ancient Greece alone, one can find them in Aristophanes and Aristotle, Plato and Plutarch. How, all these works ask us, does literature shape the character of the young citizen? What moral weight do its forms and structures have? This, we might say without distortion, is *the* dominant question asked about literature in the Western aesthetic tradition. And it is asked, when it is asked well, in a manner that does not neglect the literary form of the text. In fact, one of the greatest contributions of both Plato and Aristotle to aesthetics was their subtle account of the ways in which literary forms themselves convey a content, a view of what is worth taking seriously, and what the world is like.

What could someone mean by saying that these questions are not aesthetic? Such a claim can be seriously supported only by defending a picture of the aesthetic that has had a relatively narrow and recent history in the Western tradition, namely the Kantian and post-Kantian formalist tradition, according to which the proper aesthetic attitude is one that abstracts from all practical interests. Kant's own thought on this topic is complex and susceptible of multiple interpretations. But his claim that beauty gives pleasure without interest has certainly led many people to suppose that he was urging us to look at art without thinking of any practical questions at all, including very general questions, such as what is worth caring for, what is just and good. More recently, formalist aestheti-cians such as Bloomsbury writers Clive Bell and Roger Fry advocated that sort of detach-ment as characteristic of a truly aesthetic response.[15] In a famous example supplied by their ally, aesthetician Edward Bullough, people caught in the fog will usually prove unable to look at the fog aesthetically, because they are preoccupied with their safety.[16] They will succeed in doing so only if they can suspend their practical interests in safety and well-being, and attend to the pure color and shape that surround them. George Will needs to defend such a view to make sense of his claims. On other more common views of the aesthetic, political criticism is a central part of aesthetic attention.

Is the formalist view an adequate view of the aesthetic? It has a certain intuitive appeal. It seems true that if I am preoccupied with how to get out of the fog, there are many features of its shape, color, and form to which I am probably not attending. Similarly, if I am reading Ellison's novel as a set of instructions on how to bring about racial harmony, or Dickens' *Hard Times* as a blueprint for labor reform, much will elude me. Ellison described his novel as "a raft of hope, perception, and entertainment"; the person who ignores the entertainment loses a crucial dimension of the perception and hope. But this does not mean that the texture of Dickens' or Ellison's language is not profoundly moral and political, aimed at creating a community of a certain sort and at acknowledging certain parts of the human world as worthy of our attention and love.

Most great aesthetic theorists in the Western tradition have ultimately rejected the extreme formalist view. The long list includes Plato, Aristotle, the Stoics, Hegel, Nietzsche, Tolstoy, and fine present-day theorists such as Arthur Danto, Nelson Goodman, and Richard Wollheim. Ironically, it includes, as well, the Renaissance humanists who shaped the canon of literary classics that conservative theorists defend: for these thinkers saw their focus on the Greeks and Romans as part of the "political agenda" of reacting against medieval scholasticism and promoting a more human-centered view of the world.

One can at least comprehend how one might look at a Monet canvas in the way Bell and Bullough recommend – although I doubt that it is the most richly rewarding way to look, if it neglects ways in which Monet's forms express joy, and serenity, and even a certain ideal of community. One can at least comprehend what it might mean to listen to a Mahler symphony that way – though, once again, it seems that one would lose much by refusing the music's invitation to feel compassion, disgust, despair, and triumphant joy, and one would certainly be doing violence to Mahler's own self-conception, which seems a remarkably fruitful one. (He repeatedly speaks in letters of the ways in which his works address questions about the meaning of life and seek to create a compassionate, nonhierarchical community.) It is at least possible to look at dances of some modern choreographers in this way – though, once again, one would, I think, be missing a great deal that is both ethical and political, for example Martha Graham's narrative investigations of myth, sexuality, and ethical conflict.

But it is next to impossible to see what it could mean to read a drama of Sophocles, or a novel of Dickens or George Eliot, in the detached way. It is impossible to care about the characters and their well-being in the way the text invites, without having some very definite political and moral interests awakened in oneself – interests, for example, in the just treatment of workers and in the reform of education. Both Dickens and Eliot frequently address the reader, alluding to such common interests. This commitment to the making of a social world, and of a deliberative community to think critically about it, is what makes the adventure of reading so fascinating, and so urgent.

There was a brief moment in the recent history of literary criticism when it did seem possible and desirable to hold such concerns in abeyance. This was the moment of the flourishing of the so-called New Criticism, which held (to simplify) that when one read a poem one should bring nothing external to that reading – no historical and social context, no questions of one's own about life and how to live it.[17] Not surprisingly, this movement produced its best work in the area of lyric poetry, and even there only by a degree of inconsistency – for critics did allow themselves to ask what a word could have meant in 1786, say, and did permit themselves the extraneous knowledge that a certain other meaning came into being only in 1925. If they had not done so they would have produced gibberish. Other elements of context crept back in, as did normal human concerns about love and death, meaning and emptiness. Indeed, claims were ultimately made about the political meaning of literary irony and complexity. But even in its more elastic version, this movement had a difficult time doing justice to complex narrative works with a social dimension. For this reason it was resisted all along by some of the finest minds in the field, among them British moral critic F. R. Leavis and American social thinker Lionel Trilling. Both of these men had a political agenda. Trilling's *The Liberal Imagination* made explicit his own commitment to liberalism and democracy, and argued brilliantly that the novel as genre is committed to liberalism in its very form, in the way in which it shows respect for the individuality and the privacy of each human mind. He connected his criticism of the fiction of Henry James very closely with his general social criticism. *The Liberal Imagination* juxtaposes essays on James with essays on contemporary social issues.

What Wayne Booth and many other contemporary critics are doing today, feminist critics prominently among them, is to continue such approaches and to render them more sophisticated by asking more subtle questions about the ways in which works construct desire and thought, inviting the imagination to be active in these or those ways. Such a critical stance sometimes leads the critic to be harsh toward famous works of literature. Thus Wayne Booth argues that Rabelais's works display a contemptuous and cruel attitude to women, and that such an attitude is intrinsic not only to certain characters, but also to the works as a whole and their humor. Booth finds Rabelais distasteful because of this lack of empathy, and reports that he can no longer really enjoy the work's humor now that he has come to see it in this critical light, as tinged with cruelty. He is therefore probably somewhat less likely to teach and recommend the works, though in his book he does continue to "teach" them in this critical spirit.

On the other hand, considerations of empathy more frequently lead to an expansion of the traditional list of works read, as critics, searching for accounts of the experience of silenced people, discover powerful accounts of that experience that have previously been overlooked. A representative example of this type of criticism is the article "In the Waiting Room," by the young feminist critic Judith Frank. In the first portion of her article, Frank, a scholar of eighteenth-century English literature who teaches at Amherst College, describes her own teaching of unfamiliar works by women. She notes that these works focused on the vicissitudes of the female body in a way unparalleled, not surprisingly, in male works of that period. Three of them, in fact, dealt with breast cancer – one being Fanny Burney's journal account of her mastectomy, "an operation performed during the eighteenth century with only a wine cordial as anesthesia." Frank's brilliant idea of setting her account of curricular controversies in the context of a vivid, unsentimental, and powerful account of her own radiation treatment for breast cancer – diagnosed the semester after she taught the three nonstandard works alluding to breast cancer – reminds her reader vividly of the fact that this historically and ethically situated kind of criticism responds to an age-old conception of what gives literature its importance in human life. "… isn't that, after all," she asks, "what many people think good literature should do: sustain us when we're weak, deepen our understanding of history, expand our sense of what it's possible to think and feel?" She makes us ask why we might suspect a teacher who assigns the three nonstandard works of having a "political agenda": is it political to acknowledge the bodies of women and the illnesses to which women are subject, and apolitical to deny such recognition? Is criticism political only when it asks us to look and see, acknowledging what we might not have acknowledged before, and apolitical when it does not invite such acknowledgment?

The move to include noncanonical works and to scrutinize the ways in which such works construct desire and recognition does not necessarily lead to "delegitimizing Western civilization," as George Will fears. Says Frank,

Despite the picture Will paints of contemporary academic life, I did not whine to my colleagues that Shakespeare and Milton don't talk about breast cancer; nor did I, deciding that the lack of a poetic treatment of breast cancer in their works makes them bad writers, demand that my department replace our courses in Shakespeare and Milton with courses on Maria Edgeworth and Audre Lorde. Rather, like many of my colleagues, I taught the noncanonical alongside the canonical: Edgeworth and Burney, for example, alongside Defoe, Richardson, Fielding, Smollett, and Sterne. Will is anxious about the wholesale destruction of Western civilization, I think, because canon revision reveals the canon to be a social institution rather than a self-evidently sublime entity unsoiled by the grime of human interest.

If literature is a representation of human possibilities, the works of literature we choose will inevitably respond to, and further develop, our sense of who we are and might be.

Once we start to think of literature this way, we notice something else: that the New Critics' decision *not* to concern themselves with the social and historical dimensions of literary works was itself a political act, an act of a quietistic type. Turning to the ethical interpretation of a standard text, Frank defends an interpretation of Defoe's *Robinson Crusoe* that links it closely to its own historical context, one in which moral issues involved in colonialism and slavery were hotly debated. As Frank puts it, "You need to do a lot of work to ignore the historical context of *Robinson Crusoe*, no matter how mythically it presents itself." The willful choice to remain ignorant of such issues, and to treat the work as distant myth, betrays a certain stance, a stance of detachment from concrete human problems. The detachment of the Bloomsbury formalists was less innocent of politics than it might at first seem. Indeed, it seems evident, when one studies the writings of Bell, Fry, and other members of the Bloomsbury group, that their stance was closely connected with Bloomsbury's own complicated political stance, radical in matters of sex and aristocratic in matters of taste and education. The idea was that the cultivation and defense of fine-tuned, detached aesthetic responses allowed them to rise above everyday moral judgments (and thus to protect unconventional forms of sexual life), but also to neglect reformist proposals of the day that focused on the education of the masses, concentrating instead on the cultivation of small elite communities of friends. (The Bloomsbury ideal was closely linked not only to disdain for the working classes but also, frequently, to anti-Semitism and other forms of ethnic and racial prejudice. These prejudices also infect much of the New Criticism.) There is of course no reason why the political attitudes of Bloomsbury or the related ideas of the New Criticism should not be found in the literary classroom. We all learn most from a curriculum that contains dissent and difference, an interaction of opposing views. Even in the process of coming to grips with one work in a single class we should seek out a plurality of contrasting judgments. And different classrooms will properly differ greatly, as they foster approaches with political dimensions of many different types. The important thing to recognize is that we don't avoid the political dimension by pretending it isn't there; and insofar as we do, we drain the works, especially narrative works, of much of their meaning and urgency. This sort of frank debate about the moral content of art has been a staple of the Western tradition, in both philosophy and literature. There is no reason why it should not continue to make our teaching of literature more truly Socratic. The addition of new works will enhance our understanding both of history and of human beings. A critical examination of more standard works will yield new insights – frequently (as in the case of *Robinson Crusoe*) by revealing a dimension of unease or criticism in the text that a more morally detached style of criticism might have missed.

World Citizenship, Relativism, and Identity Politics

What, if anything, should worry us in the current political criticism? It is not a cause for concern that some political critics are more radical than Wayne Booth and Lionel Trilling, just as some are more conservative. It would be dull if all academics were liberals; criticism, like moral and political philosophy, profits from vigorous debate. It is far more healthy for students to hear debates between opposing views than for them to hear only refined talk about a poem's irony, divorced from any historical or ethical considerations.

Nor is it a cause for grave concern, ultimately, that many contemporary critics espouse forms of moral relativism deriving from French postmodernist philosophy, denying the objectivity of value judgments. One may certainly take issue with the conclusions of these critics, and find fault with their arguments. On the whole, philosophers thinking about truth and objectivity have not been very impressed by the arguments of the postmodernist critics, even when they defend versions of relativism on other grounds. The full assessment of these issues requires an arduous engagement with arguments, frequently technical in nature, drawn from the philosophy of physics, the philosophy of mathematics, and the philosophy of language. Any scholar who moves between philosophical debates on these issues and the related debates in literary theory cannot help noticing a difference in sophistication and in complexity of argument. (Literature is not the only field guilty of lapses in conceptual clarity: when economists talk about values, they are equally likely to espouse a naive form of relativism that would not withstand philosophical scrutiny.) We should demand more philosophical rigor in literary discussions of relativism, which otherwise risk superficiality and triviality.

But to ask for more rigor is not to say that relativist positions should be ignored or dismissed. The humanities classroom ought to contain vigorous debate between relativists and antirelativists of many kinds, just as between conservatives and liberals. When carried on at a high level, such a debate about the objectivity of value judgments enriches our understanding of alternatives in a useful way.

Such reflections about the philosophical shortcomings of literary teaching suggest that the teaching of literature can prepare world citizens better if it becomes more truly Socratic, more concerned with self-critical argument and with the contribution of philosophy. Interdisciplinary teaching, such as the work done at St. Lawrence by Grant Cornwell of the Philosophy Department and Eve Stoddard of the English Department, is an especially good way of promoting this rigor, both in the work of faculty and in their undergraduate teaching. Any literature classroom in which views of deconstructionist critics are discussed or exemplified should also contain some basic analysis of the arguments for and against various forms of cultural relativism. This can most easily be done in a climate of interdisciplinary dialogue and debate, in which literature teachers can observe the way these issues are handled by philosophers in courses on issues ranging from ethics to the philosophy of science, and in which the philosophers become aware of the subtle issues involved in discussions of literary interpretation. There is indeed a risk that our newly theory-conscious departments of literature will produce an outpouring of bad philosophy on these issues, both in research and in teaching. Interdisciplinary dialogue is the best way to prevent this from happening more than it already has.

Interdisciplinary dialogue about literature takes a variety of forms on today's campuses. Many introductory courses in "world civilization" or "Western civilization" bring philosophers together with literary scholars for the discussion of central literary texts. Such courses are most successful if they give the faculty support for course-development time, during which they can talk together and bring the resources of their disciplines to their common readings. Faculty also frequently team-teach courses at a higher level, integrating the perspectives of different disciplines. And finally, faculty may join in interdisciplinary dialogue outside the classroom, in ways that shape their classroom teaching. At St. Lawrence, the interdisciplinary faculty seminar, which focused extensively on theoretical issues of relativism, influenced the design and the methods of each individual faculty member's departmental courses. Such approaches need strong support, since without them the facile relativism that many undergraduates bring to the classroom is likely to remain unexamined and the goals of world citizenship to that extent unfulfilled.

The really grave cause for concern in the current teaching of literature, however, is not the presence of defective arguments, which can easily be criticized. It is, instead, the prevalence of an approach to literature that questions the very possibility of a sympathy that takes one outside one's group, and of common human needs and interests as a basis for that sympathy. The goal of producing world citizens is profoundly opposed to the spirit of identity politics, which holds that one's primary affiliation is with one's local group, whether religious or ethnic or based on sexuality or gender. Much teaching of literature in the current academy is inspired by the spirit of identity politics. Under the label "multiculturalism" – which can refer to the appropriate recognition of human diversity and cultural complexity – a new antihumanist view has sometimes emerged, one that celebrates difference in an uncritical way and denies the very possibility of common interests and understandings, even of dialogue and debate, that take one outside one's own group. In the world-citizen version of multiculturalism, the ethical argument for adding a work such as *Invisible Man* to the curriculum will be Ellison's own argument: that our nation has a history of racial obtuseness and that this work helps all citizens to perceive racial issues with greater clarity. In the identity-politics version of multiculturalism, by contrast, the argument in favor of *Invisible Man* will be that it affirms the experience of African-American students. This view denies the possibility of the task Ellison set himself: "of revealing the human universals hidden within the plight of one who was both black and American."

These different defenses of literature are connected with different conceptions of democracy. The world-citizen view insists on the need for all citizens to understand differences with which they need to live; it sees citizens as striving to deliberate and to understand across these divisions. It is connected with a conception of democratic debate as deliberation about the common good. The identity-politics view, by contrast, depicts the citizen body as a marketplace of identity-based interest groups jockeying for power, and views difference as something to be affirmed rather than understood. Indeed, it seems a bit hard to blame literature professionals for the current prevalence of identity politics in the academy, when these scholars simply reflect a cultural view that has other, more powerful sources. Dominant economic views of rationality within the political culture have long powerfully promoted the idea that democracy is merely a marketplace of competing interest groups, without any common goals and ends that can be rationally deliberated. Economics has a far more pervasive and formative influence on our lives than does French literary theory, and it is striking that conservative critics who attack the Modern Language Association are slow to criticize the far more powerful sources of such anticosmopolitan ideas when they are presented by market economists. It was no postmodernist, but Milton Friedman, who said that about matters of value, "men can ultimately only fight."[18] This statement is false and pernicious. World citizens should vigorously criticize these ideas wherever they occur, insisting that they lead to an impoverished view of democracy.

An especially damaging consequence of identity politics in the literary academy is the belief, which one encounters in both students and scholars, that only a member of a particular oppressed group can write well or, perhaps, even read well about that group's experience. Only female writers understand the experience of women; only African-American writers understand black experience. This claim has a superficial air of plausibility, since it is hard to deny that members of oppressed groups frequently do know things about their lives that other people do not know. Neither individuals or groups are perfect in self-knowledge, and a perceptive outsider may sometimes see what a person immersed in an experience fails to see. But in general, if we want to understand the situation of a group, we do well to begin with the best that has been written by members of that group. We must, however, insist that when we do so it may be possible for us to expand our own understanding – the strongest reason for including such works in the curriculum. We could learn nothing from such works if it were impossible to cross group boundaries in imagination.

Literary interpretation is indeed superficial if it preaches the simplistic message that we are all alike under the skin. Experience and culture shape many aspects of what is "under the skin," as we can easily see if we reflect and read. It is for this reason that literature is so urgently important for the citizen, as an expansion of sympathies that real life cannot cultivate sufficiently. It is the political promise of literature that it can transport us, while remaining ourselves, into the life of another, revealing similarities but also profound differences between the life and thought of that other and myself and making them comprehensible, or at least more nearly comprehensible. Any stance toward criticism that denies that possibility seems to deny the very possibility of literary experience as a human social good. We should energetically oppose these views wherever they are found, insisting on the world-citizen, rather than the identity-politics, form of multiculturalism as the basis for our curricular efforts.

Literature makes many contributions to human life, and the undergraduate curriculum should certainly reflect this plurality. But the great contribution literature has to make to the life of the citizen is its ability to wrest from our frequently obtuse and blunted imaginations an acknowledgment of those who are other than ourselves, both in concrete circumstances and even in thought and emotion. As Ellison put it, a work of fiction may contribute "to defeat this national tendency to deny the common humanity shared by my character and those who might happen to read of his experience."[19] This contribution makes it a key element in higher education.

We are now trying to build an academy that will overcome defects of vision and receptivity that marred the humanities departments of earlier eras, an academy in which no group will be invisible in Ellison's sense. That is in its way a radical political agenda; it is always radical, in any society, to insist on the equal worth of all human beings, and people find all sorts of ways to avoid the claim of that ideal, much though they may pay it lip service. The current agenda is radical in the way that Stoic world citizenship was radical in a Rome built on hierarchy and rank, in the way that the Christian idea of love of one's neighbor was and is radical, in a world anxious to deny our common membership in the kingdom of ends or the kingdom of heaven. We should defend that radical agenda as the only one worthy of our conception of democracy and worthy of guiding its future.

Notes

1 The issues of this chapter are treated at greater length in Martha C. Nussbaum, *Poetic Justice: The Literary Imagination in Public Life* (Boston: Beacon Press, 1996).

2 Ralph Ellison, *Invisible Man* (New York: Random House, 1992), pp. 563, 566, 3.

3 Ibid., p. 572.

4 Ibid., pp. xxiv–xxv, xxvi.

5 See Nussbaum, *Poetic Justice*, for Dickens' discussion of this case.

6 See Lionel Trilling, *The Liberal Imagination* (New York: Scribner's, 1953).

7 Jean-Jacques Rousseau, *Emile, or On Education*, trans. Allan Bloom (New York: Basic Books, 1979), p. 224.

8 On this phenomenon, see Charles Taylor, *Sources of the Self: The Making of the Modern Identity* (Cambridge, Mass.: Harvard University Press, 1989); also Ian Watt, *The Rise of the Novel* (Berkeley: University of California Press, 1957).

9 The original Stoics were critical of most literature of their time, since they believed that it usually exaggerated the importance of circumstances for human well-being. But this aspect of their view is logically independent of their interest in sympathetic perception, which naturally led them to take an interest in cultivating the imagination.

10 Walt Whitman, "By Blue Ontario's Shore."

11 Wayne Booth, *The Company We Keep: An Ethics of Fiction* (Berkeley: University of California Press, 1988).

12 See Stanley Cavell, *The Claim of Reason: Wittgenstein, Skepticism, Morality, and Tragedy* (New York: Oxford University Press, 1976).

13 See Judith Frank, "In the Waiting Room: Canons, Communities, 'Political Correctness,'" in *Wild Orchids and Trotsky: Messages from American Universities*, ed. Mark Edmundson (New York: Penguin, 1993), pp. 125–149.

14 George Will, *Newsweek*, April 22, 1991.

15 Clive Bell, *Art* (London: Chatto & Windus, 1913); Roger Fry, *Transformations* (London: Chatto & Windus, 1926).

16 Edward Bullough, "Psychical Distance as a Factor in Art and as an Aesthetic Principle," *British Journal of Psychology* 5 (1912): 87–98.

17 W. K. Wimsatt and Monroe C. Beardsley, "The Intentional Fallacy," *Sewanee Review* 54 (1946); also Cleanth Brooks, *The Well-Wrought Urn* (New York: Harcourt Brace, 1947).

18 Milton Friedman, "The Methodology of Positive Economics," reprinted in Daniel M. Hausman, ed., *The Philosophy of Economics* (Cambridge: Cambridge University Press, 1984), p. 212.

19 Ellison, *Invisible Man*, p. xxvi.

CHAPTER 9

Theory in Practice
Relation and Responsibility:
A Levinasian Reading of King Lear

Kent Lehnhof

Kent Lehnhof teaches English at Chapman University and writes on Milton, Shakespeare, Spenser, and Sidney. In this essay, he explores the applicability of the ethical philosophy of Emmanuel Levinas to *King Lear*. He argues that Levinas's idea that self and other are inseparable in the ethical relationship is evident in Lear's actions towards his daughters. The relation to the other defines the tragic situation in which Lear finds himself, and the play, according to Lehnhof, does not resolve the problem that the relation to the other inserts into human life.

To escape the "there is," one must not be posed but deposed; to make an act of deposition, in the sense one speaks of deposed kings. This deposition of sovereignty by the ego is the social relationship with the Other, the dis-inter-ested relation.

(Emmanuel Levinas)[1]

The late philosopher Emmanuel Levinas (1905–95) is frequently celebrated as one of the twentieth century's most astute and insightful readers of Husserl and Heidegger. Yet Levinas was also an attentive reader of Shakespeare. He specifically mentions Shakespeare when talking of his early influences, and he includes the English playwright in a list of authors whose art he admires.[2] Levinas's great work *Otherwise than Being* (1974) alludes to both *Hamlet* and *Macbeth* on its very first page, and his collected works contain more references to Shakespeare than to any other author, save Dostoyevsky. Indeed, Levinas refers to Shakespeare so frequently in the lectures from 1946 and 1947 published under the title *Time and the Other* that he feels compelled at one point to pause and beg pardon for having "overindulged" himself. The self-deprecating gesture,

Original publication details: Kent Lehnhof, "A Levinasian Reading of *King Lear*."
Modern Philology 111.3, pp. 485–509. University of Chicago Press, 2014.
Reproduced with permission from University of Chicago Press and K. Lehnhof.

of course, does not prevent him from going on to say more about Shakespeare, nor does it really apologize for anything. Less an apology than a justification, Levinas excuses his literary allusiveness by provocatively suggesting that Shakespeare is at the center of all philosophical activity. "It sometimes seems to me," Levinas says, "that the whole of philosophy is only a meditation of Shakespeare."[3]

Although Levinas is not alone in ascribing a philosophical thickness to Shakespeare's oeuvre, what makes his claim especially intriguing (aside from its arresting hyperbole) is the kind of philosophizing it takes the plays to be performing. For by way of his recurrent allusions, Levinas would make Shakespeare proximate to his own philosophical position that the "I" cannot exist apart from the other, that the self comes into being only in and through the interpersonal relation. At first glance, this might seem an easy thing to say of an early modern author, since it is commonplace to describe identity in the early modern era as a relational construct, arising from any number of social networks or situations. But Levinas's claims about subjectivity and Shakespeare go well beyond our work on the self-constituting effects of kinship, ethnicity, sex, rank, and profession. As Alphonso Lingis notes, Levinas's ideas about intersubjectivity are nothing short of "anarchic."[4] They have profoundly changed our reading of philosophy, and they can change our reading of Shakespeare as well. To demonstrate what I mean, I propose to use Levinas to put philosophical pressure on Shakespeare's dramatization of human relatedness in *The Tragedy of King Lear* (1607–8). Even though Levinas does not discuss *Lear* at length in any of his published work, this difficult philosopher and this difficult play have much to say to one another.[5] As I will show, Levinas can be fruitfully brought to bear on Shakespeare's great tragedy, generating fresh and productive ideas about its most pivotal moments, its most perplexing questions, and its most popular interpretations. In addition, Levinas can provide a useful frame for discussing the nature of the response the stage play requires of us, both as audience members and literary critics. Levinas, I suggest, goes some distance toward helping us think what it might mean to "speak what we feel, not what we ought to say" (5.3.299).[6]

The difficult relation between self and other that lies at the heart of Shakespeare's stagecraft is both the core and crux of Levinas's phenomenology. Its primacy is expressed in Levinas's oft-repeated assertion that ethics – not ontology – is "first philosophy." Ethics must come first, Levinas explains, because the "I" does not emerge as an existent until after the arrival of *autrui* (the other person, someone other than myself). Were it not for the other, nothing would oppose the notion that all is an extension of the self. *Autrui*, however, explodes this egoistic delusion by confronting me with that which cannot be reduced or assimilated to myself. At every moment, the other overflows and destroys all thoughts I can think of him. Or, as Levinas puts it, "He escapes my grasp by an essential dimension, even if I have him at my disposal."[7] In his absolute alterity, the other reveals to me the boundaries of my being and in this manner constitutes me as a subject. I become an ego inasmuch as I am demarcated or delimited as such by the presence of the other.

But the self that is so constituted is also (and immediately) called into question. I cannot freely pursue my own interests in the face of the other, for the nudity and neediness I see in the face of the other lays claim to all that I would consume, control, or possess in such a pursuit. Arresting all egoism, the encounter with the other makes me responsible – not because I accept responsibility – but because the mere existence of the other makes this responsibility incumbent upon me. For Levinas, the essence of this responsibility is service. The face of the other commands me to give all that I have, to not merely be, but be for the other. Though I can try to ignore this summons, I can never "unhear" or silence it. According to Levinas, responsibility is the inexorable condition of human subjectivity. "To be" is always already to be "ordained," to be called to a long and difficult life of service.

Paradoxically, this inexhaustible ordination does not diminish my subjectivity but actually invests it. Because I am the only one who can fulfill my obligation to the other, my obligation endows me with absolute individuality – what Levinas terms the "supreme dignity of the unique." As Levinas writes, "I am I in the sole measure that I am responsible, a non-interchangeable I. I can substitute myself for everyone, but no one can substitute himself for me. Such is my inalienable identity of subject."[8] Moreover, the other person who gives me my identity also gives me my world, affording it a reality it could not otherwise possess. As Levinas explains, the exteriority of the world depends upon there being more to it than just me. Because the other provides me with the category of "not-me" that is the essence of exteriority, the other makes my world real. I know it to be actual rather than illusory exactly to the extent that I have it in common with the other.

All told, these ideas about exteriority, intersubjectivity, and infinite responsibility are quite difficult and carry with them some disturbing implications. However, I concur with Levinas that they are central to much of Shakespeare. Especially in *King Lear* – with its unflinching focus on interpersonal bonds "which are too intrince t'unloose" (2.2.69) – Shakespeare explores what it means to be in relation to the other and to be responsible for the other. The stage for this examination is set in the very first scene, for the starting point for *Lear*, as for Levinas, is the traumatic encounter with one who cannot be made same-as-me.

When the drama begins, Lear is blithely doing what being does: seeking its own interests, maintaining its own existence, apprehending and assimilating the world unto itself. And for the purposes of personal enrichment, Goneril and Regan elect to play along. Venally performing the obsequious parts to which they have been assigned, they dissemble their otherness and present themselves as obedient extensions of Lear's self. Their hypocrisy enables the king's fantasies of self-sovereignty, and things move along smoothly enough. But with her bare "nothing," Cordelia abruptly brings to an end this inauthentic play of the same. As Gayatri Spivak observes, Cordelia's answer to the question, "What can you say to draw / A third more opulent than your sisters?" derails everything – the meter as well as the moment.

CORDELIA. Nothing my lord. [six syllables of silence]
LEAR.   Nothing? [eight syllables of silence]
CORDELIA. Nothing. [eight syllables of silence]
LEAR.   Nothing will come of nothing. Speak again.
                                    (1.1.83–88)[9]

As an answer to Lear's question, Cordelia's reply is incomprehensible, irrecuperable. The king cannot bend it to his will. To borrow from Levinas, we might say that Cordelia here exceeds her father's grasp by an essential dimension, even when he has her at his disposal.

Of course, Lear is not alone in his perplexity. For the better part of four hundred years, audiences, actors, and critics have struggled to make sense of Cordelia's comportment in the love contest, worrying over her words and wondering about her motives. Some have suggested that she acts as she does because she is confused, either too innocent or too naïve to know what is expected of her. Others have regarded her as obstinate or passive-aggressive, refusing to play her father's game because it demeans her and devalues love. Still others have seen her as intentionally hurtful, provoking her father so as to expose his arrogance and pride.[10] What makes it so hard to settle upon a single interpretation is the strange way in which all seem to apply. As oxymoronic as it might be, Cordelia is humble, high-minded, and hostile – all at the same time. Yet this contradictory condition is precisely what Levinas identifies as the principal modality of the other. To look upon the other is to see both mastery and abjection – or, rather, mastery in abjection, since what gives the other power over me is precisely his nudity, destitution, and poverty. Such is Cordelia's situation in the play's opening scene. Standing before her father in the place of the inassimilable other, Cordelia confronts the king with a dispossessing defenselessness and a commanding vulnerability. She overwhelms him with what Levinas calls "the resistance of what has no resistance – the ethical resistance."[11]

Whereas Goneril and Regan use rhetorical figures and theatrical masks to conceal themselves, Cordelia does not suppress her alterity. Instead of offering her father empty words, she offers him herself. For, whatever else Cordelia's bare "nothing" might mean, it is first and foremost an exposure: an opening of herself to the examination, indignation, and authority of the king. By way of her one-word answer, Cordelia as much as says: "You have asked me to declare my love, but I can say nothing beyond what I am. My answer is myself. Behold me here." This is not rhetoric but revelation.

But if Cordelia's response is a revelation, it is an unwelcome one, for it interrupts the egotistical exercise the king is attempting to oversee. Her plainness upends everything by inverting in an instant the power relations that structure his contest. Having expended all his political capital to make himself the center of attention, Lear finds himself supplanted by a daughter whose powerlessness comprises a more compelling claim to that place. Her vulnerability speaks more loudly than his majesty, obliging him to attend to her. And in that moment of attention, Lear instantly knows himself to be a usurper, responsible to the one before him.[12] Rather than respond with care, however, Lear responds with rage. His anger is quite obviously an evasion, an attempt to duck his responsibility by casting blame on Cordelia. As Sears Jayne remarks, Lear reacts with "that violence which characterizes the actions of people who are stung by the consciousness of their own guilt."[13] The perverse logic of Lear's passion goes something like this: "You have made me angry, so you must be in the wrong. Were I the offender, I would be feeling contrition. Instead, I am feeling outrage, which is the natural response to unjust treatment. Thus, the emotions you have made me feel prove that I am the victim here, the one to whom redress must be made." In the palpable force of his anger, the king would validate his neglect of Cordelia, and the intensity of his ire is the measure of his self-betrayal, showing the lengths to which he must go to ignore the accountability he feels. Lear must crowd out his sense of responsibility with all-consuming anger if he is to persist on his selfish path.

And persist he does. From one moment to the next, Lear disowns his daughter and leaves her without a dowry, as if he could relinquish his responsibility by renouncing his paternity. Even when stripped of her filial status, though, Cordelia continues to stand before her father in the primary ethical relation of the-one-before-the-other. Her upright and exposed face is a perpetual reproof, a vision so searing that Lear cannot stand to look upon it. "Hence, and avoid my sight!" he roars (1.1.122). To elude the obligations otherness imposes upon him, Lear turns away from the face in which he has seen it:

> Thou hast her, France. Let her be thine, for we
> Have no such daughter, nor shall ever see,
> That face of hers again.
>
> (1.1.260–62)

Rather than heed Kent's call to "See better, Lear," the king forswears forever the sight of his youngest daughter (1.1.156). While it is common for critics to parley these repeated references to sight into an overarching trope about eyesight and insight, Paul Alpers is right to remind us that looking in this play is primarily a form of connection, not perception. To look upon someone is to enter into relation with him or her. Thus, when Lear turns away from Cordelia what he rejects is not abstract moral truth but "actual human relationships that give rise to moral obligations."[14] The king does not want to look on his daughter because he perceives in her naked face a naked command.

The pattern established with Cordelia repeats itself throughout the opening acts. Each time the king encounters alterity, he tries to escape the claim it makes on him, first by raging against the other, and then by demanding that he or she be removed from his field of vision. When Kent, for example, presents himself as "the true blank of thine eye," Lear tries not to look (1.1.157). He orders Kent to absent himself ("Out of my sight!" [1.1.155]) and then banishes him under penalty of death. Later, when Goneril and Regan cast off their false faces and reveal themselves as they really are, Lear showers them with curses. He cannot countenance his daughters the second they stop pretending to be the same as him. By this time, though, the king has surrendered his scepter and can no longer banish them as he has done Kent and Cordelia. Consequently, he exiles himself. Rather than submit to others, Lear takes to the heath, vainly seeking what Levinas terms "the salvation of a hermit."[15] Before Lear will be for the other, he will try to be without the other, as if he could return – through sheer force of will – to an imaginary state prior to the arrival of the other and the claims he makes.

It is a fool's errand, destined to fail. There can be no "I" without the other, and Shakespeare suggests as much when the king, in his isolation, increasingly loses hold of himself and his world. Try as he might, Lear cannot keep it together. His sides come unbound. His tears pour forth. His sorrows rise up. His heart breaks into a hundred thousand flaws. For a materialist critic like Margreta de Grazia, this dissolution demonstrates the degree to which early modern personhood is tied to property, such that "what *one* is depends on what one *owns*."[16] Thus, the sovereign who surrenders his crown and kingdom becomes a nobody or nothing: what the fool witheringly calls "an O without a figure" (1.4.158). Though this reading is both insightful and compelling, our appreciation for the identity effects of the objective relation in *Lear* should not overshadow the importance of the intersubjective one, especially since Lear's self-stability is so closely connected to his proximity to others. It is when Lear tries to live outside of all interrelation that he feels his sanity slipping away, giving theatrical expression to Levinas's statement that "the self cannot survive by itself alone, cannot find meaning within its own being-in-the-world, within the ontology of sameness."[17] As Lear flees from the answerability that is uniquely his own, he retreats from the one thing that both dignifies and defines him. He declines from the "supreme dignity" and "inalienable identity" of the one who is answerable to the ignominy and anonymity of one who is but "Lear's shadow" (1.4.196). Moreover, as Lear recoils from the alterity that is the condition of his exteriority, he causes his world to collapse upon itself. Out on the heath, the tempest without merges with the tempest within, for Lear has turned away from the human other who divides the interior from the exterior, giving shape and meaning to each. The tenuous reality of Lear's world out on the heath is a direct consequence of his refusal to occupy it with another.

Of course, Lear cannot really regress to a state prior to the other. (The other always already precedes the ego.) But inasmuch as *Lear* imagines this possibility, it suggestively ties identity and exteriority to interrelation, indicating that both self and world would slip away without the other. In his self-imposed solipsism, Lear is stripped of subjectivity and set adrift in a formless, faceless universe that threatens to swallow him up. If he is to be brought back, the stage play intimates, it must be by way of the other person – the shivering fool, the naked beggar, the blinded father, the suffering servant, the downcast daughter – each of whom summons Lear back to himself by summoning him back to his obligation.

Many are the points of contact with Levinas's work, where interrelation is said to deliver the self from the horrors of impersonal existence. Levinas refers to this state of being-less being as the "*il y a*" (the "there is") and associates it with panic and dread. He maintains, however, that one does not escape "the anonymous and senseless rumbling of being" by asserting one's self but by deposing one's self, "in the sense one speaks of deposed kings."[18] This idea of deposition has obvious significance for Shakespeare's play. Indeed, *Lear* can be seen to revolve around two types of deposition: one political and one ethical. The political deposition takes place early on, when Lear abdicates his throne and Goneril and Regan conspire to seize even the limited authority he would retain. Lear's ethical deposition, however, is another matter altogether. Nevertheless, this is the one toward which the play presses, pushing us to consider what it might mean to depose the ego and enter into disinterested relation with the other.

A number of critics have addressed the play's searching exploration of interrelation. Among the most insightful is Stanley Cavell, who seeks to understand why Lear turns away from characters like Kent and Cordelia, who quite plainly love him. Cavell ultimately concludes that the old man does not want to be loved – cannot bear to be loved – because love presents itself to him as a demand. Were he to acknowledge the affection of others, the king would be bound to deserve and reciprocate it. But this burden seems too large to bear, so Lear endeavors to avoid loving interrelation and all who offer it.[19] This argument is elegant, and much of it can be harmonized with my own interpretation. Nevertheless, I hesitate to accede to the principle of reciprocity that Cavell uses to explain the relations of love and responsibility in *Lear*. By tying interpersonal obligation to the offer and acceptance of love, Cavell effectively makes the answerability of the king contingent upon the actions of the other. Lear is bound to love where he is loved, but where he is not loved, his obligations are much less clear. Cavell's reading, in other words, circumscribes personal responsibility within a network of symmetrical and mutually reinforcing demands, implicitly limiting Lear's obligation only to those who love him. The king must care for Cordelia, but he owes little (if anything) to Regan, Edmund, and Cornwall.

I find Shakespeare's play to be more exacting than this. If we apply a strictly reciprocal logic to the tragic action, it is difficult to fault Lear for hating the daughters who have betrayed him. Yet it seems clear to me that we are meant to wince when Lear savagely curses Goneril and then Regan. Their mistreatment of him does not condone his mistreatment of them. And truly, if the actions of the most virtuous characters in the play are to teach us anything, it is that commitment can have nothing to do with calculation or conditionality. The Fool, Kent, and Cordelia all give themselves to one who cannot be said to deserve their devotion, and their actions are approved for this very reason. If we are to give proper value to the play's most meaningful characters and moments, we must acknowledge that what they have in common is an unqualified altruism quite apart from all thoughts of reciprocity and all systems of exchange. This, I believe, is the ethical standard to which the play holds us.

Such extreme selflessness perhaps runs counter to our notions of justice and fairness, but for Levinas it is the only ethical response. He is adamant that my relation to the other is not a quid pro quo.[20] According to Levinas, my obligation to *autrui* has nothing to do with his behavior toward me. It is our relation that commands me, anterior to and irrespective of all action he might undertake. And since this summons inheres as long as I am in relation to the other, my obligation to him is endless. At no point can I limit it by saying "I have done enough" or "I have done my part" or "I am more sinned against than sinning."

To be clear, Levinas does not rule out justice and fairness. Quite the contrary, Levinas asserts that my obligation to all others (and not just the other currently before me) compels me to arbitrate between competing interests and pursue a course of justice. Similarly, there are considerations that intervene and require justice even for me. But the "I" who is obliged to seek justice for others can never do so for itself, for it is impossible for the self to give weight to its own interests over and against the interests of the other. While it might be reasonable to expect that my face commands the other just as his face commands me, or to assume that the claims he makes on me are counterbalanced by the claims I make on him, Levinas insists that the "I" cannot experience its interrelatedness from the outside, as a symmetry or reciprocity. The face of the other, Levinas frequently says, addresses me from an insuperable "height" or "elevation." He and I are never on equal footing. Before the other, I can know nothing but my own obligation.

According to Levinas, this radically asymmetrical relation brings the self into being. But some have objected that it must also bring the self unto destruction. Paul Ricoeur, for example, contends that the claim that the "I" can never be equal to the other leads inevitably to self-loathing, while the corollary claim that the "I" must give all to the other leads just as surely to self-annihilation.[21] Significantly, a number of literary critics have seen Shakespeare's play as moving in the same direction. According to Richard Halpern, the tragedy imposes such impossible interpersonal demands upon its characters that self-destruction is the only viable response. In his view, the characters of *Lear* live and move in a zero-sum economy that does not allow for rational conservation. Consequently, what is ultimately "chosen" by the play as the most adequate response to its world of scarcity and struggle is aristocratic *dépense* or "self-destructive expenditure." If we are to credit Halpern's interpretation, we must conclude that all signs in *Lear* point toward aggressive self-annihilation.[22]

Yet Levinas insists that suicide is no answer to answerability and advises, more generally, that "my responsibility for all can and has to manifest itself also in limiting itself."[23] Paradoxically, the basis for this self-limiting is the limitlessness of my responsibility. If the "I" is to support a responsibility that extends uninterruptedly into eternity and embraces an infinity of others, it must have a care for itself. The self must preserve and maintain itself if it is to have anything to give (in the first place) and if it is to continue being able to give (in the second place). Or as Jamie Ferreira puts it, we can speak of self-surrender without requiring self-annihilation because "the counter-weight to GIVING ALL is ALWAYS GIVING."[24] If responsibility is understood to be infinite, then it cannot be discharged in the matter of a moment, no matter how spectacular that moment might be.

There are, to be sure, a number of spectacular moments of self-sacrifice in Shakespeare's play. And it is true that Lear turns to "self-destructive expenditure" when his initial attempts to browbeat, banish, and turn his back on the other fail to give him the relief he seeks. In spite of his act 1 evasions, the king simply cannot escape the neighbor whose nudity and neediness overmaster him. Even in the wilderness, Lear is unmistakably summoned. Edgar runs onstage, and Lear must confess: "Thou art the thing itself. Unaccommodated man is no more but such a poor, bare, forked animal as thou art" (3.4.95–97).[25] So piercing is Poor Tom's poverty that Lear is compelled to respond. This time, however, he does not resort to anger or exile. Rather, he starts ripping off his raiment, literally exposing himself to feel what wretches feel. "Off, off, you lendings!" he bellows, "Come, unbutton here" (3.4.97–98). Lear's desperate disrobing seems to be of a different order than his anger and self-estrangement. Yet Lear's self-exposure is no less of an evasion, for it is clear that the king is not undressing to relieve Edgar (to whom he does not offer the cast-off clothing) but to relieve himself. As was the case with Lear's wrath, his divestment turns out to be just another dodge, an attempt to put melodrama in the place of meaningful service. It is as if the king believes he can escape his obligation by making himself just as destitute (and therefore just as commanding) as the beggar before him. Or as if he can acquit himself of a lifetime of responsibility by performing one grand, self-destructive gesture. Instead of submitting himself, Lear magnificently attempts to undo himself.[26]

Gloucester tries to escape his ordination in analogous fashion. Upon finally owning up to the enormity of his individual responsibility, Gloucester despairs of ever being equal to it and resolves to cast off his burden – as Lear has cast off his clothing – in one extravagant, self-consuming act. Bestowing his wealth upon a beggar, he hurls himself (as he supposes) off a cliff. Though Gloucester presents this intended suicide as a protest on the part of all humanity, such a sacrifice would benefit nobody but him. Taking his cue from Hamlet, who would "his quietus make / With a bare bodkin" (3.1.77–78), Gloucester embraces self-slaughter as a strategy for paying off or canceling his account.[27] By leaping into oblivion, Gloucester hopes to end not only his life but also his answerability.

If we attend to these scenes, however, we can see that Shakespeare's play does not permit self-sacrifice to take the place of true surrender any more than Levinas does. When Lear undresses and Gloucester falls face-first, the futility and absurdity of their actions is apparent. It cannot be the case that these self-destructive acts are "chosen" by the play when they have put so many in mind of the temper tantrums of young children and the buffoonery of circus clowns.[28] Even if Gloucester and Lear want to bow out in a blaze of glory, the play will not let them. Self-sacrifice, or *dépense*, is not allowed as a final answer. Each of these suffering selves must pick himself up and keep going.[29] Indeed, it is this relentless drive that makes the play so poignant and so powerful. The summons to be otherwise works ceaselessly on Gloucester and Lear, such that they cannot ignore their ordination, even if they will not altogether assume it. Pricked again and again by their encounters with the other, the play's protagonists are pitched relentlessly forward, lurching toward transcendence.

This ragged trajectory has often been plotted along an axis of empathy or fellow feeling. Christian and humanist readings alike have long held that Shakespeare's Lear achieves redemption insofar as his torments teach him to feel what others feel.[30] In these interpretations, the king is said to take his first stumbling steps toward self-knowledge and salvation in 3.2, when he conceives a compassionate concern for the fool. The tender scene certainly seems like a turning point. We are out on the heath. The king is contending with the elements in self-righteous fury. The apocalyptic annihilation for which he has been calling appears imminent. But then his glance falls on the fool. The sight of the boy, skin-soaked and shivering, cuts Lear to the quick. He stops his shouting and says, "My wits begin to turn." Though many have taken these lines to announce a turn for the worse (Lear is really losing it now!), what follows is not the stuff of madness. For the first time in the play, Lear sets aside his obsessive interest in his own injuries and attends to the needs of another: "Come on, my boy. How dost, my boy? Art cold?" (3.2.66–67). As he addresses himself to the plight of the fool, Lear speaks with more reason and moderation than he has for some time. He also regains enough understanding to seek shelter from the storm. He conducts the fool to an outbuilding and invites him to enter, even offering him priority of place: "In, boy; go first" (3.4.26). Then, before taking shelter himself, Lear pauses to pray. Kneeling in the mud, the king pours out his heart to the houseless and the unfed, exhorting himself to "to take physic" and "expose thyself to feel what wretches feel" (3.4.26–34). It is a poignant moment, and many have taken it to express the overarching message of the play: namely, that compassion can cure us.

Levinas, however, is adamant that empathy is no achievement, and his critique of fellow feeling gives us reason to think twice about interpretations applauding Lear's emergent desire to identify with others. In Levinas's view, to see one's neighbor as one's self is not to respond to him but to totalize him, to make him an instance of one's own categories. Empathy in this respect is but "egology": an approach that reduces the other to an analogue of the self. This tiresome play of the same, Levinas maintains, cannot emancipate anyone – which is what we see when Shakespeare's king seizes upon Tom o' Bedlam as a second self, or partner in sorrows.

When Poor Tom rushes onstage, his wildness and weirdness are utterly astonishing. Lear, however, strives to close the gap between the stranger and himself by asserting an essential similarity. As if to blunt the force of Edgar's alterity, Lear equates the beggar's condition with his own.

> Didst thou give all to thy two daughters,
> And art thou come to this?
> ....
> Has his daughters brought him to this pass?
> Couldst thou save nothing? Wouldst thou give 'em all?
> (3.4.47–48, 59–60)

Though Kent objects that Poor Tom has no daughters, Lear is undeterred in his identification. He will not allow that Edgar's situation might exceed his own: "Death, traitor! Nothing could have subdued nature / To such a lowness but his unkind daughters" (3.4.65–66). Lear's approach is all wrong, and not just on points of fact. By comprehending Edgar's suffering within the circumference of his own, Lear effectively denies Edgar's difference and makes himself the model for all misfortune. Staged like this, Lear's empathy looks a lot like narcissism.[31] It is unseemly, and it does nothing to deliver

Lear from the solitude of being that manifests itself in this play as madness. When Lear cozies up to Poor Tom as to a known quantity, his mental state precipitously declines. Before long, he is removing all his clothes – a sure sign of madness in Shakespeare's day.[32] As a corrective, then, to the conventional view that *Lear* is all about empathy, we ought to acknowledge that though the king comes to think of others as of himself, this is not enough to heal him. Indeed, it is in a fit of fellow feeling that Lear strips himself naked and provides conclusive proof that he is mad.

This is not to say that empathy is given no value in Shakespeare's play. (As egocentric as it may be, Lear's empathy is at least an attempt at relation.) It is to say, however, that empathy's limitations are everywhere implied. As Jonathan Dollimore remarks, the king who commits himself to the cause of "windowless poverty" after coming to "feel what wretches feel," draws attention to the difficulty of seeking social justice in fellow feeling: the majority is bound to remain poor, naked, and wretched if a king must share the suffering of his subjects in order to "care."[33] In the end, empathy cannot produce an ethical society – or even prevent an unethical one. As Levinas explains, empathy is incapable of preventing bad acts because its ethical effects diminish as soon as we tell ourselves that some people are not "really" the same as us, that some people are not as fully human as are we.[34] This is what the Nazis claimed of the Jews, and this is what Lear claims of his "pelican daughters" (3.4.70). Lear feels justified in offering violence to Regan and Goneril because he has determined that they are not persons but predators (wolves, foxes, serpents, curs). As is evident in the king's chilling "Then kill, kill, kill, kill, kill, kill!" (4.5.177), empathy is an inadequate ground for ethics because it is too easily qualified or set aside. If Lear is to be brought more fully into the realm of the ethical, something more will be required. Instead of encountering the neighbor as an alter ego (to be given equal consideration), Lear must encounter him as an other (to be given all). What is needed is not empathy but awe.[35]

If we look at the moments wherein Lear is most authentically connected to other people, what we see is not empathy or understanding but profound embarrassment, even shame. The king is furthest from the mark when he feels "at home" with others: when he experiences the other as familiar, accommodating, or companionable. However, he comes closest to the play's ideal when he feels overwhelmed or at a loss – when his interactions are so disturbing, disarming, and dispossessing that he knows not what to do or say. This ethical discomfiture is most evident in his act 4 encounter with Cordelia, and it is for this reason that their reunion is rightly regarded as *Lear*'s highest moment.

Suffused as it is with gentle tones and soft music, the scene is unlike any other in the play.[36] Some of its elements, however, are familiar. When Lear rouses from sleep, Cordelia offers herself to him as she previously did in the love contest, inviting his gaze and subjecting herself to it. "Sir, do you know me?" (4.6.41), and "O look upon me, sir" (4.6.50). Lear shrinks back, confessing that Cordelia has ample cause to hate him. Her gentle reply is no more than a murmur: "No cause, no cause" (4.6.68). Like the "nothing" of act 1 that it echoes, Cordelia's "no cause" performs the literal operation of negation or denial. Yet the meaning of her words surpasses their linguistic function.[37] Analysis always feels inadequate to Cordelia's utterance because its meaning, as Levinas would say, lies not in the said (*le dit*) but in the saying (*le dire*). What gives "no cause" its significance is not only the content it communicates but also the approach it enacts. Her words will always be in excess of interpretation because Cordelia is not using signs so much as she is making herself a sign, delivering herself to her father in that discursive attitude of sustained exposure and incessant offer that Levinas calls "the very signifyingness of signification."[38]

Where Cordelia's self-exposure pitched Lear into a fiery passion in act 1, it works differently on him in act 4. What we see now is not rage but responsiveness. When Cordelia bows her head to receive his blessing, Lear does not hold his hand over her in the gesture of authority but kneels before her in a posture of humility. This action, as Richard McCoy points out, revisits an earlier instance in which Lear has kneeled sarcastically to beg a daughter for food, bed, and raiment. There, the action was cruelly derisive and was rebuked as such ("Good sir, no more. These are unsightly tricks" [2.2.321–22]). But when Lear takes to his knees in act 4, the gesture seems genuine.[39] His submissiveness is so stirring, so sublime, that A. C. Bradley finds the scene "almost a profanity to touch."[40]

When Margreta de Grazia looks upon this scene, she sees a man whose misfortunes have stripped him of selfhood. In his "*not* having," de Grazia writes, Lear is reduced to "*non*-being."[41] Levinas, however, would see things differently. For Levinas, the king who kneels before Cordelia has not been plunged into "non-being" but has been moved "beyond being." He has not ceased to be so much as he has begun to "be-otherwise." This state of self-surrender is what Lear – and his play – has been groping toward from the very beginning. It is more than empathy, more than self-sacrifice, more than loving reciprocity. Edgar refers to it as "ripeness" (5.2.11), but Levinas calls it "passivity" – by which he does not mean inertia or apathy but rather a readiness to be moved by the other, to be called by him without anticipating or presuming to know what is required.[42] This passivity, Adriaan Peperzak writes, "is lived in the humility of a devotion that is not planned but undergone." It is the way of transcendence, but it is also the way of suffering. "To live for others is to suffer, and even to suffer gratuitously, without meaning, for nothing, because only such a passion unquestioningly realizes the unchosen, entirely disinterested character of transcendent passivity."[43]

Kent, Cordelia, and the Fool appear to inhabit this exhausting ethical space from the outset. They are, in Levinasian terms, hostage to the other: obsessed, afflicted, wounded, burdened. But what about Lear? The trajectory of the tragedy is shaped by his struggle to enter into the ethical. But does this arc eventually complete itself? The question is vexing, for the transcendent encounter of act 4 is followed by the cruel crosses of act 5, sorely testing the passivity Lear appeared to assume. At times, the king seems to relapse into his old evasions. When Cordelia, for example, wants to go see these daughters and these sisters, Lear's anxious "No, no, no, no" calls to mind his earlier attempts to turn away from the face of the other (5.3.8). At other times, his responsiveness seems too tied to Cordelia. Though Lear will stop at nothing to succor his youngest, he can treat others, such as Kent and Gloucester, with apparent apathy and insensitivity. And even his intense devotion to Cordelia is alarming, since Lear's bearing toward her oscillates uncomfortably between submissiveness and possessiveness. The final act forces us to wonder whether Lear has truly given himself to the ethical relation or whether he has merely adopted more subtle means to monopolize Cordelia's affection and attention.[44]

In the instant before his heart breaks, Lear gives us reason to believe he is sincerely answering his ordination, and our hope that this is so attests to the play's success in impressing upon us its exacting ethical vision. The king's attentiveness to Cordelia's inert form, as Michael Holahan has shown, is an exquisite example of ethical perception and responsiveness.[45] And it is true, as Maynard Mack affirms, that Lear dies with no regard for himself. He draws his last breath "with his whole being launched toward another."[46] Yet this altruistic posture is undermined by several of Lear's last lines, some of which signal delusion ("This feather stirs. She lives" [5.3.239]), others indifference ("Prithee, away" [5.3.242]), and others wrath ("A plague upon you, murderers, traitors all" [5.3.243]). The play drives toward an ideal of ethical interrelation and absolute responsibility, but how close does the king come? After all is said and done, what we have witnessed remains enigmatic. Like the irreducible other, the tragedy resists our efforts to thematize its content or comprehend its meaning.[47]

But even as the play frustrates our understanding, it requires our response. This requirement is especially acute in the case of Cordelia, for the king is not the only one caught up in the face-to-face encounter with her. As the drama draws to a close, Lear exhorts every person in the theater to cast eyes on his daughter: "Do you see this? Look on her. Look, her lips, / Look there, look there" (5.3.285–86).[48] In performance, it is not uncommon for the actor playing Lear to turn his body and speak these lines directly to the audience, rotating and elevating Cordelia's inert form so as to present it to the seated spectators. The staging feels right, for in his last lines the king offers to each of us the daughter who has repeatedly offered herself to him. Yet what do we see if we obey Lear's injunction and look? We see, to be sure, a beloved daughter who is dead, but we also see an actor who is dressed up and dissimulating. "Beholders are asked to see what may not exist," Holahan writes, "for this is and is not Cordelia. Her character now appears only in an actor's body's mimicry of a past life – a striking union of death and theatrical illusion."[49] The "Cordelia" we are asked to consider is a theatrical construct: a person masked in a dramatic character. To what degree, then, can we live up to Lear's final command and look on, lament, and love this virtuous girl? Is it even possible for us to submit ourselves to a simulation?

Cavell believes that it is. Even as he concedes that our acknowledgment of Cordelia cannot be completed, Cavell downplays the difference between acknowledging a theatrical character and acknowledging an actual person. In both instances, he says, the difficulty lies in presenting ourselves to others to be recognized and commanded by them. Since dramatic characters do not and cannot take cognizance of us, this self-presentation seems especially difficult in the theater. But Cavell maintains that the problem inheres in every interrelation. Bound up within our own egos, you and I never occupy the same site. Thus, what is the case inside the theater is also the case outside of it. It is true that we cannot put ourselves in the presence of a theatrical character, but we cannot put ourselves in the presence of a real person, either. But though I cannot put myself in your presence, I can put myself in your present – and I do so by making your present mine. By suspending my egocentric perspective and surrendering the moment to you, I can make the present yours and put myself in it. This is how we acknowledge another person, and this is how we acknowledge Cordelia.[50]

Cavell's argument makes sense, but it depends on the elision of the actor. If we are to talk about surrendering ourselves to Cordelia's present, we must use the plural, for when Cordelia is before us there are two "presents" present. There is the present of the girl who is trying to help her father, and there is the present of the actor who is trying to enact the assigned role. Can we make one present without the other? Can we concentrate on Cordelia to the exclusion of the actor? The actor's "present" would seem to persist, no matter how enthusiastically we embrace the illusion. Were the actor to stumble, or sneeze, or say something surprising, we would instantly be aware of her "present," not Cordelia's. The actor in this scene is invisible to us only to the extent that she conforms to the expectations we are constantly applying to her. But if she should surpass, disappoint, or alter our idea of who Cordelia is and how Cordelia should act, the actor and her agency are immediately on our minds. How can the actor not exist in this scenario, if we are perpetually overseeing her and her actions?

As audience members, we may want to give ourselves entirely to Cordelia, but a part of us will always be attentive to the actor: to her skill in simulating loss (How believable this is!), to her success in evoking our wonder (What a remarkable performance!) – even to her safety in the final scene (Is the actor playing Lear going to be able to carry her safely?). The artificiality of the event intrudes. It divides our attention and makes us see double. Knowing that this is a simulation, we cannot fully commit ourselves to the characters on the stage. We may feel their grief and pain, but our experience of it is diminished by the knowledge that it is dissembled. Thus, at the same time that *King Lear* demands our response, it also constrains it. The play preaches the importance of an ethical openness it does not altogether allow.

Lear calls attention to the inadequacy of our response when he staggers onstage with Cordelia's lifeless body. His rebuke indicts the audience as well as the actors/characters at his side:

> Howl, howl, howl, howl! O, you are men of stones.
> Had I your tongues and eyes, I'd use them so
> That heaven's vault should crack.
>
>   (5.3.231–33)

As Marianne Novy observes, no spectator can respond accordingly, and our inability is profoundly embarrassing. For Novy, this unsettling insufficiency instills within each of us a keen sense of isolation. As we watch on in silence while Lear bursts his lungs and then his heart, we come to feel a sharp separation not only from the characters onstage but also from our fellow spectators. Nevertheless, Novy insists that this feeling of isolation ultimately gives way to a sense of solidarity. I cannot know if you and I are feeling the same thing, and I cannot deny that neither of us is feeling enough, but the simple fact that we are both feeling something (whatever it is) attests to a basic connectedness that, finally, fashions us into a community of care. "The one consolation that [Shakespeare] offers – and in a theater it is a significant one – is that we feel each other's loss because of our basic connection." Although our emotional response to Lear's tragedy will never rise to the height it deserves, it is – at least for Novy – enough to knit us together.[51]

The connectedness that Novy envisions, however, is hard to see onstage. At the close of the play, the surviving characters remain painfully and awkwardly apart. Albany tries to establish some form of sociality, but his proposal to reconstitute the realm under the joint rule of Kent and Edgar falls flat. Kent is intent on suicide, while Edgar makes no answer at all. Who will rule the kingdom and what will become of it are left as open questions, muddled even more by the fact that the play's final speech, which would customarily spoken by the royal successor, is inconsistently assigned to Albany in the Quarto and to Edgar in the Folio.[52] In a certain sense, this incertitude is apt: the nomination of a new king is hardly relevant, for the kingdom he would inherit has disintegrated. No longer a society, Albion is now a number of atomistic individuals, aloof and embarrassed. Their dissociation is distressing, and it prods us to consider a number of difficult questions concerning ethics, sociality, and politics. Among other things, we are brought to wonder whether the ethical relation can coalesce into – or even coexist with – the political relation. In a play world that places such weight on intersubjectivity and individual responsibility, is politics even possible?

Lear appears to answer in the negative, seemingly because politics – as imagined in the play – would put limits on responsibilities that are limitless. Even though Lear's regime instills within its subjects a sense of exorbitant duty, the expression of this duty (whether sincere or not) is too narrow. All devotion is directed at the king, who is officially enthroned as the singular other, the one whose plenipotent voice drowns out every other summons. By restricting responsiveness to the royal court, the monarchial structure of *Lear* would elide the existence and ignore the neediness of the non-regal other. Moreover, by channeling altruism into the well-defined and well-worn conventions of courtly service, the play's political system would distance its subjects from the unpredictable passivity that is the essence of the ethical. Court forms are too rigid, insisting upon choreographed behaviors and chivalric displays instead of openness and sincerity.

Even the king is too constrained by the monarchial model, inasmuch as his royal office subsumes his self in such a way as to inure him to the "elevation" of *autrui* and impedes him from responding as a flesh-and-blood individual to the other before him. The king is not an "I" but a "we," and the metaphysical plurality of his person inhibits him from assuming the ethical stance of the one-for-the-other. This difficulty is evident in the very first scene, as Lear slips in and out of the third person, recurrently using the royal "we" to make personal demands.[53] His erratic usage is indicative of his inability to separate his self from his scepter, an inability that confuses his conversation and complicates his approach to the other. To truly address himself to the other, a king would have to extract himself from his office: he would have to speak in the first person. Henry V attempts something of the sort on the eve of the battle at Agincourt, but he butts up against political impossibility. To enter into relation, a king must do more than borrow a cloak. He must truly depose himself before the other, which would seem to leave us – at least in the case of *Lear* – without a prince and without a polity.

Simon Critchley denies that ethics and politics are incommensurable, claiming to the contrary that an ethics of individual responsibility exists "for the sake of politics."[54] This may well be true, but Shakespeare's tragedy is silent on how it could be so. Aside from the evils of anarchy, the play does not present an alternative to monarchy. There is no purer ethico-political system waiting in the wings, ready to step in and save the gored state. Instead of trying to sketch out a political situation in which individual responsibility could be actualized and honored, *Lear* simply abandons politics altogether. The drama that begins with royal edicts and courtly ceremony concludes with stateless sincerity and direct address. At play's end, there is neither king nor kingdom – only responsibility. The relentless pursuit of the ethical pulls the play away from its political underpinnings, perhaps positing politics as antiethical.

But if *Lear*'s emphasis on individual responsibility leaves us without a recognizable political system, it also leaves us without a recognizable ethical system. Though the play thrusts us into the realm of the ethical (*l'éthique*), this realm does not resolve into an ethics (*une éthique*).[55] Or, to put it another way, the drama does not yield up or yield to a set of general rules capable of determining the proper course of action anterior to or outside of the event. Categorical imperatives cannot tell us what Cordelia ought to do when asked to profess her love, or what Lear ought to do when betrayed by his eldest daughters, or what Edgar ought to do when solicited by his suicidal father. Clearly, these characters must respond to the other, but the quality of their response remains rooted in the moment, deeply infixed in "ripeness" and "feeling" rather than in precepts and rules. With a few notable exceptions (e.g., the treachery of Edmund, the cruelty of Cornwall and Regan), the challenging emotional landscape of this play is not to be navigated by a priori ethical precepts – which is one of the many reasons it feels so Levinasian to me. Whereas someone like Kant envisions ethics as a matter of principle, such that uprightness consists of accepting and enacting impersonal, rational rules, Levinas believes it is unconscionably reductive to regard the other or my relation to him as universal instances or generic abstractions. The other is neither an instance nor an abstraction: he is who he is. Consequently, the ethical experience must be personal and particular, not principled.[56] Levinas argues – and I think *Lear* is in broad agreement – that one cannot resort to preconceived imperatives if one is to respond authentically. Rather, what one must do is resign oneself to a thoroughgoing passivity in which responsiveness is determined wholly in the moment, entirely by the other.

   After all, this is exactly what the play calls for at the close. As Edgar (or is it Albany?) speaks the last lines of the play, he affirms the necessity of an exhaustively personal response that goes far beyond our sense of what "should" be said in such a situation.

> The weight of this sad time we must obey,
> Speak what we feel, not what we ought to say.
> The oldest hath borne most. We that are young
> Shall never see so much, nor live so long.
>   (5.3.298–302)

Platitudes are too paltry for what we have witnessed. If we are to do justice to the suffering and exposedness of those before us, we must offer more than our conventional expressions of consolation. We must bravely enter that unscripted, self-delivering realm of discourse that Levinas calls "conversation" and that Shakespeare calls "speaking what we feel."[57]

   But perhaps I go too far in giving such ethical weight to a stage play written and presented primarily as an entertainment. In spite of the early moderns' enthusiasm for poetry's ability to delight and to instruct, art and ethics are not identical. In fact, the distance between them can be such that we might wonder whether they are ever in alignment, whether art can ever bring about an ethical end. If the ethical is imagined as an encounter with radical alterity, what can be the value of the simulation? On this question, Levinas is equivocal, if not contradictory. On the one hand, he distrusts art as an escape or an evasion. Art can give us selfish pleasure and enable our flight from the real world, thereby offering us false transcendence. In this respect, art is an idol: a lifeless object put in place of the other. On the other hand, Levinas openly acknowledges his philosophical debts to the great authors of Russia and western Europe and frequently refers to their literary works in his own writings. (The most obvious example is the line from *The Brothers Karamazov* that Levinas adopts as his motto, quoting it no less than twelve times in his published work.)[58] The best authors, Levinas will say, not only recognize and resist art's idolatrous potential but also wrestle with core philosophical questions, such as the meaning of life and the meaning of the human. In this way, the best art can prepare one for authors like Plato and Kant. What is more, it can also model the way out of being. According to Levinas, good art can imitate a form of ethical discourse by continually interrupting itself and calling itself into question.[59]

   King Lear, it would seem, does this in spades. The tragedy assails us in our unknowing. At play's end, we are baffled and bewildered – and compelled to speak even so. But what can we say? Or, to put a finer point on the question, what can we say that will not violate the terms of our speaking? Can we speak in a way that does not reduce or thematize? If it is true that great literature, like *Lear*, can imitate a form of ethical discourse, is it possible for literary criticism to do the same? As I draw this essay to a close, I would like to touch briefly on this question by considering how a Levinasian perspective might influence not only our experience of the drama but also our critical reception of it. In doing so, I make what is admittedly a perilous leap from stage plays to scripture, proposing to think about Levinas's approach to the Talmud as both a mode and model of literary criticism.[60]

Though Levinas took pains to separate his Talmudic writings from his philosophical writings (e.g., publishing each with different publishers), both endeavors are characterized by an antipathy toward totalization. With regard to scripture, Levinas unsurprisingly insists that the commentator's task is not to solve, settle, or decipher the text. He speaks instead of "renewal." "The life of the Talmudist," Levinas writes, "is nothing but the permanent renewal of the letter through the intelligence."[61] No amount of erudition or historical contextualization or critical knowledge can substitute for the unceasing work of asking questions of the text, since anything other than this has the effect of turning the text into a dead letter, an academic artifact containing obscurities without interest. For Levinas, the truth of the Talmud is inextricable from the light each individual sheds upon it; consequently, Talmudic thought must needs foster a dynamic pluralism – not to delight in relativism but to honor the infinite density of the Word, which requires the multiplicity of persons to express itself and unfold in the course of time.[62]

While it might seem like the worst kind of bardolatry to say that Shakespearean criticism could or should follow Levinas's Talmudic pattern, I am nonetheless attracted to a hermeneutic that favors renewal over resolution. Such an approach would oppose an analytic order that tries to contract a plenitude of responses into a handful of "right" readings and that tramples individuality underfoot in its expectation that all informed readers and audience members respond alike. Such an approach would recognize that agreement and unicity can dry up the wellsprings of meaning and significance and would embrace instead the unsettling effects of multiplicity and plurality, which do not appease us with a self-satisfying sense of knowledge but send us back to the text, obsessed and enthralled. Such an approach would begin to resemble what Simon Critchley, in a slightly different context, calls "dissensual emancipatory praxis": a relentless disturbing of the idyll of consensus, not to do away with consensus (or criticism) but to bring about its endless betterment.[63] The ethical possibilities toward which Levinas directs us (if only indirectly) are to be realized in a literary criticism that does not thematize but throws open, upsetting our apprehension in such a way as to reaffirm the richness of the text and the range and depth of responses it can draw forth. This kind of criticism would not be defined by dogmatism but would depend instead upon the incessant questioning of all: the disciple as well as the master. This criticism would strive to keep our responsiveness from rigidifying into a stultifying totality. It would aim at something akin to "the permanent renewal of the text through the intelligence."

And perhaps no stage play lends itself to this type of criticism as readily as Shakespeare's *King Lear*. With its challenging portrayal of our intersubjective situation and the infinite responsibility to which this puts us, the play text ushers us into a distressed and difficult realm of relation. To experience this tragedy is to be called into question: to be both traumatized and summoned. It is difficult to ignore this state of ordination, even though it most certainly exceeds us. We think and talk and write about the play with particular energy because it is in and through our responsiveness that we begin to uphold our noninterchangeable obligation and in this manner approximate the ethical ideal at the heart of the play.

Literary criticism as an act of ethical responsiveness? Speak what we feel, indeed.

Notes

The origins of this essay trace back to an undergraduate honors thesis written in 1994 at Brigham Young University under the direction of Richard Duerden and Bruce Young. It was presented in revised form at the 2007 meeting of the Shakespeare Association of America in a seminar organized by Douglas Trevor and Kristen Poole. Its current state owes a great deal to the generosity and insight of several anonymous readers.

1 Emmanuel Levinas, *Ethics and Infinity*, trans. Richard A. Cohen (Pittsburgh: Duquesne University Press, 1985), 52.

2 Ibid., 22, and Emmanuel Levinas, "Reality and Its Shadow," trans. Alphonso Lingis, in *The Levinas Reader*, ed. Seán Hand (Oxford: Blackwell, 1989), 138.

3 Emmanuel Levinas, *Time and the Other*, trans. Richard A. Cohen (Pittsburgh: Duquesne University Press, 1987), 72.

4 Alphonso Lingis, "Translator's Introduction," in Emmanuel Levinas, *Otherwise than Being: Or Beyond Essence*, trans. Alphonso Lingis (Pittsburgh: Duquesne University Press, 2006), xx.

5 For other readings of *Lear* informed by Levinas, see Seán Lawrence, "The Difficulty of Dying in *King Lear*," *English Studies in Canada* 31 (2005): 35–52; and James Kearney, "'This Is Above All Strangeness': *King Lear*, Ethics, and the Phenomenology of Recognition," *Criticism* 54 (2012): 455–67. Both of these essays, which I unfortunately did not discover until late in the writing of my own essay, relate to mine in interesting ways. For additional interpretations of Shakespeare influenced by Levinas, see Geoff Baker, "Other Capital: Investment, Return, Alterity, and *The Merchant of Venice*," *Upstart Crow* 22 (2002): 21–36; Jeremy Tambling, "Levinas and *Macbeth*'s 'Strange Images of Death,'" *Essays in Criticism* 54 (2004): 351–72; David Ruiter, "Harry's (In)Human Face," in *Spiritual Shakespeares*, ed. Ewan Fernie (London: Routledge, 2005), 50–72; Steven Shankman, "The Idea of Europe, Levinas, and Shakespeare's *The Merchant of Venice*," in *Engaging Europe: Rethinking a Changing Continent*, ed. Evlyn Gould and George J. Sheridan Jr. (Lanham, MD: Rowman & Littlefield, 2005), 63–78; and Seán Lawrence, "Listening to Lavinia: Emmanuel Levinas's Saying and Said in *Titus Andronicus*," in *Through a Glass Darkly: Suffering, the Sacred, and the Sublime in Literature and Theory*, ed. Holly Faith Nelson, Lynn R. Szabo, and Jens Zimmermann (Waterloo, ON: Wilfrid Laurier University Press, 2010), 57–69.

6 All quotations come from *The Tragedy of King Lear* (the Folio version) as reprinted in *The Norton Shakespeare: Based on the Oxford Edition*, ed. Stephen Greenblatt et al. (New York: Norton, 1997). Though I refer to F rather than Q, I do not think my reading is significantly affected by the choice of texts.

7 Emmanuel Levinas, *Totality and Infinity: An Essay on Exteriority*, trans. Alphonso Lingis (Pittsburgh: Duquesne University Press, 1988), 39.

8 Levinas, *Ethics and Infinity*, 101.

9 Gayatri Chakravorty Spivak, "Ethics and Politics in Tagore, Coetzee, and Certain Scenes of Teaching," *Diacritics* 32 (2002): 20.

10 It is impossible to cite all the relevant readings, so a few representatives will have to suffice. Stanley Cavell is among those who see Cordelia's reply as an expression of confusion. Richard Halpern is less forgiving, emphasizing the cruelty of Cordelia's words and relating them to the more vicious revenges of Goneril and Regan. Eugene England tries to recuperate the painfulness of Cordelia's response by portraying her as a therapist/savior who only hurts her father to heal him. See Stanley Cavell, *Disowning Knowledge in Seven Plays of Shakespeare*, updated ed. (Cambridge University Press, 2003), 62–64; Richard Halpern, *The Poetics of Primitive Accumulation: English Renaissance Culture and the Genealogy of Capital* (Ithaca, NY: Cornell University Press, 1991), 248–49; and Eugene England, "Cordelia and Paulina: Shakespeare's Healing Dramatists," *Literature and Belief* 2 (1982): 69–82.

11 Levinas, *Totality and Infinity*, 199.

12 "What is … a solitary individual," Levinas asks, "if not a growing tree without regard for all that it cuts off and destroys, absorbing the nourishment, the air and the sun, a being which is fully justified in its nature and its being? What is an individual if not a usurper? What does the advent

of conscience mean …, if not the discovery of cadavers at my side and my horror of existing as a murderer?" (Levinas, quoted in Adriaan T. Peperzak, "Judaism and Philosophy in Levinas," *International Journal for Philosophy of Religion* 40 [1996]: 135).

13   Sears Jayne, "Charity in *King Lear*," *Shakespeare Quarterly* 15 (1964): 278.

14   Paul J. Alpers, "*King Lear* and the Theory of the 'Sight Pattern,'" in *In Defense of Reading: A Reader's Approach to Literary Criticism*, ed. Reuben A. Brower and Richard Poirier (New York: Dutton, 1962), 135.

15   Levinas, quoted in Peperzak, "Judaism and Philosophy in Levinas," 135.

16   Margreta de Grazia, "The Ideology of Superfluous Things: *King Lear* as Period Piece," in *Subject and Object in Renaissance Culture*, ed. Margreta de Grazia, Maureen Quilligan, and Peter Stallybrass (Cambridge University Press, 1996), 34.

17   Levinas, quoted in M. Jamie Ferreira, "'Total Altruism' in Levinas's 'Ethics of the Welcome,'" *Journal of Religious Ethics* 29 (2001): 462.

18   See the epigraph to this essay, and n. 1 above.

19   Cavell, *Disowning Knowledge*, 57–62.

20   We gain a sense of Levinas's commitments here by noting that he distrusts and distances himself from the word "love" that is central to Cavell's analysis precisely because it implies reciprocity and familiarity. Levinas prefers instead "the harsh name for what we call love of one's neighbor," namely, "responsibility for my neighbor" (Emmanuel Levinas, *Entre Nous: On Thinking-of-the-Other*, trans. Michael B. Smith and Barbara Harshav [New York: Columbia University Press, 1998], 103).

21   Paul Ricoeur, *Oneself as Another*, trans. Kathleen Blamey (University of Chicago Press, 1992). For a concise summary of Ricoeur's critique, see Ferreira, "'Total Altruism,'" 451–52.

22   Halpern, *Poetics of Primitive Accumulation*, 264.

23   Levinas, *Ethics and Infinity*, 121–22, and *Otherwise than Being*, 128.

24   Ferreira, "'Total Altruism,'" 454.

25   In these lines, we might find the rudiments of an early modern rationale for Levinas's claim that *autrui* is always and only human. Perplexed by his anthropocentric stance, several of Levinas's critics have asked why the "I" is not also ordained by the alterity of animals, or even plants. Though Levinas answers religiously (the human other bears "the trace of God," whereas plants and animals do not), the human exceptionalism established in Lear's speech is different. As Laurie Shannon has shown, it is a negative exceptionalism, predicated upon the underprovisioned condition of humankind. Whereas nonhuman animals are naturally "coated," the human creature Lear considers is uniquely naked, compelled to case himself in secondhand skins, or "lendings." Given Levinas's insistence on the essential nudity of *autrui*, Lear's vision of "unaccommodated man" seems relevant. As Shannon remarks, the "poor, bare, forked animal" we are made to see in the play raises the question of whether any animal other than the human may fairly be deemed "naked." See Laurie Shannon, "Poor, Bare, Forked: Animal Sovereignty, Human Negative Exceptionalism, and the Natural History of *King Lear*," *Shakespeare Quarterly* 60 (2009): 168–96.

26   Act 3's "Off, off, you lendings! Come, unbutton here" is revisited in act 5 when Lear asks of an attendant, "Pray you, undo this button. Thank you, sir" (5.2.84). Making the same basic request, but in a much calmer register, the king signals a shift in his character. This shift is even more significant if we take Lear to be making the request for Cordelia, rather than himself. In most productions, the king tugs at his own constricting collar when he speaks these lines, but he could be fumbling with Cordelia's. He is, after all, trying to resuscitate her, and undoing a button at her neckline would be commensurate with this. If staged like this, the scene would show a subtle yet striking reversal. The man who once tried to "unbutton" to escape his answerability now unbuttons to administer aid to another.

27   In the early modern period, a paid-off account was marked *Quietus est* ("laid to rest"), as the Norton edition states in a footnote to *Hamlet* (1706 n. 9).

28   Janet Adelman sees in Lear's actions "the rage of an abandoned infant." G. Wilson Knight remarks that the king's "tremendous soul" is "incongruously geared to a puerile intellect." According to Knight, "Lear is mentally a child; in passion, a Titan." For Jan Kott, both Lear and Gloucester are "too ridiculous" to be tragic: they are "clowns who do not yet know they are clowns." Nowhere is this more apparent than in Gloucester's attempt to end his life. The attempted suicide, Kott

writes, "is merely a circus somersault on an empty stage ... the classic expression of buffoonery." See Janet Adelman, *Suffocating Mothers: Fantasies of Maternal Origin in Shakespeare's Plays, "Hamlet" to "The Tempest"* (New York: Routledge, 1992), 118; G. Wilson Knight, *The Wheel of Fire: Essays in Interpretation of Shakespeare's Sombre Tragedies* (London: Oxford University Press, 1930), 177, 179; and Jan Kott, *Shakespeare Our Contemporary*, trans. Boleslaw Taborski (Garden City, NY: Doubleday, 1964), 90, 177, 117.

29 On this point, see also Lawrence, "Difficulty of Dying in *King Lear*."

30 Paul Siegel epitomizes the Christian approach, while Wendell Berry exemplifies the humanist approach. Jonathan Dollimore provides a useful overview of both Christian and humanist readings in *Radical Tragedy* before rejecting each for misguidedly mystifying the suffering of Lear and others. See Paul N. Siegel, "Adversity and the Miracle of Love in *King Lear*," *Shakespeare Quarterly* 6 (1955): 325–36; Wendell Berry, "The Uses of Adversity," *Sewanee Review* 115 (2007): 211–38; and Jonathan Dollimore, *Radical Tragedy: Religion, Ideology and Power in the Drama of Shakespeare and His Contemporaries* (University of Chicago Press, 1984), 189–95.

31 On this point, see also Kearney, "'This Is Above All Strangeness,'" 458–59.

32 See Michael MacDonald, *Mystical Bedlam: Madness, Anxiety, and Healing in Seventeenth-Century England* (Cambridge University Press, 1981), 130.

33 Dollimore, *Radical Tragedy*, 191.

34 See Hilary Putnam, "Levinas and Judaism," in *The Cambridge Companion to Levinas*, ed. Simon Critchley and Robert Bernasconi (Cambridge University Press, 2002), 35.

35 On the subject of sympathy versus awe, Jean Marsden's work is suggestive. She observes that an English obsession with sympathy in the second half of the eighteenth century led to extensive revisions of *Lear*. "Here we can find," Marsden writes, "an attempt to bring Shakespeare into the realm of sympathy, to recast his tragedies in a form that inspired not awe but 'fellow-feeling'" (Jean Marsden, "Shakespeare and Sympathy," in *Shakespeare and the Eighteenth Century*, ed. Peter Sabor and Paul Yachnin [Aldershot: Ashgate, 2008], 29).

36 Music is explicitly indicated in Q, where the Doctor says: "Louder the music there!" (Q 4.21.23).

37 Alpers eloquently describes Cordelia's words as "almost speechless gestures – the verbal equivalents of simple physical contact" ("*King Lear* and the Theory of the 'Sight Pattern,'" 150).

38 Levinas, *Otherwise than Being*, 5.

39 Richard C. McCoy, "'Look upon Me, Sir': Relationships in *King Lear*," *Representations* 81 (2003): 50–51.

40 A. C. Bradley, *Shakespearean Tragedy: Lectures on "Hamlet," "Othello," "King Lear," and "Macbeth,"* 2nd ed. (London: Macmillan, 1905), 285.

41 De Grazia, "Ideology of Superfluous Things," 21.

42 I adapt this phrasing from Catherine Chalier, "The Philosophy of Emmanuel Levinas and the Hebraic Tradition," in *Ethics as First Philosophy: The Significance of Emmanuel Levinas for Philosophy, Literature and Religion*, ed. Adriaan T. Peperzak (New York: Routledge, 1995), 8.

43 Adriaan T. Peperzak, "Transcendence," in *Ethics as First Philosophy*, 191.

44 For readings that draw out the darker aspects of Lear's demeanor and Cordelia's commitment, see Adelman, *Suffocating Mothers*, 121–29; and Maureen Quilligan, *Incest and Agency in Elizabeth's England* (Philadelphia: University of Pennsylvania Press, 2005), 213–35.

45 Michael Holahan, "'Look, Her Lips': Softness of Voice, Construction of Character in *King Lear*," *Shakespeare Quarterly* 48 (1997): 406–31.

46 Maynard Mack, *"King Lear" in Our Time* (Berkeley: University of California Press, 1965), 100.

47 This is not to equate *King Lear* with *Autrui*. It is simply to note that the economy of the same interrupted by the other is also interrupted by our experience of *Lear*.

48 These lines appear only in F.

49 Holahan, "'Look, Her Lips,'" 412.

50 See Cavell, *Disowning Knowledge*, 97–110.

51 Marianne Novy, *Love's Argument: Gender Relations in Shakespeare* (Chapel Hill: University of North Carolina Press, 1984), 163.

52 Contemporary critics tend to see Edgar as the more suitable successor (as implied in F), but Richard Dutton and Tom Clayton show that there is a case to be made for Albany as well. See

Richard Dutton, *"King Lear, The Triumphs of Reunited Britannia* and 'The Matter of Britain,'" *Literature and History* 12 (1986): 146–47; and Tom Clayton, "'The Injuries That They Themselves Procure': Justice Poetic and Pragmatic, and Aspects of the Endplay, in *King Lear*," in *"King Lear":* *New Critical Essays*, ed. Jeffrey Kahan (New York: Routledge, 2008), 198–203.

53 See Jerry Wasserman, "'And Every One Have Need of Other': Bond and Relationship in *King Lear*," *Mosaic* 9 (1976): 22.

54 Simon Critchley, "Five Problems in Levinas's View of Politics and the Sketch of a Solution to Them," *Political Theory* 32 (2004): 182.

55 I am indebted to John Llewelyn for the distinction between *l'éthique* and *une éthique*. See John Llewelyn, "In the Name of Philosophy," *Research in Phenomenology* 28 (1998): 39.

56 In contrasting Kant and Levinas, I lean heavily on the ideas and phrasing of Hilary Putnam. See Putnam, "Levinas and Judaism," 54–55.

57 "To approach the Other in conversation is to welcome his expression, in which at each instant he overflows the idea a thought would carry away from it. It is therefore to *receive* from the Other beyond the capacity of the I.... The relation with the Other, or Conversation, is a non-allergic relation, an ethical relation" (Levinas, *Totality and Infinity*, 51).

58 "We are all guilty of all and for all men before all, and I more than the others" (Fyodor Dostoyevsky, *The Brothers Karamazov*, trans. Constance Garnett [New York: New American Library, 1957], 264).

59 For useful summaries of Levinas's statements on art, see C. Fred Alford, "The Opposite of Totality: Levinas and the Frankfurt School," *Theory and Society* 31 (2002): 238–39; and Gerald L. Bruns, "The Concepts of Art and Poetry in Emmanuel Levinas's Writings," in Critchley and Bernasconi, *Cambridge Companion to Levinas*, 206–33.

60 As Jill Robbins demonstrates in her admirable study of Levinas and literature, it is virtually impossible to cull a coherent theory of literary criticism from Levinas's thought and practice. By turning to his Talmudic writings, I oversimplify the situation and draw what might be unpardonable parallels. Nevertheless, I hope that the suggestiveness of the maneuver will make up for its recklessness. See Jill Robbins, *Altered Realities: Levinas and Literature* (University of Chicago Press, 1999).

61 Emmanuel Levinas, *Nine Talmudic Readings*, trans. Annette Aronowicz (Bloomington: Indiana University Press, 1990), 79.

62 This paragraph is drawn from Catherine Chalier, "Levinas and the Talmud," trans. Annette Aronowicz, in Critchley and Bernasconi, *Cambridge Companion to Levinas*, 103–4.

63 Critchley uses the term in a discussion of Levinas and politics. Noting that government tends to become tyrannical when left to itself, Critchley commends the way Levinas's ethical ideas can cultivate forms of "dissensual emancipatory praxis" that "work against the consensual idyll of the state, not in order to do away with the state or consensus, but to bring about its endless betterment" ("Five Problems in Levinas's View of Politics," 183).

CHAPTER 10

Theory in Practice
The Baby or the Violin: Ethics and Femininity in the Fiction of Alice Munro

Naomi Morgenstern

Naomi Morgenstern is an Assistant Professor in the Department of English at the University of Toronto. She has published essays on Willa Cather, Toni Morrison, E. L. Doctorow, and feminist and psychoanalytic theory.

Doing this in the name of the good, and even more in the name of the good of the other, is something that is far from protecting us not only from guilt but also from all kinds of inner catastrophes.

– Jacques Lacan

Ahhhh! No Lessons. No lessons ever!

– Alice Munro

When asked in a 1982 interview whether or not she "embed[s] lessons in [her] stories," Alice Munro objected in no uncertain terms (Hancock 223). And surely no one would want to call Alice Munro a "moral" writer. Her narrators and central characters provocatively resist final acts of judgment, leaving readers confronted by the complexities and impossibilities that characterize the ethical.[1] The name *morality*, Derek Attridge has recently suggested, is often given to "specific obligations governing concrete situations in a social context, which require the greatest possible control of outcomes," whereas ethical demands involve "responsibility" and "obligation," but also "unpredictability and risk" (28).[2] Munro's stories represent the risks of the ethical (the possibility that the call from the other has been misidentified; the possibility that the other's otherness has been compromised in the work of responding; the risk that the subject of

Original publication details: Naomi Morgenstern, "The Baby or the Violin: Ethics and Femininity in the Fiction of Alice Munro." *Lit: Literature Interpretation Theory*, 14.2, pp. 69–97. Reproduced with permission from Taylor & Francis.

an ethical intervention will never recover herself) even as they insist on giving us nothing but "specific obligations" and "concrete situations."

Take, for example, the recent "Post and Beam." Lorna, a young married woman with two children, is visited by her needy cousin Polly. Already weighed down with responsibility and fantasizing of escape, Lorna wants to be able to think of Polly and her other relatives back home as "some people she knew and liked but was not responsible for" (103). "You should live your own life," Lorna tells her older cousin with exasperation (100). But when Lorna and her husband and children go away for the weekend, leaving the houseguest behind, Lorna is tormented by the thought – the very definitive image – of a Polly who will have committed suicide in their absence. Lorna will have failed Polly; she will not have responded to her call. For Lorna, it is as if others are at risk if one refuses to take responsibility for them (which is, of course – just to complicate matters – sometimes the case). In the car on the way home Lorna tries to reason her way out of responsibility for Polly. After all, Polly is an adult; Lorna has children of her own to care for. But "No sooner had she put the argument in place than she felt the body knock against the door as they tried to push it open. The deadweight, the gray body. The body of Polly who had been given nothing at all" (105).

Lorna's attempt to reason her way out of concern for her cousin is disrupted by something which has the feel of exteriority: "No sooner had she put the argument in place than she felt the body knock against the door as they tried to push it open" (105). Munro's words here demand careful attention: Lorna's call to responsibility is experienced as the uncannily intentional "knock" on the door given by a corpse. This corpse, moreover, has been put into motion by the subject's attempt to respond (by opening the door). Lorna's image (for it is, after all, *her* corpse – *her* conjuration) figures the call of responsibility as a call from beyond; the dead body of Polly knocks against Lorna's reasoning, even as it is Lorna's concerned pushing that sets the body in motion. Lorna is more than aware of the "neurotic," "primitive," childish nature of her fears and their tendency to discount the otherness of others even as they overcome her with concern. Nevertheless, she cannot shake the knocking of the corpse and so decides to make a "bargain" on the drive home (109). What will she, Lorna, have to sacrifice, so that Polly will survive her betrayal? When Lorna returns home, Polly is more than all right. She stands strongly independent and may even have taken up with the "friend of the family," Lionel, who had represented Lorna's own fantastic possibilities of escape, a possible shadowy affair (106). What Lorna realizes is that others exist independently of her fantasy life and psychic economy. She looks out on the backyard at her husband, Brendan, at Polly, at Lionel, at her daughter Elizabeth, at their mundanely pleasant interactions, their otherness, their separateness, the fact that they are all temporarily happy without her. It is both something of a miracle and the simplest of truths: "How had that happened? [...] A scene so ordinary and amazing come about as if by magic. Everybody happy" (108).

The end of "Post and Beam" tells us, with a jolt, that this all happened long ago (something we both know and do not know as we read the story) and that Lorna will continue to make bargains. In other words, she will repeatedly confuse herself with others: "It was a long time ago that this happened. In North Vancouver, when they lived in the post-and-beam house. When she was twenty-four years old and new to bargaining" (109). Why, then, Munro's story leads us to ask, does the ethical insight – that the other exists beyond the self – need to be repeated? Why does it fail to sustain itself? Munro's stories, I will argue, offer us more than one answer. First of all, they suggest that we

cannot but live in the stories we tell ourselves; if confusing life with literary narrative is
a mistake, it is also an inevitable one (Munro's stories insist on this again and again).[3]
The unmaking and remaking of a subject and the world she inhabits are a repeated
process in Munro's fiction. But the stories do not allow us to stop here; the ethical insight
is also impossible to maintain because this simple truth – that the other is radically
exterior – is simultaneously false. And this is why many have contended that ethics are
"impossible" or "paradoxical." ("It is on the basis of the thinking of a certain impossibility,"
writes Jill Robbins, "that the ethical becomes legible" [xv].) How can one reach out to
the other without doing violence to their otherness in the very attempt to fold them into
the self's understanding? How can an encounter with alterity not do violence to the
encountering subject (ethical responsibility, writes Emmanuel Levinas, "requires subjectivity as an irreplaceable hostage [...] my being that belongs to me and not to another
is undone" [qtd. in Keenan 20])?[4] Would the subject be capable of ethical response if he
or she were not already the subject of a constitutive alterity? "If the settled patterns of
my mental world," writes Derek Attridge, "have been so freed up that the truly other
finds a welcome, my subjectivity will have been altered in some degree, and thus – especially
if the cumulative effect of such events is taken into account – the self too can be said to be a
creation of the other" (21). In "Post and Beam" Lorna realizes that her life itself is already
the bargain, a compromise, a giving up, not discrete in itself; she is inhabited by otherness.
Where in one's life story could one hope to locate a time or space outside of dependence and
responsibility?

   Lorna's back and forth between a registration of the absolute exteriority of the call to
responsibility and a refusal to recognize the other's radical exteriority (the reduction of
all others to characters in the drama of the subject's responsibility) defines a compelling
engagement with the complexities of the ethical. "Can there be something," Levinas
asks, "as strange as an experience of the absolutely exterior, as contradictory in its terms
as a heteronomous experience [...] whose movement unto the other is not recuperated
in identification, does not return to its point of departure [?]" ("Trace of the Other"
348). Munro's characters experience ethical crisis as an encounter with demands that
cannot be comfortably located or coherently translated, and this is part of their appeal
and their sophistication. It is not easy to describe who or what one responds to in the
ethical moment ("Exactly *to* whom we are responsible or answerable in this situation is
one of the questions I shall have to leave unaddressed," writes Attridge [27]; "A fragility
at the limit of non-being," is one of the ways Levinas finds to describe that which calls
one to responsibility [*Totality* 258]), but in Munro's fiction the relationship established
by ethical responsibility resists the banality of an economic exchange – of needs and
their satisfaction; of knowledge and understanding – between two intentionalities figured as equal partners. The call of the other in "Post and Beam" is indissociable from the
force exerted by the same; the call is as much Lorna's as is her attempt to reason a way
out of responsibility. In this respect the story suggests that the possibility of an ethical
response is linked to the violence of an attempt to contain the other's otherness within
an economy of the same. But as Jacques Derrida writes in his commentary on Levinas,
"the irreducible violence of the relation to the other, is at the same time nonviolence,
since it opens the relation to the other" ("Violence" 128–29).

   Alice Munro's stories of ethical crisis, then, depict characters responding – or failing
to respond – to calls defined by their ambiguous intentionality and potential meaninglessness. Hesitating on the border between the mechanical and the human, the physiological and the intentional, or the outside and the inside of the psyche, these calls put

language, and hence being, into question. In what follows, I want to elaborate on the relationship between ethics and intersubjectivity in Munro's fiction by focusing on two stories in which a dreaming woman is called, quite literally, to responsibility by cries that verge on the inhuman: that of a yowling, nameless woman in "Meneseteung," and a screaming infant, who also happens to be the narrator, in "My Mother's Dream." While dreams are usually taken to be the "royal road" to the individual's unconscious, in Munro's narratives, I claim, dreams fleetingly register the other's otherness. In reading "Meneseteung" and "My Mother's Dream" together, then, I am insisting on their specific registration of an ethical dilemma. These stories explore the impossibility of the ethical and the crises of responsibility generated by ethical relations, and they address the question of why it is that the ethical insight – that the other exists beyond the self – needs to be repeated. In addition, I want to pay particular attention to the ways in which these stories inflect ethical encounters with crises of gendered subjectivity. In Munro's stories, sexual difference is never left behind, but neither is it simply mapped onto the opposition between self and other. "Meneseteung" presents us with what I will call an ethical "primal scene" that threatens conventional femininity and its accompanying limited and calculable acts of generosity, while "My Mother's Dream" explores the relationship between object loss, lack, and gendered subjecthood. Re-reading the classical psychoanalytic account, Munro provocatively suggests that "femininity" reconsidered may coincide with the relational itself. These are feminist stories, I argue, that repeatedly refuse to think of ethical questions as separable from embodied life (although, of course, this does not mean that involving the body provides any simple answers). Munro's stories, I suggest, can be read to expose the mystical and somewhat desperate fiction (woman and man as "opposite" sexes) that has been crucial to notions of alterity promised by the metaphysics of presence.

Recently critics have argued that while Munro herself is no theorist, her writing speaks powerfully to feminism and to literary theory.[5] While concurring with this assessment, I add that Munro's stories have much to contribute to contemporary efforts to think about literariness and ethics.[6] Intriguingly, Magdalene Redekop's study of Munro's fiction ends (except for the postscript) with an insistent repetition of the word "responsibility." "Meneseteung," she argues, defines "an explicit *responsibility* – that of the contemporary woman writer to the voices of the past. It is a *responsibility*, however, that is linked to the writer's *responsibility* to her craft [...] The writer's *responsibility*, in turn, is linked by Munro to our *responsibilities* in the real world that contains a river called the 'Meneseteung'" (228; italics mine). This insistence, then, is my starting point for a consideration of gender and ethics in the fiction of Alice Munro.[7]

"Meneseteung"

In "Meneseteung" an unnamed narrator tells the story of a nineteenth-century Canadian woman poet, Almeda Roth, who is the author of a single conventional book of poems entitled *Offerings*. Five years after the publication of her book, Almeda is contemplating the possibility of marriage to her neighbor, the widower Jarvis Poulter. But Almeda awakens from a dream one night to hear a horrible racket: a fight between a drunken man and woman and what might be a call for help. Knowing that she must do something, Almeda only goes back to sleep. She is re-awakened by the "sorrowful" voice of a crow (505). There is a woman's body lying up against her back gate. Almeda assumes that the

woman is dead, and that she, Almeda, has failed to take responsibility for her. She goes
to Jarvis Poulter for help. The woman, it turns out, is not dead at all. She heaves herself
up onto all fours and calls out inarticulately. Ultimately, she is shooed off the premises
by Mr. Poulter, who would preclude, or at least contain, Almeda's encounter with otherness. He is a proper and "productive" subject, possessed of a "lively commercial spirit";
"Stop it. Gwan home, now. Gwan home, where you belong," he says to the woman (513,
507). But if the woman retreats to where she "belongs" (even in this almost allegorical
story one only glimpses otherness), where Almeda "belongs" is forever unsettled.

Far from welcoming, then, what another nineteenth-century poet called the "merge"
(Walt Whitman's "Who need be afraid of the merge?" 31) and the interchangeability of
"you" and "I" ("And what I assume, you shall assume" 25), Almeda's daily life in what
was once the "wilds of Canada West" reproduces rigid structures of distinction:

> Almeda Roth's house faces on Dufferin Street, which is a street of considerable respectabil-
> ity. On this street, merchants, a mill owner, an operator of salt wells have their houses. But
> Pearl Street, which her back windows overlook and back gate opens onto, is another story.
> Workmen's houses are adjacent to hers. Small but decent row houses – that is all right.
> Things deteriorate toward the end of the block, and the next, last one becomes dismal.
> Nobody but the poorest people, the unrespectable and undeserving poor, would live there
> at the edge of a boghole (drained since then), called the Pearl Street Swamp. Bushy and
> luxuriant weeds grow there, makeshift shacks have been put up, there are piles of refuse and
> debris and crowds of runty children, slops are slung from doorways. The town tries to
> compel these people to build privies, but they would just as soon go in the bushes [...] It is
> said that even the town constable won't go down Pearl Street on a Saturday night. (497)

This passage describes the face of respectability set in opposition to the abject body with
its functions, needs, and desires ("boghole," "Swamp," "Bushy and luxuriant weeds,"
"runty children," "slops"). Munro forges a connection, here, between denying one's
own embodiment and dehumanizing others (a familiar and convenient psychopolitical
maneuver according to which only others have bodies that are messy, reproduce, decay,
and die). But this does not mean that the entire world beyond Almeda's psyche is only
the projection of Almeda's psyche. And, I would contend, "Meneseteung" is most
compelling insofar as it is *not* a psychological tale, or rather insofar as it allegorizes the
necessary limitations of such a narration. Instead, the narrator tells us that Almeda
Roth's back gate opens onto "another story": not "reality" but a potentially new center;
not incoherence and unviability itself, but rather what might throw one version of coherence into crisis. It is when this crisis occurs, when the closed system is interrupted, that
we can locate an ethical moment in the text.[8]

It is the encounter between Almeda and the nameless woman that constitutes the
primary ethical scene in "Meneseteung." Moreover, this primary scene is also a *primal*
scene, both because it is propped on the familiar psychoanalytic primal scene (Almeda
witnesses and fantasizes an enigmatic encounter between a man and woman that is
both puzzlingly erotic and perceived as violent), and because it so clearly delineates
a structure – the subject's glimpse of the other's otherness – that can serve as an
"origin" for exploring ethics in Munro's fiction. If the psychoanalytic primal scene is
classically a "solution" to explain away a childhood enigma, this ethical primal scene is a
crisis that disturbs language, identity, and recognizable social relations. The nameless
woman appears on the threshold of Almeda's world and "asks" for something, demands
something, beyond what Almeda knows and is accustomed to giving. If Almeda only

glimpses the other's otherness, she is simultaneously overexposed. The "call" is strangely impersonal, verging on the inhuman (Levinas writes of the "wild barbarian character of alterity" ["Trace" 345]), and Almeda's subjecthood is taken "hostage" in the encounter. Almeda will never be the same again.[9]

"Meneseteung" narrates the request for a radical "gift": Almeda Roth is asked to give something more, something that exceeds those conventionally feminine offerings she is accustomed to giving. Almeda writes in the preface to her book, *Offerings*, that her poems stand in the place of embroidery; we are told she suffers a "tendency toward fancy iced cakes and decorated tarts" (500), and on a certain hot Saturday in August she makes "*little* jars of grape jelly" for they "will make fine Christmas presents, or *offerings* to the sick" (503). "Meneseteung," that is to say, presents us with an ethical demand (what I am calling the *gift* as opposed to the *offering*) that disrupts and exceeds the gendered economy of daily life in nineteenth-century Ontario. Almeda is called on to be responsible for another, and this initiates a crisis in her very being and arguably in the very coherence of the linguistic/symbolic order as such (Blanchot writes: "*My* responsibility for the Other presupposes an overturning such that it can only be marked by a change in the status of 'me,' a change in time and perhaps in language. Responsibility, which withdraws me from my order – perhaps from all orders and from order itself – responsibility, which separates me from myself [...]" [25]). Almeda begins to write a masterwork that will never – *could* never – assume form, and she simultaneously goes over to the "other" side, becoming indistinguishable from the other she failed to help. Almeda is ultimately relegated to the margins of social coherence and viability.[10]

What distinguishes the call to responsibility in this story (and recalls similar structures in other stories by Munro) is the liminal state in which the subject of ethical crisis experiences the call to responsibility. Thus it is in between waking and sleeping, and in a semi-drugged condition, that Almeda Roth experiences her encounter with the other woman. Almeda still sleeps in her childhood bedroom in the back of the house. Her window opens out onto Pearl Street. One hot August night, after having begun the preparations for making grape jelly, Almeda goes to sleep with her window open: "When she wakes up, the night seems fiery hot and full of threats. She lies sweating on her bed, and she has the impression that the noises she hears are knives and saws and axes – all angry implements chopping and jabbing and boring within her head. But it isn't true" (504).[11] The noises are not *just* in Almeda's head. The unconscious is outside. The scene gradually shapes itself into a more and more recognizable primal encounter that "confuses" sexuality and violence: "just the two figures come on and grapple, and break loose again and finally fall down against Almeda's fence. The sound they make becomes very confused – gagging, vomiting, grunting, pounding. Then a long, vibrating, choking sound of pain and self-abasement, self-abandonment, which could come from either or both of them" (505).[12]

In addition to being a primal scene, however, this scene is both a fantastic beating scene and a scene of real sexual violence: "Two voices gradually distinguish themselves – a rising and falling howling cry and a steady throbbing low-pitched stream of abuse that contains all those words which Almeda associates with danger and depravity and foul smells and disgusting sights. Someone – the person crying out 'Kill me! Kill me now!' – is being beaten. A woman is being beaten [...] Yet there is something taunting and triumphant about her cry. There is something theatrical about it" (504).[12] Here then is Almeda's dilemma: "Is that the sound of murder she has heard? What is to be done, what is she to do? She must light a lantern, she must go downstairs and light a lantern – she must go out into the yard, she must go downstairs. Into the yard. The lantern" (505). Almeda knows what she "must" do – and in this sense there is no dilemma – and then she falls asleep.

Almeda wakes the next morning to the sound of a "big crow" talking in a "disapproving but unsurprised way [...] 'Wake up and move the wheelbarrow!' it says to her scolding, and she understands that it means something else by 'wheelbarrow' – something foul and sorrowful. Then she is awake and sees that there is no such bird" (505).[13] "Meneseteung," in other words, suggests that the call of another can only be heard by something other than consciousness, by something "beyond" one's self-sufficient fictions, even as a return to sleep also constitutes a flight (*"What is it that wakes the sleeper?"* writes Lacan, "Is it not, *in* the dream, another reality?" [58]). Almeda looks out the window and sees "a body." Significantly, Almeda cannot see the body's face. The other woman will not emerge as another subject, instead this body is all body, all animal; it is grotesque ("Smelling of vomit. Urine, drink, vomit" [506]), and yet unsettlingly aestheticizable ("the haunch showing a bruise as big as a sunflower" [506]). Almeda "runs away" to Poulter's house for help. "There is the body of a woman," she says (506). Poulter and Almeda enter the Roth yard to encounter the body. Its existence exceeds any fantastic need Almeda might have had to conjure it up. "Of course the body is still there. Hunched up, half bare, the same as before" (507). While Almeda feels compelled to express that the unconscious or possibly even dead woman lying against her fence is in some way her responsibility, Poulter shows no qualms about treating the anonymous woman like an animal and with absolute disgust and disdain. But then the woman "speaks" for herself:

> Now a startling thing happens. The body heaves itself onto all fours, the head is lifted – the hair all matted with blood and vomit – and the woman begins to bang this head, hard and rhythmically, against Almeda Roth's picket fence. As she bangs her head, she finds her voice and lets out an openmouthed yowl, full of strength and what sounds like an anguished pleasure. (507)

One might read this moment ("she bangs her head, she finds her voice") as a parody of feminist aspiration, or perhaps as a dark version of Whitman's "barbaric yawp." One witnesses here a scandalous moment of masochistic pleasure lodged in a speaking and insistent body that Almeda cannot claim and "celebrate" (as in Whitman's "I celebrate myself"). The woman who "bangs her head" and "finds her voice," I would argue, represents a crisis in the symbolic order. The yowling woman represents a plenitude that exists on the periphery; she is literally banging her head on that which divides. And this plenitude includes the body, the specifically female body (this encounter also marks the onset of Almeda's menstruation), the lives that might feature in other stories that would be differently centered, and that scandalous sexuality which does not know pleasure from pain. It also includes the call of an other, the call to be responsible for an other, to recognize what disrupts one's singular economy.

In 1929 V. N. Volosinov argued that there was only one use of the human voice that could be said to be asocial, prior to signification: "The animal cry, the pure response to pain in the organism, is bereft of accent; it is a purely natural phenomenon. For such a cry, the social atmosphere is irrelevant, and therefore it does not contain even the germ of sign formation" (21–22). Otherwise, Volosinov held, all signs were ideological and the "individual consciousness" was "ideological through and through" (22). But

"Meneseteung" encourages us to hesitate before making such binary distinctions: the cry of pain on one side, the entirety of human signification on the other. For Volosinov's cry, like the voice in Munro's story, destabilizes the symbolic, revealing that its apparent closure is merely contingent. If bodies speak, language also must be said to have a body, and this is why there can be no absolutely unique voice (so much for the idealized rendering of finding one's own voice: everything begins with reproduction). Furthermore, it is because of this irreducible destabilization that there is always something new to be said, something not yet signified, a cry from beyond.[14] If Munro's stories explore the potential collapse of language into sheer materiality (a collapse that takes place on the border of the human and the animal, the human and the machine, the living and the dead), they also recognize this space as generative and ethical. The cry from beyond is simultaneously a cry from the internal border of language, from that in language which, without precedent or preparation, is nevertheless at home in language ("an at home that is given, or, rather, loaned, allotted, advanced before every contract, in the 'anachronism of a debt preceding the loan'" [Derrida, *Adieu* 99]).

After the woman stumbles off, Almeda will retreat into her house, consume several drops of "nerve medicine" in her tea, and, in an account resembling "The Yellow Wallpaper" (another story about madness, freedom, and responsibility for others who are also the self), she will begin to hallucinate: "A lot of things to watch. For every one of these patterns, decorations seems charged with life, ready to move and flow and alter. Or possibly to explode. Almeda Roth's occupation throughout the day is to keep an eye on them" (510). What was once decorous, decorative, and feminine is in danger of exploding (we are reminded earlier in the story that single men never decorate their houses). Almeda now imagines "one very great poem that will contain everything [...] Stars and flowers and birds and trees and angels in the snow and dead children at twilight – that is not the half of it. You have to get in the obscene racket on Pearl Street and the polished toes of Jarvis Poulter's boot and the plucked chicken haunch with its blue-black flower" (510–11). Her *Leaves of Grass* would be "Meneseteung": "All this can be borne only if it is channeled into a poem, and the word *channeled* is appropriate, because the name of the poem will be – it *is* – 'The Meneseteung.' The name of the poem is the name of the river. No, in fact it is the river, the Meneseteung, that is the poem – " (511). Almeda no longer thinks of "what could be done for that woman" (and the wording and perspective here are crucial), nor does she imagine herself as Jarvis Poulter's wife "keeping [his] dinner warm and hanging his long underwear on the line" (511). That she no longer thinks of either of these relations suggests that the order and divisions that delimit and give form to Almeda's world have been suspended. We are beyond the home economics of cooking and laundry and traditional self-sacrificing femininity and even beyond a calculable model of responsibility (doing for others). Almeda could be said to inhabit the space of "a dissident and inventive rupture with respect to tradition, authority, orthodoxy, rule, or doctrine"; the space, in other words, in which responsibility can be found.[15]

In fact, Almeda would already seem to have *become* the overembodied other. "On her way through the kitchen, she walks through the pool of grape juice. She knows that she will have to mop it up, but not yet, and she walks upstairs leaving purple footprints and smelling her escaping blood and the sweat of her body that has sat all day in the closed room" (511). But neither this, nor her hallucinatory state, alarms her. "For she hasn't thought that crocheted roses could float away or that tombstones could hurry down the street. She doesn't mistake that for reality, and neither does she mistake anything else for reality, and that is how she knows that she is sane" (512). But to be sane, of course, *is* to mistake a familiar order for reality, and in this sense insanity is intimately bound up with the possibility of ethical relations. Even as Almeda fails the other woman, her crisis must be said to be an ethical one. There has been a suspension of the closed story, a suspension of cultural coherence, without which an ethical encounter cannot be said to have taken place. Ethics, in "Meneseteung," is indistinguishable from insanity, from being out of one's (own) mind.[16]

In the wake of their abortive courtship, Almeda Roth and Jarvis Poulter go on to lead separate lives and die separate deaths. The local newspaper, the *Vidette*, describes Almeda's end:

> She had become, in the eyes of those unmindful of her former pride and daintiness, a familiar eccentric, or even, sadly, a figure of fun [...] Her last illness was of mercifully short duration. She caught cold, after having become thoroughly wet from a ramble in the Pearl Street bog. (It has been said that some urchins chased her into the water, and such is the boldness and cruelty of some of our youth, and their observed persecution of this lady, that the tale cannot be entirely discounted.) (512)

One must note here how completely Almeda has become the other, one of those not quite distinguishable characters of Pearl Street. Almeda has gone out her back door never to return, recalling, in the end, both the old, drunken "Queen Aggie" and, of course, the nameless, faceless, yowling figure. Instead of refusing the other, failing to hear the other, constructing a coherence based on his or her exclusion, Almeda opts for a more Whitmanesque "solution" ("I am the man, I suffered, I was there"). While to *become* the other is certainly not what anyone would want to call ethical, Munro's story insists on marking the ethical as a crisis for language, for social structures, and for the individual being's coherence.

Almeda is called to responsibility more than once: "Wake up and move the wheelbarrow!" says the crow. But as the reader schooled in dreams and close reading will notice, this discordant signifier that calls Almeda does not come from her own psychic store of the day's fragments. It comes instead from a story in the *Vidette* and/or from the narrator's reconstructed history. We are told at the very beginning of the story of "Queen Aggie": "They get her into a wheelbarrow and trundle her all over town, then dump her into a ditch to sober her up" (496). The "wheelbarrow" stands metonymically for the other woman in her otherness and in her abject embodiment. Perhaps this is one more "clue" as to the unreliability of the narrator; she gives herself away in making the other's "dream" (Almeda's) her own. But more intriguingly, I would suggest, since the wheelbarrow is "beyond" Almeda, it also disrupts our illusion that she is a discrete individual. "The responsibility with which I am charged is not mine," writes Blanchot, "and makes me no longer myself" (13). "Wheelbarrow" (the word itself) conveys, within Munro's story, the very interruption of the sovereign subject that constitutes a call to ethics.[17]

"My Mother's Dream"

"Meneseteung" is not the only Alice Munro story in which a character is called to responsibility from within a dream. "My Mother's Dream," which stages a conflict between two who would presume to be sovereign subjects (they are referred to as "monsters"), also includes such a call. In the dream a very young baby has been left out overnight by its mother ("and perhaps it was not last night but a week or month ago that she had done this" [294]), and the call comes, strikingly, as a silence (prior to the dream, the baby has done nothing but scream – the baby could even be said to have been holding its mother hostage to this scream). In reading the ethical encounter that takes place in "My Mother's Dream," however, I also want to pay particular attention to this story's explicit suggestion that the encounter coincides with an origin for sexual difference. Munro's story succeeds, I suggest, in combining an enquiry into the ethical relation with a feminist critique of the modern sex/gender system.

In Freud's myth of the origin of sexual difference, both the boy and the girl must address the crisis of lack. For the boy, time is the way out. He cannot have his pleasure now, but he can defer it: someday he will be like his father and have a love object like his mother. So the story goes. The girl, on the other hand, has no way out. She can deny "reality" and insist on her own masculinity ("The hope of some day obtaining a penis in spite of everything and so of becoming like a man may persist to an incredibly late age and may become a motive for strange and otherwise unaccountable actions" [Freud, "Some Psychical Consequences" 337]); she can suffer in woundedness, or she can take up a masculine identification that allows her to regard other women with scorn and contempt. There is certainly no "authentic" feminine position to be found here, and this, of course, is what feminists have both despised Freud for and precisely what they have found most insightful in his work. (Freud was recuperated for feminism with Juliet Mitchell's influential claim and productive misreading: psychoanalysis is not a prescription for, but rather a description of, the patriarchal unconscious.) How, then, do we take a loss? After all, Freud insists, we are profoundly conservative creatures. Our very development as subjects paradoxically consists in a series of "vigorous attempts" to recreate the past ("On Narcissism" 95). We never give up a pleasure, a satisfaction, an object, without the most tremendous resistance. "The opposition [to loss] can be so intense," Freud claims, "that a turning away from reality takes place and a clinging to the object through the medium of a hallucinatory wishful psychosis" ("Mourning and Melancholia" 253). The enigma of femininity for Freud is thus, I would claim, the enigma of lack. How do women put up with it? And what do they really want anyway? While there is a certain slippage in my account (between loss-of-the-other and self-loss or loss-of-wholeness), it is precisely the interrelatedness of object loss and lack, I argue, that Alice Munro addresses so profoundly in "My Mother's Dream."

Recent feminist and queer explorations of psychoanalytic theory have reread Freud's account by pointing to a peculiar and culturally dominant equation: the opposition between self and other is understood as being equivalent to the opposition between the sexes. Judith Butler asks, "But why is sexual difference the primary guarantor of loss in our psychic lives? And can all separation and loss be traced back to that structuring loss of the other sex by which we emerge as this sexed being in the world?" (164–65). Similarly, Michael Warner wonders, "why is gender assumed to be our only access to alterity?" (200). He asserts: "the assumption that gender is the phenomenology of difference itself [...] is a staggeringly primitive confusion" (200). In "My Mother's Dream," Munro, too, retells Freud's story of assuming a sexed identity. But while continuing to associate femaleness with loss, "My Mother's Dream" also suggests that the "feminine" "choice" of loss or lack is a choice akin to a life drive, a will to survive. Annihilation, on the one hand, and triumph, on the other, are by implication the more "masculine" options.[18] The oldest of misogynist associations of women with death may actually be an intolerance of the other's ability to *survive* precisely as a subject of lack.

It is not incidental, I would add, that "My Mother's Dream" is narrated from an impossible position. The narrator narrates from, or at least knows of, "her" intrauterine existence, and "her" life as a pre-verbal non-subject. Indeed, the story is haunted by the possibility that its narrator may very well be a *dead* baby. But it is precisely by speaking in fiction from this impossible place, as I hope to show, that Munro can restage both the birth of the (sexed) subject and the origin of human relatedness (the ethical).

We begin the story in the dream. The dreamer, Jill, looks out from a high spacious house onto a snowy world ("snow had settled overnight on the luxury of summer" [293]). The dreamer has the sense that there is something she has forgotten. She goes outside and remembers: "She had left a baby out there somewhere, before the snow had fallen" (294). She is overcome with horror. And it is "as if" she is awakening from a dream within the dream. She awakens "to a knowledge of her responsibility and mistake" (294). She awakens within the dream a second time (in fact, the states of waking and sleeping are decidedly uncertain from the very start) and discovers that the baby is alive and asleep in its crib. The baby becomes "her" baby: "Red hair like her own on her perfectly safe and unmistakable baby" (295). The dream is simultaneously a wish fulfilled (to have no demand made of her, to have no responsibility, no relation to the baby) and a realization of Jill's most intense fear: she has killed the baby, and is thus utterly and forever responsible for its being. Freud writes at length on dreaming about the death of those we love, but in Munro's story it is the death wish that makes "love" possible. It is by encountering the loss of her child that the mother claims the child, becomes its mother, for the *first* time. Freud writes of childhood development and object love that "the finding of an object is in fact a refinding of it" (*Three Essays* 145). Munro could be said to explore this paradox non-developmentally and from the other side: the only object one can "have" is a "lost" one.[19] In fact, in a provocative way the story contains an alternative trajectory in which the baby *does* die, and the story is narrated by this dead baby. This is an illusion (and a radical figuration of the call from beyond) that the completion of the tale both dismisses and sustains: in the end the narrator refers to herself as a "ghost." In this alternative version the mother's first "awakening" within the dream would be the true one. And this mother, who comes to pass as the most normal of mothers, would then be a murderer. Thus in Munro, dreams *can* concern responsibility for another (which needs to be contemplated since, as Freud tells us, there is no such thing as an altruistic dream; dreams, like children, are entirely egoistic), and this is in part because they explore the unconscious that is "outside." While Almeda Roth is "awakened" by the "racket on Pearl Street," Jill will later refer to her sister-in-law as having "got[ten] into the wrong part of the dream" (329). Munro's dreams, in other words, rehearse the paradoxes of the ethical: the egoistic closure of the dream may simultaneously open up a space in which otherness can be encountered.

"My Mother's Dream" concerns a battle between mother and newborn; the dream itself is the culmination of the battle. The narrator of Munro's story asserts, "We were monsters to each other. Jill and I" (321). In "My Monster/My Self," Barbara Johnson comments, "The idea that a mother can loathe, fear, and reject her baby has until recently been one of the most repressed of psychoanalytical insights, although it is of course already implicit in the story of Oedipus, whose parents cast him out as an infant to die" (149–50). In Munro's story, the mother and baby must each give up a fantastic omnipotence to find the other; death (paradoxically a more radical interrelatedness – absolute responsibility for the other) is the only other option. Thus if Freud finds it necessary to provide us with an origin for sexual difference, Munro offers us an origin for what is "only natural": motherhood. "My Mother's Dream" is one of the stories in which Munro empties out and questions the naturalness of maternal desire.[20] But what kind of mother or non-mother or pre-mother is Jill? She certainly has her desires and they are not (in a traditional patriarchal heterosexualizing trajectory of a woman's life) what they are supposed to be. While getting married, Jill fantasizes about pancakes and bacon, and at her husband's wake she is dreaming of a burger and mayonnaise. Munro codes orality as female and often presents food as the currency of eroticized exchange between mother and daughter (one could look, for example, at the oral seduction that takes place in an earlier story, "Royal Beatings"). But Munro, I would suggest, is also playing with and re-materializing that idealizing question: "what does a woman want?" If woman is classically an enigma ("throughout history people have banged their heads against the riddle of the nature of femininity," writes Freud [*Three Essays* 146]), Munro assures us that Jill is merely a "puzzle," and to anybody who would bother to be concerned she is a "dull" one. Jill's other desire is her violin. It is with the violin, not the baby, that she has a seemingly natural rapport ("She was sure that she and some violin were naturally, fatefully connected, and would have come together without human help" [310]). While it is suggested that it is the baby who first rejects the mother ("I refused to take my mother's breast. I screamed blue murder. The big stiff breast might just as well have been a snouted beast rummaging in my face" [314]), the mother does not seem to mind. In fact, she experiences her relationship to her violin, as opposed to the baby, as the "responsibility" that she has taken on in life.

Not surprisingly, the baby, while consistently rejecting her mother, also has an incredibly antagonistic relationship to her mother's instrument (the sign, or sound, of her mother's desire and self-possession). This baby wants to have her cake and eat it too: she wants both to reject her mother and make an absolute claim on her. After the baby's birth, Jill tries to play the violin again: "I woke without a whimper of discontent. No warning, no buildup. Just a shriek, a waterfall of shrieks descended on the house a cry unlike any cry I'd managed before. The letting loose of a new flood of unsuspected anguish, a grief that punished the world with its waves full of stones, the volley of woe sent down from the windows of the torture chamber" (317–18). The impossible baby narrator thus verbalizes her prelinguistic intentions: "My crying is a knife to cut out of her life all that isn't useful. To me" (319). And although the daughter narrates, it is hard not to identify with Jill. The baby's demands are absolute (as babies' demands are); they constitute an "assault" with the power to "annihilate" ("Responsibility," writes Jill Robbins, "feels like persecution, if it is not ethics" [16]). With absolutely no exaggeration one can make the claim that the baby in this text is figured as an axe-wielding psychopathic murderer, as well as a pale, sweet, fuzzy-headed darling wearing plastic pants with a pattern of butterflies.[21]

The end of the story finds the baby and the violin quite literally in the same place: shoved under the couch. Jill significantly rescues the baby first; although she will go on to play the violin again, professionally and quite successfully. Jill, as I have argued, claims her baby and thus becomes a mother only after suffering the baby's loss in the dream. Whereas the loss of Jill's husband (who is killed in World War II, almost immediately after their marriage) is described as the loss of an "extension [with] lighted rooms showing up full of a bewildering sort of splendor," the loss of the baby threatens to eliminate Jill's internal constitutive space: "There would never be any room in her for anything else. No room for anything" (306, 295).[22] Moreover, the mother curiously feels all the more sorrow for the baby as a pre-desiring, pre-subject, who does not even know that it is her, its mother, that it lacks: "The sorrow that came to my mother was the sorrow of the baby's waiting and not knowing it waited for her, its only hope, when she had forgotten all about it. So small and new a baby that could not even turn away from the snow. She could hardly breathe for her sorrow" (293–94). The baby is a subject on the edge, both tyrant and victim. This is not, however, because the baby has not yet established a self/other distinction, but rather because the distinction is dangerously absolute. Thus her cry, or lack thereof, is strangely impersonal. Blanchot's articulation of Levinasian responsibility calls out for application to the maternal and specifically to "My Mother's Dream": "There is a cry for help, addressed not to me in particular, not to anyone in particular, but to me as anyone – anyone can help – and my anonymity in the situation, far from offering an excuse to ignore the plea, implicates me directly" (22). With this implication comes, in Munro's story, a crucial identification: While the mother feels overwhelming guilt, it is also hard to distinguish her from her infant (thus complicating, precisely as it establishes, responsibility for the other). Who, for example, is it that can "hardly breathe for her sorrow"?

Munro thus suggests that motherhood has to *happen* – or has to be imagined as happening. Maternal subjectivity cannot merely be assigned to the "natural" and taken for granted. For as we know, what gets assigned to the "natural" tends to return and haunt us as monstrous. There is a crucial sense, then, in which Jill is "Everymother" who must negotiate between her self and that other who is both other and self. Yet, as I have suggested, there is an alternative trajectory here, and there is also a significant third player (and it is not the father). With this other trajectory the normal (good enough?) mother and the murderer come ominously close to being interchangeable.[23]

When the baby is born she does not choose her mother. Instead, it is the powerless, "nervous wreck" of an aunt, Iona, who becomes the baby's "chosen home" (314). Iona, as honorary mother, goes from being "the most negligible to being the most important person in the house" (315). She is the only one who can save the others from the baby's potentially annihilating cries: "Touched or spoken to by a non-Iona, I cried. Put down to sleep, not rocked by Iona, I cried myself into exhaustion and slept for ten minutes and woke ready to go at it again. I had no good times or fussy times. I had the Iona-times and the Iona-desertion-times, which might become – oh, worse and worse – the other-people times, mostly Jill-times" (315). Jill, the "real" mother, reads baby books. Iona, the substitute, performs effective mothering. This structure, which is repeated in other Munro stories, challenges the unquestioned primacy of the maternal: here the substitute comes first.

But eventually the dreaded day comes, and, as a result of the other sister-in-law's manipulations, Iona is whisked off for an overnight trip. Jill is left alone with the baby. Exhausted and unable to escape the baby's cries, Jill eventually takes out her violin: "In a way she does me honor. No more counterfeit soothing, no more pretend lullabies or concern for tummy-ache, no petsy-wetsy whatsamatter. Instead she will play Mendelssohn's Violin Concerto" (323). It is after midnight. Jill is nearly mad and definitively exhausted. She goes rummaging for some strong headache medicine and finds a prescription drug: "my cries coming down at her like the clamor of birds of prey over a gurgling river [...] and she thinks, *Yes*" (327). In addition to dosing herself, Jill shaves a tiny bit of the pill off and sprinkles it over the milk. In the drugged sleep that follows, Jill dreams the dream of the story's title, the dream of her dead and then not dead baby. The white snow is the pill dust.

If Jill almost kills her baby (and it is by chance or accident that she does not), Iona will return home to discover a baby who is "dead." Munro brilliantly depicts a psychic coincidence, a mutual crisis at the site of motherhood. Iona returns home early. She is worried that she has "lost" the baby (which she has – from now on Jill will be its mother). And her fear about her own traumatic loss takes the form of accusing Jill of murder. Meanwhile, of course, Jill has come terribly close to being a murderer:

> Iona ducked past her and ran up the stairs. Now she's screaming. *Dead. Dead. Murderer.* She knows nothing about the pills. So why does she scream "Murderer"? It's the blanket. She sees the blanket pulled up right over my head [...] It has not taken her any time, not half a second, to get from "dead" to "murderer." It's an immediate flying leap [...] "You've killed my baby," Iona is screaming at her. Jill doesn't correct her – she doesn't say, *Mine.* (328)

A structure like this one in which Jill's and Iona's fantasies, their fears and desires, collide (Jill wants to "lose" a baby and finds one, while Iona suffers precisely the loss she dreads) certainly destabilizes an easy distinction between sleep (fantasy) and awakening (reality). And indeed, when Jill finds the baby that Iona, in her hysteria, literally hides, it is "just as in the dream she comes upon a live baby, not a little desiccated nutmeg-headed corpse" (333). Iona is depicted at the end of the story in all her mad desperation, whereas Jill has "awakened" to motherhood, responsibility, and a living baby. Pointedly, however, Munro does not discredit what Iona perceived:

> She said I felt stiff. Then she said not stiff but heavy. So heavy, she said, she instantly thought I could not be alive. A lump, a dead weight. I think there is something to this. I don't believe that I was dead, or that I came back from the dead, but I do think that I was at a distance, from which I might or might not have come back. I think that the outcome was not certain and that *will* was involved. It *was up to me*, I mean, to go one way or the other. (337; italics mine)

This is the curious "choice" that I referred to at the beginning of this discussion. The baby "chooses" survival; she chooses the "half a loaf" of love and maternal competence that she will receive from Jill over Iona's wholeness. In fact, the narrator goes farther and asserts that it was at this moment, when she gave up the battle with her mother, that she assumed her sexed identity:

> To me it seems that it was only then that I became female. I know that the matter was decided long before I was born and was plain to everybody else since the beginning of my life, but I believe that it was only at the moment when I decided to come back, when I gave up the fight against my mother (which must have been a fight for something like her total surrender) and when in fact I chose survival over victory (death would have been victory), that I took on my female nature. And to some extent Jill took on hers. Sobered and grateful, not even able to risk thinking about what she'd just escaped, she took on loving me, because the alternative to loving was disaster. (337–38)

In Munro's primal scene of sexed identity the assumption of femininity takes place without a man in sight! This shouldn't surprise us, as Freud was of course able to conceptualize sexual difference only from within a fantasy of sameness, working, as many have, from the assumption that the subject is primarily male. But, more seriously, Munro's scene intriguingly suggests that sexed identity is taken on *between* mother and daughter. Mother and daughter mutually become female in their choice to give up, to lose out, which is also the choice of survival. They both accept the lack, which means that they will have a relationship ("this being-together as separation precedes or exceeds society, collectivity, community" writes Derrida ["Violence" 95]). Indeed, it is the irreducibility of this mutual lack that makes relationship possible, and this is why I would insist that even here, between mother and daughter, Munro gives us access to the complexities of an ethical encounter.

There is, however, another figuration of lack in "My Mother's Dream," one that belongs (if one can speak of a lack as belonging) neither to Jill nor to her daughter. It belongs to Iona. We are told early in the story that Iona has been subjected to shock treatments that "have blown a hole in her discretion" (presumably accomplishing precisely what they were not supposed to accomplish, leaving her less regulatable, less controllable than before) (314). And we encounter this lack again when Iona loses the baby: "she seems to be trying to squeeze the bundle of me into a new terrifying hole in the middle of her body" (328). With this "hole" Munro suggests that if femaleness is associated with lack or loss, there is more than one version of this story. If self-loss is the price some women have paid in exchange for a place in the social order (and one might think here of the "hole" in the middle of Iona's name), another loss names the only access that there is to (inter)subjectivity.

Conclusion

"My Mother's Dream" presents one with almost too much theoretical weight. It is the story of a mother becoming a mother (and of the very substitutive nature of what we think of as primary), of a sexed identity being taken on, and of choosing life over death.[24] Much more might also be said about the specificity of ethics and the mother–child relation in Alice Munro's fiction (the "unnatural" mother, it could be argued, is Munro's paradigmatic ethical subject). One could also explore her interest in the writer's responsibility to those whom he or she represents (by considering, for example, the markedly irresponsible ex-husband writer in "Material" who manages arguably ethical feats of representation). One could even interrogate the ethics of intertextuality (by looking at, among other instances, Munro's reimagining of "The Grandmother" from O'Connor's "A Good Man is Hard to Find"). I have tried in this essay, however, to focus on the representation of a specific ethical crisis in which the coherence of the subject is called into question from beyond. In "Meneseteung" and "My Mother's Dream" (as well as in "Post and Beam" and others), an ethical encounter is inseparable from an encounter with the frayed edge of meaning (an edge that we might refer to as being "beyond" the social contract of intelligible communication but which we could also describe as coming before or always at work *within* such intelligibility). This inseparability in Munro's stories recalls what Jill Robbins refers to as "thinking responsibility as a relation to the trace" (31). The enigma that these stories help us to articulate is that of a subject for whom the failure to respond to these violently absolute and uncertain cries would be experienced as an irrecoverable loss.

If Munro's stories insist upon difficult ethical readings, however, it must be added that their humor and particularity just as insistently deflate any overly ambitious design or account. In "Lichen," for example, Stella's desperate ex-husband David finds younger and younger women in an attempt to deny his own aging. He invents others in order to preclude his relationship to mortality, which he manages to read as a personal insult. Sexual difference, for this character, displaces or prevents the possibility of an ethical relation. But rather inconveniently for David, the person at the very end of life in this story is not a woman, but Stella's ninety-three-year-old father. Stella's father is the source of yet another call from beyond, from a place that borders on the inhuman:

> Her father said, "David?" The sound seemed to come from a wet cave deep inside him, to be unshaped by lips or jaws or tongue [...] Up through this neck came further sounds, a conversational offering. It was the core of each syllable that was presented, a damp vowel barely held in shape by surrounding consonants. (380–81)

But for all he knows and does not know ("David knows what he's doing. This is the interesting part of it, he thinks, and has said" [379]), David will not give up. He flees to a phone booth to call his latest obsession. Unable to get through to her, he tries her ex-boyfriend and even imagines disguising his voice on the phone. David is shaking, sweating, praying, and still there is no answer. David is ultimately addressed by an impersonal voice from beyond in the familiar guise of the telephone operator: "Sir? Do you want to keep on trying?" (380). Munro's achievement at moments like this is to represent the pathos and comedy of language hesitating on the border between meaningless, mechanical repetition, and forceful poignancy. The call to responsibility here (or the call to depart from irresponsibility: "Do you want to keep on trying?") comes from a voice whose materiality disrupts its presence; the "accidental" significance of the operator's rote phrase generates the humor and the gravity of an inner catastrophe without which there is no chance for ethics.[25]

Notes

1   In "The Children Stay," for example, Pauline reflects on her decision to leave her young daughters to run away with her lover. "Her children have grown up. They don't hate her. For going away or staying away. They don't forgive her, either. Perhaps they wouldn't have forgiven her anyway, but it would have been for something different" (213). In other words, there may well have been permanent consequences for the very personhood of the young daughters (they don't, after all, forgive their mother), but quite possibly (even inevitably) she would have failed them otherwise. Such refusals to judge are further complicated, however, by the fact that we cannot simply attribute their insight or blindness either to the narrator or to the ostensible subject herself. (Does Pauline's reflection offer us a reliable resistance to moralizing, or is it a guilty mother's attempt at rationalization?)

2   See also Buell, Newton, and Robbins.

3   "It would be unfortunate [...] to confuse the materiality of the signifier with the materiality of what it signifies," writes Paul De Man, but "it is very difficult not to conceive of the pattern of one's past and future existence in accordance with temporal and spatial schemes that belong to fictional narratives and not to the world. This does not mean that fictional narratives are not part of the world and of reality; their impact may well be all too strong for comfort" (11).

4   Robbins offers a valuable account of the evolving concept of ethics in Levinas' work:

> Whereas *Totality and Infinity* described the putting into question of the self in the presence of the other, *Otherwise than Being* describes the self as always already worked over, traumatized and dispossessed by the other. In the later work, ethics does not happen to a self or a subject. The conception of responsibility and ethics that emerges is nonvoluntaristic and nonvolitional. It chooses me before I choose it. (xv)

5   For theoretical readings of Munro's stories as well as for more general commentary on the relationship between Munro's fiction and literary theory see Heble, Howells, Houston, and Redekop. Redekop claims that "Munro has no overt feminist agenda [and] she cannot speak the language of literary theory, [still], Munro's stories have a lot to teach theorists writing today" (xii); Heble remarks that while he would "not suggest that Munro is on the cutting edge of literary theory [...] In one way or another, her stories *themselves* signal to us that they are moving away from the myth of the transparency of linguistic representation" (13). Houston reads "Meneseteung" as a Lacanian story about language compensating for and covering over lack, and Howells appeals to a Derridean account of the supplement in her overview of Munro's fiction: "instead of placing the supplement at the end [Howells is writing of a shift she claims takes place in Munro's style in the collections of the 1980s], supplementarity pervades the whole narrative [...] unsettling the story at every stage of its telling" (11).

6   For general accounts of the relationship between literature and ethics in contemporary criticism and theory see Buell and Harpham. Buell has argued that ethics may "become the paradigm-defining concept that textuality was for the 1970s and historicism for the 1980s" (7), and Harpham claims "if the battles of literary theory are won on the playing fields of ethics, this is because literary theory, as a kind of oxymoron, has always already accepted the responsibility of otherness, just as literature itself bears the burden of managing the encounter between language and the world" (404).

7   Critics have begun to explore how Munro's apparently realist fiction repeatedly and characteristically disrupts itself; and it is precisely these interruptions, I would suggest, that could be said to constitute the ethical dimension of her work. See particularly Heble and Howells on the "disruption" that characterizes Munro's fiction. Heble offers an overview of those critics who explore Munro's "departure from traditional mimetic realism" (15–17).

8   Another such "interruption" occurs at the end of "Simon's Luck" where Rose is shocked to learn of Simon's death. She has run away from her love affair with Simon – run away from the possibility of being deserted – only to discover belatedly that she has, in a sense, been the deserter. Starring in a television show in which nothing awful ever happens, Rose, the actress, is also starring in the story of her own life. Playing the role of one who has used up her power, she must vigilantly defend herself against the powerlessness of the relational:

> People watching trusted that they would be protected from predictable disasters, also from those shifts of emphasis that throw the story line open to question, the disarrangements which demand new judgements and solutions, and throw the windows open on inappropriate unforgettable scenery.
>   Simon's dying struck Rose as that kind of disarrangement. It was preposterous, it was unfair, that such a chunk of information should have been left out, and that Rose even at this late date could have thought herself the only person who could seriously lack power. (212–13)

9   "Meneseteung" reads as an account of why there could not have been a female Walt Whitman, "hankering, gross, mystical, nude," poet of the body as well as of the soul, who could claim "The scent of these arm-pits is aroma finer than prayer [...] If I worship any particular thing it shall be some of the spread of my body" (Whitman 43, 49). Almeda Joynt Roth, unlike Walt Whitman, cannot write of a radical democracy that includes silenced peoples and silenced parts of the self (the body and its appetites). Roth cannot do this and survive as a coherent (feminine) subject. Among other things, she is presumably lacking in Whitman's highly gendered self-promotional capacities.

10   "Meneseteung" cites so-called "Anglo-American" feminist criticism in recovering a "lost" woman writer, but it also engages with "French" feminist theorists and the connection between writing and embodiment. In fact this doubleness is encoded in the story's very title, which is the name of a lost text (Almeda Roth's presumably never written, never-published masterpiece) but which also translates as something like "embodied voice" or "blood speech": menesetueng = menses + tongue.

11 One might recall here the similarity to "The Dream and the Primal Scene," the text in which Freud most extensively explores the primal scene, although not, of course, a primal scene of ethics. The Wolfman's notorious dream is also a dream of suddenly waking and being arrested by what is just outside the window.

12 For more on fantastic beating scenes that are also scenes of real (and potentially sexual) violence see Munro's earlier "Royal Beatings," in which both a child and a father are beaten, the female child in a perpetual or habitual present tense, the father in the past of a told and re-told narration.

13 Redekop has noted the allusion to "The Raven" in "Meneseteung" (225), and we might also want to consider the relevance of Poe's "The Philosophy of Composition," for Munro's story pointedly and ironically rewrites the infamous death of the "beautiful" woman: "'There goes your dead body!'" exclaims Jarvis Poulter, our "hero," as the drunken, disheveled, abject, "other" woman stumbles off. I would like to suggest, however, that "Meneseteung"'s most significant nineteenth-century American intertext is Melville's "Bartleby, the Scrivener." For in Melville's story, as in Munro's, an enigmatic other poses an impossible ethical demand that throws the sovereign subjecthood of the organizing consciousness, and ultimately of every individual ("Ah, Bartleby! Ah, humanity!") into question. Bartleby's "call," like that of "Meneseteung"'s nameless woman, verges disconcertingly on the meaningless. Both stories also resonate with Levinas' discussion of the ethical "moment": "A face is imposed on me without my being able to be deaf to its appeal nor to forget it, that is, without my being able to cease to be held responsible for its wretchedness. Consciousness loses its first place" (Levinas, "Trace" 352).

14 "By definition, if the other is the other, and if all speech is for the other, no logos as absolute knowledge can *comprehend* dialogue and the trajectory toward the other. This incomprehensibility, this rupture of logos is not the beginning of irrationalism but the wound or inspiration which opens speech and then makes possible every logos or every rationalism" ("Violence" 98).

15 See Derrida, *The Gift of Death* 27.

16 Coral Ann Howells suggests that the scene Almeda witnesses (the "fight" that goes on just outside her back window) is a sexual primal scene that the innocent, childlike Victorian heroine cannot read: "in her innocence [Almeda] interprets as murder [...] the sounds of sex" (109–10). But to read the story this way is to leave out the other woman in her otherness. As an ethical story "Meneseteung" is neither "merely" psychological nor concerned solely with sexuality. Almeda feels that she is responsible, feels ashamed that she had not even realized that the woman was alive.

17 The same Old English word (*beran*) gives us, suggestively, the words "barrow," "bear," "born," and "bier." There is something unbearable, "Meneseteung" seems to know, about the call to ethical responsibility.

18 The appeal of death in this scenario is an appeal with a recognizable history. Addressing the specifically masculine crises of Mary Shelley's *Frankenstein*, Francis Ferguson writes: "While the sublime raises the specter of the annihilation of the self, even such annihilation looks like a consolidation beside the constant stretching necessary to any self that attempts to honor the various claims on its attention and affection" (111).

19 "Who loves the *stranger*? Whom else is there to love?" (Derrida, *Adieu* 105).

20 See Redekop on the "multiplication of surrogate maternal figures" in Munro's fiction (4).

21 "A work conceived in its ultimate nature requires a radical generosity of the same who in the work goes unto the other. It then requires an *ingratitude* of the other. Gratitude would in fact be the *return* of the movement to its origin" (Levinas, "Trace" 349).

22 The suggestion that losing the baby, failing to respond to its [silent] cry, would leave the mother with no more room gives us another way to understand Levinas' suggestion that "the relationship with another puts me into question, empties me of myself, and does not let off emptying me – uncovering for me ever new resources" ("Trace" 350). Loss would leave Munro's mother with no more room (the loss of lack).

23 In fact, Munro proposes that it may only be chance that separates the two. See also "Miles City, Montana": "'What I can't get over,' said Andrew, 'is how you got the signal. It's got to be some kind of extra sense that mothers have.' Partly I wanted to believe that, to bask in my extra sense. Partly I wanted to warn him – to warn everybody – never to count on it" (407). Munro's fiction challenges us to think about responsibility *and* radical contingency.

24   It is also a story about dreams. In fact, "My Mother's Dream" would seem both to refer to and rewrite Freud's famous dream of the "burning child" (which concerns a father's responsibility for his dead son and the relationship between external stimuli and fantasy life) and analyses of this "simple" dream (really, says Freud, there is not much to say about it) by Lacan, Zizek, Shengold, Felman, Caruth, and others. His son has died and an exhausted father finally goes to sleep. He leaves an older man to watch over his dead child, but the watchman himself dozes off, knocking a candle onto the child's body. Instead of waking immediately (seeing the light, hearing the noise), as one might expect him to do, the father sleeps on momentarily and dreams that his son has come to his side reproachfully: "Father, don't you see I'm burning?" ("The Psychology of Dream Processes" 653). The father dreams of a responsibility in the form of his son's reproach ("Father, don't you see I'm burning?") that would simultaneously restore to him the son he has so painfully lost. Munro's mother is luckier. She awakens to a loss, femininity, that allows her to claim her child. Cathy Caruth writes: "the dream reveals how the very consciousness of the father as father, as the one who wishes to see his child alive again so much that he sleeps in spite of the burning corpse, is linked inextricably to the impossibility of adequately responding to the plea of the child in its death. The bond to the child, the sense of responsibility, is in its essence tied to the impossibility of recognizing the child in its potential death" (103).

25   In her most recently published story, Munro once again utilizes liminal voices which could be said to hesitate between the human and the inhuman, the intentional and the mechanical, and she does so in an exploration of the relationship between ethics and the craft of fiction writing. The young writer/narrator figure in "Family Furnishings" listens to the story of her father's cousin's mother's death and hears something new: "And the minute that I heard it, something happened. It was as if a trap had snapped shut to hold these words in my head. I did not exactly understand what use I would have for them. I knew only how they jolted me and released me, right away, to breathe a different kind of air, available only to myself" (74). Even as the narrator cannot process the message she receives (which is crucially the story of both a missed and an experienced ethical insight), in a sense, it is with this message that she becomes a writer for the first time. We hear another liminal voice at the very end of the story. The sounds of a baseball game on the radio at the back of a shop: "I did not think of the story that I would write about Alfrida – not of that in particular – but of the work I wanted to do, which seemed more like grabbing something out of the air than like constructing stories. The cries of the crowd came to me like big heartbeats, full of sorrows, lovely, formal-sounding waves, with their distant, almost inhuman assent and lamentation" (77). In this story, then, irresponsibility and responsibility cross paths (absolute indifference to the other can become indistinguishable from the very ability to register the other's voice). The ethical and the liminal voice clearly remain a preoccupation in Munro's work.

Works Cited

Attridge, Derek. "Innovation, Literature, Ethics: Relating to the Other." *PMLA* 114 (1999): 20–31.

Blanchot, Maurice. *The Writing of the Disaster*. Trans. Ann Smock. Lincoln: U of Nebraska P, 1986.

Buell, Lawrence. "Introduction. In Pursuit of Ethics." *PMLA* 114 (1999): 7–19.

Butler, Judith. *The Psychic Life of Power: Theories in Subjection*. Stanford: Stanford UP, 1997.

Caruth, Cathy. *Unclaimed Experience: Trauma, Narrative, and History*. Baltimore: Johns Hopkins UP, 1996.

De Man, Paul. "The Resistance to Theory." *The Resistance to Theory*. Minneapolis: U of Minnesota P, 1986. 3–21.

Derrida, Jacques. *Adieu to Emmanuel Levinas*. Trans. Michael Naas and Pascale-Anne Brault. Stanford: Stanford UP, 1999.

Derrida, Jacques. *The Gift of Death*. Trans. David Willis. Chicago: U of Chicago P, 1995.

Derrida, Jacques. "Violence and Metaphysics: An Essay on the Thought of Emmanuel Levinas." *Writing and Difference*. Trans. Alan Bass. Chicago: U of Chicago P, 1980. 79–153.

Ferguson, Frances. *Solitude and the Sublime: Romanticism and the Aesthetics of Individuation*. New York: Routledge, 1992.

Freud, Sigmund. "The Dream and the Primal Scene." *From the History of an Infantile Neurosis*. 1918 [1914]. Trans. James Strachey. London: Hogarth, 1955. Vol. 17 of *The Standard Edition of the Complete Psychological Works*. 24 vols. 29–47.

Freud, Sigmund. "Mourning and Melancholia." 1917 [1915]. *On Metapsychology*. Vol. 11 of *The Penguin Freud Library*. Trans. James Strachey. New York: Penguin, 1991. 245–68.

Freud, Sigmund. "On Narcissism: an Introduction." 1914. *On Metapsychology*. Vol. 11 of *The Penguin Freud Library*. Trans. James Strachey. New York: Penguin, 1991. 59–98.

Freud, Sigmund. "The Psychology of Dream Processes." *The Interpretation of Dreams*. 1900. Vol. 4 of *The Penguin Freud Library*. Trans. James Strachey. New York: Penguin, 1991. 652–783.

Freud, Sigmund. "Some Psychical Consequences of the Anatomical Distinction Between the Sexes." *On Sexuality*. Vol. 7 of *The Penguin Freud Library*. Trans. James Strachey. New York: Penguin, 1991.

Freud, Sigmund. "Three Essays on the Theory of Sexuality" *On Sexuality* 1905. Vol. 7 of *The Penguin Freud Library*. Trans. James Strachey. New York: Penguin, 1991. 45–169.

Hancock, Geoffrey. "Alice Munro." *Canadian Writers at Work: Interviews with Geoff Hancock*. Toronto: Oxford UP, 1987. 187–224.

Harpham, Geoffrey Galt. "Ethics." *Critical Terms for Literary Study*. Ed. Frank Lentricchia and Thomas McLaughlin. 2nd ed. Chicago: U of Chicago P, 1995. 387–404.

Heble, Ajay. *The Tumble of Reason: Alice Munro's Discourse of Absence*. Toronto: U of Toronto P, 1994.

Houston, Pam. "A Hopeful Sign: The Making of Metonymic Meaning in Munro's 'Meneseteung'". *Kenyon Review* 14.4 (1992): 79–92.

Howells, Coral Ann. *Alice Munro*. Manchester: Manchester UP, 1998.

Johnson, Barbara. "My Monster/My Self." *A World of Difference*. Baltimore: Johns Hopkins UP, 1987. 144–54.

Keenan, Thomas. *Fables of Responsibility: Aberrations and Predicaments in Ethics and Politics*. Stanford: Stanford UP, 1997.

Lacan, Jacques. "Tuchè and Automaton." *The Four Fundamental Concepts of Psycho-Analysis*. Ed. Jacques-Alain Miller. Trans. Alan Sheridan. New York: Norton, 1978. 53–64.

Levinas, Emmanuel. *Totality and Infinity: An Essay on Exteriority*. Trans. A. Lingis. Pittsburgh: Duquesne UP, 1969.

Levinas, Emmanuel. "The Trace of the Other." Trans. A. Lingis. *Deconstruction in Context*. Ed. Mark C. Taylor. Chicago: U of Chicago P, 1986. 345–59.

Melville, Herman. "Bartleby." 1853. *Billy Budd, Sailor and Other Stories*. New York: Penguin, 1986. 1–46.

Mitchell, Juliet. *Psychoanalysis and Feminism: Freud, Reich, Laing and Women*. New York: Random House, 1974.

Munro, Alice. "Alice Munro." *Canadian Writers at Work: Interviews with Geoff Hancock*. Toronto: Oxford UP, 1987. 187–224.

Munro, Alice. "The Children Stay." *The Love of a Good Woman*. Toronto: McClleland, 1998. 181–214.

Munro, Alice. "Family Furnishings." *The New Yorker* 23 July 2001. 64–77.

Munro, Alice. "Lichen." *Selected Stories*. Toronto: Penguin, 1998. 362–85.

Munro, Alice. "Material." *Selected Stories*. Toronto: Penguin, 1998. 100–18.

Munro, Alice. "Meneseteung." *Selected Stories*. Toronto: Penguin, 1998. 492–514.

Munro, Alice. "Miles City, Montana." *Selected Stories*. Toronto: Penguin, 1998. 386–407.

Munro, Alice. "My Mother's Dream." *The Love of a Good Woman*. Toronto: McClleland, 1998. 293–340.

Munro, Alice. "Post and Beam." *The New Yorker* 11 Dec. 2000. 96–109.

Munro, Alice. "Royal Beatings." *Selected Stories*. Toronto: Penguin, 1998. 119–42.

Munro, Alice. "Simon's Luck." *Selected Stories*. Toronto: Penguin, 1998. 190–213.

Newton, Adam Zachary, *Narrative Ethics*. Cambridge: Harvard UP, 1995.

Redekop, Magdalene. *Mothers and Other Clowns: The Stories of Alice Munro*. London: Routledge, 1992.

Robbins, Jill. *Altered Reading: Levinas and Literature*. Chicago: U of Chicago P, 1999.

Volosinov, V. N. *Marxism and the Philosophy of Language*. 1929. Trans. Ladislav Matejka and I. R. Titunic. New York: Seminar, 1973.

Warner, Michael. "Homo-Narcissism; or, Heterosexuality." *Engendering Men: The Question of Male Feminist Criticism*. Ed. J. A. Boone and M. Cadden. New York: Routledge, 1990. 190–206.

Whitman, Walt. *Leaves of Grass*. 1855. Ed. Malcolm Cowley. New York: Penguin, 1986.

PART FOUR
Post-Structuralism

CHAPTER 1

Introduction
The Class of 1968 – Post-Structuralism par lui-même

Julie Rivkin and Michael Ryan

Opposition ceases its labor and difference begins its play.
Gilles Deleuze, *Nietzsche and Philosophy*

The moment of transgression is the key moment of practice: we can speak of practice wherever there is a transgression of systematicity.
Julia Kristeva, "The System and the Speaking Subject"

The March 22nd Movement[1] is engaged in three sorts of disturbance; it belongs to the crisis of the university and to the social crisis; but its proper arena … is the transformation of the relationship between what is desired and what is given, between potential energy and the machinery of society. Its location in relation to the first two kinds of disturbance and its attempt to respond to them situates it like any other group within the order of politics, an institution which has as its function (like the others though more particularly) the regulation of the flow of energy within the system. But in as much as the March 22nd Movement increases the third kind of disturbance, its work was that of undoing, an anti-political kind of work, carrying out not the reinforcement but the dissolution of the system.
Jean-François Lyotard, *Adrift After Marx and Freud*

The French Communist Party has often played the role of a kind of bourgeois superego: it stands for the moral principles which it accuses the ruling class of respecting in theory, only to betray them in practice.

Guy Hocquenghem, *Homosexual Desire*

Hence there is a major role for students, youth who are disqualified [from capitalist production] in advance, voluntarily or not, as well as all types of social groups, of regional communities, ethnic or linguistic, because, by the process of the centralization and technocratic pyramidization of the system, they fall into marginality, into the periphery, into the zone of disaffection and irresponsibility. Excluded from the game, their revolt henceforth aims at the rules of the game.…
    It is no longer then a question of an internal, dialectical negativity in the mode of production, but a refusal, pure and simple, of production as the general axiomatic of social

Literary Theory: An Anthology, Third Edition. Edited by Julie Rivkin and Michael Ryan.
© 2017 John Wiley & Sons, Ltd. Published 2017 by John Wiley & Sons, Ltd.

relations. Without any doubt, the refusal is hidden in wage and union demands; in mid-stream it is transposed into a carefully asphyxiated and channeled radical negation by the Parties and the Unions, for whom, just as for the system itself, economic demands are the ideal means of control and manipulation. This is what gives the new left or hippie move-ment its meaning. Not the open revolt of a few, but the immense, latent defection, the endemic, masked resistance of a silent majority, but one nostalgic for the spoken word and for violence. Something in all men profoundly rejoices in seeing a car burn.

Jean Baudrillard, *The Mirror of Production*

Even signs must burn…. The catastrophic situation opened up by May '68 is not over.

Jean Baudrillard, *The Political Economy of the Sign*

Structuralism, which is best represented by the work of anthropologist Claude Lévi-Strauss, literary critic Roland Barthes, and Marxist philosopher Louis Althusser, uses linguistics to find order everywhere, from kinship systems to fashion. Its successor, Post-Structuralism, uses linguistics to argue that all such orders are founded on an essential endemic disorder in language and in the world that can never be mastered by any structure or semantic code that might assign it a meaning. Structuralism dominated French intel-lectual life in the late 1950s and early 1960s, but even as it reigned, a counter-movement was in the making from the early 1960s onward, one that was less interested in knowing how systems worked than in finding out how they might be undone, so that the energies and potentials that they held in place might be liberated and used to construct an alto-gether different kind of society. If Structuralism, despite the left political credentials of its most noteworthy practitioners, was methodologically conservative, a description of stable structures which seemed an argument on behalf of their universality or eternity, Post-Structuralism would be self-consciously radical, a putting in question or play of the meth-ods rational thought traditionally uses to describe the world. If Structuralists saw signs as windows to a trans-empirical world of crystalline order, of identities of form that main-tained themselves over time and outside history, of codes of meaning that seemed exempt from the differences entailed by the contingencies of living examples, Post-Structuralists claim all such orders are strategies of power and social control, ways of ignoring reality rather than understanding it. It was time, they argued, to burn down the signs and with the signs, all the orders of meaning and/or reality that signs help maintain.

The first works of what would eventually be called Post-Structuralism began to appear in the early 1960s, and they reflected the growing influence on French thought of Friedrich Nietzsche (whose works had been recently translated into French), a thinker whose value for younger French philosophers had to do with his rejection of both the rationalist tradition of objective description and the idealist tradition which dissolved empirical world events into non-empirical or hidden meanings or truths. Another major counter-Structuralist influence was Martin Heidegger, a German thinker whose work had been highly influential in France since the 1940s (especially in the work of Jean-Paul Sartre, whose *Being and Nothingness* is in many ways a pre-text of Post-Structuralism in that it elaborates on themes – such as the foundationlessness of foundations – that would become major assumptions of such Post-Structuralist thinkers as Jacques Derrida). Michel Foucault's *Madness and Unreasonableness* (*Folie et déraison*, translated as *Madness and Civilization*, 1961)[2] set the tone for the new tendency in French thought by noting how classical reason constructed itself by banishing alternative "nonsensical" modes of thought and labeling them as "madness." People previ-ously considered mystics were suddenly in need of incarceration, and that switch was due to the invention of Reason as a guiding category for the Enlightenment. Reason assisted nascent capitalism by permitting utility or usefulness to be calculated and objects and people to be identified, assigned categories, and controlled.

Another major early Post-Structuralist book, Gilles Deleuze's *Nietzsche and Philosophy* (1962), brought attention to Nietzsche's subversion of the rationalist ideal of knowledge and his caustic critique of Christian civilization's habit of locating spiritual meaning in everything. The material world is a play of forces in contention, not something that conceals spirit or meaning. It cannot be understood using rational categories like "subject," or "object," or "will," or "truth," because all categories necessarily "lie." By grasping the world of forces in differential flux, categories translate flux into stable identities, things that have nothing to do with the world. All our thinking is fiction making, making metaphors that substitute stability for the inherent instability of existence, meaning for the eternally returning sameness of a material world that conceals no spiritual sense and that ultimately resists being translated into ideas or ideals like justice or truth or sin and redemption. Nietzsche's ideal philosopher-artist learns to accept this state of affairs, to refuse to assign meaning to things, to avoid categorization, to accept the groundlessness of all our ways of thinking, to throw himself into the play of the world and dance with it.

Deleuze's book was pathbreaking because it presented Nietzsche's hitherto ignored critique of three of the major assumptions of Structuralism: the notion that knowable structures underlie empirical events, the assumption that knowledge operates according to procedures that are axiomatic or not open to question, and the belief that reality is not radically contingent, not a play of forces without order or a series of accidents or events without meaning or logical sequence. It was as if a new door had been opened. The Structuralist desire to find knowable orders everywhere, to break down the flow of the world into unities that could be understood as so many languages or orders of meaning, found itself faced with a disturbing alternative. For the moment, however, that alternative could be ignored. Deleuze's book was a marginal philosophical monograph, not a scandal, and Foucault's book was written in a Heideggerian style that placed it on the margins of then mainstream French debate, which was consumed with the study of signs and structures. Structuralism continued to hold sway and to speak in the voice and style of high reason. Order, meaning, categorization, grammars, logic, et cetera – all continued to circulate as the dominant themes in French intellectual debates.

Everything changed in 1966 with the publication of another book by Foucault – *Words and Things* (*Les Mots et les Choses*, translated as *The Order of Things*). Foucault's style is now more within the Structuralist mainstream, and rather than speak about the expelled others of rationalism, he examines rationalism itself historically and shows how it comes into being and changes over time. Reason could no longer claim to be a light switched on at one go somewhere in the seventeenth century that continues to illuminate everything we do and think in the same consistent manner, locating an objective order in empirical events. The very notion of such an order, Foucault argues, was itself an historical invention, one that required the systematic displacement of earlier ways of knowing that did not make classificatory cuts in the world and that thought and spoke of the world as an order of resemblances and interconnected parts one of which was language itself. The invention of Reason in the "Classical Age," from the seventeenth to the eighteenth centuries, institutes a separation between words and things, language and the world, and turns language into a means of representation of a world now conceived as a world apart, as identifiable objects that differ from other separate objects and can be assigned proper names. From this point on, reason consists, Foucault argues, of historically evolving discursive procedures, from the classificatory divisions of the eighteenth century to the nineteenth century's emphasis on utility or usefulness or functionality. It is a set of representational techniques or languages, of discursive practices which form rules of consistency amongst themselves in historically evolving regimes of knowledge, what Foucault calls "epistemes." The known world characterized by legible signs of embodied meaning and resemblances between parts that was in existence until the seventeenth century gives way over time to a rationally analyzed and mastered object world of separated parts in functional subordination to each other. And that order becomes a way of justifying society's system of exchange, the way it allows goods and money or money and human labor to be differentiated and equated, made into profitable orders. Strategies of knowledge and strategies of capitalization are complicit.

Foucault's book establishes themes that will reemerge in the work of other Post-Structuralist thinkers, from Jacques Derrida to Jean Baudrillard. Perhaps the idea that is most crucial to their common endeavors is that there is a prior realm (either in history or in language or outside rationalist Western society) where language and world are not yet separated, where the cut that separates knower from world, word from thing, signifier from signified in order to establish rational knowledge in the form of an equivalence of meaning (word = thing, signifier = signified), has not yet occurred. There the play of ambivalence in language, its uncut potential for creating a multiplicity of possible lateral or transverse meanings that exceed all rational binary orders (identity/non-identity, etc.), is still available, still not separated from the material world of which language is a part. Words and things are still the same, as yet not ordered into a classificatory difference between signifier and signified within the order of reason. The act of reason that turns language into a representation of a world apart and the knowing subject into someone separate from the field of vision he masters with representation has yet to occur. After the cut, what reason creates (representation, meaning, knowledge as knowable order, equivalence of signifier and signified, etc.) will necessarily be surrounded by what it banishes. And within reason there will be as a result a murmur of disturbance, the sound of what reason would call nonsense and unreason but that might also simply be called the intertwining of language and world that is the ground of reason: "If language exists, it is because below the level of identities and differences, there is the foundation provided by continuities, resemblances, repetitions, and natural criss-crossings. Resemblance, excluded from knowledge since the early seventeenth century, still constitutes the outer edge of language: the ring surrounding the domain of that which can be analyzed, reduced to order, and known. Discourse dissipates the murmur, but without it it could not speak." After *Words and Things*, French thinkers began to see signification not as a gateway to structure but as a way of constructing repressive orders of knowledge and meaning as well as an apparatus for repressing anti-structuring forces. Signification was not a path to knowledge but a servant of cultural regimes that imposed repressive categorical orders on the world.[3]

Foucault's pathbreaking work intersected with parallel changes that were underway in French psychoanalysis, literature, and politics. Psychoanalysis had been present in French intellectual life long before the 1960s, but it took on an especially crucial role in the development of Post-Structuralism in 1966, when Jacques Lacan published his magisterial *Ecrits* (*Writings*). Language was no longer to be considered a representation of psychology; rather, language was, for Lacan, what made psychology or self-identity possible. We become human subjects or selves through our entry into the Symbolic Order of our culture, that language of norms and roles that assigns us a sense of who we are by telling us what we cannot be. Around the same time in the mid-1960s, alternative theories of madness from the Anglophone world (the work of David Cooper and R. D. Laing) began to have an impact on French thinking. Cooper and Laing's anti-psychiatry reconceived schizophrenia positively as providing access to potentially higher or more complex modes of cognition, and they argued that normality is itself pathological. An alternative tradition regarding schizophrenia was already present in French intellectual life since the Surrealist movement of the 1930s. The work of Georges Bataille and Antonin Artaud, writers of the 1930s and 1940s, in the mid-1960s began to enjoy a revival. Outside civilized structure, according to Bataille, lay not what rationalism calls madness but rather something else entirely, a realm of symbolic exchange that puts the orders of Reason in question. So-called civilized life, Bataille argues, is no different from primitive life; it is founded on sacrifice, the expulsion of the "accursed share," or cursed portion of ourselves that is bodily and material. The accursed share takes the form of forbidden eroticism (incest), excrement, and death (the return to material nature of human life). All are the object of taboos that constitute Western civilization under the sign of rational utility, repression of matter, a cut that separates culture from nature, and the reign of religions of transcendence. The structures of meaning in primitive societies are no different from those in modern society (a point also made by Lévi-Strauss in *The Savage Mind*); symbolic exchange is premised on a reciprocity of gifts rather than the equivalence of commodity exchange, and it permits the waste of surplus to preserve social cohesion rather than allowing the unequal division and accumulation of the surplus as in capitalism. The way primitive societies arrange their economies around a point of "sovereignty," someone who owns so much that he can have everyone to lunch and give away too much, thus initiating a round of reciprocal gift-giving, represents a positive kind of "general expenditure" that stands at odds with the "restricted expenditure" that emerges as capitalism, one that requires that all acquiesce to a norm of usefulness or utility in place of play, rational meaning in place of gay nonsense.[4]

Bataille and others such as Pierre Klossowski were fascinated by figures of excess and criminality like the Marquis de Sade, who drew attention to the violence at the heart of Western rational normality, the sacrifices everyone must make (of themselves and of their "excess" desires) in order to become good citizens. One can see how this line of thinking linked up with that of Foucault to provide the basis for a critique of the way modern societies rationalize or normalize the world. Such societies come into being historically by constructing an ideal of Reason that licenses the definition of alternatives to the societies as "madness." The madman, the criminal, and the experimental writer, the very types whose idiosyncrasy a rationalist procedure like Structuralism could not take into account because they are the anomaly whose expulsion defines the order sought in the Structuralist method, the unexplainably different counter-example or outside that could never be inside because its negativity allowed the positivity of the inside to define itself, began to attract new attention. That Nietzsche defined himself as such a poet-philosopher began suddenly to make sense to a variety of thinkers. Perhaps rationalism and art were merely different ways of using language?

It was in the experimental literature of writers like Mallarmé, Lautréamont, and Artaud especially that the new French thinkers began to see an alternative current to the rationalism and repression that characterized both Structuralism and modern culture in general. If Structuralism harnessed signifiers to signifieds, the differential play of empirical signs to consistent unities, latent structures, and codified orders, and if that buttoning down of language onto structure and meaning was part and parcel of the way rational capitalism maintained a repressive social regime which depended on a particular signification (construction) of reality and a particular subjection (both as becoming a self and becoming subject to a regime of self-sacrifice), then the new thinking would instead try to find out how all those unities and structures might be undone, come unraveled as principles of cognitive and social order, by unharnessing the signifying potential of the signifier itself and with it all the heterogeneous elements that capitalist signification worked to restrain in the world signified. A new politics of the signifier began to emerge in the journal *Tel Quel* (literally, "Just As It Is")[5] especially, which devoted many pages to the new generation of Post-Structuralist thinkers like Julia Kristeva and Jacques Derrida.

The publication in 1967 of Derrida's three books, *Of Grammatology*, *Writing and Difference*, and *Speech and Phenomenon*, marks another major turn in the evolution of Post-Structuralism. Derrida's critique of Western rationalism includes Lévi-Strauss's Structuralism, and Derrida finds an alternative to that tradition in the very artist/ renegades, such as Bataille and Artaud, who were being championed by the *telquellistes*.

Derrida's principal quarrel is with the metaphysical tradition in philosophy, which he calls "logocentrism," because it takes for granted the founding authority of reason or the *logos* (mind). *Logos* in Greek can also mean speech as well as meaning, so when Derrida criticizes logocentrism, he has in mind something more complicated than simple rational thought. He notices that in philosophy from Plato down to Husserl, speech, meaning, and thought are conceived as almost a natural weld, a continuum without joints or artic- ulation. They are seen as being one full and complete substance amongst whose parts there is almost no difference, no spaces of articulation between parts. The mind's aware- ness of meaning or ideas in its own internal voice of consciousness is, according to Derrida, a repeatedly referred to norm of authenticity, authority, and truthfulness in metaphysics. We know what truth is because our mind tells us what it is, and we can trust that voice of reason because it is closer than any other form of signification to ideas as they occur in the mind. Such other forms of signification as writing are mere substitu- tions, repetitions of a more original substance of truth, ideation, mental speech, and meaning. Throughout the history of philosophy, writing is banished from the realm of truth into a pure exterior. But, Derrida asks (and this question is the essence of his criti- cal strategy called "deconstruction"), what justifies the distinction between inside and outside, intelligible and physical, speech and writing? Doesn't there have to be a prior act of expulsion, setting in opposition, and differentiation in order for the supposed ground and absolute foundation of truth in the voice of the mind thinking the presence of truth to itself to come into being? If philosophy is about intelligibility, doesn't that require a prior distinction between what is intelligible and what is sensible or material or physical or graphical? Isn't the ground of truth, which should have no further ground, itself derived, an effect of something more primordial? And if that is the case, what is that more primordial thing?

The *logos* speaks not only truth but authority. It is always a command. And it is so, Derrida claims, because it is founded on an instability and a deficiency that it must control and conceal at all costs. It is not, according to Derrida, what it claims to be – a self-sufficient and complete identity of thought or meaning or idea in the internal voice of consciousness. At work underneath that supposed identity is a process of difference that makes identity possible but which itself can never assume the form of a knowable iden- tity. To understand what Derrida means by this, recall Saussure's claim that in language there are no full terms, only differences. There are no self-identical terms in language that stand on their own; language consists of differences, not identities. Derrida applies this "diacritical" principle to everything. All being and all thought is similarly differential, he claims. Everything that exists as an object or a thing, that can be present to our minds and known, is so only in so much as it is different from something else, and to think its identity as what it is (one of the tasks that philosophy sets for itself), one must suppress and ignore the differentiating process that constitutes it. Similarly, when we think or reason philosophically, we try to grasp an idea or a concept of something, but since we exist in time, such a concept or idea can exist only in a kind of movement of temporalization, moving from past to present to future. It is always split apart by difference, always requires a process of self-repetition to maintain the illusion of permanent presence, and such repetition insinuates difference into the heart of the presence of the idea in the mind.

We can never arrest that movement of difference and have a stable, self-identical moment of thought that would hold onto something, grasp both its presence to the mind and its present-ness or here-and-now-ness, outside of that movement. That movement is itself a constant and irreducible differing that does not lend itself to self-identity. What is present in the mind is derived from something else that cannot be known as such, as a graspable presence or identity, a category that does not spill over into other differences that are infinite. Difference between things and difference or deferment in time, according to Derrida, precedes and makes possible the momentary ever movable identities and present experiences, the seemingly stable categories, concepts, and ideas we are able to have in our minds.

In order to be able to begin with a ground of identity and authority that establishes a criterion of what is true, philosophy must always have a second beginning that precedes the first, an act of opposition and differentiation that expels such things as artifice, representation, metaphor, empty substitutes, non-identity, difference, and writing into an outside that then allows an inside to be established. The outside is then subordinated in opposition to the inside. As a result, identity, truth, meaning, the voice of consciousness, et cetera, are seen by philosophy as the superior and original terms, and artifice, writing, substitution, difference, non-identity, and the rest are seen as inferior, secondary, derived, added on, merely supplementary in relation to a prior truth. Philosophy, in other words, relies on a sleight of hand, a maneuver of substitution that places its real origin in difference outside its desired origin in identity (of truth, of reason, of ideas welded to the mind in the *logos*, etc.). It says that substitution is secondary to an original, more authentic moment of truth, but in order to found that moment, it must substitute truth for the more original act of differentiation that constitutes philosophy's supposedly original identity (of meaning to the mind, of truth to reason, etc.). If substitution is how metaphysics defines writing, then it must begin in writing, not in the speech of the mind and the awareness of truth.

Derrida persistently asks the following question of philosophy: if philosophy must begin in this way, with an act of differentiation, then isn't what it begins by declaring secondary and additional already at work in its foundation, at its point of origin? Isn't difference more original than identity? And doesn't this mean that all the values established by that initial differentiation or setting in opposition are questionable? Is substitution really outside and below authenticity if authenticity comes into being through an act of substitution? Is the non-truth of mere representation really secondary to the substance of truth in the voice of consciousness if a certain "re-," a certain doubling or turning is required in order for the substance of truth to establish itself precisely as not being representation, as something which is immediately and always also "the expulsion of representation"? Is signification and the differential processes that make it work really entirely opposite to a "nature" or a "reality" that is sufficient unto itself and not in need of signification or of the differential process that articulates terms and creates meaning, reference, and a world signified if our knowledge of reality, thought, being, and meaning can only occur within the differential movement that we normally attribute to external signification, to a signification that is supposedly external and additive to thought, truth, ideas, reality, meaning, and the rest?

One cannot, Derrida contends, speak of truth without signification, without those processes of substitution (of a signifier for a signified) and differentiation (of the signifier from the signified and from other signifiers) and repetition (of the original differentiation in an opposition that situates it as the subordinate and devalued term) and non–identity (of the original truth with itself because its "self" is entirely other than itself, being difference) that are "essential" to the making of meaning in language. And if this is so, then there is no more truth as logocentrism has conceived or thought of it: something whose essence is defined precisely by its exemption from a relationship of differentiation to something else that originally defines what it "is," or that is prior to repetition, being the ground that gives rise to repetition in representation and is itself a cause prior to all acts of repetition, or that is outside of substitution, the replacement of something original and authentic by a mere stand–in, or that is entirely self–sufficient and one with itself, not needing supplementary assistance to be what it is from something outside its orbit, an opposed term which might have to be there for it to be what it (supposedly) is. No truth without falsity, Nietzsche said, for similar reasons. The supposed essential unity and self–sufficient completeness of thought, meaning, or idea welded to the voice of consciousness in the internal realm of the mind which served as the gold standard for metaphysics suddenly looks like what it claimed to be exempt from – a myth, a story, a fiction, a metaphor, an act of differential signification, a piece of writing without any real referent that is not itself differential.

Derrida examines how writing especially is conceived in Western thought as a threat to the *logos*/speech/truth ideal. Writing is a substitute for speech, a repetition of the voice of the mind. Writing is an external addition or supplement to a truth that could just as easily do without its assistance. At stake here in the opposition between mind and the graphic of the written sign are, according to Derrida, all the oppositions that dominate Western thought – mind and matter, spirit and world, intelligibility and sensibility, interior and exterior, culture and nature, the true and the false, good and evil, the authentic and the artificial, et cetera. Derrida argues that such oppositional thinking is only possible on the basis of what it banishes as secondary to all of its values. Writing, which for Derrida is another name for *différance*, is more primordial than speech, truth, presence, et cetera. Its movement makes all of these ideals possible. Without difference and repetition, there could be no truth and no opposition between truth and falsity as such. Something external must be declared external, and that something is precisely what can never possess the qualities of truth (presence, self–identity, immediate intelligibility, etc.). Yet without it, without the exteriority of the signifier that allows a mythic internal realm of intelligibility to be constituted, there would be no concept of truth.

With other Post-Structuralist philosophers like Deleuze, Derrida writes a death sentence for two of the more durable philosophic traditions of the European West – Platonism and Hegelianism. Hegelianism was rampant in France since the late 1930s, and it allowed Sartre and Lacan to define their undertakings. Both Platonism and Hegelianism absorb the material or empirical world into ideal meanings or truths that stand outside history and the contingencies of specific social locations. For Derrida (as for Deleuze), critical philosophy reverses and displaces this hierarchy. From now on, the contingencies and indeterminacies of the empirical world (and for the French "empirical" means more the play of sensible or material existence than the mental experience of objects), would be seen as primary. Ideas are merely effects of operations such as repetition and difference that do not possess an ontological status as "things" or as "events." They make all such things and events possible while never being able to assume thingly or eventual form. Like the most basic forces of physics, they can be known only through the effects they generate, and they never appear to our minds (little Kodak cameras that they are) as picturable presences easily known and understood. They are beyond the kind of mastery both Hegel and Plato so easily assumed was possible.

Deleuze, in *Difference and Repetition* (1968) and *The Logic of Meaning* (1969), elaborates on his own earlier work on Nietzsche's concepts of play and the differences of force that constitute reality. The first book evolves a counter-ontology to the Platonic tradition. Whereas Plato privileges Ideas (universal rational concepts such as Beauty and Justice) over their mode of appearance, their surfaces in the material world (what Plato called "Simulacra"), Deleuze gives privilege to the surfaces, the depth-less appearances. There are no universal ideas, only appearances, but even these can no longer be called appearances, since they do not make anything appear; they are all that is. A scholar of Bergson, the philosopher of the *durée* or duration, Deleuze promotes becoming, the processes of material life, over being, the ideal of a static, unitary ontological substance that stands outside history and representation. *The Logic of Meaning* is about how sense or meaning (the French word for meaning is *sens*) depends on non-sense. Below the unities of language (what makes sense) are asemantic or nonsensical processes that do not permit a differentiation (opposition) between the world of matter and the world of language or between the realm of signifiers (appearance, simulacra) and that of meaning (depth). The two are threaded together, and making sense of the world is belied by a counter-movement that moves meaning towards non-meaning, sense towards non-sense. Like other Post-Structuralists, Deleuze takes heed of the work of Louis Hjelmslev, which provides an alternative to Saussure in that it argues that form and expression, the matter to be stated and the way it is stated, constitute a continuum. One cannot divide language into an intelligible realm of signifieds and a material realm of signifiers; they are all one thing, though shaped differently in different places. There is in other words no "metalanguage," a language that stands outside of and in opposition to the rest of language, a clearing where reason can operate without getting entangled immediately in semiotic thorns. And clearly also, there are no structures or depths that exist outside or beyond surface manifestations, providing meaning to what is otherwise merely simulacral. There are only simulacra, only surface manifestations. And structure, like meaning, is one of them. When one supposedly moves from signifier to signified, sign to meaning, one merely moves from one surface to another, one part of the world to another. There is no outside. (Arguably, this is what Derrida meant when he announced that "*il n'y a pas de hors texte*," or "there is no outside to the text," if by text we mean world, by which we mean language, at least any world we might know or inhabit).

Kristeva is probably the thinker who most clearly embodies the radical spirit of *Tel Quel*. In *Semeiotike: Towards a Semanalysis* (1969) and *Revolution in Poetic Language* (1974), she joins aesthetic to political radicalism. In the first, she links Marx's notion of production to semiotics and presents the work of Mikhail Bakhtin, especially his concept of dialogic ambivalence, to French readers for the first time. In *Poetic Language*, she argues that writers like Lautréamont, by undermining the orders of signification (which she associates with thetic statements that assume a separation of subject and predicate in a thesis statement such as "I know x"), tap into a well of as yet unordered language processes and unarticulated sounds to generate new possibilities for thought and for society, greater freedom to signify and greater liberation from the capitalist regime of utility, functionality, and work. Every literary text is a phenotext that orders the unruly and potentially infinitely multiple elements of language (the genotext) into discrete, bounded identities of meaning and signification. But that well or *chora* (which is also a locus of libidinal energy) always threatens to erupt and disturb the orders made from it. Experimental literature engages in deliberate disturbances of those orders. It is therefore revolutionary in that it questions the stability of capitalist reality and subjectivity in so much as both are discursively created events, separate identities fabricated thetically. Such literature draws attention to the excesses, the heterogeneous elements, that must be cut off and curtailed if civilization is to found itself (as a regime of necessary repression through forms of representation).

The theorists and writers of *Tel Quel* were not alone in their radicalism. Across the world, a "New Left" critical of capitalism and a "counter-culture" critical of Western rationalism was emerging throughout the 1960s. The new radical politics of the mid- to late 1960s stood opposed to such long-standing institutions of the more orthodox left as the Communist Party of France (PCF), a powerful institution which regularly earned the vote of a quarter of the electorate, and the unions (which the leftists argued were instruments of domination because they limited worker claims to a share of the pie rather than extending those demands to a more fundamental transformation of the social system). The new style of radical politics favored the Nietzschean play of Situationist "happenings" over the dour seriousness of the Communist Party officialdom, contested a multiplicity of repressions (of women, of sexual energy, of desire in general, of ethnic and national minorities, etc.), and were skeptical of the single economic repression decreed as "determining in the last instance" by the "scientific analysis" of the Party philosophers such as Louis Althusser. Althusser's work, from *For Marx* (1965) to *Reading Capital* (1968), despite its allegiance to a materialism that was in the process of being displaced by Post-Structuralism, could itself in certain respects be considered part of the new movement. Although he locates himself within "Structuralist" parameters, he is deeply influenced by Lacan, especially in his anti-humanist theory of how human subjectivity is formed and shaped by institutions and by discursive practices. We live in ideology, blinded by an "imaginary" consciousness that prevents us from gaining access to objective truth about our historical and class situation. (For a selection from Althusser and more on his theory of ideology, see Part Six.) If in his allegiance to such objectivist notions of science he remains Structuralist, in his theory of how different points in the social system "overdetermine" each other in an unstable and decentered manner, such that each has some autonomy from the others, Althusser moves over towards Post-Structuralism and helps enable the new movement's focus on the way "superstructure" can play a determining role on "infrastructure." Perhaps more importantly for the student movement, his thinking helped insert a studious and non-sloganeering reconsideration of Marx's texts into everyday intellectual discussions of the mid-1960s and helped shape the general radical climate that made the student revolt of 1968 possible.

The new radicals critiqued the politics of representation, the idea that anyone, any party especially, can speak for and represent or stand in for the mass of people and the multiplicity of their desires, needs, and aspirations. There began to emerge a counter-political ideal of "autonomy" that took root in Italy particularly (in such writers as

Antonio Negri – from *Marx Beyond Marx* to *The Savage Anomaly* – and in such organi-zations as *Autonomia*). According to this new political model, the material energies and creative potentials of people take precedence over the dictates of the traditional Communist Party. Those energies and potentials, not the Party leaders, should guide political change. This democratic critique of political representation intersected cru-cially with two major historical events in the spring of 1968 – the Soviet invasion of Czechoslovakia to suppress the "Prague Spring," a movement of democratization that was a precursor of the democratic revolutions of 1989 that swept Stalinism out of power in Eastern Europe and the former Soviet Republics, and the student uprisings in Paris (and around the world) that same spring, uprisings usually referred to as "May '68." May '68 really began on March 22, when students at the University of Paris at Nanterre rose up against the authority of the university. That uprising soon spread to the streets and attracted the participation of workers, who went on wildcat strikes in support of the students. But the movement was ultimately repressed by the government, which was supported by the unions and the PCF. That move by the Party had a profound effect on a generation of student radicals, most of whom would from that point on be either anti-Marxist or post-Marxist.[6]

If they were not already, of course, they would also be Post-Structuralist, since the death of Structuralism as an intellectual movement with any real claim on the allegiance of the most important new thinkers in French thought might be located at or around 1968. The new movement found one of its most eloquent political voices in one of its eldest members – Gilles Deleuze. With his collaborator of the 1970s, Felix Guattari, Deleuze becomes one of the most interesting and creative political Post-Structuralists. While the weld of Marx, Freud, and poetic Modernism in *Tel Quel* in some respects inaugurates Post-Structuralism understood as a form of cultural politics, it remained for Deleuze and Guattari to take the additional step of going beyond Marx and Freud. With Guy Hocquenghem's *Homosexual Desire* (1972), Jean-François Lyotard's *Adrift After Marx and Freud* (1973), Jean Baudrillard's *The Mirror of Production* (1973), Julia Kristeva's *Revolution in Poetic Language* (1974), Luce Irigaray's *Speculum of the Other Woman* (1974), Hélène Cixous's *The Newly Born Woman* (1975), and Michel Foucault's *Discipline and Punish* (1975), their *The Anti-Oedipus: Capitalism and Schizophrenia* (1972) marks the beginning (in writing at least) of political Post-Structuralism. We will discuss it in conjunction with their later *A Thousand Plateaus: Capitalism and Schizophrenia* (1980).

Against the then-prevalent psychoanalytic myth of Oedipus, which describes desire as originating in absence or lack (of access to the forbidden mother), Deleuze and Guattari instead propose a positive concept of desire as a productive activity. But Deleuze and Guattari go much further than a critique of orthodox Freudian psychoanalysis. They also announce a new set of concepts for understanding the world and our place within it. We are all machines, they argue, and the institutions we make for ourselves such as the family and the state are also machines that take the desiring-production of humanity and process it in useful ways for a particular social regime. The Oedipal family is useful for capitalism because it represses desires that might be in excess of the limits the utilitarian capitalist system requires. In order to work functionally, we have to desire efficiently. But desire is innately reckless and inefficient, an energistics without bounds, and it should be understood as just one segment in larger flows of energy and matter that constitute the world as a mobile, varying, multiple flux with different strata that make up planes of consistency. We exist within such planes as lines of flight that can either escape or be captured and pinned down by signifying regimes, semantic orders that assign us meanings and identities as "boy" or "girl" or "businessman" or "wife." All such stabilizations or codings constitute territorializations in that they establish boundaries of identity that restrain temporarily the movement of the flows and the lines of flight. They hold them in place (a territory), but deterritorialization is a more powerful force, and everything eventually breaks apart and flows anew, only once again to be recaptured and reterritorialized by another social regime of signification, made useful and meaningful at the same time. Capitalism represents a supreme form of deterritorialization in regard to the molar (large-scale) institutions of feudalism; it set free energies and desires that had been overcoded and restrained by the Catholic Church and the feudal economy. But capitalism itself is a form of territorialization, and it is always threatened by even more molecular or small-scale movements of energy, matter, and desire, flows that threaten to overwhelm its temporary codifications and territorializations. Schizophrenia represents the repressed underside of capitalist normality, the energy and productive potential that it must constrain in order to fabricate useful citizens and productive workers.

What Deleuze and Guattari propose is a radical new materialism. Thought no longer stands outside matter and understands it as an object of cognition. Thought is a move within matter itself. Rather than have a mind and a body, we are all bodies that are part of the general "body without organs" that is what used previously to be called "the world" or "nature" or "matter." We are all part of this primordial substance that is unarticulated into identities or objects or selves, but that can be cut up in various ways by signification, which must be understood as a practical material action in/on the world. Indeed, rather than think of history as a succession of modes of economic production, Deleuze and Guattari suggest that we think of it as a succession of signifying regimes, ways of ordering the flows of matter and of desiring-production using "*mots d'ordre*," or command words. Representation as philosophy has traditionally conceived of it – as something outside matter that embodies rational meaning – does not exist. Representation is itself a body, a line of flight, an act of territorialization or deterritorialization depending on its use or result. There is no difference then between signifier and signified; both are on the same material plane; both flow and are transformed multiply and endlessly. The way signifying orders and the world of desiring production interact is entirely contingent and unpredictable. Deleuze and Guattari frequently rely on analogies to contemporary mathematical theory, especially the theory of catastrophe or chaos, and describe flows as approaching "boundaries" or "thresholds" or "limits" that they either stay within, maintaining a temporary and mobile consistency, or move beyond, destroying that consistency and mutating to form another. Those thresholds are also the points of contact between things or between lines of flight; things are not so much outside each other and in contact, as in perpetual horizontal linkage with other things. No maps can be drawn of such a world; the map would merely be one more linkage, and its mastery merely one more hooking up laterally with things it can never master from a superior position of vertical mastery.

The politics Deleuze and Guattari espouse is perfectly in keeping with the spirit of the students in May '68. It is at once personal and public, micrological and macrological. And it is unabashedly utopian. Of the many social movements unleashed by 1968, feminism and gay liberation were probably among the most significant. Workers had a voice already in the unions and parties, but gays and women had no such organizations and no legitimate route of access to public debate. Nineteen-sixty-eight changed all of that, and two of the most important books of the post-1968 era are Hocquenghem's *Homosexual*

Desire and Irigaray's *Speculum*. Hocquenghem's book is exemplary of Post-Structuralism in that it begins with what is expelled or marginalized by civilization, in this case, homosexuality, and resituates it at the heart of civilization itself. Civilization is phallocentric and Oedipal, a heterosexual codification that expels non-heterosexual practices and identities. Essentially paranoiac, civilization founds itself by locating its enemies, its others that must be banished if its own categories are to be stable and grounded. In a Foucauldian manner, Hocquenghem notices how science pathologizes homosexuality and thereby licenses the penal subordination of gay sexuality to heterosexual norms. The homosexual person is seen as deficient or ill in this light. But it is only by engaging in such violent expulsion that civilized heterosexual normality can come into being. Drawing on Deleuze and Guattari's gay manifesto *Anti-Oedipus*, Hocquenghem argues that this fear of homosexuality is simply a way of dealing with the subversive transversality of desire, the way all sexuality exists on a continuum of possibilities, none of which is more valuable or natural than another. He cites *The Anti-Oedipus* at the close of his book: "We are heterosexual statistically or in a molar sense, homosexual personally (whether we are aware of it or not), and finally transsexual in an elementary or molecular sense."[7]

   Both in *Speculum* and in *This Sex Which Is Not One* (1977), Irigaray elaborates a Post-Structuralist theory of feminist separatism. In Western philosophy, women have been portrayed as matter, body, physicality, fluidity, boundarylessness, irrationality, artificiality, and the like. Women are the other or opposite, the mirror image, of all the positive values male-dominated Western philosophy privileges, from reason and truth to identity and authenticity. Irigaray plays on the word "speculation," which in philosophy refers to the process of reasoning, especially the metaphysical process of going "beyond" empirical appearances to talk about concepts like "being" and "becoming," or "truth" and "infinity." Such abstraction from concrete particularity and bodily materiality is, according to Irigaray, quintessentially male. Man must separate from the bloody origin in the mother and elevate himself above such matter if he is to attain a psychological identity predicated on masculine principles and ideals. By constructing their own subjective identity, man also projects matter, the matter that includes him, into a position of objectivity, entirely separate and apart from him. This is a gesture of power and control, and the other, Irigaray notes, becomes his "speculum" or mirror, that which confirms his self-identity. That other is woman in general, which Irigaray construes as linked essentially to bodily and material life. *Mater* is like *matrix*, the ground of philosophical speculation, because they are the same matter. Man seeks to extract himself from matter and to dominate it using concepts. All Western philosophy, including Freud's psychoanalysis, thus positions woman in a subordinate place in relation to the male subject (of knowledge and of mastery of matter). There can be no theory of the subject, as she puts it, that is not masculine.

   We must elude the opposition, Irigaray suggests, especially in *This Sex*. She proposes that women step outside the system of male equivalence (which is the system of philosophic equivalence – between sign and thing, subject and object, truth and matter, etc. – as such). They must fall back on themselves, value their own bodies instead of despising them as the male tradition has urged. Female bodies amongst themselves, clitoral lips touching each other in an aphallic caress – this is the sexual model Irigaray proposes as an alternative to the male one of penetration, which is as much cognitive or philosophic as phallic. Stop being the mirror of men, she urges; stop pretending to be "feminine."

Hélène Cixous in *The Newly Born Woman* offers a similar argument. Women must abandon the male phallocentric tradition of thinking of the world in oppositions between active and passive, nature and culture, father and mother, *logos* and pathos, form and matter, man and woman. We must instead think (or write, since we are now outside traditional thinking) the transverse ambivalence that underlies all of these oppositions. Cixous argues that only a particular kind of experimental writing, what she calls *écriture féminine* or feminine writing, can achieve this end. Feminine writing is not the exclusive domain of women; "male" writers like Joyce also practice it. Cixous's writing is itself an embodiment of such a new practice in that it crosses the line between the public or thetic and the personal or autobiographical. She writes philosophically of her own life experience, and of philosophy in a personal manner. The purpose of such writing practice is to reconnect with the world of matter that male speculation projected into a realm of intelligible objectivity: "Let us simultaneously imagine a general change in all the structures of training, education, and supervision – hence in the structures of reproduction of ideological results. And let us imagine a real liberation of sexuality, that is to say, a transformation of each one's relationship to his or her body (and to the other body), an approximation to the vast, material, organic, sensuous universe that we are."[8]

While one strand of Post-Structuralists reconfigured Western assumptions regarding gender identity and sexuality, another set about pursuing the radical implications of the new theories of representation and signification. If the orders of society were fabricated by signs (rather than being the hidden meanings signs embodied), how did such signs work and how did they accomplish their goals? In a long line of books, from *The System of Objects* (1968) to *The Transparency of Evil* (1990), Jean Baudrillard examines the way in which capitalism has shifted from being a mode of production to being a mode of signification. The real is no longer a matter of production or of productive forces and relations; rather, it has been replaced by simulation models that tell us who we are and shape what will pass for reality. Baudrillard espouses an immediatist politics appropriate to the student movement of 1968, which demanded an immediate total revolution of society, in place of the deferred change or gradual amelioration sought by the unions and the left parties. As a professor at Nanterre, Baudrillard was, as it were, at the heart of the uprising, and his thinking was profoundly shaped by it. As our epigraphs from his work indicate, that work is unique in that it self-consciously adopts the pose of the aesthetic *provocateur*, the poet-cum-outsider-cum-criminal that had become the ideal of at least one part of his generation. He is alone among them in speaking, as it were, with cobblestones. No other thinker of the "class of 1968" would say how nice it is to see a car burn. Or say that signs must also be burned. And then set about developing a burning style that leaves most of the assumptions, platitudes, certainties, and values of his and of any other generation for that matter in ruins. Baudrillard is the closest to Nietzsche's later style of provocative polemic of all the writers we discuss here.

Baudrillard's first book, *The System of Objects*, appeared, appropriately, in 1968. It lays out one of his central themes: modes of signification have taken the place of reality. About the shaping of desire and identity by advertising, *System* describes a world in which material needs have given way to codified equivalences between commodities and personal identity. Capitalist production has ceded primacy to the process of reproduction through the marketing of goods, and that marketing is entirely semiotic. The code dominates our lives and tells us who we are. There is no reality apart from it. Baudrillard would extend this argument in *Consumer Society* (1970) and *For a Critique of the Political Economy of the Sign* (1972), but his most scandalous book of this early period is *The*

Mirror of Production (1973), an extended critique of Marx and of Marxism. Marx, he argues, merely holds up a mirror to capitalism by adopting its categories, such as "production." By doing so, Marx mortgages everyone's lives to the capitalist-rationalist ideals of deferred gratification and functional usefulness. Reform socialists (to this day) argue that the goal of social revolution is a shorter working day; Baudrillard argues that it should be the abolition of work as capitalism knows and imposes it – a system of equivalence that equates human lives with monetary signs and exchange values. No contradiction at the heart of production of the kind Marx adduced (between workers and owners, or between productive forces and productive relations) will end this system; only dismantling the code of signification itself (which is what defines capitalist production itself as a set of equations between money, time, and human life) will bring about change. Against the subsumption of all the radical energies opposed to this rationalist social system into parties or unions that as much control and restrain as direct them, Baudrillard proposes a negative strategy of disaffection, a withdrawal of support, a revolt against the code of valuation as such:

> All the institutions of "advanced democracy," all "social achievements" in regard to personal growth, culture, individual and collective creativity, all of this is, as it has always been, simply the privilege of those with private property, the true right of the few. And for everyone else there are day-care centers and nurseries, institutions of social control in which productive forces are deliberately neutralized. For the system no longer needs universal productivity; it requires only that everyone play the game. This leads to the paradox of social groups who are compelled to fight for a place in the circuit of work and of productivity, the paradox of generations who are left out or placed off limits by the very development of the productive forces.... Revolt emerged against the integration of labor power as a factor of production. The new social groups, de facto dropouts, on the contrary, proved the incapacity of the system to "socialize the society" in its traditionally strategic level, to dynamically integrate them, even by violent contradiction at the level of production. And it is on the basis of their *total irresponsibility* that these marginal generations carry on the revolt.

It is in this book as well that Baudrillard provides a capsule portrait of the artist radical:

> The cursed poet, non-official art, and utopian writings in general, by giving a current and immediate content to man's liberation, should be the very speech of communism, its direct prophecy. They are only its bad conscience precisely because in them something of man is *immediately* realized, because they object without pity to the "political" dimension of the revolution, which is merely the dimension of its final postponement. They are the equivalent, at the level of discourse, of the wild [*sauvage*, wild or uncontrolled] social movements [of May '68] that were born in a symbolic situation of rupture (symbolic – which means non-universalized, non-dialectical, non-rationalized in the mirror of an imaginary objective history).

The Mirror of Production describes society in a manner that will influence Foucault's theory of the carceral or disciplinary society. For Baudrillard, society consists of very little else than institutions of social control and discipline. Like the Italian radical thinkers of his generation, especially Negri, he argues that the discipline of the factory floor has merely spread to all of society.

The work of Jean-François Lyotard very quickly after 1968 acquired the political tone established that year (what might be called "revolutionary optimism"). In *Discourse/Figures*

(1971) he argues for a deconstructive understanding of figuration or rhetoricity as the spatial representation which makes the discursive ordering of objects possible while simultaneously undermining and precluding all rational intelligibility. Figuration can never be incorporated into a discursive order of oppositions that pose signifiers as standing opposite to meanings. That would itself be an act of figuration, a display in space. Discourse can thus never internalize figuration to its system of order, yet without figuration, no discursive order would be possible. Lyotard is also concerned in this book with noting how the world of objects usually thought to be "grasped" by concepts somehow remains outside rational conceptuality and can never be reduced to it. As Bill Readings puts it: "The object resists being reduced to the state of mere equivalence to its meaning within a system of signification, and the figural marks this resistance, the sense that we cannot 'say' everything about an object, that an object always in some sense remains 'other' to any discourse we may maintain about it, has a singularity in excess of any meanings we may assign to it."[9] Finally, art, Lyotard claims with Nietzsche, makes knowledge possible. True knowers are supreme fabricators; the aesthetic cannot be separated from the epistemic.

Lyotard's *Dérive à partir de Marx et Freud* (*Adrift After Marx and Freud*) (1973) gives voice to the post- or anti-Marxism that would become a commonplace of French Post-Structuralist thought in the 1970s. Already in *Discourse/Figures*, Lyotard had linked figuration to desire and to the operations of the unconscious, what he would in a later book call a "libidinal economy."[10] In this book, social and political institutions like capitalism or the Party are described as mechanisms for restraining desires potentially in excess of socially acceptable limits. The task of radical politics is to liberate those desires. Lyotard accords priority to experimental art, which works radically with visual figuration itself rather than making it subordinate to meaning, over the traditional sloganizing of the Left, which gives primacy to meaning over the artifice of figuration.

Already one can begin to glimpse the outlines of what might be called a "general program" of Post-Structuralism: against meaning, figuration, against rigid structure, free play, against conceptuality, the resistance of the object, against identity, endless difference, against identity again, the relation to the other in general,[11] against making sense, the making sense of sense by non-sense, against universality, the irreducible singularity of the event, against signification, significatory multiplicity and excess, against representation conceived as the embodiment of meaning, the same representation conceived as a perpetual leftover which can never become the other within a binary oppositional order of meaning without generating one more representation (forever outside the semantic order), against rationality, the differential flux of life that is a-rational and beyond reason (and which contains reason), against the dialectic, the endless mediation of everything by everything else, against normality and good citizenship, the good madman or the positive criminal, against the repression required for civilized life, liberation, against the Party, the people, against authority, the authorship of authority by dictatorial rhetorics and regimes of discipline that lack all justification other than force and power, against the mind and ideas, the body and the matter that encompass both the mind and ideas, against transcendence, irreducible immanence or here and now within-the-world-ness, against the social system, all the forces of desire that the system must either expel or curtail in order to be itself. And so on.

Michel Foucault in the 1970s and 1980s broadened his historical critique of Western regimes of knowledge and Western social institutions such as the hospital to include what he called the general disciplinary power that saturates society as a whole and shapes our lives. Foucault's master work of 1975, *Oversee and Punish: The Birth of the Prison*

(*Surveiller et punir: naissance de la prison*, translated as *Discipline and Punish*), is a history of the emergence in modern times of a "carceral" or disciplinary society in which overt forms of public punishment of the kind that characterized the eighteenth century have given way to practices of self-discipline learned in institutions such as schools. Anxiety over behaving well has replaced fear of being publicly dismembered or burned. We have become our own prison guards, according to Foucault, and have learned to mold our behavior in accordance with the needs of modern capitalism. The bourgeois ideal of individual freedom, he argues, is an illusion, a way of loosening the tethers so that we can run faster and better, like useful social machines. Moreover, the modern knowledge disciplines that seem the embodiment of scientific reason are merely, Foucault argues, exercises in social power, ways to impose order on society by constructing personal or social identities and decreeing or normalizing "appropriate" behavior. If the heterosexual family is needed to produce useful citizens, then homosexuality, which had not been previously identified as a "pathology," will be so identified, and it along with other alternative forms of non-reproductive sexuality will be scientifically branded as "perversions" and banished from normality. The three volumes of Foucault's *History of Sexuality* (1976, 1984) dislocate how gender has been traditionally conceived as a stable, ontologically grounded cluster of acceptable identities by arguing that sexuality and sexual practices have been the objects of disciplinary power/knowledge that have "scientifically" constructed ideals of propriety by excising and rendering unwelcome sexual practices that earlier ages had no trouble accommodating. Foucault's most provocative example is sexual love between men in ancient Greece, a practice celebrated by none other than Plato, the philosopher most fondly turned to by many contemporary social conservatives who oppose equal rights for gays and lesbians.

Baudrillard's work of the late 1970s and 1980s, especially *Symbolic Exchange and Death* (1976), portrays signification as having so replaced reality that now one can say that the world is entirely simulational, entirely generated by semiotic models that have no referent in a supposedly "real world." All of our desires are codified and manipulated as fashion; all of our thought is saturated with semiotic equations that make critique (the pose of standing outside the system and opposing it) futile; detached from any referent in the world, capitalist signs refer only to other signs within a closed system. Baudrillard's later work, especially *Seduction* (1979), *Simulacra and Simulations* (1981), *The Fatal Strategies* (1983), and *The Gulf War Did Not Happen* (1991),[12] has attracted a great deal of attention amongst philosophers, cultural critics, and artists (who perhaps have come to recognize in his deliberately provocative style a version of their own aesthetic radicalism). Baudrillard's work is the most resiliently leftist and political of his "class." Indeed, thirty years later, it is difficult to imagine that someone still manages to write so ably and accurately in the style of 1968.

In 1979, Post-Structuralism changed names, but, as any Post-Structuralist will tell you, when names change, things change. Post-Structuralism (a term used mostly in the Anglophone academy) found itself being replaced by a new word (actually an old word transplanted from America to France and back again). That word was "Post-Modernism." Lyotard published a book that year entitled *The Post-Modern Condition: A Report on Knowledge* in which he calls the contemporary historical situation in which the old West European master narratives of progressive subjective enlightenment and rational liberation (Liberal Humanism and Marxism especially) no longer apply to a world of micronarratives that could not be dominated by any single legitimating metanarrative. Instead, a criterion of scientific and economic performativity or usefulness and technical/economic effectiveness has replaced the old rationalist ideal of a legitimating metalanguage, and it is linked to the growing power of corporations. By controlling scientific research, they are setting the terms of what would be construed as useful knowledge (and by implication, of what would be construed as true). Truth is no longer the possession of a rational subject, nor is it a property of a reality that would be described objectively using objective scientific methods. Rather it is determined by the effectivity of knowledge within a particular economic situation dominated by corporations that have the power both to shape the world and to say what counts as scientific truth regarding that world. What will count as true is what is useful from their point of view. For example, tests on drugs that provide justification for marketability will be deemed true; tests that provide contrary results will be avoided. So long as people continue to smoke and buy cigarettes, it will be true that they are not banishable; which is to say, only tests proving their non-banishability will be deemed true.

"Modernity" is a term common more in Germany than in France or the Anglophone intellectual world as a name for the post-feudal era, which German thinkers like Jürgen Habermas think of as one of progressive enlightenment or rationalization. Our world has come increasingly under the sway of reason in the form of rational laws and procedures, although defects remain that might be corrected if we were able to rationally discuss the issues together and achieve a consensus about remedying them. By choosing the word "Post-Modernism" or "Post-Modernity" to name the contemporary era, Lyotard was implicitly criticizing Habermas. Throughout the 1970s, while Habermas had been arguing in favor of the priority of Reason over discourse, Lyotard had been arguing in books like *Pagan Lessons* (1977) that all we have is discourse or narratives. Reason or rationality might be one language game, one narrative among others, but it is no more than that. In typical Post-Structuralist fashion, Lyotard branded "consensus" the ultimate form of totalitarianism, an attempt to cut off the play of discursive interaction by monologically and authoritatively imposing a model of undifferentiated unity on a field of discussion that can never be closed off or bound in. Discursive linkages are not amenable to domination by ideals of rational meaning. To determine that meaning would simply create one more discursive linkage, another narrative, and so on. Litigations settle disputes between discussants, but according to Lyotard, we live in what he calls "differends," situations of discussion that are irresolvable. No conclusion or simple judgment that terminates discussion and argument can be achieved.

The books in which Lyotard makes these arguments are *Just Gaming* (*Au Fuste*, 1979) and *The Differend* (1984). Lyotard takes up the obvious questions an anti-Post-Structuralist would propose: what about justice and ethics? How do you deal with these issues in a world that is nothing but narratives and language games? Lyotard's answer is "you don't." Let them be. Decide by not deciding, and by not deciding, you leave the questions open and you continue talking. Injustice is the closing off of debate and the subordination of the other. It is the imposition on an object, even a horrifying object like Auschwitz, of a meaning or of a category. The category and the meaning necessarily, by virtue of their preponderance and their presence in our minds and in our discourse, make the object disappear. Auschwitz loses its horror even as we attempt to do honor to the horror, to name it as such. There are things, Lyotard contends, that cannot be named, and they are the things most deserving of being honored by non-presentation and silence. Post-Modernism in art, Lyotard contends, consists of trying to present the non-presentable, but that places it outside the habitual regimes of representation that we take for granted in our everyday lives and our everyday rationality.

By a very circuitous route, we are back to the initial issue between Structuralism and Post-Structuralism, that of words and things, names and objects, categories and the world categorized. The problem with Structuralism in general, Lyotard would contend, is that it is an act of violence against an object such as Auschwitz, a reduction of complexity to simplicity, of something differential and problematic to a simple identity of structure that may have nothing to do with what the objects themselves are about or have to say. Why not instead acknowledge that one is always within narrative and pursue the narratives, ask for more stories, fill out the blanks on the same horizontal plane as the event or object itself? Might that not be more a way of "doing it justice"? One might be tempted to add that a law against such things as Auschwitz is always also a helpful additional piece of narrative, but Lyotard would reply that such laws existed before the event and they made no difference; what matters is creating a general discourse or web of arguments that becomes so strong in all cultures that such things simply become practical (which is to say, narrative) impossibilities, stories which can no longer be told because they no longer convince. Laws are just one discursive tool for shaping the world; persuasive narration is another, perhaps more effective, one. Trust in the ability of narratives to persuade and to generate new beliefs, Lyotard would argue, rather than falling back on the bad rationalist habit of authoritatively and violently declaring what a supposedly separate reality is or should be, without taking any decisive, which is to say, convincingly argued, well-narrated steps to change that reality's potential for taking such violent forms.

Marxists have made something of a cottage industry out of denouncing Post-Structuralism, and for good reason.[13] It places political Marxism, that of the Leninist parties and the trade unions, on the defensive and lays claim to a more challenging political imperative, the demand of the immediate revolution, as opposed to the deferred reform. It also places theoretical Marxism in jeopardy by noting the resemblance between its categories and those of the rationalist-utilitarian tradition Marxism seeks to displace. Marxism, according to Post-Structuralism, is no longer a critical philosophy, one that can stand apart and offer something new. But then, at least according to Post-Structuralists like Baudrillard, such an external critical position is an impossibility in any event. We are all within, and when we seem without, in a position of critical transcendence where we can speak in a metalanguage of reason, we are simply looking at the world through glass, and the glass prevents us from touching anything. It is a matter of shattering the glass, of reinserting ourselves into the world and then of asking, now what? How do we change the shape of things without laying claim to an external instance of power like the Party or resorting to a world-transcending foundation of rational authority like Reason or Truth. As Derrida notes in *Specters of Marx* (1993), Post-Structuralist deconstruction is in some respects the next logical step in Marxism, but as such and as what it has to be, it is also necessarily a step away from Marxism towards what Derrida calls a "New International," a program for change that ranges from family dynamics to global institutional politics. It is indeed a "general program," if a Post-Marxist one.

It consists of putting aside all of our concepts and categories regarding knowledge and being and of starting over, possibly from a number of different places at once. One place would be Derrida: to note that all thought is in identities (discrete categories), but that one needs difference to make such identities. So why not reexamine what it means to talk about the world in terms of identities, such as, say, an individual or a free speech or a meaning or a war or a corporation or a worker (which one?) or a woman or the school or the global economy? Can we reword these categories in terms of difference?

And how might that change our thinking? Another place would be Deleuze and Guattari: to note that we are energy that connects up with, bounces off, and is invested in the things around us, which are parts of grids or schemas that temporarily stabilize the general flows of energy that traverse all of us. How are those energies coded, directed, shaped, et cetera? How does the signifying regime we are within allow an order to come about from all of the potentially explosive energy that is in society? Another place would be Kristeva: to note that the foundation of our being and our knowledge is a thesis, a separation of subject and object. How might we reconfigure that relationship? Is it innate or mandatory? Or can we look to avant-garde literature and find there lessons in how it might provide glimpses of an alternative world, one perhaps beyond work and utility and the kinds of meaning that our founding theses bring about? Another place would be Irigaray: to ask how the most everyday categories of thought and action are imbued with phallocratic values and ideals. How might we work beyond the phallic model into some other site of sexualized thinking that would bring into play all the values and ideals the phallocratic tradition represses? Another place would be Lyotard: to note that our moral assumptions exist nowhere outside discursive procedures (memories of lessons in good behavior, sermons, laws, discussions, arguments, confessions, rebukes, bad news, good news, etc.). And if reason is itself such a procedure, how might we discuss and change those moral ideals without granting one party a trump that allows it to claim to be more rational?[14] How do "enlightened" people talk to neo-Nazis without betraying the morality of discussion and laying claim to enlightenment, an extra-discursive point of rationality? Another place would be Foucault or Baudrillard: to note that codes have taken over our lives, that we simulate models of good behavior even when we feel most original. How can we lay claim to the codes, undo the equations between money and human lives or between good behavior and codified social repression that anathematizes and stigmatizes the outsiders, the minorities, the criminals, the poor, those who do not live up to "our" expectations, those of the people on the inside of that simulation model of "the good"?

One might say that a paradigm shift has occurred, but that would itself be to remain within the world that has shifted. We are not in a new paradigm. Rather, there are no paradigms or models of knowledge that stand apart from the world and outside the play of its movements (repetition, difference, spacing, energetics, agonistics or antagonism, aesthetics or figuration, etc.). We are simply in the world we have always been in without knowing it, without being able to know it because we were preoccupied with one move (cognition in language) within that world and because the world somehow, even though we can describe it from within (the planetarium of knowledge), cannot be known (summed up in identitarian categories that stand outside, etc.). It can only be lived in knowingly.

Notes

1   The March 22nd Movement was the student group at the University of Nanterre led by Daniel Cohn-Bendit that ignited the student and worker uprisings in the Spring of 1968 in Paris.

2   We will occasionally provide alternative translations of French titles when it seems relevant. Here, for example, the standard English translation misses one meaning of Foucault's original title, his use of the word "*déraison*," which intimates his sense that madness represents a kind of "unreason," or even more actively "undoing of reason." The French title also alludes to the verb "*déraisonner*," to talk nonsense.

3   We could even apply this idea to Post-Structuralism itself. Jacques Derrida, for example, notes a resemblance and makes an analogy between the linguistic notion of difference and another process of differentiation that he sees operating in conceptuality or knowledge as well as in the world of entities. Derrida's project of deconstruction might thus be said to be founded on a "mere" metaphorical comparison, which might at first seem to disprove his argument, if it was not a perfect confirmation of the argument.

4   A crucial, much-discussed book in this regard is Marcel Mauss's *The Gift*.

5   *Tel Quel's* collaborative volume *Théorie d'ensemble* (1968) is something of a manifesto for the journal's theory of a revolutionary signifying practice that would disturb existing orders and make possible new worlds of thought and being.

6   By the mid-1970s, some of them, who became known as the "New Philosophers," would become polemicists against the possibility that the PCF might become part of a coalition government with the Socialist Party.

7   Gilles Deleuze and Felix Guattari, *The Anti-Oedipus* (Minneapolis: University of Minnesota Press, 1983), p. 149.

8   Hélène Cixous, *The Newly Born Woman* (Minneapolis: University of Minnesota Press, 1986), p. 83.

9   Bill Readings, *Introducing Lyotard: Art and Politics* (London and New York: Routledge, 1991), p. 4.

10   *Economie Libidinale* (Paris: Minuit, 1974). Translated as *Libidinal Economy* (Bloomington: Indiana University Press, 1994).

11   The "other" is a term that can name other people or other things, but it also implies the idea of a relation beyond oneself (identifiable as a subject) or beyond something (identifiable as an object) to something or someone else. We all appear to be identities, to possess selves, but the mark of "other" people is on us in the form of relations or experiences we have had with them. Similarly, no object stands apart from some relation to a field of perception containing other objects in which it is situated. The relation to the other in general, Post-Structuralists contend, is irreducible.

12   This piece, widely condemned by Marxists as rightist, was in fact first published in the French leftist newspaper *Libération*.

13   The Marxist critique is itself something of a lesson in Post-Structuralism in that it operates at the level of signification and subordinates reality to the dictates of its code. Marxists apply the word "postmodernism" to the latest stage of capitalism, and declare that capitalism is postmodernism. Then, they apply the same word "postmodernism" to Post-Structuralism and call it "Post-modernism." Consequently, Post-Structuralism must be the latest stage of capitalism, since they share a name. One has to forget, of course, everything that radical anti-capitalist Post-Structuralist thinkers from Foucault to Baudrillard have written if one is to believe this, which makes it somewhat insubstantial as an argument.

    The metaphors Marxists use in their denunciations are somewhat sinister. Eagleton speaks of getting Post-Structuralism in his "sights," Jameson of "tracking" (as in hunting?) it, and Simpson of "shock therapy." One must bear in mind that "reform socialists" of the sort a Marxist like Eagleton celebrates as an alternative to the "ultra-leftism" of Post-Structuralism are in the bad habit (at least in Spain) of literally getting ultra-leftist Basque separatists in the sights of their death squads. As Post-Structuralists suggest, one might want to be more careful about one's metaphors.

14   See Michael Ryan, "The Joker's Not Wild: Critical Theory and Social Policing," in *Politics and Culture: Working Hypotheses for a Post-Revolutionary Society* (London: Macmillan, 1989; Baltimore: Johns Hopkins University Press, 1989).

CHAPTER 2

The Will to Power

Friedrich Nietzsche

Nietzsche died before being able to complete what was to be his major work, *The Will to Power* (1885–6). In it, he argues that the essential drive in all life is a yearning for mastery. Nietzsche links this yearning to knowledge. When we know the world, we master its temporally fluid and spatially diverse reality by fixing identities with words. For Nietzsche, philosophical courage consists of being able to tolerate the nonidentical and meaningless character of existence without having to resort to words that posit identities or meanings in things. The world merely exists (what he calls the "eternal return" of the same), and there is no theological origin or conclusion to history. This skepticism regarding the likelihood of a separate spiritual realm in existence carries over into Post-Structuralism, which also questions the more secular versions of this ideal of transcendence, especially the notion that the realm of meaning is essentially distinct from the realm of signification. When the Post-Structuralists declare that there is no "transcendental signified," they are echoing Nietzsche's claim that there is teleology, no theological origin or goal to the world.

499

"Thinking" in primitive conditions (pre-organic) is the crystallization of forms, as in the case of crystal. – In *our* thought, the essential feature is fitting new material into old schemas ("Procrustes" = bed), *making* equal what is new.

500

… The same equalizing and ordering force that rules in the idioplasm, rules also in the incorporation of the outer world: our sense perceptions are already the result of this assimilation and equalization in regard to *all* the past in us; they do not follow directly upon the "impression" –

Original publication details: Friedrich Nietzsche, from *The Will to Power*, trans. Walter Kaufmann, sections 449 to 517, 542–543, and 552. Random House, 1967. Reproduced with permission from Random House, Inc.

501

All thought, judgment, perception, considered as comparison, has as its precondition a "*positing* of equality," and earlier still a "*making* equal." The process of making equal is the same as the process of incorporation of appropriated material in the amoeba.

511

Equality and similarity.

1. The coarser organ sees much apparent equality;
2. the mind *wants* equality, i.e., to subsume a sense impression into an existing series: in the same way as the body *assimilates* inorganic matter.

Toward an understanding of logic: *the will to equality is the will to power* – the belief that something is thus and thus (the essence of *judgment*) is the consequence of a will that things as much as possible *shall be* equal.

512

Logic is bound to the condition: assume there are identical cases. In fact, to make possible logical thinking and inferences, this condition must first be treated fictitiously as fulfilled. That is: the will to logical truth can be carried through only after a fundamental *falsification* of all events is assumed. From which it follows that a drive rules here that is capable of employing both means, firstly falsification, then the implementation of its own point of view: logic does *not* spring from the will to truth.

513

The inventive force that invented categories labored in the service of our needs, namely of our need for security, for quick understanding on the basis of signs and sounds, for means of abbreviation: "substance," "subject," "object," "being," "becoming" have nothing to do with metaphysical truths. –

It is the powerful who made the names of things into law, and among the powerful it is the greatest artists in abstraction who created the categories.

514

A morality, a mode of living tried and *proved* by long experience and testing, at length enters consciousness as a law, as *dominating* – And therewith the entire group of related values and states enters into it: it becomes venerable, unassailable, holy, true; it is part of its development that its origin should be forgotten – That is a sign it has become master –

Exactly the same thing could have happened with the categories of reason: they could have prevailed, after much groping and fumbling, through their relative utility – There came a point when one collected them together, raised them to consciousness as a whole – and when one commanded them, i.e., when they had the effect of a command – From then on, they counted as a priori, as beyond experience, as irrefutable. And yet perhaps they represent nothing more than the expediency of a certain race and species – their utility alone is their "truth" –

515

Not "to know" but to schematize – to impose upon chaos as much regularity and form as our practical needs require....

516

We are unable to affirm and to deny one and the same thing: this is a subjective empirical law, not the expression of any "necessity" but only of an inability.

If, according to Aristotle, the law of contradiction is the most certain of all principles, if it is the ultimate and most basic, upon which every demonstrative proof rests, if the principle of every axiom lies in it; then one should consider all the more rigorously what *presuppositions* already lie at the bottom of it. Either it asserts something about actuality, about being, as if one already knew this from another source; that is, as if opposite attributes *could* not be ascribed to it. Or the proposition means: opposite attributes *should* not be ascribed to it. In that case, logic would be an imperative, not to know the true, but to posit and arrange a world that shall be called true by us.

In short, the question remains open: are the axioms of logic adequate to reality or are they a means and measure for us to *create* reality, the concept "reality," for ourselves? – To affirm the former one would, as already said, have to have a previous knowledge of being – which is certainly not the case. The proposition therefore contains no *criterion of truth*, but an *imperative* concerning that which *should* count as true....

517

In order to think and infer it is necessary to assume beings: logic handles only formulas for what remains the same. That is why this assumption would not be proof of reality: "beings" are part of our perspective. The "ego" as a being (– not affected by becoming and development).

The fictitious world of subject, substance, "reason," etc., is needed – : there is in us a power to order, simplify, falsify, artificially distinguish. "Truth" is the will to be master over the multiplicity of sensations: – to classify phenomena into definite categories. In this we start from a belief in the "in-itself" of things (we take phenomena as *real*).

The character of the world in a state of becoming as incapable of formulation, as "false," as "self-contradictory." Knowledge and becoming exclude one another. Consequently, "knowledge" must be something else: there must first of all be a will to make knowable, a kind of becoming must itself create the deception of beings ...

542

If the character of existence should be false – which would be possible – what would truth, all our truth, be then? – An unconscionable falsification of the false? The false raised to a higher power? –

543

In a world that is essentially false, truthfulness would be an antinatural tendency: such a tendency could have meaning only as a means to a higher power of falsehood. In order for a world of the true, of being, to be invented, the truthful man would first have to be created (including the fact that such a man believes himself "truthful").

Simple, transparent, not in contradiction with himself, durable, remaining always the same, without wrinkle, fold, concealment, form: a man of this kind conceives a world of being as "God" in his own image.

For truthfulness to be possible, the whole sphere of man must be very clean, small, and respectable; advantage in every sense must be with the truthful man. – Lies, deception, dissimulation must arouse astonishment – ...

552

When one has grasped that the "subject" is not something that creates effects, but only a fiction, much follows.

It is only after the model of the subject that we have invented the reality of things and projected them into the medley of sensations. If we no longer believe in the effective subject, then belief also disappears in effective things, in reciprocation, cause and effect between those phenomena that we call things.

There also disappears, of course, the world of effective atoms: the assumption of which always depended on the supposition that one needed subjects.

At last, the "thing-in-itself" also disappears, because this is fundamentally the conception of a "subject-in-itself." But we have grasped that the subject is a fiction. The antithesis "thing-in-itself" and "appearance" is untenable; with that, however, the concept "appearance" also disappears.

If we give up the effective subject, we also give up the object upon which effects are produced. Duration, identity with itself, being are inherent neither in that which is called subject nor in that which is called object: they are complexes of events apparently durable in comparison with other complexes – e.g., through the difference in tempo of the event (rest–motion, firm–loose: opposites that do not exist in themselves and that actually express only variations in degree that from a certain perspective appear to be opposites. There are no opposites: only from those of logic do we derive the concept of opposites – and falsely transfer it to things).

If we give up the concept "subject" and "object," then also the concept "substance" – and as a consequence also the various modifications of it, e.g., "matter," "spirit," and other hypothetical entities, "the eternity and immutability of matter," etc. We have got rid of *materiality*.

From the standpoint of morality, the world is false. But to the extent that morality itself is a part of this world, morality is false.

Will to truth is a making firm, a making true and durable, an abolition of the false character of things, a reinterpretation of it into beings. "Truth" is therefore not something there, that might be found or discovered – but something that must be created and that gives a name to a process, or rather to a will to overcome that has in itself no end – introducing truth, as a *processus in infinitum*, an active determining – not a becoming conscious of something that is in itself firm and determined. It is a word for the "will to power."

Life is founded upon the premise of a belief in enduring and regularly recurring things; the more powerful life is, the wider must be the knowable world to which we, as it were, attribute being. Logicizing, rationalizing, systematizing as expedients of life.

Man projects his drive to truth, his "goal" in a certain sense, outside himself as a world that has being, as a metaphysical world, as a "thing-in-itself," as a world already in existence. His needs as creator to invent the world upon which he works, anticipate it; this anticipation (this "belief" in truth) is his support …

Man seeks "the truth": a world that is not self-contradictory, not deceptive, does not change, a *true* world – a world in which one does not suffer; contradiction, deception, change – causes of suffering! He does not doubt that a world as it ought to be exists; he would like to seek out the road to it. (Indian critique: even the "ego" as apparent, as not real.)

Whence does man here derive the concept reality? – Why is it that he derives *suffering* from change, deception, contradiction? and why not rather his happiness? –

Contempt, hatred for all that perishes, changes, varies – whence comes this valuation of that which remains constant? Obviously, the will to truth is here merely the desire for a world of the constant.

The senses deceive, reason corrects the errors; consequently, one concluded, reason is the road to the constant; the least sensual ideas must be closest to the "true world." – It is from the senses that most misfortunes come – they are deceivers, deluders, destroyers. –

Happiness can be guaranteed only by being; change and happiness exclude one another. The highest desire therefore contemplates unity with what has being. This is the formula for: the road to the highest happiness.

In summa: the world as it ought to be exists; this world, in which we live, is an error – this world of ours ought not to exist.

Belief in what has being is only a consequence: the real *primum mobile* is disbelief in becoming, mistrust of becoming, the low valuation of all that becomes –

What kind of man reflects in this way? An unproductive, suffering kind, a kind weary of life. If we imagine the opposite kind of man, he would not need to believe in what has being; more, he would despise it as dead, tedious, indifferent –

The belief that the world as it ought to be is, really exists, is a belief of the unproductive who do *not desire to create a world* as it ought to be. They posit it as already available, they seek ways and means of reaching it. "Will to truth" – *as the failure of the will to create….*

Whoever is incapable of laying his will into things, lacking will and strength, at least lays some *meaning* into them, i.e., the faith that there is a will in them already.

It is a measure of the degree of strength of will to what extent one can do without meaning in things, to what extent one can endure to live in a meaningless world *because one organizes a small portion of it oneself….*

Overthrowing of philosophers through the destruction of the world of being: intermediary period of nihilism: before there is yet present the strength to reverse values and to deify becoming and the apparent world as the only world, and to call them good …

CHAPTER 3

What Is Becoming?

Gilles Deleuze

Gilles Deleuze was one of the most prolific and influential French philosophers of the 1960s and 1970s. Like other figures of the time, he emphasized the complexity of thought, of literature, and of the world. He developed new abstract models for the world (the difference between "book" and "rhizome," for example) that sought to capture a sense of the instability in existence – that it consists as much of becoming and change as of being and stability. Conceiving of the world in this way renders our old vocabularies less useful and invites the creation of new terms such as "territory" and "deterritorialization" to account for how human life changes over time (see *A Thousand Plateaus*).

Alice and *Through the Looking-Glass* involve a category of very special things: events, pure events. When I say "Alice becomes larger," I mean that she becomes larger than she was. By the same token, however, she becomes smaller than she is now. Certainly, she is not bigger and smaller at the same time. She is larger now; she was smaller before. But it is at the same moment that one becomes larger than one was and smaller than one becomes. This is the simultaneity of a becoming whose characteristic is to elude the present. Insofar as it eludes the present, becoming does not tolerate the separation or the distinction of before and after, or of past and future. It pertains to the essence of becoming to move and to pull in both directions at once: Alice does not grow without shrinking, and vice versa. Good sense affirms that in all things there is a determinable sense or direction [*sens*]; but paradox is the affirmation of both senses or directions at the same time.

Plato invites us to distinguish between two dimensions: (1) that of limited and measured things, of fixed qualities, permanent or temporary which always presuppose pauses and rests, the fixing of presents, and the assignation of subjects (for example, a particular subject having a particular largeness or a particular smallness at a particular moment); and (2) a pure becoming without measure, a veritable becoming-mad, which never rests. It moves in both directions at once. It always eludes the present, causing future and past, more and less, too much and not enough to coincide in the simultaneity of a rebellious

Original publication details: Gilles Deleuze, "What Is Becoming?" from *The Logic of Sense*, pp. 1–3. Columbia University Press, 1989. Reproduced with permission from Columbia University Press.

Literary Theory: An Anthology, Third Edition. Edited by Julie Rivkin and Michael Ryan.
© 2017 John Wiley & Sons, Ltd. Published 2017 by John Wiley & Sons, Ltd.

matter. "'Hotter' never stops where it is but is always going a point further, and the same applies to 'colder,' where as definite quality is something that has stopped going on and is fixed"; "... the younger becoming older than the older, the older becoming younger than the younger – but they can never finally become so; if they did they would no longer be becoming, but would be so."

We recognize this Platonic dualism. It is not at all the dualism of the intelligible and the sensible, of Idea and matter, or of Ideas and bodies. It is a more profound and secret dualism hidden in sensible and material bodies themselves. It is a subterranean dualism between that which receives the action of the Idea and that which eludes this action. It is not the distinction between the Model and the copy, but rather between copies and simulacra. Pure becoming, the unlimited, is the matter of the simulacrum insofar as it eludes the action of the Idea and insofar as it contests *both* model *and* copy at once. Limited things lie beneath the Ideas; but even beneath things, is there not still this mad element which subsists and occurs on the other side of the order that Ideas impose and things receive? Sometimes Plato wonders whether this pure becoming might not have a very peculiar relation to language. This seems to be one of the principal meanings of the *Cratylus*. Could this relation be, perhaps, essential to language, as in the case of a "flow" of speech, or a wild discourse which would incessantly slide over its referent, without ever stopping? Or might there not be two languages and two sorts of "names," one designating the pauses and rests which receive the action of the Idea, the other expressing the movements or rebel becomings? Or further still, is it not possible that there are two distinct dimensions internal to language in general – one always concealed by the other, yet continuously coming to the aid of, or subsisting under, the other?

The paradox of this pure becoming, with its capacity to elude the present, is the paradox of infinite identity (the infinite identity of both directions or senses at the same time – of future and past, of the day before and the day after, of more and less, of too much and not enough, of active and passive, and of cause and effect). It is language which fixes the limits (the moment, for example, at which the excess begins), but it is language as well which transcends the limits and restores them to the infinite equiva- lence of an unlimited becoming ("A red–hot poker will burn you if you hold it too long; and ... if you cut your finger *very* deeply with a knife, it usually bleeds"). Hence the reversals which constitute Alice's adventures: the reversal of becoming larger and becoming smaller – "which way, which way?" asks Alice, sensing that it is always in both directions at the same time, so that for once she stays the same, through an optical illusion; the reversal of the day before and the day after, the present always being eluded – "jam tomorrow and jam yesterday – but never jam *to–day*"; the reversal of more and less: five nights are five times hotter than a single one, "but they must be five times as cold for the same reason"; the reversal of active and passive: "do cats eat bats?" is as good as "do bats eat cats?"; the reversal of cause and effect: to be punished before having committed a fault, to cry before having pricked oneself, to serve before having divided up the servings.

All these reversals as they appear in infinite identity have one consequence: the contesting of Alice's personal identity and the loss of her proper name. The loss of the proper name is the adventure which is repeated throughout all Alice's adventures. For the proper or singular name is guaranteed by the permanence of *savoir*. The latter is embodied in general names designating pauses and rests, in substantives and adjectives, with which the proper name maintains a constant connection. Thus the personal self requires God and the world in general. But when substantives and adjectives begin to dissolve, when the names of pause and rest are carried away by the verbs of pure becoming and slide into the language of events, all identity disappears from the self, the world, and God. This is the test of *savoir* and recitation which strips Alice of her identity. In it words may go awry, being obliquely swept away by the verbs. It is as if events enjoyed an irreality which is communicated through language to the *savoir* and to persons. For personal uncertainty is not a doubt foreign to what is happening, but rather an objective structure of the event itself, insofar as it moves in two directions at once, and insofar as it fragments the subject following this double direction. Paradox is initially that which destroys good sense as the only direction, but it is also that which destroys common sense as the assignation of fixed identities.

CHAPTER 4

Différance[1]

Jacques Derrida

In his 1968 essay, "Différance," Derrida describes the process of spatial and temporal movement that he claims makes all thought and all reality possible. To justify it, he draws on the work of Saussure, Heidegger, and Nietzsche. He also alludes to the work of the pre-Socratic philosophers such as Anaximander.

Saussure argued that there is no substance in language. All language consists of differences. In language there are only forms, not substances, and by that he meant that all apparently substantive units of language are generated by other things that lie outside them, but these external characteristics are actually internal to their make-up. A "form" is something external that shapes material into a particular identity or substance. All elements of language have identity only in so much as they are produced by a network of differences, and each element will itself consist of further differentiations, endlessly.

Derrida contends that thought and our perception of reality are governed by similar processes. Traditional philosophy held that we see actual presences and substances in the world and that our ideas have presence and substance that guarantees their truthfulness. Derrida set about demonstrating that ideas especially are like units of language; they are generated by difference; they have no substance apart from the networks of differences (each bearing the traces of other elements and other differences) that generate them as effects. But of course, as in language, those processes that generate them do not have a palpable or graspable presence of their own. Like forms, they are empty, nonpresent, and nonsubstantive.

In this essay, he uses two axes to talk about the work of difference that produces presence as an effect that the mind then mistakenly assumes is a substance that guarantees truthfulness. The first is time. When we think of anything, we cannot grasp it in the "present moment," because that present moment is always passing away. Presence is shadowed by the death of presence, its shuttling past the mind into the oblivion of the past. Similarly, any current present moment bears in it the future present moments toward

Original publication details: Jacques Derrida, "Différance" from *Speech and Phenomena and Other Essays on Husserl's Theory of Signs*, trans. David B. Allison, pp. 142–149. Northwestern University Press, 1973. Reprinted with permission from Northwestern University Press, University of Nebraska Press, and Editions Seuil.

which it is moving. The differences between these "presents" constitute the "present" we attempt to grasp as something substantive before our minds. The second axis is space, and the same process of difference haunts the idea of a spatially determinate identity of presence. Any spatially locatable object of thought or idea has an identity or presence of its own only by differing from other things.

Another term for this operation of difference that shadows presence is "trace." All ideas and all objects of thought and perception bear the trace of other things, other moments, other "presences." To bear the trace of other things is to be shadowed by "alterity," which literally means "otherness."

Derrida concludes this essay by evoking the pre-Socratic notion of the "sumploke" or "confluence of being." What the concept of differance leads to is a sense that everything in existence is relationally connected. We can sort it out into parts, but we should not assume those parts are pure and original or that they are pure identities. They are the effects of other processes of relation and differentiation. Derrida will elsewhere argue that what this means is that all things are signs and that all reality is "textual," in that all parts refer to or signify other parts, which are themselves signifiers of other parts. If we bear in mind the traditional definition of writing as the sign of a sign (the written sign of mental speech), then all reality is in a sense *graphic*, a form of writing. At the origin of thought is not a purely present idea but rather what Derrida calls "archi-writing," and by that he means the process he here describes as the spatio-temporal movement of "differance."

Derrida brings Saussure's notion of difference to bear on philosophical concepts. Like signs in language, he argues, they too are given identity by their differences from one another. He famously notes that philosophical oppositions such as the intelligible and the sensible, nature and culture, the ideal and physical, etc. can be shown to be produced by differance. Many literary critics have mistakenly limited deconstruction to this "undoing of binary opposition," but the questioning of oppositions is only one part of Derrida's undertaking, which aims to put in question the values and assumptions of the metaphysical philosophical tradition.

The verb "to differ" [*différer*] seems to differ from itself. On the one hand, it indicates difference as distinction, inequality, or discernibility; on the other, it expresses the interposition of delay, the interval of a *spacing* and *temporalizing* that puts off until "later" what is presently denied, the possible that is presently impossible. Sometimes the *different* and sometimes the *deferred* correspond [in French] to the verb "to differ." This correlation, however, is not simply one between act and object, cause and effect, or primordial and derived.

In the one case "to differ" signifies nonidentity; in the other case it signifies the order of the *same*. Yet there must be a common, although entirely differant[2] [*différante*], root within the sphere that relates the two movements of differing to one another. We provisionally give the name *differance* to this *sameness* which is not *identical*: by the silent writing of its *a*, it has the desired advantage of referring to differing, *both* as spacing/temporalizing and as the movement that structures every dissociation.

As distinct from difference, differance thus points out the irreducibility of temporalizing (which is also temporalization – in transcendental language which is no longer adequate here, this would be called the constitution of primordial temporality – just as the term "spacing" also includes the constitution of primordial spatiality). Differance is not simply active (any more than it is a subjective accomplishment); it rather indicates the middle voice, it precedes and sets up the opposition between passivity and activity. With its *a*, differance more properly refers to what in classical language would be called the origin or production of differences and the differences between differences, the *play* [*jeu*] of differences. Its locus and operation will therefore be seen wherever speech appeals to difference.

Differance is neither a *word* nor a *concept*. In it, however, we shall see the juncture rather than the summation – of what has been most decisively inscribed in the thought of what is conveniently called our "epoch": the difference of forces in Nietzsche, Saussure's principle of semiological difference, differing as the possibility of [neurone] facilitation,[3] impression and delayed effect in Freud, difference as the irreducibility of the trace of the other in Levinas, and the ontic-ontological difference in Heidegger. Reflection on this last determination of difference will lead us to consider differance as the *strategic* note or connection – relatively or provisionally *privileged* – which indicates the closure of presence, together with the closure of the conceptual order and denomination, a closure that is effected in the functioning of traces.

I SHALL SPEAK, THEN, OF A LETTER – the first one, if we are to believe the alphabet and most of the speculations that have concerned themselves with it.

I shall speak then of the letter *a*, this first letter which it seemed necessary to introduce now and then in writing the word "difference." This seemed necessary in the course of writing about writing, and of writing within a writing whose different strokes all pass, in certain respects, through a gross spelling mistake, through a violation of the rules governing writing, violating the law that governs writing and regulates its conventions of propriety. In fact or theory we can always erase or lessen this spelling mistake, and, in each case, while these are analytically different from one another but for practical purposes the same, find it grave, unseemly, or, indeed, supposing the greatest ingenuousness, amusing. Whether or not we care to quietly overlook this infraction, the attention we give it beforehand will allow us to recognize, as though prescribed by some mute irony, the inaudible but displaced character of this literal permutation. We can always act as though this makes no difference. I must say from the start that my account serves less to justify this silent spelling mistake, or still less to excuse it, than to aggravate its obtrusive character.

On the other hand, I must be excused if I refer, at least implicitly, to one or another of the texts that I have ventured to publish. Precisely what I would like to attempt to some extent (although this is in principle and in its highest degree impossible, due to essential *de jure* reasons) is to bring together an *assemblage* of the different ways I have been able to utilize – or, rather, have allowed to be imposed on me – what I will provisionally call the word or concept of differance in its new spelling. It is literally neither a word nor a concept, as we shall see. I insist on the word "assemblage" here for two reasons: on the one hand, it is not a matter of describing a history, of recounting the steps, text by text, context by context, each time showing which scheme has been able to impose this graphic disorder, although this could have been done as well; rather, we are concerned with the *general system of all these schemata*. On the other hand, the word "assemblage" seems more apt for suggesting that the kind of bringing together proposed here has the structure of an interlacing, a weaving, or a web, which would allow the different threads and different lines of sense or force to separate again, as well as being ready to bind others together.

In a quite preliminary way, we now recall that this particular graphic intervention was conceived in the writing-up of a question about writing; it was not made simply to shock the reader or grammarian. Now, in point of fact, it happens that this graphic difference (the *a* instead of the *e*), this marked difference between two apparently vocalic notations, between vowels, remains purely graphic: it is written or read, but it is not heard. It cannot be heard, and we shall see in what respects it is also beyond the order of under-standing. It is put forward by a silent mark, by a tacit monument, or, one might even say, by a pyramid – keeping in mind not only the capital form of the printed letter but also that passage from Hegel's *Encyclopaedia* where he compares the body of the sign to an Egyptian pyramid. The *a* of differance, therefore, is not heard; it remains silent, secret, and discreet, like a tomb.[4]

It is a tomb that (provided one knows how to decipher its legend) is not far from sign-aling the death of the king.

It is a tomb that cannot even be made to resonate. For I cannot even let you know, by my talk, now being spoken before the Société Française de Philosophie, which difference I am talking about at the very moment I speak of it. I can only talk about this graphic difference by keeping to a very indirect speech about writing, and on the condition that I specify each time that I am referring to difference with an *e* or differance with an *a*. All of which is not going to simplify matters today, and will give us all a great deal of trouble when we want to understand one another. In any event, when I do specify which differ-ence I mean – when I say "with an *e*" or "with an *a*" – this will refer irreducibly to a *written text*, a text governing my talk, a text that I keep in front of me, that I will read, and toward which I shall have to try to lead your hands and eyes. We cannot refrain here from going by way of a written text, from ordering ourselves by the disorder that is produced therein – and this is what matters to me first of all.

Doubtless this pyramidal silence of the graphic difference between the *e* and the *a* can function only within the system of phonetic writing and within a language or grammar historically tied to phonetic writing and to the whole culture which is inseparable from it. But I will say that it is just this – this silence that functions only within what is called phonetic writing – that points out or reminds us in a very opportune way that, contrary to an enormous prejudice, there is no phonetic writing. There is no purely and strictly phonetic writing. What is called phonetic writing can only function – in principle and *de jure*, and not due to some factual and technical inadequacy – by incorporating non-phonetic "signs" (punctuation, spacing, etc.); but when we examine their structure and necessity, we will quickly see that they are ill described by the concept of signs. Saussure had only to remind us that the play of difference was the functional condition, the con-dition of possibility, for every sign; and it is itself silent. The difference between two phonemes, which enables them to exist and to operate, is inaudible. The inaudible opens the two present phonemes to hearing, as they present themselves. If, then, there is no purely phonetic writing, it is because there is no purely phonetic phone. The difference that brings out phonemes and lets them be heard and understood [*entendre*] itself remains inaudible.

It will perhaps be objected that, for the same reasons, the graphic difference itself sinks into darkness, that it never constitutes the fullness of a sensible term, but draws out an invisible connection, the mark of an inapparent relation between two spectacles. That is no doubt true. Indeed, since from this point of view the difference between the *e* and the *a* marked in "differance" eludes vision and hearing, this happily suggests that we must here let ourselves be referred to an order that no longer refers to sensibility.

But we are not referred to intelligibility either, to an ideality not fortuitously associated with the objectivity of *theorein* or understanding. We must be referred to an order, then, that resists philosophy's founding opposition between the sensible and the intelligible. The order that resists this opposition, that resists it because it sustains it, is designated in a movement of differance (with an *a*) between two differences or between two letters. This differance belongs neither to the voice nor to writing in the ordinary sense, and it takes place, like the strange space that will assemble us here for the course of an hour, *between* speech and writing and beyond the tranquil familiarity that binds us to one and to the other, reassuring us sometimes in the illusion that they are two separate things.

Now, HOW AM I TO SPEAK OF the *a* of differance? It is clear that it cannot be *exposed*. We can expose only what, at a certain moment, can become *present*, manifest; what can be shown, presented as a present, a being-present in its truth, the truth of a present or the presence of a present. However, if differance is (I also cross out the "is") what makes the presentation of being-present possible, it never presents itself as such. It is never given in the present or to anyone. Holding back and not exposing itself, it goes beyond the order of truth on this specific point and in this determined way, yet is not itself concealed, as if it were something, a mysterious being, in the occult zone of a non-knowing. Any exposition would expose it to disappearing as a disappearance. It would risk appearing, thus disappearing.

Thus, the detours, phrases, and syntax that I shall often have to resort to will resemble – will sometimes be practically indiscernible from – those of negative theology. Already we had to note that differance is *not*, does not exist, and is not any sort of being-present (*on*). And we will have to point out everything that it *is not*, and, consequently, that it has neither existence nor essence. It belongs to no category of being, present or absent. And yet what is thus denoted as differance is not theological, not even in the most negative order of negative theology. The latter, as we know, is always occupied with letting a supraessential reality go beyond the finite categories of essence and existence, that is, of presence, and always hastens to remind us that, if we deny the predicate of existence to God, it is in order to recognize him as a superior, inconceivable, and ineffable mode of being. Here there is no question of such a move, as will be confirmed as we go along. Not only is differance irreducible to every ontological or theological – onto-theological – reappropriation, but it opens up the very space in which onto-theology – philosophy – produces its system and its history. It thus encompasses and irrevocably surpasses onto-theology or philosophy.

For the same reason, I do not know where to begin to mark out this assemblage, this graph, of differance. Precisely what is in question here is the requirement that there be a *de jure* commencement, an absolute point of departure, a responsibility arising from a principle. The problem of writing opens by questioning the *arche*. Thus what I put forth here will not be developed simply as a philosophical discourse that operates on the basis of a principle, of postulates, axioms, and definitions and that moves according to the discursive line of a rational order. In marking out differance, everything is a matter of strategy and risk. It is a question of strategy because no transcendent truth present outside the sphere of writing can theologically command the totality of this field. It is hazardous because this strategy is not simply one in the sense that we say that strategy orients the tactics according to a final aim, a *telos* or the theme of a domination, a mastery or an ultimate reappropriation of movement and field. In the end, it is a strategy without finality. We might call it blind tactics or empirical errance, if the value of empiricism did not itself derive all its meaning from its opposition to philosophical responsibility. If there is a certain errance in the tracing-out of differance, it no longer follows the line of logico-philosophical speech or that of its integral and symmetrical opposite, logico-empirical speech. The concept of *play* [*jeu*] remains beyond this opposition; on the eve and aftermath of philosophy, it designates the unity of chance and necessity in an endless calculus.

By decision and, as it were, by the rules of the game, then, turning this thought around, let us introduce ourselves to the thought of differance by way of the theme of strategy or stratagem. By this merely strategic justification, I want to emphasize that the efficacy of this thematics of differance very well may, and even one day must, be sublated, i.e., lend itself, if not to its own replacement, at least to its involvement in a series of events which in fact it never commanded. This also means that it is not a theological thematics.

I will say, first of all, that differance, which is neither a word nor a concept, seemed to me to be strategically the theme most proper to think out, if not master (thought being here, perhaps, held in a certain necessary relation with the structional limits of mastery), in what is most characteristic of our "epoch." I start off, then, strategically, from the place and time in which "we" are, even though my opening is not justifiable in the final account, and though it is always on the basis of differance and its "history" that we can claim to know who and where "we" are and what the limits of an "epoch" can be.

Although "difference" is neither a word nor a concept, let us nonetheless attempt a simple and approximative semantic analysis which will bring us in view of what is at stake [*en vue de l'enjeu*]. We do know that the verb "to differ" [*différer*] (the Latin verb *differre*) has two seemingly quite distinct meanings; in the *Littré* dictionary, for example, they are the subject of two separate articles. In this sense, the Latin *differre* is not the simple translation of the Greek *diapherein*; this fact will not be without consequence for us in tying our discussion to a particular language, one that passes for being less philosophical, less primordially philosophical, than the other. For the distribution of sense in the Greek *diapherein* does not carry one of the two themes of the Latin *differre*, namely, the action of postponing until later, of taking into account, the taking-account of time and forces in an operation that implies an economic reckoning, a detour, a respite, a delay, a reserve, a representation – all the concepts that I will sum up here in a word I have never used but which could be added to this series: *temporalizing*. "To differ" in this sense is to temporalize, to resort, consciously or unconsciously, to the temporal and temporalizing mediation of a detour that suspends the accomplishment or fulfillment of "desire" or "will," or carries desire or will out in a way that annuls or tempers their effect. We shall see, later, in what respects this temporalizing is also a temporalization and spacing, is space's becoming-temporal and time's becoming-spatial, is "primordial constitution" of space and time, as metaphysics or transcendental phenomenology would call it in the language that is here criticized and displaced.

The other sense of "to differ" [*différer*] is the most common and most identifiable, the sense of not being identical, of being other, of being discernible, etc. And in "differents," whether referring to the alterity of dissimilarity or the alterity of allergy or of polemics, it is necessary that interval, distance, *spacing* occur among the different elements and occur actively, dynamically, and with a certain perseverance in repetition.

But the word "difference" (with an *e*) could never refer to differing as temporalizing or to difference as *polemos*. It is this loss of sense that the word differance (with an *a*) will have to schematically compensate for. Differance can refer to the whole complex of its meanings at once, for it is immediately and irreducibly multivalent, something which will be important for the discourse I am trying to develop. It refers to this whole complex of meanings not only when it is supported by a language or interpretive context (like any signification), but it already does so somehow of itself. Or at least it does so more easily by itself than does any other word: here the *a* comes more immediately from the present participle [*différant*] and brings us closer to the action of "differing" that is in progress, even before it has produced the effect that is constituted as different or resulted in difference (with an *e*). Within a conceptual system and in terms of classical requirements, differance could be said to designate the productive and primordial constituting causality, the process of scission and division whose differings and differences would be the constituted products or effects. But while bringing us closer to the infinitive and active core of differing, "differance" with an *a* neutralizes what the infinitive denotes as simply active, in the same way that "parlance" does not signify the simple fact of speaking, of speaking to or being spoken to. Nor is resonance the act of resonating. Here in the usage of our language we must consider that the ending -*ance* is undecided between active and passive. And we shall see why what is designated by "differance" is neither simply active nor simply passive, that it announces or rather recalls something like the middle voice, that it speaks of an operation which is not an operation, which cannot be thought of either as a passion or as an action of a subject upon an object, as starting from an agent or from a patient, or on the basis of, or in view of, any of these *terms*. But philosophy has perhaps commenced by distributing the middle voice, expressing a certain intransitiveness, into the active and the passive voice, and has itself been constituted in this repression.

How are differance as temporalizing and differance as spacing conjoined?

Let us begin with the problem of signs and writing – since we are already in the midst of it. We ordinarily say that a sign is put in place of the thing itself, the present thing – "thing" holding here for the sense as well as the referent. Signs represent the present in its absence; they take the place of the present. When we cannot take hold of or show the thing, let us say the present, the being-present, when the present does not present itself, then we signify, we go through the detour of signs. We take up or give signs; we make signs. The sign would thus be a deferred presence. Whether it is a question of verbal or written signs, monetary signs, electoral delegates, or political representatives, the movement of signs defers the moment of encountering the thing itself, the moment at which we could lay hold of it, consume or expend it, touch it, see it, have a present intuition of it. What I am describing here is the structure of signs as classically determined, in order to define – through a commonplace characterization of its traits – signification as the differance of temporalizing. Now this classical determination presupposes that the sign (which defers presence) is conceivable only *on the basis of* the presence that it defers and *in view of* the deferred presence one intends to reappropriate. Following this classical semiology, the substitution of the sign for the thing itself is both *secondary* and *provisional*: it is second in order after an original and lost presence, a presence from which the sign would be derived. It is provisional with respect to this final and missing presence, in view of which the sign would serve as a movement of mediation.

In attempting to examine these secondary and provisional aspects of the substitute, we shall no doubt catch sight of something like a primordial differance. Yet we could no longer even call it primordial or final, inasmuch as the characteristics of origin, beginning, *telos*, *eschaton*, etc., have always denoted presence – *ousia*, *parousia*, etc. To question the secondary and provisional character of the sign, to oppose it to a "primordial" differance, would thus have the following consequences:

(1)   Differance can no longer be understood according to the concept of "sign," which has always been taken to mean the representation of a presence and has been constituted in a system (of thought or language) determined on the basis of and in view of presence.

(2)   In this way we question the authority of presence or its simple symmetrical contrary, absence or lack. We thus interrogate the limit that has always constrained us, that always constrains us – we who inhabit a language and a system of thought – to form the meaning of being in general as presence or absence, in the categories of being or beingness (*ousia*). It already appears that the kind of questioning we are thus led back to is, let us say, the Heideggerian kind, and that differance *seems* to lead us back to the ontic-ontological difference. But permit me to postpone this reference. I shall only note that between differance as temporalizing-temporalization (which we can no longer conceive within the horizon of the present) and what Heidegger says about temporalization in *Sein und Zeit* (namely, that as the transcendental horizon of the question of being it must be freed from the traditional and metaphysical domination by the present or the now) – between these two there is a close, if not exhaustive and irreducibly necessary, interconnection.

But first of all, let us remain with the semiological aspects of the problem to see how differance as temporalizing is conjoined with differance as spacing. Most of the semiological or linguistic research currently dominating the field of thought (whether due to the results of its own investigations or due to its role as a generally recognized regulative model) traces its genealogy, rightly or wrongly, to Saussure as its common founder. It was Saussure who first of all set forth the *arbitrariness of signs* and the *differential character* of signs as principles of general semiology and particularly of linguistics. And, as we know, these two themes – the arbitrary and the differential – are in his view inseparable. Arbitrariness can occur only because the system of signs is constituted by the differences between the terms, and not by their fullness. The elements of signification function not by virtue of the compact force of their cores but by the network of oppositions that distinguish them and relate them to one another. "Arbitrary and differential" says Saussure "are two correlative qualities."

As the condition for signification, this principle of difference affects the *whole sign*, that is, both the signified and the signifying aspects. The signified aspect is the concept, the ideal sense. The signifying aspect is what Saussure calls the material or physical (e.g., acoustical) "image." We do not here have to enter into all the problems these definitions pose. Let us only cite Saussure where it interests us:

> The conceptual side of value is made up solely of relations and differences with respect to the other terms of language, and the same can be said of its material side … . Everything that has been said up to this point boils down to this: in language there are only differences. Even more important: a difference generally implies positive terms between which the difference is set up; but in language there are only differences *without positive terms*. Whether we take the signified or the signifier, language has neither ideas nor sounds that existed before the linguistic system, but only conceptual and phonic differences that have issued from the system. The idea or phonic substance that a sign contains is of less importance than the other signs that surround it.[5]

The first consequence to be drawn from this is that the signified concept is never present in itself, in an adequate presence that would refer only to itself. Every concept is necessarily and essentially inscribed in a chain or a system, within which it refers to another and to other concepts, by the systematic play of differences. Such a play, then – differance – is no longer simply a concept, but the possibility of conceptuality, of the conceptual system and process in general. For the same reason, differance, which is not a concept, is not a mere word; that is, it is not what we represent to ourselves as the calm and present self-referential unity of a concept and sound [*phonie*]. We shall later discuss the consequences of this for the notion of a word.

The difference that Saussure speaks about, therefore, is neither itself a concept nor one word among others. We can say this *a fortiori* for differance. Thus we are brought to make the relation between the one and the other explicit.

Within a language, within the *system* of language, there are only differences. A taxonomic operation can accordingly undertake its systematic, statistical, and classificatory inventory. But, on the one hand, these differences *play a role* in language, in speech as well, and in the exchange between language and speech. On the other hand, these differences are themselves *effects*. They have not fallen from the sky ready made; they are no more inscribed in a *topos noētos* than they are prescribed in the wax of the brain. If the word "History" did not carry with it the theme of a final repression of differance, we could say that differences alone could be "historical" through and through and from the start.

What we note as *differance* will thus be the movement of play that "produces" (and not by something that is simply an activity) these differences, these effects of difference. This does not mean that the differance which produces differences is before them in a simple and in itself unmodified and indifferent present. Differance is the nonfull, non-simple "origin"; it is the structured and differing origin of differences.

Since language (which Saussure says is a classification) has not fallen from the sky, it is clear that the differences have been produced; they are the effects produced, but effects that do not have as their cause a subject or substance, a thing in general, or a being that is somewhere present and itself escapes the play of difference. If such a presence were implied (quite classically) in the general concept of cause, we would therefore have to talk about an effect without a cause, something that would very quickly lead to no longer talking about effects. I have tried to indicate a way out of the closure imposed by this system, namely, by means of the "trace." No more an effect than a cause, the "trace" cannot of itself, taken outside its context, suffice to bring about the required transgression.

As there is no presence before the semiological difference or outside it, we can extend what Saussure writes about language to signs in general: "Language is necessary in order for speech to be intelligible and to produce all of its effects; but the latter is necessary in order for language to be established; historically, the fact of speech always comes first."[6]

Retaining at least the schema, if not the content, of the demand formulated by Saussure, we shall designate by the term *differance* the movement by which language, or any code, any system of reference in general, becomes "historically" constituted as a fabric of differences. Here, the terms "constituted," "produced," "created," "movement," "historically," etc., with all they imply, are not to be understood only in terms of the language of metaphysics, from which they are taken. It would have to be shown why the concepts of production, like those of constitution and history, remain accessories in this respect to what is here being questioned; this, however, would draw us too far away today, toward the theory of the representation of the "circle" in which we seem to be enclosed. I only use these terms here, like many other concepts, out of strategic convenience and in order to prepare the deconstruction of the system they form at the point which is now most decisive. In any event, we will have understood, by virtue of the very circle we appear to be caught up in, that differance, as it is written here, is no more static than genetic, no more structural than historical. Nor is it any less so. And it is completely to miss the point of this orthographical impropriety to want to object to it on the basis of the oldest of metaphysical oppositions – for example, by opposing some generative point of view to a structuralist-taxonomic point of view, or conversely. These oppositions do not pertain in the least to differance; and this, no doubt, is what makes thinking about it difficult and uncomfortable.

If we now consider the chain to which "differance" gets subjected, according to the context, to a certain number of nonsynonymic substitutions, one will ask why we resorted to such concepts as "reserve," "protowriting," "prototrace," "spacing," indeed to "supplement" or "*pharmakon*," and, before long, to "hymen," etc.[7]

Let us begin again. Differance is what makes the movement of signification possible only if each element that is said to be "present," appearing on the stage of presence, is related to something other than itself but retains the mark of a past element and already lets itself be hollowed out by the mark of its relation to a future element. This trace relates no less to what is called the future than to what is called the past, and it constitutes what is called the present by this very relation to what it is not, to what it absolutely is not; that is, not even to a past or future considered as a modified present. In order for it to be, an interval must separate it from what it is not; but the interval that constitutes it in the present must also, and by the same token, divide the present in itself, thus dividing, along with the present, everything that can be conceived on its basis, that is, every being – in particular, for our metaphysical language, the substance or subject. Constituting itself, dynamically dividing itself, this interval is what could be called *spacing*; time's becoming-spatial or space's becoming-temporal (*temporalizing*). And it is this constitution of the present as a "primordial" and irreducibly nonsimple, and, therefore, in the strict sense nonprimordial, synthesis of traces, retentions, and protentions (to reproduce here, analogically and provisionally, a phenomenological and transcendental language that will presently be revealed as inadequate) that I propose to call protowriting, prototrace, or difference. The latter (is) (both) spacing (and) temporalizing.[8]

Given this (active) movement of the (production of) difference without origin, could we not, quite simply and without any neographism, call it *differentiation*? Among other confusions, such a word would suggest some organic unity, some primordial and homogeneous unity, that would eventually come to be divided up and take on difference as an event. Above all, formed on the verb "to differentiate," this word would annul the economic signification of detour, temporalizing delay, "deferring." I owe a remark in passing to a recent reading of one of Koyré's texts entitled "Hegel at Jena."[9] In that text, Koyré cites long passages from the Jena *Logic* in German and gives his own translation. On two occasions in Hegel's text he encounters the expression "*differente Beziehung*." This word (*different*), whose root is Latin, is extremely rare in German and also, I believe, in Hegel, who instead uses *verschieden* or *ungleich*, calling difference *Unterschied* and qualitative variety *Verschiedenheit*. In the Jena *Logic*, he uses the word *different* precisely at the point where he deals with time and the present. Before coming to Koyré's valuable remark, here are some passages from Hegel, as rendered by Koyré:

The infinite, in this simplicity is – as a moment opposed to the self-identical – the negative. In its moments, while the infinite presents the totality to (itself) and in itself, (it is) excluding in general, the point or limit; but in this, its own (action of) negating, it relates itself immediately to the other and negates itself. The limit or moment of the present (*der Gegenwart*), the absolute "this" of time or the now, is an absolutely negative simplicity absolutely excluding all multiplicity from itself, and by this very fact is absolutely determined; it is not an extended whole or *quantum* within itself (and) which would in itself also have an undetermined aspect or qualitative variety, which of itself would be related, indifferently (*gleichguldig*) or externally to another but on the contrary, this is an absolutely different relation of the simple.[10]

And Koyré specifies in a striking note: "Different relation *differente Beziehung*. We could say: differentiating relation." And on the following page, from another text of Hegel, we can read: "*Diese Beziehung ist Gegenwart, als eine differente Beziehung*" (This relation is [the] present, as a different relation). There is another note by Koyré: "The term '*different*' is taken here in an active sense."

Writing "differing" or "differance" (with an *a*) would have had the utility of making it possible to translate Hegel on precisely this point with no further qualifications – and it is a quite decisive point in his text. The translation would be, as it always should be, the transformation of one language by another. Naturally, I maintain that the word "differance" can be used in other ways, too; first of all, because it denotes not only the activity of primordial difference but also the temporalizing detour of deferring. It has, however, an even more important usage. Despite the very profound affinities that differance thus written has with Hegelian speech (as it should be read), it can, at a certain point, not exactly break with it, but rather work a sort of displacement with regard to it. A definite rupture with Hegelian language would make no sense, nor would it be at all likely; but this displacement is both infinitesimal and radical. I have tried to indicate the extent of this displacement elsewhere; it would be difficult to talk about it with any brevity at this point.

Differences are thus "produced" – differed – by differance. But *what* differs, or *who* differs? In other words, *what is* differance? With this question we attain another stage and another source of the problem.

What differs? Who differs? What is differance?

If we answered these questions even before examining them as questions, even before going back over them and questioning their form (even what seems to be most natural and necessary about them), we would fall below the level we have now reached. For if we accepted the form of the question in its own sense and syntax ("What?," "What is?," "Who is?"), we would have to admit that differance is derived, supervenient, controlled, and ordered from the starting point of a being-present, one capable of being something, a force, a state, or power in the world, to which we could give all kinds of names: a *what*, or being-present as a *subject*, a *who*. In the latter case, notably, we would implicitly admit that the being-present (for example, as a self-present being or consciousness) would eventually result in differing: in delaying or in diverting the fulfillment of a "need" or "desire," or in differing from itself. But in none of these cases would such a being-present be "constituted" by this differance.

Now if we once again refer to the semiological difference, what was it that Saussure in particular reminded us of? That "language [which consists only of differences] is not a function of the speaking subject." This implies that the subject (self-identical or even conscious of self-identity, self-conscious) is inscribed in the language, that he is a "function" of the language. He becomes a *speaking* subject only by conforming his speech – even in the aforesaid "creation," even in the aforesaid "transgression" – to the system of linguistic prescriptions taken as the system of differences, or at least to the general law of differance, by conforming to that law of language which Saussure calls "language without speech." "Language is necessary for the spoken word to be intelligible and so that it can produce all of its effects."[11]

If, by hypothesis, we maintain the strict opposition between speech and language, then differance will be not only the play of differences within the language but the relation of speech to language, the detour by which I must also pass in order to speak, the silent token I must give, which holds just as well for linguistics in the strict sense as it does for general semiology; it dictates all the relations between usage and the formal schema, between the message and the particular code, etc. Elsewhere I have tried to suggest that this differance within language, and in the relation between speech and language, forbids the essential dissociation between speech and writing that Saussure, in keeping with tradition, wanted to draw at another level of his presentation. The use of language or the employment of any code which implies a play of forms – with no determined or invariable substratum – also presupposes a retention and protention of differences, a spacing and temporalizing, a play of traces. This play must be a sort of inscription prior to writing, a protowriting without a present origin, without an *arche*. From this comes the systematic crossing-out of the *arche* and the transformation of general semiology into a grammatology, the latter performing a critical work upon everything within semiology – right down to its matrical concept of signs – that retains any metaphysical presuppositions incompatible with the theme of differance.

We might be tempted by an objection: to be sure, the subject becomes a *speaking* subject only by dealing with the system of linguistic differences; or again, he becomes a *signifying* subject (generally by speech or other signs) only by entering into the system of differences. In this sense, certainly, the speaking or signifying subject would not be self-present, insofar as he speaks or signifies, except for the play of linguistic or semiological differance. But can we not conceive of a presence and self-presence of the subject before speech or its signs, a subject's self-presence in a silent and intuitive consciousness?

Such a question therefore supposes that prior to signs and outside them, and excluding every trace and differance, something such as consciousness is possible. It supposes, moreover, that, even before the distribution of its signs in space and in the world, consciousness can gather itself up in its own presence. What then is consciousness? What does "consciousness" mean? Most often in the very form of "meaning" ["*vouloir dire*"], consciousness in all its modifications is conceivable only as self-presence, a self-perception of presence. And what holds for consciousness also holds here for what is called subjective existence in general. Just as the category of subject is not and never has been conceivable without reference to presence as *hypokeimenon* or *ousia*, etc., so the subject as consciousness has never been able to be evinced otherwise than as self-presence. The privilege accorded to consciousness thus means a privilege accorded to the present; and even if the transcendental temporality of consciousness is described in depth, as Husserl described it, the power of synthesis and of the incessant gathering-up of traces is always accorded to the "living present."

This privilege is the ether of metaphysics, the very element of our thought insofar as it is caught up in the language of metaphysics. We can only de-limit such a closure today by evoking this import of presence, which Heidegger has shown to be the onto-theological determination of being. Therefore, in evoking this import of presence, by an examination which would have to be of a quite peculiar nature, we question the absolute privilege of this form or epoch of presence in general, that is, consciousness as meaning [*vouloir dire*] in self-presence.

We thus come to posit presence – and, in particular, consciousness, the being-next-to-itself consciousness – no longer as the absolutely matrical form of being but as a "determination" and an "effect." Presence is a determination and effect within a system which is no longer that of presence but that of differance; it no more allows the opposition between activity and passivity than that between cause and effect or in-determination and determination, etc. This system is of such a kind that even to designate consciousness as an effect or determination – for strategic reasons, reasons that can be more or less clearly considered and systematically ascertained – is to continue to operate according to the vocabulary of that very thing to be delimited.

Before being so radically and expressly Heideggerian, this was also Nietzsche's and Freud's move, both of whom, as we know, and often in a very similar way, questioned the self-assured certitude of consciousness. And is it not remarkable that both of them did this by starting out with the theme of differance?

This theme appears almost literally in their work, at the most crucial places. I shall not expand on this here; I shall only recall that for Nietzsche "the important main activity is unconscious" and that consciousness is the effect of forces whose essence, ways, and modalities are not peculiar to it. Now force itself is never present; it is only a play of differences and quantities. There would be no force in general without the difference between forces; and here the difference in quantity counts more than the content of quantity, more than the absolute magnitude itself.

> Quantity itself therefore is not separable from the difference in quantity. The difference in quantity is the essence of force, the relation of force with force. To fancy two equal forces, even if we grant them opposing directions, is an approximate and crude illusion, a statistical dream in which life is immersed, but which chemistry dispels.[12]

Is not the whole thought of Nietzsche a critique of philosophy as active indifference to difference, as a system of reduction or adiaphoristic repression? Following the same logic – logic itself – this does not exclude the fact that philosophy lives *in* and *from* differance, that it thereby blinds itself to the *same*, which is not the identical. The same is precisely differance (with an *a*), as the diverted and equivocal passage from one difference to another, from one term of the opposition to the other. We could thus take up all the coupled oppositions on which philosophy is constructed, and from which our language lives, not in order to see opposition vanish but to see the emergence of a necessity such that one of the terms appears as the differance of the other, the other as "differed" within the systematic ordering of the same (e.g., the intelligible as differing from the sensible, as sensible differed; the concept as differed-differing intuition, life as differing-differed matter; mind as differed-differing life; culture as differed-differing nature; and all the terms designating what is other than *physis* – *technē*, *nomos*, society, freedom, history, spirit, etc. – as *physis* differed or *physis* differing: *physis in différance*). It is out of the unfolding of this "same" as differance that the sameness of difference and of repetition is presented in the eternal return.

In Nietzsche, these are so many themes that can be related with the kind of symptomatology that always serves to diagnose the evasions and ruses of anything disguised in its difference. Or again, these terms can be related with the entire thematics of active interpretation, which substitutes an incessant deciphering for the disclosure of truth as a presentation of the thing itself in its presence, etc. What results is a cipher without truth, or at least a system of ciphers that is not dominated by truth value, which only then becomes a function that is understood, inscribed, and circumscribed.

We shall therefore call differance this "active" (in movement) discord of the different forces and of the differences between forces which Nietzsche opposes to the entire system of metaphysical grammar, wherever that system controls culture, philosophy, and science.

It is historically significant that this diaphoristics, understood as an energetics or an economy of forces, set up to question the primacy of presence qua consciousness, is also the major theme of Freud's thought; in his work we find another diaphoristics, both in the form of a theory of ciphers or traces and an energetics. The questioning of the authority of consciousness is first and always differential.

The two apparently different meanings of differance are tied together in Freudian theory: differing [*le différer*] as discernibility, distinction, deviation, diastem, *spacing*; and deferring [*le différer*] as detour, delay, relay, reserve, *temporalizing*. I shall recall only that:

(1) The concept of trace (*Spur*), of facilitation (*Bahnung*), of forces of facilitation are, as early as the composition of the *Entwurf*, inseparable from the concept of difference. The origin of memory and of the psyche as a memory in general (conscious or unconscious) can only be described by taking into account the difference between the facilitation thresholds, as Freud says explicitly. There is no facilitation [*Bahnung*] without difference and no difference without a trace.

(2) All the differences involved in the production of unconscious traces and in the process of inscription (*Niederschrift*) can also be interpreted as moments of differance, in the sense of "placing on reserve." Following a schema that continually guides Freud's thinking, the movement of the trace is described as an effort of life to protect itself by *deferring* the dangerous investment, by constituting a reserve (*Vorrat*). And all the conceptual oppositions that furrow Freudian thought relate each concept to the other like movements of a detour, within the economy of differance. The one is only the other deferred, the one differing from the other. The one is the other in differance, the one is the differance from the other. Every apparently rigorous and irreducible opposition (for example that between the secondary and primary) is thus said to be, at one time or another, a "theoretical fiction." In this way again, for example (but such an example covers everything or communicates with everything), the difference between the pleasure principle and the reality principle is only difference as detour (*Aufschieben, Aufschub*). In *Beyond the Pleasure Principle*, Freud writes

> Under the influence of the ego's instincts of self-preservation, the pleasure principle is replaced by the reality principle. This latter principle does not abandon the intention of ultimately obtaining pleasure, but it nevertheless demands and carries into effect the postponement of satisfaction, the abandonment of a number of possibilities of gaining satisfaction and the temporary toleration of unpleasure as a step on the long indirect road (*Aufschub*) to pleasure.[13]

Here we touch on the point of greatest obscurity, on the very enigma of differance, on how the concept we have of it is divided by a strange separation. We must not hasten to make a decision too quickly. How can we conceive of differance as a systematic detour which, within the element of the same, always aims at either finding again the pleasure or the presence that had been deferred by (conscious or unconscious) calculation, and, *at the same time*, how can we, on the other hand, conceive of differance as the relation to an impossible presence as an expenditure without reserve, as an irreparable loss of presence, an irreversible wearing-down of energy, or indeed as a death instinct and a relation to the absolutely other that apparently breaks up any economy? It is evident – it is evidence itself – that system and nonsystem, the same and the absolutely other, etc., cannot be conceived *together*.

If differance is this inconceivable factor, must we not perhaps hasten to make it evident, to bring it into the philosophical element of evidence, and thus quickly dissipate its mirage character and illogicality, dissipate it with the infallibility of the calculus we know well – since we have recognized its place, necessity, and function within the structure of differance? What would be accounted for philosophically here has already been taken into account in the system of differance as it is here being calculated. I have tried elsewhere, in a reading of Bataille,[14] to indicate what might be the establishment of a rigorous, and in a new sense "scientific," *relating* of a "restricted economy" – one having nothing to do with an unreserved expenditure, with death, with being exposed to nonsense, etc. – to a "general economy" or system that, so to speak, *takes account of* what is unreserved. It is a relation between a differance that is accounted for and a differance that fails to be accounted for, where the establishment of a pure presence, without loss, is one with the occurrence of absolute loss, with death. By establishing this relation between a restricted and a general system, we shift and recommence the very project of philosophy under the privileged heading of Hegelianism.

The economic character of differance in no way implies that the deferred presence can always be recovered, that it simply amounts to an investment that only temporarily and without loss delays the presentation of presence, that is, the perception of gain or the gain of perception. Contrary to the metaphysical, dialectical, and "Hegelian" interpretation of the economic movement of differance, we must admit a game where whoever loses wins and where one wins and loses each time. If the diverted presentation continues to be somehow definitively and irreducibly withheld, this is not because a particular present remains hidden or absent, but because differance holds us in a relation with what exceeds (though we necessarily fail to recognize this) the alternative of presence or absence. A certain alterity – Freud gives it a metaphysical name, the unconscious – is definitively taken away from every process of presentation in which we would demand for it to be shown forth in person. In this context and under this heading, the unconscious is not, as we know, a hidden, virtual, and potential self-presence. It is differed – which no doubt means that it is woven out of differences, but also that it sends out, that it delegates, representatives or proxies; but there is no chance that the mandating subject "exists" somewhere, that it is present or is "itself," and still less chance that it will become conscious. In this sense, contrary to the terms of an old debate, strongly symptomatic of the metaphysical investments it has always assumed, the "unconscious" can no more be classed as a "thing" than as anything else; it is no more of a thing than an implicit or masked consciousness. This radical alterity, removed from every possible mode of presence, is characterized by irreducible aftereffects, by delayed effects. In order to describe them, in order to read the traces of the "unconscious" traces (there are no "conscious" traces), the language of presence or absence, the metaphysical speech of phenomenology, is in principle inadequate.

The structure of delay (*retardement: Nachträglichkeit*) that Freud talks about indeed prohibits our taking temporalization (temporalizing) to be a simple dialectical complication of the present; rather, this is the style of transcendental phenomenology. It describes the living present as a primordial and incessant synthesis that is constantly led back upon itself, back upon its assembled and assembling self, by retentional traces and protentional openings. With the alterity of the "unconscious," we have to deal not with the horizons of modified presents – past or future – but with a "past" that has never been nor will ever be present, whose "future" will never be produced or reproduced in the form of presence. The concept of trace is therefore incommensurate with that of retention, that of the becoming-past of what had been present. The trace cannot be conceived – nor, therefore, can differance – on the basis of either the present or the presence of the present.

A past that has never been present: with this formula Emmanuel Levinas designates (in ways that are, to be sure, not those of psychoanalysis) the trace and the enigma of absolute alterity, that is, the Other [*autrui*]. At least within these limits, and from this point of view, the thought of differance implies the whole critique of classical ontology undertaken by Levinas. And the concept of trace, like that of differance, forms – across these different traces and through these differences between traces, as understood by Nietzsche, Freud, and Levinas (these "authors' names" serve only as indications) – the network that sums up and permeates our "epoch" as the de-limitation of ontology (of presence).

The ontology of presence is the ontology of beings and beingness. Everywhere, the dominance of beings is solicited by differance – in the sense that *sollicitare* means, in old Latin, to shake all over, to make the whole tremble. What is questioned by the thought of differance, therefore, is the determination of being in presence, or in beingness. Such a question could not arise and be understood without the difference between Being and beings opening up somewhere. The first consequence of this is that differance is not. It is not a being-present, however excellent, unique, principal, or transcendent one makes it. It commands nothing, rules over nothing, and nowhere does it exercise any authority. It is not marked by a capital letter. Not only is there no realm of differance, but differance is even the subversion of every realm. This is obviously what makes it threatening and necessarily dreaded by everything in us that desires a realm, the past or future presence of a realm. And it is always in the name of a realm that, believing one sees it ascend to the capital letter, one can reproach it for wanting to rule.

Does this mean, then, that differance finds its place within the spread of the onti-contological difference, as it is conceived, as the "epoch" conceives itself within it, and particularly "across" the Heideggerian meditation, which cannot be gotten around?

There is no simple answer to such a question.

In one particular respect, differance is, to be sure, but the historical and epochal *deployment* of Being or of the ontological difference. The *a* of differance marks the *movement* of this deployment.

And yet, is not the thought that conceives the *meaning* or *truth* of Being, the determination of differance as ontic-ontological difference – difference conceived within the horizon of the question of *Being* – still an intrametaphysical effect of differance? Perhaps the deployment of differance is not only the truth or the epochality of Being. Perhaps we must try to think this *unheard-of* thought, this silent tracing, namely, that the history of Being (the thought of which is committed to the Greco-Western logos), as it is itself produced across the ontological difference, is only one epoch of the *diapherein*. Then we could no longer even call it an "epoch," for the concept of epochality belongs within history understood as the history of Being. Being has always made "sense," has always been conceived or spoken of as such, only by dissimulating itself in beings; thus, in a particular and very strange way, differance (is) "older" than the ontological difference or the truth of Being. In this age it can be called the play of traces. It is a trace that no longer belongs to the horizon of Being but one whose sense of Being is borne and bound by this play; it is a play of traces or differance that has no meaning and is not, a play that does not belong. There is no support to be found and no depth to be had for this bottomless chessboard where being is set in play.

It is perhaps in this way that the Heraclitean play of the *hen diapheron heautoi*, of the one differing from itself, of what is in difference with itself, already becomes lost as a trace in determining the *diapherein* as ontological difference.

To think through the ontological difference doubtless remains a difficult task, a task whose statement has remained nearly inaudible. And to prepare ourselves for venturing beyond our own logos, that is, for a differance so violent that it refuses to be stopped and examined as the epochality of Being and ontological difference, is neither to give up this passage through the truth of Being, nor is it in any way to "criticize," "contest," or fail to recognize the incessant necessity for it. On the contrary, we must stay within the difficulty of this passage; we must repeat this passage in a rigorous reading of metaphysics, wherever metaphysics serves as the norm of Western speech, and not only in the texts of "the history of philosophy." Here we must allow the trace of whatever goes beyond the truth of Being to appear/disappear in its fully rigorous way. It is a trace of something that can never present itself; it is itself a trace that can never be presented, that is, can never appear and manifest itself as such in its phenomenon. It is a trace that lies beyond what profoundly ties fundamental ontology to phenomenology. Like differance, the trace is never presented as such. In presenting itself it becomes effaced; in being sounded it dies away, like the writing of the *a*, inscribing its pyramid in differance.

We can always reveal the precursive and secretive traces of this movement in metaphysical speech, especially in the contemporary talk about the closure of ontology, i.e., through the various attempts we have looked at (Nietzsche, Freud, Levinas) – and particularly in Heidegger's work.

The latter provokes us to question the essence of the present, the presence of the present.

What is the present? What is it to conceive the present in its presence?

Let us consider, for example, the 1946 text entitled "Der Spruch des Anaximander." Heidegger there recalls that the forgetting of Being forgets about the difference between Being and beings:

> But the point of Being (*die Sache des Seins*) is to be the Being *of* beings. The linguistic form of this enigmatic and multivalent genitive designates a genesis (*Genesis*), a provenance (*Herkunft*) of the *present* from presence (*des Anwesenden aus dem Anwesen*). But with the unfolding of these two, the essence (*Wesen*) of this provenance remains hidden (*verborgen*). Not only is the essence of this provenance not thought out, but neither is the simple relation between presence and present (*Anwesen und Anwesenden*).
>
> Since the dawn, it seems that presence and being-present are each separately something. Imperceptibly, presence becomes itself a present.... The essence of presence (*Das Wesen des Anwesens*), and thus the difference between presence and present, is forgotten. *The forgetting of Being is the forgetting of the difference between Being and beings.*[15]

In recalling the difference between Being and beings (the ontological difference) as the difference between presence and present, Heidegger puts forward a proposition, indeed, a group of propositions; it is not our intention here to idly or hastily "criticize" them but rather to convey them with all their provocative force.

Let us then proceed slowly. What Heidegger wants to point out is that the difference between Being and beings, forgotten by metaphysics, has disappeared without leaving a trace. The very trace of difference has sunk from sight. If we admit that differance (is) (itself) something other than presence and absence, if it *traces*, then we are dealing with the forgetting of the difference (between Being and beings), and we now have to talk about a disappearance of the trace's trace. This is certainly what this passage from "Der Spruch des Anaximander" seems to imply:

> The forgetting of Being is a part of the very essence of Being, and is concealed by it. The forgetting belongs so essentially to the destination of Being that the dawn of this destination begins precisely as an unconcealment of the *present* in its *presence*. This means: the history of Being begins by the forgetting of Being, in that Being retains its essence, its difference from beings. Difference is wanting; it remains forgotten. Only what is differentiated – the present and presence (*das Anwesende und das Anwesen*) – becomes uncovered, but not *insofar as* it is differentiated. On the contrary, the matinal trace (*die frühe Spur*) of difference effaces itself from the moment that presence appears as a being-present (*das Anwesen und ein Anwesendes erscheint*) and finds its provenance in a supreme (being)-present (*in einem höchsten Anwesenden*).[16]

The trace is not a presence but is rather the simulacrum of a presence that dislocates, displaces, and refers beyond itself. The trace has, properly speaking, no place, for effacement belongs to the very structure of the trace. Effacement must always be able to overtake the trace; otherwise it would not be a trace but an indestructible and monumental substance. In addition, and from the start, effacement constitutes it as a trace – effacement establishes the trace in a change of place and makes it disappear in its appearing, makes it issue forth from itself in its very position. The effacing of this early trace (*die frühe Spur*) of difference is therefore "the same" as its tracing within the text of metaphysics. This metaphysical text must have retained a mark of what it lost or put in reserve, set aside. In the language of metaphysics the paradox of such a structure is the inversion of the metaphysical concept which produces the following effect: the present becomes the sign of signs, the trace of traces. It is no longer what every reference refers to in the last instance; it becomes a function in a generalized referential structure. It is a trace, and a trace of the effacement of a trace.

In this way the metaphysical text is *understood*; it is still readable, and remains to be read. It proposes both the monument and the mirage of the trace, the trace as simultaneously traced and effaced, simultaneously alive and dead, alive as always to simulate even life in its preserved inscription; it is a pyramid.

Thus we think through, without contradiction, or at least without granting any pertinence to such contradiction, what is perceptible and imperceptible about the trace. The "matinal trace" of difference is lost in an irretrievable invisibility, and yet even its loss is covered, preserved, regarded, and retarded. This happens in a text, in the form of presence.

Having spoken about the effacement of the matinal trace, Heidegger can thus, in this contradiction without contradiction, consign or countersign the sealing of the trace. We read on a little further:

The difference between Being and beings, however, can in turn be experienced as something forgotten only if it is already discovered with the presence of the present (*mit dem
Anwesen des Anwesenden*) and if it is thus sealed in a trace (*so eine Spur geprägt hat*) that
remains preserved (*gewahrt bleibt*) in the language which Being appropriates.[17]

Further on still, while meditating upon Anaximander's τό χρεών, translated as *Brauch*
(sustaining use), Heidegger writes the following:

> Dispensing accord and deference (*Fug und Ruch verfügend*), our sustaining use frees the
> present (*das Anwesende*) in its sojourn and sets it free every time for its sojourn. But by the
> same token the present is equally seen to be exposed to the constant danger of hardening in
> the insistence (*in das blosse Beharren verhärtet*) out of its sojourning duration. In this way
> sustaining use (*Brauch*) remains itself and at the same time an abandonment (*Aushändigung*:
> handing-over) of presence (*des Anwesens*) *in den Un-fug*, to discord (disjointedness).
> Sustaining use joins together the dis- (*Der Brauch fügt das Un-*).[18]

And it is at the point where Heidegger determines *sustaining use* as *trace* that the question
must be asked: can we, and how far can we, think of this trace and the *dis-* of differance
as *Wesen des Seins*? Doesn't the *dis* of differance refer us beyond the history of Being,
beyond our language as well, and beyond everything that can be named by it? Doesn't
it call for – in the language of being – the necessarily violent transformation of this
language by an entirely different language?

Let us be more precise here. In order to dislodge the "trace" from its cover (and whoever believes that one tracks down some *thing*; one tracks down tracks), let us continue
reading this passage:

> The translation of τό χρεών "sustaining use" (*Brauch*) does not derive from cogitations of
> an etymologico-lexical nature. The choice of the word "sustaining use" derives from an
> antecedent translation (*Übersetzen*) of the thought that attempts to conceive difference in
> the deployment of Being (*im Wesen des Seins*) toward the historical beginning of the forget-
> ting of Being. The word "sustaining use" is dictated to thought in the apprehension
> (*Erfahrung*) of the forgetting of Being. τό χρεών properly names a trace (*Spur*) of what
> remains to be conceived in the word "sustaining use," a trace that quickly disappears
> (*alsbald verschwindet*) into the history of Being, in its world-historical unfolding as Western
> metaphysics.[19]

How do we conceive of the outside of a text? How, for example, do we conceive of what
stands opposed to the text of Western metaphysics? To be sure, the "trace that quickly
disappears into the history of Being, ... as Western metaphysics," escapes all the
determinations, all the names it might receive in the metaphysical text. The trace is
sheltered and thus dissimulated in these names; it does not appear in the text as the
trace "itself." But this is because the trace itself could never itself appear as such.
Heidegger also says that difference can never appear *as such*: "Lichtung des
Unterschiedes kann deshalb auch nicht bedeuten, dass der Unterschied als der
Unterschied erscheint." There is no essence of differance; not only can it not allow
itself to be taken up into the *as such* of its name or its appearing, but it threatens the
authority of the *as such* in general, the thing's presence in its essence. That there is no
essence of differance at this point also implies that there is neither Being nor truth to
the play of writing, *insofar as* it involves differance.

For us, differance remains a metaphysical name; and all the names that it receives from our language are still, so far as they are names, metaphysical. This is particularly so when they speak of determining differance as the difference between presence and present (*Anwesen/Anwesend*), but already and especially so when, in the most general way, they speak of determining differance as the difference between Being and beings. "Older" than Being itself, our language has no name for such a differance. But we "already know" that if it is unnameable, this is not simply provisional; it is not because our language has still not found or received this *name*, or because we would have to look for it in another language, outside the finite system of our language. It is because there is no *name* for this, not even essence or Being – not even the name "differance," which is not a name, which is not a pure nominal unity, and continually breaks up in a chain of different substitutions.

"There is no name for this": we read this as a truism. What is unnameable here is not some ineffable being that cannot be approached by a name; like God, for example. What is unnameable is the play that brings about the nominal effects, the relatively unitary or atomic structures we call names, or chains of substitutions for names. In these, for example, the nominal effect of "differance" is itself involved, carried off, and reinscribed, just as the false beginning or end of a game is still part of the game, a function of the system.

What we do know, what we could know if it were simply a question of knowing, is that there never has been and never will be a unique word, a master name. This is why thinking about the letter *a* of differance is not the primary prescription, nor is it the prophetic announcement of some imminent and still unheard-of designation. There is nothing kerygmatic about this "word" so long as we can perceive its reduction to a lower-case letter.

There will be no unique name, not even the name of Being. It must be conceived without *nostalgia*; that is, it must be conceived outside the myth of the purely maternal or paternal language belonging to the lost fatherland of thought. On the contrary, we must *affirm* it – in the sense that Nietzsche brings affirmation into play – with a certain laughter and with a certain dance.

After this laughter and dance, after this affirmation that is foreign to any dialectic, the question arises as to the other side of nostalgia, which I will call Heideggerian *hope*. I am not unaware that this term may be somewhat shocking. I venture it all the same, without excluding any of its implications, and shall relate it to what seems to me to be retained of metaphysics in "Der Spruch des Anaximander," namely, the quest for the proper word and the unique name. In talking about the "first word of Being" (*das frühe Wort des Seins*: τὸ χρεών), Heidegger writes,

> The relation to the present, unfolding its order in the very essence of *presence*, is unique (*ist eine einzige*). It is pre-eminently incomparable to any other relation; it belongs to the uniqueness of Being itself (*Sie gehört zur Einzigkeit des Seins selbst*). Thus, in order to name what is deployed in Being (*das Wesende des Seins*), language will have to find a single word, the unique word (*ein einziges, das einzige Wort*). There we see how hazardous is every word of thought (every thoughtful word: *denkende Wort*) that addresses itself to Being (*das dem Sein zugesprochen wird*). What is hazarded here, however, is not something impossible, because Being speaks through every language; everywhere and always.[20]

Such is the question: the marriage between speech and Being in the unique word, in the finally proper name. Such is the question that enters into the affirmation put into play

by differance. The question bears (upon) each of the words in this sentence: "Being /
speaks / through every language; / everywhere and always /."

Notes

1   This essay appeared originally in the *Bulletin de la Société française de philosophie*, LXII, No. 3
    (July–September, 1968), pp. 73–101. Derrida's remarks were delivered as a lecture at a meeting of
    the Société at the Sorbonne, in the Amphithéâtre Michelet, on January 27, 1968, with Jean Wahl
    presiding. Professor Wahl's introductory and closing remarks have not been translated. The essay
    was reprinted in *Théorie d'ensemble*, a collection of essays by Derrida and others, published by
    Editions Seuil in 1968. It is reproduced here by permission of Editions Seuil.

2   [The reader should bear in mind that "differance," or difference with an *a*, incorporates two
    significations: "to differ" and "to defer." – Trans.]

3   [For the term "facilitation" (*frayage*) in Freud, cf. "Project for a Scientific Psychology" in *The
    Complete Psychological Works of Sigmund Freud*, 24 vols (New York and London: Macmillan, 1964)
    I, p. 300, n. 4 by the translator, James Strachey: "The word 'facilitation' as a rendering of the
    German '*Bahnung*' seems to have been introduced by Sherrington a few years after the *Project* was
    written. The German word, however, was already in use." The sense that Derrida draws upon
    here is stronger in the French or German, that is, the opening-up or clearing-out of a pathway. In
    the context of the "Project for a Scientific Psychology I," facilitation denotes the conduction
    capability that results from a difference in resistance levels in the memory and perception circuits
    of the nervous system. Thus, lowering the resistance threshold of a contact barrier serves to "open
    up" a nerve pathway and "facilitates" the excitatory process for the circuit. Cf. also J. Derrida,
    L'Ecriture et la différence, ch. VII, "Freud et la scène de l'écriture" (Paris: Seuil, 1967), esp.
    pp. 29–305. – Trans.]

4   [On "pyramid" and "tomb" see J. Derrida, "Le Puits et la pyramide," in *Hegel et la pensée moderne*
    (Paris: Presses Universitaires de France, 1970), esp. pp. 44–5. – Trans.]

5   Ferdinand de Saussure, *Cours de linguistique générale*, ed. C. Bally and A. Sechehaye (Paris: Payot,
    1916); English translation by Wade Baskin, *Course in General Linguistics* (New York: Philosophical
    Library, 1959), pp. 117–18, 120.

6   Saussure, *Course in General Linguistics*, p. 18.

7   [On "supplement" see *Speech and Phenomena*, ch. 7, pp. 88–104. Cf. also Derrida, *De la gramma-
    tologie* (Paris: Editions de Minuit, 1967). On "*pharmakon*" see Derrida, "La Pharmacie de Platon,"
    Tel Quel, No. 32 (Winter 1967), pp. 17–59; No. 33 (Spring 1968), pp. 4–48. On "hymen" see
    Derrida, "La Double séance," *Tel Quel*, No. 41 (Spring 1970), pp. 3–43; No. 42 (Summer 1970),
    pp. 3–45. "La Pharmacie de Platon" and "La Double séance" have been reprinted in a recent text
    of Derrida, *La Dissémination* (Paris: Editions du Seuil, 1972). – Trans.]

8   [Derrida often brackets or "crosses out" certain key terms taken from metaphysics and logic, and
    in doing this, he follows Heidegger's usage in *Zur Seinsfrage*. The terms in question no longer have
    their full meaning, they no longer have the status of a purely signified content of expression – no
    longer, that is, after the deconstruction of metaphysics. Generated out of the play of differance,
    they still retain a vestigial trace of sense, however, a trace that cannot simply be gotten around
    (*incontournable*). An extensive discussion of all this is to be found in *De la grammatologie*,
    pp. 31–40. – Trans.]

9   Alexandre Koyré, "Hegel à Iena," *Revue d'histoire et de philosophie religieuse*, XIV (1934), pp. 420–58;
    reprinted in Koyré, *Etudes d'histoire de la pensée philosophique* (Paris: Armand Colin, 1961),
    pp. 135–73.

10 Koyré, *Etudes d'histoire*, pp. 153–4. [The quotation from Hegel (my translation) comes from
    "Jenenser Logik, Metaphysik, und Naturphilosophie," *Sämtliche Werke* (Leipzig: F. Meiner,
    1925), XVIII, p. 202. Koyré reproduces the original German text on pp. 153–4, n. 2. – Trans.]

11 Saussure, *Course in General Linguistics*, p. 37.

12 G. Deleuze, *Nietzsche et la philosophie* (Paris: Presses Universitaires de France, 1970), p. 49.

13 Freud, *Complete Psychological Works*, XVIII, p. 10.
14 Derrida, *L'Ecriture et la différence*, pp. 369–407.
15 Martin Heidegger, *Holzwege* (Frankfurt: V. Klostermann, 1957), pp. 335–6. [All translations of quotations from *Holzwege* are mine. – Trans.]
16 Ibid., p. 336.
17 Ibid.
18 Ibid., pp. 339–40.
19 Ibid., p. 340.
20 Ibid., pp. 337–8.

CHAPTER 5

That Dangerous Supplement

Jacques Derrida

In *Of Grammatology* (1967), Derrida evoked the metaphor of "writing" to characterize the primordial process of differentiation he saw interrupting the categories of the metaphysical tradition in philosophy – identity, essence, presence, being, et cetera. The metaphysical tradition usually operated as a hierarchy of terms. One set of terms was designated as more original, morally superior, conceptually prior, axiomatic, et cetera, while the other was characterized by terms suggesting loss, a falling away, depletion, derivation, imitation, et cetera. On the one side was presence, life, wholeness, identity, nature, et cetera; on the other absence, death, dissolution, non-identity, artifice, technology, representation. Writing was always characterized as inauthentic, not the real thing, a mere substitute, while speech conveyed the immediate presence of the living mind; it was therefore more likely to be associated with authenticity, nature, and truth. For Jean-Jacques Rousseau, therefore, the most original form of language is speech; writing for him is a degradation that corrupts the purity of speech. Only speech can convey pure truth that is not prey to deviation or falseness.

Derrida sees the distinction between speech and writing as a template for metaphysics. Metaphysics differentiated between values and ideas associated with truth (identity, presence, nature, immediacy, originality, etc.) and those associated with non-truth (difference, absence, artifice, mediation, repetition, imitation, etc.). But according to Derrida, difference is in fact primary and gives rise to identity. Therefore, all the hierarchies of value that found metaphysics fall apart. Bringing about such a collapse of hierarchical values through a close textual analysis is called deconstruction, the term Derrida used to characterize his method of reading. In the case of Rousseau, it consists of demonstrating that the speech Rousseau thought to be at the origin of language must, in fact, be characterized in terms associated in Rousseau's own text with writing such as articulation (which assumes the difference between terms that are articulated or related through connection). Rousseau's ideal speech cannot exist without articulation; no speech is

Original publication details: Jacques Derrida, "That Dangerous Supplement" from *Of Grammatology*, trans. G.C. Spivak, pp. 141–164. Johns Hopkins University Press, 1977. Reproduced with permission from Johns Hopkins University Press.

Literary Theory: An Anthology, Third Edition. Edited by Julie Rivkin and Michael Ryan.

possible without a distinction between vowels and consonants. Difference is therefore more primordial than the presence Rousseau imagined at the origin of language as a pure speech devoid of all the characteristics of writing. To an extent, speaking metaphorically, writing precedes speech (if by "writing," we mean "différance"). What this means is that one cannot do as metaphysics does and divide the world categorically into nature and technique, origin and imitation, identity and alterity, et cetera. Differentiation is more prior than all of these categories, and there is no identity, origin, nature, or truth of differentiation. To try to locate an origin, a presence, a nature, or a truth that would serve as a solid ground for constructing a metaphysical hierarchy of values is a bit like tossing a buoy overboard from a rowboat in the middle of the ocean and declaring "There is the center of the ocean."

In this selection from *Of Grammatology*, Derrida examines the use of the term "supplement" in Rousseau. Rousseau characterizes writing as a supplement to speech. It is added on to speech in order to make it more widely useful, but in doing so, it suggests there is a fault or lack in speech. It is not as complete or full in itself as Rousseau imagines. Language can cover greater distances in the form of writing; it no longer requires the immediate presence of the speaker. But for Rousseau, such presence is the gold standard of truth. A mere supplement that is added on as an artificial technological representation in the form of dead letters on the page cannot really convey such truth. Yet without the help of this addition, speech-as-truth would be limited in range and usefulness. Speech needs writing, but by adding writing, it depletes the superior value of truth. This strange logic (whereby a helpful addition points out a lack or deficiency in the supposedly superior original) attracts Derrida's attention because it points to the fault in all of metaphysics – that it proclaims things like speech to be superior (because they are more present, more natural, more immediate, more self-identical, etc.) but it simultaneously points out a deficiency in the superior value. It is not self-sufficient; it requires an other; it is therefore caught up in differentiation. Derrida sees this shuttling between original-that-requires-supplementation and supplement-that-is-non-original as a version of the *différance* or differentiation that disturbs metaphysics' founding values of presence, identity, and authenticity. In Rousseau, original speech is never intact in itself, a pure identity. In a primordial sense, it requires something different from itself to supplement it. It is primordially dependent on something other. Writing is chosen as a metaphor for this shuttling of difference between the supposedly self-identical and the other it needs in order to be self-identical because each part of a written sentence has identity only in relation to all the other parts.

How people will cry out against me! I hear from afar the shouts of that false wisdom which is ever dragging us onwards, counting the present as nothing, and pursuing without a pause a future which flies as we pursue, that false wisdom which removes us from our place and never brings us to any other.

— Emile

All the papers which I have collected to fill the gaps in my memory and to guide me in my undertaking, have passed into other hands, and will never return to mine.

— Confessions

I have implied it repeatedly: the praise of living speech, as it *preoccupies* Lévi-Strauss's discourse, is faithful to only one particular motif in Rousseau. This motif comes to terms with and is organized by its contrary: a perpetually reanimated mistrust with regard to the so-called full speech. In the spoken address, presence is at once promised and refused. The speech that Rousseau raised above writing is speech as it should be or rather as it *should have been*. And we must pay attention to that mode, to that tense which relates us to presence within living colloquy. *In fact*, Rousseau had tested the concealment within speech itself, in the mirage of its immediacy. He had recognized and analyzed it with incomparable acumen. We are dispossessed of the longed-for presence in the gesture of language by which we attempt to seize it. To the experience of the "robber robbed" that Starobinski admirably describes in *L'oeil vivant* [Paris, 1961], Jean Jacques is subjected not only in the play of the mirror image which "captures his reflection and exposes his presence" (p. 109). It lies in wait for us from the first word. The speculary dispossession which at the same time institutes and deconstitutes me is also a law of language. It operates as a power of death in the heart of living speech: a power all the more redoubtable because it opens as much as it threatens the possibility of the spoken word.

Having in a certain way recognized this power which, inaugurating speech, dislocates the subject that it constructs, prevents it from being present to its signs, torments its language with a complete writing, Rousseau is nevertheless more pressed to exorcise it than to assume its necessity. That is why, straining toward the reconstruction of presence, he valorizes and disqualifies writing at the same time. At the same time; that is to say, in one divided but coherent movement. We must try not to lose sight of its strange unity. Rousseau condemns writing as destruction of presence and as disease of speech. He rehabilitates it to the extent that it promises the reappropriation of that of which speech allowed itself to be dispossessed. But by what, if not already a writing older than speech and already installed in that place?

The first movement of this desire is formulated as a theory of language. The other governs the experience of the writer. In the *Confessions*, when Jean-Jacques tries to explain how he became a writer, he describes the passage to writing as the restoration, by a certain absence and by a sort of calculated effacement, of presence disappointed of itself in speech. To write is indeed the only way of keeping or recapturing speech since speech denies itself as it gives itself. Thus an *economy of signs* is organized. It will be equally disappointing, closer yet to the very essence and to the necessity of disappointment. One cannot help wishing to master absence and yet we must always let go. Starobinski describes the profound law that commands the space within which Rousseau must move:

> How will he overcome the misunderstanding that prevents him from expressing himself according to his true value? How escape the risks of improvised speech? To what other mode of communication can he turn? By what other means manifest himself? Jean-Jacques chooses to be *absent* and to *write*. Paradoxically, he will hide himself to show himself better, and he will confide in written speech: "I would love society like others, if I were not sure of showing myself not only at a disadvantage, but as completely different from what I am. The part that I have taken of *writing and hiding myself* is precisely the one that suits me. If I were present, one would never know what I was worth" (*Confessions*). The admission is singular and merits emphasis: Jean-Jacques breaks with others, only to present himself to them in written speech. Protected by solitude, he will turn and re-turn his sentences at leisure.[1]

Let us note that the economy is perhaps indicated in the following: the operation that substitutes writing for speech also replaces presence by value: to the *I am* or to the *I am present* thus sacrificed, a *what* I am or a *what I am worth* is *preferred*. "If I were present, one would never know what I was worth." I renounce my present life, my present and concrete existence in order to make myself known in the ideality of truth and value. A well-known schema. The battle by which I wish to raise myself above my life even while I retain it, in order to enjoy recognition, is in this case within myself, and writing is indeed the phenomenon of this battle.

Such would be the writing lesson in Jean-Jacques' existence. The act of writing would be essentially – and here in an exemplary fashion – the greatest sacrifice aiming at the greatest symbolic reappropriation of presence. From this point of view, Rousseau knew that death is not the simple outside of life. Death by writing also inaugurates life. "I can certainly say that I never began to live, until I looked upon myself as a dead man" (*Confessions*, Book 6 [p. 236]). As soon as one determines it within the system of this economy, is not the sacrifice – the "literary suicide" – dissipated in the *appearance*? Is it anything but a symbolic reappropriation? Does it not renounce the *present* and the *proper* in order to master them better in their meaning, in the ideal form of truth, of the presence of the present and of the proximity or property of the proper? We would be obliged to decide that a ruse and an appearance are necessary if in fact we were to abide by these concepts (sacrifice, expenditure, renunciation, symbol, appearance, truth, etc.) which determine what we here call economy in terms of truth and appearance, starting from the opposition presence/absence.

But the work of writing and the economy of differance will not be dominated by this classical conceptuality, this ontology, or this epistemology. On the contrary, these furnish its hidden premises. Differance does not *resist* appropriation, it does not impose an exterior limit upon it. Differance began by *broaching* alienation and it ends by leaving reappropriation *breached*. Until death. Death is the movement of differance to the extent that that movement is necessarily finite. This means that differance makes the opposition of presence and absence possible. Without the possibility of differance, the desire of presence as such would not find its breathing-space. That means by the same token that this desire carries in itself the destiny of its non-satisfaction. Differance produces what it forbids, makes possible the very thing that it makes impossible.

If differance is recognized as the obliterated origin of absence and presence, major forms of the disappearing and the appearing of the entity, it would still remain to be known if being, before its determination into absence or presence, is already implicated in the thought of differance. And if differance as the project of the mastery of the entity should be understood with reference to the sense of being. Can one not think the converse? Since the sense of being is never produced as history outside of its determination as presence, has it not always already been caught within the history of metaphysics as the epoch of presence? This is perhaps what Nietzsche wanted to write and what resists the Heideggerian reading of Nietzsche; *differance* in its *active* movement – *what* is comprehended in the concept of *differance* without exhausting it – is what not only precedes metaphysics but also extends beyond the thought of being. The latter speaks *nothing other than* metaphysics, even if it exceeds it and thinks it as what it is within its closure.

From/Of Blindness to the Supplement

In terms of this problematical scheme, we must therefore think Rousseau's experience and his theory of writing together, the accord and the discord that, under the name of writing, relate Jean-Jacques to Rousseau, uniting and dividing his proper name. On the side of experience, a recourse to literature as reappropriation of presence, that is to say, as we shall see, of Nature; on the side of theory, an indictment against the negativity of the letter, in which must be read the degeneracy of culture and the disruption of the community.

If indeed one wishes to surround it with the entire constellation of concepts that shares its system, the word *supplement* seems to account for the strange unity of these two gestures.

In both cases, in fact, Rousseau considers writing as a dangerous means, a menacing aid, the critical response to a situation of distress. When Nature, as self-proximity, comes to be forbidden or interrupted, when speech fails to protect presence, writing becomes necessary. It must *be added* to the word urgently. I have identified in advance one of the forms of this *addition*; speech being natural or at least the natural expression of thought, the most natural form of institution or convention for signifying thought, writing is added to it, is adjoined, as an image or representation. In that sense, it is not natural. It diverts the immediate presence of thought to speech into representation and the imagination. This recourse is not only "bizarre," but dangerous. It is the addition of a technique, a sort of artificial and artful ruse to make speech present when it is actually absent. It is a violence done to the natural destiny of the language:

> Languages are made to be spoken, writing serves only as a supplement to speech. … Speech represents thought by conventional signs, and writing represents the same with regard to speech. Thus the art of writing is nothing but a mediated representation of thought.

Writing is dangerous from the moment that representation there claims to be presence and the sign of the thing itself. And there is a fatal necessity, inscribed in the very functioning of the sign, that the substitute make one forget the vicariousness of its own function and make itself pass for the plenitude of a speech whose deficiency and infirmity it nevertheless only *supplements*. For the concept of the supplement – which here determines that of the representative image – harbors within itself two significations whose cohabitation is as strange as it is necessary. The supplement adds itself, it is a surplus, a plenitude enriching another plenitude, the *fullest measure* of presence. It cumulates and accumulates presence. It is thus that art, *technè*, image, representation, convention, etc., come as supplements to nature and are rich with this entire cumulating function. This kind of supplementarity determines in a certain way all the conceptual oppositions within which Rousseau inscribes the notion of Nature to the extent that it *should* be self-sufficient.

But the supplement supplements. It adds only to replace. It intervenes or insinuates itself *in-the-place-of*; if it fills, it is as if one fills a void. If it represents and makes an image, it is by the anterior default of a presence. Compensatory [*suppléant*] and vicarious, the supplement is an adjunct, a subaltern instance which *takes-(the)-place* [*tient-lieu*]. As substitute, it is not simply added to the positivity of a presence, it produces no relief, its place is assigned in the structure by the mark of an emptiness. Somewhere, something can be filled up of *itself*, can accomplish itself, only by allowing itself to be filled through sign and proxy. The sign is always the supplement of the thing itself.

This second signification of the supplement cannot be separated from the first. We shall constantly have to confirm that both operate within Rousseau's texts. But the inflexion varies from moment to moment. Each of the two significations is by turns effaced or becomes discreetly vague in the presence of the other. But their common function is shown in this: whether it adds or substitutes itself, the supplement is *exterior*, outside of the positivity to which it is super-added, alien to that which, in order to be replaced by it, must be other than it. Unlike the *complement*, dictionaries tell us, the supplement is an "*exterior* addition" (Robert's *French Dictionary*).

According to Rousseau, the negativity of evil will always have the form of supplementarity. Evil is exterior to nature, to what is by nature innocent and good. It supervenes upon nature. But always by way of compensation for [*sous l'espèce de la suppléance*] what *ought to* lack nothing at all in itself.

Thus presence, always natural, which for Rousseau more than for others means maternal, *ought to be* self-sufficient. Its *essence*, another name for presence, may be read through the grid of this ought to be [*ce conditionnel*]. Like Nature's love, "there is no substitute for a mother's love," says *Emile*.[2] It is in no way *supplemented*, that is to say it does not have to be supplemented, it suffices and is self-sufficient; but that also means that it is irreplaceable; what one would substitute for it would not equal it, would be only a mediocre makeshift. Finally it means that Nature does not supplement *itself* at all; Nature's supplement does not proceed from Nature, it is not only inferior to but other than Nature.

Yet all education, the keystone of Rousseauist thought, will be described or presented as a system of substitution [*suppléance*] destined to reconstitute Nature's edifice in the most natural way possible. The first chapter of *Emile* announces the function of this pedagogy. Although there is no substitute for a mother's love, "it is better that the child should suck the breast of a healthy nurse rather than of a petted mother, if he has any further evil to fear from her who has given him birth" (ibid.) [p. 12]. It is indeed culture or cultivation that must supplement a deficient nature, a deficiency that cannot by definition be anything but an accident and a deviation from Nature. Culture or cultivation is here called habit; it is necessary and insufficient from the moment when the substitution of mothers is no longer envisaged only "from the physiological point of view":

> Other women, or even other animals, may give him the milk she denies him, but there is no substitute for a mother's love. The woman who nurses another's child in place of her own is a bad mother; how can she be a good nurse? She may become one in time; use [habit] will overcome nature … (ibid.).

Here the problems of natural right, of the relationship between Nature and Society, the concepts of alienation, alterity, and corruption, are adapted most spontaneously to the pedagogic problem of the substitution of mothers and children:

> And this affection when developed has its drawbacks, which should make every sensible woman afraid to put her child out to nurse. Is she prepared to divide her mother's rights, or rather to abdicate them in favor of a stranger; to see her child loving another as much as and more than herself … (ibid.).

If, premeditating the theme of writing, I began by speaking of the substitution of mothers, it is because, as Rousseau will himself say, "more depends on this than you realize."

> How emphatically would I speak if it were not so hopeless to keep struggling in vain on behalf of a real reform. More depends on this than you realize. Would you restore all men to their primal duties, begin with the mothers; the results will surprise you. Every evil

follows in the train of this first sin; the whole moral order is disturbed, nature is quenched in every breast ... (p. 18) [p. 13].

Childhood is the first manifestation of the deficiency which, in Nature, calls for substitution [*suppléance*]. Pedagogy illuminates perhaps more crudely the paradoxes of the supplement. How is a natural weakness possible? How can Nature ask for forces that it does not furnish? How is a child possible in general?

> *First Maxim.* – Far from being too strong, children are not strong enough for all the claims of nature. Give them full use of such strength as they have and which they will not abuse. *Second Maxim.* – Help them and supply what they lack, in intelligence or in strength, whenever the need is of the body (p. 50) [p. 35].

All the organization of, and all the time spent in, education will be regulated by this necessary evil: "supply [*suppléer*] ... [what] ... is lacking" and to replace Nature. It must be done as little and as late as possible. "One of the best rules of good farming [*culture*] is to *keep things back* as much as possible" (p. 274) [p. 193]. "Give nature time to work before you *take over her business* [act in her place – *agir à sa place*]" (p. 102; italics added) [p. 71].

Without childhood, no supplement would ever appear in Nature. The supplement is here both humanity's good fortune and the origin of its perversion. The health of the human race:

> Plants are fashioned by cultivation, and men by education. If man were born big and strong, his size and strength would be useless to him until he had learned to use them; they would create a prejudice against him, by not allowing others to think of assisting him; and, left to himself, he would die miserably before knowing his needs. We complain of the state of infancy; we do not see that, if man had not begun by being a child, the human race would have perished (p. 67).

The threat of perversion:

> While the Author of nature has given children the active principle, He takes care that it shall do little harm by giving them small power to use it. But as soon as they can think of people as tools that they are responsible for activating, they use them to carry out their wishes and to *supplement* their own weakness. This is how they become tiresome, masterful, imperious, naughty, and unmanageable; a development which does not spring from a natural love of power, but one which gives it to them, for it does not need much experience to realize how pleasant it is to act through the hands of others and to move the world by simply moving the tongue (p. 49; italics added) [p. 34].

The supplement will always be the moving of the tongue or acting through the hands of others. In it everything is brought together: progress as the possibility of perversion, regression toward an evil that is not natural and that adheres to the power of substitution that permits us to absent ourselves and act by proxy, through representation, through the hands of others. Through the written [*par écrit*]. This substitution always has the form of the sign. The scandal is that the sign, the image, or the representer, become forces and make "the world move."

This scandal is such, and its evil effects are sometimes so irreparable, that the world seems to turn the wrong way (and we shall see later what such a *catastrophe* can signify for Rousseau); then Nature becomes the supplement of art and society. It is the moment when evil seems incurable: "As the child does not know how to be cured, let him know how to be ill. The one art takes the place of [*supplée*] the other and is often more successful; it is the art of nature" (p. 31) [p. 22]. It is also the moment when maternal nature, ceasing to be loved, as she ought to be, for herself and in an immediate proximity ("O Nature! O my mother! behold me under thy protection alone! Here there is no cunning or knavish mortal to thrust himself between me and thee." [*Confession*, Book 12] [p. 669]) becomes the substitute for another love and for another attachment:

> The contemplation of Nature always had a very great attraction for his heart; he found there a supplement to the attachments that he needed; but he would have left the supplement for the thing, if he had had the choice, and he was reduced to converse with the plants only after vain efforts to converse with human beings (*Dialogues*, p. 794).

That botany becomes the supplement of society is more than a catastrophe. It is the catastrophe of the catastrophe. For in Nature, the plant is the most *natural* thing. It is natural *life*. The mineral is distinguished from the vegetable in that it is a dead and useful Nature, servile to man's industry. When man has lost the sense and the taste of true natural riches – plants – he rummages in the entrails of his mother and risks his health:

> The Mineral Kingdom has nothing in itself either amiable or attractive; its riches, enclosed in the breast [womb – *sein*] of the earth, seem to have been removed from the gaze of man in order not to tempt his cupidity; they are there like a reserve to serve one day as a *supplement* to the true wealth which is more within his grasp, and for which he loses taste according to the extent of his corruption. Then he is compelled to call in industry, to struggle, and to labor to alleviate his miseries; he searches the entrails of earth; he goes seeking to its center, at the risk of his life and at the expense of his health, for imaginary goods in place of the real good which the earth offers of herself if he knew how to enjoy it. *He flies from the sun and the day, which he is no longer worthy to see.*[3]

Man has thus put out his eyes, he blinds himself by the desire to rummage in these entrails. Here is the horrible spectacle of the punishment that follows the crime, in sum a simple substitution:

> He buries himself alive, and does well, not being worthy of living in the light of day. There quarries, pits, forges, furnaces, a battery of anvils, hammers, smoke and fire, succeed to the fair images of his rustic labors. The wan faces of the unhappy people who languish in the poisonous vapors of mines, of black forgemen, of hideous cyclops, are the spectacle which the working of the mine substitutes, in the heart [womb] of the earth for that of green fields and flowers, the azure sky, amorous shepherds and robust laborers upon its surface.[4]

Such is the scandal, such the catastrophe. The supplement is what neither Nature nor Reason can tolerate. Neither Nature, our "common mother" (*Reveries*, p. 1066) [p. 143], nor the reason which is reasonable, if not reasoning (*De l'état de nature*, [*Pléiade*, vol. 3], p. 478). And had they not done everything to avoid this catastrophe, to protect themselves from this violence and to guard and keep us from this fatal crime? "so that," says the second *Discourse* precisely of mines, "it looks as if nature had taken pains to keep the fatal secret from us" (p. 172) [p. 200]. And let us not forget that the violence that takes us toward the entrails of the earth, the moment of mine-blindness, that is, of metallurgy, is the origin of society. For according to Rousseau, as we shall often confirm, agriculture, marking the organization of civil society, assumes the beginning of metallurgy. Blindness thus produces that which is born at the same time as society: the languages, the regulated substitution of signs for things, the order of the supplement. One goes *from blindness to the supplement*. But the blind person cannot see, in its origin, the very thing he produces to supplement his sight. *Blindness to the supplement* is the law. And especially blindness to its concept. Moreover, it does not suffice to locate its functioning in order to *see* its meaning. The supplement has no sense and is given to no intuition. We do not therefore make it emerge out of its strange penumbra. We speak its reserve.

Reason is incapable of thinking this double infringement upon Nature: that there is *lack* in Nature and that *because of that very fact* something *is added* to it. Yet one should not say that Reason is *powerless to think this*; it is constituted by that lack of power. It is the principle of identity. It is the thought of the self-identity of the natural being. It cannot even determine the supplement as its other, as the irrational and the non-natural, for the supplement comes *naturally* to put itself in Nature's place. The supplement is the image and the representation of Nature. The image is neither in nor out of Nature. The supplement is therefore equally dangerous for Reason, the natural health of Reason.

Dangerous supplement. These are the words that Rousseau uses in the *Confessions*. He uses them in a context which is only apparently different, and in order to explain, precisely, a "condition almost unintelligible and inconceivable [to reason]": "In a word, between myself and the most passionate lover there was only one, but that an essential, point of distinction, which makes my condition almost unintelligible and inconceivable" (*Pléiade*, vol. 1, [p. 111]).

If we lend to the text below a paradigmatic value, it is only provisional and does not prejudge what the discipline of a future reading might rigorously determine. No model of reading seems to me at the moment ready to measure up to this text – which I would like to read as a *text* and not as a document. Measure up to it fully and rigorously, that is, beyond what already makes the text most legible, and more legible than has been so far thought. My only ambition will be to draw out of it a signification which that presumed future reading will not be able to dispense with [*faire économie*]; the economy of a written text, circulating through other texts, leading back to it constantly, conforming to the element of a language and to its regulated functioning. For example, what unites the word "supplement" to its concept was not invented by Rousseau and the originality of its functioning is neither fully mastered by Rousseau nor simply imposed by history and the language, by the history of the language. To speak of the writing of Rousseau is to try to recognize what escapes these categories of passivity and activity, blindness and responsibility. And one cannot abstract from the written text to rush to the signified it *would mean*, since the signified is here the text itself. It is so little a matter of looking for a *truth signified* by these writings (metaphysical or psychological truth: Jean-Jacques' life behind his work) that if the texts that interest us *mean* something, it is the engagement and the appurtenance that encompass existence and writing in the same *tissue*, the same *text*. The same is here called supplement, another name for differance.

Here is the irruption of the dangerous supplement in Nature, between nature and nature, between natural innocence as *virginity* and natural innocence as *pucelage**: "In a

---

* "*Pucelage*" is the more earthy French word for the actual physical fact of sexual intactness, in the female the membrane itself. Rousseau applies the word to his own case with some derision, contrasting it to the spiritual innocence of true "virginity."

word, between myself and the most passionate lover there was only one, but that an essential, point of distinction, which makes my condition almost unintelligible and inconceivable." Here, the lineation should not hide the fact that the following paragraph is destined to explain the "only one point of distinction" and the "almost unintelligible and inconceivable" "condition." Rousseau elaborates:

> I had returned from Italy not quite the same as I had entered it, but as, perhaps, no one of my age had ever returned from it. I had brought back, not my virginity but my *pucelage*. I had felt the progress of years; my restless temperament had at last made itself felt, and its first outbreak, quite involuntary, had caused me alarm about my health in a manner which shows better than anything else the innocence in which I had lived up to that time. Soon reassured, I learned that dangerous means of assisting it [*ce dangereux supplément*], which cheats Nature and saves up for young men of my temperament many forms of excess at the expense of their health, strength, and, sometimes, their life (*Pléiade*, I, pp. 108–09 [p. 111]).

We read in *Emile* (Book IV): "If once he acquires this dangerous habit [*supplément*] he is ruined" [p. 299]. In the same book, it is also a question of "mak[ing] up ... by trading on ... inexperience" [*suppléer en gagnant de vitesse sur l'experience*; literally "supplement-ing by out-distancing experience"] (p. 437) [p. 315], and of the "mind, which reinforces [*supplée*] ... the bodily strength" (p. 183) [p. 129].

The experience of auto-eroticism is lived in anguish. Masturbation reassures ("soon reassured") only through that culpability traditionally attached to the practice, obliging children to assume the fault and to interiorize the threat of castration that always accom-panies it. Pleasure is thus lived as the irremediable loss of the vital substance, as exposure to madness and death. It is produced "at the expense of their health, strength, and, sometimes, their life." In the same way, the *Reveries* will say, the man who "searches the entrails of earth ... goes seeking to its center, at the risk of his life and at the expense of his health, for imaginary goods in place of the real good which the earth offers of herself if he knew how to enjoy it" (*Pléiade*, vol. 1, 1067 [p. 145]).

And indeed it is a question of the imaginary. The supplement that "cheats" maternal "nature" operates as writing, and as writing it is dangerous to life. This danger is that of the image. Just as writing opens the crisis of the living speech in terms of its "image," its painting or its representation, so onanism announces the ruin of vitality in terms of imaginary seductions:

> This vice, which shame and timidity find so convenient, possesses, besides a great attrac-tion for lively imaginations – that of being able to dispose of the whole sex as they desire, and to make the beauty which tempts them minister to their pleasures, without being obliged to obtain its consent [*Confessions*, p. 111].

The dangerous supplement, which Rousseau also calls a "fatal advantage," is properly *seductive*; it leads desire away from the good path, makes it err far from natural ways, guides it toward its loss or fall and therefore it is a sort of lapse or scandal (*scandalon*). It thus destroys Nature. But the scandal of Reason is that nothing seems more natural than this destruction of Nature. It is myself who exerts myself to separate myself from the force that Nature has entrusted to me: "Seduced by this fatal advantage, I did my best to destroy the good constitution which Nature had restored to me, and [to] which I had allowed time to strengthen itself." We know what importance *Emile* gives to time, to the slow maturation of natural forces. The entire art of pedagogy is a calculated patience, allowing the work of Nature time to come to fruition, respecting its rhythm and the order of its stages. The dangerous supplement destroys very quickly the forces that Nature has slowly constituted and accumulated. In "out-distancing" natural experience, it runs non-stop [*brûle les étapes* – literally "burns the halting-points"] and consumes energy without possibility of recovery. As I shall confirm, like the sign it bypasses the presence of the thing and the duration of being.

The dangerous supplement breaks with Nature. The entire description of this moving away from Nature has a *scene* [*théâtre*]. The *Confessions* stage the evocation of the dangerous supplement at the moment when it is a question of making visible a distancing which is neither the same nor an other; Nature draws away at the same time as the Mother, or rather "Mamma," who already signified the disappearance of the true mother and has substituted herself in the well-known ambiguous manner. It is therefore now a question of the distance between Mamma and the person she called "Little one."[5] As *Emile* says, all evil comes from the fact that "women have ceased to be mothers, they do not and will not return to their duty" (p. 18) [p. 14]. A certain absence, then, of a certain sort of mother. And the experience of which we speak is such as to reduce that absence as much as to maintain it. A *furtive* experience, that of a thief who needs invisibility: that the mother be invisible and not see. These lines are often quoted:

> I should never have done, if I were to enter into the details of all the follies which the remembrance of this dear mamma caused me to commit when I was no longer in her presence. How often have I kissed my bed, since she had slept in it; my curtains, all the furniture of my room, since they belonged to her, and her beautiful hand had touched them; even the floor, on which I prostrated myself, since she had walked upon it! Sometimes, even in her presence, I was guilty of extravagances, which only the most violent love seemed capable of inspiring. At table one day, just when she had put a piece of food into her mouth, I exclaimed that I saw a hair in it; she put back the morsel on her plate, and I eagerly seized and swallowed it.[6] In a word, between myself and the most passionate lover there was only one, but that an essential, point of distinction, which makes my condition almost unintelligible and inconceivable … [A little above, we read] I only felt the full strength of my attachment when I no longer saw her (p. 107) [pp. 110–11]

The Chain of Supplements

The discovery of the dangerous supplement will be next cited *among* these "follies," but it will still retain a privilege; Rousseau evokes it after the others and as a sort of explanation of the state inconceivable to reason. For it is not the question of diverting total enjoyment toward a particular substitute, but now of experiencing it or miming it *directly and in its totality*. It is no longer a question of kissing the bed, the floor, the curtains, the furniture, etc., not even of "swallowing" the "piece … [that] she had put into her mouth," but of "dispos[ing] of the whole sex as … [one] desire[s]."

I remarked that the stage of this theater was not only a setting in the generally understood sense: an ensemble of accessories. The topographic disposition of the experience is not unimportant. Jean-Jacques is in the house of Madame de Warens; close enough to *Mamma* to see her and to nourish his imagination upon her but with the possibility of a partition. It is at the moment when the mother disappears that substitution becomes possible and necessary. The play of maternal presence or absence, this alteration of perception and imagination must correspond to an organization of space; the text argues as follows:

> Add to this habit the circumstances of my position, living as I was with a beautiful woman, caressing her image in the bottom of my heart, seeing her continually throughout the day, surrounded in the evening by objects which reminded me of her, sleeping in the bed in which I knew she had slept! What causes for excitement! Many a reader, who reflects upon them, no doubt already considers me as half-dead! Quite the contrary; that which ought to have destroyed me was just the thing that saved me, at least for a time. Intoxicated with the charm of living with her, with the ardent desire of spending my life with her, I always saw in her, whether she were absent or present, a tender mother, a beloved sister, a delightful friend, and nothing more. … She was for me the only woman in the world; and the extreme sweetness of the feelings with which she inspired me did not allow my senses time to awake for others, and protected me against her and all her sex.

This experience was not an event marking an archaic or adolescent period. Not only did it construct or sustain a particular hidden foundation, an edifice of significations. It remained an active obsession whose "present" is constantly reactivated and constituted in its turn, until the end of Jean-Jacques Rousseau's "life" and "text." A little later, a little further on in the text of the *Confessions* (Book IV),[7] "a little incident, which I find some difficulty in relating," [p. 150] is related to us. The encounter with a man "addicted to the same vice." Terrified, Jean-Jacques runs away, "trembling as if" he had just "committed a crime." "The recollection of this incident cured me of it for a long time" [p. 151].

For a long time? Rousseau will never stop having recourse to, and accusing himself of, this onanism that permits one to be himself affected by providing himself with presences, by summoning absent beauties. In his eyes it will remain the model of vice and perversion. Affecting oneself by another presence, one *corrupts* oneself [makes oneself other] by oneself [*on s'altère soi-même*]. Rousseau neither wishes to think nor can think that this alteration does not simply happen to the self, that it is the self's very origin. He must consider it a contingent evil coming from without to affect the integrity of the subject. But he cannot give up what immediately restores to him the other desired presence; no more than one can give up language. This is why, in this respect as well, as he says in the *Dialogues* [*Pléiade*, vol. 1] (p. 800), "to the end of his life he will remain an aged child."

The restitution of presence by language, restitution at the same time symbolic and immediate. This contradiction must be thought. Immediate experience of restitution because as experience, as consciousness or conscience, *it dispenses with passage through the world*. What is touching is touched, auto-affection gives itself as pure autarchy. If the presence that it then gives itself is the substitutive symbol of another presence, it has never been possible to desire that presence "in person" before this play of substitution and this symbolic experience of auto-affection. The thing itself does not appear outside of the symbolic system that does not exist without the possibility of auto-affection. Experience of *immediate* restitution, also because it *does not wait*. It is satisfied then and there and in the moment. If it waits, it is not because the other makes it wait. Pleasure seems no longer to be deferred. "Why give oneself so much trouble in a hope remote from so poor and uncertain a success, when one can, from the very instant …" (*Dialogues*).

But what is no longer deferred is also absolutely deferred. The presence that is thus delivered to us in the present is a chimera. Auto-affection is a pure speculation. The sign, the image, the representation, which come to supplement the absent presence are the illusions that sidetrack us. To culpability, to the anguish of death and castration, is added or rather is assimilated the experience of frustration. *Donner le change* ["sidetrack-ing" or, "giving money"]: in whatever sense it is understood, this expression describes the recourse to the supplement admirably. In order to explain his "dislike" for "common prostitutes," Rousseau tells us that in Venice, at thirty-one, the "propensity which had modified all my passions" (*Confessions*, p. 41) [p. 35][8] has not disappeared: "I had not lost the pernicious habit of satisfying my wants [*donner le change*]" (p. 316) [p. 289].

The enjoyment of the *thing itself* is thus undermined, in its act and in its essence, by frustration. One cannot therefore say that it has an essence or an act (*eidos, ousia, energeia*, etc.). Something promises itself as it escapes, gives itself as it moves away, and strictly speaking it cannot even be called presence. Such is the constraint of the supple-ment, such, exceeding all the language of metaphysics, is this structure "almost incon-ceivable to reason." *Almost* inconceivable: simple irrationality, the opposite of reason, are less irritating and waylaying for classical logic. The supplement is maddening because it is neither presence nor absence and because it consequently breaches both our pleasure and our virginity. "... abstinence and enjoyment, pleasure and wisdom, escaped me in equal measure" (*Confessions*, p. 12).

Are things not complicated enough? The symbolic is the immediate, presence is absence, the nondeferred is deferred, pleasure is the menace of death. But one stroke must still be added to this system, to this strange economy of the supplement. In a cer-tain way, it was already legible. A terrifying menace, the supplement is also the first and surest protection; against that very menace. This is why it cannot be given up. And sexual auto-affection, that is auto-affection in general, neither begins nor ends with what one thinks can be circumscribed by the name of masturbation. The supplement has not only the power of *procuring* an absent presence through its image; procuring it for us through the proxy [*procuration*] of the sign, it holds it at a distance and masters it. For this pres-ence is at the same time desired and feared. The supplement transgresses and at the same time respects the interdict. This is what also permits writing as the supplement of speech; but already also the spoken word as writing in general. Its economy exposes and protects us at the same time according to the play of forces and of the differences of forces. Thus, the supplement is dangerous in that it threatens us with death, but Rousseau thinks that it is not at all as dangerous as "cohabitation with women." Pleasure *itself*, without symbol or suppletory, that which would accord us (to) pure presence itself, if such a thing were possible, would be only another name for death. Rousseau says it:

> Enjoyment! Is such a thing made for man? Ah! If I had ever in my life tasted the delights of
> love even once in their plenitude, I do not imagine that my frail existence would have been
> sufficient for them, I would have been dead in the act (*Confessions*, Book VIII).

If one abides by the universal evidence, by the necessary and a priori value of this proposition in the form of a sigh, one must immediately recognize that "cohabitation with women," hetero-eroticism, can be lived (effectively, really, as one believes it can be said) only through the ability to reserve within itself its own supplementary protection. In other words, between auto-eroticism and hetero-eroticism, there is not a frontier but an economic distribution. It is within this general rule that the differences are mapped out. This is Rousseau's general rule. And before trying – what I do not pretend to be doing here – to encompass the pure singularity of Rousseau's economy or his writing, we must carefully raise and articulate between them all the structural or essential necessities on their different levels of generality.

It is from a certain determined representation of "cohabitation with women" that Rousseau had to have recourse throughout his life to that type of dangerous supplement that is called masturbation and that cannot be separated from his activity as a writer. To the end. Thérèse – the Thérèse of whom we can speak, Thérèse in the text, whose name and "life" belong to the writing we read – experienced it at her cost. In Book XII of the *Confessions*, at the moment when "I must speak without reserve," the "two reasons combined" of certain "resolutions" is confided to us:

> I must speak without reserve. I have never concealed either my poor mamma's faults or my own. I must not show greater favor to Thérèse either; and, pleased as I am to render honor to one who is so dear to me, neither do I wish to conceal her faults, if so be that an involuntary change in the heart's affections is really a fault. I had long since observed that her affection for me had cooled. ... I was conscious again of an unpleasantness, the effects of which I had formerly felt when with mamma; and the effect was the same with Thérèse. Let us not look for perfections which are not to be found in nature; it would be the same with any other woman whatsoever. ... My situation, however, was at that time the same, and even aggravated by the animosity of my enemies, who only sought to find me at fault. I was afraid of a repetition; and, not desiring to run the risk of it, I preferred to condemn myself to strict continence, than to expose Thérèse to the risk of finding herself in the same condition again. Besides, I had observed that intercourse with women distinctly aggravated my ill-health. ... These two reasons combined caused me to form resolutions which I had sometimes been very inconsistent in keeping, but in which I had persevered with greater firmness for the last three or four years (p. 595) [pp. 616–17].

In the *Manuscrit de Paris*, after "distinctly aggravated my ill-health!" we read: "the corresponding vice, of which I have never been able to cure myself completely, appeared to me to produce less injurious results. These two reasons combined ...."[9]

This perversion consists of preferring the sign and protects me from mortal expenditure. To be sure. But this apparently egotistical economy also functions within an entire system of moral representation. Egotism is redeemed by a culpability, which determines auto-eroticism as a fatal waste and a wounding of the self by the self. But as I thus harm only myself, this perversion is not truly condemnable. Rousseau explains it in more than one letter. Thus: "With that exception and [the exception of] vices that have always done harm to me alone, I can expose to all eyes a life irreproachable in all the secrets of my heart" (to M. de Saint-Germain, 2–26–70). "I have great vices, but they have never harmed anyone but me" (to M. Le Noir, 1–15–72).[10]

Jean-Jacques could thus look for a supplement to Thérèse only on one condition: that the system of supplementarity in general be already open in its possibility, that the play of substitutions be already operative for a long time and that *in a certain way Thérèse herself be already a supplement*. As Mamma was already the supplement of an unknown mother, and as the "true mother" herself, at whom the known "psychoanalyses" of the case of Jean-Jacques Rousseau stop, was also in a certain way a supplement, from the first trace, and even if she had not "truly" died in giving birth. Here is the chain of supplements. The name Mamma already designates one:

> Ah, my Thérèse! I am only too happy to possess you, modest and healthy, and not to find what I never looked for. [The question is of "maidenhood" [*pucelage*] which Thérèse has just

confessed to have lost in innocence and by accident.] At first I had only sought amusement; I now saw that I had found more and gained a companion. A little intimacy with this excellent girl, a little reflection upon my situation, made me feel that, while thinking only of my pleasures, I had done much to promote my happiness. *To supply the place of* my extinguished ambition, I needed a lively sentiment which should *take complete possession of* [literally "fill" – *remplit*] my heart. In a word, I needed a successor to mamma. As I should never live with her again, I wanted someone to live with her pupil, in whom I might find the simplicity and docility of heart which she had found in me. I felt it neecssary that the gentle tranquillity of private and domestic life *should make up* to me for the loss of the brilliant career which I was renouncing. When I was quite alone, I felt a void in my heart, which it only needed another heart *to fill.* Destiny had deprived me of, or, at least in part, alienated me from, that heart for which Nature had formed me. From that moment I was alone; for *with me it has always been everything or nothing. I found in Thérèse the substitute [supplément] that I needed.*[11]

Through this sequence of supplements a necessity is announced: that of an infinite chain, ineluctably multiplying the supplementary mediations that produce the sense of the very thing they defer: the mirage of the thing itself, of immediate presence, of originary perception. Immediacy is derived. That all begins through the intermediary is what is indeed "inconceivable [to reason]."

The Exorbitant. Question of Method

"For me there has never been an intermediary between everything or nothing." The intermediary is the mid-point and the mediation, the middle term between total absence and the absolute plenitude of presence. It is clear that mediacy is the name of all that Rousseau wanted opinionatedly to efface. This wish is expressed in a deliberate, sharp, thematic way. It does not have to be deciphered. Jean-Jacques recalls it here at the very moment when he is spelling out the supplements that are linked together to replace a mother or a Nature. And here the supplement occupies the middle point between total absence and total presence. The play of substitution fills and marks a determined lack. But Rousseau argues as if the recourse to the supplement – here to Thérèse – was going to appease his impatience when confronted with the intermediary: "From that moment I was alone; for me there has never been an intermediary between everything and nothing. I found in Thérèse the substitute that I needed." The virulence of this concept is thus appeased, as if one were able to *arrest it*, domesticate it, tame it.

This brings up the question of the usage of the word "supplement": of Rousseau's situation within the language and the logic that assures to this word or this concept sufficiently *surprising* resources so that the presumed subject of the sentence might always say, through using the "supplement," more, less, or something other than what he *would mean [voudrait dire]*. This question is therefore not only of Rousseau's writing but also of our reading. We should begin by taking rigorous account of this *being held within [prise]* or this *surprise*: the writer writes *in* a language and *in* a logic whose proper system, laws, and life his discourse by definition cannot dominate absolutely. He uses them only by letting himself, after a fashion and up to a point, be governed by the system. And the reading must always aim at a certain relationship, unperceived by the writer, between what he commands and what he does not command of the patterns of the language that he uses. This relationship is not a certain quantitative distribution of shadow and light, of weakness or of force, but a signifying structure that critical reading should *produce*.

What does produce mean here? In my attempt to explain that, I would initiate a justi-fication of my principles of reading. A justification, as we shall see, entirely negative, outlining by exclusion a space of reading that I shall not fill here: a task of reading.

To produce this signifying structure obviously cannot consist of reproducing, by the effaced and respectful doubling of commentary, the conscious, voluntary, intentional relationship that the writer institutes in his exchanges with the history to which he belongs thanks to the element of language. This moment of doubling commentary should no doubt have its place in a critical reading. To recognize and respect all its classical exigencies is not easy and requires all the instruments of traditional criticism. Without this recognition and this respect, critical production would risk developing in any direction at all and authorize itself to say almost anything. But this indispensable guardrail has always only *protected*, it has never *opened*, a reading.

Yet if reading must not be content with doubling the text, it cannot legitimately trans-gress the text toward something other than it, toward a referent (a reality that is meta-physical, historical, psychobiographical, etc.) or toward a signified outside the text whose content could take place, could have taken place outside of language, that is to say, in the sense that we give here to that word, outside of writing in general. That is why the meth-odological considerations that we risk applying here to an example are closely dependent on general propositions that we have elaborated above; as regards the absence of the referent or the transcendental signified. *There is nothing outside of the text* [there is no outside-text; *il n'y a pas de horstexte*]. And that is neither because Jean-Jacques' life, or the existence of Mamma or Thérèse *themselves*, is not of prime interest to us, nor because we have access to their so-called "real" existence only in the text and we have neither any means of altering this, nor any right to neglect this limitation. All reasons of this type would already be sufficient, to be sure, but there are more radical reasons. What we have tried to show by following the guiding line of the "dangerous supplement," is that in what one calls the real life of these existences "of flesh and bone," beyond and behind what one believes can be circumscribed as Rousseau's text, there has never been anything but writing; there have never been anything but supplements, substitutive significations which could only come forth in a chain of differential references, the "real" supervening, and being added only while taking on meaning from a trace and from an invocation of the supplement, etc. And thus to infinity, for we have read, *in the text*, that the absolute present, Nature, that which words like "real mother" name, have always already escaped, have never existed; that what opens meaning and language is writing as the disappear-ance of natural presence.

Although it is not commentary, our reading must be intrinsic and remain within the text. That is why, in spite of certain appearances, the locating of the word *supplement* is here not at all psychoanalytical, if by that we understand an interpretation that takes us outside of the writing toward a psychobiographical signified, or even toward a general psychological structure that could rightly be separated from the signifier. This method has occasionally been opposed to the traditional doubling commentary; it could be shown that it actually comes to terms with it quite easily. *The security with which the commentary considers the self-identity of the text, the confidence with which it carves out its contour, goes hand in hand with the tranquil assurance that leaps over the text toward its presumed content, in the direction of the pure signified.* And in effect, in Rousseau's case, psychoanalytical studies like those of Dr. Laforgue transgress the text only after having read it according to the most current methods. The reading of the literary "symptom" is most banal, most academic, most naive. And once one has thus blinded oneself to the very tissue of the "symptom," to its proper texture, one cheerfully exceeds it toward a psychobiographical signified whose link with the literary signifier then becomes perfectly extrinsic and contingent. One recognizes the other aspect of the same gesture when, in general works on Rousseau, in a package of classical shape that gives itself out to be a synthesis that faithfully restores, through commentary and compilation of themes, the totality of the work and the thought, one encounters a chapter of biographical and psychoanalytical cast on the "problem of sexuality in Rousseau," with a reference in an Appendix to the author's medical case-history.

If it seems to us in principle impossible to separate, through interpretation or commentary, the signified from the signifier, and thus to destroy writing by the writing that is yet reading, we nevertheless believe that this impossibility is historically articulated. It does not limit attempts at deciphering in the same way, to the same degree, and according to the same rules. Here we must take into account the history of the text in general. When we speak of the writer and of the encompassing power of the language to which he is subject, we are not only thinking of the writer in literature. The philosopher, the chronicler, the theoretician in general, and at the limit everyone writing, is thus taken by surprise. But, in each case, the person writing is inscribed in a determined textual system. Even if there is never a pure signified, there are different relationships as to that which, from the signifier, *is presented* as the irreducible stratum of the signified. For example, the philosophical text, although it is in fact always written, includes, precisely as its philosophical specificity, the project of effacing itself in the face of the signified content which it transports and in general teaches. Reading should be aware of this project, even if, in the last analysis, it intends to expose the project's failure. The entire history of texts, and within it the history of literary forms in the West, should be studied from this point of view. With the exception of a thrust or a point of resistance which has only been very lately recognized as such, literary writing has, almost always and almost everywhere, according to some fashions and across very diverse ages, lent itself to this *transcendent* reading, in that search for the signified which we here put in question, not to annul it but to understand it within a system to which such a reading is blind. Philosophical literature is only one example within this history but it is among the most significant. And it interests us particularly in Rousseau's case. Who at the same time and for profound reasons produced a philosophical literature to which belong *The Social Contract* and *La nouvelle Héloise*, and chose to live by literary writing; by a writing which would not be exhausted by the message – philosophical or otherwise – which it could, so to speak, deliver. And what Rousseau has said, as philosopher or as psychologist, of writing in general, cannot be separated from the system of his own writing. We should be aware of this.

This poses formidable problems. Problems of outlining in particular. Let me give three examples.

(1)   If the course I have followed in the reading of the "supplement" is not merely psychoanalytical, it is undoubtedly because the habitual psychoanalysis of literature begins by putting the literary signifier as such within parentheses. It is no doubt also because psychoanalytic theory itself is for me a collection of texts belonging to my history and my culture. To that extent, if it marks my reading and the writing of my interpretation, it does not do so as a principle or a truth that one could abstract from the textual system that I inhabit in order to illuminate it with complete neutrality. In a certain way, I am *within* the history of psychoanalysis as I am *within* Rousseau's text. Just as Rousseau drew upon a

language that was already there – and which is found to be somewhat our own, thus assuring us a certain minimal readability of French literature – in the same way we operate today within a certain network of significations marked by psychoanalytic theory, even if we do not master it and even if we are assured of never being able to master it perfectly.

But it is for another reason that this is not even a somewhat inarticulate psychoanalysis of Jean-Jacques Rousseau. Such a psychoanalysis is already obliged to have located all the structures of appurtenance within Rousseau's text, all that is not unique to it – by reason of the encompassing power and the already-thereness of the language or of the culture – all that could be inhabited rather than produced by writing. Around the irreducible point of originality of this writing an immense series of structures, of historical totalities of all orders, are organized, enveloped, and blended. Supposing that psychoanalysis can by rights succeed in outlining them and their interpretations, supposing that it takes into account the entire history of metaphysics – the history of that Western metaphysics that entertains relationships of cohabitation with Rousseau's text, it would still be necessary for this psychoanalysis to elucidate the law of its own appurtenance to metaphysics and Western culture. Let us not pursue this any further. We have already measured the difficulty of the task and the element of frustration in our interpretation of the supplement. We are sure that something irreducibly Rousseauist is captured there but we have carried off, at the same time, a yet quite unformed mass of roots, soil, and sediments of all sorts.

(2)   Even supposing that Rousseau's text can be rigorously isolated and articulated within history in general, and then within the history of the sign "supplement," one must still take into consideration many other possibilities. Following the appearances of the word "supplement" and of the corresponding concept or concepts, we traverse a certain path within Rousseau's text. To be sure, this particular path will assure us the economy of a synopsis. But are other paths not possible? And as long as the totality of paths is not effectively exhausted, how shall we justify this one?

(3)   In Rousseau's text, after having indicated – by anticipation and as a prelude – the function of the sign "supplement," I now prepare myself to give special privilege, in a manner that some might consider exorbitant, to certain texts like the *Essay on the Origin of Languages* and other fragments on the theory of language and writing. By what right? And why these short texts, published for the most part after the author's death, difficult to classify, of uncertain date and inspiration?

To all these questions and within the logic of their system, there is no satisfying response. In a certain measure and in spite of the theoretical precautions that I formulate, my choice is in fact *exorbitant*.

But what is the exorbitant?

I wished to reach the point of a certain exteriority in relation to the totality of the age of logocentrism. Starting from this point of exteriority, a certain deconstruction of that totality which is also a traced path, of that orb (*orbis*) which is also orbitary (*orbita*), might be broached. The first gesture of this departure and this deconstruction, although subject to a certain historical necessity, cannot be given methodological or logical intraorbitary assurances. Within the closure, one can only judge its style in terms of the accepted oppositions. It may be said that this style is empiricist and in a certain way that would be correct. The *departure* is radically empiricist. It proceeds like a wandering thought on the possibility of itinerary and of method. It is affected by nonknowledge as by its future and it *ventures out* deliberately.

I have myself defined the form and the vulnerability of this empiricism. But here the very concept of empiricism destroys itself. To *exceed* the metaphysical orb is an attempt to get out of the orbit (*orbita*), to think the entirety of the classical conceptual oppositions, particularly the one within which the value of empiricism is held: the opposition of philosophy and non-philosophy, another name for empiricism, for this incapability to sustain on one's own and to the limit the coherence of one's own discourse, for being produced as truth at the moment when the value of truth is shattered, for escaping the internal contradictions of skepticism, etc. *The thought of this historical opposition between philosophy and empiricism is not simply empirical and it cannot be thus qualified without abuse and misunderstanding.*

Let us make the diagram more specific. What is exorbitant in the reading of Rousseau? No doubt Rousseau, as I have already suggested, has only a very relative privilege in the history that interests us. If we merely wished to situate him within this history, the attention that we accord him would be clearly disproportionate. But that is not our intention. We wish to identify a decisive articulation of the logocentric epoch. For purposes of this identification Rousseau seems to us to be most revealing. That obviously supposes that we have already prepared the exit, determined the repression of writing as the fundamental operation of the epoch, read a certain number of texts but not all of them, a certain number of Rousseau's texts but not all of them. This avowal of empiricism can sustain itself only by the strength of the question. The opening of the question, the departure from the closure of a self-evidence, the putting into doubt of a system of oppositions, all these movements necessarily have the form of empiricism and of errancy. At any rate, they cannot be described, *as to past norms*, except in this form. No other trace is available, and as these errant questions are not absolute beginnings in every way, they allow themselves to be effectively reached, on one entire surface, by this description which is also a criticism. We must begin *wherever we are* and the thought of the trace, which cannot not take the scent into account, has already taught us that it was impossible to justify a point of departure absolutely. *Wherever we are*: in a text where we already believe ourselves to be.

Let us narrow the arguments down further. In certain respects, the theme of supplementarity is certainly no more than one theme among others. It is in a chain, carried by it. Perhaps one could substitute something else for it. *But it happens that this theme describes the chain itself, the being-chain of a textual chain, the structure of substitution, the articulation of desire and of language, the logic of all conceptual oppositions taken over by Rousseau*, and particularly the role and the function, in his system, of the concept of Nature. It tells us in a text what a text is, it tells us in writing what writing it, in Rousseau's writing it tells us Jean-Jacques' desire, etc. If we consider, according to the axial proposition of this essay, that there is nothing outside the text, our ultimate justification would be the following: the concept of the supplement and the theory of writing designate textuality itself in Rousseau's text in an indefinitely multiplied structure – *en abyme* [*in an abyss*] – to employ the current phrase. And we shall see that this abyss is not a happy or unhappy accident. An entire theory of the structural necessity of the abyss will be gradually constituted in our reading; the indefinite process of supplementarity has always already *infiltrated* presence, always already inscribed there the space of repetition and the splitting of the self. Representation *in the abyss* of presence is not an accident of presence; the desire of presence is, on the contrary, born from the abyss (the indefinite multiplication) of representation, from the representation of representation, etc. The supplement itself is quite exorbitant, in every sense of the word.

Thus Rousseau inscribes textuality in the text. But its operation is not simple. It tricks with a gesture of effacement, and strategic relations like the relationships of force among the two movements form a complex design. This design seems to us to be represented in the handling of the concept of the supplement. Rousseau cannot utilize it at the same time in all the virtualities of its meaning. The way in which he determines the concept and, in so doing, lets himself be determined by that very thing that he excludes from it, the direction in which he bends it, here as addition, there as substitute, now as the positivity and exteriority of evil, now as a happy auxiliary, all this conveys neither a passivity nor an activity, neither an unconsciousness nor a lucidity on the part of the author. Reading should not only abandon these categories – which are also, let us recall in passing, the founding categories of metaphysics – but should produce the law of this relationship to the concept of the supplement. It is certainly a production, because I do not simply duplicate what Rousseau thought of this relationship. The concept of the supplement is a sort of blind spot in Rousseau's text, the not-seen that opens and limits visibility. But the production, if it attempts to make the not-seen accessible to sight, does not leave the text. It has moreover only believed it was doing so by illusion. It is contained in the transformation of the language it designates, in the regulated exchanges between Rousseau and history. We know that these exchanges only take place by way of the language and the text, in the infrastructural sense that we now give to that word. And what we call production is necessarily a text, the system of a writing and of a reading which we know is ordered around its own blind spot. We know this a priori, but only now and with a knowledge that is not a knowledge at all.

Notes

1 *La transparence et l'obstacle* [Paris, 1958] p. 154. Naturally, I can only cite Rousseau's interpreters to indicate borrowings or to circumscribe a debate. But it goes without saying that every reader of Rousseau is guided by the admirable edition of the *Oeuvres complètes* now in progress at the "Bibliothèques de la Pléiade," and by the masterful work of Messrs. [François] Bouchardy, [Pierre] Burgelin, [Jean-Daniel] Candaux, [Robert] Derathé, [Jean] Fabre, [Michel] Foucault, [Bernard] Gagnebin, [Henri] Gouhier, [Bernard] Groethuysen, [Bernard] Guyon, [Robert] Osmont, [Georges] Poulet, [Marcel] Raymond, [Sven] Stelling-Michaud and, here especially, Jean Starobinski.

2 Edition Garnier, p. 17. My references are to the *Oeuvres complètes* (Pléiade edition) only in cases where the text has been published in one of the three volumes that have currently appeared. Other works will be cited from the Garnier editions. Of the *Essay on the Origin of Languages*, which we cite from the 1817 Bélin edition, I indicate, for the sake of convenience, only the numbers of the chapters.

3 *Rêveries.* Septième Promenade (*Pléiade* I, pp. 1066–67) [pp. 144–45]. Italics added. It may be objected that the animal represents a natural life even more animated than the plant, but one can only deal with it dead. "The study of animals is nothing without anatomy" (p. 1068) [p. 146].

4 Ibid. Without looking for a principle of reading there, I refer, out of curiosity and from among many other possible examples, to what Karl Abraham says of the Cyclops, of the fear of being blind, of the eye, of the sun, of masturbation etc. in *Oeuvres complètes*, tr. Ilse Barande [and E. Grin (Payot, 1965)] II, pp. 18 f. Let us recall that in a sequence of Egyptian mythology, Seth, helper of Thoth (god of writing here considered as a brother of Osiris), kills Osiris by trickery (cf. Vandier, op. cit., p. 46). Writing, auxiliary and suppletory, kills the father and light in the same gesture (Cf. supra, p. 101, 328–29 n. 31).

5 "'Little one' was my name; 'Mama' was hers; and we always remained 'Little one' and 'Mama,' even when advancing years had almost obliterated the difference between us. I find that these two names give a wonderfully good idea of the tone of our intercourse, of the simplicity of our manners, and, above all, of the mutual relation of our hearts. For me she was the tenderest of mothers, who

never sought her own pleasure, but always what was best for me; and if sensuality entered at all into her attachment for me, it did not alter its character, but only rendered it more enchanting, and intoxicated me with the delight of having a young and pretty mamma whom it was delightful to me to caress – I say caress in the strictest sense of the word, for it never occurred to her to be sparing of kisses and the tenderest caresses of a mother, and it certainly never entered my mind to abuse them. It will be objected that, in the end, we had relations of a different character; I admit it, but I must wait a little – I cannot say all at once" (p. 106) [p. 109]. Let us add this sentence from Georges Bataille: "I am myself the 'little one,' I have only a hidden place" (*Le petit* [2d edition (Paris, 1963), p. 9]).

6   This passage is often cited, but has it ever been analyzed for itself? The Pléiade editors of the *Confessions*, Gagnebin and Raymond, are no doubt right in being cautious, as they are, systematically and inevitably, of what they call psychiatry (note p. 1281. This same note checks off very usefully all the texts where Rousseau recalls his "follies" or "extravagances.") But this caution is not legitimate, it seems to me, except to the extent that it concerns the abuse – which has hitherto no doubt been confounded with the use – of psychoanalytic reading, and where it does not prescribe the duplication of the usual commentary which has rendered this kind of text most often unreadable. We must distinguish here between, on the one hand, the often hasty and careless, but often also enlightening, analyses by Dr. René Laforgue ("Etude sur J.-J. Rousseau," in *Revue française de psychanalyse*, I, ii [1927], pp. 370 f.; and *Psychopathologie de l'échec* [1944], [Paris], pp. 114 f.), which moreover do not consider the texts I have just cited, and, on the other hand, an interpretation which would take into more rigorous account, at least in principle, the teachings of psychoanalysis. That is one of the directions in which Jean Starobinski's fine and careful analyses are engaged. Thus, in *L'oeil vivant*, the sentence that has given us pause is reinscribed within an entire series of examples of analogous substitution, borrowed mostly from the *Nouvelle Héloise*; this one for example, among other "erotic fetishes": "All the parts of your scattered dress present to my ardent imagination those of your body that they conceal. This delicate headdress which sets off the large blond curls which it pretends to cover; this happy bodice shawl against which at least once I shall not have to complain; this elegant and simple gown which displays so well the taste of the wearer; these dainty slippers that a supple foot fills so easily; this corset so slender which touches and embraces ... what an enchanting form ... in front two gentle curves ... oh voluptuous sight ... the whalebone has yielded to the force of the impression ... delicious imprints, let me kiss you a thousand times!" (p. 147 [tr. Judith H. McDowell (University Park and London, 1968), pp. 122–23].

But do the singularity of these substitutions and the articulation of these displacements hold the attention of the interpreter? I wonder if, too concerned with reacting against a reductionist, causalist, dissociative psychology, Starobinski does not in general give too much credit to a totalitarian psychoanalysis of the phenomenological or existentialist style. Such a psychoanalysis, diffusing sexuality in the totality of behavior, perhaps risks blurring the cleavages, the differences, the displacements, the fixations of all sorts that structure that totality. Do the place or the places of sexuality not disappear in the analysis of global behavior, as Starobinski recommends: "Erotic behavior is not a fragmentary given; it is the manifestation of a total individual, and it is as such that it ought to be analyzed. Whether it is to neglect it or to make it a privileged subject of study, one cannot limit exhibitionism to the sexual 'sphere': the entire personality is revealed there, with some of its fundamental 'existential choices.'" (*La transparence et l'obstacle*, pp. 210–11. A note refers us to the *Phénoménologie de la perception* of [Maurice] Merleau-Ponty [(Paris, 1945); *Phenomenology of Perception*, tr. Colin Smith (New York, 1965)]). And does one not, in this way, risk determining the pathological in a very classic manner, as "excess" thought within "existential" categories: "In the perspective of a global analysis, it will appear that certain primary givens of consciousness constitute at the same time the source of Rousseau's speculative thought, and the source of his folly. But these given-sources are not morbid by themselves. It is only because they are lived in an excessive manner, that the malady declares itself and is developed. ... The morbid development will realize the caricatural placing in evidence of a fundamental 'existential' question that consciousness was not able to dominate" (p. 253).

7   Page 165 [p. 171].

8   In these celebrated pages of the first Book of the *Confessions*, Rousseau compares the first experiences of reading ("secret and ill-chosen reading") to the first discoveries of auto-eroticism. Not that

the "filthy and licentious [books]" encouraged him in it. Quite the contrary. "Chance aided my modest disposition so well, that I was more than thirty years old before I set eyes upon any of those dangerous books which a fine lady finds inconvenient because they can only be read with one hand" (p. 40) [p. 40]. Without these "dangerous books," Jean-Jacques gives himself to other dangers. The continuation of the paragraph which closes thus is well known: "It is sufficient for me to have defined the origin and first cause of a propensity which has modified all my passions, and which, restraining them by means of themselves, has always made me slow to act, owing to my excessive impetuosity in desire" (p. 41) [p. 41]. The intention and the letter of this passage should be related to another page of the *Confessions* (p. 444 [p. 459]. Cf. also the editors' note), and to the page from which I quote these lines: "for I have always had a fancy for reading while eating, if I am alone; it supplies the want of society. I devour alternately a page and a morsel. It seems as if my book were dining with me" (p. 269) [p. 278].

9 See editors' note, p. 1569. [The English translation includes the sentence quoted in the Pléiade note on p. 617.]

10 [*Correspondance générale de J.-J. Rousseau* (Paris, 1934), vol. 19, p. 242, vol. 20, p. 122, the latter actually addressed to M. de Sartine, Lieutenant-general of police.]. See also the *Confessions* (p. 109, editors' note).

11 Pages 331–32 [pp. 340–41] (italics added), Starobinski (*La transparence et l'obstacle*, p. 221) and the editors of the *Confessions* (p. 332, n.1) justly relate the use of the word "supplement" to what is made of it on p. 109 [p. 111] ("dangerous means of assisting it" [a literal translation would be "dangerous supplement"]).

CHAPTER 6

The Death of the Author

Roland Barthes

Jacques Derrida's works of 1967, especially *Of Grammatology*, changed the direction of French thinking regarding literature. It had been concerned with the implications of Saussure's linguistics (that literary works have hidden orders or structures; that signs are embedded in discourses; that the relation between words and things is unstable). After 1967, literary theorists such as Roland Barthes became preoccupied with pursuing the implications of Derrida's theories. One implication was that the traditional French educational concern with "great writers" should be reconsidered. If what Derrida claimed was true, then the author was just one point of reference for a text. He argued that one cannot arrest the flow of signifying possibilities that a literary text generates. A text refers in multiple directions, and those possibilities cannot be summed up in or limited to the life of the author. This idea frees up the reader to work on a text, ferreting out strands of significance that the author herself may not have been aware of, actively producing readings.

In his story Sarrasine, Balzac, speaking of a castrato disguised as a woman, writes this sentence: "It was Woman, with her sudden fears, her irrational whims, her instinctive fears, her unprovoked bravado, her daring and her delicious delicacy of feeling." Who is speaking in this way? Is it the story's hero, concerned to ignore the castrato concealed beneath the woman? Is it the man Balzac, endowed by his personal experience with a philosophy of Woman? Is it the author Balzac, professing certain "literary" ideas of femininity? Is it universal wisdom? or romantic psychology? It will always be impossible to know, for the good reason that all writing is itself this special voice, consisting of several indiscernible voices, and that literature is precisely the invention of this voice, to which we cannot assign a specific origin: literature is that neuter, that composite, that oblique into which every subject escapes, the trap where all identity is lost, beginning with the very identity of the body that writes.

Probably this has always been the case: once an action is recounted, for intransitive ends, and no longer in order to act directly upon reality – that is, finally external to any function but the very exercise of the symbol – this disjunction occurs, the voice loses its origin,

Original publication details: Roland Barthes, "The Death of the Author" from *Rustle of Language*, trans. Richard Howard, pp. 49–55. Farrar, Straus, Giroux, 1986. English translation copyright © 1986 by Richard Howard. Reproduced with permission from Hill & Wang, a division of Farrar, Straus and Giroux, LLC.

Literary Theory: An Anthology, Third Edition. Edited by Julie Rivkin and Michael Ryan.
© 2017 John Wiley & Sons, Ltd. Published 2017 by John Wiley & Sons, Ltd.

the author enters his own death, writing begins. Nevertheless, the feeling about this phenomenon has been variable; in primitive societies, narrative is never undertaken by a person, but by a mediator, shaman or speaker, whose "performance" may be admired (that is, his mastery of the narrative code), but not his "genius." The author is a modern figure, produced no doubt by our society insofar as, at the end of the middle ages, with English empiricism, French rationalism and the personal faith of the Reformation, it discovered the prestige of the individual, or, to put it more nobly, of the "human person." Hence it is logical that with regard to literature it should be positivism, resume and the result of capitalist ideology, which has accorded the greatest importance to the author's "person." The author still rules in manuals of literary history, in biographies of writers, in magazine interviews, and even in the awareness of literary men, anxious to unite, by their private journals, their person and their work; the image of literature to be found in contemporary culture is tyrannically centered on the author, his person, his history, his tastes, his passions; criticism still consists, most of the time, in saying that Baudelaire's work is the failure of the man Baudelaire, Van Gogh's work his madness, Tchaikovsky's his vice: the explanation of the work is always sought in the man who has produced it, as if, through the more or less transparent allegory of fiction, it was always finally the voice of one and the same person, the author, which delivered his "confidence."

Though the Author's empire is still very powerful (recent criticism has often merely consolidated it), it is evident that for a long time now certain writers have attempted to topple it. In France, Mallarmé was doubtless the first to see and foresee in its full extent the necessity of substituting language itself for the man who hitherto was supposed to own it; for Mallarmé, as for us, it is language which speaks, not the author: to write is to reach, through a preexisting impersonality – never to be confused with the castrating objectivity of the realistic novelist – that point where language alone acts, "performs," and not "oneself": Mallarmé's entire poetics consists in suppressing the author for the sake of the writing (which is, as we shall see, to restore the status of the reader.) Valery, encumbered with a psychology of the Self, greatly edulcorated Mallarmé's theory, but, turning in a preference for classicism to the lessons of rhetoric, he unceasingly questioned and mocked the Author, emphasized the linguistic and almost "chance" nature of his activity, and throughout his prose works championed the essentially verbal condition of literature, in the face of which any recourse to the writer's inferiority seemed to him pure superstition. It is clear that Proust himself, despite the apparent psychological character of what is called his analyses, undertook the responsibility of inexorably blurring, by an extreme subtilization, the relation of the writer and his characters: by making the narrator not the person who has seen or felt, nor even the person who writes, but the person who will write (the young man of the novel – but, in fact, how old is he, and who is he? – wants to write but cannot, and the novel ends when at last the writing becomes possible), Proust has given modern writing its epic: by a radical reversal, instead of putting his life into his novel, as we say so often, he makes his very life into a work for which his own book was in a sense the model, so that it is quite obvious to us that it is not Charlus who imitates Montesquiou, but that Montesquiou in his anecdotal, historical reality is merely a secondary fragment, derived from Charlus. Surrealism lastly – to remain on the level of this prehistory of modernity – surrealism doubtless could not accord language a sovereign place, since language is a system and since what the movement sought was, romantically, a direct subversion of all codes – an illusory subversion, moreover, for a code cannot be destroyed, it can only be "played with"; but by abruptly violating expected meanings (this was the famous surrealist "jolt"), by entrusting to the hand the responsibility of writing as fast as possible what the head itself ignores (this was automatic writing), by accepting the principle and the experience of a collective writing, surrealism helped secularize the image of the Author. Finally, outside of literature itself (actually, these distinctions are being superseded), linguistics has just furnished the destruction of the Author with a precious analytic instrument by showing that utterance in its entirety is a void process, which functions perfectly without requiring to be filled by the person of the interlocutors: linguistically, the author is never anything more than the man who writes, just as I is no more than the man who says I: language knows a "subject," not a "person," end this subject, void outside of the very utterance which defines it, suffices to make language "work," that is, to exhaust it.

The absence of the Author (with Brecht, we might speak here of a real "alienation:" the Author diminishing like a tiny figure at the far end of the literary stage) is not only a historical fact or an act of writing: it utterly transforms the modern text (or – what is the same thing – the text is henceforth written and read so that in it, on every level, the Author absents himself). Time, first of all, is no longer the same. The Author, when we believe in him, is always conceived as the past of his own book: the book and the author take their places of their own accord on the same line, cast as a before and an after: the Author is supposed to feed the book – that is, he pre-exists it, thinks, suffers, lives for it; he maintains with his work the same relation of antecedence a father maintains with his child. Quite the contrary, the modern writer (scriptor) is born simultaneously with his text; he is in no way supplied with a being which precedes or transcends his writing, he is in no way the subject of which his book is the predicate; there is no other time than that of the utterance, and every text is eternally written here and now. This is because (or: it follows that) to write can no longer designate an operation of recording, of observing, of representing, of "painting" (as the Classic writers put it), but rather what the linguisticians, following the vocabulary of the Oxford school, call a performative, a rare verbal form (exclusively given to the first person and to the present), in which utterance has no other content than the act by which it is uttered: something like the / Command of kings or the I Sing of the early bards; the modern writer, having buried the Author, can therefore no longer believe, according to the "pathos" of his predecessors, that his hand is too slow for his thought or his passion, and that in consequence, making a law out of necessity, he must accentuate this gap and endlessly "elaborate" his form; for him, on the contrary, his hand, detached from any voice, borne by a pure gesture of inscription (and not of expression), traces a field without origin – or which, at least, has no other origin than language itself, that is, the very thing which ceaselessly questions any origin.

We know that a text does not consist of a line of words, releasing a single "theological" meaning (the "message" of the Author-God), but is a space of many dimensions, in which are wedded and contested various kinds of writing, no one of which is original: the text is a tissue of citations, resulting from the thousand sources of culture. Like Bouvard and Pecuchet, those eternal copyists, both sublime and comical and whose profound absurdity precisely designates the truth of writing, the writer can only imitate a gesture forever anterior, never original; his only power is to combine the different kinds of writing, to oppose some by others, so as never to sustain himself by just one of them; if he wants to express himself, at least he should know that the internal "thing" he claims to "translate" is itself only a readymade dictionary whose words can be explained (defined) only by other words, and so on ad infinitum: an experience which occurred in an exemplary fashion to the young De Quincey, so gifted in Greek that in order to translate into that dead language certain absolutely modern ideas and images, Baudelaire tells us, "he created for it a standing dictionary much more complex and extensive than the one which results from the vulgar patience of purely literary themes" (Paradis Artificiels). Succeeding the Author, the writer no longer contains within himself passions, humors, sentiments, impressions, but that enormous dictionary, from which he derives a writing which can know no end or halt: life can only imitate the book, and the book itself is only a tissue of signs, a lost, infinitely remote imitation.

Once the Author is gone, the claim to "decipher" a text becomes quite useless. To give an Author to a text is to impose upon that text a stop clause, to furnish it with a final signification, to close the writing. This conception perfectly suits criticism, which can then take as its major task the discovery of the Author (or his hypostases: society, history, the psyche, freedom) beneath the work: once the Author is discovered, the text is "explained:' the critic has conquered; hence it is scarcely surprising not only that, historically, the reign of the Author should also have been that of the Critic, but that criticism (even "new criticism") should be overthrown along with the Author. In a multiple writing, indeed, everything is to be distinguished, but nothing deciphered; structure can be followed, "threaded" (like a stocking that has run) in all its recurrences and all its stages, but there is no underlying ground; the space of the writing is to be traversed, not penetrated: writing ceaselessly posits meaning but always in order to evaporate it: it proceeds to a systematic exemption of meaning. Thus literature (it would be better, henceforth, to say writing), by refusing to assign to the text (and to the world as text) a "secret:' that is, an ultimate meaning, liberates an activity which we might call counter-theological, properly revolutionary, for to refuse to arrest meaning is finally to refuse God and his hypostases, reason, science, the law.

Let us return to Balzac's sentence: no one (that is, no "person") utters it: its source, its voice is not to be located; and yet it is perfectly read; this is because the true locus of writing is reading. Another very specific example can make this understood: recent investigations (J.P. Vernant) have shed light upon the constitutively ambiguous nature of Greek tragedy, the text of which is woven with words that have double meanings, each character understanding them unilaterally (this perpetual misunderstanding is precisely what is meant by "the tragic"); yet there is someone who understands each word in its duplicity, and understands further, one might say, the very deafness of the characters speaking in front of him: this someone is precisely the reader (or here the spectator). In this way is revealed the whole being of writing: a text consists of multiple writings, issuing from several cultures and entering into dialogue with each other, into parody, into contestation; but there is one place where this multiplicity is collected, united, and this place is not the author, as we have hitherto said it was, but the reader: the reader is the very space in which are inscribed, without any being lost, all the citations a writing consists of; the unity of a text is not in its origin, it is in its destination; but this destination can no longer be personal: the reader is a man without history, without biography, without psychology; he is only that someone who holds gathered into a single field all the paths of which the text is constituted. This is why it is absurd to hear the new writing condemned in the name of a humanism which hypocritically appoints itself the champion of the reader's rights. The reader has never been the concern of classical criticism; for it, there is no other man in literature but the one who writes. We are now beginning to be the dupes no longer of such antiphrases, by which our society proudly champions precisely what it dismisses, ignores, smothers or destroys; we know that to restore to writing its future, we must reverse its myth: the birth of the reader must be ransomed by the death of the Author.

Translated by Richard Howard

CHAPTER 7

From Work to Text

Roland Barthes

In the aftermath of Jacques Derrida's work, French thinking about literature changed. Emphasis shifted from the way literary texts contained a hidden order or structure to the way literary texts generate semantic references that exceed the bounds of standard notions of meaning. In one famous passage, Derrida pointed out that Rousseau's works referred not just to Rousseau's life but also to all the other things that life referred to. Endless referentiality could only be stopped by an arbitrary decision based on conventions (academic rules about what constitutes "proper" meaning, for example). Why was this the case? Because language was made possible by a texture of differences between terms none of which could have identity apart from those differences. That texture is what Derrida calls "textuality" or simply "text." There is, he remarked famously, no outside to the text. What he meant was that one could not declare a meaning or referent or truth finally achieved that would not itself be subject to further reference, a further dissemination of meanings because to be what it is, it had to be different from something else – endlessly. Relations prevail over identities, and there are no identities without relations. For example, in the 1960s, it was accepted wisdom that the meaning of Joseph Conrad's *Heart of Darkness* was that colonialism was a bad thing. But those declaring that meaning were all for the most part white men who lived in the countries most responsible for colonialism. They were themselves signifiers of cultural assumptions that were themselves signifiers of colonial history (and so on back in time and into culture). They therefore ignored the work's racism and its implicit endorsement of a more severe colonialism than the one that was represented as failing in the novel. By pushing meaning and reference further, by opening the work to multiple possible interpretations, further layers and levels of meaning become evident. Complicate simplicity – that might be a good slogan for the import of the concept of the "text" in literary theory at this point of time in the late 1960s and early 1970s when Derrida's work was having its greatest influence on writers such as Barthes in France.

Original publication details: Roland Barthes, "From Work to Text" from *Rustle of Language*, trans. Richard Howard, pp. 56–64. Farrar, Straus, Giroux, 1986. English translation copyright © 1986 by Richard Howard. Reproduced with permission from Hill & Wang, a division of Farrar, Straus and Giroux, LLC.

Literary Theory: An Anthology, Third Edition. Edited by Julie Rivkin and Michael Ryan.
© 2017 John Wiley & Sons, Ltd. Published 2017 by John Wiley & Sons, Ltd.

A change has lately occurred, or is occurring, in our idea of language and consequently of the (literary) work which owes to that language at least its phenomenal existence. This change is obviously linked to the present development of (among other disciplines) linguistics, anthropology, Marxism, psychoanalysis (the word *link* is used here in a deliberately neutral manner: no determination is being invoked, however multiple and dialectical). The transformation of the notion of the work does not necessarily derive from the internal renewal of each of these disciplines, but rather from their intersection at the level of an object which traditionally proceeds from none of them. We might say, as a matter of fact, that *interdisciplinary* activity, today so highly valued in research, cannot be achieved by the simple confrontation of specialized branches of knowledge; the interdisciplinary is not a comfortable affair: it begins *effectively* (and not by the simple utterance of a pious hope) when the solidarity of the old disciplines breaks down – perhaps even violently, through the shocks of fashion – to the advantage of a new object, a new language, neither of which is precisely this discomfort of classification which permits diagnosing a certain mutation. The mutation which seems to be affecting the notion of the work must not, however, be overestimated; it is part of an epistemo-logical shift, more than of a real break of the kind which in fact occurred in the last century upon the appearance of Marxism and Freudianism; no new break has occurred since, and we might say that for the last hundred years we have been involved in a repeti-tion. What History, our History, allows us today is merely to displace, to vary, to tran-scend, to repudiate. Just as Einsteinian science compels us to include within the object studied the *relativity of reference points*, so the combined action of Marxism, Freudianism, and structuralism compels us, in literature, to relativize the relations of *scriptor*, reader, and observer (critic). Confronting the *work* – a traditional notion, long since, and still today, conceived in what we might call a Newtonian fashion – there now occurs the demand for a new object, obtained by a shift or a reversal of previous categories. This object is the *Text*. I know that this word is fashionable (I myself am compelled to use it frequently), hence suspect in some quarters; but this is precisely why I should like to review the main propositions at whose intersection the Text is located, as I see it; the word *proposition* must here be understood more grammatically than logically: these are speech-acts, not arguments, "hints," approaches which agree to remain metaphorical. Here are these propositions: they concern method, genres, the sign, the plural, filiation, reading, pleasure.

(1)   The text must not be understood as a computable object. It would be futile to attempt a material separation of works from texts. In particular, we must not permit ourselves to say: the work is classical, the text is avant-garde; there is no question of establishing a trophy in modernity's name and declaring certain literary productions *in* and *out* by reason of their chronological situation: there can be "Text" in a very old work, and many products of contemporary literature are not texts at all. The difference is as follows: the work is a fragment of substance, it occupies a portion of the spaces of books (for example, in a library). The Text is a methodological field. The opposition may recall (though not reproduce term for term) a distinction proposed by Lacan: "reality" is shown [*se montre*], the "real" is proved [*se démontre*]; in the same way, the work is seen (in bookstores, in card catalogues, on examination syllabuses), the text is demonstrated, is spoken according to certain rules (or against certain rules); the work is held in the hand, the text is held in language: it exists only when caught up in a discourse (or rather it is Text for the very reason that it knows itself to be so); the Text is not the decomposition

of the work, it is the work which is the Text's imaginary tail. Or again: *the Text is experienced only in an activity, in a production*. It follows that the Text cannot stop (for example, at a library shelf); its constitutive moment is *traversal* (notably, it can traverse the work, several works).

(2)   Similarly, the Text does not stop at (good) literature; it cannot be caught up in a hierarchy, or even in a simple distribution of genres. What constitutes it is on the contrary (or precisely) its force of subversion with regard to the old classifications. How to classify Georges Bataille? Is this writer a novelist, a poet, an essayist, an economist, a philosopher, a mystic? The answer is so uncertain that handbooks of literature generally prefer to leave Bataille out; as a matter of fact, Bataille has written texts, or even, perhaps, always one and the same text. If the Text raises problems of classification (moreover, this is one of its "social" functions), it is because it always implies a certain experience of limits. Thibaudet used to speak (but in a very restricted sense) of limit-works (such as Chateaubriand's *Life of Rancé*, a work which indeed seems to us to be a "text"): the Text is what is situated at the limit of the rules of the speech-act (rationality, readability, etc.). This notion is not rhetorical, we do not resort to it for "heroic" postures: the Text attempts to locate itself very specifically *behind* the limit of the *doxa* (is not public opinion, constitutive of our democratic societies, powerfully aided by mass communications – is not public opinion defined by its limits, its energy of exclusion, its *censorship?*); taking the word literally, we might say that the Text is always *paradoxical*.

(3)   The text is approached and experienced in relation to the sign. The work closes upon a signified. We can attribute two modes of signification to this signified: either it is claimed to be apparent, and the work is then the object of a science of the letter, which is philology; or else this signified is said to be secret and final, and must be sought for, and then the work depends upon a hermeneutics, an interpretation (Marxist, psychoanalytic, thematic, etc.); in short, the work itself functions as a general sign, and it is natural that it should represent an institutional category of the civilization of the Sign. The Text, on the contrary, practices the infinite postponement of the signified, the Text is dilatory; its field is that of the signifier; the signifier must not be imagined as "the first part of the meaning," its material vestibule, but rather, on the contrary, as its *aftermath*; similarly, the signifier's *infinitude* does not refer to some notion of the ineffable (of an unnamable signified) but to a notion of *play*; the engendering of the perpetual signifier (in the fashion of a perpetual calendar) in the field of the Text is not achieved by some organic process of maturation, or a hermeneutic process of "delving deeper," but rather by a serial movement of dislocations, overlappings, variations; the logic governing the Text is not comprehensive (trying to define what the work "means") but metonymic; the activity of associations, contiguities, cross-references coincides with a liberation of symbolic energy (if it failed him, man would die). The work (in the best of cases) is *moderately* symbolic (its symbolics runs short, i.e., stops); the Text is *radically* symbolic: *a work whose integrally symbolic nature one conceives, perceives, and receives is a text*. The Text is thus restored to language; like language, it is structured but decentered, without closure (let us note, to answer the scornful suspicion of "fashion" sometimes lodged against structuralism, that the epistemological privilege nowadays granted to language derives precisely from the fact that in it [language] we have discovered a paradoxical idea of structure: a system without end or center).

(4) The Text is plural. This does not mean only that it has several meanings but that it fulfills the very plurality of meaning: an *irreducible* (and not just acceptable) plurality. The Text is not coexistence of meaning, but passage, traversal; hence, it depends not on an interpretation, however liberal, but on an explosion, on dissemination. The plurality of the Text depends, as a matter of fact, not on the ambiguity of its contents, but on what we might call the stereographic plurality of the signifiers which weave it (etymologically, the text is a fabric): the reader of the Text might be compared to an idle subject (who has relaxed his image-repertoire): this fairly empty subject strolls (this has happened to the author of these lines, and it is for this reason that he has come to an intense awareness of the Text) along a hillside at the bottom of which flows a wadi (I use the word to attest to a certain alienation); what he perceives is multiple, irreducible, issuing from heterogeneous, detached substances and levels: lights, colors, vegetation, heat, air, tenuous explosions of sound, tiny cries of birds, children's voices from the other side of the valley, paths, gestures, garments of inhabitants close by or very far away; all these incidents are half identifiable: they issue from known codes, but their combinative operation is unique, it grounds the stroll in a difference which cannot be repeated except as *difference*. This is what happens in the Text: it can be Text only in its difference (which does not mean its individuality); its reading is semelfactive (which renders any inductive-deductive science of texts illusory: no "grammar" of the text) and yet entirely woven of quotations, references, echoes: cultural languages (what language is not cultural?), antecedent or contemporary, which traverse it through and through, in a vast stereophony. The intertextuality in which any text is apprehended, since it is itself the intertext of another text, cannot be identified with some *origin* of the text: to seek out the "sources," the "influences" of a work is to satisfy the myth of filiation; the quotations a text is made of are anonymous, irrecoverable, and yet *already read*: they are quotations without quotation marks. The work disturbs no monistic philosophy (there are antagonistic ones, as we know); for such a philosophy, plurality is Evil. Hence, confronting the work, the Text might indeed take for its motto the words of the man possessed by devils: "My name is legion, for we are many" (Mark 5:9). The plural or demonic texture which sets the Text in opposition to the work may involve profound modifications of reading, precisely where monologism seems to be the law: certain "texts" of Scripture, traditionally adopted by theological (historical or anagogical) monism, may lend themselves to a diffraction of meanings (i.e., finally, to a materialist reading), while the Marxist interpretation of the work, hitherto resolutely monistic, may become more materialist by pluralizing itself (if, of course, Marxist "institutions" permit this).

(5) The work is caught up in a process of filiation. What is postulated are a *determination* of the world (of the race, then of History) over the work, a *consecution* of works among themselves, and an *appropriation* of the work to its author. The author is reputed to be the father and the owner of his work; literary science thus teaches us to *respect* the manuscript and the author's declared intentions, and society postulates a legality of the author's relation to his work (this is the "author's rights," actually a recent affair, not legalized in France until the time of the Revolution). The Text, on the other hand, is read without the Father's inscription. The metaphor of the Text is here again detached from the metaphor of the work; the latter refers to the image of an *organism* which grows by vital expansion, by "development" (a significantly ambiguous word: biological and rhetorical); the metaphor of the Text is that of the *network*; if the Text expands, it is by the effect of a combinative operation, of a systematics (an image, moreover, close to the

views of contemporary biology concerning the living being); no vital "respect" is therefore due to the Text: it can be *broken* (moreover, this is what the Middle Ages did with two nonetheless authoritarian texts: Scripture and Aristotle); the Text can be read without its father's guarantee; the restoration of the intertext paradoxically abolishes inheritance. It is not that the Author cannot "return" in the Text, in his text, but he does so, one might say, as a guest; if he is a novelist, he inscribes himself there as one of his characters, drawn as a figure in the carpet; his inscription is no longer privileged, paternal, alethic, but ludic: he becomes, one can say, a paper author; his life is no longer the origin of his fables, but a fable concurrent with his life; there is a reversion of the work upon life (and no longer the contrary); the work of Proust and Genet permits us to read their lives as a text: the word *bio-graphy* regains a strong, etymological meaning; and thereby the sincerity of the speech-act, a veritable "cross" of literary ethics, becomes a false problem: the *I* that writes the text is never anything but a paper *I*.

(6)   The work is ordinarily the object of consumption; I intend no demagoguery by referring to what is called a consumer culture, but we must recognize that today it is the work's "quality" (which ultimately implies an appreciation of "taste") and not the actual operation of reading which can make differences between books: "cultivated" reading is not structurally different from reading on trains. The Text (if only by its frequent "unreadability") decants the work (if it permits it at all) from its consumption and recuperates it as play, task, production, practice. This means that the Text requires an attempt to abolish (or at least to diminish) the distance between writing and reading, not by intensifying the reader's projection into the work, but by linking the two together into one and the same signifying practice. The distance that separates reading from writing is historical. In the period of strongest social division (before the instauration of democratic cultures), reading and writing were *equally* class privileges: Rhetoric, the great literary code of that time, taught *writing* (even if what was ordinarily produced were discourses, not texts); it is significant that the advent of democracy reversed the watchword: the (secondary) school prides itself on teaching *reading* and no longer writing. In fact, *reading*, in the sense of *consuming*, is not *playing* with the text. "Playing" must be taken here in all the polysemy of the term: the text itself "plays" (like a door that "plays" back and forth on its hinges; like a fishing rod in which there is some "play"); and the reader plays twice over: he *plays at* the Text (ludic meaning), he seeks a practice which reproduces it; but, so that this practice is not reduced to a passive, interior *mimesis* (the Text being precisely what resists this reduction), he *plays* the Text; we must not forget that *play* is also a musical term; the history of music (as practice, not as "art") is, moreover, quite parallel to that of the Text; there was a time when, active amateurs being numerous (at least within a certain class), "to play" and "to listen" constituted a virtually undifferentiated activity; then two roles successively appeared: first of all, that of the *interpreter*, to which the bourgeois public (though it could still play a little itself: this is the entire history of the piano) delegated its playing; then that of the (passive) amateur who listens to music without being able to play it (the piano has effectively been replaced by the record); we know that today post-serial music has disrupted the role of the "interpreter," who is asked to be in a sense the co-author of the score which he completes rather than "expresses." The Text is a little like a score of this new kind: it solicits from the reader a practical collaboration. A great novation this, for who *executes* the work? (Mallarmé raised this question: he wanted the audience to *produce* the book.) Today only the critic executes the work (pun intended). The reduction of reading to consumption is

obviously responsible for the "boredom" many feel in the presence of the modern ("unreadable") text, the avant-garde film or painting: to be bored means one cannot produce the text, play it, release it, *make it go*.

(7) This suggests one final approach to the Text: that of pleasure. I do not know if a hedonist aesthetic ever existed (eudaemonist philosophies are certainly rare). Of course, a pleasure of the work (of certain works) exists; I can enjoy reading and rereading Proust, Flaubert, Balzac, and even – why not? – Alexandre Dumas; but this pleasure, however intense, and even when it is released from any prejudice, remains partly (unless there has been an exceptional critical effort) a pleasure of consumption: for, if I can read these authors, I also know that I cannot *rewrite* them (that one cannot, today, write "like that"); and this rather depressing knowledge suffices to separate me from the production of these works, at the very moment when their distancing founds my modernity (to be modern – is this not really to know that one cannot begin again?). The Text is linked to delectation, i.e., to pleasure without separation. Order of the signifier, the Text participates in its way in a social utopia; before History (supposing that History does not choose barbarism), the Text fulfills if not the transparency of social relations, at least the transparency of language relations: it is the space in which no language prevails over any other, where the languages circulate (retaining the *circular* meaning of the word).

These few propositions do not necessarily constitute the articulation of a Theory of the Text. This is not merely the consequence of the presenter's inadequacies (moreover, in many points he has merely recapitulated what is being investigated and developed around him). This is a consequence of the fact that a Theory of the Text cannot be satisfied with a metalinguistic exposition: the destruction of meta-language, or at least (for it may be necessary to resort to it provisionally) calling it into question, is part of the theory itself: discourse on the Text should itself be only text, research, textual activity, since the Text is that *social* space which leaves no language safe, outside, and no subject of the speech-act in a situation of judge, master, analyst, confessor, decoder: the theory of the Text can coincide only with a practice of writing.

CHAPTER 8

Writing

Barbara Johnson

An American school of deconstructive criticism developed out of Jacques Derrida's work. Its leading proponents were Paul de Man and J. Hillis Miller. While Derrida sought to dislocate the assumptions of metaphysics in philosophy, these critics were concerned with the dislocation of naïve assumptions about meaning in literary texts. Texts are figural or rhetorical, and they refer endlessly to other texts, not to a knowable presence of truth or to determinable meanings that might, as the New Critics assumed, be said to constitute "universals." In this selection, Barbara Johnson, a student of de Man and herself a leading practitioner of American deconstruction, explains how the French concern with "writing" is linked to the deconstructive project.

How is it that the word "writing" has come to be considered a critical term? Isn't "writing" simply one of those aspects of literature that can be taken for granted? Isn't it merely the medium through which a reader encounters words on a page – for example, these?

Every essay in this volume communicates to some extent *by means of* the very thing it is talking *about*. Nowhere is this more obvious than in the case of writing. An essay about writing, therefore, is an unclosable loop: it is an attempt to comprehend that which it is comprehended by. The non-Euclidean logic of such reciprocal inclusion has often itself been an object of attention in recent theoretical discussions of writing. That is only one of the consequences that the study of writing has entailed.

Writing about writing is hardly a new phenomenon, however. From Omar Khayyám's moving finger to Rousseau's trembling hand, from the broken tables of Moses to the purloined letters of Poe and Alice Walker, from Borges's encyclopedia to Wordsworth's lines left upon a seat in a yew tree, images of writing in writing testify to an enduring fascination with the mechanics and materiality of the written word. A comprehensive treatment of the question of writing is obviously beyond the scope of the present essay. I will therefore concentrate on a particular recent moment of reflection about

Original publication details: Barbara Johnson, "Writing" from *Critical Terms for Literary Study*, ed. Frank Lentricchia and Thomas McLaughlin, pp. 39–47. University of Chicago Press, 1990. Reprinted with permission from University of Chicago Press.

Literary Theory: An Anthology, Third Edition. Edited by Julie Rivkin and Michael Ryan.

writing – the theoretical "revolution" in France in 1967 – which has had a decisive impact upon the shape of literary studies today.

Writing (*l'écriture*) came to philosophical, psychoanalytic, and literary prominence in France in the 1960s, primarily through the work of Jacques Derrida, Roland Barthes, and other writers who were at that time associated with the journal *Tel Quel*. Philippe Sollers, in a "Program" that heads the group's collective theoretical volume, proclaimed in 1967: "A comprehensive theory arising out of a thought about the practice of writing cries out for elaboration." Writing, it seemed, was to become the key to all mythologies. The sudden spectacular interest in writing sprang from many different sources, some of which I will outline quickly here.

As early as 1953, in *Writing Degree Zero*, Roland Barthes had investigated the paradoxical relationship that existed in the nineteenth century in France between the development of a concept of Literature (with a capital *L*) and the growing sense of a breakdown in the representational capacities of language. Literature was in some ways being exalted as a substitute religion, but it was a religion whose high priests seemed only to proclaim the obscurity, imperfection, or unreliability of their own medium. The proper names associated with the elaboration of *both* sides of this phenomenon are Flaubert and Mallarmé. These writers, says Barthes, *constructed* the object Literature in the very act of announcing its death. In later essays, Barthes lays out a theory of literature based on a split between the classic notion of a *work* (*œuvre*) – considered as a closed, finished, reliable representational *object* – and the modern notion of a *text* – considered as an open, infinite *process* that is both meaning-generating and meaning-subverting. "Work" and "text" are thus not two different kinds of object but two different ways of viewing the written word. What interests Barthes is the *tension* between the concept of Literature and the concept of textuality. While Literature is seen as a series of discrete and highly meaningful Great Works, textuality is the manifestation of an open-ended, heterogeneous, disruptive force of signification and erasure that transgresses all closure – a force that is operative even within the Great Works themselves.

Closure versus subversion, product versus practice, meaning-containing object versus significance-scattering process: Barthes' theory of writing owes a great deal, as we shall see, both to Marxism and to psychoanalysis. But the *Tel Quel* writers' involvement with Marxism and psychoanalysis takes on its particular coloring, strangely enough, through the mediation of Saussurian linguistics. How does this happen?

In his *Course in General Linguistics* (first published by his students in 1916, with new editions in 1948 and 1966), Ferdinand de Saussure mapped out a science of linguistics based not on the historical ("diachronic") development of families of languages but on the structural ("synchronic") properties of language "as such," frozen in time as a *system*. This "structuralist" perspective, also developed in the 1950s in anthropology by Claude Lévi-Strauss, involves viewing the system as a set of relations among elements governed by rules. The favorite analogy for such systems is chess: whatever the particular properties of an individual "man" (ivory, wood, plastic), the "man" is involved in a system of moves and relations that can be known and manipulated in themselves. From the structural point of view, there is no difference between ivory and plastic. There is difference between king, queen, and knight, or between white and black.

Saussure's most enduring contribution has been his description of the *sign* as the unit of the language system. The sign is composed of two parts: a mental image or concept (the "signified"), and a phonic or graphic vehicle (the "signifier"). The sign is thus both conceptual and material, sense and sound, spirit and letter at once. The existence of numerous languages indicates that the relation between the signifier and the signified in any given sign is arbitrary (there is no natural resemblance between sound and idea), but once fixed, that relation becomes a convention that cannot be modified at will by any individual speaker. By thus deciding that what is relevant to a structural study of language is neither history ("diachrony") nor reality (the "referent") but rather the system of differential relations among signs, Saussure set up a tremendously enabling, as well as limiting, heuristic perspective for analysis. And by asserting that signs signify not as independently meaningful units corresponding to external objects but as elements whose value is generated by their difference from neighboring elements in the system, Saussure put forth a notion of *difference* (not identity) as the origin of meaning.

Saussure's suspension of interest in history and the external world would seem to place him at the farthest remove from Marxism. But theorists of writing saw a connection between the signifier/signified relation and the materialism/idealism relation: If the signifier was the material condition of the existence of ideas, then the privileging of the signified resembled the fetishization of commodities resulting from bourgeois idealism's blindness to labor and to the material conditions of economic existence. The liberation of the signifier, the rebellion against idealist repressions, and the unleashing of the forces of difference and desire against the law and order of identity were all part of the program for change that developed in France in the 1960s. Whether linguistic materiality and economic materiality are linked *only* by analogy, or whether there is some profound interimplication between them, is still a subject for debate today. But whatever the case, the repressive return to order that followed the strikes and demonstrations in France in May 1968 squelched the optimism of those who might have believed in any simple connection between liberating the signifier and changing the class structure of society.

The understanding of what it might mean to liberate the signifier also had roots in the psychoanalytic theory of Jacques Lacan. For many years prior to the 1966 publication of his *Ecrits* (*Writings*), Lacan had been conducting a seminar in which he attempted to work out a radically new way of reading Freud. What he emphasized in Freud's writing was the discovery that "the unconscious is structured like a language." The unconscious is *structured*. It is not a reservoir of amorphous drives and energies but a system of articulations through which repressed ideas return in displaced form. Freud's comparison of a dream to a rebus is extended as an analogy for all effects of the unconscious: just as each element in a rebus must be translated separately in order to decipher the total message, so each element in a dream is a knot of associations that must be explored without regard for the dream's surface coherence. Dreams, slips of the tongue, parapraxes, hysterical symptoms, and other expressions of the unconscious are for Lacan manifestations of a "signifying chain," a structure of associations that resembles an unconscious foreign language. Consciousness attempts to disregard this language in order to control and define the identity of the self, but the psychoanalyst's task is to attempt to hear that language despite the ego's efforts to scramble it. Using the terminology of Saussure, Lacan calls the units of unconscious expression "signifiers," linked to repressed "signifieds." But the search for the signified can only take the form of a sliding along the chain of signifiers. In other words, there is no one-to-one link between signifier and signified but rather an "effect of signified" generated by the movement from one signifier to another. Freud never comes to the end of his dream analyses, never "solves" their enigma, but it feels as though something like insight is achieved by following out the dreamer's chains of associations.

Lacan's troubling of Saussure's one-to-one link between signifiers and signifieds actually turns out to have its counterpart in Saussure's own work. Beginning in 1964, Jean Starobinski began publishing strange notebooks in which Saussure attempted to prove that certain late Latin poems contained hidden proper names anagrammatically dispersed throughout their texts. The poems, in other words, contained extra signifiers, readable only to those in the know. Whether or not these anagrams were a secret key to late Latin poetics, the notion that the signifier could take the lead in creating poetic effects appealed to students of poetry. Saussure's anagrams prompted Julia Kristeva, among others, to theorize an anagrammatic (or paragrammatic) functioning in poetic language as such.

The claim that signifiers can generate effects even when the signified is unknown serves as the basis for Lacan's famous reading of Poe's story "The Purloined Letter." In that story, an unscrupulous minister steals a compromising letter from the queen under the unsuspecting eyes of the king. An amateur detective, Dupin, is commissioned by the stymied prefect of police to get the letter back. Dupin suspects that the minister has hidden the letter in plain sight, just as it had been when he stole it. Dupin then repeats the minister's act and steals the letter back for the queen. Lacan emphasizes the way in which the characters' actions are determined by the position of the letter among them. Neither the letter's contents (the never-revealed "signified") nor the individual identities of the people (the psychological equivalent of Saussure's ivory and wood chessmen) determine the course of the plot. It is the movement of the letter that dictates the characters' actions.

The rebus, the anagram, and the letter are clearly all manifestations of *writing*. They are graphic, articulated, material instantiations of systems of marks that simultaneously obscure and convey meaning. They are also something other than mere transcriptions of the spoken word. In other words, they are not examples of *phonetic* writing. It is this "something other" that must be kept in mind as we now turn to the work of the most important French theorist of writing, Jacques Derrida.

It was in 1967 that Derrida published three major books devoted to the question of writing: *Writing and Difference, Of Grammatology*, and *Speech and Phenomena*. Derrida's project in these writings is to reevaluate the structuring principles of Western metaphysics. Western philosophy, writes Derrida, has analyzed the world in terms of binary oppositions: mind vs. body, good vs. evil, man vs. woman, presence vs. absence. Each of these pairs is organized hierarchically: the first term is seen as higher or better than the second. According to Derrida, the opposition between speech and writing has been structured similarly: speech is seen as immediacy, presence, life, and identity, whereas writing is seen as deferment, absence, death, and difference. Speech is primary; writing secondary. Derrida calls this privileging of speech as self-present meaning "logocentrism."

In his three volumes of 1967, Derrida gives rigorous attention to the paradox that the Western tradition (the "Great Books") is filled with *writings* that privilege *speech*. By closely analyzing those writings, Derrida attempts to uncover the ways in which the Great Books rebel against their own stated intention to say that speech is better than writing. What his analyses reveal is that even when a text *tries* to privilege speech as immediacy, it cannot completely eliminate the fact that speech, like writing, is based on a *différance* (a Derridean neologism meaning both "deferment" and "difference") between signifier and signified inherent in the sign. Speakers do not beam meanings directly from one mind to another. Immediacy is an illusion. Properties normally associated with writing inevitably creep into a discussion designed to privilege speech. Thus, for example, although Saussure wishes to treat speech as primary and writing as secondary for an understanding of language, he describes language as a "dictionary in the head" or as "linear" – a spatial term more applicable to writing than to speech. Or, to take another example, when Socrates tells Phaedrus that proper teaching must take place orally rather than in writing, he nevertheless ends up describing the truths such teaching is supposed to reach as being "*inscribed* in the soul." Because a gap of heterogeneity and distance is fundamental to the structure of language, Derrida sees "speech" as being ultimately structured like "writing." This emphasis on writing as the more originary category is designed to counter the history of logocentrism and to track the functioning of *différance* in structures of signification.

Many literary texts seem in fact to stage some version of this encounter between the search for spoken immediacy or identity and the recourse to writing and difference. The following poem by Edward Taylor (ca. 1642–1729), for example, does not seem to expect to end up talking about writing:

Meditation 6

Am I thy gold? Or purse, Lord, for thy wealth,
  Whether in mine or mint refined for thee?
I'm counted so, but count me o'er thyself,
  Lest gold washed face, and brass in heart I be.
  I fear my touchstone touches when I try
  Me and my counted gold too overly.

Am I new minted by thy stamp indeed?
  Mine eyes are dim; I cannot clearly see.
Be thou my spectacles that I may read
  Thine image and inscription stamped on me.
  If thy bright image do upon me stand,
  I am a golden angel in thy hand.

Lord, make my soul thy plate, thine image bright
  Within the circle of the same enfile
And on its brims in golden letters write
  Thy superscription in an holy style.
  Then I shall be thy money, thou my horde:
  Let me thy angel be, be thou my Lord.

Written in a style of extended metaphor known as the metaphysical conceit, this poem sets out to express spiritual value in terms of material value (gold). The most obvious figure for the conjunction between the spiritual and the material is the word "angel," which means both a heavenly being and an old English coin. Through this spiritual/material alloy, the poem attempts to make human value both derive from and coincide with divine value, to eliminate the space of difference or distance between the human and the divine.

The poem is composed of a series of questions and imperatives addressed to God. While these aim to alleviate doubt, difference, and distance, they seem only to widen the gap they attempt to close. Am I gold or purse? value-object or container? the poet asks. He then pursues the first possibility, only to stumble upon a new inside/outside opposition: "Lest gold washed face, and brass in heart I be." The gold begins to resemble a sign, with no guaranteed correlation between face (signifier) and heart (signified). The becoming-sign process continues in the second stanza, where the speaker is "stamped" with an image and an inscription. The speaker is now a reader, and what he reads is himself. God has become an image, and a corrective lens. In the final stanza, the text ("inscription") that was dimly decipherable in the second stanza turns out not yet to have been written. While the poem still yearns for a perfectly reciprocal container/contained relation ("I shall be thy money, thou my horde"), this relation now requires the active intervention of writing ("in golden letters write / Thy superscription"). In his increasingly aggressive submissiveness, the speaker tries to order God to take his place as the writer.

From metal to image to letters, from touching to reading to writing, from counted to almost-read to not-yet-written, the speaker seems to be farther away from coincidence with God at the end than he was at the beginning. The mediating elements only increase the *différance*. Yet this *différance* is also the space of the poem's existence. The speaker cannot *write* his way into an immediacy that would eliminate writing. Nor can he write himself into a submissiveness great enough to overtake the fact that it is he, not God, who writes. His conceit will never succeed in erasing the "conceit" of writing itself.

The logic of writing is thus a double logic: writing is called upon as a necessary remedy for *différance*, but at the same time it *is* the very *différance* for which a remedy must be sought. In Derrida's analyses of writing, this logic is called the logic of the *supplément*. In French, the word *supplément* means both an "addition" and a "substitute." To say that "A is a *supplément* to B" is thus to say something ambiguous. Addition and substitution are not exactly contradictory, but neither can they be combined in the traditional logic of identity. In the poem, the inscriptions, images, and even spectacles function as *suppléments:* they are at once additions and substitutes simultaneously bridging and widening the gap between God and the speaker. Some sense of the way in which supplementary logic differs from the binary logic of identity ($A = A$) and noncontradiction ($A \neq$ not A) may be derived from the following list. In this list, all statements are to be taken as *simultaneously* equivalent to the statement "A is a *supplément* to B." (In terms of the Taylor poem, say B = the presence of, or coincidence with, God; and A = writing).

A is added to B.
A substitutes for B.
A is a superfluous addition to B.
A makes up for the absence of B.
A usurps the place of B.
A makes up for B's deficiency.
A corrupts the purity of B.
A is necessary so that B can be restored.
A is an accident alienating B from itself.
A is that without which B would be lost.
A is that through which B is lost.
A is a danger to B.
A is a remedy to B.
A's fallacious charm seduces one away from B.
A can never satisfy the desire for B.
A protects against direct encounter with B.

Supplementary logic is not only the logic *of* writing – it is also a logic that can only really exist *in* writing. That is, it is a nonintuitive logic that inheres (Lacan would say, "in-sists") in a text as a system of traces. Like an algebraic equation with more than one unknown, supplementary logic cannot be held in the head but must be worked out in external form. It is no accident that the word "differential" is central both to calculus and to Derrida's theory of writing.

Derrida's theory of writing turns out to have been, in fact, a theory of reading. The epigraph to his *Writing and Difference* is a quotation from Mallarmé: "Le tout sans nouveauté qu'un espacement de la lecture" ("All without innovation except for a certain spacing-out of reading"). What does it mean to introduce "space" into reading? For Mallarmé, it means two things. It means giving a signifying function to the materiality – the blanks, the typefaces, the placement on the page, the punctuation – of writing. And it also means tracking syntactic and semantic ambiguities in such a way as to generate multiple, often conflicting, meanings out of a single utterance. The "meaning" of a Mallarmé text, like that of a dream, cannot be grasped intuitively as a whole but must be worked out rigorously by following each strand in a network of relations. What Derrida generalizes and analyzes in other writings is this "spacing" that Mallarmé attempts to maximize. In his reading of Plato's *Phaedrus*, for instance, Derrida follows the ambiguity of the word *pharmakon*, which Plato uses to describe writing itself. If *pharmakon* can mean both "poison" and "remedy," what does it mean to call writing a *pharmakon*? As Derrida points out, translators of Plato have rendered this word by choosing to favor one side or the other of the ambiguity according to the context. They have subordinated its ambiguity to their notion of what makes the most sense. They have thus subordinated "writing" as spacing and ambiguity to "speech" as single intention. The ambiguity of the poison/remedy relation is tamed thereby into something far less unsettling. "Sense" is achieved, however, at a cost. To know the difference between poison and remedy may be reassuring, but that reassurance may well make it difficult to come to grips with the meaning of Socrates' death.

Thus "reading," for Derrida, involves following the "other" logics of structures of signification inscribed in writing that may or may not be in conformity with traditional logics of meaning, identity, consciousness, or intention. It involves taking seriously the elements that a standard reading disregards, overlooks, or edits out. Just as Freud rendered dreams and slips of the tongue *readable* rather than dismissing them as mere nonsense or error, so Derrida sees signifying force in the gaps, margins, figures, echoes, digressions, discontinuities, contradictions, and ambiguities of a text. When one writes, one writes more than (or less than, or other than) one thinks. The reader's task is to read what is written rather than simply attempt to intuit what might have been meant.

The possibility of reading materiality, silence, space, and conflict within texts has opened up extremely productive ways of studying the politics of language. If each text is seen as presenting a major claim that attempts to dominate, erase, or distort various "other" claims (whose traces nevertheless remain detectable to a reader who goes against the grain of the dominant claim), then "reading" in its extended sense is deeply involved in questions of authority and power. One field of conflict and domination in discourse that has been fruitfully studied in this sense is the field of sexual politics. Alice Jardine, in *Gynesis* (1985), points out that since logocentric logic has been coded as "male," the "other" logics of spacing, ambiguity, figuration, and indirection are often coded as "female," and that a critique of logocentrism can enable a critique of "phallocentrism" as well. A theory and practice of female writing (*écriture féminine*) has been developed in France by such writers as Hélène Cixous and Luce Irigaray, who have attempted to write the specificity of female biological and ideological difference. While Cixous, Irigaray, and others work on the relations between writing and the body, many feminists on both sides of the Atlantic have been interested in the gender implications of the relations between writing and silence. In *The Madwoman in the Attic* (1979), Sandra Gilbert and Susan Gubar show how nineteenth-century women writers struggle for authorship against the silence that has already been prescribed for them by the patriarchal language they must both use and transform. Adrienne Rich also explores the traces of women's silence in a collection of essays entitled *On Lies, Secrets, and Silence* (1979). These and other works have as their project the attempt to read the suppressed, distorted, or disguised messages that women's writing has encoded. They require a reading strategy that goes beyond apparent intentions or surface meanings, a reading that takes full advantage of writing's capacity to preserve that which cannot yet, perhaps, be deciphered.

The writings of Western male authorities have often encoded the silence, denigration, or idealization not only of women but also of other "others." Edward Said, in *Orientalism* (1978), analyzes the discursive fields of scholarship, art, and politics in which the "Oriental" is projected as the "other" of the European. By reading against the grain of the writers' intentions, he shows how European men of reason and benevolence could inscribe a rationale for oppression and exploitation within their very discourse of Enlightenment....

Suggested Readings

Abel, Elizabeth, ed. 1982. *Writing and Sexual Difference*.
Barthes, Roland. [1953] 1967. *Writing Degree Zero*.
Derrida, Jacques. [1967a] 1978. *Of Grammatology*.
Derrida, Jacques. [1967b] 1973. *Speech and Phenomena*.
Derrida, Jacques. [1967c] 1973. *Writing and Difference*.
Gates, Henry Louis, Jr., ed. 1986. *"Race," Writing, and Difference*.
Ong, Walter, 1982. *Orality and Literacy*.

CHAPTER 9

Theory in Practice
Lear's After-Life

John Joughin

Currently an administrator at the University of East London, John Joughin is a leading Shakespeare scholar whose books include *Shakespeare and National Culture* (1997), *Philosophical Shakespeares* (2000), and *The New Aestheticism* (2003). In this essay, he uses Derrida and deconstructive analysis to explore the complexity of meaning in *King Lear*.

I

It is true that, with respect to the disaster, one dies too late.
(Maurice Blanchot, *The Writing of the Disaster*)[1]

What does it mean to speak of the afterlife of a literary text? And why do some texts retain an enduring significance while others simply fade away? The survival of one text over another clearly depends on its sustained ability to unsettle existing conventions and to defamiliarize habitual perceptions, and in the case of canonical texts, such as Shakespeare, this is clearly a transformative potential which is retained over a considerable period of time. In this respect, of course, the afterlife of any given text is directly dependent on its critical life, its ability to draw generations of readers back to crucial points of analysis or interpretative ambiguity. In tracking back across Shakespeare's critical heritage and dipping into the closely contested editorial squabbles of years gone by, one unearths a series of textual disputes and dilemmas which open out into questions which remain unanswered to this day. In confronting the unlikely resurrection of Hermione at the end of *The Winter's Tale*, or the confusion surrounding the whereabouts of Lady Macbeth's 'missing children', the critic encounters a form of inexplicable alterity or otherness which exceeds his or her intellectual grasp, rather than providing the grounded repleteness of a 'meaningful' solution.[2] In the case of a dramatic text, the

Original publication details: John Joughin, "Lear's Afterlife." *Shakespeare Survey* 55 (2002), pp. 67–81. Annual Bibliography of English Language and Literature. Cambridge University Press, 2002. Reproduced with permission from Cambridge University Press.

qualitative newness of a play's afterlife is clearly also linked in quite complex ways to our experience of a play in performance; often these are moments of affective intensity which linger on after the play and force us to re-evaluate our preconceptions concerning how an individual scene might be construed. In these and a multitude of other ways then, there is clearly an implicit *recognition* that the value of a literary text is that it serves to remind us of the limits of our comprehension even as it functions to sharpen our response. Yet the question remains: why do some literary afterlives prove more enduring than others? And if a key aspect of our engagement with literary and dramatic texts is the sense in which they continue to resist a definitive explanation, then why, or in what sense, can this aspect of literary experience still be said to remain distinctive or meaningful?

In some respects *Lear* remains the exemplary text through which to explore precisely these types of issues, insofar as our enduring fascination with the play seems to be inextricably linked to a sense of incomprehension and anxiety concerning its transgression of most conventional thresholds of taste and decorum. In other words, *Lear*'s position as a text which takes us beyond conventional expectations – sometimes to the point of incredulity – has the merit of offering us a type of critical degree zero against which to press *any* claims to meaningful interpretation. Such is the extent of the 'wildness' of the play's formal disintegration that for many critics there is something simultaneously implausible and unactable about Shakespeare's text which borders on barbarism. For the nineteenth-century critic Charles Lamb, *Lear* approximates to a type of disaster 'painful and disgusting', 'beyond all art' and 'essentially impossible to be represented on a stage'.[3] And Lamb's disparagement is already hinted at in the Preface to Samuel Johnson's edition of the play, where he is compulsively drawn back to *Lear*'s unreality, and repeatedly confronts the dilemma of 'proving' its exceptions. Here, for example, is Johnson on Gloucester's blinding:

> I am not able to apologize with equal plausibility for the extrusion of Gloucester's eyes, which seems an act too horrid to be endured in dramatic exhibition, and such as must always compel the mind to relieve its distress by incredulity.[4]

For Johnson the fascination of witnessing these and other improbabilities is that from the very outset they transfix us *even as* they keep the audience in a state of perpetual tumult:

> General Observation. The tragedy of *Lear* is deservedly celebrated among the dramas of Shakespeare. There is perhaps no play which keeps the attention so strongly fixed; which so much agitates our passions and interests our curiosity. The artful involutions of distinct interests, the striking opposition of contrary characters, the sudden changes of fortune, and the quick succession of events, fill the mind with a perpetual tumult of indignation, pity, and hope.[5]

Here and elsewhere in his Preface to the play, something clearly snags on Johnson's reading consciousness as he witnesses a series of events which in their 'artful involution' defy 'reasonable explanation', even as they then serve to heighten his perception of the drama to the point of extreme discomfort. Well over a century later, A. C. Bradley confirms *Lear*'s surplus effect in similar terms, observing that the play is simply

> too huge for the stage ... the immense scope of the work; the mass and variety of intense experience which it contains; the interpenetration of sublime imagination, piercing pathos, and humour almost as moving as the pathos; the vastness of the convulsion both of nature and of human passion.[6]

As Philip Armstrong comments, these and other critical encounters with the play testify to an 'excess that overflows generic boundaries'; it is as if 'there must be in the play something more than the play, which returns upon the spectator'[7] – and here perhaps Johnson's use of the term '*involution*', both in the process of 'involving', but also in the literal sense of 'involute' – suggesting a 'tight coil' or 'curled spiral' waiting to recoil upon the spectator – might betray more than it could possibly know.

In this article I want to try to unpack the significance of one such after-effect: the '*pietà*-like' image of Lear holding the dead Cordelia in his arms, a scene of 'pity and hope' which has continued to haunt critics, editors and spectators of the play alike. Such is the affective intensity of the scene that it seems to retain an almost totemic significance, particularly for directors of the play, who invariably recall the incident in their programme notes, as if to somehow exorcise its affect. Here, for example, is Barrie Rutter, founder and director of the Northern Broadsides theatre company, offering a 'behind the scenes' glimpse of the genesis of his recent touring production of the play:

> So there we were in Salts Mills in 1993, rehearsing *Merry Wives*: pigeons flying around the wooden beams of the spinning lobby on the fifth floor, and Shakespeare's comedy giving us all a lot of fun. Suddenly, I stop rehearsals and say, 'Wouldn't it be terrific if Lear walked the whole length of this room carrying the dead Cordelia, saying "Howl, howl howl"?' I turned round and the merry wives with Mistress Quickly (Polly Hemingway, Elizabeth Estensen and Ishia Bennison) all had tears rolling down their cheeks. 'Yes', they croaked in unison.
>
> I've hung on to that image for six years, and now have a chance to use it. As a touring company, of course, we have to adapt to different venues and each theatre or space will see the equivalent of 'the long walk'.[8]

Rutter's comments testify to the fact that in performance (even, indeed, in rehearsal), there is something 'out of joint', ob-scene or extra about the 'unbearable spectacle' of Lear carrying Cordelia across the stage at the end of the play. Rutter's 'advance recollection' of the scene confirms a type of 'spectral effect' insofar as Derrida reminds us that: 'a specter is always a *revenant*. One cannot control its comings and goings because *it begins by coming back*'.[9] An analogous form of temporal dislocation is already anticipated by the position of the scene in the play itself, so that, as R. A. Foakes reminds us, strictly speaking Cordelia's death comes '*after* the end' of the play (or at least follows the formal completion of the drama with the deaths of Goneril, Regan and Edmund);[10] on the other hand, without the episode that comes after and disrupts the play's formal unity, *Lear* would somehow be incomplete. These and other types of disturbance that 'add only to replace' confirm the contradictory logic of what Derrida would term the scene's supplementarity.[11] In the process, as Foakes observes: 'the final scene stretches out Lear's suffering beyond the point at which to have died would have been fitting'.[12] Repeated but always singular, the recurring agony of Cordelia's death confirms *Lear* as a tale that can never be told but is in some sense crucial to our experience of the play.[13] The untimeliness of the scene and its excessive affect, as well as its proximity to death and the compulsion of critics to repeat their engagement with the scene ever since, clearly takes us into the territory of Freud's notion of the *Unheimlich* or uncanny.[14] It is quite simply a spectacle of 'inexpressible horror' or, as Lear himself puts it: 'Howl, howl, howl …'.

One should hardly be surprised, then, that in confronting the unendurable excess of the scene and in an attempt to make the play 'fit' for consumption, the solution of early editors and adaptors was to 'regularize' the ending of the play in order to confirm *Lear* as a formal comedy more in keeping with its original source material. Nahum Tate's 'New-modelling' of the story with Edgar and Cordelia married off as a 'celestial Pair' and Lear living on into happy retirement is the obvious example. Yet traditionally, from Tate's 1681 production onwards, even in its absence, the scene troubled critics and editors of the play. For Samuel Johnson, for example, there is a lasting sense of injustice surrounding Cordelia's death, the reverberations of which carry far beyond the theatrical experience itself:

> Shakespeare has suffered the virtue of Cordelia to perish in a just cause, contrary to the natural ideas of justice, to the hope of the reader, and, what is yet more strange, to the faith of the chronicles ... A play in which the wicked prosper and the virtuous miscarry may doubtless be good, because it is a just representation of the common events of human life; but since all reasonable beings naturally love justice, I cannot be easily persuaded that the observation of justice makes a play worse; or that, if other excellencies are equal, the audience will not always rise better pleased from the final triumph of persecuted virtue.
>
> In the present case the public has decided. Cordelia, from the time of Tate, has always retired with victory and felicity. And, if my sensations could add anything to the general suffrage, I might relate, I was many years ago so shocked by Cordelia's death that I know not whether I ever endured to read again the last scenes of the play till I undertook to revise them as editor.[15]

In teasing out the implications of Johnson's response I would want to argue that something like the residue of the supplementary affect we noted above now re-surfaces in a critical context, and that as a consequence Johnson's appeal to 'the natural idea of justice' begins to sound a bit strained. The moment comes when Johnson the critic adopts the position of a spectator. Crucially, the critic cannot help conceding that in performance, just as the scene is unfit, it fits – so even as Cordelia's death scene flouts any 'justifiable' moral schema, it remains 'a *just* representation of the common events of human life'. In some respects, then, the episode constitutes a potentially transgressive or 'critical' location precisely *because* of its lack of fit or indeterminacy. In the process it is as if the disjointure between moral ideal and dramatic practice itself remarks a type of discordant 'truth' about the actual predicament of moral life. Of course the predictable disavowal follows, insofar as Johnson is quick to remind the reader that 'all reasonable beings naturally love justice'; yet in the course of attempting to justify his own position Johnson feels bound to concede that:

> this conduct [suffering the virtue of Cordelia to perish in a just cause, contrary to the natural ideas of justice] is justified by the Spectator, who blames Tate for giving Cordelia success and happiness in his alteration and declares that, in his opinion, *the tragedy has lost half its beauty*.[16]

Somewhat confusingly, then, it might be said that there are two types of 'truth' to be had here: the idealized 'truth' which depends on the formalized convention of Cordelia's recovery; and the disconcerting authenticity of the unfit yet somehow more 'just' spectacle of her 'perish[-ing] in a just cause'. The reference to the justification 'by the Spectator' is now made even more explicit, and as soon as Johnson switches to this perspective he finds himself admitting that the playwright's work sustains its relative exclusivity (its 'tragic beauty' if you like), by 'authenticating' a claim to validity that is somehow unique. The fact that this truth claim simultaneously also exceeds the restrictive demands of empirical truth which governed the neo–classical criticism of the period is, I would want to argue, precisely the point. Johnson's remarks serve to remind us that, in performance, Cordelia's death presents us with a type of untheorizable excess; such moments threaten the critic with a relinquishment of intellectual control – the mind full of 'perpetual torment' no doubt – yet it is precisely here that the ethical demand of the play is finally disclosed. The event-like relation of performance constitutes an irruptive excess – something that 'happens' outside an a priori grid of expectations and refuses the foreclosure of conventional attempts to explain it away. As a result 'justice' is revealed as a type of acategorical category: one which at once complies with and deviates from the formal aesthetics of which it is part.

As we have seen, witnessed in performance the force of this encountered otherness ensures that the viewing subject experiences a sense of ungrounding and disorientation, so that for Rutter we might recall that the dislocation of the 'long walk' recurs outside of the rehearsal space ('Suddenly I stop rehearsals'), though still somehow within it, as – 'in character' but beside themselves with pity – the 'merry wives' shed tears and croak their affirmation of witness. As Robert Eaglestone observes: 'It is in these [uncanny] moments when our sense of our selves and our relation to the *logos* is interrupted and put into question that the ethics of literature are at their clearest.'[17] In occupying the same time as the characters, we effectively 'live through' a sequence of moments with them, and while we cannot actually put ourselves in the 'presence' of characters during perfor-mance, in acknowledging their specificity as particular individuals, as Stanley Cavell reminds us: 'we are in, or can put ourselves in, their *present*'.[18] Characters and audience confront this form of the encountered other on an almost nightly basis. Moreover, in performance, the unendurable excess of incidents like Cordelia's death retains a 'com-plex and shaming power': a sense of witness, for the audience that views them.

We might begin to speak here then of the ethics of interpretation, in a twofold sense: not just in the sense of our encounter with otherness in performance where we are presented with what we might term after Levinas and Derrida 'the irreducible otherness of the other', but also in terms of the act of criticism itself, insofar as it demonstrates a willingness to 'promote' the unexpected or the *unheimlich* 'within the material it examines'.[19] Alert to those same 'artful involutions' that continue to disrupt and plague philosophical idealism with the very impossibility of their representation – in endlessly repositioning us and in being open to a form of otherness which both attracts and defies our comprehension – this process of interpretation is necessarily open-ended, for as Eaglestone puts it: 'There can be no final reading, no last word.'[20] In this regard, an ethical reading is also, as Maurice Blanchot reminds us, an act of testimony, a form of reading which is no longer passive, but is passivity's reading:

> Finally, there is the reading that is no longer passive, but is passivity's reading. It is without pleasure, without joy; it escapes both comprehension and desire. It is like the nocturnal vigil, that 'inspiring' insomnia when, all having been said, 'Saying' is heard, and the testi-mony of the last witness pronounced.[21]

Blanchot's incomprehension in the face of disaster is, perhaps, not so far removed from Johnson's 'perpetual tumult of indignation, pity, and hope', yet even as we live on *after*, or survive the disaster itself, we might ask what type of justice would actually be possible in such a violently unjust world? In the case of Cordelia's death, the ethical demand of the scene seems to lurk within the uncanniness of the acts of testimony we have briefly reviewed above, even as they then serve as a palpable reminder that in some profound sense in being drawn back as witnesses we are both absent and present – this is doubtless why the scene continues to transfix us so powerfully. Yet is it possible that our continued *fascination* with *Lear*'s closing scene – its haunting afterlife, if you like – almost sustains a 'micrology' of our relation to the play itself, that each time the scene is performed, it secretes the truth of an ethical exigency – a 'felt contact at a distance' – that offers, and then refuses us, the chance of redemption? These moments of affective intensity clearly 'live on' in performance and thus in a fundamental sense constitute the 'afterlife' of Shakespeare's play. Yet in merely testifying to the fact that we continue to survive the unendurable, can *Lear*'s 'artful involutions' then still be said to retain their transformative potential against all the odds, or is there simply a limit to the play's afterlife? And – to return to the question I opened with – how, in these circumstances, can *Lear* then still be said to remain distinctive or meaningful?

II

We come after, and that is the nerve of our condition.
(George Steiner, *Language and Silence*)[22]

These questions arguably become even more pressing for a modern audience, who 'live on' after the horrific events of the twentieth century. After all, in this context, as R. A. Foakes reminds us, *Lear*'s apparently 'passive indifference to suffering' is all too depressingly familiar:

> Its [*King Lear*'s] exposure of the horror of torture and suffering no longer seems outrageous in the context of concentration camps, napalm bombs, anti-personnel mines, and acts of terrorism such as have become familiar in report to everyone … It has seemed to some the play of our time in being open to nihilistic interpretation as showing not the potentially heroic journey or pilgrimage of Man through life, but rather a progression towards despair or mere nothingness.[23]

From Foakes's perspective then, the danger is that by now, however sympathetically we might view the play, we are simply inured to *Lear*'s displays of cruelty. Yet ultimately, this seems to me to be a rather complacent position to take. In a certain sense Foakes is clearly right to remind us that *Lear* is 'to some the play of our time in being open to nihilistic interpretation', but might this not also run the risk of universalizing an encounter which finally resists universalization? While there has been a tendency for critics to suggest that our culture could be 'valued' according to the nature of our engagement with this play alone – and here of course Foakes's sense of *Lear* as our contemporary consciously echoes Jan Kott's hugely influential *Shakespeare Our Contemporary* – I would want to argue that this actually oversimplifies the nature of our relation to the play. Paradoxically of course, as I've already suggested above, the fact is that Shakespeare's play constitutes a type of exemplary text precisely *because* it continues to remind us of the limits of our attempts to engage in meaningful interpretation. In teasing out the implications of this, we might push the argument on a stage further and say that the paradox is that *Lear* can still remain 'valuable' for us *only* in its wider perception that modern culture is increasingly found to be lacking in value; and thus, in the same process, *Lear*'s 'value' is somehow simultaneously to survive the experience of outliving its own utility. In this respect the notion of *Lear* being 'our contemporary' clearly stands in need of some fuller interrogation, especially insofar as it echoes recent philosophical debates concerning the problem of nihilism. There are several possible ways of responding to nihilism, yet *Lear*'s delineation of the problem comes uncannily close to the experience of those philosophers who suffer a sense of belatedness in surviving the catastrophic history in which they continue to find themselves implicated. For thinkers such as Theodor Adorno for example, 'living on' after events such as the Holocaust, is bound up with a sense of unjustifiable survivorhood and in such a context there is something inhuman, not just in surviving disaster, but in attempting to theorize it. In the opening section of his 'Meditations on metaphysics' in *Negative Dialectics* Adorno is forced to wonder

> whether after Auschwitz you can go on living – especially whether one who escaped by accident, one who by rights should have been killed, may go on living.[24]

For Adorno then, the 'despair and or mere nothingness' to which Foakes alludes is at once a tangible yet still somehow 'unreal' feature of our modern existence. In these circumstances, 'survival' is directly complicit with an epistemological regime it outlives, but which it now also in some sense necessarily continues to inhabit. For those who practise philosophy this means negotiating the realization that philosophy was always already non-redemptive; it 'lives on', we live on (precisely) because 'the moment to realise it was missed'. Or as Adorno puts it:

> survival calls for the coldness, the basic principles of bourgeois subjectivity, without which there could have been no Auschwitz; this is the drastic guilt of him who was spared. By way of atonement he will be plagued by dreams such as that he is no longer living at all, that he was sent to the ovens in 1944 and his whole existence since has been imaginary, an emanation of the insane wish of a man killed twenty years earlier.
>
> Thinking men and artists have not infrequently described a sense of being not quite there, of not playing along, a feeling as if they were not themselves at all, but a kind of spectator.[25]

For those who 'come after', then, bearing witness once again confirms the uncanny sense 'of being not quite there'. And again of course, it is difficult not to hear in these lines the key trope of Lear's own journey, a character who also crucially in some sense lives life belatedly, and for whom enduring finitude entails the discovery of an identity which is now directly predicated on the loss of identity:

LEAR   ... Who is it that can tell me who I am?
FOOL   Lear's shadow.[26]

In either form, survival constitutes a type of haunting and Lear is a shadow or a shade of what he once was. Fittingly enough, of course, in *Lear* characters reside 'out o'th'grave' having long outstayed their welcome. In such a world as this, the only wonder is that, as Kent puts it on the king's eventual demise: 'he hath endured so long; / He but usurped his life' (5.3.315–16). Indeed, in some sense, as Francis Barker reminds us, under the conditions existing in the play: 'one is never more truly oneself than when speaking of oneself as not oneself'.[27] In 'coming after' we are confronted with a play which refuses the comfort of narrative continuity and settled identity, and in a world lacking the 'existential balm' of religion Shakespearian tragedy already offers us a shadow narrative of the despair and nihilism of late modernity.[28] The shared 'disappointment' of a post-religious world and of a post-metaphysical philosophy is one of a spectral afterlife where there is an inability to reconcile metaphysical speculation with experience.[29] We are presented instead with a world of acute discontinuity and self-misrecognition and the failure of religion or philosophy to make any significant or practical difference. The lack of an antidote to this situation takes us to the precipice of what Nietzsche would term 'the last form of nihilism' which: 'includes disbelief in any metaphysical world and forbids itself any belief in a *true* world', in having reached this standpoint:

> one grants the reality of becoming as the *only* reality, forbids oneself every kind of clandes-tine access to after-worlds and false divinities – but *cannot endure this world though one does not want to deny it*.[30]

In this climate, as the British philosopher Simon Critchley puts it, the challenge for a newly attenuated philosophical enterprise is to locate 'a meaning to human finitude without recourse to anything that transcends that finitude'.[31] Baldly stated, there is no redemption, nor can there be, at least not for us, not yet …

Yet enduring finitude means that there is always an unsettled moment of the 'post' or an aftermath and in raising contemporary questions concerning our disenchantment with metaphysics, even the most recent adaptations of the play continue to confirm Foakes's sense of *Lear*'s 'openness' to nihilistic interpretation. Unsurprisingly perhaps, these reworkings of the Lear myth are often tales of survival and traumatic memory too. In Jane Smiley's *A Thousand Acres*, for example, amidst a revisionist reading which transports Lear to the mid-West of America we are offered a sub-text concerning the 'recovered memory' of paternal abuse and incest,[32] while in the recent Dogme 95 film *The King is Alive* (2000) directed by Kristian Levring, a group of tourists find them-selves abandoned in a disused mining village in the middle of the Namibian desert. In a setting which aptly evokes a sense of depletion and exhausted resource, the survivors attempt a memorial reconstruction of *Lear*, presumably in an attempt to utilize drama in order to sustain a mutually recognizing community. Yet the power of performance is reduced, as one unwilling participant is told: 'You don't have to worry, you know. Nobody has to fall in love and everybody gets to die in the end.' Digitally shot with hand-held cameras according to Dogme house-rules, the film's visual feel accentuates intimacy but also conveys the alienation and distance of docudrama. And in a further twist we are confronted with a group of recognizably Shakespearian actors, including David Calder and Janet McTeer, in the process of learning to unlearn their parts, characters who liter-ally might be said to play along 'by not playing along'.

In several recent reviews *The King is Alive* is cast as resembling Beckett, thus indi-rectly substantiating Foakes's observation that Shakespearian tragedy might still more properly be construed as 'a kind of parallel' to the twentieth-century Theatre of the Absurd. For, as Foakes rightly implies, not the least disconcerting aspect of *Lear*'s timely untimeliness is that it could just as easily be read alongside plays like *Waiting for Godot* and *Endgame*.[33] Shakespeare's dramaturgy, like Beckett's, is littered with characters that seem to teeter on the abyss of survival, endlessly enduring an 'experience of the limit': characters who are 'unable to go on, unable not to go on',[34] and where the need to con-front an unreconciled gap between theory and practice, action and word, in part also closely mirrors the practical failure of philosophy or art to change or transform the world. Moreover, in the case of each playwright – Beckett and Shakespeare – we might say that we are faced with the possibility that drama has lost its therapeutic function and its ability to rekindle community.

In the course of contemplating these questions in their Shakespearian context one is inevitably drawn back here to the seminal work of Stanley Cavell (another early reader of Beckett's *Endgame*) who in the very midst of his groundbreaking analysis of *Lear* offers the following despairing aside on the relation that 'currently' obtains between tragedy and modern life:

> Since we are ineluctably actors in what is happening, nothing can be present to us to which we are not present. Of course we can still know, more than ever, what is going on. But then we always could, more or less. What we do not now know is what there is to acknowledge, what it is I am to make present, what I am to make myself present to. I know there is inex-plicable pain and death everywhere, and now if I ask myself why I do nothing the answer must be, I choose not to.[35]

Caught up (at a distance) in the same cold-war hostilities as Beckett and Kott, in its original form, as Richard Halpern reminds us, Cavell's *Lear* essay inevitably 'bears the marks of its historical moment (1967)' as 'the death and suffering to which Cavell refers is exemplified primarily, as he makes clear, in the Vietnam War'[36] – scenes of suffering which, we might remember at the time, appeared on television screens on an almost nightly basis, and to which, as Halpern adds: 'as citizen and intellectual he [Cavell] feels opposed – yet in regard to which he finds himself choosing the course of paralysis or inaction'.[37]

Yet curiously, of course, insofar as the problem of 'spectatorship' to which Cavell alludes here relates to a form of distance, it is simultaneously a form of distance which results from 'our' almost omnipresent proximity to suffering – a proximity which in its very intimacy breeds a type of passivity. In such a context there is something indifferent in the encounter itself. And the tragedy of course is that, in the very act of watching, as Cavell reminds us, 'we absent ourselves' from incidents of pain and death. In short, even in 'seeing' we could ultimately be said to avoid the confusion of contact, for as Cavell himself puts it: 'What we do not now know is what there is to acknowledge, what it is I am to make present, what I am to make myself present to.'[38] In glossing the fuller drift of this passage from Cavell, Richard Halpern offers the following summation:

> Modernity, Cavell argues, has inverted the traditional relation between tragic theatre and the world. Theater [sic] used to be a privileged place in which we could witness human suffering without actually being obliged to intervene in it; we could be, as Cavell puts it, ethically 'present' to tragic characters without actually being in their presence. Now, how-ever, passive indifference to suffering has become the norm, and so theatrical spectatorship is no longer a special case but depressingly ubiquitous.[39]

There is no simple outside to this situation, even as we continue to inhabit it. Yet for a culture which is in some sense post-metaphysical the key problem remains that, as Cavell's comments imply (and as we saw earlier with Adorno), philosophy and art are now inevitably complicit with the very process they would otherwise be expected to overcome. During his reading of *Lear* Cavell maintains his own complex sense of indi-vidual indictment, maintaining a watchful almost Adornian-like vigilance over the fact that in this context there is something inhuman not just in surviving disaster, but in surviving disaster and failing to confront it.[40] In this respect then, as Jay Bernstein notes, Adorno, Cavell, Beckett (*and* I would want to add *Lear*) each indirectly circle around similar problems:

> How can art stop being a pain-killer yet be appropriate to what makes all response inappropriate and still, still authenticate the call of the things of this unworldly world? How can it make a promise that is not complicit with what has undone all promises or kept them too well?[41]

If actual events have now shattered the basis upon which the task of thinking might be reconciled with experience,[42] and if theatre in its modernity falls short of empathy, the problem remains that if we choose the path of paralysis and inaction we must also finally absent ourselves from pain and death. I would simply wish to counter that, in pushing this oscillation between contact and distance to another kind of ultimate limit, in these circumstances Cordelia's death nevertheless remains a 'special case'.

III

> *Last witness, end of history, close of a period, turning point, crisis – or, end of (meta-physical) philosophy.*
>
> (Maurice Blanchot, *The Writing of the Disaster*)[43]

In the course of 'opposing' a redemptive reading of *Lear* Stanley Cavell offers the following observation:

> Is this a Christian play? The question is very equivocal. When it is answered affirmatively, Cordelia is viewed as a Christ figure whose love redeems nature and transfigures Lear. So far as this is intelligible to me, I find it false both to the experience of the play and to the fact that it *is* a play. *King Lear* is not illustrated theology (anyway, which theology is thought to be illustrated, what understanding of atonement, redemption, etc., is thought to be figured?), and nature and Lear are not touched, but run out. If Cordelia exemplifies Christ, it is at the moment of crucifixion, not resurrection.[44]

Without wanting to reinstall a theological component to suffering (although, doubt-less, as Cavell's comments suggest, there almost always inevitably is one), I would want to argue that in the face of contemporary 'indifference to suffering', our enduring fascination with the image of Cordelia in Lear's arms is that, against all the odds, it continues to sustain a form of (secular) transfiguration from which there is no option of turning away, and which still seems to touch us with what Blanchot evocatively terms a 'grasping contact':

> *The image*
> Why fascination? Seeing implies distance, the decision that causes separation, the power not to be in contact and to avoid the confusion of contact. Seeing means that this separation has nonetheless become an encounter. But what happens when what you see, even though from a distance, seems to touch you with a grasping contact, when the manner of seeing is a sort of touch, when seeing is a *contact* at a distance? What happens when what is seen imposes itself on your gaze, as though the gaze had been seized, touched, put in contact

with appearance? Not an active contact, not the initiative and action that might still remain in a true touch; rather, the gaze is drawn, absorbed into an immobile movement and a depth without depth. What is given to us by contact at a distance is the image, and fascination is passion for the image.

What fascinates us, takes away our power to give it meaning, abandons its 'perceptible' nature, abandons the world, withdraws to the near side of the world and attracts us there, no longer reveals itself to us and yet asserts itself in a presence alien to the present in time and to presence in space ... Fascination is ... vision that is no longer the possibility of seeing, but the impossibility of not seeing, impossibility that turns into seeing, that preserves – always and always – in a vision that does not end: a dead gaze, a gaze that has become the ghost of an eternal vision.[45]

Blanchot's 'contact at a distance' is not an 'active contact' but neither is it the passive proximity of indifference rehearsed in Cavell's sense of our own individual participation in a 'generalized abdication' from responsibility. Crucially, as Jay Bernstein reminds us, for Blanchot, in yielding 'a passion for the image', fascination confronts us with 'the precedence of the object' or, as Blanchot himself puts it, 'seeing is a sort of touch'.[46] In its very duration the image of Lear holding Cordelia yields something of this complex phenomenology to its audience, manifesting 'a depth without depth' which only in the actual process of closing unfolds itself on uncertain surfaces, as a series of pressing intangibles which barely disclose themselves as: 'breath, mist and stain(ing)' or the 'chance' of a 'feather stirring' (cf. 5.3.260, 264). Such is the auratic potential of the scene that it fixes our gaze, yet insofar as it demands our attention, it does so without ever quite relinquishing itself to us, and in doing so it 'imposes itself on the gaze' as an enduring image. In the process it is as though 'the gaze had been seized, touched, put in contact with appearance'.[47]

Of course, in some sense the scene offers us a distorted perspective, and in the process of breathing life into a stone, the brutal fact of the matter might well be that she dies and he lives. Yet Lear's preoccupation with Cordelia's corpse also confirms an 'aestheticization of suffering' which, whilst it is barely recoverable, and remains beyond comprehension, still exists in such close proximity and in such extreme circumstances that the manner of 'seeing' itself asserts an irreducible alterity which in its partial redemption sustains the 'touch' of the other. And the distinction between 'seeing' and reading remains crucial here, as in performance, beyond the detached objectivities of editorial hindsight, what fixes us is precisely the memory of what Samuel Johnson protests himself unable to rewitness and yet is bound to disavow: 'I was many years ago so shocked by Cordelia's death that I know not whether I ever endured to read again the last scenes of the play till I undertook to revise them as editor.' We might say that Cordelia's death confirms what Blanchot terms 'the impossibility of not seeing', so that however much Johnson opts for it, the 'choice' of turning away does not ever really enter into the equation. Even as fascination maintains its endless recurring 'contact at a distance', then, it is also inextricably intertwined with what Blanchot elsewhere terms last-witness, and which in the present extract confirms itself as a form of spectatorship which 'asserts itself in a presence alien to the present in time and to presence in space', from which finally there is no absenting oneself. In short, our fascination with Cordelia's death confirms the 'conduct' of turning and last witness as an incessant testament which is just and fitting though never quite *justified* by the spectator. It preserves 'a vision that does not end', an image which Rutter 'hangs on to for six years'. Its moment of memorial is momentous, and it remains a compulsive trope both in terms of the decisive or critical point it retains in the play's overall dramatic structure, but also in its confirmation of an 'ethical exigency' which eventually proves impossible to avoid or eliminate.

IV

Finished, it's finished, nearly finished, it must be nearly finished ...

(Samuel Beckett, *Endgame*)[48]

Art or philosophy, or any form of practice is bound to be inadequate, an inappropriate response to the now infinite disaster ... but we are always standing somewhere, talking; so winding up, having done with art and meaning is less easy than it appears: the habit of meaning is hard to break. Maybe, but who are we to say, the task of ending meaning is infinite too (maybe that is the disaster – too), an uncompletable task; perhaps we can be stopped, but not finish.

(Jay Bernstein on *Endgame*)[49]

In some form, one might say that *Lear*'s Theatre of the Absurd, like Beckett's, ends as it begins, by eking out its own utter sense of incompletion. The untimeliness of Beckett's world, and of 'our' world, is almost wholly in keeping with *Lear*'s. In the case of *Endgame* we are confronted with an apocalyptic terrain to rival *Lear*'s, as we witness a 'master' and his 'servant' entombed in what appears to be a type of nuclear bunker where the survivors hang on to the last vestiges of 'human contact'. And in Beckett's drama, as in Shakespeare's, while writing the disaster maintains its endless unendurability, it also sustains its own form of 'waning intensity'.[50] Amidst their overwhelming sense of disenchantment the plays somehow retain an ethical impulse, so that a utopian glimmer that things could be otherwise, however paltry, just about remains intact. In this respect, at least, as Bernstein observes: 'having done with art and meaning is less easy than it appears: the habit of meaning is hard to break'.

For my part though, the strain at the end of *Lear* also sustains a utopian impulse and in doing so is eventually probably more Adornian than Cavellian in terms of its overall ethical trajectory. Adorno's thought, like Beckett's, is often caricatured as securing nothing more or less than a fatalistic pessimism of the intellect, yet even amidst disenchantment and indifference, the 'seismic' potential of Adorno's philosophy resides in its willingness to sustain a 'standpoint of redemption' against all the odds.[51] For Adorno, as for Cavell, it is true to say that there is eventually 'no conceivable standpoint from which the disaster might be named or articulated',[52] yet as Max Pensky reminds us, in addressing those things that fall by the wayside Adorno's work simultaneously responds to 'an ethical intuition, according to which the repressed other – the nonidentical – can reappear within the ruins of a dominant discourse' and the wreckage of its unassimilated material.[53] Eventually then we might say that Beckett's art, like Adorno's philosophy, 'survives its own apocalypse' in that, although art and philosophy will always come too late, in the very process of witnessing its own demise it holds on to the possibility that 'one day it will arrive in time'.[54] In this respect, for Adorno, as Simon Critchley puts it:

> the reality or unreality of redemption hardly matters. What is important is the messianic demand [of redemption] and not whether this demand is underwritten by some guarantee of redemption.[55]

Adorno of course does not attempt a reading of *Lear*, yet if we were to extend the logic of his position, in reading the runes of Shakespeare's play in the face of despair but also from a 'standpoint of redemption', we could say that, even in death, *Lear*'s 'messianic demand' is maintained. In no small part, as I have intimated above, it continues to be sustained by the ungraspable image of Cordelia, of which there is no letting go. Of course such a reading would expose us only to 'a universe of greys', a type of future past which oscillates between the despair of being 'too late' in the 'hope against hope' of affirmation, and in holding on to a 'not yet' which is finally unfulfillable.[56] There is evidently no straightforward sense in which this finally underwrites either an act of overcoming or a form of restoration. Yet by the final scene of Shakespeare's play, of course, this is precisely Lear's 'place'. And, when they are culled from their original theatrical context, it is perhaps unsurprising that his own 'last' words read very much like a fragmented series of recalcitrant one liners from Beckett:

> *not yet*
> 'Why then she lives.'
> 'if it be so ...'
> 'stay a little. Ha?'
> 'What is't thou sayst?'
> 'Do you see this?'
>   (5.3.261, 263, 269,
>   270, 308)

> *too late*
> 'she's gone for ever'
> 'She's dead as earth'
> 'now she's gone for ever'
> 'No, no, no life!'
> 'Never, never, never, never, never'
>   (5.3.257, 259, 268, 304, 307)

Caught between hope and despair, Lear holding Cordelia confirms the broken halves of a type of dialectical image that will never finally add up. Or as Lear puts it:

'I might have saved her; now she's gone for ever' (5.3.268)

Fittingly of course it is an 'image of horror' and as such it remains constitutively incomplete and unfulfillable in its very failure to reconcile a felt discrepancy between thought and experience. Yet just as *Lear*'s closing scene necessarily remains incomprehensible, it also retains its ethical imperative in sustaining its evocative demand that it must somehow still be construed for the sake of future action.[57] In this sense, at least, the play's ultimate scene of departure maintains its currency. And the line '*now* she's gone forever' might just as easily be turned back against itself, in being said to 'forever' occupy the moment of the '*now*'. Alongside Lear, each one of us hangs on to this. Nothing more and nothing less. It is the play's endlessly recurring afterimage – a moment of last witness which suddenly unexpectedly resurrects its close contact at a distance:

> Do you see this? Look on her: look, her lips,
> Look there, look there! *He dies*
>   (5.3.308-9)

V

Metaphysics must know how to wish.[58]

(Theodor Adorno, *Negative Dialectics*)

So where does this leave those who come after? How does one go on? And what form might that future action take? Fittingly of course *Lear* remains equivocal to the last:

> EDGAR: The weight of this sad time we must obey,
> Speak what we feel, not what we ought to say.
> The oldest hath borne most we that are young
> Shall never see so much, nor live so long.
> *Exeunt with a dead march.* (5.3.322–5)

In the closing lines of the play 'feeling' and 'speaking', rather than feeling and seeing, are cast in tantalizing proximity. Perhaps then it is a form of obligation, a 'speaking' that eventually comes from learning by heart? Let me expand briefly on what it might mean to say this.

When I worked with a group of students on these lines recently, several of them noticed a resemblance to the well-known fourth stanza of Laurence Binyon's poem 'For the Fallen':

> They shall grow not old, as we that are left grow old:
> Age shall not weary them, nor the years condemn.
> At the going down of the sun and in the morning
> We will remember them.[59]

Doubtless it was the time of year, as we were studying the play just after the Remembrance Sunday services commemorating the anniversary of Armistice Day and held annually across Britain in memory of those who have sacrificed their lives for peace. Of course, in Binyon's stanza, in surviving the disaster, it is we who come after, we who are left to grow old and weary while our predecessors are forever young and immortalized as a consequence. In Edgar's speech, however long we have got left, in outliving those that 'we' survive, those who are left will never live so long as those who are now also in some sense immortalized. So on an intuitive level at least the students' sense of a correspondence between the two stanzas seems absolutely right. Yet something continues to trouble me in the comparison.

Even in the short term of growing old, can we never live up to our elders who are old but forever young? And even while they remain beyond reproof, as Binyon implies, will the unlived lives of our ancestors in turn effectively condemn us? Does this mean that there is no learning from experience? In suggesting that: 'we that are young / Shall never see so much, nor live so long', Edgar's speech is earthbound in that it constitutes a reflection from within experience that inaugurates a degree of responsibility for those who come after. And we need to live the conditionality of our inheritance, however fraught with difficulty that 'living' might be. Perhaps a clue resides in the words of the obligation that precede *Lear*'s last testament?

> The weight of this sad time we must obey,
> Speak what we feel, not what we ought to say.

As Foakes reminds us in his gloss on the line, there seems to be a conscious echo of *Lear*'s opening scene here: 'in 1.1, Goneril and Regan spoke dutifully what they *ought to say*'.[60] But now we might notice that in closing there is also the more substantial temporal duty or 'obedience', which precedes what we merely 'ought' to say: 'The weight of this sad time *we must obey*' – a duty, that is to say, which is beyond mere public duty, and one which arguably marks an ethical turning point in coming after but now lying beyond the empty rhetoric which attended the official investment of power and responsibility at the beginning of the play. The outcome is discordant; yet it also arguably re-marks the recognition that 'the obligations imposed by the dead *are* the obligations we discover and renegotiate in life'[61] – a form of ethical demand that lives on in our day-to-day commitments and continues to inform our relations with others in its development beyond the unredeemable lament of Binyon's in memoriam.

Of course, as Foakes observes elsewhere:

> The last line [of the play] remains enigmatic, since saying what one feels (Lear in his rages? Goneril and Regan expressing their lust for Edmund?) may be just as damaging as saying what one ought to say (Goneril and Regan speaking by the rules in the opening scene?).[62]

For her part, we might remember that, during the opening scene, Cordelia effectively enacted an 'articulated silence',[63] rehearsing what she felt by opting out of linguistic exchange in taking the side of things against language; thereby indirectly acknowledging the inequality of those speech acts which are based on dissimulation, and where even in speaking 'true', people will say anything – the 'dutiful ought' of Goneril and Regan in pledging their allegiance. In contrast the articulated silence of loving and being silent is one which in refusing justification and suffering false accusation is willing to risk the consequence:

LEAR	But goes thy heart with this?
CORDELIA	Ay, my good lord.
LEAR	So young and so untender?
CORDELIA	So young, my lord, and true.
LEAR	Well, let it be so. Thy truth then be thy dower
	(1.1.105–9)

It is not merely that, as Foakes suggests, Cordelia 'thought she had to conceal her feelings' in the opening scene.[64] Rather, to love and to suffer the love of dutiful silence, which is still to be felt as such and to be dutiful, is a type of learning by heart which despite its unhappiness refuses to heave its heart into its mouth (1.1.91–2).

This is not to hypostasize the experience of suffering or to universalize its significance, but rather to suggest that the facticity of suffering 'makes a virtue out of limitation' and resides in an openness to corrigibility. Here the difference between thinking and saying cannot be merely anticipated, so that – as the philosopher Gillian Rose puts it:

> To grow in love-ability is to accept the boundaries of oneself and others, while remaining vulnerable, woundable, around the bounds[65]

– an ability that Cordelia exhibits from the start. And, unlikely as it seems, a morsel of this sentiment still survives in the play's closing stanza, even after the enduring memory of her death at the end of the play. As a consequence, we are bound to acknowledge it, for its obligation is an ob-ligature, a binding-up, or bond, to which we are still bound.[66]

However constrictive and unrelenting it might now seem to be, this is 'true' even of Tate's imposed comedic ending to the play, which unwittingly secretes its own testament to provisionality and improvization even as it strives to forget the fact of that which will not be forgotten. After all, Tate's original Dedication actually hinges on its own admission of an impossible juggling act. In the course of defending his 'New-modelling of this story ... whereof I had no Ground in my Author' he protests that he was 'wract with no small Fears for so bold a change', and although he locates his main justification for the 're-modelling' of the play in its performance, protesting the change 'well received by the audience', he feels bound to add one further 'theoretical' disclaimer:

> Neither is it of so Trivial an Undertaking to make a Tragedy end happily, for 'tis more difficult to save than 'tis to Kill: The Dagger and Cup of Poison are always in Readiness; but to bring the Action to the last Extremity, and then by probable means to recover All, will require the Art and Judgement of a Writer, and cost him many a Pang in the Performance.[67]

Is it too fanciful to hear a trace of regretful over-compensation in Tate's account of his 'accomplishment'? In 'hindsight', perhaps the trick will be in preserving the spirit of Tate's ethical intuition – his acknowledgement that *"tis more difficult to save than 'tis to Kill"* – against the formal reconciliation that he finally opts for. Yet the admission of '*probable means*' remains improbable. Faced with discordancy Tate opts for resolution, but the trace of protestation – *"tis more difficult to save...to bring the Action to the last Extremity, and then by probable means to recover All"* – almost saves Tate's wishful thinking as a wishful need, acknowledging a part of truth which exceeds his grasp yet remains tantalising within reach. I would want to re-style Tate's 'improvement' of *Lear* as a comedy finally recast as a drama of misrecognition, where, to read Tate in the spirit of Gillian Rose reading Hegel,

> the drama of misrecognition ... ensues at every stage and transition of the work – a ceaseless comedy, according to which our aims and outcomes constantly mismatch each other, and provoke yet another revised aim, action and discordant outcome.[68]

If we accept the comic possibility of the impossible recursion that admits that it is more difficult to save than it is to kill, even as Tate would rather save us from doing so, then it – the comic possibility – still potentially saves us. For then we uphold 'ceaseless comedy' against mere comic closure. And if we do not, we deny any attempt to imagine it otherwise.

In some ways *Lear*'s aesthetic, like Beckett's and Adorno's, still undoubtedly presents us with a universe of greys. And this means that those who survive are left to express the unimaginable. In this respect art and philosophy can only offer some small consolation, so that, as Adorno observes,

> Perennial suffering has as much right to expression as a tortured man has to scream; hence it may have been wrong to say that after Auschwitz you could no longer write poems.[69]

To which *Lear* responds:

Howl, howl, howl, howl! (5.3.255)

Yet only once the formal propriety of *Lear*'s comedy is measured in the totality of its non-fulfilment can a responsible criticism also then begin to contemplate things as they actually 'are'. The trick of course will be in preserving this ethical demand without reconciling ourselves to the barbarism which would deny vulnerability (even in its partial admission of truth) and then merely confirm *Lear* as a formal comedy and have done with the rest.

Notes

1 Maurice Blanchot, *The Writing of the Disaster*, trans. Ann Smock (Lincoln and London, 1995), p. 4.

2 Indeed, as I have argued elsewhere, it is precisely in escaping 'reasonable explanation' that Shakespeare's open-ended resistance to conceptual control might finally prove to be a far more crucial resource for critical thought, providing a form of access to the 'literary conditions' of philosophical questioning itself. See John J. Joughin, 'Philosophical Shakespeares: an introduction', in John J. Joughin, ed., *Philosophical Shakespeares* (London and New York, 2000), pp. 1–17.

3 Charles Lamb, 'On the Tragedies of Shakespeare (1810–11)', in Frank Kermode, ed., *Shakespeare: King Lear* (Basingstoke, 1992), pp. 42–3.

4 Samuel Johnson, 'Preface and Notes to *King Lear* (1765)', in Kermode, ed., *Shakespeare: King Lear*, p. 28.

5 Johnson, 'Preface', p. 27.

6 A. C. Bradley, *Shakespearean Tragedy: Lectures on Hamlet, Othello, King Lear, Macbeth* (Basingstoke, 1992), p. 211.

7 See Philip Armstrong, 'Uncanny Spectacles: Psychoanalysis and the Texts of *King Lear*', *Textual Practice*, 8: 3 (1994), 414–34; p. 416. I'm grateful to Armstrong for alerting me to Bradley's comments. As Armstrong's essay demonstrates there is a clear link to psychoanalytic theory here, particularly in relation to the play's staging of 'excessive affect'. I do not pursue that line of enquiry myself, although I will want to follow Armstrong in touching briefly upon Freud's sense of the 'uncanny'. For the time being though I would want to note that a more explicit link could be established between psychoanalytical criticism and the province of aesthetics; Freud himself makes the connection clear enough when he argues in the opening lines of his essay that: 'aesthetics is understood to mean not merely the theory of beauty but the theory of the qualities of feeling'; see Sigmund Freud, 'The Uncanny', in James Strachey, ed., *Complete Psychological Works*, vol. 17, Standard Edition (London, 1963), pp. 217–56, p. 219.

8 Barrie Rutter, 'Rutter Writes', in programme notes for Northern Broadsides touring production of *King Lear* (1999), no pagination.

9 Jacques Derrida, *Specters of Marx: The State of the Debt, the Work of Mourning and the New International*, trans. Peggy Kamuf (New York and London, 1994), p. 11 (Derrida's emphasis).

10 R. A. Foakes, 'Introduction', in W. Shakespeare, *King Lear*, ed. R. A. Foakes (Walton-on-Thames, 1997), p. 72; also compare Stephen Booth, *King Lear, Macbeth, Indefinition and Tragedy* (New Haven, 1983), p. 11.

11 Jacques Derrida, *Of Grammatology*, trans. Gayatri Chakravorty Spivak (Baltimore and London, 1976), pp. 141–64, and compare Andrew Bennett and Nicholas Royle who offer an accessible and provocative overview of the paradoxical logic of literary endings in their *Introduction to Literature, Criticism and Theory* (Hemel Hempstead, 1999), pp. 251–9; see esp. pp. 253–4.

12 R. A. Foakes, *Hamlet versus Lear: Cultural Politics and Shakespeare's Art* (Cambridge, 1993), p. 211.

13 Again compare Bennett and Royle, *Introduction to Literature*, p. 254.

14 Freud, 'The Uncanny', *passim*.

15 Johnson, 'Preface', 27–9; p. 28.

16 Johnson, 'Preface', 28, (Johnson's emphasis).

17 Robert Eaglestone, *Ethical Criticism: Reading After Levinas* (Edinburgh, 1997), p. 175.

18 See Stanley Cavell, *Disowning Knowledge in Six Plays of Shakespeare* (Cambridge, 1987), p. 108, Cavell's emphasis. I'm also directly indebted here to Stephen Mulhall's exposition of Cavell in *Stanley Cavell: Philosophy's Recounting of the Ordinary* (Oxford, 1994), esp. pp. 198–9.

19 I am grateful to Terence Hawkes for clarifying this distinction; compare his incisive account of 'The Heimlich Manoeuvre', *Textual Practice*, 8: 2 (1994), 302–16; cf. esp. p. 312.

20 Eaglestone, *Ethical Criticism*, p. 179.

21 Maurice Blanchot, *The Writing of the Disaster*, trans. Ann Smock (Lincoln and London, 1995), p. 101; also cited in Eaglestone, *Ethical Criticism*, p. 175.

22 George Steiner, *Language and Silence* (London, 1985), p. 22.

23 Foakes, 'Introduction', 2.

24 Theodor W. Adorno, *Negative Dialectics*, trans. E. B. Ashton (London, 1990), p. 363.

25 *Ibid*.

26 William Shakespeare, *King Lear*, ed. Foakes, 1.4.221–2. All subsequent quotations from the play are taken from this edition.

27 Francis Barker, *The Culture of Violence: Essays on Tragedy and History* (Manchester, 1993), p. 15.

28 Though of course, 'historicizing' *Lear*'s percipient untimeliness presents us with another set of problems. In 'coming after' we are clearly confronted with a memory which refuses sequential narrativization. As such, we are confronted with what Lyotard terms an 'improper achronological effect', one which is nonetheless entirely contemporary in that it results from the *continued shock* of 'unassimilated traumatic experience'; see Jean-François Lyotard, *Heidegger and 'The Jews'*, trans. Andreas Michel and Mark Roberts (Minneapolis, 1990), p. 16. For a fuller explication of Lyotard, to which I am directly indebted here, compare Nicola King, '"We come after": Remembering the Holocaust', in Roger Luckhurst and Peter Marks, eds., *Literature and the Contemporary: Fictions and Theories of the Present* (Harlow, 1999), pp. 94–108, p. 97; I am also grateful to King for suggesting the epigraph for this section of the paper.

29 See Simon Critchley, *Very Little ... Almost Nothing* (London and New York, 1997), pp. 1–28, esp. p. 2, I am indebted here and above to Critchley for providing some key distinctions concerning the problem of nihilism.

30 Friedrich Nietzsche, *The Will to Power*, trans. W. Kaufmann and R. J. Hollingdale (New York, 1968), p. 13; also cited by Critchley in *Very Little*, pp. 7–8.

31 See Critchley, *Very Little, passim*.

32 For a fuller exposition see Roger Luckhurst, 'Memory Recovered/Recovered Memory', in Luckhurst and Marks, eds, *Literature and the Contemporary*, pp. 80–93, esp. 86–7.

33 Foakes, in Foakes, ed., *King Lear*, p. 2.

34 Again compare Critchley, *Very Little*, p. 23.

35 Cavell, *Disowning Knowledge*, pp. 116–17, also cited in Richard Halpern, *Shakespeare Among the Moderns* (Ithaca and London, 1997), p. 108. Elsewhere in the *Lear* essay of course Cavell draws a rather different distinction between spectatorship and character and the ability of the theatre to disclose the uneven (and potentially redemptive relationship) between the theatricalization and literalization of our relations with others. What though, I wonder, would Cavell make of Levring's *The King is Alive* which, in self-consciously aping the so called reality-TV format of survival shows like *Big Brother* and *Survivor*, is already all too literally implicated in dramatizing the theatricalization of its relationships with others. This makes for a particularly complex turn of Cavell's sense of the theatricalization of existence which I have not got time to examine here.

36 Halpern, *Shakespeare Among the Moderns*, p. 108.

37 Halpern, *Shakespeare Among the Moderns*, p. 108.

38 Cavell, *Disowning Knowledge*, pp. 116–17.

39 Halpern, *Shakespeare Among the Moderns*, p. 108.

40 Although Halpern insists that 'Cavell's use of "we" ... both indicts him as an individual and absolves him as a mere participant in a generalized abdication', see Halpern, *Shakespeare Among the Moderns*, p. 109.

41 See Jay Bernstein, 'Philosophy's Refuge: Adorno in Beckett', in David Wood, ed., *Philosophers' Poets* (London and New York, 1990), pp. 177–91; p. 183.

42 Compare Critchley, *Very Little, passim*.

43 Blanchot, *The Writing of the Disaster*, p. 101.

44 Cavell, *Disowning Knowledge*, p. 73.

45   Maurice Blanchot, *The Gaze of Orpheus* in *The Station Hill Blanchot Reader: Fiction and Literary Essays*, ed. George Quasha (Barrytown, New York, 1998), pp. 412–13; also cited in Jay Bernstein, 'Fragment, Fascination, Damaged Life: "The Truth about Hedda Gabler"', in Max Pensky, ed., *The Actuality of Adorno: Critical Essays on Adorno and the Postmodern* (Albany, New York, 1997), pp. 154–82; pp. 156–7. I should note that my understanding of Blanchot (though not my reading of *Lear*) is considerably indebted to Jay Bernstein at this point and in the arguments that follow, cf. esp. pp. 156–8.

46   Bernstein, 'Fragment, Fascination, Damaged Life', p. 157.

47   Again compare Bernstein, 'Fragment'.

48   Samuel Beckett, *Endgame* (London, 1964), p. 12.

49   Bernstein, 'Philosophy's Refuge', p. 183.

50   I owe this phrase to Critchley, *Very Little*, p. 27.

51   For a more detailed unpacking of the full paradox of Adorno's 'standpoint' in this respect see Critchley, *Very Little*, pp. 18–23.

52   See Theodor Adorno, *Aesthetic Theory*, trans. C. Lenhardt (London, 1984), p. 354, but also compare the 'finale' to Adorno's *Minima Moralia: Reflections from Damaged Life* (London, 1978), p. 247.

53   See Max Pensky, 'Editor's Introduction: Adorno's Actuality', in Max Pensky, ed., *The Actuality of Adorno: Critical Essays on Adorno and the Postmodern* (Albany, New York, 1997), pp. 1–21, see esp. p. 6 and p. 19, n. 8.

54   See Pensky, 'Editor's Introduction', p. 10; and compare Eva Geulen, 'Theodor Adorno on Tradition', in Pensky, ed., *The Actuality of Adorno*, pp. 183–93, esp. p. 186.

55   Critchley, *Very Little*, p. 19.

56   Again of course the register here is also Adornian. For a fuller explication of these 'temporal vocabularies' and for an explication of their significance for Adorno's work to which I'm indebted see Pensky, 'Editor's Introduction', p. 10 and Guelen, 'Theodor Adorno on Tradition', p. 186.

57   Again compare Critchley, *Very Little*, p. 19.

58   Adorno, *Negative Dialectics*, p. 407.

59   Laurence Binyon, 'For the Fallen' in Helen Gardner, ed., *The New Oxford Book of English Verse* (Oxford, 1972), p. 831.

60   Foakes, in Foakes, ed., *King Lear*, p. 392; Foakes's emphasis.

61   I borrow this formulation directly from Wendy Wheeler who makes use of it in an intriguing discussion of Graham's Swift's, *Last Orders*. See Wendy Wheeler, 'Melancholic Modernity and Contemporary Grief: The Novels of Graham Swift', in Luckhurst and Marks, eds., *Literature and the Contemporary*, pp. 63–79, p. 78. Though I should note that both Wheeler and I are indebted in turn to the work of the philosopher Gillian Rose. Compare especially Gillian Rose, *Mourning Becomes the Law: Philosophy and Representation* (Cambridge, 1996).

62   Foakes, 'Introduction', p. 79.

63   I borrow this phrase from Barker, *The Culture of Violence*, p. 11.

64   Foakes, in Foakes, ed., *King Lear*, p. 392.

65   Gillian Rose, *Love's Work* (London, 1995), p. 98.

66   Again I'm grateful to Wendy Wheeler for pointing out the 'tie' between obligation and ligature, see Wheeler, 'Melancholic Modernity', in Luckhurst and Marks, eds., *Literature and the Contemporary*, p. 76.

67   Nahum Tate, 'Dedication and Prologue to *King Lear* (1681)', in Kermode, ed., *Shakespeare: King Lear*, pp. 25–6.

68   Rose, *Mourning Becomes the Law*, p. 72.

69   Adorno, *Negative Dialectics*, p. 362.

CHAPTER 10

Theory in Practice
Allegories of Reading in Alice Munro's "Carried Away"

Miriam Marty Clark

The Post-Structuralist and deconstructive approach to literature pays attention more to multiplicity than to singularity, the highly specific plurality of meanings than to meaning's universality, and the webbed texture of discourses than to the unity of a single text or discourse. Noting that Alice Munro's fiction interrupts the placid illusion of realism whereby we assume words equal things, Miriam Marty Clark describes the complexity of Munro's fiction, the way she draws our attention to the instability of representation rather than to its certainty of success. The figure for complexity in the fiction is the library, a place of endless reference from book to book that allows us to imagine a simple accessible version of truth regarding our lives but does not necessarily guarantee its safe delivery.

Much has already been said about the relation – "intimate and profound" (Blodgett 1) – of Alice Munro's art to life. In finely layered, minutely observed stories which she herself calls "autobiographical in form" (*Lives* n. pag.), Munro tracks a long, recursive passage out of girlhood in small towns along the Ottawa Valley of Canada. Marking at every turn the tangled connection between past and present, she plots the bitterness and satisfactions of family love, the inscrutability of private lives, and the stubborn calculus of social relations not only in fictional towns like Jubilee and Hanratty but later in Toronto and Vancouver, in affluent suburbs and middle-class marriages.

Hers is a fiction, as Ajay Heble points out, that continues both to invite and to sustain reading within a realist tradition. In the last decade, however, a growing body of critical work has focused attention on the ways in which Munro's stories problematize the very mode they inhabit, undoing the illusion of transparency and advancing in reflexive, opaque, often difficult ways on the unstable worlds of narrative, memory, and writing

Original publication details: Miriam Marty Clark, "Allegories of Reading in Alice Munro's 'Carried Away.'" *Contemporary Literature* 37.1, pp. 49–61. University of Wisconsin Press, 1996. Reproduced with permission from the University of Wisconsin Press.

itself. Ildikó de Papp Carrington's extensive tracking of Munro's allusions and meta-phors, James Carscallen's elaboration of patterns (of names, of symbols, of tropes) across volumes, Magdalene Redekop's identification of suppressed maternal imagery, E. D. Blodgett's reasoning about narrative strategies and narrative selves, Heble's own persuasive argument for language's dual nature as "a form of representation" in Munro's work but also as a "system of signs" (5) – all emphasize in new ways the multiplicity and complexity of the stories. At the same time, most of these accounts acknowledge as both the first and the final pleasure of Munro's fiction what Redekop calls simply "a pleasure of recognition" (3), the undiminished if not uncomplicated presence of life in art.

In this essay, however, I want to trace a different and neglected relation, of books to books, considering how Munro's fiction is "linked," in Foucault's productive terms, "to the vast world of print and develops within the recognizable institution of writing" (91). The stories in *Friend of My Youth* (1990) and *Open Secrets* (1994) dismantle – not for the first time in Munro's career but more extensively than before – the foundations of realist narra-tive, figuring or disclosing the many texts in the one and so refiguring the linked practices of writing and reading. The terms of these later stories shift markedly from work to text, from memory and expressive evocation to language, from readerliness toward writerliness. In this essay I want to describe that shift more fully, turning finally to one story, "Carried Away," which addresses allegorically the politics of the library and the ethics of reading.

The vast world of print, the lively and troubling presence of the library, is manifest in Munro's fiction from early on: nowhere is the irreducible plurality of narrative fully sup-pressed or long hidden from view. Carrington has established Munro's recurrent allusiveness to Homer, the Bible, Shakespeare, Hardy, and others, arguing finally that these references serve to dramatize and master fundamental ambivalences within the stories (*Controlling*). But "allu-sion" does not adequately describe these stories' lodgings at the intersection of many texts or their abundant furnishings in books, letters, scandalous doggerel, and best-loved verses. All of Munro's towns have libraries, "Walls of printed pages, evidence of so many created worlds" (99), Del Jordan thinks in *Lives of Girls and Women*; they have newspapers, Great Books groups, and encyclopedia salesmen marketing Knowledge to wartime farmers flush with cash.

And the stories are often *about* readers. They are the young protagonists of Munro's female bildungsromans – Del of *Lives of Girls and Women*, Rose of *The Beggar Maid* – reading everything in the library, intuiting the future in girls' magazines and old medical texts, in Brontë novels and lines by Tennyson. Later, they are Rose and her friend Jocelyn on the maternity ward in "Mischief" (*Beggar*), reading Gide and Santayana to distinguish themselves from the gabbling housewives around them. They are middle-aged women on the verge of feminist awakening, taking courses, opening bookstores, growing fat on dusty Russian novels, on "skimpy-looking books by Czechs or Japanese or Rumanians" (*Friend* 112), and on rows of Penguin paperbacks.

But if books are accorded a central place in Munro's towns – in the library, the school-room, and the church – the place of reading is nevertheless marginal. Reading occupies a space normally taken up in adults by sexual passion, domestic responsibility, and eco-nomic productivity. "She ... had outgrown the habit," Del says of her friend Naomi; "This was the normal thing in Jubilee; reading books was something like chewing gum, a habit to be abandoned when the seriousness and satisfactions of adult life took over. It persisted mostly in unmarried ladies, would have been shameful in a man" (*Lives* 99). The habit hangs on in librarians and teachers, like "dry and wooden and innocent" Miss Farris (*Lives* 102) and ineffectual Arthur Comer, living vicariously through histories and mysteries in "Something I've Been Meaning to Tell You" (*Something*). It persists in eccentrics like Rose's father, who repairs furniture and has a shed full of books, and Del's mother, for whom the Great Books discussion group is one way of reckoning her own lost possibilities. For women who take up reading in the course of self-awakening, the practice gives way soon enough, of necessity, to real work, editing or teaching or producing television.

Even for the young, reading never has the pure purposefulness of silence, exile, and cunning. It isn't only that it smacks of peculiarity, uselessness, memory work. To read seriously is to stand both within and outside culture, at the center and at the margins. To take to heart the texts taught in school, to advance in earnest on the shelves of books in the Town Hall library, is to enter into a complicated and sometimes oppositional relation to the community that has established those institutions and authorizes reading. And the books that offer a way out of the ungrammatical, unilluminated world of home always threaten to turn with unwelcome irony or incomprehension on the familiar. Reading Katherine Mansfield's "The Garden Party" for a school assignment, for example, Rose becomes as enraged by Mansfield's uncomprehending treatment of the poor as she is irritated by her stepmother's stupidity about literature.

Furthermore, other texts come into characters' lives and into the stories themselves with less than epiphanic clarity. Like all allusions, these carry their own libidinal energies, their own troubling imperatives and interrogations; they trail multiple hermeneutic possibilities and unrestricted powers of foretelling and explaining. A performance of *The Pied Piper* in "Changes and Ceremonies" (*Lives*) is no mere fairy tale but provides occasion for an upwelling of adolescent sexual fervor, the transformation of childish boy-girl hostility into the "anarchy" and "mystery" of sexual feeling. At the same time, the operetta based on Browning's poem carries a darker plot of money and social class, only barely glimpsed by the narrator and never smoothly folded into the "meaning" of the story. The unresolved, unaddressed, almost unacknowledged tale of exploited labor and its fearful consequences (the piper, unpaid by the mayor and the corporation of Hamlin, leads the children of the town away forever) stands as a troubling remainder, a lingering disequilibrium.

For readers of, as well as readers in, these stories, other texts have increasingly this kind of anarchic force, a power to create gaps and uncertainties, to proliferate meanings and unravel the very processes of meaning-making and realist representation. In some early stories Munro's impulse seems to be to circumscribe closely the symbolic operations of other texts, their convergences, their inscription and thematization as acts of reading. They are ritualized as ceremony, drama, rhyme; they are enshrined in fancy bindings or housed in libraries where they operate under special regulations. "PENALTY FOR IMPROPER USE $100" the sign in the Jubilee public library warns (*Lives* 98), not far from the table where Del Jordan and her friend linger over suggestive passages in a favorite historical romance. Other texts are preemptively interpreted, or moved, with all their polyvalences and hermeneutic possibilities, outside the plot, so that what happens to people "in stories" is distinct from, even if it bears an ironic or illuminating resemblance to, what happens to people in the "real world" Munro defines. Even so, the boundaries prove illusory, easily breached as the energies of other texts flow relentlessly back across them into the stories.

But Munro's more recent fiction foregrounds and thematizes its own plurality, addressing itself directly to prior texts and other discourses. Her mode of address is by turns archaeological and allegorical: in the one, prior texts are excavated and considered – as fossils, as fragments – at the site of the story; in the other, the act of reading becomes itself the subject of narration. In the stories of *Friend of My Youth*, Munro strips away some of the thick description of character and community that marked her earlier work and makes an archaeological exploration of the discursive and textual character of her narratives and of the multiple acts of narration within them. In other texts – Hardy novels, forgotten letters, small-town papers – she locates the unstable, discursive, and infinitely regressive infrastructures of her stories, denaturalizing realist representation and deconstructing its premises from within. "Meneseteung," a writer's story, and a reader's, is only one such exploration and figuration. The story moves away from, rather than toward, a coherent narrative of the life of Almeda Joynt Roth, a nineteenth-century "poetess" and madwoman. Prowling in what are simultaneously the foundations and the ruins of the realist text, her narrator – a would-be biographer – sifts through the documents, both actual and imaginary, out of which such a story might be made. These include the newspaper (an insinuating weekly, the *Vidette*), a book of poems, an autobiographical preface, a photograph, a note, a tombstone. Almeda Roth appears first, last, and only as text; the story begins when the narrator comes upon the book of poems and ends as she clears the overgrown tombstone marked simply "Meda."

Working from reports in the *Vidette*, the narrator recuperates and parodies the language of the nineteenth century and the small frontier town; she draws on the language of the poetess with its high tones and its barely repressed sexual yearnings. Out of these she writes the story of Almeda, her brief courtship in middle age by Jarvis Poulter, a salt producer, and her descent into madness. Hers is a madness of textuality, a breakdown into words and the pure inescapableness of words:

> Almeda in her observations cannot escape words. She may think she can, but she can't. Soon this glowing and swelling begins to suggest words – not specific words but a flow of words somewhere, just about ready to make themselves known to her. Poems, even. Yes, again, poems. Or one poem. Isn't that the idea – one very great poem that will contain everything and, oh, that will make all the other poems, the poems she has written, inconsequential, mere trial and error, mere rags? Stars and flowers and birds and trees and angels in the snow and dead children at twilight – that is not the half of it. You have to get in the obscene racket of Pearl Street and the polished toe of Jarvis Poulter's boot and the plucked-chicken haunch with its blue-black flower. Almeda is a long way now from human sympathies or fears or cozy household considerations.

Almeda does not, the narrator concludes, mistake this flux for reality, "and neither does she mistake anything else for reality, and that is how she knows that she is sane" (*Friend* 70).

By showing a character constructed out of the discourses of the past and particularly the discourses of gender, Munro moves representation, if not subjectivity itself, out of the realm of nature and experience and into the realm of discursive practice. Nowhere is the language of gender construction more forcefully at work than in the obituaries of Almeda Roth and Jarvis Poulter, which the narrator places side by side near the end of the story. Almeda's emphasizes her qualities of sensitivity, eloquence, "pride," "daintiness," "decorum," duty, womanliness, charity, and "unfailing ... faith" (71). Jarvis's, on the other hand, emphasizes his "industry," "productivity," and "employment to our town" (72). Here, as elsewhere, the effect is political as the narrator excavates from the realist text buried narratives of gender, class struggle, and economic violence.

In "Carried Away," Munro turns from the archaeological to the allegorical in her exploration of the politics of reading and the practices of realist writing. At the outset a brief synopsis of the story's fairly complicated plot may be helpful. Set in Carstairs,

Ontario, at the height of industrial capitalism, between 1917 and the mid-1950s, "Carried Away" begins when Louisa, once a traveling saleswoman but now the town librarian, starts receiving romantic letters from Jack Agnew, a soldier off to war. Jack identifies himself to her as a reader – first of Zane Grey, later of what he calls "History and Travel" books – and he tells Louisa that he has watched and admired her in the library, that he daydreams about her at her work. "*I think of you up on a stool at the Library reaching to put a book away,*" he writes, "*and I come up and put my hands on your waist and lift you down, and you turning around inside my arms as if we agreed about everything*" (*Open* 11). Though she can't remember or picture him, Louisa responds to his letters, sends him the photograph he asks for, and waits hopefully for his return.

In the story's second section, Louisa tells a salesman named Jim Frarey about the letters. We learn from her account that when Jack came home after the war he married someone else, saying nothing to Louisa but leaving on her desk at the library a scrap of paper on which he had written the words, "*I was engaged before I went over-seas.*" "No name," Munro notes, "not his or hers" (18). Jim offers his own affable interpretation – that, thinking he might never return from the war, Jack Agnew "got a little carried away" (18) – and then he takes Louisa upstairs to bed, where she gives up her virginity.

The third section of the story recounts Jack's death in a grisly accident in the saw-milling operation at Doud's organ and piano factory where he worked. The section is told from the point of view of Arthur Doud, owner of the factory and son of the man who founded not only Doud's but the Carstairs public library. It is Arthur who takes charge after Jack is decapitated. He picks up the severed head, carrying it back to the body and calling (irrationally, he later thinks) for the doctor. Later he visits the widow, who asks him to return Jack's library books – borrowed but not checked out. In the library Arthur meets Louisa, whose unresolved interest in Jack (only ever known to her as text – letter and newspaper) is revealed in the questions she asks Arthur about the circumstances surrounding the accident. Never a reader himself, Arthur begins coming to the library many evenings after Jack's death, adopting Jack's faintly voyeuristic atti-tude toward the librarian. Eventually, almost inexplicably, Arthur and Louisa marry. Together they raise a son and run the factory through the depression into the prosper-ous mid-century.

At this point the story takes a remarkable turn. Many years later, after Arthur's death, Louisa encounters Jack Agnew – alive and well! – at a city park where a union rally is being held. They give radically divergent accounts of the past: in hers (which is also, at this point, ours) he dies spectacularly; in his, he has become a prominent labor organizer and a public figure. Munro herself has commented on this divergence, noting that ini-tially she "had a pretty realistic story going about World War I, small-town industry, the kind of accidents they had, the boss, the workers. But all the time I felt a parallel story going in which the accident never happened and another reality developed" ("Contributors'" 371).

I want to argue that what this story generates is not parallel realities but two simulta-neous and ultimately irreconcilable allegories of reading. In one, Jack Agnew is the figure of the reader. His borrowing is unauthorized, his gaze illicit, his use of the library both politically and erotically charged. Under the beneficent portrait of old Mr. Doud, he finds not the cultural legacy that the Douds – like their Carnegie counterparts – had envisioned but the language of class struggle and the seeds of revolution in books like H. G. Wells's *Mankind in the Making*, Bertrand Russell's *The Practice and Theory of*

Bolshevism, and G. K. Chesterton's *What's Wrong with the World*, which ends with an unflinchingly revolutionary proposition. "Because there should be a redistribution of property," Chesterton writes, "there shall be a revolution" (214).

Jack's origins are not working class but precapitalist. His father is a fisherman and a gardener, a "lone wolf" (5) uninvolved in the accelerating production (of organs and pianos, then of player pianos, then bowling alley lanes and radar cases, too) and consumption (of washing machines and new cars and kitchen appliances) in which the town is caught up between the wars. He lives by agricultural time and his own rhythms and so stands in striking contrast to those who, like his son, are governed by the posted rules (the story lists them) and the factory whistle, which blows at six "for many to get up," then again "for work to start at seven and at twelve for dinnertime and at one in the afternoon for work to recommence, and then at five-thirty for the men to lay down their tools and go home" (25).

For all his reading, Jack Agnew lives by the factory whistle and dies by the machine. His decapitation literalizes the fragmentation and alienation of life under a rationalized labor process, the mutilation of the laborer into a fragment of a man. It figures the estrangement of intellectual life – the life of the reader and the revolutionary – from the life of the body, its labor and its wages. When his blood pours mightily onto the sawdust floor of the factory, the names and dark energies of the revolutionary texts seem to pour with it.

After Jack's death, Arthur Doud becomes a reader himself – "almost accidentally," he remarks, as if by contact with the dead man's head and his unreturned library books. In Arthur, however, reading is a bourgeois practice; it soothes and confirms rather than incites. He spends his evenings in the library reading the same magazines that come to his home, satisfied and peaceful beneath his father's gaze. "*A Believer*," the inscription below the portrait notes without irony, "*in Progress, Culture, and Education*" (28).

In the end, Jack's spilled blood forms an underground tide, a narrative energy which cannot be stemmed but wells up with a force that literally ruptures the story with Jack's reappearance. The repressed and appropriated energies of revolution return to compel the narrative out of linear time, to reverse its irreversible premise, to force a rereading and a rewriting of the past. These energies are powerful enough to disrupt both realist practice and the practices that have governed reading and interpretation into the twentieth century.

At the same time, a second allegory unfolds under the sign of the book. Its governing metaphor is not the decapitation (with its significant echo in Louisa's loss of maidenhead) but the library, which functions to organize and reproduce culture and to authorize reading. "*My name is Jack Agnew*," the first letter from overseas reads, "*and my card is in the drawer*" (4).

For Louisa, books are commodities before they are a library. "*There is no interesting story*," she tells Jack. "*My parents are both dead. My father worked for Eaton's in Toronto in the Furniture Department, and after his death my mother worked there too in Linens. And I also worked there for a while in Books. Perhaps you could say Eaton's was our Douds*" (5). Jim Frarey, who after Jack's seductions and betrayals is the one to take Louisa to bed, also deals in books as commodities. He "sold typewriters and office equipment and books," Munro writes, "and all sorts of stationery supplies" (13).

As commodities, books take their place wholly within capitalist modes of production and consumption. They anticipate – as the piano factory does, metaphorically – the incorporation of aesthetic production into commodity production generally, which

Fredric Jameson takes as the tendency of modernism and the settled circumstance of postmodernism. Arthur Doud's first romantic considerations of Louisa (which contrast strikingly with Jack Agnew's fantasy of intellectual and erotic union in the library) turn in part on hiring and wages. For Arthur, attractiveness is also construed as commodity; "style" and "looking well" can be bought by a shrewd consumer, even one on a librarian's wage. "She was not a young woman anymore," he thinks, "but she maintained an eye-catching style. He remembered that years ago when they had hired her, he had thought that she got herself up very soberly. Her hair was not bobbed in those days. ... He tried to think how much she was paid. Not much, certainly. She kept herself looking well on it. And where did she live? In one of the boarding houses – the one with the schoolteachers? No, not there. She lived in the Commercial Hotel" (35).

If books, as commodities, find their quarter in the Commercial Hotel, the library has its proper lodging in the Town Hall, where capitalism and civic duty conspire to create a place in which reading is authorized and writing – even writing about revolution and the redistribution of property – is rendered harmless under headings of Fiction and Non Fiction, History and Travel. Beneath the pink-cheeked portrait of the library's founder, the great civilizing influence of capital is extended and class struggle is transformed into True Friendship with the Working Man.

With Jack's death, Arthur Doud assumes the mantle of the reader. He reauthorizes reading, returning the stolen books and establishing a presence of his own, "genial," he thinks, "reassuring, and, above all, natural" (31). At the same time he domesticates into bourgeois marriage with Louisa the erotic energies circulating at the library. The surplus – the erotic, the revolutionary, the hidden and spilled – funds a renegotiation of patriarchal power for postwar capitalism. If his father operated with a kind of heroic paternalism, by "whims and decrees" (31), Arthur comes during those evenings at the library to see himself not as the impostor he once feared being but as a new kind of man, a public servant: dignified, fair, and philanthropic. He also becomes, not coincidentally, an exemplary consumer. After thinking about the town's demands – for hockey uniforms and war memorials, road maintenance and Sunday School buildings – Arthur notes:

> Expectations at home were not lacking either. Bea [Arthur's daughter] was agitating to go away to private school and Mrs. Feare had her eye on some new mixing apparatus for the kitchen, also a new washing machine. All the trim on the house was due to be painted this year. All that wedding-cake decoration that consumed paint by the gallon. And in the midst of this what had Arthur done but order himself a new car – a Chrysler sedan.
>
> It was necessary – he had to drive a new car. He had to drive a new car, Bea had to go away to school, Mrs. Feare had to have the latest, and the trim had to be as fresh as Christmas snow. Else they would lose respect, they would lose confidence, they would start to wonder if things were going downhill. And it could be managed, with luck it could all be managed. (32)

The same surplus reads out quite differently, and more dramatically, as female hysteria. The unauthorized and the anarchic, read under the sign of the feminine as erotic desire – evoked by Jack's letters and frustrated by his death, then repressed, domesticated – emerge with dizzying force twice in Louisa's life, once just after her encounter with Jim Frarey and a second time, many years later. The first time, Munro writes that Louisa "felt herself whirling around in an irresistible way, as if the mattress had turned into a child's top and was carrying her off" (20).

The second time, the experience begins with anxiety, "a faintly sickening, familiar agitation" (43) after a visit to a doctor in the city. Soon Louisa is disoriented, confused. Jack Agnew appears, not dead at all but white-haired and wrinkled, a union man (martyrdom being modulated into trade unionism in this gesture) and famous, to make a puzzling pronouncement: "Love never dies" (48). Jim Frarey appears too, from the back, in a crowd of Mennonites. "Oh, what kind of a trick was being played on her, or what kind of trick was she playing on herself!" Munro writes.

> She was dizzy and humiliated. She would not have it. …
>
>   No wonder she was feeling clammy. She had gone under a wave, which nobody else had noticed. You could say anything you liked about what had happened – but what it amounted to was going under a wave. She had gone under and through it and was left with a cold sheen on her skin, a beating in her ears, a cavity in her chest, and revolt in her stomach. It was anarchy she was up against – a devouring muddle. Sudden holes and impromptu tricks and radiant vanishing consolations. (49–50)

Carrington has recently made a convincing case for this scene as a hallucination, the "psychological aftermath" of the factory accident ("What's in a Title?" 555). I want to go further, to suggest again that this is only one of the two stories unfolding in Munro's text. This one marks as female and symptomatic – and so appropriates, explains, and contains – the anarchic force which both drives and violently ruptures narrative in that other, simultaneous, allegory of reading.

Finally, nothing more fully activates the plurality of these readings of reading than this, that while one of the two allegories splits the narrative irretrievably open – and not into epiphanic clarity but into a devouring muddle several paragraphs before the end of the story – the other continues, acknowledging reading's powers and subverting its dangers by renaming them. It preserves the linear integrity of the narrative and pushes toward closure under a Hardy-esque rubric (invoked early in the story and late) of accident or fate. "She believed," Munro writes of Louisa at the end, "in the swift decision, the unforeseen intervention, the uniqueness of her fate" (51).

Closure is a less interesting matter here, it seems to me, than reading's end. To be the reader in this text is to occupy the space where repression and anarchy contend. Once the narrative is no longer suspended between allegories of reading, it vacates its ethical premises and recedes in the final paragraphs of the story toward one-dimensionality. Hysteria subsides into nostalgia as Louisa envisions the solid houses and mature trees of long ago, the blinkered horses pulling sleighs out from the city into the blankness of the country. Fate moves forward, unresisted, toward death.

"There is no document of civilization," Walter Benjamin contends in a well-known formulation, "which is not at the same time a document of barbarism" (256);[1] cultural treasures – borne forward from generation to generation, whether in martial triumph or enlightened philanthropy – are inevitably, often invisibly, tainted by oppression and anonymous toil. For a sustained moment in "Carried Away," Munro brings both civilization and the barbarism that is its dark other, its necessary condition, fully into view. At the same time, perhaps paradoxically, she preserves from earlier stories a sense of the liberatory and subversive power of books and reading. In a crucial instant the continuum of history and its expression as narrative are briefly, lavishly ruptured, laying bare the nature of the library and all the acts of reading it shelters and signifies.

Auburn University

Note

1   This statement appears in "Theses on the Philosophy of History" (1940), as cited. Benjamin makes the same observation in his essay "Eduard Fuchs, Collector and Historian" (1937), published in *One-Way Street*, trans. Edmund Jephcott and Kingsley Shorter (London: NLB, 1979) 349–86.

Works Cited

Benjamin, Walter. *Illuminations*. Trans. Harry Zohn. Ed. Hannah Arendt. New York: Schocken, 1968.

Blodgett, E. D. *Alice Munro*. Boston: Twayne, 1988.

Carrington, Ildikó de Papp. *Controlling the Uncontrollable: The Fiction of Alice Munro*. DeKalb: Northern Illinois UP, 1989.

Carrington, Ildikó de Papp. "What's in a Title?: Alice Munro's 'Carried Away.'" *Studies in Short Fiction* 30 (1993): 555–64.

Carscallen, James. *The Other Country: Patterns in the Writing of Alice Munro*. Toronto: ECW, 1993.

Chesterton, G. K. *What's Wrong with the World*. 1910. New York: Sheed & Ward, 1956.

Foucault, Michel. "Fantasia of the Library." *Language, Counter-memory, Practice*. Trans. Donald F. Bouchard and Sherry Simon. Ed. Donald F. Bouchard. Ithaca, NY: Cornell UP, 1977. 87–109.

Heble, Ajay. *The Tumble of Reason: Alice Munro's Discourse of Absence*. Toronto: U of Toronto P, 1994.

Munro, Alice. *The Beggar Maid: Stories of Flo and Rose*. 1979. New York: Vintage, 1991.

Munro, Alice. "Contributors' Notes." *Best American Stories* 1992. Ed. Robert Stone and Katrina Kenison. New York: Houghton, 1992. 371.

Munro, Alice. *Friend of My Youth*. New York: Knopf, 1990.

Munro, Alice. *Lives of Girls and Women*. 1971. New York: Plume, 1983.

Munro, Alice. *Open Secrets*. New York: Knopf, 1994.

Munro, Alice. *Something I've Been Meaning to Tell You*. 1974. New York: Plume, 1987.

Redekop, Magdalene. *Mothers and Other Clowns: The Stories of Alice Munro*. New York: Routledge, 1992.

PART FIVE
Psychoanalysis and Psychology

CHAPTER 1

Introduction
Strangers to Ourselves: Psychoanalysis

Julie Rivkin and Michael Ryan

A picture of the human mind as a unified whole that can achieve full awareness of itself has been central to Western thought since the seventeenth century. The "cogito" or thinking self defines our humanity and our civility, our difference from animals chained to blind nature and uncontrollable instincts. In the early part of the twentieth century, the assurance of that self-description was disturbed by Sigmund Freud's book, *The Interpretation of Dreams* (1900), which described a discovery that would become the centerpiece of a new discipline called psychoanalysis. His discovery was that the human mind contains a dimension that is only partially accessible to consciousness and then only through indirect means such as dreams or neurotic symptoms. The "unconscious," as he called it, is a repository of repressed desires, feelings, memories, and instinctual drives, many of which, according to Freud, have to do with sexuality and violence. In subsequent books and studies such as *Beyond the Pleasure Principle*, "A Case of Infantile Neurosis," *Three Essays on Sexuality*, *The Ego and the Id*, and *The Psychopathology of Everyday Life*, Freud argued that our mental lives derive largely from biological drives, that the highest achievements and ideals of civilization are inseparable from instinctual urges towards pleasure, constancy, and the release of excitation and energy. As each child grows and enters first the family then society, he or she learns to repress those instinctual drives and the conscious desires they instigate and to mold aggressive and sexual impulses as well as an initially grandiose sense of self to the demands of life with others. Repression is essential to civilization, the conversion of animal instinct into civil behavior, but such repression creates what might be called a second self, a stranger within, a place where all that cannot for one reason or another be expressed or realized in civil life takes up residence. This, for Freud, explains why people experience what he calls "uncanny" feelings of doubleness that consist of a sense that something strange coexists with what is most familiar inside ourselves. It also explains why we compulsively repeat certain gestures, desires, experiences, and self-induced situations that might be quite distressing but also compellingly unavoidable. We cannot help but do so because they are brought about by forces and drives within ourselves over which we exercise very little conscious control because they arise from something or somewhere that is beyond our control – the unconscious.

Literary Theory: An Anthology, Third Edition. Edited by Julie Rivkin and Michael Ryan.
© 2017 John Wiley & Sons, Ltd. Published 2017 by John Wiley & Sons, Ltd.

Freud discovered the unconscious by studying patients with neurotic symptoms which pointed towards unresolved conflicts between unconscious inclinations or feelings and the repressive demands of the ego or conscious self. He noticed that such patients engaged in behavior that frequently embodied desires or fears (persistent phobic anxiety about animals, for example) whose repetitiveness suggested that the patient was in the grip of something outside his awareness or her control. Freud borrowed from his teacher Josef Breuer a method of analysis whereby patients would say whatever came to their minds regardless of how seemingly meaningless or unpertinent. In this way, he found that patients divulged thoughts and feelings that had been kept repressed in the unconscious and hidden from the patient's own conscious view. One patient, for example, experienced a recurring fear of animals that turned out, through his free associations or thoughts, to refer to his childhood fear of his father, something he had repressed and forgotten.

In studying his patients, Freud realized that the unconscious often expresses itself in the form of dreams, since at night during sleep the vigilance of the repressive ego in regard to unconscious desire is stilled. Dreams, Freud found, express wishes or desires that cannot find expression in waking life precisely because they are at odds with the requirements of the ego, which itself merely registers the requirements of the larger society. Unconscious wishes can find expression in dreams because dreams distort the unconscious material and make it appear different from itself and more acceptable to consciousness. The "dream work" displaces unacceptable material onto acceptable images, condenses several different though related unconscious elements into a single image, and turns drives into their opposites, so that they can elude censorship. A dream about not being able to serve a smoked salmon dinner to a friend might turn out to have nothing to do with dining but instead might refer to a wish not to help the friend gain weight and become more attractive to one's husband, who that very day, before the dream, mentioned how attractive he found the friend to be precisely because of her plumpness.

A similar process is at work, Freud discovered, in neurotic symptoms. They frequently displace desires, or anxieties, or drive energies that are unconscious onto expressive activities or compulsive thoughts. Such symptoms perform a variety of translative procedures on unconscious material, from compromise formation (the construction of an indirect expression that allows release of unacceptable drive energy while nonetheless honoring the imperatives of repression) to inversion (the conversion into its opposite of a desire or impulse). For example, someone raised in a strongly religious way that proscribes sexual activity may perform forbidden sexual acts ritualistically so as to seem to be respecting the norm while nonetheless attaining satisfaction. Or someone who feels great animosity towards a cold and distant mother may convert that feeling into its opposite, a fantasy that all women are themselves hostile and therefore unworthy of his love.

Other important terms in the study of symptom formation are fixation, splitting, introjection, and projection. Anxiety about entry into an adult world perceived as threatening of a too-fragile sense of self or anxiety that awakens either troubling memories or drive energies will propel some people to fixate at an early state of development. They will remain attached to early forms of emotional life and sexual activity that are usually surpassed in the transition to adulthood. In some instances, for example, people who fear the passage to genital sexuality will continue to find gratification from other parts of their bodies or other activities than genital sex. Splitting is a way of dealing with anxiety by dividing the object of anxiety in two, one bearing all the negative feeling while the other embodies all the positive feelings one wishes to substitute for the anxieties the object or situation provokes. Children may, for example, direct all of their aggression or hostility towards one parent while idealizing the other, and such splitting may be as much a response to the trajectory of their own drive energies as to external parental behavior. Finally, introjection and projection are terms used to describe how the self shapes itself by adapting models from outside itself and externalizes its own feelings by assigning them to others. If introjection brings in something from someone else, creating an ideal of that person within oneself, projection throws out something from within oneself and makes it seem as if it is a trait of someone else.

Freud spent most of his life studying the boundary and the dynamic movements between the conscious self or ego and the unconscious, which he later came to call the id. The id is the site of the energy of the mind, energy that Freud characterized as a combination of sexual libido and other instincts, such as aggression, that propel the human organism through life, moving it to grow, develop, and eventually to die. That primary process of life is entirely irrational, and it cannot distinguish images and things, reasonable objects and unreasonable or socially unacceptable ones. It is the secondary processes of the mind, lodged in the ego and superego or conscience, that bring reason, order, logic, and social acceptability to the otherwise uncontrolled and potentially harmful realm of the biological drives. But, according to Freud, the drives of the unconscious, though repressed, can never be quelled entirely. They emerge in dreams, and, when the rational part of the mind fails to handle them successfully, in the seemingly irrational behavior that is neurotic symptomatology (the fears, unjustified anxieties, and compulsive behaviors that indicate something out of joint in a personality). When conscious control breaks down altogether and drives and unconscious content are expressed directly, without any mediation by consciousness, one is in the realm of psychosis or schizophrenia, which Freud distinguished from neurosis by saying that neurosis maintains the relationship to an external reality while in psychosis that relationship breaks down altogether.

Freud insisted that sexuality was evident throughout life, from childhood on. The energy of sexuality is far from exclusively genital; it can also be anal or oral, Freud noted, and it can also be displaced onto fetish objects or substitutes that replace early desired objects with ones that avoid anxiety or are responses to trauma. In one famous case study, Freud analyzed an obsessional neurotic (known as the "Wolf Man" because of a dream he had about wolves in a tree staring at him) who developed a sexually invested fondness for military dress and regimen in response to early traumatic experiences regarding his sexual identity. His anxiety provoked him to displace his sexual drive away from human objects and onto fetish substitutes.

At the core of Freud's sexual theory is the so-called "Oedipus Complex," something Freud believed all children experience as a rite of passage to adult gender identity. As befitted his time, Freud was primarily concerned with the Oedipal trajectory of the male child (hence Oedipus rather than, say, Clytemnestra or Medea). All male children, Freud argued, experience an early attachment to the mother that is sexual in nature. Only the father's intervention, separating mother from child, prevents incest. All civilization is founded on the prohibition expressed in the father's intervention. The male child learns to give up his initial "pre-Oedipal" desire for and attachment to the mother; instead, he identifies with the father (instead of longing to be the father with his mother) and learns to desire other women than the mother. He becomes an adult male heterosexual (Freud's implicit norm). Similarly, the female child experiences an early desire for the father which takes the form of a simultaneous desire to *be* her mother, to take her place as the father's sexual object, but she too learns to relinquish that desire and to identify with her mother and to seek other objects outside the family. The crucial process in gender formation is identification, the molding of a self from equations made between oneself and external objects through the internalization of images or models of those objects.

Psychoanalytic theory after Freud divides into two strands, one called object relations, the other neo-Freudianism. While object relations theory favors a model that does without instincts almost altogether and concentrates instead on the way the self interacts with its social world, especially the initial world of primary caretakers such as the mother, neo-Freudian theory in the work of Jacques Lacan especially argues that the instinctual drives and the unconscious are more essential to psychoanalytic work than the ego, which Lacan sees as a mirage that can never fully know and master the unconscious.

The theory of identification, which places greater emphasis on social relations at the expense of the instinctual drives, was especially appealing to the object relations school of psychoanalysis that came into being after World War II in Britain and America and is associated with such names as Melanie Klein, R. W. D. Fairbairn, D. W. Winnicott, and Margaret Mahler. It is concerned less with the battle between the ego and the instinctual drives, a notion that some of the theorists reject outright, than it is with the way the relations between the child and its objects, especially the mother, during the pre-Oedipal period, shape its personality. The contours of self-identity are given or shaped by that primary relationship, by whether or not it is distant, cold, and frustrating, for example, or overwhelming and engulfing. The child's ability to separate successfully from its primary unity with the mother by building self-boundaries and appropriate mental representations of an external object world will determine what kind of personality he or she will possess – be it one yearning for fusion with objects that never fully satisfy its yearning or one dominated by a feeling of being compelled to flee from relationships that threaten to overwhelm its fragile self-boundaries.

Unlike Freud, object relations theorists consider the ego to be a major part of (if not the entire) personality. How it manages to construct an internal world for itself made up of introjected fantasy objects or projections of destructive feelings onto the world during the "pre-Oedipal" stage of development is more important for such theorists than the later Oedipal stage of passage into adult gender identity. Some consider the original separation from the mother to be a primary frustration or basic fault that can never be assuaged; life's longings are defined by its schema. Others like Margaret Mahler see the relation to the mother more positively as providing a "beacon" that allows the child to emerge into the world from a primary symbiotic state. And others like Melanie Klein see the child constructing a world for itself through fantasies that allow it to distinguish its destructive from its affectionate feelings through introjection/projection and the splitting between good and bad internal objects. For a child, the mother consists of "part objects" like the breast or the face. Ultimately, the child learns to engage in "reparation," the restoration of whole objects and good relations that its own destructive impulses sundered during the process of separation, individuation, and growth. While object relations theory has been criticized for at times advancing an overly optimistic picture of "adaptation" of a debatably coherent "self" to an unproblematic "environment," it has also inspired such pathbreaking work as Klaus Theweleit's *Male*

Fantasies, a study of pre-Nazi literature that locates the origins of Nazism in a particular psychological formation that perceived women, communists, and Jews as external equivalents of internal boundary-threatening urges that had to be either violently expelled or regimented.

Neo-Freudianism enjoyed great popularity in France in the 1960s and 1970s and continues to be a viable school of literary criticism. In the 1950s and 1960s, Jacques Lacan developed a structuralist theory of psychoanalysis based on the linguistic theory of Saussure. Against object relations theory, Lacan argues that the ego is constructed through imaginary percepts and narcissistic fantasies, and it remains blind to its determination by the drives, the unconscious, and its placement and construction in/by language. Before language assigns us an "I," we possess no sense of self. It is language that gives us identity. The unified self posited by object relations theory is an illusion. The child begins as fragmented drives, percepts, and attachments that eventually congeal into an imaginary identity at the "mirror stage" of development. It is through the child's original symbiotic relationship with the mother that he/she develops a false narcissistic sense of unity. The child assumes the mother is himself, and his primary desire is for her desire (of him). Desire and its realization only appear immediate, however, and what Lacan calls the Real, an impossible wholeness of self, plenitude of desire satisfaction (*jouissance*), and continuity of signifier and signified or word and object, is never possible. The mother is a congeries of part objects (*l'objet petit a*) and partial fulfillments like the breast, and the whole we imaginarily seek and imagine we have when we construct egos for ourselves or seek desired objects that embody our fantasies of wholeness is merely a way of concealing from ourselves the initial fissure or *béance* that separation from the mother installs permanently within our being. Indeed, our being is not founded on the mythic identity of the ego; rather it is founded on what Lacan calls our initial lack-of-being (*manque-à-être*), the initial experience of being ripped out of an original imaginary fullness of being and separated from the object – the mother – that provided us with it. More real is our overdetermination by the drives, the unconscious, and the Symbolic Order of our culture, the social languages that identify us and lend us identities, all of which exceed consciousness and never assume the form of knowable or conscious identity (which, for Lacan, is always fantasmatic). Our identity is given to us from outside, and we are constitutively alienated. The imaginary or narcissistic character of all desire merely conceals this basic fault, this radical alterity or otherness, in human existence.

The mirror stage of dyadic symbiosis with the mother must be left behind as the child develops and enters that social world. The shattering of it occurs when the child is confronted with the father's "no," which is to say, with the incest taboo that declares the mother an inappropriate object. The bar forbidding access to the mother is akin to the bar that separates signifier from signified or word from thing. Within language, we have no access to real objects. So also, children have no access to the real mother after a certain point in development. They only have signifiers of her which they can either accept realistically or which they can overvalue and fetishize (developing neurotic symptoms in consequence). If a child accepts separation from the mother (the Law of the Father), s/he (though mostly "he," one always suspects, with Lacan) then learns to accept his/her place in the Symbolic Order, that symbolic language which assigns social roles and dictates proper behavior in society. That order is like a language, since it is defined as relations between terms (mother/father, mother/son, etc.) and by a lexicon that assigns meaning or identity according to the binary opposition of presence or absence (of terms). With the initiation of the Symbolic, the original desire for the mother is repressed, and Lacan compares this to the way the signified is made absent by the signifier, and is always beneath the bar in Saussure's algorithm: S/s. The acceptance of repression and the entry into the Symbolic is itself comparable to language in that once one learns to name something, one accepts separation from it; by naming, one sacrifices the object, since the presence of the sign/word is the absence of the signified thing. The naming of objects separates one from them. The arrival of the Symbolic and the shattering of the Imaginary thus consists of the installation of a combined linguistic/psychological separation of the child both from its initial object, the mother, and from the undifferentiated matter of natural existence. We learn to be social, to have social identities, by learning to say no, to sacrifice or give up both the initial contact one has with the natural world and with one's first human objects. The mother's body is barred, and the desire for it is placed under the bar of the signifier and enters the unconscious. The small "o" other or initial object becomes the large "O" Other of the symbolic unconscious; it acquires meaning as what one cannot have and as that whose absence dictates the form of all subsequent desires, all the signifiers we pursue as hoped-for fillers for an initial unfillable absence. That bar can never be crossed, and all our desires throughout life will consist of attempts to come to terms with this separation, our "lack-of-being." The other side of the bar can enter our consciousness only in the form of substitutes, as metaphors that can indicate it only as/in its absence because the unconscious can never be present to the mind (except through substitute signifiers). Similarly, all desire is inherently metaphoric, inherently a matter of a substitute object that stands in for the initially absent mother object, and because no metaphor can embody what we ultimately desire when we desire anything, we are condemned to slide along a chain of signifiers each of which is a metonymy, a part standing in for the whole we (always) miss. Thus, unlike object relations theory, which assumes a whole self is possible that would be transparent to itself and would be defined by a healthy ego, Lacan thinks that we are constitutively split from ourselves and that we can never possibly attain wholeness in the world of objects. That is a delusion of the ego (and of ego psychology, he would add, somewhat polemically). What we can learn is to accept frustration and to come to acknowledge the lack that defines our being. We exist in a chain of signifiers of desires that never arrive at the Real, the ever-absent cause of desire which is the undifferentiatedness of nature, something we can never have access to from within society except through signifiers that distance it (substitute for it) as they name it.

Psychoanalytic literary criticism begins with Freud himself, whose "The Uncanny," in part a reading of Hoffman's horror story "The Sandman," can be said to inaugurate the critical genre. Freud notices that literary texts are like dreams; they embody or express unconscious material in the form of complex displacements and condensations. The same rule that he prescribes for dream interpretation, however, also applies to literature: it is not a direct translation of the unconscious into symbols that "stand for" unconscious meanings. Rather, literature displaces unconscious desires, drives, and motives into imagery that might bear no resemblance to its origin but that nonetheless permits it to achieve release or expression. Literature, as fiction, might even be said to demonstrate these very processes of representation-through-indirection at work. For Freud in "The Uncanny," fear of castration takes the form not of a literal image, but of a metaphoric substitute that displaces the protagonist's anxiety onto a fear of losing his eyes, a fear that is available for interpretation only because language displays the latent connection.

Freud and many later psychoanalytic critics were concerned with what they thought was the primary anxiety of patriarchal culture, the male child's fears as he moves from presexual childhood to sexual adulthood, a trajectory that necessarily crosses the sexual relationship between his mother and his father. All of Nathaniel Hawthorne's fiction, for example, might be read in this light as embodying the Oedipal conflict between a son and a threatening father (as between Reverend Dimmesdale and Chillingsworth in *The Scarlet Letter*). As object relations theory shifts attention towards the pre-Oedipal realm, however, so also does later psychoanalytic criticism focus more on the relational dynamics of psychosexual development and on children's relations to their mothers in patrocentric cultures that assign child-rearing work to women. Klaus Theweleit in *Male Fantasies*, for example, studies the representations of violence against women in literature by German ex-soldiers from World War I who would eventually become major supporters of Nazism and interprets them as expressions of hostility against mothers. The literary works are characterized by images of fear in regard to women perceived as being too powerful, fear that is displaced onto anxieties about having one's self-boundaries overwhelmed by a "red flood" of Bolshevism. Nazism would be the German response to that political threat of communist revolution, an erection of a rigid social order that was the equivalent of the psychological defense these males constructed to guard themselves against personal dissolution, what Theweleit calls "body armor." Theweleit sees the relation to the mother as more determining of these men's psychological identities than that to the father, who tends to be a peripheral figure in the literature. At stake in the literature is not an ego that does battle with a paternal superego or with unconscious urges for pleasure that meet repression; rather the literature depicts a self that never fully formed, never acquired a healthy relation to the world, because of abusive child-rearing practices in German society at the time. It is this that accounts for the enormous representational violence against women who might be construed as similarly maternal and similarly abusive of self-identity.

Lacanian criticism shifts attention to language and sees it and the unconscious as almost identical. Human desire is carried by signifiers which stand in for a lack that can never be filled in. It is in the signifiers then, in language itself, that the unconscious, what of the unconscious one can know, resides. Processes of signification of the kind that are frozen temporarily in works of literature constitute the human subject and determine the shape of its life – whether one neurotically and repetitively pursues the same signifier of a possibly completely fulfilled desire (a particular kind of sexual partner) or whether one renounces such pursuits and accommodates oneself to a more mundane destiny, for example. Such fulfillment is, of course, for Lacan, an impossibility; so literature always enacts the way the chain of signifiers simply eternally displaces an end to signification, the arrival of a real referent that would be the fulfillment of desire and the end of its displacement along a chain.

For example, Hemingway's novel *A Farewell to Arms* hinges on a play on words in the title. About a wounded soldier who has an affair with a nurse who dies in the end while giving birth to their child (itself stillborn), *Arms* is about both bodily "arms" (as in the sexual embrace) and military "arms" (as in the guns that wound Jake, the hero). He wishes to escape from the military into the arms of the maternal Catherine, but he is obliged to say farewell to her arms in the end. The novel maps out the trajectory of development as Lacan describes it: the male child must learn to renounce the imaginary moment of fulfilled desire with the mother in order to accept separation and to enter the Symbolic Order. The bifurcating meanings of "arms" indicate a split in the narrative subject (the narrator shifts from "we" to "I" throughout) that testifies to the split within all human subjectivity between the conscious self and the unconscious that determines that self and between the desiring self and the ultimately impossible fulfillment of that desire (in a return to the mother's arms). The imaginary identity (of self/(m)other) must be given up, and separation (the duality of meaning implied by the fact that one can only have metaphors and not real things or complete fulfillment) accepted.[1]

Note

1   See Ben Stoltzfus, *Lacan and Literature: Purloined Pretexts* (Albany: SUNY Press, 1996), from whom we purloined this reading of the novel.

CHAPTER 2

The Interpretation of Dreams

Sigmund Freud

When it was published in 1900, Freud's *Interpretation of Dreams* launched an entirely new idea and a new discipline of human knowledge. The idea was that the mind harbors wishes or desires that lie outside awareness but that nevertheless manifest themselves at night in dreams. Dreams, when read or interpreted as a rebus or puzzle, instead of being taken literally, turn out to be translations into semi-conscious form of unconscious material. Such material is generally in the unconscious because it has been repressed, or driven from consciousness by a mental censor that judges what is fit for expression. Things unfit for expression (at the time of Freud's work) were ideas or desires having to do, for example, with sexuality. But not all dreams were of a sexual character. In the central dream analyzed in this selection, Freud, for example, has a dream that expresses an egotistical wish that his work be properly recognized.

The Dream of the Botanical Monograph

I had written a monograph on a certain plant. The book lay before me and I was at the moment turning over a folded colored plate. Bound up in each copy there was a dried specimen of the plant, as though it had been taken from a herbarium.

Analysis

That morning I had seen a new book in the window of a book-shop, bearing the title *The Genus Cyclamen* – evidently a *monograph* on that plant.

Cyclamens, I reflected, were my *wife's favorite flowers* and I reproached myself for so rarely remembering to *bring her flowers*, which was what *she* liked. – The subject of "*bringing*

Original publication details: Sigmund Freud, from *The Interpretation of Dreams*, trans. James Strachey, pp. 169–173, 277–292, 295–296, 302–309. Basic Books, Inc., 1956. Reproduced with permission from Basic Books.

Literary Theory: An Anthology, Third Edition. Edited by Julie Rivkin and Michael Ryan.
© 2017 John Wiley & Sons, Ltd. Published 2017 by John Wiley & Sons, Ltd.

flowers" recalled an anecdote which I had recently repeated to a circle of friends and which I had used as evidence in favor of my theory that forgetting is very often determined by an unconscious purpose and that it always enables one to deduce the secret intentions of the person who forgets. A young woman was accustomed to receiving a bouquet of flowers from her husband on her birthday. One year this token of his affection failed to appear, and she burst into tears. Her husband came in and had no idea why she was crying till she told him that to-day was her birthday. He clasped his hand to his head and exclaimed: "I'm so sorry, but I'd quite forgotten. I'll go out at once and fetch *your flowers*." But she was not to be consoled; for she recognized that her husband's forgetfulness was a proof that she no longer had the same place in his thoughts as she had formerly. – This lady, Frau L., had met my wife two days before I had the dream, had told her that she was feeling quite well and enquired after me. Some years ago she had come to me for treatment.

I now made a fresh start. Once, I recalled, I really *had* written something in the nature of a *monograph on a plant*, namely a dissertation on the *coca-plant*, which had drawn Karl Koller's attention to the anaesthetic properties of cocaine. I had myself indicated this application of the alkaloid in my published paper, but I had not been thorough enough to pursue the matter further. This reminded me that on the morning of the day after the dream – I had not found time to interpret it till the evening – I had thought about cocaine in a kind of daydream. If ever I got glaucoma, I had thought, I should travel to Berlin and get myself operated on, incognito, in my friend's [Fliess's] house, by a surgeon recommended by him. The operating surgeon, who would have no idea of my identity, would boast once again of how easily such operations could be performed since the introduction of cocaine; and I should not give the slightest hint that I myself had had a share in the discovery. This phantasy had led on to reflections of how awkward it is, when all is said and done, for a physician to ask for medical treatment for himself from his professional colleagues. The Berlin eye-surgeon would not know me, and I should be able to pay his fees like anyone else. It was not until I had recalled this daydream that I realized that the recollection of a specific event lay behind it. Shortly after Koller's discovery, my father had in fact been attacked by glaucoma; my friend Dr Königstein, the ophthalmic surgeon, had operated on him; while Dr Koller had been in charge of the cocaine anaesthesia and had commented on the fact that this case had brought together all of the three men who had had a share in the introduction of cocaine.

My thoughts then went on to the occasion when I had last been reminded of this business of the cocaine. It had been a few days earlier, when I had been looking at a copy of a *Festschrift* in which grateful pupils had celebrated the jubilee of their teacher and laboratory director. Among the laboratory's claims to distinction which were enumerated in this book I had seen a mention of the fact that Koller had made his discovery there of the anaesthetic properties of cocaine. I then suddenly perceived that my dream was connected with an event of the previous evening. I had walked home precisely with Dr Königstein and had got into conversation with him about a matter which never fails to excite my feelings whenever it is raised. While I was talking to him in the entrance-hall, Professor *Gärtner* [Gardener] and his wife had joined us; and I could not help congratulating them both on their *blooming* looks. But Professor Gärtner was one of the authors of the *Festschrift* I have just mentioned, and may well have reminded me of it. Moreover, the Frau L., whose disappointment on her birthday I described earlier, was mentioned – though only, it is true, in another connection – in my conversation with Dr Königstein.

I will make an attempt at interpreting the other determinants of the content of the dream as well. There was *a dried specimen of the plant* included in the monograph, as though it had been a *herbarium*. This led me to a memory from my secondary school. Our headmaster once called together the boys from the higher forms and handed over the school's herbarium to them to be looked through and cleaned. Some small worms – book-worms – had found their way into it. He does not seem to have had much confidence in my helpfulness, for he handed me only a few sheets. These, as I could still recall, included some Crucifers. I never had a specially intimate contact with botany. In my preliminary examination in botany I was also given a Crucifer to identify – and failed to do so. My prospects would not have been too bright, if I had not been helped out by my theoretical knowledge. I went on from the Cruciferae to the Compositae. It occurred to me that artichokes were Compositae, and indeed I might fairly have called them *my favorite flowers*. Being more generous than I am, my wife often brought me back these favorite flowers of mine from the market.

I saw the monograph which I had written *lying before me*. This again led me back to something. I had had a letter from my friend [Fliess] in Berlin the day before in which he had shown his power of visualization; "I am very much occupied with your dream-book. *I see it lying finished before me and I see myself turning over its pages.*" How much I envied him his gift as a seer! If only I could have seen it lying finished before me!

The folded colored plate. While I was a medical student I was the constant victim of an impulse only to learn things out of *monographs*. In spite of my limited means, I succeeded in getting hold of a number of volumes of the proceedings of medical societies and was enthralled by their *colored plates*. I was proud of my hankering for thoroughness. When I myself had begun to publish papers, I had been obliged to make my own drawings to illustrate them and I remembered that one of them had been so wretched that a friendly colleague had jeered at me over it. There followed, I could not quite make out how, a recollection from very early youth. It had once amused my father to hand over a book with *colored plates* (an account of a journey through Persia) for me and my eldest sister to destroy. Not easy to justify from the educational point of view! I had been five years old at the time and my sister not yet three; and the picture of the two of us blissfully pulling the book to pieces (leaf by leaf, like an *artichoke*, I found myself saying) was almost the only plastic memory that I retained from that period of my life. Then, when I became a student, I had developed a passion for collecting and owning books, which was analogous to my liking for learning out of monographs: *a favorite hobby*. (The idea of "*favorite*" had already appeared in connection with cyclamens and artichokes.) I had become a *bookworm*. I had always, from the time I first began to think about myself, referred this first passion of mine back to the childhood memory I have mentioned. Or rather, I had recognized that the childhood scene was a "screen memory" for my later bibliophile propensities.

And I had early discovered, of course, that passions often lead to sorrow. When I was seventeen I had run up a largish account at the bookseller's and had nothing to meet it with; and my father had scarcely taken it as an excuse that my inclinations might have chosen a worse outlet. The recollection of this experience from the later years of my youth at once brought back to my mind the conversation with my friend Dr Königstein. For in the course of it we had discussed the same question of my being blamed for being too much absorbed in my *favorite hobbies*.

For reasons with which we are not concerned, I shall not pursue the interpretation of this dream any further, but will merely indicate the direction in which it lay. In the course of the work of analysis I was reminded of my conversation with Dr Königstein, and I was brought to it from more than one direction. When I take into account the topics touched upon in that conversation, the meaning of the dream becomes intelligible to me. All the trains of thought starting from the dream – the thoughts about my wife's and my own favorite flowers, about cocaine, about the awkwardness of medical treatment among colleagues, about my preference for studying monographs and about my neglect of certain branches of science such as botany – all of these trains of thought, when they were further pursued, led ultimately to one or other of the many ramifications of my conversation with Dr Königstein. Once again the dream, like the one we first analyzed – the dream of Irma's injection – turns out to have been in the nature of a self-justification, a plea on behalf of my own rights. Indeed, it carried the subject that was raised in the earlier dream a stage further and discussed it with reference to fresh material that had arisen in the interval between the two dreams. Even the apparently indifferent form in which the dream was couched turns out to have had significance. What it meant was: "After all, I'm the man who wrote the valuable and memorable paper (on cocaine)," just as in the earlier dream I had said on my behalf: "I'm a conscientious and hard-working student." In both cases what I was insisting was: "I may allow myself to do this." ...

The Dream-work

Every attempt that has hitherto been made to solve the problem of dreams has dealt directly with their *manifest* content as it is presented in our memory. All such attempts have endeavored to arrive at an interpretation of dreams from their manifest content or (if no interpretation was attempted) to form a judgement as to their nature on the basis of that same manifest content. We are alone in taking something else into account. We have introduced a new class of psychical material between the manifest content of dreams and the conclusions of our enquiry: namely, their *latent* content, or (as we say) the "dream-thoughts," arrived at by means of our procedure. It is from these dream-thoughts and not from a dream's manifest content that we disentangle its meaning. We are thus presented with a new task which had no previous existence: the task, that is, of investigating the relations between the manifest content of dreams and the latent dream-thoughts, and of tracing out the processes by which the latter have been changed into the former.

The dream-thoughts and the dream-content are presented to us like two versions of the same subject-matter in two different languages. Or, more properly, the dream-content seems like a transcript of the dream-thoughts into another mode of expression, whose characters and syntactic laws it is our business to discover by comparing the original and the translation. The dream-thoughts are immediately comprehensible, as soon as we have learnt them. The dream-content, on the other hand, is expressed as it were in a pictographic script, the characters of which have to be transposed individually into the language of the dream-thoughts. If we attempted to read these characters according to their pictorial value instead of according to their symbolic relation, we should clearly be led into error. Suppose I have a picture-puzzle, a rebus, in front of me. It depicts a house with a boat on its roof, a single letter of the alphabet, the figure of a running man whose head has been conjured away, and so on. Now I might be misled into raising objections and declaring that the picture as a whole and its component parts are nonsensical. A boat has no business to be on the roof of a house, and a headless man cannot run. Moreover, the man is bigger than the house; and if the whole picture is intended to represent a landscape, letters of the alphabet are out of place in it since such objects do not occur in nature.

But obviously we can only form a proper judgement of the rebus if we put aside criticisms such as these of the whole composition and its parts and if, instead, we try to replace each separate element by a syllable or word that can be represented by that element in some way or other. The words which are put together in this way are no longer nonsensical but may form a poetical phrase of the greatest beauty and significance. A dream is a picture-puzzle of this sort and our predecessors in the field of dream-interpretation have made the mistake of treating the rebus as a pictorial composition: and as such it has seemed to them nonsensical and worthless.

The work of condensation

The first thing that becomes clear to anyone who compares the dream-content with the dream-thoughts is that a work of *condensation* on a large scale has been carried out. Dreams are brief, meagre and laconic in comparison with the range and wealth of the dream-thoughts. If a dream is written out it may perhaps fill half a page. The analysis setting out the dream-thoughts underlying it may occupy six, eight or a dozen times as much space. This relation varies with different dreams; but so far as my experience goes its direction never varies. As a rule one underestimates the amount of compression that has taken place, since one is inclined to regard the dream-thoughts that have been brought to light as the complete material, whereas if the work of interpretation is carried further it may reveal still more thoughts concealed behind the dream. I have already had occasion to point out that it is in fact never possible to be sure that a dream has been completely interpreted. Even if the solution seems satisfactory and without gaps, the possibility always remains that the dream may have yet another meaning. Strictly speaking, then, it is impossible to determine the amount of condensation.

There is an answer, which at first sight seems most plausible, to the argument that the great lack of proportion between the dream-content and the dream-thoughts implies that the psychical material has undergone an extensive process of condensation in the course of the formation of the dream. We very often have an impression that we have dreamt a great deal all through the night and have since forgotten most of what we dreamt. On this view, the dream which we remember when we wake up would only be a fragmentary remnant of the total dream-work; and this, if we could recollect it in its entirety, might well be as extensive as the dream-thoughts. There is undoubtedly some truth in this: there can be no question that dreams can be reproduced most accurately if we try to recall them as soon as we wake up and that our memory of them becomes more and more incomplete towards evening. But on the other hand it can be shown that the impression that we have dreamt a great deal more than we can reproduce is very often based on an illusion, the origin of which I shall discuss later. Moreover the hypothesis that condensation occurs during the dream-work is not affected by the possibility of dreams being forgotten, since this hypothesis is proved to be correct by the quantities of ideas which are related to each individual piece of the dream which has been retained. Even supposing that a large piece of the dream has escaped recollection, this may merely have prevented our having access to another group of dream-thoughts. There is no justification for supposing that the lost pieces of the dream would have related to the same thoughts which we have already reached from the pieces of the dream that have survived.[1]

In view of the very great number of associations produced in analysis to each individual element of the content of a dream, some readers may be led to doubt whether, as a matter of principle, we are justified in regarding as part of the dream-thoughts all the associations that occur to us during the subsequent analysis – whether we are justified, that is, in supposing that all these thoughts were already active during the state of sleep and played a part in the formation of the dream. Is it not more probable that new trains of thought have arisen in the course of the analysis which had no share in forming the dream? I can only give limited assent to this argument. It is no doubt true that some trains of thought arise for the first time during the analysis. But one can convince oneself in all such cases that these new connections are only set up between thoughts which were already linked in some other way in the dream-thoughts. The new connections are, as it were, loop-lines or short-circuits, made possible by the existence of other and deeper-lying connecting paths. It must be allowed that the great bulk of the thoughts which are revealed in analysis were already active during the process of forming the dream; for, after working through a string of thoughts which seem to have no connection with the formation of a dream, one suddenly comes upon one which is represented in its content and is indispensable for its interpretation, but which could not have been reached except by this particular line of approach. I may here recall the dream of the botanical mono-graph, which strikes one as the product of an astonishing amount of condensation, even though I have not reported its analysis in full.

How, then, are we to picture psychical conditions during the period of sleep which precedes dreams? Are all the dream-thoughts present alongside one another? or do they occur in sequence? or do a number of trains of thought start out simultaneously from different centers and afterwards unite? There is no need for the present, in my opinion, to form any plastic idea of psychical conditions during the formation of dreams. It must not be forgotten, however, that we are dealing with an *unconscious* process of thought, which may easily be different from what we perceive during purposive reflection accom-panied by consciousness.

The unquestionable fact remains, however, that the formation of dreams is based on a process of condensation. How is that condensation brought about?

When we reflect that only a small minority of all the dream-thoughts revealed are represented in the dream by one of their ideational elements, we might conclude that condensation is brought about by *omission*: that is, that the dream is not a faithful transla-tion or a point-for-point projection of the dream-thoughts, but a highly incomplete and fragmentary version of them. This view, as we shall soon discover, is a most inadequate one. But we may take it as a provisional starting-point and go on to a further question. If only a few elements from the dream-thoughts find their way into the dream-content, what are the conditions which determine their selection?

In order to get some light on this question we must turn our attention to those elements of the dream-content which must have fulfilled these conditions. And the most favorable material for such an investigation will be a dream to the construction of which a particularly intense process of condensation has contributed. I shall accordingly begin by choosing for the purpose the dream which I have already recorded.

The dream of the botanical monograph

Content of the Dream. – *I had written a monograph on an (unspecified) genus of plants. The book lay before me and I was at the moment turning over a folded colored plate. Bound up in the copy there was a dried specimen of the plant.*

The element in this dream which stood out most was the *botanical monograph*. This arose from the impressions of the dream-day: I had in fact seen a monograph on the genus Cyclamen in the window of a book-shop. There was no mention of this genus in the content of the dream; all that was left in it was the monograph and its relation to botany. The "botanical monograph" immediately revealed its connection with the *work upon cocaine* which I had once written. From "cocaine" the chains of thought led on the one hand to the *Festschrift* and to certain events in a University laboratory, and on the other hand to my friend Dr Königstein, the eye-surgeon, who had had a share in the introduction of cocaine. The figure of Dr Königstein further reminded me of the interrupted conversation which I had had with him the evening before and of my various reflections upon the payment for medical services among colleagues. This conversation was the actual currently active instigator of the dream; the monograph on the cyclamen was also a currently active impression, but one of an indifferent nature. As I perceived, the "botanical monograph" in the dream turned out to be an "intermediate common entity" between the two experiences of the previous day: it was taken over unaltered from the indifferent impression and was linked with the psychically significant event by copious associative connections.

Not only the compound idea, "botanical monograph," however, but each of its components, "botanical" and "monograph" separately, led by numerous connecting paths deeper and deeper into the tangle of dream-thoughts. "Botanical" was related to the figure of Professor *Gärtner* [Gardener], the *blooming* looks of his wife, to my patient *Flora* and to the lady [Frau L.] of whom I had told the story of the forgotten flowers. Gärtner led in turn to the laboratory and to my conversation with Königstein. My two patients [Flora and Frau L.] had been mentioned in the course of this conversation. A train of thought joined the lady with the flowers to my wife's *favorite flowers* and thence to the title of the monograph which I had seen for a moment during the day. In addition to these, "botanical" recalled an episode at my secondary school and an examination while I was at the University. A fresh topic touched upon in my conversation with Dr Königstein – my favorite hobbies – was joined, through the intermediate link of what I jokingly called *my favorite flower*, the artichoke, with the train of thought proceeding from the forgotten flowers. Behind "artichokes" lay, on the one hand, my thoughts about Italy and, on the other hand, a scene from my childhood which was the opening of what have since become my intimate relations with books. Thus "botanical" was a regular nodal point in the dream. Numerous trains of thought converged upon it, which, as I can guarantee, had appropriately entered into the context of the conversation with Dr Königstein. Here we find ourselves in a factory of thoughts where, as in the "weaver's masterpiece," –

> Ein Tritt tausend Fäden regt,
> Die Schifflein herüber hinüber schiessen,
> Die Fäden ungesehen fliessen,
> Ein Schlag tausend Verbindungen schlägt.[2]

So, too, "monograph" in the dream touches upon two subjects: the one-sidedness of my studies and the costliness of my favorite hobbies.

This first investigation leads us to conclude that the elements "botanical" and "monograph" found their way into the content of the dream because they possessed copious contacts with the majority of the dream-thoughts, because, that is to say, they constituted "nodal points" upon which a great number of the dream-thoughts converged, and because they had several meanings in connection with the interpretation of the dream. The explanation of this fundamental fact can also be put in another way: each of the elements of the dream's content turns out to have been "overdetermined" – to have been represented in the dream-thoughts many times over.

We discover still more when we come to examine the remaining constituents of the dream in relation to their appearance in the dream-thoughts. The *colored plate* which I was unfolding led to a new topic, my colleagues' criticisms of my activities, and to one which was already represented in the dream, my favorite hobbies; and it led, in addition, to the childhood memory in which I was pulling to pieces a book with colored plates. The *dried specimen of the plant* touched upon the episode of the herbarium at my secondary school and specially stressed that memory.

The nature of the relation between dream-content and dream-thoughts thus becomes visible. Not only are the elements of a dream determined by the dream-thoughts many times over, but the individual dream-thoughts are represented in the dream by several elements. Associative paths lead from one element of the dream to several dream-thoughts, and from one dream-thought to several elements of the dream. Thus a dream is not constructed by each individual dream-thought, or group of dream-thoughts, finding (in abbreviated form) separate representation in the content of the dream – in the kind of way in which an electorate chooses parliamentary representatives; a dream is constructed, rather, by the whole mass of dream-thoughts being submitted to a sort of manipulative process in which those elements which have the most numerous and strongest supports acquire the right of entry into the dream-content – in a manner analogous to election by *scrutin de liste*. In the case of every dream which I have submitted to an analysis of this kind I have invariably found these same fundamental principles confirmed: the elements of the dream are constructed out of the whole mass of dream-thoughts and each one of those elements is shown to have been determined many times over in relation to the dream-thoughts.

It will certainly not be out of place to illustrate the connection between dream-content and dream-thoughts by a further example, which is distinguished by the specially ingenious interweaving of their reciprocal relations. It is a dream produced by one of my patients – a man whom I was treating for claustrophobia. It will soon become clear why I have chosen to give this exceptionally clever dream-production the title of

A lovely dream

He was driving with a large party to X Street, in which there was an unpretentious inn. (This is not the case.) There was a play being acted inside it. At one moment he was audience, at another actor. When it was over they had to change their clothes so as to get back to town. Some of the company were shown into rooms on the ground floor and others into rooms on the first floor. Then a dispute broke out. The ones up above were angry because the ones down below were not ready, and they could not come downstairs. His brother was up above and he was down below and he was angry with his brother because they were so much pressed. (This part was obscure.) Moreover, it had been decided and arranged even when they first arrived who was to be up above and who was to be down below. Then he was walking by himself up the rise made by X Street in the direction of town. He walked with such difficulty and so laboriously that he seemed glued to the spot. An elderly gentleman came up to him and began abusing the King of Italy. At the top of the rise he was able to walk much more easily.

His difficulty in walking up the rise was so distinct that after waking up he was for some time in doubt whether it was a dream or reality.

We should not think very highly of this dream, judging by its manifest content. In defiance of the rules, I shall begin its interpretation with the portion which the dreamer described as being the most distinct.

The difficulty which he dreamt of and probably actually experienced during the dream – the laborious climbing up the rise accompanied by dyspnoea – was one of the symptoms which the patient had in fact exhibited years before and which had at that time been attributed, along with certain other symptoms, to tuberculosis. (The probability is that this was hysterically simulated.) The peculiar sensation of inhibited movement that occurs in this dream is already familiar to us from dreams of exhibiting and we see once more that it is material available at any time for any other representational purpose. The piece of the dream-content which described how the climb began by being difficult and became easy at the end of the rise reminded me, when I heard it, of the masterly introduction to Alphonse Daudet's *Sappho*. That well-known passage describes how a young man carries his mistress upstairs in his arms; at first she is as light as a feather, but the higher he climbs the heavier grows her weight. The whole scene foreshadows the course of their love-affair, which was intended by Daudet as a warning to young men not to allow their affections to be seriously engaged by girls of humble origin and a dubious past.[3] Though I knew that my patient had been involved in a love-affair which he had recently broken off with a lady on the stage, I did not expect to find my guess at an interpretation justified. Moreover the situation in *Sappho* was the *reverse* of what it had been in the dream. In the dream the climbing had been difficult to begin with and had afterwards become easy; whereas the symbolism in the novel only made sense if something that had been begun lightly ended by becoming a heavy burden. But to my astonishment my patient replied that my interpretation fitted in very well with a piece he had seen at the theater the evening before. It was called *Rund um Wien* [*Round Vienna*] and gave a picture of the career of a girl who began by being respectable, who then became a *demi-mondaine* and had *liaisons* with men in high positions and so "*went up in the world*," but who ended by "*coming down in the world*." The piece had moreover reminded him of another, which he had seen some years earlier, called *Von Stufe zu Stufe* [*Step by Step*], and which had been advertised by a poster showing a staircase with a flight of *steps*.

To continue with the interpretation. The actress with whom he had had this latest, eventful *liaison* had lived in X Street. There is nothing in the nature of an inn in that street. But when he was spending part of the summer in Vienna on the lady's account he had put up [German "*abgestiegen*," literally "*stepped down*"] at a small hotel in the neighborhood. When he left the hotel he had said to his cab-driver: "Anyhow I'm lucky not to have picked up any vermin." (This, incidentally, was another of his phobias.) To this the driver had replied: "How could anyone put up at such a place! It's not a hotel, it's only an *inn*."

The idea of an inn at once recalled a quotation to his mind:

> Bei einem *Wirte* wundermild,
> Da war ich jüngst zu Gaste.[4]

The host in Uhland's poem was an *apple-tree*; and a second quotation now carried on his train of thought:

FAUST: (*mit der Jüngen tanzend*):
               Einst hatt' ich *einen schönen Traum*;
               Da sah ich einen *Apfelbaum*,
               Zwei schöne Äpfel glänzten dran,
               Sie reizten mich, *ich stieg hinan.*
DIE SCHÖNE: Der Äpfelchen begehrt ihr sehr,
               Und schon vom Paradiese her.
               Von Freuden fühl' ich mich bewegt,
               Dass auch mein Garten solche trägt.[5]

There cannot be the faintest doubt what the apple-tree and the apples stood for. Moreover, lovely breasts had been among the charms which had attracted the dreamer to his actress.

The context of the analysis gave us every ground for supposing that the dream went back to an impression in childhood. If so, it must have referred to the wet-nurse of the dreamer, who was by then a man almost thirty years old. For an infant the breasts of his wet-nurse are nothing more nor less than an inn. The wet-nurse, as well as Daudet's Sappho, seem to have been allusions to the mistress whom the patient had recently dropped.

The patient's (elder) brother also appeared in the content of the dream, the brother being up *above* and the patient himself *down below*. This was once again the *reverse* of the actual situation; for, as I knew, the brother had lost his social position while the patient had maintained his. In repeating the content of the dream to me, the dreamer had avoided saying that his brother was up above and he himself "on the ground floor." That would have put the position too clearly, since here in Vienna if we say someone is "*on the ground floor*" we mean that he has lost his money and his position – in other words, that he has "*come down in the world*." Now there must have been a reason for some of this part of the dream being represented by its *reverse*. Further, the reversal must hold good of some other relation between dream-thoughts and dream-content as well; and we have a hint of where to look for this reversal. It must evidently be at the end of the dream, where once again there was a *reversal* of the difficulty in going upstairs as described in *Sappho*. We can then easily see what reversal is intended. In *Sappho* the man carried a woman who was in a sexual relation to him; in the dream-thoughts the position was *reversed*, and a woman was carrying a man. And since this can only happen in childhood, the reference was once more to the wet-nurse bearing the weight of the infant in her arms. Thus the end of the dream made a simultaneous reference to *Sappho* and to the wet-nurse.

Just as the author of the novel, in choosing the name "Sappho," had in mind an allusion to Lesbian practices, so too the pieces of the dream that spoke of people "*up above*" and "*down below*" alluded to phantasies of a sexual nature which occupied the patient's mind and, as suppressed desires, were not without a bearing on his neurosis. (The interpretation of the dream did not itself show us that what were thus represented in the dream were phantasies and not recollections of real events; an analysis only gives us the *content* of a thought and leaves it to us to determine its reality. Real and imaginary events appear in dreams at first sight as of equal validity; and that is so not only in dreams but in the production of more important psychical structures.)

A "large party" meant, as we already know, a secret. His brother was simply the representative (introduced into the childhood scene by a "retrospective phantasy") of all his later rivals for a woman's affection. The episode of the gentleman who abused the King of Italy related once again, via the medium of a recent and in itself indifferent experience, to people of lower rank pushing their way into higher society. It was just as though the child at the breast was being given a warning parallel to the one which Daudet had given to young men.[6]

To provide a third opportunity for studying condensation in the formation of dreams, I will give part of the analysis of another dream, which I owe to an elderly lady undergoing psycho-analytic treatment. As was to be expected from the severe anxiety-states from which the patient suffered, her dreams contained a very large number of sexual thoughts, the first realization of which both surprised and alarmed her. Since I shall not be able to pursue the interpretation of the dream to the end, its material will appear to fall into several groups without any visible connection.

The May-beetle[7] dream

Content of the Dream. – *She called to mind that she had two may-beetles in a box and that she must set them free or they would suffocate. She opened the box and the may-beetles were in an exhausted state. One of them flew out of the open window; but the other was crushed by the casement while she was shutting it at someone's request. (Signs of disgust.)*

Analysis. – Her husband was temporarily away from home, and her fourteen-year-old daughter was sleeping in the bed beside her. The evening before, the girl had drawn her attention to a moth which had fallen into her tumbler of water; but she had not taken it out and felt sorry for the poor creature next morning. The book she had been reading during the evening had told how some boys had thrown a cat into boiling water, and had described the animal's convulsions. These were the two precipitating causes of the dream – in themselves indifferent.

She then pursued the subject of *cruelty to animals* further. Some years before, while they were spending the summer at a particular place, her daughter had been very cruel to animals. She was collecting butterflies and asked the patient for some *arsenic* to kill them with. On one occasion a moth with a pin through its body had gone on flying about the room for a long time; another time some caterpillars which the child was keeping to turn into chrysalises starved to death. At a still more tender age the same child used to tear the wings off *beetles* and butterflies. But to-day she would be horrified at all these cruel actions – she had grown so kind-hearted.

The patient reflected over this contradiction. It reminded her of another contradiction, between appearance and character, as George Eliot displays it in *Adam Bede*: one girl who was pretty, but vain and stupid, and another who was ugly, but of high character; a nobleman who seduced the silly girl, and a working man who felt and acted with true nobility. How impossible it was, she remarked, to recognize that sort of thing in people! Who would have guessed, to look at *her*, that she was tormented by sensual desires?

In the same year in which the little girl had begun collecting butterflies, the district they were in had suffered from a serious plague of *may-beetles*. The children were furious with the beetles and *crushed* them unmercifully. At that time my patient had seen a man who tore the wings off may-beetles and then ate their bodies. She herself had been born in *May* and had been married in *May*. Three days after her marriage she had written to her parents at home saying how happy she was. But it had been far from true.

The evening before the dream she had been rummaging among some old letters and had read some of them – some serious and some comic – aloud to her children. There had been a most amusing letter from a piano-teacher who had courted her when she was a girl, and another from an admirer *of noble birth*.[8]

She blamed herself because one of her daughters had got hold of a "bad" book by Maupassant.[9] The *arsenic* that the girl had asked for reminded her of the *arsenic pills* which restored the Duc de Mora's youthful strength in [Daudet's] *Le Nabab*.

"Set them free" made her think of a passage in the *Magic Flute*:

> Zur Liebe kann ich dich nicht zwingen,
> Doch geb ich dir *die Freiheit* nicht.[10]

"May-beetles" also made her think of Kätchen's words:

> Verliebt ja wie ein *Käfer* bist du mir.[11]

And in the middle of all this came a quotation from *Tannhäuser*:

> Weil du von *böser Lust* beseelt …[12]

She was living in a perpetual worry about her absent husband. Her fear that something might happen to him on his journey was expressed in numerous waking phantasies. A short time before, in the course of her analysis, she had lighted among her unconscious thoughts upon a complaint about her husband "growing senile." The wishful thought concealed by her present dream will perhaps best be conjectured if I mention that, some days before she dreamt it, she was horrified, in the middle of her daily affairs, by a phrase in the imperative mood which came into her head and was aimed at her husband: "Go and hang yourself!" It turned out that a few hours earlier she had read somewhere or other that when a man is hanged he gets a powerful erection. The wish for an erection was what had emerged from repression in this horrifying disguise. "Go and hang your-self!" was equivalent to: "Get yourself an erection at any price!" Dr Jenkins's arsenic pills in *Le Nabab* fitted in here. But my patient was also aware that the most powerful aphrodisiac, cantharides (commonly known as "Spanish flies"), was prepared from *crushed beetles*. This was the drift of the principal part of the dream's content.

The opening and shutting of *windows* was one of the main subjects of dispute between her and her husband. She herself was aerophilic in her sleeping habits; her husband was aerophobic. *Exhaustion* was the chief symptom which she complained of at the time of the dream….

The work of condensation in dreams is seen at its clearest when it handles words and names. It is true in general that words are treated in dreams as though they were concrete things, and for that reason they are apt to be combined in just the same way as presentations of concrete things. Dreams of this sort offer the most amusing and curious neologisms.

On one occasion a medical colleague had sent me a paper he had written, in which the importance of a recent physiological discovery was, in my opinion, overestimated, and in which, above all, the subject was treated in too emotional a manner. The next night I dreamt a sentence which clearly referred to this paper: "*It's written in a positively norek-dal style.*" The analysis of the word caused me some difficulty at first. There could be no doubt that it was a parody of the [German] superlatives "*kolossal*" and "*pyramidal*";

but its origin was not so easy to guess. At last I saw that the monstrosity was composed of the two names "Nora" and "Ekdal" – characters in two well-known plays of Ibsen's. [*A Doll's House* and *The Wild Duck*.] Some time before, I had read a newspaper article on Ibsen by the same author whose latest work I was criticizing in the dream....

VI

Early this morning, between dreaming and waking, I experienced a very nice example of verbal condensation. In the course of a mass of dream-fragments that I could scarcely remember, I was brought up short, as it were, by a word which I saw before me as though it were half written and half printed. The word was "*erzefilisch*," and it formed part of a sentence which slipped into my conscious memory apart from any context and in complete isolation: "That has an *erzefilisch* influence on the sexual emotions." I knew at once that the word ought really to have been "*erzieherisch*" ["educational"]. And I was in doubt for some time whether the second "*e*" in "*erzefilisch*" should not have been an "*i*."[13] In that connection the word "syphilis" occurred to me and, starting to analyze the dream while I was still half asleep, I racked my brains in an effort to make out how that word could have got into my dream, since I had nothing to do with the disease either personally or professionally. I then thought of "*erzehlerisch*" [another nonsense word], and this explained the "*e*" of the second syllable of "*erzefilisch*" by reminding me that the evening before I had been asked by our governess [*Erzieherin*] to say something to her on the problem of prostitution, and had given her Hesse's book on prostitution in order to influence her emotional life – for this had not developed quite normally; after which I had talked [*erzählt*] a lot to her on the problem. I then saw all at once that the word "syphilis" was not to be taken literally, but stood for "poison" – of course in relation to sexual life. When translated, therefore, the sentence in the dream ran quite logically: "My talk [*Erzählung*] was intended to have an educational [*erzieherisch*] influence on the emotional life of our governess [*Erzieherin*]; but I fear it may at the same time have had a poisonous effect." "*Erzefilisch*" was compounded from "*erzäh-*" and "*erzieh-*."

The verbal malformations in dreams greatly resemble those which are familiar in paranoia but which are also present in hysteria and obsessions. The linguistic tricks performed by children, who sometimes actually treat words as though they were objects and moreover invent new languages and artificial syntactic forms, are the common source of these things in dreams and psycho-neuroses alike.

The analysis of the nonsensical verbal forms that occur in dreams is particularly well calculated to exhibit the dream-work's achievements in the way of condensation. The reader should not conclude from the paucity of the instances which I have given that material of this kind is rare or observed at all exceptionally. On the contrary, it is very common. But as a result of the fact that dream-interpretation is dependent upon psycho-analytic treatment, only a very small number of instances are observed and recorded and the analyses of such instances are as a rule only intelligible to experts in the pathology of the neuroses. Thus a dream of this kind was reported by Dr von Karpinska (1914) containing the nonsensical verbal form: "*Svingnum elvi*." It is also worth mentioning those cases in which a word appears in a dream which is not in itself meaningless but which has lost its proper meaning and combines a number of other meanings to which it is related in just the same way as a "meaningless" word would be. This is what occurred, for instance, in the ten-year-old boy's dream of a "category" which was recorded by Tausk (1913). "Category" in that case meant "female genitals" and to "categorate" meant the same as "to micturate."

Where spoken sentences occur in dreams and are expressly distinguished as such from thoughts, it is an invariable rule that the words spoken in the dream are derived from spoken words remembered in the dream-material. The text of the speech is either retained unaltered or expressed with some slight displacement. A speech in a dream is often put together from various recollected speeches, the text remaining the same but being given, if possible, several meanings, or one different from the original one. A spoken remark in a dream is not infrequently no more than an allusion to an occasion on which the remark in question was made.[14]

The work of displacement

In making our collection of instances of condensation in dreams, the existence of another relation, probably of no less importance, had already become evident. It could be seen that the elements which stand out as the principal components of the manifest content of the dream are far from playing the same part in the dream-thoughts. And, as a corollary, the converse of this assertion can be affirmed: what is clearly the essence of the dream-thoughts need not be represented in the dream at all. The dream is, as it were, differently centered from the dream-thoughts – its content has different elements as its central point. Thus in the dream of the botanical monograph, for instance, the central point of the dream-content was obviously the element "botanical"; whereas the dream-thoughts were concerned with the complications and conflicts arising between colleagues from their professional obligations, and further with the charge that I was in the habit of sacrificing too much for the sake of my hobbies. The element "botanical" had no place whatever in this core of the dream-thoughts, unless it was loosely connected with it by an antithesis – the fact that botany never had a place among my favorite studies. In my patient's *Sappho* dream the central position was occupied by climbing up and down and being up above and down below; the dream-thoughts, however, dealt with the dangers of sexual relations with people of an inferior social class. So that only a single element of the dream-thoughts seems to have found its way into the dream-content, though that element was expanded to a disproportionate extent. Similarly, in the dream of the may-beetles, the topic of which was the relations of sexuality to cruelty, it is true that the factor of cruelty emerged in the dream-content; but it did so in another connection and without any mention of sexuality, that is to say, divorced from its context and consequently transformed into something extraneous. Once again, in my dream about my uncle, the fair beard which formed its center-point seems to have had no connection in its meaning with my ambitious wishes which, as we saw, were the core of the dream-thoughts. Dreams such as these give a justifiable impression of "displacement." In complete contrast to these examples, we can see that in the dream of Irma's injection the different elements were able to retain, during the process of constructing the dream, the approximate place which they occupied in the dream-thoughts. This further relation between the dream-thoughts and the dream-content, wholly variable as it is in its sense or direction, is calculated at first to create astonishment. If we are considering a psychical process in normal life and find that one out of its several component ideas has been picked out and has acquired a special degree of vividness in consciousness, we usually regard this effect as evidence that a specially high amount of psychical value – some particular degree of interest – attaches to this predominant idea. But we now discover that, in the case of the different elements of the dream-thoughts, a value of this kind does not persist or is disregarded in the process of dream-formation. There is never any doubt as to which of the elements of the dream-thoughts have the highest psychical value; we learn that by direct judgement. In the course of the formation of a dream these essential elements, charged, as they are, with intense interest, may be treated as though they were of small value, and their place may be taken in the dream by other elements, of whose small value in the dream-thoughts there can be no question. At first sight it looks as though no attention whatever is paid to the psychical intensity[15] of the various ideas in making the choice among them for the dream, and as though the only thing considered is the greater or less degree of multiplicity of their determination. What appears in dreams, we might suppose, is not what is *important* in the dream-thoughts but what occurs in them several times over. But this hypothesis does not greatly assist our understanding of dream-formation, since from the nature of things it seems clear that the two factors of multiple determination and inherent psychical value must necessarily operate in the same sense. The ideas which are most important among the dream-thoughts will almost certainly be those which occur most often in them, since the different dream-thoughts will, as it were, radiate out from them. Nevertheless a dream can reject elements which are thus both highly stressed in themselves and reinforced from many directions, and can select for its content other elements which possess only the second of these attributes.

In order to solve this difficulty we shall make use of another impression derived from our enquiry [in the previous section] into the overdetermination of the dream-content. Perhaps some of those who have read that enquiry may already have formed an independent conclusion that the overdetermination of the elements of dreams is no very important discovery, since it is a self-evident one. For in analysis we start out from the dream-elements and note down all the associations which lead off from them; so that there is nothing surprising in the fact that in the thought-material arrived at in this way we come across these same elements with peculiar frequency. I cannot accept this objection; but I will myself put into words something that sounds not unlike it. Among the thoughts that analysis brings to light are many which are relatively remote from the kernel of the dream and which look like artificial interpolations made for some particular purpose. That purpose is easy to divine. It is precisely *they* that constitute a connection, often a forced and far-fetched one, between the dream-content and the dream-thoughts; and if these elements were weeded out of the analysis the result would often be that the component parts of the dream-content would be left not only without overdetermination but without any satisfactory determination at all. We shall be led to conclude that the multiple determination which decides what shall be included in a dream is not always a primary factor in dream-construction but is often the secondary product of a psychical force which is still unknown to us. Nevertheless multiple determination must be of importance in choosing what particular elements shall enter a dream, since we can see that a considerable expenditure of effort is used to bring it about in cases where it does not arise from the dream-material unassisted.

It thus seems plausible to suppose that in the dream-work a psychical force is operating which on the one hand strips the elements which have a high psychical value of their intensity, and on the other hand, by *means of overdetermination*, creates from elements of low psychical value new values, which afterwards find their way into the dream-content. If that is so, *a transference and displacement of psychical intensities* occurs in the process of dream-formation, and it is as a result of these that the difference between the text of the dream-content and that of the dream-thoughts comes about. The process which we are here presuming is nothing less than the essential portion of the dream-work; and it deserves to be described as "dream-displacement." Dream-displacement and dream-condensation are the two governing factors to whose activity we may in essence ascribe the form assumed by dreams.

Nor do I think we shall have any difficulty in recognizing the psychical force which manifests itself in the facts of dream-displacement. The consequence of the displacement is that the dream-content no longer resembles the core of the dream-thoughts and that the dream gives no more than a distortion of the dream-wish which exists in the unconscious. But we are already familiar with dream-distortion. We traced it back to the censorship which is exercised by one psychical agency in the mind over another. Dream-displacement is one of the chief methods by which that distortion is achieved. *Is fecit cui profuit.*[16] We may assume, then, that dream-displacement comes about through the influence of the same censorship – that is, the censorship of endopsychic defence.[17]

The question of the interplay of these factors – of displacement, condensation and overdetermination – in the construction of dreams, and the question which is a dominant factor and which a subordinate one – all of this we shall leave aside for later investigation. But we can state provisionally a second condition which must be satisfied by those elements of the dream-thoughts which make their way into the dream: *they must escape the censorship imposed by resistance*. And henceforward in interpreting dreams we shall take dream-displacement into account as an undeniable fact.

Notes

1 The occurrence of condensation in dreams has been hinted at by many writers. Du Prel has a passage in which he says it is absolutely certain that there has been a process of condensation of the groups of ideas in dreams. (C. Du Prel, *Die Philosophie der Mystik* (Leipzig, 1885), p. 85.)

2 [" ... a thousand threads one treadle throws, / Where fly the shuttles hither and thither, / Unseen the threads are knit together, / And an infinite combination grows." Goethe, *Faust*, Part I [Scene 4] (Bayard Taylor's translation).]

3 [*Footnote added* 1911:] What I have written below in the section on symbolism about the significance of dreams of climbing throws light upon the imagery chosen by the novelist.

4 [Literally: "I was lately a guest at an *inn* with a most gentle host." (Uhland, *Wanderlieder*, 8, "Einkehr.")]

5 ["FAUST (*dancing with the Young Witch*): *A lovely dream* once came to me, / And I beheld an *apple-tree*, / On which two lovely apples shone; / They charmed me so, I *climbed thereon*. THE LOVELY WITCH: Apples have been desired by you, / Since first in Paradise they grew; / And I am moved with joy to know / That such within my garden grow." Goethe, *Faust*, Part I [Scene 21, Walpurgisnacht] (Bayard Taylor's translation, slightly modified).]

6 The imaginary nature of the situation relating to the dreamer's wet-nurse was proved by the objectively established fact that in his case the wet-nurse had been his mother. I may recall in this connection the anecdote of the young man who regretted that he had not made better use of his opportunities with his wet-nurse. A regret of the same kind was no doubt the source of the present dream.

7 [The commoner English equivalent for the German "*Maikäfer*" is "cockchafer." For the purposes of this dream, however, a literal translation is to be preferred.]

8 This had been the true instigator of the dream.

9 An interpolation is required at this point: "books of that kind are *poison* to a girl." The patient herself had dipped into forbidden books a great deal when she was young.

10 [Fear not, to love I'll ne'er compel thee; Yet 'tis too soon to *set thee free*. (Sarastro to Pamina in the *Finale* to Act I. – E. J. Dent's translation.)]

11 ["You are madly in love with me." Literally: "You are in love with me like a *beetle*." From Kleist's *Kätchen von Heilbronn*, IV, 2.] – A further train of thought led to the same poet's *Penthesilea*, and to the idea of *cruelty* to a lover.

12 [Literally: "Because thou wast inspired by such *evil pleasure*." This is presumably a recollection of the opening phrase of the Pope's condemnation reported by Tannhäuser in the last scene of the opera. The actual words are: "Hast du so böse Lust getheilt" – "Since thou hast shared such evil pleasure."]

13 [This ingenious example of condensation turns upon the pronunciation of the second syllable – the stressed syllable – of the nonsense word. If it is "*ze*," it is pronounced roughly like the English "say," thus resembling the second syllable of "*erzählen*" and of the invented "*erzehlerisch*." If it is "*zi*," it is pronounced roughly like the English "tsee," thus resembling the second syllable of "*erzieherisch*," as well as (less closely) the first syllable of "syphilis."]

14 [*Footnote added* 1909:] Not long ago I found a single exception to this rule in the case of a young man who suffered from obsessions while retaining intact his highly developed intellectual powers. The spoken words which occurred in his dreams were not derived from remarks which he had heard or made himself. They contained the undistorted text of his obsessional thoughts, which in his waking life only reached his consciousness in a modified form.

15 *Psychical* intensity or value or the degree of interest of an idea is of course to be distinguished from *sensory* intensity or the intensity of the image presented.

16 [The old legal tag: "He did the deed who gained by it."]

17 [*Footnote added* 1909:] Since I may say that the kernel of my theory of dreams lies in my derivation of dream-distortion from the censorship, I will here insert the last part of a story from *Phantasien eines Realisten* [*Phantasies of a Realist*] by "Lynkeus" (Vienna, 2nd edition, 1900 [1st edition, 1899]), in which I have found this principal feature of my theory once more expounded. The title of the story is "Träumen wie Wachen" ["Dreaming like Waking"]:

> "About a man who has the remarkable attribute of never dreaming nonsense....
>
> "This splendid gift of yours, for dreaming as though you were waking, is a consequence of your virtues, of your kindness, your sense of justice, and your love of truth; it is the moral serenity of your nature which makes me understand all about you."
>
> "But when I think the matter over properly," replied the other, "I almost believe that everyone is made like me, and that no one at all ever dreams nonsense. Any dream which one can remember clearly enough to describe it afterwards – any dream, that is to say, which is not a fever-dream – must *always* make sense, and it cannot possibly be otherwise. For things that were mutually contradictory could not group themselves into a single whole. The fact that time and space are often thrown into confusion does not affect the true content of the dream, since no doubt neither of them are of significance for its real essence. We often do the same thing in waking life. Only think of fairy tales and of the many daring products of the imagination, which are full of meaning and of which only a man without intelligence could say: 'This is nonsense, for it's impossible.' "
>
> "If only one always knew how to interpret dreams in the right way, as you have just done with mine!" said his friend.
>
> "That is certainly no easy task; but with a little attention on the part of the dreamer himself it should no doubt always succeed. – You ask why it is that for the most part it does *not* succeed? In you other people there seems always to be something that lies concealed in your dreams, something unchaste in a special and higher sense, a certain secret quality in your being which it is hard to follow. And that is why your dreams so often seem to be without meaning or even to be nonsense. But in the deepest sense this is not in the least so; indeed, it cannot be so at all – for it is always the same man, whether he is awake or dreaming."

CHAPTER 3

The Uncanny

Sigmund Freud

In this famous essay from 1914, Freud attempts to account for strange coincidences in life (such as repeatedly returning to the same place without seeming to intend to do so). These "uncanny" moments, he argues, are in fact manifestations of the work of our unconscious mind. We are two people – our conscious self and the "other" self that prompts and inspires us to actions that often seem against our better, more rational will. That other self is as much us as us. It is driven by feelings, yearnings, and needs that result from our past experiences, experiences that necessarily get erased from consciousness and pass into unconsciousness as we move through life. Those records remain, and they remain active if they have not been dealt with properly. You did not fulfill a dream in your youth? A feeling of frustration and yearning in that regard may continue to drive you later in life. And often, you will have no clue where it's coming from. It just happens. Such, according to Freud, is the uncanny work of the unconscious. That is why he was attracted to stories of possession, doubles, and automatons. Often, we ourselves are our own double; we are possessed (by ourselves); and we behave as if part of us were on automatic pilot, driving us forward, apparently outside and often against our conscious will.

I

IT is only rarely that a psycho-analyst feels impelled to investigate the subject of aesthetics, even when aesthetics is understood to mean not merely the theory of beauty but the theory of the qualities of feeling. He works in other strata of mental life and has little to do with the subdued emotional impulses which, inhibited in their aims and dependent on a host of concurrent factors, usually furnish the material for the study of aesthetics. But it does occasionally happen that he has to interest himself in some particular province of that subject; and this province usually proves to be a rather remote one, and one which has been neglected in the specialist literature of aesthetics.

Original publication details: Sigmund Freud, "The Uncanny" from *The Standard Edition of the Complete Psychological Works*, trans. James Strachey, pp. 217–252. Hogarth Press, 1955.
Reproduced with permission from The Random House Group Ltd, Perseus Books and Marsh Agency on behalf of Sigmund Freud Copyrights.

The subject of the 'uncanny'[1] is a province of this kind. It is undoubtedly related to what is frightening – to what arouses dread and horror; equally certainly, too, the word is not always used in a clearly definable sense, so that it tends to coincide with what excites fear in general. Yet we may expect that a special core of feeling is present which justifies the use of a special conceptual term. One is curious to know what this common core is which allows us to distinguish as 'uncanny' certain things which lie within the field of what is frightening.

As good as nothing is to be found upon this subject in comprehensive treatises on aesthetics, which in general prefer to concern themselves with what is beautiful, attractive and sublime – that is, with feelings of a positive nature – and with the circumstances and the objects that call them forth, rather than with the opposite feelings of repulsion and distress. I know of only one attempt in medico-psychological literature, a fertile but not exhaustive paper by Jentsch (1906). But I must confess that I have not made a very thorough examination of the literature, especially the foreign literature, relating to this present modest contribution of mine, for reasons which, as may easily be guessed, lie in the times in which we live;[2] so that my paper is presented to the reader without any claim to priority.

In his study of the 'uncanny' Jentsch quite rightly lays stress on the obstacle presented by the fact that people vary so very greatly in their sensitivity to this quality of feeling. The writer of the present contribution, indeed, must himself plead guilty to a special obtuseness in the matter, where extreme delicacy of perception would be more in place. It is long since he has experienced or heard of anything which has given him an uncanny impression, and he must start by translating himself into that state of feeling, by awakening in himself the possibility of experiencing it. Still, such difficulties make themselves powerfully felt in many other branches of aesthetics; we need not on that account despair of finding instances in which the quality in question will be unhesitatingly recognized by most people.

Two courses are open to us at the outset. Either we can find out what meaning has come to be attached to the word 'uncanny' in the course of its history; or we can collect all those properties of persons, things, sense-impressions, experiences and situations which arouse in us the feeling of uncanniness, and then infer the unknown nature of the uncanny from what all these examples have in common. I will say at once that both courses lead to the same result: the uncanny is that class of the frightening which leads back to what is known of old and long familiar. How this is possible, in what circumstances the familiar can become uncanny and frightening, I shall show in what follows. Let me also add that my investigation was actually begun by collecting a number of individual cases, and was only later confirmed by an examination of linguistic usage. In this discussion, however, I shall follow the reverse course.

The German word '*unheimlich*' is obviously the opposite of '*heimlich*' ['homely'], '*heimisch*' ['native'] – the opposite of what is familiar; and we are tempted to conclude that what is 'uncanny' is frightening precisely because it is *not* known and familiar. Naturally not everything that is new and unfamiliar is frightening, however; the relation is not capable of inversion. We can only say that what is novel can easily become frightening and uncanny; some new things are frightening but not by any means all. Something has to be added to what is novel and unfamiliar in order to make it uncanny.

On the whole, Jentsch did not get beyond this relation of the uncanny to the novel and unfamiliar. He ascribes the essential factor in the production of the feeling of uncanniness to intellectual uncertainty; so that the uncanny would always, as it were, be something one does not know one's way about in. The better orientated in his environment a person is, the less readily will he get the impression of something uncanny in regard to the objects and events in it.

It is not difficult to see that this definition is incomplete, and we will therefore try to proceed beyond the equation 'uncanny' = 'unfamiliar'. We will first turn to other languages. But the dictionaries that we consult tell us nothing new, perhaps only because we ourselves speak a language that is foreign. Indeed, we get an impression that many languages are without a word for this particular shade of what is frightening.

I should like to express my indebtedness to Dr. Theodor Reik for the following excerpts: –

LATIN: (K. E. Georges, *Deutschlateinisches Wörterbuch*, 1898). An uncanny place: *locus suspectus*; at an uncanny time of night: *intempesta nocte*.

GREEK: (Rost's and Schenkl's Lexikons). ξένος (i.e. strange, foreign).

ENGLISH: (from the dictionaries of Lucas, Bellows, Flügel and Muret-Sanders). Uncomfortable, uneasy, gloomy, dismal, uncanny, ghastly; (of a house) haunted; (of a man) a repulsive fellow.

FRENCH: (Sachs-Villatte). *Inquiétant, sinistre, lugubre, mal à son aise.*

SPANISH: (Tollhausen, 1889). *Sospechoso, de mal agüero, lúgubre, siniestro.*

The Italian and Portuguese languages seem to content themselves with words which we should describe as circumlocutions. In Arabic and Hebrew 'uncanny' means the same as 'daemonic', 'gruesome'.

Let us therefore return to the German language. In Daniel Sanders's *Wörterbuch der Deutschen Sprache* (1860, **1**, 729), the following entry, which I here reproduce in full, is to be found under the word '*heimlich*'. I have laid stress on one or two passages by italicizing them.[3]

Heimlich, adj., subst. *Heimlichkeit* (pl. *Heimlichkeiten*): I. Also *heimelich, heimelig*, belonging to the house, not strange, familiar, tame, intimate, friendly, etc.

(*a*) (Obsolete) belonging to the house or the family, or regarded as so belonging (cf. Latin *familiaris*, familiar): *Die Heimlichen*, the members of the household; *Der heimliche Rat* (Gen. xli, 45; 2 Sam. xxiii. 23; 1 Chron. xii. 25; Wisd. viii. 4), now more usually *Geheimer Rat* [Privy Councillor].

(*b*) Of animals: tame, companionable to man. As opposed to wild, e.g. 'Animals which are neither wild nor *heimlich*', etc. 'Wild animals … that are trained to be *heimlich* and accustomed to men.' 'If these young creatures are brought up from early days among men they become quite *heimlich*, friendly' etc. – So also: 'It (the lamb) is so *heimlich* and eats out of my hand.' 'Nevertheless, the stork is a beautiful, *heimelich* bird.'

(*c*) Intimate, friendlily comfortable; the enjoyment of quiet content, etc., arousing a sense of agreeable restfulness and security as in one within the four walls of his house.[4] 'Is it still *heimlich* to you in your country where strangers are felling your woods?' 'She did not feel too *heimlich* with him.' 'Along a high, *heimlich*, shady path …, beside a purling, gushing and babbling woodland brook.' 'To destroy the *Heimlichkeit* of the home.' 'I could not readily find another spot so intimate and *heimlich* as this.' 'We pictured it so comfortable, so nice, so cosy and *heimlich*.' 'In quiet *Heimlichkeit*, surrounded by close walls.' 'A careful housewife, who knows how to make a pleasing *Heimlichkeit* (*Häuslichkeit* [domesticity]) out of the smallest means.' 'The man who till recently had been so strange to him now seemed to him all the more *heimlich*.' 'The protestant land-owners do not feel … *heimlich* among their catholic inferiors.' 'When it grows *heimlich* and still, and the evening quiet alone watches over your cell.' 'Quiet, lovely and *heimlich*, no place more fitted for their rest.' 'He did not feel at all *heimlich* about it.' – Also, [in compounds] 'The place was so peaceful, so lonely, so shadily-*heimlich*.' 'The in- and outflowing waves of the current, dreamy and lullaby-*heimlich*.' Cf. in especial *Unheimlich* [see below]. Among Swabian Swiss authors in especial, often as a trisyllable: 'How *heimelich* it seemed to Ivo again of an evening, when he was at home.' 'It was so *heimelig* in the house.' 'The warm room and the *heimelig* afternoon.' 'When a man feels in his heart that he is so small and the Lord so great – that is what is truly *heimelig*.' 'Little by little they grew at ease and *heimelig* among themselves.' 'Friendly *Heimeligkeit*.' 'I shall be nowhere more *heimelich* than I am here.' 'That which comes from afar ... assuredly does not live quite *heimelig* (*heimatlich* [at home], *freundnachbarlich* [in a neighbourly way]) among the people.' 'The cottage where he had once sat so often among his own people, so *heimelig*, so happy.' 'The sentinel's horn sounds so *heimelig* from the tower, and his voice invites so hospitably.' 'You go to sleep there so soft and warm, so wonderfully *heim'lig*.' *– This form of the word deserves to become general in order to protect this perfectly good sense of the word from becoming obsolete through an easy confusion with* II [see below]. Cf: '"*The Zecks* [a family name] *are all 'heimlich'*." (in sense II) " '*Heimlich'? ... What do you understand by 'heimlich'?' "Well, ... they are like a buried spring or a dried-up pond. One cannot walk over it without always having the feeling that water might come up there again." "Oh, we call it 'unheimlich'; you call it 'heimlich'. Well, what makes you think that there is something secret and untrustworthy about this family?"* ' (Gutzkow).

(*d*) Especially in Silesia: gay, cheerful; also of the weather.

II. Concealed, kept from sight, so that others do not get to know of or about it, withheld from others. To do something *heimlich*, i.e. behind someone's back; to steal away *heimlich*; *heimlich* meetings and appointments; to look on with *heimlich* pleasure at someone's discomfiture; to sigh or weep *heimlich*; to behave *heimlich*, as though there was something to conceal; *heimlich* love-affair, love, sin; *heimlich* places (which good manners oblige us to conceal) (1 Sam. v. 6). 'The *heimlich* chamber' (privy) (2 Kings x. 27.). Also, 'the *heimlich* chair'. 'To throw into pits or *Heimlichkeiten*'. – 'Led the steeds *heimlich* before Laomedon.' – 'As secretive, *heimlich*, deceitful and malicious towards cruel masters ... as frank, open, sympathetic and helpful towards a friend in misfortune.' 'You have still to learn what is *heimlich* holiest to me.' 'The *heimlich* art' (magic). 'Where public ventilation has to stop, there *heimlich* machinations begin.' 'Freedom is the whispered watchword of *heimlich* conspirators and the loud battle-cry of professed revolutionaries.' 'A holy, *heimlich* effect.' 'I have roots that are most *heimlich*, I am grown in the deep earth.' 'My *heimlich* pranks.' 'If he is not given it openly and scrupulously he may seize it *heimlich* and unscrupulously.' 'He had achromatic telescopes constructed *heimlich* and secretly.' 'Henceforth I desire that there should be nothing *heimlich* any longer between us.' – To discover, disclose, betray someone's *Heimlichkeiten*; 'to concoct *Heimlichkeiten* behind my back'. 'In my time we studied *Heimlichkeit*.' 'The hand of understanding can alone undo the powerless spell of the *Heimlichkeit* (of hidden gold).' 'Say, where is the place of concealment ... in what place of hidden *Heimlichkeit*?' 'Bees, who make the lock of *Heimlichkeiten*' (i.e. sealing-wax). 'Learned in strange *Heimlichkeiten*' (magic arts).

For compounds see above, I*c*. Note especially the negative '*un*-': eerie, weird, arousing gruesome fear: 'Seeming quite *unheimlich* and ghostly to him.' 'The *unheimlich*, fearful hours of night.' 'I had already long since felt an *unheimlich*, even gruesome feeling.' 'Now I am beginning to have an *unheimlich* feeling.' ... 'Feels an *unheimlich* horror.' '*Unheimlich* and motionless like a stone image.' 'The *unheimlich* mist called hill-fog.' 'These pale youths are *unheimlich* and are brewing heaven knows what mischief.' '"*Unheimlich*" is the name for everything that ought to have remained ... secret and hidden but has come to light' (Schelling). – 'To veil the divine, to surround it with a certain *Unheimlichkeit*.' – *Unheimlich* is not often used as opposite to meaning II (above).

What interests us most in this long extract is to find that among its different shades of meaning the word '*heimlich*' exhibits one which is identical with its opposite, '*unheimlich*'.

What is *heimlich* thus comes to be *unheimlich*. (Cf. the quotation from Gutzkow: 'We call it "*unheimlich*"; you call it "*heimlich*".') In general we are reminded that the word '*heimlich*' is not unambiguous, but belongs to two sets of ideas, which, without being contradictory, are yet very different: on the one hand it means what is familiar and agreeable, and on the other, what is concealed and kept out of sight.[5] '*Unheimlich*' is customarily used, we are told, as the contrary only of the first signification of '*heimlich*', and not of the second. Sanders tells us nothing concerning a possible genetic connection between these two meanings of *heimlich*. On the other hand, we notice that Schelling says something which throws quite a new light on the concept of the *Unheimlich*, for which we were certainly not prepared. According to him, everything is *unheimlich* that ought to have remained secret and hidden but has come to light.

Some of the doubts that have thus arisen are removed if we consult Grimm's dictionary. (1877, **4**, Part 2, 873 ff.)

We read:

Heimlich; adj. and adv. *vernaculus, occultus*; MHG. heimelich, heimlich.
(P. 874.) In a slightly different sense: 'I feel *heimlich*, well, free from fear.' ...
[3] (*b*) *Heimlich* is also used of a place free from ghostly influences ... familiar, friendly, intimate.
(P. 875: *β*) Familiar, amicable, unreserved.
4. *From the idea of 'homelike', 'belonging to the house', the further idea is developed of something withdrawn from the eyes of strangers, something concealed, secret; and this idea is expanded in many ways* ...
(P. 876.) 'On the left bank of the lake there lies a meadow *heimlich* in the wood.' (Schiller, *Wilhelm Tell*, I. 4.)... Poetic licence, rarely so used in modern speech ... *Heimlich* is used in conjunction with a verb expressing the act of concealing: 'In the secret of his tabernacle he shall hide me *heimlich*.' (Ps. xxvii. 5.) ... *Heimlich* parts of the human body, *pudenda* ... 'the men that died not were smitten on their *heimlich* parts.' (1 Samuel v. 12.) ...
(*c*) Officials who give important advice which has to be kept secret in matters of state are called *heimlich* councillors; the adjective, according to modern usage, has been replaced by *geheim* [secret] ... 'Pharaoh called Joseph's name "him to whom secrets are revealed"' (*heimlich* councillor). (Gen. xli. 45.)
(P. 878.) 6. *Heimlich*, as used of knowledge – mystic, allegorical: a *heimlich* meaning, *mysticus, divinus, occultus, figuratus*.
(P. 878.) *Heimlich* in a different sense, as withdrawn from knowledge, unconscious ... *Heimlich* also has the meaning of that which is obscure, inaccessible to knowledge ... 'Do you not see? They do not trust us; they fear the *heimlich* face of the Duke of Friedland.' (Schiller, *Wallensteins Lager*, Scene 2.)
9. *The notion of something hidden and dangerous, which is expressed in the last paragraph, is still further developed, so that 'heimlich' comes to have the meaning usually ascribed to 'unheimlich'.* Thus: 'At times I feel like a man who walks in the night and believes in ghosts; every corner is *heimlich* and full of terrors for him'. (Klinger, *Theater*, 3. 298.)

Thus *heimlich* is a word the meaning of which develops in the direction of ambivalence, until it finally coincides with its opposite, *unheimlich*. *Unheimlich* is in some way or other a sub-species of *heimlich*. Let us bear this discovery in mind, though we cannot yet rightly understand it, alongside of Schelling's[6] definition of the *Unheimlich*. If we go on to examine individual instances of uncanniness, these hints will become intelligible to us.

II

When we proceed to review the things, persons, impressions, events and situations which are able to arouse in us a feeling of the uncanny in a particularly forcible and definite form, the first requirement is obviously to select a suitable example to start on. Jentsch has taken as a very good instance 'doubts whether an apparently animate being is really alive; or conversely, whether a lifeless object might not be in fact animate'; and he refers in this connection to the impression made by wax-work figures, ingeniously constructed dolls and automata. To these he adds the uncanny effect of epileptic fits, and of manifestations of insanity, because these excite in the spectator the impression of automatic, mechanical processes at work behind the ordinary appearance of mental activity. Without entirely accepting this author's view, we will take it as a starting-point for our own investigation because in what follows he reminds us of a writer who has succeeded in producing uncanny effects better than anyone else.

Jentsch writes: 'In telling a story, one of the most successful devices for easily creating uncanny effects is to leave the reader in uncertainty whether a particular figure in the story is a human being or an automaton, and to do it in such a way that his attention is not focused directly upon his uncertainty, so that he may not be led to go into the matter and clear it up immediately. That, as we have said, would quickly dissipate the peculiar emotional effect of the thing. E. T. A. Hoffmann has repeatedly employed this psychological artifice with success in his fantastic narratives.'

This observation, undoubtedly a correct one, refers primarily to the story of 'The Sand-Man' in Hoffmann's *Nachtstücken*,[7] which contains the original of Olympia, the doll that appears in the first act of Offenbach's opera, *Tales of Hoffmann*. But I cannot think – and I hope most readers of the story will agree with me – that the theme of the doll Olympia, who is to all appearances a living being, is by any means the only, or indeed the most important, element that must be held responsible for the quite unparalleled atmosphere of uncanniness evoked by the story. Nor is this atmosphere heightened by the fact that the author himself treats the episode of Olympia with a faint touch of satire and uses it to poke fun at the young man's idealization of his mistress. The main theme of the story is, on the contrary, something different, something which gives it its name, and which is always re-introduced at critical moments: it is the theme of the 'Sand-Man' who tears out children's eyes.

This fantastic tale opens with the childhood recollections of the student Nathaniel. In spite of his present happiness, he cannot banish the memories associated with the mysterious and terrifying death of his beloved father. On certain evenings his mother used to send the children to bed early, warning them that 'the Sand-Man was coming'; and, sure enough, Nathaniel would not fail to hear the heavy tread of a visitor, with whom his father would then be occupied for the evening. When questioned about the Sand-Man, his mother, it is true, denied that such a person existed except as a figure of speech; but his nurse could give him more definite information: 'He's a wicked man who comes when children won't go to bed, and throws handfuls of sand in their eyes so that they jump out of their heads all bleeding. Then he puts the eyes in a sack and carries them off to the half-moon to feed his children. They sit up there in their nest, and their beaks are hooked like owls' beaks, and they use them to peck up naughty boys' and girls' eyes with.'

Although little Nathaniel was sensible and old enough not to credit the figure of the Sand-Man with such gruesome attributes, yet the dread of him became fixed in his heart. He determined to find out what the Sand-Man looked like; and one evening, when the Sand-Man was expected again, he hid in his father's study. He recognized the visitor as the lawyer Coppelius, a repulsive person whom the children were frightened of when he occasionally came to a meal; and he now identified this Coppelius with the dreaded Sand-Man. As regards the rest of the scene, Hoffmann already leaves us in doubt whether what we are witnessing is the first delirium of the panic-stricken boy, or a succession of events which are to be regarded in the story as being real. His father and the guest are at work at a brazier with glowing flames. The little eavesdropper hears Coppelius call out: 'Eyes here! Eyes here!' and betrays himself by screaming aloud. Coppelius seizes him and is on the point of dropping bits of red-hot coal from the fire into his eyes, and then of throwing them into the brazier, but his father begs him off and saves his eyes. After this the boy falls into a deep swoon; and a long illness brings his experience to an end. Those who decide in favour of the rationalistic interpretation of the Sand-Man will not fail to recognize in the child's phantasy the persisting influence of his nurse's story. The bits of sand that are to be thrown into the child's eyes turn into bits of red-hot coal from the flames; and in both cases they are intended to make his eyes jump out. In the course of another visit of the Sand-Man's, a year later, his father is killed in his study by an explosion. The lawyer Coppelius disappears from the place without leaving a trace behind.

Nathaniel, now a student, believes that he has recognized this phantom of horror from his childhood in an itinerant optician, an Italian called Giuseppe Coppola, who at his university town, offers him weather-glasses for sale. When Nathaniel refuses, the man goes on: 'Not weather-glasses? not weather-glasses? also got fine eyes, fine eyes!' The student's terror is allayed when he finds that the proffered eyes are only harmless spectacles, and he buys a pocket spy-glass from Coppola. With its aid he looks across into Professor Spalanzani's house opposite and there spies Spalanzani's beautiful, but strangely silent and motionless daughter, Olympia. He soon falls in love with her so violently that, because of her, he quite forgets the clever and sensible girl to whom he is betrothed. But Olympia is an automaton whose clock-work has been made by Spalanzani, and whose eyes have been put in by Coppola, the Sand-Man. The student surprises the two Masters quarrelling over their handiwork. The optician carries off the wooden eyeless doll; and the mechanician, Spalanzani, picks up Olympia's bleeding eyes from the ground and throws them at Nathaniel's breast, saying that Coppola had stolen them from the student. Nathaniel succumbs to a fresh attack of madness, and in his delirium his recollection of his father's death is mingled with this new experience. 'Hurry up! hurry up! ring of fire!' he cries. 'Spin about, ring of fire – Hurrah! Hurry up, wooden doll! lovely wooden doll, spin about – .' He then falls upon the professor, Olympia's 'father', and tries to strangle him.

Rallying from a long and serious illness, Nathaniel seems at last to have recovered. He intends to marry his betrothed, with whom he has become reconciled. One day he and she are walking through the city market-place, over which the high tower of the Town Hall throws its huge shadow. On the girl's suggestion, they climb the tower, leaving her brother, who is walking with them, down below. From the top, Clara's attention is drawn to a curious object moving along the street. Nathaniel looks at this thing through Coppola's spy-glass, which he finds in his pocket, and falls into a new attack of madness. Shouting 'Spin about, wooden doll!' he tries to throw the girl into the gulf below. Her brother, brought to her side by her cries, rescues her and hastens down with her to safety. On the tower above, the madman rushes round, shrieking 'Ring of fire, spin about!' – and we know the origin of the words. Among the people who begin to gather below there comes forward the figure of the lawyer Coppelius, who has suddenly returned. We may suppose that it was his approach, seen through the spy-glass, which threw Nathaniel into his fit of madness. As the onlookers prepare to go up and overpower the madman, Coppelius laughs and says: 'Wait a bit; he'll come down of himself.' Nathaniel suddenly stands still, catches sight of Coppelius, and with a wild shriek 'Yes! "Fine eyes – fine eyes"!' flings himself over the parapet. While he lies on the paving-stones with a shattered skull the Sand-Man vanishes in the throng.

This short summary leaves no doubt, I think, that the feeling of something uncanny is directly attached to the figure of the Sand-Man, that is, to the idea of being robbed of one's eyes, and that Jentsch's point of an intellectual uncertainty has nothing to do with the effect. Uncertainty whether an object is living or inanimate, which admittedly applied to the doll Olympia, is quite irrelevant in connection with this other, more striking instance of uncanniness. It is true that the writer creates a kind of uncertainty in us in the beginning by not letting us know, no doubt purposely, whether he is taking us into the real world or into a purely fantastic one of his own creation. He has, of course, a right to do either; and if he chooses to stage his action in a world peopled with spirits, demons and ghosts, as Shakespeare does in *Hamlet*, in *Macbeth* and, in a different sense, in *The Tempest* and *A Midsummer-Night's Dream*, we must bow to his decision and treat his setting as though it were real for as long as we put ourselves into his hands. But this uncertainty disappears in the course of Hoffmann's story, and we perceive that he intends to make us, too, look through the demon optician's spectacles or spy-glass – perhaps, indeed, that the author in his very own person once peered through such an instrument. For the conclusion of the story makes it quite clear that Coppola the optician really *is* the lawyer Coppelius[8] and also, therefore, the Sand-Man.

There is no question therefore, of any intellectual uncertainty here: we know now that we are not supposed to be looking on at the products of a madman's imagination, behind which we, with the superiority of rational minds, are able to detect the sober truth; and yet this knowledge does not lessen the impression of uncanniness in the least degree. The theory of intellectual uncertainty is thus incapable of explaining that impression.

We know from psycho-analytic experience, however, that the fear of damaging or losing one's eyes is a terrible one in children. Many adults retain their apprehensiveness in this respect, and no physical injury is so much dreaded by them as an injury to the eye. We are accustomed to say, too, that we will treasure a thing as the apple of our eye. A study of dreams, phantasies and myths has taught us that anxiety about one's eyes, the fear of going blind, is often enough a substitute for the dread of being castrated. The self-blinding of the mythical criminal, Oedipus, was simply a mitigated form of the punishment of castration – the only punishment that was adequate for him by the *lex talionis*. We may try on rationalistic grounds to deny that fears about the eye are derived from the fear of castration, and may argue that it is very natural that so precious an organ as the eye should be guarded by a proportionate dread. Indeed, we might go further and say that the fear of castration itself contains no other significance and no deeper secret than a justifiable dread of this rational kind. But this view does not account adequately for the substitutive relation between the eye and the male organ which is seen to exist in dreams and myths and phantasies; nor can it dispel the impression that the threat of being castrated in especial excites a peculiarly violent and obscure emotion, and that this emotion is what first gives the idea of losing other organs its intense colouring. All further doubts are removed when we learn the details of their 'castration complex' from the analysis of neurotic patients, and realize its immense importance in their mental life.

Moreover, I would not recommend any opponent of the psycho-analytic view to select this particular story of the Sand-Man with which to support his argument that anxiety about the eyes has nothing to do with the castration complex. For why does Hoffmann bring the anxiety about eyes into such intimate connection with the father's death? And why does the Sand-Man always appear as a disturber of love? He separates the unfortunate Nathaniel from his betrothed and from her brother, his best friend; he destroys the second object of his love, Olympia, the lovely doll; and he drives him into suicide at the moment when he has won back his Clara and is about to be happily united to her. Elements in the story like these, and many others, seem arbitrary and meaningless so long as we deny all connection between fears about the eye and castration; but they become intelligible as soon as we replace the Sand-Man by the dreaded father at whose hands castration is expected.[9]

We shall venture, therefore, to refer the uncanny effect of the Sand-Man to the anxiety belonging to the castration complex of childhood. But having reached the idea that we can make an infantile factor such as this responsible for feelings of uncanniness, we are encouraged to see whether we can apply it to other instances of the uncanny. We find in the story of the Sand-Man the other theme on which Jentsch lays stress, of a doll which appears to be alive. Jentsch believes that a particularly favourable condition for awakening uncanny feelings is created when there is intellectual uncertainty whether an object is alive or not, and when an inanimate object becomes too much like an animate one. Now, dolls are of course rather closely connected with childhood life. We remember that in their early games children do not distinguish at all sharply between living and inanimate objects, and that they are especially fond of treating their dolls like live people. In fact, I have occasionally heard a woman patient declare that even at the age of eight she had still been convinced that her dolls would be certain to come to life if she were to look at them in a particular, extremely concentrated, way. So that here, too, it is not difficult to discover a factor from childhood. But, curiously enough, while the Sand-Man story deals with the arousing of an early childhood fear, the idea of a 'living doll' excites no fear at all; children have no fear of their dolls coming to life, they may even desire it. The source of uncanny feelings would not, therefore, be an infantile fear in this case, but rather an infantile wish or even merely an infantile belief. There seems to be a contradiction here; but perhaps it is only a complication, which may be helpful to us later on.

Hoffmann is the unrivalled master of the uncanny in literature. His novel, *Die Elixire des Teufels* [*The Devil's Elixir*], contains a whole mass of themes to which one is tempted to ascribe the uncanny effect of the narrative;[10] but it is too obscure and intricate a story for us to venture upon a summary of it. Towards the end of the book the reader is told the facts, hitherto concealed from him, from which the action springs; with the result, not that he is at last enlightened, but that he falls into a state of complete bewilderment. The author has piled up too much material of the same kind. In consequence one's grasp of the story as a whole suffers, though not the impression it makes. We must content ourselves with selecting those themes of uncanniness which are most prominent, and with seeing whether they too can fairly be traced back to infantile sources. These themes are all concerned with the phenomenon of the 'double', which appears in every shape and in every degree of development. Thus we have characters who are to be considered identical because they look alike. This relation is accentuated by mental processes leaping from one of these characters to another – by what we should call telepathy – , so that the one possesses knowledge, feelings and experience in common with the other. Or it is marked by the fact that the subject identifies himself with someone else, so that he is in doubt as to which his self is, or substitutes the extraneous self for his own. In other words, there is a doubling, dividing and interchanging of the self. And finally there is the constant recurrence of the same thing[11] – the repetition of the same features or character-traits or vicissitudes, of the same crimes, or even the same names through several consecutive generations.

The theme of the 'double' has been very thoroughly treated by Otto Rank (1914). He has gone into the connections which the 'double' has with reflections in mirrors, with shadows, with guardian spirits, with the belief in the soul and with the fear of death; but he also lets in a flood of light on the surprising evolution of the idea. For the 'double' was originally an insurance against the destruction of the ego, an 'energetic denial of the power of death', as Rank says; and probably the 'immortal' soul was the first 'double' of the body. This invention of doubling as a preservation against extinction has its counter-part in the language of dreams, which is fond of representing castration by a doubling or multiplication of a genital symbol.[12] The same desire led the Ancient Egyptians to develop the art of making images of the dead in lasting materials. Such ideas, however, have sprung from the soil of unbounded self-love, from the primary narcissism which dominates the mind of the child and of primitive man. But when this stage has been surmounted, the 'double' reverses its aspect. From having been an assurance of immortality, it becomes the uncanny harbinger of death.

The idea of the 'double' does not necessarily disappear with the passing of primary narcissism, for it can receive fresh meaning from the later stages of the ego's develop-ment. A special agency is slowly formed there, which is able to stand over against the rest of the ego, which has the function of observing and criticizing the self and of exercising a censorship within the mind, and which we become aware of as our 'conscience'. In the pathological case of delusions of being watched, this mental agency becomes isolated, dissociated from the ego, and discernible to the physician's eye. The fact that an agency of this kind exists, which is able to treat the rest of the ego like an object – the fact, that is, that man is capable of self-observation – renders it possible to invest the old idea of a 'double' with a new meaning and to ascribe a number of things to it – above all, those things which seem to self-criticism to belong to the old surmounted narcissism of earliest times.[13]

But it is not only this latter material, offensive as it is to the criticism of the ego, which may be incorporated in the idea of a double. There are also all the unfulfilled but possible futures to which we still like to cling in phantasy, all the strivings of the ego which adverse external circumstances have crushed, and all our suppressed acts of volition which nourish in us the illusion of Free Will.[14] [Cf. Freud, 1901b, Chapter XII (B).]

But after having thus considered the *manifest* motivation of the figure of a 'double', we have to admit that none of this helps us to understand the extraordinarily strong feeling of something uncanny that pervades the conception; and our knowledge of pathological mental processes enables us to add that nothing in this more superficial material could account for the urge towards defence which has caused the ego to project that material outward as something foreign to itself. When all is said and done, the quality of uncan-niness can only come from the fact of the 'double' being a creation dating back to a very early mental stage, long since surmounted – a stage, incidentally, at which it wore a more friendly aspect. The 'double' has become a thing of terror, just as, after the collapse of their religion, the gods turned into demons.[15]

The other forms of ego–disturbance exploited by Hoffmann can easily be estimated along the same lines as the theme of the 'double'. They are a harking-back to particular phases in the evolution of the self-regarding feeling, a regression to a time when the ego had not yet marked itself off sharply from the external world and from other people. I believe that these factors are partly responsible for the impression of uncanniness, although it is not easy to isolate and determine exactly their share of it.

The factor of the repetition of the same thing will perhaps not appeal to everyone as a source of uncanny feeling. From what I have observed, this phenomenon does undoubtedly, subject to certain conditions and combined with certain circumstances, arouse an uncanny feeling, which, furthermore, recalls the sense of helplessness experienced in some dream-states. As I was walking, one hot summer afternoon, through the deserted streets of a provincial town in Italy which was unknown to me, I found myself in a quarter of whose character I could not long remain in doubt. Nothing but painted women were to be seen at the windows of the small houses, and I hastened to leave the narrow street at the next turning. But after having wandered about for a time without enquiring my way, I suddenly found myself back in the same street, where my presence was now beginning to excite attention. I hurried away once more, only to arrive by another *détour* at the same place yet a third time. Now, however, a feeling overcame me which I can only describe as uncanny, and I was glad enough to find myself back at the piazza I had left a short while before, without any further voyages of discovery. Other situations which have in common with my adventure an unintended recurrence of the same situation, but which differ radically from it in other respects, also result in the same feeling of helplessness and of uncanniness. So, for instance, when, caught in a mist perhaps, one has lost one's way in a mountain forest, every attempt to find the marked or familiar path may bring one back again and again to one and the same spot, which one can identify by some particular landmark. Or one may wander about in a dark, strange room, looking for the door or the electric switch, and collide time after time with the same piece of furniture – though it is true that Mark Twain succeeded by wild exaggeration in turning this latter situation into something irresistibly comic.[16]

If we take another class of things, it is easy to see that there, too, it is only this factor of involuntary repetition which surrounds what would otherwise be innocent enough with an uncanny atmosphere, and forces upon us the idea of something fateful and inescapable when otherwise we should have spoken only of 'chance'. For instance, we naturally attach no importance to the event when we hand in an overcoat and get a cloak-room ticket with the number, let us say, 62; or when we find that our cabin on a ship bears that number. But the impression is altered if two such events, each in itself indifferent, happen close together – if we come across the number 62 several times in a single day, or if we begin to notice that everything which has a number – addresses, hotel rooms, compartments in railway trains – invariably has the same one, or at all events one which contains the same figures. We do feel this to be uncanny. And unless a man is utterly hardened and proof against the lure of superstition, he will be tempted to ascribe a secret meaning to this obstinate recurrence of a number; he will take it, perhaps, as an indication of the span of life allotted to him.[17] Or suppose one is engaged in reading the works of the famous physiologist, Hering, and within the space of a few days receives two letters from two different countries, each from a person called Hering, though one has never before had any dealings with anyone of that name. Not long ago an ingenious scientist (Kammerer, 1919) attempted to reduce coincidences of this kind to certain laws, and so deprive them of their uncanny effect. I will not venture to decide whether he has succeeded or not.

How exactly we can trace back to infantile psychology the uncanny effect of such similar recurrences is a question I can only lightly touch on in these pages; and I must refer the reader instead to another work,[18] already completed, in which this has been gone into in detail, but in a different connection. For it is possible to recognize the dominance in the unconscious mind of a 'compulsion to repeat' proceeding from the instinctual impulses and probably inherent in the very nature of the instincts – a compulsion powerful enough to overrule the pleasure principle, lending to certain aspects of the mind their daemonic character, and still very clearly expressed in the impulses of small children; a compulsion, too, which is responsible for a part of the course taken by the analyses of neurotic patients. All these considerations prepare us for the discovery that whatever reminds us of this inner 'compulsion to repeat' is perceived as uncanny.

Now, however, it is time to turn from these aspects of the matter, which are in any case difficult to judge, and look for some undeniable instances of the uncanny, in the hope that an analysis of them will decide whether our hypothesis is a valid one.

In the story of 'The Ring of Polycrates',[19] the King of Egypt turns away in horror from his host, Polycrates, because he sees that his friend's every wish is at once fulfilled, his every care promptly removed by kindly fate. His host has become 'uncanny' to him. His own explanation, that the too fortunate man has to fear the envy of the gods, seems obscure to us; its meaning is veiled in mythological language. We will therefore turn to another example in a less grandiose setting. In the case history of an obsessional neurotic,[20] I have described how the patient once stayed in a hydropathic establishment and benefited greatly by it. He had the good sense, however, to attribute his improvement not to the therapeutic properties of the water, but to the situation of his room, which immediately adjoined that of a very accommodating nurse. So on his second visit to the establishment he asked for the same room, but was told that it was already occupied by an old gentleman, where-upon he gave vent to his annoyance in the words: 'I wish he may be struck dead for it.' A fortnight later the old gentleman really did have a stroke. My patient thought this an 'uncanny' experience. The impression of uncanniness would have been stronger still if less time had elapsed between his words and the untoward event, or if he had been able to report innumerable similar coincidences. As a matter of fact, he had no difficulty in producing coincidences of this sort; but then not only he but every obsessional neurotic I have observed has been able to relate analogous experiences. They are never surprised at their invariably running up against someone they have just been thinking of, perhaps for the first time for a long while. If they say one day 'I haven't had any news of so-and-so for a long time', they will be sure to get a letter from him the next morning, and an accident or a death will rarely take place without having passed through their mind a little while before. They are in the habit of referring to this state of affairs in the most modest manner, saying that they have 'presentiments' which 'usually' come true.

One of the most uncanny and wide-spread forms of superstition is the dread of the evil eye, which has been exhaustively studied by the Hamburg oculist Seligmann (1910–11). There never seems to have been any doubt about the source of this dread. Whoever possesses something that is at once valuable and fragile is afraid of other people's envy, in so far as he projects on to them the envy he would have felt in their place. A feeling like this betrays itself by a look[21] even though it is not put into words; and when a man is prominent owing to noticeable, and particularly owing to unattractive, attributes, other people are ready to believe that his envy is rising to a more than usual degree of intensity and that this intensity will convert it into effective action. What is feared is thus a secret intention of doing harm, and certain signs are taken to mean that that intention has the necessary power at its command.

These last examples of the uncanny are to be referred to the principle which I have called 'omnipotence of thoughts', taking the name from an expression used by one of my patients.[22] And now we find ourselves on familiar ground. Our analysis of instances of the uncanny has led us back to the old, animistic conception of the universe. This was characterized by the idea that the world was peopled with the spirits of human beings; by the subject's narcissistic overvaluation of his own mental processes; by the belief in the omnipotence of thoughts and the technique of magic based on that belief; by the attribution to various outside persons and things of carefully graded magical powers, or '*mana*'; as well as by all the other creations with the help of which man, in the unrestricted narcissism of that stage of development, strove to fend off the manifest prohibitions of reality. It seems as if each one of us has been through a phase of individual development corresponding to this animistic stage in primitive men, that none of us has passed through it without preserving certain residues and traces of it which are still capable of manifesting themselves, and that everything which now strikes us as 'uncanny' fulfils the condition of touching those residues of animistic mental activity within us and bringing them to expression.[23]

At this point I will put forward two considerations which, I think, contain the gist of this short study. In the first place, if psycho-analytic theory is correct in maintaining that every affect belonging to an emotional impulse, whatever its kind, is transformed, if it is repressed, into anxiety, then among instances of frightening things there must be one class in which the frightening element can be shown to be something repressed which *recurs*. This class of frightening things would then constitute the uncanny; and it must be a matter of indifference whether what is uncanny was itself originally frightening or whether it carried some *other* affect. In the second place, if this is indeed the secret nature of the uncanny, we can understand why linguistic usage has extended *das Heimliche* ['homely'] into its opposite, *das Unheimliche*; for this uncanny is in reality nothing new or alien, but something which is familiar and old-established in the mind and which has become alienated from it only through the process of repression. This reference to the factor of repression enables us, furthermore, to understand Schelling's definition of the uncanny as something which ought to have remained hidden but has come to light.

It only remains for us to test our new hypothesis on one or two more examples of the uncanny.

Many people experience the feeling in the highest degree in relation to death and dead bodies, to the return of the dead, and to spirits and ghosts. As we have seen some languages in use to-day can only render the German expression 'an *unheimlich* house' by 'a *haunted* house'. We might indeed have begun our investigation with this example, perhaps the most striking of all, of something uncanny, but we refrained from doing so because the uncanny in it is too much intermixed with what is purely gruesome and is in part over-laid by it. There is scarcely any other matter, however, upon which our thoughts and feelings have changed so little since the very earliest times, and in which discarded forms have been so completely preserved under a thin disguise, as our relation to death. Two things account for our conservatism: the strength of our original emotional reaction to death and the insufficiency of our scientific knowledge about it. Biology has not yet been able to decide whether death is the inevitable fate of every living being or whether it is only a regular but yet perhaps avoidable event in life.[24] It is true that the statement 'All men are mortal' is paraded in text-books of logic as an example of a general proposition;

but no human being really grasps it, and our unconscious has as little use now as it ever had for the idea of its own mortality.[25] Religions continue to dispute the importance of the undeniable fact of individual death and to postulate a life after death; civil governments still believe that they cannot maintain moral order among the living if they do not uphold the prospect of a better life hereafter as a recompense for mundane existence. In our great cities, placards announce lectures that undertake to tell us how to get into touch with the souls of the departed; and it cannot be denied that not a few of the most able and penetrating minds among our men of science have come to the conclusion, especially towards the close of their own lives, that a contact of this kind is not impossible. Since almost all of us still think as savages do on this topic, it is no matter for surprise that the primitive fear of the dead is still so strong within us and always ready to come to the surface on any provocation. Most likely our fear still implies the old belief that the dead man becomes the enemy of his survivor and seeks to carry him off to share his new life with him. Considering our unchanged attitude towards death, we might rather enquire what has become of the repression, which is the necessary condition of a primitive feeling recurring in the shape of something uncanny. But repression is there, too. All supposedly educated people have ceased to believe officially that the dead can become visible as spirits, and have made any such appearances dependent on improbable and remote conditions; their emotional attitude towards their dead, moreover, once a highly ambiguous and ambivalent one, has been toned down in the higher strata of the mind into an unambiguous feeling of piety.[26]

We have now only a few remarks to add – for animism, magic and sorcery, the omnipotence of thoughts, man's attitude to death, involuntary repetition and the castration complex comprise practically all the factors which turn something frightening into something uncanny.

We can also speak of a living person as uncanny, and we do so when we ascribe evil intentions to him. But that is not all; in addition to this we must feel that his intentions to harm us are going to be carried out with the help of special powers. A good instance of this is the '*Gettatore*',[27] that uncanny figure of Romanic superstition which Schaeffer, with intuitive poetic feeling and profound psycho-analytic understanding, has transformed into a sympathetic character in his *Josef Montfort*. But the question of these secret powers brings us back again to the realm of animism. It was the pious Gretchen's intuition that Mephistopheles possessed secret powers of this kind that made him so uncanny to her.

> Sie fühlt dass ich ganz sicher ein Genie,
> Vielleicht sogar der Teufel bin.[28]

The uncanny effect of epilepsy and of madness has the same origin. The layman sees in them the working of forces hitherto unsuspected in his fellow-men, but at the same time he is dimly aware of them in remote corners of his own being. The Middle Ages quite consistently ascribed all such maladies to the influence of demons, and in this their psychology was almost correct. Indeed, I should not be surprised to hear that psycho-analysis, which is concerned with laying bare these hidden forces, has itself become uncanny to many people for that very reason. In one case, after I had succeeded – though none too rapidly – in effecting a cure in a girl who had been an invalid for many years, I myself heard this view expressed by the patient's mother long after her recovery.

Dismembered limbs, a severed head, a hand cut off at the wrist, as in a fairy tale of Hauff's,[29] feet which dance by themselves, as in the book by Schaeffer which I mentioned above – all these have something peculiarly uncanny about them, especially when, as in the last instance, they prove capable of independent activity in addition. As we already know, this kind of uncanniness springs from its proximity to the castration complex. To some people the idea of being buried alive by mistake is the most uncanny thing of all. And yet psycho-analysis has taught us that this terrifying phantasy is only a transformation of another phantasy which had originally nothing terrifying about it at all, but was qualified by a certain lasciviousness – the phantasy, I mean, of intra-uterine existence.[30]

There is one more point of general application which I should like to add, though, strictly speaking, it has been included in what has already been said about animism and modes of working of the mental apparatus that have been surmounted; for I think it deserves special emphasis. This is that an uncanny effect is often and easily produced when the distinction between imagination and reality is effaced, as when something that we have hitherto regarded as imaginary appears before us in reality, or when a symbol takes over the full functions of the thing it symbolizes, and so on. It is this factor which contributes not a little to the uncanny effect attaching to magical practices. The infantile element in this, which also dominates the minds of neurotics, is the over-accentuation of psychical reality in comparison with material reality – a feature closely allied to the belief in the omnipotence of thoughts. In the middle of the isolation of war-time a number of the English *Strand Magazine* fell into my hands; and, among other somewhat redundant matter, I read a story about a young married couple who move into a furnished house in which there is a curiously shaped table with carvings of crocodiles on it. Towards evening an intolerable and very specific smell begins to pervade the house; they stumble over something in the dark; they seem to see a vague form gliding over the stairs – in short, we are given to understand that the presence of the table causes ghostly crocodiles to haunt the place, or that the wooden monsters come to life in the dark, or something of the sort. It was a naïve enough story, but the uncanny feeling it produced was quite remarkable.

To conclude this collection of examples, which is certainly not complete, I will relate an instance taken from psycho-analytic experience; if it does not rest upon mere coincidence, it furnishes a beautiful confirmation of our theory of the uncanny. It often happens that neurotic men declare that they feel there is something uncanny about the female genital organs. This *unheimlich* place, however, is the entrance to the former *Heim* [home] of all human beings, to the place where each one of us lived once upon a time and in the beginning. There is a joking saying that 'Love is home-sickness'; and whenever a man dreams of a place or a country and says to himself, while he is still dreaming: 'this place is familiar to me, I've been here before', we may interpret the place as being his mother's genitals or her body.[31] In this case too, then, the *unheimlich* is what was once *heimisch*, familiar; the prefix '*un*' ['un-'] is the token of repression.[32]

III

In the course of this discussion the reader will have felt certain doubts arising in his mind; and he must now have an opportunity of collecting them and bringing them forward.

It may be true that the uncanny [*unheimlich*] is something which is secretly familiar [*heimlich-heimisch*], which has undergone repression and then returned from it, and that everything that is uncanny fulfils this condition. But the selection of material on this basis does not enable us to solve the problem of the uncanny. For our proposition is clearly not convertible. Not everything that fulfils this condition – not everything that recalls repressed desires and surmounted modes of thinking belonging to the prehistory of the individual and of the race – is on that account uncanny.

Nor shall we conceal the fact that for almost every example adduced in support of our hypothesis one may be found which rebuts it. The story of the severed hand in Hauff's fairy tale certainly has an uncanny effect, and we have traced that effect back to the castration complex; but most readers will probably agree with me in judging that no trace of uncanniness is provoked by Herodotus's story of the treasure of Rhampsinitus, in which the master-thief, whom the princess tries to hold fast by the hand, leaves his brother's severed hand behind with her instead. Again, the prompt fulfilment of the wishes of Polycrates undoubtedly affects us in the same uncanny way as it did the king of Egypt; yet our own fairy stories are crammed with instantaneous wish-fulfilments which produce no uncanny effect whatever. In the story of 'The Three Wishes', the woman is tempted by the savoury smell of a sausage to wish that she might have one too, and in an instant it lies on a plate before her. In his annoyance at her hastiness her husband wishes it may hang on her nose. And there it is, dangling from her nose. All this is very striking but not in the least uncanny. Fairy tales quite frankly adopt the animistic standpoint of the omnipotence of thoughts and wishes, and yet I cannot think of any genuine fairy story which has anything uncanny about it. We have heard that it is in the highest degree uncanny when an inanimate object – a picture or a doll – comes to life; nevertheless in Hans Andersen's stories the household utensils, furniture and tin soldiers are alive, yet nothing could well be more remote from the uncanny. And we should hardly call it uncanny when Pygmalion's beautiful statue comes to life.

Apparent death and the re-animation of the dead have been represented as most uncanny themes. But things of this sort too are very common in fairy stories. Who would be so bold as to call it uncanny, for instance, when Snow-White opens her eyes once more? And the resuscitation of the dead in accounts of miracles, as in the New Testament, elicits feelings quite unrelated to the uncanny. Then, too, the theme that achieves such an indubitably uncanny effect, the unintended recurrence of the same thing, serves other and quite different purposes in another class of cases. We have already come across one example in which it is employed to call up a feeling of the comic; and we could multiply instances of this kind. Or again, it works as a means of emphasis, and so on. And once more: what is the origin of the uncanny effect of silence, darkness and solitude? Do not these factors point to the part played by danger in the genesis of what is uncanny, notwithstanding that in children these same factors are the most frequent determinants of the expression of fear [rather than of the uncanny]? And are we after all justified in entirely ignoring intellectual uncertainty as a factor, seeing that we have admitted its importance in relation to death?

It is evident therefore, that we must be prepared to admit that there are other elements besides those which we have so far laid down as determining the production of uncanny feelings. We might say that these preliminary results have satisfied *psycho-analytic* interest in the problem of the uncanny, and that what remains probably calls for an *aesthetic* enquiry. But that would be to open the door to doubts about what exactly is the value of our general contention that the uncanny proceeds from something familiar which has been repressed.

We have noticed one point which may help us to resolve these uncertainties: nearly all the instances that contradict our hypothesis are taken from the realm of fiction, of imaginative writing. This suggests that we should differentiate between the uncanny that we actually experience and the uncanny that we merely picture or read about.

What is *experienced* as uncanny is much more simply conditioned but comprises far fewer instances. We shall find, I think, that it fits in perfectly with our attempt at a solution, and can be traced back without exception to something familiar that has been repressed. But here, too, we must make a certain important and psychologically significant differentiation in our material, which is best illustrated by turning to suitable examples.

Let us take the uncanny associated with the omnipotence of thoughts, with the prompt fulfilment of wishes, with secret injurious powers and with the return of the dead. The condition under which the feeling of uncanniness arises here is unmistakable. We – or our primitive forefathers – once believed that these possibilities were realities, and were convinced that they actually happened. Nowadays we no longer believe in them, we have *surmounted* these modes of thought; but we do not feel quite sure of our new beliefs, and the old ones still exist within us ready to seize upon any confirmation. As soon as something *actually happens* in our lives which seems to confirm the old, discarded beliefs we get a feeling of the uncanny; it is as though we were making a judgement something like this: 'So, after all, it is *true* that one can kill a person by the mere wish!' or, 'So the dead *do* live on and appear on the scene of their former activities!' and so on. Conversely, anyone who has completely and finally rid himself of animistic beliefs will be insensible to this type of the uncanny. The most remarkable coincidences of wish and fulfilment, the most mysterious repetition of similar experiences in a particular place or on a particular date, the most deceptive sights and suspicious noises – none of these things will disconcert him or raise the kind of fear which can be described as 'a fear of something uncanny'. The whole thing is purely an affair of 'reality-testing', a question of the material reality of the phenomena.[33]

The state of affairs is different when the uncanny proceeds from repressed infantile complexes, from the castration complex, womb-phantasies, etc.; but experiences which arouse this kind of uncanny feeling are not of very frequent occurrence in real life. The uncanny which proceeds from actual experience belongs for the most part to the first group [the group dealt with in the previous paragraph]. Nevertheless the distinction between the two is theoretically very important. Where the uncanny comes from infantile complexes the question of material reality does not arise; its place is taken by psychical reality. What is involved is an actual repression of some content of thought and a return of this repressed content, not a cessation of *belief in the reality* of such a content. We might say that in the one case what had been repressed is a particular ideational content, and in the other the belief in its (material) reality. But this last phrase no doubt extends the term 'repression' beyond its legitimate meaning. It would be more correct to take into account a psychological distinction which can be detected here, and to say that the animistic beliefs of civilized people are in a state of having been (to a greater or lesser extent) *surmounted* [rather than repressed]. Our conclusion could then be stated thus: an uncanny experience occurs either when infantile complexes which have been repressed are once more revived by some impression, or when primitive beliefs which have been surmounted seem once more to be confirmed. Finally, we must not let our predilection for smooth solutions and lucid exposition blind us to the fact that these two classes of uncanny experience are not always sharply distinguishable. When we consider that primitive beliefs are most intimately connected with infantile complexes, and are, in fact, based on them, we shall not be greatly astonished to find that the distinction is often a hazy one.

The uncanny as it is depicted in *literature*, in stories and imaginative productions, merits in truth a separate discussion. Above all, it is a much more fertile province than the uncanny in real life, for it contains the whole of the latter and something more besides, something that cannot be found in real life. The contrast between what has been repressed and what has been surmounted cannot be transposed on to the uncanny in fiction without profound modification; for the realm of phantasy depends for its effect on the fact that its content is not submitted to reality-testing. The somewhat paradoxical result is that *in the first place a great deal that is not uncanny in fiction would be so if it happened in real life; and in the second place that there are many more means of creating uncanny effects in fiction than there are in real life.*

The imaginative writer has this licence among many others, that he can select his world of representation so that it either coincides with the realities we are familiar with or departs from them in what particulars he pleases. We accept his ruling in every case. In fairy tales, for instance, the world of reality is left behind from the very start, and the animistic system of beliefs is frankly adopted. Wish-fulfilments, secret powers, omnipotence of thoughts, animation of inanimate objects, all the elements so common in fairy stories, can exert no uncanny influence here; for, as we have learnt, that feeling cannot arise unless there is a conflict of judgement as to whether things which have been 'surmounted' and are regarded as incredible may not, after all, be possible; and this problem is eliminated from the outset by the postulates of the world of fairy tales. Thus we see that fairy stories, which have furnished us with most of the contradictions to our hypothesis of the uncanny, confirm the first part of our proposition – that in the realm of fiction many things are not uncanny which would be so if they happened in real life. In the case of these stories there are other contributory factors, which we shall briefly touch upon later.

The creative writer can also choose a setting which though less imaginary than the world of fairy tales, does yet differ from the real world by admitting superior spiritual beings such as daemonic spirits or ghosts of the dead. So long as they remain within their setting of poetic reality, such figures lose any uncanniness which they might possess. The souls in Dante's *Inferno*, or the supernatural apparitions in Shakespeare's *Hamlet*, *Macbeth* or *Julius Caesar*, may be gloomy and terrible enough, but they are no more really uncanny than Homer's jovial world of gods. We adapt our judgement to the imaginary reality imposed on us by the writer, and regard souls, spirits and ghosts as though their existence had the same validity as our own has in material reality. In this case too we avoid all trace of the uncanny.

The situation is altered as soon as the writer pretends to move in the world of common reality. In this case he accepts as well all the conditions operating to produce uncanny feelings in real life; and everything that would have an uncanny effect in reality has it in his story. But in this case he can even increase his effect and multiply it far beyond what could happen in reality, by bringing about events which never or very rarely happen in fact. In doing this he is in a sense betraying us to the superstitiousness which we have ostensibly surmounted; he deceives us by promising to give us the sober truth, and then after all overstepping it. We react to his inventions as we would have reacted to real experiences; by the time we have seen through his trick it is already too late and the author has achieved his object. But it must be added that his success is not unalloyed. We retain a feeling of dissatisfaction, a kind of grudge against the attempted deceit. I have noticed this particularly after reading Schnitzler's *Die Weissagung* [*The Prophecy*] and similar stories which flirt with the supernatural. However, the writer has one more means which he can use in order to avoid our recalcitrance and at the same time to improve his chances of success. He can keep us in the dark for a long time about the precise nature of the presuppositions on which the world he writes about is based, or he can cunningly and ingeniously avoid any definite information on the point to the last. Speaking generally, however, we find a confirmation of the second part of our proposition – that fiction presents more opportunities for creating uncanny feelings than are possible in real life.

Strictly speaking, all these complications relate only to that class of the uncanny which proceeds from forms of thought that have been surmounted. The class which proceeds from repressed complexes is more resistant and remains as powerful in fiction as in real experience, subject to one exception. The uncanny belonging to the first class – that proceeding from forms of thought that have been surmounted – retains its character not only in experience but in fiction as well, so long as the setting is one of material reality; but where it is given an arbitrary and artificial setting in fiction, it is apt to lose that character.

We have clearly not exhausted the possibilities of poetic licence and the privileges enjoyed by story-writers in evoking or in excluding an uncanny feeling. In the main we adopt an unvarying passive attitude towards real experience and are subject to the influence of our physical environment. But the story-teller has a *peculiarly* directive power over us; by means of the moods he can put us into, he is able to guide the current of our emotions, to dam it up in one direction and make it flow in another, and he often obtains a great variety of effects from the same material. All this is nothing new, and has doubtless long since been fully taken into account by students of aesthetics. We have drifted into this field of research half involuntarily, through the temptation to explain certain instances which contradicted our theory of the causes of the uncanny. Accordingly we will now return to the examination of a few of those instances.

We have already asked why it is that the severed hand in the story of the treasure of Rhampsinitus has no uncanny effect in the way that the severed hand has in Hauff's story. The question seems to have gained in importance now that we have recognized that the class of the uncanny which proceeds from repressed complexes is the more resistant of the two. The answer is easy. In the Herodotus story our thoughts are concentrated much more on the superior cunning of the master-thief than on the feelings of the princess. The princess may very well have had an uncanny feeling, indeed she very probably fell into a swoon; but *we* have no such sensations, for we put ourselves in the thief's place, not in hers. In Nestroy's farce, *Der Zerrissene* [*The Torn Man*], another means is used to avoid any impression of the uncanny in the scene in which the fleeing man, convinced that he is a murderer, lifts up one trapdoor after another and each time sees what he takes to be the ghost of his victim rising up out of it. He calls out in despair, 'But I've only killed *one* man. Why this ghastly multiplication?' We know what went before this scene and do not share his error, so what must be uncanny to him has an irresistibly comic effect on us. Even a 'real' ghost, as in Oscar Wilde's *Canterville Ghost*, loses all power of at least arousing *gruesome* feelings in us as soon as the author begins to amuse himself by being ironical about it and allows liberties to be taken with it. Thus we see how independent emotional effects can be of the actual subject-matter in the world of fiction. In fairy stories feelings of fear – including therefore uncanny feelings – are ruled out altogether. We understand this, and that is why we ignore any opportunities we find in them for developing such feelings.

Concerning the factors of silence, solitude and darkness, we can only say that they are actually elements in the production of the infantile anxiety from which the majority of human beings have never become quite free. This problem has been discussed from a psycho-analytic point of view elsewhere.[34]

List of Abbreviations

G.S. = Freud, *Gesammelte Schriften* (12 vols.), Vienna, 1924–34
G.W. = Freud, *Gesammelte Werke* (18 vols.), London, from 1940
C.P. = Freud, *Collected Papers* (5 vols.), London, 1924–50
Standard Ed. = Freud, *Standard Edition* (24 vols.), London, from 1953

Notes

1 [The German word, translated throughout this paper by the English 'uncanny', is '*unheimlich*', literally 'unhomely'. The English term is not, of course, an exact equivalent of the German one.]
2 [An allusion to the first World War only just concluded.]
3 [In the translation which follows in the text above, a few details, mainly giving the sources of the quotations, have been omitted. For purposes of reference, we reprint in an Appendix the entire extract from Sanders's Dictionary exactly as it is given in German in Freud's original paper except that a few minor misprints have been put right.]
4 [It may be remarked that the English 'canny', in addition to its more usual meaning of 'shrewd', can mean 'pleasant', 'cosy'.]
5 [According to the Oxford English Dictionary, a similar ambiguity attaches to the English 'canny', which may mean not only 'cosy' but also 'endowed with occult or magical powers'.]
6 [In the original version of the paper (1919) only, the name 'Schleiermacher' was printed here, evidently in error.]
7 Hoffmann's *Sämtliche Werke*, Grisebach Edition, 3. [A translation of 'The Sand-Man' is included in *Eight Tales of Hoffmann*, translated by J. M. Cohen, London, Pan Books, 1952.]
8 Frau Dr. Rank has pointed out the association of the name with '*coppella*' = crucible, connecting it with the chemical operations that caused the father's death; and also with '*coppo*' = eye-socket. [Except in the first (1919) edition this footnote was attached, it seems erroneously, to the first occurrence of the name Coppelius on this page.]
9 In fact, Hoffmann's imaginative treatment of his material has not made such wild confusion of its elements that we cannot reconstruct their original arrangement. In the story of Nathaniel's childhood, the figures of his father and Coppelius represent the two opposites into which the father-imago is split by his ambivalence; whereas the one threatens to blind him – that is, to castrate him – , the other, the 'good' father, intercedes for his sight. The part of the complex which is most strongly repressed, the death-wish against the 'bad' father, finds expression in the death of the 'good' father, and Coppelius is made answerable for it. This pair of fathers is represented later, in his student days, by Professor Spalanzani and Coppola the optician. The Professor is in himself a member of the father-series, and Coppola is recognized as identical with Coppelius the lawyer. Just as they used before to work together over the secret brazier, so now they have jointly created the doll Olympia; the Professor is even called the father of Olympia. This double occurrence of activity in common betrays them as divisions of the father-imago: both the mechanician and the optician were

the father of Nathaniel (and of Olympia as well). In the frightening scene in childhood, Coppelius, after sparing Nathaniel's eyes, had screwed off his arms and legs as an experiment; that is, he had worked on him as a mechanician would on a doll. This singular feature, which seems quite outside the picture of the Sand-Man, introduces a new castration equivalent; but it also points to the inner identity of Coppelius with his later counterpart, Spalanzani the mechanician, and prepares us for the interpretation of Olympia. This automatic doll can be nothing else than a materialization of Nathaniel's feminine attitude towards his father in his infancy. Her fathers, Spalanzani and Coppola, are, after all, nothing but new editions, reincarnations of Nathaniel's pair of fathers. Spalanzani's otherwise incomprehensible statement that the optician has stolen Nathaniel's eyes (see above), so as to set them in the doll, now becomes significant as supplying evidence of the identity of Olympia and Nathaniel. Olympia is, as it were, a dissociated complex of Nathaniel's which confronts him as a person, and Nathaniel's enslavement to this complex is expressed in his senseless obsessive love for Olympia. We may with justice call love of this kind narcissistic, and we can understand why someone who has fallen victim to it should relinquish the real, external object of his love. The psychological truth of the situation in which the young man, fixated upon his father by his castration complex, becomes incapable of loving a woman, is amply proved by numerous analyses of patients whose story, though less fantastic, is hardly less tragic than that of the student Nathaniel.

   Hoffmann was the child of an unhappy marriage. When he was three years old, his father left his small family, and was never united to them again. According to Grisebach, in his biographical introduction to Hoffmann's works, the writer's relation to his father was always a most sensitive subject with him.

10   [Under the rubric 'Varia' in one of the issues of the *Internationale Zeitschrift für Psychoanalyse* for 1919 (5, 308), the year in which the present paper was first published, there appears over the initials 'S.F.' a short note which it is not unreasonable to attribute to Freud. Its insertion here, though strictly speaking irrelevant, may perhaps be excused. The note is headed: 'E. T. A. Hoffmann on the Function of Consciousness' and it proceeds: 'In *Die Elixire des Teufels* (Part II, p. 210, in Hesse's edition) – a novel rich in masterly descriptions of pathological mental states – Schönfeld comforts the hero, whose consciousness is temporarily disturbed, with the following words: "And what do you get out of it? I mean out of the particular mental function which we call consciousness, and which is nothing but the confounded activity of a damned toll-collector – excise-man – deputy-chief customs officer, who has set up his infamous bureau in our top storey and who exclaims, whenever any goods try to get out: 'Hi! hi! exports are prohibited ... they must stay here ... here, in this country. ...'"']

11   [This phrase seems to be an echo from Nietzsche (e.g. from the last part of *Also Sprach Zarathustra*). In Chapter III of *Beyond the Pleasure Principle* (1920*g*), *Standard Ed.*, **18**, 22, Freud puts a similar phrase 'the perpetual recurrence of the same thing' into inverted commas.]

12   [Cf. *The Interpretation of Dreams*, *Standard Ed.*, **5**, 357.]

13   I believe that when poets complain that two souls dwell in the human breast, and when popular psychologists talk of the splitting of people's egos, what they are thinking of is this division (in the sphere of ego-psychology) between the critical agency and the rest of the ego, and not the antithesis discovered by psycho-analysis between the ego and what is unconscious and repressed. It is true that the distinction between these two antitheses is to some extent effaced by the circumstance that foremost among the things that are rejected by the criticism of the ego are derivatives of the repressed. – [Freud had already discussed this critical agency at length in Section III of his paper on narcissism (1914*c*), and it was soon to be further expanded into the 'ego-ideal' and 'super-ego' in Chapter XI of his *Group Psychology* (1921*c*) and Chapter III of *The Ego and the Id* (1923*b*) respectively.]

14   In Ewers's *Der Student von Prag*, which serves as the starting-point of Rank's study on the 'double', the hero has promised his beloved not to kill his antagonist in a duel. But on his way to the duelling-ground he meets his 'double', who has already killed his rival.

15   Heine, *Die Götter im Exil*.

16   [Mark Twain, *A Tramp Abroad*, London, 1880, **1**, 107.]

17   [Freud had himself reached the age of 62 a year earlier, in 1918.]

18 [This was published a year later as *Beyond the Pleasure Principle* (1920*g*). The various manifesta-
    tions of the 'compulsion to repeat' enumerated here are enlarged upon in Chapters II and III of
    that work. The 'compulsion to repeat' had already been described by Freud as a clinical phenomenon,
    in a technical paper published five years earlier (1914*g*).]
19 [Schiller's poem based on Herodotus.]
20 'Notes upon a Case of Obsessional Neurosis' (1909*d*) [*Standard Ed.*, **10**, 234].
21 ['The evil eye' in German is '*der böse Blick*', literally 'the evil look'.]
22 [The obsessional patient referred to just above – the 'Rat Man' (1909*d*), *Standard Ed.*, **10**, 233 f.]
23 Cf. my book *Totem and Taboo* (1912–13), Essay III, 'Animism, Magic and the Omnipotence of
    Thoughts', where the following footnote will be found: 'We appear to attribute an "uncanny"
    quality to impressions that seek to confirm the omnipotence of thoughts and the animistic mode
    of thinking in general, after we have reached a stage at which, in our *judgment*, we have abandoned
    such beliefs.' [*Standard Ed.*, **13**, 86.]
24 [This problem figures prominently in *Beyond the Pleasure Principle* (1920*g*), on which Freud was
    engaged while writing the present paper. See *Standard Ed.*, **18**, 44 ff.]
25 [Freud had discussed the individual's attitude to death at greater length in the second part of his
    paper 'Thoughts for the Times on War and Death' (1915*b*).]
26 Cf. *Totem and Taboo* [*Standard Ed.*, **13**, 66].
27 [Literally 'thrower' (of bad luck), or 'one who casts' (the evil eye). – Schaeffer's novel was
    published in 1918.]
28 [She feels that surely I'm a genius now, – Perhaps the very Devil indeed!
        Goethe, *Faust*, Part I (Scene 16),
        (Bayard Taylor's translation).]
29 [*Die Geschichte von der abgehauenen Hand* ('The Story of the Severed Hand').]
30 [See Section VIII of Freud's analysis of the 'Wolf Man' (1918*b*), above.]
31 [Cf. *The Interpretation of Dreams* (1900*a*), *Standard Ed.*, **5**, 399.]
32 [See Freud's paper on 'Negation' (1925*h*).]
33 Since the uncanny effect of a 'double' also belongs to this same group it is interesting to observe
    what the effect is of meeting one's own image unbidden and unexpected. Ernst Mach has related
    two such observations in his *Analyse der Empfindungen* (1900, 3). On the first occasion he was not
    a little startled when he realized that the face before him was his own. The second time he formed
    a very unfavourable opinion about the supposed stranger who entered the omnibus, and thought
    'What a shabby-looking school-master that man is who is getting in!' – I can report a similar
    adventure. I was sitting alone in my *wagon-lit* compartment when a more than usually violent jolt
    of the train swung back the door of the adjoining washing-cabinet, and an elderly gentleman in a
    dressing-gown and a travelling cap came in. I assumed that in leaving the washing-cabinet, which
    lay between the two compartments, he had taken the wrong direction and come into my compart-
    ment by mistake. Jumping up with the intention of putting him right, I at once realized to my
    dismay that the intruder was nothing but my own reflection in the looking-glass on the open door.
    I can still recollect that I thoroughly disliked his appearance. Instead, therefore, of being *frightened*
    by our 'doubles', both Mach and I simply failed to recognize them as such. Is it not possible,
    though, that our dislike of them was a vestigial trace of the archaic reaction which feels the
    'double' to be something uncanny?
34 [See the discussion of children's fear of the dark in Section V of the third of Freud's *Three Essays*
    (1905*d*), *Standard Ed.*, **7**, 224 *n.*]

Works Cited

Freud, S. (1900a) *Die Traumdeutung*, Vienna. *G.S.*, 2–3; *G.W.*, 2–3. (33, 35, 51–2, 102, 103, 128, 152, 156,
    235, 245) [*Trans.: The Interpretation of Dreams*, London and New York, 1955; *Standard Ed.*, 4–5.]
Freud, S. (1901b) *Zur Psychopathologie des Alltagslebens*, Berlin, 1904. *G.S.*, 4; *G.W.*, 4. (148, 236, 272)
    [*Trans.: The Psychopathology of Everyday Life*, *Standard Ed.*, 6.]

Freud, S. (1905d) *Drei Abhandlungen zur Sexualtheorie,* Vienna. *G.S.,* 5, 3; *G.W.,* 5, 29. (5, 81, 106, 115, 126, 133, 177, 182, 252) [*Trans.: Three Essays on the Theory of Sexuality,* London, 1949; *Standard Ed.,* 7, 125.]

Freud, S. (1909d) 'Bemerkungen über einen Fall von Zwangsneurose', *G.S.,* 8, 269; *G.W.,* 7, 381. (75, 103, 123, 149, 195, 239, 240) [*Trans.:* 'Notes upon a Case of Obsessional Neurosis', *C.P.,* 3, 293; *Standard Ed.,* 10, 155.]

Freud, S. (1912–13) *Totem und Tabu,* Vienna, 1913. *G.S.,* 10, 3; *G.W.,* 9. (6, 59, 114, 218, 241, 243, 262) [*Trans.: Totem and Taboo,* London, 1950; New York, 1952; *Standard Ed.,* 13, 1.]

Freud, S. (1914c) 'Zur Einführung des Narzissmus', *G.S.,* 6, 155; *G.W.,* 10, 138. (6, 53, 129, 136, 194, 236) [*Trans.:* 'On Narcissism: an Introduction', *C.P.,* 4, 30; *Standard Ed.,* 14.]

Freud, S. (1914*g*) 'Weitere Ratschläge zur Technik der Psychoanalyse: II. Erinnern, Wiederholen und Durcharbeiten', *G.S.,* 6, 109; *G.W.,* 10, 126. (159, 239) [*Trans.:* 'Recollecting, Repeating and Working Through (Further Recommendations on the Technique of Psycho-Analysis, II)', *C.P.,* 2, 366; *Standard Ed.,* 12.]

Freud, S. (1915b) 'Zeitgemässes über Krieg und Tod', *G.S.,* 10, 315; *G.W.,* 10, 324. (242) [*Trans.:* 'Thoughts for the Times on War and Death', *C.P.,* 4, 288; *Standard Ed.,* 14.]

Freud, S. (1918b [1914]) 'Aus der Geschichte einer infantilen Neurose', *G.S.,* 8, 439; *G.W.,* 12, 29. (123, 126, 166, 178, 198, 201, 244) [*Trans.:* 'From the History of an Infantile Neurosis', *C.P.,* 3, 473; *Standard Ed.,* 17, 3.]

Freud, S. (1920*g*) *Jenseits des Lustprinzips,* Vienna. *G.S.,* 6, 191; *G.W.,* 13, 3. (86, 194, 218, 234, 238, 242) [*Trans.: Beyond the Pleasure Principle,* London, 1950; *Standard Ed.,* 18, 7.]

Freud, S. (1921c) *Massenpsychologie und Ich-Analyse,* Vienna. *G.S.,* 6, 261; *G.W.* 13, 73. (27, 236) [*Trans.: Group Psychology and the Analysis of the Ego,* London, 1922; New York, 1940; *Standard Ed.,* 18, 69.]

Freud, S. (1923b) *Das Ich und das Es,* Vienna. *G.S.,* 6, 353; *G.W.,* 13, 237. (6, 102, 182, 194, 236) [*Trans.: The Ego and the Id,* London, 1927; *Standard Ed.,* 19.]

Freud, S. (1925*h*) 'Die Verneinung', *G.S.,* 11, 3; *G.W.,* 14, 11. (81, 245) [*Trans.:* 'Negation', *C.P.,* 5, 181; *Standard Ed.,* 19.]

Grimm, J. and W. (1877) *Deutsches Wörterbuch,* 4, Leipzig. (225–6)

Jentsch, E. (1906) 'Zur Psychologie des Unheimlichen', *Psychiat.-neurol. Wschr.,* 8, 195. (219–21, 226–7)

Kammerer, P. (1919) *Das Gesetz der Serie,* Vienna. (238)

Mach, E. (1900) *Die Analyse der Empfindung,* 2nd ed., Jena. (248)

Rank, O. (1914) 'Der Doppelgänger', *Imago,* 3, 97. (234–6)

Sanders, D. (1860) *Wörterbuch der Deutschen Sprache,* Leipzig. (221–5, 253–6)

Seligmann, S. (1910–11) *Der böse Blick und Verwandtes,* Berlin. (240)

CHAPTER 4

Group Psychology and the Analysis
of the Ego

Sigmund Freud

In this essay from 1921, Freud put forth an important concept for later psychoanalysis – identification. The child's ability to internalize representations of caregivers and others in its immediate social environment lies at the heart of later object relations theory. It seeks to account for the social character of the self, the way it is built up from relations with others. Freud here also hints at a more sociological version of the very dubious ideas of "castration" and of "castration complex," ideas that mistakenly turn historically specific and local cultural anecdotes about threats issued to children into psychological and anthropological principles. In that sociological account, what Freud calls "castration anxiety" would be seen as a misinterpretation or misnaming of an anxiety any young person feels as he or she undergoes the passage into sexual adulthood. The anxiety over loss has to do more with an anxiety over being able to fulfill the demands of the social ideal of adult sexual identity. One way of achieving an adult identity is to identify with the father or mother and to attempt to emulate them.

Identification is known to psycho-analysis as the earliest expression of an emotional tie with another person. It plays a part in the early history of the Oedipus complex. A little boy will exhibit a special interest in his father; he would like to grow like him and be like him, and take his place everywhere. We may say simply that he takes his father as his ideal. This behavior has nothing to do with a passive or feminine attitude towards his father (and towards males in general); it is on the contrary typically masculine. It fits in very well with the Oedipus complex, for which it helps to prepare the way.

Original publication details: Sigmund Freud, "Group Psychology and the Analysis of the Ego" from
The Standard Edition of the Complete Psychological Works, trans. James Strachey. Hogarth Press, 1922, 1959.
Copyright © 1922, 1959 by the Institute of Psycho-Analysis and Angela Richards.
Copyright © 1959 by Sigmund Freud Copyrights Ltd. Copyright © 1959 by James Strachey.
Reproduced with permission from Random House Group Ltd, W.W. Norton & Company, Inc.
and the Marsh Agency on behalf of Sigmund Freud Copyrights.

Literary Theory: An Anthology, Third Edition. Edited by Julie Rivkin and Michael Ryan.
© 2017 John Wiley & Sons, Ltd. Published 2017 by John Wiley & Sons, Ltd.

At the same time as this identification with his father, or a little later, the boy has begun to develop a true object-cathexis towards his mother according to the attachment [anaclitic] type. He then exhibits, therefore, two psychologically distinct ties: a straight-forward sexual object-cathexis towards his mother and an identification with his father which takes him as his model. The two subsist side by side for a time without any mutual influence or interference. In consequence of the irresistible advance towards a unification of mental life, they come together at last; and the normal Oedipus complex originates from their confluence. The little boy notices that his father stands in his way with his mother. His identification with his father then takes on a hostile coloring and becomes identical with the wish to replace his father in regard to his mother as well. Identification, in fact, is ambivalent from the very first; it can turn into an expression of tenderness as easily as into a wish for someone's removal. It behaves like a derivative of the first, *oral* phase of the organization of the libido, in which the object that we long for and prize is assimilated by eating and is in that way annihilated as such. The cannibal, as we know, has remained at this standpoint; he has a devouring affection for his enemies and only devours people of whom he is fond.[1]

The subsequent history of this identification with the father may easily be lost sight of. It may happen that the Oedipus complex becomes inverted, and that the father is taken as the object of a feminine attitude, an object from which the directly sexual instincts look for satisfaction; in that event the identification with the father has become the precursor of an object-tie with the father. The same holds good, with the necessary substitutions, of the baby daughter as well.

It is easy to state in a formula the distinction between an identification with the father and the choice of the father as an object. In the first case one's father is what one would like to *be*, and in the second he is what one would like to *have*. The distinction, that is, depends upon whether the tie attaches to the subject or to the object of the ego. The former kind of tie is therefore already possible before any sexual object-choice has been made. It is much more difficult to give a clear meta-psychological representation of the distinction. We can only see that identification endeavors to mold a person's own ego after the fashion of the one that has been taken as a model.

Let us disentangle identification as it occurs in the structure of a neurotic symptom from its rather complicated connections. Supposing that a little girl (and we will keep to her for the present) develops the same painful symptom as her mother – for instance, the same tormenting cough. This may come about in various ways. The identification may come from the Oedipus complex; in that case it signifies a hostile desire on the girl's part to take her mother's place, and the symptom expresses her object-love towards her father, and brings about a realization, under the influence of a sense of guilt, of her desire to take her mother's place: "You wanted to be your mother, and now you *are* – anyhow so far as your sufferings are concerned." This is the complete mechanism of the structure of a hysterical symptom. Or, on the other hand, the symptom may be the same as that of the person who is loved; so, for instance, Dora[2] imitated her father's cough. In that case we can only describe the state of things by saying *that identification has appeared instead of object-choice, and that object-choice has regressed to identification.* We have heard that identification is the earliest and original form of emotional tie; it often happens that under the conditions in which symptoms are constructed, that is, where there is repres-sion and where the mechanisms of the unconscious are dominant, object-choice is turned back into identification – the ego assumes the characteristics of the object. It is noticeable that in these identifications the ego sometimes copies the person who is not loved and sometimes the one who is loved. It must also strike us that in both cases the identification is a partial and extremely limited one and only borrows a single trait from the person who is its object.

There is a third particularly frequent and important case of symptom formation, in which the identification leaves entirely out of account any object-relation to the person who is being copied. Supposing, for instance, that one of the girls in a boarding school has had a letter from someone with whom she is secretly in love which arouses her jealousy, and that she reacts to it with a fit of hysterics; then some of her friends who know about it will catch the fit, as we say, by mental infection. The mechanism is that of identification based upon the possibility or desire of putting oneself in the same situation. The other girls would like to have a secret love affair too, and under the influence of a sense of guilt they also accept the suffering involved in it. It would be wrong to suppose that they take on the symptom out of sympathy. On the contrary, the sympathy only arises out of the identification, and this is proved by the fact that infection or imitation of this kind takes place in circumstances where even less pre-existing sympathy is to be assumed than usually exists between friends in a girls' school. One ego has perceived a significant analogy with another upon one point – in our example upon openness to a similar emotion; an identification is thereupon constructed on this point, and, under the influence of the pathogenic situation, is displaced on to the symptom which the one ego has produced. The identification by means of the symptom has thus become the mark of a point of coincidence between the two egos which has to be kept repressed.

What we have learned from these three sources may be summarized as follows. First, identification is the original form of emotional tie with an object; secondly, in a regressive way it becomes a substitute for a libidinal object-tie, as it were by means of introjection of the object into the ego; and thirdly, it may arise with any new perception of a common quality shared with some other person who is not an object of the sexual instinct. The more important this common quality is, the more successful may this partial identification become, and it may thus represent the beginning of a new tie.

Notes

1   See my *Three Essays* [*Standard Edition*, 7 (1905), p. 198] and Abraham, "The First Pregenital Stage of the Libido," *Selected Papers on Psycho-Analysis* (London, 1927), ch. XII.
2   In my "Fragment of an Analysis of a Case of Hysteria," *Standard Edition*, 7 (1905), pp. 82–3.

CHAPTER 5

The Mirror Stage as Formative of the Function of the I as Revealed in Psychoanalytic Experience

Jacques Lacan

Jacques Lacan's *Ecrits* (1966) was the most influential work of Structuralist psychoanalysis. Lacan's work constitutes a rebuke to ego or self psychology and a return to Freud's belief in the power of the unconscious in human life. Yet his work also rewrites Freud in important ways. He inserts the self into culture. We are all shaped by the Symbolic Order into which we are born, an order that determines our gender identity and our place in our families. When we learn to make symbols, we also learn to separate from our ambient childhood world of objects and achieve an independent selfhood that is experienced as loss. That lack can never be filled, and all human desire circulates around it, yearning to hark back to the lost unity. Lacan calls such yearning and the kind of consciousness it provokes the Imaginary. It is the narcissistic part of the mind that defines ego activity. Lacan placed great emphasis on Freud's contention that the ego deludes itself into thinking it controls the mind. What the ego cannot reach or know is the Real, the realm of the drives, the instincts, and the unconscious processes that shape our selves but that cannot be known by a mind that constitutes itself as the effacement of such determination. In this famous essay from 1949, Lacan describes his concept of the self as a delusory construct plagued in its very constitution by imaginary identifications with a spurious sense of wholeness or unity. Lacan's polemic is directed against those ego psychologists who were just beginning in England and America to explore the possibility that psychoanalysis should focus on the whole complex of the self in its social setting rather than on the dynamic interrelations between consciousness and the unconscious.

Original publication details: Jacques Lacan: "The Mirror Stage as Formative of the I" from *Ecrits: A Selection by Jacques Lacan*, trans. Alan Sheridan, pp. 1–7. Norton, 1977. Copyright © 1966 by Éditions du Seuil. English translation copyright © 1977 Tavistock Publications.

Literary Theory: An Anthology, Third Edition. Edited by Julie Rivkin and Michael Ryan.
© 2017 John Wiley & Sons, Ltd. Published 2017 by John Wiley & Sons, Ltd.

The conception of the mirror stage that I introduced at our last congress, thirteen years ago, has since become more or less established in the practice of the French group. However, I think it worthwhile to bring it again to your attention, especially today, for the light it sheds on the formation of the *I* as we experience it in psychoanalysis. It is an experience that leads us to oppose any philosophy directly issuing from the *Cogito*.

Some of you may recall that this conception originated in a feature of human behaviour illuminated by a fact of comparative psychology. The child, at an age when he is for a time, however short, outdone by the chimpanzee in instrumental intelligence, can nevertheless already recognize as such his own image in a mirror. This recognition is indicated in the illuminative mimicry of the *Aha-Erlebnis*, which Köhler sees as the expression of situational apperception, an essential stage of the act of intelligence.

This act, far from exhausting itself, as in the case of the monkey, once the image has been mastered and found empty, immediately rebounds in the case of the child in a series of gestures in which he experiences in play the relation between the movements assumed in the image and the reflected environment, and between this virtual complex and the reality it reduplicates – the child's own body, and the persons and things, around him.

This event can take place, as we have known since Baldwin, from the age of six months, and its repetition has often made me reflect upon the startling spectacle of the infant in front of the mirror. Unable as yet to walk, or even to stand up, and held tightly as he is by some support, human or artificial (what, in France, we call a '*trotte-bébé*'), he nevertheless overcomes, in a flutter of jubilant activity, the obstructions of his support and, fixing his attitude in a slightly leaning-forward position, in order to hold it in his gaze, brings back an instantaneous aspect of the image.

For me, this activity retains the meaning I have given it up to the age of eighteen months. This meaning discloses a libidinal dynamism, which has hitherto remained problematic, as well as an ontological structure of the human world that accords with my reflections on paranoiac knowledge.

We have only to understand the mirror stage *as an identification*, in the full sense that analysis gives to the term: namely, the transformation that takes place in the subject when he assumes an image – whose predestination to this phase-effect is sufficiently indicated by the use, in analytic theory, of the ancient term *imago*.

This jubilant assumption of his specular image by the child at the *infans* stage, still sunk in his motor incapacity and nursling dependence, would seem to exhibit in an exemplary situation the symbolic matrix in which the *I* is precipitated in a primordial form, before it is objectified in the dialectic of identification with the other, and before language restores to it, in the universal, its function as subject.

This form would have to be called the Ideal-I,[1] if we wished to incorporate it into our usual register, in the sense that it will also be the source of secondary identifications, under which term I would place the functions of libidinal normalization. But the important point is that this form situates the agency of the ego, before its social determination, in a fictional direction, which will always remain irreducible for the individual alone, or rather, which will only rejoin the coming-into-being (*le devenir*) of the subject asymptotically, whatever the success of the dialectical syntheses by which he must resolve as *I* his discordance with his own reality.

The fact is that the total form of the body by which the subject anticipates in a mirage the maturation of his power is given to him only as *Gestalt*, that is to say, in an exteriority in which this form is certainly more constituent than constituted, but in which it appears to him above all in a contrasting size (*un relief de stature*) that fixes it and in a symmetry that inverts it, in contrast with the turbulent movements that the subject feels are animating him. Thus, this *Gestalt* – whose pregnancy should be regarded as bound up with the species, though its motor style remains scarcely recognizable – by these two aspects of its appearance, symbolizes the mental permanence of the *I*, at the same time as it prefigures its alienating destination; it is still pregnant with the correspondences that unite the *I* with the statue in which man projects himself, with the phantoms that dominate him, or with the automaton in which, in an ambiguous relation, the world of his own making tends to find completion.

Indeed, for the *imagos* – whose veiled faces it is our privilege to see in outline in our daily experience and in the penumbra of symbolic efficacity[2] – the mirror-image would seem to be the threshold of the visible world, if we go by the mirror disposition that the *imago of one's own body* presents in hallucinations or dreams, whether it concerns its individual features, or even its infirmities, or its object-projections; or if we observe the role of the mirror apparatus in the appearances of the *double*, in which psychical realities, however heterogeneous, are manifested.

That a *Gestalt* should be capable of formative effects in the organism is attested by a piece of biological experimentation that is itself so alien to the idea of psychical causality that it cannot bring itself to formulate its results in these terms. It nevertheless recognizes that it is a necessary condition for the maturation of the gonad of the female pigeon that it should see another member of its species, of either sex; so sufficient in itself is this condition that the desired effect may be obtained merely by placing the individual within reach of the field of reflection of a mirror. Similarly, in the case of the migratory locust, the transition within a generation from the solitary to the gregarious form can be obtained by exposing the individual, at a certain stage, to the exclusively visual action of a similar image, provided it is animated by movements of a style sufficiently close to that characteristic of the species. Such facts are inscribed in an order of homeomorphic identification that would itself fall within the larger question of the meaning of beauty as both formative and erogenic.

But the facts of mimicry are no less instructive when conceived as cases of heteromorphic identification, in as much as they raise the problem of the signification of space for the living organism – psychological concepts hardly seem less appropriate for shedding light on these matters than ridiculous attempts to reduce them to the supposedly supreme law of adaptation. We have only to recall how Roger Caillois (who was then very young, and still fresh from his breach with the sociological school in which he was trained) illuminated the subject by using the term '*legendary psychasthenia*' to classify morphological mimicry as an obsession with space in its derealizing effect.

I have myself shown in the social dialectic that structures human knowledge as paranoiac[3] why human knowledge has greater autonomy than animal knowledge in relation to the field of force of desire, but also why human knowledge is determined in that 'little reality' (*ce peu de réalité*), which the Surrealists, in their restless way, saw as its limitation. These reflections lead me to recognize in the spatial captation manifested in the mirror-stage, even before the social dialectic, the effect in man of an organic insufficiency in his natural reality – in so far as any meaning can be given to the word 'nature'.

I am led, therefore, to regard the function of the mirror-stage as a particular case of the function of the *imago*, which is to establish a relation between the organism and its reality – or, as they say, between the *Innenwelt* and the *Umwelt*.

In man, however, this relation to nature is altered by a certain dehiscence at the heart of the organism, a primordial Discord betrayed by the signs of uneasiness and motor unco-ordination of the neo-natal months. The objective notion of the anatomical incompleteness of the pyramidal system and likewise the presence of certain humoral residues of the maternal organism confirm the view I have formulated as the fact of a real *specific prematurity of birth* in man.

It is worth noting, incidentally, that this is a fact recognized as such by embryologists, by the term *foetalization*, which determines the prevalence of the so-called superior apparatus of the neurax, and especially of the cortex, which psycho-surgical operations lead us to regard as the intra-organic mirror.

This development is experienced as a temporal dialectic that decisively projects the formation of the individual into history. The *mirror stage* is a drama whose internal thrust is precipitated from insufficiency to anticipation – and which manufactures for the subject, caught up in the lure of spatial identification, the succession of phantasies that extends from a fragmented body-image to a form of its totality that I shall call orthopaedic – and, lastly, to the assumption of the armour of an alienating identity, which will mark with its rigid structure the subject's entire mental development. Thus, to break out of the circle of the *Innenwelt* into the *Umwelt* generates the inexhaustible quadrature of the ego's verifications.

This fragmented body – which term I have also introduced into our system of theoretical references – usually manifests itself in dreams when the movement of the analysis encounters a certain level of aggressive disintegration in the individual. It then appears in the form of disjointed limbs, or of those organs represented in exoscopy, growing wings and taking up arms for intestinal persecutions – the very same that the visionary Hieronymus Bosch has fixed, for all time, in painting, in their ascent from the fifteenth century to the imaginary zenith of modern man. But this form is even tangibly revealed at the organic level, in the lines of 'fragilization' that define the anatomy of phantasy, as exhibited in the schizoid and spasmodic symptoms of hysteria.

Correlatively, the formation of the *I* is symbolized in dreams by a fortress, or a stadium – its inner arena and enclosure, surrounded by marshes and rubbish-tips, dividing it into two opposed fields of contest where the subject flounders in quest of the lofty, remote inner castle whose form (sometimes juxtaposed in the same scenario) symbolizes the id in a quite startling way. Similarly, on the mental plane, we find realized the structures of fortified works, the metaphor of which arises spontaneously, as if issuing from the symptoms themselves, to designate the mechanisms of obsessional neurosis – inversion, isolation, reduplication, cancellation and displacement.

But if we were to build on these subjective givens alone – however little we free them from the condition of experience that makes us see them as partaking of the nature of a linguistic technique – our theoretical attempts would remain exposed to the charge of projecting themselves into the unthinkable of an absolute subject. This is why I have sought in the present hypothesis, grounded in a conjunction of objective data, the guiding grid for a *method of symbolic reduction*.

It establishes in the *defences of the ego* a genetic order, in accordance with the wish formulated by Miss Anna Freud, in the first part of her great work, and situates (as against a frequently expressed prejudice) hysterical repression and its returns at a more archaic stage than obsessional inversion and its isolating processes, and the latter in turn as preliminary to paranoic alienation, which dates from the deflection of the specular *I* into the social *I*.

This moment in which the mirror-stage comes to an end inaugurates, by the identification with the *imago* of the counterpart and the drama of primordial jealousy (so well brought out by the school of Charlotte Bühler in the phenomenon of infantile *transitivism*), the dialectic that will henceforth link the *I* to socially elaborated situations.

It is this moment that decisively tips the whole of human knowledge into mediatization through the desire of the other, constitutes its objects in an abstract equivalence by the co-operation of others, and turns the I into that apparatus for which every instinctual thrust constitutes a danger, even though it should correspond to a natural maturation – the very normalization of this maturation being henceforth dependent, in man, on a cultural mediation as exemplified, in the case of the sexual object, by the Oedipus complex.

In the light of this conception, the term primary narcissism, by which analytic doctrine designates the libidinal investment characteristic of that moment, reveals in those who invented it the most profound awareness of semantic latencies. But it also throws light on the dynamic opposition between this libido and the sexual libido, which the first analysts tried to define when they invoked destructive and, indeed, death instincts, in order to explain the evident connection between the narcissistic libido and the alienating function of the *I*, the aggressivity it releases in any relation to the other, even in a relation involving the most Samaritan of aid.

In fact, they were encountering that existential negativity whose reality is so vigorously proclaimed by the contemporary philosophy of being and nothingness.

But unfortunately that philosophy grasps negativity only within the limits of a self-sufficiency of consciousness, which, as one of its premises, links to the *méconnaissances* that constitute the ego, the illusion of autonomy to which it entrusts itself. This flight of fancy, for all that it draws, to an unusual extent, on borrowings from psychoanalytic experience, culminates in the pretention of providing an existential psychoanalysis.

At the culmination of the historical effort of a society to refuse to recognize that it has any function other than the utilitarian one, and in the anxiety of the individual confronting the 'concentrational'[4] form of the social bond that seems to arise to crown this effort, existentialism must be judged by the explanations it gives of the subjective impasses that have indeed resulted from it; a freedom that is never more authentic than when it is within the walls of a prison; a demand for commitment, expressing the impotence of a pure consciousness to master any situation; a voyeuristic-sadistic idealization of the sexual relation; a personality that realizes itself only in suicide; a consciousness of the other that can be satisfied only by Hegelian murder.

These propositions are opposed by all our experience, in so far as it teaches us not to regard the ego as centred on the *perception–consciousness system*, or as organized by the 'reality principle' – a principle that is the expression of a scientific prejudice most hostile to the dialectic of knowledge. Our experience shows that we should start instead from the *function of méconnaissance* that characterizes the ego in all its structures, so markedly articulated by Miss Anna Freud. For, if the *Verneinung* represents the patent form of that function, its effects will, for the most part, remain latent, so long as they are not illuminated by some light reflected on to the level of fatality, which is where the id manifests itself.

We can thus understand the inertia characteristic of the formations of the *I*, and find there the most extensive definition of neurosis – just as the captation of the subject by the situation gives us the most general formula for madness, not only the madness that lies behind the walls of asylums, but also the madness that deafens the world with its sound and fury.

The sufferings of neurosis and psychosis are for us a schooling in the passions of the soul, just as the beam of the psychoanalytic scales, when we calculate the tilt of its threat to entire communities, provides us with an indication of the deadening of the passions in society.

At this junction of nature and culture, so persistently examined by modern anthropology, psychoanalysis alone recognizes this knot of imaginary servitude that love must always undo again, or sever.

For such a task, we place no trust in altruistic feeling, we who lay bare the aggressivity that underlies the activity of the philanthropist, the idealist, the pedagogue, and even the reformer.

In the recourse of subject to subject that we preserve, psychoanalysis may accompany the patient to the ecstatic limit of the '*Thou art that*', in which is revealed to him the cipher of his mortal destiny, but it is not in our mere power as practitioners to bring him to that point where the real journey begins.

Notes

1   Throughout this article I leave in its peculiarity the translation I have adopted for Freud's *Ideal-Ich* [i.e., 'je-idéal'], without further comment, other than to say that I have not maintained it since.
2   Cf. Claude Lévi-Strauss, *Structural Anthropology*, Chapter X.
3   Cf. 'Aggressivity in Psychoanalysis', p. 8 and *Écrits*, p. 180.
4   '*Concentrationnaire*', an adjective coined after World War II (this article was written in 1949) to describe the life of the concentration-camp. In the hands of certain writers it became, by extension, applicable to many aspects of 'modern' life [Tr.].

CHAPTER 6

Transitional Objects and Transitional Phenomena[1]

D.W. Winnicott

D. W. Winnicott was an English psychoanalyst who specialized in object relations theory. His books include *Playing and Reality* (1971) and *The Child and the Family* (1957).

A Study of the First *Not-me* Possession[2]

Introduction

IT IS WELL KNOWN that infants as soon as they are born tend to use fist, fingers, thumbs in stimulation of the oral erotogenic zone, in satisfaction of the instincts at that zone, and also in quiet union. It is also well known that after a few months infants of either sex become fond of playing with dolls, and that most mothers allow their infants some special object and expect them to become, as it were, addicted to such objects.

There is a relationship between these two sets of phenomena that are separated by a time interval, and a study of the development from the earlier into the later can be profitable, and can make use of important clinical material that has been somewhat neglected.

The First Possession

Those who happen to be in close touch with mothers' interests and problems will be already aware of the very rich patterns ordinarily displayed by babies in their use of the first *Not-Me* possession. These patterns, being displayed, can be subjected to direct observation.

There is a wide variation to be found in a sequence of events which starts with the new-born infant's fist-in-mouth activities, and that leads eventually on to an attachment to a teddy, a doll or soft toy, or to a hard toy.

Original publication details: D.W. Winnicott, "Transitional Objects and Transitional Phenomena" from *Playing and Reality*, pp. 229–242. Basic Books, 1980. Reproduced with permission from Taylor & Francis.

It is clear that something is important here other than oral excitement and satisfaction, although this may be the basis of everything else. Many other important things can be studied, and they include:

> The nature of the object.
> The infant's capacity to recognize the object as *Not-Me*.
> The place of the object – outside, inside, at the border.
> The infant's capacity to create, think up, devise, originate, produce an object.
> The initiation of an affectionate type of object relationship.

I have introduced the terms 'transitional object' and 'transitional phenomena' for designation of the intermediate area of experience, between the thumb and the teddy bear, between the oral erotism and true object relationship, between primary creative activity and projection of what has already been introjected, between primary unawareness of indebtedness and the acknowledgement of indebtedness ('Say: ta!').

By this definition an infant's babbling or the way an older child goes over a repertoire of songs and tunes while preparing for sleep come within the intermediate area as transitional phenomena, along with the use made of objects that are not part of the infant's body yet are not fully recognized as belonging to external reality.

It is generally acknowledged that a statement of human nature is inadequate when given in terms of interpersonal relationships, even when the imaginative elaboration of function, the whole of fantasy both conscious and unconscious, including the repressed unconscious, is allowed for. There is another way of describing persons that comes out of the researches of the past two decades, that suggests that of every individual who has reached to the stage of being a unit (with a limiting membrane and an outside and an inside) it can be said that there is an *inner reality* to that individual, an inner world which can be rich or poor and can be at peace or in a state of war.

My claim is that if there is a need for this double statement, there is need for a triple one; there is the third part of the life of a human being, a part that we cannot ignore, an intermediate area of *experiencing*, to which inner reality and external life both contribute. It is an area which is not challenged, because no claim is made on its behalf except that it shall exist as a resting-place for the individual engaged in the perpetual human task of keeping inner and outer reality separate yet inter-related.

It is usual to refer to 'reality-testing', and to make a clear distinction between apperception and perception. I am here staking a claim for an intermediate state between a baby's inability and growing ability to recognize and accept reality. I am therefore studying the substance of *illusion*, that which is allowed to the infant, and which in adult life is inherent in art and religion. We can share a respect for *illusory experience*, and if we wish we may collect together and form a group on the basis of the similarity of our illusory experiences. This is a natural root of grouping among human beings. Yet it is a hall-mark of madness when an adult puts too powerful a claim on the credulity of others, forcing them to acknowledge a sharing of illusion that is not their own.

I hope it will be understood that I am not referring exactly to the little child's teddy bear nor to the infant's first use of the fist (thumb, fingers). I am not specifically studying the first object of object relationships. I am concerned with the first possession, and with the intermediate area between the subjective and that which is objectively perceived.

Development of a Personal Pattern

There is plenty of reference in psycho-analytic literature to the progress from 'hand to mouth' to 'hand to genital', but perhaps less to progress leading to the handling of truly '*Not-Me*' objects. Sooner or later in an infant's development there comes a tendency on the part of the infant to weave other-than-me objects into the personal pattern. To some extent these objects stand for the breast, but it is not especially this point that is under discussion.

In the case of some infants the thumb is placed in the mouth while fingers are made to caress the face by pronation and supination movements of the forearm. The mouth is then active in relation to the thumb, but not in relation to the fingers. The fingers caressing the upper lip, or some other part, may be or may become more important than the thumb engaging the mouth. Moreover this caressing activity may be found alone, without the more direct thumb-mouth union. (Freud, 1905. Hoffer, 1949.)

In common experience one of the following occurs, complicating an auto-erotic experience such as thumb-sucking:

1. with the other hand the baby takes an external object, say a part of a sheet or blanket, into the mouth along with the fingers; or
2. somehow or other the bit of cloth[3] is held and sucked, or not actually sucked. The objects used naturally include napkins and (later) handkerchiefs, and this depends on what is readily and reliably available; or
3. the baby starts from early months to pluck wool and to collect it and to use it for the caressing part of the activity.[4] Less commonly, the wool is swallowed, even causing trouble; or
4. mouthing, accompanied by sounds of 'mum-mum', babbling,[5] anal noises, the first musical notes and so on.

One may suppose that thinking, or fantasying, gets linked up with these functional experiences.

All these things I am calling *transitional phenomena*. Also, out of all this (if we study any one infant) there may emerge some thing or some phenomenon — perhaps a bundle of wool or the corner of a blanket or eiderdown, or a word or tune, or a mannerism, which becomes vitally important to the infant for use at the time of going to sleep, and is a defence against anxiety, especially anxiety of depressive type. (Illingworth, 1951.) Perhaps some soft object or cot cover has been found and used by the infant, and this then becomes what I am calling a *transitional object*. This object goes on being important. The parents get to know its value and carry it round when travelling. The mother lets it get dirty and even smelly, knowing that by washing it she introduces a break in continuity in the infant's experience, a break that may destroy the meaning and value of the object to the infant.

I suggest that the pattern of transitional phenomena begins to show at about 4–6–8–12 months. Purposely I leave room for wide variations.

Patterns set in infancy may persist into childhood, so that the original soft object continues to be absolutely necessary at bed-time or at time of loneliness or when a depressed mood threatens. In health, however, there is a gradual extension of range of interest, and eventually the extended range is maintained, even when depressive anxiety is near. A need for a specific object or a behaviour pattern that started at a very early date may reappear at a later age when deprivation threatens.

This first possession is used in conjunction with special techniques derived from very early infancy, which can include or exist apart from the more direct autoerotic activities. Gradually in the life of an infant teddies and dolls and hard toys are acquired. Boys to some extent tend to go over to use hard objects, whereas girls tend to proceed right ahead to the acquisition of a family. It is important to note, however, that *there is no noticeable difference between boy and girl in their use of the original Not-Me possession*, which I am calling the transitional object.

As the infant starts to use organized sounds (mum, ta, da) there may appear a 'word' for the transitional object. The name given by the infant to these earliest objects is often significant, and it usually has a word used by the adults partly incorporated in it. For instance, 'baa' may be the name, and the 'b' may have come from the adult's use of the word 'baby' or 'bear'.

I should mention that sometimes there is no transitional object except the mother herself. Or an infant may be so disturbed in emotional development that the transition state cannot be enjoyed, or the sequence of objects used is broken. The sequence may nevertheless be maintained in a hidden way.

Summary of Special Qualities in the Relationship

1. The infant assumes rights over the object, and we agree to this assumption. Nevertheless some abrogation of omnipotence is a feature from the start.
2. The object is affectionately cuddled as well as excitedly loved and mutilated.
3. It must never change, unless changed by the infant.
4. It must survive instinctual loving, and also hating, and, if it be a feature, pure aggression.
5. Yet it must seem to the infant to give warmth, or to move, or to have texture, or to do something that seems to show it has vitality or reality of its own.
6. It comes from without from our point of view, but not so from the point of view of the baby. Neither does it come from within; it is not an hallucination.
7. Its fate is to be gradually allowed to be decathected, so that in the course of years it becomes not so much forgotten as relegated to limbo. By this I mean that in health the transitional object does not 'go inside' nor does the feeling about it necessarily undergo repression. It is not forgotten and it is not mourned. It loses meaning, and this is because the transitional phenomena have become diffused, have become spread out over the whole intermediate territory between 'inner psychic reality' and 'the external world as perceived by two persons in common', that is to say, over the whole cultural field.

At this point my subject widens out into that of play, and of artistic creativity and appreciation, and of religious feeling, and of dreaming, and also of fetishism, lying and stealing, the origin and loss of affectionate feeling, drug addiction, the talisman of obsessional rituals, etc.

Relationship of the Transitional Object to Symbolism

It is true that the piece of blanket (or whatever it is) is symbolical of some part-object, such as the breast. Nevertheless the point of it is not its symbolic value so much as its actuality. Its not being the breast (or the mother) is as important as the fact that it stands for the breast (or mother).

When symbolism is employed the infant is already clearly distinguishing between fantasy and fact, between inner objects and external objects, between primary creativity and perception. But the term transitional object, according to my suggestion, gives room for the process of becoming able to accept difference and similarity. I think there is use for a term for the root of symbolism in time, a term that describes the infant's journey from the purely subjective to objectivity; and it seems to me that the transitional object (piece of blanket, etc.) is what we see of this journey of progress towards experiencing.

It would be possible to understand the transitional object while not fully understanding the nature of symbolism. It seems that symbolism can only be properly studied in the process of the growth of an individual, and that it has at the very best a variable meaning. For instance, if we consider the wafer of the Blessed Sacrament, which is symbolic of the body of Christ, I think I am right in saying that for the Roman Catholic community it *is* the body, and for the Protestant community it is a *substitute*, a reminder, and is essentially not, in fact, actually the body itself. Yet in both cases it is a symbol.

A schizoid patient asked me, after Christmas, had I enjoyed eating her at the feast. And then, *had I really eaten her or only in fantasy*. I knew that she could not be satisfied with either alternative. Her split needed the double answer.

Clinical Description of a Transitional Object

For anyone in touch with parents and children, there is an infinite quantity and variety of illustrative clinical material.[6] The following illustrations are given merely to remind readers of similar material in their own experiences.

Two Brothers: Contrast in Early Use of Possessions

Distortion in use of transitional object. X, now a healthy man, has had to fight his way towards maturity. The mother 'learned how to be a mother' in her management of X when he was an infant and she was able to avoid certain mistakes with the other children because of what she learned with him. There were also external reasons why she was anxious at the time of her rather lonely management of X when he was born. She took her job as a mother very seriously and she breast-fed X for seven months. She feels that in his case this was too long and he was very difficult to wean. He never sucked his thumb or his fingers and when she weaned him 'he had nothing to fall back on'. He had never had the bottle or a dummy or any other form of feeding. He had a very strong and early *attachment to the mother herself*, as a person, and it was her actual person that he needed.

From twelve months he adopted a rabbit which he would cuddle and his affectionate regard for the rabbit eventually transferred to real rabbits. This particular rabbit lasted till he was five or six years old. It could be described as a *comforter*, but it never had the true quality of a transitional object. It was never, as a true transitional object would have been, more important than the mother, an almost inseparable part of the infant. In the case of this particular boy the kind of anxieties which were brought to a head by the weaning at seven months later produced asthma, and only gradually did he conquer this. It was important for him that he found employment far away from the home town. His attachment to his mother is still very powerful. He comes within the wide definition of the term normal, or healthy. This man has not married.

Typical use of transitional object. X's younger brother, Y, has developed in quite a straightforward way throughout. He now has three healthy children of his own. He was fed at the breast for four months and then weaned without difficulty.[7] Y sucked his thumb in the early weeks and this again 'made weaning easier for him than for his older brother'. Soon after weaning at five to six months he adopted the end of the blanket where the stitching finished. He was pleased if a little bit of the wool stuck out at the corner and with this he would tickle his nose. This very early became his 'Baa'; he invented this word for it himself as soon as he could use organized sounds. From the time when he was about a year old he was able to substitute for the end of the blanket a soft green jersey with a red tie. This was not a 'comforter' as in the case of the depressive older brother, but a 'soother'. It was a sedative which always worked. This is a typical example of what I am calling a *Transitional Object*. When Y was a little boy it was always certain that if anyone gave him his 'Baa' he would immediately suck it and lose anxiety, and in fact he would go to sleep within a few minutes if the time for sleep were at all near. The thumb-sucking continued at the same time, lasting until he was three or four years old, and he remembers thumb-sucking and a hard place on one thumb which resulted from it. He is now interested (as a father) in the thumb-sucking of his own children and their use of 'Baas'.

The story of seven ordinary children in this family brings out the points, arranged for comparison in the table below.

		Thumb	Transitional Object		Type of Child
X	Boy	O	Mother	Rabbit (comforter)	Mother-fixated
Y	Boy	+	'Baa'	Jersey (soother)	Free
Twins	Girl	O	Dummy	Donkey (friend)	Late maturity
	Boy	O	'Ee'	Ee (protective)	Latent psychopathic
Children of Y	Girl	O	'Baa'	Blanket (reassurance)	Developing well
	Girl				
	Boy	+	Thumb	Thumb (satisfaction)	" "
		+	'Mimis'*	Objects (sorting)	" "

* Innumerable similar soft objects distinguished by colour, length, width, and early subjected to sorting and classification.

In consultation with a parent it is often valuable to get information about the early techniques and possessions of all the children of the family. This starts the mother on a comparison of her children one with another, and enables her to remember and compare their characteristics at an early age.

Information can often be obtained from a child in regard to transitional objects; for instance, Angus (11 years 9 months) told me that his brother 'has tons of teddies and things' and 'before that he had little bears', and he followed this up with a talk about his own history. He said he never had teddies. There was a bell rope which hung down, a tag end of which he would go on hitting, and so go off to sleep. Probably in the end it fell, and that was the end of it. There was, however, something else. He was very shy about this. It was a purple rabbit with red eyes. 'I wasn't fond of it. I used to throw it around. Jeremy has it now. I gave it to him. I gave it to Jeremy because it was naughty. It *would* fall off the chest of drawers. *It still visits me. I like it to visit me.*' He surprised himself when he drew the purple rabbit. It will be noted that this eleven-year-old boy with the ordinary good reality-sense of his age spoke as if lacking in reality-sense when describing the transitional object's qualities and activities. When I saw the mother later she expressed surprise that Angus remembered the purple rabbit. She easily recognized it from the coloured drawing.

I deliberately refrain from giving more case material here, particularly as I wish to avoid giving the impression that what I am reporting is rare. In practically every case history there is something to be found that is interesting in the transitional phenomena, or in their absence (cf. Stevenson, Olive, 1954).

Theoretical Study

There are certain comments that can be made on the basis of accepted psycho-analytic theory.

1.   The transitional object stands for the breast, or the object of the first relationship.
2.   The transitional object antedates established reality-testing.
3.   In relation to the transitional object the infant passes from (magical) omnipotent control to control by manipulation (involving muscle erotism and coordination pleasure).
4.   The transitional object may eventually develop into a fetish object and so persist as a characteristic of the adult sexual life. (See Wulff's development of the theme.)
5.   The transitional object may, because of anal-erotic organization, stand for faeces (but it is not for this reason that it may become smelly and remain unwashed).

Relationship to Internal Object (Klein)

It is interesting to compare the transitional object concept with Melanie Klein's concept of the internal object. The transitional object is *not an internal object* (which is a mental concept) – it is a possession. Yet it is not (for the infant) an external object either.

The following complex statement has to be made. The infant can employ a transitional object when the internal object is alive and real and good enough (not too persecutory). But this internal object depends for its qualities on the existence and aliveness and behaviour of the external object (breast, mother figure, general environmental care). Badness or failure of the latter indirectly leads to deadness or to a persecutory quality of internal object. After a persistence of failure of the external object the internal object fails to have meaning to the infant, and then, and then only, does the transitional object become meaningless too. The transitional object may therefore stand for the 'external' breast, but *indirectly* so, through standing for an 'internal' breast.

The transitional object is never under magical control like the internal object, nor is it outside control as the real mother is.

Illusion–Disillusionment

In order to prepare the ground for my own positive contribution to this subject I must put into words some of the things that I think are taken too easily for granted in many psycho-analytic writings on infantile emotional development, although they may be understood in practice.

There is no possibility whatever for an infant to proceed from the pleasure-principle to the reality principle or towards and beyond primary identification (see Freud, 1923, p. 14),[8] unless there is a good enough mother.[9] The good enough 'mother' (not necessarily the infant's own mother) is one who makes active adaptation to the infant's needs, an active adaptation that gradually lessens, according to the infant's growing ability to account for failure of adaptation and to tolerate the results of frustration. Naturally the infant's own mother is more likely to be good enough than some other person, since this active adaptation demands an easy and unresented preoccupation with the one infant; in fact, success in infant care depends on the fact of devotion, not on cleverness or intellectual enlightenment.

The good-enough mother, as I have stated, starts off with an almost complete adaptation to her infant's needs, and as time proceeds she adapts less and less completely, gradually, according to the infant's growing ability to deal with her failure.

The infant's means of dealing with this maternal failure include the following:

> The infant's experience, often repeated, that there is a time limit to frustration. At first, naturally, this time limit must be short.
> A growing sense of process.
> The beginnings of mental activity.
> The employment of auto-erotic satisfactions.
> Remembering, reliving, fantasying, dreaming; the integrating of past, present, and future.

If all goes well the infant can actually come to gain from the experience of frustration, since incomplete adaptation to need makes objects real, that is to say hated as well as loved. The consequence of this is that *if all goes well* the infant can be disturbed by a close adaptation to need that is continued too long, not allowed its natural decrease, since exact adaptation resembles magic and the object that behaves perfectly becomes no better than an hallucination. Nevertheless *at the start* adaptation needs to be almost exact, and unless this is so it is not possible for the infant to begin to develop a capacity to experience a relationship to external reality, or even to form a conception of external reality.

Illusion and the Value of Illusion

The mother, at the beginning, by an almost 100 per cent adaptation affords the infant the opportunity for the *illusion* that her breast is part of the infant. It is, as it were, under magical control. The same can be said in terms of infant care in general, in the quiet times between excitements. Omnipotence is nearly a fact of experience. The mother's eventual task is gradually to disillusion the infant, but she has no hope of success unless at first she has been able to give sufficient opportunity for illusion.

In another language, the breast is created by the infant over and over again out of the infant's capacity to love or (one can say) out of need. A subjective phenomenon develops in the baby which we call the mother's breast.[10] The mother places the actual breast just there where the infant is ready to create, and at the right moment.

From birth, therefore, the human being is concerned with the problem of the relationship between what is objectively perceived and what is subjectively conceived of, and in the solution of this problem there is no health for the human being who has not been started off well enough by the mother. *The intermediate area to which I am referring is the area that is allowed to the infant between primary creativity and objective perception based on reality-testing.* The transitional phenomena represent the early stages of the use of illusion, without which there is no meaning for the human being in the idea of a relationship with an object that is perceived by others as external to that being.

The idea illustrated in *Fig.* 19 is this: that at some theoretical point early in the development of every human individual an infant in a certain setting provided by the mother is capable of conceiving of the idea of something which would meet the growing need which arises out of instinctual tension. The infant cannot be said to know at first what is to be created. At this point in time the mother presents herself. In the ordinary way she gives her breast and her potential feeding urge. The mother's adaptation to the infant's needs, when good enough, gives the infant the *illusion* that there is an external reality that corresponds to the infant's own capacity to create. In other words, there is an overlap between what the mother supplies and what the child might conceive of. To the observer the child perceives what the mother actually presents, but this is not the whole truth. The infant perceives the breast only in so far as a breast could be created just there and then. There is no interchange between the mother and the infant. Psychologically the infant takes from a breast that is part of the infant, and the mother gives milk to an infant that is part of herself. In psychology, the idea of interchange is based on an illusion.

In *Fig.* 20 a shape is given to the area of illusion, to illustrate what I consider to be the main function of the transitional object and of transitional phenomena. The transitional object and the transitional phenomena start each human being off with what will always be important for them, i.e. a neutral area of experience which will not be challenged. *Of the transitional object it can be said that it is a matter of agreement between us and the baby that we will never ask the question 'Did you conceive of this or was it presented to you from*

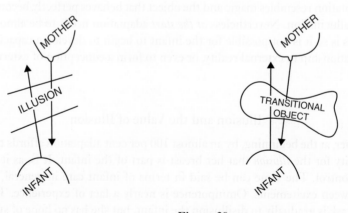

Figure 19   Figure 20

without?' The important point is that no decision on this point is expected. The question is not to be formulated.

This problem, which undoubtedly concerns the human infant in a hidden way at the beginning, gradually becomes an obvious problem on account of the fact that the mother's main task (next to providing opportunity for illusion) is disillusionment. This is preliminary to the task of weaning, and it also continues as one of the tasks of parents and educators. In other words, this matter of *illusion* is one which belongs inherently to human beings and which no individual finally solves for himself or herself, although a *theoretical* understanding of it may provide a *theoretical* solution. If things go well, in this gradual disillusionment process, the stage is set for the frustrations that we gather together under the word weaning; but it should be remembered that when we talk about the phenomena (which Klein has specifically illuminated) that cluster round weaning we are assuming the underlying process, the process by which opportunity for illusion and gradual disillusionment is provided. If illusion-disillusionment has gone astray the infant cannot attain to so normal a thing as weaning, nor to a reaction to weaning, and it is then absurd to refer to weaning at all. The mere termination of breast feeding is not a weaning.

We can see the tremendous significance of weaning in the case of the normal child. When we witness the complex reaction that is set going in a certain child by the weaning process we know that this is able to take place in that child because the illusion-disillusionment process is being carried through so well that we can ignore it while discussing actual weaning.

It is assumed here that the task of reality-acceptance is never completed, that no human being is free from the strain of relating inner and outer reality, and that relief from this strain is provided by an intermediate area of experience which is not challenged (arts, religion, etc.) (cf. Riviere, 1936). This intermediate area is in direct continuity with the play area of the small child who is 'lost' in play.

In infancy this intermediate area is necessary for the initiation of a relationship between the child and the world, and is made possible by good enough mothering at the early critical phase. Essential to all this is continuity (in time) of the external emotional environment and of particular elements in the physical environment such as the transitional object or objects.

The transitional phenomena are allowable to the infant because of the parents' intuitive recognition of the strain inherent in objective perception, and we do not challenge the infant in regard to subjectivity or objectivity just here where there is the transitional object.

Should an adult make claims on us for our acceptance of the objectivity of his subjective phenomena we discern or diagnose madness. If, however, the adult can manage to enjoy the personal intermediate area without making claims, then we can acknowledge our own corresponding intermediate areas, and are pleased to find examples of overlapping, that is to say common experience between members of a group in art or religion or philosophy.

I wish to draw particular attention to the paper by Wulff, referred to above, in which clinical material is given illustrating exactly that which I am referring to under the heading of transitional objects and transitional phenomena. There is a difference between my point of view and that of Wulff which is reflected in my use of this special term and his use of the term 'fetish object'. A study of Wulff's paper seems to show that in using the word fetish he has taken back to infancy something that belongs in ordinary theory to the sexual perversions. I am not able to find in his article sufficient room for the consideration of the child's transitional object as a healthy early experience. Yet I do consider that transitional phenomena are healthy and universal. Moreover if we extend the use of the word fetish to cover normal phenomena we shall perhaps be losing some of the value of the term.

I would prefer to retain the word fetish to describe the object that is employed on account of a *delusion* of a maternal phallus. I would then go further and say that we must keep a place for the *illusion* of a maternal phallus, that is to say, an idea that is universal and not pathological. If we shift the accent now from the object on to the word illusion we get near to the infant's transitional object; the importance lies in the concept of illusion, a universal in the field of experience.

Following this, we can allow the transitional object to be potentially a maternal phallus but originally the breast, that is to say, the thing created by the infant and at the same time provided from the environment. In this way I think that a study of the infant's use of the transitional object and of transitional phenomena in general may throw light on the origin of the fetish object and of fetishism. There is something to be lost, however, in working backwards from the psychopathology of fetishism to the transitional phenomena which belong to the beginnings of experience and which are inherent in healthy emotional development.

Summary

Attention is drawn to the rich field for observation provided by the earliest experiences of the healthy infant as expressed principally in the relationship to the first possession.

This first possession is related backwards in time to auto-erotic phenomena and fist- and thumb-sucking, and also forwards to the first soft animal or doll and to hard toys. It is related both to the external object (mother's breast) and to internal objects (magically introjected breast), but is distinct from each.

The transitional objects and transitional phenomena belong to the realm of illusion which is at the basis of initiation of experience. This early stage in development is made possible by the mother's special capacity for making adaptation to the needs of her infant, thus allowing the infant the illusion that what the infant creates really exists.

This intermediate area of experience, unchallenged in respect of its belonging to inner or external (shared) reality, constitutes the greater part of the infant's experience and throughout life is retained in the intense experiencing that belongs to the arts and to religion and to imaginative living, and to creative scientific work.

A positive value of illusion can therefore be stated.

An infant's transitional object ordinarily becomes gradually decathected, especially as cultural interests develop.

In psychopathology:

Addiction can be stated in terms of regression to the early stage at which the transitional phenomena are unchallenged.

Fetishism can be described in terms of a persistence of a specific object or type of object dating from infantile experience in the transitional field, linked with the delusion of a maternal phallus.

Pseudologia fantastica and thieving can be described in terms of an individual's unconscious urge to bridge a gap in continuity of experience in respect of a transitional object.

Notes

1 Based on a paper read before the British Psycho-Analytical Society on 30th May, 1951. *Int. J. Psycho-Anal.*, Vol. XXXIV, 1953.

2 It is necessary to stress that the word used here is 'possession' and not 'object'. In the typed version distributed to members I did in fact use the word 'object' (instead of 'possession') in one place by mistake, and this led to confusion in the discussion. It was pointed out that the first *Not–Me object*

is usually taken to be the breast. The reader's attention is drawn to the use of the word 'transitional' in many places by Fairbairn (1952, p. 35.).

3   A recent example is the blanket-doll of the child in the film *A Two-year-old Goes to Hospital* by James Robertson (Tavistock Clinic), cf. also Robertson *et al.* (1952).

4   Here there could possibly be an explanation for the use of the term 'wool-gathering', which means: inhabiting the transitional or intermediate area.

5   cf. Scott (1955).

6   There are excellent examples in the one article I have found on this same subject. Wulff ('Fetishism and Object Choice in Early Childhood', *Psychoanal. Quart.*, 1946, 15, p. 450) is clearly studying this same phenomenon, but he calls the objects 'fetish objects'. It is not clear to me that this term is correct, and I discuss this below. I did not actually know of Wulff's paper until I had written my own, but it gave me great pleasure and support to find the subject had already been considered worthy of discussion by a colleague. See also Abraham (1916) and Lindner (1879).

7   The mother had 'learned from her first child that it was a good idea to give one bottle feed while breast feeding', that is, to allow for the positive value of substitutes for herself, and by this means she achieved easier weaning than with X.

8   See also Freud (1921), p. 65.

9   One effect, and the main effect, of failure of the mother in this respect at the start of an infant's life, is discussed clearly (in my view) by Marion Milner (1952, p. 181). She shows that because of the mother's failure there is brought about a premature ego development, with precocious sorting out of a bad from a good object. The period of illusion (or my Transitional Phase) is disturbed. In analysis or in various activities in ordinary life an individual can be seen to be going on seeking the valuable resting-place of illusion. Illusion in this way has its positive value. See also Freud (1950).

10   I include the whole technique of mothering. When it is said that the first object is the breast, the word 'breast' is used, I believe, to stand for the technique of mothering as well as for the actual flesh. It is not impossible for a mother to be a good-enough mother (in my way of putting it) with a bottle for the actual feeding. If this wide meaning of the word 'breast' is kept in mind, and maternal technique is seen to be included in the total meaning of the term, then there is a bridge forming between the wording of Melanie Klein's statement of early history and that of Anna Freud. The only difference left is one of dates, which is in fact an unimportant difference which will automatically disappear in the course of time.

References

Freud, Sigmund (1923). *The Ego and the Id*. Standard Edition, Vol. 19.

Hoffer, Willi (1949). Mouth, Hand, and Ego-Integration. *Psychoanal. Study Child*, 3/4.

Klein, Melanie (1932). *The Psycho-Analysis of Children*. Rev. edn. London: Hogarth Press and the Institute of Psycho-Analysis, 1949.

Milner, M. (1952). Aspects of Symbolism in Comprehension of the Not-Self. *Int. J. Psycho-Anal.*, 33.

Riviere, Joan (1936). On the Genesis of Psychical Conflict in Earliest Infancy. *Int. J. Psycho-Anal.*, 17.

Stevenson, O. (1954). The First Treasured Possession: A Study of the Part Played by specially Loved Objects and Toys in the Lives of Certain Children. *Psychoanal. Study Child*, 9.

Wulff, M. (1946). Fetishism and Object Choice in Early Childhood . *Psychoanal. Quart.*, 15.

CHAPTER 7

Trauma Studies and the Literature of the US South

Lisa Hinrichsen

Lisa Hinrichsen is Assistant Professor of English at the University of Arkansas. She is currently revising a manuscript on the roles trauma, fantasy, and misrecognition play in modern and contemporary southern literature. She holds a PhD in English from Boston University.

Southern literature and its criticism have long recognized the roles that memory, trauma, and history play in the development of culture, but criticism about "the mind of the South" has historically been problematic: riddled by Oedipal anxieties and fascinations, much of this work has served to replay and reinforce the notion that, as Faulkner put it, "The past is never dead. It's not even past" (81).[1] Yet in the wake of postmodern and postcolonial studies, gender studies, and trauma and memory studies, southern studies has recently begun to reexamine its own historical construction, representation, and development, questioning notions of self-identity, history, and community, and complicating what it means to remember. Drawing on trauma studies, which bequeaths a theoretical framework and methodology to southern studies' key concepts of "memory" and "history," has been an increasingly popular move, especially within the theoretically inflected "New Southern Studies."[2] This essay briefly historicizes and surveys the rise of contemporary trauma theory, notes the impact that these theories have had on southern literary criticism, evaluates the role that depictions of injury play in the literature of the South, and assesses the usefulness of trauma theory for understanding events such as slavery, segregation, racism, and political violence. To historicize and contextualize trauma means recognizing the fissures within the concept and understanding the limitations of it as a descriptive term and organizing category. While the term "trauma" originally had a physical meaning – it comes from the ancient Greek word for "wound" and

Original publication details: Lisa Hinrichsen, "Trauma Studies and the Literature of the US South." *Literature Compass* 10.8 (2013), pp. 605–617. Reproduced with permission from John Wiley & Sons.

Literary Theory: An Anthology, Third Edition. Edited by Julie Rivkin and Michael Ryan.
© 2017 John Wiley & Sons, Ltd. Published 2017 by John Wiley & Sons, Ltd.

its primary denotation is invasive bodily injury – in modernity, through the work of Jean-Martin Charcot, Pierre Janet, Joseph Breuer, and Sigmund Freud, it accrued mental as well as physical meanings and came to refer to both individual and collective processes. As Judith Herman (1992) has noted, trauma has had a history of "episodic amnesia" because "the subject provokes such intense controversy that it periodically becomes anathema" (7); as she remarks, it periodically erupts into public consciousness in conjunction with certain charged social and political movements.

As a history of the term reveals, trauma is a concept closely tied to modernity. The professional codification of the concept came largely from four main branches of medical thinking: Anglo-American legal medicine, French studies on hysteria, German social medicine, and modern war psychiatry (Lerner and Micale 21). The modern understanding of trauma can be traced to the work of the British physician John Erichsen, who during the 1860s identified signs of trauma (somatic symptoms, repetitive behaviors) in victims suffering from the emotional aftershocks of railway accidents; the Berlin neurologist Paul Oppenheim subsequently gave this psychic state the name 'traumatic neurosis' (Leys 3). Much of the early work on trauma emerges from work on hysteria by Charcot and Janet, and later by Breuer and Freud in their *Studies on Hysteria* (1895), which formed part of the reorientation of the human and medical sciences away from somatically based models and toward psychological models of subjectivity.

A revised understanding arose in conjunction with the violent outbreak of World War I and the subsequent large numbers of returning soldiers with mental disorders. Composed during the war, Freud's *Beyond the Pleasure Principle* (1920) explores the issue of internal versus external assault on the ego and renders a definition of trauma through military metaphors: "We describe as 'traumatic' any excitations from outside which are powerful enough to break through the protective shield," Freud wrote, provoking "a disturbance on a large scale in the functioning of the organism's energy and [setting] in motion every possible defensive measure" (33). Yet, arguably, Freud's most significant discussion on the subject occurs in *Moses and Monotheism* (1939), written while he was living in exile in England after the outbreak of World War II. Here, Freud, acutely aware of the complex temporal aspects of trauma, compares the "forgetting" of monotheism in Judaism to the latency of the man who walks away from a train accident, physically unharmed but suffering from belated psychical and motor symptoms. *Moses and Monotheism* also marks a methodological shift: Freud develops the beginnings of an understanding of trauma not as an individual but as a collective phenomenon, a move debated in contemporary theoretical work, and struggles to explain its transgenerational persistence.

The origin of contemporary trauma studies can be dated to 1980, when the American Psychiatric Association officially recognized Post-Traumatic Stress Disorder (PTSD). As Judith Herman and Anne Whitehead argue, the formal acknowledgment of PTSD was the result of aggressive political campaigning by Vietnam veterans seeking to raise public awareness about the ongoing psychological effects of combat exposure. As Whitehead writes, this was a significant cultural moment, marking widespread recognition that "a psychiatric disorder could be wholly environmentally determined and that a traumatic event occurring in adulthood could have lasting psychological consequences" (2004, 2). "Trauma theory," as a distinct field of humanistic study that sought to understand the literary, cultural, and ethical implications of trauma, began to emerge in the early 1990s. At a cultural moment in which literary theory was seen as being irrelevant or indifferent to "real-world" issues of history, politics, and ethics, trauma theory gained ubiquity as a way to reinvigorate humanistic work with ethical and political potency. Cathy Caruth (1995, 1996), Shoshana Felman (1992, 2002), and Geoffrey Hartman (1994, 1996) became early investigators of the relationship between trauma and literature, examining the ways in which psychoanalytical theory and literature engage in a complex dialogue about how injury is experienced, remembered, and represented. Felman and Dori Laub's *Testimony: Crisis of Witnessing in Literature, Psychoanalysis and History* (1992) and Caruth's *Trauma: Explorations in Memory* (1995) were two landmark edited volumes that sought to make trauma studies an interdisciplinary dialogue that could combine work by literary critics, sociologists, archivists, filmmakers, and psychiatrists; Caruth's *Unclaimed Experience: Trauma, Narrative and History* (1996) followed, quickly becoming a seminal publication in an emerging field (the term "trauma theory" [72] first appears in *Unclaimed Experience*). Meanwhile, psychologists and literary critics were engaged in expanding Holocaust studies with new psychological and literary dimensions, drawing attention to issues of transference, sublimity, working through and acting out, and deferred meaning. Work by Dominick La Capra (1996, 1998, 2000), James E. Young (1988, 1993), Eric Santner (1993), Robert Jay Lifton (2000), Marianne Hirsch (1997, 2012), and Michael Rothberg (2000, 2009), among others, sought to understand how the Holocaust as a traumatic event makes fundamental demands on representation.

Caruth's and Felman's work echoes the definition of trauma in the American Psychiatric Association's *Diagnostic and Statistical Manual of Mental Disorders* and builds on the work of scientist Bessel A. Van der Kolk and a selective reading of Freud, while also utilizing deconstructive and poststructuralist models of reading. As such, their work opens itself to larger critiques over the role dissociation plays in the experience of trauma, the validity of importing medical models into literary models, and the way in which the American Psychiatric Association's definition of PTSD participates in a process that converts what is often a social and political problem into an individual psychopathology. For Caruth, trauma fundamentally involves a crisis of representation, and her work emphasizes poststructuralist tropes of difficulty, rupture, aporia, and impossibility, positioning the traumatic experience as radically displaced, unable to be integrated into schemes of prior knowledge, instead remaining positioned *between* times: trauma is, in her definition, "not known in the first instance" and "not locatable in the simple violent or original event in an individual's past, but rather in the way that its very unassimilated nature – the way it was precisely *not known* in the first instance – returns to haunt the survivor later on" (4). Both Caruth's and Felman's work insists on an opposition between traumatic event and narrative possibility; together they emphasize the need for a changed critical – and ethical – practice and a new mode of reading and listening, in which intersubjectivity plays a key role in bearing witness to how wound becomes voice (Caruth ix). As Felman writes in *Testimony: Crises of Witnessing in Literature, Psychoanalysis, and History*, bearing witness demands an act of testimony, which, as she sees it, encompasses "the political dimension of oppression and the ethical dimension of resistance" (12).

Despite criticism of their work – Susannah Radstone, for example, has critiqued its underlying model of subjectivity and its relation to theories of referentiality and representation, and Ruth Leys, in *Trauma: A Genealogy* (2000), has vehemently argued against what she sees as Caruth's universalization of the concept and her effacement of the distinction between victims and perpetrators – it has come to form the dominant model of trauma studies. The continued importance of Caruth's and Felman's work lies in the way they elaborate and revise Freudian concepts in line with deconstructionist and poststructuralist modes of reading. Some of the many literary and cultural studies texts that draw on and respond to Caruth's and Felman's claims include Anne Whitehead's *Trauma Fiction* (2004), Laurie Vickroy's *Trauma and Survival in Contemporary Fiction* (2002), E. Ann Kaplan's *Trauma Culture: The Politics of Terror and Loss in Media and Literature* (2005), Leigh Gilmore's *The Limits of Autobiography: Trauma and Testimony* (2001), Nancy K. Miller and Jason Tougaw's edited volume *Extremities: Trauma, Testimony, and Community* (2002), Judith Greenberg's collection *Trauma at Home: After 9/11* (2003), Deborah M. Horovitz's *Literary Trauma: Sadism, Memory, and Sexual Violence in American Women's Fiction* (2000), Michelle Balaev's *The Nature of Trauma in American Novels* (2012), Sarah Anderson's *Readings of Trauma, Madness, and the Body* (2012), Julie Goodspeed-Chadwick's *Modernist Women Writers and War: Trauma and the Female Body in Djuana Barnes, H.D., and Gertrude Stein* (2011), Jennifer L. Griffiths' *Traumatic Possessions: The Body and Memory in African American Women's Writing and Performance* (2009), Anne Rothe's *Popular Trauma Culture: Selling the Pain of Others in the Mass Media* (2011) and Ann Cvetkovich's *An Archive of Feelings: Trauma, Sexuality, and Lesbian Public Cultures* (2003).

As these titles reveal, trauma theory has been adopted not only by scholars working on the politics and aesthetics of literary form but also more broadly by scholars examining issues of public culture, mass media, and the politics of gender, race, and sexuality. The field has long been critically self-reflective, and a surplus of work explores anew the history of the concept. Texts such as Mark Micale and Paul Lerner's *Traumatic Pasts* (2001) and Roger Luckhurst's *The Trauma Question* (2008) outline with more detail the manner in which trauma has been historically constructed and contingent on social context, and work by Jeffrey Alexander (2004, 2012) and Arthur Neal (1998) examine trauma's relation to discourses of nationalism, imperialism, and politics. Kali Tal's *Worlds of Hurt: Reading the Literatures of Trauma* (1995) draws on a feminist politics that underscores how systemic violence shapes everyday life; Tal discusses critical approaches to Holocaust testimony, literature by Vietnam War veterans, and published testimonies by female survivors of incest and child abuse, focusing on social appropriations of individual testimonies. Similarly, in *Serial Killers: Death and Life in America's Wound Culture* (1998), Mark Seltzer examines the formation of the public sphere around the pathological visualization of suffering and violence. One of the results of this profusion of work on trauma has been the tendency to see victimhood everywhere: in *Hystories* (1998), for example, Elaine Showalter criticizes the hysterical "victim" culture in the United States, and in *Post-Traumatic Culture: Injury and Interpretation in the Nineties* (1998), Kirby Farrell investigates how trauma functions as an "enabling fiction, an explanatory tool for managing unquiet minds in an overwhelming world" (x).

The surge of interest in theories of collective trauma have also raised questions regarding the universality and limits of victimhood. Beginning with Maurice Halbwachs' conception of *collective memory* (1925), Freud's musings in *Moses and Monotheism*, the work of Kai Erikson (1976), Arthur G. Neal (1998) and Ron Eyerman (2001) and Pierre Nora's conceptualization of *lieux de mémoire* (1984–1992), and extending to contemporary work such as Paul Connerton's *How Societies Remember* (1989) and Jeffrey Alexander's *Trauma: A Social Theory* (2012), which draws attention to postcolonial trauma and civil institutions, the concepts of collective trauma and collective memory have remained a contentious issue. While some theorists assume an unproblematic translation from individual to collective trauma, others caution that a simple metaphorical extension may be both intellectually reductive and politically irresponsible. While critics like Dominick LaCapra in *Writing History, Writing Trauma* (2000) employ the psychoanalytic categories of "acting out" (Freud's term for behavior marked by repetitive, unconscious actions, and fantasies) and "working through" (repetition altered by interpretation, capable of arresting unconscious repetitions) to analyze collective responses to historical events such as the Holocaust, there remain a number of theoretical loose ends in conceptualizations of collective trauma: how exactly is injury mediated among a collective group? Is collective or communal violence perhaps best seen as a political and ideological issue rather than a psychological one?

Finally, the definition of trauma has been further complicated by popular culture's extension of its psychoanalytical definition – what Jeffrey C. Alexander has called trauma's "embeddedness in everyday life and language" (2) – and its untethered use as a metaphor for the "memoro-politics" of a wide variety of psychic and cultural struggles, which often divert focus away from the individual. The feminist psychotherapist Laura S. Brown, for example, has argued that traumatic experiences of people of color, women, gays and lesbians, lower-class people, and people with disabilities often go unrecognized because current definitions are based on the experiences of dominant groups in Western society. Brown stresses the need to expand our understanding from sudden catastrophic events to "insidious trauma," by which she means "the traumatogenic effects of oppression that are not necessarily overtly violent or threatening to bodily well-being at the given moment but that do violence to the soul and spirit" (107). The result is a revitalized focus on what surrounds suffering: politics, communities, institutions, experiences, and environments, marking a movement away from a problematic politics in which certain types of pain are privileged.

Trauma and the U.S. South

Despite the complications of defining and historicizing trauma, several studies have gestured toward the potential usefulness of trauma studies in articulating the South as a site of particular cultural and psychological conflict. The U.S. South has long been seen as a terrain of trauma, a space where American violence is projected and "contained," and its history is marked by removals and diasporas, including Native American genocide and dispossession; the slavery, migration, and displacement of African Americans; legacies of forced, unpaid labor; and brutal deeds and violent institutions. The sense that lost histories still linger is vividly felt in the sense of inherited historical consciousness in contemporary southern writing. As Barbara Ladd states,

> Memory continues to be important in the determination of southernists to interpret or reproduce orality and performance, to attend to what writing erases or elides, and especially to attend to what United States historiography (plain and literary) has obscured in its commitment to cultural naturalism (1636).

In bequeathing a sense of grounding specificity and locality to trauma as a general concept, southern studies scholars have been conceptualizing the differing functions of temporal and spatial memorials (narrative, ritual, history, monuments); uncovering and articulating the political uses of mourning; exploring the relationship between cultural memory and cultural amnesia; examining forms of aesthetic representation and memorialization; and articulating the power of countermemories in the political and narrative history of the South. The vocabulary and paradigms of trauma studies, when rooted in the historical and cultural specificity of southern space and place, have enabled further theorizing of the field's longstanding key concepts of memory and history, though there is still a great deal of work to be done, especially in relation to the diversity and complexity of identities and histories found in the region.

Scholars within southern studies have long been attentive to personal and historical trauma but have not always named it as such. Historian C. Vann Woodward's sense of the "burden" of southern history (1993) and its experience of defeat frames southerners as fundamentally permeated with historical consciousness. Other historians, such as C. Hugh Holman, in his *The Immoderate Past: The Southern Writer and History* (1977) and Louis D. Rubin (1989) note a particularly southern preoccupation with memory. Texts such as Anne Goodwyn Jones and Susan Donaldson's edited collection *Haunted Bodies: Gender and Southern Texts* (1997), the work of Patricia Yaeger in *Dirt and Desire: Reconstructing Southern Women's Writing, 1930–1990* (2000), and the sociologist Avery F. Gordon's *Ghostly Matters: Haunting and the Sociological Imagination* (1996) find articulation for trauma's eerie ability to escape our ability to rationalize or analyze it by using the language of the supernatural, the grotesque, and the spectacular, describing its effects through metaphors of "haunting."

More recently, Fitzhugh Brundage, in *Where These Memories Grow: History, Memory, and Southern Identity* (2000) and *The Southern Past: A Clash of Race and Memory* (2005), examines the meaning and use of the southern past, underscoring the political and ideological work of certain versions of history – especially ones that privilege the Civil War, defining it as traumatic for white southerners – in establishing White racial privilege and power, while also noting how black countermemories fueled the Civil Rights movement. Wolfgang Schivelbusch, in *The Culture of Defeat: On National Trauma, Mourning, and Recovery* (2003), details the state of the South after the Civil War, which he positions as a "national trauma" akin to France in the wake of the Franco-Prussian War and Germany following World War I, and notes how, in the aftermath of military defeat, myths of cultural superiority, such as nostalgic plantation legends, flourish as means of explaining the experience of loss. As Tara McPherson notes in *Reconstructing Dixie* (2003), these modes of imaginative fantasy continue to resonate, for the South "remains at once the site of the trauma of slavery and also the mythic location of a vast nostalgia industry" (3). Simultaneously a geographical space and an imaginative site, the U.S. South forms a locus for examining the relationship of social and individual memory to structures of power, including the discursive construction of experience.

While a large body of criticism has devoted itself to the way that the Civil War and Lost Cause mythologies have "haunted" the South and its literature, theories of memory, and trauma have been a productive part of other aspects of the discourse surrounding the South. Work on the plantation as a site of memory, such as Jessica Adams' *Wounds of Returning* (2007), reveals how the landscape of the "postslavery plantation," as a site of cultural trauma, has been transformed by tourism and consumer culture (5). Elizabeth Christine Russ's *The Plantation in the Postslavery Imagination* (2009) emphasizes how plantation-era modes of being and thinking refuse historical boundaries, affecting several generations. Other work has attended to how literature has memorialized and aestheticized violent historical events: Harriet Pollack and Christopher Metress's edited collection *Emmett Till in Literary Memory and Imagination* (2008) takes a paramount moment in racial history as its focal point, exploring how Till's brutal murder has been rendered by writers such as William Bradford Huie, James Baldwin, Langston Hughes, Gwendolyn

Brooks, Audre Lorde, Anne Moody, Nicolas Guillén, Aimé Césaire, Bebe Moore Campbell, and Lewis Nordan; Metress stresses how Emmett Till's murder functions as what Ron Eyerman in his work on slavery and African American identity calls a "cultural trauma" or "tear in the social fabric" (Metress 17). The aesthetic impact of Till's traumatic murder has also been explored by Ted Atkinson in "Hellhound on His Trail: Faulknerian Blood-guilt and the Traumatized Form of Lewis Nordan's *Wolf Whistle*" (2011); here, Atkinson argues that Nordan's surreal, defamiliarized style reflects "the limiting and haunting historical and cultural narratives that the author is compelled to rehearse," including, but not limited to, negotiating the long shadow of Faulkner's influence on what it means to tell about the South. Other key historical traumas and their impact on southern literature have also been explored: David A. Davis (2011), for example, has examined Katherine Anne Porter's "Pale Horse, Pale Rider," and its rendering of the Influenza Pandemic of 1918; Daniel Y. Kim (2009) has explored the impact of the Korean War in Susan Choi's *The Foreign Student*; Julie Buckner Armstrong (2011) has investigated the impact of Mary Turner's lynching on a range of literature, journalism, and artistic representation, including the "Kabnis" section of Jean Toomer's *Cane* and Angelina Weld Grimké's short story "Goldie"; and Lisa Hinrichsen (2008) has detailed the influence of the Vietnam War in Bobbie Ann Mason's *In Country*.

Additional work has veered from focusing on how specific historical traumas have been registered to examining larger issues of social structures, economies, and aesthetics. A notable special issue of *The Southern Literary Journal* in the Spring of 2008, edited by Minrose Gwin, focused on history, memory, and forgetting, and essays by Ruth Salvaggio, Susan V. Donaldson, Daniel Cross Turner, Rebecca Mark, Pearl McHaney, and others drew attention to issues of intertextuality, nostalgia, melancholia, and sublimination in southern literature and cinema, while also underscoring the impact of trauma studies as a critical approach. Melanie Benson Taylor's work on the trauma of capitalism in *Disturbing Calculations: The Economics of Identity in Postcolonial Southern Literature, 1912–2002* (2008) examines how structures of calculations and numbers, historically indebted to the traumatic history of the South as a site of capitalism and colonialism, function to determine social and racial hierarchies and establish individual worth and identity, perpetuating traumatic patterns; and, in *Reconstructing the Native South: American Indian Literature and the Lost Cause* (2012), Benson examines Native American removal, economic dispossession, and recuperation, underscoring the way that southern literary criticism has long tended to omit and obscure the story of American Indians in the South, forming modes of traumatic erasure. Michael Kreyling focuses on topic of memory in *The South That Wasn't There: Postsouthern Memory and History* (2010). Building upon Martyn Bone's work on the "postsouthern" and Scott Romine's work on the mechanically reproduced and media-made "post-South," Kreyling explores a diversity of texts and films in which memory and history take center stage, probing difficult issues such as the applicability of Holocaust and trauma studies to the narrative remembrance of slavery and the role that collective memory plays in key canonical texts like Toni Morrison's *Beloved*. More recently, Daniel Cross Turner's *Southern Crossings: Poetry, Memory, and the Transcultural South* (2012), examines the work of a variety of southern poets, from Robert Penn Warren and James Dickey to Betty Adcock, and Charles Wright, Yusef Komunyakaa, and Natasha Trethewey, reconceiving in the process theories of collective remembrance on regional, national, and transnational levels, while examining trauma alongside other modes of memory, including nostalgia, primal and cartographic memory, and countermemory.

Trauma theory's privileging of the testimonial power of literature resonates with the emphasis in southern studies on the aesthetic power of certain forms of literature that bear witness to difficult histories. As Felman and Laub argue in *Testimony*, in order to address "the consequent, ongoing, as yet unresolved crisis of history," one must turn to literature, for "literature becomes a witness, and perhaps the only witness, to the crisis within history which precisely cannot be articulated, witnessed in the given categories of history itself" (xviii). Neo–slave narratives, such as Edward P. Jones' *The Known World* (2003), Sherley Anne Williams' *Dessa Rose* (1986), Valerie Martin's *Property* (2003), and Octavia E. Butler's *Kindred* (1979) revise both the content and form of the historical record as they raise postmodern questions about how that record has been constructed through erasure. Works such as William Styron's *The Confessions of Nat Turner* (1967), Alex Haley's *Roots* (1976), and Ernest Gaines's *The Autobiography of Miss Jane Pittman* (1971) turn back to the past to probe the origins and consequences of racial violence. Literary memoirs, such as Lillian Smith's *Killers of the Dream* (1949) and Anne Moody's *Coming of Age in Mississippi* (1968) assert the impact of traumatic historical events on individual memories. Contemporary texts like Morrison's *Beloved* (1987) have become magnets for work on trauma: there has been a surge of work that addresses *Beloved*'s portrayal of physical and emotional injury and the relationship between individual recovery and the complex sociopolitical heritage that the novel registers in aesthetically inventive ways. Critics such as J. Brooks Bouson (1999) have focused on how Morrison utilizes literary techniques that mirror at a formal level the effects of trauma, noting the novel's insistence on circling back to violent events, and its disrupted timeline, structures of belatedness, and withholding of important information, as well as its literalization of the haunting past through a ghost. Roger Luckhurst, author of *The Trauma Question* (2008), addresses *Beloved*'s status as "a formative text in literary trauma studies" (90), and Evelyn Jaffe Schreiber's *Race, Trauma and Home in the Novels of Toni Morrison* (2010) examines issues of slavery and inherited trauma in Morrison's novels, paying particular attention to the "core cultural trauma of slavery" (1).

The work of William Faulkner has also frequently been read through the lens of trauma theory: Greg Forter, in "Freud, Faulkner, Caruth: Trauma and the Politics of Literary Form" (2007) and "Faulkner, Trauma, and the Uses of Crime Fiction" (2007), details Faulkner's relationship to trauma theory. Richard Godden's work, in *William Faulkner: An Economy of Complex Words* (2007) and *Fictions of Labor: William Faulkner and the South's Long Revolution* (1997) marks how Faulkner's late fiction registers the economic and racial traumas of the South's delayed modernization; in both books, Godden links stylistic aspects of Faulkner's writing to a generative social trauma – a labor trauma – which constitutes its formal core. And in *"Not Even Past": Race, Historical Trauma, and Subjectivity in Faulkner, Larsen, and Van Vechten* (2010), Dorothy Stringer examines William Faulkner's *Sanctuary* and *Requiem for a Nun* (1951), drawing upon the work of Judith Butler, Joan Riviere, and Freud to illuminate how these novels stage fantasies about race and gender and illustrate the racialization of trauma as a discursive phenomenon. In Stringer's reading, Faulkner frames slavery and institutionalized anti–Black racism as key structural determinants of national history and individual identity.

Issues of collective memory have long been a focal point in southern studies, as each generation of Americans since the Civil War has had to deal with the structural and generational memory of slavery. Whereas dominant (White) culture holds the collective memory of slavery as a moral, political, or economic wrong righted by the Civil War and a century of activism that followed, African Americans hold countermemories based on ongoing experiences of discrimination. As Leigh Anne Duck has powerfully articulated in *The Nation's Region: Southern Modernism, Segregation, and U.S. Nationalism* (2006), White southerners have relied upon an identity narrative closely bound to specific modes of memorializing the past in ways that block and prevent ethical modes of witnessing. As she demonstrates, strategies of White southern public memorialization have historically "cast purportedly traditional values, including White supremacy, as immutable elements in a culture that maintained an anomalous relationship to time" (159). The construction of the South as backwards, damaged, and anti-modern was part of larger national interests that necessitated seeing the region as the figure of an otherness to the nation at large, and as a site where national racist practice and ideology could be contained and localized. The South's supposedly specific identity crisis is thus part and parcel of a larger national obsession with racial trauma, White victimization, and American "innocence."

Thus, scholars such as Deborah Cohn and Jon Smith (2004) have reminded us that though the South has long been seen as the exception within American exceptionalism – and as a particular space of trauma – it is necessary to "look away" from an insular view of the South to instead explore links between the South and developing countries with similar economic histories of belated capitalist modernization, slavery, and exploitation of labor and raw materials. In recent years, southern studies has embraced work which sets trauma in transatlantic terms: Dave Eggers' post-Katrina novel *Zeitoun* (2009), which centers on a Syrian immigrant and his American-born family; Erna Brodber's diasporic novel *Louisiana* (1994), which features connections between the U.S. South and the Caribbean; and Cynthia Shearer's *The Celestial Jukebox* (2004), which intertwines the stories of a Chinese-American grocer and a young African immigrant and sets them against a soundtrack of American melodies that compose a global pop culture. Scholars such as Maureen Ryan have explored how novels like Lan Cao's *Monkey Bridge* (1997) draw parallels between traumatic experience in South Vietnam and the U.S. South, and work has been done on other writers who have confronted the trauma of the Vietnam War – Jayne Anne Phillips, James Webb, Winston Groom, Barry Hannah, and Robert Olen Butler – through a particularly southern lens. Meanwhile, Deborah Cohn, in *History and Memory in the Two Souths: Recent Southern and Spanish American Fiction* (1999) and George Handley, in *Postslavery Literature in the Americas: Family Portraits in Black and White* (2000), have explored interconnections based on shared traumatic histories between the U.S. South, Latin America, and the Caribbean.

Furthermore, New Orleans, with its African, French, Spanish, Caribbean foundations, and transatlantic history, has been a site of national trauma and global anguish in the wake of Hurricane Katrina (2005). The growing collection of post-Katrina literature, which offers opportunities for scholars working with trauma theory, includes John Biguenet's acclaimed plays, *Rising Water* (2006) and *Shotgun* (2009); Tom Piazza's novel *City of Refuge* (2008) and his post-Katrina polemic *Why New Orleans Matters* (2005); James Lee Burke's novel *The Tin Roof Blowdown* (2007), as well as his short story collection *Jesus Out to Sea* (2007); Jesmyn Ward's novel *Salvage the Bones* (2011); Chris Rose's essay collection *1 Dead in Attic* (2005, 2007); inventive memoirs such as Jerry Ward's *The Katrina Papers: A Journal of Trauma and Recovery* (2009) and Joshua Clark's *Heart Like Water* (2007); poetry by Raymond McDaniel, Patricia Smith, and Katie Ford; as well as numerous collections, such as Jarret Lofstead and Joe Longo's *Life in the Wake: Fiction from Post-Katrina New Orleans* (2007). A wave of graphic novels has also emerged, forming innovative visual and narrative responses to the problem of writing trauma: Brad Benischek's *Revacuation* (2007), Mat Johnson's *Dark Rain* (2011), and Josh Neufeld's *A.D.: New Orleans After the Deluge* (2009) are notable. Many of these plays, poems, essays, memoirs, and graphic novels make political as well as aesthetic statements, highlighting the failed crisis management, the endemic racial and economic inequity, the lasting environmental damage, and the mix of carelessness and compassion that defined the human response to the disaster and contributed to its traumatic impact.

Theories of the Global South and conceptualizations of the U.S. South as a postcolonial space, when combined with a focus on trauma, stress the need to rethink some fundamental aspects of current theories, for trauma has been a category largely codified by Western medical and psychological institutions and grounded in events and processes of Western modernity. Though Cathy Caruth wrote that in "a catastrophic age" such as ours, "trauma itself may provide the very link between cultures" and between disparate historical experiences (1995, 11), there has been insufficient exploration of how Western theoretical and diagnostic models translate into non-Western contexts, and how conceptions of memory in non-Western contexts challenge and revise dominant Western conceptions. If, as Caruth argues, "history is precisely the way we are implicated in each other's traumas" (*Unclaimed* 24), then Western histories are, some scholars suggest, tied up with histories of colonial trauma. While two collections of essays, *Trauma and Dissociation in a Cross-Cultural Perspective: Not Just a North American Phenomenon* (2006) and *Honoring Differences: Cultural Issues in the Treatment of Trauma and Loss* (1999, 2010, 2011), have explored the relationship between cultural difference and trauma, and postcolonial critics and theorists like Jill Bennett, Sam Durrant, Linda Hutcheon, David Lloyd, and Rebecca Saunders have suggested theorizing colonization in terms of the infliction of a collective trauma, effectively reconceptualizing postcolonialism as a post-traumatic cultural formation, scholars within southern studies have just started to explore these interconnections.

Despite trauma's conceptual thorniness and complicated history, southern studies seems set to foster sustained engagement with it. As scholars of the U.S. South continue to explore the Global South, moving away from an outdated model of regional exceptionalism, the plantation, as site and source of traumatic inheritance, will continue to be a focal interest, as will further conceptualizing collective cultural trauma. Comparative work will necessitate additional investigations of what trauma means across an array of cultural, historical, political, and social experiences. As myths about the monolithic homogeneity of "the South" continue to be deconstructed, the internal diversity of the region will foster complex modes of thinking about the relationship between racial and ethnic identity and trauma, especially in regard to African American and Native American identity. Added studies will also need to be done on late 20th and early 21st century experiences that are still being narrated – Katrina, 9/11, and continued experiences of racial, sexual, and economic trauma. As southern studies increasingly focuses on issues of mass media, including cinema, and its reception, there will likely be work on what Alison Landsberg terms "prosthetic memory," or memory enabled by mass cultural communication and commodification. Without a doubt, however, southern literary studies' continued commitment to the importance of language, and to the specificity of historical time and place, will continue to cultivate nuanced work on how literature configures and refigures trauma through the aesthetic power of narrative.

Notes

*   Correspondence: English Department, University of Arkansas, 333 Kimpel Hall, Fayetteville, AR
    72701, USA. Email: lhinrich@uark.edu
1   Quoted in *Requiem for a Nun* (1950). See also W.J. Cash's *The Mind of the South* (1941).
2   The New Southern Studies originates in Houston A. Baker, Jr. and Dana Nelson's call in a 2001
    special issue of *American Literature* on "Violence, the Body, and 'The South'" for a "new Southern
    studies […] that welcomes intellectual, multiparticipant, and revisionary complexity," and that
    embraces "the complication of old borders and terrains, [and] wishes to construct and survey a new
    scholarly map of 'The South.'" (243). This call has been continued in work published in the
    University of Georgia Press's New Southern Studies series, in publications such as Kathryn McKee
    and Annette Trefzer's special issue of *American Literature* on "Global Contexts, Local Literatures:
    The New Southern Studies" (2006), and in book-length projects such as Jon Smith and Deborah
    Cohn's edited collection *Look Away! The U.S. South in New World Studies* (2004). These projects
    rely upon a destabilized view of the South, positioning it as a porous, dynamic construct, rather
    than as an insular and contained space with fixed cultural and geographical demarcations.

Works Cited

Adams, Jessica. *Wounds of Returning: Race, Memory, and Property on the Postslavery Plantation*. Chapel
    Hill: The University of North Carolina Press, 2007.
Alexander, Jeffrey C. *Trauma: A Social Theory*. Cambridge: Polity Press, 2012.
Alexander, Jeffrey C., et al. *Cultural Trauma and Collective Identity*. Berkeley: University of California
    Press, 2004.
Anderson, Sarah. *Readings of Trauma, Madness, and the Body*. New York: Palgrave MacMillan, 2012.
Armstrong, Julie Buckner. *Mary Turner and the Memory of Lynching*. Athens, GA: U of Georgia Press,
    2011.
Atkinson, Ted. 'Hellhound on His Trail: Faulknerian Blood-guilt and the Traumatized Form of Lewis
    Nordan's *Wolf Whistle*'. *The Southern Literary Journal*. 44.1 (Fall 2011): 19–36.
Baker, Houston A. Jr., and Dana D. Nelson. 'Preface: Violence, the Body and "The South"'. *American
    Literature* 73 (2001): 243.
Balaev, Michelle. *The Nature of Trauma in American Novels*. Evanston, IL: Northwestern UP, 2012.
Benischek, Brad. *Revacuation*. New Orleans: Press Street, 2007.
Benson, Melanie. *Disturbing Calculations: The Economics of Identity in Postcolonial Southern Literature,
    1912–2002*. Athens: University of Georgia Press, 2008.
Biguenet, John. *Rising Water*. Unpublished, 2006.
Biguenet, John. *Shotgun*. New York: Dramatists Play Service, 2009.
Bouson, J. Brooks. *Quiet as It's Kept: Shame, Trauma, and Race in the Novels of Toni Morrison*. SUNY
    Press, 1999.
Brodber, Erna. *Louisiana*. London: New Beacon Books, 1994.
Brundage, W. Fitzhugh. *The Southern Past: A Clash of Race and Memory*. Cambridge: Harvard UP,
    2005.
Brundage, W. Fitzhugh, ed. *Where These Memories Grow: History, Memory, and Southern Identity*.
    Chapel Hill: U of North Carolina P, 2000.
Breuer, Joseph, and Sigmund Freud. *Studies on Hysteria*. New York: Basic Books, 2000.
Brown, Laura S. 'Not Outside the Range: One Feminist Perspective on Psychic Trauma'. *Explorations
    in Memory*. Ed. Cathy Caruth. Baltimore: Johns Hopkins UP, 1995. 100–112.
Burke, James Lee. *Jesus Out to Sea*. New York: Simon and Schuster, 2007.
Burke, James Lee. *The Tin Roof Blowdown*. New York: Simon and Schuster, 2007.
Butler, Octavia. *Kindred*. New York: Doubleday, 1979.
Cao, Lan. *Monkey Bridge*. New York: Penguin, 1997.
Caruth, Cathy, ed. *Trauma: Explorations in Memory*. Baltimore: Johns Hopkins UP, 1995.

Caruth, Cathy. *Unclaimed Experience: Trauma, Narrative, and History*. Baltimore: Johns Hopkins UP, 1996.

Cash, W.J. *The Mind of the South*. New York: Knopf, 1941.

Clark, Joshua. *Heart Like Water: Surviving Katrina and Life in Its Disaster Zone*. New York: Free Press, 2007.

Cohn, Deborah. *History and Memory in the Two Souths: Recent Southern and Spanish American Fiction*. Nashville: Vanderbilt UP, 1999.

Connerton, Paul. *How Societies Remember*. Cambridge : Cambridge UP, 1989.

Craps, Stef, and Michael Rothberg, eds. Transcultural Negotiations of Holocaust Memory. Spec. issue of *Criticism: A Quarterly for Literature and the Arts* 53.4 (2011).

Craps, Stef, 'Wor(l)ds of Grief: Traumatic Memory and Literary Witnessing in Cross-Cultural Perspective.' *Textual Practice* 24.1 (2010): 51–68.

Cvetkovich, Ann. *An Archive of Feelings: Trauma, Sexuality, and Lesbian Public Feelings*. Durham: Duke UP, 2003.

Davis, David A. 'The Forgotten Apocalypse: Katherine Anne Porter's 'Pale Horse, Pale Rider,' Traumatic Memory, and the Influenza Pandemic of 1918'. *The Southern Literary Journal*. 43.2. (Spring 2011). 55–74.

Duck, Leigh Anne. *The Nation's Region: Southern Modernism, Segregation, and U.S. Nationalism*. Athens: University of Georgia Press, 2006.

Eggers, Dave. *Zeitoun*. San Francisco: McSweeney's, 2009.

Eyerman, Ron. *Cultural Trauma: Slavery and the Formation of African American Identity*. Cambridge: Cambridge UP, 2001.

Farrell, Kirby. *Post-Traumatic Culture: Injury and Interpretation in the Nineties*. Baltimore: Johns Hopkins UP, 1998.

Faulkner, William. *Requiem for a Nun*. New York: Random House, 1951.

Felman, Shoshana, and Dori Laub, M.D. *Testimony: Crises of Witnessing in Literature, Psychoanalysis, and History*. New York: Routledge, 1992.

Felman, Shoshana, and Dori Laub, M.D. *The Juridical Unconscious: Trials and Traumas in the Twentieth Century*. Cambridge, MA: Harvard UP, 2002.

Forter, Greg. 'Faulkner, Trauma, and the Uses of Crime Fiction', in *A Companion to William Faulkner* (ed R. C. Moreland), Malden, MA, USA: Blackwell Publishing, 2007a. doi: 10.1002/9780470996881. ch23.

Forter, Greg. 'Freud, Faulkner, Caruth: Trauma and the Politics of Literary Form'. *Narrative* 15(3), (2007b). 259–285.

Freud, Sigmund. *Beyond the Pleasure Principle*. Trans. Ed. James Strachey. New York: Norton, 1961.

Freud, Sigmund. *Moses and Monotheism*. Trans. Katherine Jones. New York: Vintage, 1939.

Gaines, Ernest. *The Autobiography of Miss Jane Pittman*. New York: Dial Press, 1971.

Gilmore, Leigh. *The Limits of Autobiography: Trauma and Testimony*. Ithaca: Cornell UP, 2001.

Godden, Richard. *Fictions of Labor: William Faulkner and the South's Long Revolution*. New York and Cambridge: Cambridge UP, 1997.

Godden, Richard. *Williams Faulkner: An Economy of Complex Words*. Princeton, NJ: Princeton UP, 2007.

Goodspeed-Chadwick, Julie. *Modernist Women Writers and War: Trauma and the Female Body in Djuna Barnes, H.D., and Gertrude Stein*. Baton Rouge: Louisiana State UP, 2011.

Gordon, Avery. *Ghostly Matters: Haunting and the Sociological Imagination*. Minneapolis: University of Minnesota Press, 1996.

Greenberg, Judith. *Trauma at Home: After 9/11*. Lincoln: University of Nebraska Press, 2003.

Griffiths, Jennifer L. *Traumatic Possessions: The Body and Memory in African American Women's Writing and Performance*. Charlottesville, VA: U of Virginia P, 2009.

Halbwachs, Maurice. *The Collective Memory*. Trans. Francis J Ditter, Jr. and Vida Yazdi Ditter. New York: Harper and Row, 1925.

Haley, Alex. *Roots*. New York: Doubleday, 1976.

Handley, George. *Postslavery Literatures in the Americas: Family Portraits in Black and White*. Charlottesville: University of Virginia Press, 2000.

Hartman, Geoffrey. 'On Traumatic Knowledge and Literary Studies'. *New Literary History*. 26.3 (1995).

Herman, Judith. *Trauma and Recovery*. New York: Perseus, 1992.

Hinrichsen, Lisa. "I Can't Believe It Was Really Real': Violence, Vietnam, and Bringing War Home in Bobbie Ann Mason's *In Country'*. *The Southern Literary Journal* 40.2 (2008). 232–248.

Hirsch, Marianne. *Family Frames: Photography, Narrative and Postmemory*. Cambridge: Harvard UP, 1997.

Hirsch, Marianne. *The Generation of Postmemory: Visual Culture After the Holocaust*. New York: Columbia UP, 2012.

Holman, C. Hugh. *The Immoderate Past: The Southern Writer and History*. Athens: The University of Georgia Press, 1977.

Horovitz, Deborah M. *Literary Trauma: Sadism, Memory, and Sexual Violence in American Women's Fiction*. Albany, NY: SUNY Press, 2000.

Johnson, Mat. *Dark Rain: A New Orleans Story*. New York: Vertigo, 2011.

Jones, Anne Goodwyn, and Susan V. Donaldson, eds. *Haunted Bodies: Gender and Southern Texts*. Charlottesville and London: University Press of Virginia, 1997.

Jones, Edward P. *The Known World*. New York: Amistad/HarperCollins, 2003.

Kaplan, E. Ann. *Trauma Culture: The Politics of Terror and Loss in Media and Literature*. New Brunswick, NJ: Rutgers UP, 2005.

Kim, Daniel Y. "Bled In, Letter by Letter': Translation, Postmemory, and the Subject of Korean War: History in Susan Choi's *The Foreign Student'*. *American Literary History* 21.3 (2009): 550–583.

Kreyling, Michael. *The South That Wasn't There: Postsouthern Memory and History*. Baton Rouge: Louisiana State UP, 2010.

LaCapra, Dominick. *History and Memory After Auschwitz*. Ithaca, NY: Cornell UP, 1998.

LaCapra, Dominick. *Representing the Holocaust: History, Theory, Trauma*. Ithaca, NY: Cornell UP, 1996.

LaCapra, Dominick. *Writing History, Writing Trauma*. Baltimore: The Johns Hopkins UP, 2000.

Ladd, Barbara. 'Literary Studies: The Southern United States, 2005'. *PMLA*. No. 5. Volume 120, 2005. 1628–1639.

Landsberg, Alison. *Prosthetic Memory: The Transformation of American Remembrance in the Age of Mass Culture*. New York: Columbia UP, 2004.

Lerner, Paul, and Mark Micale. *Traumatic Pasts: History, Psychiatry, and Trauma in the Modern Age, 1870–1931*. Oxford: Oxford UP, 2001.

Leys, Ruth. *Trauma: A Genealogy*. Chicago: University of Chicago Press, 2000.

Lifton, Robert Jay. *The Nazi Doctors: Medical Killing and the Psychology of Genocide*. New York: Basic Books, 2000.

Lofstead, Jarrett and Joe, Longo. *Life in the Wake: Fiction from Post-Katrina New Orleans*. New Orleans, LA: NOLAFugees Press, 2007.

Luckhurst, Roger. *The Trauma Question*. London: Routledge, 2008.

Martin, Valerie. *Property*. New York: Nan A. Talese/Doubleday, 2003.

McPherson, Tara. *Reconstructing Dixie: Race, Gender, and Nostalgia in the Imagined South*. Durham: Duke UP, 2003.

Miller, Nancy K., and Jason Tougaw. *Extremities: Trauma, Testimony, and Community*. Champaign, IL: University of Illinois Press, 2002.

Moody, Anne. *Coming of Age in Mississippi*. New York: Dial Press, 1968.

Morrison, Toni. *Beloved*. New York: Knopf, 1987.

Nader, Kathleen, Nancy Dubrow, and B. Hudnall Stamm. *Honoring Differences: Cultural Issues in the Treatment of Trauma and Loss*. New York: Routledge, 1999.

Neal, Arthur G. *National Trauma and Collective Memory: Major Events in the American Century*. Armonk, N.Y.: M.E. Sharpe, 1998.

Neufeld, Josh. *A.D.: New Orleans After the Deluge*. New York: Pantheon Graphic Novels, 2009.

Nora, Pierre ed. *Les Lieux de mémoire*. Seven volumes. Paris: Edition Gallimard, 1984–1992.

Piazza, Tom. *City of Refuge*. New York: Harper Collins, 2008.

Piazza, Tom. *Why New Orleans Matters*. New York: Harper Collins, 2005.

Pollack, Harriet, and Christopher Metress, eds. *Emmett Till in Literary Memory and Imagination*. Baton Rouge: Louisiana State UP, 2008.

Rhoades, George F., and Vedat Sar, Eds. *Trauma and Dissociation in a Cross-Cultural Perspective: Not Just a North American Phenomenon*. New York: Routledge, 2006.

Rose, Chris. *1 Dead in Attic*. New Orleans, LA: CR Books, 2005.

Rose, Chris. *1 Dead in Attic*. New York, NY: Simon and Schuster, 2007.

Rothberg, Michael. *Multidirectional Memory: Remembering the Holocaust in the Age of Decolonization*. Stanford: Stanford UP, 2009.

Rothberg, Michael. *Traumatic Realism: The Demands of Holocaust Representation*. Minneapolis: University of Minnesota Press, 2000.

Rothe, Anne. *Popular Trauma Culture: Selling the Pain of Others in the Mass Media*. New Brunswick, NJ: Rutgers UP, 2011.

Rubin, Louis D. *The Edge of the Swamp: A Study in the Literature and Society of the Old South*. Baton Rouge: Louisiana State UP, 1989.

Russ, Elizabeth Christine. *The Plantation in the Postslavery Imagination*. New York: Oxford UP, 2009.

Santner, Eric. *Stranded Objects: Mourning, Memory and Film in Postwar Germany*. Ithaca: Cornell UP, 1993.

Schreiber, Evelyn Jaffe. *Race, Trauma, and Home in the Novels of Toni Morrison*. Baton Rouge: Louisiana State UP, 2010.

Seltzer, Mark. *Serial Killers: Death and Life in America's Wound Culture*. New York: Routledge, 1998.

Schivelbusch, Wolfgang. *The Culture of Defeat: On National Trauma, Mourning, and Recovery*. Translated by Jefferson Chase. New York: Metropolitan Books, 2003.

Shearer, Cynthia. *The Celestial Jukebox*. Berkeley, CA: Counterpoint Press, 2004.

Showalter, Elaine. *Hystories: Hysterical Epidemics and Modern Media*. New York: Columbia UP, 1998.

Smith, Jon, and Deborah Cohn. *Look Away! The U.S. South in New World Studies*. Durham: Duke UP, 2004.

Smith, Lillian. *Killers of the Dream*. New York: Norton, 1949.

Stringer, Dorothy. *"Not Even Past": Race, Historical Trauma, and Subjectivity in Faulkner, Larsen, and Van Vechten*. New York: Fordham UP, 2010.

Styron, William. *The Confessions of Nat Turner*. New York: Random House, 1967.

Tal, Kali. *Worlds of Hurt: Reading the Literatures of Trauma*. Cambridge: Cambridge UP, 1995.

Taylor, Melanie Benson. *Reconstructing the Native South: American Indian Literature and the Lost Cause*. Athens: University of Georgia Press, 2012.

Turner, Daniel Cross. *Southern Crossings: Poetry, Memory, and the Transcultural South*. Knoxville: University of Tennessee Press, 2012.

Vickroy, Laurie. *Trauma and Survival in Contemporary Fiction*. Charlottesville: University of Virginia Press, 2002.

Ward, Jerry. *The Katrina Papers: A Journal of Trauma and Recovery*. New Orleans, LA: UNO Press, 2009.

Ward, Jesmyn. *Salvage the Bones*. New York: Bloomsbury, 2011.

Whitehead, Anne. *Trauma Fiction*. Edinburgh: Edinburgh UP, 2004.

Williams, Sherley Anne. *Dessa Rose*. New York: William Morrow, 1986.

Woodward, C. Vann. *The Burden of Southern History*. Baton Rouge: Louisiana State UP, 1993.

Yaeger, Patricia. *Dirt and Desire: Reconstructing Southern Women's Writing, 1930–1990*. Chicago: University of Chicago Press, 2000.

Young, James E. *Writing and Rewriting the Holocaust*. Bloomington: Indiana UP, 1988.

Young, James E. *The Texture of Memory*. New Haven: Yale UP, 1993.

CHAPTER 8

Theory in Practice
King Lear: *The Transference of the Kingdom*

Jeffrey Stern

Jeffrey Stern is a research and clinical graduate of the Institute for Psychoanalysis, and a member of the faculty. He is a lecturer in the University of Chicago's psychiatry department and a member of the psychiatry faculty at Rush University, where he lectures on Shakespeare and film.

I

The transference of Lear's kingdom occasions the very tragedy it is designed to prevent.[1] Lear's plan is to avoid future strife between his three daughters by publishing their several dowers – that is, by dividing his kingdom among them – and divesting himself of power. It has been a convention of criticism since Coleridge to regard the plan as foolish, even absurd, but Harry Jaffa has demonstrated convincingly that it is the strategy of a leader skilled in the complexities of *Realpolitik*.[2] By placing the favored Cordelia between Goneril and Regan in the center of the kingdom and bequeathing to her the lion's share of the land and power, Lear reduces the likelihood that his elder, dangerous daughters will be able either to attack one another or to join in league against Cordelia and her disturbingly foreign husband.

The plan, however, is not only public and political but personal and psychological, not only (indeed, I think, not crucially) about the division of the state and the loss of his lands but rather about the division of the self and the loss of his heart – of Cordelia. The time compels Lear to give away the child whose minority has allowed him to defy the concerns of age. He associates the loss of this child with the loss of life itself. Following her marriage he will "crawl toward death" (1.1.41).[3] He does not wish to let her go. Although his "last and least," she is his "joy" (ll. 82, 83). Division of the kingdom and divestiture are the means by which he can outwit time's demand and prevent her departure. He will ransom his kingdom for his love. By giving Cordelia her portion while he

Original publication details: Jeffrey Stern, "*King Lear*: The Transference of the Kingdom." *Shakespeare Quarterly* 41.3 (Autumn 1990), pp. 299–308. Reproduced with permission from Johns Hopkins University Press.

Literary Theory: An Anthology, Third Edition. Edited by Julie Rivkin and Michael Ryan.
© 2017 John Wiley & Sons, Ltd. Published 2017 by John Wiley & Sons, Ltd.

lives, he will block her passage across the sea with a husband[4] and keep her in Britain with him to rule. He would "set [his] rest / On [Cordelia's] kind nursery" (ll. 123–24).

Yet, like Hamlet, Lear delays. Each daughter's portion has been decided: Kent and Gloucester discuss the shares planned for Cornwall and Albany:

KENT   I thought the King had more affected the Duke of Albany than Cornwall.
GLOUCESTER   It did always seem so to us; but now, in the division of the kingdom, it
              appears not which of the dukes he values most, for equalities are so
              weigh'd that curiosity in neither can make choice of either's moi'ty.
              (ll. 1–7)

Burgundy is fully aware of what Cordelia's husband shall receive:

> Most royal Majesty,
> I crave no more than hath your Highness offer'd,
> Nor will you tender less.
> (ll. 194–96)

Nonetheless, the "great rivals in [his] youngest daughter's love" (l. 46) have long in his court made their amorous sojourn and still require answer. Stanley Cavell, in his beautiful essay "The Avoidance of Love," points out that divestiture would leave Lear powerless – and thus feeling shamefully unworthy of love.[5] Lear's plan requires another turn of the screw: a master stroke to regain the prestige that in divesting he must lose. Thus he conceives the love trial.[6]

This ceremony, which is to precede the announcement of the name of Cordelia's husband and in which dowers are exchanged for vows of love, is, in its staging and its intended effect, that of a marriage, preeminently a marriage to Cordelia.[7] Her suitors do not attend. Pledging her truth of love to Lear, she will in effect be plighting her troth to him, thereby nullifying, annulling, as it were, the force if not the fact of her vows to Burgundy. Lear's will be the prior, the ultimate claim of her affection as well as of her allegiance. The same will obtain for Goneril and Regan: he will give his lands to their husbands after the daughters have sworn a husband's prerogative to him. That which Lear describes, then, as his "darker purpose" (l. 36) is, in effect, to regain by marrying its new queen(s) the kingdom he has renounced.

By making his daughters' portions depend on their professions of love to him rather than upon loving actions, Lear seeks ultimately to establish a new dispensation in which words will not merely symbolize but will equal deeds; for to retain his royal authority without the lands that would underwrite it, he requires a kingdom in which merely to possess the "name, and all th' addition to a king" (l. 136) will be to be a king in deed.

If language is to be taken not as symbolic but as literal action, it follows that the child who loves best will say best, that speech is a fair (indeed the only possible) measure of love. By such logic, Lear's decision to award the most ample third of his kingdom to the best-spoken child is reasonable. Naturally, he expects this child to be Cordelia. He has reason to think so: "Her voice was ever soft, / Gentle, and low, an excellent thing in woman" (5.3.276–77).

Regan and Goneril are eager to participate in the trial because if words no longer depend on deeds, if action no longer joins signifier and signified, rhetoric alone will be power, and their claims, by definition, will be as valid as those of Cordelia. They may gain most by speaking best; loving will have fallen beside the point. This is why Cordelia is angry. In a game in which to speak love is everything, her love itself will mean nothing. To speak it would be to equate it qualitatively with the love of her sisters, would be, in other words, to lie. Indeed, only a lie, in the sense of only words emptied of their significance, can win. So Cordelia says nothing.

Critics have both praised Cordelia's devotion to truth and blamed her proud obstinacy. Those who blame her assume that Lear's plan is a sound one and that if she had humored him, the play would have been comic and, one presumes, short. Let me take a moment to say that I think not. Had Shakespeare been required to write this play following the success of Lear's plan (i.e., Cordelia marries Burgundy and sets up housekeeping with her father), the outcome would have been the same: his rage at Cordelia is not a function of her bad behavior but of his inability to tolerate the waning of his strength and influence, a consequence of the fact (and not the form) of her marriage and the changes in his relations to her it mandates. No amount of solicitousness from Cordelia could protect him ultimately from the jealous conviction that he is no longer preeminent in her love, that rival claimants are being honored at his expense. Indeed, I think that what we see in Lear's outrage over Goneril's malicious neglect is a fast-forwarded version of what he would eventually feel even in the entirely devoted care of Cordelia, because his rage is fundamentally a rage against Time, a rage against the dying of the light. Inevitably he would break with her (perhaps following her decision to accompany her husband to the Continent – though the reason hardly matters), after which Lear would flee in fury to Goneril for recompense. Seeing her chance, Goneril would use her father's power and influence to prepare a campaign with Regan against Cordelia before discarding Lear and launching the play we know. My point is that Lear's tragedy is crucially one of character, not circumstance, and that in time his fate, like murder, will out.

Returning then to the opposing conceptions of Cordelia, I would say that discussions regarding her either as proudly obstinate or valiant for truth nevertheless beg the question of Lear's reaction – which cannot be thought to follow necessarily from what Cordelia says. However startled and displeased he is by her answer, he has other options – especially inasmuch as it is her "bond" speech, rather than what clearly strike him as her not-very-sweet "nothings," that precipitates his rage. "Good my Lord," she says,

> You have begot me, bred me, lov'd me. I
> Return those duties back as are right fit,
> Obey you, love you, and most honor you.
> Why have my sisters husbands, if they say
> They love you all? Happily, when I shall wed,
> That lord whose hand must take my plight shall carry
> Half my love with him, half my care and duty.
> Sure I shall never marry like my sisters,
> To love my father all.
>
> (1.1.96–104)

Jaffa points out that Lear might well laud her truth as precisely the response he seeks (as, in effect, the correct answer to the riddle of the three caskets that Portia's deceased father asks his daughter's suitors in *The Merchant of Venice*), the plain leaden truth that unlocks the secret to love's golden treasure.[8] Moreover, Cordelia's attack on her sisters' claim that while they have husbands they can love their father all implies a defense of the authenticity of her own love. She alone is unmarried, hence bound at this time entirely to Lear. If it can be asked why Cordelia might not compromise her truth in the service of her love, it seems warranted to ask why might not Lear, in the interest of the plan upon which he has staked his kingdom and indeed his very life, interpret her words to his own advantage?

The answer, I believe, is that Lear finds love on Cordelia's terms intolerable precisely because these terms require that he accept all he has sought to deny. By insisting that marriage must divide her love, Cordelia insists that he accept the validity of her union to another – thus, in effect, that he accept time's tragic news of loss and change, of difference; that he recognize that the future requires giving up the past; that he see that he cannot give her away and demand all of her love, renounce his kingdom and remain a king, crawl toward death and live forever. Wishing, even saying, otherwise will not make it so. He will not endow such a truth with his name: dower it. Rather he disavows it and disinherits her – even as he banishes Kent, who swears by that truth – awarding her prize instead to the dream-sustaining rhetoric of Goneril and Regan. They have spoken well; if he is to achieve his desire, he must affirm that what they mean is what they have said.

His decision to retain the name but to forsake the function of king, and at the same time to make his daughters his mothers, inverts the oedipal law of culture, which requires the sacrifice of the incestuous object as the condition of participation in the social order. Thus he engenders a dispensation not of wish-fulfillment but of empty words and primitive, even monstrous, hunger. Figuring himself in terms of "the barbarous Scythian, / Or he that makes his generation messes / To gorge his appetite" (ll. 116–18), he commands Cornwall and Albany to "digest" (l. 28) Cordelia's portion between them.[9] Not fantasy but falseness comes to rule. Edmund appears the true son by forging letters, Goneril deceives her husband, and both sisters dishonor their father in violation of their claims of love. Lear's commands cease to be translated into deeds that satisfy his wishes. The Fool tells him he is "an O without a figure" (1.4.189–90) – as Goneril and Regan literalize when they "disquantity [his] train" (l. 245) from the one-hundred knights in his retinue to none. When his words lose all of their force, when he is to have no follower who would act on them, Lear flees into the storm and into madness.

Where the love trial failed, madness appears to succeed in reinvesting his voice with power. He exhorts the storm to rage and, as if in answer to his command, it does. At his word a joint stool becomes Goneril, the hovel a courtroom; he is "every inch a king" (4.6.107). Yet even madness cannot protect him from his distress over Cordelia's truth of love divided between father and husband. It is this truth that lies behind his fearful misogyny – his sense of woman as monstrously double: "Down from the waist they are Centaurs, / Though women all above. / But to the girdle do the gods" – does a father – "inherit, / Beneath is all the fiends'" (ll. 124–27) – is all a husband's, is all France's: "There's hell, there's darkness, there is the sulphurous pit, / Burning, scalding …" (ll. 128–29). Female sexuality seems to Lear thus because it represents the key to his daughter's unbearable desire of the other, of France. Thus he characterizes it horribly in imagery associated with syphilis, in terms, that is, of the venereal infection Shakespeare's countrymen called the French disease.[10]

Yet, as he had by means of the love trial, Lear tries madly to transform the source of his distress into one of comfort. As it is Cordelia's sexuality that threatens him, he would convince himself of its virtue. Having been betrayed by the artificial affection of Goneril and Regan, he appears fantastically "bedecked with weeds" (4.6.80 s.d.) in the place of Cordelia's champion, the Fool, to advocate natural – that is, sexual – relations. He is "even / The natural fool of fortune" (ll. 190–91). He would forgive Gloucester his crime: "Thou shalt not die. Die for adultery? No" (l. 111). And he would do so because sexual activity is natural: "The wren goes to't, and the small gilded fly / Does lecher in my sight" (ll. 112–13) – though of course it is not Gloucester's adultery that threatens Lear but Cordelia's: for adultery is how he experiences her marriage to France and its betrayal of her union to him, a union that he hoped the love trial would sacrilize. He would "Let copulation thrive" (l. 114) that the very cause of his loss of Cordelia's protection might provide protection in the form of male children – bastard sons? – who would rally to his defense: "To't, luxury, pell-mell, for I lack soldiers" (l. 117). Such children he thinks would take better care of him than his own ungrateful progeny: "for Gloucester's bastard son / Was kinder to his father than my daughters / Got 'tween the lawful sheets" (ll. 114–16). But the idea of the begetting of his daughters inevitably evokes the intolerable idea of sexuality as the secret of woman's essentially divided, her essentially duplicitous nature:

> Behold yond simp'ring dame,
> Whose face between her forks presages snow,
> That minces virtue, and does shake the head
> To hear of pleasure's name;
> The fitchew, nor the soiled horse, goes to't
> With a more riotous appetite.
> (ll. 120–25)

It is precisely the fear of a secret, ineluctable nature within his daughter that plagues another of Shakespeare's tragic fathers, Brabantio, the fear of a secret doubleness that would compel Desdemona to be ruled by another authority. Brabantio claims she is entirely "opposite to marriage" (1.2.68), "A maiden never bold; / Of spirit so still and quiet that her motion / Blush'd at herself" (1.3.96–98) and insists it can only be witchcraft that allows her to fall in love with what she fears to look on. Yet Desdemona's speech to her father before the Senate is nearly Cordelia's to Lear before the court: "I do perceive here a divided duty," she tells him:

> To you I am bound for life and education;
> My life and education both do learn me
> How to respect you. You are the lord of duty;
> I am hitherto your daughter. But here's my husband,
> And so much duty as my mother show'd
> To you, preferring you before her father,
> So much I challenge that I may profess
> Due to the Moor my lord.
> (ll. 183–91)

And as does Lear, Brabantio conceives of the desire of his daughter for a husband as monstrous. Thus when the empathic if not honest Iago[11] tells Brabantio, "an old black ram / Is tupping your white ewe" (1.1.89–90), that Brabantio will have his daughter "cover'd with a Barbary horse" (l. 112), as if she were the centaur of Lear's tortured fantasy, Brabantio says the elopement described is "not unlike my dream" (l. 143).

Madly Lear reasons that if he would possess his daughter's love – compete, that is, with a husband – he must be a husband, must "die bravely, like a smug bridegroom" (4.6.198), as he says he will when Cordelia's soldiers announce that she is near. He imagines he has done so: when he awakens, he cannot remember "where [he] did lodge" (4.7.70) the previous – the fantasized wedding – night but thinks he is in France – that is, in the place of Cordelia's husband, the son-in-law whom he would have stolen upon and killed. His fantasy leaves him once again burning – this time with unutterable shame, the physical hell of his unsweetened imagination having become a moral one: he is "bound / Upon a wheel of fire, that [his] own tears / Do scald like molten lead" (ll. 47–49), for he believes his incestuous thoughts – thoughts he cannot distinguish from deeds – have killed her: "You are a spirit, I know. When did you die?" (l. 50). Cordelia's living presence makes possible his awakening as if from death itself – "You do me wrong to take me out o' th' grave" (l. 46) – for it absolves him of his terrible guilt. So too her loving forgiveness disabuses him of his madness ("The great rage, / You see, is kill'd in him" [ll. 80–81]) and fills him with joy because it reawakens his original fantasy of their union: "Come, let's away to prison. / We two alone will sing like birds i' th' cage" (5.3.8–9). They are not in France but in Lear's "own kingdom" (4.7.78). France himself has disappeared. The "wall'd prison" (5.3.18) to which Lear imagines they will escape is a kind of faery land where they will live, as it were, gathered within the artifice of eternity, singing, praying, telling old tales, overseeing and outliving "packs and sects of great ones, / That ebb and flow by th' moon" (ll. 18–19); taking upon them the secrets of the forbidden, "the mystery of things" (l. 16), with the license of heaven – as if they were "God's spies" (l. 17). "Upon such sacrifices," Lear tells his child, "the gods themselves throw incense" (ll. 20–21).

Lear's experience has transformed the rhetoric and intention though not the nature of his desire. Where he had sought to bribe Cordelia for her pledge of love, now he speaks exquisitely of his own love, and he no longer cares either for the name or "all th' addition to a king" (1.1.136). The magical vision and communion of lovers will make world enough of prison. Cavell writes:

> he has found at the end a way to have what he has wanted from the beginning … partnership in a mystic marriage … it is their love itself which [for Lear] has the meaning of sacrifice. As though the ideas of love and of death are interlocked in his mind – and in particular of death as a payment or placation for the granting of love.[12]

It must be. It is this love that cannot sustain or be sustained by the world, that sacrifices the world to itself. This love, by collapsing the difference between father, husband, and son, and between wife, mother, and daughter, collapses the difference upon which linguistic, psychic, and social structure depends. At the end Lear can no longer distinguish Cordelia's breath from the stillness, her voice from the silence, her life from her death. His words collapse into the action they can no longer symbolize: he dies like a bridegroom on the body of his child – the play's cruel justice an expression of Freud's law of culture: for the wages of incest are death.

II

I think that to say all of this is, nonetheless, to leave much unsaid about the nature of Lear's desire and about the nature of desire in the play. What he wants from Cordelia – certainly until he becomes floridly psychotic – is not sexual but maternal, as Kahn has seen. He would "marry" Cordelia in order to assure her maternal care. Indeed, it is his failure to find such care from his daughters that leads to his rage and madness. It is his professed desire to "set [his] rest / On her kind nursery" (1.1.23–24), and he becomes enraged over Cordelia's refusal to promise him the limitless devotion he requires. The Fool chides him for making his elder daughters his mothers, and the daughters infuriate him further by withholding the maternal responsiveness he demands. He would have Goneril feed him on the instant he commands – "Let me not stay a jot for dinner; go get it ready" (1.4.9–10) – and is shaken when she doesn't smile at him: "How now, daughter? What makes that frontlet on? / You are too much of late i' th' frown!" (ll. 186–87). The "weary negligence" (1.3.13) with which she and her retainers attend him leaves him doubting his very identity: "This is not Lear. / Does Lear walk thus? Speak thus? Where are his eyes?" (1.4.222–23); and her insistence that he "disquantity his train" (l. 245) unleashes his curses. For denying him a mother's care, he would deny her the very capacity to bear children, urging that Nature convey into her womb sterility and "dry up in her the organs of increase" (l. 276). Fleeing to Regan in hopes of sympathy and redress, he discovers – as children often discover of the parent they hope will take their part – that she is entirely in league with Goneril. Having exhausted all hope of reintegration into a world of maternal love, he flees into the storm calling on the thunder to "Strike flat the thick rotundity o' th' world! / Crack nature's molds, all germains spill at once, / That makes ingrateful man" (3.2.79). Denied mothering, his rage is such that he would destroy the round maternal belly of the very earth itself and abort its gestating contents.

The storm lays bare his need for maternal care: cold, wet, furious, and raving, he is, on the heath, the very image of the child the Fool accused him of being, and it is in this regressed condition that he finally finds a version of the attention he has sought – finds it not from his daughters but from the maternal males who tend him there. Kent, Gloucester, and the Fool deliver him to shelter and then dry, change, feed, warm, and soothe him before finally getting him to sleep.

Lear's transference of the kingdom thus seems engendered by and surely to engender in him, indeed in his kingdom, a transference in the psychoanalytic sense: that is, an awakening in the present of powerful infantile feelings and attitudes. In psychoanalysis, transference reenacts what the analysand cannot or will not remember about his or her psychological past. It is thus the source of the self's lost knowledge. Lear's transference of the kingdom, seen in the light of the psychological transference behavior it generates, also points, I would suggest, toward earlier conflicts that the exigencies of the time have remobilized. If we regard Lear's transference of the kingdom as linked to his transference crisis over the loss of Cordelia, and if we interpret this crisis, as the play asks us to do, in terms of a loss of mothering – or to put it more precisely, a loss of functions a mother would perform – our psychoanalytic question must be: what does the loss of Cordelia repeat?

Of course the play offers nothing about Lear's own mother, nor about his early life. But we do know that the woman who replaces the mother in the structure of his psychological history[13] – the mother of his children – is dead. Given the fact that Cordelia never invokes her mother's memory, nor for that matter does Goneril, Regan, or anyone but Lear (who mentions her only once), it seems that Shakespeare means us to suppose she has long been absent from their lives. Indeed, Lear's words to his "last and least" encourage us to imagine that Cordelia has replaced her mother in Lear's affection. This would seem to explain Lear's extraordinary love for this child, and something of his father-of-the-bride's wish not to give her up. Nonetheless I think it fails to make sense of the fact that he has "ever but slenderly known himself" (1.1.294–95), or of the extraordinary extent of his distress in the face of her marriage, or of the violence and implacability of his rage following what he experiences as her denial of him.

I would argue that Lear's proneness to rage and shame, his inability to tolerate the division of Cordelia's affection, and his fragmentation in the face of her perceived betrayal are evidence of what Heinz Kohut would call a deficit in the self, or what literary critics, also thinking of pathological narcissism, of pride, have traditionally called a tragic flaw. And this deficit stands as a scar or trace of the earliest relationship with the mother (or whatever caretaker stood in her place). Thus it is interesting that Lear calls the madness he feels "swell[ing] up toward [his] heart" "this mother" (2.4.55).[14] For it is as a consequence of the earliest mother-child matrix that the child's secure sense of self is established. Kohut sees such a self as a consequence of the mother's loving admiration – the gleam in her eye in the face of "his-majesty-the-baby's" grandiose exhibitionistic display of himself.[15]

As a result of this maternal responsiveness to the infant, this "mirroring" by the need-satisfying (m)other, which Kohut calls the "self-object,"[16] the child develops the internal psychic structure to regulate self-esteem. A failure of this required responsiveness inhibits such development, and hence inhibits the development of a cohesive self. In the absence of such psychological completeness, the child continues to depend on others to provide the mirroring he or she requires to maintain a narcissistic homeostasis. Kohut thus explains the extraordinary need of people with such deficits – people who, like Lear, might be said but slenderly to know themselves – for the admiration of others. Thus it is that Shakespeare's quintessentially narcissistic King Lear surrounds himself with loving – male – companions like Kent and the Fool whose devotion is absolute, and whose nature is not, like that of Lear's daughters, to divide; neither has wife or children, and the hallmark of each is loyalty: the Fool is a fool for love: he is faithful and will tarry. And thus it is that when Lear is refused the responsiveness he requires, when he is not mirrored, his sense of self begins to fade: "Does any here know me?" (1.4.222) he asks. "Who is it that can tell me who I am?" (l. 226). He has become, the Fool tells him, "Lear's shadow" (l. 227).

Inasmuch as self-objects perform crucially self-regulating functions, they are jealously regarded. Even small fluctuations in their attentiveness unsettle the equilibrium of the self and are experienced as evidence of bad faith. Indeed the subject's failure to control the self-object is felt as tantamount to a failure to control a part of his own body and gives rise to a painful sense of psychic fragmentation, which manifests itself as rage.[17] The loss of such objects is inevitably traumatic, and even their death is experienced unconsciously as evidence of betrayal, of willful abandonment, a common fantasy of bereaved children. It is not surprising then that Lear's sole mention of his dead wife elaborates a fantasy of her infidelity. He says that if Regan is not glad to see him when he meets her at Gloucester's, he will "divorce me from thy mother's tomb, / Sepulchring an adultress" (2.4.129–30).

The story then that frames the story of Lear's traumatic loss of Cordelia in the play is thus a barely spoken story of the loss of her mother, and the trace, perhaps, of an unspoken story of lost maternal responsiveness in his own childhood. Unlike the loss of Cordelia, however, the story of this second loss, the loss of Lear's wife, contains the resolution to the crisis of narcissism that is implicit for Lear in its structure. This is because it leaves Lear with a new self-object in the person of Cordelia, a self-object argu-ably better positioned to protect his fragile narcissistic equilibrium than could a wife whose love, of necessity, was divided between husband and children. Cordelia, with no mother to require a bond of "half [her] love ... half [her] care and duty" (1.1.102), is bound in love entirely to Lear. He is thus never so happy as in the presence of this child – she whom he calls "our joy" (l. 82) – and it is not difficult to understand the anxious terror with which he confronts her impending loss to him in marriage: the loss of Cordelia threatens him with the loss of an irreplaceable (mirroring/maternal) self-object. This is to say it threatens Lear with a catastrophic loss of self, with, in effect, the loss of his mind – exactly the whirlwind it reaps.

Notes

1 I am deeply indebted to Drs. Arnold Goldberg, Henry Seidenberg, Jarl Dyrud, and Jerry Winer for their thoughts and encouragement during the writing of this essay; to Professors David Bevington and Richard Strier; and especially to my father, Richard Stern.

2 "The Limits of Politics: *King Lear*, Act I, scene i" in *Shakespeare's Politics*, Allan Bloom with Harry V. Jaffa (New York: Basic Books, 1964), pp. 113–45.

3 All quotations of Shakespeare are from *The Complete Works of Shakespeare*, David Bevington, ed. (Glenview, Ill.: Scott, Foresman, 1980).

4 Jaffa argues persuasively that it is Burgundy whose status is that of the favored suitor (pp. 124–25). Thus Lear's plan specifically blocks her crossing to France with Burgundy.

5 "The Avoidance of Love: A Reading of *King Lear*" in *Must We Mean What We Say?* (New York: Charles Scribner's Sons, 1969), pp. 267–353, esp. p. 289.

6 Jaffa argues that the trial is a strategy to trap Goneril and Regan into accepting portions they might otherwise have been unwilling to take (pp. 128–29). But I think this is at best no more than its manifest rationale.

7 See Lynda E. Boose, "The Father and the Bride in Shakespeare," *PMLA*, 97 (1982), 325–47. See also Arpad Pauncz, "Psychopathology of Shakespeare's 'King Lear'," *American Imago*, 9 (1952), 57–78.

8 pp. 128–29.

9 Coppélia Kahn writes,

> The play is full of oral rage: it abounds in fantasies of biting and devouring, and more specifically, fantasies of parents eating children and children eating parents. … When Cordelia doesn't feed [Lear] with love, he thinks angrily of eating *her*.

See her wonderful essay "The Absent Mother in *King Lear*" in *Rewriting the Renaissance: The Discourses of Sexual Difference in Early Modern Europe*, Margaret W. Ferguson, Maureen Quilligan, and Nancy J. Vickers, eds. (Chicago: Univ. of Chicago Press, 1986), pp. 33–49, esp. pp. 41–42.

10 Anthony Burgess feels that the astonishing misogyny of these lines reflects a collapse of Shakespeare's control of Lear's character and suspects the poet himself may have been suffering from syphilis at the time he wrote *King Lear* (*Shakespeare* [London: Jonathan Cape, 1970], pp. 186, 220–22).

11 Stephen Greenblatt writes that "what [sociologist] Professor [Daniel] Lerner calls 'empathy' Shakespeare calls 'Iago'" (*Renaissance Self-Fashioning: From More to Shakespeare* [Chicago: Univ. of Chicago Press, 1980], p. 225).

12 pp. 297–98 (cited in n. 5, above).

13 See Sigmund Freud, "The Theme of the Three Caskets," *The Standard Edition of the Complete Psychological Works of Sigmund Freud*, 23 vols., ed. James Strachey (London: The Hogarth Press, 1966), Vol. 12, 289–301.

14 Kahn argues that as a result of Lear's loss of maternal care, the repressed feminine component of his nature returns. Thus he is humiliated that "women's weapons, water drops, stain [his] man's cheeks" and he identifies his malaise as "*hysterica passio*" (from the Greek *hustera*, womb) – a condition brought on, it was thought, by a wandering womb. Lear would restore his "climbing sorrow," the mother's part, the womb, to its proper element "below" (pp. 33–34). The idea of

Lear's rage at an uncontrollable womb within himself helps to explain his wish to destroy the creative power of Goneril's womb and Nature's.

15   *The Analysis of the Self* (New York: International Univs. Press, 1971). See especially Chapter 5, "Types of Mirror Transferences," pp. 105–32.

16   Kohut defines self-objects as "objects [that is, other people] which are themselves experienced as part of the self." The control a small child, for example, expects to have "over such (self-object) others is then closer to the concept of the control which a grownup expects to have over his own body and mind than to the concept of the control which he expects to have over others" (pp. xiv, 26–27).

17   pp. 27, 33.

CHAPTER 9

Theory in Practice
The Weirdest Scale on Earth: Elizabeth Bishop and Containment

Lee Zimmerman

Lee Zimmerman's study of Elizabeth Bishop's poetry takes an object relations perspective. Rather than focus on the tension between primitive drives and an embattled ego trying to deal with them (the Freudian model), Zimmerman examines instead the use of language to negotiate the boundary between self and other. He focuses especially on Bishop's poems about children engaging with mothers or mother figures. Dr. Zimmerman teaches twentieth-century American Literature at Hofstra University and is the editor of the journal *Twentieth Century Literature*.

At the heart of "In the Waiting Room" – the first poem in Elizabeth Bishop's last book – lies the recollection of a terrifying childhood experience:

> the sensation of falling off
> the round, turning world
> into cold, blue-black space.
> (160)[1]

This experience has been characterized by many readers, following Helen Vendler, as "vertigo" (1977, 37), and though Vendler herself construes vertigo as "metaphysical doubt," I would like to take a harder look at what is at stake in this childhood memory, which inaugurates a volume whose last line concedes the persistence of beginnings: "(A yesterday I find almost impossible to lift)" (181). What other sense can we make of this early "falling off"?

Original publication details: Lee Zimmerman, "The Weirdest Scale on Earth: Elizabeth Bishop and Containment." *American Imago* 61.4 (Winter 2004), pp. 495–518. Reproduced with permission from Johns Hopkins University Press.

One way to pursue this question is to consider the passage as a stark instance of one of Bishop's crucial tropes: the destabilizing threat of what, in the poem following "In the Waiting Room," Bishop's Crusoe calls "weird scale" (164). Highlighting the way that "throughout her work Bishop loves juggling relative sizes," James Merrill points out that in "Crusoe in England" "Crusoe's flute appropriately plays 'the weirdest scale on earth'" (1989, 256). Merrill's formulation, however, seems to me a little too cheerful, by contrast with the darker sense informing Vendler's observation that "Bishop's poems ... put into relief the continuing vibration between two frequencies – the domestic and the strange" (1977, 32). But of the important early readings, perhaps David Kalstone's most clearly evokes the threat posed by such "juggling" and "continuing vibration": the "odd, habitual changes of scale" (1977, 13) in Bishop's poems, Kalstone asserts, reflect "an effort at reconstituting the world as if it were in danger of being continually lost" (12).

Focusing on this trope of instability in "In the Waiting Room" and some related work, I would like to explore the threat that impels Bishop's weird scale. We can call this the threat of "loss" that many critics have come to recognize as central to Bishop's writing.[2] In trying to enrich our sense of how her work explores what "loss" means, I shall have recourse to a psychoanalytic perspective, albeit one that cuts against the Lacanian grain of many previous readings of Bishop, drawing instead on the object-relational formulations of D. W. Winnicott and W. R. Bion.[3]

This tradition envisions the role of language very differently from that ascribed to it by Lacan. As Jane Flax maintains in her lucid contrast of Lacan and Winnicott, since for Lacan language "is not self-created, it must be alien and alienating. Language and its laws are seen as imposed on the subject from the 'outside' – by a culture that is 'alien'" (1990, 96–97). For Winnicott, in contrast, culture, including language, can occupy a "potential space" between inner and outer worlds that is neither purely subjective nor purely objective; given a "good-enough" presentation of the external world, the individual "*can* creatively transform what is given in part by bringing something of inner reality to the process" (Flax 1990, 119).

Barbara Schapiro points out that "much of the current clinical research ... would seem to belie Lacan's view of the primacy of language in the construction of subjectivity" (1994, 22). She marshals many recent theorists who share Daniel Stern's view that "the word is given to the infant from the outside, by the mother, but there exists a thought for it to be given to.... It occupies a midway position between the infant's subjectivity and the mother's objectivity [and thus] is a union experience" (qtd. in Schapiro 1994, 23).[4] Christopher Bollas, as Peter Rudnytsky summarizes him, "subsumes a theory of language, the alpha and omega for Lacanians, within an object relational framework, which recognizes that nonverbal affects precede linguistic representations" (1993, xvi–xvii). For Lacan, all human beings come to language in the same way, as something fixed and non-negotiable; for Winnicott and his colleagues, our encounter with language participates in an already existing *relationship* between self and world that is, necessarily, different for each of us.

Crucial to this approach is that the *conditions* of our earliest relationships shape how we experience language and other cultural formations. Winnicott sees "cultural experience" as being located in the "*potential space* between the individual and the environment (originally the object)" (1967, 100), and he claims this "intermediate area" or "transitional" realm is indispensable for "the perpetual human task of keeping inner and outer reality separate yet related" (1953, 2). Marion Milner likewise stresses those very early "moments when the original 'poet' in each of us created the outside world for us, by finding the familiar in the unfamiliar" (1955, 18). But the possibility of this intermediate area where moments of poetic originality can occur depends (at least in part) on the external environment. Winnicott's "potential space happens only *in rela-tion to a feeling of confidence* on the part of the baby ... related to the dependability of the mother-figure or environmental elements" (1967, 100), and Milner's focus is on "the internal and external conditions that make it possible to find the familiar in the unfamiliar" (1955, 16).

Bion's notion of "containment" provides, in my view, an especially illuminating way of posing these "conditions" and exploring how they animate Bishop's work. Before undertaking any further theoretical elaboration, though, I would like to consider in more detail the ubiquity in Bishop's writing of the trope of instability. An oft-quoted instance concerns her admiration for Darwin:

> reading Darwin one admires the beautiful solid case being built up out of his endless, heroic observations, almost unconscious or automatic – and then comes a sudden relaxa-tion, a forgetful phrase, and one feels that strangeness of his undertaking, sees the lonely young man, his eyes fixed on facts and minute details, sinking or sliding giddily off into the unknown.[5] (1966, 288)

This is pretty obviously also a self-portrait, but the anxiety implicit in such sinking or sliding into the unknown is veiled here – or isn't really – by the "giddiness." Writing to herself, Bishop is more forthright about the danger of such sliding off, as is suggested by two entries Kalstone cites from her shipboard journal on her first, disorienting, trip to Europe, in 1935: she sees something in the water as "*men on rafts*, poor wretches, cling-ing to a board or two" (Kalstone 1989, 20), and twice at dinner is "overtaken by an awful feeling of deathly physical and mental *illness* – something that seems 'after' me. It is as if one were whirled off from all the world and the interests of the world in a sort of cloud – dark, sulphurous gray – of melancholia" (21).[6]

Kalstone notes how this 1935 experience of sinking and sliding anticipates the late, very ungiddy, "In the Waiting Room," but – if we accept that such disorientation is related to Merrill's "juggling," Vendler's "continuous vibration," and Kalstone's "odd, habitual changes of scale" – we can begin to see its threat lurking just about everywhere in Bishop's work. Her first volume presents "The Unbeliever," who firmly shuts out the external world, sleeping "on top of his mast / with his eyes closed tight," anxious about a Darwinian sinking or sliding, as he dreams, "I must not fall. / The spangled sea below wants me to fall / ... it wants to destroy us all" (22). "Sleeping on the Ceiling" begins with a disorienting shift in scale –

> It is so peaceful on the ceiling!
> It is the place de la Concorde.
> The little crystal chandelier
> is off, the fountain is in the dark
>   (29)

– as does "The Man-Moth," whose first line, in the act of offering a setting, dislo-cates: "Here, above" (14). The title of that poem, too, uneasily commingles the small (moth) with the medium (man) with the large (the title is taken from a "misprint for mammoth"). That such weirdness of scale expresses troubled early relationships seems all but explicit at the start of "Chemin de Fer":

> Alone on the railroad track
> I walked with pounding heart.
> The ties were too close together
> or maybe too far apart.
>
> (8)

The connection between vexed early "ties" and subsequent instability concludes "At the Fishhouses," in the second volume, where knowledge of the external world derives from "rocky breasts" and is thus imagined as undependable, not merely "flowing," but, more troublingly, "flown," having left no substantiating trace (66). In "Sandpiper," in the third book, the bird's panic reflects this absence; knowing "that every so often the world is bound to shake," that on his beach "a sheet / of interrupting water comes and goes," he obsessively observes the grains of sand ("no detail too small") and, like Darwin, is "preoccupied, / looking for something, something, something" (131). And in the last volume, in addition to "In the Waiting Room," we find Crusoe's island of weird scale, also a place of giant waves where "the world [is] bound to shake" so violently, in volcanic eruptions, that the volcanoes' heads are "blown off," dependable scale dissolves, and thought itself cannot reconstitute things:

> Well, I had fifty-two
> miserable, small volcanoes I could climb
> with a few slithery strides –
> volcanoes dead as ash heaps.
> I used to sit on the edge of the highest one
> and count the others standing up,
> naked and leaden, with their heads blown off.
> I'd think that if they were the size
> I thought volcanoes should be, then I had
> become a giant;
> and if I had become a giant
> *I couldn't bear to think* what size
> the goats and turtles were,
> or the gulls, or the overlapping rollers.
>
> (162; italics added)

Such weirdness of scale seems to derive not only from "rocky breasts" or from violent explosions or from sinking and sliding away, but also from the kind of cultural representations that structure Bishop's early experience. In her prose memoir "Primer Class," she recalls the start of her formal education, an early experience of being presented with the external forms of a culture. Already haunted by her parentlessness – "I used to ask Grandmother … to promise me not to die before I came home" from school (6)[7] – young Elizabeth seems hungry for meaningful symbols but also thwarted by them. She is fascinated by "long columns of numbers, handwritten," but they remain "a mystery I never solved when I went to Primer Class in Nova Scotia!" (4). She is drawn to "two rolled-up maps, one of Canada and one of the whole world" (10), and wants to meet these symbolic representations half-way – in a potential space where her own agency is accommodated, and she is allowed playfully to "snap them up, and pull them down again, and touch all the countries and provinces with my own hands."

These first lessons don't, however, mediate between the internal world and the external one or help the students discover the familiar in the unfamiliar: "we didn't sit about socially, and build things, or crayon, or play, or quarrel. We sat one behind the other in a line of small, bolted-down desks and chairs" (4). Elizabeth never does get her hands on the maps, and soon these rigid representations of identity and place serve only to confuse, as scale turns weird: "I got the general impression that Canada was the same size as the world, which somehow or other fitted in it, or the other way around" (10).

A dominant strain in the critical response to Bishop's trope of instability – reflecting some postmodern and feminist valorizations of indeterminacy – celebrates it as her resistance to repressive, inflexible structures of meaning. Barbara Page contends that, "against the finality of closure, Bishop asserted her preference for unofficial and unstable positionings" (1993, 210). Bonnie Costello parses her "antimimetic manipulations of perspective and scale ... which challenge visual and conceptual frames" (1991, 5). For Susan McCabe, Bishop's poetry "dismantles the notion of the traditional self as it confesses to a disunified self" (1994, xvi), a position echoed in David Jarraway's Žižekian claim that Bishop "proposes to turn a blind eye to universalist (i.e. natural, normal) notions of selfhood, constructing in their place hypothetical (i.e. synthetic, artificial) versions, whose endlessly rhetorical prospect makes true selfhood ... unattainable" (1998, 250). Lee Edelman's influential essay on "In the Waiting Room" concludes that "the critical desire to locate or to define or to frame any literal inside for that voice [the '*oh!* of pain'] to emerge from has been discredited as ideological blindness, a hierarchical gesture" (1985, 107).

It is certainly true, as such readings suggest, that Bishop's work resists authoritarian and universalist structures, and remains alive to the vitality of the particular and unpredictable. There *is* some giddiness to sliding away, as her last poem, "Sonnet," insists, slyly sexualizing and celebrating as "Freed" the "rainbow-bird ... flying wherever / it feels like, gay!" (192). But to do justice to this freedom one must also take into account what threatens it. In her shipboard diary, as we have seen, Bishop equates being "whirled off from the world" with "melancholia" and "*homesickness*"; and as Kalstone observes, "disorientation and the threat of abandonment are very close in her mind" (1989, 21).

What has forsaken Bishop, then, is what Edelman and many others don't allow for: an external structure that is not *by definition* alienating and repressive. Brett Millier sees in her work "the simultaneous realization of selfhood and the awful otherness of the inevitable world" (1993, 23), and even Vendler seems to take for granted "the fact that one's house always *is* inscrutable" (1977, 33). But how much of the world *is* inevitable, and why is otherness self-evidently only awful? Is one's house necessarily *only* inscrutable, affording no possibility of, in Milner's phrase, "finding the familiar in the unfamiliar"?

Millier and Vendler are hardly "Lacanian," but even they accept Lacan's premise of the fixity of the symbolic order – an assumption strangely at odds with the frequent postmodern celebrations of indeterminacy. Jane Flax interrogates the way Lacan "assumes that if something is not self-created, it must be alien and alienating" (1990, 96), and contrasts his view with the relational one, "more compatible with postmodernism than Freud and Lacan" in that it doesn't "require a fixed ... view of 'human nature'" (110). For Winnicott and his British colleagues, again, much depends upon the particulars of one's early relations with others, who may respond either in a way that imposes rigid structure and thus alienates or in one that, to a good-enough degree, negotiates with the individual's emerging disposition and thus shapes a self *capable* of giddily resisting closure or "flying wherever / it feels like."[8] The "permanent gap between subject and Other, self and culture," that Flax rightly imputes to Lacan can, she argues, instead be rethought as a "space" (126–27) where disposition flourishes in some dependable relation to a not too inflexibly positioned other.

To the limited extent that object relational perspectives have been taken up by literary and critical theorists, Winnicott is now a central figure. But as important to many psychoanalysts is the work of W. R. Bion, whose notion of "containment" I find especially helpful in thinking about the fragility of potential space – that is, about the possibilities and anxieties of weird scale – in Bishop's work.[9] For Bion, an infant's often overwhelmingly intense internal states need to be made tolerable by the mother by being taken in and returned to the infant in a more bearable form. This is the basis for constructing a relationship between inside and outside, and hence also for thinking and experiencing. Bion describes how containment operates in a psychoanalytic session:

> When the patient strove to rid himself of fears of death which were felt to be too powerful for his personality to contain he split off his fears and put them into me, the idea apparently being that if they were allowed to repose there long enough they would undergo modification by my psyche and could then be safely reintrojected.... An understanding mother is able to experience the feeling of dread that this baby was striving to deal with by projective identification, and yet retain a balanced outlook. (1959, 103–4)

So-called "normal development" thus involves a caretaker with a state of mind that Bion calls "maternal reverie" and who engages in *active* mirroring:

> Normal development follows if the relationship between the infant and breast permits the infant to project a feeling, say, that it is dying into the mother and to reintroject it after its sojourn in the breast has made it tolerable to the infant psyche. If projection is not accepted by the mother the infant feels that its feeling that it is dying is stripped of such meaning as it has. It therefore reintrojects, not a fear of dying made tolerable, but a nameless dread. (1962b, 116)

As glossed by Hanna Segal, maternal reverie is the origin of the emerging self's experience of "mental stability":

> When an infant has an intolerable anxiety he deals with it by projecting it into the mother. The mother's response is to acknowledge the anxiety and do whatever is necessary to relieve the infant's distress. The infant's perception is that he has projected something intolerable into his object, but the object was capable of containing it.... He can then reintroject not only his original anxiety but an anxiety modified by having been contained. He also introjects an object capable of containing ... anxiety. The containment of anxiety by an external object capable of understanding is a beginning of mental stability. (1981, 134–35)

Although containment is originally presymbolic, Bion's view of early relations implies that language itself, far from constituting an inevitable structure of alienation, is one medium through which containment can be achieved, while containment is reciprocally one form by which the meaningful use of language can be achieved.[10] Bion writes of a patient who was "trying to 'contain' his emotions within a form of words.... The words that should have represented the meaning the man wanted to express were fragmented by the emotional forces to which he wished to give only verbal expression: the verbal formulation could not 'contain' his emotions" (1970, 94). The failure of containment thus leads not only to an intense mental state being "stripped of such meaning as it has" with a consequent disruption of "mental stability," but also to what Bion calls "nameless dread" or to what Winnicott analogously calls "unthinkable anxiety," an "acute confusional state" also resulting from maternal absence (1967, 97).[11] In turn, the world itself no longer seems to be dependably there, as "the patient feels surrounded not so much by real objects, things-in-themselves, but by bizarre objects that are … stripped of their meaning" (Bion 1962a, 99).

Bishop is not alone among her poetic kin in exploring this terrain. In "Of Modern Poetry," Wallace Stevens describes the challenge of a modern poem in terms that evoke an infant's predicament. It has to develop some sense of meaningful space – to "construct a new stage" – and to "learn the speech of the place," "face the men," and "meet / The women of the time" (1990, 174–75). But the poem functions at once as the infant and as the infant's first good object. In mirroring itself, in being able to "repeat / Exactly, that which it wants to hear," it has "expressed / … an emotion as of two people, as of two / Emotions becoming one." By such responsiveness, the poem "gives / Sounds passing through sudden rightness, wholly / Containing the mind." Poetry as an art of containment lies at the heart, too, of James Merrill's *The Changing Light at Sandover*, where God B reveals to DJ and JM their true subject: "*MY SON MICHAEL LIT UP YOUR MINDS MY SON / GABRIEL TURNED THEM TO THE DARK FORCE WE / CONTAIN*" (1982, 493).

But though she is not unique in this respect, Bishop is surely among the poets most consistently and originally engaged by such issues. When she says that "There are times … when I really start to wonder what holds me together – awful times" (qtd. in Wehr 1981, 325), and in her notebook ascribes to a severed arm the words, "this is what it means to be really 'alone in the world'" (Page 1993, 197), we can sense how the "loss" so often taken to be central to her work is experienced as a failure of containment.[12] And when readers repeatedly stress that Bishop's world is "populated by people and things whose ties to one another [are] tenuous at best and at worst nonexistent" (Lombardi 1995, 103), that her "great subject" is "discovering the strangeness, the unreality of our reality" (Ashbery 1977, 8), they are intuiting that such failure of containment produces a world of Bionian "bizarre objects."

Bishop's most explicit writing about her difficult early relations with her mother is the autobiographical story "In the Village," the "vital center," as Kalstone puts it, "from which many of Bishop's poem's radiate" (1977, 16). The story concerns her mother's return from a sanitarium to the Nova Scotia village where, her father having died when she was an infant, Elizabeth has been living with her maternal grandparents and aunts. Her mother can't cope and soon must leave again, for another sanitarium, where she remains for good; at the age of five, Bishop has seen her mother for the last time. The story's exposition starkly presents the destabilizing family history: "First" the mother "had come home, with her child. Then she had gone away again, alone, and left the child. Then she had come home. Then she had gone away again, with her sister; and now she was home again" (1984, 252).

In the beginning was "a scream," as the story's first words tell us, one that seems to have permeated nature itself and the narrator's perceiving consciousness: "A scream, the echo of a scream, hangs over that Nova Scotian village. No one hears it; it hangs there forever, a slight stain in those pure blue skies…. The scream hangs like that, unheard, in memory – in the past, in the present, and those years between" (251). Woven into the fabric of perception – partly constituting the narrator's world – the scream is quietly associated in that first paragraph with weirdness of scale: its "pitch would be the pitch of my village. Flick the lightning rod on top of the church steeple with your fingernail and you will hear it." (You would have to be gigantic, or the church miniaturized, to play upon its string instrument so casually.)

The mother is experienced primarily as the source of this scream. She is being fitted for a new purple dress, having decided, finally, to "come out of [the] black" (251) she has been wearing since her husband's death five years earlier. (Her tenuous presence for the child reflects her own uncontained grief.) Both drawn to and wary of the mother, the child stands "in the doorway, watching" (252). The negotiation between self and world fails:

> The dress was all wrong. She screamed.
> The child vanishes.
>
> (253)

Bishop's almost desperate flatness of tone here, as in the introductory family history ("First she had come home ..."), might suggest the intensity of the child's feelings, but rather than the mother accepting and returning them in "tolerable" form, the mother herself is overcome. Whereas containment might have constructed a potential space, an explosion undermines its possibility, and the child's intense feelings are, in Bion's phrase, "stripped of ... meaning." The world, in turn, vanishes, doesn't seem to be really and dependably and usefully there, a disorienting condition that persists, as the scream, "alive forever" (251), becomes the very "pitch of [the] village."

"In the Village" thus presents a scream-stained world where, the child having emotionally vanished, external objects are tenuously present or are stripped of meaning and become "bizarre." Just as in "Primer Class," where maps served not to locate but to disorient, here once again the symbolic order mystifies:

> "There's that mourning coat she got the first winter," says my aunt.
> But always I think they are saying "morning." Why, in the morning did one put on black? How early in the morning did one begin? (254)

Mother's china is "painfully desirable" but "broken," and the "innocent and small" grains of rice it bears on its surface seem present but "aren't really there," a hidden absence augmented by the rigid (and patriarchally inflected) imposition of language: "My aunt says that she has heard they write the Lord's Prayer" on the grains (256).

Other objects associated with the mother likewise are "bizarre," fail to help constitute the sense of a relatively stable, meaningful presence. The material for her new dress threatens to explode: "The purple stuff lies on a table.... Oh, look away before it moves by itself, or makes a sound; before it echoes, echoes, what it has heard!" (258–59). The mother's creative power having been withheld, the child is compelled to "abscond with a little ivory stick," her mother's embroidery tool, but her anxiety about its reality precludes her making use of it: "To keep it forever I bury it under the bleeding heart by the crab-apple tree, but it is never found again" (257). Substitute sources of maternal creativity and containment are likewise scream-stained. The dressmaker puts things together, helps the outside world "fit" the self, but with "a bosom full of needles" (258) she hardly offers a "breast" (in Bion's explanation of containment) in which the child's "feeling that it is dying" can "sojourn" and thus be "made ... tolerable to the infant psyche." Even though the needles are "to make nests with," the possibility of violence seems nigh, and, indeed, the child sniffs infanticide in the air: "A gray kitten once lay on the treadle of her sewing machine, where she rocked it as she sewed, like a baby in a cradle, but it got hanged on the belt.... But another gray-and-white one lies now by the arm of the machine in imminent danger of being sewn into a turban."

If danger is in the air, sadness spills over into the food; nourishment itself is infused with pain, and Bishop is a long way from a world where her fears can be modified and "safely reintrojected": "My grandmother is sitting in the kitchen stirring potato mash for tomorrow's bread and crying into it. She gives me a spoonful and it tastes wonderful but wrong. In it I think I taste my grandmother's tears" (259). Anything so problematically introjected can't be left at home. When the child goes out and looks in a shop window, she sees in "something new" the old, devastating story of her parents: "In the other window is something new: shoes, single shoes, summer shoes, each sitting on top of its own box with its mate beneath it, inside, in the dark" (262). And when she ventures beyond the village to the pasture, the natural world, seemingly at first a safe haven, finally is "stripped of such meaning as it has": "For a while I entertain the idea of not going home today at all, of staying safely here in the pasture all day, playing in the brook and climbing on the squishy, moss-covered hummocks in the swampy part. But an immense, sibilant, glistening loneliness suddenly faces me" (265).[13]

The few times Bishop writes of even earlier experience with her mother reflect this anxiety about containment. Her memory of a "first ride on a swan boat ... at the age of three" centers on a "live swan" who bit the finger of her still-mourning mother (1952, 282). Rather than giving shape to, and thus making bearable, the intensity of feeling – if we can read the swan's bite as expressing Bishop's own early (oral) rage, a biting of the hand that failed really to feed her – all her mother does is bleed, the inside seeping out beyond a containing boundary (both her skin and the black glove), in muted anticipation, perhaps, of the scream.

But if the scream persists in "In the Village," it is not the only sound that does. When the child "vanishes," she heads to Nate's blacksmith shop and its "beautiful sound" (252), the "Clang" of metal being worked into shape. The clang can't erase the scream from memory, but it at least offers the prospect of another sort of interaction. The scream signals a self shattered by the intensity of its feelings; the clang sounds the *shaping* of elemental forces, as Nate neither denies nor is overcome by them. The mother's final breakdown and return to the sanitarium is precipitated by a fire that destroys part of a nearby barn; a fire is present at Nate's too, but, rather than going uncontained, it is made meaningful, focused in the forge. Nate controls it with bellows, and when the "coals blow red and wild," he doesn't scream but "laughs."[14]

The smithy is but a temporary refuge. Soon the child is removed from the Nova Scotia village to live in Worcester, Massachusetts, with her father's parents, a period Bishop writes about in her prose memoir "The Country Mouse" (1984). This transplantation offers no escape from the threat of the scream, as "there was something ominous, threatening, lowering in the air" (17), but the most immediate threat isn't an explosion but its opposite, suffocation. From the start, a rigid, conventionalized external world imposes itself on the child: "I had been brought back unconsulted and against my wishes to the house my father had been born in, to be saved from a life of poverty and provincialism." These new caretakers themselves seem depersonalized, a "surprising set of extra grandparents" who "until a few weeks ago [were] no more than names." Indeed, their oppressiveness takes the form of an inflexible symbolic order, generic (and gendered) phrases that displace, rather than negotiate, individual identity and thus produce a "depressing" sense of unreality:

> if only Grandma hadn't such a confusing way of talking. It was almost as if we were playing house. She would speak of "grandma" and "little girls" and "fathers" and "being good" – things I had never before considered in the abstract, or rarely in the third person. In particular, there seemed to be much, much more to being a "little girl" than I had realized: the prospect was beginning to depress me. (16)

What might have served as a "transitional object" (Winnicott 1953, 2) – something the child experiences as both under its control *and* having objective existence, thus enabling meaningful relations between inside and outside – is colonized. Instead of making possible a "finding of the familiar in the unfamiliar," Bishop's doll isn't a transitional object but a bizarre one, "stripped of meaning." The grandmother asks:

> "Where's your doll? Where's *Drusilla?*"
> Oh dear. I had dolls, back home in Nova Scotia; I was even quite fond of one or two of them. But Grandma had found them all in no condition to go traveling in Pullmans. She had bought me the best our country store could provide, and made her a checked dress herself. And when I had been reluctant to name her, she had even given her that unappealing name. The doll (I couldn't say that name) was totally uninteresting.... I could scarcely conceal my real feelings about her. But that seemed to be one of Grandma's ideas: a "little girl" should carry a doll when she went traveling. (Bishop 1984, 16)

The child herself becomes a kind of doll. As it did for her mother, being literally ill-fitted to the world yields what Winnicott might call "unthinkable anxiety": "The dressmaker came.... She made me four hideous dresses, too long, too dark, and with decorations made from leftovers of Grandma's dresses. (Forty-three years later I can scarcely bear to think of those dresses.) ... Then Grandma decided I should have long hair and braids, like 'nice little girls'" (29).

The consequences of enforcing upon the child such generic and unresponsive cultural forms emerge as "The Country Mouse" culminates in the waiting-room episode reworked later in "In the Waiting Room." Like the explosive scream, such rigid forms preclude a *relationship* between self and world that might make both seem real. Language having been presented as alienating, when the child is left to *read* she feels an "absolute and utter desolation" (33); but she doesn't *feel* this feeling (it isn't contained) so much as she is *defined* by it: "I felt ... *myself*.... I felt *I,I,I*." To be is to be desolate, to be and no one else. For the child here, being someone doesn't derive from being both like and unlike others, but from sheer differentiation; she has the "awful sensation" that "'You are you.... You are not Beppo, or the chestnut tree, or Emma, you are *you* and you are going to be *you* forever.'" Insofar as she feels herself to be *"one* of them," this isn't a self-substantiating connection, but a usurpation by external forms such as that of a "nice little girl"; the only alternative to "utter desolation" (if it is one) is Winnicott's "false self" (1960, 140): "'You're in for it now,' something said. How had I got tricked into such a false position? I would be like that woman opposite who smiled at me so falsely" (Bishop 1984, 33). The memoir ends with the child vanishing into desolation or into its double, falsity: she is either uncontained ("It was like coasting downhill, this thought, only much worse") or else rigidly quashed (this thought "quickly smashed into a tree").

Which is worse, the catastrophe of being uncontained or the falsity of being a nice little girl? Nameless dread or the dread of being named? The attempt to represent this dilemma is extended in "In the Waiting Room." As the first poem in *Geography III*, Bishop's last and most directly autobiographical book, it evinces a concern with origins, though these origins are destabilized and destabilizing. The volume's epigraph, from a schooltext "First Lessons in Geography," frames the issue: can earliest contact with otherness (e.g., maps, representation) offer a sense of location? Initially, the series of questions in the lesson is answered, but soon – as it turns to the volcano, a violent threat to containment – unanswered questions proliferate dizzyingly:

> In what direction is the Volcano? The
> Cape? The Bay? The Lake? The Straight?
> The Mountains? The Isthmus?
> What is in the East? In the West? In the
> South? In the North? In the Northwest?
> In the Southeast? In the Northeast?
> In the Southwest?
>
> (1983, 157)

This vertiginous list ends the epigraph, as "First Lessons" leaves a student wondering: where am I? "In the Waiting Room" expands this question: if I don't know *where* I am, how do I know *who* I am?[15]

It is important that such questions emerge in a waiting room. Whereas "potential space" is a way of describing a realm in which self and world can find each other, a waiting room is a zone where time is killed and nothing is supposed to happen; it is not a place of interplay "between me-extensions and the not-me" (Winnicott 1967, 100), but a nowhere that excludes both.

Winnicott holds that potential space arises only from "a confidence related to the dependability of the mother figure or environmental elements" (100), but it is the very absence of such confidence that marks Bishop's experience here. Indeed, one of the ways that "In the Waiting Room" exceeds "The Country Mouse" is in its closer examination of how the child's initial reading of *National Geographic* suggests this absence. In the memoir, the "desolation" is triggered when the child merely "looked at the magazine cover" (32), while the poem details the photographs she "carefully / studied" (159), photographs that, for all their exoticism, evoke an uncannily familiar – or *familial* – history and set of anxieties. "A dead man on a pole" conjures her fatherlessness, while the bizarre caption, "Long Pig," pretending but really failing to explain, suggests the inexplicability of such a loss, the failure to make it nameable or thinkable through containment. The image of "Babies with pointed heads / wound round and round with string" evokes the imposition of thwarting external forms upon the emerging self and the dread of being named – that is, defined as a nice little girl – in such a context. The grown women are similarly thwarted, "with necks / wound round and round with wire / like the necks of light bulbs," a condition that produces an "undependable" maternal presence, not breasts in which infantile fears can, as Bion puts it, "sojourn" and be "made tolerable," but rather, in Bishop's own words, breasts that are "horrifying" and "awful."

This anxiety about maternal containment, indeed, is the ground note of the child's reading, evident in the first photograph she encounters, underlying all the others:

> the inside of a volcano,
> black, and full of ashes;
> then it was spilling over
> in rivulets of fire.
>
> (159)

"First Lessons in Geography" defines Earth as "The planet or body on which we live," but here the planet/body doesn't help to constitute an initial potential space, an interplay, and thus a sorting out, of inside and outside; rather, the inside explodes out, the intensity isn't made bearable, the original object, we might say, doesn't shape but rather screams. Something wound tightly with wire might well want to unwind with a vengeance, to blow its top.[16]

Confronted by this "spilling over," by her whole dislocating history, the child tries to keep things in place, to sort inside from out, to attend to a series of boundaries: "And then I looked at the cover: / the yellow margins, the date." But the initial failure of containment is repeated as "Suddenly, from inside, / came an *oh!* of pain" (160): another eruption, another shattering of language and its meanings, another scream. Although the "*oh!*" was "not very loud," it "could have / got loud and worse" (161), just as the original scream "was not even loud to begin with, perhaps" (251). As Edelman (1985) emphasizes, the source of the "*oh!*" is crucially indeterminate;[17] it came "from inside" the office, was "Aunt Consuelo's voice," but just as the mother's scream came "to live forever" in Bishop's memory, so too this exclamation "was *me*: / my voice, in my mouth." As with the volcano, meaningful relations between inside and outside dissolve, questions of place are revealed to be questions of identity, and the unthinkable cry of pain causes the child to vanish:

> the sensation of falling off
> the round, turning world
> into cold, blue-black space
>
> .....
>
> The waiting room was bright
> and too hot. It was sliding
> beneath a big black wave,
> another, and another.
>
> (160–61)

To "stop / the sensation," the child resorts to language and number, to a symbolic order of absolute demarcation: "I said to myself: three days / and you'll be seven years old." But at what cost? Even if language is not by definition alienating, in this context being culturally positioned is as estranging as falling, and, again, the only alternative to nameless dread is the dread of being rigidly named. To stop falling, Bishop reassures herself, "you are an *I*, / you are an *Elizabeth*," but to be "*an* I" or "*an* Elizabeth" is to be just an example, to be no one in particular, to be not herself but "one of *them*," a placement experienced as arbitrary and "awful": "*Why* should you be one, too?" she wonders:

> Why should I be my aunt,
> or me, or anyone?

What similarities –
boots, hands, the family voice
I felt in my throat, or even
the *National Geographic*
and those awful hanging breasts –
held us all together
or made us just one?[18]

(161)

Coming in out of the cold, blue-black, isolating space means renouncing any degree of the crucial difference necessary for relatedness. Self and others, inside and outside, aren't *related* but are "just one," a realization Bishop is loathe to confront, as she "scarcely dared to look" at the other people in the waiting room "to see what it was I was" (160). If she *is* the others (if they are "all just one"), she isn't *like* them, a distinction she quietly insists on by calling this experience of ostensible kinship "unlikely." Indeed, as unthinkable as vanishing is, "nothing / stranger could ever happen" than this being relocated in the social world. What is "unlikely" and "strange" is just what might *seem* to fend off strangeness, so Bishop goes back and forth. After the initial falling off the world, she comes back to be one of them, but then again the world slides away, "beneath a big black wave" (161), and, once more, at the poem's end, it comes back. If "The [First World] War was on" in that outside world, with intense forces going uncontained, the poem makes us see how containment's failure has loosed an even earlier war from her childhood. The waiting room is the antipode of Winnicott's "resting-place for the individual engaged in the perpetual human task of keeping inner and outer reality separate yet interrelated" (1953, 2) – a room where the failure of containment precludes such an intertwining, not a potential space but the nowhere of war.

In tracing how "In the Waiting Room" seems to hover between nameless dread and the dread of being named, I have elided the distinction between "the child" and the adult poet, between the events recalled and the act of writing about them. To some degree, the poem itself asks us to do this: adopting a childlike trimeter and a humble, sometimes markedly childlike diction ("grown-up people" [159]), the poet pretends to sound seven years old, and the poem keeps its focus entirely on the child's experience as it unfolds – in contrast, say, to "Crusoe in England," structured by the distance between past experience, on the island, and the present scene of recounting it, in England. But we can't think "In the Waiting Room" is too invested in this pretense (and couldn't think so even if, like "The Moose," it was cast in the present tense). Indeed, the transparency of the pretense is crucial. The child "didn't know any / word" (161) for her predicament, but the poet knows the poem's words; the child remains in the nowhere of the waiting room, neither in nor out, but the poet's stanzas – the term derives from the Italian for "room" – form a potential space where the inner world can find language, a place for "the perpetual human task of keeping inner and outer reality separate yet interrelated." If young Elizabeth continues to suffer from the failure of containment, the older Bishop, as poet, keeps up that perpetual task (and we might think again of how Merrill sees her "juggling relative sizes"): the task of writing her way between nameless dread and the dread of being named.

Department of English
Hofstra University
Hempstead, NY 11549
Englzz@Hofstra.edu

Notes

1   All quotations from Bishop's poems are to *The Complete Poems* (1983), with page numbers included in the text.

2   Brett Millier summarizes Bishop's history of loss: "As a child, she had lost her father before she knew him, when he died of Bright's disease eight months after she was born. Her mother was deeply disoriented by her husband's death and spent the next five years in and out of mental institutions until, in 1916, she was diagnosed as permanently insane. Her five-year-old daughter would never see her again. Little Elizabeth had managed … to construct herself a secure world in the home of her maternal grandparents in Great Village, Nova Scotia. But her father's wealthy Boston family, worried that their only grandchild would grow up backward there among the ignorant, uprooted her a year later, and she began what would become a lifetime of living as guest in other people's homes. In 1967, the most secure of these guest homes, in Petropolis, Brazil, was violently disrupted when her hostess, friend, and lover of fifteen years suffered a breakdown and committed suicide, and Bishop was once again cast out" (1990, 233; see also Millier 1993).

3   In working with this kind of psychoanalysis, I do not mean to shift attention away from Bishop's poems and prose to her biography. I am not aiming, that is, to trace the *sources* of the trope of instability, but rather to ponder its underappreciated suggestiveness. The events of Bishop's life and her responses to them perhaps have a role in the argument, but only insofar as these are the explicit concerns of her writing. Thus, if I am going against the grain of much previous psychoanalytic work on Bishop, I think I am going *with* the grain of her own work.

4   Schapiro is quoting from Stern (1985, 172).

5   The previous sentence of this letter refers to the "surrealism of everyday life," and what I've called the trope of instability – especially weirdness of scale – can certainly be read as Bishop's witty engagement with the literary strategy of surrealism. Indeed, it can be read tellingly in a number of ways. By stressing the anxiety implicit in weird scales, I'm hoping to help us grow more acute to the complexities of Bishop's attitude and tone, certainly not trying to obscure the playfulness and bravery that are never too separable from anxiety and terror in her work.

6   Kalstone is quoting from the Bishop notebooks at Vassar College Library.

7   Unless otherwise indicated, all citations from Bishop's prose are to *The Collected Prose* (1984), with page references included in the text.

8   Winnicott stresses that the "capacity to be alone" depends upon an early sense of maternal presence: "Although many types of experience go to the establishment of the capacity to be alone, there is one that is basic …; *this experience is that of being alone, as an infant and small child, in the presence of mother*. Thus the basis of the capacity to be alone is a paradox; it is the experience of being alone while someone else is present" (1958, 30).

9   As Rudnytsky comments, both in Britain and the United States "the perspective on psychoanalysis adopted by most academics has been filtered through the French postmodernist lens of Jacques Lacan, rather than the humanist lens of the English Winnicott. There must be ten literary critics conversant with Lacan's *Écrits* for every one who has read Winnicott's *Playing and Reality*" (1993, xi). For an overview of the British object relations tradition out of which Bion and Winnicott both emerge, see also Greenberg and Mitchell (1983).

10 As James S. Grotstein emphasizes: "it is important to differentiate Bion's conception of containment from the mirroring mother as denoted by Lacan, Winnicott, and Kohut…. Bion's conception is of an elaborated primary process activity which acts like a *prism* to refract the intense hue of the infant's screams into the components of the color spectrum, so to speak, so as to sort them out and relegate them to a hierarchy of importance and mental action. Thus, containment for Bion is a very active process – which involves feeling, thinking, organizing, and acting" (1981, 134*n*).

11 R. D. Hinshelwood, whose *Dictionary* has informed my discussion of containment, writes that "nameless dread" is "a term first used by Karin Stephen" in 1941, and "was later given a fuller and specific meaning by Bion to describe a state of meaningless fear that comes about in the context of an infant with a mother incapable of 'reverie'" (1989, 349). I wonder whether Bion fixed on this sort of melodramatic term as a reminder of the predicament of trying to give the nameless a name.

12   This failure of containment is aptly summarized in Alan Williamson's (implicitly Bionian) observation that "if Bishop characteristically distanced emotion, it was partly because emotion for her – and especially feelings of despair, loneliness, apprehension – tended to become immense and categorical, insusceptible to rational or, in poetry, to structural counter-argument" (1983, 96).

13   Contrast this child going forth with Whitman's, who also wonders "whether that which appears so is so, or is it all flashes and specks?" but who finally believes in his real connection to things. Rather than screaming, the mother in "There Was a Child Went Forth" is characterized by her "mild words"; rather than one with broken china, there is a "mother at home quietly placing the dishes on the supper-table." Vendler cites Whitman's poem as another instance of the "momentary vertigo" (38) she finds in "In the Waiting Room," but while the comparison is suggestive it serves in my view to highlight the crucial differences between the two children going forth.

14   Patricia Yeager perceives in the story "the alienating necessity – for the woman writer – of escaping from the mother's scream into the father's speech" (1988, 136). This formulation typifies the way Lacanian-inflected readings assume a fixed set of conditions: the mother can only scream, the father's speech is necessarily alienating, and gender determines the child's response. Although it is true that Winnicott gives insufficient attention to gender (see Flax 1990, 120–26, and Kahane 1993), all of Yeager's assumptions are debatable, as I have argued above.

15   Perhaps the paradigmatic posing of this question in American literature occurs in *Huckleberry Finn*. Having been (falsely) told that an agonizing episode of separation from Huck was really a dream, Jim replies, "'Is I *me*, or who *is* I? Is I heah, or whah *is* I? Now dat's what I wants to know'" (1885, 103).

16   Marilyn Lombardi writes, "Like the volcanoes that the child finds pictured in her magazine, Bishop's own mother threatened to erupt in unpredictable ways; emotionally numb one moment, she would spill over in rivulets of fiery, hysterical emotion the next" (1995, 27).

17   Edelman's reading is acute, especially in its parsing of how issues of gender inflect Bishop's predicament, though he assumes that language by definition alienates or objectifies the self. Thus, he interprets the "*Oh!*" not merely as the cry "against that text" she is reading that it surely is (though it is not self-evidently against the text *as* a text, but rather against a particular *kind* of language), but also as "a cry of the female refusal of position in favor of disposition" (107), a view that seems to me to underestimate what is at stake in Bishop's very ungiddy "falling."

18   As this passage suggests, and as Edelman and others emphasize, the dread of being "one of *them*" is the dread of being defined as a (heterosexual) "woman" (or, as in "The Country Mouse," a "nice little girl") by a patriarchal cultural system. Even if, as I have implied, gender is not the only structure that can be rigidly imposed, it is certainly a crucial one in Bishop's experience of this dilemma.

References

Ashbery, John. 1977. Second Presentation of Elizabeth Bishop. *World Literature Today* 51–1:9–11.

Bion, W. R. 1959. Attacks on Linking. In Bion 1967, pp. 93–109.

Bion, W. R. 1962a. *Learning from Experience*. Rpt. in Bion 1977.

Bion, W. R. 1962b. A Theory of Thinking. In Bion 1967, pp. 110–19.

Bion, W. R. 1967. *Second Thoughts: Selected Papers on Psycho-Analysis*. London: Heinemann.

Bion, W. R. 1970. *Attention and Interpretation*. Rpt. in Bion 1977.

Bion, W. R. 1977. *Seven Servants*. New York: Aronson.

Bishop, Elizabeth. 1952. From "What the Young Man Said to the Psalmist." In Schwartz and Estess 1983, p. 282.

Bishop, Elizabeth. 1966. The "Darwin" Letter. In Schwartz and Estess 1983, p. 288.

Bishop, Elizabeth. 1983. *The Complete Poems, 1927–1979*. New York: Farrar, Straus and Giroux.

Bishop, Elizabeth. 1984. *The Collected Prose*. Ed. Robert Giroux. New York: Farrar, Straus and Giroux.

Costello, Bonnie. 1991. *Elizabeth Bishop: Questions of Mastery*. Cambridge, MA: Harvard University Press.

Edelman, Lee. 1985. The Geography of Gender: Elizabeth Bishop's "In the Waiting Room." In Lombardi 1993, pp. 91–107.

Flax, Jane. 1990. *Thinking Fragments: Psychoanalysis, Feminism, and Postmodernism in the Contemporary West*. Berkeley: University of California Press.

Greenberg, Jay, and Stephen Mitchell. 1983. *Object Relations in Psychoanalytic Theory*. Cambridge, MA: Harvard University Press.

Grotstein, James S. 1981. *Splitting and Projective Identification*. New York: Aronson.

Hinshelwood, R. D. 1989. *A Dictionary of Kleinian Thought*. London: Free Association Books.

Jarraway, David R. 1998. "O Canada!": The Spectral Lesbian Poetics of Elizabeth Bishop. *PMLA*, 113:243–57.

Kahane, Claire. 1993. Gender and Voice in Transitional Phenomena. In Rudnytsky 1993, pp. 278–91.

Kalstone, David. 1977. Elizabeth Bishop: Questions of Memory, Questions of Travel. In Schwartz and Estess 1983, pp. 3–31.

Kalstone, David. 1989. *Becoming a Poet: Elizabeth Bishop with Marianne Moore and Robert Lowell*. Ed. Robert Hemenway. New York: Farrar.

Lombardi, Marilyn May. ed. 1993. *Elizabeth Bishop: The Geography of Gender*. Charlottesville: University Press of Virginia.

Lombardi, Marilyn May. 1995. *The Body and the Song: Elizabeth Bishop's Poetics*. Carbondale: Southern Illinois University Press.

McCabe, Susan. 1994. *Elizabeth Bishop: Her Poetics of Loss*. University Park: Penn State University Press.

Merrill, James. 1982. *The Changing Light at Sandover*. New York: Atheneum.

Merrill, James. 1989. Afterword. In Kalstone 1989, pp. 251–62.

Millier, Brett. 1990. Elusive Mastery: The Drafts of Elizabeth Bishop's "One Art." In Lombardi 1993, pp. 233–43.

Millier, Brett. 1993. *Elizabeth Bishop: Life and the Memory of It*. Berkeley: University of California Press.

Milner, Marion. 1955. The Role of Illusion in Symbol Formation. In Rudnytsky 1993, pp. 13–39.

Page, Barbara. 1993. Off-Beat Claves, Oblique Realities: The Key West Notebooks of Elizabeth Bishop. In Lombardi 1993, pp. 196–211.

Rudnytsky, Peter L., ed. 1993. *Transitional Objects and Potential Spaces: Literary Uses of D. W. Winnicott*. New York: Columbia University Press.

Schapiro, Barbara Ann. 1994. *Literature and the Relational Self*. New York: New York University Press.

Schwartz, Lloyd, and Sybil P. Estess, eds. 1983. *Elizabeth Bishop and Her Art*. Ann Arbor: University of Michigan Press.

Segal, Hanna. 1981. *The Work of Hanna Segal*. New York: Aronson.

Stern, Daniel. 1985. *The Interpersonal World of the Infant*. New York: Basic Books.

Stevens, Wallace. 1990. *The Palm at the End of the Mind*. New York: Vintage.

Twain, Mark. 1885. *The Adventures of Huckleberry Finn*. Berkeley: University of California Press, 1995.

Vendler, Helen. 1977. Domestication, Domesticity, and the Otherworldly. In Schwartz and Estess 1983, pp. 32–48.

Wehr, Wesley. 1981. Elizabeth Bishop: Conversations and Class Notes. *Antioch Review*, 39:319–28.

Whitman, Walt. 1959. *Complete Poetry and Selected Prose*. Boston: Houghton Mifflin.

Williamson, Alan. 1983. *A Cold Spring*: The Poet of Feeling. In Schwartz and Estess 1983, pp. 96–108.

Winnicott, D. W. 1953. Transitional Objects and Transitional Phenomena. In Winnicott 1971, pp. 1–25.

Winnicott, D. W. 1958. The Capacity to Be Alone. In Winnicott 1965, pp. 29–36.

Winnicott, D. W. 1960. Ego Distortion in Terms of True and False Self. In Winnicott 1965, pp. 140–52.

Winnicott, D. W. 1965. *The Maturational Processes and the Facilitating Environment: Studies in the Theory of Emotional Development*. New York: International Universities Press.

Winnicott, D. W. 1967. The Location of Cultural Experience. In Winnicott 1971, pp. 95–103.

Winnicott, D. W. 1971. *Playing and Reality*. London: Routledge.

Yaeger, Patricia. 1988. *Honey-Mad Women: Emancipatory Strategies in Women's Writing*. New York: Columbia University Press.

CHAPTER 10

Theory in Practice
The Uncontrollable: The Underground Stream

Ildiko de Papp Carrington

Alice Munro's stories, according to Ildiko de Papp Carrington, depict a tension between a culture of self-control and a reality of emotional eruption. In Munro's fiction, people pay a price for such restraint in the form of violence that breaks the cultural regime of control apart and gives expression to tormented feelings and negative energies. Violence is pervasive in Munro's world, from the beating of children to the murder of those with disabilities by mean children. Carrington focuses on Freud's essay "A Child Is Being Beaten" and discusses it in relation to Munro's stories about child-beating, especially her famous "Royal Beatings."

The basic values of the Scotch–Irish Protestant culture in which Munro grew up provide a key to understanding why the events watched by the detached observers in her fiction are so often secret and concealed. One central value of this culture is dramatized by a brief passage in "A Better Place Than Home" (1979), an uncollected story that served as the basis for "1847," Munro's CBC screenplay about the Irish immigrants of the 1840s.[1] One of its two Catholic protagonists, James Thompson, is a young Irishman emigrating to Canada. During the first storm at sea, James and all the other passengers rush up on deck. Terrified of drowning, the Catholic passengers are crying, vomiting, and praying, frantically calling on "Saint Patrick, Saint Christopher, Saint Michael, and the Mother of God." But the "Protestant family," James observes, "did not weep or pray or vomit, but crouched together and held themselves tight in their Protestant way" (115). This cultural contrast vividly dramatizes the almost superhuman physical and emotional self-control of the "tight" Protestant family.

The descendants of these Canadian Protestant immigrants still define both physical and emotional tightness as desirable. They exhibit what could be termed *claustrophilia*.

Original publication details: Ildiko de Papp Carrington, "The Uncontrollable: The Underground Stream" from *Controlling the Uncontrollable: The Fiction of Alice Munro*, pp. 33–70. Northern Illinois University Press, 1989. Reproduced with permission from Northern Illinois University Press.

For example, Munro describes physical tightness as a necessary ingredient of her arrangements for writing. When she writes, she sits facing a "wall" that "slop[es] down in front" of her; thus, she is "very closed in. Very tight." She explains, "I like it that way" ("Interview": Hancock, 110). Elsewhere she suggests, "It's like being inside a warm wooden place" (Slopen, 77). This physically closed setting also suggests emotional tightness, repression valued as a primary virtue. To be unrepressed is to be outside the tightly closed-in community. Thus, it is significant that Harry Brooke, the babbling protagonist of "The Edge of Town" (1955), lives where he does, geographically, as well as emotionally, on the periphery of the community that views him with deep distrust and suspicion because he fails to subscribe to their ethos of silent repression. That Harry once owned a bookstore and is "a great reader of books" about Spiritualism is bad enough (369). But what the town cannot "trust" is his "naked and discomfiting talk" about those books. The adjective "naked" shows that even talk can be a form of shameful exposure. "Among the raw bony faces of the Scotch-Irish, with their unspeaking eyes, the face of Harry was a flickering light, an unsteady blade; his exaggerated flowering talk ran riot amongst barren statements and silences" (371). Such stubborn silences also characterized Munro's Scotch-Presbyterian grandfather, whom she describes in "Working for a Living" as a man who "lived a life of discipline, silence, privacy," a man who almost "never talked" to his son (15, 14). In "Winter Wind" the narrator describes her grandmother in very similar terms, as a woman who "had schooled herself" never to "lose control" (SIB, 206, 204). And in "The Stone in the Field" the narrator's painfully shy maiden aunts lead a life of hard, silent, and unremitting toil and consider any decision contrary to this ethos, even the purchase of labor-saving farm machinery, "a sign of an alarming ... lack of propriety and self-control" (MJ, 29).

But Munro repeatedly reveals that such rigidly silent repression and self-control have their limits. From time to time, the taut surface is shattered by violent emotional outbursts.[2] "[T]hese people are very controlled ... on the surface, very *very* careful. Life is very circumscribed and then occasionally something – well, Gothic – will happen." When it does, "there will be an incident that is a kind of outbreak. ..." This incident "will be perhaps a murder, a fire[,] ... something very black, very horrible" (Untitled, 171, 170, 171). In a later interview she has defined these Gothic incidents as "big bustings-out and grotesque crime. ... There's always this sort of boiling life going on" ("Interview": Hancock, 93). One clue to the nature of this "boiling life" is the "junkyard" in "The Edge of Town," "where the wrecked cars lie overturned" (368). Similarly, in *Lives of Girls and Women* the local young men bust out by drinking "like fish" and driving "like fools" (195); gory accidents are the inevitable results. The narrator of "Home," as she returns to the family farm in southwestern Ontario where she grew up, also notes these appalling accidents: "drunks on Saturday nights manage regularly to disembowel and decapitate themselves ..." (134). Musing on the reasons for their suicidal speeding, she refers to "*[a]n underground stream that surfaces in the murderous driving* ..." (142). This image of a subterranean force suddenly splitting the earth and bursting forth in an uncontrolled and destructive fury is a metaphor for the violently "boiling life" that resists repression. The relative infrequency of these outbursts makes them all the more terrifyingly shameful when they do occur. Such an eruption first appears in one of Munro's early uncollected stories, "At the Other Place." A detailed analysis of this revealing story illuminates the techniques and themes developed in many later major stories.

Published in September 1955 under her maiden name, Alice Laidlaw, "At the Other Place" is narrated by a retrospective first-person narrator who is a preadolescent girl in the time frame of the story. During a Sunday picnic with her family "at the other place," the poor sheep farm where her father and his brother, Uncle Bert, grew up, the girl hears a conversation between her parents that reminds her of an earlier episode involving the uncle and his wife, Aunt Thelma. The flashback to the earlier episode is preceded by a description of the narrator's parents, which not only contrasts them to Bert and Thelma but also introduces their arrival. The uncle and aunt disrupt the pleasant picnic in a climactic scene of horrible quarreling.

At the beginning of the story, the girl describes the elaborate food her mother has prepared for the picnic and her mother's appearance in a rose dress and pink makeup. In contrast, her father looks stiff and uncomfortable in his Sunday best, but "in the fields ... he was sure and powerful, a little more than life-size" (131). This difference between the narrator's parents emphasizes the clearly defined "sexual polarity" that Munro says "feels good" ("Name," 69): the conventional social role of the feminine, food-preparing, pink mother and the masculine self-confidence and power of the farmer-father in his working element, the fields. But in the marriage of Uncle Bert and Aunt Thelma, this conventional sexual difference is significantly reversed. He, too, is a farmer, but his "hungry, watchful, distempered" wife runs the show when he threshes, when he taps maple trees, and even when he is "dealing with his oldest neighbor," whom she forces him to cheat. Uncle Bert "did not go against her in anything." The narrator's description of red-faced, weather-beaten Aunt Thelma, wearing "a man's leather jacket" and always carrying a phallic stick, suggests that she has figuratively castrated her "miserable" husband. Not only powerfully male but also ferociously sadistic, she beats her children regularly, "with a leather belt or a halter strap" ("At the Other Place," 132).

In their picnic conversation the parents tell an anecdote about Uncle Bert watching Aunt Thelma thrash a dog with a horsewhip. Bert and Thelma apparently were not yet married, for this episode is identified as occurring the "first time" that Uncle Bert brought Thelma to the farm; the family dog, who "didn't like strangers round the barn," had nipped her on the ankle. As the narrator's father recalls his brother's behavior, he is very puzzled: "Bert just stood and watched her. That was a queer thing to see" (132). What is "queer," of course, is that Bert is not at all repelled by this violence in his future wife. His silence makes him Thelma's accomplice in her sadism. This revealing anecdote reminds the narrator of another significant episode in which she, too, watched her aunt in blindly brutal action.

The point of view from which this memory is narrated, the powerful emotional connotations of what the narrator sees and describes, the interpretive comments that the retrospective, older narrator makes about her experience, and the connection between this remembered experience and the reason behind the quarrel at the story's climax – all these significant elements in this story are either repeated or developed with variations in many later, major stories. In his discussion of Munro's earlier stories, Robert Thacker has pointed out that "'At the Other Place' is the first story in which the narrator's voice reveals two personae," a child's and a "more mature" person's (4).[3] In the remembered scene, however, the child's physical position gives the story's simple title an additional meaning that defines the narrator's point of view not as that of a protagonist but as that of a witness. She is in "the other place" of a first-person narrator, the position of a peripheral character quite literally on the edge of the action, looking in at and watching the frightening adult characters. "I was with Marjory, my oldest cousin, and we were looking in the window of the back kitchen, watching Aunt Thelma punish ... Alma ..." (132). What happens then is narrated in a way that allows the reader to comprehend far more than the young Peeping Tom, peering in through a split in a concealing surface, can understand. Her innocent eye sees, but she records without fully articulated comprehension. Aunt Thelma

> was excited, and sucked her breath in …; she rocked on her feet to the rhythm of the blows, and her face was dark and glowing with the blood underneath. Uncle Bert came in; she was out of breath and let Alma run away. She and Uncle Bert stood looking at each other; her face looked blind, and seemed to throb with blood coming up in it; his was ashamed and desperate, but it reflected the look in hers – and in the moment of this look they seemed to me so alien and frightful that I did not need to have Marjory drag me away from the window. (132)

Both the narrator's frightened reaction to the adults' exchanged and naked "look" and Marjory's dragging her away emphasize the subliminal sexual connotations of Thelma's orgasmic rocking and throbbing and Bert's instinctive but unwilling complicity in her sadistic excitement. Seeing Marjory's "sly pale face," the narrator "angrily" asks her cousin why she is laughing. Marjory's evasive reply, "I'm older than you are," prompts the retrospective narrator, older than both of them, to interject a very important insight: "[F]rom that time on I knew there was something here I could not understand, a secret, an ugly bondage" (132). But the precise meaning of the obviously sexual "bondage" in this scene is left undefined, and is deeply confused, both by Alma's role and by her mother's masculinity.

After this flashback Aunt Thelma, ravaged by terminal cancer, suddenly arrives at the picnic with Uncle Bert and their children. The narrator remarks that she and her siblings "did not know Death to see it but were afraid of her in a different way than ever before" (132). This somewhat heavy-handed personification of death in Thelma's terrifying figure, her face "the dirty yellowish color of an old bruise" and her skin hanging "slack from the bones," begins a series of such symbolic characters in Munro's early fiction (132). These symbolic figures are "Old Bram," the scissors-man in "The Time of Death" (1956); the mysterious hypnotist in "A Trip to the Coast" (1961); and Joe Phippen, the paranoid old hermit in "Images" (1968) (Ross, 118). More significant, this description also juxtaposes the image of shameful sexual excitement with the frightening image of death: the narrator's two memories of Aunt Thelma's blind, throbbing face and of her dying face, drained of its excitedly glowing blood, are recalled one after the other.

The climax of this story is a second terrible scene between the uncle and the aunt, once again witnessed by the narrator and once again not completely comprehended. It is introduced by Marjory telling the narrator that she has to nurse her mother. Humiliated by her helplessness in the face of impending death, Aunt Thelma is now weak enough for her husband to humiliate *her*, for usurping his masculine role throughout their marriage and holding him in lifelong bondage. Although she still has her symbolic stick, she holds it up "shakily"; she has become powerless. In a quarrel about how many of the sheep on the farm belong to his wife, Uncle Bert yells at her in a voice "full of rage and loathing," a "terrible, hating, vengeful voice," mocking her and laughing "straight into her face" (133). Horrified by this eruption, the narrator's parents drag their children away from the scene, just as Marjory dragged the watching narrator away from the window. The shameful revelations of this second drama are clearly the explosive consequence of the first one, typical of Bert and Thelma's marriage. The children are bursting with bewildered questions, but their parents refuse to answer. Hastily piling their family into the truck, they drive home "in the sunlight, the golden air of July," an ironic contrast to the dark scene of sadistic humiliation, revenge, and impending death that they have left behind them (133).

This slightly clumsy, but immensely powerful, early story can be seen as the proto-type of many major Munro stories, for it contains many of the characteristic elements that recur in her later work. These include a watcher, a sense of something secret, a sudden revelation of the secret, and a struggle to control the threatening results of this revelation. The watcher is either a character – a retrospective first-person narrator or a third-person observer – or the omniscient author. The secret is something either shame-ful or frightening or both, temporarily concealed from the watching character. The most typical secret is often a combination of death and sex, the impending death of a family member or the character's apprehension of her or his own mortality or sexuality. A sudden split in the concealing surface reveals this secret through an unexpected event or experience that threatens the character's control. Struggling to maintain or regain control, the character may attempt to control the threatening external or internal forces, to dominate a relationship with another character, or often to do both.

For the purposes of this study, I have divided Munro's stories into four large and occasionally overlapping groups. They overlap mainly because, as already indicated, the inevitability of death hovers over much of Munro's fiction.[4] Haunted by her mother's death, Munro believes that it imbued her with "a great sense of fatality" and evoked a "tremendous guilt" ("What Is," 18; "Name," 70).[5] This sense of fatality, however, pro-duces her compulsion to watch life: "[T]he thing I most want to do," she says, "is *look* at things, and see the way everything is. And I only have a few years to do that. The collec-tion of molecules that is me isn't going to be here very long" ("Name," 71). But often what she makes her characters look at is ghosts. She peoples her fiction not only with the ghosts of dead mothers, as many critics have pointed out, but also with those of acciden-tally killed children and young people. Unlike Del in "Baptizing," who fights against drowning, six of her characters actually drown, and the literal or metaphorical image of a drowned corpse reappears in story after story, from *Lives of Girls and Women* to *The Progress of Love*, and "Meneseteung." Thus, even when these deaths do not constitute the major plot elements, they create a backdrop that intensifies the struggles of the living characters in the foreground. For thirty years – from "The Time of Death" (1956), through "Heirs of the Living Body" (1971), "Memorial" (1974), and "Accident" (1977), and right on to her most recent stories, "The Ferguson Girls Must Never Marry" (1982), "Miles City, Montana" (1985), and "Circle of Prayer" (1986) – Munro's fiction has been full of funerals. For her, death is one of those "intense ... moments of experi-ence" in which she can "zero in" on life (Slopen, 76).

But death is by no means the only recurrent topic in her fiction. In discussing the fiction of other writers, Munro has made an important observation that characterizes her own work, too:

> I disagree with this picture of writing that you progress from one book to the next and that you do different things, you open up new areas of your consciousness and for your readers, and that it's supposed to be a kind of step-ladder. ... It may be that you ... have to go back over and over again and mine the same material and look at it in different ways, or in the same way, and sometimes you get to it and sometimes you don't. ("Real Material," 12)

As the list of characteristic elements in her stories suggests, Munro recognizes that she returns to "the same material": "I've been writing the same kind of stories all along"

(Adachi, D3). She repeatedly returns to her sudden revelations of the submerged but rock-hard realities of life, certain sets of situations that threaten her characters' sense of control over their lives. Because her emphasis upon controlling these essentially uncontrollable realities is the central, paradoxical theme of her work, I have classified her stories into four groups according to the specific source of the external or internal power that threatens her narrators' or protagonists' sense of control. By comparing her techniques in these stories, I will show that, although the basic material of her stories remains much the same, she changes and develops her methods, especially those methods that connect her retrospective split point of view with her recurrent splitting metaphors.

In the first group is a series of stories about different characters – major male protagonists as well as female ones – presented from both the first-person and the third-person points of view. These characters observe, and sometimes participate in, external violence – not only beatings and murders but also accidents that end the lives of children. In this group of stories, the common element is the eruption of either deliberate or accidental violence that, like an underground stream that splits the earth, suddenly bursts through the seemly surface of everyday behavior. These frightening eruptions make the characters lose control of themselves or of the events in their lives, but then they struggle to regain it somehow. This pattern of eruptions, which can be traced through the thirty-nine years of Munro's fiction, climaxes in two of the stories in *The Progress of Love*, "Fits" and "Miles City, Montana." This is the group of stories I will discuss in this chapter.

In the second, and chronologically earlier group, to be discussed in chapter 3, is a series of stories told by the same first-person narrator, the unnamed little girl who appears in three stories in *Dance of the Happy Shades* and who reappears as Del Jordan, the retrospective narrator of *Lives of Girls and Women*. Like the watching narrator in "At the Other Place," who not only senses the power of both sexuality and natural death but also apprehends them in a particularly frightening synergistic combination, Del repeatedly sees these two centrally defining human experiences as closely related forces. Although both are, of course, internal forces, she sees them as terrifying powers loose in the world, powers that she must try to understand and, through understanding, somehow to control. Thus the fear of losing control and the importance of trying to maintain or regain it constitute a thematic similarity that these stories share with the first group. The two groups also have an important metaphorical similarity. "Images" (1968), one of the three stories narrated by Ben Jordan's daughter in *Dance of the Happy Shades*, and the interrelated stories of the novel narrated by Del Jordan are linked by a repeated metaphorical pattern, which reappears in the later stories of the first group. The function of this pattern, which equates the power of both sexuality and death with electric power or lightning, is analogous to the function of the pattern of eruptions that Munro repeatedly uses in the stories about violence. They both split open surfaces to reveal what is hidden inside or underneath. This analogous function is an important key to comprehending what Munro repeatedly demonstrates about sexuality, a dangerous power that threatens her characters' control.

But there are also major differences between these two groups of stories. In the first group, Munro uses different characters and also manipulates point of view in steadily more complicated and ironic ways than in the earlier Del stories. The second group, the Del stories, is also linked both thematically and metaphorically to the third and fourth groups of stories, both of which extend from Munro's first collection to her most recent collected and uncollected stories. To analyze and emphasize these important thematic and metaphorical links, I will discuss the Del stories out of chronological order. Because

Del is a writer-figure ironically ambivalent both about sexuality and her relationship to her mother, Del is Munro's most significant character. This double ambivalence and the deep internal struggles it creates in Del as a woman and as a writer link her thematically with the narrators and protagonists in both earlier and later stories.

Because Munro is much more interested in the psychological paradoxes of internal violence than in the final simplicity of external force, the third group of stories is by far the largest group. It consists mainly, though not completely, of stories about ambivalent characters struggling for power, primarily the power to control sexual encounters, love affairs, and marriages. But the situations that expose these characters' internal vulnerability sometimes also include aging or the ultimate humiliation of approaching death, especially as it affects sexuality. The vulnerability of these characters is revealed by their exposure either to sexual scenes or to scenes in which others are trying or failing to achieve control. The metaphorical link between some of these stories and *Lives of Girls and Women* is that the loss of control or the failure to achieve control is repeatedly equated with drowning, as in the climactic river scene of the novel. Thus, in this group of stories the question of control is often the humiliating question of *being* controlled by the power of sexual desire and the sexual partner. Most of the characters thus humiliated are deeply ambivalent female narrators or protagonists who abdicate their power. Like Del, they are ambivalent because a part of them wants to be controlled by the man but at the same time another part struggles for self-assertion against such control. At the conclusion of several of these stories, however, the question of which sex is in control is shown to be "beside the point" (SIB, 190). As at the end of "At the Other Place," death is in control. However, in Munro's most recent collection, *The Progress of Love*, the question sometimes has a new answer, for, although she continues to create deeply ambivalent female characters, there are also humiliated male characters and some controlling female ones. But the concept of control is shown to be ironically illusory in "White Dump" and in her satiric novella, "A Queer Streak." This third group of stories will be discussed in chapter 4.

The final group of stories is about parents and daughters, mainly mothers and daughters. These stories also examine the humiliations caused by the loss of control, but these losses repeatedly involve a daughter's failure to achieve emotional distance from her obsessive relationship with her mother. It is only in some of her most recent stories, the title stories in *The Moons of Jupiter* and *The Progress of Love*, that Munro grants these daughter-characters the emotional freedom that they seek. In these stories the daughters have become middle-aged mothers with adult daughters of their own. This last group of stories will be discussed in chapter 5.

In discussing these four major groups of stories, I will take the same freedom to slide up and down the time axis that Munro gives her retrospective narrators and protagonists. As already indicated, my basis of classification is, therefore, not primarily chronological but thematic and metaphorical. So I will not discuss the stories in Munro's six books in strict chronological order; neither will I discuss every story in every book. But within the four groups of stories that I have defined, I will generally discuss the works in chronological order, though sometimes I will also range back and forth within closely related thematic clusters in a given group to illuminate significant relationships between them. One such cluster, for example, consists of three stories in three different collections: "Lives of Girls and Women" (LGW), "Wild Swans" (WDY), and "Jesse and Meribeth" (PL) are all about adolescent sexual curiosity. Occasionally I will also discuss key stories more than once to illustrate different sets of relationships between them.

In adopting this type of organization, I will be following Munro's practice in yet another way, spatially as well as temporally. She has a uniquely nonlinear method of reading other writers' stories: "I can start reading them anywhere; from beginning to end, from end to beginning, from any point in between in either direction." The result of this non-linear reading is that she goes "into" a story "and move[s] back and forth ... and stay[s] in it for a while," as if the story were "like a house," a "structure" that "encloses space and makes connections between one enclosed space and another ..." ("What Is Real," 5). I will demonstrate the unity of Munro's fiction by making such connections myself, not only between the spaces or rooms in her carefully constructed story-houses but also between the structures of those she has built in similar architectural styles.

The shameful pattern of watching beatings and murderous humiliations that is introduced in "At the Other Place" recurs briefly in "The Ottawa Valley" (1974), and much more significantly in "Royal Beatings" (1977), "Executioners" (1974), and "Fits" (1986). Although both *Lives of Girls and Women* and *Who Do You Think You Are?* begin with a story in which a child is beaten – "The Flats Road" and "Royal Beatings," respectively – there is a significant difference: the beating episodes in "The Flats Road" are not watched by Del, the narrator. She only hears Uncle Benny's "stories" of how Madeleine, his teenage mail-order wife, beats Diane, her daughter (LGW, 22). Even though Diane has visible "bruises on her legs," at the end of the story Del's mother suggests, "Uncle Benny could have made up the beatings" (18, 26–27). This ambiguity about what happened disappears in "The Ottawa Valley," where, as in "At the Other Place," the first-person narrator actually watches her aunt beat her children. Aunt Lena's name is very similar to both Aunt Thelma's and Madeleine's, and Aunt Lena's physique and personality also resemble Thelma's. Lena has "arms ... as long and strong as a man's," dominates her husband, and beats her children (SIB, 232). Like both Uncle Bert and Uncle Benny, Uncle James, Lena's husband, "never held [the children] back from being beaten, never protested" (233). Sometimes Aunt Lena dwindles to "an unthreatening dark shape," holding a child on her lap, but when the visiting first-person narrator watches her beat her howling children, the scene repeats the earlier one in "At the Other Place" in two key ways: in the presence of the watching observer and in the humiliation evoked (238). The narrator comments that, although her cousins soon forgot Aunt Lena's beatings, "[w]ith me, such a humiliation could last for weeks, or forever" (232). Although the word *humiliation* has many meanings in this story, as I will show in chapter 5, the phrase "such a humiliation" restricts the meaning in this sentence to the humiliation of being beaten. It is this meaning that recurs in "Royal Beatings," the opening story in *Who Do You Think You Are?*, first published on 14 March 1977, in the *New Yorker*.

If the watching narrator in "The Ottawa Valley" is one of Munro's personae, the eternal duration of the humiliation with which the narrator identifies is confirmed by the second reappearance of the character that she watches, the beaten child. But in "Royal Beatings," which Munro has defined as "a *big* breakthrough story, a kind of story that [she] didn't intend to write at all," the narrative method she uses to describe the child's beatings changes in several significant ways ("Real Material," 21). First, in contrast to "At the Other Place" and "The Ottawa Valley," where she describes the beatings in the past tense, in "Royal Beatings" she uses the present tense, with present progressive verbs narrating the actual action: "her father is ... cracking the belt at her ..." (WDY, 17). The psychological effect created by this use of the "dramatic Present" is defined by

Otto Jespersen in *Essentials of English Grammar:* "the speaker … forgets all about time and recalls what he is recounting as vividly as if it were now present before his eyes" (238, 239). The significance of Jespersen's reference to the speaker's eyes is emphasized by Munro's revealing comment on the beating scene: "I just wanted to look at it and think about it and it was a drama in my mind" ("Interview": Hancock, 101). Thus, the point of view has also changed, for the author herself is the watching narrator here. In contrast to the first-person narrators Munro uses in the two earlier stories, in "Royal Beatings" she uses a split third-person point of view. The speaker, therefore, is not Rose, the child being beaten, but the narrating author who is watching her as the drama of the relived memory of the beating is synchronized with its narration. The dreamlike nature of this memory is suggested by Munro's reference to "Royal Beatings" as "the story about the child being beaten" ("Interview": Hancock, 101); this phrase echoes the title of Freud's essay about beating fantasies, "A Child Is Being Beaten." That Munro consciously conceived of the memory of the beating as Rose's repeatedly relived fantasy is indicated not only by her description of the beating scene as a mental drama but also by her use of the present tense and the third person for its narration.

The third and most important difference between this story and the two earlier ones is that Rose, the child being beaten, is no longer a minor character but the protagonist. In significant correlation with this difference, the parents' roles have also been reversed. Although Flo, Rose's stepmother, instigates the beating because she wants Rose punished for verbally humiliating her, it is Rose's father who beats her while Flo watches. This double change, however, does not alter one basic similarity between the reactions of the two sets of parents in this story and in "At the Other Place." Both stories suggest that the adults' behavior reveals something shameful about them. At the beginning of "Royal Beatings," Rose thinks, "she could not stand to know anymore, about her father, or about Flo; she pushed any discovery aside with embarrassment and dread" (3). But because of the shift in point of view, the shameful revelations in this story include a significant addition to the adults' behavior: Rose's pleasurable complicity in her own beating.

In his essay "A Child Is Being Beaten," Freud discusses the genesis of such masochism in the "high degree of pleasure and … pleasurable, auto-erotic gratification" associated with girls' beating fantasies (173). In the first stage of these fantasies, as in "At the Other Place" and "The Ottawa Valley," a girl watches another child being beaten by an adult. In later stages, as in "Royal Beatings," she watches *herself* being beaten by her father. The change in the identity of the beating adult clarifies the secret significance of both Aunt Thelma's and Aunt Lena's powerful masculinity: they are fathers in disguise. The second stage of the beating fantasies, "the most important and the most momentous" (179), Freud defines as "a meeting-place between the sense of guilt and sexual love. *It is not only the punishment for the forbidden genital relation, but also the regressive substitute for it*, and from this latter source it derives the libidinal excitation which is from this time attached to it, and which finds its outlet in onanistic acts. Here for the first time we have the essence of masochism" (184). The similarities and differences between "At the Other Place" and "Royal Beatings" illustrate these two stages vividly.

In both stories the beating is administered in almost exactly the same way, with sexual overtones of almost orgasmic release. When Aunt Thelma beat Alma, her daughter, "[s]he was swinging the belt and it flew out of her hand, so she used the flat of her hands against the sides of Alma's head" (132). When Rose's father beats her, he too begins with his belt, then switches to his hands: "Her father is … cracking the belt at her when he can, then abandoning it and using his hands. Bang over the ear, then bang over the other ear" (WDY, 17). Just as the narrator in "At the Other Place" observes Aunt Thelma's sadistic pleasure, so Rose observes the same feeling building up in her father as she watches his reaction to Flo's accusations against her. She sees the appalling revelations in his face: "It fills with hatred and pleasure. Rose sees that and knows it. Is that just a description of anger, should she see his eyes filling up with anger? No. Hatred is right. Pleasure is right. His face loosens and changes and grows younger ..." as he "starts to loosen his belt" (16). The combination of these two loosening actions is highly suggestive.

The other two participants also experience a release charged with guilt because it is felt and defined in sexually suggestive terms. After instigating and watching the sickening family charade, Flo becomes very solicitous. The cold cream she brings Rose, the tempting snack that she prepares and takes to Rose in her bedroom, and the acrobatic tricks that she later performs to amuse the family all reveal her guilt about the pleasure that she has derived from Rose's beating.

But Rose's masochistic pleasure is the most significant because it is the new element in this story and because it is both psychological and physical. During the beating she splits in half to become observer and observed, listening to her own "willing sound of humiliation and defeat," and watching herself playing her father's "victim with a self-indulgence that arouses, and maybe hopes to arouse, his final, sickened contempt" (17). The key word here, *self-indulgence*, with its autoerotic connotations, also suggests the true nature of Rose's intensely sensual enjoyment of her sweet snack. At first she tries to resist the miserable temptation to eat the sandwiches, chocolate cookies, and chocolate milk, but soon she is "roused and troubled ... by the smell of salmon, the anticipation of crisp chocolate. ..." Finally, "in helpless corruption," with chocolate syrup smeared on her fingers, she eats everything, "though she sniffles with shame" (19). The highly ambiguous connotations of *roused, corruption*, and *shame* do not suggest a simple, childish appetite. And Rose succumbs to its pleasurable gratification much as her father, seduced by Flo, succumbs to the pleasure of beating his daughter.

After the beating and its aftermath are both over, the family members "feel a queer lassitude, a convalescent indolence, not far off satisfaction," that, as their mutual embarrassment evaporates, gradually mellows into "a feeling of permission, relaxation, even a current of happiness ..." (19, 20). These distinctly postcoital interpretations by the ironic, omniscient narrator, who, along with Rose, has watched the royal beating, are further intensified by the story's narrative structure. The story begins with Flo's threat to Rose, "You are going to get one Royal Beating," but she does not carry out her threat of punishment immediately (1). Instead, Flo's conversation with a visitor to her store introduces the story of Becky Tyde, a dwarf deformed by polio, and Becky's late father, the prosperous English butcher who once owned a large brick house, a slaughterhouse, and an orchard. The much discussed parallels between this story and the story of Rose's beating, which it interrupts, are derived from two subtly intertwined sets of similarities.[6]

The first set of similarities connects Flo's steaming resentment of her stepdaughter's verbal skills and the community's envy and resentment of the well-to-do outsider. After Becky contracted polio and became deformed, Tyde kept her out of school: "He didn't want people gloating" (7). The second set of similarities emerges from the rumors that the ignorant community manufactures when its itch to gloat is frustrated. The community's malicious fantasies about Tyde and his daughter explicitly emphasize the elements only subliminally suggested by Rose's sensually self-indulgent complicity in her beating.

These rumors include tales not only of beatings but also of incest, pregnancy, and infanticide to explain why Becky was deformed and why she never left the house. Telling these "lurid" tales about Becky and Tyde, Flo "regretfully" admits, "It was all lies in all probability" (7). The adverb suggests that Flo would dearly love the stories to be true, for Tyde, with his prosperity and his position, has the same effect on the community as Rose has on Flo. Before calling in Rose's father to beat her *for* her, Flo angrily asks, "Who do you think you are?" (13). Symbolically, the community asked Tyde exactly the same angry question when it, too, decided to call in somebody to beat him on its behalf, powerful surrogates to cut him and his pretensions of superiority down to size. "Three useless young men" were "got together, by more influential" members of the community to give Tyde "a horsewhipping in the interests of public morality" (7). Flo uses an analogous moral argument when she accuses Rose of teaching Brian, her brother, dirty words. Both arguments are transparently trumped-up rationalizations to justify persecution, for Rose silently protests that Flo has been "telling the grossest sort of lies, twisting everything to suit herself," just as the townspeople told lies about Tyde, distorting everything to suit themselves about him (15). When he later died as a result of the vicious beating that symbolically reduced him to the source of his resented wealth, bloody "*Butcher's meat*," the three young men received prison sentences; but these sentences were merely more pretense, for the men were soon released and even given jobs (8).

In an essay entitled "What Is Real?" Munro has identified the story of Tyde's beating as "a big chunk of reality," a true "story out of an old newspaper," that shows "the dark side of human nature, the beast let loose, the evil we can run up against in communities and families" (36). But she characteristically rejects a didactic purpose in inserting this chunk of terrible reality into her story. "I don't do it to show anything," she protests. "I put this story at the heart of my story because I need it there and it belongs there. It is the black room at the centre of the house," the "structure which encloses the soul of my story," and all the other rooms lead "to and away from" this evil black room (36). This metaphor of the house with the central black room shows why Munro uses the Tyde story to interrupt the scene of Rose's beating: to emphasize both the psychological and the perversely theatrical parallels between them. Like the theatrical beating of Rose by her father, the trial and the abbreviated punishment of the three horsewhippers constitute a "farce" (WDY, 9). Both of these episodes are farcical performances in which every participant plays a preassigned role. So in the case of Rose's beating, these roles are not the "savage and splendid" ones that Rose imagines at the beginning of the story, when she childishly fantasizes about a royal beating, witnessed by "a crowd of formal spectators" (1). Freud comments on the "artistic superstructure of day-dreams, ... of great significance for the life of the person concerned, [which] had grown up over the masochistic beating-phantasy. The function of this superstructure was to make possible a feeling of gratified excitation ..." (185). But in Rose's case this gratified excitation is soon replaced by a shameful reality devoid of all "dignity" (WDY, 1).

Rose thinks of her father as "king of the royal beatings," but this fantasy image is ironically exploded when she overhears him quote from *The Tempest* (1). Gassed in World War I, he constantly coughs and mutters to himself in the shed where he works. Here she overhears him speak Prospero's lines, "The cloud-capped towers, the gorgeous palaces" (4). Although Rose does not recognize the passage, the allusion to Prospero deepens Munro's irony by emphasizing the difference between *The Tempest* and the sordid farce in which Rose's father performs. Prospero is the rightful Duke of Milan, so when he uses his magic powers to punish his wicked enemies, his revenge *is* a royal beating that the usurpers richly deserve. This subtle contrast between a powerful, aristocratic magician and a chronically ill man manipulated by his wife emphasizes Munro's ironic point that a similar release of tension in "real life" swiftly degenerates from a "gorgeous" fantasy into something shabby and shameful, into *farce noire*, a vengeful triumph of the underground id (1).

This emphasis on the shameful release from analogous tensions hidden under the surface of family and community life also characterizes the aftermath of the beating, the story's epilogue, and Munro's further comments on her story. After the beating, Flo and Rose's father discuss the old men who sit in front of Flo's store. To explain the presence of the planet Venus in the evening sky, the old men make up their own fantasies: they say it is an American airship. The ignorant old men have "never heard of the planet Venus," and, Rose knows, neither has Flo (20). Just as the old men do not recognize what they are looking at, neither do the members of Rose's family recognize what they are doing. Venus is the goddess of sexual love, and there is a shameful and secretly sexual component in the sadomasochistic family farce in which all three participate. Although my references to Freud's analysis of masochistic fantasies are not meant to suggest that Munro had Freud consciously in mind, this final allusion to Venus, combined with the genesis of the tense family situation in "a dream ... go[ing] back and back into other dreams, ... maddeningly dim ... and familiar and elusive," reinforces a sexual interpretation of the dark underground of family relationships (WDY, 11).

In the epilogue, set in the present, Hat Nettleton, one of the horse-whippers egged on to get Tyde, and Flo, who egged on Rose's father and originally told her Tyde's story, are both residents in the county home for the aged. Like the formidable Aunt Thelma in "At the Other Place," the two ferocious characters have both been diminished by old age. When Rose hears Nettleton interviewed on the radio, she thinks that if she could tell Flo about the interview, Flo would have "her worst suspicions gorgeously confirmed" (22). But the completely senile Flo no longer talks or listens to anyone, although she occasionally bites her nurse, and Nettleton, although cackling with belligerent obscenity, does not say anything at all about the long-ago Tyde affair. Thus, because both characters are confined and reduced, the parallels between them continue.

Munro's further comments on the story make it clear that her psychological purpose in writing it is to control *her* worst suspicions about the shameful, hidden secrets of human nature by turning their confirmation into art: "Who told me to write [Tyde's] story? Who feels any need of it before it's written? I do. I do, so that I might grab off this piece of horrid reality and install it where I see fit, even if Hat Nettleton and his friends are still around to make me sorry" ("What Is Real?," 36).

Munro's comment implies that the desire for revenge is always burning in "the beast let loose," and this beast breaks out even more violently in a story published three years earlier, "Executioners" ("What Is Real?," 36). Here again, the watching narrator's primary emotion begins as humiliation; here again, as Sandra Djwa has pointed out, the narrative structure of the story develops a thematic parallel between two situations (186); here again, the metaphors emphasize the sudden bursting out of what was rigidly repressed; and here again, the final irony is generated by allusions to literary concepts of dignity.

Helena, the retrospective first-person narrator of "Executioners," is humiliated by her classmates' taunts about her clothes; like the narrator of "Walker Brothers Cowboy," she is overdressed by her ladylike mother. Helena puts herself into an even more humiliating situation, however, by condescending to a bootlegger's son, Howard Troy, a retarded classmate so unteachable that both teachers and students simply ignore him. By giving him a piece of paper and a pencil, Helena brings herself to his attention.

She soon regrets her deed. Howard begins to waylay her and to torment her with sexual taunts: "*You want to fuck*" (SIB, 142). This obscenity is the spoken equivalent of the dirty words on the sidewalk in "Walker Brothers Cowboy." In the story's epilogue, Helena, now an elderly widow, tries to explain how deeply the word *fuck* humiliated her in the past:

> It used to be a word that could be thrown against you, that could bring you to an absolute stop. Humiliation was promised, but was perhaps already there, was contained in the hearing, the being stopped, having to acknowledge. Shame could choke you. … quantities of greasy shame, … indigestible bad secrets. The vulnerability which is in itself a shame. We are shamefully made. (142–43)

Convinced that only she is vulnerable to such torment, Helena never tells anyone what is happening. But of course her silence and rigid repression do not work: "it had to be concealed and blotted out, stamped out, quick, quick, but I could never get it all, the knowledge, the memory, it was running underground and spurting out at another place in my mind" (143). Like the "*underground stream that surfaces in the murderous driving*" of the drunken rural drivers in "Home" (a story published in 1974, the same year as "Executioners"), this subterranean urge surfaces in murderous thoughts (142): Helena imagines horribly sadistic punishments for Howard.

Her sadistic fantasies are closely connected to her description of her relationship with the family of Robina, her mother's sinister maid. There is a deeply rankling enmity between Stump Troy, Howard's legless father, crippled in a mill accident, and Jimmy and Duval, Robina's brothers. Stump and the brothers are "rivals, or fallen-out accomplices, in the bootlegging business" (148). After Robina tells Helena how much her brothers hate Stump Troy, Helena thinks of how much she hates Howard. Helena's relationship with Jimmy and Duval suggests the hidden reason for her violent reaction to Howard's sexual taunts: he knows what she wants. When Jimmy and Duval tickle her "to make [her] break into screams of jittery pleasure," call her their "girl friend," and "play-[fight] over [her], each of them grabbing [her] from the other and trapping [her] in a hard hug," her reaction to these mock battles for her possession is obviously sexual (147). That reaction is the unacknowledged reason for her fantasy about stabbing Howard: then "all kinds of pus, venomous substances, would spurt and flow, everything would leak away" (149). Her fantasy of revenge combines an image of Howard's suffering with an act of denial through projection, in which his tortured body becomes her tortured mind. What she is really describing is the foul purging of her own ambivalent hatred, her guilty lust not only for vengeance but for denial.

In the very next sentence after this fantasy, in a sudden associative leap forward in time, the two parts of the plot are fused (Djwa, 185–86). Helena narrates: "The fire filled the house the way blood fills a boil. It seemed every minute ready to burst, but the skin still held" (SIB, 149). Robina, who knows that her brothers have committed arson to transform *their* fantasies of revenge into reality, watches the Troys' burning house "in a great state of excitement. She trembled and crackled, she was like a burning beam herself" (150). This scarlet simile links Robina not only with the burning house but also with the blood-filled boil of hate that is Helena's mind. Like Helena fantasizing about Howard's horrible punishment, Robina, who has only one arm herself, licks her chops with sadistic relish over the legless Stump trapped in the blazing house: "He's not going to walk out of there, is he?" (151). This gloating question echoes Helena's earlier description of how she walked past Howard when he called "fuck" after her: "I walked past him with … my breath drawn, just like somebody walking through a wall of flame" (142). As the burning house collapses, this simile leaps into reality. Howard, whose initial attempt to rescue his father has been prevented, has been watching the fire helplessly, but suddenly he rushes into the collapsing house and dies with his father.

As the epilogue transfers the reader to the present, Helena's sense of complicity in the bootleggers' revenge is still festering in her mind. Although she tries to drown her memory in whiskey, to her Calvinistic conscience the fire still seems an eruption of her own secret desire: she wished and she watched. Like the constantly replayed beating in "Royal Beatings," the fire will continue burning in her mind as long as she or anybody else "who could have remembered it" is alive (155). Confession, therefore, is not catharsis.

The Homeric allusions in the names of Helena and Troy and in the burning of the house also function in much the same ironic way as the allusions to *The Tempest* and the theatrical metaphors do in "Royal Beatings." Helena is not a beautiful queen fought over by the Greeks and Trojans but an overdressed and sexually confused schoolgirl "play-fought" over by two bootleggers (147). The burning of the Troys' house is not the fabled destruction of the topless towers of Ilium, but an act of arson committed against a legless man and his retarded son. Howard's rush into the burning house is "far too late to save anybody," although those onlookers who interpret his action as a second desperate attempt to rescue his father see him as "heroic" (152). This adjective ironically links Howard with the semidivine hero Aeneas, who carried his crippled old father, Anchises, out of the burning ruins of Troy. Anchises was crippled by a lightning bolt for boasting of the love of Venus, Aeneas's mother. It is almost as if Munro were rewriting "A Basket of Strawberries," once again to reject Mr. Torrance's far-fetched fantasies about a classical dreamworld. Howard does not found a new empire, no one composes a classical epic about him, and no one has any definitive "explanations" of what he has done (152). But the pathetic difference between Vergil's hero and the retarded, but crazily courageous, Howard subtly shifts the reader's final sympathies from Helena to Howard. And through this completely unexpected shift, these allusions emphasize the same shameful irony that the fantasizing theatricality of "Royal Beatings" does. In both stories, the final result is murder.

Munro has defined the genesis of her stories as her desire to get "*at* some kind of emotional core that [she] want[s] to investigate" or to approach "something that is mysterious and important" ("What Is," 17; Untitled, 178). These three stories – "At the Other Place," "Royal Beatings," and "Executioners" – all get at the same violent and mysterious emotional core, and although "Royal Beatings," unlike the other two, is written in the third person, the role of the watching observer is clear both in the repeated splits in Rose's perception and in the author's comments. As already illustrated, Rose not only watches herself performing at the time but, from the retrospective vantage point of a later time, she or the narrating author also comments on what has happened earlier. At the critical moment, for instance, just before Rose's father begins beating her, the narration is interrupted to describe Rose's thoughts in the future: "She has since wondered about murders, and murderers. Does the thing have to be carried through … to prove … that such a thing can happen, that there is nothing that can't happen …?" (WDY, 16). When the interrupted beating scene is resumed, Rose is seeking "rescue" by staring down at the kitchen linoleum instead of at her father's shamefully excited face as he removes his belt. But she sees that "the patterns of linoleum can leer up at you, treachery is the other side of dailiness" (16). The startling personification in this interpretive hindsight emphasizes the scene's sexual significance: not the mother but the *father* beats the daughter. The displacement of the leer from the father's far too naked face to a much safer, disguised location – the linoleum – seems to be an observation from the point of view of the generalizing narrator rather than of Rose. The distance of this narrator from Rose suggests a frightening answer to Rose's question about murders: when the rigid dailiness is shattered, anything *can* happen, including murder.[7]

Murder also shatters the decent daily surface in a story in Munro's latest collection, *The Progress of Love*. In "Fits" (1986), as in "Royal Beatings" and "Executioners," the narrative structure develops a thematic parallel between several situations, and here again Munro's images and metaphors dramatize a violent emotional eruption. But the manipulation of point of view is something definitely different from both the retrospective first-person point of view in "Executioners" and the third-person point of view in "Royal Beatings." The third-person male protagonist of "Fits," Robert Kuiper, does not observe the violence. Instead, Peg, his wife, delivering some eggs to their neighbors, Walter and Nora Weebles, discovers their corpses. Walter has murdered his wife and then shot himself. But instead of being narrated directly, Peg's experience is related indirectly from Robert's point of view.

Robert's role as an observer is defined in the beginning of the story: he is described as an outsider in Gilmore, the rural community on Lake Huron where the action is set. Although his father used to own stores in Gilmore, Robert does not settle there until his father dies and he himself is over forty. After Peg's discovery, he gradually reconstructs her experience from several direct and indirect sources. "He picture[s] what happened" from what he is told by her; by the constable to whom she initially reports her discovery; by Karen, Peg's co-worker; and by various other characters, including Clayton, one of Peg's teenage sons from her first marriage (PL, 111). Thus, the "many abominable details" of what Peg must have seen in the Weebles' bedroom are *doubly* distanced by being filtered through the point of view of an outsider and a secondhand observer, a witness who observes not the murder scene itself but only the bloodstained observer returned from that scene (130).

Robert first hears what has happened from the constable who has already investigated the Weebles' house. Then rushing to the store where Peg works, Robert sees that her coat is smeared with blood. Karen, Peg's co-worker, tells him that Peg also left bloody footprints when she entered the store. Later, at home, he observes his wife: "Robert was watching her, from time to time. He would have said that he was watching to see … if she seemed numb, or strange, or showed a quiver. … But in fact he was watching her just because there was no sign of such difficulty and because he knew there wouldn't be" (124). The repetition of the word *watching* emphasizes Robert's role as a third-person observer. He is not surprised by his wife's behavior because he has always considered her calm and "self-contained" (109). His limited knowledge of the Weebles also underscores their seemly self-control; he knew them only as a good-looking, well-dressed, fairly affluent retired couple who lived in an immaculate house.

The other characters with whom Robert discusses the Weebles all speculate about various possible reasons for the catastrophe, such as imminent financial ruin or terminal illness, but all these speculations prove false. Although there seems to be no explanation, Clayton, Peg's son, insists that his mother was not "surprised" that the Weebles "could do it" (125). When she insists that she *was* surprised, Clayton suddenly reminds her of the terrible quarrels that she used to have with his father, from whom she is divorced. During these quarrels Clayton "used to lie in bed and think" that one of his parents "was going to come and kill [him] with a knife" (126).

At this point Munro has the listening Robert interject a metaphorical comment that suggests his function as not only an observer but also a narrator. His comment explains the title of the story, "Fits," and defines the parallel between the Weebles' marriage and Peg's marriage to Dave, her first husband. Robert tells Clayton, "[I]t's like an earthquake or a volcano. It's that kind of happening. It's a kind of fit. People can take a fit like the earth takes a fit. But it only happens once in a long while. It's a freak occurrence" (126). This metaphor of an earthquake splitting the earth or a volcano erupting is like the "underground stream" in "Home," the leering linoleum in "Royal Beatings," and the bursting boil in "Executioners."[8] But Clayton rejects the freakishness of earthquakes and volcanoes and insists, "If you want to call that a fit, you'd have to call it a periodic fit. Such as people have, married people have" (126). Although this remark could also describe the fits of two earlier married couples, Aunt Thelma and Uncle Bert in "At the Other Place," and Rose's father and stepmother in "Royal Beatings," a comparison of these two couples and the Weebles shows that the reasons for their "fits" become more mysterious. In "At the Other Place," at least one reason is perfectly clear; in "Royal Beatings," the reason is only subliminally suggested; in "Fits" it not only remains mysterious but mirrors the mysteriousness of the two other relationships.

After his conversation with Peg and Clayton, Robert goes for a long walk, during which he recalls his relationship with Lee, his lover before his marriage to Peg. Just as violence erupted through the deceptively ordinary surface of the Weebles' marriage and of Peg and Dave's, so an earthquake "split open" Lee and Robert's relationship. "[T]hey found themselves saying the cruellest things to each other that they could imagine," and they said these things with "loathing," the same noun Munro used to describe Uncle Bert's hatred of his dying wife (127). And just as the face of Rose's father "fills with hatred and pleasure" as he prepares to inflict pain upon her (WDY, 16), so Robert and Lee "trembled with murderous pleasure, … they exulted in wounds inflicted but also in wounds received …" (PL, 128). Here the separation between verbal and specifically sexual sadism quickly dissolves, for Robert remembers that their volcanic quarrel culminated in making love "with a self-conscious brutality," after which "they were enormously and finally sick of each other …" (128).[9] Extrapolating from his own experience, therefore, he imagines that something similar must have occurred between Peg and Dave, who abandoned his family to work in the Arctic.

But during these reminiscences on his walk, Robert is still worrying about what Peg told him that she saw outside the Weebles' bedroom. She said that she saw Walter's "leg stretched out into the hall," and then she entered the room (125). Having heard the constable's description of the murder scene before he heard Peg's, Robert knows that she has lied to him on this point. But to increase the suspense of her narration, Munro delays until the very end of her story Robert's memory of the constable's description of the bedroom scene.

Worrying about Peg's false story, Robert slowly approaches what he eventually recognizes as an auto junkyard full of wrecked cars almost completely buried in deep drifts of frozen snow. These "[t]wisted" and "gutted" cars, piled crazily on top of each other, recall the junkyard full of wrecked cars in "The Edge of Town" and the drunken accidents in "Home" (131). Here Munro develops the buried cars into a complex symbol. Robert's doubly distanced point of view, combined with his slow, puzzled approach to the junkyard, emphasizes the many layers of mystery concealing the true nature not only of the Weebles but also of his "preternaturally reserved" wife (Duchêne, 109).

When he began his walk, Robert noticed curious townspeople driving by the Weebles' house. These drivers "seemed joined to their cars, making some new kind of monster that came poking around in a brutally curious way" (PL, 126). Now in the deep snow covering the auto junkyard, he sees "a new kind of glitter under the trees" (130). Through the repetition of the phrase "new kind," Munro suggests the metaphorical function of the junkyard. The "congestion of shapes, with black holes in them, and unmatched arms or petals reaching up to the lower branches of the trees" seem monstrous (130). As Robert approaches, he at first cannot identify these vaguely human shapes: "They did not look like anything, except perhaps a bit like armed giants half collapsed, frozen in combat. … He kept waiting for an explanation, and not getting one, until he got very close. He was so close he could almost have touched one of these monstrosities before he saw that they were just old cars" (130–31). His puzzled curiosity about the "new kind of glitter" finally satisfied, he then remembers what the constable told him: Walter Weebles blew off his head. "What was left of it was laying out in the hall" (131). This description links Walter's mangled corpse with the anthropomorphic car wrecks buried in the snow, a fusion foreshadowed by the earlier link between the "brutally curious" neighbors and their cars. But the murderous Walter and his neighbors are not the only monsters loose in the story.

Going home to his wife, Robert suddenly realizes that she has seen Walter's shattered skull, *not* his leg. "That was not what anybody turning at the top of the stairs would see and would have to step over, step through, … to go into the bedroom to look at the rest of what was there" (131). This realization forces the reader to reinterpret Robert's picture of Peg. He has seen her as "reserved" and "self-contained," with "a scrubbed, youthful look," created not only by her schoolgirlish wardrobe but also by her earnest participation in cultural courses at the local high school (108, 109). He has read her neat notes on Prince Henry the Navigator, whose "*importance … was in the inspiration and encouragement of other explorers for Portugal, even though he did not go on voyages himself*" (109). But ironically, this description applies to Walter and Peg as well as to Prince Henry and the Portuguese explorers, for Walter inspired Peg's exploration of his bedroom. All the townspeople expect Peg to be "absolutely shattered" by her experience, but, on the contrary, she was so fascinated by what Walter had done that she wanted to see more of it (120). So, instead of screaming and running away, she stepped through whatever remained of Walter's exploded head and entered the bedroom to look at Nora's corpse. That is how her feet and coat got bloodstained. Although incapable of Walter's physical violence, Peg was thus exhibiting a much more violent form of the same brutal curiosity that her neighbors exhibited later on. Along with Robert, the reader is forced to figure this all out like a detective, for, like Walter's mysteriously hidden motives and like the anthropomorphic monsters in the snow, Peg's real nature is buried and frozen, rigid and deeply repressed. Only when Clayton reminds her of her quarrels with his father does the watching Robert see her expression of "steady, helpless, unapologetic pain" (126). This expression is as close as she comes to revealing to Robert the eruptions in her past life, the emotional upheavals that occurred when she, like Walter, suddenly lost control. This superbly crafted story, in which the peripheral point of view is reinforced by the central symbol, is the climax of Munro's collected stories about murderous violence.

Although Walter's suicide and the anthropomorphic wrecked cars in "Fits" suggest the psychological ambiguity of any distinction between deliberate and accidental violence, the second type of story about external violence is the accident story. In a significant group of seven stories – "The Time of Death" (1956), "Memorial" (1974), "Accident" (1977), "Wood" (1980), "Circle of Prayer" (1986), "Monsieur les Deux Chapeaux" (1985), and "Miles City, Montana" (1985) – accidents symbolize the sudden, violent eruption of a different world into the controlled daily one. Only in "Circle of Prayer" is the accident not the main pivot of the plot. Although not all the accidents are fatal, the characters who die are all children; thus the shock is intensified. In different ways the surviving characters in all these stories try to reestablish their shattered sense of control.

Munro's technique in "Time of Death" resembles, although in a limited way, the subtly indirect method just discussed in "Fits." Originally published in the *Canadian Forum*, this story is not narrated directly but pieced together nonchronologically by an omniscient author. Like the Weebles murder-suicide, the pivotal event of the story, the fatal scalding of retarded Benny Parry, happens before the story begins and is never actually described. Instead, Munro gives the reader three reactions to the child's death – by Leona, his mother; Patricia, his sister; and a neighbor, Allie McGee – and a concluding description of the frozen small-town setting by the omniscient author. At the beginning of the story, Allie briefly and ironically observes Leona's reaction to her son's death. Allie's perspective, similar to Robert's internal and peripheral angle in "Fits," defines Allie as the watcher in this story, noting Leona's self-defensive lies and evasions but saying nothing, just as Robert says nothing to his wife about her lies.

It is nine-year-old Patricia's reaction, delayed until the story's climax, that dramatizes the terrible price of self-control. Unlike her mother, who has hysterics almost immediately and therefore bounces back to normality, Patricia, who feels responsible for Benny's death because she was boiling the water that scalded him, exerts formidable self-control and succeeds in repressing her guilt until the visit of Brandon, the scissors-man. Because Benny was fond of the old man, Patricia associates the two of them. When she hears Brandon coming down the road with "his unintelligible chant, mournful and shrill, and so strange that you would think … that there was a madman loose in the world," she begins "to scream …" (DHS, 98). Because she has tried very hard to act "the way a grown-up does," and to be the careful mother to her siblings that the slovenly Leona is not, her terror of something completely uncontrolled in the world shatters her: she turns into "a wretched little animal insane with rage or fear" (92, 99). The sharp contrast between Leona's and Patricia's reactions makes this early story about self-control memorable, although Munro has criticized it as "a kind of imitation Southern story" and has noted both its lack of complexity and the lack of "compassion" for Leona ("Real Material," 23; Untitled, 181).

"Memorial," published eighteen years later in 1974, handles the same subject of accidental death in an infinitely more complicated and sophisticated fashion. Set in an affluent, suburban Vancouver home in the 1960s, this satirical story is narrated mainly, but not completely, from the point of view of Eileen, the aunt of seventeen-year-old Douglas, who has just been killed in a freakish car crash. Like Robert in "Fits" and Allie in "The Time of Death," Eileen is a third-person observer, on the periphery of the main action, watching her trendy sister, June, and her wealthy brother-in-law, Ewart, on the day of their son's funeral or "memorial." Like Allie, silently critical of Leona, Eileen is inwardly disapproving of the psychological jargon June uses in her determined efforts to demonstrate self-control despite her son's death. In the past, the two sisters have quarreled about June's compulsion to control everything, and Eileen has tried "to turn June's own language against her" by insisting, "Order is an anal perversion" (SIB, 210). Now, however, she expects June's body to "have loosened, in her grief, ... her voice" to "have grown uncertain, or been silenced" (208).

But on the morning of her son's funeral, June chats on the telephone in "a cheerful buoyant matter-of-fact voice" in which Eileen disapprovingly discerns "some lively insistence on control" (209). She suspects that both her sister, still confidently mouthing the clichés of pop psychology she acquired in college, and Ewart, her earnest husband, see the funeral as "[a]n occasion to display ... [their] values" (214), and Eileen recognizes that their "earnestness was no joke. Here was a system of digestion which found everything to its purposes," including the terror of "accidental death," which it "accepted, chewed and altered, assimilated, destroyed" (216). Eileen admits that "[w]ithout religion" it is impossible to face "the fact of ... death," and even with it, "it [can]not be done" (215). Nevertheless, she is "offended" when a passage from *The Prophet* is read at Douglas's memorial service (221). She rejects this "modern equivalent of piety" as a fraudulent attempt to conceal and control the harsh facts of accidental death, which she compares to being struck by "lightning" (221, 215). "People die; they suffer, they die. ... Illness and accidents. They ought to be respected, not explained. Words are all shameful. They ought to crumble in shame" (221). In this critical mood, she rejects all words, even though she was a literature major in college. She decides that "[s]ilence" is "the only possible thing" because, listening to her sister's determined psychobabble, she feels that speaking any words at all is pretending to have control and therefore perpetrating some kind of verbal and emotional "fraud" (221).

If this story ended here, the contrast between the two sisters' attitudes would be clearly defined. But in her insistence on complexity, clear definition is exactly what Munro wishes to avoid. Therefore, the story continues to a very ironic conclusion in which the contrast between the two sisters, unlike the contrast between Leona and Patricia Parry, is deliberately blurred by the sudden and repeatedly dissonant intrusion of another point of view, that of an omniscient narrator who evokes the reader's criticism of the highly critical Eileen.[10] Munro has commented that "there's a kind of smugness" about Eileen's "point of view" in this story ("Real Material," 24). This smugness is what she wants her reader to recognize when she introduces an ironically observing narrator. This narrator temporarily becomes the second watcher in the story when, on the night of the funeral, Eileen permits the drunk and grieving Ewart to make love to her in his car.

During the love scene, Eileen notices that Ewart keeps repeating her name, but her question, "What did Ewart mean by that name, what was Eileen to him?," is not immediately answered (SIB, 224). Instead, an omniscient narrator intrudes with a series of generalizations in the plural and in the present tense: "Women have to wonder. Pinned down not too comfortably on a car seat ... they will still look for clues, and store things up in a hurry to be considered later. They have to believe that more is going on than seems to be going on; that is part of the trouble" (224). In discussing such interruptions of narration from a character's point of view, Cohn points out in *Transparent Minds* that "the most emphatic of all marks of narratorial disparity" is "a gnomic generalization" (150).[11] Here the disparity is between what Eileen has been telling herself about how totally different she is from June and what the author now tells the reader. This disparity effectively throws into confusion not only everything that Eileen has already made the reader believe, but also her answer to the question about what she means to her brother-in-law when he makes loves to her: "What Eileen meant to Ewart, she would tell herself later, was confusion. The opposite of June, wasn't that what she was?. ... Eileen ... comes out of the same part of the world accidents come from. He lies in her to acknowledge, to yield – but temporarily, safely – to whatever has got his son, whatever cannot be spoken of in his house" (SIB, 224).

Eileen's subjective point of view returns in this narrated monologue, but immediately afterwards the omniscient narrator intrudes again. Cohn explains that "narrated monologues ... tend to commit the narrator to attitudes of sympathy or irony. Precisely because they cast the language of a subjective mind into the grammar of objective narration, they amplify emotional notes, but also throw into ironic relief all false notes struck by a figural mind" (117). These false notes are "most clearly in evidence when narrated monologues show up in a pronouncedly authorial milieu, framed by explicit commentary" (118). That is precisely what happens here as the narrator critically examines Eileen's future thoughts: "So Eileen, with her fruitful background of reading, her nimble habit of analysis (material and direction different from June's, but the habit not so different, after all), can later explain and arrange it for herself. Not knowing, never knowing, if that is not all literary, fanciful" (SIB, 224). Eileen has been contrasting her study of literature to her sister's psychology major, but now the deflating narrator describes their resulting mental habits as "not so different, after all." Then the narrator increases the disparity between herself and Eileen even farther by emphasizing Eileen's fatuous mistake in investing Ewart's words with meaning. This error, the narrator's generalization points out, once again in the present tense, is one commonly committed by women who would naturally love to believe that their own "woman's body" is uniquely significant (224). But it is not: "Before and during the act [men] seem to invest this body with certain individual powers, they will say its name in a way that indicates something particular, something unique, that is sought for. Afterwards it appears that they have changed their minds, they wish it understood that such bodies are interchangeable. Women's bodies" (224–25).

Eileen is unaware of her mistaken attempt at self-definition because it lies in the future. Thus her delusion is a piece of information shared only by the subtly mocking narrator and the sadly nodding reader. But when Eileen tries to apologize to June the next morning, Eileen becomes aware of the terrible unreliability of her own verbal attempt to control her present situation. When Eileen says, "I haven't helped you the way I meant to," she cringes at the unintentional irony of her words. "No sooner was that sentence out than it flung itself inside out and grinned at her. This was a day when there was nothing she could say that would work" (225). And glimpsing her face in the mirror, she is guiltily surprised by the discrepancy between her inner thoughts and her outward, "wonderfully appropriate look of tactfulness and concern" as she listens to her sister describe her son's freakish death (226).

Through these double splits in point of view – shifting from Eileen in the present to the ironically omniscient narrator in the future, and then splitting Eileen in half by having her look at her false reflection in the mirror – Munro suggests that the compulsive drive to define, explain, and thus control the uncontrollable, the terrifying "part of the world accidents come from," is not limited just to June and to her obvious misuse of language (224). The situation is more complicated than that. Eileen also uses language spuriously, to inflate herself and her sexual favors with false and smugly fanciful significance by concealing the true nature of what happens between herself and her sister's husband. Thus, she has no real moral right to criticize because, without fully realizing it, she is just as confused about herself as her sister is.

"Accident," a story originally published three years after "Memorial," is similar to "Memorial" in two ways: a son is accidentally killed, as if suddenly struck by lightning, and an ironically omniscient narrator comments on the characters' reactions to this eruption of confusion and violence into their lives. But in "Accident" there are two central characters instead of one. Frances Wright, a high-school music teacher in Hanratty, and Ted Makkavala, a married colleague, are carrying on an adulterous love affair. They both believe it is a well-concealed secret, but the omniscient narrator gleefully informs the reader that it is not a secret at all. In this story there are thus really three clearly defined points of view, Frances's, Ted's, and that of the omniscient author, who is the watcher.

In discussing her own fiction, Margaret Atwood has defined the advantages of using such a triple point of view. Two characters, she says,

> can … think for themselves, and what they think won't always be what [another character] thinks of *them*. If I like, I can add in yet another point of view, that of the omniscient author, … yet another voice within the [story]. The omniscient author can claim to know things about the characters that even they don't know, thus letting the reader know these things as well. (426)

In "Accident" Munro introduces such a fully developed, alternating, multiple point of view and thus creates exactly the kind of situation that Atwood defines. The omniscient author watches Frances and Ted and keeps interrupting their internal comments with her own ironic reflections. Her purpose is to show how mistaken they are in what they believe about the townspeople of Hanratty, about each other, and – most significantly – about themselves. This narrator functions throughout the story, rather than just at the conclusion, as in "Memorial." By interjecting these ironic revelations, she emphasizes the uncontrolled repercussions of the fatal accident that permanently alters the lives of Frances and Ted.

In the opening scene, narrated from Frances's third-person point of view, Frances "shamefully" eavesdrops outside Ted's science classroom. Although she hears only a normal schoolroom pattern of "order and acquiescence," Frances feels "a familiar pressure, of longing or foreboding, that strange lump of something you can feel sometimes in music or a landscape, barely withheld, promising to burst and reveal itself, but it doesn't, it dissolves and goes away" (MJ, 79). However, this time the lump does burst, in an accident that kills two children, and this foreshadowing metaphor of bursting and revelation clearly links this story with the ones already discussed.

The reasons motivating the lovers' belief that their relationship is a secret constitute another link between this story and the later "Fits." Like Robert, Frances and Ted are outsiders, although in Frances's case this role is merely the result of her four years of study at an out-of-town conservatory. "It is in imagining her affair to be a secret," the omniscient author explains, "that Frances shows, most clearly, a lack of small-town instincts, a trust and recklessness she is unaware of; this is what people mean when they say of her that it sure shows that she has been away" (80). It shows in "the outsider's innocent way of supposing herself unobserved as she dashes from one place to another around town …" (81). Ted actually is an outsider, not only from a "frontier settlement" in Northern Ontario but also from an intellectual Finnish family "banished from Finland" for their political activities (96, 98). During the main time frame of the narrative, 1943, Ted is "considered an enemy alien" in Canada, and he is "proud of it" (98). By characterizing both protagonists in this way, Munro sharpens the irony of her narrator's comment that the high-school secretary, "[l]ike almost everybody else in town, … had known about [Frances and Ted] for some time" (86).

This secretary interrupts their excited preparations for intercourse in a school storeroom. While undressing, Frances has been remembering their previous encounters in the same place, associating them with "lightning, a crazy and shattering, painful kind of lust," and admiring Ted's "ruddy cheerful penis, upright and workmanlike" (85, 86). But when the secretary yells through the door, "Mr. Makkavala! ... Your son's been killed!," Frances sees him unmanned, "that workman ... losing color [and] ...drooping ..." (87). This sudden physiological change symbolizes a more shattering and painful kind of lightning, Bobby's sudden death and Ted's consequent loss of control over his life.

The following scene is narrated from Ted's third-person point of view. When Bobby Makkavala and another boy tied their sleds to the back of a car, they were accidentally run over. The other boy has died, but Bobby is still alive, although obviously dying. As Ted and Greta, his wife, wait helplessly in the hospital, Ted thinks, "Everything was changed" (87). Struggling to exercise some control over this unbelievably changed world in which his only son can die, he suddenly thinks of bargaining with God to let Bobby live. He will give up Frances in exchange for his son: "by not even thinking about her, by willing her to stop existing in his life, he could increase Bobby's chances, hold off his death" (88). The terrible irony of Ted's desperate maneuvering for control is that he is an atheist. After his son's death, he himself realizes this irony: he tells Frances "his thoughts of bargains" to illustrate "the way the most rational mind can relapse and grovel" (89).

In the next scene, narrated once again from Frances's point of view, she callously rages against Bobby because she believes that the accident will end her relationship with Ted. "She felt fury at that child, at his stupidity, at his stupid risk, ... his breaking through into other people's lives, into her life" (94). This metaphor of "breaking through" connects Frances's present reaction with her initial apprehension of something ready to "burst and reveal itself" (79). Almost as if she intuited Ted's attempt to bargain with God, she believes that Greta and Ted will be reunited by their shared grief and that she will not see him anymore. But she is mistaken, for exactly the opposite happens. This plot structure embodies Munro's main point about the effect of Bobby's death on Ted, his sense of losing control of his life.

After Bobby's funeral, Ted boasts to Frances of how he imposed his will upon Greta's huge, bossy, devoutly Lutheran family, who descended en masse from Northern Ontario. Although the clan insisted on bringing a Finnish Lutheran pastor to the funeral, Ted proudly tells Frances that at the grave he outshouted the family, wailing in Finnish, to read the "few memorial paragraphs" that he had written (101). He did not allow "that pack of maniacs" any hymns or prayers (102). But by narrating this scene from Frances's point of view, Munro reveals that Ted's conscious motives in confessing his temporary irrationality in the hospital are not his real motives. He confesses to emphasize his swiftly restored rationality and his decisiveness. "I knew I couldn't show a moment's hesitation" (102). But underneath his confession and boasting, Frances clearly observes his selfish and frightened egotism: "He did it all for himself, Frances was thinking. He wasn't thinking of Greta for a moment. Or of Bobby. He was thinking of himself and his beliefs and not giving in to his enemies. That was what mattered to him. She could not help seeing this and she did not like it" (103). Immediately after his boasting, Ted insists on making love, even though Frances is "not ready"; he is "too intent to notice" how she feels, for, like Ewart in "Memorial," he sees the act as another way to reassert his control (103).

In the next scene, the omniscient author adds her own ironic comments on Ted's motives in an interview with his principal. When the principal tries to elicit some pro forma promise from Ted to terminate his affair, Ted furiously announces that he is going to divorce Greta and marry Frances: "My mind was made up long ago." The narrator wryly observes, "He believed that was true" (104). And Frances feels the same skepticism when he later insists that he would have married her in any case, accident or no accident: "But it didn't seem so to Frances, and she wondered if he said it just because he could not bear the thought of anything being set in motion outside his control – and so wastefully, so cruelly ..." (106). In an interview, Munro has defined "Accident" as a story about "love ... suddenly catapulted into having to be real ..." ("Visit," 13). Because the accident is the cruel catapult, Frances's part in Ted's frantic decision remains "ambiguous" (MJ, 106).

But in an epilogue "nearly thirty years later," when Frances returns to Hanratty for another funeral, she meets the man who accidentally ran over Bobby (107). She is forced to admit that Bobby's death gave her Ted and their marriage, but she pushes this admission out of her mind as "too ugly" and "monstrous" (109). Even a generation after the event, the eruption of accidental violence into life's routine orderliness is so intensely frightening that it cannot be faced. The dark parentheses of the two funerals, the alternating points of view, and the intruding, ironic narrator all emphasize Ted's self-deluding attempts to convince himself and Frances that, after only a momentary loss, he has regained full control of his life.[12]

Munro's comments on "Wood," another story in which an accident is the pivotal plot element, emphasize the same loss of control. Describing Roy Fowler, the main character in this uncollected *New Yorker* story, she has said: "The man's accident when he's alone in the woods brings him out of that ordinary world of control and inquisitiveness and into a completely different world" ("Interview": Hancock, 90). Like Robert in "Fits" and Ted in "Accident," Roy is an outsider, not so much in Logan, Ontario, where he lives, as in the huge and "closeknit clan" into which he has married but to which he has not contributed any children. "As a rule," he notes, "they don't take much notice of people who aren't like themselves" ("Wood," 46). He is a woodcutter who classifies and catalogues the trees in every bush or forest because he wants to exert control. "Roy's thoughts about wood are covetous and nearly obsessive. ... He would like to map every bush he sees, get it in his mind, know what is there" (48). His inquisitiveness, like Munro's documentary urge, constitutes part of his desire for control. Very proud of his experienced knowledge of the bush, he "thinks that there is very little danger in going tree cutting alone if you know what you are doing" (47). Knowing that includes the self-vigilance of constant awareness: "In the bush it isn't good to let your mind wander or your worries intrude" (48).

But, ironically, that is exactly what Roy does when old Percy Marshall, a local character, tells him a confused rumor that another, unidentified man has secured a lucrative contract for cutting the same trees that Roy has received the owner's verbal permission to cut. Initially Roy considers the "possibility" that Percy may "have got [the story] badly twisted," but in his eagerness to cut some of the promised trees, he forgets this suspicion (50). Even though it has begun to snow, he hurries out into the bush alone to begin cutting.

As a result of these psychological and physical conditions, Roy has an accident. Hurrying over the rough, snow-covered, hummocky ground, he slips, falls, and breaks his ankle. Unable to walk, he has "to abandon his axe and his chain saw and get down on his hands and knees and crawl" (53). Munro has emphasized that what is "important to [her] in the story is what his experience is like when he is crawling back trying to get to the truck" ("Interview": Hancock, 90). He has quite literally split the concealing surface in his fall, his "feet … plung[ing] through a cover of snowy brush to the ground, … farther down than he expected" (52). Then, as he slowly and painfully crawls over "rotten leaves and dirt," hatless and gloveless in the steadily falling snow, he is gradually forced to accept the reality of his situation, to stop "believing in an order of things in which [his accident] couldn't happen" (53). Beginning "to feel almost light-headed," he becomes increasingly detached from his worries: "Nobody knows what anybody else is thinking about or how anybody else is feeling. … Nobody knows how others see themselves" (54). This generalization introduces a significant split in his self-perception. He backs off to look at himself and at how this absurd accident has occurred. As he sees a hawk or a buzzard circling above him, "its eye on him" in his exposed and potentially vulnerable situation, he suddenly realizes how his generalization about other people applies to him (54). Because he momentarily sees himself as the watching bird sees him, he also sees what the rumormongers have been thinking about him.

Percy's rumor about the unidentified woodcutter with the contract is about "Roy himself" (54). Percy has simply distorted the story of Roy's agreement with the owner of the bush because "[e]verything that involves money, in this county, gets talked up, distorted, … turned into a story" (54). By not recognizing himself in Percy's "big fable," Roy has ironically and very painfully lost control of himself in the very setting in which he has been the most confident of both his mental and physical control (54). It is almost a case of hubris, but there is no tragedy.

The concluding paragraph of the story pulls sharply away from Roy to emphasize this thematic irony. An omniscient author, distancing herself from her protagonist, observes:

> Roy's mind operates very economically at this moment – perhaps more selectively than ever before. It manages to turn everything to good account. It no longer dwells on the foolish-ness of the accident but triumphs in the long, successful crawl and the approach to the truck. (He is on his way again.) It cancels out any embarrassment at his having been so mistaken; it pushes out any troubling detection of waste and calamity; it ushers in a decent sense of victory. Safe. (54)

This ironic conclusion, with its emphasis on Roy's rejection of "waste and calamity" and on his triumphant reassertion of control, leaves him in a state of mind very similar to Ted's when he deluded himself about his motives for marrying Frances: "he could not bear the thought of anything being set in motion outside his control – and so wastefully …" (MJ, 106). In both stories, published three years apart ("Accident" appeared in *Toronto Life* in November 1977; "Wood," in the *New Yorker* on 24 November 1980), the ironic distance of the omniscient narrator from her protagonists emphasizes their loss of control as something so terrifying that they unconsciously deny it.[13]

Accidents occur in the background of other stories. For instance, Sandy Desmond drowns in "Something I've Been Meaning to Tell You," and Frank McArter drowns in "Walking on Water." But in Munro's first three non-interrelated collections – *Dance of the Happy Shades, Something I've Been Meaning To Tell You,* and *The Moons of Jupiter* – there is only one major accident story apiece. In contrast, *The Progress of Love* includes three such stories: "Circle of Prayer," "Monsieur les Deux Chapeaux," and "Miles City, Montana." Interviewed upon the publication of this collection, Munro commented that her "way of thinking … embraces randomness pretty well" (Kolson, 4C). The increased number of accidents suggests her intensified concentration on life's frightening fragility. The randomness of accidents represents the most frightening fact of life, its uncontrollability.[14]

In "Circle of Prayer," originally published in the *Paris Review*, the fatal accident is not the central plot element, for the story describes the disintegration of a marriage two years before the accident. But, although Trudy, the central character, initially manages to come to terms with the loss of Dan, her husband, the accident later forces her to confront the finality of this loss as something almost like a death. To unify her story, Munro establishes the parallels between these two losses in several subtle ways. When Dan leaves Trudy for a woman whom he meets by chance and who exploits him, he destroys his marriage in what he himself initially recognizes as "a middle-aged fit" (PL, 265). Similarly, when their daughter's drunk or stoned friend, fifteen-year-old Tracy Lee, accidentally drives a truck into a tree, she, too, is "self-destructive" and "stupid" (259). After Dan's defection Trudy keeps three objects in a jug, her engagement and wedding rings and a valuable jet necklace Dan's mother has willed to Robin, their daughter. In the opening scene of the story, when Trudy discovers that this necklace is missing, she immediately suspects what Robin has done with it, and, in a fit of destructive rage, throws the heavy jug across Robin's room. Robin says that her mother "could have killed" her, and eventually Trudy admits the truth of this accusation (255). By starting her story with this jug-throwing scene, Munro shows that Trudy, like Dan and Tracy Lee, is capable of fits of uncontrolled and potentially dangerous behavior. When the necklace is buried with Tracy Lee, its loss becomes a symbolic burial of Dan and Trudy's dead marriage.

The circumstances under which the necklace ends up in the dead girl's coffin not only emphasize the parallel between the two types of deaths but also demonstrate, once again, the crucial importance of trying to assert control in an uncontrollable world. The "crying" and "shivering" teenage girls who attend Tracy Lee's funeral-home visitation file past her open coffin. As they do, they sing what they believe to be "an old hymn" (263). Although it is actually a song from a movie, the carpe diem theme of its lyrics explains their naive mistake. When they reach the coffin, they strip off their jewelry – rings, bracelets, earrings, necklaces, and chains – and drop them all in, "flashing and sparkling down on the dead girl. ..." With unconscious irony, they all behave as if this were "a religious ceremony," and the bereaved family gratefully agrees: "It was like church" (263). Like Eileen in "Memorial," the girls, including Robin, find it impossible to face death without any religious faith. Trying to fill the frightening emptiness created by the sudden and accidental death of one of their own peers, they rediscover a ritual reminiscent of many pre-Christian burial practices. Thus they form the first circle of prayer around the coffin.

This circle's adult counterpart is the "Circle of Prayer" that Trudy's friend, Janet, tells her about on the morning of the funeral. Janet suggests that Judy join the women in this circle to pray for the return of the necklace and Dan, her husband. To this suggestion, Trudy replies: "I'll just go down on my knees right now and pray. ... that I get the necklace back and I get Dan back, and why do I have to stop there? I can pray that Tracy Lee never died. I can pray that she comes back to life. Why didn't her mother ever think of that?" (269–70). Although later Trudy not only apologizes for this outburst but even asks another character whether *he* prays, her sarcastic rejection of prayer completes the many parallels between Tracy Lee's death and the death of Trudy and Dan's marriage. In different ways, both losses are the results of random accidents, beyond anything but symbolic control.

In "Monsieur les Deux Chapeaux" this compulsion to control the frightening uncontrollability of life becomes the lifelong obsession of Colin, the protagonist, after a fatal accident, or rather what momentarily appears to be one. In the climactic flashback that concludes the story, Colin believes that he has accidentally killed Ross, his younger brother. Although he soon finds out that Ross was only pretending to be dead, this childhood trauma of imagining himself a murderer shapes his adult life. He becomes what Cain, the first fratricide, protests to God he cannot be: Colin – the name is symbolically similar to Cain – becomes his brother's keeper.

In the opening scene, the principal of the school where Colin teaches and Ross does occasional yard work asks Colin, "Is that your brother out there?" (PL, 56). This question echoes the one God asked the guilty Cain: "Where is Abel, thy brother?" The principal's query is prompted by the fact that Ross, while clipping the school grass, is wearing two hats, one on top of the other. A French teacher also notices the two hats and dubs Ross "Monsieur les Deux Chapeaux," but when she later mentions seeing him, Ross denies what he was doing. "You're seeing things. You got double vision" (69). In a symbolical sense, however, it is Colin, not Ross, who wears two hats; it is also Colin, not the French teacher, who has double vision because he is constantly watching his brother, the "secret weight on" his life (66).

Initially Ross's weird behavior and his proneness to car accidents seem to be the only reasons for Colin's hovering protectiveness. But gradually Munro builds up to the revelation of something "horrible" that occurred in the past and "could've been tragic" (74). These suspenseful allusions to the past are embedded in a discussion of something dangerous that Ross is doing in the present, installing an engine in a car not big enough for it. The French teacher warns Colin that the powerful engine "will simply break the drive shaft" and "literally flip [the car] over" (70). Colin is anxious not only to prevent Ross from doing this but also to avoid hurting his feelings by criticizing him.

The climactic flashback at the end of the story reveals that Colin's protectiveness is not only the result but, paradoxically, also the cause of the traumatic event that shaped his life. When the two brothers and several young boys find a rifle and start playing with it, Colin grabs it to prevent Ross from doing something dangerous. Somehow the gun goes off, there are screams and shouts, and in the confusion Colin sees "Ross lying on the ground, on his back, with his arms flung out, a dark stain spilled out from the top of his head" (77). This description also echoes Abel's death, whose "blood crieth unto [God] from the ground." But what Colin imagines to be blood is actually a puddle of water, for Ross is only feigning death: "The bullet hadn't come near him" (77).

In the final scene of the flashback, Colin is sitting on a bridge girder. From this perch above nothingness, he sees "all the jumble of his life, and other people's lives ..., rolled back, just like a photograph split and rolled back, so it shows what was underneath all along. Nothing" (81–82). Like so many other Munro characters at the moment of crisis, Colin feels not only completely dissociated from himself but also suddenly separated from the safe world, whose surface he has broken through. "How silly it was that he should have a name and it should be Colin. ... His life had split open, and nothing had to be figured out anymore" (82). But then a crowd of people arrives, with the living and laughing Ross in tow, shouting, "I ain't dead, Colin!" and calling him to come down (82). As Colin obeys, "sick with the force of things coming back to life," and trying not to think about what has nearly happened, he knows "that to watch out for something like that happening – to Ross, and to himself – [is] going to be his job in life from then on" (83). Thus he becomes one of Munro's watchers, but in an almost saintly sense: he stays permanently split, permanently double. The final irony is that the new identity shaped by his brother's unintentionally cruel hoax is the exact opposite of Cain's, but marks him nonetheless.

The dramatic culmination of these stories about accidents is "Miles City, Montana," the only accident story with a first-person narrator who is not only the mother of a small child threatened by a fatal accident but also a writer. In this tightly unified story, the retrospective narrator – who seems to be speaking in the actual present – tells the stories of two accidents occurring twenty years apart. The later story, which she dates in the summer of 1961, is framed within her confused childhood memory of the other event, a boy's accidental drowning. The two stories are associatively linked by a third memory: the narrator remembers helping her farmer father rescue stranded turkeys who "had managed to crowd to higher ground and avoid drowning" in a rainstorm that flooded the fields (PL, 94). In the first accident, Steve Gauley fell into a flooded gravel pit; his father did not watch him, and even his "fatherhood seemed accidental ..." (85). In the later accident, the narrator's little girl, Meg, falls into the deep end of a public pool in Miles City when nobody is watching her, but she comes up swimming and is swiftly rescued by Andrew, her father. These two accidents are focused in parallel images of a father carrying a child. The story opens with this ominous sentence: "My father came across the field carrying the body of the boy who had been drowned" (84). When Andrew rescues Meg, he also carries her. But the narrator's role in these two incidents is radically different. In the first story she is a six-year-old child who has partially seen and partially imagined a dark and indelible image of death: the corpse of another child, a motherless little boy, whose "hair and clothes were mud-colored," whose nostrils and ears "were plugged up with greenish mud" (84). In the second story she is the mother of a three-year-old child who has escaped drowning. The associative link, however, is not merely the common theme of drowning but the painful paradox of parents as the begetters of death, a paradox that the narrator discovers as a result of the change in her role from watching child to writing parent.

In the first drowning story, the six-year-old child attends the drowned boy's funeral. Holding "a white narcissus" and wearing innocent white stockings, she stands "removed from" her hymn-singing parents. "[W]atching" them, she feels "a furious and sickening disgust" (86). Thirty years separate this narrator from the narrator of "At the Other Place," removed from the adults and watching them, but she, too, remembers seeing them as grossly sexual beings. Although her parents are decorously dressed for the formal occasion, she is disgusted by their "bloated power" and by what she insists on imagining under their dark clothes: their "lumpy shapes," their "coarseness, ... hairiness, [and] ... horrid secretions," all of which fill her with "a thin, familiar misgiving" (86).

After Meg's rescue from the swimming pool, the narrator suddenly understands what this dimly perceived "misgiving" really meant. As a child she had suspected that her parents were not her protection from death but some kind of threat. Now she and her husband, Andrew, have become a threat to their own children. Trying to imagine what Meg's death and its aftermath would have been like, "a blind sinking and shifting," she tells herself that it is "shameful" to place her "finger on the wire to get the safe shock, feeling a bit of what it's like, then pulling back" (103). These metaphors dramatically combine three forms of splitting: "sinking" suggests drowning, "shifting" suggests an earthquake, and "the wire" suggests electricity, lightning in its safely controlled form. That is why the narrator tells herself that her imagination is shameful: to do what the writer does, "changing from a participant into an observer," is to play with lightning, to arrange "patterns and destinies" like God ("Author's Commentary," 125). It is shameful for another reason, too. This deliberate exercise of the writer's controlling imagination reveals an appalling fact: just as Andrew has always suspected, his wife, the narrator, "really" is "a secret monster of egotism" because she can contemplate the death of her own child (PL, 91). Recognizing this fact makes her remember her parents at the funeral once again, and now she feels that her parents consented to her own death simply by the act of begetting her: "Their big, stiff, dressed-up bodies did not stand between me and sudden death, or any kind of death. They gave consent. So it seemed. They gave consent to the death of children and to my death ... by the very fact that they had made children – they had made me" (103). Their hypocritical hymn-singing at the funeral only made things worse because it denied or attempted to conceal the frightening facts.

The narrator thus sees the treacherous world of sudden and accidental death, where children can drown in "clear blue water," as a world into which parents thrust their children simply by begetting them and exposing them to inevitable mortality (102). In retrospect, the scene in "Accident" in which Ted loses his erection as he hears the premature announcement of his son's death becomes a paradigm of the paradox explicitly developed here: sexual desire sows the seeds not only of new life but also of death. Children are forced to trust their parents, but their parents have thrust them into a trap.

Thus, even though baby Meg blithely observes, "I didn't drown," and even though her parents exult in their luck, "Miles City, Montana" seems the most deeply pessimistic of this group of stories in which accidents are the pivotal plot elements (102). The dimly persistent image of the drowned boy haunting the background of the two earlier stories already mentioned – the memory of little Sandy Desmond in "Something I've Been Meaning to Tell You," and of young Frank McArter in "Walking on Water" – now comes into focus as the central image (SIB, 7, 90). Meg's escape from tragedy on a sunny summer day does *not* mean that life is not a tragedy. Although the narrator longs for the right of children to be "free, to live a new, superior kind of life," she knows that they are "caught in the snares of vanquished grownups, with their sex and funerals" (PL, 104).

These close links between the shocking power of death and the literal shock of electric power and between sex and funerals constitute a recurrent thematic pattern in Munro's work. As already shown, she describes sexual excitement and impending death on the same page in both "At the Other Place" and "Accident" and sex and a funeral on the very same day in "Memorial." The electric metaphor first occurs in "Images," where the shocking power of death is perceived as electric power, and both this metaphor and the close link between death significantly recur in *Lives of Girls and Women*, at the climax of which Del, the narrator, is nearly drowned immediately after intercourse.

Notes

1   The sources for Munro's documentary script were Susanna Moodie and an Irish couple's diary and letters (Adachi D3).
2   In "The Fiction of Alice Munro," Hallvard Dahlie compares Munro to Flannery O'Connor in their shared "vision" of "worlds ... suddenly violated by ... some unexpected force or event" (58). See also Andrew Stubbs (56) and Catherine Sheldrick Ross (112).
3   Although Miss Abelhart, the protagonist of "The Dimensions of a Shadow," is not a narrator, she is actually Munro's first split character, for her imaginary other self, the male student, is in many ways a younger persona.

4   Eileen Dombrowski defines Munro's first three books as illustrations of her "vision" of "life as slipping away in a relentless movement toward death" (21). See also the conclusion of John Orange's essay: "At the centre of the maze is death …" (97).

5   The second phrase is not Munro's own, but when Ken Murch interviewed her for *Chatelaine* in August 1975 and remarked, "Many of your stories seem to involve the tremendous guilt over the death of someone," she agreed: "Yes … you're very perceptive. … That's probably the thing with my mother… yes" ("Name," 70).

6   Critics disagree on the meaning of the parallels between the beatings in this story and even on the question of whether there are any parallels. They also have somewhat different interpretations of the theatrical metaphors. See Lawrence Mathews, 185–87; Warwick, 211; Barry Cameron, viii; Hallvard Dahlie, "Alice Munro and Her Works," 248–9; J. R. (Tim) Struthers, "Alice Munro's Fictive Imagination," 109–10; and Martin, *Alice Munro: Paradox and Parallel*, 104–6.

7   In "'The Other Side of Dailiness,'" York quotes this passage about the linoleum as an illustration of the paradox that "even familiar objects are not man's familiars" (51). In "'Gulfs' and 'Connections,'" she sees the father in this scene as "a hate-filled child beater" (141).

8   Compare "A Trip to the Coast" where the child May thinks: "If her grandmother capitulated [to the hypnotist] it would be as unsettling an event as an earthquake …" (DHS, 188).

9   The phrase "with a self-conscious brutality" occurs in the original version of "Fits" in *Grand Street* 5 (1986): 58, but Munro deleted it from the revised version in *The Progress of Love*. Compare the fight and the violent copulation in "Meneseteung," *New Yorker*, 11 Jan. 1988: 33–34.

10 Lorna Irvine emphasizes "the opposition between" the two sisters and ignores the story's ironic conclusion ("Changing," 104–5). Although Margaret Anne Fitzpatrick recognizes that the "vice [Eileen] accuses her sister of turns out to be her own," Fitzpatrick does not discuss the shifts in point of view that reveal this "projection" (19).

11 Although Dorrit Cohn's discussion in this passage is about a first-person point of view, her comment is applicable to sudden shifts from a limited third-person point of view.

12 W. R. Martin, who criticizes this story as one about "naked, unrefined sexual desire," does not recognize the triple point of view Munro uses in its narration (*Alice Munro: Paradox and Parallel*, 138).

13 James Carscallen includes an analysis of "Wood" in "The Shining House," 93–94, 97–100. W. R. Martin also discusses this story in *Alice Munro: Paradox and Parallel*, 168–70.

14 Accidents continue to play a key role in two later, uncollected *New Yorker* stories. In "Oh, What Avails" (1987), Morris Fordyce is blinded in one eye as the result of a childhood accident. Scorned as "Deadeye Dick" and rejected by the woman he loves, he remains a bachelor all his life. In "Five Points" (1988), Cornelius Zendt is so badly injured in a salt-mine accident that he can no longer work at the mine and often has to "lie on the livingroom floor, coping with the pain" (34). His wife copes by taking a lover.

Bibliography

In each category, entries are listed chronologically by date of publication.

Primary Sources

Stories

Laidlaw, Alice. "The Dimensions of a Shadow." *Folio* Apr. 1950: [4–10].

Munro, Alice. "A Basket of Strawberries." *Mayfair* Nov. 1953: 32–33, 78–80, 82.

Laidlaw, Alice. "At the Other Place." *Canadian Forum* Sept. 1955: 131–33.

Munroe [*sic*], Alice. "The Edge of Town." *Queen's Quarterly* 62 (1955): 368–80.

Laidlaw, Alice. "The Time of Death." *Canadian Forum* June 1956: 63–66.

Munro, Alice. "The Trip to the Coast." *Ten for Wednesday Night*. Ed. Robert Weaver. Toronto: McClelland and Stewart, 1961. 74–92.

Munro, Alice. *Dance of the Happy Shades.* New York: McGraw-Hill, 1968. Includes "Walker Brothers Cowboy," "The Shining Houses," "Images," "Thanks for the Ride," "The Office" (revised), "An Ounce of Cure," "The Time of Death" (revised), "Day of the Butterfly" ("Good-By, Myra" revised), "Boys and Girls," "Postcard," "Red Dress – 1946," "Sunday Afternoon," "A Trip to the Coast" (revised), "The Peace of Utrecht" (revised), and "Dance of the Happy Shades."

Munro, Alice. *Lives of Girls and Women.* Toronto: McGraw-Hill Ryerson, 1971. Includes "The Flats Road, "Heirs of the Living Body," "Princess Ida," "Age of Faith," "Changes and Ceremonies," "Lives of Girls and Women," "Baptizing," and "Epilogue: The Photographer."

Munro, Alice. "Home." *New Canadian Stories: 74.* Ed. and introd. David Helwig and Joan Harcourt. Ottawa: Oberon, 1974. 133–53.

Munro, Alice. *Something I've Been Meaning To Tell You.* Toronto: McGraw-Hill Ryerson, 1974. Includes "Something I've Been Meaning To Tell You," "Material," "How I Met My Husband" (revised), "Walking on Water," "Forgiveness in Families," "Tell Me Yes or No," "The Found Boat," "Executioners," "Marrakesh," "The Spanish Lady," "Winter Wind," "Memorial," and "The Ottawa Valley."

Munro, Alice. "Royal Beatings." *New Yorker* 14 Mar. 1977: 36–44.

Munro, Alice. "Accident." *Toronto Life* Nov. 1977: 61, 87–90, 92–95, 149–50, 153–56, 159–60, 162–65, 167, 169–73.

Munro, Alice. "Wild Swans." *Toronto Life* Apr. 1978: 52–53, 124–25.

Munro, Alice. *Who Do You Think You Are?* Toronto: Macmillan, 1978 [*The Beggar Maid: Stories of Flo and Rose* in the United States]. Includes "Royal Beatings" (revised), "Privilege" (revised), "Half a Grapefruit" (revised), "Wild Swans," "The Beggar Maid" (revised), "Mischief" (revised), "Providence" (revised), "Simon's Luck" ("Emily" revised), "Spelling" (revised and expanded), and "Who Do You Think You Are?"

Munro, Alice. "A Better Place Than Home." *The Newcomers: Inhabiting a New Land.* Ed. Charles E. Israel. Toronto. McClelland and Stewart, 1979. 113–24.

Munro, Alice. "The Stone in the Field." *Saturday Night* Apr. 1979: 40–45.

Munro, Alice. "Wood." *New Yorker* 24 Nov. 1980: 46–54.

Munro, Alice. "The Ferguson Girls Must Never Marry." *Grand Street* 1.3 (1982): 27–64.

Munro, Alice. *The Moons of Jupiter.* Toronto: Macmillan, 1982. Includes "Chaddeleys and Flemings: I Connection (revised) and II The Stone in the Field" (revised), "Dulse" (revised), "The Turkey Season" (revised), "Accident," "Bardon Bus," "Prue," "Labor Day Dinner," "Mrs. Cross and Mrs. Kidd," "Hard-Luck Stories," "Visitors," and "The Moons of Jupiter" (revised).

Munro, Alice. "Miles City, Montana." *New Yorker* 14 Jan. 1985: 30–40.

Munro, Alice. "Monsieur les Deux Chapeaux." *Grand Street* 4.3 (1985): 7–33.

Munro, Alice. "A Queer Streak. Part One: Anonymous Letters." *Granta* 17 (1985): 187–212.

Munro, Alice. "Fits." *Grand Street* 5.2 (1986): 36–61.

Munro, Alice. "A Queer Streak. Part Two: Possession." *Granta* 18 (1986): 201–19.

Munro, Alice. "White Dump." *New Yorker* 28 July 1986: 25–39, 42–43.

Munro, Alice. "Circle of Prayer." *Paris Review* 100 (1986): 31–51.

Munro, Alice. *The Progress of Love.* Toronto: McClelland and Stewart, 1986. Includes "The Progress of Love" (revised), "Lichen," "Monsieur les Deux Chapeaux," "Miles City, Montana" (revised), "Fits" (revised), "The Moon in the Orange Street Skating Rink" (revised), "Jesse and Meribeth" ("Secrets Between Friends," revised), "Eskimo," "A Queer Streak" (revised), "Circle of Prayer," and "White Dump" (revised).

Munro, Alice. "Oh, What Avails." *New Yorker* 16 Nov. 1987: 42–52, 55–56, 58–59, 62, 64–65, 67.

Munro, Alice. "Meneseteung." *New Yorker* 11 Jan. 1988: 28–38.

Munro, Alice. "Five Points." *New Yorker* 14 Mar. 1988: 34–43.

Articles and Letters

Munro, Alice. "Author's Commentary." *Sixteen by Twelve: Short Stories by Canadian Writers.* Ed. John Metcalf. Toronto: Ryerson, 1970. 125–26.

Munro, Alice. "What is Real?" *Canadian Forum* Sept. 1982: 5, 36. (Republished in *Making It New: Contemporary Canadian Stories*. Ed. John Metcalf. Toronto: Methuen, 1982. 223–26).

Interviews

Munro, Alice. Untitled Interview with Alice Munro. Appendix. "The Early Short Stories of Alice Munro." Jill M. Gardiner. M.A. Thesis, New Brunswick U, 1973. 169–82. [Untitled]

Munro, Alice. "Name: Alice Munro. Occupation: Writer." *Chatelaine*. By Ken Murch. Aug. 1975: 42–3, 69–72. ["Name"]

Munro, Alice. "What Is: Alice Munro." *For Openers: Conversation with Twenty-four Canadian Writers*. With Alan Twigg. Madeira Park, B.C.: Harbour, 1981. 13–20. ["What Is"]

Munro, Alice. "An Interview with Alice Munro." *Canadian Fiction Magazine*. By Geoff Hancock. 43 (1982): 75–114. ["Interview": Hancock]

Munro, Alice. "A Visit with Alice Munro." *Monday Magazine* [Victoria]. By Stephen Scobie. 19–25 Nov. 1982: 12–13. ["Visit"]

Munro, Alice. "The Real Material: An Interview with Alice Munro." By J. R. (Tim) Struthers. *Probable Fictions: Alice Munro's Narrative Acts*. Ed. Louis K. MacKendrick. Downsview, Ont.: ECW, 1983. 5–36. ["Real Material"]

Secondary Sources

Adachi, Ken. "Alice Munro Puts Her Pen to Script for CBC-TV Drama." *Toronto Star* 6 Jan. 1978: D3.

Atwood, Margaret. "Writing the Male Character." *This Magazine* Sept. 1982: 4–10. Republished in *Second Words: Selected Critical Prose*. Boston: Beacon, 1984. 412–30.

Cameron, Barry. Introduction. *Making It New: Contemporary Canadian Stories*. Ed. John Metcalf. Toronto: Methuen, 1982. vii–x.

Carscallen, James. "The Shining House: A Group of Stories." Miller 85–101.

Cohn, Dorrit. *Transparent Minds: Narrative Modes for Presenting Consciousness in Fiction*. Princeton: Princeton UP, 1978.

Dahlie, Hallvard. "The Fiction of Alice Munro." *Ploughshares* 4.3 (1978): 56–71.

Dahlie, Hallvard. "Alice Munro and Her Works." *Canadian Writers and Their Works*. Ed. Robert Lecker, Jack David, and Ellen Quigley. Fiction Series 7. Toronto: ECW, 1985. 215–56.

Djwa, Sandra. "Deep Caves and Kitchen Linoleum: Psychological Violence in the Fiction of Alice Munro." *Violence in the Canadian Novel Since 1960/dans le roman Canadien depuis 1960*. Ed. Virginia Harger-Grinling and Terry Goldie. St. John's: Memorial University of Newfoundland. 1981. 177–90.

Dombrowski, Eileen. "'Down to Death': Alice Munro and Transcience." *University of Windsor Review* 14.1 (1978): 21–29.

Duchêne, Anne. "Respect for the Facts." Rev. of *The Progress of Love*, by Alice Munro. *Times Literary Supplement* 30 Jan. 1987: 109.

Fitzpatrick, Margaret Anne. "'Projection' in Alice Munro's *Something I've Been Meaning To Tell You*." Miller 15–20.

Freud, Sigmund. "A Child Is Being Beaten." *Collected Papers*. Ed. Ernest Jones. Trans. Alix and James Strachey. New York: Basic Books, 1959. II, 172–201.

Irvine, Lorna. "Changing Is the Word I Want." MacKendrick 99–111.

Jespersen, Otto. *Essentials of English Grammar*. New York: Holt, 1933.

Kolson, Ann. "Writing Was Her Secret." *The Philadelphia Inquirer* 7 Nov. 1986: 1C, 4C.

MacKendrick, Louis K. ed. *Probable Fictions: Alice Munro's Narrative Acts*. Downsview, Ont.: ECW, 1983.

Martin, W. R. *Alice Munro: Paradox and Parallel*. Edmonton: U of Alberta P, 1987.

Mathews, Lawrence. "*Who Do You Think You Are?*: Alice Munro's Art of Disarrangement." MacKendrick 181–93.

Miller, Judith, ed. *The Art of Alice Munro: Saying the Unsayable*. Waterloo: U of Waterloo P, 1984.

Orange, John. "Alice Munro and A Maze of Time." MacKendrick 83–98.

Ross, Catherine Sheldrick. "'At least part legend': The Fiction of Alice Munro." MacKendrick 112–26.

Slopen, Beverley. "PW Interviews Alice Munro." *Publisher's Weekly* 22 Aug. 1986: 76–77.

Struthers, J. R. (Tim). "Alice Munro's Fictive Imagination." Miller 103–12.

Stubbs, Andrew. "Fictional Landscape: Mythology and Dialectic in the Fiction of Alice Munro." *World Literature Written in English* 23 (1984): 53–62.

Warwick, Susan J. "Growing Up: The Novels of Alice Munroe." *Essays on Canadian Writing* 29 (1984): 204–25.

York, Lorraine M. "'The Other Side of Dailiness': The Paradox of Photography in Alice Munro's Fiction." *Studies in Canadian Literature* 8 (1983): 49–60.

PART SIX

Marxism, Critical Theory, History

CHAPTER 1

Introduction
Starting with Zero

Julie Rivkin and Michael Ryan

Marxism derives from the work of Karl Marx, a German philosopher who lived in Paris and London in the middle of the nineteenth century, a time of severe industrialization that was creating a new class of industrial workers that he called the "proletariat." When Marx wrote his major works *The German Ideology* (1846), *The Manifesto of the Communist Party* (1848), and *Capital* (1867), the ideals of socialism (that wealth should be distributed more equitably, that class differences should be abolished, that society should be devoted to providing for everyone's basic needs, etc.) were emerging in counterpoint to the principles and realities of industrial capitalism – individual freedom in economic matters, an intractable inequality in the distribution of wealth, severe class differentiation, and brutal poverty for those without property. It was also a time of revolution. Across Europe in 1848, monarchies were challenged by democratic uprisings, and colonized nations struggled for independence. In 1870–1, workers seized power in Paris, and the Commune briefly established an egalitarian alternative to capitalism. It was a time when "bourgeois" society itself, which was organized around the ideal of the private accumulation of wealth in an economy unhampered by state regulation, was being challenged for the first time. That Marx was deeply influenced by his historical context is itself a lesson in Marxist methodology. According to Marx, we are all situated historically and socially, and our social and historical contexts mean that our lives are "determined," which simply means that they are concrete and specific and "determinate." They are material, historical, and social. This is as true of literature as it is of human beings: literature is not, according to Marxist criticism, the expression of universal or eternal ideas, as the New Critics claimed, nor is it, as the Russian Formalists claimed, an autonomous realm of aesthetic or formal devices and techniques that act independently of their material setting in society and history. Rather, literature is in the first instance a social phenomenon, and as such, it cannot be studied independently of the social relations, the economic forms, and the political realities of the time in which it was written.

Marxist literary criticism has traditionally been concerned with studying the embeddedness of a work within its historical, social, and economic contexts. Some Marxist criticism argues that literature reflects unproblematically the values and ideals of the class in dominance. In order to make it onto the stage at all, Shakespeare's plays had

Literary Theory: An Anthology, Third Edition. Edited by Julie Rivkin and Michael Ryan.

somehow to address (which is to say, accept and further) the values and ideals of monar-chial English culture. Shakespeare's history plays all celebrate kingship not because he was a political conservative but because the material context of literary production places limits on what can and cannot be said or expressed at a particular historical moment. Shakespeare could not have expressed counter-monarchial ideas and still been "Shakespeare," that is, someone hired to produce plays for the king's court. All literature is in this respect "determined" by economics, by the translation into cultural limitations and imperatives of the sheer weight of how material life in a society is conducted. Those limitations range from the choosing of what will or will not be published to the implanted selection procedures that readers inherit from schooling within a culture and that shape what and how they read (whether or not they can even understand the language of a play like *Lear*, for example).

This "reflectionist" approach to literature has been supplanted by critical approaches that emphasize the complexity of the relationships between literature and its social context. While some contemporary Marxist critics continue to emphasize the role of literature and of culture in reproducing class society, others look for ways in which literature undermines or subverts the dominant ideologies of the culture simply because all inegalitarian societies contain contradictions between their professed egalitarianism (freedom for all, for example) and their unequal reality, and those contradictions manifest themselves in the cultural products of the society. One function of literature is to offer those on the economic losing end in any given society images that assure them that their situation of relative deprivation is the natural result of fair play and fair rules, not of systematic dispossession that is a structural feature of the society. In Shakespeare's plays, for example, the lower-class characters, though likeable and comic for the most part, seem to deserve their lower-class status. Their speech and patterns of thought suggest less refined natures than those possessed by their "betters," who usually happen to be aristocrats. The plays legitimate class division.

But literature also displays signs of contradictions (between classes, between ideolo-gies and realities) that threaten society from within and are put on display in literature. No matter how much it spuriously resolves contradictions in society between the rich and the poor or between an ideal of "freedom" and a reality of economic enslavement, literature must also show them forth for all to see. According to this approach, all attempts to naturalize social divisions reveal their artificiality, and all ideological resolutions put their "imaginary" quality on display. In Shakespeare's plays, for example, the nobility may consistently triumph, but the very necessity of depicting such triumph over adversaries suggests that there is trouble, rather than peace and universal content-ment, in the society. In the effort to reassure the nobility, the plays draw attention both to divisions in society and to the need on the part of those in power to make those divisions seem easily resolvable. The very effort suggests that the class differences harbor potential dangers for the rule of the aristocracy.

British Marxism has evolved in two different directions. Influenced less by dialectical theory, it has developed in much more historicist directions. Raymond Williams, for many years the sole practitioner of Marxist literary studies on either side of the Atlantic, helped to foster a concern in British Marxist literary criticism with the evolu-tion of literature in relation to social, political, and economic changes. Terry Eagleton has refined this historicist approach by linking literary form to social ideology. According to Eagleton, literary form is itself ideological and laden with political mean-ings. In his book, *Criticism and Ideology* (1977), Eagleton argued that as one moves from the nineteenth into the twentieth century, works of literature provide different and differently ideological pictures of the social universe both in their content and in the way they are written. The organic form of the Romantics suggested a virtuously cohesive society in which class difference is an accepted feature of life, while T. S. Eliot's fragmented Modernist poetic form embodies his reactionary sense that modern democratic life represents a falling away from a good cultural tradition based on conservative values.

Another school of British Marxism, called Cultural Materialism, draws on Post-Structuralist and gender theory. Cultural Materialist scholars such as Alan Sinfield take issue with the idea that literature reflects and promotes social power or embodies in an unproblematic way the interests of a ruling class. All power structures are contingent; that is, they lack a logical ground or a natural foundation and are dependent on assistance from cultural narratives that assure their legitimacy. Such narratives strive for plausibility, but they must work against the contingency of the institutions they defend, a contingency that leaves them open to counter-narratives that suggest different social possibilities. Moreover, all class-divided societies project into culture the instabilities on which they are built. Those instabilities register in literary works as dissidence and as dissonance. The narratives of such works usually evoke social adversaries in order to quell them, as, for example, Edmund in *King Lear* is evoked as a pretender to power but ultimately killed by "true" nobles. He represents a dissident presence in the social world of the era, a new class of merchants, small businessmen, and industrialists who were struggling for power against the reigning nobility. His presence in the play, moreover, produces dissonance within the play's discourse. True, "virtue" (the ideological term the nobility used to anoint itself with the right to rule) triumphs in the end, but it can do so only by evoking vice and by giving it time on stage. Even as the play asserts the right of the nobility to rule, it evokes the reality that such rule was being contested at the time. By having the defeat of Edmund hang solely on an act of violence (Edgar, the true noble, defeats him in combat), the play also draws attention to the fact that the nobility's claim to legitimacy is tenuous, a matter of force, not virtue.

Another strand of Marxism arose in Germany in the mid-twentieth century and is usually referred to as "Critical Theory." It comprised the work of Walter Benjamin, Theodor Adorno, Ernst Bloch, Herbert Marcuse, and others. They were fascinated by the way society and culture consisted of parts in necessary relationship to one another such that a change in one area meant changes in another inevitably. In this "dialectical" way of theorizing about society and culture, those relations were often conceived as being antagonistic, dissonant, or contradictory. An example of relational change would be the way the growth of huge amounts of wealth in one sector of the population under capitalism meant the relative deprivation of another large group, and this imbalance gave rise to cultural forms that were also unbalanced. High art captured the best of human imagination for a few, while banal popular culture fed the under-nourished masses a gruel of rote, repetitive, intellectually depleted forms of "entertainment" that kept them happy and kept them from complaining overly much about the unequal situation in which they lived. Yet because they were dialecticians, the Critical Theorists located negations within the seeming unity of capitalist culture. High art negated the banal reality of capitalism by assigning value to things other than commodities or money. Art therefore could progressively point ahead in a utopian manner to a society founded on non-utilitarian principles where activities could, like art, be ends in themselves rather than slavishly dutiful work for the benefit of someone in economic power.

Marxism is one form of historical criticism, but it is not the only one. Back when New Criticism was getting itself named new, one kind of traditional criticism that it was replacing was historical. This historical work might or might not be governed by a specific theory of history – such as, for example, Marxism – but it would invariably see the historical as a context for the study of the literary work. Historical background, historical context: the language of a traditional historicism saw the literary work in the foreground and history in the background, with the task of the critic being to connect the two. The literary work might represent or refer to the historical context; the critic would make sense of the literary work by researching the history to which it referred. Without such background information, how could the reader understand anything from the wars fought in a Shakespeare play to the property laws that governed the plot of an Austen novel? One notable consequence was that a literary critic needed to read a good deal of non-literary work, and the critic's enterprise led to the historical archive. Biographical, social, cultural, political – there were as many possibilities as there were schools of historical study, and the literary critic might share with his colleague in history a knowledge of certain eras or institutions that could make him look like an early advocate of interdisciplinarity. Indeed, such was the accusation of the New Critics, who were interested in distinguishing and clarifying the uniquely literary nature of their enterprise, and in sending the historians, sociologists, and biographers of literary study off to their separate fields of study. But history has returned to literary study, and like any repressed entity, it has done so with a vengeance. Literary study today is pervasively historical.

The first return of history falls under the denomination of New Historicism. New Historicism distinguished itself from its antecedents largely because of the way in which the concept of history it assumed had passed through a Post-Structuralist critique. What such a critique makes explicit is the textuality of history, the way in which history is only available as a collection of discourses and the way history is itself relational and web-like (much like a text). Foucault and Derrida are the Post-Structuralist thinkers who most influenced this critical approach. Foucault's histories of everything from madness to sexuality are histories of the discourses that have constructed the past. And Derrida's theory of supplementarity denaturalized the referent by converting it from a thing into a web of relations. New Historians see the historical as textual, and one effect is to create a new relationship between the historical and the literary text. Because both are representations, a term very important to the New Historians (so much so that it is the title of a New Historical journal), neither one is closer to the "truth" of history. History is not some unmediated reality out there, some stable background that the literary text reflects or refers to; it is not a context. Rather, it is like the literary text itself – of a different genre, granted, but no less a discourse or a web of relations. Such a view might seem to undo the privilege of the literary text or of "history" – depending on whether someone valorizes an aesthetic distinction or an ontological one – but it does make it possible to study relations between texts both literary and historical and discover how they trace certain patterns and negotiate various kinds of cultural meaning.

What kinds of patterns interest the New Historian? Influenced at once by Foucauldian and Marxist theories of history, the New Historian focuses on issues of power – with a particular interest in the ways in which power is maintained by unofficial means such as the theatricality of royal display in the Court. The cultural materialists argued that all power is fragile, subject to undermining by dissident elements within a society, and they believed that literature inadvertently displays the fissures in power, the moments of subversion where the precariousness of power is most palpable. Responding to their critique, New Historicist Stephen Greenblatt argued that subversion itself was a ruse of power. His essay, entitled "Invisible Bullets," referred to a ploy of English colonists, who characterized the diseases ravaging Native populations as God-sent punishment for disobedience to their colonial masters; in Greenblatt's argument, the containment of subversion was like the "invisible bullets" of germ warfare used to contain Native resistance. A playwright like Shakespeare might evoke the undermining of royal power in his *Henry* plays, but in the end, such undermining merely serves the ends of reinforcing that power all the more forcefully. At a certain point, subversion and containment were almost the catch-phrases of New Historicism.

Another preoccupation of New Historicism is with the circulation of discourses both within and through various texts. Any text itself will have a mode of circulation – it will have a place within an economic system – but it will also serve to circulate certain discourses. To see the discourses circulating in a particular era, one needs to see not only their literary manifestation but also their presence in other kinds of cultural representations. The New Historian is selective in an approach to the archive; the historical text that illuminates a pattern might be a single manifesto or conduct book, a broadside or a periodical. All texts might be called interventions in such patterns, in that they do not merely reflect but have effects on the cultural situation they represent. A New Historicist essay will often put the same reading practices into play for all the texts it studies, with the non-literary subject to the same close reading as the literary.

The turn to history is a crucial part of the current scene in literary study and is one conducted under the aegis of many critical approaches. Feminism and gender studies, post-colonialism and ethnic studies: the categories of analysis are themselves historical, and in the anti-essentialism of the moment few would be willing to adopt a vocabulary without historicizing it. Historicism in literary study received a highly visible revival with the creation of New Historicism, but in some sense the wider success of historicism is evidenced in the ways historicism has entered almost every other critical approach from C. L. R. James's study of the revolution in Haiti, *The Black Jacobins*, to Gerald Vizenor's work on nostalgic imagery of the "vanishing" Native Americans, *Native Poses,* to Paul Gilroy's account of a circum-Atlantic African cultural diaspora in "Black Atlantic."

A historian recently characterized his discipline as one in which knowledge is presumed to be diachronic, across time, to use the vocabulary introduced by Saussure. Saussure himself focused on a synchronic mode of analysis, we might note. Historicism today is, in fact, both diachronic and synchronic. That is, many contemporary historicist critics draw on the synchronic analysis of Saussure and his structuralist heirs, who show "reality" to be constituted of systems of signs, realms of discourse that work to construct a version of the real. Understanding "history" as discursively produced allows one to consider the source of a given discourse, its genealogy, to use a term important to Foucault, and along with its source the perspective it might serve. In a recent film entitled *The Official Story*, an Argentinian woman who teaches history in a high school is brought face to face with the discrepancy between history as she is teaching it, as her government wants her to teach it, with all of its occlusions, and history as she is living it. Reading between the lines of "the official story," she discovers an alternative discourse being produced by the mothers of the disappeared (victims of Argentina's right-wing military dictatorship), a discourse that inhabits her own family, however much the official story denies its existence. Or to cite a different example, in a preface to Frederick

Douglass's *Narrative*, Wendell Phillips recounts the fable of "The Man and the Lion" in which the Lion complains that he would not be so misrepresented "when the lions write history." Frederick Douglass, a fugitive slave for whom literacy itself was against the law, was Wendell Phillips's lion, and he was writing history. Presumably the disappeared can tell no stories. No more can lions. But the metaphor of their missing stories is another way to mark the place of alternative discourses, alternative histories, of all the historical work yet to be done in the ever-expanding processes of writing the past.

CHAPTER 2

The Philosophic and Economic Manuscripts of 1844

Karl Marx

Private property is a concept in Marx that has been widely misunderstood. By private property, Marx did not mean things like cars, houses, bank accounts, and businesses. He meant instead the product of human labor that is seized by the owners of capital and converted into their exclusive private property as accumulated wealth. Marx saw human life as an active process of creation and production. Humans act on nature, transforming it to suit their needs. Human life is creative active life. In early human existence, humans only needed to produce food to survive, but as human civilization developed (another product of human creativity), human needs expanded. Now, humans needed to produce dwellings, institutions such as governments, and manufactured goods such as pottery and roofing tiles that could be used in food storage and building. Advance again two thousand years in time, and humans were producing clothes, pots and pans, cutlery, furniture, iron goods, and horse carriages. Usually, these produced goods belonged to those who made them. Small shops did the manufacture. But with time, as the human population expanded and civilization grew, more produced goods were needed, and new human inventions such as steam power made their production on a mass scale possible. Humans, separated from farms and the ability to grow their own food, had to sell their labor to the owners of capital who employed them making things in the new factories. The creative activity of humans now was in the service of someone else (it had become "alien" or "estranged"). And the product of human labor now belonged to the owner of the factory rather than to the workers. The product of human labor had become "privatized."

That is what Marx means by private property. The products of human creative labor belong to someone other than those who made them. Under the rules of capitalism, the factory owner owns what others make for him in return for wages.

Original publication details: Karl Marx, "The Economic and Philosophic Manuscripts" from *The Marx–Engels Reader*, trans. Robert C. Tucker, pp. 52–71. W.W. Norton, 1972. Reproduced with permission from W.W. Norton & Company Inc.

In his early manuscripts, Marx develops this theory, but because they were not made available until 1932, well after the Russian Revolution of 1917, which attempted to transform Russia into a Marxist society that abolished "private property," the Russian communists instead tried to abolish private property in the colloquial sense, taking homes and businesses away from people.

Estranged Labour[1]

We have proceeded from the premises of political economy. We have accepted its language and its laws. We presupposed private property, the separation of labour, capital and land, and of wages, profit of capital and rent of land – likewise division of labour, competition, the concept of exchange-value, etc. On the basis of political economy itself, in its own words, we have shown that the worker sinks to the level of a commodity and becomes indeed the most wretched of commodities; that the wretchedness of the worker is in inverse proportion to the power and magnitude of his production; that the necessary result of competition is the accumulation of capital in a few hands, and thus the restoration of monopoly in a more terrible form; that finally the distinction between capitalist and land-rentier, like that between the tiller of the soil and the factory-worker, disappears and that the whole of society must fall apart into the two classes – the property-*owners* and the propertyless *workers*.

Political economy proceeds from the fact of private property, but it does not explain it to us. It expresses in general, abstract formulae the *material* process through which private property actually passes, and these formulae it then takes for *laws*. It does not *comprehend* these laws – i.e., it does not demonstrate how they arise from the very nature of private property. Political economy does not disclose the source of the division between labour and capital, and between capital and land. When, for example, it defines the relationship of wages to profit, it takes the interest of the capitalists to be the ultimate cause; i.e., it takes for granted what it is supposed to evolve. Similarly, competition comes in everywhere. It is explained from external circumstances. As to how far these external and apparently fortuitous circumstances are but the expression of a necessary course of development, political economy teaches us nothing. We have seen how, to it, exchange itself appears to be a fortuitous fact. The only wheels which political economy sets in motion are *avarice* and the *war amongst the avaricious – competition*.

Precisely because political economy does not grasp the connections within the movement, it was possible to counterpose, for instance, the doctrine of competition to the doctrine of monopoly, the doctrine of craft-liberty to the doctrine of the corporation, the doctrine of the division of landed property to the doctrine of the big estate – for competition, craft-liberty and the division of landed property were explained and comprehended only as fortuitous, premeditated and violent consequences of monopoly, the corporation, and feudal property, not as their necessary, inevitable and natural consequences.

Now, therefore, we have to grasp the essential connection between private property, avarice, and the separation of labour, capital and landed property; between exchange and competition, value and the devaluation of men, monopoly and competition, etc.; the connection between this whole estrangement and the *money*-system.

Do not let us go back to a fictitious primordial condition as the political economist does, when he tries to explain. Such a primordial condition explains nothing. He merely pushes the question away into a grey nebulous distance. He assumes in the form of fact, of an event, what he is supposed to deduce – namely, the necessary relationship between two things – between, for example, division of labour and exchange. Theology in the same way explains the origin of evil by the fall of man: that is, it assumes as a fact, in historical form, what has to be explained.

We proceed from an *actual* economic fact.

The worker becomes all the poorer the more wealth he produces, the more his production increases in power and range. The worker becomes an ever cheaper commodity the more commodities he creates. With the *increasing value* of the world of things proceeds in direct proportion the *devaluation* of the world of men. Labour produces not only commodities; it produces itself and the worker as a *commodity* – and does so in the proportion in which it produces commodities generally.

This fact expresses merely that the object which labour produces – labour's product – confronts it as *something alien*, as a *power independent* of the producer. The product of labour is labour which has been congealed in an object, which has become material: it is the *objectification* of labour. Labour's realization is its objectification. In the conditions dealt with by political economy this realization of labour appears as *loss of reality* for the workers; objectification as *loss of the object* and *object-bondage*; appropriation as *estrangement*, as *alienation*.[2]

So much does labour's realization appear as loss of reality that the worker loses reality to the point of starving to death. So much does objectification appear as loss of the object that the worker is robbed of the objects most necessary not only for his life but for his work. Indeed, labour itself becomes an object which he can get hold of only with the greatest effort and with the most irregular interruptions. So much does the appropriation of the object appear as estrangement that the more objects the worker produces the fewer can he possess and the more he falls under the dominion of his product, capital.

All these consequences are contained in the definition that the worker is related to the *product of his labour* as to an *alien* object. For on this premise it is clear that the more the worker spends himself, the more powerful the alien objective world becomes which he creates over-against himself, the poorer he himself – his inner world – becomes, the less belongs to him as his own. It is the same in religion. The more man puts into God, the less he retains in himself. The worker puts his life into the object; but now his life no longer belongs to him but to the object. Hence, the greater this activity, the greater is the worker's lack of objects. Whatever the product of his labour is, he is not. Therefore the greater this product, the less is he himself. The *alienation* of the worker in his product means not only that his labour becomes an object, an *external* existence, but that it exists *outside him*, independently, as something alien to him, and that it becomes a power of its own confronting him; it means that the life which he has conferred on the object confronts him as something hostile and alien.

Let us now look more closely at the *objectification*, at the production of the worker; and therein at the *estrangement*, the *loss* of the object, his product.

The worker can create nothing without *nature*, without the *sensuous external world*. It is the material on which his labor is manifested, in which it is active, from which and by means of which it produces.

But just as nature provides labor with the *means of life* in the sense that labour cannot *live* without objects on which to operate, on the other hand, it also provides the *means of life* in the more restricted sense – i.e., the means for the physical subsistence of the *worker* himself.

Thus the more the worker by his labour *appropriates* the external world, sensuous nature, the more he deprives himself of *means of life* in the double respect: first, that the sensuous external world more and more ceases to be an object belonging to his labour – to be his labour's *means of life*; and secondly, that it more and more ceases to be *means of life* in the immediate sense, means for the physical subsistence of the worker.

Thus in this double respect the worker becomes a slave of his object, first, in that he receives an *object of labour*, i.e., in that he receives *work*; and secondly, in that he receives *means of subsistence*. Therefore, it enables him to exist, first, as a *worker;* and, second, as a *physical subject*. The extremity of this bondage is that it is only as a *worker* that he continues to maintain himself as a *physical subject*, and that it is only as a *physical subject* that he is a *worker*.

(The laws of political economy express the estrangement of the worker in his object thus: the more the worker produces, the less he has to consume; the more values he creates, the more valueless, the more unworthy he becomes; the better formed his product, the more deformed becomes the worker; the more civilized his object, the more barbarous becomes the worker; the mightier labour becomes, the more powerless becomes the worker; the more ingenious labour becomes, the duller becomes the worker and the more he becomes nature's bondsman.)

Political economy conceals the estrangement inherent in the nature of labour by not considering the direct relationship between the worker (labour) *and production*. It is true that labour produces for the rich wonderful things – but for the worker it produces privation. It produces palaces – but for the worker, hovels. It produces beauty – but for the worker, deformity. It replaces labour by machines – but some of the workers it throws back to a barbarous type of labour, and the other workers it turns into machines. It produces intelligence – but for the worker idiocy, cretinism.

The direct relationship of labour to its produce is the relationship of the worker to the objects of his production. The relationship of the man of means to the objects of production and to production itself is only a *consequence* of this first relationship – and confirms it. We shall consider this other aspect later.

When we ask, then, what is the essential relationship of labour we are asking about the relationship of the *worker* to production.

Till now we have been considering the estrangement, the alienation of the worker only in one of its aspects, i.e., the worker's *relationship to the products of his labour*. But the estrangement is manifested not only in the result but in the *act of production* – within the *producing activity* itself. How would the worker come to face the product of his activity as a stranger, were it not that in the very act of production he was estranging himself from himself? The product is after all but the summary of the activity of production. If then the product of labour is alienation, production itself must be active alienation, the alienation of activity, the activity of alienation. In the estrangement of the object of labour is merely summarized the estrangement, the alienation, in the activity of labour itself.

What, then, constitutes the alienation of labour?

First, the fact that labour is *external* to the worker, i.e., it does not belong to his essential being; that in his work, therefore, he does not affirm himself but denies himself, does not feel content but unhappy, does not develop freely his physical and mental energy but mortifies his body and ruins his mind. The worker therefore only feels himself outside his work, and in his work feels outside himself. He is at home when he is not working, and when he is working he is not at home. His labour is therefore not voluntary, but coerced; it is *forced labour*. It is therefore not the satisfaction of a need; it is merely a *means* to satisfy needs external to it. Its alien character emerges clearly in the fact that as soon as no physical or other compulsion exists, labour is shunned like the plague. External labour, labour in which man alienates himself, is a labour of self-sacrifice, of mortification. Lastly, the external character of labour for the worker appears in the fact that it is not his own, but someone else's, that it does not belong to him, that in it he belongs, not to himself, but to another. Just as in religion the spontaneous activity of the human imagination, of the human brain and the human heart, operates independently of the individual – that is, operates on him as an alien, divine or diabolical activity – in the same way the worker's activity is not his spontaneous activity. It belongs to another; it is the loss of his self.

As a result, therefore, man (the worker) no longer feels himself to be freely active in any but his animal functions – eating, drinking, procreating, or at most in his dwelling and in dressing-up, etc.; and in his human functions he no longer feels himself to be anything but an animal. What is animal becomes human and what is human becomes animal.

Certainly eating, drinking, procreating, etc., are also genuinely human functions. But in the abstraction which separates them from the sphere of all other human activity and turns them into sole and ultimate ends, they are animal.

We have considered the act of estranging practical human activity, labour, in two of its aspects. (1) The relation of the worker to the *product of labour* as an alien object exercising power over him. This relation is at the same time the relation to the sensuous external world, to the objects of nature as an alien world antagonistically opposed to him. (2) The relation of labour to the *act of production* within the *labour* process. This relation is the relation of the worker to his own activity as an alien activity not belonging to him; it is activity as suffering, strength as weakness, begetting as emasculating, the worker's *own* physical and mental energy, his personal life or what is life other than activity – as an activity which is turned against him, neither depends on nor belongs to him. Here we have *self-estrangement*, as we had previously the estrangement of the *thing*.

We have yet a third aspect of *estranged labour* to deduce from the two already considered.

Man is a species being, not only because in practice and in theory he adopts the species as his object (his own as well as those of other things), but – and this is only another way of expressing it – but also because he treats himself as the actual, living species; because he treats himself as a *universal* and therefore a free being.

The life of the species, both in man and in animals, consists physically in the fact that man (like the animal) lives on inorganic nature; and the more universal man is compared with an animal, the more universal is the sphere of inorganic nature on which he lives. Just as plants, animals, stones, the air, light, etc., constitute a part of human consciousness in the realm of theory, partly as objects of natural science, partly as objects of art – his spiritual inorganic nature, spiritual nourishment which he must first prepare to make it palatable and digestible – so too in the realm of practice they constitute a part of human life and human activity. Physically man lives only on these products of nature, whether they appear in the form of food, heating, clothes, a dwelling, or whatever it may be. The universality of man is in practice manifested precisely in the universality which makes all nature his *inorganic* body – both inasmuch as nature is (1) his direct means of life, and (2) the material, the object, and the instrument of his life-activity. Nature is man's *inorganic body* – nature, that is, in so far as it is not itself the human body. Man *lives* on nature – means that nature is his *body*, with which he must remain in continuous intercourse if he is not to die. That man's physical and spiritual life is linked to nature means simply that nature is linked to itself, for man is a part of nature.

In estranging from man (1) nature, and (2) himself, his own active functions, his life-activity, estranged labour estranges the *species* from man. It turns for him the *life of the species* into a means of individual life. First it estranges the life of the species and individual life, and secondly it makes individual life in its abstract form the purpose of the life of the species, likewise in its abstract and estranged form.

For in the first place labour, *life-activity, productive life* itself, appears to man merely as a *means* of satisfying a need – the need to maintain the physical existence. Yet the productive life is the life of the species. It is life-engendering life. The whole character of a species – its species character – is contained in the character of its life-activity; and free, conscious activity is man's species character. Life itself appears only as *a means to life*.

The animal is immediately identical with its life-activity. It does not distinguish itself from it. It is *its life-activity*. Man makes his life-activity itself the object of his will and of his consciousness. He has conscious life-activity. It is not a determination with which he directly merges. Conscious life-activity directly distinguishes man from animal life-activity. It is just because of this that he is a species being. Or it is only because he is a species being that he is a Conscious Being, i.e., that his own life is an object for him. Only because of that is his activity free activity. Estranged labour reverses this relationship, so that it is just because man is a conscious being that he makes his life-activity, his *essential* being, a mere means to his *existence*.

In creating an *objective world* by his practical activity, in *working-up* inorganic nature, man proves himself a conscious species being, i.e., as a being that treats the species as its own essential being, or that treats itself as a species being. Admittedly animals also produce. They build themselves nests, dwellings, like the bees, beavers, ants, etc. But an animal only produces what it immediately needs for itself or its young. It produces one-sidedly, whilst man produces universally. It produces only under the dominion of immediate physical need, whilst man produces even when he is free from physical need and only truly produces in freedom therefrom. An animal produces only itself, whilst man reproduces the whole of nature. An animal's product belongs immediately to its physical body, whilst man freely confronts his product. An animal forms things in accordance with the standard and the need of the species to which it belongs, whilst man knows how to produce in accordance with the standard of every species, and knows how to apply everywhere the inherent standard to the object. Man therefore also forms things in accordance with the laws of beauty.

It is just in the working-up of the objective world, therefore, that man first really proves himself to be a *species being*. This production is his active species life. Through and because of this production, nature appears as *his* work and his reality. The object of labour is, therefore, the *objectification of man's species life*: for he duplicates himself not only, as in consciousness, intellectually, but also actively, in reality, and therefore he contemplates himself in a world that he has created. In tearing away from man the object of his production, therefore, estranged labour tears from him his *species life*, his real species objectivity, and transforms his advantage over animals into the disadvantage that his inorganic body, nature, is taken from him.

Similarly, in degrading spontaneous activity, free activity, to a means, estranged labour makes man's species life a means to his physical existence.

The consciousness which man has of his species is thus transformed by estrangement in such a way that the species life becomes for him a means.

Estranged labour turns thus:

(3) *Man's species being*, both nature and his spiritual species property, into a being *alien* to him, into a *means* to his *individual existence*. It estranges man's own body from him, as it does external nature and his spiritual essence, his *human* being.

(4) An immediate consequence of the fact that man is estranged from the product of his labour, from his life-activity, from his species being is the *estrangement of man* from *man*. If a man is confronted by himself, he is confronted by the *other* man. What applies to a man's relation to his work, to the product of his labour and to himself, also holds of a man's relation to the other man, and to the other man's labour and object of labour.

In fact, the proposition that man's species nature is estranged from him means that one man is estranged from the other, as each of them is from man's essential nature.[3]

The estrangement of man, and in fact every relationship in which man stands to himself, is first realized and expressed in the relationship in which a man stands to other men.

Hence within the relationship of estranged labour each man views the other in accordance with the standard and the position in which he finds himself as a worker.

We took our departure from a fact of political economy – the estrangement of the worker and his production. We have formulated the concept of this fact – *estranged, alienated* labour. We have analysed this concept – hence analysing merely a fact of political economy.

Let us now see, further, how in real life the concept of estranged, alienated labour must express and present itself.

If the product of labour is alien to me, if it confronts me as an alien power, to whom, then, does it belong?

If my own activity does not belong to me, if it is an alien, a coerced activity, to whom, then, does it belong?

To a being *other* than me.

Who is this being?

The *gods*? To be sure, in the earliest times the principal production (for example, the building of temples, etc., in Egypt, India and Mexico) appears to be in the service of the gods, and the product belongs to the gods. However, the gods on their own were never the lords of labour. No more was *nature*. And what a contradiction it would be if, the more man subjugated nature by his labour and the more the miracles of the gods were rendered superfluous by the miracles of industry, the more man were to renounce the joy of production and the enjoyment of the produce in favour of these powers.

The *alien* being, to whom labour and the produce of labour belongs, in whose service labour is done and for whose benefit the produce of labour is provided, can only be *man* himself.

If the product of labour does not belong to the worker, if it confronts him as an alien power, this can only be because it belongs to some *other man than the worker*. If the worker's activity is a torment to him, to another it must be *delight* and his life's joy. Not the gods, not nature, but only man himself can be this alien power over man.

We must bear in mind the above-stated proposition that man's relation to himself only becomes *objective* and *real* for him through his relation to the other man. Thus, if the product of his labour, his labour *objectified*, is for him an *alien*, hostile, powerful object independent of him, then his position towards it is such that someone else is master of this object, someone who is alien, hostile, powerful, and independent of him. If his own activity is to him an unfree activity, then he is treating it as activity performed in the service, under the dominion, the coercion and the yoke of another man.

Every self-estrangement of man from himself and from nature appears in the relation in which he places himself and nature to men other than and differentiated from himself. For this reason religious self-estrangement necessarily appears in the relationship of the layman to the priest, or again to a mediator, etc., since we are here dealing with the intellectual world. In the real practical world self-estrangement can only become manifest through the real practical relationship to other men. The medium through which estrangement takes place is itself *practical*. Thus through estranged labour man not only engenders his relationship to the object and to the act of production as to powers that are alien and hostile to him; he also engenders the relationship in which other men stand to his production and to his product, and the relationship in which he stands to these other men. Just as he begets his own production as the loss of his reality, as his punishment; just as he begets his own product as a loss, as a product not belonging to him; so he begets the dominion of the one who does not produce over production and over the product. Just as he estranges from himself his own activity, so he confers to the stranger activity which is not his own.

Till now we have only considered this relationship from the standpoint of the worker and later we shall be considering it also from the standpoint of the non-worker.

Through *estranged, alienated labour*, then, the worker produces the relationship to this labour of a man alien to labour and standing outside it. The relationship of the worker to labour engenders the relation to it of the capitalist, or whatever one chooses to call the master of labour. *Private property* is thus the product, the result, the necessary consequence, of *alienated labour*, of the external relation of the worker to nature and to himself.

Private property thus results by analysis from the concept of *alienated labour* – that is, of *alienated man*, of estranged labour, of estranged life, of *estranged* man.

True, it is as a result of the *movement of private property* that we have obtained the concept of *alienated labour* (*of alienated life*) from political economy. But on analysis of this concept it becomes clear that though private property appears to be the source, the cause of alienated labour, it is really its consequence, just as the gods *in the beginning* are not the cause but the effect of man's intellectual confusion. Later this relationship becomes reciprocal.

Only at the very culmination of the development of private property does this, its secret, re-emerge, namely, that on the one hand it is the *product* of alienated labour, and that secondly it is the *means* by which labour alienates itself, the *realization of this alienation*.

This exposition immediately sheds light on various hitherto unsolved conflicts.

(1) Political economy starts from labour as the real soul of production; yet to labour it gives nothing, and to private property everything. From this contradiction Proudhon has concluded in favour of labour and against private property. We understand, however, that this apparent contradiction is the contradiction of *estranged labour* with itself, and that political economy has merely formulated the laws of estranged labour.

We also understand, therefore, that *wages* and *private property* are identical: where the product, the object of labour pays for labour itself, the wage is but a necessary consequence of labour's estrangement, for after all in the wage of labour, labour does not appear as an end in itself but as the servant of the wage. We shall develop this point later, and meanwhile will only deduce some conclusions.

A *forcing-up of wages* (disregarding all other difficulties, including the fact that it would only be by force, too, that the higher wages, being an anomaly, could be maintained) would therefore be nothing but *better payment for the slave*, and would not conquer either for the worker or for labour their human status and dignity.

Indeed, even the *equality of wages* demanded by Proudhon only transforms the relationship of the present-day worker to his labour into the relationship of all men to labour. Society is then conceived as an abstract capitalist.

Wages are a direct consequence of estranged labour, and estranged labour is the direct cause of private property. The downfall of the one aspect must therefore mean the downfall of the other.

(2) From the relationship of estranged labour to private property it further follows that the emancipation of society from private property, etc., from servitude, is expressed in the *political* form of the *emancipation of the workers*; not that *their* emancipation alone was at stake but because the emancipation of the workers contains universal human emancipation – and it contains this, because the whole of human servitude is involved in the relation of the worker to production, and every relation of servitude is but a modification and consequence of this relation.

Just as we have found the concept of *private property* from the concept of *estranged, alienated labour* by *analysis*, in the same way every *category* of political economy can be evolved with the help of these two factors; and we shall find again in each category, e.g., trade, competition, capital, money, only a *definite* and *developed expression* of the first foundations.

Before considering this configuration, however, let us try to solve two problems.

(1) To define the general *nature of private property*, as it has arisen as a result of estranged labour, in its relation to *truly human, social property*.

(2) We have accepted the *estrangement of labour*, its *alienation*, as a fact, and we have analysed this fact. How, we now ask, does *man* come to *alienate*, to estrange, *his labour?* How is this estrangement rooted in the nature of human development? We have already gone a long way to the solution of this problem by *transforming* the question as to the *origin of private property* into the question as to the relation of *alienated labour* to the course of humanity's development. For when one speaks of *private property*, one thinks of being concerned with something external to man. When one speaks of labour, one is directly concerned with man himself. This new formulation of the question already contains its solution.

As to (1): The general nature of private property and its relation to truly human property.

Alienated labour has resolved itself for us into two elements which mutually condition one another, or which are but different expressions of one and the same relationship. *Appropriation* appears as *estrangement*, as *alienation*; and *alienation* appears as *appropriation*, *estrangement* as true *enfranchisement*.

We have considered the one side – *alienated* labour in relation to the *worker* himself, i.e., the *relation of alienated labour to itself.* The *property-relation of the non-worker to the worker and to labour* we have found as the product, the necessary outcome of this relation of alienated labour. *Private property*, as the material, summary expression of alienated labour, embraces both relations – the *relation of the worker to work, to the product of his labour and to the non-worker*, and the relation of the *non-worker to the worker and to the product of his labour.*

Having seen that in relation to the worker who *appropriates* nature by means of his labour, this appropriation *appears* as estrangement, his own spontaneous activity as activity for another and as activity of another, vitality as a sacrifice of life, production of the object as loss of the object to an alien power, to an *alien* person – we shall now consider the relation to the worker, to labour and its object of this person who is *alien* to labour and the worker.

First it has to be noticed, that everything which appears in the worker as an *activity of alienation, of estrangement*, appears in the non-worker as a *state of alienation, of estrangement*.

Secondly, that the worker's *real, practical attitude* in production and to the product (as a state of mind) appears in the non-worker confronting him as a *theoretical* attitude.

Thirdly, the non-worker does everything against the worker which the worker does against himself; but he does not do against himself what he does against the worker.

Let us look more closely at these three relations.[4]

Private Property and Communism

Re. p. XXXIX. The antithesis of *propertylessness* and *property* so long as it is not compre-hended as the antithesis of *labour* and *capital*, still remains an antithesis of indifference, not grasped in its *active connection*, its *internal* relation – an antithesis not yet grasped as a *contradiction*. It can find expression in this *first* form even without the advanced devel-opment of private property (as in ancient Rome, Turkey, etc.). It does not yet *appear* as having been established by private property itself. But labour, the subjective essence of private property as exclusion of property, and capital, objective labour as exclusion of labour, constitute *private property* as its developed state of contradiction – hence a dynamic relationship moving inexorably to its resolution.

Re. the same page. The transcendence of self-estrangement follows the same course as self-estrangement. *Private property* is first considered only in its objective aspect – but nevertheless with labour as its essence. Its form of existence is therefore *capital*, which is to be annulled "as such" (Proudhon). Or a *particular form* of labour – labour levelled down, parcelled, and therefore unfree – is conceived as the source of private property's *pernicious-ness* and of its existence in estrangement from men; for instance, *Fourier*, who, like the physiocrats, also conceived *agricultural labour* to be at least the *exemplary* type, whilst *Saint-Simon* declares in contrast that *industrial labour* as such is the essence, and now also aspires to the *exclusive* rule of the industrialists and the improvement of the workers' condition. Finally, *communism* is the *positive* expression of annulled private property – at first as *universal* private property. By embracing this relation as a *whole*, communism is:

(1)   In its first form only a *generalization* and *consummation* of this relationship. It shows itself as such in a twofold form: on the one hand, the dominion of *material* property bulks so large that it wants to destroy *everything* which is not capable of being possessed by all as *private property*. It wants to abstract *by force* from talent, etc. For it the sole purpose of life and existence is direct, physical *possession*. The category of *labourer* is not done away with, but extended to all men. The relationship of private property persists as the relationship of the community to the world of things. Finally, this movement of counterposing universal private property to private property finds expression in the bestial form of counterposing to *marriage* (certainly a *form of exclusive private property*) the *community of women*, in which a woman becomes a piece of *communal* and *common* property. It may be said that this idea of the *community of women* gives away the *secret* of

this as yet completely crude and thoughtless communism. Just as the woman passes from marriage to general prostitution,[5] so the entire world of wealth (that is, of man's objective substance) passes from the relationship of exclusive marriage with the owner of private property to a state of universal prostitution with the community. In negating the *personality* of man in every sphere, this type of communism is really nothing but the logical expression of private property, which is this negation. General envy constituting itself as a power is the disguise in which *avarice* re-establishes itself and satisfies itself, only in *another* way. The thoughts of every piece of private property – inherent in each piece as such – are *at least* turned against all *wealthier* private property in the form of envy and the urge to reduce to a common level, so that this envy and urge even constitute the essence of competition. The crude communism is only the consummation of this envy and of this levelling-down proceeding from the *preconceived* minimum. It has a *definite, limited* standard. How little this annulment of private property is really an appropriation is in fact proved by the abstract negation of the entire world of culture and civilization, the regression to the *unnatural* simplicity of the *poor and undemanding* man who has not only failed to go beyond private property, but has not yet even attained to it.

The community is only a community of *labour*, and an equality of *wages* paid out by the communal capital – the *community* as the universal capitalist. Both sides of the relationship are raised to an *imagined* universality – *labour* as a state in which every person is put, and *capital* as the acknowledged universality and power of the community.

In the approach to *woman* as the spoil and handmaid of communal lust is expressed the infinite degradation in which man exists for himself, for the secret of this approach has its *unambiguous*, decisive, *plain* and undisguised expression in the relation of *man* to *woman* and in the manner in which the *direct* and *natural* procreative relationship is conceived. The direct, natural, and necessary relation of person to person is the *relation of man to woman*. In this *natural* relationship of the sexes man's relation to nature is immediately his relation to man, just as his relation to man is immediately his relation to nature – his own *natural* function. In this relationship, therefore, is *sensuously manifested*, reduced to an observable *fact*, the extent to which the human essence has become nature to man, or to which nature has to him become the human essence of man. From this relationship one can therefore judge man's whole level of development. It follows from the character of this relationship how much *man* as a *species being*, as *man*, has come to be himself and to comprehend himself; the relation of man to woman is *the most natural* relation of human being to human being. It therefore reveals the extent to which man's *natural* behaviour has become *human*, or the extent to which the *human* essence in him has become a *natural* essence – the extent to which his *human nature* has come to be *nature to him*. In this relationship is revealed, too, the extent to which man's *need* has become a *human* need; the extent to which, therefore, the *other* person as a person has become for him a need – the extent to which he in his individual existence is at the same time a social being. The first positive annulment of private property – *crude* communism – is thus merely one *form* in which the vileness of private property, which wants to set itself up as the *positive community, comes to the surface*.

(2)   Communism (a) of a political nature still – democratic or despotic; (b) with the annulment of the state, yet still incomplete, and being still affected by private property (i.e., by the estrangement of man). In both forms communism already knows itself to be re-integration or return of man to himself, the transcendence of human self-estrangement; but since it has not yet grasped the positive essence of private property, and just as

little the *human* nature of need, it remains captive to it and infected by it. It has, indeed, grasped its concept, but not its essence.

(3)   *Communism* as the *positive* transcendence of *private property*, or *human self-estrangement*, and therefore as the real *appropriation of the human* essence by and for man; communism therefore as the complete return of man to himself as a *social* (i.e., human) being – a return become conscious, and accomplished within the entire wealth of previous development. This communism, as fully-developed naturalism, equals humanism, and as fully-developed humanism equals naturalism; it is the *genuine* resolution of the conflict between man and nature and between man and man – the true resolution of the strife between existence and essence, between objectification and self-confirmation, between freedom and necessity, between the individual and the species. Communism is the riddle of history solved, and it knows itself to be this solution.

The entire movement of history is, therefore, both its *actual* act of genesis (the birth act of its empirical existence) and also for its thinking consciousness the *comprehended* and *known* process of its *coming-to-be*. That other, still immature communism, meanwhile, seeks an *historical* proof for itself – a proof in the realm of the existent – amongst disconnected historical phenomena opposed to private property, tearing single phases from the historical process and focussing attention on them as proofs of its historical pedigree (a horse ridden hard especially by Cabet, Villegardelle, etc.). By so doing it simply makes clear that by far the greater part of this process contradicts its claims, and that, if it has once been, precisely its being in the *past* refutes its pretension to being *essential*.

That the entire revolutionary movement necessarily finds both its empirical and its theoretical basis in the movement of *private property* – in that of the economy, to be precise – is easy to see.

This *material*, immediately *sensuous* private property is the material sensuous expression of *estranged human* life. Its movement – production and consumption – is the *sensuous* revelation of the movement of all production hitherto – i.e., the realization or the reality of man. Religion, family, state, law, morality, science, art, etc., are only *particular* modes of production, and fall under its general law. The positive transcendence of *private property* as the appropriation of *human* life is, therefore, the positive transcendence of all estrangement – that is to say, the return of man from religion, family, state, etc., to his *human*, i.e., *social* mode of existence. Religious estrangement as such occurs only in the realm of *consciousness*, of man's inner life, but economic estrangement is that of *real life*; its transcendence therefore embraces both aspects. It is evident that the *initial* stage of the movement amongst the various peoples depends on whether the true and for them *authentic* life of the people manifests itself more in consciousness or in the external world – is more ideal or real. Communism begins from the outset (*Owen*) with atheism; but atheism is at first far from being *communism*; indeed, it is still mostly an abstraction.

The philanthropy of atheism is therefore at first only *philosophical*, abstract, philanthropy, and that of communism is at once *real* and directly bent on *action*.

We have seen how on the premise of positively annulled private property man produces man – himself and the other man; how the object, being the direct embodiment of his individuality, is simultaneously his own existence for the other man, the existence of the other man, and that existence for him. Likewise, however, both the material of labour and man as the subject, are the point of departure as well as the result of the movement (and precisely in this fact, that they must constitute the *point of departure*, lies the historical *necessity* of private property). Thus the *social* character is the general character of the whole movement: *just as* society itself produces *man as man*, so is society *produced* by him. Activity and consumption, both in their content and in their *mode of existence*, are *social: social* activity and *social* consumption; the *human* essence of nature first exists only for *social* man; for only here does nature exist for him as a *bond* with *man* – as his existence for the other and the other's existence for him – as the life-element of the human world; only here does nature exist as the *foundation* of his own *human* existence. Only here has what is to him his *natural* existence become his *human* existence, and nature become man for him. Thus *society* is the consummated oneness in substance of man and nature – the true resurrection of nature – the naturalism of man and the humanism of nature both brought to fulfilment.

Notes

1   *Die Entfremdete Arbeit*. [In some other translations this phrase appears as "alienated labour." – *R. T.*]
2   "Alienation" – *Entausserung*. An alternative and perhaps better translation of *Entausserung* would be "externalization." The term translated "estrangement" in the above passage is *Entfremdung*. [*R. T.*]
3   "Species nature" (and, earlier, "species being") – *Gattungswesen*; "man's essential nature" – *menschlichen Wesen*.
4   At this point the first manuscript breaks off unfinished.
5   Prostitution is only a *specific* expression of the *general* prostitution of the *labourer*, and since it is a relationship in which falls not the prostitute alone, but also the one who prostitutes – and the latter's abomination is still greater – the capitalist, etc., also comes under this head. [*Marx*]

CHAPTER 3

The German Ideology

Karl Marx

In this early work (1846), Marx retells the story of human history from the perspective of who owns and who works. In this selection, he argues against a group of mid-nineteenth-century German thinkers who saw the world as an embodiment of spiritual ideas. Marx believed that there was no such thing as spirit. All life consists of physical or material processes. And human consciousness is part of those physical processes.

Men can be distinguished from animals by consciousness, by religion, or anything else you like. They themselves begin to distinguish themselves from animals as soon as they begin to produce their means of subsistence, a step which is conditioned by their physical organization. By producing their means of subsistence men are indirectly producing their actual material life.

The way in which men produce their means of subsistence depends first of all on the nature of the actual means of subsistence they find in existence and have to reproduce. This mode of production must not be considered simply as being the reproduction of the physical existence of the individuals. Rather it is a definite form of activity of these individuals, a definite form of expressing their life, a definite *mode of life* on their part. As individuals express their life, so they are. What they are, therefore coincides with their production, both with *what* they produce and with *how* they produce. The nature of individuals thus depends on the material conditions determining their production.

This production only makes its appearance with the *increase of population*. In its turn this presupposes the *intercourse* [*Verkehr*] of individuals with one another. The form of this intercourse is again determined by production.

The relations of different nations among themselves depend upon the extent to which each has developed its productive forces, the division of labor and internal intercourse. This statement is generally recognized. But not only the relation of one nation to others, but also the whole interval structure of the nation itself depends on the stage of

Original publication details: Karl Marx, "The German Ideology: Part 1," *from The Marx–Engels Reader*, second edition, trans. Robert C. Tucker, pp. 110–164. W.W. Norton, 1978. Reproduced with permission from W.W. Norton & Company Inc.

Literary Theory: An Anthology, Third Edition. Edited by Julie Rivkin and Michael Ryan.
© 2017 John Wiley & Sons, Ltd. Published 2017 by John Wiley & Sons, Ltd.

development reached by its production and its internal and external intercourse. How far the productive forces of a nation are developed is shown most manifestly by the degree to which the division of labor has been carried. Each new productive force, insofar as it is not merely a quantitative extension of productive forces already known (for instance the bringing into cultivation of fresh land), causes a further development of the division of labor.

The division of labor inside a nation leads at first to the separation of industrial and commercial from agricultural labor, and hence to the separation of *town* and *country* and to the conflict of their interests. Its further development leads to the separation of commercial from industrial labor. At the same time through the division of labor inside these various branches there develop various divisions among the individuals cooperating in definite kinds of labor. The relative position of these individual groups is determined by the methods employed in agriculture, industry, and commerce (patriarchalism, slavery, estates, classes). These same conditions are to be seen (given a more developed intercourse) in the relations of different nations to one another.

The various stages of development in the division of labor are just so many different forms of ownership, i.e., the existing stage in the division of labor determines also the relations of individuals to one another with reference to the material, instrument, and product of labor.

The first form of ownership is tribal [*Stammeigentum*] ownership. It corresponds to the undeveloped stage of production, at which a people lives by hunting and fishing, by the rearing of beasts, or, in the highest stage, agriculture. In the latter case it presupposes a great mass of uncultivated stretches of land. The division of labor is at this stage still very elementary and is confined to a further extension of the natural division of labor existing in the family. The social structure is, therefore, limited to an extension of the family; patriarchal family chieftains, below them the members of the tribe, finally slaves. The slavery latent in the family only develops gradually with the increase of populations, the growth of wants, and with the extension of external relations, both of war and of barter.

The second form is the ancient communal and State ownership which proceeds especially from the union of several tribes into a city by agreement or by conquest, and which is still accompanied by slavery. Beside communal ownership we already find movable, and later also immovable, private property developing, but as an abnormal form subordinate to communal ownership. The citizens hold power over their laboring slaves only in their community, and on this account alone, therefore, they are bound to the form of communal ownership. It is the communal private property which compels the active citizens to remain in this spontaneously derived form of association over against their slaves. For this reason the whole structure of society based on this communal ownership, and with it the power of the people, decays in the same measure as, in particular, immovable private property evolves. The division of labor is already more developed. We already find the antagonism of town and country; later the antagonism between those states which represent town interests and those which represent country interests, and inside the towns themselves the antagonism between industry and maritime commerce. The class relation between citizens and slaves is now completely developed.... .

The third form of ownership is feudal or estate property. If antiquity started out from the town and its little territory, the Middle Ages started out from the *country*. This different starting-point was determined by the sparseness of the political at that time, which was scattered over a large area and which received no large increase from the conquerors. In contrast to Greece and Rome, feudal development at the outset, therefore, extends over a territory, prepared by the Roman conflicts and the spread of agriculture; at first associated with them. The last centuries of the declining Roman Empire and its conquest by the barbarians destroyed a number of productive forces; agriculture had declined, industry had decayed for want of a market, trade had died out or been violently suspended, the rural and urban population had decreased. From these conditions and the mode of organization of the conquest determined by them, feudal property developed under the influence of the Germanic military constitution. Like tribal and communal ownership, it is based again on a community; but the directly producing class standing over against it is not, as in the case of the ancient community, the slaves, but the enserfed small peasantry. As soon as feudalism is fully developed, there also arises antagonism to the towns. The hierarchical structure of landownership, and the armed bodies of retainers associated with it, gave the nobility power over the serfs. This feudal organization was, just as much as the ancient communal ownership, an association against a subjected producing class; but the form of association and the relation to the direct producers were different because of the different conditions of production.

This feudal system of landownership had its counterpart in the *towns* in the shape of corporative property, the feudal organization of trades. Here property consisted chiefly in the labor of each individual person. The necessity for association against the organized robber nobility, the need for communal covered markets in an age when the industrialist was at the same time a merchant, the growing competition of the escaped serfs swarming into the rising towns, the feudal structure of the whole country, these combined to bring about the *guilds*. The gradually accumulated small capital of individual craftsmen and their stable numbers, as against the growing population, evolved the relation of journeyman and apprentice, which brought into being in the towns a hierarchy similar to that in the country.

Thus the chief form of property during the feudal epoch consisted on the one hand of landed property with serf labor chained to it, and on the other of the labor of the individual with small capital commanding the labor of journeymen. The organization of both was determined by the restricted conditions of production – the small-scale and primitive cultivation of the land, and the craft type of industry. There was little division of labor in the heyday of feudalism. Each country bore in itself the antithesis of town and country; the division into estates was certainly strongly marked; but apart from the differentiation of princes, nobility, clergy and peasants in the country and masters, journeymen, apprentices and soon also the rabble of casual laborers in the towns, no division of importance took place. In agriculture it was rendered difficult by the strip-system beside which the cottage industry of the peasants themselves emerged. In industry there was no division of labor at all in the individual trades themselves, and very little between them. The separation of industry and commerce was found already in existence in older towns; in the newer it only developed later, when the towns entered into mutual relations.

The grouping of larger territories into feudal kingdoms was a necessity for the landed nobility as for the towns. The organization of the ruling class, the nobility, had, therefore, everywhere a monarch at its head.

The fact is, therefore, that definite individuals who are productively active in a definite way enter into these definite social and political relations. Empirical observation must in each separate instance bring out empirically, all without mystification and speculation, the connection of the social and political structure with production. The social structure and the State are continually evolving out of the life process of definite individuals, but of individuals, not as they may appear in their own or other people's imagination, but as they *really* are; i.e., as they operate, produce materially, and hence as they work under specific material limits, presuppositions and conditions independent of their will.

The production of ideas, of conceptions, of consciousness is at first directly interwoven with the material activities and the material intercourse of men, the language of real life. Conceiving, thinking, the mental intercourse of men, appear at this stage as the direct efflux of their material behavior. The same applies to mental production as expressed in the language of politics, laws, morality, religion, metaphysics, etc., of a people. Men are the producers of their conceptions, ideas, etc. – real active men, as they are conditioned by a particular development of their productive forces and of the intercourse corresponding to these, up to its furthest forms. Consciousness can never be anything else than conscious existence, and the existence of men is their actual life-process. If in all ideology men and their circumstances appear upside-down as in a *camera obscura*, this phenomenon arises just as much from their historical life-process as the inversion of objects on the retina does from their physical life-process.

In direct contrast to German philosophy which descends from heaven to earth, here we ascend from earth to heaven. That is to say, we do not set out from what men say, imagine, conceive, nor from men as narrated, thought of, imagined, conceived, in order to arrive at men in the flesh. We set out from real, active men, and on the basis of their real life-process we demonstrate the development of the ideological reflexes and echoes of this life-process. The phantoms formed in the human brain are also, necessarily, sublimates of their material life-process, which is empirically verifiable and bound to material premises. Morality, religion, metaphysics, all the rest of ideology and their corresponding forms of consciousness, thus no longer retain the semblance of independence. They have no history, no development; but men, developing their material production and their material intercourse, alter, along with this their real existence, their thinking and the products of their thinking. Life is not determined by consciousness, but consciousness by life. In the first method of approach the starting-point is consciousness taken as the living individual; in the second method, which conforms to real life, it is the real living individuals themselves, and consciousness is considered solely as *their* consciousness.... .

The ideas of the ruling class are in every epoch the ruling ideas: i.e., the class which is the ruling *material* force of society, is at the same time its ruling *intellectual* force. The class which has the means of material production at its disposal has control at the same time over the means of material production, so that thereby, generally speaking, the ideas of those who lack the means of mental production are subject to it. The ruling ideas are nothing more than the ideal expression of the dominant material relationships, the dominant material relationships grasped as ideas; hence of the relationships which make the one class the ruling one, therefore, the ideas of its dominance. The individuals composing the ruling class possess among other things consciousness, and therefore think. Insofar, therefore, as they rule as a class and determine the extent and compass of an epoch, it is self-evident that they do this in its whole range, hence among other things rule also as thinkers, as producers of ideas, and regulate the production and distribution of the ideas of their age: thus their ideas are the ruling ideas of the epoch. For instance, in an age and in a country where royal power, aristocracy, and bourgeoisie are contending for mastery and where, therefore, mastery is shared, the doctrine of the separation of powers proves to be the dominant idea and is expressed as an "eternal law."

The division of labor, which we have already seen above as one of the chief forces of history up till now, manifests itself also in the ruling class as the division of mental and material labor, so that inside this class one part appears as the thinkers of the class (its active, conceptive ideologists, who make the perfecting of the illusion of the class about itself their chief source of livelihood), while the others' attitude to these ideas and illusions is more passive and receptive, because they are in reality the active members of this class and have less time to make up illusions and ideas about themselves. Within this class this cleavage can even develop into a certain opposition and hostility between the two parts, which, however, in the case of a practical collision, in which the class itself is endangered, automatically comes to nothing, in which case there also vanishes the semblance that the ruling ideas were not the ideas of the ruling class and had a power distinct from the power of this class. The existence of revolutionary ideas in a particular period presupposes the existence of a revolutionary class; about the premises for the latter sufficient has already been said above.

If now in considering the course of history we detach the ideas of the ruling class from the ruling class itself and attribute to them an independent existence, if we confine ourselves to saying that these or those ideas were dominant at a given time, without bothering ourselves about the conditions of production and the producers of these ideas, if we thus ignore the individuals and world conditions which are the source of the ideas, we can say, for instance, that during the time that the aristocracy was dominant, the concepts honor, loyalty, etc., were dominant, during the dominance of the bourgeoisie the concepts freedom, equality, etc. The ruling class itself on the whole imagines this to be so. This conception of history, which is common to all historians, particularly since the eighteenth century, will necessarily come up against the phenomenon that increasingly abstract ideas hold sway, i.e., ideas which increasingly take on the form of universality. For each new class which puts itself in the place of one ruling before it, is compelled, merely in order to carry through its aim, to represent its interest as the common interest of all the members of society, that is, expressed an ideal form: it has to give its ideas the form of universality, and represent them as the only rational, universally valid ones. The class making a revolution appears from the very start, if only because it is opposed to a *class*, not as a class but as the representative of the whole of society; it appears as the whole mass of society confronting the one ruling class.[1] It can do this because, to start with, its interest really is more connected to the common interest of all other non-ruling classes, because under the pressure of hitherto existing conditions its interest has not yet been able to develop as the particular interest of a particular class. Its victory, therefore, benefits also many individuals of the other classes which are not winning a dominant position, but only insofar as it now puts these individuals in a position to raise themselves into the ruling class. When the French bourgeoisie overthrew the power of the aristocracy, it thereby made it possible for many proletarians to raise themselves above the proletariat, but only insofar as they became bourgeois. Every new class, therefore, achieves its hegemony only on a broader basis than that of the class ruling previously, whereas the opposition of the non-ruling class against the new ruling class develops all the more sharply and profoundly. Both these things determine the fact that the struggle to be waged against this new ruling class, in its turn, aims at a more decided and radical negation of the previous conditions of society than could all previous classes which sought to rule.

This whole semblance, that the rule of a certain class is only the rule of certain ideas, comes to a natural end, of course, as soon as class rule in general ceases to be the form in which society is organized, that is to say, as soon as it is no longer necessary to represent a particular interest as general or the "general interest" as ruling.

Note

1 Marginal note by Marx: "Universality corresponds to (1) the class versus the estate, (2) the competition, world-wide intercourse, etc., (3) the great numerical strength of the ruling class, (4) the illusion of the *common* interests (in the beginning this illusion is true), (5) the delusion of the ideologists and the division of labor."

CHAPTER 4

Theses on the Philosophy of History

Walter Benjamin

Walter Benjamin was one of the most important Marxist thinkers of the twentieth century. Both highly speculative in his approach as well as extremely perceptive regarding the intersection of art and popular culture, he wrote essays that have continued to inspire scholars concerned with combating the tendency towards Fascism in human nature and with understanding how such things as technology transform our concepts and practices of literature and art. His well-known "The Work of Art in the Age of Mechanical Reproduction" argues that the new media that make art easily reproducible change its cultural value and deprive it of the aura that allowed it to be a sign of cultural status and hieratic value. The new medium of film, Benjamin argued, in a move that prefigured some findings of neuroscience, changes our ways of thinking and seeing. In this essay on the concept of history, he notes that political positions such as those of the Social Democrats assume a particular picture of how history moves through time. At the time in the 1920s and 1930s, the parliamentary Left (the Social Democrats mainly) were at odds with the Right (the Nazis). The Marxists (the Spartacists) had been repressed in 1919, clearing the way for the rise of the revolutionary conservative movement called Nazism. The Social Democrats did not perceive the danger the Nazis posed. They conceived of history as moving progressively forward. The working class could therefore make accommodations with capitalists because their lives were slowly improving through better working conditions and higher wages. The Marxists (who Benjamin refers to as Historical Materialists) felt history was not progressive. Rather, the continuity of history could be broken by a state of exception of the kind the Nazis represented. The working class also had to think of history as in the present, as a moment of breaking, if it was to liberate itself from capitalism.

Original publication details: Walter Benjamin, "Theses on History" from *Illuminations*, pp. 253–264. Shocken Books, 1955. Reproduced with permission from HMH Co.

Literary Theory: An Anthology, Third Edition. Edited by Julie Rivkin and Michael Ryan.
© 2017 John Wiley & Sons, Ltd. Published 2017 by John Wiley & Sons, Ltd.

I

The story is told of an automaton constructed in such a way that it could play a winning game of chess, answering each move of an opponent with a countermove. A puppet in Turkish attire and with a hookah in its mouth sat before a chessboard placed on a large table. A system of mirrors created the illusion that this table was transparent from all sides. Actually, a little hunchback who was an expert chess player sat inside and guided the puppet's hand by means of strings. One can imagine a philosophical counterpart to this device. The puppet called "historical materialism" is to win all the time. It can easily be a match for anyone if it enlists the services of theology, which today, as we know, is wizened and has to keep out of sight.

II

"One of the most remarkable characteristics of human nature," writes Lotze, "is, along-side so much selfishness in specific instances, the freedom from envy which the present displays toward the future." Reflection shows us that our image of happiness is thoroughly colored by the time to which the course of our own existence has assigned us. The kind of happiness that could arouse envy in us exists only in the air we have breathed, among people we could have talked to, women who could have given themselves to us. In other words, our image of happiness is indissolubly bound up with the image of redemption. The same applies to our view of the past, which is the concern of history. The past carries with it a temporal index by which it is referred to redemption. There is a secret agreement between past generations and the present one. Our coming was expected on earth. Like every generation that preceded us, we have been endowed with a *weak* Messianic power, a power to which the past has a claim. That claim cannot be settled cheaply. Historical materialists are aware of that.

III

A chronicler who recites events without distinguishing between major and minor ones acts in accordance with the following truth: nothing that has ever happened should be regarded as lost for history. To be sure, only a redeemed mankind receives the fullness of its past – which is to say, only for a redeemed mankind has its past become citable in all its moments. Each moment it has lived becomes a *citation à l'ordre du jour* – and that day is Judgment Day.

IV

*Seek for food and clothing first, then
the Kingdom of God shall be added unto you.*

— Hegel, 1807

The class struggle, which is always present to a historian influenced by Marx, is a fight for the crude and material things without which no refined and spiritual things could exist. Nevertheless, it is not in the form of the spoils which fall to the victor that the latter make their presence felt in the class struggle. They manifest themselves in this struggle as courage, humor, cunning, and fortitude. They have retroactive force and will constantly call in question every victory, past and present, of the rulers. As flowers turn toward the sun, by dint of a secret heliotropism the past strives to turn toward that sun which is rising in the sky of history. A historical materialist must be aware of this most inconspicuous of all transformations.

V

The true picture of the past flits by. The past can be seized only as an image which flashes up at the instant when it can be recognized and is never seen again. "The truth will not run away from us": in the historical outlook of historicism these words of Gottfried Keller mark the exact point where historical materialism cuts through historicism. For every image of the past that is not recognized by the present as one of its own concerns threatens to disappear irretrievably. (The good tidings which the historian of the past brings with throbbing heart may be lost in a void the very moment he opens his mouth.)

VI

To articulate the past historically does not mean to recognize it "the way it really was" (Ranke). It means to seize hold of a memory as it flashes up at a moment of danger. Historical materialism wishes to retain that image of the past which unexpectedly appears to man singled out by history at a moment of danger. The danger affects both the content of the tradition and its receivers. The same threat hangs over both: that of becoming a tool of the ruling classes. In every era the attempt must be made anew to wrest tradition away from a conformism that is about to overpower it. The Messiah comes not only as the redeemer, he comes as the subduer of Antichrist. Only that historian will have the gift of fanning the spark of hope in the past who is firmly convinced that *even the dead* will not be safe from the enemy if he wins. And this enemy has not ceased to be victorious.

VII

Consider the darkness and the great cold
In this vale which resounds with mysery.

— Brecht, THE THREEPENNY OPERA

To historians who wish to relive an era, Fustel de Coulanges recommends that they blot out everything they know about the later course of history. There is no better way of characterizing the method with which historical materialism has broken. It is a process of empathy whose origin is the indolence of the heart, *acedia*, which despairs of grasping and holding the genuine historical image as it flares up briefly. Among medieval theologians it was regarded as the root cause of sadness. Flaubert, who was familiar with it, wrote: "*Peu de gens devineront combien il a fallu être triste pour ressusciter Carthage.*"[1]

The nature of this sadness stands out more clearly if one asks with whom the adherents of historicism actually empathize. The answer is inevitable: with the victor. And all rulers are the heirs of those who conquered before them. Hence, empathy with the victor invariably benefits the rulers. Historical materialists know what that means. Whoever has emerged victorious participates to this day in the triumphal procession in which the present rulers step over those who are lying prostrate. According to traditional practice, the spoils are carried along in the procession. They are called cultural treasures, and a historical materialist views them with cautious detachment. For without exception the cultural treasures he surveys have an origin which he cannot contemplate without horror. They owe their existence not only to the efforts of the great minds and talents who have created them, but also to the anonymous toil of their contemporaries. There is no document of civilization which is not at the same time a document of barbarism. And just as such a document is not free of barbarism, barbarism taints also the manner in which it was transmitted from one owner to another. A historical materialist therefore dissociates himself from it as far as possible. He regards it as his task to brush history against the grain.

VIII

The tradition of the oppressed teaches us that the "state of emergency" in which we live is not the exception but the rule. We must attain to a conception of history that is in keeping with this insight. Then we shall clearly realize that it is our task to bring about a real state of emergency, and this will improve our position in the struggle against Fascism. One reason why Fascism has a chance is that in the name of progress its opponents treat it as a historical norm. The current amazement that the things we are experiencing are "still" possible in the twentieth century is *not* philosophical. This amazement is not the beginning of knowledge – unless it is the knowledge that the view of history which gives rise to it is untenable.

IX

Mein Flügel ist zum Schwung bereit,
ich kehrte gern zurück,
denn blieb ich auch lebendige Zeit,
ich hätte wenig Glück.

– Gerhard Scholem, "Gruss vom Angelus"[2]

A Klee painting named "Angelus Novus" shows an angel looking as though he is about to move away from something he is fixedly contemplating. His eyes are staring, his mouth is open, his wings are spread. This is how one pictures the angel of history. His face is turned toward the past. Where we perceive a chain of events, he sees one single catastrophe which keeps piling wreckage upon wreckage and hurls it in front of his feet. The angel would like to stay, awaken the dead, and make whole what has been smashed. But a storm is blowing from Paradise; it has got caught in his wings with such violence that the angel can no longer close them. This storm irresistibly propels him into the future to which his back is turned, while the pile of debris before him grows skyward. This storm is what we call progress.

X

The themes which monastic discipline assigned to friars for meditation were designed to turn them away from the world and its affairs. The thoughts which we are developing here originate from similar considerations. At a moment when the politicians in whom the opponents of Fascism had placed their hopes are prostrate and confirm their defeat by betraying their own cause, these observations are intended to disentangle the political worldlings from the snares in which the traitors have entrapped them. Our consideration proceeds from the insight that the politicians' stubborn faith in progress, their confidence in their "mass basis," and, finally, their servile integration in an uncontrollable apparatus have been three aspects of the same thing. It seeks to convey an idea of the high price our accustomed thinking will have to pay for a conception of history that avoids any complicity with the thinking to which these politicians continue to adhere.

XI

The conformism which has been part and parcel of Social Democracy from the beginning attaches not only to its political tactics but to its economic views as well. It is one reason for its later breakdown. Nothing has corrupted the German working class so much as the notion that it was moving with the current. It regarded technological developments as the fall of the stream with which it thought it was moving. From there it was but a step to the illusion that the factory work which was supposed to tend toward technological progress constituted a political achievement. The old Protestant ethics of work was resurrected among German workers in secularized form. The Gotha Program[3] already bears traces of this confusion, defining labor as "the source of all wealth and all culture." Smelling a rat, Marx countered that "... the man who possesses no other property than his labor power" must of necessity become "the slave of other men who have made themselves the owners...." However, the confusion spread, and soon thereafter Josef Dietzgen proclaimed: "The savior of modern times is called work. The ... improvement ... of labor constitutes the wealth which is now able to accomplish what no redeemer has ever been able to do." This vulgar-Marxist conception of the nature of labor bypasses the question of how its products might benefit the workers while still not being at their disposal. It recognizes only the progress in the mastery of nature, not the retrogression of society; it already displays the technocratic features later encountered in Fascism. Among these is a conception of nature which differs ominously from the one in the Socialist utopias before the 1848 revolution. The new conception of labor amounts to the exploitation of nature, which with naïve complacency is contrasted with the exploitation of the proletariat. Compared with this positivistic conception, Fourier's fantasies, which have so often been ridiculed, prove to be surprisingly sound. According to Fourier, as a result of efficient cooperative labor, four moons would illuminate the earthly night, the ice would recede from the poles, sea water would no longer taste salty, and beasts of prey would do man's bidding. All this illustrates a kind of labor which, far from exploiting nature, is capable of delivering her of the creations which lie dormant in her womb as potentials. Nature, which, as Dietzgen puts it, "exists gratis," is a complement to the corrupted conception of labor.

XII

We need history, but not the way a spoiled loafer
in the garden of knowledge needs it.

         – Nietzsche, OF THE USE AND ABUSE OF HISTORY

Not man or men but the struggling, oppressed class itself is the depository of historical knowledge. In Marx it appears as the last enslaved class, as the avenger that completes the task of liberation in the name of generations of the downtrodden. This conviction, which had a brief resurgence in the Spartacist group,[4] has always been objectionable to Social Democrats. Within three decades they managed virtually to erase the name of Blanqui, though it had been the rallying sound that had reverberated through the preceding century. Social Democracy thought fit to assign to the working class the role of the redeemer of future generations, in this way cutting the sinews of its greatest strength. This training made the working class forget both its hatred and its spirit of sacrifice, for both are nourished by the image of enslaved ancestors rather than that of liberated grandchildren.

XIII

Every day our cause becomes clearer and people get smarter.

         – Wilhelm Dietzgen, DIE RELIGION DER SOZIALDEMOKRATIE

Social Democratic theory, and even more its practice, have been formed by a conception of progress which did not adhere to reality but made dogmatic claims. Progress as pictured in the minds of Social Democrats was, first of all, the progress of mankind itself (and not just advances in men's ability and knowledge). Secondly, it was something boundless, in keeping with the infinite perfectibility of mankind. Thirdly, progress was regarded as irresistible, something that automatically pursued a straight or spiral course. Each of these predicates is controversial and open to criticism. However, when the chips are down, criticism must penetrate beyond these predicates and focus on something that they have in common. The concept of the historical progress of mankind cannot be sundered from the concept of its progression through a homogeneous, empty time. A critique of the concept of such a progression must be the basis of any criticism of the concept of progress itself.

XIV

Origin is the goal.

         – Karl Kraus, WORTE IN VERSEN, Vol. I

History is the subject of a structure whose site is not homogeneous, empty time, but time filled by the presence of the now [*Jetztzeit*].[5] Thus, to Robespierre ancient Rome was a past charged with the time of the now which he blasted out of the continuum of history. The French Revolution viewed itself as Rome reincarnate. It evoked ancient Rome the way fashion evokes costumes of the past. Fashion has a flair for the topical, no matter where it stirs in the thickets of long ago; it is a tiger's leap into the past. This jump, however, takes place in an arena where the ruling class gives the commands. The same leap in the open air of history is the dialectical one, which is how Marx understood the revolution.

XV

The awareness that they are about to make the continuum of history explode is characteristic of the revolutionary classes at the moment of their action. The great revolution introduced a new calendar. The initial day of a calendar serves as a historical time-lapse camera. And, basically, it is the same day that keeps recurring in the guise of holidays, which are days of remembrance. Thus the calendars do not measure time as clocks do; they are monuments of a historical consciousness of which not the slightest trace has been apparent in Europe in the past hundred years. In the July revolution an incident occurred which showed this consciousness still alive. On the first evening of fighting it turned out that the clocks in towers were being fired on simultaneously and independently from several places in Paris. An eye-witness, who may have owed his insight to the rhyme, wrote as follows:

> Qui le croirait! on dit, qu'irrités contre l'heure
> De nouveaux Josués au pied de chaque tour,
> Tiraient sur les cadrans pour arrêter le jour.[6]

XVI

A historical materialist cannot do without the notion of a present which is not a transition, but in which time stands still and has come to a stop. For this notion defines the present in which he himself is writing history. Historicism gives the "eternal" image of the past; historical materialism supplies a unique experience with the past. The historical materialist leaves it to others to be drained by the whore called "Once upon a time" in historicism's bordello. He remains in control of his powers, man enough to blast open the continuum of history.

XVII

Historicism rightly culminates in universal history. Materialistic historiography differs from it as to method more clearly than from any other kind. Universal history has no theoretical armature. Its method is additive; it musters a mass of data to fill the homogeneous, empty time. Materialistic historiography, on the other hand, is based on a constructive principle. Thinking involves not only the flow of thoughts, but their arrest as well. Where thinking suddenly stops in a configuration pregnant with tensions, it gives that configuration a shock, by which it crystallizes into a monad. A historical materialist approaches a historical subject only where he encounters it as a monad. In this structure he recognizes the sign of a Messianic cessation of happening, or, put differently, a revolutionary chance in the fight for the oppressed past. He takes cognizance of it in order to blast a specific era out of the homogeneous course of history – blasting a specific life out of the era or a specific work out of the lifework. As a result of this method the lifework is preserved in this work and at the same time canceled[7]; in the lifework, the era; and in the era, the entire course of history. The nourishing fruit of the historically understood contains time as a precious but tasteless seed.

XVIII

"In relation to the history of organic life on earth," writes a modern biologist, "the paltry fifty millennia of *homo sapiens* constitute something like two seconds at the close of a twenty-four-hour day. On this scale, the history of civilized mankind would fill one-fifth of the last second of the last hour." The present, which, as a model of Messianic time, comprises the entire history of mankind in an enormous abridgment, coincides exactly with the stature which the history of mankind has in the universe.

A

Historicism contents itself with establishing a causal connection between various moments in history. But no fact that is a cause is for that very reason historical. It became historical posthumously, as it were, through events that may be separated from it by thousands of years. A historian who takes this as his point of departure stops telling the sequence of events like the beads of a rosary. Instead, he grasps the constellation which his own era has formed with a definite earlier one. Thus he establishes a conception of the present as the "time of the now" which is shot through with chips of Messianic time.

B

The soothsayers who found out from time what it had in store certainly did not experience time as either homogeneous or empty. Anyone who keeps this in mind will perhaps get an idea of how past times were experienced in remembrance – namely, in just the same way. We know that the Jews were prohibited from investigating the future. The Torah and the prayers instruct them in remembrance, however. This stripped the future of its magic, to which all those succumb who turn to the soothsayers for enlightenment. This does not imply, however, that for the Jews the future turned into homogeneous, empty time. For every second of time was the strait gate through which the Messiah might enter.

Notes

1   "Few will be able to guess how sad one had to be in order to resuscitate Carthage."
2   *My wing is ready for flight,*
                             I would like to turn back.
                             If I stayed timeless time,
                             I would have little luck.

3   The Gotha Congress of 1875 united the two German Socialist parties, one led by Ferdinand Lassalle, the other by Karl Marx and Wilhelm Liebknecht. The program, drafted by Liebknecht and Lassalle, was severely attacked by Marx in London. See his "Critique of the Gotha Program."

4   Leftist group, founded by Karl Liebknecht and Rosa Luxemburg at the beginning of World War I in opposition to the pro-war policies of the German Socialist party, later absorbed by the Communist party.

5   Benjamin says "*Jetztzeit*" and indicates by the quotation marks that he does not simply mean an equivalent to *Gegenwart*, that is, present. He clearly is thinking of the mystical *nunc stans*.

6   Who would have believed it! we are told that new Joshuas
    at the foot of every tower, as though irritated with
    time itself, fired at the dials in order to stop the day.

7   The Hegelian term *aufheben* in its threefold meaning: to preserve, to elevate, to cancel.

CHAPTER 5

Structures and the Habitus

Pierre Bourdieu

In this selection from his *Outline of a Theory of Practice* (1972), Marxist social theorist Pierre Bourdieu describes how social practices replicate social structures. We live inside structures that guide behavior in such a way that an implied social order is maintained by our own actions. Dating practices, for example, replicate the heteronormative assumptions of most societies, while associated practices such as dowries or even engagement rings replicate assumptions regarding gender.

Bourdieu's argument is classically dialectical. According to dialectical reasoning, any system operates on the basis of presuppositions, and the action of the system re-posits or replicates those presuppositions. For Marxist dialecticians, this means that the assumptions that allow capitalism to operate – especially the divorce of workers from the product of their labor (which becomes the private property of the capitalist) and the greater power of the capitalist over workers in terms of accumulated wealth – are reproduced through the normal operations of capitalism, which would never suddenly make workers wealthy and capitalists penurious. Bourdieu sees such dialectical operations in all social action. In his highly regarded *Distinction* (1979), for example, a study of taste, he noted that the local culture of each social class trains inhabitants in particular kinds of taste regarding cultural goods. Practicing those tastes effectively helps maintain one's status or lack of it in the hierarchy of cultural locations and goods.

A False Dilemma: Mechanism and Finalism

The structures constitutive of a particular type of environment (e.g. the material conditions of existence characteristic of a class condition) produce *habitus*, systems of durable, transposable *dispositions*,[1] structured structures predisposed to function as structuring structures, that is, as principles of the generation and structuring of practices and representations which can be objectively "regulated" and "regular" without in any way being the product of obedience to rules, objectively adapted to their goals

Original publication details: Pierre Bourdieu, "Structures and the Habitus" from *Outline of a Theory of Practice*, pp. 72–95. Cambridge University Press, 1977.

Literary Theory: An Anthology, Third Edition. Edited by Julie Rivkin and Michael Ryan.
© 2017 John Wiley & Sons, Ltd. Published 2017 by John Wiley & Sons, Ltd.

without presupposing a conscious aiming at ends or an express mastery of the operations necessary to attain them and, being all this, collectively orchestrated without being the product of the orchestrating action of a conductor.

Even when they appear as the realization of the explicit, and explicitly stated, purposes of a project or plan, the practices produced by the habitus, as the strategy-generating principle enabling agents to cope with unforeseen and ever-changing situations, are only apparently determined by the future. If they seem determined by anticipation of their own consequences, thereby encouraging the finalist illusion, the fact is that, always tending to reproduce the objective structures of which they are the product, they are determined by the past conditions which have produced the principle of their production, that is, by the actual outcome of identical or interchangeable past practices, which coincides with their own outcome to the extent (*and only to the extent*) that the objective structures of which they are the product are prolonged in the structures within which they function. Thus, for example, in the interaction between two agents or groups of agents endowed with the same habitus (say A and B), everything takes place as if the actions of each of them (say, a_1 for A) were organized in relation to the reactions they call forth from any agent possessing the same habitus (say, b_1, B's reaction to a_1) so that they objectively imply anticipation of the reaction which these reactions in turn call forth (say a_2, the reaction to b_1). But the teleological description according to which each action has the purpose of making possible the reaction to the reaction it arouses (individual A performing action a_1, e.g. a gift or challenge, in order to make individual B produce action b_1, a counter-gift or riposte, so as to be able to perform action a_2, a stepped-up gift or challenge) is quite as naive as the mechanistic description which presents the action and the riposte as moments in a sequence of programmed actions produced by a mechanical apparatus. The habitus is the source of these series of moves which are objectively organized as strategies without being the product of a genuine strategic intention – which would presuppose at least that they are perceived as one strategy among other possible strategies.[2]

It is necessary to abandon all theories which explicitly or implicitly treat practice as a mechanical reaction, directly determined by the antecedent conditions and entirely reducible to the mechanical functioning of pre-established assemblies, "models" or "rôles" – which one would, moreover, have to postulate in infinite number, like the chance configurations of stimuli capable of triggering them from outside, thereby condemning oneself to the grandiose and desperate undertaking of the anthropologist, armed with fine positivist courage, who recorded 480 elementary units of behaviour in twenty minutes' observation of his wife in the kitchen.[3] But rejection of mechanistic theories in no way implies that, in accordance with another obligatory option, we should bestow on some creative free will the free and wilful power to constitute, on the instant, the meaning of the situation by projecting the ends aiming at its transformation, and that we should reduce the objective intentions and constituted significations of actions and works to the conscious and deliberate intentions of their authors.

Jean-Paul Sartre deserves credit for having given an ultra-consistent formulation of the philosophy of action accepted, usually implicitly, by all those who describe practices as strategies explicitly oriented by reference to purposes explicitly defined by a free project[4] or even, with some interactionists, by reference to the anticipated cues as to the reaction to practices. Thus, refusing to recognize anything resembling durable dispositions, Sartre makes each action a sort of unprecedented confrontation between the subject and the world. This is clearly seen in the passages in *Being and Nothingness* where he confers on the awakening of revolutionary consciousness – a sort of "conversion" of consciousness produced by a sort of imaginary variation – the power to create the meaning of the present by creating the revolutionary future which negates it: "For it is necessary to reverse the common opinion and acknowledge that it is not the harshness of a situation or the sufferings it imposes that lead people to conceive of another state of affairs in which things would be better for everybody. It is on the day that we are able to conceive of another state of affairs, that a new light is cast on our trouble and our suffering and we *decide* that they are unbearable."[5] If the world of action is nothing other than this universe of interchangeable possibles, entirely dependent on the decrees of the consciousness which creates it and hence totally devoid of *objectivity*, if it is moving because the subject chooses to be moved, revolting because he chooses to be revolted, then emotions, passions, and actions are merely games of bad faith, sad farces in which one is both bad actor and good audience: "It is not by chance that materialism is serious; it is not by chance that it is found at all times and places as the favourite doctrine of the revolutionary. This is because revolutionaries are serious. They come to know themselves first in terms of the world which oppresses them ... The serious man is 'of the world' and has no resource in himself. He does not even imagine any longer the possibility of *getting out* of the world ... he is in *bad faith*."[6] The same incapacity to encounter "seriousness" other than in the disapproved form of the "spirit of seriousness" can be seen in an analysis of emotion which, significantly, is separated by *L'imaginaire* (*Psychology of the Imagination*) from the less radically subjectivist descriptions in *Sketch for a Theory of the Emotions*: "What will make me decide to choose the magical aspect or the technical aspect of the world? It cannot be the world itself, for this in order to be manifested waits to be discovered. Therefore it is necessary that the for-itself in its project must choose being the one by whom the world is revealed as magical or rational; that is, the for-itself must as a free project of itself give to itself rational or magical existence. It is responsible for either one, for the for-itself can *be* only if it has chosen itself. Therefore the for-itself appears as the free foundation of its emotions as of its volitions. My fear *is* free and manifests my freedom."[7] Such a theory of action was inevitably to lead to the desperate project of a transcendental genesis of society and history (the *Critique de la raison dialectique*) to which Durkheim seemed to be pointing when he wrote in *The Rules of Sociological Method*: "It is because the imaginary offers the mind no resistance that the mind, conscious of no restraint, gives itself up to boundless ambitions and believes it possible to construct, or rather reconstruct, the world by virtue of its own strength and at the whim of its desires."[8]

No doubt one could counterpose to this analysis of Sartrian anthropology the numerous texts (found especially in the earliest and the latest works) in which Sartre recognizes, for example, the "passive syntheses" of a universe of already constituted significations or expressly challenges the very principles of his philosophy, such as the passage in *Being and Nothingness* in which he seeks to distinguish his position from the *instantanéiste* philosophy of Descartes[9] or a sentence from the *Critique de la raison dialectique* in which he announces the study of "agentless actions, totalizer-less productions, counter-finalities, infernal circularities".[10] The fact remains that Sartre rejects with visceral repugnance "those gelatinous realities, more or less vaguely haunted by a supra-individual consciousness, which a shamefaced organicism still seeks to retrieve, against all likelihood, in the rough, complex but clear-cut field of passive activity in which there are individual organisms and inorganic material realities",[11] and that he leaves no room for everything that, as much on the side of the things of the world as on the side of the agents, might seem to blur the sharp line his rigorous dualism seeks to maintain between the pure transparency of the subject and the mineral opacity of the thing. Within this logic, "objective" sociology can grasp only "the sociality of inertia", that is, for example, the class reduced to *inertia*, hence to impotence, class as a thing, an essence, "congealed" in its being, i.e. in its "having been": "Class seriality makes the individual (whoever he is and whatever the class) a being who defines himself as a humanized thing … The other form of class, that is, the group totalizing in a *praxis*, is born at the heart of the passive form and as its negation."[12] The social world, the site of these compromises between thing and meaning which define "objective meaning" as meaning-made-thing and dispositions as meaning-made-body, is a positive challenge to someone who can only live in the pure, transparent universe of consciousness or individual "praxis". The only limit this artificialism recognizes to the freedom of the ego is that which freedom sets itself by the free abdication of a pledge or the surrender of bad faith, the Sartrian name for alienation, or the submission imposed on it by the alienating freedom of the alter ego in the Hegelian struggles between master and slave. Seeing "in social arrangments only artificial and more or less arbitrary combinations", as Durkheim puts it,[13] without a second thought he subordinates the transcendence of the social – reduced to "the reciprocity of constraints and autonomies" – to the "transcendence of the ego", as the early Sartre used to put it: "In the course of this action, the individual discovers the dialectic as rational transparency, inasmuch as he produces it, and as absolute necessity inasmuch as it escapes him, in other words, *quite simply*, inasmuch as others produce it; finally, precisely insofar as he recognizes himself in overcoming his needs, he recognizes the law which others impose on him in overcoming their own (recognizes it: this does not mean that he submits to it), he recognizes his own autonomy (inasmuch as it can be used by another and daily is, bluffs, manoeuvres, etc.) as a foreign power and the autonomy of others as the inexorable law which allows him to coerce them."[14] The transcendence of the social can only be the effect of recurrence, that is to say, in the last analysis, of *number* (hence the importance accorded to the "series"), or of the "materialization of recurrence" in cultural objects;[15] alienation consists in the free abdication of freedom in favour of the demands of "worked upon matter": "the 19th century worker *makes himself what he is*, that is, he practically and rationally determines the order of his expenditure – hence he decides in his free praxis – and by his freedom he makes himself what he was, what he is, what he must be: a machine whose wages represent no more than its running costs… Class-being as practico-inert being comes to men by men through the passive syntheses of worked upon matter."[16] Elsewhere, affirmation of the "logical" primacy of "individual praxis", constituent Reason, over history, constituted Reason, leads Sartre to pose the problem of the genesis of society in the same terms as those employed by the theoreticians of the social contract: "History determines the content of human relationships in its totality and these relationships … relate back to everything. But it is not History which *causes* there to be human relationships in general. It is not the problems of organization and division of labour that have caused relations to be set up between those *initially separate* objects, men."[17] Just as for Descartes "creation is continuous", as Jean Wahl puts it, "because time is not" and because extended substance does not contain within itself the power to subsist – God being invested with the ever-renewed task of recreating the world *ex nihilo* by a free decree of his will – so the typically Cartesian refusal of the viscous opacity of "objective potentialities" and objective meaning leads Sartre to entrust to the absolute initiative of individual or collective "historical agents", such as the Party, the hypostasis of the

Sartrian subject, the indefinite task of tearing the social whole, or the class, out of the inertia of the "practico-inert". At the end of his immense imaginary novel of the death and resurrection of freedom, with its twofold movement, the "externalization of internality", which leads from freedom to alienation, from consciousness to the materialization of consciousness, or, as the title puts it, "from praxis to the practico–inert", and the "internalization of externality" which, by the abrupt shortcuts of the awakening of consciousness and the "fusion of consciousnesses", leads "from the group to history", from the reified state of the alienated group to the authentic existence of the historical agent, consciousness and thing are as irremediably separate as they were at the outset, without anything resembling an institution or a socially constituted agent ever having been observed or constructed. The appearances of a dialectical discourse (or the dialectical appearances of the discourse) cannot mask the endless oscillation between the in-itself and the for-itself, or in the new language, between materiality and praxis, between the inertia of the group reduced to its "essence", i.e. to its outlived past and its necessity (abandoned to sociologists) and the continuous creation of the free collective project, seen as a series of acts of commitment indispensable for saving the group from annihilation in pure materiality.[18]

It is, of course, never ruled out that the responses of the habitus may be accompanied by a strategic calculation tending to carry on quasi-consciously the operation the habitus carries on in a quite different way, namely an estimation of chances which assumes the transformation of the past effect into the expected objective. But the fact remains that these responses are defined first in relation to a system of objective potentialities, immediately inscribed in the present, things to do or not to do, to say or not to say, in relation to a *forthcoming* reality which – in contrast to the future conceived as "absolute possibility" (*absolute Möglichkeit*), in Hegel's sense, projected by the pure project of a "negative freedom" – puts itself forward with an urgency and a claim to existence excluding all deliberation. To eliminate the need to resort to "rules", it would be necessary to establish in each case a complete description (which invocation of rules allows one to dispense with) of the relation between the habitus, as a socially constituted system of cognitive and motivating structures, and the socially structured situation in which the agents' *interests* are defined, and with them the objective functions and subjective motivations of their practices. It would then become clear that, as Weber indicated, the juridical or customary rule is never more than a *secondary principle* of the determination of practices, intervening when the primary principle, interest, fails.[19]

Symbolic – that is, *conventional* and *conditional* – stimulations, which act only on condition they encounter agents conditioned to perceive them, tend to impose themselves unconditionally and necessarily when inculcation of the arbitrary abolishes the arbitrariness of both the inculcation and the significations inculcated. The world of urgencies and of goals already achieved, of uses to be made and paths to be taken, of objects endowed with a "permanent teleological character", in Husserl's phrase, tools, instruments and institutions, the world of practicality, can grant only a conditional freedom – *liberet si liceret* – rather like that of the magnetic needle which Leibniz imagined actually enjoyed turning northwards. If one regularly observes a very close correlation between the scientifically constructed *objective probabilities* (e.g. the chances of access to a particular good) and *subjective aspirations* ("motivations" or "needs") or, in other terms, between the *a posteriori* or *ex post* probability known from past experience and the *a priori* or *ex ante* probability attributed to it, this is not because agents consciously adjust their aspirations to an exact evaluation of their chances of success, like a player regulating his bets as a function of perfect information as to his chances of winning, as one implicitly presupposes whenever, forgetting the "everything takes place as if", one *proceeds as if* game theory or the calculation of probabilities, each constructed *against* spontaneous dispositions, amounted to anthropological descriptions of practice.

Completely reversing the tendency of objectivism, we can, on the contrary, seek in the scientific theory of probabilities (or strategies) not an anthropological model of practice, but the elements of a *negative description* of the implicit logic of the *spontaneous interpretation of statistics* (e.g. the prospensity to privilege early experiences) which the scientific theory necessarily contains because it is explicitly constructed against that logic. Unlike the estimation of probabilities which science constructs methodically on the basis of controlled experiments from data established according to precise rules, practical evaluation of the likelihood of the success of a given action in a given situation brings into play a whole body of wisdom, sayings, commonplaces, ethical precepts ("that's not for the likes of us") and, at a deeper level, the unconscious principles of the *ethos* which, being the product of a learning process dominated by a determinate type of objective regularities, determines "reasonable" and "unreasonable" conduct for every agent subjected to those regularities.[20] "We are no sooner acquainted with the impossibility of satisfying any desire", says Hume in *A Treatise of Human Nature*, "than the desire itself vanishes." And Marx in the *Economic and Philosophical Manuscripts*: "If I have no money for travel, I have no *need*, i.e. no real and self-realizing need, to travel. If I have a vocation to study, but no money for it, I have *no* vocation to study, i.e. no *real, true* vocation."

Because the dispositions durably inculcated by objective conditions (which science apprehends through statistical regularities as the probabilities objectively attached to a group or class) engender aspirations and practices objectively compatible with those objective requirements, the most improbable practices are excluded, either totally without examination, as *unthinkable*, or at the cost of the *double negation* which inclines agents to make a virtue of necessity, that is, to refuse what is anyway refused and to love the inevitable. The very conditions of production of the ethos, *necessity made into a virtue*, are such that the expectations to which it gives rise tend to ignore the restriction to which the validity of any calculus of probabilities is subordinated, namely that the conditions of the experiments should not have been modified. Unlike scientific estimations, which are corrected after each experiment in accordance with rigorous rules of calculation, practical estimates give disproportionate weight to early experiences: the structures characteristic of a determinate type of conditions of existence, through the economic and social necessity which they bring to bear on the relatively autonomous universe of family relationships, or more precisely, through the mediation of the specifically familial manifestations of this external necessity (sexual division of labour, domestic morality, cares, strife, tastes, etc.), produce the structures of the habitus which become in turn the basis of perception and appreciation of all subsequent experience. Thus, as a result of the *hysteresis effect* necessarily implied in the logic of the constitution of habitus, practices are always liable to incur negative sanctions when the environment with which they are actually confronted is too distant from that to which they are objectively fitted. This is why generation conflicts oppose not age-classes separated by natural properties, but habitus which have been produced by different *modes of generation*, that is, by conditions of existence which, in imposing different definitions of the impossible, the possible, and the probable, cause one group to experience as natural or reasonable practices or aspirations which another group finds unthinkable or scandalous, and vice versa.

Structures, Habitus and Practices

The habitus, the durably installed generative principle of regulated improvisations, produces practices which tend to reproduce the regularities immanent in the objective conditions of the production of their generative principle, while adjusting to the demands inscribed as objective potentialities in the situation, as defined by the cognitive and motivating structures making up the habitus. It follows that these practices cannot be directly deduced either from the objective conditions, defined as the instantaneous sum of the stimuli which may appear to have directly triggered them, or from the conditions which produced the durable principle of their production. These practices can be accounted for only by relating the objective *structure* defining the social conditions of the production of the habitus which engendered them to the conditions in which this habitus is operating, that is, to the *conjuncture* which, short of a radical transformation, represents a particular state of this structure. In practice, it is the habitus, history turned into nature, i.e. denied as such, which accomplishes practically the relating of these two systems of relations, in and through the production of practice. The "unconscious" is never anything other than the forgetting of history which history itself produces by incorporating the objective structures it produces in the second natures of habitus: "... in each of us, in varying proportions, there is part of yesterday's man; it is yesterday's man who inevitably predominates in us, since the present amounts to little compared with the long past in the course of which we were formed and from which we result. Yet we do not sense this man of the past, because he is inveterate in us; he makes up the unconscious part of ourselves. Consequently we are led to take no account of him, any more than we take account of his legitimate demands. Conversely, we are very much aware of the most recent attainments of civilization, because, being recent, they have not yet had time to settle into our unconscious."[21]

Genesis amnesia is also encouraged (if not entailed) by the objectivist apprehension which, grasping the product of history as an *opus operatum*, a *fait accompli*, can only invoke the mysteries of pre-established harmony or the prodigies of conscious orchestration to account for what, apprehended in pure synchrony, appears as objective meaning, whether it be the internal coherence of works or institutions such as myths, rites, or bodies of law, or the objective co-ordination which the concordant or conflicting practices of the members of the same group or class at once manifest and presuppose (inasmuch as they imply a community of dispositions).

Each agent, wittingly or unwittingly, willy nilly, is a producer and reproducer of objective meaning. Because his actions and works are the product of a *modus operandi* of which he is not the producer and has no conscious mastery, they contain an "objective intention", as the Scholastics put it, which always outruns his conscious intentions. The schemes of thought and expression he has acquired are the basis for the *intentionless invention* of regulated improvisation. Endlessly overtaken by his own words, with which he maintains a relation of "carry and be carried", as Nicolaï Hartmann put it, the virtuoso finds in the *opus operatum* new triggers and new supports for the *modus operandi* from which they arise, so that his discourse continuously feeds off itself like a train bringing along its own rails.[22] If witticisms surprise their author no less than their audience, and impress as much by their retrospective necessity as by their novelty, the reason is that the *trouvaille* appears as the simple unearthing, at once accidental and irresistible, of a buried possibility. It is because subjects do not, strictly speaking, know what they are doing that what they do has more meaning than they know. The habitus is the universalizing mediation which causes an individual agent's practices, without either explicit reason or signifying intent, to be none the less "sensible" and "reasonable". That part of practices which remains obscure in the eyes of their own producers is the aspect by which they are objectively adjusted to other practices and to the structures of which the principle of their production is itself the product.[23]

One of the fundamental effects of the orchestration of habitus is the production of a commonsense world endowed with the *objectivity* secured by consensus on the meaning (*sens*) of practices and the world, in other words the harmonization of agents' experiences and the continuous reinforcement that each of them receives from the expression, individual or collective (in festivals, for example), improvised or programmed (commonplaces, sayings), of similar or identical experiences. The homogeneity of habitus is what – within the limits of the group of agents possessing the schemes (of production and interpretation) implied in their production – causes practices and works to be immediately intelligible and foreseeable, and hence taken for granted. This practical comprehension obviates the "intention" and "intentional transfer into the Other" dear to the phenomenologists, by dispensing, for the ordinary occasions of life, with close analysis of the nuances of another's practice and tacit or explicit inquiry ("What do you *mean*?") into his intentions. Automatic and impersonal, significant without intending to signify, ordinary practices lend themselves to an understanding no less automatic and impersonal: the picking up of the objective intention they express in no way implies "reactivation" of the "lived" intention of the agent who performs them.[24] "Communication of consciousnesses" presupposes community of "unconsciouses" (i.e. of linguistic and cultural competences). The deciphering of the objective intention of practices and works has nothing to do with the "reproduction" (*Nachbildung*, as the early Dilthey puts it) of lived experiences and the reconstitution, unnecessary and uncertain, of the personal singularities of an "intention" which is not their true origin.

The objective homogenizing of group or class habitus which results from the homogeneity of the conditions of existence is what enables practices to be objectively harmonized without any intentional calculation or conscious reference to a norm and mutually adjusted *in the absence of any direct interaction* or, *a fortiori*, explicit co-ordination. "Imagine", Leibniz suggests, "two clocks or watches in perfect agreement as to the time. This may occur in one of three ways. The first consists in mutual influence; the second is to appoint a skilful workman to correct them and synchronize them at all times; the third is to construct these clocks with such art and precision that one can be assured of their subsequent agreement."[25] So long as, retaining only the first or at a pinch the second hypothesis, one ignores the true principle of the conductorless orchestration which gives regularity, unity, and systematicity to the practices of a group or class, and this even in the absence of any spontaneous or externally imposed organization of individual projects, one is condemned to the naive artificialism which recognizes no other principle unifying a group's or class's ordinary or extraordinary action than the conscious co-ordination of a conspiracy.[26] If the practices of the members of the same group or class are more and better harmonized than the agents know or wish, it is because, as Leibniz puts it, "following only [his] own laws", each "nonetheless agrees with the other".[27] The habitus is precisely this immanent law, *lex insita*, laid down in each agent by his earliest upbringing, which is the precondition not only for the co-ordination of practices but also for practices of co-ordination, since the corrections and adjustments the agents themselves consciously carry out presuppose their mastery of a common code and since undertakings of collective mobilization cannot succeed without a minimum of concordance between the habitus of the mobilizing agents (e.g. prophet, party leader, etc.) and the dispositions of those whose aspirations and world-view they express.

So it is because they are the product of dispositions which, being the internalization of the same objective structures, are objectively concerted that the practices of the members of the same group or, in a differentiated society, the same class are endowed with an objective meaning that is at once unitary and systematic, transcending subjective intentions and conscious projects whether individual or collective.[28] To describe the process of objectification and orchestration in the language of *interaction* and mutual adjustment is to forget that the interaction itself owes its form to the objective structures which have produced the dispositions of the interacting agents and which allot them their relative positions in the interaction and elsewhere. Every confrontation between agents in fact brings together, in an *interaction* defined by the *objective structure* of the relation between the groups they belong to (e.g. a boss giving orders to a subordinate, colleagues discussing their pupils, academics taking part in a symposium), systems of dispositions (carried by "natural persons") such as a linguistic competence and a cultural competence and, through these habitus, all the objective structures of which they are the product, structures which are active only when *embodied* in a competence acquired in the course of a particular history (with the different types of bilingualism or pronunciation, for example, stemming from different modes of acquisition).[29]

Thus, when we speak of class habitus, we are insisting, against all forms of the occasionalist illusion which consists in directly relating practices to properties inscribed in the situation, that "interpersonal" relations are never, except in appearance, *individual-to-individual* relationships and that the truth of the interaction is never entirely contained in the interaction. This is what social psychology and interactionism or ethnomethodology forget when, reducing the objective structure of the relationship between the assembled individuals to the conjunctural structure of their interaction in a particular situation and group, they seek to explain everything that occurs in an experimental or observed interaction in terms of the experimentally controlled characteristics of the situation, such as the relative spatial positions of the participants or the nature of the channels used. In fact it is their present and past positions in the social structure that biological individuals carry with them, at all times and in all places, in the form of dispositions which are so many marks of *social position* and hence of the social distance between objective positions, that is, between social persons conjuncturally brought together (in physical space, which is not the same thing as social space) and correlatively, so many reminders of this distance and of the conduct required in order to "keep one's distance" or to manipulate it strategically, whether symbolically or actually, to reduce it (easier for the dominant than for the dominated), increase it, or simply maintain it (by not "letting oneself go", not "becoming familiar", in short, "standing on one's dignity", or on the other hand, refusing to "take liberties" and "put oneself forward", in short "knowing one's place" and staying there).

Even those forms of interaction seemingly most amenable to description in terms of "intentional transfer into the Other", such as sympathy, friendship, or love, are dominated (as class homogamy attests), through the harmony of habitus, that is to say, more precisely, the harmony of ethos and tastes – doubtless sensed in the imperceptible cues of body *hexis* – by the objective structure of the relations between social conditions. The illusion of mutual election or predestination arises from ignorance of the social conditions for the harmony of aesthetic tastes or ethical leanings, which is thereby perceived as evidence of the ineffable affinities which spring from it.

In short, the habitus, the product of history, produces individual and collective practices, and hence history, in accordance with the schemes engendered by history. The system of dispositions – a past which survives in the present and tends to perpetuate itself into the future by making itself present in practices structured according to its principles, an internal law relaying the continuous exercise of the law of external necessities (irreducible to immediate conjunctural constraints) – is the principle of the continuity and regularity which objectivism discerns in the social world without being able to give them a rational basis. And it is at the same time the principle of the transformations and regulated revolutions which neither the extrinsic and instantaneous determinisms of a mechanistic sociologism nor the purely internal but equally punctual determination of voluntarist or spontaneist subjectivism are capable of accounting for.

It is just as true and just as untrue to say that collective actions produce the event or that they are its product. The conjuncture capable of transforming practices objectively co-ordinated because subordinated to partially or wholly identical objective necessities, into *collective action* (e.g. revolutionary action) is constituted in the dialectical relationship between, on the one hand, a *habitus*, understood as a system of lasting, transposable dispositions which, integrating past experiences, functions at every moment as a *matrix of perceptions, appreciations, and actions* and makes possible the achievement of infinitely diversified tasks, thanks to analogical transfers of schemes permitting the solution of similarly shaped problems, and thanks to the unceasing corrections of the results obtained, dialectically produced by those results, and on the other hand, an *objective event* which exerts its action of conditional stimulation calling for or demanding a determinate response, only on those who are disposed to constitute it as such because they are endowed with a determinate type of dispositions (which are amenable to reduplication and reinforcement by the "awakening of class consciousness", that is, by the direct or indirect possession of a discourse capable of securing symbolic mastery of the practically mastered principles of the class habitus). Without ever being totally co-ordinated, since they are the product of "causal series" characterized by different structural durations, the dispositions and the situations which combine synchronically to constitute a determinate conjuncture are never wholly independent, since they are engendered by the objective structures, that is, in the last analysis, by the economic bases of the social formation in question. The hysteresis of habitus, which is inherent in the social conditions of the reproduction of the structures in habitus, is doubtless one of the foundations of the structural lag between opportunities and the dispositions to grasp them which is the cause of missed opportunities and, in particular, of the frequently observed incapacity to think historical crises in categories of perception and thought other than those of the past, albeit a revolutionary past.

If one ignores the dialectical relationship between the objective structures and the cognitive and motivating structures which they produce and which tend to reproduce them, if one forgets that these objective structures are themselves products of historical practices and are constantly reproduced and transformed by historical practices whose productive principle is itself the product of the structures which it consequently tends to reproduce, then one is condemned to reduce the relationship between the different social agencies (*instances*), treated as "different translations of the same sentence" – in a Spinozist metaphor which contains the truth of the objectivist language of "articulation" – to the logical formula enabling any one of them to be derived from any other. The unifying principle of practices in different domains which objectivist analysis would assign to separate "sub-systems", such as matrimonial strategies, fertility strategies, or economic choices, is nothing other than the habitus, the locus of practical realization of the "articulation" of fields which objectivism (from Parsons to the structuralist readers of Marx) lays out side by side without securing the means of discovering the real principle of the structural homologies or relations of transformation objectively established between them (which is not to deny that the structures are objectivities irreducible to their manifestation in the habitus which they produce and which tend to reproduce them). So long as one accepts the canonic opposition which, endlessly reappearing in new forms throughout the history of social thought, nowadays pits "humanist" against "structuralist" readings of Marx, to declare diametrical opposition to subjectivism is not genuinely to *break* with it, but to fall into the fetishism of social laws to which objectivism consigns itself when in establishing between structure and practice the relation of the virtual to the actual, of the score to the performance, of essence to existence, it merely substitutes for the creative man of subjectivism a man subjugated to the dead laws of a natural history. And how could one underestimate the strength of the ideological couple subjectivism/objectivism when one sees that the critique of the *individual* considered as *ens realissimum* only leads to his being made an epiphenomenon of hypostatized structure, and that the well-founded assertion of the primacy of objective relations results in products of human action, the structures, being credited with the power to develop in accordance with their own laws and to determine and overdetermine other structures?

Just as the opposition of language to speech as mere execution or even as a preconstructed object masks the opposition between the objective relations of the language and the dispositions making up linguistic competence, so the opposition between the structure and the individual against whom the structure has to be won and endlessly rewon stands in the way of construction of the dialectical relationship between the structure and the dispositions making up the habitus.

If the debate on the relationship between "culture" and "personality" which dominated a whole era of American anthropology now seems so artificial and sterile, it is because, amidst a host of logical and epistemological fallacies, it was organized around the relation between two complementary products of the same realist, substantialist representation of the scientific object. In its most exaggerated forms, the theory of "basic personality" tends to define personality as a miniature replica (obtained by "moulding") of the "culture", to be found in all members of the same society, except deviants. Cora Du Bois's celebrated analyses on the Alor Island natives provide a very typical example of the confusions and contradictions resulting from the theory that "culture" and personality can each be deduced from the other: determined to reconcile the anthropologist's conclusions, based on the postulate that the same influences produce the same basic personality, with her own clinical observations of four subjects who seem to her to be "highly individual characters", each "moulded by the specific factors in his individual fate", the psychoanalyst who struggles to find individual incarnations of the basic personality is condemned to recantations and contradictions.[30] Thus, she can see Mangma as "the most typical" of the four ("his personality corresponds to the basic personality structure") after having written: "It is difficult to decide how typical Mangma is. I would venture to say that if he were typical, the society could not continue to exist." Ripalda, who is passive and has a strong super-ego, is "atypical". So is Fantan, who has "the strongest character formation, devoid of inhibitions toward women" (extreme heterosexual inhibition being the rule), and "differs from the other men as much as a city-slicker differs from a farmer". The fourth, Malekala, whose biography is typical at every point, is a well-known prophet who tried to start a revivalist movement, and his personality seems to resemble that of Ripalda, another sorcerer who, as we have seen, is described as atypical. All this is capped by the analyst's observation that "characters such as Mangma, Ripalda and Fantan can be found in any society". Anthony F. Wallace, from whom this critique is taken,[31] is no doubt right in pointing out that the notion of modal personality has the advantage of avoiding the illogicalities resulting from indifference to differences (and thus to statistics) usually implicit in recourse to the notion of basic personality. But what might pass for a mere refinement of the measuring and checking techniques used to test the validity of a theoretical construct amounts in fact to the substitution of one object for another: a system of hypotheses as to the *structure* of personality, conceived as a homeostatic system which changes by reinterpreting external pressures in accordance with its own logic, is replaced by a simple description of the central tendency in the distribution of the values of a variable, or rather a combination of variables. Wallace thus comes to the tautological conclusion that in a population of Tuscarora Indians, the modal personality type defined by reference to twenty-seven variables is to be found in only 37 per cent of the subjects studied. The construction of a class *ethos* may, for example, make use of a reading of statistical regularities treated as *indices*, without the principle which unifies and explains these regularities being reducible to the regularities in which it manifests itself. In short, failing to see in the notion of "basic personality" anything other than a way of pointing to a directly observable "datum", i.e. the "personality type" shared by the greatest number of members of a given society, the advocates of this notion cannot, in all logic, take issue with those who submit this theory to the test of statistical critique, in the name of the same realist representation of the scientific object.

The habitus is the product of the work of inculcation and appropriation necessary in order for those products of collective history, the objective structures (e.g. of language, economy, etc.) to succeed in reproducing themselves more or less completely, in the form of durable dispositions, in the organisms (which one can, if one wishes, call individuals) lastingly subjected to the same conditionings, and hence placed in the same material conditions of existence. Therefore sociology treats as identical all the biological individuals who, being the product of the same objective conditions, are the supports of the same habitus: social class, understood as a system of objective determinations, must be brought into relation not with the individual or with the "class" as a *population*, i.e. as an aggregate of enumerable, measurable biological individuals, but with the class habitus, the system of dispositions (partially) common to all products of the same structures. Though it is impossible for *all* members of the same class (or even two of them) to have had the same experiences, in the same order, it is certain that each member of the same class is more likely than any member of another class to have been confronted with the situations most frequent for the members of that class. The objective structures which science apprehends in the form of statistical regularities (e.g. employment rates, income curves, probabilities of access to secondary education, frequency of holidays, etc.) inculcate, through the direct or indirect but always convergent experiences which give a social environment its *physiognomy*, with its "closed doors", "dead ends", and limited "prospects", that "art of assessing likelihoods", as Leibniz put it, of anticipating the objective future, in short, the sense of reality or realities which is perhaps the best-concealed principle of their efficacy.

In order to define the relations between class, habitus and the organic individuality which can never entirely be removed from sociological discourse, inasmuch as, being given immediately to immediate perception (*intuitus personae*), it is also socially designated and recognized (name, legal identity, etc.) and is defined by a *social trajectory* strictly speaking irreducible to any other, the habitus could be considered as a subjective but not individual system of internalized structures, schemes of perception, conception, and action common to all members of the same group or class and constituting the precondition for all objectification and apperception: and the objective co-ordination of practices and the sharing of a world-view could be founded on the perfect impersonality and inter-changeability of singular practices and views. But this would amount to regarding all the practices or representations produced in accordance with identical schemes as impersonal and substitutable, like singular intuitions of space which, according to Kant, reflect none of the peculiarities of the individual ego. In fact, it is in a relation of homology, of diversity within homogeneity reflecting the diversity within homogeneity characteristic of their social conditions of production, that the singular habitus of the different members of the same class are united; the homology of world-views implies the systematic differences which separate singular world-views, adopted from singular but concerted standpoints. Since the history of the individual is never anything other than a certain specification of the collective history of his group or class, *each individual system of dispositions* may be seen as a *structural variant* of all the other group or class habitus, expressing the difference between trajectories and positions inside or outside the class. "Personal" style, the particular stamp marking all the products of the same habitus, whether practices or works, is never more than a *deviation* in relation to the *style* of a period or class so that it relates back to the common style not only by its conformity – like Phidias, who, according to Hegel, had no "manner" – but also by the difference which makes the whole "manner".

The principle of these individual differences lies in the fact that, being the product of a chronologically ordered series of structuring determinations, the habitus, which at every moment structures in terms of the structuring experiences which produced it the structuring experiences which affect its structure, brings about a unique integration, dominated by the earliest experiences, of the experiences statistically common to the members of the same class. Thus, for example, the habitus acquired in the family underlies the structuring of school experiences (in particular the reception and assimilation of the specifically pedagogic message), and the habitus transformed by schooling, itself diversified, in turn underlies the structuring of all subsequent experiences (e.g. the reception and assimilation of the messages of the culture industry or work experiences), and so on, from restructuring to restructuring.

Springing from the encounter in an integrative organism of relatively independent causal series, such as biological and social determinisms, the habitus makes coherence and necessity out of accident and contingency: for example, the equivalences it establishes between positions in the division of labour and positions in the division between the sexes are doubtless not peculiar to societies in which the division of labour and the division between the sexes coincide almost perfectly. In a class society, all the products of a given agent, by an essential *overdetermination*, speak inseparably and simultaneously of his class – or, more, precisely, his position in the social structure and his rising or falling trajectory – and of his (or her) body – or, more precisely, all the properties, always socially qualified, of which he or she is the bearer – sexual properties of course, but also physical properties, praised, like strength or beauty, or stigmatized.

The Dialectic of Objectification and Embodiment

So long as the work of education is not clearly institutionalized as a specific, autonomous practice, and it is a whole group and a whole symbolically structured environment, without specialized agents or specific moments, which exerts an anonymous, pervasive pedagogic action, the essential part of the *modus operandi* which defines practical mastery is transmitted in practice, in its practical state, without attaining the level of discourse. The child imitates not "models" but other people's actions. Body *hexis* speaks directly to the motor function, in the form of a pattern of postures that is both individual and systematic, because linked to a whole system of techniques involving the body and tools, and charged with a host of social meanings and values: in all societies, children are particularly attentive to the gestures and postures which, in their eyes, express every-thing that goes to make an accomplished adult – a way of walking, a tilt of the head, facial expressions, ways of sitting and of using implements, always associated with a tone of voice, a style of speech, and (how could it be otherwise?) a certain subjective experience. But the fact that schemes are able to pass from practice to practice without going through discourse or consciousness does not mean that acquisition of the habitus comes down to a question of mechanical learning by trial and error. Unlike an incoherent series of figures, which can be learnt only gradually, through repeated attempts and with continu-ous predictable progress, a numerical series is mastered more easily because it contains a structure which makes it unnecessary to memorize all the numbers one by one: in verbal products such as proverbs, sayings, maxims, songs, riddles, or games; in objects, such as tools, the house, or the village; or again, in practices such as contests of honour, gift exchanges, rites, etc., the material which the Kabyle child has to assimilate is the product of the systematic application of principles coherent in practice,[32] which means, that in all this endlessly redundant material, he has no difficulty in grasping the *rationale* of what are clearly series and in making it his own in the form of a principle generating conduct organized in accordance with the same rationale.

Experimental analyses of learning which establish that "neither the formation nor the application of a concept requires conscious recognition of the common elements or relationship involved in the specific instances"[33] enable us to understand the dialectic of objectification and incorporation whereby the systematic objectifications of systematic dispositions tend in their turn to give rise to systematic dispositions: when faced with series of symbols – Chinese characters (Hull) or pictures varying simultaneously the colour, nature, and number of the objects represented (Heidbreder) – distributed into classes with arbitrary but objectively based names, subjects who are unable to state the principle of classification nonetheless attain higher scores than they would *if they were guessing at random*, thereby demonstrating that they achieve a practical mastery of the classificatory schemes which in no way implies symbolic mastery – i.e. conscious recog-nition and verbal expression – of the processes practically applied. Albert B. Lord's analysis of the acquiring of structured material in a natural environment, based on his study of the training of the *guslar*, the Yugoslav bard, entirely confirms the experimental findings: the practical mastery of what Lord calls "the formula", that is, the capacity to improvise by combining "formulae", sequences of words "regularly employed under the same metrical conditions to express a given idea",[34] is acquired through sheer familiari-zation, "by hearing the poems",[35] without the learner's having any sense of learning and subsequently manipulating this or that formula or any set of formulae:[36] the constraints of rhythm are internalized at the same time as melody and meaning, without being attended to for their own sake.

Between apprenticeship through simple familiarization, in which the apprentice insensibly and unconsciously acquires the principles of the "art" and the art of living – including those which are not known to the producer of the practices or works imitated, and, at the other extreme, explicit and express transmission by precept and prescription, every society provides for *structural exercises* tending to transmit this or that form of practical mastery. Such are the riddles and ritual contests which test the "sense of ritual language" and all the games, often structured according to the logic of the wager, the challenge or the combat (duels, group battles, target-shooting, etc.), which require the boys to set to work, in the mode of "let's pretend", the schemes generating the strategies of honour.[37] Then there is daily participation in gift exchanges and all their subtleties, which the boys derive from their rôle as messengers and, more especially, as intermediaries between the female world and the male world. There is silent observation of the discussions in the men's assembly, with their effects of eloquence, their rituals, their strategies, their ritual strategies and strategic uses of ritual. There are the interactions with their relatives, which lead them to explore the structured space of objective kin relationships in all directions by means of *reversals* requiring the person who saw himself and behaved as a nephew of his father's brother to see himself and behave as a paternal uncle towards his brother's son, and thus to acquire mastery of the transformational schemes which permit the passage from the system of dispositions attached to one position to the system appropriate to the symmetrically opposite position. There are the lexical and grammatical commutations ("I" and "you" designating the same person according to the relation to the speaker) which instil the sense of the interchangeability of positions and of reciprocity as well as a sense of the limits of each. And, at a deeper level, there are the relationships with the mother and the father, which, by their dyssymmetry in antagonistic complementarity, constitute one of the opportunities to internalize, inseparably, the schemes of the *sexual division of labour* and of the *division of sexual labour*.

But it is in the dialectical relationship between the body and a space structured according to the mythico-ritual oppositions that one finds the form par excellence of the structural apprenticeship which leads to the em-bodying of the structures of the world, that is, the appropriating by the world of a body thus enabled to appropriate the world. In a social formation in which the absence of the symbolic-product-conserving techniques associated with literacy retards the objectification of symbolic and particularly cultural capital, inhabited space – and above all the house – is the principal locus for the objectification of the generative schemes; and, through the intermediary of the divisions and hierarchies it sets up between things, persons, and practices, this tangible classifying system continuously inculcates and reinforces the taxonomic principles underlying all the arbitrary provisions of this culture.[38] Thus, as we have seen, the opposition between the sacred of the right hand and the sacred of the left hand, between *nif* and *ḥaram*, between man, invested with protective, fecundating virtues, and woman, at once sacred and charged with maleficent forces, and, correlatively, between religion (male) and magic (female), is reproduced in the spatial division between male space, with the place of assembly, the market, or the fields, and female space, the house and its garden, the retreats of *ḥaram*. To discover how this spatial organization (matched by a temporal organization obeying the same logic) governs practices and representations – far beyond the frequently described rough divisions between the male world and the female world, the assembly and the fountain, public life and intimacy – and thereby contributes to the durable imposition of the schemes of perception, thought, and action, it is necessary to grasp the dialectic of objectification and embodiment in the privileged locus of the space of the house and the earliest learning processes.

This analysis of the relationship between the objectified schemes and the schemes incorporated or being incorporated presupposes a structural analysis of the social organization of the internal space of the house and the relation of this internal space to external space, an analysis which is not an end in itself but which, precisely on account of the (dangerous) affinity between objectivism and all that is already objectified, is the only means of fully grasping the structuring structures which, remaining obscure to themselves, are revealed only in the objects they structure. The house, an *opus operatum*, lends itself as such to a deciphering, but only to a deciphering which does not forget that the "book" from which the children learn their vision of the world is read with the body, in and through the movements and displacements which make the space within which they are enacted as much as they are made by it.

The interior of the Kabyle house, rectangular in shape, is divided into two parts by a low wall: the larger of these two parts, slightly higher than the other, is reserved for human use; the other side, occupied by the animals, has a loft above it. A door with two wings gives access to both rooms. In the upper part is the hearth and, facing the door, the weaving loom. The lower, dark, nocturnal part of the house, the place of damp, green, or raw objects – water jars set on the benches on either side of the entrance to the stable or against the "wall of darkness", wood, green fodder – the place too of natural beings – oxen and cows, donkeys and mules – and natural activities – sleep, sex, birth – and also of death, is opposed to the high, light-filled, noble place of humans and in particular of the guest, fire and fire-made objects, the lamp, kitchen utensils, the rifle – the attribute of the manly point of honour (*nif*) which protects female honour (*ḥurma*) – the loom, the symbol of all protection, the place also of the two specifically cultural activities per-formed within the house, cooking and weaving. The meaning objectified in things or places is fully revealed only in the practices structured according to the same schemes which are organized in relation to them (and vice versa). The guest to be honoured (*qabel*, a verb also meaning "to stand up to", and "to face the east") is invited to sit in front of the loom. The opposite wall is called the wall of darkness, or the wall of the invalid: a sick person's bed is placed next to it. The washing of the dead takes place at the entrance to the stable. The low dark part is opposed to the upper part as the female to the male: it is the most intimate place within the world of intimacy (sexuality, fertility). The opposition between the male and the female also reappears in the opposition between the "master" beam and the main pillar, a fork open skywards.

Thus, the house is organized according to a set of homologous oppositions – fire: water :: cooked:raw :: high:low :: light:shade :: day:night :: male:female :: *nif:ḥurma* :: fertilizing:able to be fertilized. But in fact the same oppositions are established between the house as a whole and the rest of the universe, that is, the male world, the place of assembly, the fields, and the market. It follows that each of these two parts of the house (and, by the same token, each of the objects placed in it and each of the activities carried out in it) is in a sense qualified at two degrees, first as female (nocturnal, dark, etc.) inso-far as it partakes of the universe of the house, and secondarily as male or female insofar as it belongs to one or the other of the divisions of that universe. Thus, for example, the proverb "Man is the lamp of the outside, woman the lamp of the inside" must be taken to mean that man is the true light, that of the day, and woman the light of darkness, dark brightness; and we also know that she is to the moon as man is to the sun. But one or the other of the two systems of oppositions which define the house, either in its internal organization or in its relationship with the external world, is brought to the foreground, depending on whether the house is considered from the male point of view or the female point of view: whereas for the man, the house is not so much a place he enters as a place he comes out of, movement inwards properly befits the woman.[39]

All the actions performed in a space constructed in this way are immediately qualified symbolically and function as so many structural exercises through which is built up practical mastery of the fundamental schemes, which organize magical practices and representations: going in and coming out, filling and emptying, opening and shutting, going leftwards and going rightwards, going westwards and going eastwards, etc. Through the magic of a world of objects which is the product of the application of the same schemes to the most diverse domains, a world in which each thing speaks metaphorically of all the others, each practice comes to be invested with an objective meaning, a meaning with which practices – and particularly rites – have to reckon at all times, whether to evoke or revoke it. The construction of the world of objects is clearly not the sovereign operation of consciousness which the neo-Kantian tradition conceives of; the mental structures which construct the world of objects are constructed in the practice of a world of objects constructed according to the same structures.[40] The mind born of the world of objects does not rise as a subjectivity confronting an objectivity: the objective universe is made up of objects which are the product of objectifying operations structured according to the very structures which the mind applies to it. The mind is a metaphor of the world of objects which is itself but an endless circle of mutually reflecting metaphors.

All the symbolic manipulations of body experience, starting with displacements within a mythically structured space, e.g. the movements of going in and coming out, tend to impose the *integration* of the body space with cosmic space by grasping in terms of the same concepts (and naturally at the price of great laxity in logic) the relationship between man and the natural world and the complementarity and opposed states and actions of the two sexes in the division of sexual work and sexual division of work, and hence in the work of biological and social reproduction. For example, the opposition between movement outwards towards the fields or the market, towards the production and circulation of goods, and movement inwards, towards the accumulation and con- sumption of the products of work, corresponds symbolically to the opposition between the male body, self-enclosed and directed towards the outside world, and the female body, resembling the dark, damp house, full of food, utensils, and children, which is entered and left by the same inevitably soiled opening.[41]

The opposition between the *centrifugal*, male orientation and the *centripetal*, female orientation, which, as we have seen, is the true principle of the organization of domestic space, is doubtless also the basis of the relationship of each of the sexes to their "psyche", that is, to their bodies and more precisely to their sexuality. As in every society dominated by male values – and European societies, which assign men to politics, history, or war and women to the hearth, the novel, and psychology, are no exception – the specifically male relation to sexuality is that of *sublimation*, the symbolism of honour tending at once to refuse any direct expression of sexuality and to encourage its transfigured manifesta- tion in the form of manly prowess: the men, who are neither conscious of nor concerned with the female orgasm but seek the affirmation of their potency in repetition rather than prolongation of the sexual act, are not unaware that, through the intermediary of the female gossip that they both fear and despise, the eyes of the group always threaten their intimacy. As for the women, it is true to say, with Erikson, that male domination tends to "restrict their verbal consciousness"[42] so long as this is taken to mean not that they are forbidden all talk of sex, but that their discourse is dominated by the male values of virility, so that all reference to specifically female sexual "interests" is excluded from this aggressive and shame-filled cult of male potency.

Psychoanalysis, the disenchanting product of the disenchantment of the world, which leads to a domain of signification that is mythically overdetermined to be constituted *as such*, forgets and causes it to be forgotten that one's own body and other people's bodies are only ever perceived through categories of perception which it would be naive to treat as sexual, even if, as is attested by the women's laughter during conversations, and the interpretations they give of graphic symbols – mural paintings, pottery or carpet designs, etc. – these categories always relate back, sometimes very concretely, to the opposition between the biologically defined properties of the two sexes. As naive as it would be to reduce to their strictly sexual dimension the countless acts of diffuse incul- cation through which the body and the world tend to be set in order, by means of a symbolic manipulation of the relation to the body and to the world aiming to impose what has to be called, in Melanie Klein's term, a "body geography", a particular case of geography, or better, cosmology.[43] The child's initial relation to its father or mother, or in other terms, to the paternal body and maternal body, which offers the most dramatic opportunity to experience all the fundamental oppositions of mythopoeic practice, cannot be found as the basis of the acquisition of the principles of the structuring of the ego and the world, and in particular of every homosexual and heterosexual relationship, except insofar as that initial relation is set up with objects whose sex is defined symbolically and not biologically. The child constructs its *sexual identity*, the major element in its social identity, at the same time as it constructs its image of the division of work between the sexes, out of the same socially defined set of inseparably biological and social indices. In other words, the awakening of consciousness of sexual identity and the incorporation of the dispositions associated with a determinate social definition of the social functions incumbent on men and women come hand in hand with the adoption of a socially defined vision of the sexual division of labour.

Psychologists' work on the perception of sexual differences makes it clear that children establish clear-cut distinctions very early (about age five) between male and female functions, assigning domestic tasks to women and mothers and economic activities to men and fathers. Everything suggests that the awareness of sexual differences and the distinction between paternal and maternal functions are constituted simultaneously. From the numerous analyses of the differential perception of mother and father it may be gathered that the father is generally seen as more competent and more severe than the mother, who is regarded as "kinder" and more affectionate than the father and is the object of a more emotional and more agreeable relationship. In fact, as Emmerich very rightly points out, underlying all these differences is the fact that children attribute more power to the father than to the mother.

It is not hard to imagine the weight that must be brought to bear on the construction of self-image and world-image by the opposition between masculinity and femininity when it constitutes the fundamental principle of division of the social and symbolic world. As is emphasized by the twofold meaning of the world *nif*, sexual potency insepa- rable from social potency, what is imposed through a certain social definition of maleness (and, by derivation, of femaleness), is a political mythology which governs all bodily experiences, not least sexual experiences themselves. Thus, the opposition between male sexuality, public and sublimated, and female sexuality, secret and, so to speak, "alienated" (with respect to Erikson's "utopia of universal genitality", i.e. the "utopia of full orgasmic reciprocity") is only a specification of the opposition between the extraversion of politics or public religion and the introversion of psychology or private magic, made up for the most part of rites aimed at domesticating the male partners.

Bodily *hexis* is political mythology realized, *em-bodied*, turned into a permanent disposition, a durable manner of standing, speaking, and thereby of *feeling* and *thinking*. The oppositions which mythico–ritual logic makes between the male and the female and which organize the whole system of values reappear, for example, in the gestures and movements of the body, in the form of the opposition between the straight and the bent, or between assurance and restraint. "The Kabyle is like the heather, he would rather break than bend." The man of honour's pace is steady and determined. His way of walking, that of a man who knows where he is going and knows he will arrive in time, whatever the obstacles, expresses strength and resolution, as opposed to the hesitant gait (*thikli thamahmahth*) announcing indecision, half-hearted promises (*awal amahmah*), the fear of commitments and the incapacity to fulfil them. At the same time it is a *measured* pace: it contrasts as much with the haste of the man who "throws his feet up as high as his head", "walks along with great strides", "dances" – running being weak and frivolous conduct – as it does with the sluggishness of the man who "trails along". The manly man stands up straight and honours the person he approaches or wishes to welcome by looking him right in the eyes; ever on the alert, because ever threatened, he lets nothing that happens around him escape him, whereas a gaze that is up in the clouds or fixed on the ground is the mark of an irresponsible man, who has nothing to fear because he has no responsibilities in his group. Conversely, a woman is expected to walk with a slight stoop, looking down, keeping her eyes on the spot where she will next put her foot, especially if she happens to have to walk past the *thajma'th*; her gait must avoid the excessive swing of the hips which comes from a heavy stride; she must always be girdled with the *thimehremth*, a rectangular piece of cloth with yellow, red, and black stripes worn over her dress, and take care that her headscarf does not come unknotted, revealing her hair. In short, the specifically feminine virtue, *lahia*, modesty, restraint, reserve, orients the whole female body downwards, towards the ground, the inside, the house, whereas male excellence, *nif*, is asserted in movement upwards, outwards, towards other men.

If all societies and, significantly, all the "totalitarian institutions", in Goffman's phrase, that seek to produce a new man through a process of "deculturation" and "reculturation" set such store on the seemingly most insignificant details of *dress, bearing*, physical and verbal *manners*, the reason is that, treating the body as a memory, they entrust to it in abbreviated and practical, i.e. mnemonic, form the fundamental principles of the arbitrary content of the culture. The principles em-bodied in this way are placed beyond the grasp of consciousness, and hence cannot be touched by voluntary, deliberate transformation, cannot even be made explicit; nothing seems more ineffable, more incommunicable, more inimitable, and, therefore, more precious, than the values given body, *made* body by the transubstantiation achieved by the hidden persuasion of an implicit pedagogy, capable of instilling a whole cosmology, an ethic, a metaphysic, a political philosophy, through injunctions as insignificant as "stand up straight" or "don't hold your knife in your left hand".[44] The logic of scheme transfer which makes each technique of the body a sort of *pars totalis*, predisposed to function in accordance with the fallacy *pars pro toto*, and hence to evoke the whole system of which it is a part, gives a very general scope to the seemingly most circumscribed and circumstantial observances. The whole trick of pedagogic reason lies precisely in the way it extorts the essential while seeming to demand the insignificant: in obtaining the respect for form and forms of respect which constitute the most visible and at the same time the best-hidden (because most "natural") manifestation of submission to the established order, the incorporation of the arbitrary abolishes what Raymond Ruyer calls "lateral possibilities", that is, all the eccentricities and deviations which are the small change of madness. The concessions of *politeness* always contain *political* concessions. The term *obsequium* used by Spinoza to denote the "constant will" produced by the conditioning through which "the State fashions us for its own use and which enables it to survive"[45] could be reserved to designate the public testimonies of recognition which every group expects of its members (especially at moments of co-option), that is, the symbolic taxes due from individuals in the exchanges which are set up in every group between the individuals and the group. Because, as in gift exchange, the exchange is an end in itself, the tribute demanded by the group generally comes down to a matter of trifles, that is, to symbolic rituals (rites of passage, the ceremonials of etiquette, etc.), formalities and formalisms which "cost nothing" to perform and seem such "natural" things to demand ("It's the least one can do ...": "It wouldn't cost him anything to ...") that abstention amounts to a refusal or a challenge.[46]

Through the habitus, the structure which has produced it governs practice, not by the processes of a mechanical determinism, but through the mediation of the orientations and limits it assigns to the habitus's operations of invention.[47] As an acquired system of generative schemes objectively adjusted to the particular conditions in which it is constituted, the habitus engenders all the thoughts, all the perceptions, and all the actions consistent with those conditions, and no others. This paradoxical product is difficult to conceive, even inconceivable, only so long as one remains locked in the dilemma of determinism and freedom, conditioning and creativity (like Chomsky, for example, who thought the only escape from Bloomfieldian behaviourism lay in seeking "freedom" and "creativity" in the "structure" – i.e. the "nature" – of the human mind). Because the habitus is an endless capacity to engender products – thoughts, perceptions, expressions, actions – whose limits are set by the historically and socially situated conditions of its production, the conditioned and conditional freedom it secures is as remote from a creation of unpredictable novelty as it is from a simple mechanical reproduction of the initial conditionings.[48]

Notes

1   The word *disposition* seems particularly suited to express what is covered by the concept of habitus (defined as a system of dispositions). It expresses first the *result of an organizing action*, with a meaning close to that of words such as structure; it also designates a *way of being*, a *habitual state* (especially of the body) and, in particular, a *predisposition, tendency, propensity*, or *inclination*. [The semantic cluster of "disposition" is rather wider in French than in English, but as this note – translated literally – shows, the equivalence is adequate. Translator.]

2   The most profitable strategies are usually those produced, on the hither side of all calculation and in the illusion of the most "authentic" sincerity, by a habitus objectively fitted to the objective structures. These strategies without strategic calculation procure an important secondary advantage for those who can scarcely be called their authors – the social approval accruing from apparent disinterestedness.

3   "Here we confront the distressing fact that the sample episode chain under analysis is a fragment of a larger segment of behavior which in the complete record contains some 480 separate episodes. Moreover, it took only twenty minutes for these 480 behavior stream events to occur. If my wife's rate of behavior is roughly representative of that of other actors, we must be prepared to deal with an inventory of episodes produced at the rate of some 20,000 per sixteen-hour day per actor ... In a population consisting of several hundred actor-types, the number of different episodes in the total repertory must amount to many millions during the course of an annual cycle" (M. Harris, *The Nature of Cultural Things* (New York: Random House, 1964), pp. 74–5).

4   See A. Touraine, *Sociologie de l'action*, Paris: Seuil, 1965, and "La raison d'être d'une sociologie de l'action", *Revue Française de Sociologie*, 7 (October–December 1966), pp. 518–27.

5   J.-P. Sartre, *L'etre et le néant* (Paris: Gallimard, 1943), p. 510 (*Being and Nothingness* (London: Methuen, 1957), pp. 434–5 [translation emended]); see also Sartre, "Répose à Lefort", *Les Temps Modernes*, no. 89 (April 1963), pp. 1571–1629.

6   *L'être et le néant*, p. 669; *Being and Nothingness*, p. 580.

7   *L'être et le néant*, p. 521; *Being and Nothingness*, p. 445.

8   E. Durkheim, *Les règles de la méthode sociologique*, 18th ed. (Paris: PUF, 1973), p. 18; English trans. *The Rules of Sociological Method* (New York: Free Press, 1964), p. 17.

9   *L'être et le néant*, p. 543; *Being and Nothingness*, p. 465.

10 *Critique de la raison dialectique* (Paris: Gallimard, 1960), p. 161.

11 *Critique*, p. 305.

12 *Critique*, p. 357.

13 *Règles*, p. 19; *Rules*, p. 18.

14 *Critique*, p. 133.

15 *Critique*, pp. 234 and 281.

16 *Critique*, p. 294.

17 *Critique*, p. 179.

18 Can one avoid attributing to the permanence of a habitus the constancy with which the objective intention of the Sartrian philosophy (despite its language) asserts itself against the subjective intentions of its author, that is, against a permanent project of "conversion", a project never more manifest and manifestly sincere than in certain anathemas which would perhaps be less violent if they were not redolent of conscious or unconscious self-critique? (Thus, for example, one needs to bear in mind the famous analysis of the café waiter for a full appreciation of a sentence such as this: "To all those who take themselves for angels, their neighbour's activities seem absurd, because such people presume to transcend the human enterprise by refusing to take part in it": *Critique*, pp. 182–3). And when, in his analysis of the relationship between Flaubert and the bourgeoisie, Sartre makes the awakening of consciousness the basis of an existence and an oeuvre, he testifies that it is not sufficient to become aware of class condition in order to be liberated from the lasting dispositions it produces (see P. Bourdieu, "Champ du pouvoir, champ intellectuel et habitus de classe", *Scolies*, 1 (1971), pp. 7–26, esp. pp. 12–14).

19 See the whole chapter entitled "Rechtsordnung, Konvention und Sitte", in which Max Weber analyses the differences and transitions between custom, convention, and law (*Wirtschaft und Gesellschaft* (Cologne and Berlin: Kiepenhauer und Witsch, 1964), vol. 1, pp. 240–50, esp. pp. 246–9; English trans. "Law, Convention and Custom", *Economy and Society*, ed. G. Roth and C. Wittich (New York: Bedminster Press, 1968), 1, pp. 319–33).

20 "We call this subjective, variable probability – which sometimes excludes doubt and engenders a certainty *sui generis* and which at other times appears as no more than a vague glimmer – *philosophical probability*, because it refers to the exercise of the higher faculty whereby we comprehend the order and the rationality of things. All reasonable men have a confused notion of similar probabilities; this then determines, or at least justifies, those unshakable beliefs we call *common sense*" (A. Cournot, *Essai sur les fondements de la connaissance et sur les caractères de la critique philosophique* (Paris: Hachette, 1922; 1st ed., 1851), p. 70).

21 E. Durkheim, *L'évolution pédagogique en France* (Paris: Alcan, 1938), p. 16.

22 R. Ruyer, *Paradoxes de la conscience et limites de l'automatisme* (Paris: Albin Michel, 1966), p. 136.

23 This universalization has the same limits as the objective conditions of which the principle generating practices and works is the product. The objective conditions exercise simultaneously a universalizing effect and a particularizing effect, because they cannot homogenize the agents whom they determine and whom they constitute into an objective group, without distinguishing them from all the agents produced in different conditions.

24 One of the merits of subjectivism and moralism is that the analyses in which it condemns, as inauthentic, actions subject to the objective solicitations of the world (e.g. Heidegger on everyday existence and "*das Man*" or Sartre on the "spirit of seriousness") demonstrate, *per absurdum*, the

impossibility of the authentic existence that would gather up all pregiven significations and objective determinations into a project of freedom. The *purely ethical* pursuit of authenticity is the privilege of the leisured thinker who can afford to dispense with the economy of thought which "inauthentic" conduct allows.

25 G. W. Leibniz, "Second éclaircissement du système de la communication des substances" (1696), in *Oeuvres philosophiques*, ed. P. Janet (Paris: de Lagrange, 1866), vol. II, p. 548.

26 Thus, ignorance of the surest but best-hidden foundation of group or class integration leads some (e.g. Aron, Dahl, etc.) to deny the unity of the dominant class with no other proof than the impossibility of establishing empirically that the members of the dominant class have an explicit *policy*, expressly imposed by explicit co-ordination, and others (Sartre, for example) to see the awakening of class consciousness – a sort of revolutionary cogito bringing the class into existence by constituting it as a "class for itself" – as the only possible foundation of the unity of the dominated class.

27 Leibniz, "Second éclaircissement", p. 548.

28 Were such language not dangerous in another way, one would be tempted to say, against all forms of subjectivist voluntarism, that class unity rests fundamentally on the "class unconscious". The awakening of "class consciousness" is not a primal act constituting the class in a blaze of freedom; its sole efficacy, as with all actions of symbolic reduplication, lies in the extent to which it brings to consciousness all that is implicitly assumed in the unconscious mode in the class habitus.

29 This takes us beyond the false opposition in which the theories of acculturation have allowed themselves to be trapped, with, on the one hand, the *realism of the structure* which represents cultural or linguistic contacts as contacts between cultures or languages, subject to generic laws (e.g. the law of the restructuring of borrowings) and specific laws (those established by analysis of the structures specific to the languages or cultures in contact) and on the other hand the *realism of the element*, which emphasizes the contacts between the *societies* (regarded as populations) involved or, at best, the structures of the relations between those societies (domination, etc.).

30 *The People of Alor*, Minneapolis: University of Minnesota Press, 1944.

31 *Culture and Personality* (New York: Random House, 1965), p. 86.

32 If illiterate societies seem to have a particular bent for the structural games which fascinate the anthropologist, their purpose is often quite simply mnemonic: the remarkable homology to be observed in Kabylia between the structure of the distribution of the families in the village and the structure of the distribution of graves in the cemetery (Aït Hichem, Tizi Hibel) clearly makes it easier to locate the traditionally anonymous graves (with expressly transmitted landmarks added to the structural principles).

33 B. Berelson and G. A. Steiner, *Human Behavior* (New York: Harcourt, Brace and World, 1964), p. 193.

34 *The Singer of the Tales* (Cambridge, Mass.: Harvard University Press, 1960), p. 30.

35 *Ibid.* p. 32.

36 *Ibid.* p. 24.

37 Thus, in the game of *qochra*, which the children play in early spring, the cork ball (the *qochra*) which is fought for, passed and defended, is the practical equivalent of woman. In the course of the game the players must both defend themselves against it and, possessing it, defend it against those trying to take it away. At the start of the match, the leader of the game repeatedly asks, "Whose daughter is she?" but no one will volunteer to be her father and protect her: a daughter is always a liability for men. And so lots have to be drawn for her, and the unlucky player who gets her must accept his fate. He now has to protect the ball against the attacks of all the others, while at the same time trying to pass it on to another player; but he can only do so in an honourable, approved way. A player whom the "father" manages to touch with his stick, telling him "She's your daughter", has to acknowledge defeat, like a man temporarily obliged to a socially inferior family from whom he has taken a wife. For the suitors the temptation is to take the prestigious course of abduction, whereas the father wants a marriage that will free him from guardianship and allow him to re-enter the game. The loser of the game is excluded from the world of men; the ball is tied under his shirt so that he looks like a girl who has been got pregnant.

38 It is said that formerly the women used to go to market alone; but they are so talkative that the market went on until the market time of the following week. So the men turned up one day with

sticks and put an end to their wives' gossiping ... It can be seen that the "myth" "explains" the present division of space and work by invoking the "evil nature" of women. When a man wants to say that the world is topsy-turvy, he says that "the women are going to market".

39 A full presentation of the analysis of the internal structure of the Kabyle house, of which it has only been possible to give the indispensable outline here, can be found in P. Bourdieu, *Esquisse d'une théorie de la pratique* (Paris and Geneva: Librairie Droz, 1972), pp. 45–69.

40 This means to say that the "learning by doing" hypothesis, associated with the name of Arrow (see K. J. Arrow, "The Economic Implications of Learning by Doing", *Review of Economic Studies*, 29, 3, no. 80 (June 1962), pp. 155–73) is a particular case (whose particularity needs to be specified) of a very general law: every made product – including symbolic products such as works of art, games, myths, etc. – exerts by its very functioning, particularly by the use made of it, an educative effect which helps to make it easier to acquire the dispositions necessary for its adequate use.

41 Erikson's analyses of the Yoruk might be interpreted in the same light (see E. H. Erikson, "Observations on the Yoruk: Childhood and World Image" (University of California Publications in American Archaeology and Ethnology, vol. 35, no. 10, Berkeley: University of California Press, 1943), pp. 257–302).

42 E. H. Erikson, "Childhood and Tradition in Two American Tribes", in *The Psychoanalytic Study of the Child* (New York: International Universities Press, 1945), vol. I, pp. 319–50.

43 *Contributions to Psycho-analysis 1921–1945* (London: Hogarth Press, 1948), p. 109n1 and p. 260n1.

44 Every group entrusts to bodily automatisms those principles most basic to it and most indispensable to its conservation. In societies which lack any other recording and objectifying instrument, inherited knowledge can survive only in its embodied state. Among other consequences, it follows that it is never detached from the body which bears it and which – as Plato noted – can deliver it only at the price of a sort of gymnastics intended to evoke it: *mimesis*. The body is thus continuously mingled with all the knowledge it reproduces, which can never have the objectivity and distance stemming from objectification in writing.

45 A. Matheron, *Individu et société chez Spinoza* (Paris: Editions de Minuit, 1969), p. 349.

46 Thus, practical mastery of what are called the rules of politeness, and in particular the art of adjusting each of the available formulae (e.g. at the end of a letter) to the different classes of possible addressees, presupposes the implicit mastery, hence the recognition, of a set of oppositions constituting the implicit axiomatics of a determinate political order: in the example considered these are (in France) the opposition between men and women, the former requiring "homage", the latter "salutations" or "sentiments"; the opposition between the older and the younger; the opposition between the personal, or private, and the impersonal – with administrative or business letters; and finally the hierarchical opposition between superiors, equals, and inferiors, which governs the subtle grading of marks of respect.

47 One of the reasons for the use of the term habitus is the wish to set aside the common conception of habit as a mechanical assembly or preformed programme, as Hegel does when in the *Phenomenology of Mind* he speaks of "habit as dexterity".

48 For a sociological application of these analyses, see P. Bourdieu, "Avenir de classe et causalité du probable", *Revue Française de Sociologie*, 15, (January–March 1974), pp. 3–42. English translation forthcoming.

CHAPTER 6

Ideology and Ideological State Apparatuses

Louis Althusser

Louis Althusser was the leading Structuralist Marxist philosopher in France in the 1960s. His books included *For Marx* (1965) and *Lenin and Philosophy* (1971). In this his most famous essay, published in 1968, he describes ideology, which traditionally had been characterized as a species of "false consciousness," as a set of practices and institutions that sustain an individual's imaginary relationship to his or her material conditions of existence.

Ideology is a "Representation" of the Imaginary Relationship of Individuals to their Real Conditions of Existence

In order to approach my central thesis on the structure and functioning of ideology, I shall first present two theses, one negative, the other positive. The first concerns the object which is "represented" in the imaginary form of ideology, the second concerns the materiality of ideology.

THESIS I: Ideology represents the imaginary relationship of individuals to their real conditions of existence.

We commonly call religious ideology, ethical ideology, legal ideology, political ideology, etc., so many "world outlooks." Of course, assuming that we do not live one of these ideologies as the truth (e.g. "believe" in God, Duty, Justice, etc....), we admit that the ideology we are discussing from a critical point of view, examining it as the ethnologist examines the myths of a "primitive society," that these "world outlooks" are largely imaginary, i.e. do not "correspond to reality."

Original publication details: Louis Althusser, "Ideology and Ideological State Apparatuses" from *Lenin and Philosophy*, trans. B. Brewster, pp. 85–125. New Left Books, 1971. Reproduced with permission from Éditions La Découverte and the publishers, Verso.

However, while admitting that they do not correspond to reality, i.e. that they constitute an illusion, we admit that they do make allusion to reality, and that they need only be "interpreted" to discover the reality of the world behind their imaginary representation of that world (ideology = *illusion/allusion*).

There are different types of interpretation, the most famous of which are the *mechanistic* type, current in the eighteenth century (God is the imaginary representation of the real King), and the "*hermeneutic*" interpretation, inaugurated by the earliest Church Fathers, and revived by Feuerbach and the theologico-philosophical school which descends from him, e.g. the theologian Barth (to Feuerbach, for example, God is the essence of real Man). The essential point is that on condition that we interpret the imaginary transposition (and inversion) of ideology we arrive at the conclusion that in ideology "men represent their real conditions of existence to themselves in an imaginary form."

Unfortunately, this interpretation leaves one small problem unsettled: why do men "need" this imaginary transposition of their real conditions of existence in order to "represent to themselves" their real conditions of existence?

The first answer (that of the eighteenth century) proposes a simple solution: Priests or Despots are responsible. They "forged" the Beautiful Lies so that, in the belief that they were obeying God, men would in fact obey the Priests and Despots, who are usually in alliance in their imposture, the Priests acting in the interests of the Despots or *vice versa*, according to the political positions of the "theoreticians" concerned. There is therefore a cause for the imaginary transposition of the real conditions of existence: that cause is the existence of a small number of cynical men who base their domination and exploitation of the "people" on a falsified representation of the world which they have imagined in order to enslave other minds by dominating their imaginations.

The second answer (that of Feuerbach, taken over word for word by Marx in his *Early Works*) is more "profound," i.e. just as false. It, too, seeks and finds a cause for the imaginary transposition and distortion of men's real conditions of existence, in short, for the alienation in the imaginary of the representation of men's conditions of existence. This cause is no longer Priests or Despots, nor their active imagination and the passive imagination of their victims. This cause is the material alienation which reigns in the conditions of existence of men themselves. This is how, in *The Jewish Question* and elsewhere, Marx defends the Feuerbachian idea that men make themselves an alienated (= imaginary) representation of their conditions of existence because these conditions of existence are themselves alienating (in the *1844 Manuscripts*: because these conditions are dominated by the essence of alienated society – "*alienated labor*").

All these interpretations thus take literally the thesis which they presuppose, and on which they depend, i.e. that what is reflected in the imaginary representation of the world found in an ideology is the conditions of existence of men, i.e. their real world.

Now I can return to a thesis which I have already advanced: it is not their real conditions of existence, their real world, that "men" "represent to themselves" in ideology, but above all it is their relation to those conditions of existence which is represented to them there. It is this relation which is at the center of every ideological, i.e. imaginary, representation of the real world. It is this relation that contains the "cause" which has to explain the imaginary distortion of the ideological representation of the real world. Or rather, to leave aside the language of causality, it is necessary to advance the thesis that it is the *imaginary nature of this relation* which underlies all the imaginary distortion that we can observe (if we do not live in its truth) in all ideology.

To speak in a Marxist language, if it is true that the representation of the real conditions of existence of the individuals occupying the posts of agents of production, exploitation, repression, ideologization and scientific practice, does in the last analysis arise from the relations of production, and from relations deriving from the relations of production, we can say the following: all ideology represents in its necessarily imaginary distortion not the existing relations of production (and the other relations that derive from them), but above all the (imaginary) relationship of individuals to the relations of production and the relations that derive from them. What is represented in ideology is therefore not the system of the real relations which govern the existence of individuals, but the imaginary relation of those individuals to the real relations in which they live.

If this is the case, the question of the "cause" of the imaginary distortion of the real relations in ideology disappears and must be replaced by a different question: why is the representation given to individuals of their (individual) relation to the social relations which govern their conditions of existence and their collective and individual life necessarily an imaginary relation? And what is the nature of this imaginariness? Posed in this way, the question explodes the solution by a "clique,"[1] by a group of individuals (Priests or Despots) who are the authors of the great ideological mystification, just as it explodes the solution by the alienated character of the real world. We shall see why later in my exposition. For the moment I shall go no further.

THESIS II: Ideology has a material existence.

I have already touched on this thesis by saying that the "ideas" or "representations," etc., which seem to make up ideology do not have an ideal (*idéale* or *idéelle*) or spiritual existence, but a material existence. I even suggested that the ideal (*idéale, idéelle*) and spiritual existence of "ideas" arises exclusively in an ideology of the "idea" and of ideology, and let me add, in an ideology of what seems to have "founded" this conception since the emergence of the sciences, i.e. what the practicians of the sciences represent to themselves in their spontaneous ideology as "ideas," true or false. Of course, presented in affirmative form, this thesis is unproven. I simply ask that the reader be favorably disposed towards it, say, in the name of materialism. A long series of arguments would be necessary to prove it.

This hypothetical thesis of the not spiritual but material existence of "ideas" or other "representations" is indeed necessary if we are to advance in our analysis of the nature of ideology. Or rather, it is merely useful to us in order the better to reveal what every at all serious analysis of any ideology will immediately and empirically show to every observer, however critical.

While discussing the ideological State apparatuses and their practices, I said that each of them was the realization of an ideology (the unity of these different regional ideologies – religious, ethical, legal, political, aesthetic, etc. being assured by their subjection to the ruling ideology). I now return to this thesis: an ideology always exists in an apparatus, and its practice, or practices. This existence is material.

Of course, the material existence of the ideology in an apparatus and its practices does not have the same modality as the material existence of a paving-stone or a rifle. But, at the risk of being taken for a Neo-Aristotelian (NB Marx had a very high regard for Aristotle), I shall say that "matter is discussed in many senses," or rather that it exists in different modalities, all rooted in the last instance in "physical" matter.

Having said this, let me move straight on and see what happens to the "individuals" who live in ideology, i.e. in a determinate (religious, ethical, etc.) representation of the world whose imaginary distortion depends on their imaginary relation to their conditions of existence, in other words, in the last instance, to the relations of production and to class relations (ideology = an imaginary relation to real relations). I shall say that this imaginary relation is itself endowed with a material existence.

Now I observe the following.

An individual believes in God, or Duty, or Justice, etc. This belief derives (for everyone, i.e. for all those who live in an ideological representation of ideology, which reduces ideology to ideas endowed by definition with a spiritual existence) from the ideas of the individual concerned, i.e. from him as a subject with a consciousness which contains the ideas of his belief. In this way, i.e. by means of the absolutely ideological "conceptual" device (*dispositif*) thus set up (a subject endowed with a consciousness in which he freely forms or freely recognizes ideas in which he believes), the (material) attitude of the subject concerned naturally follows.

The individual in question behaves in such and such a way, adopts such and such a practical attitude, and, what is more, participates in certain regular practices which are those of the ideological apparatus on which "depend" the ideas which he has in all consciousness freely chosen as a subject. If he believes in God, he goes to Church to attend Mass, kneels, prays, confesses, does penance (once it was material in the ordinary sense of the term) and naturally repents and so on. If he believes in Duty, he will have the corresponding attitudes, inscribed in ritual practices "according to the correct principles." If he believes in Justice, he will submit unconditionally to the rules of the Law, and may even protest when they are violated, sign petitions, take part in a demonstration, etc.

Throughout this schema we observe that the ideological representation of ideology is itself forced to recognize that every "subject" endowed with a "consciousness" and believing in the "ideas" that his "consciousness" inspires in him and freely accepts, must "*act* according to his ideas," must therefore inscribe his own ideas as a free subject in the actions of his material practice. If he does not do so, "that is wicked."

Indeed, if he does not do what he ought to do as a function of what he believes, it is because he does something else, which, still as a function of the same idealist scheme, implies that he has other ideas in his head as well as those he proclaims, and that he acts according to these other ideas, as a man who is either "inconsistent" ("no one is willingly evil") or cynical, or perverse.

In every case, the ideology of ideology thus recognizes, despite its imaginary distortion, that the "ideas" of a human subject exist in his actions, or ought to exist in his actions, and if that is not the case, it lends him other ideas corresponding to the actions (however perverse) that he does perform. This ideology talks of actions: I shall talk of actions inserted into *practices*. And I shall point out that these practices are governed by the *rituals* in which these practices are inscribed, within the *material existence of an ideological apparatus*, be it only a small part of that apparatus: a small mass in a small church, a funeral, a minor match at a sports club, a school day, a political party meeting, etc.

Besides, we are indebted to Pascal's defensive "dialectic" for the wonderful formula which will enable us to invert the order of the notional schema of ideology. Pascal says more or less: "Kneel down, move your lips in prayer, and you will believe." He thus scandalously inverts the order of things, bringing, like Christ, not peace but strife, and in addition something hardly Christian (for woe to him who brings scandal into the world!) – scandal itself. A fortunate scandal which makes him stick with Jansenist defiance to a language that directly names the reality.

I will be allowed to leave Pascal to the arguments of his ideological struggle with the religious ideological State apparatus of his day. And I shall be expected to use a more directly Marxist vocabulary, if that is possible, for we are advancing in still poorly explored domains.

I shall therefore say that, where only a single subject (such and such an individual) is concerned, the existence of the ideas of his belief is material in that *his ideas are his material actions inserted into material practices governed by material rituals which are themselves defined by the material ideological apparatus from which derive the ideas of that subject*. Naturally, the four inscriptions of the adjective "material" in my proposition must be affected by different modalities: the materialities of a displacement for going to mass, of kneeling down, of the gesture of the sign of the cross, or of the *mea culpa*, of a sentence, of a prayer, of an act of contrition, of a penitence, of a gaze, of a hand-shake, of an external verbal discourse or an "internal" verbal discourse (consciousness), are not one and the same materiality. I shall leave on one side the problem of a theory of the differences between the modalities of materiality.

It remains that in this inverted presentation of things, we are not dealing with an "inversion" at all, since it is clear that certain notions have purely and simply disappeared from our presentation, whereas others on the contrary survive, and new terms appear.

DISAPPEARED: the term *ideas*.
SURVIVE: the terms *subject, consciousness, belief, actions*.
APPEAR: the terms *practices, rituals, ideological apparatus*.

It is therefore not an inversion or overturning (except in the sense in which one might say a government or a glass is overturned), but a reshuffle (of a non-ministerial type), a rather strange reshuffle, since we obtain the following result.

Ideas have disappeared as such (insofar as they are endowed with an ideal or spiritual existence), to the precise extent that it has emerged that their existence is inscribed in the actions of practices governed by rituals defined in the last instance by an ideological apparatus. It therefore appears that the subject acts insofar as he is acted by the following system (set out in the order of its real determination): ideology existing in a material ideological apparatus, prescribing material practices governed by a material ritual, which practices exist in the material actions of a subject acting in all consciousness according to his belief.

But this very presentation reveals that we have retained the following notions: subject, consciousness, belief, actions. From this series I shall immediately extract the decisive central term on which everything else depends: the notion of the *subject*.

And I shall immediately set down two conjoint theses:

1.   there is no practice except by and in an ideology;
2.   there is no ideology except by the subject and for subjects.

I can now come to my central thesis.

Ideology Interpellates Individuals as Subjects

This thesis is simply a matter of making my last proposition explicit: there is no ideology except by the subject and for subjects. Meaning, there is no ideology except for concrete subjects, and this destination for ideology is only made possible by the subject: meaning, *by the category of the subject* and its functioning.

By this I mean that, even if it only appears under this name (the subject) with the rise of bourgeois ideology, above all with the rise of legal ideology,[2] the category of the subject (which may function under other names: e.g., as the soul in Plato, as God, etc.) is the constitutive category of all ideology, whatever its determination (regional or class) and whatever its historical date – since ideology has no history.

I say: the category of the subject is constitutive of all ideology, but at the same time and immediately I add that *the category of the subject is only constitutive of all ideology insofar as all ideology has the function (which defines it) of "constituting" concrete individuals as subjects*. In the interaction of this double constitution exists the functioning of all ideology, ideology being nothing but its functioning in the material forms of existence of that functioning.

In order to grasp what follows, it is essential to realize that both he who is writing these lines and the reader who reads them are themselves subjects, and therefore ideological subjects (a tautological proposition), i.e. that the author and the reader of these lines both live "spontaneously" or "naturally" in ideology in the sense in which I have said that "man is an ideological animal by nature."

That the author, insofar as he writes the lines of a discourse which claims to be scientific, is completely absent as a "subject" from "his" scientific discourse (for all scientific discourse is by definition a subject-less discourse, there is no "Subject of science" except in an ideology of science) is a different question which I shall leave on one side for the moment.

As St Paul admirably put it, it is in the "Logos," meaning in ideology, that we "live, move and have our being." It follows that, for you and for me, the category of the subject is a primary "obviousness" (obviousnesses are always primary): it is clear that you and I are subjects (free, ethical, etc....). Like all obviousnesses, including those that make a word "name a thing" or "have a meaning" (therefore including the obviousness of the "transparency" of language), the "obviousness" that you and I are subjects – and that that does not cause any problems – is an ideological effect, the elementary ideological effect.[3] It is indeed a peculiarity of ideology that it imposes (without appearing to do so, since these are "obviousnesses") obviousnesses as obviousnesses, which we cannot *fail to recognize* and before which we have the inevitable and natural reaction of crying out (aloud or in the "still, small voice of conscience"): "That's obvious! That's right! That's true!"

At work in this reaction is the ideological function which is one of the two functions of ideology as such (its inverse being the function of *misrecognition – méconnaissance*).

To take a highly "concrete" example, we all have friends who, when they knock on our door and we ask, through the door, the question "Who's there?," answer (since "it's obvious") "It's me." And we recognize that "it is him," or "her." We open the door, and "it's true, it really was she who was there." To take another example, when we recognize somebody of our (previous) acquaintance ((re)-*connaissance*) in the street, we show him that we have recognized him (and have recognized that he has recognized us) by saying to him "Hello, my friend," and shaking his hand (a material ritual practice of ideological recognition in everyday life – in France, at least; elsewhere, there are other rituals).

In this preliminary remark and these concrete illustrations, I only wish to point out that you and I are *always already* subjects, and as such constantly practice the rituals of ideological recognition, which guarantee for us that we are indeed concrete, individual, distinguishable and (naturally) irreplaceable subjects. The writing I am currently executing and the reading you are currently[4] performing are also in this respect rituals of ideological recognition, including the "obviousness" with which the "truth" or "error" of my reflections may impose itself on you.

But to recognize that we are subjects and that we function in the practical rituals of the most elementary everyday life (the hand-shake, the fact of calling you by your name, the fact of knowing, even if I do not know what it is, that you "have" a name of your own, which means that you are recognized as a unique subject, etc.) – this recognition only gives us the "consciousness" of our incessant (eternal) practice of ideological recognition – its consciousness, i.e. its *recognition* – but in no sense does it give us the (scientific) *knowledge* of the mechanism of this recognition. Now it is this knowledge that we have to reach, if you will, while speaking in ideology, and from within ideology we have to outline a discourse which tries to break with ideology, in order to dare to be the beginning of a scientific (i.e. subjectless) discourse on ideology.

Thus in order to represent why the category of the "subject" is constitutive of ideology, which only exists by constituting concrete subjects as subjects, I shall employ a special mode of exposition: "concrete" enough to be recognized, but abstract enough to be thinkable and thought, giving rise to a knowledge.

As a first formulation I shall say: *all ideology hails or interpellates concrete individuals as concrete subjects*, by the functioning of the category of the subject.

This is a proposition which entails that we distinguish for the moment between concrete individuals on the one hand and concrete subjects on the other, although at this level concrete subjects only exist insofar as they are supported by a concrete individual.

I shall then suggest that ideology "acts" or "functions" in such a way that it "recruits" subjects among the individuals (it recruits them all), or "transforms" the individuals into subjects (it transforms them all) by that very precise operation which I have called *interpellation* or hailing, and which can be imagined along the lines of the most commonplace everyday police (or other) hailing: "Hey, you there!"[5]

Assuming that the theoretical scene I have imagined takes place in the street, the hailed individual will turn round. By this mere one-hundred-and-eighty-degree physical conversion, he becomes a *subject*. Why? Because he has recognized that the hail was "really" addressed to him, and that "it was *really him* who was hailed" (and not someone else). Experience shows that the practical telecommunication of hailings is such that they hardly ever miss their man: verbal call or whistle, the one hailed always recognizes that it is really him who is being hailed. And yet it is a strange phenomenon, and one which cannot be explained solely by "guilt feelings," despite the large numbers who "have something on their consciences."

Naturally for the convenience and clarity of my little theoretical theater I have had to present things in the form of a sequence, with a before and an after, and thus in the form of a temporal succession. There are individuals walking along. Somewhere (usually behind them) the hail rings out: "Hey, you there!" One individual (nine times out of ten it is the right one) turns round, believing/suspecting/knowing that it is for him, i.e. recognizing that "it really is he" who is meant by the hailing. But in reality these things happen without any succession. The existence of ideology and the hailing or interpellation of individuals as subjects are one and the same thing.

I might add: what thus seems to take place outside ideology (to be precise, in the street), in reality takes place in ideology. What really takes place in ideology seems therefore to take place outside it. That is why those who are in ideology believe themselves by definition outside ideology: one of the effects of ideology is the practical *denial* of the ideological character of ideology by ideology: ideology never says, "I am ideological." It is necessary to be outside ideology, i.e. in scientific knowledge, to be able to say: I am in ideology (a quite exceptional case) or (the general case): I was in ideology. As is well known, the accusation of being in ideology only applies to others, never to oneself (unless one is really a Spinozist or a Marxist, which, in this matter, is to be exactly the same thing). Which amounts to saying that ideology *has no outside* (for itself), but at the same time *that it is nothing but outside* (for science and reality).

Spinoza explained this completely two centuries before Marx, who practiced it but without explaining it in detail. But let us leave this point, although it is heavy with consequences, consequences which are not just theoretical, but also directly political, since, for example, the whole theory of criticism and self-criticism, the golden rule of the Marxist-Leninist practice of the class struggle, depends on it.

Thus ideology hails or interpellates individuals as subjects. As ideology is eternal, I must now suppress the temporal form in which I have presented the functioning of ideology, and say: ideology has always-already interpellated individuals as subjects; which amounts to making it clear that individuals are always-already interpellated by ideology as subjects, which necessarily leads us to one last proposition: *individuals are always-already subjects.* Hence individuals are "abstract" with respect to the subjects which they always-already are. This proposition might seem paradoxical.

That an individual is always-already a subject, even before he is born, is nevertheless the plain reality, accessible to everyone and not a paradox at all. Freud shows that individuals are always "abstract" with respect to the subjects they always-already are, simply noting the ideological ritual that surrounds the expectation of a "birth," that "happy event." Everyone knows how much and in what way an unborn child is expected. Which amounts to saying, very prosaically, if we agree to drop the "sentiments," i.e. the forms of family ideology (paternal/maternal/conjugal/fraternal) in which the unborn child is expected: it is certain in advance that it will bear its father's name, and will therefore have an identity and be irreplaceable. Before its birth, the child is therefore always-already a subject, appointed as a subject in and by the specific familial ideological configuration in which it is "expected" once it has been conceived. I hardly need add that this familial ideological configuration is, in its uniqueness, highly structured, and that it is in this implacable and more or less "pathological" (presupposing that any meaning can be assigned to that term) structure that the former subject-to-be will have to "find" "its" place, i.e., "become" the sexual subject (boy or girl) which it already is in advance. It is clear that this ideological constraint and pre-appointment, and all the rituals of rearing and then education in the family, have some relationship with what Freud studied in the forms of the pre-genital and genital "stages" of sexuality, i.e. in the "grip" of what Freud registered by its effects as being the unconscious. But let us leave this point, too, to one side... .

Let me summarize what we have discovered about ideology in general.

The duplicate mirror-structure of ideology ensures simultaneously:

1. the interpellation of "individuals" as subjects;
2. their subjection to the Subject;[6]

3.   the mutual recognition of subjects and Subject, the subjects' recognition of each other, and finally the subject's recognition of himself;[7]
4.   the absolute guarantee that everything really is so, and that on condition that the subjects recognize what they are and behave accordingly, everything will be all right: Amen – *"So be it."*

Result: caught in this quadruple system of interpellation as subjects, of subjection to the Subject, of universal recognition and of absolute guarantee, the subjects "work," they "work by themselves" in the vast majority of cases, with the exception of the "bad subjects" who on occasion provoke the intervention of one of the detachments of the (repressive) State apparatus. But the vast majority of (good) subjects work all right "all by themselves," i.e. by ideology (whose concrete forms are realized in the Ideological State Apparatuses [ISAs]). They are inserted into practices governed by the rituals of the ISAs. They "recognize" the existing state of affairs (*das Bestehende*), that "it really is true that it is so and not otherwise," and that they must be obedient to God, to their conscience, to the priest, to de Gaulle, to the boss, to the engineer, that thou shalt "love thy neighbour as thyself," etc. Their concrete, material behavior is simply the inscription in life of the admirable words of the prayer: "Amen – *So be it.*"

Yes, the subjects "work by themselves." The whole mystery of this effect lies in the first two moments of the quadruple system I have just discussed, or, if you prefer, in the ambiguity of the term *subject*. In the ordinary use of the term, subject in fact means: (1) a free subjectivity, a center of initiatives, author of and responsible for its actions; (2) a subjected being who submits to a higher authority, and is therefore stripped of all freedom except that of freely accepting his submission. This last note gives us the meaning of this ambiguity, which is merely a reflection of the effect which produces it: the individual *is interpellated as a (free) subject in order that he shall (freely) accept his subjection*, i.e. in order that he shall make the gestures and actions of his subjection "all by himself." *There are no subjects except by and for their subjection.* That is why they "work all by themselves."

"*So be it! …*" This phrase which registers the effect to be obtained proves that it is not "naturally" so ("naturally": outside the prayer, i.e. outside the ideological intervention). This phrase proves that it *has* to be so if things are to be what they must be, and let us let the words slip: if the reproduction of the relations of production is to be assured, even in the processes of production and circulation, every day, in the "consciousness," i.e. in the attitudes of the individual subjects occupying the posts which the socio-technical division of labor assigns to them in production, exploitation, repression, ideologization, scientific practice, etc. Indeed, what is really in question in this mechanism of the mirror recognition of the Subject and of the individuals interpellated as subjects, and of the guarantee given by the Subject to the subjects if they freely accept their subjection to the Subject's "commandments"? The reality in question in this mechanism, the reality which is necessarily *misrecognized* (*méconnue*) in the very forms of recognition (ideology = misrecognition/ignorance) is indeed, in the last resort, the reproduction of the relations of production and of the relations deriving from them.

Notes

1   I use this very modern term deliberately. For even in Communist circles, unfortunately, it is a commonplace to "explain" some political deviation (left or right opportunism) by the action of a "clique."

2 Which borrowed the legal category of "subject in law" to make an ideological notion: man is by nature a subject.

3 Linguists and those who appeal to linguistics for various purposes often run up against difficulties which arise because they ignore the action of the ideological effects in all discourses – including even scientific discourses.

4 NB: this double "currently" is one more proof of the fact that ideology is "eternal," since these two "currentlys" are separated by an indefinite interval; I am writing these lines on April 6, 1969, you may read them at any subsequent time.

5 Hailing as an everyday practice subject to a precise ritual takes a quite "special" form in the policeman's practice of "hailing," which concerns the hailing of "suspects."

6 By "Subject," Althusser means the deity. [Eds.]

7 Hegel is (unknowingly) an admirable "theoretician" of ideology insofar as he is a "theoretician" of Universal Recognition who unfortunately ends up in the ideology of Absolute Knowledge. Feuerbach is an astonishing "theoretician" of the mirror connexion, who unfortunately ends up in the ideology of the Human Essence. To find the material with which to construct a theory of the guarantee, we must turn to Spinoza.

CHAPTER 7

Right of Death and Power over Life

Michel Foucault

In this famous essay, Michel Foucault introduced the concept of "biopower." In the past sovereigns assumed the right to decide life or death in regard to their subjects. With time, that right has diminished, but, according to Foucault, power over life merely shifted mode of operation and became more insidious and pervasive, operating now through mechanisms of knowledge such as police reports or psychiatric examinations and through the disciplinary management of bodies for purposes that seem positive and enabling such as work.

For a long time, one of the characteristic privileges of sovereign power was the right to decide life and death. In a formal sense, it derived no doubt from the ancient *patria potestas* that granted the father of the Roman family the right to "dispose" of the life of his children and his slaves; just as he had given them life, so he could take it away. By the time the right of life and death was framed by the classical theoreticians, it was in a considerably diminished form. It was no longer considered that this power of the sovereign over his subjects could be exercised in an absolute and unconditional way, but only in cases where the sovereign's very existence was in jeopardy: a sort of right of rejoinder. If he were threatened by external enemies who sought to overthrow him or contest his rights, he could then legitimately wage war, and require his subjects to take part in the defense of the state; without "directly proposing their death," he was empowered to "expose their life": in this sense, he wielded an "indirect" power over them of life and death.[1] But if someone dared to rise up against him and transgress his laws, then he could exercise a direct power over the offender's life: as punishment, the latter would be put to death. Viewed in this way, the power of life and death was not an absolute privilege: it was conditioned by the defense of the sovereign, and his own survival. Must we follow Hobbes in seeing it as the transfer to the prince of the natural right possessed by every individual to defend his life even if this meant the death of others? Or should it be regarded as a specific right that was manifested with the formation of that new juridical

Original publication details: Michel Foucault, "Right of Death and Power over Life" from *History of Sexuality*, trans. Robert Hurley, pp. 133–159. Random House and Editions Gallimard, 1978. Reproduced with permission from Penguin UK and Georges Borchardt, Inc., for Editions Gallimard.

Literary Theory: An Anthology, Third Edition. Edited by Julie Rivkin and Michael Ryan.
© 2017 John Wiley & Sons, Ltd. Published 2017 by John Wiley & Sons, Ltd.

being, the sovereign?[2] In any case, in its modern form – relative and limited – as in its ancient and absolute form, the right of life and death is a dissymmetrical one. The sovereign exercised his right of life only by exercising his right to kill, or by refraining from killing; he evidenced his power over life only through the death he was capable of requiring. The right which was formulated as the "power of life and death" was in reality the right to *take* life or *let* live. Its symbol, after all, was the sword. Perhaps this juridical form must be referred to a historical type of society in which power was exercised mainly as a means of deduction (*prélèvement*), a subtraction mechanism, a right to appropriate a portion of the wealth, a tax of products, goods and services, labor and blood, levied on the subjects. Power in this instance was essentially a right of seizure: of things, time, bodies, and ultimately life itself; it culminated in the privilege to seize hold of life in order to suppress it.

Since the classical age the West has undergone a very profound transformation of these mechanisms of power. "Deduction" has tended to be no longer the major form of power but merely one element among others, working to incite, reinforce, control, monitor, optimize, and organize the forces under it: a power bent on generating forces, making them grow, and ordering them, rather than one dedicated to impeding them, making them submit, or destroying them. There has been a parallel shift in the right of death, or at least a tendency to align itself with the exigencies of a life-administering power and to define itself accordingly. This death that was based on the right of the sovereign is now manifested as simply the reverse of the right of the social body to ensure, maintain, or develop its life. Yet wars were never as bloody as they have been since the nineteenth century, and all things being equal, never before did regimes visit such holocausts on their own populations. But this formidable power of death – and this is perhaps what accounts for part of its force and the cynicism with which it has so greatly expanded its limits – now presents itself as the counterpart of a power that exerts a positive influence on life, that endeavors to administer, optimize, and multiply it, subjecting it to precise controls and comprehensive regulations. Wars are no longer waged in the name of a sovereign who must be defended; they are waged on behalf of the existence of everyone; entire populations are mobilized for the purpose of wholesale slaughter in the name of life necessity: massacres have become vital. It is as managers of life and survival, of bodies and the race, that so many regimes have been able to wage so many wars, causing so many men to be killed. And through a turn that closes the circle, as the technology of wars has caused them to tend increasingly toward all-out destruction, the decision that initiates them and the one that terminates them are in fact increasingly informed by the naked question of survival. The atomic situation is now at the end point of this process: the power to expose a whole population to death is the underside of the power to guarantee an individual's continued existence. The principle underlying the tactics of battle – that one has to be capable of killing in order to go on living – has become the principle that defines the strategy of states. But the existence in question is no longer the juridical existence of sovereignty; at stake is the biological existence of a population. If genocide is indeed the dream of modern powers, this is not because of a recent return of the ancient right to kill; it is because power is situated and exercised at the level of life, the species, the race, and the large-scale phenomena of population.

On another level, I might have taken up the example of the death penalty. Together with war, it was for a long time the other form of the right of the sword; it constituted the reply of the sovereign to those who attacked his will, his law, or his person. Those who died on the scaffold became fewer and fewer, in contrast to those who died in wars.

But it was for the same reasons that the latter became more numerous and the former more and more rare. As soon as power gave itself the function of administering life, its reason for being and the logic of its exercise – and not the awakening of humanitarian feelings – made it more and more difficult to apply the death penalty. How could power exercise its highest prerogatives by putting people to death, when its main role was to ensure, sustain, and multiply life, to put this life in order? For such a power, execution was at the same time a limit, a scandal, and a contradiction. Hence capital punishment could not be maintained except by invoking less the enormity of the crime itself than the monstrosity of the criminal, his incorrigibility, and the safeguard of society. One had the right to kill those who represented a kind of biological danger to others.

One might say that the ancient right to *take* life or *let* live was replaced by a power to *foster* life or *disallow* it to the point of death. This is perhaps what explains that disqualification of death which marks the recent wane of the rituals that accompanied it. That death is so carefully evaded is linked less to a new anxiety which makes death unbearable for our societies than to the fact that the procedures of power have not ceased to turn away from death. In the passage from this world to the other, death was the manner in which a terrestrial sovereignty was relieved by another, singularly more powerful sovereignty; the pageantry that surrounded it was in the category of political ceremony. Now it is over life, throughout its unfolding, that power establishes its dominion; death is power's limit, the moment that escapes it; death becomes the most secret aspect of existence, the most "private." It is not surprising that suicide – once a crime, since it was a way to usurp the power of death which the sovereign alone, whether the one here below or the Lord above, had the right to exercise – became, in the course of the nineteenth century, one of the first conducts to enter into the sphere of sociological analysis; it testified to the individual and private right to die, at the borders and in the interstices of power that was exercised over life. This determination to die, strange and yet so persistent and constant in its manifestations, and consequently so difficult to explain as being due to particular circumstances or individual accidents, was one of the first astonishments of a society in which political power had assigned itself the task of administering life.

In concrete terms, starting in the seventeenth century, this power over life evolved in two basic forms; these forms were not antithetical, however; they constituted rather two poles of development linked together by a whole intermediary cluster of relations. One of these poles – the first to be formed, it seems – centered on the body as a machine: its disciplining, the optimization of its capabilities, the extortion of its forces, the parallel increase of its usefulness and its docility, its integration into systems of efficient and economic controls, all this was ensured by the procedures of power that characterized the *disciplines: an anatomo-politics of the human body*. The second, formed somewhat later, focused on the species body, the body imbued with the mechanics of life and serving as the basis of the biological processes: propagation, births and mortality, the level of health, life expectancy and longevity, with all the conditions that can cause these to vary. Their supervision was effected through an entire series of interventions and *regulatory controls: a biopolitics of the population*. The disciplines of the body and the regulations of the population constituted the two poles around which the organization of power over life was deployed. The setting up, in the course of the classical age, of this great bipolar technology – anatomic and biological, individualizing and specifying, directed toward the performances of the body, with attention to the processes of life – characterized a power whose highest function was perhaps no longer to kill, but to invest life through and through.

The old power of death that symbolized sovereign power was now carefully supplanted by the administration of bodies and the calculated management of life. During the classical period, there was a rapid development of various disciplines – universities, secondary schools, barracks, workshops; there was also the emergence, in the field of political practices and economic observation, of the problems of birthrate, longevity, public health, housing, and migration. Hence there was an explosion of numerous and diverse techniques for achieving the subjugation of bodies and the control of populations, marking the beginning of an era of "biopower." The two directions taken by its development still appeared to be clearly separate in the eighteenth century. With regard to discipline, this development was embodied in institutions such as the army and the schools, and in reflections on tactics, apprenticeship, education, and the nature of societies, ranging from the strictly military analyses of Marshal de Saxe to the political reveries of Guibert or Servan. As for population controls, one notes the emergence of demography, the evaluation of the relationship between resources and inhabitants, the constructing of tables analyzing wealth and its circulation: the work of Quesnay, Moheau, and Süssmilch. The philosophy of the "Ideologists," as a theory of ideas, signs, and the individual genesis of sensations, but also a theory of the social composition of interests – Ideology being a doctrine of apprenticeship, but also a doctrine of contracts and the regulated formation of the social body – no doubt constituted the abstract discourse in which one sought to coordinate these two techniques of power in order to construct a general theory of it. In point of fact, however, they were not to be joined at the level of a speculative discourse, but in the form of concrete arrangements (*agencements concrets*) that would go to make up the great technology of power in the nineteenth century: the deployment of sexuality would be one of them, and one of the most important.

This bio-power was without question an indispensable element in the development of capitalism; the latter would not have been possible without the controlled insertion of bodies into the machinery of production and the adjustment of the phenomena of population to economic processes. But this was not all it required; it also needed the growth of both these factors, their reinforcement as well as their availability and docility; it had to have methods of power capable of optimizing forces, aptitudes, and life in general without at the same time making them more difficult to govern. If the development of the great instruments of the state, as *institutions* of power, ensured the maintenance of production relations, the rudiments of anatomo- and bio-politics, created in the eighteenth century as *techniques* of power present at every level of the social body and utilized by very diverse institutions (the family and the army, schools and the police, individual medicine and the administration of collective bodies), operated in the sphere of economic processes, their development, and the forces working to sustain them. They also acted as factors of segregation and social hierarchization, exerting their influence on the respective forces of both these movements, guaranteeing relations of domination and effects of hegemony. The adjustment of the accumulation of men to that of capital, the joining of the growth of human groups to the expansion of productive forces and the differential allocation of profit, were made possible in part by the exercise of bio-power in its many forms and modes of application. The investment of the body, its valorization, and the distributive management of its forces were at the time indispensable.

One knows how many times the question has been raised concerning the role of an ascetic morality in the first formation of capitalism; but what occurred in the eighteenth century in some Western countries, an event bound up with the development of capitalism, was a different phenomenon having perhaps a wider impact than the new morality;

this was nothing less than the entry of life into history, that is, the entry of phenomena peculiar to the life of the human species into the order of knowledge and power, into the sphere of political techniques. It is not a question of claiming that this was the moment when the first contact between life and history was brought about. On the contrary, the pressure exerted by the biological on the historical had remained very strong for thousands of years; epidemics and famine were the two great dramatic forms of this relationship that was always dominated by the menace of death. But through a circular process, the economic – and primarily agricultural – development of the eighteenth century, and an increase in productivity and resources even more rapid than the demographic growth it encouraged, allowed a measure of relief from these profound threats: despite some renewed outbreaks, the period of great ravages from starvation and plague had come to a close before the French Revolution; death was ceasing to torment life so directly. But at the same time, the development of the different fields of knowledge concerned with life in general, the improvement of agricultural techniques, and the observations and measures relative to man's life and survival contributed to this relaxation: a relative control over life averted some of the imminent risks of death. In the space for movement thus conquered, and broadening and organizing that space, methods of power and knowledge assumed responsibility for the life processes and undertook to control and modify them. Western man was gradually learning what it meant to be a living species in a living world, to have a body, conditions of existence, probabilities of life, an individual and collective welfare, forces that could be modified, and a space in which they could be distributed in an optimal manner. For the first time in history, no doubt, biological existence was reflected in political existence; the fact of living was no longer an inaccessible substrate that only emerged from time to time, amid the randomness of death and its fatality; part of it passed into knowledge's field of control and power's sphere of intervention. Power would no longer be dealing simply with legal subjects over whom the ultimate dominion was death, but with living beings, and the mastery it would be able to exercise over them would have to be applied at the level of life itself; it was the taking charge of life, more than the threat of death, that gave power its access even to the body. If one can apply the term *bio-history* to the pressures through which the movements of life and the processes of history interfere with one another, one would have to speak of *bio-power* to designate what brought life and its mechanisms into the realm of explicit calculations and made knowledge-power an agent of transformation of human life. It is not that life has been totally integrated into techniques that govern and administer it; it constantly escapes them. Outside the Western world, famine exists, on a greater scale than ever; and the biological risks confronting the species are perhaps greater, and certainly more serious, than before the birth of microbiology. But what might be called a society's "threshold of modernity" has been reached when the life of the species is wagered on its own political strategies. For millennia, man remained what he was for Aristotle: a living animal with the additional capacity for a political existence; modern man is an animal whose politics places his existence as a living being in question.

This transformation had considerable consequences. It would serve no purpose here to dwell on the rupture that occurred then in the pattern of scientific discourse and on the manner in which the twofold problematic of life and man disrupted and redistributed the order of the classical episteme. If the question of man was raised – insofar as he was a specific living being, and specifically related to other living beings – the reason for this is to be sought in the new mode of relation between history and life: in this dual position of life that placed it at the same time outside history, in its biological environment, and inside human historicity, penetrated by the latter's techniques of knowledge and power. There is no need either to lay further stress on the proliferation of political technologies that ensued, investing the body, health, modes of subsistence and habitation, living conditions, the whole space of existence.

Another consequence of this development of bio-power was the growing importance assumed by the action of the norm, at the expense of the juridical system of the law. Law cannot help but be armed, and its arm, *par excellence*, is death; to those who transgress it, it replies, at least as a last resort, with that absolute menace. The law always refers to the sword. But a power whose task is to take charge of life needs continuous regulatory and corrective mechanisms. It is no longer a matter of bringing death into play in the field of sovereignty, but of distributing the living in the domain of value and utility. Such a power has to qualify, measure, appraise, and hierarchize, rather than display itself in its murderous splendor; it does not have to draw the line that separates the enemies of the sovereign from his obedient subjects; it effects distributions around the norm. I do not mean to say that the law fades into the background or that the institutions of justice tend to disappear, but rather that the law operates more and more as a norm, and that the judicial institution is increasingly incorporated into a continuum of apparatuses (medical, administrative, and so on) whose functions are for the most part regulatory. A normalizing society is the historical outcome of a technology of power centered on life. We have entered a phase of juridical regression in comparison with the pre-seventeenth-century societies we are acquainted with; we should not be deceived by all the Constitutions framed throughout the world since the French Revolution, the Codes written and revised, a whole continual and clamorous legislative activity: these were the forms that made an essentially normalizing power acceptable.

Moreover, against this power that was still new in the nineteenth century, the forces that resisted relied for support on the very thing it invested, that is, on life and man as a living being. Since the last century, the great struggles that have challenged the general system of power were not guided by the belief in a return to former rights, or by the age-old dream of a cycle of time or a Golden Age. One no longer aspired toward the coming of the emperor of the poor, or the kingdom of the latter days, or even the restoration of our imagined ancestral rights; what was demanded and what served as an objective was life, understood as the basic needs, man's concrete essence, the realization of his potential, a plenitude of the possible. Whether or not it was Utopia that was wanted is of little importance; what we have seen has been a very real process of struggle; life as a political object was in a sense taken at face value and turned back against the system that was bent on controlling it. It was life more than the law that became the issue of political struggles, even if the latter were formulated through affirmations concerning rights. The "right" to life, to one's body, to health, to happiness, to the satisfaction of needs, and beyond all the oppressions or "alienations," the "right" to rediscover what one is and all that one can be, this "right" – which the classical juridical system was utterly incapable of comprehending – was the political response to all these new procedures of power which did not derive, either, from the traditional right of sovereignty.

This is the background that enables us to understand the importance assumed by sex as a political issue. It was at the pivot of the two axes along which developed the entire political technology of life. On the one hand it was tied to the disciplines of the body: the harnessing, intensification, and distribution of forces, the adjustment and economy of energies. On the other hand, it was applied to the regulation of populations, through all the far-reaching effects of its activity. It fitted in both categories at once, giving rise to infinitesimal surveillances, permanent controls, extremely meticulous orderings of space, indeterminate medical or psychological examinations, to an entire micro-power concerned with the body. But it gave rise as well to comprehensive measures, statistical assessments, and interventions aimed at the entire social body or at groups taken as a whole. Sex was a means of access both to the life of the body and the life of the species. It was employed as a standard for the disciplines and as a basis for regulations. This is why in the nineteenth century sexuality was sought out in the smallest details of individual existences; it was tracked down in behavior, pursued in dreams; it was suspected of underlying the least follies, it was traced back into the earliest years of childhood; it became the stamp of individuality – at the same time what enabled one to analyze the latter and what made it possible to master it. But one also sees it becoming the theme of political operations, economic interventions (through incitements to or curbs on procreation), and ideological campaigns for raising standards of morality and responsibility: it was put forward as the index of a society's strength, revealing of both its political energy and its biological vigor. Spread out from one pole to the other of this technology of sex was a whole series of different tactics that combined in varying proportions the objective of disciplining the body and that of regulating populations.

Whence the importance of the four great lines of attack along which the politics of sex advanced for two centuries. Each one was a way of combining disciplinary techniques with regulative methods. The first two rested on the requirements of regulation, on a whole thematic of the species, descent, and collective welfare, in order to obtain results at the level of discipline; the sexualization of children was accomplished in the form of a campaign for the health of the race (precocious sexuality was presented from the eighteenth century to the end of the nineteenth as an epidemic menace that risked compromising not only the future health of adults but the future of the entire society and species); the hysterization of women, which involved a thorough medicalization of their bodies and their sex, was carried out in the name of the responsibility they owed to the health of their children, the solidity of the family institution, and the safeguarding of society. It was the reverse relationship that applied in the case of birth controls and the psychiatrization of perversions: here the intervention was regulatory in nature, but it had to rely on the demand for individual disciplines and constraints *(dressages)*. Broadly speaking, at the juncture of the "body" and the "population," sex became a crucial target of a power organized around the management of life rather than the menace of death.

The blood relation long remained an important element in the mechanisms of power, its manifestations, and its rituals. For a society in which the systems of alliance, the political form of the sovereign, the differentiation into orders and castes, and the value of descent lines were predominant; for a society in which famine, epidemics, and violence made death imminent, blood constituted one of the fundamental values. It owed its high value at the same time to its instrumental role (the ability to shed blood), to the way it functioned in the order of signs (to have a certain blood, to be of the same blood, to be prepared to risk one's blood), and also to its precariousness (easily spilled, subject to drying up, too readily mixed, capable of being quickly corrupted). A society of blood – I was tempted to say, of "sanguinity" – where power spoke *through* blood: the honor of war, the fear of famine, the triumph of death, the sovereign with his sword, executioners, and tortures; blood was *a reality with a symbolic function*. We, on the other hand, are in a society of "sex," or rather a society "with a sexuality": the mechanisms of power are addressed to the body, to life, to what causes it to proliferate, to what reinforces the species, its stamina, its ability to dominate, or its capacity for being used. Through the themes of health, progeny, race, the future of the species, the vitality of the social body, power spoke *of* sexuality and *to* sexuality; the latter was not a mark or a symbol, it was an object and a target. Moreover, its importance was due less to its rarity or its precariousness than to its insistence, its insidious presence, the fact that it was everywhere an object of excitement and fear at the same time. Power delineated it, aroused it, and employed it as the proliferating meaning that had always to be taken control of again lest it escape; it was *an effect with a meaning-value*. I do not mean to say that a substitution of sex for blood was by itself responsible for all the transformations that marked the threshold of our modernity. It is not the soul of two civilizations or the organizing principle of two cultural forms that I am attempting to express; I am looking for the reasons for which sexuality, far from being repressed in the society of that period, on the contrary was constantly aroused. The new procedures of power that were devised during the classical age and employed in the nineteenth century were what caused our societies to go from *a symbolics of blood* to *an analytics of sexuality*. Clearly, nothing was more on the side of the law, death, transgression, the symbolic, and sovereignty than blood; just as sexuality was on the side of the norm, knowledge, life, meaning, the disciplines, and regulations.

Sade and the first eugenists were contemporary with this transition from "sanguinity" to "sexuality." But whereas the first dreams of the perfecting of the species inclined the whole problem toward an extremely exacting administration of sex (the art of determining good marriages, of inducing the desired fertilities, of ensuring the health and longevity of children), and while the new concept of race tended to obliterate the aristocratic particularities of blood, retaining only the controllable effects of sex, Sade carried the exhaustive analysis of sex over into the mechanisms of the old power of sovereignty and endowed it with the ancient but fully maintained prestige of blood; the latter flowed through the whole dimension of pleasure – the blood of torture and absolute power, the blood of the caste which was respected in itself and which nonetheless was made to flow in the major rituals of parricide and incest, the blood of the people, which was shed unreservedly since the sort that flowed in its veins was not even deserving of a name. In Sade, sex is without any norm or intrinsic rule that might be formulated from its own nature; but it is subject to the unrestricted law of a power which itself knows no other law but its own; if by chance it is at times forced to accept the order of progressions carefully disciplined into successive days, this exercise carries it to a point where it is no longer anything but a unique and naked sovereignty: an unlimited right of all-powerful monstrosity.

While it is true that the analytics of sexuality and the symbolics of blood were grounded at first in two very distinct regimes of power, in actual fact the passage from one to the other did not come about (any more than did these powers themselves) without overlappings, interactions, and echoes. In different ways, the preoccupation with blood and the law has for nearly two centuries haunted the administration of sexuality. Two of these interferences are noteworthy, the one for its historical importance, the other for the problems it poses. Beginning in the second half of the nineteenth century, the thematics of blood was sometimes called on to lend its entire historical weight toward revitalizing the type of political power that was exercised through the devices of sexuality. Racism took shape at this point (racism in its modern, "biologizing," statist form): it was then that a whole politics of settlement *(peuplement)*, family, marriage, education, social hierarchization, and property, accompanied by a long series of permanent interventions at the level of the body, conduct, health, and everyday life, received their color and their justification from the mythical concern with protecting the purity of the blood and ensuring the triumph of the race. Nazism was doubtless the most cunning and the most naïve (and the former because of the latter) combination of the fantasies of blood and the paroxysms of a disciplinary power. A eugenic ordering of society, with all that implied in the way of extension and intensification of micro-powers, in the guise of an unrestricted state control *(étatisation)*, was accompanied by the oneiric exaltation of a superior blood; the latter implied both the systematic genocide of others and the risk of exposing oneself to a total sacrifice. It is an irony of history that the Hitlerite politics of sex remained an insignificant practice while the blood myth was transformed into the greatest blood bath in recent memory.

At the opposite extreme, starting from this same end of the nineteenth century, we can trace the theoretical effort to reinscribe the thematic of sexuality in the system of law, the symbolic order, and sovereignty. It is to the political credit of psychoanalysis – or at least, of what was most coherent in it – that it regarded with suspicion (and this from its inception, that is, from the moment it broke away from the neuropsychiatry of degenerescence) the irrevocably proliferating aspects which might be contained in these power mechanisms aimed at controlling and administering the everyday life of sexuality: whence the Freudian endeavor (out of reaction no doubt to the great surge of racism that was contemporary with it) to ground sexuality in the law – the law of alliance, tabooed consanguinity, and the Sovereign-Father, in short, to surround desire with all the trappings of the old order of power. It was owing to this that psychoanalysis was – in the main, with a few exceptions – in theoretical and practical opposition to fascism. But this position of psychoanalysis was tied to a specific historical conjuncture. And yet, to conceive the category of the sexual in terms of the law, death, blood, and sovereignty – whatever the references to Sade and Bataille, and however one might gauge their "subversive" influence – is in the last analysis a historical "retro-version." We must conceptualize the deployment of sexuality on the basis of the techniques of power that are contemporary with it.

People are going to say that I am dealing in a historicism which is more careless than radical; that I am evading the biologically established existence of sexual functions for the benefit of phenomena that are variable, perhaps, but fragile, secondary, and ultimately superficial; and that I speak of sexuality as if sex did not exist. And one would be entitled to object as follows: "You claim to analyze in detail the processes by which women's bodies, the lives of children, family relationships, and an entire network of social relations were sexualized. You wish to describe that great awakening of sexual concern since the eighteenth century and our growing eagerness to suspect the presence of sex in everything. Let us admit as much and suppose that the mechanisms of power were in fact used more to arouse and 'excite' sexuality than to repress it. But here you remain quite near to the thing you no doubt believe you have gotten away from; at bottom, when you point out phenomena of diffusion, anchorage, and fixation of sexuality, you are trying to reveal what might be called the organization of 'erotic zones' in the social body; it may well be the case that you have done nothing more than transpose to the level of diffuse processes mechanisms which psychoanalysis has identified with precision at the level of the individual. But you pass over the thing on the basis of which this sexualization was able to develop and which psychoanalysis does not fail to recognize – namely, sex. Before Freud, one sought to localize sexuality as closely as possible: in sex, in its reproductive functions, in its immediate anatomical localizations; one fell back upon a biological minimum: organ, instinct, and finality. You, on the other hand, are in a symmetrical and inverse position: for you, there remain only groundless effects, ramifications without roots, a sexuality without a sex. What is this if not castration once again?"

Here we need to distinguish between two questions. First, does the analysis of sexuality necessarily imply the elision of the body, anatomy, the biological, the functional? To this question, I think we can reply in the negative. In any case, the purpose of the present study is in fact to show how deployments of power are directly connected to the body – to bodies, functions, physiological processes, sensations, and pleasures; far from the body having to be effaced, what is needed is to make it visible through an analysis in which the biological and the historical are not consecutive to one another, as in the evolutionism of the first sociologists, but are bound together in an increasingly complex fashion in accordance with the development of the modern technologies of power that take life as their objective. Hence I do not envisage a "history of mentalities" that would take account of bodies only through the manner in which they have been perceived and given meaning and value; but a "history of bodies" and the manner in which what is most material and most vital in them has been invested.

Another question, distinct from the first one: this materiality that is referred to, is it not, then, that of sex, and is it not paradoxical to venture a history of sexuality at the level of bodies, without there being the least question of sex? After all, is the power that is exercised through sexuality not directed specifically at that element of reality which is "sex," sex in general? That sexuality is not, in relation to power, an exterior domain to which power is applied, that on the contrary it is a result and an instrument of power's designs, is all very well. But as for sex, is it not the "other" with respect to power, while being the center around which sexuality distributes its effects? Now, it is precisely this idea of sex *in itself* that we cannot accept without examination. Is "sex" really the anchorage point that supports the manifestations of sexuality, or is it not rather a complex idea that was formed inside the deployment of sexuality? In any case, one could show how this idea of sex took form in the different strategies of power and the definite role it played therein.

All along the great lines which the development of the deployment of sexuality has followed since the nineteenth century, one sees the elaboration of this idea that there exists something other than bodies, organs, somatic localizations, functions, anatomo-physiological systems, sensations, and pleasures; something else and something more, with intrinsic properties and laws of its own: "sex." Thus, in the process of hysterization of women, "sex" was defined in three ways: as that which belongs in common to men and women; as that which belongs, *par excellence*, to men, and hence is lacking in women; but at the same time, as that which by itself constitutes woman's body, ordering it wholly in terms of the functions of reproduction and keeping it in constant agitation through the effects of that very function. Hysteria was interpreted in this strategy as the movement of sex insofar as it was the "one" and the "other," whole and part, principle and lack. In the sexualization of childhood, there was formed the idea of a sex that was both present (from the evidence of anatomy) and absent (from the standpoint of physiology), present too if one considered its activity, and deficient if one referred to its reproductive finality; or again, actual in its manifestations, but hidden in its eventual effects, whose pathological seriousness would only become apparent later. If the sex of the child was still present in the adult, it was in the form of a secret causality that tended to nullify the sex of the latter (it was one of the tenets of eighteenth- and nineteenth-century medicine that precocious sex would eventually result in sterility, impotence, frigidity, the inability to experience pleasure, or the deadening of the senses); by sexualizing childhood, the idea was established of a sex characterized essentially by the interplay of presence and absence, the visible and the hidden; masturbation and the effects imputed to it were thought to reveal in a privileged way this interplay of presence and absence, of the visible and the hidden.

In the psychiatrization of perversions, sex was related to biological functions and to an anatomo-physiological machinery that gave it its "meaning," that is, its finality; but it was also referred to an instinct which, through its peculiar development and according to the objects to which it could become attached, made it possible for perverse behavior patterns to arise and made their genesis intelligible. Thus "sex" was defined by the interlacing of function and instinct, finality and signification; moreover, this was the form in which it was manifested, more clearly than anywhere else, in the model perversion, in that "fetishism" which, from at least as early as 1877, served as the guiding thread for analyzing all the other deviations. In it one could clearly perceive the way in which the instinct became fastened to an object in accordance with an individual's historical adherence and biological inadequacy. Lastly, in the socialization of procreative behavior, "sex" was described as being caught between a law of reality (economic necessity being its most abrupt and immediate form) and an economy of pleasure which was always attempting to circumvent that law – when, that is, it did not ignore it altogether. The most notorious of "frauds," coitus interruptus, represented the point where the insistence of the real forced an end to pleasure and where the pleasure found a way to surface despite the economy dictated by the real. It is apparent that the deployment of sexuality, with its different strategies, was what established this notion of "sex"; and in the four major forms of hysteria, onanism, fetishism, and interrupted coition, it showed this sex to be governed by the interplay of whole and part, principle and lack, absence and presence, excess and deficiency, by the function of instinct, finality, and meaning, of reality and pleasure.

The theory thus generated performed a certain number of functions that made it indispensable. First, the notion of "sex" made it possible to group together, in an artificial unity, anatomical elements, biological functions, conducts, sensations, and pleasures, and it enabled one to make use of this fictitious unity as a causal principle, an omnipresent meaning, a secret to be discovered everywhere: sex was thus able to function as a unique signifier and as a universal signified. Further, by presenting itself in a unitary fashion, as anatomy and lack, as function and latency, as instinct and meaning, it was able to mark the line of contact between a knowledge of human sexuality and the biological sciences of reproduction; thus, without really borrowing anything from these sciences, excepting a few doubtful analogies, the knowledge of sexuality gained through proximity a guarantee of quasi-scientificity; but by virtue of this same proximity, some of the contents of biology and physiology were able to serve as a principle of normality for human sexuality. Finally, the notion of sex brought about a fundamental reversal; it made it possible to invert the representation of the relationships of power to sexuality, causing the latter to appear, not in its essential and positive relation to power, but as being rooted in a specific and irreducible urgency which power tries as best it can to dominate; thus the idea of "sex" makes it possible to evade what gives "power" its power; it enables one to conceive power solely as law and taboo. Sex – that agency which appears to dominate us and that secret which seems to underlie all that we are, that point which enthralls us through the power it manifests and the meaning it conceals, and which we ask to reveal what we are and to free us from what defines us – is doubtless but an ideal point made necessary by the deployment of sexuality and its operation. We must not make the mistake of thinking that sex is an autonomous agency which secondarily produces manifold effects of sexuality over the entire length of its surface of contact with power. On the contrary, sex is the most speculative, most ideal, and most internal element in a deployment of sexuality organized by power in its grip on bodies and their materiality, their forces, energies, sensations, and pleasures.

It might be added that "sex" performs yet another function that runs through and sustains the ones we have just examined. Its role in this instance is more practical than theoretical. It is through sex – in fact, an imaginary point determined by the deployment of sexuality – that each individual has to pass in order to have access to his own intelligibility (seeing that it is both the hidden aspect and the generative principle of meaning), to the whole of his body (since it is a real and threatened part of it, while symbolically constituting the whole), to his identity (since it joins the force of a drive to the singularity of a history). Through a reversal that doubtless had its surreptitious beginnings long ago – it was already making itself felt at the time of the Christian pastoral of the flesh – we have arrived at the point where we expect our intelligibility to come from what was for many centuries thought of as madness; the plenitude of our body from what was long considered its stigma and likened to a wound; our identity from what was perceived as an obscure and nameless urge. Hence the importance we ascribe to it, the reverential fear with which we surround it, the care we take to know it. Hence the fact that over the centuries it has become more important than our soul, more important almost than our life; and so it is that all the world's enigmas appear frivolous to us compared to this secret, minuscule in each of us, but of a density that makes it more serious than any other. The Faustian pact, whose temptation has been instilled in us by the deployment of sexuality, is now as follows: to exchange life in its entirety for sex itself, for the truth and the sovereignty of sex. Sex is worth dying for. It is in this (strictly historical) sense that sex is indeed imbued with the death instinct. When a long while ago the West discovered love, it bestowed on it a value high enough to make death acceptable; nowadays it is sex that claims this equivalence, the highest of all. And while the deployment of sexuality permits the techniques of power to invest life, the fictitious point of sex, itself marked by that deployment, exerts enough charm on everyone for them to accept hearing the grumble of death within it.

By creating the imaginary element that is "sex," the deployment of sexuality established one of its most essential internal operating principles: the desire for sex – the desire to have it, to have access to it, to discover it, to liberate it, to articulate it in discourse, to formulate it in truth. It constituted "sex" itself as something desirable. And it is this desirability of sex that attaches each one of us to the injunction to know it, to reveal its law and its power; it is this desirability that makes us think we are affirming the rights of our sex against all power, when in fact we are fastened to the deployment of sexuality that has lifted up from deep within us a sort of mirage in which we think we see ourselves reflected – the dark shimmer of sex.

"It is sex," said Kate in *The Plumed Serpent*. "How wonderful sex can be, when men keep it powerful and sacred, and it fills the world! like sunshine through and through one!"

So we must not refer a history of sexuality to the agency of sex; but rather show how "sex" is historically subordinate to sexuality. We must not place sex on the side of reality, and sexuality on that of confused ideas and illusions; sexuality is a very real historical formation; it is what gave rise to the notion of sex, as a speculative element necessary to its operation. We must not think that by saying yes to sex, one says no to power; on the contrary, one tracks along the course laid out by the general deployment of sexuality. It is the agency of sex that we must break away from, if we aim – through a tactical reversal of the various mechanisms of sexuality – to counter the grips of power with the claims of bodies, pleasures, and knowledges, in their multiplicity and their possibility of resistance. The rallying point for the counterattack against the deployment of sexuality ought not to be sex-desire, but bodies and pleasures.

"There has been so much action in the past," said D. H. Lawrence, "especially sexual action, a wearying repetition over and over, without a corresponding thought, a corresponding realization. Now our business is to realize sex. Today the full conscious realization of sex is even more important than the act itself."

Perhaps one day people will wonder at this. They will not be able to understand how a civilization so intent on developing enormous instruments of production and destruction found the time and the infinite patience to inquire so anxiously concerning the actual state of sex; people will smile perhaps when they recall that here were men – meaning ourselves – who believed that therein resided a truth every bit as precious as the one they had already demanded from the earth, the stars, and the pure forms of their thought; people will be surprised at the eagerness with which we went about pretending to rouse from its slumber a sexuality which everything – our discourses, our customs, our institutions, our regulations, our knowledges – was busy producing in the light of day and broadcasting to noisy accompaniment. And people will ask themselves why we were so bent on ending the rule of silence regarding what was the noisiest of our preoccupations. In retrospect, this noise may appear to have been out of place, but how much stranger will seem our persistence in interpreting it as but the refusal to speak and the order to remain silent. People will wonder what could have made us so presumptuous; they will look for the reasons that might explain why we prided ourselves on being the first to grant sex the importance we say is its due and how we came to congratulate ourselves for finally – in the twentieth century – having broken free of a long period of harsh repression, a protracted Christian asceticism, greedily and fastidiously adapted to the imperatives of bourgeois economy. And what we now perceive as the chronicle of a censorship and the difficult struggle to remove it will be seen rather as the centuries-long rise of a complex deployment for compelling sex to speak, for fastening our attention and concern upon sex, for getting us to believe in the sovereignty of its law when in fact we were moved by the power mechanisms of sexuality.

People will be amused at the reproach of pansexualism that was once aimed at Freud and psychoanalysis. But the ones who will appear to have been blind will perhaps be not so much those who formulated the objection as those who discounted it out of hand, as if it merely expressed the fears of an outmoded prudishness. For the first, after all, were only taken unawares by a process which had begun long before and by which, unbeknown to them, they were already surrounded on all sides; what they had attributed solely to the genius of Freud had already gone through a long stage of preparation; they had gotten their dates wrong as to the establishment, in our society, of a general deployment of sexuality. But the others were mistaken concerning the nature of the process; they believed that Freud had at last, through a sudden reversal, restored to sex the rightful share which it had been denied for so long; they had not seen how the good genius of Freud had placed it at one of the critical points marked out for it since the eighteenth century by the strategies of knowledge and power, how wonderfully effective he was – worthy of the greatest spiritual fathers and directors of the classical period – in giving a new impetus to the secular injunction to study sex and transform it into discourse.

We are often reminded of the countless procedures which Christianity once employed to make us detest the body; but let us ponder all the ruses that were employed for centuries to make us love sex, to make the knowledge of it desirable and everything said about it precious. Let us consider the stratagems by which we were induced to apply all our skills to discovering its secrets, by which we were attached to the obligation to draw out its truth, and made guilty for having failed to recognize it for so long. These devices are what ought to make us wonder today. Moreover, we need to consider the possibility that one day, perhaps, in a different economy of bodies and pleasures, people will no longer quite understand how the ruses of sexuality, and the power that sustains its organization, were able to subject us to that austere monarchy of sex, so that we became dedicated to the endless task of forcing its secret, of exacting the truest of confessions from a shadow.

The irony of this deployment is in having us believe that our "liberation" is in the balance.

Notes

1 Samuel von Pufendorf, *Le Droit de la nature* (French trans., 1734), p. 445.
2 "Just as a composite body can have properties not found in any of the simple bodies of which the mixture consists, so a moral body, by virtue of the very union of persons of which it is composed, can have certain rights which none of the individuals could expressly claim and whose exercise is the proper function of leaders alone." Pufendorf, *Le Droit de la nature*, p. 452.

CHAPTER 8

Homo Sacer

Giorgio Agamben

Giorgio Agamben is an Italian philosopher whose works include *The Open* (2004), *Homo Sacer* (2004), and *State of Exception* (2004).

Introduction

The Greeks had no single term to express what we mean by the word "life." They used two terms that, although traceable to a common etymological root, are semantically and morphologically distinct: *zoē*, which expressed the simple fact of living common to all living beings (animals, men, or gods), and *bios*, which indicated the form or way of living proper to an individual or a group. When Plato mentions three kinds of life in the *Philebus*, and when Aristotle distinguishes the contemplative life of the philosopher (*bios theōrētikos*) from the life of pleasure (*bios apolaustikos*) and the political life (*bios politikos*) in the *Nichomachean Ethics*, neither philosopher would ever have used the term *zoē* (which in Greek, significantly enough, lacks a plural). This follows from the simple fact that what was at issue for both thinkers was not at all simple natural life but rather a qualified life, a particular way of life. Concerning God, Aristotle can certainly speak of a *zoē aristē kai aidios*, a more noble and eternal life (*Metaphysics*, 1072b, 28), but only insofar as he means to underline the significant truth that even God is a living being (similarly, Aristotle uses the term *zoē* in the same context – and in a way that is just as meaningful – to define the act of thinking). But to speak of a *zoē politikē* of the citizens of Athens would have made no sense. Not that the classical world had no familiarity with the idea that natural life, simple *zoē* as such, could be a good in itself. In a passage of the *Politics*, after noting that the end of the city is life according to the good, Aristotle expresses his awareness of that idea with the most perfect lucidity:

> This [life according to the good] is the greatest end both in common for all men and for each man separately. But men also come together and maintain the political community in view of simple living, because there is probably some kind of good in the mere fact of living

Original publication details: Giorgio Agamben, "Introduction" and "The Paradox of Sovereignty," from *Homo Sacer*, trans. Daniel Heller-Roazen, pp. 1–29. Stanford University Press, 1998.
Reproduced with permission from the Board of Trustees of the Leland Stanford Jr. University.

Literary Theory: An Anthology, Third Edition. Edited by Julie Rivkin and Michael Ryan.
© 2017 John Wiley & Sons, Ltd. Published 2017 by John Wiley & Sons, Ltd.

itself [*kata to zēn auto monon*]. If there is no great difficulty as to the way of life [*kata ton bion*], clearly most men will tolerate much suffering and hold on to life [*zoē*] as if it were a kind of serenity [*euēmeria*, beautiful day] and a natural sweetness. (1278b, 23–31)

In the classical world, however, simple natural life is excluded from the *polis* in the strict sense, and remains confined – as merely reproductive life – to the sphere of the *oikos*, "home" (*Politics*, 1252a, 26–35). At the beginning of the *Politics*, Aristotle takes the greatest care to distinguish the *oikonomos* (the head of an estate) and the *despotēs* (the head of the family), both of whom are concerned with the reproduction and the subsistence of life, from the politician, and he scorns those who think the difference between the two is one of quantity and not of kind. And when Aristotle defined the end of the perfect community in a passage that was to become canonical for the political tradition of the West (1252b, 30), he did so precisely by opposing the simple fact of living (*to zēn*) to politically qualified life (*to eu zēn*): *ginomenē men oun tou zēn heneken, ousa de tou eu zēn*, "born with regard to life, but existing essentially with regard to the good life" (in the Latin translation of William of Moerbeke, which both Aquinas and Marsilius of Padua had before them: *facta quidem igitur vivendi gratia, existens autem gratia bene vivendi*).

It is true that in a famous passage of the same work, Aristotle defines man as a *politikon zōon* (*Politics*, 1253a, 4). But here (aside from the fact that in Attic Greek the verb *bionai* is practically never used in the present tense), "political" is not an attribute of the living being as such, but rather a specific difference that determines the genus *zōon*. (Only a little later, after all, human politics is distinguished from that of other living beings in that it is founded, through a supplement of politicity [*policità*] tied to language, on a community not simply of the pleasant and the painful but of the good and the evil and of the just and the unjust.)

Michel Foucault refers to this very definition when, at the end of the first volume of *The History of Sexuality*, he summarizes the process by which, at the threshold of the modern era, natural life begins to be included in the mechanisms and calculations of State power, and politics turns into *biopolitics*. "For millennia," he writes, "man remained what he was for Aristotle: a living animal with the additional capacity for political existence; modern man is an animal whose politics calls his existence as a living being into question" (*La volonté*, p. 188).

According to Foucault, a society's "threshold of biological modernity" is situated at the point at which the species and the individual as a simple living body become what is at stake in a society's political strategies. After 1977, the courses at the Collège de France start to focus on the passage from the "territorial State" to the "State of population" and on the resulting increase in importance of the nation's health and biological life as a problem of sovereign power, which is then gradually transformed into a "government of men" (*Dits et écrits*, 3: 719). "What follows is a kind of bestialization of man achieved through the most sophisticated political techniques. For the first time in history, the possibilities of the social sciences are made known, and at once it becomes possible both to protect life and to authorize a holocaust." In particular, the development and triumph of capitalism would not have been possible, from this perspective, without the disciplinary control achieved by the new bio-power, which, through a series of appropriate technologies, so to speak created the "docile bodies" that it needed.

Almost twenty years before *The History of Sexuality*, Hannah Arendt had already analyzed the process that brings *homo laborans* – and, with it, biological life as such – gradually to occupy the very center of the political scene of modernity. In *The Human Condition*,

Arendt attributes the transformation and decadence of the political realm in modern societies to this very primacy of natural life over political action. That Foucault was able to begin his study of biopolitics with no reference to Arendt's work (which remains, even today, practically without continuation) bears witness to the difficulties and resistances that thinking had to encounter in this area. And it is most likely these very difficulties that account for the curious fact that Arendt establishes no connection between her research in *The Human Condition* and the penetrating analyses she had previously devoted to totalitarian power (in which a biopolitical perspective is altogether lacking), and that Foucault, in just as striking a fashion, never dwelt on the exemplary places of modern biopolitics: the concentration camp and the structure of the great totalitarian states of the twentieth century.

Foucault's death kept him from showing how he would have developed the concept and study of biopolitics. In any case, however, the entry of *zoē* into the sphere of the *polis* – the politicization of bare life as such – constitutes the decisive event of modernity and signals a radical transformation of the political-philosophical categories of classical thought. It is even likely that if politics today seems to be passing through a lasting eclipse, this is because politics has failed to reckon with this foundational event of modernity. The "enigmas" (Furet, *L'Allemagne nazi*, p. 7) that our century has proposed to historical reason and that remain with us (Nazism is only the most disquieting among them) will be solved only on the terrain – biopolitics – on which they were formed. Only within a biopolitical horizon will it be possible to decide whether the categories whose opposition founded modern politics (right/left, private/public, absolutism/democracy, etc.) – and which have been steadily dissolving, to the point of entering today into a real zone of indistinction – will have to be abandoned or will, instead, eventually regain the meaning they lost in that very horizon. And only a reflection that, taking up Foucault's and Benjamin's suggestion, thematically interrogates the link between bare life and politics, a link that secretly governs the modern ideologies seemingly most distant from one another, will be able to bring the political out of its concealment and, at the same time, return thought to its practical calling.

One of the most persistent features of Foucault's work is its decisive abandonment of the traditional approach to the problem of power, which is based on juridico–institutional models (the definition of sovereignty, the theory of the State), in favor of an unprejudiced analysis of the concrete ways in which power penetrates subjects' very bodies and forms of life. As shown by a seminar held in 1982 at the University of Vermont, in his final years Foucault seemed to orient this analysis according to two distinct directives for research: on the one hand, the study of the *political techniques* (such as the science of the police) with which the State assumes and integrates the care of the natural life of individuals into its very center; on the other hand, the examination of the *technologies of the self* by which processes of subjectivization bring the individual to bind himself to his own identity and consciousness and, at the same time, to an external power. Clearly these two lines (which carry on two tendencies present in Foucault's work from the very beginning) intersect in many points and refer back to a common center. In one of his last writings, Foucault argues that the modern Western state has integrated techniques of subjective individualization with procedures of objective totalization to an unprecedented degree, and he speaks of a real "political 'double bind,' constituted by individualization and the simultaneous totalization of structures of modern power" (*Dits et écrits*, 4: 229–32).

Yet the point at which these two faces of power converge remains strangely unclear in Foucault's work, so much so that it has even been claimed that Foucault would have consistently refused to elaborate a unitary theory of power. If Foucault contests the traditional approach to the problem of power, which is exclusively based on juridical models ("What legitimates power?") or on institutional models ("What is the State?"), and if he calls for a "liberation from the theoretical privilege of sovereignty" in order to construct an analytic of power that would not take law as its model and code, then where, in the body of power, is the zone of indistinction (or, at least, the point of intersection) at which techniques of individualization and totalizing procedures converge? And, more generally, is there a unitary center in which the political "double bind" finds its *raison d'être*? That there is a subjective aspect in the genesis of power was already implicit in the concept of *servitude volontaire* in Étienne de La Boétie. But what is the point at which the voluntary servitude of individuals comes into contact with objective power? Can one be content, in such a delicate area, with psychological explanations such as the suggestive notion of a parallelism between external and internal neuroses? Confronted with phenomena such as the power of the society of the spectacle that is everywhere transforming the political realm today, is it legitimate or even possible to hold subjective technologies and political techniques apart?

Although the existence of such a line of thinking seems to be logically implicit in Foucault's work, it remains a blind spot to the eye of the researcher, or rather something like a vanishing point that the different perspectival lines of Foucault's inquiry (and, more generally, of the entire Western reflection on power) converge toward without reaching.

The present inquiry concerns precisely this hidden point of intersection between the juridico-institutional and the biopolitical models of power. What this work has had to record among its likely conclusions is precisely that the two analyses cannot be separated, and that the inclusion of bare life in the political realm constitutes the original – if concealed – nucleus of sovereign power. *It can even be said that the production of a biopolitical body is the original activity of sovereign power.* In this sense, biopolitics is at least as old as the sovereign exception. Placing biological life at the center of its calculations, the modern State therefore does nothing other than bring to light the secret tie uniting power and bare life, thereby reaffirming the bond (derived from a tenacious correspondence between the modern and the archaic which one encounters in the most diverse spheres) between modern power and the most immemorial of the *arcana imperii.*

If this is true, it will be necessary to reconsider the sense of the Aristotelian definition of the *polis* as the opposition between life (*zēn*) and good life (*eu zēn*). The opposition is, in fact, at the same time an implication of the first in the second, of bare life in politically qualified life. What remains to be interrogated in the Aristotelian definition is not merely – as has been assumed until now – the sense, the modes, and the possible articulations of the "good life" as the *telos* of the political. We must instead ask why Western politics first constitutes itself through an exclusion (which is simultaneously an inclusion) of bare life. What is the relation between politics and life, if life presents itself as what is included by means of an exclusion?

The structure of the exception delineated in the first part of this book appears from this perspective to be consubstantial with Western politics. In Foucault's statement according to which man was, for Aristotle, a "living animal with the additional capacity for political existence," it is therefore precisely the meaning of this "additional capacity" that must be understood as problematic. The peculiar phrase "born with regard to life, but existing essentially with regard to the good life" can be read not only as an implication of being born (*ginomenē*) in being (*ousa*), but also as an inclusive exclusion (an *exceptio*) of *zoē* in the *polis*, almost as if politics were the place in which life had to transform itself into good life and in which what had to be politicized were always already bare life. In Western politics, bare life has the peculiar privilege of being that whose exclusion founds the city of men.

It is not by chance, then, that a passage of the *Politics* situates the proper place of the *polis* in the transition from voice to language. The link between bare life and politics is the same link that the metaphysical definition of man as "the living being who has language" seeks in the relation between *phonē* and *logos*:

> Among living beings, only man has language. The voice is the sign of pain and pleasure, and this is why it belongs to other living beings (since their nature has developed to the point of having the sensations of pain and pleasure and of signifying the two). But language is for manifesting the fitting and the unfitting and the just and the unjust. To have the sensation of the good and the bad and of the just and the unjust is what is proper to men as opposed to other living beings, and the community of these things makes dwelling and the city. (1253a, 10–18)

The question "In what way does the living being have language?" corresponds exactly to the question "In what way does bare life dwell in the *polis*?" The living being has *logos* by taking away and conserving its own voice in it, even as it dwells in the *polis* by letting its own bare life be excluded, as an exception, within it. Politics therefore appears as the truly fundamental structure of Western metaphysics insofar as it occupies the threshold on which the relation between the living being and the *logos* is realized. In the "politicization" of bare life – the metaphysical task *par excellence* – the humanity of living man is decided. In assuming this task, modernity does nothing other than declare its own faithfulness to the essential structure of the metaphysical tradition. The fundamental categorial pair of Western politics is not that of friend/enemy but that of bare life/political existence, *zoē/bios*, exclusion/inclusion. There is politics because man is the living being who, in language, separates and opposes himself to his own bare life and, at the same time, maintains himself in relation to that bare life in an inclusive exclusion.

The protagonist of this book is bare life, that is, the life of *homo sacer* (sacred man), who *may be killed and yet not sacrificed*, and whose essential function in modern politics we intend to assert. An obscure figure of archaic Roman law, in which human life is included in the juridical order [*ordinamento*][1] solely in the form of its exclusion (that is, of its capacity to be killed), has thus offered the key by which not only the sacred texts of sovereignty but also the very codes of political power will unveil their mysteries. At the same time, however, this ancient meaning of the term *sacer* presents us with the enigma of a figure of the sacred that, before or beyond the religious, constitutes the first paradigm of the political realm of the West. The Foucauldian thesis will then have to be corrected or, at least, completed, in the sense that what characterizes modern politics is not so much the inclusion of *zoē* in the *polis* – which is, in itself, absolutely ancient – nor simply the fact that life as such becomes a principal object of the projections and calculations of State power. Instead the decisive fact is that, together with the process by which the exception everywhere becomes the rule, the realm of bare life – which is originally situated at the margins of the political order – gradually begins to coincide with the political realm, and exclusion and inclusion, outside and inside, *bios* and *zoē*, right and fact, enter into a zone of irreducible indistinction. At once excluding bare life from and capturing it within the political order, the state of exception actually constituted, in its very separateness, the hidden foundation on which the entire political system rested. When its borders begin to be blurred, the bare life that dwelt there frees itself in the city and becomes both subject and object of the conflicts of the political order, the one place for both the organization of State power and emancipation from it. Everything happens as if, along with the disciplinary process by which State power makes man as a living being into its own specific object, another process is set in motion that in large measure corresponds to the birth of modern democracy, in which man as a living being presents himself no longer as an *object* but as the *subject* of political power. These processes – which in many ways oppose and (at least apparently) bitterly conflict with each other – nevertheless converge insofar as both concern the bare life of the citizen, the new biopolitical body of humanity.

If anything characterizes modern democracy as opposed to classical democracy, then, it is that modern democracy presents itself from the beginning as a vindication and liberation of *zoē*, and that it is constantly trying to transform its own bare life into a way of life and to find, so to speak, the *bios* of *zoē*. Hence, too, modern democracy's specific aporia: it wants to put the freedom and happiness of men into play in the very place – "bare life" – that marked their subjection. Behind the long, strife-ridden process that leads to the recognition of rights and formal liberties stands once again the body of the sacred man with his double sovereign, his life that cannot be sacrificed yet may, nevertheless, be killed. To become conscious of this aporia is not to belittle the conquests and accomplishments of democracy. It is, rather, to try to understand once and for all why democracy, at the very moment in which it seemed to have finally triumphed over its adversaries and reached its greatest height, proved itself incapable of saving *zoē*, to whose happiness it had dedicated all its efforts, from unprecedented ruin. Modern democracy's decadence and gradual convergence with totalitarian states in post-democratic spectacular societies (which begins to become evident with Alexis de Tocqueville and finds its final sanction in the analyses of Guy Debord) may well be rooted in this aporia, which marks the beginning of modern democracy and forces it into complicity with its most implacable enemy. Today politics knows no value (and, consequently, no nonvalue) other than life, and until the contradictions that this fact implies are dissolved, Nazism and fascism – which transformed the decision on bare life into the supreme political principle – will remain stubbornly with us. According to the testimony of Robert Antelme, in fact, what the camps taught those who lived there was precisely that "calling into question the quality of man provokes an almost biological assertion of belonging to the human race" (*L'éspèce humaine*, p. 11).

The idea of an inner solidarity between democracy and totalitarianism (which here we must, with every caution, advance) is obviously not (like Leo Strauss's thesis concerning the secret convergence of the final goals of liberalism and communism) a historiographical claim, which would authorize the liquidation and leveling of the enormous differences that characterize their history and their rivalry. Yet this idea must nevertheless be strongly maintained on a historico-philosophical level, since it alone will allow us to orient ourselves in relation to the new realities and unforeseen convergences of the end of the millennium. This idea alone will make it possible to clear the way for the new politics, which remains largely to be invented.

In contrasting the "beautiful day" (*euēmeria*) of simple life with the "great difficulty" of political *bios* in the passage cited above, Aristotle may well have given the most beautiful formulation to the aporia that lies at the foundation of Western politics. The 24 centuries that have since gone by have brought only provisional and ineffective solutions. In carrying out the metaphysical task that has led it more and more to assume the form of a biopolitics, Western politics has not succeeded in constructing the link between *zoē* and *bios*, between voice and language, that would have healed the fracture. Bare life remains included in politics in the form of the exception, that is, as something that is included solely through an exclusion. How is it possible to "politicize" the "natural sweetness" of *zoē*? And first of all, does *zoē* really need to be politicized, or is politics not already contained in *zoē* as its most precious center? The biopolitics of both modern totalitarianism and the society of mass hedonism and consumerism certainly constitute answers to these questions. Nevertheless, until a completely new politics – that is, a politics no longer founded on the *exceptio* of bare life – is at hand, every theory and every praxis will remain imprisoned and immobile, and the "beautiful day" of life will be given citizenship only either through blood and death or in the perfect senselessness to which the society of the spectacle condemns it.

Carl Schmitt's definition of sovereignty ("Sovereign is he who decides on the state of exception") became a commonplace even before there was any understanding that what was at issue in it was nothing less than the limit concept of the doctrine of law and the State, in which sovereignty borders (since every limit concept is always the limit between two concepts) on the sphere of life and becomes indistinguishable from it. As long as the form of the State constituted the fundamental horizon of all communal life and the political, religious, juridical, and economic doctrines that sustained this form were still strong, this "most extreme sphere" could not truly come to light. The problem of sovereignty was reduced to the question of who within the political order was invested with certain powers, and the very threshold of the political order itself was never called into question. Today, now that the great State structures have entered into a process of dissolution and the emergency has, as Walter Benjamin foresaw, become the rule, the time is ripe to place the problem of the originary structure and limits of the form of the State in a new perspective. The weakness of anarchist and Marxian critiques of the State was precisely to have not caught sight of this structure and thus to have quickly left the *arcanum imperii* aside, as if it had no substance outside of the simulacra and the ideologies invoked to justify it. But one ends up identifying with an enemy whose structure one does not understand, and the theory of the State (and in particular of the state of exception, which is to say, of the dictatorship of the proletariat as the transitional phase leading to the stateless society) is the reef on which the revolutions of our century have been shipwrecked.

This book, which was originally conceived as a response to the bloody mystification of a new planetary order, therefore had to reckon with problems – first of all that of the sacredness of life – which the author had not, in the beginning, foreseen. In the course of the undertaking, however, it became clear that one cannot, in such an area, accept as a guarantee any of the notions that the social sciences (from jurisprudence to anthropology) thought they had defined or presupposed as evident, and that many of these notions demanded – in the urgency of catastrophe – to be revised without reserve.

PART ONE

The Logic of Sovereignty

§1 The Paradox of Sovereignty

1.1. The paradox of sovereignty consists in the fact the sovereign is, at the same time, outside and inside the juridical order. If the sovereign is truly the one to whom the juridical order grants the power of proclaiming a state of exception and, therefore, of suspending the order's own validity, then "the sovereign stands outside the juridical order and, nevertheless, belongs to it, since it is up to him to decide if the constitution is to be suspended *in toto*" (Schmitt, *Politische Theologie*, p. 13). The specification that the sovereign is "*at the same time* outside and inside the juridical order" (emphasis added) is not insignificant: the sovereign, having the legal power to suspend the validity of the law, legally places himself outside the law. This means that the paradox can also be formulated this way: "the law is outside itself," or: "I, the sovereign, who am outside the law, declare that there is nothing outside the law [*che non c'è un fuori legge*]*."

The topology implicit in the paradox is worth reflecting upon, since the degree to which sovereignty marks the limit (in the double sense of end and principle) of the juridical order will become clear only once the structure of the paradox is grasped. Schmitt presents this structure as the structure of the exception (*Ausnahme*):

> The exception is that which cannot be subsumed; it defies general codification, but it simultaneously reveals a specifically juridical formal element: the decision in absolute purity. The exception appears in its absolute form when it is a question of creating a situation in which juridical rules can be valid. Every general rule demands a regular, everyday frame of life to which it can be factually applied and which is submitted to its regulations. The rule requires a homogeneous medium. This factual regularity is not merely an "external presupposition" that the jurist can ignore; it belongs, rather, to the rule's immanent validity. There is no rule that is applicable to chaos. Order must be established for juridical order to make sense. A regular situation must be created, and sovereign is he who definitely decides if this situation is actually effective. All law is "situational law." The sovereign creates and guarantees the situation as a whole in its totality. He has the monopoly over the final decision. Therein consists the essence of State sovereignty, which must therefore be properly juridically defined not as the monopoly to sanction or to rule but as the monopoly to decide, where the word "monopoly" is used in a general sense that is still to be developed. The decision reveals the essence of State authority most clearly. Here the decision must be distinguished from the juridical regulation, and (to formulate it paradoxically) authority proves itself not to need law to create law. ... The exception is more interesting than the regular case. The latter proves nothing; the exception proves everything. The exception does not only confirm the rule; the rule as such lives off the exception alone. A Protestant theologian who demonstrated the vital intensity of which theological reflection was still capable in the nineteenth century said: "The exception explains the general and itself. And when one really wants to study the general, one need only look around for a real exception. It brings everything to light more clearly than the general itself. After a while, one becomes disgusted with the endless talk about the general – there are exceptions. If they cannot be explained, then neither can the general be explained. Usually the difficulty is not noticed, since the general is thought about not with passion but only with comfortable superficiality. The exception, on the other hand, thinks the general with intense passion." (*Politische Theologie*, pp. 19–22)

It is not by chance that in defining the exception Schmitt refers to the work of a theologian (who is none other than Søren Kierkegaard). Giambattista Vico had, to be sure, affirmed the superiority of the exception, which he called "the ultimate configuration of facts," over positive law in a way which was not so dissimilar: "An esteemed jurist is, therefore, not someone who, with the help of a good memory, masters positive law [or the general complex of laws], but rather someone who, with sharp judgment, knows how to look into cases and see the ultimate circumstances of facts that merit equitable consideration and exceptions from general rules" (*De antiquissima*, chap. 2). Yet nowhere in the realm of the juridical sciences can one find a theory that grants such a high position to the exception. For what is at issue in the sovereign exception is, according to Schmitt, the very condition of possibility of juridical rule and, along with it, the very meaning of State authority. Through the state of exception, the sovereign "creates and guarantees the situation" that the law needs for its own validity. But what is this "situation," what is its structure, such that it consists in nothing other than the suspension of the rule?

ℵ The Vichian opposition between positive law (*ius theticum*) and exception well expresses the particular status of the exception. The exception is an element in law that transcends positive law in the form of its suspension. The exception is to positive law what negative theology is to positive theology. While the latter affirms and predicates determinate qualities of God, negative (or mystical) theology, with its "neither … nor …," negates and suspends the attribution to God of any predicate whatsoever. Yet negative theology is not outside theology and can actually be shown to function as the principle grounding the possibility in general of anything like a theology. Only because it has been negatively presupposed as what subsists outside any possible predicate can divinity become the subject of a predication. Analogously, only because its validity is suspended in the state of exception can positive law define the normal case as the realm of its own validity.

1.2. The exception is a kind of exclusion. What is excluded from the general rule is an individual case. But the most proper characteristic of the exception is that what is excluded in it is not, on account of being excluded, absolutely without relation to the rule. On the contrary, what is excluded in the exception maintains itself in relation to the rule in the form of the rule's suspension. *The rule applies to the exception in no longer applying, in withdrawing from it.* The state of exception is thus not the chaos that precedes order but rather the situation that results from its suspension. In this sense, the exception is truly, according to its etymological root, *taken outside* (*ex-capere*), and not simply excluded.

It has often been observed that the juridico-political order has the structure of an inclusion of what is simultaneously pushed outside. Gilles Deleuze and Félix Guattari were thus able to write, "Sovereignty only rules over what it is capable of interiorizing" (Deleuze and Guattari, *Mille plateaux*, p. 445); and, concerning the "great confinement" described by Foucault in his *Madness and Civilization*, Maurice Blanchot spoke of society's attempt to "confine the outside" (*enfermer le dehors*), that is, to constitute it in an "interiority of expectation or of exception." Confronted with an excess, the system interiorizes what exceeds it through an interdiction and in this way "designates itself as exterior to itself" (*L'entretien infini*, p. 292). The exception that defines the structure of sovereignty is, however, even more complex. Here what is outside is included not simply by means of an interdiction or an internment, but rather by means of the suspension of the juridical order's validity – by letting the juridical order, that is, withdraw from the exception and abandon it. The exception does not subtract itself from the rule; rather, the rule, suspending itself, gives rise to the exception and, maintaining itself in relation to the exception, first constitutes itself as a rule. The particular "force" of law consists in this capacity of law to maintain itself in relation to an exteriority. We shall give the name *relation of exception* to the extreme form of relation by which something is included solely through its exclusion.

The situation created in the exception has the peculiar characteristic that it cannot be defined either as a situation of fact or as a situation of right, but instead institutes a paradoxical threshold of indistinction between the two. It is not a fact, since it is only created through the suspension of the rule. But for the same reason, it is not even a juridical case in point, even if it opens the possibility of the force of law. This is the ultimate meaning of the paradox that Schmitt formulates when he writes that the sovereign decision "proves itself not to need law to create law." What is at issue in the sovereign exception is not so much the control or neutralization of an excess as the creation and definition of the very space in which the juridico-political order can have validity. In this sense, the sovereign exception is the fundamental localization (*Ortung*), which does not limit itself to distinguishing what is inside from what is outside but instead traces a threshold (the state of exception) between the two, on the basis of which outside and inside, the normal situation and chaos, enter into those complex topological relations that make the validity of the juridical order possible.

The "ordering of space" that is, according to Schmitt, constitutive of the sovereign *nomos* is therefore not only a "taking of land" (*Landesnahme*) – the determination of a juridical and a territorial ordering (of an *Ordnung* and an *Ortung*) – but above all a "taking of the outside," an exception (*Ausnahme*).

ℵ Since "there is no rule that is applicable to chaos," chaos must first be included in the juridical order through the creation of a zone of indistinction between outside and inside, chaos and the normal situation – the state of exception. To refer to something, a rule must both presuppose and yet still establish a relation with what is outside relation (the nonrelational). The relation of exception thus simply expresses the originary formal structure of the juridical relation. In this sense, the sovereign decision on the exception is the originary juridico-political structure on the basis of which what is included in the juridical order and what is excluded from it acquire their meaning. In its archetypal form, the state of exception is therefore the principle of every juridical localization, since only the state of exception opens the space in which the determination of a certain juridical order and a particular territory first becomes possible. As such, the state of exception itself is thus essentially unlocalizable (even if definite spatiotemporal limits can be assigned to it from time to time).

The link between localization (*Ortung*) and ordering (*Ordnung*) constitutive of the "*nomos* of the earth" (Schmitt, *Das Nomos*, p. 48) is therefore even more complex than Schmitt maintains and, at its center, contains a fundamental ambiguity, an unlocalizable zone of indistinction or exception that, in the last analysis, necessarily acts against it as a principle of its infinite dislocation. One of the theses of the present inquiry is that in our age, the state of exception comes more and more to the foreground as the fundamental political structure and ultimately begins to become the rule. When our age tried to grant the unlocalizable a permanent and visible localization, the result was the concentration camp. The camp – and not the prison – is the space that corresponds to this originary structure of the *nomos*. This is shown, among other things, by the fact that while prison law only constitutes a particular sphere of penal law and is not outside the normal order, the juridical constellation that guides the camp is (as we shall see) martial law and the state of siege. This is why it is not possible to inscribe the analysis of the camp in the trail opened by the works of Foucault, from *Madness and Civilization* to *Discipline and Punish*.

As the absolute space of exception, the camp is topologically different from a simple space of confinement. And it is this space of exception, in which the link between localization and ordering is definitively broken, that has determined the crisis of the old "*nomos* of the earth."

1.3.   The validity of a juridical rule does not coincide with its application to the individual case in, for example, a trial or an executive act. On the contrary, the rule must, precisely insofar as it is general, be valid independent of the individual case. Here the sphere of law shows its essential proximity to that of language. Just as in an occurrence of actual speech, a word acquires its ability to denote a segment of reality only insofar as it is also meaningful in its own not-denoting (that is, as *langue* as opposed to *parole*, as a term in its mere lexical consistency, independent of its concrete use in discourse), so the rule can refer to the individual case only because it is in force, in the sovereign exception, as pure potentiality in the suspension of every actual reference. And just as language presupposes the nonlinguistic as that with which it must maintain itself in a virtual relation (in the form of a *langue* or, more precisely, a grammatical game, that is, in the form of a discourse whose actual denotation is maintained in infinite suspension) so that it may later denote it in actual speech, so the law presupposes the nonjuridical (for example, mere violence in the form of the state of nature) as that with which it maintains itself in a potential relation in the state of exception. *The sovereign exception (as zone of indistinction between nature and right) is the presupposition of the juridical reference in the form of its suspension.* Inscribed as a presupposed exception in every rule that orders or forbids something (for example, in the rule that forbids homicide) is the pure and unsanctionable figure of the offense that, in the normal case, brings about the rule's own transgression (in the same example, the killing of a man not as natural violence but as sovereign violence in the state of exception).

ℵ Hegel was the first to truly understand the presuppositional structure thanks to which language is at once outside and inside itself and the immediate (the nonlinguistic) reveals itself to be nothing but a presupposition of language. "Language," he wrote in the *Phenomenology of Spirit*, "is the perfect element in which interiority is as external as exteriority is internal" (see *Phänomenologie des Geistes*, pp. 527–29). We have seen that only the sovereign decision on the state of exception opens the space in which it is possible to trace borders between inside and outside and in which determinate rules can be assigned to determinate territories. In exactly the same way, only language as the pure potentiality to signify, withdrawing itself from every concrete instance of speech, divides the linguistic from the nonlinguistic and allows for the opening of areas of meaningful speech in which certain terms correspond to certain denotations. Language is the sovereign who, in a permanent state of exception, declares that there is nothing outside language and that language is always beyond itself. The particular structure of law has its foundation in this presuppositional structure of human language. It expresses the bond of inclusive exclusion to which a thing is subject because of the fact of being in language, of being named. To speak [*dire*] is, in this sense, always to "speak the law," *ius dicere*.

1.4.   From this perspective, the exception is situated in a symmetrical position with respect to the example, with which it forms a system. Exception and example constitute the two modes by which a set tries to found and maintain its own coherence. But while the exception is, as we saw, an *inclusive exclusion* (which thus serves to include what is excluded), the example instead functions as an *exclusive inclusion*. Take the case of the grammatical example (Milner, "L'exemple," p. 176): the paradox here is that a single utterance in no way distinguished from others of its kind is isolated from them precisely insofar as it belongs to them. If the syntagm "I love you" is uttered as an example of a performative speech act, then this syntagm both cannot be understood as in a normal context and yet still must be treated as a real utterance in order for it to be taken as an example. What the example shows is its belonging to a class, but for this very reason the example steps out of its class in the very moment in which it exhibits and delimits it (in the case of a linguistic syntagm, the example thus *shows* its own signifying and, in this way, suspends its own meaning). If one now asks if the rule applies to the example, the answer is not easy, since the rule applies to the example only as to a normal case and obviously not as to an example. The example is thus excluded from the normal case not because it does not belong to it but, on the contrary, because it exhibits its own belonging to it. The example is truly a *paradigm* in the etymological sense: it is what is "shown beside," and a class can contain everything except its own paradigm.

The mechanism of the exception is different. While the example is excluded from the set insofar as it belongs to it, the exception is included in the normal case precisely because it does not belong to it. And just as belonging to a class can be shown only by an example – that is, outside of the class itself – so non-belonging can be shown only at the center of the class, by an exception. In every case (as is shown by the dispute between anomalists and analogists among the ancient grammarians), exception and example are correlative concepts that are ultimately indistinguishable and that come into play every time the very sense of the belonging and commonality of individuals is to be defined. In every logical system, just as in every social system, the relation between outside and inside, strangeness and intimacy, is this complicated.

א The *exceptio* of Roman court law well shows this particular structure of the exception. The *exceptio* is an instrument of the defendant's defense that, in the case of a judgment, functions to neutralize the conclusiveness of the grounds proffered by the plaintiff and thus to render the normal application of the *ius civile* impossible. The Romans saw it as a form of exclusion directed at the application of the *ius civile* (*Digesta*, 44. 1. 2; Ulpianus, 74: *Exceptio dicta est quasi quaedam exclusio, quae opponi actioni solet ad excludendum id, quod in intentionem condemnationemve deductum est*, "It is said to be an exception because it is almost a kind of exclusion, a kind of exclusion that is usually opposed to the trial in order to exclude what was argued in the *intentio* and the *condemnatio*"). In this sense, the *exceptio* is not absolutely outside the law, but rather shows a contrast between two juridical demands, a contrast that in Roman law refers back to the opposition between *ius civile* and *ius honorarium*, that is, to the law introduced by the magistrate to temper the excessive generality of the norms of civil law.

In its technical expression in the law of the Roman court, the *exceptio* thus takes the form of a conditional negative clause inserted between the *intentio* and the *condemnatio*, by means of which the condemnation of the defendant is subordinated to the nonexistence of the fact excepted by both *intentio* and *condemnatio* (for example: *si in ea re nihil malo A. Agerii factum sit neque fiat*, "if there has not been malice"). The case of the exception is thus excluded from the application of the *ius civile* without, however, thereby calling into question the belonging of the case in point to the regulative provision. The sovereign exception represents a further dimension: it displaces a contrast between two juridical demands into a limit relation between what is inside and what is outside the law.

It may seem incongruous to define the structure of sovereign power, with its cruel factual implications, by means of two innocuous grammatical categories. Yet there is a case in which the linguistic example's decisive character and ultimate indistinguishability from the exception show an unmistakable involvement with the power of life and death. We refer to the episode in *Judges* 12: 6 in which the Galatians recognize the fleeing Ephraimites, who are trying to save themselves beyond the Jordan, by asking them to pronounce the word "Shibboleth," which the Ephraimites pronounce "Sibboleth" ("The men of Gilead said unto him, 'Art thou an Ephraimite?' If he said, 'Nay'; then they said unto him, 'Say now Shibboleth': and he said Sibboleth: for he could not frame to pronounce it right. Then they took him, and slew him at the passages of Jordan"). In the Shibboleth, example and exception become indistinguishable: "Shibboleth" is an exemplary exception or an example that functions as an exception. (In this sense, it is not surprising that there is a predilection to resort to exemplary punishment in the state of exception.)

1.5. Set theory distinguishes between membership and inclusion. A term is included when it is part of a set in the sense that all of its elements are elements of that set (one then says that *b* is a subset of *a*, and one writes it $b \subset a$). But a term may be a member of a set without being included in it (membership is, after all, the primitive notion of set theory, which one writes $b \in a$), or, conversely, a term may be included in a set without being one of its members. In a recent book, Alain Badiou has developed this distinction in order to translate it into political terms. Badiou has membership correspond to presentation, and inclusion correspond to representation (re-presentation). One then says that a term *is a member of* a situation (in political terms, these are single individuals insofar as they belong to a society). And one says that a term is *included* in a situation if it is represented in the metastructure (the State) in which the structure of the situation is counted as one term (individuals insofar as they are recodified by the State into classes, for example, or into "electorates"). Badiou defines a term as *normal* when it is both presented and represented (that is, when it both is a member and is included), as *excrescent* when it is represented but not presented (that is, when it is included in a situation without being a member of that situation), and as *singular* when it is presented but not represented (a term that is a member without being included) (*L'être*, pp. 95–115).

What becomes of the exception in this scheme? At first glance, one might think that it falls into the third case, that the exception, in other words, embodies a kind of membership without inclusion. And this is certainly Badiou's position. But what defines the character of the sovereign claim is precisely that it applies to the exception in no longer applying to it, that it includes what is outside itself. The sovereign exception is thus the figure in which singularity is represented as such, which is to say, insofar as it is unrepresentable. What cannot be included in any way is included in the form of the exception. In Badiou's scheme, the exception introduces a fourth figure, a threshold of indistinction between excrescence (representation without presentation) and singularity (presentation without representation), something like a paradoxical inclusion of membership itself. *The exception is what cannot be included in the whole of which it is a member and cannot be a member of the whole in which it is always already included.* What emerges in this limit figure is the radical crisis of every possibility of clearly distinguishing between membership and inclusion, between what is outside and what is inside, between exception and rule.

ℵ Badiou's thought is, from this perspective, a rigorous thought of the exception. His central category of the event corresponds to the structure of the exception. Badiou defines the event as an element of a situation such that its membership in the situation is undecidable from the perspective of the situation. To the State, the event thus necessarily appears as an excrescence. According to Badiou, the relation between membership and inclusion is also marked by a fundamental lack of correspondence, such that inclusion always exceeds membership (theorem of the point of excess). The exception expresses precisely this impossibility of a system's making inclusion coincide with membership, its reducing all its parts to unity.

From the point of view of language, it is possible to assimilate inclusion to sense and membership to denotation. In this way, the fact that a word always has more sense than it can actually denote corresponds to the theorem of the point of excess. Precisely this disjunction is at issue both in Claude Lévi-Strauss's theory of the constitutive excess of the signifier over the signified ("there is always a lack of equivalence between the two, which is resolvable for a divine intellect alone, and which results in the existence of a superabundance of the signifier over the signifieds on which it rests" [Introduction à Mauss, p. xlix]) and in Émile Benveniste's doctrine of the irreducible opposition between the semiotic and the semantic. The thought of our time finds itself confronted with the structure of the exception in every area. Language's sovereign claim thus consists in the attempt to make sense coincide with denotation, to stabilize a zone of indistinction between the two in which language can maintain itself in relation to its *denotata* by abandoning them and withdrawing from them into a pure *langue* (the linguistic "state of exception"). This is what deconstruction does, positing undecidables that are infinitely in excess of every possibility of signification.

1.6.   This is why sovereignty presents itself in Schmitt in the form of a decision on the exception. Here the decision is not the expression of the will of a subject hierarchically superior to all others, but rather represents the inscription within the body of the *nomos* of the exteriority that animates it and gives it meaning. The sovereign decides not the licit and illicit but the originary inclusion of the living in the sphere of law or, in the words of Schmitt, "the normal structuring of life relations," which the law needs. The decision concerns neither a *quaestio iuris* nor a *quaestio facti*, but rather the very relation between law and fact. Here it is a question not only, as Schmitt seems to suggest, of the irruption of the "effective life" that, in the exception, "breaks the crust of a mechanism grown rigid through repetition" but of something that concerns the most inner nature of the law. The law has a regulative character and is a "rule" not because it commands and proscribes, but because it must first of all create the sphere of its own reference in real life and *make that reference regular*. Since the rule both stabilizes and presupposes the conditions of this reference, the originary structure of the rule is always of this kind: "If (a real case in point, e.g.: *si membrum rupsit*), then (juridical consequence, e.g.: *talio esto*)," in which a fact is included in the juridical order through its exclusion, and transgression seems to precede and determine the lawful case. That the law initially has the form of a *lex talionis* (*talio*, perhaps from *talis*, amounts to "the thing itself") means that the juridical order does not originally present itself simply as sanctioning a transgressive fact but instead constitutes itself through the repetition of the same act without any sanction, that is, as an exceptional case. This is not a punishment of this first act, but rather represents its inclusion in the juridical order, violence as a primordial juridical fact (*permittit enim lex parem vindictam*, "for the law allows equitable vengeance" [Pompeius Festus, *De verborum significatione*, 496. 15]). In this sense, the exception is the originary form of law.

The cipher of this capture of life in law is not sanction (which is not at all an exclusive characteristic of the juridical rule) but guilt (not in the technical sense that this concept has in penal law but in the originary sense that indicates a being-in-debt: *in culpa esse*), which is to say, precisely the condition of being included through an exclusion, of being in relation to something from which one is excluded or which one cannot fully assume.

Guilt refers not to transgression, that is, to the determination of the licit and the illicit, but to the pure force of the law, to the law's simple reference to something. This is the ultimate ground of the juridical maxim, which is foreign to all morality, according to which ignorance of the rule does not eliminate guilt. In this impossibility of deciding if it is guilt that grounds the rule or the rule that posits guilt, what comes clearly to light is the indistinction between outside and inside and between life and law that characterizes the sovereign decision on the exception. The "sovereign" structure of the law, its peculiar and original "force," has the form of a state of exception in which fact and law are indistinguishable (yet must, nevertheless, be decided on). Life, which is thus obliged, can in the last instance be implicated in the sphere of law only through the presupposition of its inclusive exclusion, only in an *exceptio*. There is a limit-figure of life, a threshold in which life is both inside and outside the juridical order, and this threshold is the place of sovereignty.

The statement "The rule lives off the exception alone" must therefore be taken to the letter. Law is made of nothing but what it manages to capture inside itself through the inclusive exclusion of the *exceptio*: it nourishes itself on this exception and is a dead letter without it. In this sense, the law truly "has no existence in itself, but rather has its being in the very life of men." The sovereign decision traces and from time to time renews this threshold of indistinction between outside and inside, exclusion and inclusion, *nomos* and *physis*, in which life is originarily excepted in law. Its decision is the position of an undecidable.

א Not by chance is Schmitt's first work wholly devoted to the definition of the juridical concept of guilt. What is immediately striking in this study is the decision with which the author refutes every technico-formal definition of the concept of guilt in favor of terms that, at first glance, seem more moral than juridical. Here, in fact, guilt is (against the ancient juridical proverb "There is no guilt without rule") first of all a "process of inner life," which is to say, something essentially "intrasubjective," which can be qualified as a real "ill will" that consists in "knowingly positing ends contrary to those of the juridical order" (*Über Schuld*, pp. 18–24, 92).

It is not possible to say whether Benjamin was familiar with this text while he was writing "Fate and Character" and "Critique of Violence." But it remains the case that his definition of guilt as an originary juridical concept unduly transferred to the ethico-religious sphere is in perfect agreement with Schmitt's thesis – even if Benjamin's definition goes in a decisively opposed direction. For Benjamin, the state of demonic existence of which law is a residue is to be overcome and man is to be liberated from guilt (which is nothing other than the inscription of natural life in the order of law and destiny). At the heart of the Schmittian assertion of the juridical character and centrality of the notion of guilt is, however, not the freedom of the ethical man but only the controlling force of a sovereign power (*katechon*), which can, in the best of cases, merely slow the dominion of the Antichrist.

There is an analogous convergence with respect to the concept of character. Like Benjamin, Schmitt clearly distinguishes between character and guilt ("the concept of guilt," he writes, "has to do with an *operari*, and not with an *esse*" [*Über Schuld*, p. 46]). Yet in Benjamin, it is precisely this element (character insofar as it escapes all conscious willing) that presents itself as the principle capable of releasing man from guilt and of affirming natural innocence.

1.7.   If the exception is the structure of sovereignty, then sovereignty is not an exclusively political concept, an exclusively juridical category, a power external to law

(Schmitt), or the supreme rule of the juridical order (Hans Kelsen): it is the originary structure in which law refers to life and includes it in itself by suspending it. Taking up Jean-Luc Nancy's suggestion, we shall give the name *ban* (from the old Germanic term that designates both exclusion from the community and the command and insignia of the sovereign) to this potentiality (in the proper sense of the Aristotelian *dynamis*, which is always also *dynamis mē energein*, the potentiality not to pass into actuality) of the law to maintain itself in its own privation, to apply in no longer applying. The relation of exception is a relation of ban. He who has been banned is not, in fact, simply set outside the law and made indifferent to it but rather *abandoned* by it, that is, exposed and threatened on the threshold in which life and law, outside and inside, become indistinguishable. It is literally not possible to say whether the one who has been banned is outside or inside the juridical order. (This is why in Romance languages, to be "banned" originally means both to be "at the mercy of" and "at one's own will, freely," to be "excluded" and also "open to all, free.") It is in this sense that the paradox of sovereignty can take the form "There is nothing outside the law." *The originary relation of law to life is not application but Abandonment.* The matchless potentiality of the *nomos*, its originary *"force of law,"* is that it holds life in its ban by abandoning it. This is the structure of the ban that we shall try to understand here, so that we can eventually call it into question.

א The ban is a form of relation. But precisely what kind of relation is at issue here, when the ban has no positive content and the terms of the relation seem to exclude (and, at the same time, to include) each other? What is the form of law that expresses itself in the ban? The ban is the pure form of reference to something in general, which is to say, the simple positing of relation with the nonrelational. In this sense, the ban is identical with the limit form of relation. A critique of the ban will therefore necessarily have to put the very form of relation into question, and to ask if the political fact is not perhaps thinkable beyond relation and, thus, no longer in the form of a connection.

Note

1 "Order" renders the Italian *ordinamento*, which carries the sense not only of order but of political and juridical rule, regulation, and system. The word *ordinamento* is also the Italian translation of Carl Schmitt's *Ordnung*. Where the author refers to *ordinamento* as *Ordnung*, the English word used is the one chosen by Schmitt's translators, "ordering." – Trans.

Works Cited

Antelme, Robert. *L'espèce humaine*. Paris: Gallimard, 1994. (*The Human Race*. Trans. Jeffrey Haight and Annie Mahler. Malboro, Vt.: Malboro Press, 1992.)

Badiou, Alain. *L'être et l'événement*. Paris: Seuil, 1988.

Benveniste, Émile. *Le vocabulaire des institutions indo-européennes*. Vol. 2. Paris: Minuit, 1969. (*Indo-European Language and Society*. Trans. Elizabeth Palmer. Coral Gables: University of Florida Press, 1973.)

Blanchot, Maurice. *L'entretien infini*. Paris: Gallimard, 1969. (*The Infinite Conversation*. Trans. Susan Hanson. Minneapolis: University of Minnesota Press, 1993.)

Deleuze, Gilles, and Félix Guattari. *Mille plateaux*. Paris: Minuit, 1980. (*A Thousand Plateaus: Capitalism and Schizophrenia*. Trans. Brian Massumi. Minneapolis: University of Minnesota Press, 1987.)

Foucault, Michel. *Dits et écrits*. Vols. 3–4. Paris: Gallimard, 1994.

Furet, François, ed. *L'Allemagne nazi et le génocide juif*. Paris: Seuil, 1985. (*Unanswered Questions: Nazi Germany and the Genocide of the Jews*. New York: Schocken, 1989.)

Hegel, Georg Wilhelm Friedrich. *Phänomenologie des Geistes*. In G. W. F. Hegel, *Werke in zwanzig Bänden*, vol. 3. Frankfurt: Suhrkamp, 1971. (*Phenomenology of Spirit*. Trans. A. V. Miller. Oxford: Oxford University Press, 1977.)

Lévi-Strauss, Claude. "Introduction à l'œuvre de Marcel Mauss." In Marcel Mauss, *Sociologie et anthropologie*. Paris: Presses Universitaire de France, 1950.

Milner, J.-C. "L'exemple et la fiction." In *Transparence et opacité: Littérature et sciences cognitives*, ed. Tibor Papp and Pierre Pira. Paris: Cerf, 1988.

Nancy, Jean-Luc. *L'impératif catégorique*. Paris: Flammarion, 1983. ("Abandoned Being." In Jean-Luc Nancy, *The Birth to Presence*, trans. Brian Holmes. Stanford, Calif.: Stanford University Press, 1993.)

Schmitt, Carl. *Das Nomos von der Erde*. Berlin: Duncker & Humbolt, 1974.

Schmitt, Carl. *Politische Theologie, Vier Kapitel zur Lehre von der Souveränität*. Munich–Leipzig: Duncker & Humbolt, 1922. (*Political Theology: Four Chapters on the Concept of Sovereignty*. Trans. George Schwab. Cambridge, Mass.: MIT Press, 1985.)

Schmitt, Carl. *Über Schuld und Schuldarten, Eine terminologische Untersuchung*. Breslau: Schletter, 1910.

CHAPTER 9

New Historicisms

Louis Montrose

The New Historicism was a reaction against Post-Structuralism as well as a further iteration of some of its assumptions. Post-Structuralism (especially "Deconstruction") had focused on literary texts without any consideration of history. And deconstruction especially seemed to deny the possibility of any reference from text to extra-textual world. The New Historicists (especially Stephen Greenblatt and Catherine Gallagher) renewed a sense of the importance of history to literary studies. The New Historicists were "new" because they eschewed traditional fact-based historiography and focused instead on the way text and context are interwoven. History is itself textual in the sense that many forms of power depend on signification to be effective. Michel Foucault's work on "panopticism," the way discipline is maintained in modern capitalist societies without the need for force, was especially influential on their work.

I

In the 1980s, literary studies in the American academy came to be centrally concerned with the historical, social, and political conditions and consequences of literary production and interpretation. From a multiplicity of sometimes convergent and sometimes incompatible perspectives, the writing and reading of texts, as well as the processes by which they are circulated and categorized, analyzed and taught, are now being construed as historically determined and determining modes of cultural work. What have often been taken to be self-contained aesthetic and academic issues are being reunderstood as inextricably linked to other social discourses, practices, and institutions; and such overdetermined and unstable linkages are apprehended as constitutive of the ideological field within which individual subjectivities and collective structures are mutually shaped.

In various combinations and with varying degrees of consistency and effectiveness, the intellectual forces identifiable as new historicism or cultural poetics, cultural materialism,

Original publication details: Louis Montrose, "New Historicisms" from *Redrawing the Boundaries*, ed. Stephen Greenblatt, pp. 392–418. Modern Language Association, 1992.

Literary Theory: An Anthology, Third Edition. Edited by Julie Rivkin and Michael Ryan.
© 2017 John Wiley & Sons, Ltd. Published 2017 by John Wiley & Sons, Ltd.

feminism, and revisionist forms of Marxism have been engaged in redrawing the boundaries and restructuring the content of English and American literary studies during the
past decade. My assigned task in this essay is to discuss "the new historicism." I place this
term inside quotation marks to indicate my resistance to its now-conventional representation within critical discourse as a fixed and homogeneous body of doctrines and techniques. As such, the new historicism is the invention of its critics and commentators. The
motives and methods of this invention are part of my present concern. But I also, and
primarily, wish to discuss some of the heterogeneous and changing dimensions of the
work frequently designated as new historicist and to situate it within the larger field configured by the mutually conditioning forces I have enumerated.

The critical forces I have conveniently if simplistically labeled as new historicism or
cultural poetics, cultural materialism, feminism, and Marxism have in common a concern
at once to affirm and to problematize the connections between literary and other discourses, the dialectic between the text and the world. In recent years, these forces have
challenged, with considerable success, the dominant paradigms of New Critical rhetorical
analysis and positivist historical scholarship in Anglo-American literary criticism. The
enabling conditions of this challenge have been various in their origins and complex in
their interactions (Boose; W. Cohen; Gallagher, "Marxism"; Wayne, "Power, Politics").
Here I shall merely suggest three factors that appear to be of widespread relevance. First,
there has been taking place, for some time, an opening of the profession of English to
scholars whose gender, ethnicity, religious or class origins, political allegiances, or sexual
preferences (or some combination of these) complicate their participation in the cultural
and ideological traditions enshrined in the canonical works they study and teach.
Experiences of exclusion or otherness may, of course, provoke a compensatory embrace of
the dominant culture, a desire for acceptance and assimilation; but they may also (and,
perhaps, simultaneously) provoke attitudes of resistance or contestation. Such divided
and dissonant positions may provide vantage points for the appropriation and critique of
particular canonical texts – and, more important, for an appropriation and critique of the
constitutive categories and normative procedures of literary studies. Second, the reorientation in the field under way since at least the beginning of the 1980s is largely the work
of critics whose values were formed while they were students during the culturally experimental and politically turbulent 1960s. The burgeoning of the women's movement
and of feminism during the 1970s, when most of them were seeking to establish their
careers, had a profound social, institutional, and intellectual impact on this generation of
critics – although, of course, the contours and consequences of that impact varied enormously, not only with the gender but also with the particular gender identities and
attitudes of individuals and subgroups. In general, these critics responded to the radically
altered sociopolitical climate of the 1980s – and, perhaps, for some of them, to the uneasy
comfort they had now achieved within its academic establishment – with work that confronted ideologies and cultural politics of other times and places but resisted the articulation of its own assumptions and commitments. Third, the modes of criticism to which I
have referred have variously reacted against and contributed to the intellectual ferment of
the past two decades. Such ferment, summed up in the word *theory*, has challenged the
assumptions and procedures of normative discourses in several academic disciplines. And
in our own discipline, it has shaken if not undermined the aesthetic, moral, and ontological principles that prescribe the ideological dispositions of traditional literary studies.
The theoretical field of poststructuralism is inhabited by a multiplicity of unstable, variously conjoined and conflicting discourses. Among the principles some of them share are

a problematization of those processes by which meaning and value are produced and grounded; a shift from an essential or immanent to a historical, contextual, and conjunctural model of signification; and a general suspicion of closed systems, totalities, and universals.

In the United States, feminism and the women's movement have provided, in recent years, the most powerful infusions of intellectual and social energy into the practices of cultural critique, both written and lived. Across the disciplines, feminist theory and practice have called attention to the discursive construction of gender and sexuality and of social and domestic relations generally, and to the role of such constructs in the formation and regulation of exploitative social and cultural relations. In turn, this perspective has foregrounded the different subject positions from which readers interpret texts and from which they may negotiate or resist inscription into the positions constructed for them by the texts that they read. During the past decade, feminist analyses of discourses that construct and regulate hierarchies of gender and sexuality have increased in cultural and historical specificity; and, at the same time, they have analyzed with increasing subtlety the shifting articulations of gender and sexuality with each other and with the discourses of class and ethnicity. Such scholarship has explored the ways in which women's voices are marginalized, suppressed, ventriloquized, or appropriated in various literary and dramatic works – and in previous commentaries on those works; and it has spurred the recovery of marginalized or suppressed texts written by women. These projects have challenged liberal humanist claims that the literary and critical canons embody an essential and inclusive range of human experience and expression. By seeking openly and collectively to connect the spheres of critical practice, academic policy, and sociopolitical activity, feminist academics have demystified claims that scholarship and the academy stand apart from or above the interests, biases, and struggles of material existence; they have, as well, provided a model for the mutual articulation of intellectual, professional, and social concerns.

The recent revival of interest in historical, social, and political questions in literary and cultural studies is also, no doubt, a response to the acceleration in the forgetting of history that seems to characterize an increasingly technocratic and commodified American academy and society. A primary task for those who profess the humanities must be to disabuse students of the notion that history is what's over and done with; to bring them to a realization that they themselves live *in* history and that the form and pressure of history are made manifest in their subjective thoughts and actions, in their beliefs and desires. Of course, there is more than one way to implement a return to history. Disturbed by "the erosion of historical consciousness" in our society, the chair of the National Endowment for the Humanities has written that "by reaching into the past, we affirm our humanity. And we inevitably come to the essence of it. Because we cannot encompass the totality of other lives and times, we strip away the thousand details of existence and come to its heart" (Cheney, *American Memory* 7, 6). To resolve history into a simple antinomy of myriad expendable details and a single irreducible essence is precisely to refuse history – to refuse history by utterly effacing its *constitutive* differences, by effacing those complex historical formations in which not only the details but also the essences are produced, revised, challenged, and transformed. The emergent social-political-historical orientation in literary studies is characterized by an antireflectionist perspective on cultural work, by a shift in emphasis from the aesthetic analysis of verbal *artifacts* to the ideological analysis of discursive *practices*, and by an understanding of meaning as situationally and provisionally constructed. This orientation is pervasively concerned with writing, reading, and teaching as modes of *action*. And such academic concerns with the sociopolitical instrumentality of cultural and intellectual work are themselves forms of a sociopolitical praxis – although of highly variable and always conjunctural import and efficacy.

This general reorientation in literary and cultural studies is the unhappy subject of J. Hillis Miller's 1986 Presidential Address to the Modern Language Association. In his speech, Miller noted with some dismay – and with some hyperbole – that

> literary study in the past few years has undergone a sudden, almost universal turn away from theory in the sense of an orientation toward language as such and has made a corresponding turn toward history, culture, society, politics, institutions, class and gender conditions, the social context, the material base. ("Triumph" 283)

By such a formulation, Miller polarizes the discursive and the social domains. However, the prevailing tendency across cultural studies has been to emphasize their reciprocity and mutual constitution: on the one hand, the social is understood to be discursively constructed; and on the other, language use is understood to be necessarily dialogical, to be socially and materially determined. Thus Fredric Jameson can retheorize a Marxist concept of the social by appropriating a poststructuralist concept of the textual. He writes that history as material necessity " – Althusser's 'absent cause,' Lacan's 'Real' – is *not* a text, for it is fundamentally non-narrative and non-representational; what can be added, however, is the proviso that history is inaccessible to us except in textual form" (*Political Unconscious* 82). Miller identifies "theory" exclusively with domesticated varieties of deconstruction, conformable to formalist critical traditions in the United States. Theory so construed he privileges ethically and epistemologically in relation to what he scorns as "ideology" – an impassioned and delusional condition that "the critics and antagonists of deconstruction on the so-called left and so-called right" ("Triumph" 289) are said to share. Although his polemic indiscriminately (though hardly unintentionally) lumps them with the academy's intellectually and politically reactionary forces, the various modes of sociopolitical and historical criticism have not only been challenged and influenced by the theoretical developments of the past two decades but have been vitally engaged in their definition and direction. And one such direction is the understanding that "theory" does not reside serenely above "ideology" but rather is mired within it.

Miller's categorical opposition of "reading" to cultural critique, of "theory" to the discourses of "history, culture, society, politics, institutions, class and gender conditions," seems to me not only an oversimplification of both sets of terms but also a suppression of their points of contact and compatibility. The propositions and techniques of deconstruction are employed as powerful tools of ideological analysis when they are trained on the overdetermined and hierarchically structured binary oppositions that constitute the central tradition in Western thought. Derrida himself has suggested that "deconstructive readings and writings are concerned not only with ... discourses, with conceptual and semantic contents. ... Deconstructive practices are also and first of all political and institutional practices" ("But, beyond" 168). The notorious Derridean aphorism "*Il n'y a pas de hors-texte*" may be invoked to abet an escape from the necessities of history, to sanction a self-abandonment to the indeterminate pleasures and/or terrors of the text. However, the phrase may also be construed in terms of the Jamesonian "proviso that history is inaccessible to us except in textual form." That is to say, it may signify the pervasive ideological force of discourse in general and, in particular, the specific ideological force of those discourses that seek to reduce the work of discourse to the mere reflection of an ontologically prior, essential or empirical reality.

Traditionally, *ideology* has referred to the system of ideas, values, and beliefs common to any social group; in recent years, this vexed but indispensable term has come to be associated with the processes by which social subjects are formed, re-formed, and enabled to perform in an apparently meaningful world. In the well-known formulation of Althusser's essay "Ideology and Ideological State Apparatuses," "Ideology is a 'Representation' of the Imaginary Relationship of Individuals to their Real Conditions of Existence," a representation that "Interpellates Individuals as Subjects" (Althusser, *Lenin* 162, 170; Eagleton, *Ideology: An Introduction*). Representations of the world in written discourse participate in the construction of the world: they are engaged in shaping the modalities of social reality and in accommodating their writers, performers, readers, and audiences to multiple and shifting subject positions within the world that they themselves both constitute and inhabit. In such terms, our professional practice is, like our subject matter, a production of ideology. By this I mean that it bears traces of the professor's values, beliefs, and experiences – his or her socially constructed subjectivity – and also that it actively – if not always consciously, and rarely consistently – instantiates those values, beliefs and experiences. Like anyone else's, my readings of cultural texts cannot but be partial – by which I mean incapable of offering an exhaustive description, a complete explanation; but also incapable of offering any description or explanation that is disinterested, that is located at some Archimedean point outside the history I study, in some ideal space that transcends the coordinates of gender, ethnicity, class, age, and profession that plot my own shifting and potentially contradictory subject positions. In its pursuit of knowledge and virtue, the academic profession of literature is necessarily impure. From this perspective, any claim for what Miller calls an "orientation to language *as such*" (my emphasis) is itself – always already – an orientation to language that is being produced from a position *within* "history, culture, society, politics, institutions, class and gender conditions."

II

In an essay published in 1986, I attempted briefly to articulate and scrutinize some of the theoretical, methodological, and political assumptions and implications of the kind of work produced since the late 1970s by those Renaissance specialists (including myself) who were then coming to be labeled as "new historicists" (Montrose, "Renaissance"). The focus of such work had been on a refiguration of the sociocultural field within which now-canonical Renaissance literary and dramatic works had been originally produced, on situating them in relation not only to various other genres and modes of writing from beyond the literary canon but also to other cultural domains, including the social practices and political institutions of early modern England (Goldberg, *James I*; Greenblatt; Montrose; Mullaney; Wayne; Whigham). The dominant mode of interpretation in English literary studies had long been to combine techniques of formal and rhetorical analysis with the elaboration of relatively self-contained histories of "ideas" or of literary genres and topoi – histories abstracted from their social matrices. In addition to such literary histories, we may note two other traditional practices of "history" in English literary studies. One comprises those commentaries on political commonplaces in which the dominant ideology – the unreliable machinery of sociopolitical legitimation – is celebrated by the historical critic as being the morally, intellectually, and aesthetically satisfying structure of understanding and belief, the stable and coherent world picture, that is shared by all members of the social body. The canonical literary works of the period in question are then discovered to reproduce, by synecdoche, the lucid organic form inhabited by the spirit of the age. The other historical practice is an erudite antiquarian scholarship that, by treating texts as elaborate ciphers, seeks to fix the meaning of fictional characters and actions in their reference to specific historical persons and events. Though sometimes reproducing the methodological shortcomings of such older idealist and empiricist modes of historical criticism, but often appropriating their prodigious scholarly labors to good effect, the newer historical criticism could claim to be new in refusing unexamined distinctions between "literature" and "history," between "text" and "context," in resisting a tendency to posit and privilege an autonomous individual – whether an author or a work – to be set against a social or literary background.

In his introduction to a 1982 essay collection, Stephen J. Greenblatt distinguished what he dubbed the "new historicism," both from an older, reflectionist, and positivist literary historical scholarship and from New Critical formalism. He commented that "Renaissance literary works are no longer regarded either as a fixed set of texts that are set apart from all other forms of expression and that contain their own determinate meanings or as a stable set of reflections of historical facts that lie beyond them" (Introduction 6). Furthermore, he suggested that the contours of art and literature are socially and historically configured: distinctions "between artistic production and other kinds of social production ... are not intrinsic to the texts; rather they are made up and constantly redrawn by artists, audiences, and readers." We might now add that the very identities, expectations, and practices associated with the positions termed artist, audience, and reader are themselves "made up and constantly redrawn" by the discursive processes in which they are engaged and that condition their own engagement with texts. Such a reciprocal fashioning is emphasized in Tony Bennett's concept of the "reading formation," described as

> an attempt to identify the determinations which, in operating on both texts and readers, mediate the relations between text and context, connecting the two and providing the mechanisms through which they productively interact in representing context not as a set of extra-discursive relations but as a set of intertextual and discursive relations which produce readers for texts and texts for readers. ... Texts, readers and contexts ... are variable functions within a discursively ordered set of relations. Different reading formations ... produce their own texts, their own readers and their own contexts. (74)

This concept implicates critics in historically and institutionally situated roles as privileged readers, whose specialized though hardly disinterested knowledge constitutes the past that they undertake to elucidate. From this perspective, a new historicism, or cultural poetics, must be positioned within our own reading formation.

The symbolic anthropology of Clifford Geertz conspicuously influenced work identifiable as new historicism, or cultural poetics, produced during the later 1970s and early 1980s (*Interpretation*; *Local Knowledge*; *Negara*). Geertz himself seems to have been engaged in a liberal humanist response to the quantifying scientism of American social science, on the one hand, and to the totalizing theoretical discourses of structuralism and Marxism, on the other. For Geertz,

> the term "culture" ... denotes an historically transmitted pattern of meanings embodied in symbols, a system of inherited conceptions expressed in symbolic forms by means of which men communicate, perpetuate, and develop their knowledge about and attitudes toward life. (*Interpretation* 89)

In Geertzian symbolic anthropology, culture is the medium of semiosis, "a set of control mechanisms – plans, recipes, rules, instructions ... – for the governing of behavior" (44); a system of codes regulates social life by "governing" the production of those ensembles of conventions, practices, and artifacts to which the word *culture* is often loosely applied. It is a version of what Marshall Sahlins has called "the symbolic or meaningful" concept of culture, in which "human action in the world is to be understood as mediated by the cultural design, which gives order at once to practical experience, customary practice, and the relationship between the two" (*Culture* viii, 55).

Geertz's work offered to literary critics and cultural historians not so much a powerful *theory* of culture as an exemplary and eminently literary *method* for narrating culture in action, culture as lived in the performances and narratives of individual and collective human actors. Geertz called his rhetorically self-conscious ethnographic practice "thick description" (*Interpretation* 3–30). "It is explication I am after," he avers, "construing social expressions on their surface enigmatical" (5). The ethnographer's enterprise is "like that of the literary critic" (9) – and, we might add, like that of a New Critic. Thus he describes his "concept of culture" in a metaphysical conceit:

> Believing ... that man is an animal suspended in webs of significance he himself has spun, I take culture to be those webs, and the analysis of it to be therefore not an experimental science in search of law but an interpretive one in search of meaning. (5)

"Thick description" might be more accurately described as "interpretive narration": it seizes on an event, performance, or other practice and, through the interrogation of its minute particulars, seeks to reveal the ethos of an alien culture.

Unsurprisingly, Geertz's method and style have probably been more admired and imitated beyond the discipline of anthropology than within it. Anthropologists of various persuasions have been sharply critical of Geertz's tendency to sublimate the dynamics of material struggle into the forms of collective imagination; of what some see as his impressionistic descriptions of alien worldviews; and of the isolated or fragmentary "local knowledge" produced by thick description, its failure to relate "'cultural texts' ... to each other or to general processes of economic and social change" (Walters 551–52; see also Asad; Shankman; Crapanzano).

Geertz focuses on indigenous cultural meanings rather than on general social laws, on cultural cohesion rather than on social struggle. The latter interpretive bias – and its consequences for the work of social historians and literary critics influenced by Geertzian symbolic anthropology – has been the subject of considerable recent criticism, trenchantly summarized in Roger Keesing's remark that "cultures are webs of mystification as well as signification. We need to ask who *creates* and who *defines* cultural meanings, and to what ends" (161–62; see also LaCapra, *Soundings*; Pecora; Biersack). In other words, critique of the Geertzian mode of analysis concentrates on the ways in which a cultural poetics suppresses or subsumes a cultural politics.

III

In a typical new-historicist essay or book chapter, the Geertzian model of thick description is evident in the initial deployment of an exemplary anecdote as a strategy of cultural and historical estrangement. In some examples of new-historicist work, such anecdotes may be elaborated into the interpretive units from which a sustained argument emerges; in others, the method may seem merely fashionable and formulaic, a vaguely associative accumulation of historical curiosities. Thus Walter Cohen characterizes new-historicist method (or, perhaps, antimethod) as "arbitrary connectedness": "The strategy is governed methodologically by the assumption that any one aspect of a society is related to any other. No organizing principle determines these relationships" (34). And in order to describe this phenomenon, Dominick LaCapra offers the generous choice of "facile associationism, juxtaposition, or pastiche ... weak montage, or, if you prefer, cut-and-paste bricolage" (*Soundings* 193). New-historicist work has been particularly susceptible to such responses because it has frequently failed to theorize its method or its model of culture in any sustained way. Proceeding on the basis of tacit and perhaps inconsistent notions about cultural dynamics, new-historicist studies may sometimes seem to imply that the objects they analyze are connected merely by a principle of cultural contingency or by the wit of the critic ("arbitrary connectedness"); or, on the contrary, that they have a necessary connection that is grounded in a principle of cultural determinism ("containment").

Having first called his critical project a "cultural poetics" in *Renaissance Self-Fashioning* (4–5), Greenblatt returns to and develops the term in *Shakespearean Negotiations*. This enterprise is now defined as a "study of the collective making of distinct cultural practices and inquiry into the relations among these practices"; its relevant concerns are "how collective beliefs and experiences were shaped, moved from one medium to another, concentrated in manageable aesthetic form, offered for consumption [and] how the boundaries were marked between cultural practices understood to be art forms and other, contiguous, forms of expression" (5). Described, in conspicuously formalist and structuralist terms, as a study of distinctions among "*contiguous* ... forms of expression" (my emphasis), cultural poetics tends to emphasize structural relations at the expense of sequential processes; in effect, it orients the axis of intertextuality synchronically, as the text of a cultural system, rather than diachronically, as the text of an autonomous literary history.

One of the implications of Greenblatt's formulation – an implication already present in the widespread early new-historicist reliance on Geertzian notions of culture – is that "art forms and other, contiguous, forms of expression" are expressive of some underlying causal principle or generative and restrictive cultural code, that they are thus organically related to one another, and that this genetic relationship among practices is manifested in their surface articulation as a tropological system. Thus Greenblatt writes in the essay "Fiction and Friction":

> The relation I wish to establish between medical and theatrical practice is not one of cause and effect or source and literary realization. We are dealing rather with a shared code, a set of interlocking tropes and similitudes that function not only as objects but as the conditions of representation. (*Shakespearean* 86)

The cultural model implicit in such new-historicist work seems to have its origins in a cross between Geertzian and Foucauldian conceptual schemes: specifically, between Geertz's integrative sense of culture, his construal of culture as a localized and collective system of symbols, and Foucault's early epistemic history, which elucidates similitudes and rejects causality "in order to establish those diverse converging, and sometimes divergent, but never autonomous series that enable us to circumscribe the 'locus' of an event, the limits to its fluidity and the conditions of its emergence" (Foucault, "Discourse" 230). Some elements of new-historicist critical practice that have puzzled or irritated its critics may be explicable (though not, therefore, always or easily defensible) as consequences of this implicit cultural model. Certain examples of new-historicist work imply that a culture is a shared system of symbols expressive of a cohesive and closed (a "restricted" or "sutured") ideology. The problematic or contested consequences of such a model tend to suggest its affinities with formalist modes of analysis. They include the methodological assumption of tropological rather than causal relations among new historicism's objects of study; the emphasis on culture as a text, on the discursivity of material life and of social and political relations; the critic's self-imposed limitation to the study of synchronic intracultural processes, exemplified in particular texts and textualized performances; and the apparent incompatibility of the cultural paradigm with the dynamics of ideological resistance, conflict, and change.

The terms in which the problematic of ideology and resistance came to be posed in new-historicist studies of the Renaissance – terms that have now become widely established in other fields of specialization – are those of a simplistic, reductive, and hypostatized opposition between "containment" and "subversion." These terms – which appear to be residues of a cold war ideology that had pernicious consequences in both international and domestic policy – prove once again to be wholly inadequate instruments of analysis and debate. Nevertheless, they are significant indicators of a shift of perspective within Anglo-American literary criticism and its ambient political culture. As the problem of ideology has become an acceptable and even a central topic of critical discourse in the American academy, so the emphases in sociocultural analysis have shifted from unity, reciprocity, and consent to difference, domination, and resistance. It is precisely this shift of emphasis from canonicity and consensus to diversity and contestation that, during the past decade, has been the focus of the national debate about the direction of the humanities – a debate that has been waged on the campuses and on the best-seller lists, in the public media and in the policy statements and funding priorities of government agencies. It is within the context of these cultural politics – and as their displacement – that the "new historicism" has been constituted as an academic site of ideological struggle between containment and subversion. This struggle may be reduced to the following scenario. Critics who emphasize the possibilities for the effective agency of individual or collective subjects against forms of domination, exclusion, and assimilation have energetically contested critics who stress the capacity of the early modern state, as personified in the monarch, to *contain* apparently subversive gestures, or even to *produce* them precisely in order to contain them. According to a now-notorious argument in Greenblatt's essay "Invisible Bullets," the ability of the dominant order to generate subversion so as to use it to its own ends marks "the very condition of power" (45). Thus a generalized argument for the "containment of subversion" is itself subversive of arguments for the agency of subjects, which it reduces to the illusory and delusive effects of a dominant order. The binary logic of subversion-containment produces a closed conceptual structure of reciprocally defining and dependent terms, terms that are complementary and mutually complicit.

One can readily see that the larger assumptions and implications of a "containment" position concerning the operations of ideology might be suspect or even alarming, not only to traditionalists who cherish liberal humanist ideals of individual self-determination but also to those cultural critics who have a stake in making their own discursive practice a direct intervention in the process of ideological reproduction. At its extreme, the "containment of subversion" position suggests a reading of Foucault that emphasizes the discontinuity of history and the inescapable subjection of subjects; it makes no theoretical space for change or for contestation. Such a position might be said to reinstate the Elizabethan world picture, but now transposed into the ironic mode. Recent commentators have, with increasing frequency, seized on the provocative argument of "Invisible Bullets," misleadingly ascribed to the essay the claims of a cultural law, and then inaccurately represented it as the central tenet of the new historicism – sometimes using it to characterize the work of those who have been explicitly engaged in contesting Greenblatt's thesis. Such assertions gain credibility and authority simply from their frequent repetition in print; nevertheless, subscription to the "containment hypothesis" in no way characterizes the work of all those writers identified as new historicists, any more than it characterizes all of Greenblatt's work – or, for that matter, all of Foucault's.

The putatively Foucauldian new-historicist argument for the dominant's production and containment of subversion is pungently characterized by Frank Lentricchia as "a prearranged theatre of struggle set upon the substratum of a monolithic agency which produces 'opposition' as one of its delusive political effects" ("Foucault's Legacy" 234). However, such a strict containment argument oversimplifies Foucault's subtle, flexible, and dynamic conception of power by suggesting that the volatile and contingent relations of power that saturate social space are actually determined by the crystallization of power in the state apparatus. Foucault emphasizes that

> power's condition of possibility ... must not be sought in the primary existence of a central point, in a unique source of sovereignty from which secondary and descendent forms would emanate; it is the moving substrate of force relations which, by virtue of their inequality, constantly engender states of power, but the latter are always local and unstable. (*History* 1: 93)

For Foucault, power is never monolithic; and power relations always imply multiple sites not only of power but also of resistance. He writes that such sites of resistance are of variable configuration, intensity, and effectiveness:

> The strictly relational character of power relationships ... depends on a multiplicity of points of resistance: these play the role of adversary, target, support, or handle in power relations. ... Resistance ... can only exist in the strategic field of power relations. But this does not mean that they are only a reaction or rebound, forming with respect to the basic domination an underside that is in the end always passive, doomed to perpetual defeat. ... The points, knots, or focuses of resistance are spread over time and space at varying densities. ... Are there no great radical ruptures, massive binary divisions, then? Occasionally, yes. But more often one is dealing with mobile and transitory points of resistance, producing cleavages in a society that shift about, fracturing unities and effecting regroupings, furrowing across individuals themselves. ... It is doubtless the strategic codification of these points of resistance that makes a revolution possible, somewhat similar to the way in which the state relies on the institutional integration of power relationships. (1: 95–96)

Foucault's flexible conception of power relations may accommodate local instances of a subversion that is produced for containment, but it also acknowledges revolutionary social transformations and other possible modalities of power and resistance. If, on the one hand, ideological dominance can never be monolithic, total, and closed, then, on the other hand, revolutionary upheavals occur relatively rarely; modes and instances of resistance – subversions, contestations, transgressions, appropriations – tend to be local and dispersed in their occurrences, variable and limited in their consequences. Thus one need look no further than Foucault's own work for confirmation of the hopeless inadequacy of subversion-containment as an explanatory model for the dynamism and specificity of relations of power, and for the necessity to make more subtle discriminations among the modalities of resistance and among their various conditions of possibility.

Within the context of the containment-subversion debate, my own position has been that a closed and static, monolithic and homogeneous notion of ideology must be replaced by one that is heterogeneous and unstable, permeable and processual. Raymond Williams's invaluable *Marxism and Literature* theorizes ideology in just such dynamic and dialogic terms. By emphasizing "interrelations between movements and tendencies both within and beyond a specific and effective dominance" (121), Williams clarifies the existence, at any point in time, of residual and emergent, oppositional and alternative values, meanings, and practices. The shifting conjunctures of such "movements and tendencies" may create conceptual sites within the ideological field from which the dominant can be contested, and against which it must be continuously redefined and redefended – and so, perforce, continuously transformed. An ideological dominance is qualified by the specific conjunctures of ethnic, gender, class, profession, age, and other social positions occupied by individual cultural producers; by the heterogeneous positionality of the spectators, auditors, and readers who consume, appropriate, and resist cultural productions; and by the relative autonomy – the properties, possibilities, and limitations – of the cultural medium being worked. In other words, allowance must be made for the manifold mediations involved in the production, reproduction, and appropriation of an ideological dominance: for the collective, sectional, and individual agency of the state's subjects, and for the resources, conventions, and modes of production and distribution of the representational forms that they employ. In its emphasis on a dynamic, agonistic, and temporal model of culture and ideology – a ceaseless contest among dominant and subordinate positions, a ceaseless interplay of continuity and change, of identity and difference – such a perspective opens cultural poetics to history.

Such binary terms as *containment* and *subversion, dominance* and *contestation* are always dialectical and relative; their configuration, content, and effect are produced in specific and changing conjunctures. During the 1940s and 1950s, literary-historical scholarship was much concerned to demonstrate the ideological orthodoxy of such canonical authors as Shakespeare. In the climate of recent cultural politics, however, it has become fashionable for critics to affirm their favorite canonical literary works to be "subversive" of their own canonicity. Frequently, such claims are based on analyses that are less historical and dialectical than formal and immanent, implying that "subversiveness" is an essence secreted in particular texts or classes of texts. However, as Jonathan Dollimore points out in his introduction to *Political Shakespeare*:

Nothing can be intrinsically or essentially subversive in the sense that prior to the event subversiveness can be more than potential; in other words it cannot be guaranteed a priori, independent of articulation, context and reception. Likewise the mere thinking of

a radical idea is not what makes it subversive: typically it is the context of its articulation:
to whom, how many and in what circumstances; one might go further and suggest that
not only does the idea have to be conveyed, it has also actually to be used to refuse authority *or* be seen by authority as capable and likely of being so used. It is, then, somewhat
misleading to speak freely and only of "subversive thought"; what we are concerned with
… is a social *process*. (13)

Crucial here is the concept of a "context of … articulation," which must include not
only the social effectivity of a particular notion, formulation, or action but also the
historical and social specificity of its subsequent representations; in other words, it
must include the context of articulation – or, following Tony Bennett, what we might
also call the reading formation – within which we retrospectively inscribe, identify, and
interpret "subversion." Ideology can be said to exist only as it is instantiated in particular
cultural forms and practices, including those traditionally categorized as literature and
as criticism. All texts are ideologically marked, however multivalent or inconsistent that
inscription may be. And if the ideological status of texts in the literary canon is necessarily overdetermined and unstable, it is so precisely as a condition and consequence of
their canonicity. If, for example, I characterize *Hamlet* as a "complex" text, I am not
reverting to an aesthetics of immanence, unity, and closure; rather, I am describing the
transformation of a *text* into an open, changing, and contradictory *discourse* that is
cumulatively produced and appropriated within history and within a history of other
productions and appropriations. In so historically and socially sedimented a textual
space – an always-occupied space that signifies to a historically and ideologically sited
reader – so many cultural codes converge and interact that ideological coherence and
stability are scarcely possible.

IV

In "Renaissance Literary Studies and the Subject of History," I did not characterize new
historicism as a school, movement, or program but merely as an emergent historical
orientation within our field of study. It seemed to me then that those identified with this
orientation, by themselves or by others, were heterogeneous in their critical practices
and, for the most part, reluctant to theorize those practices. The very lack of such explicit
articulations was itself symptomatic of the residual elements of empiricism, formalism,
and humanism that undermined attempts to distinguish any new critical paradigm from
an older one. Furthermore – and in marked contrast to both their feminist and Marxist
contemporaries in the United States and their cultural materialist colleagues in
Britain – American male academics producing new-historicist work in Renaissance
studies during the past decade tended to displace and contain the cultural politics of
their own practice by at once foregrounding relations of power and confining them to the
English past that was presently under study. In Britain – where class barriers remain
more clearly articulated than in the United States; where, too, radical politics enjoy
stronger traditions; and where the coercive pressure of the state on centralized educational institutions and practices has for some time been direct and intense – there has
been a polemical emphasis by cultural materialist critics on the uses to which a historical
present puts its versions of the national past (see Dollimore and Sinfield, "Culture" and
Political Shakespeare). Such scholars have been concerned with the processes by which

the canon of English Authors and Works incorporated into English culture and into the British educational system has helped to forge the ideology of the dominant social class and to perpetuate its hegemony. Cultural materialism derives its name, principles, and politics from the later, Gramsci-inspired work of Raymond Williams. In their brief, programmatic foreword to *Political Shakespeare*, Jonathan Dollimore and Alan Sinfield propound "a combination of historical context, theoretical method, political commitment and textual analysis" (vii) as the four principles of cultural materialism. Among these, explicit "political commitment" of the sort they suggest – "socialist and feminist commitment [that] confronts the conservative categories in which most criticism has hitherto been conducted" – is conspicuously absent from the American new-historicist work with which they align their own. Analogous projects in the United States have been more feminist or Marxist than new historicist.

A complex amalgam of geographical, social, ethnic, institutional, and gender-specific factors were at work in producing, in the work of American new historicists, a domesticated Foucauldian emphasis on historical and cultural discontinuities, on the radical and fascinating otherness of the Renaissance. To the degree that it recuperated in practice the critical traditions and values that it (sometimes nostalgically) repudiated in principle, the emergent new historicism may have been perceived by some discomfited English professors as more palatable than the Marxist and feminist projects with which it was ambiguously linked. Such a response may partially explain the rapid installation of "The New Historicism" as the newest academic orthodoxy, its rapid assimilation and varying appropriations by the fractious "interpretive community" of Renaissance literary studies – and, too, the waves of opposition and attack following almost immediately on its canonization. Certainly, some who have been identified as exemplary new historicists now enjoy the material and symbolic tokens of academic success; and any number of clearly labeled new-historicist dissertations, conferences, and publications testify to an institutional authority and prestige. However, it remains unclear whether this "ism," with its appeal to our commodifying cult of the "new," will have been more than another passing intellectual fancy in what Jameson would call the academic marketplace under late capitalism. The new historicism has not yet faded from the academic scene, nor has it quietly taken its place in the assortment of critical approaches on the interpreter's shelf. But neither has it become any clearer that "the new historicism" designates any agreed-on intellectual and institutional program. There has been no coalescence of the various identifiably new-historicist practices into a systematic and authoritative interpretive paradigm, nor does the emergence of such a paradigm seem either likely or desirable. Instead, what we have been witnessing is the convergence of various special interests on an unstable signifier: *New historicism* has been constituted as a terminological site of intense debate, of multiple appropriations and contestations, not only within Renaissance studies but in other areas of literary criticism, in history and anthropology, and within the cross-disciplinary space of cultural studies.

During the past decade, as some historians and anthropologists have become increasingly concerned with the cognitive and ideological importance of narrative forms and rhetorical strategies, literary theory has come to exert an unprecedented extradisciplinary influence in the humanities and interpretive social sciences. For example, in a discussion of recent controversies in history, Lynn Hunt characterizes that discipline as "an ongoing tension between stories that have been told and stories that might be told. In this sense, it is more useful to think of history as an ethical and political practice than as an epistemology with a clear ontological status" ("History" 103). And, in anthropology, the ambiguous status of the ethnographer as participant-observer of the alien culture that is the object of study has been reproblematized by a focus on textual and ideological dimensions of ethnographic discourse (Clifford and Marcus; Marcus and Fischer; Wagner). It should be noted, however, that such trends have also met with considerable hostility from some historians and anthropologists, and that the opposition manifests a range of positions analogous to those critical of poststructuralist and new-historicist directions in literary studies. For example, some scholars in the tradition of empiricist Marxist historiography have produced their own version of the opposition between textuality and materiality; and having done so, they are compelled to insist on the logical and the political priority of the latter term (Fox-Genovese). At the other end of the political-intellectual spectrum, guardians of the Humanist tradition engage in an idealist and essentialist polemic against poststructuralist, textualist, and new-historicist modes of historiography (Himmelfarb).

Much of the most interesting work now being produced within our discipline is by younger scholars whose graduate studies have endowed them with a poststructuralist sensitivity to both the *instability* and the *instrumentality* of representation. In their dissertations and publications, these younger scholars are synthesizing elements of the engaged theoretical discourses of feminism, Marxism, postcolonialism, and gay and lesbian studies. Some of this work demonstrates that avowedly new-historicist perspectives are compatible with, and enabling of, such projects of cultural-political analysis and critique. It seems to me, however, that although it is sometimes construed as a cultural-political project unto itself, the merely academic phenomenon of new historicism is incommensurable with the worldwide social movements articulated by feminist, Marxist, postcolonial, and gay and lesbian discourses. A partial explanation of why *new historicism* has been at once so central and so contested a term may lie in the relative availability of new-historicist methods for deployment in projects of widely varying or obscure ideological direction.

Right-wing critics in the academy, the popular press, and the federal government have yoked new historicism with Marxism and feminism in an unholy trinity bent on sullying, with its political credo of race, class, and gender, the enduring and universal concerns of the great authors and works (D. Brooks; Cheney, *Humanities*; Pechter; Will). At the same time, some self-identified Marxist critics have been actively indicting new historicism for its reluctance to address processes of historical change, for its evasion of political commitments, for its tendency to confine its analyses to the texts of men working within the dominant discourse, and thus for its inadequate attention to the marginalized or suppressed voices of the colonized and the commons, as well as those of women (W. Cohen; Gallagher, "Marxism"; Holstun; Porter "Are We Being Historical" and "History"). While some scholars, including both women and men, are fruitfully combining new-historicist and feminist perspectives in their research and teaching, others have represented these projects in terms of a gender-specific antagonism. This hostility seems to have its origin in a complex amalgam of gender politics, intellectual antipathies between new historicism and modes of psychoanalytic and essentialist feminism, and professional and institutional rivalries symptomatic of the academy at large. New historicist work by men has been indicted for its effacements, objectifications, marginalizations, and appropriations of feminist discourses and/or of women (Boose; P. Erickson; Neely, "Constructing"; J. Newton; Waller). Whatever the critical practice of particular new historicists, there has never seemed to me to be any *necessary* problem of theoretical, methodological, or political incompatibility between new historicism and materialist and historicist modes of feminist criticism. And, indeed, work that is both feminist and new historicist is increasingly evident in many areas of literary and cultural studies. While some see new historicism as one of several modes of criticism engaged in constructing a theoretically informed, poststructuralist problematic of historical study, others see it as aligned with a neopragmatist and cynically professionalist reaction against all claims for the theorization of practice and all calls for an oppositional cultural politics. If some see new-historicist preoccupation with ideology and social context as threatening to traditional idealist and humanist values, others see a new-historicist delight in anecdote, narrative and "thick description" as an imperialistic will to appropriate *all* of culture at the domain of literary criticism – to construe the world as an aesthetic macrotext to be cleverly interpreted by means of a formalist cultural poetics.

Inhabiting the discursive spaces currently traversed by the term *new historicism* are some of the most complex, persistent, and unsettling problems that professors of literature attempt to confront or to evade – among them the conflict between essentialist and historically specific perspectives on the category of literature and its relations with other discourses; the possible relations between cultural practices and social, political, and economic institutions and processes; the consequences of poststructuralist theories of textuality for historical or materialist criticism; the means by which ideologies are produced, sustained, and contested; the operations that construct, maintain, destabilize, and alter subjectivity through the shifting conjunctures of multiple subject positions. My point is not that "the new historicism" as a definable project, or the work of individuals identified by themselves or by others as new historicists, can provide even provisional answers to each of these questions but rather that "the new historicism" is currently being invoked in order to bring such problems into play, and to stake out, or to hunt down, specific positions on the ideological terrain mapped by them.

The poststructuralist orientation to history now emerging in literary studies I characterize chiastically, as a reciprocal concern with the historicity of texts and the textuality of histories. By the *historicity of texts*, I mean to suggest the historical specificity, the social and material embedding, of all modes of *writing* – including not only the texts that critics study but also the texts in which we study them; thus, I also mean to suggest the historical, social, and material embedding of all modes of *reading*. By the *textuality of histories*, I mean to suggest, in the first place, that we can have no access to a full and authentic past, to a material existence that is unmediated by the textual traces of the society in question; and, furthermore, that the survival of those traces rather than others cannot be assumed to be merely contingent but must rather be presumed to be at least partially consequent on subtle processes of selective preservation and effacement – processes like those that have produced the traditional humanities curriculum. In the second place, those victorious traces of material and ideological struggle are themselves subject to subsequent mediations when they are construed as the "documents" on which those who profess the humanities ground their own descriptive and interpretive texts. As Hayden White and others have forcefully reminded us, such textual histories and ethnographies necessarily although incompletely constitute, in their own narrative and rhetorical forms, the past or alien actions and meanings – the "history" or "culture" – to which they offer access.

In *After the New Criticism*, Lentricchia links "the antihistorical impulses of formalist theories of literary criticism" with monolithic and teleological theories of history (xiii–xiv) – visions of history that, in their unity, totality, and inexorability, can be grounded only on essentialist or metaphysical premises. I assume that among such visions of history belongs not only the great code of Christian figural and eschatological history but also the master narrative of classical Hegelian Marxism. The latter has been characterized by Jameson as "history now conceived in its vastest sense of the sequence of modes of production and the succession and destiny of the various human social formations"; this he projects as the "untranscendable horizon" of interpretive activity, subsuming "apparently antagonistic or incommensurable critical operations, assigning them an undoubted sectoral validity within itself, and thus at once cancelling and preserving them" (*Political Unconscious* 75, 10). (Perhaps we should now add, as a bathetic coda to the history of grand historical narratives, the recent pop theory that, with the collapse of totalitarian Communist regimes in eastern Europe, History as such has suddenly ended – the end having come somewhat short of the Marxian trajectory, in the supposed universal embrace of liberal democracy and consumer capitalism.) One of the most powerful theoretical challenges to the Marxian master narrative has come from within the Marxist tradition itself, in the post-Marxist analysis of Ernesto Laclau and Chantal Mouffe. In the polemical introduction to *Hegemony and Socialist Strategy*, they write that

> there is not *one* discourse and *one* system of categories through which the "real" might speak without mediations. In operating deconstructively within Marxist categories, we do not claim to be writing "universal history," to be inscribing our discourse as a moment of a single, linear process of knowledge. Just as the era of normative epistemologies has come to an end, so too has the era of universal discourses. (3)

Accordingly, "the rejection of privileged points of rupture and the confluence of struggles into a unified political space, and the acceptance, on the contrary, of the plurality and indeterminacy of the social, seem to us the two fundamental bases from which a new political imaginary can be constructed" (152). Similarly, against the monstrous marriage of unhistoricized formalisms and totalized history, Lentricchia opposes the multiplicity of "histories," characterized by "forces of heterogeneity, contradiction, fragmentation, and difference" (*New Criticism* xiv). It seems to me that the various modes of what could be called poststructuralist historical criticism – including new historicism or cultural poetics, as well as modes of revisionist, or post-, Marxism – can be characterized by such a shift from History to histories.

The conjunction of the terms *new historicism* and *cultural poetics* points to the characteristic mixture, in exemplary new-historicist work, of historicist and formalist, materialist and textualist or tropological, interests and analytical techniques (Liu, "Power"; Wayne, "New Historicism"). As I have suggested, this mixture is sometimes criticized as being – and may sometimes merely be – the symptom of a fundamentally antimaterialist, residual, or recuperative formalism. But it has also demonstrated the potential for development in the direction of a genuinely materialist and historicist formalism – a historical analysis of what Jameson calls "the ideology of form," which is inseparable from a historical analysis of the form of ideology. "The ideology of form and the form of ideology"; "the historicity of texts and the textuality of histories": if such chiastic formulations are in fashion today – when, in the wake of deconstruction, referentiality has become so vexed and tropology so conspicuous – it may be because they figure forth from within discourse itself the model of a reciprocally constitutive and transformative relation between the discursive and material domains. Rejecting "the distinction between discursive and non-discursive practices," Laclau and Mouffe have asserted that "every object is constituted as an object of discourse, insofar as no object is given outside every discursive condition of emergence." They hasten to add that "the fact that every object is constituted as an object of discourse has *nothing to do* with whether there is a world external to thought, or with the realism / idealism opposition"; against the assumption that discourse is merely mental in character, they affirm "the *material* character of every discursive structure" (109, 110). One important implication for literary studies is the possibility of transcending the formalist-historicist opposition in a new mode of textualist-materialist critical practice:

> The main consequence of a break with the discursive/extra-discursive dichotomy is an abandonment of the thought/reality opposition, and hence a major enlargement of the field of those categories which can account for social relations. Synonymy, metonymy, metaphor are not forms of thought that add a second sense to a primary, constitutive literality of social relations; instead, they are part of the primary terrain itself in which the social is constituted. (110)

From a perspective that affirms *figuration* to be *materially* constitutive of society and history, the reorientation in literary studies of which Hillis Miller has complained – the turn from "language as such … toward history, culture, society, politics, institutions" – might be better construed as a widening and deepening of our central scholarly concern with language and reading. Literary criticism has for some time been making its traditional analytical strengths useful to new transdisciplinary projects of cultural analysis, and it has been doing so by studying the ways in which discursive forms and processes constitute "history, culture, society, politics, institutions."

V

Recent invocations of *history* (which, like *power*, is a term now in constant danger of hypostatization) have often appeared to be responses to – or, in certain cases, nothing more than positivistic retrenchments against – various structuralist and poststructuralist formalisms that have seemed, to some, to question the very possibility of historical understanding and historical experience; that have threatened to dissolve history into what Perry Anderson has suggested is an antinomy of objectivist determinism and subjectivist free play, an antinomy that allows no possibility for historical agency on the part of individual or collective human subjects (*In the Tracks*). *Subject*, both a grammatical and a political term, has come into widespread use not merely as a fashionable synonym for *the individual* but precisely as a means of emphasizing that individuals and the very concept of the individual are historically constituted in language and society. Although it continues to thrive in the mass media, in political rhetoric, and in undergraduate essays, the freely self-creating and world-creating individual of so-called bourgeois humanism has, for quite some time, been defunct in the texts of academic theory. Against the beleaguered category of the historical agent, contending armies of theory have opposed the specters of structural determinism and poststructural contingency – the latter tartly characterized by Anderson as "subjectivism without a subject" (54). We now behold, on the one hand, the implacable code, and on the other, the slippery signifier – the contemporary equivalents of Predestination and Fortune.

Anderson remarks that the "one master-problem around which *all* contenders have revolved" on the battlefield of contemporary social theory is "the nature of the relationships between structure and subject in human history and society" (33). Variations on this problematic might juxtapose structure to history or to practice; might oppose system or totality, on the one hand, to strategy or agency, on the other. And, indeed, one such version has characterized the interplay of current historical-social-political orientations to English and American literary studies in the form of containment versus subversion. As I have already suggested, such formulations are no more adequate to our own situation than to that of Elizabethan England. I believe that we should resist the reductive tendency to formulate our conceptual terms in binary oppositions; rather, we should construe them as joined in a mutually constitutive, recursive, and transformative *process*.

I have in mind here such recent work in social theory as Anthony Giddens's concept of *structuration*:

> The structural properties of social systems are both the medium and the outcome of the practices that constitute those systems. ...
> Rules and resources are drawn upon by actors in the production of interaction, but are thereby also reconstituted through such interaction. (*Central Problems* 69, 71)

Pierre Bourdieu's concept of *habitus*:

> Systems of durable, transposable *dispositions*, structured structures predisposed to function as structuring structures, that is, as principles of the generation and structuring of practices and representations. ... (*Outline* 72)

and Marshall Sahlins's concept of the *structure of the conjuncture*:

> History is culturally ordered, differently so in different societies, according to meaningful schemes of things. The converse is also true: cultural schemes are historically ordered, since to a greater or lesser extent the meanings are revalued as they are practically enacted. ...
> By the "structure of the conjuncture" I mean the practical realization of the cultural categories in a specific historical context, as expressed in the interested action of the historical agents. (*Islands* vii, xiv)

With such perspectives in mind, we might entertain the following propositions: that the processes of subjectification and structuration are both interdependent and ineluctably historical; that the apparent systematicity of society is produced, adjusted, and transformed by means of the interactive social practices of individuals and groups; and that there is no necessary relationship between the intentions of actors and the outcomes of their actions – in other words, that their effectivity is conjunctural or situational and, to varying degrees, contingent. The possibilities for action are always socially and historically situated, always limited and limiting. Nevertheless, collective structures may enable as well as constrain individual agency; and they may be potentially enabling precisely when they are experienced by the subject as multiple, heterogeneous, and even contradictory in their imperatives. Paul Smith articulates such a concept of agency:

> The symbolic realm, the *place* where we are in language and in social formations and which is also the *process* whereby we fit into them, *constructs* the ideological. ... Resistance does take place, but it takes place only within a social context which has already construed

subject-positions for the human agent. The place of that resistance has, then, to be glimpsed somewhere in the interstices of the subject-positions which are offered in any social formation. More precisely, resistance must be regarded as the by-product of contradictions in and among subject-positions. ... Resistance is best understood as a specific twist in the dialectic between individuation and ideological interpellation. (25)

The possibility of social and political agency cannot be based on the illusion that consciousness is a condition somehow beyond ideology. However, the very process of subjectively *living* the contradictions *within* or *among* ideological formations may allow us to experience facets of our own subjection at shifting internal distances – to read, as in a refracted light, one fragment of our ideological inscription by means of another. A reflexive knowledge so partial and unstable may, nevertheless, provide subjects with a means of empowerment as agents. Thus my invocation of the term *subject* is meant to suggest an equivocal process of *subjectification*: on the one hand, it shapes individuals as loci of consciousness and initiators of action, endowing them with *subjectivity* and with the capacity for agency; and, on the other hand, it positions, motivates, and constrains them within – it *subjects them to* – social networks and cultural codes, forces of necessity and contingency, that ultimately exceed their comprehension or control.

The refiguring of the relation between the verbal and the social, between the text and the world, involves a rejection of some still-prevalent, alternative idealist, empiricist, and materialist conceptions of literature: as an autonomous aesthetic, moral, or intellectual order that transcends the shifting and conflicting pressures of material needs and interests; as a collection of inert discursive records of "real events"; as the superstructural reflection produced by a determining economic base. Recent theories of textuality have argued persuasively that the referent of a linguistic sign cannot be fixed, that the meaning of a text cannot be stabilized. However, writing and reading are always historically and socially situated events, performed *in* the world and *upon* the world by ideologically situated individual and collective human agents. In any situation of signification, the theoretical indeterminacy of the signifying process is delimited by the historical specificity of discursive practices, by the constraints and resources of the reading formation within which that signification takes place. The project of a new sociohistorical criticism in literary studies is, then, to analyze the interplay of culture-specific discursive practices, including those by which cultural canons are formed and reformed. By such discursive means, versions of the real, of history, are experienced, deployed, reproduced, and by such means they may also be appropriated, contested, transformed.

Any collective critical project must be mindful that it, too, is a social practice that participates in the very interplay of interests and perspectives that it seeks to analyze. All academic texts selectively constitute the objects of their literary-historical knowledge, and do so on frequently unexamined and inconsistent grounds. Integral to any genuinely new-historicist project, however, must be a realization and acknowledgment that our analyses necessarily proceed from our own historically, socially, and institutionally shaped vantage points and that the pasts we reconstruct are, at the same time, the textual constructs of critics who are, ourselves, historical subjects. Our comprehension and representation of the texts of the past proceed by a mixture of estrangement and appropriation, as a reciprocal conditioning by the discourses of the past and our discourses about the past (McCanles; LaCapra, "Rethinking"). Scholarship actively constructs and delimits its object of study, and the scholar is historically positioned vis-à-vis that object. Thus, a historical criticism that seeks to recover meanings that are in any final or absolute sense authentic, correct, and complete is pursuing an illusion. It also becomes necessary to historicize the present as well as the past, and to historicize the dialectic between them – those pressures by which the past has shaped the present and the present reshapes the past. Such a critical practice constitutes a dialogue between a *poetics* and a *politics* of culture.

Since the beginning of the 1980s – the period marked, according to Miller, by the lurch of literary studies "toward history, culture, society, politics, institutions, class and gender conditions, the social context, the material base" – segments of the American political establishment, the mass media, and the neoconservative intelligentsia have been attacking what they represent as the degradation of literature and the humanities within the academy, and of cultural production and performance in society at large, as a result of the leftist agendas of professors and artists. In the very process of mobilizing their attack, these forces have made manifest their own agendas for the policing of education and the arts. The campaign for curricular reform pursued by the National Endowment for the Humanities has played on a widespread anxiety about the perceived demise of "traditional values" since the permissive 1960s. Under the successive leadership of William Bennett and Lynne V. Cheney, the NEH has focused on the preservation of curricula reflecting the dominant culture and the maintenance of syllabi that emphasize the putative stability, cohesion, and inclusiveness of American values and beliefs. A succession of official NEH reports, which have been endorsed in numerous editorials and popular commentaries, have sought to discredit cultural analyses that stress alternative and oppositional perspectives in history, politics, class, race, gender, and sexuality.

Whatever other responses it may provoke, the hostile attention paid from beyond the groves of academe to developments in literary theory, curriculum, and pedagogy confirms that the academy is perceived as a site for the contestation as well as for the reproduction of ideological dominants; that there may be something important at stake in our reading, teaching, and revision of the literary canon; and that, if we suddenly discover ourselves to be culturally and institutionally empowered, we are now compelled to choose if, when, and how to employ that power. The politics of the academy extend beyond what we casually refer to as "academic politics": the study and teaching of cultural poetics are enmeshed in a larger cultural politics that is without disinterested parties, without objective positions. Nevertheless, the claim to just such disinterestedness, like the naive appeal beyond interpretation to "the text itself," is a means of legitimating the dominant interest. By our choices, not only of what to read but of how to read, we may bring to our students and to ourselves a heightened awareness that we are engaged in a politics of reading, a sharper sense of our own historicity, an apprehension of our own positions within a regime of power and knowledge that at once sustains us and constrains us. It is by reconstruing "literature" within an unstable and agonistic field of verbal and social practices – by redrawing the boundaries of literary study, and then by transgressing those boundaries – that we may articulate the humanities as a site of intellectually and socially significant work in the historical present.[1]

Note

1   Portions of this essay have appeared under the title "Professing the Renaissance: The Poetics and Politics of Culture" in the book *The New Historicism*, edited by H. Aram Veeser, published by Routledge in 1989.

Selected Bibliography

This list of suggestions for further reading contains a number of studies exemplifying new-historicist and related modes of recent literary criticism. I have selected only books, emphasized collections and anthologies rather than single-author volumes, and included representative work in fields of literary study outside the English Renaissance.

Greenblatt, Stephen J. *Renaissance Self-Fashioning: From More to Shakespeare*. Chicago: U of Chicago P, 1980. A seminal study in the cultural poetics of identity formation in Tudor and Jacobean England.

Greenblatt, Stephen J., ed. *Representing the English Renaissance*. Berkeley: U of California P, 1988. An anthology of essays on sixteenth- and seventeenth-century English culture and ideology, reprinted from the journal *Representations*. Many of the articles are characteristic of new-historicist methods and themes.

Hunt, Lynn, ed. *The New Cultural History*. Berkeley: U of California P, 1989. A stimulating collection of original essays on current methods and topics in the practice of cultural history, by scholars from the United States, Britain, and France.

Levinson, Marjorie, Marilyn Butler, Jerome McGann, and Paul Hamilton. *Rethinking Historicism: Critical Readings in Romantic History*. Oxford: Blackwell, 1989. A collection of revisionist studies of English Romanticism by British and American critics.

Michaels, Walter Benn, and Donald E. Pease, eds. *The American Renaissance Reconsidered: Selected Papers from the English Institute*, 1982–83. Baltimore: Johns Hopkins UP, 1985. Revisionist studies of canonical and noncanonical American Renaissance writers in relation to nineteenth-century socioeconomic issues, and of the critical history of the American Renaissance in relation to twentieth-century ideologies.

Patterson, Lee, ed. *Literary Practice and Social Change in Britain*, 1380–1530. The New Historicism: Studies in Cultural Poetics 8. Berkeley: U of California P, 1990. Critical historicist essays on writing practices in late medieval England and on the discipline of medieval studies.

Veeser, H. Aram, ed. *The New Historicism*. New York: Routledge, 1989. A lively collection of analytical and polemical essays from a variety of critical and disciplinary perspectives, on the genealogy, methods, and politics of the new historicism.

Works Cited

Althusser, Louis. *Lenin and Philosophy and Other Essays*. Trans. Ben Brewster. New York: Monthly Rev., 1971.

Anderson. Perry. *In the Tracks of Historical Materialism*. Chicago: U of Chicago P. 1984.

Arac, Jonathan, and Barbara Johnson, eds. *Consequences of Theory: Selected Papers from the English Institute, 1987–88*. Baltimore: Johns Hopkins UP, 1991.

Asad, Talal. "Anthropological Conceptions of Religion: Reflections on Geertz." *Man* 18 (1983): 237–59.

Bennett, Tony. "Texts in History: The Determinations of Readings and Their Texts." *Post-structuralism and the Question of History*. Ed. Derek Attridge, Geoff Bennington, and Robert Young. Cambridge: Cambridge UP, 1987. 63–81.

Biersack, Aletta. "Local Knowledge, Local History: Geertz and Beyond." Hunt, *New Cultural History* 72–96.

Boose, Lynda E. "The Family in Shakespeare Studies; or, Studies in the Family of Shakespeareans; or, The Politics of Politics." *Renaissance Quarterly* 40 (1987): 707–42.

Bourdieu, Pierre. *Outline of a Theory of Practice*. Trans. Richard Nice. Cambridge: Cambridge UP, 1977.

Brooks, David. "From Western Lit to Westerns as Lit." *Wall Street Journal* 2 Feb. 1988: 36.

Cheney, Lynne V. *American Memory: A Report on the Humanities in the Nation's Public Schools*. Washington: NEH, 1987.

Cheney, Lynne V. *Humanities in America: A Report to the President, the Congress, and the American People*. Washington: NEH, 1988.

Clifford, James, and George E. Marcus, eds. *Writing Culture: The Poetics and Politics of Ethnography*. Berkeley: U of California P, 1986.

Cohen, Walter. "Political Criticism of Shakespeare." Howard and O'Connor 18–46.

Crapanzano, Vincent. "Hermes's Dilemma: The Masking of Subversion in Ethnographic Description." Clifford and Marcus 50–76.

Derrida, Jacques. "But, beyond ...: Open Letter to Anne McClinstock and Rob Nixon." Trans. Peggy Kamuf. *Critical Inquiry* 13 (1986): 155–70.

Dollimore, Jonathan, and Alan Sinfield. "Culture and Textuality: Debating Cultural Materialism." *Textual Practice* 4 (1990): 91–100.

Dollimore, Jonathan, and Alan Sinfield, eds. *Political Shakespeare: New Essays in Cultural Materialism*. Ithaca UP: Cornell, 1985.

Eagleton, Terry. *Ideology: An Introduction*. London: Verso, 1991.

Erickson, Peter. "Rewriting the Renaissance, Rewriting Ourselves." *Shakespeare Quarterly* 38 (1987): 327–37.

Foucault, Michel. 'The Discourse on Language." *The Archaeology of Knowledge*. Trans. Alan Sheridan. New York: Pantheon, 1972. 215–37.

Foucault, Michel. *The History of Sexuality: An Introduction*. Trans. Robert Hurley. New York: Pantheon, 1978. Vol. 1 of *The History of Sexuality*. 3 vols. 1978–86.

Fox-Genovese, Elizabeth. "Literary Criticism and the Politics of New Historicism." Veeser 213–24.

Gallagher, Catherine. "Marxism and the New Historicism." Veeser 37–48.

Geertz, Clifford. *The Interpretation of Cultures: Selected Essays*. New York: Basic, 1973.

Geertz, Clifford. *Local Knowledge: Further Essays in Interpretive Anthropology*. New York: Basic, 1983.

Geertz, Clifford. *Negara: The Theatre State in Nineteenth-Century Bali*. Princeton: Princeton UP, 1980.

Giddens, Anthony. *Central Problems in Social Theory: Action, Structure, and Contradiction in Social Analysis*. Berkeley: U of California P, 1979.

Goldberg, Jonathan. *James I and the Politics of Literature: Jonson, Donne, and Their Contemporaries*. Baltimore: Johns Hopkins UP, 1983.

Greenblatt, Stephen J. Introduction. *The Forms of Power and the Power of Forms in the Renaissance*. Spec. issue of *Genre* 15.1–2 (1982): 3–6.

Greenblatt, Stephen J. "Invisible Bullets: Renaissance Authority and Its Subversion." Dollimore and Sinfield, *Political Shakespeare* 18–47 .

Greenblatt, Stephen J. *Marvelous Possessions: The Wonder of the New World*. Chicago: U of Chicago P, 1991.

Greenblatt, Stephen J. *Renaissance Self-Fashioning: From More to Shakespeare*. Chicago: U of Chicago P, 1980.

Greenblatt, Stephen J, ed. *Representing the English Renaissance*. Berkeley: U of California P, 1988.

Greenblatt, Stephen J. *Shakespearean Negotiations: The Circulation of Social Energy in Renaissance England*. Berkeley: U of California P, 1988.

Greenblatt, Stephen J. "Towards a Poetics of Culture." *Southern Review* [Australia] 20 (1987): 3–15. Rpt. in Veeser 1–14.

Himmelfarb, Gertrude. *The New History and the Old: Critical Essays and Reappraisals*. Cambridge: Harvard UP, 1987.

Holstun, James. "Ranting at the New Historicism." *English Literary Renaissance* 19 (1989): 189–225.

Howard, Jean E., and Marion F. O'Connor. *Shakespeare Reproduced: The Text in History and Ideology*. New York: Methuen, 1987.

Hunt, Lynn "History as Gesture; or, The Scandal of History." Arac and Johnson 91–107 .

Hunt, Lynn, ed. *The New Cultural History*. Berkeley: U of California P, 1989.

Jameson, Fredric. *The Political Unconscious: Narrative as a Socially Symbolic Act*. Ithaca: Cornell UP, 1981.

Keesing, Roger M. "Anthropology as Interpretive Quest." *Current Anthropology* 28 (1987): 161–76.

LaCapra, Dominick. "Rethinking Intellectual History and Reading Texts." *Rethinking Intellectual History*. Ithaca: Cornell UP, 1983. 23–71.

LaCapra, Dominick. *Soundings in Critical Theory*. Ithaca: Cornell UP, 1989.

Laclau, Ernesto, and Chantal Mouffe. *Hegemony and Socialist Strategy: Towards a Radical Democratic Politics*. Trans. Winston Moore and Paul Cammack. London: Verso. 1985.

Lentricchia, Frank. *After the New Criticism*. Chicago: U of Chicago P, 1980.

Lentricchia, Frank. "Foucault's Legacy." Veeser 231–42.

Liu, Alan. "The Power of Formalism: The New Historicism." *ELH* 56 (1989): 721–71.

Marcus, George E., and Michael J. Fischer, eds. *Anthropology as Cultural Critique: An Experimental Moment in the Human Sciences*. Chicago: U of Chicago P, 1986.

McCanles, Michael. "The Authentic Discourse of the Renaissance." *Diacritics* 10 (1980): 77–87.

Miller, J. Hillis. "Presidential Address 1986. The Triumph of Theory, the Resistance to Reading, and the Question of the Material Base." *PMLA* 102 (1987): 281–91.

Montrose, Louis. "'Eliza, Queene of Shepheardes' and the Pastoral of Power." *English Literary Renaissance* 10 (1980): 153–82.

Montrose, Louis. "Of Gentlemen and Shepherds: The Politics of Elizabethan Pastoral Form." *ELH* 50 (1983): 415–59.

Montrose, Louis. "'The Place of a Brother' in *As You Like It:* Social Process and Comic Form." *Shakespeare Quarterly* 32 (1981): 28–54.

Montrose, Louis. "The Purpose of Playing: Reflections on a Shakespearean Anthropology." *Helios ns* 7 (1980): 51–74.

Montrose, Louis. "Renaissance Literary Studies and the Subject of History." *English Literary Renaissance* 16 (1986): 5–12.

Montrose, Louis. "'Shaping Fantasies': Figurations of Gender and Power in Elizabethan Culture." *Representations* 2 (1983): 61–94.

Mullaney, Steven. "Lying like the Truth: Riddle, Representation, and Treason in Renaissance England." *ELH* 47 (1980): 32–48.

Mullaney, Steven. *The Place of the Stage: License, Play, and Power in Renaissance England*. Chicago: U of Chicago P, 1988.

Mullaney, Steven. "Strange Things, Gross Terms, Curious Customs: The Rehearsal of Cultures in the Late Renaissance." *Representations* 3 (1983): 40–67.

Neely, Carol T. "Constructing the Subject: Feminist Practice and New Renaissance Discourses." *English Literary Renaissance* 18 (1988): 5–18.

Newton, Judith. "History as Usual?: Feminism and the 'New Historicism.'" *Cultural Critique* 9 (1988): 87–121.

Pechter, Edward. "The New Historicism and Its Discontents: Politicizing Renaissance Drama." *PMLA* 102 (1987): 292–303.

Pecora, Vincent P. "The Limits of Local Knowledge." Veeser 243–76.

Porter, Carolyn. "Are We Being Historical Yet?" *South Atlantic Quarterly* 87 (1988): 743–86.

Porter, Carolyn. "History and Literature: 'After the New Historicism.'" *New Literary History* 21 (1990): 253–72.

Sahlins, Marshall. *Culture and Practical Reason*. Chicago: U of Chicago P, 1975.

Sahlins, Marshall. *Islands of History*. Chicago: U of Chicago P, 1985.

Shankman, Paul. "The Thick and the Thin: On the Interpretive Theoretical Program of Clifford Geertz." *Current Anthropology* 25 (1984): 262–79.

Smith. Paul. *Discerning the Subject*. Minneapolis: U of Minnesota P, 1988.

Veeser, H. Aram, ed. *The New Historicism*. New York: Routledge, 1989.

Wagner, Roy. *The Invention of Culture*. Rev. ed. Chicago: U of Chicago P, 1981.

Waller, Marguerite. "Academic Tootsie: The Denial of Difference and the Difference It Makes." *Diacritics* 17 (1987): 2–20.

Walters, Ronald G. "Signs of the Times: Clifford Geertz and Historians." *Social Research* 47 (1980): 537–56.

Wayne, Don E. "New Historicism." *Literature and Criticism: A New Century Guide*. Ed. Kelsall et al. London: Routledge, 1990.

Wayne, Don E. *Penshurst: The Semiotics of Place and the Poetics of History*. Madison: U of Wisconsin P, 1984.

Wayne, Don E. "Power, Politics, and the Shakespearean Text." Howard and O'Connor 47–67 .

Whigham, Frank. *Ambition and Privilege: The Social Tropes of Elizabethan Courtesy Theory*. Berkeley: U of California P, 1984.

Will, George. "Literary Politics." *Newsweek* 22 Apr. 1991: 72.

Williams, Raymond. *Marxism and Literature*. Oxford: Oxford UP, 1977.

CHAPTER 10

Theory in Practice
Reason and Need: King Lear and the Crisis of the Aristocracy

Rosalie Colie

Rosalie Colie's essay is a good example of traditional literary historiography. She considers Shakespeare's play in relation to events of the time. In this case, those events consisted of the decline of the aristocracy, as a new mercantile social class began to emerge in the late sixteenth and early seventeenth centuries. Whilst the aristocracy relied largely on held land and its income to maintain their lifestyle (which did not involve work), the new merchants were entrepreneurs, investors, bankers, traders, and small industrialists who worked and made their own money. The laws of inheritance left many aristocrats without land, since property went to the eldest son in each family. So there was a downward movement economically on the part of many aristocrats. At the same time, the merchant class sought to increase its status by purchasing honors and titles. The identity of the aristocracy and its social ascendancy began to become unstable and precarious. Tensions mounted and, by the middle of the seventeenth century, a revolution occurred against the monarchy and the aristocratic class. *King Lear* resonates with these issues, as some undeserving sons strive to rise and take property from their elder, more legitimate brothers, and an aristocrat deals with the loss of power, land, and authority.

No; he's a yeoman that has a gentleman to his son; for he's a mad yeoman that sees his son a gentleman before him. (3.6.12–14)

When every case in law is right;
No squire in debt, nor no poor knight … (3.2.85–6)

Prithee, tell him, so much the rent of his land comes to … (1.4.140–1)

Original publication details: Rosalie Colie, "Reason and Need: *King Lear* and the Crisis of the Aristocracy" from *Some Facets of "King Lear": Essays in Prismatic Criticism*, ed. Rosalie Colie and F.T. Flahiff, pp. 185–220. University of Toronto Press, 1978. Reproduced with permission from University of Toronto Press.

Love cools, friendship falls off, brothers divide: in cities, mutinies; in countries, discord; in palaces, treason; and the bond crack'd 'twixt son and father. (1.2.110–14)

... unnaturalness between the child and the parent; death, dearth, dissolutions of ancient amities; divisions in state; menaces and maledictions against King and nobles; needless diffidences, banishment of friends, dissipation of cohorts, nuptial breaches, and I know not what. (1.2.151–6)

These comments from *King Lear* show some of the topsy-turvyness in the social order that informs the play, which has often been criticized as if its tragedy sprang from the simple disruption of an hieratic, orderly, customary society in which each man knew his place and responsibilities and kept to them both, in which duty and deference were expected and exacted in proportion to a man's known social and political status. According to one interpretation of *Lear* (as of many Shakespearean and other Renaissance dramas) the plot itself, with its manifold difficulties and sufferings, results from the deliberate abrogation of responsibility by the ruler. This Love-jovian or Tillyardian view has ruled for some time in criticism of the English Renaissance,[1] and only recently has it begun to be criticized, both by literary students who find in the abrogations of degree, priority, and place a less than necessary cause for tragic, or even significant action; and by historians who have consistently found the English Renaissance (like any other historical 'period') full of inconsistency, anomaly, disorder, and disruption.[2] Without quarrelling deeply with the Tillyardian notion of *the* Elizabethan world-picture, I want to pillage from quite a different historical scheme to illustrate some aspects of the social tensions involved in *King Lear*; that is, from Lawrence Stone's *Crisis of the Aristocracy, 1558–1641*, a rich, suggestive analysis of a major social class over a long period of time.[3]

Mr Stone's 'crisis' was a prolonged affair,[4] during which the aristocracy, although it never lost its favourable position in English society, lost its relative importance and was forced to alter its own self-image from that of an entrenched chivalric and 'feudal' group, with particular military obligations of service and general obligations of largesse, to that of a group involved in private lives and obligations precariously facing the problems of an expanding economy and a society increasingly articulate. Although the Tudors elevated themselves above their erstwhile peers, they came out of the aristocratic class and shared, as a family, some of the social and personal problems of that class.

Yet they sought to identify themselves with their state and its administration. Thus public policy underlined their differences from the nobility rather than their likenesses, and the English nobility found itself, like its European cousins, increasingly threatened by the centralizing efforts of the state. Chiefly, the court set out to gentle the armigerous aristocracy, to disarm them in all kinds of ways – by charming the nobles to live at court and to involve themselves in a growing bureaucracy;[5] by cutting the number of armed servants and thus the private military power long enjoyed by local noblemen; by educating the nobility to the gentle pursuits of humanistic learning and artistic patronage; by allowing and even encouraging the greater participation of women in social life – especially at its centre, the court itself. In many ways, central governments sought to domesticate the aristocracy; the aristocracy, too, found some pleasure and satisfaction in domesticating itself – in building houses according to new patterns; in making collections of paintings, sculpture, furniture, and books.

Withal, the aristocracy was faced with the particular problem of self-definition. Those who had given up the sword for the chamberer's graces found their relation to the sovereign somewhat altered: under Elizabeth and James, noble courtiers accustomed to deference themselves had to learn the importance of deferring to a monarch. The greater the family from which a courtier came, the greater the deference the monarch seemed to require. The more opulent a subject's house, the more he was expected to put it at his sovereign's service. In various rather touching ways, noblemen attempted to show their difference from other men. The great 'prodigy houses,' most of them built by Lords Treasurer, of whom Stone so amusingly speaks,[6] were for a while a major proof of class grandeur. With their ancient outlet in militarism gradually being closed off, noblemen and gentlemen tended to substitute the code of honour for the chivalric values. The older system of armigerous behaviour was superseded not only by modern technology and ordnance, but also by modern social arrangements: there was less and less place for the serious tournament or the trial-by-combat, as judicial settlements were otherwise reached. So a nobleman's word came to be defended and upheld by a complicated system of swordsmanship, based on the peculiar anomaly of the long, showy, dangerous rapier, which belonged neither to the old world of weaponry nor to the new. The rapier duel was an invention of a group of men trying to set themselves off socially from the 'others'; the weapon itself, carrying on a social tradition of archaism, was brilliantly and obviously nonfunctional as a practical weapon in an ordnance world.[7]

Another method by which noblemen set themselves off was dress. As Stone puts it, the acid test of living nobly was to have the money to spend liberally, to dress elegantly, and to entertain lavishly.[8] The portraits of the royal favourites, Leicester, Essex, Ralegh, and Buckingham, give some proof of the expense involved in looking the peacock courtier or the 'compleat' Queen.[9] Against such expenditure, even the conservative authors of the homilies sounded their injunctions: preachers never ceased to bewail the ruinous and frivolous preoccupation of the rich with their apparel.[10]

> Thou art a lady;
> If only to go warm were gorgeous,
> Why, nature needs not what thou gorgeous wear'st,
> Which scarcely keeps thee warm
>
> (2.4.269–72)

Lear says to Goneril, whose costume we can imagine from the opulent ladies portrayed in Renaissance pictures; and Kent's rage at Oswald – 'a tailor made thee!' – records his anger at the upstarts who imitated their social betters.

Conspicuous expenditure and consumption were frequent causes of ruin for aristocratic families: 'Put not your finger in mortar,' Coke wrote, having observed the financial difficulties incurred by many great builders. Critics of gorgeous apparel noted that men 'weare their lands upon their backes.'[11] Yet these particular modes of setting themselves off from other men did not protect the aristocracy from imitation by social inferiors: noble ladies were offended by the liquefaction of merchant capital that could be heard in the rustle of city wives' skirts. Satirical literature of the period is full of upstarts, crow and popinjay, 'nobodies' who deck themselves in the costumes and manners of their betters. Ralegh himself, though an intermittent profiteer from the arbitrary system of favourites, was in effect such a 'nobody': he rose by his wits, his imagination, and his *sprezzatura*, and he fell for the same qualities. Ralegh had exceptional talent and exceptional personality; the Osrics, Oswalds, and Parolleses of Shakespeare's world are permitted no such virtues. Their showiness is just that: they are the froth thrown up by a roiled social system. Clearly, then, garb and retinue were insufficient protections from social intrusion, and dressed-up nobodies offered a real critique of the methods by which noblemen defended themselves against encroachments upon their rank and exclusive privileges. One can recognize at once the superficiality of distinctions as separate from function, while acknowledging that as function declined, such distinctions seemed ever more necessary. Barred from the automatic recognition conferred by its old sumptuary monopolies,[12] the aristocracy had to find in just such attitudes, attributes, and costumes a substitute means of self-definition, even of self-identification. The sociological impor-tance of the nobility's self-concentration is obvious – and it carried economic implications as well, as shoals of craftsmen, jewellers, tailors, silkworkers, cabinetmakers, stonecarvers, architects, and so on, were called upon to support the aristocratic self-image in England.[13] The lavish expenditure characteristic of the medieval noble way of life was simple, as many commentators remarked,[14] compared to the new ways a nobleman might spend his money – the new commerce, the New World, and the aristocratic need for show accounted for remarkable outlays of income.

Although these signs of aristocracy were important and obvious at the time, they were by no means the only problems an aristocrat faced. Over the long span of time from the accession of Henry VII to the outbreak of the Civil War, there was obviously a slackening in the deference automatically due to a lord: the war itself is one gross measure of the change in aristocratic weight in the nation's social world. Other changes took place as well: for one thing, as Stone stresses, even among the aristocracy there was a consider-able decline in paternal authority. Very few children adopted the social views Edmund attributed to Edgar, that 'sons at perfect age, and fathers declin'd, the father should be as ward to the son, and the son manage his revenue' (1.2.72–4), but the case of poor Sir Brian Annesley, whose daughters sued to declare him insane that they might get his estate,[15] is relevant to the general problem and perhaps even to the play of *King Lear*. In spite of marked deference shown parents by their children in England, it is clear that over the century and a half of the Renaissance, fathers lost their unquestioned authority in the disposition of their children's lives and fortunes. Legal requirements came to protect, particularly, daughters. In other cases, fathers took a more active interest in their children's individual personalities and welfare, in particular permitting them to marry with greater attention to need and temperament; often, too, fathers provided so gener-ously for daughters and younger sons (in some cases, for bastards as well) that support for entailed estates was severely jeopardized.[16] As general respect for the individual came to be recognized, paternal authority counted for less; as ideals of social egalitarianism grew more widespread, aristocratic authority counted for less too. All the same, the class was, and remained, particularly privileged. Their crisis, such as it was, was as nothing to the difficulties suffered by the rural and urban poor, some of whom were not even privi-leged to recognize a 'crisis' in their affairs: life was certainly problematical for many segments of what is now called the middle class. But the nobility did face changes that unsettled many individuals within the class, if not the class itself. Against this particular set of problems, especially in their psychological manifestations, I want to look at *King Lear*. It is a play deeply rooted in its own period, a play which draws some of its power from the playwright's insight into the peculiar aristocratic situation of the time in which it was written, the situation Lawrence Stone has been at such pains to delineate.[17]

Before beginning on that task itself, I must assert something else, obvious enough. This play will not provide a proof-text for the aristocratic crisis (if that is what it was). Indeed, the adjustments described in Stone's book are too drawn out to have been compressed into one literary work – although, for a critic dissatisfied with a 'crisis' lasting for nearly a century, perhaps the concentration of the play more nearly justifies the use of that term. There is, of course, much in the general aristocratic social situation that is *not* in *King Lear*: for one thing, the play does not dwell topically on a major problem occupying the nobility and their advisers, namely, education; for another, though it exploits the question in its metaphors, it does not overtly deal with economics. In the play, actual economics are vague: the curious anachronisms of this play are uncompromised by discussions of pounds, shillings, pence, guineas, rose-nobles, and so on: but it is difficult not to read from this play a profound critique of habits of quantification induced by a commercial revolution. Though certainly questions of deference, of privatism, of personal and class ethos are of the utmost significance, *King Lear* is something very much greater, very much more complex, than a mere sketch in play-form of the psycho-social problems of new-style sovereigns and magnates. As these essays exist to proclaim, *King Lear* is made up of so much that to isolate one strand of its meaning is dangerously to oversimplify its multifoliate richness. The play is only in the highest sense an historical 'source,' testifying but fitfully to the problems historians must face head on. Indeed *King Lear* handles what might be called sociological materials very unevenly; at some points, the text is amazingly allusive, vague, and generalized; at others, remarkably direct and precise. The problem of being 'noble' is no less complicated than many of the purely literary problems this book deals with: the poet is sometimes astonishingly exact in what is here taken as data, and at other times hazy. But the playwright is nonetheless remarkable for what he saw in his society – and furthermore in a segment of society not naturally 'his' – and in his efficient translation into *literary* structures of the social structure of these problems. Indeed, he used many social paradigms in the terms of his given literary schemes and paradigms: he was able to treat his society, then, as he treated many other non-literary materials, as something to be rendered in the terms of his craft. What is remarkable, too, is that the playwright dealt analytically, even-handedly, and problematically with social problems, even as he consistently did with literary problems, and, thus, with the same striking insight and originality. If one may turn things about somewhat, the hypothesis might be offered that the play gives us, in its own laying out of social problems untouched by the benefits of modern analytical techniques, one bulwark to Lawrence Stone's massive analytic reconstruction of aristocratic society.

Within the play, historical structures are oddly treated. First of all, English 'history' is telescoped. According to chronicle-myth, the troubles of the Lear family did not end with the king's death; his daughters quarrelled fatally, and Cordelia's sons (imagine Cordelia with her sons!) did too. A train of Celtic king-figures had to reign before the historical Edgar could join the kingdom under a single strong rule.[18] The very names of the major figures in this play serve to fuse the layers of the English past – Lear and his daughters come from the catalogue of British royalty; Edgar and his wicked brother bear Anglo-Saxon names, one of them of the greatest significance in the roster of English kings; Gloucester was a Plantagenet royal title until the fifteenth century and would again become a royal title; the earls of Kent were local noblemen who had died out early in the sixteenth century; the title revived under Elizabeth in 1572. Albany and Cornwall were imaginable titles in the English Renaissance;[19] the earls of Cornwall had been both Plantagenets and Piers Gaveston; the kings of Scotland descended from a darkling Duke of Cornwall, and Albany was one of James I's titles as well.[20] The names 'Albany' and

'Cornwall' are realistic enough, then, but they recall something as well of Arthurian intermarriage. These names reverberate symbolically with English historical meaning; they do for the vertical range of time past what Edgar and Kent between them do for the horizontal range, across the social estates, of English speech, as those figures shift their dialects to offer a schematic section of the local and class languages of the nation. But Shakespeare was careful, too, in his use of title: he observed the rules of precedence, so that the blood royal takes precedence over all others, dukes take precedence over earls, and earls over the rest of the play's population.[21]

By such simple means, then, great implications are suggested. For all its moments of exact social observation and commentary, *King Lear* is surrounded by questions neither directly met nor directly answered. The action is mysteriously sited both in time and in place. The great rituals of the first scene echo with reverberations of something far deeper than specific reason or policy. We never know the practical details about the kingdom Lear rules and divides. Where does Lear hold court? Where was his palace before he went to lodge with his daughters in turn? That palace vanishes like Prospero's: indeed, except for Dover, we never know where anything takes place. In 1 *Henry* IV, the rebels divide the kingdom precisely, even arguing about its boundaries – Lear simply draws on a great map we never see. Obviously Gloucester's 'little' house (apparently a small castle of the old nobility rather than a great house of the new, but even so, peculiarly situated: 'for many miles about / There's scarce a bush' [2.4.303–4]) lies within the district allotted to Regan, for Cornwall becomes, Gloucester says, his 'patron.' Where Regan's house is in relation to it, or Goneril's in relation to either, we do not discover: simply, Lear's palace dissolves with his power, and the 'court' is concentrated on where power subsequently is rather than in a specific town or at a specific seat.

Other things are odd, too. Letters pass at an amazing rate from hand to hand – but there is no hint of how they do so. Nor do we know why the Gentleman (evidently the messenger between Cordelia and Kent) so readily trusts Kent on the heath; simply, we must accept that two good-hearted people, devoted to the king and Cordelia, trust one another on sight and do each other's offices willingly for that trust. All we know is that letters and people pass from here and there to Dover; even a beggar can lead a blind man to that critical port.

As with geography, so with other things: much is left unclear. Did Oswald do the act of darkness with Goneril, and if he did, why was he so willing to act as go-between for his mistress and Edmund? What happens to the Fool in fact and (more critical even) what kind of 'journey' must Kent go on, at the end of the play? Albany is left sole ruler of the kingdom, a position to which, judging from the first speech of the play, he had aspired; but without explanation or anything like the ritual fuss of the first act he resigns his rule first to Lear, then to Edgar. Most important of all, does Lear die thinking Cordelia dead or alive – can we tell, or should we try to tell? Within these areas of non-definition, of vagueness and mystery, the lives of King Lear and his three daughters, of the Earl of Gloucester and his two sons, of Kent, the Fool, and the rest are nonetheless lived to an extraordinary degree within the terms of sixteenth-century English society. Maynard Mack has pointed to one thematic and poetic gamut operating in this play, that from morality abstraction to naturalistic imitation of actions; the play moves along another gamut, from ritual and myth to an extremely practical and accurate grasp of local affairs.[22] There are things in this huge, difficult, and shocking play that become a little clearer when we apply to it some of the categories laid out by Stone's paradigm of the English aristocracy in the Renaissance.

Indeed, the more we look at the play, the more clearly we can see in it Stone's schema for the problems of the aristocracy. As he put it, 'the aristocratic ethic [*sic*] is one of voluntary service to the State, generous hospitality, clear class distinctions, social stability, tolerant indifference to the sins of the flesh, inequality of opportunity based on the accident of inheritance, arrogant self-confidence, a paternalist and patronizing attitude towards economic dependants and inferiors, and an acceptance of the grinding poverty of the lower classes as part of the natural order of things.'[23] These values are striking illuminations of the value-system of the play. For one thing, Kent's extraordinary loyalty to the king is a mark of his commitment to the aristocratic ethos. His behaviour within the play, evidently, is no less consistently loyal than his behaviour before the play began:

> My life I never held but as a pawn
> To wage against thine enemies.
>   (1.1.155–6)

As a private person Lear assumes the hospitality and generosity of his daughters; and Gloucester's touching confidence that Cornwall cannot mean either his extreme rudeness to the old king or his cruelty to Gloucester's own person is based on his view of the unchangeable relation between host and guest – 'You are my guests,' he says (3.7.31) and 'I am your host' (3.7.39). The class distinctions of the play are clear enough, although the play's action in part consists in showing how tenuous they are when faith is bad. Gloucester's tenant comes on stage, it seems, solely to demonstrate how greatly Gloucester's landlordism attached the loyalty of his dependants; Lear shows gentleness, even on the heath, to his dependant, the Fool. Gloucester's repetitious *sententiae* about the breaking of social bonds are one measure of the limitations of his imagination – he recognizes that social bonds are being broken around him, but not why that is so. For him, as for the composers of the homilies, the social order 'ought' to remain constant, even when he sees it fall into disruption. Hence Gloucester's defencelessness against the deceptions of his son and the brutality of his lieges. Both Gloucester and Kent, adherents of the old aristocratic mores, are tolerant of the sins of the flesh, as we learn in the play's opening interlude; the Fool conforms to the manners of his social betters when, at the end of act 1, he suggests his love-play with the castle maids.

The problems raised by the inequality of inheritance are twice dramatized and very differently stressed. Lear takes a 'modern' solution to his predicament, the absence of a male heir: he divides his kingdom justly among his co-heiresses, attempting to prevent strife later. Gloucester, on the other hand, acts as the old aristocrat would, not noticing, until he thinks himself betrayed by Edgar, the injustice of what Stone calls 'the winner-take-all doctrine of primogeniture';[24] Edmund's bastardy-speech is, in fact, not a paradox only: it bespeaks a new and fairer view of individual worth in rejecting the automatic second-classness of bastards. These aristocrats are all arrogant, in different personal idioms; Kent never entirely forgets who he is, even when he is stocked for his apparent presumption to Cornwall. Cornwall is wantonly confident of his own power and safety among his servants, as he mutilates his elderly, aristocratic host. Goneril and Regan are high-handed with all others; both Lear and Cordelia are extravagantly high-minded and proud. As Sigurd Burckhardt has beautifully pointed out, Lear's absolute trust in his own and other people's 'word' is an outmoded social habit, but one entirely appropriate to his rank and style.[25] Of the noblemen, only Edgar demonstrates his independent awareness of the plight of the kingdom's poor – and yet this same Edgar, companion of poverty, becomes the champion of the whole kingdom, on whose swordsmanship the national virtue must be risked. He ranges along the whole social scale, from beggar and Bedlamite, doubly outcast, to the rituals of high-born conflict.

As against the 'paternalistic and patronizing attitude toward economic dependants and acceptance of the grinding poverty of the lower classes as part of the natural order of things,' one must note that Stone's aristocrats were also astonishingly open-handed.[26] Their testamentary charities may not have reached the standards set by the middle class[27] in this period, but their daily and weekly support of the poor and of other odd folk was both steady and generous.[28] In his dealings with the Fool and with Tom, Lear shows some of that characteristic paternalism – in his case, the more poignant because of his personal problems as a father. From his behaviour to the Fool, we can realize both Lear's automatic aristocratic kindness and his personal gentleness:

> My wits begin to turn.
> Come on, my boy. How dost, my boy? Art cold?
> I am cold myself. Where is this straw, my fellow?
> The art of our necessities is strange,
> And can make vile things precious. Come, your hovel.
> Poor Fool and knave, I have one part in my heart
> That's sorry yet for thee.
>
> (3.2.67–73)

Finally, in the king's awareness of the plight of the truly poor in his kingdom, lies his achievement of a responsibility which, without his tribulations, he might never have won. There is nothing in the past life of King Lear – indeed, nothing in the play itself – to suggest that 'the people' were important in either the private or the public economy of the nation or of its rulers. Of all Shakespeare's political plays (in which I include all his late tragedies), this one most overtly closes off considerations of subjects, populace, and the non-noble life. In the history plays, in the other tragedies, there is much reference made to the people, English, Scottish, Danish, Roman, even Cypriot; in both *Hamlet* and *Macbeth* we are ever aware of potential rebellion against the centres of power. In *King Lear*, though, the great ones fight out their battles within their own class, and such realization as the audience has of other groups is skimpy and schematic. The more remarkable, then, that from this background and in this setting, King Lear, having renounced his kingdom, comes to realize, at the stretch of his extremity, what it means to be really poor. In his 'houseless poverty' speech ring the echoes of a common configuration of ideas of poverty, charity, clothing, and food:[29]

> Poor naked wretches, whereso'er you are,
> That bide the pelting of this pitiless storm,
> How shall your houseless heads and unfed sides,
> Your loop'd and window'd raggedness, defend you
> From seasons such as these? O! I have ta'en
> Too little care of this. Take physic, Pomp;
> Expose thyself to feel what wretches feel,
> That thou mayst shake the superflux to them,
> And show the Heavens more just.
>
> (3.4.28–36)

As in so much else, Gloucester echoes both the king's predicament and his insight; in his blindness, exposed to the miseries the Bedlam beggar illustrates for him, he says, too:

> Heavens, deal so still!
> Let the superfluous and lust-dieted man,
> That slaves your ordinance, that will not see
> Because he does not feel, feel your power quickly;
> So distribution should undo excess,
> And each man have enough.
>
> (4.1.66–71)

Both old men began the play securely enclosed in their own convictions of rightness and security; both undergo indescribable psychological torment, Gloucester paying with his eyes for not having 'seen' aright, Lear with his reason for not having understood how to be a proper parent. Both emerge from their class-bound view to 'see feelingly,' as kings and aristocrats were generally spared from seeing and feeling, what it meant to be a plain poor man in the kingdoms of this world. Both men are remarkably modernized by their sufferings, enlarged from the conscriptions of their social status. It comes with some irony that these undefended old men reach their new insights, their astonishing sympathies, under the guidance and by means of the emblematic beggar who seems to them 'the thing itself; unaccommodated man,' but whose unaccommodated state is simply a disguise.

To say that Lear and Gloucester achieve some of their greatness because they break out of the limitations of high-born assumptions does scant justice to the richness of their experience. Yet no more than in real life can this play be presented by some abstraction or social paradigm. In different ways, Lear, Gloucester, and Kent are old-fashioned aristocrats, theirs the noble ethos in the process of erosion during the Renaissance; equally, Albany, Cornwall, Goneril, Regan, and Edmund are domesticated in a 'new' world of power and might, which they intend to keep well within their own control. But just because we prefer Lear, Kent, and Gloucester to the scheming members of the next generation, we cannot explain the play by the glib assumption that Shakespeare asserted his characteristic conservatism by the play's means, praising an old if outmoded way of life for its moral symmetry and beauty; nor can we claim that human virtues are assigned to the old way, vices consigned to the new. Like Shakespeare's other great plays, *King Lear* deals in problems and problematics: neither way of life is sanctified, neither is regarded as an unqualified success.

This play begins with the situation feared by all men, kings and noblemen alike, with an inheritance to leave behind them, the absence of a male – that is, an obvious – heir. The number of noble families that died out in the period between Elizabeth's accession and the outbreak of the Civil War was frighteningly large.[30] Of royal families, the Tudors themselves died out, and in spite of Henry II's quiverful of sons, the Valois died out too. For a time Philip II feared to die without a male heir; the Stuarts survived by the puny breath of James VI; the nearly-royal Oranges twice just escaped heirlessness, both times at a period critical to the Netherlands' turbulent history. Great families had to worry about male issue, and kings more than others. Shakespeare followed his sources in providing King Lear with no male heir, but he stressed that critical fact not at all, though his sources, including the earlier play, make much of it. We see, then, the king coping with his problem and deciding to deal with his three daughters as co-heiresses. This is not an English or French royal habit – or, at least, not a modern habit, though Charlemagne had split his kingdom three ways long before Lear treats his girls in a thoroughly modern manner, as noblemen and commercial grandees without sons had begun to treat their daughters. Shakespeare followed these same sources in making the king relinquish sovereignty before his own death, and Lear's reason for doing so makes political sense in either a primitive or an early modern kingdom. Lear wanted to be sure, before he died, that his division of the kingdom was acceptable both to his beneficiaries and to the subjects over whom, after all, the girls with their husbands would rule. The division was proclaimed in public, before the lords and with the acquiescence of daughters and sons-in-law, 'that future strife / May be prevented now' (1.1.44–5). As a generation of students has written in criticism of this play, Lear's unwisdom is 'proved' by just this gesture – no king 'ought' to relinquish rule before it has formally ended with his mortal death. Historical rulers were not so obedient to this regulation as critical orthodoxy would suggest – against the rule there are several counter-cases. Not only was there no rule against abdication – Charles V, after all, voluntarily gave up his great Empire; Mary Stuart had perforce abdicated; though Shakespeare's Richard II may have been an anointed king, the playwright does not conceal his unfitness to rule, all the same – but also Lear was unlucky. In cases where a male heir lacked, was young, or was weak, political disruption could be expected, as Machiavelli taught; it could be argued that in trying to secure assent to the division of his kingdom, Lear showed foresight of an unexpected sort.[31]

Although Lear never complains of having only daughters, his assumption that continuance is crucial emerges clearly from his speeches to his daughters: he says to Goneril, 'to thine and Albany's issues / Be this perpetual' (1.1.66–7), and to Regan, 'To thee and thine, hereditary ever, / Remain this ample third of our fair kingdom' (1.1.79–80). The significance of his later cursing Goneril with sterility becomes even more profound when we consider his preoccupation with issue.[32] Apparently, too, Lear was less satisfied with one son-in-law than with the other. In the first words of the play, Kent says, 'I thought the King had more affected the Duke of Albany than Cornwall' (a preference which does the king credit, after all); later we hear of 'inevitable' dissent between the sons-in-law. But, as Gloucester says, Lear had resolved for strict justice between the dukes –

> It did always seem so to us; but now, in the division of the kingdom, it appears not which of the Dukes he values most; for equalities are so weigh'd that curiosity in neither can make choice of either's moiety. (1.1.3–7)

In the first scene, the emotional weight of Lear's imposition of the competitive declarations of love for him tends to overbear the fact that, in spite of his psychological inequity, his division of the kingdom was 'just.' He divided the land into three rich parts, intending for his favourite child a third evidently not larger, but 'more opulent,' than those assigned her sisters. There is in the ritual charting of the new rule more than the suggestion that, before he allowed his psychological needs expression in the competition, Lear had taken thought for the political needs of the nation: he was not, in fact, dividing his kingdom solely in response to his daughters' declarations of devotion.

Looked at in the context of contemporary behaviour, Lear's solution for his kingdom was in line with modern aristocratic providence about rule, and with modern aristocratic treatment of daughters, by which the strongly paternalist father strove to provide generously for their futures.[33] The difficulty with Lear's situation is that it did not allow for the roles both of ruler and of father; he did not recognize his situation as unique – though Charlemagne, another dimly historical ruler in Elizabethan imaginations, divided his kingdom into three, British and English rulers customarily did not. But there is an interesting record of aristocratic division of wealth: consideration of daughters' material prosperity often contributed to the financial difficulty of noble families, some of which collapsed at the centre because of generosity in dowries and jointure-arrangements. By treating his kingdom as if it were simply 'his land,' an estate, Lear threatened his land, his 'country,' at its centre, too. It might be said that Lear's kingdom *figuratively* came to grief just because of his generous division of it among his heiresses. To say this, though, is to offer material substitutes for eventuations in the play sufficiently grounded in character and psychology, to say nothing of the ritual folklore of the deed itself. We do not need to know that, as a matter of economic and social fact, great holdings were often dissolved by division among children, especially female children, to realize that there is something fatal in Lear's act of division; but the modern relevance of that problematic gesture deepens the play's reference to a felt reality. One simplistic observation might be that in making Lear regard his kingdom as his property, Shakespeare made his profoundest comment on kingly misapprehension of rule and on ancient modes of governing.

Just the same, in at least two ways, Lear's disposition of the kingdom *did* observe modern rules of prudence and justice. In many ways doubtless more important, Lear must be ranged with the conservative noblemen of the play as an adherent, even a blinkered adherent, of the old ethos, dependent upon its values and profoundly endangered by their abrogation. His notion of *himself*, if not of his daughters and his kingdom, is entirely in terms of the old modes: though divesting himself of 'the sway Revenue, execution' of kingship, Lear chooses to retain 'only,' as he says, 'The name and all th'addition to a king' (1.1.136). In practice, what this means is that Lear wants to spend his latter days surrounded by his familiar household and the signs of his former greatness (in this case, a retinue of a hundred armed knights, a clever Fool, and whatever servants he may require for his personal needs), domiciled with his daughters by turn, on a perpetual royal progress. Under normal circumstances, this arrangement could very well have been made for an old patriarch and even for a self-retired king, at his life's end turning in legitimately upon private and familial pleasures. Furthermore, a great social figure would have had a household – witness Catherine of Aragon after her repudiation, or Mary Stuart in her detention – distinguished by a train of retainers. Retainers were not only a sign of an aristocrat's prestige but a defence of his prerogatives.[34] The sovereign often attempted to cut down on retaining because of its potential danger, but no ex-king could imagine himself entirely without retainers, simply to show his rank. One deep theme of this play is the *meaning* of deference to those who expected it as their due. The significance of *King Lear* would be greatly lessened if we could not understand what it meant to the king, to his children, to his nobles and servants, that men were deferred to according to their rank in society. From the vantage-point of the aristocratic ethos, there was nothing odd about Lear's wanting to maintain the 'exhibition' of his former greatness, even after he had delegated its great function to others. From the point of view of the new functionalism, equally, there was nothing peculiar about Goneril's and Regan's attempts to cut down their father's retinue: Elizabeth never allowed Mary Stuart a quota of *armed* servants.

Since so much of the struggle between early modern rulers and their nobility was over the monopoly on violence, it is obvious that retainers were looked at darkly by the sovereign.[35] The physical inconvenience and danger surrounding a retinue was one thing, the *psychological* importance of such a train was another. Rulers intent on their own security were unlikely to tolerate a mighty subject surrounded by proofs of his power; a retinue was, as Lear called it in that quantitative language so characteristic of his utterance before the storm, the 'addition' by which a grandee could reckon his importance.

Thus when Goneril says, 'His knights grow riotous,' Elizabethans would scarcely have found her remark incredible – if they knew of Sir Richard Cholmley's liveried retainers, who sneaked into the kitchen and speared the meat out of the pot with their daggers,[36] they might well have sympathized with her. On the face of it, her complaint carried weight; her insistence on the retainers' 'rank and not-to-be-endured riots' was hardly different from Henry's or Elizabeth's. Goneril was, by her father's donation, sovereign in her portion of the country, and certainly in her house. As sovereign, she simply acted the efficient ruler striving for order in her palace and, by extension, her kingdom:

> A hundred knights!
> 'Tis politic and safe to let him keep
> At point a hundred knights; yes, that on every dream,
> Each buzz, each fancy, each complaint, dislike,
> He may enguard his dotage with their powers,
> And hold our lives in mercy.
>
> (1.4.332–7)

Later, as the size of Lear's retinue is ruthlessly cut down (only thirty-five or thirty-six of his knights join the king's forces at Dover), Regan states the general argument against a mobile retinue in a speech far more neutral and sensible, in social terms, than it is usually considered:

> what! fifty followers
> Is it not well? What should you need of more?
> Yea, or so many, sith that both charge and danger
> Speak 'gainst so great a number? *How, in one house,*
> *Should many people, under two commands,*
> *Hold amity? 'Tis hard; almost impossible.*
>
> (2.4.239–44; italics mine)

The objections the daughters raised against the knights were those of a practical, modern, civilizing, rationalizing social orderliness; their objections were, in fact, received opinion. Further, from Goneril's remarks about Lear's servitors, we realize what sort of household *she* kept:

> Hear me, my Lord.
> What need you five-and-twenty, ten, or five,
> To follow in *a house where twice so many*
> Have a command to tend you?
>
> (2.4.262–5; italics mine)

From this hint, we may assume that Goneril's house was – in contrast to Gloucester's isolated little house, typical of the parochial older nobility – a truly 'great' house, a palace, a prodigy house; she had a staff of at least fifty servants, from whom a sufficient number could always be spared to tend to her father's needs.[37] With this glimpse into Goneril's milieu, we suddenly see the degree of pride, of self-indulgence, involved in the lives lived by 'these daughters and these sisters.' They have their modern ways of conspicuous consumption no less grandiose than their father's old-fashioned train – and far more centred on themselves, on their own comforts and the projected image of their own greatness. Coupled with the fact that Shakespeare makes us witnesses to Goneril's complotting with Oswald to offend the king ('Put on what weary negligence you please' [1.3.13]), this glimpse into her values and manner of living makes us realize that her objections to Lear's knights are *not* simply those of a sovereign lady intent on maintaining civil peace. Indeed, just as with Edmund, at first sympathetically presented and only later revealed as the cheat he is, the playwright is careful to deny Goneril her claims to justification in this respect. So also with Cornwall, commanding that Kent and Oswald put up their swords – 'Keep peace, upon your lives: / He dies that strikes again' (2.2.48–9) – his words are those of any sensible ruler concerned for civil order.[38] We might take them at face value if we were not in the next act to see how Cornwall behaves when he thinks the monopoly on violence securely his. Shakespeare never leaves us long in doubt about these 'new' statesmen.

That Lear's knights *were* troublesome, we have only Goneril's authority; when we hear Regan linking Edgar and the knights, an association clearly false, we must wonder about the knights' behaviour altogether. Of Lear's 'riotous' train, only a single gentle figure says anything at all, and what he says is, it seems, a remarkable understatement of the actual situation:

> My Lord, I know not what the matter is; but, to my judgment, your Highness is not entertain'd with that ceremonious affection as you were wont; there's a great abatement of kindness appears as well in the general dependants as in the Duke himself also and your daughter. (1.4.60–5)

'Ceremonious affection' is entirely absent from this house, as we know from Goneril's planning with Oswald to withhold deference from her father. Gradually we realize the symbolic importance of withholding the ceremony normally due a father and a king: Goneril seeks to destroy the old man's sense of himself long before king-killing becomes part of the action.

Goneril and Regan were, of course, afraid of something other than mere inconvenience; they were afraid that their father, invested with his military power, might discover their aims and seek to stop them by turning that power against them. Their eagerness to strip Lear of his symbols of personal greatness is one thing; but it was quite another matter, a matter of pure power, to want out of the way those hundred knights who might have made up a Lear faction. Since the remnant of the retinue *did* join Cordelia at Dover, if Oswald's words are accurate, we may assume that at least those knights knew the proper duty of their allegiance and followed it.

One problem of the Tudor monarchs was that, like King Lear, they lacked soldiers. In times of crisis, Elizabeth had to depend upon a very mixed army, composed of trained bands, pressmen[39] (some little better than the crew gathered by Falstaff), and the cohorts of her great lords contributed as private trains, in the old-fashioned way, to the sovereign's cause.[40] During the period studied by Stone, loyalty was never entirely diverted from the great lords to the Crown, for all of Henry VIII's statutes and propaganda of the 'Faerie Queene'; the dutiful behaviour of Lear's knights was still quite understandable to a Jacobean audience. As far as the play itself is concerned, though, the knights barely appear; they are a shadow-retinue, whose importance depends entirely upon the director's, not upon the playwright's, injunctions. Their behaviour is undefined, largely attributed them by the daughters' unreliable words. Lear is effectively stripped of his strong bodyguard, left destitute and alone save for his Fool and a disguised servant.

He has not forgotten the orthodox meaning of his retinue, however, as on the heath he recruits the Bedlam beggar as its replacement – 'You, sir, I entertain for one of my hundred' (3.6.80). That his retinue wore his colours is evident from his next remark to Tom, famous for its beautifully learned associations: 'only I do not like the fashion of your garments: you will say they are Persian; but let them be chang'd' (3.6.80–3). It is important to notice throughout these scenes, the great gentleness of the king. While he has control of his retainers, he never thinks to call them in his own defence against the extraordinary behaviour of his daughters, never thinks of himself as the leader of a band of *armed* men. For all his childishness, his irascibility, his arrogance, Lear is a civilized man, thinking himself in a civilized country. He lets his defenders slip away from him as if their 'real' function had never crossed his mind. Indeed, for him, the knights *were* simply a means of signalling his dignity to himself and others, never defences against his nearest kin.

The astonishing breaches in decorum in this play are not so immediately obvious to us as to an audience trained in the deference society. When Oswald refuses to stop at the king's command, when he identifies the king as 'My Lady's father,' the shock was almost as severe to the audience as to the defenceless and unprepared Lear. That Oswald 'would not' do the king's bidding utterly shatters Lear; when he finds his servant stocked, he says,

> They durst not do't,
> They could not, would not do't; *'tis worse than murther,*
> To do upon respect such violent outrage.
> (2.4.22–4; italics mine)

Lear's awareness of criminal degree is imperfect, one might say; because, as Kent sits outside the house in which Gloucester's mutilation is soon to take place, we shortly realize how insignificant, beside that crime, the stocking of the king's servant is. But at the time, that punishment is part of the ruthless imposition of their will and rule on Lear and his kingdom that the daughters' party puts into effect. Lear must learn that he is no longer sovereign in Britain; his daughters undertake to teach him.

Of course Lear was arbitrary. Sovereigns were – and could count on absolute deference, even in their tantrums. Hence Lear's fury at Kent's gainsaying him, his attack on Kent in terms of the feudal bond – 'Hear me, recreant! / On thine allegiance, hear me!' It is one measure of Shakespeare's art that we come to see Lear's autocratic demands for his dinner naturalistically, as the signs of the childish greed in an old man, rather than as one automatic prerogative of royal position.[41] Goneril has, after all, commanded that dinner be made ready; why should not the king, hungry from hunting, have it when he likes? That Goneril orders her *servants* to slight the king shows how far she was willing to go, disgracing him, her kin, her father, before outsiders; Regan, literally, went further to show Lear incivility. When he rushes from Goneril's house to hers, Lear could expect (as any sovereign could) to be received. But Regan did what only a few landowners dared to do to Elizabeth; she left her house empty, so that the king was unable to rest on his progress. That she could do such a thing, unthinkable either to a father or to a sovereign, makes it less incredible that Regan could take such an active part in the blinding of her host shortly after.

In terms of the deference society, Kent's behaviour is interesting. He is round with the king, but obviously loyal and dutiful. With Oswald he is violent, outraged that a

'clotpoll' should so treat a king, outraged that his clotpoll should so flout *him*, even when
he is in disguise. When Cornwall makes to stock him, Kent cannot believe that such a
punishment, from which noblemen were securely exempt, could possibly be meted out
to him; both he and Gloucester remonstrate with Cornwall in vain, urging him not to
punish the king's servant.[42] Kent' reaction, like his overreaction to Oswald, is a remnant
of his own aristocratic experience. Such things simply cannot be done to a man like him.
That they are somehow prepares us for the outrage done Gloucester within doors.

    Indeed, in spite of the control he achieves at stress–points, Kent's reactions are not
always under his own control. His outburst against Oswald is that of the old aristocrat,
against the falsity of a cowardly, braggart 'new' man, a nobody, a butterfly made by a
tailor – 'That such a slave as this should wear a sword!'[43] Kent too lacks deference, lacks
'reverence' for those apparently his superiors; his gorgeous rudeness to Cornwall may
endear him to the audience, but it brings him to suffer punishments expressly forbidden to
be applied to aristocrats. Still, no servingman Caius could speak as Kent spoke to the Duke
and Duchess of Cornwall. For all his willing self-degradation in the service of his degraded
king, Kent has difficulty in maintaining his servant role, although the violent language
he uses to Oswald is certainly matched by other historical noblemen and gentlemen.[44]
That difficulty shows in one very interesting context: Kent evidently did not share his
master's fellow-feeling for the Bedlam beggar, who later says of him that he, 'having seen
me in my worst estate, / Shunn'd my abhorr'd society' (5.3.209–10). When he comes to
recognize in the beggar his old friend's son, Kent is joyously reconciled to Edgar – but a
remnant of his fastidiousness remained during their time of common disguise.

    The question of rank is relevant also to the 'punishment' of Gloucester. Though
noblemen could be, and were, put under attainder and executed for treason, they could
not be hanged, as Regan suggested, and certainly could not be blinded. Neither were
they properly subject to the summary 'justice' meted out by Cornwall (who was himself
uneasy about it [3.7.24–7]). The blinding of Gloucester is shocking dramatically,
humanly, and socially: the First Servant's reaction to the deed sprang from his outraged
sense of decorum as well as from his shock at the cruelty of the deed. The Servant is
interesting: he dares give an order to his lord –

Hold your hand, my Lord.
I have serv'd you ever since I was a child,
But better service have I never done you
Than now to bid you hold.
(3.7.71–4; italics mine; cf. 4.2.73–8)

'Ever since I was a child': the Servant's devotion to Cornwall, which should have been
automatic, could only be broken by the horror of what he was forced to witness, this
wanton brutality against an old man, a peer, and his master's host. To Regan the Servant
speaks as boldly,

If you did wear a beard upon your chin
I'd shake it on this quarrel,
(3.7.75–6)

which causes Cornwall, in turn stunned by the disruption of received decorum in his
train, to cry, 'My villain!' Unthinkable – 'My villain!' Obviously Cornwall and Regan,

recognizing their youth, power, and strength, think themselves immune from opposition and above social regulations; but that they too live within the conventions of deference is shown by their shock that a 'peasant' should 'stand up thus!' Regan is never more herself than when she stabs the man, and from behind. For Regan, as she makes plain later, is sovereign and intends to make the most of her independence. She and her husband simply take over Gloucester's house; later, in the rivalry for Edmund, she plays her advantageous widowhood against Goneril. Her 'rights' are in her own gift, and she can 'invest' Edmund with them so that he then 'compeers the best' (5.3.69–70). Regan knows her power and uses her precedence for her own ends.

The rise of Edmund, the bastard, the nobody, the new man, is indeed spectacular. He appears at the beginning, acknowledged but unprovided, a victim of his father's callousness to his predicament. Gloucester says of him, quite calmly, 'He hath been out nine years, and away he shall again,' never thinking that a nice-looking young man (who also happened to be his son) might prefer to stay 'in,' at court.[45] To Cordelia's and Edgar's disinheritance Edmund stands as emblem: we see in Gloucester's carelessness toward this child of his flesh (whose mother he does not even name) a failure of paternity which slightly prepares us for the king's abrupt rejection of his child and for Gloucester's speedy rejection of Edgar later. Cordelia is, of course, incapable of policy altogether, and Edgar's dissimulations trouble him; Edmund's nature, on the contrary, mates with his condition to make of him a natural machiavel, a new man, outside the customary values, as careless of privileged lives as his father had been of Edmund's unprivileged existence. Edmund follows his version of 'nature,' an impartial naturalistic goddess who, with other gods unnamed, stands up for bastards. At first, it seems to be only 'land,' or position, that he wants – and Edgar's, not his father's. That is, as a bastard he wishes simply to stand in his brother's legitimate place, content at the time simply to be his father's heir.[46] That Gloucester took it for granted that an heir he must have, is evident from his remarks to Edmund at Edgar's supposed treachery. Like King Lear and like Henry VIII (who, despairing of a legitimate son, for a while considered legitimating the Duke of Richmond), Gloucester knew the importance of male issue. Thus he can say, almost without thinking, 'of my land, ... I'll work the means / To make thee capable' (2.1.83–5), acknowledging both the need for an heir and the legal difficulties involved in such a transfer of rights. It turns out that Edmund need not – perhaps could not – wait out his father's natural life; perceiving the means, he betrays Gloucester, and Cornwall takes over the punishment of the old man's 'treason,' sequestering his estates and awarding them to Edmund, who by his father's attainder becomes Goneril's 'most dear Gloucester.' The young simply cancel out the older generation; later, we can read Albany's re-alliance from his refusal to accept Edmund's new title and his references to the old Earl as 'Gloucester.' Once an earl, why not more? So Edmund makes his loves to the two queens, evidently indifferent to their relative charms.[47] As the example of the Earl of Essex attests, if one is granted private privileges by a ruler, it is an easy temptation to fancy one's self as ruler. When Edmund sees the two women dead before him, he says with a pardonable pride but an unpardonable self-centredness, 'Yet Edmund was belov'd' – with never a word to spare for them.

Edmund brutally illustrates the ambitious ethos of the new man (in this respect he is unlike Essex and his aristocratic crew, rather men failed in their ranks than new men aspiring to greater noble position); Edmund is the natural talent unsupported by background who makes his way into the chancy world of Renaissance opportunity. Without respect for the privileged, he nonetheless covets their privileges; his parallel at a lower rank is the opportunist Oswald, a clothes rack, a mock-man, a braggart soldier, a go-between. Whatever can be done for his advancement, Oswald does, in ways that have their real analogue in the disoriented men of Essex's train. Oswald's view of the world as made for him emerges from his horrible remarks just before he blunders upon his own death. Seeing the blind Gloucester, on whose head a price has been set, he cries:

> A proclaim'd prize! Most happy!
> That eyeless head of thine was first fram'd flesh
> To raise my fortunes.
>
> (4.6.227–9)

'To raise *my* fortunes'! After this, the audience can see him dispatched without the least qualm. 'Advancement' and 'fortune' are associated with this whole party: Goneril promises Oswald advancement; Edmund purchases the murder of Lear and Cordelia. To his tool, the Captain, he says,

> One step I have advanc'd thee; if thou dost
> As this instructs thee, thou dost make thy way
> To noble fortunes; know thou this, that men
> Are as the time is; to be tender-minded
> Does not become a sword; thy great employment
> Will not bear question; either say thou'lt do't,
> Or thrive by other means.
>
> (5.3.29–35)

Actually, the 'other means' of thriving is illustrated in the play. When he asks Tom to direct him to Dover, Gloucester gives him a purse, at that point speaking of aristocratic charity not as an automatic duty, but in terms of social justice (4.1.70–1); when he believes himself on the point of dying, he gives Tom another purse, 'in it a jewel / Well worth a poor man's taking' (4.6.28–9). At the end of his 'every inch a king' speech, Lear in turn gives money to the blinded Gloucester, whose condition he recognizes – 'No eyes in your head, nor no money in your purse?' (4.6.146–7) – before he admits to recognizing the man himself: 'I know thee well enough; thy name is Gloucester' (4.6.179). The almsgiving of both Lear and Gloucester has become something more meaningful than that largesse traditional to aristocrats: Gloucester at least begins to speak in full awareness of what destitution means, and to realize in personal terms what money can do for a beggar (4.1.76–7), and Lear has made his astonishing remarks about his poor subjects, about those denied justice by their poverty, and about 'the thing itself.'

For the old men, the realization that some men are poor comes as an immense revelation. Unlike them, and in spite of his naïveté about his brother's motives, Edgar possesses remarkable social experience for a young aristocrat. His description of Bedlam beggars may argue a mere sightseeing visit to a madhouse, but his knowing how beggars 'Enforce their charity' (2.3.9–20) and are 'whipp'd from tithing to tithing, and stock-punish'd, and imprison'd' (3.4.137–9) suggests that he has already paid considerable attention to contemporary customs outside the normal purview of the heir to an earldom. This sort of knowledge, got we know not how, argues for Edgar's ultimate fitness to rule the kingdom: he will not, one assumes, take 'Too little care of this.' As king he will be, it is implied, a just judge, a 'justicer' in reality for whom 'Robes and furr'd gowns' shall not 'hide all,' fulfilling the ancient duties ascribed to an earl, or 'Iudex.'[48]

Edgar may seem surprisingly democratic in this respect, but he is impeccably trained in the old aristocratic ethos – his training offers one explanation, indeed, of how he was so easily duped by his half-brother, from whom he could not imagine treachery; and why he was unable to do his father hurt, sorely though that father had hurt him. Edgar's nature makes him the ideal *preux chevalier* to challenge Edmund; in that short episode of trial-by-combat, when Edmund receives his mortal wound, much is involved. First, Edmund is arrested for 'capital treason' on a charge familiar enough in sixteenth-century England, adultery with the Queen. Second, he is to prove himself by an old-fashioned and quintessentially aristocratic method, the formal trial-at-arms outmoded in the late sixteenth century as a customary proof. The modern equivalent of this sort of combat was the duel, a far more private affair than Edgar's challenge to Edmund; treason trials were judicial, carried on *in camera*. The anachronism stresses the play's archaism; further, it sets the struggle between factions into a simple morality-context, where virtue must be victorious. With this episode we are back in the world of chivalry of which we have heard nothing in the play and to which, under normal circumstances, Edmund the bastard could never have aspired. The new man, intent only on the main chance, ought to have looked on such an outmoded, hazardous process with contempt – but Edmund found himself subtly flattered by being party to such a procedure, the signature, after all, of the aristocratic life which he had usurped.[49] From his answer to Edgar's formal challenge we can hear how attracted Edmund was to the idea of himself as a 'real' aristocrat, the true inheritor of this beautiful, dangerous, elaborate ritual:

> In wisdom I should ask thy name;
> But since thy outside looks so fair and war-like,
> And that thy tongue some say of breeding breathes,
> What safe and nicely I might well delay
> By rule of knighthood, I disdain and spurn ...
>
> (5.3.141–5)

Edmund adapts his language to the archaic formalities of chivalric address; his behaviour assimilates to that of the nobleman born. In this hour of his greatest danger, Edmund is at least offered a chance to act with the full dignity of the high-born, to take up the class-legacy his father did not leave him. Evidently, too, there is something purgative about this gesture; though he speaks to Edgar with a condescension disallowed by the real facts ('If thou'rt noble, / I do forgive thee' [5.3.165–7]) he admits his guilt and acknowledges the ironic justice of fortune's wheel, to which he was bound from the beginning (5.3.173–4). He resolves to do 'some good' by sending to stop the execution of Lear and Cordelia, and is borne off to die with some dignity before that terrible *pietà* of parent and child takes place.

Beside the bodies of Goneril and Regan, the bodies of Cordelia and Lear come to lie. Before our eyes, the greatest family in England is brought to its end. What every patriarch feared – even Lear, who could invoke sterility upon Goneril – has come to pass. From 'the promis'd end,' or 'image of that horror' the survivors must build back to some restoration of order, of justice. Kent refuses the commission of the kingdom, resigning his share to Edgar; Albany, who has begun the play ambitious for rule, is glad to relinquish its responsibility; Edgar, who never wished any such thing, lives to rule, his father's surviving son and godson to the dead king. A dynasty has ended, and a different rule is about to begin.

We do not know what the reign will be like: we can only assume that Edgar, having profited from knowing 'The worst' in his own experience, his father's, and his godfather's, having travelled the long road from the heath to the combat at Dover, from destitution to sovereignty, will rule as a Lear 'improv'd.' Just as at the play's beginning we are given no hint of what went before the day of division, at the play's end we are given no warranty of the future, but are simply asked to commit ourselves to Edgar's experience, sense of justice, and human-kindness. As the play began, *in medias res*, without explanation or motivation offered, to present us with the agonizing exemplum of the complexity of human life and human intents, inexplicable often even to the actors themselves, so it ends without explanation, prophecy, or promise.

That contemporary social problems were analysed and exploited to make up much of the substance of this play may strike us as astonishing, although readers of Shakespeare's history plays will not be surprised at this further link between them and *King Lear*. Some of the elements of the aristocratic 'crisis' – for example, primogeniture, retinue and service, exhibition of power, and actual power – are obvious enough in plot and theme; but other aspects of the problem, on their face less apparent in society, as well as less prominent in the play, turn out to be crucial. I have spoken of the importance of deference to both old and new aristocrats; Stone regards the decline of respect to the nobility as one of the major social changes that class had to face,[50] and, obviously, monarchs had to come to terms, after 1647, with the regicidal ideas subjects could afford to entertain. Stone gives many reasons for the decline of automatic deference to aristocrats – the passing of aristocratic military power, the relative rise of the gentry and the commercial classes with respect to the nobility, the creation of a 'rival' ethos involving prudence and frugality rather than openhandedness and magnificence, the venality of some noblemen and the wickedness of others, together with a communications system that permitted open criticism of such foibles and faults. Shakespeare, of course, concentrates, translates, and transvalues this process of devaluation in dramatic and symbolic rather than realistic or reportorial terms. For example, the terrible poignancy of the play's situation is heightened by the fact that it is Lear's daughters who, instead of jealously guarding the prerogatives of their rank and family (as would have been the normal 'real' behaviour of even unloving daughters), so calculatingly rob Lear of the deference due him. But 'rule' enforces high stakes: in his private capacity, Lear might expect family solidarity, but as ruler he risked great dangers particularly from members of his family.

A rather silly way of speaking of this play is to suggest that it dramatizes, as no other piece of literature in the period does, the actual decline of paternal authority that Stone has tried to measure in the English Renaissance.[51] Some of the power noble fathers exercised over their children, as we have seen, they themselves relinquished, and did so gladly for the children's sake. Some of the decline in parental authority is related to the gradual softening of behaviour between the generations, as noblemen allowed themselves a greater preoccupation with private pleasures and satisfactions. This tendency toward privatism – symbolically crucial in the play, and ironically expressed in Lear's joy at the prospect of sharing his prison with Cordelia – is apparent also in his early speeches, when he clearly looked forward to retirement in his daughters' houses, especially Cordelia's: 'I lov'd her most, and thought to set my rest / On her kind nursery' (1.1.123–4). Unlike Richard II, whose preference for private pleasure brought an end to his rule, King Lear had evidently fulfilled his public obligations during his reign; but that he could take such pleasure in withdrawing from public power is one mark of the period in which this play was written, rather than the primitive period in which it is supposed to have taken place. Obviously, Lear thinks that he has come to deserve the delights of retirement on his own terms.

In England, a mark of respect paid parents by their children was kneeling for their blessing: in a sermon of 1629, far later than this play, Donne wrote, 'Children kneele to aske blessing of Parents in England, but where else?' Still later, Evelyn commented on the childish dutifulness of grown children before their parents.[52] Against such a background, Lear's cursing his daughters (Cordelia, 1.1.108–20; Goneril, 1.4.284–98; 2.4.147,163–9), and his denial of benison to Cordelia (1.1.264–5) gain great force, and bring the play out of its Celtic pre-christianity into the sixteenth century; so also does his bitter mockery of the forgiveness Regan counsels him to ask of Goneril:

> Ask her forgiveness?
> Do you but mark *how this becomes the house*:
> 'Dear daughter, I confess that I am old;
> Age is unnecessary: on my knees I beg
> That you'll vouchsafe me raiment, bed, and food.'
> (2.4.153–7; italics mine)

The king's gesture of kneeling to his children is not just a momentary criticism of the children's behaviour to him, but also a confirmation of the Fool's sharp words, that he has made '[his] daughters [his] mothers,' and must kneel to them to supplicate the elemental support that fathers without question provide for their children and can in turn expect from them.[53] From Cordelia, much later, he does receive raiment, bed, and food: she becomes his real mother, on whose kind nursery he can set his brief rest. Not only that, Cordelia asserts her daughterhood the while, by asking the blessing he had withheld from her when they parted –

> O! look upon me, Sir,
> And hold your hand in benediction o'er me,
> (4.7.57–8)

she says, cancelling out the harshness of that last exchange. And Lear, as befits the moral and social dependant, kneels to her, a gesture which her dutiful daughterhood cannot permit: 'No, Sir, you must not kneel' (4.7.59). He is still her father and, for her, still king as well (4.7.44). The significance of these gestures of reconciliation sticks in Lear's mind, so that when Edmund's guard carries him and Cordelia off to prison, he welcomes the respite from warlike life and plans, in the safety of the birdcage endlessly to recapitulate his reunion with Cordelia:

> When thou dost ask me blessing, I'll kneel down,
> And ask of thee forgiveness: so we'll live,
> And pray, and sing, and tell old tales, and laugh
> At gilded butterflies ...
> (5.3.10–13)[54]

The old man's union with his child is, in fact, their fusion: each as parent blesses the other, who asks blessing as a child. The paternal and filial functions, so long misused, skewed, and uncommunicated in the play, finally interchange to become one. When it is too late to do more than assert their value, the old bonds are confirmed and made stronger than ever.

Lear becomes reconciled to his child, and to his own paternity. Stable values are corroborated as he comes to rest, for a tragically brief moment, confident of the security of Cordelia's 'bond.' In other ways, Lear shows traces of 'modern' attitudes toward sexuality and paternity, some pleasant and some unpleasant. Although the play's skilful arrangements with its secondary plot both corroborate and counterpoint the main plot, in one social respect Lear and Gloucester, so often alike, differ markedly. Betrayed as he is by the fruit of his adultery, Gloucester might have been expected to denounce aristocratic licence. Not so, however; the harshest comments on sexuality come from Edgar, puritanical in his view of his father's behaviour, and from Lear, who suffers an extraordinary revulsion from sexuality altogether. Although, presumably, aristocratic tolerance of sexual laxity remained greater than that of other social classes, it too underwent some stiffening over the period of the Renaissance, in part because marriages had more to do with love than hitherto, in part because women emerged as a stronger social force within the class, and in part because real pressure was exerted on the nobility by chaplains, ministers, and disapproving puritan commentators on sexual habits.[55] Lear's attacks on Goneril's sexuality, his comments on the 'rascal beadle' standing in for lustful humanity at large, and his backhanded encomium of adultery and luxury all testify to his obsession with his own begetting, but also represent the greater preoccupation of noblemen with the question of sexual standards, earlier rarely considered at all. As a whole, the play condemns sexual licence and casts doubt on the values of sexuality: Gloucester suffers extremely for his early adultery, and their sexuality is one mark of the monstrousness and inhumanity of Goneril, Regan, and Edmund.

In quite a different range of language, another major theme of *King Lear* is tied to the problems of an aristocracy caught between an old ethos of unreckoned generosity, magnificence, and carelessness, and new values stressing greater providence, frugality, and even calculation. The economic alterations characteristic of the period struck the aristocracy, as everyone else; noblemen made various kinds of compromise with new economic exigencies – dowries and jointures, for example, were initiated as prudential arrangements; some noblemen were faced with choosing between imposing higher rents and receiving still the unqualified reverence of grateful tenants. Old-fashioned aristocrats tended to maintain old ways, with their concomitant bonds of service, in the teeth of economic difficulty; newfangled lords often put their relations with their dependants upon a businesslike basis unknown earlier.[56]

We might well expect Goneril, Regan, and Edmund to think quantitatively – to fractionate and even annihilate Lear's retinue, to set prices on Gloucester's head and Lear's and Cordelia's lives; we might expect, too, that Oswald and the Captain should seek their material advancement by the deaths of these great ones. Such people represent and act out their lives in terms of the material values of both power and accounting. They can always go one arithmetical step farther – 'What need one?' 'Till noon! till night, my Lord; and all night'; 'Hang him instantly.' – 'Pluck out his eyes.' They know the minimum and the maximum – Goneril calculates to the last, assuring her mortally wounded lover that he had not had to answer the challenge of 'An unknown opposite.' Their naked calculation reduces all human values to quantitative measurement and thus easily loses sight of the 'need' underlying such values, to slip easily over into the utmost barbarity. But the fractionating by Goneril and Regan of their father's train, after all, echoes the same habit of mind and spirit exercised by the king himself, who set a price on his daughters' love and divided his kingdom in relation to their assertions of quantitative devotion. Again and again, characters take account, reckon their own and others' emotions: even the saintly Cordelia (perhaps pedagogically) speaks to her father of bonds and fractions – half her love for her husband, half left with her father. Gloucester tells Kent that Edgar is 'no dearer in [his] account' than Edmund; Kent speaks metaphorically of fee, as does the Fool later. For Lear, bestowing his disinherited daughter as a bad investment, Cordelia's 'price is fallen'; for France, brought up to admire magnanimity, 'She is herself a dowry.' Later, when Goneril's husband tells her she is not 'worth the dust which the rude wind / Blows in your face' (4.2.30–1), we realize how much he has begun to learn of calculation's values. Finally, the language of number is dissolved into paradoxes of 'all' and 'nothing,' thereby running out into areas of meaninglessness and incalculability. Need cannot be reasoned, or measured – nor can love, fidelity, or truth. It takes Lear a long time to come to that lesson: on his way to it, he can still say to Goneril,

> Thy fifty yet doth double five-and-twenty,
> And thou art twice her love,
>
> (2.4.261–2)

only to hear Regan ask a moment after, 'What need one?' Reduced to nothing, he has reached the point of non-support implied when the Fool asked Kent, 'Prithee, tell him, so much the rent of his land comes to' (1.4.140–1) – that is, to nothing. Lear, like Gloucester, passes through a stage of thought involving 'distribution' and 'superflux,' the language of justice in which he arraigns his daughters and criticizes the exercise of authority. He must evidently pass through that stage, which is after all simply another kind of reasoning of need (exposed in Goneril's hard statement of power, 'Who can arraign me for't?')[57] to realize that there are senses, good and bad, in which 'None does offend, none, I say, none' (4.6.170) – and in which even those with cause to harm or punish reject the bargaining code implied by the concept of 'cause': 'No cause, no cause.'

In all kinds of ways, in many ranges of expression and of art, this play passes through ordinary human experience to insist upon the greatness and the abyss of human life. From the simplest, and often the silliest, aspects of human behaviour, its morality is made to open upon an almost metaphysical amplitude. The play forces upon us a realization of the limitations of being human, as well as of humanity's potentiality for transcending and even transvaluing itself. In one particular literary type, the figure of the Fool, we have an example of this transfiguration from naturalistic representation to reverberating symbol. Fools, as the books assure us,[58] were typical appendages of both medieval and Renaissance courts. Interestingly enough, in England James I (famous for his fools and his foolishness, though perhaps not yet for the latter when this play was first put on) was the last English monarch to patronize professional fools; they too went out in the peculiar, muted modernization of life resulting from the War and the Interregnum. Of the figures in the play, the Fool most of all moves along the gamut from morality to naturalism: the Fool speaks both *in propria persona* and in the stylized persona of the official fool, sometimes 'all-licens'd' and satirical, sometimes sad and despondent, sometimes mixing modes of actuality and metaphor. His 'prophecy' is one such mixture (3.2.81–95); at first he seems to project a utopian world 'When priests are more in word than matter,' at other times a world upside down in unpleasantness – 'When brewers mar their malt with water.' From that point on, the prophecy jumbles ideal with deformed elements, and we are never sure what the measuring-rod is. Why should it be better, or worse, if 'No heretics' are 'burn'd, but wenches' suitors'? Though it would indeed be utopian if 'No squire' were 'in debt, nor no poor knight,' and if usurers could 'tell their gold i' th' field' secure from theft, still it is an imperfect England that harbours usurers at all; there is, too, no particular virtue in bawds' and whores' building churches. The world of the Fool's prophecy is no schematic world of handy-dandy, where evil systematically replaces good or good evil: the Fool recognizes, even in this utterance, that the world in which he lives is deeply confused. His words to Kent in the stocks, too, both the prose comment on fortune and favour and the little poem reiterating the theme, seem to say that wise men ought not to follow declining patrons; yet he calls those who fly such patrons 'knaves' and insists with pride upon his own 'foolish' loyalty to his powerless lord. The Fool knows the ways of Goneril and Regan – and rejects them. Perhaps it is not so grotesque, after all, that he is one of the justicers of the crazy King's Bench which arraigns Goneril, the joint-stool in a symbolic gesture whose meaning the real woman could never recognize. Like Erasmus' Folly, Lear's Fool knows truth from fiction, and knows their complicated interdependence as well.

The Fool disappears – from the play as from English courts, and for just the reason Lear's Fool gives: 'Lords and great ones' usurp his monopoly. The Fool's comment is extremely shrewd. For a time folly was the monopoly, granted by monarchs, as the exclusive privilege of fools, but as the social distinctions upon which such regulated mockery depended fell away, so everyone 'snatched' at all privilege, even the dubious one of folly. Along with the gentleman and yeoman of the riddle, even a king can be a fool. When that happens, deference offers no defence against folly, and professional fools must be got rid of.

Lear becomes, by his own admission, a fool – an old king, caught in the conflict of one ethos with another, trying to be fair by the new standards and yet relying on the privileges granted by the old, becomes a child again, with all the nonsense and the clarity of a child. He fails in the impossible task of doing right by a double standard he cannot even define, but after he *has* failed, he comes to understand, reject, and transcend those standards to assert a vision even truer than the normal ones, a reason purer than the customary assessments of either need or logic, and a charity greater than even royal munificence could show. One way we can perceive Lear's poignant predicament and accomplishment is to reckon it by the real problems that faced his peers, as Stone's book enables us to do. Shakespeare has not let Lear off easily; as so often, the playwright, for all that his heart lay with the old mores of abundance, kindness, and carelessness, scrupulously shows the problems and limits of such a code. Magnanimous noblemen were careless of costs, wasted human potential in their easy acceptance of the old customs. Ambitious 'new' noblemen may have corrected some of the errors of their conservative elders – but the cost of their correction, as this play demonstrates, is prohibitive. We are forced to acknowledge that there is a crisis of values in this play, and that neither ethos will do – and, though there is no doubt which side the playwright preferred, he was too scrupulous to present the problem simply as a morality, or simply as a conservative argument for 'order' and 'degree.' He saw both the practical rightness of the position Goneril, Regan, and Edmund abused, and the social grace of the position Lear and Gloucester exploited. But however we come to love and pity the old aristocrats, we know that their unconsidered acceptance of their own values was too expensive, in terms of their own families. Those lapsing fathers counted on unexamined social custom for protection against everything, even against the mysteries of hard hearts and calculating brains. The moral weight of the play comes down decisively with the advocates of old values, but not without having hesitated long enough to show how crucially those values fell short.

Notes

1 E.M.W. Tillyard *The Elizabethan World Picture* (London 1943); A.O. Lovejoy *The Great Chain of Being* (Cambridge, Mass. 1936); E.W. Talbert *The Problem of Order* (Chapel Hill 1958).

2 For example, Sigurd Burckhardt *Shakespearean Meanings* (Princeton 1968) 117, 137, 150; Nicholas Brooke *Shakespeare's Early Tragedies* (London 1968) especially pp. 8–10; Wilbur Sanders *The Dramatist and the Received Idea* (Cambridge 1968); and Herbert Howarth, *The Tiger's Heart* (New York 1970) 165–91, especially 168–73 for *King Lear*. As for 'historians,' *all* serious students of the period accept, even embrace, its anomalousness.

3 (Oxford 1965); see my brief review, *Renaissance News* XIX (1966) 48–54.

4 Stone's notion of so long a 'crisis' has been criticized; for my purposes, that criticism proved helpful in showing how the play's focus demonstrates such a crisis more schematically and intensely than historical documents covering a hundred-year period. That is, 'crisis' may be the wrong word for Stone's book, but it *is* the right word for *King Lear*.

5 Stone *Crisis* chap 8; and G.E. Aylmer *The King's Servants* (London 1961) chap 5.

6 *Crisis* 549–55; and in a still-unpublished lecture on English country houses.

7 *Crisis* 242–50; Sheldon P. Zitner, 'Hamlet: Duellist,' *University of Toronto Quarterly* XXXIX (1969) 1–18. See also Vincentio Saviolo *His Practice* (London 1595); and George Silver *Paradoxes of Defence* (London 1599).

8 *Crisis* 50.

9 Ibid 562–6; *A Discourse of the Common Weal of England* ed. Elizabeth Lamond (Cambridge 1929) 82–3; *The Household Papers of Henry Percy, Ninth Earl of Northumberland* ed. G.R. Batho (London 1962) 63, 108, 114.

10 *Certaine Sermons* (London 1595) Part II, 6: 'Against excess of apparell'; see also Lawrence Humfrey *The Nobles, or the Nobilitye* (London 1563) III: 'Of Apparel'; Philip Stubbs *The Anatomie of Abuses* (London 1585) 6–7, 16–38; Robert Greene *A Quip for an Upstart Courtier or, A quaint dispute between Velvet breeches and Cloth breeches* (London 1620); William Harrison *Description of England* ed. F.J. Furnivall (London 1877) I, 168–72. For appropriate illustration, see Roy Strong *Portraits of Queen Elizabeth I* (Oxford 1963); and *The English Icon: Elizabethan and Jacobean Portraiture* (London and New York 1969).

11 James Cleland *Propaideia, or the Institution of a Young Noble Man* (Oxford 1607) 214–17.

12 Stone *Crisis* 28–9.

13 Ibid 184–8, 547–86.

14 Hieronimus Osorius *A Discourse of Civill, and Christian Nobilitie* (London 1576) 27ff; *Cyvile and Uncyvile Life* (London 1579) 12; Gervase Markham *A Health to the Gentlemanly Profession of Servingmen* Roxburghe Library ed. 1868 (London 1598) 126–31.

15 *King Lear* ed. Kenneth Muir, xliii, n1.

16 Stone *Crisis* 170–5.

17 See *Renaissance News* XIX (1966) 48–54. I do not want to seem to take the play as reportage on current political and social conditions: see the debate between Allan Bloom and Harry Jaffa on one side, and Sigurd Burckhardt on the other, in *American Political Science Review* LIV (1960) 130–66, 457–73.

18 See F.T. Flahiff, below.

19 Stone *Crisis* 99, and personal communication to the author.

20 Thomas Milles *The Catalogue of Honor* (London 1610) 20.

21 See Sir William Segar *Honor, Military, and Civill* (London 1602) 113, 122, 220.

22 '*King Lear*' in Our Time (Berkeley 1965) 47–8, 56, 166–8; W.B.C. Watkins *Shakespeare and Spenser* (Princeton 1966) 83; William Frost, 'Shakespeare's Rituals and the Opening of *King Lear*,' *Hudson Review* X (1958) 577–85.

23   *Crisis* 9.

24   Ibid 182.

25   *Shakespearean Meanings* 239–40.

26   *Crisis* 42–9, 50, 187 ff.

27   Ibid 44–7, referring to W.K. Jordan's voluminous work. As Stone points out, although noble testamentary charities were relatively smaller than those of the merchant class, or the whole 'middle' class, there was some reason for this apparent limit on almsgiving by the facts of noble inheritance. All noblemen, in effect, had fixed heirs with respect to the bulk of their estates, and middle-class patriarchs, with no such restrictions on legacies, were free to dispose of their estates as they wished, or as they thought God wished.

28   See Ibid 47–8, for some samples of noble support to others.

29   *Cyvile and Uncyvile Life* 35, for charity properly bestowed on beggars; Humfrey *The Nobles* II, on liberality; III, on apparel, and on beggars.

30   Stone *Crisis* 167–9, 171.

31   The division is all the same ambivalent, though: apparently Lear had already divided his kingdom among his co-heiresses, reserving simply the part 'more opulent' for his favourite daughter. Otherwise, principally to prevent potential strife between these sons-in-law, the division appears to have been conceived as just. The relation of the rhetorical contest among the daughters, then, to the original political division remains, like so much else in the play, mysterious and irrational.

32   See Stone *Crisis* 167, 197.

33   Ibid 170–5.

34   Ibid 201–17; *Cyvile and Uncyvile Life* 34–9; Markham *Health* passim; Harrison *Description of England* lxxi, 134–5.

35   Stone *Crisis* 238–57; Wallace MacCaffrey *The Shaping of the Elizabethan Regime* (Princeton 1968) 330–71; see also Humfrey *The Nobles* III, for distinctions between necessary and unnecessary servants; and Harrison *Description of England* 134–5, for idle servingmen.

36   Stone *Crisis* 211–12.

37   Stone *Crisis* 549–65; Harrison *Description of England* 267–77, for princes' palaces.

38   Stone *Crisis* 201, 215–50.

39   See Lear's remark, 'There's your press money' (4.6.86–7), which suggests that, however dimly, he knew he needed some defence.

40   For cohorts, see Stone *Crisis* 203–6.

41   For royal meals, see Aylmer *King's Servants* 26–32.

42   Stone *Crisis* 54 speaks of aristocratic punishment; *King Lear* ed. Muir, 77, note to 2.2.133 for punishments to servants in great households.

43   It is worth noting that Kent does not actually fight with Oswald, but uses his sword only to beat him. He is ready, however, to take on Edmund, 'goodman boy,' who enters with his noble rapier drawn.

44   See Stone *Crisis* 224 for examples.

45   For a sensitive reading of Edmund's nature and role in the play, see Julian Markels *Pillar of the World* (Columbus, Ohio 1968) 104–6; also H.A. Mason *Shakespeare's Tragedies of Love* (London 1970) 184–94; Arnold Kettle, 'From Hamlet to Lear,' in *Shakespeare in a Changing World* ed. Arnold Kettle (London 1964) 158–71.

46   For some of the disabilities of bastards, see B.G. Lyons, above; and John Ferne *The Blazon of Gentrie* (London 1586). A bastard might not inherit from his father without the father's specific and deliberate designation by gift or by testament; even a legitimated bastard might not sit at his legitimate brother's table except by invitation. These regulations had become old fashioned by 1586, however, and in many noble families bastards were generously treated.

47   Although her behaviour indicates more feeling for Edmund than do her words, Regan's argument for marrying him rests on the fact that it is more 'convenient' for her to do so than for the still-married Goneril.

48   Segar *Honor* 220 on earls: '*Elderman, id est, Iudex*'.

49   Ferne *Gentrie* 308–12; Segar *Honor* 113.

50   Stone *Crisis* 747–53.

51 Ibid 591–3.

52 Quoted in ibid 592.

53 See, for example, Robert Cleaver *A Godlie Forme of Household Government* (London 1598) for the duties of parents to children and of children to parents.

54 This quotation actually has one of the few direct references to 'the court' – 'Who's in, who's out' – in the entire play.

55 See Stone *Crisis* 660–9; and *Certaine Sermons*, homily against adultery.

56 Stone *Crisis* 273–334, for estate management.

57 F.T. Flahiff has written, in an unpublished paper, about the separation in this play of judgment and power: Lear's arraignment of his daughters on the heath is purely symbolic, and the blinding of Gloucester is done without the ceremony of justice.

58 Enid Welsford *The Fool* (London 1935); Barbara Swain *Fools and Folly during the Middle Ages and the Renaissance* (New York 1932).

CHAPTER 11

Theory in Practice
Social Class in Alice Munro's "Sunday Afternoon" and "Hired Girl"

Isla Duncan

Many of Alice Munro's stories concern the lives of poor people, and several concern moments of tension between them and those with more money and social power. In this essay, British scholar Isla Duncan discusses two stories that focus on clashes between social classes and explores changes Munro made in one of the stories to sharpen its social criticism. Dr. Duncan teaches Canadian Literature and contemporary women's writing at the University of Chichester.

In an interview with Alice Munro published over twenty years ago, Geoff Hancock suggests to the writer that her stories 'contain a veiled social commentary', adding that there is a 'kind of class system at work' in which 'we go down the ladder in Hanratty to the other side of the tracks' (Hancock 1987: 205).[1] In reply, Munro explains that when she returned to her homeland, Huron County, having spent a long time away from it in British Columbia, she became instantly aware of and 'awfully interested in' class differences (p. 206). That class distinctions matter to some of her readers is richly illustrated in an anecdote Munro tells Hancock about the student who, during a seminar on *Lives of Girls and Women* (1971) taught by a friend of Munro, declared that 'the class should know that Alice Munro came from the wrong side of the tracks' (Hancock 1987: 206).

The arrogance and petty-minded snobbery displayed by this attitude are recurring traits in the less attractive Munrovian characters, from her earliest fiction to her most recent. There are several instances of what Hancock refers to as 'social commentary' in *The Beggar Maid* (1980), for example in the title story, where Patrick dismisses Rose's home town as a 'dump' (Munro 1980: 91) and does not disguise his contempt for it and for Rose's family. In 'Chaddeleys and Flemings: Connection', from *The Moons of Jupiter*

Original publication details: Isla Duncan, "Social Class in Alice Munro's 'Sunday Afternoon' and 'Hired Girl'" from *British Journal of Canadian Studies* 22.1, pp. 15–30. Liverpool University Press, 2009. Reproduced with permission from Liverpool University Press.

(1982), Richard, a character similar to Patrick, wants his wife (the narrator) to be 'amputated from [a past] which seemed to him such shabby baggage' (Munro 1982: 13). He is derogatory about her accent, her native town and the relatives who come to visit her, referring to her aunt as 'a pathetic old tart' (p. 17). Munro's continuing concern with social class is evident in later fiction, most notably in 'Family Furnishings' from *Hateship, Friendship, Courtship, Loveship, Marriage* (2001), a story whose female narrator chronicles events in 'a ramshackle background' that her fiancé disapproves of, regarding all 'failures in life … as lapses' (Munro 2001: 87).

The writer's humble upbringing in Wingham, Ontario, is chronicled by Munro herself (notably in 'Working for a Living'), while further insights are gleaned from biographies and the thought-provoking memoir, published in 2003, by Munro's eldest daughter. From such sources we learn that before leaving for university, the young Alice Laidlaw worked as a maid for a family in Rosedale, an affluent neighbourhood in Toronto. This family also owned a summer cottage on an island in Georgian Bay, near Pointe au Baril (Thacker 2005: 82). Munro explains to Catherine Sheldrick Ross that when working for her rich employers, she 'felt set apart from the people around [her], and the experience sharpened [her] sense of class differences' (Ross 1992: 46). The writer also confides to Eleanor Wachtel: 'It was probably a very important experience that way, because I saw all sorts of class things… Being a servant in a household … you see things about you and them – the barrier – which totally surprised me' (Wachtel 1991: 49).

The 'barrier' between wealthy employer and poor servant is explored in 'Hired Girl', a story anthologised in *The View from Castle Rock* (2006) but first published twelve years previously in the *New Yorker*. Munro's revisions of this story are worthy of detailed analysis, for, as I shall argue, they reveal not only her sedulous craft, but also her purposeful desire to make social class and its concomitant inequities a more salient theme in the later work. In its depiction of the narrator's fierce resentment of her status, and her calculated antagonism towards her employer, the narrative differs from Munro's earlier treatment of the 'social embarrassment' (Coldwell 1983: 537) that coming from a poor family causes characters such as Del, Rose, Janet and the unnamed narrator of 'Family Furnishings'.

In *Remnants of Nation: On Poverty Narratives by Women* (2001), Roxanne Rimstead argues that, while Munro in her fiction often 'draws attention to poverty and cross-class experiences', she does so with 'a distanced gaze' (Rimstead 2001: 105), from a position that is intended 'to control and survey the scene of poverty for its representational and aesthetic impact' (p. 216).[2] In this respect, Rimstead asserts, her perspective is unlike that of Margaret Laurence, whose fictive portrayals of the poor are more political, and more engaging of the reader's empathy. It seems to Rimstead that Laurence, in, for example, *The Diviners* (1974), invites the reader to share in the sense of outrage at the poverty that is being described, and the social injustices exposed as unacceptable. Rimstead's remarks on the 'distanciation' of Munro's gaze (p. 105) are more pertinent to Munro's earlier work, particularly *The Beggar Maid* (1980), where the protagonist Rose is shown playing 'an onlooker's part' (Munro 1980: 42) in the theatrical presentation of a past variously transformed or disguised, or offered as diversion to a dinner party audience (p. 91). In her acquiescence to the 'obedient image' (p. 85) of a less vulgar self, prescribed by rich, snobbish Patrick, Rose does not question why his family needs their ostentatious wealth, their abundant luxury; instead, she awkwardly pretends to be at ease amid such surroundings (pp. 86–8), even although, as the narrator explains, she 'was destroying herself', allowing her accent to 'be eliminated, her friends … discredited and removed' (p. 85).

In 'Hired Girl', there is little evidence of this self-conscious shame about a less privileged background. Indeed, in her revision of the story, for *The View of Castle Rock*, Munro presents a narrator who regales her addressee with 'poverty narratives': these, however, are not delivered for their aesthetic value, but as weapons of instruction and retaliation. In terms of its setting and characterisation, the story is reminiscent of a much earlier piece, 'Sunday Afternoon'. Although it is sometimes cited, briefly, as exemplary of her early fiction, 'Sunday Afternoon' has not attracted sustained critical attention. George Woodcock, in his essay on realism in Munro's fiction, describes the story as a 'little social study, highly class-conscious for a Canadian writer' (Woodcock 1986: 240). The class-consciousness is immediately discernible in the story's first paragraph, in the presentation of the employer, Mrs Gannett, as leisured and glamorous: 'flashing the polished cotton skirts of a flowered sundress', she enters the kitchen where her maid, Alva, is 'washing glasses', and delivers instructions on what and how to serve the guests, 'the usual people' who have arrived for lunch (Munro 1968: 161).

The incongruity of Alva in Mrs Gannett's world is systematically developed in a series of discrepant juxtapositions and contrasts. Thus, the 'tones of shrill and happy outrage' Alva hears from the patio, where the guests are drinking freely, make her keenly aware that she is not permitted 'to show a little relaxation and excitement' (p. 163). The narrator's wry, bathetic observation, that 'Of course, she was not drinking, except out of the bottoms of glasses' (p. 163) conjures up the image of an unaccustomed luxury, guiltily snatched. Alva keenly feels her own gaucheness, in her utility uniform, and in the 'heavy, purposeful, plebeian sound' her 'white Cuban-heeled shoes [make] on the stones of the patio ... in contrast to the sandals and pumps' (p. 164); the description of the room she occupies, tellingly above the garage, continues the theme of inconsonance, for it is the 'only place in the house where you could find things unmatched, unrelated to each other' (p. 167). The stark distinction between the servant's life and that of her employer is encapsulated in two successive sentences: 'She could not actually leave the house; Mrs Gannett might want her for something. And she could not go outside; they were out there' (p. 165). The sentences are similarly constructed, for both consist of coordinate clauses, the first expressing a negation, the second explaining it. By such construction, Munro conveys two antitheses: between freedom and incarceration, and between inside and outside.

The story is told by an extradiegetic narrator, but there are several occasions when Alva becomes the subject of the focalisation, such as when the reader learns of how Mrs Gannett summons her maid, using her voice like a bell: 'It was queer to hear her call this, in the middle of talking to someone, and then begin laughing again; it seemed as if she had a mechanical voice, even a button she pushed, for Alva' (p. 164). The informality of diction ('it was queer'), the use of the proximal deictic 'this', and the reformulation in the similes, are all hallmarks of free indirect discourse, and they serve to instantiate Alva's perspective on events. It is clear from glimpses of this perspective that Alva feels she is of little consequence, a sort of inanimate labour-saving device available to order.

Alva is further belittled at the story's conclusion, when she is the subject of the sexual advances of Mrs Gannett's cousin, although the interpretation of this encounter, as with many endings in Munro narratives, is indeterminate. The narrator explains that Alva is somehow 'eased' by 'the stranger's touch' (p. 170) and excited by the prospect of meeting the young man once again, at the Gannetts' cottage, later in the summer. The reader may be heartened by the protagonist's pleasure in a new 'lightness and confidence she had not known in this house' (p. 170); Ildiko de Papp Carrington, however, reads Alva's experience as further evidence of inequality in the relationship between privileged class and servant (Carrington 1989: 105), and I would agree. The story ends on the word 'humiliation': Alva is described as looking forward to a 'tender spot, a new and still mysterious humiliation', and this description surely undermines the confidence she feels after the 'stranger's touch' (Munro 1968: 170). A closer study of Alva's meeting with the amorous young man exposes vestiges of both social and sexual inequality.

The nameless cousin is from 'Mrs Gannett's side of the family' which, as noted at the start of the narrative, is 'the right side' (p. 161); interestingly, he is twice referred to, in the space of four lines, as 'Mrs Gannett's cousin', the repeated relational term somehow reinforcing his social credentials. He has his cousin's peremptory authority, one he flirtatiously wields, demanding that Alva 'Say thanks' (p. 170) when he passes her a glass to wash. After he has kissed her, he returns to the patio, to the outside Alva is excluded from, walking 'with the rather graceful, mocking stealth of some slight people' (p. 170). Even in such a brief vignette one can discern the assured and practised condescension that Alva is subject to throughout the narrative.

This early story, in its depiction of the barrier between privileged employer and underprivileged servant, foreshadows the fuller exploration of that relationship in 'Hired Girl'. Its narrator is a more complex, and more substantially developed character than Alva. At the very outset, she makes it clear that she is not comfortable with the role of maid, that she resents her status, and dislikes her affluent employer, Mrs Montjoy. In the revised version of 'Hired Girl', published over a decade after its first appearance in *New Yorker*, Munro intensifies the narrator's feelings of discomfort and antipathy; she widens the chasm between employer and maid, holding up to scrutiny and ridicule the mores and social pretensions of Mrs Montjoy and her summer cottage guests. It is primarily through the commentary of her feisty, sharp-eyed narrator that Munro can more critically examine that chasm.

There are several differences between the *New Yorker* version of 'Hired Girl' (1994) and the one published in the anthology *The View from Castle Rock* (2006). Drawing on the disciplines of literary linguistics, pragmatics and politeness theory, I consider these differences, focusing on the presentation of Mrs Montjoy and her treatment of the narrator; the narrator's interaction with other characters; her commentary on her status and situation, and the nature of her self-knowledge at the conclusion. In her revision of this narrative, Munro, I shall argue, sharpens the narrator's consciousness of class difference, making it a more salient theme for the reader.

The authority of the employer and the passivity of the employee are reflected in the syntax of the initiating sentence – 'Mrs Montjoy was showing me how to put the pots and pans away' (Munro 1994: 228) – in which Mrs Montjoy is the subject, the narrator the indirect object.[3] The reader learns that the narrator had been collected from Pointe au Baril station some days before and had been brought to the island by boat. The unflattering description of Mrs Montjoy is common to both versions, but while in the first the narrator concedes that her employer's 'commonest expression [was] one of impatience held *decently* in check' (Munro 1994: 82, emphasis added), in the second the judgement is harsher, for the 'impatience [is] *barely* held in check' (Munro, 2006: 229, emphasis added). The difference in adverbial choice is sufficient to suggest that the woman's 'impatience' verges on irascibility. It is during the journey from Pointe au Baril that Mrs Montjoy asks the narrator if she is 'Feeling a tad sick?' (p. 229), a question that differs from that of the earlier version, in the addition of 'a tad', an adverbial that in speech act theory would be categorised as a 'hedge', a qualification or toning down of an utterance.

The *Oxford English Dictionary* determines the status label of this lexical item, when it means 'a little' or 'slightly', as '*colloq.* (orig. and chiefly *N. Amer.*)', its first recorded usage being in 1940.[4] All the citations given are from US or Canadian sources; most of the later ones exemplify the same facetious understatement discernible in Mrs Montjoy's question.

In both versions of the story, the narrator notes that this question is accompanied by 'the briefest possible smile … like the signal for a smile, when the occasion did not warrant the real thing' (Munro 1994: 82, and 2006: 229). The inappropriateness that the narrator implies derives from the fact that Mrs Montjoy is flouting one of the four maxims of conversation that, according to the philosopher H.P. Grice, express the general cooperative principle in language (Levinson 1983: 101–18). The four maxims in Grice's theory of conversational implicature (the additional levels of meaning beyond the semantic meaning of the words uttered) refer to quantity, quality, relation and manner; in the context of Mrs Montjoy's question, quality is the pertinent term.

> *The maxim of quality*
> Try to make your contribution one that is true, specifically:
> Do not say what you believe to be false.
> Do not say that for which you lack adequate evidence.
> (Levinson 1983: 101)

The shivering narrator is holding on to the sides of a boat 'flung out on the choppy evening waters of Georgian Bay' (Munro 2006: 229). It is clear that she is unwell; yet Mrs Montjoy makes her jocular, pseudosolicitous enquiry, perhaps, the narrator suspects, because she senses fear rather than nausea. In any case, she has flouted the maxim of quality, firstly by asking a question whose answer she must know, and, secondly, by deliberately qualifying and diminishing her concern, to the extent that it is difficult to construe as heartfelt. The fleeting, perfunctory smile seems to undermine the genuineness of 'Feeling a tad sick?' a question that is pragmatically anomalous because it 'contradicts the standard quality implicature, that one believes what one asserts and [that] when one asks a question, one may standardly be taken to be asking sincerely' (Levinson 1983: 105). I would argue that the insertion of the informal, hedging, and often intentionally ironic 'a tad' serves to expose this character's insincerity.

There is abundant evidence, in both versions of the narrative, that Mrs Montjoy regards the narrator as someone of little consequence, merely a maid hired for summer help. In the later version, Munro makes the older woman's attitude towards her maid seem more functionalist; for example, when the narrator overhears Mrs Montjoy talk to a guest about the problems they share, keeping domestic staff happy, she remembers her comment: 'So you just make allowances … You do the best with them you can' (Munro 2006: 237). In the same scene in the *New Yorker* story, the statement of resignation reads: 'You do the best you can' (Munro 1994: 84). The third person pronoun reference reduces the humanity of the subjects, presenting them as an undifferentiated mass. Another remarkable instance of Mrs Montjoy's tendency to refer to her maid as inconsequential occurs in a scene when she helps her husband find a book that he has mislaid. She advises him, correctly, that he has left it in the living-room, where the narrator is working. Because she has picked it up, and is eagerly reading it, Mr Montjoy thanks her, remarking on the 'queer kind of book' that he considers it to be (it is Isak Dinesen's *Seven Gothic Tales*).

At this point, his wife enters the room, declaring: 'We'll have to get out of the way here and let her get on with the vacuuming' (Munro 2006: 242). In the *New Yorker*, Mrs Montjoy's words are: 'We'll have to get out of the way here – Elsa has to get on with the vacuuming' (Munro 1994: 85). There are two noteworthy points to be made here, and both serve to substantiate my claim that, in her later presentation of Mrs Montjoy, Munro wishes to accentuate her lack of empathy, her superiority and her rudeness.

First of all, the reader will note that, in the earlier version of the story, the narrator has a forename that is not retained in the later one. This subsequent anonymity is, I will argue, of particular importance when the narrator is addressed by one of Mrs Montjoy's flirtatious male guests. For the moment, it is the use of the third person pronoun that merits my attention. As the writer has decided that her narrator will be nameless, she has to opt for pronominal reference, but its use in this scene is marked. The syntax of the utterance makes it even more so, for, while in the earlier version, the narrator is the subject of the second clause, in the second she has become the object, a change in syntactic relations that reduces the narrator's agency.

The use of the third person pronoun in this speech event is revealing. The situation consists of two speakers, with a third party present, who is spoken of by one of the interlocutors. In his discussion of deixis, the general term for the various lexical and grammatical features that relate utterances to contexts, Lyons reminds us of the exact nature of the grammatical category, third person, in relation to first and second:

> It is important to note that only the speaker [first person] and the addressee [second person] are participating in the drama. The term 'third person' is negatively defined with respect to 'first person' and 'second person': it does not correlate with any positive participant role. (Lyons 1977: 638)

In *Personal Pronouns in Present-day English* (1996), the first book-length analysis of the subject, the British linguist Katie Wales examines third person forms and speech roles. She notes that there are many kinds of communication, in various contexts, when the role of listener is shared between third party and addressee, and that what distinguishes the latter from the former is that the addressee knows s/he is being addressed. Wales explains that '[t]his third party may be referred to exophorically, for some reason, by the speaker' (Wales 1996: 54). In the social code of politeness, Wales observes, a person's name is preferred to the pronoun, when the referent is present; when the speaker breaches this code, s/he may do so out of embarrassment, or perhaps animosity (p. 44). When Mrs Montjoy refers to her maid exophorically, excluding her from any 'positive participant role', she breaks a fundamental maxim of politeness. This is not because she is embarrassed, or feeling particularly inimical, but because she regards the young woman as irrelevant, to the company and to the conversation.

Like Mrs Gannett in 'Sunday Afternoon', Mrs Montjoy is also anxious to establish the boundary between the hired girl's milieu and that of the family and guests. The narrator is quickly made to understand that, when she is not working, she cannot occupy the same space as the adults she serves. When she carries her own meal out to the deck from the kitchen, she is reminded by her employer, with elliptical urgency: 'Three plates there? Oh, yes, two out on the deck and yours in here. Right?' (Munro 2006: 237). The proximal deictic, 'here' represents, as it did for Alva, the domestic sphere where the maid belongs. This particular episode, new to the 2006 version of 'Hired Girl', further illustrates the elaborate demarcation between the territories of servant and employer that seems more sharply defined in Munro's revision.

In her permitted interaction with Mrs Montjoy's ten-year-old daughter, Mary Anne, the narrator can express her resentment at this delimitation; what Munro remembers, from her own experience, as a 'setting apart' from others. When she is asked by the younger girl about the sports she is best at, the narrator begins, 'Everybody I know works too hard to do any sports' (p. 238), and then she launches into a detailed account of the poverty-stricken, work-beleaguered lives of people in her hometown. Her 'exaggerations or near lies' (p. 239) allow her to give vent to a sense of injustice at the chasm in wealth and opportunity between her own class and that of the Montjoy family. While in the earlier version the narrator acknowledges that her hometown had once boasted a tennis court and a golf course 'in the thirties' (Munro 1994: 84), in the revision the period is more precisely named 'the Depression' (Munro 2006: 239), the initial capital indicating its historical importance as a time of industrial and financial decline. The referential term 'the thirties' does not have the same emotive impact.

It is in order to achieve maximum impact on the young and impressionable Mary Anne that the narrator dramatises and exaggerates the hardships of her own way of life. But she also recognises that another purpose is to 'make clear the differences' (p. 241) between her home circumstances and those of her employer's daughter. It is this urge to differentiate between one way of life (characterised by affluence and privilege) and another (characterised by penury and denial) that, I think, furnishes evidence of a less objective, more empathetic view of poverty. Roxanne Rimstead maintains that Munro's 'gaze … towards the poor' is 'so distancing' as to suggest 'powerlessness and neutrality' (Rimstead 2001: 105); in addition, she opines that her protagonist's or narrator's recollections of an impoverished upbringing are a source of 'primarily personal shame, melancholy or aesthetic enthralment', rather than as 'matters of political importance and community alliances' (p. 215). But in 'Hired Girl' there is little vestige of the narrator's shame or sadness; on the contrary, she fulminates against her listener's ignorance of how less fortunate people, namely, the self-sufficient people of her community, cope with privation.

She succeeds in stimulating her listener's conscience, as well as her inventiveness: '"That isn't fair," said Mary Anne. "That's awful. I didn't know people could eat dandelion leaves." But then she brightened. "Why don't they go and catch some fish?"' (p. 240). The equivalent passage in the 1994 story is exactly the same, except for one revealing verb phrase: by substituting 'brightened' for 'added', in the original, Munro makes Mary Anne's suggestion seem like part of an entertaining parlour game, where the most imaginative ideas are awarded points for ingenuity. Try as she might, the young girl cannot envisage the kind of poverty that the narrator describes, for it is so far outwith her cosseted experience. While the narrator acknowledges that her tales are exaggerated, she is certain that 'not one of these statements – even the one about the dandelion leaves – was completely a lie' (p. 239).

The narrator's intention to widen the gulf between two households, between two classes, is confirmed in the following statement, the climax to her evocative description of the family kitchen at home:

[I]t seemed as if I had to protect it from contempt – as if I had to protect a whole precious and intimate though hardly pleasant way of life from contempt. Contempt was what I imagined to be always waiting, swinging along on live wires, just under the skin and just behind the perceptions of people like the Montjoys. (p. 240)

The corresponding section from the 1994 version reads:

> [I]t seemed that I had to protect it from contempt – that I had to protect a whole precious and intimate though often unpleasant way of life from contempt, which I supposed to be nourished in the icy hearts of people like the Montjoys. (Munro 1994: 85)

Munro has effected important changes in her revision. Firstly, she has made the word 'contempt' stand out: this she has done by using a rhetorical device called anadiplosis, which is the repetition of the last word of one clause at the beginning of the following clause (Corbett and Connors 1999: 392). Because the normal sequence of clause elements (subject–verb) is subsequently reversed, the word 'contempt', the object, is foregrounded, as it is not in the original. Indeed, attention is somewhat deflected in the *New Yorker* version, as a result of the reformulation initiated by the dash. Another change worth commenting upon is the greater elaboration of the *source* of the contempt. While Munro originally locates it in the 'icy hearts of people like the Montjoys', where it is 'nourished', in her revision she presents the contempt as pervasive, a latent, reflexive reaction, always there beneath the surface.

I believe that the changes that Munro has wrought in this scene underscore the narrator's angry defensiveness of her own class, and they heighten her antipathy towards wealthy, privileged people she thinks have no understanding of, or respect for, her class. The hired girl is presented as a more politically motivated spokeswoman for her family and class, endeavouring to ascribe dignity to their struggles.

In the narrator's interaction with some of Mrs Montjoy's summer guests, their lack of respect is clearly discernible. Her encounter with the 'courtly' Mr Hammond exposes the same kind of patronising sexual arrogance displayed by the employer's cousin in 'Sunday Afternoon'. The changes Munro has made in her revision intensify the conde-scension. In the earlier story, the character, having entered the kitchen for more gin, addresses the narrator firstly as 'Minnie' but, after being told by his wife that Minnie is not her name, addresses her, several times thereafter, as 'Elsa'. In the revised version, as I explained above, the narrator is purposefully nameless; so the correct forename is not given, although Mr Hammond is informed that he is mistaken in calling the young girl 'Minnie'. He continues to do so, however, speaking 'in an artificial, dreamy voice' that the narrator recognises as 'deeply sceptical and sophisticated' (p. 246, p. 247). In his first few addresses to the narrator, he uses what he thinks is her forename five times; over 20 per cent of his spoken words consist of the vocative. Such a high proportion of these nominal elements is unusual, in an exchange between strangers.

In a corpus-based paper he describes as 'a more focused treatment of vocatives in present-day English' (Leech 1999: 108), the grammarian and linguist Geoffrey Leech sub-divides vocatives into semantic categories. The address form 'Minnie' would be termed a 'familiarised first name' and it is the vocative type that predominates in the linguistic corpora amassed by Leech and his colleagues. In his analysis, he notes that 'familiarising vocatives, including first-name address, typically signal acquaintanceship or friendship' (p. 116). In this scene from 'Hired Girl', the vocative is linguistically marked, for its repetition is excessive, and it is used by an addresser who is *unknown* to the addressee. Sara Mills points out that while first names are exchanged between inter-locutors on equal terms, 'those in asymmetrical power relations will use differential naming patterns' (Mills 1995: 110). Such asymmetry certainly exists in the relationship between the young maid and the much older, more sophisticated, wealthy man whose meals she serves. I would argue that Munro, in her revision, portrays the character of Mr Hammond as more patronising, and more inappropriately flirtatious, so that the asymmetry is magnified. In the *New Yorker* story, he similarly overuses the vocative, but he addresses the hired girl by her given forename when told, and when he reverts to 'Minnie', he appears to do so because he is inebriated. There is not the same sustained, mocking condescension in his manner.

Immediately following the episode in the kitchen, the narrator recounts another belittling experience at the hands of the Montjoys' guests. As she heads to her room in the boathouse, she meets a couple of young guests, girls her own age, who are returning from their swim. By their behaviour towards the narrator, they make plain their belief in their social superiority. The *New Yorker* version reads: 'They stepped aside when they saw me but did not quite stop laughing. They made way for my body without looking at me' (Munro 1994: 87). The revised version is as follows: 'They stepped aside politely, not to drip water on me, but did not stop laughing. Making way for my body without a glance at my face" (Munro 2006: 248). The changes are not radical but they do make more of the guests' dismissive attitude towards the maid. For example, in the earlier version, the adverb 'quite', termed a 'downtoner' by Quirk et al. (1990: 597), denotes that the laughter does not cease but it is diminished; in the latter excerpt, however, there is no attempt to suppress it. In both versions, the narrator comments on the girls' failure to make eye contact with her, but in the passage immediately above, the rudeness appears more of a slight, for the supplementive clause on its own separates the ignoring from the stepping aside, somehow making it more of a consequent and conscious act.

The narrator's commentary on her relationship with Mrs Montjoy, her family and her guests, constitutes a remarkably accurate assessment of her social status in the household. She not only identifies material differences between her own rural background and the affluent world of the summer cottage in Georgian Bay, but she also becomes aware of attitudinal differences, noting how strange it is that Mrs Montjoy's daughter should bemoan her intelligence, when, in the narrator's township, clever boys are more likely to be looked on with suspicion, even disparaged as 'sissies' (Munro 2006: 231). Although she acknowledges that she feels incongruous in the island setting, sensing the ubiquitous presence of 'an indolent reminder. *Not for you*', she will not admit to feeling 'humbled or lonely, or that [she] was a real servant' (p. 232). One assertion she makes towards the end of the narrative epitomises both her pride and her astute self-awareness; after reflecting on the hypocrisy of her behaviour towards Mrs Montjoy, the narrator declares, 'I did not have the grace or fortitude to be a servant' (p. 252). In the earlier version, the verb phrase is contracted ('didn't') and the negation thus reduced in force. Furthermore, in her revision, Munro separates the statement in a paragraph of its own, according it greater prominence, making it seem a confident, even defiant summation.

The reflective narrator perceives, in this display of assurance, a desire for 'equality, even with a person I did not like' (p. 252). The assurance derives mostly from the narrator's sense of intellectual superiority over Mrs Montjoy, expressed early in the story, when she reveals her understanding of the allusion, in the name of the family boat, to Nausicaa in Homer's *Odyssey*, a name Mrs Montjoy mistakenly believes is 'for some character in Shakespeare' (p. 230). The narrator makes further discoveries that enhance her feeling of power, and lessen for her the disparity in status between servant and employer. Firstly, having learnt that Mrs Montjoy's senile mother does not recognise her own daughter, she takes perverse pleasure in telling her so (p. 236). She also feigns ignorance about the death of her employer's older daughter, delicately eliciting details of the tragedy from Mrs Montjoy, all the while knowing she is being hypocritical. The narrator later evaluates her action in the confession: 'Cruelty was a thing I could not recognise in myself. I thought I was blameless here, and in my dealings with the family' (p. 252). The deictic 'here' oddly jars with the past tense verbs, its incongruity serving to distinguish her present candour from her former deceit.

The conclusion of the story published in *The View from Castle Rock* differs from that published in New Yorker. Both versions end with the scene in the boathouse, on the narrator's last Sunday, when she is unexpectedly visited by Mr Montjoy, who brings her the gift of his book, *Seven Gothic Tales*. In both versions, Munro conveys her narrator's awkwardly expressed gratitude, and then her swift appropriation of what she feels is rightfully hers, something that 'had always belonged to me' (1994: 88; 2006: 254). In the earlier version, Munro inserts a flashback, several paragraphs from the end, in which the narrator recalls a conversation with Mary Anne, who, in an attempt at affiliation, had explained to her that her father 'used to be poor like you'. The attempt fails, however, for the narrator refuses to 'give anybody whose father had been a doctor the credit for being poor' (1994: 88). This flashback is omitted entirely from the revised version, and its omission removes blatant evidence of the narrator's inverted prejudice, snobbery just as deplorable as Mrs Montjoy's hauteur.

In both conclusions the reader might leave with a less favourable impression of the narrator's behaviour: in the *New Yorker* story her resentment of Mr Montjoy's working-class roots seems extreme, while in the more recent story it is her peevish self-absorption that comes across, in her dismissal of 'the person who interested me least, whose regard meant the least to me' (2006: 254). But in her later version, I believe, Munro somewhat mitigates her narrator's churlishness, for in the instances of reflection can be glimpsed a pleasing humility. Thinking on Mr Montjoy's reasons for giving her the book, the narrator observes: 'Drunk or not, I see him now as pure of motive, leaning against the boathouse wall. A person who could think me worthy of this gift. Of this book' (p. 254). This self-deprecation comes much later, after the admission of 'alarm [and] resentment' at 'having a little corner of myself come to light' (p. 254). At the time, the narrator resents the possibility that she might have betrayed any vulnerability, any commonality with a member of the Montjoy family; as an older narrator, she seems able to acknowledge a kindness, and think less of the motivation behind it. This more measured evaluation serves to deepen the narrator's psychological complexity; more importantly, its reasonableness somehow authenticates the narrator's beliefs about class, which were expressed in the diatribe to Mary Anne, and in the incisive commentary on her wealthy, privileged employers and their peers. For in her retrospective wisdom she has not retracted, and does not retract a thing, nor is she afflicted by 'a sensation of moral paralysis', that, according to Roxanne Rimstead, often dissipates 'emotions such as anger, shame or resentment' (Rimstead 2001: 105) at the conclusions of Munro's poverty narratives.

The changes that Munro effects in the second version of 'Hired Girl' produce a narrator who is unlikely to hear, as Alva does in 'Sunday Afternoon', the 'plebeian sound' her footwear makes, and who freely admits that she is unsuited to the role of serving others she considers rude and uninformed, people who hold sway over her by virtue of their social category. In her revision, Munro intensifies and makes salient the class distinctions evident in the earlier *New Yorker* version, presenting them 'as matters of political importance and community alliances' (Rimstead 2001: 215). The resulting narrative is a much more incisive, more critical social commentary that could not be described as 'veiled'.

Notes

1 The place-name 'Hanratty' in *The Beggar Maid* (1980), like 'Jubilee' in *Lives of Girls and Women* (1972), is assumed to be the fictional version of Wingham, Munro's birthplace.
2 Frank Davey has commented on Roxanne Rimstead's argument; see Davey 2003–2004.
3 In order to distinguish clearly between the two versions of the story, I use the publication dates of 2006 and 1994.
4 *The Oxford English Dictionary Online*, http://dictionary.oed.com/cgi/entry, accessed 4.11.2007.

References

Carrington, Ildiko de Papp, 1989, *Controlling the Uncontrollable: The Fiction of Alice Munro* (DeKalb, IL: University of Northern Illinois Press).

Coldwell, Joan, 1983, 'Munro, Alice', in William Toye (ed.), *The Oxford Companion to Canadian Literature* (Toronto, ON: Oxford University Press).

Corbett, Edward P.J. and Robert Connors, 1999, *Classical Rhetoric for the Modern Student* (New York, NY: Oxford University Press).

Davey, Frank, 2003–2004, 'Class, "Family Furnishings" and Munro's Early Fiction', *Open Letter*, 11:9–12:1 (Fall–Winter), 79–88.

Hancock, Geoff, 1987, *Canadian Writers at Work* (Toronto, ON: Oxford University Press).

Laurence, Margaret, 1974, *The Diviners* (London: Macmillan).

Leech, Geoffrey, 1999, 'The Distribution and Function of Vocatives in American and British English', in Hilde Hasselgård and Signe Oksefjell (eds), *Out of Corpora: Studies in Honour of Stig Johansson* (Amsterdam: Rodopi), 108–121.

Levinson, Stephen C., 1983, *Pragmatics* (Cambridge: Cambridge University Press).

Lyons, John, 1977, *Semantics*, vol. 2 (Cambridge: Cambridge University Press).

McCulloch, Jeanne and Mona Simpson, 1994, 'Alice Munro: The Art of Fiction', *Paris Review*, 131, 227–64.

Mills, Sara, 1995, *Feminist Stylistics* (London: Routledge).

Munro, Alice, 1957, 'Sunday Afternoon', *Canadian Forum* (September), 127–30.

Munro, Alice, 1968, *Dance of the Happy Shades* (Toronto, ON: Ryerson Press).

Munro, Alice, 1971, *Lives of Girls and Women* (Toronto, ON: McGraw-Hill Ryerson).

Munro, Alice, 1980, *The Beggar Maid* (London: Allen Lane).

Munro, Alice, 1981, 'Working for a Living', *Grand Street*, 1:1, 9–37.

Munro, Alice, 1982, *The Moons of Jupiter* (Toronto, ON: Macmillan).

Munro, Alice, 1994, 'Hired Girl', *The New Yorker* (11 April), 82–8.

Munro, Alice, 2001, *Hateship, Friendship, Courtship, Loveship, Marriage* (Toronto, ON: McClelland and Stewart).

Munro, Alice, 2006, *The View from Castle Rock* (Toronto, ON: McClelland and Stewart).

Munro, Sheila, 2001, *Lives of Mothers and Daughters: Growing up with Alice Munro* (Toronto, ON: McClelland and Stewart).

Quirk, Randolph, Sidney Greenbaum, Geoffrey Leech and Jan Svartnik, 1990, *A Comprehensive Grammar of the English Language* (London: Longman).

Rimstead, Roxanne, 2001, *Remnants of Nation: On Poverty Narratives by Women* (Toronto, ON: University of Toronto Press).

Ross, Catherine Sheldrick, 1992, *Alice Munro: A Double Life* (Toronto, ON: ECW Press).

Thacker, Robert, 2005, *Alice Munro: Writing Her Lives* (Toronto, ON: McClelland and Stewart).

Wachtel, Eleanor, 1991, 'An Interview with Alice Munro', *Brick*, 40, 48–53.

Wales, Katie, 1996, *Personal Pronouns in Present-day English* (Cambridge: Cambridge University Press).

Woodcock, George, 1986, 'The Plots of Life: The Realism of Alice Munro', *Queen's Quarterly*, 93:2, 235–50.

CHAPTER 12

Theory in Practice
Elizabeth Bishop, Modernism, and the Left

Betsy Erkkila

Elizabeth Bishop wrote poetry that was highly formal, well-crafted, and controlled, yet she also took on topics such as imperialism, racism, economic inequality, and war. In "A Miracle for Breakfast," she describes the hardship of the Great Depression of the 1930s. In "Brazil, January 1603," she describes imperialism from the perspective of the indigenous people. And "Roosters" is a poem about militarism and war. Betsy Erkkila traces Bishop's development in relation to the institutional and cultural Left of her era. Bishop distanced herself from the spirit of mandatory leftism that prevailed in the 1930s, but by the 1960s, she was writing poems such as "Twelve O'Clock News" that mocked the American effort to subdue other nations such as Vietnam by military means, and she was conducting interviews with Black Panthers, a radical African-American organization.

> *Even if one were tempted*
> *to literary interpretations*
> *such as: life/death, right/wrong, male/female*
> *– such notions would have resolved, dissolved, straight off*
> *in that watery, dazzling dialectic.*
>
> Elizabeth Bishop, "Santarém"

> *Every new tendency in art has begun with a rebellion.*
>
> Leon Trotsky, "Art and Politics"

Given the critical construction of Elizabeth Bishop as a subsidiary in the school of Marianne Moore, "a modest expert" (Moore 354), an "unassuming," "pleasant," "charming" poet of "restraint, calm, and proportion" (Jarrell 498–99), a soft and dreamy poet who is "not likely" to be hailed as "a giant among the moderns" (Lowell 497), an "utterly feminine" poet of "mild and affectionate brooding over what she has seen"

Original publication details: Betsy Erkkila, "Elizabeth Bishop, Modernism, and the Left." *American Literary History* 8.2 (Summer 1996), pp. 284–310. Oxford University Press, 1996. Reproduced with permission from Oxford University Press.

(Alvarez 325), "a poet's poet's poet" (John Ashbery), and an essentially "private" poet (Millier 67), to talk about Bishop in a political context at all is to challenge traditional – and gendered – readings not only of Bishop but of literary modernism itself. Adrienne Rich's important 1983 essay "The Eye of the Outsider: Elizabeth Bishop's *Complete Poems, 1927–1979*," which argues that Bishop's "experience of outsiderhood … linked with the essential outsiderhood of a lesbian identity" enabled her "to perceive other kinds of outsiders and to identify, or try to identify, with them" (127), has triggered a new interest in the sexual "politics" of Bishop's writing. As in Brett C. Millier's 1993 biography of Bishop, however, recent critics have continued to emphasize the essentially formal, aesthetic, private, and psychological dimensions of her work.[1] Perhaps attempting to wrest Bishop from earlier "objective" approaches, these critics have erected "subjectivity," "self-expression," and the "private poet" as the true badge of Bishop's seriousness, worth, and status as a major poet. Grounded in Romantic, bourgeois conceptions of the poet and the author, in the predominant psychoanalytic paradigms for reading lyric poetry, and in the gendered (including feminist) emphasis on self-expression as an essentially female mode, these newer approaches reinstate rather than challenge traditional distinctions between poetry and politics, private and public. Yet a close reading of Bishop's work problematizes the binarisms – literature/politics, formalism/social consciousness, modernism/leftism, high culture/popular culture, subjectivity/objectivity, private/public, male/female – that have characteristically governed our reading and writing of modernist literary history.

This essay will try to unfix the "selective tradition" (Williams 32) and the settled binaries we have come to associate with modernism by locating Bishop's work within the debates about the relation between literary modernism and the American – and international – Left.[2] Though she set herself against both the mythic narratives of literary modernism and the grand political narratives of the American Left, Bishop was deeply affected by the literary and political radicalism of the 1930s. Her insistence on the technical qualities "necessary to any art, to me" (qtd. in Millier 413) and the essential distinction between "politics" and "good poetry" (Millier 301) has kept us from recognizing how often her poems – even her more aestheticized and abstract early poems – take as their subjects class consciousness, race and gender struggle, the culture of the commodity and the machine, the relations of capital, property, and homelessness, and the conflict between the dominant narratives of the West and the "others" – women, lesbians, blacks, Cubans, Indians, the lower classes, the body, nature – that those narratives subjugate and colonize.

Bishop recalled that, as a student at Vassar College in the early '30s, she had admired W. H. Auden's ability to write leftist and politically knowledgeable poetry with "dazzling" technical skill ("'Work!'" 18; "From 'A Brief Reminiscence'"). While Bishop was herself a socialist and at one time an anarchist, she sought to avoid what she called the political-consciousness writing of the time by finding models not in Auden's work but in the seemingly more objective and nonpolitical work of T. S. Eliot, Wallace Stevens, and Moore. She said, "I stood up for T. S. Eliot when everybody else was talking about James T. Farrell. The atmosphere in Vassar was left-wing; it was the popular thing" ("Interview" 8).

Like later critical constructions of modernist literary history, Bishop misremembers her literary genealogy, erasing her own political engagements of the time. If she defended Eliot against Farrell, as a student at Vassar she published the story "Then Came the Poor," which seems closer to Farrell in its representation of class conflict and the coming of the Red Revolution.[3] Published in 1933 in *Con Spirito*, an experimental journal Bishop founded at Vassar with Mary McCarthy, Muriel Rukeyser, and Eleanor Clark, the story comically depicts the luxurious excesses of a rich New England family whose members flee the revolution with three cars and all their "goods" but forget their daughter. The daughter puts on worker's overalls and appears to want to join the revolution, but the story – and the revolution – end anticlimactically with "a wild, magnificent lawn-party" (4) as the workers discover her father's wine cellar and drunkenly redistribute the family property. The daughter, nevertheless, moves back into the house with several workers as part of the social redistribution. In its ironic detailing of the excesses of privilege, consumerism, and the "New England Ancestry," its vague yearning for communality and an alternative social order, and its simultaneous fascination with and withdrawal from the redemptive possibilities of social revolution, the story characterizes the class perspective and ambivalence about class struggle that would inform Bishop's verse.

Although Bishop never wrote the topical poetry we associate with the social-consciousness writing of the '30s, her work registers the "revolutionary" effects of the time as a crisis of the subject, of knowledge, of signification, and of the possibility of meaning itself. While some of Bishop's early poems – "The Colder the Air," "Wading at Wellfleet," and "Paris, 7 A.M." – seem metaphorized to the point of obscurity, others, such as the "The Map" and "The Imaginary Iceberg," engage '30s debates about the relation between art and life, form and history. "The Map" appears to endorse the necessary separation between artifice and history: "More delicate than the historians' are the mapmakers' colors." But, like the "Imaginary Iceberg," which "stands and stares" upon a "floating field" and "shifting stage" (*Complete Poems* 4), interrogative and continually self-revising mode of representation in "The Map" suggests the historicity of both creation and interpretation, subject and object. "Are they assigned, or can the countries pick their colors?" the speaker asks (*Complete Poems* 3), problematizing the notion of any transparent or unmediated relation between countries and the geographies – aesthetic, political, ethnographic, or otherwise – by which they have been mapped. Complicating the truth claims of '30s debates about the relation between aesthetics and politics, Bishop suggests that the mapmaker's art, like any art, is historically embedded and that history is, correspondingly, always and already mapped and interpreted.

"I was very aware of the Depression," Bishop said. "[S]ome of my family were much affected by it. After all, anybody who went to New York and rode the Elevated could see that things were wrong. But I had lived with poor people and knew something of poverty at firsthand" ("Interview" 294). While Bishop was, technically speaking, neither a Lukacian nor a Brechtian, a radical realist or a radical experimentalist, several of her early poems attempt to rearticulate traditional verse forms and a symbolist and surrealist aesthetics in a form of radical social and cultural critique. In a notebook dated 1934–37, Bishop describes looking out the window on a rainy day and hallucinating one of the raindrops as a "lonely, magnificent human eye, wrapped in its own tear." The image combines naturalistic detail with surrealistic perspective in what she would later call "glimpses of the always-more-successful surrealism of everyday life" (Letter to Anne Stevenson).

In "A Miracle for Breakfast," which Bishop described as "my Depression poem," "my 'social conscious' poem, a poem about hunger" ("Interview" 13), she conjoins the contemporary politics of want, a surrealist perspective, and the sestina form to represent the class struggle and hunger of the Depression. A group of people wait in the streets for "a man" and his "servant" to distribute coffee and loaves of bread "from a certain balcony":

> He stood for a minute alone on the balcony
> looking over our heads toward the river.
> A servant handed him the makings of a miracle,
> consisting of one lone cup of coffee
> and one roll, which he proceeded to crumb,
> his head, so to speak, in the clouds – along with the sun.
>
> Was the man crazy? What under the sun
> was he trying to do, up there on his balcony!
> Each man received one rather hard crumb,
> which some flicked scornfully into the river,
> and, in a cup, one drop of the coffee.
> Some of us stood around, waiting for the miracle.
>
>   (*Complete Poems* 18)

Associating the historical struggle between rich and poor in the Depression-era US with the monarchical and feudal orders of the past, the biblical miracle of the bread and blood of Christ, and Romantic mythologies of natural plenitude, the poem ironically critiques not only the American myth of abundance but also myths of natural providence or religio-spiritual grace. The failure of man, God, nature, or America to provide is reinforced by the formal constraints of the sestina form, whose repetition of end words suggests the almost ritualistic repetition of the class struggle through time and the miracle's failure to transpire either in the natural, feudal, or religio-spiritual orders of the past or in the putatively democratic order of the present. An understated envoi associates the American dream – and the failure of progressive history – with the phantasm and perversity of the surreal: "We licked up the crumb and swallowed the coffee. / A window across the river caught the sun / as if the miracle were working, on the wrong balcony" (*Complete Poems* 19).

"I think that it is in the city alone, maybe New York alone, that one gets in this country these sudden intuitions into the whole of contemporaneity" (Notebook), Bishop noted while she was living in New York City after graduation from Vassar. "Love Lies Sleeping," first published in the *Partisan Review* in 1938 side by side with John Dos Passos's proletarian story "Migratory Worker," represents a powerful, though understated, protest against the invasiveness and pain of the city, the industrial work-place, and modern technology. Ironically combining the traditional form of the aubade with a surrealist poetics and modern urban critique, "Love Lies Sleeping" breaks down the distinction between dream and reality, body and city, the surreal and everyday life. The "coupling" tracks, "neon shapes," "twitching signs," and "exploding" sounds of the city penetrate and become indistinguishable from the dream life, the body, the erotic, and the "coupling" lovers themselves. The artificial and potentially poisonous figure of the city as a "little chemical 'garden' in a jar" reverses the myth of the garden – and the West. Both the landscape and the industrial workplace become spaces of physical and psychological violence that terrorize the workers even in their sleep:

> The sparrows hurriedly begin their play.
> Then, in the West, "Boom!" and a cloud of smoke.
> "Boom!" and the exploding ball
> of blossom blooms again.

> (And all the employees who work in plants
> where such a sound says "Danger," or once said "Death,"
> turn in their sleep and feel
> the short hairs bristling
>
> on backs of necks.) The cloud of smoke moves off.
> (*Complete Poems* 16–17)

As for Walter Benjamin's Baudelaire, the "shock experience" of the modern city is at the center of Bishop's early work (163). But while the conflict between "Spleen" and "Ideal" distances this "shock" in Baudelaire, Bishop's work rejects any vertical leap toward the "Ideal." As the title of the poem and its surreal "coupling" of trains and lovers suggests, love itself becomes locked in the urban economies of capital and consumption. "[Y]ou will dine well / on his heart, on his, and his" (*Complete Poems* 17), says the lover to the city, anticipating the more cynical refrain of "Varick Street" (1947), where the economics of capital becomes constitutive of the love relation: "*And I shall sell you sell you / sell you of course, my dear, and you'll sell me*" (*Complete Poems* 75).

"Love Lies Sleeping" ends by conjoining psyche and city in the gaze of a drunken or dead man:

> the city grows down into his open eyes
> inverted and distorted. No. I mean
> distorted and revealed,
> if he sees it at all.
> (*Complete Poems* 17)

The poem's conjunction of waking, the city, modern technology, and death seems curiously reminiscent of the proletarian poem "Dilemma of a Dead Man about to Wake Up," which appeared in Stanley Burnshaw's *The Iron Land* (1936). Burnshaw's lines "The dynamos whir in the sheds of steel. / The powerhouse of steel distributes pain – " (76) share Bishop's perception of the physical and psychic "pain" and "daily murdering hands" (Burnshaw 76) of the new technological landscape. Although Burnshaw's realistic and proletarian aesthetics contrasts with Bishop's symbolism and surrealism, both poems protest against urbanization, mechanization, the industrial workplace, and the new technologies of iron and steel.

Bishop's relationship with the New York intellectuals and the *Partisan Review*, where much of her work in the '30s appeared, was cordial but distant. "I'm a 'Radical,' of course," she wrote to Frani Blough in 1938, but her radicalism did not encompass either the Trotskyist politics of the *Partisan Review* editors (Phillip Rahv, William Phillips, Dwight MacDonald, and Mary McCarthy) or their high modernist faith in the role of the artist and the intellectual in the modern world. Although Bishop refers to her daily reading of Russian Marxist criticism in a 1936 letter to Moore, her distrust of the doctrinaire in all party ideology – Left, Right, or center – and her firsthand experience of the desecrations of Communism and the Popular Front during a trip to Spain in 1936, set her against all forms of Communist party ideology. In "Lullaby for the Cat," an unpublished 1937 lyric, she playfully mocked the idealistic rhetoric and wildly utopian faith of many on the American Left: "Darling Minnow, drop that frown, / Just cooperate, / Not a kitten shall be drowned / In the Marxist State" (*Complete Poems* 204).

Although she sympathized with the *Partisan Review* editors' distinction, after 1937, between literature and practical politics, she did not share their correspondingly exalted notion of the oppositional role of art and artist in the modern world. Her comic evocation of Moore as a kind of good witch of modernist decorum in "Invitation to Miss Marianne Moore" (1948) and her later evocation of Ezra Pound as a pitiable and tragically deluded nursery-rhyme Jack in "Visits to St. Elizabeths" (1957) both enact this resistance. In the mid '30s, however, she herself began to move toward an increasingly self-conscious attempt to give her work more social weight and significance. Her notebooks of the time speculate on the uses she might make of contemporary events reported in the New York *Daily News*. Her short story "The Sea and Its Shore" was published as the lead story in a volume that *New Masses* literary editor Horace Gregory – in an attempt to articulate a more inclusive Popular Front poetics – presented as a kind of contemporary American writing that is not necessarily "useful" for the purposes of "immediate political action" (14) but is nevertheless dialectically engaged in and with the history of its time. In 1938 a selection of Bishop's '30s poems ("The Unbeliever," "Quai d'Orleans," and "Late Air") appeared along with Trotsky's important essay "Art and Politics" in the *Partisan Review*.

At the very moment, in fact, when the *Partisan Review* editors began to move away from realism and proletarianism toward the high modernist canon of Eliot, Kafka, Joyce, Proust, William Butler Yeats, and others, Bishop was moving away from the Eurocentric aesthetics of her early poems toward a more socially embedded and class-conscious art. This move was reinforced geographically in 1938 when she retreated from the centers of literary power in New York and bought a house with Louise Crane in Key West, Florida. "The town was absolutely broke then," Bishop said. "Everybody lived on the W. P. A. I seemed to have a taste for impoverished places in those days" ("Interview" 16). Amid the racially mixed and economically depressed landscape of Key West, Bishop moved toward an even more emphatic social and political focus, as she turned away from symbolist and surrealist aesthetics toward an experimental use of popular forms (nursery rhymes, lullabies, songs) and the aesthetics of everyday life she began to define in the materially conditioned and commemorative art of "The Monument" (1939):

> The monument's an object, yet those decorations,
> carelessly nailed, looking like nothing at all,
> give it away as having life, and wishing;
> wanting to be a monument, to cherish something.
> The crudest scroll-work says "commemorate."
>   (*Collected Poetry* 24)

Bishop's essay "Gregorio Valdes," written to commemorate the death of the Key West Cuban factory worker and painter in 1939, is at once a proletarian portrait and an attempt to define a popular, communal, working-class art:

> The first painting I saw by Gregorio Valdes was in the window of a barbershop on Duval Street, the main street of Key West. The shop is in a block of cheap liquor stores, shoeshine parlors and poolrooms, all under a long wooden awning shading the sidewalk. The picture leaned against a cardboard advertisement for Eagle Whiskey, among other window decorations of red-and-green crepe-paper rosettes and streamers left over from Christmas and the announcement of an operetta at the Cuban school – all covered with dust and fly spots and littered with termites' wings. (*Collected Prose* 51)

Bishop makes no grand claims for Valdes, a cigar factory worker, an ice cream peddler, a photographer, a sign painter, a painter: "Gregorio was not a great painter at all, and although he certainly belongs to the class of painters we call 'primitive,' sometimes he was not even a good 'primitive'" (*Collected Prose* 58). Almost all his paintings are "copies of photographs or of reproductions of other pictures," Bishop tells us, but when he "copied" "from a photograph of something he knew and liked, such as palm trees, he managed to make just the right changes in perspective and coloring to give it a peculiar and captivating freshness, flatness, and remoteness" (*Collected Prose* 58) (see Fig. 1). Through the work of Valdes Bishop defines a literal, mimetic, working-class art that is both embedded in the material conditions of Key West life and that nevertheless slips almost imperceptibly through the local knowledges and desire of the factory worker/ sign painter/painter into a kind of magical realism, a perspective that is "mysterious," uncanny, and alluring. In doing so Bishop perhaps comes closer to negotiating the putative conflict between proletarianism and aesthetics than other more earnest commentators on the respective claims of politics and art, such as Rahv at the *Partisan Review* or Mike Gold at the *New Masses*.

Figure 1 Paintings by Gregorio Valdes reproduced in Elizabeth Bishop's commemorative article "Gregorio Valdes, 1879–1939," which was published in the *Partisan Review* in the summer issue of 1939.

While the *Partisan Review* editors were wondering – in the same issue in which Bishop's Valdes essay appeared – whether Henry James rather than Walt Whitman might be "more relevant to the present and future of American writing" ("Situation in American Writing" 25), as they turned increasingly to Europe, and particularly to Paris, as site and source of modern art's renewal, Bishop was seeking to achieve some of the uncanny literalism of Valdes in the local ground of Key West: its "flat" landscape, its impoverished and primarily Cuban inhabitants, its class struggles, and its forms of communal art. In "Jerónimo's House" (1941), Bishop presents the speaker as a figure at once of dispossession, local inventiveness, and survival:

> My house, my fairy
>   palace, is
> of perishable
>   clapboards with
> three rooms in all,
>   my gray wasps' nest
> of chewed-up paper
>   glued with spit.
>   (*Complete Poems* 34)

The spare, nursery rhyme lines underscore the artifice and flimsiness of this home as "fairy palace" "glued with spit," which, with its plastic ferns, leftover Christmas decorations, pink tissue-paper roses, and painted and repainted decor represents a form of communal or mass art that enables adaptability to and survival against the material conditions of continual displacement and dispossession:

> When I move
> I take these things,
>   not much more, from
> my shelter from
>   the hurricane
>   (*Complete Poems* 34).[4]

Rather than privileging class in a classically Marxist analysis, Bishop focuses on the intimate, interdependent, but also strained relations between blacks, whites, and Hispanics, servants and masters, rich and poor, woman and woman in the complex social landscape of Key West. "Cootchie" (1941) and "Faustina, or Rock Roses" (1947), both based on persons Bishop actually knew in Key West, represent the class and race struggle not as a struggle between a prototypically male worker and employer in the workplace, but as a struggle between master and servant, white and black, that takes place between women in the home. As in Bishop's Brazil poems, these Key West poems conjoin active displacements in scale and perspective with a dialectical representation that poses contradictory, alternative, and resistant points of view. In "Faustina, or Rock Roses," the relationship between an enfeebled and dying white woman and her "sinister kind" servant, Faustina, is represented from the not always distinguishable points of view of the narrator, a visitor (Bishop), the dying woman, and Faustina herself. When a question is posed about the relationship between the white woman and her black Cuban servant, it proliferates, like the poem's perspective, into a "dazzling dialectic," refusing to pose any single or simple answer to the simultaneous affection, dependency, hate, and fear – the "dream of protection and rest?" or "the very worst, / the unimaginable nightmare?" – that informs the relationship between master and servant. "There is," as the poem says, "no way of telling. / The eyes say only either" (*Complete Poems* 73–74).

In 1945 Bishop wrote to Houghton Mifflin about her first volume of poems *North & South* (1946): "The fact that none of these poems deal directly with the war, at a time when so much war poetry is being published, will, I am afraid, leave me open to reproach" (*One Art* 125). She asked that her publisher insert a "disclaimer" at the front of *North & South* that reads: "Most of these poems were written, or partly written, before 1942." Despite the disclaimer, tropes of militarism and violence, sometimes accompanied by dim predictions of apocalypse and doom, pervade the volume, informing even the seemingly natural landscapes of "Florida," "Little Exercise," "The Fish," and "Late Air." Moreover, Bishop admitted that her 1941 poem "Roosters" was inspired by events of the war. "In the first part," she wrote to Moore in 1940, "I was thinking of Key West, and also of those aerial views of dismal little towns in Finland and Norway, when the Germans took over, and their atmosphere of poverty" (*One Art* 96). More than an antiwar poem, "Roosters" is a stark and unsparing evocation of the impulses toward brutality, domination, and colonial conquest that motivated World War II and were in evidence in Key West as well as in Fascist-dominated Europe. Like Virginia Woolf's *Three Guineas* (1938) and H. D.'s *Trilogy* (1944–46), it is also an angry protest against the patriarchal orders in which war, militarism, fascism, and violence are grounded. Crowing "uncontrolled, traditional cries" in the "gun-metal" dawn, Bishop's cocks

> planned to command and terrorize the rest,
>
> the many wives
> who lead hens' lives
> of being courted and despised;
>
> deep from raw throats
> a senseless order floats
> all over town. A rooster gloats
>
> over our beds
> from rusty iron sheds
> and fences made from old bedsteads,
>
> over our churches
> where the tin rooster perches,
> over our little wooden northern houses
>   (*Complete Poems* 35–36)

Insisting on the relationship between the cocks who "command and terrorize" women in the private sphere and the "senseless order" of war, militarism, and violence in the public sphere, "Roosters" is also a kind of veiled "coming out" poem in which Bishop registers her personal protest against the "senseless order" of marriage and heterosexuality that "floats / all over town" and "gloats" over the bed of lesbian love. "Roosters, what are you projecting?" the speaker asks,

> what right have you to give
> commands and tell us how to live,
>
> cry "Here!" and "Here!"
> and wake us here where are
> unwanted love, conceit and war?
>   (*Complete Poems* 36)

The speaker's questions protest against the scenes of private and public violation – of "unwanted love, conceit and war" – to which she is awakened by the heterosexual order of the rooster as cock or phallus.[5]

The continued influence of the '30s on Bishop's social and political perspective is particularly evident in her 1944 poem "Songs for a Colored Singer." During that decade she had met and become friendly with Billie Holiday, and she said that her four "Songs for a Colored Singer" were written for music with "Billie Holiday in mind" ("Interview" 296). At the time the poem was written, Bishop was beginning to experiment with the more personal lyric expression of female subjectivity and sexuality, specifically lesbian sexuality, that would inform the poems of *A Cold Spring* (1955).[6] Making use of blues rhythms, the black vernacular, lullaby, the popular song, Bishop's "Songs for a Colored Singer" speaks not only *for* but *as* and *through* a black blues-woman. As such the poem is emblematic of the ways Bishop's work refuses to distinguish between "private" and "public" as separate and discrete realms. Whereas Bishop's earlier poems evoke rather than resolve or call for a change in the dynamics of race, class, and gender relations, "Songs for a Colored Singer" not only describes the material conditions of black, specifically black female, oppression but also calls for – and indeed prophesies – the transformation of black sorrow and tears into "seeds" of black revolution, "beating, beating on the ground" (*Complete Poems* 50).

In *North & South* "Songs for a Colored Singer" appears just before the final poem "Anaphora," which records a fall into time and history as the dream of earthly plenitude, perhaps associated with the promise of the Left and the hopes of the '30s, "instantly, instantly falls / victim of long intrigue,"

> suffers our uses and abuses,
> sinks through the drift of bodies,
> sinks through the drift of classes
> to evening to the beggar in the park
>   (*Complete Poems* 52)

Coming just before the seemingly pessimistic reading of the possibilities of class revolution in "Anaphora," "Songs for a Colored Singer" suggests that the real revolution, if it comes, will be propelled not by class but by the "black seeds" and "conspiring root" of race struggle: "They're too real to be a dream" (*Complete Poems* 50–51).

In 1951 Bishop moved to Brazil, where she would live for 16 years with her aristocratic Brazilian lover, Lota de Macedo Soares. As many proletarian writers and radicals of the '30s, including the editors of the *Partisan Review*, were retreating into the consoling ideologies of Americanism, the New Criticism, and the Cold War, Bishop focused in her Brazil poems on a densely textured intersection of race, class, and gender ideologies with the politics of colonialism and colonial conquest in the New World. This focus set Bishop apart from many of the white North American poets writing during the '50s and early '60s. At a time when Rich's poems were still informed by the allusive and symbolic structures of high formalism, when the Beat poets were affirming an insistently white male ethos of "cock" and "cunt" and "endless balls" (Ginsberg 9), and when the confessional poems of Robert Lowell, Anne Sexton, Sylvia Plath, John Berryman, and others were focusing on the dark interiors of self as historical allegory, Bishop's poems seem at once more postmodern and more postcolonial in their focus on "questions" of cultural encounter, difference, knowledge, and representation.

Questions of Travel (1965), which bears on its cover a map of the *Nuevo Mundo* drawn from the *Cosmographia* of the sixteenth-century cartographer Sebastian Munster (see Fig. 2), opens with scenes of colonial encounter not only between Old World and New but between North and South America. In "Arrival at Santos," the first poem in the

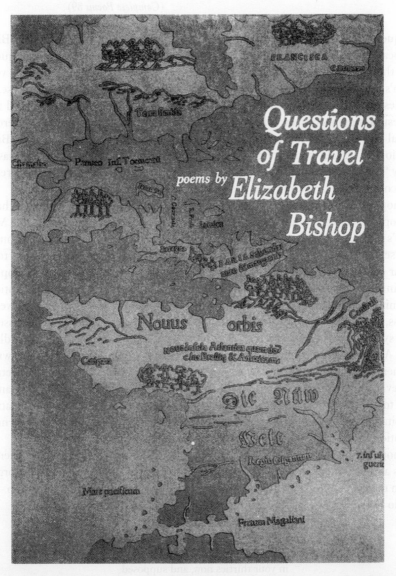

Figure 2 Cover of Bishop's *Questions of Travel* (1965), which bears a map of the *Nuevo Mondo* drawn from the *Cosmographia* of the sixteenth-century cartographer Sebastian Munster.

"Brazil" section, Bishop mocks her own imperialist and, to use Edward Said's term, "Orientalist" gestures as a white middle-class North American woman. Encountering a Brazil that resists her imaginary – and colonizing – desire for an erotic and exotic other, she asks:

> Oh, tourist,
> is this how this country is going to answer you
>
> and your immodest demands for a different world,
> and a better life, and complete comprehension
> of both at last, and immediately,
> after eighteen days of suspension?
>
> (*Complete Poems* 89)

This question, about the colonizing relation of North to South America and Bishop's own location within these structures of dominance, is at the center of the questions about the politics and problematics of cultural encounter that inform the volume. Bishop's dialectical approach to cultural encounter – her willingness to reverse, question, destabilize, and ironize the gaze of the colonizer, including her own, and thus to pose resistant points of view – keeps her Brazil poems from becoming mere exercises in political and aesthetic tourism.[7] The question of aestheticization underlies Bishop's "questions of travel," subverting any easy slide into what Robert von Hallberg has called literary "tourism" (62–92) and what Millier calls Bishop's "wholly esthetic appreciation of the country, the landscape, and the people" (274).

Bishop arrived in Brazil when the former fascist dictator, Getúlio Vargas, had just been popularly elected to a second term as president. Under Vargas's former rule Macedo Soares's father, a wealthy aristocratic newspaper owner and a leftist, was imprisoned and exiled several times. In the post-World War II period, however, Vargas began to court popular discontent and the Left as a means of regaining political power. Bishop's residence in Brazil in the '50s and '60s coincided with a period of rapid industrialization and modernization, runaway inflation, and an increasingly violent struggle between the landless, impoverished, and mostly illiterate urban and rural masses and an essentially feudal system of land ownership by a few powerful aristocrats. As a white middle-class North American woman living with an aristocratic Brazilian woman who owned an apartment on Copacabana Beach in Rio de Janeiro and a country estate in Petrópolis with several servants, Bishop was a benefactor of the system. She was simultaneously drawn to the communal rhythms and seemingly harmonious race and class relations of precapitalist Brazil and repelled by the massive poverty, illiteracy, and governmental corruption that were the marks of the old patrimonial system.

Bishop's ambivalence, and the mounting tensions in the countryside between land-owners and peasants that would give rise to Francisco Julião's radical peasant organizations in the late '50s, is evident in "Manuelzinho," a poem – according to Bishop – about Macedo Soares's relationship with her impoverished and illiterate gardener:

> Half squatter, half tenant (no rent) –
> a sort of inheritance; white,
> in your thirties now, and supposed
> to supply me with vegetables,
> but you don't; or you won't; or you can't

> get the idea through your brain –
> the world's worst gardener since Cain.
>   (*Complete Poems* 96)

Although the account is given from the point of view of an aristocratic "friend of the writer," who expresses the affectionate, familial, hereditary, and strained relations between landlord and tenant, the poem's sympathies appear to be on the side of the resistant and carnivalesque figure of Manuelzinho, who refuses to play the landlord's game of mine and yours.[8] "[I]mprovident as the dawn," Manuelzinho's gardens fail to produce, his paths (or his father's or his grandfather's) traverse the master's "property," and when he comes to settle his "accounts" – "with two old copybooks, / one with flowers on the cover, / the other with a camel" – his "numbers mount to millions" with an excess of zeros (*Complete Poems* 98). While the master speaks in the poem, her voice is ironized not only by the poem's descriptions of hunger, poverty, sickness, and death but also by the endlessly inventive folk energies of Manuelzinho, who doesn't, or "won't," or "can't" submit to the master's demands for order, boundaries, and control.

Despite Bishop's engagement with political problems in Brazil, critics have continued to stress the essentially apolitical nature of her work. "'Suicide of a Moderate Dictator,'" writes Thomas Travisano of Bishop's unpublished verse response to Vargas's suicide in 1954, "represents a category for which examples exist only in Bishop's unpublished *oeuvre*: the political poem" ("'With an eye'" 613). "[W]hether from temperament, or from the insoluble puzzle of redefining her use of the lyric," writes Lorrie Goldensohn, "the leap from imagined to actual public event, the move from the fancied to the historic somehow was not possible" (239). Commenting on several unpublished Bishop poems addressing issues of slavery ("A Trip to the Mines"), poverty ("Capricorn"), infant mortality ("A Baby Found in the Garbage"), inflation and government corruption ("Brasil, 1959"), and Vargas's suicide ("a report in verse & prose"), Victoria Harrison also observes: "With irony and hope, mockery and earnestness, Bishop entered the political fray, though privately, since she published none of this writing either in Brazil or in the United States" (166). Millier similarly describes "Brasil, 1959" as "the sort of poem that Elizabeth could never write and that she condemned when other poets did" (301). It shows "her attempts at and her frustrations with trying to speak in poetry about Brazil as a political entity. She is far more comfortable with a personal point of departure" (300).

While Bishop did not publish her poems on Vargas's suicide, slavery in the mines, or social conditions under Juscelino Kubitschek's government, she did, in fact, write them. And it is simply not true to say that Bishop did not "speak in poetry about Brazil as a political entity." Bishop's focus is, however, local and immediate, embedded in the economic relations and social, sexual, and political practices of everyday life. If she never published her journalistic poems about Vargas, Kubitschek, and Jânio Quadros, she did publish "The Burglar of Babylon," a folk ballad based on newspaper accounts, about Micuçu, "a burglar and killer" whose pursuit by soldiers she watched from her balcony. "The Burglar of Babylon" registers the disruptive social effects of industrialization and modernization on the Brazilian masses, the "hysterics" of the military (who shoot each other with "tommy guns"), and the apparent indifference of the rich (who watch "through binoculars") in their response to the endless cycle of poverty, military violence, and crime that repeats itself, like the ballad's refrain: "On the fair green hills of Rio / There grows a fearful stain: / The poor who come to Rio / And can't go home again" (*Complete Poems* 117) (see Fig. 3).

Figure 3 Photograph of the *favelas* (slums) in the hills above Rio de Janeiro, which appeared in Bishop's Time-Life book on *Brazil* (1962).

As in "The Burglar of Babylon," which juxtaposes modern technologies of surveillance and violence with folk traditions and mass poverty in the Rio slums, Bishop's Brazil poems insist on the material conditions and social embeddedness of race, class, gender, and colonial ideologies: the imperialist relation of North to South America in "Arrival at Santos" and "Questions of Travel"; the (hetero)sexual and racial politics of colonial conquest in "Brazil, January 1, 1502"; the relations of property and propertylessness in "Squatter's Children" and "Twelfth Morning; Or What You Will"; the dialectics of class dominance and resistance in "Manuelzinho"; hunger, child prostitution, and homelessness in "Going to the Bakery"; the "soiled and thirsty" conditions of village life in "Under the Window: Ouro Prêto"; and the murder of beggars in "The Pink Dog." These material conditions and "lived" social relations of dominance and subordination appear to remain the same as the country changes political regimes from Left to center to Right during the '50s and '60s. Indeed, as recent reports of the shooting of eight homeless children by military police on the streets of Rio de Janeiro suggest, despite the putative return to democratic government in 1985 (after 21 years of military dictatorship), not much has changed for "The poor who come to Rio / And can't go home again."

Bishop's reputation as apolitical modernist has also tended to erase or mute the fact that after 1960 – when Quadros was elected to the presidency and Macedo Soares went to work (for free) as Rio park designer for Carlos Lacerda, the right-wing governor of Guanabara – she and Macedo Soares moved from the margins to the very center of the increasingly polarized conflict between Left and Right in Brazil. In an April 1962 letter to the *New Republic*, Bishop addressed the question of US Cold War policy in Brazil. Registering "a strong protest against" the article "Which Revolution for Brazil?" by Brazilian correspondent Louis L. Wiznitzer, she criticizes "the distorted view it gives your American readers of the Brazilian situation and its personalities." She corrects Wiznitzer's notion that Quadros – who had unexpectedly resigned the presidency in 1961 after only seven months in office – was about to return to power; she defends Lacerda against charges of terrorism and political blackmail, which "exactly follow the line of Communist propaganda here"; and she questions Wiznitzer's assertion that "in the past 12 months the masses of people have been made politically conscious" (qtd. in Bishop, Letter). "It is because, in their poverty and misery, they are still politically completely ignorant," Bishop responds, "that they are at the mercy of political opportunists – and malicious tale-spreaders like Mr. Wiznitzer." Although Bishop turned down an offer to write a regular "Brazil letter" for the *New Republic*, her desire to explain Brazil to North American readers, "to make Brazil seem less remote and less an object of picturesque fancy" ("Interview" 19), is evident not only in her poetry but in her prose translation of *The Diary of "Helena Morely"* (1957), her Time-Life book *Brazil* (1962), her translations of Brazilian poets and prose writers (including several anonymous "sambas" from Carnival), her *Anthology of Twentieth-Century Brazilian Poetry* (1972), which she co-edited with Emanuel Brasil, and a collection of essays on Brazil entitled *Black Beans and Diamonds*, which she planned but never published.

Two years after *Brazil* was published, the leftist João Goulart, who had succeeded Quadros as president in 1961, was overthrown by a military coup in order to avert the possibility of a communist takeover. At the time of the coup, Bishop, who had consistently opposed militarism and totalitarianism on the Left and the Right – in both Khrushchev's Russia and Eisenhower's America – found herself in the contradictory position of supporting a military government that, with the help of the political police of her friend Lacerda, was arresting and torturing known or suspected communist organizers in the name of economic stabilization and democracy. Like many in Brazil, Bishop appeared to believe (or hope) that military rule under the leadership of General Castelo Branco was only a temporary stage on the way to restoring popularly elected government. But by 1965, in a *New York Times Magazine* article, she noted that "a conviction … of 'betrayal' seems to be the attitude of both rich and poor" ("On the Railroad" 86). The article criticizes the army coup, Lacerda, the "shabby" conditions and "general decrepitude" of Rio, the shortages and inflation, and the "national disgrace" of the "political arrests" and "torture" conducted by the military government ("On the Railroad" 30, 84–86).[9]

In Bishop's view the political situation in Brazil was largely responsible for the emotional stress that led to the death of Macedo Soares – an apparent suicide – in 1967. After Macedo Soares's death Bishop returned to the US of the '60s. Although she continued to write about Brazil for the rest of her life, in her final collection of poems, *Geography III* (1976), she turned to a more autobiographical focus on her personal past. Recent critical accounts have used this volume to foreground a subjective and apolitical trajectory for Bishop's life and work. As David Kalstone writes of *Geography III*: "The time and the space these poems lay claim to are more peculiarly Elizabeth Bishop's own – less geological, less historical, less vastly natural; her poems are more openly inner land-scapes than ever before" (31).[10]

To get this reading, however, several clear markers need to be erased. The title *Geography III* draws attention to the subject's location within a larger historical world, and the front cover depicts a surveyor's level, a globe, books, ink, and other instruments for mapping the earth's surface, boundaries, and inhabitants (see Fig. 4). On the back cover John Ashbery comments that Bishop's poetry "renders obsolete" the "artificial distinctions" between "a public and a private poet." The volume opens with a series of questions, taken from *First Lessons in Geography* (1884), which further draw attention to the questions of geographical location, mapping, and representation, and the fluid and shifting boundaries between private and public, subject and object, map-maker and world. Even in these seemingly more personal poems, Bishop maps her subject's tempo-ral, geographical, and historical location, returning over and over again to scenes of cultural encounter with otherness, whether in the form of the young girl's encounter during World War I with "those awful hanging breasts" (7) of the "black, naked women" (4) in *National Geographic* in "In the Waiting Room"; or Crusoe's recollection of his "still / un-rediscovered, un-renamable" (9) island in "Crusoe in England"; or the communal and ultimately utopian social encounter with a "grand, otherworldly" (30) "she"-moose in "The Moose."

Figure 4 Cover of Bishop's *Geography III* (1976), which bears images of the instruments and historical effects of geographical mapping.

Insisting on the essentially personal signature of *Geography III*, most critics have (mis)read "12 O'Clock News" by moving what is literally on the margins of the poem (the description of the objects on a desk) to the center of the poem and completely ignoring the content of the poem's prose paragraphs, which mock the Cold War politics and imperial gaze of a newscaster attempting to describe "the lay of the land and the present situation" of a "small, backward country, one of the most backward left in the world today" (*Complete Poems* 174). It is unclear, finally, whether the poem alludes to US foreign policy in South America, Southeast Asia, Africa, or elsewhere. The point seems to be that any "small, backward country" – or even the contents of a desk – will fit the seemingly objective but in fact politically inflected geography of the newscaster's Cold War script.

Although Bishop said she was, in 1966, "much more interested in social problems and politics now than I was in the '30s" ("Interview" 9), she opposed some of the more self-indulgent and, in her terms, vulgar cultural and social forms of the '60s revolution. While she believed that some form of radical literary response to the times was necessary, she did not believe that flow poetry, confessionalism, or the work of the beat writers was it. In a letter to Lowell, Bishop commented on the even greater need for a revolutionary poetic articulation in the present than in the past: "[I]t's terribly hard to find the exact and right and surprising enough, or un-surprising enough, point at which to revolt now[.] The beats have just fallen back on an old corpse-strewn or monument-strewn battle-field – the real protest I suspect is something quite different – (If only I could find it …)."

In seeking that exact "point at which to revolt," Bishop was drawn to the black revolution as it was being propelled by Huey Newton, Eldridge Cleaver, Kathleen Cleaver, and the Black Panther Party in California. In February 1969 Bishop interviewed Kathleen Cleaver with the intent of writing an article or poem on her and the Black Panther Party for the *New York Review of Books*. The interview is in some sense anomalous, corresponding with nothing we know – or think we need to know – about Bishop, modernism, and the Left. Perhaps, however, it is a good place to conclude for it returns us to the revolutionary moment of "Then Came the Poor," only now Bishop's confrontation is with the black rather than the Red revolution, the time is the '60s rather than the '30s, and the subject is the new rather than the old Left.

At the time that the interview took place, Kathleen Cleaver had gone underground because her husband, Eldridge Cleaver, had been jailed. On one level this 30-page interview, which has never been published and is half-owned by Bishop and Cleaver, seems like a profound and at times even comic study in cultural dissonance as Cleaver seeks to (re)educate Bishop in the politics of race, colonialism, and the black revolution in lengthy, angry, and sometimes eloquent passages, and Bishop responds politely and monosyllabically – Yes; Yes; Yes. This cultural dissonance is nowhere more evident than in the fact that the phrase "Right on! Right on!" which punctuates Cleaver's language – and which was the powerful and fisted cry and symbol of black revolution at the time – is transcribed by Bishop and her friend, Roxanne Cumming, as "Ride on, Ride on," as if the black struggle was about a train ride rather than a revolution.

Perhaps we should marvel that the interview took place at all. As so often in Bishop's work, the encounter and the struggle is not between two men but between two women, one a seeming representative, in her own words, "of the eastern establishment to everyone here, and definitely passee" (Letter to James Merrill), and the other an articulate representative of the black revolution, a high-ranking member of the Black Panther Party, a recent candidate for the California Assembly, and one of the most prominent black women in the country.

Both women seem to agree on the general failures of the American system – institutional, educational, economic, racial, and political – and that a social revolution is at hand. Moreover, there are moments when real exchange seems to take place, as when Bishop listens intently to Cleaver's explanation of the origins of the notion of blacks as a colonized people in the US, and they both realize they share an admiration for Frantz Fanon's *The Wretched of the Earth* (1963). Or when they debate whether race (Cleaver) or economics (Bishop) is at the source of oppression and poverty in Brazil. Or when Bishop corrects Cleaver's generalizations about race, slavery, and colonialism in Brazil. "The Catholic Church was much more benevolent towards the slaves than the Protestant Church," Cleaver argues. "Oh, that isn't true – ," Bishop responds, "It was just as bad" (Cleaver 13).

Cleaver responds enthusiastically to Bishop's description of Palmares, a slave republic in Brazil. "It was a separate republic," says Bishop, "built by runaway slaves in the North of Brazil which held out for over 60 years against the combined forces of Portugal and Holland. I'm trying to write a piece about it for my book on Brazil." "That's out of sight," Cleaver responds. "Not many people know about it. I'm trying to gather material on it now," Bishop says. "Course not," Cleaver agrees, "because any history that says that the Black man was in a position of power has been deleted" (Cleaver 29–30). When Bishop sent a transcribed copy of the interview to Cleaver a few months later, she wondered if "Mrs. Cleaver" "would come in for a drink some evening" so that she could get to know her better "in a more informal visit."

In the poem "Santarém," published shortly before her death in 1979, Bishop writes of the dazzlingly dialectical "conflux of two rivers, Tapajós, Amazon," in the ancient town of Santarém:

> Here only two
> and coming together. Even if one were tempted
> to literary interpretations
> such as: life/death, right/wrong, male/female
> – such notions would have resolved, dissolved, straight off
> in that watery, dazzling dialectic.
>
> (*Complete Poems* 185)

Like the politically inflected and dazzlingly dialectical poetry that Bishop began to write under the influence of '30s radicalism and continued to write throughout her life, Bishop's interview with Cleaver does not fit the binarized "literary interpretations" of Bishop's life and work as a modernist poet. And yet, it is finally precisely because it does not fit that it forces us to press beyond the binarisms – Right/Left, aesthetics/politics, high culture/popular culture, modernism/proletarianism, poetry/revolution, male/female, white/black – that have governed literary interpretations not only of Bishop's life and work but of the, yes, similarly "watery" and dazzlingly dialectical relation of modernism and the Left.

Notes

1   See, e.g., Kalstone. In the introduction to her 1993 collection *Elizabeth Bishop: The Geography of Gender*, Marilyn May Lombardi writes: "This anthology gathers together the work of pioneering scholars in the field, critics who are exploring the psychosexual tensions within Bishop's vision and

the uncanny way her poetics of dislocation challenge our assumptions about placement and orientation" (4). Although their approaches are quite different, like Lee Edelman's ground-breaking 1985 essay "The Geography of Gender: Elizabeth Bishop's 'In the Waiting Room,'" recent books by Diehl, Goldensohn, and Harrison all emphasize "psychosexual tensions" as what Harrison calls "the personal ground springs" of Bishop's work (73). In his important study *Elizabeth Bishop: Her Artistic Development*, Thomas Travisano stresses "the vital role of history in Bishop's work" (123), but, he notes, "Her readings are in private and cultural history, not political history" (132). Harrison similarly argues that by enacting "subject-subject relations in their dailiness" Bishop "avoids ideological stances" (11, 16); and Goldensohn asserts that "[n]either war nor politics was ever her ostensible subject" (182).

2   In *The Politics of Modernism*, Raymond Williams notes that "the extraordinary innovations" of nineteenth-century social realism were themselves regarded as a vanguard of modernism until the "moment of Modernism" was fixed in the "selective tradition" we have come to associate with the work of Marcel Proust, Franz Kafka, and James Joyce (32).

3   See also Bishop's story "Chimney Sweepers." For a discussion of Bishop in relation to '30s debates about the role of the poet, see Palattella.

4   Bishop is drawn over and over to instances of a socially embedded aesthetics of local invention and folk art: "a bamboo church of Jesuit baroque: / three towers, five silver crosses" in "Questions of Travel" (*Complete Poems* 94); Manuelzinho's painted hat, "limbs" "draped in blueprints," and "two old copybooks, / one with flowers on the cover, / the other with a camel" in "Manuelzinho" (*Complete Poems* 98–99); the "fire balloons" in "The Armadillo" (*Complete Poems* 103); "the rows of cans" arranged "so that they softly say: ESSO–SO–SO–SO" in "Filling Station" (*Complete Poems* 128); Crusoe's "home-made flute" in "Crusoe in England" (*Complete Poems* 164); "an empty wasps' nest … / small, exquisite, clean matte white, / and hard as stucco," in "Santarém" (*Complete Poems* 186–87).

5   For a detailed discussion of "Roosters" in the context of World War II, see Schweik 213–41; see also Erkkila 125–28 for a discussion of the political and specifically lesbian dimensions of the poem.

6   See, e.g., Goldensohn's discussion of Bishop's unpublished lesbian aubade, "It is marvellous to wake up together" (27–52). See also Erkkila 137–41 for a discussion of the female and lesbian-centered focus of *A Cold Spring*.

7   In his discussion of "Dialectic in General," Kenneth Burke includes among his "definitions of dialectic" "any development (in organisms, works of art, stages of history) got by the interplay of various factors that mutually modify one another, and may be thought of as voices in a dialogue or roles in a play, with each voice or role in its partiality contributing to the development of the whole; or the placement of one thought or thing in terms of its opposite" (403).

8   Manuelzinho is a perfect example of the carnivalesque – the "boundless world" of "folk carnival humor" – as it is described by Mikhail Bakhtin in his introduction to *Rabelais and His World* (4). Bishop's "queer" interest in figures who refuse to be contained by Western, rationalistic bounds is particularly evident in "The Riverman," where she speaks from the point of view of an Amazonian villager who has, in effect, crossed over into the magical spirit world beyond life and death (*Complete Poems* 105–09).

9   See also Bishop's translation of the 1965 "Sambas" critical of the "rightest revolution" and conditions under the government of Castelo Branco reprinted in *Ploughshares*.

10 This emphasis on the "inner" landscape of Bishop's work is also evident in Helen Vendler's observation that "Bishop's mother, confined for life in a hospital for the insane[,] … remained the inaccessible blank at the center of all Bishop's travel" (829). In their introduction to *Elizabeth Bishop and Her Art*, Lloyd Schwartz and Sybil P. Estess note that all the critical essays in their collection "dovetail in their common underlying conviction of Bishop's powerful moral, psychological, and emotional force" (xviii). In his introduction to *Elizabeth Bishop: Modern Critical Views*, Harold Bloom also focuses on Bishop's "poetry of deep subjectivity" (1). See also Goldensohn; Diehl; Millier; and the essays collected by Lombardi in *The Geography of Gender*.

Works Cited

Alvarez, A. "Imagism and Poetesses." *Kenyon Review* 19 (1957): 321–26.

Bakhtin, Mikhail. *Rabelais and His World*. Trans. Helene Iswolsky. Cambridge: MIT P, 1968.

Benjamin, Walter. "On Some Motifs in Baudelaire." *Illuminations*. Ed. Hannah Arendt. Trans. Harry Zohn. New York: Schocken, 1962. 155–200.

Bishop, Elizabeth. "Chimney Sweepers." *Vassar Review* 19 (1933): 8+.

Bishop, Elizabeth. *The Collected Prose*. Ed. Robert Giroux. New York: Farrar, 1984.

Bishop, Elizabeth. *The Complete Poems: 1927–1979*. New York: Farrar, 1983.

Bishop, Elizabeth. "From 'A Brief Reminiscence and a Brief Tribute.'" *Elizabeth Bishop and Her Art*. Ed. Lloyd Schwartz and Sybil P. Estess. Under Discussion 1. Ann Arbor: U of Michigan P, 1983. 308.

Bishop, Elizabeth. *Geography III*. New York: Noonday-Farrar, 1976.

Bishop, Elizabeth. "An Interview with Elizabeth Bishop." *Shenandoah* 17 (1966): 3–29.

Bishop, Elizabeth. Letter. *New Republic* 30 Apr. 1962: 22.

Bishop, Elizabeth. Letter to Anne Stevenson. 8 Jan. 1964. Washington University, St. Louis.

Bishop, Elizabeth. Letter to Frani Blough. 7 Feb. 1938. Vassar College, Poughkeepsie, NY.

Bishop, Elizabeth. Letter to James Merrill. 27 Feb. 1969. Vassar College, Poughkeepsie, NY.

Bishop, Elizabeth. Letter to Kathleen Cleaver. 11 Apr. 1969. Vassar College, Poughkeepsie, NY.

Bishop, Elizabeth. Letter to Marianne Moore. 21 Aug. 1936. Rosenbach Museum and Library, Philadelphia.

Bishop, Elizabeth. Letter to Robert Lowell. 25 June 1961. Houghton Library, Cambridge, MA. bMS Am 1905 (183).

Bishop, Elizabeth. *North & South*. Boston: Houghton, 1946.

Bishop, Elizabeth. Notebook (1934–37), ms. Vassar College, Poughkeepsie, NY.

Bishop, Elizabeth. "On the Railroad Named Delight." *New York Times Magazine* 7 Mar. 1965: 30+.

Bishop, Elizabeth. *One Art: Letters, Selected and Edited*. Ed. Robert Giroux. New York: Farrar, 1994.

Bishop, Elizabeth. "Sambas." *Ploughshares* 2 (1975): 171.

Bishop, Elizabeth. "Then Came the Poor." *Con Spirito* 1 (1933): 2+.

Bishop, Elizabeth. "'The Work!': A Conversation with Elizabeth Bishop." *Ploughshares* 3 (1977): 11–29.

Bloom, Harold. Introduction. *Elizabeth Bishop*. Ed. Bloom. New York: Chelsea, 1985. 1–3.

Burke, Kenneth. *A Grammar of Motives*. New York: Prentice-Hall, 1945.

Burnshaw, Stanley. *The Iron Land: A Narrative*. Philadelphia: Centaur, 1936.

Cleaver, Kathleen. Interview. With Elizabeth Bishop. Ts. Vassar College, Poughkeepsie, NY.

Diehl, Joanne Feit. *Elizabeth Bishop and Marianne Moore: The Psychodynamics of Creativity*. Princeton: Princeton UP, 1993.

Edelman, Lee. "The Geography of Gender: Elizabeth Bishop's 'In the Waiting Room.'" *Contemporary Literature* 26 (1985): 179–96.

Erkkila, Betsy. *The Wicked Sisters: Women Poets, Literary History, and Discord*. New York: Oxford UP, 1992.

Ginsberg, Allen. *Howl and Other Poems*. San Francisco: City Lights, 1956.

Goldensohn, Lorrie. *Elizabeth Bishop: The Biography of a Poetry*. New York: Columbia UP, 1992.

Gregory, Horace. Introduction. *New Letters in America*. Ed. Gregory Clark and Eleanor Clark. New York: Norton, 1937. 9–16.

Harrison, Victoria. *Elizabeth Bishop's Poetics of Intimacy*. New York: Cambridge UP, 1993.

Jarrell, Randall. "The Poet and His Public." *Partisan Review* 13.4 (1946): 488–500.

Kalstone, David. *Becoming a Poet: Elizabeth Bishop with Marianne Moore and Robert Lowell*. Ed. Robert Hemenway. New York: Farrar, 1989.

Lombardi, Marilyn May, ed. *Elizabeth Bishop: The Geography of Gender*. Charlottesville: UP of Virginia, 1993.

Lowell, Robert. "Thomas, Bishop, and Williams." *Sewanee Review* 55 (1946): 493–503.

Millier, Brett C. *Elizabeth Bishop: Life and the Memory of It*. Berkeley: U of California P, 1993.

Moore, Marianne. "A Modest Expert." *The Nation* 28 Sept. 1946: 354.

Palattella, John. "'That Sense of Constant Re-adjustment': The Great Depression and the Provisional Politics of Bishop's *North & South.*" *Contemporary Literature* 34 (1993): 18–43.

Rich, Adrienne. "The Eye of the Outsider: Elizabeth Bishop's *Complete Poems, 1927–1979.*" *Blood, Bread, and Poetry: Selected Prose 1979–1985.* New York: Norton, 1986. 124–35.

Schwartz, Lloyd, and Sybil P. Estess, eds. Introduction. *Elizabeth Bishop and Her Art.* Ed. Schwartz and Estess. Under Discussion 1. Ann Arbor: U of Michigan P, 1983. xvii–xix.

Schweik, Susan. *A Gulf So Deeply Cut: American Women Poets and the Second World War.* Madison: U of Wisconsin P, 1991.

"The Situation in American Writing." *Partisan Review* 6.4 (1939): 25–51.

Travisano, Thomas J. *Elizabeth Bishop: Her Artistic Development.* Charlottesville: UP of Virginia, 1988.

Travisano, Thomas J. "'With an eye of Flemish accuracy': An Afterword." *Georgia Review* 46 (1992): 612–16.

Vendler, Helen. "The Poems of Elizabeth Bishop." *Critical Inquiry* 13 (1987): 825–38.

von Hallberg, Robert. *American Poetry and Culture, 1945–1980.* Cambridge: Harvard UP, 1985.

Williams, Raymond. *The Politics of Modernism: Against the New Conformists.* London: Verso, 1989.

PART SEVEN

Gender Studies and Queer Theory

CHAPTER 1

Introduction
Feminist Paradigms / Gender Effects

Julie Rivkin and Michael Ryan

Contemporary feminist literary criticism begins as much in the women's movement of the late 1960s and early 1970s as it does in the academy. Its antecedents go back much further, of course, whether one takes Virginia Woolf's *A Room of One's Own* or an even earlier text as a point of departure (Maggie Humm cites *Inanna*, a text written 2000 years before the Bible, which presents the fate of a goddess who questions sexual discourse). Feminist criticism's self-transformations over the past several decades as it engages with both critiques from within and encounters from without – encounters with psychoanalysis, Marxism, Post-Structuralisms, ethnic studies, post-colonial theory, Lesbian and Gay Studies, Queer Theory – have produced a complex proliferation of work not easily subsumed to a single description. The title of the collection of essays – *Conflicts in Feminism*[1] – speaks to the situation of feminist criticism: equality versus difference, cultural feminism versus Post-Structuralist feminism, essentialism versus social constructionism. Feminism *and* gender theory? Feminism *or* gender theory? Feminism with ethnic specificity or with other crossings? Feminism national or feminism international? If the student of literature in the early 1970s was moved to ask why is there not a *feminist* criticism, the student of literary theory in the next century might well be moved to shift the emphasis and ask but why is there not *a* feminist criticism? The frustrations of proliferation can also be construed as the pains of progress, and if the tone of feminist criticism has lost the celebratory solidarity of its early days, it has gained a much-needed complexity of analysis. An analysis of gender that "ignores" race, class, nationality, and sexuality is one that assumes a white, middle-class, heterosexual woman inclined towards motherhood as the subject of feminism; only by questioning the status of the subject of feminism – "woman" – does a feminist criticism avoid replicating the masculinist cultural error of taking the dominant for the universal.

For the women's movement of the 1960s and early 1970s the subject of feminism was women's experience under patriarchy, the long tradition of male rule in society which silenced women's voices, distorted their lives, and treated their concerns as peripheral. To be a woman under such conditions was in some respects not to exist at all. "When We Dead Awaken" seemed to Adrienne Rich a justified title for an address regarding women at the Modern Language Association in 1970.[2] With other noteworthy feminists of the 1960s and 1970s like Germaine Greer (*The Female Eunuch*) and Kate Millett (*Sexual*

Literary Theory: An Anthology, Third Edition. Edited by Julie Rivkin and Michael Ryan.
© 2017 John Wiley & Sons, Ltd. Published 2017 by John Wiley & Sons, Ltd.

Politics), Rich inspired into life a school of feminist literary criticism that took the history of women's oppression and the silencing of their voices as twin beacons to guide its work. But how was that history to be interpreted, those voices to be read? Were they the voices of fellow beings who shared a common biology or ontology? Or were history and social context so constitutive of all being that no thing called "woman" could be said to exist outside them? Was "woman" something to be escaped from or into?

Early on, feminist scholars realized that the "canon" taught in schools was overwhelmingly male. To be a woman graduate student in the 1960s was to hear recognizably male points of view, some of which were noticeably misogynist, declared to be "universal." Were there no women writers, then, aside from George Eliot and Jane Austen, Willa Cather or Emily Dickinson? And how were feminist scholars to deal with the canon? Elaine Showalter set about reconstructing a history of women writers (*A Literature of Their Own*). Judith Fetterley took up the question of how women are represented in "great" American literature (*The Resisting Reader*). And Sandra Gilbert and Susan Gubar examined the issue of what it meant for women writers to seek entry to a tradition dominated by images that did such violence to women (*The Madwoman in the Attic*).

The movement very quickly leapt across ethnic and gender boundaries (if indeed, given Rich's work both on her own ethnicity and her own gender difference, it might not be said to always have been across such boundaries). African-American feminist scholars like Mary Helen Washington, Barbara Smith, and bell hooks depicted a history of African-American women's experience along the twin axes of race and gender that had a unique specificity. Lesbian feminist critics like Bonnie Zimmerman and Susan Griffin reconstructed a hidden tradition of lesbian writing and explored the experience of radical alterity within a heterosexist world. Feminist literary scholarship in the 1970s and early 1980s was a rich, sometimes vexed, sometimes convivial, world in which words like "sisterhood" had a certain currency.

This early period is sometimes described as having two stages, one concerned with the critique of misogynist stereotypes in male literature, the other devoted to the recovery of a lost tradition and to the long labor of historical reconstruction. Banished from education and from public life, women writers had found refuge in literary forms despised by men, in diaries and letters and in sentimental fiction. Feminist scholars began to notice how the seemingly disinterested aesthetic categories that imbued literary scholarship in the academy automatically disqualified such writing from consideration for inclusion in the canon.

The mid-1980s are in retrospect a moment of great change in feminist criticism. What is called "French feminism" – essentially the work of Julia Kristeva, Luce Irigaray, and Hélène Cixous – began to have an impact on how feminist scholars thought about their work and about the assumptions that inspired it. "Woman," that unproblematic "character" of feminist stories about the world, suddenly became a matter of interpretation. Gender, rather than be the sight line that allowed one to trace woman's banishment from an androcentric culture, might instead be a construct of culture, something written into the psyche by language. Liberal and radical feminists had been in disagreement since the 1970s regarding the direction the women's movement should take – toward a deeper identification with a female "essence" or toward a departure from the way women had been made to be by patriarchy, the very thing radical feminists construed as essentially female. That difference now gained volatility within feminist literary critical discussions, and two perspectives began to form, one "constructionist" or accepting of the idea that gender is made by culture in history, the other "essentialist," more inclined to the idea that gender reflects a natural difference between men and women that is as much psychological, even linguistic, as it is biological. And there was no possible meeting of minds between the two, for each necessarily denied the other. Feminism was suddenly feminisms.

Each perspective derived support from different theoretical sources, and both, curiously enough, found support in French Post-Structuralism. The essentialists looked to the work of feminist psychoanalyst Nancy Chodorow (*The Reproduction of Mothering*), ethical philosopher Carol Gilligan (*In a Different Voice*), and French feminist philosopher Luce Irigaray (*Speculum of the Other Woman* and *This Sex Which Is Not One*) and argued that women's physical differences alone (birthing, lactation, menstruation, etc.) make them more connected with matter or with the physical world than men. Luce Irigaray distinguishes between blood and sham, between the direct link to material nature in women's bodies and the flight from such contact that is the driving force of male abstraction, its pretense to be above matter and outside of nature (in civilization). She notes how matter (which she links etymologically to maternity and to the matrix, the space that is the prop for male philosophical speculation or abstract thinking) is irreducible to male Western conceptuality; outside and making possible, yet impossible to assimilate to male reason, matter is what makes women women, an identity and an experience of their own, forever apart from male power and male concepts.

Women, essentialists argued, are innately capable of offering a different ethics from men, one more attuned to preserving the earth from destruction by weapons devised by men. Men must abstract themselves from the material world as they separate from mothers in order to acquire a license to enter the patriarchate, and they consequently adopt a violent and aggressive posture towards the world left behind, which is now construed as an "object." The primary matter they must separate from is the mother, who for them represents the tie to nature that must be overcome by the cut into abstraction that inaugurates civilization as men understand it (a set of abstract rules for assigning identities, appropriate social roles and the like that favor male power over women). Women, on the other hand, are not required to separate from the mother as they acquire a gender identity; they simply identify with the closest person to them as they grow up, their own mother. No cut is required, no separation that launches a precarious journey towards a fragile "identity" predicated on separation that simply denies its links to the physical world. Essentialist feminists argued that men think in terms of rights when confronted with ethical issues, while women think in terms of responsibilities to others. Women are more caring because their psychological and physical ties to physical being remain unbroken.

While one strand of essentialist theory finds common ground with Post-Structuralism around the body (that which male-defined reason must transcend but which includes and exceeds it always), another finds in Post-Structuralism an argument against all identity. What lies outside male reason is precisely everything such reason abhors – contradiction, non-identity, fluidity, non-rationality, illogicality, mixing of genres, etcetera. Domination through categorical analysis (the violent cut of distinction) is impossible in the realm of matter where things flow into one another and are unamenable to philosophical opposition. Woman names this non-identity, and her language, what the French feminists call *écriture féminine* or feminine writing, is exercised in a heterogeneous style that deliberately undermines all the hierarchical orders of male rationalist philosophy by breaking from the ideal of coherent meaning and good rational style. (It should be noted that for writers like Cixous, feminine writing also characterizes the work of male writers like Joyce.)

The constructivist position took inspiration from the Marxist theory of the social construction of individual subjectivity (Althusser) and from the Post-Structuralist idea that language writes rather than reflects identities. Gender identity is no less a construction of patriarchal culture than the idea that men are somehow superior to women; both are born at the same time and with the same stroke of the pen. The psychology or identity that feminist essentialists think is different from men's is merely the product of conditioning under patriarchy, a conditioning to be caring, relational, and maternal that may make women seem more ethical than men, but a conditioning nonetheless. The constructionists worried that the essentialists were taking an effect to be a cause, interpreting the subordination of women as women's nature. What must change, they contended, is not the way androcentric culture traps and stifles a woman's identity that should be liberated into separation, but rather the way all gender, both male and female, is fabricated. Marxist feminists especially noted that much of what the essentialists took to be signs of a good female nature were in fact attributes assigned women in capitalist culture to make them better domestic laborers, better angels in the house.

At its most radical, the constructivist counter-paradigm embraces such categories as performativity, masquerade, and imitation, which are seen as cultural processes that generate gender identities that only appear to possess a pre-existing natural or material substance. Of more importance than physical or biological difference might be psychological identity (across a range from "masculine" to "feminine," from aggressivity and self-assertiveness to emotional flexibility and psychological relationality). Women can be just as much "masculine" as men, and biological men might simply be "masculine" (or pretend to be such) only out of obedience to cultural codes. Feminist critics like Judith Butler began to argue in the mid-1980s that all gender is "performative," an imitation of a code that refers to no natural substance. Masculine means not feminine as much as it means anything natural. Susan Jeffords in *The Remasculinization of American Culture* notices, for example, that male masculinity in US culture after the Vietnam War is constructed through an expulsion of emotional traits associated with femininity.

The encounter with psychoanalysis has been crucial to the development of contemporary feminist thinking about literature and culture. Millett attacked Freud's most noteworthy mistakes regarding women, but later feminists have argued that the engagement with psychoanalysis should not be one entirely of rejection. Juliet Mitchell has argued that what is important about Freud is the theory of engendering. Gender is socially constructed, and although Freud's own account is patriarchal, other accounts are possible, as are other ways of constructing human subjectivity. While Freud favored the Oedipal drama of gender inscription, whereby the father's intervention between mother and son initiates the separation that preserves civilization, feminists have urged that greater attention be given the pre-Oedipal period, one shaped by the child's relationship with its mother (at least in traditional households in which men work and women do domestic labor). In the mother–child relationship might be found more of the constituents of identity (as object relations psychoanalytic theory claims) than are given during the later Oedipal stage. This shift in attention has the virtue of displacing a central theoretical premise of patriarchal culture – that fathers determine sexual identity – but it broaches the dangerous possibility of reducing a sociological postulate – mothering – to a biological destiny. Is "mothering" constructed within patriarchy as the other of "fathering" (understood as non-domestic labor), or is it a value, an ideal, and a human relationship that offers a way out of patriarchy, a different voice and perhaps even a different language?

Feminist literary criticism moves with time from the criticism of writing by men and the exploration of writing by women to a questioning of what it means at all to engage with or in language. If all language carries worlds within it, assumptions and values that lie embedded in the simplest of utterances, then how can women take up such language, the language of patriarchy, and hope to use it to forge a better world for women? Or is language neutral, an indifferent instrument that can be wielded in any number of socially constructive ways? And what does it mean here to speak of "a better world for women"? Is that not to nominate into an indifferent identity a splintered multiplicity of women's lives around the world and around any one community or society? And if feminism, in its inspiration, is about the painful particularities of any one person's experience, their right to be heard despite centuries of deafness and deliberate, systematic muting, then how can it especially name into silence voices that know no language with which to speak? Shouldn't women especially know what it means to need to speak and be denied a language with which to speak? Yet isn't to speak for "other" women, women outside the glow of the tent lights of highly literate literary culture, even if it is to take up their cause and stand in for them at the podium of history, to do what men have always done for women? How can language be given when it takes so much away? Yet a woman was stoned to death on March 30, 1997, for being in the company of someone not of her "kin." If silence is complicity, what form should speech take in such a situation? Should it adopt the language of rights, the one created by men? Or is there a different construction of the problem, one less abstract, made more angry by painful experience, that is more appropriately "feminist"?

At its outer boundary, the feminist literary criticism that arose in the 1960s and 1970s in the US and the Commonwealth countries discovers the conditions as well as the limits of its own possibility in language and in literacy. And by looking beyond the boundary it encounters its own origin in the pain of denied speech and the presumption of assigned speech. There as well, perhaps, from the achieved vantage of an international, transethnic, parasexual perspective, it discovers a field of work that takes it back beyond its own beginning in the emergence from silence into language – to undo the silence of those who still do not speak.

In 1969 a revolution occurred. It seemed small at first, but like many other small gestures of rebellion, it represented the first significant fissure in the crystalline edifice of a certain social order. Ultimately that fissure widened, and in spreading broke the system that defined what otherwise might have been a night's fun as a gesture of rebellion. In retrospect, the fact that a group of gays, lesbians, and transvestites should resist undergoing the by-then routine procedure of being harassed and arrested by the New York police seems fairly happenstance. But something much bigger was at stake in the riot that occurred that night. That something was the regime of what Adrienne Rich calls "compulsory heterosexuality." That regime had as a major correlate (if not presupposition) the banishment of alternative sexual practices and the violation of bearers of nonheterosexual gender identities. If women were to be compelled to be child-productive wives by the dominant social group of heterosexual men, then women's friendships would be deemed suspicious, and lesbianism would be enjoined. If men were to behave in accordance with the dictates of compulsory heterosexuality and not engage in sexual practices that placed the reigning code of heterosexual masculinity in question, then their friendships too would be suspect, and male homosexuality would also be forbidden. Those guilty of daring to challenge this social and cultural regime – Oscar Wilde comes to mind – would be the objects of calumny, if not of overt violence. And all of this would be called "normality" while all of "that" would be stigmatized as "perversion." That science and medicine were complicit in this regime only says once again, in case it needs repeating, that science and medicine could do to rethink their founding rationalist criteria and their principles of social constitution, two things that always coexist but whose coexistence science always has trouble recognizing.

The emergence of a Gay and Lesbian Liberation Movement in the late 1960s and early 1970s intersected necessarily with the work of feminists who were concerned with issues of sexuality and of gender identity. For a time, the two movements seemed to share a common ground; women and gays were objects of oppression by a dominant male heterosexual group. But in other respects (and in hindsight), there were grounds for difference.

In the 1980s, feminism began to change direction. For some time, feminist theorists had been discussing the idea that there might be a difference within feminism proper between biological sexual identity (the physical difference that makes women women and men men) and gender identity. If biological sexual identity belonged to nature and could allow a general class of "women" to be identified as "not male," gender identity seemed more subject to the contingencies of culture and history, more something constructed in and variable across society and through history. It might not lend itself to an opposition such as that between "man" and "woman." The generality of the category "women" might in fact conceal and suppress differentiations between women in regard to choice of sexual object, sexual practices, and psychological identities, some of which might be "masculine." While a masculine woman would for feminists of the 1970s be "male-identified," for the emerging Gender Studies and Gay/Lesbian theories of the 1980s, such a person might simply be one of a variety of possible gender and sexual locations, an intersection of biology and culture, or physicality and psychology that is not easily identified (and certainly not easily vilified). The path-breaking work of anthropologists like Gayle Rubin and historians like Alan Bray and Michel Foucault bore out the point that gender is variable: in history and between societies, there is variation between different ways of practicing sex and being one gender or another. Sexual practices like anal intercourse, intercourse between women, fellatio, and cunnilingus are coded differently across different societies and throughout history. Anal intercourse and fellatio between men were common in fifth-century Greek society, and only later (in the late nineteenth century, according to Foucault) would they be "discovered" to be signs of an identifiable "perversion." Christianity stands between the two dates or sites and probably has a great deal to do with how non-reproductive sexual practices became stigmatized over time.

Gay and lesbian scholars during the 1970s and 1980s began to peel away the layers of prejudice that had made it almost impossible, before the Stonewall riot, to study the history of gay and lesbian writing or to analyze how gays and lesbian life and experience were distorted in cultural history. Some of this early work included Guy Hocquenghem's examination of the psychology of homophobia, Jeffrey Weeks's history of "coming out," Richard Dyer's exploration of representations of gays and lesbians in film, Terry Castle's study of "things not fit to be mentioned" in eighteenth-century literature, Lillian Faderman's work on love between women in the Renaissance, the Combahee River Collective's manifesto for African-American lesbians, Andrew Britton's rebuttal of normative homophobia on the intellectual Left, Adrienne Rich's celebrated statement against "compulsory heterosexuality," Sharon O'Brien's exploration of Willa Cather's problematic attitude towards her own lesbianism, John D'Emilio's history of how homosexuals were minoritized in US culture, and Jeffrey Escoffier's analysis of the need for a gay revolution equivalent to the socialist one against capitalism. One of the more attention-getting publications during this period was the translation of the first volume of Foucault's *History of Sexuality* (1978). Foucault's argument that "homosexuality" is a social, medical, and ontological category invented in the late nineteenth century and imposed on sexual practices that prior to that point had enjoyed an absence of such "scientific" scrutiny provided impetus to the idea that modern heterocentric gender culture founds itself on the anathemizing of non-reproductive sexual alternatives that are in fact everywhere present in human society.

In the mid- to late 1970s and into the early 1980s, a new field of Gender Studies constituted itself in conjunction with Gay and Lesbian Studies. It turned its attention on all gender formations, both heterosexual and homosexual. Gender scholars found that heterosexuality can be understood as forming a continuum with homosexuality in that such ideals as heterosexual masculinity seem inseparable from a "panic" component, an apotropaic move or turn away from a certain homosexuality that helps construct heterosexuality. In *Between Men* (1985), Eve Sedgwick notices that male heterosexual desire is always modeled on another male's desire and always has a "homosocial" cast. The male bonding that sutures patriarchy is necessarily homophilic and forms a continuum with homosexuality.

More so than Gay Studies, Lesbian Studies has demonstrated a tendency towards separatism, perhaps because as women, lesbians suffer a double oppression. (If one factors in ethnic prejudice, as in the case of Gloria Anzaldua (*Borderlands / La Frontera*), the sense of pain grows exponentially.) A separatist strand of Lesbian Studies was theorized by Monique Wittig ("The Straight Mind," 1980) and Luce Irigaray (in her *This Sex Which Is Not One* (1977; English translation, 1985)). Lesbian women, Irigaray argues, can only exist as such in a world of their own apart from patrocentric culture. The difference of Lesbian Studies from feminism also began to be marked at this time. Judith Butler's *Gender Trouble* (1990) made the argument against enclosing Lesbian Studies within feminism emphatic by deconstructing the very notion of an identity of "woman" and demonstrating that all gender identity is a performance, an apparent substance that is an effect of a prior act of imitation. That same year Eve Kosofsky Sedgwick published her celebrated theoretical analysis of "closeting" (*Epistemology of the Closet*). Building on her earlier work, Sedgwick contends that one cannot logically separate men-loving-men within patriarchy from homosexuality. Sedgwick's work demonstrates the significance of Post-Structuralist thinking for Gender Theory, since it underscores the contingency of all supposedly axiomatic oppositions as that between homosexuality and heterosexuality. Sexuality and gender are variable and indeterminate; they do not align with simple polarities and can take multiple, highly differentiated forms. In 1994, Lee Edelman's *Homo-graphesis* brought deconstructive theory to bear on the question of gay identity and the issue of recognizability. The gay is a "homograph," someone who simulates the "normality" of masculinity or heterosexuality only to displace them as grounding ontological categories.

In the mid- to late 1980s, Acquired Immune Deficiency Syndrome killed many people in the gay community. Queer Theory, which emerged around this time, is in some respects a response to the epidemic, both a way of providing gays and lesbians with a common term around which to unite and a more radical way of calling attention to the issues raised by them. Queer Theory adopted a term of stigmatization ("queer" being a derogatory name for a gay or lesbian person) and turned it against the perpetrator by transforming it into a token of pride. The shift in name also indicates a shift in analytic strategy, for now gay and lesbian theorists began to explore the "queerness" of supposedly "normal" sexual culture. The controversy over the photographs of Robert Mapplethorpe, some of which depict aspects of the gay sadomasochistic subculture, helped focus attention on the mendacity of a heterosexual sex–gender system that condemned as "perversion" in others what it practiced on a routine basis in its own homes. The work of Michael Moon and Paul Morrison is especially compelling in this regard. Morrison suggests that one reason Mapplethorpe's pictures of men in leather bound with chains sitting in living rooms and looking very normal, almost like dinner guests awaiting their cue to head for the table, were so disturbing to the dominant heterosexual community is that they draw attention to the discipline and coercion operative in those living rooms. That discipline is normal, whereas the gay mimesis or enactment of such violence in the routines of sadism or masochism is stigmatized.[3] In a similar fashion, Moon uses Freud's notion of the "uncanny," the disturbing other within, to intimate that routine male heterosexual identity is premised on violent competition between men that has a sadistic component. Where we draw the lines between normal and non-normal is, Moon suggests, entirely contingent.

Gender Studies, Gay/Lesbian Studies, and Queer Theory have delineated three broad areas of work in literary and cultural theory. First, the examination of the history of the oppression of gays, lesbians, and practitioners of sexualities other than those deemed normal by the dominant heterosexual group. Second, the exploration of the counter-cultures of gay and lesbian writing that existed in parallel fashion with the dominant heterosexual culture. And third, the analysis of the instability and indeterminacy of all gender identity, such that even "normal" heterosexuality itself might be seen as a kind of panicked closure imposed on a variable, contingent, and multiple sexuality whose mobility and potentiality is signaled by the worlds of possibility opened up by gays and lesbians.

Notes

1 Marianne Hirsch and Evelyn Fox Keller, eds., *Conflicts in Feminism* (New York and London: Routledge, 1990).

2 Adrienne Rich, "When We Dead Awaken: Writing as Re-Vision," in *On Lies, Secrets Silence: Selected Prose 1966–1978* (New York: Norton, 1979).

Acknowledgments are an inadequate expression of how much this essay, like most, is the product of many minds. They are also necessary to free others of the responsibility for what is ultimately a personal vision of a collective conversation. I want to free and thank the following persons: Tom Anderson and Arlene Gorelick, with whom I co-authored the essay from which this one evolved; Rayna Reiter, Larry Shields, Ray Kelly, Peggy White, Norma Diamond, Randy Reiter, Frederick Wyatt, Anne Locksley, Juliet Mitchell, and Susan Harding, for countless conversations and ideas; Marshall Sahlins, for the revelation of anthropology; Lynn Eden, for sardonic editing; the members of Women's Studies 340/004, for my initiation into teaching; Sally Brenner, for heroic typing; Susan Lowes, for incredible patience; and Emma Goldman, for the title.

3 Paul Morrison, "Coffee Table Sex," *Genders*, no. 11 (Fall 1991), pp. 17–34.

CHAPTER 2

The Traffic in Women

Gayle Rubin

This 1975 essay by feminist anthropologist Gayle Rubin quickly became a key text of feminist argument in the 1970s. At that time, feminists were trying to find their place in relation to three of the dominant schools of thought on the academic Left – Freudian psychoanalysis, Structural anthropology, and Marxism. Rubin's essay notes the points of helpful contact for feminists with these schools as well as the moments of dissonance.

The literature on women – both feminist and anti-feminist – is a long rumination on the question of the nature and genesis of women's oppression and social subordination. The question is not a trivial one, since the answers given it determine our visions of the future, and our evaluation of whether or not it is realistic to hope for a sexually egalitarian society. More importantly, the analysis of the causes of women's oppression forms the basis for any assessment of just what would have to be changed in order to achieve a society without gender hierarchy. Thus, if innate male aggression and dominance are at the root of female oppression, then the feminist program would logically require either the extermination of the offending sex, or else a eugenics project to modify its character. If sexism is a by-product of capitalism's relentless appetite for profit, then sexism would wither away in the advent of a successful socialist revolution. If the world historical defeat of women occurred at the hands of an armed patriarchal revolt, then it is time for Amazon guerrillas to start training in the Adirondacks.

It lies outside the scope of this paper to conduct a sustained critique of some of the currently popular explanations of the genesis of sexual inequality – theories such as the popular evolution exemplified by *The Imperial Animal*, the alleged overthrow of prehistoric matriarchies, or the attempt to extract all of the phenomena of social subordination

Original publication details: Gayle Rubin, "The Traffic in Women" from *Toward an Anthropology of Women*, ed. Rayna Reiter. Monthly Review Press, 1975. Reproduced with permission from Duke University Press and G. Rubin.

from the first volume of *Capital*. Instead, I want to sketch some elements of an alternate explanation of the problem.

Marx once asked: "What is a Negro slave? A man of the black race. The one explanation is as good as the other. A Negro is a Negro. He only becomes a slave in certain relations. A cotton spinning jenny is a machine for spinning cotton. It becomes capital only in certain relations. Torn from these relationships it is no more capital than gold in itself is money or sugar is the price of sugar."[1] One might paraphrase: What is a domesticated woman? A female of the species. The one explanation is as good as the other. A woman is a woman. She only becomes a domestic, a wife, a chattel, a playboy bunny, a prostitute, or a human dictaphone in certain relations. Torn from these relationships, she is no more the helpmate of man than gold in itself is money ... etc. What then are these relationships by which a female becomes an oppressed woman? The place to begin to unravel the system of relationships by which women become the prey of men is in the overlapping works of Claude Lévi-Strauss and Sigmund Freud. The domestication of women, under other names, is discussed at length in both of their œuvre. In reading through these works, one begins to have a sense of a systematic social apparatus which takes up females as raw materials and fashions domesticated women as products. Neither Freud nor Lévi-Strauss sees his work in this light, and certainly neither turns a critical glance upon the processes he describes. Their analyses and descriptions must be read, therefore, in something like the way in which Marx read the classical political economists who preceded him.[2] Freud and Lévi-Strauss are in some sense analogous to Ricardo and Smith: They see neither the implications of what they are saying, nor the implicit critique which their work can generate when subjected to a feminist eye. Nevertheless, they provide conceptual tools with which one can build descriptions of the part of social life which is the locus of the oppression of women, of sexual minorities, and of certain aspects of human personality within individuals. I call that part of social life the "sex/gender system," for lack of a more elegant term. As a preliminary definition, a "sex/gender system" is the set of arrangements by which a society transforms biological sexuality into products of human activity, and in which these transformed sexual needs are satisfied.

The purpose of this essay is to arrive at a more fully developed definition of the sex/gender system, by way of a somewhat idiosyncratic and exegetical reading of Lévi-Strauss and Freud. I use the word "exegetical" deliberately. The dictionary defines "exegesis" as a "critical explanation or analysis; especially, interpretation of the Scriptures." At times, my reading of Lévi-Strauss and Freud is freely interpretive, moving from the explicit content of a text to its presuppositions and implications. My reading of certain psychoanalytic texts is filtered through a lens provided by Jacques Lacan, whose own interpretation of the Freudian scripture has been heavily influenced by Lévi-Strauss.[3]

I will return later to a refinement of the definition of a sex/gender system. First, however, I will try to demonstrate the need for such a concept by discussing the failure of classical Marxism to fully express or conceptualize sex oppression. This failure results from the fact that Marxism, as a theory of social life, is relatively unconcerned with sex. In Marx's map of the social world, human beings are workers, peasants, or capitalists; that they are also men and women is not seen as very significant. By contrast, in the maps of social reality drawn by Freud and Lévi-Strauss, there is a deep recognition of the place of sexuality in society, and of the profound differences between the social experience of men and women.

Marx

There is no theory which accounts for the oppression of women – in its endless variety and monotonous similarity, cross-culturally and throughout history – with anything like the explanatory power of the Marxist theory of class oppression. Therefore, it is not surprising that there have been numerous attempts to apply Marxist analysis to the question of women. There are many ways of doing this. It has been argued that women are a reserve labor force for capitalism, that women's generally lower wages provide extra surplus to a capitalist employer, that women serve the ends of capitalist consumerism in their roles as administrators of family consumption, and so forth.

However, a number of articles have tried to do something much more ambitious – to locate the oppression of women in the heart of the capitalist dynamic by pointing to the relationship between housework and the reproduction of labor. To do this is to place women squarely in the definition of capitalism, the process in which capital is produced by the extraction of surplus value from labor by capital.[4]

Briefly, Marx argued that capitalism is distinguished from all other modes of production by its unique aim: the creation and expansion of capital. Whereas other modes of production might find their purpose in making useful things to satisfy human needs, or in producing a surplus for a ruling nobility, or in producing to insure sufficient sacrifice for the edification of the gods, capitalism produces capital. Capitalism is a set of social relations – forms of property, and so forth – in which production takes the form of turning money, things, and people into capital. And capital is a quantity of goods or money which, when exchanged for labor, reproduces and augments itself by extracting unpaid labor, or surplus value, from labor and into itself.

> The result of the capitalist production process is neither a mere produce (use-value) nor a commodity, that is, a use-value which has exchange-value. Its result, its product, is the creation of surplus-value for capital, and consequently the actual transformation of money or commodity into capitals.[5]

The exchange between capital and labor which produces surplus value, and hence capital, is highly specific. The worker gets a wage; the capitalist gets the things the worker has made during his or her time of employment. If the total value of the things the worker has made exceeds the value of his or her wage, the aim of capitalism has been achieved. The capitalist gets back the cost of the wage, plus an increment – surplus value. This can occur because the wage is determined not by the value of what the laborer makes, but by the value of what it takes to keep him or her going – to reproduce him or her from day to day, and to reproduce the entire work force from one generation to the next. Thus, surplus value is the difference between what the laboring class produces as a whole, and the amount of that total which is recycled into maintaining the laboring class.

> The capital given in exchange for labor power is converted into necessaries, by the consumption of which the muscles, nerves, bones, and brains of existing laborers are reproduced, and new laborers are begotten … the individual consumption of the laborer, whether it proceed within the workshop or outside it, whether it be part of the process of production or not, forms therefore a factor of the production and reproduction of capital; just as cleaning machinery does.[6]
>
> Given the individual, the production of labor-power consists in his reproduction of himself or his maintenance. For his maintenance he requires a given quantity of the means

of subsistence.... Labor-power sets itself in action only by working. But thereby a definite quantity of human muscle, brain, nerve, etc., is wasted, and these require to be restored.[7]

The amount of the difference between the reproduction of labor power and its products depends, therefore, on the determination of what it takes to reproduce that labor power. Marx tends to make that determination on the basis of the quantity of commodities – food, clothing, housing, fuel – which would be necessary to maintain the health, life, and strength of a worker. But these commodities must be consumed before they can be sustenance, and they are not immediately in consumable form when they are purchased by the wage. Additional labor must be performed upon these things before they can be turned into people. Food must be cooked, clothes cleaned, beds made, wood chopped, etc. Housework is therefore a key element in the process of the reproduction of the laborer from whom surplus value is taken. Since it is usually women who do housework, it has been observed that it is through the reproduction of labor power that women are articulated into the surplus value nexus which is the sine qua non of capitalism.[8] It can be further argued that since no wage is paid for housework, the labor of women in the home contributes to the ultimate quantity of surplus value realized.

Women are oppressed in societies which can by no stretch of the imagination be described as capitalist. In the Amazon valley and the New Guinea Highlands, women are frequently kept in their place by gang rape when the ordinary mechanisms of masculine intimidation prove insufficient. "We tame our women with the banana," said one Mundurucu man.[9] The ethnographic record is littered with practices whose effect is to keep women "in their place" – men's cults, secret initiations, arcane male knowledge, etc. And pre-capitalist, feudal Europe was hardly a society in which there was no sexism. Capitalism has taken over, and rewired notions of male and female which predate it by centuries. No analysis of the reproduction of labor power under capitalism can explain foot-binding, chastity belts, or any of the incredible array of Byzantine, fetishized indignities, let alone the more ordinary ones, which have been inflicted upon women in various times and places. The analysis of the reproduction of labor power does not even explain why it is usually women who do domestic work in the home, rather than men.

In this light it is interesting to return to Marx's discussion of the reproduction of labor. What is necessary to reproduce the worker is determined in part by the biological needs of the human organism, in part by the physical conditions of the place in which it lives, and in part by cultural tradition. Marx observed that beer is necessary for the reproduction of the English working class, and wine necessary for the French.

> [T]he number and extent of his [the worker's] so-called necessary wants, as also the modes of satisfying them, are themselves the product of historical development, and depend therefore to a great extent on the degree of civilization of a country, more particularly on the conditions under which, and consequently on the habits and degree of comfort in which, the class of free laborers has been formed. In contradistinction therefore to the case of other commodities, there enters into the determination of the value of labor-power a historical and moral element.[10]

It is precisely this "historical and moral element" which determines that a "wife" is among the necessities of a worker, that women rather than men do housework, and that capitalism is heir to a long tradition in which women do not inherit, in which women do not lead, and in which women do not talk to god. It is this "historical and moral element" which presented capitalism with a cultural heritage of forms of masculinity and femininity. It is within this "historical and moral element" that the entire domain of sex, sexuality, and sex oppression is subsumed. And the briefness of Marx's comment only serves to emphasize the vast area of social life which it covers and leaves unexamined. Only by subjecting this "historical and moral element" to analysis can the structure of sex oppression be delineated.

Engels

In *The Origin of the Family, Private Property, and the State*, Engels sees sex oppression as part of capitalism's heritage from prior social forms. Moreover, Engels integrates sex and sexuality into his theory of society. *Origin* is a frustrating book. Like the nineteenth-century tomes on the history of marriage and the family which it echoes, the state of the evidence in *Origin* renders it quaint to a reader familiar with more recent developments in anthropology. Nevertheless, it is a book whose considerable insight should not be overshadowed by its limitations. The idea that the "relations of sexuality" can and should be distinguished from the "relations of production" is not the least of Engels' intuitions:

> According to the materialistic conception, the determining factor in history is, in the final instance, the production and reproduction of immediate life. This again, is of a twofold character: on the one hand, the production of the means of existence, of food, clothing, and shelter and the tools necessary for that production; on the other side, the production of human beings themselves, the propagation of the species. The social organization under which the people of a particular historical epoch and a particular country live is determined by both kinds of production: by the stage of development of labor on the one hand, and of the family on the other.[11]

This passage indicates an important recognition – that a human group must do more than apply its activity to reshaping the natural world in order to clothe, feed, and warm itself. We usually call the system by which elements of the natural world are transformed into objects of human consumption the "economy." But the needs which are satisfied by economic activity even in the richest, Marxian sense, do not exhaust fundamental human requirements. A human group must also reproduce itself from generation to generation. The needs of sexuality and procreation must be satisfied as much as the need to eat, and one of the most obvious deductions which can be made from the data of anthropology is that these needs are hardly ever satisfied in any "natural" form, any more than are the needs for food. Hunger is hunger, but what counts as food is culturally determined and obtained. Every society has some form of organized economic activity. Sex is sex, but what counts as sex is equally culturally determined and obtained. Every society also has a sex gender system – a set of arrangements by which the biological raw material of human sex and procreation is shaped by human, social intervention and satisfied in a conventional manner, no matter how bizarre some of the conventions may be.[12]

The realm of human sex, gender, and procreation has been subjected to, and changed by, relentless social activity for millennia. Sex as we know it – gender identity, sexual desire and fantasy, concepts of childhood – is itself a social product. We need to under-stand the relations of its production, and forget, for a while, about food, clothing, automobiles, and transistor radios. In most Marxist tradition, and even in Engels' book, the concept of the "second aspect of material life" has tended to fade into the background, or to be incorporated into the usual notions of "material life." Engels' suggestion has never been followed up and subjected to the refinement which it needs. But he does indicate the existence and importance of the domain of social life which I want to call the sex/gender system.

Other names have been proposed for the sex/gender system. The most common alternatives are "mode of reproduction" and "patriarchy." It may be foolish to quibble about terms, but both of these can lead to confusion. All three proposals have been made in order to introduce a distinction between "economic" systems and "sexual" systems, and to indicate that sexual systems have a certain autonomy and cannot always be explained in terms of economic forces. "Mode of reproduction," for instance, has been proposed in opposition to the more familiar "mode of production." But this terminology links the "economy" to production, and the sexual system to "reproduction." It reduces the richness of either system, since "productions" and "reproductions" take place in both. Every mode of production involves reproduction – of tools, labor, and social relations. We cannot relegate all of the multi-faceted aspects of social reproduction to the sex system. Replacement of machinery is an example of reproduction in the economy. On the other hand, we cannot limit the sex system to "reproduction" in either the social or biological sense of the term. A sex/gender system is not simply the reproductive moment of a "mode of production." The formation of gender identity is an example of production in the realm of the sexual system. And a sex/gender system involves more than the "relations of procreation," reproduction in the biological sense.

The term "patriarchy" was introduced to distinguish the forces maintaining sexism from other social forces, such as capitalism. But the use of "patriarchy" obscures other distinctions. Its use is analogous to using capitalism to refer to all modes of production, whereas the usefulness of the term "capitalism" lies precisely in that it distinguishes between the different systems by which societies are provisioned and organized. Any society will have some system of "political economy." Such a system may be egalitarian or socialist. It may be class stratified, in which case the oppressed class may consist of serfs, peasants, or slaves. The oppressed class may consist of wage laborers, in which case the system is properly labeled "capitalist." The power of the term lies in its implication that, in fact, there are alternatives to capitalism.

Similarly, any society will have some systematic ways to deal with sex, gender, and babies. Such a system may be sexually egalitarian, at least in theory, or it may be "gender stratified," as seems to be the case for most or all of the known examples. But it is important – even in the face of a depressing history – to maintain a distinction between the human capacity and necessity to create a sexual world, and the empirically oppressive ways in which sexual worlds have been organized. Patriarchy subsumes both meanings into the same term. Sex/gender system, on the other hand, is a neutral term which refers to the domain and indicates that oppression is not inevitable in that domain, but is the product of the specific social relations which organize it.

Finally, there are gender-stratified systems which are not adequately described as patriarchal. Many New Guinea societies (Enga, Maring, Bena Bena, Huli, Melpa, Kuma, Gahuku Gama, Fore, Marind Anim, ad nauseam) are viciously oppressive to women. But the power of males in these groups is not founded on their roles as fathers or patriarchs, but on their collective adult maleness, embodied in secret cults, men's houses, warfare, exchange networks, ritual knowledge, and various initiation procedures. Patriarchy is a specific form of male dominance, and the use of the term ought to be confined to the Old Testament-type pastoral nomads from whom the term comes, or groups like them. Abraham was a Patriarch – one old man whose absolute power over wives, children, herds, and dependents was an aspect of the institution of fatherhood, as defined in the social group in which he lived.

Whichever term we use, what is important is to develop concepts to adequately describe the social organization of sexuality and the reproduction of the conventions of sex and gender. We need to pursue the project Engels abandoned when he located the subordination of women in a development within the mode of production.[13] To do this, we can imitate Engels in his method rather than in his results. Engels approached the task of analyzing the "second aspect of material life" by way of an examination of a theory of kinship systems. Kinship systems are and do many things. But they are made up of, and reproduce, concrete forms of socially organized sexuality. Kinship systems are observable and empirical forms of sex/gender systems.

Kinship

(On the part played by sexuality in the transition from ape to "man.")

To an anthropologist, a kinship system is not a list of biological relatives. It is a system of categories and statuses which often contradict actual genetic relationships. There are dozens of examples in which socially defined kinship statuses take precedence over biology. The Nuer custom of "woman marriage" is a case in point. The Nuer define the status of fatherhood as belonging to the person in whose name cattle bridewealth is given for the mother. Thus, a woman can be married to another woman, and be husband to the wife and father of her children, despite the fact that she is not the inseminator.[14]

In pre-state societies, kinship is the idiom of social interaction, organizing economic, political, and ceremonial, as well as sexual, activity. One's duties; responsibilities, and privileges *vis-à-vis* others are defined in terms of mutual kinship or lack thereof. The exchange of goods and services, production and distribution, hostility and solidarity, ritual and ceremony, all take place within the organizational structure of kinship. The ubiquity and adaptive effectiveness of kinship has led many anthropologists to consider its invention, along with the invention of language, to have been the developments which decisively marked the discontinuity between semi-human hominids and human beings.[15]

While the idea of the importance of kinship enjoys the status of a first principle in anthropology, the internal workings of kinship systems have long been a focus for intense controversy. Kinship systems vary wildly from one culture to the next. They contain all sorts of bewildering rules which govern whom one may or may not marry. Their internal complexity is dazzling. Kinship systems have for decades provoked the anthropological imagination into trying to explain incest taboos, cross-cousin marriage, terms of descent, relationships of avoidance or forced intimacy, clans and sections, taboos on names – the diverse array of items found in descriptions of actual kinship systems. In the nineteenth century, several thinkers attempted to write comprehensive accounts of the nature and history of human sexual systems.[16] One of these was *Ancient Society*, by Lewis Henry Morgan. It was this book which inspired Engels to write *The Origin of the Family, Private Property, and the State*. Engels' theory is based upon Morgan's account of kinship and marriage.

In taking up Engels' project of extracting a theory of sex oppression from the study of kinship, we have the advantage of the maturation of ethnology since the nineteenth century. We also have the advantage of a peculiar and particularly appropriate book, Lévi-Strauss' *The Elementary Structures of Kinship*. This is the boldest twentieth-century version of the nineteenth-century project to understand human marriage. It is a book in which kinship is explicitly conceived of as an imposition of cultural organization upon the facts of biological procreation. It is permeated with an awareness of the importance of sexuality in human society. It is a description of society which does not assume an abstract, genderless human subject. On the contrary, the human subject in Lévi-Strauss' work is always either male or female, and the divergent social destinies of the two sexes can therefore be traced. Since Lévi-Strauss sees the essence of kinship systems to lie in an exchange of women between men, he constructs an implicit theory of sex oppression. Aptly, the book is dedicated to the memory of Lewis Henry Morgan.

> "Vile and precious merchandise"
> *Monique Wittig*

The Elementary Structures of Kinship is a grand statement on the origin and nature of human society. It is a treatise on the kinship systems of approximately one-third of the ethnographic globe. Most fundamentally, it is an attempt to discern the structural principles of kinship. Lévi-Strauss argues that the application of these principles (summarized in the last chapter of *Elementary Structures*) to kinship data reveals an intelligible logic to the taboos and marriage rules which have perplexed and mystified Western anthropologists. He constructs a chess game of such complexity that it cannot be recapitulated here. But two of his chess pieces are particularly relevant to women – the "gift" and the incest taboo, whose dual articulation adds up to his concept of the exchange of women.

Elementary Structures is in part a radical gloss on another famous theory of primitive social organization, Mauss' *Essay on the Gift*.[17] It was Mauss who first theorized as to the significance of one of the most striking features of primitive societies: the extent to which giving, receiving, and reciprocating gifts dominates social intercourse. In such societies, all sorts of things circulate in exchange – food, spells, rituals, words, names, ornaments, tools, and dowers.

> Your own mother, your own sister, your own pigs, your own yams that you have piled up, you may not eat. Other people's mothers, other people's sisters, other people's pigs, other people's yams that they have piled up, you may eat.[18]

In a typical gift transaction, neither party gains anything. In the Trobriand Islands, each household maintains a garden of yams and each household eats yams. But the yams a household grows and the yams it eats are not the same. At harvest time, a man sends the yams he has cultivated to the household of his sister; the household in which he lives is provisioned by his wife's brother.[19] Since such a procedure appears to be a useless one from the point of view of accumulation or trade, its logic has been sought elsewhere. Mauss proposed that the significance of gift giving is that it expresses, affirms, or creates a social link between the partners of an exchange. Gift giving confers upon its participants a special relationship of trust, solidarity, and mutual aid. One can solicit a friendly relationship in the offer of a gift; acceptance implies a willingness to return a gift and a confirmation of the relationship. Gift exchange may also be the idiom of competition and rivalry. There are many examples in which one person humiliates another by giving more than can be reciprocated. Some political systems, such as the Big Man systems of Highland New Guinea, are based on exchange which is unequal on the material plane. An aspiring Big Man wants to give away more goods than can be reciprocated. He gets his return in political prestige.

Although both Mauss and Lévi-Strauss emphasize the solidary aspects of gift exchange, the other purposes served by gift giving only strengthen the point that it is a ubiquitous means of social commerce. Mauss proposed that gifts were the threads of social discourse, the means by which such societies were held together in the absence of specialized governmental institutions. "The gift is the primitive way of achieving the peace that in civil society is secured by the state…. Composing society, the gift was the liberation of culture."[20]

Lévi-Strauss adds to the theory of primitive reciprocity the idea that marriages are a most basic form of gift exchange, in which it is women who are the most precious of gifts. He argues that the incest taboo should best be understood as a mechanism to insure that such exchanges take place between families and between groups. Since the existence of incest taboos is universal, but the content of their prohibitions variable, they cannot be explained as having the aim of preventing the occurrence of genetically close matings. Rather, the incest taboo imposes the social aim of exogamy and alliance upon the biological events of sex and procreation. The incest taboo divides the universe of sexual choice into categories of permitted and prohibited sexual partners. Specifically, by forbidding unions within a group it enjoins marital exchange between groups.

> The prohibition on the sexual use of a daughter or a sister compels them to be given in marriage to another man, and at the same time it establishes a right to the daughter or sister of this other man…. The woman whom one does not take is, for that very reason, offered up.[21]
>
> The prohibition of incest is less a rule prohibiting marriage with the mother, sister, or daughter, than a rule obliging the mother, sister, or daughter to be given to others. It is the supreme rule of the gift….[22]

The result of a gift of women is more profound than the result of other gift transactions, because the relationship thus established is not just one of reciprocity, but one of kinship. The exchange partners have become affines, and their descendants will be related by blood: "Two people may meet in friendship and exchange gifts and yet quarrel and fight in later times, but intermarriage connects them in a permanent manner."[23] As is the case with other gift giving, marriages are not always so simply activities to make peace. Marriages may be highly competitive, and there are plenty of affines who fight each other. Nevertheless, in a general sense the argument is that the taboo on incest results in a wide network of relations, a set of people whose connections with one another are a kinship structure. All other levels, amounts, and directions of exchange – including hostile ones – are ordered by this structure. The marriage ceremonies recorded in the ethnographic literature are moments in a ceaseless and ordered procession in which women, children, shells, words, cattle names, fish, ancestors, whales' teeth, pigs, yams, spells, dances, mats, etc., pass from hand to hand, leaving as their tracks the ties that bind. Kinship is organization, and organization gives power. But who is organized?

If it is women who are being transacted, then it is the men who give and take them who are linked, the women being a conduit of a relationship rather than a partner to it.[24] The exchange of women does not necessarily imply that women are objectified, in the modern sense, since objects in the primitive world are imbued with highly personal qualities. But it does imply a distinction between gift and giver. If women are the gifts, then it is men who are the exchange partners. And it is the partners, not the presents, upon whom reciprocal exchange confers its quasi-mystical power of social linkage. The relations of such a system are such that women are in no position to realize the benefits of their own circulation. As long as the relations specify that men exchange women, it is men who are the beneficiaries of the product of such exchanges – social organization.

> The total relationship of exchange which constitutes marriage is not established between a man and a woman, but between two groups of men, and the woman figures only as one of the objects in the exchange, not as one of the partners…. This remains true even when the girl's feelings are taken into consideration, as, moreover, is usually the case. In acquiescing to the proposed union, she precipitates or allows the exchange to take place, she cannot alter its nature.[25]

To enter into a gift exchange as a partner, one must have something to give. If women are for men to dispose of, they are in no position to give themselves away.

> "What woman," mused a young Northern Melpa man, "is ever strong enough to get up and say, 'Let us make *moka*, let us find wives and pigs, let us give our daughters to men, let us wage war, let us kill our enemies!' No indeed not! … they are little rubbish things who stay at home simply, don't you see?"[26]

What women indeed! The Melpa women of whom the young man spoke can't get wives, they *are* wives, and what they get are husbands, an entirely different matter. The Melpa women can't give their daughters to men, because they do not have the same rights in their daughters that their male kin have, rights of bestowal (although *not* of ownership).

The "exchange of women" is a seductive and powerful concept. It is attractive in that it places the oppression of women within social systems, rather than in biology. Moreover, it suggests that we look for the ultimate locus of women's oppression within the traffic in women, rather than within the traffic in merchandise. It is certainly not difficult to find ethnographic and historical examples of trafficking in women. Women are given in marriage, taken in battle, exchanged for favors, sent as tribute, traded, bought, and sold. Far from being confined to the "primitive" world, these practices seem only to become more pronounced and commercialized in more "civilized" societies. Men are of course also trafficked – but as slaves, hustlers, athletic stars, serfs, or as some other catastrophic social status, rather than as men. Women are transacted as slaves, serfs, and prostitutes, but also simply as women. And if men have been sexual subjects – exchangers – and women sexual semi-objects – gifts – for much of human history, then many customs, clichés, and personality traits seem to make a great deal of sense (among others, the curious custom by which a father gives away the bride)….

The exchange of women is also a problematic concept. Since Lévi-Strauss argues that the incest taboo and the results of its application constitute the origin of culture, it can be deduced that the world historical defeat of women occurred with the origin of culture, and is a prerequisite of culture. If his analysis is adopted in its pure form, the feminist program must include a task even more onerous than the extermination of men; it must attempt to get rid of culture and substitute some entirely new phenomena on the face of the earth. However, it would be a dubious proposition at best to argue that if there were no exchange of women there would be no culture, if for no other reason than that culture is, by definition, inventive. It is even debatable that "exchange of women" adequately describes all of the empirical evidence of kinship systems. Some cultures, such as the Lele and the Kuma, exchange women explicitly and overtly. In other cultures, the exchange of women can be inferred. In some – particularly those hunters and gatherers excluded from Lévi-Strauss' sample – the efficacy of the concept becomes altogether questionable. What are we to make of a concept which seems so useful and yet so difficult?

The "exchange of women" is neither a definition of culture nor a system in and of itself. The concept is an acute, but condensed, apprehension of certain aspects of the social relations of sex and gender. A kinship system is an imposition of social ends upon a part of the natural world. It is therefore "production" in the most general sense of the term: a molding, a transformation of objects (in this case, people) to and by a subjective purpose. It has its own relations to production, distribution, and exchange, which include certain "property" forms in people. These forms are not exclusive private property rights, but rather different sorts of rights that various people have over other people. Marriage transactions – the gifts and material which circulate in the ceremonies marking a marriage – are a rich source of data for determining exactly who has which rights in whom. It is not difficult to deduce from such transactions that in most cases women's rights are considerably more residual than those of men.

Kinship systems do not merely exchange women. They exchange sexual access, genealogical statuses, lineage names and ancestors, rights and people – men, women, and children – in concrete systems of social relationships. These relationships always include certain rights for men, others for women. "Exchange of women" is a shorthand for expressing that the social relations of a kinship system specify that men have certain rights in their female kin, and that women do not have the same rights either to themselves or to their male kin. In this sense, the exchange of women is a profound perception of a system in which women do not have full rights to themselves. The exchange of women becomes an obfuscation if it is seen as a cultural necessity and when it is used as the single tool with which an analysis of a particular kinship system is approached.

If Lévi-Strauss is correct in seeing the exchange of women as a fundamental principle of kinship, the subordination of women can be seen as a product of the relationships by which sex and gender are organized and produced. The economic oppression of women is derivative and secondary. But there is an "economics" of sex and gender, and what we need is a political economy of sexual systems. We need to study each society to determine the exact mechanisms by which particular conventions of sexuality are produced and maintained. The "exchange of women" is an initial step toward building an arsenal of concepts with which sexual systems can be described.

Deeper into the Labyrinth

More concepts can be derived from an essay by Lévi-Strauss, "The Family," in which he introduces other considerations into his analysis of kinship. In *The Elementary Structures of Kinship*, he describes rules and systems of sexual combination. In "The Family," he raises the issue of the preconditions necessary for marriage systems to operate. He asks what sort of "people" are required by kinship systems, by way of an analysis of the sexual division of labor.

Although every society has some sort of division of tasks by sex, the assignment of any particular task to one sex or the other varies enormously. In some groups, agriculture is the work of women, in others, the work of men. Women carry the heavy burdens in some societies, men in others. There are even examples of female hunters and warriors, and of men performing child-care tasks. Lévi-Strauss concludes from a survey of the division of labor by sex that it is not a biological specialization, but must have some other purpose. This purpose, he argues, is to insure the union of men and women by making the smallest viable economic unit contain at least one man and one woman.

> The very fact that it [the sexual division of labor] varies endlessly according to the society selected for consideration shows that ... it is the mere fact of its existence which is mysteriously required, the form under which it comes to exist being utterly irrelevant, at least from the point of view of any natural necessity ... [T]he sexual division of labor is nothing else than a device to institute a reciprocal state of dependency between the sexes.[27]

The division of labor by sex can therefore be seen as a "taboo": a taboo against the sameness of men and women, a taboo dividing the sexes into two mutually exclusive categories, a taboo which exacerbates the biological differences between the sexes and thereby *creates* gender. The division of labor can also be seen as a taboo against sexual arrangements other than those containing at least one man and one woman, thereby enjoining heterosexual marriage.

The argument in "The Family" displays a radical questioning of all human sexual arrangements, in which no aspect of sexuality is taken for granted as "natural" (Hertz constructs a similar argument for a thoroughly cultural explanation of the denigration of left-handedness).[28] Rather, all manifest forms of sex and gender are seen as being constituted by the imperatives of social systems. From such a perspective, even *The Elementary Structures of Kinship* can be seen to assume certain preconditions. In purely logical terms, a rule forbidding some marriages and commanding others presupposes a rule enjoining marriage. And marriage presupposes individuals who are disposed to marry.

It is of interest to carry this kind of deductive enterprise even further than Lévi-Strauss does, and to explicate the logical structure which underlies his entire analysis of kinship. At the most general level, the social organization of sex rests upon gender, obligatory heterosexuality, and the constraint of female sexuality.

Gender is a socially imposed division of the sexes. It is a product of the social relations of sexuality. Kinship systems rest upon marriage. They therefore transform males and females into "men" and "women," each an incomplete half which can only find wholeness when united with the other. Men and women are, of course, different. But they are not as different as day and night, earth and sky, yin and yang, life and death. In fact, from the standpoint of nature, men and women are closer to each other than either is to anything else – for instance, mountains, kangaroos, or coconut palms. The idea that men and women are more different from one another than either is from anything else must come from somewhere other than nature. Furthermore, although there is an average difference between males and females on a variety of traits, the range of variation of those traits shows considerable overlap. There will always be some women who are taller than some men, for instance, even though men are on the average taller than women. But the idea that men and women are two mutually exclusive categories must arise out of something other than a nonexistent "natural" opposition.[29] Far from being an expression of natural differences, exclusive gender identity is the suppression of natural similarities. It requires repression: in men, of whatever is the local version of "feminine" traits; in women, of the local definition of "masculine" traits. The division of the sexes has the effect of repressing some of the personality characteristics of virtually everyone, men and women. The same social system which oppresses women in its relations of exchange, oppresses everyone in its insistence upon a rigid division of personality.

Furthermore, individuals are engendered in order that marriage be guaranteed. Lévi-Strauss comes dangerously close to saying that heterosexuality is an instituted process. If biological and hormonal imperatives were as overwhelming as popular mythology would have them, it would hardly be necessary to insure heterosexual unions by means of economic interdependency. Moreover, the incest taboo presupposes a prior, less artic-ulate taboo on homosexuality. A prohibition against some heterosexual unions assumes a taboo against non-heterosexual unions. Gender is not only an identification with one sex; it also entails that sexual desire be directed toward the other sex. The sexual division of labor is implicated in both aspects of gender – male and female it creates them, and it creates them heterosexual. The suppression of the homosexual component of human sexuality, and by corollary, the oppression of homosexuals, is therefore a product of the same system whose rules and relations oppress women....

In fact, the situation is not so simple, as is obvious when we move from the level of generalities to the analysis of specific sexual systems. Kinship systems do not merely encourage heterosexuality to the detriment of homosexuality. In the first place, specific forms of heterosexuality may be required. For instance, some marriage systems have a rule of obligatory cross-cousin marriage. A person in such a system is not only hetero-sexual, but "cross-cousin-sexual." If the rule of marriage further specifies matrilateral cross-cousin marriage, then a man will be "mother's-brother's-daughter-sexual" and a woman will be "father's-sister's-son-sexual."

On the other hand, the very complexities of a kinship system may result in particular forms of institutionalized homosexuality. In many New Guinea groups, men and women are considered to be so inimical to one another that the period spent by a male child *in utero* negates his maleness. Since male life force is thought to reside in semen, the boy can overcome the malevolent effects of his fetal history by obtaining and consuming semen. He does so through a homosexual partnership with an older male kinsman.[30]

In kinship systems where bridewealth determines the statuses of husband and wife, the simple prerequisites of marriage and gender may be overridden. Among the Azande, women are monopolized by older men. A young man of means may, however, take a boy as wife while he waits to come of age. He simply pays a bridewealth (in spears) for the boy, who is thereby turned into a wife.[31] In Dahomey, a women could turn herself into a husband if she possessed the necessary bridewealth.[32]

The institutionalized "transvesticism" of the Mohave permitted a person to change from one sex to the other. An anatomical man could become a woman by means of a special ceremony, and an anatomical woman could in the same way become a man. The transvestite then took a wife or husband of her/his own anatomical sex and opposite social sex. These marriages, which we would label homosexual, were heterosexual ones by Mohave standards, unions of opposite socially defined sexes. By comparison with our society, this whole arrangement permitted a great deal of freedom. However, a person was not permitted to be some of both genders – he/she could be either male or female, but not a little of each.[33]

In all of the above examples, the rules of gender division and obligatory heterosexuality are present even in their transformations. These two rules apply equally to
the constraint of both male and female behavior and personality. Kinship systems
dictate some sculpting of the sexuality of both sexes. But it can be deduced from *The
Elementary Structures of Kinship* that more constraint is applied to females when
they are pressed into the service of kinship than to males. If women are exchanged,
in whatever sense we take the term, marital debts are reckoned in female flesh.
A woman must become the sexual partner of some man to whom she is owed as
return on a previous marriage. If a girl is promised in infancy, her refusal to participate as an adult would disrupt the flow of debts and promises. It would be in the
interests of the smooth and continuous operation of such a system if the woman in
question did not have too many ideas of her own about whom she might want to
sleep with. From the standpoint of the system, the preferred female sexuality would
be one which responded to the desire of others, rather than one which actively
desired and sought a response.

This generality, like the ones about gender and heterosexuality, is also subject to
considerable variation and free play in actual systems. The Lele and the Kuma provide
two of the clearest ethnographic examples of the exchange of women. Men in both
cultures are perpetually engaged in schemes which necessitate that they have full control
over the sexual destinies of their female kinswomen. Much of the drama in both societies
consists in female attempts to evade the sexual control of their kinsmen. Nevertheless,
female resistance in both cases is severely circumscribed.[34]

One last generality could be predicted as a consequence of the exchange of women
under a system in which rights to women are held by men. What would happen if our
hypothetical woman not only refused the man to whom she was promised, but asked for
a woman instead? If a single refusal were disruptive, a double refusal would be insurrectionary. If each woman is promised to some man, neither has a right to dispose of
herself. If two women managed to extricate themselves from the debt nexus, two other
women would have to be found to replace them. As long as men have rights in women
which women do not have in themselves, it would be sensible to expect that homosexuality
in women would be subject to more suppression than in men.

In summary, some basic generalities about the organization of human sexuality can be
derived from an exegesis of Lévi-Strauss' theories of kinship. These are the incest taboo,
obligatory heterosexuality, and an asymmetric division of the sexes. The asymmetry of
gender – the difference between exchanger and exchanged – entails the constraint of
female sexuality. Concrete kinship systems will have more specific conventions, and
these conventions vary a great deal. While particular socio-sexual systems vary, each one
is specific, and individuals within it will have to conform to a finite set of possibilities.
Each new generation must learn and become its sexual destiny, each person must be
encoded with its appropriate status within the system. It would be extraordinary for
one of us to calmly assume that we would conventionally marry a mother's brother's
daughter, or a father's sister's son. Yet there are groups in which such a marital future is
taken for granted.

Anthropology, and descriptions of kinship systems, do not explain the mechanisms by
which children are engraved with the conventions of sex and gender. Psychoanalysis, on
the other hand, is a theory about the reproduction of kinship. Psychoanalysis describes
the residue left within individuals by their confrontation with the rules and regulations
of sexuality of the societies to which they are born.

Psychoanalysis and Its Discontents

The battle between psychoanalysis and the women's and gay movements has become legendary. In part, this confrontation between sexual revolutionaries and the clinical establishment has been due to the evolution of psychoanalysis in the United States, where clinical tradition has fetishized anatomy. The child is thought to travel through its organismic stages until it reaches its anatomical destiny and the missionary position. Clinical practice has often seen its mission as the repair of individuals who somehow have become derailed en route to their "biological" aim. Transforming moral law into scientific law, clinical practice has acted to enforce sexual convention upon unruly participants. In this sense, psychoanalysis has often become more than a theory of the mechanisms of the reproduction of sexual arrangements; it has been one of those mechanisms. Since the aim of the feminist and gay revolts is to dismantle the apparatus of sexual enforcement, a critique of psychoanalysis has been in order....

The organization of sex and gender once had functions other than itself – it organized society. Now, it only organizes and reproduces itself. The kinds of relationships of sexuality established in the dim human past still dominate our sexual lives, our ideas about men and women, and the ways we raise our children. But they lack the functional load they once carried. One of the most conspicuous features of kinship is that it has been systematically stripped of its functions – political, economic, educational, and organizational. It has been reduced to its barest bones – *sex and gender*.

Human sexual life will always be subject to convention and human intervention. It will never be completely "natural," if only because our species is social, cultural, and articulate. The wild profusion of infantile sexuality will always be tamed. The confrontation between immature and helpless infants and the developed social life of their elders will probably always leave some residue of disturbance. But the mechanisms and aims of this process need not be largely independent of conscious choice. Cultural evolution provides us with the opportunity to seize control of the means of sexuality, reproduction, and socialization, and to make conscious decisions to liberate human sexual life from the archaic relationships which deform it. Ultimately, a thorough-going feminist revolution would liberate more than women. It would liberate forms of sexual expression, and it would liberate human personality from the straitjacket of gender.

> "Daddy, daddy, you bastard, I'm through."
>
> *Sylvia Plath*

In the course of this essay I have tried to construct a theory of women's oppression by borrowing concepts from anthropology and psychoanalysis. But Lévi-Strauss and Freud write within an intellectual tradition produced by a culture in which women are oppressed. The danger in my enterprise is that the sexism in the tradition of which they are a part tends to be dragged in with each borrowing. "We cannot utter a single destructive proposition which has not already slipped into the form, the logic, and the implicit postulations of precisely what it seeks to contest."[35] And what slips in is formidable. Both psychoanalysis and structural anthropology are, in one sense, the most sophisticated ideologies of sexism around.[36]

For instance, Lévi-Strauss sees women as being like words, which are misused when they are not "communicated" and exchanged. On the last page of a very long book, he observes that this creates something of a contradiction in women, since women are at the same time "speakers" and "spoken." His only comment on this contradiction is this:

> But woman could never become just a sign and nothing more, since even in a man's world she is still a person, and since insofar as she is defined as a sign she must be recognized as a generator of signs. In the matrimonial dialogue of men, woman is never purely what is spoken about; for if women in general represent a certain category of signs, destined to a certain kind of communication, each woman preserves a particular value arising from her talent, before and after marriage, for taking her part in a duet. In contrast to words, which have wholly become signs, woman has remained at once a sign and a value. *This explains why the relations between the sexes have preserved that affective richness, ardour and mystery which doubtless originally permeated the entire universe of human communications.*[37]

This is an extraordinary statement. Why is he not, at this point, denouncing what kinship systems do to women, instead of presenting one of the greatest rip-offs of all time as the root of romance?

A similar insensitivity is revealed within psychoanalysis by the inconsistency with which it assimilates the critical implications of its own theory. For instance, Freud did not hesitate to recognize that his findings posed a challenge to conventional morality:

> We cannot avoid observing with critical eyes, and we have found that it is impossible to give our support to conventional sexual morality or to approve highly of the means by which society attempts to arrange the practical problems of sexuality in life. We can demonstrate with ease that what the world calls its code of morals demands more sacrifices than it is worth, and that its behavior is neither dictated by honesty nor instituted with wisdom.[38]

Nevertheless, when psychoanalysis demonstrates with equal facility that the ordinary components of feminine personality are masochism, self-hatred, and passivity,[39] a similar judgment is not made. Instead, a double standard of interpretation is employed. Masochism is bad for men, essential to women. Adequate narcissism is necessary for men, impossible for women. Passivity is tragic in man, while lack of passivity is tragic in a woman.

It is this double standard which enables clinicians to try to accommodate women to a role whose destructiveness is so lucidly detailed in their own theories. It is the same inconsistent attitude which permits therapists to consider lesbianism as a problem to be cured, rather than as the resistance to a bad situation that their own theory suggests.[40]

There are points within the analytic discussions of femininity where one might say, "This is oppression of women," or "We can demonstrate with ease that what the world calls femininity demands more sacrifices than it is worth." It is precisely at such points that the implications of the theory are ignored, and are replaced with formulations whose purpose is to keep those implications firmly lodged in the theoretical unconscious. It is at these points that all sorts of mysterious chemical substances, joys in pain, and biological aims are substituted for a critical assessment of the costs of femininity. These substitutions are the symptoms of theoretical repression, in that they are not consistent with the usual canons of psychoanalytic argument. The extent to which these rationalizations of femininity go against the grain of psychoanalytic logic is strong evidence for the extent of the need to suppress the radical and feminist implications of the theory of femininity (Deutsch's discussions are excellent examples of this process of substitution and repression).

The argument which must be woven in order to assimilate Lévi-Strauss and Freud into feminist theory is somewhat tortuous. I have engaged it for several reasons. First, while neither Lévi-Strauss nor Freud questions the undoubted sexism endemic to the systems they describe, the questions which ought to be posed are blindingly obvious. Secondly, their work enables us to isolate sex and gender from "mode of production," and to counter a certain tendency to explain sex oppression as a reflex of economic forces. Their work provides a framework in which the full weight of sexuality and marriage can be incorporated into an analysis of sex oppression. It suggests a conception of the women's movement as analogous to, rather than isomorphic with, the working-class movement, each addressing a different source of human discontent. In Marx's vision, the working-class movement would do more than throw off the burden of its own exploitation. It also had the potential to change society, to liberate humanity, to create a classless society. Perhaps the women's movement has the task of effecting the same kind of social change for a system of which Marx had only an imperfect apperception. Something of this sort is implicit in Wittig – the dictatorship of the Amazon *guerillères* is a temporary means for achieving a genderless society.

The sex/gender system is not immutably oppressive and has lost much of its traditional function. Nevertheless, it will not wither away in the absence of opposition. It still carries the social burden of sex and gender, of socializing the young, and of providing ultimate propositions about the nature of human beings themselves. And it serves economic and political ends other than those it was originally designed to further.[41] The sex/gender system must be reorganized through political action.

Finally, the exegesis of Lévi-Strauss and Freud suggests a certain vision of feminist politics and the feminist utopia. It suggests that we should not aim for the elimination of men, but for the elimination of the social system which creates sexism and gender. I personally find a vision of an Amazon matriarchate, in which men are reduced to servitude or oblivion (depending on the possibilities for parthenogenetic reproduction), distasteful and inadequate. Such a vision maintains gender and the division of the sexes. It is a vision which simply inverts the arguments of those who base their case for inevitable male dominance on ineradicable and significant biological differences between the sexes. But we are not only oppressed as women, we are oppressed by having to be women, or men as the case may be. I personally feel that the feminist movement must dream of even more than the elimination of the oppression of women. It must dream of the elimination of obligatory sexualities and sex roles. The dream I find most compelling is one of an androgynous and genderless (though not sexless) society, in which one's sexual anatomy is irrelevant to who one is, what one does, and with whom one makes love.

The Political Economy of Sex

It would be nice to be able to conclude here with the implications for feminism and gay liberation of the overlap between Freud and Lévi-Strauss. But I must suggest, tentatively, a next step on the agenda: a Marxian analysis of sex/gender systems. Sex/gender systems are not ahistorical emanations of the human mind; they are products of historical human activity.

We need, for instance, an analysis of the evolution of sexual exchange along the lines of Marx's discussion in *Capital* of the evolution of money and commodities. There is an economics and a politics to sex/gender systems which is obscured by the concept of "exchange of women." For instance, a system in which women are exchangeable only for one another has different effects on women than one in which there is a commodity equivalent for women.

> That marriage in simple societies involves an "exchange" is a somewhat vague notion that has often confused the analysis of social systems. The extreme case is the exchange of "sisters," formerly practiced in parts of Australia and Africa. Here the term has the precise dictionary meaning of "to be received as an equivalent for," "to give and receive recipro- cally." From quite a different standpoint the virtually universal incest prohibition means that marriage systems necessarily involve "exchanging" siblings for spouses, giving rise to a reciprocity that is purely notational. But in most societies marriage is mediated by a set of intermediary transactions. If we see these transactions as simply implying immediate or long-term reciprocity, then the analysis is likely to be blurred.... The analysis is further limited if one regards the passage of property simply as a symbol of the transfer of rights, for then the nature of the objects handed over ... is of little importance.... Neither of these approaches is wrong; both are inadequate.[42]

There are systems in which there is no equivalent for a woman. To get a wife, a man must have a daughter, a sister, or other female kinswoman in whom he has a right of bestowal. He must have control over some female flesh. The Lele and Kuma are cases in point. Lele men scheme constantly in order to stake claims in some as yet unborn girl, and scheme further to make good their claims.[43] A Kuma girl's marriage is determined by an intricate web of debts, and she has little say in choosing her husband. A girl is usually married against her will, and her groom shoots an arrow into her thigh to sym- bolically prevent her from running away. The young wives almost always do run away, only to be returned to their new husbands by an elaborate conspiracy enacted by their kin and affines.[44]

In other societies, there is an equivalent for women. A woman can be converted into bridewealth, and bridewealth can be in turn converted into a woman. The dynamics of such systems vary accordingly, as does the specific kind of pressure exerted upon women. The marriage of a Melpa woman is not a return for a previous debt. Each transaction is self-contained, in that the payment of a bridewealth in pigs and shells will cancel the debt. The Melpa woman therefore has more latitude in choosing her husband than does her Kuma counterpart. On the other hand, her destiny is linked to bridewealth. If her husband's kin are slow to pay, her kin may encourage her to leave him. On the other hand, if her consanguineal kin are satisfied with the balance of payments, they may refuse to back her in the event that she wants to leave her husband. Moreover, her male kinsmen use the bridewealth for their own purposes, in *moka* exchange and for their own marriages. If a woman leaves her husband, some or all of the bridewealth will have to be returned. If, as is usually the case, the pigs and shells have been distributed or promised, her kin will be reluctant to back her in the event of marital discord. And each time a woman divorces and remarries, her value in bridewealth tends to depreciate. On the whole, her male consanguines will lose in the event of a divorce, unless the groom has been delinquent in his payments. While the Melpa woman is freer as a new bride than a Kuma woman, the bridewealth system makes divorce difficult or impossible.[45]

In some societies, like the Nuer, bridewealth can only be converted into brides. In others, bridewealth can be converted into something else, like political prestige. In this case, a woman's marriage is implicated in a political system. In the Big Man systems of Highland New Guinea, the material which circulates for women also circulates in the exchanges on which political power is based. Within the political system, men are in constant need of valuables to disburse, and they are dependent upon input. They depend not only upon their immediate partners, but upon the partners of their partners, to several degrees of remove. If a man has to return some bridewealth he may not be able to give it to someone who planned to give it to someone else who intended to use it to give a feast upon which his status depends. Big Men are therefore concerned with the domestic affairs of others, whose relationship with them may be extremely indirect. There are cases in which headmen intervene in marital disputes involving indirect trading partners in order that *moka* exchanges not be disrupted.[46] The weight of this entire system may come to rest upon one woman kept in a miserable marriage.

In short, there are other questions to ask of a marriage system than whether or not it exchanges women. Is the woman traded for a woman, or is there an equivalent? Is this equivalent only for women, or can it be turned into something else? If it can be turned into something else, is it turned into political power or wealth? On the other hand, can bridewealth be obtained only in marital exchange, or can it be obtained from elsewhere? Can women be accumulated through amassing wealth? Can wealth be accumulated by disposing of women? Is a marriage system part of a system of stratification?[47]

These last questions point to another task for a political economy of sex. Kinship and marriage are always parts of total social systems, and are always tied into economic and political arrangements.

> Lévi-Strauss ... rightly argues that the structural implications of a marriage can only be understood if we think of it as one item in a whole series of transactions between kin groups. So far, so good. But in none of the examples which he provides in his book does he carry this principle far enough. The reciprocities of kinship obligation are not merely symbols of alliance, they are also economic transactions, political transactions, charters to rights of domicile and land use. No useful picture of "how a kinship system works" can be provided unless these several aspects or implications of the kinship organization are considered simultaneously.[48]

Among the Kachin, the relationship of a tenant to a landlord is also a relationship between a son-in-law and a father-in-law. "The procedure for acquiring land rights of any kind is in almost all cases tantamount to marrying a woman from the lineage of the lord."[49] In the Kachin system, bridewealth moves from commoners to aristocrats, women moving in the opposite direction.

> From an economic aspect the effect of matrilateral cross-cousin marriage is that, on balance, the headman's lineage constantly pays wealth to the chief's lineage in the form of bridewealth. The payment can also, from an analytical point of view, be regarded as a rent paid to the senior landlord by the tenant. The most important part of this payment is in the form of consumer goods – namely cattle. The chief converts this perishable wealth into imperishable prestige through the medium of spectacular feasting. The ultimate consumers of the goods are in this way the original producers, namely, the commoners who attend the feast.[50]

In another example, it is traditional in the Trobriands for a man to send a harvest gift – *urigubu* – of yams to his sister's household. For the commoners, this amounts to a simple circulation of yams. But the chief is polygamous, and marries a woman from each subdistrict within his domain. Each of these subdistricts therefore sends *urigubu* to the chief, providing him with a bulging storehouse out of which he finances feasts, craft production, and *kula* expeditions. This "fund of power" underwrites the political system and forms the basis for chiefly power.[51]

In some systems, position in a political hierarchy and position in a marriage system are intimately linked. In traditional Tonga, women married up in rank. Thus, low-ranking lineages would send women to higher-ranking lineages. Women of the highest lineage were married into the "house of Fiji," a lineage defined as outside the political system. If the highest-ranking chief gave his sister to a lineage other than one which had no part in the ranking system, he would no longer be the highest-ranking chief. Rather, the lineage of his sister's son would outrank his own. In times of political rearrangement, the demotion of the previous high-ranking lineage was formalized when it gave a wife to a lineage which it had formerly outranked. In traditional Hawaii, the situation was the reverse. Women married down, and the dominant lineage gave wives to junior lines. A paramount would either marry a sister or obtain a wife from Tonga. When a junior lineage usurped rank, it formalized its position by giving a wife to its former senior line.

There is even some tantalizing data suggesting that marriage systems may be implicated in the evolution of social strata, and perhaps in the development of early states. The first round of the political consolidation which resulted in the formation of a state in Madagascar occurred when one chief obtained title to several autonomous districts through the vagaries of marriage and inheritance.[52] In Samoa, legends place the origin of the paramount title – the *Tafa'ifa* – as a result of intermarriage between ranking members of four major lineages. My thoughts are too speculative, my data too sketchy, to say much on this subject. But a search ought to be undertaken for data which might demonstrate how marriage systems intersect with large-scale political processes like state-making. Marriage systems might be implicated in a number of ways: in the accumulation of wealth and the maintenance of differential access to political and economic resources; in the building of alliances; in the consolidation of high-ranking persons into a single closed strata of endogamous kin.

These examples – like the Kachin and the Trobriand ones – indicate that sexual systems cannot, in the final analysis, be understood in complete isolation. A full-bodied analysis of women in a single society, or throughout history, must take *everything* into account: the evolution of commodity forms in women, systems of land tenure, political arrangements, subsistence technology, etc. Equally important, economic and political analyses are incomplete if they do not consider women, marriage, and sexuality. Traditional concerns of anthropology and social science – such as the evolution of social stratification and the origin of the state – must be reworked to include the implications of matrilateral cross-cousin marriage, surplus extracted in the form of daughters, the conversion of female labor into male wealth, the conversion of female lives into marriage alliances, the contribution of marriage to political power, and the transformations which all of these varied aspects of society have undergone in the course of time.

This sort of endeavor is, in the final analysis, exactly what Engels tried to do in his effort to weave a coherent analysis of so many of the diverse aspects of social life. He tried to relate men and women, town and country, kinship and state, forms of property, systems of land tenure, convertibility of wealth, forms of exchange, the technology of food production, and forms of trade, to name a few, into a systematic historical account. Eventually, someone will have to write a new version of *The Origin of the Family, Private Property, and the State*, recognizing the mutual interdependence of sexuality, economics, and politics without underestimating the full significance of each in human society.

Notes

1 Karl Marx, *Wage Labor and Capital* (New York: International Publishers, 1971), p. 28.

2 Louis Althusser and Etienne Balibar, *Reading Capital* (London: New Left Books, 1970), pp. 11–69.

3 Moving between Marxism, structuralism, and psychoanalysis produces a certain clash of episte-mologies. In particular, structuralism is a can from which worms crawl out all over the epistemo-logical map. Rather than trying to cope with this problem, I have more or less ignored the fact that Lacan and Lévi-Strauss are among the foremost living ancestors of the contemporary French intellectual revolution (see Michel Foucault, *The Order of Things* (New York, 1970)). It would be fun, interesting, and, if this were France, essential, to start my argument from the center of the structuralist maze and work my way out from there, along the lines of a "dialectical theory of signifying practices" (see Robert Hefner, "The *Tel Quel* Ideology: Material Practice Upon Material Practice," *Substance* 8 (1974), pp. 127–38).

4 Margaret Benston, "The Political Economy of Women's Liberation," *Monthly Review* 21, no. (1969), pp. 13–27; Mariarosa Dalla Costa and Selma James, *The Power of Women and the Subversion of the Community* (Bristol: Falling Wall Press, 1972); Isabel Larguia and John Dumoulin, "Towards a Science of Women's Liberation," *NACLA Newsletter* 6, no. 10 (1972), pp. 3–20; Ira Gerstein, "Domestic Work and Capitalism," *Radical America* 7, nos 4 and 5 (1973), pp. 101–28; Lise Vogel, "The Earthly Family," *Radical America* 7, nos 4 and 5 (1973), pp. 9–50; Wally Secombe, "Housework Under Capitalism," *New Left Review* 83 (1973), pp. 3–24; Jean Gardiner, "Political Economy of Female Labor in Capitalist Society," unpublished manuscript; M. and J. Rowntree, "More on the Political Economy of Women's Liberation," *Monthly Review* 21, no. 8 (1970), pp. 26–32.

5 Karl Marx, *Theories of Surplus Value*, Part 1 (Moscow: Progress Publishers, 1969), p. 399.

6 Karl Marx, *Capital*, vol. 1 (New York: International Publishers, 1972), p. 572.

7 Ibid., p. 171.

8 A lot of the debate on women and housework has centered around the question of whether or not housework is "productive" labor. Strictly speaking, housework is not ordinarily "productive" in the technical sense of the term (I. Gough, "Marx and Productive Labor," *New Left Review* 76 (1972), pp. 47–72; Marx, *Theories of Surplus Value*, pp. 387–413). But this distinction is irrelevant to the main line of the argument. Housework may not be "productive," in the sense of directly producing surplus value and capital, and yet be a crucial element in the production of surplus value and capital by the capitalist. But to explain women's usefulness to capitalism is one thing. To argue that this usefulness explains the genesis of the oppression of women is quite another. It is precisely at this point that the analysis of capitalism ceases to explain very much about women and the oppression of women.

9 Robert Murphy, "Social Structure and Sex Antagonism," *Southwestern Journal of Anthropology* 15, no. 1 (1959), pp. 81–96.

10 Marx, *Capital*, p. 171.

11 Frederick Engels, *The Origin of the Family, Private Property, and the State* (New York: International Publishers, 1972), pp. 71–2.

12 That some of them are pretty bizarre, from our point of view, only demonstrates the point that sexuality is expressed through the intervention of culture. (See Clellan Ford and Frank Beach, *Patterns of Sexual Behavior* (New York: Harper, 1972).) Some examples may be chosen from among the exotica in which anthropologists delight.

Among the Banaro, marriage involves several socially sanctioned sexual partnerships. When a woman is married, she is initiated into intercourse by the sib-friend of her groom's father. After bearing a child by this man, she begins to have intercourse with her husband. She also has an institutionalized partnership with the sib-friend of her husband. A man's partners include his wife, the wife of his sib-friend, and the wife of his sib-friend's son. (See Richard Thurnwald, "Banaro Society," *Memoirs of the American Anthropological Association* 3, no. 4 (1916), pp. 251–391.) Multiple intercourse is a more pronounced custom among the Marind Anim. At the time of marriage the bride has intercourse with all of the members of the groom's clan, the groom coming last. Every major festival is accompanied by a practice known as otiv-bombari, in which semen is collected for ritual purposes. A few women have intercourse with many men, and the resulting semen is collected in coconut-shell buckets. A Marind male is subjected to multiple homosexual intercourse during initiation (J. Van Baal, *Dema* (The Hague: Nijhoff, 1966)). Among the Etoro, heterosexual intercourse is taboo for between 205 and 260 days a year (Raymond Kelly, "Witchcraft and Sexual Relations: An Exploration of the Social and Semantic Implications of the Structure of Belief," paper read at the 73rd Annual Meeting of the American Anthropological Association, Mexico City). In much of New Guinea, men fear copulation and think that it will kill them if they engage in it without magical precautions (R. M. Glasse, "The Mask of Venery," paper read at the 70th annual meeting of the American Anthropological Association, New York City, December 1971; M. J. Meggitt, "Male–Female Relationships in the Highlands of Australian New Guinea," *American Anthropologist* 66, no. 4, part 2 (1972), pp. 204–24). Usually, such ideas of feminine pollution express the subordination of women. But symbolic systems contain internal contradictions, whose logical extensions sometimes lead to inversions of the propositions on which a system is based. In New Britain, men's fear of sex is so extreme that rape appears to be feared by men rather than women. Women run after the men, who flee from them, women are the sexual aggressors, and it is bridegrooms who are reluctant (Jane C. Goodale and Ann Chowning, "The Contaminating Woman," paper read at the 70th annual meeting of the American Anthropological Association, 1971). Other interesting sexual variations can be found in Yalmon ("On the Purity of Women in the Castes of Ceylon and Malabar," *Journal of the Royal Anthropological Institute* 93, no. 1 (1963), pp. 25–58) and K. Gough ("The Nayars and the Definition of Marriage," *Journal of the Royal Anthropological Institute* 89 (1959), pp. 23–4).

13   Engels thought that men acquired wealth in the form of herds and, wanting to pass this wealth to their own children, overthrew "mother right" in favor of patrilineal inheritance. "The overthrow of mother right was the *world historical defeat of the female sex*. The man took command in the home also; the woman was degraded and reduced to servitude; she became the slave of his lust and a mere instrument for the production of children" (Engels, *Origin of the Family*, pp. 120–1; italics in original). As has been often pointed out, women do not necessarily have significant social authority in societies practicing matrilineal inheritance (David Schneider and Kathleen Gough (eds.), *Matrilineal Kinship* (Berkeley: University of California Press, 1961)).

14   E. E. Evans-Pritchard, *Kinship and Marriage Among the Nuer* (London: Oxford University Press, 1951), pp. 107–9.

15   Marshall Sahlins, "The Origin of Society," *Scientific American* 203, no. 3 (1960), pp. 76–86; Frank Livingstone, "Genetics, Ecology, and the Origins of Incest and Exogamy," *Current Anthropology* 10, no. 1 (1969), pp. 45–9; Claude Lévi-Strauss, *The Elementary Structures of Kinship* (Boston: Beacon Press, 1969).

16   See Elizabeth Fee, "The Sexual Politics of Victorian Social Anthropology," *Feminist Studies* (Winter/Spring 1973), pp. 23–9.

17   See Marshall Sahlins, *Stone Age Economics* (Chicago: Aldine Atherton, 1972), ch. 4.

18   Claude Lévi-Strauss, *The Elementary Structures of Kinship* (Boston: Beacon Press, 1969), p. 27.

19   Bronislaw Malinowski, *The Sexual Life of Savages* (London: Routledge, 1929).

20   Sahlins, *Stone Age Economics*, pp. 169, 175.

21   Lévi-Strauss, *Elementary Structures*, p. 51.

22   Ibid., p. 481.

23   Best, cited in Lévi-Strauss, *Elementary Structures*, p. 481.

24   "What, would you like to marry your sister? What is the matter with you? Don't you want a brother-in-law? Don't you realize that if you marry another man's sister and another man marries your sister, you will have at least two brothers-in-law, while if you marry your own sister you will have none? With whom will you hunt, with whom will you garden, whom will you go visit?" (Arapesh, cited in Lévi-Strauss, *Elementary Structures*, p. 485).

25   Lévi-Strauss, *Elementary Structures*, p. 161. This analysis of society as based on bonds between men by means of women makes the separatist responses of the women's movement thoroughly intelligible. Separatism can be seen as a mutation in social structure, as an attempt to form social groups based on unmediated bonds between women. It can also be seen as a radical denial of men's "rights" in women and as a claim by women of rights in themselves.

26 Marilyn Strathern, *Women In Between* (New York: Seminar, 1971), p. 161.

27 Claude Lévi-Strauss, "The Family," in H. Shapiro (ed.), *Man, Culture, and Society* (London: Oxford University Press, 1971), pp. 347–8.

28 Robert Hertz, *Death and the Right Hand* (Glencove, 1960).

29 "The woman shall not wear that which pertaineth unto a man neither shall a man put on a woman's garment: for all that do so *are* abomination unto the Lord they God" (Deuteronomy 22:5; emphasis not mine).

30 Kelly, "Witchcraft and Sexual Relations"; Van Baal, *Dema*; F. E. Williams, *Papuans of the Trans-Fly* (Oxford: Clarendon, 1936).

31 E. E. Evans-Pritchard, "Sexual Inversion Among the Azande," *American Anthropologist* 72 (1970), pp. 1428–34.

32 Melville Herskovitz, "A Note on 'Woman Marriage' in Dahomey," *Africa* 10, no. 3 (1937), pp. 335–41.

33 George Devereaux, "Institutionalized Homosexuality Among Mohave Indians," *Human Biology* 9 (1937), pp. 498–529; Douglas McMurtrie, "A Legend of Lesbian Love Among North American Indians," *Urologic and Cutaneous Review* (April, 1914), pp. 192–3; David Sonenschein, "Homosexuality as a Subject of Anthropological Investigation," *Anthropological Quarterly* 2 (1966), pp. 73–82.

34 Mary Douglas, *The Lele of Kasai* (London: Oxford University Press, 1963); Marie Reay, *The Kuma* (London: Cambridge University Press, 1959).

35 Jacques Derrida, "Structure, Sign, and Play," in R. Macksey and E. Donatio (eds.), *The Structuralist Controversy* (Baltimore: Johns Hopkins University Press, 1972), p. 250.

36 Parts of Wittig's *Les Guerillères* (New York: Avon, 1973) appear to be tirades against Lévi-Strauss and Lacan. For instance:

> Has he not indeed written, power and the possession of women leisure and the enjoyment of women? He writes that you are currency, an item of exchange. He writes, barter, barter, possession and acquisition of women and merchandise. Better for you to see your guts in the sun and utter the death rattle than to live a life that anyone can appropriate. What belongs to you on this earth? Only death. No power on earth can take that away from you. And – consider, explain, tell yourself – if happiness consists in the possession of something, then hold fast to this sovereign happiness – to die. (pp. 115–16; see also pp. 106–7; 113–14; 134)

The awareness of French feminists of Lévi-Strauss and Lacan is most clearly evident in a group called "Psychoanalyse et Politique," which defined its task as a feminist use and critique of Lacanian psychoanalysis.

37 Lévi-Strauss, *Elementary Structures*, p. 496; my italics.

38 Sigmund Freud, *A General Introduction to Psychoanalysis* (Garden City, NY: Garden City Publishing Company, 1943), pp. 376–7.

39 "Every woman adores a fascist" – Sylvia Plath.

40 One clinician, Charlotte Wolff (*Love Between Women* (London: Duckworth, 1971)) has taken the psychoanalytic theory of womanhood to its logical extreme and proposed that lesbianism is a healthy response to female socialization.

> Women who do not rebel against the status of object have declared themselves defeated as persons in their own right. (p. 65)
>   The lesbian girl is the one who, by all means at her disposal, will try to find a place of safety inside and outside the family, through her fight for equality with the male. She will not, like other women, play up to him: indeed, she despises the very idea of it. (p. 59)
>   The lesbian was and is unquestionably in the avant-garde of the fight for equality of the sexes, and for the psychical liberation of women. (p. 66)

It is revealing to compare Wolff's discussion with the articles on lesbianism in Marmor, *Sexual Inversion* (London: Basic Books, 1965).

41 John Finley Scott, "The Role of Collegiate Sororities in Maintaining Class and Ethnic Endogamy," *American Sociological Review* 30, no. 4 (1965), pp. 415–26.

42 Jack Goody and S. J. Tambiah, *Bridewealth and Dowry* (Cambridge: Cambridge University Press, 1973), p. 2.

43 Douglas, *The Lele of Kasai*.

44 Reay, *The Kuma*.

45 Strathern, *Women In Between*.

46 Ralph Bulmer, "Political Aspects of the Moka Ceremonial Exchange System Among the Kyaka People of the Western Highlands of New Guinea," *Oceania* 31, no. 1 (1969), pp. 1–13.

47 Another line of inquiry would compare bridewealth systems to dowry systems. Many of these questions are treated in Goody and Tambiah, *Bridewealth and Dowry*.

48 Edmund Leach, *Rethinking Anthropology* (New York: Humanities Press, 1971), p. 90.

49 Ibid., p. 88.

50 Ibid., p. 89.

51 Bronislaw Malinowski, "The Primitive Economics of the Trobriand Islanders," in T. Harding and B. Wallace, eds., *Cultures of the Pacific* (New York: Free Press, 1970).

52 Henry Wright, personal communication.

CHAPTER 3

Compulsory Heterosexuality and Lesbian Experience

Adrienne Rich

A major American poet as well as cultural critic, Adrienne Rich was both a writer and a feminist/lesbian activist. In her writing, she examines the power of patriarchy over women and promotes their resistance to it. She also helped separate the lesbian movement from the feminist movement. In this major essay from 1980, she discusses the separateness of lesbian experience and participates in the critique of the feminist movement of the 1960s and 1970s for having ignored or marginalized lesbians. Her resonant title underscores one of the major contributions of the essay: to point out that heterosexuality is not "normal," rather, it is a compulsory form of behavior often imposed in the past on those who do not identify with it.

I

Biologically men have only one innate orientation – a sexual one that draws them to women, – while women have two innate orientations, sexual toward men and reproductive toward their young.[1]

I was a woman terribly vulnerable, critical, using femaleness as a sort of standard or yard-stick to measure and discard men. Yes – something like that. I was an Anna who invited defeat from men without ever being conscious of it. (But I am conscious of it. And being conscious of it means I shall leave it all behind me and become – but what?) I was stuck fast in an emotion common to women of our time, that can turn them bitter, or Lesbian, or solitary. Yes, that Anna during that time was …[2]

The bias of compulsory heterosexuality, through which lesbian experience is perceived on a scale ranging from deviant to abhorrent or simply rendered invisible, could be illustrated from many texts other than the two just preceding. The assumption made by

Original publication details: Adrienne Rich, "Compulsory Heterosexuality and Lesbian Experience" from *Blood, Bread, & Poetry: Selected Prose*, pp. 23–75. W.W. Norton, 1986. Reproduced with permission from W.W. Norton.

Literary Theory: An Anthology, Third Edition. Edited by Julie Rivkin and Michael Ryan.

Rossi, that women are "innately" sexually oriented only toward men, and that made by Lessing, that the lesbian is simply acting out of her bitterness toward men, are by no means theirs alone; these assumptions are widely current in literature and in the social sciences.

I am concerned here with two other matters as well: first, how and why women's choice of women as passionate comrades, life partners, co-workers, lovers, community has been crushed, invalidated, forced into hiding and disguise; and second, the virtual or total neglect of lesbian existence in a wide range of writings, including feminist scholarship. Obviously there is a connection here. I believe that much feminist theory and criticism is stranded on this shoal.

My organizing impulse is the belief that it is not enough for feminist thought that specifically lesbian texts exist. Any theory or cultural/political creation that treats lesbian existence as a marginal or less "natural" phenomenon, as mere "sexual preference," or as the mirror image of either heterosexual or male homosexual relations is profoundly weakened thereby, whatever its other contributions. Feminist theory can no longer afford merely to voice a toleration of "lesbianism" as an "alternative life style" or make token allusion to lesbians. A feminist critique of compulsory heterosexual orientation for women is long overdue. In this exploratory paper, I shall try to show why.

I will begin by way of examples, briefly discussing four books that have appeared in the last few years, written from different viewpoints and political orientations, but all presenting themselves, and favorably reviewed, as feminist.[3] All take as a basic assumption that the social relations of the sexes are disordered and extremely problematic, if not disabling, for women; all seek paths toward change. I have learned more from some of these books than from others, but on this I am clear: each one might have been more accurate, more powerful, more truly a force for change had the author dealt with lesbian existence as a reality and as a source of knowledge and power available to women, or with the institution of heterosexuality itself as a beachhead of male dominance.[4] In none of them is the question ever raised as to whether, in a different context or other things being equal, women would *choose* heterosexual coupling and marriage; heterosexuality is presumed the "sexual preference" of "most women," either implicitly or explicitly. In none of these books, which concern themselves with mothering, sex roles, relationships, and societal prescriptions for women, is compulsory heterosexuality ever examined as an institution powerfully affecting all these, or the idea of "preference" or "innate orientation" even indirectly questioned.

In *For Her Own Good: 150 Years of the Experts' Advice to Women* by Barbara Ehrenreich and Deirdre English, the authors' superb pamphlets *Witches, Midwives and Nurses: A History of Women Healers* and *Complaints and Disorders: The Sexual Politics of Sickness* are developed into a provocative and complex study. Their thesis in this book is that the advice given to American women by male health professionals, particularly in the areas of marital sex, maternity, and child care, has echoed the dictates of the economic market-place and the role capitalism has needed women to play in production and/or reproduction. Women have become the consumer victims of various cures, therapies, and normative judgments in different periods (including the prescription to middle-class women to embody and preserve the sacredness of the home – the "scientific" romanticization of the home itself). None of the "experts'" advice has been either particularly scientific or women-oriented; it has reflected male needs, male fantasies about women, and male interest in controlling women – particularly in the realms of sexuality and motherhood – fused with the requirements of industrial capitalism. So much of this book is so devastatingly informative and is written with such lucid feminist wit, that I kept waiting as I read for the basic proscription against lesbianism to be examined. It never was.

This can hardly be for lack of information. Jonathan Katz's *Gay American History*[5] tells us that as early as 1656 the New Haven Colony prescribed the death penalty for lesbians. Katz provides many suggestive and informative documents on the "treatment" (or torture) of lesbians by the medical profession in the nineteenth and twentieth centuries. Recent work by the historian Nancy Sahli documents the crackdown on intense female friendships among college women at the turn of the present century.[6] The ironic title *For Her Own Good* might have referred first and foremost to the economic imperative to heterosexuality and marriage and to the sanctions imposed against single women and widows – both of whom have been and still are viewed as deviant. Yet, in this often enlightening Marxist-feminist overview of male prescriptions for female sanity and health, the economics of prescriptive heterosexuality go unexamined.[7]

Of the three psychoanalytically based books, one, Jean Baker Miller's *Toward a New Psychology of Women*, is written as if lesbians simply do not exist, even as marginal beings. Given Miller's title, I find this astonishing. However, the favorable reviews the book has received in feminist journals, including *Signs* and *Spokeswoman*, suggest that Miller's heterocentric assumptions are widely shared. In *The Mermaid and the Minotaur: Sexual Arrangements and the Human Malaise*, Dorothy Dinnerstein makes an impassioned argument for the sharing of parenting between women and men and for an end to what she perceives as the male/female symbiosis of "gender arrangements," which she feels are leading the species further and further into violence and self-extinction. Apart from other problems that I have with this book (including her silence on the institutional and random terrorism men have practiced on women – and children – throughout history,[8] and her obsession with psychology to the neglect of economic and other material realities that help to create psychological reality), I find Dinnerstein's view of the relations between women and men as "a collaboration to keep history mad" utterly ahistorical. She means by this a collaboration to perpetuate social relations which are hostile, exploitative, and destructive to life itself. She sees women and men as equal partners in the making of "sexual arrangements," seemingly unaware of the repeated struggles of women to resist oppression (their own and that of others) and to change their condition. She ignores, specifically, the history of women who – as witches, *femmes seules*, marriage resisters, spinsters, autonomous widows, and/or lesbians – have managed on varying levels *not* to collaborate. It is this history, precisely, from which feminists have so much to learn and on which there is overall such blanketing silence. Dinnerstein acknowledges at the end of her book that "female separatism," though "on a large scale and in the long run wildly impractical," has something to teach us: "Separate, women could in principle set out to learn from scratch – undeflected by the opportunities to evade this task that men's presence has so far offered – what intact self-creative humanness is."[9] Phrases like "intact self-creative humanness" obscure the question of what the many forms of female separatism have actually been addressing. The fact is that women in every culture and throughout history *have* undertaken the task of independent, nonheterosexual, woman-connected existence, to the extent made possible by their context, often in the belief that they were the "only ones" ever to have done so. They have undertaken it even though few women have been in an economic position to resist marriage altogether, and even though attacks against unmarried women have ranged from aspersion and mockery to deliberate gynocide, including the burning and torturing of millions of widows and spinsters during the witch persecutions of the fifteenth, sixteenth, and seventeenth centuries in Europe.

Nancy Chodorow does come close to the edge of an acknowledgment of lesbian existence. Like Dinnerstein, Chodorow believes that the fact that women, and women only, are responsible for child care in the sexual division of labor has led to an entire social organization of gender inequality, and that men as well as women must become primary carers for children if that inequality is to change. In the process of examining, from a psychoanalytic perspective, how mothering by women affects the psychological development of girl and boy children, she offers documentation that men are "emotionally secondary" in women's lives, that "women have a richer, ongoing inner world to fall back on ... men do not become as emotionally important to women as women do to men."[10] This would carry into the late twentieth century Smith-Rosenberg's findings about eighteenth- and nineteenth-century women's emotional focus on women. "Emotionally important" can, of course, refer to anger as well as to love, or to that intense mixture of the two often found in women's relationships with women – one aspect of what I have come to call the "double life of women" (see below). Chodorow concludes that because women have women as mothers, "the mother remains a primary internal object [*sic*] to the girl, so that heterosexual relationships are on the model of a nonexclusive, second relationship for her, whereas for the boy they re-create an exclusive, primary relationship." According to Chodorow, women "have learned to deny the limitations of masculine lovers for both psychological and practical reasons."[11]

But the practical reasons (like witch burnings, male control of law, theology, and science, or economic nonviability within the sexual division of labor) are glossed over. Chodorow's account barely glances at the constraints and sanctions which historically have enforced or ensured the coupling of women with men and obstructed or penalized women's coupling or allying in independent groups with other women. She dismisses lesbian existence with the comment that "lesbian relationships do tend to re-create mother-daughter emotions and connections, but most women are heterosexual" (implied: more mature, having developed beyond the mother-daughter connection?). She then adds: "This heterosexual preference and taboos on homosexuality, in addition to objective economic dependence on men, make the option of primary sexual bonds with other women unlikely – though more prevalent in recent years."[12] The significance of that qualification seems irresistible, but Chodorow does not explore it further. Is she saying that lesbian existence has become more *visible* in recent years (in certain groups), that economic and other pressures have changed (under capitalism, socialism, or both), and that consequently more women are rejecting the heterosexual "choice"? She argues that women want children because their heterosexual relationships lack richness and intensity, that in having a child a woman seeks to re-create her own intense relationship with her mother. It seems to me that on the basis of her own findings, Chodorow leads us implicitly to conclude that heterosexuality is *not* a "preference" for women, that, for one thing, it fragments the erotic from the emotional in a way that women find impoverishing and painful. Yet her book participates in mandating it. Neglecting the covert socializations and the overt forces which have channeled women into marriage and heterosexual romance, pressures ranging from the selling of daughters to the silences of literature to the images of the television screen, she, like Dinnerstein, is stuck with trying to reform a man-made institution – compulsory heterosexuality – as if, despite profound emotional impulses and complementarities drawing women toward women, there is a mystical/biological heterosexual inclination, a "preference" or "choice" which draws women toward men.

Moreover, it is understood that this "preference" does not need to be explained unless through the tortuous theory of the female Oedipus complex or the necessity for species reproduction. It is lesbian sexuality which (usually, and incorrectly, "included" under male homosexuality) is seen as requiring explanation. This assumption of female hetero-sexuality seems to me in itself remarkable: it is an enormous assumption to have glided so silently into the foundations of our thought.

The extension of this assumption is the frequently heard assertion that in a world of genuine equality, where men are nonoppressive and nurturing, everyone would be bisexual. Such a notion blurs and sentimentalizes the actualities within which women have expe-rienced sexuality; it is a liberal leap across the tasks and struggles of here and now, the continuing process of sexual definition which will generate its own possibilities and choices. (It also assumes that women who have chosen women have done so simply because men are oppressive and emotionally unavailable, which still fails to account for women who continue to pursue relationships with oppressive and/or emotionally unsatisfying men.) I am suggesting that heterosexuality, like motherhood, needs to be recognized and studied as a *political institution* – even, or especially, by those individuals who feel they are, in their personal experience, the precursors of a new social relation between the sexes.

II

If women are the earliest sources of emotional caring and physical nurture for both female and male children, it would seem logical, from a feminist perspective at least, to pose the following questions: whether the search for love and tenderness in both sexes does not originally lead toward women; *why in fact women would ever redirect that search*; why species survival, the means of impregnation, and emotional/erotic relationships should ever have become so rigidly identified with each other; and why such violent strictures should be found necessary to enforce women's total emotional, erotic loyalty and subservience to men. I doubt that enough feminist scholars and theorists have taken the pains to acknowledge the societal forces which wrench women's emotional and erotic energies away from themselves and other women and from woman-identified values. These forces, as I shall try to show, range from literal physical enslavement to the disguising and distorting of possible options.

I do not assume that mothering by women is a "sufficient cause" of lesbian existence. But the issue of mothering by women has been much in the air of late, usually accompa-nied by the view that increased parenting by men would minimize antagonism between the sexes and equalize the sexual imbalance of power of males over females. These discussions are carried on without reference to compulsory heterosexuality as a phenomenon, let alone as an ideology. I do not wish to psychologize here, but rather to identify sources of male power. I believe large numbers of men could, in fact, undertake child care on a large scale without radically altering the balance of male power in a male-identified society.

In her essay "The Origin of the Family," Kathleen Gough lists eight characteristics of male power in archaic and contemporary societies which I would like to use as a frame-work: "men's ability to deny women sexuality or to force it upon them; to command or exploit their labor to control their produce; to control or rob them of their children; to confine them physically and prevent their movement; to use them as objects in male transactions; to cramp their creativeness; or to withhold from them large areas of the society's knowledge and cultural attainments."[13] (Gough does not perceive these power characteristics as specifically enforcing heterosexuality, only as producing sexual inequality.) Below, Gough's words appear in italics; the elaboration of each of her categories, in brackets, is my own.

Characteristics of male power include *the power of men*

1. *to deny women* [their own] *sexuality* – [by means of clitoridectomy and infibulation; chastity belts; punishment, including death, for female adultery; punishment, including death, for lesbian sexuality; psychoanalytic denial of the clitoris; strictures against masturbation; denial of maternal and postmenopausal sensuality; unnecessary hysterectomy; pseudolesbian images in the media and literature; closing of archives and destruction of documents relating to lesbian existence]

2. *or to force it* [male sexuality] *upon them* – [by means of rape (including marital rape) and wife beating; father-daughter, brother-sister incest; the socialization of women to feel that male sexual "drive" amounts to a right;[14] idealization of heterosexual romance in art, literature, the media, advertising, etc.; child marriage; arranged marriage; prostitution; the harem; psychoanalytic doctrines of frigidity and vaginal orgasm; pornographic depictions of women responding pleasurably to sexual violence and humiliation (a subliminal message being that sadistic heterosexuality is more "normal" than sensuality between women)]

3. *to command or exploit their labor to control their produce* – [by means of the institutions of marriage and motherhood as unpaid production; the horizontal segregation of women in paid employment; the decoy of the upwardly mobile token woman; male control of abortion, contraception, sterilization, and child-birth; pimping; female infanticide, which robs mothers of daughters and contributes to generalized devaluation of women]

4. *to control or rob them of their children* – [by means of father right and "legal kidnapping";[15] enforced sterilization; systematized infanticide; seizure of children from lesbian mothers by the courts; the malpractice of male obstetrics; use of the mother as "token torturer"[16] in genital mutilation or in binding the daughter's feet (or mind) to fit her for marriage]

5. *to confine them physically and prevent their movement* – [by means of rape as terrorism, keeping women off the streets; purdah; foot binding; atrophying of women's athletic capabilities; high heels and "feminine" dress codes in fashion; the veil; sexual harassment on the streets; horizontal segregation of women in employment; prescriptions for "full-time" mothering at home; enforced economic dependence of wives]

6. *to use them as objects in male transactions* – [use of women as "gifts"; bride price; pimping; arranged marriage; use of women as entertainers to facilitate male deals – e.g., wife-hostess, cocktail waitress required to dress for male sexual titillation, call girls, "bunnies," geisha, *kisaeng* prostitutes, secretaries]

7. *to cramp their creativeness* – [witch persecutions as campaigns against midwives and female healers, and as pogrom against independent, "unassimilated" women;[17] definition of male pursuits as more valuable than female within any culture, so that cultural values become the embodiment of male subjectivity; restriction of female self-fulfillment to marriage and motherhood; sexual exploitation of women by male artists and teachers; the social and economic disruption of women's creative aspirations;[18] erasure of female tradition][19]

8. *to withhold from them large areas of the society's knowledge and cultural attainments –* [by means of noneducation of females; the "Great Silence" regarding women and particularly lesbian existence in history and culture;[20] sex-role tracking which deflects women from science, technology, and other "masculine" pursuits; male social/professional bonding which excludes women; discrimination against women in the professions]

These are some of the methods by which male power is manifested and maintained. Looking at the schema, what surely impresses itself is the fact that we are confronting not a simple maintenance of inequality and property possession, but a pervasive cluster of forces, ranging from physical brutality to control of consciousness, which suggests that an enormous potential counterforce is having to be restrained.

Some of the forms by which male power manifests itself are more easily recognizable as enforcing heterosexuality on women than are others. Yet each one I have listed adds to the cluster of forces within which women have been convinced that marriage and sexual orientation toward men are inevitable – even if unsatisfying or oppressive – components of their lives. The chastity belt; child marriage; erasure of lesbian existence (except as exotic and perverse) in art, literature, film; idealization of heterosexual romance and marriage – these are some fairly obvious forms of compulsion, the first two exemplifying physical force, the second two control of consciousness. While clitoridectomy has been assailed by feminists as a form of woman torture,[21] Kathleen Barry first pointed out that it is not simply a way of turning the young girl into a "marriageable" woman through brutal surgery. It intends that women in the intimate proximity of polygynous marriage will not form sexual relationships with each other, that – from a male, genital-fetishist perspective – female erotic connections, even in a sex-segregated situation, will be literally excised.[22]

The function of pornography as an influence on consciousness is a major public issue of our time, when a multibillion-dollar industry has the power to disseminate increasingly sadistic, women-degrading visual images. But even so-called soft-core pornography and advertising depict women as objects of sexual appetite devoid of emotional context, without individual meaning or personality – essentially as a sexual commodity to be consumed by males. (So-called lesbian pornography, created for the male voyeuristic eye, is equally devoid of emotional context or individual personality.) The most pernicious message relayed by pornography is that women are natural sexual prey to men and love it, that sexuality and violence are congruent, and that for women sex is essentially masochistic, humiliation pleasurable, physical abuse erotic. But along with this message comes another, not always recognized: that enforced submission and the use of cruelty, if played out in heterosexual pairing, is sexually "normal," while sensuality between women, including erotic mutuality and respect, is "queer," "sick," and either pornographic in itself or not very exciting compared with the sexuality of whips and bondage.[23] Pornography does not simply create a climate in which sex and violence are interchangeable; *it widens the range of behavior considered acceptable from men in heterosexual intercourse –* behavior which reiteratively strips women of their autonomy, dignity, and sexual potential, including the potential of loving and being loved by women in mutuality and integrity.

In her brilliant study *Sexual Harassment of Working Women: A Case of Sex Discrimination*, Catharine A. MacKinnon delineates the intersection of compulsory heterosexuality and economics. Under capitalism, women are horizontally segregated by gender and occupy a structurally inferior position in the workplace. This is hardly news, but MacKinnon raises the question why, even if capitalism "requires some collection of individuals to occupy low-status, low-paying positions … such persons must be biologically female," and goes on to point out that "the fact that male employers often do not hire qualified women, *even when they could pay them less than men* suggests that more than the profit motive is implicated" [emphasis added].[24] She cites a wealth of material documenting the fact that women are not only segregated in low-paying service jobs (as secretaries, domestics, nurses, typists, telephone operators, child-care workers, waitresses), but that "sexualization of the woman" is part of the job. Central and intrinsic to the economic realities of women's lives is the requirement that women will "market sexual attractiveness to men, who tend to hold the economic power and position to enforce their predilections." And MacKinnon documents that "sexual harassment perpetuates the interlocked structure by which women have been kept sexually in thrall to men at the bottom of the labor market. Two forces of American society converge: men's control over women's sexuality and capital's control over employees' work lives."[25] Thus, women in the workplace are at the mercy of sex as power in a vicious circle. Economically disadvantaged, women – whether waitresses or professors – endure sexual harassment to keep their jobs and learn to behave in a complaisantly and ingratiatingly heterosexual manner because they discover this is their true qualification for employment, whatever the job description. And, MacKinnon notes, the woman who too decisively resists sexual overtures in the workplace is accused of being "dried up" and sexless, or lesbian. This raises a specific difference between the experiences of lesbians and homosexual men. A lesbian, closeted on her job because of heterosexist prejudice, is not simply forced into denying the truth of her outside relationships or private life. Her job depends on her pretending to be not merely heterosexual, but a heterosexual *woman* in terms of dressing and playing the feminine, deferential role required of "real" women.

MacKinnon raises radical questions as to the qualitative differences between sexual harassment, rape, and ordinary heterosexual intercourse. ("As one accused rapist put it, he hadn't used 'any more force than is usual for males during the preliminaries.'") She criticizes Susan Brownmiller[26] for separating rape from the mainstream of daily life and for her unexamined premise that "rape is violence, intercourse is sexuality," removing rape from the sexual sphere altogether. Most crucially she argues that "taking rape from the realm of 'the sexual,' placing it in the realm of 'the violent,' allows one to be against it without raising any questions about the extent to which the institution of heterosexuality has defined force as a normal part of 'the preliminaries.'"[27] "Never is it asked whether, under conditions of male supremacy, the notion of 'consent' has any meaning."[28]

The fact is that the workplace, among other social institutions, is a place where women have learned to accept male violation of their psychic and physical boundaries as the price of survival; where women have been educated – no less than by romantic literature or by pornography – to perceive themselves as sexual prey. A woman seeking to escape such casual violations along with economic disadvantage may well turn to marriage as a form of hoped-for protection, while bringing into marriage neither social nor economic power, thus entering that institution also from a disadvantaged position. MacKinnon finally asks:

> What if inequality is built into the social conceptions of male and female sexuality, of masculinity and femininity, of sexiness and heterosexual attractiveness? Incidents of sexual harassment suggest that male sexual desire itself may be aroused by female vulnerability.…

Men feel they can take advantage, so they want to, so they do. Examination of sexual harassment, precisely because the episodes appear commonplace, forces one to confront the fact that sexual intercourse normally occurs between economic (as well as physical) unequals ... the apparent legal requirement that violations of women's sexuality appear out of the ordinary before they will be punished helps prevent women from defining the ordinary conditions of their own consent.[29]

Given the nature and extent of heterosexual pressures – the daily "eroticization of women's subordination," as MacKinnon phrases it[30] – I question the more or less psychoanalytic perspective (suggested by such writers as Karen Horney, H. R. Hayes, Wolfgang Lederer, and, most recently, Dorothy Dinnerstein) that the male need to control women sexually results from some primal male "fear of women" and of women's sexual insatiability. It seems more probable that men really fear not that they will have women's sexual appetites forced on them or that women want to smother and devour them, but that women could be indifferent to them altogether, that men could be allowed sexual and emotional – therefore economic – access to women *only* on women's terms, otherwise being left on the periphery of the matrix.

The means of assuring male sexual access to women have recently received searching investigation by Kathleen Barry.[31] She documents extensive and appalling evidence for the existence, on a very large scale, of international female slavery, the institution once known as "white slavery" but which in fact has involved, and at this very moment involves, women of every race and class. In the theoretical analysis derived from her research, Barry makes the connection between all enforced conditions under which women live subject to men: prostitution, marital rape, father-daughter and brother-sister incest, wife beating, pornography, bride price, the selling of daughters, purdah, and genital mutilation. She sees the rape paradigm – where the victim of sexual assault is held responsible for her own victimization – as leading to the rationalization and acceptance of other forms of enslavement where the woman is presumed to have "chosen" her fate, to embrace it passively, or to have courted it perversely through rash or unchaste behavior. On the contrary, Barry maintains, "female sexual slavery is present in ALL situations where women or girls cannot change the conditions of their existence; where regardless of how they got into those conditions, e.g., social pressure, economic hardship, misplaced trust or the longing for affection, they cannot get out; and where they are subject to sexual violence and exploitation."[32] She provides a spectrum of concrete examples, not only as to the existence of a widespread international traffic in women, but also as to how this operates – whether in the form of a "Minnesota pipeline" funneling blonde, blue-eyed midwestern runaways to Times Square, or the purchasing of young women out of rural poverty in Latin America or Southeast Asia, or the providing of *maisons d'abattage* for migrant workers in the eighteenth arrondissement of Paris. Instead of "blaming the victim" or trying to diagnose her presumed pathology, Barry turns her floodlight on the pathology of sex colonization itself, the ideology of "cultural sadism" represented by the pornography industry and by the overall identification of women primarily as "sexual beings whose responsibility is the sexual service of men."[33]

Barry delineates what she names a "sexual domination perspective" through whose lens sexual abuse and terrorism of women by men has been rendered almost invisible by treating it as natural and inevitable. From its point of view, women are expendable as long as the sexual and emotional needs of the male can be satisfied. To replace this perspective of domination with a universal standard of basic freedom for women from gender-specific violence, from constraints on movement, and from male right of sexual and emotional access is the political purpose of her book. Like Mary Daly in *Gyn/ Ecology*, Barry rejects structuralist and other cultural-relativist rationalizations for sexual torture and anti-woman violence. In her opening chapter, she asks of her readers that they refuse all handy escapes into ignorance and denial. "The only way we can come out of hiding, break through our paralyzing defenses, is to know it all – the full extent of sexual violence and domination of women.... In *knowing*, in facing directly, we can learn to chart our course out of this oppression, by envisioning and creating a world which will preclude sexual slavery."[34]

"Until we name the practice, give conceptual definition and form to it, illustrate its life over time and in space, those who are its most obvious victims will also not be able to name it or define their experience."

But women are all, in different ways and to different degrees, its victims; and part of the problem with naming and conceptualizing female sexual slavery is, as Barry clearly sees, compulsory heterosexuality.[35] Compulsory heterosexuality simplifies the task of the procurer and pimp in world-wide prostitution rings and "eros centers," while, in the privacy of the home, it leads the daughter to "accept" incest/rape by her father, the mother to deny that it is happening, the battered wife to stay on with an abusive husband. "Befriending or love" is a major tactic of the procurer, whose job it is to turn the runaway or the confused young girl over to the pimp for seasoning. The ideology of heterosexual romance, beamed at her from childhood out of fairy tales, television, films, advertising, popular songs, wedding pageantry, is a tool ready to the procurer's hand and one which he does not hesitate to use, as Barry documents. Early female indoctrination in "love" as an emotion may be largely a Western concept; but a more universal ideology concerns the primacy and uncontrollability of the male sexual drive. This is one of many insights offered by Barry's work:

> As sexual power is learned by adolescent boys through the social experience of their sex drive, so do girls learn that the locus of sexual power is male. Given the importance placed on the male sex drive in the socialization of girls as well as boys, early adolescence is probably the first significant phase of male identification in a girl's life and development.... As a young girl becomes aware of her own increasing sexual feelings ... she turns away from her heretofore primary relationships with girlfriends. As they become secondary to her, recede in importance in her life, her own identity also assumes a secondary role and she grows into male identification.[36]

We still need to ask why some women never, even temporarily, turn away from "heretofore primary relationships" with other females. And why does male identification – the casting of one's social, political, and intellectual allegiances with men – exist among lifelong sexual lesbians? Barry's hypothesis throws us among new questions, but it clarifies the diversity of forms in which compulsory heterosexuality presents itself. In the mystique of the overpowering, all-conquering male sex drive, the penis-with-a-life-of-its-own, is rooted the law of male sex right to women, which justifies prostitution as a universal cultural assumption on the one hand, while defending sexual slavery within the family on the basis of "family privacy and cultural uniqueness" on the other.[37] The adolescent male sex drive, which, as both young women and men are taught, once triggered cannot take responsibility for itself or take no for an answer, becomes, according to Barry, the norm and rationale for adult male sexual behavior: a condition of *arrested sexual development*. Women learn to accept as natural the inevitability of this "drive" because they receive it as dogma. Hence, marital rape; hence, the Japanese wife resignedly packing her husband's suitcase for a weekend in the *kisaeng* brothels of Taiwan; hence, the psychological as well as economic imbalance of power between husband and wife, male employer and female worker, father and daughter, male professor and female student.

The effect of male identification means

> internalizing the values of the colonizer and actively participating in carrying out the colonization of one's self and one's sex.... Male identification is the act whereby women place men above women, including themselves, in credibility, status, and importance in most situations, regardless of the comparative quality the women may bring to the situation.... Interaction with women is seen as a lesser form of relating on every level.[38]

What deserves further exploration is the doublethink many women engage in and from which no woman is permanently and utterly free: However woman-to-woman relationships, female support networks, a female and feminist value system are relied on and cherished, indoctrination in male credibility and status can still create synapses in thought, denials of feeling, wishful thinking, a profound sexual and intellectual confusion.[39] I quote here from a letter I received the day I was writing this passage: "I have had very bad relationships with men – I am now in the midst of a very painful separation. I am trying to find my strength through women – without my friends, I could not survive." How many times a day do women speak words like these or think them or write them, and how often does the synapse reassert itself?

Barry summarizes her findings:

> Considering the arrested sexual development that is understood to be normal in the male population, and considering the numbers of men who are pimps, procurers, members of slavery gangs, corrupt officials participating in this traffic, owners, operators, employees of brothels and lodging and entertainment facilities, pornography purveyors, associated with prostitution, wife beaters, child molesters, incest perpetrators, johns (tricks) and rapists, one cannot but be momentarily stunned by the enormous male population engaging in female sexual slavery. The huge number of men engaged in these practices should be cause for declaration of an international emergency, a crisis in sexual violence. But what should be cause for alarm is instead accepted as normal sexual intercourse.[40]

Susan Cavin, in a rich and provocative, if highly speculative, dissertation, suggests that patriarchy becomes possible when the original female band, which includes children but ejects adolescent males, becomes invaded and outnumbered by males; that not patriarchal marriage, but the rape of the mother by the son, becomes the first act of male domination. The entering wedge, or leverage, which allows this to happen is not just a simple change in sex ratios; it is also the mother-child bond, manipulated by adolescent males in order to remain within the matrix past the age of exclusion. Maternal affection is used to establish male right of sexual access, which, however, must ever after be held by force (or through control of consciousness) since the original deep adult bonding is that of woman for woman.[41] I find this hypothesis extremely suggestive, since one form of false consciousness which serves compulsory heterosexuality is the maintenance of a mother-son relationship between women and men, including the demand that women provide maternal solace, nonjudgmental nurturing, and compassion for their harassers, rapists, and batterers (as well as for men who passively vampirize them).

But whatever its origins, when we look hard and clearly at the extent and elaboration of measures designed to keep women within a male sexual purlieu, it becomes an inescapable question whether the issue feminists have to address is not simple "gender inequality" nor the domination of culture by males nor mere "taboos against homosexuality," but the enforcement of heterosexuality for women as a means of assuring male right of physical, economic, and emotional access.[42] One of many means of enforcement is, of course, the rendering invisible of the lesbian possibility, an engulfed continent which rises fragmentedly into view from time to time only to become submerged again. Feminist research and theory that contribute to lesbian invisibility or marginality are actually working against the liberation and empowerment of women as a group.[43]

The assumption that "most women are innately heterosexual" stands as a theoretical and political stumbling block for feminism. It remains a tenable assumption partly because lesbian existence has been written out of history or catalogued under disease, partly because it has been treated as exceptional rather than intrinsic, partly because to acknowledge that for women heterosexuality may not be a "preference" at all but something that has had to be imposed, managed, organized, propagandized, and maintained by force is an immense step to take if you consider yourself freely and "innately" heterosexual. Yet the failure to examine heterosexuality as an institution is like failing to admit that the economic system called capitalism or the caste system of racism is maintained by a variety of forces, including both physical violence and false consciousness. To take the step of questioning heterosexuality as a "preference" or "choice" for women – and to do the intellectual and emotional work that follows – will call for a special quality of courage in heterosexually identified feminists, but I think the rewards will be great: a freeing-up of thinking, the exploring of new paths, the shattering of another great silence, new clarity in personal relationships.

Notes

1   Alice Rossi, "Children and Work in the Lives of Women," paper delivered at the University of Arizona, Tuscon, February 1976.

2   Doris Lessing, *The Golden Notebook*, 1962 (New York: Bantam, 1977), p. 480.

3   Nancy Chodorow, *The Reproduction of Mothering* (Berkeley: University of California Press, 1978); Dorothy Dinnerstein, *The Mermaid and the Minotaur: Sexual Arrangements and the Human Malaise* (New York: Harper & Row, 1976); Barbara Ehrenreich and Deirdre English, *For Her Own Good: 150 Years of the Experts' Advice to Women* (Garden City, N.Y.: Doubleday, Anchor, 1978); Jean Baker Miller, *Toward a New Psychology of Women* (Boston: Beacon, 1976).

4   I could have chosen many other serious and influential recent books, including anthologies, which would illustrate the same point: e.g., *Our Bodies, Ourselves*, the Boston Women's Health Book Collective's best seller (New York: Simon and Schuster, 1976), which devotes a separate (and inadequate) chapter to lesbians, but whose message is that heterosexuality is most women's life preference; Berenice Carroll, ed., *Liberating Women's History: Theoretical and Critical Essays* (Urbana: University of Illinois Press, 1976), which does not include even a token essay on the lesbian presence in history, though an essay by Linda Gordon, Persis Hunt, *et al.* notes the use by male historians of "sexual deviance" as a category to discredit and dismiss Anna Howard Shaw, Jane Addams, and other feminists ("Historical Phallacies: Sexism in American Historical Writing"); and Renate Bridenthal and Claudia Koonz, eds., *Becoming Visible: Women in European History* (Boston: Houghton Mifflin, 1977), which contains three mentions of male homosexuality but no materials that I have been able to locate on lesbians. Gerda Lerner, ed., *The Female Experience: An American Documentary* (Indianapolis: Bobbs-Merrill, 1977), contains an abridgment of two lesbian-feminist-

position papers from the contemporary movement but no other documentation of lesbian existence. Lerner does note in her preface, however, how the charge of deviance has been used to
fragment women and discourage women's resistance. Linda Gordon, in *Woman's Body, Woman's
Right: A Social History of Birth Control in America* (New York: Viking, Grossman, 1976), notes
accurately that "it is not that feminism has produced more lesbians. There have always been many
lesbians, despite the high levels of repression; and most lesbians experience their sexual preference as innate" (p. 410).

[A.R., 1986: I am glad to update the first annotation in this footnote. "*The New" Our Bodies,
Ourselves* (New York: Simon and Schuster, 1984) contains an expanded chapter on "Loving
Women: Lesbian Life and Relationships" and furthermore emphasizes *choices* for women through-
out – in terms of sexuality, health care, family, politics, etc.]

5   Jonathan Katz, ed., *Gay American History: Lesbians and Gay Men in the U.S.A.* (New York:
    Thomas Y. Crowell, 1976).

6   Nancy Sahli, "Smashing Women's Relationships before the Fall," *Chrysalis: A Magazine of
    Women's Culture* 8 (1979): 17–27.

7   This is a book which I have publicly endorsed. I would still do so, though with the above caveat.
    It is only since beginning to write this article that I fully appreciated how enormous is the unasked
    question in Ehrenreich and English's book.

8   See, for example, Kathleen Barry, *Female Sexual Slavery* (Englewood Cliffs, N.J.: Prentice-Hall,
    1979); Mary Daly, *Gyn/Ecology: The Metaethics of Radical Feminism* (Boston: Beacon, 1978);
    Susan Griffin, *Woman and Nature: The Roaring inside Her* (New York: Harper & Row, 1978);
    Diana Russell and Nicole van de Ven, eds., *Proceedings of the International Tribunal of Crimes
    against Women* (Millbrae, Calif.: Les Femmes, 1976); and Susan Brownmiller, *Against Our Will:
    Men, Women and Rape* (New York: Simon and Schuster, 1975); *Aegis: Magazine on Ending Violence
    against Women* (Feminist Alliance against Rape, P.O. Box 21033, Washington, D.C. 20009).

    [A.R., 1986: Work on both incest and on woman battering has appeared in the 1980s which
    I did not cite in the essay. See Florence Rush, *The Best-kept Secret* (New York: McGraw-Hill,
    1980); Louise Armstrong, *Kiss Daddy Goodnight: A Speakout on Incest* (New York: Pocket
    Books, 1979); Sandra Butler, *Conspiracy of Silence: The Trauma of Incest* (San Francisco: New
    Glide, 1978); F. Delacoste and F. Newman, eds., *Fight Back!: Feminist Resistance to Male Violence*
    (Minneapolis: Cleis Press, 1981); Judy Freespirit, *Daddy's Girl: An Incest Survivor's Story*
    (Langlois, Ore.: Diaspora Distribution, 1982); Judith Herman, *Father-Daughter Incest* (Cambridge,
    Mass.: Harvard University Press, 1981); Toni McNaron and Yarrow Morgan, eds., *Voices in the
    Night: Women Speaking about Incest* (Minneapolis: Cleis Press, 1982); and Betsy Warrior's richly
    informative, multipurpose compilation of essays, statistics, listings, and facts, the *Battered Women's
    Directory* (formerly entitled *Working on Wife Abuse*), 8th ed. (Cambridge, Mass.: 1982).]

9   Dinnerstein, p. 272.

10 Chodorow, pp. 197–198.

11 *Ibid.*, pp. 198–199.

12 *Ibid.*, p. 200.

13 Kathleen Gough, "The Origin of the Family," in *Toward an Anthropology of Women*, ed. Rayna
    [Rapp] Reiter (New York: Monthly Review Press, 1975), pp. 69–70.

14 Barry, pp. 216–219.

15 Anna Demeter, *Legal Kidnapping* (Boston: Beacon, 1977), pp. xx, 126–128.

16 Daly, pp. 139–141, 163–165.

17 Barbara Ehrenreich and Deirdre English, *Witches, Midwives and Nurses: A History of Women
    Healers* (Old Westbury, N.Y.: Feminist Press, 1973); Andrea Dworkin, *Woman Hating* (New York:
    Dutton, 1974), pp. 118–154; Daly, pp. 178–222.

18 See Virginia Woolf, *A Room of One's Own* (London: Hogarth, 1929), and *id.*, *Three Guineas* (New
    York: Harcourt Brace, [1938] 1966); Tillie Olsen, *Silences* (Boston: Delacorte, 1978); Michelle
    Cliff, "The Resonance of Interruption," *Chrysalis: A Magazine of Women's Culture* 8 (1979):
    29–37.

19 Mary Daly, *Beyond God the Father* (Boston: Beacon, 1973), pp. 347–351; Olsen, pp. 22–46.

20 Daly, *Beyond God the Father*, p. 93.

21 Fran P. Hosken, "The Violence of Power: Genital Mutilation of Females," *Heresies: A Feminist Journal of Art and Politics* 6 (1979): 28–35; Russell and van de Ven, pp. 194–195.

    [A.R., 1986: See especially "Circumcision of Girls," in Nawal El Saadawi, *The Hidden Face of Eve: Women in the Arab World* (Boston: Beacon, 1982), pp. 33–43.]

22 Barry, pp. 163–164.

23 The issue of "lesbian sadomasochism" needs to be examined in terms of dominant cultures' teachings about the relation of sex and violence. I believe this to be another example of the "double life" of women.

24 Catharine A. MacKinnon, *Sexual Harassment of Working Women: A Case of Sex Discrimination* (New Haven, Conn.: Yale University Press, 1979), pp. 15–16.

25 *Ibid.*, p. 174.

26 Brownmiller, *op. cit.*

27 MacKinnon, p. 219. Susan Schecter writes: "The push for heterosexual union at whatever cost is so intense that ... it has become a cultural force of its own that creates battering. The ideology of romantic love and its jealous possession of the partner as property provide the masquerade for what can become severe abuse" (*Aegis: Magazine on Ending Violence against Women* [July–August 1979]: 50–51).

28 MacKinnon, p. 298.

29 *Ibid.*, p. 220.

30 *Ibid.*, p. 221.

31 Barry, *op. cit.*

    [A.R., 1986: See also Kathleen Barry, Charlotte Bunch, and Shirley Castley, eds., *International Feminism: Networking against Female Sexual Slavery* (New York: International Women's Tribune Center, 1984).]

32 Barry, p. 33.

33 *Ibid.*, p. 103.

34 *Ibid.*, p. 5.

35 *Ibid.*, p. 100.

    [A.R., 1986: This statement has been taken as claiming that "all women are victims" purely and simply, or that "all heterosexuality equals sexual slavery." I would say, rather, that all women are affected, though differently, by dehumanizing attitudes and practices directed at women as a group.]

36 *Ibid.*, p. 218.

37 *Ibid.*, p. 140.

38 *Ibid.*, p. 172.

39 Elsewhere I have suggested that male identification has been a powerful source of white women's racism and that it has often been women already seen as "disloyal" to male codes and systems who have actively battled against it (Adrienne Rich, "Disloyal to Civilization: Feminism, Racism, Gynephobia," in *On Lies, Secrets, and Silence: Selected Prose, 1966–1978* [New York: W. W. Norton, 1979]).

40 Barry, p. 220.

41 Susan Cavin, "Lesbian Origins" (Ph.D. diss., Rutgers University, 1978), unpublished, ch. 6.

    [A.R., 1986: This dissertation was recently published as *Lesbian Origins* (San Francisco: Ism Press, 1986).]

42 For my perception of heterosexuality as an economic institution I am indebted to Lisa Leghorn and Katherine Parker, who allowed me to read the unpublished manuscript of their book *Woman's Worth: Sexual Economics and the World of Women* (London and Boston: Routledge & Kegan Paul, 1981).

43 I would suggest that lesbian existence has been most recognized and tolerated where it has resembled a "deviant" version of heterosexuality – e.g., where lesbians have, like Stein and Toklas, played heterosexual roles (or seemed to in public) and have been chiefly identified with male culture. See also Claude E. Schaeffer, "The Kuterai Female Berdache: Courier, Guide, Prophetess and Warrior," *Ethnohistory* 12, no. 3 (Summer 1965): 193–236. (Berdache: "an individual of a definite physiological sex [m. or f.] who assumes the role and status of the opposite sex and who is

viewed by the community as being of one sex physiologically but as having assumed the role and status of the opposite sex" [Schaeffer, p. 231].) Lesbian existence has also been relegated to an upper-class phenomenon, an elite decadence (as in the fascination with Paris salon lesbians such as Renée Vivien and Natalie Clifford Barney), to the obscuring of such "common women" as Judy Grahn depicts in her *The Work of a Common Woman* (Oakland, Calif.: Diana Press, 1978) and *True to Life Adventure Stories* (Oakland, Calif.: Diana Press, 1978).

CHAPTER 4

The Laugh of the Medusa

Hélène Cixous

Hélène Cixous is a French literary scholar, feminist philosopher, and fiction writer. Her most famous work, "The Laugh of the Medusa," was published in 1976.

I shall speak about women's writing: about *what it will do*. Woman must write her self: must write about women and bring women to writing, from which they have been driven away as violently as from their bodies – for the same reasons, by the same law, with the same fatal goal. Woman must put herself into the text – as into the world and into history – by her own movement.

The future must no longer be determined by the past. I do not deny that the effects of the past are still with us. But I refuse to strengthen them by repeating them, to confer upon them an irremovability the equivalent of destiny, to confuse the biological and the cultural. Anticipation is imperative.

Since these reflections are taking shape in an area just on the point of being discovered, they necessarily bear the mark of our time – a time during which the new breaks away from the old, and, more precisely, the (feminine) new from the old (*la nouvelle de l'ancien*). Thus, as there are no grounds for establishing a discourse, but rather an arid millennial ground to break, what I say has at least two sides and two aims: to break up, to destroy; and to foresee the unforeseeable, to project.

I write this as a woman, toward women. When I say "woman," I'm speaking of woman in her inevitable struggle against conventional man; and of a universal woman subject who must bring women to their senses and to their meaning in history. But first it must be said that in spite of the enormity of the repression that has kept them in the "dark" – that dark which people have been trying to make them accept as their attribute – there is, at this time, no general woman, no one typical woman. What they have *in common* I will say. But what strikes me is the infinite richness of their individual constitutions: you can't talk about *a* female sexuality, uniform, homogeneous, classifiable into codes – any

Original publication details: Helene Cixous, "The Laugh of the Medusa" from *The Signs Reader: Women, Gender, and Scholarship,* trans. Keith and Paula Cohen, ed. Elizabeth Abel and Emily Abel, pp. 279–297. University of Chicago Press, 1983. Complete and unabridged.

Literary Theory: An Anthology, Third Edition. Edited by Julie Rivkin and Michael Ryan.

more than you can talk about one unconscious resembling another. Women's imaginary is inexhaustible, like music, painting, writing: their stream of phantasms is incredible.

I have been amazed more than once by a description a woman gave me of a world all her own which she had been secretly haunting since early childhood. A world of searching, the elaboration of a knowledge, on the basis of a systematic experimentation with the bodily functions, a passionate and precise interrogation of her erotogeneity. This practice, extraordinarily rich and inventive, in particular as concerns masturbation, is prolonged or accompanied by a production of forms, a veritable aesthetic activity, each stage of rapture inscribing a resonant vision, a composition, something beautiful. Beauty will no longer be forbidden.

I wished that that woman would write and proclaim this unique empire so that other women, other unacknowledged sovereigns, might exclaim: I, too, overflow; my desires have invented new desires, my body knows unheard-of songs. Time and again I, too, have felt so full of luminous torrents that I could burst – burst with forms much more beautiful than those which are put up in frames and sold for a stinking fortune. And I, too, said nothing, showed nothing; I didn't open my mouth. I didn't repaint my half of the world. I was ashamed. I was afraid, and I swallowed my shame and my fear. I said to myself: You are mad! What's the meaning of these waves, these floods, these outbursts? Where is the ebullient, infinite woman who, immersed as she was in her naïveté, kept in the dark about herself, led into self-disdain by the great arm of parental-conjugal phallocentrism, hasn't been ashamed of her strength? Who, surprised and horrified by the fantastic tumult of her drives (for she was made to believe that a well-adjusted normal woman has a … divine composure), hasn't accused herself of being a monster? Who, feeling a funny desire stirring inside her (to sing, to write, to dare to speak, in short, to bring out something new), hasn't thought she was sick? Well, her shameful sickness is that she resists death, that she makes trouble.

And why don't you write? Write! Writing is for you, you are for you; your body is yours, take it. I know why you haven't written. (And why I didn't write before the age of twenty-seven.) Because writing is at once too high, too great for you, it's reserved for the great – that is, for "great men"; and it's "silly." Besides, you've written a little, but in secret. And it wasn't good, because it was in secret, and because you punished yourself for writing, because you didn't go all the way; or because you wrote, irresistibly, as when we would masturbate in secret, not to go further, but to attenuate the tension a bit, just enough to take the edge off. And then as soon as we come, we go and make ourselves feel guilty – so as to be forgiven; or to forget, to bury it until the next time.

Write, let no one hold you back, let nothing stop you: not man; not the imbecilic capitalist machinery, in which publishing houses are the crafty, obsequious relayers of imperatives handed down by an economy that works against us and off our backs; and not *yourself.* Smug-faced readers, managing editors, and big bosses don't like the true texts of women – female-sexed texts. That kind scares them.

I write woman: woman must write woman. And man, man. So only an oblique consideration will be found here of man; it's up to him to say where his masculinity and femininity are at: this will concern us once men have opened their eyes and seen themselves clearly.[1]

Now women return from afar, from always: from "without," from the heath where witches are kept alive; from below, from beyond "culture"; from their childhood which men have been trying desperately to make them forget, condemning it to "eternal rest." The little girls and their "ill-mannered" bodies immured, well-preserved, intact unto themselves, in the mirror. Frigidified. But are they ever seething underneath! What an effort it takes – there's no end to it – for the sex cops to bar their threatening return. Such a display of forces on both sides that the struggle has for centuries been immobilized in the trembling equilibrium of a deadlock.

Here they are, returning, arriving over and again, because the unconscious is impregnable. They have wandered around in circles, confined to the narrow room in which they've been given a deadly brainwashing. You can incarcerate them, slow them down, get away with the old Apartheid routine, but for a time only. As soon as they begin to speak, at the same time as they're taught their name, they can be taught that their territory is black: because you are Africa, you are black. Your continent is dark. Dark is dangerous. You can't see anything in the dark, you're afraid. Don't move, you might fall. Most of all, don't go into the forest. And so we have internalized this horror of the dark.

Men have committed the greatest crime against women. Insidiously, violently, they have led them to hate women, to be their own enemies, to mobilize their immense strength against themselves, to be the executants of their virile needs. They have made for women an antinarcissism! A narcissism which loves itself only to be loved for what women haven't got! They have constructed the infamous logic of antilove.

We the precocious, we the repressed of culture, our lovely mouths gagged with pollen, our wind knocked out of us, we the labyrinths, the ladders, the trampled spaces, the bevies – we are black and we are beautiful.

We're stormy, and that which is ours breaks loose from us without our fearing any debilitation. Our glances, our smiles, are spent; laughs exude from all our mouths; our blood flows and we extend ourselves without ever reaching an end; we never hold back our thoughts, our signs, our writing; and we're not afraid of lacking.

What happiness for us who are omitted, brushed aside at the scene of inheritances; we inspire ourselves and we expire without running out of breath, we are everywhere!

From now on, who, if we say so, can say no to us? We've come back from always.

It is time to liberate the New Woman from the Old by coming to know her – by loving her for getting by, for getting beyond the Old without delay, by going out ahead of what the New Woman will be, as an arrow quits the bow with a movement that gathers and separates the vibrations musically, in order to be more than her self.

I say that we must, for, with a few rare exceptions, there has not yet been any writing that inscribes femininity; exceptions so rare, in fact, that, after plowing through literature across languages, cultures, and ages,[2] one can only be startled at this vain scouting mission. It is well known that the number of women writers (while having increased very slightly from the nineteenth century on) has always been ridiculously small. This is a useless and deceptive fact unless from their species of female writers we do not first deduct the immense majority whose workmanship is in no way different from male writing, and which either obscures women or reproduces the classic representations of women (as sensitive – intuitive – dreamy, etc.)[3]

Let me insert here a parenthetical remark. I mean it when I speak of male writing. I maintain unequivocally that there is such a thing as *marked* writing; that, until now, far more extensively and repressively than is ever suspected or admitted, writing has been run by a libidinal and cultural – hence political, typically masculine – economy; that this is a locus where the repression of women has been perpetuated, over and over, more or less consciously, and in a manner that's frightening since it's often hidden or adorned with the mystifying charms of fiction; that this locus has grossly exaggerated all the signs of sexual opposition (and not sexual difference), where woman has never *her* turn to speak – this being all the more serious and unpardonable in that writing is precisely *the very possibility of change*, the space that can serve as a springboard for subversive thought, the precursory movement of a transformation of social and cultural structures.

Nearly the entire history of writing is confounded with the history of reason, of which it is at once the effect, the support, and one of the privileged alibis. It has been one with the phallocentric tradition. It is indeed that same self-admiring, self-stimulating, self-congratulatory phallocentrism.

With some exceptions, for there have been failures – and if it weren't for them, I wouldn't be writing (I-woman, escapee) – in that enormous machine that has been operating and turning out its "truth" for centuries. There have been poets who would go to any lengths to slip something by at odds with tradition – men capable of loving love and hence capable of loving others and of wanting them, of imagining the woman who would hold out against oppression and constitute herself as a superb, equal, hence "impossible" subject, untenable in a real social framework. Such a woman the poet could desire only by breaking the codes that negate her. Her appearance would necessarily bring on, if not revolution – for the bastion was supposed to be immutable – at least harrowing explosions. At times it is in the fissure caused by an earthquake, through that radical mutation of things brought on by a material upheaval when every structure is for a moment thrown off balance and an ephemeral wildness sweeps order away, that the poet slips something by, for a brief span, of woman. Thus did Kleist expend himself in his yearning for the existence of sister-lovers, maternal daughters, mother-sisters, who never hung their heads in shame. Once the palace of magistrates is restored, it's time to pay: immediate bloody death to the uncontrollable elements.

But only the poets – not the novelists, allies of representationalism. Because poetry involves gaining strength through the unconscious and because the unconscious, that other limitless country, is the place where the repressed manage to survive: women, or as Hoffmann would say, fairies.

She must write her self, because this is the invention of a *new insurgent* writing which, when the moment of her liberation has come, will allow her to carry out the indispensable ruptures and transformations in her history, first at two levels that cannot be separated.

a) Individually. By writing her self, woman will return to the body which has been more than confiscated from her, which has been turned into the uncanny stranger on display – the ailing or dead figure, which so often turns out to be the nasty companion, the cause and location of inhibitions. Censor the body and you censor breath and speech at the same time.

Write your self. Your body must be heard. Only then will the immense resources of the unconscious spring forth. Our naphtha will spread, throughout the world, without dollars – black or gold – nonassessed values that will change the rules of the old game.

To write. An act which will not only "realize" the decensored relation of woman to her sexuality, to her womanly being, giving her access to her native strength; it will give her back her goods, her pleasures, her organs, her immense bodily territories which have been kept under seal; it will tear her away from the superegoized structure in which she has always occupied the place reserved for the guilty (guilty of everything, guilty at every turn: for having desires, for not having any; for being frigid, for being "too hot"; for not being both at once; for being too motherly and not enough; for having children and for not having any; for nursing and for not nursing...) – tear her away by means of this research, this job of analysis and illumination, this emancipation of the marvelous text of her self that she must urgently learn to speak. A woman without a body, dumb, blind, can't possibly be a good fighter. She is reduced to being the servant of the militant male, his shadow. We must kill the false woman who is preventing the live one from breathing. Inscribe the breath of the whole woman.

b) An act that will also be marked by woman's *seizing* the occasion to *speak*, hence her shattering entry into history, which has always been based *on her suppression*. To write and thus to forge for herself the antilogos weapon. To become *at will* the taker and initiator, for her own right, in every symbolic system, in every political process.

It is time for women to start scoring their feats in written and oral language.

Every woman has known the torment of getting up to speak. Her heart racing, at times entirely lost for words, ground and language slipping away – that's how daring a feat, how great a transgression it is for a woman to speak – even just open her mouth – in public. A double distress, for even if she transgresses, her words fall almost always upon the deaf male ear, which hears in language only that which speaks in the masculine.

It is by writing, from and toward women, and by taking up the challenge of speech which has been governed by the phallus, that women will confirm women in a place other than that which is reserved in and by the symbolic, that is, in a place other than silence. Women should break out of the snare of silence. They shouldn't be conned into accepting a domain which is the margin or the harem.

Listen to a woman speak at a public gathering (if she hasn't painfully lost her wind). She doesn't "speak," she throws her trembling body forward; she lets go of herself, she flies; all of her passes into her voice, and it's with her body that she vitally supports the "logic" of her speech. Her flesh speaks true. She lays herself bare. In fact, she physically materializes what she's thinking; she signifies it with her body. In a certain way she *inscribes* what she's saying, because she doesn't deny her drives the intractable and impassioned part they have in speaking. Her speech, even when "theoretical" or political, is never simple or linear or "objectified," generalized: she draws her story into history.

There is not that scission, that division made by the common man between the logic of oral speech and the logic of the text, bound as he is by his antiquated relation – servile, calculating – to mastery. From which proceeds the niggardly lip service which engages only the tiniest part of the body, plus the mask.

In women's speech, as in their writing, that element which never stops resonating, which, once we've been permeated by it, profoundly and imperceptibly touched by it, retains the power of moving us – that element is the song: first music from the first voice of love which is alive in every woman. Why this privileged relationship with the voice? Because no woman stockpiles as many defenses for countering the drives as does a man. You don't build walls around yourself, you don't forego pleasure as "wisely" as he. Even if phallic mystification has generally contaminated good relationships, a woman is never far from "mother" (I mean outside her role functions: the "mother" as nonname and as source of goods). There is always within her at least a little of that good mother's milk. She writes in white ink.

Woman for women. – There always remains in woman that force which produces/is produced by the other – in particular, the other woman. *In* her, matrix, cradler; herself giver as her mother and child; she is her own sister-daughter. You might object, "What about she who is the hysterical offspring of a bad mother?" Everything will be changed once woman gives woman to the other woman. There is hidden and always ready in woman the source; the locus for the other. The mother, too, is a metaphor. It is necessary and sufficient that the best of herself be given to woman by another woman for her to be able to love herself and return in love the body that was "born" to her. Touch me, caress me, you the living no-name, give me my self as myself. The relation to the "mother," in terms of intense pleasure and violence, is curtailed no more than the relation to child-hood (the child that she was, that she is, that she makes, remakes, undoes, there at the point where, the same, she others herself). Text: my body – shot through with streams of song; I don't mean the overbearing, clutchy "mother" but, rather, what touches you, the equivoice that affects you, fills your breast with an urge to come to language and launches your force; the rhythm that laughs you; the intimate recipient who makes all metaphors possible and desirable; body (body? bodies?), no more describable than god, the soul, or the Other; that part of you that leaves a space between yourself and urges you to inscribe in language your woman's style. In women there is always more or less of the mother who makes everything all right, who nourishes, and who stands up against separation; a force that will not be cut off but will knock the wind out of the codes. We will rethink woman-kind beginning with every form and every period of her body. The Americans remind us, "We are all Lesbians"; that is, don't denigrate woman, don't make of her what men have made of you.

Because the "economy" of her drives is prodigious, she cannot fail, in seizing the occasion to speak, to transform directly and indirectly *all* systems of exchange based on masculine thrift. Her libido will produce far more radical effects of political and social change than some might like to think.

Because she arrives, vibrant, over and again, we are at the beginning of a new history, or rather of a process of becoming in which several histories intersect with one another. As subject for history, woman always occurs simultaneously in several places. Woman un-thinks[4] the unifying, regulating history that homogenizes and channels forces, herding contradictions into a single battlefield. In woman, personal history blends together with the history of all women, as well as national and world history. As a militant, she is an integral part of all liberations. She must be farsighted, not limited to a blow-by-blow interaction. She foresees that her liberation will do more than modify power relations or toss the ball over to the other camp; she will bring about a mutation in human relations, in thought, in all praxis: hers is not simply a class struggle, which she carries forward into a much vaster movement. Not that in order to be a woman-in-struggle(s) you have to leave the class struggle or repudiate it; but you have to split it open, spread it out, push it forward, fill it with the fundamental struggle so as to prevent the class struggle, or any other struggle for the liberation of a class or people, from operating as a form of repression, pretext for postponing the inevitable, the staggering alteration in power relations and in the production of individualities. This alteration is already upon us – in the United States, for example, where millions of night crawlers are in the process of undermining the family and disintegrating the whole of American sociality.

The new history is coming; it's not a dream, though it does extend beyond men's imagination, and for good reason. It's going to deprive them of their conceptual orthopedics, beginning with the destruction of their enticement machine.

It is impossible to *define* a feminine practice of writing, and this is an impossibility that will remain, for this practice can never be theorized, enclosed, coded – which doesn't mean that it doesn't exist. But it will always surpass the discourse that regulates the phallocentric system; it does and will take place in areas other than those subordinated to philosophico-theoretical domination. It will be conceived of only by subjects who are breakers of automatisms, by peripheral figures that no authority can ever subjugate.

Hence the necessity to affirm the flourishes of this writing, to give form to its movement, its near and distant byways. Bear in mind to begin with (1) that sexual opposition, which has always worked for man's profit to the point of reducing writing, too, to his laws, is only a historico-cultural limit. There is, there will be more and more rapidly pervasive now, a fiction that produces irreducible effects of femininity. (2) That it is through ignorance that most readers, critics, and writers of both sexes hesitate to admit or deny outright the possibility or the pertinence of a distinction between feminine and masculine writing. It will usually be said, thus disposing of sexual difference: either that all writing, to the extent that it materializes, is feminine; or, inversely – but it comes to the same thing – that the act of writing is equivalent to masculine masturbation (and so the woman who writes cuts herself out a paper penis); or that writing is bisexual, hence neuter, which again does away with differentiation. To admit that writing is precisely working (in) the in-between, inspecting the process of the same and of the other without which nothing can live, undoing the work of death – to admit this is first to want the two, as well as both, the ensemble of the one and the other, not fixed in sequences of struggle and expulsion or some other form of death but infinitely dynamized by an incessant process of exchange from one subject to another. A process of different subjects knowing one another and beginning one another anew only from the living boundaries of the other: a multiple and inexhaustible course with millions of encounters and transformations of the same into the other and into the in-between, from which woman takes her forms (and man, in his turn; but that's his other history).

In saying "bisexual, hence neuter," I am referring to the classic conception of bisexuality, which, squashed under the emblem of castration fear and along with the fantasy of a "total" being (though composed of two halves), would do away with the difference experienced as an operation incurring loss, as the mark of dreaded sectility.

To this self-effacing, merger-type bisexuality, which would conjure away castration (the writer who puts up his sign: "bisexual written here, come and see," when the odds are good that it's neither one nor the other), I oppose the *other bisexuality* on which every subject not enclosed in the false theater of phallocentric representationalism has founded his/her erotic universe. Bisexuality: that is, each one's location in self (*répérage en soi*) of the presence – variously manifest and insistent according to each person, male or female – of both sexes, nonexclusion either of the difference or of one sex, and, from this "self-permission," multiplication of the effects of the inscription of desire, over all parts of my body and the other body.

Now it happens that at present, for historico-cultural reasons, it is women who are opening up to and benefiting from this vatic bisexuality which doesn't annul differences but stirs them up, pursues them, increases their number. In a certain way, "woman is bisexual"; man – it's a secret to no one – being poised to keep glorious phallic monosexuality in view. By virtue of affirming the primacy of the phallus and of bringing it into play, phallocratic ideology has claimed more than one victim. As a woman, I've been clouded over by the great shadow of the scepter and been told: idolize it, that which you cannot brandish. But at the same time, man has been handed that grotesque and scarcely enviable destiny (just imagine) of being reduced to a single idol with clay balls. And consumed, as Freud and his followers note, by a fear of being a woman! For, if psychoanalysis was constituted from woman, to repress femininity (and not so successful a repression at that – men have made it clear), its account of masculine sexuality is now hardly refutable; as with all the "human" sciences, it reproduces the masculine view, of which it is one of the effects.

Here we encounter the inevitable man-with-rock, standing erect in his old Freudian realm, in the way that, to take the figure back to the point where linguistics is conceptualizing it "anew," Lacan preserves it in the sanctuary of the phallos (φ) "sheltered" from *castration's lack*! Their "symbolic" exists, it holds power – we, the sowers of disorder, know it only too well. But we are in no way obliged to deposit our lives in their banks of lack, to consider the constitution of the subject in terms of a drama manglingly restaged, to reinstate again and again the religion of the father. Because we don't want that. We don't fawn around the supreme hole. We have no womanly reason to pledge allegiance to the negative. The feminine (as the poets suspected) affirms: "... And yes," says Molly, carrying *Ulysses* off beyond any book and toward the new writing; "I said yes, I will Yes."

The Dark Continent is neither dark nor unexplorable. – It is still unexplored only because we've been made to believe that it was too dark to be explorable. And because they want to make us believe that what interests us is the white continent, with its monuments to Lack. And we believed. They riveted us between two horrifying myths: between the Medusa and the abyss. That would be enough to set half the world laughing, except that it's still going on. For the phallologocentric sublation[5] is with us, and it's militant, regenerating the old patterns, anchored in the dogma of castration. They haven't changed a thing: they've theorized their desire for reality! Let the priests tremble, we're going to show them our sexts!

Too bad for them if they fall apart upon discovering that women aren't men, or that the mother doesn't have one. But isn't this fear convenient for them? Wouldn't the worst be, isn't the worst, in truth, that women aren't castrated, that they have only to stop listening to the Sirens (for the Sirens were men) for history to change its meaning? You only have to look at the Medusa straight on to see her. And she's not deadly. She's beautiful and she's laughing.

Men say that there are two unrepresentable things: death and the feminine sex. That's because they need femininity to be associated with death; it's the jitters that gives them a hard-on! for themselves! They need to be afraid of us. Look at the trembling Perseuses moving backward toward us, clad in apotropes. What lovely backs! Not another minute to lose. Let's get out of here.

Let's hurry: the continent is not impenetrably dark. I've been there often. I was overjoyed one day to run into Jean Genêt. It was in *Pompes funèbres*.[6] He had come there led by his Jean. There are some men (all too few) who aren't afraid of femininity.

Almost everything is yet to be written by women about femininity: about their sexuality, that is, its infinite and mobile complexity, about their eroticization, sudden turn-ons of a certain miniscule-immense area of their bodies; not about destiny, but about the adventure of such and such a drive, about trips, crossings, trudges, abrupt and gradual awakenings, discoveries of a zone at one time timorous and soon to be forthright. A woman's body, with its thousand and one thresholds of ardor – once, by smashing yokes and censors, she lets it articulate the profusion of meanings that run through it in every direction – will make the old single-grooved mother tongue reverberate with more than one language.

We've been turned away from our bodies, shamefully taught to ignore them, to strike them with that stupid sexual modesty; we've been made victims of the old fool's game: each one will love the other sex. I'll give you your body and you'll give me mine. But who are the men who give women the body that women blindly yield to them? Why so few texts? Because so few women have as yet won back their body. Women must write through their bodies, they must invent the impregnable language that will wreck partitions, classes, and rhetorics, regulations and codes, they must submerge, cut through, get beyond the ultimate reserve-discourse, including the one that laughs at the very idea of pronouncing the word "silence," the one that, aiming for the impossible, stops short before the word "impossible" and writes it as "the end."

Such is the strength of women that, sweeping away syntax, breaking that famous thread (just a tiny little thread, they say) which acts for men as a surrogate umbilical cord, assuring them – otherwise they couldn't come – that the old lady is always right behind them, watching them make phallus, women will go right up to the impossible.

When the "repressed" of their culture and their society returns, it's an explosive, *utterly* destructive, staggering return, with a force never yet unleashed and equal to the most forbidding of suppressions. For when the Phallic period comes to an end, women will have been either annihilated or borne up to the highest and most violent incandescence. Muffled throughout their history, they have lived in dreams, in bodies (though muted), in silences, in aphonic revolts.

And with such force in their fragility; a fragility, a vulnerability, equal to their incomparable intensity. Fortunately, they haven't sublimated; they've saved their skin, their energy. They haven't worked at liquidating the impasse of lives without futures. They have furiously inhabited these sumptuous bodies: admirable hysterics who made Freud succumb to many voluptuous moments impossible to confess, bombarding his Mosaic statue with their carnal and passionate body words, haunting him with their inaudible and thundering denunciations, dazzling, more than naked underneath the seven veils of modesty. Those who, with a single word of the body, have inscribed the vertiginous immensity of a history which is sprung like an arrow from the whole history of men and from biblico-capitalist society, are the women, the supplicants of yesterday, who come as forebears of the new women, after whom no intersubjective relation will ever be the same. You, Dora, you the indomitable, the poetic body, you are the true "mistress" of the Signifier. Before long your efficacity will be seen at work when your speech is no longer suppressed, its point turned in against your breast, but written out over against the other.

In body. – More so than men who are coaxed toward social success, toward sublimation, women are body. More body, hence more writing. For a long time it has been in body that women have responded to persecution, to the familial-conjugal enterprise of domestication, to the repeated attempts at castrating them. Those who have turned their tongues 10,000 times seven times before not speaking are either dead from it or more familiar with their tongues and their mouths than anyone else. Now, I-woman am going to blow up the Law: an explosion henceforth possible and ineluctable; let it be done, right now, *in* language.

Let us not be trapped by an analysis still encumbered with the old automatisms. It's not to be feared that language conceals an invincible adversary, because it's the language of men and their grammar. We mustn't leave them a single place that's any more theirs alone than we are.

If woman has always functioned "within" the discourse of man, a signifier that has always referred back to the opposite signifier which annihilates its specific energy and diminishes or stifles its very different sounds, it is time for her to dislocate this "within," to explode it, turn it around, and seize it; to make it hers, containing it, taking it in her own mouth, biting that tongue with her very own teeth to invent for herself a language to get inside of. And you'll see with what ease she will spring forth from that "within" – the "within" where once she so drowsily crouched – to overflow at the lips she will cover the foam.

Nor is the point to appropriate their instruments, their concepts, their places, or to begrudge them their position of mastery. Just because there's a risk of identification doesn't mean that we'll succumb. Let's leave it to the worriers, to masculine anxiety and its obsession with how to dominate the way things work – knowing "how it works" in order to "make it work." For us the point is not to take possession in order to internalize or manipulate, but rather to dash through and to "fly."[7]

Flying is woman's gesture – flying in language and making it fly. We have all learned the art of flying and its numerous techniques; for centuries we've been able to possess anything only by flying; we've lived in flight, stealing away, finding, when desired, narrow passageways, hidden crossovers. It's no accident that *voler* has a double meaning, that it plays on each of them and thus throws off the agents of sense. It's no accident: women take after birds and robbers just as robbers take after women and birds. They (*illes*)[8] go by, fly the coop, take pleasure in jumbling the order of space, in disorienting it, in changing around the furniture, dislocating things and values, breaking them all up, emptying structures, and turning propriety upside down.

What woman hasn't flown/stolen? Who hasn't felt, dreamt, performed the gesture that jams sociality? Who hasn't crumbled, held up to ridicule, the bar of separation? Who hasn't inscribed with her body the differential, punctured the system of couples and opposition? Who, by some act of transgression, hasn't overthrown successiveness, connection, the wall of circumfusion?

A feminine text cannot fail to be more than subversive. It is volcanic; as it is written it brings about an upheaval of the old property crust, carrier of masculine investments; there's no other way. There's no room for her if she's not a he. If she's a her-she, it's in order to smash everything, to shatter the framework of institutions, to blow up the law, to break up the "truth" with laughter.

For once she blazes *her* trail in the symbolic, she cannot fail to make of it the chaosmos of the "personal" – in her pronouns, her nouns, and her clique of referents. And for good reason. There will have been the long history of gynocide. This is known by the colonized peoples of yesterday, the workers, the nations, the species off whose backs the history of men has made its gold; those who have known the ignominy of persecution derive from it an obstinate future desire for grandeur; those who are locked up know better than their jailers the taste of free air. Thanks to their history, women today know (how to do and want) what men will be able to conceive of only much later. I say woman overturns the "personal," for if, by means of laws, lies, blackmail, and marriage, her right to herself has been extorted at the same time as her name, she has been able, through the very movement of mortal alienation, to see more closely the inanity of "propriety," the reductive stinginess of the masculine-conjugal subjective economy, which she doubly resists. On the one hand she has constituted herself necessarily as that "person" capable of losing a part of herself without losing her integrity. But secretly, silently, deep down inside, she grows and multiplies, for, on the other hand, she knows far more about living and about the relation between the economy of the drives and the management of the ego than any man. Unlike man, who holds so dearly to his title and his titles, his pouches of value, his cap, crown, and everything connected with his head, woman couldn't care less about the fear of decapitation (or castration), adventuring, without the masculine temerity, into anonymity, which she can merge with without annihilating herself: because she's a giver.

I shall have a great deal to say about the whole deceptive problematic of the gift. Woman is obviously not that woman Nietzsche dreamed of who gives only in order to.[9]

Who could ever think of the gift as a gift-that-takes? Who else but man, precisely the one who would like to take everything?

If there is a "propriety of woman," it is paradoxically her capacity to depropriate unselfishly: body without end, without appendage, without principal "parts." If she is a whole, it's a whole composed of parts that are wholes, not simple partial objects but a moving, limitlessly changing ensemble, a cosmos tirelessly traversed by Eros, an immense astral space not organized around any one sun that's any more of a star than the others.

This doesn't mean that she's an undifferentiated magma, but that she doesn't lord it over her body or her desire. Though masculine sexuality gravitates around the penis, engendering that centralized body (in political anatomy) under the dictatorship of its parts, woman does not bring about the same regionalization which serves the couple head/genitals and which is inscribed only within boundaries. Her libido is cosmic, just as her unconscious is worldwide. Her writing can only keep going, without ever inscribing or discerning contours, daring to make these vertiginous crossings of the other(s) ephemeral and passionate sojourns in him, her, them, whom she inhabits long enough to look at from the point closest to their unconscious from the moment they awaken, to love them at the point closest to their drives: and then further, impregnated through and through with these brief, identificatory embraces, she goes and passes into infinity. She alone dares and wishes to know from within, where she, the outcast, has never ceased to hear the resonance of fore-language. She lets the other language speak – the language of 1,000 tongues which knows neither enclosure nor death. To life she refuses nothing. Her language does not contain, it carries; it does not hold back, it makes possible. When id is ambiguously uttered – the wonder of being several – she doesn't defend herself against these unknown women whom she's surprised at becoming, but derives pleasure from this gift of alterability. I am spacious, singing flesh, on which is grafted no one knows which I, more or less human, but alive because of transformation.

Write! and your self-seeking text will know itself better than flesh and blood, rising, insurrectionary dough kneading itself, with sonorous, perfumed ingredients, a lively combination of flying colors, leaves, and rivers plunging into the sea we feed. "Ah, there's her sea," he will say as he holds out to me a basin full of water from the little phallic mother from whom he's inseparable. But look, our seas are what we make of them, full of fish or not, opaque or transparent, red or black, high or smooth, narrow or bankless; and we are ourselves sea, sand, coral, seaweed, beaches, tides, swimmers, children, waves.... More or less wavily sea, earth, sky – what matter would rebuff us? We know how to speak them all.

Heterogeneous, yes. For her joyous benefit she is erogenous; she is the erotogeneity of the heterogeneous: airborne swimmer, in flight, she does not cling to herself: she is dispersible, prodigious, stunning, desirous and capable of others, of the other woman that she will be, of the other woman she isn't, of him, of you.

Woman be unafraid of any other place, of any same, or any other. My eyes, my tongue, my ears, my nose, my skin, my mouth, my body-for-(the)-other – not that I long for it in order to fill up a hole, to provide against some defect of mine, or because, as fate would have it, I'm spurred on by feminine "jealousy"; not because I've been dragged into the whole chain of substitutions that brings that which is substituted back to its ultimate object. That sort of thing you would expect to come straight out of "Tom Thumb," out of the *Penisneid* whispered to us by old grandmother ogresses, servants to their father-sons. If they believe, in order to muster up some self-importance, if they really need to believe that we're dying of desire, that we are this hole fringed with desire for their penis – that's their immemorial business. Undeniably (we verify it at our own expense – but also to our amusement), it's their business to let us know they're getting a hard-on, so that we'll assure them (we the maternal mistresses of their little pocket signifier) that they still can, that it's still there – that men structure themselves only by being fitted with a feather. In the child it's not the penis that the woman desires, it's not that famous bit of skin around which every man gravitates. Pregnancy cannot be traced back, except within the historical limits of the ancients, to some form of fate, to those mechanical substitutions brought about by the unconscious of some eternal "jealous woman"; not to penis envies; and not to narcissism or to some sort of homosexuality linked to the ever-present mother! Begetting a child doesn't mean that the woman or the man must fall ineluctably into patterns or must recharge the circuit of reproduction. If there's a risk there's not an inevitable trap: may women be spared the pressure, under the guise of consciousness-raising, of a supplement of interdictions. Either you want a kid or you don't – *that's your business*. Let nobody threaten you; in satisfying your desire, let not the fear of becoming the accomplice to a sociality succeed the old-time fear of being "taken." And man, are you still going to bank on everyone's blindness and passivity, afraid lest the child make a father and, consequently, that in having a kid the woman land herself more than one bad deal by engendering all at once child – mother – father – family? No; it's up to you to break the old circuits. It will be up to man and woman to render obsolete the former relationship and all its consequences, to consider the launching of a brand-new subject, alive, with defamilialization. Let us demater-paternalize rather than deny woman, in an effort to avoid the co-optation of procreation, a thrilling era of the body. Let us defetishize. Let's get away from the dialectic which has it that the only good father is a dead one, or that the child is the death of his parents. The child is the other, but the other without violence, bypassing loss, struggle. We're fed up with the reuniting of bonds forever to be severed, with the litany of castration that's handed down and genealogized. We won't advance backward anymore; we're not going to repress something so simple as the desire for life. Oral drive, anal drive, vocal drive – all these drives are our strengths, and among them is the gestation drive – just like the desire to write: a desire to live self from within, a desire for the swollen belly, for language, for blood. We are not going to refuse, if it should happen to strike our fancy, the unsurpassed pleasures of pregnancy which have actually been always exaggerated or conjured away – or cursed – in the classic texts. For if there's one thing that's been repressed here's just the place to find it: in the taboo of the pregnant woman. This says a lot about the power she seems invested with at the time, because it has always been suspected, that, when pregnant, the woman not only doubles her market value, but – what's more important – takes on intrinsic value as a woman in her own eyes and, undeniably, acquires body and sex.

There are thousands of ways of living one's pregnancy; to have or not to have with that still invisible other a relationship of another intensity. And if you don't have that particular yearning, it doesn't mean that you're in any way lacking. Each body distributes in its own special way, without model or norm, the nonfinite and changing totality of its desires. Decide for yourself on your position in the arena of contradictions, where pleasure and reality embrace. Bring the other to life. Women know how to live detachment; giving birth is neither losing nor increasing. It's adding to life an other. Am I dreaming? Am I mis-recognizing? You, the defenders of "theory," the sacrosanct yes-men of Concept, enthroners of the phallus (but not of the penis):

Once more you'll say that all this smacks of "idealism," or what's worse, you'll splutter that I'm a "mystic."

And what about the libido? Haven't I read the "Signification of the Phallus"? And what about separation, what about that bit of self for which, to be born, you undergo an ablation – an ablation, so they say, to be forever commemorated by your desire?

Besides, isn't it evident that the penis gets around in my texts, that I give it a place and appeal? Of course I do. I want all. I want all of me with all of him. Why should I deprive myself of a part of us? I want all of us. Woman of course has a desire for a "loving desire" and not a jealous one. But not because she is gelded; not because she's deprived and needs to be filled out, like some wounded person who wants to console herself or seek vengeance: I don't want a penis to decorate my body with. But I do desire the other for the other, whole and entire, male or female; because living means wanting everything that is, everything that lives, and wanting it alive. Castration? Let others toy with it. What's a desire originating from a lack? A pretty meager desire.

The woman who still allows herself to be threatened by the big dick, who's still impressed by the commotion of the phallic stance, who still leads a loyal master to the beat of the drum: that's the woman of yesterday. They still exist, easy and numerous victims of the oldest of farces; either they're cast in the original silent version in which, as titanesses lying under the mountains they make with their quivering, they never see erected that theoretic monument to the golden phallus looming, in the old manner, over their bodies. Or, coming today out of their *infans* period and into the second, "enlightened" version of their virtuous debasement, they see themselves suddenly assaulted by the builders of the analytic empire and, as soon as they've begun to formulate the new desire, naked, nameless, so happy at making an appearance, they're taken in their bath by the new old men, and then, whoops! Luring them with flashy signifiers, the demon of interpretation – oblique, decked out in modernity – sells them the same old handcuffs, baubles, and chains. Which castration do you prefer? Whose degrading do you like better, the father's or the mother's? Oh, what pwetty eyes, you pwetty little girl. Here, buy my glasses and you'll see the Truth-Me-Myself tell you everything you should know. Put them on your nose and take a fetishist's look (you are me, the other analyst – that's what I'm telling you) at your body and the body of the other. You see? No? Wait, you'll have everything explained to you, and you'll know at last which sort of neurosis you're related to. Hold still, we're going to do your portrait, so that you can begin looking like it right away.

Yes, the naives to the first and second degree are still legion. If the New Women, arriving now, dare to create outside the theoretical, they're called in by the cops of the signifier, fingerprinted, remonstrated, and brought into the line of order that they are supposed to know; assigned by force of trickery to a precise place in the chain that's always formed for the benefit of a privileged signifier. We are pieced back to the string which leads back, if not to the Name-of-the-Father, then, for a new twist, to the place of the phallic-mother.

Beware, my friend, of the signifier that would take you back to the authority of a signified! Beware of diagnoses that would reduce your generative powers. "Common" nouns are also proper nouns that disparage your singularity by classifying it into species. Break out of the circles; don't remain within the psychoanalytic closure. Take a look around, then cut through!

And if we are legion, it's because the war of liberation has only made as yet a tiny breakthrough. But women are thronging to it. I've seen them, those who will be neither dupe nor domestic, those who will not fear the risk of being a woman; will not fear any risk, any desire, any space still unexplored in themselves, among themselves and others or anywhere else. They do not fetishize, they do not deny, they do not hate. They observe, they approach, they try to see the other woman, the child, the lover – not to strengthen their own narcissism or verify the solidity or weakness of the master, but to make love better, to invent.

Other love. – In the beginning are our differences. The new love dares for the other, wants the other, makes dizzying, precipitous flights between knowledge and invention. The woman arriving over and over again does not stand still; she's everywhere, she exchanges, she is the desire-that-gives. (Not enclosed in the paradox of the gift that takes nor under the illusion of unitary fusion. We're past that.) She comes in, comes-in-between herself me and you, between herself me and you, between the other me where one is always infinitely more than one and more than me, without the fear of ever reaching a limit; she thrills in our becoming. And we'll keep on becoming! She cuts through defensive loves, motherages, and devourations: beyond selfish narcissism, in the moving, open, transitional space, she runs her risks. Beyond the struggle-to-the-death that's been removed to the bed, beyond the love-battle that claims to represent exchange, she scorns at an Eros dynamic that would be fed by hatred. Hatred: a heritage, again, a remainder, a duping subservience to the phallus. To love, to watch-think-seek the other in the other, to despecularize, to unhoard. Does this seem difficult? It's not impossible, and this is what nourishes life – a love that has no commerce with the apprehensive desire that provides against the lack and stultifies the strange; a love that rejoices in the exchange that multiplies. Wherever history still unfolds as the history of death, she does not tread. Opposition, hierarchizing exchange, the struggle for mastery which can end only in at least one death (one master – one slave, or two nonmasters ≠ two dead) – all that comes from a period in time governed by phallocentric values. The fact that this period extends into the present doesn't prevent woman from starting the history of life somewhere else. Elsewhere, she gives. She doesn't "know" what she's giving, she doesn't measure it; she gives, though, neither a counterfeit impression nor something she hasn't got. She gives more, with no assurance that she'll get back even some unexpected profit from what she puts out. She gives that there may be life, thought, transformation. This is an "economy" that can no longer be put in economic terms. Wherever she loves, all the old concepts of management are left behind. At the end of a more or less conscious computation, she finds not her sum but her differences. I am for you what you want me to be at the moment you look at me in a way you've never seen me before: at every instant. When I write, it's everything that we don't know we can be that is written out of me, without exclusions, without stipulation, and everything we will be calls us to the unflagging, intoxicating, unappeasable search for love. In one another we will never be lacking.

University of Paris VIII – Vincennes

Notes

1   Men still have everything to say about their sexuality, and everything to write. For what they have said so far, for the most part, stems from the opposition activity/passivity, from the power relation between a fantasized obligatory virility meant to invade, to colonize, and the consequential phantasm of woman as a "dark continent" to penetrate and to "pacify." (We know what "pacify" means in terms of scotomizing the other and misrecognizing the self.) Conquering her, they've made haste to depart from her borders, to get out of sight, out of body. The way man has of getting out of himself and into her whom he takes not for the other but for his own, deprives him, he knows, of his own bodily territory. One can understand how man, confusing himself with his penis and rushing

in for the attack, might feel resentment and fear of being "taken" by the woman, of being lost in her, absorbed, or alone.

2 I am speaking here only of the place "reserved" for women by the Western world.

3 Which works, then, might be called feminine? I'll just point out some examples: one would have to give them full readings to bring out what is pervasively feminine in their significance. Which I shall do elsewhere. In France (have you noted our infinite poverty in this field? – the Anglo-Saxon countries have shown resources of distinctly greater consequence), leading through what's come out of the twentieth century – and it's not much – the only inscriptions of femininity that I have seen were by Colette, Marguerite Duras, ... and Jean Genêt.

4 "*Dé-pense*," a neologism formed on the verb *penser*, hence "unthinks," but also "spends" (from *dèpenser*) (translator's note).

5 Standard English term for the Hegelian *Aufhebung*, the French *la relève*

6 Jean Genêt, *Pompes funèbres* (Paris, 1948), p. 185.

7 Also, "to steal." Both meanings of the verb *voler* are played on, as the text itself explains in the following paragraph (translator's note).

8 *Illes* is a fusion of the masculine pronoun *ils*, which refers back to birds and robbers, with the feminine pronoun *elles*, which refers to women (translator's note).

9 Reread Derrida's text, "Le Style de la femine," in *Nietzsche aujourd'hui* (Paris: Union Générale d'Editions, Coll. 10/18), where the philosopher can be seen operating an *Aufhebung* of all philosophy in its systematic reducing of woman to the place of seduction: she appears as the one who is taken for; the bait in person, all veils unfurled, the one who doesn't give but who gives only in order to (take).

CHAPTER 5

Imitation and Gender Insubordination

Judith Butler

Judith Butler's 1982 book, *Gender Trouble*, helped initiate the new field of Gender Studies. In it, she argued that gender identity is fabricated through identification with cultural ideals of masculinity and femininity that are repetitively performed into being. Freud had noticed that identity is formed through the internalization of images of parents. Butler transposes this model to the way culture provides images of gender identity to its members. By repeating those images in the daily performances of life, we seem to approximate an identity that is stable and complete, but because such identity arises through imitation and repetition, there are always gaps of uncertainty and incompleteness that render gender inherently unstable as a category.

Here is something like a confession which is meant merely to thematize the impossibility of confession: As a young person, I suffered for a long time, and I suspect many people have, from being told, explicitly or implicitly, that what I "am" is a copy, an imitation, a derivative example, a shadow of the real. Compulsory heterosexuality sets itself up as the original, the true, the authentic; the norm that determines the real implies that "being" lesbian is always a kind of miming, a vain effort to participate in the phantasmatic plenitude of naturalized heterosexuality which will always and only fail.[1] And yet, I remember quite distinctly when I first read in Esther Newton's *Mother Camp: "Female" Impersonators in America*[2] that drag is not an imitation or a copy of some prior and true gender; according to Newton, drag enacts the very structure of impersonation by which any *gender* is assumed. Drag is not the putting on of a gender that belongs properly to some other group, i.e. an act of expropriation or appropriation that assumes that gender is the rightful property of sex, that "masculine" belongs to "male" and "feminine" belongs to "female." There is no "proper" gender, a gender proper to one sex rather than another, which is in some sense that sex's cultural property. Where that notion of the "proper" operates, it is always and only improperly installed as the effect of a compulsory system. Drag constitutes the mundane way in which genders are appropriated, theatricalized, worn, and done; it implies that all gendering is a kind of impersonation

Original publication details: Judith Butler, "Imitation and Gender Insubordination" from *Inside/Out*, ed. Diana Fuss, pp. 13–31. Routledge, 1991. Reproduced with permission from Taylor & Francis.

Literary Theory: An Anthology, Third Edition. Edited by Julie Rivkin and Michael Ryan.
© 2017 John Wiley & Sons, Ltd. Published 2017 by John Wiley & Sons, Ltd.

and approximation. If this is true, it seems, there is no original or primary gender that drag imitates, but *gender is a kind of imitation for which there is no original*; in fact, it is a kind of imitation that produces the very notion of the original as an *effect* and consequence of the imitation itself. In other words, the naturalistic effects of heterosexualized genders are produced through imitative strategies; what they imitate is a phantasmatic ideal of heterosexual identity, one that is produced by the imitation as its effect. In this sense, the "reality" of heterosexual identities is performatively constituted through an imitation that sets itself up as the origin and the ground of all imitations. In other words, heterosexuality is always in the process of imitating and approximating its own phantasmatic idealization of itself—*and failing*. Precisely because it is bound to fail, and yet endeavors to succeed, the project of heterosexual identity is propelled into an endless repetition of itself. Indeed, in its efforts to naturalize itself as the originally heterosexuality must be understood as a compulsive and compulsory repetition that can only produce the *effect* of its own originality; in other words, compulsory heterosexual identities, those ontologically consolidated phantasms of "man" and "woman," are theatrically produced effects that posture as grounds, origins, the normative measure of the real.[3]

Reconsider then the homophobic charge that queens and butches and femmes are imitations of the heterosexual real. Here "imitation" carries the meaning of "derivative" or "secondary," a copy of an origin which is itself the ground of all copies, but which is itself a copy of nothing. Logically, this notion of an "origin" is suspect, for how can something operate as an origin if there are no secondary consequences which retrospectively confirm the originality of that origin? The origin requires its derivations in order to affirm itself as an origin, for origins only make sense to the extent that they are differentiated from that which they produce as derivatives. Hence, if it were not for the notion of the homosexual as copy, there would be no construct of heterosexuality *as* origin. Heterosexuality here presupposes homosexuality. And if the homosexual as copy *precedes* the heterosexual as origin, then it seems only fair to concede that the copy comes before the origin, and that homosexuality is thus the origin, and heterosexuality the copy.

But simple inversions are not really possible. For it is only *as* a copy that homosexuality can be argued to *precede* heterosexuality as the origin. In other words, the entire framework of copy and origin proves radically unstable as each position inverts into the other and confounds the possibility of any stable way to locate the temporal or logical priority of either term.

But let us then consider this problematic inversion from a psychic/political perspective. If the structure of gender imitation is such that the imitated is to some degree produced – or, rather, *re*produced – by imitation (see again Derrida's inversion and displacement of mimesis in "The Double Session"), then to claim that gay and lesbian identities are implicated in heterosexual norms or in hegemonic culture generally is not to *derive* gayness from straightness. On the contrary, *imitation* does not copy that which is prior, but produces and *inverts* the very terms of priority and derivativeness. Hence, if gay identities are implicated in heterosexuality, that is not the same as claiming that they are determined or derived from heterosexuality, and it is not the same as claiming that that heterosexuality is the only cultural network in which they are implicated. These are, quite literally, *inverted* imitations, ones which invert the order of imitated and imitation, and which, in the process, expose the fundamental dependency of "the origin" on that which it claims to produce as its secondary effect.

What follows if we concede from the start that gay identities as derivative inversions are in part defined in terms of the very heterosexual identities from which they are differentiated? If heterosexuality is an impossible imitation of itself, an imitation that performatively constitutes itself as the original, then the imitative parody of "heterosexuality" – when and where it exists in gay cultures – is always and only an imitation of an imitation, a copy of a copy, for which there is no original. Put in yet a different way, the parodic or imitative effect of gay identities works neither to copy nor to emulate heterosexuality, but rather, to expose heterosexuality as an incessant and *panicked* imitation of its own naturalized idealization. That heterosexuality is always in the act of elaborating itself is evidence that it is perpetually at risk, that is, that it "knows" its own possibility of becoming undone: hence, its compulsion to repeat which is at once a foreclosure of that which threatens its coherence. That it can never eradicate that risk it attests to its profound dependency upon the homosexuality that it seeks fully to eradicate and never can or that it seeks to make second, but which is always already there as a prior possibility.[4] Although this failure of naturalized heterosexuality might constitute a source of pathos for heterosexuality itself – what its theorists often refer to as its constitutive malaise – it can become an occasion for a subversive and proliferating parody of gender norms in which the very claim to originality and to the real is shown to be the effect of a certain kind of naturalized gender mime.

It is important to recognize the ways in which heterosexual norms reappear within gay identities, to affirm that gay and lesbian identities are not only structured in part by dominant heterosexual frames, but that they are *not* for that reason *determined* by them. They are running commentaries on those naturalized positions as well, parodic replays and resignifications of precisely those heterosexual structures that would consign gay life to discursive domains of unreality and unthinkability. But to be constituted or structured in part by the very heterosexual norms by which gay people are oppressed is not, I repeat, to be claimed or determined by those structures. And it is not necessary to think of such heterosexual constructs as the pernicious intrusion of "the straight mind" one that must be rooted out in its entirety. In a way, the presence of heterosexual constructs and positionalities in whatever form in gay and lesbian identities presupposes that there is a gay and lesbian repetition of straightness, a recapitulation of straightness – which is itself a repetition and recapitulation of its own ideality – within its own terms, a site in which all sorts of resignifying and parodic repetitions become possible. The parodic replication and resignification of heterosexual constructs within non-heterosexual frames brings into relief the utterly constructed status of the so-called original, but it shows that heterosexuality only constitutes itself as the original through a convincing act of repetition. The more that "act" is expropriated, the more the heterosexual claim to originality is exposed as illusory.

Although I have concentrated in the above on the reality-effects of gender practices, performances, repetitions, and mimes, I do not mean to suggest that drag is a "role" that can be taken on or taken off at will. There is no volitional subject behind the mime who decides, as it were, which gender it will be today. On the contrary, the very possibility of becoming a viable subject requires that a certain gender mime be already underway. The "being" of the subject is no more self-identical than the "being" of any gender; in fact, coherent gender, achieved through an apparent repetition of the same, produces as its *effect* the illusion of a prior and volitional subject. In this sense, gender is not a performance that a prior subject elects to do, but gender is *performative* in the sense that it constitutes as an effect the very subject it appears to express. It is a *compulsory* performance in the sense that acting out of line with heterosexual norms brings with it ostracism, punishment, and violence, not to mention the transgressive pleasures produced by those very prohibitions.

To claim that there is no performer prior to the performed, that the performance is performative, that the performance constitutes the appearance of a "subject" as its effect is difficult to accept. This difficulty is the result of a predisposition to think of sexuality and gender as "expressing" in some indirect or direct way a psychic reality that precedes it. The denial of the *priority* of the subject, however, is not the denial of the subject; in fact, the refusal to conflate the subject with the psyche marks the psychic as that which exceeds the domain of the conscious subject. This psychic excess is precisely what is being systematically denied by the notion of a volitional "subject" who elects at will which gender and/or sexuality to be at any given time and place. It is this excess which erupts within the intervals of those repeated gestures and acts that construct the apparent uniformity of heterosexual positionalities, indeed which compels the repetition itself, and which guarantees its perpetual failure. In this sense, it is this excess which, within the heterosexual economy, implicitly includes homosexuality, that perpetual threat of a disruption which is quelled through a reenforced repetition of the same. And yet, if repetition is the way in which power works to construct the illusion of a seamless heterosexual identity, if heterosexuality is compelled to *repeat itself* in order to establish the illusion of its own uniformity and identity, then this is an identity permanently at risk, for what if it fails to repeat, or if the very exercise of repetition is redeployed for a very different performative purpose? If there is, as it were, always a compulsion to repeat, repetition never fully accomplishes identity. That there is a need for a repetition at all is a sign that identity is not self-identical. It requires to be instituted again and again, which is to say that it runs the risk of becoming de-instituted at every interval.

So what is this psychic excess, and what will constitute a subversive or de-instituting repetition? First, it is necessary to consider that sexuality always exceeds any given performance, presentation, or narrative which is why it is not possible to derive or read off a sexuality from any given gender presentation. And sexuality may be said to exceed any definitive narrativization. Sexuality is never fully "expressed" in a performance or practice; there will be passive and butchy femmes, femmy and aggressive butches, and both of those, and more, will turn out to describe more or less anatomically stable "males" and "females." There are no direct expressive or causal lines between sex, gender, gender presentation, sexual practice, fantasy and sexuality. None of those terms captures or determines the rest. Part of what constitutes sexuality is precisely that which does not appear and that which, to some degree, can never appear. This is perhaps the most fundamental reason why sexuality is to some degree always closeted, especially to the one who would express it through acts of self-disclosure. That which is excluded for a given gender presentation to "succeed" may be precisely what is played out sexually, that is, an "inverted" relation, as it were, between gender and gender presentation, and gender presentation and sexuality. On the other hand, both gender presentation and sexual practices may corollate such that it appears that the former "expresses" the latter, and yet both are jointly constituted by the very sexual possibilities that they exclude.

This logic of inversion gets played out interestingly in versions of lesbian butch and femme gender stylization. For a butch can present herself as capable, forceful, and all-providing, and a stone butch may well seek to constitute her lover as the exclusive site of erotic attention and pleasure. And yet, this "providing" butch who seems *at first* to replicate a certain husband-like role, can find herself caught in a logic of inversion whereby that "providingness" turns to a self-sacrifice, which implicates her in the most ancient trap of feminine self-abnegation. She may well find herself in a situation of radical need, which is precisely what she sought to locate, find, and fulfill in her femme lover. In effect, the butch inverts into the femme or remains caught up in the specter of that inversion, or takes pleasure in it. On the other hand, the femme who, as Amber Hollibaugh has argued, "orchestrates" sexual exchange,[5] may well eroticize a certain dependency only to learn that the very power to orchestrate that dependency exposes her own incontrovertible power, at which point she inverts into a butch or becomes caught up in the specter of that inversion, or perhaps delights in it.

Psychic Mimesis

What stylizes or forms an erotic style and/or a gender presentation – and that which makes such categories inherently unstable – is a set of *psychic identifications* that are not simple to describe. Some psychoanalytic theories tend to construe identification and desire as two mutually exclusive relations to love objects that have been lost through prohibition and/or separation. Any intense emotional attachment thus divides into either wanting to have someone or wanting to be that someone, but never both at once. It is important to consider that identification and desire can coexist, and that their formulation in terms of mutually exclusive oppositions serves a heterosexual matrix. But I would like to focus attention on yet a different construal of that scenario, namely, that "wanting to be" and "wanting to have" can operate to differentiate mutually exclusive positionalities internal to lesbian erotic exchange. Consider that identifications are always made in response to loss of some kind, and that they involve a certain *mimetic practice* that seeks to incorporate the lost love within the very "identity" of the one who remains. This was Freud's thesis in "Mourning and Melancholia" in 1917 and continues to inform contemporary psychoanalytic discussions of identification.[6]

For psychoanalytic theorists Mikkel Borch-Jacobsen and Ruth Leys, however, identification and, in particular, identificatory mimetism, *precedes* "identity" and constitutes identity as that which is fundamentally "other to itself." The notion of this Other *in* the self, as it were, implies that the self/Other distinction is *not* primarily external (a powerful critique of ego psychology follows from this); the self is from the start radically implicated in the "Other." This theory of primary mimetism differs from Freud's account of melancholic incorporation. In Freud's view, which I continue to find useful, incorporation – a kind of psychic miming – is a response to, and refusal of, *loss*. Gender as the site of such psychic mimes is thus constituted by the variously gendered Others who have been loved and lost, where the loss is suspended through a melancholic and imaginary incorporation (and preservation) of those Others into the psyche. Over and against this account of psychic mimesis by way of incorporation and melancholy, the theory of primary mimetism argues an even stronger position in favor of the non-self identity of the psychic subject. Mimetism is not motivated by a drama of loss and wishful recovery, but appears to precede and constitute desire (and motivation) itself, in this sense; mimetism would be prior to the possibility of loss and the disappointments of love.

Whether loss or mimetism is primary (perhaps an undecidable problem), the psychic subject is nevertheless constituted internally by differentially gendered Others and is, therefore, never, as a gender, self-identical.

In my view, the self only becomes a self on the condition that it has suffered a separation (grammar fails us here, for the "it" only becomes differentiated through that separation), a loss which is suspended and provisionally resolved through a melancholic incorporation of some "Other." That "Other" installed in the self thus establishes the permanent incapacity of that itself to achieve self-identity; it is as it were always already disrupted by that Other; the disruption of the Other at the heart of the self is the very condition of that self's possibility.[7]

Such a consideration of psychic identification would vitiate the possibility of any stable set of typologies that explain or describe something like gay or lesbian identities. And any efforts to supply one – as evidenced in Kaja Silverman's recent inquiries into male homosexuality – suffer from simplification, and conform, with alarming ease, to the regulatory requirements of diagnostic epistemic regimes. If incorporation in Freud's sense in 1914 is an effort to *preserve* a lost and loved object and to refuse or postpone the recognition of loss and, hence, of grief, then to become *like* one's mother or father or sibling or other early "lovers" may be an act of love and/or a hateful effort to replace or displace. How would we "typologize" the ambivalence at the heart of mimetic incorporations such as these?[8]

How does this consideration of psychic identification return us to the question, what constitutes a subversive repetition? How are troublesome identifications apparent in cultural practices? Well, consider the way in which heterosexuality naturalizes itself through setting up certain illusions of continuity between sex, gender, and desire. When Aretha Franklin sings, "you make me feel like a natural woman," she seems at first to suggest that some natural potential of her biological sex is actualized by her participation in the cultural position of "woman" as object of heterosexual recognition. Something in her "sex" is thus expressed by her "gender" which is then fully known and consecrated within the heterosexual scene. There is no breakage, no discontinuity between "sex" as biological facticity and essence, or between gender and sexuality. Although Aretha appears to be all too glad to have her naturalness confirmed, she also seems fully and paradoxically mindful that that confirmation is never guaranteed, that the effect of naturalness is only achieved as a consequence of that moment of heterosexual recognition. After all, Aretha sings, you make me feel like a natural woman, suggesting that this is a kind of metaphorical substitution, an act of imposture, a kind of sublime and momentary participation in an ontological illusion produced by the mundane operation of heterosexual drag.

But what if Aretha were singing to me? Or what if she were singing to a drag queen whose performance somehow confirmed her own?

How do we take account of these kinds of identifications? It's not that there is some kind of *sex* that exists in hazy biological form that is somehow *expressed* in the gait, the posture, the gesture; and that some sexuality then expresses both that apparent gender or that more or less magical sex. If gender is drag, and if it is an imitation that regularly produces the ideal it attempts to approximate, then gender is a performance that *produces* the illusion of an inner sex or essence or psychic gender core; it *produces* on the skin, through the gesture, the move, the gait (that array of corporeal theatrics understood as gender presentation), the illusion of an inner depth. In effect, one way that genders gets naturalized is through being constructed as an inner psychic or physical *necessity*. And yet, it is always a surface sign, a signification on and with the public body that produces this illusion of an inner depth, necessity, or essence that is somehow magically, causally expressed.

To dispute the psyche as *inner depth*, however, is not to refuse the psyche altogether. On the contrary, the psyche calls to be rethought precisely as a compulsive repetition, as that which conditions and disables the repetitive performance of identity. If every performance repeats itself to institute the effect of identity, then every repetition requires an interval between the acts, as it were, in which risk and excess threaten to disrupt the identity being constituted. The unconscious is this excess that enables and contests every performance, and which never fully appears within the performance itself. The psyche is not "in" the body, but in the very signifying process through which that body comes to appear it is the lapse in repetition as well as its compulsion, precisely what the performance seeks to deny and that which compels it from the start.

To locate the psyche within this signifying chain as the instability of all iterability is not the same as claiming that it is [an] inner core that is awaiting its full and liberatory expression. On the contrary, the psyche is the permanent failure of expression a failure that has its values, for it impels repetition and so reinstates the possibility of disruption. What then does it mean to pursue disruptive repetition within compulsory heterosexuality?

Although compulsory heterosexuality often presumes that there is first a sex that is expressed through a gender and then through a sexuality, it may now be necessary fully to invert and displace that operation of thought. If a regime of sexuality mandates a compulsory performance of sex then it may be only through that performance that the binary system of gender and the binary system of sex come to have intelligibility at all. It may be that the very categories of sex of sexual identity of gender are produced or maintained in the *effects* of this compulsory performance, effects which are disingenuously renamed as causes, origins, disingenuously lined up within a causal or expressive sequence that the heterosexual norm produces to legitimate itself as the origin of all sex. How then to expose the causal lines as retrospectively and performatively produced fabrications, and to engage gender itself as an inevitable fabrication, to fabricate gender in terms which reveal every claim to the origin, the inner, the true, and the real as nothing other than the effects of *drag*, whose subversive possibilities ought to be played and replayed to make the "sex" of gender into a site of insistent political play? Perhaps this will be a matter of working sexuality *against* identity even against gender, and of letting that which cannot fully appear in any performance persist in its disruptive promise.

Notes

1 Although miming suggests that there is a prior model which is being copied it can have the effect of exposing that prior model as purely phantasmatic. In Jacques Derrida's "The Double Session" in *Dissemination*, trans. Barbara Johnson (Chicago: University of Chicago Press, 1981) he considers the textual effect of the mime in Mallarmé's "Mimique." There Derrida argues that the mime does not imitate or copy some prior phenomenon, idea, or figure but constitutes – some might say *performatively* – the phantasm of the original in and through the mime:

> He represents nothing, imitates nothing, does not have to conform to any prior referent with the aim of achieving adequation or verisimilitude. One can here foresee an objection: since the mime imitates nothing, reproduces nothing, opens up in its origin the very thing he is tracing out, presenting, or producing, he must be the very movement of truth. Not, of course, truth in the form of adequation between the representation and the present of the thing itself or between the imitator and the imitated but truth as the present unveiling of the present ... But this is not the case ... we are faced then with mimicry imitating nothing: faced so to

speak with a double that couples no simple, a double that nothing anticipates, nothing at least that is not itself already double. There is no simple reference ... This speculum reflects no reality: it produces mere "reality-effects" ... In this speculum with no reality in this mirror of a mirror a difference or dyad does exist since there are mimes and phantoms. But it is a difference without reference or rather reference without a referent, without any first or last unit, a ghost that is the phantom of no flesh ... (p. 206)

2   Esther Newton, *Mother Camp: "Female" Impersonators in America* (Chicago: University of Chicago Press, 1972).

3   In a sense one might offer a redescription of the above in Lacanian terms. The sexual "positions" of heterosexually differentiated "man" and "woman" are part of the *Symbolic*, that is an ideal embodiment of the Law of sexual difference which constitutes the object of imaginary pursuits but which is always thwarted by the "real." These symbolic positions for Lacan are by definition impossible to occupy even as they are impossible to resist as the structuring telos of desire. I accept the former point and reject the latter one. The imputation of universal necessity to such positions simply encodes compulsory heterosexuality at the level of the Symbolic and the "failure" to achieve it is implicitly lamented as a source of heterosexual pathos.

4   Of course, it is Eve Kosofsky Sedgwick's *Epistemology of the Closet* (Berkeley: University of California Press, 1990) which traces the subtleties of this kind of panic in Western heterosexual epistemes.

5   Amber Hollibaugh and Cherrie Moraga, "What We're Rollin Around in Bed With: Sexual Silences in Feminism," in Ann Snitow, Christine Stansell, and Sharon Thompson, eds, *Powers of Desire: The Politics of Sexuality* (New York: Monthly Review Press, 1983), pp. 394–405.

6   Mikkel Borch-Jacobsen, *The Freudian Subject* (Stanford: Stanford University Press, 1988); for citations of Ruth Leys's work, see the following two endnotes.

7   For a very fine analysis of primary mimetism with direct implications for gender formation, see Ruth Leys, "The Real Miss Beauchamp: The History and Sexual Politics of the Multiple Personality Concept," in Judith Butler and Joan W. Scott, eds, *Feminists Theorize the Political* (New York and London: Routledge, 1992). For Leys, a primary mimetism or suggestibility requires that the "self" from the start is constituted by its incorporations; the effort to differentiate oneself from that by which one is constituted is, of course, impossible, but it does entail a certain "incorporative violence," to use her term. The violence of identification is in this way in the service of an effort at differentiation, to take the place of the Other who is, as it were, insulted at the foundation of the self. That this replacement, which seeks to be a displacement, fails, and must repeat itself endlessly, becomes the trajectory of one's psychic career.

8   Here again, I think it is the work of Ruth Leys which will clarify some of the complex questions of gender constitution that emerge from a close psychoanalytic consideration of imitation and identification. Her forthcoming book manuscript will doubtless galvanize this field: *The Subject of Imitation*.

CHAPTER 6

Global Identities: Theorizing Transnational Studies of Sexuality

Inderpal Grewal and Caren Kaplan

Inderpal Grewal teaches gender and sexuality studies at Yale University. Caren Kaplan is Professor of American Studies at the University of California, Davis. Kaplan is the author of *Questions of Travel* (1996). Grewal's books include *Transnational America* (2005) and *Theorizing NGOs* (2014). Together they have written *An Introduction to Women's Studies* (2005) and *Scattered Hegemonies* (1994).

In modernity, identities inevitably become global. Indeed, few things remain local in the aftermath of the rise of capitalism. Just as goods and people come to circulate in new ways, so too identities emerge and come into specific relations of circulation and expansion. In this globalized framework of encounter and exchange, sexual identities are similar to other kinds of identities in that they are imbued with power relations. These power relations are connected to inequalities that result from earlier forms of globalization, but they have also generated new asymmetries. Our task is to examine both the specificities and the continuities within the globalization of sexual identities at the present juncture.

For the most part, throughout the twentieth century, what we might call politically "progressive" studies of sexuality emerged as a result of identity politics and social movements. Increasingly, with the rise of ethnic and postcolonial studies and the growing emphasis on diaspora in American studies, the scholarship on sexuality is globalized.[1] Yet thinking simply about global identities does not begin to get at the complex terrain of sexual politics that is at once national, regional, local, even "cross-cultural" and hybrid. In many works on globalization, the "global" is seen either as a homogenizing influence or as a neocolonial movement of ideas and capital from West to non-West.[2] Debates on the nature of global identities have suggested the inadequacy of understanding globalization simply through political economy or through theories of "Western" cultural imperialism and have pushed us to probe further the

Original publication details: Inderpal Grewal and Caren Kaplan, "Global Identities: Theorizing Transnational Studies of Sexuality." *GLQ: A Journal of Lesbian and Gay Studies* 7.4 (2001), pp. 663–679. Duke University Press, 2001. Reproduced with permission from Duke University Press.

Literary Theory: An Anthology, Third Edition. Edited by Julie Rivkin and Michael Ryan.
© 2017 John Wiley & Sons, Ltd. Published 2017 by John Wiley & Sons, Ltd.

relationship between globalization and culture.[3] Yet how do we understand these emerging identities, given the divergent theories regarding the relationship between globalization and cultural formations? Can these identities be called "global identities," or is some other term more useful?

In light of the problems that some scholars have pointed out with the rhetoric of diversity and globality with respect to sexual identity, such that these discourses produce a "monumentalist gay identity" and elide "radical sexual difference," the term *transnational* seems to us more helpful in getting to the specifics of sexualities in postmodernity.[4] As we have argued elsewhere, the term *transnational* can address the asymmetries of the globalization process.[5] Yet it has become so ubiquitous in cultural, literary, and critical studies that much of its political valence seems to have become evacuated. Is this a function of globalization in its cultural aspects, of the ways in which it has become a truism that everyone and everything are always already displaced and hence "transnational"? Or is it a function of the modernist search for novelty and innovation leading to the adoption of a seemingly new term for a global world? Perhaps these two tendencies are intertwined, and this term works at this point because it has become "real" or "appropriate" in some way that it would do us good to examine. By thinking about the many ways in which the term is being rearticulated, we can understand the rhetorical imperative that underlies such uses. Since terms and critical practices are neither authentic nor pure, we do not wish to argue that one use is more correct than another. Rather, we need to examine the circulation of this term and its regulation through institutional sites, such as academic publishing, conference panels and papers, and academic personnel matters. By doing so, we can begin to understand how the study of sexuality remains bound by disciplinary constraints. A more interdisciplinary and transnational approach that addresses inequalities as well as new formations can begin more adequately to explore the nature of sexual identities in the current phase of globalization.

We can identify several primary ways in which the term *transnational* does a particular kind of work in the U.S. academy in general. First, it circulates widely as a more useful term to describe migration at the present time. This is the application that we find most often at work in anthropology, for example, in the work that theorizes migration as a transnational process.[6] In emphasizing labor migration, this approach leaves out other factors in the globalization of labor. We can also identify an application in the notion of "transnational flows," a concept that sometimes ignores inequities as well as those aspects of modernity that seem fixed or immobile.[7] Some Marxist commentators prefer the term *flexible* over the term *flow*, since it ties globalization to flexible accumulation in current capitalism.[8]

A second use of *transnational* is to signal the demise or irrelevance of the nation-state in the current phase of globalization.[9] A related "borderless world" argument suggests that cultures are more and more important or relevant than nations and that identities are linked to cultures more than to nations or to the institutions of the nation-state.[10] In this approach, the concept of transnational does not have to concern itself with the postcolonial state; that is, it erases political economy as well as new forms of governmentality. As Victoria Bernal has put it so powerfully, "Embracing globalization and transnationalism as forces that render the nation inconsequential may appeal to anthropologists and humanities scholars in part because it allows them to conveniently ignore the ambivalent and troubling postcolonial state in favor of more sympathetic social forms."[11] Thus, by eliminating the postcolonial nation-state, flows of people and shifts in culture appear to be almost inevitable and strangely ahistorical.

A third use of *transnational* that has become visible recently is as a synonym for *diasporic*. In this increasingly common usage, which follows on the current use of *transnational* as a term that describes cross-border migration, any reference to materials or evidence or texts from a region outside the United States is coded as "diasporic."[12] And everyone in the United States is believed to be diasporic in some way. Often diasporics come to be figured as always in resistance to the nation-state in which they are located.[13] In this formulation, diasporic groups can be best understood through the politics of cultural identity or cultural citizenship. Thus subcultures of immigration and migration are always already diasporas. Here we are not arguing that people are better understood simply through the politics of the local. Rather, we are pointing to the mystification and romanticization of displacement that often accompany this formulation.[14]

A fourth use of *transnational* is to designate a form of neocolonialism. In this approach, *transnational* is a deeply problematic term, because it appears to be completely imbricated in the movements of transnational capital.[15] That is, the argument goes, globalization involves rapid movements of finance capital and thus facilitates a global economy in which transnational corporations have trampled on and destroyed local formations. In our view, this approach may inadvertently mystify what existed before the advent of late capitalism, whereas we would argue that earlier phases of globalization produced their own inequalities. Certainly, transnational capital is creating new forms of inequality and continuing older asymmetries. Consequently, a long historical viewpoint, indeed multiple views for many sites, is necessary.

A fifth use of *transnational* signals what has been called the NGOization of social movements.[16] In the wake of several decades of U.N. conferences on women, the emergence of global feminism as a policy and an activist arena, and the rise of human rights initiatives that enact new forms of governmentality, the term *transnational* has been adopted to stand for all of the above. Thus we find more and more references to "transnationalism from below" or to transnational women's movements (with *transnational* supplanting *global*).[17] Such a shift in usage is interesting and significant, since it signals an alternative to the problematic of the "global" and the "international" as it was articulated primarily by Western or Euro-American second-wave feminists as well as by multinational corporations, for which "becoming global" marks an expansion into new markets. Our response to this specific development is that we need to trace the histories of such movements through the modern period to understand how they have been tied to colonial processes and to imperialism. Thus such usage relied on a universal subject of feminism, while *transnational* could signal cultural and national difference. However, it is important to remain alert to these national and international histories, which are embedded in every so-called transnational social movement, regardless of the intention of committed individuals and organizations.

If we have pointed out some of the ways in which *transnational* is used so ubiquitously at the present moment, it is not to suggest that we should abandon the term on the grounds that it has been overused to the point of meaning nothing in particular. Since ignoring transnational formations has left studies of sexualities without the tools to address questions of globalization, race, political economy, immigration, migration, and geopolitics, it is important to bring questions of transnationalism into conversation with the feminist study of sexuality. The history of the way in which sexuality has been studied and described needs to be better understood. Many scholars working on sexuality have begun to identify how separate spheres of study have arisen as a result of the disciplinary divides in the U.S. academy. In this context, critical practices are at a bit of an impasse, relying heavily on conventional disciplinary approaches that are unable to address some key issues and problems.

What are these separate spheres? The first divide is the separation of sexuality from the study of race, class, nation, religion, and so on. If Western, Judeo-Christian culture has viewed sexuality as the other within each individual, the study of sexuality in the U.S. academy has been limited by the inability of the human sciences to address this feared aspect of human life. In general, in the social sciences sexuality has been discussed at length only as an attribute of "primitive" cultures – exerting a strong fascination and producing an enormous literature that continues to this day. As anthropologists begin to study their "own" cultures, we have begun to see some shifts in this dynamic. But the legacies of the rise of the human sciences remain. And the Western body stands as the normative body in scholarly discourse and in public policy.

We have to turn to the rise of biomedicine and the emergence of eugenics, gynecology, endocrinology, genetics, and psychology to understand fully the social and political stakes in viewing sexuality as distinct from race, class, nation, and other factors in modernity. Gender and sexual difference have become understood as attributes of bodies unmarked in any other way, despite copious evidence that all of these modern identities are interconnected. The binary gender model is so pervasive and universalized that it has become naturalized. In most queer studies in the United States, destabilization of gender binarism seems to remain in the zone of gender permutation or diversity rather than including considerations of histories of political economies and forms of governmentality.[18] For instance, if we can argue that historical analysis shows us that concepts of gender difference in medieval China were quite different from those in medieval Islamic cultures, we will begin to understand that the legacies of these traditions with attendant identities and practices produce new kinds of subjects in the present moment. Here we have to pause to note that we are not arguing that cultural specificity leads to complete difference. Rather, we want to add to this model of cultural difference a consideration of power, history, and analyses of contact and change.

In the study of sexuality in a transnational frame, we need a mapping of different medical traditions, conceptions of the body, scientific discourses, and, last but not least, political economies of the family. Such a mapping requires us to rethink the reliance on the family as a primary locus of difference and inequality. The family has been primarily treated as an entity that emerges in the context of a public-private split and as a result of divisions of labor. Internationalizing the public-private split and patriarchal divisions of labor has not changed the content of the scholarship much. Many of these approaches to the family produce representations of a heteronormative unit, a universal patriarchy, and, very often, a victimized and unified subject of feminism. If class comes to the fore in these analyses, sexuality remains in the realm of the exploitation and control of women via reproduction or trafficking. This emphasis on the family as a universal category of analysis also enables an allied mode of universalizing, that is, psychoanalytic criticism.

Psychoanalysis is a powerful mode of interpretation that has struggled with its universalizing tendencies.[19] That is, many psychoanalytic critiques admit to cultural limitations in the model but find it impossible to depart from it. If sexual desire is always already understood as produced in and through the family, then it would be difficult to detach it from a psychoanalytic approach. The family is an important figure in modernity, but it is not the only site of subject production. We want to argue that the study of sexuality in a transnational frame must be detached from psychoanalysis as a primary method in order to resist the universalization of the Western body as sexual difference. Psychoanalysis is a powerful interpretive tool, but it has become a form of biomedicine and cannot be utilized in ignorance of its own power structures.

Recently, new versions of psychoanalysis have sought to lift the cultural blinders from earlier work. These new works focus on the nation or the community as the family to provide new examples from diverse places. Although in recent years there has emerged an interest in expanding and rearticulating the notion of family and kinship, for the most part psychoanalytic cultural criticism may be of limited usefulness. Its Eurocentric biases can often be marshaled to reproduce nationalist formations.[20] Even Lacanian psychoanalysis cannot shake off its reliance on the modern European family as a central structuring metaphor. As we have said, this type of family may not make sense to people in other cultures and nation-states, nor can desire be understood solely in Western psychoanalytic terms. At the very least, the psychoanalytic framework may have to be different where relations between family and state are not the same as in the wealthier welfare states or where psychoanalysis is not medicalized or professionalized, as it is in Europe and North America.

The second instance of separated spheres that we wish to examine concerns the demarcation in the United States of international area studies from American studies. As Tani E. Barlow has argued, international area studies was implicated in the production of Cold War cultural and political knowledges about other cultures and nations.[21] American studies comes from a 1930s Marxist, popular-front effort to critique and oppose capitalism. During the conservative backlash of the Cold War, it was co-opted and became articulated as American exceptionalism. At that point, the whiteness of "American" studies became distinguishable from what was later called "ethnic studies." The emergence of ethnic studies has to be understood as a response to this conservative retrenching of an otherwise limited but more radical initial vision. So both international area studies and American studies as we know them today are Cold War productions generated to manage and negotiate the tensions that arose after the Second World War and during decolonization worldwide, that is, in distinction to the emergence of other nationalisms.

One consequence of these divisions has been that comparative work in international area studies and American studies remains bound by the nation-state. Although an analytic position of the comparison studies mode has given us some useful insights, it naturalizes and reproduces the nationalist basis of modern scholarship.[22] By questioning the distinctness of areas presupposed by the comparative framework and by respecting the specificities of historical and cultural conjectures, we might enable new insights into the workings of gender and patriarchy across various borders rather than simply within the parameters of the state or the nation. The changing nature of migrations, global flows of media, and capital demands a different notion of transdisciplinary scholarship.

How does the institutional divide between international area studies and American studies affect contemporary studies of sexuality? The academic study of sexuality that can be linked to the emergence of gay and lesbian politics of identity and new queer formations has focused on U.S. and European examples, with the primary emphasis on white, middle-class life.[23] Thus the disciplinary divides that emerge out of other political arenas are played out on campus and off, that is, in academic as well as in "community-based" or activist locations. As a result, much of the experience-based literature rearticulates the divide between a sexuality-based lesbian or gay or queer culture or identity and one that is based on race or class or ethnicity.[24] In recent years, both "articulation" theory and "intersectionality" approaches have attempted to resolve this problem by arguing for complex or hybrid subjects.[25] That is, the nationalist basis of these academic disciplinary formations has participated in producing sexual subjects as nationalist subjects or as cultural-nationalist subjects. A related issue that we are not going to dwell on here but that we have discussed elsewhere is the nature of the cosmopolitan subject as a mystified national subject in the guise of a "world" or global citizen.[26]

A third divide that we would like to bring up can be characterized as the tradition-modernity split. Following postcolonial studies, much has been said about this primary binary of Western culture. What is noteworthy, however, is the reemergence of this split in the international study of sexuality. As we noted above, nationalist biases and geopolitics contribute to this binary formulation, in which the United States and Europe are figured as modern and thus as the sites of progressive social movements, while other parts of the world are presumed to be traditional, especially in regard to sexuality. If any countries or nations depart from this model, it is because they are interpellated by "primitivism." In general, the United States and Europe come to be seen as unified sites of "freedom" and "democratic choice" over and against locations characterized by oppression.

In our work on female sexual surgeries and the global and cultural feminist discourse of "female genital mutilation" (FGM), we have argued that the tradition-modernity binary is foundational and even modern in that sexual subjects are produced as traditional in order to create feminist modern subjects.[27] Thus the global feminist is one who has free choice over her body and a complete and intact rather than a fragmented or surgically altered body, while the traditional female subject of patriarchy is forcibly altered, fragmented, alienated from her innate sexuality, and deprived of choices or agency. As we have discussed in relation to the film text by Alice Walker and Pratibha Parmar, *Warrior Marks*, freedom of choice in this nexus of modernity is marked by "coming out" as a lesbian. This is a complicated example, but suffice it to say at this juncture that a feminist and lesbian cosmopolitanism emerges over and against rural, African and Islamic "barbarism" in the name of saving "traditional women" from their own families. Although we see plenty of events and instances in the United States, for example, in which violence is enacted against gays and lesbians, against transgendered people, and against women, the displacement of the victims of sexualized violence to the Third World needs more discussion.

Another example of the tradition-modernity divide at work in the study of sexuality can be found in the literature on migration and refugee asylum. In such work, the process of migration to the United States, Europe, and other metropolitan locations is figured as the movement from repression to freedom.[28] That is, "backward," often rural subjects flee their homes and/or patriarchal families or violent, abusive situations to come to the modern metropolis, where they can express their true nature as sexual identity in a state of freedom. This narrative is a hallowed one in domestic "coming-out" discourses as well as in a burgeoning international human rights arena. Refugee asylum in the United States, for instance, produces gay and lesbian subjects through a political and legal articulation of such narratives. Some recent research suggests that it is virtually impossible to stay in the country without deploying such a narrative, thereby questioning its "natural" origins.[29] Further inquiry into this international context of immigration and asylum would need to focus on the ways in which the state becomes involved in producing sexual identities in an era of globalization. This is why we are arguing that a cultural or psychoanalytic understanding of so-called global lesbian and gay movements is inadequate. Nation-states, economic formations, consumer cultures, and forms of governmentality all work together to produce and uphold subjectivities and communities.

It is these kinds of examples and considerations that lead us to believe that we cannot think of sexual subjects as purely oppositional or resistant to dominant institutions that produce heteronormativity. In other words, as many have pointed out, queer subjects are not always already avant-garde for all time and in all places. For example, lesbian sexuality and practices in many sites have to struggle against patriarchal formations, while gay male sexualities may not. Our point is that, again, universalized models of resistance with idealized tropes or politics of identity obscure rather than elucidate the terrain of subjectivity in postmodernity.

A fourth link in this chain of examples of separate spheres is the global-local divide. In the context of globalization and some kinds of transnational studies, the local is seen as working against or in resistance to the global. That is, local and global constitute two separate spheres that never contaminate each other. The global-local divide is a tempting device for many cultural critics, but, like all the other binaries we are discussing, this one obscures important aspects of post-modernity, not the least of which is that the local is often constituted through the global, and vice versa.[30] It is also a model that hails critics because of its liberatory and resistance qualities. In this formulation, the local serves as the space of oppositional consciousness and generates practices of resistance, and the global serves as an oppressive network of dominant power structures. In various critical engagements with this global-local binary, lesbian, gay, and queer theorists have argued that the site of the local destabilizes the homogenizing tendencies of global gay formations.[31] There is another formulation that advocates the globalizing of Euro-American identity politics of sexuality along the lines that we have discussed above, that is, to advance human rights and freedom of choice.

We think that there is another way to look at the tension between these heavily mediated practices that appear to signal "local" or "global." We would advocate a mode of study that adopts a more complicated model of transnational relations in which power structures, asymmetries, and inequalities become the conditions of possibility of new subjects. For example, we could look at the way social and political movements are cosmopolitan and class-based, generating new sites of power rather than simply forms of resistance.[32] We could also investigate the empowering practices of consumption and engagements with media and new technologies that create new subjects that trouble the model of rights and citizenship. Above all, there should be much more attention to the power relations of travel – contacts and transactions of all kinds – that are part of the knowledge production through which subjects are constituted. The social aspects of sexuality are always embedded in the material histories of these encounters and must be addressed in nuanced ways.

In many ways we are addressing the problem of writing history, a problem foregrounded by many theorists and critics working in gay and lesbian and queer studies.[33] That is, subjects are produced by the writing of history itself and thus may always be marked by a belated recognition or identification that is always already in the terms of the present. While we can see this problem at work in the representation of the past, we are not always as aware of the limits of representation in the present. This problem of the present is especially egregious when we look at other cultures near or far. That is, identity politics have structured our view so profoundly that we literally cannot see the link between representation and subject formation in the ways that we are calling for vis-à-vis a transnational framework. Actually, what we are really grappling with here is not just representation; it is also the emergence of new forms of governmentality with an entire repertoire of strategies, regulatory practices, and instrumentalities linking the state to bodies. Thus representation is always linked to production, consumption, and regulation.[34]

Most of the identities we can recognize have emerged during the era of modernity encompassing the rise of capitalism and the nation-state in the context of imperialism. Our point is that sexual subjects are produced not just by the politics of identity or social movements but by the links between various institutions that accompany these social movements. Furthermore, we need to probe these connections and circuits to see how identities are upheld or made possible by institutions linked to the state. We find it problematic that in much work on sexual identities the state seldom has a hand in enabling these identities.[35] Most discussions of the state focus on queer or gay resistance to state-sanctioned heterosexism. While most states seem to oppose all forms of sexuality that are not related to reproduction or marriage, there have been cases where states (or institutions within states) have not been so uniformly in opposition. Although there is increasing discussion of the ways in which communities might be affected by institutions such as schools or the military, other state-linked or related institutions, such as universities and census boards, or institutions of the market, such as advertising, financial flows, and banks, are not often discussed in work on sexualities or sexual identities. Instead, communities seem to be simply produced by culture or by a culturalist notion of history, and by *culture* we mean in both the Arnoldian and the anthropological sense. This idea of culture signals a means of distinguishing between and ranking groups or seeing cultural formations as aesthetic categories.

What, then, is a transnational practice of the study of sexuality? There is a great deal of very exciting and useful work coming out of both interdisciplinary and disciplinary sites. Journals such as *GLQ* and *positions* have taken the lead in publishing new approaches, and there have been a plethora of conferences, workshops, and panels where these intersections have been increasingly evident.[36] Other institutional sites – such as centers for the study of sexuality or for gay, lesbian, and transgender studies; women's studies; gender studies; ethnic studies; and other interdisciplinary initiatives – are encouraging new scholarship and fostering various dialogues. Sexuality studies, like feminist and gender studies, is an increasingly important area of work in all kinds of disciplinary formations as well.

In our work on the film text of *Warrior Marks*, we began the project of creating a transnational framework for the study of sexual surgeries. We started by examining the ways in which colonial and postcolonial discourses of modernity and tradition have structured feminist and lesbian-feminist cultural production and identity politics as well as policy and activism in the Clinton era. Other parts of this long-term project include examinations of refugee asylum and other human rights practices and legal-juridical discourses that produce sexed subjects and identities. Another valence concerns the deployment of FGM discourse in social activism around infant sex assignment practices. Here the complicated issues involve the emergence of an intersex movement in the United States and the complexities of resisting recent biomedical practices by relying on notions of a natural body, conventions of sexual and gender difference, and colonial notions of tradition, barbarism, and mutilation. There is more that we can say about this project, but for now we would argue that the study of biomedicine must incorporate the kind of transnational frame that we are calling for in this essay.

Another area that engages not only our work but the work of many other scholars is travel and tourism.[37] As feminists in colonial and postcolonial discourse studies have argued, the emergence of travel in the modern period has been constitutive of many forms of orientalism and other ethnocentrisms.[38] Power differentials are always implicated in the activity of travel. Imperialism enabled forms of travel and exploration that produced circuits and flows of power and desire through which new forms of otherness and exoticism arose. From the "sotadic" zone in Richard Burton's travel narratives to Roland Barthes's "empire of signs" (not to forget Isabelle Eberhardt's peregrinations in male attire in North Africa), sexuality has been a primary subject of travel writing.[39] While over the last fifteen years both feminist and postcolonial critics have written extensively about travel in the era of imperialism, the field has been plagued by many of the critical limits that we have delineated here. In gay and lesbian and queer studies, the discussion of travel follows the parameters that we have critiqued thus far, for instance, the positioning of gay and lesbian travelers as transcending colonial power relations or functioning as agents of resistance.

Tourism is linked both to the colonial history of travel and to new forms of globalization in late capitalism. From global trafficking of women to sex tourism, the topic of tourism provides a window onto specific connections among nationalism, political economy, and cultural formations. The debate about global trafficking and sex tourism in certain locales, such as Thailand, Sri Lanka, and the Caribbean, for example, tends to portray sex workers as downtrodden victims of their patriarchies and "underdeveloped" economies. The figure of the "Third World prostitute," male or female, adult or child, is structured by the fantasy of rescue.[40] As Spivak's formulation argues, it is the old colonial project of saving the brown woman from her own kind – in these instances, we can expand this formulation to various subjects of capitalism and patriarchy, although there are important differences among these linked subjects.[41] There has been a lot of new work on these circuits of labor and desire, but much more needs to be done, especially in terms of media and visual culture.

We are also interested in new kinds of studies of migration and immigration that trouble the narratives of movement from oppression to freedom that we have already mentioned. Migration within nations as well as across different kinds of national boundaries has been studied in different disciplines; however, we need to pay attention to the different kinds of boundaries that are crossed or that cannot be crossed, and by whom. For instance, the family-based categories for immigration into the United States are profoundly antigay and -lesbian, but they also assume models of the family based on a hierarchy of nations and cultures. Other nation-states have enacted laws requiring HIV testing for entry as well as other invasive and homophobic practices. Here nationalism, gender, sexuality, and geopolitics must be considered, along with the political economy that underlies the regulation of immigration at the current moment.

One of the best examples of the issues we are raising here is the production of HIV/AIDS discourses over the last two decades. In this field we can discern a massive shift from the separate spheres to which we have been referring to the new forms of global and transnational policy discussions that have been created in response to this emergency. We see also the interconnections among state policies, nationalist agendas, pharmaceutical corporate practices, biomedical institutions, and the varied sexual subjects, cultures, and practices that become visible and targeted in new ways. The discourse of the modern nation-state's heteronormative family and of sexuality as the purview of males has been disrupted by the circulation of discourses of viruses, consumer actions, treatment strategies, theories of origins, and new sexual subjects. This example enables us to see the limits of the separate spheres approach as well as the interconnections that transnational subjects engender.

In conclusion, we would like to return to the five points with which we began our discussion of the circulation of the term *transnational*. We pointed out the limits of current uses of the term and linked these uses to articulations of knowledge formations. These limits include the production of various kinds of separate spheres or binaries, which prevent an approach to the study of sexuality that would usefully enable us to examine some of the areas of study that we have mentioned. Although other such topics can be considered, we have raised a few here as a contribution to a discussion that can build a bridge between the fields of global and transnational studies and those of sexuality, gender, women's, ethnic, and cultural studies in the U.S. academy. Such interdisciplinary work will enable us to understand global identities at the present time and to examine complicities as well as resistances in order to create the possibility of critique and change.

Notes

The text published here was delivered as an inaugural lecture at the Center for the Study of Gender and Sexuality at New York University on 12 February 2001. We would like to thank Carolyn Dinshaw for her encouragement and support of this project. We would also like to thank the audiences at the NYU Center for the Study of Gender and Sexuality, the University of Maastricht workshop "Gender, Ethnicity, and Globalization," and the Center for the Study of Sexual Cultures at the University of California, Berkeley, for terrific comments and feedback.

1   See Jasbir Kaur Puar, "Global Circuits: Transnational Sexualities and Trinidad," *Signs* 26 (2001): 1039–65; Martin F. Manalansan IV, "Diasporic Deviants/Divas: How Filipino Gay Transmigrants 'Play with the World,'" in *Queer Diasporas*, ed. Cindy Patton and Benigno Sánchez-Eppler (Durham: Duke University Press, 2000), 183–203; Yukiko Hanawa, ed., "Circuits of Desire," special issue of *positions* 2, no. 1 (1994); Elizabeth A. Povinelli and George Chauncey, eds., "Thinking Sexuality Transnationally," special issue of *GLQ* 5, no. 4 (1999); Phillip Brian Harper et al., eds., "Queer Transexions of Race, Nation, and Gender," special issue of *Social Text*, nos. 52–53 (1997); and Engin F. Isin and Patricia K. Wood, *Citizenship and Identity* (London: Sage, 1999).

2   For an influential account of this approach to globalization see Richard J. Barnet and John Cavanagh, *Global Dreams: Imperial Corporations and the New World Order* (New York: Touchstone, 1994); see also George Ritzer, *The McDonaldization of Society* (Thousand Oaks, Calif.: Pine Forge, 1993).

3   See Mike Featherstone, ed., *Global Culture* (London: Sage, 1990); Stuart Hall, "The Question of Cultural Identity," in *Modernity and Its Futures*, ed. Stuart Hall, David Held, and Tony McGrew (Cambridge: Polity, 1992), 274–316; Anthony D. King, ed., *Culture, Globalization, and the World System* (Minneapolis: University of Minnesota Press, 1997); and Fredric Jameson and Masao Miyoshi, eds., *The Cultures of Globalization* (Durham: Duke University Press, 1998).

4   See Lisa Rofel, "Qualities of Desire: Imagining Gay Identities in China," *GLQ* 5 (1999): 451–74.

5   See Inderpal Grewal and Caren Kaplan, "Introduction: Transnational Feminist Practices and Questions of Postmodernity," in *Scattered Hegemonies: Postmodernity and Transnational Feminist Practices*, ed. Inderpal Grewal and Caren Kaplan (Minneapolis: University of Minnesota Press, 1994), 1–33.

6   See Linda Basch, Nina Glick Schiller, and Cristina Szanton Blanc, eds., *Nations Unbound: Transnational Projects, Postcolonial Predicaments, and Deterritorialized Nation-States* (Langhorne, Pa.: Gordon and Breach, 1994).

7   See Arjun Appadurai, *Modernity at Large: Cultural Dimensions of Globalization* (Minneapolis: University of Minnesota Press, 1999); Ulf Hannerz, *Transnational Connections* (London: Routledge, 1996); and Scott Lash and John Urry, *Economies of Signs and Space* (London: Sage, 1994).

8   See David Harvey, *The Condition of Postmodernity: An Enquiry into the Origins of Cultural Change* (Oxford: Blackwell, 1989).

9   See Appadurai, *Modernity at Large*.

10   See Hannerz, *Transnational Connections*.

11   Victoria Bernal, "The Nation and the World: Reflections on Nationalism in a Transnational Era," unpublished manuscript, 2001.

12   This usage is evident at conferences such as the American Studies Association meetings, as well as other meetings of humanities or social science academic organizations such as the American Anthropological Association. See also David L. Eng, *Racial Castration: Managing Masculinity in Asian America* (Durham: Duke University Press, 2001).

13   See Paul Gilroy, *The Black Atlantic: Modernity and Double Consciousness* (Cambridge, Mass.: Harvard University Press, 1993).

14   See Caren Kaplan, *Questions of Travel: Postmodern Discourses of Displacement* (Durham: Duke University Press, 1996).

15   See Lisa Lowe and David Lloyd, eds., *The Politics of Culture in the Shadow of Capital* (Durham: Duke University Press, 1997).

16   We take this phrase from Sabine Lang, "The NGOization of Feminism," in *Transitions, Translations, Environments: Feminisms in International Politics*, ed. Joan W. Scott, Cora Kaplan, and Debra Keates (New York: Routledge, 1997), 101–20.

17   See Teresa Carillo, "Cross-Border Talk: Transnational Perspectives on Labor, Race, and Sexuality," in *Talking Visions: Multicultural Feminism in a Transnational Age*, ed. Ella Shohat (New York: New Museum for Modern Art; Cambridge, Mass.: MIT Press, 1998), 391–412.

18   Although *The Lesbian and Gay Studies Reader*, ed. Henry Abelove, Michèle Aina Barale, and David M. Halperin (New York: Routledge, 1993), broke new ground in important ways, many of the essays in it focus on this approach to gender diversity. Since then, other publications have attempted to address this problem. See Gerald Hunt, ed., *Laboring for Rights: Unions and Sexual Diversity across Nations* (Philadelphia: Temple University Press, 1999); Amy Gluckman and Betsy Reed, eds., *Homo Economics: Capitalism, Community, and Lesbian and Gay Life* (New York: Routledge, 1997); Erica Rand, *Barbie's Queer Accessories* (Durham: Duke University Press, 1995); Donald Morton, ed., *The Material Queer: A LesBiGay Cultural Studies Reader* (Boulder, Colo.: Westview, 1996); and Roger N. Lancaster and Micaela di Leonardo, eds., *The Gender/Sexuality Reader: Culture, History, Political Economy* (New York: Routledge, 1997).

19   For a trenchant critique of such work see Gayatri Chakravorty Spivak, "French Feminism in an International Frame," in *In Other Worlds: Essays in Cultural Politics* (New York: Routledge, 1988), 134–53.

20   For instance, in the context of South Asian studies see the work of Ashis Nandy, *The Intimate Enemy: Loss and Recovery of Self under Colonialism* (Delhi: Oxford University Press, 1983).

21   Tani E. Barlow, "Colonialism's Career in Postwar China Studies," *positions* 1, no. 1 (1993): 224–67.

22   See Inderpal Grewal, *Home and Harem: Nation, Gender, Empire, and the Cultures of Travel* (Durham: Duke University Press, 1996); and Inderpal Grewal, Akhil Gupta, and Aihwa Ong, eds., introduction to "Asian Transnationalities," special issue of *positions* 7 (1999): 653–66.

23   Many writers have pointed out that analyses of race are often absent from works by gay and lesbian scholars. See Audre Lorde, *Sister/Outsider* (Trumansburg, N.Y.: Crossing, 1984); bell hooks, *Yearning: Race, Gender, and Cultural Politics* (Boston: South End, 1990); and Cherríe Moraga and Gloria Anzaldúa, *This Bridge Called My Back: Writings by Radical Women of Color* (Watertown, Mass.: Persephone, 1981). An example of work that does not address the relation between sexuality and race or ethnicity is Corey K. Creekmur and Alexander Doty, eds., *Out in Culture: Gay, Lesbian, and Queer Essays on Popular Culture* (Durham: Duke University Press, 1995). In the very influential *Lesbian and Gay Studies Reader*, most of the essays focus on Europe and North America, although some address the relationship among sexuality, sexual identities, and race. Lancaster and di Leonardo's anthology *The Gender/Sexuality Reader* provides a more cross-cultural perspective.

24   See Patton and Sánchez-Eppler, *Queer Diasporas*; Emilie L. Bergmann and Paul Julian Smith, eds., *¿Entiendes? Queer Readings, Hispanic Writings* (Durham: Duke University Press, 1995); Russell Leong, ed., *Asian American Sexualities: Dimensions of the Gay and Lesbian Experience* (New York: Routledge, 1996); and David Eng and Alice Hom, eds., *Q & A: Queer in Asian America* (Philadelphia: Temple University Press, 1998).

25   For articulation theory see Lawrence Grossberg, ed., "On Postmodernism and Articulation: An Interview with Stuart Hall," *Journal of Communication Inquiry* 10, no. 2 (1986): 45–60. For inter-sectional theory see Kimberlé Crenshaw, "Mapping the Margins: Intersectionality, Identity Politics, and Violence against Women of Color," in *After Identity: A Reader in Law and Culture*, ed. Dan Danielson and Karen Engle (New York: Routledge, 1995), 332–54.

26   See Kaplan, *Questions of Travel*; and Caren Kaplan, "Hillary Clinton's Orient: Cosmopolitan Travel and Global Feminist Subjects," *Meridians: Feminism, Race, Transnationalism* 2 (2001): 219–40.

27   See Inderpal Grewal and Caren Kaplan, "Warrior Marks: Global Womanism's Neo-Colonial Discourse in a Multicultural Context," *Camera Obscura* 39 (1996): 5–33.

28   See Olivia Espin, *Women Crossing Boundaries: A Psychology of Immigration and Transformations of Sexuality* (New York: Routledge, 1999).

29   See Inderpal Grewal, *Transnational America: Gender, Nation, and Diaspora* (Durham: Duke University Press, forthcoming).

30   See Rob Wilson and Wimal Dissanayake, eds., *Global/Local: Cultural Production and the Transnational Imaginary* (Durham: Duke University Press, 1996).

31   Katie King, "Local and Global: AIDS Activism and Feminist Theory," *Camera Obscura* 28 (1992): 79–100.

32   Lash and Urry, *Economies of Signs and Space*; Manuel Castells, *The Rise of the Network Society* (Cambridge, Mass.: Blackwell, 1996).

33   See Michel Foucault, *The History of Sexuality* (New York: Pantheon, 1978); David M. Halperin, "Is There a History of Sexuality?" *History and Theory* 28 (1989): 257–74; Halperin, "How to Do the History of Male Homosexuality," *GLQ* 6 (2000): 87–124; John D'Emilio, "Capitalism and Gay Identity," in *Powers of Desire: The Politics of Sexuality*, ed. Ann Snitow, Christine Stansell, and Sharon Thompson (New York: Monthly Review Press, 1983), 100–113; Carolyn Dinshaw, *Getting Medieval: Sexualities and Communities, Pre- and Postmodern* (Durham: Duke University Press, 1999); and Donna Penn, "Queer: Theorizing Politics and History," *Radical History Review*, no. 62 (1995): 28–30.

34   See Stuart Hall, *introduction to Representation: Cultural Representations and Signifying Practices*, ed. Stuart Hall (London: Sage, 1997), 1–11.

35   For work that does address the state in the context of transnationality see M. Jacqui Alexander, "Erotic Autonomy as a Politics of Decolonization: An Anatomy of Feminist and State Practice in the Bahamas Tourist Economy," in *Feminist Genealogies, Colonial Legacies, Democratic Futures*, ed. M. Jacqui Alexander and Chandra Talpade Mohanty (New York: Routledge, 1997), 63–100.

36   See Hanawa, "Circuits of Desire," in which some essays utilize approaches that engage with circulations of identity and sexuality. See also Povinelli and Chauncey, "Thinking Sexuality Transnationally"; and Harper et al., "Queer Transexions of Race, Nation, and Gender."

37   See Puar, "Global Circuits"; and Alexander, "Erotic Autonomy as a Politics of Decolonization."

38   See Mary Louise Pratt, *Imperial Eyes: Travel Writing and Transculturation* (New York: Routledge, 1992); Ella Shohat, "Gender and the Culture of Empire: Toward a Feminist Ethnography of the Cinema," *Quarterly Review of Film and Video*, no. 131 (1991): 45–84; Lisa Lowe, *Critical Terrains: French and British Orientalisms* (Ithaca: Cornell University Press, 1991); Reina Lewis, *Gendering Orientalism: Race, Femininity, and Representation* (London: Routledge, 1996); Grewal, *Home and Harem*; Anne McClintock, *Imperial Leather: Race, Gender, and Sexuality in the Colonial Context* (New York: Routledge, 1995); and Sara Mills, *Discourses of Difference: An Analysis of Travel Writing and Colonialism* (New York: Routledge, 1991).

39   See Richard Phillips, "Travelling Sexualities: Richard Burton's Sotadic Zone," in *Writes of Passage: Reading Travel Writing*, ed. James Duncan and Derek Gregory (London: Routledge, 1999), 70–91; and Phillips, "Imaginative Geographies and Sexuality Politics: The City, the

Country, and the Age of Consent," in *De-centring Sexualities: Politics and Representations beyond the Metropolis*, ed. Richard Phillips, Diane Watt, and David Shuttleton (London: Routledge, 2000). Primary works include Richard F. Burton, *The Book of the Thousand Nights and a Night*, 6 vols. (New York: Limited Editions Club, 1934); Roland Barthes, *The Empire of Signs*, trans. Richard Howard (New York: Farrar, Straus and Giroux, 1982); and Isabelle Eberhardt, *The Passionate Nomad: The Diary of Isabelle Eberhardt* (Boston: Beacon, 1988).

40 See Kamala Kempadoo and Jo Doezema, eds., *Global Sex Workers: Rights, Resistance, and Redefinition* (New York: Routledge, 1998).

41 See Gayatri Chakravorty Spivak, "Can the Subaltern Speak?" in *Marxism and the Interpretation of Culture*, ed. Cary Nelson and Lawrence Grossberg (Urbana: University of Illinois Press, 1988), 271–313.

CHAPTER 7

Women Workers and Capitalist Scripts

Chandra Talpade Mohanty

Chandra Talpade Mohanty teaches English at Cornell University. Her books include *Feminism Without Borders* (2003) and *Third World Women and the Politics of Feminism* (1991).

We dream that when we work hard, we'll be able to clothe our children decently, and still have a little time and money left for ourselves. And we dream that when we do as good as other people, we get treated the same, and that nobody puts us down because we are not like them.... Then we ask ourselves, "How could we make these things come true?" And so far we've come up with only two possible answers: win the lottery, or organize. What can I say, except I have never been lucky with numbers. So tell this in your book: tell them it may take time that people think they don't have, but they have to organize! ... Because the only way to get a little measure of power over your own life is to do it collectively, with the support of other people who share your needs.

Irma, a Filipina worker in the Silicon Valley, California[1]

Irma's dreams of a decent life for her children and herself, her desire for equal treatment and dignity on the basis of the quality and merit of her work, her conviction that collective struggle is the means to "get a little measure of power over your own life," succinctly capture the struggles of poor women workers in the global capitalist arena. In this essay, I want to focus on the exploitation of poor Third-World women, on their agency as workers, on the common interests of women workers based on an understanding of shared location and needs, and on the strategies/practices of organizing that are anchored in and lead to the transformation of the daily lives of women workers.

This has been an especially difficult essay to write – perhaps because the almost-total saturation of the processes of capitalist domination makes it hard to envision forms of feminist resistance which would make a real difference in the daily lives of poor women workers. However, as I began to sort through the actions, reflections, and analyses by and about women workers (or wage laborers) in the capitalist economy,

Original publication details: Chandra Talpade Mohanty, "Women Workers and Capitalist Scripts" from *Feminist Approaches to Theory and Methodology*, ed. Sharlene Hesse-Biber, Christina Martin, and Robin Lydenberg, pp. 364–387. Oxford University Press, 1999. Reproduced with permission from Oxford University Press.

I discovered the dignity of women workers' struggles in the face of overwhelming odds. From these struggles we can learn a great deal about processes of exploitation and domination as well as about autonomy and liberation.

A recent study tour to Tijuana, Mexico, organized by Mary Tong of the San Diego-based Support Committee for Maquiladora Workers, confirmed my belief in the radical possibilities of cross-border organizing, especially in the wake of NAFTA. Exchanging ideas, experiences, and strategies with Veronica Vasquez, a twenty-one-year-old Maquila worker fighting for her job, for better working conditions, and against sexual harassment, was as much of an inspiration as any in writing this essay. Veronica Vasquez, along with ninety-nine former employees of the Tijuana factory Exportadora Mano de Obra, S.A. de C.V., has filed an unprecedented lawsuit in Los Angeles, California, against the U.S. owner of Exportadora, National O-Ring of Downey, demanding that it be forced to follow Mexican labor laws and provide workers with three months' back pay after shutting down company operations in Tijuana in November 1994. The courage, determination, and analytical clarity of these young Mexican women workers in launching the first case to test the legality of NAFTA suggest that in spite of the global saturation of processes of capitalist domination, 1995 was a moment of great possibility for building cross-border feminist solidarity.[2]

Over the years, I have been preoccupied with the limits as well as the possibilities of constructing feminist solidarities across national, racial, sexual, and class divides. Women's lives as workers, consumers, and citizens have changed radically with the triumphal rise of capitalism in the global arena. The common interests of capital (e.g., profit, accumulation, exploitation, etc.) are somewhat clear at this point. But how do we talk about poor Third-World women workers' interests, their agency, and their (in)visibility in so-called democratic processes? What are the possibilities for democratic citizenship for Third-World women workers in the contemporary capitalist economy? These are some of the questions driving this essay. I hope to clarify and analyze the location of Third-World women workers and their collective struggles in an attempt to generate ways to think about mobilization, organizing, and conscientization transnationally.

This essay extends the arguments I have made elsewhere regarding the location of Third-World women as workers in a global economy.[3] I write now, as I did then, from my own discontinuous locations: as a South Asian anticapitalist feminist in the U.S. committed to working on a truly liberatory feminist practice which theorizes and enacts the potential for a cross-cultural, international politics of solidarity; as a Third-World feminist teacher and activist for whom the psychic economy of "home" and of "work" has always been the space of contradiction and struggle; and as a woman whose middle-class struggles for self-definition and autonomy outside the definitions of daughter, wife, and mother mark an intellectual and political genealogy that led me to this particular analysis of Third-World women's work.

Here, I want to examine the analytical category of "women's work," and to look at the historically specific *naturalization* of gender and race hierarchies through this category. An international division of labor is central to the establishment, consolidation, and maintenance of the current world order: global assembly lines are as much about the production of people as they are about "providing jobs" or making profit. Thus, naturalized assumptions about *work* and *the worker* are crucial to understanding the sexual politics of global capitalism. I believe that the relation of local to global processes of colonization and exploitation, and the specification of a process of cultural and ideological homogenization across national borders, in part through the creation of the consumer as "the" citizen under advanced capitalism, must be crucial aspects of any comparative feminist project. This definition of the citizen-consumer depends to a large degree on the definition and disciplining of producers/workers on whose backs the citizen-consumer gains legitimacy. It is the worker/producer side of this equation that I will address. Who are the workers that make the citizen-consumer possible? What role do sexual politics play in the ideological creation of this worker? How does global capitalism, in search of ever-increasing profits, utilize gender and racialized ideologies in crafting forms of women's work? And, does the social location of particular women as workers suggest the basis for common interests and potential solidarities across national borders?

As global capitalism develops and wage labor becomes the hegemonic form of organizing production and reproduction, class relations within and across national borders have become more complex and less transparent.[4] Thus, issues of spatial economy – the manner by which capital utilizes particular spaces for differential production and the accumulation of capital and, in the process, transforms these spaces (and peoples) – gain fundamental importance for feminist analysis.[5] In the aftermath of feminist struggles around the right to work and the demand for equal pay, the boundaries between home/family and work are no longer seen as inviolable (of course these boundaries were always fluid for poor and working-class women). Women are (and have always been) in the workforce, and we are here to stay. In this essay, I offer an analysis of certain historical and ideological transformations of gender, capital, and work across the borders of nation-states,[6] and, in the process, develop a way of thinking about the common interests of Third-World women workers, and in particular about questions of agency and the transformation of consciousness.

Drawing specifically on case studies of the incorporation of Third-World women into a global division of labor at different geographical ends of the new world order, I argue for a historically delineated category of "women's work" as an example of a productive and necessary basis for feminist cross-cultural analysis.[7] The idea I am interested in invoking here is not "the work that women do" or even the occupations that they/we happen to be concentrated in, but rather the ideological construction of jobs and tasks in terms of notions of appropriate femininity, domesticity, (hetero)sexuality, and racial and cultural stereotypes. I am interested in mapping these operations of capitalism across different divides, in tracing the naturalization of capitalist processes, ideologies, and values through the way women's work is *constitutively* defined – in this case, in terms of gender and racial parameters. One of the questions I explore pertains to the way gender identity (defined in domestic, heterosexual, familial terms) structures the nature of the work women are allowed to perform or precludes women from being "workers" altogether.

While I base the details of my analysis in geographically anchored case studies, I am suggesting a comparative methodology which moves beyond the case-study approach and illuminates global processes which inflect and draw upon indigenous hierarchies, ideologies, and forms of exploitation to consolidate new modes of colonization (what we refer to in the introductory chapter as "recolonization"). The local and the global are indeed connected through parallel, contradictory, and sometimes converging relations of rule which position women in different and similar locations as workers.[8] I agree with feminists who argue that class struggle, narrowly defined, can no longer be the only basis for solidarity among women workers. The fact of being women with particular racial, ethnic, cultural, sexual, and geographical histories has everything to do with our definitions and identities as workers. A number of feminists have analyzed the division between production and reproduction, and the construction of ideologies of womanhood in terms of public/private spheres. Here, I want to highlight a) the persistence of patriarchal definitions of womanhood in the arena of wage labor; b) the versatility and specificity of capitalist exploitative processes providing the basis for thinking about potential common interests and solidarity between Third-World women workers; and c) the challenges for collective organizing in a context where traditional union methods (based on the idea of the class interests of the male worker) are inadequate as strategies for empowerment.

If, as I suggest, the logic of a world order characterized by a transnational economy involves the active construction and dissemination of an image of the "Third World/racialized, or marginalized woman worker" that draws on indigenous histories of gender and race inequalities, and if this worker's identity is coded in patriarchal terms which define her in relation to men and the heterosexual, conjugal family unit, then the model of class conflict between capitalists and workers needs to be recrafted in terms of the interests (and perhaps identities) of Third-World women workers. Patriarchal ideologies, which sometimes pit women against men within and outside the home, infuse the material realities of the lives of Third-World women workers, making it imperative to reconceptualize the way we think about working-class interests and strategies for organizing. Thus, while this is not an argument for just recognizing the "common experiences" of Third-World women workers, it *is* an argument for recognizing (concrete, not abstract) "common interests" and the potential bases of cross-national solidarity – a common context of struggle. In addition, while I choose to focus on the "Third World" woman worker, my argument holds for white women workers who are also racialized in similar ways. The argument then is about a *process* of gender and race domination, rather than about the *content* of "Third World." Making Third-World women workers visible in this gender, race, class formation involves engaging a capitalist script of subordination and exploitation. But it also leads to thinking about the possibilities of emancipatory action on the basis of the reconceptualization of Third-World women as agents rather than victims.

But why even use "Third World," a somewhat problematic term which many now consider outdated? And why make an argument which privileges the social location, experiences, and identities of Third-World women workers, as opposed to any other group of workers, male or female? Certainly, there are problems with the term "Third World." It is inadequate in comprehensively characterizing the economic, political, racial, and cultural differences *within* the borders of Third-World nations. But in comparison with other similar formulations like "North/South" and "advanced/under-developed nations," "Third World" retains a certain heuristic value and explanatory specificity in relation to the inheritance of colonialism and contemporary neocolonial economic and geopolitical processes that the other formulations lack.[9]

In response to the second question, I would argue that at this time in the development and operation of a "new" world order, Third-World women workers (defined in this context as both women from the geographical Third World and immigrant and indigenous women of color in the U.S. and Western Europe) occupy a specific social location in the international division of labor which *illuminates* and *explains* crucial features of the capitalist processes of exploitation and domination. These are features of the social world that are usually obfuscated or mystified in discourses about the "progress" and "development" (e.g., the creation of jobs for poor, Third-World women as the marker of economic and social advancement) that is assumed to "naturally" accompany the triumphal rise of global capitalism. I do not claim to explain *all* the relevant features of the social world or to offer a *comprehensive* analysis of capitalist processes of recolonization. However, I am suggesting that Third-World women workers have a potential identity in common, an identity as *workers* in a particular division of labor at this historical moment. And I believe that exploring and analyzing this potential commonality across geographical and cultural divides provides both a way of reading and understanding the world and an explanation of the consolidation of inequities of gender, race, class, and (hetero) sexuality, which are necessary to envision and enact transnational feminist solidarity.[10]

The argument that multinationals position and exploit women workers in certain ways does not originate with me. I want to suggest, however, that in interconnecting and comparing some of these case studies, a larger theoretical argument can be made about the category of women's work, specifically about the Third-World woman as worker, at this particular historical moment. I think this intersection of gender and work, where the very definition of work draws upon and reconstructs notions of masculinity, femininity, and sexuality, offers a basis of cross-cultural comparison and analysis which is grounded in the concrete realities of women's lives. I am not suggesting that this basis for comparison exhausts the *totality* of women's experience cross-culturally. In other words, because similar ideological constructions of "women's work" make cross-cultural analysis possible, this does not automatically mean women's lives are the *same*, but rather that they are *comparable*. I argue for a notion of political solidarity and common interests, defined as a community or collectivity among women workers across class, race, and national boundaries which is based on shared material interests and identity and common ways of reading the world. This idea of political solidarity in the context of the incorporation of Third-World women into a global economy offers a basis for cross-cultural comparison and analysis which is grounded in history and social location rather than in an ahistorical notion of culture or experience. I am making a choice here to focus on and analyze the *continuities* in the experiences, histories, and strategies of survival of these particular workers. But this does not mean that differences and discontinuities in experience do not exist or that they are insignificant. The focus on continuities is a *strategic* one – it makes possible a way of reading the operation of capital from a location (that of Third-World women workers) which, while forming the bedrock of a certain kind of global exploitation of labor, remains somewhat invisible and undertheorized.

Gender and Work: Historical and Ideological Transformations

"Work makes life sweet," says Lola Weixel, a working-class Jewish woman in Connie Field's film "The Life and Times of Rosie the Riveter." Weixel is reflecting on her experience of working in a welding factory during World War II, at a time when large numbers of U.S. women were incorporated into the labor force to replace men who were fighting the war. In one of the most moving moments in the film, she draws attention to what it meant to her and to other women to work side by side, to learn skills and craft products, and to be paid for the work they did, only to be told at the end of the war that they were no longer needed and should go back to being girlfriends, housewives, and mothers. While the U.S. state propaganda machine was especially explicit on matters of work for men and women, and the corresponding expectations of masculinity/ femininity and domesticity in the late 1940s and 1950s, this is no longer the case in the 1990s. Shifting definitions of public and private, and of workers, consumers and citizens no longer define wage-work in visibly masculine terms. However, the dynamics of job competition, loss, and profit-making in the 1990s are still part of the dynamic process that spelled the decline of the mill towns of New England in the early 1900s and that now pits "American" against "immigrant" and "Third-World" workers along the U.S./ Mexico border or in the Silicon Valley in California. Similarly, there are continuities between the women-led New York garment-workers strike of 1909, the Bread and Roses (Lawrence textile) strike of 1912, Lola Weixel's role in union organizing during WWII, and the frequent strikes in the 1980s and 1990s of Korean textile and electronic workers, most of whom are young, single women.[11] While the global division of labor in 1995 looks quite different from what it was in the 1950s, ideologies of women's work, the meaning and value of work for women, and women workers' struggles against exploitation remain central issues for feminists around the world. After all, women's labor has always been central to the development, consolidation, and reproduction of capitalism in the U.S.A. and elsewhere.

In the United States, histories of slavery, indentured servitude, contract labor, self-employment, and wage-work are also simultaneously histories of gender, race, and (hetero)sexuality, nested within the context of the development of capitalism. Thus, women of different races, ethnicities, and social classes had profoundly different, though interconnected, experiences of work in the economic development from nineteenth-century economic and social practices (slave agriculture in the South, emergent industrial capitalism in the Northeast, the hacienda system in the Southwest, independent family farms in the rural Midwest, Native American hunting/gathering and agriculture) to wage-labor and self-employment (including family businesses) in the late-twentieth century. In 1995, almost a century after the Lowell girls lost their jobs when textile mills moved South to attract non-unionized labor, feminists are faced with a number of profound analytical and organizational challenges in different regions of the world. The material, cultural, and political effects of the processes of domination and exploitation which sustain what is called the New World Order (NWO)[12] are devastating for the vast majority of people in the world – and most especially for impoverished and Third-World women. Maria Mies argues that the increasing division of the world into consumers and producers has a profound effect on Third-World women workers, who are drawn into the international division of labor as workers in agriculture; in large-scale manufacturing industries like textiles, electronics, garments, and toys; in small-scale manufacturing of consumer goods like handicrafts and food processing (the informal sector); and as workers in the sex and tourist industries.[13]

The values, power, and meanings attached to being either a consumer or a producer/worker vary enormously depending on where and who we happen to be in an unequal global system. In the 1990s, it is, after all, multinational corporations that are the hallmark of global capitalism. In an analysis of the effects of these corporations on the new world order, Richard Barnet and John Cavanagh characterize the global commercial arena in terms of four intersecting webs: the Global Cultural Bazaar (which creates and disseminates images and dreams through films, television, radio, music, and other media), the Global Shopping Mall (a planetary supermarket which sells things to eat, drink, wear, and enjoy through advertising, distribution, and marketing networks), the Global Workplace (a network of factories and workplaces where goods are produced, information processed, and services rendered), and, finally, the Global Financial Network (the international traffic in currency transactions, global securities, etc.).[14] In each of these webs, racialized ideologies of masculinity, femininity, and sexuality play a role in constructing the legitimate consumer, worker, and manager. Meanwhile, the psychic and social disenfranchisement and impoverishment of women continues. Women's bodies and labor are used to consolidate global dreams, desires, and ideologies of success and the good life in unprecedented ways.

Feminists have responded directly to the challenges of globalization and capitalist modes of recolonization by addressing the sexual politics and effects on women of a) religious fundamentalist movements within and across the boundaries of the nation-state; b) structural adjustment policies (SAPs); c) militarism, demilitarization, and violence against women; d) environmental degradation and land/sovereignty struggles of indigenous and native peoples; and e) population control, health, and reproductive policies and practices.[15] In each of these cases, feminists have analyzed the effects on women as workers, sexual partners, mothers and caretakers, consumers, and transmitters and transformers of culture and tradition. Analysis of the ideologies of masculinity and femininity, of motherhood and (hetero)sexuality and the understanding and mapping of agency, access, and choice are central to this analysis and organizing. Thus, while my characterization of capitalist processes of domination and recolonization may appear somewhat overwhelming, I want to draw attention to the numerous forms of resistance and struggle that have also always been constitutive of the script of colonialism/capitalism. Capitalist patriarchies and racialized, class/caste-specific hierarchies are a key part of the long history of domination and exploitation of women, but struggles against these practices and vibrant, creative, collective forms of mobilization and organizing have also always been a part of our histories. In fact, like Jacqui Alexander and a number of other authors in this collection, I attempt to articulate an emancipatory discourse and knowledge, one that furthers the cause of feminist liberatory practice. After all, part of what needs to change within racialized capitalist patriarchies is the very concept of work/labor, as well as the naturalization of heterosexual masculinity in the definition of "the worker."

Teresa Amott and Julie Matthaei, in analyzing the U.S. labor market, argue that the intersection of gender, class, and racial-ethnic hierarchies of power has had two major effects:

> First, disempowered groups have been concentrated in jobs with lower pay, less job security, and more difficult working conditions. Second, workplaces have been places of extreme segregation, in which workers have worked in jobs only with members of their same racial-ethnic, gender, and class group, even though the particular racial-ethnic group and gender assigned to a job may have varied across firms and regions.[16]

While Amott and Matthaei draw attention to the sex-and-race typing of jobs, they do not *theorize* the relationship between this job typing and the social identity of the workers concentrated in these low-paying, segregated, often unsafe sectors of the labor market. While the economic history they chart is crucial to any understanding of the race-and-gender basis of U.S. capitalist processes, their analysis begs the question of whether there is a connection (other than the common history of domination of people of color) between *how* these jobs are defined and *who* is sought after for the jobs.

By examining two instances of the incorporation of women into the global economy (women lacemakers in Narsapur, India, and women in the electronics industry in the Silicon Valley) I want to delineate the interconnections between gender, race, and ethnicity, and the ideologies of work which locate women in particular exploitative contexts.

The contradictory positioning of women along class, race, and ethnic lines in these two cases suggests that, in spite of the obvious geographical and sociocultural differences between the two contexts, the organization of the global economy by contemporary capital positions these workers in very similar ways, effectively reproducing and trans-forming locally specific hierarchies. There are also some significant continuities between homework and factory work in these contexts, in terms of both the inherent ideologies of work as well as the experiences and social identities of women as workers. This ten-dency can also be seen in the case studies of black women workers (of Afro-Caribbean, Asian, and African origin) in Britain, especially women engaged in homework, factory work, and family businesses.

Housewives and Homework: The Lacemakers of Narsapur

Maria Mies's 1982 study of the lacemakers of Narsapur, India, is a graphic illustration of how women bear the impact of development processes in countries where poor peas-ant and tribal societies are being "integrated" into an international division of labor under the dictates of capital accumulation. Mies's study illustrates how capitalist pro-duction relations are built upon the backs of women workers defined as *housewives*. Ideologies of gender and work and their historical transformation provide the necessary ground for the exploitation of the lacemakers. But the definition of women as house-wives also suggests the heterosexualization of women's work – women are always defined in relation to men and conjugal marriage. Mies's account of the development of the lace industry and the corresponding relations of production illustrates fundamental trans-formations of gender, caste, and ethnic relations. The original caste distinctions between the feudal warrior castes (the landowners) and the Narsapur (poor Christians) and Serepalam (poor Kapus/Hindu agriculturalists) women are totally transformed through the development of the lace industry, and a new caste hierarchy is effected.

At the time of Mies's study, there were sixty lace manufacturers, with some 200,000 women in Narsapur and Serepalam constituting the work force. Lacemaking women worked six to eight hours a day, and ranged in age from six to eighty. Mies argues that the expansion of the lace industry between 1970 and 1978 and its integration into the world market led to class/caste differentiation within particular communities, with a masculinization of all nonproduction jobs (trade) and a total feminization of the produc-tion process. Thus, men sold women's products and lived on profits from women's labor. The polarization between men and women's work, where men actually defined them-selves as exporters and businessmen who invested in women's labor, bolstered the social and ideological definition of women as housewives and their work as "leisure time activity." In other words, work, in this context, was grounded in sexual identity, in concrete definitions of femininity, masculinity, and heterosexuality.

Two particular indigenous hierarchies, those of caste and gender, interacted to pro-duce normative definitions of "women's work." Where, at the onset of the lace indus-try, Kapu men and women were agricultural laborers and it was the lower-caste Harijan women who were lacemakers, with the development of capitalist relations of produc-tion and the possibility of caste/class mobility, it was the Harijan women who were agricultural laborers while the Kapu women undertook the "leisure time" activity of lacemaking. The caste-based ideology of seclusion and purdah was essential to the extraction of surplus value. Since purdah and the seclusion of women is a sign of higher caste status, the domestication of Kapu laborer women – where their (lacemaking) activity was tied to the concept of the "women sitting in the house" was entirely within the logic of capital accumulation and profit. Now, Kapu women, not just the women of feudal, landowning castes, are in purdah as housewives producing for the world market.

Ideologies of seclusion and the domestication of women are clearly sexual, drawing as they do on masculine and feminine notions of protectionism and property. They are also heterosexual ideologies, based on the normative definition of women as wives, sisters, and mothers – always in relation to conjugal marriage and the "family." Thus, the caste trans-formation and separation of women along lines of domestication and nondomestication (Kapu housewives vs. Harijan laborers) effectively links the work that women do with their sexual and caste/class identities. Domestication works, in this case, because of the persistence and legitimacy of the ideology of the housewife, which defines women in terms of their place within the home, conjugal marriage, and heterosexuality. The opposi-tion between definitions of the "laborer" and of the "housewife" anchors the invisibility (and caste-related status) of work; in effect, it defines women as *non-workers*. By defini-tion, housewives cannot be workers or laborers; housewives make male breadwinners and consumers possible. Clearly, ideologies of "women's place and work" have real material force in this instance, where spatial parameters construct and maintain gendered and caste-specific hierarchies. Thus, Mies's study illustrates the concrete effects of the social definition of women as housewives. Not only are the lacemakers invisible in census fig-ures (after all, their work is leisure), but their definition as housewives makes possible the definition of men as "breadwinners." Here, class and gender proletarianization through the development of capitalist relations of production, and the integration of women into the world market is possible because of the history and transformation of indigenous caste and sexual ideologies.

Reading the operation of capitalist processes from the position of the housewife/worker who produces for the world market makes the specifically gendered and caste/class opposition between laborer and the non-worker (housewife) visible. Moreover, it makes it possible to acknowledge and account for the hidden costs of women's labor. And finally, it illuminates the fundamentally *masculine* definition of laborer/worker in a con-text where, as Mies says, men live off women who are the producers. Analyzing and transforming this masculine definition of labor, which is the mainstay of capitalist patri-archal cultures, is one of the most significant challenges we face. The effect of this defi-nition of labor is not only that it makes women's labor and its costs invisible, but that it undercuts women's agency by defining them as victims of a process of pauperization or of "tradition" or "patriarchy," rather than as agents capable of making their own choices.

In fact, the contradictions raised by these choices are evident in the lace-makers' responses to characterizations of their own work as "leisure activity." While the fact that they did "work" was clear to them and while they had a sense of the history of their own pauperization (with a rise in prices for goods but no corresponding rise in wages), they were unable to explain how they came to be in the situation they found themselves. Thus, while some of the contradictions between their work and their roles as housewives and mothers were evident to them, they did not have access to an analysis of these contradictions which could lead to a) seeing the complete picture in terms of their exploitation; b) strategizing and organizing to transform their material situations; or c) recognizing their common interests as women workers across caste/class lines. As a matter of fact, the Serepelam women defined their lacemaking in terms of "housework" rather than wage-work, and women who had managed to establish themselves as petty commodity producers saw what they did as entrepreneurial: they saw themselves as selling *products* rather than *labor*. Thus, in both cases, women internalized the ideologies that defined them as nonworkers. The isolation of the work context (work done in the house rather than in a public setting) as well as the internalization of caste and patriarchal ideologies thus militated against organizing as *workers*, or as *women*. However, Mies suggests that there were cracks in this ideology: the women expressed some envy toward agricultural laborers, whom the lacemakers saw as enjoying working together in the fields. What seems necessary in such a context, in terms of feminist mobilization, is a recognition of the fact that the identity of the housewife needs to be transformed into the identity of a "woman worker or working woman." Recognition of common interests as housewives is very different from recognition of common interests as women and as workers.

Immigrant Wives, Mothers, and Factory Work: Electronics Workers in the Silicon Valley

My discussion of the U.S. end of the global assembly line is based on studies by Naomi Katz and David Kemnitzer (1983) and Karen Hossfeld (1990) of electronics workers in the so-called Silicon Valley in California. An analysis of production strategies and processes indicates a significant ideological redefinition of normative ideas of factory work in terms of the Third-World, immigrant women who constitute the primary workforce. While the lacemakers of Narsapur were located as *housewives* and their work defined as *leisure time activity* in a very complex international world market, Third-World women in the electronics industry in the Silicon Valley are located as *mothers*, *wives*, and *supplementary* workers. Unlike the search for the "single" woman assembly worker in Third-World countries, it is in part the ideology of the "married woman" which defines job parameters in the Valley, according to Katz and Kemnitzer's data.

Hossfeld also documents how existing ideologies of femininity cement the exploitation of the immigrant women workers in the Valley, and how the women often use this patriarchal logic against management. Assumptions of "single" and "married" women as the ideal workforce at the two geographical ends of the electronics global assembly line (which includes South Korea, Hong Kong, China, Taiwan, Thailand, Malaysia, Japan, India, Pakistan, the Philippines, and the United States, Scotland, and Italy)[17] are anchored in normative understandings of femininity, womanhood, and sexual identity. The labels are predicated on sexual difference and the institution of heterosexual marriage and carry connotations of a "manageable" (docile?) labor force.[18]

Katz and Kemnitzer's data indicates a definition and transformation of women's work which relies on gender, race, and ethnic hierarchies already historically anchored in the U.S. Further, their data illustrates that the construction of "job labels" pertaining to Third-World women's work is closely allied with their sexual and racial identities. While Hossfeld's more recent study reinforces some of Katz and Kemnitzer's conclusions, she focuses more specifically on how "contradictory ideologies about sex, race, class, and nationality are used as forms of both labor control and labor resistance in the capitalist workplace today."[19] Her contribution lies in charting the operation of gendered ideologies in the structuring of the industry and in analyzing what she calls "refeminization strategies" in the workplace.

Although the primary workforce in the Valley consists of Third-World and newly immigrant women, substantial numbers of Third-World and immigrant men are also employed by the electronics industry. In the early 1980s, 70,000 women held 80 to 90 percent of the operative or laborer jobs on the shop floor. Of these, 45 to 50 percent were Third-World, especially Asian, immigrants. White men held either technician or supervisory jobs. Hossfeld's study was conducted between 1983 and 1986, at which time she estimates that up to 80 percent of the operative jobs were held by people of color, with women constituting up to 90 percent of the assembly workers. Katz and Kemnitzer maintain that the industry actively seeks sources of cheap labor by deskilling production and by using race, gender, and ethnic stereotypes to "attract" groups of workers who are "more suited" to perform tedious, unrewarding, poorly paid work. When interviewed, management personnel described the jobs as a) unskilled (as easy as a recipe); b) requiring tolerance for tedious work (Asian women are therefore more suited); and c) supplementary activity for women whose main tasks were mothering and housework.

It may be instructive to unpack these job labels in relation to the immigrant and Third-World (married) women who perform these jobs. The job labels recorded by Katz and Kemnitzer need to be analyzed as definitions of *women's work*, specifically as definitions of *Third-World/immigrant women's work*. First, the notion of "unskilled" as easy (like following a recipe) and the idea of tolerance for tedious work both have racial and gendered dimensions. Both draw upon stereotypes which infantilize Third-World women and initiate a nativist discourse of "tedium" and "tolerance" as characteristics of non-Western, primarily agricultural, premodern (Asian) cultures. Secondly, defining jobs as supplementary activity for *mothers* and *housewives* adds a further dimension: sexual identity and appropriate notions of heterosexual femininity as marital domesticity. These are not part-time jobs, but they are defined as supplementary. Thus, in this particular context, (Third-World) women's work needs are defined as temporary.

While Hossfeld's analysis of management logic follows similar lines, she offers a much more nuanced understanding of how the gender and racial stereotypes prevalent in the larger culture infuse worker consciousness and resistance. For instance, she draws attention to the ways in which factory jobs are seen by the workers as "unfeminine" or not "ladylike." Management exploits and reinforces these ideologies by encouraging women to view femininity as contradictory to factory work, by defining their jobs as secondary and temporary, and by asking women to choose between defining themselves as women or as workers. Womanhood and femininity are thus defined along a domestic, familial model, with work seen as supplemental to this primary identity. Significantly, although 80 percent of the immigrant women in Hossfeld's study were the largest annual income producers in their families, they still considered men to be the breadwinners.

Thus, as with the exploitation of Indian lacemakers as "housewives," Third-World/ immigrant women in the Silicon Valley are located as "mothers and homemakers" and only secondarily as workers. In both cases, men are seen as the real breadwinners. While (women's) work is usually defined as something that takes place in the "public" or production sphere, these ideologies clearly draw on stereotypes of women as homebound. In addition, the *invisibility* of work in the Indian context can be compared to the *temporary/secondary* nature of work in the Valley. Like the Mies study, the data compiled by Hossfeld and Katz and Kemnitzer indicate the presence of local ideologies and hierarchies of gender and race as the basis for the exploitation of the electronics workers. The question that arises is: How do women understand their own positions and construct meanings in an exploitative job situation?

Interviews with electronics workers indicate that, contrary to the views of management, women do not see their jobs as temporary but as part of a life-time strategy of upward mobility. Conscious of their racial, class, and gender status, they combat their devaluation as workers by increasing their income: by job-hopping, overtime, and moonlighting as pieceworkers. Note that, in effect, the "homework" that Silicon Valley workers do is performed under conditions very similar to the lacemaking of Narsapur women. Both kinds of work are done in the home, in isolation, with the worker paying her own overhead costs (like electricity and cleaning), with no legally mandated protections (such as a minimum wage, paid leave, health benefits, etc.). However, clearly the meanings attached to the work differ in both contexts, as does the way we understand them.

For Katz and Kemnitzer the commitment of electronics workers to class mobility is an important assertion of self. Thus, unlike in Narsapur, in the Silicon Valley, homework has an entrepreneurial aspect for the women themselves. In fact, in Narsapur, women's work turns the men into entrepreneurs! In the Valley, women take advantage of the contradictions of the situations they face as *individual workers*. While in Narsapur, it is purdah and caste/class mobility which provides the necessary self-definition required to anchor women's work in the home as leisure activity, in the Silicon Valley, it is a specifically *American* notion of individual ambition and entrepreneurship which provides the necessary ideological anchor for Third-World women.

Katz and Kemnitzer maintain that this underground economy produces an *ideological* redefinition of jobs, allowing them to be defined as *other than* the basis of support of the historically stable, "comfortable," white, metropolitan working class. In other words, there is a clear connection between low wages and the definition of the job as supplementary, and the fact that the lifestyles of people of color are defined as different and cheaper. Thus, according to Katz and Kemnitzer, *women* and *people of color* continue to be "defined out" of the old industrial system and become targets and/or instruments of the ideological shift away from class towards national/ethnic/gender lines.[20] In this context, ideology and popular culture emphasize the *individual maximization* of options for personal success. Individual success is thus severed from union activity, political struggle, and collective relations. Similarly, Hossfeld suggests that it is the racist and sexist management logic of the needs of "immigrants" that allows the kind of exploitative labor processes that she documents.[21] However, in spite of Katz and Kemnitzer's complex analysis of the relationship of modes of production, social relations of production, culture, and ideology in the context of the Silicon Valley workers, they do not specify why it is *Third-World women* who constitute the primary labor force. Similarly, while Hossfeld provides a nuanced analysis of the gendering of the workplace and the use of racial and gendered logic to consolidate capitalist accumulation, she also sometimes separates "women" and "minority workers" (Hossfeld, p. 176), and does not specify why it is women of color who constitute the major labor force on the assembly lines in the Valley. In distinguishing between women and people of color, Katz and Kemnitzer tend to reproduce the old conceptual divisions of gender and race, where women are defined primarily in terms of their gender and people of color in terms of race. What is excluded is an *interactive* notion of gender and race, whereby women's gendered identity is grounded in race and people of color's racial identities are gendered.

I would argue that the data compiled by Katz and Kemnitzer and Hossfeld does, in fact, explain why Third-World women are targeted for jobs in electronics factories. The explanation lies in the redefinition of work as temporary, supplementary, and unskilled, in the construction of women as mothers and homemakers, and in the positioning of femininity as contradictory to factory work. In addition, the explanation also lies in the specific definition of Third-World, immigrant women as docile, tolerant, and satisfied with substandard wages. It is the ideological redefinition of women's work that provides the necessary understanding of this phenomenon. Hossfeld describes some strategies of resistance in which the workers utilize against management the very gendered and racialized logic that management uses against them. However, while these tactics may provide some temporary relief on the job, they build on racial and gender stereotypes which, in the long run, can be and are used against Third-World women.

Daughters, Wives, and Mothers: Migrant Women Workers in Britain

> Family businesses have been able to access minority women's labor power through media-
> tions of kinship and an appeal to ideologies which emphasize the role of women in the
> home as wives and mothers and as keepers of family honor.[22]

In a collection of essays exploring the working lives of black and minority women inside and outside the home, Sallie Westwood and Parminder Bhachu focus on the benefits afforded the British capitalist state by the racial and gendered aspects of migrant women's labor. They point to the fact that what has been called the "ethnic economy" (the way migrants draw on resources to survive in situations where the combined effects of a hostile, racist environment and economic decline serve to oppress them) is also fundamentally a gendered economy. Statistics indicate that Afro-Caribbean and non-Muslim Asian women have a higher full-time labor participation rate than white women in the U.K. Thus, while the perception that black women (defined, in this case, as women of Afro-Caribbean, Asian, and African origin) are mostly concentrated in part-time jobs is untrue, the *forms* and *patterns* of their work lives within the context of homework and family firms, businesses where the entire family is involved in earning a living, either inside or outside the home bears examination. Work by British feminist scholars (Phizacklea 1983, Westwood 1984, 1988, Josephides 1988, and others) suggests that familial ideologies of domesticity and heterosexual marriage cement the economic and social exploitation of black women's labor within family firms. Repressive patriarchal ideologies, which fix the woman's role in the family are grounded in inherited systems of inequality and oppression in Black women's cultures of origin. And these very ideologies are reproduced and consolidated in order to provide the glue for profit-making in the context of the racialized British capitalist state.

For instance, Annie Phizacklea's work on Bangladeshi homeworkers in the clothing industry in the English West Midlands illuminates the extent to which family and community ties, maintained by women, are crucial in allowing this domestic subcontracting in the clothing industry to undercut the competition in terms of wages and long workdays and its cost to women workers. In addition, Sallie Westwood's work on Gujarati women factory workers in the East Midlands hosiery industry suggests that the power and creativity of the shop-floor culture – which draws on cultural norms of femininity, masculinity and domesticity, while simultaneously generating resistance and solidarity among the Indian and white women workers – is, in fact, anchored in Gujarati cultural inheritances. Discussing the contradictions in the lives of Gujarati women within the home and the perception that male family members have of their work as an extension of their family roles (not as a path to financial independence), Westwood elaborates on the continuities between the ideologies of domesticity within the household, which are the result of (often repressive) indigenous cultural values and practices, and the culture of the shopfloor. Celebrating each other as daughters, wives, and mothers is one form of generating solidarity on the shopfloor – but it is also a powerful refeminization strategy, in Hossfeld's terms.

Finally, family businesses, which depend on the cultural and ideological resources and loyalties within the family to transform ethnic "minority" women into workers committed to common familial goals, are also anchored in women's roles as daughters, wives, mothers, and keepers of family honor (Josephides 1988, Bhachu 1998). Women's work in family business is unpaid and produces dependencies that are similar to those of homeworkers whose labor, although paid, is invisible. Both are predicated on ideologies of domesticity and womanhood which infuse the spheres of production and reproduction. In discussing Cypriot women in family firms, Sasha Josephides cites the use of familial ideologies of "honor" and the construction of a "safe" environment outside the public sphere as the bases for a definition of femininity and womanhood (the perfect corollary to a paternal, protective definition of masculinity) that allows Cypriot women to see themselves as workers for their family, rather than as workers for themselves. All conflict around the question of work is thus accommodated within the context of the family. This is an important instance of the privatization of work, and of the redefinition of the identity of women workers in family firms as doing work that is a "natural extension" of their familial duties (not unlike the lacemakers). It is their identity as mothers, wives, and family members that stands in for their identity as workers. Parminder Bhachu's work with Punjabi Sikhs also illustrates this fact. Citing the growth of small-scale entrepreneurship among South Asians as a relatively new trend in the British economy, Bhachu states that women workers in family businesses often end up losing autonomy and reenter more traditional forms of patriarchal dominance where men control all or most of the economic resources within the family: "By giving up work, these women not only lose an independent source of income, and a large network of often female colleagues, but they also find themselves sucked back into the kinship system which emphasizes patrilaterality."[23] Women thus lose a "direct relationship with the productive process," thus raising the issue of the invisibility (even to themselves) of their identity as workers.

This analysis of migrant women's work in Britain illustrates the parallel trajectory of their exploitation as workers within a different metropolitan context than the U.S. To summarize, all these case studies indicate ways in which ideologies of domesticity, femininity, and race form the basis of the construction of the notion of "women's work" for Third-World women in the contemporary economy. In the case of the lacemakers, this is done through the definition of homework as leisure time activity and of the workers themselves as housewives. As discussed earlier, indigenous hierarchies of gender and caste/class make this definition possible. In the case of the electronics workers, women's work is defined as unskilled, tedious, and supplementary activity for mothers and homemakers. It is a specifically American ideology of individual success, as well as local histories of race and ethnicity that constitute this definition. We can thus contrast the *invisibility* of the lacemakers as workers to the *temporary* nature of the work of Third-World women in the Silicon Valley. In the case of migrant women workers in family firms in Britain, work becomes an extension of familial roles and loyalties, and draws upon cultural and ethnic/racial ideologies of womanhood, domesticity, and entrepreneurship to consolidate patriarchal dependencies. In all these cases, ideas of *flexibility*, *temporality*, *invisibility*, and *domesticity* in the naturalization of categories of work are crucial in the construction of Third-World women as an appropriate and cheap labor force. All of the above ideas rest on stereotypes about gender, race, and poverty, which, in turn, characterize Third-World women as workers in the contemporary global arena.

Eileen Boris and Cynthia Daniels claim that "homework belongs to the decentralization of production that seems to be a central strategy of some sectors and firms for coping with the international restructuring of production, consumption, and capital accumulation."[24] Homework assumes a significant role in the contemporary capitalist global economy. The discussion of homework performed by Third-World women in the three geographical spaces discussed above – India, U.S.A., and Britain – suggests something specific about capitalist strategies of recolonization at this historical juncture. Homework emerged at the same time as factory work in the early nineteenth century in the U.S., and, as a system, it has always reinforced the conjoining of capitalism and patriarchy. Analyzing the homeworker as a wage laborer (rather than an entrepreneur who controls both her labor and the market for it) dependent on the employer for work which is carried out usually in the "home" or domestic premises, makes it possible to understand the *systematic* invisibility of this form of work. What allows this work to be so fundamentally exploitative as to be invisible as a form of work are ideologies of domesticity, dependency, and (hetero)sexuality, which designate women – in this case, Third-World women – as primarily housewives/mothers and men as economic supporters/breadwinners. Homework capitalizes on the equation of home, family, and patriarchal and racial/cultural ideologies of femininity/masculinity with work. This is work done at home, in the midst of doing housework, childcare, and other tasks related to "homemaking," often work that never ceases. Characterizations of "housewives," "mothers," and "homemakers" make it impossible to see home-workers as workers earning regular wages and entitled to the rights of workers. Thus, not just their *production*, but homeworkers' *exploitation* as workers, can, in fact, also remain invisible, contained within domestic, patriarchal relations in the family. This is a form of work that often falls outside accounts of wage labor, as well as accounts of household dynamics.[25]

Family firms in Britain represent a similar ideological pattern, within a different class dynamic. Black women imagine themselves as entrepreneurs (rather than as wage laborers) working for the prosperity of their families in a racist society. However, the work they do is still seen as an extension of their familial roles and often creates economic and social dependencies. This does not mean that women in family firms never attain a sense of autonomy, but that, as a system, the operation of family business exploits Third-World women's labor by drawing on and reinforcing indigenous hierarchies in the search for upward mobility in the (racist) British capitalist economy. What makes this form of work in the contemporary global capitalist arena so profoundly exploitative is that its invisibility (both to the market, and sometimes to the workers themselves) is premised on deeply ingrained sexist and racist relationships within and outside heterosexual kinship systems. This is also the reason why changing the gendered relationships that anchor homework, and organizing homeworkers becomes such a challenge for feminists.

The analysis of factory work and family business in Britain and of homework in all three geographical locations raises the question of whether homework and factory work would be defined in these particular ways if the workers were single women. In this case, the construct of the *worker* is dependant on gender ideologies. In fact, the idea of work or labor as necessary for the psychic, material, and spiritual survival and development of women workers is absent. Instead, it is the identity of women as housewives, wives, and mothers (identities also defined outside the parameters of work) that is assumed to provide the basis for women's survival and growth. These Third-World women are defined out of the labor/capital process as if work in their case isn't necessary for economic, social, psychic autonomy, independence, and self-determination – a nonalienated relation to work is a conceptual and practical impossibility in this situation.

Common Interests/Different Needs: Collective Struggles of Poor Women Workers

Thus far, this essay has charted the ideological commonalities of the exploitation of (mostly) poor Third-World women workers by global capitalist economic processes in different geographical locations. The analysis of the continuities between factory work and homework in objectifying and domesticating Third-World women workers such that their very identity as *workers* is secondary to familial roles and identities, and predicated on patriarchal and racial/ethnic hierarchies anchored in local/indigenous *and* transnational processes of exploitation exposes the profound challenges posed in organizing women workers on the basis of common interests. Clearly, these women are not merely victims of colonizing, exploitative processes – the analysis of the case studies indicates different levels of consciousness of their own exploitation, different modes of resistance, and different understandings of the contradictions they face, and of their own agency as workers. While the essay thus far lays the groundwork for conceptualizing the common interests of women workers based on an understanding of shared location and needs, the analysis foregrounds processes of *repression* rather than forms of *opposition*. How have poor Third-World women organized as workers? How do we conceptualize the question of "common interests" based in a "common context of struggle," such that women are agents who make choices and decisions that lead to the transformation of consciousness and of their daily lives as workers?

As discussed earlier, with the current domination in the global arena of the arbitrary interests of the market and of transnational capital, older signposts and definitions of capital/labor or of "the worker" or even of "class struggle" are no longer totally accurate or viable conceptual or organizational categories. It is, in fact, the predicament of poor working women and their experiences of survival and resistance in the creation of new organizational forms to earn a living and improve their daily lives that offers new possibilities for struggle and action.[26] In this instance, then, the experiences of Third-World women workers are relevant for understanding and transforming the work experiences and daily lives of poor women everywhere. The rest of this essay explores these questions by suggesting a working definition of the question of the common interests of Third-World women workers in the contemporary global capitalist economy, drawing on the work of feminist political theorist Anna G. Jonasdottir.

Jonasdottir explores the concept of women's interests in participatory democratic political theory. She emphasizes both the formal and the content aspects of a theory of social and political interests that refers to "different layers of social existence: agency and the needs/desires that give strength and meaning to agency."[27] Adjudicating between political analysts who theorize common interests in formal terms (i.e., the claim to actively "be among," to choose to participate in defining the terms of one's own existence, or acquiring the conditions for choice), and those who reject the concept of interests in favor of the concept of (subjective) individualized, and group-based "needs and desires," (the consequences of choice), Jonasdottir formulates a concept of the common interests of women that emphasizes the former, but is a combination of both perspectives. She argues that the formal aspect of interest (an active "being among") is crucial: "Understood historically, and seen as emerging from people's lived experiences, interests about basic processes of social life are divided systematically between groups of people in so far as their living conditions are systematically different. Thus, historically and socially defined, interests can be characterized as 'objective.'"[28] In other words, there are systematic material and historical bases for claiming Third-World women workers have common interests. However, Jonasdottir suggests that the second aspect of theorizing interest, the satisfaction of needs and desires (she distinguishes between agency and the result of agency) remains a open question. Thus, the *content* of needs and desires from the point of view of interest remains open for subjective interpretation. According to Jonasdottir, feminists can acknowledge and fight on the basis of the (objective) common interests of women in terms of active representation and choices to participate in a democratic polity, while at the same time not reducing women's common interests (based on subjective needs and desires) to this formal "being among" aspect of the question of interest. This theorization allows us to acknowledge common interests and potential agency on the basis of systematic aspects of social location and experience, while keeping open what I see as the deeper, more fundamental question of understanding and organizing around the needs, desires, and choices (the question of critical, transformative consciousness) in order to transform the material and ideological conditions of daily life. The latter has a pedagogical and transformative dimension which the former does not.

How does this theorization relate to conceptualizations of the common interests of Third-World women workers? Jonasdottir's distinction between agency and the result of agency is a very useful one in this instance. The challenges for feminists in this arena are a) understanding Third-World women workers as having objective interests in common as workers (they are thus agents and make choices as workers); and b) recognizing the contradictions and dislocations in women's own consciousness of themselves as workers, and thus of their needs and desires – which sometimes militate *against* organizing on the basis of their common interests (the results of agency). Thus, work has to be done here in analyzing the links between the social location and the historical and current experiences of domination of Third-World women workers on the one hand, and in theorizing and enacting the common *social identity* of Third-World women workers on the other. Reviewing the forms of collective struggle of poor, Third-World women workers in relation to the above theorization of common interests provides a map of where we are in this project.

In the case of women workers in the free-trade zones in a number of countries, trade unions have been the most visible forum for expressing the needs and demands of poor women. The sexism of trade unions, however, has led women to recognize the need for alternative, more democratic organizational structures, and to form women's unions (as in Korea, China, Italy, and Malaysia)[29] or to turn to community groups, church committees, or feminist organizations. In the U.S., Third-World immigrant women in electronics factories have often been hostile to unions which they recognize as clearly modeled in the image of the white, male, working-class American worker. Thus, church involvement in immigrant women workers' struggles has been a important form of collective struggle in the U.S.[30]

Women workers have developed innovative strategies of struggle in women's unions. For instance, in 1989, the Korean Women Workers Association staged an occupation of the factory in Masan. They moved into the factory and lived there, cooked meals, guarded the machines and premises, and effectively stopped production.[31] In this form of occupation of the work premises, the processes of daily life become constitutive of resistance (also evident in the welfare rights struggles in the U.S.A.) and opposition is anchored in the systematic realities of the lives of poor women. It expresses not only their common interests as workers, but acknowledges their social circumstance as *women* for whom the artificial separation of work and home has little meaning. This "occupation" is a strategy of collective resistance that draws attention to poor women worker's *building community* as a form of survival.

Kumudhini Rosa makes a similar argument in her analysis of the "habits of resistance" of women workers in Free Trade Zones (FTZ) in Sri Lanka, Malaysia, and the Philippines.[32] The fact that women live and work together in these FTZs is crucial in analyzing the ways in which they build community life, share resources and dreams, provide mutual support and aid on the assembly line and in the street, and develop individual and collective habits of resistance. Rosa claims that these forms of resistance and mutual aid are anchored in a "culture of subversion" in which women living in patriarchal, authoritarian households where they are required to be obedient and disciplined, acquire practice in "concealed forms of rebelling" (86). Thus, women workers engage in "spontaneous" strikes in Sri Lanka, "wildcat" strikes in Malaysia, and "sympathy" strikes in the Philippines. They also support each other by systematically lowering the production target, or helping slow workers to meet the production targets on assembly lines. Rosa's analysis illustrates recognition of the common interests of women workers at a formal "being among" level. While women are conscious of the contradictions of their daily lives as women and as workers, and enact their resistance, they have not organized actively to identify their collective needs and to transform the conditions of their daily lives.

While the earlier section on the ideological construction of work in terms of gender and racial/ethnic hierarchies discussed homework as one of the most acute forms of exploitation of poor Third-World women, it is also the area in which some of the most creative and transformative collective organizing has occurred. The two most visibly successful organizational efforts in this arena are the Working Women's Forum (WWF) and SEWA (Self Employed Women's Association) in India, both registered as independent trade unions, and focusing on incorporating homeworkers, as well as petty traders, hawkers, and laborers in the informal economy into their membership.[33]

There has also been a long history of organizing homeworkers in Britain. Discussing the experience of the West Yorkshire Homeworking Group in the late 1980s, Jane Tate states that "a homework campaign has to work at a number of levels, in which the personal interconnects with the political, the family situation with work, lobbying Parliament with small local meetings.... In practical terms, the homeworking campaigns have adopted a way of organising that reflects the practice of many women's groups, as well as being influenced by the theory and practice of community work. It aims to bring out the strength of women, more often in small groups with a less formal structure and organisation than in a body such as a union."[34] Issues of race, ethnicity, and class are central in this effort since most of the homeworkers are of Asian or

Third-World origin. Tate identifies a number of simultaneous strategies used by the West Yorkshire Group to organize homeworkers: pinpointing and making visible the "real" employer (or the real enemy), rather than directing organizational efforts only against local subsidiaries; consumer education and pressure, which links the buying of goods to homeworker struggles; fighting for a code of work practice for suppliers by forming alliances between trade unions, women's, and consumer groups; linking campaigns to the development of alternative trade organizations (for instance, SEWA); fighting for visibility in international bodies like the ILO; and, finally, developing transnational links between local grass-roots homeworker organizations – thus, sharing resources, strategies, and working toward empowerment. The common interests of homeworkers are acknowledged in terms of their daily lives as workers and as women – there is no artificial separation of the "worker" and the "homemaker" or the "housewife" in this context. While the West Yorkshire Homeworking Group has achieved some measure of success in organizing homeworkers, and there is a commitment to literacy, consciousness-raising, and empowerment of workers, this is still a feminist group that organizes women workers (rather than the impetus for organization emerging from the workers themselves – women workers organizing). It is in this regard that SEWA and WWF emerge as important models for poor women workers organizations.

Swasti Mitter discusses the success of SEWA and WWF in terms of: a) their representing the potential for organizing powerful women workers' organizations (the membership of WWF is 85,000 and that of SEWA is 46,000 workers) when effective strategies are used; and b) making these "hidden" workers visible as *workers* to national and international policy makers. Both WWF and SEWA address the demands of poor women workers, and both include a development plan for women which includes leadership training, child care, women's banks, and producer's cooperatives which offer alternative trading opportunities. Renana Jhabvala, SEWA's secretary, explains that, while SEWA was born in 1972 in the Indian labor movement and drew inspiration from the women's movement, it always saw itself as a part of the cooperative movement, as well. Thus, struggling for poor women workers' rights always went hand-in-hand with strategies to develop alternative economic systems. Jhabvala states, "SEWA accepts the co-operative principles and sees itself as part of the co-operative movement attempting to extend these principles to the poorest women.... SEWA sees the need to bring poor women into workers' co-operatives. The co-operative structure has to be revitalised if they are to become truely workers' organisations, and thereby mobilise the strength of the co-operative movement in the task of organising and strengthening poor women."[35] This emphasis on the extension of cooperative (or democratic) principles to poor women, the focus on political and legal literacy, education for critical and collective consciousness, and developing strategies for collective (and sometimes militant) struggle *and* for economic, social, and psychic development makes SEWA's project a deeply feminist, democratic, and transformative one. Self-employed women are some of the most disenfranchised in Indian society – they are vulnerable economically, in caste terms, physically, sexually, and in terms of their health, and, of course, they are socially and politically invisible. Thus, they are also one of the most difficult constituencies to organize. The simultaneous focus on collective struggle for equal rights and justice (struggle against) coupled with economic development on the basis of cooperative, democratic principles of sharing, education, self-reliance, and autonomy (struggle for) is what is responsible for SEWA's success at organizing poor, home-based, women workers. Jhabvala summarizes this when she says, "The combination of trade union and co-operative power makes it possible not only to defend members but to present an ideological alternative. Poor women's co-operatives are a new phenomenon. SEWA has a vision of the co-operative as a form of society which will bring about more equal relationships and lead to a new type of society."[36]

SEWA appears to come closest to articulating the common interests and needs of Third-World women workers in the terms that Jonasdottir elaborates. SEWA organizes on the basis of the objective interests of poor women workers – both the trade union and cooperative development aspect of the organizational strategies illustrate this. The status of poor women workers as workers and as citizens entitled to rights and justice is primary. But SEWA also approaches the deeper level of the articulation of needs and desires based on recognition of subjective, collective interests. As discussed earlier, it is this level of the recognition and articulation of common interest that is the challenge for women workers globally. While the common interests of women workers as *workers* have been variously articulated in the forms of struggles and organization reviewed above, the transition to identifying common needs and desires (the *content* aspect of interest) of Third-World women workers, which leads potentially to the construction of the *identity* of Third-World women workers, is what remains a challenge – a challenge that perhaps SEWA comes closest to identifying and addressing.

I have argued that the particular location of Third-World women workers at this moment in the development of global capitalism provides a vantage point from which to a) make particular practices of domination and recolonization visible and transparent, thus illuminating the minute and global processes of capitalist recolonization of women workers, and b) understand the commonalities of experiences, histories, and identity as the basis for solidarity and in organizing Third-World women workers transnationally. My claim, here, is that the definition of the social identity of women as workers is not only class-based, but, in fact, in this case, must be grounded in understandings of race, gender, and caste histories and experiences of work. In effect, I suggest that homework is one of the most significant, and repressive forms of "women's work" in contemporary global capitalism. In pointing to the ideology of the "Third-World woman worker" created in the context of a global division of labor, I am articulating differences located in specific histories of inequality, i.e., histories of gender and caste/class in the Narsapur context, and histories of gender, race, and liberal individualism in the Silicon Valley and in Britain.

However, my argument does not suggest that these are *discrete* and *separate* histories. In focusing on women's work as a particular form of Third-World women's exploitation in the contemporary economy, I also want to foreground a particular history that third- and first-world women seem to have in common: the logic and operation of capital in the contemporary global arena. I maintain that the interests of contemporary transnational capital and the strategies employed enable it to draw upon indigenous social hierarchies and to construct, reproduce, and maintain ideologies of masculinity/femininity, technological superiority, appropriate development, skilled/unskilled labor, etc. Here I have argued this in terms of the category of "women's work," which I have shown to be grounded in an ideology of the Third-World women worker. Thus, analysis of the location of Third-World women in the new international division of labor must draw upon the histories of colonialism and race, class and capitalism, gender and patriarchy, and sexual and familial figurations. The analysis of the ideological definition and redefinition of women's work thus indicates a political basis for common struggles and it is this particular forging of the political unity of Third-World women workers that I would like to endorse. This is in opposition to ahistorical notions of the common experience, exploitation, or strength of Third-World women or between third- and first-world women, which serve to naturalize normative Western feminist categories of self and other. If Third-World women are to be seen as the *subjects of theory and of struggle*, we must pay attention to the specificities of their/our common *and* different histories.

In summary, this essay highlights the following analytic and political issues pertaining to Third-World women workers in the global arena: 1) it writes a particular group of women workers into history and into the operation of contemporary capitalist hegemony; 2) it charts the links and potential for solidarity between women workers across the borders of nation-states, based on demystifying the ideology of the masculinized worker; 3) it exposes a domesticated definition of Third-World women's work to be in actuality a strategy of global capitalist recolonization; 4) it suggests that women have common interests as workers, not just in transforming their work lives and environments, but in redefining home spaces so that homework is recognized as work to earn a living rather than as leisure of supplemental activity; 5) it foregrounds the need for feminist libera- tory knowledge as the basis of feminist organizing and collective struggles for economic and political justice; 6) it provides a working definition of the common interests of Third-World women workers based on theorizing the common social identity of Third- World women as women/workers; and finally, 7) it reviews the habits of resistance, forms of collective struggle, and strategies of organizing of poor, Third-World women workers. Irma is right when she says that "the only way to get a little measure of power over your own life is to do it collectively, with the support of other people who share your needs." The question of defining common interests and needs such that the identity of Third-World women workers forms a potentially revolutionary basis for struggles against capitalist recolonization, and for feminist self-determination and autonomy, is a complex one. However, as maquiladora worker Veronica Vasquez and the women in SEWA demonstrate, women are already waging such struggles. The end of the twentieth century may be characterized by the exacerbation of the sexual politics of global capitalist domination and exploitation, but it is also suggestive of the dawning of a renewed politics of hope and solidarity.

Notes

Even after a number of new beginnings and revisions, this essay remains work in progress. I have come to the conclusion that this is indicative of both my own level of thinking about these issues as well as the current material and ideological conditions which position Third-World women wage-laborers in con- tradictory ways. I would like to thank Jacqui Alexander for careful, systematic, and patient feedback on this essay. The essay would not have been possible without Satya Mohanty's pertinent and incisive critique, and his unstinting emotional and intellectual support. My students at Hamilton College and colleagues at various institutions where I have presented sections of this argument are responsible for whatever clarity and lucidity the essay offers – thanks for keeping me on my toes. It is my involvement with the staff and board members of Grassroots Leadership of North Carolina that has sharpened my thinking about the struggles of poor and working people, and about the politics of solidarity and hope it engenders. Finally, it was Lisa Lowe, and then Mary Tong of the Support Committee for Maquiladora Workers, who brought the cross-border organizing of Veronica Vasquez and other workers to my atten- tion. I thank all these organizers for teaching me and for the grassroots organizing work they continue to do in the face of great odds.

1   See Karen Hossfeld, "United States: Why Aren't High-Tech Workers Organised?" in Women Working Worldwide, eds., *Common Interests: Women Organising in Global Electronics* (London: Tavistock), pp. 33–52, esp. pp. 50–51.

2   See "Tijuanans Sue in L.A. after Their Maquiladora Is Closed," by Sandra Dribble, in *The San Diego Union-Tribune*, Friday, December 16, 1994. The Support Committee for Maquiladora Workers promotes cross-border organizing against corporate impunity. This is a San Diego-based volunteer effort of unionists, community activists, and others to assist workers in building auto-nomous organizations and facilitating ties between Mexican and U.S. workers. The Committee, which is coordinated by Mary Tong, also sees its task as educating U.S. citizens about the realities of life, work, and efforts for change among maquiladora workers. For more information write the Support Committee at 3909 Centre St., #210, San Diego, CA 92103.

3   See my essay, "Cartographies of Struggle: Third World Women and the Politics of Feminism," in Mohanty, Russo, and Torres, eds. *Third World Women and The Politics of Feminism*, (Bloomington: Indiana University Press, 1991), especially p. 39, where I identified five provisional historical, polit-ical, and discursive junctures for understanding Third-World feminist politics: "decolonization and national liberation movements in the third world, the consolidation of white, liberal capitalist patriarchies in Euro-America, the operation of multinational capital within a global economy, ... anthropology as an example of a discourse of dominance and self-reflexivity, ... (and) storytelling or autobiography (the practice of writing) as a discourse of oppositional consciousness and agency." This essay represents a continuation of one part of this project: the operation of multinational capital and the location of poor Third-World women workers.

4   See the excellent analysis in Teresa L. Amott and Julie A. Matthaei, *Race, Gender and Work: A Multicultural Economic History of Women in the United States* (Boston: South End Press, 1991), esp. pp. 22–23.

5   See Bagguley, Mark-Lawson, Shapiro, Urry, Walby, and Warde, *Restructuring: Place, Class and Gender* (London: Sage Publications, 1990).

6   Joan Smith has argued, in a similar vein, for the usefulness of a world-systems-theory approach (seeing the various economic and social hierarchies and national divisions around the globe as part of a singular systematic division of labor, with multiple parts, rather than as plural and autonomous national systems) which incorporates the notion of the "household" as integral to understanding the profoundly gendered character of this systemic division of labor. While her analysis is useful in historicizing and analyzing the idea of the household as the constellation of relationships that makes the transfer of wealth possible across age, gender, class, and national lines, the ideologies of mascu-linity, femininity, and heterosexuality that are internal to the concept of the household are left curiously intact in her analysis – as are differences in understandings of the household in different cultures. In addition, the impact of domesticating ideologies in the sphere of production, in con-structions of "women's work" are also not addressed in Smith's analysis. While I find this version of the world-systems approach useful, my own analysis attempts a different series of connections and theorizations. See Joan Smith, "The Creation of the World We Know: The World-Economy and the Re-creation of Gendered Identities," in V. Moghadam, ed., *Identity Politics and Women: Cultural Reassertions in International Perspective* (Boulder: Westview Press, 1994), pp. 27–41.

7   The case studies I analyze are: Maria Mies, *The Lacemakers of Narsapur, Indian Housewives Produce for the World Market* (London: Zed Press, 1982); Naomi Katz and David Kemnitzer, "Fast Forward: the Internationalization of the Silicon Valley," in June Nash and M. P. Fernandez-Kelly, *Women, Men, and the International Division of Labor* (Albany: SUNY Press, 1983), pp 273–331; Katz and Kemnitzer, "Women and Work in the Silicon Valley," in Karen Brodkin Sacks, *My Troubles Are Going to Have Trouble with Me: Everyday Trials and Triumphs of Women Workers* (New Brunswick, NJ: Rutgers University Press, 1984), pp 193–208; and Karen J. Hossfeld, "'Their Logic Against Them:' Contradictions in Sex, Race, and Class in the Silicon Valley," in Kathryn Ward, ed., *Women Workers and Global Restructuring* (Ithaca: Cornell University Press, 1990), pp. 149–178. I also draw on case studies of Black women workers in the British context in Sallie Westwood and Parminder Bhachu, eds., *Enterprising Women* (New York: Routledge, 1988).

8   See my discussion of "relations of rule" in "Cartographies." There has been an immense amount of excellent feminist scholarship on women and work and women and multinationals in the last

decade. In fact, it is this scholarship which makes my argument possible. Without the analytic and political insights and analyses of scholars like Aihwa Ong, Maria Patricia Fernandez-Kelly, Lourdes Beneria and Martha Roldan, Maria Mies, Swasti Mitter, and Sallie Westwood, among others, my attempt to understand and stitch together the lives and struggles of women workers in different geographical spaces would be sharply limited. This essay builds on arguments offered by some of these scholars, while attempting to move beyond particular cases to an integrated analysis which is not the same as the world-systems model. See especially Nash and Fernandez-Kelly, *Women, Men and the International Division of Labor; Ward, ed., Women Workers and Global Restructuring; Review of Radical Political Economics*, vol. 23, no. 3–4, (Fall/Winter 1991) special issue on "Women in the International Economy"; Harriet Bradley, *Men's Work, Women's Work* (Minneapolis: University of Minnesota Press, 1989); Lynne Brydon and Sylvia Chant, *Women in the Third World, Gender Issues in Rural and Urban Areas* (New Brunswick, NJ: Rutgers University Press, 1989).

9 See Ella Shohat and Robert Stam, *Unthinking Eurocentrism: Multiculturalism and the Media* (London and New York: Routledge, 1994), esp. pp. 25–27. In a discussion of the analytic and political problems involved in using terms like "Third World," Shohat and Stam draw attention to the adoption of "third world" at the 1955 Bandung Conference of "non-aligned" African and Asian nations, an adoption which was premised on the solidarity of these nations around the anticolonial struggles in Vietnam and Algeria. This is the genealogy of the term that I choose to invoke here.

10 My understanding and appreciation of the links between location, experience, and social identity in political and intellectual matters grows out of numerous discussions with Satya Mohanty. See especially his essay, "Colonial Legacies, Multicultural Futures: Relativism, Objectivity, and the Challenge of Otherness," in *PMLA*, January 1995, pp. 108–117. See also Paula Moya's essay in this collection for further discussion of these issues.

11 Karen Brodkin Sacks, "Introduction," in Karen Brodkin Sacks and D. Remy, eds., *My Troubles Are Going to Have Trouble with Me*, esp. pp. 10–11.

12 Jeremy Brecher, "The Hierarch's New World Order – and Ours," in Jeremy S. Brecher et al., eds., *Global Visions, Beyond the New World Order* (Boston: South End Press, 1993), pp. 3–12.

13 See Maria Mies, *Patriarchy and Accumulation on a World Scale: Women in the International Division of Labor* (London: Zed Press, 1986), pp. 114–15.

14 Richard J. Barnet and John Cavanagh, *Global Dreams: Imperial Corporations and the New World Order* (New York: Simon and Shuster, 1994), esp. pp. 25–41.

15 For examples of cross-national feminist organizing around these issues, see the following texts: Gita Sahgal and Nira Yuval Davis, eds., *Refusing Holy Orders, Women and Fundamentalism in Britain* (London: Virago, 1992); Valentine M. Moghadam, *Identity Politics and Women, Cultural Reassertions and Feminisms in International Perspective* (Boulder: Westview Press, 1994); *Claiming Our Place, Working the Human Rights System to Women's Advantage* (Washington D.C.: Institute for Women, Law and Development, 1993); Sheila Rowbotham and Swasti Mitter, eds., *Dignity and Daily Bread: New Forms of Economic Organizing among Poor Women in the Third World and the First* (New York: Routledge, 1994); and Julie Peters and Andrea Wolper, eds., *Women's Rights, Human Rights: International Feminist Perspectives* (New York: Routledge, 1995).

16 Amott and Matthaei, eds., *Race, Gender and Work*, pp. 316–17.

17 *Women Working Worldwide, Common Interests*, ibid.

18 Aihwa Ong's discussion of the various modes of surveillance of young Malaysian factory women as a way of discursively producing and constructing notions of feminine sexuality is also applicable in this context, where "single" and "married" assume powerful connotations of sexual control. See Aihwa Ong, *Spirits of Resistance and Capitalist Discipline: Factory Women in Malaysia* (Albany: SUNY Press, 1987).

19 Hossfeld, "Their Logic Against Them," p. 149. Hossfeld states that she spoke to workers from at least thirty Third-World nations (including Mexico, Vietnam, the Philippines, Korea, China, Cambodia, Laos, Thailand, Malaysia, Indonesia, India, Pakistan, Iran, Ethiopia, Haiti, Cuba, El Salvador, Nicaragua, Guatemala, Venezuela, as well as southern Europe, especially Portugal and Greece). It may be instructive to pause and reflect on the implications of this level of racial

and national diversity on the shop floor in the Silicon Valley. While all these workers are defined as "immigrants," a number of them as recent immigrants, the racial, ethnic, and gender logic of capitalist strategies of recolonization in this situation locate all the workers in similar relationships to the management, as well as to the U.S. state.

20 Assembly lines in the Silicon Valley are often divided along race, ethnic, and gender lines, with workers competing against each other for greater productivity. Individual worker choices, however imaginative or ambitious, do not transform the system. Often they merely undercut the historically won benefits of the metropolitan working class. Thus, while moonlighting, overtime, and job-hopping are indications of individual modes of resistance, and of an overall strategy of class mobility, it is these very aspects of worker's choices which supports an underground domestic economy which evades or circumvents legal, institutionalized, or contractual arrangements that add to the indirect wages of workers.

21 Hossfeld, "Their Logic Against Them," p. 149: "You're paid less because women are different than men" or "Immigrants need less to get by."

22 Westwood and Bhachu, "Introduction," *Enterprising Women*, p. 5. See also, in the same collection, Annie Phizacklea, "Entrepreneurship, Ethnicity and Gender," pp. 20–33; Parminder Bhachu, "Apni Marzi Kardhi, Home and Work: Sikh Women in Britain," pp. 76–102; Sallie Westwood, "Workers and Wives: Continuities and Discontinuities in the Lives of Gujarati Women," pp. 103–31; and Sasha Josephides, "Honor, Family, and Work: Greek Cypriot Women Before and After Migration," pp. 34–57.

23 P. Bhachu, "Apni Marzi Kardhi, Home and Work," p. 85.

24 For a thorough discussion of the history and contemporary configurations of homework in the U.S., see Eileen Boris and Cynthia R. Daniels, eds., *Homework, Historical and Contemporary Perspectives on Paid Labor at Home* (Urbana: University of Illinois Press, 1989). See especially the "Introduction," pp. 1–12; M. Patricia Fernandez-Kelly and Anna García, "Hispanic Women and Homework: Women in the Informal Economy of Miami Los Angeles," pp. 165–82; and Sheila Allen, "Locating Homework in an Analysis of the Ideological and Material Constraints on Women's Paid Work," pp. 272–91.

25 Allen, "Locating Homework."

26 See Rowbotham and Mitter, "Introduction," in Rowbotham and Mitter, eds., *Dignity and Daily Bread*.

27 Anna G. Jonasdottir, "On the Concept of Interest, Women's Interests, and the Limitations of Interest Theory," in Kathleen Jones and Anna G. Jonasdottir, eds., *The Political Interests of Gender* (London: Sage Publications, 1988), pp. 33–65, esp. p. 57.

28 Ibid., p. 41.

29 See Women Working Worldwide, eds., *Common Interests*.

30 Ibid., p. 38.

31 Ibid., p. 31.

32 Kumudhini Rosa, "The Conditions and Organisational Activities of Women in Free Trade Zones: Malaysia, Philippines and Sri Lanka, 1970–1990," in Rowbotham and Mitter, eds., *Dignity and Daily Bread*, pp. 73–99, esp. p. 86.

33 Swasti Mitter, "On Organising Women in Causalized Work: A Global Overview," in Rowbotham and Mitter, eds., *Dignity and Daily Bread*, pp. 14–52, esp. p. 33.

34 Jane Tate, "Homework in West Yorkshire," in Rowbotham and Mitter, eds., *Dignity and Daily Bread*, pp. 193–217, esp. p. 203.

35 Renana Jhabvala, "Self-Employed Women's Association: Organising Women by Struggle and Development," in Rowbotham and Mitter, eds., *Dignity and Daily Bread*, pp. 114–38, esp. p. 116.

36 Ibid., p. 135.

CHAPTER 8

"I Would Rather Be a Cyborg Than a Goddess": Becoming Intersectional in Assemblage Theory

Jasbir Puar

Jasbir Puar teaches Women's and Gender Studies at Rutgers University. Her books include *Terrorist Assemblages* (2007) and *Interspecies* (2011).

"Grids happen" writes Brian Massumi, at a moment in *Parables for the Virtual* where one is tempted to be swept away by the endless affirmative becomings of movement, flux, and potential, as opposed to being pinned down by the retroactive positioning of identity (2002, 8). For the most part, Massumi has been less interested in how grids happen than in asking how they can un-happen, or not happen. What the tension between the two purportedly opposing forces signals, at this junction of scholarly criticism, might be thought of as a dialogue between theories that deploy the subject as a primary analytic frame, and those that highlight the forces that make subject formation tenuous, if not impossible or even undesirable. I have seen this tension manifest acutely in my own work on intersectionality and assemblage theory. On the one hand I have been a staunch advocate of what is now commonly known as an intersectional approach: analyses that foreground the mutually co-constitutive forces of race, class, sex, gender, and nation. Numerous feminist thinkers consider intersectionality the dominant paradigm through which feminist theory has analyzed difference; Leslie McCall argues that intersectionality might be considered "the most important theoretical contribution that women's studies, in conjunction with other fields, has made so far" (McCall 2005, 1771). Intersectional analysis is now a prevalent approach in queer theory.[1] At the same time, encountering a poststructuralist fatigue with the

Original publication details: Jasbir Puar, "I Would Rather Be a Cyborg than a Goddess: Becoming Intersectional in Assemblage Theory." *philoSOPHIA*, 2.1. State University of New York Press, 2012. Reproduced with permission from State University of New York and J. Paur.

now-predictable yet still necessary demands for subject recognition, I also argued in my book, *Terrorist Assemblages: Homonationalism in Queer Times*, that intersectionality as an intellectual rubric and a tool for political intervention must be supplemented – if not complicated and reconceptualized – by a notion of assemblage. Following Massumi on the "retrospective ordering" of identities such as "gender, race, and sexual orientation" which "back-form their reality," in *Terrorist Assemblages* I write, "[I]ntersectional identities and assemblages must remain as interlocutors in tension ... intersectional identities are the byproducts of attempts to still and quell the perpetual motion of assemblages, to capture and reduce them, to harness their threatening mobility" (Puar 2007, 213). Subject positioning on a grid is never self-coinciding; positioning does not precede movement but rather it is induced by it; epistemological correctives cannot apprehend ontological becomings; the complexity of process is continually mistaken for a resultant product.[2]

Since the publication of *Terrorist Assemblages*, in response to anxieties about my apparent prescription to leave intersectionality behind (as if one could), I have often been asked to elaborate on the political usages of assemblages and assemblage theory. A prominent concept in the work of Gilles Deleuze and Felix Guattari, assemblage seems to inspire doubt about its political "applicability," while intersectionality seems to hold fast as a successful tool for political and scholarly transformation. Part of the assumption at work in these queries is that representation, and its recognized subjects, is the dominant, primary, or most efficacious platform of political intervention, while a Deleuzian nonrepresentational, non-subject-oriented politics is deemed impossible. Perhaps these queries also reveal concerns about how they might be somehow incompatible or even oppositional, despite the fact that intersectionality and assemblage are not analogous in terms of content, utility, or deployment. As analytics, they may not be reconcilable. Yet they need not be oppositional but rather, I argue, frictional.

In what follows, I offer some preliminary thoughts on the limits and possibilities of intersectionality and assemblage and what might be gained by thinking them through and with each other. What are the strengths of each in the realms of theory, political organizing, legal structures, and method? Through highlighting the convivial crossings of these two differentiated but not oppositional genealogies, I offer some thoughts on epistemological correctives in feminist knowledge production – which has been driven, sometimes single-mindedly, by the mandate of intersectional analysis – to see what kinds of futures are possible for feminist theorizing. I reread the formative concept that fueled the metaphoric invocation of intersectionality, specifically Kimberlé Crenshaw's use of the traffic intersection, to show where intersectionality, as that which retroactively forms the grid and positions on it, and assemblage, as that which is prior to, beyond, or past the grid, not so much intersect (though I am tempted to make the pun) but rather resonate with each other. That is to say, what follows aspires to an affirmative, convivial conversation between what have generally been construed as oppositional sets of literatures: that of women of color intersectional feminist theory, and feminist theory that has been invested in postrepresentational, posthuman, or postsubject conceptualizations of the body. My aim here, then, is not to evaluate the limits and potentials of intersectionality for the sake of refining intersectionality itself, nor to weigh in on debates about whether intersectionality is "outmoded and outdated" (Taylor et al. 2011, 3), but to put intersectionality in tandem with assemblage to see how they might be thought together.

Intersectionality and Its Discontents

It has been more than twenty years since Kimberlé Crenshaw wrote her groundbreaking piece titled, "Demarginalizing the Intersection of Race and Sex: A Black Feminist Critique of Antidiscrimination Doctrine, Feminist Theory, and Antiracist Politics" (1989), which, along with her 1991 piece "Mapping the Margins: Intersectionality, Identity Politics, and Violence against Women of Color," went on to become seminal texts for the theorization of intersectionality. The twentieth anniversary was marked by a number of special journal issues, edited books, and conferences commemorating Crenshaw's contribution and discussing the impact of intersectional feminist theorizing, perhaps generating a resurgence of interest in the topic, as anniversaries are wont to do. As activist and theoretical discourse about "difference" developed over several decades by black feminists in the United States such as Audre Lorde, bell hooks, Angela Davis, and The Combahee River Collective, the term *intersectionality* was introduced by and became solidified as a feminist heuristic through Crenshaw's analysis of U.S. antidiscrimination legal doctrine. Crenshaw mapped out three forms of intersectional analysis she deemed crucial: structural (addressing the intersection of racism and patriarchy in relation to battering and rape of women); political (addressing the intersection of antiracist organizing and feminist organizing); and representational (addressing the intersection of racial stereotypes and gender stereotypes, particularly in the case of 2 Live Crew). Her intervention into mutually exclusive identity paradigms is one of rethinking identity politics from within, in particular, from within systemic legal exclusions.[3]

While Crenshaw specifically targeted the elisions of both critical race paradigms and gender normative paradigms, intersectionality emerged from the struggles of second wave feminism as a crucial black feminist intervention challenging the hegemonic rubrics of race, class, and gender within predominantly white feminist frames. Pedagogically, since the emergence and consolidation of intersectionality from the 1980s on, it has been deployed more forcefully as a feminist intervention to disrupt whiteness and less so as a critical race intervention to disrupt masculinist frames. Thus, precisely in the act of performing this intervention, what is also produced is an ironic reification of sexual difference as a/the foundational one that needs to be disrupted. Sexual and gender difference is understood as the constant from which there are variants, just as women of color are constructed in dominant feminist generational narratives as the newest arrivals among the subjects of feminism. This pedagogical deployment has had the effect of re-securing the centrality of the subject positioning of white women.

How is this possible? The theory of intersectionality argues that all identities are lived and experienced as intersectional – in such a way that identity categories themselves are cut through and unstable – and that all subjects are intersectional whether or not they recognize themselves as such. In the succinct words of Arun Saldanha, using Venn diagrams to illustrate his point, "The theory of intersectionality holds that there is no actual body that is a member of only one set" (Saldanha 2010, 289). But what the method of intersectionality is most predominantly used to qualify is the *specific difference* of "women of color," a category that has now become, I would argue, simultaneously emptied of specific meaning in its ubiquitous application and yet overdetermined in its deployment. In this usage, intersectionality always produces an Other, and that Other is always a Woman of Color (now on referred to as WOC, to underscore the overdetermined emptiness of its gratuitousness), who must invariably be shown to be resistant, subversive, or articulating a grievance.[4] More pointedly, it is the difference of African American women that dominates this genealogy of the term *women of color*. Indeed, Crenshaw is clear that she centralizes "black women's experience" and posits "black women as the starting point" of her analysis (Crenshaw 1991, 1243). Thus, the insistent consolidation of intersectionality as a dominant heuristic may well be driven by anxieties about maintaining the "integrity" of a discrete black feminist genealogy, one that might actually obfuscate how intersectionality is thought of and functions differently in different strands of black feminist and women of color feminist thought. For example, while Crenshew's work is about disrupting and reconciling what are perceived to be irreconcilable binary options of gender and race, Audre Lorde's seminal piece "Age, Race, Class, and Sex: Women Redefining Difference" from 1984 reads as a dynamic, affectively resonant postulation of inchoate and sometimes contradictory intersectional subjectivities.[5]

This ironic othering of WOC through an approach that meant to alleviate such othering is exacerbated by the fact that intersectionality has become cathected to the field of women's studies as the paradigmatic frame through which women's lives are understood and theorized, a problem reified by both WOC feminists and white feminists.[6] McCall notes that "feminists are perhaps alone in the academy in the extent to which they have embraced intersectionality … as itself a central category of analysis" (McCall 2005, 1771). This claim to intersectionality as the dominant feminist method can be produced with such insistence that an interest in exploring other frames, for example assemblage, is rendered problematic and even produces WOC feminists invested in multiple genealogies as "race-traitors."[7] This accusation of course reinforces the implicit understanding that intersectionality is a tool to diagnose specifically *racial difference*. Despite decades of feminist theorizing on the question of difference, difference continues to be "difference from," that is, the difference from "white woman." Distinct from a frame that privileges "difference within," "difference from" produces difference as a contradiction rather than as a recognizing it as a perpetual and continuous process of splitting. This is also then an ironic reification of racial difference. Malini Johar Schueller, for example, argues that most scholarship on WOC is produced by WOC, while many white feminists, although hailing intersectionality as a self-evident, primary methodological rubric, continue to produce scholarship that presumes gender difference as foundational. Writes Schueller: "While women of color theorize about a particular group of women, many white feminists continue to theorize about gender/sexuality/women in general." And later: "Indeed, it has become almost a given that works in gender and sexuality studies acknowledge multiple axes of oppression or invoke the mantra of race, class, gender and sexuality" (Schueller 2005, 64).[8] Much like the language of diversity, the language of intersectionality, its very invocation, it seems, largely substitutes for intersectional analysis itself. What I have elsewhere called "diversity management" can more rigorously be described as a "tendency to displace the concept of intersectionality from any political practice and socio-economic context by translating it into a merely theoretical abstraction of slipping signifiers of identity" (Erel et al. 2011, 66).

Political practice and socioeconomic context are shifting metrics that require a historicization of the "event" of intersectionality, its emergence, and the thought that it moved and generated. Further questions about practice and context arise when intersectionality is situated within the changing historical and economic landscape of neoliberal capitalism and identity. What does an intersectional critique look like – or more to the point, what does it do – in an age of neoliberal pluralism, absorption, and accommodation of all kinds of differences? If it is the case that intersectionality has been "mainstreamed" in the last two decades – a way to manage difference that colludes with dominant forms of liberal multiculturalism – is the qualitative force of the interpellation of "difference itself" altered or uncertain? Should intersectionality have to account for anything beyond the context of the legal doctrine from which it was developed? Let me qualify that my concern is not about the formative, generative, and necessary intervention of Crenshaw's work, but about both the changed geopolitics of reception (one that purports to include rather than exclude difference) as well as a tendency toward reification in the deployment of intersectional method. Has intersectionality become, as Schueller implies, an alibi for the re-centering of white liberal feminists? What is a poststructuralist theory of intersectionality that might address liberal multicultural and "postracial" discourses of inclusion that destabilize the WOC as a mere enabling prosthetic to white feminists?

Such questions about time, history, and the shifts from exclusion to inclusion also bring to the fore the dynamics of the spatialization of intersectional analyses. If, as Avtar Brah and Ann Phoenix have argued, "old debates about the category woman have assumed new critical urgency" (Brah and Phoenix 2004, 76) in the context of recent historical events, such as September 11th and the occupation of Afghanistan and Iraq, transnational and postcolonial scholars point out that the categories privileged by intersectional analysis do not necessarily traverse national and regional boundaries nor genealogical exigencies, presuming and producing static epistemological renderings of categories themselves across historical and geopolitical locations. Indeed, many of the cherished categories of the intersectional mantra – originally starting with race, class, gender, now including sexuality, nation, religion, age, and disability – are the products of modernist colonial agendas and regimes of epistemic violence, operative through a Western/Euro-American epistemological formation through which the notion of discrete identity has emerged. Joseph Massad quite astutely points out, in his refinement of Foucauldian framings of sexuality, that the colonial project deployed "sexuality" as a concept that was largely internalized within intellectual and juridical realms but was not distilled as a widespread hegemonic project. While one might worry, then, about the development and adaptation of the terms *gay* or *lesbian* or the globalization of the term *queer*, Massad highlights the graver problem of the generalization and assumed transparency of the term *sexuality* itself – a taken for granted category of the modernist imperial project, not only an imposed epistemological frame, but also ontologically presumptuous – or in fact, an epistemological capture of an ontologically irreducible becoming (Massad 2009).

These problems of epistemic violence are reproduced in feminist and gay and lesbian human rights discourses, as intesectionality is now widely understood as a policy-friendly paradigm. In her piece detailing the incorporation of the language and the conceptual frame of intersectionality into UN and NGO forums, Nira Yuval-Davis points out: "The analysis and methodology of intersectionality, especially in UN-related bodies is just emerging and often suffers from analytic confusions that have already been tackled by feminist scholars who have been working on these issues for longer" (Yuval-Davis 2006, 206). Yuval-Davis also notes that the relatively recent spread of intersection-ality in Europe has largely been attributed to its amenability to policy discussions, an attribution she argues elides the work on migrant feminisms in Europe and particularly the scholarly interventions of black British feminists in the 1970s. To further complicate the travels of intersectional theorizing, in the United States intersectionality came from a very specific set of social movements, whereas in Europe, where the term is currently being widely taken up, the interest in intersectionality does not emerge from social movements (and in fact, as Yuval-Davis points out, with the exception perhaps of Britain, the efforts of migrant women to challenge dominant feminist frames went largely ignored). Rather, this newfound interest in intersectionality signals a belated recognition of the need to theorize racial difference; it also functions as a method for European women's studies to "catch up institutionally" with U.S. women's studies. The category "nation" therefore appears to be the least theorized and acknowledged of intersectional categories, transmitted through a form of globalizing transparency. The United States is reproduced as the dominant site of feminist inquiry through the use of intersectionality as a heuristic to teach difference. Thus, the Euro-American bias of women's studies and history of feminism is ironically reiterated via intersectionality, eliding the main intervention of transnational and postcolonial feminist scholars since the 1990s, which has been, in part, about destabilizing the nation-centered production of the category WOC (Kaplan and Grewal 1994).

The issues I have sketched out reflect issues about knowledge production and suggest that intersectionality is a viable corrective to epistemological violence, should these limitations regarding subject positioning be addressed. But a different critique suggests that intersectionality functions as a problematic reinvestment in the humanist subject, in particular, the "subject X." Rey Chow has produced the most damning critique of what she calls "poststructuralist significatory incarceration," seriously questioning whether the marginalized subject is still a viable site from which to produce politics, much less whether the subject is a necessary precursor for politics (Chow 2006, 53). "Difference" produces new subjects of inquiry that then infinitely multiply exclusion in order to promote inclusion. Difference now precedes and defines identity. Part of Chow's concern is that poststructuralist efforts to attend to the specificity of Others has become a universalizing project that is always beholden to the self-referentiality of the "center," ironically given that intersectionality functions as a call for and a form of antiessentialism (Brah and Phoenix 2004, 76). The poststructuralist fatigue Chow describes is contingent on the following temporal sequencing: Subject X may be different in content, but shows up, time and again, as the same in form. (Examples might be found in the relatively recent entrance of both "trans" identity and "disability" into the intersectional fray.)

Cyborgs and Other Companionate Assemblages

The literature on intersectionality has been bolstered by the focus on representational politics; scholars concerned with the impact and development of representational politics rarely come into dialogue with those convinced of the nonrepresentational referent of "matter itself." There has yet to be a serious interrogation of how these theories on matter and mattering might animate conceptualizations of intersectionality. I am speaking broadly of the work of Donna Haraway, Elizabeth Grosz, Elizabeth Wilson, Karan Barad, Patricia Clough, Dianne Currier, Claire Colebrook, Vicky Kirby, Miriam Fraser, and Luciana Parisi, to name a few. While this group is an artificial construction of my own making and reflects many divergent interests and different theoretical orientations, a few noteworthy commonalities run across them. Divested from subject formation (but for different reasons than Chow), these feminist scholars in science and technology studies, some inflected by posthumanism, others by Deleuzian thought, have generally argued that the liminality of bodily matter cannot be captured by intersectional subject positioning. They proffer instead the notion that bodies are unstable entities that cannot be seamlessly disaggregated into identity formations. Elizabeth Grosz, for example, foregrounding its spatial and temporal essentializations, calls intersectionality "a gridlock model that fails to account for the mutual constitution and indeterminacy of embodied configurations of gender, sexuality, race, class, and nation" (Grosz 1994). They can be loosely described as feminist materialists or feminists invested in de-centering linguistic signification and social constructionism that still takes a division between matter and discourse as the starting point for deconstructive critique.[9]

Haraway has arguably been the most influential of this group. In a leading text from this literature she famously stated, as the very last line in her groundbreaking 1985 essay "A Manifesto for Cyborgs" that she would rather be a cyborg than a goddess, favoring the postmodern technologized figure of techno-human over the reclamation of a racialized, matriarchal past, thus implicitly invoking this binary between intersectionality and assemblage (Haraway 1985). Several theorists have critiqued Haraway's use of the trope of "woman of color" to denote a cyborg par excellence, including Chela Sandoval and Schueller (who has argued that women of color function as a prosthetic to the cyborg myth, which, as I point out earlier, is not unlike how WOC function in relation to intersectionality) (Sandoval 2000; Schueller 2005). Even though Haraway's cyborgs are meant to undermine binaries – of humans and animals, of humans and machines, and of the organic and inorganic – a cyborg actually inhabits the intersection of body and technology. Dianne Currier writes: "In the construction of a cyborg, technologies are added to impact upon, and at some point intersect with a discrete, non-technological 'body.' … Thus, insofar as the hybrid cyborg is forged in the intermeshing of technology with a body, in a process of addition, it leaves largely intact those two categories – (human) body and technology – that preceded the conjunction." Currier argues that despite intending otherwise, the theorization of cyborgs winds up unwittingly "reinscribing the cyborg into the binary logic of identity which Haraway hopes to circumvent" (Currier 2003, 323). Haraway does not actually approach a human/animal/machine nexus, though more recent theorizations of the nature/culture divide, by Luciana Parisi for example, demarcate the biophysical, the biocultural, and the biodigital (Parisi 2004, 12). Still, the question of how the body is materialized, rather than what the body signifies, is the dominant one in this literature.

"Assemblage" is actually an awkward translation of the French term *agencement*. The original term in Deleuze and Guattari's work is not the French word *assemblage*, but *agencement*, a term that means design, layout, organization, arrangement, and relations – the focus being not on content but on relations, relations of patterns (Phillips 2006, 108). In *agencement*, as John Phillips explains, specific *connections with* other concepts is precisely what gives them their meaning. Concepts do not prescribe relations, nor do they exist prior to them; rather, relations of force, connection, resonance, and patterning give rise to concepts. As Phillips writes, the priority is neither to "the state of affairs [what one might call essence] nor the statement [enunciation or expression of that essence] but rather of their connection, which implies the production of a sense that exceeds them and of which, transformed, they now form parts" (ibid., 108). The French and English definitions of assemblage, however, both refer to a collection of things, a combination of items and the fact of assembling. The problematic that haunts this traversal from French theoretical production to U.S. academic usage is about the generative effects of this "mistranslation." Phillips argues that the enunciation of *agencement* as assemblage might be "justified as a further event of *agencement* (assemblage) were it not for the tendency of discourses of knowledge to operate as statements *about* states of affairs" (ibid., 109).

One productive way of approaching this continental impasse would be to ask not necessarily what assemblages are, but rather, what assemblages do. What does assemblage as a conceptual frame do, and what does their theoretical deployment as such do? What is a practice of *agencement*? For current purposes, assemblages are interesting because they de-privilege the human body as a discrete organic thing. As Haraway notes, the body does not end at the skin. We leave traces of our DNA everywhere we go, we live with other bodies within us, microbes and bacteria, we are enmeshed in forces, affects, energies, we are composites of information. Assemblages do not privilege bodies as human, nor as residing within a human animal/nonhuman animal binary. Along with a de-exceptionalizing of human bodies, multiple forms of matter can be bodies – bodies of water, cities, institutions, and so on. Matter is an actor. Following Karen Barad on her theory of performative metaphysics, matter is not a "thing" but a doing. In particular, Barad challenges dominant notions of performativity that operate through an implicit distinction between signification and that which is signified, stating that matter does not materialize through signification alone. Writes Barad:

> A performative understanding of discursive practices challenges the representationalist belief in the power of words to represent preexisting things. Performativity, properly construed, is not an invitation to turn everything (including material bodies) into words; on the contrary, performativity is precisely a contestation of the excessive power granted to language to determine what is real. Hence, in ironic contrast to the monism that takes language to be the stuff of reality, performativity is actually a contestation of the unexamined habits of mind that grant language and other forms of representation more power in determining our ontologies than they deserve (Barad 2003, 802).[10]

Barad's is a posthumanist framing that questions the boundaries between human and nonhuman, matter and discourse, and interrogates the practices through which these boundaries are constituted, stabilized, and destabilized. Signification is only one element of many that give a substance both meaning and capacity. In his book *A New Philosophy of Society: Assemblage Theory and Social Complexity*, Manuel DeLanda undertakes the radical move to "make language last" (DeLanda 2006, 16). In this post-poststructuralist framing, essentialism, which is usually posited as the opposite of social constructionism, is now placed squarely within the realms of signification and language, what DeLanda and others have called "linguistic essentialism." Karen Barad writes: "Language has been granted too much power. The linguistic turn, the semiotic turn, the interpretative turn, the cultural turn; it seems that at every turn lately every 'thing' is turned into language or some other form of cultural representation.... There is an important sense in which the only thing that does not seem to matter anymore is matter" (Barad 2003, 801). Categories – race, gender, sexuality – are considered events, actions, and encounters between bodies, rather than simply entities and attributes of subjects. Situated along a "vertical and horizontal axis," assemblages come into existence within processes of deterritorialization and reterritorialization. In *A Thousand Plateaus*, Deleuze and Guattari problematize a model that produces a constant in order to establish its variations. Instead, they argue, assemblages foreground no constants but rather "variation to variation" and hence the event-ness of identity (Deleuze and Guattari 1987). DeLanda thus argues that race and gender are situated as attributes only within a study of "the pattern of recurring links, as well as the properties of those links" (DeLanda 2006, 56). Using the notion of assemblage (note the translation of *agencement* as "arrangement" here), Guattari elaborates the limits of "molar" categories such as class:

> Take the notion of class, or the class struggle. It implies that there are perfectly delimited sociological objects: bourgeoisie, proletariat, aristocracy.... But these entities become hazy in the many interzones, the intersections of the petite bourgeoisie, the aristocratic bourgeoisie, the aristocracy of the proletariat, the lumpenproletariat, the nonguaranteed elite.... The result: an indeterminacy that prevents the social field from being mapped out in a clear and distinct way, and which undermines militant practice. Now the notion of arrangement can be useful here, because it shows that social entities are not made up of bipolar oppositions. Complex arrangements place parameters like race, sex, age, nationality, etc., into relief. Interactive crossings imply other kinds of logic than that of two-by-two class oppositions. Importing this notion of arrangement to the social field isn't just a gratuitous theoretical subtlety. But it might help to configure the situation, to come up with cartographies capable of identifying and eluding certain simplistic conceptions concerning class struggle. (Guattari 2009, 26)

Re-reading Intersectionality as Assemblage

One of Crenshaw's foundational examples – that of the traffic intersection – does indeed describe intersectionality as an event. Crenshaw writes, "Consider an analogy to traffic in an intersection, coming and going in all four directions. Discrimination, like traffic through an intersection, may flow in one direction, and it may flow in another. If an accident happens in an intersection, it can be caused by cars traveling from any number of directions and, sometimes, from all of them." And later: "But it is not always easy to reconstruct an accident: Sometimes the skid marks and the injuries simply indicate that they occurred simultaneously, frustrating efforts to determine which driver caused the harm. In these cases the tendency seems to be that no driver is held responsible, no treatment is administered, and the involved parties simply get back in their cars and zoom away" (Crenshaw 1989, 149).

As Crenshaw indicates in this description, identification is a process; identity is an encounter, an event, an accident, in fact. Identities are multicausal, multidirectional, liminal; traces aren't always self-evident. The problem of how the two preexisting roads come into being notwithstanding, there is emphasis on motion rather than gridlock, on how the halting of motion produces the demand to locate. The accident itself indicates the entry of the standardizing needs of the juridical; is there a crime taking place? How does one determine who is at fault? As a metaphor, then, intersectionality is a more porous paradigm than the standardization of method inherent to a discipline has allowed it to be; the institutionalization of women's studies in the United States has led to demands for a subject/s (subject X, in fact) and a method.

However animated the scene of the accident at the traffic intersection might read, it still remains, I would argue, primarily trapped within the logic of identity. I want to turn now to a moment in Brian Massumi's *Parables for the Virtual* where he reads an incident of domestic violence through what he calls the "home event-space" (Massumi 2002, 81). For him, the event is not defined as a discrete act or series of actions or activities, but rather the "folding of dimensions of time into each other" (ibid., 15). This folding of dimensions of time is a result of the "conversion of surface distance into intensity [which] is also the conversion of the materiality of the body into an event" (ibid., 14). Interested in the claim regarding a purported increase in domestic violence during Super Bowl Sunday, Massumi writes:

> The home entry of the game, at its crest of intensity, upsets the fragile equilibrium of the household. The patterns of relations between household bodies is reproblematized. The game event momentarily interrupts the pattern of extrinsic relations generally obtaining between domestic types, as typed by gender. A struggle ensues: a gender struggle over clashing codes of sociality, rights to access to portions of the home and its contents, and rituals of servitude. The sociohistorical home place converts into an event space. The television suddenly stands out from the background of the furnishings, imposing itself as a catalytic part-subject, arraying domestic bodies around itself according to the differential potentials generally attaching to their gender type. For a moment, everything is up in the air – and around the TV set, and between the living room and the kitchen. In proximity to the TV, words and gestures take on unaccustomed intensity. Anything could happen. The male body, sensing the potential, transduces the heterogeneity of the elements of the situation into a reflex readiness to violence. The "game" is rigged by the male's already-constituted propensity to strike. The typical pattern of relations is re-imposed in the unity of movement of hand against face. The strike expresses the empirical reality of situation: recontainment by the male-dominated power formation of the domestic. The event short-circuits. The event is recapture. The home event-space is back to the place it was: a container of asymmetric relations between terms already constituted according to gender. Folding back onto domes-tication. Coded belonging, no becoming. (ibid., 80–81)

So what transpires in this assemblage of the event-space? There is an intensifi-cation of the body's relation to itself (one definition of affect), produced not only by the significance of the game, Super Bowl Sunday, but by the bodily force and energy given over to this significance. The difference between signification and significance (sense, value, force) is accentuated. There is a focus on the patterns of relations – not the entities themselves, but the patterns within which they are arranged with each other. The placements within the space itself have not necessarily altered, but the intensified relations have given new capacities to the entities ("The television sud-denly stands out"). Not Assemblage, but *Agencement*. "Household" bodies are not organic bodies alone: the television is an actor, a matter with force, conveying (not deterministically, but suggestively) who moves where and how and when. The televi-sion is an affective conductor: "In proximity to the TV, words and gestures take on an unaccustomed intensity." There is a sense of potentiality, a becoming. "Anything could happen." It is a moment of deterritorialization, a line of flight, something not available for immediate capture – "everything is up in the air," and quite literally, the air is charged with possibility. Intersectional identity comes into play, as the (white) male is always already ideologically coded as more prone to violence. Finally, the strike happens: the hand against face. The line of flight is reterritorialized, forward into the social script, a closing off of one becoming, routed into another assemblage.

Massumi writes: "The point of bringing up this issue is not to enter the debate on whether there is an empirically provable causal link between professional sports and violence against women. The outpouring of verbal aggression provoked by the mere suggestion that there was a link is enough to establish the theoretical point in question here: that what the mass media transmit is not fundamentally image-content but event-potential" (Massumi 2002, 269n5). Thus, this reading of Massumi's is not a textual analysis of the possibility that watching violent television produces violence, or violent subjects. It is not a theory of spectatorship identification, but of affective intensification: the meeting of technology (good old television, no need to always privilege the Internet), bodies, matter, molecular movements, and energetic transfers. Massumi has been criticized for aestheticizing violence, but I would argue that what he conveys so well is the interplay between signification and significance, movement and capture, matter and meaning, affect and identity. Unlike Crenshaw's accident at the traffic intersection, the focus here is not on whether there is a crime taking place, nor determining who is at fault, but rather asking, what are the affective conditions necessary for the event-space to unfold? In the most basic of feminist terms, we can read Massumi's interest in unraveling the script as offering a different way of thinking about the questions, what causes domestic violence and how can we prevent it?

There's obviously much more to say about such an example; certainly one can note (once again) that Massumi also presumes sex/gender differentiation as the primary one that locates bodies on the grid. But in rereading Massumi's example, one sees, as Saldanha argues, using the Deleuzian concepts of "molar" and "molecular" differences, that intersectionality as a concept "is only meant for the molar 'level' … molecular forces continually upset the topological localizability of a body" (Saldanha 2010, 290). In closing, and as an effort to signpost the lines of flight this essay cannot fully follow given space restrictions, my own concerns about intersectional frameworks go far beyond rethinking its contextual specificity (this is not only about epistemological incongruence or correctives, but more importantly, ontological irreducibility). As I have argued in *Terrorist Assemblages*: "No matter how intersectional our models of subjectivity, no matter how attuned to locational politics of space, place, and scale, these formulations – these fine tunings of intersectionality, as it were, that continue to be demanded – may still limit us if they presume the automatic primacy and singularity of the disciplinary subject and its identitarian interpellation" (Puar 2007, 206). My interest in interrogating the predominance of subjecthood itself is driven precisely by the limitations of poststructuralist critique that Rey Chow foregrounds, the concerns about the nature/culture divide and questions of language and matter that the technoscience and materialist feminists have outlined, and the attention to power and affect that assemblage theorists centralize.

I want to make one final connection between intersectionality, assemblage, and the debates on disciplinary societies and societies of control, derived from the work of Michel Foucault and Deleuze's extension of it. While discipline works at the level of identity, control works at the level of intensity; identity is a process involving an intensification of habituation, thus discipline and control are mutually entwined, though not necessarily compatible, with each other. In the 2007 English translation of Michel Foucault's 1977–78 lectures titled *Security, Territory, and Population*, Foucault distinguishes between disciplinary mechanisms and security apparatuses, what Deleuze would later come to call "control societies." On the disciplinary organization of multiplicity, Foucault writes: "Discipline is a mode of individualization of multiplicities rather than something that constructs an edifice of multiple elements on the basis of individuals who are worked on as, first of all, individuals" (Foucault 2007, 12). Many relations between discipline (exclusion and inclusion) and control (modulation, tweaking) have been proffered: one, as various overlapping yet progressive stages of market capitalism and governmentality; two, as coexisting models and exercises of power; three, control as an effect of disciplinary apparatuses – control as the epitome of a disciplinary society par excellence (in that disciplinary forms of power exceed their sites to reproduce everywhere); and finally, as Foucault suggests above, disciplinary frames as a form of control and as a response to the proliferation of control.

It seems to me, and I pose these as speculative points that I continue to think through, that intersectional critique has both intervened in the legal and capitalist structures that demand the fixity of the rights-bearing subject and has also simultaneously reproduced the disciplinary demands of that subject formation. As Norma Alarcon presciently asked, in 1984, in her response to the publication of *This Bridge Called My Back*, are we going to make a subject of the whole world? (Alarcon 1990, 361). If, as Brah and Phoenix argue, "a key feature of feminist analysis of intersectionality is ... decentering ... the normative subject of feminism" (Brah and Phoenix 2004, 78), then how do feminist thinkers address the problem that the construct of the subject is itself already normative? At this productive impasse, then, is this conundrum: the heuristic of intersectionality has produced a tremendous amount of work on WOC while concomitantly excusing white feminists from this work, re-centering gender and sexual difference as foundational and primary – indeed, this amplification of knowledge has in some senses been at the cost of WOC. Yet "we" (this "we" always under duress and contestation) might be reaching a poststructuralist fatigue around the notion of the subject itself. The limits of the epistemological corrective are encountered.

Therefore, to dismiss assemblages in favor of retaining intersectional identitarian frameworks is to dismiss how societies of control tweak and modulate bodies as matter, not predominantly through signification or identity interpellation but rather through affective capacities and tendencies. It is also to miss that assemblages encompass not only ongoing attempts to destabilize identities and grids, but also the forces that continue to mandate and enforce them. That is to say, grid making is a recognized process of *agencement*. But to render intersectionality as an archaic relic of identity politics bypasses entirely the possibility that for some bodies – we can call them statistical outliers, or those consigned to premature death, or those once formerly considered useless bodies or bodies of excess – discipline and punish may well still be a primary apparatus of power. There are different conceptual problems posed by each; intersectionality attempts to comprehend political institutions and their attendant forms of social normativity and disciplinary administration, while assemblages, in an effort to reintroduce politics into the political, asks what is prior to and beyond what gets established. So one of the big payoffs for thinking through the intertwined relations of intersectionality and assemblages is that it can help us produce more roadmaps of precisely these not quite fully understood relations between discipline and control.

To return to the title of this piece, and the juxtaposition that Haraway (unfortunately, but presciently) renders, would I really rather be a cyborg than a goddess? The former hails the future in a teleological technological determinism – culture – that seems not only overdetermined, but also exceptionalizes our current technologies. The latter – nature – is embedded in the racialized matriarchal mythos of feminist reclamation narratives. Certainly it sounds sexier, these days, to lay claim to being a cyborg than a goddess. But why disaggregate the two when there surely must be cyborgian goddesses in our midst? Now that is a becoming-intersectional assemblage that I could really appreciate.

– Rutgers University

Notes

1   For a comprehensive overview of these debates in queer theory, see Taylor et al., 2011.
2   For the full reading of Massumi on movement and my interpretation of it regarding debates on intersectionality, see Puar 2007, 211–26.
3   Disrupting hegemonic frames of race and gender seems to be the initial impetus for many intersectional analyses, while other oppressions follow; for example, the Combahee River Collective writes: "A combined anti-racist and anti-sexist position drew us together initially, and as we developed politically we addressed ourselves to heterosexism and economic oppression under capitalism" (Combahee River Collective, The Combahee River Collective Statement, 1979).
4   My point here is simple: intersectionality rarely refers to work on white subjects, with the important exception of white working-class women. And more generally it rarely refers to work addressing privileged subjects, for example, white upper-class men. While the study of these subjects may well indeed involve an intersectional analysis or approach, the claim to the term itself is sutured to a referent that leads to racial essentialization.
5   As Lorde writes, "As a forty-nine-year-old Black lesbian feminist socialist mother of two, including one boy, and a member of an interracial couple …" (1984, 120).
6   This is despite the fact that there are wide geopolitical differences in the interest in intersectionality. As someone who works with graduate students at Rutgers, I encounter a variety of uneven responses to the importance of intersectionality, determined in part by variations among women's and gender studies programs and geographical regions – from students who are well schooled in the lexicon of intersectionality and presume a taken-for-grantedness of its necessity, to those who have never encountered it in their undergraduate schooling.
7   This is an observation based on responses to my work as well as anecdotal evidence from several WOC with whom I have discussed these issues.
8   Schueller's overall project examines the use of racial analogy as way of restabilizing white women as the proper subject of feminism, what she terms "incorporation by analogy."
9   There have been many varied strands of materialist feminism and not all of these thinkers would describe themselves as such. For a good overview of what has been recently hailed as "the new materialisms," see the Introduction to Coole and Frost 2010.
10 While I find Barad very useful in thinking about how performativity has come to signal a predominantly linguistic process, the danger of her notion of "ontological realism" is that the effort to destabilize linguist essentialism may well privilege an essentialized truth produced through matter, a sort of ontological essentialism or materialist essentialism that uses a linguistic frame – performativity – to shore up the durational temporalities of matter. A similar conundrum appears in the work of Jane Bennet's *Vibrant Matter: A Political Ecology of Things*. Her otherwise instructive theorization of the vitality of matter is undercut, in my opinion, by the use of "agency" as something that can be accorded to certain forms of matter. Agency as it has historically been deployed refers to the capacities of the liberal humanist subject, an anthropocentric conceptualization of movement.

References

Alarcon, Norma. 1990. The theoretical subject(s) of *This bridge called my back* and Anglo-American feminism. In *Making face, making soul/hacienda caras: Creative and critical perspectives by feminists of color*, ed. Gloria Anzaldua, 356–69. San Francisco: Aunt Lute Books.

Barad, Karen. 2003. Posthumanist performativity: Toward an understanding of how matter comes to matter. *Signs: Journal of Women in Culture and Society* 28, no. 3: 801–31.

Brah, Avitar, and Ann Phoenix. 2004. Ain't I a woman: Revisiting intersectionality. *Journal of International Women's Studies* 3: 75–86.

Chow, Rey. 2006. *The age of the world target*. Durham: Duke University Press.

Combahee River Collective. 1979. The Combahee River collective statement.

Coole, Diana, and Samantha Frost. 2010. *New materialisms: Ontology, agency, and politics*. Durham: Duke University Press.

Crenshaw, Kimberlé Williams. 1989. Demarginalizing the intersection of race and sex: A black feminist critique of antidiscrimination doctrine, feminist theory and antiracist politics. *The University of Chicago Legal Forum Volume 1989: Feminism in the Law: Theory, Practice and Criticism*: 139–67.

Crenshaw, Kimberlé Williams. 1991. Mapping the margins: Intersectionality, identity Politics, and violence against women of color. *Stanford Law Review* 6: 1241–99.

Currier, Dianne. 2003. Feminist technological futures: Deleuze and body/technology assemblages. *Feminist Theory* 3: 321–38.

DeLanda, Manuel. 2006. *A new philosophy of society: Assemblage theory and social complexity*. London and New York: Continuum.

Deleuze, Gilles, and Felix Guattari. 1987. *A thousand plateaus*. Trans. Brian Massumi. Minneapolis: University of Minnesota Press.

Erel, Umut, Jin Haritaworn, Encarnacion Gutierrez Rodriguez, and Christian Klesse. 2011. On the depoliticisation of intersectionality talk: Conceptualising multiple oppressions in critical sexuality studies. In *Theorizing intersectionality and sexuality*, ed. Yvette Taylor, Sally Hines, and Mark E. Casey, 56–78. New York: Palgrave MacMillan.

Foucault, Michel. 2007. *Security, territory, population: Lectures at the collège de France, 1977–78*. Trans. Graham Burchell. New York: Picador.

Grosz, Elizabeth. 1994. *Volatile bodies: Toward a corporeal feminism*. Indianapolis: University of Indiana Press.

Guattari, Felix. 2009. I am an idea-thief. In *Soft subversions: Texts and interviews 1977–1985*, ed. Sylvere Lotringer, trans. Chet Wiener and Emily Wittman, 22–33. Los Angeles: Semiotext(e).

Haraway, Donna. 1985. Manifesto for cyborgs: Science, technology, and socialist feminism in the 1980s. *Socialist Review* 80: 65–108.

Kaplan, Caren, and Inderpal Grewal. 1994. *Scattered hegemonies: Postmodernity and transnational feminist practices*. Minneapolis: University of Minnesota Press.

Lorde, Audre. 1984. *Sister outsider: Essays and speeches*. Berkeley: Crossing Press.

Massad, Joseph. 2009. How not to study gender in the Arab world. Lecture at Oberlin College.

Massumi, Brian. 2002. *Parables for the virtual: Affect, movement, sensation*. Durham: Duke University Press.

McCall, Leslie. 2005. The complexity of intersectionality. *Signs: Journal of Women in Culture and Society* 30, no. 3: 1771–1800.

Parisi, Luciana. 2004. *Abstract sex: Philosophy, technology, and mutations of desire*. London and New York: Continuum.

Phillips, John. 2006. *Agencement/assemblage. Theory, Culture and Society* 23, no. 2–3: 108–109.

Puar, Jasbir K. 2007. *Terrorist assemblages: Homonationalism in queer times*. Durham: Duke University Press.

Saldanha, Arun. 2010. Politics and difference. In *Taking place: Non-representational theories and human geography*, ed. Ben Anderson and Paul Harrison, 283–303. Surrey, UK, and Burlington, VT: Ashgate Publishing.

Sandoval, Chela. 2000. *The methodology of the oppressed*. Minneapolis: University of Minnesota Press.

Schueller, Malini Johar. 2005. Analogy and (white) feminist theory: Thinking race and the color of the cyborg Body. *Signs: Journal of Women in Culture and Society* 30, no. 1: 63–92.

Taylor, Yvette, Sally Hines, and Mark E. Casey, eds. 2011. *Theorizing intersectionality and sexuality*. New York: Palgrave MacMillan.

Yuval-Davis, Nira. 2006. Intersectionality and feminist politics. *European Journal of Women's Studies* 13, no. 3: 193–209.

CHAPTER 9

Epistemology of the Closet

Eve Kosofsky Sedgwick

Eve Sedgwick's *Epistemology of the Closet* (1990) is part of the body of scholarship and theory that grew especially in the 1980s and 1990s around the issue of gay and lesbian representation in literature. Sedgwick's work is important for the way it conceives of that issue in terms of the question of knowledge and secrecy. Important in her work as well is the argument that sexuality and gender do not match up in any easily identifiable manner. As many gay theorists noted regarding the US Supreme Court's rulings against homosexuals, the very "unnatural" sexual practices that supposedly distinguish gays from straights are practiced by many heterosexual couples.

Historically, the framing of *Epistemology of the Closet* begins with a puzzle. It is a rather amazing fact that, of the very many dimensions along which the genital activity of one person can be differentiated from that of another (dimensions that include preference for certain acts, certain zones or sensations, certain physical types, a certain frequency, certain symbolic investments, certain relations of age or power, a certain species, a certain number of participants, etc. etc. etc.), precisely one, the gender of object choice, emerged from the turn of the century, and has remained, as *the* dimension denoted by the now ubiquitous category of "sexual orientation." This is not a development that would have been foreseen from the viewpoint of the fin de siècle itself, where a rich stew of male algolagnia, child-love, and autoeroticism, to mention no more of its components, seemed to have as indicative a relation as did homosexuality to the whole, obsessively entertained problematic of sexual "perversion" or, more broadly, "decadence." Foucault, for instance, mentions the hysterical woman and the masturbating child, along with "entomologized" sexological categories such as zoophiles, zooerasts, auto-monosexualists, and gynecomasts, as typifying the new sexual taxonomies, the *"specification of individuals"* that facilitated the modern freighting of sexual definition with epistemological and power relations.[1] True as his notation is, it suggests without beginning to answer the further question: why the category of "the masturbator," to choose only one example,

Original publication details: Eve Kosofsky Sedgwick, "Epistemology of the Closet" from *Epistemology of the Closet*, pp. 8–13, 27–35. University of California Press, 1990. Reproduced with permission from University of California Press.

Literary Theory: An Anthology, Third Edition. Edited by Julie Rivkin and Michael Ryan.
© 2017 John Wiley & Sons, Ltd. Published 2017 by John Wiley & Sons, Ltd.

should by now have entirely lost its diacritical potential for specifying a particular kind of person, an identity, at the same time as it continues to be true – becomes increasingly true – that, for a crucial strain of Western discourse, in Foucault's words "the homosexual was now a species."[2] So, as a result, is the heterosexual, and between *these* species the human species has come more and more to be divided. *Epistemology of the Closet* does not have an explanation to offer for this sudden, radical condensation of sexual categories; instead of speculating on its causes, the book explores its unpredictably varied and acute implications and consequences.

At the same time that this process of sexual specification or species-formation was going on, the book will argue, less stable and identity-bound understandings of sexual choice also persisted and developed, often among the same people or interwoven in the same systems of thought. Again, the book will not suggest (nor do I believe there currently exists) any standpoint of thought from which the rival claims of these minoritizing and universalizing understandings of sexual definition could be decisively arbitrated as to their "truth." Instead, the performative effects of the self-contradictory discursive field of force created by their overlap will be my subject. And, of course, it makes every difference that these impactions of homo/heterosexual definition took place in a setting, not of spacious emotional or analytic impartiality, but rather of urgent homophobic pressure to devalue one of the two nominally symmetrical forms of choice.

As several of the formulations above would suggest, one main strand of argument in this book is deconstructive, in a fairly specific sense. The analytic move it makes is to demonstrate that categories presented in a culture as symmetrical binary oppositions – heterosexual/homosexual, in this case – actually subsist in a more unsettled and dynamic tacit relation according to which, first, term B is not symmetrical with but subordinated to term A; but, second, the ontologically valorized term A actually depends for its meaning on the simultaneous subsumption and exclusion of term B; hence, third, the question of priority between the supposed central and the supposed marginal category of each dyad is irresolvably unstable, an instability caused by the fact that term B is constituted as at once internal and external to term A. Harold Beaver, for instance, in an influential 1981 essay sketched the outlines of such a deconstructive strategy:

> The aim must be to reverse the rhetorical opposition of what is "transparent" or "natural" and what is "derivative" or "contrived" by demonstrating that the qualities predicated of "homosexuality" (as a dependent term) are in fact a condition of "heterosexuality"; that "heterosexuality," far from possessing a privileged status, must itself be treated as a dependent term.[3]

To understand these conceptual relations as irresolvably unstable is not, however, to understand them as inefficacious or innocuous. It is at least premature when Roland Barthes prophesies that "once the paradigm is blurred, utopia begins: meaning and sex become the objects of free play, at the heart of which the (polysemant) forms and the (sensual) practices, liberated from the binary prison, will achieve a state of infinite expansion."[4] To the contrary, a deconstructive understanding of these binarisms makes it possible to identify them as sites that are *peculiarly* densely charged with lasting potentials for powerful manipulation – through precisely the mechanisms of self-contradictory definition or, more succinctly, the double bind. Nor is a deconstructive analysis of such definitional knots, however necessary, at all sufficient to disable them. Quite the opposite: I would suggest that an understanding of their irresolvable instability has been continually available, and has continually lent discursive authority, to antigay as well as to gay cultural forces of this century. Beaver makes an optimistic prediction that "by disqualifying the autonomy of what was deemed spontaneously immanent, the whole sexual system is fundamentally decentred and exposed."[5] But there is reason to believe that the oppressive sexual system of the past hundred years was if anything born and bred (if I may rely on the pith of a fable whose value doesn't, I must hope, stand or fall with its history of racist uses) in the briar patch of the most notorious and repeated decenterings and exposures.

These deconstructive contestations can occur, moreover, only in the context of an entire cultural network of normative definitions, definitions themselves equally unstable but responding to different sets of contiguities and often at a different rate. The master terms of a particular historical moment will be those that are so situated as to entangle most inextricably and at the same time most differentially the filaments of other important definitional nexuses. In arguing that homo/heterosexual definition has been a presiding master term of the past century, one that has the same, primary importance for all modern Western identity and social organization (and not merely for homosexual identity and culture) as do the more traditionally visible cruxes of gender, class, and race, I'll argue that the now chronic modern crisis of homo/heterosexual definition has affected our culture through its ineffaceable marking particularly of the categories secrecy/disclosure, knowledge/ignorance, private/public, masculine/feminine, majority/minority, innocence/initiation, natural/artificial, new/old, discipline/terrorism, canonic/noncanonic, wholeness/decadence, urbane/provincial, domestic/foreign, health/illness, same/different, active/passive, in/out, cognition/paranoia, art/kitsch, utopia/apocalypse, sincerity/sentimentality, and voluntarity/addiction.[6] And rather than embrace an idealist faith in the necessarily, immanently self-corrosive efficacy of the contradictions inherent to these definitional binarisms, I will suggest instead that contests for discursive power can be specified as competitions for the material or rhetorical leverage required to set the terms of, and to profit in some way from, the operations of such an incoherence of definition.

Perhaps I should say something about the project of hypothesizing that certain binarisms that structure meaning in a culture may be "ineffaceably marked" by association with this one particular problematic – ineffaceably even when invisibly. Hypothesizing is easier than proving, but indeed I cannot imagine the protocol by which such hypotheses might be *tested*; they must be deepened and broadened – not the work of one book – and used, rather than proved or disproved by a few examples. The collecting of instances of each binarism that would appear to "common sense" to be unmarked by issues of homo/heterosexual definition, though an inexhaustibly stimulating heuristic, is not, I believe, a good test of such a hypothesis. After all, the particular kinds of skill that might be required to produce the most telling interpretations have hardly been a valued part of the "common sense" of this epistemologically cloven culture. If a painstaking process of accumulative reading and historical de- and recontextualization does not render these homologies resonant and productive, that is the only test they can directly fail, the only one they need to pass.

The structure of the present book has been markedly affected by this intuition – by a sense that the cultural interrogations it aims to make imperative will be trivialized or evacuated, at this early stage, to the degree that their procedures seem to partake of the a priori. I've wanted the book to be inviting (as well as imperative) but resolutely non-algorithmic. A point of the book is *not to know* how far its insights and projects are generalizable, not to be able to say in advance where the semantic specificity of these issues gives over to (or: itself structures?) the syntax of a "broader" or more abstractable critical project. In particular, the book aims to resist in every way it can the deadening pretended knowingness by which the chisel of modern homo/heterosexual definitional crisis tends, in public discourse, to be hammered most fatally home....

> *Axiom 2 The study of sexuality is not coextensive with the study of gender; correspondingly, antihomophobic inquiry is not coextensive with feminist inquiry. But we can't know in advance how they will be different.*

Sex, gender, sexuality: three terms whose usage relations and analytical relations are almost irremediably slippery. The charting of a space between something called "sex" and something called "gender" has been one of the most influential and successful undertakings of feminist thought. For the purposes of that undertaking, "sex" has had the meaning of a certain group of irreducible, biological differentiations between members of the species *Homo sapiens* who have XX and those who have XY chromosomes. These include (or are ordinarily thought to include) more or less marked dimorphisms of genital formation, hair growth (in populations that have body hair), fat distribution, hormonal function, and reproductive capacity. "Sex" in this sense – what I'll demarcate as "chromosomal sex" – is seen as the relatively minimal raw material on which is then based the social construction of *gender*. Gender, then, is the far more elaborated, more fully and rigidly dichotomized social production and reproduction of male and female identities and behaviors – of male and female *persons* – in a cultural system for which "male/female" functions as a primary and perhaps model binarism affecting the structure and meaning of many, many other binarisms whose apparent connection to chromosomal sex will often be exiguous or nonexistent. Compared to chromosomal sex, which is seen (by these definitions) as tending to be immutable, immanent in the individual, and biologically based, the meaning of gender is seen as culturally mutable and variable, highly relational (in the sense that each of the binarized genders is defined primarily by its relation to the other), and inextricable from a history of power differentials between genders. This feminist charting of what Gayle Rubin refers to as a "sex/gender system,"[7] the system by which chromosomal sex is turned into, and processed as, cultural gender, has tended to minimize the attribution of people's various behaviors and identities to chromosomal sex and to maximize their attribution to socialized gender constructs. The purpose of that strategy has been to gain analytic and critical leverage on the female-disadvantaging social arrangements that prevail at a given time in a given society, by throwing into question their legitimate ideological grounding in biologically based narratives of the "natural."

"Sex" is, however, a term that extends indefinitely beyond chromosomal sex. That its history of usage often overlaps with what might, now, more properly be called "gender" is only one problem. ("I can only love someone of my own sex." Shouldn't "sex" be "gender" in such a sentence? "M. saw that the person who approached was of the opposite sex." Genders – insofar as there are two and they are defined in contradistinction to one another – may be said to be opposite; but in what sense is XX the opposite of XY?) Beyond chromosomes, however, the association of "sex," precisely through the physical body, with reproduction and with genital activity and sensation keeps offering new challenges to the conceptual clarity or even possibility of sex/gender differentiation. There is a powerful argument to be made that a primary (or *the* primary) issue in gender differentiation and gender struggle is the question of who is to have control of women's (biologically) distinctive reproductive capability. Indeed, the intimacy of the association between several of the most signal forms of gender oppression and "the facts" of women's bodies and women's reproductive activity has led some radical feminists to question, more or less explicitly, the usefulness of insisting on a sex/gender distinction. For these reasons, even usages involving the "sex/gender system" within feminist theory are able to use "sex/gender" only to delineate a problematical *space* rather than a crisp distinction. My own loose usage in this book will be to denominate that problematized space of the sex/gender system, the whole package of physical and cultural distinctions between women and men, more simply under the rubric "gender." I do this in order to reduce the likelihood of confusion between "sex" in the sense of "the space of differences between male and female" (what I'll be grouping under "gender") and "sex" in the sense of sexuality.

For meanwhile the whole realm of what modern culture refers to as "sexuality" and *also* calls "sex" – the array of acts, expectations, narratives, pleasures, identity-formations, and knowledges, in both women and men, that tends to cluster most densely around certain genital sensations but is not adequately defined by them – that realm is virtually impossible to situate on a map delimited by the feminist-defined sex/gender distinction. To the degree that it has a center or starting point in certain physical sites, acts, and rhythms associated (however contingently) with procreation or the potential for it, "sexuality" in this sense may seem to be of a piece with "chromosomal sex": biologically necessary to species survival, tending toward the individually immanent, the socially immutable, the given. But to the extent that, as Freud argued and Foucault assumed, the distinctively sexual nature of human sexuality has to do precisely with its excess over or potential difference from the bare choreographies of procreation, "sexuality" might be the very opposite of what we originally referred to as (chromosomal-based) sex: it could occupy, instead, even more than "gender" the polar position of the relational, the social/symbolic, the constructed, the variable, the representational (see Figure 1). To note that, according to these different findings, *something* legitimately called sex or sexuality is all over the experiential and conceptual map is to record a problem less resolvable than a necessary choice of analytic paradigms or a determinate slippage of semantic meaning; it is rather, I would say, true to quite a range of contemporary worldviews and intuitions to find that sex/sexuality *does* tend to represent the full spectrum of positions between the most intimate and the most social, the most predetermined and the most aleatory, the most physically rooted and the most symbolically infused, the most innate and the most learned, the most autonomous and the most relational traits of being.

If all this is true of the definitional nexus between sex and sexuality, how much less simple, even, must be that between sexuality and gender. It will be an assumption of this study that there is always at least the potential for an analytic distance between gender and sexuality, even if particular manifestations or features of particular sexualities are among the things that plunge women and men most ineluctably into the discursive, institutional, and bodily enmeshments of gender definition, gender relation, and gender inequality. This, too, has been posed by Gayle Rubin:

> I want to challenge the assumption that feminism is or should be the privileged site of a
> theory of sexuality. Feminism is the theory of gender oppression. ... Gender affects the
> operation of the sexual system, and the sexual system has had gender-specific manifestations.
> But although sex and gender are related, they are not the same thing.[8]

Biological	Cultural
Essential	Constructed
Individually immanent	Relational

Constructivist Feminist Analysis

chromosomal sex ————————————————— gender
                                        gender inequality

Radical Feminist Analysis

chromosomal sex

reproductive relations ————————————— reproductive relations

sexual inequality   sexual inequality

Foucault-influenced Analysis

chromosomal sex ———————— reproduction ———————— sexuality

Figure 1 Some Mappings of Sex, Gender, and Sexuality.

This book will hypothesize, with Rubin, that the question of gender and the question of sexuality, inextricable from one another though they are in that each can be expressed only in the terms of the other, are nonetheless not the same question, that in twentieth-century Western culture gender and sexuality represent two analytic axes that may productively be imagined as being as distinct from one another as, say, gender and class, or class and race. Distinct, that is to say, no more than minimally, but nonetheless usefully.

Under this hypothesis, then, just as one has learned to assume that every issue of racial meaning must be embodied through the specificity of a particular class position – and every issue of class, for instance, through the specificity of a particular gender position – so every issue of gender would necessarily be embodied through the specificity of a particular sexuality, and vice versa; but nonetheless there could be use in keeping the analytic axes distinct.

An objection to this analogy might be that gender is *definitionally* built into determinations of sexuality, in a way that neither of them is definitionally intertwined with, for instance, determinations of class or race. It is certainly true that without a concept of gender there could be, quite simply, no concept of homo- or heterosexuality. But many other dimensions of sexual choice (auto- or alloerotic, within or between generations, species, etc.) have no such distinctive, explicit definitional connection with gender; indeed, some dimensions of sexuality might be tied, not to gender, but *instead* to differences or similarities of race or class. The definitional narrowing-down in this century of sexuality as a whole to a binarized calculus of *homo-* or *hetero*sexuality is a weighty fact but an entirely historical one. To use that fait accompli as a reason for analytically conflating sexuality per se with gender would obscure the degree to which the fact itself requires explanation. It would also, I think, risk obscuring yet again the extreme intimacy with which all these available analytic axes do after all mutually constitute one another: to assume the distinctiveness of the *intimacy* between sexuality and gender might well risk assuming too much about the definitional *separability* of either of them from determinations of, say, class or race.

It may be, as well, that a damaging bias toward heterosocial or heterosexist assumptions inheres unavoidably in the very concept of gender. This bias would be built into any gender-based analytic perspective to the extent that gender definition and gender identity are necessarily relational between genders – to the extent, that is, that in any gender system, female identity or definition is constructed by analogy, supplementarity, or contrast to male, or vice versa. Although many gender-based forms of analysis do involve accounts, sometimes fairly rich ones, of intragender behaviors and relations, the ultimate definitional appeal in any gender-based analysis must necessarily be to the diacritical frontier between different genders. This gives heterosocial and heterosexual relations a conceptual privilege of incalculable consequence. Undeniably, residues, markers, tracks, signs referring to that diacritical frontier between genders are everywhere, as well, internal to and determinative of the experience of each gender and its intragender relations; gender-based analysis can never be dispensed with in even the most purely intragender context. Nevertheless it seems predictable that the analytic bite of a purely gender-based account will grow less incisive and direct as the distance of its subject from a social interface between different genders increases. It is unrealistic to expect a close, textured analysis of same-sex relations through an optic calibrated in the first place to the coarser stigmata of gender difference.[9] The development of an alternative analytic axis – call it sexuality – might well be, therefore, a particularly urgent project for gay/lesbian and antihomophobic inquiry.

It would be a natural corollary to Axiom 2 to hypothesize, then, that gay/lesbian and antihomophobic inquiry still has a lot to learn from asking questions that feminist inquiry has learned to ask – but only so long as we don't demand to receive the same answers in both interlocutions. In a comparison of feminist and gay theory as they currently stand, the newness and consequent relative underdevelopment of gay theory are seen most clearly in two manifestations. First, we are by now very used to asking as feminists what we aren't yet used to asking as antihomophobic readers: how a variety of forms of oppression intertwine systemically with each other; and especially how the person who is disabled through one set of oppressions may *by the same positioning* be enabled through others. For instance, the understated demeanor of educated women in our society tends to mark both their deference to educated men and their expectation of deference from women and men of lower class. Again, a woman's use of a married name makes graphic at the same time her subordination as a woman and her privilege as a presumptive heterosexual. Or, again, the distinctive vulnerability to rape of women of all races has become in this country a powerful tool for the racist enforcement by which white people, including women, are privileged at the expense of Black people of both genders. That one is *either* oppressed *or* an oppressor, or that if one happens to be both, the two are not likely to have much to do with each other, still seems to be a common assumption, however, in at any rate male gay writing and activism,[10] as it hasn't for a long time been in careful feminist work.

Indeed, it was the long, painful realization, *not* that all oppressions are congruent, but that they are *differently* structured and so must intersect in complex embodiments that was the first great heuristic breakthrough of socialist-feminist thought and of the thought of women of color.[11] This realization has as its corollary that the comparison of different axes of oppression is a crucial task, not for any purpose of ranking oppressions, but to the contrary because each oppression is likely to be in a uniquely indicative relation to certain distinctive nodes of cultural organization. The *special* centrality of homophobic oppression in the twentieth century, I will be arguing, has resulted from its inextricability from the question of knowledge and the processes of knowing in modern Western culture at large.

The second and perhaps even greater heuristic leap of feminism has been the recognition that categories of gender and, hence, oppressions of gender can have a structuring force for nodes of thought, for axes of cultural discrimination, whose thematic subject isn't explicitly gendered at all. Through a series of developments structured by the deconstructive understandings and procedures sketched above, we have now learned as feminist readers that dichotomies in a given text of culture as opposed to nature, public as opposed to private, mind as opposed to body, activity as opposed to passivity, etc. etc., are, under particular pressures of culture and history, likely places to look for implicit allegories of the relations of men to women; more, that to fail to analyze such nominally ungendered constructs in gender terms can itself be a gravely tendentious move in the gender politics of reading. This has given us ways to ask the question of gender about texts even where the culturally "marked" gender (female) is not present as either author or thematic.

The dichotomy heterosexual/homosexual, as it has emerged through the last century of Western discourse, would seem to lend itself peculiarly neatly to a set of analytic moves learned from this deconstructive moment in feminist theory. In fact, the dichotomy heterosexual/homosexual fits the deconstructive template much more neatly than male/female itself does, and hence, importantly differently. The most dramatic difference between gender and sexual orientation – that virtually all people are publicly and unalterably assigned to one or the other gender, and from birth – seems if anything to mean that it is, rather, sexual orientation, with its far greater potential for rearrangement, ambiguity, and representational doubleness, that would offer the apter deconstructive object. An essentialism of sexual object-choice is far less easy to maintain, far more visibly incoherent, more visibly stressed and challenged at every point in the culture than any essentialism of gender. This is not an argument for any epistemological or ontological privileging of an axis of sexuality over an axis of gender; but it is a powerful argument for their potential distinctness one from the other.

Even given the imperative of constructing an account of sexuality irreducible to gender, however, it should already be clear that there are certain distortions necessarily built into the relation of gay/lesbian and antihomophobic theory to a larger project of conceiving a theory of sexuality as a whole. The two can after all scarcely be coextensive. And this is true not because "gay/lesbian and antihomophobic theory" would fail to cover heterosexual as well as same-sex object-choice (any more than "feminist theory" would fail to cover men as well as women), but rather because, as we have noted, sexuality extends along so many dimensions that aren't well described in terms of the gender of object-choice at all. Some of these dimensions are habitually condensed under the rubrics of object-choice, so that certain discriminations of (for instance) *act* or of (for another instance) *erotic localization* come into play, however implicitly and however incoherently, when categories of object-choice are mobilized. One used, for instance, to hear a lot about a high developmental stage called "heterosexual genitality," as though cross-gender object-choice automatically erased desires attaching to mouth, anus, breasts, feet, etc.; a certain anal-erotic salience of male homosexuality is if anything increasingly strong under the glare of heterosexist AIDS-phobia; and several different historical influences have led to the de-genitalization and bodily diffusion of many popular, and indeed many lesbian, understandings of lesbian sexuality. Other dimensions of sexuality, however, distinguish object-choice quite differently (e.g., human/animal, adult/child, singular/plural, autoerotic/alloerotic) or are not even about object choice (e.g., orgasmic/nonorgasmic, noncommercial/commercial, using bodies only/using manufactured objects, in private/in public, spontaneous/scripted).[12] Some of these other dimensions of sexuality have had high diacritical importance in different historical contexts (e.g., human/animal, autoerotic/alloerotic). Others, like adult/child object choice, visibly do have such importance today, but without being very fully subsumed under the hetero/homosexual binarism. Still others, including a host of them I haven't mentioned or couldn't think of, subsist in this culture as nondiacritical differences, differences that seem to make little difference beyond themselves – except that the hyperintensive structuring of sexuality in our culture sets several of them, for instance, at the exact border between legal and illegal. What I mean at any rate to emphasize is that the implicit condensation of "sexual theory" into "gay/lesbian and antihomophobic theory," which corresponds roughly to our by now unquestioned reading of the phrase "sexual orientation" to mean "gender of object-choice," is at the very least damagingly skewed by the specificity of its historical placement.

Notes

1 Michel Foucault, *History of Sexuality: An Introduction*, trans. Robert Hurley (New York: Random House, 1980), pp. 105, 43.

2 Ibid., p. 43.

3 Harold Beaver, "Homosexual Signs," *Critical Inquiry* 8 (Autumn 1981): 115.

4 *Roland Barthes by Roland Barthes*, trans. Richard Howard (New York: Hill and Wang, 1977), p. 133.

5 Beaver, "Homosexual Signs," pp. 115–16.

6 My casting of all these definitional nodes in the form of binarisms, I should make explicit, has to do not with a mystical faith in the number two but, rather, with the felt need to schematize in some consistent way the treatment of social vectors so exceedingly various. The kind of falsification necessarily performed on each by this reduction cannot, unfortunately, itself be consistent. But the scope of the kind of hypothesis I want to pose does seem to require a drastic reductiveness, at least in its initial formulations.

7 Gayle Rubin, "The Traffic in Women: Notes on the 'Political Economy' of Sex," in Rayna R. Reiter (ed.), *Toward an Anthropology of Women* (New York: Monthly Review Press, 1975), pp. 157–210.

8 Rubin, "Thinking Sex: Notes for a Radical Theory of the Politics of Sexuality." In Carole S. Vance, ed., *Pleasure and Danger: Exploring Female Sexuality* (Boston: Routledge, 1984), pp. 307–8.

9 For valuable related discussions, see Katie King, "The Situation of Lesbianism as Feminism's Magical Sign: Contests for Meaning and the US Women's Movement, 1968–1972," in *Communication* 9 (1986): 65–91. Special issue, "Feminist Critiques of Popular Culture," ed. Paula A. Treichler and Ellen Wartella, 9: 65–91; and Teresa de Lauretis, "Sexual Indifference and Lesbian Representation," *Theatre Journal* 40 (May 1988): 155–77.

10 Gay male-centered work that uses more complex models to investigate the intersection of different oppressions includes Gay Left Collective (eds.), *Homosexuality: Power and Politics* (London: Allison & Busby, 1980); Paul Hoch, *White Hero Black Beast: Racism, Sexism, and the Mask of Masculinity* (London: Pluto, 1979); Guy Hocquenghem, *Homosexual Desire*, trans. Daniella Dangoor (London: Allison & Busby, 1978); Mario Mieli, *Homosexuality and Liberation: Elements of a Gay Critique*, trans. David Fernbach (London: Gay Men's Press, 1980); D. A. Miller, *The Novel and the Police* (Berkeley and Los Angeles: University of California Press, 1988); Michael Moon, " 'The Gentle Boy from the Dangerous Classes': Pederasty, Domesticity, and Capitalism in Horatio Alger," *Representations*, no. 19 (Summer 1987): 87–110; Michael Moon, *Disseminating Whitman* (Cambridge, Mass.: Harvard University Press, 1990); and Jeffrey Weeks, *Sexuality and its Discontents: Meanings, Myths and Modern Sexualities* (London: Longman, 1980).

11 The influential socialist-feminist investigations have included Michèle Barrett, *Women's Oppression Today: Problems in Marxist Feminist Analysis* (London: Verso, 1980); Zillah Eisenstein (ed.), *Capitalist Patriarchy and the Case for Socialist Feminism* (New York: Monthly Review Press, 1979); and Juliet Mitchell, *Women's Estate* (New York: Vintage, 1973). On the intersections of racial with gender and sexual oppressions, see, for example, Elly Bulkin, Barbara Smith, and Minnie Bruce Pratt, *Yours in Struggle: Three Feminist Perspectives on Anti-Semitism and Racism* (New York: Long Haul Press, 1984); Bell Hooks [Gloria Watkins], *Feminist Theory: From Margin to Center* (Boston: South End Press, 1984); Katie King, "Audre Lorde's Lacquered Layerings: The Lesbian Bar as a Site of Literary Production," *Cultural Studies* 2, no. 3 (1988): 321–42; Audre Lorde, *Sister Outsider: Essays and Speeches* (Trumansburg, NY: The Crossing Press, 1984); Cherríe Moraga, *Loving in the War Years: Lo que nunca paso por sus labios* (Boston: South End Press, 1983); Cherríe Moraga and Gloria Anzaldua (eds.), *This Bridge Called My Back: Writings by Radical Women of Color* (Watertown: Persephone, 1981; rpt. edn., New York: Kitchen Table: Women of Color Press, 1984); and Barbara Smith (ed.), *Home Girls: A Black Feminist Anthology* (New York: Kitchen Table: Women of Color Press, 1983). Good overviews of several of these intersections as they relate to women and in particular to lesbians, can be found in Ann Snitow, Christine Stansell, and Sharon Thompson (eds.), *The Powers of Desire: The Politics of Sexuality* (New York: Monthly Review/New Feminist Library, 1983); Vance, *Pleasure and Danger*; and de Lauretis, "Sexual Indifference."

12 This list owes something to Rubin, "Thinking Sex," esp. pp. 281–2.

CHAPTER 10

Queers, Read This

Queer Nation

The modern gay and lesbian movement began with the Stonewall revolt in New York in 1969. Gays and lesbians and transgender people rejected police harassment, which had been common up to that moment. Seldom have single events changed history so vividly or effectively. However, by the late 1980s, the gay and lesbian movement that grew in the 1970s and 1980s was considered by many younger gay and lesbian activists to be too moderate and too assimilationist. The goal, they felt, was not to be "accepted" by straight heterosexual society. They rejected straight culture with its assumption that heterosexuality was the norm but that "deviants" were welcome. "Be nice to deviants" was not enough of a rallying cry for the younger generation. So they embraced their difference and became queer, adopting a pejorative term that had been used for decades to stigmatize as "other" anyone who departed from the dominant heterosexual paradigm. Rather than seek acceptance by a straight culture that was assumed to be normal, queers began to dismantle the assumptions that sustained that culture, rejecting the idea that gender had to be an identity or that there was anything that might be a norm in regard to either sex or gender. Queers celebrate the free-floating transitivity of gender forms and practices, and their work over the past several decades has been instrumental in adding transgender, bi, and queer to the diversity flag: LGBTQ. The pamphlet that follows was distributed at the 1990 Pride March in New York City.

A Leaflet Distributed at Pride March in NY Published Anonymously by Queers June, 1990

How can I tell you. How can I convince you, brother, sister that your life is in danger: That everyday you wake up alive, relatively happy, and a functioning human being, you are committing a rebellious act. You as an alive and functioning queer are a revolutionary.

There is nothing on this planet that validates, protects or encourages your existence. It is a miracle you are standing here reading these words. You should by all rights be

Original publication details: Queer Nation, "Queers Read This." Queer Nation, 1990.

dead. Don't be fooled, straight people own the world and the only reason you have been spared is you're smart, lucky or a fighter.

Straight people have a privilege that allows them to do whatever they please and fuck without fear. But not only do they live a life free of fear; they flaunt their freedom in my face. Their images are on my TV, in the magazine I bought, in the restaurant I want to eat in, and on the street where I live. I want there to be a moratorium on straight marriage, on babies, on public displays of affection among the opposite sex and media images that promote heterosexuality. Until I can enjoy the same freedom of movement and sexuality, as straights, their privilege must stop and it must be given over to me and my queer sisters and brothers. Straight people will not do this voluntarily and so they must be forced into it. Straights must be frightened into it. Terrorized into it. Fear is the most powerful motivation. No one will give us what we deserve. Rights are not given they are taken, by force if necessary. It is easier to fight when you know who your enemy is. Straight people are your enemy. They are your enemy when they don't acknowledge your invisibility and continue to live in and contribute to a culture that kills you. Every day one of us is taken by the enemy. Whether it's an AIDS death due to homophobic government inaction or a lesbian bashing in an all-night diner (in a supposedly lesbian neighborhood).

An Army of Lovers cannot Lose

Being queer is not about a right to privacy; it is about the freedom to be public, to just be who we are. It means everyday fighting oppression; homophobia, racism, misogyny, the bigotry of religious hypocrites and our own self-hatred. (We have been carefully taught to hate ourselves.) And now of course it means fighting a virus as well, and all those homo-haters who are using AIDS to wipe us off the face of the earth. Being queer means leading a different sort of life. It's not about the mainstream, profit-margins, patriotism, patriarchy or being assimilated. It's not about executive directors, privilege and elitism. It's about being on the margins, defining ourselves; it's about gender-fuck and secrets, what's beneath the belt and deep inside the heart; it's about the night. Being queer is "grass roots" because we know that everyone of us, every body, every cunt, every heart and ass and dick is a world of pleasure waiting to be explored. Everyone of us is a world of infinite possibility. We are an army because we have to be. We are an army because we are so powerful. (We have so much to fight for; we are the most precious of endangered species.) And we are an army of lovers because it is we who know what love is. Desire and lust, too. We invented them. We come out of the closet, face the rejection of society, face firing squads, just to love each other! Every time we fuck, we win. We must fight for ourselves (no one else is going to do it) and if in that process we bring greater freedom to the world at large then great. (We've given so much to that world: democracy, all the arts, the concepts of love, philosophy and the soul, to name just a few gifts from our ancient Greek Dykes, Fags.) Let's make every space a Lesbian and Gay space. Every street a part of our sexual geography. A city of yearning and then total satisfaction. A city and a country where we can be safe and free and more. We must look at our lives and see what's best in them, see what is queer and what is straight and let that straight chaff fall away! Remember there is so, so little time. And I want to be a lover of each and every one of you. Next year, we march naked.

Anger

"The strong sisters told the brothers that there were two important things to remember about the coming revolutions, the first is that we will get our asses kicked. The second, is that we will win."

I'm angry. I'm angry for being condemned to death by strangers saying, "You deserve to die" and "AIDS is the cure." Fury erupts when a Republican woman wearing thousands of dollars of garments and jewelry minces by the police lines shaking her head, chuckling and wagging her finger at us like we are recalcitrant children making absurd demands and throwing temper tantrum when they aren't met. Angry while Joseph agonizes over $8,000 a over for AZT which might keep him alive a little longer and which makes him sicker than the disease he is diagnosed with. Angry as I listen to a man tell me that after changing his will five times he's running out of people to leave things to. All of his best friends are dead. Angry when stand in a sea of quilt panels, or go to a candlelight march or attend yet another memorial service. I will not march silently with a fucking candle and I want to take that goddamned quilt and wrap myself in it and furiously rend it and my hair and curse every god religion ever created. I refuse to accept a creation that cuts people down in the third decade of their life.

It is cruel and vile and meaningless and everything I have in me rails against the absurdity and I raise my face to the clouds and a ragged laugh that sounds more demonic than joyous erupts from my throat and tears stream down my face and if this disease doesn't kill me, I may just die of frustration. My feet pound the streets and Peter's hands are chained to a pharmaceutical company's reception desk while the receptionist looks on in horror and Eric's body lies rotting in a Brooklyn cemetery and I'll never hear his flute resounding off the walls of the meeting house again. And I see the old people in Tompkins Square Park huddled in their long wool coats in June to keep out the cold they perceive is there and to cling to whatever little life has left to offer them. I'm reminded of the people who strip and stand before a mirror each night before they go to bed and search their bodies for any mark that might not have been there yesterday. A mark that this scourge has visited them.

And I'm angry when the newspapers call us "victims" and sound alarms that "it" might soon spread to the "general population." And I want to scream "Who the fuck am I?" And I want to scream at New York Hospital with its yellow plastic bags marked "isolation linen", "ropa infecciosa" and its orderlies in latex gloves and surgical masks skirting the bed as if its occupant will suddenly leap out and douse them with blood and semen giving them too the plague.

And I'm angry at straight people who sit smugly wrapped in their self-protective coat of monogamy and heterosexuality confident that this disease has nothing to do with them because "it" only happens to "them." And the teenage boys who upon spotting my Silence = Death button begin chanting "Faggot's gonna die" and I wonder, who taught them this? Enveloped in fury and fear, I remain silent while my button mocks me every step of the way. And the anger I fell when a television program on the quilt gives profiles of the dead and the list begins with a baby, a teenage girl who got a blood transfusion, an elderly baptist minister and his wife and when they finally show a gay man, he's described as someone who knowingly infected teenage male prostitutes with the virus. What else can you expect from a faggot?

I'm angry.

Queer Artists

Since time began, the world has been inspired by the work of queer artists. In exchange, there has been suffering, there has been pain, there has been violence. Throughout history, society has struck a bargain with its queer citizens: they may pursue creative careers, if they do it discreetly. Through the arts queers are productive, lucrative, entertaining and even uplifting. These are the clear-cut and useful by-products of what is otherwise considered antisocial behavior. In cultured circles, queers may quietly coexist with an otherwise disapproving power elite.

At the forefront of the most recent campaign to bash queer artists is Jesse Helms, arbiter of all that is decent, moral, christian and amerikan. For Helms, queer art is quite simply a threat to the world. In his imaginings, heterosexual culture is too fragile to bear up to the admission of human or sexual diversity. Quite simply, the structure of power in the Judeo-Christian world has made procreation its cornerstone. Families having children assures consumers for the nation's products and a work force to produce them, as well as a built-in family system to care for its ill, reducing the expense of public healthcare systems.

ALL NON-PROCREATIVE BEHAVIOR IS CONSIDERED A THREAT, from homosexuality to birth control to abortion as an option. It is not enough, according to the religious right, to consistently advertise procreation and heterosexuality … it is also necessary to destroy any alternatives. It is not art Helms is after.… IT IS OUR LIVES! Art is the last safe place for lesbians and gay men to thrive. Helms knows this, and has developed a program to purge queers from the one arena they have been permitted to contribute to our shared culture.

Helms is advocating a world free from diversity or dissent. It is easy to imagine why that might feel more comfortable to those in charge of such a world. It is also easy to envision an amerikan landscape flattened by such power. Helms should just ask for what he is hinting at: State sponsored art, art of totalitarianism, art that speaks only in christian terms, art which supports the goals of those in power, art that matches the sofas in the Oval Office. Ask for what you want, Jesse, so that men and women of conscience can mobilize against it, as we do against the human rights violations of other countries, and fight to free our own country's dissidents.

If you're Queer,

Queers are under siege.

Queers are being attacked on all fronts and I'm afraid it's ok with us.

In 1969, there were 50 "Queer Bashings" in the month of May alone. Violent attacks, 3,720 men, women and children died of AIDS in the same month, caused by a more violent attack – government inaction, rooted in society's growing homophobia. This is institutionalized violence, perhaps more dangerous to the existence of queers because the attackers are faceless. We allow these attacks by our own continued lack of action against them. AIDS has affected the straight world and now they're blaming us for AIDS and using it as a way to justify their violence against us. They don't want us anymore. They will beat us, rape us and kill us before they will continue to live with us. What will it take for this not to be ok? Feel some rage. If rage doesn't empower you, try fear. If that doesn't work, try panic.

Shout It!

Be proud. Do whatever you need to do to tear yourself away from your customary state of acceptance. Be free. Shout.

In 1969, Queers fought back. In 1990, Queers say ok. Next year, will we be here?

I Hate ...

I hate Jesse Helms. I hate Jesse Helms so much I'd rejoice if he dropped down dead. If someone killed him I'd consider it his own fault.

I hate Ronald Reagan, too, because he mass-murdered my people for eight years. But to be honest, I hate him even more for eulogizing Ryan White without first admitting his guilt, without begging forgiveness for Ryan's death and for the deaths of tens of thousands of other PWA's – most of them queer. I hate him for making a mockery of our grief.

I hate the fucking Pope, and I hate John fucking Cardinal fucking O'Connor, and I hate the whole fucking Catholic Church. The same goes for the Military, and especially for Amerika's Law Enforcement Officials – the cops – state sanctioned sadists who brutalize street transvestites, prostitutes and queer prisoners. I also hate the medical and mental health establishments, particularly the psychiatrist who convinced me not to have sex with men for three years until we (meaning he) could make me bisexual rather than queer. I also hate the education profession, for its share in driving thousands of queer teens to suicide every year. I hate the "respectable" art world; and the entertainment industry, and the mainstream media, especially The New York Times. In fact, I hate every sector of the straight establishment in this country – the worst of whom actively want all queers dead, the best of whom never stick their necks out to keep us alive.

I hate straight people who think they have anything intelligent to say about "outing." I hate straight people who think stories about themselves are "universal" but stories about us are only about homosexuality. I hate straight recording artists who make their careers off of queer people, then attack us, then act hurt when we get angry and then deny having wronged us rather than apologize for it. I hate straight people who say, "I don't see why you feel the need to wear those buttons and t-shirts. I don't go around telling the whole world I'm straight."

I hate that in twelve years of public education I was never taught about queer people. I hate that I grew up thinking I was the only queer in the world, and I hate even more that most queer kids still grow up the same way. I hate that I was tormented by other kids for being a faggot, but more that I was taught to feel ashamed for being the object of their cruelty, taught to feel it was my fault. I hate that the Supreme Court of this country says it's okay to criminalize me because of how I make love. I hate that so many straight people are so concerned about my goddamned sex life. I hate that so many twisted straight people become parents, while I have to fight like hell to be allowed to be a father. I hate straights.

Where Are You Sisters?

I wear my pink triangle everywhere. I do not lower my voice in public when talking about lesbian love or sex. I always tell people I'm a lesbian. I don't wait to be asked about my "boyfriend." I don't say it's "no one's business."

I don't do this for straight people. Most of them don't know what the pink triangle even means. Most of them couldn't care less that my girlfriend and I are totally in love or having a fight on the street. Most of them don't notice us no matter what we do. I do what I do to reach other lesbians. I do what I do because I don't want lesbians to assume I'm a straight girl. I am out all the time, everywhere, because I WANT TO REACH YOU. Maybe you'll notice me, maybe we'll start talking, maybe we'll exchange numbers, maybe we'll become friends. Maybe we won't say a word but our eyes will meet and I will imagine you naked, sweating, openmouthed, your back arched as I am fucking you. And we'll be happy to know we aren't the only ones in the world. We'll be happy because we found each other, without saying a word, maybe just for a moment. But no.

You won't wear a pink triangle on that linen lapel. You won't meet my eyes if I flirt with you on the street. You avoid me on the job because I'm "too" out. You chastise me in bars because I'm "too political." You ignore me in public because I bring "too much" attention to "my" lesbianism. But then you want me to be your lover, you want me to be your friend, you want me to love you, support, you, fight for "OUR" right to exist.

Where Are You?

You talk, talk, talk about invisibility and then retreat to your homes to nest with your lovers or carouse in a bar with pals and stumble home in a cab or sit silently and politely by while your family, your boss, your neighbors, your public servants distort and disfigure us, deride us and punish us. Then home again and you feel like screaming. Then you pad your anger with a relationship or a career or a party with other dykes like you and still you wonder why we can't find each other, why you feel lonely, angry, alienated.

Get Up, Wake Up Sisters!!

Your life is in your hands.

When I risk it all to be out, I risk it for both of us. When I risk it all and it works (which it often does if you would try it), I benefit and so do you. When it doesn't work, I suffer and you do not.

But girl you can't wait for other dykes to make the world safe for you. STOP waiting for a better more lesbian future! The revolution could be here if we started it.

Where are you sisters? I'm trying to find you, I'm trying to find you. How come I only see you on Gay Pride Day?

We're OUT, Where the fuck are YOU?

When Anyone Assaults You for being Queer, It is Queer Bashing. Right?

A crowd of 50 people exit a gay bar as it closes. Across the street, some straight boys are shouting "Faggots" and throwing beer bottles at the gathering, which outnumbers them by 10 to 1. Three queers make a move to respond, getting no support from the group. Why did a group this size allow themselves to be sitting ducks?

Tompkins Square Park, Labor Day. At an annual outdoor concert/drag show, a group of gay men were harassed by teens carrying sticks. In the midst of thousands of gay men and lesbians, these straight boys beat two gay men to the ground, then stood around triumphantly laughing amongst themselves. The emcee was alerted and warned the crowd from the stage, "You girls be careful. When you dress up it drives the boys crazy," as if it were a practical joke inspired by what the victims were wearing rather than a pointed attack on anyone and everyone at that event.

What would it have taken for that crowd to stand up to its attackers?

After James Zappalorti, an openly gay man, was murdered in cold blood on Staten Island this winter, a single demonstration was held in protest. Only one hundred people came. When Yuseuf Hawkins, a black youth, was shot to death for being on "white turf" in Bensonhurst, African Americans marched through that neighborhood in large numbers again and again. A black person was killed BECAUSE HE WAS BLACK, and people of color throughout the city recognized it and acted on it. The bullet that hit Hawkins was meant for a black man, ANY black man. Do most gays and lesbians think that the knife that punctured Zappalorti's heart was meant only for him?

The straight world has us so convinced that we are helpless and deserving victims of the violence against us, that queers are immobilized when faced with a threat. BE OUTRAGED! These attacks must not be tolerated. DO SOMETHING. Recognize that any act of aggression against any member of our community is an attack on every member of the community. The more we allow homophobes to inflict violence, terror and fear on our lives, the more frequently and ferociously we will be the object of their hatred. Your immeasurably valuable, because unless you start believing that, it can easily be taken from you. If you know how to gently and efficiently immobilize your attacker, then by all means, do it. If you lack those skills, then think about gouging out his fucking eyes, slamming his nose back into his brain, slashing his throat with a broken bottle – do whatever you can, whatever you have to, to save your life!

reeuQ yhW

Queer!

Ah, do we really have to use that word? It's trouble. Every gay person has his or her own take on it. For some it means strange and eccentric and kind of mysterious. That's okay, we like that. But some gay girls and boys don't. They think they're more normal than strange. And for others "queer" conjures up those awful memories of adolescent suffering. Queer. It's forcibly bittersweet and quaint at best – weakening and painful at worst. Couldn't we just use "gay" instead? It's a much brighter word and isn't it synonymous with "happy?" When will you militants grow up and get over the novelty of being different?

Why Queer

Well, yes, "gay" is great. It has its place. But when a lot of lesbians and gay men wake up in the morning we feel angry and disgusted, not gay. So we've chosen to call ourselves queer. Using "queer" is a way of reminding us how we are perceived by the rest of the world. It's a way of telling ourselves we don't have to be witty and charming people who keep our lives discreet and marginalized in the straight world. We use queer as gay men loving lesbians and lesbians loving being queer.

Queer, unlike GAY, doesn't mean MALE.

And when spoken to other gays and lesbians it's a way of suggesting we close ranks, and forget (temporarily) our individual differences because we face a more insidious common enemy. Yeah, QUEER can be a rough word but it is also a sly and ironic weapon we can steal from the homophobe's hands and use against him.

No Sex Police

For anyone to say that coming out is not part of the revolution is missing the point. Positive sexual images and what they manifest saves lives because they affirm those lives and make it possible for people to attempt to live as self-loving instead of self-loathing. As the famous "Black is beautiful" slogan changed many lives, so does "Read my lips" affirm queerness in the face of hatred and invisibility as displayed in a recent governmental study of suicides that states at least one third of all teen suicides are Queer kids. This is further exemplified by the rise in HIV transmission among those under 21.

We are most hated as queers for our sexualness, that is, our physical contact with the same sex. Our sexuality and sexual expression are what makes us most susceptible to physical violence. Our difference, our otherness, our uniqueness can either paralyze us or politicize us. Hopefully, the majority of us will not let it kill us.

Queer Space

Why in the world do we let heteros into queer clubs? Who gives a fuck if they like us because we "really know how to party?" WE HAVE TO IN ORDER TO BLOW OFF THE STEAM THEY MAKE US FEEL ALL THE TIME! They make out wherever they please, and take up too much room on the dance floor doing ostentatious couples dances. They wear their heterosexuality like a "Keep Out" sign, or like a deed of ownership.

Why the fuck do we tolerate them when they invade our space like it's their right? Why do we let them shove heterosexuality – a weapon their world wields against us – right in our faces in the few public spots where we can be sexy with each other and not fear attack?

It's time to stop letting the straight people make all the rules. Let's start by posting this sign outside every queer club and bar:

Rules of Conduct for Straight People

1. Keep your display of affection (kissing, handholding, embracing) to a minimum. Your sexuality is unwanted and offensive to many here. 2. If you must slow dance, be as inconspicuous as possible. 3. Do not gawk or stare at lesbians or gay men, especially bull dykes or drag queens. We are not your entertainment. 4. If you cannot comfortably deal with someone of the same sex making a pass at you, get out. 5. Do not flaunt your heterosexuality. Be Discreet. Risk being mistaken for a lezzie or a homo. 6. If you feel these rules are unfair, go fight homophobia in straight clubs, or: 7. Go Fuck Yourself.

I Hate Straights

I have friends. Some of them are straight.

Year after year, I see my straight friends. I want to see them, to see how they are doing, to add newness to our long and complicated histories, to experience some continuity. Year after year I continue to realize that the facts of my life are irrelevant to them and that I am only half listened to, that I am an appendage to the doings of a greater world, a world of power and privilege, of the laws of installation, a world of exclusion. "That's not true," argue my straight friends. There is the one certainty in the politics of power: those left out of it beg for inclusion, while the insiders claim that they already are. Men do it to women, whites do it to blacks, and everyone does it to queers. The main dividing line, both conscious and unconscious, is procreation ... and that magic word – Family. Frequently, the ones we are born into disown us when they find out who we really are, and to make matters worse, we are prevented from having our own. We are punished, insulted, cut off, and treated like seditionaries in terms of child rearing, both damned if we try and damned if we abstain. It's as if the propagation of the species is such a fragile directive that without enforcing it as if it were an agenda, humankind would melt back into the primeval ooze.

I hate having to convice straight people that lesbians and gays live in a war zone, that we're surrounded by bomb blasts only we seem to hear, that our bodies and souls are heaped high, dead from fright or bashed or raped, dying of grief or disease, stripped of our personhood.

I hate straight people who can't listen to queer anger without saying "hey, all straight people aren't like that. I'm straight too, you know," as if their egos don't get enough stroking or protection in this arrogant, heterosexist world. Why must we take care of them, in the midst of our just anger brought on by their fucked up society?! Why add the reassurance of "Of course, I don't mean you. You don't act that way." Let them figure out for themselves whether they deserve to be included in our anger.

But of course that would mean listening to our anger, which they almost never do. They deflect it, by saying "I'm not like that" or "Now look who's generalizing" or "You'll catch more flies with honey ... " or "If you focus on the negative you just give out more power" or "you're not the only one in the world who's suffering." They say "Don't yell at me, I'm on your side" or "I think you're overreacting" or "BOY, YOU'RE BITTER."

They've taught us that good queers don't get mad. They've taught us so well that we not only hide our anger from them, we hide it from each other. WE EVEN HIDE IT FROM OURSELVES. We hide it with substance abuse and suicide and overarhcieving in the hope of proving our worth. They bash us and stab us and shoot us and bomb us in ever increasing numbers and still we freak out when angry queers carry banners or signs that say BASH BACK. For the last decade they let us die in droves and still we thank President Bush for planting a fucking tree, applaud him for likening PWAs to car accident victims who refuse to wear seatbelts. LET YOURSELF BE ANGRY. Let yourself be angry that the price of our visibility is the constant threat of violence, anti-queer violence to which practically every segment of this society contributes. Let yourself feel angry that THERE IS NO PLACE IN THIS COUNTRY WHERE WE ARE SAFE, no place where we are not targeted for hatred and attack, the self-hatred, the suicide – of the closet. The next time some straight person comes down on you for being angry, tell them that until things change, you don't need any more evidence that the world turns at your expense. You don't need to see only hetero couple grocery shopping on your TV ... You don't want any more baby pictures shoved in your face until you can have or keep your own. No more weddings, showers, anniversaries, please, unless they are our own brothers and sisters celebrating. And tell them not to dismiss you by saying "You have rights," "You have privileges," "You're overreacting," or "You have a victim's mentality." Tell them "GO AWAY FROM ME, until YOU can change." Go away and try on a world without the brave, strong queers that are its backbone, that are its guts and brains and souls. Go tell them go away until they have spent a month walking hand in hand in public with someone of the same sex. After they survive that, then you'll hear what they have to say about queer anger.

Otherwise, tell them to shut up and listen.

CHAPTER 11

Sex in Public

Lauren Berlant and Michael Warner

Lauren Berlant teaches English at the University of Chicago and is co-editor of *Critical Inquiry*. Her books include *The Anatomy of National Fantasy* (1991) and *The Queen of America Goes to Washington* (1997). Michael Warner teaches English at Yale University. His books include *Fear of a Queer Planet* (1993) and *The Letters of the Republic* (1990).

1.   There Is Nothing More Public Than Privacy

A paper titled "Sex in Public" teases with the obscurity of its object and the twisted aim of its narrative. In this paper we will be talking not about the sex people already have clarity about, nor identities and acts, nor a wildness in need of derepression; but rather about sex as it is mediated by publics.[1] Some of these publics have an obvious relation to sex: pornographic cinema, phone sex, "adult" markets for print, lap dancing. Others are organized around sex, but not necessarily sex *acts* in the usual sense: queer zones and other worlds estranged from heterosexual culture, but also more tacit scenes of sexuality like official national culture, which depends on a notion of privacy to cloak its sexualization of national membership.

The aim of this paper is to describe what we want to promote as the radical aspirations of queer culture building: not just a safe zone for queer sex but the changed possibilities of identity, intelligibility, publics, culture, and sex that appear when the heterosexual couple is no longer the referent or the privileged example of sexual culture. Queer social practices like sex and theory try to unsettle the garbled but powerful norms supporting that privilege – including the project of normalization that has made heterosexuality hegemonic – as well as those material practices that, though not explicitly sexual, are implicated in the hierarchies of property and propriety that we will describe as heteronormative.[2] We open with two scenes of sex in public.

Original publication details: Lauren Berlant and Michael Warner, "Sex in Public." *Critical Inquiry* 24.2, Intimacy (Winter 1998), pp. 547–566. University of Chicago Press, 1998. Reproduced with permission from University of Chicago Press and L. Berlant.

Literary Theory: An Anthology, Third Edition. Edited by Julie Rivkin and Michael Ryan.
© 2017 John Wiley & Sons, Ltd. Published 2017 by John Wiley & Sons, Ltd.

Scene 1

In 1993 *Time* magazine published a special issue about immigration called "The New Face of America."[3] The cover girl of this issue was morphed via computer from head shots representing a range of U.S. immigrant groups: an amalgam of "Middle Eastern," "Italian," "African," "Vietnamese," "Anglo-Saxon," "Chinese," and "Hispanic" faces. The new face of America is supposed to represent what the modal citizen will look like when, in the year 2004, it is projected, there is no longer a white statistical majority in the United States. Naked, smiling, and just off-white, *Time*'s divine Frankenstein aims to organize hegemonic optimism about citizenship and the national future. *Time*'s theory is that by the twenty-first century interracial reproductive sex will have taken place in the United States on such a mass scale that racial difference itself will be finally replaced by a kind of family feeling based on blood relations. In the twenty-first century, *Time* imagines, hundreds of millions of hybrid faces will erase American racism altogether: the nation will become a happy racial monoculture made up of "one (mixed) blood."[4]

The publication of this special issue caused a brief flurry of interest but had no important effects; its very banality calls us to understand the technologies that produce its ordinariness. The fantasy banalized by the image is one that reverberates in the law and in the most intimate crevices of everyday life. Its explicit aim is to help its public process the threat to "normal" or "core" national culture that is currently phrased as "the problem of immigration."[5] But this crisis image of immigrants is also a *racial mirage* generated by a white-dominated society, supplying a specific phobia to organize its public so that a more substantial discussion of exploitation in the United States can be avoided and then remaindered to the part of collective memory sanctified not by nostalgia but by mass aversion. Let's call this the amnesia archive. The motto above the door is Memory Is the Amnesia You Like.

But more than exploitation and racism are forgotten in this whirl of projection and suppression. Central to the transfiguration of the immigrant into a nostalgic image to shore up core national culture and allay white fears of minoritization is something that cannot speak its name, though its signature is everywhere: national heterosexuality. National heterosexuality is the mechanism by which a core national culture can be imagined as a sanitized space of sentimental feeling and immaculate behavior, a space of pure citizenship. A familial model of society displaces the recognition of structural racism and other systemic inequalities. This is not entirely new: the family form has functioned as a mediator and metaphor of national existence in the United States since the eighteenth century.[6] We are arguing that its contemporary deployment increasingly supports the governmentality of the welfare state by separating the aspirations of national belonging from the critical culture of the public sphere and from political citizenship.[7] Immigration crises have also previously produced feminine icons that function as prostheses for the state – most famously, the Statue of Liberty, which symbolized seamless immigrant assimilation to the metaculture of the United States. In *Time*'s face it is not symbolic femininity but practical heterosexuality that guarantees the monocultural nation.

The nostalgic family values covenant of contemporary American politics stipulates a privatization of citizenship and sex in a number of ways. In law and political ideology, for example, the fetus and the child have been spectacularly elevated to the place of sanctified nationality. The state now sponsors stings and legislation to purify the internet on behalf of children. New welfare and tax "reforms" passed under the cooperation between the

Contract with America and Clintonian familialism seek to increase the legal and economic privileges of married couples and parents. Vouchers and privatization rezone education as the domain of parents rather than citizens. Meanwhile, senators such as Ted Kennedy and Jesse Helms support amendments that refuse federal funds to organizations that "promote, disseminate, or produce materials that are obscene or that depict or describe, in a patently offensive way, sexual or excretory activities or organs, including but not limited to obscene depictions of sadomasochism, homo-eroticism, the sexual exploitation of children, or individuals engaged in sexual intercourse."[8] These developments, though distinct, are linked in the way they organize a hegemonic national public around sex. But because this sex public officially claims to act only in order to protect the zone of heterosexual privacy, the institutions of economic privilege and social reproduction informing its practices and organizing its ideal world are protected by the spectacular demonization of any represented sex.

Scene 2

In October 1995, the New York City Council passed a new zoning law by a forty-one to nine vote. The Zoning Text Amendment covers adult book and video stores, eating and drinking establishments, theaters, and other businesses. It allows these businesses only in certain areas zoned as nonresidential, most of which turn out to be on the waterfront. Within the new reserved districts, adult businesses are disallowed within five hundred feet of another adult establishment or within five hundred feet of a house of worship, school, or day-care center. They are limited to one per lot and in size to ten thousand square feet. Signs are limited in size, placement, and illumination. All other adult businesses are required to close within a year. Of the estimated 177 adult businesses in the city, all but 28 may have to close under this law. Enforcement of the bill is entrusted to building inspectors.

A court challenge against the bill was brought by a coalition that also fought it in the political process, formed by anticensorship groups such as the New York Civil Liberties Union (NYCLU), Feminists for Free Expression, People for the American Way, and the National Coalition Against Censorship as well as gay and lesbian organizations such as the Lambda Legal Defense Fund, the Empire State Pride Agenda, and the AIDS Prevention Action League. (An appeal was still pending as of July 1997.) These latter groups joined the anticensorship groups for a simple reason: the impact of rezoning on businesses catering to queers, especially to gay men, will be devastating. All five of the adult businesses on Christopher Street will be shut down, along with the principal venues where men meet men for sex. None of these businesses have been targets of local complaints. Gay men have come to take for granted the availability of explicit sexual materials, theaters, and clubs. That is how they have learned to find each other; to map a commonly accessible world; to construct the architecture of queer space in a homophobic environment; and, for the last fifteen years, to cultivate a collective ethos of safer sex. All of that is about to change. Now, gay men who want sexual materials or who want to meet other men for sex will have two choices: they can cathect the privatized virtual public of phone sex and the internet; or they can travel to small, inaccessible, little-trafficked, badly lit areas, remote from public transportation and from any residences, mostly on the waterfront, where heterosexual porn users will also be relocated and where the risk of violence will consequently be higher.[9] In either case, the result will be a sense of isolation and diminished expectations for queer life, as well as an attenuated capacity for political community. The nascent lesbian sexual culture, including the Clit Club and the only video rental club catering to lesbians, will also disappear. The impact of the sexual purification of New York will fall unequally on those who already have fewest publicly accessible resources.

2. Normativity and Sexual Culture

Heterosexuality is not a thing. We speak of heterosexual culture rather than heterosexuality because that culture never has more than a provisional unity.[10] It is neither a single Symbolic nor a single ideology nor a unified set of shared beliefs.[11] The conflicts between these strands are seldom more than dimly perceived in practice, where the givenness of male-female sexual relations is part of the ordinary rightness of the world, its fragility masked in shows of solemn rectitude. Such conflicts have also gone unrecognized in theory, partly because of the metacultural work of the very category of heterosexuality, which consolidates as *a sexuality* widely differing practices, norms, and institutions; and partly because the sciences of social knowledge are themselves so deeply anchored in the process of normalization to which Foucault attributes so much of modern sexuality.[12] Thus when we say that the contemporary United States is saturated by the project of constructing national heterosexuality, we do not mean that national heterosexuality is anything like a simple monoculture. Hegemonies are nothing if not elastic alliances, involving dispersed and contradictory strategies for self-maintenance and reproduction.

Heterosexual culture achieves much of its metacultural intelligibility through the ideologies and institutions of intimacy. We want to argue here that although the intimate relations of private personhood appear to be the realm of sexuality itself, allowing "sex in public" to appear like matter out of place, intimacy is itself publicly mediated, in several senses. First, its conventional spaces presuppose a structural differentiation of "personal life" from work, politics, and the public sphere.[13] Second, the normativity of heterosexual culture links intimacy only to the institutions of personal life, making them the privileged institutions of social reproduction, the accumulation and transfer of capital, and self-development. Third, by making sex seem irrelevant or merely personal, heteronormative conventions of intimacy block the building of nonnormative or explicit public sexual cultures. Finally, those conventions conjure a mirage: a home base of prepolitical humanity from which citizens are thought to come into political discourse and to which they are expected to return in the (always imaginary) future after political conflict. Intimate life is the endlessly cited *elsewhere* of political public discourse, a promised haven that distracts citizens from the unequal conditions of their political and economic lives, consoles them for the damaged humanity of mass society, and shames them for any divergence between their lives and the intimate sphere that is alleged to be simple personhood.

Ideologies and institutions of intimacy are increasingly offered as a vision of the good life for the destabilized and struggling citizenry of the United States, the only (fantasy) zone in which a future might be thought and willed, the only (imaginary) place where good citizens might be produced away from the confusing and unsettling distractions and contradictions of capitalism and politics. Indeed, one of the unforeseen paradoxes of national-capitalist privatization has been that citizens have been led through heterosexual culture to identify both themselves *and their politics* with privacy.

In the official public, this involves making sex private; reintensifying blood as a psychic base for identification; replacing state mandates for social justice with a privatized ethics of responsibility, charity, atonement, and "values"; and enforcing boundaries between moral persons and economic ones.[14]

A complex cluster of sexual practices gets confused, in heterosexual culture, with the love plot of intimacy and familialism that signifies belonging to society in a deep and normal way. Community is imagined through scenes of intimacy, coupling, and kinship; a historical relation to futurity is restricted to generational narrative and reproduction.[15] A whole field of social relations becomes intelligible as heterosexuality, and this privatized sexual culture bestows on its sexual practices a tacit sense of rightness and normalcy. This sense of rightness – embedded in things and not just in sex – is what we call heteronormativity. Heteronormativity is more than ideology, or prejudice, or phobia against gays and lesbians; it is produced in almost every aspect of the forms and arrangements of social life: nationality, the state, and the law; commerce; medicine; and education; as well as in the conventions and affects of narrativity, romance, and other protected spaces of culture. It is hard to see these fields as heteronormative because the sexual culture straight people inhabit is so diffuse, a mix of languages they are just developing with premodern notions of sexuality so ancient that their material conditions feel hardwired into personhood.

But intimacy has not always had the meaning it has for contemporary heteronormative culture. Along with Foucault and other historians, the classicist David Halperin, for example, has shown that in ancient Athens sex was a transitive act rather than a fundamental dimension of personhood or an expression of intimacy. The verb for having sex appears on a late antique list of things that are not done in regard to or through others: "namely, speaking, singing, dancing, fist-fighting, competing, hanging oneself, dying, being crucified, diving, finding a treasure, having sex, vomiting, moving one's bowels, sleeping, laughing, crying, talking to the gods, and the like."[16] Halperin points out that the inclusion of fucking on this list shows that sex is not here "knit up in a web of mutuality."[17] In contrast, modern heterosexuality is supposed to refer to relations of intimacy and identification with other persons, and sex acts are supposed to be the most intimate communication of them all.[18] The sex act shielded by the zone of privacy is the affectional nimbus that heterosexual culture protects and from which it abstracts its model of ethics, but this utopia of social belonging is also supported and extended by acts less commonly recognized as part of sexual culture: paying taxes, being disgusted, philandering, bequeathing, celebrating a holiday, investing for the future, teaching, disposing of a corpse, carrying wallet photos, buying economy size, being nepotistic, running for president, divorcing, or owning anything "His" and "Hers."

The elaboration of this list is a project for further study. Meanwhile, to make it and to laugh at it is not immediately to label any practice as oppressive, uncool, or definitive. We are describing a constellation of practices that everywhere disperses heterosexual privilege as a tacit but central organizing index of social membership. Exposing it inevitably produces what we have elsewhere called a "wrenching sense of recontextualization," as its subjects, even its gay and lesbian subjects, begin to piece together how it is that social and economic discourses, institutions, and practices that don't feel especially sexual or familial collaborate to produce as a social norm and ideal an extremely narrow context for living.[19] Heterosexual culture cannot recognize, validate, sustain, incorporate, or remember much of what people know and experience about the cruelty of normal culture even to the people who identify with it.

But that cruelty does not go unregistered. Intimacy, for example, has a whole public environment of therapeutic genres dedicated to witnessing the constant failure of heterosexual ideologies and institutions. Every day, in many countries now, people testify to their failure to sustain or be sustained by institutions of privacy on talk shows, in scandal journalism, even in the ordinary course of mainstream journalism addressed to middlebrow culture. We can learn a lot from these stories of love plots that have gone astray: about the ways quotidian violence is linked to complex pressures from money, racism, histories of sexual violence, cross-generational tensions. We can learn a lot from listening to the increasing demands on love to deliver the good life it promises. And we can learn from the extremely punitive responses that tend to emerge when people seem not to suffer enough for their transgressions and failures.

Maybe we would learn too much. Recently, the proliferation of evidence for heterosexuality's failings has produced a backlash against talk-show therapy. It has even brought William Bennett to the podium; but rather than confessing his transgressions or making a complaint about someone else's, we find him calling for boycotts and for the suppression of heterosexual therapy culture altogether. Recognition of heterosexuality's daily failures agitates him as much as queerness. "We've forgotten that civilization depends on keeping some of this stuff under wraps," he said. "This is a tropism toward the toilet."[20]

But does civilization need to cover its ass? Or does heterosexual culture actually secure itself through banalizing intimacy? Does belief that normal life is actually possible *require* amnesia and the ludicrous stereotyping of a bottom-feeding culture apparently inadequate to intimacy? On these shows no one ever blames the ideology and institutions of heterosexuality. Every day, even the talk-show hosts are newly astonished to find that people who are committed to hetero intimacy are nevertheless unhappy. After all is said and done, the prospects and promises of heterosexual culture still represent the optimism for optimism, a hope to which people apparently have already pledged their consent – at least in public.

Recently, Biddy Martin has written that some queer social theorists have produced a reductive and pseudoradical antinormativity by actively repudiating the institutions of heterosexuality that have come to oversaturate the social imaginary. She shows that the kinds of arguments that crop up in the writings of people like Andrew Sullivan are not just right-wing fantasies. "In some queer work," she writes, "the very fact of attachment has been cast as only punitive and constraining because already socially constructed.... Radical anti-normativity throws out a lot of babies with a lot of bathwater.... An enormous fear of ordinariness or normalcy results in superficial accounts of the complex imbrication of sexuality with other aspects of social and psychic life, and in far too little attention to the dilemmas of the average people that we also are."[21]

We think our friend Biddy might be referring to us, although in this segment she cites no one in particular. We would like to clarify the argument. To be against heteronormativity is not to be against norms. To be against the processes of normalization is not to be afraid of ordinariness. Nor is it to advocate the "existence without limit" she sees as produced by bad Foucauldians ("EH," p. 123). Nor is it to decide that sentimental identifications with family and children are waste or garbage, or make people into waste or garbage. Nor is it to say that any sex called "lovemaking" isn't lovemaking; whatever the ideological or historical burdens of sexuality have been, they have not excluded, and indeed may have entailed, the ability of sex to count as intimacy and care. What we have been arguing here is that the space of sexual culture has become obnoxiously cramped from doing the work of maintaining a normal metaculture. When Biddy Martin calls us to recognize ourselves as "average people," to relax from an artificially stimulated "fear of normalcy," the image of average personhood appears to be simply descriptive ("EH," p. 123). But its averageness is also normative, in exactly the sense that Foucault meant by "normalization": not the imposition of an alien will, but a distribution around a statistically imagined norm. This deceptive appeal of the average remains heteronormative, measuring deviance from the mass. It can also be consoling, an expression of a utopian desire for unconflicted personhood. But this desire cannot be satisfied in the current conditions of privacy. People feel that the price they must pay for social membership and a relation to the future is identification with the heterosexual life narrative; that they are individually responsible for the rages, instabilities, ambivalences, and failures they experience in their intimate lives, while the fractures of the contemporary United States shame and sabotage them everywhere. Heterosexuality involves so many practices that are not sex that a world in which this hegemonic cluster would not be dominant is, at this point, unimaginable. We are trying to bring that world into being.

3.   Queer Counterpublics

By queer culture we mean a world-making project, where "world," like "public," differs from community or group because it necessarily includes more people than can be identified, more spaces than can be mapped beyond a few reference points, modes of feeling that can be learned rather than experienced as a birthright. The queer world is a space of entrances, exits, unsystematized lines of acquaintance, projected horizons, typifying examples, alternate routes, blockages, incommensurate geographies.[22] World making, as much in the mode of dirty talk as of print-mediated representation, is dispersed through incommensurate registers, by definition *unrealizable* as community or identity. Every cultural form, be it a novel or an after-hours club or an academic lecture, indexes a virtual social world, in ways that range from a repertoire of styles and speech genres to referential metaculture. A novel like Andrew Holleran's *Dancer from the Dance* relies much more heavily on referential metaculture than does an after-hours club that survives on word of mouth and may be a major scene because it is only barely coherent *as* a scene. Yet for all their differences, both allow for the concretization of a queer counterpublic. We are trying to promote this world-making project, and a first step in doing so is to recognize that queer culture constitutes itself in many ways other than through the official publics of opinion culture and the state, or through the privatized forms normally associated with sexuality. Queer and other insurgents have long striven, often dangerously or scandalously, to cultivate what good folks used to call criminal intimacies. We have developed relations and narratives that are only recognized as intimate in queer culture: girlfriends, gal pals, fuckbuddies, tricks. Queer culture has learned not only how to sexualize these and other relations, but also to use them as a context for witnessing intense and personal affect while elaborating a public world of belonging and transformation. Making a queer world has required the development of kinds of intimacy that bear no necessary relation to domestic space, to kinship, to the couple form, to property, or to the nation. These intimacies *do* bear a necessary relation to a counterpublic – an indefinitely accessible world conscious of its subordinate relation. They are typical both of the inventiveness of queer world making and of the queer world's fragility.

Nonstandard intimacies would seem less criminal and less fleeting if, as used to be the case, normal intimacies included everything from consorts to courtiers, friends, amours, associates, and coconspirators.[23] Along with the sex it legitimates, intimacy has been privatized; the discourse contexts that narrate true personhood have been segregated from those that represent citizens, workers, or professionals.

This transformation in the cultural forms of intimacy is related both to the history of the modern public sphere and to the modern discourse of sexuality as a fundamental human capacity. In *The Structural Transformation of the Public Sphere*, Habermas shows that the institutions and forms of domestic intimacy made private people private, members of the public sphere of private society rather than the market or the state. Intimacy grounded abstract, disembodied citizens in a sense of universal humanity. In *The History of Sexuality*, Foucault describes the personalization of sex from the other direction: the confessional and expert discourses of civil society continually posit an inner personal essence, equating this true personhood with sex and surrounding that sex with dramas of secrecy and disclosure. There is an instructive convergence here in two thinkers who otherwise seem to be describing different planets.[24] Habermas overlooks the administrative and normalizing dimensions of privatized sex in sciences of social knowledge because he is interested in the norm of a critical relation between state and civil society. Foucault overlooks the critical culture that might enable transformation of sex and other private relations; he wants to show that modern epistemologies of sexual personhood, far from bringing sexual publics into being, are techniques of isolation; they identify persons as normal or perverse, for the purpose of medicalizing or otherwise administering them as individuals. Yet both Habermas and Foucault point to the way a hegemonic public has founded itself by a privatization of sex and the sexualization of private personhood. Both identify the conditions in which sexuality seems like a property of subjectivity rather than a publicly or counterpublicly accessible culture.

Like most ideologies, that of normal intimacy may never have been an accurate description of how people actually live. It was from the beginning mediated not only by a structural separation of economic and domestic space but also by opinion culture, correspondence, novels, and romances; Rousseau's *Confessions* is typical both of the ideology and of its reliance on mediation by print and by new, hybrid forms of life narrative. Habermas notes that "subjectivity, as the innermost core of the private, was always oriented to an audience,"[25] adding that the structure of this intimacy includes a fundamentally contradictory relation to the economy:

> To the autonomy of property owners in the market corresponded a self-presentation of human beings in the family. The latter's intimacy, apparently set free from the constraint of society, was the seal on the truth of a private autonomy exercised in competition. Thus it was a private autonomy denying its economic origins ... that provided the bourgeois family with its consciousness of itself.[26]

This structural relation is no less normative for being imperfect in practice. Its force is to prevent the recognition, memory, elaboration, or institutionalization of all the nonstandard intimacies that people have in everyday life. Affective life slops over onto work and political life; people have key self-constitutive relations with strangers and acquaintances; and they have eroticism, if not sex, outside of the couple form. These border intimacies give people tremendous pleasure. But when that pleasure is called sexuality, the spillage of eroticism into everyday social life seems transgressive in a way that provokes normal aversion, a hygienic recoil even as contemporary consumer and media cultures increasingly trope toiletward, splattering the matter of intimate life at the highest levels of national culture.

In gay male culture, the principal scenes of criminal intimacy have been tearooms, streets, sex clubs, and parks – a tropism toward the public toilet.[27] Promiscuity is so heavily stigmatized as nonintimate that it is often called anonymous, whether names are used or not. One of the most commonly forgotten lessons of AIDS is that this promiscuous intimacy turned out to be a lifesaving public resource. Unbidden by experts, gay people invented safer sex; and, as Douglas Crimp wrote in 1987

> we were able to invent safe sex because we have always known that sex is not, in an epidemic or not, limited to penetrative sex. Our promiscuity taught us many things, not only about the pleasures of sex, but about the great multiplicity of those pleasures. It is that psychic preparation, that experimentation, that conscious work on our own sexualities that has allowed many of us to change our sexual behaviors – something that brutal "behavioral therapies" tried unsuccessfully for over a century to force us to do – very quickly and very dramatically.... All those who contend that gay male promiscuity is merely sexual *compulsion* resulting from fear of intimacy are now faced with very strong evidence against their prejudices.... Gay male promiscuity should be seen instead as a positive model of how sexual pleasures might be pursued by and granted to everyone if those pleasures were not confined within the narrow limits of institutionalized sexuality.[28]

AIDS is a special case, and this model of sexual culture has been typically male. But sexual practice is only one kind of counterintimacy. More important is the critical practical knowledge that allows such relations to count as intimate, to be not empty release or transgression but a common language of self-cultivation, shared knowledge, and the exchange of inwardness.

Queer culture has found it necessary to develop this knowledge in mobile sites of drag, youth culture, music, dance, parades, flaunting, and cruising – sites whose mobility makes them possible but also renders them hard to recognize as world making because they are so fragile and ephemeral. They are paradigmatically trivialized as "lifestyle." But to understand them only as self-expression or as a demand for recognition would be to misrecognize the fundamentally unequal material conditions whereby the institutions of social reproduction are coupled to the forms of hetero culture.[29] Contexts of queer world making depend on parasitic and fugitive elaboration through gossip, dance clubs, softball leagues, and the phone-sex ads that increasingly are the commercial support for print-mediated left culture in general.[30] Queer is difficult to entextualize *as* culture.

This is particularly true of intimate culture. Heteronormative forms of intimacy are supported, as we have argued, not only by overt referential discourse such as love plots and sentimentality but materially, in marriage and family law, in the architecture of the domestic, in the zoning of work and politics. Queer culture, by contrast, has almost no institutional matrix for its counterintimacies. In the absence of marriage and the rituals that organize life around matrimony, improvisation is always necessary for the speech act of pledging, or the narrative practice of dating, or for such apparently noneconomic economies as joint checking. The heteronormativity in such practices may seem weak and indirect. After all, same-sex couples have sometimes been able to invent versions of such practices. But they have done so only by betrothing themselves to the couple form and its language of personal significance, leaving untransformed the material and ideological conditions that divide intimacy from history, politics, and publics. The queer project we imagine is not just to destigmatize those average intimacies, not just to give access to the sentimentality of the couple for persons of the same sex, and definitely not to certify as properly private the personal lives of gays and lesbians.[31] Rather, it is to support forms of affective, erotic, and personal living that are public in the sense of accessible, available to memory, and sustained through collective activity.

Because the heteronormative culture of intimacy leaves queer culture especially dependent on ephemeral elaborations in urban space and print culture, queer publics are also peculiarly vulnerable to initiatives such as Mayor Rudolph Giuliani's new zoning law. The law aims to restrict any counterpublic sexual culture by regulating its economic conditions; its effects will reach far beyond the adult businesses it explicitly controls. The gay bars on Christopher Street draw customers from people who come there because of its sex trade. The street is cruisier because of the sex shops. The boutiques that sell freedom rings and "Don't Panic" T-shirts do more business for the same reasons. Not all of the thousands who migrate or make pilgrimages to Christopher Street use the porn shops, but all benefit from the fact that some do. After a certain point, a quantitative change is a qualitative change. A critical mass develops. The street becomes queer. It develops a dense, publicly accessible sexual culture. It therefore becomes a base for nonporn businesses, like the Oscar Wilde Bookshop. And it becomes a political base from which to pressure politicians with a gay voting bloc.

No group is more dependent on this kind of pattern in urban space than queers. If we could not concentrate a publicly accessible culture somewhere, we would always be outnumbered and overwhelmed. And because what brings us together is sexual culture, there are very few places in the world that have assembled much of a queer population without a base in sex commerce, and even those that do exist, such as the lesbian culture in Northampton, Massachusetts, are stronger because of their ties to places like the West Village, Dupont Circle, West Hollywood, and the Castro. Respectable gays like to think that they owe nothing to the sexual subculture they think of as sleazy. But their success, their way of living, their political rights, and their very identities would never have been possible but for the existence of the public sexual culture they now despise. Extinguish it, and almost all *out* gay or queer culture will wither on the vine. No one knows this connection better than the right. Conservatives would not so flagrantly contradict their stated belief in a market free from government interference if they did not see this kind of hyper-regulation as an important victory.

The point here is not that queer politics needs more free-market ideology, but that heteronormative forms, so central to the accumulation and reproduction of capital, also depend on heavy interventions in the regulation of capital. One of the most disturbing fantasies in the zoning scheme, for example, is the idea that an urban locale is a community of shared interest based on residence and property. The ideology of the neighborhood is politically unchallengeable in the current debate, which is dominated by a fantasy that sexual subjects only reside, that the space relevant to sexual politics is the neighborhood. But a district like Christopher Street is not just a neighborhood affair. The local character of the neighborhood depends on the daily presence of thousands of nonresidents. Those who actually live in the West Village should not forget their debt to these mostly queer pilgrims. And we should not make the mistake of confusing the class of citizens with the class of property owners. Many of those who hang out on Christopher Street—typically young, queer, and African American—couldn't possibly afford to live there. Urban space is always a host space. The right to the city extends to those who use the city.[32] It is not limited to property owners. It is not because of a fluke in the politics of zoning that urban space is so deeply misrecognized; normal sexuality requires such misrecognitions, including their economic and legal enforcement, in order to sustain its illusion of humanity.

4.   Tweaking and Thwacking

Queer social theory is committed to sexuality as an inescapable category of analysis, agitation, and refunctioning. Like class relations, which in this moment are mainly visible in the polarized embodiments of identity forms, heteronormativity is a fundamental motor of social organization in the United States, a founding condition of unequal and exploitative relations throughout even straight society. Any social theory that miscomprehends this participates in their reproduction.

The project of thinking about sex in public does not only engage sex when it is disavowed or suppressed. Even if sex practice is not the object domain of queer studies, sex is everywhere present. But where is the tweaking, thwacking, thumping, sliming, and rubbing you might have expected – or dreaded – in a paper on sex? We close with two scenes that might have happened on the same day in our wanderings around the city. One afternoon, we were riding with a young straight couple we know, in their station wagon. Gingerly, after much circumlocution, they brought the conversation around to vibrators. These are people whose reproductivity governs their lives, their aspirations, and their relations to money and entailment, mediating their relations to everyone and everything else. But the woman in this couple had recently read an article in a women's magazine about sex toys and other forms of nonreproductive eroticism. She and her husband did some mail-order shopping and have become increasingly involved in what from most points of view would count as queer sex practices; their bodies have become disorganized and exciting to them. They said to us: you're the only people we can talk to about this; to all of our straight friends this would make us perverts. In order not to feel like perverts, they had to make *us* into a kind of sex public.

Later, the question of aversion and perversion came up again. This time we were in a bar that on most nights is a garden-variety leather bar, but that, on Wednesday nights, hosts a sex performance event called "Pork." Shows typically include spanking, flagellation, shaving, branding, laceration, bondage, humiliation, wrestling – you know, the usual: amateur, everyday practitioners strutting for everyone else's gratification, not unlike an academic conference. This night, word was circulating that the performance was to be erotic vomiting. This sounded like an appetite spoiler, and the thought of leaving early occurred to us but was overcome by a simple curiosity: what would the foreplay be like? Let's stay until it gets messy. Then we can leave.

A boy, twentyish, very skateboard, comes on the low stage at one end of the bar, wearing lycra shorts and a dog collar. He sits loosely in a restraining chair. His partner comes out and tilts the bottom's head up to the ceiling, stretching out his throat. Behind them is an array of foods. The top begins pouring milk down the boy's throat, then food, then more milk. It spills over, down his chest and onto the floor. A dynamic is established between them in which they carefully keep at the threshold of gagging. The bottom struggles to keep taking in more than he really can. The top is careful to give him just enough to stretch his capacities. From time to time a baby bottle is offered as a respite, but soon the rhythm intensifies. The boy's stomach is beginning to rise and pulse, almost convulsively.

It is at this point that we realize we cannot leave, cannot even look away. No one can. The crowd is transfixed by the scene of intimacy and display, control and abandon, ferocity and abjection. People are moaning softly with admiration, then whistling, stomping, screaming encouragements. They have pressed forward in a compact and intimate group. Finally, as the top inserts two, then three fingers in the bottom's throat, insistently offering his own stomach for the repeated climaxes, we realize that we have never seen such a display of trust and violation. We are breathless. But, good academics that we are, we also have some questions to ask. Word has gone around that the boy is straight. We want to know: What does that mean in this context? How did you discover that this is what you want to do? How did you find a male top to do it with? How did you come to do it in a leather bar? Where else do you do this? How do you feel about your new partners, this audience?

We did not get to ask these questions, but we have others that we can pose now, about these scenes where sex appears more sublime than narration itself, neither redemptive nor transgressive, moral nor immoral, hetero nor homo, nor sutured to any axis of social legitimation. We have been arguing that sex opens a wedge to the transformation of those social norms that require only its static intelligibility or its deadness as a source of meaning.[33] In these cases, though, paths through publicity led to the production of nonheteronormative bodily contexts. They intended nonheteronormative worlds because they refused to pretend that privacy was their ground; because they were forms of sociability that unlinked money and family from the scene of the good life; because they made sex the consequence of public mediations and collective self-activity in a way that made for unpredicted pleasures; because, in turn, they attempted to make a context of support for their practices; because their pleasures were not purchased by a redemptive pastoralism of sex, nor by mandatory amnesia about failure, shame, and aversion.[34]

We are used to thinking about sexuality as a form of intimacy and subjectivity, and we have just demonstrated how limited that representation is. But the heteronormativity of U.S. culture is not something that can be easily rezoned or disavowed by individual acts of will, by a subversiveness imagined only as personal rather than as the basis of public-formation, nor even by the lyric moments that interrupt the hostile cultural narrative that we have been staging here. Remembering the utopian wish behind normal intimate life, we also want to remember that we aren't married to it.

Notes

1 On public sex in the standard sense, see Pat Califia, *Public Sex: The Culture of Radical Sex* (Pittsburgh, 1994). On acts and identities, see Janet E. Halley, "The Status/Conduct Distinction in the 1993 Revisions to Military Antigay Policy: A Legal Archaeology," GLQ 3 (1996): 159–252. The classic political argument for sexual derepression as a condition of freedom is put forth in Herbert Marcuse, *Eros and Civilization: A Philosophical Inquiry into Freud* (Boston, 1966). In contemporary prosex thought inspired by volume 1 of Michel Foucault's *The History of Sexuality*, the denunciation of "erotic injustice and sexual oppression" is situated less in the freedom of individuals than in analyses of the normative and coercive relations between specific "populations" and the institutions created to manage them (Gayle Rubin, "Thinking Sex: Notes for a Radical Theory of the Politics of Sexuality," in *Pleasure and Danger: Exploring Female Sexuality*, ed. Carole S. Vance [Boston, 1984], p. 275). See also Michel Foucault, *The History of Sexuality: An Introduction*, vol. 1 of *The History of Sexuality*, trans. Robert Hurley (New York, 1978).

2 By heteronormativity we mean the institutions, structures of understanding, and practical orientations that make heterosexuality seem not only coherent – that is, organized as a sexuality – but also privileged. Its coherence is always provisional, and its privilege can take several (sometimes contradictory) forms: unmarked, as the basic idiom of the personal and the social; or marked as a natural state; or projected as an ideal or moral accomplishment. It consists less of norms that could be summarized as a body of doctrine than of a sense of rightness produced in contradictory manifestations – often unconscious, immanent to practice or to institutions. Contexts that have

little visible relation to sex practice, such as life narrative and generational identity, can be het-eronormative in this sense, while in other contexts forms of sex between men and women might *not* be heteronormative. Heteronormativity is thus a concept distinct from heterosexuality. One of the most conspicuous differences is that it has no parallel, unlike heterosexuality, which organizes homosexuality as its opposite. Because homosexuality can never have the invisible, tacit, society-founding rightness that heterosexuality has, it would not be possible to speak of "homonormativity" in the same sense. See Michael Warner, "Fear of a Queer Planet," *Social Text*, no. 29 (1991): 3–17.

3   See *Time*, special issue, "The New Face of America," Fall 1993. This analysis reworks materials in Lauren Berlant, *The Queen of America Goes to Washington City: Essays on Sex and Citizenship* (Durham, N.C., 1997), pp. 200–208.

4   For a treatment of the centrality of "blood" to U.S. nationalist discourse, see Bonnie Honig, *No Place Like Home: Democracy and the Politics of Foreignness* (forthcoming).

5   See, for example, William J. Bennett, *The De-Valuing of America: The Fight for Our Culture and Our Children* (New York, 1992); Peter Brimelow, *Alien Nation: Common Sense about America's Immigration Disaster* (New York, 1995); and William A. Henry III, *In Defense of Elitism* (New York, 1994).

6   On the family form in national rhetoric, see Jay Fliegelman, *Prodigals and Pilgrims: The American Revolution against Patriarchal Authority, 1750–1800* (Cambridge, 1982), and Shirley Samuels, *Romances of the Republic: Women, the Family, and Violence in the Literature of the Early American Nation* (New York, 1996). On fantasies of genetic assimilation, see Robert S. Tilton, *Pocahontas: The Evolution of an American Narrative* (Cambridge, 1994), pp. 9–33, and Elise Lemire, "Making Miscegenation" (Ph.D. diss., Rutgers University, 1996).

7   The concept of welfare state governmentality has a growing literature. For a concise statement, see Jürgen Habermas, "The New Obscurity: The Crisis of the Welfare State and the Exhaustion of Utopian Energies," *The New Conservatism: Cultural Criticism and the Historians' Debate*, trans. Shierry Weber Nicholsen (Cambridge, Mass., 1989), pp. 48–70. Michael Warner has discussed the relation between this analysis and queer culture in his "Something Queer about the Nation-State," in *After Political Correctness: The Humanities and Society in the 1990s*, ed. Christopher Newfield and Ronald Strickland (Boulder, Colo., 1995), pp. 361–71.

8   *Congressional Record*, 101st Cong., 1st. sess., 1989, 135, pt. 134:12967.

9   Political geography in this way produces systematic effects of violence. Queers are forced to find each other in untrafficked areas because of the combined pressures of propriety, stigma, the closet, and state regulation such as laws against public lewdness. The same areas are known to gay-bashers and other criminals. And they are disregarded by police. The effect is to make both violence and police neglect seem like natural hazards, voluntarily courted by queers. As the 1997 documentary film *Licensed to Kill* illustrates, antigay violence has been difficult to combat by legal means: vic-tims are reluctant to come forward in any public and prosecutorial framework, while bashers can appeal to the geographic circumstances to implicate the victims themselves. The legal system has helped to produce the violence it is called upon to remedy.

10 See Eve Kosofsky Sedgwick, *Epistemology of the Closet* (Berkeley, 1992).

11 Gay and lesbian theory, especially in the humanities, frequently emphasizes psychoanalytic or psychoanalytic-style models of subject-formation, the differences among which are significant and yet all of which tend to elide the difference between the categories male/female and the pro-cess and project of heteronormativity. Three propositional paradigms are relevant here: those that propose that human identity itself is fundamentally organized by gender identifications that are hardwired into infants; those that equate the clarities of gender identity with the domination of a relatively coherent and vertically stable "straight" ideology; and those that focus on a phallocen-tric Symbolic order that produces gendered subjects who live out the destiny of their positioning in it. The psychoanalytic and philosophical insights and limits of these models (which, we feel, underdescribe the practices, institutions, and incongruities of heteronormativity) require further engagement. For the time being, these works stand in as the most challenging relevant archive: Judith Butler, *Bodies that Matter: On the Discursive Limits of "Sex"* (New York, 1993); Luce Irigaray, *Speculum of the Other Woman*, trans. Gillian C. Gill (Ithaca, N.Y., 1985) and *This Sex*

Which Is Not One, trans. Catherine Porter and Carolyn Burke (Ithaca, N.Y., 1985); Teresa de Lauretis, *The Practice of Love: Lesbian Sexuality and Perverse Desire* (Bloomington, Ind., 1994); Kaja Silverman, *Male Subjectivity at the Margins* (New York, 1992); and Monique Wittig, *The Straight Mind and Other Essays* (Boston, 1992). Psychoanalytic work on sexuality does not always latch acts and inclinations to natural or constructed "identity": see, for example, Leo Bersani, *Homos* (Cambridge, Mass., 1995) and "Is the Rectum a Grave?" in *AIDS: Cultural Analysis/ Cultural Activism*, ed. Douglas Crimp (Cambridge, Mass., 1988).

12   The notion of metaculture we borrow from Greg Urban. See Greg Urban, *A Discourse-Centered Approach to Culture: Native South American Myths and Rituals* (Austin, Tex., 1991) and *Noumenal Community: Myth and Reality in an Amerindian Brazilian Society* (Austin, Tex., 1996). On normalization, see Foucault, *Discipline and Punish: The Birth of the Prison*, trans. Alan Sheridan (New York, 1979), pp. 184–85 and *The History of Sexuality*, p. 144. Foucault derives his argument here from the revised version of Georges Canguilhem, *The Normal and the Pathological*, trans. Carolyn R. Fawcett and Robert S. Cohen (New York, 1991).

13   Here we are influenced by Eli Zaretsky, *Capitalism, the Family, and Personal Life* (New York, 1986), and Stephanie Coontz, *The Social Origins of Private Life: A History of American Families, 1600–1900* (London, 1988), though heteronormativity is a problem not often made visible in Coontz's work.

14   On privatization and intimacy politics, see Berlant, *The Queen of America Goes to Washington City*, pp. 1–24 and "Feminism and the Institutions of Intimacy," in *The Politics of Research*, ed. E. Ann Kaplan and George Levine (New Brunswick, N.J., 1997), pp. 143–61; Honig, *No Place Like Home*; and Rosalind Pollack Petchesky, "The Body as Property: A Feminist Re-vision," in *Conceiving the New World Order: The Global Politics of Reproduction*, ed. Faye D. Ginsburg and Rayna Rapp (Berkeley, 1995), pp. 387–406. On privatization and national-capitalism, see David Harvey, *The Condition of Postmodernity: An Enquiry into the Origins of Cultural Change* (Oxford, 1989), and Mike Davis, *City of Quartz: Excavating the Future in Los Angeles* (New York, 1992).

15   This language for community is a problem for gay historiography. In otherwise fine and important studies such as Esther Newton's *Cherry Grove, Fire Island: Sixty Years in America's First Gay and Lesbian Town* (Boston, 1993), or Elizabeth Lapovsky Kennedy and Madeline D. Davis's *Boots of Leather, Slippers of Gold: The History of a Lesbian Community* (New York, 1993), or even George Chauncey's *Gay New York: Gender, Urban Culture, and the Makings of the Gay Male World, 1890–1940* (New York, 1994), community is imagined as whole-person, face-to-face relations – local, experiential, proximate, and saturating. But queer worlds seldom manifest themselves in such forms. Cherry Grove – a seasonal resort depending heavily on weekend visits by New Yorkers – may be typical less of a "gay and lesbian town" than of the way queer sites are specialized spaces in which transits can project alternative worlds. John D'Emilio's *Sexual Politics, Sexual Communities: The Making of a Homosexual Minority in the United States, 1940–1970* is an especially interesting example of the imaginative power of the idealization of local community for queers: the book charts the separate tracks of political organizing and local scenes such as bar life, showing that when the "movement" and the "subculture" began to converge in San Francisco, the result was a new formation with a new utopian appeal: "A 'community,'" D'Emilio writes, "was in fact forming around a shared sexual orientation" (John D'Emilio, *Sexual Politics, Sexual Communities: The Making of a Homosexual Minority in the United States, 1940–1970* [Chicago, 1983], p. 195). D'Emilio (wisely) keeps scare quotes around "community" in the very sentence declaring it to exist in fact.

16   Artemidorus, *Oneirocritica* 1.2, quoted in David M. Halperin, "Sex before Sexuality: Pederasty, Politics, and Power in Classical Athens," in *Hidden from History: Reclaiming the Gay and Lesbian Past*, ed. Martin Bauml Duberman, Martha Vicinus, and Chauncey (New York, 1989), p. 49.

17   Halperin, "Sex before Sexuality," p. 49.

18   Studies of intimacy that do not assume this "web of mutuality," either as the self-evident nature of intimacy or as a human value, are rare. Roland Barthes's *A Lover's Discourse: Fragments*, trans. Richard Howard (New York, 1978), and Niklas Luhmann's *Love as Passion*, trans. Jeremy Gaines and Doris L. Jones (Cambridge, Mass., 1986) both try, in very different ways, to describe analytically the production of intimacy. More typical is Anthony Giddens's attempt to theorize intimacy

as "pure relationship" in *The Transformation of Intimacy: Sexuality, Love, and Eroticism in Modern Societies* (Cambridge, 1992). There, ironically, it is "the gays who are the pioneers" in separating the "pure relationship" of love from extraneous institutions and contexts such as marriage and reproduction.

19   Berlant and Warner, "What Does Queer Theory Teach Us about *X*?" *PMLA* 110 (May 1995): 345.

20   Bennett, quoted in Maureen Dowd, "Talk Is Cheap," *New York Times*, 26 Oct. 1995, p. A25.

21   Biddy Martin, "Extraordinary Homosexuals and the Fear of Being Ordinary," *Differences* 6 (Summer–Fall 1994): 123; hereafter abbreviated "EH."

22   In some traditions of social theory, the process of world making as we describe it here is seen as common to all social actors. See, for example, Alfred Schutz's emphasis on the practices of typification and projects of action involved in ordinary knowledge of the social in *The Phenomenology of the Social World*, trans. George Walsh and Frederick Lehnert (Evanston, Ill., 1967). Yet in most contexts the social world is understood, not as constructed by reference to types or projects, but as instantiated whole in a form capable of reproducing itself. The family, the state, a neighborhood, the human species, or institutions such as school and church – such images of social being share an appearance of plenitude seldom approached in contexts of queer world making. However much the latter might resemble the process of world construction in ordinary contexts, queer worlds do not have the power to represent a taken-for-granted social existence.

23   See, for example, Alan Bray, "Homosexuality and the Signs of Male Friendship in Elizabethan England," History Workshop 29 (Spring 1990): 1–19; Laurie J. Shannon, "Emilia's Argument: Friendship and 'Human Title' in *The Two Noble Kinsmen*," *ELH* 64 (Fall 1997); and *Passions of the Renaissance*, trans. Arthur Goldhammer, ed. Roger Chartier, vol. 3 of *A History of Private Life*, ed. Philippe Ariès and Georges Duby (Cambridge, Mass., 1989).

24   On the relation between Foucault and Habermas, we take inspiration from Tom McCarthy, *Ideals and Illusions* (Cambridge, Mass., 1991), pp. 43–75.

25   Habermas, *The Structural Transformation of the Public Sphere: An Inquiry into a Category of Bourgeois Society*, trans. Thomas Burger and Frederick Lawrence (Cambridge, Mass., 1991), p. 49.

26   Ibid., p. 46.

27   On the centrality of semipublic spaces like tearooms, bathrooms, and bathhouses to gay male life, see Chauncey, *Gay New York*, and Lee Edelman, "Tearooms and Sympathy, or, Epistemology of the Water Closet," in *Nationalisms and Sexualities*, ed. Andrew Parker et al. (New York, 1992), pp. 263–84. The spaces of both gay and lesbian semipublic sexual practices are investigated in *Mapping Desire: Geographies of Sexualities*, ed. David Bell and Gill Valentine (New York, 1995).

28   Douglas Crimp, "How to Have Promiscuity in an Epidemic," *October*, no. 43 (Winter 1987): 253.

29   The notion of a demand for recognition has been recently advanced by a number of thinkers as a way of understanding multicultural politics. See, for example, Axel Honneth, *The Struggle for Recognition: The Moral Grammar of Social Conflicts*, trans. Joel Anderson (Cambridge, 1995), or *Multiculturalism: Examining the Politics of Recognition*, ed. Amy Gutmann (Princeton, N.J., 1994). We are suggesting that although queer politics does contest the terrain of recognition, it cannot be conceived as a politics of recognition *as opposed to* an issue of distributive justice; this is the distinction proposed in Nancy Fraser's "From Redistribution to Recognition? Dilemmas of Justice in a 'Postsocialist' Age," *New Left Review*, no. 212 (July–Aug. 1995): 68–93; rept. in her *Justice Interruptus: Critical Reflections on the "Postsocialist" Condition* (New York, 1997).

30   See Sedgwick, *Epistemology of the Closet*, and Yvonne Zipter, *Diamonds Are a Dyke's Best Friend: Reflections, Reminiscences, and Reports from the Field on the Lesbian National Pastime* (Ithaca, N.Y., 1988).

31   Such a politics is increasingly recommended within the gay movement. See, for example, Andrew Sullivan, *Same-Sex Marriage, Pro and Con* (New York, 1997); Michelangelo Signorile, *Life Outside: The Signorile Report on Gay Men, Sex, Drugs, Muscles, and the Passages of Life* (New York, 1997); Gabriel Rotello, *Sexual Ecology: AIDS and the Destiny of Gay Men* (New York, 1997); William N. Eskridge, Jr., *The Case for Same-Sex Marriage: From Sexual Liberty to Civilized Commitment* (New York, 1996); *Same-Sex Marriage: The Moral and Legal Debate*, ed. Robert M. Baird and Stuart E. Rosenbaum (Amherst, N.Y., 1996); and Mark Strasser, *Legally Wed: Same-Sex Marriage and the Constitution* (Ithaca, N.Y., 1997).

32   The phrase "the right to the city" is Henri Lefebvre's, from his *Le Droit à la ville* (Paris, 1968); trans. Eleonore Kofman and Elizabeth Lebas, under the title "The Right to the City," *Writings on Cities* (Oxford, 1996), pp. 147–59. See also Manuel Castells, *The City and the Grassroots* (Berkeley, 1983).

33   On deadness as an affect and aspiration of normative social membership, see Berlant, "Live Sex Acts (Parental Advisory: Explicit Material)," *The Queen of America Goes to Washington City*, pp. 59–60, 79–81.

34   The classic argument against the redemptive sex pastoralism of normative sexual ideology is made in Bersani, "Is the Rectum a Grave?"; on redemptive visions more generally, see his *The Culture of Redemption* (Cambridge, Mass., 1990).

CHAPTER 12

Naturally Queer

Myra Hird

Sociologist Myra Hird's essay introduces us to the "new materialism," a movement across the social sciences that treats the boundaries between the human and the biological as fluid. As Hird notes, we humans are populated by bacteria with which we interact in ways that do not respect the boundaries that are usually expected to exist between entities. Moreover, our heterosexual reproductive paradigm is minoritarian when considered in the context of the numerous pan-sexual forms of reproduction with which we live in close proximity. Nature is not a static thing in relation to which cultural fluidity is measured; rather biology itself is fluid in ways that provoke a questioning of our static habits of thought and action in regard to gender identity and reproduction.

Transgressing boundaries is a hallmark of queer theory and research. The analysis of boundary transgressions is usually framed as the purview of culture, with living and non-living matter figured as the stubborn, inert, 'outside' to transgressive potential. This short paper aims to suggest nonlinear biology as a potent lens with which to explore particular boundary transgressions associated with queer theory including the autonomy of the self, embodiment and sexual difference.

Queerying Sexual Difference

Non-linear biology provides a wealth of evidence to confound static notions of sexual difference.[1] Human bodies, like those of other living organisms, are only 'sexed' from a particularly narrow perspective. The *vast* majority of cells in human bodies are intersex (and this category itself is only possible by maintaining a division between 'female' and 'male' chromosomes), with only egg and sperm cells counting as sexually dimorphic. *Most* of the reproduction that we undertake in our lifetimes has nothing to do with 'sex'. The cells in our bodies engage in constant, energetic reproduction in the form of *recombination* (cutting and patching of DNA strands), *merging* (fertilization of cells), *meiosis* (cell division by halving chromosome number, for instance in making sperm and eggs),

Original publication details: Myra Hird, "Naturally Queer." *Feminist Theory* 5, pp. 85–89. Sage, 2004. Reproduced with permission from Sage and M. Hird.

and *mitosis* (cell division with maintenance of cell number). Nor does reproduction take place between discrete 'selves', as many cultural analyses would have it. Indeed, only by taking our skin as a definitive impenetrable boundary are we able to see our bodies as discrete selves.[2] Our human bodies are more accurately 'built from a mass of interacting selves ... the self is not only corporeal but corporate' (Sagan, 1992: 370). Our cells also provide asylum for a variety of bacteria, viruses and countless genetic fragments. And none of this reproduction requires any bodily contact with another human being. Moreover, there is no linear relationship between sexual dimorphism and sexual reproduction. Male sea horses, pipe fish and hares get pregnant. Many species are male and female simultaneously, or sequentially. Many types of fish change sex back and forth depending on environmental conditions (see Rothblatt, 1995).

Indeed, what I would call our bodily state of sexual *indifference* is founded upon an entire evolutionary legacy. During most of our evolutionary heritage, our ancestors reproduced without sex. Currently, most of the organisms in four out of the five kingdoms do not require sex for reproduction. Imagine *The Joy of Sex* for plants, fungi, and bacteria. *Schizophyllum*, for instance, has more than 28,000 sexes. And sex among these promiscuous mushrooms is literally a 'touch-and-go' event, leading Laidman to conclude that for fungi there are 'so many genders, so little time ...' (2000: 1–3). Thus, sexual 'difference' might be culturally significant, but this term obscures the much more prevalent sex diversity among living matter.

Queerying Technology

Whether cultural analyses trumpet technology as the future site of new ways of living, or caution the perceived headlong rush toward technological dependence in the absence of sustained ethical consideration, these analyses tend to tacitly assume technology to be the cache of human beings. But as Arthur Clarke points out, 'we never invent anything that nature hasn't tried out millions of years earlier' (2000: 333). At a basic level, life itself is, and has always been, 'technological' in the very real sense that bacteria, protoctists and animals incorporate external structural materials into their bodies (see Margulis and Sagan, 1997). And it is particularly in relation to technology that I begin my ode to bacteria. Bacteria have been around for about three billion years. Sagan is right to argue that 'bacteria are biochemically and metabolically far more diverse than all plants and animals put together' (1992: 377). On their curriculum vitae, bacteria can boast the ability to detect light, produce alcohol, and convert various gases and minerals (see Margulis and Sagan, 1997). The ancestors of all living things, bacteria are, indisputably, the supreme chemists in the history of this planet. They, and not hippies, were the first beings to grow on nothing but sun, water and air. But that's not all. Bacteria also invented all major forms of metabolism, multicellularity, nanotechnology (controlling molecules in ways that continue to elude scientists), and metallurgy. They are the single most important living beings to maintain the biosphere, and they have even figured out a way to successfully resist death. As Margulis and Sagan note:

> Bacteria and protoctists set the stage. They, not animals, introduced DNA recombination, locomotion, reproduction leading to exponential growth, photosynthesis, boil-proof spores. They, not animals, pioneered symbiosis and the organization of individuals from multicellular collectives. They invented intracellular motility (including mitosis), complex developmental

cycles, meiosis, sexual fusion, individuality, and programmed death. The prokaryotic microbes, not animals or plants, still run all the geochemical cycles that make the planet habitable. The protoctists, in their new status as individuals form coevolved bacterial communities, invented resistant cysts, skeletons and shells, gender behaviours, cell-to-cell communication, lethal toxins, and many other processes later co-opted by animals. Animals were preceded by bacteria and protoctists, not by chemicals. The animal explosion has a long microbial fuse. (1995: 160)

Bacteria also seriously raise the queering bar through their abilities to cross species barriers and perform hypersex. Current controversy over the use of animal cell and organ 'donation' (no one, as far as I know, has ever asked the pigs for their consent) is old hat for bacteria. The equivalent to this bacterial ability in human animals would be a 'man with red hair and freckles wak[ing] up, after a swim with his brunette boyfriend and dog, with brown hair, a tail and floppy ears' (Margulis and Sagan, 1997: 53). Bacteria long ago cornered the market on 'trans', whether transduction or transfection.[3] Bacteria are not lumbered with quaint ideas about sexual reproduction to exchange genes, and will avidly exchange genes with just about any living organism (including our not-so-autonomous human bodies). Much of the 'brave new world' of reproductive technologies is human mimicry of well-worn, millions of years old bacterial practices. And, within bacterial being, the female/male, sex/gender distinction has no meaning (Margulis and Sagan, 1997). Since bacteria recognize and avidly embrace diversity, they do not discriminate on the basis of 'sex' or 'gender' differences at all.

Queerying Boundaries

One of the founding aims of queer theory is to challenge normative boundaries, between what is 'normal' and 'abnormal', 'heterosexual' and 'homosexual' and so on. My 'ode to bacteria' might suggest that while I may have queered human notions of technology, I have re-established a boundary/binary between 'human' and 'bacteria'. However, my central point here is that bacteria are us. Put another way, 'we' live in a symbiotic relationship with bacteria, and when we say 'human' we necessarily mean, at a physical level, bacteria as well (as well as a host of other matter such as viruses, thread worms and so on). Thus, in non-linear biology, the penultimate embodiment of queer may be bodies themselves. Take, for example, Donna Haraway's (2001) *Mixotricha paradoxa*, a minute single-celled organism that lives in symbiotic relationship with five other organisms in the gut of the South Australian termite. For *Mixotricha paradoxa*, as for *Homo sapiens*, the key boundary is between the self and other, or as Haraway puts it 'the one and the many' (2001: 82). Recent research on chimerism and mosaicism within human and other animals further troubles the notion of material autonomy.[4]

Beyond the autonomy of the (human) self, non-linear biology might help us to re-think other boundaries such as the distinction between humans and primates, and living and non-living matter more generally. As Sarah Franklin notes, 'trading organismic distinction for pan-species genetic information flow pulls the rug out from under the sex/gender system as we know it' (1995: 69). Non-linear biology also provides a growing catalogue of homosexual, transgender, and non-reproductive heterosexual behaviour in animals that defies the traditional homosexual/heterosexual boundary. Gay parenting, lesbianism, homosexuality, sex-changing, and other behaviours in animals are prevalent in living matter. It is at least curious that queer theory does not devote more space to the abundant queer behaviour of most of the living matter on this planet.

Conclusion

If queer critiques 'have fallen into old and familiar patterns [then one way this] ubiquitous gravitation to culture' might be averted is by studying the queerness of matter (Wilson, 1996: 50). We may no longer be certain that it is nature that remains static and culture that evinces limitless malleability. Non-linear biology stands to make a significant contribution to queer discussions of the constitution, boundaries and technologies of 'sex', 'gender', and 'sexuality'.

Notes

1   For a longer account of queerying sexual difference, technology and boundaries, see Hird (2003).
2   Lewis Thomas puts it more directly: from the point of view of the mitochondria in our bodies (which occupy as much volume in themselves as the rest of us), we 'could be taken for a very large, motile colony of respiring bacteria, operating a complex system of nuclei, microtubules, and neurons for the pleasure and sustenance of their families, and running, at the moment, a typewriter' (1974: 72).
3   Humans tend to think of agency as requiring intentionality born of subjectivity, but if we use Karen Barad's (1998) definition of 'agency as an enactment rather than something someone has' we get a different picture. To deny all forms of non-human matter agency reminds me of Descartes' humanocentric claim that dogs do not suffer pain.
4   See for example Pearson (2002) and Strain et al. (1998).

References

Barad, K. (1998) 'Getting Real: Technoscientific Practices and the Materialization of Reality', *differences: A Journal of Feminist Cultural Studies* 10(2): 87–128.

Clarke, A. (2000) *Greetings, Carbon-based Bipeds!* London: HarperCollins.

Franklin, S. (1995) 'Romancing the Helix: Nature and Scientific Discovery', pp. 63–77 in L. Pearce and J. Stacey (eds) *Romance Revisited*. London: Lawrence and Wishart.

Haraway, D. (2001) 'More than Metaphor', pp. 91–6 in M. Mayberry, B. Subramaniam and L. Weasel (eds) *Feminist Science Studies*. New York: Routledge.

Hird, M.J. (2003) 'From the Culture of Matter to the Matter of Culture', *Sociological Research Online*, 8(1). http://www.socresonline.org.uk/8/1/hird.html

Laidman, J. (2000) 'Reproduction a Touch-and-go Thing for Fungus', *Nature* 24: 1–3.

Margulis, L. and D. Sagan (1995) *What is Life?* Berkeley and Los Angeles: University of California Press.

Margulis, L. and D. Sagan (1997) *What is Sex?* New York: Simon and Schuster.

Pearson, H. (2002) 'Dual Identities', *Nature* 417: 10–11.

Rothblatt, M. (1995) *The Apartheid of Sex*. New York: Crown Publishers.

Sagan, D. (1992) 'Metametazoa: Biology and Multiplicity', pp. 362–85 in J. Crary and S. Kwinter (eds) *Incorporations*. New York: Urzone Books.

Strain, L., J. Dean, M. Hamilton and D. Bonthron (1998) 'A True Hermaphrodite Chimera Resulting from Embryo Amalgamation after in vitro Fertilization', *The New England Journal of Medicine* 338(3): 166–9.

Thomas, L. (1974) *The Lives of a Cell*. New York: The Viking Press.

Wilson, E. (1996) 'On the Nature of Neurology', *Hysteric Body and Medicine* 49–63.

CHAPTER 13

Cruising Utopia: "Introduction" and "Queerness as Horizon: Utopian Hermeneutics in the Face of Gay Pragmatism"

José Esteban Muñoz

José Esteban Muñoz (1967–December 4, 2013) was an American academic in the fields of performance studies, visual culture, Queer Theory, cultural studies, and critical theory. His book *Disidentifications: Queers of Color and the Performance of Politics* (1999) examines queer and racial minority issues from a performance studies perspective. His second book, *Cruising Utopia: The Then and There of Queer Futurity*, was published by NYU Press in 2009. He also co-edited *Pop Out: Queer Warhol* (1996) with Jennifer Doyle and Jonathan Flatley, and *Everynight Life: Culture and Dance in Latin/o America* (1997) with Celeste Fraser Delgado. Muñoz was Professor in, and former Chair of, the Department of Performance Studies at New York University's Tisch School of the Arts.

Introduction

Feeling Utopia

A map of the world that does not include utopia is not worth glancing at.

– Oscar Wilde

Queerness is not yet here. Queerness is an ideality. Put another way, we are not yet queer. We may never touch queerness, but we can feel it as the warm illumination of a horizon imbued with potentiality. We have never been queer, yet queerness exists for us as an ideality that can be distilled from the past and used to imagine a future. The future is queerness's domain. Queerness is a structuring and educated mode of desiring that

Original publication details: José Esteban Muñoz, from *Cruising Utopia*, pp. 1–48. New York University Press, 2009.

Literary Theory: An Anthology, Third Edition. Edited by Julie Rivkin and Michael Ryan.
© 2017 John Wiley & Sons, Ltd. Published 2017 by John Wiley & Sons, Ltd.

allows us to see and feel beyond the quagmire of the present. The here and now is a prison house. We must strive, in the face of the here and now's totalizing rendering of reality, to think and feel a *then and there*. Some will say that all we have are the pleasures of this moment, but we must never settle for that minimal transport; we must dream and enact new and better pleasures, other ways of being in the world, and ultimately new worlds. Queerness is a longing that propels us onward, beyond romances of the negative and toiling in the present. Queerness is that thing that lets us feel that this world is not enough, that indeed something is missing. Often we can glimpse the worlds proposed and promised by queerness in the realm of the aesthetic. The aesthetic, especially the queer aesthetic, frequently contains blueprints and schemata of a forward-dawning futurity. Both the ornamental and the quotidian can contain a map of the utopia that is queerness. Turning to the aesthetic in the case of queerness is nothing like an escape from the social realm, insofar as queer aesthetics map future social relations. Queerness is also a performative because it is not simply a being but a doing for and toward the future. Queerness is essentially about the rejection of a here and now and an insistence on potentiality or concrete possibility for another world.

Queerness as Horizon

Utopian Hermeneutics in the Face of Gay Pragmatism

for John

I begin this chapter on futurity and a desire that is utopian by turning to a text from the past – more specifically, to those words that emanate from the spatiotemporal coordinate Bloch referred to as the no-longer-conscious, a term that attempts to enact a more precise understanding of the work that the past does, what can be understood as the performative force of the past. A 1971 issue of the gay liberation journal *Gay Flames* included a manifesto by a group calling itself Third World Gay Revolution. The text, titled "What We Want, What We Believe," offered a detailed list of demands that included the abolition of capital punishment, the abolishment of institutional religion, and the end of the bourgeois family. The entire list of sixteen demands culminated with a request that was especially radical and poignant when compared to the anemic political agenda that dominates contemporary LGBT politics in North America today.

> 16.) We want a new society – a revolutionary socialist society. We want liberation of humanity, free food, free shelter, free clothing, free transportation, free health care, free utilities, free education, free art for all. We want a society where the needs of the people come first.
> We believe that all people should share the labor and products of society, according to each one's needs and abilities, regardless of race, sex, age or sexual preferences. We believe the land, technology and the means of production belong to the people, and must be shared by the people collectively for the liberation of all.[1]

When we consider the extremely pragmatic agenda that organizes LGBT activism in North America today, the demand "we want a new society" may seem naive by the present's standards. Many people would dismiss these demands as impractical or merely utopian. Yet I contend that there is great value in pulling these words from the no-longer-conscious to arm a critique of the present. The use of "we" in this manifesto can be mistakenly read as the "we" implicit in the identity politics that emerged after the Third World Gay Revolution group. Such a reading would miss the point. This "we" does not speak to a merely identitarian logic but instead to a logic of futurity. The "we" speaks to a "we" that is "not yet conscious," the future society that is being invoked and addressed at the same moment. The "we" is not content to describe who the collective is but more nearly describes what the collective and the larger social order could be, what it should be. The particularities that are listed – "race, sex, age or sexual preferences" – are not things in and of themselves that format this "we"; indeed the statement's "we" is "regardless" of these markers, which is not to say that it is beyond such distinctions or due to these differences but, instead, that it is *beside* them. This is to say that the field of utopian possibility is one in which multiple forms of belonging in difference adhere to a belonging in collectivity.

Such multiple forms of belonging-in-difference and expansive critiques of social asymmetries are absent in the dominant LGBT leadership community and in many aspects of queer critique. One manifesto from today's movement that seems especially representative of the anemic, short-sighted, and retrograde politics of the present is "All Together Now (A Blueprint for the Movement),"[2] a text written by pro-gay-marriage lawyer Evan Wolfson that appeared on his website, freedomtomarry.org. Wolfson's single-minded text identifies the social recognition and financial advantages offered by traditional marriage pacts as the key to what he calls "freedom." Freedom for Wolfson is mere inclusion in a corrupt and bankrupt social order. Wolfson cannot critique the larger ideological regime that represents marriage as something desirable, natural, and good. His assimilationist gay politics posits an "all" that is in fact a few: queers with enough access to capital to imagine a life integrated within North American capitalist culture. It goes almost without saying that the "all" invoked by the gay lawyer and his followers are normative citizen-subjects with a host of rights only afforded to some (and not all) queer people. Arguments against gay marriage have been articulated with great acumen by Lisa Duggan and Richard Kim.[3] But it is Wolfson's invocation of the term *freedom* that is most unsettling.

Wolfson and his website's rhetoric degrade the concept of freedom. Homonormative cultural and political lobbyists such as Wolfson have degraded the political and conceptual force of concepts such as freedom in the same way that the current political regime of the United States has degraded the term *liberation* in the case of recent Middle Eastern foreign policy. I invoke Wolfson here not so much as this chapter's problem or foil but merely as a recent symptom of the erosion of the gay and lesbian political imagination. Wolfson represents many homonormative interests leading the contemporary LGBT movement toward the goal of "naturalizing" the flawed and toxic ideological formation known as marriage. The aping of traditional straight relationality, especially marriage, for gays and lesbians announces itself as a pragmatic strategy when it is in fact a deeply ideological project that is hardly practical. In this way gay marriage's detractors are absolutely right: gay marriage is not natural – but then again, neither is marriage for any individual.

A similar but more nuanced form of what I am referring to as gay pragmatic thought can be seen in Biddy Martin's work, especially her psychoanalytically inspired diagnosis that queer critique suffers from an androcentric bias in which queerness presents itself as the "extraordinary" while at the same time fleeing the charge of being "ordinary." Being ordinary and being married are both antiutopian wishes, desires that automatically rein themselves in, never daring to see or imagine the not-yet-conscious. This line of thought that I am identifying as pragmatic is taken from its vernacular register. I am not referring to the actual philosophical tradition of American pragmatism of Charles Peirce, William James, or John Dewey. But the current gay political strategy I am describing does share an interest in empiricism with that school. Gay pragmatic organizing is in direct opposition to the idealist thought that I associate as endemic to a forward-dawning queerness that calls on a no-longer-conscious in the service of imagining a futurity.

The not-quite-conscious is the realm of potentiality that must be called on, and insisted on, if we are ever to look beyond the pragmatic sphere of the here and now, the hollow nature of the present. Thus, I wish to argue that queerness is not quite here; it is, in the language of Italian philosopher Giorgio Agamben, a potentiality.[4] Alain Badiou refers to that which follows the event as the thing-that-is-not-yet-imagined,[5] and in my estimation queerness too should be understood to have a similar valence. But my turn to this notion of the not-quite-conscious is again indebted to Bloch and his massive three-volume text *The Principle of Hope*.[6] That treatise, both a continuation and an amplification of German idealist practices of thought, is a critical discourse – which is to say that it does not avert or turn away from the present. Rather, it critiques an autonaturalizing temporality that we might call *straight time*. Straight time tells us that there is no future but the here and now of our everyday life.[7] The only futurity promised is that of reproductive majoritarian heterosexuality, the spectacle of the state refurbishing its ranks through overt and subsidized acts of reproduction. In *No Future*, Lee Edelman advises queers that the future is "kid stuff."[8] Although I believe that there is a lot to like about Edelman's polemic – mostly its disdain for the culture of the child – I ultimately want to speak for a notion of queer futurity by turning to Bloch's critical notion of utopia.

It is equally polemical to argue that we are not quite queer yet, that queerness, what we will really know as queerness, does not yet exist. I suggest that holding queerness in a sort of ontologically humble state, under a conceptual grid in which we do not claim to always already know queerness in the world, potentially staves off the ossifying effects of neoliberal ideology and the degradation of politics brought about by representations of queerness in contemporary popular culture.

A posterior glance at different moments, objects, and spaces might offer us an anticipatory illumination of queerness. We cannot trust in the manifestations of what some people would call queerness in the present, especially as embodied in the pragmatic debates that dominate contemporary gay and lesbian politics. (Here, again, I most pointedly mean U.S. queers clamoring for their right to participate in the suspect institution of marriage and, maybe worse, to serve in the military.) None of this is to say that there are not avatars of a queer futurity, both in the past and the present, especially in sites of cultural production. What I am suggesting is that we gain a greater conceptual and theoretical leverage if we see queerness as something that is not yet here. In this sense it is useful to consider Edmund Husserl, phenomenology's founder, and his invitation to look to horizons of being.[9] Indeed to access queer visuality we may need to squint, to strain our vision and force it to see otherwise, beyond the limited vista of the here and now.

To critique an overarching "here and now" is not to turn one's face away from the everyday. Roland Barthes wrote that the mark of the utopian is the quotidian.[10] Such an argument would stress that the utopian is an impulse that we see in everyday life. This impulse is to be glimpsed as something that is extra to the everyday transaction of heteronormative capitalism. This quotidian example of the utopian can be glimpsed in utopian bonds, affiliations, designs, and gestures that exist within the present moment. Turning to the New York School of poetry, a moment that is one of the cultural touchstones for my research, we can consider a poem by James Schuyler that speaks of a hope and desire that is clearly utopian. The poem, like most of Schuyler's body of work, is clearly rooted in an observation of the affective realm of the present. Yet there is an excess that the poet also conveys, a type of affective excess that presents the enabling force of a forward-dawning futurity that is queerness. In the poem "A photograph," published in 1974 in the collection *Hymn to Life*, a picture that resides on the speaker's desk sparks a recollection of domestic bliss.

A photograph
Shows you in a London
room; books, a painting,
your smile, a silky
tie, a suit. And more.
It looks so like you
and I see it every day
(here, on my desk)
which I don't you. Last
Friday was grand.
We went out, we came
back, we went wild. You
slept. Me too. The pup
woke you and you dressed
and walked him. When
you left, I was sleeping.
When I woke there was
just time to make the
train to a country dinner
and talk about ecstasy.
Which I think comes in
two sorts: that which you
Know "Now I am ecstatic"
Like my strange scream
last Friday night. And
another kind, that you
know only in retrospect:
"Why, that joy I felt
and didn't think about
when his feet were in
my lap, or when I looked
down and saw his slanty
eyes shut, that too was
ecstasy. Nor is there
necessarily a downer from
it." Do I believe in
the perfectibility of
man? Strangely enough,
(I've known unhappiness enough) I
do. I mean it.
I really do believe
future generations can
live without the intervals of anxious

fear we know between our
bouts and strolls of
ecstasy. The struck ball
finds the pocket. You
smile some years back
in London, I have
known ecstasy and calm:
haven't you too? Let's
try to understand, my
handsome friend who
wears his nose awry.[11]

The speaker remembers the grandness of an unspectacular Friday in which he and his addressee slept in and then scrambled to catch a train to a dinner out in the country. He attempts to explain the ecstasy he felt that night, indicating that one moment of ecstasy, a moment he identifies as being marked both by self-consciousness and oblivi-ousness, possesses a potentially transformative charge. He then considers another moment of ecstasy in retrospect, a looking back at a no-longer-conscious that provides an affective enclave in the present that staves off the sense of "bad feelings" that mark the affective disjuncture of being queer in straight time.

The moment in the poem of deeper introspection – beginning "Do I believe in / the perfectibility of / man?" – is an example of a utopian desire inspired by queer relational-ity. Moments of queer relational bliss, what the poet names as ecstasies, are viewed as having the ability to rewrite a larger map of everyday life. When "future generations" are invoked, the poet is signaling a queerness to come, a way of being in the world that is glimpsed through reveries in a quotidian life that challenges the dominance of an affective world, a present, full of anxiousness and fear. These future generations are, like the "we" invoked in the manifesto by the Third World Gay Revolution group, not an identitarian formulation but, instead, the invocation of a future collectivity, a queerness that registers as the illumination of a horizon of existence.

The poem speaks of multiple temporalities and the affective mode known as ecstasy, which resonates alongside the work of Martin Heidegger. In *Being and Time* Heidegger reflects on the activity of timeliness and its relation to *ekstatisch* (ecstasy), signaling for Heidegger the ecstatic unity of temporality – Past, Present, and Future.[12] The ecstasy the speaker feels and remembers in "A photograph" is not consigned to one moment. It steps out from the past and remarks on the unity of an expansive version of temporality; hence, future generations are invoked. To know ecstasy in the way in which the poem's speaker does is to have a sense of timeliness's motion, to understand a temporal unity that is important to what I attempt to describe as the time of queerness. Queerness's time is a stepping out of the linearity of straight time. Straight time is a self-naturalizing temporality. Straight time's "presentness" needs to be phenomenologically questioned, and this is the fundamental value of a queer utopian hermeneutics. Queerness's ecstatic and horizonal temporality is a path and a movement to a greater openness to the world.

It would be difficult to mistake Schuyler's poem for one of Frank O'Hara's upbeat reveries. O'Hara's optimism is a contagious happiness within the quotidian that I would also describe as having a utopian quality. Schuyler's poetry is not so much about opti-mism but instead about a hope that is distinctly utopian and distinctly queer. The poem imagines another collective belonging, an enclave in the future where readers will not be beset with feelings of nervousness and fear. These feelings are the affective results of being outside of straight time. He writes from a depressive position, "(I've known un- / happiness enough)," but reaches beyond the affective force-field of the present.

Hope for Bloch is an essential characteristic of not only the utopian but also the human condition. Thus, I talk about the human as a relatively stable category. But queerness in its utopian connotations promises a human that is not yet here, thus disrupting any ossified understanding of the human. The point is to stave off a gay and lesbian anti-utopianism that is very much tainted with a polemics of the pragmatic rights discourse that in and of itself hamstrings not only politics but also desire. Queerness as utopian formation is a formation based on an economy of desire and desiring. This desire is always directed at that thing that is not yet here, objects and moments that burn with anticipation and promise. The desire that propels Schuyler's "A photograph" is born of the no-longer-conscious, the rich resonance of remembrance, distinct pleasures felt in the past. And thus past pleasures stave off the affective perils of the present while they enable a desire that is queer futurity's core.

Queerness is utopian, and there is something queer about the utopian. Fredric Jameson described the utopian as the oddball or the maniac.[13] Indeed, to live inside straight time and ask for, desire, and imagine another time and place is to represent and perform a desire that is both utopian and queer. To participate in such an endeavor is not to imagine an isolated future for the individual but instead to participate in a hermeneutic that wishes to describe a collective futurity, a notion of futurity that functions as a historical materialist critique. In the two textual examples I have employed we see an overt utopianism that is explicit in the Third World Gay Revolution manifesto, and what I am identifying as a *utopian impulse* is perceivable in Schuyler's poetry. One requires a utopian hermeneutic to see an already operative principle of hope that hums in the poet's work. The other text, the manifesto, does another type of performative work; it *does* utopia.

To "read" the performative, along the lines of thought first inaugurated by J. L. Austin, is implicitly to critique the epistemological.[14] Performativity and utopia both call into question what is epistemologically there and signal a highly ephemeral ontological field that can be characterized as a *doing in futurity*. Thus, a manifesto is a call to a doing in and for the future. The utopian impulse to be gleaned from the poem is a call for "doing" that is a becoming: the becoming of and for "future generations." This rejection of the here and now, the ontologically static, is indeed, by the measure of homonormative codes, a maniacal and oddball endeavor. The queer utopian project addressed here turns to the fringe of political and cultural production to offset the tyranny of the homonormative. It is drawn to tastes, ideologies, and aesthetics that can only seem odd, strange, or indeed queer next to the muted striving of the practical and normalcy-desiring homosexual.

The turn to the call of the no-longer-conscious is not a turn to normative historical analysis. Indeed it is important to complicate queer history and understand it as doing more than the flawed process of merely evidencing. Evidencing protocols often fail to enact real hermeneutical inquiry and instead opt to reinstate that which is known in advance. Thus, practices of knowledge production that are content merely to cull selectively from the past, while striking a pose of positivist undertaking or empirical knowledge retrieval, often nullify the political imagination. Jameson's Marxian dictate "always historicize"[15] is not a methodological call for empirical data collection. Instead, it is a dialectical injunction, suggesting we animate our critical faculties by bringing the past to bear on the present and the future. Utopian hermeneutics offer us a refined lens to view queerness, insofar as queerness, if it is indeed not quite here, is nonetheless intensely relational with the past.

The present is not enough. It is impoverished and toxic for queers and other people who do not feel the privilege of majoritarian belonging, normative tastes, and "rational" expectations. (I address the question of rationalism shortly). Let me be clear that the idea is not simply to turn away from the present. One cannot afford such a maneuver, and if one thinks one can, one has resisted the present in favor of folly. The present must be known in relation to the alternative temporal and spatial maps provided by a perception of past and future affective worlds.

Utopian thinking gets maligned for being naively romantic. Of course, much of it has been naive. We know that any history of actualized utopian communities would be replete with failures. No one, other than perhaps Marx himself, has been more cognizant about this fact than Bloch. But it is through this Marxian tradition, not beside or against it, that the problem of the present is addressed. In the following quotation we begin to glimpse the importance of the Marxian tradition for the here and now.

> Marxism, above all, was first to bring a concept of knowledge into the world that essentially refers to Becomeness, but to the tendency of what is coming up; thus for the first time it brings future into our conceptual and theoretical grasp. Such recognition of tendency is necessary to remember, and to open up the No-Longer-Conscious.[16]

Thus we see Bloch's model for approaching the past. The idea is not to attempt merely to represent it with simplistic strokes. More nearly, it is important to call on the past, to animate it, understanding that the past has a performative nature, which is to say that rather than being static and fixed, the past does things. It is in this very way that the past is performative. Following a Blochian thread, it seems important to put the past into play with the present, calling into view the tautological nature of the present. The present, which is almost exclusively conceived through the parameters of straight time, is a self-naturalizing endeavor. Opening up a queer past is enabled by Marxian ideological tactics. Bloch explains that

> Marxism thus rescued the rational core of utopia and made it concrete as well as the core of the still idealistic tendency of dialectics. Romanticism does not understand utopia, not even its own, but utopia that has become concrete understands Romanticism and makes inroads into it, in so far as archaic material in its archetypes and work, contain a not yet voiced, undischarged element.[17]

Bloch invites us to look to this no-longer-conscious, a past that is akin to what Derrida described as the trace. These ephemeral traces, flickering illuminations from other times and places, are sites that may indeed appear merely romantic, even to themselves. Nonetheless they assist those of us who wish to follow queerness's promise, its still unrealized potential, to see something else, a component that the German aesthetician would call *cultural surplus*. I build on this idea to suggest that the surplus is both cultural and *affective*. More distinctly, I point to a queer feeling of hope in the face of hopeless heteronormative maps of the present where futurity is indeed the province of normative reproduction. This hope takes on the philosophical contours of idealism.

A queer utopian hermeneutic would thus be queer in its aim to look for queer relational formations within the social. It is also about this temporal project that I align with queerness, a work shaped by its idealist trajectory; indeed it is the work of not settling for the present, of asking and looking beyond the here and now. Such a hermeneutic would then be *epistemologically and ontologically humble* in that it would not claim the epistemological certitude of a queerness that we simply "know" but, instead, strain to activate the no-longer-conscious and to extend a glance toward that which is forward-dawning, anticipatory illuminations of the not-yet-conscious. The purpose of such temporal maneuvers is to wrest ourselves from the present's stultifying hold, to know our queerness as a belonging in particularity that is not dictated or organized around the spirit of political impasse that characterizes the present.

Jameson has suggested that for Bloch the present is provincial.[18] This spatialization of time makes sense in relation to the history of utopian thought, most famously described as an island by Thomas More. To mark the present as provincial is not to ridicule or demean the spots on queerness's map that do not signify as metropolitan. The here and now has an opposite number, and that would be the then and there. I have argued that the *then* that disrupts the tyranny of the *now* is both past and future. Along those lines, the here that is unnamed yet always implicit in the metropolitan hub requires the challenge of a there that can be regional or global. The transregional or the global as modes of spatial organization potentially displace the hegemony of an unnamed here that is always dominated by the shadow of the nation-state and its mutable and multiple corporate interests. While *globalization* is a term that mostly defines a worldwide system of manu-factured asymmetry and ravenous exploitation, it also signals the encroaching of the there on the here in ways that are worth considering.

The Third World Gay Revolution group was an organization that grew out of the larger Gay Liberation Front at roughly the same time that the Radicalesbians also spun off from the larger group in the spring/summer of 1970. Although they took the name Third World Gay Revolution, the group's members have been described by a recent historian as people of color.[19] Their own usage of the term "Third World" clearly connotes their deep identification with the global phenomenon that was decolonization. It is therefore imperative to remember this moment from the no-longer-conscious that transcended a gay and lesbian activist nationalist imaginary. For Heidegger "time and space are not co-ordinate. Time is prior to space."[20] If time is prior to space, then we can view both the force of the no-longer-conscious and the not-yet-here as potentially bearing on the *here* of naturalized space and time. Thus, at the center of cultural texts such as the manifesto "All Together Now (A Blueprint for the Movement)" we find an ideological document, and its claim to the pragmatic is the product of a short-sighted here that fails to include anything but an entitled and privileged world. The there of queer utopia cannot simply be that of the faltering yet still influential nation-state.

This is then to say that the distinctions between here and there, and the world that the here and now organizes, are not fixed – they are already becoming undone in relation to a forward-dawning futurity. It is important to understand that a critique of our homo-sexual present is not an attack on what many people routinely name as lesbian or gay but, instead, an appraisal of how queerness is still forming, or in many crucial ways formless. Queerness's form is utopian. Ultimately, we must insist on a queer futurity because the present is so poisonous and insolvent. A resource that cannot be discounted to know the future is indeed the no-longer-conscious, that thing or place that may be extinguished but not yet discharged in its utopian potentiality.

Bloch explains the Kantian nature of his project as the "saving" of a "rationalist core." It is worth remarking that Kant's rationalism is not merely held up in this instance; indeed *rationalism itself is refunctioned*. No longer is rationalism the ruler used by univer-salism to measure time and space. In Bloch's work rationalism is transformed via a political urgency. Rationalism is not dismissed but is instead unyoked from a politics of the pragmatic. Herbert Marcuse discussed the "irrational element in rationality" as an important component of industrial society's nature. Irrationality flourishes in "established institutions" – marriage is perhaps one of the very best examples of an institution that hampers rational advancement and the not-yet-imagined versions of freedom that heteronormative and homonormative culture proscribe.[21] In Marcuse's analysis the advancements in rationality made by technological innovations were counteracted by gay pragmatic political strategies that tell us not to dream of other spatial/temporal coordinates but instead to dwell in a broken-down present. This homosexual pragmatism takes on the practical contours of the homonormativity so powerfully described by Lisa Duggan in her treatise on neoliberalism, *The Twilight of Equality?*[22] Within the hermeneutical scope of a queer utopian inquiry rationalism is reignited with an affective spark of idealist thought.

Abstract utopias are indeed dead ends, too often vectoring into the escapist disavowal of our current moment. But a turn to what Bloch calls the no-longer-conscious is an essential route for the purpose of arriving at the not-yet-here. This maneuver, a turn to the past for the purpose of critiquing the present, is propelled by a desire for futurity. Queer futurity does not underplay desire. In fact it is all about desire, desire for both larger semiabstractions such as a better world or freedom but also, more immediately, better relations within the social that include better sex and more pleasure. Some theorists of postmodernity, such as David Harvey, have narrated sex radicalism as a turning away from a politics of the collectivity toward the individualistic and the petty.[23] In his *A Brief History of Neoliberalism* Harvey plots what he views as the condition of neoliberalism. In his account, "The narcissistic exploration of self, sexuality and identity became the leitmotif of bourgeois urban culture." In this account, the hard-fought struggles for sexual liberation are reduced to a "demand for lifestyle diversification." Harvey's critique pits the "working-class and ethnic immigrant New York" against elites who pursue "lifestyle diversification."[24] The experiences of working-class or ethnic-racial queers are beyond his notice or interest. Harvey's failing is a too-common error for some, but not all, members of a recalcitrant, unreconstructed North American left. The rejection of queer and feminist politics represented by Harvey and other reductive left thinkers is a deviation away from the Frankfurt School's interest in the transformative force of *eros* and its implicit relationship to political desire. The failings and limits of commentators such as Harvey have certainly made queer and utopian thinkers alike wary of left thought. Thus, I suggest a turn to previous modes of Marxian philosophy, such as the work of Marcuse or Bloch. The point is not to succumb to the phobic panic that muddles left thinking or to unimaginative invocations of the rationalism cited by neoliberal gays and lesbians. The point is once again to pull from the past, the no-longer-conscious, described and represented by Bloch today, to push beyond the impasse of the present.

I swerve away from my critique of the failures of imagination in the LGBT activist enterprises to Harvey for a very specific purpose. Harvey represented a fairly more expansive and nuanced critique in his previous work on postmodernity, writing that was thoughtfully critiqued by queer theorists such as Judith Halberstam.[25] But Harvey's work has become, like that of many Marxist scholars, all too ready to dismiss or sacrifice questions of sexuality and gender. Furthermore, these mostly white writers have, as in the example I cited in the preceding paragraph, been quick to posit race and class as real antagonisms within a larger socioeconomic struggle and sexuality and gender as merely "lifestyle diversification." In many ways they are performing a function that is the direct opposite of white neoliberal queers who studiously avoid the question of ethnic, racial, class, ability, or gender difference. This correspondence is representative of a larger political impasse that I understand as being the toll of pragmatic politics and antiutopian thought.

Concrete utopias remake rationalism, unlinking it from the provincial and pragmatic politics of the present. Taking back a rationalist core, in the way in which Bloch suggests we do in relation to romanticism, is to insist on an ordering of life that is not dictated by the spatial/temporal coordinates of straight time, a time and space matrix in which, unfortunately, far too many gays, lesbians, and other purportedly "queer" people reside.

To see queerness as horizon is to perceive it as a modality of ecstatic time in which the temporal stranglehold that I describe as straight time is interrupted or stepped out of. Ecstatic time is signaled at the moment one feels ecstasy, announced perhaps in a scream or grunt of pleasure, and more importantly during moments of contemplation when one looks back at a scene from one's past, present, or future. Opening oneself up to such a perception of queerness as manifestation in and of ecstatic time offers queers much more than the meager offerings of pragmatic gay and lesbian politics. Seeing queerness as horizon rescues and emboldens concepts such as freedom that have been withered by the touch of neoliberal thought and gay assimilationist politics. Pragmatic gay politics present themselves as rational and ultimately more doable. Such politics and their proponents often attempt to describe themselves as not being ideological, yet they are extremely ideological and, more precisely, are representative of a decayed ideological institution known as marriage. Rationalism need not be given over to gay neoliberals who attempt to sell a cheapened and degraded version of freedom. The freedom that is offered by an LGBT position that does not bend to straight time's gravitational pull is akin to one of Heidegger's descriptions of freedom as unboundness. And more often than not the "rhetorical" deployment of the pragmatic leads to a *not-doing*, an anti-performativity. Doing, performing, engaging the performative as force of and for futurity is queerness's bent and ideally the way to queerness.[26]

Notes

1   Third World Gay Revolution, "Manifesto of the Third World Gay Revolution," in *Out of the Closets: Voices of Gay Liberation*, ed. Karla Jay and Allen Young (New York: New York University Press, 1992), 367.

2   Evan Wolfson, "All Together Now (A Blueprint for the Movement)," *Advocate*, September 11, 2001; available online at http://www.freedomtomarry.org/evan_wolfson/by/all_together_now.php (accessed February 6, 2009).

3   See Lisa Duggan, "Holy Matrimony!" *Nation*, March 15, 2004, available online at http://www.thenation.com/doc/20040315/duggan; and Lisa Duggan and Richard Kim, "Beyond Gay Marriage," *Nation*, July 18, 2005, available online at http://www.thenation.com/doc/20050718/kim.

4   Giorgio Agamben, *Potentialities: Collected Essays in Philosophy*, ed. and trans. Daniel Heller-Roazen (Stanford, CA: Stanford University Press, 1999).

5   Alain Badiou, *Being and Event* (London: Continuum, 2005).

6   Ernst Bloch, *The Principle of Hope*, trans. Neville Plaice, Stephen Plaice, and Paul Knight, 3 vols. (Cambridge, MA: MIT Press, 1995).

7   Here I draw from Judith Halberstam's notion of time and normativity that she mines from a critique of David Harvey. I see her alerting us to a normative straight temporality that underscores heterosexual and heteronormative life and constructs straight space. My notion of time or critique

of a certain modality of time is interested in the way in which a queer utopian hermeneutic wishes to interrupt the linear temporal ordering of past, present, and future. See Judith Halberstam, *In a Queer Time and Place: Transgender Bodies, Subcultural Lives* (New York: New York University Press, 2005).

8 Lee Edelman, *No Future: Queer Theory and the Death Drive* (Durham, NC: Duke University Press, 2004).

9 Edmund Husserl, *Ideas Pertaining to a Pure Phenomenology and to a Phenomenological Philosophy*, trans. R. Rojcewicz (New York: Springer, 1991).

10 Roland Barthes, *Sade, Fourier, Loyola* (New York: Hill and Wang, 1976), 23.

11 James Schuyler, *Collected Poems* (New York: Farrar, Straus and Giroux, 1993), 186–187.

12 Martin Heidegger, *Being and Time*, trans. Joan Stambaugh (Albany: State University of New York Press, 1996), 329.

13 Fredric Jameson, *Archaeologies of the Future: The Desire Called Utopia and Other Science Fictions* (New York: Verso, 2005), 10.

14 J. L. Austin, *How to Do Things with Words* (Cambridge, MA: Harvard University Press, 1962).

15 Fredric Jameson, *The Political Unconscious: Narrative as a Socially Symbolic Act* (Ithaca, NY: Cornell University Press, 1981).

16 Bloch, *Principle of Hope*, 1:141.

17 Ibid.

18 Fredric Jameson, *Marxism and Form: Twentieth-Century Dialectical Theories of Literature* (Princeton, NJ: Princeton University Press, 1972).

19 Terrence Kissack, "Freaking Fag Revolutionaries: New York's Gay Liberation Front, 1969–1971," *Radical History Review* 62 (1995): 104–135.

20 This economical summary is drawn from Michael Inwood's useful book: Michael Inwood, *Heidegger: A Very Short Introduction* (Oxford: Oxford University Press, 2000), 121.

21 Herbert Marcuse, *One-Dimensional Man: Studies in the Ideology of Advanced Industrial Society* (Boston: Beacon, 1964), 17.

22 Lisa Duggan, *The Twilight of Equality? Neoliberalism, Cultural Politics, and the Attack on Democracy* (Boston: Beacon, 2003).

23 David Harvey, *A Brief History of Neo-Liberalism* (Oxford: Oxford University Press, 2005).

24 Ibid, 46–47.

25 Halberstam, *In a Queer Time and Place*.

26 This chapter benefited from Fred Moten's thoughtful suggestions and generous attention. I am also grateful for excellent feedback from Joshua Chambers-Letson, Lisa Duggan, Anna McCarthy, Tavia Nyong'o, Shane Vogel, an audience at the University of California, Santa Cruz, and this volume's editors. John Andrews offered me the gift of extremely generative conversations during the writing of this essay. I only partially acknowledge my gratitude by dedicating it to him.

CHAPTER 14

Theory in Practice
Queer Lear: A Gender Reading of King Lear

Michael Ryan

Michael Ryan teaches in the Department of Film and Media Arts at Temple University. His books include *Marxism and Deconstruction* (1982), *Camera Politica* (1988), and *The Human Animal: How Science Explains Politics* (Academica.edu). In this essay, he explores the possibility that the initial presentation of *King Lear* on St. Stephen's Night, 1606, at the court of King James, means that the play was intended to flatter the queer king. The play's gender dynamics can be interpreted as slyly alluding to queer themes.

King Lear was first presented at King James's court on St. Stephen's night, 1606. King James had been monarch of England since 1603, when he arrived from Scotland upon the death of his predecessor, Queen Elizabeth I. He was a controversial figure at the time the play was staged for his entertainment. He brought with him from Scotland assumptions about the distribution of power between monarch and people that were throwbacks to an earlier feudal political culture. He lived in a plain Christian way that shocked an English court used to a refined style of speech and gentility of behavior. His court consumed twice as much as that of his predecessor, prompting a fight with Parliament, which was paying the bills. And he was openly queer. He lived apart from his wife and child and lavished gifts – including Sir Walter Raleigh's last estate – on his young male lovers. Alan Bray's *Homosexuality in Renaissance England* cites one contemporary account, the *Memoirs* of Lucy Hutchinson, which describes James's court as full of "fools and bawds, mimics and catamites" who engaged in "debaucheries." "Mimics" is a word for actors and "catamites" a contemporary term for queers. The London theater was, like James's court, a locus of the queer subculture of early seventeenth-century England. Parents were afraid to see their sons become involved with the institution for fear they might be "corrupted." Given that *King Lear* was performed by a queer acting troupe at a queer court, it is possible that the play inscribes within itself a link between these two queer subcultural sites. If so, then those moments in the play that might be interpreted as making sly queer allusions – the Fool's remark that one should

Reproduced by permission of the author.

Literary Theory: An Anthology, Third Edition. Edited by Julie Rivkin and Michael Ryan.
© 2017 John Wiley & Sons, Ltd. Published 2017 by John Wiley & Sons, Ltd.

not trust "a boy's love," which was so controversial it was excised from the Folio edition – take on an additional significance. Indeed, we will argue the play is something of a queer Valentine's Day card from William Shakespeare to King James I.

What might one expect of a play written and acted by a queer theater company for presentation to an audience of drunk queers? Perhaps a play with touching scenes of male love, a fair amount of ribald queer humor, plenty of crowd-pleasing bashing of heterosexuality, some mockingly campy excessive gender behavior, and expressions of skepticism regarding the easy installation of gender traits such as masculinity and femininity in biologically male or female bodies. But how do we know that Shakespeare would even have wanted to please King James rather than slyly subvert his controversial political positions that seemed to trample on traditional English "liberties"?

It can be argued that the play endorses James's political worldview in a rather flattering way. When James assumed the throne, he brought with him arcane feudal ideas about the right of kings to rule their lands autocratically. He compared his rule to that of God over his human family, and he expected as much reverence and obedience from his people. But this feudal idea was out of step with the emerging economic and social reality in England, a land in which a new merchant class was displacing the old nobility. The merchants insisted on a role in governing the country through Parliament. They felt the king should not have absolute power. They argued with James over prerogative (who should make laws) and sustenance (who should pay to support the king's court). Lear is initially portrayed as a representative of a feudal order whose assumptions would have been pleasing to the new king of England. Lear uses words like "recreant" and "vassal" that identify him as feudal, and he expects his daughters to play by feudal rules of fealty and duty. His tragedy is that they, like the parliamentarians, have stopped doing so. His successor – Edgar – is opposed by an illegitimate pretender with characteristics that evoke the new capitalist class. He wishes to prosper and rise, and he rejects feudal customs. That all the characters associated with the breach of feudal norms and with the values of the new capitalist class are killed suggests that the play is fairly straightforward in its political allegiance. It sides with James against the parliamentarians.

But *King Lear* also engages in more strikingly personal forms of flattery towards the new king. James was a rash and imperious ruler who was given to delivering intemperate, oath-filled lectures to Parliament when they did not meet his wishes or provide monies to support a court lifestyle that cost twice what it had under Elizabeth. The king also had difficulties with the people he ruled. His right to demand housing and food for himself and his numerous notoriously ill-mannered retainers while making his rounds of the country in pursuit of the hunt, something he preferred to sitting at court in London, provoked complaints. One day, one of his favorite hunting hounds disappeared and returned with a note around his neck begging the king to depart, since he and his followers were eating up the countryside: "[I]t will please his Majestie to go back to London … all our provision is spent already and we are not able to entertain him longer."

The parallels with *Lear* scarcely need underscoring. It is a play about rebellion against a king that hinges on a denial of hospitality. Lear assumes that those who owe him "service" will provide food and shelter to his retinue of knights and courtiers, who are given to "pranks," debauchery, and drink. The negative characters in the play refer to them as a "disordered rabble" that make "servants of their betters." James was well known to dislike the duties of office, and Lear's first act in the play is to divest himself of the "cares of state" in order to go hunting, James's favorite diversion. The religious James valued the Christian ideal of "plain" speech that imitated Christ's simple parables, and the play privileges such speech in the character of Kent as well as, ultimately, in Lear himself ("I am a very foolish, fond old man / ... And, to deal plainly"). James himself resembled Kent, who like James swears a great deal and shuns pomp, and like Kent, who cares little what people think of his bad manners, James was blunt rather than politic. His disgruntled behavior during his extravagant welcoming procession in 1603 was so obvious it offended his new subjects.

The shift in the play from an initial language of flattery, circumlocution, and courtly elegance to one of simple Christian plainness by the end can be seen as a figural rendering of the changes James brought about in Elizabethan court culture. In keeping with the Christian ideal of plainness, he dressed simply and saw an absence of Christian virtue in those who dressed luxuriously. He disliked the extravagant dress of the likes of Raleigh and kept his clothes until they were completely worn out, a practice which seems to be echoed in Lear's own disregard for dress when he is on the heath. Of all the meanings of Lear's gesture of undressing, one is the rejection of the Elizabethan court style, with its emphasis on external appearances as opposed to the inner Christian virtues James favored. James's intemperateness as well as his penchant for oaths also seem to be echoed in Lear's behavior and in his oath-filled speeches with their references to classical mythology, a characteristic of James's own literary works. James loved "fooleries," and his court was the first English court and the last European one to have a Fool and was full of jokes and pranks, much like the court of Lear, in which a Fool plays a prominent role. Fond of masques and burlesques, James staged scenes with comic or moral effects of the kind Lear arranges for his daughters' mock trial. The daughters' behavior seems all the more reprehensible given Lear's generosity towards them, and indeed, James himself was caught in a similar dilemma: known for his extreme, indeed reckless, generosity, he also had trouble getting those responsible for his upkeep to cover his financial needs. Finally, James and his Scottish followers were looked upon by many in much the same way as Lear's followers are by Goneril: they sought to govern their "betters."

The link between Lear and James becomes more evident if one compares the play with *Basilikon Doron*, James's advice book to his son, an English-language version of which appeared shortly after he assumed power in 1603, and with his *Demonologie* (also 1603). In many respects, *Basilikon* provides both a thematic and linguistic dictionary for *King Lear*. Given the importance of the word "plain" and the value of plainness in the play, it is important that James's book begins with a sonnet that argues that kings should "Reward the just, be stedfast, true, and plaine." James returns to the virtue of plainness on numerous occasions ("be plaine and truthful") and contrasts it with "the filthy vice of Flattery, the pest of all Princes." It is as if he has Lear himself in mind when he counsels his son to "love them best, that are plainest with you, and disguise not the trueth for all their kinne." In Act 2, Scene 2, Kent confronts Cornwall and announces: "Sir, 'tis my occupation to be plain." He mocks ornate and elaborate speech: "Sir, in good sooth, in sincere verity, / Under the allowance of your great aspect, / Whose influence, like the wreath of radiant fire, / On flickering Phoebus' front." Cornwall complains of Kent's plain speaking: "He cannot flatter, he, / An honest mind and plain, he must speak the truth!" One can hear a welcoming chuckle from the loyal James's supporters in the court audience for the play on St. Stephen's Night. They would no doubt have gotten the anti-Elizabethan joke.

Plainness is a necessary virtue of a good monarch, according to James, as is control over sexual appetites, something Kent and Edgar demonstrate positively, and Goneril and Regan negatively. James writes: "[H]e cannot be thought worthie to rule and command others, that cannot rule … his owne proper affections and unreasonable appetites." James, in terms that echo the sexual advice Edgar delivers to Lear, tells his son to "abstain from fornication" and to avoid "the filthy vice of adultery," and warns of women who use "their painted preened fashion, [to] serve for baites to filthie lecherie." As if he were counseling Goneril, who places private interest over national security ("I had rather lose the battle than that sister / Should loosen him and me"), James says the king should subject "his owne private affections and appetites to the weale and standing of his subiectes, ever thinking the common interesse his cheefest particulare." He uses the same terms Shakespeare uses to characterize Cordelia (who "was a queen over her passion") when he promotes Temperance which "shall as a Queene, command all the affections and passion." Shakespeare also seems to have James in mind when he has Lear take note of poverty and advocate charity on the part of wealthy nobles: "O, I have ta'en / Too little care of this! Take physic, pomp; / Expose thyself to feel what wretches feel, / That thou mayst shake the superflux to them / And show the heavens more just." James advises his son to "embrace the quarrel of the poore and distressed … care for the pleasure of none, neither spare ye any paines in your own person, to see their wrongs redressed." Finally, James condemns disobedience of parents in terms ("a thing monstrous," "unnatural") that echo the play: "I had rather not be a Father, and childlesse, then be a Father of wicked children." Lear gives vent to a similar feeling when he says he "would divorce me from thy mother's tomb, / Sepulch'ring an adult'ress." Like Shakespeare, James refers to parental authority and filial loyalty as the "order of nature" and characterizes writing against parents as an "unpardonable crime."

In *Demonologie*, James describes the power of devils to "transport from one place to another a solid body" and speaks in the same passage of the possibility of falling "from an high and stay rock." One is reminded, of course, of Edgar and Gloucester at Dover, where Edgar speaks of a "fiend" standing next to Gloucester before his mock fall. The "foul fiend" is an imaginary symptom of Edgar's feigned madness, but the fiend also represents disobedience and the danger of broken contracts: "Take heed o' the foul fiend. Obey thy parents; keep thy word's justice." The first mention of the fiend coincides with Lear's banishment by his daughters. Later in the play, the associations are more ominously demonic. "See thyself, devil," Albany says to Goneril. "Proper deformity shows not in the fiend / So horrid as in woman." In *Demonologie*, James is particularly critical of women who are prone to become witches and succumb to the "greedy desire" for power or for "worldly riches … their whole practices are either to hurt men and their goods." Shakespeare, in his depiction of Goneril and Regan, would seem to agree.

Shakespeare uses the character of Lear to ingratiate himself with the new ruler of the land in which he did business. James himself had brought a gift of cloth for the playwright upon his ascension to the throne, and Shakespeare seems to return the favor in this play by painting a flattering portrait of a tragic king whose resemblance to James would easily have been clear to those in the audience at court on St. Stephen's Night, 1606. But Shakespeare might also be said to take the king's side in a number of quarrels in which he was engaged and thereby to help further royal power at a time when it was vigorously debated in England. Perhaps the most significant of those disputes concerned the character of monarchical rule itself, whether it should be absolute or limited by law and by Parliament.

In *The True Lawe of Free Monarchies* (1598), James, still king of Scotland at the time, makes a statement that would not sit well in England, the land over which he would become king five years later. Arguing that kings rule at God's behest and therefore are deserving of absolute obedience, he writes: "the King is above the Law.… And therefore general lawes, made publikly in Parlamente, may uppon knowne respects to the King by his authoritie be mittigated, and suspended upon causes onely knowne to him." To the English, who had fought hard to secure their liberties against monarchical power of just this kind and who believed in the sanctity of the common law tradition, that well of legal precedents that was binding on all, including the king, such statements were troubling, if not alarming. The future Chief Justice of Common Pleas, Edward Coke, was especially disturbed. In 1607 he would advise Parliament: "There is a maxim. The common law hath admeasured the King's prerogative." James, in Coke's eyes and in those of many other Englishmen, was wrong.

In an encounter famous in legal history for establishing the superiority of law to political power, Coke entered into a direct argument with James concerning Fuller's Case, which concerned the rights of dissident Puritans. James's loyalists, who felt that judges were "delegates" of the king and therefore that the king was the ultimate judge in all matters, wanted to force the Puritans to testify under an inquisitorial oath that deprived them of their common law rights. As Chief Justice of the Common Pleas Court that fought for jurisdiction with the loyalists' Ecclesiastical High Commission regarding the judgment of lay matters, Coke disagreed, and the issue came before James. When the loyalists claimed that the ultimate decision lay with the king, Coke replied: "The King cannot take any cause out of any of his courts and give judgment upon it himself." James accused Coke of speaking foolishly and said he reserved the power to decide jurisdictional issues, adding that he "would ever protect the common law." Coke responded: "The common law protecteth the King." At this point, James accused him of treason. "The King protecteth the law, and not the law the King," he declared. To which Coke replied "The King should not be under man, but under God and the Laws." He nevertheless flung himself at the king's feet and seemed to submit. But the next week he commenced once again to issue rulings at odds with the Commission.

I recount this anecdote to give a sense of what the discursive ambience was at the time *Lear* was written. The topics of monarchical power and judicial authority were publicly discussed and debated. The limits of monarchical power were at stake, and the conflict between king and Parliament would eventually lead to civil war and the overthrow of the monarchy in mid-century. James's *True Lawe* is an argument against such rebellion. James begins by warning his audience of just how abusive monarchical rule can be. The monarch will, James warns, quoting the book of Samuel, take your sons and make them servants, take your daughters and make them "Cookes and Bakers," take your fields and give them to his servants, "take the tenth of your seede ... and give it to his Eunuches," and "all that ye possess shall serve his private use and inordinate appetite." He concludes "and ye shall be his servants." If one weren't aware that one was reading a work by a reigning monarch, one might at this point think that the author was Guy Fawkes himself trying to raise a following. It suggests that kings do abuse their power, and it quite accurately and vividly describes those abuses.

Yet by quoting scripture, James places the question of monarchical rule within the frame of the paradoxical parables of the Bible, parables whose very incomprehensibility serves to reinforce God's ultimate authority, his transcendence of mere worldly logic. "Yet it shall not be lawful to you to cast it off," James argues of monarchy, because absolute rule is "the ordinance of God" and "your selves have chosen him unto you, thereby renouncing for ever all privileges, by your willing consent," especially that one which would allow people to "call backe unto your selves againe that power" given to the king. In other words, despite all the great abuses of monarchical power that have just been so vividly depicted, you will have to put up with it. As in biblical parables in general, which argue that one has to learn to accept rough treatment at the hands of God since it is for one's own good, one must, according to James, also put up with abusive kings, because the king is a step down from God. Hence, he has the loyal people say to Samuel: "Al your speeches and hard conditions shal not skarre us, but we wil take the good and evill of it upon us, and we will be content to bear whatsoever burthen it shall please our King to lay upon us." If the king is bad, God will judge him – but no one else shall. He has the "power to judge [his people] but to be judged only by God."

The king, for James, is like a father in a family. If the people must fear the king "as their judge," they must love him "as their father." To displace the king through rebellion is to invert "the order of all law and reason," so that "the commanded may be made to command their commander, the judged to judge their Judge, and they that are governed to governe their time about their lord & governer." Obedience is the "duty his children owe to" a father, and hence also to a king. It would be "monstrous and unnatural to his sons to rise up against" either father or king. Fittingly, rebels who claim a higher allegiance to the commonwealth, "as to a Mother," are condemned. James concludes the text by denouncing what he twice, using language echoed in *Lear*, refers to as "monstrous and unnatural rebellions" against an absolute monarch. It is wrong for one party to break a contract "except that first a lawful trial and cognition be had by the ordinary judge of the breakers thereof."

What *Lear* depicts is in many ways what James describes and denounces – a "monstrous" and "unnatural" rebellion against both paternal and monarchical power. The play literalizes James's metaphors. Lear is both father and king; the rebels are his daughters. They invert the right order of government when they "command the commander" and refuse him "the duty his children owe to him." They enter into a contract – land in exchange for love and hospitality – and break it unilaterally. Regan's language of rebellion recalls the legal language of arguments in favor of parliamentary prerogative: "In my right, / By me invested, he compeers the best."

It is as if Shakespeare had James's concluding argument in mind when he has Lear summon his daughters forth for an imaginary trial, which enacts the lawful reinstatement of the appropriate judge so that "cognition" can be taken of "the breakers." If Shakespeare would seem to take James's part in his argument with Parliament, he also seems, especially in the trial scene, to take his side in his debate with the common law judges, especially Coke. "You are o' the commission; / Sit you too," Lear tells Kent. This is not the first reference in the play to the Ecclesiastical Commission that supported James's claim to absolute authority over the common law judges. Already in Act 3, Scene 2, Lear speaks favorably of "These dreadful summoners," a reference to the police or summoners who served warrants for the Ecclesiastical Commission or court. Given James's antipathy to the common law judges, it is probably of some significance that the trial scene concludes with Lear's cry "Corruption in the place! / False justicer!"

But what are we to make of Lear's vision of a judge and a thief as interchangeable and of his provocative suggestion that judges favor the wealthy over the poor? It is one of the most subversive statements in the play. Yet like the mock trial scene, it is framed by an implicit pledge of allegiance to James's absolutist position regarding the superiority of monarchical power to the common law. Coke was one judge who had become quite wealthy while in office, and justices of the peace, upholders of the common law, were great obstructers of the poor relief James advocated. The 1590s were a time of harvest failures and of famine. As a result of the enclosure of common land for the sake of more profitable pasturing, more and more farm laborers turned to vagrancy, giving rise to laws regarding poor relief and charity. James was a promoter of charity, and the Statute of 1604 was meant to provide such relief on a more uniform basis. Its implementation was overseen by his Privy Council, but it met with a resistant negligence on the part of justices of the peace, who were in charge of tax collecting and the enforcement of statutes on the local level, even when prodded "by extraordinary directions derived from the prerogative power of his Majesty by proclamations, letters, and commission." Perhaps this is why one of the most sympathetic characters in the play, Edgar as Tom, mentions charity twice: "Do poor Tom some charity ... The country gives me proof and precedent / Of Bedlam beggars who with roaring voices / ... Enforce their charity."

Other seemingly subversive statements by Lear can be interpreted in a similar manner as pleas for James's positions. When Lear speaks of "the great image of authority; / A dog's obeyed in office," he refers not to the king, whose position as a divinely ordained ruler was above "office," but rather to the holders of political office – the parliamentarians – who circumvented the king's wishes. And the "Robes and furred gowns" that "hide all" vices in the following lines refer to the Elizabethan courtiers, like Raleigh, who James loathed. If Shakespeare is critical of judges and of justices in a way that echoes James's absolutist positions, the one positive reference to justices in the play also endorses James's position regarding the superiority of divine and monarchial justice to common law human justice. Of the quick death of Cornwall after Gloucester's blinding, Albany says: "This shows you are above, / You justicers, that these our nether crimes / So speedily can venge!" Heavenly not earthly judges are the guardians of justice in the play. The rebels are also subject to "the judgement of the heavens, that makes us tremble." "The gods are just," Edgar remarks, after having vanquished Edmund and set right the kingdom. He is presented as an instrument of divine justice, while also evincing a natural royalty. The force of someone endowed with royal power ("thy very gait did prophesy / A royal nobleness") is needed because legal measures are subject to the contingencies of broken agreements and the failure of judges. "[T]he laws are mine, not thine," Goneril claims defiantly, "Who can arraign me for 't?" A divine judge, James might respond, and in his place, a king or would-be king like Edgar. The play thus endorses James's position that the right order of justice moves from God to king to judge. Human law is subject to divine law as represented in the king.

The critique of justice and of judges in the play legitimates absolute monarchical rule by warning of its abuses in order better to plead for its divinely ordained necessity. "[W]e will resign to him, / ... our absolute power," Albany says of Lear at the end. Rather than directly advocate such power, however, the play enacts a subversive vision of inversion and disorder whose ultimate purpose is to reinforce the need for that which is overturned and to further James's argument in favor of absolute monarchial power. Initially, monarchical rule is presented negatively. Lear rules in an abusive manner. In a single scene, he banishes his favorite courtier and deprives his favorite daughter of her dowry. He is intolerant of dissent and commands absolute obedience. His behavior seems "rash," but it is also typical of how kings should be allowed to behave, according to James, and still, like a father, command obedience. Kent's and Cordelia's remarkable fidelity in the face of the king's abusive exercise of monarchical power would seem to reinforce this idea. Kings may be rash, the play argues, but we must, like Kent and Cordelia, obey them absolutely nonetheless. Even the infirmity and fury of a king, like that of a father, must, according to James, be "borne." Even as a madman, Lear is told, somewhat illogically and paradoxically, "You are a royal one, and we obey you."

Shakespeare in the characters of Lear and Kent clearly wanted to create a flattering portrait of the new king. Little surprise then that he also paints a flattering gender portrait of the queer monarch. The play begins on a homosocial note that very quickly veers into an at least jokingly queer suggestiveness. "I thought the King had more affected the Duke of Albany than Cornwall," Kent remarks, drawing attention to the relation between male affection and affairs of state. The remark hints at the rashness and indecisiveness in Lear that will result in the destruction of the state; like a woman – as she is coded in Renaissance culture – he will act on the basis more of emotion than reason. The intimation that a man might behave like a woman seems to evoke a further crossing of genders when Kent says to Gloucester "I cannot conceive you." He means he doesn't understand his male companion, but Gloucester picks up on the sexual meaning: "Sir, this young fellow's mother could; whereupon she grew round-wombed." The possible reference to sodomy, which likely provoked a burst of laughter in the queer court audience, is as quickly erased as it is evoked, and it is deflected into a heteronormative framework. That maneuver befits a culture dominated by the discourse and rituals of compulsory heterosexuality, which are enacted in the ensuing dowry scene, a culture that in its religion and its law was hostile to such homosexual acts as sodomy. As a result, homosexuality only appears in the play in glimpses whose fleetingness, like a pun, suggests repression as much as expression. One might even say that by evoking it in this opening dialogue, which is played out of view of the more public events that follow, Shakespeare is noting the behind the scenes or closeted quality of life in the queer subculture to which he, like James (they both lived apart from their wives in well-known queer sites), probably belonged.

The play depicts a crisis in heteronormativity, an institution centered on an ideal of male masculinity which finds an enabling and confirming other in female femininity. That social institution is depicted as dangerous to heterosexual men because women can refuse to confirm masculinity, assume masculine qualities themselves, and effeminize men. The play offers a cure for the failings of the heteronormative model in retraction into an all-male world from the troubled heterosexual sphere. In the mad scenes on the heath, a mock theater is created that offers therapy in the form of love between men, a love laced with queer allusiveness.

The play portrays heterosexuality as a weakness that has harmful effects on men. It makes men prone to incest and to the domination of women's lives for the sake of male vanity. "Better thou / Hadst not been born than not t'have pleased me better," Lear says to Cordelia in a line that is not meant to evoke sympathy from the audience. The incestuous character of his demands on his daughters is made evident when Cordelia points out that his desire for expressions of affection trespasses upon the rights of a husband. Later, he accuses his daughters of opposing "the bolt / Against my coming in." Heterosexuality is dangerous for men because it is founded on an instability: while it would seem to assure a man's identity as a masculine male, it leaves the man dependent on feminine women for certification. Rather than be an identity, heterosexuality consists of a relation or an exchange, whereby male masculinity is confirmed by its other, the feminine – submissive and passive – woman. It is what it is not. Cordelia's "Nothing" in response to Lear's demands for tokens of affection exemplifies this dilemma. At the limit where the heterosexual male and the heterosexual female meet, there is always a margin of error where something needed can be lacking, where a required repetition that confirms by recognizing fails to occur. As the Fool reminds Lear several times, without heterosexual confirmation, Lear himself is nothing – "an O without a figure." Which is to say, given the slang meaning of nothing (vagina), he resembles a passive woman.

If women are the soft spot of the heteronormative regime, its point of proof as well as of vulnerability, it is because the exchange relationship that characterizes that system is reversible. Men can be feminized by masculine women. In a world shaped by the dictates of heteronormativity, the feminization of men by women results in a depletion of personal power and social authority. If one cannot "command service" both as domestic and as sexual labor, one should not rule. In a world organized around aggressive relations between contending sites of male power – a fact emphasized in the play in references to possible strife between such players as Albany and Cornwall – the need to survive as masculine men dictates the subordination of weak characteristics such as tearful emotionality and the privileging of strong ones such as a capacity for martial combat. That these characteristics should be assumed in heteronormative culture to be distributed along biological gender lines is not surprising. What is innovative about the play is that it suggests that those characteristics may not be distributed along the lines of sexual object choice. Kent and Edgar, the strong masculine men who save the kingdom, apparently love men not women.

In the play, a dangerous and destructive feminization of men occurs when women assume traditionally masculine powers. This places the masculinity of men like Lear, who are dependent on confirmation by feminine women of their masculine identity under the heteronormative regime, in jeopardy. Their feminization is figured in the play as madness – a loss of the reason that distinguishes masculinity from emotional and bodily femininity. Within the Renaissance bodily code, Lear's loss of temper and rash actions based on momentary emotions are coded as female. Fittingly, in relinquishing his power to his daughters and thereby masculinizing them, he says that he will follow a "monthly course," a reference to menstruation. By entering the realm of uncontrolled bodily and emotional processes, he abandons the realm of principle, reason, and law – the realm assigned men in the play and in patriarchal culture generally. He breaks his quasi-legal agreement with Burgundy to provide land as dowry for Cordelia, and he subverts the principles of fairness and justice by depriving her of everything for nothing. The price he pays for behaving like a woman is to become a woman.

When his Fool speaks of him as "nothing," he adds a sexual spin to Lear's loss of power: "Thou hast pared thy wit o' both sides and left nothing i' the middle. Here comes one o' the parings." The use of "Nothing" for the thing in the middle (of Lear's legs) suggests that Lear will be obliged to adopt a "feminine" sexual posture of passivity to penetration, and indeed, Goneril, who assumes masculine phallic proportions as a result of the territory and power Lear attributes to her, makes him bend to her will in a manner that Albany characterizes in symbolically sexual terms when he says to Goneril: "How far your eyes may pierce I cannot tell." The Fool's preparation of the encounter between father and daughter is more explicitly sexual: "[T]hou mad'st thy daughters thy mothers ... thou gav'st them the rod and putt'st down thine own breeches." The image of punishment suggests the submissive sexual position and the feminization of the heterosexual man deprived of masculine power. He can now be had from behind by his phallic daughter's "rod." Earlier, the Fool had compared the division of Lear's kingdom to the breaking of an egg into two ends or crowns: "Why, after I have cut the egg i' th' middle and eat up the meat, the two crowns of the egg. When thou clovest thy crown i' th' middle and gav'st away both parts, thou bor'st thine ass on thy back o'er the dirt." "Ass" refers to servant ("Thy asses are gone about [getting your horses]," the Fool tells Lear at one point), and because servants were used sexually by their masters in Renaissance England (as suggested by the trial of the Earl of Castlehaven), the image, in addition to social inversion, also suggests the adoption of a submissive sexual posture in regard to someone more powerful, someone who would be quite literally on Lear's back. Something similar is implied by Lear's statement "Persuade me rather to be slave and sumpter / To this detested groom." A sumpter is a pack animal, but the term also carries the connotation of putting something (or someone) on one's back. That someone, of course, is Goneril, who now possesses the quality of firmness ("marble-hearted fiend") Lear lacks. When he wishes sterility upon her, he more or less completes her sex-change operation, and when she taunts her husband with "milky gentleness," she assumes masculine power in her own household. It is at this point in the play that the Fool's sexual taunts most concern castration and the loss of sexual power on Lear's part: "She ... / Shall not be a maid long, unless things be cut shorter." "I am ashamed," Lear says, "That thou hast power to shake my manhood thus." And he is described as suffering an "eyeless rage."

One consequence of the instability of heterosexuality in the play is a parallel structuring of relationships between men and women on one side and men and men on the other. The dangerously feminizing dependence inscribed in heterosexuality provokes a rejection of women, the agents of feminization, and a separation of the heroic male characters from the danger heterosexual women represent. As a result, the emotional needs and dependencies that leave a heterosexual male vulnerable to feminization within a heteronormative culture that proscribes "woman's tears" on a man's face and that mandates a more aggressive, emotionally sanitized martial posture towards the world in order to achieve heteronormative masculinity are transferred into the realm of explicitly homosocial and implicitly heterosexual male relations where feminine emotion in men is acceptable and masculinity is not endangered by dependence on unreliable and untrustworthy women. Lear, by virtue of a passage through healing male love, moves from pathological heterosexuality ("I have sworn. I am firm") to an acceptance of his own "infirmity." If emotional vulnerability is disallowed to men under the regime of heteronormative heterosexuality, it is permitted and even expected in love relations between men of the kind Edgar and Lear and Lear and Kent experience.

Edgar and Kent, the two characters most capable of masculine strength, are also those most associated with a healing queer autarchy in regard to women. Kent says he is "not so young ... to love a woman for singing, nor so old to dote on her for anything." Edgar repeatedly warns against heterosexual attachments. He articulates the play's critique of heterosexuality when as Tom, in speaking of having "served the lust of my mistress' heart," he equates heterosexuality with demonic possession by the "foul fiend." His and Kent's dislike of women offers the failed king a safe exit from heteronormativity by providing a queer model of masculinity that serves as a redemptive alternative to heterosexuality. Kent stands up to bullying by Goneril and Regan, while Edgar's decisive capacity for martial violence against Edmund distinguishes his masculinity from that of the effeminized old king, who in one crucial moment is incapable of saying what violence he will wreak on his daughters: "I will have such revenges on you both / That all the world shall – I will do such things – / What they are yet I know not." In Edgar and Kent, Shakespeare offers figures of queer masculinity that counteract the harmful effects of women on heterosexual men in the play.

If the phallic woman feminizes Lear, deprives him of power, and transforms him into a sexual servant, Lear discovers in Kent someone who subordinates himself to Lear in both a political and a sexual manner. "What wouldst thou?" Lear asks him. "Service," Kent replies. "Service" has throughout the play the dual meaning of obedient labor

("The dear father ... commands ... service") and sexual labor ("one that wouldst be a bawd in way of good service," "To thee a woman's services are due"). In queer love relations, the feminized heterosexual male can be repositioned in a dominant masculine posture if he receives "service" from another male. While such plays on words like "service" seem less obvious to us now, in court on St. Stephen's Night, 1606, they would have been quite clear to the queers in the audience, including King James himself. Indeed, such a pun provides a perfect metaphor for the closet in which those queers lived – an obvious meaning and a hidden meaning, one straight, one queer, that would have perfectly summed up their experience of the world.

Edgar is the character who is most representative of a queer masculinity that heals Lear and the state (much as James imagined himself healing an England harmed by his female predecessor, the Goneril-like man-woman Elizabeth I). Like Kent, Edgar is markedly non-heterosexual; he doesn't even talk about women, at least while sane, and while insane, all he talks about is why one should avoid them. Lear learns from him not to trust women in the way that he has up to that point. Edgar also offers the king the possibility of being placed in a subordinate feminine sexual position without suffering humiliation. Edgar undergoes with Lear an experience of liquefaction that is a metaphor for queer intercourse. He and Lear are naked in the rain together, and when Lear sheds his clothes and joins Edgar in nakedness (save for Edgar's blanket), the visual display evokes a queer public sex encounter, as does Edgar's vocabulary of possession, which at the time was associated with sodomy. "Sodomites" or queers were often linked to witches, were-people, and evil spells, and Edgar's mad speeches are full of such allusions: "Flibbertigibbet ... squinnies the eye and makes the harelip ... aroint thee, witch." Lear immediately develops an affectionate attachment to the "learned Theban" and will not let him go. His characterization of Edgar as an "Athenian" slyly situates their encounter within the homoerotic Greek tradition of master and pupil, and indeed, Lear adopts a student's posture towards the younger man, a posture in keeping with the prevailing image of homosexuality at the time as a relationship between an older man and a younger one or "Ganymede." That James's lovers all were quite young would have made the allusion all the more visible and appealing to the court audience.

Water is also a metaphor for the dissolving of masculine heterosexual identity by women and for the overwhelming of reason by eyeless emotion. That a figure like water with two quite opposed meanings might exist at the heart of the play is to be expected, since identity forms itself out of undifferentiated matter, and the play depicts a loss of identity and a return to matter (humankind's bare forked animal condition). To lose the "additions" that make one a king is to fall back into that state of undifferentiated nothing in which social identity dissolves and masculinity and femininity merge. It is a fitting condition for Lear, who has lost his masculine heterosexual identity and been feminized by masculine women. But water also suggests the progressive instability and fluidity of gender, as does the metaphor of theatricality and role-playing. Edgar's acting suggests his malleability and the possibility of a change in identity. In a similar way, all Lear has to do is take off his clothes, allow himself to be soaked, and he is transformed from mad emasculated hetero to gayly happy homo. From dissolution a new identity can be formed, and Lear's new identity is, like Edgar's, a queer one. He can now be as feminine as he wants with his beloved "Athenian." No one will stigmatize or punish him. He is with people who love him, and they are all men. The free-floating, contingent, and theatrical quality of gender becomes a resource for redemption.

Nevertheless, in the end, Lear is repositioned in relation to a woman, Cordelia. Does the play evoke queerness only to abandon it? Does it succumb to closeting in the end in ultimate deference to heterosexual norms?

That Cordelia is a part played by a boy actor and that her character forms a continuum with a healing homosocial male companion – the Fool – suggests how cannily Shakespeare inserts a queer subtext into this play, one that would have allowed the court audience to see a literal story of queer love while nevertheless respecting the rules of heteronormativity by endorsing the theatrical convention and the mimetic illusion that a boy is a woman. With Kent and Edgar, the Fool is a figure suggestive of homosexuality who was likely played by a boy. Called a "pretty knave" upon entering, he is a male correlate of Cordelia, who is referred to later as Lear's "fool": "And my poor fool is hanged." It is possible, since the Fool and Cordelia do not appear in the same scenes and since the disappearance of the Fool from the play is the play's one structural flaw, that the same boy actor played both roles. Both are romanticized figures of affection untainted by expediency, another quality that suggests continuity between them. The Fool remains loyal to Lear when it is foolish to do so, even in his own cynical terms. And Cordelia accepts loss for the king's gain, even after he has imposed great losses on her. Their generosity recalls James's own reckless generosity towards those he loved. The two characters represent a gift economy at odds with the harsh exchange economy of the parliamentarians who were hounding James over the high cost of his court, an exchange economy present in the opening act of the play, when Lear demands a return for his investment in his daughters. In one sense, Lear's tragedy is that he becomes too like the parliamentarians, and he is saved by the very James-like gift-giving generosity of the Fool and of Cordelia.

The continuity between the Fool and Cordelia suggests some of the complexity of queer experience at the time as well as its closeted character, while also embodying the difficult representational strategies Shakespeare was obliged to adopt in telling his queer story. A play about the benefits of homosexuality in a queer-repressive heteronormative culture must necessarily try to have it both ways – displaying yet hiding – while having it neither way in the pure form. Its queer argument is necessarily oblique and double-voiced, a mix of metaphor and literal image. Cordelia in death metaphorically fulfills Lear's sexual desires (that they die in each other's arms should at least evoke the possibility of the Renaissance coding of death as sex). But literally, of course, on St. Stephen's Night, she would have been a boy dressed as a woman in the arms of an older man, a visual signal the queer king and his young queer lover would have had to be blind not to notice.

Despite its closeted quality, the play's ending is noteworthy for its emotionality. In contrast to their earlier fear of taint by women's tears, the men seem to cry in abundance. Their hearts burst asunder, and their love for each other is manifest. Lear's "I am firm" no longer seems to have a place. The pathological masculinity he initially represents is now replaced by a new gender identity that includes femininity. If women have been like men in the play, men now become like women, and no one seems to mind. Culturally certified traits shuttle back and forth. The play is at its most gender-radical when it seems to suggest that those traits have no biological home in physical gender. Lear's transformation from hyper-hetero male at the outset to infirm, emotionally vulnerable femme queer by the end is a way of insisting that gender has no bio-ontology. Masculinity is not the exclusive province of men, nor is femininity exclusive to women.

King Lear concludes on a note of aristocratic queer romanticism ("Speak what we feel, not what we ought to say") that privileges dissonant subjectivity over social convention, the pride of the closet over the mandates of compulsory heterosexuality. It does so, I would argue, because Shakespeare himself no doubt experienced the play's equivocal subject position, which is inwardly queer and outwardly straight. As we know James to have been queer yet married, we know Edgar to love men, yet he must, like James, stand up in a public forum at the end of the play and pretend to submit to the customs and assumptions of heteronormativity. That no sign of that mandate is evident (no woman is present in the final scene) suggests just how grudgingly it is accepted. But it is there nonetheless, inscribed in the anti-sodomy laws and in the religious culture that could not tolerate queer coupling. Only in such enclaves as the theater and the court was a queer subculture possible because only under assumed roles or with the permission of the king could men act out their love for one other. The hovel – hidden and out of view – to which the Edgar and Lear retreat is the appropriate spatial metaphor for that closeted condition, just as madness provides the hidden language of queers in the play, a way for queer love to speak itself without censorship or judgment. That James's queer court was known for staging plays like *Lear* says something about the necessary theatricality of queerness at the time, that it had to be enacted under the guise of madness, role-playing, and boy-to-woman drag. The real tragedy of *Lear* is that of the queer who must live out the forms of heteronormativity, acting all the time, while yet experiencing feelings that must remain silent.

That straight-passing was so mandatory in so closeted a culture allows us to understand the double-voiced character of the play. Ostensibly a tragedy about a king who is mistreated by women, it is also a coded message to King James on St. Stephen's Night, 1606, expressing sympathy for the drubbing James was taking from the English Parliament regarding sustenance and expressing – what shall we call it? – queer love for the beset monarch in troubled times. Lear's crown at the end prominently contains darnel weed, which evokes the Darnel of the house of Tudor, James's family, as well as the name of James's queer father, Lord Darnel. Darnel blossoms are red and white. It is as if Shakespeare, in the final image of the sadly mad yet beloved king, were sending the beset king and fellow queer a Valentine or a Get Well card in the form of a play that to the audience at court on St. Stephen's Night would have seemed riotously funny, emotionally evocative, and slyly queer. Cheer up, James. Things could be worse. Mwah! Love you, Will.

CHAPTER 15

Theory in Practice
Elizabeth Bishop's "Queer Birds": Vassar, Con Spirito, and the Romance of Female Community

Betheny Hicok

Bethany Hicok is the author of *Elizabeth Bishop's Brazil* (2016) and *Degrees of Freedom: American Women Poets and the Women's College, 1905–1955* (2008). A professor of English at Westminster College, she teaches courses in modern poetry, modernism, critical theory, gender studies, and interdisciplinary studies focusing on genetics and literature, utopias, and Ancient Greek ideas of justice.

"We demand nothing but fresh conception." Thus began the manifesto of *Con Spirito*, the rebel literary magazine Elizabeth Bishop and some of her fellow students started at Vassar in February 1933. "Frankly we are more interested in experimental than in traditional writing," they continued on the front page of their first issue. "Anything – politics, science, art, music, philosophy – anything that is spontaneous, that is lively" (Editorial 1). Bishop's co-conspirators were an impressive group of women, including Mary McCarthy, Eleanor and Eunice Clark, Frani Blough, Margaret Miller, and probably Muriel Rukeyser.[1] According to McCarthy, Bishop had come up with the name *Con Spirito* for the magazine, "a pun joining the musical notation meaning 'with zest' to the announcement of a conspiracy" (226). The original intent of *Con Spirito* was to provide an alternative to the college's established literary magazine, *The Vassar Review*. Or, as Bishop had put it somewhat more strongly in a letter to Donald Stanford, *Con Spirito*'s aim was "to startle the college and kill the traditional magazine" (*One Art* 13). Betsy Erkkila has mentioned *Con Spirito* in passing as a "striking" example of a successful collaboration among women who are positioned in competition with other women in a "struggle" for literary territory (*Wicked Sisters* 100). Paying attention to struggles such

Original publication details: Bethany Hicok, "Elizabeth Bishop's 'Queer Birds': Vassar, Con Spirito, and the Romance of Female Community." *Contemporary Literature* 40.2, pp. 286–310. University of Wisconsin Press, 1999. Reproduced with permission from the University of Wisconsin Press.

Literary Theory: An Anthology, Third Edition. Edited by Julie Rivkin and Michael Ryan.
© 2017 John Wiley & Sons, Ltd. Published 2017 by John Wiley & Sons, Ltd.

as these, Erkkila argues, provides a richer reading of literary history, one that can account for the differences among women (4). The editorial in the first issue of *Con Spirito*, however, also aligns these women in collaboration against a male-dominated literary tradition and particularly challenges the stereotypes of college-educated women put forward by the literary press.

Con Spirito was also a conspiracy, a clandestine and anonymous meeting of literary minds, in an attempt to create a space of freedom for the imagination within the boundaries of the women's college community and the larger literary world. Although it was short-lived (the magazine folded in November 1933 after only three issues), *Con Spirito* provided an important forum for the developing talents of its writers. Two of Bishop's *Con Spirito* pieces, "Then Came the Poor" and "Hymn to the Virgin," became her first professional publications when they appeared without significant changes in *The Magazine* in 1934. McCarthy took issues of *Con Spirito* to impress Malcolm Cowley at *The New Republic* when she was looking for review assignments (McCarthy 262). T. S. Eliot praised the magazine when he came to the Vassar campus in May 1933 (Fountain and Brazeau 51). Of the seven co-conspirators, four went on to establish successful literary careers: Bishop, McCarthy, Eleanor Clark, and Rukeyser. But beyond its importance as a professional vehicle, *Con Spirito* provided a space of possibility for Bishop, who had not yet come to terms with her lesbian sexuality or her literary ambition. In a limited sense, I will argue, *Con Spirito* allowed Bishop to "come out" as both a writer and, perhaps much more provisionally, a lesbian. Moreover, the *Con Spirito* writers seemed to share a fantasy of a productive female community, an idea of community that I will argue in the last part of my essay remained a powerful structuring fantasy in Bishop's work. Hence the idea of literary community that I pursue through my reading of Bishop's experience at Vassar allows me to suggest new ways to see the enclosure fantasies that have long been noted by critics as an important feature of Bishop's work. These enclosure fantasies – among them the boarding house, the prison, and the island – serve as spaces of "possibility" in Bishop's work that provide a challenge to the fixed ideas of both gender and literary identity that she found constrained the artist in the 1930s.

Before moving to the inner spaces defined by Bishop's early writing in *Con Spirito* and beyond, I would like to examine the larger territory defined by the *Con Spirito* writers in their bid for literary power at the college. This bid, as I have suggested, involved a dual challenge to the boundaries of literary and sexual convention both inside and outside the Vassar community. In the first issue of *Con Spirito*, for example, the writers responded to an editorial that had appeared in the January 1933 issue of *The American Spectator*, a literary magazine that had recently been founded by Theodore Dreiser, Eugene O'Neill, James Branch Cabell, Ernest Boyd, and George Jean Nathan. *The Spectator* had criticized Smith and Vassar "girls" for wanting to be "carbon copies of men," called their professors "desiccated old maids," and lamented the loss of "femininity" in the educated woman. Here *The Spectator* adopted the position put forward by theories of sexology that defined the independent college woman and all-female communities of the 1920s and 1930s as deviant (Smith-Rosenberg 265).

Although many college women graduated, married, and had children, the pervasive discourse labeled independent women "unnatural," because it was thought that their education would interfere with their becoming wives and mothers, roles assumed to be "natural" to their sex. In this sense, as Carroll Smith-Rosenberg has argued, their choices "violated normal gender categories" (265). *The Spectator* editorial had suggested that a woman's intellectual productivity would interfere with her reproductivity (hence the characterization of Vassar's female professors as "desiccated old maids"). Theories of sexology also attached masculine physical characteristics to independent women. The Viennese neurologist Richard von Krafft-Ebing, for example, had invented a new category in the nineteenth century for women who took on men's roles, the Mannish Lesbian (Smith-Rosenberg 272). The Mannish Lesbian symbolized social disorder and perversion not so much because of her sexual orientation but because of her rejection of traditional feminine roles and her desire for "male privileges and power" (Smith-Rosenberg 271). With this sexual classification, Krafft-Ebing connected women's independence "to cross-dressing, sexual perversion, and borderline hermaphroditism" (272). Krafft-Ebing's theories continued to have an enormous impact on early twentieth-century ideas about college women. George Jean Nathan's familiarity with such theories of sexology seems evident in his *Spectator* article "The Theatre," where he complained that lesbians, or as he put it, women "who are of the sexual disposition of the Aeolian-Greek island colonizers," were ruining the theater with their "masculine hardness and chill undertone." He concluded, "you cannot cast Sappho as Cinderella, or as Juliet" (2).[2] Finally, women's college communities were portrayed in terms of metaphors of disease and contagion and became in the words of one educator "'the great breeding ground' of lesbianism" (Faderman 49).[3] These attitudes toward women's colleges and independent women in general permeated a great deal of writing in the twenties and thirties.

Con Spirito writers responded to and challenged this discourse of biological determinism. At the beginning of their first editorial, the *Con Spirito* editors argued that, while they might seem "by the very launching of this publication to have become the prototype of desiccated womanhood," they felt confident that their "intellectual venture" would not interfere with their ability to have children (Editorial 1), just as they presumed that "the literary dalliance" of *The Spectator* writers had not "interfered with their lawful begetting of infants" (1). At the end of their editorial, the *Con Spirito* editors further challenged the myth that aligned womanhood with motherhood by claiming the magazine as their child, a child they would need to keep nourished with "forward-looking" writing or it would die; they thus demonstrated that they could produce children through the male channels of productivity and thereby distance themselves from reproduction. As they appropriated the productive power of men, the *Con Spirito* editors stepped confidently over the boundary that *The Spectator* had established between feminine and masculine spheres. In other words, they made "gender trouble" in the ways that Judith Butler suggests by calling into question "those naturalized and reified notions of gender that support masculine hegemony and heterosexist power" (33–34).

The *Con Spirito* editors further challenged these fixed categories by appropriating certain aspects of masculine style, thereby calling attention to the performative aspects of masculinity. McCarthy describes, for example, how the idea for *Con Spirito* got started in the "smoking room" of Cushing Hall at Vassar. Some of the *Con Spirito* editors liked to think they were a tough bunch. Bishop, McCarthy, and others sat around puffing and debating, "several sort of droll characters," and made up bawdy rhymes, which were "mostly borrowed from men's colleges" (Fountain and Brazeau 43). While *Con Spirito*'s response to *The Spectator* and adoption of masculine style challenged fixed ideas about gender categories, the battle between *Con Spirito* and *The Vassar Review* tended to reinforce the discourse of male writers engaged in what Nina Baym has called "melodramas of beset manhood" (63–80).[4] According to Baym, masculine writers perceived themselves as beset by "flagrantly bad best-sellers written by women" that threatened their "integrity and livelihood" (70) and responded to this perceived threat by creating a fiction about the woman author. In this melodrama, the woman author is excluded from the canon and becomes the creator not of art but of "conventional works" (77). The *Con Spirito* writers used similar language in their criticism of *The Vassar Review*. The *Review* was "tame," according to McCarthy (257). Bishop called it "dull and old-fashioned" ("Interview" 293), and she makes the connections between gender and quality even clearer in her letter to Donald Stanford, with which she enclosed copies of *Con Spirito* with this note: "There are some very poor things in them – but for college writing, particularly women's college writing, I think they're pretty good" (*One Art* 13). Here Bishop repeats the logic of the melodrama. While proud of the writing in *Con Spirito*, Bishop aligns poor writing with women in particular rather than college literary magazines in general. *Con Spirito* writers seemed to want to put distance between themselves and what they saw as the more "feminine" *Vassar Review*, especially since this official college magazine had rejected their avant-garde work (Jessup 17).

The editors' various accounts of *Con Spirito*'s formation suggest that they imagined themselves to be part of a subversive underground. Eunice Clark calls *Con Spirito* the "counter-establishment blast" and describes their efforts as "a tiny part of a worldwide literary revolution stretching, in variegated forms, from Walt Whitman to *Finnegans Wake*" (Jessup 17). Bishop's title for the magazine, which contains "an almost Joycean palimpsest of meaning" for Clark, emphasizes both collective action and secrecy, the pleasure associated with music, something done "with spirit," and the danger associated with subversion and any close alliance among women (Jessup 17). To add to the conspiratorial atmosphere, the magazine was published anonymously. Even the *Con Spirito* editors didn't know who wrote what, except by guessing: "manuscripts for submission were put, unsigned, on a wooden chair, to be read and argued over," McCarthy recalls (258). In addition, the makeup of the editorial board was a secret to the campus. The co-conspirators advertised the magazine "by posters we nailed up on trees in the dark of night" (258). They claimed they had "darkened [themselves] in anonymity" in order to avoid the *Review*'s "aristocratic" policies, not, as they put it, because they wanted to "wallow with impunity in 'communism and copulations'" (Editorial 1). But here, of course, the editors themselves brought together in their denial radical politics and illicit sexuality.

All this emphasis on secrecy plays on the danger associated with women's colleges. Educators worried that "the invert" could lure other women into a life of perversion, because the woman-centered, secretive community of the women's college provided a perfect haven for such activity (Smith-Rosenberg 280). The language of sexology and popular psychology had linked such an alliance with sexuality, danger, and perversion. These Vassar "girls" had rejected their reproductive roles, according to the logic of *The Spectator*, in order to be productive, and in so doing had cast off their femininity to adopt masculine style; they were therefore professional as well as sexual outcasts. McCarthy describes the college's reaction to *Con Spirito* in terms that maintain this alliance between literary "outsiderhood" and sexual "outsiderhood." When *Con Spirito* first came out in February 1933, it caused a tremendous stir on campus, not so much because of the writing in the magazine, according to McCarthy, although *Con Spirito*'s focus on the experimental made it different in every way from the *Review*, but because it was "unsigned": "That was the outrage, the shameful crime, treated as such even by some of the faculty, who breathed the word 'anonymous' as though it were married to the word 'letter,' denoting something so scurrilous that it dared not sign its name" (258). McCarthy's allusion to Hawthorne suggests that she identifies with a group that has been cast out. While the tone registers outrage, it also indicates a romance of sorts, one that seemed to be shared by others in the group.

Read in the context of McCarthy's comment, Bishop's poem "A Word with You," published in the second issue of *Con Spirito*, becomes less the "panicky" fear of being identified with "outsiderhood" that Adrienne Rich sees in the poem than a controlled, satirical account of a women's college and the speaker's identification with a "select group" of outsiders:[5]

> Look out! there's that damned ape again
> sit silently until he goes,
> or else forgets the things he knows
> (whatever they are) about us, then
> we can begin to talk again.
>
> (2)[6]

The poem goes on to list a whole zoo full of animals that appear to be watching over and squawking about the couple who are trying to talk. The poem continues:

> You see
>
> how hard it is, you understand
> this nervous strain in which we live –
> Why just one luscious adjective
> infuriates the whole damned band
> and they're squabbling for it....

In this remarkably sophisticated poem, Bishop seems to connect the suspicion and scrutiny with which relationships were monitored in women's colleges in the 1930s with the production of words. The production of "one luscious adjective" creates a furor among the animals, much as *Con Spirito* had when it first appeared. Bishop's poem also suggests the contradictory positions of the women's college in the thirties. While providing a place for women to come together and form a sense of community, encouraging an atmosphere of free expression, women's colleges also harshly policed and censored that same expression. As Barbara Solomon has noted, a woman could be expelled from college not only "for staying out all night with a man" but also "for having too 'intense' a relationship with another woman" (162).[7] The poem's ending reflects the kind of paranoia that such policies might produce:

> Quick! there's the cockatoo! he heard!
> (He can't bear any form of wit.)
> – Please watch out that you don't get bit;
> there's not a thing escapes that bird.
> Be silent, – now the ape has overheard.

But Bishop's tone, and the zoolike atmosphere, suggests that she turned panic and paranoia into a double-edged wit that sliced through the dullness that she felt surrounded her.

While it could be argued that "A Word with You" re-creates the limitations of the women's college in the 1930s, as well as *Con Spirito*'s resistance to them, Bishop's story "Seven-Days Monologue," also published in the second issue of *Con Spirito*, appears to provide a spatial metaphor for the working out of these conflicts. The setting for this story, related in a series of seven diary entries, is the female community of the boarding house. The conflict in the story centers around the landlady, who is a source of both fascination and obsession for the narrator; for much of the story, for instance, the narrator is trying to remember or find out the landlady's name: "She is large, looming seriously now into my life, but unlabelled" (3). She is also a dangerous maternal presence who possesses the house. In "September 2nd" the narrator notes:

> Now I am suspicious of the landlady. Every time I see her I see "the house" floating over her head, like St. Paul with his church. I think she feels it there all the time: high and narrow and dark, its long stairways, black turns and lighted halls, fire-escapes and shut, white doors. We are all closed behind them, over her head, spidery legs and arms, little buttony heads. (4)

If those shut white doors lining dark, narrow passages remind one of a series of closets, the image of the landlady dressed in lavender provided earlier in the monologue seems a fairly obvious clue that Bishop's story has something to do with lesbian sexuality. As Lillian Faderman has pointed out, the color lavender was commonly used by lesbians as a code word for community in the 1930s (106). The narrator, identified as a "female lodger" about midway through the story, is fascinated by the landlady, who is described as the matriarch of this community: "There she sits on the sofa, like an ancient unculled pearl in a battered shell. She is constantly bedewed with perspiration and invariably wears a lavendar dress" (4). Bishop twice uses the color "lavendar" as a description in her story, each time in a section charged with eroticism. While this code word may not have been obvious to a straight person in 1933, it might have been to another lesbian. I am fully aware that Bishop was quite reticent about her sexuality, because of the consequences such a confession could have for her career and her life, but to those who understood and sympathized with her position, she seems to have been quite open. And "Seven-Days Monologue," even at this early date, seems a limited kind of "coming out" to me.

In "September 4th," the narrator describes how the landlady comes into her bedroom and sits down on the bed:

> Early this morning she came into the room like a thunder-cloud with a silver lining, her smiling face above all the rest of the *lavendarishness* and vastness, and a long white slit down the side where her dress had burst open.... I mustn't forget those feet: how her shoes have shaped themselves around them, how they bulged out and over and made themselves at home. There was something very compatible about her face and feet; you can look from one to the other without the slightest feeling of discrepancy. (4; emphasis added)

In this rather witty passage, the narrator mixes the grotesque with eroticism. The sexologists called the lesbian (and the educated woman) grotesque because she crossed acceptable gender boundaries. The idea that the women's college could be a "breeding ground" for lesbian sexuality indicates the concern over permeable boundaries, the idea that the women's college was a body that could be invaded by disease and thereby destroyed. The only hope against such a possible contagion was to police the borders and expel those who threatened them. In such a context this large and uncontainable landlady may represent the "excess" of same-sex desire – that is, what falls outside the boundaries of what can be narrated and thereby labeled within a story.[8]

The introduction of a heterosexual subplot immediately following this passage reinforces such a reading, since the description is so unappetizing as to suggest rejection. In this section, the narrator, whose gender up to this point has not been clear, is identified as a "female lodger." She is visited by a man:

> It was hot as hell; we quarrelled slowly, back and forth, until I wanted to push him off the fire-escape and leave him to the mercies of the alley-cats. The air was rigid; people's voices outside held to the same accent, on and on. The smell of their suppers was deathly, as if it would stick in their throats and choke them. I never thought the church steeple clock would have dared to strike the hour – or if it did it would declaim it like a death sentence and seal us all in leaden immobility.

While their quarrel mimics sexual intercourse, it could hardly be described as pleasurable. Heterosexuality is associated here with rigidness, death, argument, stale food, lack of motion, "leaden immobility." Heterosexuality is the death knell in this story and requires quite literally a shower to cleanse it: "Finally, thank God, it rained, a wonderful rain, almost like mercury, fluid and metallic" (4). While female sexuality is associated with the grotesque and the fluidity of boundaries in the figure of the landlady, it carries both pleasure and danger, eroticism and power.[9] It is the landlady and the desire to know (about) her that drives both the narrator's desire and the reader's in this story.

In its adoption of the boarding house as an experimental space to test the boundaries and limits of both literary and sexual possibility, Bishop's story might be thought of in terms of the kinds of enclosure fantasies that have been noted in Bishop criticism.[10] Langdon Hammer has recently called Bishop's dream house in "The End of March" the most important of these enclosures and has pointed out not only its provisional nature but its potential as a site of possibility. Hammer, using the object-relations theory of D. W. Winnicott, has argued that the dream house, like Bishop's correspondence, creates a kind of "potential space" or "third area," which allows her to establish an "intimate relation" between poet and reader ("Useless Concentration" 173). In this way, Hammer notes the "collaborative structure" not only of Bishop's correspondence but of her poetry as well (173).[11]

This "potential space" in Bishop's work also might be productively considered in terms of Mary Russo's discussion of such a space in her study of carnival theory and the female grotesque. Russo argues that female pilots such as Amelia Earhart created a kind of "provisional space" for taking risks through the "practice of stunting," which came to be defined as an "abnormal and increasingly liminal activity with regard to official flying" (22). In a theoretical sense, Russo argues, stunting is "a tactic for groups or individuals in a certain risky situation in which a strategy is not possible.... As a temporal category, the tactic, or in Earhart's terms, the practice of stunting, belongs to the improvisational, to the realm of what is possible in the moment" (22). The space created by such a practice is not, Russo is quick to point out, that boundless and "transcendent space associated with the Kantian sublime" (11). It is rather a space that "emerges within the very constrained spaces of normalization." This practice of stunting strikes me as very much an aspect of the "improvisational" nature of *Con Spirito*'s formation, a practice as I have already suggested that emerged out of the normalizing discourse of the period that closely aligned literary ambition with sexual perversion. Such stunting can be heard in the language Bishop and McCarthy used to describe *Con Spirito*'s formation. For example, both of them tell of going to Signor Bruno's, a speakeasy in Poughkeepsie, in order to discuss the magazine. They drank "dreadful" red wine out of white coffee cups and got "slightly high" (McCarthy 258; "Interview" 293). Such descriptions underscore the improvisational as well as the risky behavior (drinking during Prohibition) that marked so much of the discourse surrounding *Con Spirito*. The dialogue of improvisation continued even after Bishop graduated. In a letter to Bishop from co-conspirator Frani Blough, with whom Bishop corresponded until her death, Blough discusses the possibilities of an opera that she and Bishop were planning to write together. Blough was in graduate school studying music in New York and Bishop was traveling in France. In this letter, Blough imagines an improvisational community of artists who might transform the world of opera with their innovative ideas:

> Opera needs to start all over again, it seems to me, and the best thing to do is sweep away the Wagnerian debris and start as though the whole thing were quite a new idea, had by a few select people sitting around after dinner, then polished up.... I think satire could work very well in this sort of medium.... Something really funny and amusing and not heavy.... Also it would be a thing that a group of people could do with very little more preparation than an evening of quartet playing. Do come home and lend your able advice.[12]

Blough's description sounds very much like what *Con Spirito* had turned out to be – "quite a new idea, had by a few select people sitting around after dinner, then polished up."

Bishop reproduced this improvisational space in her poetry. The boarding house, for instance, appears as an isolated space of community where a "grotesque" assortment of creatures assemble under the landlady's roof in "A Summer's Dream," a later poem that Bishop published in *A Cold Spring* (1955):

> To the sagging wharf
> few ships could come.
> The population numbered
> two giants, an idiot, a dwarf,
>
> a gentle storekeeper
> asleep behind his counter,
> and our kind landlady –
> the dwarf was her dressmaker.
> (*Complete Poems* 62)

Bishop's assemblage of a community of grotesques not only suggests the discourse that labeled lesbians as outside and therefore perverse in relation to "normal," heterosexual womanhood but also echoes the theme of difference and outsiderhood shared by the women of *Con Spirito*. At the end of "Seven-Days Monologue," the narrator identifies and brings together her community of outsiders. Describing herself in terms similar to the landlady in the passage about St. Paul, she aligns herself with that subject position:

> Damn it all – I'm the Bird-Catcher, that's it. I must start going around balancing innumerable small silver-gilt bird-cages on my head and arms, to catch them in, and keep them all singing in the closet.

The image contains elements that have distinguished Bishop's poetry and prose throughout her career: the collection of a "little society" within an enclosed space, a sense of the absurd, and what Jeredith Merrin has called Bishop's "obsession with trans-mogrification" (154). In Bishop's work, Merrin argues, "everything is always turning into something else" (153). This pleasure in changeability is inseparable from Bishop's "gayness," which Merrin defines as "her questioning of gender boundaries" in her work, "and the exploration (however oblique and shrouded) of the pleasures and anxieties of same-sex love" (154).

As the Bird-Catcher, the narrator takes on the role of the landlady, entrapping her prey, and so she lives the role assigned her by the sexologists, the role of a grotesque who can lure others into the closet with her. Like the color lavender, "birds" (or sometimes "queer birds") was a code word for lesbians in the 1930s (Faderman 106), and its use here intensifies the sense that Bishop is identifying and establishing a community of society's deviants. At the end of the story this sense of a possible lesbian community becomes closely associated with the idea of literary community. "The Bird-Catcher" not only attempts to lure others to her but distributes phallic symbols, among other objects, to all her friends, each of whom is identified by an initial letter that corresponds to the first letters of the names of the *Con Spirito* women:

> One box of various articles to hand around, for conversational purposes only. The fans and tweezers and an occasional hat-pin for M. The anvil and hammer and the beautiful knives and forks for F. And a couple of genuine phallic symbols for E., nothing else. A new box of tricks.[13]

The Bird-Catcher distributes the props and designates the players in this theater of the absurd in a parody of the way that Bishop, according to Eleanor Clark, might have "gather[ed] her little society" at Vassar (Fountain and Brazeau 37).

Bishop's *Con Spirito* story "Then Came the Poor" also creates a kind of provisional space for community, but this time through a discourse of class politics, which would have been familiar to the *Con Spirito* writers. At the time, a number of the co-conspirators, including Bishop, were interested in socialist politics. However, Bishop found their commitment to real change shallow, for, as Blough recalled later, their theories "weren't grounded firmly enough in any action for them to last very long," and they would have been horrified at the idea of revolution, although that was "the bottom line" (Fountain and Brazeau 50). "Then Came the Poor," according to Blough, was Bishop's response to this lack of commitment. But Bishop's story is more than just a send-up of what Blough calls a "childish" view of politics bandied about at Vassar. In the 1930s, when radical politics became the acceptable form of protest in intellectual circles, it served Bishop, at least in part, not as an answer for what was wrong with the world but as a narrative "cover" for a different story, the story of same-sex love.

In "Then Came the Poor," the narrator's aristocratic family abandons their home after a communist takeover, forgetting the narrator, who had wanted to stay behind any-way, in their rush to get away. As the mob takes over and "ransacks" the house, they dress up in the clothing of the departed aristocrats, while the narrator dresses down in some old clothes he finds in the barn. Now dressed as a stableboy, the narrator successfully passes as one of the crowd and enters the house. In her recent article on Bishop and the left, Betsy Erkkila identifies the narrator in "Then Came the Poor" as female ("Elizabeth Bishop" 286). But there is very little in the story to indicate that this is the case, since the narrator is never named. There is no clear designation of gender in the story until the narrator dresses up as a stableboy. At that point, he is perceived as male by the other characters. It is this gender ambiguity and the ability to put on and take off gender identity that is important to Bishop and key to this story. This is consistent with Bishop's reluctance to align herself with fixed positions.[14]

Once inside the house, the narrator encounters a series of "scenes." Because of their erotic charge, their connection to parental objects and rooms, and the positioning of the narrator as voyeur in relationship to each of the scenes, they can be read as "primal" scenes that stage a reverse of what Freud has described as a family romance fantasy. The family romance, which is both a class fantasy and a sexual one, is a wish-fulfillment fantasy with two principal aims – erotic and ambitious (Freud 299). In the typical romance fantasy, the child imagines that in getting rid of his own parents who are of low birth, he is free to replace them with those who occupy a higher social station. He does this by imagining a series of primal scenes in order to alter the conditions of his birth. In keeping with the socialist leanings of *Con Spirito*, Bishop's fantasy works in reverse.

In the first "scene" described in Bishop's story, the narrator sees two women in the hall, "fighting over the remains of a roasted chicken, both pulling" (4). On the "greasy and muddy" marble floor, the women are trampling red roses underfoot, the same red roses that the narrator had observed earlier in the story in association with objects belonging to the mother. The narrator explains that "people were coming and going in excited groups, pointing and grabbing and exclaiming, some of them dressed in fantastic costumes put together from the wardrobes of my departed family." Here, a scene that seems meant to portray the workings of greed becomes erotically charged by the roses, a metaphor for the female body and sometimes for the female genitals themselves.[15] The representation of women as petty, squabbling over the "remains" of some meager food, brings to mind the squabbling animals in "A Word with You" and could perhaps be read in terms of Bishop's disdain for *The Vassar Review*.

The chicken scene, with its disturbing representations of women, can be connected to two later "scenes" viewed by the narrator as he makes his way through the house. In a later scene, an old woman sits on the drawing-room floor "in a ring of dirty petticoats…, carefully unhooking the cut glass pendants from the chandelier…. She was bedecked and a'dazzle from top to toe" (4). Finally, the narrator arrives at the mother's bedroom, where he sees that "[i]n mother's French bed, canopied with lime-colored satin, some-one had put two filthy babies to sleep." Female sexuality in these scenes is associated with something not quite clean, something, in fact, sordid. The two women, fighting over the chicken on a "greasy and muddy floor," trample the roses underfoot, while the old woman in her dirty petticoat greedily ransacks the chandelier. Two "filthy" babies fall asleep amid the lime-colored drapery of the mother's French bed.

A very different but related scene interrupts this wallowing femininity. Here is how the narrator describes it:

> From father's large bathroom came loud laughter, splashings and slappings. I looked in and discovered two naked men jumping in and out of the shower and bath, throwing powder and bathsalts at each other, spitting shining spouts of water out the window into the sunlight and onto their amused friends below. (4)

This decidedly campy scene, which is unmistakably homoerotic, gains meaning only retroactively, during the lottery at the end of the story. During the lottery, the men are drawing lots to see who will live in the narrator's house. As they do so, they call out the name of a man, Jacob Kaffir. Bishop's description of him at once labels him as other: he is dark, "the color of a well used penny," and wears a fez. The narrator describes him as "an amazing little man," similar to the character in "A Flight of Fancy," a short story Bishop published in her high school literary magazine. He represents the elflike creatures in Bishop's earlier stories that seem to signal some entrance into a kind of parallel universe, a fantasy world where some expression of same-sex desire becomes possible. Jacob acts as a similar bridge figure in "Then Came the Poor." He has no family, and so in order to get a room in the house, he must choose someone with whom to live. Like two men cruising each other in a bar, Jacob and the narrator exchange suggestive signals:

> I caught Jacob's eye and smiled as hard as I could, raising my forefinger like a man saying "One, next the wall," in a restaurant.
> "Him?" Jacob shouted. "He live with me. O.K. to you?"
> "You bet," I said. "Well it may be sort of fun for a while," I thought.
> Apparently Jacob had the same idea. "We'll have fun, huh?" he said, waving an empty bottle at me, and he gave me a wink I could almost hear.
> "Seems like home already, don't it."

Although the narrator's attitude toward the situation is ironic, the "sexual undertones" in this passage, as James Longenbach has pointed out, are unmistakable, especially given the earlier bath scene (470).

The scenes in this story that involve women, like the chicken scene discussed above, have the same erotic power but are much more fraught with dangers and difficulties, while in the father's bathroom the men are having good, clean fun and ejaculating out the window. The presence of the maternal hovering over the three scenes that involve women – or, in the cases of the chicken fight and the French bed, the absent mother – seems to disturb the representation of these scenes, so that it is only with two men and the space they occupy that Bishop can effectively distance herself from the taint of "femininity" and come briefly to some sort of space of "pure" pleasure, represented by their joyful "masculinity."

Bishop's fantasy of female community (expressed throughout her *Con Spirito* writing in terms of literary ambition, fear of a feminine taint, sexual perversion, and cross-dressing) continued to be part of her work throughout her career, attesting to the persistence of the discourse of perversion surrounding literary ambition and lesbian sexuality. Bishop's 1938 story "In Prison," for example, brings together ideas of gender ambiguity, literary influence, female community, and lesbian sexuality. Langdon Hammer has suggested that "In Prison" is a metaphor for life in the closet ("New Elizabeth Bishop" 144).

Provisional spaces such as these can be found in Bishop's work throughout her career, but they are strikingly present in her well-known "Crusoe in England," published at the end of her career, although it is important to note that notebook entries from 1934 demonstrate that ideas for this poem are connected to the Vassar years and the discourse of the 1930s. Immediately following graduation from Vassar in 1934, Bishop stayed on Cuttyhunk Island in Massachusetts for several weeks. The landlord of her temporary home by the sea was Mr. Wuthenaur, a man who wanted to "simplify life" all the time, and his behavior led Bishop to consider writing a poem about "making things in a pinch – & how it looks sad when the emergency is over."[16] The idea was finally published in 1972 as "Crusoe in England." David Kalstone has written that the poems in *Geography III*, of which "Crusoe in England" is one, "revisit her earlier poems as Bishop herself once visited tropical and polar zones, and ... they refigure her work in wonderful ways" (252). Bishop's "Crusoe in England" refigures the ideas of female community found in the *Con Spirito* work.

"Crusoe in England," like "In Prison," narrates the fantasy of a community both found and lost during the course of the poem. Alone on the island and oppressed by solitude, Crusoe has

> nightmares of other islands
> stretching away from mine, infinities
> of islands, islands spawning islands,
> like frogs' eggs turning into polliwogs
> of islands....
> (*Complete Poems* 165)

The images Bishop uses here are reminiscent of those I have already discussed that describe the lesbian who was supposed to be simultaneously sterile – the "desiccated old maid" – and associated with a "breeding ground" for producing more of her kind.

This is an island that repeats in one sense the representations of lesbian community that Gabriele Griffith has argued were common to the early part of the twentieth century (11). These representations create an image of lesbians "as the only one in their community, as isolated individuals ... intended to arouse pity rather than condemnation." This isolated figure is precisely the one we see as Crusoe sits dangling his legs over the edge of a volcano: "I often gave way to self-pity," he tells us:

> "Do I deserve this? I suppose I must.
> I wouldn't be here otherwise. Was there
> a moment when I actually chose this?

If Crusoe is one of a kind, so is everything else on this island:

> The sun set in the sea; the same odd sun
> rose from the sea,
> and there was one of it and one of me.
> The island had one kind of everything....
> (163)

Crusoe's loneliness is alleviated temporarily, just as it is in Defoe's *Robinson Crusoe*, by the arrival of Friday. But while Crusoe in Defoe's colonial account is only able to construct Friday, the "savage," as a slave, even though he is clearly fond of him, Bishop's Crusoe calls Friday a "friend":

> Just when I thought I couldn't stand it
> another minute longer, Friday came.
> (Accounts of that have everything all wrong.)
> Friday was nice.
> Friday was nice, and we were friends.
> If only he had been a woman!
> I wanted to propagate my kind,
> and so did he, I think, poor boy.
> He'd pet the baby goats sometimes,
> and race with them, or carry one around.
> – Pretty to watch; he had a pretty body.
> (165–66)

The narrator's elusiveness about the nature of his relationship with Friday and the cryptic phrase "(Accounts of that have everything all wrong)" suggest that the relationship between the two men was one of mutual desire. Immediately following this parenthetical comment, however, Crusoe utters what must be the most banal sentence in the world: "Friday was nice." He then repeats it in the next line and adds, "and we were friends," as if this would somehow explain the confusion.

Bishop wrote the poem long after she had read *Robinson Crusoe* and only reread the novel after she had written the poem, so she relies on a hazy memory of the book to re-create her Crusoe. It was the idea of the desert island and making things do in an emergency that appealed to her. But it is clearly also the relationship between Friday and Crusoe that fascinated Bishop. In Defoe's account, Crusoe "civilizes" Friday and teaches him English. In Bishop's poem, Crusoe does not try to convert Friday. They are friends, on equal terms with each other. But immediately following these lines, Crusoe cries out, "If only he had been a woman! / I wanted to propagate my kind, / and so did he, I think, poor boy." Bishop thereby adds a new factor to this story of Crusoe and Friday, a marriage plot that legitimizes Crusoe's feelings for Friday. As in "Seven-Days Monologue," however, Crusoe ultimately rejects the heterosexual narrative. Lorrie Goldensohn suggests in her reading of this passage that it is important to pay attention to "the pressure of [Bishop's] particular experience behind and within the poem," the suicide of her Brazilian lover Lota de Macedo Soares, and the desire she expressed in numerous letters to have children that she and Soares could raise together (*Elizabeth Bishop* 78). I would agree with this reading in part. But this stanza, with its qualifying and hedging, also suggests other ways of reading the phrase "I wanted to propagate my kind." What Crusoe dwells on at the end of the stanza is Friday's body. Friday was, after all, "Pretty to watch; he had a pretty body." Immediately following these lines, Crusoe and Friday are taken off the island and returned to England. In the last two stanzas of the poem, Crusoe – surrounded by his island possessions – is living on what he describes as "another island," England. There is no reason why he should not have found a woman in England, but the poem makes clear that he has stayed with Friday. The poem ends with the weight of loss: "And Friday, my dear Friday, died of measles / seventeen years ago come March" (166).

Loss is registered in the person of Friday. Crusoe took Friday "home" to England, and he died there. Certainly a tenuous connection can be made here, as Goldensohn does, between Friday's death and Soares's suicide, but leaving it there would ignore some of the complexity of the idea of "home." Her "home" in Brazil with Soares was perhaps the closest Bishop ever got to a sense of real belonging, and yet when she and Soares broke up, she found it more and more difficult to make a life there. Soares was her "home" in Brazil, not the country itself or the house she had bought, however much she tried to make it so. Much like Crusoe in Defoe's account, Crusoe in Bishop's finds a sense of purpose, of "home," when Friday arrives. The original title of the poem was "Crusoe at Home" (Millier 366), which suggests that Bishop had initially thought of the poem in terms of an investigation of Crusoe's relationship to the idea of "home," or at least an ironic commentary on ideas of "home." In this sense Crusoe finds a home with Friday much in the same way that the narrator in "Then Came the Poor" finds a home with Jacob. Here again, as in that early story, an ambiguous but erotically charged relationship is represented through an investigation of the complex connections between two male personae. Joanne Feit Diehl has argued that "Crusoe in England" is "Bishop's most extreme poetic instance of gender-crossing fused with eroticism" (20). It is here within this space that the desire to "propagate my kind" is most strongly expressed.

In "Crusoe in England," as in many of Bishop's stories and poems, we are presented with a circumscribed world in which a lonely individual or a societal misfit contacts another like himself and for a brief period finds a home. The circumscribed world of the island, like the prison, the boarding house, or the communal house in "Then Came the Poor," represents a landscape in which the poet, the woman, the orphan, or the lesbian can contact others like herself and form a community. It may represent that limited but also "capacious" space of the closet that Timothy Morris has suggested "resonates throughout [Bishop's] work" (125). Hence Bishop's sense of community and influence cannot be thought of apart from the desire to "propagate [her] kind," to create a language that would begin to speak of lesbian desire. Crusoe's phrase "I wanted to propagate my kind" cannot be interpreted simply as an expression of the biological urge of a childless poet to have children. Spoken by a character created by a lesbian poet wise to the homoeroticism of Defoe's original text, Crusoe's statement becomes a challenge to the biological determinism that hindered the careers of literary women of Bishop's generation. Crusoe's statement refers not simply to reproductive power but to productive power – the power to write, to influence future generations, and to build community.

Bishop's ideas of community and her own place in it might be productively considered in light of an essay she published at Vassar. Interested in the workings of time in the novel, Bishop offers us yet another spatial metaphor. Disturbed from her studies by a sound outside, she writes that she looked out her window and noticed the birds "going South" ("Time's Andromedas" 102). They were "spread across a wide swath of sky, each rather alone" and yet connected by an "invisible thread." It was "within this fragile network," Bishop writes, that "they possessed the sky." As I have suggested throughout this essay, Bishop built this fragile network at Vassar and maintained it in suggestive ways in the poetry and prose she published throughout her life. It is by establishing this connection that I have attempted to momentarily catch hold of the "invisible thread" that connected Bishop to a larger community of writers and artists who attempted, however briefly, to "possess the sky."

Mount St. Clare College

Notes

I would like to thank the Susan B. Anthony Center at the University of Rochester for a grant that enabled me to travel to Vassar College to work with the Elizabeth Bishop Papers. I would also like to thank Nancy MacKechnie, Curator of Rare Books and Manuscripts, Special Collections of Vassar College Libraries, for providing access to the papers and for her help when I was researching this article, and Frani Blough Muser for permission to quote from her letter to Bishop.

1   Rukeyser's participation in the group is uncertain. McCarthy wrote in her memoir that she thought Rukeyser was part of the group but was unable to identify anything she wrote for the magazine, except perhaps for a verse account of T. S. Eliot's visit to campus in May 1933 entitled "Lecture by Mr. Eliot." This verse account does look stylistically like Rukeyser's work.

2   *The Spectator* printed an article by the leading sexologist in British and American circles, Havelock Ellis, on the front page of the same issue. Although Ellis's article ("The Physician and Sex") was not specifically about "inversion," its presence here would seem not only to confirm the popularity of Ellis within the literary community but to authenticate *The Spectator*'s views on educated women. Nathan's familiarity with the theories of the sexologists is also evident in a play he wrote in 1933 that parodied Noel Coward's *Design for Living*. Called *Design for Loving*, Nathan's play featured a hermaphrodite, an onanist, a flagellant, a transvestite, a male homosexual, a lesbian, and another woman with "tribade tendencies" among its cast of characters (Faderman 104).

3   Smith-Rosenberg notes that "articles complaining of lesbianism in women's colleges, clubs, prisons, and reformatories – wherever women gathered – became common" after World War I as progressive women reformers gained more power (280).

4   See also Andreas Huyssen's "Mass Culture as Woman," in which Huyssen argues that in modernist discourse "mass culture is somehow associated with woman while real, authentic culture remains the prerogative of men" (47), and Sandra Gilbert and Susan Gubar's massive study of male modernist rage against women writers, *No Man's Land*.

5   In "The Eye of the Outsider," Rich reads this poem as one that illustrates Bishop's divided sense of self at this time. The poem, she argues, is "a tense, panicky, one-sided conversation during which a whole menagerie gets out of control" (128).

6   I quote here from the *Con Spirito* version of "A Word with You," which was reprinted in *The Complete Poems* (218–19).

7   Novels of the 1920s reflected the fear that intimacy between women could carry severe consequences. In Wanda Fraiken Neff's 1928 roman à clef *We Sing Diana*, the protagonist says of women's colleges: "Intimacies between two girls were watched with keen, distrustful eyes. Among one's classmates, one looked for the bisexual type, the masculine girl searching for a feminine counterpart, and one ridiculed their devotions" (199).

8   It is possible that the landlady is also a parody of the "aging Lady in Lavender," a persona for the independent woman that appeared in male literature of the 1920s, who "preyed upon the innocence of young girls, teaching them to fear men and their own sexual impulses" (Smith-Rosenberg 282).

9   As Carole Vance argues, "Sexuality is simultaneously a domain of restriction, repression, and danger as well as a domain of exploration, pleasure, and agency" (1).

10   Thomas Travisano, one of the first critics to LABEL 11 aspect of Bishop's work, refers to these spaces as "fables of enclosure" (18).

11   David Bromwich also notes the conversational nature of Bishop's work and the risks she is willing to take to communicate with the "readers she cares for" (160).

12   Letter from Frani Blough Muser to Elizabeth Bishop, 7 Oct. 1935 (Elizabeth Bishop Papers, Vassar College Box 16, 1935–47).

13   Bishop's story complements a brief play by Frani Blough in the same issue, "The Bacchae, or Revelling Women." The play is a satire of D. H. Lawrence (called Dionysius H. Lawrence here) and his "colony" of followers, including Katherine Mansfield, Mabel Dodge Luhan, Lady Ottoline Morrel, Aldous Huxley, and Richard Aldington. Lawrence enters carrying the "sweetly Phallic symbol" aloft, while the chorus of women sings his praises: "You are good. You are beautiful. You are tortured. We claim you as our own" (2). Later Aldington and Huxley enter in drag.

14   For another reading of this story in relationship to Bishop and the politics of the left, see Palatella.

15   For excellent discussions of the rose metaphor in Bishop, see Costello and Goldensohn, "Body's Roses."

16   Entry dated July 1934, Notebooks: 1934–37 (Elizabeth Bishop Papers, Vassar College Folder 72A.3).

Works Cited

Baym, Nina. "Melodramas of Beset Manhood: How Theories of American Fiction Exclude Women Authors." *The New Feminist Criticism: Essays on Women, Literature & Theory*. Ed. Elaine Showalter. New York: Pantheon, 1985. 63–80.

Bishop, Elizabeth. *The Complete Poems: 1927–1979*. New York: Farrar, 1983.

Bishop, Elizabeth. Elizabeth Bishop Papers. Vassar College Library Special Collections, Poughkeepsie, New York.

Bishop, Elizabeth. "A Flight of Fancy." *Blue Pencil* Dec. 1929: 22–26.

Bishop, Elizabeth. "Hymn to the Virgin." *Con Spirito* 1.2 (Apr. 1933): 3.

Bishop, Elizabeth. "In Prison." *The Collected Prose*. Ed. Robert Giroux. New York: Farrar, 1984. 181–91.

Bishop, Elizabeth. "An Interview with Elizabeth Bishop." With Ashley Brown. *Elizabeth Bishop and Her Art*. Ed. Lloyd Schwartz and Sybil P. Estess. Ann Arbor: U of Michigan P, 1983. 289–302.

Bishop, Elizabeth. *One Art: Letters*. Ed. Robert Giroux. New York: Farrar, 1994.

Bishop, Elizabeth. "Seven-Days Monologue." *Con Spirito* 1.2 (Apr. 1933): 3–4.

Bishop, Elizabeth. "Then Came the Poor." *Con Spirito* 1.1 (Feb. 1933): 2 + .

Bishop, Elizabeth. "Time's Andromedas." *Vassar Journal of Undergraduate Studies* 7 (May 1933): 102–20.

Bishop, Elizabeth. "A Word with You." *Con Spirito* 1.2 (Apr. 1933): 2.

Blough, Frani. "The Bacchae, or Revelling Women." *Con Spirito* 1.2 (Apr. 1933): 2.

Bromwich, David. "Elizabeth Bishop's Dream-Houses." *Raritan* 4.1 (1984): 77–94.

Butler, Judith. *Gender Trouble: Feminism and the Subversion of Identity*. New York: Routledge, 1990.

Costello, Bonnie. "Attractive Mortality." Lombardi 126–52.

Diehl, Joanne Feit. "Bishop's Sexual Poetics." Lombardi 17–45.

Editorial. *American Spectator* 1.3 (Jan. 1933): 1.

Editorial. *Con Spirito* 1.1 (Feb. 1933): 1.

Ellis, Havelock. "The Physician and Sex." *American Spectator* 1.1 (Nov. 1932): 1.

Erkkila, Betsy. "Elizabeth Bishop, Modernism, and the Left." *American Literary History* 8 (1996): 284–310.

Erkkila, Betsy. *The Wicked Sisters: Women Poets, Literary History and Discord*. New York: Oxford UP, 1992.

Faderman, Lillian. *Odd Girls and Twilight Lovers: A History of Lesbian Life in Twentieth-Century America*. New York: Penguin, 1991.

Fountain, Gary, and Peter Brazeau. *Remembering Elizabeth Bishop: An Oral Biography*. Amherst: U of Massachusetts P, 1994.

Gilbert, Sandra, and Susan Gubar. *No Man's Land: The Place of the Woman Writer in the Twentieth Century*. Vol. 1. New Haven, CT: Yale UP, 1988.

Goldensohn, Lorrie. "The Body's Roses: Race, Sex, and Gender in Elizabeth Bishop's Representations of Self." Lombardi 70–90.

Freud, Sigmund. "Family Romances." 1908. *The Freud Reader*. Ed. Peter Gay. New York: Norton, 1989. 297–300.

Goldensohn, Lorrie. *Elizabeth Bishop: The Biography of a Poetry*. New York: Columbia UP, 1992.

Griffith, Gabriele. *Heavenly Love? Lesbian Images in Twentieth Century Women's Writing*. Manchester, Eng.: Manchester UP, 1993.

Hammer, Langdon. "The New Elizabeth Bishop." *Yale Review* 82.1 (1994): 135–49.

Hammer, Langdon. "Useless Concentration: Life and Work in Elizabeth Bishop's Letters and Poems." *American Literary History* 9 (1997): 162–80.

Huyssen, Andreas. "Mass Culture as Woman." *After the Great Divide: Modernism, Mass Culture, Postmodernism*. Bloomington: Indiana UP, 1986. 44–62.

Jessup, Eunice Clark. "Memoirs of Literatae and Socialists 1929–1933." *Vassar Quarterly* 55 (1979): 16–17.

Kalstone, David. *Becoming a Poet: Elizabeth Bishop with Marianne Moore and Robert Lowell*. Ed. Robert Hemenway. New York: Noonday, 1989.

Lombardi, Marilyn May, ed. *Elizabeth Bishop: The Geography of Gender*. Charlottesville: UP of Virginia, 1993.

Longenbach, James. "Elizabeth Bishop's Social Conscience." *English Literary History* 62 (1995): 467–86.

McCarthy, Mary. *How I Grew*. San Diego: Harcourt, 1986.

Merrin, Jeredith. "Elizabeth Bishop: Gaiety, Gayness, and Change." Lombardi 153–72.

Millier, Brett C. *Elizabeth Bishop: Life and the Memory of It*. Berkeley: U of California P, 1993.

Morris, Timothy. *Becoming Canonical in American Poetry*. Urbana: U of Illinois P, 1995.

Nathan, George Jean. "The Theatre." *American Spectator* 1.1 (Nov. 1932): 2.

Neff, Wanda Fraiken. *We Sing Diana*. Boston: Houghton, 1928.

Palatella, John. "That Sense of Constant Re-adjustment': The Great Depression and the Provisional Politics of Elizabeth Bishop's *North & South*." *Contemporary Literature* 34 (1993): 18–43.

Rich, Adrienne. "The Eye of the Outsider: Elizabeth Bishop's Complete Poems, 1927–1979." *Blood, Bread, and Poetry: Selected Prose 1979–1985*. New York: Norton, 1986. 124–35.

Rukeyser, Muriel. "Lecture by Mr. Eliot." *Con Spirito* 2.1 (Nov. 1933): 2.

Russo, Mary. *The Female Grotesque: Risk, Excess and Modernity*. New York: Routledge, 1994.

Smith-Rosenberg, Carroll. "The New Woman as Androgyne: Social Disorder and Gender Crisis, 1870–1936." *Disorderly Conduct: Visions of Gender in Victorian America*. New York: Knopf, 1985. 245–96.

Solomon, Barbara Miller. *In the Company of Educated Women: A History of Women and Higher Education in America*. New Haven, CT: Yale UP, 1985.

Travisano, Thomas. *Elizabeth Bishop: Her Artistic Development*. Charlottesville: UP of Virginia, 1988.

Vance, Carole S. "Pleasure and Danger: Toward a Politics of Sexuality." *Pleasure and Danger: Exploring Female Sexuality*. Ed. Carole S. Vance. Boston: Routledge, 1984.

Rich, Adrienne. "The Eye of the Outsider: Elizabeth Bishop's Complete Poems, 1927–1979." Blood, Bread, and Poetry: Selected Prose 1979–1985. New York: Norton, 1986. 124–35.

Rukeyser, Muriel. "Lecture by Mr. Eliot." Con Spirito 2.1 (Nov. 1933): 2

Russo, Mary. The Female Grotesque: Risk, Excess and Modernity. New York: Routledge, 1994.

Smith-Rosenberg, Carroll. "The New Woman as Androgyne: Social Disorder and Gender Crisis, 1870–1936." Disorderly Conduct: Visions of Gender in Victorian America. New York: Knopf, 1985. 245–96.

Solomon, Barbara Miller. In the Company of Educated Women: A History of Women and Higher Education in America. New Haven, CT: Yale UP, 1985.

Travisano, Thomas. Elizabeth Bishop: Her Artistic Development. Charlottesville: UP of Virginia, 1988

Vance, Carole S. "Pleasure and Danger: Toward a Politics of Sexuality." Pleasure and Danger: Exploring Female Sexuality. Ed. Carole S. Vance. Boston: Routledge, 1984.

PART EIGHT

Ethnic, Indigenous, Post-Colonial, and Transnational Studies

CHAPTER 1

Introduction
English Without Shadows: Literature on a World Scale

Julie Rivkin and Michael Ryan

"English," the name given to the literary tradition of a body of work produced in the dialect of the southeastern region of an island off the west coast of Europe, supplanted the "Classics," the literature of two Mediterranean peninsulas dating back to over two thousand years ago, as the body of texts used in the cultural training of young professional men in Great Britain in the late nineteenth century. Instead of Homer, Aeschylus, Pindar, Seneca, and Cicero, men in training now read Shakespeare, Milton, Pope, Wordsworth, and Eliot. This change might have been inconsequential enough had Great Britain not been the center of a global empire. But because of that imperial status, "English" soon became a very power-ful global cultural institution. Most of you reading this book will be doing so in the context of an "English Department" at an institution of higher learning. Those of you not doing so in such a context will probably be doing so for related reasons: either because you are in a literature department where the language in use is English even if the literature in question is not (is Australian or Canadian, say) or because the largest publishing market for literary discussions of any kind is in English even though your native language is something else.

While during the age of empire English the language was providing large parts of the world with a cultural, political, and economic *lingua franca* (as also French and Spanish) and English the cultural institution providing a supposedly universal set of ideals for proper living, people's lives were being changed and people's bodies moved in ways that made for painful and brutal contrasts to the benign values the English literary tradition supposedly fostered. The enslavement and displacement of large numbers of Africans to the Caribbean and North America is only the most powerful and violent example of such a counter-reality. The violence done by empire (with the US slave system being considered here a kind of internal imperialism) generated the negative energies that would eventually end empire and which have been the seeds out of which alternatives to "English" have grown.

That English the language and English the cultural institution are inseparable from the experience of empire does not mean that English is or was in itself an imperial under-taking. It was indeed used to help create a more "literate" and, one might argue, docile class of colonized subjects capable of co-administering empire, and English (the literary tradition and the conjoined academic institution) has for a long time and for reasons of

Literary Theory: An Anthology, Third Edition. Edited by Julie Rivkin and Michael Ryan.
© 2017 John Wiley & Sons, Ltd. Published 2017 by John Wiley & Sons, Ltd.

empire occupied a central place in literature departments in many parts of the world. The cultural misconstrual of the local for the universal could only endure for so long, however, and English's status for some time has also been changing, as indigenous literatures, from Australia to Africa to North America, have emerged to assume equal standing with or to displace entirely the English tradition. Those changes are bound up with the end of official empire and the transfer of political, if not always economic power, to formerly colonialized peoples in the latter half of the twentieth century.

These historical developments wrought great changes in literature and in the discussion and teaching of literature. Entire bodies of writing emerged out of the imperial front, that line of contact between colonizer and colonized which is characterized as much by reciprocal envy and adulation as by reciprocal fear and resentment. On the one side of that front stand works like Forster's *Passage to India* or Kipling's *Kim*, while on the other stand such works as Rhys's *Wide Sargasso Sea* or Kincaid's *A Small Place*. Each colonized nation also produced its own body of literature that dealt with the imperial experience or attempted to define a post-imperial sense of national and cultural identity, with the works of African writers such as Wole Soyinka and Ngugi wa Thiong'o being exemplary in this regard. In places like the United States, the former slave population of displaced Africans has given rise to a literary tradition of its own, many works of which, from the poetry of Langston Hughes to the novels of Toni Morrison, seek to make sense of their history and their continuing experience of racism. And throughout the world, peoples in diasporic situations of dispersal sought to establish a sense of cultural and ethnic identity within locales like England itself, where the majority ethnic group tended to control the production of mainstream culture.

The 1960s are once again a time of enormous transformation. English in England expanded to include the literature of the Commonwealth, while in the former colonies like the Caribbean it began to be displaced by indigenous traditions. In the US, it came to embrace the long-ignored tradition of African-American writing in the form of Afro-American programs. Such changes in institutional shape and disciplinary self-definition both fostered and were brought about by new developments in literary criticism. Scholars emerged who were less interested in the European tradition and more interested in post-colonial writers like V. S. Naipaul or Nadine Gordimer.

If English was losing some of its institutional power, it was also being cast in a new light as a result of these developments. No longer could it present itself as a repository of good values or of appropriate style if those values were connected, albeit metonymically rather than metaphorically, to imperial violence or if that style could be shown to be the result of a history of the forced displacement of other linguistic forms which had the misfortune alone of being practiced by people with smaller or no guns. Scholars began to take note of the fact that many great works of English literature promoted beliefs and assumptions regarding other geographic regions and other ethnic groups – from Shakespeare's Caliban to Brontë's Mrs. Rochester – that created the cultural preconditions for and no doubt enabled the work of empire. The promotion of such beliefs and assumptions in literature, Edward Said noted in his pathbreaking *Orientalism* (1978), was just one part of larger processes of discursive construction in a variety of forms of writing, from novels to scholarly treatises on geography and philology, that represented other peoples (in Said's example, the people of "the Orient") as less civilized or less capable and as needing Western paternalist assistance. Any attention to processes of domination usually spurs an interest in counter-processes of resistance, and as interest in colonial and post-colonial literature increased in the 1980s, attention turned, especially in the work of Homi Bhabha and in the collective volume *The Empire Writes Back* (1989), to the complex interface between colonizer and colonized, an interface that Bhabha found characterized as much by a subversive work of parody and mimicry as by straightforward domination. Later work along these lines, especially Paul Gilroy's *The Black Atlantic* (1993), has moved away from inter-national or inter-ethnic demarcations and towards an understanding of the para-national and trans-regional flows of culture. From the Caribbean to New York to London, black cultural influences and migrations tend not to heed traditional literary boundary lines, and these new realities demand new modes of non-national critical thinking.

Much of the early work in this rather large and diverse area of ethnic, post-colonial, and international studies was shaped by categories that have since been rethought by scholars in the field whose critical perspective is shaped by Structuralism, Feminism, and Post-Structuralism. While early anti-imperialist thinkers like DuBois and Fanon resorted to unproblematic notions of ethnic identity or to ideals of a traditional "people's culture," later thinkers have pointed out the isomorphism of racist and racialist ideologies as well as the mistake of assuming the unproblematic existence of such things as ethnic identities where fluctuation, change, and temporary blood-line settlements are more likely to be the case. Others have contended that recourse to a supposedly more authentic traditional culture as a counterpoint to imperial or neocolonial domination merely reduces the complex history of cultural change to an inaccurate folkloric myth and selectively privileges quaint "tribal" practices which are misconstrued as original and without history. Feminists have noted that there would be no ethnic identity without the forced containment and channeling of women's reproductive capacities along consanguine family and clan lines and that the privileging of ideals of ethnic or national cultural identity conceals internal fissures of gender and sexual domination. And Post-Structuralists in the field suggest that other concepts of identity, from the nation or the ethnic group to the national culture, are no longer relevant to a transnational, migratory, and diasporic world culture. What the experience of geographic displacement teaches is that all the supposedly stable equations of place, ethnos, and national political institution are imaginary constructs which displace displacement by substituting for the history of permanent migratory dislocation an ontologizing image of home or of a homeland, a proper place where a spuriously pure ethnos can authenticate itself.

The recent critical attention to such concepts as exile, home, and diaspora as much reflects the influence of Post-Structuralism's reexamination of taken-for-granted notions of identity as it does the experience of writers and theorists of African, Asian, or Caribbean descent who live in former imperial centers like Britain. DuBois first formulated the problematic nature of such experience when he spoke of "twoness," the twin experience of being both American and black, loyal to a nation while yet a victim of its prejudice against the minority ethnic group. For Fanon, the problem of twoness reappeared in a different guise, that of travelers to the imperial center from the colonized periphery who adopted the imperial culture as their own out of a sense of the inferiority of their own native culture. Since they wrote and since the emergence of new generations of people whose immigrant ethnic roots do not conflict with a sense of at-homeness in an imperial center like England, twoness gives way to a bilateral sense of parallel cultures and to a sense of multiple belongings, plural identities with no one more standard or normal or appropriate than another. And with that change of experience comes, of course, the possibility of multiple languages – not Creole or English, as Fanon noticed, but Creole and English.

What does all of this mean for English, for English as an academic institution that still in many places consists of the teaching of *the* national tradition century by century? It has meant the creation of new slots for an African-American specialist or a post-colonial specialist. And it has meant the reconceptualization of at least twentieth-century English literature to include Commonwealth literature and the emergence of new ways of organizing the American literary canon so that it includes more African and other voices (the much praised Heath Anthology). But if one source of empire was the national parochialism embodied in the ideal of the teaching of one's national literature alone and one result of the new ethnic, post-colonial, and international criticism is a sense of how all national literatures, especially those with global connections or with apparently singular ethnic roots, always cast shadows and are therefore always shadowed by their others, from Caliban to Mrs. Rochester to Beloved, then perhaps English itself should be reconsidered as a project of knowledge limited by national and linguistic boundaries. The national parochialism of empire continues as the national parochialism of "international competition," with each nation or ethnic group's imaginary sanctity and identity upheld by just the kind of national literary traditions and academic literary institutions that made English English. But by piercing its others and walking with its shadows, English also generated a migratory and cultural reciprocity that means that the future of English in England at least is necessarily multicultural and multiethnic (if not polylingual). It is also, Paul Gilroy would argue, transgeographical, a culture without national boundaries that thrives on lateral connections and syncretisms, a culture where in-betweenness replaces identity as the defining trope of cultural production. And such a new English is in some respects a model (shades of empire) for a new kind of Literature Department, one that would be at once national, international, and non-national or non-ethnic, one in which students might become as familiar with African as with English literature and learn thereby, not falsely universal values or accurately parochial national traditions, but the complex reality of difference.

Ethnicity and race emerged as an important new approach to literary study in the late 1960s and early 1970s in the Anglophone academy. Writers from a diverse range of ethnic minority perspectives – African American, Asian American, Hispanic American, Native American, etcetera – had been actively engaged with the problem of representing the experiences and the lives of the Anglo-American majority's "others." Writers such as Langston Hughes, Frank Chin, John Joseph Mathews, and Américo Paredes reflected in prose and in fiction on the conditions of minority ethnic life in a society dominated by another ethnic group's cultural vision and social interests. But it was not until the 1970s that courses and programs began to appear that consolidated a sense of the importance of representing the literatures of minority populations in the academy.

African-American literature was the first to achieve widespread representation in the academy. The Civil Rights Movement and the Black Arts Movement created a new cultural impetus that led to new courses and programs in African-American literature in the 1970s. Such courses and programs constituted in their mere presence a theoretical statement; as Henry Louis Gates observes, "Unlike almost every other literary tradition, the Afro-American literary tradition was generated as a response to eighteenth- and nineteenth-century allegations that persons of African descent did not, and could not, create literature" (*Figures in Black*, 25).

Among the first wave of African-American literary scholars in the US were Charles Davis, Mary Helen Washington, Barbara Christian, Darwin Turner, and Alan Ramperstad. Their work was soon followed by the work of scholars trained in the new critical approaches and literary theories of the 1970s and 1980s, critics such as Henry Louis Gates, Hortense Spillers, Hazel Carby, Valerie Smith, and Houston Baker. These critics developed a widely ranging body of scholarship, with some of its projects of revision and cultural recovery paralleling the projects of feminist criticism. Some critics concentrated on historical African-American literary movements such as the Harlem Renaissance; others studied the interface of white racism and black literary and cultural response throughout American history; others blended analyses of African-American musical culture with literary study. In some sense their work on culture is inseparable from that of the African-American writers whose work extended the very literary tradition now receiving such attention. The emergence of writers such as Amiri Baraka, Ishmael Reed, Toni Morrison, Edgar Wideman, and Alice Walker helped to further the new school of African-American literary criticism.

The Civil Rights Movement resulted as well in the emergence of movements for equal rights and equal status by other ethnic groups, such as Native Americans and Hispanic Americans, and academic departments or programs devoted to the cultures of these groups quickly took shape. By the 1980s, a recognizable body of scholarship on Asian-American writing had also developed. Each of these new approaches was aided by the emergence of important new writers within each of their fields of study – Gerald Vizenor, Leslie Silko, and Louise Erdrich in Native American, Rudolfo Anaya and Sandra Cisneros in Chicano, and Maxine Hong Kingston and Amy Tan in Asian American.

The emergence of Native-American literary studies coincides roughly with the renaissance in Native-American literature initiated in 1968 with the publication of M. Scott Momaday's *House Made of Dawn*. The American Indian Movement in the late 1960s and early 1970s also drew attention to long-suppressed issues relating to the Native-American presence in the mainstream culture defined and shaped by Anglo-American needs and concerns. Much of the early critical work by Kimberley Blaeser and Paula Gunn Allen on indigenous literature was concerned with preserving the religious, mythic, and oral dimensions of Native culture. The success and popularity of Leslie Marmon Silko's work, especially her novel *Ceremony*, worked to maintain that folkloric focus. Scholars such as Arnold Krupat drew on contemporary critical models in studying Native literature, but it was not until the 1990s that younger scholars versed in newer critical approaches, such as Robert Dale Parker and Carlton Smith, began to frame an understanding of such literature in contemporary theoretical terms. Their efforts are aided by the fact that more recent writers, such as Louise Erdrich and Thomas King, are more concerned with realist depictions of contemporary indigenous American life or with Postmodern filterings of Native experience. Gerald Vizenor has been especially instrumental in merging a sensitive appreciation for Native tradition with impressive meditations on the relevance of Post-Structuralist theories to an accurate description of the complex cultural mediations through which Native life must be seen. Indeed, it is fair to say that Vizenor, like his counterpart Gómez-Peña, is one of the most brilliant theoreticians of contemporary American culture.

Latino and Chicano critics have also moved beyond the early folkloric emphasis of critics such as Paredes, whose *With His Pistol in His Hand* (1958) was one of the first works of Chicano cultural studies, and they have come to incorporate into their work the most advanced critical theories. The work of Latino and Chicano scholarship has focused extensively on the concept of the border, given the locus of Chicano life along the vexed border between the US and Mexico. In its bilingualism, its invocation of a new geography, its attention to (im)migration, Chicano studies has its own particular contributions to ethnic studies. Post-Structuralist concepts of territoriality and hybridity were well suited to the work of Chicano theorists, and those concepts were incorporated into a critical vocabulary specific to Chicano studies. "Border theory," as it came to be called, drew on Post-Structuralist theories of contingency, hybridity, and territoriality in analyzing literary works by such writers as Helena Maria Viramontes and Ana Castillo. In addition, Chicana cultural theorists allied themselves very early on with African-American feminists to create a practically hybrid cultural movement. The collection by Chicana feminists and African-American writers and critics – *This Bridge Called My Back* (1981) – was one of the most famous early texts of the feminist movement. One of its participants – Gloria Anzaldúa – went on to write an important text of border theory – *Borderlands/La Frontera* (1987), a multilingual account of growing up along the border. Contemporary Chicano critics and theorists include such names as Guillermo Bomez-Peña, Renato Rosaldo, Hector Calderón, Ramón Saldívar, José David Saldívar, Juan Bruce-Novoa, and Norma Alarcón.

The successful emergence of popular Asian-American writers such as Maxine Hong Kingston and Amy Tan in the 1980s was predicated in part on the efforts of the Combined Asian Resources Project in the 1970s and on the publication of *Aiiieeeee! An Anthology of Asian-American Writers* in 1974. What these efforts exposed was the tremendous multiplicity within the term "Asian American," which encompasses Chinese (themselves a diverse group), Japanese, Korean, Pacific, South Asian, Vietnamese, and other Asian Americans. This enormous diversity also drew attention to the fact that while the category of ethnic studies takes a domestic location in the US, its existence is a product of transnational processes like colonialism, slavery, and immigration that have produced ethnic and racial diversities. It is perhaps not surprising that questions of cultural pluralism and ethnic identity-within-difference often come to the foreground as important concerns of writers from these Asian ethnic traditions. A not uncommon title of a critical essay on Asian-American literature as a result is "The Ambivalent American." With the erosion of segregation in the US in the post-Civil Rights Movement era, more and more Asian Americans have been assimilating into the Anglo-dominated cultural "mainstream." Indeed, many works of fiction such as, perhaps most famously, *The Joy Luck Club* (1976) make this change its principal focus. Perhaps because their own life experiences, like those of Chicanos and Native peoples, have been fissured by the recent experience of immigration, exclusion, linguistic difference, and the ongoing experience of living on the fault-line between an unself-consciously dominant ethnic culture and their own marginalized culture, many Asian-American critics find Post-Structuralist theories of hybridity, difference, and ambivalence to be helpful in their work. Critics such as Shirley Geok-Lin Lim have also challenged the ideal of ethnic homogeneity that the dominant Anglo group fosters in order to dilute and, ultimately, destroy singular and different ethnic cultures.

Critics like Geok-Lin have not been content to affirm the necessity of identity-within-difference in an ethnically plural society. Many ethnic studies scholars have begun to question the implicit assumptions that allow a white-dominated ethnic culture to present "color-blindness" as a norm for non-whites. The norm of whiteness became an object of critical study by the 1990s. Historian Theodore Allen in *The Invention of the White Race* (1994) and sociologist David Roediger in *The Wages of Whiteness* (1999) argued that the cultural category of whiteness came into being as a response to the presence of feared ethnic others such as African Americans in the United States. The category allowed for both self-identification and communal collusion against the feared "others."

These scholarly findings gave rise to a new body of literary and cultural scholarship on whiteness by such scholars as Dana Nelson and Ruth Frankenburg.

The last two decades have seen the rise of an explicitly theoretical body of writing on race. In the 1990s, scholars such as Anthony Appiah (in *In My Father's House* (1992)) drew attention to scientific evidence to the effect that biological genetic differences did not sort themselves out into evenly distinguishable "races." Race is more a cultural and social category than a natural, genetic, or biological one. Different external traits such as skin color are not indices of separate racial identities. They are more akin to differences in hair color. Nevertheless, race does, as Cornell West argued, "matter." African Americans are, according to Toni Morrison, the "pariahs" of US society. The dominant US white group's culture is marked by traces of those whose violation has been a precondition of that group's cohesiveness both economically and culturally. As a result, there is, as Morrison, argues, an "Africanist" presence, unacknowledged but palpable, in American literature. Many in the reparations movement argued that the same is true of the US economy, which grew and expanded in the early nineteenth century as a result of the unpaid labor of African slaves.

Looking backward as well as forward, the new scholarship on race has also focused critical attention on some of the early theorists of race. Pre-eminent among them is W. E. B. DuBois, whose work on a "racial concept" constituted the first real critique of a scientific racism inherited from the nineteenth century. That is, until DuBois, race was understood as a biological category, and in keeping with a social Darwinist perspective, this biological and essentialist view was also a justification for white supremacy. DuBois's movement towards a cultural understanding of race coincided with his sense of the historical sources of racial domination, and his work would be extremely important for a number of contemporary theorists, most notably Appiah and Henry Louis Gates.

One strand of the critical work on race came not out of the field of literary study, but rather out of the field of law. Critical race theory, adopted now by cultural critics as well as legal theorists, was an outgrowth of the critical legal studies movement and an important contribution to the new thinking about race. The founders of the movement are Derrick Bell, Richard Delgado, and Alan Freeman, and their work, which dates back to the mid-seventies, has been followed by that of a number of other legal scholars, including Kimberlé Crenshaw, Angela Harris, Charles Lawrence, Mari Matsuda, and Patricia Williams. Critical race theorists emphasize the ways in which racism is normalized in US culture, such that the principles of liberalism are not adequate to address its distortions. In particular, critical race theorists question the view that color-blind or "formal" conceptions of equality can actually remedy the effects of a pervasive and deeply rooted social racism. Critical race theorists extend the early work of DuBois on a social rather than biological concept of race. Among the theorists working on the cultural construction of race are the sociologists Michael Omi and Howard Winant, and their concept of racial formation shows how conceptions of race are invariably linked to political projects, political projects which change across time and which work to change racial formations. For example, the current discourse of color-blindness, which might seem to echo the civil rights language of Martin Luther King, is in fact used today to justify an anti-affirmative action conservative agenda. The concept of racial formation thus has a pragmatist dimension, linked as it is to the political effects of a particular discourse of race.

Ethnic literary scholars face tasks similar to those that faced feminists – the constitution of a history or tradition and the examination, using the best methodological tools available, of the works of writers operating within the cultural framework of an ethnic group whose existence is defined by internal exclusion. Not surprisingly, these critics tend to focus on questions of identity and of representation. What does it mean to hold national citizenship and to belong to an ethnic group whose features and whose culture exist to one side of a mainstream that seems blissfully unaware of its own hegemony? How can any one person represent "their" ethnic culture? What is the identity of a culture torn between traditional values and contemporary changes that could be represented? And for whom and for what reason does such representation, generally in the mainstream culture, occur? As the size of non-Anglo ethnic populations in the US grows and as the culture becomes less hegemonically white and Anglo, a different set of concerns will no doubt begin to emerge. That change is greatly aided by the work of the various ethnic scholars whose work we present in this section.

CHAPTER 2

Orientalism

Edward Said

In 1977, Palestinian scholar Edward Said published *Orientalism* and helped launch a new field of "Post-Colonial" studies. Influenced by the French historian Michel Foucault, Said set out to describe the discourse that arose in colonialist countries to account for the worlds they colonized. The study of the "Orient" was, according to Said, a way of not only legitimizing imperialism but also assisting its supervision and management. Scholarly knowledge had an imperial purpose. From the perspective of the metropole, colonized subjects became stereotypes whose absorption into discursive tropes made them more readily available to an imperial gaze that deprived them of a point of view of their own, of agency in the management of their own lives, and of human rights.

Introduction

I

On a visit to Beirut during the terrible civil war of 1975–1976 a French journalist wrote regretfully of the gutted downtown area that "it had once seemed to belong to … the Orient of Chateaubriand and Nerval."[1] He was right about the place, of course especially so far as a European was concerned. The Orient was almost a European invention, and had been since antiquity a place of romance, exotic beings, haunting memories and landscapes, remarkable experiences. Now it was disappearing; in a sense it had happened, its time was over. Perhaps it seemed irrelevant that Orientals themselves had something at stake in the process, that even in the time of Chateaubriand and Nerval Orientals had lived there, and that now it was they who were suffering; the main thing for the European visitor was a European representation of the Orient and its contemporary fate, both of which had a privileged communal significance for the journalist and his French readers.

Original publication details: Edward Said, from *Orientalism*, pp. 1–45. Pantheon, 1978. Reproduced with permission from Knopf Doubleday Publishing Group, a division of Penguin Random House LLC.

Literary Theory: An Anthology, Third Edition. Edited by Julie Rivkin and Michael Ryan.
© 2017 John Wiley & Sons, Ltd. Published 2017 by John Wiley & Sons, Ltd.

Americans will not feel quite the same about the Orient, which for them is much more likely to be associated very differently with the Far East (China and Japan, mainly). Unlike the Americans, the French and the British – less so the Germans, Russians, Spanish, Portuguese, Italians, and Swiss – have had a long tradition of what I shall be calling *Orientalism*, a way of coming to terms with the Orient that is based on the Orient's special place in European Western experience. The Orient is not only adjacent to Europe; it is also the place of Europe's greatest and richest and oldest colonies, the source of its civilizations and languages, its cultural contestant, and one of its deepest and most recurring images of the Other. In addition, the Orient has helped to define Europe (or the West) as its contrasting image, idea, personality, experience. Yet none of this Orient is merely imaginative. The Orient is an integral part of European *material* civilization and culture. Orientalism expresses and represents that part culturally and even ideologically as a mode of discourse with supporting institutions, vocabulary, scholarship, imagery, doctrines, even colonial bureaucracies and colonial styles. In contrast, the American understanding of the Orient will seem considerably less dense, although our recent Japanese, Korean, and Indochinese adventures ought now to be creating a more sober, more realistic "Oriental" awareness. Moreover, the vastly expanded American political and economic role in the Near East (the Middle East) makes great claims on our understanding of that Orient.

It will be clear to the reader (and will become clearer still throughout the many pages that follow) that by Orientalism I mean several things, all of them, in my opinion, interdependent. The most readily accepted designation for Orientalism is an academic one, and indeed the label still serves in a number of academic institutions. Anyone who teaches, writes about, or researches the Orient – and this applies whether the person is an anthropologist, sociologist, historian, or philologist – either in its specific or its general aspects, is an Orientalist, and what he or she does is Orientalism. Compared with *Oriental studies* or *area studies*, it is true that the term *Orientalism* is less preferred by specialists today, both because it is too vague and general and because it connotes the high-handed executive attitude of nineteenth-century and early-twentieth-century European colonialism. Nevertheless books are written and congresses held with "the Orient" as their main focus, with the Orientalist in his new or old guise as their main authority. The point is that even if it does not survive as it once did, Orientalism lives on academically through its doctrines and theses about the Orient and the Oriental.

Related to this academic tradition, whose fortunes, transmigrations, specializations, and transmissions are in part the subject of this study, is a more general meaning for Orientalism. Orientalism is a style of thought based upon an ontological and epistemological distinction made between "the Orient" and (most of the time) "the Occident." Thus a very large mass of writers, among whom are poets, novelists, philosophers, political theorists, economists, and imperial administrators, have accepted the basic distinction between East and West as the starting point for elaborate theories, epics, novels, social descriptions, and political accounts concerning the Orient, its people, customs, "mind," destiny, and so on. *This* Orientalism can accommodate Aeschylus, say, and Victor Hugo, Dante and Karl Marx. A little later in this introduction I shall deal with the methodological problems one encounters in so broadly construed a "field" as this.

The interchange between the academic and the more or less imaginative meanings of Orientalism is a constant one, and since the late eighteenth century there has been a considerable, quite disciplined – perhaps even regulated – traffic between the two. Here I come to the third meaning of Orientalism, which is something more historically and materially defined than either of the other two. Taking the late eighteenth century as a very roughly defined starting point Orientalism can be discussed and analyzed as the corporate institution for dealing with the Orient – dealing with it by making statements about it, authorizing views of it, describing it, by teaching it, settling it, ruling over it: in short, Orientalism as a Western style for dominating, restructuring, and having authority over the Orient. I have found it useful here to employ Michel Foucault's notion of a discourse, as described by him in *The Archaeology of Knowledge* and in *Discipline and Punish*, to identify Orientalism. My contention is that without examining Orientalism as a discourse one cannot possibly understand the enormously systematic discipline by which European culture was able to manage – and even produce – the Orient politically, sociologically, militarily, ideologically, scientifically, and imaginatively during the post-Enlightenment period. Moreover, so authoritative a position did Orientalism have that I believe no one writing, thinking, or acting on the Orient could do so without taking account of the limitations on thought and action imposed by Orientalism. In brief, because of Orientalism the Orient was not (and is not) a free subject of thought or action. This is not to say that Orientalism unilaterally determines what can be said about the Orient, but that it is the whole network of interests inevitably brought to bear on (and therefore always involved in) any occasion when that peculiar entity "the Orient" is in question. How this happens is what this book tries to demonstrate. It also tries to show that European culture gained in strength and identity by setting itself off against the Orient as a sort of surrogate and even underground self.

Historically and culturally there is a quantitative as well as a qualitative difference between the Franco-British involvement in the Orient and – until the period of American ascendancy after World War II – the involvement of every other European and Atlantic power. To speak of Orientalism therefore is to speak mainly, although not exclusively, of a British and French cultural enterprise, a project whose dimensions take in such disparate realms as the imagination itself, the whole of India and the Levant, the Biblical texts and the Biblical lands, the spice trade, colonial armies and a long tradition of colonial administrators, a formidable scholarly corpus, innumerable Oriental "experts" and "hands," an Oriental professorate, a complex array of "Oriental" ideas (Oriental despotism, Oriental splendor, cruelty, sensuality), many Eastern sects, philosophies, and wisdoms domesticated for local European use – the list can be extended more or less indefinitely. My point is that Orientalism derives from a particular closeness experienced between Britain and France and the Orient, which until the early nineteenth century had really meant only India and the Bible lands. From the beginning of the nineteenth century until the end of World War II France and Britain dominated the Orient and Orientalism; since World War II America has dominated the Orient, and approaches it as France and Britain once did. Out of that closeness, whose dynamic is enormously productive even if it always demonstrates the comparatively greater strength of the Occident (British, French, or American), comes the large body of texts I call Orientalist.

It should be said at once that even with the generous number of books and authors that I examine, there is a much larger number that I simply have had to leave out. My argument, however, depends neither upon an exhaustive catalogue of texts dealing with the Orient nor upon a clearly delimited set of texts, authors, and ideas that together make up the Orientalist canon. I have depended instead upon a different methodological alternative – whose backbone in a sense is the set of historical generalizations I have so far been making in this Introduction – and it is these I want now to discuss in more analytical detail.

II

I have begun with the assumption that the Orient is not an inert fact of nature. It is not merely *there*, just as the Occident itself is not just *there* either. We must take seriously Vico's great observation that men make their own history, that what they can know is what they have made, and extend it to geography: as both geographical and cultural entities – to say nothing of historical entities – such locales, regions, geographical sectors as "Orient" and "Occident" are man-made. Therefore as much as the West itself, the Orient is an idea that has a history and a tradition of thought, imagery, and vocabulary that have given it reality and presence in and for the West. The two geographical entities thus support and to an extent reflect each other.

Having said that, one must go on to state a number of reasonable qualifications. In the first place, it would be wrong to conclude that the Orient was *essentially* an idea, or a creation with no corresponding reality. When Disraeli said in his novel *Tancred* that the East was a career, he meant that to be interested in the East was something bright young Westerners would find to be an all-consuming passion; he should not be interpreted as saying that the East was *only* a career for Westerners. There were – and are – cultures and nations whose location is in the East, and their lives, histories, and customs have a brute reality obviously greater than anything that could be said about them in the West. About that fact this study of Orientalism has very little to contribute, except to acknowledge it tacitly. But the phenomenon of Orientalism as I study it here deals principally, not with a correspondence between Orientalism and Orient, but with the internal consistency of Orientalism and its ideas about the Orient (the East as career) despite or beyond any correspondence, or lack thereof, with a "real" Orient. My point is that Disraeli's statement about the East refers mainly to that created consistency, that regular constellation of ideas as the pre-eminent thing about the Orient, and not to its mere being, as Wallace Stevens's phrase has it.

A second qualification is that ideas, cultures, and histories cannot seriously be understood or studied without their force, or more precisely their configurations of power, also being studied. To believe that the Orient was created – or, as I call it, "Orientalized" – and to believe that such things happen simply as a necessity of the imagination, is to be disingenuous. The relationship between Occident and Orient is a relationship of power, of domination, of varying degrees of a complex hegemony, and is quite accurately indicated in the title of K. M. Panikkar's classic *Asia and Western Dominance*.[2] The Orient was Orientalized not only because it was discovered to be "Oriental" in all those ways considered commonplace by an average nineteenth-century European, but also because it *could be* – that is, submitted to being – *made* Oriental. There is very little consent to be found, for example, in the fact that Flaubert's encounter with an Egyptian courtesan produced a widely influential model of the Oriental woman; she never spoke of herself, she never represented her emotions, presence, or history. *He* spoke for and represented her. He was foreign, comparatively wealthy, male, and these were historical facts of domination that allowed him not only to possess Kuchuk Hanem physically but to speak for her and tell his readers in what way she was "typically Oriental." My argument is that Flaubert's situation of strength in relation to Kuchuk Hanem was not an isolated instance. It fairly stands for the pattern of relative strength between East and West, and the discourse about the Orient that it enabled.

This brings us to a third qualification. One ought never to assume that the structure of Orientalism is nothing more than a structure of lies or of myths which, were the truth about them to be told, would simply blow away. I myself believe that Orientalism is more particularly valuable as a sign of European-Atlantic power over the Orient than it is as a veridic discourse about the Orient (which is what, in its academic or scholarly form, it claims to be). Nevertheless, what we must respect and try to grasp is the sheer knitted-together strength of Orientalist discourse, its very close ties to the enabling socio-economic and political institutions, and its redoubtable durability. After all, any system of ideas that can remain unchanged as teachable wisdom (in academies, books, congresses, universities, foreign-service institutes) from the period of Ernest Renan in the late 1840s until the present in the United States must be something more formidable than a mere collection of lies. Orientalism, therefore, is not an airy European fantasy about the Orient, but a created body of theory and practice in which, for many generations, there has been a considerable material investment. Continued investment made Orientalism, as a system of knowledge about the Orient, an accepted grid for filtering through the Orient into Western consciousness, just as that same investment multiplied – indeed, made truly productive – the statements proliferating out from Orientalism into the general culture.

Gramsci has made the useful analytic distinction between civil and political society in which the former is made up of voluntary (or at least rational and noncoercive) affiliations like schools, families, and unions, the latter of state institutions (the army, the police, the central bureaucracy) whose role in the polity is direct domination. Culture, of course, is to be found operating within civil society, where the influence of ideas, of institutions, and of other persons works not through domination but by what Gramsci calls consent. In any society not totalitarian, then, certain cultural forms predominate over others, just as certain ideas are more influential than others; the form of this cultural leadership is what Gramsci has identified as *hegemony*, an indispensable concept for any understanding of cultural life in the industrial West. It is hegemony, or rather the result of cultural hegemony at work, that gives Orientalism the durability and the strength I have been speaking about so far. Orientalism is never far from what Denys Hay has called the idea of Europe,[3] a collective notion identifying "us" Europeans as against all "those" non-Europeans, and indeed it can be argued that the major component in European culture is precisely what made that culture hegemonic both in and outside Europe: the idea of European identity as a superior one in comparison with all the non-European peoples and cultures. There is in addition the hegemony of European ideas about the Orient, themselves reiterating European superiority over Oriental backwardness, usually overriding the possibility that a more independent, or more skeptical, thinker might have had different views on the matter.

In a quite constant way, Orientalism depends for its strategy on this flexible *positional* superiority, which puts the Westerner in a whole series of possible relationships with the Orient without ever losing him the relative upper hand. And why should it have been otherwise, especially during the period of extraordinary European ascendancy from the late Renaissance to the present? The scientist, the scholar, the missionary, the trader, or the soldier was in, or thought about, the Orient because he *could be there*, or could think about it, with very little resistance on the Orient's part. Under the general heading of knowledge of the Orient, and within the umbrella of Western hegemony over the Orient during the period from the end of the eighteenth century, there emerged a complex Orient suitable for study in the academy, for display in the museum, for reconstruction in the colonial office, for theoretical illustration in anthropological, biological, linguistic, racial, and historical theses about mankind and the universe, for instances of economic and sociological theories of development, revolution, cultural personality, national or religious character. Additionally, the imaginative examination of things Oriental was based more or less exclusively upon a sovereign Western consciousness out of whose unchallenged centrality an Oriental world emerged, first according to general ideas about who or what was an Oriental, then according to a detailed logic governed not simply by empirical reality but by a battery of desires, repressions, investments, and projections. If we can point to great Orientalist works of genuine scholarship like Silvestre de Sacy's *Chrestomathie arabe* or Edward William Lane's *Account of the Manners and Customs of the Modern Egyptians*, we need also to note that Renan's and Gobineau's racial ideas came out of the same impulse, as did a great many Victorian pornographic novels (see the analysis by Steven Marcus of "The Lustful Turk"[4]).

And yet, one must repeatedly ask oneself whether what matters in Orientalism is the general group of ideas overriding the mass of material – about which who could deny that they were shot through with doctrines of European superiority, various kinds of racism, imperialism, and the like, dogmatic views of "the Oriental" as a kind of ideal and unchanging abstraction? – or the much more varied work produced by almost uncountable individual writers, whom one would take up as individual instances of authors dealing with the Orient. In a sense the two alternatives, general and particular, are really two perspectives on the same material: in both instances one would have to deal with pioneers in the field like William Jones, with great artists like Nerval or Flaubert. And why would it not be possible to employ both perspectives together, or one after the other? Isn't there an obvious danger of distortion (of precisely the kind that academic Orientalism has always been prone to) if either too general or too specific a level of description is maintained systematically?

My two fears are distortion and inaccuracy, or rather the kind of inaccuracy produced by too dogmatic a generality and too positivistic a localized focus. In trying to deal with these problems I have tried to deal with three main aspects of my own contemporary reality that seem to me to point the way out of the methodological or perspectival difficulties I have been discussing, difficulties that might force one, in the first instance, into writing a coarse polemic on so unacceptably general a level of description as not to be worth the effort, or in the second instance, into writing so detailed and atomistic a series of analyses as to lose all track of the general lines of force informing the field, giving it its special cogency. How then to recognize individuality and to reconcile it with its intelligent, and by no means passive or merely dictatorial, general and hegemonic context?

III

I mentioned three aspects of my contemporary reality: I must explain and briefly discuss them now, so that it can be seen how I was led to a particular course of research and writing.

1. *The distinction between pure and political knowledge.* It is very easy to argue that knowledge about Shakespeare or Wordsworth is not political whereas knowledge about contemporary China or the Soviet Union is. My own formal and professional designation is that of "humanist," a title which indicates the humanities as my field and therefore the unlikely eventuality that there might be anything political about what I do in that field. Of course, all these labels and terms are quite unnuanced as I use them here, but the general truth of what I am pointing to is, I think, widely held. One reason for saying that

a humanist who writes about Wordsworth, or an editor whose specialty is Keats, is not involved in anything political is that what he does seems to have no direct political effect upon reality in the everyday sense. A scholar whose field is Soviet economics works in a highly charged area where there is much government interest, and what he might produce in the way of studies or proposals will be taken up by policymakers, government officials, institutional economists, intelligence experts. The distinction between "humanists" and persons whose work has policy implications, or political significance can be broadened further by saying that the former's ideological color is a matter of incidental importance to politics (although possibly of great moment to his colleagues in the field, who may object to his Stalinism or fascism or too easy liberalism), whereas the ideology of the latter is woven directly into his material indeed, economics, politics, and sociology in the modern academy are ideological sciences – and therefore taken for granted as being "political."

Nevertheless the determining impingement on most knowledge produced in the contemporary West (and here I speak mainly about the United States) is that it be nonpolitical, that is, scholarly, academic, impartial, above partisan or small-minded doctrinal belief. One can have no quarrel with such an ambition in theory, perhaps, but in practice the reality is much more problematic. No one has ever devised a method for detaching the scholar from the circumstances of life, from the fact of his involvement (conscious or unconscious) with a class, a set of beliefs, a social position, or from the mere activity of being a member of a society. These continue to bear on what he does professionally, even though naturally enough his research and its fruits do attempt to reach a level of relative freedom from the inhibitions and the restrictions of brute, everyday reality. For there is such a thing as knowledge that is less, rather than more, partial than the individual (with his entangling and distracting life circumstances) who produces it. Yet this knowledge is not therefore automatically nonpolitical.

Whether discussions of literature or of classical philology are fraught with – or have unmediated – political significance is a very large question that I have tried to treat in some detail elsewhere.[5] What I am interested in doing now is suggesting how the general liberal consensus that "true" knowledge is fundamentally nonpolitical (and conversely, that overtly political knowledge is not "true" knowledge) obscures the highly if obscurely organized political circumstances obtaining when knowledge is produced. No one is helped in understanding this today when the adjective "political" is used as a label to discredit any work for daring to violate the protocol of pretended suprapolitical objectivity. We may say, first, that civil society recognizes a gradation of political importance in the various fields of knowledge. To some extent the political importance given a field comes from the possibility of its direct translation into economic terms; but to a greater extent political importance comes from the closeness of a field to ascertainable sources of power in political society. Thus an economic study of long-term Soviet energy potential and its effect on military capability is likely to be commissioned by the Defense Department, and thereafter to acquire a kind of political status impossible for a study of Tolstoi's early fiction financed in part by a foundation. Yet both works belong in what civil society acknowledges to be a similar field, Russian studies, even though one work may be done by a very conservative economist, the other by a radical literary historian. My point here is that "Russia" as a general subject matter has political priority over nicer distinctions such as "economics" and "literary history," because political society in Gramsci's sense reaches into such realms of civil society as the academy and saturates them with significance of direct concern to it.

I do not want to press all this any further on general theoretical grounds: it seems to me that the value and credibility of my case can be demonstrated by being much more specific, in the way, for example, Noam Chomsky has studied the instrumental connection between the Vietnam War and the notion of objective scholarship as it was applied to cover state-sponsored military research.[6] Now because Britain, France, and recently the United States are imperial powers, their political societies impart to their civil societies a sense of urgency, a direct political infusion as it were, where and whenever matters pertaining to their imperial interests abroad are concerned. I doubt that it is controversial, for example, to say that an Englishman in India or Egypt in the later nineteenth century took an interest in those countries that was never far from their status in his mind as British colonies. To say this may seem quite different from saying that all academic knowledge about India and Egypt is somehow tinged and impressed with, violated by, the gross political fact – and yet *that is what I am saying* in this study of Orientalism. For if it is true that no production of knowledge in the human sciences can ever ignore or disclaim its author's involvement as a human subject in his own circumstances, then it must also be true that for a European or American studying the Orient there can be no disclaiming the main circumstances of *his* actuality: that he comes up against the Orient as a European or American first, as an individual second. And to be a European or an American in such a situation is by no means an inert fact. It meant and means being aware, however dimly, that one belongs to a power with definite interests in the Orient, and more important, that one belongs to a part of the earth with a definite history of involvement in the Orient almost since the time of Homer.

Put in this way, these political actualities are still too undefined and general to be really interesting. Anyone would agree to them without necessarily agreeing also that they mattered very much, for instance, to Flaubert as he wrote *Salammbô*, or to H. A. R. Gibb as he wrote *Modern Trends in Islam*. The trouble is that there is too great a distance between the big dominating fact, as I have described it, and the details of everyday life that govern the minute discipline of a novel or a scholarly text as each is being written. Yet if we eliminate from the start any notion that "big" facts like imperial domination can be applied mechanically and deterministically to such complex matters as culture and ideas, then we will begin to approach an interesting kind of study. My idea is that European and then American interest in the Orient was political according to some of the obvious historical accounts of it that I have given here, but that it was the culture that created that interest, that acted dynamically along with brute political, economic, and military rationales to make the Orient the varied and complicated place that it obviously was in the field I call Orientalism.

Therefore, Orientalism is not a mere political subject matter or field that is reflected passively by culture, scholarship, or institutions; nor is it a large and diffuse collection of texts about the Orient; nor is it representative and expressive of some nefarious "Western" imperialist plot to hold down the "Oriental" world. It is rather a *distribution* of geopolitical awareness into aesthetic, scholarly, economic, sociological, historical, and philological texts; it is an *elaboration* not only of a basic geographical distinction (the world is made up of two unequal halves, Orient and Occident) but also of a whole series of "interests" which, by such means as scholarly discovery, philological reconstruction, psychological analysis, landscape and sociological description, it not only creates but also maintains; it *is*, rather than expresses, a certain *will* or *intention* to understand, in some cases to control, manipulate, even to incorporate, what is a manifestly different (or alternative and novel) world; it is, above all, a discourse that is by no means in direct, corresponding relationship with political power in the raw, but rather is produced and exists in an uneven exchange with various kinds of power, shaped to a degree by the exchange with power political (as with a colonial or imperial establishment), power intellectual (as with reigning sciences like comparative linguistics or anatomy, or any of the modern policy sciences), power cultural (as with orthodoxies and canons of taste, texts, values), power moral (as with ideas about what "we" do and what "they" cannot do or understand as "we" do). Indeed, my real argument is that Orientalism is – and does not simply represent – a considerable dimension of modern political-intellectual culture, and as such has less to do with the Orient than it does with "our" world.

Because Orientalism is a cultural and a political fact, then, it does not exist in some archival vacuum; quite the contrary, I think it can be shown that what is thought, said, or even done about the Orient follows (perhaps occurs within) certain distinct and intellectually knowable lines. Here too a considerable degree of nuance and elaboration can be seen working as between the broad superstructural pressures and the details of composition, the facts of textuality. Most humanistic scholars are, I think, perfectly happy with the notion that texts exist in contexts, that there is such a thing as intertextuality, that the pressures of conventions, predecessors, and rhetorical styles limit what Walter Benjamin once called the "overtaxing of the productive person in the name of … the principle of 'creativity,'" in which the poet is believed on his own, and out of his pure mind, to have brought forth his work.[7] Yet there is a reluctance to allow that political, institutional, and ideological constraints act in the same manner on the individual author. A humanist will believe it to be an interesting fact to any interpreter of Balzac that he was influenced in the *Comédie humaine* by the conflict between Geoffroy Saint-Hilaire and Cuvier, but the same sort of pressure on Balzac of deeply reactionary monarchism is felt in some vague way to demean his literary "genius" and therefore to be less worth serious study. Similarly – as Harry Bracken has been tirelessly showing – philosophers will conduct their discussions of Locke, Hume, and empiricism without ever taking into account that there is an explicit connection in these classic writers between their "philosophic" doctrines and racial theory, justifications of slavery, or arguments for colonial exploitation.[8] These are common enough ways by which contemporary scholarship keeps itself pure.

Perhaps it is true that most attempts to rub culture's nose in the mud of politics have been crudely iconoclastic; perhaps also the social interpretation of literature in my own field has simply not kept up with the enormous technical advances in detailed textual analysis. But there is no getting away from the fact that literary studies in general, and American Marxist theorists in particular, have avoided the effort of seriously bridging the gap between the superstructural and the base levels in textual, historical scholarship; on another occasion I have gone so far as to say that the literary-cultural establishment as a whole has declared the serious study of imperialism and culture off limits.[9] For Orientalism brings one up directly against that question – that is, to realizing that political imperialism governs an entire field of study, imagination, and scholarly institutions – in such a way as to make its avoidance an intellectual and historical impossibility. Yet there will always remain the perennial escape mechanism of saying that a literary scholar and a philosopher, for example, are trained in literature and philosophy respectively, not in politics or ideological analysis. In other words, the specialist argument can work quite effectively to block the larger and, in my opinion, the more intellectually serious perspective.

Here it seems to me there is a simple two-part answer to be given, at least so far as the study of imperialism and culture (or Orientalism) is concerned. In the first place, nearly every nineteenth-century writer (and the same is true enough of writers in earlier periods) was extraordinarily well aware of the fact of empire: this is a subject not very well studied, but it will not take a modern Victorian specialist long to admit that liberal cultural heroes like John Stuart Mill, Arnold, Carlyle, Newman, Macaulay, Ruskin, George Eliot, and even Dickens had definite views on race and imperialism, which are quite easily to be found at work in their writing. So even a specialist must deal with the knowledge that Mill, for example, made it clear in *On Liberty* and *Representative Government* that his views there could not be applied to India (he was an India Office functionary for a good deal of his life, after all) because the Indians were civilizationally, if not racially, inferior. The same kind of paradox is to be found in Marx, as I try to show in this book. In the second place, to believe that politics in the form of imperialism bears upon the production of literature, scholarship, social theory, and history writing is by no means equivalent to saying that culture is therefore a demeaned or denigrated thing. Quite the contrary: my whole point is to say that we can better understand the persistence and the durability of saturating hegemonic systems like culture when we realize that their internal constraints upon writers and thinkers were *productive*, not unilaterally inhibiting. It is this idea that Gramsci, certainly, and Foucault and Raymond Williams in their very different ways have been trying to illustrate. Even one or two pages by Williams on "the uses of the Empire" in *The Long Revolution* tell us more about nineteenth-century cultural richness than many volumes of hermetic textual analyses.[10]

Therefore I study Orientalism as a dynamic exchange between individual authors and the large political concerns shaped by the three great empires – British, French, American – in whose intellectual and imaginative territory the writing was produced. What interests me most as a scholar is not the gross political verity but the detail, as indeed what interests us in someone like Lane or Flaubert or Renan is not the (to him) indisputable truth that Occidentals are superior to Orientals, but the profoundly worked over and modulated evidence of his detailed work within the very wide space opened up by that truth. One need only remember that Lane's *Manners and Customs of the Modern Egyptians* is a classic of historical and anthropological observation because of its style, its enormously intelligent and brilliant details, not because of its simple reflection of racial superiority, to understand what I am saying here.

The kind of political questions raised by Orientalism, then, are as follows: What other sorts of intellectual, aesthetic, scholarly, and cultural energies went into the making of an imperialist tradition like the Orientalist one? How did philology, lexicography, history, biology, political and economic theory, novel-writing, and lyric poetry come to the service of Orientalism's broadly imperialist view of the world? What changes, modulations, refinements, even revolutions take place within Orientalism? What is the meaning of originality, of continuity, of individuality, in this context? How does Orientalism transmit or reproduce itself from one epoch to another? In fine, how can we treat the cultural, historical phenomenon of Orientalism as a kind of *willed human work* – not of mere unconditioned ratiocination – in all its historical complexity, detail, and worth without at the same time losing sight of the alliance between cultural work, political tendencies, the state, and the specific realities of domination? Governed by such concerns a humanistic study can responsibly address itself to politics *and* culture. But this is not to say that such a study establishes a hard-and-fast rule about the relationship between knowledge and politics. My argument is that each humanistic investigation must formulate the nature of that connection in the specific context of the study, the subject matter, and its historical circumstances.

2. *The methodological question.* In a previous book I gave a good deal of thought and analysis to the methodological importance for work in the human sciences of finding and formulating a first step, a point of departure, a beginning principle.[11] A major lesson I learned and tried to present was that there is no such thing as a merely given, or simply available, starting point: beginnings have to be made for each project in such a way as to *enable* what follows from them. Nowhere in my experience has the difficulty of this lesson been more consciously lived (with what success – or failure – I cannot really say) than in this study of Orientalism. The idea of beginning, indeed the act of beginning, necessarily involves an act of delimitation by which something is cut out of a great mass of material, separated from the mass, and made to stand for, as well as be, a starting point, a beginning; for the student of texts one such notion of inaugural delimitation is Louis Althusser's idea of the *problematic*, a specific determinate unity of a text, or group of texts, which is something given rise to by analysis.[12] Yet in the case of Orientalism (as opposed to the case of Marx's texts, which is what Althusser studies) there is not simply the problem of finding a point of departure, or problematic, but also the question of designating which texts, authors, and periods are the ones best suited for study.

It has seemed to me foolish to attempt an encyclopedic narrative history of Orientalism, first of all because if my guiding principle was to be "the European idea of the Orient" there would be virtually no limit to the material I would have had to deal with; second because the narrative model itself did not suit my descriptive and political interests; third, because in such books as Raymond Schwab's *La Renaissance orientale*, Johann Fück's *Die Arabischen Studien in Europa bis in den Anfang des 20. Jahrhunderts*, and more recently, Dorothee Metlitzki's *The Matter of Araby in Medieval England*[13] there already exist encyclopedic works on certain aspects of the European-Oriental encounter such as make the critic's job, in the general political and intellectual context I sketched above, a different one.

There still remained the problem of cutting down a very fat archive to manageable dimensions, and more important, outlining something in the nature of an intellectual order within that group of texts without at the same time following a mindlessly chronological order. My starting point therefore has been the British, French, and American experience of the Orient taken as a unit, what made that experience possible by way of historical and intellectual background, what the quality and character of the experience has been. For reasons I shall discuss presently I limited that already limited (but still inordinately large) set of questions to the Anglo-French-American experience of the Arabs and Islam, which for almost a thousand years together stood for the Orient. Immediately upon doing that, a large part of the Orient seemed to have been eliminated – India, Japan, China, and other sections of the Far East – not because these regions were not important (they obviously have been) but because one could discuss Europe's experience of the Near Orient, or of Islam, apart from its experience of the Far Orient. Yet at certain moments of that general European history of interest in the East, particular parts of the Orient like Egypt, Syria, and Arabia cannot be discussed without also studying Europe's involvement in the more distant parts, of which Persia and India are the most important; a notable case in point is the connection between Egypt and India so far as eighteenth- and nineteenth-century Britain was concerned. Similarly the French role in deciphering the Zend-Avesta, the pre-eminence of Paris as a center of Sanskrit studies during the first decade of the nineteenth century, the fact that Napoleon's interest in the Orient was contingent upon his sense of the British role in India: all these Far Eastern interests directly influenced French interest in the Near East, Islam, and the Arabs.

Britain and France dominated the Eastern Mediterranean from about the end of the seventeenth century on. Yet my discussion of that domination and systematic interest does not do justice to (*a*) the important contributions to Orientalism of Germany, Italy, Russia, Spain, and Portugal and (*b*) the fact that one of the important impulses toward the study of the Orient in the eighteenth century was the revolution in Biblical studies stimulated by such variously interesting pioneers as Bishop Lowth, Eichhorn, Herder, and Michaelis. In the first place, I had to focus rigorously upon the British-French and later the American material because it seemed inescapably true not only that Britain and France were the pioneer nations in the Orient and in Oriental studies, but that these vanguard positions were held by virtue of the two greatest colonial networks in pre-twentieth-century history; the American Oriental position since World War II has fit – I think, quite self-consciously – in the places excavated by the two earlier European powers. Then too, I believe that the sheer quality, consistency, and mass of British, French, and American writing on the Orient lifts it above the doubtless crucial work done in Germany, Italy, Russia, and elsewhere. But I think it is also true that the major steps in Oriental scholarship were first taken in either Britain and France, then elaborated upon by Germans. Silvestre de Sacy, for example, was not only the first modern and institutional European Orientalist, who worked on Islam, Arabic literature, the Druze religion, and Sassanid Persia; he was also the teacher of Champollion and of Franz Bopp, the founder of German comparative linguistics. A similar claim of priority and subsequent pre-eminence can be made for William Jones and Edward William Lane.

In the second place – and here the failings of my study of Orientalism are amply made up for – there has been some important recent work on the background in Biblical scholarship to the rise of what I have called modern Orientalism. The best and the most illuminatingly relevant is E. S. Shaffer's impressive *"Kubla Khan" and The Fall of Jerusalem*,[14] an indispensable study of the origins of Romanticism, and of the intellectual activity underpinning a great deal of what goes on in Coleridge, Browning, and George Eliot. To some degree Shaffer's work refines upon the outlines provided in Schwab, by articulating the material of relevance to be found in the German Biblical scholars and using that material to read, in an intelligent and always interesting way, the work of three major British writers. Yet what is missing in the book is some sense of the political as well as ideological edge given the Oriental material by the British and French writers I am principally concerned with; in addition, unlike Shaffer I attempt to elucidate subsequent developments in academic as well as literary Orientalism that bear on the connection between British and French Orientalism on the one hand and the rise of an explicitly colonial-minded imperialism on the other. Then too, I wish to show how all these earlier matters are reproduced more or less in American Orientalism after the Second World War.

Nevertheless there is a possibly misleading aspect to my study, where, aside from an occasional reference, I do not exhaustively discuss the German developments after the inaugural period dominated by Sacy. Any work that seeks to provide an understanding of academic Orientalism and pays little attention to scholars like Steinthal, Müller, Becker, Goldziher, Brockelmann, Nöldeke – to mention only a handful – needs to be reproached, and I freely reproach myself. I particularly regret not taking more account of the great scientific prestige that accrued to German scholarship by the middle of the nineteenth century, whose neglect was made into a denunciation of insular British scholars by George Eliot. I have in mind Eliot's unforgettable portrait of Mr. Casaubon in *Middlemarch*. One reason Casaubon cannot finish his Key to All Mythologies is, according to his young cousin Will Ladislaw, that he is unacquainted with German scholarship.

For not only has Casaubon chosen a subject "as changing as chemistry: new discoveries are constantly making new points of view": he is undertaking a job similar to a refutation of Paracelsus because "he is not an Orientalist, you know."[15]

Eliot was not wrong in implying that by about 1830, which is when *Middlemarch* is set, German scholarship had fully attained its European pre-eminence. Yet at no time in German scholarship during the first two-thirds of the nineteenth century could a close partnership have developed between Orientalists and a protracted, sustained *national* interest in the Orient. There was nothing in Germany to correspond to the Anglo-French presence in India, the Levant, North Africa. Moreover, the German Orient was almost exclusively a scholarly, or at least a classical, Orient: it was made the subject of lyrics, fantasies, and even novels, but it was never actual, the way Egypt and Syria were actual for Chateaubriand, Lane, Lamartine, Burton, Disraeli, or Nerval. There is some significance in the fact that the two most renowned German works on the Orient, Goethe's *Westöstlicher Diwan* and Friedrich Schlegel's *Über die Sprache und Weisheit der Indier*, were based respectively on a Rhine journey and on hours spent in Paris libraries. What German Oriental scholarship did was to refine and elaborate techniques whose application was to texts, myths, ideas, and languages almost literally gathered from the Orient by imperial Britain and France.

Yet what German Orientalism had in common with Anglo-French and later American Orientalism was a kind of intellectual *authority* over the Orient within Western culture. This authority must in large part be the subject of any description of Orientalism, and it is so in this study. Even the name *Orientalism* suggests a serious, perhaps ponderous style of expertise; when I apply it to modern American social scientists (since they do not call themselves Orientalists, my use of the word is anomalous), it is to draw attention to the way Middle East experts can still draw on the vestiges of Orientalism's intellectual position in nineteenth-century Europe.

There is nothing mysterious or natural about authority. It is formed, irradiated, disseminated; it is instrumental, it is persuasive; it has status, it establishes canons of taste and value; it is virtually indistinguishable from certain ideas it dignifies as true, and from traditions, perceptions, and judgments it forms, transmits, reproduces. Above all, authority can, indeed must, be analyzed. All these attributes of authority apply to Orientalism, and much of what I do in this study is to describe both the historical authority in and the personal authorities of Orientalism.

My principal methodological devices for studying authority here are what can be called *strategic location*, which is a way of describing the author's position in a text with regard to the Oriental material he writes about, and *strategic formation*, which is a way of analyzing the relationship between texts and the way in which groups of texts, types of texts, even textual genres, acquire mass, density, and referential power among themselves and thereafter in the culture at large. I use the notion of strategy simply to identify the problem every writer on the Orient has faced: how to get hold of it, how to approach it, how not to be defeated or overwhelmed by its sublimity, its scope, its awful dimensions. Everyone who writes about the Orient must locate himself vis-à-vis the Orient; translated into his text, this location includes the kind of narrative voice he adopts, the type of structure he builds, the kinds of images, themes, motifs that circulate in his text – all of which add up to deliberate ways of addressing the reader, containing the Orient, and finally, representing it or speaking in its behalf. None of this takes place in the abstract, however. Every writer on the Orient (and this is true even of Homer) assumes some Oriental precedent, some previous knowledge of the Orient, to which he refers and on which he relies. Additionally, each work on the Orient *affiliates* itself with other works, with audiences, with institutions, with the Orient itself. The ensemble of relationships between works, audiences, and some particular aspects of the Orient therefore constitutes an analyzable formation – for example, that of philological studies, of anthologies of extracts from Oriental literature, of travel books, of Oriental fantasies – whose presence in time, in discourse, in institutions (schools, libraries, foreign services) gives it strength and authority.

It is clear, I hope, that my concern with authority does not entail analysis of what lies hidden in the Orientalist text, but analysis rather of the text's surface, its exteriority to what it describes. I do not think that this idea can be overemphasized. Orientalism is premised upon exteriority, that is, on the fact that the Orientalist, poet or scholar, makes the Orient speak, describes the Orient, renders its mysteries plain for and to the West. He is never concerned with the Orient except as the first cause of what he says. What he says and writes, by virtue of the fact that it is said or written, is meant to indicate that the Orientalist is outside the Orient, both as an existential and as a moral fact. The principal product of this exteriority is of course representation: as early as Aeschylus's play *The Persians* the Orient is transformed from a very far distant and often threatening Otherness into figures that are relatively familiar (in Aeschylus's case, grieving Asiatic women). The dramatic immediacy of representation in *The Persians* obscures the fact that the audience is watching a highly artificial enactment of what a non-Oriental has made into a symbol for the whole Orient. My analysis of the Orientalist text therefore places emphasis on the evidence, which is by no means invisible, for such representations *as representations*, not as "natural" depictions of the Orient. This evidence is found just as prominently in the so-called truthful text (histories, philological analyses, political treatises) as in the avowedly artistic (i.e., openly imaginative) text. The things to look at are style, figures of speech, setting, narrative devices, historical and social circumstances, *not* the correctness of the representation nor its fidelity to some great original. The exteriority of the representation is always governed by some version of the truism that if the Orient could represent itself, it would; since it cannot, the representation does the job, for the West, and *faute de mieux*, for the poor Orient. "Sie können sich nicht vertreten, sie müssen vertreten werden," as Marx wrote in *The Eighteenth Brumaire of Louis Bonaparte*.

Another reason for insisting upon exteriority is that I believe it needs to be made clear about cultural discourse and exchange within a culture that what is commonly circulated by it is not "truth" but representations. It hardly needs to be demonstrated again that language itself is a highly organized and encoded system, which employs many devices to express, indicate, exchange messages and information, represent, and so forth. In any instance of at least written language, there is no such thing as a delivered presence, but a *re-presence*, or a representation. The value, efficacy, strength, apparent veracity of a written statement about the Orient therefore relies very little, and cannot instrumentally depend, on the Orient as such. On the contrary, the written statement is a presence to the reader by virtue of its having excluded, displaced, made supererogatory any such *real thing* as "the Orient." Thus all of Orientalism stands forth and away from the Orient: that Orientalism makes sense at all depends more on the West than on the Orient, and this sense is directly indebted to various Western techniques of representation that make the Orient visible, clear, "there" in discourse about it. And these representations rely upon institutions, traditions, conventions, agreed-upon codes of understanding for their effects, not upon a distant and amorphous Orient.

The difference between representations of the Orient before the last third of the eighteenth century and those after it (that is, those belonging to what I call modern Orientalism) is that the range of representation expanded enormously in the later period. It is true that after William Jones and Anquetil-Duperron, and after Napoleon's Egyptian expedition, Europe came to know the Orient more scientifically, to live in it with greater authority and discipline than ever before. But what mattered to Europe was the expanded scope and the much greater refinement given its techniques for receiving the Orient. When around the turn of the eighteenth century the Orient definitively revealed the age of its languages – thus outdating Hebrew's divine pedigree – it was a group of Europeans who made the discovery, passed it on to other scholars, and preserved the discovery in the new science of Indo-European philology. A new powerful science for viewing the linguistic Orient was born, and with it, as Foucault has shown in *The Order of Things*, a whole web of related scientific interests. Similarly William Beckford, Byron, Goethe, and Hugo restructured the Orient by their art and made its colors, lights, and people visible through their images, rhythms, and motifs. At most, the "real" Orient provoked a writer to his vision; it very rarely guided it.

Orientalism responded more to the culture that produced it than to its putative object, which was also produced by the West. Thus the history of Orientalism has both an internal consistency and a highly articulated set of relationships to the dominant culture surrounding it. My analyses consequently try to show the field's shape and internal organization, its pioneers, patriarchal authorities, canonical texts, doxological ideas, exemplary figures, its followers, elaborators, and new authorities; I try also to explain how Orientalism borrowed and was frequently informed by "strong" ideas, doctrines, and trends ruling the culture. Thus there was (and is) a linguistic Orient, a Freudian Orient, a Spenglerian Orient, a Darwinian Orient, a racist Orient – and so on. Yet never has there been such a thing as a pure, or unconditional, Orient; similarly, never has there been a nonmaterial form of Orientalism, much less something so innocent as an "idea" of the Orient. In this underlying conviction and in its ensuing methodological conse-quences do I differ from scholars who study the history of ideas. For the emphases and the executive form, above all the material effectiveness, of statements made by Orientalist discourse are possible in ways that any hermetic history of ideas tends completely to scant. Without those emphases and that material effectiveness Orientalism would be just another idea, whereas it is and was much more than that. Therefore I set out to examine not only scholarly works but also works of literature, political tracts, journalistic texts, travel books, religious and philological studies. In other words, my hybrid perspective is broadly historical and "anthropological," given that I believe all texts to be worldly and circumstantial in (of course) ways that vary from genre to genre, and from historical period to historical period.

Yet unlike Michel Foucault, to whose work I am greatly indebted, I do believe in the determining imprint of individual writers upon the otherwise anonymous collective body of texts constituting a discursive formation like Orientalism. The unity of the large ensemble of texts I analyze is due in part to the fact that they frequently refer to each other: Orientalism is after all a system for citing works and authors. Edward William Lane's *Manners and Customs of the Modern Egyptians* was read and cited by such diverse figures as Nerval, Flaubert, and Richard Burton. He was an authority whose use was an imperative for anyone writing or thinking about the Orient, not just about Egypt: when Nerval borrows passages verbatim from *Modern Egyptians* it is to use Lane's authority to assist him in describing village scenes in Syria, not Egypt. Lane's authority and the opportunities provided for citing him discriminately as well as indiscriminately were there because Orientalism could give his text the kind of distributive currency that he acquired. There is no way, however, of understanding Lane's currency without also understanding the peculiar features of *his* text; this is equally true of Renan, Sacy, Lamartine, Schlegel, and a group of other influential writers. Foucault believes that in general the individual text or author counts for very little; empirically, in the case of Orientalism (and perhaps nowhere else) I find this not to be so. Accordingly my analyses employ close textual readings whose goal is to reveal the dialectic between individual text or writer and the complex collective formation to which his work is a contribution.

Yet even though it includes an ample selection of writers, this book is still far from a complete history or general account of Orientalism. Of this failing I am very conscious. The fabric of as thick a discourse as Orientalism has survived and functioned in Western society because of its richness: all I have done is to describe parts of that fabric at certain moments, and merely to suggest the existence of a larger whole, detailed, interesting, dotted with fascinating figures, texts, and events. I have consoled myself with believing that this book is one installment of several, and hope there are scholars and critics who might want to write others. There is still a general essay to be written on imperialism and culture; other studies would go more deeply into the connection between Orientalism and pedagogy, or into Italian, Dutch, German, and Swiss Orientalism, or into the dynamic between scholarship and imaginative writing, or into the relationship between administrative ideas and intellectual discipline. Perhaps the most important task of all would be to undertake studies in contemporary alternatives to Orientalism, to ask how one can study other cultures and peoples from a libertarian, or a nonrepressive and nonmanipulative, perspective. But then one would have to rethink the whole complex problem of knowledge and power. These are all tasks left embarrassingly incomplete in this study.

The last, perhaps self-flattering, observation on method that I want to make here is that I have written this study with several audiences in mind. For students of literature and criticism, Orientalism offers a marvelous instance of the interrelations between society, history, and textuality; moreover, the cultural role played by the Orient in the West connects Orientalism with ideology, politics, and the logic of power, matters of relevance, I think, to the literary community. For contemporary students of the Orient, from university scholars to policymakers, I have written with two ends in mind: one, to present their intellectual genealogy to them in a way that has not been done; two, to criticize – with the hope of stirring discussion – the often unquestioned assumptions on which their work for the most part depends. For the general reader, this study deals with matters that always compel attention, all of them connected not only with Western conceptions and treatments of the Other but also with the singularly important role played by Western culture in what Vico called the world of nations. Lastly, for readers in the so-called Third World, this study proposes itself as a step towards an understanding not so much of Western politics and of the non-Western world in those politics as of the *strength* of Western cultural discourse, a strength too often mistaken as merely decorative or "superstructural." My hope is to illustrate the formidable structure of cultural domination and, specifically for formerly colonized peoples, the dangers and temptations of employing this structure upon themselves or upon others.

The three long chapters and twelve shorter units into which this book is divided are intended to facilitate exposition as much as possible. Chapter One, "The Scope of Orientalism," draws a large circle around all the dimensions of the subject, both in terms of historical time and experiences and in terms of philosophical and political themes.

Chapter Two, "Orientalist Structures and Restructures," attempts to trace the development of modern Orientalism by a broadly chronological description, and also by the description of a set of devices common to the work of important poets, artists, and scholars. Chapter Three, "Orientalism Now," begins where its predecessor left off, at around 1870. This is the period of great colonial expansion into the Orient, and it culminates in World War II. The very last section of Chapter Three characterizes the shift from British and French to American hegemony; I attempt there finally to sketch the present intellectual and social realities of Orientalism in the United States.

3. The personal dimension. In the *Prison Notebooks* Gramsci says: "The starting-point of critical elaboration is the consciousness of what one really is, and is 'knowing thyself as a product of the historical process to date, which has deposited in you an infinity of traces, without leaving an inventory." The only available English translation inexplicably leaves Gramsci's comment at that, whereas in fact Gramsci's Italian text concludes by adding, "therefore it is imperative at the outset to compile such an inventory."[16]

Much of the personal investment in this study derives from my awareness of being an "Oriental" as a child growing up in two British colonies. All of my education, in those colonies (Palestine and Egypt) and in the United States, has been Western, and yet that deep early awareness has persisted. In many ways my study of Orientalism has been an attempt to inventory the traces upon me, the Oriental subject, of the culture whose domination has been so powerful a factor in the life of all Orientals. This is why for me the Islamic Orient has had to be the center of attention. Whether what I have achieved is the inventory prescribed by Gramsci is not for me to judge, although I have felt it important to be conscious of trying to produce one. Along the way, as severely and as rationally as I have been able, I have tried to maintain a critical consciousness, as well as employing those instruments of historical, humanistic, and cultural research of which my education has made me the fortunate beneficiary. In none of that, however, have I ever lost hold of the cultural reality of, the personal involvement in having been constituted as, "an Oriental."

The historical circumstances making such a study possible are fairly complex, and I can only list them schematically here. Anyone resident in the West since the 1950s, particularly in the United States, will have lived through an era of extraordinary turbulence in the relations of East and West. No one will have failed to note how "East" has always signified danger and threat during this period, even as it has meant the traditional Orient as well as Russia. In the universities a growing establishment of area-studies programs and institutes has made the scholarly study of the Orient a branch of national policy. Public affairs in this country include a healthy interest in the Orient, as much for its strategic and economic importance as for its traditional exoticism. If the world has become immediately accessible to a Western citizen living in the electronic age, the Orient too has drawn nearer to him, and is now less a myth perhaps than a place crisscrossed by Western, especially American, interests.

One aspect of the electronic, postmodern world is that there has been a reinforcement of the stereotypes by which the Orient is viewed. Television, the films, and all the media's resources have forced information into more and more standardized molds. So far as the Orient is concerned, standardization and cultural stereotyping have intensified the hold of the nineteenth-century academic and imaginative demonology of "the mysterious Orient." This is nowhere more true than in the ways by which the Near East is grasped. Three things have contributed to making even the simplest perception of the Arabs and Islam into a highly-politicized, almost raucous matter: one, the history of popular anti-Arab and anti-Islamic prejudice in the West, which is immediately reflected in the history of Orientalism; two the struggle between the Arabs and Israeli Zionism, and its effects upon American Jews as well as upon both the liberal culture and the population at large; three, the almost total absence of any cultural position making it possible either to identify with or dispassionately to discuss the Arabs or Islam. Furthermore, it hardly needs saying that because the Middle East is now so identified with Great Power politics, oil economics, and the simple-minded dichotomy of freedom-loving, democratic Israel and evil, totalitarian, and terroristic Arabs, the chances of anything like a clear view of what one talks about in talking about the Near East are depressingly small.

My own experiences of these matters are in part what made me write this book. The life of an Arab Palestinian in the West, particularly in America, is disheartening. There exists here an almost unanimous consensus that politically he does not exist, and when it is allowed that he does, it is either as a nuisance or as an Oriental. The web of racism, cultural stereotypes, political imperialism, dehumanizing ideology holding in the Arab or the Muslim is very strong indeed, and it is this web which every Palestinian has come to feel as his uniquely punishing destiny. It has made matters worse for him to remark that no person academically involved with the Near East – no Orientalist, that is – has ever in the United States culturally and politically identified himself whole-heartedly with the Arabs; certainly there have been identifications on some level, but they have never taken an "acceptable" form as has liberal American identification with Zionism, and all too frequently they have been radically flawed by their associa-tion either with discredited political and economic interests (oil-company and State Department Arabists, for example) or with religion.

The nexus of knowledge and power creating "the Oriental" and in a sense obliterating him as a human being is therefore not for me an exclusively academic matter. Yet it is an *intellectual* matter of some very obvious importance. I have been able to put to use my humanistic and political concerns for the analysis and description of a very worldly matter, the rise, development, and consolidation of Orientalism. Too often literature and culture are presumed to be politically, even historically innocent; it has regularly seemed otherwise to me, and certainly my study of Orientalism has convinced me (and I hope will convince my literary colleagues) that society and literary culture can only be understood and stud-ied together. In addition, and by an almost inescapable logic, I have found myself writing the history of a strange, secret sharer of Western anti-Semitism. That anti-Semitism and, as I have discussed it in its Islamic branch, Orientalism resemble each other very closely is a historical, cultural, and political truth that needs only to be mentioned to an Arab Palestinian for its irony to be perfectly understood. But what I should like also to have contributed here is a better understanding of the way cultural domination has operated. If this stimulates a new kind of dealing with the Orient, indeed if it eliminates the "Orient" and "Occident" altogether, then we shall have advanced a little in the process of what Raymond Williams has called the "unlearning" of "the inherent dominative mode."[17]

The Scope of Orientalism

… le génie inquiet et ambitieux de Européens … impatient d'employer les nouveaux instruments de leur puissance …

– Jean-Baptiste-Joseph Fourier, *Préface historique* (1809),
Description de l'Égypte

I: Knowing the Oriental

On June 13, 1910, Arthur James Balfour lectured the House of Commons on "the problems with which we have to deal in Egypt." These, he said, "belong to a wholly different category" than those "affecting the Isle of Wight or the West Riding of Yorkshire." He spoke with the authority of a long-time member of Parliament, former private secretary to Lord Salisbury, former chief secretary for Ireland, former secretary for Scotland, former prime minister, veteran of numerous overseas crises, achievements, and changes. During his involvement in imperial affairs Balfour served a monarch who in 1876 had been declared Empress of India; he had been especially well placed in positions of uncommon influence to follow the Afghan and Zulu wars, the British occupation of Egypt in 1882, the death of General Gordon in the Sudan, the Fashoda Incident, the battle of Omdurman, the Boer War, the Russo-Japanese War. In addition his remarkable social eminence, the breadth of his learning and wit – he could write on such varied subjects as Bergson, Handel, theism, and golf – his education at Eton and Trinity College, Cambridge, and his apparent command over imperial affairs all gave considerable authority to what he told the Commons in June 1910. But there was still more to Balfour's speech, or at least to his need for giving it so didactically and moralistically. Some members were questioning the necessity for "England in Egypt," the subject of Alfred Milner's enthusiastic book of 1892, but here designating a once-profitable occupation that had become a source of trouble now that Egyptian nationalism was on the rise and the continuing British presence in Egypt no longer so easy to defend. Balfour, then, to inform and explain.

Recalling the challenge of J. M. Robertson, the member of Tyneside, Balfour himself put Robertson's question again: "What right have you to take up these airs of superiority with regard to people whom you choose to call Oriental?" The choice of "Oriental" was canonical; it had been employed by Chaucer and Mandeville, by Shakespeare, Dryden, Pope, and Byron. It designated Asia or the East, geographically, morally, culturally. One could speak in Europe of an Oriental personality, an Oriental atmosphere, an Oriental tale, Oriental despotism, or an Oriental mode of production, and be understood. Marx had used the word, and now Balfour was using it; his choice was understandable and called for no comment whatever.

> I take up no attitude of superiority. But I ask [Robertson and anyone else] … who has even the most superficial knowledge of history, if they will look in the face the facts with which a British statesman has to deal when he is put in a position of supremacy over great races like the inhabitants of Egypt and countries in the East. We know the civilization of Egypt better than we know the civilization of any other country. We know it further back; we know it more intimately; we know more about it. It goes far beyond the petty span of the history of our race, which is lost in the prehistoric period at a time when the Egyptian civilisation had already passed its prime. Look at all the Oriental countries. Do not talk about superiority or inferiority.

Two great themes dominate his remarks here and in what will follow: knowledge and power, the Baconian themes. As Balfour justifies the necessity for British occupation of Egypt, supremacy in his mind is associated with "our" knowledge of Egypt and not principally with military or economic power. Knowledge to Balfour means surveying a civilization from its origins to its prime to its decline – and of course, it means *being able to do that*. Knowledge means rising above immediacy, beyond self, into the foreign and distant. The object of such knowledge is inherently vulnerable to scrutiny; this object is a "fact" which, if it develops, changes, or otherwise transforms itself in the way that civilizations frequently do, nevertheless is fundamentally, even ontologically stable. To have such knowledge of such a thing is to dominate it, to have authority over it. And authority here means for "us" to deny autonomy to "it" – the Oriental country – since we know it and it exists, in a sense, *as* we know it. British knowledge of Egypt *is* Egypt for Balfour, and the burdens of knowledge make such questions as inferiority and superiority seem petty ones. Balfour nowhere denies British superiority and Egyptian inferiority; he takes them for granted as he describes the consequences of knowledge.

> First of all, look at the facts of the case. Western nations as soon as they emerge into history show the beginnings of those capacities for self-government ... having merits of their own ... You may look through the whole history of the Orientals in what is called, broadly speaking, the East, and you never find traces of self-government. All their great centuries – and they have been very great – have been passed under despotisms, under absolute government. All their great contributions to civilisation – and they have been great – have been made under that form of government. Conqueror has succeeded conqueror; one domination has followed another; but never in all the revolutions of fate and fortune have you seen one of those nations of its own motion establish what we, from a Western point of view, call self-government. That is the fact. It is not a question of superiority and inferiority. I suppose a true Eastern sage would say that the working government which we have taken upon ourselves in Egypt and elsewhere is not a work worthy of a philosopher – that it is the dirty work, the inferior work, of carrying on the necessary labour.

Since these facts are facts, Balfour must then go on to the next part of his argument.

> Is it a good thing for these great nations – I admit their greatness – that this absolute government should be exercised by us? I think it is a good thing. I think that experience shows that they have got under it far better government than in the whole history of the world they ever had before, and which not only is a benefit to them, but is undoubtedly a benefit to the whole of the West ... We are in Egypt not merely for the sake of Egyptians, though we are there for their sake; we are there also for the sake of Europe at large.

Balfour produces no evidence that Egyptians and "the races with whom we deal" appreciate or even understand the good that is being done them by colonial occupation. It does not occur to Balfour, however, to let the Egyptian speak for himself, since presumably any Egyptian who would speak out is more likely to be "the agitator [who] wishes to raise difficulties" than the good native who overlooks the "difficulties" of foreign domination. And so, having settled the ethical problems, Balfour turns at last to the practical ones. "If it is our business to govern, with or without gratitude, with or without the real and genuine memory of all the loss of which we have relieved the population [Balfour by no means implies, as part of that loss, the loss or at least the indefinite postponement of Egyptian independence] and no vivid imagination of all the benefits which we have given to them; if that is our duty, how is it to be performed?" England exports "our very best to these countries." These selfless administrators do their work "amidst tens of thousands of persons belonging to a different creed, a different race, a different discipline, different conditions of life." What makes their work of governing possible is their sense of being supported at home by a government that endorses what they do. Yet

> directly the native populations have that instinctive feeling that those with whom they have got to deal have not behind them the might, the authority, the sympathy, the full and ungrudging support of the country which sent them there, those populations lose all that sense of order which is the very basis of their civilisation, just as our officers lose all that sense of power and authority, which is the very basis of everything they can do for the benefit of those among whom they have been sent.

Balfour's logic here is interesting, not least for being completely consistent with the premises of the entire speech. England knows Egypt; Egypt is what England knows; England knows that Egypt cannot have self-government; England confirms that by occupying Egypt; for the Egyptians, Egypt is what England has occupied and now governs; foreign occupation therefore becomes "the very basis" of contemporary Egyptian civilization; Egypt requires, indeed insists upon, British occupation. But if the special intimacy between governor and governed in Egypt is disturbed by Parliament's doubts at home, then "the authority of what ... is the dominant race – and as I think ought to remain the dominant race – has been undermined." Not only does English prestige suffer; "it is vain for a handful of British officials – endow them how you like, give them all the qualities of character and genius you can imagine – it is impossible for them to carry out the great task which in Egypt, not we only, but the civilised world have imposed upon them."[1]

As a rhetorical performance Balfour's speech is significant for the way in which he plays the part of, and represents, a variety of characters. There are of course "the English," for whom the pronoun "we" is used with the full weight of a distinguished, powerful man who feels himself to be representative of all that is best in his nation's history. Balfour can also speak for the civilized world, the West, and the relatively small corps of colonial officials in Egypt. If he does not speak directly for the Orientals, it is because they after all speak another language; yet he knows how they feel since he knows their history, their reliance upon such as he, and their expectations. Still, he does speak for them in the sense that what they might have to say, were they to be asked and might they be able to answer, would somewhat uselessly confirm what is already evident: that they are a subject race, dominated by a race that knows them and what is good for them better than they could possibly know themselves. Their great moments were in the past; they are useful in the modern world only because the powerful and up-to-date empires have effectively brought them out of the wretchedness of their decline and turned them into rehabilitated residents of productive colonies.

Egypt in particular was an excellent case in point, and Balfour was perfectly aware of how much right he had to speak as a member of his country's parliament on behalf of England, the West, Western Civilization, about modern Egypt. For Egypt was not just another colony: it was the vindication of Western imperialism; it was, until its annexation by England, an almost academic example of Oriental backwardness; it was to become the triumph of English knowledge and power. Between 1882, the year in which England occupied Egypt and put an end to the nationalist rebellion of Colonel Arabi, and 1907 England's representative in Egypt, Egypt's master, was Evelyn Baring (also known as "Over-baring"), Lord Cromer. On July 30, 1907, it was Balfour in the Commons who had supported the project to give Cromer a retirement prize of fifty thousand pounds as a reward for what he had done in Egypt. Cromer *made* Egypt, said Balfour:

> Everything he has touched he has succeeded in ... Lord Cromer's services during the past quarter of a century have raised Egypt from the lowest pitch of social and economic degradation until it now stands among Oriental nations, I believe, absolutely alone in its prosperity, financial and moral.[2]

How Egypt's moral prosperity was measured, Balfour did not venture to say. British exports to Egypt equaled those to the whole of Africa; that certainly indicated a sort of financial prosperity, for Egypt and England (somewhat unevenly) together. But what really mattered was the unbroken, all-embracing Western tutelage of an Oriental country, from the scholars, missionaries, businessmen, soldiers, and teachers who prepared and then implemented the occupation to the high functionaries like Cromer and Balfour who saw themselves as providing for, directing, and sometimes even forcing Egypt's rise from Oriental neglect to its present lonely eminence.

If British success in Egypt was as exceptional as Balfour said, it was by no means an inexplicable or irrational success. Egyptian affairs had been controlled according to a general theory expressed both by Balfour in his notions about Oriental civilization and by Cromer in his management of everyday business in Egypt. The most important thing about the theory during the first decade of the twentieth century was that it worked, and worked staggeringly well. The argument, when reduced to its simplest form, was clear, it was precise, it was easy to grasp. There are Westerners, and there are Orientals. The former dominate; the latter must be dominated, which usually means having their land occupied, their internal affairs rigidly controlled, their blood and treasure put at the disposal of one or another Western power. That Balfour and Cromer, as we shall soon see, could strip humanity down to such ruthless cultural and racial essences was not at all an indication of their particular viciousness. Rather it was an indication of how streamlined a general doctrine had become by the time they put it to use – how streamlined and effective.

Unlike Balfour, whose theses on Orientals pretended to objective universality, Cromer spoke about Orientals specifically as what he had ruled or had to deal with, first in India, then for the twenty-five years in Egypt during which he emerged as the paramount consul-general in England's empire. Balfour's "Orientals" are Cromer's "subject races," which he made the topic of a long essay published in the *Edinburgh Review* in January 1908. Once again, knowledge of subject races or Orientals is what makes their management easy and profitable: knowledge gives power, more power requires more knowledge, and so on in an increasingly profitable dialectic of information and control. Cromer's notion is that England's empire will not dissolve if such things as militarism and commercial egotism at home and "free institutions" in the colony (as opposed to British government "according to the Code of Christian morality") are kept in check. For if, according to Cromer, logic is something "the existence of which the Oriental is disposed altogether to ignore," the proper method of ruling is not to impose ultrascientific measures upon him or to force him bodily to accept logic. It is rather to understand his limitations and "endeavor to find, in the contentment of the subject race, a more worthy and, it may be hoped, a stronger bond of union between the rulers and the ruled." Lurking everywhere behind the pacification of the subject race is imperial might, more effective for its refined understanding and infrequent use than for its soldiers, brutal tax gatherers, and incontinent force. In a word, the Empire must be wise; it must temper its cupidity with selflessness, and its impatience with flexible discipline.

> To be more explicit, what is meant when it is said that the commercial spirit should be under some control is this – that in dealing with Indians or Egyptians, or Shilluks, or Zulus, the first question is to consider what these people, who are all, nationally speaking, more or less *in statu pupillari*, themselves think is best in their own interests, although this is a point which deserves serious consideration. But it is essential that each special issue should be decided mainly with reference to what, by the light of Western knowledge and experience tempered by local considerations, we conscientiously think is best for the subject race, without reference to any real or supposed advantage which may accrue to England as a nation, or – as is more frequently the case – to the special interests represented by some one or more influential classes of Englishmen. If the British nation as a whole persistently bears this principle in mind, and insists sternly on its application, though we can never create a patriotism akin to that based on affinity of race or community of language, we may perhaps foster some sort of cosmopolitan allegiance grounded on the respect always accorded to superior talents and unselfish conduct, and on the gratitude derived both from favours conferred and from those to come. There may then at all events be some hope that the Egyptian will hesitate before he throws in his lot with any future Arabi ... Even the Central African savage may eventually learn to chant a hymn in honour of Astraea Redux, as represented by the British official who denies him gin but gives him justice. More than this, commerce will gain.[3]

How much "serious consideration" the ruler ought to give proposals from the subject race was illustrated in Cromer's total opposition to Egyptian nationalism. Free native institutions, the absence of foreign occupation, a self-sustaining national sovereignty: these unsurprising demands were consistently rejected by Cromer, who asserted unambiguously that "the real future of Egypt ... lies not in the direction of a narrow nationalism, which will only embrace native Egyptians ... but rather in that of an enlarged cosmopolitanism."[4] Subject races did not have it in them to know what was good for them. Most of them were Orientals, of whose characteristics Cromer was very knowledgeable since he had had experience with them both in India and Egypt. One of the convenient things about Orientals for Cromer was that managing them, although circumstances might differ slightly here and there, was almost everywhere nearly the same.[5] This was, of course, because Orientals were almost everywhere nearly the same.

Now at last we approach the long-developing core of essential knowledge, knowledge both academic and practical, which Cromer and Balfour inherited from a century of modern Western Orientalism: knowledge about and knowledge of Orientals, their race, character, culture, history, traditions, society, and possibilities. This knowledge was effective: Cromer believed he had put it to use in governing Egypt. Moreover, it was tested and unchanging knowledge, since "Orientals" for all practical purposes were a Platonic essence, which any Orientalist (or ruler of Orientals) might examine, understand, and expose. Thus in the thirty-fourth chapter of his two-volume work *Modern Egypt*, the magisterial record of his experience and achievement, Cromer puts down a sort of personal canon of Orientalist wisdom:

> Sir Alfred Lyall once said to me: "Accuracy is abhorrent to the Oriental mind. Every Anglo-Indian should always remember that maxim." Want of accuracy, which easily degenerates into untruthfulness, is in fact the main characteristic of the Oriental mind.

The European is a close reasoner; his statements of fact are devoid of any ambiguity; he is a natural logician, albeit he may not have studied logic; he is by nature sceptical and requires proof before he can accept the truth of any proposition; his trained intelligence works like a piece of mechanism. The mind of the Oriental, on the other hand, like his picturesque streets, is eminently wanting in symmetry. His reasoning is of the most slipshod description. Although the ancient Arabs acquired in a somewhat higher degree the science of dialectics, their descendants are singularly deficient in the logical faculty. They are often incapable of drawing the most obvious conclusions from any simple premises of which they may admit the truth. Endeavor to elicit a plain statement of facts from any ordinary Egyptian. His explanation will generally be lengthy, and wanting in lucidity. He will probably contradict himself half-a-dozen times before he has finished his story. He will often break down under the mildest process of cross-examination.

Orientals or Arabs are thereafter shown to be gullible, "devoid of energy and initiative," much given to "fulsome flattery," intrigue, cunning, and unkindness to animals; Orientals cannot walk on either a road or a pavement (their disordered minds fail to understand what the clever European grasps immediately, that roads and pavements are made for walking); Orientals are inveterate liars, they are "lethargic and suspicious," and in everything oppose the clarity, directness, and nobility of the Anglo-Saxon race.[6] Cromer makes no effort to conceal that Orientals for him were always and only the human material he governed in British colonies. "As I am only a diplomatist and an administrator, whose proper study is also man, but from the point of view of governing him," Cromer says, "... I content myself with noting the fact that somehow or other the Oriental generally acts, speaks, and thinks in a manner exactly opposite to the European."[7] Cromer's descriptions are of course based partly on direct observation, yet here and there he refers to orthodox Orientalist authorities (in particular Ernest Renan and Constantin de Volney) to support his views. To these authorities he also defers when it comes to explaining why Orientals are the way they are. He has no doubt that *any* knowledge of the Oriental will confirm his views, which, to judge from his description of the Egyptian breaking under cross-examination, find the Oriental to be guilty. The crime was that the Oriental was an Oriental, and it is an accurate sign of how commonly acceptable such a tautology was that it could be written without even an appeal to European logic or symmetry of mind. Thus any deviation from what were considered the norms of Oriental behavior was believed to be unnatural; Cromer's last annual report from Egypt consequently proclaimed Egyptian nationalism to be an "entirely novel idea" and "a plant of exotic rather than of indigenous growth."[8]

We would be wrong, I think, to underestimate the reservoir of accredited knowledge, the codes of Orientalist orthodoxy, to which Cromer and Balfour refer everywhere in their writing and in their public policy. To say simply that Orientalism was a rationalization of colonial rule is to ignore the extent to which colonial rule was justified in advance by Orientalism, rather than after the fact. Men have always divided the world up into regions having either real or imagined distinction from each other. The absolute demarcation between East and West, which Balfour and Cromer accept with such complacency, had been years, even centuries, in the making. There were of course innumerable voyages of discovery; there were contacts through trade and war. But more than this, since the middle of the eighteenth century there had been two principal elements in the relation between East and West. One was a growing systematic knowledge in Europe about the Orient, knowledge reinforced by the colonial encounter as well as by the widespread interest in the alien and unusual, exploited by the developing sciences of ethnology, comparative anatomy, philology, and history; furthermore, to this systematic knowledge was added a sizable body of literature produced by novelists, poets, translators, and gifted travelers. The other feature of Oriental-European relations was that Europe was always in a position of strength, not to say domination. There is no way of putting this euphemistically. True, the relationship of strong to weak could be disguised or mitigated, as when Balfour acknowledged the "greatness" of Oriental civilizations. But the essential relationship, on political, cultural, and even religious grounds, was seen – in the West, which is what concerns us here – to be one between a strong and a weak partner.

Many terms were used to express the relation: Balfour and Cromer, typically, used several. The Oriental is irrational, depraved (fallen), childlike, "different"; thus the European is rational, virtuous, mature, "normal." But the way of enlivening the relationship was everywhere to stress the fact that the Oriental lived in a different but thoroughly organized world of his own, a world with its own national, cultural, and epistemological boundaries and principles of internal coherence. Yet what gave the Oriental's world its intelligibility and identity was not the result of his own efforts but rather the whole complex series of knowledgeable manipulations by which the Orient was identified by the West. Thus the two features of cultural relationship I have been discussing come together. Knowledge of the Orient, because generated out of strength, in a sense *creates* the Orient, the Oriental, and his world. In Cromer's and Balfour's language the Oriental is depicted as something one judges (as in a court of law), something one studies and depicts (as in a curriculum), something one disciplines (as in a school or prison), something one illustrates (as in a zoological manual). The point is that in each of these cases the Oriental is *contained* and *represented* by dominating frameworks. Where do these come from?

Cultural strength is not something we can discuss very easily – and one of the purposes of the present work is to illustrate, analyze, and reflect upon Orientalism as an exercise of cultural strength. In other words, it is better not to risk generalizations about so vague and yet so important a notion as cultural strength until a good deal of material has been analyzed first. But at the outset one can say that so far as the West was concerned during the nineteenth and twentieth centuries, an assumption had been made that the Orient and everything in it was, if not patently inferior to, then in need of corrective study by the West. The Orient was viewed as if framed by the classroom, the criminal court, the prison, the illustrated manual. Orientalism, then, is knowledge of the Orient that places things Oriental in class, court, prison, or manual for scrutiny, study, judgment, discipline, or governing.

During the early years of the twentieth century, men like Balfour and Cromer could say what they said, in the way they did, because a still earlier tradition of Orientalism than the nineteenth-century one provided them with a vocabulary, imagery, rhetoric, and figures with which to say it. Yet Orientalism reinforced, and was reinforced by, the certain knowledge that Europe or the West literally commanded the vastly greater part of the earth's surface. The period of immense advance in the institutions and content of Orientalism coincides exactly with the period of unparalleled European expansion; from 1815 to 1914 European direct colonial dominion expanded from about 35 percent of the earth's surface to about 85 percent of it.[9] Every continent was affected, none more so than Africa and Asia. The two greatest empires were the British and the French; allies and partners in some things, in others they were hostile rivals.

In the Orient, from the eastern shores of the Mediterranean to Indochina and Malaya, their colonial possessions and imperial spheres of influence were adjacent, frequently overlapped, often were fought over. But it was in the Near Orient, the lands of the Arab Near East, where Islam was supposed to define cultural and racial characteristics, that the British and the French encountered each other and "the Orient" with the greatest intensity, familiarity, and complexity. For much of the nineteenth century, as Lord Salisbury put it in 1881, their common view of the Orient was intricately problematic: "When you have got a ... faithful ally who is bent on meddling in a country in which you are deeply interested – you have three courses open to you. You may renounce – or monopolize – or share. Renouncing would have been to place the French across our road to India. Monopolizing would have been very near the risk of war. So we resolved to share."[10]

And share they did, in ways that we shall investigate presently. What they shared, however, was not only land or profit or rule; it was kind of intellectual power I have been calling Orientalism. In a sense Orientalism was a library or archive of information commonly and, in some of its aspects, unanimously held. What bound the archive together was a family of ideas[11] and a unifying set of values proven in various ways to be effective. These ideas explained the behavior of Orientals; they supplied Orientals with a mentality, a genealogy, an atmosphere; most important, they allowed Europeans to deal with and even to see Orientals as a phenomenon possessing regular characteristics. But like any set of durable ideas, Orientalist notions influenced the people who were called Orientals as well as those called Occidental, European, or Western; in short, Orientalism is better grasped as a set of constraints upon and limitations of thought than it is simply as a positive doctrine. If the essence of Orientalism is the ineradicable distinction between Western superiority and Oriental inferiority, then we must be prepared to note how in its development and subsequent history Orientalism deepened and even hardened the distinction. When it became common practice during the nineteenth century for Britain to retire its administrators from India and elsewhere once they had reached the age of fifty-five, then a further refinement in Orientalism had been achieved; no Oriental was ever allowed to see a Westerner as he aged and degenerated, just as no Westerner needed ever to see himself, mirrored in the eyes of the subject race, as anything but a vigorous, rational, ever-alert young Raj.[12]

Orientalist ideas took a number of different forms during the nineteenth and twentieth centuries. First of all, in Europe there was a vast literature about the Orient inherited from the European past. What is distinctive about the late eighteenth and early nineteenth centuries, which is where this study assumes modem Orientalism to have begun, is that an Oriental renaissance took place, as Edgar Quinet phrased it.[13] Suddenly it seemed to a wide variety of thinkers, politicians, and artists that a new awareness of the Orient, which extended from China to the Mediterranean, had arisen. This awareness was partly the result of newly discovered and translated Oriental texts in languages like Sanskrit, Zend, and Arabic; it was also the result of a newly perceived relationship between the Orient and the West. For my purposes here, the keynote of the relationship was set for the Near East and Europe by the Napoleonic invasion of Egypt in 1798, an invasion which was in many ways the very model of a truly scientific appropriation of one culture by another, apparently stronger one. For with Napoleon's occupation of Egypt processes were set in motion between East and West that still dominate our contemporary cultural and political perspectives. And the Napoleonic expedition, with its great collective monument of erudition, the *Description de l'Egypte*, provided a scene or setting for

Orientalism, since Egypt and subsequently the other Islamic lands were viewed as the live province, the laboratory, the theater of effective Western knowledge about the Orient. I shall return to the Napoleonic adventure a little later.

With such experiences as Napoleon's the Orient as a body of knowledge in the West was modernized, and this is a second form in which nineteenth- and twentieth-century Orientalism existed. From the outset of the period I shall be examining there was everywhere amongst Orientalists the ambition to formulate their discoveries, experiences, and insights suitably in modern terms, to put ideas about the Orient in very close touch with modern realities. Renan's linguistic investigations of Semitic in 1848, for example, were couched in a style that drew heavily for its authority upon contemporary comparative grammar, comparative anatomy, and racial theory; these lent his Orientalism prestige and – the other side of the coin – made Orientalism vulnerable, as it has been ever since, to modish as well as seriously influential currents of thought in the West. Orientalism has been subjected to imperialism, positivism, utopianism, historicism, Darwinism, racism, Freudianism, Marxism, Spenglerism. But Orientalism, like many of the natural and social sciences, has had "paradigms" of research, its own learned societies, its own Establishment. During the nineteenth century the field increased enormously in prestige, as did also the reputation and influence of such institutions as the Société asiatique, the Royal Asiatic Society, the Deutsche Morgenländische Gesellschaft, and the American Oriental Society. With the growth of these societies went also an increase, all across Europe, in the number of professorships in Oriental studies; consequently there was an expansion in the available means for disseminating Orientalism. Orientalist periodicals, beginning with the *Fundgraben des Orients* (1809), multiplied the quantity of knowledge as well as the number of specialties.

Yet little of this activity and very few of these institutions existed and flourished freely, for in a third form in which it existed, Orientalism imposed limits upon thought about the Orient. Even the most imaginative writers of an age, men like Flaubert, Nerval, or Scott, were constrained in what they could either experience of or say about the Orient. For Orientalism was ultimately a political vision of reality whose structure promoted the difference between the familiar (Europe, the West, "us") and the strange (the Orient, the East, "them"). This vision in a sense created and then served the two worlds thus conceived. Orientals lived in their world, "we" lived in ours. The vision and material reality propped each other up, kept each other going. A certain freedom of intercourse was always the Westerner's privilege; because his was the stronger culture, he could penetrate, he could wrestle with, he could give shape and meaning to the great Asiatic mystery, as Disraeli once called it. Yet what has, I think, been previously overlooked is the constricted vocabulary of such a privilege, and the comparative limitations of such a vision. My argument takes it that the Orientalist reality is both antihuman and persistent. Its scope, as much as its institutions and all-pervasive influence, lasts up to the present.

But how did and does Orientalism work? How can one describe it all together as a historical phenomenon, a way of thought, a contemporary problem, and a material reality? Consider Cromer again, an accomplished technician of empire but also a beneficiary of Orientalism. He can furnish us with a rudimentary answer. In "The Government of Subject Races" he wrestles with the problem of how Britain, a nation of individuals, is to administer a wide-flung empire according to a number of central principles. He contrasts the "local agent," who has both a specialist's knowledge of the native and an Anglo-Saxon individuality, with the central authority at home in London. The former may "treat subjects of local interest in a manner calculated to damage, or even to jeopardize, Imperial interests. The central authority is in a position to obviate any danger arising from this cause." Why? Because this authority can "ensure the harmonious working of the different parts of the machine" and "should endeavour, so far as is possible, to realise the circumstances attendant on the government of the dependency."[14] The language is vague and unattractive, but the point is not hard to grasp. Cromer envisions a seat of power in the West, and radiating out from it towards the East a great embracing machine, sustaining the central authority yet commanded by it. What the machine's branches feed into it in the East – human material, material wealth, knowledge, what have you – is processed by the machine, then converted into more power. The specialist does the immediate translation of mere Oriental matter into useful substance: the Oriental becomes, for example, a subject race, an example of an "Oriental" mentality, all for the enhancement of the "authority" at home. "Local interests" are Orientalist special interests, the "central authority" is the general interest of the imperial society as a whole. What Cromer quite accurately sees is the management of knowledge by society, the fact that knowledge – no matter how special – is regulated first by the local concerns of a specialist, later by the general concerns of a social system of authority. The interplay between local and central interests is intricate, but by no means indiscriminate.

In Cromer's own case as an imperial administrator the "proper study is also man," he says. When Pope proclaimed the proper study of mankind to be man, he meant all men, including "the poor Indian"; whereas Cromer's "also" reminds us that certain men, such as Orientals, can be singled out as the subject for *proper* study. The proper study – in this sense – of Orientals is Orientalism, properly separate from other forms of knowledge, but finally useful (because finite) for the material and social reality enclosing all knowledge at any time, supporting knowledge, providing it with uses. An order of sovereignty is set up from East to West, a mock chain of being whose clearest form was given once by Kipling:

> Mule, horse, elephant, or bullock, he obeys his driver, and the driver his sergeant, and the sergeant his lieutenant, and the lieutenant his captain, and the captain his major, and the major his colonel, and the colonel his brigadier commanding three regiments, and the brigadier his general, who obeys the Viceroy, who is the servant of the Empress.[15]

As deeply forged as is this monstrous chain of command, as strongly managed as is Cromer's "harmonious working," Orientalism can also express the strength of the West and the Orient's weakness – as seen by the West. Such strength and such weakness are as intrinsic to Orientalism as they are to any view that divides the world into large general divisions, entities that coexist in a state of tension produced by what is believed to be radical difference.

For that is the main intellectual issue raised by Orientalism. Can one divide human reality, as indeed human reality seems to be genuinely divided, into clearly different cultures, histories, traditions, societies, even races, and survive the consequences humanly? By surviving the consequences humanly, I mean to ask whether there is any way of avoiding the hostility expressed by the division, say, of men into "us" (Westerners) and "they" (Orientals). For such divisions are generalities whose use historically and actually has been to press the importance of the distinction between some men and some other men, usually towards not especially admirable ends.

Notes

Introduction

1 Thierry Desjardins, *Le Martyre du Liban* (Paris: Plon, 1976), p. 14.

2 K. M. Panikkar, *Asia and Western Dominance* (London: George Allen & Unwin, 1959).

3 Denys Hay, *Europe: The Emergence of an Idea*, 2nd ed. (Edinburgh: Edinburgh University Press, 1968).

4 Steven Marcus, *The Other Victorians: A Study of Sexuality and Pornography in Mid-Nineteenth Century England* (1966; reprint ed., New York: Bantam Books, 1967), pp. 200–19.

5 See my *Criticism Between Culture and System* (Cambridge, Mass.: Harvard University Press, forthcoming).

6 Principally in his *American Power and the New Mandarins: Historical and Political Essays* (New York: Pantheon Books, 1969) and *For Reasons of State* (New York: Pantheon Books, 1973).

7 Walter Benjamin, *Charles Baudelaire: A Lyric Poet in the Era of High Capitalism*, trans. Harry Zohn (London: New Left Books, 1973), p. 71.

8 Harry Bracken, "Essence, Accident and Race," *Hermathena* 116 (Winter 1973): 81–96.

9 In an interview published in *Diacritics* 6, no. 3 (Fall 1976): 38.

10 Raymond Williams, *The Long Revolution* (London: Chatto & Windus, 1961), pp. 66–7.

11 In my *Beginnings: Intention and Method* (New York: Basic Books, 1975).

12 Louis Althusser, *For Marx*, trans. Ben Brewster (New York: Pantheon Books, 1969), pp. 65–7.

13 Raymond Schwab, *La Renaissance orientale* (Paris: Payot, 1950); Johann W. Fück, *Die Arabischen Studien in Europa bis in den Anfang des 20. Jahrhunderts* (Leipzig: Otto Harrassowitz, 1955); Dorothee Metlitzki, *The Matter of Araby in Medieval England* (New Haven, Conn.: Yale University Press, 1977).

14 E. S. Shaffer, *"Kubla Khan" and The Fall of Jerusalem: The Mythological School in Biblical Criticism and Secular Literature, 1770–1880* (Cambridge: Cambridge University Press, 1975).

15 George Eliot, *Middlemarch: A Study of Provincial Life* (1872; reprint ed., Boston: Houghton Mifflin Co., 1956), p. 164.

16 Antonio Gramsci, *The Prison Notebooks: Selections*, trans. and ed. Quintin Hoare and Geoffrey Nowell Smith (New York: International Publishers, 1971), p. 324. The full passage, unavailable in the Hoare and Smith translation, is to be found in Gramsci, *Quaderni del Carcere*, ed. Valentino Gerratana (Turin: Einaudi Editore, 1975), 2: 1363.

17 Raymond Williams, *Culture and Society, 1780–1950* (London: Chatto & Windus, 1958), p. 376.

The Scope of Orientalism

1 This and the preceding quotations from Arthur James Balfour's speech to the House of Commons are from Great Britain, *Parliamentary Debates* (Commons), 5th ser., 17 (1910): 1140–46. See also A. P. Thornton, *The Imperial Idea and Its Enemies: A Study in British Power* (London: Macmillan & Co., 1959), pp. 357–60. Balfour's speech was a defense of Eldon Gorst's policy in Egypt; for a discussion of that see Peter John Dreyfus Mellini, "Sir Eldon Gorst and British Imperial Policy in Egypt," unpublished Ph.D. dissertation, Stanford University, 1971.

2 Denis Judd, *Balfour and the British Empire: A Study in Imperial Evolution, 1874–1932* (London: MacMillan & Co., 1968), p. 286. See also p. 292: as late as 1926 Balfour spoke – without irony – of Egypt as an "independent nation."

3 Evelyn Baring, Lord Cromer, *Political and Literary Essays, 1908–1913* (1913; reprint ed., Freeport, N.Y.: Books for Libraries Press, 1969), pp. 40, 53, 12–14.

4 Ibid., p. 171.

5 Roger Owen, "The Influence of Lord Cromer's Indian Experience on British Policy in Egypt 1883–1907," in *Middle Eastern Affairs, Number Four: St. Antony's Papers Number 17*, ed. Albert Hourani (London: Oxford University Press, 1965), pp. 109–39.

6 Evelyn Baring, Lord Cromer, *Modern Egypt* (New York: Macmillan Co., 1908), 2: 146–67. For a British view of British policy in Egypt that runs totally counter to Cromer's, see Wilfrid Scawen

Blunt, *Secret History of the English Occupation of Egypt: Being a Personal Narrative of Events* (New York: Alfred A. Knopf, 1922). There is a valuable discussion of Egyptian opposition to British rule in Mounah A. Khouri, *Poetry and the Making of Modern Egypt, 1882–1922* (Leiden: E. J. Brill, 1971).

7   Cromer, *Modern Egypt*, 2: 164.

8   Cited in John Marlowe, *Cromer in Egypt* (London: Elek Books, 1970), p. 271.

9   Harry Magdoff, "Colonialism (1763–c. 1970)," *Encyclopaedia Britannica*, 15th ed. (1974), pp. 893–4. See also D. K. Fieldhouse, *The Colonial Empires: A Comparative Survey from the Eighteenth Century* (New York: Delacorte Press, 1967), p. 178.

10 Quoted in Afaf Lutfi al-Sayyid, *Egypt and Cromer: A Study in Anglo-Egyptian Relations* (New York: Frederick A. Praeger, 1969), p. 3.

11 The phrase is to be found in Ian Hacking, *The Emergence of Probability: A Philosophical Study of Early Ideas About Probability, Induction and Statistical Inference* (London: Cambridge University Press, 1975), p. 17.

12 V. G. Kiernan, *The Lords of Human Kind: Black Man, Yellow Man, and White Man in an Age of Empire* (Boston: Little, Brown & Co., 1969), p. 55.

13 Edgar Quinet, *Le Génie des religions*, in *Oeuvres complètes* (Paris: Paguerre, 1857), pp. 55–74.

14 Cromer, *Political and Literary Essays*, p. 35.

15 See Jonah Raskin, *The Mythology of Imperialism* (New York: Random House, 1971), p. 40.

CHAPTER 3

An Image of Africa:
Racism in Conrad's *Heart of Darkness*

Chinua Achebe

The mid-twentieth century witnessed a remarkable turn in human history, as the colonized peoples of Africa, Asia, and Europe revolted against their colonial oppressors and achieved independence. That major change led to a reconsideration of the culture that helped sustain colonialism. Joseph Conrad's *Heart of Darkness* had been taught as an example of an interesting narrative form, and nobody seemed to notice that it was a remarkably racist and quite reactionary text. Conrad, a reactionary monarchist, may have been capable of great narrative irony, but he was also capable of depicting Africans as sub-human animals whose "darkness" he summoned as a taunt against European liberal opponents of colonialism. He was critical of weak-kneed colonialism, which he measured negatively against an ideal of a more manly and true imperialism. Nigerian writer, Chinua Achebe, was raised under colonial rule and experienced the mistreatment accorded native Africans under imperial rule. His take on Conrad is therefore very different from that of those who celebrated his narrative irony.

It was a fine autumn morning at the beginning of this academic year such as encouraged friendliness to passing strangers. Brisk youngsters were hurrying in all directions, many of them obviously freshmen in their first flush of enthusiasm. An older man, going the same way as I, turned and remarked to me how very young they came these days. I agreed. Then he asked me if I was a student too. I said no, I was a teacher. What did I teach? African literature. Now that was funny, he said, because he never had thought of Africa as having that kind of stuff, you know. By this time I was walking much faster. "Oh well," I heard him say finally, behind me, "I guess I have to take your course to find out."

A few weeks later I received two very touching letters from high school children in Yonkers, New York, who – bless their teacher – had just read *Things Fall Apart*. One of them was particularly happy to learn about the customs and superstitions of an African tribe.

Original publication details: Chinua Achebe, "An Image of Africa," from *The Chancellor's Lecture Series, 1974–5*, printed in *The Massachusetts Review* (1976), pp. 782–794. Amherst 1976. Reproduced with permission from The Wylie Agency (UK) Ltd.

Literary Theory: An Anthology, Third Edition. Edited by Julie Rivkin and Michael Ryan.
© 2017 John Wiley & Sons, Ltd. Published 2017 by John Wiley & Sons, Ltd.

I propose to draw from these rather trivial encounters rather heavy conclusions which at first sight might seem somewhat out of proportion to them: But only at first sight.

The young fellow from Yonkers, perhaps partly on account of his age but I believe also for much deeper and more serious reasons, is obviously unaware that the life of his own tribesmen in Yonkers, New York, is full of odd customs and superstitions and, like everybody else in his culture, imagines that he needs a trip to Africa to encounter those things.

The other person being fully my own age could not be excused on the grounds of his years. Ignorance might be a more likely reason; but here again I believe that something more willful than a mere lack of information was at work. For did not that erudite British historian and Regius Professor at Oxford, Hugh Trevor Roper, pronounce a few years ago that African history did not exist?

If there is something in these utterances more than youthful experience, more than a lack of factual knowledge, what is it? Quite simply it is the desire – one might indeed say the need – in Western psychology to set Africa up as a foil in Europe, a place of negations at once remote and vaguely familiar in comparison with which Europe's own state of spiritual grace will be manifest.

This need is not new: which should relieve us of considerable responsibility and perhaps make us even willing to look at this phenomenon dispassionately. I have neither the desire nor, indeed, the competence to do so with the tools of the social and biological sciences. But, I can respond, as a novelist, to one famous book of European fiction, Joseph Conrad's *Heart of Darkness*, which better than any other work I know displays that Western desire and need which I have just spoken about. Of course, there are whole libraries of books devoted to the same purpose, but most of them are so obvious and so crude that few people worry about them today. Conrad, on the other hand, is undoubt-edly one of the great stylists of modern fiction and a good storyteller into the bargain. His contribution therefore falls automatically into a different class – permanent literature – read and taught and constantly evaluated by serious academics. *Heart of Darkness* is indeed so secure today that a leading Conrad scholar has numbered it "among the half-dozen greatest short novels in the English language."[1] I will return to this critical option in due course because it may seriously modify my earlier suppositions about who may or may not be guilty in the things of which I will now speak.

Heart of Darkness projects the image of Africa as "the other world," the antithesis of Europe and therefore of civilization, a place where a man's vaunted intelligence and refinement are finally mocked by triumphant bestiality. The book opens on the River Thames, tranquil, resting peacefully "at the decline of day after ages of good service done to the race that peopled its banks." But the actual story takes place on the River Congo, the very antithesis of the Thames. The River Congo is quite decid-edly not a River Emeritus. It has rendered no service and enjoys no old-age pension. We are told that "going up that river was like travelling back to the earliest beginning of the world."

Is Conrad saying then that these two rivers are very different, one good, the other bad? Yes, but that is not the real point. What actually worries Conrad is the lurking hint of kinship, of common ancestry. For the Thames, too, "has been one of the dark places of the earth." It conquered its darkness, of course, and is now at peace. But if it were to visit its primordial relative, the Congo, it would run the terrible risk of hearing grotesque, suggestive echoes of its own forgotten darkness, and of falling victim to an avenging recrudescence of the mindless frenzy of the first beginnings.

I am not going to waste your time with examples of Conrad's famed evocation of the African atmosphere. In the final consideration it amounts to no more than a steady, ponderous, fake-ritualistic repetition of two sentences, one about silence and the other about frenzy. An example of the former is "It was the stillness of an implacable force brooding over an inscrutable intention" and of the latter, "The steamer toiled along slowly on the edge of a black and incomprehensible frenzy." Of course, there is a judicious change of adjective from time to time so that instead of "inscrutable," for example, you might have "unspeakable," etc., etc.

The eagle-eyed English critic, F. R. Leavis, drew attention nearly thirty years ago to Conrad's "adjectival insistence upon inexpressible and incomprehensible mystery." That insistence must not be dismissed lightly, as many Conrad critics have tended to do, as a mere stylistic flaw. For it raises serious questions of artistic good faith. When a writer, while pretending to record scenes, incidents and their impact, is in reality engaged in inducing hypnotic stupor in his readers through a bombardment of emotive words and other forms of trickery much more has to be at stake than stylistic felicity. Generally, normal readers are well armed to detect and resist such underhand activity. But Conrad chose his subject well – one which was guaranteed not to put him in conflict with the psychological predisposition of his readers or raise the need for him to contend with their resistance. He chose the role of purveyor of comforting myths.

The most interesting and revealing passages in *Heart of Darkness* are, however, about people. I must quote a long passage from the middle of the story in which representatives of Europe in a steamer going down the Congo encounter the denizens of Africa:

> We were wanderers on a prehistoric earth, on an earth that wore the aspect of an unknown planet. We could have fancied ourselves the first of men taking possession of an accursed inheritance, to be subdued at the cost of profound anguish and of excessive toil. But suddenly, as we struggled round a bend, there would be a glimpse of rush walls, of peaked grass-roofs, a burst of yells, a whirl of black limbs, a mass of hands clapping, of feet stamping, of bodies swaying, of eyes rolling, under the droop of heavy and motionless foliage. The steamer toiled along slowly on the edge of a black and incomprehensible frenzy. The prehistoric man was cursing us, praying to us, welcoming us – who could tell? We were cut off from the comprehension of our surroundings; we glided past like phantoms, wondering and secretly appalled, as sane men would be before an enthusiastic outbreak in a madhouse. We could not remember because we were travelling in the night of first ages, of those ages that are gone, leaving hardly a sign – and no memories.
>
> The earth seemed unearthly. We are accustomed to look upon the shackled form of a conquered monster, but there – there you could look at a thing monstrous and free. It was unearthly, and the men were – No, they were not inhuman. Well, you know, that was the worst of it – this suspicion of their not being inhuman. It would come slowly to one. They howled and leaped, and spun, and made horrid faces; but what thrilled you was just the thought of your remote kinship with this wild and passionate uproar. Ugly. Yes, it was ugly enough; but if you were man enough you would admit to yourself that there was in you just the faintest trace of a response to the terrible frankness of that noise, a dim suspicion of there being a meaning in it which you – you so remote from the night of first ages – could comprehend.

Herein lies the meaning of *Heart of Darkness* and the fascination it holds over the Western mind: "What thrilled you was just the thought of their humanity – like yours.... Ugly."

Having shown us Africa in the mass, Conrad then zeros in on a specific example, giving us one of his rare descriptions of an African who is not just limbs or rolling eyes:

> And between whiles I had to look after the savage who was fireman. He was an improved specimen; he could fire up a vertical boiler. He was there below me, and, upon my word, to look at him was as edifying as seeing a dog in a parody of breeches and a feather hat, walking on his hind legs. A few months of training had done for that really fine chap. He squinted at the steam gauge and at the water gauge with an evident effort of intrepidity – and he had filed his teeth, too, the poor devil, and the wool of his pate shaved into queer patterns, and three ornamental scars on each of his cheeks. He ought to have been clapping his hands and stamping his feet on the bank, instead of which he was hard at work, a thrall to strange witchcraft, full of improving knowledge.

As everybody knows, Conrad is a romantic on the side. He might not exactly admire savages clapping their hands and stamping their feet but they have at least the merit of being in their place, unlike this dog in a parody of breeches. For Conrad, things (and persons) being in their place is of the utmost importance.

Towards the end of the story, Conrad lavishes great attention quite unexpectedly on an African woman who has obviously been some kind of mistress to Mr. Kurtz and now presides (if I may be permitted a little imitation of Conrad) like a formidable mystery over the inexorable imminence of his departure:

> She was savage and superb, wild-eyed and magnificent ... She stood looking at us without a stir and like the wilderness itself, with an air of brooding over an inscrutable purpose.

This Amazon is drawn in considerable detail, albeit of a predictable nature, for two reasons. First, she is in her place and so can win Conrad's special brand of approval; and second, she fulfills a structural requirement of the story; she is a savage counterpart to the refined, European woman with whom the story will end:

> She came forward, all in black with a pale head, floating towards me in the dusk. She was in mourning.... She took both my hands in hers and murmured, "I had heard you were coming" ... She had a mature capacity for fidelity, for belief, for suffering.

The difference in the attitude of the novelist to these two women is conveyed in too many direct and subtle ways to need elaboration. But perhaps the most significant difference is the one implied in the author's bestowal of human expression to the one and the withholding of it from the other. It is clearly not part of Conrad's purpose to confer language on the "rudimentary souls" of Africa. They only "exchanged short grunting phrases" even among themselves but mostly they were too busy with their frenzy. There are two occasions in the book, however, when Conrad departs somewhat from his practice and confers speech, even English speech, on the savages. The first occurs when cannibalism gets the better of them:

> "Catch 'im," he snapped, with a bloodshot widening of his eyes and a flash of sharp white teeth – "catch 'im. Give 'im to us." "To you, eh?" I asked; "what would you do with them?" "Eat 'im!" he said curtly ...

The other occasion is the famous announcement:

> Mistah Kurtz – he dead.

At first sight, these instances might be mistaken for unexpected acts of generosity from Conrad. In reality, they constitute some of his best assaults. In the case of the cannibals, the incomprehensible grunts that had thus far served them for speech suddenly proved inadequate for Conrad's purpose of letting the European glimpse the unspeakable craving in their hearts. Weighing the necessity for consistency in the portrayal of the dumb brutes against the sensational advantages of securing their conviction by clear, unambiguous evidence issuing out of their own mouth, Conrad chose the latter. As for the announcement of Mr. Kurtz's death by the "insolent black head of the doorway," what better or more appropriate *finis* could be written to the horror story of that wayward child of civilization who willfully had given his soul to the powers of darkness and "taken a high seat amongst the devils of the land" than the proclamation of his physical death by the forces he had joined?

It might be contended, of course, that the attitude to the African in *Heart of Darkness* is not Conrad's but that of his fictional narrator, Marlow, and that far from endorsing it Conrad might indeed be holding it up to irony and criticism. Certainly, Conrad appears to go to considerable pains to set up layers of insulation between himself and the moral universe of his story. He has, for example, a narrator behind a narrator. The primary narrator is Marlow but his account is given to us through the filter of a second, shadowy person. But if Conrad's intention is to draw a *cordon sanitaire* between himself and the moral and psychological malaise of his narrator, his care seems to me totally wasted because he neglects to hint however subtly or tentatively at an alternative frame of reference by which we may judge the actions and opinions of his characters. It would not have been beyond Conrad's power to make that provision if he had thought it necessary. Marlow seems to me to enjoy Conrad's complete confidence – a feeling reinforced by the close similarities between their careers.

Marlow comes through to us not only as a witness of truth, but one holding those advanced and humane views appropriate to the English liberal tradition which required all Englishmen of decency to be deeply shocked by atrocities in Bulgaria or the Congo of King Leopold of the Belgians or wherever. Thus Marlow is able to toss out such bleeding-heart sentiments as these:

> They were all dying slowly – it was very clear. They were not enemies, they were not criminals, they were nothing earthly now – nothing but black shadows of disease and starvation, lying confusedly in the greenish gloom. Brought from all the recesses of the coast in all the legality of time contracts, lost in uncongenial surroundings, fed on unfamiliar food, they sickened, became inefficient, and were then allowed to crawl away and rest.

The kind of liberalism espoused here by Marlow/Conrad touched all the best minds of the age in England, Europe, and America. It took different forms in the minds of different people but almost always managed to sidestep the ultimate question of equality between white people and black people. That extraordinary missionary, Albert Schweitzer, who sacrificed brilliant careers in music and theology in Europe for a life of service to Africans in much the same area as Conrad writes about, epitomizes the ambivalence. In a comment which I have often quoted but must quote one last time Schweitzer says: "The African is indeed my brother but my junior brother." And so he proceeded to build a hospital appropriate to the needs of junior brothers with standards of hygiene reminiscent of medical practice in the days before the germ theory of disease came into being.

Naturally, he became a sensation in Europe and America. Pilgrims flocked, and I believe still flock even after he has passed on, to witness the prodigious miracle in Lamberene, on the edge of the primeval forest.

Conrad's liberalism would not take him quite as far as Schweitzer's, though. He would not use the word "brother" however qualified; the farthest he would go was "kinship." When Marlow's African helmsman falls down with a spear in his heart he gives his white master one final disquieting look.

> And the intimate profundity of that look he gave me when he received his hurt remains to this day in my memory – like a claim of distant kinship affirmed in a supreme moment.

It is important to note that Conrad, careful as ever with his words, is not talking so much about *distant kinship* as about someone *laying a claim* on it. The black man lays a claim on the white man which is well-nigh intolerable. It is the laying of this claim which frightens and at the same time fascinates Conrad, "… the thought of their humanity – like yours … Ugly."

The point of my observations should be quite clear by now, namely, that Conrad was a bloody racist. That this simple truth is glossed over in criticism of his work is due to the fact that white racism against Africa is such a normal way of thinking that its manifestations go completely undetected. Students of *Heart of Darkness* will often tell you that Conrad is concerned not so much with Africa as with the deterioration of one European mind caused by solitude and sickness. They will point out to you that Conrad is, if anything, less charitable to the Europeans in the story than he is to the natives. A Conrad student told me in Scotland last year that Africa is merely a setting for the disintegration of the mind of Mr. Kurtz.

Which is partly the point: Africa as setting and backdrop which eliminates the African as human factor. Africa as a metaphysical battlefield devoid of all recognizable humanity, into which the wandering European enters at his peril. Of course, there is a preposterous and perverse kind of arrogance in thus reducing Africa to the role of props for the breakup of one petty European mind. But that is not even the point. The real question is the dehumanization of Africa and Africans which this age-long attitude has fostered and continues to foster in the world. And the question is whether a novel which celebrates this dehumanization, which depersonalizes a portion of the human race, can be called a great work of art. My answer is: No, it cannot. I would not call that man an artist, for example, who composes an eloquent instigation to one people to fall upon another and destroy them. No matter how striking his imagery or how beautiful his cadences fall such a man is no more a great artist than another may be called a priest who reads the mass backwards or a physician who poisons his patients. All those men in Nazi Germany who lent their talent to the service of virulent racism whether in science, philosophy or the arts have generally and rightly been condemned for their perversions. The time is long overdue for taking a hard look at the work of creative artists who apply their talents, alas often considerable as in the case of Conrad, to set people against people. This, I take it, is what Yevtushenko is after when he tells us that a poet cannot be a slave trader at the same time, and gives the striking example of Arthur Rimbaud who was fortunately honest enough to give up any pretenses to poetry when he opted for slave trading. For poetry surely can only be on the side of man's deliverance and not his enslavement; for the brotherhood and unity of all mankind and against the doctrines of Hitler's master races or Conrad's "rudimentary souls."

Last year was the 50th anniversary of Conrad's death. He was born in 1857, the very year in which the first Anglican missionaries were arriving among my own people in Nigeria. It was certainly not his fault that he lived his life at a time when the reputation of the black man was at a particularly low level. But even after due allowances have been made for all the influences of contemporary prejudice on his sensibility, there remains still in Conrad's attitude a residue of antipathy to black people which his peculiar psychology alone can explain. His own account of his first encounter with a black man is very revealing:

> A certain enormous buck nigger encountered in Haiti fixed my conception of blind, furious, unreasoning rage, as manifested in the human animal to the end of my days. Of the nigger I used to dream for years afterwards.

Certainly, Conrad had a problem with niggers. His inordinate love of that word itself should be of interest to psychoanalysts. Sometimes his fixation on blackness is equally interesting as when he gives us this brief description:

> A black figure stood up, strode on long black legs, waving long black arms.[2]

as though we might expect a black figure striding along on black legs to have *white* arms! But so unrelenting is Conrad's obsession.

As a matter of interest Conrad gives us in *A Personal Record* what amounts to a companion piece to the buck nigger of Haiti. At the age of sixteen Conrad encountered his first Englishman in Europe. He calls him "my unforgettable Englishman" and describes him in the following manner:

> [his] calves exposed to the public gaze ... dazzled the beholder by the splendor of their marble-like condition and their rich tone of young ivory ... The light of a headlong, exalted satisfaction with the world of men ... illumined his face ... and triumphant eyes. In passing he cast a glance of kindly curiosity and a friendly gleam of big, sound, shiny teeth ... his white calves twinkled sturdily.[3]

Irrational love and irrational hate jostling together in the heart of that tormented man. But whereas irrational love may at worst engender foolish acts of indiscretion, irrational hate can endanger the life of the community. Naturally, Conrad is a dream for psychoanalytic critics. Perhaps the most detailed study of him in this direction is by Bernard C. Meyer, M.D. In this lengthy book, Dr. Meyer follows every conceivable lead (and sometimes inconceivable ones) to explain Conrad. As an example, he gives us long disquisitions on the significance of hair and hair-cutting in Conrad. And yet not even one word is spared for his attitude to black people. Not even the discussion of Conrad's antisemitism was enough to spark off in Dr. Meyer's mind those other dark and explosive thoughts. Which only leads one to surmise that Western psychoanalysts must regard the kind of racism displayed by Conrad as absolutely normal despite the profoundly important work done by Frantz Fanon in the psychiatric hospitals of French Algeria.

Whatever Conrad's problems were, you might say he is now safely dead. Quite true. Unfortunately, his heart of darkness plagues us still. Which is why an offensive and totally deplorable book can be described by a serious scholar as "among the half dozen greatest short novels in the English language," and why it is today perhaps the most commonly prescribed novel in the twentieth-century literature courses in our own English Department here. Indeed the time is long overdue for a hard look at things.

There are two probable grounds on which what I have said so far may be contested. The first is that it is no concern of fiction to please people about whom it is written. I will go along with that. But I am not talking about pleasing people. I am talking about a book which parades in the most vulgar fashion prejudices and insults from which a section of mankind has suffered untold agonies and atrocities in the past and continues to do so in many ways and many places today. I am talking about a story in which the very humanity of black people is called in question. It seems to me totally inconceivable that great art or even good art could possibly reside in such unwholesome surroundings.

Secondly, I may be challenged on the grounds of actuality. Conrad, after all, sailed down the Congo in 1890 when my own father was still a babe in arms, and recorded what he saw. How could I stand up in 1975, fifty years after his death and purport to contradict him? My answer is that as a sensible man I will not accept just any traveller's tales solely on the grounds that I have not made the journey myself. I will not trust the evidence even of a man's very eyes when I suspect them to be as jaundiced as Conrad's. And we also happen to know that Conrad was, in the words of his biographer, Bernard C. Meyer, "notoriously inaccurate in the rendering of his own history."[4]

But more important by far is the abundant testimony about Conrad's savages which we could gather if we were so inclined from other sources and which might lead us to think that these people must have had other occupations besides merging into the evil forest or materializing out of it simply to plague Marlow and his dispirited band. For as it happened, soon after Conrad had written his book an event of far greater consequence was taking place in the art world of Europe. This is how Frank Willett, a British art historian, describes it:

> Gaugin had gone to Tahiti, the most extravagant individual act of turning to a non-European culture in the decades immediately before and after 1900, when European artists were avid for new artistic experiences, but it was only about 1904–5 that African art began to make its distinctive impact. One piece is still identifiable; it is a mask that had been given to Maurice Vlaminck in 1905. He records that Derain was "speechless" and "stunned" when he saw it, bought it from Vlaminck and in turn showed it to Picasso and Matisse, who were also greatly affected by it. Ambroise Vollard then borrowed it and had it cast in bronze ... The revolution of twentieth century art was under way![5]

The mask in question was made by other savages living just north of Conrad's River Congo. They have a name, the Fang people, and are without a doubt among the world's greatest masters of the sculptured form. As you might have guessed, the event to which Frank Willett refers marked the beginning of cubism and the infusion of new life into European art that had run completely out of strength.

The point of all this is to suggest that Conrad's picture of the people of the Congo seems grossly inadequate even at the height of their subjection to the ravages of King Leopold's International Association for the Civilization of Central Africa. Travellers with closed minds can tell us little except about themselves. But even those not blinkered, like Conrad, with xenophobia, can be astonishingly blind.

Let me digress a little here. One of the greatest and most intrepid travellers of all time, Marco Polo, journeyed to the Far East from the Mediterranean in the thirteenth century and spent twenty years in the court of Kublai Khan in China. On his return to

Venice he set down in his book entitled *Description of the World* his impressions of the peoples and places and customs he had seen. There are at least two extraordinary omissions in his account. He says nothing about the art of printing unknown as yet in Europe but in full flower in China. He either did not notice it at all or if he did, failed to see what use Europe could possibly have for it. Whatever reason, Europe had to wait another hundred years for Gutenberg. But even more spectacular was Marco Polo's omission of any reference to the Great Wall of China nearly 4000 miles long and already more than 1000 years old at the time of his visit. Again, he may not have seen it; but the Great Wall of China is the only structure built by man which is visible from the moon![6] Indeed, travellers can be blind.

As I said earlier, Conrad did not originate the image of Africa which we find in his book. It was and is the dominant image of Africa in the Western imagination and Conrad merely brought the peculiar gifts of his own mind to bear on it. For reasons which can certainly use close psychological inquiry, the West seems to suffer deep anxieties about the precariousness of its civilization and to have a need for constant reassurance by comparing it with Africa. If Europe, advancing in civilization, could cast a backward glance periodically at Africa trapped in primordial barbarity, it could say with faith and feeling: There go I but for the grace of God. Africa is to Europe as the picture is to Dorian Gray – a carrier onto whom the master unloads his physical and moral deformities so that he may go forward, erect and immaculate. Consequently, Africa is something to be avoided just as the picture has to be hidden away to safeguard the man's jeopardous integrity. Keep away from Africa, or else! Mr. Kurtz of *Heart of Darkness* should have heeded that warning and the prowling horror in his heart would have kept its place, chained to its lair. But he foolishly exposed himself to the wild irresistible allure of the jungle and lo! the darkness found him out.

In my original conception of this talk I had thought to conclude it nicely on an appropriately positive note in which I would suggest from my privileged position in African and Western culture some advantages the West might derive from Africa once it rid its mind of old prejudices and began to look at Africa not through a haze of distortions and cheap mystification but quite simply as a continent of people – not angels, but not rudimentary souls either – just people, often highly gifted people and often strikingly successful in their enterprise with life and society. But as I thought more about the stereotype image, about its grip and pervasiveness, about the willful tenacity with which the West holds it to its heart; when I thought of your television and the cinema and newspapers, about books read in schools and out of school, of churches preaching to empty pews about the need to send help to the heathen in Africa, I realized that no easy optimism was possible. And there is something totally wrong in offering bribes to the West in return for its good opinion of Africa. Ultimately, the abandonment of unwholesome thoughts must be its own and only reward. Although I have used the word *willful* a few times in this talk to characterize the West's view of Africa it may well be that what is happening at this stage is more akin to reflex action than calculated malice. Which does not make the situation more, but less, hopeful. Let me give you one last and really minor example of what I mean.

Last November the *Christian Science Monitor* carried an interesting article written by its Education Editor on the serious psychological and learning problems faced by little children who speak one language at home and then go to school where something else is spoken. It was a wide-ranging article taking in Spanish-speaking children in this country, the children of migrant Italian workers in Germany, the quadrilingual phenomenon in Malaysia and so on. And all this while the article speaks unequivocally about *language*. But then out of the blue sky comes this:

> In London there is an enormous immigration of children who speak Indian or Nigerian dialects, or some other native language.[7]

I believe that the introduction of *dialects*, which is technically erroneous in the context, is almost a reflex action caused by an instinctive desire of the writer to downgrade the discussion to the level of Africa and India. And this is quite comparable to Conrad's withholding of language from his rudimentary souls. Language is too grand for these chaps; let's give them dialects. In all this business a lot of violence is inevitably done to words and their meaning. Look at the phrase "native language" in the above excerpt. Surely the only native language possible in London is Cockney English. But our writer obviously means something else – something Indians and Africans speak.

Perhaps a change will come. Perhaps this is the time when it can begin, when the high optimism engendered by the breathtaking achievements of Western science and industry is giving way to doubt and even confusion. There is just the possibility that Western man may begin to look seriously at the achievements of other people. I read in the papers the other day a suggestion that what America needs at this time is somehow to bring back the extended family. And I saw in my mind's eye future African Peace Corps Volunteers coming to help you set up the system.

Seriously, although the work which needs to be done may appear too daunting, I believe that it is not one day too soon to begin. And where better than at a University?

Notes

1   Albert J. Guerard, Introduction to *Heart of Darkness* (New York: New American Library, 1950), p. 9.
2   Jonah Raskin, *The Mythology of Imperialism* (New York: Random House, 1971), p. 143.
3   Bernard C. Meyer, M.D., *Joseph Conrad: A Psychoanalytic Biography* (Princeton, N.J.: Princeton University Press, 1967), p. 30.
4   *Ibid.*, p. 30.
5   Frank Willett, *African Art* (New York: Praeger, 1971), pp. 35–36.
6   About the omission of the Great Wall of China I am indebted to *The Journey of Marco Polo* as recreated by artist Michael Foreman, published by *Pegasus* Magazine, 1974.
7   *Christian Science Monitor*, Nov. 25, 1974, p. 11.

CHAPTER 4

Three Women's Texts and a Critique of Imperialism

Gayatri Chakravorty Spivak

Gayatri Chakravorty Spivak has written widely on Post-Colonialism, feminism, and Post-Structuralist literary theory. In this 1986 essay, she criticizes American feminists for ignoring the figure of Bertha Mason in Charlotte Brontë's *Jane Eyre*, and she offers an alternative to the dominant liberal individualism of US feminism that takes the historical reality of imperialism and colonialism into account.

It should not be possible to read nineteenth-century British literature without remembering that imperialism, understood as England's social mission, was a crucial part of the cultural representation of England to the English. The role of literature in the production of cultural representation should not be ignored. These two obvious "facts" continue to be disregarded in the reading of nineteenth-century British literature. This itself attests to the continuing success of the imperialist project, displaced and dispersed into more modern forms.

If these "facts" were remembered, not only in the study of British literature but in the study of the literatures of the European colonizing cultures of the great age of imperialism, we would produce a narrative, in literary history, of the "worlding" of what is now called "the Third World." To consider the Third World as distant cultures, exploited but with rich intact literary heritages waiting to be recovered, interpreted, and curricularized in English translation fosters the emergence of "the Third World" as a signifier that allows us to forget that "worlding," even as it expands the empire of the literary discipline.[1]

It seems particularly unfortunate when the emergent perspective of feminist criticism reproduces the axioms of imperialism. A basically isolationist admiration for the literature of the female subject in Europe and Anglo-America establishes the high feminist norm. It is supported and operated by an information-retrieval approach

Original publication details: Gayatri Chakravorty Spivak, "Three Women's Texts and a Critique of Imperialism" from *Race, Writing and Difference*, ed. H.L. Gates, pp. 262–80. University of Chicago Press, 1987. Reproduced with permission from Gayatri Chakravorty Spivak.

Literary Theory: An Anthology, Third Edition. Edited by Julie Rivkin and Michael Ryan.
© 2017 John Wiley & Sons, Ltd. Published 2017 by John Wiley & Sons, Ltd.

to "Third World" literature which often employs a deliberately "nontheoretical" methodology with self-conscious rectitude.

In this essay, I will attempt to examine the operation of the "worlding" of what is today "the Third World" by what has become a cult text of feminism: *Jane Eyre*.[2] I plot the novel's reach and grasp, and locate its structural motors. I read *Wide Sargasso Sea* as *Jane Eyre*'s reinscription and *Frankenstein* as an analysis – even a deconstruction – of a "worlding" such as *Jane Eyre*'s.[3]

I need hardly mention that the object of my investigation is the printed book, not its "author." To make such a distinction is, of course, to ignore the lessons of deconstruction. A deconstructive critical approach would loosen the binding of the book, undo the opposition between verbal text and the bio-graphy of the named subject "Charlotte Brontë," and see the two as each other's "scene of writing." In such a reading, the life that writes itself as "my life" is as much a production in psychosocial space (other names can be found) as the book that is written by the holder of that named life – a book that is then consigned to what *is* most often recognized as genuinely "social": the world of publication and distribution.[4] To touch Brontë's "life" in such a way, however, would be too risky here. We must rather strategically take shelter in an essentialism which, not wishing to lose the important advantages won by US mainstream feminism, will continue to honor the suspect binary oppositions – book and author, individual and history – and start with an assurance of the following sort: my readings here do not seek to undermine the excellence of the individual artist. If even minimally successful, the readings will incite a degree of rage against the imperialist narrativization of history, that it should produce so abject a script for her. I provide these assurances to allow myself some room to situate feminist individualism in its historical determination rather than simply to canonize it as feminism as such.

Sympathetic US feminists have remarked that I do not do justice to Jane Eyre's subjectivity. A word of explanation is perhaps in order. The broad strokes of my presuppositions are that what is at stake, for feminist individualism in the age of imperialism, is precisely the making of human beings, the constitution and "interpellation" of the subject not only as individual but as "individualist."[5] This stake is represented on two registers: childbearing and soul making. The first is domestic-society-through-sexual-reproduction cathected as "companionate love"; the second is the imperialist project cathected as civil-society-through-social-mission. As the female individualist, not-quite/not-male, articulates herself in shifting relationship to what is at stake, the "native female" as such (*within* discourse, *as* a signifier) is excluded from any share in this emerging norm.[6] If we read this account from an isolationist perspective in a "metropolitan" context, we see nothing there but the psychobiography of the militant female subject. In a reading such as mine, in contrast, the effort is to wrench oneself away from the mesmerizing focus of the "subject-constitution" of the female individualist.

To develop further the notion that my stance need not be an accusing one, I will refer to a passage from Roberto Fernández Retamar's "Caliban."[7] José Enrique Rodó had argued in 1900 that the model for the Latin American intellectual in relationship to Europe could be Shakespeare's Ariel.[8] In 1971 Retamar, denying the possibility of an identifiable "Latin American Culture," recast the model as Caliban. Not surprisingly, this powerful exchange still excludes any specific consideration of the civilizations of the Maya, the Aztecs, the Incas, or the smaller nations of what is now called Latin America. Let us note carefully that, at this stage of my argument, this "conversation" between Europe and Latin America (without a specific consideration of the political economy of the "worlding" of the "native") provides a sufficient thematic description of our attempt to confront the ethnocentric and reverse-ethnocentric benevolent double bind (that is, considering the "native" as object for enthusiastic information-retrieval and thus denying its own "worlding") that I sketched in my opening paragraphs.

In a moving passage in "Caliban," Retamar locates both Caliban and Ariel in the postcolonial intellectual:

> There is no real Ariel–Caliban polarity: both are slaves in the hands of Prospero, the foreign magician. But Caliban is the rude and unconquerable master of the island, while Ariel, a creature of the air, although also a child of the isle, is the intellectual.
>
> The deformed Caliban – enslaved, robbed of his island, and taught the language by Prospero – rebukes him thus: "You taught me language, and my profit on't / Is, I know how to curse." ["C," pp. 28, 11]

As we attempt to unlearn our so-called privilege as Ariel and "seek from [a certain] Caliban the honor of a place in his rebellious and glorious ranks," we do not ask that our students and colleagues should emulate us but that they should attend to us ("C," p. 72). If, however, we are driven by a nostalgia for lost origins, we too run the risk of effacing the "native" and stepping forth as "the real Caliban," of forgetting that he is a name in a play, an inaccessible blankness circumscribed by an interpretable text.[9] The stagings of Caliban work alongside the narrativization of history: claiming to *be* Caliban legitimizes the very individualism that we must persistently attempt to undermine from within.

Elizabeth Fox-Genovese, in an article on history and women's history, shows us how to define the historical moment of feminism in the West in terms of female access to individualism.[10] The battle for female individualism plays itself out within the larger theater of the establishment of meritocratic individualism, indexed in the aesthetic field by the ideology of "the creative imagination." Fox-Genovese's presupposition will guide us into the beautifully orchestrated opening of *Jane Eyre*.

It is a scene of the marginalization and privatization of the protagonist: "There was no possibility of taking a walk that day…. Out-door exercise was now out of the question. I was glad of it," Brontë writes (*JE*, p. 9). The movement continues as Jane breaks the rules of the appropriate topography of withdrawal. The family at the center withdraws into the sanctioned architectural space of the withdrawing room or drawing room; Jane inserts herself – "I slipped in" – into the margin – "A small breakfast-room *adjoined* the drawing room" (*JE*, p. 9; my emphasis).

The manipulation of the domestic inscription of space within the upwardly mobilizing currents of the eighteenth- and nineteenth-century bourgeoisie in England and France is well known. It seems fitting that the place to which Jane withdraws is not only not the withdrawing room but also not the dining room, the sanctioned place of family meals. Nor is it the library, the appropriate place for reading. The breakfast room "contained a book-case" (*JE*, p. 9). As Rudolph Ackerman wrote in his *Repository* (1823), one of the many manuals of taste in circulation in nineteenth-century England, these low bookcases and stands were designed to "contain all the books that may be desired for a sitting-room without reference to the library."[11] Even in this already triply off-center place, "having drawn the red moreen curtain nearly close, I [Jane] was shrined in double retirement" (*JE*, pp. 9–10).

Here in Jane's self-marginalized uniqueness, the reader becomes her accomplice: the reader and Jane are united – both are reading. Yet Jane still preserves her odd privilege, for she continues never quite doing the proper thing in its proper place. She cares little for reading what is *meant* to be read: the "letter-press." *She* reads the pictures. The power of this singular hermeneutics is precisely that it can make the outside inside. "At intervals, while turning over the leaves of my book, I studied the aspect of that winter afternoon." Under "the clear panes of glass," the rain no longer penetrates, "the drear November day" is rather a one-dimensional "aspect" to be "studied," not decoded like the "letter-press" but, like pictures, deciphered by the unique creative imagination of the marginal individualist (*JE*, p. 10).

Before following the track of this unique imagination, let us consider the suggestion that the progress of *Jane Eyre* can be charted through a sequential arrangement of the family/counter-family dyad. In the novel, we encounter, first, the Reeds as the legal family and Jane, the late Mr. Reed's sister's daughter, as the representative of a near incestuous counter-family; second, the Brocklehursts, who run the school Jane is sent to, as the legal family and Jane, Miss Temple, and Helen Burns as a counter-family that falls short because it is only a community of women; third, Rochester and the mad Mrs. Rochester as the legal family and Jane and Rochester as the illicit counter-family. Other items may be added to the thematic chain in this sequence: Rochester and Céline Varens as structurally functional counter-family; Rochester and Blanche Ingram as dissimulation of legality – and so on. It is during this sequence that Jane is moved from the counter-family to the family-in-law. In the next sequence, it is Jane who restores full family status to the as-yet-incomplete community of siblings, the Riverses. The final sequence of the book is a *community of families*, with Jane, Rochester, and their children at the center.

In terms of the narrative energy of the novel, how is Jane moved from the place of the counter-family to the family-in-law? It is the active ideology of imperialism that provides the discursive field.

(My working definition of "discursive field" must assume the existence of discrete "systems of signs" at hand in the socius, each based on a specific axiomatics. I am identifying these systems as discursive fields. "Imperialism as social mission" generates the possibility of one such axiomatics. How the individual artist taps the discursive field at hand with a sure touch, if not with transhistorical clairvoyance, in order to make the narrative structure move I hope to demonstrate through the following example. It is crucial that we extend our analysis of this example beyond the minimal diagnosis of "racism.")

Let us consider the figure of Bertha Mason, a figure produced by the axiomatics of imperialism. Through Bertha Mason, the white Jamaican Creole, Brontë renders the human/animal frontier as acceptably indeterminate, so that a good greater than the letter of the Law can be broached. Here is the celebrated passage, given in the voice of Jane:

> In the deep shade, at the further end of the room, a figure ran backwards and forwards. What it was, whether beast or human being, one could not … tell: it grovelled, seemingly, on all fours; it snatched and growled like some strange wild animal: but it was covered with clothing, and a quantity of dark, grizzled hair, wild as a mane, hid its head and face. [*JE*, p. 295]

In a matching passage, given in the voice of Rochester speaking *to* Jane, Brontë presents the imperative for a shift beyond the Law as divine injunction rather than human motive. In the terms of my essay, we might say that this is the register not of mere marriage or sexual reproduction but of Europe and its not-yet-human Other, of soul making. The field of imperial conquest is here inscribed as Hell:

> "One night I had been awakened by her yells … it was a fiery West Indian night…."
>
> "'This life,' said I at last, 'is hell! – this is the air – those are the sounds of the bottomless pit! *I have a right* to deliver myself from it if I can…. Let me break away, and go home to God!'…"
>
> "A wind fresh from Europe blew over the ocean and rushed through the open casement: the storm broke, streamed, thundered, blazed, and the air grew pure…. It was true Wisdom that consoled me in that hour, and showed me the right path…."
>
> "The sweet wind from Europe was still whispering in the refreshed leaves, and the Atlantic was thundering in glorious liberty…."
>
> "'Go,' said Hope, 'and live again in Europe…. You have done all that God and Humanity require of you.'" [*JE*, pp. 310–11; my emphasis]

It is the unquestioned ideology of imperialist axiomatics, then, that conditions Jane's move from the counter-family set to the set of the family-in-law. Marxist critics such as Terry Eagleton have seen this only in terms of the ambiguous *class* position of the governess.[12] Sandra Gilbert and Susan Gubar, on the other hand, have seen Bertha Mason only in psychological terms, as Jane's dark double.[13]

I will not enter the critical debates that offer themselves here. Instead, I will develop the suggestion that nineteenth-century feminist individualism could conceive of a "greater" project than access to the closed circle of the nuclear family. This is the project of soul making beyond "mere" sexual reproduction. Here the native "subject" is not almost an animal but rather the object of what might be termed the terrorism of the categorical imperative.

I am using "Kant" in this essay as a metonym for the most flexible ethical moment in the European eighteenth century. Kant words the categorical imperative, conceived as the universal moral law given by pure reason, in this way: "In all creation every thing one chooses and over which one has any power, may be used *merely as means;* man alone, and with him every rational creature, is an *end in himself*." It is thus a moving displacement of Christian ethics from religion to philosophy. As Kant writes: "With this agrees very well the possibility of such a command as: *Love God above everything, and thy neighbor as thyself*. For as a command it requires respect for a law which *commands love* and does not leave it to our own arbitrary choice to make this our principle."[14]

The "categorical" in Kant cannot be adequately represented in determinately grounded action. The dangerous transformative power of philosophy, however, is that its formal subtlety can be travestied in the service of the state. Such a travesty in the case of the categorical imperative can justify the imperialist project by producing the following formula: *make* the heathen into a human so that he can be treated as an end in himself.[15] This project is presented as a sort of tangent in *Jane Eyre*, a tangent that escapes the closed circle of the *narrative* conclusion. The tangent narrative is the story of St. John Rivers, who is granted the important task of concluding the *text*.

At the novel's end, the *allegorical* language of Christian psychobiography – rather than the textually constituted and seemingly *private* grammar of the creative imagination which we noted in the novel's opening – marks the inaccessibility of the imperialist project as such to the nascent "feminist" scenario. The concluding passage of *Jane Eyre* places St. John Rivers within the fold of *Pilgrim's Progress*. Eagleton pays no attention to this but accepts the novel's ideological lexicon, which establishes St. John Rivers' hero-ism by identifying a life in Calcutta with an unquestioning choice of death. Gilbert and Gubar, by calling *Jane Eyre* "Plain Jane's progress," see the novel as simply replacing the male protagonist with the female. They do not notice the distance between sexual reproduction and soul making, both actualized by the unquestioned idiom of imperialist presuppositions evident in the last part of *Jane Eyre*:

> Firm, faithful, and devoted, full of energy, and zeal, and truth, [St. John Rivers] labours for his race.... His is the sternness of the warrior Greatheart, who guards his pilgrim convoy from the onslaught of Apollyon.... His is the ambition of the high master-spirit[s] ... who stand without fault before the throne of God; who share the last mighty victories of the Lamb; who are called, and chosen, and faithful. [*JE*, p. 455]

Earlier in the novel, St. John Rivers himself justifies the project: "My vocation? My great work? ... My hopes of being numbered in the band who have merged all ambitions in the glorious one of bettering their race – of carrying knowledge into the realms of ignorance – of substituting peace for war – freedom for bondage – religion for superstition – the hope of heaven for the fear of hell?" (*JE*, p. 376). Imperialism and its territorial and subject-constituting project are a violent deconstruction of these oppositions.

When Jean Rhys, born on the Caribbean island of Dominica, read *Jane Eyre* as a child, she was moved by Bertha Mason: "I thought I'd try to write her a life."[16] *Wide Sargasso Sea*, the slim novel published in 1965, at the end of Rhys' long career, is that "life."

I have suggested that Bertha's function in *Jane Eyre* is to render indeterminate the boundary between human and animal and thereby to weaken her entitlement under the spirit if not the letter of the Law. When Rhys rewrites the scene in *Jane Eyre* where Jane hears "a snarling, snatching sound, almost like a dog quarrelling" and then encounters a bleeding Richard Mason (*JE*, p. 210), she keeps Bertha's humanity, indeed her sanity as critic of imperialism, intact. Grace Poole, another character originally in *Jane Eyre*, describes the incident to Bertha in *Wide Sargasso Sea*: "So you don't remember that you attacked this gentleman with a knife? ... I didn't hear all he said except 'I cannot interfere legally between yourself and your husband'. It was when he said 'legally' that you flew at him'" (*WSS*, p. 150). In Rhys' retelling, it is the dissimulation that Bertha discerns in the word "legally" – not an innate bestiality – that prompts her violent *reaction*.

In the figure of Antoinette, whom in *Wide Sargasso Sea* Rochester violently renames Bertha, Rhys suggests that so intimate a thing as personal and human identity might be determined by the politics of imperialism. Antoinette, as a white Creole child growing up at the time of emancipation in Jamaica, is caught between the English imperialist and the black native. In recounting Antoinette's development, Rhys reinscribes some thematics of Narcissus.

There are, noticeably, many images of mirroring in the text. I will quote one from the first section. In this passage, Tia is the little black servant girl who is Antoinette's close companion: "We had eaten the same food, slept side by side, bathed in the same river. As I ran, I thought, I will live with Tia and I will be like her.... When I was close I saw the jagged stone in her hand but I did not see her throw it.... We stared at each other, blood on my face, tears on hers. It was as if I saw myself. Like in a looking glass" (*WSS*, p. 38).

A progressive sequence of dreams reinforces this mirror imagery. In its second occurrence, the dream is partially set in a *hortus conclusus*, or "enclosed garden" – Rhys uses the phrase (*WSS*, p. 50) – a Romance rewriting of the Narcissus topos as the place of encounter with Love.[17] In the enclosed garden, Antoinette encounters not Love but a strange threatening voice that says merely "in here," inviting her into a prison which masquerades as the legalization of love (*WSS*, p. 50).

In Ovid's *Metamorphoses*, Narcissus' madness is disclosed when he recognizes his Other as his self: "Iste ego sum."[18] Rhys makes Antoinette see her *self* as her Other, Brontë's Bertha. In the last section of *Wide Sargasso Sea*, Antoinette acts out *Jane Eyre's* conclusion and recognizes herself as the so-called ghost in Thornfield Hall: "I went into the hall again with the tall candle in my hand. It was then that I saw her – the ghost. The woman with streaming hair. She was surrounded by a gilt frame but I knew her" (*WSS*, p. 154). The gilt frame encloses a mirror: as Narcissus' pool reflects the selfed Other, so this "pool" reflects the Othered self. Here the dream sequence ends, with an invocation of none other than Tia, the Other that could not be selfed, because the fracture of imperialism rather than the Ovidian pool intervened. (I will return to this difficult point.) "That was the third time I had my dream, and it ended.... I called 'Tia' and jumped and woke" (*WSS*, p. 155). It is now, at the very end of the book, that Antoinette/Bertha can say: "Now at last I know why I was brought here and what I have to do" (*WSS*, pp. 155–6). We can read this as her having been brought into the England of Brontë's novel: "This cardboard house" – a book between cardboard covers – "where I walk at night is not England" (*WSS*, p. 148). In this fictive England, she must play out her role, act out the transformation of her "self" into that fictive Other, set fire to the house and kill herself, so that Jane Eyre can become the feminist individualist heroine of British fiction. I must read this as an allegory of the general epistemic violence of imperialism, the construction of a self-immolating colonial subject for the glorification of the social mission of the colonizer. At least Rhys sees to it that the woman from the colonies is not sacrificed as an insane animal for her sister's consolation.

Critics have remarked that *Wide Sargasso Sea* treats the Rochester character with understanding and sympathy.[19] Indeed, he narrates the entire middle section of the book. Rhys makes it clear that he is a victim of the patriarchal inheritance law of entailment rather than of a father's natural preference for the firstborn: in *Wide Sargasso Sea*, Rochester's situation is clearly that of a younger son dispatched to the colonies to buy an heiress. If in the case of Antoinette and her identity, Rhys utilizes the thematics of Narcissus, in the case of Rochester and his patrimony, she touches on the thematics of Oedipus. (In this she has her finger on our "historical moment." If, in the nineteenth century, subject-constitution is represented as childbearing and soul making, in the twentieth century psychoanalysis allows the West to plot the itinerary of the subject from Narcissus [the "imaginary"] to Oedipus [the "symbolic"]. This subject, however, is the normative male subject. In Rhys' reinscription of these themes, divided between the female and the male protagonist, feminism and a critique of imperialism become complicit.)

In place of the "wind from Europe" scene, Rhys substitutes the scenario of a suppressed letter to a father, a letter which would be the "correct" explanation of the tragedy of the book.[20] "I thought about the letter which should have been written to England a week ago. Dear Father ..." (*WSS*, p. 57). This is the first instance: the letter not written. Shortly afterward:

> Dear Father. The thirty thousand pounds have been paid to me without question or condition. No provision made for her (that must be seen to).... I will never be a disgrace to you or to my dear brother the son you love. No begging letters, no mean requests. None of the

furtive shabby manoeuvres of a younger son. I have sold my soul or you have sold it, and after all is it such a bad bargain? The girl is thought to be beautiful, she is beautiful. And yet ... [*WSS*, p. 59]

This is the second instance: the letter not sent. The formal letter is uninteresting; I will quote only a part of it:

> Dear Father, we have arrived from Jamaica after an uncomfortable few days. This little estate in the Windward Islands is part of the family property and Antoinette is much attached to it.... All is well and has gone according to your plans and wishes. I dealt of course with Richard Mason.... He seemed to become attached to me and trusted me completely. This place is very beautiful but my illness has left me too exhausted to appreciate it fully. I will write again in a few days' time. [*WSS*, p. 63]

And so on.

Rhys' version of the Oedipal exchange is ironic, not a closed circle. We cannot know if the letter actually reaches its destination. "I wondered how they got their letters posted," the Rochester figure muses. "I folded mine and put it into a drawer of the desk.... There are blanks in my mind that cannot be filled up" (*WSS*, p. 64). It is as if the text presses us to note the analogy between letter and mind.

Rhys denies to Brontë's Rochester the one thing that is supposed to be secured in the Oedipal relay: the Name of the Father, or the patronymic. In *Wide Sargasso Sea*, the character corresponding to Rochester has no name. His writing of the final version of the letter to his father is supervised, in fact, by an image of the *loss* of the patronymic: "There was a crude bookshelf made of three shingles strung together over the desk and I looked at the books, Byron's poems, novels by Sir Walter Scott, *Confessions of an Opium Eater* ... and on the last shelf, *Life and Letters of* ... The rest was eaten away" (*WSS*, p. 63).

Wide Sargasso Sea marks with uncanny clarity the limits of its own discourse in Christophine, Antoinette's black nurse. We may perhaps surmise the distance between *Jane Eyre* and *Wide Sargasso Sea* by remarking that Christophine's unfinished story is the tangent to the latter narrative, as St. John Rivers' story is to the former. Christophine is not a native of Jamaica; she is from Martinique. Taxonomically, she belongs to the category of the good servant rather than that of the pure native. But within these borders, Rhys creates a powerfully suggestive figure.

Christophine is the first interpreter and named speaking subject in the text. "The Jamaican ladies had never approved of my mother, 'because she pretty like pretty self' Christophine said," we read in the book's opening paragraph (*WSS*, p. 15). I have taught this book five times, once in France, once to students who had worked on the book with the well-known Caribbean novelist Wilson Harris, and once at a prestigious institute where the majority of the students were faculty from other universities. It is part of the political argument I am making that all these students blithely stepped over this paragraph without asking or knowing what Christophine's patois, so-called incorrect English, might mean.

Christophine is, of course, a commodified person. "'She was your father's wedding present to me'" explains Antoinette's mother, "'one of his presents'" (*WSS*, p. 18). Yet Rhys assigns her some crucial functions in the text. It is Christophine who judges that black ritual practices are culture-specific and cannot be used by whites as cheap remedies for social evils, such as Rochester's lack of love for Antoinette. Most important, it is Christophine alone whom Rhys allows to offer a hard analysis of Rochester's actions, to challenge him in a face-to-face encounter. The entire extended passage is worthy of comment. I quote a brief extract:

> "She is Creole girl, and she have the sun in her. Tell the truth now. She don't come to your house in this place England they tell me about, she don't come to your beautiful house to beg you to marry with her. No, it's you come all the long way to her house – it's you beg her to marry. And she love you and she give you all she have. Now you say you don't love her and you break her up. What you do with her money, eh?" [And then Rochester, the white man, comments silently to himself] Her voice was still quiet but with a hiss in it when she said "money." [*WSS*, p. 130]

Her analysis is powerful enough for the white man to be afraid: "I no longer felt dazed, tired, half hypnotized, but alert and wary, ready to defend myself" (*WSS*, p. 130).

Rhys does not, however, romanticize individual heroics on the part of the oppressed. When the Man refers to the forces of Law and Order, Christophine recognizes their power. This exposure of civil inequality is emphasized by the fact that, just before the Man's successful threat, Christophine had invoked the emancipation of slaves in Jamaica by proclaiming: "No chain gang, no tread machine, no dark jail either. This is free country and I am free woman" (*WSS*, p. 131).

As I mentioned above, Christophine is tangential to this narrative. She cannot be contained by a novel which rewrites a canonical English text within the European novel-istic tradition in the interest of the white Creole rather than the native. No perspective *critical* of imperialism can turn the Other into a self, because the project of imperialism has always already historically refracted what might have been the absolutely Other into a domesticated Other that consolidates the imperialist self.[21] The Caliban of Retamar, caught between Europe and Latin America, reflects this predicament. We can read Rhys' reinscription of Narcissus as a thematization of the same problematic.

Of course, we cannot know Jean Rhys' feelings in the matter. We can, however, look at the scene of Christophine's inscription in the text. Immediately after the exchange between her and the Man, well before the conclusion, she is simply driven out of the story, with neither narrative nor characterological explanation or justice. "'Read and write I don't know. Other things I know.' She walked away without looking back" (*WSS*, p. 133).

Indeed, if Rhys rewrites the madwoman's attack on the Man by underlining of the misuse of "legality," she cannot deal with the passage that corresponds to St. John Rivers' own justification of his martyrdom, for it has been displaced into the current idiom of modernization and development. Attempts to construct the "Third World Woman" as a signifier remind us that the hegemonic definition of literature is itself caught within the history of imperialism. A full literary reinscription cannot easily flour-ish in the imperialist fracture or discontinuity, covered over by an alien legal system masquerading as Law as such, an alien ideology established as only Truth, and a set of human sciences busy establishing the "native" as self-consolidating Other.

In the Indian case at least, it would be difficult to find an ideological clue to the planned epistemic violence of imperialism merely by rearranging curricula or syllabi within existing norms of literary pedagogy. For a later period of imperialism – when the constituted colonial subject has firmly taken hold – straightforward experiments of comparison can be undertaken, say, between the functionally witless India of *Mrs. Dalloway*, on the one hand, and literary texts produced in India in the 1920s, on the other. But the first half of the nineteenth century resists questioning through literature or literary criticism in the narrow sense, because both are implicated in the project of producing Ariel. To reopen the fracture without succumbing to a nostalgia for lost origins, the literary critic must turn to the archives of imperial governance.

In conclusion, I shall look briefly at Mary Shelley's *Frankenstein*, a text of nascent feminism that remains cryptic, I think, simply because it does not speak the language of feminist individualism which we have come to hail as the language of high feminism within English literature. It is interesting that Barbara Johnson's brief study tries to rescue this recalcitrant text for the service of feminist autobiography.[22] Alternatively, George Levine reads *Frankenstein* in the context of the creative imagination and the nature of the hero. He sees the novel as a book about its own writing and about writing itself, a Romantic allegory of reading within which Jane Eyre as unself-conscious critic would fit quite nicely.[23]

I propose to take *Frankenstein* out of this arena and focus on it in terms of that sense of English cultural identity which I invoked at the opening of this essay. Within that focus we are obliged to admit that, although *Frankenstein* is ostensibly about the origin and evolution of man in society, it does not deploy the axiomatics of imperialism.

Let me say at once that there is plenty of incidental imperialist sentiment in *Frankenstein*. My point, within the argument of this essay, is that the discursive field of imperialism does not produce unquestioned ideological correlatives for the narrative structuring of the book. The discourse of imperialism surfaces in a curiously powerful way in Shelley's novel, and I will later discuss the moment at which it emerges.

Frankenstein is not a battleground of male and female individualism articulated in terms of sexual reproduction (family and female) and social subject-production (race and male). That binary opposition is undone in Victor Frankenstein's laboratory – an artificial womb where both projects are undertaken simultaneously, though the terms are never openly spelled out. Frankenstein's apparent antagonist is God himself as Maker of Man, but his real competitor is also woman as the maker of children. It is not just that his dream of the death of mother and bride and the actual death of his bride are associated with the visit of his monstrous homoerotic "son" to his bed. On a much more overt level, the monster is a bodied "corpse," unnatural because bereft of a determinable childhood: "No father had watched my infant days, no mother had blessed me with smiles and caresses; or if they had, all my past was now a blot, a blind vacancy in which I distinguished nothing" (*F*, pp. 57, 115). It is Frankenstein's own ambiguous and miscued understanding of the real motive for the monster's vengefulness that reveals his own competition with woman as maker:

> I created a rational creature and was bound towards him to assure, as far as was in my power, his happiness and well-being. This was my duty, but there was another still paramount to that. My duties towards the beings of my own species had greater claims to my attention because they included a greater proportion of happiness or misery. Urged by this view, I refused, and I did right in refusing, to create a companion for the first creature. [*F*, p. 206]

It is impossible not to notice the accents of transgression inflecting Frankenstein's demolition of his experiment to create the future Eve. Even in the laboratory, the woman-in-the-making is not a bodied corpse but "a human being." The (il)logic of the metaphor bestows on her a prior existence which Frankenstein aborts, rather than an anterior death which he reembodies: "The remains of the half-finished creature, whom

I had destroyed, lay scattered on the floor, and I almost felt as if I had mangled the living flesh of a human being" (*F*, p. 163).

In Shelley's view, man's hubris as soul maker both usurps the place of God and attempts – vainly – to sublate woman's physiological prerogative.[24] Indeed, indulging a Freudian fantasy here, I could urge that, if to give and withhold to/from the mother a phallus is *the* male fetish, then to give and withhold to/from the man a womb might be the female fetish.[25] The icon of the sublimated womb in man is surely his productive brain, the box in the head.

In the judgment of classical psychoanalysis, the phallic mother exists only by virtue of the castration-anxious son; in *Frankenstein*'s judgment, the hysteric father (Victor Frankenstein gifted with his laboratory – the womb of theoretical reason) cannot produce a daughter. Here the language of racism – the dark side of imperialism understood as social mission – combines with the hysteria of masculism into the idiom of (the withdrawal of) sexual reproduction rather than subject-constitution. The roles of masculine and feminine individualists are hence reversed and displaced. Frankenstein cannot produce a "daughter" because "she might become ten thousand times more malignant than her mate ... [and because] one of the first results of those sympathies for which the demon thirsted would be children, and a race of devils would be propagated upon the earth who might make the very existence of the species of man a condition precarious and full of terror" (*F*, p. 158). This particular narrative strand also launches a thoroughgoing critique of the eighteenth-century European discourses on the origin of society through (Western Christian) man. Should I mention that, much like Jean-Jacques Rousseau's remark in his *Confessions*, Frankenstein declares himself to be "by birth a Genevese" (*F*, p. 31)?

In this overly didactic text, Shelley's point is that social engineering should not be based on pure, theoretical, or natural-scientific reason alone, which is her implicit critique of the utilitarian vision of an engineered society. To this end, she presents in the first part of her deliberately schematic story three characters, childhood friends, who seem to represent Kant's three-part conception of the human subject: Victor Frankenstein, the forces of theoretical reason or "natural philosophy"; Henry Clerval, the forces of practical reason or "the moral relations of things"; and Elizabeth Lavenza, that aesthetic judgment – "the aerial creation of the poets" – which, according to Kant, is "a suitable mediating link connecting the realm of the concept of nature and that of the concept of freedom ... (which) promotes ... *moral* feeling" (*F*, pp. 37, 36).[26]

This three-part subject does not operate harmoniously in *Frankenstein*. That Henry Clerval, associated as he is with practical reason, should have as his "design ... to visit India, in the belief that he had in his knowledge of its various languages, and in the views he had taken of its society, the means of materially assisting the progress of European colonization and trade" is proof of this, as well as part of the incidental imperialist sentiment that I speak of above (*F*, pp. 151–2). I should perhaps point out that the language here is entrepreneurial rather than missionary:

> He came to the university with the design of making himself complete master of the Oriental languages, as thus he should open a field for the plan of life he had marked out for himself. Resolved to pursue no inglorious career, he turned his eyes towards the East as affording scope for his spirit of enterprise. The Persian, Arabic, and Sanskrit languages engaged his attention. [*F*, pp. 66–7]

But it is of course Victor Frankenstein, with his strange itinerary of obsession with natural philosophy, who offers the strongest demonstration that the multiple perspectives of the three-part Kantian subject cannot co-operate harmoniously. Frankenstein creates a putative human subject out of natural philosophy alone. According to his own miscued summation: "In a fit of enthusiastic madness I created a rational creature" (*F*, p. 206). It is not at all farfetched to say that Kant's categorical imperative can most easily be mistaken for the hypothetical imperative – a command to ground in cognitive comprehension what can be apprehended only by moral will – by putting natural philosophy in the place of practical reason.

I should hasten to add here that just as readings such as this one do not necessarily accuse Charlotte Brontë the named individual of harboring imperialist sentiments, so also they do not necessarily commend Mary Shelley the named individual for writing a successful Kantian allegory. The most I can say is that it is possible to read these texts, within the frame of imperialism and the Kantian ethical moment, in a politically useful way. Such an approach presupposes that a "disinterested" reading attempts to render transparent the interests of the hegemonic readership. (Other "political" readings – for instance, that the monster is the nascent working class – can also be advanced.)

Frankenstein is built in the established epistolary tradition of multiple frames. At the heart of the multiple frames, the narrative of the monster (as reported by Frankenstein to Robert Walton, who then recounts it in a letter to his sister) is of his almost learning, clandestinely, to be human. It is invariably noticed that the monster reads *Paradise Lost* as true history. What is not so often noticed is that he also reads Plutarch's *Lives*, "the histories of the first founders of the ancient republics," which he compares to "the patriarchal lives of my protectors" (*F*, pp. 123, 124). And his *education* comes through "Volney's *Ruins of Empires*," which purported to be a prefiguration of the French Revolution, published after the event and after the author had rounded off his theory with practice (*F*, p. 113). It is an attempt at an enlightened universal secular, rather than a Eurocentric Christian, history, written from the perspective of a narrator "from below," somewhat like the attempts of Eric Wolf or Peter Worsley in our own time.[27]

This Caliban's education in (universal secular) humanity takes place through the monster's eavesdropping on the instruction of an Ariel – Safie, the Christianized "Arabian" to whom "a residence in Turkey was abhorrent" (*F*, p. 121). In depicting Safie, Shelley uses some commonplaces of eighteenth-century liberalism that are shared by many today: Safie's Muslim father was a victim of (bad) Christian religious prejudice and yet was himself a wily and ungrateful man not as morally refined as her (good) Christian mother. Having tasted the emancipation of woman, Safie could not go home. The confusion between "Turk" and "Arab" has its counterpart in present-day confusion about Turkey and Iran as "Middle Eastern" but not "Arab."

Although we are a far cry here from the unexamined and covert axiomatics of imperialism in *Jane Eyre*, we will gain nothing by celebrating the time-bound pieties that Shelley, as the daughter of two antievangelicals, produces. It is more interesting for us that Shelley differentiates the Other, works at the Caliban/Ariel distinction, and *cannot* make the monster identical with the proper recipient of these lessons. Although he had "heard of the discovery of the American hemisphere and *wept with Safie* over the helpless fate of its original inhabitants," Safie cannot reciprocate his attachment. When she first catches sight of him, "Safie, unable to attend to her friend [Agatha], rushed out of the cottage" (*F*, pp. 114 [my emphasis], 129).

In the taxonomy of characters, the Muslim-Christian Safie belongs with Rhys' Antoinette/Bertha. And indeed, like Christophine the good servant, the subject created by the fiat of natural philosophy is the tangential unresolved moment in *Frankenstein*.

The simple suggestion that the monster is human inside but monstrous outside and only provoked into vengefulness is clearly not enough to bear the burden of so great a historical dilemma.

At one moment, in fact, Shelley's Frankenstein does try to tame the monster, to humanize him by bringing him within the circuit of the Law. He "repair[s] to a criminal judge in the town and … relate[s his] history briefly but with firmness" – the first and disinterested version of the narrative of Frankenstein – "marking the dates with accuracy and never deviating into invective or exclamation…. When I had concluded my narration I said, 'This is the being whom I accuse and for whose seizure and punishment I call upon you to exert your whole power. It is your duty as a magistrate'" (*F*, pp. 189, 190). The sheer social reasonableness of the mundane voice of Shelley's "Genevan magistrate" reminds us that the absolutely Other cannot be selfed, that the monster has "properties" which will not be contained by "proper" measures:

> "I will exert myself [he says], and if it is in my power to seize the monster, be assured that he shall suffer punishment proportionate to his crimes. But I fear, from what you have yourself described to be his properties, that this will prove impracticable; and thus, while every proper measure is pursued, you should make up your mind to disappointment." [*F*, p. 190]

In the end, as is obvious to most readers, distinctions of human individuality themselves seem to fall away from the novel. Monster, Frankenstein, and Walton seem to become each other's relays. Frankenstein's story comes to an end in death; Walton concludes his own story within the frame of his function as letter writer. In the *narrative* conclusion, he is the natural philosopher who learns from Frankenstein's example. At the end of the *text*, the monster, having confessed his guilt toward his maker and ostensibly intending to immolate himself, is borne away on an ice raft. We do not see the conflagration of his funeral pile – the self-immolation is not consummated in the text: he too cannot be contained by the text. In terms of narrative logic, he is "lost in darkness and distance" (*F*, p. 211) – these are the last words of the novel – into an existential temporality that is coherent with neither the territorializing individual imagination (as in the opening of *Jane Eyre*) nor the authoritative scenario of Christian psychobiography (as at the end of Brontë's work). The very relationship between sexual reproduction and social subject-production – the dynamic nineteenth-century topos of feminism-in-imperialism – remains problematic within the limits of Shelley's text and, paradoxically, constitutes its strength.

Earlier, I offered a reading of woman as womb holder in *Frankenstein*. I would now suggest that there is a framing woman in the book who is neither tangential, nor encircled, nor yet encircling. "Mrs. Saville," "excellent Margaret," "beloved Sister" are her address and kinship inscriptions (*F*, pp. 15, 17, 22). She is the occasion, though not the protagonist, of the novel. She is the feminine *subject* rather than the female individualist: she is the irreducible *recipient*-function of the letters that constitute *Frankenstein*. I have commented on the singular appropriative hermeneutics of the reader reading with Jane in the opening pages of *Jane Eyre*. Here the reader must read with Margaret Saville in the crucial sense that she must *intercept* the recipient-function, read the letters *as* recipient, in order for the novel to exist.[28] Margaret Saville does not respond to close the text as frame. The frame is thus simultaneously not a frame, and the monster can step "beyond the text" and be "lost in darkness." Within the allegory of our reading, the place of both the English lady and the unnamable monster are left open by this great flawed text. It is satisfying for a postcolonial reader to consider this a noble resolution for a nineteenth-century English novel. This is all the more striking because, on the anecdotal level, Shelley herself abundantly "identifies" with Victor Frankenstein.[29]

I must myself close with an idea that I cannot establish within the limits of this essay. Earlier I contended that *Wide Sargasso Sea* is necessarily bound by the reach of the European novel. I suggested that, in contradistinction, to reopen the epistemic fracture of imperialism without succumbing to a nostalgia for lost origins, the critic must turn to the archives of imperialist governance. I have not turned to those archives in these pages. In my current work, by way of a modest and inexpert "reading" of "archives," I try to extend, outside of the reach of the European novelistic tradition, the most powerful suggestion in *Wide Sargasso Sea:* that *Jane Eyre* can be read as the orchestration and staging of the self-immolation of Bertha Mason as "good wife." The power of that sugges-tion remains unclear if we remain insufficiently knowledgeable about the history of the legal manipulation of widow-sacrifice in the entitlement of the British government in India. I would hope that an informed critique of imperialism, granted some attention from readers in the First World, will at least expand the frontiers of the politics of reading.

Notes

1   My notion of the "worlding of a world" upon what must be assumed to be uninscribed earth is a vulgarization of Martin Heidegger's idea; see "The Origin of the Work of Art," *Poetry, Language, Thought*, trans. Albert Hofstadter (New York, 1977), pp. 17–87.

2   See Charlotte Brontë, *Jane Eyre* (New York, 1960); all further references to this work, abbreviated *JE*, will be included in the text.

3   See Jean Rhys, *Wide Sargasso Sea* (Harmondsworth, 1966); all further references to this work, abbreviated *WSS*, will be included in the text. And see Mary Shelley, *Frankenstein; or, The Modern Prometheus* (New York, 1965); all further references to this work, abbreviated *F*, will be included in the text.

4   I have tried to do this in my essay "Unmaking and Making in *To the Lighthouse*," in *Women and Language in Literature and Society*, ed. Sally McConnell-Ginet, Ruth Borker, and Nelly Furman (New York, 1980), pp. 310–27.

5   As always, I take my formula from Louis Althusser, "Ideology an Ideological State Apparatuses (Notes towards an Investigation)," *"Lenin and Philosophy" and Other Essays*, trans. Ben Brewster (New York, 1971), pp. 127–86. For an acute differentiation between the individual and individual-ism, see V. N. Vološinov, *Marxism and the Philosophy of Language*, trans. Ladislav Matejka and I. R. Titunik, Studies in Language, vol. 1 (New York, 1973), pp. 93–4 and 152–3. For a "straight" analysis of the roots and ramifications of English "individualism," see C. B. MacPherson, *The Political Theory of Possessive Individualism: Hobbes to Locke* (Oxford, 1962). I am grateful to Jonathan Rée for bringing this book to my attention and for giving a careful reading of all but the very end of the present essay.

6   I am constructing an analogy with Homi Bhabha's powerful notion of "not-quite/not-white" in his "Of Mimicry and Man: The Ambiguity of Colonial Discourse," *October* 28 (Spring 1984): 132. I should also add that I use the word "native" here in reaction to the term "Third World Woman." It cannot, of course, apply with equal historical justice to both the West Indian and the Indian contexts nor to contexts of imperialism by transportation.

7   See Roberto Fernández Retamar, "Caliban: Notes towards a Discussion of Culture in Our America," trans. Lynn Garafola, David Arthur McMurray, and Robert Márquez, *Massachusetts Review* 15 (Winter–Spring 1974): 7–72; all further references to this work, abbreviated "C," will be included in the text.

8   See José Enrique Rodó, *Ariel*, ed. Gordon Brotherston (Cambridge, 1967).

9   For an elaboration of "an inaccessible blankness circumscribed by an interpretable text," see my "Can the Subaltern Speak?" *Marxism and the Interpretation of Culture*, ed. Cary Nelson (Urbana, Ill., 1988).

10 See Elizabeth Fox-Genovese, "Placing Women's History in History," *New Left Review* 133 (May–June 1982): 5–29.

11 Rudolph Ackerman, *The Repository of Arts, Literature, Commerce, Manufactures, Fashions, and Politics* (London, 1823), p. 310.

12 See Terry Eagleton, *Myths of Power: A Marxist Study of the Brontës* (London, 1975); this is one of the general presuppositions of his book.

13 See Sandra M. Gilbert and Susan Gubar, *The Madwoman in the Attic: The Woman Writer and the Nineteenth-Century Literary Imagination* (New Haven, Conn., 1979), pp. 360–2.

14 Immanuel Kant, *Critique of Practical Reason, the "Critique of Pure Reason," the "Critique of Practical Reason" and Other Ethical Treatises, the "Critique of Judgement,"* trans. J. M. D. Meiklejohn et al. (Chicago, 1952), pp. 328, 326.

15 I have tried to justify the reduction of sociohistorical problems to formulas or propositions in my essay "Can the Subaltern Speak?" The "travesty" I speak of does not befall the Kantian ethic in its purity as an accident but rather exists within its lineaments as a possible supplement. On the register of the human being as child rather than heathen, my formula can be found, for example, in "What Is Enlightenment?" in Kant, *"Foundations of the Metaphysics of Morals," "What Is Enlightenment?" and a Passage from "The Metaphysics of Morals,"* trans. and ed. Lewis White Beck (Chicago, 1950). I have profited from discussing Kant with Jonathan Rée.

16 Jean Rhys, in an interview with Elizabeth Vreeland, quoted in Nancy R. Harrison, *Jean Rhys and the Novel as Women's Text* (Chapel Hill, NC, 1988). This is an excellent, detailed study of Rhys.

17 See Louise Vinge, *The Narcissus Theme in Western European Literature Up to the Early Nineteenth Century*, trans. Robert Dewsnap et al. (Lund, 1967), ch. 5.

18 For a detailed study of this text, see John Brenkman, "Narcissus in the Text," *Georgia Review* 30 (Summer 1976): 293–327.

19 See, e.g., Thomas F. Staley, *Jean Rhys: A Critical Study* (Austin, Tex. 1979), pp. 108–16; it is interesting to note Staley's masculist discomfort with this and his consequent dissatisfaction with Rhys' novel.

20 I have tried to relate castration and suppressed letters in my "The Letter As Cutting Edge," in *Literature and Psychoanalysis; The Question of Reading: Otherwise*, ed. Shoshana Felman (New Haven, Conn., 1981), pp. 208–26.

21 This is the main argument of my "Can the Subaltern Speak?"

22 See Barbara Johnson, "My Monster/My Self," *Diacritics* 12 (Summer 1982): 2–10.

23 See George Levine, *The Realistic Imagination: English Fiction from Frankenstein to Lady Chatterley* (Chicago, 1981), pp. 23–35.

24 Consult the publications of the Feminist International Network for the best overview of the current debate on reproductive technology.

25 For the male fetish, see Sigmund Freud, "Fetishism," *The Standard Edition of the Complete Psychological Works of Sigmund Freud*, ed. and trans. James Strachey et al., 24 vols. (London, 1953–74), 21:152–7. For a more "serious" Freudian study of *Frankenstein*, see Mary Jacobus, "Is There a Woman in This Text?" *New Literary History* 14 (Autumn 1982): 117–41. My "fantasy" would of course be disproved by the "fact" that it is more difficult for a woman to assume the position of fetishist than for a man; see Mary Ann Doane, "Film and the Masquerade: Theorising the Female Spectator," *Screen* 23 (Sept.–Oct. 1982): 74–87.

26 Kant, *Critique of Judgement*, trans. J. H. Bernard (New York, 1951), p. 39.

27 See [Constantin François Chasseboeuf de Volney], *The Ruins; or, Meditations on the Revolutions of Empires*, trans. pub. (London, 1811). Johannes Fabian has shown us the manipulation of time in "new" secular histories of a similar kind; see *Time and the Other: How Anthropology Makes Its Object* (New York, 1983). See also Eric R. Wolf, *Europe and the People without History* (Berkeley and Los Angeles, 1982), and Peter Worsley, *The Third World*, 2nd edn. (Chicago, 1973); I am grateful to Dennis Dworkin for bringing the latter book to my attention. The most striking ignoring of the monster's education through Volney is in Gilbert's otherwise brilliant "Horror's Twin: Mary Shelley's

Monstrous Eve," *Feminist Studies* 4 (June 1980): 48–73. Gilbert's essay reflects the absence of race-determinations in a certain sort of feminism. Her present work has most convincingly filled in this gap; see, e.g., her recent piece on H. Rider Haggard's *She* ("Rider Haggard's Heart of Darkness," *Partisan Review* 50, no. 3 [1983]: 444–53).

28 "A letter is always and *a priori* intercepted,... the 'subjects' are neither the senders nor the receivers of messages.... The letter is constituted ... by its interception" (Jacques Derrida, "Discussion," after Claude Rabant, "Il n'a aucune chance de l'entendre," in *Affranchissement: Du transfert et de la lettre*, ed. René Major [Paris, 1981], p. 106; my translation). Margaret Saville is not made to appropriate the reader's "subject" into the signature of her own "individuality."

29 The most striking "internal evidence" is the admission in the "Author's Introduction" that, after dreaming of the yet-unnamed Victor Frankenstein figure and being terrified (through, yet not quite through, him) by the monster in a scene she later reproduced in Frankenstein's story, Shelley began her tale "on the morrow ... with the words 'It was on a dreary night of November'" (*F*, p. xi). Those are the opening words of chapter 5 of the finished book, where Frankenstein begins to recount the actual making of his monster (see *F*, p. 56).

CHAPTER 5

Playing in the Dark

Toni Morrison

Novelist Toni Morrison brought her intelligence to bear on questions of literary criticism in *Playing in the Dark* (1992), a series of lectures in which she took up the question of the place of African Americans in American literature. Drawing in this selection on the work of sociologist Orlando Patterson, who argues that the American concept of liberty depended for its definition on the existence of African slavery in America, she discusses the way the literature of the European-descended White population takes an "Africanist" presence for granted.

> *I am moved by fancies that are curled*
> *Around these images, and cling:*
> *The notion of some infinitely gentle*
> *Infinitely suffering thing.*
>
> T. S. Eliot,
> *"Preludes, IV"*

These chapters put forth an argument for extending the study of American literature into what I hope will be a wider landscape. I want to draw a map, so to speak, of a critical geography and use that map to open as much space for discovery, intellectual adventure, and close exploration as did the original charting of the New World – without the mandate for conquest. I intend to outline an attractive, fruitful, and provocative critical project, unencumbered by dreams of subversion or rallying gestures at fortress walls.

I would like it to be clear at the outset that I do not bring to these matters solely or even principally the tools of a literary critic. As a reader (before becoming a writer) I read as I had been taught to do. But books revealed themselves rather differently to me as a writer. In that capacity I have to place enormous trust in my ability to imagine others and my willingness to project consciously into the danger zones such others may represent for me. I am drawn to the ways all writers do this: the way Homer renders a heart-eating cyclops so that our hearts are wrenched with pity; the way Dostoevsky compels intimacy

Original publication details: Toni Morrison, "Playing in the Dark" from *Playing in the Dark*. Harvard University Press, 1992. Reproduced with permission from International Creative Management.

with Svidrigailov and Prince Myshkin. I am in awe of the authority of Faulkner's Benjy, James's Maisie, Flaubert's Emma, Melville's Pip, Mary Shelley's Frankenstein – each of us can extend the list.

I am interested in what prompts and makes possible this process of entering what one is estranged from – and in what disables the foray, for purposes of fiction, into corners of the consciousness held off and away from the reach of the writer's imagination. My work requires me to think about how free I can be as an African-American woman writer in my genderized, sexualized, wholly racialized world. To think about (and wrestle with) the full implications of my situation leads me to consider what happens when other writers work in a highly and historically racialized society. For them, as for me, imagining is not merely looking or looking at; nor is it taking oneself intact into the other. It is, for the purposes of the work, *becoming*.

My project rises from delight, not disappointment. It rises from what I know about the ways writers transform aspects of their social grounding into aspects of language, and the ways they tell other stories, fight secret wars, limn out all sorts of debates blanketed in their text. And rises from my certainty that writers always know, at some level, that they do this.

For some time now I have been thinking about the validity or vulnerability of a certain set of assumptions conventionally accepted among literary historians and critics and circulated as "knowledge." This knowledge holds that traditional, canonical American literature is free of, uninformed, and unshaped by the four-hundred-year-old presence of, first, Africans and then African-Americans in the United States. It assumes that this presence – which shaped the body politic, the Constitution, and the entire history of the culture – has had no significant place or consequence in the origin and development of that culture's literature. Moreover, such knowledge assumes that the characteristics of our national literature emanate from a particular "Americanness" that is separate from and unaccountable to this presence. There seems to be a more or less tacit agreement among literary scholars that, because American literature has been clearly the preserve of white male views, genius, and power, those views, genius, and power are without relationship to and removed from the overwhelming presence of black people in the United States. This agreement is made about a population that preceded every American writer of renown and was, I have come to believe, one of the most furtively radical impinging forces on the country's literature. The contemplation of this black presence is central to any understanding of our national literature and should not be permitted to hover at the margins of the literary imagination.

These speculations have led me to wonder whether the major and championed characteristics of our national literature – individualism, masculinity, social engagement versus historical isolation; acute and ambiguous moral problematics; the thematics of innocence coupled with an obsession with figurations of death and hell – are not in fact responses to a dark, abiding, signing Africanist presence. It has occurred to me that the very manner by which American literature distinguishes itself as a coherent entity exists because of this unsettled and unsettling population. Just as the formation of the nation necessitated coded language and purposeful restriction to deal with the racial disingenuousness and moral frailty at its heart, so too did the literature, whose founding characteristics extend into the twentieth century, reproduce the necessity for codes and restriction. Through significant and underscored omissions, startling contradictions, heavily nuanced conflicts, through the way writers peopled their work with the signs and bodies of this presence – one can see that a real or fabricated Africanist presence was crucial to their sense of Americanness. And it shows.

My curiosity about the origins and literary uses of this carefully observed, and carefully invented, Africanist presence has become an informal study of what I call American Africanism. It is an investigation into the ways in which a nonwhite, Africanlike (or Africanist) presence or persona was constructed in the United States, and the imaginative uses this fabricated presence served. I am using the term "Africanism" not to suggest the larger body of knowledge on Africa that the philosopher Valentine Mudimbe means by the term "Africanism," nor to suggest the varieties and complexities of African people and their descendants who have inhabited this country. Rather I use it as a term for the denotative and connotative blackness that African peoples have come to signify, as well as the entire range of views, assumptions, readings, and misreadings that accompany Eurocentric learning about these people. As a trope, little restraint has been attached to its uses. As a disabling virus within literary discourse, Africanism has become, in the Eurocentric tradition that American education favors, both a way of talking about and a way of policing matters of class, sexual license, and repression, formations and exercises of power, and meditations on ethics and accountability. Through the simple expedient of demonizing and reifying the range of color on a palette, American Africanism makes it possible to say and not say, to inscribe and erase, to escape and engage, to act out and act on, to historicize and render timeless. It provides a way of contemplating chaos and civilization, desire and fear, and a mechanism for testing the problems and blessings of freedom. The United States, of course, is not unique in the construction of Africanism. South America, England, France, Germany, Spain – the cultures of all these countries have participated in and contributed to some aspect of an "invented Africa." None has been able to persuade itself for long that criteria and knowledge could emerge outside the categories of domination. Among Europeans and the Europeanized, this shared process of exclusion – of assigning designation and value – has led to the popular and academic notion that racism is a "natural," if irritating, phenomenon. The literature of almost all these countries, however, is now subject to sustained critiques of its racialized discourse. The United States is a curious exception, even though it stands out as being the oldest democracy in which a black population accompanied (if one can use that word) and in many cases preceded the white settlers. Here in that nexus, with its particular formulations, and in the absence of real knowledge or open-minded inquiry about Africans and African-Americans, under the pressures of ideological and imperialistic rationales for subjugation, an American brand of Africanism emerged: strongly urged, thoroughly serviceable, companionably ego-reinforcing, and pervasive. For excellent reasons of state – because European sources of cultural hegemony were dispersed but not yet valorized in the new country – the process of organizing American coherence through a distancing Africanism became the operative mode of a new cultural hegemony.

These remarks should not be interpreted as simply an effort to move the gaze of African-American studies to a different site. I do not want to alter one hierarchy in order to institute another. It is true that I do not want to encourage those totalizing approaches to African-American scholarship which have no drive other than the exchange of dominations – dominant Eurocentric scholarship replaced by dominant Afrocentric scholarship. More interesting is what makes intellectual domination possible; how knowledge is transformed from invasion and conquest to revelation and choice; what ignites and informs the literary imagination, and what forces help establish the parameters of criticism.

Above all I am interested in how agendas in criticism have disguised themselves and, in so doing, impoverished the literature it studies. Criticism as a form of knowledge is capable of robbing literature not only of its own implicit and explicit ideology but of its ideas as well; it can dismiss the difficult, arduous work writers do to make an art that becomes and remains part of and significant within a human landscape. It is important to see how inextricable Africanism is or ought to be from the deliberations of literary criticism and the wanton, elaborate strategies undertaken to erase its presence from view.

What Africanism became for, and how it functioned in, the literary imagination is of paramount interest because it may be possible to discover, through a close look at literary "blackness," the nature – even the cause – of literary "whiteness." What is it *for*? What parts do the invention and development of whiteness play in the construction of what is loosely described as "American"? If such an inquiry ever comes to maturity, it may provide access to a deeper reading of American literature – a reading not completely available now, not least, I suspect, because of the studied indifference of most literary criticism to these matters.

One likely reason for the paucity of critical material on this large and compelling subject is that, in matters of race, silence and evasion have historically ruled literary discourse. Evasion has fostered another, substitute language in which the issues are encoded, foreclosing open debate. The situation is aggravated by the tremor that breaks into discourse on race. It is further complicated by the fact that the habit of ignoring race is understood to be a graceful, even generous, liberal gesture. To notice is to recognize an already discredited difference. To enforce its invisibility through silence is to allow the black body a shadowless participation in the dominant cultural body. According to this logic, every well-bred instinct argues *against noticing* and forecloses adult discourse. It is just this concept of literary and scholarly moeurs (which functions smoothly in literary criticism, but neither makes nor receives credible claims in other disciplines) that has terminated the shelf life of some once extremely well-regarded American authors and blocked access to remarkable insights in their works.

These moeurs are delicate things, however, which must be given some thought before they are abandoned. Not observing such niceties can lead to startling displays of scholarly lapses in objectivity. In 1936 an American scholar investigating the use of Negro so-called dialect in the works of Edgar Allan Poe (a short article clearly proud of its racial equanimity) opens this way: "Despite the fact that he grew up largely in the south and spent some of his most fruitful years in Richmond and Baltimore, Poe has little to say about the darky."[1]

Although I know this sentence represents the polite parlance of the day, that "darky" was understood to be a term more acceptable than "nigger," the grimace I made upon reading it was followed by an alarmed distrust of the scholar's abilities. If it seems unfair to reach back to the thirties for samples of the kind of lapse that can occur when certain manners of polite repression are waived, let me assure you equally egregious representations of the phenomenon are still common.

Another reason for this quite ornamental vacuum in literary discourse on the presence and influence of Africanist peoples in American criticism is the pattern of thinking about racialism in terms of its consequences on the victim – of always defining it assymetrically from the perspective of its impact on the object of racist policy and attitudes. A good deal of time and intelligence has been invested in the exposure of racism and the horrific results on its objects. There are constant, if erratic, liberalizing efforts to legislate these matters. There are also powerful and persuasive attempts to analyze the origin and fabrication of racism itself, contesting the assumption that it is an inevitable, permanent, and eternal part of all social landscapes. I do not wish to disparage these inquiries. It is precisely because of them that any progress at all has been accomplished in matters of racial discourse. But that well-established study should be joined with another, equally important one: the impact of racism on those who perpetuate it. It seems both poignant and striking how avoided and unanalyzed is the effect of racist inflection on the subject. What I propose here is to examine the impact of notions of racial hierarchy, racial exclusion, and racial vulnerability and availability on nonblacks who held, resisted, explored, or altered those notions. The scholarship that looks into the mind, imagination, and behavior of slaves is valuable. But equally valuable is a serious intellectual effort to see what racial ideology does to the mind, imagination, and behavior of masters.

Historians have approached these areas, as have social scientists, anthropologists, psychiatrists, and some students of comparative literature. Literary scholars have begun to pose these questions of various national literatures. Urgently needed is the same kind of attention paid to the literature of the western country that has one of the most resilient Africanist populations in the world – a population that has always had a curiously intimate and unhingingly separate existence within the dominant one. When matters of race are located and called attention to in American literature, critical response has tended to be on the order of a humanistic nostrum – or a dismissal mandated by the label "political." Excising the political from the life of the mind is a sacrifice that has proven costly. I think of this erasure as a kind of trembling hypochondria always curing itself with unnecessary surgery. A criticism that needs to insist that literature is not only "universal" but also "race-free" risks lobotomizing that literature, and diminishes both the art and the artist.

I am vulnerable to the inference here that my inquiry has vested interests; that because I am an African-American and a writer I stand to benefit in ways not limited to intellectual fulfillment from this line of questioning. I will have to risk the accusation because the point is too important: for both black and white American writers, in a wholly racialized society, there is no escape from racially inflected language, and the work writers do to unhobble the imagination from the demands of that language is complicated, interesting, and definitive.

Like thousands of avid but nonacademic readers, some powerful literary critics in the United States have never read, and are proud to say so, *any* African-American text. It seems to have done them no harm, presented them with no discernible limitations in the scope of their work or influence. I suspect, with much evidence to support the suspicion, that they will continue to flourish without any knowledge whatsoever of African-American literature. What is fascinating, however, is to observe how their lavish exploration of literature manages *not* to see meaning in the thunderous, theatrical presence of black surrogacy – an informing, stabilizing, and disturbing element – in the literature they do study. It is interesting, not surprising, that the arbiters of critical power in American literature seem to take pleasure in, indeed relish, their ignorance of African-American texts. What is surprising is that their refusal to read black texts – a refusal that makes no disturbance in their intellectual life – repeats itself when they reread the traditional, established works of literature worthy of their attention.

It is possible, for example, to read Henry James scholarship exhaustively and never arrive at a nodding mention, much less a satisfactory treatment, of the black woman who lubricates the turn of the plot and becomes the agency of moral choice and meaning in *What Maisie Knew*. Never are we invited to a reading of "The Beast in the Jungle" in which that figuration is followed to what seems to me its logical conclusion. It is hard to think of any aspect of Gertrude Stein's *Three Lives* that has not been covered, except the exploratory and explanatory uses to which she puts the black woman who holds center stage in that work. The urgency and anxiety in Willa Cather's rendering of black characters are liable to be missed entirely; no mention is made of the problem that race causes in the technique and the credibility of her last novel, *Sapphira and the Slave Girl*. These critics see no excitement or meaning in the tropes of darkness, sexuality, and desire in Ernest Hemingway or in his cast of black men. They see no connection between God's grace and Africanist "othering" in Flannery O'Connor. With few exceptions, Faulkner criticism collapses the major themes of that writer into discursive "mythologies" and treats the later works – whose focus is race and class – as minor, superficial, marked by decline.

An instructive parallel to this willed scholarly indifference is the centuries-long, hysterical blindness to feminist discourse and the way in which women and women's issues were read (or unread). Blatant sexist readings are on the decline, and where they still exist they have little effect because of the successful appropriation by women of their own discourse.

National literatures, like writers, get along the best way they can, and with what they can. Yet they do seem to end up describing and inscribing what is really on the national mind. For the most part, the literature of the United States has taken as its concern the architecture of a *new white man*. If I am disenchanted by the indifference of literary criticism toward examining the range of that concern, I do have a lasting resort: the writers themselves.

Writers are among the most sensitive, the most intellectually anarchic, most representative, most probing of artists. The ability of writers to imagine what is not the self, to familiarize the strange and mystify the familiar, is the test of their power. The languages they use and the social and historical context in which these languages signify are indirect and direct revelations of that power and its limitations. So it is to them, the creators of American literature, that I look for clarification about the invention and effect of Africanism in the United States.

My early assumptions as a reader were that black people signified little or nothing in the imagination of white American writers. Other than as objects of an occasional bout of jungle fever, other than to provide local color or to lend some touch of verisimilitude or to supply a needed moral gesture, humor, or bit of pathos, blacks made no appearance at all. This was a reflection, I thought, of the marginal impact that blacks had on the lives of the characters in the work as well as the creative imagination of the author. To imagine or write otherwise, to situate black people throughout the pages and scenes of a book like some government quota, would be ludicrous and dishonest.

But then I stopped reading as a reader and began to read as a writer. Living in a racially articulated and predicated world, I could not be alone in reacting to this aspect of the American cultural and historical condition. I began to see how the literature I revered, the literature I loathed, behaved in its encounter with racial ideology. American literature could not help being shaped by that encounter. Yes, I wanted to identify those moments when American literature was complicit in the fabrication of racism, but equally important, I still wanted to see when literature exploded and undermined it. Still, those were minor concerns. Much more important was to contemplate how Africanist personae, narrative, and idiom moved and enriched the text in self-conscious ways, to consider what the engagement meant for the work of the writer's imagination.

How does literary utterance arrange itself when it tries to imagine an Africanist other? What are the signs, the codes, the literary strategies designed to accommodate this encounter? What does the inclusion of Africans or African-Americans do to and for the "work." As a reader my assumption had always been that nothing "happens": Africans and their descendants were not in any sense that matters, *there*; and when they were there, they were decorative – displays of the agile writer's technical expertise. I assumed that since the author was not black, the appearance of Africanist characters or narrative or idiom in a work could never be *about* anything other than the "normal," unracialized, illusory white world that provided the fictional backdrop. Certainly no American text of the sort I am discussing was ever written *for* black people – no more than *Uncle Tom's Cabin* was written for Uncle Tom to read or be persuaded by. As a writer reading, I came to realize the obvious: the subject of the dream is the dreamer. The fabrication of an Africanist persona is reflexive; an extraordinary meditation on the self; a powerful exploration of the fears and desires that reside in the writerly conscious. It is an astonishing revelation of longing, of terror, of perplexity, of shame, of magnanimity. It requires hard work *not* to see this.

It is as if I had been looking at a fishbowl – the glide and flick of the golden scales, the green tip, the bolt of white careening back from the gills; the castles at the bottom, surrounded by pebbles and tiny, intricate fronds of green; the barely disturbed water, the flecks of waste and food, the tranquil bubbles traveling to the surface – and suddenly I saw the bowl, the structure that transparently (and invisibly) permits the ordered life it contains to exist in the large world. In other words, I began to rely on my knowledge of how books get written, how language arrives; my sense of how and why writers abandon or take on certain aspects of their project. I began to rely on my understanding of what the linguistic struggle requires of writers and what they make of the surprise that is the inevitable concomitant of the act of creation. What became transparent were the self-evident ways that Americans choose to talk about themselves through and within a sometimes allegorical, sometimes metaphorical, but always choked representation of an Africanist presence. I have made much here of a kind of willful critical blindness – a blindness that, if it had not existed, could have made these insights part of our routine literary heritage. Habit, manners, and political agenda have contributed to this refusal of critical insight. A case in point is Willa Cather's *Sapphira and the Slave Girl*, a text that has been virtually jettisoned from the body of American literature by critical consensus. References to this novel in much Cather scholarship are apologetic, dismissive, even cutting in their brief documentation of its flaws – of which there are a sufficient number. What remains less acknowledged is the source of its flaws and the conceptual problems that the book both poses and represents. Simply to assert the failure of Cather's gifts, the exhaustion of her perception, the narrowing of her canvas, evades the obligation to look carefully at what might have caused the book to fail – if "failure" is an intelligent term to apply to any fiction. (It is as if the realms of fiction and reality were divided by a line that, when maintained, offers the possibility of winning but, when crossed, signals the inevitability of losing.)

I suspect that the "problem" of *Sapphira and the Slave Girl* is not that it has a weaker vision or is the work of a weaker mind. The problem is trying to come to terms critically and artistically with the novel's concerns: the power and license of a white slave mistress over her female slaves. How can that *content* be subsumed by some other meaning? How can the story of a white mistress be severed from a consideration of race and the violence entailed in the story's premise? If *Sapphira and the Slave Girl* neither pleases nor engages us, it may be enlightening to discover why. It is as if this last book – this troublesome, quietly dismissed novel, very important to Cather – is not only about a fugitive but is itself a fugitive from its author's literary estate. It is also a book that describes and inscribes its narrative's own fugitive flight from itself. Our first hint of this flight appears in the title, *Sapphira and the Slave Girl*. The girl referred to is named Nancy. To have called the book "Sapphira and Nancy" would have lured Cather into dangerous deep water. Such a title would have clarified and drawn attention immediately to what the novel obscures even as it makes a valiant effort at honest engagement: the sycophancy of white identity. The story, briefly, is this.

Sapphira Colbert, an invalid confined to her chair and dependent on slaves for the most intimate services, has persuaded herself that her husband is having or aching to have a liaison with Nancy, the pubescent daughter of her most devoted female slave. It is clear from the beginning that Mistress Colbert is in error: Nancy is pure to the point of vapidity; Master Colbert is a man of modest habits, ambition, and imagination. Sapphira's suspicions, fed by her feverish imagination and by her leisure to have them, grow and luxuriate unbearably. She forms a plan. She will invite a malleable lecherous nephew, Martin, to visit and let his nature run its course: Nancy will be seduced. The purpose of arranging the rape of her young servant is to reclaim, for purposes not made clear, the full attentions of her husband.

Interference with these plans comes from Sapphira's daughter, Rachel, estranged from her mother primarily for her abolitionist views but also, we are led to believe, because Sapphira does not tolerate opposition. It is Rachel who manages to effect Nancy's escape to the north and freedom, with the timid help of her father, Mr. Colbert. A reconciliation of all of the white characters takes place when the daughter loses one of her children to diphtheria and is blessed with the recuperation of the other. The reconciliation of the two key black characters is rendered in a postscript in which many years later Nancy returns to see her aged mother and recount her post-flight adult narrative to the author, a child witnessing the return and the happiness that is the novel's dénouement. The novel was published in 1940, but has the shape and feel of a tale written or experienced much earlier.

This précis in no way does justice to the novel's complexities and its problems of execution. Both arise, I believe, not because Cather was failing in narrative power, but because of her struggle to address an almost completely buried subject: the interdependent working of power, race, and sexuality in a white woman's battle for coherence.

In some ways this novel is a classic fugitive slave narrative: a thrilling escape to freedom. But we learn almost nothing of the trials of the fugitive's journey because the emphasis is on Nancy's fugitive state within the house *before her escape*. And the real fugitive, the text asserts, is the slave mistress. Furthermore, the plot escapes the author's control and, as its own fugitive status becomes clear, is destined to point to the hopelessness of excising racial considerations from formulations of white identity.

Escape is the central focus of Nancy's existence on the Colbert farm. From the moment of her first appearance, she is forced to hide her emotions, her thoughts, and eventually her body from pursuers. Unable to please Sapphira, plagued by the jealousy of the darker-skinned slaves, she is also barred from help, instruction, or consolation from her own mother, Till. That condition could only prevail in a slave society where the mistress can count on (and an author can believe the reader does not object to) the complicity of a mother in the seduction and rape of her own daughter. Because Till's loyalty to and responsibility for her mistress is so primary, it never occurs and need not occur to Sapphira that Till might be hurt or alarmed by the violence planned for her only child. That assumption is based on another – that slave women are not mothers; they are "natally dead," with no obligations to their offspring or their own parents.

This breach startles the contemporary reader and renders Till an unbelievable and unsympathetic character. It is a problem that Cather herself seems hard put to address.

She both acknowledges and banishes this wholly unanalyzed mother–daughter relationship by inserting a furtive exchange between Till and Rachel in chapter 10:

> … Till asked in a low, cautious murmur: "You ain't heard nothin', Miss Rachel?"
>
> "Not yet. When I do hear, I'll let you know. I saw her into good hands, Till. I don't doubt she's in Canada by this time, amongst English people."
>
> "Thank you, mam, Miss Rachel. I can't say no more. I don't want them niggers to see me cryin'. If she's up there with the English folks, she'll have some chance."[2]

The passage seems to come out of nowhere because there has been nothing in a hundred or so pages to prepare us for such maternal concern. "You ain't heard nothin'?" Till asks of Rachel. Just that – those four words – meaning: Is Nancy all right? Did she arrive safely? Is she alive? Is anybody after her? All of these questions lie in the one she does manage to ask. Surrounding this dialogue is the silence of four hundred years. It leaps out of the novel's void and out of the void of historical discourse on slave parent–child relationships and pain. The contemporary reader is relieved when Till finally finds the language and occasion to make this inquiry about the fate of her daughter. But nothing more is made of it. And the reader is asked to believe that the silence surrounding the inquiry as well as its delay are due to Till's greater concern about her status among dark-skinned "field" niggers. Clearly Cather was driven to create the exchange not to rehabilitate Till in our readerly eyes but because at some point the silence became an unbearable violence, even in a work full of violence and evasion. Consider the pressures exerted by the subject: the need to portray the faithful slave; the compelling attraction of exploring the possibilities of one woman's absolute power over the body of another woman; confrontation with an uncontested assumption of the sexual availability of black females; the need to make credible the bottomless devotion of the person on whom Sapphira was dependent. It is after all *hers*, this slave woman's body, in a way that her own invalid flesh is not. These fictional demands stretch to breaking all narrative coherence. It is no wonder that Nancy cannot think up her own escape and must be urged into taking the risk.

Nancy has to hide her interior life from hostile fellow slaves *and* her own mother. The absence of camaraderie between Nancy and the other slave women turns on the device of color fetish – the skin-color privilege that Nancy enjoys because she is lighter than the others and therefore enviable. The absence of mother love, always a troubling concern of Cather's, is connected to the assumption of a slave's natal isolation. These are bizarre and disturbing deformations of reality that normally lie mute in novels containing Africanist characters, but Cather does not repress them altogether. The character she creates is at once a fugitive within the household and a sign of the sterility of the fiction-making imagination when there is no available language to clarify or even name the source of unbelievability.

Interestingly, the other major cause of Nancy's constant state of flight is wholly credible: that she should be unarmed in the face of the nephew's sexual assault and that she alone is responsible for extracting herself from the crisis. We do not question her vulnerability. What becomes titillating in this wicked pursuit of innocence – what makes it something other than an American variant of *Clarissa* – is the racial component. The nephew is not even required to court or flatter Nancy. After an unsuccessful reach for her from the branches of a cherry tree, he can, and plans to simply arrive wherever she is sleeping. And since Sapphira has ordered her to sleep in the hall on a pallet, Nancy is forced to sneak away in the dark to quarters where she may be, but is not certain to be, safe.

Other than Rachel, the pro-abolitionist, Nancy has access to no one to whom she can complain, explain, object, or from whom she can seek protection. We must accept her total lack of initiative, for there are no exits. She has no recourse – except in miserable looks that arouse Rachel's curiosity.

Nor is there any law, if the nephew succeeds in the rape, to entertain her complaint. If she becomes pregnant as a result of the violence, the issue is a boon to the economy of the estate, not an injury to it. There is no father or, in this case, "stepfather" to voice a protest on Nancy's behalf, since honor was the first thing stripped from the man. He is a "capon," we are told, given to Till so that she will have no more children and can give her full attention and energy to Mistress Sapphira.

Rendered voiceless, a cipher, a perfect victim, Nancy runs the risk of losing the reader's interest. In a curious way, Sapphira's plotting, like Cather's plot, is without reference to the characters and exists solely for the ego-gratification of the slave mistress. This becomes obvious when we consider what would have been the consequences of a successful rape. Given the novel's own terms, there can be no grounds for Sapphira's thinking that Nancy can be "ruined" in the conventional sense. There is no question of marriage to Martin, to Colbert, to anybody. Then, too, why would such an assault move her slave girl outside her husband's interest? The probability is that it would secure it. If Mr Colbert is tempted by Nancy the chaste, is there anything in slavocracy to make him disdain Nancy the unchaste?

Such a breakdown in the logic and machinery of plot construction implies the powerful impact race has on narrative – and on narrative strategy. Nancy is not only the victim of Sapphira's evil, whimsical scheming. She becomes the unconsulted, appropriated ground of Cather's inquiry into what is of paramount importance to the author: the reckless, unabated power of a white woman gathering identity unto herself from the wholly available and serviceable lives of Africanist others. This seems to me to provide the coordinates of an immensely important moral debate.

This novel is not a story of a mean, vindictive mistress; it is the story of a desperate one. It concerns a troubled, disappointed woman confined to the prison of her defeated flesh, whose social pedestal rests on the sturdy spine of racial degradation; whose privileged gender has nothing that elevates it except color, and whose moral posture collapses with-out a whimper before the greater necessity of self-esteem, even though the source of that esteem is a delusion. For Sapphira too is a fugitive in this novel, committed to escape: from the possibility of developing her own adult personality and her own sensibilities, from her femaleness; from motherhood; from the community of women; from her body.

She escapes the necessity of inhabiting her own body by dwelling on the young, healthy, and sexually appetizing Nancy. She has transferred its care into the hands of others. In this way she escapes her illness, decay, confinement, anonymity, and physical powerlessness. In other words, she has the leisure and the instruments to construct a self; but the self she constructs must be – is conceivable only as – white. The surrogate black bodies become her hands and feet, her fantasies of sexual intimacy with her husband and not inconsiderably, her sole source of love.

If the Africanist characters and their condition are removed from the text of *Sapphira and the Slave Girl* we will not have a Miss Havisham immured or in flames. We have nothing: no process of deranged self-construction that can take for granted acquiescence in so awful an enterprise; no drama of limitless power. Sapphira can hide far more successfully than Nancy. She can, and does, remain outside the normal requirements of adult womanhood because of the infantilized Africanist population at her disposal.

The final fugitive in Cather's novel is the novel itself. The plot's own plotting to free the endangered slave girl (of no apparent interest, as we have seen, to the girl's mother or her slave associates) is designed for quite other purposes. It functions as a means for the author to meditate on the moral equivalence of free white women and enslaved black women. The fact that these equations are designed as mother–daughter pairings and relationships leads to the inescapable conclusion that Cather was dreaming and redreaming her problematic relationship with her own mother.

The imaginative strategy is a difficult one at best, an impossible one in the event – so impossible that Cather permits the novel to escape from the pages of fiction into nonfiction. For narrative credibility she substitutes her own determination to force the equation. It is an equation that must take place outside the narrative.

Sapphira and the Slave Girl turns at the end into a kind of memoir, the author's recollection of herself as a child witnessing the return, the reconciliation, and an imposed "all rightness" in untenable, outrageous circumstances. The silenced, acquiescent Africanist characters in the narrative are not less muzzled in the epilogue. The reunion – the drama of it, like its narrative function – is no more the slave characters' than their slave lives have been. The reunion is literally stage-managed for the author, now become a child. Till agrees to wait until little Willa is at the doorway before she permits herself the first sight she has had of her daughter in twenty-five years.

Only with Africanist characters is such a project thinkable: delayed gratification for the pleasure of a (white) child. When the embrace is over, Willa the white child accompanies the black mother and daughter into their narrative, listening to the dialogue but intervening in it at every turn. The shape and detail and substance of their lives are hers, not theirs. Just as Sapphira has employed these surrogate, serviceable black bodies for her own purposes of power without risk so the author employs them in behalf of her own desire for a *safe* participation in loss, in love, in chaos, in justice.

But things go awry. As often happens, characters make claims, impose demands of imaginative accountability over and above the author's will to contain them. Just as Rachel's intervention foils Sapphira's plot, so Cather's urgent need to know and understand this Africanist mother and daughter requires her to give them center stage. The child Cather listens to Till's stories, and the slave, silenced in the narrative, has the final words of the epilogue.

Yet even, or especially, here where the novel ends Cather feels obliged to gesture compassionately toward slavery. Through Till's agency the elevating benevolence of the institution is invoked. Serviceable to the last, this Africanist presence is permitted speech only to reinforce the slaveholders' ideology, in spite of the fact that it subverts the entire premise of the novel. Till's voluntary genuflection is as ecstatic as it is suspicious.

In returning to her childhood, at the end of her writing career, Cather returns to a very personal, indeed private experience. In her last novel she works out and toward the meaning of female betrayal as it faces the void of racism. She may not have arrived safely, like Nancy, but to her credit she did undertake the dangerous journey.

Notes

1   Killis Campbell, "Poe's Treatment of the Negro and of the Negro Dialect," *Studies in English* 16 (1936), p. 106.
2   Willa Cather, *Sapphira and the Slave Girl* (New York: Alfred A. Knopf, 1940), p. 49.

CHAPTER 6

A Small Place

Jamaica Kincaid

Jamaica Kincaid's *A Small Place* (1988) addresses the question of what might be called "secondary colonialism." Secondary colonialism occurs when inhabitants of wealthy, highly developed northern or western countries convert poorer, formerly colonial, usually southern and eastern countries into sites or objects of useful pleasure. Tourism is the most obvious example of such colonization, but it might also be said to assume more symbolic forms, as when the inhabitants of such poorer countries or the places themselves are converted into occasions for the creation of cultural meaning or the achievement of self-fulfillment by secondary colonists. E. M. Forster's *A Passage to India* is a clear example of such symbolic conversion.

If you go to Antigua as a tourist, this is what you will see. If you come by aeroplane you will land at the V. C. Bird International Airport. Vere Cornwall (V. C.) Bird is the Prime Minister of Antigua. You may be the sort of tourist who would wonder why a Prime Minister would want an airport named after him – why not a school, why not a hospital, why not some great public monument? You are a tourist and you have not yet seen a school in Antigua, you have not yet seen the hospital in Antigua, you have not yet seen a public monument in Antigua. As your plane descends to land, you might say, What a beautiful island Antigua is – more beautiful than any of the other islands you have seen, and they were very beautiful, in their way, but they were much too green, much too lush with vegetation, which indicated to you, the tourist, that they got quite a bit of rainfall, and rain is the very thing that you, just now, do not want, for you are thinking of the hard and cold and dark and long days you spent working in North America (or, worse, Europe), earning some money so that you could stay in this place (Antigua) where the sun always shines and where the climate is deliciously hot and dry for the four to ten days you are going to be staying there; and since you are on your holiday, since you are a tourist, the thought of what it might be like for someone who had to live day in day out in a place that suffers constantly from drought, and so has to watch carefully every drop of fresh water used (while at the

Original publication details: Jamaica Kincaid, from *A Small Place*, pp. 3–14. Farrar, Straus & Giroux, 1988. Copyright © 1988 by Jamaica Kincaid. Reproduced with permission from Farrar, Straus and Giroux, LLC.

Literary Theory: An Anthology, Third Edition. Edited by Julie Rivkin and Michael Ryan.
© 2017 John Wiley & Sons, Ltd. Published 2017 by John Wiley & Sons, Ltd.

same time surrounded by a sea and an ocean – the Caribbean Sea on one side, the Atlantic Ocean on the other), must never cross your mind.

You disembark from your plane. You go through customs. Since you are a tourist, a North American or European – to be frank, white and not an Antiguan black returning to Antigua from Europe or North America with cardboard boxes of much needed cheap clothes and food for relatives, you move through customs swiftly, you move through customs with ease. Your bags are not searched. You emerge from customs into the hot, clean air: immediately you feel cleansed, immediately you feel blessed (which is to say special); you feel free. You see a man, a taxi driver; you ask him to take you to your destination; he quotes you a price. You immediately think that the price is in the local currency, for you are a tourist and you are familiar with these things (rates of exchange) and you feel even more free, for things seem so cheap, but then your driver ends by saying, "In US currency." You may say, "Hmmmm, do you have a formal sheet that lists official prices and destinations?" Your driver obeys the law and shows you the sheet, and he apologizes for the incredible mistake he has made in quoting you a price off the top of his head which is so vastly different (favoring him) from the one listed. You are driven to your hotel by this taxi driver in his taxi, a brand-new Japanese-made vehicle. The road on which you are traveling is a very bad road, very much in need of repair. You are feeling wonderful, so you say, "Oh, what a marvelous change these bad roads are from the splen-did highways I am used to in North America." (Or, worse, Europe.) Your driver is reck-less; he is a dangerous man who drives in the middle of the road when he thinks no other cars are coming in the opposite direction, passes other cars on blind curves that run uphill, drives at sixty miles an hour on narrow, curving roads when the road sign, a rust-ing, beat-up thing left over from colonial days, says 40 MPH. This might frighten you (you are on your holiday; you are a tourist); this might excite you (you are on your holiday; you are a tourist), though if you are from New York and take taxis you are used to this style of driving: most of the taxi drivers in New York are from places in the world like this. You are looking out the window (because you want to get your money's worth); you notice that all the cars you see are brand-new, or almost brand-new, and that they are all Japanese made. There are no American cars in Antigua – no new ones, at any rate; none that were manufactured in the last ten years. You continue to look at the cars and you say to yourself, Why, they look brand-new, but they have an awful sound, like an old car – a very old, dilapidated car. How to account for that? Well, possibly it's because they use leaded gasoline in these brand-new cars whose engines were built to use non-leaded gasoline, but you musn't ask the person driving the car if this is so, because he or she has never heard of unleaded gasoline. You look closely at the car; you see that it's a model of a Japanese car that you might hesitate to buy; it's a model that's very expensive; it's a model that's quite impractical for a person who has to work as hard as you do and who watches every penny you earn so that you can afford this holiday you are on. How do they afford such a car? And do they live in a luxurious house to match such a car? Well, no. You will be surprised, then, to see that most likely the person driving this brand-new car filled with the wrong gas lives in a house that, in comparison, is far beneath the status of the car; and if you were to ask why you would be told that the banks are encouraged by the government to make loans available for cars, but loans for houses not so easily avail-able; and if you ask again why, you will be told that the two main car dealerships in Antigua are owned in part or outright by ministers in government. Oh, but you are on holiday and the sight of these brand-new cars driven by people who may or may not have really passed their driving test (there was once a scandal about driving licenses for sale) would not really stir up these thoughts in you. You pass a building sitting in a sea of dust and you think, It's some latrines for people just passing by, but when you look again you see the building has written on it PIGOTT'S SCHOOL. You pass the hospital, the Holberton Hospital, and how wrong you are not to think about this, for though you are a tourist on your holiday, what if your heart should miss a few beats? What if a blood vessel in your neck should break? What if one of those people driving those brand-new cars filled with the wrong gas fails to pass safely while going uphill on a curve and you are in the car going in the opposite direction? Will you be comforted to know that the hospital is staffed with doctors that no actual Antiguan trusts; that Antiguans always say about the doctors, "I don't want them near me"; that Antiguans refer to them not as doctors but as "the three men" (there are three of them); that when the Minister of Health himself doesn't feel well he takes the first plane to New York to see a real doctor; that if any one of the ministers in government needs medical care he flies to New York to get it?

It's a good thing that you brought your own books with you, for you couldn't just go to the library and borrow some. Antigua used to have a splendid library but in The Earthquake (everyone talks about it that way – The Earthquake; we Antiguans, for I am one, have a great sense of things, and the more meaningful the thing, the more meaningless we make it) the library building was damaged. This was in 1974, and soon after that a sign was placed on the front of the building saying, THIS BUILDING WAS DAMAGED IN THE EARTHQUAKE OF 1974. REPAIRS ARE PENDING. The sign hangs there, and hangs there more than a decade later, with its unfulfilled promise of repair, and you might see this as a sort of quaintness on the part of these islanders, these people descended from slaves – what a strange, unusual perception of time they have. REPAIRS ARE PENDING, and here it is many years later, but perhaps in a world that is twelve miles long and nine miles wide (the size of Antigua) twelve years and twelve minutes and twelve days are all the same. The library is one of those splendid old buildings from colonial times, and the sign telling of the repairs is a splendid old sign from colonial times. Not very long after The Earthquake Antigua got its independence from Britain, making Antigua a state in its own right and Antiguans are so proud of this that each year, to mark the day, they go to church and thank God, a British God, for this. But you should not think of the confusion that must lie in all that and you must not think of the damaged library. You have brought your own books with you, and among them is one of those new books about economic history, one of those books explaining how the West (meaning Europe and North America after its conquest and settlement by Europeans) got rich: the West got nothing and then under-valued labor, for generations, of the people like me you see walking around you in Antigua but from the ingenuity of small shopkeepers in Sheffield and Yorkshire and Lancashire, or wherever; and what a great part the invention of the wristwatch played in it, for there was nothing noble-minded men could not do when they discovered they could slap time on their wrists just like that (isn't that the last straw; for not only did we have to suffer the unspeakableness of slavery, but the satisfaction to be had from "We made you bas-tards rich" is taken away, too), and so you needn't let that slightly funny feeling you have from time to time about exploitation, oppression, domination develop into full-fledged unease, discomfort; you could ruin your holiday. They are not responsible for what you have; you owe them nothing; in fact, you did them a big favor, and you can provide one hundred examples. For here you are now, passing by Government House. And here you are now, passing by the Prime Minister's Office and the Parliament Building, and over-looking these, with a splendid view of St John's Harbour, the American Embassy. If it were not for you, they would not have Government House, and Prime Minister's Office, and Parliament Building and embassy of powerful country. Now you are passing a mansion, an extraordinary house painted the color of old cow dung, with more aerials and antennas attached to it than you will see even at the American Embassy. The people who live in this house are a merchant family who came to Antigua from the Middle East less than twenty years ago. When this family first came to Antigua, they sold dry goods door to door from suitcases they carried on their backs. Now they own a lot of Antigua; they regularly lend money to the government, they build enormous (for Antigua), ugly (for Antigua), concrete buildings in Antigua's capital, St John's, which the government then rents for huge sums of money; a member of their family is the Antiguan Ambassador to Syria; Antiguans hate them. Not far from this mansion is another mansion, the home of a drug smuggler. Everybody knows he's a drug smuggler, and if just as you were driving by he stepped out of his door your driver might point him out to you as the notorious person that he is, for this drug smuggler is so rich people say he buys cars in tens – ten of this one, ten of that one and that he bought a house (another mansion) near Five Islands, contents included, with cash he carried in a suitcase: three hundred and fifty thousand American dollars, and, to the surprise of the seller of the house, lots of American dollars were left over. Overlooking the drug smuggler's mansion is yet another mansion, and leading up to it is the best paved road in all of Antigua – even better than the road that was paved for the Queen's visit in 1985 (when the Queen came, all the roads that she would travel on were paved anew, so that the Queen might have been left with the impression that riding in a car in Antigua was a pleasant experience). In this mansion lives a woman sophisticated people in Antigua call Evita. She is a notorious woman. She's young and beautiful and the girlfriend of somebody very high up in the government. Evita is notorious because her relationship with this high government official has made her the owner of boutiques and property and given her a say in cabinet meetings, and all sorts of other privileges such a relationship would bring a beautiful young woman.

Oh, but by now you are tired of all this looking, and you want to reach your destination – your hotel, your room. You long to refresh yourself; you long to eat some nice lobster, some nice local food. You take a bath, you brush your teeth. You get dressed again; as you get dressed, you look out the window. That water – have you ever seen anything like it? Far out, to the horizon, the color of the water is navy-blue; nearer, the water is the color of the North American sky. From there to the shore, the water is pale, silvery, clear, so clear that you can see its pinkish-white sand bottom. Oh, what beauty! Oh, what beauty! You have never seen anything like this. You are so excited. You breathe shallow. You breathe deep. You see a beautiful boy skimming the water, godlike, on a Windsurfer. You see an incredibly unattractive, fat, pastrylike-fleshed woman enjoying a walk on the beautiful sand with a man, an incredibly unattractive, fat, pastrylike-fleshed man; you see the pleasure they're taking in their surroundings. Still standing, looking out the window, you see yourself lying on the beach, enjoying the amazing sun (a sun so powerful and yet so beautiful, the way it is always overhead as if on permanent guard, ready to stamp out any cloud that dares to darken and so empty rain on you and ruin your holiday; a sun that is your personal friend). You see yourself taking a walk on that beach, you see yourself meeting new people (only they are new in a very limited way, for they are people just like you). You see yourself eating some delicious, locally grown food. You see yourself, yourself ... You must not wonder what exactly happened to the contents of your lavatory when you flushed it. You must not wonder where your bath water went when you pulled out the stopper. You must not wonder what happened when you brushed your teeth. Oh, it might all end up in the water you are thinking of taking a swim in; the contents of your lavatory might, just might, graze gently against your ankle as you wade carefree in the water, for you see, in Antigua, there is no proper sewage-disposal system. But the Caribbean Sea is very big and the Atlantic Ocean is even bigger; it would amaze even you to know the number of black slaves this ocean has swallowed up. When you sit down to eat your delicious meal, it's better that you don't know that most of what you are eating came off a plane from Miami. And before it got on a plane in Miami, who knows where it came from? A good guess is that it came from a place like Antigua first, where it was grown dirt-cheap, went to Miami, and came back. There is a world of something in this, but I can't go into it right now.

The thing you have always suspected about yourself the minute you become a tourist is true: A tourist is an ugly human being. You are not an ugly person all the time; you are not an ugly person ordinarily; you are not an ugly person day to day. From day to day, you are a nice person. From day to day, all the people who are supposed to love you on the whole do. From day to day, as you walk down a busy street in the large and modern and prosperous city in which you work and live, dismayed, puzzled (a cliche, but only a cliche can explain you) at how alone you feel in this crowd, how awful it is to go unnoticed, how awful it is to go unloved, even as you are surrounded by more people than you could possibly get to know in a lifetime that lasted for millennia, and then out of the corner of your eye you see someone looking at you and absolute pleasure is written all over that person's face, and then you realize that you are not as revolting a presence as you think you are (for that look just told you so). And so, ordinarily, you are a nice person, an attractive person, a person capable of drawing to yourself the affection of other people (people just like you), a person at home in your own skin (sort of; I mean, in a way; I mean, your dismay and puzzlement are natural to you, because people like you just seem to be like that, and so many of the things people like you find admirable about yourselves – the things you think about, the things you think really define you – seem rooted in these feelings): a person at home in your own house (and all its nice house things), with its nice back yard (and its nice back-yard things), at home on your street, your church, in community activities, your job, at home with your family, your relatives, your friends – you are a whole person. But one day, when you are sitting somewhere, alone in that crowd, and that awful feeling of displacedness comes over you, and really, as an ordinary person you are not well equipped to look too far inward and set yourself aright, because being ordinary is already so taxing, and being ordinary takes all you have out of you, and though the words "I must get away" do not actually pass across your lips, you make a leap from being that nice blob just sitting like a boob in your amniotic sac of the modern experience to being a person visiting heaps of death and ruin and feeling alive and inspired at the sight of it; to being a person lying on some faraway beach, your stilled body stinking and glistening in the sand, looking like something first forgotten, then remembered, then not important enough to go back for; to being a person marveling at the harmony (ordinarily, what you would say is the backwardness) and the union these other people (and they are other people) have with nature. And you look at the things they can do with a piece of ordinary cloth, the things they fashion out of cheap, vulgarly colored (to you) twines, the way they squat down over a hole they have made in the ground, the hole itself is something to marvel at, and since you are being an ugly person this ugly but joyful thought will swell inside you: their ancestors were not clever in the way yours were and not ruthless in the way yours were, for then would it not be you who would be in harmony with nature and backwards in that charming way? An ugly thing, that is what you are when you become a tourist, an ugly, empty thing, a stupid thing, a piece of rubbish pausing here and there to gaze at this and taste that, and it will never occur to you that the people who inhabit the place in which you have just paused cannot stand you, that behind their closed doors they laugh at your strangeness (you do not look the way they look); the physical sight of you does not please them; you have bad manners (it is their custom to eat their food with their hands; you try eating their way, you look silly; you try eating the way you always eat, you look silly); they do not like the way you speak (you have an accent); they collapse helpless from laughter, mimicking the way they imagine you must look as you carry out some everyday bodily function. They do not like you. *They do not like me!* That thought never actually occurs to you. Still, you feel a little uneasy. Still you feel a little foolish. Still, you feel a little out of place. But the banality of your own life is very real to you; it drove you to this extreme, spending your days and your nights in the company of people who despise you, people you do not like really, people you would not want to have as your actual neighbor. And so you must devote yourself to puzzling out how much of what you are told is really, really true (Is ground-up bottle glass in peanut sauce really a delicacy around here, or will it do just what you think ground-up bottle glass will do? Is this rare, multicolored, snout-mouthed fish really an aphrodisiac, or will it cause you to fall asleep permanently?). Oh, the hard work all of this is, and is it any wonder, then, that on your return home you feel the need of a long rest, so that you can recover from your life as a tourist?

That the native does not like the tourist is not hard to explain. For every native of every place is a potential tourist, and every tourist is a native of somewhere. Every native everywhere lives a life of overwhelming and crushing banality and boredom and desperation and depression, and every deed, good and bad, is an attempt to forget this. Every native would like to find a way out, every native would like a rest, every native would like a tour. But some natives – most natives in the world – cannot go anywhere. They are too poor. They are too poor to go anywhere. They are too poor to escape the reality of their lives; and they are too poor to live properly in the place where they live, which is the very place you, the tourist, want to go – so when the natives see you, the tourist, they envy you, they envy your ability to leave your own banality and boredom, they envy your ability to turn their own banality and boredom into a source of pleasure for yourself.

CHAPTER 7

Disjuncture and Difference in the Global Cultural Economy

Arjun Appadurai

Modern global culture is characterized by "disjuncture," according to Arjun Appadurai, Professor of Media, Culture, and Education at New York University. Things hold together in new ways that depart from traditional anchors such as regional geography and ethnic identity, and individual lives are complexly influenced and shaped by modes of understanding and living that are provided by the media, culture, and finance.

The central problem of today's global interactions is the tension between cultural homogenization and cultural heterogenization. A vast array of empirical facts could be brought to bear on the side of the 'homogenization' argument, and much of it has come from the left end of the spectrum of media studies (Hamelink, 1983; Mattelart, 1983; Schiller, 1976), and some from other, less appealing, perspectives (Gans, 1985; Iyer, 1988). Most often, the homogenization argument subspeciates into either an argument about Americanization, or an argument about 'commoditization', and very often the two arguments are closely linked. What these arguments fail to consider is that at least as rapidly as forces from various metropolises are brought into new societies they tend to become indigenized in one or other way: this is true of music and housing styles as much as it is true of science and terrorism, spectacles and constitutions. The dynamics of such indigenization have just begun to be explored in a sophisticated manner (Barber, 1987; Feld, 1988; Hannerz, 1987, 1989; Ivy, 1988; Nicoll, 1989; Yoshimoto, 1989), and much more needs to be done. But it is worth noticing that for the people of Irian Jaya, Indonesianization may be more worrisome than Americanization, as Japanization may be for Koreans, Indianization for Sri Lankans, Vietnamization for the Cambodians, Russianization for the people of Soviet Armenia and the Baltic Republics. Such a list of alternative fears to Americanization could be greatly expanded, but it is not a shapeless

Original publication details: Arjun Appadurai, "Disjuncture and Difference in the Global Cultural Economy." *Theory, Culture & Society* 7 (1990), pp. 295–310. Sage.

inventory: for polities of smaller scale, there is always a fear of cultural absorption by polities of larger scale, especially those that are nearby. One man's imagined community (Anderson, 1983) is another man's political prison.

This scalar dynamic, which has widespread global manifestations, is also tied to the relationship between nations and states, to which I shall return later in this essay. For the moment let us note that the simplification of these many forces (and fears) of homogenization can also be exploited by nation-states in relation to their own minorities, by posing global commoditization (or capitalism, or some other such external enemy) as more 'real' than the threat of its own hegemonic strategies.

The new global cultural economy has to be understood as a complex, overlapping, disjunctive order, which cannot any longer be understood in terms of existing center-periphery models (even those that might account for multiple centers and peripheries). Nor is it susceptible to simple models of push and pull (in terms of migration theory) or of surpluses and deficits (as in traditional models of balance of trade), or of consumers and producers (as in most neo-Marxist theories of development). Even the most complex and flexible theories of global development which have come out of the Marxist tradition (Amin, 1980; Mandel, 1978; Wallerstein, 1974; Wolf, 1982) are inadequately quirky, and they have not come to terms with what Lash and Urry (1987) have recently called 'disorganized capitalism'. The complexity of the current global economy has to do with certain fundamental disjunctures between economy, culture and politics which we have barely begun to theorize.[1]

I propose that an elementary framework for exploring such disjunctures is to look at the relationship between five dimensions of global cultural flow which can be termed: (a) ethnoscapes; (b) mediascapes; (c) technoscapes; (d) finanscapes; and (e) ideoscapes.[2] I use terms with the common suffix scape to indicate first of all that these are not objectively given relations which look the same from every angle of vision, but rather that they are deeply perspectival constructs, inflected very much by the historical, linguistic and political situatedness of different sorts of actors: nation-states, multinationals, diasporic communities, as well as sub-national groupings and movements (whether religious, political or economic), and even intimate face-to-face groups, such as villages, neighborhoods and families. Indeed, the individual actor is the last locus of this perspectival set of landscapes, for these landscapes are eventually navigated by agents who both experience and constitute larger formations, in part by their own sense of what these landscapes offer. These landscapes thus, are the building blocks of what, extending Benedict Anderson, I would like to call 'imagined worlds', that is, the multiple worlds which are constituted by the historically situated imaginations of persons and groups spread around the globe (Appadurai, 1989). An important fact of the world we live in today is that many persons on the globe live in such imagined 'worlds' and not just in imagined communities, and thus are able to contest and sometimes even subvert the 'imagined worlds' of the official mind and of the entrepreneurial mentality that surround them. The suffix scape also allows us to point to the fluid, irregular shapes of these landscapes, shapes which characterize international capital as deeply as they do international clothing styles.

By 'ethnoscape', I mean the landscape of persons who constitute the shifting world in which we live: tourists, immigrants, refugees, exiles, guestworkers and other moving groups and persons constitute an essential feature of the world, and appear to affect the politics of and between nations to a hitherto unprecedented degree. This is not to say that there are not anywhere relatively stable communities and networks, of kinship, of friendship, of work and of leisure, as well as of birth, residence and other filiative forms.

But it is to say that the warp of these stabilities is everywhere shot through with the woof of human motion, as more persons and groups deal with the realities of having to move, or the fantasies of wanting to move. What is more, both these realities as well as these fantasies now function on larger scales, as men and women from villages in India think not just of moving to Poona or Madras, but of moving to Dubai and Houston, and refugees from Sri Lanka find themselves in South India as well as in Canada, just as the Hmong are driven to London as well as to Philadelphia. And as international capital shifts its needs, as production and technology generate different needs, as nation-states shift their policies on refugee populations, these moving groups can never afford to let their imaginations rest too long, even if they wished to.

By 'technoscape', I mean the global configuration, also ever fluid, of technology, and of the fact that technology, both high and low, both mechanical and informational, now moves at high speeds across various kinds of previously impervious boundaries. Many countries now are the roots of multinational enterprise: a huge steel complex in Libya may involve interests from India, China, Russia and Japan, providing different components of new technological configurations. The odd distribution of technologies, and thus the peculiarities of these technoscapes, are increasingly driven not by any obvious economies of scale, of political control, or of market rationality, but of increasingly complex relationships between money flows, political possibilities and the availability of both low and highly-skilled labor. So, while India exports waiters and chauffeurs to Dubai and Sharjah, it also exports software engineers to the United States (indentured briefly to Tata-Burroughs or the World Bank), then laundered through the State Department to become wealthy 'resident aliens', who are in turn objects of seductive messages to invest their money and know-how in federal and state projects in India. The global economy can still be described in terms of traditional 'indicators' (as the World Bank continues to do) and studied in terms of traditional comparisons (as in Project Link at the University of Pennsylvania), but the complicated technoscapes (and the shifting ethnoscapes), which underlie these 'indicators' and 'comparisons' are further out of the reach of the 'queen of the social sciences' than ever before. How is one to make a meaningful comparison of wages in Japan and the United States, or of real estate costs in New York and Tokyo, without taking sophisticated account of the very complex fiscal and investment flows that link the two economies through a global grid of currency speculation and capital transfer?

Thus it is useful to speak as well of 'finanscapes', since the disposition of global capital is now a more mysterious, rapid and difficult landscape to follow than ever before, as currency markets, national stock exchanges, and commodity speculations move mega-monies through national turnstiles at blinding speed, with vast absolute implications for small differences in percentage points and time units. But the critical point is that the global relationship between ethnoscapes, technoscapes and finanscapes is deeply disjunctive and profoundly unpredictable, since each of these landscapes is subject to its own constraints and incentives (some political, some informational and some techno-environmental), at the same time as each acts as a constraint and a parameter for movements in the other. Thus, even an elementary model of global political economy must take into account the shifting relationship between perspectives on human movement, technological flow, and financial transfers, which can accommodate their deeply disjunctive relationships with one another.

Built upon these disjunctures (which hardly form a simple, mechanical global 'infra-structure' in any case) are what I have called 'mediascapes' and 'ideoscapes', though the latter two are closely related landscapes of images. 'Mediascapes' refer both to the distribution of the electronic capabilities to produce and disseminate information (newspapers, magazines, television stations, film production studios, etc.), which are now available to a growing number of private and public interests throughout the world; and to the images of the world created by these media. These images of the world involve many complicated inflections, depending on their mode (documentary or entertainment), their hardware (electronic or pre-electronic), their audiences (local, national or transnational) and the interests of those who own and control them. What is most important about these mediascapes is that they provide (especially in their television, film and cassette forms) large and complex repertoires of images, narratives and 'ethnoscapes' to viewers throughout the world, in which the world of commodities and the world of 'news' and politics are profoundly mixed. What this means is that many audiences throughout the world experience the media themselves as a complicated and interconnected repertoire of print, celluloid, electronic screens and billboards. The lines between the 'realistic' and the fictional landscapes they see are blurred, so that the further away these audiences are from the direct experiences of metropolitan life, the more likely they are to construct 'imagined worlds' which are chimerical, aesthetic, even fantastic objects, particularly if assessed by the criteria of some other perspective, some other 'imagined world'.

'Mediascapes', whether produced by private or state interests, tend to be image-centered, narrative-based accounts of strips of reality, and what they offer to those who experience and transform them is a series of elements (such as characters, plots and textual forms) out of which scripts can be formed of imagined lives, their own as well as those of others living in other places. These scripts can and do get disaggregated into complex sets of metaphors by which people live (Lakoff and Johnson, 1980) as they help to constitute narratives of the 'other' and proto-narratives of possible lives, fantasies which could become prologemena to the desire for acquisition and movement.

'Ideoscapes' are also concatenations of images, but they are often directly political and frequently have to do with the ideologies of states and the counter-ideologies of movements explicitly oriented to capturing state power or a piece of it. These ideoscapes are composed of elements of the Enlightenment world-view, which consists of a concatenation of ideas, terms and images, including 'freedom', 'welfare', 'rights', 'sovereignty', 'representation' and the master-term 'democracy'. The master-narrative of the Enlightenment (and its many variants in England, France and the United States) was constructed with a certain internal logic and presupposed a certain relationship between reading, representation and the public sphere (for the dynamics of this process in the early history of the United States, see Warner, 1990). But their diaspora across the world, especially since the nineteenth century, has loosened the internal coherence which held these terms and images together in a Euro-American master-narrative, and provided instead a loosely structured synopticon of politics, in which different nation-states, as part of their evolution, have organized their political cultures around different 'keywords' (Williams, 1976).

As a result of the differential diaspora of these keywords, the political narratives that govern communication between elites and followings in different parts of the world involve problems of both a semantic and a pragmatic nature: semantic to the extent that words (and their lexical equivalents) require careful translation from context to context in their global movements; and pragmatic to the extent that the use of these words by political actors and their audiences may be subject to very different sets of contextual conventions that mediate their translation into public politics. Such conventions are not only matters of the nature of political rhetoric (viz. what does the aging Chinese leadership mean when it refers to the dangers of hooliganism? What does the South Korean leadership mean when it speaks of 'discipline' as the key to democratic industrial growth?).

These conventions also involve the far more subtle question of what sets of communicative genres are valued in what way (newspapers versus cinema for example) and what sorts of pragmatic genre conventions govern the collective 'readings' of different kinds of text. So, while an Indian audience may be attentive to the resonances of a political speech in terms of some key words and phrases reminiscent of Hindi cinema, a Korean audience may respond to the subtle codings of Buddhist or neo-Confucian rhetorical strategy encoded in a political document. The very relationship of reading to hearing and seeing may vary in important ways that determine the morphology of these different 'ideoscapes' as they shape themselves in different national and transnational contexts. This globally variable synaesthesia has hardly even been noted, but it demands urgent analysis. Thus 'democracy' has clearly become a master-term, with powerful echoes from Haiti and Poland to the Soviet Union and China, but it sits at the center of a variety of ideoscapes (composed of distinctive pragmatic configurations of rough 'translations' of other central terms from the vocabulary of the Enlightenment). This creates ever new terminological kaleidoscopes, as states (and the groups that seek to capture them) seek to pacify populations whose own ethnoscapes are in motion, and whose mediascapes may create severe problems for the ideoscapes with which they are presented. The fluidity of ideoscapes is complicated in particular by the growing diasporas (both voluntary and involuntary) of intellectuals who continuously inject new meaning-streams into the discourse of democracy in different parts of the world.

This extended terminological discussion of the five terms I have coined sets the basis for a tentative formulation about the conditions under which current global flows occur: *they occur in and through the growing disjunctures between ethnoscapes, technoscapes, finanscapes, mediascapes and ideoscapes.* This formulation, the core of my model of global cultural flow, needs some explanation. First, people, machinery, money, images, and ideas now follow increasingly non-isomorphic paths: of course, at all periods in human history, there have been some disjunctures between the flows of these things, but the sheer speed, scale and volume of each of these flows is now so great that the disjunctures have become central to the politics of global culture. The Japanese are notoriously hospitable to ideas and are stereotyped as inclined to export (all) and import (some) goods, but they are also notoriously closed to immigration, like the Swiss, the Swedes and the Saudis. Yet the Swiss and Saudis accept populations of guestworkers, thus creating labor diasporas of Turks, Italians and other circum-mediterranean groups. Some such guestworker groups maintain continuous contact with their home-nations, like the Turks, but others, like high-level South Asian migrants tend to desire lives in their new homes, raising anew the problem of reproduction in a deterritorialized context.

Deterritorialization, in general, is one of the central forces of the modern world, since it brings laboring populations into the lower class sectors and spaces of relatively wealthy societies, while sometimes creating exaggerated and intensified senses of criticism or attachment to politics in the home-state. Deterritorialization, whether of Hindus, Sikhs, Palestinians or Ukrainians, is now at the core of a variety of global fundamentalisms, including Islamic and Hindu fundamentalism. In the Hindu case for example (Appadurai and Breckenridge, forthcoming) it is clear that the overseas movement of Indians has been exploited by a variety of interests both within and outside India to create a complicated network of finances and religious identifications, in which the problems of cultural reproduction for Hindus abroad has become tied to the politics of Hindu fundamentalism at home.

At the same time, deterritorialization creates new markets for film companies, art impressarios and travel agencies, who thrive on the need of the deterritorialized population for contact with its homeland. Naturally, these invented homelands, which constitute the mediascapes of deterritorialized groups, can often become sufficiently fantastic and one-sided that they provide the material for new ideoscapes in which ethnic conflicts can begin to erupt. The creation of 'Khalistan', an invented homeland of the deterritorialized Sikh population of England, Canada and the United States, is one example of the bloody potential in such mediascapes, as they interact with the 'internal colonialisms' (Hechter, 1974) of the nation-state. The West Bank, Namibia and Eritrea are other theaters for the enactment of the bloody negotiation between existing nation-states and various deterritorialized groupings.

The idea of deterritorialization may also be applied to money and finance, as money managers seek the best markets for their investments, independent of national boundaries. In turn, these movements of monies are the basis of new kinds of conflict, as Los Angelenos worry about the Japanese buying up their city, and people in Bombay worry about the rich Arabs from the Gulf States who have not only transformed the prices of mangoes in Bombay, but have also substantially altered the profile of hotels, restaurants and other services in the eyes of the local population, just as they continue to do in London. Yet, most residents of Bombay are ambivalent about the Arab presence there, for the flip side of their presence is the absence of friends and kinsmen earning big money in the Middle East and bringing back both money and luxury commodities to Bombay and other cities in India. Such commodities transform consumer taste in these cities, and also often end up smuggled through air and sea ports and peddled in the gray markets of Bombay's streets. In these gray markets, some members of Bombay's middle-classes and of its lumpenproletariat can buy some of these goods, ranging from cartons of Marlboro cigarettes, to Old Spice shaving cream and tapes of Madonna. Similarly gray routes, often subsidized by the moonlighting activities of sailors, diplomats, and airline stewardesses who get to move in and out of the country regularly, keep the gray markets of Bombay, Madras and Calcutta filled with goods not only from the West, but also from the Middle East, Hong Kong and Singapore.

It is this fertile ground of deterritorialization, in which money, commodities and persons are involved in ceaselessly chasing each other around the world, that the mediascapes and ideoscapes of the modern world find their fractured and fragmented counterpart. For the ideas and images produced by mass media often are only partial guides to the goods and experiences that deterritorialized populations transfer to one another. In Mira Nair's brilliant film, *India Cabaret*, we see the multiple loops of this fractured deterritorialization as young women, barely competent in Bombay's metropolitan glitz, come to seek their fortunes as cabaret dancers and prostitutes in Bombay, entertaining men in clubs with dance formats derived wholly from the prurient dance sequences of Hindi films. These scenes cater in turn to ideas about Western and foreign women and their 'looseness', while they provide tawdry career alibis for these women. Some of these women come from Kerala, where cabaret clubs and the pornographic film industry have blossomed, partly in response to the purses and tastes of Keralites returned from the Middle East, where their diasporic lives away from women distort their very sense of what the relations between men and women might be. These tragedies of displacement could certainly be replayed in a more detailed analysis of the relations between the Japanese and German sex tours to Thailand and the tragedies of the sex trade in Bangkok, and in other similar loops which tie together fantasies about the other, the conveniences and seductions of travel, the economics of global trade and the brutal mobility fantasies that dominate gender politics in many parts of Asia and the world at large.

While far more could be said about the cultural politics of deterritorialization and the larger sociology of displacement that it expresses, it is appropriate at this juncture to bring in the role of the nation-state in the disjunctive global economy of culture today. The relationship between states and nations is everywhere an embattled one. It is possible to say that in many societies, the nation and the state have become one another's projects. That is, while nations (or more properly groups with ideas about nationhood) seek to capture or co-opt states and state power, states simultaneously seek to capture and monopolize ideas about nationhood (Baruah, 1986; Chatterjee, 1986; Nandy, 1989). In general, separatist, transnational movements, including those which have included terror in their methods, exemplify nations in search of states: Sikhs, Tamil Sri Lankans, Basques, Moros, Quebecois, each of these represent imagined communities which seek to create states of their own or carve pieces out of existing states. States, on the other hand, are everywhere seeking to monopolize the moral resources of community, either by flatly claiming perfect coevality between nation and state, or by systematically museumizing and representing all the groups within them in a variety of heritage politics that seems remarkably uniform throughout the world (Handler, 1988; Herzfeld, 1982; McQueen, 1988). Here, national and international mediascapes are exploited by nation-states to pacify separatists or even the potential fissiparousness of all ideas of difference. Typically, contemporary nation-states do this by exercising taxonomical control over difference; by creating various kinds of international spectacle to domesticate difference; and by seducing small groups with the fantasy of self-display on some sort of global or cosmopolitan stage. One important new feature of global cultural politics, tied to the disjunctive relationships between the various landscapes discussed earlier, is that state and nation are at each's throats, and the hyphen that links them is now less an icon of conjuncture than an index of disjuncture. This disjunctive relationship between nation and state has two levels: at the level of any given nation-state, it means that there is a battle of the imagination, with state and nation seeking to cannibalize one another. Here is the seed-bed of brutal separatisms, majoritarianisms that seem to have appeared from nowhere, and micro-identities that have become political projects within the nation-state. At another level, this disjunctive relationship is deeply entangled with the global disjunctures discussed throughout this essay: ideas of nationhood appear to be steadily increasing in scale and regularly crossing existing state boundaries: sometimes, as with the Kurds, because previous identities stretched across vast national spaces, or, as with the Tamils in Sri Lanka, the dormant threads of a transnational diaspora have been activated to ignite the micro-politics of a nation-state.

In discussing the cultural politics that have subverted the hyphen that links the nation to the state, it is especially important not to forget its mooring in the irregularities that now characterize 'disorganized capital' (Lash and Urry, 1987; Kothari, 1989). It is because labor, finance and technology are now so widely separated that the volatilities that underlie movements for nationhood (as large as transnational Islam on the one hand, or as small as the movement of the Gurkhas for a separate state in the North-East of India) grind against the vulnerabilities which characterize the relationships between states. States find themselves pressed to stay 'open' by the forces of media, technology, and travel which had fueled consumerism throughout the world and have increased the craving, even in the non-Western world, for new commodities and spectacles. On the other hand, these very cravings can become caught up in new ethnoscapes, mediascapes, and eventually, ideoscapes, such as 'democracy' in China, that the state cannot tolerate as threats to its own control over ideas of nationhood and 'people-hood'. States throughout the world are under siege, especially where contests over the ideoscapes of democracy are fierce and fundamental, and where there are radical disjunctures between ideoscapes and technoscapes (as in the case of very small countries that lack contemporary technologies of production and information); or between ideoscapes and finanscapes (as in countries, such as Mexico or Brazil where international lending influences national politics to a very large degree); or between ideoscapes and ethnoscapes (as in Beirut, where diasporic, local and translocal filiations are suicidally at battle); or between ideoscapes and mediascapes (as in many countries in the Middle East and Asia) where the lifestyles represented on both national and international TV and cinema completely overwhelm and undermine the rhetoric of national politics: in the Indian case, the myth of the law-breaking hero has emerged to mediate this naked struggle between the pieties and the realities of Indian politics, which has grown increasingly brutalized and corrupt (Vachani, 1989).

The transnational movement of the martial-arts, particularly through Asia, as mediated by the Hollywood and Hongkong film industries (Zarilli, forthcoming) is a rich illustration of the ways in which long-standing martial arts traditions, reformulated to meet the fantasies of contemporary (sometimes lumpen) youth populations, create new cultures of masculinity and violence, which are in turn the fuel for increased violence in national and international politics. Such violence is in turn the spur to an increasingly rapid and amoral arms trade which penetrates the entire world. The worldwide spread of the AK-47 and the Uzi, in films, in corporate and state security, in terror, and in police and military activity, is a reminder that apparently simple technical uniformities often conceal an increasingly complex set of loops, linking images of violence to aspirations for community in some 'imagined world'.

Returning then to the 'ethnoscapes' with which I began, the central paradox of ethnic politics in today's world is that primordia, (whether of language or skin color or neighborhood or of kinship) have become globalized. That is, sentiments whose greatest force is in their ability to ignite intimacy into a political sentiment and turn locality into a staging ground for identity, have become spread over vast and irregular spaces, as groups move, yet stay linked to one another through sophisticated media capabilities. This is not to deny that such primordia are often the product of invented traditions (Hobsbawm and Ranger, 1983) or retrospective affiliations, but to emphasize that because of the disjunctive and unstable interplay of commerce, media, national policies and consumer fantasies, ethnicity, once a genie contained in the bottle of some sort of locality (however large) has now become a global force, forever slipping in and through the cracks between states and borders.

But the relationship between the cultural and economic levels of this new set of global disjunctures is not a simple one-way street in which the terms of global cultural politics are set wholly by, or confined wholly within, the vicissitudes of international flows of technology, labor and finance, demanding only a modest modification of existing neo-Marxist models of uneven development and state-formation. There is a deeper change,

itself driven by the disjunctures between all the landscapes I have discussed, and constituted by their continuously fluid and uncertain interplay, which concerns the relationship between production and consumption in today's global economy. Here I begin with
Marx's famous (and often mined) view of the fetishism of the commodity, and suggest
that this fetishism has been replaced in the world at large (now seeing the world as one,
large, interactive system, composed of many complex sub-systems) by two mutually
supportive descendants, the first of which I call production fetishism, and the second of
which I call the fetishism of the consumer.

By production fetishism I mean an illusion created by contemporary transnational
production loci, which masks translocal capital, transnational earning-flows, global
management and often faraway workers (engaged in various kinds of high-tech putting
out operations) in the idiom and spectacle of local (sometimes even worker) control,
national productivity and territorial sovereignty. To the extent that various kinds of Free
Trade Zone have become the models for production at large, especially of high-tech
commodities, production has itself become a fetish, masking not social relations as such,
but the relations of production, which are increasingly transnational. The locality (both
in the sense of the local factory or site of production and in the extended sense of the
nation-state) becomes a fetish which disguises the globally dispersed forces that actually
drive the production process. This generates alienation (in Marx's sense) twice intensified, for its social sense is now compounded by a complicated spatial dynamic which is
increasingly global.

As for the fetishism of the consumer, I mean to indicate here that the consumer has
been transformed, through commodity flows (and the mediascapes, especially of advertising, that accompany them) into a sign, both in Baudrillard's sense of a simulacrum
which only asymptotically approaches the form of a real social agent; and in the sense of
a mask for the real seat of agency, which is not the consumer but the producer and the
many forces that constitute production. Global advertising is the key technology for the
worldwide dissemination of a plethora of creative, and culturally well-chosen, ideas of
consumer agency. These images of agency are increasingly distortions of a world of
merchandising so subtle that the consumer is consistently helped to believe that he or
she is an actor, where in fact he or she is at best a chooser.

The globalization of culture is not the same as its homogenization, but globalization
involves the use of a variety of instruments of homogenization (armaments, advertising
techniques, language hegemonies, clothing styles and the like), which are absorbed into
local political and cultural economies, only to be repatriated as heterogeneous dialogues
of national sovereignty, free enterprise, fundamentalism, etc. in which the state plays an
increasingly delicate role: too much openness to global flows and the nation-state is
threatened by revolt – the China syndrome; too little, and the state exits the international
stage, as Burma, Albania and North Korea, in various ways have done. In general, the
state has become the arbiter of this *repatriation of difference* (in the form of goods, signs,
slogans, styles, etc.). But this repatriation or export of the designs and commodities of
difference continuously exacerbates the 'internal' politics of majoritarianism and homogenization, which is most frequently played out in debates over heritage.

Thus the central feature of global culture today is the politics of the mutual effort of
sameness and difference to cannibalize one another and thus to proclaim their successful hijacking of the twin Enlightenment ideas of the triumphantly universal and the
resiliently particular. This mutual cannibalization shows its ugly face in riots, in refugee-
flows, in state-sponsored torture and in ethnocide (with or without state support).

Its brighter side is in the expansion of many individual horizons of hope and fantasy, in the global spread of oral rehydration therapy and other low-tech instruments of well-being, in the susceptibility even of South Africa to the force of global opinion, in the inability of the Polish state to repress its own working-classes, and in the growth of a wide range of progressive, transnational alliances. Examples of both sorts could be multiplied. The critical point is that both sides of the coin of global cultural process today are products of the infinitely varied mutual contest of sameness and difference on a stage characterized by radical disjunctures between different sorts of global flows and the uncertain landscapes created in and through these disjunctures.

Notes

A longer version of this essay appears in *Public Culture* 2 (2), Spring 1990. This longer version sets the present formulation in the context of global cultural traffic in earlier historical periods, and draws out some of its implications for the study of cultural forms more generally.

1   One major exception is Fredric Jameson, whose (1984) essay on the relationship between postmodernism and late capitalism has in many ways, inspired this essay. However, the debate between Jameson (1986) and Ahmad (1987) in *Social Text* shows that the creation of a globalizing Marxist narrative, in cultural matters, is difficult territory indeed. My own effort, in this context, is to begin a restructuring of the Marxist narrative (by stressing lags and disjunctures) that many Marxists might find abhorrent. Such a restructuring has to avoid the dangers of obliterating difference within the 'third world', of eliding the social referent (as some French postmodernists seem inclined to do) and of retaining the narrative authority of the Marxist tradition, in favor of greater attention to global fragmentation, uncertainty and difference.
2   These ideas are argued more fully in a book I am currently working on, tentatively entitled *Imploding Worlds: Imagination and Disjuncture in the Global Cultural Economy*.

References

Ahmad, A. (1987) 'Jameson's Rhetoric of Otherness and the "National Allegory"', *Social Text* 17: 3–25.
Amin, S. (1980) *Class and Nation: Historically and in the Current Crisis*. New York and London: Monthly Review.
Anderson, B. (1983) *Imagined Communities: Reflections on the Origin and Spread of Nationalism*. London: Verso.
Appadurai, A. (1989) 'Global Ethnoscapes: Notes and Queries for a Transnational Anthropology', in R.G. Fox (ed.), *Interventions: Anthropology of the Present*.
Appadurai, A. and Breckenridge, C.A. (forthcoming) *A Transnational Culture in the Making: The Asian Indian Diaspora in the United States*. London: Berg.
Barber, K. (1987) 'Popular Arts in Africa', *African Studies Review* 30(3).
Baruah, S. (1986) 'Immigration, Ethnic Conflict and Political Turmoil, Assam 1979–1985', *Asian Survey* 26 (11).
Chatterjee, P. (1986) *Nationalist Thought and the Colonial World: A Derivative Discourse*. London: Zed Books.
Feld, S. (1988) 'Notes on World Beat', *Public Culture* 1(1): 31–7.
Gans, Eric (1985) *The End of Culture: Toward a Generative Anthropology*. Berkeley: University of California.
Hamelink, C. (1983) *Cultural Autonomy in Global Communications*. New York: Longman.
Handler, R. (1988) *Nationalism and the Politics of Culture in Quebec*. Madison: University of Wisconsin.
Hannerz, U. (1987) 'The World in Creolization,' *Africa* 57(4): 546–59.

Hannerz, U. (1989) 'Notes on the Global Ecumene', *Public Culture* 1(2): 66–75.

Hechter, M. (1974) *Internal Colonialism: The Celtic Fringe in British National Development, 1536–1966*. Berkeley and Los Angeles: University of California.

Herzfeld, M. (1982) *Ours Once More: Folklore, Ideology and the Making of Modern Greece*. Austin: University of Texas.

Hobsbawm, E. and Ranger, T. (eds) (1983) *The Invention of Tradition*. New York: Columbia University Press.

Ivy, M. (1988) 'Tradition and Difference in the Japanese Mass Media', *Public Culture* 1(1): 21–9.

Iyer, P. (1988) *Video Night in Kathmandu*. New York: Knopf.

Jameson, F. (1984) 'Postmodernism, or the Cultural Logic of Late Capitalism', *New Left Review* 146 (July–August): 53–92.

Jameson, F. (1986) 'Third World Literature in the Era of Multi-National Capitalism', *Social Text* 15 (Fall): 65–88.

Kothari, R. (1989) *State Against Democracy: In Search of Humane Governance*. New York: New Horizons.

Lakoff, G. and Johnson, M. (1980) *Metaphors We Live By*. Chicago and London: University of Chicago.

Lash, S. and Urry, J. (1987) *The End of Organized Capitalism*. Madison: University of Wisconsin.

McQueen, H. (1988) 'The Australian Stamp: Image, Design and Ideology', *Arena* 84 Spring: 78–96.

Mandel, E. (1978) *Late Capitalism*. London: Verso.

Mattelart, A. (1983) *Transnationals and Third World: The Struggle for Culture*. South Hadley, MA: Bergin and Garvey.

Nandy, A. (1989) 'The Political Culture of the Indian State', *Daedalus* 118(4): 1–26.

Nicoll, F. (1989) 'My Trip to Alice', *Criticism, Heresy and Interpretation (CHAI)*, 3: 21–32.

Schiller, H. (1976) *Communication and Cultural Domination*. White Plains, NY: International Arts and Sciences.

Vachani, L. (1989) 'Narrative, Pleasure and Ideology in the Hindi Film: An Analysis of the Outsider Formula', MA thesis, The Annenberg School of Communication, The University of Pennsylvania.

Wallerstein, I. (1974) *The Modern World-System* (2 volumes). New York and London: Academic Press.

Warner, M. (1990) *The Letters of the Republic: Publication and the Public Sphere*. Cambridge, MA: Harvard.

Williams, R. (1976) *Keywords*. New York: Oxford.

Wolf, E. (1982) *Europe and the People Without History*. Berkeley: University of California.

Yoshimoto, M. (1989) 'The Postmodern and Mass Images in Japan', *Public Culture* 1(2): 8–25.

Zarilli, P. (Forthcoming) 'Repositioning the Body: An Indian Martial Art and its Pan-Asian Publics' in C.A. Breckenridge, (ed.), *Producing the Postcolonial: Trajectories to Public Culture in India*.

CHAPTER 8

Cultural Identity and Diaspora

Stuart Hall

A leading figure in the field of Cultural Studies, Stuart Hall in this essay argues that the cultural and ethnic identities summoned as alternatives to colonial imposition are made complicated by differences and are never simple. Hall is famous for his work with the "Birmingham School" of cultural studies in England and is associated with the study of the role of the media in maintaining the power of dominant economic and social groups.

A new cinema of the Caribbean is emerging, joining the company of the other 'Third Cinemas'. It is related to, but different from the vibrant film and other forms of visual representation of the Afro-Caribbean (and Asian) 'blacks' of the diasporas of the West – the new post-colonial subjects. All these cultural practices and forms of representation have the black subject at their centre, putting the issue of cultural identity in question. Who is this emergent, new subject of the cinema? From where does he/she speak? Practices of representation always implicate the positions from which we speak or write – the positions of *enunciation*. What recent theories of enunciation suggest is that, though we speak, so to say 'in our own name', of ourselves and from our own experience, nevertheless who speaks, and the subject who is spoken of, are never identical, never exactly in the same place. Identity is not as transparent or unproblematic as we think. Perhaps instead of thinking of identity as an already accomplished fact, which the new cultural practices then represent, we should think, instead, of identity as a 'production', which is never complete, always in process, and always constituted within, not outside, representation. This view problematises the very authority and authenticity to which the term, 'cultural identity', lays claim.

We seek, here, to open a dialogue, an investigation, on the subject of cultural identity and representation. Of course, the 'I' who writes here must also be thought of as, itself, 'enunciated'. We all write and speak from a particular place and time, from a history and a culture which is specific. What we say is always 'in context', *positioned*. I was born into and spent my childhood and adolescence in a lower-middle-class family in Jamaica. I have lived all my adult life in England, in the shadow of the black diaspora – 'in the belly of the beast'. I write against the background of a lifetime's work in cultural studies. If the paper

Original publication details: Stuart Hall "Cultural Identity and Diaspora." *Framework* (no. 36), (1989), pp. 222–237. Reproduced with permission from *Framework*.

seems preoccupied with the diaspora experience and its narratives of displacement, it is worth remembering that all discourse is 'placed', and the heart has its reasons.

There are at least two different ways of thinking about 'cultural identity'. The first position defines 'cultural identity' in terms of one, shared culture, a sort of collective 'one true self', hiding inside the many other, more superficial or artificially imposed 'selves', which people with a shared history and ancestry hold in common. Within the terms of this definition, our cultural identities reflect the common historical experiences and shared cultural codes which provide us, as 'one people', with stable, unchanging and continuous frames of reference and meaning, beneath the shifting divisions and vicissitudes of our actual history. This 'oneness', underlying all the other, more superficial differences, is the truth, the essence, of 'Caribbeanness', of the black experience. It is this identity which a Caribbean or black diaspora must discover, excavate, bring to light and express through cinematic representation.

Such a conception of cultural identity played a critical role in all the post-colonial struggles which have so profoundly reshaped our world. It lay at the centre of the vision of the poets of 'Negritude', like Aimee Ceasire and Leopold Senghor, and of the Pan-African political project, earlier in the century. It continues to be a very powerful and creative force in emergent forms of representation amongst hitherto marginalised peoples. In post-colonial societies, the rediscovery of this identity is often the object of what Frantz Fanon once called a

> passionate research ... directed by the secret hope of discovering beyond the misery of today, beyond self-contempt, resignation and abjuration, some very beautiful and splendid era whose existence rehabilitates us both in regard to ourselves and in regard to others.

New forms of cultural practice in these societies address themselves to this project for the very good reason that, as Fanon puts it, in the recent past,

> Colonisation is not satisfied merely with holding a people in its grip and emptying the native's brain of all form and content. By a kind of perverted logic, it turns to the past of oppressed people, and distorts, disfigures and destroys it.[1]

The question which Fanon's observation poses is, what is the nature of this 'profound research' which drives the new forms of visual and cinematic representation? Is it only a matter of unearthing that which the colonial experience buried and overlaid, bringing to light the hidden continuities it suppressed? Or is a quite different practice entailed – not the rediscovery but the *production* of identity. Not an identity grounded in the archaeology, but in the *re-telling* of the past?

We should not, for a moment, underestimate or neglect the importance of the act of imaginative rediscovery which this conception of a rediscovered, essential identity entails. 'Hidden histories' have played a critical role in the emergence of many of the most important social movements of our time – feminist, anti-colonial and anti-racist. The photographic work of a generation of Jamaican and Rastafarian artists, or of a visual artist like Armet Francis (a Jamaican-born photographer who has lived in Britain since the age of eight) is a testimony to the continuing creative power of this conception of identity within the emerging practices of representation. Francis's photographs of the peoples of The Black Triangle, taken in Africa, the Caribbean, the USA and the UK, attempt to reconstruct in visual terms 'the underlying unity of the black people whom colonisation and slavery distributed across the African diaspora.' His text is an act of imaginary reunification.

Crucially, such images offer a way of imposing an imaginary coherence on the experience of dispersal and fragmentation, which is the history of all enforced diasporas. They do this by representing or 'figuring' Africa as the mother of these different civilisations. This Triangle is, after all, 'centred' in Africa. Africa is the name of the missing term, the great aporia, which lies at the centre of our cultural identity and gives it a meaning which, until recently, it lacked. No one who looks at these textural images now, in the light of the history of transportation, slavery and migration, can fail to understand how the rift of separation, the 'loss of identity', which has been integral to the Caribbean experience only begins to be healed when these forgotten connections are once more set in place. Such texts restore an imaginary fullness or plentitude, to set against the broken rubric of our past. They are resources of resistance and identity, with which to confront the fragmented and pathological ways in which that experience has been reconstructed within the dominant regimes of cinematic and visual representation of the West.

There is, however, a second, related but different view of cultural identity. This second position recognises that, as well as the many points of similarity, there are also critical points of deep and significant *difference* which constitute 'what we really are'; or rather – since history has intervened – 'what we have become'. We cannot speak for very long, with any exactness, about 'one experience, one identity', without acknowledging its other side – the ruptures and discontinuities which constitute, precisely, the Caribbean's 'uniqueness'. Cultural identity, in this second sense, is a matter of 'becoming' as well as of 'being'. It belongs to the future as much as to the past. It is not something which already exists, transcending place, time, history and culture. Cultural identities come from somewhere, have histories. But, like everything which is historical, they undergo constant transformation. Far from being eternally fixed in some essentialised past, they are subject to the continuous 'play' of history, culture and power. Far from being grounded in a mere 'recovery' of the past, which is waiting to be found, and which, when found, will secure our sense of ourselves into eternity, identities are the names we give to the different ways we are positioned by, and position ourselves within, the narratives of the past.

It is only from this second position that we can properly understand the traumatic character of 'the colonial experience'. The ways in which black people, black experiences, were positioned and subject-ed in the dominant regimes of representation were the effects of a critical exercise of cultural power and normalisation. Not only, in Said's 'Orientalist' sense, were we constructed as different and other within the categories of knowledge of the West by those regimes. They had the power to make us see and experience *ourselves* as 'Other'. Every regime of representation is a regime of power formed, as Foucault reminds us, by the fatal couplet, 'power/knowledge'. But this kind of knowledge is internal, not external. It is one thing to position a subject or set of peoples as the Other of a dominant discourse. It is quite another thing to subject them to that 'knowledge', not only as a matter of imposed will and domination, by the power of inner compulsion and subjective con-formation to the norm. That is the lesson – the sombre majesty – of Fanon's insight into the colonising experience in *Black Skin, White Masks*.

This inner expropriation of cultural identity cripples and deforms. If its silences are not resisted, they produce, in Fanon's vivid phrase, 'individuals without an anchor, without horizon, colourless, stateless, rootless – a race of angels'.[2] Nevertheless, this idea of otherness as an inner compulsion changes our conception of 'cultural identity'. In this perspective, cultural identity is not a fixed essence at all, lying unchanged outside history and culture. It is not some universal and transcendental spirit inside us on which history has made no fundamental mark. It is not once-and-for-all. It is not a fixed origin to which we can make some final and absolute Return. Of course, it is not a mere phantasm either. It is *something* – not a mere trick of the imagination. It has its histories – and histories have their real, material and symbolic effects. The past continues to speak to us. But it no longer addresses us as a simple, factual 'past', since our relation to it, like the child's relation to the mother, is always-already 'after the break'. It is always constructed through memory, fantasy, narrative and myth. Cultural identities are the points of identification, the unstable points of identification or suture, which are made, within the discourses of history and culture. Not an essence but a *positioning*. Hence, there is always a politics of identity, a politics of position, which has no absolute guarantee in an unproblematic, transcendental 'law of origin'.

This second view of cultural identity is much less familiar, and more unsettling. If identity does not proceed, in a straight, unbroken line, from some fixed origin, how are we to understand its formation? We might think of black Caribbean identities as 'framed' by two axes or vectors, simultaneously operative: the vector of similarity and continuity; and the vector of difference and rupture. Caribbean identities always have to be thought of in terms of the dialogic relationship between these two axes. The one gives us some grounding in, some continuity with, the past. The second reminds us that what we share is precisely the experience of a profound discontinuity: the peoples dragged into slavery, transportation, colonisation, migration, came predominantly from Africa – and when that supply ended, it was temporarily refreshed by indentured labour from the Asian subcontinent. (This neglected fact explains why, when you visit Guyana or Trinidad, you see, symbolically inscribed in the faces of their peoples, the paradoxical 'truth' of Christopher Columbus's mistake: you *can* find 'Asia' by sailing west, if you know where to look!) In the history of the modern world, there are few more traumatic ruptures to match these enforced separations from Africa – already figured, in the European imaginary, as 'the Dark Continent'. But the slaves were also from different countries, tribal communities, villages, languages and gods. African religion, which has been so profoundly formative in Caribbean spiritual life, is precisely *different* from Christian monotheism in believing that God is so powerful that he can only be known through a proliferation of spiritual manifestations, present everywhere in the natural and social world. These gods live on, in an underground existence, in the hybridised religious universe of Haitian voodoo, pocomania, Native pentacostalism, Black baptism, Rastafarianism and the black Saints Latin American Catholicism. The paradox is that it was the uprooting of slavery and transportation and the insertion into the plantation economy (as well as the symbolic economy) of the Western world that 'unified' these peoples across their differences, in the same moment as it cut them off from direct access to their past.

Difference, therefore, persists – in and alongside continuity. To return to the Caribbean after any long absence is to experience again the shock of the 'doubleness' of similarity and difference. Visiting the French Caribbean for the first time, I also saw at once how different Martinique is from, say, Jamaica: and this is no mere difference of topography or climate. It is a profound difference of culture and history. And the difference *matters*. It positions Martiniquains and Jamaicans as *both* the same *and* different. Moreover, the boundaries of difference are continually repositioned in relation to different points of reference. Vis-a-vis the developed West, we are very much 'the same'. We belong to the marginal, the underdeveloped, the periphery, the 'Other'. We are at the outer edge, the 'rim', of the metropolitan world – always 'South' to someone else's *El Norte*.

At the same time, we do not stand in the same relation of the 'otherness' to the metropolitan centres. Each has negotiated its economic, political and cultural dependency differently. And this 'difference', whether we like it or not, is already inscribed in our cultural identities. In turn, it is this negotiation of identity which makes us, vis-a-vis other Latin American people, with a very similar history, different – Caribbeans, *les Antilliennes* ('islanders' to their mainland). And yet, vis-a-vis one another, Jamaican, Haitian, Cuban, Guadeloupean, Barbadian, etc ...

How, then, to describe this play of 'difference' within identity? The common history – transportation, slavery, colonisation – has been profoundly formative. For all these societies, unifying us across our differences. But it does not constitute a common *origin*, since it was, metaphorically as well as literally, a translation. The inscription of difference is also specific and critical. I use the word 'play' because the double meaning of the metaphor is important. It suggests, on the one hand, the instability, the permanent unsettlement, the lack of any final resolution. On the other hand, it reminds us that the place where this 'doubleness' is most powerfully to be heard is 'playing' within the varieties of Caribbean musics. This cultural play could not therefore be represented, cinematically, as a simple, binary opposition – 'past/present', 'them/us'. Its complexity exceeds this binary structure of representation. At different places, times, in relation to different questions, the boundaries are re-sited. They become, not only what they have, at times, certainly been – mutually excluding categories, but also what they sometimes are – differential points along a sliding scale.

One trivial example is the way Martinique both *is* and *is not* 'French'. It is, of course, a *department* of France, and this is reflected in its standard and style of life, Fort de France is a much richer, more 'fashionable' place than Kingston – which is not only visibly poorer, but itself at a point of transition between being 'in fashion' in an Anglo-African and Afro-American way – for those who can afford to be in any sort of fashion at all. Yet, what is distinctively 'Martiniquais' can only be described in terms of that special and peculiar supplement which the black and mulatto skin adds to the 'refinement' and sophistication of a Parisian-derived *haute couture:* that is, a sophistication which, because it is black, is always transgressive.

To capture this sense of difference which is not pure 'otherness', we need to deploy the play on words of a theorist like Jacques Derrida. Derrida uses the anomalous 'a' in his way of writing 'difference' – *differance* – as a marker which sets up a disturbance in our settled understanding or translation of the word/concept. It sets the word in motion to new meanings without erasing the *trace* of its other meanings. His sense of *differance*, as Christopher Norris puts it, thus

> remains suspended between the two French verbs 'to differ' and 'to defer' (postpone), both of which contribute to its textual force but neither of which can fully capture its meaning. Language depends on difference, as Saussure showed ... the structure of distinctive propositions which make up its basic economy. Where Derrida breaks new ground ... is in the extent to which 'differ' shades into 'defer' ... the idea that meaning is always deferred, perhaps to this point of an endless supplementarity, by the play of signification.[3]

This second sense of difference challenges the fixed binaries which stablise meaning and representation and show how meaning is never finished or completed, but keeps on moving to encompass other, additional or supplementary meanings, which, as Norris puts it elsewhere,[4] 'disturb the classical economy of language and representation'.

Without relations of difference, no representation could occur. But what is then constituted within representation is always open to being deferred, staggered, serialised.

Where, then, does identity come in to this infinite postponement of meaning? Derrida does not help us as much as he might here, though the notion of the 'trace' goes some way towards it. This is where it sometimes seems as if Derrida has permitted his profound theoretical insights to be reappropriated by his disciples into a celebration of formal 'playfulness', which evacuates them of their political meaning. For if signification depends upon the endless repositioning of its differential terms, meaning, in any specific instance, depends on the contingent and arbitrary stop – the necessary and temporary 'break' in the infinite semiosis of language. This does not detract from the original insight. It only threatens to do so if we mistake this 'cut' of identity – this *positioning*, which makes meaning possible – as a natural and permanent, rather than an arbitrary and contingent 'ending' – whereas I understand every such position as 'strategic' and arbitrary, in the sense that there is no permanent equivalence between the particular sentence we close, and its true meaning, as such. Meaning continues to unfold, so to speak, beyond the arbitrary closure which makes it, at any moment, possible. It is always either over- or under-determined, either an excess or a supplement. There is always something 'left over'.

It is possible, with this conception of 'difference', to rethink the positionings and repositionings of Caribbean cultural identities in relation to at least three 'presences', to borrow Aimee Cesaire's and Leopold Senghor's metaphor: *Presence Africaine, Presence Europeenne,* and the third, most ambiguous, presence of all – the sliding term, *Presence Americain.* Of course, I am collapsing, for the moment, the many other cultural 'presences' which constitute the complexity of Caribbean identity (Indian, Chinese, Lebanese etc). I mean America, here, not in its 'first-world' sense – the big cousin to the North whose 'rim' we occupy, but in the second, broader sense: America, the 'New World', *Terra Incognita.*

Presence Africaine is the site of the repressed. Apparently silenced beyond memory by the power of the experience of slavery, Africa was, in fact present everywhere: in the everyday life and customs of the slave quarters, in the languages and patois of the plantations, in names and words, often disconnected from their taxonomies, in the secret syntactical structures through which other languages were spoken, in the stories and tales told to children, in religious practices and beliefs, in the spiritual life, the arts, crafts, musics and rhythms of slave and post-emancipation society. Africa, the signified which could not be represented directly in slavery, remained and remains the unspoken, unspeakable 'presence' in Caribbean culture. It is 'hiding' behind every verbal inflection, every narrative twist of Caribbean cultural life. It is the secret code with which every Western text was 're-read'. It is the ground-bass of every rhythm and bodily movement. *This* was – is – the 'Africa' that 'is alive and well in the diaspora'.[5]

When I was growing up in the 1940s and 1950s as a child in Kingston, I was surrounded by the signs, music and rhythms of this Africa of the diaspora, which only existed as a result of a long and discontinuous series of transformations. But, although almost everyone around me was some shade of brown or black (Africa 'speaks'!), I never once heard a single person refer to themselves or to others as, in some way, or as having been at some time in the past, 'African'. It was only in the 1970s that this Afro-Caribbean identity became historically available to the great majority of Jamaican people, at home and abroad. In this historic moment, Jamaicans discovered themselves to be 'black' – just as, in the same moment, they discovered themselves to be the sons and daughters of 'slavery'.

This profound cultural discovery, however, was not, and could not be, made directly, without 'mediation'. It could only be made *through* the impact on popular life of the post-colonial revolution, the civil rights struggles, the culture of Rastafarianism and the music of reggae – the metaphors, the figures or signifiers of a new construction of 'Jamaican-ness'. These signified a 'new' Africa of the New World, grounded in an 'old' Africa: – a spiritual journey of discovery that led, in the Caribbean, to an indigenous cultural revolution; this is Africa, as we might say, necessarily 'deferred' – as a spiritual, cultural and political metaphor.

It is the presence/absence of Africa, in this form, which has made it the privileged signifier of new conceptions of Caribbean identity. Everyone in the Caribbean, of whatever ethnic background, must sooner or later come to terms with this African presence. Black, brown, mulatto, white – all must look *Presence Africaine* in the face, speak its name. But whether it is, in this sense, an *origin* of our identities, unchanged by four hundred years of displacement, dismemberment, transportation, to which we could in any final or literal sense return, is more open to doubt. The original 'Africa' is no longer there. It too has been transformed. History is, in that sense, irreversible. We must not collude with the West which, precisely, normalises and appropriates Africa by freezing it into some timeless zone of the primitive, unchanging past. Africa must at last be reckoned with by Caribbean people, but it cannot in any simple sense be merely recovered.

It belongs irrevocably, for us, to what Edward Said once called an 'imaginative geography and history',[6] which helps 'the mind to intensify its own sense of itself by dramatising the difference between what is close to it and what is far away'. It 'has acquired an imaginative or figurative value we can name and feel'.[7] Our belongingness to it constitutes what Benedict Anderson calls 'an imagined community'.[8] To *this* 'Africa', which is a necessary part of the Caribbean imaginary, we can't literally go home again.

The character of this displaced 'homeward' journey – its length and complexity – comes across vividly, in a variety of texts. Tony Sewell's documentary archival photographs, Garvey's Children: the Legacy of Marcus Garvey, tells the story of a 'return' to an African identity which went, necessarily, by the long route – through London and the United States. It 'ends', not in Ethiopia but with Garvey's statue in front of the St Ann Parish Library in Jamaica: not with a traditional tribal chant but with the music of Burning Spear and Bob Marley's Redemption Song. This is our long journey home. Derek Bishton's courageous visual and written text, *Black Heart Man* – the story of the journey of a *white* photographer 'on the trail of the promised land' – starts in England, and goes, through Shashemene, the place in Ethiopia to which many Jamaican people have found their way on their search for the Promised Land, and slavery; but it ends in Pinnacle, Jamaica, where the first Rastafarian settlement was established, and 'beyond' – among the dispossessed of 20th-century Kingston and the streets of Handsworth, where Bishton's voyage of discovery first began. These symbolic journies are necessary for us all – and necessarily circular. This is the Africa we must return to – but 'by another route': what Africa has *become* in the New World, what we have made of 'Africa': 'Africa' – as we re-tell it through politics, memory and desire.

What of the second, troubling, term in the identity equation – the European presence? For many of us, this is a matter not of too little but of too much. Where Africa was a case of the unspoken, Europe was a case of that which is endlessly speaking – and endlessly speaking *us*. The European presence interrupts the innocence of the whole discourse of 'difference' in the Caribbean by introducing the question of power. 'Europe' belongs irrevocably to the play of power, to the lines of force and consent, to the role of the *dominant*, in Caribbean culture. In terms of colonialism, underdevelopment, poverty and the racism of colour, the European presence is that which, in visual representation, has positioned the black subject within its dominant regimes of representation: the colonial discourse, the literatures of adventure and exploration, the romance of the exotic, the ethnographic and travelling eye, the tropical languages of tourism, travel brochure and Hollywood and the violent, pornographic languages of *ganja* and urban violence.

Because *Presence Europeenne* is about exclusion, imposition and expropriation, we are often tempted to locate that power as wholly external to us – an extrinsic force, whose influence can be thrown off like the serpent sheds its skin. What Frantz Fanon reminds us, in *Black Skin, White Masks*, is how this power has become a constitutive element in our own identities.

> The movements, the attitudes, the glances of the other fixed me there, in the sense in which a chemical solution is fixed by a dye. I was indignant; I demanded an explanation. Nothing happened. I burst apart. Now the fragments have been put together again by another self.[9]

This 'look', from – so to speak – the place of the Other, fixes us, not only in its violence, hostility and aggression, but in the ambivalence of its desire. This brings us face to face, not simply with the dominating European presence as the site or 'scene' of integration where those other presences which it had actively disaggregated were recomposed – re-framed, put together in a new way; but as the site of a profound splitting and doubling – what Homi Bhaba has called 'the ambivalent identifications of the racist world ... the 'otherness' of the self inscribed in the perverse palimpsest of colonial identity.'[10]

The dialogue of power and resistance, of refusal and recognition, with and against *Presence Europeenne* is almost as complex as the 'dialogue' with Africa. In terms of popular cultural life, it is nowhere to be found in its pure, pristine state. It is always-already fused, syncretised, with other cultural elements. It is always-already creolised – not lost beyond the Middle Passage, but ever-present: from the harmonics in our musics to the ground-bass of Africa, traversing and intersecting our lives at every point. How can we stage this dialogue so that, finally, we can place it, without terror or violence, rather than being forever placed by it? Can we ever recognise its irreversible influence, whilst resisting its imperialising eye? The enigma is impossible, so far, to resolve. It requires the most complex of cultural strategies. Think, for example, of the dialogue of every Caribbean filmmaker or writer, one way or another, with the dominant cinemas and literature of the West – the complex relationship of young black British filmmakers with the 'avant-gardes' of European and American filmmaking. Who could describe this tense and tortured dialogue as a one way trip?

The Third, 'New World' presence, is not so much power, as ground, place, territory. It is the juncture-point where the many cultural tributaries meet, the 'empty' land (the European colonisers emptied it) where strangers from every other part of the globe collided. None of the people who now occupy the islands – black, brown, white, African, European, American, Spanish, French, East Indian, Chinese, Portuguese, Jew, Dutch – originally 'belonged' there. It is the space where the creolisations and assimilations and syncretisms were negotiated. The New World is the third term – the primal scene – where the fateful/fatal encounter was staged between Africa and the West. It also has to be understood as the place of many, continuous displacements: of the original pre-Columbian inhabitants, the Arawaks, Caribs and Amerindians, permanently displaced from their homelands and decimated; of other peoples displaced in different ways from Africa, Asia and Europe; the displacements of slavery, colonisation and conquest. It stands for the endless ways in which Caribbean people have been destined to 'migrate'; it is the signifier of migration itself – of travelling, voyaging and return as fate, as destiny; of the Antillean as the prototype of the modern or postmodern New World nomad, continually moving between centre and periphery. This preoccupation with movement and migration Caribbean cinema shares with many other 'Third Cinemas', but it is one of our defining themes, and it is destined to cross the narrative of every film script or cinematic image.

Presence Americaine continues to have its silences, its suppressions. Peter Hulme, in his essay on 'Islands of Enchantment'[11] reminds us that the word 'Jamaica' is the Hispanic form of the indigenous Arawak name – 'land of wood and water' – which Columbus's re-naming ('Santiago') never replaced. The Arawak presence remains today a ghostly one, visible in the islands mainly in museums and archeological sites, part of the barely knowable or usable 'past'. Hulme notes that it is not represented in the emblem of the Jamaican National Heritage Trust, for example, which chose instead the figure of Diego Pimienta, 'an African who fought for his Spanish masters against the English invasion of the island in 1655' – a deferred, metonymic, sly and sliding representation of Jamaican identity if ever there was one! He recounts the story of how Prime Minister Edward Seaga tried to alter the Jamaican coat-of-arms, which consists of two Arawak figures holding a shield with five pineapples, surmounted by an alligator. 'Can the crushed and extinct Arawaks represent the dauntless character of Jamaicans? Does the low-slung, near extinct crocodile, a cold-blooded reptile, symbolise the warm, soaring spirit of Jamaicans?' Prime Minister Seaga asked rhetorically.[12] There can be few political statements which so eloquently testify to the complexities entailed in the process of trying to represent a diverse people with a diverse history through a single, hegemonic 'identity'. Fortunately, Mr Seaga's invitation to the Jamaican people, who are overwhelmingly of African descent, to start their 'remembering' by first 'forgetting' something else, got the comeuppance it so richly deserved.

The 'New World' presence – America, *Terra Incognita* – is therefore itself the beginning of diaspora, of diversity, of hybridity and difference, what makes Afro-Caribbean people already people of a diaspora. I use this term here metaphorically, not literally: diaspora does not refer us to those scattered tribes whose identity can only be secured in relation to some sacred homeland to which they must at all costs return, even if it means pushing other people into the sea. This is the old, the imperialising, the hegemonising, form of 'ethnicity'. We have seen the fate of the people of Palestine at the hands of this backward-looking conception of diaspora – and the complicity of the West with it. The diaspora experience as I intend it here is defined, not by essence or purity, but by the recognition of a necessary heterogeneity and diversity; by a conception of 'identity' which lives with and through, not despite, difference; by *hybridity*. Diaspora identities are those which are constantly producing and reproducing themselves anew, through transformation and difference. One can only think here of what is uniquely – 'essentially' – Caribbean: precisely the mixes of colour, pigmentation, physiognomic type; the 'blends' of tastes that is Caribbean cuisine; the aesthetics of the 'cross-overs', of 'cut-and-mix', to borrow Dick Hebdige's telling phrase, which is the heart and soul of black music. Young black cultural practitioners and critics in Britain are increasingly coming to acknowledge and explore in their work this 'diaspora aesthetic' and its formations in the post-colonial experience:

Across a whole range of cultural forms there is a 'syncretic' dynamic which critically appro-priates elements from the master-codes of the dominant culture and 'creolises' them, disarticulating given signs and re-articulating their symbolic meaning. The subversive force of this hybridising tendency is most apparent at the level of language itself where Creoles, patois and black English decentre, destabilise and carnivalise the linguistic domination of 'English' – the nation-language of master-discourse – through strategic inflections, re-accentuations and other performative moves in semantic, syntactic and lexical codes.[13]

It is because this New World is constituted for us as place, a narrative of displacement, that it gives rise so profoundly to a certain imaginary plenitude, recreating the endless desire to return to 'lost origins', to be one again with the mother, to go back to the begin-ning. Who can ever forget, when once seen rising up out of that blue-green Caribbean, those islands of enchantment. Who has not known, at this moment, the surge of an overwhelming nostalgia for lost origins, for 'times past? And yet, this 'return to the beginning' is like the imaginary in Lacan – it can neither be fulfilled nor requited, and hence is the beginning of the symbolic, of representation, the infinitely renewable source of desire, memory, myth, search, discovery – in short, the reservoir of our cinematic narratives.

We have been trying, in a series of metaphors, to put in play a different sense of our relationship to the past, and thus a different way of thinking about cultural identity, which might constitute new points of recognition in the discourses of the emerging Caribbean cinema and black British cinemas. We have been trying to theorise identity as constituted, not outside but within representation; and hence of cinema, not as a second-order mirror held up to reflect what already exists, but as that form of represen-tation which is able to constitute us as new kinds of subjects, and thereby enable us to discover places from which to speak. Communities, Benedict Anderson argues in *Imagined Communities* are to be distinguished, not by their falsity/genuineness, but by the style in which they are imagined.[14] This is the vocation of modern black cinemas: by allowing us to see and recognise the different parts and histories of ourselves, to construct those points of identification, those positionalities we call in retrospect our 'cultural identities'.

> We must not therefore be content with delving into the past of a people in order to find coherent elements which will counteract colonialism's attempts to falsify and harm … A national culture is not a folk-lore, nor an abstract populism that believes it can discover a people's true nature. A national culture is the whole body of efforts made by a people in the sphere of thought to describe, justify and praise the action through which that people has created itself and keeps itself in existence.[15]

Notes

1   Frantz Fanon, 'On National Culture', in *The Wretched of the Earth*, London 1963, p170.
2   *Ibid.*, p176.
3   Christopher Norris, *Deconstruction: Theory and Practice*, London 1982, p32.
4   Christopher Norris, *Jacques Derrida*, London 1987, p15.
5   Stuart Hall, *Resistance Through Rituals*, London 1976.
6   Edward Said, *Orientalism*, London 1985, p55.
7   *Ibid.*

8   Benedict Anderson, *Imagined Communities: Reflections on the Origin and Rise of Nationalism*, London 1982.

9   Frantz Fanon, *Black Skin, White Masks*, London 1986, p109.

10 Homi Bhabha, 'Foreword' to Fanon, *ibid.*, xv.

11 In *New Formations*, no.3, Winter 1987.

12 *Jamaica Hansard*, vol.9, 1983–4, p363. Quoted in Hulme, *ibid*.

13 Kobena Mercer, 'Diaspora Culture and the Dialogic Imagination', in M. Cham and C. Watkins (eds), *Blackframes: Critical Perspectives on Black Independent Cinema*, 1988, p57.

14 Anderson, *op.cit.*, p15.

15 Fanon, *op.cit.*, 1963, p188.

CHAPTER 9

Translation, Empiricism, Ethics

Lawrence Venuti

Lawrence Venuti, Professor of English at Temple University, works in early modern literature, Anglophone and foreign-language poetic traditions, translation theory and history, and literary translation. He is the author of *Our Halcyon Dayes: English Prerevolutionary Texts and Postmodern Culture* (1989); *The Translator's Invisibility: A History of Translation* (1995, 2008); *The Scandals of Translation: Towards an Ethics of Difference* (1998); and *Translation Changes Everything: Theory and Practice* (2013). He is the editor of the anthology of essays *Rethinking Translation: Discourse, Subjectivity, Ideology* (1992) and of *The Translation Studies Reader* (2000, 2004, 2012), a survey of translation theory from antiquity to the present.

My case study is drawn from the work of a contemporary translator, Arthur Goldhammer, who is currently a senior affiliate of the Center for European Studies at Harvard University. During the past thirty years, Goldhammer has written English versions of over a hundred French texts in art history, literary theory and history, and philosophy and history of science. By far the bulk of his work falls in the field of social history, monographs and edited volumes by such historians as Philippe Ariès, Georges Duby, Emmanuel Le Roy Ladurie, Jacques Le Goff, and Pierre Nora. It would be no exaggeration to say that countless readers are greatly in Goldhammer's debt.

This remark, however, is an honorific cliché when said of any translator's work, and it sheds no light on what is at stake in translating. We might rather ask, In what does a reader's debt to a translator consist, a debt that clearly exceeds any translation fee (which is paid, in any case, by a publisher)? Can the debt to Goldhammer be reduced to his making intelligible to Anglophones over a hundred French texts? Is it possible to think of translation as a gift that does not incur a debt or participate in a contract, whether with a publisher or a reader? In what would the translator's gift consist and how can it be appreciated beyond debt or contract, whether to the foreign text or culture or to the receiving culture? Can answers to these questions lead to thinking

Original publication details: Lawrence Venuti, "Translation, Empiricism, Ethics." *Profession* (2010), pp. 72–81. Modern Language Association of America. Reproduced with permission from the Modern Language Association of America.

Literary Theory: An Anthology, Third Edition. Edited by Julie Rivkin and Michael Ryan.
© 2017 John Wiley & Sons, Ltd. Published 2017 by John Wiley & Sons, Ltd.

about translation that removes, diminishes, or perhaps redefines the neglect and misunderstanding that it continues to suffer today?

These questions consider translation vis-à-vis Jacques Derrida's exploration of the paradoxes involved in gift giving. Goldhammer, like most professional translators, is likely to see such speculation as irrelevant. "Translation is hard enough," he has said, "without hamstringing yourself with theoretical *partis pris*" (*How to Do Things*). In lectures where he has set out his own understanding of his approach, his gambit is to analyze verbal choices from various translations. "Together," he tells his audience, "we can walk through some of the questions distilled from daily practice" (*Translating*). The examples he gathers – all instances of outright error or failures to transfer the precise nuance of a word or phrase – point to one overriding question, namely, whether the translation reproduces the style of a literary text or the meaning of a scholarly text. A telling metaphor reveals the concepts underlying Goldhammer's approach. Translation, he asserts, is "like fielding a ground ball: it's almost impossible to explain in words how you do it, and anyone who tried to follow such a description would look pretty foolish on the ballfield. But any spectator can see when the job is being done well" (*Translating*).

This metaphor does assume a theory, the epistemology known as empiricism. According to Antony Easthope's succinct but dissenting account (88–89), empiricism might be said to consist of three key assumptions:

> A real object or process is not constructed for knowledge but given, autonomous from the knowing subject, and on observation that object or process yields a knowledge that is free of illusion and prejudice.
> The linguistic and cultural forms by which reality is known are transparent and do not materially affect the subject's observation or knowledge.
> The subject too is not constructed but autonomous from any process of construction, always free to know, so that knowledge derives from the correspondence between subject and object.

In line with these assumptions, Goldhammer asserts that a good translation can be instantly perceived as such by any reader, and this union of knowing subject and object of knowledge is unmediated by the subject's cultural formation, so that the nature and value of the translation need no description, explanation, or justification, which in any case are "almost impossible" to provide and in the end "pretty foolish."

Insofar as empiricism is characteristic of British and American cultural traditions, emerging with such thinkers as Francis Bacon, Thomas Hobbes, and John Locke and evident, as Easthope shows, not only in philosophical speculation but also in history, poetry, and literary journalism, it produces a distinctively anglocentric image of translation – commonsensical, pragmatic, ultimately anti-intellectual. Under scrutiny, its limitations become apparent. If it is valid, one must wonder why academics, publishers, and readers have not recognized translation as a valuable cultural practice by rewarding it at tenure-and-promotion considerations, issuing a steady stream of translated texts, and reading them with an informed appreciation of their status as second-order creations, as translations. One must wonder why as a rule academics fail to remark on the translations that they use in their research and teaching, going so far as to quote and comment on the translation as if it were the source text. Goldhammer is an extremely accomplished translator, but he cannot present an account of his work that illuminates it for his colleagues, his publishers, or his readers, and so he is powerless to remedy the continuing marginality of translation or to improve its effectiveness as an essential practice in cross-cultural exchange.

Empiricism is a central problem here because it gives rise to a concept of language as direct expression or reference, leading to an instrumental model of translation as the reproduction or transfer of an invariant contained in or caused by the source text, whether its form, its meaning, or its effect. In *An Essay concerning Human Understanding* (1689), Locke assumed the instrumental model in describing translation as "chang[ing] two words of the same signification one for the other" (3.4.9), where the "same signification" refers to a semantic invariant. Instrumentalism continues to guide a great deal of translation practice and research as well as translator training. It is the dominant understanding of translation everywhere today, even among scholars who look at their work as far removed from empiricism because deliberately or explicitly grounded in other theoretical discourses.

To advance the understanding of translation, we must replace instrumentalism by thinking that is hermeneutic. On the materialist assumption that language is creation thickly mediated by linguistic and cultural determinants, a hermeneutic model treats translation as an interpretation of the source text whose form, meaning, and effect are seen as variable, subject to inevitable transformation during the translating process. This is to suggest not that no formal or semantic correspondence exists between the source and translated texts but that any such correspondence results from an interpretive labor that is decisively determined by the translating language and culture. Translating never gives back the source text unaltered. It can only inscribe an interpretation, one among many possibilities, through lexical and syntactic choices that can alter source-textual features like meter and tone, point of view and characterization, narrative and genre, terminology and argument.

The translator inscribes an interpretation by applying a third category, which mediates between the source language and culture, on the one hand, and the receiving language and culture, on the other, a method of transforming the source text into the translation. This third category I call an interpretant, deriving it from Charles Peirce's semiotics. Peirce makes clear that the interpretant constitutes a "mediating representation" between a "sign" or signifier and its "object," where the object is itself a representation, a content or signified (53–54; cf. Eco, *Theory* 69). In Peirce's theory, as Umberto Eco observes, "a sign can *stand for* something else to somebody only because this 'standing-for' relation is mediated by an interpretant" (15). As examples of interpretants, Eco lists a dictionary definition, an encyclopedia entry, a visual image, and a translation into other language, showing that the interpretant functions as a means of performing a semantic analysis: it is a code or theme that invests the sign with a certain intelligibility by transforming it into another chain of signifiers ("Peirce's Notion" 1469; see also Eco, *Theory* 70–71). Eco's discussion becomes somewhat misleading when he lists a translation as an interpretant, insofar as every translation, as I am arguing, requires the application of an interpretant as an essential condition of its existence. With this qualification we can see that interpretants too can precipitate an endless chain of interpretants, codes used to analyze the interpretants in processes like translation.

Peirce himself suggestively compares the notion of an interpretant to translation. He remarks that he relies on this notion "because it fulfills the office of an interpreter, who says that a foreigner says the same thing which he himself says" (53–54). Note that here the interpreter does not merely interpret or orally translate a foreigner's speech but "says" in some unspecified way that his interpretation has met the formal requirement of adequacy or equivalence. An interpretant, it would seem, might be not only thematic in relating a signifier to a signified but formal in indicating the structural nature of the relation.

In translation, the interpretant is a principle of mediation and transformation that is both formal and thematic. Formal interpretants include a concept of equivalence, such as a semantic correspondence based on current dictionary definitions, or a concept of style, a distinctive lexicon and syntax related to a genre. Thematic interpretants are codes: they may be specific values, beliefs, and representations; a discourse in the sense of a relatively coherent body of concepts, problems, and arguments; or a particular interpretation of the source text that has been articulated independently in commentary. Interpretants are fundamentally intertextual and interdiscursive, rooted primarily in the receiving situation even if they incorporate source-cultural materials to some extent. The translator's application of interpretants recontextualizes the source text, replacing intertextual and interdiscursive relations in the source language and culture with relations in the translating language and culture that are built into the translation.

To explore the usefulness of the hermeneutic model, I consider Goldhammer's 1992 translation *The Village of Cannibals*. The French text is the historian Alain Corbin's account of the social and political motives behind an incident of rural violence in nineteenth-century France: a nobleman in the Dordogne was tortured and burned to death by a crowd of peasants. Goldhammer, while making adjustments that conform to the structural features and linguistic norms of English, generally maintained a semantic correspondence according to current French-English dictionaries in a transparent style characteristic of British and American academic history. In fact, his choices recast Corbin's writing in a recognizably academic form. Thus Goldhammer used such formulaic words and phrases as "flourished," "played a crucial role," and "the crux of the matter," all of which are free renderings that deviate from the French text. The word "flourished," employed in the sentence "This myth flourished through much of the nineteenth century," renders "se révélera d'une grande solidité" (in a closer version, "will exhibit great stability"), while the phrase "played a crucial role" renders "constitue un élément décisif" ("constitutes a decisive element") (*Village of Cannibals* 3; *Village des cannibales* 11). Similarly, "the crux of the matter" was used to translate the French word "l'essentiel," which can be Englished as "the essential [thing]" or "the essential [point]" without adopting an academic formula (7, 12; 16, 22). These departures point to Goldhammer's application of a specific formal interpretant in his translation: the stylistic conventions of academic historical writing in anglophone cultures.

Similar conventions underlie Goldhammer's handling of Corbin's frequent use of the term *l'imaginaire*, although here a thematic interpretant can also be perceived: the philosophical code of empiricism. *L'imaginaire* can be closely rendered into English as "the imaginary," but Goldhammer consistently replaced it with such words as "image," "imagination," "imagery," "fancy," even "propaganda" (see *Village des cannibales* 12, 13, 33, 37, 124, 134, 141, 150; *Village of Cannibals* 4, 5, 20, 55, 89, 97, 102, 109). Thus Corbin's assertion that "Il faut le massacre pour que se réalise pleinement la métamorphose ou, plutôt, pour que s'opère la totale incarnation des figures hostiles imposées par l'imaginaire" (66) might be given a close rendering as follows:

The slaughter was necessary for the metamorphosis to be fully achieved or, better, for the total incarnation of the hostile figures imposed by the imaginary to take place.

Goldhammer, however, translated freely:

> It took a murder to bring about the full metamorphosis of the "Prussian" from figure of the imagination to incarnation of evil. (46)

In replacing *l'imaginaire* with "the imagination" and related words, Goldhammer's translation draws the sharp distinctions between fact and fiction, truth and falsehood, reality and appearance on which empiricist epistemologies are based.

Yet Corbin's use of the term *l'imaginaire* can be interpreted very differently, according to a materialist genealogy. This genealogy would stretch back at least to Jacques Lacan's 1949 essay "The Mirror Stage As Formative of the Function of the I," where the first moment in the formation of human identity is called the "imaginary phase" but is nonetheless real, "an ontological structure of the human world" that establishes the basis for the subsequent construction of subjectivity through interpersonal relationships and in language (2). During the 1960s, this psychoanalytic concept was given a social application, when Louis Althusser relied on Lacan to rethink the Marxist concept of ideology, not as political ideas or false consciousness but as a representation embodied in social practices, at once imaginary and lived, active in forming class identities and in mystifying real social relations ("Ideology" and "Marxism"). At roughly the same time, the political theorist Cornelius Castoriadis formulated the imaginary as a concept of social analysis that bears even more directly on Corbin's use of the term. The "social imaginary," according to Castoriadis, "is not an image *of*. It is the unceasing and essentially *undetermined* (social-historical and psychical) creation of figures / forms / images, on the basis of which alone there can ever be a question *of* something" (3). In Castoriadis's thinking, the materialism assigned to the concept by Lacan and Althusser comes to the fore such that the imaginary not only is indistinguishable from but also creates reality. Corbin's argument that the murdered nobleman came to embody the peasants' social imaginary might thus be seen as giving the concept the same ontological status that it has in Castoriadis's work.

Philippe Carrard has criticized Goldhammer's translation for its departures from Corbin's French text, particularly in "simplifying his theoretical apparatus" (81). The matter is more complicated, because Goldhammer's translation cannot be judged simply as inaccurate or incorrect. He has offered an interpretation that is neither incompetent nor arbitrary by applying a distinctive set of formal and thematic interpretants. His interpretation included the idea that, as he put it in an interview, Corbin is not "a particularly theoretically self-conscious historian" but rather one who takes "a more literary, intuitive approach." Corbin himself examined Goldhammer's translation in unusual detail, sending the translator five pages of handwritten notes. Goldhammer explained that "nearly all the comments had to do with the 'weight' and 'coloration' of specific word choices. [Corbin] didn't raise any issues of theoretical interpretation / misinterpretation" (Message).

Accustomed as we are to disallowing authorial intent as a reliable standard of interpretation, we might well be suspicious of Corbin's assessment of the translation. Yet the fact remains that whether Corbin deploys the concept of *l'imaginaire* with rigorous consistency can be questioned, primarily because the historical incident he addresses raises the issue of delusion. It involved a false attribution to the victim: the crowd of peasants accused the nobleman of shouting "Vive la République!" and of being a Prussian, although at the murderers' trial neither accusation was found to be true. Corbin argues that the nobleman was transformed into a scapegoat by the peasants' social imaginary, a contradictory ensemble of antiaristocratic, antirepublican, and proimperial sentiments, but he occasionally uses the term *fantasmes* ("fantasies") to describe the gap between their collective anxieties and the identity and actions of their victim (e.g., see Corbin, *Village des cannibales* 119, 120). Goldhammer has in effect chosen to emphasize Corbin's use of terms like *fantasmes* instead of assigning a specifically French conceptual density or intertextual relation to his use of *l'imaginaire*. In setting up this choice as the equivalent of the French text, the translator has performed the "abstraction" that Althusser saw in empiricist truth claims, a procedure in which essential data are separated from the inessential on the basis of a privileged epistemology and in which a real object is reduced to a partial object of knowledge (Althusser and Balibar 34–43).

Goldhammer's translation thus reflects a deep investment in empiricist discourse. On the one hand, the assumption that language is transparent communication led Goldhammer to reject any jargon that too noticeably departed from current Standard English, the most familiar form of the language and therefore the most seemingly transparent. On the other hand, the assumption that historical writing discovers an objective truth based on facts led him to avoid theoretical concepts that posited the difficulty, if not impossibility, of distinguishing between textuality and reality and that thereby put into question the historian's objectivity. He inscribed the French text with the empiricism that continues to dominate British and American academic history and informs his own instrumental theory of translation.

How, then, should Goldhammer's translation be evaluated? The instrumental model is of no help here. The invariant that it assumes is contained in or caused by the source text – its form, meaning, or effect – becomes the sole criterion of accuracy and therefore fundamentally determines the value of the translation. Yet Corbin's text, particularly his use of the term *l'imaginaire*, can support at least two conflicting interpretations inscribed by two different translations. The hermeneutic model offers a more incisive and comprehensive account, because it treats any formal and semantic correspondence as partial and contingent: partial, because it is incomplete in re-creating the source text and slanted toward the receiving language and culture; contingent, because it is fixed by one among other possible interpretations, each of which establishes a criterion of accuracy that varies among receiving cultural constituencies, social situations, and historical moments.

Because translating always submits the source text to a transformation, a translation cannot be evaluated merely through a comparison to that text without taking into account the cultural and social conditions of the translator's interpretation. The evaluation must be shifted to a different level, a level that seems to me properly ethical: in inscribing an interpretation in the source text, a translation can stake out an ethical position and thereby perform an ideological function in relation to competing interpretations. Here I draw on Alain Badiou's thinking, specifically his concept of an ethics that challenges institutionalized knowledges and communitarian interests and pursues cultural innovation and social equality. Badiou's ethics raises a number of questions, not the least of which is his antipathy toward the communitarian, as if every social grouping were exclusionary or repressive, enforcing conformity and domination (73–74). I want precisely to worry this point in his thinking, treating as unethical not knowledge that serves any communitarian interest whatsoever but only knowledge affiliated with a group that has achieved such dominance in an institution as to exclude or marginalize the competing knowledge of other groups. A translation in the human sciences, then, might be evaluated according to its impact, potential or real, on academic disciplines in the translating culture; according to whether it challenges the styles, genres, and discourses that have gained disciplinary authority; according to whether it stimulates innovative thinking, research, and writing and alters the course of the institution.

I would therefore question translators who conceive of their role as the importation of foreign thinking without affecting the smooth operation of the academic institutions where that thinking is to be received. Goldhammer has advocated such a role, arguing that "scholarly prose is written for consumption primarily by a scholarly community, and the translator must respect the linguistic norms of the target community" (*Translating*). But Goldhammer has done much more: he has assimilated Corbin's French text to the styles and discourses that are invested with the greatest authority among British and American academic historians. His translation professes a greater sense of responsibility toward this audience than toward Corbin's project or French historical discourses. This is the crucial sense in which anglophone academic historians are in Goldhammer's debt.

The mostly positive reviews that greeted the translation, reviews that favorably received Corbin's work and only rarely mentioned Goldhammer's, demonstrate that the translation was successful according to the empiricist terms that the translator shared with his main academic audience. In a typical review that appeared in the *Times Literary Supplement*, Robert Tombs, a specialist in French history at Cambridge University, praised Corbin's text as providing a "startling picture of some of the grim realities of rural life, narrated simply and sensitively, and translated plainly, so that the horrors of the act of retribution still emerge starkly amid the theoretical exegesis." Tombs's investment in empiricist history is evident in his preference for a "simple" narration that is not complicated by "theoretical exegesis." To call Goldhammer's translation "plain" also fits this bill, given its seeming transparency, but Tombs seems entirely unaware of the strongly assimilative nature of the English version, which reduces the term "plain" to a naive understatement.

Let us rather imagine a translator who assumes an oppositional stance in his or her work, a translator who is an intellectual in Edward Said's sense, "skeptical, engaged, unremittingly devoted to rational investigation and moral judgment" (20), refusing any complacency or quiescence in relation to authoritative cultural and social institutions like the academy and the publishing industry – even when the translator is employed by them. This translator will be constantly alert to the differences that comprise foreign languages, texts, and cultures, constantly engaged in signaling those differences to constituencies and institutions in the receiving situation, and constantly inventive in finding the linguistic and cultural means to make a productive difference in that situation. Such a translator gives us the basis of a relentless interrogation of the academic status quo. The resulting translation is not given or recognized as a gift, whether to the foreign text and culture or to the receiving situation, and it is not written with the expectation of a reward, insofar as it aims at a radical questioning of the rewarding institution, of the hierarchy of values, beliefs, and representations housed in that institution. This translation – need I say? – is not likely to be received with gratitude, which it does not seek, but it may construct a new intellectual community that did not previously exist and that, when the translation has done its interrogative work, will set it aside, its work done, its critical moment past. Is this translation with a hammer, initiating a transvaluation that establishes a new critical orthodoxy? Or is this translation that is self-consuming, that sacrifices itself in its very reception, eventually superseded? Can it be both, so that we remain trapped in yet another cliché, although now revised, the notion that translation is a thankless task?

Works Cited

Althusser, Louis. "Ideology and Ideological State Apparatuses." *"Lenin and Philosophy" and Other Essays*. Trans. Ben Brewster. London: Monthly Rev., 1970. 127–86. Print.

Althusser, Louis. "Marxism and Humanism." *For Marx*. Trans. Ben Brewster. London: New Left, 1977. 219–47. Print.

Althusser, Louis, and Étienne Balibar. *Reading Capital*. Trans. Ben Brewster. London: New Left, 1970. Print.

Badiou, Alain. *Ethics: An Essay on the Understanding of Evil*. Trans. Peter Hallward. London: Verso, 2001. Print.

Carrard, Philippe. "Taming the New History: Alain Corbin and the Politics of Translation." *History of the Human Sciences* 6 (1993): 79–90. Print.

Castoriadis, Cornelius. *The Imaginary Institution of Society*. Trans. Kathleen Blamey. Cambridge: MIT P, 1998. Print.

Corbin, Alain. *Le village des cannibales*. Paris: Aubier, 1990. Print.

Corbin, Alain. *The Village of Cannibals: Rage and Murder in France, 1870*. Trans. Arthur Goldhammer. Cambridge: Harvard UP, 1992. Print.

Derrida, Jacques. *Given Time: 1: Counterfeit Money*. Trans. Peggy Kamuf. Chicago: U of Chicago P, 1972. Print.

Easthope, Antony. *Englishness and National Culture*. London: Routledge, 1999. Print.

Eco, Umberto. "Peirce's Notion of Interpretant." *MLN* 91 (1976): 1457–72. Print.

Eco, Umberto. *A Theory of Semiotics*. Bloomington: Indiana UP, 1976. Print.

Goldhammer, Arthur. *How to Do Things with Style*. 24 Jan. 1997. Center for European Studies, Harvard U, n.d. Web. 9 Feb. 2010.

Goldhammer, Arthur. Message to the author. 4 Oct. 2004. E-mail.

Goldhammer, Arthur. *Translating Subtexts: What the Translator Must Know*. Center for European Studies, Harvard U, n.d. Web. 9 Feb. 2010.

Lacan, Jacques. *Écrits: A Selection*. Trans. Alan Sheridan. New York: Norton, 1977. Print.

Locke, John. *An Essay concerning Human Understanding*. Ed. Peter H. Nidditch. Oxford: Oxford UP, 1975. Print.

Peirce, Charles S. *The Writings of Charles S. Peirce: A Chronological Edition, 1867–1871*. Vol. 2. Ed. Edward C. Moore. Bloomington: Indiana UP, 1984. Print.

Said, Edward W. *Representations of the Intellectual*. New York: Random, 1994. Print.

Tombs, Robert. "Roasting a Fine Pig." *Times Literary Supplement* 16 Oct. 1992: 22. Print.

CHAPTER 10

Theory in Practice
National Messianism and English Choreography in King Lear

Jaecheol Kim

Jaecheol Kim holds a PhD in English from the University of Buffalo. He is an Assistant Professor of English at Hansung University, Seoul.

Through a close reading of Shakespeare's King Lear, *this essay surveys English nationalism in a very specific moment – at the time of King James's accession and his propagation of the Union of kingdoms, which was soon followed by his edict of "Naturalization of the Scots". This political claim of the Scottish monarch was in conflict with his English subjects' allegiance to English nationhood, thus creating an ambiguous allegiance between the two. Shakespeare, as James's English subject, had to negotiate between the absolutist claim of the Union propagated by the Scottish monarch and his own allegiance to English territory. Thus how this ruptured consciousness creates textual-national ambiguities in Shakespeare's play and how his political negotiation develops what Hans Kohn calls "national messianism" are the most important concerns in this essay. In* King Lear, *along with Cordelia's redemptive features, if the national messianic craving is expressed through regional identity, it is through Kent. In early-modern literature, Kent, which includes Canterbury (the locus of the national shrine) was often a geographical symbol of essential Englishness. The regional topography of Kent expresses past English identity as uncompromised by Scottish contamination. This chorographical allegiance to English regional territory properly explains the reason why at the end of the play the stage heavily gravitates toward Dover – the end of Kent/England – embodying all the national messianic images. The Shakespearean geopolitics represented in* King Lear *thus negotiates the huge gap between the Scottish monarch's absolutist rhetoric of Union and English nationhood forming a national ambiguity.*

Original publication details: Jaecheol Kim, "National Messianism and English Choreography in *King Lear*" from *English Studies* 94.6, pp. 685–703. Taylor & Francis, 2013. Reproduced with permission from Taylor & Francis.

In short, the substance of national*ism* as such is always morally, politically, humanly ambiguous.[1]

ALBION: "Etymology" [OE. Albion, f. L. Albion, -nis (Pliny), Gr. (Ptolemy): Celtic *Albio, gen. Albionis, whence Ir.-Gael. Alba, gen. Alban Scotland (cf. med.L. Albania: see ALBANIAN a.1); usu. referred to *albho- (L. albus) white, the allusion being to the white cliffs of Britain.] [f. med.L. Albania Scotland (Ir. Alba, gen. Alban) + -AN.]

ALBANIAN: "Etymology" A. adj. Of or pertaining to Scotland. B. n. A Scot. So Albanic (ælbænk) a. [cf. Ir. Albanach, Gael. Albannech], Scottish.[2]

I. Nation, Nature and *Natio*: "The King Falls from Bias of Nature"

King Lear is a *camera obscura* that creates upside-down images of King James's political propagation of Union. Unearthing the rich subtext of the play, Marie Axton and her followers have demonstrated that *King Lear* was produced in the heavy referential web of James's claim of Union (1603) and responds to the absolutist request by representing a territorial division and civil wars.[3] James's claim of Union is epitomized as follows:

Hath not God first united these two *Kingdomes* [England and Scotland] both in Language, Religion, and similitude of maners? Yea, hath he not made us all in one Island, compassed with one Sea, and of it selfe by *nature* so indivisible, as almost those that were borderers themselves on the late Borders, cannot distinguish, nor know, or discerne their owne limits? These two Countries being separated neither by Sea, nor great River, Mountaine, nor other strength of *nature*, but onely by little small brookes, or demolished little walles, so as rather they were divided in apprehension, then in effect. And now in the end and fulnesse of time united, the right and title of both in my Person, alike lineally descended of both the *Crownes*, whereby it is now become like a little World within it selfe, being intrenched and fortified round about with a *naturall*, and yet admirable strong pond or ditch, whereby all the former feares of this *Nation* are now quite cut off.[4]

In James's political rhetoric, kingdom, nation and nature are one indistinguishable entity. Thus there should be only one law, faith, language, parliament, king and nation in the Kingdom. Insofar as the accession of James himself reconciled all royal and national bodies of Britain and because there is no marked territorial-topographical distinction within the British Isles, the nation is one natural geographical body. This absolutist request rhetorically displaces Scottish alterities, equating "Crown" with "Nation" or his "Person" with the natural "Country". This propagation soon develops into his proclamation of "Naturalization" of the Scots. Yet, for James's English subjects, this anti-nationalist claim, wearing absolutist rhetoric, was hardly acceptable; it was *unnatural* for his English-born subjects. James's claim was close to empty rhetoric without any powerful political-fiscal support along with legal bindings. The House of Commons rejected this claim for two reasons: first, they "did not want the Scots equal in rights with native born Englishmen"; and next they "objected to discard 'ancient and honorable name England'".[5] If we say the Union was achieved, it was done without the consent of the English Parliament. James, after all, only assumed the title "King of Britain" by "proclamation" rather than legal "statue" following Francis Bacon's advice: the proclaimed title could thus be used in letters or other treaties, though not in "any legal proceeding, instrument or assurance".[6] Behind Parliament's refusal of James's proclamation of naturalization of the Scots, which inevitably accompanied his claim of Union, existed a very vexed question the House of Commons raised – "was the object of allegiance King or soil?"[7] This phrase explicitly summarizes the ambiguities or split allegiance between the Scottish monarch's argument and his English subjects' loyalty to English nationhood, which is metonymically expressed as "soil". The Albanian Prince's propagation, after all, betrays the huge chasm between "monarchy" and "nation" or between "king's body" and "national soil", which he wanted his English subjects to resolve, or at least, to negotiate. This national-political context of *King Lear* is crucial because it causes, as we shall see, the geopolitical problems Shakespeare's British tragedy, performed before James, reveals.

From the very drawing up of the curtain, the question of territorial division is discussed by Lear head-on; the play directly engages the issue of Union, only reversing it. Even though Shakespeare stages the keen national-political issue of the Jacobean claim, critics have had difficulty in determining Shakespeare's attitude toward Jacobean politics. Victor Turner argues that for a certain sense of *communitas* to be established, a temporary suspension or destruction of it is required.[8] *King Lear*, in this respect, creates a prerequisite suspension of the communality or order suggested by absolutism by staging territorial division and civil wars. In other words, this division-of-the-kingdom tragedy ultimately asserts, as Annabel Patterson and Leah Marcus's readings suggest, the necessity of territorial Union and the acceptance of James's Scottish subjects by the English people. Yet, of course, Shakespeare's work cannot simply be reduced to a political propaganda of absolutism, as it expresses its own polemics against Jacobean politics. As Franco Moretti's reading of the play persuasively shows, Shakespeare's text attempts to deconsecrate monarchial sovereignty, betraying the irrationality of absolutism *per se*.[9] These bifurcated critical responses to *King Lear* show, then, the play's self-contradictory attitudes toward the accession of the Scottish monarch. They also reveal the fact that *King Lear* is uncomfortably poised between British monarchy and English nationhood, King's blood lineage and English soil, the Scottish monarch's absolutist claim and the English Parliament's dissention against it. But most importantly, this ambiguous political allegiance mainly evokes the huge gulf for Englishmen between, as Axton puts it, "what [they] felt" and "what [they] ought to say"[10] in the presence of the Albanian (Scottish) monarch and his political claims, which Shakespeare, as an English subject, probably had to negotiate as well.

James, expecting this controversy, as suggested in his Parliament speech excerpted in the foregoing text, connects the essentially distinct discourses of "Kingdom" and "Nation" with the word "nature": he argues that the British Kingdom as a unified entity is nature regained. In this political context, the word "nature" for English subjects becomes the most ambiguous entity, evoking and embracing all the Scottish alterities insofar as it is associated with the issue of Union and naturalization of the Scots. Therefore, in *King Lear*, a "British" tragedy in which Shakespeare erases the word "England" and all its derivatives under this heated debate of Union, it is worthwhile to explore as well the semantic features of words such as "nature" and the "nation" in it – in particular, their irreducible ambiguities. Edmund argues,

> Thou, *nature*, art my goddess. To thy law
> My services are bound. Wherefore should I

> Stand in the plague of custom and permit
> The curiosity of *nations* to deprive me
> For that I am some twelve or fourteen moonshines
> Lag of a brother? Why "bastard"? Wherefore "base"?
> (1.2.1–6; emphasis added)[11]

As suggested in Edmund's evil invocation the most recurrent motif of the tragedy is birth (*natio*) to which words such as "propinquity" (1.1.112), "property" (1.1.112), "bond" (1.1.91) and "nations" (1.2.4) are articulated. *Natio*, as its shared etymology of "nation" and "nature", becomes the thematic joint of the play insofar as the text and subtexts of *King Lear* discuss in depth the questions of "birth" and "property" (with the motif of primogeniture) along with "nature" and "nationhood" (with the motif of unnatural national-territorial division). In the time of Shakespeare, the concept of *natio* was strongly attached to the sense of nation as well as to the notions of kinship or household. Shakespeare's *tour de force* in the tragedy is his conflation of the problems of nation, commonweal and public sphere in the main plot, with problems of household, private property and private sphere in its sub-plot. Thus the word "nation" in the excerpt is multiply determined, suggesting family lineage, primogeniture, given order, law and state. Nonetheless, despite the presumed harmony between "nation" and "nature" together with their shared etymological root, in the very heart of the play's poetic *agon* resides an antagonism between them; "O ruined piece of nature!" (4.5.127) properly expresses the poetic complication of the play.

In addition, Edmund's phrases illustrate the antithetical signification structure of primal words. In the sixteenth- to seventeenth-century English language, "natural" embraces two contradictory meanings at the same time, both concerning the birth-right: it signifies "Of the transfer of a privilege, property, etc.: according to right of heredity"; and "Of a person: related genetically but not legally to his or her father; born outside marriage, illegitimate".[12] As this semantic ambiguity develops in the play, *King Lear*'s tragic complication largely resides in Gloucester's bastard becoming a "Loyal and natural boy" (2.1.83). The significations of *natio* (birth) are heavily contaminated to the extent that they are irresolvable. This creates the irreducibly double-edged semantic conditions of the play; as in the final scene of the play, when, after poisoning Regan, Goneril calls the poison "medicine" (5.3.90), the state of "nature" becomes both "cure" and "poison" (*pharmakon*) in the play.

The signification problem of nature (*natio*) thus symptomatically expresses the problems of nation (*natio*) on a subtextual level. While James, as I have discussed above, tried to bridge in vain the crevice between his notion of Britain as a unified *nation/nature* and his English subjects' political allegiances to English soil, the play, on the contrary, creates an irreducible sense of antinomy between "nature" and "nationhood". More strikingly, Edmund, embodying all these iconoclastic social drives, claims, "Let me, if not by birth, have lands by wit. / All with me's meet that I can fashion fit" (1.2.160–1). In *King Lear*, *natio* could be not something naturally given by birth; it is manipulative, mercurial and artfully fashioned and negotiated. In my reading, the semantic dissociation between "nation" and "nature" lies at the heart of *King Lear*'s national argument. James based his claim of Union on his steadfast rhetorical fusion of royal lineage, nature and nation, but Shakespeare's play, like the deep-down heart of James's English subjects, does not conceive "Britain" or "Albion" as something naturally given as nation. Thus I take as the central claim of the play Gloucester's bitter remark – "The King falls from bias of nature" (1.2.101–2), which most directly expresses the schism between monarchy and sense of nationness. As we shall see in the next section of this essay, this oppressed nationhood in the tragedy generates apocalyptic narrative and messianic waiting – which is expressed chorographically rather than in religious or metaphysical terms. This is because messianic narrative is another facet of James's rhetoric of Union, and for Shakespeare it is the best literary device to represent the rise of the Scottish national alterities and the ambiguities that they create at the same time. The complex semantic ambiguities the play develops are now translated into national or topographical messianism.

II. Topography, *Topos* and *Telos*: Kent and National Messianism

Expecting a huge "eclipse", in which "nature finds itself scourg'd" and "the King falls from bias of nature", Gloucester, who facing the end, cannot but look back, laments that "We have seen the best of our time" (1.2.95–103).[13] Of course, by discussing *King Lear* in relation to apocalypse, I am not suggesting that Shakespeare develops a Christian narrative in a pagan setting. The play radically denies the Christian endings of its sources; as Stephen Greenblatt's source study of the play powerfully shows, the play creates religiously redemptive imagery, but at the same time it produces a critical distance from it, finally questioning it: the rich religious imagery of the play creates a sense of self-consciously committed fraud.[14] On this basis, my question develops further: if the play consciously invokes spiritual or idealist belief only to reject it, how does the play generate or evoke its almost religious senses of human emancipation? In other words, if, for instance, Edgar's demonic possession is the play's acknowledged "self-fashioning" and if men's anxiety about the huge eclipse merely betrays their "foppery" (1.2.108), what creates the play's pseudo-religious impulses or drives? To answer this question, I suggest that we need to understand *King Lear*'s metaphysical desire, including its apocalyptic and messianic narrative, first politically, then nationally and finally chorographically or topographically. My answer is already hinted at by Benedict Anderson, who claims that nation replaced the huge religious sense of community and hence is akin to religion.[15]

Hans Kohn traces the roots of nationalism among European societies back to their Judeo-Greek cultural heritages. He claims that "Three essential traits of modern nationalism originated with the Hebrew: the idea of the chosen people, the emphasis on a common stock of memory of the past and of hopes for the future, and finally national messianism".[16] The case of early-modern England was not an exception; nationalist discourses since the reign of Elizabeth had developed eschatological messianism. Richard Helgerson and Andrew Escobedo argue that the English narratives in this time were essentially nationalist as well as apocalyptic: this is largely because messianism itself was the most important rhetorical device at the time of the Tudor Reformation, which distinguished England from Catholic states.[17] Shakespeare's *King Lear*, as we shall see, restores this Tudor apocalypticism in a geopolitical way, contextualizing James's political chiliasm.

Escobedo suggests that, in the Tudor apocalyptic messianism produced during the Elizabethan era, the Queen was frequently a figure of Christ and many authors repeated discourses of historical ending. And the 1540s and 50s were the apex of apocalyptic chiliasm, which developed a very worldly idea that "the prophecy of St. John will be fulfilled in the English history, defeating anti-Christ papacy".[18] This historical ending, however, is never achieved in Elizabethan apocalyptic literatures. The reason is pretty simple: once a narrative or an event is already fully realized and uncovered, it cannot be apocalyptic (*apo* + *kaluptein*, to uncover) anymore. In other words, a narrative could be apocalyptic or messianic only when the real event of historical completion is still deferred and interminable, not achieved. Thus, as Escobedo argues, the apocalyptic visions of Foxe and Spenser, in this time, were inevitably narratives of deferral.[19]

This Tudor deferral becomes crucial for understanding Jacobean literature because one of James's political strategies was to appropriate this visionary literary tradition and to proclaim the advent of prophesied historical completion by his "Person" and national "Union". He states, for example, "I have ever ... kept Peace and amity with all, which hath been so far tied to my person, as at my coming here you are witnesses I found the State embarked in a great and tedious war, and only by mine arrival here, and by the Peace in my Person, is now amity kept, where war was before, which is no small blessing to a Christian Common-wealth".[20] James thus took advantage of Tudor national messianism, which seems essentially chiliastic or millenary, believing the end of history will be earthly and national rather than heavenly or religious. He equates his "coming" or "arrival" with the Advent: indeed, "the Peace", which "God hath so long ever since [his] Birth bestowed upon [him]", was his personal property as well as a blessing to the "Common-wealth". This new Jacobean national millennium, however, could not be achieved without the completion of Union; he continues, "Union of two ancient and famous Kingdomes" is "the other inward Peace annexed to my Person".[21] James fashioned himself as a Christ figure, and the accomplishment of the Union was another essential earthly requirement for the chiliasm associated with his personal "arrival". James thus believed that "Britain" as a nation is the historical completion. This is Jacobean chiliasm, which he develops by appropriating Elizabethan Protestant nationalism. It seems that, with his eschatological narrative, Shakespeare attempts to graft his pre-Christian play onto James's political discourse of Union: the territorial division and civil wars in an imminent doomsday of Britain that the play depicts are a reversed image of James's chiliasm. For the original sin of Lear – another figure of Brutus, who first divided the land into three – being redeemed and happily reunified by James was a very widely circulating pro-absolutist discourse of that time.[22]

Yet Shakespeare never simply repeats the absolutist argument in the play; on the contrary, he most radically refigures the apocalyptic cast in an English nationalist context rather than in favour of the monarch. A more important motif in relation to time in *King Lear* is that, because the sense of chronological history is heavily reorganized due to messianic narrative, the redemptive images of the play are not concerned with time and history, but rather with geography and space. Thus I want to propose that *King Lear* should be read as a "chorography". Even though recently a number of critics have addressed the play's cartographical features, critics still have failed to point out its regionally represented historiography which shows chorographical allegiance to regional English territories.[23] As we shall see, the truly radical features of the play derive from Shakespeare's fashioning of regional-topographical allegiance in the tragedy.

In the play, the Dukes of Albany and Cornwall and the French King, who claim their own portions of Lear's land, express national alterities. These three Otherly Celtic national bodies take higher political titles and power: as a king or dukes, their titles outrank and overpower the two English Earls – Kent and Gloucester. This localized identity fashioning is interesting enough: as Edmund Spenser and Raphael Holinshed's sources depict, the traditional tale of Lear is all pre-Roman Celtic history, while in *King Lear*, the titles of Earl of Kent and Gloucester are English ones only known after the eleventh-to twelfth-century English history.[24] The representation of two earls in the play, Shakespeare's own invention not found in his sources, thus compromises the tragedy's ahistorical all-Britonic narrative of national-origin with an infiltration of English national consciousness. Thus, the play, highlighting these two loyal English earls, defines the most threatening political identities as the foreign national powers of Albany, Cornwall and France. However, we might also be able to consider them as Celtic nationalities within the British Isles, because Shakespeare's struggle with French national identity is simply resolved. The King of France is actually a dummy and easily silenced at the end of the play. Though we hear about his landing in Dover, the English/British soil doesn't let him in. In the Quarto version of the text, he returns to France immediately after his landing because of "Something he left imperfect in the state" (Q.17.3), and in the Folio version, even more conveniently, he is entirely absent after the beginning of the play. Insofar as the King of France is a present *absence*, Shakespeare's British play qualifies the national struggle of the play between Englishness and Celticism within the British Isles, and if the play creates national and messianic narrative, inevitably, it is limited to British topographies.

Admittedly, in the tragedy, all the redemptive ideas focus on Cordelia. If she is alive, for Lear, it "does redeem all sorrows" (5.3.240), and Kent's receipt of a letter from Cordelia marks the beginning of messianic waiting and the deferral of narrative termination. But behind this pseudo-theological fashioning of Cordelia exist complex national-regional implications. One of Shakespeare's poetic feats in *King Lear* is his mediation of Cordelia with Lear's most loyal subject, Kent. He, along with Edgar, signifies another proper masculine power in the destroyed *patria* (fatherland), which is endangered and engendered as a feminine entity without any male heir, only with the wicked "pelican daughters" (3.4.70) of the old king. Thus, if Cordelia represents in the play both the only proper heir of Lear and, metaphorically, the English nation, Kent is her masculine displacement. This reading is supported by regional metaphors indicating her intricate connection with Kent. Recently, Valerie Traub very persuasively showed that, in *King Lear*, anatomical discourses usually articulate and metaphorize the cartographical discourses,[25] and this observation makes us read the close anatomical-topographical association between Cordelia and Kent in the text. It is noteworthy that Kent is the counterpart of Eubulus in *Gorboduc* and Perillus in *King Leir*, two of Shakespeare's sources,[26] but the regional and topographical fashioning of his loyalty is Shakespeare's own invention, stressing his/its Englishness. When Cordelia is unfairly treated by Lear, Kent feels the invasion of an arrowhead in "the region of [his] heart" (1.1.143) and *Cor*-delia's suffocated *heart* – as she says, "I cannot heave / my heart into my mouth" (1.1.89–90) – expresses the regional heart of Englishness – Kent. As absent *presences*, in the beginning of the play, they are banished from Lear's eyes, but they ever shadow Lear. In the final scene of the play, Kent plaintively says, "from your [Lear's] first of difference and decay / Have follow'd your sad step" (5.3.263–4); but this phrase is equally applicable to Lear's Fool, who doubles as Cordelia.[27] Their repressed (thus absent or displaced) but surely present Englishness actually rules the entire narrative.

More importantly, if Cordelia's identities are linked with a certain regional English geography, her stubborn will to remain a virgin – "sure I shall never marry like my sisters" (1.1.101) – requires more exploration because whenever early modern literature depicts or stages virginity, it is never a mere coincidence. Louis Montrose argues in his reading of *A Midsummer Night's Dream* that, in the reign of Queen Elizabeth, the state tried to appropriate the Virgin cult, redirecting it into the power of the nation-state, and in that course Elizabeth's virginity became the national icon of conquering power outwardly and of the unconquerable fortress internally.[28] For instance, Raleigh states, "Her Majesty hereby shall confirme and strengthen the opinions of al nations ... the Dominion and Empire of the *Amazones*, those women shall hereby heare the name of a virgin, which is not onely able to defend her owne territories and her neighbors, but also to invade and conquere so great Empyres and so farre removed".[29] This national implication of Elizabeth's virginity suffuses Spenser's Tudor national messianism in *The Faerie Queene* with his virgin characters like Britomart and Belphoebe. If Cordelia expresses this lost virgin national icon of Queen Elizabeth, who unified the senses of royal lineage and English nationhood more firmly than James did, it is Kent who topographically or regionally expresses Cordelia's virginity as a national bulwark. In the Jacobean era, as chorographically depicted in *The Roaring Girl*, a phrase such as "The purity of your wench would I fain try; she seems like Kent unconquered" seems an axiomatic expression.[30] For Shakespeare's Say, Kent was the "*bona terra*" (*2H6* 4.7.47), which cannot be the origin of rebels such as Jack Cade, as he cites a phrase of Caesar, Kent

> Is termed the civil'st place of all [the] isle;
> Sweet is the country, because full of riches,
> The people liberal, valiant, active, wealthy.
> (*2H6* 4.7.54–6)

These kinds of description of Kent are often found in Elizabethan-Jacobean chorography: for example, William Camden describes Kent as a virgin territory, quoting from an unknown Latin source that "this County [Kent] was never conquered, ... but by concluding of a peace subjected themselves to the dominion of the Conquerour, retaining to themselves all their liberties, immunities, and customs which they had and used before time".[31] In addition, as Camden records, Kent is a territory which retains the memory of the Queen Elizabeth and her optic national power; in particular, "Greenwich was our late Queene Elizabeth, who heere, most happily borne to see the light by the resplendent brightnesse of her roiall vertue, enlightned all England".[32] If Queen Elizabeth as the unconquerable national body is geo-symbolically represented on English soil, it is by Kent. *King Lear*'s almost chorographical allegiance to Kent could be examined in more depth. In Elizabethan-Jacobean chorographies, the land as a personified agency of historical speeches was a persistent motif. This kind of localized loyalty was, according to Helgerson, usually against monarchial authority and stressed national-regional identities.[33] Then, if Kent speaks as a personified entity, what it would be like is a very intriguing question, and Michael Drayton's *Poly-Olbion* gives the best answer to it: it represents Kent as an eloquent nationalist speaker of English history. Especially when the poet describes the lands, rivers, mountains, villages, towns of Kent in Book XVIII, his pro-English jingoism is manifest. The land of Kent, especially the River Medway, recounts a long list of Anglo-Saxon victories over the French, the Irish, the Welsh and, in particular, the Scottish. The tedious national chauvinism amounts to almost 650 lines and continues until

> the Kentish Nymphs doe interrupt her song,
> By letting *Medway* knowe shee tarried had too long
> Upon this warlike troupe.[34]

Drayton's ideologically laden political topography of Kent is summarized by the song of River Stour:

> O noble *Kent*, quoth he, this praise doth thee belong,
> The hard'st to be controld, impatient test of wrong.
> Who, when the *Norman* first with pride and horror sway'd,
> Threw'st off the servile yoke upon *English* lay'd;
> And with a high resolve, most bravely didst restore
> That libertie so long enjoy'd by thee before.
> §. Not Suffring forraine Lawes should thy free Customes bind,
> Then onely showd'st thy selfe of th'ancient *Saxon* kind.
> Of all the *English* Shires be thou surnam'd the Free,
> §. And formost ever plac't, when they shall reckoned bee.
> And let this Towne, which Chiefe of thy rich Country is,
> Of all the *British* Sees be still *Metropolis*.[35]

Along with its unconquerable virginity, Kent is essentially the Anglo-Saxon ethnic territory, which even "restore[s]" the national liberty from "forraine Lawes"; this regional account of Shakespeare's contemporary might best explain why in *King Lear* national messianism is centralized around Kent. The county of Kent contains a radical utopian egalitarianism: in the foregoing text, the word "Customes" should be noted; when it is used in the context of Kent and its regional economy, it signifies an old habit of the Kentish "gavelkind". Camden interprets it as "Give all kinne, by which they are not so bound by Copyhold, customarie tenures, or Tenant-right, as in other parts of England, but in maner every man is a free-holder and hath some part of his owne to live upon", and he continues, "For lands of this nature are equally divided among the male children or, if there be no sonnes, among the daughters".[36] This notion of gavelkind is also well depicted in William Lambarde's *A Perambulation of Kent*. For Lambarde, Kent is a land for yeomanry and common people because of this custom and "it is agreed by all men, that there were never any bondmen (or villaines, as the law calleth them) in Kent".[37] Obviously, behind the textual body of *King Lear* lie uncomfortable social feuds derived from unequal habits of property distribution, including bastardization, against which Edmund rises, and peasant rebellion, which Regan is conscious of as she exclaims, "A peasant stands up thus!" (3.7.78), slaying Gloucester's servant. If so, the Kentish egalitarian custom called gavelkind is suitable to resolve all the problems revolving around questions of property that the tragedy raises and this might be one of the reasons Kent becomes the topographical backdrop of the play. This utopian vision, along with its virgin regional territory uncontaminated by any other nationhood, is why Kent can enjoy the status of "Chiefe" and "Metropolis" above all other counties.[38] With these geopolitical implications, in *King Lear*, Kent as a person and geographical locus embodies all the messianic anticipations and becomes at once *topos* and *telos* of the tragedy.

III. *Alba*, Albion and Albany: "Wherefore to Dover?"

Toward the end of *King Lear*, the stage gravitates heavily toward Dover, a small port/fort in Kent: the narrative trajectory moves southward as if it wants to escape a threatening alterity from the north. Like his representations of Kent, Dover itself is Shakespeare's own rendering of his sources. Dover in the play is associated with redemptive images by Gloucester in act 3 scene 3; it is the place where the demented King can have "welcome and protection" (3.6.46). It is also the place where Lear's company can "boast / To have well-armed friends" (3.7.17–18) and "preparation stands / in expectation of them" (4.3.22–3). From these phrases, we vaguely assume that Dover is where Cordelia's French forces encamp and that they can defeat Edmund's British powers. Yet still this is an unnatural reading given the nationalist impulse we have already surveyed because, according to this reading, Frenchness is welcomed over Britishness or Englishness. The reason for this geographical centralization into Dover, not just into Kent as an unspecified locus of Englishness, anyhow, is not very explicitly stated in the text, and when Cornwall and Regan interrogate Gloucester to locate Lear, they repeat the phrase "Wherefore to Dover?" three times (3.7.50, 51, 53). Yet Gloucester's response to them is not sufficient to fully grasp Shakespeare's geopolitics. The answer to this spatial centralization is only hinted at by Gloucester in the subsequent act:

> There is a cliff, whose high and bending head
> Looks fearfully in the confined deep.
> Bring me but to the very brim of it,
> And I'll repair the misery thou dost bear
> With something rich about me: from that place
> I shall no leading need.
>
>   (4.1.67–72)

Blind Gloucester, guided by his son Edgar, treads a historical way to Dover. His destination, from which he "shall no leading need", suggests that the doomsday is displaced from history to the specific regional locus. Richard Halpern observes the literalized *de casibus* motif in the cliff and argues that "as a machine for producing sublimity", the cliff of Dover "creates values through its destruction".[39] It thus erases the boundary between a certain value and nil, also destruction and redemption, creating an irreducible ambiguity. What my reading focuses on with regard to Shakespeare's geopolitics of Dover, then, is the coexistence of essential English nationhood and the most threatening Scottish-Celtic alterity within the geopolitics of this. As I shall demonstrate, Dover, as a culturally and nationally liminal place, is an in-between place where the *heimlich* sense of English belonging and its exposure to the *unheimlich* existence of others coexist. More specifically, in the context of James's claim of Union, Dover is a locus in which the absolutist claim of British Kingdom and people's chorographical allegiance to English nationhood is negotiated. Also, for English subjects, including Shakespeare, it is a literary venue in which they can bridge the huge cleft between "what [Englishmen] felt" and "what [Englishmen] ought to say" to their Scottish monarch.

In order to show this, first, we need to explore Dover's affiliation with Kent-Englishness. In Gloucester's foregoing speech, even though the play does not clearly indicate the beginning point of Gloucester and Edgar's "pilgrimage" (5.3.187), Edgar is now in disguise as a "Bedlam beggar" (2.2.171) – clearly indicating his London suburban subjectivity. It is most probable that they pass the old Watling Street, which overlaps the way from Southwark to Canterbury – the setting of Chaucer's *Canterbury Tales*. Thus they pace through the long English literary tradition as well as the heart of Kent. No wonder Kent is the region of the national shrine, Canterbury, which might contextualize their "pilgrimage". This properly Kentish way to Dover trodden by Edgar and

Gloucester represents the geopolitical identities of loyal Cordelia and the Earl of Kent – the national-regional purity of the land and of egalitarian utopian vision.

Indeed, their final destination, around the "cliff [of Dover], whose high and bending head / Looks fearfully in the confined deep" (4.1.67–8), invokes an enormous Shakespearean English national fantasy. In *The Comedy of Errors*, Dromio of Syracuse explains the essential quality of "England" with this "chalky cliff" in a humorous comparison to Nell's teeth (*CE* 3.2.124–7). The cliff of Dover is the "fortress built by Nature for herself" (*R2* 2.1.43), which John of Gaunt praises, depicting the most vivid (but still questionable) Englishness in the entire English canon. It is the palisade protecting exclusive English identity from other nationalities and cultures. Facing the sea and Calais in France, it is a territory which suggests the geographical boundedness of the British Isles and its clear division from Continental influences. When it comes to Franco-Norman power, as Lambarde's *Perambulation of Kent* proudly records, during the time of the French invasion of 1216 Dover was the only unconquered of England's Cinque ports, and in the next year the great victory of Hubert de Burgh, who was "Constable" and "Earle of Kent", over the French naval force saved the English realm from "forreigne servitude".[40] The national import of the Dover Cliff is rephrased in *Cymbeline* as

> Neptune's park, ribbed and paled in
> With rocks unscalable and roaring waters,
> With sands that will not bear your enemies' boats.
>   (*C* 3.1.19–21)

Dover, then, as a national locus, is at once a British *port* facing Continental nations across the sea and an English *fort* against foreign invasions. Following Matthew Paris, Lambarde epitomizes the geopolitics of Dover as "*Clavis, & Repagulum totius Regni*, the verie locke and keye of the whole Realme of England":[41] it is a synecdochic expression of English nationhood as such, uncompromised by other nationalities.

Given this cultural fantasy, if it is *natio* that is unnaturalized from the very beginning of the play, as stated in Edmund's evil invocation, it is not surprising that this national place becomes the proper place of cure and redemption in *King Lear*. Dover thus becomes the literary locus where all tragic tensions should be resolved; where all the disguised and self-fashioned identities of Edgar, Kent and Edmund should be restored; where all the lost reasons and orders should be regained. Dover appears to be the proper stronghold of English values against the Celtic contaminations of Cornwall and Albany. In addition, given that *King Lear* was written in the time of James's propagation of Union, Dover is the place at which English subjects can speak in terms of what Englishmen really felt concerning the Albanian Prince and his devouring Scottish subjects.

In *King Lear*, however, the influence of Scottish invasion is stronger than the English subject's ability to maintain the clear-cut semantic tenor of this national locale. We must note that this symbolic location also signifies the most exclusive and xenophobic British national epithet, deriving from its white cliff – Albion. This exclusive English as well as British name is derived from the Gaelic etymology of *alba*, which it mainly relates to the Scottish monarch – Albany. Given that the tragedy presupposes a British history before the Arthurian legend, the word "Albion" itself thus evokes the British (rather than English) myth of historical origin. The Dover cliff, therefore, defines the British Isles in terms of Albion-Scottishness (or Britishness) rather than Englishness. The place becomes eponymous for Scottish terrain and the geopolitics of Dover thus uncannily satisfies James's request – Union under the name of Albion or Britain. Indeed "Sith God hath made al under one, / Let Albione now al-be-one"[42] was the most dreadful political claim of that time, rigorously rejected by James's English subjects. The Shakespearean geopolitics of Dover is thus politically and semantically riven: the Janus-faced national-cultural imports of Dover never neatly dovetail with one another. This liminal location tries to satisfy both essential Englishness and the request of the Albanian monarch at the same time.

This political-national schism has clear narrative effects: it causes the notoriously unresolved ending of the play, staged "near Dover". The most mysterious feature of the play, created by these multiple semantic ambiguities, is that Dover, as a Kentish region, as well as its Albion cliff never actually appears in the play. Both the signification of the cliff and its national implications are under deferral and dissemination. This symbolic location is heard about, desired, imaginarily created (by Edgar) and believed in (by Gloucester), but its presence is always already deferred. Toward the end of the narrative, we hear Cordelia's French forces landed on Dover, but the stage only ever resides *near* Dover. The chimerical nature of Dover has already been fully analyzed by Jonathan Goldberg, following post-structural linguistic philosophy,[43] but my point has more to do with nation and geography in relation to the illusive national messianism Dover creates. In *King Lear*, Dover itself is at once English and British territory – satisfying English nationalism and James's absolutist request at the same time – but Shakespeare stages Dover as an alien "French camp". Demented Lear says in Dover, most confusingly, "Am I in France?" (4.6.69). After Edgar's imaginary creation of the cliff of Dover, which is a reality for Gloucester's imagination, Edgar says, "I know not how conceit may rob / The treasury of life" (4.5.43–4). In his understanding, the idea of reaching an essential nationness as well as the proper *telos* of history could be even a "conceit", just as Edmund "can fashion" his birthright (1.2.161). In *King Lear* nation is no longer a nature or con-genital *natio* but a manipulative creation. This is the reason why Dover, as an iconic symbol of proper nationness, is out of representation and *absent*, only creating its *effects*. This is how Shakespearean national tragedy topographically and chorographically responds to James's claim of Britain as a unified nature and nation.

IV. The Duke of Albany and *Macbeth*: "Is This the Promised End?"

Shakespeare's tragic rendering of the Lear story, however, fashions the Duke of Albany in general as a good-hearted figure, surviving to the end of the narrative. Cornish iden-tity, however, is simply silenced with the premature death of Cornwall. This is under-standable given that, in the Shakespearean era, the Cornish identity was already largely subsumed into England. Thus the existence of the Duke of Albany alone becomes the national alterity to the end of the tragedy, evoking the accession of James, who had held the title of Duke of Albany from February to July 1567. Shakespeare could not have been more careful in this context. Inevitably, in *King Lear*, the Duke of Albany, suggesting an adjective sense of Scottishness, becomes a very complicated character, who causes divi-sion of land and at the same time re-establishes the lost order in England at the end of the narrative.

The clear difference between the Quarto and Folio versions of the text is that, in the Quarto version, which was performed before the King during the Christmas holidays, the closing speech falls upon Albany while in the Folio version the lost order is established by Edgar. Michael Warren summarizes his political interpretation of the textual-editorial variations as follows:

> In Q, Edgar remains an immature young man and ends the play devastated by his experience, while Albany stands as the modest, diffident, but strong and morally upright man. In F Edgar grows into a potential ruler, a well intentioned resolute man in a harsh world, while Albany, a weaker man, abdicates his responsibilities. In neither text is the prospect for the country a matter of great optimism, but the vision seems bleaker and darker in F, where the young Edgar, inexperienced in rule, faces the future with little support.[44]

Warren suggests that Shakespeare tried to establish the superiority of Englishness over Scottishness in the later version of the play – given that we can regard the Folio version as a later and more revised edition. Even though it creates a more extreme "image of … horror" (5.3.238), in the Folio version, Shakespeare does not let Albany establish the national order. The editorial differences between the Quarto and Folio versions seem to express the crevice between the political allegiance to the Scottish-origin monarch and English nationhood. The editorial trajectory of *King Lear* fully signifies the textual unrest that derives from the alterity between the British crown and English identity. This negotiation continues until Shakespeare finishes staging *Macbeth*. In this play, Shakespeare negotiates the authorities of the Scottish Kingdom and the English nation better than in *King Lear*. In *Macbeth*, by tracing the English royal line back to Banquo, he acknowledges James's Scottish lineage as English regal right. However, at the same time, English power, which is not contaminated by Scottish witchcraft, establishes order in morbid Scotland. The return of Malcolm and Macduff from England with an exorcizing power "Unknown to woman" (*M* 4.3.127) and shielded by Siward is nothing but the return of overriding English nationalism. The poet satisfies the national desire only with an ostensible exclamation – "Hail, King of Scotland!" (*M* 5.11.25).

Notes

1 Nairn, 348.
2 *Oxford English Dictionary* (*OED*).
3 Axton, 131–47. Marie Axton's discussion has influenced critics interested in censorship. For example, Annabel Patterson's reading deals with the issue of Union and the textual unrest expressed in the play (64–73). Leah Marcus, based on the subtitle of the Quarto version of the text ("played before the kings majestie at Whitehall upon S. Stephens night in Christmas Holidayes' in the year of 1606"), argues that the play was produced before James on St. Stephen's Night, a day of charity and granting hospitality. Marcus understands the play as an extended political exemplum promoting charity toward the Scottish monarch and his Scottish subjects (148–59).
4 Excerpted from James's speech of March 1603, delivered in the Upper House (James, 271–2; emphasis added).
5 Axton, 134.
6 Francis Bacon quoted in Willson, 252.
7 For the House of Commons's rejection of James's claim, see Axton, 134–5; and Willson, 251–8.
8 Turner, 231–71.
9 Franco Moretti argues, based on the play's representation of division of territory as a "darker purpose" acting against all reason, the political purpose of English tragedies from *Gorboduc* to *Lear* is ultimately the deconsecration of monarchial sovereignty.

10 Axton, 142. This phrase is from the closing speech of the play – "Speak what we feel, not what we ought to say" (5.3.299).

11 All citations to and quotations from William Shakespeare's texts are taken from *The Norton Shakespeare* and appear parenthetically in the text. The following abbreviations are used for plays other than *King Lear*: *C* (*Cymbeline*); *CE* (*The Comedy of Errors*); *2H6* (*Henry VI, Part II*); *M* (*Macbeth*); *R2* (*Richard II*). Being conscious of the marked differences between the Quarto and Folio versions of *King Lear*, I have used the parallel text in the Norton edition. This essay is mainly founded on the Folio version and when I need to cite the Quarto version, I indicate it with a "Q." The proper names of the play follow the conflated text edited by Barbara L. Lewalski in the Norton text.

12 *OED*, "Natural."

13 Joseph Wittreich's work exhaustively analyzes the apocalyptic framework in *King Lear* by reading Shakespeare's two British tragedies, *King Lear* and *Macbeth*, in apocalyptic frameworks.

14 See "Shakespeare and the Exorcists" in Greenblatt, 94–128. Also a number of writers have pointed out the play's self-conscious rejection of religious redemption. For example, for Sigmund Freud, Cordelia forms an illusory sense of redemption but she is actually a Goddess of Death in disguise (291–301). A. C. Bradley says, "The 'gods,' it seems, do *not* show their approval by 'defending' their own from adversity or death, or by giving them power and prosperity" (326). For Jonathan Dollimore, the play's radical feature resides in its rejection of any idealist or humanist value in its final scene (202–3).

15 See chapter titled "Cultural Roots" in Anderson, 9–37.

16 Kohn, 11. Also Liah Greenfeld argues that the sense of chosen people of the Old Testament provided the most important rhetorical basis for English nationalism at the time of the Reformation. It was "the language in which they could express the novel consciousness of nationality, for which no language had existed before" (Greenfeld, 52).

17 See "Apocalyptics and Apologetics" in Helgerson, 249–68; Escobedo; Haller.

18 Escobedo, 85.

19 Ibid., 83.

20 James, 270.

21 Ibid., 270–1.

22 Anthony Munday's pageant, *The Triumphs of Re-United Britannia*, is well discussed by Axton in this regard. In the pageant, Brutus's sin, his division of land, is now redeemed by James, creating a motif of *felix culpa* (Axton, 136–7). This kind of political motif which praises James's Union of territory continued until the King's death in 1625. For example, Ben Jonson's masque, "The Fortunate Isles, and Their Union," (1624) typically reveals this motif.

23 Critics have read *King Lear* as a cartographical narrative pointing out Lear's mapping desire saying "Give me the map" (1.1.35). For example, Valerie Traub discusses the play's identification of anatomical science with cartographical representations. She argues that "the circulation and diffusion of western European anatomical illustrations, voyage illustrations, and maps around the end of the sixteenth century – when voyages of discovery, colonization, and trade were occurring at an unprecedented rate – resulted in a new graphic idiom, the spatializing logic of which *King Lear* appropriates, and to which it adds" (53). Bruce Avery discusses the "rhetorical purpose" of the cartographical scene in the play. According to Avery, the map in *King Lear* owes "its ability to possession" and represents "power" and "becomes as important as the territory that forms the actual possession" (51); thus it becomes the means through which Lear "intends to retain psychological control over" his daughters (52). However, critics have seldom discussed *King Lear*'s intertextual correlations with chorographical writings, and my point of discussion in this essay is how the localized narrative of *King Lear* articulates national concerns which are particularly represented in messianic anticipation.

24 See Holinshed, 1–3; Spenser, 2.10.27–32.

25 Traub, 42–4.

26 Passim.

27 The identification of Cordelia with the Fool is now generally accepted as a theatrical tradition. This dual role is suggested in phrases such as "since my young lady's going into France, sir, the

fool hath much pined away" (1.4.63) or "But who is with him? / None but the Fool, who labours to outjest His heart-struck injuries" (3.1.7–8).

28   See Montrose, 77–87. Leonard Tennenhouse also demonstrates in his reading of *Titus* the relation between national territory and virgin body. According to him, because Elizabeth, with her aristocratic virgin body, is usually identified with the body of nation-state, Tudor dramas cannot be more political than when they deal with an aristocratic virgin (111–12).

29   *Discovery of Guiana* quoted in Montrose, 78.

30   Middleton and Dekker, 2.1.324–6.

31   "Kent" in Camden.

32   Ibid.

33   See the chapter entitled "The Land Speak" in Helgerson, 105–48. Richard Helgerson argues that "The needs of cartographic representation [in early modern English chorography] are such that, for it to be successful, information concerning such matters as royal patronage or sovereignty must be pushed to the side," and "It strengthened the sense of both local and national identity at the expense of an identity based on dynastic loyalty" (114).

34   Drayton, 18.653–5.

35   Ibid., 5.729–40.

36   "Kent" in Camden. Joan Thirsk's classical account of "younger son" singles out Kent as a location of gavelkind. According to her, "Kentish gentry still held much land by gavelkind tenure, and many continued to uphold the spirit and the letter of this custom, resisting any attempt at change" (Thirsk, 340). In this light, Richard Wilson discusses one of *King Lear*'s sources – the property bequest of Brian Annesley, who had three daughters, last one named Cordelia. According to Wilson, many features of Lear himself reflect Annesley's property devise case. This source study is relevant to my reading since Annesley had his property in Kent and thus his property was "subject to the antique custom of gavelkind" (Wilson, 215). More recently Ronald W. Cooley has rehearsed this argument, by contextualizing *Lear*'s Kent in the very heavy discursive referential web of Jacobean property bequest. According to him, "As an aristocrat" the Earl of Kent "sees the dynastic disadvantage of a divided legacy, and protests Lear's division of the kingdom; as a 'man of Kent' he displays the independence and individualism that divided legacies had promoted" (Cooley, 334). However, Wilson and Cooley largely disregard the national and metropolitan identities which Kent represents and especially the messianic anticipation revolving around Dover, which I shall soon discuss.

37   Lambarde, 7.

38   As the *OED* suggests, the word "metropolis" began to be used in order to indicate a chief town with an archbishop in the fourteenth century. Yet it gradually began to manifest colonial connotations. See *OED*, "Metropolis" and "Metropolitan."

39   Halpern, 268.

40   Lambarde, 139–40.

41   Ibid., 138.

42   Robert Pont's *De unione britanniae* quoted in Patterson, 65.

43   Jonathan Goldberg argues that the impossible signification of Dover suggests the endless division between the signifier and signified. In this sense, "the limits that 'Dover' represents in the text are the limits of representation themselves" (134).

44   Warren, 35.

References

Anderson, Benedict. *Imagined Communities: Reflection on the Origin and Spread of Nationalism*. London: Verso, 1991.

Avery, Bruce. "Gelded Continents and Plenteous Rivers: Cartography as Rhetoric in Shakespeare." In *Playing the Globe: Genre and Geography in English Renaissance Drama*, edited by John Gillies and Virginia Mason Vaughan. Cranbury, NJ: Associated University Press, 1998.

Axton, Marie. *The Queen's Two Bodies: Drama and the Elizabethan Succession*. London: Royal Historical Society, 1977.

Bradley, A. C. *Shakespearean Tragedy*. New York: Macmillan, 1949.

Camden, William. *Britannia*. Translated by Philemon Holland and edited by Dana F. Sutton. *The Philological Museum*. The University of Birmingham. [4 January 2011]. Available from http://www.philological.bham.ac.uk/cambrit.

Cooley, Ronald W. "Kent and Primogeniture in *King Lear*." *Studies in English Literature 1500–1900* 48 (2008): 327–48.

Dollimore, Jonathan. *Radical Tragedy: Religion, Ideology and Power in the Drama of Shakespeare and his Contemporaries*. Durham, NC: Duke University Press, 2004.

Drayton, Michael. *Poly-Olbion*. In *The Works of Michael Drayton*, edited by J. Hebel. Oxford: Shakespeare Head Press, 1961.

Escobedo, Andrew. *Nationalism and Historical Loss in Renaissance England: Foxe, Dee, Spenser, Milton*. Ithaca, NY: Cornell University Press, 2004.

Freud, Sigmund. "The Theme of the Three Caskets." In *The Standard Edition of the Complete Psychological Works of Sigmund Freud*, edited by James Strachey and Anna Freud. Vol. 12. London: Hogarth Press, 1978.

Goldberg, Jonathan. "Perspectives: Dover Cliff and the Conditions of Representation." In *Shakespeare's Hand*. Minneapolis: University of Minnesota Press, 2003.

Greenblatt, Stephen. *Shakespearean Negotiations*. Berkeley: University of California Press, 1988.

Greenfeld, Liah. *Nationalism: Five Roads to Modernity*. Cambridge, MA: Harvard University Press, 1992.

Haller, William. *The Elect Nation: The Meaning and Relevance of Foxe's Book of Martyrs*. New York: Harper & Row, 1963.

Halpern, Richard. *The Poetics of Primitive Accumulation: English Renaissance Culture and the Genealogy of Capital*. Ithaca, NY: Cornell University Press, 1991.

Helgerson, Richard. *Forms of Nationhood: The Elizabethan Writing of England*. Chicago, IL: University of Chicago Press, 1992.

Holinshed, Raphael. *Shakespeare's Holinshed: Source of Shakespeare's History Plays*, King Lear, Cymbeline, and Macbeth. Edited by Richard Hosley. New York: G. P. Putnam's Sons, 1963.

James, I (King). *The Political Works of James I*. Edited by Charles H. McIlwain. New York: Russell & Russell, 1965.

Jonson, Ben. "The Fortunate Isles, and Their Union." In *Ben Jonson: The Complete Masques*, edited by Stephen Orgel. New Haven, CT: Yale University Press, 1969.

King Leir. Edited by Tiffany Stern. London: Routledge, 2003.

Kohn, Hans. *Nationalism: Its Meaning and History*. Princeton, NJ: D. Van Nostrand, 1965.

Lambarde, William. *A Perambulation of Kent: Conteining the Description, Hystorie, and Customes*. London: Chatham, 1826.

Marcus, Leah. *Puzzling Shakespeare: Local Reading and its Discontents*. Berkeley: University of California Press, 1988.

Middleton, Thomas, and Thomas Dekker. *The Roaring Girl*. In *English Renaissance Drama*, edited by David Bevington. New York: Norton, 2002.

Montrose, Louis. "*A Midsummer Night's Dream* and the Shaping Fantasies of Elizabethan Culture: Gender, Power, and Form." In *Rewriting the Renaissance: The Discourse of Sexual Difference in Early Modern Europe*, edited by Margaret W. Ferguson. Chicago, IL: University of Chicago Press, 1987.

Moretti, Franco. "'A Huge Eclipse': Tragic Form and the Deconsecration of Sovereignty." *Genre* 15 (1982): 7–40.

Nairn, Tom. *The Break-Up of Britain: Crisis and Neo-Nationalism*. London: NLB, 1977.

Norton, Thomas, and Thomas Sackville. *Gorboduc, or, Ferrex and Porrex*. Edited by Irby B. Cauthen, Jr. Lincoln, NE: Nebraska University Press, 1970.

Oxford English Dictionary Online. Oxford University Press. [cited 14 March 2000]. Available from http://www.oed.com.

Patterson, Annabel. *Censorship and Interpretation: The Conditions of Writing and Reading in the Early Modern England*. Madison: University of Wisconsin Press, 1984.

Shakespeare, William. *The Norton Shakespeare*. Edited by Stephen Greenblatt et al. New York: Norton, 1997.

Spenser, Edmund. *The Faerie Queene*. Edited by Thomas P. Roche, Jr. London: Penguin, 1987.

Tennenhouse, Leonard. *Power on Display: The Politics of Shakespeare's Genres*. New York: Methuen, 1986.

Thirsk, Joan. *The Rural Economy of England: Collected Essays*. London: Hambledon, 1984.

Traub, Valerie. "The Nature of Norms in Early Modern England: Anatomy, Cartography, *King Lear*." *South Central Review* 26 (2009): 42–81.

Turner, Victor. *Dramas, Fields, and Metaphors: Symbolic Action in Human Society*. Ithaca, NY: Cornell University Press, 1974.

Warren, Michael. "Quarto and Folio *King Lear* and the Interpretation of Albany and Edgar." In *Critical Essays on Shakespeare's King Lear*, edited by Jay L. Halio. New York: G. K. Hall, 1996.

Willson, D. Harris. *King James VI and I*. Oxford: Alden, 1956.

Wilson, Richard. *Will Power: Essay on Shakespearean Authority*. Detroit, MI: Wayne State University Press, 1993.

Wittreich, Joseph. *"Images of That Horror:" History, Prophecy, and Apocalypse in King Lear*. San Marino, CA: The Huntington Library, 1984.

CHAPTER 11

Theory in Practice
Elizabeth Bishop's "Brazil, January 1, 1502" and Max Jacob's "Etablissement d'une communauté au Brésil": A Study of Transformative Interpretation and Influence

Sylvia Henneberg

Sylvia Henneberg is a Professor of English at Morehead State University. Her research focuses primarily on contemporary women's poetry. She has published on Adrienne Rich, Elizabeth Bishop, May Sarton, and Judy Grahn as well as on Emily Dickinson. Her book, *The Creative Crone: Aging and the Poetry of May Sarton and Adrienne Rich* (2010), examines the work of two major contemporary women poets to show how they confront aging.

Elizabeth Bishop's misgivings about free translation are well known to scholars of her work. Fearful of misappropriating creations not her own, her preference was to translate cautiously and literally.[1] In her unpublished *Remarks on Translation – (Of poetry, mostly)*, she enumerates several "complaints about translations," including "inaccuracy – the wrong word" and "using three words – or more – when one would do" (2). She offers the following advice: "When a word is repeated – *repeat* it! (Just because English has more words than any other language except Russian – doesn't mean we have to use them all....) When a line is repeated – repeat it – and also – stick to the *structure*." Translations were to be handled, as she wrote in a letter to Anne Stevenson, "with a minimum of bloodletting or seepage" (qtd. in Lombardi, 138). Even Robert Lowell's *Imitations* (1961), a body of work that, as most critics agree, is best understood as creative personalized reinterpretation of French poems rather than free translation, triggered discomfort

Original publication details: Sylvia Henneberg, "Elizabeth Bishop's 'Brazil, January 1, 1502' and Max Jacob's 'Etablissement d'une communauté au Brésil': A Study of Transformative Interpretation and Influence." *Texas Studies in Literature and Language* 45.4, *Intertextual Variations* (Winter 2003), pp. 337–351. Reproduced with permission from University of Texas Press.

Literary Theory: An Anthology, Third Edition. Edited by Julie Rivkin and Michael Ryan.
© 2017 John Wiley & Sons, Ltd. Published 2017 by John Wiley & Sons, Ltd.

in Bishop. Responding to *Imitations* in several letters that emphasized to Lowell the importance of fidelity to rhyme, meter, and poetic intent, she concluded with the comment: "I just can't decide how 'free' one has the right to be with the poet's intentions" (qtd. in Kalstone, 205).[2]

Despite such reservations about writings akin to free translation, Bishop did engage in what might be called transformative interpretation of poems in other languages. Her "Invitation to Marianne Moore," based on Pablo Neruda's elegy "Alberto Rojas Giménez viene volando," is one of the better known examples. The connection between one of Bishop's most important poems, "Brazil, January 1, 1502" (1960), and the French Modernist poet Max Jacob's "Etablissement d'une communauté au Brésil" ["Foundation of a Religious Community in Brazil"] (1921), however, remains unexplored. It is possible that both poets independently drew on the 1502 map of Brazil that was to be reprinted in Bishop's Time Inc. book *Brazil* (1962). Perhaps the striking similarities one notices, particularly the depiction of Brazil as garden landscape appearing in the map and in both poems, can be traced back to that coincidence. However, given not only the many affinities between their two poems but also the ways in which Bishop seems to respond and react to Jacob's piece, it seems more likely that "Etablissement" became part of the extensive reading on Brazil Bishop did before writing her poem. A study, therefore, of Bishop's reconfiguration of Jacob's poem serves two important purposes: on the one hand, it calls attention to a frequently overlooked influence on Bishop's poetry. On the other, it broadens our understanding of Bishop's strategies of transformative interpretation as a creative means of interacting with and building on existing foreign poetry without, for as much, engaging in the free translation of which she was so deeply skeptical.

Reading Bishop's published letters and biography, one can easily come away with the impression that the poet was not altogether fond of France and its culture. A tragic car accident in Burgundy, acute attacks of asthma during her sojourns in Paris, and too many visits to the American Hospital in Neuilly led her to exclaim in a letter to Marianne Moore, dated November 24, 1937: "I hope I never see the place again." Bishop, it seems, came to associate many of the traumas of her life – loss, loneliness, illness, injury, the inability to write, and even alcoholism (for she had developed what Brett Millier calls "an unfortunate fondness for Pernod" [93]) – with French culture and surroundings. It is telling that after several visits in the mid- and late 1930s, she never returned.

Although she seemed to be at odds with all things French, Bishop must have been somewhat interested in the French Cubist poet Max Jacob (1876–1944). Engaging with his work enough to publish literal translations of four of his poems in 1950, she may have also been inspired by some of his titles, experiments, and themes.[3] Both Bishop and Jacob have a poem titled "Chemin de Fer" ["Railway"]; both have many titles evoking the concepts of travel and geography; Bishop's "Roosters" is reminiscent of Jacob's "Le coq et la perle" ["The Rooster and the Pearl"]; Bishop's title "One Art" resembles Jacob's "Art intime" ["Private Art"]; and her "Exchanging Hats" bears resemblance to his "La tante, la tarte et le chapeau" ["The Aunt, the Tart, and the Hat"]. Beyond titles, the surrealist experiment seen in "The Man-Moth" recalls one of Jacob's most important collections, *Le cornet à dés* (1917) [*The Dice Cup*]. Moreover, Bishop's recurrent attempts to conceptualize the relationship between home and travel in such poems as "Questions of Travel" and "Arrival at Santos" are reflected in several of Jacob's poems including "Voyages" ["Trips"]. Bishop and Jacob again have a common denominator in that they repeatedly expressed their frustrated inability to know marginalized peoples, as in Bishop's "Manuelzinho" and Jacob's "La mendiante de Naples" ["The Beggar Woman of Naples"].[4]

The extent to which such connections can be used to develop a deeper understanding of Jacob's influence on Bishop remains to be seen.[5] However, there is no question about the importance of the relationship between Jacob's "Etablissement d'une communauté au Brésil" ["Foundation of a Religious Community in Brazil"] (1921) and Bishop's "Brazil, January 1, 1502" (1960). In these two poems the setting, plot, and dramatic development toward crisis all yield significant parallels. Just as important are the ways in which Bishop reacts to and departs from Jacob's model, crafting a piece that redirects and sharpens Jacob's critique of imperialism. It is such transformative interpretation of a fairly obscure poem by Max Jacob, then, that has contributed to one of most important poems Bishop ever wrote.

Formally, the two poems are different enough. Jacob's "Etablissement" is made up of grammatically complete sentences that are strongly marked by internal rhyme and cast in classic alexandrine lines punctuated by regularly recurring heroic couplets. Though similar in overall length and stanzaic structure, Bishop's "Brazil" consists of free verse whose cumulative descriptive phrases disregard conventional syntax. Irregular in length, casual in tone, the lines of this poem follow no regular rhyme scheme but rely on such devices as alliteration, repetition, and enumeration, all of which are almost entirely absent from Jacob's poem.

While the formal elements of the two poems have little in common, their respective openings usher in strong thematic affinities. The two poems begin as follows:

> On fut reçu par la fougère et l'ananas
> L'antilope craintif sous l'ipécacuanha.
> Le moine enlumineur quitta son aquarelle
> Et le vaisseau n'avait pas replié son aile
> Que cent abris légers fleurissaient la forêt.
> Les nonnes laboraient. L'une d'elles pleurait
> Trouvant dans une lettre un sujet de chagrin
> Un moine intempérant s'enivrait de raisin.
> Et l'on priait pour le pardon de ce péché
> On cueillait des poisons à la cime des branches
> Et les moines vanniers tressaient des urnes blanches.
> Un forçat évadé qui vivait de la chasse
>
> Fut guéri de ses plaies et touché de la grâce:
> Devenu saint, de tous les autres adoré,
> Il obligeait les fauves à leur lécher les pieds.
> Et les oiseaux du ciel, les bêtes de la terre
> Leur apportaient à tous les objets nécessaires.
> Un jour on eut un orgue au creux de murs crépis
> Des troupeaux de moutons qui mordaient les épis
> Un moine est borrelier, l'autre est distillateur
> Le dimanche après vêpre on herborise en chœur.
>   (stanza 1, Jacob's "Etablissement")

> We were received by ferns and pineapple
> The timid antelope beneath the ipecacuanha.
> The monk abandoned his illumination
> And the vessel had scarcely folded its wings
> When a hundred simple shelters flowered in the forest.

The nuns labored. One of them wept
Finding in a letter occasion for shame
An intemperate monk became drunk on grape wine.
And we prayed for his sin to be pardoned
We plucked potions from the tips of the boughs
And the basket-making monks plaited white urns.
An escaped convict who survived on hunting
Was cured of his wounds and blessed by grace:
Became a saint, worshipped by all others,
And compelled wild creatures to lick their feet.
And the birds in the sky, the beasts of the earth
Brought them all that they needed.
One day an organ was housed in the hollow of the rough walls
Herds of sheep nibbled the ears of corn
One monk is a saddler, the other a distiller
On Sundays, after vespers, we botanize as we chant.

                                                         (translation[6])

Januaries, Nature greets our eyes
exactly as she must have greeted theirs:
every square inch filling in with foliage –
big leaves, little leaves, and giant leaves,
blue, blue-green, and olive,
with occasional lighter veins and edges,
or a satin underleaf turned over;
monster ferns
in silver-gray relief,
and flowers, too, like giant water lilies
up in the air – up, rather, in the leaves –
purple, yellow, two yellows, pink,
rust red and greenish white;
solid but airy; fresh as if just finished
and taken off the frame.

                                        (stanza 1, Bishop's "Brazil")

Both poems are set in Brazil; both evoke a period of colonization when Christians arrived on foreign soil and began to call it their own. The openings are very similar in that they both portray nature as eagerly welcoming its invaders. Jacob's poem begins with "We were received by ferns and pineapple, / the timid antelope beneath the ipecacuanha" ["On fut reçu par la fougère et l'ananas / L'antilope craintif sous l'ipécacuanha"],[7] and Bishop's opens, "Nature greets our eyes / exactly as she must have greeted theirs" – the intruders'. Seductively lush and abundant, landscape and nature are quickly understood as existing for the sole purpose of serving the white man.

    Such fecundity and splendor lure the Christians into a false sense of harmony with their surroundings. Blinded by the Edenic vision of "wild creatures lick[ing] their feet" ["Il obligeait les fauves à leur lécher les pieds"] and "the birds in the sky, the beasts of the earth" supplying "all that they needed" ["Et les oiseaux du ciel, les bêtes de la terre / Leurs apportaient à tous les objets nécessaires"], the monks and nuns of Jacob's poem fail to understand that their peace derives not from the welcome nature extends to them but from the ideals they import and impose on it. In Bishop's "Brazil," the Portuguese conquistadors do not appear until the last stanza; however, the poet implies from the beginning that nature's plenty blinds them in similar ways. The saturation of the surroundings, conveyed by Bishop's rich visual detail and her repeated emphasis on color, makes it impossible for these people (as well as for any visitor who came after them) to see anything but the "purple, yellow, two yellows, pink, / rust red and greenish white" vegetation. Despite or precisely because of their voyeurism, they do not recognize that they are violating this earth, domesticating it by means of their own cultural codes. What they see is a luxurious aesthetic tapestry – something they could simply "[take] off the frame" and use as they see fit – not a complex political reality.

Tracing a plot whose three cornerstones are white Christian invasion of Brazil, appropriation of land and nature, and confrontation with nonwhite peoples, both poems stage a dramatically rising tension before moving into the climactic battle. "Etablissement" foreshadows the violent events by repeatedly invoking sin. Jacob mentions a nun who weeps, "Finding in a letter occasion for shame" ["Trouvant dans une lettre un sujet de chagrin"], "An intemperate monk [who] became drunk on grape wine" ["Un moine intempérant s'enivrait de raisin"], and "An escaped convict who survived on hunting" ["Un forçat évadé qui vivait de la chasse"]. The sense of impending doom is at its strongest when, in stanza two, Jacob charges the atmosphere with such an exaggerated sense of bliss that the very walls he evokes threaten to crumble:

> Saluez le manguier et bénissez la mangue
> La flûte du crapaud vous parle dans sa langue
> Les autels sont parés de fleurs vraiment étranges
> Leurs parfums attiraient le sourire des anges,
> Des sylphes, des esprits blottis dans la forêt
> Autour des murs carrés de la communauté.
> (from stanza 2, Jacob's "Etablissement")

> Hail to the mango tree and blessed be its flesh
> The flute of the toad speaks to you in its tongue
> The altars are decked with astonishing flowers
> Their fragrance made the angels smile,
> Sylphs, spirits huddled in the forest
> All around the square walls of the community.
> (translation)

This vision of Brazil, the poem's parodic tone makes clear, is unsustainable. Peaceful, pastoral, and paradisal beyond all plausibility, the descriptions create in the reader an expectation of collapse and doom.

Like Jacob, Bishop strategically builds toward the confrontation at the end of her poem. As Barbara Page has observed, her title, "Brazil, January 1, 1502," denotes the date of the naming of Rio de Janeiro by a party of Portuguese colonists and thus already represents an appropriative act that presages the ensuing violence (40). The final battle is further prepared for by Bishop's deliberate yoking of nature and culture in stanza two:

> A blue-white sky, a simple web,
> backing for feathery detail:
> brief arcs, a pale-green broken wheel,
> a few palms, swarthy, squat, but delicate;

> and perching there in profile, beaks agape,
> the big symbolic birds keep quiet,
> each showing only half his puffed and padded,
> pure-colored or spotted breast.
>   (from stanza 2, Bishop's "Brazil")

Just as Jacob lets not nature alone but "a hundred simple shelters flower in the forest" ["cent abris légers fleurissaient la forêt"] in his poem, so human traces stemming from the colonists, the "pale-green broken wheel," become part of the "feathery detail" that otherwise consists of palms and birds in Bishop's. In both cases, the landscape is thus marked as violated, its purity compromised by outside influences.

Paralleling Jacob, Bishop invokes sin to foreshadow the ending of the poem, capitalizing "Sin" and placing it in a prominent position in the middle of stanza two:

> Still in the foreground there is Sin:
> five sooty dragons near some massy rocks.
> The rocks are worked with lichens, gray moonbursts
> splattered and overlapping,
> threatened from underneath by moss
> in lovely hell-green flames,
> attacked above
> by scaling-ladder vines, oblique and neat,
> "one leaf yes and one leaf no" (in Portuguese).
> The lizards scarcely breathe; all eyes
> are on the smaller, female one, back-to,
> her wicked tail straight up and over,
> red as a red-hot wire.
>   (from stanza 2, Bishop's "Brazil")

Here, the mention of "Sin," just like that of the broken wheel, interrupts the descriptions of nature and calls attention to imperialist presence. Nature itself is hardly sinful; instead, lizards that seem like "dragons" with "wicked tails," moss that is likened to "hell-green flames" capable of "attack," and birds that appear as "symbolic," in some cases (sinfully) "spotted," are all European constructions, New World nature seen through the lens of Old World myth. Reconfiguring nature as deliciously sinful *"femme fatale,"* as Thomas Travisano puts it (139), Bishop prepares her contrast with the real sin at the end of the poem, the ravaging of the landscape and its population.

If Jacob's most effective device for developing such dramatic tension is his persona's exaggerated vocal praise of his New World surroundings, Bishop's is the ominous silence she creates up to her poem's final stanza. The "beaks agape" of the birds seem frozen, the pun on *"Still* in the foreground there is Sin" spreads a hushed atmosphere, and her "lizards scarcely breathe." Brazil's nature is lying in wait, nearing the boiling point. Like Jacob's, it is suspended but ready to explode.

The rising tension leads to a violent confrontation between Christians and nonwhite peoples in both poems. Jacob reaches this climax at the end of stanza two; Bishop does so in her final stanza:

> Or voici qu'un matin quand l'Aurore saignante
> Fit la nuée plus pure et plus fraîche la plante
> La forêt où la vigne au cèdre s'unissait,

Parut avoir la teigne. Un nègre paraissait
Puis deux, puis cent, puis mille et l'herbe en était teinte
Et le Saint qui pouvait dompter les animaux
Ne put rien sur ces gens qui furent ses bourreaux.
La tête du couvent roula dans l'herbe verte
Et des moines détruits la place fut déserte
Sans que rien dans l'azur ne frémit de la mort.

(from stanza 2, Jacob's "Etablissement")

Now one morning when a dawn bleeding red
Purified the storm cloud and refreshed all vegetation
The forest where the cedar vines entwined,
Seemed infected with ringworm. A negro appeared
Then two, then a hundred, then a thousand, then the grass was tainted
And the saint who could tame wild animals
Could not avail against these people, his torturers.
The head of the convent rolled in the green grass
And, once the monks were dead, the place was deserted
Without anything in the sky trembling with death.

(translation)

Just so the Christians, hard as nails,
tiny as nails, and glinting,
in creaking armor, came and found it all,
not unfamiliar:
no lovers' walks, no bowers,
no cherries to be picked, no lute music,
but corresponding, nevertheless,
to an old dream of wealth and luxury
already out of style when they left home –
wealth, plus a brand-new pleasure.
Directly after Mass, humming perhaps
L'Homme armé or some such tune,
they ripped away into the hanging fabric,
each out to catch an Indian for himself –
those maddening little women who kept calling,
calling to each other (or had the birds waked up?)
and retreating, always retreating, behind it.

(stanza 3, Bishop's "Brazil")

In "Etablissement," the aggressors are identified as Negroes who emerge from the forest and multiply by the thousands: "The forest where the cedar vines entwined, / Seemed infected with ringworm. A negro appeared / Then two, then a hundred, then a thousand, then the grass was tainted" ["La forêt où la vigne au cèdre s'unissait, / Parut avoir la teigne. Un nègre paraissait / Puis deux, puis cent, puis mille et l'herbe en était teinte"]. The victims, in turn, are the monks; even the convict-turned-saint "Could not avail against these people, his torturers" ["Ne put rien sur ces gens qui furent ses bourreaux"]. Far from positioning himself on the side of the victims, however, Jacob introduces a subtle irony that destabilizes easy assumptions about the Negro as degraded and the Christian as noble. To the speaker and the religious community, the Negroes may appear like a ringworm infection that taints their Edenic space with sin. To the reader, however, they are presented as a natural force, an embodiment of the Brazilian forest materializing to repel the Christians from a place to which they have no right. The Christians are portrayed with the same sense of irony. While they see themselves as righteous, a perception that is indicated as religious words like "saint," "monk," and "convent" reinforce one another during the moment of crisis, Jacob does little to strengthen his reader's sympathy for them.

Like Jacob, Bishop finds confrontation inevitable, and like him, she stages it to develop a critique of imperialist intervention.[8] However, Bishop chooses to voice this shared concern in much more explicit terms. To do so, she introduces several important variations on Jacob's poem. First, she reverses the positions of the Christians in "Brazil." The Portuguese colonists assume the role of brutalizing offenders as they "[rip] away into the hanging fabric." They are cold-blooded torturers, for, as Bishop makes clear, they are not simply attacking for some vaguely justified reason; rather, they are intent on experiencing illicit stimulation, "a brand-new pleasure" they cannot get at home. Bishop calls them "Christians" once, but far from stressing their religious devotion, she evokes the term only to contrast and replace it with military imagery that recasts them as belligerent soldiers. Indeed, they become the savages whose morality Bishop questions by calling attention, as many have pointed out, to their suspicious yoking of religion and war: "Directly after Mass, [they are] humming perhaps / *L'Homme armé* or some such tune." Their brutality does not, however, gain them an unequivocal position of power. Careful not to make them appear valiant, Bishop ridicules them, reducing them to "Christians, hard as nails, / tiny as nails, and glinting, / in creaking armor." While Jacob made it difficult to pity his Christians, Bishop makes it impossible. Once indicted and belittled by the poet, the dwarfed intruders cannot begin to measure up to the awe and dignity commanded by, say, Brazil's "monster ferns." For all their violence, these tin soldiers remain impotent.

The second way in which Bishop formulates a more direct critique of imperialist appropriation is by reconfiguring the gender dynamics of Jacob's poem. Unlike "Etablissement," where all female presence, notably that of the nuns, disappears from the battle scene, the indigenous people who appear in the climactic moment of "Brazil" are specifically identified as women. These women are prey in the eyes of the Portuguese conquistadors; unwilling or unable to fight even in self-defense, they retreat from the hostility of their predators. Their retreat does not, however, represent defeat. Matching and surpassing Jacob's strategy of linking nature and nonwhites, Bishop aligns these native women with their surroundings, connecting them with the female lizard, merging their cries with the birds', and anchoring them securely in the protective tapestry of nature. "[C]alling to each other," they break the poem's silence as they rely on values of communion and a politics of inclusion that destabilizes the strategies of their stalkers. To be sure, these aggressors still advance, but because they fight individually, "each out to catch an Indian for himself," they always remain on the margins of both the women's and their own community. Clearly, then, Bishop shares Jacob's focus on the disruption and destruction caused by imperialist intrusion. However, she expands that focus by linking sexual exploitation to geographic imperialism and by highlighting the ways in which such invasiveness might well expose the aggressors' weaknesses more clearly than those of the the victims.[9]

In a third key variation on Jacob's poem, Bishop's "Brazil" moves away from considerations of how imperialism might affect its perpetrators so as to examine its impact on the land and its people. Transforming Jacob's "Negroes" who violently attack a holy mission into "Indians" who are pursued through no fault of their own, Bishop positions her speaker squarely on the side of the beleaguered natives. "Etablissement" reveals the fate of the Christian monks whose deaths culminate in the "head of the convent" ["La tête du couvent"] "roll[ing] in the green grass" ["roula dans l'herbe verte"]. The Negroes, however, suddenly vanish, as does their forest, and while the last stanza provides insight into the life of the surviving speaker long after the events, we learn no more about Brazil in the aftermath of the crisis. Bishop denies her speaker (and us) the escape from the Brazilian perspective that Jacob allows his speaker, keeping her poem firmly situated in the country, among its natives. Each stride her Christians take to penetrate into the forest is directly counteracted by her Indians' retreating steps, creating a perpetual limbo that leaves us suspended in Brazil. Underscoring this suspension, Bishop leads us away from definitive victories or defeats, alluding to violence but skillfully withdrawing her profuse color imagery once its only logical use would be to suggest blood. Ironically, such resistance to closure calls attention to the scope of the country's violation. Imperialism, the poem argues, must be seen as an ongoing cycle of advance and retreat causing obvious but also insidious violations whose costs are as elusive as they are high. Just as the generalizing use of the plural in "Januaries" in the poem's opening suggests an impact so far-reaching that 1502 and the present are forever linked, so Bishop's unresolved ending indicates that imperialist acts have caused Brazil and its inhabitants to suffer far beyond what can be assessed accurately or immediately.

In what is perhaps her most significant move to both share and sharpen Jacob's concerns about the consequences of imperialism, Bishop aligns her persona with Jacob's and then repositions that voice in order to propose a constructive model for dealing with issues of guilt and complicity. The similarities between the two personae are apparent enough as both are clearly relating an event from which they have gained considerable distance. Jacob's persona has long returned home, as his last stanza implies:

> C'est ainsi que vêtu d'innocence et d'amour
> J'avançais en traçant mon travail chaque jour
> Priant Dieu et croyant à la beauté des choses
> Mais le rire cruel, les soucis qu'on m'impose
> L'argent et l'opinion, la bêtise d'autrui
> Ont fait de moi le dur bourgeois qui signe ici.
> (stanza 3, Jacob's "Etablissement")

> Thus it was that I, clad in innocence and love
> Moved along laying out my task each day
> Praying to God and believing in the beauty of things
> But the cruel jeers, the troubles that are laid upon me
> The money and people's opinions, the foolishness of others
> Have made me the harsh bourgeois who attests to this.
> (translation)

Bishop's, a visitor-tourist who re-imagines the events of Brazil in 1502, is even more removed from the actual events. In both cases, however, passing time does little to deflect the speakers' complicity. Jacob's cannot be exonerated as he was part of a religious community whose presence led to mass slaughter. Though the speaker of "Brazil" was never a participant or even a direct witness, Bishop takes care to overlay this visitor's critical and historical distance to imperialism with recurrent intimations of her implication in it. On the one hand, her persona is clearly aware of wrongly imposed reconstructions of

Brazil; on the other, she is as seduced by the land as were the settlers in 1502. Unable to resist the desire to mark this exotic earth as her own, she still applies her ideals and vocabulary to capture its images.[10]

The shared complicity and guilt of the personae, however, result in disparate responses. Far from developing a sense of responsibility, Jacob's speaker falls into a resignation that makes it impossible for him to see beyond his own person. Rather than considering his deeds and what he might do to atone for them, he focuses on his own suffering in the wake of the community's failure: "But the cruel jeers, the troubles that are laid upon me / The money and people's opinion, the foolishness of others / Have made me the harsh bourgeois who attests to this" ["Mais le rire cruel, les soucis qu'on m'impose / L'argent et l'opinion, la bêtise d'autrui / Ont fait de moi le dur bourgeois qui signe ici"]. Steeped in effusive self-pity and bitterness, he sees himself as an innocent victim, an essentially good and God-fearing man who has been hardened by the circumstances of his life. Imperialism becomes a personal tragedy that is answered by a narcissistic retreat into the self.

Jacob makes his persona so thoroughly unlikable that it becomes clear that the poet is not condoning but indicting his escape from complicity. Bishop, however, moves beyond simply exposing fruitless ways of dealing with guilt, illustrating not how one can lapse into repressing and denying one's implication in the processes of imperialism but, rather, how one might face such implication. Her main strategy for doing so consists of transforming the self-centered persona in "Etablissement" into the sympathetic voice in "Brazil." By the end of the poem, Bishop's speaker has aligned herself with the Indian women and seems to join them as they retreat into the depths of the receding forest. The imperialist guilt of Bishop's visitor-tourist, like that of Jacob's, leads to retreat, but her retreat signals not a withdrawal into the self but a cautious affiliation with the embattled women. Bishop thus closes "Brazil" by establishing a useful, if imperfect, basis for acknowledging guilt and complicity, one that involves interacting and engaging with the violated land and its natives on their terms. Significantly, Bishop's ironic assurance that "Nature greets our eyes / exactly as she must have greeted theirs" attests to the capacity for insight of her speaker, whereas the mock-peaceful skies in Jacob's post-battle scene stress the blindness of his.

Without further investigation, the full extent of Jacob's influence on Bishop will remain unclear. However, it seems likely that as she was working on "Brazil," he and his poem came to her attention. Drawing on "Etablissement," Bishop developed, redirected, and politicized the critique of imperialism she found in Jacob. Her response to the model poem sheds important light on Bishop's strategies of building on existing foreign poetry to voice her own concerns more clearly and may, in the present case, serve to inform and confirm the increasing number of studies that seek to adjust the long-held misperception of Bishop's poetry as apolitical.[11] Given the relationship between the two poems, it is moreover perhaps time to admit Max Jacob to a more central position in the arena of Bishop studies. To be sure, "Brazil, January 1, 1502" is not literal or free translation – something, as we have seen, Bishop always associated with some measure of "bloodletting or seepage." In line with the anti-imperialist sentiment of "Brazil, January 1, 1502," she did not rip into the fabric of "Etablissement d'une communauté au Brésil" to create her own poem. But like the Portuguese conquerors who came to Brazil, she too was seduced into making use of a rich texture she beheld, crafting anew a work of art in a double-stitched pattern of transformative interpretation.

Morehead State University
Morehead, Kentucky

Notes

1   In the introduction to her collection of translations from the Portuguese, *An Anthology of Twentieth-Century Brazilian Poetry* (1972), she confirmed this position by showing herself proud of her and her fellow translators' successful attempts at self-effacement, commenting that "The editors feel that the translators have done extremely well, keeping close to the texts and yet managing to produce 'poems' preserving many of the characteristics of the originals" (xv). As Victoria Harrison observes, Bishop would only translate what lent itself to literal translation, and she saw her translations from the Portuguese as her "duty for Brazilian letters" (letter to May Swenson, 30 Dec. 1963, qtd. in Harrison, 174).

2   For a discussion of Bishop's concern with Lowell's translations, see David Kalstone's *Becoming a Poet: Elizabeth Bishop with Marianne Moore and Robert Lowell* (203–8).

3   Four literal translations, "Rainbow," "Patience of an Angel," "Banks," and "Hell is Graduated," appear in Bishop's *The Complete Poems: 1927–1979* and were first published in the May 1950 issue of *Poetry*.

4   Some translations of titles here are generally established and accepted; others are mine.

5   The biographical parallels, though very possibly coincidental, warrant some attention. Bishop shared Jacob's tendency toward timidity, self-hatred, addiction, depression, and restlessness. Both poets were homosexual, and while Bishop never went so far as to refer to her lesbianism as "an atrocious accident, a tear in the robe of humanity" (Jacob, qtd. in Huffington, 58), she, like Jacob, did not feel comfortable displaying her sexual identity in her writings. With varying success, both poets attempted to separate the public and the private, and both have been described as impersonal and masked. Though Jacob evolved into a recluse and Bishop did not, his retreat from Paris to the small French village of Saint-Benoît-sur-Loire parallels Bishop's period in Brazil and her lifelong discomfort with the bustling life of New York City. Repeatedly writing about travel, the two poets moreover shared an inability or reluctance to live sedentary, stable lives with regular jobs, which resulted, in both cases, in frequent shuttling between several base locations. In their respective poetic practices, both poets concentrated on form and detail, and the scholarly community has, in both cases, vacillated between claiming them as surrealists, modernists, and postmodernists.

6   In my translation of Jacob's "Etablissement d'une communauté au Brésil," I am indebted to David Burnett's *Transfusions: Poems from the French*. Special thanks also to Jed Deppman, who was enormously helpful to the translation and understanding of this poem. I have made every attempt to translate as literally as possible.

7   According to the *Oxford English Dictionary* the ipecacuanha is a South American shrub that possesses emetic, diaphoretic, and purgative properties. The Dutch and the Portuguese brought it home from the coasts of Brazil.

8   One can assume that Jacob stands behind the critique in his poem and that he was, indeed, opposed to imperialist gestures. Although he passionately believed in the value of converting people to Christianity and openly serving God, he was firmly convinced that it was wrong to impose his beliefs. A Jew who, following a vision in 1909, became a devout Catholic, Jacob wanted to serve as a model to the people surrounding him, but only by letting religion take an indirect effect on them. In *La Défense de Tartufe*, Jacob lists several rules he seeks to follow in his life. The fourth rule reads: "ne pas se vanter de sa religion parce que c'est se servir de Dieu pour une attitude, et pourtant ne pas s'en cacher, donc ne pas mettre les perles devant les pourceaux" ["do not flaunt your religion, for that is using God for the sake of appearance only. Yet do not hide it; in other words, don't throw pearls before swine"]. His fifth rule is: "ne prêcher que les gens convertissables" ["preach only to those who may be converted"]. And the sixth runs: "donner à tous l'exemple de la vie modèle, pour faire indirectement l'éloge d'une religion si admirable" ["live a model life, and in so doing, give indirect praise to an excellent religion"] (qtd. in Billy, 32–33; translations mine). Bishop appears to have been similarly sensitive about appropriative impositions. When Time, Inc. proceeded to make numerous excisions from the *Brazil* volume she had painstakingly prepared for the new Life World Library, her reactions were little short of violent. "Their idea," she protested in a letter written to May Swenson in 1962, "is to present their own undisturbed pre-conceptions of a country" (qtd. in Millier, 328). In a letter to Lowell, dated 1960, she expressed the difficulty of using the Brazilian "accumulation of exotic or picturesque or charming detail"

while maintaining the distance and respect that a "New Englander herring-choker bluenoser" owes the country (*One Art*, 383–84).

9   For a reading of the bird-women as victorious, see Page's "Nature, History, and Art in Elizabeth Bishop's 'Brazil, January 1, 1502'" and Lynn Keller and Cristanne Miller's "Emily Dickinson, Elizabeth Bishop, and the Rewards of Indirection."

10   Commenting on Bishop's own complicity, Robert Dale Parker argues, "She describes the creation of Brazil in violence and rape, and yet also pays homage to the cultural and bodily trauma of its birth, because that trauma begets the identity and heritage of the place she loves" (97).

11   For examples of studies that highlight Bishop's political dimensions, see James Longenbach's article "Elizabeth Bishop's Social Conscience" or Camille Roman's *Elizabeth Bishop's World War II – Cold War View*.

Works Cited

Billy, André. *Poètes d'Aujourd'hui: Max Jacob*. Paris: Editions Pierre Seghers, 1960.

Bishop, Elizabeth. *Brazil*. New York: Time-Life Books, 1962.

Bishop, Elizabeth. *The Complete Poems 1927–1979*. New York: Farrar, Straus and Giroux, 1983.

Bishop, Elizabeth. *One Art: Letters, Selected and Edited*. Ed. Robert Giroux. New York: Noonday Press, 1994.

Bishop, Elizabeth. *Remarks on Translation – (Of poetry, mostly)*. Elizabeth Bishop Papers. Ms. 54.12. Vassar College Libraries, Special Collections. Poughkeepsie, N.Y.

Bishop, Elizabeth, and Emanuel Brasil, eds. *An Anthology of Twentieth-Century Brazilian Poetry*. Middleton: Wesleyan University Press, 1972.

Goldensohn, Lorrie. *Elizabeth Bishop: The Biography of a Poet*. New York: Columbia University Press, 1992.

Harrison, Victoria. *Elizabeth Bishop's Poetics of Intimacy*. Cambridge: Cambridge University Press, 1993.

Huffington, Arianna Stassinopoulos. *Picasso: Creator and Destroyer*. New York: Simon and Schuster, 1988.

Jacob, Max. "Etablissement d'une communauté au Brésil." *Le Laboratoire central: Poésies*. Paris: Au Sans Pareil, 1921.

Jacob, Max. Ballades suivi de Visions infernales, Fond de l'eau, Sacrifice impérial, Rivage, Les Pénitents en maillots roses. Paris: Editions Gallimard, 1970.

Jacob, Max. "Foundation of a community in Brazil." Trans. David Burnett. *Transfusions: Poems from the French*. Newcastle upon Tyne: Tynside Free Press, 1995.

Jacob, Max. *Le Cornet à dés* (1917). Paris: Editions Gallimard, 1945.

Kalstone, David. *Becoming a Poet: Elizabeth Bishop with Marianne Moore and Robert Lowell*. New York: Farrar, Straus, and Giroux, 1989.

Keller, Lynn, and Christanne Miller. "Emily Dickinson, Elizabeth Bishop, and the Rewards of Indirection." *New England Quarterly* 57 (Dec. 1984): 533–53.

Lombardi, Marilyn May. *The Body and the Song: Elizabeth Bishop's Poetics*. Carbondale: Southern Illinois University Press, 1995.

Longenbach, James. "Elizabeth Bishop's Social Conscience." *ELH* 62 (Summer 1995): 467–86.

Millier, Brett C. *Elizabeth Bishop: Life and the Memory of It*. Berkeley: University of California Press, 1993.

Page, Barbara. "Nature, History, and Art in Elizabeth Bishop's 'Brazil, January 1, 1502.'" *Perspectives on Contemporary Literature* 14 (1988): 39–46.

Parker, Robert Dale. *The Unbeliever: The Poetry of Elizabeth Bishop*. Urbana: University of Illinois Press, 1988.

Roman, Camille. *Elizabeth Bishop's World War II – Cold War View*. New York: Palgrave, 2001.

Travisano, Thomas J. *Elizabeth Bishop: Her Artistic Development*. Charlottesville: University Press of Virginia, 1988.

CHAPTER 12

Theory in Practice

Annals of Ice: Formations of Empire, Place and History in John Galt and Alice Munro

Katie Trumpener

Katie Trumpener compares a fiction about the colonization of Canada – John Galt's *Bogle Corbet*, which was written in the early nineteenth century and which depicts the imperial arrival in Canada of European emigrants and colonialists – with Alice Munro's *Lives of Girls and Women*, written in the late twentieth century, which examines the same geographic and cultural terrain as Galt's novel but from the perspective of the legacies of successful colonization.

Nineteenth-century Scots were disproportionately involved in the British Empire as army officers, administrators, engineers, settlers – and writers. John Galt and William 'Tiger' Dunlop in Upper Canada, Thomas McCulloch in Nova Scotia, Thomas Pringle in the Cape and Thomas McCombie in Australia wrote pioneering literary works in and about Britain's new colonies, established new frameworks for colonial life and spread an empire-wide vogue for Scottish literature.

From the nineteenth century onward, indeed, Canada's English-language writers closely followed Scottish literary prototypes; Canadian literature was filled with Scottish character types (from ministers to crofters) and modelled on Scottish literary genres (from historical novel to dialect poetry) (Gittings 1995; Waterston 2003). Writers of Scottish heritage, moreover, played a pre-eminent role in the literary life of Anglophone Canada; as late as the 1960s and 1970s, Margaret Laurence, Alice Munro, Mavis Gallant and Margaret Atwood were hailed as harbingers of a new national literature. Yet while steeped in Scottish cultural and literary narratives, Munro and Laurence wrote to correct long-standing Scottish views of Canada itself. This chapter reads Scotland's

Original publication details: Katie Trumpener, "Annals of Ice: Formations of Empire, Place, and History in John Galt and Alice Munro" from *Scottish Literature and Postcolonial Theory: Comparative Texts and Critical Perspectives*, ed. Michael Gardiner, Graeme Macdonald, and Niall O'Gallagher, pp. 43–56. Edinburgh University Press, 2011.

most complex nineteenth-century colonial novel, Galt's half-forgotten 1831 *Bogle Corbet, or the Emigrants*, against Munro's fiction. Galt and Munro inhabit very different temporal, political and literary moments, yet describe the same area, in present-day Ontario, while sharing an interest in the local texture of historical experience, using annalistic accretion to ground new forms of historical fiction.

Galt arrived in Upper Canada in 1826 to supervise development of the Huron Tract, a million acres of largely uninhabited, previously unsurveyed land adjoining Lake Huron. He founded the towns of Guelph and Goderich – experiences he fictionalised once back in Britain. Munro claims lineal and literary descent from Scottish Romanticism. Her ancestors migrated to Upper Canada from Scotland in 1818 and, beginning in the 1840s, homesteaded on the Huron Tract. Munro grew up (and still lives) near Goderich.

In describing the same region, Galt and Munro frame it very differently. Galt's Bogle Corbet moves to Canada in a doomed attempt to escape politics and history: from the political unrest of the Jamaica plantations, the social transformations accompanying Scotland's Industrial Revolution, the failure of Jacobin politics. Yet these traumas continue to haunt the new colony. Munro's Ontario, in turn, is haunted by its own nineteenth-century settlement history, the legacy of colonists like Galt. *Bogle Corbet* at once allegorises Galt's own involvement with imperial political economy, and develops a far-reaching model of imperial exchange, consciousness and guilt; it both recapitulates and complicates Galt's earlier novelistic annals of Scottish life. Munro's interest is less in imperial morality than in colonial self-understanding and epistemology, as they shape contemporary life and potentially complicate nationalist or postcolonial notions of cultural reclamation.

Galt and Munro's accounts are overlapping yet asymmetrical. This asymmetry is reflected in the structure of this comparative chapter, which begins by detailing Galt's activities as a 'coloniser' in Upper Canada, highlighting the complexity of his historical circumstances, motivations and relationship to British and colonial authority. If Galt's administrative work in Upper Canada might exemplify a distinctive Scottish colonial idealism, his setbacks and disappointments discernibly shaped *Bogle Corbet* as an anti-imperial novel. The chapter then develops a rather different framework for Munro's fiction, and reads against the literary politics of Canadian nationalism (itself consciously reorienting a long Scottish-Canadian literary tradition). Yet Munro also adapts and refashions the Galtian novel of place, implicitly rejoining Galt's inquiry into the relationship between history and neurosis, time and place, empire and nation.

Long before he became an official colonist or colonial chronicler, Galt had, as a political commentator and lobbyist, followed – and, from London, interceded in – Canadian affairs, publishing a 1807 'Statistical Account of Upper Canada' and, during the 1820s, repeatedly petitioning Parliament on behalf of Upper Canada claimants loyal to the Crown throughout the colony's 1812 American invasion and suffering damages from the invading American army. In 1825, Galt gained the lasting gratitude of Mohawk chief John Brant by securing parliamentary approval for a land claim by the Six Nations Indians, recognising their 1812 allegiance to Britain (Timothy 1977: 97). Yet other Loyalists, despite Galt's efforts, remained unrecompensed. During the colony's initial British settlement, two-sevenths of Upper Canada's land became vast 'crown and clergy reserves', set aside for public works and Protestant church use. Galt unsuccessfully proposed that the colony compensate loyalists by selling reserve land. Later, he spear-headed a move by London investors to create the Canada Company, a joint stock company, incorporated by Parliament in 1826, to buy up Upper Canada reserve lands for development and resale to emigrants.

Appointed as the Company's first Canadian superintendent, Galt sailed for North America, inspected pre-existing settlements in upstate New York, then began developing the Huron Tract: surveying, laying connective roads, building schools, receiving settlers. On St George's Day, 1827, Galt joined his woodsmen in the rainy bush, and with a ceremonial axe-stroke began tree-felling and bush clearance, founding Guelph as a new company town, sixty miles west of present-day Toronto. His report to London treats the date as happy coincidence, yet later autobiographical writings underscore his conscious choice of date – and the name Guelph, honouring Britain's royal family – to create origin myths (Stelter 1985). Soon after, on the shore of Lake Huron, Galt established Goderich, named for Fredrick Robinson, Viscount Goderich, the Canada Company's most influential parliamentary champion. Today Goderich is a small town of 8,000 while Guelph, currently a university town of over 100,000, retains many of its original limestone buildings, and a statue of Galt in front of City Hall.

On 4 August 2008, Guelph celebrated its first annual John Galt Day. But before dawn, anarchists splashed red paint on Galt's statue, an action memorialised on several anarchist websites. As one explains, the Canada Company settlement took place

> at the expense of indigenous populations. John Galt was actively engaged in that process and helped lay the foundation for genocide of unimaginable proportions. John Galt's own words foretold the horrific consequences of the Canada Companies [sic] agenda of genocide on the day he ceremonially felled the first tree in the founding of the city of Guelph. He wrote that 'the tree fell with a crash of accumulating thunder, as if ancient nature were alarmed at the entrance of social man into her innocent solitudes with his sorrows, his follies and his crimes' (the *Autobiography of John Galt*, pp. 58–9). To celebrate John Galt is to celebrate the foundation of colonization and genocide among other follies and crimes of European men. ('Anarchists' 2008)

Such rhetoric positions Galt as a genocidal conqueror, a Canadian Christopher Columbus. Galt indeed supported land development in Upper Canada, envisioning a colony where Scottish and British emigrants could regain self-sufficiency. Yet he was also an early champion of indigenous land claims and government transparency.

As the tree-felling passage from his *Autobiography* suggests, Galt was no naïve memoirist, needing postcolonial reading-against-the-grain to explicate unconscious subtexts of colonial guilt. His novelistic corpus, likewise, is consistently, overtly concerned with imperialism's historical meaning and psychic consequences. In Upper Canada, amid the practical work of planning, surveying and building, Galt informed his London publisher that he envisioned a novel or series set in Upper Canada, tentatively titled *The Settlers, or Tales of Guelph* (Waterston 1977a: 2). As actually written, *Bogle Corbet* became Galt's most explicit, sustained meditation on the British imperial project; its final volume chronicles the founding of an ill-fated Upper Canada settlement.

Galt's own stay in Upper Canada ended abruptly and badly. From the outset, the Family Compact (the colony's nepotistic, wealthy, reactionary oligarchy) viewed him with enmity. Determined to extirpate republican politics, the Compact repeatedly persecuted radicals like William Lyon Mackenzie (later to foment the 1837 Upper Canada Rebellion); resolved to establish Anglican primacy in the colony, this Anglican elite not only ignored Presbyterian and Methodist claims but also falsified census data about the colonists' religious make-up. Galt, in contrast, advocated religious tolerance and actively recruited Catholic settlers; Upper Canada's reformers and radicals publicly (although sometimes without his approval) claimed him as an ally.

In 1827, Galt faced an acute humanitarian crisis, when 135 indigent Scottish settlers, fleeing a failed colony in Caracas, unexpectedly arrived at the Huron Tract, sent on from Philadelphia by the British Consul. The Tract was always envisioned as a commercial venture, designed for emigrants with means to purchase their own land. The 'La Guayrans' refugees (half of them children), in contrast, arrived penniless, yet in urgent need of food, shelter and medicine, which Galt supplied using money owed to the government. Already critical of Galt's political involvement, the Compact now charged him with usurping government functions – and denounced him to Canada Company shareholders in London. The Company, in turn, urged Galt to mollify the Compact, spend less time and money developing colonial infrastructure, eliminate charitable spending and sell more land; in their view, Galt's ambitions, social vision and poor book-keeping threatened the Company's viability.

Galt was recalled to London in 1829, fired by the Company and landed in debtors' prison. He never returned to North America (Timothy 1977; Nash-Graham 1984; Lee 2004). Yet he retained direct and indirect involvement with Canada, in 1834 co-founding the British American Land Company, and sending his three sons to settle in Canada. All three became influential figures, one as Huron County registrar, another as Ontario Chief Justice, and the youngest, Sir Alexander Tilloch Galt, as secretary and commissioner of the British American Land Company, Upper Canada parliamen-tarian, Inspector-General of Canada and Canada's first federal Finance Minister. He remains best remembered as a Father of Confederation, who lobbied for Canada's 1867 constitution, then for its enshrinement of minority religious rights (Timothy 1977; Skelton 1966).

John Galt, in contrast, is not usually remembered as a Father of Canadian Literature. Yet from his London debtors' prison, he drafted two contrasting novels about Scottish emigration to North America. Both the chipper narrator of Galt's best-selling *Lawrie Todd, or The Settlers in the Wood* (1830) and *Bogle Corbet*'s depressive narrator lead emigrant parties from the West of Scotland. Lawrie Todd founds a successful settlement in upstate New York. Once Corbet's party arrive in Upper Canada, most reject his oligarchic leadership, while he disowns them.

Together, these novels represent a paradoxical coda to Galt's collectively titled 'Tales of the West'. Overlapping temporally with Scott's Waverley Novels, anticipating novel cycles by John and Michael Banim, Honoré de Balzac, Anthony Trollope, Benito Pérez Galdos and Émile Zola, Galt's novel sequence measures the depth and breadth of regional history, describing crucial historical developments from various sociological, temporal and geopolitical perspectives (Trumpener 2005, 2007; Duncan 2007). Galt's early novels repeatedly experimented with annalistic structure, as an alternative to Scott's epic history. *Annals of the Parish* (1821) and *The Provost* (1822) describe Scotland's economic and political modernisation from the contrasting vantage points of a senti-mental small-town clergyman and a Machiavellian small-town political operator. *Annals* suggests the accretion of a single place over time; *The Provost* tracks the emptying out of place and tradition.

Each of Scott's Waverley Novels describes a crisis or turning point in Scottish history. Yet cumulatively they evoke a deep, rich, unbroken national history. 'Tales of the West' has the opposite effect. Its novels describe key events and developments from various interested perspectives, determined by occupation, class and political ideology. Cumulatively, the series creates a multi-faceted mosaic. A sense of sentimental recupera-tion permeates some novels. Yet others convey a pessimistic or depressive sense of gloom, tragedy and social dissolution. The sequence should act accretively, conveying a detailed, historically ramified sense of place. Instead, it questions Scotland's place – and future – in the world. For the 'Tales' position Scotland simultaneously as an early casualty and economic node of Britain's nascent empire. *The Entail* (1820) presents Scotland's Union with Britain – and nineteenth-century Scottish fears of cultural, political and economic disenfranchisement – as consequences of Scotland's disastrous attempt to establish its own Central American colony. Its supply lines sabotaged by the English, the Darien colony rapidly collapsed, precipitating the collapse of the Scottish economy – and, in Galt's eyes, the Act of Union. Scotland's bid to become an imperial power paradoxically reduced it to a *de facto* colony.

Yet in many more indirect ways, too, Scottish cultural tradition becomes subordinated to a new imperial logic. *The Provost* describes Scotland's economic and political modernisation process, and its widespread disenfranchisements, as by-products of local power-grabs by emerging mercantile oligarchs. *The Last of the Lairds* (1826) shows agents of empire inaugurating parallel changes; a Scottish 'nabob', returning from India with an ill-gotten colonial fortune, gradually displaces an enfeebled local aristocracy, awakening local nostalgia for more traditional stewardship.

In *Bogle Corbet*, most ambitiously, Scotland appears as part of a worldwide imperial-industrial circuit. Born in Jamaica into a Scottish planter's family and nursed there by a devoted slave, Corbet comes of age in Lowland textile mills, where Jacobin weavers inadvertently precipitate the industrial revolution yet fail to foment domestic revolution. Later, in London, Corbet observes corrupt old India hands capitalising the industrialisation process. In the novel's final third, he accompanies to Upper Canada a settlement party of politically disillusioned Jacobin weavers, old Lowland acquaintances.

As it nears the North American continent, the emigrants' ship encounters a vast iceberg. At least at first sight, its frozen sublimity emblematises Canada's chilly, unfathomable, pristine vastness. Within the imperial system Galt's novel sketches, Canada initially represents a place of new beginnings and utopian renewal, proffering refuge for political dissidents, those sickened by the taint of mills and money. Yet only hours later, the passengers shudder as their ship passes Anticosta Island, where it almost founders, amid the 'roaring tempest' (Waterston 1977b: 26). In 1828, real-life mariners shipwrecked on Anticosta Island had been forced into cannibalism, as newspapers reported worldwide. Now, in a novel whose protagonist originates in Jamaica and ends in Upper Canada, the spectre of cannibalism (and the Shakespearean conjunction of 'tempest' / shipwreck) suggests subterranean links between present-day settlement in Britain's latest Canadian colony and Christopher Columbus's much earlier voyages of conquest. Columbus's first log, describing his discovery of the Caribbean, famously emphasises its Edenic qualities. Yet logs of his subsequent voyages show cannibalism fears rapidly tainting the party's interactions with indigenes – and precipitating pre-emptive genocide.

Galt's settlers shed no blood and only once glimpse Indians, salmon-fishers grouped in tableau. None the less, *Bogle Corbet* echoes the template of cultural encounter that Columbus established and Shakespeare allegorised. Veterans of empire and revolutionary upheaval come to Upper Canada to be made whole, to start again. Yet they carry with them repressed traumas, blighted dreams, deep moral exhaustion. Already at their approach, the landscape mirrors back their own suppressed violence. At first sighting, the iceberg embodies stasis. Yet it threatens to overwhelm the ship as it approaches, appearing like a 'whole dreadful continent' before violently sundering 'with undescribable crashing' (22); even in its fragments, it remains menacing, until the vessel slips into the safety of the seaway. Still shaken, Corbet finds the accompanying change in water colour 'portentous', probably 'a consequence of some great internal turbulence' (23).

Corbet's own inner turbulence, buried fears of insurrection, and insistence on re-establishing class 'distinction' (77) will dog Upper Canada's newest settlement. As old acquaintances and old radicals, the settlers refuse to bend to Corbet's will. Some, seduced by the idea of representative government, pre-emptively stage what Corbet terms 'a mutiny' (58), forsaking the British colony for the American republic. Others stay in Upper Canada, yet retain inconvenient political hopes. Before leaving Scotland, the settlers determined to build a village and live 'in community' (66). Now, clearing the bush, many begin to believe that their labours entitle them to their own farms. Corbet, they insist, has no moral right to dispose of communal property, for 'this wild country was ta'en from the Indians, who have the best right to the land, if anyone has a right' (73). From their Jacobin perspective, Corbet's authority has little foundation; in North America, private property is built on expropriation.

As a colonial administrator, Galt took responsibility for the 'La Guayrans', fleeing one failed settlement, continent, empire for another. In Nova Scotia, contemporary satirists Thomas McCulloch and Thomas Chandler Haliburton evoked the spectre of Scottish emigrants circulating among colonies, restless and increasingly rootless wanderers. Early nineteenth-century Scottish commentaries like John Leyden's 'Scenes of Infancy. Descriptive of Teviotdale' (1803) and late twentieth-century Scottish-Canadian novels like Margaret Laurence's *The Diviners* (1974) and Alistair MacLeod's *No Great Mischief* (1999), repeatedly linked such circulation to indigenous disenfranchisement; in an imperial domino effect, Highland disasters and clearances led directly, causally, to the displacements and genocides of Canada's First Nations (Trumpener 1997).

Bogle Corbet explores a related but finally different problem. As a colonial administrator, John Galt battled local oligarchs. None the less, *Bogle Corbet* persistently conflates colonial administrator with oligarch. In the bush, the settlement leader becomes the *de facto* government, forcing other settlers to conform or flee. Yet even as Corbet grumbles about 'malcontents', battles their attempts at self-sufficiency, and triumphs at their subordination, he also falls into paralysing 'depression' (79), having ruined not only their old dreams of sovereign equality but also his own. Like many Galt novels, *Bogle Corbet* turns on its narrator's self-interest, self-delusion, bad faith and false consciousness. In Scots, 'bogle' means both bogeyman and scarecrow. A child – and increasingly a tool – of empire, Bogle Corbet becomes a hollow man, malign yet haunted. Canada can bring no new beginning, only an ill-fated transposition of imperial inequity, guilt and violence into yet another place. Galt's novelistic œuvre explores the complex geopolitical layering of colonial and historical experience. As *Bogle Corbet* demonstrates, the contradictions of colonial experience necessitate mechanisms for historical amnesia – and authorise a guilt-stricken, hence paranoid reading of colonial landscapes. Yet Galt is interested less in Canada's history of indigenous dispossession – or indeed in any facet of its prior history – than its ability to serve as a staging ground and social laboratory for the moral problems generated by empire as a whole.

In the 1820s and 1830s, McCulloch and Haliburton worried over Nova Scotia's mercantile links to the Caribbean and slavery, and its proximity to American industrial capitalism (envisioned by Haliburton as a genocidal abattoir for wage-labourers and poor Irish immigrants). The first volume of *Bogle Corbet* makes similar links – between Jamaica and Scotland, between slavery and industrialisation. Yet Upper Canada is important to Galt not as an economic link in the imperial or capitalist economy but as a *tabula rasa*, an isolated, empty stage on which settlers imported from older parts of the empire can play out now-ingrained, imperially tainted social dynamics.

Bogle Corbet diagrams imperial alienation in psycho-dynamic terms that anticipate Joseph Conrad, Jean-Paul Sartre, Frantz Fanon and George Lamming's 1954 novel *The Emigrants*. What it does not and cannot provide, consequently, is a history of Canada itself. Galt's 'Tales of the West' provides a cumulative, complex account of Scotland's history in the context of empire. *Bogle Corbet* is a covert historical novel, yet any sense of ongoing history dissipates once protagonists (and readers) reach the St Lawrence. In Upper Canada, history only repeats itself, in symbolic re-enactment of battles fought elsewhere – in and about the British Empire. Overdetermined, overshadowed by this prior history, the colony cannot develop an autochthonous, let alone annalistic history.

Latter-day Canadian nationalists had difficulty reconciling Galt's vision of Canada with their own agendas. The 1960s' and 1970s' surge in Canadian cultural nationalism was accompanied by a literary boom characterised by a resurgence of historical fiction, using narrative templates pioneered by Scott (and popular with nineteenth-century Canadian novelists and readers), now often placed in more experimental modes. Leonard Cohen, Margaret Atwood, Michael Ondaatje, Anne Hébert, Margaret Laurence, James Reaney, Marian Engel, Timothy Findley and Antonine Maillet reanimated colonial literary sources, questioning the adequacy of transmitted documents or the colonial archives to capture the full range of Canadian historical experience.

Meanwhile, Canadian scholars began rediscovering colonial literary history, republishing key nineteenth-century literary works (Lecker 1992). McClelland & Stewart's New Canadian Library virtually created a new Canadian canon and teaching canon. Yet its 1977 paperback reissue of *Bogle Corbet* (as Volume 135 in the New Canadian Library) involved severe abridgment. The 1831 London original had encompassed three volumes; McClelland & Stewart's reprint consisted solely of the third volume (beginning, with little preparation, *in medias res*). The nationalist mandate of the New Canadian Library (as of McClelland & Stewart, 'the Canadian publishers') apparently made such truncation acceptable. Ignoring the original's preoccupation with Canada's connection to other imperial sites (Jamaica, Scotland, India), the New Canadian Library produced a *Bogle Corbet* concerned solely with Canadian experience, yet in the process rendered almost incomprehensible – and largely failing to find new readers (Trumpener 1997). *Bogle's* latter-day 'editor', University of Guelph English professor Elizabeth Waterston, subsequently celebrated Galt's *Annals* as formative for Canadian writing (1985b) – and discounted *Bogle* as a 'sour novel' (2003: 97).

During the Romantic period, Scottish writers attempted to impart literary fullness to places, languages and cultures not fully comprehensible or comprehended in English letters' prior history. Yet the nineteenth-century Scottish reading public thought of Canada as a place to which relatives, and sometimes whole local communities, had departed, never to return. It was hence a place of fantasy and projection, but above all loss. Like Scottish literary nationalism before it, mid-twentieth-century Canadian literary nationalism came to understand itself as counter-acting a long history of trivialising or elegiac representations. Canada was presented as neither a void nor a distant tomb but the place of real life, worthy of literary attention. Canadian literary nationalism thus unconsciously mimicked Scottish literary strategies of self-assertion even as it challenged British – and Scottish – views of Canada. Laurence's *The Diviners* (1974), for instance, argued for a new Canadian social contract by evoking traumatic memories of the Highland Clearances; read postcolonially, however, Laurence's narrative offers a utopian vision of Britain's dispossessed Scots grasping their structural analogies to – and hence literally embracing – Canada's dispossessed Native and Méti population.

Laurence's plot of female self-emancipation drew heavily on Munro's 1971 break-through novel, *Lives of Girls and Women*, a subtler interrogation and integration of Scottish models. In the early nineteenth century, Munro's family, the Laidlaws, emi-grated to Upper Canada; while back in Scotland, two Laidlaw relatives assumed key roles in Romantic literary culture. Their cousin James Hogg, illiterate until the age of 40, spent his early life as a shepherd and his later life as an unconventional literary lion, championed (and patronised) by Walter Scott, publishing poetry and fascinatingly unorthodox novels, and participating in the circle around *Blackwood's Edinburgh Magazine*. In 1820, when one émigré Laidlaw sent a letter from Upper Canada, urging Scottish relatives to join them, Hogg printed it in *Blackwood's*, with a letter of his own (Thacker 2005: 15). Hogg's mother, Margaret Laidlaw, steeped in oral tradition, became a key source for Scott's revision of *Minstrelsy of the Scottish Border*, although famously upbraiding Scott for publishing – and hence ruining – works "'made for singin' and no for prentin" (Hogg 1999b: 38).

Only in middle age did Munro discover her own genealogical links to Hogg and his mother. By then, Munro and, in her wake, her father Robert Laidlaw had already published fiction based on oral family sources. Written with Munro's encouragement and published posthumously in 1979, Laidlaw's historical novel, *The McGregors: A Novel of an Ontario Pioneer Family*, drew on Laidlaw family stories of homesteading in the Huron Tract. Eight years earlier, *Lives of Girls and Women* had positioned itself as a historical novel of the recent past.

In a series of short stories linking into a first-person *Bildungsroman*, *Lives'* narrator, Del Jordan, describes her girlhood in the small Ontario town of Jubilee. During the 1970s and 1980s, Canadian literary historians pointed to *Lives* (as to short story cycles by Duncan Campbell Scott, Stephen Leacock, Mordecai Richler, Laurence and Gallant) to argue the linked short story sequence as a quintessential Canadian or indigenous post-colonial form. W. H. New (1987) offered a more complex formulation, suggesting that the modern story cycle both extended and departed from nineteenth-century colonial 'sketches'.

Yet Romantic-era Scottish experiments with narrative scale suggest alternative pre-cedents; tale sequences, the annalistic novel and the novel sequence offer varying ways to slice and recombine time. *Lives of Girls and Women* not only develops a self-consciously idiosyncratic variation of the Galtian annalistic novel, but also repeatedly meditates on the historiographic problems in representing a community's history. On one level, Munro's novel explores ever further reaches of the Joycean concentric world Del imag-ines, as a girl, stretching from 'The Flats Road, Jubilee, Wawanash County, Ontario' to 'The Solar System, The Universe' (Munro 1983: 9). On another level, the novel memo-rialises a series of neighbours, relatives, friends and lovers whose idiosyncrasies and life philosophies consecutively, cumulatively shape Del's consciousness, while reconstruct-ing a sequence of discrete historical micro-periods – the Depression, World War II, the 1950s – experienced from the perspective of the provinces, ostensibly removed from world-historical events. In the temporal gaps between chapters, as in the new vantage point each chapter introduces, the novel underscores the limitations of its own preten-sions to historical coverage.

Del spends her early childhood on the Flats Road, a semi-rural no-man's-land between the bush and Jubilee. Uncle Benny, Del's semi-literate neighbour, embodies that liminality.

His intimate, semi-intuitive relationship to the wilderness is offset by his inability to use a map, surmount his chaotic personal life or envision a larger social order. Del's own relationship to the world veers uneasily between a pitying sympathy with Uncle Benny's plight, anxiety about her own semi-pariah status (her critical mind trapped in an embarrassingly female body), and a precarious sense of intellectual entitlement (particularly once her autodidactic mother moves into Jubilee and sells encyclopedias).

Lives' ethical and aesthetic crux is the problem of giving literary voice to those unable to describe themselves. Munro advocates a Galtian immersion in regional history; Del remains sceptical. A key story/chapter, 'Heirs of the Living Body', describes the obsessive attempt of Del's great-uncle Craig, former township clerk, to compile retrospective annals of the parish, the authoritative early history of the county. To Del's irreverent young eyes, the project is dogged by his completism and unreflexive sense of history.

> I wanted to hear about how Jenkin's Bend was named, after a young man killed by a falling tree just a little way up the road; he had been in this country less than a month. Uncle Craig's grandfather ... had given the young man's name to it, for what else would such a young man, a bachelor, have to be remembered by?
>   'Where was he killed?'
>   'Up the road, not a quarter of a mile.'
>   'Can I go see where?'
>   'There's nothing marked. That's not the sort of thing they put a marker up for.'
>   Uncle Craig looked at me with disapproval; he was not moved to curiosity. He often thought me flighty and stupid and I did not care much; there was something large and impersonal about his judgment that left me free.   (Munro 1983: 25)

Absorbed in, made impersonal by, his mandate to chronicle, Uncle Craig leaves all domestic drudgery and familial upkeep to his sisters. In his household, male and female spheres of experience rarely overlap. Men focus on a wide historical view; women, relegated to current burdens and pleasures, treat male privilege with mocking deference. Yet when her great-uncle dies, Del inherits his uncompleted magnum opus, with the expectation that she will finish it. Unwilling to subordinate her writerly energies to his vision of history, she stows it under her bed, then in the basement, where damp renders it illegible, unsalvageable.

If this sodden manuscript fuels inchoate guilt, the novel we hold – the novel Del grows up to write for us – offers an expanded settlement history on the traces Uncle Craig laid out, foregrounding not the political and economic history made by Jubilee's men but the private lives of women and other insignificants (Godard 1984). Uncle Craig's grandfather named a town for a man killed by a tree; Uncle Craig finds the man, even his place of death, unworthy of a marker. In nineteenth-century Huron Township, one of Munro's family was killed by a falling tree; Munro's works repeatedly rework this elusive episode, paradigmatic for problems of commemoration and reconstruction (Carrington 1996; Gittings 1997). History, she insists, happens everywhere and to everyone, whether or not their lives are deemed worthy of record. *Lives* undertakes a compassionate, collective, compensatory chronicle, in the tradition of Thomas Gray's 1751 'Elegy Written in a Country Churchyard', recording the 'short and simple annals of the poor', or of Galt's *Annals*, working to comprehend the logic, desperation and dignity of provincial lives.

As an implicit *Künstlerroman*, moreover, *Lives* explores the ways a flat, uninflected, unrecorded, apparently inconsequential place not only produces but also necessitates literature. Munro greatly admired James Agee's 1941 *Now Let Us Praise Famous Men* (Sheila Munro 2001: 38), famously obsessed by the ethics of description. *Lives* too underscores how class, education, gender and generation implicitly divide the novelist from her subjects and the shame, self-consciousness and uncertainty this gap engenders. The act of writing, none the less, is ethically imperative. Even if its subjects do not welcome description, they have an inalienable right to be described. They may harbour a deep-rooted suspicion of map-making, even literacy itself. Yet fiction's cosmologies counteract their sense of unmooring in the universe.

Del's early taste is Gothic – and *Lives* itself is conceived in terms drawn partly from Southern Gothic (William Faulkner, Flannery O'Connor, Eudora Welty, Carson McCullers, Harper Lee), as from historical novels (*War and Peace*, Sigrid Undset's *Kristin Lavransdatter, Gone with the Wind*). Yet Munro's sense of novelistic form and temporality is also inflected by the experimental fictional forms of Scottish Romanticism, Scottish novelists' attempts to reanimate Scottish Enlightenment obsessions with stadialist history, to correlate geological, cultural and historical time scales. In *Lives* and subsequent short-story novel *Who Do You Think You Are?* (*The Beggar Maid*, 1978), Munro foregrounds the inherent novelistic tension between thick description, evoking particular moments or junctures, and the arc of narrative development. In Munro's narratives of girlhood development, each phase is important, concrete, yet takes on final meaning in retrospect and memory, after yielding to a subsequent dispensation.

Galt's 'Tales of the West' return repeatedly, obsessively, to the same region of Scotland, examined from different historical and sociological vantage points – including, finally, an imperial perspective which saw it as only one of many interdependent places. Munro's œuvre attempts a similarly comprehensive, multi-faceted survey. Like Galt, she has simultaneously immersed herself in local history (studying diaries, chronicles and newspapers) and tried to pull away from local perspectives, placing her locale in a much larger cosmology.

Munro's 1994 short-story collection *Open Secrets* involves perspectival experiments, exploring Ontario's history in annalistic layers. A key story, 'A Wilderness Station', recapitulates this project by assembling the history of one locale across successive eras. Such collation involves significant overlaps of character and collective memory, but also highlights lacunae, a drift towards forgetfulness. The story's early sections detail a widely noted tragedy, from the settlement's first epoch: a man's death – or murder – beneath a falling tree. Yet by the story's epilogue, decades later, the episode is incompletely remembered, half-legendary, the initial protagonist recalled as an eccentric bit-player. With its telescoping, collapsing and overlapping temporal slices, 'A Wilderness Station' demonstrates the layering of the past, the triumphs and failures of historical reconstruction; a human story struggles to re-emerge from distance and document, then becomes obscure again.

Other works foreground the relationship between Munro's mode of historical fiction and early nineteenth-century Scottish experimental novels, including those of Hogg. *Friend of My Youth* (1990) chronicles Munro's personal pilgrimage back to Scotland, in search of such antecedents; *The View from Castle Rock*, a speculative, fictionalised family memoir, episodically follows Munro's emigrating Laidlaw ancestors in the other direction, from Scotland to Canada, pondering the accidents which established Munro's eventual line of descent, the nature of family memory.

Such meditations are deepened in *View*'s final story, 'What Do You Want to Know For?', whose narrator evokes years of drives across southern Ontario with her geologist husband. Nominally quests for geological formations, and hence navigated with special physiographic maps (showing deep formations, alongside rivers, towns and township boundaries), these repeated journeys change the travellers' sense of their home's location, shifting and deepening their grasp of proximate places. The story ponders the land and (as the couple search for, then investigate a country churchyard) the human record, with echoes of Gray's 'Churchyard', Galt's *Annals* and Scott's 1816 *Old Mortality*.

Romantic-era British naturalists developed a new sense of 'locale', a symbiotic biotope fostering specific plants and animals. By analogue, Martha Bohrer argues, British intellectuals use locale to comprehend social ecology; George Crabbe's *The Borough* (1810), Mary Mitford's *Our Village* (1824–32) and Galt's *Annals* thus understand town, parish and village as human biotopes, microcosms (Bohrer 2003, 2007). Munro's story reunites these senses of locale, reconciling the scales of human and geological history.

> The landscape here is a record of ancient events. It was formed by the advancing, stationary, and retreating ice. The ice has staged its conquests and retreats here several times, withdrawing for the last time about fifteen thousand years ago.   (Munro 2006: 318)

The process of geological formation separates adjacent pieces of landscape. Like history, geology involves uneven development, creates particular figure-ground relationships.

> Kame moraines show where a heap of dead ice sat, cut off from the rest of the moving glacier, earth-stuff pouring through all its holes and crevices. Or sometimes it shows where two lobes of ice pulled apart, and the crevice filled in … wild and bumpy, unpredictable, with a look of chance and secrets.   (Munro 2006: 321)

In the eighteenth century, from Europe's distance, Voltaire dismissed New France as a few leagues of ice: 'quelques arpents de glace en Canada'. In the late twentieth century, indigenous literati worked to effect Canada's literary reclamation, reassembling a New Canadian Library. For many years, Munro has been one of the three-member advisory board of the New Canadian Library, functioning literally as a keeper of the Canadian canon. *Lives of Girls and Women*, too, participated in the project of nationalist retrieval. Yet, as this chapter's comparative and historical character has demonstrated, Munro's recent fiction pushes beyond a nationalist sense of Canadian terrain to think about deep formation in local and transatlantic terms.

Bogle Corbet sailed for Canada searching for the end of history, an escape from historical and economic pressures, the plantation system, the industrial revolution. Yet he carries that local/world history with him, re-enacts it in the New World, and ends his story sunk into himself. At the dark heart of Joseph Conrad's Congo is the horror of an inhuman colonial trade in commodities and lives. At the icy heart of Corbet's Canada is a white void, reflecting back the moral hollowness of imperial, industrial Europe.

The anarchists who paint-bombed Galt's statue targeted the wrong man. Yet *Bogle Corbet* does encapsulate both the project of colonial literature and its necessary failure. The novel is intermittently attentive to natural landscapes, how weather, climate and countryside shape world-view. Yet where Galt's West of Scotland is annalistically layered and socially complex, ascertainable only through a multiplicity of vantage-points and temporal scales, Galt's Upper Canada functions primarily as an allegorical mirror, emblematising settlers' inability to leave their pasts behind, their failure to arrive.

Traversing the same geographical and literary ground, almost 200 years later, Munro finds an accreted, rich, half-buried record of human life, the annalistic micro-histories of the parish dwarfed only by the accreted, epoch-spanning natural-historical record. In their different ways, Galt and Munro each carve annals of ice. Yet their relationship remains oblique. And despite repeated calls to read them side by side (Craig 1981; Gittings 1995), so does the larger relationship between colonial and postcolonial literature. Meanwhile, the once provocative notion that postcolonial writers literally rewrite or unwrite colonial narratives has proved applicable mainly to a few famous, fiercely corrective alternative versions (Jean Rhys's 1966 *Wide Sargasso Sea*; Margaret Atwood's 1970 *Journals of Susanna Moodie*; J. M. Coetzee's 1986 *Foe*) now so over-taught that they appear calculating, as if designed to secure hyper-canonical status for themselves.

This chapter has modelled a different approach. Both colonial and postcolonial writing, it suggests, reach their greatest profundity not where they refunction specific metropolitan stories but when they understand their particular places as echo chambers or palimpsests, channelling a host of histories, narrative traditions and possible social forms. The relationship between metropolitan, colonial and postcolonial literature may not represent a direct line of descent or filiation – nor even rebuttal. Galt and Munro do think about place in relationship to models that earlier texts provide – but their interest is in utilising these texts' still-unrealised formal, linguistic, political and philosophical possibilities. In Galt's case, moreover, the 'coloniser' is simultaneously a withering critic of empire. Galt depicts Canada as empty. Yet this betokens not an annihilating colonial gaze so much as a symptomatic reading of imperial fatigue. Munro, in turn, grapples not with Galt's content but with his formal innovations, not with his ignorance, pre-emptory dismissal or suppression of Canadian history, but with the myriad possibilities his novels open up – for local history, a corrective, complex historiography, new forms of fictional meditation.

Bibliography

'Anarchists paint bomb statue of John Galt' (2008). Available at http://www.anarchist-news.org/?q=node/4655, accessed 10 October 2010.

Bohrer, Martha (2003), 'Tales of Locale: *The Natural History of Selbourne and Castle Rackrent*', *Modern Philogy*, 100:3 (February), pp. 393–416.

Bohrer, Martha (2007), 'Thinking Locally: Novelistic Worlds in Provincial Fiction' in Richard Maxwell and Katie Trumpener (eds), *Cambridge Companion to Fiction in the Romantic Period*, Cambridge: Cambridge University Press, pp. 89–106.

Carrington, Ildiko de Papp (1996), 'Double-talking Devils: Alice Munro's "A Wilderness Station"', *Essays on Canadian Writing*, 58 (Spring), pp. 71–93.

Craig, Cairns (1981), 'Peripheries', *Cencrastus*, 9, pp. 3–9.

Duncan, Ian (2007), *Scott's Shadow: The Novel in Romantic Edinburgh*, Princeton: Princeton University Press.

Galt, John (1831), *Bogle Corbet*, 3 vols, London: Henry Colburn & Richard Bentley.

Galt, John (1977), *Bogle Corbet*, ed. Elizabeth Waterston, Toronto: McClelland & Stewart.

Gittings, Christopher E. (1995), 'Canada and Scotland: Conceptualizing "Postcolonial" Spaces', *Essays on Canadian Writing*, 56:1 (Fall), pp. 135–61.

Gittings, Christopher E. (1997), 'Constructing a Scots-Canadian Ground: Family History and Cultural Translation in Alice Munro', *Studies in Short Fiction*, 34: 1 (Winter), pp. 27–37.

Godard, Barbara (1984), '"Heirs of the Living Body": Alice Munro and the Question of a Female Aesthetic', in Judith Miller (ed.), *The Art of Alice Munro: Saying the Unsayable*, Waterloo: University of Waterloo Press, pp. 43–71.

Hogg, James (1999b), *Anecdotes of Walter Scott*, ed. Jill Rubinstein, Edinburgh: Edinburgh University Press.

Lecker, Robert (1992), *Canadian Canons. Essays in Literary Value*, Toronto: University of Toronto Press.

Lee, Robert C. (2004), *The Canada Company and the Huron Tract, 1826–1853*, Toronto: Natural Heritage.

Munro, Alice (1983), *Lives of Girls and Women*, New York: New American Library.

Munro, Alice (2006), *The View from Castle Rock*, New York: Knopf.

Munro, Sheila (2001), *Lives of Mothers and Daughters: Growing Up with Alice Munro*, Toronto: McClelland & Stewart.

Nash-Graham, Debra (1984), 'In the Palm of God's Hand? The Irish Catholic Experience in Mid-Nineteenth-Century Guelph', *CCHA Historical Studies*, 51, pp. 67–87.

New, William H. (1987), *Dreams of Speech and Violence: The Art of the Short Story in Canada and New Zealand*, Toronto: University of Toronto Press.

Skelton, Oscar Douglas (1966), *The Life and Times of Sir Alexander Tilloch Galt*, ed. Guy MacLean, Toronto: McClelland & Stewart.

Stelter, Gilbert A. (1985), 'John Galt as Town Booster and Builder', in Elizabeth Waterston (ed.), *John Galt: Reappraisals*, Guelph: University of Guelph Press, pp. 17–43.

Thacker, Robert (2005), *Alice Munro: Writing her Lives. A Biography*, Toronto: McClelland & Stewart.

Timothy, H. B. (1977), *The Galts: A Canadian Odyssey. Vol. I: John Galt: 1779–1839*, Toronto: McClelland & Stewart.

Trumpener, Katie (1997), *Bardic Nationalism: The Romantic Novel and the British Empire*, Princeton: Princeton University Press.

Trumpener, Katie (2005), 'The Peripheral Rise of the Novel', in Liam MacInveray and Raymond Ryan, (eds), *Ireland and Scotland: Culture and Society 1707–2000*, Dublin: Four Courts, pp. 164–82.

Trumpener, Katie (2007), 'Tales for Child Readers', in Richard Maxwell and Katie Trumpener (eds), *Cambridge Companion to Fiction in the Romantic Period*, Cambridge: Cambridge University Press, pp. 177–90.

Waterston, Elizabeth (1977a), 'Introduction', in Elizabeth Waterston (ed.). *Bogle Corbet*, Guelph: University of Guelph Press, pp. 1–7.

Waterston, Elizabeth (ed.) (1977b), *Bogle Corbet*, Toronto: McClelland & Stewart.

Waterston, Elizabeth (ed.) (1985b), *John Galt: Reappraisals*, Guelph: University of Guelph Press.

Waterston, Elizabeth (2003), *Rapt in Plaid: Canadian Literature and Scottish Tradition*, Toronto: University of Toronto Press.

PART NINE

Cognition, Emotion, Evolution, Science

CHAPTER 1

Introduction
In the Body of the Text

Julie Rivkin and Michael Ryan

The body is making a come-back. For decades, it was neglected in favor of ideology, culture, history, politics, discourse, and representation. One could see trouble ahead for these big concepts already in the 1980s, however, when Judith Butler theorized that gender was performance but immediately had to backtrack and announce that bodies mattered too. There were not enough critical or theoretical tools around in the 1980s to assist those who felt inclined to ask, if everything is constructed, what constructs construction? Where does it come from? A vague idea of "the body" offered itself, but not much came of the persnickety query.

In the 1990s and into the next century, more tools began to make themselves available, from affect theory, to evolutionary psychology, to the theory of embodied consciousness, and the body was well launched as a topic of critical conversation. The commitment on the part of theorists to cultural construction began to weaken as it became clear that the architecture of thought that allowed one to think that the body might be constructed might itself be shaped by bodily experience, that our minds function in ways that can only be explained as evolutionary adaptations grounded in biology, and that we do more than think during the course of each day. We also feel. And literature is very much about such feelings.

Let's begin with cognition. George Lakoff and Mark Johnson argued in their 1980 book, *Metaphors We Live By*, that much of our thinking is shaped by image schemas derived from our bodily experience. We go up and down in life, or we move ahead in our careers, while backing off from difficult situations. Lakoff and Johnson contended that the operations of the mind are determined by the location and orientation of the body, from up/down to in/out to forward/back. Derrida had noticed a similar tendency in philosophy to think in spatial categories – center/margin, for example. But Lakoff and Johnson argued that this tendency was inherent to all thinking because our minds are embodied. Thought is captive to its physical location and thinking is inherently spatial. We form concepts using basic image schema that are bodily in nature. Our moral and aesthetic measures and values are spatially grounded and graphed. We think of someone "highly" or consider something a "low" activity.

It is fairly easy to find examples from literature of these basic image schemes. Virginia Woolf builds *Mrs. Dalloway* around the two very different characters of Clarissa Dalloway and Septimus Smith, each of whom is linked to a particular spatial movement,

Literary Theory: An Anthology, Third Edition. Edited by Julie Rivkin and Michael Ryan.
© 2017 John Wiley & Sons, Ltd. Published 2017 by John Wiley & Sons, Ltd.

one up and one down. "What a lark! What a plunge!" Clarissa thinks now and then, mapping the novel's dual existential and emotional trajectories. Clarissa is overly sane and proper and follows conventions, while Septimus verges on mental collapse and imagines all sorts of odd things that nevertheless are true measures of the world around him. Clarissa thinks about how best to negotiate a variety of social encounters that require deft adjustments in tone and self-presentation, all the time maintaining control over one's emotions, while Septimus is the victim of involuntary fantasies that ultimately drive him to suicide. Clarissa's passage through an ordinary day is figured as flight ("What a lark!") while Septimus experiences it as a fall ("What a plunge!"), and he literally plunges to his death at the end. It is a novel with many facets, but one major one is its embodied cognitive dimension that characterizes everyday life as a pitched battle, graphed spatially as movements up or down, between involuntary emotional experiences and the control we exercise over them in order to maintain our social identities. Cognitive criticism emerged in the early 1990s in the work of Mark Turner, whose *Reading Minds* (1991) argued for attending to cognitive semantics (rather than the Chomskian concern with syntax) and for locating cognition within evolutionary biology. We know in order to survive. Our minds are able to transfer lessons from one environment into another using cognitive schema such as metaphor and metonymy. All of our concepts can be understood as emerging from the basic schemas our bodily experience provides us, and they have shapes similar to those found in rhetoric – especially metaphor. Later theorists in this critical tradition such as Patrick Hogan argue that because cognition is a universal human capacity, literature will manifest shared or common features that can be called universals. Those include the forms of "verbal art" such as assonance, symbolism, genres, and the like. David Herman studies the cognitive tools readers bring to the reading of narrative such as frames, schema, and scripts that allow sense to be made of a temporally unfolding story and sense to be made of fictional events through a matching with stored information about narrativity. Other cognitive theorists such as F. Elizabeth Hart use cognitive science to correct perceived flaws in post-structuralist accounts of literature by emphasizing the rootedness of language in the brain and of the brain in the body while making connections between the small-scale operations of language in texts with the large-scale concerns of history and ideology that preoccupy post-structuralist critics.

Cognitive literary criticism can also focus on readers and audiences, as in Ellen Spolsky's examination of how art helps to overcome the inherent "gappiness" of knowledge, the way our brains function in modules that are "domain specific" (or oriented towards a specific task), or the focus can be on characters and their interaction, as in Lisa Zunshine's study of Jane Austen's innovative depiction of characters' awareness of other characters' awareness. For example, Henry James's *The Ambassadors* hinges on the issue of faulty knowledge. Lambert Strether, sent to retrieve a young man who has been seduced by Paris (and by a *parisienne*), is unaware through much of the novel of what is going on around him in the romantic lives of his friends, while they are very much aware of his lack of awareness and orchestrate deceptions to maintain it. The reader is as duped as Strether in this fiction that depicts knowledge as situational and therefore partial, always prone to "go astray" (to evoke the name of key character – Maria Gostrey) by the angles of perspectival vision that both allow and disable it. Cognitive textual criticism often focuses on linguistics, since the rules of syntax are embedded in the brain, and our brains often follow forms or patterns that are noticeable and analyzable. These patterns can be "universal," or they can be quite specific to a historical moment. In *Shakespeare's*

Brain, for example, Mary Crane describes how Shakespeare in *Twelfth Night* uses the word "suits" (from suits of clothes to law suits to love suits) in multiple ways that resonate with issues of ideology, power, and theatricality in his culture.

The brain engages in cognitive processing, but it is also the locus of emotions. Historians have long been aware of the power of emotions in our lives. Radical rightwing political movements such as Nazism derive force from their mobilization of negative feelings against reviled adversaries. And the history of religion is a history in many instances of the struggle to regulate emotions that threaten ideals of religious sanctity or norms of ethical decorum. Emotion also always has both a class and gender dimension in that ruling men have always been able to appear more "in control" in contrast to women who are angry or distraught for reasons of social subordination, and the working class often is depicted as prone to stigmatized emotions such as envy and resentment by those further up the class ladder who can "afford" to be more moderate in their feelings and who are more prone to feelings of condescension, scorn, and derision regarding those further down the class ladder. Charles Dickens's endorsement of the moral ideals of the commercial culture in which he lived often takes the form of distinguishing poor or working-class characters who experience ugly emotions from more refined characters who regulate such emotions and adhere to bourgeois standards of taste and moderation in regard to feelings.

Affect theory begins with the perception that affect is primary in our lives. We feel before we think. Affect became an object of study in the 1960s when Silvan Tomkins first proposed that there were biologically based affects that occurred in pairs: interest–excitement, enjoyment–joy, surprise–startle, distress–anguish, anger–rage, fear–terror, and shame–humiliation. Recent fMRI studies bear out Tomkins's theory and find that there is a distinction between the physiological basis of emotion and its social dimension. Each emotion activates a different region or regions of the brain, and the degree of activation and its specific location changes according to the varying social character of the stimulus. But recent research also finds that Tomkins's affects are not in fact universal; culture and geography make for other kinds of affect.

Affect theory began to enter literary studies in the 1990s and 2000s through the work of scholars such as Eve Sedgwick, Lauren Berlant, and Brian Massumi. Massumi's contention that affect precedes cognition drew on a study that found that affective experience preceded cognitive awareness. More recent studies confirm a strong relation between the body and the way such things as fear are experienced. In one study, the rhythm of the heart as it switched from systole to diastole was linked to changes in how much fear was experienced.

Literary and cultural scholars have been actively exploring the new field of affect and emotion studies. Lauren Berlant studies the way the conservatism (or neoliberalism) that has come to dominate US public discourse over the past half century fosters a sense of optimism in working- and middle-class Americans. Yet under the economic policies sustained and fostered by that discourse, those people are less likely to thrive economically because neoliberal policies exacerbate economic inequality. Other scholars such as Ann Cvetkovich have studied the boundary between public and private feelings. Ngai Sianne describes the role of what she calls "ugly feelings" such as envy and resentment in a modern administered world of "sub" subjects. That emotion has important political ramifications is clear when Sara Ahmed explores the manipulation of hate in racist and nationalist movements.

The emergence of affect studies also is part of a larger methodological displacement occurring throughout the social and cultural sciences. One way of describing that methodological change would be to say cultural science has begun to attend to smaller scale units of analysis often characterized by a non-repetitive singularity, to complex arrays and assemblages of materials rather than to single "objects," and to aspects of reality that lack clarity and stability and are characterized instead by indeterminacy, probability, uncertainty, potentiality, emergence, virtuality, and complexity. Fields of events in motion whose direction is unpredictable and whose likely interactions are random – reality these days looks more like an ocean than a landscape. Affect and emotion are important destabilizers of the old scholarly world of cognitive objects because they draw attention to the physiological character of our lives, to the flows of feeling that course beneath and around the cognition we use to stabilize a subject position in relation to an object world that is no longer objectified but is instead in motion in us, through us, and around us, dissolving the boundary that secured a private realm of affect from the public realm of impersonal institutions, conventions, and symbols.

Evolutionary literary criticism takes its departure from the idea that all living things change form over time in response to pressure from the environment. All organisms are endowed with an ability to adapt to changing circumstances through the generation of genetic mutations. Some mutated versions of the organism survive, reproduce, and pass on the new trait, which is retained as part of the organism's subsequent genetic make-up. In perhaps the most significant mutation/adaptation for understanding our own species, sometime around 70 to 90 ka, our ancestors in Africa became capable of abstract mimetic cognition.

For a long time, evolutionary scientists thought the mutations in genes that gave rise to new traits were entirely random and accidental, but some geneticists now think that the ability to mutate in response to circumstances may be an evolved adaptation. Influenza, for example, has acquired an ability to generate multiple versions of itself when threatened. The virus makes copies of itself that are slightly different. Some of these mutated copies survive and thrive. Certain human characteristics such as Tay-Sachs Syndrome were initially adaptations designed to address an adverse environment. The lesson is that humans may also have evolved an ability to mutate in response to stressful circumstances. Our genetic self-protective system works by generating alternative versions to repair genes, for example, and this changes their make-up. It is possible, therefore, that some mutations may be "interpretive," or the result of prompts from the environment that set going changes in our genetic make-up that increase the likelihood we will adapt to the new circumstances. It is possible, some geneticists now claim, that stress on humans is like stress on viruses that make the viruses mutate to survive by generating slightly different copies of themselves. Like viruses, some early humans responsively mutated to give rise to a new more powerful form of cognition a hundred thousand years ago. As a result, they survived and reproduced, and soon most, but not all, *H. sapiens* possessed the new kind of cognitive power.

The evocation of evolutionary biology in literary and cultural studies, therefore, does not require that one pledge allegiance to a determinist view of human life that renders human effort futile. Genes are builders, but they are guided in part by signals from the environment. We can therefore change how our genetic make-up evolves by changing our niche environment. A caring environment fosters gene activation conducive to more civil forms of interaction, for example, while a harsh, survivalist environment will likely activate genes better suited to competitive behavior. Those different dispositions will then be passed on. In a sense, we can choose what version of *H. sapiens* will evolve. And that makes our debates regarding the shape of our world all the more significant.

Evolutionary theory is a powerful interpretive tool because it assumes everything in our make-up is functional. A trait would not exist if it did not aid survival in the past. That idea opens interesting possibilities for interpreting aspects of our lives that might appear meaningless, immoral, or merely embarrassing. For example, narcissism, that universal human trait, is in the light of evolution a necessary feature of our make-up. It assists survival by making self-concern a primary human motive. Lacanian psycho-analysis may therefore be off the mark in suggesting narcissism is a pathological feature of human psychological life that must be overcome if we are to achieve a mature sense of realism about life. Ordinary narcissism may be a perfectly fine feature in all of us. Without it, we might not have made it this far. Similarly, *Schadenfreude*, or pleasure in someone's else's misfortune, is likely a residue of an ancestral disposition forged at a time when early humans routinely exercised great violence against one another and needed to think of others' misfortune as beneficial. Even seemingly silly features of popular cultural life such as the Manic Pixie Dream Girl stereotype of films such as *500 Days of Summer* or television shows such as *In the Flesh* are understandable in terms of the evolved difference between men's and women's brains in regard to connectivity. Men's brains are wired back to front, emphasizing skills formed when men did the hunting and women the child-rearing, while women are wired side to side, a kind of connectivity that would allow for communicative skills needed for large amounts of time spent in a small community interacting with others. Because men dominate the production of visual culture, it is not surprising, in an evolutionary sense, that many images of women in male-run visual culture project male fantasies of an "other" completely unlike men whose "oddball" wiring might represent relief or escape from the stress-inducing mono-maniacal wiring men inherit from early human task differentiation and the eugenic effects it generated. Our moral behavior can also be interpreted in light of the adapta-tions required by successful evolution. All humans experience pleasure when someone gets their "comeuppance," payment for having broken social rules. Our cultural stories are crowded with stories of successful payback. Why? An evolutionary critic would argue that humans, in order to live together peacefully in large organized societies, had to acquire traits that made them more likely to accept the restraints on behavior imposed by social rules. Accompanying those traits was an innate sense that the breaking of rules merited punishment. All human traits and characteristics should be understood in a similar way as the results of a long evolutionary process that allowed humans to survive on earth in challenging circumstances.

Over the past several decades, evolutionary literary theory has made significant contributions to critical discussions. Joseph Carroll, Bryan Boyd, Nancy Easterlin, and Jonathan Gottschall have all written important books. Boyd's *On the Origin of Stories* (2010) describes how story-telling emerged as a human cultural practice, and he links the development to the need for the brain, as it evolved, to learn how to imagine non-empirical or play scenarios. Carroll in *Literary Darwinism* (2004) has mapped out a useful guide for performing sociobiological critical analysis using Darwinian evolution-ary theory. Easterlin's *A Biocultural Approach to Literary Theory and Interpretation* (2012) combines evolutionary, cognitive, and environmental theory in a reading of several writers such as Emily Brontë and Jean Rhys. And Gottschall's *The Rape of Troy* (2008) controversially uses Darwin's theory of sexual selection to argue that rape is a mechanism for achieving fitness or the passing on of one's genes.

When it draws on the highly controversial ideas of sociobiology such as "reproductive success" and "inclusive fitness" too uncritically, evolutionary literary theory risks committing several errors. It fails to see the historical and even the political character of nature; it mistakenly assumes there is a single universal "human nature"; and it imputes a subject (a selfish gene) to a subject-less process that works in a random, happenstance fashion that lacks the kind of intentionality slogans such as "reproductive success" impute to nature. To understand the possibly historical and political character of what sociobiologists call "nature," one need only consider gendered bodies. If women evolved smaller bodies and men larger, that process did not simply happen "naturally." Force was likely exercised against large-bodied women as men assumed dominance in early human communities, and small-bodied women likely stood a better chance of surviving. Eugenics has probably always been a feature of human evolution. Sociobiological critics avoid such an historical understanding and instead take the current state of nature as a universal that has not changed and cannot change. It is an all-determining absolute, an archetype with authority to determine who or what we are. To do so, however, they must limit the range of the authorities they cite – Darwin and the sociobiologists mostly – and avoid engaging with current ongoing scientific research, especially research that questions and is questioning the assumptions of sociobiological theology regarding sexual selection and fitness.

Sociobiological literary criticism also assumes *H. sapiens* is undifferentiated. There is a single universal "human nature." The species has ceased to evolve by mutating and splitting. Yet recent evidence suggests that there are remarkable physical differences between us. Conservatives, for example, have larger right amygdala than liberals, who have a larger anterior cingulate cortex. That physiological difference explains much of the ideological differences between the two groups. Approached scientifically rather than onto-theologically, *H. sapiens* would appear, as one would expect of any species, to be evolving by generating alternative versions of itself. There is no single "human nature" that is universal in all of us. To use the terminology of evolutionary theory, our differences are not just phenotypic; they are also genotypic. They pertain to how our genes operate, how they are arrayed, and what different biological versions of us they produce.

Contemporary science also provides a very different picture of evolutionary nature than is taken for granted by sociobiological literary criticism. It is a picture that accords more with the concepts and theories of Post-Structuralism and Postmodernism, theories that emphasize the stochastic character of change over time and the indeterminate, transformational, emergent, and complex character of any existing state of affairs. Because they are so devoted to the ideal of archetypal authority, sociobiological critics fail to grasp the indeterminacy and unpredictability of evolution itself. To deal with that unpredictability and indeterminacy, they have constructed metaphysical explanations for natural processes for which science itself provides simple physical descriptions.

For example, sociobiological genetic theory developed in the 1970s conceives of genes as selfish seekers of self-transmission through "reproductive success." Genes are conceived as bearers of heritable material and as active agents of gene transmission whose actions resemble subjective intention. The intention is to be ascendant over other competing genes and to spread heritable material as widely as possible. Mainly, it is male genes that seem to be conceptualized here, since women in accounts such as Gottschall's *Rape of Troy* are more the passive receivers of genetic material who assist competitive men in assuring fitness or reproductive success. These already ideologically freighted ideas derive from Darwin's own well-freighted early nineteenth-century cultural assumptions, such as the then-new "liberal" notion of economic life as competition and the new racial theories that saw some races as more fit than others to lead. Darwin's theory of sexual selection holds that males compete for females who choose the most fit with whom to reproduce. The peacock's display is designed to achieve reproductive success. There is therefore a gene for sexually competitive behavior that is armed with the intention to propagate itself. Alfred Russell Wallace, the man from whom Darwin pilfered the theory of natural selection, correctly thought the theory of sexual selection erroneous and felt, as recent science has borne out, that it was far more likely the peacock's display was related to self-defense.

Moreover, since these theories were developed, the genome has been unlocked and genetics has become a more refined science. Genes are no longer conceived as transits of inherited material; they are now understood to be building tools that are complexly regulated, interactive with their environment, and stochastic or probabilistic in their activation patterns. As Eva Jablonka and Marion Lamb argue in *Evolution in Four Dimensions*, how genes pass on traits is a highly contingent process that is shaped by circumstance and situation. Because there are no guarantees that a gene will give rise to a particular effect, the idea popular in the 1970s that genes seek to reproduce and pass on their material now seems dubious. Moreover, that theory mistakes an effect (that genetic material is passed on) as a cause (a desire to pass on genetic material) and injects an agent into an agent-less process. It gives rise to such fragile claims as that of Gottschall that men rape to produce offspring in order to further the pre-eminence of their genetic material over that of other men. It is more probable, given the simply physical and random manner in which nature works, that successful reproduction at some point was associated accidentally through repeated random mutation with sexual pleasure, and this accidental linkage endured and was passed on because it induced males to engage in a higher rate of reproductive activity of which one accidental consequence was that genes linking high degrees of pleasure with reproductive activity were passed on. In other words, what sociobiology sees as the metaphysical cause – a drive or intention to achieve reproductive success – might be a misreading of a structural effect of an entirely random and purely physical process. In sociobiological theory, this physical and accidental process that aligns sexual pleasure accidentally with gene transmission becomes a meta-physical account of successful agency and intention. But it is far more likely men rape for a sexual fix rather than because they have a gene that longs for competitive success and longevity over generations. Nature's simple physicality contradicts the metaphysics of agency in sociobiology.

The bases of sociobiological evolutionary literary theory are also put in question by recent research. Researchers find that there is very little evidence of sexual selection in nature. The experiment that gave rise to Bateman's Law (that accounted for gender differences in mate selection) has proven un-reproducible. The mathematical models for "inclusive fitness" (which justifies altruistic behavior towards consanguines because that assures gene transmission) have been disproven. In addition, sexual selection theory requires that females be able to tell from visual signals if males carry "good" genes, but research has proven that it is nearly impossible to tell from visual signals what the "quality" of genes are, and experimental evidence to justify the theory of sexual selection is scant. It seems more likely that the various calls and shows that some animals put on to attract mates aid the avoidance of excess in-breeding and disease rather than guarantee

Darwin's somewhat racist assumptions about superior and inferior ethnicities who carry either "good" or "bad" genes.

Evolutionary literary theory is on much more secure ground when it puts aside what one scientist termed its "crass" preoccupation with reproduction and mating and instead explores the function of literature and of art. Arts serves a social function; reading fiction has been found to increase empathy. As humans evolved, they needed to be able to live together in larger groups, and art aided that process by training human minds in the ability to imagine other's lives as similar to their own. The sense of otherness that inspired fear and prompted violence was thereby diminished. Art also provided a play model for mental activities that were beneficial to survival, such as imagining possible scenarios or life situations and planning the future.

The cognitive-evolutionary-affective turn in literary studies holds the promise of new kinds of research that connect the humanities and the sciences. The links between human behavior and brain region are clear, and it is becoming clear as well that the inter-action between our biological selves and our natural and constructed environments is crucial to both human culture and to our biological development within culture. To turn to science is not, therefore, to abandon a sense of the importance of culture or of society or, indeed, of history and politics. Nor should it be done in order to find in science an authoritative lexicon for culture. Indeed, the more one knows about the biological world, the more proximate science seems to mapping ocean currents. Change and transforma-tion are more prevalent than stasis and predictability. And that is as true of *H. sapiens* as of anything. The historical graphing of biological modifications in humanity over time, as they are evident in culture, is likely, therefore, to be an interesting new field of scholarly endeavor.

The digitization of the humanities and of the sciences will aid this work. It is now possible through university library portals to gain easy access to scientific journals. As you explore them, you will become aware that scientists are as prone to difference and debate as we humanists are. They study physical events, but often, those physical events can be interpreted in different ways. There is no easy truth to be found, therefore, on the side of science. Rather, there seems to be a continuum of endeavor as scholars of either the physical or the cultural world try to link observed events or empirical data to ideas and narratives about them. And the two worlds blend and interact in profoundly connected ways. Geneticists, for example, have become more aware of the power of symbolic inheritance and of learning environments in determining genetic outcomes, even as we realize that physical brain structure differences with genetic bases may help account for palpable differences in kinds of cultural activity. The study of those blend-ings will become increasingly important for our understanding of literature and of culture in the years ahead.

What awaits next might be called a "scientific turn" in literary and cultural studies. It will consist of consulting scientific research in such areas as cognition, emotion, and the neuroscience of evolved traits such as prejudice and empathy that play so important a role in literature and in human culture. It will not be possible for literary scholars to master fully the biochemistry of emotion in brain function, but it will be possible to link the conclusions of such studies – that certain hormones are more active in certain kinds of cognition and more present in certain kinds of brain structure, for example – to the products of human culture, which is to say, the products of the human brain. An assump-tion and a necessary conclusion of such research will be that our cultural fantasies spring directly from our evolved biology. They are not arbitrary, contingent, random, or determined in their substance by external, non-biological, cultural, social, or rhetorical forms or conventions. They are not so much ideology as they are bio-ideology.

We need to move beyond the idea that linkages of culture to matter mean that culture is now "determined" by matter. The brain itself is a realm of culture and operates in ways we would consider both semiotic and cultural. A crucial feature of our evolved neurobiology is the capacity to make mental representations. Such mental images allowed our ancestors to control negative emotions such as fear and prejudice that stood in the way of emergent sociality. By placing an image in the place of an automatic negative emotional response such as prejudice, our ancestors learned how to exercise emotional self control, and such control allowed them eventually to live together in large communities made up of both kin and non-kin. In a sense, the capacity to signify, to arrest an automatic emotional response with a sign of it, distinguished the new model human equipped with abstract mimetic abilities, a greater power of control over negative emotions, and a better chance of forming civilization from the older model early human who was still victimized by automatic negative emotional responses. What this means is that our cultural stories (which are transposed mental representations) are connected directly to differentiated neurobiological abilities that are indexed to different evolutionary locations. Our literary and cultural stories directly express a particular balance of hormones, a specific brain region structure, an array of epigenetic switches, a different evolutionary biological achievement, and a different point in a range of possible evolutionary locations graphed both spatially and temporally. We are records and archives, each one of us, of an evolutionary biological history. One meaning of literature, then, is neurobiology, and that is the case because neurobiology is itself literary; it operates most successfully when it can build complex internal signs or mental representations that narrate and quell negative automatic emotional responses that we inherited from our very violent ancestors such as *H. erectus.*

Our interpretive protocols will change as a result of turning to science as will our sense of what particular kinds of cultural representation mean. Scientific research tends towards settled, confirmable results, and while scientific theory might locate those results in different contending paradigms, the results themselves – untheorized – tend towards indisputability. The hormone NMDA is linked to prejudice and is more present in the operations of the amygdala, which is associated with negative emotional responses such as "fight or flight" and is larger in those self-identifying as political conservatives. Numerous tests confirm the result. It is beyond dispute, a matter now of settled knowledge. Such knowledge allows us to see ideology as biology in a more settled way than the protocols of hermeneutics. Movies such as *Apocalypse Now* or *Falling* Down that expresses prejudice can now be understood in a more physically grounded manner as the expressions of certain brain structure configurations or neurological hormonal distributions. Push further, and they can be understood as part of the evolutionary archive that tells us what the function in the distant past of an older part of the brain such as the amygdala was in early human history. A fantasy such as *Falling Down* in other words is not just about troubled racial relations in the present. As an expression of traits such as more expressed NMDA and an enlarged amygdala, it points to evolutionary history and shows us what race relations were like a hundred thousand years ago, when the amygdala was a younger newer feature of the human brain (it is lodged just atop the spinal column). Such scientific analysis thus gives us access to a different kind of "long history" and makes us aware of just how much "older" each of us is in that we bear within us emotional capacities forged thousands of years in the past.

This new scientific criticism should also be able to explain aesthetic differences such as why different kinds of literary and cultural representations exist on a range from highly differentiated and complex to very simple and undifferentiated, from a film such as *Hiroshima, Mon Amour* with its complex mix of forms, its differentiated depiction of others, and its reflection on the complex ethics of forgiveness, to films such as *Argo* or *Zero Dark Thirty* that engage in the narcissistic heroizing of unquestionably virtuous protagonists, project an undifferentiated racial other lacking complex traits, and play to primitive feelings of band loyalty formed around prejudice against adversaries. More complex forms of mental representation align with greater control over negative emotions, and psychologists link it to a more successfully achieved sense of a separate self free from longings for fusion. Complexity, differentiation, and reflection characterize the representational form of literary and cinematic works infused with such mental states. Less complex forms align with less self control and greater longings for a fused identity more likely to project an adversarial other against which violence could be directed. This new bio-aesthetic axis might amplify our current tools for differentiating literary forms into genres and modes and allow for a new understanding of the way mental representations transfer brain function into public cultural form.

CHAPTER 2

Embodied Literature: A Cognitive-Poststructuralist Approach to Genre

F. Elizabeth Hart

Post-Structuralism shifts attention from genre to discourse, but in doing so, Elizabeth Hart argues, it fails to consider the mediation of all cultural institutions such as literary genres by the mind. A cognitive approach to genre focuses attention on the way the categories of genre are part of an embodied human mind and makes our understanding of genre more accurately reflective of the species specificity of cognition.

I

Genre, like other formal aspects of literature, has been subjected to profound scrutiny over the past three decades' advance of postmodernism. Organizing the literary system into *kinds* – poetry, novel, drama; lyric, romance, tragedy – is no longer the transparent task it once seemed to a New Critical world steeped in classification. Within postmodernism, the poststructuralist critique of genre has focused on the fact that traditional genre theory has almost always been either merely descriptive or, worse, rigidly prescriptive, failing or not even attempting to explain the phenomenon of cross-textual patterning in literature. We see this in the various handbooks of literary terms, for instance, which continue to represent as viable the formalist definitions of genre based on literary 'type' or 'kind' with little acknowledgment of the complexities embedded in the idea of typicality.[1] Yet despite genre's lingering associations with formalism, it continues to serve as one of the means – one of the principle means – by which literary critics distinguish themselves within the humanities. After all, if a critic's job is to demonstrate the relevance of literary texts to culture, then the fact that texts relate to one another in a non-random, non-arbitrary fashion can provide necessary legitimation for the task. As a result of genre's continued usefulness in this sense, discussions about it now span the

Original publication details: F. Elizabeth Hart, "Embodied Literature: A Cognitive-Poststructuralist Approach to Genre" from *The Work of Fiction*, ed. Alan Richardson and Ellen Spolsky, pp. 85–106. Ashgate, 2004. Reproduced with permission from Taylor & Francis.

Literary Theory: An Anthology, Third Edition. Edited by Julie Rivkin and Michael Ryan.
© 2017 John Wiley & Sons, Ltd. Published 2017 by John Wiley & Sons, Ltd.

divide between traditional or formalist criticism and contemporary, especially poststructuralist, theory.

Given poststructuralism's investment in textuality, it is not surprising that poststructuralist critics consider genre worth rescuing from its formalist past. Their critiques of formalist approaches have adopted several themes. First, denying the assumption of an *essence* or stable identity for any given genre, poststructuralists disclaim the classificatory impulses of traditional theory, noting that – as a rule and not as an exception – '[E]very [literary] work deviates from any particular set of characteristics that may be attributed to its kind' (J. Snyder, 1). A second and related charge is that, far from conforming neatly to taxonomic labels (which are implied by the presence of generic essence), most texts exhibit characteristics of more than one kind of genre and sometimes even of multiple kinds. As the critic Deborah Madsen puts it, 'Essentialist genre theory assumes that a preconceived unifying principle is a sufficient basis for interpretation, classification, and evaluation, and this kind of genre theory simply does not entertain the possibility that there may exist such a thing as a multigeneric text' (8). Taxonomy as a principle is predicated on images of fixity and stasis, and because of this critics insist that a taxonomical essentialism cannot recognize, much less explain, the evolutions and transformations that mark a genre's history. '[O]ver time,' writes Madsen, 'every work combined with all others of more or less the same kind constitutes the history of the genre: the genre *is* its history of individual instances' (9).

Predictably, virtually all the poststructuralist genre critics suggest that the way to 'de-essentialize' genre is to re-cast it in terms of discourse.[2] This move has turned out to be progressive in that it limits the tendency to reify literary types and encourages instead a focus on the process of discourse formation. Such a focus emphasizes the dialectical exchange between texts and cultures and aids in addressing the questions of why patterns within texts appear to shift so continuously, and why texts themselves intersect dynamically with other texts. But even more important, conceiving of genre in terms of discourse and dialectical exchange allows for a further alignment of genre with *ideology*. Once genre has been linked to ideology in this way, it is but a short step toward claiming that the repetitions that comprise textual patterning signify not the purity of a transcendent essence but the recursions of a historically situated set of social discourses. Thus, genre retains its function of helping the literary critic to relate literary texts to culture, only now this task may be accomplished on materialist and not formalist or idealist grounds.

But while the poststructuralist move toward dialectical exchange and ideology is both useful and necessary, conceiving of genre primarily in terms of discourse reveals certain limitations that are intrinsic to poststructuralism's basic approach to discourse and to the relationship envisioned between discourse and subjectivity. One of the purposes of this essay will be to explore lacunae in poststructuralist genre theory by means of a cognitive literary theory, an orientation toward the materiality of mind and language that, as I have argued elsewhere, shows poststructuralism to be unwittingly idealist in its own right (Hart, 'Matter'). In what follows, I hope to demonstrate the difficulties of a discourse-based genre analysis and then offer, in its place, a cognitive literary critique whose precepts include an important reconfiguration of the relation between ontology and epistemology. This shift of philosophical alignment, achieved through the interdisciplinary efforts of cognitive scientists, philosophers, linguists, and literary critics, has the potential, I contend, to alter our understanding of both discourse and subjectivity and of the function of each with respect to genre. I begin by reviewing the background of cognitive literary theory, paying specific attention to the discussions of genre found in the work of the cognitive critic Ellen Spolsky. Then I examine poststructuralist genre theory in detail preparatory to a demonstration of its applicability to a literary text with a particularly problematic history of generic placement. That text is Shakespeare's *Othello*, a play that has consistently resisted categorization by the full range of genre theories, from models based on classical tragedy to twentieth-century reinterpretations of the classical and finally to more recent considerations of the play's generic status, some of which disengage it from tragedy altogether. At the essay's end, I re-examine *Othello* through the lens of what I call a 'cognitive-poststructuralism,' a cognitive literary critique that, although it may differ in terms of precepts and methods, nonetheless shares much with poststructuralism, particularly the poststructualist insight that actively links literary genre with ideology.

II

For some time now, literary scholars have been incorporating the insights of cognitive science into their work, focusing especially on recent shifts within cognitive science toward 'embodiment' models of the human brain and mind. The 'embodied mind,' according to these models, is a conception of mind as an aspect of – though not a reduction to – the biological brain insofar as the mind shares in the brain's interactivity with the body and thus with the body's physical, social, and cultural environments.[3] Literary critics are now increasingly attuned to convergences between literary and cognitive-scientific concerns, which include, to name just a few, studies of metaphor and other figurative phenomena now suspected of providing underlying structure to both thought and language; studies of the human body as a primary site of social construction; and bodily, socially, and culturally indexed approaches to epistemology. These critics have been bringing the findings of cognitive science to such literary research areas as poetics, narrative studies, rhetoric and composition, and historicist studies of literature and culture.[4] Some of the practitioners of cognitive literary theory have proven consistently sympathetic to the materialist agenda underlying poststructuralism, claiming a strong sense of affinity with the materialist basis of historicist criticism and a desire to eschew the methodologies of literary formalism.[5] Their sense of compatibility has extended in a limited way to the poststructuralist treatment of genre, which, although not yet a concentrated focus of cognitive criticism, has been the subject of incidental analyses by the cognitive literary critic Ellen Spolsky.[6] In various considerations of genre interspersed throughout her works, Spolsky has aligned herself with the poststructuralist view by citing as normative the tendencies for literary genres to be dynamic, i.e., ever-changing, and for texts to take on multiple rather than singular affinities with texts associated with other genres. She also places emphasis on the fact that *new* genres have sprung up throughout the course of literary history and that fresh generic labels are sometimes needed to mark newly perceived differences in older texts that once met the specifications of well-established criteria.[7]

But unlike the poststructuralists, whose habitual frame is restrictively epistemological, Spolsky casts her understanding of genre within a larger scope that includes both epistemological and ontological models, and she does this by appealing to an overtly materialist version of ontology made possible through cognitive theory. Spolsky's 'onto-logical epistemology,' as we might call it, holds as central axioms the notions that all knowledge is necessarily species-specific, contingent on the perceptual and cognitive apparatuses that any given species comes equipped with, and that the material character-istics of the human brain and mind determine the conditions under which humans appre-hend and make inferences about the world around them. Spolsky argues that certain aspects of the brain/mind's materiality – for instance the modularity or function-specificity of different parts of the brain, which promotes the 'gaps' in cognitive processing that she claims are the foundation for human flexibility and creativity – are largely an 'outcome of [human] evolutionary development' *(Gaps* 2). For Spolsky, this means that the materialist ontology of Charles Darwin is every bit as relevant to understanding postmodernism as are the materialist epistemologies of Jacques Derrida, Jacques Lacan, or other of the thinkers at the foundations of literary poststructuralism. Spolsky writes: 'The general shape of my claim is that nothing could be more adaptationist, more Darwinian than deconstruction and poststructuralism, since both understand structuration – the production of structures … – as an activity that happens within and in response to a specific environ-ment. It is an activity that is always already designed for cultural use but also always ready to be reused or redesigned as needed' ('Darwin' 56).[8]

Fusing together these two forms of materialism – poststructuralism and Darwinism – has the effect, Spolsky argues, of 'compromis[ing] the absoluteness of the deconstructve claim' that language and thus knowledge must be ultimately unstable, since – inevitably – ontology constrains epistemology ('Darwin' 51). Nevertheless, despite this constraint, a Darwinian materialist ontology also has the effect of 'affirm[ing] the gradience of the [deconstructive] claim' ('Darwin' 51) – that is, of actually strengthening it:

> Precisely because the human species and its ways of knowing are evolved by the accumula-tion of random mutations in interactions with changing environments rather than geneti-cally engineered for the task of knowing, it is not at all surprising that they are unstable … It is just this instability, however, that provides the possibility for advantageous flexibility. People, their ways of knowing, and their languages are *responsive* … that is, adaptable within a changing environment. ('Darwin' 52)

In other words, the representational system described here actually thrives on flexibility rather than being crippled by instability. Through this ready adaptability, the represen-tational system helps to enhance the survival capabilities of the human species. But importantly, whatever meaning inheres within such a representational system has to relinquish all resemblance to an *absolute* meaning. Human species survival 'does not mean that everyone has to understand everything or that understanding is a logically watertight, foolproof system,' Spolsky writes. 'All it has to be is *good enough*' ('Darwin' 52). In this sense, in the sense that 'good enough' understanding aptly serves where 'pure' or 'perfect' meaning proves impossible, Darwin's materialist ontology most neatly comple-ments the materialist epistemology underlying poststructuralism because *this* ontology is not a metaphysic. On the contrary, it is explicitly non-idealist: 'The variations and revisions [that characterize a flexible representational system] for both Darwin and post-structuralists are neither divinely nor benignly directed' ('Darwin' 57) but rather operate 'without the notion of an unchanging anchoring center, a set of platonic universals or literal meanings' ('Darwin' 58).

Literary genres, in Spolsky's view, are themselves symptomatic of the systematicity that underlies both poststructuralism and Darwinism, in which stability and predictability co-exist always with the potential for adaptation – and thus restructuration – in response to an immediately surrounding environment. Genres, like word meanings, or even like biological species, are *categories* that are at times stable and yet always flexible, sensitive and responsive to changing environments through what Spolsky terms 'recategorization,' the process of moving from one state of relative categorical stability to another. A theory of semantic categories is critical to any endeavor that depends for its comprehensibility on some designation of typicality, as do our handbook-style, residually formalist definitions of genre mentioned at the beginning of this essay. Yet while some genre theorists have described genre explicitly in terms of categorization,[9] none but Spolsky has focused on the need to understand semantic categories themselves as mental and not transcendent phenomena –and thus as (arguably) pre-discursive, functioning both apart from and in sync with language and having a cognitive identity apart from their expression within a semiotic system. Spolsky's analysis actively explores the idea of a cognitive framework underlying the categories that enable genre formation, finding this framework comparable to the cognitive framework underlying word meanings, and then finding *both* analogous to the mechanisms enabling biological species evolution. (Species change would thus constitute a biological example of recategorization – granting, of course, that cultural evolution takes place at a much faster rate than biological evolution.) Her introduction of the notion of re-categorization as a descriptor for the normative behaviors of genres – for the fact that genres constantly shift and adjust, and for the fact that texts are frequently multiply structured – provides what may be our most incisive vocabulary to date with which to discuss what literary genre truly 'is.'

Therefore, throughout this essay, Spolsky's descriptions of generic recategorization shall serve as the frame within which I will situate the difficulties of poststructuralist genre theory alongside those of such a historically problematic text as Shakespeare's *Othello*. In this discussion, I will attempt to add a new dimension to Spolsky's analysis by delving more deeply into the troublingly narrow definitions of 'discourse' and 'subjectivity' that poststructuralism both asserts and implies in its configurations of genre. (Again, I do this because the similarity of critical aims between poststructuralist and cognitive-poststructuralist approaches makes their differences worthy of investigation.) Nevertheless, the gist of my argument will amount to a reiteration of some of Spolsky's key insights into recategorization, to wit: 'The dynamic of categorization balances the need to understand something new in terms of something already familiar, so that old responses can be helpfully invoked, against the need to recognize and perhaps benefit from the peculiarity or specialness of the new experience' (*Gaps* 73). Accordingly, 'Making a categorization judgment … is always conditional, the making of the judgment itself an invitation to remake it' (*Gaps* 73). This perpetually 'conditional' condition of genre thus enables the development of a genuinely non-essentialist view of genre that nonetheless credits genre with a degree of structural integrity or stability. Crucially, however, whatever relative stability genre may lay claim to is directly indexed to readers' relatively stable material experiences – to their evolutionary and experientially *embodied minds*. As Spolsky puts it, '[A] genre categorization is no less than a way of organizing a competent reader's ability to pattern inferences about a text and its relations to other discourse. Precisely because genre categories are, in the mind of an experienced reader, so flexible, they are a fertile source of innovation' (*Gaps* 78). And as something that is always undergoing renovation, the genre system itself is 'a reflection of the complexity of readers' construal of the world and the ease with which that understanding can learn and change' (*Gaps* 79).

III

Poststructuralism exemplifies just the latest effort within a long and ancient tradition of attempts to understand the causes and functions of literary patterning.[10] The problem, of course, that has always haunted theorists of genre is the question of genre's status, its definition. Neo-Platonic and neo-Aristotelian discussions long ago set down the two opposing frameworks from within which this question has always been approached, alternately locating genre in abstract, transcendent categories said to exist prior to literary texts and in idealized relationship to those texts (the neo-Platonic approach), or locating genre within the literary text itself, viewing genre as a set of textual characteristics whose accumulation manifests generic unity and thus identity (the neo-Aristotelian approach). These opposing perspectives represent deductive and inductive methodologies respectively, and share a history of established and often simultaneous practice, informing the work of such eminent recent genre theorists as Northrop Frye and Alistair Fowler. Not surprisingly, the poststructuralist difficulty with both approaches is that each tends to reify genre into a *thing*, asserting or implying the timeless stability of this thing either within an abstract, transcendent category or within the text itself. But it is this tendency to essentialize genre, found in both traditions, that effectively closes off the means to explain two key features of genre that genre *critics* have often acknowledged even if formal theories of genre have not. These are, as mentioned before, the fact that genres constantly undergo change, maintaining some but not all the traits of previous texts assigned to any given neo-Platonic category; and the fact that many texts display categorical heterogeneity, or multiple genres within single texts, belying the faith in a unified generic identity implicit in a neo-Aristotelian analysis.

Poststructuralism has produced a variety of responses to the essentialism in both forms of traditional genre theory. By far the most important has been the assertion that genre is not a thing at all but a *process* and specifically a process of communication. Genre resides not within texts themselves nor in the pre-existing essential categories to which we try to assimilate texts. It resides, rather, within and around our discursive negotiations *about* texts. Notable examples of the genre-as-communication model have included Mikhail Bakhtin's concept of genre as a dialectical 'sociology' within the framework of a 'sociological poetics' (3–15) and Jonathan Culler's structuralist analogy between 'linguistic competence' and literary competence' (131–160), in which both linguistic and literary systems gain intelligibility through an abstract rule or code system, a coding claimed to be, in effect, genre. But by far the most influential of the poststructuralist perspectives has been Fredric Jameson's view that genre is a term we apply not to transcendent categories, to texts themselves, or to abstract code systems operating on texts, but to the critical *reception* of texts, which is both determined within and limited by historical and economic specificity. 'Genres are essentially literary *institutions*,' Jameson states, 'social contracts between a writer and a specific public, whose function is to specify the proper use of a particular cultural artifact' (106). Jacques Derrida similarly locates genre in the author or critic's choice of rhetorical strategy, a strategy whose malleability to suit ethical and political purposes allows for the utilitarian isolation of select trait-alliances within texts that are otherwise crisscrossed by a multiplicity of traits ('Law'). For both Jameson and Derrida, the point is not so much the traits that adhere within the text but those that only become visible under rhetorically and historically specific circumstances. Discourse thus constitutes a dialectic between textual content and those neo-Platonic categories of traditional classification, categories that, while no longer the principal object of genre study, nevertheless remain useful as labeling devices. It is thus the interpretation – by writers and readers alike – of the relations between prior texts and textual categories that determines what patterns will emerge from within the literary system and what ethical ends their emergence will serve. Again, such determinations are inescapably functions of discourse, and the genre critic's role now shifts fundamentally from describing a *thing* to describing a process of mediation *between* things.

This move from an essentialist model to a process model indexed by discourse is, of course, one of poststructuralism's familiar trademark revisions. In keeping with this characteristic move, it is but a short step from adopting a discourse model to privileging the roles of history and ideology and, as a consequence, to a model of genre that fully embraces the necessity of generic change. As Madsen writes, 'A genre is always subject to change by the new texts it generates and by each new reading of these and other texts.... [G]enres are constantly redefined, revivified, and transformed intertextually by their literary context and by their cultural contexts' (23). The poststructuralist approach actively theorizes how change can be woven into the model of genre as a kind of 'constant variable' (the oxymoron notwithstanding), something always at work *on* the literary system and therefore necessarily integral to it. Similarly, and as Madsen's remarks imply, the poststructuralist focus on the role of discourse also begets a friendlier acknowledgment of intertextuality and its effects, those effects in genre manifesting themselves in the phenomenon of the multigeneric text. The result is a model that, more so than previous ones, judiciously arbitrates between the abstract and the material components of the literary system and offers what Madsen calls '[a] concept of genre based on repetition-that-is-not-quite-identity and differences-that-are-not-entirely-unique' (27; hyphens added for readability).

IV

In this section of the essay, I would like to demonstrate how the poststructuralist model can be especially revealing on application to a canonical text like Shakespeare's *Othello*. However, I am restrained in performing this demonstration, which out of necessity requires a review of certain aspects of *Othello* criticism, by the fact that the rhetoric of literary history assumes the objective, essential existence of literary genres such as 'tragedy,' 'comedy,' 'satire,' 'romance,' and 'Roman New Comedy' that the remainder of this essay otherwise challenges. For pragmatic reasons, I must employ these labels in my attempt to portray the history of *Othello's* reception. But I also hope that this discussion will further illuminate these labels' fundamental fluidity, entailing the very lack of a stable or objective status for the genres in question that a poststructuralist (and cognitive-poststructuralist) theory seeks to expose.

Called a tragedy in its earliest Quarto and Folio versions, and almost always grouped by critics with *Hamlet*, *King Lear*, and *Macbeth*, *Othello* nevertheless violates major requirements traditionally assigned to tragedy and has been questioned – even scorned – by critics on that basis for centuries.[11] As early as the seventeenth century, the critic Thomas Rymer complained about the non-royal status of the play's title character and found the play's themes of jealousy and infidelity to be ridiculously beneath the dignity of tragedy. Others compensated for this perceived lack of dignity by developing the subcategory of the 'domestic' tragedy, thereby excusing the play from tragedy's usual necessity for high-placed protagonists and lofty themes, as well as for the cosmic and civic dimensions of the protagonist's final sacrifice. Even so, the neo-Platonic model of tragedy still requires that the protagonist be discernibly noble of spirit and that he recover a degree of his nobility – and thus our sympathy – in the moments preceding his death. That readers and viewers have always found it difficult to respect and ultimately to pity Othello after his murder of Desdemona is attested to by the sheer volume of debate in the twentieth century alone. This debate has culminated in some critics simply giving up on tragedy or at least on tragedy as the play's dominant logic, naming other generic possibilities with which to explain our stubbornly non-tragic reactions to the play. One such alternative has been suggested by Michael Bristol in his influential essay 'Charivari and the Comedy of Abjection in *Othello*,' which proposes that we revise our understanding of the play by placing it in the context of the early modern charivari, a riotous, punitive shaming ritual derived from carnival and usually practiced against the partners of unsanctioned marriages. A similar alternative has recently been offered by Pamela Brown, who in '*Othello* and Italophobia' reads the play as an example of anti-Italian and particularly anti-Venetian revenge-satire (such as we might associate with Jonson's *Volpone*). These signs of historical discomfort with the so-called tragic elements of *Othello* illustrate the play's persistent difficulties with traditional genre analysis based on comparisons to idealized notions of tragedy. Either the text or the category itself must be distorted if we are to approximate that mirror-like reflection that we would logically expect to find between texts and abstractly derived neo-Platonic categories.

Nor has the other traditional approach, the neo-Aristotelian approach, suited the peculiarities of Shakespeare's play. Text-based genre analysis assumes that the accumulation of a text's traits will *be* its genre, but this approach cannot account for textual traits that fall outside of a dominant pattern, divergent traits that might, in fact, constitute additional patterns. And so again, since the time of *Othello's* earliest commentaries, critics have consistently found the play to be infused not just with elements of tragedy but with comedy (and in a way utterly distinct from examples of tragicomedy). Thomas Rymer was but the first of many to see the outlines of Italian *commedia dell'arte* in the spectacle of a foolish old man raging over a young wife's betrayal. Moments like Othello's Act 4 declaration that he will 'chop [Desdemona] into messes' (4.1.199)[12] struck Rymer as painfully, even insultingly absurd, bordering on what he called the familiar grotesqueries of 'Harlequin and Scarramuchio,' stereotypical characters he cited directly from the Italian comedy (qtd. in Fortin, 162). Modern scholars including Susan Snyder, Leslie Fiedler, Margo Hendricks, Pamela Brown and others have identified not just these and other elements of *commedia dell'arte* but also traces of the Roman New Comedy, romance, chivalric romance, and, as mentioned a moment ago, even a species of vicious early modern satire, all woven subtly into what Snyder calls the 'comic matrix' of this presumed tragedy.[13] To further complicate a genre analysis conducted on the expectation of finding unified form, one must also consider *Othello's* repeated evocations of the medieval morality play. There was, by the mid-1970s, an entire generation of Shakespeare critics who looked upon the play's allegory of Christian struggle – Othello's temptation by the Vice-like Iago and then his descent into the very persona of 'black devil' (5.2.135) – as a kind of renegade morality tale actively competing with tragedy for control over the play.

Poststructuralism makes explicit what genre critics have often sensed but lacked, until recently, the vocabulary to articulate. That is, no two texts manifesting a given pattern are ever identical in their replications of that pattern; and the fact that texts often contain a puzzling mixture of patterns, each one a vehicle for its own ethos and perspective and each one provoking its own set of conventional responses. Discourse, the mediator within this dynamic, operates at all moments of a given text's history, from the text's inception through all of its subsequent receptions, with each moment playing its own role in shaping the perception of the text's genre. The early modern cultural discourses within which Shakespeare wrote would have required him, in effect, to reinvent tragedy as he went since these discourses' particular emphases and the nature of their intersections with each other would have served purposes absolutely unique to this play. These discourses, amply documented in the criticism of recent years, included among others the domains of global imperialism, English and Venetian military cultures, the patriarchies of civic and marital institutions, and not least, of course, the early modern discourse on race. In terms of the discourses operating on *Othello*'s long history of reception (a subject too vast to survey here), it suffices to say that re-assessments of *Othello's* generic impact are always going to be the rule rather than the exception. This is because, as the cultural materialists aptly point out, those aspects of a text that seem most relevant to a receiving audience can almost always be shown to mirror the concerns of that audience's moment – ours, for instance, when the interplay of race, gender, and colonial expansionism is of utmost concern to our cultural identity. As the critic Virginia Mason Vaughan writes, '*Othello* [is] not simply ... a product of a cultural milieu ... [it is] also ... a *maker* of cultural meanings, part of a complex negotiation between each episteme's cultural attitudes, its actors, and their audiences' (7).

V

At this juncture, I would like to step outside the discourse-driven process model of poststructuralism in order to examine, from a very different perspective, the emphasis that this model places on discourse as the mediating agent out of which genre emerges. This shift in perspective is warranted, I would argue, because of the famously impoverished scope of the term 'discourse' within the poststructuralist tradition. I refer specifically to its uses as a term synonymous with 'practice' or sometimes 'history' and its very limited claims to materiality based, as Derrida portrays it, almost entirely on the 'acoustical' dimension of the Saussurean linguistic sign ('Difference' 10). While our imaginings of the powers of discourse delineated by Michel Foucault have revolutionized literary studies in our time, many now believe that we have purchased this revolutionary model at the expense of something important. That something is vaguely and even nostalgically understood to be the agency accorded to human beings that once underlay the liberal-humanist model of language but that now slips imperceptibly between the lines of strategically evasive poststructuralist rhetoric. We find ghost traces of this lost human entity, for instance, in any number of Foucault's descriptions of discourse in *The Archaeology of Knowledge*, such as: '[D]iscourse is not the majestically unfolding manifestation of a thinking, knowing, speaking subject, but, on the contrary, a totality, in which the dispersion of the subject and his discontinuity with himself may be determined' (55). In his attempt to do what many critics now agree is necessary, namely, replace our essentialist models with a process model that gives imagery to constructivity, Foucault also, in denying a 'thinking, knowing, speaking subject,' denies the means – the phenomenal apparatus – for human knowing.

Taken literally, such statements seem to deny the efficacy and perhaps even the presence of human *minds* that enable discourse and representation. They likewise efface, if only implicitly, the fact that there must be a conceptual component to the fields of semantic categories that shape discourse and lend well-acknowledged systematicity to ideology. In practice, ironically, poststructuralist critics routinely cite 'categories' as playing a role in determining discourse and ideology. However, few such critics (at least in my own experience) have shown much awareness that the structure and formation of semantic categories and category systems pose legitimate scholarly research questions in their own right.[14] In other words, as a theory of language, poststructuralism benefits from the commonsense *assumption* of a 'thinking, knowing, speaking subject' even while, in theory, it anxiously erases the human particularities of that subjectivity in the interests of nullifying the threat of an idealist ontology. The result is that, as an intellectual system, poststructuralism has never really had to grapple with the phenomenological implications of what a thinking, knowing, and speaking subject must really be like.

I propose that adding a cognitive perspective to the poststructuralist scenario would help resolve this contradiction as well as open up the discussion to a field of semantic category research whose philosophical bases are strikingly compatible with poststructuralism. Taking as a starting point Spolsky's marriage between Darwin's materialist ontology and Derrida's materialist epistemology, I argue that a cognitive approach allows us to circumvent the assumed dangers of ontology and thereby integrate the embodied mind into Foucault's 'totality' – the social system, of which discourse is understood to be the primary shaping tool – in such a way that in speaking of 'categories' we can finally acknowledge that the human mind plays a key role in helping to construct that very discourse. The cognitive perspective I refer to stems from a rising tide of interdisciplinary studies by linguists, philosophers, anthropologists, and cognitive scientists of varying specialties, from neuroscience to cognitive and evolutionary psychology. These studies comprise what has been christened a 'second generation' of cognitive science, representing an aggressive departure from the rule-driven, computer-focused, and formally disembodied approaches to the mind that characterized earlier stages of cognitive science.[15] The radical nature of the departure that second-generation cognitive science represents cannot be overstated because it amounts to a large-scale rejection of philosophical rationalism, on whose premise regarding the split of mind from body much of Western philosophy has subsequently been built. The result has been a shift in the understanding of reason and realism from disembodied and transcendent to quite the opposite: to a new understanding of them as embodied and emergent from the mind-body's accumulated interactions. This shift in the conception of reason and realism has inspired new approaches to the full range of cognitive-scientific research questions, from brain structure to mental imaging, problem-solving, categorization, language processing, discourse comprehension, and many related functions that touch not only on cognitive science but on a variety of other interested disciplines, including literary studies.

Within this second generation of cognitive research several new emphases in linguistics have emerged. One in particular, cognitive linguistics, offers a theory of semantic categories that makes it especially relevant to the problems of genre theory that I have been attempting to outline.[16] As I have argued at some length elsewhere, cognitive linguistics proves consistently compatible with some of poststructuralism's most important philosophical limits (Hart, 'Matter'). Their similarities may seem overly general at first glance; however, they turn out to be fundamental to both programs. Both, for instance, are dedicated to an agenda of defining a post-rationalist and non-realist epistemology.[17] Both privilege metaphor as the principal conduit of information. Both require the characteristic of openness within the knowledge and language systems that they envision and from this openness declare the normative status of change and multiplicity over stasis and unity. Finally, like poststructuralism, cognitive linguistics rejects the idealism inherent in essentialist theories of representation and meaning, offering the criterion of meaning *coherence*, or functional understanding, to replace notions of objective correspondences or literal 'truth.' This criterion of coherence, one might notice, is not too far afield from Spolsky's materialist ontological standard of a non-absolutist representational system that is 'good enough' for communication purposes and therefore sufficient to ensure species survival.

In cognitive-linguistic theory, semantic categories are thought to be the results of interaction between, on the one hand, sensory and kinesthetic information taken in by the human body and, on the other, mental representations constructed from this bodily experience, minimalist representations that the linguists call 'image schemas.' Categories emerge in a bottom-to-top direction out of the projection of image schemas from structured to unstructured domains of experience, so that the most basic experiential information brought in by our bodies becomes the basis for our on-going, more abstract constructions of knowledge and experience. Knowledge and meaning, in this sense, are wholly contingent upon the body's physical and social interactions (i.e., its materiality) and on the structural replications of those interactions within the brain. The mind-embodiment that these replications encapsulate takes on the simple geometries of such sensorimotor-driven episodes as containment, collision, release, propulsion, attraction, and compulsion, to name only some.[18] These geometries are then projected, via conceptual metaphor, into additional domains of experience in order to construct new categories, to reinforce old ones, or subtly or radically to restructure already existing categories, each category itself bearing the potential to further escalate and proliferate its content into more complex and increasingly abstract categories.

Let me offer an example using the container schema, which will figure momentarily in my discussion of *Othello* in the context of its role in formulating ethnocentric ideology.[19] Mark Johnson describes containment as 'one of the most pervasive features of our bodily experience' (21). Our bodies are themselves three-dimensional containers 'into which we put certain things (food, water, air) and out of which other things emerge (food and water wastes, air, blood, etc.). From the beginning we experience constant physical containment in our surroundings.... We move in and out of rooms, clothes, vehicles, and numerous kinds of bounded spaces. We manipulate objects, placing them in containers (cups, boxes, cans, bags, etc.)' (Johnson 21). Through this experience of spatial boundedness, we develop inferences of *in-out* orientation, which, '[w]hether in one, two, or three dimensions ... involves separation, differentiation, and enclosure, [and] which implies restriction and limitation' (22). The basic outlines of a container schema might resemble a circle with a perimeter, an outside to the perimeter, and a marker within the perimeter to indicate the condition of boundedness. The results of this simple structure are our all-important concepts for *in* and *out* (and to some extent *on*). When projected onto our experiences, containment replicates itself consistently in such a way that we speak of finding ourselves 'in' abstract situations like business deals or new relationships just as easily as we refer more concretely to putting a toy 'in' a box. The center-periphery structure of the container schema projects systematically into vast domains of experience (including the tendency to think of experience in terms of 'domains'), extending even to our most esoteric experiences, as the role of the container schema in formal logic demonstrates (Johnson, 30–40). It so happens that the very notion of the 'semantic category' owes its accessibility to the container schema: a unit of meaning is thought of as a container into which semantic features gather to make up a concept.

Now, I ask, what exactly would poststructuralism gain by admitting a cognitive-linguistic (or similarly non-rationalist, non-idealist) semantics into its understanding of discourse? For one, it would gain the wider theoretical scope it needs for its formulations of discourse and representation, a scope that even its own practitioners already assume as a matter of course in their critical readings. For another, it would gain verification for its own precepts from a set of interdisciplinary fields outside of itself, this compatibility among divergent fields providing a significant and validating convergence of epistemologies. But most important, from its broader perspective – admitting of the role of at least a *materialist* ontology, in keeping with Spolsky's claims – it would acquire a wider zone within which to identify the material constraints on discourse, on texts, and ultimately on subjectivity. This latter, the search for material constraints, is not trivial since it is one of the primary concerns of all of today's historicist schools of literary studies. Yet by admitting such a semantics into its field of vision, poststructuralism would also have to commit to the idea that at least some of the material constraints on discourse, texts, and subjectivity derive from the phenomenologically 'real' effects of mind-embodiment. That is, it would have to acknowledge the way in which the human brain-mind and body's coalescent constructions are replicated in representation, discourse, and ideology; and thereby how the patterns of our experience are transmitted to literary texts and to the *systems* of literary texts that we call genres. In short, poststructuralist genre critics would have to recognize that literary genres, which they say are mediated for our awareness by discourse, are revealed as patterns to our eyes not primarily through discourse but through that which itself constructs discourse and is, more likely, the true mediator of the literary system: embodied human experience.

VI

To illustrate how mind-embodiment constructs discourse and thus serves as the medium through which genre manifests, I would like to examine the semantics underlying one of the many discourses running throughout *Othello*, the discourse and ideology of race, which has deeply influenced recent criticism of the play.[20] When discussing this play, new historicists and cultural materialists are bound by their historicist methodology to delineate the distant background of the word 'Moor,' which serves so often in *Othello* both to name the title character and to place him within the social hierarchies of Renaissance Venice. Anthony Barthelemy, who has written one of the most extensive studies, points first to the etymology of 'Moor' in Greek and Latin roots for 'black'; second, to its association with the Spanish-named region of Mauretania, an ancient name for northern Africa; and third, to its changing uses between ancient and early modern periods, in which its meaning both narrowed to refer to black Africans in particular, and widened to include both black and non-black figures of the 'Other' within the white-English-Christian imagination.[21] At various times it was used with confidence to indicate black Africans, white Africans, Muslims, Turks, Saracens, Asians, Indians, and even Native Americans. Blackness was, by ancient trope, a metaphor for evil, and black people were singled out for sinfulness in a Christian tradition that claimed a genealogical relation between African blacks and Ham, the sinful son of Noah.[22] Since Ham's sinfulness had taken a sexual form, blacks and Moors in general were stereotyped with concupiscence.[23] Their alleged over-passion, combined with the impressions that a few Englishmen had gained in actual contact with native Africans in their tribal environments, led to the charge of sub-humanness and therefore to the Moor being relegated to the status of beast. That black people were also associated directly with the Devil was true even before actual contact among nations for trade and military exploits. A record of black-coded devilry survives from the medieval cycle plays, whose texts make explicit that Vice characters and other demons wore dark-colored costumes and may even have been performed in black-face.

Critics assessing these semantics are often shocked by the faithfulness of Shakespeare's *Othello* to these stereotypes, even while also insisting that Shakespeare purposely inverts the racial metaphors by assigning the play's worst evils to a white man, Iago.[24] Iago and Roderigo's racist epithets of 'old black ram' and 'the thick-lips' (1.1.90, 68) are convincingly mitigated, some say, by representations of Othello's dignity, by Cassio's loyalty, and by the respect that the Venetian senators show for Othello in entrusting Cyprus to his care. But after witnessing Othello's steady decline into the bestial, sexual, and finally demonic dimensions of the Moor stereotype that he had at first seemed to transcend, critics - and increasingly students - tend to hear Emilia's loaded condemnation, after Desdemona's murder, as the play's finalizing statement of its racial conscience: 'O gull! O dolt! / As ignorant as dirt!' (5.2.170–1); 'O, the more angel she, / And you the blacker devil' (5.2.134–5). Vaughan aptly describes the way in which these semantics of race subtly constitute the play despite our best efforts to rationalize them: '[T]he discourse of racial difference is inescapably embedded in the play just as it was embedded in Shakespeare's culture and our own. To be totally free of racism, one would have to invent a new language with no loaded words, no color discriminations, and no associations of blackness with evil, whiteness with good' (70). We are, she writes, 'necessarily implicated in … [the] tangled web' of this discourse, made compliant with it by mere virtue of our sitting in the audience.

A cognitive-poststructuralist reading of *Othello's* racial and racist semantics might frame these tensions along the following lines. Ethnocentricity functions image-schematically by appealing to the containment schema, which, we might recall, is characterized by having a center-periphery structure. An 'I' or 'we' position occupies the center or inside of the container, while a 'you,' 'them,' or 'Other' position is projected onto or even outside the borderlands that define the container's periphery. Given the wildly various etymology of the word 'Moor,' it is obvious that the precise range of spatial-relations schemas constituting 'Others' on or outside the periphery of this container do not matter very much in maintaining the integrity of the container. In other words, the relationships between incongruent 'Others' is incidental because it is the structure of the *inside* of the container that the container schema marks for definition. That, at least, is how 'Moor' can encompass all the identities of black and white Africans, Muslims, Asians, Turks, etc., indiscriminately, while the white-English-Christian essence of the container's interior never loses its focus. Critics agree that Othello's rhetorical conversion at the end of the play from a Christian Venetian of African descent to the 'turbaned Turk' whom Othello kills for 'traduc[ing] the state' (5.2.363–4) represents the blurring of his character into that ill-distinguished, amorphous 'Other.'[25] By now, it becomes apparent that this 'Other' has been lurking all along beneath the surface imagery of a play that was only *pretending* to be about a dignified, fully human – black – man.

Ethnocentricity is still with us, of course. But the exact semantic makeup of those borderland struggles is constantly shifting with history and with fresh human experience, and the particular semantics of Shakespeare's early modern ethnocentricity have inevitably changed. The center-peripheries of today's ethnocentric schemas simply no longer match the internal logic of race in *Othello*, and this fact has had unavoidable implications for today's critical assessments of its genre. It helps explain, for instance, why critics like Michael Bristol and Pamela Brown do not even bother to address the so-called tragic elements of *Othello*, declaring instead that the play represents a cruel and obscure form of comedy that we should try to historicize on early modern terms. Brown claims, for instance, that two centuries of *Othello* criticism have 'labored to "beautify" the play, to render it "cooked" rather than cruel and raw – labor that allows us to enjoy rather than be horrified by our complicity in its violence and racism…. [This] critical labor of rendering it a civilized tragedy has caused the satire to vanish utterly, like cooking smoke' (192). Bristol's and Brown's views align neatly with what Spolsky has found among critics of autobiography, who have, Spolsky writes, consistently validated their re-categorizations of autobiographical texts by insisting on their own 'truer accounts of the way the world actually was' at the time of the texts' compositions:

> Even as they acknowledge the power of their own political contexts as provocation for their recategorizations, the implied goal of the literary historians in all these studies of autobiography is to try to understand 'distant times'; their job, as they see it, is to be open to the old text in such a way that their critical assertions reflect the state of that world. The critics, thus, suggest revisions in literary historical descriptions, claiming that the new categorizations and attendant inferences are truer accounts of the way the world actually was, and that the new category names and the implications they propose are better descriptions of the generic intentions of the authors of the texts than were available under the old category names. (*Gaps* 80).

What Bristol's, Brown's, and Spolsky's analyses together imply is that, even if *Othello* was originally conceived and performed as a tragedy,[26] today it simply *isn't a tragedy* for an increasing number of viewers and readers – certainly not from within the experience of the many who now know first-hand the social and cultural mingling of black and white, the shuffling of real and ideological identity boundaries, and today's various discourses on race and identity that were not available to the early seventeenth century. This is not to say that no one living can ever again experience *Othello* as tragic. Some do, and some continue to write critically about the tragic elements that they discern in the play. Nevertheless, the signs of *Othello*'s active recategorization are ongoing – have been ongoing for centuries – and will continue to appear so as the shifting experiences that determine human mind-embodiment beget new semantic categories that we can't avoid deploying in our attempts to place the play within the literary system.

VII

Genre conceived on these terms – determined by the shifting semantics of human cognitive systems as well as by the mediating powers of social discourse – is radically destabilized. But this destabilization is hardly random or arbitrary. After all, it derives from human mind-embodiment and as such finds its complements and its limits in human experience. My claiming this, that genre categorization and recategorization are constrained by experience and are thus non-arbitrary, does not alter or even add substantively to the content of poststructuralist critics' readings of *Othello*. However, it does imply revisions to the philosophical bases of poststructuralism that impact how we are to understand poststructuralist *subjectivity* and the nature of the agency that is inherent to the subject. We have already seen how the materialist ontology that Spolsky imports from Darwinian evolution invites a subtle turn away from the terminology of 'destabilization' to that of 'flexibility' and 'adaptability.' In essence what Spolsky posits – at the same moment that she suggests this ontological dimension to poststructuralist imagery – is an unavoidable *phenomenology* of brains and minds embedded within real bodies that offer us physical contact with a real world, a world whose edges our brains and minds represent by imposing structural constraints on the shapes that our conceptions of reality can take. This is a poststructuralism that, in the interests of finding the widest possible scope for materialism, has dissolved the strict divisions separating epistemology, ontology, and phenomenology from one another, finding that the various modalities of materiality that each one offers can complement the others, ceasing to contradict.[27]

But the epistemology of such a poststructuralism must also relinquish its absolute commitment to constructivity. Specifically, it must retreat from the position of extreme anti-realism that it has taken for decades now, a position that has become no more tenable for many literary critics than the extreme realism against which it is a reaction. I have argued elsewhere for envisioning a cognitive-based epistemological continuum that features the epistemological positions of realism and relativism as two extreme ends defining a spectrum of positions, in which all the positions in between these two extremes are actually various combinations of *both* extremes, differing only in the degree of emphasis placed on either.[28] Cognitive literary and cultural theory of any kind, predicated on the assumption that all knowledge is species-specific, uniquely occupies this epistemological spectrum, and so would a cognitive-poststructuralism like Spolsky's. A cognitive-poststructuralism would remain constructivist as a theory of knowledge and subjectivity, as do all cognitive-based literary approaches; but it would have to incorporate, as well, a certain degree of realism, though without having to embrace realism in its strongest and least plausible form. The cognitive-poststructuralist subject that emerges from this epistemological spectrum is a blend of ontological, phenomenological, and epistemological agencies. The first, the ontological, gives the subject a measure of stability but never in the idealist, essentialist, or absolute sense. The last, the epistemological, gives the subject flexibility, but its adaptiveness is never random, unmotivated, or irrelevant to its phenomenological experience. The cognitive apparatus is pre-discursive, contributing to interpretations of orders in the world (including assessments of literary orders) by enabling but also constraining representation and through the subject's own condition of being enabled and constrained *by* representation.

Genre recategorization is thus an unsurprising effect of this cognitive-poststructuralist subjectivity, recursively reproducing the non-arbitrary limits of cognition in a display of the dynamism that characterizes the individual human's involvement in representation. These conditions will always mean that genre is a non-arbitrary yet unpredictable phenomenon, indexed, as it is, to both the cognitive and the ideological apparatuses that together determine the shape of literary history.

Notes

1   See, for example, the entry under 'genre' in Cuddon, *Dictionary*: 'A French term for a kind, a literary type or class'; or in Harmon and Holman, *Handbook*: 'Used to designate the types or categories into which literary works are grouped according to form, technique, or, sometimes, subject matter. The French term means "kind," "genus," or "type."' These and other handbooks go on to note

the complexities of typing literature, some, such as Fowler, *Dictionary*, going out of their way actively to problematize genre. However, for the most part, the notion of 'type' or 'kind' is generally taken for granted.

2   See Jameson, *Political Unconscious*; Rosmarin; Cohen, 'History and Genre' and 'Do Postmodern Genres Exist?'; Frow; Snyder; and Madsen.

3   To name only some of the key studies in embodiment-oriented cognitive science in recent years: Lakoff, *Women, Fire, and Dangerous Things*; Edelman, *Bright Air, Brilliant Fire*; Kosslyn and Koenig, *Wet Mind*; Damasio, *Descartes' Error* and *Feeling of What Happens*.

4   The full range of scholarship is too broad to represent or cite here, but see Richardson's survey in this volume, 'Studies in Literature and Cognition.' See also Richardson's 'Cognitive Science' and Crane and Richardson, 'Literary Studies.'

5   To mention only the most recent book-length studies: Crane, *Shakespeare's Brain*; Spolsky, *Satisfying Skepticism*; and Richardson, *British Romanticism*.

6   Spolsky first addresses genre in her collaborative study with Schauber, *Bounds of Interpretation: Linguistic Theory and the Literary Text*; then in *Gaps in Nature*, esp. chapters 2 and 3: and most recently in 'Darwin and Derrida.' Another cognitive critic who mentions genre – although not in relation to poststructuralist theory or concerns – is Turner, who writes: 'Given the cognitive scientific study of the nature of categories, we should not be surprised to find effects of the basic level in genre categories, or prototype effects in genre categories, or metaphoric members of a genre category, or radial categories within our conception of a given genre, or a gradient from the categorical to the analogical in the ways literary works are connected, or (perhaps most obviously) family resemblance as a creator of genres, and so on. The analysis of genre theory in the light of the cognitive scientific study of conceptual connections would be a large, intricate, and important work. It is so necessary and obvious that its development as a literary critical project in the age of cognitive science seems inevitable' (150). See also Sinding, 'Assembling Spaces.'

7   Spolsky's views in this vein appear throughout her chapters on genre in *Gaps in Nature* and in 'Darwin and Derrida.'

8   The feminist philosopher Elizabeth Grosz makes similar claims in 'Darwin and Ontology.'

9   Notable examples include Cohen, who describes genres as 'open categories' ('History and Genre,' 204); and Jameson, whose assessment of the need for a theory of historically flexible categories anticipates Spolsky's genre theory and the cognitive semantic theory of categories in general: 'The older generic categories do not … die out, but persist in the half-life of the subliterary genres of mass culture.… Meanwhile, it would seem necessary to invent a new, historically reflexive, way of using categories, such as those of genre, which are so clearly implicated in the literary history and the formal production they were traditionally supposed to classify and neutrally to describe' (107). For background on cognitive semantics, see Lakoff, *Women, Fire* and Talmy, *Toward a Cognitive Semantics*, vols. 1 and 2. The latter part of this essay will more directly address the image-schema theory at the basis of cognitive semantics.

10   I am indebted for my understanding of this tradition to discussions by Cohen and Madsen in particular, whose observations I summarize but without hope of capturing the full complexities of the genre debates they outline.

11   Early modern English playwrights were notorious for mixing genres, often to profitable effect, as evidenced by the popularity of Jacobean tragicomedy. They were not, however, un-self-conscious about this mixing. Shakespeare's joke at Polonius' expense about the staging of 'pastoral-comical, historical-pastoral, tragical-historical, [and] tragical-comical-historical-pastoral' (*Hamlet*, 2.2.397–99) suggests nothing if not acute awareness of a trend that perhaps had begun to border on the incomprehensible. But the obverse of such an awareness is a cognizance of certain accepted norms. I think it is fair, therefore, to discuss an early modern norm for tragedy despite the early modern reputation for mixing.

12   All quotations of *Othello* are from Shakespeare, *Complete Works*, ed. Bevington.

13   See S. Snyder; Fiedler; Hendricks; and Brown.

14   In fact, poststructuralist critics routinely perform readings based on the open but unexplored acknowledgment that discourses are shaped by semantic categories. To give an example just from my reading in the *Othello* criticism as preparation for writing this essay: Vaughan, discussing the impact on *Othello* of its military discourses, writes: 'While the changing *categories* embedded in

sixteenth-century military discourse do not directly cause the tragedy, they do provide Iago with linguistic tools he can use with Roderigo, Cassio, and Othello' (50, emphasis added).

15 The descriptor 'second-generation cognitive science' appears throughout Lakoff and Mark Johnson's *Philosophy in the Flesh*; see esp. 75–78.

16 The other two are functional linguistics and corpus linguistics, both of which reject the theoretical commitment to '*langue*' over '*parole*' as a premise for research (associated, for instance, with Saussurean structuralism or Chomskyan generative-transformational linguistics), instead embracing actual language practice as a starting point for linguistic research.

17 This agenda is the subject of another of my articles, 'Epistemology of Cognitive Literary Studies.'

18 There is now a large body of work being generated by linguists on an international scale that examines image schemas and their resulting complexes of categories in a wide selection of languages. For literary critics and other non-linguists, however, the best introduction to the theory of image schemas (with ample examples) remains Johnson's *The Body in the Mind*. For specialists' discussions, see (to cite only a few) Lakoff; Langacker, *Foundations of Cognitive Grammar* and *Concept, Image, and Symbol;* and Goldberg, *Constructions*.

19 The container schema may turn out to be particularly salient for a variety of ideological systems, including those that inform theatrical experience. The theater historian Bruce McConachie has focused almost exclusively on this schema in his studies of American, Broadway-based Cold War drama of the 1950s. See 'Doing Things with Image Schemas' and *American Theater*.

20 To cite only a handful of the relevant studies: Hunter; Greenblatt; Berry; Neill; Loomba; and Adelman.

21 Barthelemy, 1–17. The remainder of this paragraph is indebted for its general descriptions to Barthelemy's work, along with that of Vitkus; D'Amico, and Vaughan.

22 Genesis 10.6.

23 Vitkus discusses the long-standing tradition of assigning lechery to Muslims in particular: 'In Western European texts, from the medieval to the early modern period, Islam was usually defined as a licentious religion of sensuality and sexuality' (156). Further highlighting the blurring of ethnic and racial distinctions, Vitkus also notes that the 'alleged sexual excesses of the Muslims were linked to those of the Moors or black Africans, who are frequently described ... as a people naturally given to promiscuity' (159).

24 There is some tension between those critics who localize the play's racist elements to the character of Iago and those who view these elements as woven into the play's ethical fabric, subsuming the particular agents of a racist perspective into a larger whole. A recent example of the former is Adelman, who offers a psychoanalytic reading of Iago's racist projections onto Othello and other characters.

25 'Conversion' is the term that Vitkus uses, arguing that Othello's last-minute metamorphosis into the enemy Turk resonates with English anxiety in the seventeenth century over real or imagined threats of religious conversions, from Protestantism to Catholicism and from Christianity to Islam.

26 I should stress that Brown, even more so than Bristol, takes the stand that the play was *not* conceived or received as tragedy.

27 The phenomenology I refer to here and in the following paragraph very closely resembles the 'embodied consciousness' of the French philosopher Maurice Merleau-Ponty. While there is not space in this essay to develop the Merleau-Pontyan connections to the ontological-epistemological nexus that Spolsky suggests (and which I adopt), it should be noted that Merleau-Ponty's ideas have proved influential for second-generation cognitive science. See, for instance, Varela, Thompson, and Rosch, 3–4; or Lakoff and Johnson, 97.

28 Hart, 'Epistemology of Cognitive Literary Studies.' See also Varela, Thompson, and Rosch, 238.

References

Adelman, Janet. 'Iago's Alter Ego: Race as Projection in *Othello.' Shakespeare Quarterly* 48.2 (Summer 1997): 125–44.

Bakhtin, M. M. and P. N. Medvedev, *The Formal Method in Literary Scholarship: A Critical Introduction to Sociological Poetics*. Trans. Albert J. Wehre. Cambridge: Harvard University Press, 1985.

Barthelemy, Anthony Gerard. *Black Face, Maligned Race: The Representation of Blacks in English Drama from Shakespeare to Southerne*. Baton Rouge and London: Louisiana State University Press, 1987.

Berry, Edward. 'Othello's Alienation.' *Studies in English Literature* 30.2 (1990): 315–33.

Bristol, Michael. 'Charivari and the Comedy of Abjection in *Othello*.' *Renaissance Drama* 21 (1990): 3–22.

Brown, Pamela. '*Othello* and Italophobia.' In *Shakespeare and Intertextuality: The Transition of Cultures Between Italy and England in the Early Modern Period*, ed. Michele Marrapodi. Rome: Bulzoni Editore, 2000. 179–92.

Cohen, Ralph. 'Do Postmodern Genres Exist?' *Genre* (Fall/Winter 1987): 241–258. 'History and Genre.' *New Literary History* 27.2 (Winter 1986): 203–218.

Crane, Mary Thomas. *Shakespeare's Brain: Reading With Cognitive Theory*. Princeton: Princeton University Press, 2001.

Crane, Mary Thomas and Alan Richardson. 'Literary Studies and Cognitive Science: Toward a New Interdisciplinarity.' *Mosaic* 32 (1999): 123–140.

Cuddon, J. A., ed. *A Dictionary of Literary Terms and Literary Theory*, 3rd ed. Cambridge, Mass.: Blackwell, 1991.

Culler, Jonathan. *Structuralist Poetics: Structuralism, Linguistics and the Study of Literature*. Ithaca: Cornell University Press, 1975.

Damasio, Antonio. *Descartes' Error: Emotion, Reason, and the Human Brain*. New York: Avon, 1994.

Damasio, Antonio. *The Feeling of What Happens: Body and Emotion in the Making of Consciousness*. New York: Harcourt Brace, 1999.

D'Amico, Jack. *The Moor in English Renaissance Drama*. Tampa: The University of South Florida Press, 1991.

Derrida, Jacques. 'Difference.' *Margins of Philosophy*. Trans. Alan Bass. Chicago: University of Chicago Press, 1982. 1–27. 'The Law of Genre.' Trans. Avital Ronell. *Glyph* 7 (1980): 177–232.

Edelman, Gerald. *Bright Air, Brilliant Fire: On the Matter of the Mind*. New York: Basic Books, 1992.

Fiedler, Leslie A. *The Stranger in Shakespeare*. St. Albans, Hertfordshire: Paladin, 1972.

Fortin, Rene E. 'Allegory and Genre in *Othello*.' *Genre* 4:2 (June 1971): 153–72.

Foucault, Michel. *The Archaeology of Knowledge*. Trans. A.M. Sheridan Smith. New York: Pantheon, 1972.

Fowler, Roger, ed. *Dictionary of Modern Critical Terms*. Rev. ed. New York: Routledge, 1987.

Frow, John. *Marxism and Literary History*. Cambridge: Harvard University Press, 1986.

Goldberg, Adele. *Constructions: A Construction Grammar Approach to Argument Structure*. Chicago and London: University of Chicago Press, 1995.

Greenblatt, Stephen. 'The Improvisation of Power.' In *Renaissance Self-Fashioning: From More to Shakespeare*. Chicago and London: University of Chicago Press, 1980. 222–54.

Grosz, Elizabeth. 'Darwin and Ontology.' Paper presented at the Society for Literature and Science annual conference, Buffalo, New York, October 2001.

Harmon, William H. and C. Hugh Holman, eds. *Handbook to Literature*. 7th ed. Upper Saddle River, N.J.: Prentice Hall, 1996.

Hart, F. Elizabeth. 'The Epistemology of Cognitive Literary Studies.' *Philosophy and Literature* 25.2 (October 2001): 314–34.

Hart, F. Elizabeth. 'Matter, System, and Early Modern Studies: Outlines for a Materialist Linguistics.' *Configurations* 6 (1998): 311–43.

Hendricks, Margo. '"The Moor of Venice," or the Italian on the Renaissance Stage.' *Shakespearean Tragedy and Gender*. Ed. Shirley Nelson Gamer and Madelon Sprengnether. Bloomington: Indiana University Press, 1996.

Hunter, J. K. '*Othello* and Color Prejudice.' In *Dramatic Identities and Cultural Tradition*. New York: Barnes and Noble, 1978. 31–59.

Jameson, Frederic. *The Political Unconscious: Narrative as Socially Symbolic Act*. London: Methuen, 1981.

Johnson, Mark. *The Body in the Mind: The Bodily Basis of Meaning, Imagination, and Reason*. Chicago: University of Chicago Press, 1987.

Kosslyn, Stephen M. and Oliver Koenig. *Wet Mind: The New Cognitive Neuroscience*. New York: Free Press, 1992.

Lakoff, George. *Women, Fire, and Dangerous Things: What Categories Reveal about the Mind*. Chicago: University of Chicago Press, 1987.

Lakoff, George and Mark Johnson. *Philosophy in the Flesh: The Embodied Mind and Its Challenge to Western Thought*. New York: Basic Books, 1999.

Langacker, Ronald. *Concept, Image, and Symbol: The Cognitive Basis of Grammar*. Berlin and New York: Mouton de Gruyter, 1990. *Foundations of Cognitive Grammar*. 2 vols. Stanford: Stanford University Press, 1986–91.

Loomba, Ania. *Gender, Race, Renaissance Drama*. Manchester: Manchester University Press, 1989.

Madsen, Deborah L. *Rereading Allegory: A Narrative Approach to Genre*. New York: St. Martin's Press, 1994.

McConachie, Bruce. *American Theater in the Culture of the Cold War, 1947–1962: Producing and Contesting Containment*. Iowa City: Iowa University Press (forthcoming).

McConachie, Bruce. 'Doing Things with Image Schemas: The Cognitive Turn in Theatre Studies and the Problem of Experience for Historians.' *Theatre Journal* 53 (2001): 569–594.

Neill, Michael. 'Unproper Beds: Race, Adultery, and the Hideous in *Othello*.' *Shakespeare Quarterly* 40.4 (1989): 383–412.

Richardson, Alan. *British Romanticism and the Science of the Mind*. Cambridge: Cambridge University Press, 2001.

Richardson, Alan. 'Cognitive Science and the Future of Literary Studies.' *Philosophy and Literature* 23 (1999): 157–173.

Rosmarin, Adena. *The Power of Genre*. Minneapolis: University of Minnesota Press, 1985.

Shakespeare, William. *The Complete Works of Shakespeare*. Fourth edition. Ed. David Bevington. New York: HarperCollins, 1992.

Sinding, Michael. 'Assembling Spaces: The Conceptual Structure of Allegory.' *Style* 36.3 (Fall 2002): 503–523.

Snyder, John. *Prospects of Power: Tragedy, Satire, the Essay, and the Theory of Genre*. Lexington: University Press of Kentucky, 1991.

Snyder, Susan. *The Comic Matrix of Shakespeare's Tragedies*. Princeton: Princeton University Press, 1971.

Spolsky, Ellen. *Gaps in Nature: Literary Interpretation and the Modular Mind*. Albany: SUNY Press, 1993.

Spolsky, Ellen. 'Darwin and Derrida: Cognitive Literary Theory as a Species of Post-Structuralism.' *Poetics Today* 23.1 (Spring 2002): 43–62.

Spolsky, Ellen. *Satisfying Skepticism: Embodied Knowledge in the Early Modern World*. Aldershot: Ashgate Publishing, 2001.

Spolsky, Ellen and Ellen Schauber. *The Bounds of Interpretation: Linguistic Theory and the Literary Text*. Stanford: Stanford University Press, 1986.

Talmy, Leonard. *Toward a Cognitive Semantics*, Vol. I: *Concept Structuring Systems*. Cambridge: MIT Press, 2000.

Talmy, Leonard. *Toward a Cognitive Semantics*, Vol. II: *Typology and Process in Concept Structuring*. Cambridge: MIT Press, 2000.

Turner, Mark. *Reading Minds: The Study of English in the Age of Cognitive Science*. Princeton: Princeton University Press, 1991.

Varela, Francisco J., Evan Thompson, and Eleanor Rosch. *The Embodied Mind: Cognitive Science and the Human Experience*. Cambridge: MIT Press, 1991.

Vaughan, Virginia Mason. *Othello: A Contextual History*. Cambridge: Cambridge University Press, 1994.

Vitkus, Daniel J. 'Turning Turk in *Othello*: The Conversion and Damnation of the Moor.' *Shakespeare Quarterly* 48.2 (Summer 1997): 145–76.

CHAPTER 3

Narrative Empathy

Suzanne Keane

Suzanne Keane's work is part of the move to study the confluence of affect and cognition in the brain. That our knowledge of others' pain can provoke feelings of identification and affect-sharing has been known since Aristotle, but modern neuroscience allows for a deepening of our understanding of how that happens. Mirror neurons in the brain allow us to feel other people's sufferings as our own. Keane explores the implications of these findings for the study of fiction. Reading fiction has been found to increase readers' capacity for empathy, and Keane notes that novel writers have been found to score higher for empathy than the general population. The invitation when we open a novel to see the world from someone else's point of view seems to strengthen our mind's empathetic capacities.

We are living in a time when the activation of mirror neuron areas in the brains of onlookers can be recorded as they witness another's actions and emotional reactions.[1] Contemporary neuroscience has brought us much closer to an understanding of the neural basis for human mind-reading and emotion-sharing abilities – the mechanisms underlying empathy. The activation of onlookers' mirror neurons by a coach's demonstration of technique or an internal visualization of proper form and by representations in television, film, visual art, and pornography has already been recorded.[2] Simply hearing a description of an absent other's actions lights up mirror neuron areas during fMRI imaging of the human brain.[3] The possibility that novel reading stimulates mirror neurons' activation can now, as never before, undergo neuroscientific investigation. Neuroscientists have already declared that people scoring high on empathy tests have especially busy mirror neuron systems in their brains.[4] Fiction writers are likely to be among these high-empathy individuals. For the first time we might investigate whether human differences in mirror neuron activity can be altered by exposure to art, to teaching, to literature.

This newly enabled capacity to study empathy at the cellular level encourages speculation about human empathy's positive consequences. These speculations are not new, as any student of eighteenth-century moral sentimentalism will affirm, but they dovetail

Original publication details: Suzanne Keene, "Narrative Empathy" from *Towards a Cognitive Theory of Narrative Acts*, pp. 61–93. University of Texas Press, 2010. Reproduced with permission from University of Texas Press.

with efforts on the part of contemporary virtue ethicists, political philosophers, educators, theologians, librarians, and interested parties such as authors and publishers to connect the experience of empathy, including its literary form, with outcomes of changed attitudes, improved motives, and better care and justice. Thus a very specific, limited version of empathy located in the neural substrate meets in the contemporary moment a more broadly and loosely defined, fuzzier sense of empathy as the feeling precursor to and prerequisite for liberal aspirations to greater humanitarianism. The sense of crisis stirred up by reports of stark declines in reading goes into this mix, catalyzing fears that the evaporation of a reading public leaves behind a population incapable of feeling with others. Yet the apparently threatened set of links between novel reading, experiences of narrative empathy, and altruism has not yet been proven to exist. This chapter undertakes three tasks preliminary to the scrutiny of the empathy-altruism hypothesis[5] as it might apply to experiences of narrative empathy, an argument I develop more fully in *Empathy and the Novel* (2007).[6] These tasks include: a discussion of empathy as psychologists understand and study it; a brief introduction to my theory of narrative empathy, including proposals about how narrative empathy works; and a review of the current research on the effects of specific narrative techniques on real readers.

What Is Empathy?

Empathy, a vicarious, spontaneous sharing of affect, can be provoked by witnessing another's emotional state, by hearing about another's condition, or even by reading. Mirroring what a person might be expected to feel in that condition or context, empathy is thought to be a precursor to its semantic close relative, *sympathy*. *Personal distress*, an aversive emotional response also characterized by apprehension of another's emotion, differs from empathy in that it focuses on the self and leads not to sympathy but to avoidance. The distinction between empathy and personal distress matters because empathy is associated with the moral emotion *sympathy* (also called *empathic concern)* and thus with prosocial or altruistic action.[7] Empathy that leads to sympathy is by definition other-directed, whereas an over-aroused empathic response that creates personal distress (self-oriented and aversive) causes a turning away from the provocative condition of the other. No philosophers who put stock in the morally improving experience of narrative empathy include personal distress in their theories. Because novel reading can be so easily stopped or interrupted by an unpleasant emotional reaction to a book, however, personal distress has no place in a literary theory of empathy, though it certainly contributes to aesthetic emotions, such as those Sianne Ngai describes in her important book *Ugly Feelings*.

In empathy, sometimes described as an emotion in its own right,[8] we feel what we believe to be the emotions of others.[9] Empathy is thus agreed to be both affective and cognitive by most psychologists. Empathy is distinguished in both psychology and philosophy (though not in popular usage) from *sympathy*, in which feelings *for* another occur. So, for instance, one may distinguish empathy from sympathy in this fashion:

Empathy:
I feel what you feel.
I feel your pain.

> *Sympathy*:
> I feel a supportive emotion about your feelings.
> *I feel pity for your pain.*

These examples emphasize negative emotions – pain and pity – but it should be noted from the outset that although psychological and philosophical studies of empathy have tended to gravitate toward the negative, empathy also occurs for positive feelings of happiness, satisfaction, elation, triumph, and sexual arousal.[10] All of these positive kinds of empathy play into readers' pleasure, or *jouissance*.[11]

Experts on *emotional contagion*, the communication of one's mood to others, have done a better job of studying the full range of emotional states that can be shared through our automatic mimicry of one another.[12] Indeed, primitive emotional contagion, or "the tendency to automatically mimic and synchronize facial expressions, vocalizations, postures, and movements with those of another person and consequently, to converge emotionally" (Hatfield, Cacioppo, and Rapson, 81) offers a compelling explanation of a component of our empathy as arising from our physical and social awareness of one another, from birth. Inherited traits play an important role in our disposition to experience emotional contagion,[13] but our personal histories and cultural contexts affect the way we understand automatically shared feelings.[14]

So, for instance, emotional contagion comes into play in our reactions to narrative, for we are also story-sharing creatures. The oral storyteller not only takes advantage of our tendency to share feelings socially by doing the voices and facial expressions of characters, but also tacitly trains young children and members of the wider social group to recognize and give priority to culturally valued emotional states.[15] This education does not create our feelings, but renders emotional states legible through their labels, and activates our expectations about what emotions mean. Narratives in prose and film infamously manipulate our feelings and call upon our built-in capacity to feel with others. Indeed, the early history of empathy as a subject of study emphasized both emotional contagion and aesthetic responses.

The word *empathy* appeared as a translation of *Einfühlung* in the early twentieth century. In 1909, the experimental psychologist E. B. Titchener translated as "empathy" aesthetician Theodor Lipps's term *Einfühlung* (which meant the process of "feeling one's way into" an art object or another person).[16] Notably, Titchener's 1915 elaboration of the concept in *Beginner's Psychology* exemplifies empathy through a description of a reading experience: "We have a natural tendency to feel ourselves into what we perceive or imagine. As we read about the forest, we may, as it were, become the explorer; we feel for ourselves the gloom, the silence, the humidity, the oppression, the sense of lurking danger; everything is strange, but it is to us that strange experience has come" (198). In the beginning of the twentieth century, the English novelist Vernon Lee brought *Einfühlung* and empathy to a broader literary audience. In a public lecture followed by a magazine piece in a popular journal,[17] Lee advanced a theory of aesthetic perception of form involving empathy, though not (at first) so named. Originally Lee's aesthetics focused on bodily sensations and muscular adjustments made by beholders of works of art and architecture and downplayed emotional responsiveness. By the time she revised and expanded her ideas for presentation in book form, however, Lee had adapted Lipps's understanding of empathy, a parallel development from common sources in German aesthetics.

Defining the purpose of art as, in part, "the awakening, intensifying, or maintaining of definite emotional states" (Lee 99–100), Lee makes empathy a central feature of our collaborative responsiveness (128). In an account that combines motor mimicry, memory, and psychological responsiveness to inanimate objects, Lee argues that empathy enters into "imagination, sympathy, and also into that inference from our own inner experience which has shaped all our conceptions of an outer world, and given to the intermittent and heterogeneous sensations received from without the framework of our constant and highly unified inner experience, that is to say, of our own activities and aims" (68). No sooner had the term been announced and situated so centrally in aesthetic theory for an English-language audience, however, than it received brisk challenge from high modernist quarters. The disdain of Bertolt Brecht for empathy (and his advocacy of so-called alienation effects), the embrace of difficulty by modernist poets, and the dominance of New Criticism, which taught students to avoid the affective fallacy, all interfered with the integration of empathy into literary theory until recently. Novelists and novel readers who prized experiences of emotional fusion cultivated narrative empathy throughout periods when the term was in eclipse.

How Is Empathy Studied?

The focus on our embodied experience in feminist criticism, disability studies, cognitive approaches to narrative, and some ecocriticism, draws literary studies closer to disciplines that accept the use of making measurements, doing tests and experiments, and interpreting empirical evidence. This section explains some of the methods being used by neuroscientists and developmental and social psychologists to study empathy. Developing the conversation between literature and psychology ought to benefit both disciplines, however, and the subsequent comments on what is known and especially what has not yet been tested about the effects of narrative techniques contribute to a more nuanced application of psychonarratology to questions of interest to social and developmental psychologists.

Psychologists test and record empathy in a variety of ways. Physiological measures, sometimes combined with self-report, can show the strength or weakness (or presence and absence) of empathic responses.[18] Psychologists measure changes in heart rate and skin conductance (palm sweat). They collect data on perceptible and imperceptible facial reactions, the latter captured by EMG (electromyographic) procedures.[19] They ask subjects how they feel or how they would act in certain situations, gathering responses through self-reports during or immediately after experiments and through surveys. Specialized surveys known as "empathy scales" are used to assess subjects' strength of empathic feeling.[20] Recently, Functional Magnetic Resonance Imaging (fMRI) has had a profound impact on brain science, including the study of empathy.[21]

Tania Singer and her colleagues have recently published a study in *Science* documenting empathetic responses to witnessing another's pain, supported by fMRI data. This study broke new ground in demonstrating why a person perceives that she feels another's pain, while not literally experiencing the identical sensations. Singer compared what happened in a subject's brain when she was actually shocked, when pain regions in the limbic system (the anterior cingulate cortex, the insula, the thalamus, and the somatosensory cortices) lit up on the fMRI, with what the brain looked like during observation of another's pain. When watching a loved one in the same room receiving a sharp shock, subjects showed active responses in the *affective* parts of the brain's pain matrix (in the anterior insula and anterior cingulate cortex, the lateral cerebellum, and the brain stem), but not in the somatosensory cortices of the brain. The affective brain areas responded to both real and imagined pain. A person not actually experiencing pain but observing a loved one being shocked showed brain activation of matching emotional areas, though not the sensory areas. Empathy alone did not light up the sensory areas for pain. Singer and her colleagues conclude that empathy is mediated by the part of the pain network associated with pain's affective qualities, but not its sensory qualities (Singer et al., 1157). They observed that subjects with higher scores on general empathy scales[22] "showed stronger activations in areas significantly activated when the subjects perceived their partner as being in pain" (1159). They also discovered that the same empathetic effects could be elicited without an emotional cue – in other words, subjects did not need to see their partners grimacing in pain in order to show empathic responses. An "arbitrary cue" signaling the feeling state of another was sufficient to elicit empathy (1158). This set of results affirms what neuroscientists working on mirror neurons on monkeys have theorized and what philosophers since David Hume have been saying about empathy for centuries. For the first time, brain images supporting the long-standing introspective account of empathy have been recorded.

The questions of how and why empathy works in the bodies and brains of human beings can still only be answered with theoretical speculations about the physiological substrate,[23] though the fMRI-based research described above and recent neuroscience on the shared manifold for intersubjectivity get researchers closer than they have been before. Stephanie Preston and Frans de Waal propose that witnessing or imagining another in an emotional state activates automatic representations of that same state in the onlooker, including responses in the nervous system and the body. They write that "empathy processes likely contain fast reflexive sub-cortical processes (directly from sensory cortices to thalamus to amygdala to response) and slower cortical processes (from thalamus to cortex to amygdala to response). These roughly map onto contagious and cognitive forms of empathy, respectively" (Preston and de Waal, 12). The advantages of automatic responses lie in their speediness. Joseph LeDoux has written about how fear responses in the amygdala provide a quick-and-dirty, possibly life-saving response to environmental threats, which can then be evaluated as the slightly slower cognitive evaluation of a threat kicks in (Le Doux, 168–178). What is sometimes called "primitive empathy" may work in the same way, providing a first, fast, feeling response to seeing or learning about another's emotional state, before cognitive evaluation through deliberate role taking occurs.[24]

The human capacity for primitive empathy, or the phenomenon of spontaneously matching feelings, suggests that human beings are basically similar to one another, with a limited range of variations. Psychologist Martin Hoffman, for instance, believes that the structural similarities in people's physiological and cognitive response systems cause similar feelings to be evoked by similar events (Hoffman, *Moral Development*, 62). However, Hoffman would be the first to concede that similarity itself is not enough to guarantee an empathic response. Singer and her colleagues believe that our survival depends on effective functioning in social contexts, and that feeling what others feel, empathizing, contributes to that success. They suggest that "our ability to empathize has evolved from a system for representing our internal bodily states and subjective feeling states" to ourselves (Singer et al., 1161). In other words, empathy as Singer's group understands it participates in a theory of mind that links second-order re-representations of others to the system that allows us to predict the results of emotional stimuli for ourselves. Recent research suggests a mechanism at the neural level that would enable such representations of others' actions, including facial expressions and bodily postures that may convey emotional states.[25] Contemporary neuroscience theorizes a system for representation of others' feelings that participates in the task of enabling us to understand the motives, beliefs, and thoughts of others. This work on empathy thus supports the theories of evolutionary psychology that emphasize the adaptive function of our social relations.[26] Given this basis in human shared intersubjectivity, empathy thus appears to many to be a key element in our responsiveness to others.

My work seeks to clarify why the link between narrative empathy and altruism is nonetheless so tenuous. For a novel reader who experiences either empathy or personal distress, there can be no expectancy of reciprocation involved in the aesthetic response. The very nature of fictionality renders social contracts between people and person-like characters null and void. Unlike the hostage children in Beslan who wished that Harry Potter would come to their rescue, adult readers know that fictional characters cannot offer us aid. Similarly, we accept that we cannot help them out, much as we may wish to intervene: Don't marry him, Dorothea! We may feel intense interest in characters, but incurring obligations toward them violates the terms of fictionality. That is, an empathetic response can be diverted from a prosocial outcome through interfering cognition.

The treatment of emotions and rationality as separate and dichotomous features of our experience has been challenged in recent decades. Thinking and feeling, for Antonio R. Damasio, are part of the same package.[27] In a series of academic articles and popular books, he has shown that clinical patients suffering from emotional disorders have cognitive difficulties. Ronald DeSousa has also advocated recognition of the rationality of emotions, and Joseph LeDoux's cognitive neuroscience focuses on *The Emotional Brain*. Evolutionary psychologists Leda Cosmides and John Tooby[28] speak for a growing group of scientists who believe that "one cannot sensibly talk about emotion affecting cognition because 'cognition' refers to a language for describing all of the brain's operations, including emotions and reasoning (whether deliberative or nonconscious), and not to any particular subset of operations" (Cosmides and Tooby, "Evolutionary Psychology," 98).[29] In the relatively recent field known as Cognitive Approaches to Literary Studies, where the work of LeDoux and Damasio has virtually canonical status, matters of affect are generally considered to fall under the umbrella of the term *cognitive*. Few literary cognitivists acknowledge that a psychologist might not readily accede to the centrality of emotions to cognition. The sub-disciplinary boundaries within the extremely diverse field of psychology result in different emphases and perspectives on the place of the emotions. Empathy studies have from the start challenged the division of emotion and cognition, but they have also been altered by the convictions and disciplinary affiliations of those who study empathy.

I set aside for the moment the view that emotions and cognition describe different processes of the central nervous system, for empathy itself clearly involves both feeling and thinking. Memory, experience, and the capacity to take another's perspective (all matters traditionally considered cognitive) have roles in empathy. Yet the experience of empathy in the feeling subject involves the emotions, including sensations in the body. In any case, narrative empathy invoked by reading must involve cognition, for reading itself relies upon complex cognitive operations. Yet overall, emotional response to reading is the more neglected aspect of what literary cognitivists refer to under the umbrella term *cognition*. This does not need to be so. The discipline of aesthetics, which has historical ties both to philosophy and to psychology, as well as to literary studies, has been interested for over a century in empathy as a facet of creativity and an explanation of human response to artworks.[30] In its strongest form, aesthetics' empathy describes a projective fusing with an object – which may be another person or an animal, but may also be a fictional character made of words, or even, in some accounts, inanimate things such as landscapes, artworks, or geological features.[31] The acts of imagination and projection involved in such empathy certainly deserve the label "cognitive," but the sensations, however strange, deserve to be registered as feelings. Thus I do not quarantine narrative empathy in the zone of either affect or cognition: as a process, it involves both. When texts invite readers to feel, they also stimulate readers' thinking.[32] Whether novel reading comprises a significant enough feature of the environment of literate people to play a critical role in their prosocial development remains to be seen. Even the leap between reading and empathizing can fall short, impeded by inattention, indifference, or personal distress. Readers' cognitive and affective responses do not inevitably lead to empathizing, but fiction does disarm readers of some of the protective layers of cautious reasoning that may inhibit empathy in the real world.

Narrative theorists, novel critics, and reading specialists have already singled out a small set of narrative techniques – such as the use of first-person narration and the interior representation of characters' consciousness and emotional states – as devices supporting character identification, contributing to empathetic experiences, opening readers' minds to others, changing attitudes, and even predisposing readers to altruism. In the course of reviewing the available research on this subject, I point out the gaps in our knowledge of potentially empathetic narrative techniques. No specific set of narrative techniques has yet been verified to override the resistance to empathizing often displayed by members of an in-group regarding the emotional states of others marked out as different by their age, race, gender, weight, disabilities, and so forth.[33] Human beings, like other primates, tend to experience empathy most readily and accurately for those who seem like us, as David Hume and Adam Smith predicted.[34] We may find ourselves regarding the feelings of those who seem outside the tribe with a range of emotions, but without empathy.[35] If empathetic reading experiences start a chain reaction leading to mature sympathy and altruistic behavior, as advocates of the empathy-altruism hypothesis believe, then discovering the narrative techniques involved matters. It is one thing to discover, however, that high empathizers report empathetic reading experiences, and quite another to show that empathetic reading experiences can contribute to changing a reader's disposition, motivations, and attitudes. If novels could extend readers' sense of shared humanity beyond the predictable limitations, then the narrative techniques involved in such an accomplishment should be especially prized.

A Theory of Narrative Empathy

Character identification often invites empathy, even when the fictional character and reader differ from one another in all sorts of practical and obvious ways, but empathy for fictional characters appears to require only minimal elements of identity, situation, and feeling, not necessarily complex or realistic characterization. Whether a reader's empathy or her identification with a character comes first is an open question: spontaneous empathy for a fictional character's feelings sometimes opens the way for character identification. Not all feeling states of characters evoke empathy; indeed, empathetic responses to fictional characters and situations occur more readily for negative emotions, whether or not a match in details of experience exists. Finally, readers' experiences differ from one another, and empathy with characters doesn't always occur as a result of reading an emotionally evocative fiction.

Several observations help to explain the differences in readers' responses. Most important, readers' empathic dispositions are not identical to one another. Some humans are more empathetic to real others, and some feel little empathy at all. (Some research suggests that empathizers are better readers, because their role-taking abilities allow them to more readily comprehend causal relations in stories.)[36] The timing and the context of the reading experience matters: the capacity of novels to evoke readers' empathy changes over time, and some novels may only activate the empathy of their first, immediate audience, while others must survive to reach a later generation of readers in order to garner an emotionally resonant reading. Readers' empathy for situations depicted in fiction may be enhanced by chance relevance to particular historical, economic, cultural, or social circumstances, either in the moment of first publication or in later times, fortuitously anticipated or prophetically foreseen by the novelist.

Novelists do not exert complete control over the responses to their fiction. Empathy for a fictional character does not invariably correspond with what the author appears to set up or invite. Situational empathy, which responds primarily to aspects of plot and circumstance, involves less self-extension in imaginative role taking and more recognition of prior (or current) experience. A novelist invoking situational empathy can only hope to reach readers with appropriately correlating experiences. The generic and formal choices made by authors in crafting fictional worlds play a role in inviting (or retarding) readers' empathic responses. This means that for some readers, the author's use of the formulaic conventions of a thriller or a romance novel would increase empathic resonance, while for other readers (perhaps better educated and attuned to literary effects), unusual or striking representations promote foregrounding and open the way to empathic reading.[37]

Novelists themselves often vouch for the centrality of empathy to novel reading and writing, and express belief in narrative empathy's power to change the minds and lives of readers. This belief mirrors their experiences as ready empathizers. Yet even the most fervent employers of their empathetic imaginations realize that this key ingredient of fictional worldmaking does not always transmit to readers without interference. Authors' empathy can be devoted to socially undesirable ends that may be rejected by a disapproving reader. Indeed, empathic distress at feeling with a character whose actions are at odds with a reader's moral code may be a result of successfully exercised authorial empathy. Both authors' empathy and readers' empathy have rhetorical uses, which come more readily to notice when they conflict in instances of empathic inaccuracy (discordance arising from gaps between an author's intention and a reader's experience of narrative empathy). Experiences of empathic inaccuracy may contribute to a reader's outraged sense that the author's perspective is simply wrong, while strong concord in authors' empathy and readers' empathy can be a motivating force to move beyond literary response to prosocial action. The position of the reader with respect to the author's strategic empathizing in fictional worldmaking limits these potential results. I theorize that *bounded strategic empathy* operates with an in-group, stemming from experiences of mutuality and leading to feeling with familiar others. *Ambassadorial strategic empathy* addresses chosen others with the aim of cultivating their empathy for the in-group, often to a specific end. *Broadcast strategic empathy* calls upon every reader to feel with members of a group, by emphasizing common vulnerabilities and hopes through universalizing representations.

Empathetic Narrative Techniques

Consider the commonplace that first-person fiction more readily evokes feeling responsiveness than the whole variety of third-person narrative situations. Even a college
sophomore with a few weeks' training in theoretical terms can report that within the
category of first-person narratives, empathy may be enhanced or impeded by narrative
consonance or dissonance, unreliability, discordance, an excess of narrative levels with
multiple narrators, extremes of disorder, or an especially convoluted plot. Genre, setting,
and time period may help or hinder readers' empathy. Feeling out of sorts with the
implied readership, or fitting it exactly, may make the difference between a dutiful
reading and an experience of emotional fusion.[38] Contrasting first-person with third-
person puts the question too broadly, with too many other variables, to reach a valid
conclusion. Narrative theorists can contribute specificity and subtlety to the research
into narrative empathy.

A variety of narrative techniques have been associated with empathy by narrative
theorists and discourse processing experts carrying out empirical research into literary reading. The formal devices themselves are regarded as empathic in nature by
some theorists and researchers, while for others the disposition of the reader toward
the text can be measured by inquiring about particular consequences of literary
reading. The observations made by this latter group often lead to speculations about
narrative technique. Mapping these ostensibly empathic narrative techniques draws
attention to the many aspects of narrative form that have *not yet* been associated
with readers' empathy, but which ought not to be ruled out without careful
consideration.

The most commonly nominated feature of narrative fiction to be associated with
empathy is *character identification*. Specific aspects of characterization, such as naming, description, indirect implication of traits, reliance on types, relative flatness or
roundness, depicted actions, roles in plot trajectories, quality of attributed speech, and
mode of representation of consciousness, may be assumed to contribute to the potential for character identification and thus for empathy.[39] The link between readers'
reports of character identification and their experiences of narrative empathy has not
yet been explained.

A close second for formal quality most often associated with empathy would be *narrative situation* (including point of view and perspective): the nature of the mediation
between author and reader, including the person of the narration, the implicit location
of the narrator, the relation of the narrator to the characters, and the internal or external perspective on characters, including in some cases the style of representation of
characters' consciousness.[40] Many other elements of fiction have been supposed to
contribute to readers' empathy, including the repetitions of works in series,[41] the length
of novels,[42] genre expectations,[43] vivid use of settings,[44] metanarrative commentary,[45]
and aspects of the discourse that slow readers' pace (foregrounding, uses of disorder,
etc.).[46] The confirmation of many of the hypotheses about specific narrative techniques
and empathy has yet to be undertaken in most cases, but the work that has been done *as
often* fails fully to support the commonplaces of narratology as it authenticates them.[47]
Whether this has to do with faulty experimental design, insufficient grasp of the
nuances of narrative theory, or verifiable confutations of theory has yet to be
discovered.

Character Identification

To begin with the necessary clarification, character identification is not a narrative technique (it occurs in the reader, not in the text), but a consequence of reading that may be precipitated by the use of particular techniques of characterization.[48] These qualities have not yet been investigated in a comprehensive fashion. Peter Dixon and Marisa Bortolussi emphasize aesthetic qualities of narrative that open the way to personal involvement[49] In contrast, Jèmeljan Hakemulder suggests that readers experiencing strong admiration of an author's writing style may engage less readily with the fictional world and its inhabitants (Hakemulder, *Laboratory*, 73–74). Readers' personal involvement with a fictional character may (or may not) be contingent upon the use of a particular technique or the presence of certain representational elements that meet with their approval.[50] Keith Oatley believes that readers' personal experiences of patterns of emotional response provoke sympathy for characters, especially as readers identify with characters' goals and plans.[51] David S. Miall and Don Kuiken argue that emotional experiences of literature depend upon the engagement of the literary text with the reader's experiences,[52] but they emphasize foregrounding effects at the level of literary style that shake up conventions, slow the pace, and invite more active reading that opens the way for empathy.[53] Don Kuiken's research shows that readers who linked themselves to story characters through personal experiences were more likely to report changes in self-perception, if not actual empathy.[54] Max Louwerese and Kuiken suggest that empathy may work as a gap-filling mechanism, by which a reader supplements given character traits with a fuller psychologically resonant portrait.[55] Readers' judgments about the realism of the characters are supposed to have an impact on identification,[56] and the similarity of the reader to the character is widely believed to promote identification.[57] None of these phenomena, however, inhere in particular narrative techniques contributing to character identification.

A few techniques of characterization have actually been tested for their relation to readers' emotional responsiveness or empathy. Characters' involvement in a suspenseful situation provokes physiological responses of arousal in readers even when they disdain the quality of the narrative.[58] Plot-laden action-stories have been shown to promote faster reading than narratives focusing on characters' inner lives,[59] which may suggest by contrast greater reflectiveness on the part of character-focused readers, as Hakemulder supposes (Hakemulder, *Laboratory*, 74). However, this does not account for the quick, apparently involuntary responses to particular plot situations inspired by trashy novels. Speedy reading may be a token of involvement in a character's fate, identification, and even empathy. With the exception of appraisal of causality, virtually nothing about the role of plot structure has been associated with readers' empathetic responses, or tested in controlled settings.[60] Aspects of plot structure and narration that might have a role in invoking readers' empathy include the control of timing (pace), order (anachronies), the use of nested levels of narrative (stories within stories)[61], serial narrative, strong or weak closure, the use of subsidiary (supplementary, satellite) plot events, repetition, and gaps. Since each one of these structural categories contains an array of possibilities for characterization, their neglect leaves us with an incomplete picture of the devices whose use makes character identification possible.

Many aspects of characterization familiar to narrative theorists have not yet been tested in controlled experiments, despite their nomination by theorists. The naming of characters (including the withholding of a name, the use of an abbreviation or a role-title in place of a full name, or allegorical or symbolic naming, etc.) may play a role in the potential for character identification. The descriptive language through which readers encounter characters is assumed to make a difference (content matters!), but what about grammar and syntax? Does the use of present tense (over the usual past tense) really create effects of immediacy and direct connection, as many contemporary authors believe? The old "show, don't tell" shibboleth of creative writing classes remains to be verified: direct description of a character's emotional state or circumstances by a third-person narrator may produce empathy in readers just as effectively as indirect implication of emotional states through actions and context.[62] David S. Miall has suggested in "Affect and Narrative" that characters' motives, rather than their traits, account for the affective engagement and self-projection of readers into characters, though it remains unclear when, and at which cues, readers' emotional self-involvement jump-starts the process of interpretation. Bortolussi and Dixon believe that "transparency," or the judgment of characters' behavior as sensible and practical, contributes to identification (Bortolussi and Dixon 240). This may be too simple: even traditional novels are complex, polyvocal, and various, and Wayne Booth offers this sensible caution: "What we call 'involvement' or 'sympathy' or 'identification,' is usually made up of *many reactions* to author, narrators, observers, and other characters" (Booth 158, my emphasis). Some way of accounting for the multiplicity of reactions making up a normal novel-reading experience needs to be devised in order to study the transition from distributed characterization in narrative fiction and readers' everyday synthesis of their reactions into an experience of character identification.[63]

This may mean setting aside some common value judgments about techniques. For instance, the critical preference for psychological depth expressed by the "roundness" of characters "capable of surprising in a convincing way" (Forster 78) does not preclude empathetic response to flat characters, minor characters, or stereotyped villains and antagonists. Drawing on the literature of cognitive social psychology, Richard J. Gerrig has suggested that readers are likely to make category-based judgments about fictional characters, and to emphasize attributed dispositions of characters over their actual behavior in situations.[64] This theory suggests, as Forster intuited, that flat characters – easily comprehended and recalled – may play a greater role in readers' engagement in novels than is usually understood. Fast and easy character identification suffers in theorists' accounts of the reading process, which often privilege more arduous self-extension and analogical reasoning. Patrick Colm Hogan, for instance, regards categorical empathy (with characters matching a reader's group identity) as the more prevalent form, while situational empathy, the more ethically desirable role taking, depends upon a reader's having a memory of a comparable experience, which is never guaranteed.[65] If Hogan's situational empathy alone leads to the ethics of compassion, as he has it, then quick-match categorical empathy looks weaker and more vulnerable to bias through ethnocentrism or exclusionary thinking. We do not know, however, that categorical empathy does *not* lead to compassion, no more than we know the ethical results of situational empathy for fictional characters. Neither hypothesis has yet been tested. While literary critics and professionals value novels that unsettle convictions and contest norms, readers' reactions to familiar situations and formulaic plot trajectories may underlie their genuinely empathetic reactions to predictable plot events and to the stereotyped figures that enact them.[66] The fullness and fashion by which speech, thoughts, and feelings of characters reach the reader are very often supposed by narrative theorists to enhance character identification, as I discuss below, but relatively externalized and brief statements about a character's experiences and mental state may be sufficient to invoke empathy in a reader. Novelists do not need to be reminded of the rhetorical power of understatement, or indeed of the peril of revealing too much. Indeed, sometimes the potential for character identification and readers' empathy *decreases* with sustained exposure to a particular figure's thoughts or voice.[67]

Narrative Situation

It has been a commonplace of narrative theory that an internal perspective, achieved either through first-person self-narration, through figural narration (in which the third-person narrator stays covert and reports only on a single, focal center of consciousness located in a main character), or through authorial (omniscient) narration that moves inside characters' minds, best promotes character identification and readers' empathy. Wayne Booth, for instance, writes, "*If* an author wants intense sympathy for characters who do not have strong virtues to recommend them, *then* the psychic vividness of prolonged inside views will help him" (Booth 377–378, emphasis in original). The technique also works for characters in which readers have a natural rooting interest, such as Jane Austen's heroines. Booth's detailed account of how Austen uses the inside view to promote sympathy for the flawed Emma is a classic of narrative theory (245–256). Booth asserts, "By showing most of the story through Emma's eyes, the author insures that we will travel with Emma rather than stand against her" (245). Austen, one of the early masters of narrated monologue to represent characters' consciousness, crafts smooth transitions between her narrator's generalizations about characters' mental states (psychonarration) and transcriptions of their inner thoughts, in language that preserves the tense and person of the narration.[68] Also called free indirect discourse, narrated monologue presents the character's mental discourse in the grammatical tense and person of the narrator's discourse.

Subsequent theorists have agreed that narrated monologue has a strong effect on readers' responses to characters. David Miall specifically mentions the means of providing "privileged information about a character's mind," free indirect discourse, as especially likely to cue literariness and invite empathic decentering (Miall, "Necessity," 54). Sylvia Adamson arrives independently at a similar point, arguing that narrated monologue should be understood as "empathetic narrative." In Adamson's language the representational technique and its ostensible effects fuse. *Quoted monologue* (also called interior monologue, the direct presentation of characters' thoughts in the person and tense of their speech) also has its champions, who regard the move into first-person as invariably more authentic and direct than the more mediated or double-voiced narrated monologue. *Psychonarration*, or the narrator's generalizations about the mental states or thoughts of a character, has fewer advocates, perhaps because it is associated with traditional narratives such as epics. However, both Wayne Booth and Dorrit Cohn suggest that psychonarration can powerfully invoke character identification, and Cohn points out that both poetic analogies and metaphors for feeling states (as Virginia Woolf often employs) require the use of psychonarration.[69] Despite the frequent mention of narrated monologue as the most likely to produce empathy,[70] quoted monologue and psychonarration also give a reader access to the inner life of characters. Most theorists agree that purely externalized narration tends not to invite readers' empathy.[71]

In addition to these speculations about modes of representing inner life, the person of the narration often seems likely to effect readers' responses to narrative fiction and its inhabitants. In particular, first-person fiction, in which the narrator self-narrates about his or her own experiences and perceptions, is thought to invite an especially close relationship between reader and narrative voice. For instance, Franz Stanzel believes that the choice of internal representation of the thoughts and feelings of a character in third-person fiction and the use of first-person self-narration have a particularly strong effect on readers. Novelist and literary theorist David Lodge speculates that historical and philosophical contexts may explain the preference for first-person or figural third-person narrative voice: "In a world where nothing is certain, in which transcendental belief has been undermined by scientific materialism, and even the objectivity of science is qualified by relativity and uncertainty, the single human voice, telling its own story, can seem the only authentic way of rendering consciousness" (Lodge 87). However, the existing experimental results for such an association of technique and reaction are not robust. In several studies of Dutch teenagers, W. van Peer and H. Pander Maat tested the notion that first-person narration creates a "greater illusion of closeness … allowing the reader a greater and better fusion with the world of the character."[72] They conclude, "It remains unclear why point of view has no more powerful and no more overall effect on readers, given the effort devoted by authors in order to create these devices that produce a point of view" (van Peer and Pander Maat 152). While noting that readers certainly express preferences about point of view and prefer consistency over inconsistency, they found that enhancement of sympathy for protagonists through positive internal focalization actually weakened as teenagers matured (152–154).

Lodge concedes that the first-person voice "is just as artful, or artificial, a method as writing about a character in the third-person," but he insists that it "creates an illusion of reality, it commands the willing suspension of the reader's disbelief, by modeling itself on the discourses of personal witness: the confession, the diary, autobiography, the memoir, the deposition" (Lodge 87–88). In my book I argue the opposite, that paratexts cuing readers to understand a work as fictional unleash their emotional responsiveness, in spite of fiction's historical mimicry of non-fictional, testimonial forms. My research suggests that readers' perception of a text's fictionality plays a role in subsequent empathic response, by releasing readers from the obligations of self-protection through skepticism and suspicion. Thus they may respond with greater empathy to an unreal situation and characters because of the protective fictionality, but still internalize the experience of empathy with possible later real-world responsiveness to others' needs. While a full-fledged political movement, an appropriately inspiring social context, or an emergent structure of feeling promoting change may be necessary for efficacious action to arise out of internalized experiences of narrative empathy, readers may respond in those circumstances as a result of earlier reading.

How Narrative Empathy Works: Authors and Audiences

The dispositions and beliefs of novelists themselves also belong in a thorough study of narrative empathy. Fiction writers report looking at and eavesdropping on their characters, engaging in conversations with them, struggling with them over their actions, bargaining with them, and feeling for them: characters seem to possess independent agency. In a remarkable study of fifty fiction writers, Taylor and her collaborators discovered that 92 percent of the authors reported some experience of the illusion of independent agency (IIA) and that the more successful fiction writers (those who had published) had more frequent and more intense experiences of it. Taylor hypothesizes that IIA could be related to authors' expertise in fantasy production (Taylor 361, 376–377), suggesting that it occurs more easily and spontaneously with practice, or that writers naturally endowed with creative gifts may experience it more readily. Though clearly novelists still do exercise their authority by choosing the words that end up on the page, they may experience the creative process as akin to involuntarily empathizing with a person out there, separate from themselves. Several tests administered by Taylor to her subjects support this connection. Taylor found that the fiction writers as a group scored higher than the general population on empathy (361). Using Davis's Interpersonal Reactivity Index (IRI), a frequently used empathy scale, Taylor measured her subjects' tendency to fantasize, to feel empathic concern for others, to experience personal distress in the face of others' suffering, and to engage in perspective taking (369–370). Both men and women in her sample of fiction writers scored significantly higher than Davis's reported norms for the general population, with females scoring higher in all four areas than males. Fiction writers of both genders stood out on all four subscales of Davis's IRI, but they were particularly off the charts for fantasy and perspective taking. Taylor speculates that "these two subscales tap the components of empathy that seem most conceptually related to IIA and might be seen as 'grown-up' versions of variables associated with children who have imaginary companions (pretend play and theory of mind skills)" (377).

Taylor's discoveries lead to speculation about the function of narrative empathy from the authors' perspective: *fiction writers as a group may be more empathetic than the general population*. However, we must also consider the difficulty of pinning down the difference between innate dispositions and results of practice and habitual use in groups of people; thus, *the activity of fiction writing may cultivate novelists' role-taking skills and make them more habitually empathetic*. These proposals do not imply that the actual behavior of fiction writers is any better than that of the population at large. Even the most ardent advocates of narrative ethics hesitate to argue that being a novelist correlates with being a better person, and novelists known to be nice people sometimes also exercise their empathy on behalf of nasty characters.

Most theories of narrative empathy assume that empathy can be transacted accurately from author to reader by way of a literary text (critiques of literary empathy disparage this goal as an unwholesome fantasy or projection). The comments of writers about their craft suggest the formation of a triangulated empathic bond. In this model authors' empathy contributes to the creation of textual beings designed to elicit empathic responses from readers. In fact there is no guarantee that an individual reader will respond empathetically to a particular representation. Because real people – for instance, objects of pity presented by charitable organizations – might find their position in that empathic triangle discomforting, critics of empathy claim it results in misunderstanding or worse.

From the failures of empathic individuals to question whether their assessments of the other's feelings could be off base comes a great deal of the negative reputation of empathy as a particularly invasive form of selfishness. (I impose my feelings on you and call them your feelings. Your feelings, whatever they were, undergo erasure.) Contrary to this fearful scenario, the research on empathic accuracy records the remarkable degree of correctness in human mind-reading abilities, though to be sure more cross-cultural verification of these findings would be welcome.[73] Whether from expert reading of facial cues, body language, tone of voice, context, or effective role taking on the part of the empathizer, ordinary subjects tend to do pretty well in laboratory tests of empathic accuracy. Verification can be achieved readily enough through interviews cross-checked with physical measurements and observations.

When we respond empathetically to a novel, we do not have the luxury of questioning the character: we cannot ask, Is that how you really felt? The text, however, may verify our reactions even as it elicits them. No one narrative technique assures readers that our empathic reaction precisely catches the feelings embedded in the fictional characters. For this reason, extratextual sources, such as interviews with authors, become important tools in assessing literary empathic accuracy. My term *empathic inaccuracy* describes a potential effect of narrative empathy: *a strong conviction of empathy that incorrectly identifies the feeling of a literary persona.* Empathic inaccuracy occurs when a reader responds empathetically to a fictional character at cross-purposes with an author's intentions. Authors also sometimes evoke empathy unintentionally. This accident contributes to empathic inaccuracy. Unlike in real-world, face-to-face circumstances, the novel-reading situation allows empathic inaccuracy to persist because neither author nor fictional character directly confutes it. Indeed, literary studies privilege against-the-grain interpretations of fiction that may be founded on deliberate acts of role taking that subvert the authors' apparent intentions and increase empathic inaccuracy. A reader persuaded that she has felt with a fictional character may defy the stated or implicit intentions of an author. When the author's intention matches the reader's feelings and the agreement resonates with empathic accord, then the introduction of alternative perspectives on the matter at hand may meet with disbelief or outrage. *Empathic inaccuracy*, to craft a proposal out of this circumstance, *may then contribute to a strong sense that the author's perspective is simply wrong.* This is by no means an unproductive critical stance.

For those writers who hope to reach readers with emotionally resonant representations, the struggle against empathic inaccuracy thus has two component liabilities, failure and falsity. On *failure* of narrative empathy, I propose that *while authors' empathy may be an intrinsic element of successful fictional worldmaking, its exercise does not always transmit to readers without interference.* A second form of empathic inaccuracy occurs when authors represent a practice or experience that unintentionally evokes empathy in readers, against authors' apparent or proclaimed representational goals.

Focus on the *falsity* of narrative empathy expresses the concern that experiencing narrative empathy short-circuits the impulse to act compassionately or to respond with political engagement. In this view, narrative empathy is amoral (Posner 19), a weak form of appeal to humanity in the face of organized hatred (Gourevitch 95), an obstacle to agitation for racial justice (Delgado 4–36), a waste of sentiment and encouragement of withdrawal (Williams 109), and even a pornographic indulgence of sensation acquired at the expense of suffering others (Wood 36). To some feminist and postcolonial critics, empathy loses credence the moment it appears to depend on a notion of universal human emotions, a cost too great to bear even if basic human rights depend upon it.[74] The fearful view of authors' empathy as corrupting readers by offering them others' feelings for callous consumption leads in some quarters to the depiction of empathy itself as a quality that weakens humans and makes them vulnerable to others' crudest manipulations. Narrative empathy becomes yet another example of the Western imagination's imposition of its own values on cultures and peoples that it scarcely knows, but presumes to feel with, in a cultural imperialism of the emotions. Empathic inaccuracy, in this quarrel with moral sentimentalism, then becomes evidence of the falsity of the whole enterprise of sympathetic representation.

Rather than attempting to eliminate empathic inaccuracy by arguing with or correcting readers' feeling responses, recognizing the conflict between authors' empathy and readers' empathy opens the way to an understanding of narrative empathy as rhetorical. *Both authors' empathy and readers' empathy have rhetorical uses, which may be more noticeable when they conflict in instances of empathic inaccuracy.* By using their powers of empathetic projection, authors may attempt to persuade readers to feel with them on politically charged subjects. Readers, in turn, may experience narrative empathy in ways not anticipated or intended by authors. When those readers articulate their differences with a text's or an author's apparent claims, they may call upon their own empathetic responses as a sort of witness to an alternative perspective. Arguments over empathic differences between authors and readers, or among readers with different emotional reactions to a shared text, give feeling responsiveness to fiction a status it has not often been granted in academic analyses of literature. Narrative empathy can impede or assist arguments staged in the public sphere. Indeed, the existence of empathic novel reading experiences, whether accurate or not, often enters into debates covertly. More self-consciousness about our own experiences of narrative empathy depends in part upon identifying where we stand as members of the diverse audiences reached by authors' empathic representations.

Narrative empathy intersects with identities in problematic ways. Do we respond because we belong to an in-group, or can narrative empathy call to us across boundaries of difference? Even this formulation could be read as participating in a hierarchical model of empathy. The habit of making the reactions of white, Western, educated readers home base for consideration of reader response has not yet been corrected by transnational studies of readers, though narrative theorists such as Peter J. Rabinowitz offer subtle ways of understanding the various audiences narrative fiction may simultaneously address. When the subject positions of empathizer and object of empathetic identification are removed from the suspect arrangement that privileges white Western responses to subaltern suffering, the apparent condescension of empathy can be transformed by its strategic use.

In advancing a theory of *authorial strategic empathizing* I hope to add to the theoretical understanding of the relationship among authorial audiences (comprised of those ideal readers imagined and hoped for by authors) and actual, historic audiences made up of a variety of real readers. The resources of rhetoric, with its traditional emphases on authorial tactics, textual strategies, and audience responses, appropriately match the critical needs of a theory of narrative empathy, which must account for the empathy of both authors and readers, as well as the potentially empathetic tropes and techniques of narrative texts, as discussed above. My term *strategic empathizing*, coined in slant rhyme with Gayatri Chakravorty Spivak's strategic essentializing,[75] indicates the intentional (not always efficacious) work of narrative artists to evoke emotions of audiences closer and further from the authors and subjects of representation. (That many narratives have more than one built-in audience, as Peter J. Rabinowitz and Brian Richardson have argued, I assume.[76]) Like strategic essentializing, strategic empathizing occurs when an author employs empathy in the crafting of fictional texts, in service of "a scrupulously visible political interest."[77] These interests make different demands on the various audiences that may read and respond to the invitation to emotional resonance. Thus I enquire, How does strategic narrative empathy reach readers in immediate, more distant, and totally remote audiences, where the metaphor of nearness/distance also correlates with familiarity/strangeness and sameness/otherness?

Strategic empathizing, a variety of authors' empathy, describes how authors attempt to direct an emotional transaction through a fictional work aimed at a particular audience, not necessarily including every reader who happens upon the text. *Bounded strategic empathy occurs within an in-group, stemming from experiences of mutuality, and leading to feeling with familiar others.* This kind of empathy can be called upon by the bards of the in-group, and it may indeed prevent outsiders from joining the empathic circle. Though we are prone to notice the delineations of class, gender, sexuality, and ethnicity that mark a text as for one audience and not so much for another, an effort of strategic empathizing may also be bounded by the toggle switch of experience. Either you have lost a partner, or you have not; either you have battled a life-threatening illness, or you have not; either you have been assaulted or imprisoned, or you have not. The gate swings open to invite you in, or it stays closed. Nothing prevents a reader who has not shared an experience from exercising the role-taking imagination while reading a remote or forbidding work, but some works do not extend the invitation to all potential readers. The persistent reader *may* or *may not* join the authorial audience, in Rabinowitz's term. The disinvited reader may not choose or be able to live up to the terms of the ideal audience projected by a narrative.

As Brian Richardson observes, "divergent audiences are regularly addressed in a literary work, and in many cases the disparate groups fail to mesh."[78] Sometimes a novelist writes to more than one audience simultaneously, with a hope of bridging the gap between them. Novelists with a purpose may set out to reach – and change – the attitudes and beliefs of a target audience. This ambition encourages the use of *ambassadorial strategic empathy*. It also directs an emotional transaction through a fictional work aimed at a particular audience, not necessarily including every reader who happens upon the text. Successfully exercised ambassadorial strategic empathy on the part of authors can be a powerful rhetorical tool in reaching and swaying the feelings of audiences. It may teach readers to feel with otherwise alien fictional others. *Ambassadorial strategic empathy addresses chosen others with the aim of cultivating their empathy for the in-group, often to a specific end.* Appeals for justice, recognition, and assistance often employ it. If identity and experience mark the audience of texts employing *bounded* strategic empathy, the relationship between the time of reading and the historical moment of publication delimits *ambassadorial* strategic empathy. Ambassadorial strategic empathy is time sensitive and context and issue dependent, marked by the period when a text's dissemination performs its ambassadorial duty by recruiting particular readers to a present cause through emotional fusion. Accompanying paratextual statements of intention on the part of writers and organizations make the attempt to use ambassadorial strategic empathy legible. A text's reception history, including enthusiastic accounts of rapport and conversion to the cause as well as hostility, also preserves the traces of ambassadorial strategic empathy at work. Polemical, didactic, biased, purposeful: narratives employing ambassadorial strategic empathy in order to reach and even change target audiences also meet resistance.

The judgments of literary merit that critics make about narrative fiction do not reliably correspond with evidence of a text's transaction of strategic empathy from author to target audience(s). Indeed, a narrative's popularity may simultaneously interfere with its reputation among tastemakers and vouch for its empathetic intensity for its readership. Indeed, narratives that deploy *broadcast strategic empathizing* in an attempt to reach the widest possible audience most often invite derisive judgments from cultural watchdogs. *Broadcast strategic empathy calls upon every reader to feel with members of a group, by emphasizing our common human experiences, feelings, hopes, and vulnerabilities.* Narrative empathy in the form of an author's broadcast strategic empathizing employs a universal tool (language) to reach distant others and transmit the particularities that connect a faraway subject to a feeling reader. While not all novelists seek to influence as many and as various a set of readers as their books can reach, some do, and we reliably find in their fiction opportunities for character identification emphasizing the common-alities of our embodied experiences, our psychological dispositions, and our social circumstances. The fact that many postcolonial novelists aspire to extend readers' sense of our shared humanity suggests that broadcast strategic empathy deserves attention more nuanced than refusal of empathy as an impossible goal of representation.

Unanswered Questions

In the book from which this chapter is derived, I subject to critical scrutiny the literary version of the empathy-altruism hypothesis, which holds that novel reading, by eliciting empathy, encourages prosocial action and good world citizenship. If indeed such a link could be substantiated (it has not yet been verified), then investigation of the effects of narrative techniques on real readers would have to extend beyond generalizations about character identification and a small subset of narrative situations. To the questions currently under investigation, many more may be added.

What effect (if any) does consonance (relative closeness to the related events) and dissonance (greater distance between the happening and the telling) have on readers of first-person, self-narrated fictions? Does a plural, communal narrative voice, a "we" narration, bring the reader into a perceptive circle where empathetic reactions are more readily available? Does the use of second-person "you" narration enhance the intimacy of the reading experience by drawing the reader and narrator close, or does it emphasize dissonance as it becomes clear that "you" cannot include the reader? In third-person fiction, does the use of a figural reflector, rather than an authorial (omniscient) narrator, make any difference in readers' emotional responsiveness to situations and characters?[79] Does the location of the narrator inside (or outside) the story-world affect readers' reactions to the content of the narration? Does a covert narrator, who scarcely does more than provide cues about characters' movements and speech, disinvite empathy for those characters, or invite readers to see the action with a greater sense of immediacy, as if it were a play, as Bortolussi and Dixon suggest (Bortolussi and Dixon 202)? In the most fully polyphonic novels, in which a single narrative perspective is simply not available to the reader, does readers' empathy increase, dwindle, or vary according to the page they are on?

Finally, to bring the questions back to what happens in actual readers, if a narrative situation devised to evoke empathy fails to do so, does the fault lie in the reader, or in the overestimation of the efficacy of the technique? While I am inclined to agree with Wayne Booth that no one ethical effect inheres in a single narrative device, the commen-tary on narrative form often asserts (or assumes) that a specific technique inevitably results in particular effects – political, ethical, emotional – in readers. These views, in my opinion, should be subjected to careful empirical testing before any aspect of narrative technique earns the label of "empathic." To persist in the nomination of favored techniques as empathic without attention to the full range of techniques that may be contributing to empathic effects renders the study of narrative empathy an impression-istic endeavor at best.[80]

Notes

1 On mirror neurons, see Keysers et al., "Demystifying Social Cognition" (501), and Gallese et al., "A Unifying View of the Basis of Social Cognition" (396).

2 For an overview of this research in neuroscience, see Gallese, "'Being Like Me': Self-Other Identity, Mirror Neurons, and Empathy."

3 On the neural effects of hearing narrative, see Tettamanti et al., "Listening to Action-Related Sentences" (273). Though most neuroscientists working on mirror neurons agree that the effects are strongest in real life, face-to-face interactions, what Gallese calls the "shared manifold for intersubjectivity" still operates when subjects see videos, experience virtual reality through com-puter interfaces, and simply hear narration about others. See Blakeslee (F1, F4).

4 Dr. Christian Keysers, cited in Blakeslee (F1, F4).

5 Social and developmental psychologists, philosophers of virtue ethics, feminist advocates of an ethic of caring, and many defenders of the humanities believe that empathic emotion motivates altruistic action, resulting in less aggression, less fickle helping, less blaming of victims for their misfortunes, increased cooperation in conflict situations, and improved actions on behalf of needy individuals and members of stigmatized groups. See Batson et al., "Benefits and Liabilities of Empathy-Induced Altruism" (360–370), for a discussion of the recent research on each of these results of empathy. For a warm, agent-based virtue ethics view of empathy and sympathy, see Slote, *Morals from Motives* (109–110).

6 Feeling with fictional others does not guarantee changes in the capacity to feel with real others and does not predict altruistic behavior on real others' behalf. For my argument that the transposition of the "empathy-altruism" hypothesis to experiences of narrative empathy lacks experimental sup-port, see Keen, *Empathy and the Novel* (90–92, 99, 116, 145).

7 On personal distress as aversive and empathy as a precursor to sympathy or empathic concern, see Batson, *The Altruism Question* (56–57), and "Altruism and Prosocial Behavior" (282–316); see also Eisenberg, "Emotion, Regulation, and Moral Development" (671–672), and "The Development of Empathy-Related Responding."

8 Charles Darwin's treatment of sympathy in *The Expression of the Emotions in Man and Animals* clearly includes empathy, though he does not use the term. Paul Ekman, the leading authority on facial expressions as indicators of universal human emotions, does not treat empathy as a core emo-tion, but as one of the nine starting points for emotional reactions (when we feel what others feel). See Ekman, *Emotions Revealed* (34, 37). Neuroscientist Jaak Panksepp argues that emotional sys-tems in the brain involve central affective programs comprised of neural anatomy, physiology, and chemicals. Panksepp considers empathy one of the higher sentiments (mixing lower, reflexive affects and higher cognitive processes) emerging out of the recent evolutionary expansion of the forebrain. See "Emotions as Natural Kinds within the Mammalian Brain" (142–143). For philosopher Martha C. Nussbaum, empathy comes into play as a part of compassion, which she treats as a human emotion. See *Upheavals of Thought* (327–335). For John Deigh and those work-ing at the intersection of ethics and cognitive science, empathy is one of the moral emotions.

9 For working definitions of different vicariously induced emotional states, see Eisenberg and Fabes, "Children's Disclosure of Vicariously Induced Emotions" (111). I follow Eisenberg in differentiat-ing empathy, aversive personal distress, and sympathy. Empathic response includes the possibility of personal distress, but personal distress (unlike empathy) is less likely to lead to sympathy, if it proceeds beyond evanescent shared feeling.

10 Positive forms of empathy are drastically underemphasized in the literature. See Ainslie and Monterosso, "Hyperbolic Discounting Lets Empathy Be a Motivated Process."

11 See Barthes for the distinction between the relatively easy pleasure of the readerly text and the bliss that comes when the demanding writerly text helps readers break out of their subject positions.

12 See for instance the treatment of happiness, joy, and love in Hatfield, Cacioppo, and Rapson, *Emotional Contagion*. Theodor Lipps, an important early theorist of empathy, proposed motor mimicry as an automatic response to another's expression of emotion. See Lipps, "Das Wissen von Fremden Ichen."

13 For genetic influences on prosocial acts and empathic concern, see Zahn-Waxler et al., "Empathy and Prosocial Patterns in Young MZ and DZ Twins."

14 Cultural differences implicate differences in the nature of emotional experience. Our understanding of what it means to be a person in our cultural context affects the way we experience daily emotions of pleasantness and unpleasantness, or whether we feel entitled as individuals to express a particular emotion. See Shields.

15 Oral storytelling is not isolated to preliterate cultures. Children in literate cultures also absorb cultural values and narrative styles through collaborative storytelling. See the comments on rapport and empathy in Minami and McCabe.

16 See Titchener, 181–185. See also Lipps, *Zur Einfühlung*.

17 See Lee and Anstruther-Thomson for the original journal articles.

18 Evaluation of patients who show changes in behavior as a result of brain injuries, ailments, or surgery contributes to the understanding of empathy. See Gratton and Elsinger.

19 Physiological measures have the advantage of being unaffected by the subjects' desire to present themselves favorably, as may occur in surveys, interviews, or self-reports. See Eisenberg et al., "Physiological Indices of Empathy." On deceleration of heart rate in response to negative experiences of others, see Craig. On the measurement of palmar skin conductance and heart rate in response to images of people in pain, see R. S. Lazarus et al. For a skin conductance study suggesting that empathetic arousal occurs when subjects believe a person is receiving a painful shock, see Geer and Jarmecky. On facial or gestural responses as indications of empathy, see Marcus. See also Hoffman, "The Measurement of Empathy." On EMG and other physiological measurements of emotional responses, see Cacioppo and Petty, "Just Because You're Imaging the Brain."

20 A number of empathy scales developed since the 1950s are still in use by psychologists. The Sherman-Stotland scale includes a factor (VI) measuring "fantasy empathy" for fictional characters in stories, plays, and films. See Stotland (135–156). More recent tests of emotional intelligence include the Balanced Emotional Empathy Scale (BEES) and Davis's Interpersonal Reactivity Index (IRI). On BEES, see Mehrabian. For the IRI, which has subscales in Empathic Concern, Perspective Taking, Fantasy (including narrative empathy), and Personal Distress, see Davis, "A Multidimensional Approach" and "Measuring Individual Differences." Survey methodology has its limitations, as psychologists acknowledge. Eisenberg has repeatedly observed that cultural influences such as sex-role differentiation show up more in the kinds of tests that rely on surveys and interviews and much less (or not at all) in tests using physiological methods. See Lennon and Eisenberg.

21 For a salutary caution on the interpretation of these fMRI studies, which feature such dazzling pictures and often receive quite credulous promotion in the press, see Cacioppo and Petty, "Just Because You're Imaging the Brain."

22 Singer and her colleagues employed two empathy scales, Mehrabian's Balanced Emotional Empathy Scale and Davis's Empathic Concern Scale ("Empathy for Pain," 1159).

23 The amygdala, anterior temporal cortex, and orbital frontal cortex (as well as physiological synchrony of the autonomic nervous system) are probably involved in empathy, as the evidence of emotional impairment in brain-damaged or diseased patients suggests. See Brothers; Levenson and Ruef; and Rosen et al.

24 This account is consistent with the emotion theory of neuroscientist Edmund T. Rolls, who hypothesizes that human brain mechanisms provide two routes to action, one a quick, unconscious prompt for a behavioral response (which we share with other mammals) and the other a slower, language mediated, rational planning faculty. The two routes can produce conflicting results.

25 Mirror neurons fire not only when carrying out an action but also when observing another carrying out the same action. They provide a basis for understanding primates' mind-reading, and by extension, human empathy. See Gallese et al., "The Mirror Matching System." See also Iacoboni et al.

26 See for instance Cosmides and Tooby, "Cognitive Adaptations for Social Exchange."

27 See for instance Antonio Damasio et al., "Somatic Markers and the Guidance of Behavior: Theory and Preliminary Testing." Damasio's works for general readers (*Descartes' Error, The Feeling of What Happens*, and *Looking for Spinoza*) have resulted in wide dissemination of his theories.

28 See Cosmides and Tooby, "Evolutionary Psychology and the Emotions."

29 Some neuroscientists informally refer to "cogmotions" to emphasize the fusion of the two concepts in their research. (My informant is neuroscientist Dr. Tyler S. Lorig.) Nonetheless, many experts in cognition carry out their work without regard to the emotions, and basic textbooks on cognition rarely refer to emotions. See for instance Reed's introductory college text, *Cognition: Theory and Applications*, 6th ed. Emotional states receive fleeting mention on just three pages of this text. The younger hybrid discipline of Social Cognition is more likely to reflect the understandings of affect and cognition as intertwined. See for instance Forgas.

30 The core elements of the modern concept of empathy in aesthetics can legitimately be traced to Lee, who was also a novelist. As with several key dates in psychology, rival claimants to earliest usage appear. Lipps's 1897 work on *Einfühlung* gets translated in 1909 by experimental psychologist Titchener as *empathy*. Lee drew on Lipps's work for *The Beautiful*. Freud also had Lipps's books in his library and adopted the term *Einfühlung*. See Wispé.

31 For speculations on the role of aesthetics in human evolution, see Cosmides and Tooby, "Does Beauty Build Adapted Minds?"

32 Philosopher Lawrence Blum believes that insofar as emotions of sympathy and empathy promote perspective taking, they may result in better prosocial responses than rationality alone. See Blum (122–139).

33 Some studies suggest that people with very empathetic dispositions respond more positively to members of out-groups than less empathetic people do, but, for most people, perceived similarity encourages empathy. For a classic study affirming similarity's relationship to higher empathy scores, see Krebs. On out-groups, see Sheehan et al. On similarity, see the literature review in Davis, *Empathy* (15, 96–99, 105–106, 109, 116–118).

34 On evolutionary bases for empathy for those who are like us, see Kruger; see also Hoffman, *Empathy and Moral Development* (4, 13, 206).

35 See the account of empathy's potential to replace egocentrism with ethnocentrism in Sherman.

36 On empathy as a precursor to reading comprehension, see Bourg.

37 See Miall and Kuiken, "What Is Literariness?"; see also Miall, "Beyond the Schema Given."

38 For this catalog of helps and impediments to empathetic reading of first-person fiction, I draw upon the in-class essays of the students in English 232, The Novel, composed on 20 February 2006, answering this question: "How does your recent reading experience in this course square with the notion that first-person narration is especially productive of empathetic reading? What differences in technique in the variety of first-person narrative situations might alter readers' responses?"

39 Very little empirical research has been attempted to verify the theoretical speculations about aspects of characterization that operate in readers' character identification. Bortolussi and Dixon's pioneering study *Psychonarratology* reports their findings that character actions contribute to readers' assessments of character traits, while self-evaluations provided by the narrator (description) do not. However, the test stories employed first-person narrators, so narrators' evaluations of characters in third-person fiction cannot be included in this preliminary conclusion (160–165).

40 Schneider represents narrative situation as a factor in eliciting readers' empathy and lack of representation of inner life as a likely inhibitor of it.

41 On affective responses to serial fiction, see Warhol (71–72). See also Hakemulder, *Moral Laboratory* (93, 143), drawing on Feshbach's observations of the effects of repetitive role-taking.

42 Nussbaum's empathy-inducing novels are invariably long. Writing about the character David Copperfield's reading habits in Dickens's novel of that name (1849–1850), Nussbaum comments, "He remains with [books] for hours in an intense, intimate, and loving relationship. As he imagines, dreams, and desires in their company, he becomes a certain sort of person." For Nussbaum the length of the immersion is a vital component of the process, permitting intensity, dreaming, and desiring that develops the reader's loving heart. See Nussbaum, *Love's Knowledge* (230–231).

43 Canonically, see Jameson. See also Zwaan, who compares readers' behavior when processing texts labeled as "news stories" or "narratives." Bortolussi and Dixon aptly caution that research in discourse processing has focused on broad generic distinctions rather than on narrative fiction's subgenres (253–254). For evidence of emotional responses to fictional subgenres in television, see Bryant and Zillmann, eds. Literary genre critics have been reluctant to adopt findings from mass communications research (to the extent that they are aware of them), perhaps because audiovisual (iconic) representations are assumed to be more emotionally stimulating than the verbal representations of prose narrative fiction. This assumption, however, has not been investigated systematically.

44 Feminist criticism often celebrates the power of women's writing's vividly represented spaces and places, in tandem with identity themes, to work out boundary-crossing potentials for connection, communication, and change. See for instance Friedman.

45 See the account of Nünning's remarks on empathy-inducing functions of metanarration, in Fludernik, "Metanarrative and Metafictional Commentary" (39).

46 Relevant to slower pace as potentially fostering empathy is Zillmann, who hypothesizes that the fast pace of television news stories and dramas may impede empathetic response ("Empathy," 160–161). Miall's work on foregrounding and empathy in literary texts correlates a slower reading pace with enhanced empathy.

47 See for instance van Peer's judgment in "Justice in Perspective."

48 Character identification thus exemplifies what Bortolussi and Dixon identify as readers' mental constructions, as opposed to textual features (*Psychonarratology* 28). Bortolussi and Dixon systematically measure how particular readers process specific textual features in narratives, but the experimental results bridging disciplines of discourse processing and narrative theory are still quite scanty. On their narratology, see Diengott.

49 See Dixon et al. ("Literary Processing," 5–33).

50 Writing about identification with dramatic characters, Zillman argues that the audience member's disposition precipitates empathic and counterempathic reactions and suggests that audiences must be made to care about characters one way or another. He believes that enactment of good or evil deeds by protagonists and antagonists, with opportunities for the moral appraisal of their actions, promotes strong emotional reactions. See Zillman, "Mechanisms of Emotional Involvement."

51 See Oatley, "A Taxonomy of the Emotions of Literary Response."

52 In this respect Miall and Kuiken are in accord with earlier work that demonstrates a relationship between a subject's prior similar experiences and empathy felt for another in the same situation. See Stotland.

53 See Miall and Kuiken, "What Is Literariness?" (121–138), and Miall, "Beyond the Schema Given."

54 See Kuiken et al., "Locating Self-Modifying Feelings."

55 See Louwerse and Kuiken ("Effects of Personal Involvement," 170). Their research confirms some of what Iser proposes about active reading as gap-filling (168–169).

56 For critiques of this assumption, see Konijn and Hoorn, from a discourse processing angle; see also Walsh.

57 See Klemenz-Belgardt (368); see also Jose and Brewer. Hakemulder reports on recent studies confirming the importance of personal relevance for intensity of reader response. See *Moral Laboratory* (71).

58 Wünsch cited in Hakemulder, *Moral Laboratory* (73).

59 For this reading-speed research, see Chupchik and Lazló.

60 Research into the empathy evoked by various genres of television advertisements suggests that discontinuous, nonlinear "vignette" ads discourage empathy, whereas classical, character-centered dramatic form in ads evokes viewers' empathy. See Stern.

61 For a good application of cognitive theory on levels of embedding to readers' capacity to comprehend embedded accounts of characters' mental states, see Zunshine, "Theory of Mind."

62 For a subtle treatment of the variety of techniques by which sympathy for characters may be cultivated, see Booth, *Rhetoric of Fiction* (129–133, 243–266, 274–282, 379–391). Ultimately Booth

prefers the use of an "inside view" for invoking sympathy, but he describes the full range of strate-gies that authors from the classical period to the modernists actually employ.

63 For an excellent description of readers' imaginative construction of characters, see Cohan.

64 See Gerrig, "The Construction of Literary Character." See also his account of participatory responses to fiction in *Experiencing Narrative Worlds.*

65 See Hogan, "The Epilogue of Suffering." Though this article suggests a preference for the cognitive role-taking Hogan associates with situational empathy, his later very brief treatment of readers' empathy in *Cognitive Science, Literature, and the Arts* improves on his theory by describing how emotion triggers invoke quick-and-dirty responses, as well as imaginative role-taking, neither of which need be denigrated as egocentric (186–187). For work confirming the role of lived experi-ence in spontaneous situational empathy with characters on film documentaries, see Sapolsky and Zillmann, "Experience and Empathy." Women who had given birth responded to a medical film of actual childbirth with more intense physiological reactions; otherwise, gender and related experiences had a negligible effect on empathy.

66 See Jauss (152–188), especially his summary figure, "Interaction Patterns of Identification with the Hero" (159). See also Hogan on emotions and prototypes in narrative, in *The Mind and Its Stories.*

67 For preliminary confirmation from film studies, see Andringa et al. (154–155).

68 For narrated monologue, psychonarration, and quoted monologue, see Cohn, *Transparent Minds.*

69 See Booth's discussion of traditional literature's use of "telling" in *Rhetoric of Fiction* (3–16); see also Cohn on psychonarration in *Transparent Minds.*

70 See for instance Palmer, *Fictional Minds.*

71 Three good starting points for recent work on the representation of consciousness are Fludernik's magisterial *The Fictions of Language and the Languages of Fiction;* Zunshine's *Why We Read Fiction: Theory of Mind and the Novel;* and George Butte's *I Know That You Know That I Know.*

72 Van Peer and Pander Maat designed experiments using five versions of stories, rewritten to test the relationship between positive internal focalization and readers' allocation of sympathy. See "Perspectivation" (145).

73 For a variety of essays verifying human beings' tendency accurately to identify others' feelings and states of mind, see Ickes, ed.

74 Indeed, human rights are not exempted from criticism. Some regard "the whole idea of 'universal' human rights" as a "gigantic fraud, where Western imperialist or excolonial powers try to pass off their own, very specific and localized idea of what 'rights' should be as universal, trampling roughly over everyone else's beliefs and traditions." See Howe (3).

75 See Spivak (214).

76 See Rabinowitz, *Before Reading,* and two essays by B. Richardson, "The Other Reader's Response" and "Singular Text, Multiple Implied Readers." Rabinowitz and Richardson offer subtle ways of understanding the various audiences narrative fiction may simultaneously address, and the condi-tions that pertain when we choose to join them.

77 See Spivak (214).

78 See Richardson, "The Other Reader's Response" (38).

79 Bertolussi and Dixon have done the best work on this subject, though they phrase the question differently: To what degree do readers fuse narrators and characters as a result of perceptual access to a particular character's perspective, and thus develop a rooting interest in that character and making assumptions about the narrator's and author's gender? See *Psychonarratology* (166–199).

80 This chapter is a revision of an essay that originally appeared in *Narrative* 14, no. 3 (2006): 207–236. The chapter is reprinted with permission from *Narrative.*

Works Cited

Ainslie, George, and John Monterosso. "Hyperbolic Discounting Lets Empathy Be a Motivated Process." *Behavioral and Brain Sciences* 25 (February 2002): 20–21.

Andringa, Els, et al. "Point of View and Viewer Empathy in Film." In *New Perspectives on Narrative Perspective*. Ed. Willie van Peer and Seymour Chatman. Albany, N.Y.: SUNY Press, 2001. 133–157.

Batson, C. Daniel. *The Altruism Question: Toward a Social-Psychological Answer*. Hillsdale, N.J.: Erlbaum, 1991.

Batson, C. Daniel, and Adam A. Powell. "Altruism and Prosocial Behavior." In *Handbook of Psychology, Personality and Social Psychology*, Vol. 5. Ed. Theodore Millon and Melvin J. Lerner. New York: Wiley, 2003. 463–484.

Batson, C. Daniel. "Benefits and Liabilities of Empathy-induced Altruism." In *The Social Psychology of Good and Evil*. Ed. Arthur G. Miller. New York: Guilford Press, 2004. 359–385.

Blakeslee, Sandra. "Cells That Read Minds." *New York Times* (10 January 2006): F1, F4.

Blum, Lawrence A. *Friendship, Altruism and Morality*. London and New York: Routledge and Kegan Paul, 1980.

Booth, W. *The Rhetoric of Fiction*, 2nd ed. Chicago: University of Chicago Press, 1983.

Bortolussi, Marisa, and Peter Dixon. *Psychonarratology: Foundations for the Empirical Study of Literary Response*. Cambridge and New York: Cambridge University Press, 2003.

Bourg, Tammy. "The Role of Emotion, Empathy, and Text Structure in Children's and Adults' Narrative Text Comprehension." In *Empirical Approaches to Literature and Aesthetics*. Ed. Roger J. Kreuz and Mary Sue MacNealy. Norwood, N.J.: Ablex, 1996. 241–260.

Brothers, Leslie. "A Biological Perspective on Empathy." *American Journal of Psychiatry* 146 (1989): 10–19.

Bryant, Jennings, and Dolf Zillmann. *Responding to the Screen: Reception and Reaction Processes*. Mahwah, N.J.: Erlbaum, 1991.

Butte, George. *I Know That You Know That I Know: Narrating Subjects from Moll Flanders to Marnie*. Columbus: Ohio State University Press, 2004.

Cacioppo, John T., and R. E. Petty. "Just Because You're Imaging the Brain Doesn't Mean You Can Stop Using Your Head: A Primer and Set of First Principles." *Journal of Personality and Social Psychology* 85 (October 2003): 650–661.

Chupchik, G. C., and János Lázló. "The Landscape of Time in Literary Reception: Character Experience and Narrative Action." *Cognition and Emotion* 8 (1994): 297–312.

Cohan, Steven. "Figures beyond the Text: A Theory of Readable Character in the Novel." *Novel: A Forum on Fiction* 17 (1983): 5–27.

Cohn, Dorrit. *Transparent Minds: Narrative Modes for Presenting Consciousness*. Princeton, N.J.: Princeton University Press, 1978.

Cosmides, Leda, and John Tooby. "Cognitive Adaptations for Social Exchange." In *The Adapted Mind*. Ed. J. Barkow, Leda Cosmides, and John Tooby. Oxford and New York: Oxford University Press, 1992. 163–228.

Cosmides, Leda, and John Tooby. "Does Beauty Build Adapted Minds? Toward an Evolutionary Theory of Aesthetics, Fiction and the Arts." *SubStance* 94/95 (2001): 6–27.

Cosmides, Leda, and John Tooby. "Evolutionary Psychology and the Emotions." In *Handbook of Emotions*, 2nd ed. Ed. Michael Lewis and Jeanette M. Haviland-Jones. New York: Guilford Press, 2000. 91–115.

Craig, K. D. "Physiological Arousal as a Function of Imagined, Vicarious, and Direct Stress Experiences." *Journal of Abnormal Psychology* 73 (1968): 513–520.

Damasio, Antonio R. *Descartes' Error: Emotion, Reason, and the Human Brain*. New York: Putnam, 1994.

Damasio, Antonio R. *The Feeling of What Happens: Body and Emotion in the Making of Consciousness*. San Diego: Harcourt, 1999.

Damasio, Antonio R. *Looking for Spinoza: Joy, Sorrow and the Feeling Brain*. New York: Harcourt, 2003.

Davis, Mark H. *Empathy: A Social Psychological Approach*. Boulder: Westview, 1994.

Davis, Mark H. "A Multidimensional Approach to Individual Differences in Empathy." *JSAS Catalog of Selected Documents in Psychology* 10 (1980): 85.

Davis, Mark H. "Measuring Individual Differences in Empathy: Evidence for a Multidimensional Approach." *Journal of Personality and Social Psychology* 44 (1983): 113–26.

Delgado, Richard. *The Coming Race War? and Other Apocalyptic Tales of America after Affirmative Action and Welfare*. New York: NYU Press, 1996.

Dixon, Peter, et al. "Literary Processing and Interpretation: Towards Empirical Foundations." *Poetics* 22 (1993): 5–33.

Eisenberg, Nancy. "Emotion, Regulation, and Moral Development." *Annual Review of Psychology* 51 (2000): 665–697.

Eisenberg, Nancy, and Richard A. Fabes. "Children's Disclosure of Vicariously Induced Emotions." In *Disclosure Processes in Children and Adolescents*. Ed. Ken J. Rotenberg. Cambridge and New York: Cambridge University Press, 1995. 111–134.

Eisenberg, Nancy, Richard A. Fabes, Denise Bustamante, and Robin M. Mathy. "The Development of Empathy-Related Responding." In *Moral Motivation through the Life Span*. Ed. Gustavo Carlo and Carolyn Pope Edwards. Lincoln: University of Nebraska Press, 2005. 73–117.

Eisenberg, Nancy, Richard A. Fabes, Denise Bustamante, and Robin M. Mathy. "Physiological Indices of Empathy." In *Empathy and Its Development*. Ed. Nancy Eisenberg and Janet Strayer. Cambridge and New York: Cambridge University Press, 1987. 380–385.

Ekman, Paul. *Emotions Revealed: Recognizing Faces and Feelings to Improve Communication and Emotional Life*. New York: Henry Holt, 2003.

Fludernik, Monika. *The Fictions of Language and the Languages of Fiction*. London and New York: Routledge, 1993.

Fludernik, Monika. "Metanarrative and Metafictional Commentary: From Metadiscursivity to Metanarration and Metafiction." *Poetica* 35 (2003): 1–39.

Forgas, Joseph P. Ed. *Handbook of Affect and Social Cognition*. Mahwah, N.J.: Erlbaum, 2001.

Forster, E. M. *Aspects of the Novel*. New York: Harcourt, 1927.

Friedman, Susan Stanford. *Mappings: Feminism and the Cultural Geographies of Encounter*. Princeton, N.J.: Princeton University Press, 1998.

Gallese, Vittorio, et al. "A Unifying View of the Basis of Social Cognition." *Trends in Cognitive Science* 8, no. 9 (September 2004): 396–403.

Gallese, Vittorio, et al. "'Being Like Me': Self-Other Identity, Mirror Neurons, and Empathy." In *Perspectives on Imitation: From Neuroscience to Social Science. Volume 1: Mechanisms of Imitation and Imitation in Animals*. Ed. Susan Hurley and Nick Chater. Cambridge, Mass.: MIT Press, 2005. 101–118.

Gallese, Vittorio, et al. "The Mirror Matching System: A Shared Manifold for Intersubjectivity." *Behavioral and Brain Sciences* 25 (February 2002): 35–36.

Geer, J. H., and L. Jarmecky. "The Effect of Being Responsible for Reducing Another's Pain on Subject's Response and Arousal." *Journal of Personality and Social Psychology* (1973): 232–237.

Gerrig, Richard J. "The Construction of Literary Character: A View from Cognitive Psychology." *Style* 24 (Fall 1990): 380–392.

Gerrig, Richard J. *Experiencing Narrative Worlds: On the Psychological Activities of Reading*. New Haven: Yale University Press, 1993.

Gourevitch, Philip. *We Wish to Inform You That Tomorrow We Will Be Killed with Our Families: Stories from Rwanda*. New York: Farrar, Straus, and Giroux, 1998.

Gratton, Lynn M., and Paul J. Elsinger. "High Cognition and Social Behavior: Changes in Cognitive Flexibility and Empathy after Cerebral Lesions." *Neuropsychology* 3 (1989): 175–185.

Hakemulder, Jèmeljan. *The Moral Laboratory: Experiments Examining the Effects of Reading Literature on Social Perception and Moral Self-Concept*. Utrecht Publications in General and Comparative Literature 34. Amsterdam and Philadelphia: John Benjamins, 2000.

Hatfield, Elaine, John T. Cacioppo, and Richard L. Rapson. *Emotional Contagion*. Cambridge: Cambridge University Press, 1994.

Hoffman, Martin. *Empathy and Moral Development: Implications for Caring and Justice*. Cambridge and New York: Cambridge University Press, 2000.

Hoffman, Martin. "The Measurement of Empathy." In *Measuring Emotions in Infants and Children*. Ed. C. E. Izard. Cambridge and New York: Cambridge University Press, 1982. 279–296.

Hogan, Patrick Colm. "The Epilogue of Suffering: Heroism, Empathy, Ethics." *SubStance* 30 (2001): 119–143.

Hogan, Patrick Colm. *Cognitive Science, Literature, and the Arts: A Guide for Humanists*. London and New York: Routledge, 2003.

Hogan, Patrick Colm. *The Mind and Its Stories: Narrative Universals and Human Emotion*. Cambridge: Cambridge University Press, 2003.

Howe, Stephen. *Empire: A Very Short Introduction*. Oxford and New York: Oxford, 2002.

Iacoboni, Marco, et al. "Cortical Mechanisms of Human Imitation." *Science* 286 (1999): 2526–2528.

Ickes, William. Ed. *Empathic Accuracy*. New York: Guilford, 1997.

Iser, Wolfgang. *The Act of Reading: A Theory of Aesthetic Response*. Baltimore: Johns Hopkins University Press, 1978.

Jameson, Fredric. *The Political Unconscious: Narrative as a Socially Symbolic Act*. Ithaca, N.Y.: Cornell University Press, 1981.

Jauss, Hans Robert. *Aesthetic Experience and Literary Hermeneutics*. Trans. Michael Shaw. Minneapolis, Minn.: University of Minnesota Press, 1982.

Jose, P. E., and W. F. Brewer. "Development of Story Liking: Character Identification, Suspense, and Outcome Resolution." *Developmental Psychology* 20 (1984): 911–924.

Keen, Suzanne. *Empathy and the Novel*. New York: Oxford, 2007.

Keysers, Christian, et al. "Demystifying Social Cognition: a Hebbian Perspective." *Trends in Cognitive Science* 8 (November 2004): 501–507.

Klemenz-Belgardt, Edith. "American Research of Response to Literature." *Poetics* 10 (1981): 357–380.

Konijn, Elly A., and Johan F. Hoorn. "Reality-based Genre Preferences Do Not Direct Personal Involvement." *Discourse Processes* 38 (2004): 219–246.

Krebs, Dennis. "Empathy and Altruism." *Journal of Personality and Social Psychology* 32 (1975): 1134–1146.

Kruger, Daniel J. "Evolution and Altruism: Combining Psychological Mediators with Naturally Selected Tendencies." *Evolution and Human Behavior* 24 (2003): 118–125.

Kuiken, Don, et al. "Locating Self-Modifying Feelings within Literary Reading." *Discourse Processes* 38 (2004): 267–286.

Lazarus, R. S., et al. "A Laboratory Study of Psychological Stress Produced by a Motion Picture Film." *Psychological Monographs* 76 (1962): 1–35.

LeDoux, Joseph E. *The Emotional Brain: The Mysterious Underpinnings of Emotional Life*. New York: Simon and Schuster, 1996.

Lee, Vernon [Violet Paget]. *The Beautiful: An Introduction to Psychological Aesthetics*. Cambridge: Cambridge University Press, 1913.

Lee, Vernon, and C. Anstruther-Thomson. "Beauty and Ugliness." *Contemporary Review* 72 (October 1897): 544–569 (November 1897): 669–688.

Lennon, Randy, and Nancy Eisenberg. "Gender/Age Differences in Empathy/Sympathy." In *Empathy and Its Development*. Ed. Nancy Eisenberg and Janet Strayer. Cambridge and New York: Cambridge University Press, 1987. 195–217.

Levenson, Robert, and Anna Ruef. "Physiological Aspects of Emotional Knowledge and Rapport." In *Empathic Accuracy*. Ed. William Ickes. New York: Guilford Press, 1997. 44–72.

Lipps, Theodor. "Das Wissen von Fremden Ichen." *Psychologische Untersuchungen* 1 (1906): 694–722.

Lipps, Theodor. *Zur Einfühlung*. Leipzig: Engleman, 1913.

Lodge, David. *The Modes of Modern Writing: Metaphor, Metonymy, and the Typology of Modern Literature*. Chicago: University of Chicago Press, 1977.

Louwerse, Max, and Don Kuiken. "The Effects of Personal Involvement in Narrative Discourse." *Discourse Processes* 38 (2004): 169–172.

Marcus, Robert F. "Somatic Indices of Empathy." In *Empathy and Its Development*. Ed. Nancy Eisenberg and Janet Strayer. Cambridge and New York: Cambridge University Press, 1987. 374–379.

Mehrabian, Albert. "Relations among Personality Scales of Aggression, Violence, and Empathy: Validational Evidence Bearing on the Risk of Violence Scale." *Aggressive Behavior* 23 (1997): 433–445.

Miall, David S. "Affect and Narrative: A Model of Responses to Stories." *Poetics* 17 (1988): 259–272.

Miall, David S. "Beyond the Schema Given: Affective Comprehension of Literary Narratives." *Cognition and Emotion* 3 (1989): 55–78.

Miall, David S., and Don Kuiken. "What Is Literariness? Three Components of Literary Reading." *Discourse Processes* 28 (1999): 121–138.

Minami, Masahiko, and Alyssa McCabe. "Rice Balls and Bear Hunts: Japanese and North American Family Narrative Patterns." *Journal of Child Language* 22 (1995): 423–445.

Nussbaum, Martha C. *Love's Knowledge: Essays on Philosophy and Literature*. Oxford and New York: Oxford University Press, 1990.

Nussbaum, Martha C. *Upheavals of Thought: The Intelligence of Emotions*. Cambridge: Cambridge University Press, 2001.

Oatley, Keith. "A Taxonomy of the Emotions of Literary Response and a Theory of Identification in Fictional Narrative." *Poetics* 23 (1994): 53–74.

Palmer, Alan. *Fictional Minds*. Lincoln and London: University of Nebraska Press, 2004.

Panksepp, Jaak. "Emotions as Natural Kinds within the Mammalian Brain." In *Handbook of Emotions*. Ed. Michael Lewis and Jeannette M. Haviland-Jones. 2nd ed. New York: Guilford Press, 2000. 137–156.

Posner, Richard. "Against Ethical Criticism." *Philosophy and Literature* 21 (1997): 1–27.

Preston, Stephanie D., and Frans B. M. de Waal. "Empathy: Its Ultimate and Proximate Bases." *Behavioral and Brain Sciences* 25 (February 2002): 1–20, 49–71.

Rabinowitz, Peter J. *Before Reading: Narrative Conventions and the Politics of Interpretation*. Ithaca, N.Y.: Cornell University Press, 1987.

Reed, Stephen K. Cognition: *Theory and Applications*, 6th ed. Belmont, Calif.: Wadsworth, 2004.

Richardson, Alan. "The Other Reader's Response: On Multiple, Divided, and Oppositional Audiences." *Criticism* 39, no. 1 (Winter 1997): 31–53.

Richardson, Alan. "Singular Text, Multiple Implied Readers." *Style* 41 (2007): 259–274.

Rosen, Howard J., et al. "Emotion Comprehension in the Temporal Variant of Frontotemporal Dementia." *Brain* 125 (October 2002): 2286–2295.

Sapolsky, Barry, and Dolf Zillmann. "Experience and Empathy: Affective Reactions to Witnessing Childbirth." *Journal of Social Psychology* 105 (1978): 133–144.

Schneider, Ralf. "Toward a Cognitive Theory of Literary Character: The Dynamics of Mental-Model Construction." *Style* 35 (2001): 607–642.

Sheehan, E. P., et al. "Reactions to AIDS and Other Illnesses: Reported Interactions in the Workplace." *Journal of Psychology* 123 (1989): 525–536.

Sherman, Nancy. "Empathy and Imagination." In *Philosophy of Emotions*. Midwest Studies in Philosophy, XXII. Ed. Peter French and Howard K. Wettstein. South Bend, Ind.: University of Notre Dame Press, 1998. 82–119.

Shields, Stephanie A. *Speaking from the Heart: Gender and the Social Meaning of Emotion*. Cambridge and New York: Cambridge University Press, 2002.

Singer, Tania, et al. "Empathy for Pain Involves the Affective but Not Sensory Components of Pain." *Science* 303 (20 February 2004): 1157–1162.

Slote, Michael. *Morals from Motives*. New York: Oxford University Press, 2001.

Spivak, Gayatri Chakravorty. "Subaltern Studies: Deconstructing Historiography." In *The Spivak Reader: Selected Works of Gayatri Chakravorty Spivak*. Ed. Donna Landry and Gerald MacLean. New York and London: Routledge, 1996. 203–235.

Stern, Barbara. "Classical and Vignette Television Advertising Dramas: Structural Models, Formal Analysis, and Consumer Effects." *Journal of Consumer Research* 20 (1994): 601–615.

Stotland, Ezra, et al. *Empathy, Fantasy and Helping*. Beverly Hills: Sage, 1978.

Taylor, Marjorie, et al. "The Illusion of Independent Agency: Do Adult Fiction Writers Experience Their Characters as Having Minds of Their Own?" *Imagination, Cognition and Personality* 22 (2002/2003): 361–380.

Tettamanti, Marco, et al. "Listening to Action-related Sentences Activates Fronto-parietal Motor Circuits." *Journal of Cognitive Neuroscience* 17 (February 2005): 273–281.

Titchener, E. B. *Experimental Psychology of the Thought Processes*. London: Macmillan, 1909.

Van Peer, Willie. "Justice in Perspective." In *New Perspectives on Narrative Perspective*. Ed. Willie van Peer and Seymour Chatman. Albany, N.Y.: SUNY Press, 2001. 325–338.

Van Peer, Willie, and H. Pander Maat. "Perspectivation and Sympathy: Effects of Narrative Point of View." In *Empirical Approaches to Literature and Aesthetics*. Ed. Roger J. Kreuz and Mary Sue MacNealy. Norwood, N.J.: Ablex, 1996. 143–154.

Walsh, Richard. "Why We Wept for Little Nell: Character and Emotional Involvement." *Narrative* 5 (October 1997): 306–321.

Warhol, Robyn. *Having a Good Cry: Effeminate Feelings and Pop-Culture Forms*. Columbus, Ohio: Ohio State University Press, 2003.

Williams, Raymond. *Culture and Society, 1780–1950*. Reprint with a new introduction. New York: Columbia University Press, 1983.

Wispé, Lauren. "History of the Concept of Empathy." In *Empathy and Its Development*. Ed. Nancy Eisenberg and Janet Strayer. Cambridge and New York: Cambridge University Press, 1987. 17–37.

Wood, Marcus. *Slavery, Empathy and Pornography*. Oxford and New York: Oxford, 2002.

Zahn-Waxler, Carolyn, et al. "Empathy and Prosocial Patterns in Young MZ and DZ Twins: Development and Genetic and Environmental Influences." In *Infancy to Early Childhood: Genetic and Environmental Influences on Developmental Change*. Ed. Robert M. Emde and John K. Hewitt. Oxford and New York: Oxford University Press, 2001. 141–162.

Zillmann, Dolf. "Empathy: Affect from Bearing Witness to the Emotions of Others." In *Responding to the Screen: Reception and Reaction Processes*. Ed. Dolf Zillmann and Jennings Bryant. Mahwah, N.J.: Erlbaum, 1991. 135–167.

Zillmann, Dolf. "Mechanisms of Emotional Involvement with Drama." *Poetics* 23 (1994): 33–51.

Zunshine, Lisa. "Theory of Mind and Experimental Representations of Fictional Consciousness." *Narrative* 11 (October 2003): 270–291.

Zunshine, Lisa. *Why We Read Fiction: Theory of Mind and the Novel*. Columbus: Ohio State University Press, 2006.

Zwaan, Rolf A. "Effect of Genre Expectations on Text Comprehension." *Journal of Experimental Psychology: Learning, Memory and Cognition* 20 (1994): 920–933.

CHAPTER 4

Affective Economies

Sara Ahmed

Sara Ahmed teaches Gender, Media, and Culture at Goldsmiths College and is the Director of the Centre for Feminist Research. Her books include *The Cultural Politics of Emotion* (2014), *Willful Subjects* (2014), *On Being Included* (2012), *The Promise of Happiness* (2010), and *Queer Phenomenologies* (2006).

The depths of Love are rooted and very deep in a real white nationalist's soul and spirit, no form of "hate" could even begin to compare. At least not a hate motivated by ungrounded reasoning. It is not hate that makes the average white man look upon a mixed race couple with a scowl on his face and loathing in his heart. It is not hate that makes the white house-wife throw down the daily jewspaper in repulsion and anger after reading of yet another child molester or rapist sentenced by corrupt courts to a couple of short years in prison or on parole. It is not hate that makes the white workingman curse about the latest boatload of aliens dumped on our shores to be given job preference over the white citizen who built this land. It is not hate that brings rage into the heart of a white Christian farmer when he reads of billions loaned or given away as "aid" to foreigners when he can't get the smallest break from an unmerciful government to save his failing farm. No, it's not hate. It is love.[1]

– Aryan Nations Web site

How do emotions work to align some subjects with some others and against other others? How do emotions move between bodies? In this essay, I argue that emotions play a crucial role in the "surfacing" of individual and collective bodies through the way in which emotions circulate between bodies and signs. Such an argument clearly challenges any assumption that emotions are a private matter, that they simply belong to individuals, or even that they come from within and *then* move outward toward others. It suggests that emotions are not simply "within" or "without" but that they create the very effect of the surfaces or boundaries of bodies and worlds.

For instance, in the above narrative on the Aryan Nations Web site, the role of emotions, in particular of hate and love, is crucial to the delineation of the bodies of individual subjects and the body of the nation. Here a subject (the white nationalist, the average white

Original publication details: Sara Ahmed, "Affective Economies." *Social Text* 22.2 (Summer 2004), pp. 117–139. Duke University Press, 2004. Reproduced with permission from Duke University Press.

man, the white housewife, the white working man, the white citizen, and the white Christian farmer) is presented as endangered by imagined others whose proximity threatens not only to take something away from the subject (jobs, security, wealth), but to take the place of the subject. In other words, the presence of these others is imagined as a threat to the object of love. The narrative involves a rewriting of history, in which the labor of others (migrants, slaves) is concealed in a fantasy that it is the white subject who "built this land."[2] The white subjects claim the place of hosts ("our shores") at the same time as they claim the position of the victim, as the ones who are damaged by an "unmerciful government." The narrative hence suggests that it is love for the nation that makes the white Aryans hate those whom they recognize as strangers, as the ones who are taking away the nation and the role of the Aryans in its history, as well as their future.

We might note as well that the reading of others as hateful aligns the imagined subject with rights and the imagined nation with ground. This alignment is affected by the representation of both the rights of the subject and the grounds of the nation as already under threat. *It is the emotional reading of hate that works to bind the imagined white subject and nation together.* The average white man feels "fear and loathing"; the white housewife, "repulsion and anger"; the white workingman, "curses"; the white Christian farmer, "rage." The passion of these negative attachments to others is redefined simultaneously as a positive attachment to the imagined subjects brought together through the repetition of the signifier, "white." It is the love of white, or those recognizable as white, that supposedly explains this shared "communal" visceral response of hate. *Together we hate, and this hate is what makes us together.*

This narrative is far from extraordinary. Indeed, what it shows us is the production of the ordinary. The ordinary is here fantastic. The ordinary white subject is a fantasy that comes into being through the mobilization of hate, as a passionate attachment tied closely to love. The emotion of hate works to animate the ordinary subject, to bring that fantasy to life, precisely by constituting the ordinary as in crisis, and the ordinary person as the real victim. The ordinary becomes that which is already under threat by imagined others whose proximity becomes a crime against person as well as place. The ordinary or normative subject is reproduced as the injured party: the one "hurt" or even damaged by the "invasion" of others. The bodies of others are hence transformed into "the hated" through a discourse of pain. They are assumed to "cause" injury to the ordinary white subject, such that their proximity is read as the origin of bad feeling: indeed, the implication here is that the white subject's good feelings (love, care, loyalty) are being "taken" away by the abuse of such feelings by others.

So who is hated in such a narrative of injury? Clearly, hate is distributed across various figures (in this case, the mixed-racial couple, the child molester, the rapist, aliens, and foreigners). These figures come to embody the threat of loss: lost jobs, lost money, lost land. They signify the danger of impurity, or the mixing or taking of blood. They threaten to violate the pure bodies; such bodies can only be imagined as pure by the perpetual restaging of this fantasy of violation. Note the work that is being done through this metonymic slide: mixed-race couplings and immigration become readable as (like) forms of rape or molestation: an invasion of the body of the nation, represented here as the vulnerable and damaged bodies of the white woman and child. The slide between figures constructs a relation of resemblance between the figures: what makes them alike may be their "unlikeness" from "us." Within the narrative, hate cannot be found in one figure, but works to create the very outline of different figures or objects of hate, a creation that crucially aligns the figures together and constitutes them as a "common" threat. Importantly, then, hate does not reside in a given subject or object. Hate is economic; it circulates between signifiers in relationships of difference and displacement.

In such affective economies, emotions *do things*, and they align individuals with communities – or bodily space with social space – through the very intensity of their attachments. Rather than seeing emotions as psychological dispositions, we need to consider how they work, in concrete and particular ways, to mediate the relationship between the psychic and the social, and between the individual and the collective. In particular, I will show how emotions work by sticking figures together (adherence), a sticking that creates the very effect of a collective (coherence), with reference to the figures of the asylum seeker and the international terrorist. My economic model of emotions suggests that while emotions do not positively reside in a subject or figure, they still work to bind subjects together. Indeed, to put it more strongly, the nonresidence of emotions is what makes them "binding."

Economies of Hate

Everyday language certainly constructs emotions as a form of positive residence. So I might say I "have a feeling." Or I might describe a film as "being sad." In such ways of speaking, emotions become property; something that belongs to a subject or object, which can take the form of a characteristic or quality. I want to challenge the idea that I have an emotion, or that something or somebody makes me feel a certain way. I am interested in the way emotions *involve* subjects and objects, but without residing positively within them. Indeed, emotions may only seem like a form of residence as an effect of a certain history, a history that may operate by concealing its own traces. Clearly, such an approach borrows from psychoanalysis, which is also a theory of the subject as lacking positive residence, a lack of being most commonly articulated as "the unconscious." In his essay on the unconscious, Freud introduces the notion of unconscious emotions, where an affective impulse is perceived but misconstrued, and which becomes attached to another idea.[3] What is repressed from consciousness is not the feeling as such, but the idea to which the feeling may have been first (but provisionally) connected. Psychoanalysis allows us to see that emotionality involves movements or associations whereby "feelings" take us across different levels of signification, not all of which can be admitted in the present. This is what I would call the rippling effect of emotions; they move sideways (through "sticky" associations between signs, figures, and objects) as well as backward (repression always leaves its trace in the present – hence "what sticks" is also bound up with the "absent presence" of historicity). In the opening quotation, we can see precisely how hate "slides" sideways between figures, as well as backward, by reopening past associations that allow some bodies to be read as the cause of "our hate," or as "being" hateful.

Indeed, insofar as psychoanalysis is a theory of the subject as lacking in the present, then it offers a theory of emotion as economy, *as involving relationships of difference and displacement without positive value*. That is, emotions work as a form of capital: affect does not reside positively in the sign or commodity, but is produced only as an effect of its circulation. I am using "the economic" to suggest that emotions circulate and are distributed across a social as well as psychic field. I am borrowing from the Marxian critique of the logic of capital. In *Capital*, Marx discusses how the movement of commodities and money, in the formula M-C-M (money to commodity to money), creates surplus value.[4] That is, through circulation and exchange M acquires more value. Or as he puts it, "The value originally advanced, therefore, not only remains intact while in circulation, but increases its magnitude, adds to itself a surplus-value or is valorised. *And this movement converts it into capital*."[5] I am identifying a similar logic: the movement between signs converts into affect. Marx links value with affect through the figures of the capitalist and the miser: "This boundless drive for enrichment, this passionate chase after value, is common to the capitalist, and the miser."[6] Passion drives the accumulation of capital: the capitalist is not interested in the use value of commodities, but in the "appropriation of ever more wealth."[7] What I am offering is a theory of passion not as the drive to accumulate (whether it be value, power, or meaning), but as that which is accumulated over time. Affect does not reside in an object or sign, but is an affect of the circulation between objects and signs (= the accumulation of affective value over time). Some signs, that is, increase in affective value as an effect of the movement between signs: the more they circulate, the more affective they become, and the more they appear to "contain" affect. Another way to theorize this process would be to describe "feelings" via an analogy with "commodity fetishism": feelings appear in objects, or indeed *as* objects with a life of their own, only by the concealment of how they are shaped by histories, including histories of production (labor and labor time), as well as circulation or exchange.

Of course, such an argument about affect as an economy does not respect the important Marxian distinction between use value and exchange value and hence relies on a limited analogy. In some ways, my approach may have more in common with a psychoanalytic emphasis on difference and displacement as the form or language of the unconscious, described above. Where my approach involves a departure from psychoanalysis is precisely in my refusal to identify this economy as a psychic one (although neither is it *not* a psychic one), that is, to return these relationships of difference and displacement to the signifier of "the subject." This "return" is not only clear in Freud's work, but also in Lacan's positing of "the subject" as the proper scene of absence and loss.[8] As Laplanche and Pontalis argue, if Lacan defines "the subject" as "the locus of the signifier," then it is in "a theory of the subject that the locus of the signifier settles."[9] This constitution of the subject as "settlement," even if what settles is lacking in presence, means that the suspended contexts of the signifier are delimited by the contours of the subject. In contrast, my account of hate as an affective economy shows that emotions do not positively inhabit any-body as well as any-thing, meaning that "the subject" is simply one nodal point in the economy, rather than its origin and destination. This is extremely important: it suggests that the sideways and backward movement of emotions such as hate is not contained within the contours of a subject. The unconscious is hence not the unconscious of a subject, but the failure of presence – or the failure to be present – that constitutes the relationality of subjects and objects (a relationality that works through the circulation of signs). Given this, affective economies need to be seen as social and material, as well as psychic. Indeed, if the movement of affect is crucial to the very making of a difference between "in here" and "out there," then the psychic and the social cannot be installed as proper objects. Instead, materialization, which Judith Butler describes as "the effect of boundary, fixity and surface,"[10] involves a process of intensification. In other words, the accumulation of affective value shapes the surfaces of bodies and worlds.

We could hence ask how the circulation of signs of affect shapes the materialization of collective bodies, for example the "body of the nation." We have already seen how hate slides across different figures and constitutes them as a "common threat" in what we can call "hate speech." But the slippery work of emotion cannot allow us to presume any opposition between extremist discourses and the "ordinary" work of reproducing the nation. We can take as an example the speeches on asylum seekers by the previous leader of the British Conservative Party, William Hague. Between April and June 2000, other speeches were in circulation that became "stuck" to the "asylum seekers" speech through this temporal proximity, but also through the repetition with a difference, of some *sticky words* and language. In the case of the asylum speeches, Hague's narrative is somewhat predictable. Words like *flood* and *swamped* are used, which create associations between asylum and the loss of control, as well as *dirt* and *sewage*, and hence work by mobilizing fear, or the anxiety of being "overwhelmed" by the actual or potential proximity of others. These words have recently been repeated by the current British Home Secretary, David Blunkett, who used the word *swamped* to describe the effect that children of asylum seekers would have if they were taught by local schools. When criticized, he replaced the word *swamped* with *overwhelmed*. The assumption here is that *overwhelmed* resolves the implication of *swamped*, but as we can see, it still evokes the sensation of being overtaken or taken over by others. It constructs the nation as if it was a subject, one who "could not cope" with the presence of others. Here words generate effects: they create impressions of others as those who have invaded the space of the nation, threatening its existence.

Typically, Hague in the earlier speeches differentiates between those others who are welcome and those who are not by differentiating between genuine and bogus asylum seekers. Partly, this enables the national subject to imagine its own generosity in welcoming some others. The nation is hospitable, as it allows those genuine ones to stay. And yet at the same time, it constructs some others as already hateful (as bogus) in order to define the limits or the conditions of this hospitality. The construction of the bogus asylum seeker as a figure of hate also involves a narrative of uncertainty and crisis, but an uncertainty and crisis that *make that figure do more work*. How can we tell the difference between a bogus and a genuine asylum seeker? According to the logic of this discourse, it is always possible that we might not be able to tell the difference, and that they may pass into our community. Passing functions here as a technology, which relates physical movement with identity formation: to pass through a space requires passing as a particular kind of subject, one whose difference is unmarked and unremarkable.[11] The double possibility of passing commands the nation's Right and will to keep looking for signs of difference and justifies violent forms of intrusion into the bodies of others.

Indeed, the possibility that we might not be able to tell the difference swiftly converts into the possibility that any of those incoming bodies may be bogus. In advance of their arrival, they are hence read as the cause of an injury to the national body. Now how does the presentation of asylum as injury work through the proximity between figures of hate? The figure of the bogus asylum seeker may evoke the figure of the "bogeyman," a figure who stalks the nation and haunts its capacity to secure its borders. The bogeyman could be anywhere and anyone, as a ghostlike figure in the present, who gives us nightmares about the future, as an anticipated future of injury. We see "him" again and again. Such figures of hate circulate, and indeed accumulate affective value, precisely because they do not have a fixed referent. So the figure of the bogus asylum seeker is detached from particular bodies: any incoming bodies could be bogus, such that their "endless" arrival is anticipated as the scene of "our injury."[12] *The impossibility of reducing hate to a particular body allows hate to circulate in an economic sense, working to differentiate some others from other others, a differentiation that is never "over," as it awaits for others who have not yet arrived.* Such a discourse of "waiting for the bogus" justifies the repetition of violence against the bodies of others.

Hague's speeches also produced certain effects through temporal proximity to another speech about Tony Martin, a man sentenced to life imprisonment for murdering a sixteen-year-old boy who had attempted to burgle his house in a rural area of England. One sentence of Hague's circulates powerfully. Hague argued (without reference to Martin or asylum seekers) that the law is "more interested in the rights of criminals than the rights of people who are burgled." Such a sentence evokes a history that is not declared (here "what sticks" may also be what resists literalization), and, in doing so, it positions Martin as the victim and not as a criminal. The victim of the murder is now the criminal: the crime that did not happen because of the murder (the burglary) takes the place of the murder as the true crime, and as the real injustice. This reversal of the victim-criminal relationship becomes an implicit defense of the right to kill those who unlawfully enter one's property.

The detachment of the sentence allows two cases to get stuck together: burglary and asylum, which both now become matters of the right to defense. The figure of the asylum seeker hence gets aligned with the figure of the burglar. The alignment does important work: it suggests that the asylum seeker is "stealing" something from the nation. The "characteristics" of one figure get displaced or transferred onto the other. Or we could say that it is through the association between the figures that they acquire "a life of their own," as if they contained affective quality. The burglar became a foreigner, and the asylum seeker becomes a criminal. At the same time, the body of the murderer (who is renamed as the victim)[13] becomes the body of the nation, the one whose property and well-being is under threat by the forced proximity of the other. As such, the alignment of figures works as a narrative of defense: the nation/national subject must defend itself against "invasion" by others. Such a defensive narrative is not explicitly articulated, but rather works through the "movement" between figures. The circulation does its work: it produces a differentiation between "us" and "them," whereby "they" are constituted as the cause or the justification of "our" feeling of hate. Indeed, we can see how attachment involves a sliding between pain and hate: there is a perceived injury in which the other's (burglar/bogus) proximity is felt as the violence of negation against both the body of the individual (here, the farmer) and the body of the nation.

We can see that the affectivity of hate is what makes it difficult to pin down, to locate in a body, object, or figure. This difficulty is what makes emotions such as hate work the way that they do; *it is not the impossibility of hate as such, but the mode of its operation, whereby it surfaces in the world made up of other bodies.* In other words, it is the failure of emotions to be located in a body, object, or figures that allows emotions to (re)produce or generate the effects that they do.

Fear, Bodies, and Objects

I now want to relate my model of emotion as affective economy specifically, to fear and the materialization of bodies. Significantly, fear is an emotion that is often characterized as being *about* its object and hence would not seem to work in the economic sense I have defined above. Indeed, fear has often been contrasted with anxiety insofar as fear *has* an object. For example, Stanley Rachman argues that anxiety can be described as the "tense anticipation of a threatening but vague event," or a feeling of "uneasy suspense," while fear is described as an emotional reaction "to a threat that is identifiable."[14]

I want to question this model by suggesting that fear is linked to the "passing by" of the object. We can consider, for instance, that the narrative of asylum seekers "swamping" the nation works as a narrative of fear. Fear works to create a sense of being overwhelmed: rather than being contained in an object, fear is intensified by the impossibility of containment. If the others who are feared "pass by," then the others might pass their way into the community, and could be anywhere and everywhere. Heidegger also suggests that fear is intensified when it ceases to be contained by an object that approaches. He suggests:

> That which is detrimental, as something that threatens us, is not yet within striking distance, but it is coming close. … As it draws close, this "it can, and yet it may not" becomes aggravated. We say, "It is fearsome." This implies that what is detrimental as coming-close carries with it the patent possibility that it may stay away and pass us by; but instead of lessening or extinguishing our fearing, this enhances it.[15]

Crucially, Heidegger relates fear to that which is not yet in the present, in either the spatial or temporal sense of the here and the now. Fear responds to that which is approaching rather than already here. It is the futurity of fear, which makes it possible that the object of fear, rather than arriving, might pass us by. But the passing by of the object of fear does not mean the overcoming of fear: rather, the possibility of the loss of the object that approaches makes what is fearsome all the more fearsome. If fear has an object, then fear can be contained by the object. When the object of fear threatens to pass by, then fear can no longer be contained by an object. Fear in its very relationship to an object, in the very intensity of its directedness toward that object, is intensified by the loss of its object. We could characterize this absence as about being not quite present rather than, as with anxiety, being nowhere at all. Or anxiety becomes attached to particular objects, which come to life not as the cause of anxiety but as an effect of its travels. In anxiety, one's thoughts often move quickly between different objects, a movement that works to intensify the sense of anxiety. One thinks of more and more "things" to be anxious about; the detachment from one given object allows anxiety to accumulate. In other words, anxiety tends to stick to objects. Given this, anxiety becomes an approach to objects rather than, as with fear, being produced by an object's approach. The slide between fear and anxiety is affected precisely by the "passing by" of the object.

Furthermore, fear's relationship to the potential disappearance of an object is more profound than simply a relationship to the object of fear. In other words, it is not just fear that is at stake in fear. For Freud, fears themselves may function as symptoms, as mechanisms for the defense of the ego against danger. In his essay "Inhibitions, Symptoms, and Anxiety," Freud returns to the Little Hans case. Hans had a phobic relationship to horses. Freud argues that this fear is itself a symptom that has been "put in the place" of another fear, one that much more profoundly threatens the ego: the fear of castration.[16] Hans can "manage" his fear of horses through avoidance, in a way that he could not manage his fear of the father. We might remember that in Freud's model of unconscious emotions, the affect itself is not repressed: rather, what is repressed is the idea to which the affect was attached. So the affect of fear is sustained through the displacement between objects.

The displacement between objects works also to link those objects together. Such linkages are not created by fear, but may already be in place within the social imaginary. In the Freudian model, the movement between objects is intrapsychic, and goes backward;

it refers back to the primary fear of castration. Or, to be more specific, the sideways movement between objects (in this case, the horse and the father) is itself explained as determined by a repression of the idea to which the affect was originally attached (the threat of castration).[17] I would suggest that the sideways movement between objects, which works to stick objects together as signs of threat, is shaped by multiple histories. The movement between signs does not have its origin in the psyche, but is a trace of how histories remain alive in the present.

We can consider, for instance, how the language of racism sustains fear through displacement, and how this surfaces through bodies. Take the following quote from Frantz Fanon's *Black Skin, White Masks*:

> My body was given back to me sprawled out. Distorted, recolored, clad in mourning in that white winter day. The Negro is an animal, the Negro is bad, the Negro is mean, the Negro is ugly; look, a nigger, it's cold, the nigger is shivering because he is cold, the little boy is trembling because he is afraid of the nigger, the nigger is shivering with cold, that cold that goes through your bones, the handsome little boy is trembling because he thinks that the nigger is quivering with rage, the little white boy throws himself into his mother's arms: Mama, the nigger's going to eat me up.[18]

Here, fear is felt as coldness; it makes bodies shiver with a cold that moves from the surface into the depths of the body, as a cold "that goes through your bones." Fear both envelops the bodies that feel it, as well as constructs those bodies as enveloped, as contained by it, as if it comes from outside and moves inward. In the encounter, fear does not bring the bodies together: it is not a shared feeling, but works to differentiate between white and black bodies. The white child misrecognizes the shivering of the black body as rage, and hence as the "grounds" for its fear. In other words, the other is only read as fearsome through a misrecognition, a reading that is returned by the black other through its response of fear, as a fear of the white subject's fear. This is not to say that the fear comes from the white body, as if it is the origin of that fear (and its author). Rather, fear opens up past histories that stick to the present (in the very rehearsal of childhood fantasies about "being eaten up" that "take on" the value of social norms as "truths" about the other) and allow the white body to be constructed as apart from the black body.

We might note here that fear *does something*; it reestablishes distance between bodies whose difference is read off the surface, as a reading that produces the surface (shivering, recoloring). But what is very clear here is that the object of fear remains the black man, who comes to feel the fear as his own, as threatening his existence. Fear does not come from within the subject, nor does it reside in its object: we are not afraid of others because they are fearsome. Through the circulation of signs of fear, the black other "becomes" fearsome. But doesn't this example show us that fear does get contained by an object, in this case the black man? To some extent this is right: the circulation of signs of fear does lead to containment for some, and movement for others. Here, fear gets contained in a body, which henceforth becomes an object of fear. Indeed, the white child's apparent fear does not lead to containment but an expansion; his embrace of the world is suggested by how he reestablishes himself as being-at-home (the embrace of the mother as a "return home"). It is the black subject, the one who fears the "impact" of the white child's fear, who is crushed by that fear, by being sealed into a body that takes up less space. In other words, fear works to restrict some bodies through the movement or expansion of others.

But this containment is an effect of a movement between signs, as well as bodies. Such movement depends on past histories of association: Negro, animal, bad, mean, ugly. In other words, it is the movement of fear between signs, which allows the object of fear to be generated in the present (the Negro is: an animal, bad, mean, ugly). The movement between signs is what allows others to be attributed with emotional value, in this case, as being fearsome, an attribution that depends on a history that "sticks," and which does not need to be declared. The containment is provisional: insofar as the black man is the object of fear, then he may pass by. Indeed, the physicality of his "passing by" can be associated with the passing of fear between signs: it is the movement that intensifies affect. The black man becomes even more threatening if he passes by: his proximity is imagined then as the possibility of future injury. As such, the economy of fear works to contain the bodies of others, a containment whose "success" relies on its failure, as it must keep open the very grounds of fear. In this sense, fear works as an affective economy, despite how it seems directed toward an object. Fear does not reside in a particular object or sign, and it is this lack of residence that allows fear to slide across signs, and between bodies. This sliding becomes stuck only temporarily, in the very attachment of a sign to a body, whereby a sign sticks to a body by constituting it as the object of fear, a constitution taken on by the body, encircling it with a fear that becomes its own.

The sideways movement of fear (where we have a metonymic and sticky relation between signs) is also a backward movement: objects of fear become substituted for each other over time. This substitution involves the passing by of the objects from which the subject seems to flee. Fear and anxiety create the very effect of "that which I am not," through the very affect of turning away from an object, which nevertheless threatens as it passes by or is displaced. To this extent, fear does not involve the defense of borders that already exist; rather, fear makes those borders, by establishing objects from which the subject, in fearing, can stand apart, objects that become "the not" from which the subject appears to flee. Through fear not only is the very border between self and other affected, but the relation between the objects feared (rather than simply the relation between the subject and its objects) is shaped by histories that "stick," by making some objects more than others seem fearsome.

Global Economies of Fear

We can think more precisely about the processes through which fear works to secure forms of the collective. My argument is not that there is a psychic economy of fear that then becomes social and collective: rather, the individual subject comes into being through its very alignment with the collective. *It is the very failure of affect to be located in a subject or object that allows it to generate the surfaces of collective bodies.* The complexity of the spatial and bodily politics of fear has perhaps never been so apparent in the global economies of fear since September 11. Fear is, of course, named in the very naming of terrorism: terrorists are immediately identified as agents of extreme fear, that is, those who seek to make others afraid (less mobile or less free to move) as well those who seek to cause death and destruction. As the Australian prime minister, John Howard, put it, bin Laden's "hatred" for the United States and for "a world system built on individual freedom, religious tolerance, democracy, and the international free flow of commerce" means that "he wants to spread fear, create uncertainty and promote instability, hoping that this will cause communities and countries to turn against each other."[19] Howard then reads the acts of terror as attacks not only on the mobility of international capital, but also on the mobility of the bodies of Australians, on their right "to move around the world with ease and freedom and without fear." I would like to offer an alternative reading of what moves and what sticks in fear economies, one that differentiates between forms of mobility as well as different kinds of bodily enclosure, containment, or detainment.

In the first instance, we can examine how the mobility of the bodies of subjects in the West, while presented as threatened, is also defended, along with the implicit defense of the mobility of capital in the global economy (whereby capital is constructed as "clean money" and defined against the "dirty money" of terrorism, which must be frozen or blocked). The most immediate instruction made to subjects and citizens in America, Australia, and Britain was "to go about your daily business," "to travel," "to spend or consume," and so on, as a way of refusing to be a victim of terror. Indeed, in the United States, citizens were, in effect, asked not to fear, and the nation was represented as not being afraid, as a way of showing the failure of the terrorist attacks to destroy the nation. As George W. Bush put it, "It is natural to wonder if America's future is one of fear. Some speak of an age of terror. I know there are struggles ahead and dangers to face. But this country will define our times, not be defined by them. As long as the United States is determined and strong, this will not be an age of terror."[20] The nation is constructed as having prevailed through refusing to transform its vulnerability and wounds into fear, a response that would be read, in terms of this narrative, as "determination by terror" rather than self-determination. Bush, then, in an act of self-determination, turns the act of terror into an act of war, which would seek to eliminate the source of fear and transform the world into a place where the mobility of some capital and some bodies becomes the sign of freedom and civilization. This suggests that the affect of terror was not containment, but provided the very grounds for remobilization.

This is not to say, however, that individuals and groups have not experienced fear in response to the events; the affects of fear are clear in, for example, the huge reduction in air travel. However, we need to think about this containment carefully without assuming that fear simply brings people together, or that containment is the only effect of such fear. As I have already noted, following Heidegger, the object of fear may pass by, and this structural possibility is part of the lived experience of fear. While the events did happen and did constitute an object (however much it passed by, a passing by that was already at stake in the living out of the present, given the mediatization of the event *as event*), that fear slid quickly into anxiety, in which what was at stake was not the approach of an object but an approach to an object. The approach to the event – in which it is repeated and transformed into a fetish object – involved forms of alignment, whereby individuals aligned themselves with the nation as being under attack. This, of course, repeats the process of alignment whereby the nation aligned itself with individuals as having been or being attacked.

Now, what is crucial here is not just that this alignment might restrict the mobility of individuals who now feel themselves, in a way that is personal, to be terrorist targets. Rather, given the mediating work of this alignment, experiences of fear became lived as patriotic declarations of love, which allowed home itself to be mobilized as a defense against terror. If subjects stayed at home, then homes became transformed into the symbolic space of the nation through the widespread use of American flags. This is not to say that the meaning of the flags is necessary to its circulation – as if such flags could only signify national love. Rather, we can consider how the flag is a sticky sign, whereby its stickiness allows it to stick to other "flag signs," which gives the impression of coherence (the nation as "sticking together"). The flag as a sign that has historically signified territorial conquest as well as love for the nation (patriotism) has effects in terms of the display of "withness" (whereby one is "with others" and "against other others"). George Packer, in an article in the *New York Times Magazine*, expressed this well: "As flags bloomed like flowers, I found they tapped emotion as quickly as pictures of the missing. To me, these flags didn't represent flabby complacence, but alertness, grief, resolve, even love. They evoked fellow feeling with Americans, for we had been attacked together."[21] The turning away from the object of fear hence may involve a turning toward home as a "fellow feeling." That "turning toward" involves the repetition or reiteration of signs of "fellowship." That turning could even be understood as compulsory: not to display a flag could be read as a sign of a lack of fellowship, or even as the origin of terror (to paraphrase George W. Bush, if you do not show you are "with us," you would be seen as "against us").[22]

Fear mediated by love as identification with the nation, which comes to adhere as an effect of signs of love, does not necessarily shrink bodies. The turning away from the object of fear here involves a turning toward home. Fear mediated by this form of love (love as identification) does not necessarily shrink bodies, but may even allow them to occupy more space through the identification with the collective body, which stands in for the individual body and moves on its behalf. In other words, the apparent containment of some bodies in the United States functions as a form of mobilization: staying at home allows the mobilization of bodies through the symbolic identification with the nation at war. In George W. Bush's State of the Union Address in 2002 the effect of this identification is clear: "It was as if our entire country looked into a mirror and saw our better selves."[23] Hence, the United States is defined as "caught" by its own reflection in the mirror, a "catching out" that borders on collective narcissism: self-love becomes a national love that legitimates the response to terror as the protection of loved others who are "with me," whereby "withness" is premised on signs of "likeness" and whereby likeness becomes an imperative or a condition of survival.

So if the event of terror – of seeking to cause fear – leads to a defense of the mobility of capital and the mobilization of some bodies (through both the defense of the home as nation and the identification with the nation), then who is contained through terror? Whose vulnerability is at stake? As has been well documented, the events of September 11 have been used to justify the detention of any bodies suspected of being terrorists. Not only was there immediate detention of suspects in the United States and European countries, but governments in the West have responded to the terror by enacting legislation that increases the governmental rights to detain anybody suspected of being a terrorist. The British Amendment to the Terrorism Act 2000 states that the Secretary of State may issue a certificate if he believes that the person's presence in the United Kingdom is a risk to national security or he suspects the person is an international terrorist. Here risk assessment becomes a matter of belief, and suspicion itself becomes the grounds for detention. The extension of the powers of detention is not merely symbolic, nor does it merely relate to the detention of terrorists: given the structural possibility that any body could be a terrorist, what we have reinstituted and extended is the power of detention, as such.

However, the structural possibility that anyone could be a terrorist does not translate into everybody being affected by the extension of the powers of detention in the same way. It is well documented that people have been detained because of very weak links between them and terrorist networks, often involving simple links through names, or workplace, or residence. Aristide R. Zolberg considers this process a form of racial profiling, quoting details reported in the *New Yorker*: "Of the 1,147 people detained in the United States between September 11th and November 2001, some were identified on the basis of circumstantial links with the attack, but many 'were picked up based on tips, or were people of Middle Eastern or South Asian descent who had been stopped for traffic violations or for acting suspiciously.'"[24] As Muneer Ahmad describes, after September 11, there was "an unrelenting, multi-valent assault on the bodies, psyches and rights of Arab, Muslim and South Asian immigrants."[25] Indeed, Leti Volpp suggests that the responses to September 11 facilitated "a new identity category that groups together people who appear 'Middle Eastern, Arab or Muslim.'"[26] The recognition of such groups of people as "could be terrorists" depends on stereotypes already in place, at the same time as it generates a distinct category of "the fearsome" in the present. We can recall precisely the repetition of stereotypes about the black man in the encounter described by Frantz Fanon: this repetition works by generating the other as the object of fear, a fear that is then taken on as its own.

Importantly, the word *terrorist* sticks to some bodies as it reopens past histories of naming, just as it slides into other words in the accounts of the wars in Afghanistan and Iraq (such as *fundamentalism, Islam, Arab, repressive, primitive*). Indeed, the slide of metonymy can function as an implicit argument about the causal relations between terms (such as *Islam* and *terrorism*) within the making of truths and worlds, but in such a way that it does not require an explicit statement. The work done by metonymy means that it can remake links – it can stick words like *terrorist* and *Islam* together – even when arguments are made that seem to unmake those links. Utterances like "this is not a war against Islam" coexist with descriptions such as "Islamic terrorists," which work to restick the words together and constitute their coincidence as more than simply temporal. The sliding between signs also involves "sticking" signs to bodies: the bodies who "could be terrorists" are the ones who might "look Muslim."

Given that the event became an object that allowed certain forms of violence and detention of others in the name of defense, we need to ask: what role does security play in the affective politics of fear? Importantly, security is bound up with "the not" – what is "not me" or "not us," as Michael Dillon has suggested.[27] Security is not simply about securing a border that already exists, nor is fear simply a fear of what we are not. As I argued in the previous section, anxiety and fear create the very effect of borders, and the very effect of that which "we are not," partly through how we turn away from the other, whom we imagine as the cause of our fear. Borders are constructed and indeed policed in the very feeling that they have already been transgressed: the other has to get too close, in order to be recognized as an object of fear, and in order for the object to be displaced. The transgression of the border is required in order for it to be secured as a border in the first place. This is why the politics of fear as well as hate is narrated as a border anxiety: fear speaks the language of "floods" and "swamps," of being invaded by inappropriate others, against whom the nation must defend itself. We can reflect then on the ontology of insecurity within the constitution of the political: it must be presumed that things are not secure, in and of themselves, in order to justify the imperative to make things secure.

More specifically, it is through announcing a crisis in security that new forms of security, border policing, and surveillance become justified. We only have to think about how narratives of crisis are used within politics to justify a "return" to values and traditions that are perceived to be under threat. It is not simply that these crises exist, and that fears and anxieties come into being as a necessary effect of that existence. Rather, it is the very production of the crisis that is crucial. To declare a crisis is not "to make something out of nothing": such declarations often work with real events, facts, or figures (as we can see, for example, in how the rise in divorce rates is used to announce a crisis in marriage and the family). But the declaration of crisis *reads* that fact/figure/event and transforms it into a fetish object that then acquires a life of its own, in other words, that can become the grounds for declarations of war against that which is read as the source of the threat. Through designating something as already under threat in the present, that very thing becomes installed as "the truth," which we must fight for in the future, a fight that is retrospectively understood to be a matter of life and death.

Indeed, it is fear of death – of the death of oneself, one's loved ones, one's community, and one's people – that is generated by such narratives to preserve or maintain *that which is*. So I might fear for myself, for us, or on behalf of others. Since September 11, the deaths have become symbolic of that which is under threat not only by terrorists (those who take life), but by all that the possibility of terrorism stands for, a possibility linked by some commentators to internal forms of weakness, such as secularization, multiculturalism, and the decline of social and familial ties. For example, Jerry Falwell in the United States argued, "I really believe that the pagans, and the abortionists, and the feminists, and the gays, and lesbians who are actively trying to make an alternative life style ... all of them who have tried to secularize America, I point the finger in their face and say 'you helped this happen.'"[28] In the United Kingdom, the British National Party's response to September 11 was to posit Islamicization within the United Kingdom rather than the Taliban in Afghanistan as the threat to the moral future of the nation itself: "They can turn Britain into an Islamic Republic by 2025."[29]

This attribution of the crime of terror to the weakening of religion and community posed by the presence of various others has been, of course, condemned within mainstream politics, although noticeably with less of a "disgust reaction" than how some critics of U.S. foreign policy have been received. However, at the same time, a broader set of assumptions around what would be required to defend the nation and the world (strengthening the will of the community in the face of others) both displaces and reworks the narrative logic. Instead of an internal weakness being posited as responsible for this event, we have an internal strength being posited as responsible for recovery, survival, and moving beyond fear. As George W. Bush put it, "These acts of mass murder were intended to frighten our nation into chaos and retreat. But they have failed; our country is strong."[30] The response to terror becomes a way to strengthen the bonds of the nation and the global community of free nations: the wound of terror requires "sticking together" (adherence as coherence) and using the values that made America and democracy "strong."

Indeed, the emphasis on security in George W. Bush's State of the Union Address in 2002 includes the transformation of democratic citizenship into policing: "And as government works to secure our homeland, America will continue to depend on the eyes and ears of alert citizens." Citizenship here is translated into a form of Neighborhood Watch; the citizen must "look out for suspicious others."[31] Citizenship works as a way to police the boundaries of neighborhoods. The role of citizens as police is translated as an imperative to love, in which love becomes the foundation of community, as well as the guarantor of our future: "Our country also needs citizens working to rebuild our communities. We need mentors to love children."[32] The definition of values that will allow America to prevail in the face of terror – values that have been named as freedom, love, and compassion – involves the defense of particular institutional and social forms against the danger posed by others. Such values function to define not only ideals that supposedly govern war aims and objectives but democratic norms of behavior and conduct, of what it means to be civil, a civil society, and a legitimate government. To be brought into international civil society – that is, to be not named as a "rogue state" or as part of "the axis of evil" – others must "mimic" these rules of conduct and forms of governance.[33] Henceforth, the emphasis on values, truths, and norms that will allow survival slides easily into the defense of particular social forms or institutions.

We might note here that these social forms become identified as "better" by being defined as open: liberal democracy (and with it a weak model of racial and religious tolerance as well as an apparent liberal support for "feminism") become defined as what is "good" about the United States, in opposition to the closed and fundamentalist politics of the Islamic other. Hence "respect for women" and "religious tolerance" become defined as two of the values that make America and the free world strong. Such an argument allows the war to be narrated as "saving women from religious fundamentalism": this is a familiar narrative, and one that has a long imperial history. As many feminist critics have argued, such a narrative overlooks not only the heterogeneity of other cultures – and the existence of women's resistance, and feminist networks in Islamic worlds, including in Afghanistan – but also the maintenance of gendered as well as other forms of oppression in the United States and the so-called free world.[34] We need to think about the political effects of this hierarchy between open and closed cultures and show how the constitution of open cultures involves the projection of what is closed onto others, and hence the concealment of what is closed and contained "at home."

Furthermore, the fear of degeneration as a mechanism for preserving social forms becomes associated more with some bodies than others. The threat of such others to social forms (which are the materialization of norms) is represented as the threat of turning away from the values that will guarantee survival. These various others come to embody the failure of the norm to take form; it is the proximity of such other bodies that "causes" the fear that the forms of civilization (the family, the community, the nation, and international civil society) have degenerated. Those who speak out against the "truth" of this world become aligned then with the terrorists as seeking to cause the "ruin" of the world. What is important, then, is that the narratives that seek to preserve the present through working on anxieties of death as the necessary consequence of the demise of social forms also seek to locate that anxiety in some bodies, which then take on fetish qualities as objects of fear. Such bodies engender even more fear, as they cannot be held in place as objects, and threaten to pass by. That is, we may fail to see those forms that have failed to be; it is always possible that we might not be able to tell the difference. The present hence becomes preserved by defending the community against the imagined others, who may take form in ways that cannot be anticipated, a "not-yet-ness" that means the work of defense is never over. Such a defense is generated by anxiety and fear for the future, and justifies the elimination or exclusion of that which fails to materialize in the form of the norm as a struggle for survival. Insofar as we do not know what forms other others may take, those who fail to materialize in the forms that are lived as norms, the policies of continual surveillance of emergent forms is sustained as an ongoing project of survival.

It is here that we can deepen our reflections on the role of the figure of the international terrorist within the economies of fear. Crucially, the narrative that justifies the expansion of the powers to detain others within the nation and the potential expansion of the war itself to other nations relies on the structural possibility that the terrorist "could be" anyone and anywhere. The narrative of the "could be" terrorist, in which the terrorist is the one who "hides in the shadows,"[35] has a double edge. On the one hand, the figure of the terrorist is detached from particular bodies, as a shadowy figure, "an unspecifiable may-come-to-pass."[36] But it is this could-be-ness, this detachment, which also allows the restriction on the mobility of those bodies who are read as associated with terrorism: Islam, Arab, Asian, East. Fear sticks to these bodies (and to the bodies of "rogue states") that "could be" terrorist, where the "could be" opens up the power to detain. Although such fear sticks, it also slides across such bodies; it is the structural possibility that the terrorist may pass us by that justifies the expansion of these forms of intelligence, surveillance, and the rights of detention. Fear works here to expand the mobility of some bodies and contain others precisely insofar as it does not reside positively in any one body. As Samuel Weber puts it, "When *terrorism* is defined as *international* it becomes difficult to locate, situate, personify and identify,"[37] and it is this difficulty that justifies the expansion of the powers of the state.

It is important to recognize that the figure of the international terrorist has been mobilized in close proximity to the figure of the asylum seeker. The slide between these two figures does an enormous amount of work: it assumes that those who seek asylum, who flee from terror and persecution, may be bogus insofar as they could be the very agents of terror and persecution. They, like terrorists, are identified as potential burglars: as unlawful intruders into the nation. In Australia, for example, the refusal to allow the boat *Tampa* into its waters (with its cargo of 433 asylum seekers, many of whom were from Afghanistan) was retrospectively justified on the grounds that those on board *could be* linked to Osama bin Laden. The sticking together of the figure of the asylum seeker and the international terrorist, which already evokes other figures (the burglar, the bogeyman), constructs those who are "without home" as sources of "our fear" and as reasons for new forms of border policing, whereby the future is always a threat posed by others who may pass by and pass their way into the community. The slide of metonymy works to generate or make likeness: the asylum seeker is "like" the terrorist, an agent of fear, who may destroy "our home." The slide between figures involves the containment of others, who henceforth become the objects of fear.

The containment of the bodies of others affected by this economy of fear is most chillingly and violently revealed in the literal deaths of those seeking asylum in containers, deaths that remain unmourned by the very nations who embody the hope of a future for those seeking asylum. This is a chilling reminder of what is at stake in the affective economies of fear.

Notes

My thanks to the *Social Text* collective for providing me with such helpful and engaged feedback on an earlier draft of this essay.

1   Aryan Nations, www.uiowa.edu/~policult/politick/smithson/an.htm (accessed 4 January 2001).
2   Thanks to David Eng for this point.
3   Sigmund Freud, "The Unconscious," in *The Standard Edition of the Complete Psychological Works of Sigmund Freud*, trans. James Strachey (London: Hogarth, 1964), 15:110.
4   Karl Marx, *Capital: A Critique of Political Economy*, trans. Ben Fowkes (Harmondsworth, U.K.: Penguin, 1976), 1:248.

5   Ibid., 252; emphasis mine.

6   Ibid., 254.

7   Ibid.

8   For an exploration of this argument, see Sara Ahmed, *Differences That Matter: Feminist Theory and Postmodernism* (Cambridge: Cambridge University Press, 1998), 97–98.

9   Jean Laplanche and Jean-Bernard Pontalis, *The Language of Psychoanalysis*, trans. David Nicholson-Smith (London: Karnac, 1992), 65.

10 Judith Butler, *Bodies That Matter: On the Discursive Limits of "Sex"* (New York: Routledge, 1993), 9.

11 There is a long history of work on racial passing that I cannot discuss here. For a summary, see Sara Ahmed, "Passing through Hybridity," *Theory, Culture, and Society* 16 (1999): 87–106.

12 For the British National Party, this model of "*any* body could be bogus" gets translated into "all" are, or "all" might as well be, bogus: "We will abolish the positive discrimination schemes that have made white Britons second-class citizens. We will also clamp down on the flood of asylum seekers, all of whom are either bogus or can find refuge much nearer their home countries." See the British National Party Web site, www.bnp.org.uk/policies.html#immigration (accessed 30 July 2003).

13 Aidan McGurran and Jenny Johnston, "The Homecoming: It's Too Painful: Martin's Sad Return to Farm," *Daily Mirror*, 9 August 2003, 4–5. Tony Martin was released in August 2003 and "his story" was very visible in the popular press in the United Kingdom. Tabloids concentrated very much on Martin as an "ordinary farmer" whose home was ruined. The headline on the front page of the *Mirror* sums it up: "He killed to protect his house … but now the memories are too much." The tragedy of the story is not the death of "a teenage burglar" but Martin's loss of home: "This isn't a home any more. It's a shell." Given the sticky attachment between "burglar" and "bogus asylum seeker" and between "home" and "homeland," the tragedy of the story becomes linked to the tragedy that asylum seekers represent in their very presence in the United Kingdom for "ordinary subjects" such as "farmers." In other words, the moral of the story becomes: If we let them in, they will turn the nation into a shell and take the land on which "we have worked."

14 Stanley Rachman, *Anxiety* (Howe, U.K.: Psychology Press, 1998), 2–3. See also William F. Fischer, *Theories of Anxiety* (New York: Harper and Row, 1970).

15 Martin Heidegger, *Being and Time*, trans. John Macquarrie and Edward Robinson (London: SCM Press, 1962), 180.

16 See Sigmund Freud, "Inhibitions, Symptoms, and Anxiety," in *The Standard Edition of the Complete Psychological Works of Sigmund Freud*, trans. James Strachey, vol. 20 (London: Hogarth, 1964).

17 Certainly Freud's argument about "unconscious emotions" does rely on a model of origins, or the "true connection" between an idea and a feeling; see "The Unconscious," 110.

18 Frantz Fanon, *Black Skin, White Masks*, trans. Charles Lam Markmann (London: Pluto, 1986), 114.

19 John Howard, address to the Australian Defence Association, Australian Department of Foreign Affairs, 25 October 2001, www.dfat.gov.au/icat/pm_251001_speech.html (accessed 23 July 2002).

20 George W. Bush, address to a joint session of Congress and the American people, www.whitehouse. gov/news/releases/2001/09/20010920-8.html (accessed 20 September 2001).

21 See George Packer, "Recapturing the Flag," *New York Times Magazine*, 30 September 2001, 15–16. The relationship between grief and love is crucial to this narrative: the community is brought together by how it incorporates the losses. Judith Butler suggested that public responses to the losses of September 11 work to create a distinction between grievable and ungrievable lives ("Violence, Mourning, Politics," *Feminist Theory* launch, Keynote Address, University College London, London, March 2002). Losses may be publicly mourned if the life that is lost can be recognized as "like me," whereby likeness is determined as proximity to social norms. David Eng also examines the erasure of non-normative losses in public discourses of mourning: "The rhetoric of loss of 'fathers and mothers,' 'sons and daughters,' and 'brothers and sisters' attempts to trace a smooth alignment between the nation-state and the nuclear family, the symbolics of blood relations and nationalist domesticity" ("The Value of Silence," *Theatre Journal* 54 [2002]: 90). For an examination of love and grief in relation to the politics of the nation, see "In the Name of Love" and "Queer Feelings" in my *Cultural Politics of Emotion* (Edinburgh: Edinburgh University Press, forthcoming).

22   For Arabs, Muslims, and South Asians in the United States, displaying the flag might then be read not only as a form of identification with the nation but as an attempt to "cover" any signs of difference, which might be associated with the origin of terror. Muneer Ahmad examines the "swap" between the flag and the veil in "Homeland Insecurities: Racial Violence the Day after September 11," *Social Text*, no. 72 (2002): 110.

23   George W. Bush, State of the Union address 2002, www.whitehouse.gov/news/releases/2002/01/20020129-11.html (accessed 23 July 2002).

24   Aristide R. Zolberg, "Guarding the Gates," in *Understanding September 11*, ed. Craig Calhoun, Paul Price, and Ashley Timmer (New York: New Press, 2002), 296.

25   Ahmad, "Homeland Insecurities," 99.

26   Letti Volpp, "The Citizen and the Terrorist," *UCLA Law Review* 49 (2002): 1575.

27   Michael Dillon, *The Politics of Security* (London: Routledge, 1996), 34. See also Anthony Burke, *In Fear of Security* (Annandale, New South Wales: Pluto).

28   Jerry Falwell made this comment on Pat Robertson's 700 Club on 13 September 2001. He apologized the next day for suggesting that anyone but the terrorists were responsible for the attacks but repeated the message that "the problem" was secularization, caused by the presence of illegitimate others within the nation.

29   British National Party Web site, www.bnp.org.uk (accessed 30 July 2002). Quoted in BNP leaflet "The Truth About Islam," which may be viewed at www.fairuk.org/Anti-Islam%20Supplement. pdf, released November 2001.

30   George W. Bush, Statement by the president in his address to the nation, www.whitehouse.gov/news/releases/2001/09/20010920-8.html (11 September 2001).

31   For an analysis of how Neighborhood Watch involves techniques of knowledge, which work to recognize "strangers" as "bodies out of place," see Sara Ahmed, *Strange Encounters: Embodied Others in Post-Coloniality* (London: Routledge, 2000).

32   George W. Bush, State of the Union address 2002, www.whitehouse.gov/news/releases/2002/01/20020129-11.html (accessed 23 July 2002).

33   We can consider George W. Bush's powerful utterance "you are either with us or against us" as a demand for mimicry. In this narrative, those who are not "with us" are automatically constructed as against us, whereby "againstness" is aligned with a form of terror or terrorism. That is, anyone who is not "with us" is a terrorist, is a friend of terrorists, or might as well be. To "be with," one must both give one's allegiance to the community, but one also must become lovable to that community – which means recognizable as a form of civil life. We would hence argue that the utterance "you are either with us or against us" may work not as a constative or even as a performative, but as an imperative. To be "with us" is an imperative to "be like us": if others are not to be identified as terrorists or rogue states (an identification that involves the threat of violence, as well as actual violence) they must mimic the forms of civility and supposedly democratic governance that constitute the foundations of this community. We might note here that the root of the word *assimilate* is the Latin for *likeness*. This new international community may be one that is loving, in which the imperative of love is to "make alike": likeness is not the ground of this community, but an effect. If community binds others together through the demand that others become like us, then the narrative of love converts swiftly into hatred for "unlike others."

34   For important feminist critiques of the gendered discourses in the justification of the war on terrorism, see Zilla Eisenstein, "Feminisms in the Aftermath of September 11," *Social Text*, no. 72 (2002): 79–99; and Sunera Thobani, "War and the Politics of Truth-Making," *International Journal of Qualitative Studies in Education* 16.3 (2003), 399–414.

35   George W. Bush, comments made by the president in a meeting with his national security team on 12 September, www.whitehouse.gov/response/faq-what.html (accessed 23 July 2002).

36   Brian Massumi, "Everywhere You Want to Be," in *The Politics of Everyday Fear*, ed. Brian Massumi (Minneapolis: University of Minnesota Press, 1993), 11.

37   Samuel Weber, "War, Terrorism, and Spectacle" (Paper presented at Lancaster University, December 2001).

CHAPTER 5

Human Nature and Literary Meaning

Joseph Carroll

Perhaps the major figure in evolutionary literary theory, Joseph Carroll was instrumental in creating the new field of study, starting with his book, *Evolution and Literary Theory* (1995), and continuing through *Literary Darwinism: Evolution, Human Nature, and Literature* (2004). Carroll's early work in the field consisted of rebutting the arguments of Post-Structuralism; his later work is more concerned with developing a method of Darwinian analysis that focuses on both the universals of human evolutionary nature and the specific inflections of human behavior in historical social contexts. This essay begins with a discussion of debates in evolutionary theory between evolutionary psychologists (who see human behavior as primarily adaptive) and sociobiologists (who see it motivated by a drive to achieve reproductive success so that genes can be transmitted – what is called fitness). Carroll then studies Jane Austen's *Pride and Prejudice* and analyzes how style and perspective function to reinforce evolutionary themes.

The Challenge to a Darwinian Literary Criticism

The common notion of what Darwinian literary criticism could or should do is that Darwinian critics should first look into evolutionary psychology in order to identify universal, basic forms of human behavior – human universals – and that they should then examine this or that literary text in order to demonstrate that the characters in that text behave in precisely the way that evolutionary psychologists predict people will behave. The method involved in this common notion is naïve and vulnerable to obvious objections. People in reality do not simply exemplify common, universal patterns of behavior. They have individuality that is distinguished by the peculiarities of their individual temperaments, their cultural conditioning, and their individual experiences. Cultures vary widely in the ways that they organize the common elements of the human motivational and cognitive system, and even within any given culture many people deviate drastically both from the behavioral norms that characterize that culture and

Original publication details: Joseph Carroll, "Human Nature and Literary Meaning" from
The Literary Animal, ed. B. Gottschall et al., pp. 76–106. Northwestern University Press, 2005.
Reprinted with permission from Northwestern University Press.

Literary Theory: An Anthology, Third Edition. Edited by Julie Rivkin and Michael Ryan.
© 2017 John Wiley & Sons, Ltd. Published 2017 by John Wiley & Sons, Ltd.

from the deeper underlying commonalities of human nature. Moreover, characters in literary representations are not real, living people. They are fictive fabrications that reflect the notions and beliefs and purposes of individual authors, and individual authors are themselves constrained by their larger cultural context and by the traditions and conventions of literary representation that are available to them. To treat characters as if they were actual people is to ignore the whole concept of "meaning" in literature, and to ignore meaning in literature is something like ignoring the concept of "energy" in physics or the concept of "life" in biology. It is simply to miss the point.

The deficiencies in the common notion of Darwinian literary study can easily be corrected. There is no necessity that Darwinian literary critics muddle along doing a bad job with a naïve methodology simply because they have no notion of how to do a good job. The concepts necessary for integrating Darwinian psychology and literary criticism are neither hard to understand nor difficult to use. What I propose here is to lay out a necessary minimum of analytic concepts – five in all – that must enter into any reasonably competent literary analysis informed by a Darwinian understanding of human nature. The basic concepts are these: (a) human nature as a structured hierarchy of motives (within which the motive of constructing imaginative representations holds a prominent place); (b) "point of view," or the location of meaning within three distinct centers of consciousness – that of the author, the characters, and the implied or projected audience; (c) the use of human universals as a common frame of reference in relation to which authors identify their own individual identities and their own distinct structures of meaning; (d) a set of categories for analyzing individual differences in identity; and (e) the distribution of specifically literary meaning into three chief dimensions: (i) theme (conceptual content), (ii) tone (emotional coloring), and (iii) formal organization (a concept that ranges all the way from macrostructures like plot and narrative sequencing to microstructures like phrasing, word choice, and sequences of sounds).

In the course of laying out these concepts and explaining their relations, I shall also make arguments that should be of some interest to Darwinian social scientists, whether or not they care much about literature and the other arts. I shall argue that Darwinian psychology is on the verge of achieving a paradigm – that is, a consensus about the necessary minimum of conceptual elements that enter into an understanding of "human nature." This emerging paradigm does not consist merely of a list of common basic motives or "universals." It consists both of universals, the common human elements, and of the variations among those elements that we describe as "individual differences." And the paradigm also includes an understanding of how the specifically human pattern of life history – birth, development, reproduction, and death – responds with flexible but integrated strategies to the wide range of physical and cultural conditions in which it is possible for people to subsist. Among Darwinian psychologists, there is still disagreement in all these areas, and the currently dominant school of Darwinian psychology, the school most readily identified as "evolutionary psychology," has committed itself to dead ends and fallacies in its deprecation of both individual differences and domain–general intelligence. But Darwinian social science as a whole has a diverse array of intellectually independent investigators, from many convergent disciplines – paleoanthropology, life history analysis, behavioral ecology, behavioral genetics, personality theory, and the study of intelligence, among others. Given this array of investigators eager to make advances in their own fields and to integrate those fields within the larger logic of evolutionary theory, claims that are motivated by ideology and that lack both empirical support and internal consistency are not likely to survive for long. The necessary elements for a paradigm in

Darwinian psychology are already virtually in place, and I am fairly confident that the energy of active research will in the near future sweep away the obstructions that have temporarily arisen from the premature consolidation of certain orthodox doctrines.

In order to make an argument about the structure of Darwinian literary criticism, then, I shall first need to make an argument about the current condition and future prospects of Darwinian psychology. I shall sketch out what I take to be the emerging paradigm for human nature, and I shall introduce one concept – the concept of a "cognitive behavioral system" – that is relatively unfamiliar but that is, I shall argue, indispensable to the formation of an adequate paradigm both in psychology and in literary study. Most evolutionary psychologists have paid slight attention to literature and the other arts, and some have argued that the arts have no adaptive function central to human life history goals. (See Miller, 2000a, 2000b; Pinker, 1997, 2002.) Invoking the logic of the emerging paradigm in Darwinian psychology, I shall argue that literature and the other arts do indeed have an adaptive function and that understanding this adaptive function is a prerequisite to understanding our specifically *human* nature. The effort to construct a paradigm for Darwinian literary criticism and the effort to construct a paradigm for the broader field of Darwinian psychology are thus interdependent. They need each other. Fortunately, they are both within reach, and by reaching the one, we shall also reach the other.

The central challenge for a specifically Darwinian form of literary criticism is to connect the highest levels in the organization of human nature with the most detailed and subtle aspects of literary meaning. Can we connect the basic life history goals – survival, growth, and reproduction – with the finest nuances of theme, tone, and style in the organization of literary meaning in specific works? The answer to this question will determine the success or failure of Darwinian literary criticism, and the answer is "yes, we can." The elementary principles of life history analysis enter into the organization of all literary representations, and the manner in which any given author manages those principles is a defining feature in the character and quality of that author's work. In order to give a practical illustration of these claims, in the final section of this article, I shall offer a Darwinian critical commentary on a single novel, *Pride and Prejudice*. I have selected this novel because it is one of the most familiar of all novels; it is relatively short and simple; and it is so finely realized, as an artistic construct, that it offers a good test case for the challenge of demonstrating the integral relation between life history analysis and the finest components of literary meaning.

Let me emphasize that this choice of an illustrative text is in one sense arbitrary. Any work of literature, from any period or genre, could be chosen for illustrative purposes. Darwinists have written critiques of folktales, myths, plays, poems, romance novels, realist fiction, science fiction, operas, ballets, and movies. They have written interpretive studies of, among other writers, Homer, Shakespeare, Swift, Wordsworth, Pushkin, Tchaikovsky, Walter Scott, Charlotte Brontë, George Eliot, Hans Christian Andersen, Willa Cather, Walter Pater, Zamyatin, and Dr. Seuss. There is no work of literature written anywhere in the world, at any time, by any author, that is outside the scope of a Darwinian analysis. In order to be susceptible to a Darwinian analysis, an author does not have to be a Darwinian. An author can be a pagan Greek, a Christian, a Moslem, or a Zen Buddhist. He or she can be a Brazilian tribesman, a European lady, a medieval Japanese warrior, or a Tibetan monk. He or she can be heterosexual, homosexual, bisexual, or celibate. He or she need not be average or typical, and he or she need not himself or herself embrace beliefs and attitudes that are similar to those of Darwinian psychologists or Darwinian literary critics. If Darwinism gives a true account of the human mind, and if the human mind produces all literary texts, all literary texts are susceptible to a Darwinian analysis. They are susceptible, that is, to an analysis of the constraining psychological structures that regulate the production of all imaginative artifacts.

Geneticists have often found fruit flies a convenient species for their experiments. But they do not believe or suggest that genetics applies only to fruit flies. I have written on *Pride and Prejudice* in various places, using it for various illustrative purposes. I want to be clear, then, that I do not consider *Pride and Prejudice* a particularly or specifically Darwinian text. I consider it the literary equivalent of a fruit fly. Various of my colleagues in Darwinian literary study are working on the literary equivalents of mice or nematode worms, but whatever the local subject of study, we are all contributing to the same larger field.

The Emerging Paradigm in Darwinian Psychology

The argument I shall make for what Darwinian literary critics can and should do will turn on the questions of individual differences and "domain-general" intelligence. The two main orthodox tenets of evolutionary psychology that have so far impeded the full development of a paradigm for Darwinian psychology are the repudiation or depre- cation of the significance attaching to domain-general cognitive abilities and individual differences in personality and intelligence. "Evolutionary psychology" as a distinct school – and not just as a general term covering the whole field of Darwinian psy- chology – gives overwhelming, preponderating weight to "human universals," and it envisions the mind as consisting almost exclusively of "domain-specific" cognitive mechanisms, that is, "cognitive modules" that have evolved specifically for the purpose of solving adaptive problems within a Paleolithic environment. And that ancient envi- ronment is itself conceived as a set of statistically stable physical and social conditions, the "environment of evolutionary adaptedness" (EEA). The central tenets of evolution- ary psychology as a distinct school, then, are these: (a) everyone has pretty much the same sort of mind and personality, not only in basic structures but in force or quality; (b) this one universal mind, the mind that is common to all people on earth, is "designed" (= adapted) exclusively to deal with a statistically stable environment that lasted for per- haps two million years but that in good part no longer subsists; and (c) all the significant adaptive features of that mind are "cognitive modules" designed to solve adaptive prob- lems specific to the statistical regularities of this ancient environment; domain-general intelligence is not one of these adaptive cognitive features.

This characterization of evolutionary psychology is stark, stripped of qualifications and equivocations, and it is thus far a "caricature," but the merit of a caricature is that it brings into sharp relief the signal, defining features of a physiognomy. The oddly misshapen countenance that emerges from these three starkly defined tenets is in its main outlines a true portrait. (See Cosmides and Tooby, 1994; Pinker, 1994, 1995, 1997, 2002; Symons, 1992; Tooby and Cosmides, 1992. Also see the textbooks by Barrett, Dunbar, and Lycett, 2002; Bridgeman, 2003; Buss, 1999; Gaulin and McBurney, 2001; Palmer and Palmer, 2002; Rossano, 2003.)

There are two reasons, I would suggest, that evolutionary psychologists have pro- pounded this peculiarly distorted version of human cognitive evolution. The first reason is that they have been preoccupied with opposing the Standard Social Science Model (SSSM) of the mind as a blank slate or general, all-purpose computer in which all content is produced by external (social and cultural) influences (Tooby and Cosmides, "Psychological Foundation"). Domain specificity offers an alternative to domain generality. The second reason is that they have been frightened by the association of Darwinian psychology with social Darwinism, eugenics, and the exploration of individual and group differences in behavior (the field known as "behavioral genetics"), and especially differences in intelligence. The radical environmentalism or blank-slate model that dominated the social sciences in the twentieth century was itself largely motivated by the fear or rejection of social Darwinism, eugenics, and racial theory. By emphasizing universals and domain-specific mechanisms the evolutionary psychologists have sought to effect a compromise between Darwinism and the SSSM. They have reintroduced the notion of adaptive cognitive structure into psychology, but have done so without violating the ideological taboos against acknowledging the significance of individual and group differences.

The appeal of these two advantages has been so strong that it has, since the early 1990s, blinded many Darwinian psychologists to the fundamental disadvantages of the concepts that enable the compromise. The disadvantages are that this whole complex of ideas runs counter to gross and obvious features of common experience – to the vital importance both of individual differences and of general intelligence in everyday life – and that it runs counter also to the elementary logic in the theory of natural selection. In that theory, "selection" can only work on variation, that is, "individual differences." No variation, no selection. No selection, no adaptation, and thus no evolution "by means of natural selection" (Darwin, 2003).

Since the late 1990s, evolutionary psychology has achieved sufficient substance and stability to provide a big market for popular expositions and for textbooks – for summary expositions of common findings. In about the same period – in just the past few years – the psychological ideas that so quickly congealed into a premature orthodoxy have been under increasing pressure from new and genuinely innovative research into the single most important event in human evolutionary history – the "cultural revolution" that took place some 60,000 to 30,000 years ago and that produced the first evidence of complex technology, complex forms of socioeconomic organization, and sophisticated symbolic and artistic activity. This whole research area is fraught with controversy, but there is enough agreement about some basic facts so that a compelling new vision of human evolution has been emerging – a vision that contrasts sharply with the orthodox tenets of evolutionary psychology. In this new vision, the most distinctive feature of the specifically human mind – the feature that distinguishes it most from that of its primate cousins – is the emergence of a flexible general intelligence that enables humans to adapt to variations within an environment that is itself complex and unstable. (See Chiappe, 2000; Chiappe and MacDonald, under submission; Crawford, 1998; Foley, 1996; Geary, 1998; Geary and Huffman, 2002; Irons, 1998; MacDonald, 1990, 1995b, 1997, 1998a, 1998b; Mithen, 1996, 2001; Potts, 1998; Richerson and Boyd, 2000; D. S. Wilson, 1999; E. O. Wilson, 1998.)

It is a simple fact available to common observation that humans have evolved a truly extraordinary capacity to adapt to new and different environments – and to effect these adaptations while undergoing relatively little or no actual change in their anatomical or physiological characteristics. Humans can live everywhere from polar regions to deserts to tropical rain forests; they can organize themselves socially in groups that extend from small hunter-gatherer bands to tribes, hordes, nation-states, empires, and new world orders; and they can adapt to socioeconomic ecologies that stretch from hunting and gathering to agriculture, market economies, industrial cities, and vast metropolitan regions linked digitally to a total world culture. The one crucial feature of human nature that underwrites this adaptability is domain-general intelligence, and that intelligence, along with all the distinctive features of human temperament and personal character, varies from person to person and group to group. (See Bailey, 1997, 1998; Barash, 1997; Bouchard, 1994, 1997; Buss, 1990, 1995; Eaves, Eysenck and Martin, 1989; Eysenck, 1979, 1980, 1995; Herrnstein and Murray, 1994; Jensen, 1998; MacDonald, 1990, 1995b, 1997, 1998a; Rushton, 1995; Segal, 1997, 1999; Segal and MacDonald, 1998; Seligman, 1992; D. S. Wilson, 1994, 1999.)

In the new, emerging vision of human evolution and human nature, the idea of cognitive domains has not been discarded. It has been assimilated and integrated into the larger general structure of human cognition. Cognitive domains have their place and function; they subserve cognitive activities that track constant features of the environment. The eyesight that tracks the spatio-physical world is a prime example; and language aptitude that tracks the human physical and social environment is another. But these domain-specific aptitudes are only a part of the total human cognitive repertory. Another part is general intelligence, and general intelligence subserves the basic adaptive needs of human beings. The new vision does not fall back to the old blank-slate model. It does not assume that all human motives are simply fabricated by arbitrary cultural conventions. It identifies a distinct structure of human motives and cognitive dispositions that derives from the larger logic of inclusive fitness – the logic that regulates the adaptive structure of all life on earth. The distinct structure of human motives and cognitive dispositions is that which is appropriate to a primate species that is highly social and mildly polygynous, that displays concealed ovulation, continuous female receptivity, and postmenopausal life expectancy corresponding to a uniquely extended period of childhood development, that has extraordinary aptitudes for technology, that has developed language and the capacity for peering into the minds of its conspecifics, and that displays a unique disposition for fabricating and consuming aesthetic and imaginative artifacts. So long as we bear all this in mind, we need have no fear of falling back into the structural vacuum of the blank slate – a vacuum in which the mind evolved, the mind produced culture, and culture gave all content and structure to the mind.

In the 1990s, the most important theoretical conflict within Darwinian psychology itself was the conflict between "sociobiology" on the one side and "evolutionary psychology" on the other. In its simplest terms, this conflict turned on differing views of the human motivational system. Sociobiologists tended to regard humans as "fitness maximizers." As Irons formulates the idea, "Human beings tend to behave in such a way as to maximize their genetic representation in future generations" (1979, p. 257). In its most extreme form, as in the arguments produced by Betzig, fitness maximization is conceived simply in numerical terms as a matter of leaving the greatest possible number of progeny. Evolutionary psychologists, in contrast, committed themselves to the view that humans do not care particularly about reproductive success. In their view, humans are not "fitness maximizers" but rather "adaptation executors" (Tooby and Cosmides, 1992, p. 54). That is, humans are motivated exclusively by "proximal" motives like the desire for sex. In the EEA, such motives operated reliably to maximize fitness but did not, supposedly, require that reproductive success be an active motive in its own right. In the modern world, the argument goes, birth control neatly severs the link between the proximal motive of sexual desire and the "ultimate" regulative principle of inclusive fitness. People are designed only to push the pleasure buttons in their proximal motives, not to worry about the ultimate evolutionary or adaptive rationale that produced those buttons. (See Alexander, 1979, 1987, 1990; Barkow, 1990; Betzig, 1986, 1998; Chagnon, 1979; Chagnon and Irons, 1979; Irons, 1990, 1998; MacDonald, 1995a; Symons, 1989, 1992; Turke, 1990.)

In the currently orthodox version of evolutionary psychology, the idea of humans as adaptation executors has gained a decisive victory. In so far as this concept is set in contrast to the notion of counting offspring as a monolithic human motive, the victory has been legitimate, but the idea of pushing pleasure buttons is not in itself a satisfactory account of the human motivational system. We can formulate a better, more comprehensive account of the human motivational system by integrating two concepts: (a) the concept of human life history as a cycle organized around the distribution of effort between "somatic" and "reproductive" activities, and (b) the concept of "behavioral systems."

The central categories of life history analysis are birth, growth, death, and reproduction. The organisms of all species engage in two fundamental forms of effort – the acquisition of resources (somatic effort) and the expenditure of resources in reproduction. Birth, growth, and death are somatic activities. Mating and parenting are reproductive activities. (Not all individuals of all species engage in reproductive activity, but if reproductive effort were not part of the suite of characteristics in a species, that species would become extinct within a single generation.) All the main activities in the life history of an organism are integrated and interdependent. "What an organism spends in one endeavor cannot be spent in another. Life histories, the patterns of birth, growth, and death that we see, are thus the outcome of competing costs and benefits of different activities at any point in the life cycle" (Low, 1998, p. 131). Life history analysis compares the different ways in which the logic of inclusive fitness – the maximization of reproductive success – has regulated the interplay of these large-scale principles in different species. The organization of life history traits – of size, growth rate, life span, mating behavior, number and pacing of offspring, sex ratios of offspring, and parenting strategies – enters into every aspect of a species' characteristics: into its physiology, its anatomy, and its behavior. Life history theory can thus be regarded as the overarching theory for both a macroeconomics and a microeconomics of biology. (See Alexander, 1979, p. 25, 1987, pp. 40–41; Geary, 1998, pp. 11, 199; MacDonald, 1997, p. 328; McGuire and Troisi, 1998, pp. 58–59; Low, 1998, pp. 138–40, 2000, p. 92; Ridley, 1999, pp. 12, 127–128; Trivers 1972, pp. 168–174, 1985, pp. 311–314.)

The human species has a distinct form for the organization of its life history, and the logic of this organization enters into every facet of the human behavioral and cognitive order. Humans are highly social animals with pairbonded, semi-monogamous mating systems and extraordinarily high levels of parental investment. They have upright posture, narrowed birth canals, and large brains. As a result, their reproductive economy necessarily involves motivational systems geared toward male-female pair-bonding, sustained family structures, extended kinship systems, and complex social organization. Their large brains entail long development as children so that they can acquire the information and skills necessary for successful life effort. Their long childhood requires intense child-parent attachment, male-female cooperative parenting, and extended kin networks. Their large brains present them with unique adaptive opportunities, both technological and social, and also with challenges and problems other species do not face.

The idea of "behavioral systems" has been formulated as a concept in Darwinian psychiatry, and it has emerged also, implicitly, half-consciously, as an organizing principle in orthodox versions of evolutionary psychology. In *Darwinian Psychiatry*, McGuire and Troisi define behavioral systems as coordinated suites of behavior subserving specific life goals. "The term *behavior system* refers to *functionally and causally related behavior patterns and the systems responsible for them*" (1998, p. 60). McGuire and Troisi themselves identify four specific systems: survival, reproduction, kin assistance, and reciprocation – with reciprocation serving as a generalized term for social interaction beyond the kin group. In the now numerous textbooks devoted to evolutionary psychology, very similar terms typically serve as the chapter titles for the whole sequence of chapters. For instance, in the first of the textbooks (1999), after introductory chapters on the history, theory, and methodology of evolutionary psychology, Buss has this sequence of main sections: "Problems of Survival," "Challenges of Sex and Mating," "Challenges of Parenting and Kinship," "Problems of Group Living." The organization of topics in Buss's textbook set the pattern for the subsequent textbooks, and the pattern itself tacitly underwrites the theory of behavioral systems. (Buss himself is alert to the importance of personality theory and to individual differences, and in a final section of his textbook he discusses this topic but also acknowledges that orthodox evolutionary psychologists have concentrated almost exclusively on human universals.)

By combining the idea of life history analysis with the idea of behavioral systems, we can formulate an alternative to the opposing notions of fitness maximization and adaptation execution. Despite the evidence of a few great sultans, humans are not typically motivated, in any very direct or active way, to maximize the number of their progeny. But neither are they merely puppets adequately fulfilled by the pushing of their pleasure buttons. People are neither fitness maximizers nor adaptation executors. They are highly integrated sets of behavioral systems that have been organized and directed by the logic of the human life history cycle. Human nature is organized in structured sets of behavioral systems, and these systems subserve the goals that are distributed into the basic functions of somatic and reproductive life effort. Fitness maximization is not itself an active motive, but the fundamental somatic impulses (surviving and acquiring resources, both physical and social) and the fundamental reproductive impulses (acquiring mates, having sex, producing and tending children, helping kin) are in fact direct and active motives.

The behavioral systems identified by McGuire and Troisi and by the textbook writers – survival, mating, parenting, kin relations, and social interaction – are built into the human organism. They are mediated by innate structures in the genetically conditioned features of anatomy, physiology, hormones, and neurochemistry. All of these mediating forces manifest themselves psychologically as emotions – the "basic" emotions identified by Ekman and others as universal motivating forces in human psychology (joy, sadness, fear, anger, contempt, disgust, surprise). (See Damasio, 1994; Ekman, 2003; Ekman and Davidson, 1994; Ledoux, 1996; Lewis and Haviland, 2000; MacDonald, 1995b; Panksepp, 1998.) The main behavioral systems that subserve the largest life history goals are sensitive to the appropriate stimuli, but they are latent in all conditions of life. Male sexual desire, for example, is activated by the sight of nubile females, but even a male raised in total isolation by machines would presumably have stirrings of confused sexual interest or sensation – a sense of vague, frustrated longing, accompanied by spontaneous erections and emissions, and I think it safe to predict that the first time any such hypothetically deprived male saw a nubile female, he would have a sudden and instantaneous conviction that THAT was what he had been wanting, had he only known. A woman raised in similar isolation would presumably not think to herself, "I wish to be inseminated, grow an embryo in my uterus, and produce a child, which I shall then suckle and nurture," but whatever her thoughts or longings might be, she would still grow breasts and undergo a menstrual cycle, and if she were inseminated by machines in her sleep, the growth and birth of a child, however terrifying to her ignorance, would have in it a certain natural, physical logic, and the effects would carry with them instinctive impulses and sensations. Language is an instinct (Bickerton, 1990; Pinker, 1994), but feral children can never gain fluency in speech. Maternity is an instinct, but female monkeys raised in isolation perform badly as mothers. Normal human development requires socialization, but socialization itself is channeled by innate dispositions. The behavior of a female raised in isolation is disorganized and dysfunctional, but it is not simply blank.

The total anatomical and hormonal organization of women is geared toward the bearing and raising of children. Even the massively conditioned women in Huxley's *Brave New World* feel a vague longing that can be satisfied only by a full course of hormonally mediated "pregnancy substitute." In the actual modern world, a world in which people can choose whether or not to reproduce, the overwhelming majority do choose to reproduce. Many couples who for physical reasons cannot have children go to astonishing lengths, in expense and effort, to adopt children. Evolutionary psychologists emphasizing the activation of proximal mechanisms point to the fact that not everybody wants to have children. True enough, but most people are equipped by nature with the physical and psychological attributes that are necessary to the bearing and raising of children, and the majority of people feel at some point a powerful need to activate those attributes and to fulfill the behavioral capacities they feel latent within them. If this were not the case, we would have a hard time explaining adoption and the nearly universal human practice of treating pet animals as surrogate children. (See Alcock, 2001, pp. 35–40.)

Childbearing and child-rearing are only an instance, though an important one. The larger principle is that in most cases people accede to the psychological force of the total set of motivational systems that have been implanted in them by the logic of human life history. More often than not, people have a compelling need to give full and integrated play to the whole suite of their behavioral systems. Exceptions and special cases abound, but it is a broad general truth about human nature that people have a need to activate the latent capacities of the behavioral systems that have shaped the largest features of their bodies and their minds. For most people, achieving satisfaction in life depends on the fulfillment of the emotional needs built into those systems.

The Cognitive Behavioral System

The textbook versions of evolutionary psychology are a little uncertain about what, if anything, to make of the various specifically cognitive aspects of human nature. Language can usually be inserted somewhere in the sections on social interaction, but it is less clear where one is to locate aptitudes for tool use, cognitive biases for the acquisition of organized information about plants and animals, and the production of cultural artifacts of no apparent utility, especially if these artifacts do not push simple pleasure buttons in the way that pornography does for many people. If we combine the idea of behavioral systems with a recognition of the peculiarly human attribute of domain-general intelligence, we can solve this puzzle. The human mind is an extraordinary, complex organ. It is both highly structured and flexibly responsive to contingent inputs. It solves an immense array of adaptive problems. Some of its processes develop in predictably universal ways, as in the acquisition of language, of colors, or of botanical and zoological categories. (See Atran, 1990; Brown, 1991; Cosmides and Tooby, 1994; Geary, 1998; Pinker, 1994, 1995, 1997, 2002; Tooby and Cosmides, 1992.) Other processes develop with the combinatorial fluidity that we designate as "creative" or "inventive," as in the invention of new technologies and new arts, but all new inventions and discoveries work by extending and combining the elemental cognitive components that develop spontaneously and universally in human minds, as the product of an adaptive evolutionary history, and all cultural artifacts, no matter how complex or seemingly arbitrary, are constrained by the limitations of physical nature and are both prompted and constrained by an evolved human psychology. (See Barrow, 1996; Carroll, 1995; Chiappe, 2000; Chiappe and MacDonald, under submission; Darwin, 1871; Geary, 1998; Mithen, 1996; Geary and Huffman, 2002; E. O. Wilson, 1998.)

The mind is a complex and integrated feature of human nature – sufficiently complex, structured, and integrated in its operations so that it answers to the criteria for what McGuire and Troisi identify as a "behavioral system." If we identify the mind in this way, we are adding it, as a specifically human characteristic, to the set of human behavioral systems. We identify it as having characteristic innate constraints and distinctive latent capacities elicited by appropriate releasors. The mate selection system arouses desire and fulfills it in successful coupling. The parenting system arouses concern for children and achieves fulfillment in the successful rearing of children. The social interaction system arouses desire for forming coalitions and finding a place within a status hierarchy, and achieving those goals offers pleasure and provides a sensation of satisfaction. The cognitive behavioral system arouses a need for conceptual and imaginative order, and that need fulfills itself and provides satisfaction to the mind through the formulation of concepts, the construction of religious, philosophical, or ideological beliefs, the development of scientific knowledge, and the fabrication of aesthetic and imaginative artifacts.

I have already argued that domain-general intelligence has an adaptive function; it facilitates a flexible response to a variable environment. That flexibility gives humans an advantage other animals do not have, and it presents them also with challenges and difficulties unique to the human species. Other species operate mainly by means of instinct, that is, by means of stereotyped behaviors that leave little room for conscious choice. Humans create elaborate mental models of the world and make decisions on the basis of alternative scenarios that present themselves within those models. (See E. O. Wilson, 1998.) The materials available to the mind and imagination are vast, and the combination of those materials virtually infinite. The possibility for error, uncertainty, and confusion is an ever-present fact of human mental life. Because they have an irrepressibly active and unstable mental life, humans have a special need to fabricate mental maps or models that make sense of the world and provide behavioral directives that can take the place of instinctive behavioral patterns. For these mental maps or models to be effective in providing behavioral directives, they must be emotionally saturated, imaginatively vivid. Art and cultural artifacts like religion and ideology meet this demand. They fulfill a necessary adaptive function, that of regulating the human cognitive behavioral system. The arts provide emotionally saturated images and aesthetic constructs that produce a sense of total cognitive order and that help regulate the other behavioral systems. The arts make sense of human needs and motives. They simulate subjective experience, map out social relations, evoke sexual and social interactions, depict the intimate relations of kin, and locate the whole complex and interactive array of human behavioral systems within models of the total world order. Humans have a universal and irrepressible need to fabricate this sort of order, and satisfying that need provides a distinct form of pleasure and fulfillment. (See Boyd,1998, 2001; Brown, 1991; Carroll, 1995; Cooke, 1999, 2002; Dissanayake, 1995, 2000, 2003; Fromm, 2003; Love, 2003; Storey, 1993, 1996; Scalise Sugiyama, 2001b; E. O. Wilson, 1998.)

A Diagram of Human Nature

In order to clarify the hierarchical motivational structure of human nature I have been describing here, I shall construct a diagram, with inclusive fitness at the top, as the ultimate regulative principle (but not as an active and direct motive). Active and direct motive begins at the next level down, with the organization of life effort into somatic and reproductive effort. Through this hierarchical structure, I am suggesting that over and above their specific goals and motives, many people have a generalized but distinct desire to acquire resources and also to achieve successful reproduction. Not all people have an active desire for reproductive success, but such a desire is nonetheless, I would argue, a characteristic of the species as a whole. Young men do not think only, "I want to buy a red convertible so I can attract that girl there and have sex with her." They also often think, "I'd like to become prosperous, and I'd like to get married and have a family." And young women do not think only, "I'm impressed by that guy with the red convertible. I want to arouse his sexual interest and attach him to me." They also think, "I'd like to find a prosperous, reliable man, marry him, have children, and raise a family." It is these latter, generalized inclinations that I am identifying as the somatic and reproductive motives in their own right.

Below the level of generalized desire to acquire resources and succeed in sexual reproduction, I shall place the various behavioral systems that subserve both those general motive dispositions. The specific subordinate systems identified here are systems dedicated to survival, technology, mating, parenting, kin relations, social relations, and cognitive activity. Between the somatic and reproductive levels on the one hand and these specific behavioral systems on the other, I shall place the term "development" to indicate that these various systems are activated and distributed according to the developmental program appropriate to the human species. (The mating and parenting systems operate only at specific times in the life history of a human organism, and social dispositions vary in the course of the life cycle.)

In a box under each behavioral system, I have placed a few motivational goals or directives characteristic of that system. Thus, under "Survival," there is a directive "avoid predators." Under "Mating," there is a directive "avoid incest." Under "Social," a directive "build coalitions," and so on.

In the interest of completeness, I include one behavioral system – that of "technology" – that is not mentioned in the accounts by McGuire and Troisi and the textbook writers. The disposition to construct stone tools is one of the most ancient hominid adaptations, and our modern technology is continuous with the construction of complex, multipart tools that constitutes one of the distinguishing features of the "human revolution" from perhaps 100,000 to 30,000 years ago. In one of the most elaborate efforts so far to mediate between evolutionary psychology and the idea of a domain-general intelligence, Mithen (1996) identifies technology as an integrated area of cognitive activity. He calls it a cognitive domain, but the concept as he describes it is on a structural level equivalent to what I have been calling a behavioral system.

Specific cognitive modules would be activated within the relevant behavioral systems. For instance, the cognitive modules for vision – edge and motion detection, color, depth, etc. – would be activated within the technological behavioral system and the survival system. Kin-recognition modules would be activated within the kinship system. "Face recognition" modules would be activated within all interpersonal behavioral systems (mating, parenting, kin, social interaction). Modules for regulating social exchange or cheater detection would be activated in the mating system and in the social system, and so on. If, as seems likely, the brain has specific modules geared to the construction of narratives and the recognition of aesthetically pleasing verbal patterns, those would be activated within the cognitive behavioral system. (For lists of domain-specific cognitive modules, see Carey and Spelke, 1994, p. 171; Cosmides and Tooby, 1994, p. 103; Mithen, 1996; Pinker, 1994, p. 420, 1995, p. 236, 1997, pp. 128, 315; Sperber, 1994, p. 42; Tooby and Cosmides, 1992, p. 113. For suggestions about cognitive predispositions to certain kinds of aesthetic order, see Barrow, 1996; Eibl-Eibesfeldt, 1989; Frederick Turner, 1992; M. Turner, 1996.)

One final feature of the diagram is that the box in the diagram containing behavioral systems has a list of Ekman's basic emotions at the bottom of the box, thus signifying that all behavioral systems are activated and mediated by emotion.

Meaning and Point of View in Literary Representations

Literary representation is first and foremost the representation of human behavior within some surrounding world. Creating such representations is itself a fundamental motive of human nature, and human nature is the fundamental subject of the representations. The "meaning" of a representation does not reside in the represented events. Meaning resides in the *interpretation* of events. And interpretation is always, necessarily, dependent on "point of view." "Point of view" in literary narrative is not just another technical feature in a catalog of formal literary devices. In its broadest sense, point of view is a term signifying "the locus of consciousness or experience within which any meaning takes place." Point of view is thus the term we use to designate the primary components in the social interactions constituted in and by a literary representation. There are three components in the social interactions of a literary representation: the author, the represented characters, and the audience. (See Abrams, 1986.) The primary locus of meaning for all literary works is the mind of the author. Whether consciously or unconsciously, the author provides whatever determinate meaning resides in a work, but the author also negotiates among the competing points of view within the characters in the work, and negotiates further with the point of view he or she attributes to an audience.

Authors are people talking to people about people. Most stories are about people seeking resources and reproductive success – fortune and love. But they are also about people seeking to perceive meaning in or impose meaning on the events of their own lives and the lives of every person they know. All authors seek to dominate the meaning of the story they tell, and all the characters in a story have their own version of what happens. As a rule, these versions partially overlap both with one another and with the version presented by the author, but they also often conflict. The author has final say among his or her own characters, but to control the interpretation of the story as it will be registered by the audience, the author can only persuade, manipulate, cajole, wheedle,

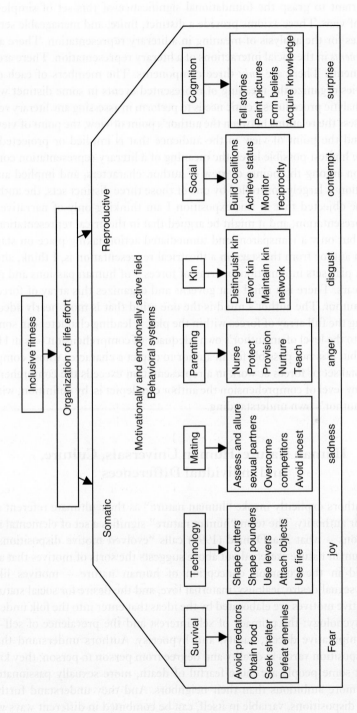

Figure 1 A Diagram of Human Nature.

intimidate, solicit, insult, flatter, bully, harangue, coax, shame, or otherwise appeal to or provoke the readers. (See Booth, 1996; Leaska, 1996, Scalise Sugiyama, 1996.)

It is important to grasp the foundational significance of this set of simple axioms about point of view. These axioms provide a distinct, finite, and manageable set of analytic categories for the analysis of meaning in a literary representation. There are *three specific components* in the social interactions of a literary representation. There are *always* three components. There are *only* three components. The members of each of these three categories organize the meaning of represented events in some distinct way. One of the chief analytic procedures a critic needs to perform in assessing any literary representation is to assess the relations between the author's point of view, the point of view of the characters, and the point of view in the audience that is implied or projected by the author. At the highest possible level, the meaning of a literary representation consists in the interaction among the points of view of author, characters, and implied audience. That interaction is largely controlled by one of those three distinct sets, the author.

It might be objected that in this exposition I am thinking only of narrative, not of theatrical representation, and it might be argued that in theatrical representations there is no author but only a transparent and unmediated action taking place on stage. The absence of an author from the stage in a theatrical representation is, I think, altogether an illusion. A play sets into motion an array of forces – of human passions and motives, desires and fears. There is a mind that governs and organizes this array of forces – the mind of the author. The author's mind is the one mind that is most nearly adequate to understanding the full array of forces within the play. A leading character can sometimes approximate to the level of an author's own adequacy of comprehension – as in Hamlet's soliloquies – but it is not possible for an author to depict a character whose comprehension of the total set of forces at work in a representation exceeds the comprehension of the author. Any level of comprehension the author can depict is, by definition, within the scope of the author's own understanding.

Human Nature, Human Universals, Culture, and Individual Differences

Almost all authors explicitly invoke "human nature" as their ultimate referent and the source of their authority. The term "human nature" signifies a set of elemental motives and dispositions – what MacDonald (1990) calls "evolved motive dispositions." The diagram of human nature sketched out above suggests the sorts of motives that are usually contained in the common conception of human nature – motives like self-preservation, sexual desire, jealousy, maternal love, and the desire for social status – and these substantive motives are elaborated by the ideas that enter into the folk understanding of ego psychology: the primacy of self-interest and the prevalence of self-serving delusion, manipulative deceit, vanity, and hypocrisy. Authors understand that each elemental disposition varies in quality and degree from person to person; they know, for instance, that some people are more fearful of death, more sexually passionate, more maternal, or more ambitious than their neighbors. And they understand further that each of these dispositions, variable in itself, can be combined in different ways with the other dispositions so as to produce the distinct configurations of individual identity. A woman might be both terrified of death and intensely protective of her children, but have little sexual desire and little social ambition – or be exactly the reverse, bold and fearless, coldly indifferent to her offspring, sexually ardent, and passionately determined to achieve high social rank. And yet again, she might be fairly bold, typically maternal, moderately amorous, and modestly ambitious.

Human universals or species-typical norms of behavior are merely behavioral patterns so firmly grounded in the logic of human life history that they are characteristic features of all known cultures. For instance, all cultures have marriage, rites of passage, social roles defined by age and sex, religious beliefs, public ceremonies, kin relations, sex taboos, medical practices, criminal codes, storytelling, jokes, and so on. (See Brown, 1991, 2000.) Universals are made up of motive dispositions that combine in relatively stable and consistent ways. The same motive dispositions can also be elaborated and organized, at higher levels of cultural complexity, in ways that vary widely from culture to culture. For instance, all cultures have marriage, but some cultures are polygynous and some monogamous; some allow divorce, and some do not. All cultures have games, but not all cultures play whist or football. All cultures have language, but not all cultures are literate; not all literate cultures have produced highly developed forms of prose fiction; and not all cultures with highly developed forms of prose fiction have produced stream-of-consciousness narrative styles.

No culture can deviate from human universals (by definition), but many individual people can and do deviate from species-typical norms of behavior. They murder their children, commit incest, fail to develop language, or otherwise behave in anomalous or dysfunctional ways. The behavior that is depicted in literary texts does not necessarily exemplify universal or species-typical behavioral patterns, but species-typical patterns form an indispensable frame of reference for the communication of meaning in literary representations. By appealing to this substratum of common human motives, authors activate a vein of common understanding in their readers. Consider maternal care and incest. Maternal care of infants is a "universal" feature of human nature, but all cultures make some provision for population control, and in cultures that do not have access to birth control and abortion, population control necessarily involves infanticide. (See Daly and Wilson, 1988; Low, 2000; Symons, 1979.) Literary authors can nonetheless depend on readers to feel the weight and value of maternal care. This is part of the common frame of reference, not just for any particular culture but for all cultures. Medea murders her own children, and Euripides can safely anticipate that the audience will react with instinctive shock and horror to the murder. So also, incest avoidance is a human universal. Different cultures define the details of incest in different ways, but certain kinds of incest are universally prohibited. No culture permits mother-son incest, and Sophocles can safely anticipate that his audience will instinctively sympathize with the revulsion of feeling that leads Oedipus to gouge out his own eyes. (See Daly and Wilson, 1990; Low, 2000; Scalise Sugiyama, 2001a.)

In the same way that each author has a unique fingerprint, he or she has also some unique configuration of identity – some individual variation of personality and experiential conditioning – and that identity defines itself in relation both to the cultural norms within which the author lives and also to the common elements of human nature. Individual identity is the basis for an author's point of view, and more often than not an author presents his or her own distinct point of view as a normative standard – as an ideal against which to judge other identities, other points of view. By appealing to "human nature," literary authors can ground their own values within what they take to be elemental realities. Sometimes, but not always, they contrast these elemental realities with the conventions of their own culture, suggesting that the conventions are shallow, perverse, artificial, unhealthy, or otherwise undesirable. (See Carroll, 1995; Jobling, 2001a, 2001b; Nesse, 1995; Nordlund, 2002.)

Some distinctions of individual difference are obvious and available to untutored common sense – for instance, distinctions of age, sex, health, attractiveness, social affiliation, social status, vocational occupation, intelligence, and honesty. (The now pat triad of class, gender, and race – the standard topics of politicized literary criticism – is an arbitrary subset of these useful categories.) Such terms, available to common sense, are also necessary to a life history analysis of the human species. The common understanding operates as an intuitive or "folk" version of life history analysis. In addition to the distinctions from this range of analysis, all critics have access to the common vocabulary for assessing temperament and personality. Differences in personality are part of the adaptive environment among which individual humans make the choices that enable them to succeed in meeting the needs of their evolved motive dispositions. In traditional, belle-lettristic or impressionistic literary criticism, differences in the quality of critical perceptions depend in good part on the acuity any given critic displays in accessing this common vocabulary. Modern personality theory has now distilled, codified, and elaborated the common vocabulary of temperament and personality, and it is very much in a literary critic's interest to become familiar with this body of empirical research. At present, the best available theory is that of the five-factor system (extraversion, neuroticism, conscientiousness, agreeableness, and imaginative and intellectual "openness"). Since this system was drawn, in the first place, from the common lexicon, it is not surprising that its categories correlate well, as a first approximation, to the depiction of characters in fiction. In order to identify the relations of authors to their own characters, the use of this common vocabulary provides an invaluable tool for a shared and delimited analytic vocabulary. (See Bouchard, 1994, 1997; Buss, 1990, 1995; Costa and Widiger, 1994; Digman, 1990; Eysenck and Eysenck, 1985; McCrae, 1992; MacDonald, 1995b, 1998b; Pervin, 1990, 2003; Pervin and John, 1999; Segal and MacDonald, 1998; Wiggins, 1996.)

The fifth factor in the five-factor personality system – imaginative or intellectual openness to experience – is the factor most closely associated with domain-general intelligence, and it is itself roughly concordant with the cognitive behavioral system. MacDonald explains, "The Openness to Experience factor taps variation in intelligence and what one might term optimal Piagetian learning – intrinsically motivated curiosity and interest in intellectual and aesthetic experience combined with imagination and creativity in these areas" (1998b, p. 126). In virtually all literature, distinctions of wit or intelligence or imaginative vitality form a central distinguishing point of reference in the discrimination among characters and in the formation of a normative or dominant authorial point of view. Authors by nature have strong cognitive behavioral systems – they would be positioned at the far end of the right tail of the bell curve distribution measuring the fifth factor – and they tend strongly to value this same quality in their characters. They tend also to invite their audiences to share in their own normative approbation of this quality.

The primary purpose of literary criticism, as an objective pursuit of true knowledge about its subject, is to identify the specific configuration of meaning in any given text or set of texts. In order to make that identification, it is necessary for the critic to have three conceptual models or templates at his or her disposal: (a) a concept of human nature (like that in the diagram earlier); (b) a concept of the cultural ecology within which any given text has been constructed; and (c) a set of categories for analyzing individual differences. In order to make analytic use of these three templates, the critic must also assess the author's own understanding of human nature, identify the author's own stance toward the cultural context, and identify the distinctive characteristics of the author's individual identity.

Life History Analysis and Cognitive Style in *Pride and Prejudice*

Before commenting on the relation of style to life history analysis in *Pride and Prejudice*, I shall take a moment to summarize the novel, as concisely as possible, for the benefit of any reader who has not read it, or who has not read it recently. The protagonist, Elizabeth Bennet, is twenty years old and the second of five daughters. Her father is a gentleman who married somewhat beneath his own social class and chose a wife for her physical charm. His wife's foolishness and vulgarity have alienated him, and he habitually engages in whimsical mockery of her. His estate is entailed to a cousin, a clergyman named Mr. Collins. When Mr. Bennet dies, Mr. Collins will inherit his estate, and Mr. Bennet's wife and five daughters will be left destitute. His wife is thus quite desperate to find rich husbands for her daughters. A wealthy and unmarried young man, Mr. Bingley, rents an estate in the Bennets' neighborhood, and his entourage includes two sisters and a friend, Mr. Darcy, who is also single and even more wealthy than Bingley. In short order, Bingley falls in love with Elizabeth Bennet's older sister, Jane, but Darcy discourages the match and persuades Bingley to leave the neighborhood. Darcy disapproves of the vulgarity of Elizabeth's mother and of her younger sisters, but he is himself nonetheless attracted to Elizabeth, whose wit and vivacity arouse his admiration. Mr. Collins, a monstrously foolish man, proposes to Elizabeth, and when she rejects him, he marries Elizabeth's best friend, Charlotte Lucas, who has little value on the marriage market and seeks only a comfortable establishment. Mr. Collins lives close to a wealthy, arrogant woman, Lady Catherine de Bourgh, who appointed him to his clerical living. Lady Catherine also happens to be Darcy's aunt, and when Elizabeth goes for an extended visit at Charlotte's new home, she again meets Darcy. He proposes to her, but does so in an insulting way, expressing his vivid sense of her social inferiority, and she angrily rejects him. In explaining her rejection, she accuses him of interfering in her sister's marriage prospects, and accuses him also of failing to meet his obligation to provide support for the son of his father's steward, Mr. Wickham, a man who grew up with Darcy. Wickham had recently been stationed with his regiment near Elizabeth's home, had become friendly with her, and had divulged his supposed mistreatment at Darcy's hands. In order to vindicate himself, Darcy writes a letter in which he explains that his own conduct to Wickham has been honorable and that Wickham is in fact a scoundrel and a prevaricator. His evidence is compelling, and Elizabeth realizes she has misjudged him. Her aunt and uncle invite her to accompany them on a vacation tour that leads them into the vicinity of Darcy's estate. They meet Darcy by accident, and his manners undergo a major change. He ceases being haughty and reserved and seeks to ingratiate himself with Elizabeth and her relatives. Elizabeth's views have also changed, and she is receptive to his address, but then she gets a letter from her sister Jane telling her that a younger sister, Lydia, has run off with Wickham, thus bringing disgrace on the whole family. Elizabeth returns home, and unbeknownst to her, Darcy finds Wickham and Lydia and bribes Wickham to marry Lydia. Elizabeth discovers this secret, and is duly grateful. When Bingley and Darcy return to Elizabeth's neighborhood, Bingley proposes to Jane and Darcy proposes, again, to Elizabeth. Both women accept the proposals, and the epilogue informs us that these two main couples live happily ever after.

Pride and Prejudice is universally recognized as a classic, and specifically as a classic distinguished by the economy of its narrative and the elegance of its style. That economy and elegance depend in large part on one central tension in the narrator's own point of view, a tension between two poles: at one pole, the tough-minded recognition of the fundamental realities of human life history, the primacy of resource acquisition and reproductive activity; and at the other pole, the determination to value individual qualities of mind and character. Austen herself grasps with a singular acuity the governing power of the somatic and reproductive foundation of human action, but virtually every character in the novel is assessed also on the basis of the quality of his or her mind. If you will refer again to the diagram of human nature, you can envision the novel as working itself out through a tension between the highest level of conscious human organization – the recognition of the primary need to acquire resources and to mate successfully – and the cognitive behavioral system. Everyone wants to marry well within the terms that are common knowledge among evolutionary sexual theorists – the women want wealth and status in their men, and the men want youth and beauty in their women. But the single most important criterion for registering personal quality in the novel is the degree to which both men and women rise above this basic standard and require also qualities of excellence in character and in mind.

The realization of character – and especially of conscientiousness – is best seen in action, in what the characters actually do. But the realization of mind is best revealed in their style – in what they say, and even more importantly, in how they say it. Austen's own style is "elegant" not in the sense of betraying effeminate delicacy or softness. It is elegant in the sense of being supple, sharp, quick, and crystal clear. It has less the quality of a brush held by a lady's gentle touch than of a finely tempered blade wielded by a hand that is strong, deft, and aggressive. The two chief characters, Elizabeth and Darcy, come to admire and love each other in good part because they share Austen's cognitive and stylistic powers. They select themselves out from the babble of folly, nonsense, and polite fatuities that make up the stylistic world of their associates, and they come to admire one another for qualities of wit and judgment that unfold themselves in sharp and serious dialogue on subjects of character, tone, and point of view. Darcy first offends Elizabeth, when they meet, by uttering some arrogant and defensive rationalizations for his own stiff behavior at a ball. (He is introverted and not very likable, but he is ultra-high on conscientiousness. Wickham, his chief rival for Elizabeth's romantic interest, is extraverted and charming but deceitful and utterly unreliable. As in many novels, one main plot line involves the long-term discrimination among superficially attractive qualities and the qualities that will wear well – a difference relevant to the basic distinction between short-term and long-term mating strategies.) Darcy first fundamentally changes Elizabeth's view of him in the letter he writes to her, after she rejects his proposal, explaining his conduct with respect to her sister's marriage prospects and his treatment of Wickham. Given the fact that he is an introvert and an intellectual, it is not surprising that he should present himself better in a letter than in a personal interview. The letter, which Austen transcribes in full, is the longest utterance he or anyone makes in the course of the novel, and if it does not display Austen's own humor – the subjects are somber, and Darcy is in no joking mood – it does display all of the precision, incisiveness, and acuity of her style. This style is itself a constant norm for the reader, and that same norm serves for all the main protagonistic characters as a measure of quality.

To take just one more of many possible examples for the signal importance of style as a measure of personal quality, Mr. Collins first introduces himself to the Bennet household in a letter that Mr. Bennet reads aloud to his family. The letter is an absolute marvel of fatuity and of pompous self-importance, and the way in which the individual family members respond to the letter reveals the quality of their own minds. Mary, the dull, plain younger sister who tries to build a niche for herself by diligent but uninspired study, thinks Mr. Collins's style rather good. Mrs. Bennet is as always simply indifferent to any quality of character or style and responds to all occasions solely on the basis of opportunistic interests. Elizabeth and her father alone register that the letter is a work of clownish absurdity. "'Can he be a sensible man, sir?'" "'No, my dear; I think not.'" (vol.1, chapter 13) In that exchange, Austen reveals the foundation of the singular affinity that Elizabeth and her father feel for one another, and the reason that they have formed an inner circle of companionship separated from all the rest of the family. Elizabeth is fond of her older sister Jane, and Jane is not vulgar, but she is so excessively sweet-tempered, so almost pathologically high on the scale of likableness, that she is incapable of any negative judgment, and thus fails to see at least half of what passes in front of her. She is, for instance, merely puzzled by the nonsense in Mr. Collins's letter, but inclined to give him full credit for good intentions.

Elizabeth and her father form an inner circle of wit and judgment, and the central figure within that circle is Austen herself. She fashions the point of view as a field of intelligence, and within this field she creates a topography in which she locates all the characters and her audience. To get a sense for how this process works, consider the famous opening sentence of the novel: "It is a truth universally acknowledged, that a single man in possession of a good fortune, must be in want of a wife." There has been considerable difference of opinion over whether that sentence is meant to be taken ironically. The issue can be resolved by reference to the modifying effect of the sentence that follows the first sentence: "However little known the feelings or views of such a man may be on his first entering a neighborhood; this truth is so well fixed in the minds of the surrounding families, that he is considered as the rightful property of some one or other of their daughters." The first sentence is a good-humored affirmation of the rules of the game. Austen identifies the basic elements that are in play in social interactions (property and mating), and she acknowledges that the configuration of elements implied in her remarks constitutes a universal pattern of human behavior: men seek to acquire resources and to use them to acquire mates, and women seek mates who are in possession of resources. But the second sentence establishes a distance between the narrator and the common view she describes. She admits of anomalies, of individual differences. The "surrounding families" operate only on the basis of generalities, and they operate without regard to the inner lives of other people. They regard the man moving into the neighborhood not as a center of consciousness – a point of view – in his own right, but rather as their own property. This is a simple and elementary failure in "theory of mind" – a failure to recognize that other people have inner lives of their own. Failures of this nature inform much of Austen's satire, and indeed of all satire. It is one of the central principles of satire. People are preoccupied with their own needs, and they treat other people as props or furniture in the self-absorbed narratives they construct about themselves. (Mrs. Bennet and Darcy's aunt, Lady Catherine de Bourgh, are signal cases in point, and chief targets of the satire.)

As it happens, in this case, the common view holds good. Bingley is in fact in want of a wife. It is nonetheless the case that in the space of two sentences Austen has established a fundamental tension between her own perspective – a perspective that takes account both of point of view and of individual differences – and the common perspective of the neighborhood. That common perspective is also the perspective of the common world outside the novel. In the course of the novel, an inner core of protagonists, civilized, cultivated, and capable of making stylistic distinctions, will ultimately constitute a small in-group that distinguishes itself from the common world of their own community. Elizabeth's aunt and uncle Gardiner belong to this inner group, and it is one of the triumphs for the ethos advanced by the novel that their cultivation and gentility of manner take precedence over their lower socioeconomic status (Mr. Gardiner is "in trade"). Austen's own point of view defines and dominates this inner group – she is its normative mind – and she tacitly invites receptive readers also to join this group. The criterion that permits a reader to join the group is the ability to read and judge the letters and conversational style of Darcy, Mr. Collins, Lady Catherine, and all the rest. Readers who pass this test of literacy succeed in segregating themselves from the common world that operates exclusively at the level of the lowest common denominators of life history analysis – the reduction of other people to general cases – and the identification of people exclusively in terms of "property."

Note that what has happened in the course of two sentences is that the author has established a set of relations among three points of view: her own, that of her characters, and that of her audience. This set of relations is not peripheral to the "meaning" of the story. By creating these relations, Austen creates an active field of communicative interaction. That is what hooks the reader, brings the reader in, rivets the reader's attention. All this happens before a single event has transpired, and before a single specific character has been introduced. To notice this is to realize that we cannot reduce the "meaning" of a story to the represented events. And even the very content of the two sentences admonishes us that if we reduce the events of the story to an exemplification of "human universals" or "species-typical behaviors," we shall have missed at least half the story. We shall in fact be on precisely the same level as the "surrounding families" personified for us, in the subsequent scene, by Mrs. Bennet. We shall be among the dullards and vulgarians who operate only on general rules and neglect to notice that every single character has a distinct center of consciousness.

Mrs. Bennet has access to a big chunk of the truth. Resources and mating do in fact form elementary building blocks in the human relations that provide the basis for stories. But in grasping this elemental reality, Mrs. Bennet neglects all other considerations of mind and character. She neglects the minds of other people, and she thus demonstrates the poverty of her own mind. The successful protagonists fully acknowledge the hard and sometimes harsh logic in the human reproductive economy, but they do so without neglecting the significance of the human mind and individual differences in identity.

Mate selection is the central behavioral system activated in this novel. That is a distinguishing, defining feature of the literary genre it exemplifies, the genre of "romantic comedy." (This genre probably provides at least half the literary biomass for the sum total of narratives in the world.) In its simplest designation, a romantic comedy is a love story that concludes in a happy marriage. Usually such stories are light in tone or enlivened with humor. But as it applies to Austen, the connotation of the words "romantic" and "comedy" could be a little misleading. There are many comical scenes, but the humor of the novel is often harsh, and the mating game is fierce and determined. Mr. Bingley's sister wants Darcy for herself and snipes incessantly, cattily, ineffectually at Elizabeth, denigrating her appearance, her temperament, her mind, and most of all her family and her social status. Miss Bingley also wants Darcy's younger sister, Georgiana, for her own brother – a liaison that would enhance her own social stand- ing – and she thus conspires with Darcy to detach Bingley from Jane Bennet. She at first expresses the warmest friendship to Jane, activating Jane's own affectionate disposition, and then coldly cuts her. Lady Catherine wants Darcy to marry her own daughter, his cousin, but her daughter is sickly and peevish, and no one but her own mother and her governess pays her any regard at all. Austen's treatment of this girl betrays a certain streak of brutality. She sacrifices Miss de Bourgh on the altar of a ruthless principle of fitness, and the only sensation Elizabeth or Austen herself express toward this poor sick girl is that of vindictive contempt; there is no hint of pity. (To get an even better feel for this streak of brutality, one should read Austen's "juvenilia," the stories she wrote as a teenager. The stories consist of a rapid series of violent and grotesque events, many of them involving characters of certifiably psychopathic disposition.) Elizabeth's own chances of successful mating are seriously endangered when her sister Lydia runs off with Wickham, thus lowering the social standing of the whole family even further. There is a real possibility that by an inevitable progression Lydia would eventually be aban- doned by Wickham and would "come on the town," living as a prostitute and in all likeli- hood dying early of disease and abuse. This doesn't happen because Darcy is determined in his choice of Elizabeth as a mate, and he exploits for his own purposes the opportunity Lydia's folly presents to him. By bribing Wickham to marry Lydia, Darcy does Elizabeth the greatest and most intimate service he could possibly do for her, and at the same time he decisively demonstrates the firmness of his commitment to her. He demonstrates that his preference for her outweighs even the disgrace of a marital association with a sluttish sister married to a reprobate of inferior birth.

The very nature of Wickham's disrepute signals the way in which resources and reproduction constitute the fundamental categories of human behavior in the novel – as they do in actual life. Wickham's evil-doing consists in two main forms of malfeasance: he leaves unpaid debts behind him, and he engages in illicit sexual liaisons with the daughters of the tradesmen and farmers in the neighborhoods he frequents. Before arriving in Elizabeth's neighborhood, he had even had the audacity to try running off with Darcy's sister. If he had succeeded, he would have damaged Darcy in his family pride and in his tenderest family feeling. He would have gained a fortune, advanced in status, and triumphed over a rival male. Darcy has good reason to resent Wickham, and this resentment renders his act of conciliation with Wickham all the more signal an instance of the self-sacrificing chivalry he displays in his commitment to Elizabeth.

Property and rank for men, and youth and beauty for women, count for much. They count almost more than anything, but within the normative perspective of the novel, they must at every point along the way be weighed in the balance of the total set of values that can be integrated within a well-proportioned economy of human life – the kind of economy that leads to the "rational" sort of happiness that Austen and Elizabeth both identify as their own central criterion of value. The total set of values that have to be given their due proportions to bring about rational happiness is not amorphous and unbounded. Sex and property, family or kin relations, parenting, social relations, and cognitive power – those are the central concerns of the book.

Next to sex and property, fidelity to kin presents itself as an urgent motivational force. Within the normative structure of values constituted by Austen's own point of view, even when family members are disgraceful and ridiculous, remaining loyal to them is a fundamental criterion of personal merit. Mr. Collins's baseness displays itself when he advises Mr. Bennet to abandon Lydia altogether after she runs off with Wickham, and Elizabeth displays her strength of character, in the epilogue, by effecting a rapprochement between Darcy and the alienated Lady Catherine, despite the insults Lady Catherine has heaped on Elizabeth herself.

The issue of parenting bulks large in the concerns of the book. The main background marriages – the marriages that serve as models or as warnings for the protagonists – are bad, either in their personal relations (as with Mr. and Mrs. Bennet) or in their parenting functions – as with both Darcy's and Elizabeth's parents. Elizabeth's mother is coarse, stupid, and frivolous, and her father is remote and detached. The situation of the family is bad, not just because of the entail but because he made a bad marriage, neglected to make the economies necessary to provide for his family after his death, neglected the discipline and education of his daughters, and failed to maintain the decorum of marital civility. (Jane and Elizabeth have educated themselves, but one chief attraction that Darcy holds for Elizabeth is that he is himself educated and holds out the promise for her of helping her to continue cultivating her own mind. Much is made of the magnificent library in his possession at his family estate.) Darcy's own parents, he says, were excellent people, but they neglected to form his temper, and they get the blame for the arrogance that first offends Elizabeth and that comes close to spoiling Darcy's ability to attract her to him, despite his wealth and rank. Mr. Collins is an oddity in part because he is a fool, a man of weak understanding, but the other half of the causal explanation is that he was raised by "an illiterate and miserly father" (vol. 1, chapter 15).

All the most intimate relations of sex, marriage, and family embed themselves within a larger social context. For this novel, one central plot question is whether Elizabeth will be accepted into the dominant social group. Her rivals hope she will not. Austen herself disparages their brittle snobbery (they laugh witlessly over the fact that she has an uncle in trade and another uncle who is a country attorney), but she also wishes for Elizabeth to gain access to the highest social level. She defines that level not only by wealth and status but by dignity and authority. One can be born into wealth and rank, but dignity and authority have to be earned by personal merit. Lady Catherine offers a self-parody of upper-class authority. Darcy is the real thing. When Elizabeth first sees Darcy's great estate, and hears his housekeeper praise his integrity and beneficence, she thinks to herself, "What praise is more valuable than the praise of an intelligent servant? As a brother, a landlord, a master, she considered how many people's happiness were in his guardianship! – How much of pleasure or pain it was in his power to bestow! – How much of good or evil must be done by him!" (vol. 3, chapter 1). Austen mocks false status – rank and wealth unsupported by education, wit, manners, and character – but she ultimately affirms the authority of legitimate social status as that is represented by the normative couple, Elizabeth and Darcy.

The chief social dynamic in the novel, the underlying social narrative, is that of a process in which dominant males marry down, selecting women of lower social rank but of superior personal quality. Conversely, women of high quality from a lower rank marry up into the higher gentry and thus integrate the standard of personal quality with the values of wealth and rank. Even Mr. Bennet, unhappily married though he is, has contributed to this process. He married a beautiful though silly woman from a social rank lower than his own. Two of his daughters are both beautiful and intelligent, and one (Elizabeth) is genuinely clever. And the two beautiful, intelligent girls both marry well, extremely well. Even Mrs. Bennet must be gratified with the results, though she understands so little of the process that produces those results.

And finally, again, in all the behavioral systems that have to be balanced in the economy of values in the novel, the cognitive system holds a place of predominating value. Mrs. Bennet contributes some heritable physical attractiveness, a matter not negligible in the total mix, but she contributes nothing of wit, and she is left almost wholly outside the scope of the inner social circle that constitutes the normative group at the end of the novel. "I wish I could say, for the sake of her family, that the accomplishment of her earnest desire in the establishment of so many of her children, produced so happy an effect as to make her a sensible, amiable, well-informed woman for the rest of her life; though perhaps it was lucky for her husband, who might not have relished domestic felicity in so unusual a form, that she was still occasionally nervous and invariably silly."

The Value of a Darwinian Literary Criticism

Previous criticism of Austen can be divided roughly into two bodies of work: (a) the traditional, common-language criticism that dominated academic literary study until the middle of the 1970s, and (b) the various forms of theory-driven criticism that emerged under the umbrella of postmodernism in the past three decades or so. The traditional criticism operates at the level of Austen's own lexicon. At its best, it makes alert observations about theme, tone, and formal organization, but its insights are impressionistic, opportunistic, and adventitious; it seeks no systematic reduction to simple principles that have large general validity. (See Bradley, 1929; C. L. Johnson, 1988; Lewes, 1859; Litz, 1965; Tanner, 1986; Van Ghent, 1953; Woolf, 1953.) At less than its best, traditional criticism consists only in otiose summary and formalistic elaboration punctuated by the occasional exercise in cranky emotional posturing. (See Butler, 1975; Duckworth, 1971; Halliday, 1960; Harding, 1940; Langland, 1984; Morgan, 1980; Mudrick, 1952; Phelan, 1989.) The positive rationale behind the revolution in theory-driven criticism is the recognition that all narratives have a surface-depth structure. Beneath the surface of local incident and occasional commentary in a narrative, there is a simpler, more basic structure of elemental motives and organizing principles. These motives and principles are the skeletal structure of the work. The business of interpretive criticism is to probe beneath the surface of common-language exposition and to find the skeletal structure. Theory-driven interpretation seeks to cut literary meaning at its joints.

The turn to theory-driven criticism answered to a manifest need, but the theoretical models that have been used, up to now, have been painfully inadequate. Deconstruction, Marxism, Freudianism, and Foucauldian political criticism have all presupposed ideas about human nature that conflict sharply with the Darwinian conception. The other main school, feminism, is less a single, coherent theory than a preoccupation about a specific subject matter – the condition of women – but the notions that cluster around this preoccupation often entail false ideas about human nature, and most feminist critics over the past thirty years have affiliated themselves with one or another of the dominant theoretical schools. All of the schools, as subsidiaries of postmodern theory, have fundamentally repudiated the idea of an innate, biologically constrained structure in the human motivational and cognitive system. Postmodern critics have sought the elemental forces of human experience in terms such as "semiosis," "textuality," "class struggle," "the Phallus," "bourgeois ideology," "desire," "discourse," "power," "gender," "dialogism," "heterosexism," "the Other," and "patriarchy," and they have contended that such terms reveal the underlying, governing forces in all literary production. In the degree to which they have succeeded in avoiding the passively reflexive character of traditional criticism, theory-driven criticism has offered distorted, skewed, and strained accounts of the elemental motives and governing principles in literary texts.

Literary criticism is both analytical and evaluative. Literary critics commit themselves to distinct concepts and to definite values. The values that animate postmodern theoretical criticism are emphatically radical, and the political critics incline either to disparage authors for their putative complicity with oppressive epistemes or, more frequently, to invest authors with their own characteristic attitudes of resentment, ideological indignation, and subversive animosity. Both the conceptual content and the political attitudes of the radical criticism are deeply alien to Austen. The conceptual content is alien to the elemental simplicity of her good sense, and the political attitudes are alien to the conservative temper of her wisdom. Many of the postmodern critics have nonetheless made some effort to assimilate Austen to an ethos of epistemological indeterminacy and political radicalism. They have sought to identify various "gaps" or "contradictions" between her overt meanings and this or that supposedly subversive implication in her style or tone. In Austen's case, particularly, these routine invocations of deconstructive formulas often appear half-hearted. The more sensitive postmodern critics evidently feel a certain queasy diffidence about pressing a case that can be made only by fabricating interpretive theses that run so clearly counter to Austen's own determinate meanings. Despite the obligatory invocation of deconstructive formulas, the bulk of commentary in the postmodern critiques blends insensibly into the thematic, tonal, and formal analyses of the traditional criticism. (See Ahearn, 1987; I. Armstrong, 1990; N. Armstrong, 1981, 1987; Auerbach, 1978; Belsey, 2002; Brownstein, 1988; Fraiman, 1989; Handler and Segal, 1990; Litvak, 1992; Newman, 1983; Newton, 1981; Poovey, 1984; Smith, 1993, 2000; Wylie, 2000.)

Darwinian literary criticism is grounded in the large facts of human evolution and human biology, facts much larger and more robust than the conceptions that characterize the various branches of postmodern theory. (See Boyd, 1998; Carroll, 1995; Dissanayake, 1995; Storey, 1996.) Darwinian psychology provides a scientifically grounded and systematic account of human nature. This is the first time in our intellectual history that we have had such a theory, but the subject of this theory – human nature itself – is the very same nature that has always animated writers and readers. Most writers historically have not had access to the evolutionary explanation for how human nature came to be what it is, but they have nonetheless had a deep intuitive understanding of human motives and human feelings. What a Darwinian social science can now do for literary criticism is to give us conscious theoretical access to the elemental forces that have impelled all human beings throughout time and that have fundamentally informed the observations and reflections of all writers and all readers. Darwinian criticism can lift us above the superficial paraphrases of traditional criticism without forcing us into the often false reductions in the postmodern conceptions of human nature. It can help us to understand the source and subject of all literary representation, and it can help us to identify the sources of exceptional power in great literary works like *Pride and Prejudice*.

The Whole Story

More could be said, in detail, about *Pride and Prejudice* – much more. I hope I have said enough to give some indication of what I have in mind by insisting that to construct an even minimally adequate account of any literary representation, we have to set up a polar tension between the highest level of reduction in life history analysis – the level of the somatic and reproductive organization of life effort – and the most fine-grained analysis of formal organization: of theme, tone, and style. I hope to have convinced you that point of view is the central locus of literary meaning because it is the dimension within which people have mental experiences. The only people who can be involved in a literary social interaction are the author, the characters, and the audience, and those three sets of people *are* involved – all three sets – always. Delineating the dynamics of that specific set of social interactions – dynamics that vary from author to author and book to book – is a fundamental and indispensable procedure in literary criticism. Darwinian literary critics who ignore this dimension of analysis might be Darwinians, but they are not literary critics, and even as Darwinians, they are missing a major part of the story.

Many Darwinian psychologists and anthropologists have been missing a major part of the larger human story – that whole part of the story that concerns itself with the evolution of the cognitive behavioral system: the fifth personality factor, "g," domain-general intelligence. They have told us a good deal about life in a supposedly stable and homogeneous EEA, but they have neglected to tell us much about the evolution and adaptive functions of the distinctively human mind. A number of Darwinian anthropologists and psychologists are now correcting that signal omission, and Darwinian literary critics should rejoice that the development of the whole field is now producing a model of human nature that converges with their needs and interests as literary critics. The benefits can be reciprocal. Darwinian psychologists and Darwinian anthropologists take human nature as their field of study. Literature can provide important information on that topic, and Darwinian literary critics can help them to gain access to that information. Practitioners on both sides will need to make some allowances for differences of idiom and method. If they make these allowances, they will benefit not just in the gain of needful information but also in a closer acquaintance with the skills and cognitive habits that constitute the characteristic strengths in each discipline.

Works Cited

Abrams, M. H. 1986. "Poetry, Theories Of." In *Princeton Encyclopedia of Poetic Terms*, edited by Alex Preminger et al., 203–14. Princeton: Princeton University Press.

Ahearn, Edward J. 1987. *Marx and Modern Fiction*. New Haven: Yale University Press.

Alcock, J. 2001. *Animal Behavior. An Evolutionary Approach*. 7th ed. Sunderland, Mass.: Sinauer.

Alexander, R. D. 1979. *Darwinism and Human Affairs*. Seattle: University of Washington Press.

Alexander, R. D. 1987. *The Biology of Moral Systems*. Hawthorne, New York: Aldine de Gruyter.

Alexander, R. D. 1989. "The Evolution of the Human Psyche." In *The Human Revolution: Behavioral and Biological Perspectives on the Origins of Modern Humans*, edited by P. Mellars and C. Stringer, 455–513. Princeton: Princeton University Press.

Alexander, R. D. 1989. "The Evolution of the Human Psyche." In *The Human Revolution: Behavioral and Biological Perspectives on the Origins of Modern Humans*, edited by P. Mellars and C. Stringer, 455–513. Princeton: Princeton University Press.

Alexander, R. D. 1990. "Epigenetic Rules and Darwinian Algorithms: The Adaptive Study of Learning and Development." *Ethology and Sociobiology* 11:241–303.

Armstrong, Nancy. 1981. "Inside Greimas's Square: Literary Characters and Cultural Constraints." In *The Sign in Music and Literature*, edited by Wendy Steiner, 52–66. Austin: University of Texas Press.

Armstrong, Nancy. 1987. *Desire and Domestic Fiction: A Political History of the Novel*. New York: Oxford University Press.

Armstrong, Isobel. 1990. Introd. to *Pride and Prejudice*, by Jane Austen. New York: Oxford University Press.

Atran, Scott. 1990. *Cognitive Foundations of Natural History: Towards an Anthropology of Science.* Cambridge: Cambridge University Press.

Auerbach, Nina. 1978. *Communities of Women: An Idea in Fiction.* Cambridge, Mass.: Harvard University Press.

Bailey, J. Michael. 1997. "Are Genetically Based Individual Differences Compatible with Species-wide Adaptations?" In *Uniting Psychology and Biology: Integrative Perspectives on Human Development,* edited by Nancy L. Segal, Glenn E. Weisfeld, and Carol C. Weisfeld, 81–100. Washington: American Psychological Association.

Bailey, J. Michael. 1998. "Can Behavior Genetics Contribute to Evolutionary Behavioral Science?" In *Handbook of Evolutionary Psychology: Ideas, Issues, Applications,* edited by Charles Crawford and Dennis L. Krebs, 211–33. Mahway, N.J.: Lawrence Erlbaum Associates.

Bailey, J. M., S. Gaulin, Y. Agyei, and B. Gladue. 1994. "Effects of Gender and Sexual Orientation on Evolutionarily Relevant Aspects of Human Mating Psychology." *Journal of Personality and Social Psychology* 66:1081–93.

Barash, D. P. 1997. "In Search of Behavioral Individuality." *Human Nature* 8:153–69.

Barkow, J. H. 1990. "Beyond the DP / DSS Controversy." *Ethology and Sociobiology* 11:341–51.

Barkow, J., L. Cosmides, and J. Tooby, eds. 1992. *The Adapted Mind.* Oxford: Oxford University Press.

Barrett, L., R. Dunbar, and J. Lycett. 2002. *Human Evolutionary Psychology.* Princeton, N.J.: Princeton University Press.

Barrow, John D. 1996. *The Artful Universe.* Oxford: Clarendon Press.

Belsey, Catherine. 2002. "Making Space: Perspective Vision and the Lacanian Real." *Textual Practice* 16:31–55.

Betzig, Laura L. 1986. *Despotism and Differential Reproduction: A Darwinian View of History.* Hawthorne, N.Y.: Aldine de Gruyter.

Betzig, Laura L. 1998. "Not Whether to Count Babies, but Which." In *Handbook of Evolutionary Psychology: Ideas, Issues, Applications,* edited by Charles Crawford and Dennis L. Krebs, 265–73. Mahway, N.J.: Lawrence Erlbaum Associates.

Bickerton, D. 1990. *Language and Species.* Chicago: University of Chicago Press.

Booth, Wayne C. 1996. "Distance and Point of View: An Essay in Classification." In *Essentials of the Theory of Fiction,* edited by Michael J. Hoffman and Patrick D. Murphy, 116–33. Durham, N.C.: Duke University Press.

Bouchard, Thomas J. 1994. "Genes, Environment, and Personality." *Science* 264:1700–1.

Bouchard, Thomas J. 1997. "The Genetics of Personality." In *Handbook of Psychiatric Genetics,* edited by Kenneth Blum and Ernest P. Noble, 267–90. Boca Raton, Fla.: CRC Press.

Boyd, Brian. 1998. "Jane, Meet Charles: Literature, Evolution, and Human Nature." *Philosophy and Literature* 22:1–30.

Boyd, Brian. 2001 "The Origin of Stories: Horton Hears a Who." *Philosophy and Literature* 25:197–214.

Bradley, A. C. 1929. *A Miscellany.* London: Macmillan.

Bridgeman, Bruce. 2003. *Psychology and Evolution: The Origins of Mind.* Thousand Oaks, Calif.: Sage.

Brown, D. E. 1991. *Human Universals.* Philadelphia: Temple University Press.

Brown, D. E. 2000. "Human Universals and Their Implications." In *Being Humans: Anthropological Universality and Particularity in Transdisciplinary Perspectives,* edited by N. Roughley, 156–74. New York: Walter de Gruyter.

Brownstein, Rachel M. 1988. "Jane Austen: Irony and Authority." *Women's Studies* 15:57–70.

Buss, D. M. 1989. "Sex Differences in Human Mate Preferences: Evolutionary Hypothesis Testing in 37 Cultures." *Behavioral and Brain Sciences* 12:1–49.

Buss, D. M. 1990. "Toward a Biologically Informed Psychology of Personality." *Journal of Personality* 58:1–16.

Buss, D. M. 1995. "Evolutionary Psychology: A New Paradigm for Psychological *Science.*" *Psychological Inquiry* 6:1–30.

Buss, D. M. 1999. *Evolutionary Psychology: The New Science of the Mind.* Boston: Allyn and Bacon.

Butler, Marilyn. 1975. *Jane Austen and the Ear of Ideas.* Oxford: Clarendon.

Carroll, J. 1995. *Evolution and Literary Theory.* Columbia: University of Missouri Press.

Chagnon, Napoleon. 1979. *Yanomamö. The Fierce People*. New York: Holt, Rinehart, and Winston.

Chagnon, Napoleon, and William Irons, eds. 1979. *Evolutionary Biology and Human Social Behavior: An Anthropological Perspective*. North Scituate, Mass.: Duxbury Press.

Chiappe, Dan. 2000. "Metaphor, Modularity, and the Evolution of Conceptual Integration." *Metaphor and Symbol* 15:137–58.

Chiappe, Dan, and Kevin MacDonald. Under submission. The Evolution of Domain-general Mechanisms in Intelligence and Learning.

Cooke, B. 1999. 'The Promise of a Biothematics." In *Sociobiology and the Arts*, edited by Jan Baptist Bedaux and Brett Cooke, 43–62. Amsterdam: Editions Rodopi.

Cooke, B. 1995 "Microplots: The Case of *Swan Lake*." *Human Nature* 6:183–96.

Cooke, B. 2002. *Human Nature in Utopia: Zamyatin's "We."* Evanston: Northwestern University Press.

Cosmides, L., and J. Tooby. 1989. "Evolutionary Psychology and the Generation of Culture, Case Study: A Computational Theory of Social Exchange," Pt 2 *Ethology and Sociobiology* 10:51–97.

Cosmides, L., and J. Tooby. 1994. "Origins of Domain Specificity: The Evolution of Functional Organization." In *Mapping the Mind: Domain Specificity in Cognition and Culture*, edited by L. Hirschfeld and S. A. Gelman, 85–116. Cambridge: Cambridge University Press.

Costa, P. T., and T. A. Widiger, eds. 2002. *Personality Disorders and the Five-Factor Model of Personality*. 2nd ed. Washington: American Psychological Association.

Crawford, Charles. 1998. "Environments and Adaptations: Then and Now." In *Handbook of Evolutionary Psychology: Ideas, Issues, Applications*, edited by Charles Crawford and Dennis L. Krebs, 275–302. Mahway, N.J.: Lawrence Erlbaum Associates.

Daly, M., and M. Wilson. 1988. *Homicide*. Hawthorne, N.Y.: Aldine.

Daly, M., and M. Wilson. 1990. "Is Parent-Offspring Conflict Sex-linked? Freudian and Darwinian Models." *Journal of Personality* 58:163–89.

Damasio, Antonio. 1994. *Descartes' Error: Emotion, Reason, and the Human Brain*. New York: G. P. Putnam.

Darwin, Charles. 1871. *The Descent of Man, and Selection in Relation to Sex*. Introd. by John Tyler Bonner and Robert M. May. Princeton: Princeton University Press, 1981.

Darwin, Charles. 1859. *On the Origin of Species by Means of Natural Selection*. Edited by Joseph Carroll. Peterborough, Ontario: Broadview, 2003.

Darwin, Charles. 1871a. *The Descent of Man, and Selection in Relation to Sex*. Introd. by John Tyler Bonner and Robert M. May. Princeton: Princeton University Press, 1981.

Darwin, Charles. 1871b. *The Descent of Man, and Selection in Relation to Sex*. London: Gibson Square, 2003.

Digman, J. M. 1990. "Personality Structure: Emergence of the Five-Factor Model." *Annual Review of Psychology* 41:417–40.

Dissanayake, E. 1988. *What Is Art For?* Seattle: University of Washington Press.

Dissanayake, E. 1995. "Chimera, Spandrel, or Adaptation: Conceptualizing Art in Human Evolution." *Human Nature* 6:99–117.

Dissanayake, E. 2000. *Art and Intimacy: How the Arts Began*. Seattle: University of Washington Press.

Dissanayake, E. 2003. "Art in Global Context: An Evolutionary/Functionalist Perspective for the Twenty-first Century." *International Journal of Anthropology* 18:245–58.

Duckworth, Alistair. 1971. *The Improvement of the Estate: A Study in Jane Austen's Novels*. Baltimore: Johns Hopkins University Press.

Eaves, L. J., H. J. Eysenck, and N. G. Martin. 1989. *Genes, Culture, and Personality: An Empirical Approach*. London: Harcourt.

Eibl-Eibesfeldt, I. 1989. *Human Ethology*. Hawthorne, N.Y.: Aldine de Gruyter.

Ekman, Paul. 2003. *Emotions Revealed: Recognizing Faces and Feelings to Improve Communication and Emotional Life*. New York: Henry Holt.

Ekman, Paul, and Richard J. Davidson, eds. 1994. *The Nature of Emotion: Fundamental Questions*. New York: Oxford University Press.

Eysenck, H. J. 1979. *The Structure and Measurement of Intelligence*. Berlin: Springer Verlag.

Eysenck, H. J. 1980. "The Biosocial Nature of Man." *Journal of Social and Biological Structures* 3:125–34.

Eysenck, H. J. 1995. *Genius: The Natural History of Creativity*. Cambridge: Cambridge University Press.

Eysenck, Hans J., and Michael W. Eysenck. 1985. *Personality and Individual Differences: A Natural Science Approach*. New York: Plenum.

Foley, Robert. 1996. "The Adaptive Legacy of Human Evolution: A Search for the Environment of Evolutionary Adaptedness." *Evolutionary Anthropology* 4:194–203.

Fraiman, Susan. 1989. "The Humiliation of Elizabeth Bennet." In *Refiguring the Father: New Feminist Readings of Patriarchy*, edited by Patricia Yaeger and Beth Kowaleski-Wallace, 168–87. Carbondale: Southern Illinois University Press.

Fromm, Harold. 2003. "The New Darwinism in the Humanities: Back to Nature Again." Pt. 2. *Hudson Review* 56:315–27.

Gaulin, Steven J. C., and Donald H. McBurney. 2001. *Psychology: An Evolutionary Approach*. Saddle River, N.J.: Prentice Hall.

Geary, D. 1998. *Male, Female: The Evolution of Human Sex Differences*. Washington, D.C.: American Psychological Association.

Geary, David C., and Kelly J. Huffman. 2002. "Brain and Cognitive Evolution Forms of Modularity and Functions of Mind." *Psychological Bulletin* 128:667–98.

Halliday, E. M. 1960. "Narrative Perspective in '*Pride and Prejudice*.'" *Nineteenth- Century Fiction* 15:65–71.

Handler, Richard, and Daniel Segal. 1990. *Jane Austen and the Fiction of Culture: An Essay on the Narration of Social Realities*. Tucson: University of Arizona Press.

Harding, D. W. 1940. "'Regulated Hatred': An Aspect in the Work of Jane Austen." *Scrutiny* 8:346–47, 351–54, 362.

Herrnstein, R. J., and C. Murray. 1994. *The Bell Curve: Intelligence and Class Structure in American Life*. New York: Free Press.

Irons, William. 1979. "Cultural and Biological Success." In *Evolutionary Biology and Human Social Behavior: An Anthropological Perspective*, edited by Napoleon A. Chagnon and William Irons, 257–72. North Scituate, Mass.: Duxbury Press.

Irons, William. 1990. "Let's Make Our Perspective Broader Rather than Narrower: A Comment on Turke's 'Which Humans Behave Adaptively, and What Does It Matter?' " *Ethology and Sociobiology* 11:361–74.

Irons, William. 1998. "Adaptively Relevant Environments Versus the Environment of Evolutionary Adaptedness." *Evolutionary Anthropology* 6:194–204.

Jensen, Arthur R. 1998. *The G Factor: The Science of Mental Ability*. Westport, Conn.: Praeger.

Jobling, Ian. 2001a. "The Psychological Foundations of the Hero-Ogre Story: A Cross-Cultural Study." *Human Nature* 12:247–72.

Jobling, Ian. 2001b. "Personal Justice and Homicide in Scott's Ivanhoe: An Evolutionary Psychological Perspective." *Interdisciplinary Literary Studies* 2:29–43.

Johnson, Claudia L. 1988. *Jane Austen: Women, Politics, and the Novel*. Chicago: University of Chicago Press.

Langland, Elizabeth. 1984. *Society in the Novel*. Chapel Hill: University of North Carolina Press.

Leaska, Mitchell A. 1996. "The Concept of Point of View." In *Essentials of the Theory of Fiction*, edited by Michael J. Hoffman and Patrick D. Murphy, 158–71. Durham, N.C.: Duke University Press.

LeDoux, Joseph. 1996. *The Emotional Brain: The Mysterious Underpinnings of Emotional Life*. New York: Simon and Schuster.

Lewes, George Henry. 1859. "The Novels of Jane Austen." *Blackwood's Magazine* 86:99–113.

Lewis, Michael, and Jeannette M. Haviland, eds. 2000. *Handbook of Emotions*. 2nd ed. New York: Guilford Press.

Litvak, Joseph. 1992. "Delicacy and Disgust, Mourning and Melancholia, Privilege and Perversity: '*Pride and Prejudice*.'" *Qui Parle* 6:35–51.

Litz, A. Walton. 1965. *Jane Austen: A Study of Her Artistic Development*. New York: Oxford University Press.

Love, Glen. 2003. *Practical Ecocriticism: Literature, Biology, and the Environment*. Charlottesville: University of Virginia Press.

Low, Bobbi S. 1998. "The Evolution of Human Life Histories." In *Handbook of Evolutionary Psychology: Ideas, Issues, Applications*, edited by Charles Crawford and Dennis L. Krebs, 131–61. Mahway, N.J.: Lawrence Erlbaum Associates.

Low, Bobbi S. 2000. *Why Sex Matters: A Darwinian Look at Human Behavior*. Princeton: Princeton University Press.

MacDonald, Kevin. 1990. "A Perspective on Darwinian Psychology: The Importance of Domain-General Mechanisms, Plasticity, and Individual Differences." *Ethology and Sociobiology* 12:449–80.

MacDonald, Kevin. 1995a. "The Establishment and Maintenance of Socially Imposed Monogamy in Western Europe." *Politics and the Life Sciences* 14:3–46.

MacDonald, Kevin. 1995b. "Evolution, the Five-Factor Model, and Levels of Personality." *Journal of Personality* 63:525–67.

MacDonald, Kevin. 1997. "Life History Theory and Human Reproductive Behavior: Environmental / Contextual Influences and Heritable Variation." *Human Behavior* 8:327–59.

MacDonald, Kevin. 1998a. "Evolution and Development." In *The Social Child*, edited by Anne Campbell and Steven Muncer, 21–49. Hove, East Sussex: Psychology Press.

MacDonald, Kevin. 1998b. "Evolution, Culture, and the Five-Factor Model." *Journal of Cross-Cultural Psychology* 29:119–49.

McCrae, Robert R., ed. 1992. "The Five-Factor Model: Issues and Applications." *Journal of Personality Special Issue*, 60.

McGuire, Michael, and Alfonso Troisi. 1998. *Darwinian Psychiatry*. New York: Oxford University Press.

Miller, Geoffrey. 1998. "How Mate Choice Shaped Human Nature: A Review of Sexual Selection and Human Evolution." In *Handbook of Evolutionary Psychology: Ideas, Issues, and Applications*, edited by Charles Crawford and Dennis Krebs, 87–129. London: Lawrence Erlbaum Associates.

Miller, Geoffrey. 2000a. "Evolution of Human Music Through Sexual Selection." In *The Origins of Music*, edited by S. Brown, B. Merker, and N. L. Wallin, 329–60. Cambridge, Mass.: Bradford/MIT Press.

Miller, Geoffrey. 2000b. *The Mating Mind: How Sexual Choice Shaped the Evolution of Human Nature*. New York: Doubleday.

Mithen, Steven J. 1990. *Thoughtful Foragers: A Study of Prehistoric Decision Making*. Cambridge: Cambridge University Press.

Mithen, Steven J. 1996. *The Prehistory of the Mind: A Search for the Origins of Art, Religion and Science*. London: Thames and Hudson.

Mithen, Steven J. 2001. "The Evolution of Imagination: An Archaeological Perspective." *Substance* 30:28–54.

Morgan, Susan. 1980. *In the Meantime: Character and Perception in Jane Austen's Fiction*. Chicago: University of Chicago Press.

Mudrick, Marvin. 1952. *Jane Austen: Irony as Defense and Discovery*. Princeton: Princeton University Press.

Nesse, Margaret. 1995. Guinevere's Choice. *Human Nature* 6:145–63.

Newman, Karen. 1983. "Can This Marriage Be Saved: Jane Austen Makes Sense of an Ending." *Journal of English Literary History* 50:693–708.

Newton, Judith Lowder. 1981. *Women, Power, and Subversion: Social Strategies in British Fiction, 1774–1860*. Athens: University of Georgia Press.

Nordlund, Marcus. 2002. "Consilient Literary Interpretation." *Philosophy and Literature* 26:312–33.

Palmer, Jack A., and Linda K. Palmer. 2002. *Evolutionary Psychology: The Ultimate Origins of Human Behavior*. Boston: Allyn and Bacon.

Panksepp, Jaak. 1998. *Affective Neuroscience: The Foundations of Human and Animal Emotions*. New York: Oxford University Press.

Pervin, Lawrence. 1990. "A Brief History of Modern Personality Theory." In *Handbook of Personality: Theory and Research*, edited by Lawrence A. Pervin, 3–18. New York: Guilford Press.

Pervin, Lawrence A., and Oliver P. John, eds. 1999. *Handbook of Personality: Theory and Research*. 2nd ed. New York: Guilford Press.

Phelan, James. 1989. *Reading People, Reading Plots: Characters, Progression, and the Interpretation of Narrative*. Chicago: University of Chicago Press.

Pinker, Steven. 1994. *The Language Instinct: How the Mind Creates Language*. New York: William Morrow.

Pinker, Steven. 1995. "Language Is a Human Instinct." In *The Third Culture: Scientists on the Edge*, edited by John Brockman, 223–38. New York: Simon and Schuster.

Pinker, Steven. 1997. *How the Mind Works*. New York: Norton.

Pinker, Steven. 2002. *The Blank Slate: The Modern Denial of Human Nature*. New York: Viking.

Poovey, Mary. 1984. *The Proper Lady and the Woman Writer: Ideology as Style in the Works of Mary Wollstonecraft, Mary Shelley, and Jane Austen*. Chicago: University of Chicago Press.

Potts, Richard. 1998. "Variability Selection in Hominid Evolution." *Evolutionary Anthropology* 7:81–96.

Richerson, Peter J., and Robert Boyd. 2000. "Climate, Culture, and the Evolution of Cognition." In *The Evolution of Cognition*, edited by Cecilia Heyes and Ludwig Huber, 329–46. Cambridge, Mass.: MIT Press.

Ridley, Matt. 1999. *Genome: Autobiography of a Species in 23 Chapters*. New York: HarperCollins.

Rossano, Matthew J. 2003. *Evolutionary Psychology: The Science of Human Behavior and Evolution*. Hoboken, N.J.: John Wiley and Sons.

Rushton, J. Philippe. 1995. *Race, Evolution, and Behavior: A Life History Perspective*. New Brunswick, N.J.: Transaction.

Scalise Sugiyama, Michelle. 1996. On the Origins of Narrative: Storyteller Bias as a Fitness-Enhancing Strategy." *Human Nature* 7:403–25.

Scalise Sugiyama, Michelle. 2001a. "Narrative Theory and Function: Why Evolution Matters." *Philosophy and Literature* 25:233–54.

Scalise Sugiyama, Michelle. 2001b. "New Science, Old Myth: An Evolutionary Critique of the Oedipal Paradigm." *Mosaic* 34:121–36.

Segal, L. 1997. "Twin Research Perspective on Human Development." In *Uniting Psychology and Biology: Integrative Perspectives on Human Development*, edited by Nancy L. Segal, Glenn E. Weisfeld, and Carol C. Weisfeld, 145–73. Washington: American Psychological Association.

Segal, L. 1999. *Entwined Lives: Twins and What They Tell Us about Human Behavior*. New York: Dutton.

Segal, Nancy L., and Kevin B. MacDonald. 1998. "Behavioral Genetics and Evolutionary Psychology: Unified Perspective on Personality Research." *Human Biology* 70:159–84.

Seligman, Daniel. 1992. *A Question of Intelligence: The IQ Debate in America*. New York: Carol.

Smith, Johanna M. 1993. "'I Am a Gentleman's Daughter': A Marxist-Feminist Reading of *Pride and Prejudice*." In *Approaches to Teaching Austen's "Pride and Prejudice,"* edited by Marcia McClintock Folsom, 67–73. New York: Modern Language Association of America.

Smith, Johanna M. 2000. "The Oppositional Reader and *Pride and Prejudice*." In *A Companion to Jane Austen Studies*, edited by Laura Cooner Lambdin and Robert Thomas Lambdin, 27–40. Westport, Conn.: Greenwood Press.

Storey, Robert. 1996. *Mimesis and the Human Animal: On the Biogenetic Foundations of Literary Representation*. Evanston, Ill.: Northwestern University Press.

Sugiyama, Lawrence. 2004. "Illness, Injury, and Disability among Shiwiar Forager- Horticulturalists: Implications of Health Risk Buffering for the Evolution of Human Life History." *American Journal of Physical Anthropology* 123:371–89.

Symons, Donald. 1979. *The Evolution of Human Sexuality*. Oxford: Oxford University Press.

Symons, Donald. 1989. "A Critique of Darwinian Anthropology." *Ethology and Sociobiology* 10:131–44.

Symons, Donald. 1992. "On the Use and Misuse of Darwinism in the Study of Human Behavior." In *The Adapted Mind: Evolutionary Psychology and the Generation of Culture*, edited by Jerome Barkow, Leda Cosmides, and John Tooby, 137–62. New York: Oxford University Press.

Tanner, Tony. 1986. *Jane Austen*. Cambridge, Mass.: Harvard University Press.

Tooby, J., and L. Cosmides. 1989. "Evolutionary Psychology and the Generation of Culture, Part I: Theoretical Considerations." *Ethology and Sociobiology* 10:29–49.

Tooby, J., and L. Cosmides. 1992. "The Psychological Foundations of Culture." In *The Adapted Mind, Evolutionary Psychology and the Generation of Culture*, edited by Jerome Barkow, Leda Cosmides, and John Tooby, 19–136. New York: Oxford University Press.

Trivers, Robert S. 1972. "Parental Investment and Sexual Selection." In *Sexual Selection and the Descent of Man 1871–1971*, edited by Bernard G. Campbell, 136–79. Chicago: Aldine.

Trivers, Robert S. 1985. *Social Evolution*. Menlo Park: Benjamin/Cummings.

Turke, Paul W. 1990. "Which Humans Behave Adaptively, and Why Does It Matter?" *Ethology and Sociobiology* 11:305–39.

Turner, F. 1992. *Natural Classicism: Essays on Literature and Science*. Charlottesville: University of Virginia Press.

Turner, Mark. 1996. *The Literary Mind*. New York: Oxford University Press.

Van Ghent, Dorothy. 1953. *The English Novel: Form and Function*. New York: Holt, Rinehart, Winston.

Wiggins, Jerry S., ed. 1996. *The Five-Factor Model of Personality: Theoretical Perspectives*. New York: Guilford Press.

Wilson, D. S. 1975. "A Theory of Group Selection." *Proceedings of the National Academy of Sciences* 72:143–46.

Wilson, D. S. 1994. "Adaptive Genetic Variation and Human Evolutionary Psychology." *Ethology and Sociobiology* 15:219–35.

Wilson, D. S. 1999. "Tasty Slice – but Where Is the Rest of the Pie?" *Evolution and Human Behavior* 20:279–87.

Wilson, E. O. 1998. *Consilience: The Unity of Knowledge*. New York: Knopf.

Woolf, Virginia. 1925. *The Common Reader: First Series*. New York: Harcourt, Brace, and World, 1953.

Wylie, Judith. 2000. "Dancing in Chains: Feminist Satire in Pride and Prejudice." *Persuasions: Journal of the Jane Austen Society of North America* 22:62–69.

CHAPTER 6

Literary Brains: Neuroscience, Criticism, and Theory

Patrick Colm Hogan

Patrick Colm Hogan teaches in the English Department at the University of Connecticut. His books include *The Politics of Interpretation* (1990), *On Interpretation* (1996, 2008), *Cognitive Science, Literature, and the Arts* (2003), and *The Mind and Its Stories* (2003).

In recent years, there has been growing interest in neuroscientific approaches to literary and other forms of humanistic study. To this point, concrete work in neurohumanities has been limited. Thus, Paul Armstrong chides literary researchers – including cognitive literary critics – for their lack of "serious engagement with neurobiology" (xiii). Much of the work that has been done falls into the broad category of what we might call "correlational criticism," which is often the initial phase of a new theoretical approach to literary analysis. In correlational criticism, the critic takes some theory – whether deconstruction or neuroscience – and finds parallels for its elements and principles in literature (e.g., Proust's treatment of memory might be seen as anticipating that of some neuroscientists, as in Lehrer's widely read book). Nonetheless, it seems clear that there are many promising research programs opening up in neurohumanities that go well beyond correlational criticism. These will undoubtedly develop much further in the coming years. The following essay aims to introduce some of these openings.

Before going on to discuss the relations between neuroscience and the humanities, however, we need to be familiar with some basic principles of neuroscience. Thus, the first section of the following essay sets out to orient readers with respect to the anatomy and function of the human brain. Such an orientation is necessarily highly selective. I have chosen those aspects of neuroanatomy and cerebral function that bear particularly on the following discussions of literature. The second section addresses specific areas of literary study that currently are benefiting from neuroscience or that promise to do so,

Original publication details: Patrick Colm Hogan, "Literary Brains: Neuroscience, Criticism, and Theory" from *Literature Compass* 11.4. John Wiley & Sons, 2014. Reproduced with permission from John Wiley & Sons.

illustrating some of these points with examples from Shakespeare. The final section addresses the practical issue of the extent to which literary critics should or should not try to become neuroscientists of literature.

Some Notes on the Brain

The brain is part of the central nervous system. In a preliminary way, it may be thought of as the organ that integrates experience and produces action. There are different ways of understanding brain organization. As the name suggests, functional neuroanatomy isolates brain regions according to what they do (their functions). Simplifying a great deal, we may first separate "sub-neocortical" (or, more briefly, "subcortical") from "neocortical" areas. The "neocortex" is the outermost region of the brain and the most recently developed in evolution. Roughly speaking, the subcortex has motivational and homeostatic functions (e.g., governing thirst). Thus, emotions such as anger are largely a function of subcortical regions. The neocortex is responsible for perception and motion, as well as the integration of information from different sense modalities. The isolation of emotional and information processing functions has fairly obvious importance for literature and the arts. (On the less evident issue of movement and aesthetic response, the reader may wish to consult Holland.)

Both the subcortex and neocortex may be further divided, first according to physical structure. Physical divisions are often roughly correlated with functional divisions; however, they are not identical. The neocortex, for example, is divided into four "lobes" – occipital (at the back), parietal (at the top), temporal (near the temples), and frontal (at the front). Visual cortex is in the occipital lobe; auditory cortex is temporal; somatosensory cortex is parietal; motor cortex is frontal.

Not all types of brain function are as intuitively obvious as those of sensory modalities. For example, there appear to be two distinct systems for spatial mapping. One system is "objective," bearing on objects' relations to one another. This is closely connected with the hippocampus (see Clark, Boutros, and Mendez 43), a subcortical structure that is very important for episodic (or autobiographical) memory. The other system is "egocentric." It organizes space in relation to the subjective situation of the perceiver, stressing particularly "peripersonal" space, the space of one's immediate vicinity (see Iacoboni 16). This may be identified as largely parietal (see Clark, Boutros, and Mendez 43; on some complications of the distributed system of peripersonal space in humans, see Schicke and citations). As we will see, recognizing these two space systems may have significant consequences for our understanding of space in literary imagination.

Some areas of the brain have what might be called "meta-functions." For example, the anterior (or forward) section of one part of the brain – called "cingulate cortex" – in effect monitors other parts of the brain for task contradictions (see Carter and colleagues). Thus, it becomes active when there is some conflict. This, in turn, motivates some attempt to resolve the conflict. One suggestion of this may be that contradictory activities or orientations (e.g., wanting to be a fashion model and wanting to eat lots of cake) must be simultaneously active in order to provoke a motivation to do something about this contradiction. In some cases, conflicts arise due to simultaneous processing of the same input in different areas of the brain. For example, sensory experiences are sent simultaneously to subcortical and neocortical areas (see LeDoux *Emotional*, 161–165). Emotional processing of the former is parallel with, though faster than, the fuller perceptual processing of the latter. Thus, the former may produce a quick fear response, while the latter determines whether or not the fear was justified ("Did I just see a snake or was it only a stick?"). In connection with this sort of contradiction, the neocortical processing may lead to *modulation* of the subcortical response (e.g., reduction of initial fear). Task contradictions and complex interactions between neocortical and subcortical responses are pervasive in literary response. Understanding them should further our understanding of literary reception.

Other divisions include that between the hemispheres. The two hemispheres of the brain are most often closely integrated, linked as they are by the *corpus callosum*. However, when the corpus callosum is severed, the hemispheres may operate separately. Even when integrated, there are some broad differences between them. Though these are usually overstated in popular accounts, they can be significant in particular areas. Rather than thinking of the right hemisphere as doing one sort of thing and the left hemisphere as doing something else, it is more productive and more accurate to think of the right hemisphere as tending to do one sort of thing in a particular functional domain and the left hemisphere as tending to do something partially different in that functional domain. For example, there are hemispheric differences in just what aspects of language are processed and how they are processed. Among other things, the right hemisphere activates a broader range of contextually irrelevant meanings for a given discourse (see Chiarello 145). In consequence, jokes that rely on puns involve right hemisphere processing such that people with right hemisphere brain damage in relevant areas may be inhibited in their ability to respond to jokes relying on puns (see Chiarello and Beeman 248). As the reference to puns suggests, at least some aspects of our verbal processing of literature rely on hemispheric differences and may be better understood in relation to those differences.

These large physical and functional regions are, of course, not solid masses. Rather, at a more fine-grained level of description, the brain comprises networks of interconnected cells. The cells themselves have their own specializations. For example, cells in visual cortex are sensitive to particular visual features, such that one cell will be activated for one type of feature (e.g., a line with a horizontal orientation), whereas another cell will be activated for another type of feature (e.g., a line with a vertical orientation). The connections between cells may be either excitatory or inhibitory. In a particular "circuit," a series of cells will activate in sequence, often inhibiting related cells that may, so to speak, "compete" with the activated cells. This simple point about the duality of neuronal operation – the fact that there are both excitatory and inhibitory connections – may have significant consequences for our conception of mental operation in literary creation, representation, and response.

Circuit activation is enabled by neurochemistry. Specifically, circuits operate by one cell communicating activation to the next cell in the circuit. That activation is generally a chemical process, and it requires neurochemical "transmitters" to proceed. Different neurochemicals have excitatory or inhibitory effects on different systems. For example, what is called the "reward system" operates through the neurotransmitter dopamine. While there are, of course, neuroanatomical components to the reward system, it is perhaps better characterized through neurochemical functionality. In phenomenological terms, the function of the "dopaminergic" reward system is the anticipatory pursuit of pleasure (see chapter three of Panksepp and Biven; Panksepp and Biven refer to this as the "SEEKING" system, rather than the "reward system"), or perhaps the anticipatory pursuit of emotional need satisfaction. The reward system is a key component of aesthetic response.

In cognitive science generally, it is common to distinguish structures, processes, and contents. Structures are the large categories or types of mental function. Processes are the operations that occur within these structures. Contents are the items on which processes operate. Thus, "memory" would be a structure (or, rather, several structures; for an overview of current understandings of memory, see Baddeley, Eysenck, and Anderson). "Storage" and "retrieval" (commitment to memory and recollection from memory) would be processes of memory. Finally, specific images or other representations (e.g., regarding what you had for lunch today) would be the contents.

In speaking of these components of *mental* architecture, we commonly have certain presuppositions about their nature. Those presuppositions may be challenged by neuroscientific research. For example, our knowledge of the way neural circuits operate affects our understanding of memory contents. Among other things, the precise configuration of a circuit may change over time; it may be affected by other circuits through activation or inhibition. Along with other research, this suggests that memory contents are not firmly fixed pictures of the past but much more malleable or less stable complexes of activation and inhibition (see Panksepp and Biven 220), changing in different circumstances. The malleable and interactive nature of memory has consequences for many aspects of literature – from creation, to representation, to response.

Moreover, research indicates that, contrary to what one might anticipate, some processes and structures, such as various emotion systems, are not fixed entirely by genetic determinants. Rather, they are significantly shaped by experience, if usually within certain limits. More precisely, there are genetic, developmental, and later, more diffuse experiential effects on structures and processes. The developmental effects are often a function of "critical period" events. These are events that occur at a pivotal point in a system's development, usually in early childhood. For example, the attachment system (the system of emotional bonding, first of all between parents and small children) is shaped by both innate propensities and by early childhood experiences. The interaction of genetics and critical period events leads to a limited range of possible outcomes – prominently differences in the degree to which one feels secure in attachment relations and the degree to which one's attachment relations are pervaded by distrust. These differences carry over into later life (see Waters, Weinfield, and Hamilton). For literary critics, it may be particularly noteworthy that critical period experiences are not wholly idiosyncratic but may manifest cultural or historical patterns.

At a methodological level, it is important to note that there are two distinct orientations in neuroscience today and cognitive science more generally. The first is the "classical" approach, which stresses abstraction and rules or recurrent patterns. The second, referred to as "situated cognition," stresses the ongoing processes of interaction with the world. Simplifying, we might say that the former focuses on constancy, while the latter emphasizes contingency and change. For example, in semantics, the former school would stress the storage of meanings in relatively stable concepts, whereas the situated approach would focus on the ways in which meanings undergo continual alterations in context (for the different case of perception, see O'Callaghan 83–86). Though often presented as alternative theories, it is perhaps best to see these as simply different interests. Classic cognitive science is like physics, interested in isolating general principles. Situated cognition is like engineering, interested in practical implementation. Both are valuable but in different ways and in different contexts. Theories of situated cognition may be particularly valuable in studying alterations of literary response, whether historical and cultural, or biographical, as a given reader's emotional reactions to literary works and cognitive understandings of those works change in the course of time.

Finally, it is important to say something about means of studying the brain. Until recent decades, the main method was "lesion study." When the brain is damaged, one may see what functions are impaired or altered. In animals, this is done systematically, with lesions induced surgically. In humans, the process is necessarily more haphazard. Someone would have a stroke or suffer some other brain injury, but then partially recover. Researchers would observe the cognitive or other alterations then correlate those alterations with neural damage identified during an autopsy after the person has died. These methods obviously left a great deal to be desired. Setting aside ethical issues, the animal studies were, of course, on nonhuman animals. In consequence, their extension to humans was often problematic. The study of stroke or brain injury did treat humans, but with messy lesions, rarely neatly confined to a single area. (On the issue of brain damage and its relation to artistic production, see for example Zaidel.)

The recent explosion of neuroscience – including the use of empirical neuroscience in the study of art and literature – is due largely to the development of non-invasive brain scanning methods. There are different methods available (for an overview, see Bookheimer). We might briefly consider two: electroencephalography (EEG) and functional magnetic resonance imaging (fMRI). EEGs measure electrical impulses. They are valuable for their fine temporal resolution (i.e., they can measure the timing of electrical changes in the brain quite well). However, they are problematic on spatial resolution (i.e., it is difficult to differentiate precise regions of change). In contrast, fMRI measures blood oxygen levels in parts of the brain. For the neocortex, it has good spatial resolution (i.e., it isolates regions of change well). However, it is less good at subcortical measures (see Panksepp and Biven 29–30), and its temporal resolution is not very fine. Other methods, such as the manipulation of neurochemicals in the brain, have other problems (e.g., localizing the effects of the neurochemicals or even getting accurate measurements of their presence in the brain [see, for example, Heinrichs 519]).

In short, while newer methods solve some problems, they commonly have their own drawbacks. Moreover, even when technical problems are resolved, it is not always clear what the results of scans mean. Consider a result from social neuroscience. Faced with an image of an out-group member (e.g., someone from another racial group), a test subject will have activation in occipital cortex, much as he or she has in seeing an image of an in-group member. However, there might also be increased activation in the insula (see Fiske, Harris, and Cuddy). What does this mean? In addition, there might be unusually low activation in medial prefrontal cortex (see Gazzaniga 204). What does that mean? The results of brain scans are not simply self-evident. They require interpretation, and the interpretation is never certain. In these cases, convergent evidence from other sources indicates that the first case is probably a response of disgust to the out-group member, and the second case is probably a lack of ordinary response to another mind. These are plausible and well-supported interpretations, but they are interpretations nonetheless, not direct observations.

The Goals of Literary Criticism and Theory and Their Relation to Neuroscience

It may seem that everyone is so fully aware of the goals of literary study that there is no point in mentioning them. However, students of literature often assume that the purpose of literary criticism and theory is simply to produce new readings of works. Things are, in fact, more complex. Clearly, interpretation is a central part of what we do in literary study. But it is not all we do. We might isolate four main purposes of literary theory and criticism: (i) aesthetic evaluation of works and the establishment of principles for such evaluation; (ii) ethical and political evaluation of works and the establishment of principles for such evaluation; (iii) isolation of broad patterns across works and explanation of those patterns; and (iv) interpretation of particular works and the establishment of principles for such interpretation.

Historically, aesthetic evaluation was perhaps the most important task on this list, though it has suffered neglect in recent years. While neuroscience has little to tell us about what the norms should be in aesthetics, it can tell us a good deal about what our tacit norms actually are. Indeed, aesthetic preference is one of the most advanced fields in neurohumanities, with research indicating that aesthetic pleasure involves both cognitive and affective components. Cognitive factors include the isolation of non-habitual patterns and approximation to category-defined prototypes or, roughly, average cases (e.g., the most beautiful face is the most average face [Langlois and Roggman]). Affective components include the reward system and perhaps the attachment system (for an overview of this research, see Hogan "Literary Aesthetics"). These findings are preliminary and clearly require elaboration and clarification. Nonetheless, they indicate that neurohumanities study in aesthetics has already developed a valuable research program. It is worth noting that this research program not only treats reception but production as well (see, for example, Zeki and Turner on creativity).

In recent decades, ethical and political evaluations have been more prominent in mainstream literary study. Literary critics and theorists are deeply concerned with the ethico-political motivations and impact of literary works, as well as the ethical and political themes developed in the works themselves. Social neuroscience is the area of research most obviously relevant to this topic. Social neuroscience, and related fields such as social psychology, may contribute to ethical and political literary study in at least two ways. First, they may alter our understanding of familiar ethical and political concepts. Second, they may introduce new concepts that alter our analyses.

Consider, for example, racism. Social neuroscience treats racism extensively. However, the neuroscientific concept of racism is somewhat different from our ordinary language notion. At a general, taxonomic level, it categorizes racism as a form of in-group/out-group definition, a broad psychological tendency that entails a range of cognitive biases and motivational preferences (for an overview of identity group definition and its consequences, see Duckitt). Second, at an operational level, it treats racism as at least in part an emotional response to individuals that need not in any way involve self-conscious, cognitive generalizations. Putting these two points together, it is perfectly possible – indeed, it is probably quite common – for a White person to have insular activation in response to a Black person and to treat him or her in a cognitively and motivationally biased way (e.g., preferring to see some White person win a particular competition) without having self-conscious beliefs or attitudes regarding Black people in general. The point has consequences for literary response to characters, to authors (thus, to aesthetic evaluation and canonization), to the reception of criticism, and other matters. Of course, racism is not the only ethical or political topic that may benefit from social neuroscience. It is simply one of many possible examples of a research program in this field. (For examples of social neuroscience and social psychology used to treat ethical and political literary analysis, see for example Aldama, Bracher, and Weik von Mossner.)

The isolation and explanation of patterns (purpose number three in the preceding list) has already made an appearance in both of the preceding categories (aesthetic and ethico-political evaluation). This is because pattern isolation and explanation are key features of neuroscience and cognitive and affective science more broadly. Indeed, one might argue that these are the most important contributions of neuroscience to literary study. This does not necessarily mean that the phenomena being explained need to have been previously unnoticed. Neuroscience may serve to explain patterns that were already familiar, but not well accounted for. For example, Hans Robert Jauss recognized that it is important for aesthetic response that a work be novel, that it deviate some from expectations, but that it not deviate too severely. Neuroscientific research on aesthetic response does not deny or radically alter this observation. Rather, it begins to explain it. For evolutionary reasons, we experience reward system activation with pattern isolation (see Vuust and Kringelbach 256 and 266, treating reward and "anticipation/prediction"). However, also for evolutionary reasons, neural activation in response to stimuli declines as experiences are repeated, becoming predictable or expected (see, for example, LeDoux *Synaptic*, 138). Moreover, the pursuit of pattern recognition without success is likely to give rise to aversive feelings, perhaps through anterior cingulate cortex activation. The interaction of these various factors predicts the phenomenon isolated by Jauss – preference for moderately novel but isolable patterns. This is not to say that neuroscientific research can in no way alter or extend Jauss's observations. To the contrary, it may further the analysis Jauss began. For example, we would expect the precise emotion systems involved and the modulation of those systems by neocortex to introduce variants and complications. Thus, high authorial reputation may lead readers to engage in processes that alter an initially negative response – for task contradiction reasons, thus in specific contexts where the different tasks (e.g., responding to the work and conforming to prestige standards) are simultaneously active.

Someone might reasonably object here that a neuroscientific account of Jauss's "aesthetic distance" (25) is not and cannot be a full explanation. It predicts only the general pattern not the details. It does not tell us why a particular author has been more or less appreciated at particular times and places. This is a perfectly reasonable comment. There are two things to say in response. First, this is where situated cognition enters. The preceding account is "classical" in the sense that it bears on recurring features of cognitive operation. The question of specific response moves us, so to speak, from physics to engineering. Writers in situated cognition stress three features of being situated: cognition is embedded, embodied, and distributed (see Robbins and Aydede). To say that cognition is embedded is to say that it is always involved with ongoing activities that are particular and contextualized. To say that it is embodied is to say that it is physically located and active, specifically active through the body. To say that it is distributed is to say that it includes interaction with a range of other people, with their particular embodiment and embodiment. Clearly, any attempt at accounting for the broad social reception of a work would need to take up not only the abstract issues but also the situated cognition. (For literary study stressing embodiment and cognition, see, for example, Wehrs; for distributed cognition and literature, see Tribble.)

This brings us to the second point raised by a neuroscientific account of Jaussian aesthetic distance. A neuroscientific account cannot explain everything about any cultural phenomenon, literary or otherwise. Even an analysis in terms of situated cognition needs to take up historical, cultural, or biographical elements, the "contents" and even the shaping, critical period experiences that are not simply given in neuroscientific analysis. For example, shifting from audience reception to authorial production, no amount of fMRI scanning would tell us about the crucial early experiences of Shakespeare that contributed to his theatrical imagination. (This would be true even if Shakespeare were around and available for an fMRI scan.) Rather, these early experiences can only be inferred through cultural and biographical study, as, for example, that undertaken by Greenblatt.

At the same time, the explanations of historians and biographers themselves seem incomplete without general explanatory principles, such as those provided by neuroscience in combination with related research and theory. For example, Greenblatt stresses Shakespeare's "dream of restoration" (see particularly 81–86) in various forms, including the reunion of separated families. Greenblatt connects restoration with painful experiences in Shakespeare's own life, experiences that give Shakespeare's works "the touch of the real" (13), in Greenblatt's phrase. Greenblatt's analysis is clearly important here. However, it is just as clearly incomplete. The touch of the real is likely to reach viewers only if there is some sort of congruence with their own sense of the real. This is one reason why it is important to recognize other patterns here, patterns that go beyond Shakespeare – for example, cross-cultural patterns in genre. One of these is the genre of parent/child separation and reunion (see Hogan *Affective*, 199–209). That genre is itself explained primarily by the neural system of attachment. Whatever one's degree of attachment security or insecurity, childhood development involves some critical period experiences of separation and reunion with caregivers. Those experiences are crucial to one's later emotional engagements with love, anxiety, and grief. (See chapter nine of Panksepp and Biven on the relation of anxiety and grief to attachment; there are different varieties of anxiety and not all are, as one might initially think, a function of the fear system [see 339–341].) Put differently, if we want to explain Shakespeare's success in family separation and reunion stories, such as *The Comedy of Errors* or *King Lear*, we need to understand the particularities of Shakespeare's experiences – for example, his own separation from his wife and children in coming to Stratford – and perhaps broad patterns in 16th century English childrearing practices. But we also need to understand the more general patterns that enable Shakespeare's experiences to resonate with those of his viewers – not only in his own time and place but in ours as well. Those patterns include both the literary genre and the (neural) emotion system that largely accounts for the genre. The recognition of the importance of interweaving cognitive and historical materials has led to the development of "cognitive historicism," one of the most prominent forms of literary study drawing on neuroscience (see, for example, Richardson and Stiles).

Finally, there is literary interpretation, the main focus of most efforts by students and professors of literature. The most obvious way of expanding interpretation is by altering the sorts of themes one may isolate in interpretation. For example, Christianity brings certain possible meanings to literary interpretation – a particular character may represent Jesus; an event may suggest resurrection. We find the same thing with psychoanalysis, where the interaction of three characters may point toward an Oedipal scenario. This "thematic innovation" is to some extent found in neuroscientific literary study as well. For example, simply by giving a non-intuitive analysis of racism, social neuroscience alters what we are likely to find in interpreting literary works. It introduces such themes as disgust-related dehumanization (where disgust limits medial prefrontal cortical response to human targets). We see this, for example, in extreme forms of misogyny and related violence. To take a literary case, it is presumably not accidental that Othello thinks of Desdemona in terms of "the slime / That sticks on filthy deeds" (V.ii.151–152) and "a cistern for foul toads" (IV.ii.61). His murder is enabled – and rendered more intuitively plausible for the audience's tacit simulation – as much by disgust as by anger, perhaps particularly disgust at female sexuality.

No less importantly, alterations in interpretation may result from how we select and organize textual information. Even such a simple matter as recognizing two spatial mapping systems may lead us to see different features of a text, thus select different phrases or scenes for interpretation. For instance, in *King Lear*, there is a strange disjunction in the forms of space implied in Lear's reunion with Cordelia. Broadly speaking, we may link the parietal system with a sense of intimacy, for it is the space of possible connectedness, of touching and being touched. The hippocampal system, in contrast, is objective and not intimate, not a matter of touching. In the context of a reunion, one would expect attachment bonds to highlight the parietal system. We find that with Cordelia. But something is amiss with Lear. The doctor asks Cordelia to "draw near" (IV.vii.23; here and below, citations of *King Lear* refer to the Quarto text), suggesting parietal space, defined by near and far, not an objective grid. Cordelia draws this space closer through the "medicine on [her] lips" that she delivers with "this kiss" (IV.vii.24–25). Her cherishing of her reunion with her father is all a matter of peripersonal space – close, even intimate contact.

Cordelia goes on to imagine and worry that he had to "hovel ... with swine" (IV.vii.37). Here, the space she imagines is specifically a substitute for home. This introduces another aspect of the neural organization of space, for home is a space of attachment bonds (on "place attachment," see Panksepp 407n.93). This suggests one fundamental, emotional organization of space, a division into the attachment-based home, on the one hand, and places of more or less intense insecurity, on the other (see Hogan *Affective* 29–31). To "hovel" is precisely the opposite of going home. Moreover, the implied disgust of hovelling "with swine" is itself the product of an emotion system directly opposed to attachment. Technically, disgust and attachment are systems with complex inhibitory relations (see Hogan *What* 45 and citations). The revulsion is salient in part because, in the hovel, there is no attachment object to inhibit disgust.

Lear's first words after waking concern being in a grave and are consistent with either a parietal or hippocampal spatial mapping. But he soon characterizes Cordelia as in Heaven and himself as in Hell – cosmological, rather than intimate or personal spaces. Cordelia aptly remarks that he is "far wide" (IV.Vii.48), a comment that now can be seen to retain its spatial meaning as well as its implications about his wandering mind. When he is somewhat recovered, he asks if he is in France (IV.vii.73), now shifting from cosmology to the equally impersonal geographical space. Perhaps the most striking expression of his alienation from the experiential space of intimacy comes when he considers his hands, the means of touching, the hands that Cordelia asks him to "hold ... in benediction o'er me" (IV.vii.56). Lear is not simply disoriented; he actually cannot experience the intimacy of contact with the space around him – so much so that he even wonders whether or not "these are my hands" (IV.vii.53). It is almost as if he had no peripersonal space at all, here suggesting a radical disturbance in attachment relations.

Part of what is going on in this scene is that Lear is having difficulty understanding what is in Cordelia's mind. Just at the moment when she is filled with tenderness and empathic feeling, he is convinced "you do not love me" (IV.vii.70). Indeed, the entire tragedy is in some ways the result of failed inter-subjective understanding, what is called "Theory of Mind." There are two sorts of Theory of Mind understanding (or misunderstanding). One is inferential; the other is a matter of "simulation" or imagining oneself in the other person's place. Simulation itself may be spontaneous or effortful (i.e., the result of a self-conscious attempt to imagine oneself in the other person's place). Perhaps because his position of authority has never required him to engage in effortful simulation and the associated empathy, Lear seems particularly unskilled at it. Nor does he seem much better at Theory of Mind inference – concluding, as he does, that Cordelia must not love him because she has "some cause" (IV.vii.72). Cordelia contrasts strikingly with Lear in this respect. In the opening act she no more engages in effortful simulation and empathy than does Lear, perhaps because of her age and circumstances. By the end of the play, however, she has developed those capacities. We see this in her profoundly empathic response to her father, and her forgiveness of him – indeed, her claim that there is nothing to forgive (IV.vii.73).

In a case such as the examination of Theory of Mind in *King Lear*, we see altered themes for interpretation along with an altered "encoding" of the text (i.e., an altered selection and organization of elements from the text). This suggests the literary value of Theory of Mind and empathy as developed in neuroscience and related fields. (For an overview of the neuroscience of empathy, see Klimecki and Singer; on Theory of Mind, see Doherty.) In keeping with this, they are two of the most influential concepts in literary neurocriticism. We see this, for example, in work by Lisa Zunshine and Suzanne Keen.

Of course, Theory of Mind does not explain everything about Lear's reunion with Cordelia. For instance, his uncertainties in this scene are bound up with another important topic of neuroscientific research, memory. Specifically, his episodic or autobiographical memory is disturbed – and it is disturbed precisely by his uncertain relation to the present. Not recognizing the place where he is or the clothes in which he finds himself, he is also uncertain that he is rightly recognizing Cordelia. The scene makes sense when we recall the importance of current experience in reconstructing past experience, that is, the contingency of memory on the conditions that evoke the memory (see Schacter 104–113). The scene may make little sense if we take memory to be a constant and precise representation, rather than a changeable neural pattern.

No less importantly, neurological research indicates that "memory" is not a single system but a number of distinct systems. Perhaps the most important of these is *emotional memory* (see LeDoux *Emotional*, 182). This is a system of "implicit" memories that, when activated, do not bring to mind explicit recollections of a past event but rather inspire an emotional response. We can infer that, even before he explicitly recognizes her, Lear's emotional memories of Cordelia have been activated. These activations produce his initial response. Placing Cordelia in Heaven is a matter of idealizing her – as one would expect from an attachment bond (which tends to foster idealization). Placing himself in Hell is an expression of his feeling of guilt – a feeling that is presumably intensified by the attachment. As these points suggest, research on memory, too, has potentially significant implications for literary study. In keeping with this, cognitive memory research has inspired literary analysis (see, for example, Rubin and Nalbantian; for a treatment of memory and literature in relation to evolutionary thought – an influential branch of cognitive and neurocognitive literary study – see chapter ten of Boyd).

Finally, in addition to changes in themes and encoding, our interpretations may be altered by just what we count as part of the text. Clearly, we do not confine ourselves to the words as printed on the page. At the very least, we incorporate a wide range of meanings, historical references, and general knowledge. In a famous essay, Stanley Fish urged, among other things, that we do and should incorporate aspects of response, including temporal changes in expectation. One may or may not accept Fish's specific claims. But his argument does indicate that it is not unreasonable to broaden one's understanding of a text beyond the context-constrained meanings. Neuroscience may be seen as giving some support to this view. Specifically, right hemisphere activations of syntactically irrelevant meanings are part of our experience of literary works. They are even to some extent a pre-dictable part of that experience. If they were not predictable, no one would ever be able to make a successful joke based on a pun. In fact, we have just considered a case of this sort – Cordelia's "far wide" (IV.vii.48). There are complex issues here as to just how these right hemisphere associations should be incorporated into the interpretation of a work or into explanations of response to works. These issues too might benefit from neuroscientific research. In any case, the literary relevance of broad, associative networks has been stressed by cognitive scientists such as Keith Oatley, as well as literary critics such as Julie Kane.

A Concluding Note on the Distinctness of Literary Study

The preceding discussion begins from the standard goals and procedures of literary study, integrating neuroscience into these. This does not mean that the contributions all go in one direction. It seems clear that literary study – like the study of other arts – can contribute to knowledge about the human mind. (I have argued for the point at length in *What Literature Teaches Us About Emotion*.) But this does not mean that literary contri-butions will be made in the form of neuroscience and according to the disciplinary procedures of the latter. Rather, it seems likely that the major contributions from literary study will be made by literary critics and theorists concentrating on what they know and do well – nuanced interpretation and evaluation of particular works, the isolation of patterns across the domain they have studied (i.e., literature), the exploration of social and historical complexities, and so on.

Among cognitivist literary critics, there is currently great enthusiasm for teaming up with neuroscientists and getting hold of fMRI equipment to run brain scans. It is undoubtedly the case that literary critics and theorists may contribute valuably to some sorts of empirical research. However, the kinds of complex interpretive issues that interest students of literature are currently not amenable to fMRI research. More generally, the enthusiasm for that research risks failing to recognize the limitations of neuroimaging and the ambiguity of its results. Certainly, we want neuroimaging research to continue and advance in literary study. Moreover, it can be valuable to add some literary scholars to the neuroscientists conducting that work (see, for example, Young and Saver for a pro-ductive collaboration; see also Starr, who admirably committed herself to learning fMRI procedures). But the brain imaging of literary response is a neuroscientific pursuit, even if it is one that takes literature as its object. Put simply, it is and will be done in neurosci-ence departments, not in literature departments. This article has been concerned with pursuits that remain fundamentally literary – pursuits engaged in by literary scholars in literature departments – even if those pursuits incorporate the findings of neuroscience into their theoretical principles and critical practices.

On a personal note, despite my enthusiasm for neuroscientific and related research, I feel it would be a great mistake if students of literature – even that subset of such students who are cognitive literary critics and theorists – were to abandon the distinctive qualities and purposes of literary study to imitate (probably badly) the more prestigious activities and interests of empirical scientists. In other words, neuroscience can help us do what we do better. Part of what we do is to contribute to the understanding of the human mind and human society. To continue and extend these contributions, the neurohumanities do not have to stop being humanities. Indeed, if they stop being humanities, anything distinctive in their contribution will stop as well.

Works Cited

Aldama, Frederick Luis. *Your Brain on Latino Comics: From Gus Arriola to Los Bros Hernandez*. Austin, TX: University of Texas Press, 2009.

Armony, Jorge and Patrik Vuilleumier, eds. *The Cambridge Handbook of Human Affective Neuroscience*. Cambridge: Cambridge University Press, 2013.

Armstrong, Paul. *How Literature Plays with the Brain: The Neuroscience of Reading and Art*. Baltimore, MD: Johns Hopkins University Press, 2013.

Baddeley, Alan, Michael Eysenck, and Michael Anderson. *Memory*. New York: Psychology Press, 2009.

Beeman, Mark and Christine Chiarello, eds. *Right Hemisphere Language Comprehension: Perspectives from Cognitive Neuroscience*. Mahwah, NJ: Lawrence Erlbaum, 1998.

Bookheimer, Susan. "Neuroimaging." In Hogan, *Cambridge*, 559–62.

Boyd, Brian. *On the Origin of Stories: Evolution, Cognition, and Fiction*. Cambridge, MA: Harvard University Press, 2009.

Bracher, Mark. *Literature and Social Justice: Protest Novels, Cognitive Politics, and Schema Criticism*. Austin, TX: University of Texas Press, 2013.

Carter, Cameron, et al. 'Anterior cingulate cortex, error detection, and the online monitoring of performance.' *Science* 280 (5364) (1 May 1998): 747–9.

Chiarello, Christine. 'On codes of meaning and the meaning of codes: semantic access and retrieval within and between hemispheres.' In Beeman and Chiarello, 141–60.

Chiarello, Christine and Mark Beeman. 'Commentary: getting the right meaning from words and sentences.' In Beeman and Chiarello, 245–51.

Clark, David, Nashaat Boutros, and Mario Mendez. *The Brain and Behavior: An Introduction to Behavioral Neuroanatomy*. 2nd ed. Cambridge: Cambridge University Press, 2005.

Doherty, Martin. *Theory of Mind: How Children Understand Others' Thoughts and Feelings*. New York: Psychology Press, 2009.

Duckitt, John H. *The Social Psychology of Prejudice*. New York: Praeger, 1992.

Fish, Stanley. 'Literature in the reader: affective stylistics.' *New Literary History* 2.1 (1970): 123–62.

Fiske, Susan, Lasana Harris, Amy Cuddy. 'Why ordinary people torture enemy prisoners.' *Science* 306 (5701) (November 26, 2004): 1482–3.

Frankish, Keith and William Ramsey, eds. *The Cambridge Handbook of Cognitive Science*. Cambridge: Cambridge University Press, 2012.

Gazzaniga, Michael. *Who's In Charge? Free Will and the Science of the Brain*. New York: Ecco, 2011.

Greenblatt, Stephen. *Will in the World: How Shakespeare Became Shakespeare*. New York: Norton, 2004.

Heinrichs, Markus, et al. 'Social stress and social approach.' In Armony and Vuilleumier, 509–32.

Hogan, Patrick Colm. *Affective Narratology: The Emotional Structure of Stories*. Lincoln, NE: University of Nebraska Press, 2011.

Hogan, Patrick Colm, ed. *The Cambridge Encyclopedia of the Language Sciences*. Cambridge: Cambridge University Press, 2011.

Hogan, Patrick Colm. 'Literary aesthetics: beauty, the brain, and *Mrs. Dalloway*.' In *Literature, Neurology, and Neuroscience: History and Modern Perspectives*. Ed. Anne Stiles, Stanley Finger, and François Boller. Amsterdam, Netherlands: Elsevier, 2013, 319–337.

Hogan, Patrick Colm. *What Literature Teaches Us About Emotion*. Cambridge: Cambridge University Press, 2011.

Holland, Norman. *Literature and the Brain*. Gainesville, FL: The PsyArt Foundation, 2009.

Iacoboni, Marco. *Mirroring People: The New Science of How We Connect with Others*. New York: Farrar, Straus and Giroux, 2008.

Jauss, Hans Robert. *Toward an Aesthetic of Reception*. Trans. Timothy Bahti. Minneapolis, MN: University of Minnesota Press, 1982.

Kane, Julie. 'Poetry as right-hemispheric language.' *Journal of Consciousness Studies* 11.5–6 (2004), 21–59.

Keen, Suzanne. *Empathy and the Novel*. Oxford: Oxford University Press, 2007.

Klimecki, Olga and Tania Singer. 'Empathy from the perspective of social neuroscience.' In Armony and Vuilleumier, 533–49.

Langlois, J. and L. Roggman. 'Attractive faces are only average.' *Psychological Science* 1 (1990): 115–21.

LeDoux, Joseph. *The Emotional Brain: The Mysterious Underpinnings of Emotional Life.* New York: Touchstone, 1996.

LeDoux, Joseph. *Synaptic Self: How Our Brains Become Who We Are.* New York: Viking, 2002.

Lehrer, Jonah. *Proust Was a Neuroscientist.* Boston, MA: Houghton Mifflin, 2008.

Nalbantian, Suzanne. *Memory in Literature: From Rousseau to Neuroscience.* New York: Palgrave Macmillan, 2003.

Oatley, Keith. *Suggestion Structure.* In Hogan, *Cambridge,* 819–20.

O'Callaghan, Casey. 'Perception'. In Frankish and Ramsey, 73–91.

Panksepp, Jaak. *Affective Neuroscience: The Foundations of Human and Animal Emotions.* Oxford: Oxford University Press, 1998.

Panksepp, Jaak and Lucy Biven. *The Archaeology of Mind: Neuroevolutionary Origins of Human Emotion.* New York: Norton, 2012.

Quart, Alissa. 'Adventures in neurohumanities.' *The Nation* (27 May 2013). Available at http://www.thenation.com/article/174221/adventures-neurohumanities#axzz2c91rPR1M (accessed 16 August 2013).

Richardson, Alan. *The Neural Sublime: Cognitive Theories and Romantic Texts.* Baltimore, MD: Johns Hopkins University Press, 2010.

Robbins, Philip and Murat Aydede. 'A short primer on situated cognition.' In *The Cambridge Handbook of Situated Cognition.* Cambridge: Cambridge University Press, 2009, 3–10.

Rubin, David. *Memory in Oral Traditions: The Cognitive Psychology of Epic, Ballads, and Counting-Out Rhymes.* New York: Oxford University Press, 1995.

Schacter, Daniel. *Searching for Memory: The Brain, the Mind, and the Past.* New York: Basic Books, 1996.

Schicke, Tobias. 'Human peripersonal space: evidence from functional magnetic resonance imaging.' *The Journal of Neuroscience* 27.14 (4 April 2007): 3616–7.

Shakespeare, William. *King Lear: A Parallel Text Edition.* Ed. René Weis. New York: Longman, 1993.

Shakespeare, William. *Othello.* Ed. Edward Pechter. New York: Norton, 2004.

Starr, G. Gabrielle. *Feeling Beauty: The Neuroscience of Aesthetic Experience.* Boston, MA: MIT Press, 2013.

Stiles, Anne. *Popular Fiction and Brain Science in the Late Nineteenth Century.* Cambridge: Cambridge University Press, 2012.

Tribble, Evelyn. 'The Dark Backward and Abysm of Time: *The Tempest* and Memory.' *College Literature* 33.1 (2006): 151–68.

Turner, Mark. *The Origin of Ideas: Blending, Creativity, and the Human Spark.* Oxford: Oxford University Press, 2014.

Vuust, P. and M. Kringelbach. 'The pleasure of music.' In *Pleasures of the Brain.* Ed. M. Kringelbach and K. Berridge. Oxford: Oxford University Press, 2010, 255–69.

Waters, Everett, Nancy Weinfield, and Claire Hamilton. 'The stability of attachment security from infancy to adolescence and early adulthood: general discussion.' *Child Development* 71.3 (2000): 703–6.

Wehrs, Donald. *Pre-Colonial Africa in Colonial African Narratives: From Ethiopia Unbound to Things Fall Apart, 1911–1958.* Burlington, VT: Ashgate, 2008.

Weik von Mossner, Alexa. *Engaging the Other: American Literature, Emotion, and the Cosmopolitan Imagination.* Austin, TX: University of Texas Press, forthcoming.

Young, Kay and Jeffrey Saver. 'The neurology of narrative.' *SubStance* 30.1/2 (2001): 72–84.

Zaidel, Dahlia. *Neuropsychology of Art: Neurological, Cognitive and Evolutionary Perspectives.* New York: Psychology Press, 2005.

Zeki, Semir. *Splendors and Miseries of the Brain: Love, Creativity, and the Quest for Human Happiness.* Chichester, West Sussex, UK: Wiley-Blackwell, 2009.

Zunshine, Lisa. *Why We Read Fiction: Theory of Mind and the Novel.* Columbus, OH: Ohio State University Press, 2006.

CHAPTER 7

Digital Humanities: Theorizing Research Practices

Ted Underwood

Digital research offers scholars of literature the possibility of grounding claims in textual evidence in new ways as a result of the digitalization of texts, Ted Underwood argues. Using data mining, scholars can now chart the use of certain words across a range of texts. Such mining can demonstrate changes in the use of certain words or word themes over time, and it can give access to commonalities across texts that would have been difficult to determine using non-digital, pencil-and-paper research.

Humanists are gearing up to have a conversation about digital research methods that will be interesting for many reasons – not least because it's oddly belated. Algorithmic mining of large electronic databases has been quietly central to the humanities for two decades. We call this practice "search," but "search" is a deceptively modest name for a complex technology that has come to play an evidentiary role in scholarship. Many of the features that seem new to us about data mining (its "bigness" or quantitative character, for instance) have been invisibly naturalized in our disciplines since humanists started using full-text search in the 1990s. Although data mining is widely framed as a novel technology now being imported to the humanities, I'll argue that it is better understood as a philosophical discourse that can help humanists think more rigorously and deliberately about existing practices of algorithmic research.

First, what does it mean to say that search plays an "evidentiary role in scholarship"? The appearance of paradox here is partly produced by the word "search" itself, which blurs boundaries between distinct technologies. Bibliographic search can be little more than an aid to memory – for instance, if a scholar is recovering the call number for a known title. Full-text search looks similar: we may even enter search terms in the same box where we would have entered a title. But the underlying technology, and its scholarly applications, are different.

Original publication details: Ted Underwood, "Digital Humanities: Theorizing Research Practices We Forgot to Theorize Twenty Years Ago." *Representations* 127.1 (Summer 2014), pp. 64–72. University of California, 2014. Reproduced with permission from University of California Press.

In practice, a full-text search is often a Boolean fishing expedition for a set of documents that may or may not exist. For instance, if I suspect that blushes are symbols of moral consciousness in nineteenth-century poetry, I can go to a database of primary sources and search for poems that contain both "blush" and "conscious." If I find enough examples, I flesh out an article. If not, I usually keep trying until I succeed. Perhaps "blush" and "shame" would work better? Here search is not just a finding aid; it's analogous to experiment – although, to be sure, there's something a bit dubious about experiments that get repeated until they produce a desired result. The search terms I have chosen encode a tacit hypothesis about the literary significance of a symbol, and I feel my hypothesis is confirmed when I get enough hits. It's possible that the article I finally write will discuss only a few of these sources, because I may not believe that the problem requires "big data." But in fact I've used algorithms to explore a big dataset, and the search process may well have shaped my way of framing the subject, or my intuitions about the representativeness of sources.

The internal mathematics of full-text search also has more in common with data mining than with bibliographic retrieval. If I do a title search for *Moby-Dick*, the results are easy to scan. But in full-text search, there are often too many matches for the user to see them all. Instead, the algorithm has to sort them according to some measure of relevance. Relevance metrics are often mathematically complex; researchers don't generally know which metric they're using; in the case of web search, the metric may be proprietary.

In short, full-text search is not a finding aid analogous to a card catalog. It's a name for a large family of algorithms that humanists have been using for several decades to test hypotheses and sort documents by relevance to their hypothesis. Simple forms of full-text search were already available in the 1970s (Lexis was an early example), but CD-ROM databases of historical sources weren't widely distributed until the 1990s. Even today, the technology may not have permeated the discipline of history as deeply as it has literary studies, since historians rely more heavily on unpublished sources. One recent study suggests, however, that humanists across a range of disciplines rely heavily on search engines, and use them for research in ways that are not very different from the way the general public uses them. (Like everyone else, we begin with Google.)[1] The scholarly consequences of search practices are difficult to assess, since scholars tend to suppress description of their own discovery process in published work.[2] But as someone who began a dissertation just before full-text databases became available, I remember that I seemed to be finishing it in a different world.

The most obvious effect of the new technology was that, like many other literary scholars in the '90s, I found myself writing about a wider range of primary sources. But I suspect that the questions scholars posed also changed to exploit the affordances of full-text search. Before 1990, narrowly defined themes were difficult to mine: there was no Library of Congress subject heading for "descriptions of work as 'energy' in British Romantic-era writing." Full-text search made that kind of topic ridiculously easy to explore. If you could associate a theme with a set of verbal tics, you could suddenly turn up dozens of citations not mentioned in existing scholarship and discover something that was easy to call "a discourse."

I remember feeling uneasy about this. The rules of the research game seemed to have changed in a way that made it impossible to lose. After all, how many sources do you need to establish the importance of a theme? Twenty? When searches were limited by networks of previous citations, that was a meaningfully high bar. But in a database containing millions of sentences, full-text search can turn up twenty examples of anything. Even at the time, it was clear that this might strengthen confirmation bias.

In hindsight, I underestimated the scope of the problem. It's true that full-text search can confirm almost any thesis you bring to it, but that may not be its most dangerous feature. The deeper problem is that sorting sources in order of relevance to your query also tends to filter out all the alternative theses you didn't bring. Search is a form of data mining, but a strangely focused form that only shows you what you already know to expect. This limitation would be a problem in any domain, but it's particularly acute in historical research, since other periods don't always organize their knowledge in ways we find intuitive. Our guesses about search terms may well project contemporary associations and occlude unfamiliar patterns of thought.

Humanists didn't spend a lot of time debating this problem in the 1990s, because search engines were usually our only mode of access to large digital collections. But in recent years, research practices have diversified, and the hermeneutic limitations of search are becoming obvious. In computer science, the subfields of data mining and machine learning have specialized in the problem of extracting knowledge from large collections.[3] They've developed a range of alternatives to search based on a more self-conscious, philosophically rigorous account of interpretation.

I realize that last sentence may be an eye-opener. Humanists tend to think of computer science as an instrumental rather than philosophical discourse. The term "data mining" makes it easy to envision the field as a collection of mining "tools." But that's not an accurate picture. The underlying language of data mining – Bayesian statistics – is a way of reasoning about interpretation that can help us approach large collections in a more principled way.[4] In particular, it emphasizes a hermeneutic spiral that will be familiar to humanists, acknowledging that we approach every question with some previous assumptions (called "prior probabilities"), as well as particular kinds of uncertainty. When we encounter new evidence, our interpretation is at once shaped by existing assumptions and (possibly) capable of reshaping them. This hermeneutic cycle is intuitive enough when we're talking about a single text; the task of data mining is to explain how it can work at the level of a collection too large to be surveyed by a single reader. All mapping strategies are going to make some assumptions about the patterns we expect to find. But some strategies are also able to reveal evidence that challenges prior assumptions.

For instance, literary scholars' habit of using keyword search to probe for intersections of themes (like "blush/shame" or "work/energy") is tacitly based on an assumption that the co-occurrence of words will reveal a connection between their meanings. This assumption is related to a model of meaning that linguists call the "distributional hypothesis," which postulates that the meaning of a word is related to its distribution across contexts.[5] This may not be a perfect model, but it has proven to be a useful one in computer science as well as literary study, and if we want to continue using it as a heuristic, there are more flexible ways to use it than iteratively guessing particular pairs of words. Algorithms based on distributional assumptions can map the language that was in practice associated with any term in a given period.[6] For instance, the word most commonly associated with "blush" in a collection of 4,820 eighteenth- and nineteenth-century volumes turns out to be not "shame" but "artless" – a detail that might interestingly complicate a scholar's assumptions about moral consciousness, if they use an exploratory strategy flexible enough to reveal it.[7] Mapping strategies like this won't replace keyword search for all purposes. When you already know what you're looking for, a search engine is the appropriate tool. But in historical scholarship, there are times when we don't know what we're looking for as well as we think.

In fact, perhaps it's already hasty to assume that the topic I'm exploring can be associated with a single word like "blush." Maybe a different term, that I can't begin to guess, was more important in this period, or maybe the social phenomena relevant to my question take shape at the intersection of many different terms. If we want a more open-ended strategy, we can map the print record by allowing an algorithm to organize the language of a collection into clusters of terms that tend to occur in the same contexts. This strategy (known as "topic modeling") is capable of revealing discursive patterns that the researcher didn't necessarily go looking for.[8]

Because topic modeling allows a word to belong to more than one "topic," it can reveal patterns of association that shift across time. Figure 1, for instance, plots occurrences of "laugh" (and words derived from that root) in eighteenth- and nineteenth-century poetry, dividing the occurrences by their association with three different algorithmically created topics.[9] It would be possible to consider each topic separately – in fact, that's how topic modeling is commonly used – but here I've added an additional twist by showing how references to laughter are so to speak passed from one topic to another over time. (The algorithm also created 117 other topics; these are only the three where "laugh-" occurred most often.) Each topic is labeled with its most common words, giving us a sense of the changing contexts where poets mention laughter. A contrast is visible between the public, satirical function of "laughter" in much eighteenth-century poetry and a different pair of contexts where laughter is associated with personal description of a sentimental or amatory kind ("sweet," "fair," "eyes"). This use of laughter for characterization is already present in the eighteenth century, but becomes more prominent as the association of laughter with public wit fades.

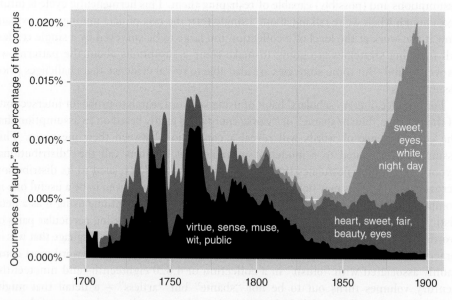

Figure 1 Occurrences of "laugh," "laughter," etc. in a collection of 13,789 volumes of poetry, divided by the topic to which each occurrence was assigned. Among 120 topics, I have plotted the three where "laugh-" occurs most often; each topic is labeled with its most frequent words.

I don't mean to imply a causal connection between these changes (for one thing, there are many other topics in the model; these three don't constitute a closed system). The illustration is only meant to show how topic modeling can generate suggestive leads. But pursued in more depth, leads become results. Matthew Jockers has used topic modeling to map nineteenth-century novels; Robert K. Nelson has used it to correlate thematic emphases in a Civil War-era newspaper with the changing fortunes of the war. Andrew Goldstone and I have used the technique to chart the rise and fall of different critical vocabularies in twentieth-century literary study.[10]

Instead of dwelling specifically on topic modeling, I want to consider the way innovations of this kind are prompting a belated conversation about algorithmic exploration in general. Topic modeling will be and should be controversial – as full-text search, actually, should have been controversial twenty years ago. Researchers can never afford to treat algorithms as black boxes that generate mysterious authority. If we're going to use algorithms in our research, we have to crack them open and find out how they work. Topic modeling, fortunately, is not proprietary, like many algorithms behind web search. Topic modeling algorithms are public, and humanists have proven to be quite capable of understanding them and changing them to fit humanistic goals.

To understand the interpretive limitations of an algorithm, one needs to understand its mathematical basis. For instance, in the most common form of topic modeling, the number of topics to be produced is one of the initial assumptions brought to the modeling process. As a consequence, the algorithm can't provide authoritative answers about the unity of any discourse, or about its boundaries. It's always possible to model the same collection with a larger or smaller number of topics, which would lump or split results differently. On the other hand, the algorithm is quite good at revealing patterns of association we might otherwise overlook.

Using algorithms for discovery raises an interesting but unfamiliar set of philosophical questions. Humanists are still more comfortable with quantitative methods when they can be presented in their familiar role as instruments of verification in the late stages of research. Using an algorithm as a source of initial leads seems perilously close to pulling a rabbit out of a hat (in spite of the fact that we've been doing this with search engines for several decades). In a recent issue of *PMLA*, for instance, Alan Liu wonders whether topic modelers aspire to the goal of "tabula rasa interpretation – the initiation of interpretation through the hypothesis-free discovery of phenomena."[11]

If this were true, it would create a real philosophical impasse. And one can certainly find technophilic rhapsodies in *Wired* magazine suggesting that we have reached that impasse: an endgame where "data" finally displaces all "theory."[12] But those rhapsodies are not well informed about the statistical models involved in data mining. It isn't the case that topic modeling (or any other data mining algorithm) pretends to be truly "hypothesis-free." A model is an abstraction created by human beings, and computer scientists have long acknowledged this.[13] The Bayesian probabilistic models now common in the discipline are especially meticulous about specifying initial interpretive assumptions.

A researcher who wants to fit a topic model to a collection of documents has to start by specifying, for instance, the number of topics she expects to find and the degree of blurriness she expects those topics to possess. In the modeling process, the computer doesn't generate insights from nothing; its calculations are rather a way of harmonizing these initial human assumptions with the complex evidence presented by the documents themselves. (To use a term of art, the computer helps us "fit" a model to the evidence.)

This mode of exploration can be more open-ended than keyword search, since assumptions about degrees of blurriness are more flexible than a specific assumption that, say, blushes will symbolize shame. But the interpretive process is still shaped and initiated by human assumptions.

I haven't had room here to make a detailed argument about the humanistic value of quantitative methods.[14] But doing that would be almost beside the point, since humanists are already mining large datasets quantitatively every time we use a web browser. The problem is that we are using search algorithms we have never theorized, and arguably using them in a strongly projective way that is at odds with historicism. Although the statistical language of computer science may seem alien to our disciplinary tradition, I think the paradoxical truth is that humanists will need to understand that language in order to design research practices that allow us to work in large collections while remaining true to our own hermeneutic principles.

This is admittedly a new kind of interdisciplinary conversation for humanists, and we may initially have a lot to learn. But we also have a lot to contribute. I've suggested that quantitative disciplines have their own useful version of hermeneutic theory, but they aren't without blind spots. The difficulty of modeling historical change, for instance, is not well understood outside the humanities. Scientists who try to model the print record over a significant time span often make assumptions about continuity that humanists would recognize as confining.[15] On this topic, and many others, a rare opportunity is emerging for a genuinely productive exchange between scientific methodology and humanistic theory.

Notes

1   Max Kemman, Martijn Kleppe, and Stef Scagliola, "Just Google It: Digital Research Practices of Humanities Scholars," *Proceedings of the Digital Humanities Congress 2012*, ed. Clare Mills, Michael Pidd, and Esther Ward (Sheffield, 2014), HRI Digital, The University of Sheffield, http://www.hrionline.ac.uk/openbook/chapter/dhc2012-kemman.

2   The invisibility of search practices is related to a pattern Lisa Gitelman has observed: "Media become authoritative as the social processes of their definition and dissemination are … forgotten"; *Always Already New: Media, History, and the Data of Culture* (Cambridge, MA, 2006), 7. For recent efforts to defamiliarize web search see René König and Miriam Rasch, eds., *Society of the Query Reader: Reflections on Web Search* (Amsterdam, 2014), Institute of Network Cultures, Hogeschool van Amsterdam, Amsterdam University of Applied Sciences, http://www.networkcultures.org/publications.

3   For a brief history of the subfield see Frans Coenen, "Data Mining: Past, Present, and Future," *Knowledge Engineering Review* 26 (2011): 25–29.

4   For a philosophical approach to this topic see Luc Bovens and Stephan Hartmann, *Bayesian Epistemology* (Oxford, 2003). A practical introduction can be found in John K. Kruschke, *Doing Bayesian Data Analysis* (Burlington, MA, 2011).

5   Magnus Sahlgren, "The Distributional Hypothesis," *Rivista di Linguistica* 20 (2008): 33–53.

6   Peter D. Turney and Patrick Pantel, "From Frequency to Meaning: Vector Space Models of Semantics," *Journal of Artificial Intelligence Research* 37 (2010): 141–88.

7   I produced this result by measuring the "cosine similarity" of word distributions over a collection of 4,820 volumes that Jordan Sellers and I assembled, with assistance from TCP-ECCO (Text Creation Partnership-Eighteenth Century Collections Online) and the Brown University Women Writers Project. Measuring cosine similarity is a simple approach; there are more sophisticated ways of using a distributional model to assess similarity between terms. (See Turney and Pantel, "From Frequency to Meaning.") Of course no single collection of volumes is perfectly representative of print culture; in practice, the best way to address questions of representativeness is often to pose the same question in multiple collections that have been selected in different ways.

8   "Topic modeling" is a name for a large family of algorithms, but the algorithm most commonly used by humanists is latent Dirichlet allocation (LDA). For an accessible humanistic introduction, see Ted Underwood, "Topic Modeling Made Just Simple Enough," *The Stone and the Shell*, April 7, 2012, http://tedunderwood.com/2012/04/07/topic-modeling-made-just-simple-enough/. For a more technical account, see David Blei, "Probabilistic Topic Models," *Communications of the ACM* 55 (2012): 77–84.

9   These 13,798 volumes of poetry were selected from a larger set of 469,000 eighteenth- and nineteenth-century volumes in the HathiTrust Digital Library. To identify the poetry in this large collection, I used tools for genre mapping described in Ted Underwood et al., "Mapping Mutable Genres in Structurally Complex Volumes," *2013 IEEE International Conference on Big Data*, 95–103, arXiv.org, Cornell University Library, http://arxiv.org/abs/1309.3323.

10 Matthew L. Jockers, *Macroanalysis: Digital Methods and Literary History* (Urbana, 2013). Robert K. Nelson, "Mining the *Dispatch*," Digital Scholarship Lab, University of Richmond, http://dsl.richmond.edu/dispatch/. Andrew Goldstone and Ted Underwood, "The Quiet Transformations of Literary Studies: What Thirteen Thousand Scholars Could Tell Us," *New Literary History* (forthcoming), preprint: https://www.ideals.illinois.edu/handle/2142/49323.

11 Alan Liu, "The Meaning of the Digital Humanities," *PMLA* 128 (2013): 414.

12 Chris Anderson, "The End of Theory: The Data Deluge Makes the Scientific Method Obsolete," *Wired*, June 23, 2008, http://www.wired.com/science/discoveries/magazine/16-07/pb_theory.

13 "Fundamentally, computer science is a science of *abstraction* – creating the right model for thinking about a problem." Alfred Aho and Jeff Ullman, *Foundations of Computer Science* (New York, 1994), 1.

14 For more examples of topic modeling, see a special issue of *Poetics* on "Topic Models and the Cultural Sciences" 41, no. 6 (2013). See also Lisa M. Rhody, "Topic Modeling and Figurative Language," *JDH: Journal of Digital Humanities* 2, no. 1 (2012), http://journalofdigitalhumanities. org/2-1/topic-modeling-and-figurative-language-by-lisa-m-rhody/.

15 Attempts to frame explicitly diachronic versions of topic modeling (like dynamic topic modeling and "topics over time") have tended to invoke dubious assumptions about historical continuity. Historians are probably better advised to rely on a simpler algorithm like generic LDA, which remains blissfully ignorant of dates and yet in practice tends to produce coherent diachronic patterns. See the appendix to Benjamin M. Schmidt, "Words Alone: Dismantling Topic Models in the Humanities," *JDH: Journal of Digital Humanities* 2, no. 1 (2012), http://journalofdigitalhumanities. org/2-1/words-alone-by-benjamin-m-schmidt/, also Xuerui Wang and Andrew McCallum, "Topics over Time: A Non-Markov Continuous-Time Model of Topical Trends," in *Proceedings of the Twelfth ACM SIGKDD International Conference on Knowledge Discovery and Data Mining* (New York, 2006), 424–33.

CHAPTER 8

Planet Hollywood

Franco Moretti

Franco Moretti, a scholar of the novel and a professor at Stanford University in the US, argues that quantitative methods can illuminate aspects of global culture such as the way Hollywood films are received and consumed around the world. Some films, Moretti finds, "play well" in certain geographic regions and less well in others.

Some time ago, while working on nineteenth-century literary markets, I was struck by how thoroughly British and French novels managed to streamline European cultural consumption: hundreds of thousands of people reading more or less the same books, and at the same time. This looked so much like the beginning of the culture industry that it suggested a little follow-up experiment – on film markets, this time. I began with the records published in *Variety*, and listed the 5 most successful American films for every year between 1986 and 1995; then I turned to non–American markets, in order to assess the extent of Hollywood's planetary diffusion. Here, the sources (*Variety International, Screen International*, and various related yearbooks) turned out to be extremely patchy, and I decided to map only those countries for which at least two years were fully documented; this made the sample a little more reliable, but unfortunately much more unbalanced: of 46 countries with 'enough' data, 25 are in Europe; Africa is almost entirely absent, as are many Asian and Latin American countries, and the demographic giants of India, China and Russia.

Big blanks. Since, however, some interesting patterns emerge, I am writing these pages anyway. Take them for what they are: initial hypotheses that should be tested against a larger, more precise set of data.

I

Figure 1: the sheer power of Hollywood. In 24 countries (the black triangles), American films make up between 75 and 90 per cent of the decade's top hits; in another 13 (the black stars) the percentage climbs above 90; in 5 cases it reaches 100. (While spending

Original publication details: Franco Moretti, "Planet Hollywood." *New Left Review* 9 (May–June 2001). Reproduced with permission from New Left Review.

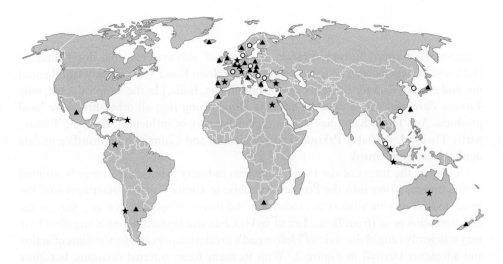

Fewest American hits (white circles):					
★ 90–100% American films	Hong Kong	6%	France	58%	South Korea 67%
▲ 75–89% American films	Serbia	33%	Bulgaria	62%	Sweden 68%
○ less than 75% American films	Malaysia	44%	Czech Republic 67%		Denmark 73%

Figure 1 US films as a percentage of top five box-office hits, 1986–95.

a year in Berlin, every now and then I checked the top ten hits of the week; always at least 9 American films, if not 10.) 'When one talks of cinema', wrote the Brazilian avant-garde director Glauber Rocha in the 1960s, 'one talks of American cinema … Every discussion of cinema made outside Hollywood must begin with Hollywood'. Indeed.

But first, a few words on those nations (the white circles) where Hollywood encounters an obstacle, and falls below 75 per cent of box-office hits. Sweden and Denmark are the core nations of Scandinavia: an area, as a dissertation by Leyvoy Joensen has shown, with a very strong regional identity, where not just Danish or Swedish novels, but Icelandic and Faroese ones had quite a criss-cross circulation. As for the Czech Republic, Serbia and Bulgaria, they are the tip of the – melting – East European iceberg: in the Czech Republic, American films accounted for less than 30 per cent of box-office hits before 1989; afterwards, they reached 76 per cent. And the same trend is visible in Slovakia and Poland (and Estonia, Romania, Slovenia: but their data were too erratic, so they don't appear in the map).

Then, France. Where the story is different; Paris was the Hollywood of the nineteenth century, its novels were read and imitated everywhere – they even invented cinema there! No wonder they hate the other Hollywood, no one likes to give up symbolic hegemony; but no one keeps it by mere force of will either, and although France knows how to protect its own market (which was twice inundated by foreign films, in the 1920s and 1940s, and twice bounced back), there is no question of its competing with Hollywood abroad. Between 1986 and 1995, only four non-American films enjoyed a large international success: *A Fish called Wanda*, *Four Weddings and a Funeral*, *Crocodile Dundee*, *The Last Emperor*: two British comedies, an Australian comedy, an American–Italian melodrama. None of them was French. In fact, none was any different from the usual Hollywood fare …

II

Scandinavia, Eastern Europe, France: all 'residual' sub-systems, that don't threaten Hollywood's hegemony. The true rival is in Asia: Hong Kong. (As I already said, I could not find enough data for the other obvious candidate, India.) In the sample decade, only *Jurassic Park* and *Speed* made it into the Hong Kong list; all other hits were local products. And Hong Kong has also its regional sphere of influence: Malaysia, Taiwan, partly Thailand, probably Pakistan and Bangladesh and China (whose insufficient data don't appear in the map).

Of course, the future of the Hong Kong film industry is not clear: it may be stunted by the incorporation into the People's Republic of China – or the exact opposite: the larger market may be a boost to production and inventiveness. Be that as it may, in the last generation or so (from Bruce Lee to Jackie Chan and beyond) Hong Kong films have very efficiently caught the wake of Hollywood's greatest export staple: the films of action and adventure charted in Figure 2.[1] With its many fuzzy internal divisions, but quite clear external borders, this is by far the most successful form both inside the US and abroad (with the exception of Europe, about which more later). South and East Asia are these films' favourite destination: they account for 50 per cent of the decade's hits in Singapore, 55 in South Korea, 65 in Indonesia, 67 in Taiwan and Thailand, 80 in Malaysia (and the sporadic data for Pakistan, India and Bangladesh confirm this pattern).

Behind this diffusion is at work one of the constants of cultural geography: stories travel well – better than other genres, anyway. It was true centuries ago, when Indian and Arab tales crossed the Mediterranean, and transformed European storytelling; it is true

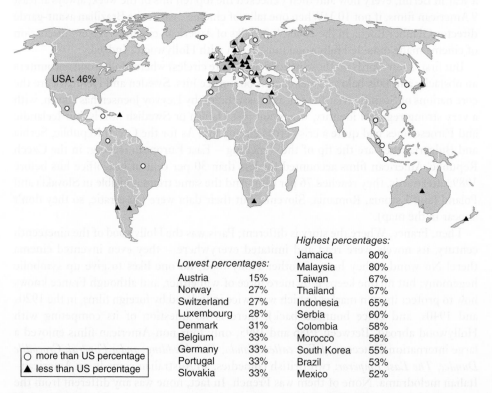

USA: 46%

Highest percentages:

Jamaica	80%
Malaysia	80%
Taiwan	67%
Thailand	67%
Indonesia	65%
Serbia	60%
Colombia	58%
Morocco	58%
South Korea	55%
Brazil	53%
Mexico	52%

Lowest percentages:

Austria	15%
Norway	27%
Switzerland	27%
Luxembourg	28%
Denmark	31%
Belgium	33%
Germany	33%
Portugal	33%
Slovakia	33%

○ more than US percentage
▲ less than US percentage

Figure 2 Action films as a percentage of top five box-office hits, 1986–95.

today, for these concatenations of striking events and hyperbolic actions (and tomorrow, with videogames: stories that never stand still, where the only thing that matters is what happens next ...). And stories travel well because they are largely *independent of language*. Within a narrative text, style and plot constitute discrete layers, and the latter can usually be translated (literally: carried across) independently from the former. (A favourite example of narrative theorists used to be, 'one can take a novel, and turn the plot into a ballet': just what happens in so many Hong Kong films.) This relative autonomy of the story-line explains the ease with which action films dispense with words, replacing them with sheer noise (explosions, crashes, gunshots, screams ...); while this brisk dismissal of language, in turn, facilitates their international diffusion. Significantly enough, in the 1920s American films were already enjoying a worldwide hegemony: what brought it to a halt was the invention of sound, which elevated language into a powerful barrier, supporting the quick take-off of the various national film industries. The abrogation of language in action films is a powerful factor in turning the tide around.

III

Next map: comedies (Figure 3). In the US, they account for 20 per cent of box-office hits; elsewhere they are usually much less successful – look at East Asia, the Mediterranean, or at the percentages indicated in the map. By contrast, even in those countries (the white circles) where Hollywood comedies are relatively more successful, the difference with the US is often insignificant.

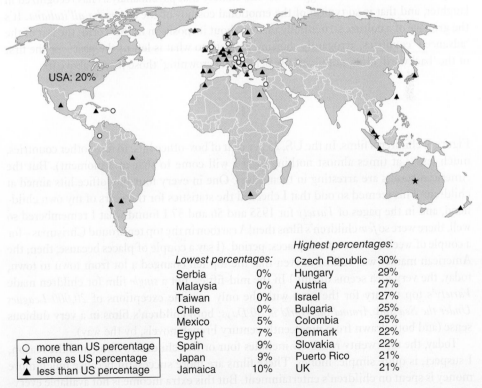

	Lowest percentages:	Highest percentages:	
		Czech Republic	30%
	Serbia 0%	Hungary	29%
	Malaysia 0%	Austria	27%
	Taiwan 0%	Israel	27%
	Chile 0%	Bulgaria	25%
	Mexico 5%	Colombia	25%
	Egypt 7%	Denmark	22%
○ more than US percentage	Spain 9%	Slovakia	22%
★ same as US percentage	Japan 9%	Puerto Rico	21%
▲ less than US percentage	Jamaica 10%	UK	21%

Figure 3 Comedies as a percentage of top five box-office hits, 1986–95.

Another rule of cultural geography: relatively speaking, comedies do *not* travel well. Compared to other French genres, the enormously popular comic novel of early nineteenth-century France, the *roman gai*, had a rather modest European diffusion. In a neat reversal of what we just saw, the main reason for this inertia is almost certainly language: since jokes and many other ingredients of comedy rely heavily on short circuits between signifier and signified, they are weakened by translation – and indeed comic films reached the apex of their world diffusion long ago, before the age of sound. Just as significant as language, however, is the fact that laughter arises out of unspoken assumptions that are buried very deep in a culture's history: and if these are not *your* assumptions, the automatic component so essential to laughter disappears. Which is interesting, we usually associate the national spirit with the sublime (*et pour cause*: unknown soldiers, torn flags, battlefields, martyrs …) yet, what makes a nation laugh turns out to be just as distinctive as what makes it cry. If not *more* distinctive, in fact: the same sublime objects reappear relentlessly from one culture to another, whereas the targets of comic aggression seem to be much more idiosyncratic, more variable. All sublime nations resemble each other, we could paraphrase *Anna Karenina*, but when they start laughing, they all do so in their own unique way.

The international weakness of Hollywood comedies, then, has much to do with their being American; or perhaps, better, with their being non-Brazilian, non-Finnish, etc. In many cases – Brazil, Argentina, Mexico, Sweden, Finland, Britain, Australia, Hong Kong – market records suggest a genuine passion for national comedies which becomes spectacular in Italy, where *every* single national hit of the sample decade was a comedy (as would be, a few years later, the biggest Italian success of all times, *Life is Beautiful*). This fixation – which began in the sixties, and apparently will never end – must have something to do with that mix of aggression and anxiety that psychoanalysis has recognized in laughter, and that is so typical of the emotional cosmos of the *commedia all'italiana*. It's the grimace of a culture structurally unsure about its position in the world: the last of the 'advanced' countries, arrogantly showing its teeth to what is left of the past – or the first of the 'backward' ones, populistically bent on 'decrowning' those placed above it?

IV

Figure 4: children's films. In the US, 25 per cent of box-office hits; in most other countries, much less – at times almost nothing (and I will come to that in a moment). But the American results are arresting in themselves. One in every four box-office hits aimed at children? This seemed so odd that I checked the statistics for the years of my own childhood, and in the pages of *Variety* for 1955 and 56 and 57 I found what I remembered so well: there were so *few* children's films then! A cartoon in the top ten around Christmas – for a couple of weeks, in a couple of places; period. (I say a couple of places because, then, the American market was still so uneven that the top ten changed a lot from town to town; today, the very idea seems quaint.) In the mid-fifties, not a *single* film for children made *Variety*'s top twenty for the year, with the only possible exceptions of *20,000 Leagues Under the Sea* and *Around the World in 80 Days*: both children's films in a very dubious sense (and both drawn from nineteenth-century French novels, by the way).

Today, the top twenty routinely includes four or five children's films, and the reason, I suspect, is quite simple: money. These films are more successful because much more money is spent on children's entertainment. But this extra income is not available everywhere, and the result is the skewed distribution of Figure 4, where the (relative) absence

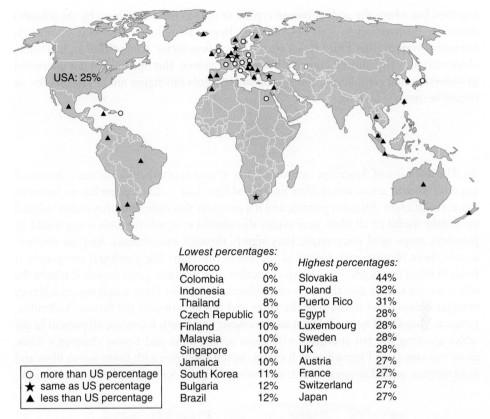

Lowest percentages:

Morocco	0%
Colombia	0%
Indonesia	6%
Thailand	8%
Czech Republic	10%
Finland	10%
Malaysia	10%
Singapore	10%
Jamaica	10%
South Korea	11%
Bulgaria	12%
Brazil	12%

Highest percentages:

Slovakia	44%
Poland	32%
Puerto Rico	31%
Egypt	28%
Luxembourg	28%
Sweden	28%
UK	28%
Austria	27%
France	27%
Switzerland	27%
Japan	27%

○ more than US percentage
★ same as US percentage
▲ less than US percentage

USA: 25%

Figure 4 Children's films as a percentage of box-office top five, 1986–95.

of the genre tends to overlap with the poverty of each given country. The correlation is not perfect, they never are (look at the data for Egypt, or Puerto Rico, or Singapore), but it seems real enough, and, incidentally, it also works *inside* the United States: studying New York videostores, my students and I discovered that the presence of children's films in Harlem and the Bronx ranged between 3 and 8 per cent; in the Upper West Side and Upper East Side, between 10 and 19 per cent. Three times higher.

'Children's films' is a sloppy definition, of course: it points to the audience, not the film – and to an audience which is moreover quite problematic. Children, after all, don't usually go to the movies by themselves and, as adults must take them, a little generic paradox ensues: whom should the film be for – the adult, or the child? Faced with this problem, the fifties offered either straightforward fairy tales (for the child: *Cinderella*, *Snow White*, even *Fantasia*), or those Jules Verne novels I mentioned earlier (which were much more successful than the fairy tales: another sign of a market directed at the adult). But today the two forms have converged, blending into a hybrid which appeals to children and adults alike: *E. T.*, *Roger Rabbit*, *Back to the Future*, the various *Star Wars* and *Indiana Jones* – these are stories designed for a new human species of savvy children and silly grown-ups (*Homo puerilis*). Their god is Steven Spielberg (and Benigni is his prophet: *Life is Beautiful* – what a childish adult wants a child to know about Auschwitz).

In one film after another (*Jaws*, *Close Encounters*, *Indiana Jones and the Temple of Doom*, *Jurassic Park*; even the uncanny detail of the girl in red, in *Schindler's List*), Spielberg has not only chosen stories in which children and adults are somehow involved together, but where the ambiguities so typical of (adult) life are defused by the (child's) desire for polarization so well described by Bruno Bettelheim. The best example is Schindler himself; this Third Reich shark turned benefactor, who offered an incredible chance to study the contradictions of historical existence. But Spielberg is not interested in understanding complicated things, and in his hands this figure out of Dostoevsky, or Brecht becomes – nothing.

V

So. The diffusion of American comedies is low almost everywhere, children's films tend to prefer wealthy areas, action films South and East Asia … Each genre has its favourite space, its different diffusion pattern, and it's precisely this difference that makes cultural geography useful (if all films were evenly distributed everywhere, these maps would be pointless: maps need unevenness, they signify through unevenness). And the unevenness is there because each region of the world functions like a cultural ecosystem: it tends to select one genre – and to reject another. It selects one genre *because* it rejects the other: setting side by side the maps of children's and action films, a striking coincidence emerges between the strength of the latter and the weakness of the former: Colombia, Jamaica, Morocco, Thailand, Malaysia, Indonesia and South Korea are all present in the tables charting the ten countries with most action films and fewest children's films. Same message from Figure 5, which charts the ten countries with *fewest* action films and most dramas: seven European countries (Portugal, Spain, Switzerland, Austria, Belgium,

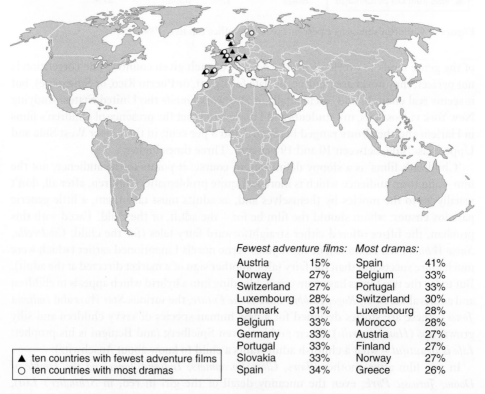

Fewest adventure films:		Most dramas:	
Austria	15%	Spain	41%
Norway	27%	Belgium	33%
Switzerland	27%	Portugal	33%
Luxembourg	28%	Switzerland	30%
Denmark	31%	Luxembourg	28%
Belgium	33%	Morocco	28%
Germany	33%	Austria	27%
Portugal	33%	Finland	27%
Slovakia	33%	Norway	27%
Spain	34%	Greece	26%

▲ ten countries with fewest adventure films
○ ten countries with most dramas

Figure 5 Countries with fewest adventure films and most dramas.

Luxembourg and Norway) are present in both lists – while five of the remaining six countries are also in Europe.[2]

We see here the Darwinian side of cultural geography: forms that *fight for space*. They fight for the limited resources of the market, and if one manages to successfully occupy one space, other forms will encounter all sorts of obstacles. In trying to explain large geographical patterns, then, the isolated case is seldom enough: the strength (or weakness) of one form can only be explained by looking at the whole system of variables at play. And with this, I turn to my last point.

VI

The nineteenth century saw a European diffusion of Anglo-French novels; the twentieth century, a planetary diffusion of American film. And the reactions to this centralized global market? Every discussion of cinema made outside Hollywood must begin with Hollywood, said Glauber Rocha. Must it also *end* with Hollywood?

Here, the history of the novel offers an interesting precedent. In his work on Brazilian novels, Roberto Schwarz has shown that the power of metropolitan models has a twofold effect on cultures of the periphery. First of all, it generates a 'disagreement between the form [which is foreign] and the material [which is local]': 'nothing is more Brazilian than these half-baked novels', he goes on, so full of 'dissonance' and 'compositional defects'. 'An impossible programme', says Masao Miyoshi of the modern Japanese novel; and similar things have been independently said just about everywhere.[3] In the case of less powerful literatures, then – which means: almost *all* literatures, inside and outside Europe – the import of foreign novels doesn't just mean that people read a lot of foreign books; it also means that local writers become uncertain of how to write *their own* novels. Market forces shape consumption *and* production too: they exert a pressure on the very form of the novel, giving rise to a genuine morphology of underdevelopment.

But this is not the whole story. Every now and then, one of those 'impossible programmes' *works*. Machado de Assis takes the 'compositional defects' of Brazilian novels, and turns them into an incredibly original narrative style. Elsewhere, the clash with the symbolic power of Western Europe produces major paradigm shifts, like the Russian novels of ideas, or Latin American magical realism (or the slightly different case of the Kafka–Joyce generation). Although these remain *exceptions*, they occur often enough to show a counter-force at work within the world literary system. The morphology of under-development is not without its surprises.

And in film? Here, reversing the tide is probably more difficult, given the stronger economic constraints (production costs, distribution monopolies, dumping practices ...), but hardly impossible. A critical reconstruction of the history of film, and of its present, will eventually offer an answer. From the viewpoint of method, however, the crucial point is the one made by Christopher Prendergast in his review of Pascale Casanova's *République mondiale des lettres*: when trying to understand the world system of culture, 'a single, generalizing description misses too much and is destined to do so, if it is offered as *the* description'.[4] This, of course, is just as true for the quantitative evidence I have used as for the study of individual directors, or film genres: the solution lies in multiple layers of description and explanation, linked together by a chain of successfully analysed 'details' (Prendergast again). God lies in the detail – perhaps. Our understanding of culture certainly does.

Notes

1   This map, and those that follow, will make use of film genres – a controversial point, given that some critics believe in the existence of genres, and others don't. Without getting into the general argument, I will just say that I belong to the first group, even more stubbornly in the case of film: if you look at a newspaper, or walk into a videostore, the reality of film genres literally leaps at you, as each film is being sold *as something*: a comedy, a film noir, science-fiction, whatever. Taxonomy here is not a scholastic pastime, it's a product of the film industry itself, which makes it easier to recognize the film, and to buy the ticket.

As for the categories I will use, I borrowed them from one section of the film industry itself – videostores. I chose an independent store in Greenwich Village, a Blockbuster store, and the *Theater for the Living Arts* catalogue, reduced their (largely coincident) categories to four large ones (Action; Comedies; Children; Dramas), and applied them to my sample.

2   'Drama' is not a very good label, I know, it sounds like a passe-partout notion designed to catch all those films that cannot fit elsewhere, but there is one sense in which it is actually appropriate: dramas have a very strong theatrical component (that's probably why they do so well in Europe, where the theatre is still a major cultural presence): the setting is often circumscribed, like the theatre – even, say, in *Forrest Gump*, where the protagonist moves around a lot, but the film is symbolically dominated by his monologue on the bus bench. Like the theatre, 'dramas' focus on language, and on its problems: *Forrest Gump* again, *Ghost, Rain Man, Dances with Wolves* (the last two titles both being translations from a different linguistic universe).

3   See my 'Conjectures on World Literature', NLR 1, Jan–Feb 2000.

4   'Negotiating World Literature', NLR 8, March–April 2001.

CHAPTER 9

Theory in Practice
According to My Bond: King Lear
and Re-Cognition

Donald C. Freeman

In this essay, Donald C. Freeman, who teaches English at the University of Southern California, argues that *King Lear* should be considered from the perspective of Lakof and Johnson's theory of embodied knowledge and cognitive metaphor. The king understands the world using a cognitive scheme of accounting and balance, but he is confronted by another cognitive metaphor – one that understands family relations as links.

An emerging theory of cognitive metaphor provides a promising basis for analysing figurative language in literary works.[1] In particular, cognitive metaphor provides accounts of language patterns that are isomorphic with larger imaginative literary structures, as well as particular interpretations that are more explicit and falsifiable than existing interpretations founded upon the language of literary works. I want to demonstrate this theory in a reading of *King Lear* that focuses on its opening scene, where metaphorical structures arise from a competition between the framing bodily experiences of balance and linking that define ways of understanding crucial to the larger patterns of the play.

1 Metaphor and Schematised Bodily Experience

The salient features of earlier research in the theory of metaphor are epitomised in the work of Samuel R. Levin, who argued in a seminal essay that, for example, to interpret a metaphor like 'a grief ago' we in effect import the semantic feature [+Time] from 'grief's' syntactic frame into the word itself; the phrase is to that extent a 'confrontation' (Levin 1964: 314) between ordinary and metaphoric language. Metaphor thus is part of a figurative language that contrasts with a 'literal', non-figurative language. According to

Original publication details: Donald C. Freeman, "According to My Bond: King Lear and Re-cognition" from *Language and Literature* 2, pp. 1–19. Sage, 1993. Reproduced with permission from Sage and Donald C. Freeman.

Literary Theory: An Anthology, Third Edition. Edited by Julie Rivkin and Michael Ryan.

this theory, 'literal' language, including 'dead' (but not literary) metaphors, is unmarked and ordinary, but figurative language, including literary (but not dead) metaphors, is deviant, foregrounded, highlighted, made strange. The 'deviance' is with respect to a language-universal set of semantic features and combinatory rules external to individual cognition. Lakoff (1987: 157–84) has characterised this view as the Objectivist position. Classically, metaphor is seen – and not only in linguistically based theories – as a deviant and parasitic structure; we characterise metaphors in terms of their deviance from ordinary non-metaphorical language.[2]

Precisely these two characterisations of metaphor – that it is a structure parasitic upon ordinary language structure and that it can be explained in terms of its deviance from semantic interpretations of ordinary, non-metaphorical language interpretable by a compositional semantics – are explicitly rejected by cognitive metaphor. The cognitive view arises from the Experientialist position (as articulated, for example, in Lakoff 1987: xv) on semantic theory. The Experientialist position claims that we create metaphor by projecting onto an abstract *target domain* the entities and structure of a concrete *source domain*, a schematised real or vicarious bodily experience. Metaphor arises from, in Johnson's (1987: xv) cogent formulation, 'embodied human understanding'. As human beings we share a range of physical experiences that take on structure and coherence from the non-propositional schemata we extract from them. Our propensity to extract these schemata is a fundamental property of mind. We project elements of the structure and components of our physical experience onto our non-physical, abstract experience. Precisely this sense of projection from schematised bodily experience constitutes the claim for metaphor as embodied human understanding.

Consider, for example, the famous line from *King Lear*, 'I am a man / More sinn'd against than sinning' (III.ii.59–60). The context, justice, makes it clear that this line epitomises Lear's sense of a higher justice, that in a truly just universe he would be no more sinned against than he had sinned, that if there were justice, Lear's sins would balance his sufferings. This notion of balance is fundamental to our idea of justice: we understand the abstraction of justice in terms of bodily balance. The concept of horizontal balance dominates both our non-verbal and verbal language about justice. Our courts decide civil lawsuits according to 'the preponderance', or greater weight, 'of the evidence'. A witness's testimony can be said to be 'biased'. Our icon for justice is a blindfolded woman holding a two-pan scale. All of these metaphors, and many more besides, having to do with such seemingly disparate notions as mathematical equality, patterns in visual art, and certain kinds of musical progression are projected from a non-verbal, non-propositional, non-representational schema of BALANCE (for general discussion of schema theory, see Johnson 1987: 18–40 and the references he cites; for discussion of musical progression and the BALANCE schema, see Freeman 1991: 153). The theory of cognitive metaphor claims that we project the elements of this schema – entities (the items that balance) and the relationships among those entities (counteraction or equality) – onto elements of our more abstract experience.

Such an explanation of 'justice' as deriving ultimately from our embodied human understanding of balance explains 'I am a man / More sinn'd against than sinning'. But the BALANCE schema also captures lines like Edgar's, 'He childed as I father'd' (III.vi.108), in which Lear's sufferings at the hands of his daughters are balanced by Edgar's sufferings at the hands of his father Gloucester (and the balance between the plot and major subplot of the play is epitomised); it captures Lear's misunderstanding of the father–child relationship, which persists even to the end, when, awakened from his sleep after he has been brought in from the heath, he implores Cordelia:

> LEAR   If you have poison for me, I will drink it.
>   I know you do not love me; for your sisters
>   Have, as I do remember, done me wrong:
>   You have some cause, they have not.
> CORDELIA   No cause, no cause.
>   (IV.vii.72–5)

Lear persists in understanding the parent–child relationship in terms of the BALANCE schema, even as Cordelia reaches beyond it. But children need no cause to wrong parents; conversely and more importantly, a child whom a parent has wronged need not balance that wrong by committing another. By no means all of the metaphors I have cited are metaphors of justice. But they do derive from a common source, the embodied, culturally reinforced experience of balance.

That source, the schema of BALANCE, underlies a richer, more important, and previously unexplained structure of metaphor in the play: that of financial accounting.[3] Terms and phrases like 'divest', 'prize me at her worth', and 'comes too short' (I.i.48, 69, 71) partake of the BALANCE schema, but they are not metaphors of justice. They can be better explained in the more densely structured, balance-based scenario[4] of financial accounting.

A second rich source of metaphor in *King Lear* is the equally simple LINKS schema, which consists of two entities joined by a bonding element. These three aspects of the LINKS schema's structure, like those of the BALANCE schema, are mapped onto a wide array of non-physical human experiences. The source of the LINKS schema arises from our literal, physical link to our biological mothers. We then proceed to, for example, a 'bonding' with our parents, our relatives, and our friends. Marriages are often celebrated with the proverb 'blest be the tie that binds,' and sometimes include the Biblical admonition, 'What therefore God hath joined, let no man put asunder' (*Matthew* 19, verse 6). People without a romantic interest are 'unattached', or free of 'entanglements'. When one event consistently follows another, we hypothesise that the two events are linked by causation. Links of divine ordination and divine love join the elements of the Great Chain which, shorn of its theology, is alive and well today (see Lakoff and Turner 1989: 160–213). The lion is still the king of the beasts, and gold is still the premier investment commodity, whereas platinum, rarer and more expensive, is merely an industrial commodity.

These two powerful perceptual structures give a local habitation and a name to previously unjustified and unrelated critical commonplaces. For example, it is a staple of Shakespearean criticism to say that in the opening scene the playwright establishes the atmosphere of a play's world. What are established, in fact, are the play's dominating schemata. In *King Lear*, Gloucester's cynical account to Kent of his sons' parentage establishes the play's competing schemata of BALANCE and LINKS. Gloucester demonstrates that like Lear, he understands parental relationships through the CHILDREN ARE FINANCIAL ASSETS metaphor, one that the audience is shortly to see played out fully in the ritual of Lear's retirement.

> His [Edmund's] breeding, Sir, hath been at my charge:
> ...
> But I have a son [Edgar], Sir, by order of law, some year elder than this, who yet is no dearer to my account:
>   (I.i.8, 18–19)

The 'charge' that Edmund's breeding constitutes for Gloucester is an analogy from estate accounting, which used the so-called 'Charge and Discharge' method, in which, Green (1930: 47) writes, 'the executor "charged" himself with the estate and "discharged" himself of disbursements properly chargeable to the estate'. Edmund, a bastard, is not a financial asset but a cost item that it has embarrassed Gloucester to acknowledge; Edgar, though not an embarrassment (a cost to Gloucester's reputation) is no more highly valued in the balance sheet of his father's affections. From the start of the play, familial LINKS are debased; children are bastards or 'by order of law'; the relationship of child to father, an important source of LINK metaphors in the play, begins with what will result in Edmund's perversion of his filial duty. Charges and accounts, sons and daughters, bastards and legal progeny (and what ought to be but are not the same thing, natural and unnatural children) – these seemingly unrelated facts of language and plot spring from the same impulses: the BALANCE and LINKS schemata.

These competing schemata structure a significant portion of the play's metaphors that traditional accounts of the play's language leave unrelated. More significantly, they and the analyses they make possible, constitute previously undiscovered empirical evidence for relating the play's figurative language to such other structural elements as narrative, plot, and particular constellations of characters. For example, many critics have found parallel structure or balance in the fact that while in the sub-plot Edmund gouges out Gloucester's eyes but Edgar redeems him to a new life, in the main plot Goneril and Regan strip Lear of his retainers but Cordelia awakens him to a restoration, however temporary, of his health, fatherhood, and kingship. But I know of nothing written about *King Lear* that uses one theoretical apparatus to *explain* this balance, the patterns of metaphor I describe, and the relationships among these levels. It is this greater explanatory power that is the major contribution to literary theory of cognitive metaphor.

2 The King's Account-books

Most accounts of *King Lear's* opening scene treat it as a trial or a love-test. Yet curiously the scene lacks elements crucial in any trial: an offence, a judge, advocates, juries, opposing parties. It is no sense an adversarial proceeding. Lear has divided his kingdom before the scene begins.[5] We find none of the legal vocabulary that Shakespeare uses so profusely in the mock trial scene (III.vi.35–83) and elsewhere in those of the sonnets and plays containing unambiguous references to trials.

Rather than a trial, what we have in the first scene of *King Lear* is a semantic frame (in the sense of Fillmore (1982)) that depends upon the structure of a quasi-legal proceeding, the auditing of financial record-books, and a more general scenario of financial accounting (the substantial evidence that Shakespeare was familiar with this subject matter is summarised in Knight 1973: 248). In financial accounting obligations are recorded both to and from the entity keeping the books. Within this scenario, centrally for Lear and less importantly for other characters, the generative metaphor (in the sense of Schön 1979: 264) that controls the scene's 'story' is CHILDREN ARE FINANCIAL ASSETS. Lear understands his daughters in the same way that he understands wealth, real property, assets, and debts. Financial assets are expected to provide a return on capital to their owners (here, their fathers). Hence an important metaphor within this framework is FILIAL LOVE IS INTEREST. Financial assets and organisations are periodically audited to see whether they are providing an adequate return, and how the return from one asset compares with that from another, so that, if need be, the investment strategy can be revised. Assets that provide better returns can be the objects of further capital investment. Assets that do not perform well are disposed of, and the money provided by the sale is re-deployed to those assets that do perform well.

Although the fundamental principles of financial accounting are the same today as they were in Shakespeare's time, some details are quite different. First, although balance sheets of a kind were kept, they were balanced out only 'when some special circumstances required the formal closing of the books' (Yamey 1949: 106). Second, audits of financial records were oral (indeed, the term 'audit' comes from the Latin *audire*, 'to hear') because when the financial audit in more or less its modern form came into existence in England in the fourteenth century, most of the participants were illiterate. The steward of another's capital recited, or 'spoke' the accounts, in the customary language, and the auditor 'heard' them. Many early account books contain notations such as the following, describing the appointment in 1456 of two auditors for the accounts of the City of Dublin: ... ther schold be from that tym forward two Audytores assignet upon the tresowrerys saud cytte, to hyr har acownt yerly ...'.[6]

The model for financial accounting and auditing with which Shakespeare and his audience probably would have been most familiar, if only by report, was the semi-annual settling of the Crown's accounts with the sheriff of every country for subventions from the Crown to the county and revenue from the county due the Crown. At this proceeding, according to a standard history:

> the treasurer representing the Exchequer read from his copy of the Great Pipe Roll [a document amounting to a national ledger] the amount due the crown from the sheriff. The Exchequer attendants placed on the checkered cloth [of the table used for the ceremony] dummy counters representing the amounts due the crown. On the near side of the checkered cloth was the sheriff. As the treasurer called the amounts the sheriff placed in the appropriate columns his tally stick, crown vouchers and money or jewels to balance the dummy counters. This settled the yearly account between the crown and sheriff.

So rich in tradition was this ceremony that it continued from the early Norman period well into the nineteenth century. Even in Shakespeare's time, this event would have been seen not merely as a settling of accounts, but a ceremony in its own right.

Just this ceremony, the hearing, or audit, of state accounts, more satisfactorily explains the curiously ritualistic character of this first major scene of the play. Much of the language crucial to Lear's expression of his 'fast intent' can be simultaneously interpreted in the semantic frames of financial accounting and of statecraft. He wishes to 'divest' himself of rule, of 'interest of territory'. He calls upon his daughters to 'tell' (i.e. count out, as well as relate) which of them 'shall we *say* doth love us most' so that he may invest[7] more parental love, which the frame asks us to understand as capital investment, according to the return on each of the three investments represented in his daughters. Each daughter is enjoined to 'speak' or 'say'. Lear will listen, or audit, as each speaks her account, and 'extend ... [his] largest bounty' where nature, natural affection, filial love, challenges, lays claim to that bounty (which again has a financial, though not an accounting, sense) with merit, with the greatest deserving. Future investment will balance past performance – as Lear perceives that performance.

Goneril is in no doubt how to demonstrate that 'merit'. Like her father, she couches the language of her declaration in financial terms. The love she bears her father is 'dearer', a word with a financial as well as an affectionate sense; that love is 'beyond what can be valued' as more conventional financial assets are appraised; it 'makes breath poor'. Regan's accounting is more concrete. She is made, she asserts, of the same 'metal' (in Shakespearean usage, normally gold metal) as her sister, and appraises herself equally ('and prize me at her worth'). But Goneril, Regan claims, 'comes too short', an idiom directly from the contemporary language of financial accounting.[8] Regan's reckoning is even more unrealistically extravagant: she professes to find happiness only in her father's love.

Underlying all of this, again, is the schema of BALANCE. Lear seeks to balance his 'bounty' against the love his daughters say they have for him; his new investment in them must balance the return he has received on his previous investments. Goneril in turn, seeks to demonstrate a highly valued love (in order to receive a highly valued piece of kingdom); Regan values herself at her sister's worth, but insists that Goneril is short in her accounts. Lear abundantly demonstrates a trait of character to which we will return: an obsession with what Johnson (1987: 95) calls 'moral mathematics' – here, the notion that the emotional costs of child-rearing can be quantified, and ought to be balanced by equally quantifiable expressions of love in a verifiable balance sheet of accounts.

Lear's version of the BALANCE schema forces Cordelia from the start into an unpalatable choice:

> Then poor Cordelia!
> And yet not so; since I am sure my love's
> More ponderous than my tongue.
> (I.i.75–7)

Compared with Regan, who 'prize[s] [herself] at [Goneril's] worth', Cordelia is both pitiably and financially poor – but she immediately rejects the financial metaphor in favour of her own version of the BALANCE schema, in which the spiritual weighs more, is more ponderous (and hence more valuable), than its literal expression. She must mediate between her father's intense desire for her to express her love in ways that allow him to maintain his account-books of filial devotion, while remaining true to her 'spiritual' notion of love. In her very first words in the play, Cordelia shows the relative value she places on feelings and words: 'What shall Cordelia speak? Love, and be silent'. For her, feelings will always outweigh words; the two can never balance; she refuses to *speak*, a word associated with the financial audit scenario, what is in effect her accounting of filial love and paternal love returned.

Hence when Lear asks Cordelia, who is the object of a financial claim[9] by her two suitors, what she can 'say to draw[10] / A third more opulent than [her] sisters? Speak' (I.i.84–5), Cordelia gives the only response possible for one who thus weighs words and feelings. She rejects the notion that a paternal gift should be 'drawn' like a salary, a usage current in Shakespeare's time. All she can *say* – all she can speak – is 'Nothing'. What counts for her is what she feels, but feelings have no place in financial audits. Understood in terms of the accounting framework that dominates this scene, Cordelia's famous silence is quite unremarkable. Cordelia's 'nothing' is understood by her father only as a number, as his bewildered response makes clear: 'Nothing will come of nothing' (I.i.89).

At this point the process of frame competition begins that undermines Lear's ceremony and results in Cordelia's being disinherited. For the BALANCE schema underlying Lear's scenario of financial accounting, Cordelia seeks to substitute a schema of LINKS. She seeks to redefine her father's understanding of family relationships as items in an accounting balance sheet into an understanding characterised in the generative metaphor FAMILY RELATIONSHIPS ARE LINKS. She begins this process with the polysemous word 'bond', which exists in both competing frames, financial and kinship:

> I love your Majesty
> According to my bond; no more nor less.
> (I.i.91–2)

From the beginning, Cordelia makes clear that she understands 'bond' in terms of her father's financial accounting scenario. In Shakespeare's time, a bond, the financial instrument, was what Shylock (*The Merchant of Venice*, I.iii.144) called a 'single bond'. It was a financial or other obligation undertaken solely on the basis of the borrower's credit, without collateral. The obligation memorialised in a single bond is not, in legal language, defeasible (performance of the obligation is the only way the debtor can discharge it; see *Black's Law Dictionary* 1981: 163). One performs under a single bond or one does not. Performance under a single bond is, in two words that come to dominate *King Lear*, all or nothing. For Cordelia, to love her father 'according to [her] bond' is to love him completely; that love can be no more (more complete than complete) nor less (partial) because of the nature of financial single bonds.

But for Cordelia the same all-or-nothing property holds of filial bonds, when this term is defined within the LINKS schema through the metaphor FILIAL RELATIONSHIPS ARE PHYSICAL LINKS. I have sketched out how the same metaphor governs our understanding of phrases like 'family ties' and 'parental bonding'. Lear cannot share the richness of Cordelia's metaphorical understanding, and replies in solely financial terms:

> Mend your speech a little,
> Lest you may mar your fortunes.
> (I.i.93–4)

Cordelia's reply partakes once again of both schemata, BALANCE and LINKS:

> Good my Lord,
> You have begot me, bred me, lov'd me: I
> Return those duties back as are right fit,
> Obey you, love you, and most honour you.
> Why have my sisters husbands, if they say
> They love you all? Happily, when I shall wed,
> That lord whose hand must take my plight shall carry
> Half my love with him, half my care and duty:
> Sure I shall never marry like my sisters,
> To love my father all.
> (I.i.94–103)

Cordelia focuses first on the physical closeness of her filial relationship with Lear, and then relates this closeness to the financial accounting frame with a verb, 'return', that can be interpreted in both frames. Links are by nature biconditional – A is linked to B if and only if B is linked to A. Within the accounting frame we speak of an investment that 'returns' such-and-such per cent. What Cordelia will 'return', she characterises as 'duties', a term that resonates in both the accounting and the links frames. That 'return' is commensurate with both the intensity of filial relationships and the balanced nature of accounts: here the most fundamental of human ties, blood relationships of begetting, breeding, loving, are expressed in the language of the wedding ceremony: obedience, love, and honour (see Rosinger 1974).

Yet the explicitly financial character of the accounting metaphor is still kept in play. For Cordelia, marriage as a bond (a human relationship) involves a 'plight' or pledge, another word interpretable within both frames, that necessarily, by the laws of both financial accounting and human development, diminishes the line of credit underlying the 'bond' of daughter to father. If a wedded daughter still loves only her father, she has falsely plighted her troth, for she has no credit left for the bond with her husband – and for Cordelia, nothing truly can come from nothing. The protestations of Goneril and Regan that they 'love [their] father all' are thus false in the same ways that Cordelia's is true – within both the accounting and the links scenarios. Lear's daughters cannot plight the half of their love that their husbands deserve without defaulting upon the bonds calling for them to 'love [Lear] all'. In both scenarios, Cordelia is 'So young, my Lord, and true' (I.i.106): i.e. both truthful, bearing a higher loyalty to her filial bond with her father, and true in the sense of having opposed to her sisters' false accounts (their 'bonds' are simultaneously pledged to two different creditors) her own true reckoning under the obligations of her financial and filial bond. In both senses, Cordelia is her family's best auditor.[11]

Characteristically, Lear interprets Cordelia's 'true' only within the financial accounting frame: 'Let it be so; thy truth then be thy dower' (I.i.107). Likewise, Burgundy expresses in financial terms the bargain he now seeks to strike for Cordelia's hand:

BURGUNDY   Most royal Majesty
          I crave no more than hath your Highness offer'd
          Nor will you tender[12] less.
LEAR   Right noble Burgundy
          When she was dear to us, we did hold her so
          But now her price is fallen.

                                        (I.i.192–6)

France, however, shares Cordelia's view that love cannot be understood as a set of accounts. After Lear offers Cordelia to Burgundy one last time, as 'herself a dowry', only to have Cordelia point up the irreconcilable conflict between balance and link: 'Since that respects and fortunes are his [Burgundy's] love, I shall not be his wife' (I.i.247–8), France, terming Cordelia 'unprized', makes clear that he loves her precisely because she does not fit Lear's balance-sheet vision, harking back to Regan's use of 'prize' as 'appraise':

               Fairest Cordelia, that art most rich, being poor;
               Most choice, forsaken; and most lov'd, despis'd!
               Thee and thy virtues here I seize upon: …
               Not all the dukes of wat'rish Burgundy
               Can buy this unpriz'd precious maid of me.

                               (I.i.249–51, 257–8)

Thus in this opening scene, Shakespeare embeds the play's major themes in the framing scenario of a financial audit, one that depends on the schema of BALANCE. Lear himself sees statecraft and fatherhood in exclusively abstract, numerical terms; Goneril and Regan give an account of their filial love in language dominated by accounting metaphors that derive from the BALANCE schema[13]; the same metaphors dominate the case pleaded unsuccessfully by Burgundy. Cordelia refutes the balance schema in its own terms; she would substitute an understanding of family relationships as arising from a schema of LINKS. For her, to say 'nothing' does not deny a daughter's love but exalts its inexpressibility; for Lear, 'nothing' is merely a nought, a book-keeping entry.

This word resonates more ambiguously for Lear as the Fool redefines it for him during his visit to Goneril:

KENT This is nothing fool.
FOOL Then 'tis like the breath of an unfee'd lawyer, you gave me nothing for't.
      Can you make no use of nothing, Nuncle?
LEAR Why no, boy; nothing can be made out of nothing.
FOOL *[to Kent]* Prithee tell him, so much the rent of his land comes to: he will not
      believe a Fool.

(I.iv.126–32)

The linguistically nimble Fool entraps Lear with a specifically financial phrase, and reminds his king of the deeper sense of the 'nothing' he now has. Lear, the great valuer, is now without value, an '0', a zero, 'without a figure' (I.iv.189–90), a king with no kingdom, a father with no daughters, a man with no standing, a cipher without a number to give it value, to whom the Fool applies Lear's own principle of accounting: 'I am better than thou art now: I am a fool, thou art nothing' (I.iv.190–1). The currency in which Lear will repay his older daughters' professions of love comes at a much higher rate of exchange than he anticipated:

FOOL But for all this, thou shalt have as many dolours for thy daughters as thou canst tell
      in a year.

(II.iv.52–3)

Lear's world is destroyed in the same terms of balance and numbers in which he sought to build it, as Goneril and Regan strip him of the numbers of his retainers:

REGAN   ... I have hope
        You [Lear] less know how to value her [Goneril's] desert
        Than she to scant her duty ...
        I cannot think my sister in the least
        Would fail her obligation.

(II.iv.135–9)

Goneril and Regan, however, indeed know how to value their father's desert; they know just the issue that will torment him most – the number of his followers. As his daughters reduce his retainers – and with them, his humanity – from the *number* one hundred to the *number* zero, it dawns on Lear that in family relationships, a deal is not necessarily a deal, irrespective of what the account-books say or what reservations are spelled out in contractual visiting arrangements:

> I gave you all –
> ...
> Made you my guardians my depositaries,
> But kept a reservation[14] to be follow'd
> With such a number.
>
> (II.iv.248, 249–51)

We recall that the Fool has already told Lear that he is 'an 0 without a figure'; now, Lear begins to realise that the 'all' he has given Regan and Goneril is being balanced – if that is the word – by nothing at all (and will come to know that Cordelia's 'nothing' is everything). With his daughters' final and specifically numerical slashes at his selfhood, 'What need you five-and-twenty? ten? or five? ... What need one?' Lear begins to see the human condition as going beyond what 'moral mathematics' or the balance sheet will justify:

> O! reason not the need; Our basest beggars
> Are in the poorest thing superfluous:
> Allow not nature more than nature needs,
> Man's life is cheap as beast's. Thou art a lady;
> If only to go warm were gorgeous,
> Why, nature needs not what thou gorgeous wear'st,
> Which scarcely keeps thee warm. But, for true need, –
> You Heavens, give me that patience, patience I need! –
>
> (II.iv.262–9)

Like Cordelia's use of 'bond' in Act I scene i, Lear's agonised 'O! reason not the need' epitomises the competition between the financial accounting and links metaphors crucial to the play's conceptual structure. Historically, 'reason' had as one of its nominal meanings a monetary reckoning.[15] The term 'need' bespeaks a link of desperate desire between Lear and 'th' name and addition of a king', represented for *this* king by the number of his retainers, which defines for Lear the nature of kingship beyond what a debit-credit, accounts-book, cost-benefit analysis would show, and represented for human beings by more than the entitlement of their mere physical requirements. For the first time, Lear begins to weigh the links of humanity more than account balances. 'True need' cannot be reasoned, accounted for, reckoned up.

3 The LINKS Schema

Early in the play, the links-based metaphors involving Lear have to do more with breaking links than with creating them. From his first entrance, Lear sees only the financial side of Cordelia's rich-languaged assertion of the 'bond' between them, and ignores her attempt to couch the father–daughter link in language that he will understand ('I return those duties back as are right fit'). Instead, Lear both physically and spiritually breaks the filial bond and denies the bonding structures of both ownership and family:

> Here I disclaim all my paternal care,
> Propinquity and property of blood,

> And as a stranger to my heart and me
> Hold thee from this for ever.
>
> (I.i.112–15)

Later, when Goneril begins the process of stripping him of his retainers, Lear seeks to destroy not only the father–daughter link, but the link of common membership in the human race – 'degenerate bastard' – and to extend this curse into the next generation, so that Goneril either may have the mother–child link denied her or have the parental link become for her an instrument of exquisite torture. Lear prays that the gods may give his own daughter a 'child of spleen' who will be 'thwart disnatured torment' to her, yet linked to her by the very constitutive linking structures that she has denied her father: nature, honour, pains and benefits, and thanks.

This severing of links is carried even further in Act II: Lear threatens to deny the bond of marriage with Regan's mother and thus his bond of fatherhood to Regan, and turns this destruction of human bonds upon himself. Lear converts his physical links of flesh and blood to Goneril to highly particularised, loathsome diseases of that same flesh and blood. The bonds that link Lear with Goneril now are only those of 'disease', 'plague', and 'corrupted blood' (II.iv.220, 222, 223). Finally, in the midst of the storm, Lear would shatter the links that hold together the world, the bonds of nature and the human race, the very 'germains' or gene-pool of life itself. He stands alone, 'the pattern of all patience', divested of links of any kind, to his daughters, to his household, to his kingdom, to the elements of the created world. Lear does not 'tax [the] elements with unkindness' (III.ii.16) because they are not of Lear's kind, they are not linked to him as his daughters should be, by gratitude, by blood, by the duty of subjects to their king.

As Lear's reintegration with the human condition begins, we likewise understand that reintegration through the schema of LINKS. As the nature of the metaphors based upon that schema begins to change, Lear first identifies himself with the Fool through shared physical needs of warmth and safety, and sees himself as linked to the Fool in suffering and sympathy:

> Come on, my boy. How dost, my boy? Art cold?
> I am cold myself. Where is this straw, my fellow?
> The art of our necessities is strange,
> And can make vile things precious. Come, your hovel.
> Poor Fool and knave, I have one part in my heart
> That's sorry yet for thee.
>
> (III.ii.68–73)

Lear demonstrates this same pattern – from physical sensation to mental feeling, from concrete to abstract, from his own physical suffering to a spiritual empathy with the suffering of another – as he begins to reverse the operative definition of kingship that has so far dominated the play: a status in which the links between a king and his subjects (and a father and his daughters) are constituted by the abstractions of courtly ceremony, of debits and credits. Lear seeks the ground of human community and kingship in the concrete links of shared physical suffering in the storm, between his nakedness and his subjects' 'loop'd and window'd raggedness' (III.iv.31), between man and man, and between a King and his subjects. When he strips off his garments in the play's climactic scene and stands naked against the elements, he is clothed in his solidarity with the physical nakedness of Tom o'Bedlam, linked to him in spiritual nakedness and vulnerability of 'unaccommodated man' before the random cruelties of the gods.

The progression is crucial. When Lear's understanding of the world in terms of the empty abstractions of the balance sheet and kingly ceremony fails him, he progressively denies first the abstract and then the physical links of fatherhood, his own marriage, his ungrateful daughters' legitimacy, their humanity and their progeny, and finally the linking structures of the created world and the human species. He then re-cognises and rebuilds his place in that world in terms of these links, bonding himself first with physical feeling (cold), then with spiritual feeling (empathy), then with individuals (the Fool), then with the rags and hunger of his kingdom's subjects ('the poor naked wretches' with 'houseless heads and unfed sides' (III.iv.28, 30)), and finally with the irreducibly human, unaccommodated, primal human condition figured in Mad Tom. This condition and bond are epitomised in Lear's 'We came crying hither' and in that 'very foolish fond old man' of Act IV, linked to Cordelia now in human mortality and imperfection.

4 On Description and Explanation

Few of the critical analyses in the foregoing are startling; indeed, Lear's restoration to humanity is an important part of any discussion of the play. Some of the financial language in *King Lear* (although not its critical significance) has been described before, as have the play's larger structural entities and the relationships between them. But to describe the play's financial language is merely that: description. What I would claim for this article as an analysis from the standpoint of cognitive metaphor is that this theory enables us not merely to describe, but to *explain* patterns of this kind, and to explain them and their interconnections at different structural levels of the play using the same theoretical apparatus. The analyses produced by a cognitive-metaphoric approach are, moreover, better grounded than earlier purely critical work.

As to the first of these assertions, cognitive metaphor proceeds on the hypothesis that '... metaphor is not just a matter of language, but of thought and reason' (Lakoff 1993: 13). The same concept, or 'activated pattern inhering in thought' (Turner 1991: 45), underlies both the dozens of examples in *King Lear* of metaphors of financial accounting that instantiate the BALANCE schema and many larger structures in the play. These would include, by way of example, the Gloucester–Edmund–Edgar subplot balanced against the main plot, and the play's balanced sets of characters: the 'unnatural' children – Edmund on one side, Goneril and Regan on the other; the rejected, despised, and then redeemed fathers – Gloucester and Lear; the 'natural' children – Edgar and Cordelia; and the good and bad servants – the Fool and Oswald. The connection between these entities and the balance-based metaphors in the text is not accidental, fortuitous, or the product of what Fish (1980: 251) criticises as responsive only to 'the pressure of the question "how do they relate?" and a relation will always be found'. The connection results from the same process, metaphoric projection from the BALANCE schema, into many distinct domains of the play: into the abstractions of Lear's idea of paternal love, and the ways in which his daughters' responses play into and resist it; into the abstractions of plot-construction, character relations, and narrative sequence; into psychological and social settings, and into many other structural elements (for discussion of these elements and cognitive-metaphoric analysis, see Wye 1992 chapters 3 and 4).

The second part of my claim for cognitive metaphor is perhaps more important. The metaphoric impulse is grounded not in intellectual abstractions but in the body that is in the mind. Because cognitive-metaphoric analysis proceeds from the elements and structure of schematised bodily experience to their projection into such abstractions as (for *King Lear*) family relationships and parental and filial love, these analytical claims can be confirmed or disconfirmed according to the accuracy with which those elements and structure and their projection are articulated. The same falsifiability applies, *mutatis mutandis*, to claims made for metaphoric projection into larger abstract structural units. In short, this analysis can be falsified if its topological analysis proves to be wrong. It can be invalidated if the patterns it posits exist only at the level of text and not in larger structural units, or if a competing candidate source domain and metaphoric projection better explains these patterns at all levels of the literary work.[16]

On this second point, we can, for example, trace a pattern of textual metaphors in *King Lear* that depend on the core metaphor LIFE IS A JOURNEY, which is based on the PATH schema: 'we came crying hither' (IV.vi.176); 'I have no way, and therefore want no eyes; I stumbled when I saw' (IV.i.18–19); 'she's [Cordelia] gone for ever ... Thou'lt come no more' (V.iii.258, 306), and many others. But very little connects this pattern of metaphoric projection in the text with larger structural elements in the play. The PATH schema entails such salient aspects as starting and terminal points and a sequence of locations that connect the beginning and the end (for discussion, see Johnson 1987: 113–17). The lives of all of *King Lear's* major characters have terminal points: most of them die. But we see little of the source points of these paths, the beginning of these journeys. A contrasting example, *Macbeth*, is not only replete with textual metaphors based on the PATH schema, but the LIFE IS A JOURNEY metaphoric projection dominates the play's plot and characters (the extreme case is Macduff, who begins the journey of his life by an alternate route to the conventional birth canal – for discussion, see D.C. Freeman forthcoming). Thus for *King Lear* we can make a principled argument *for* two candidate source domains, BALANCE and LINKS (they exist independently and the play manifests both a pattern of projections from them at the textual level and an equally rich pattern of the same projections at different levels) and *against* a third, the PATH (the play manifests a pattern of projections from it at the same level, but few if any at different levels), as the defining 'conceptual universe' (M.H. Freeman forthcoming) of the play.

Of course the choice of dominant source domains and hence of the abstract entities into which they are projected is interpretive, even if we grant the currently all-encompassing sense of that term (see Fish 1989: 320). These choices can change over time: for me, they have changed in 35 years of watching, reading and teaching *King Lear* from the SCALE schema ('Thy life's a miracle. Speak yet again ... Do but look up' [IV.vi.55, 59], and 'The worst is not / So long as we can say "This is the worst"'[IV.i.27–8], both instances of the orientational metaphors GOOD IS UP, BAD IS DOWN) to the PATH schema (in particular, the LIFE IS A JOURNEY metaphor), instantiated in the lines cited above. These changes arise from autobiography, from deepening insight, from changing views that arise from many causes. I have 're-cognised' *King Lear* several times, and I probably will do so again. But these progressive acts of 'interpretation', acts of choice, are far from being unconstrained. My choice of source domains is limited to those that are independently motivated. BALANCE, LINKS, PATH, and SCALE all lead richly documented lives as image-schemata underlying similar source domains outside *King Lear*. My choice of target domains into which a candidate source domain is projected must be consistent in form with that source domain (the source domain for 'I love you according to my bond' cannot arise from a CONTAINER schema because we do not conceive of 'bond' as having the shape of a container).

On the theory of cognitive metaphor, both my changed 'interpretations' over time and the very different 'interpretive' choices that might be made within a different interpretive community from mine are situated in the body and in bodily experience. Interpretations that depend on evidence from cognitive–metaphoric analysis are constrained both by that experience and by the requirement that the topology of that schematised experience in a metaphoric source domain be mapped into the topology of the target domain. The relative validity of particular source domains and metaphoric projection can be assessed with reference to their independent motivation and internal consistency. Of course there is no one valid God's-eye interpretation of a literary work, whether the evidence for such a claim arises from cognitive metaphor or anything else. But there is a range of plausible interpretations and a scale of valid ones. Cognitive metaphor constrains the interpretive community to the body of the embodied imagination.

Notes

1   Research for this article was conducted at the Institute of Cognitive Studies, University of California, Berkeley, while I was on sabbatical leave from the University of Southern California. I am grateful to both institutions for their support of this work, part of a longer study of cognitive metaphor in Shakespeare's major plays. Quotations from *King Lear* are taken from the Arden Shakespeare edition of the play (Muir 1985).

2   The body of recent literature on metaphor is enormous. A brief summary of this field as of a decade ago may be found in Levinson (1983: 147–62). An unsurprisingly partisan account of more recent work may be found in Lakoff forthcoming.

3   The play's financial language was noted as long ago as 1928 by Fr. Gundolf (*Shakespeare, Sein Wesen und Werk*), cited in Clemen (1951: 135), and most recently and felicitously in Colie (1974: 185–219). But these studies fail to capture two systematic relationships: first, between that language's source domain in financial accounting and the schema of BALANCE; second, between this source domain and the schema of LINKS.

4   Throughout what follows I use the term 'scenario' for what cognitive grammarians usually call a 'frame' or 'cognitive model' or 'idealised cognitive model', a way of understanding a concept or scene that structures our thinking about it.

5   Frost (1958) perceives that predictable outcomes such as the already determined awards of territory are the nature of rituals like this scene. Cordelia thus not only disrupts the ritual but, more seriously, disrupts the participants' (and the audience's) settled expectation of its outcome.

6   Reported in Brown (1905: 78).

7   Lear is to use precisely this word to describe his actions to Cornwall and Albany after he has disinherited Cordelia:

> I do invest you jointly with my power,
> Pre-eminence, and all the large effects
> That troop with majesty.
>
> (I.i.129–31)

8   See *OED. s.v.* short, III.C.8.c., 1579: 'They will all comme to short in their reckoning.'

9   Cordelia is one

> to whose young love
> The vines of France and milk of Burgundy
> Strive to be interess'd;
>
> (I.i.82–4)

'Interested' is glossed in the *OED* (1) as 'To have a right or share.' It is cognate with a noun that captures the modem sense of 'interest' as 'legal concern.'

10   A word that in Shakespeare's time also collocated with 'payment' or 'salary', just as it does today; this passage is cited in *OED* (B.I.45) for the 'payment' sense.

11   But she remains her father's daughter. When Cordelia wields executive authority late in the play she displays some of Lear's bad habits. To any of her retainers who will help the mad Lear she offers 'all [her] outward worth', (IV.iv.10) when by the link of service they should help their mistress's father (who remains, in Cordelia's view, their king as well) gratis. She seeks to balance Kent's service to her with good works of her own, a world-view he rejects with dignified irony:

> CORDELIA   O thou good Kent! how shall I live and work
>   To match thy goodness? My life will be too short
>   And every measure fail me.
> KENT   To be acknowledg'd, Madam, is o'er-paid.
>
>   (IV.vii.1–4)

12   A specifically financial sense, meaning in Shakespeare's time as well as ours 'to offer (money, etc.) in discharge of a debt or liability, especially in exact fulfilment of the requirements of the law and of the obligation'. *OED. s.v.* tender, v., 1.

13   They pledge to Lear as consideration for their inheritances a bond that Cordelia demonstrates is already half-encumbered. Cordelia's 'audit' of Lear's balance sheet demonstrates that his assets are subject to an old adage of financial audits: the troubles are usually found in the receivables.

14   A term in English property law conferring a residual right in land, such as an easement, that can have a monetary value (*Black's Law Dictionary* 1981: 1175).

15   *OED* 2c. The only citations are late fourteenth century. The same sense is not recorded for the verb, but the functional shift, from noun to verb, is one of the most general in English.

16   I am often taxed on this point with being 'totalising' or 'essentialist'. Guilty as charged. I take these terms to mean 'general, ignoring particulars that do not fit the theory.' Noam Chomsky's early work in linguistic theory is often held up to me as an example of this 'fault' (e.g. Chomsky 1957; I blush at the comparison), where he focuses on syntax and gives short shrift to semantics and pragmatics. Chomsky took the strongest position consistent with the reliable facts that he had. Subsequent research produced more, and more reliable, facts, better theoretical accounts of areas of linguistic structure that his early work ignored, etc. But the theory of government and binding, a more recent incarnation (see Chomsky 1981), bears a recognisable resemblance to its 1957 ancestor, as does a libraryful of books and articles produced in the intervening three decades. None of these developments would have been possible, in my view, had not Chomsky been an unrepentant 'totaliser' from the start. Any theory of anything worth anything begins as totalising, essentialist, and universalist, and progressively qualifies its claims as research proceeds. Among the many problems of contemporary literary 'theory' is that in seeking to keep in play exceptions and purported anomalies it explains nothing, and is less 'theory' than 'general talk'.

References

Black's Law Dictionary, 5th edn. (1981), West, St. Paul, Minnesota

Brown, R. (1905) *History of Accounting and Accountants*, Cass, London

Chomsky, N. (1957) *Syntactic Structures*, Mouton, The Hague

Chomsky, N. (1981) *Lectures on Government and Binding*, Foris, Dordrecht

Clemen, W.H. (1951) *The Development of Shakespeare's Imagery*, Harvard University Press, Cambridge, Mass

Colie, R. (1974) Reason and need: *King Lear* and the 'crisis' of the aristocracy, *Some Facets of King Lear: Essays in Prismatic Criticism*, University of Toronto Press, Toronto, 185–219

Fillmore, C. (1982) Frame semantics, in Linguistic Society of Korea, (ed.) *Linguistics in the Morning Calm*, Hanshin, Seoul, 111–38

Fish, S. (1980) *Is There a Text in This Class?*, Harvard University Press, Cambridge, Mass

Fish, S. (1989) *Doing What Comes Naturally*, Duke University Press, Durham, NC

Freeman, D.C. (1991) Songs of experience: new books on metaphor, *Poetics Today*, 12(1):145–64

Freeman, D.C. (forthcoming) 'Catch[ing] the nearest way': *Macbeth* and cognitive metaphor, in *Proceedings of the XVth International Congress of Linguists*, Quebec, August 1992

Freeman, M.H. (forthcoming) Metaphor making meaning: Dickinson's conceptual universe, in *Proceedings of the XVth International Congress of Linguists*, Quebec

Frost, W. (1958) Shakespeare's rituals, *Hudson Review* 10(4):577–85

Green, W. (1930) *History and Survey of Accountancy*, Standard Text Press, Brooklyn, NY

Johnson, M. (1987) *The Body in the Mind*, University of Chicago Press, Chicago

Knight, W.N. (1973) *Shakespeare's Hidden Life: Shakespeare at the Law, 1585–1595*, Mason and Lipscomb, New York

Lakoff, G. (1987) *Women, Fire, and Dangerous Things*, University of Chicago Press, Chicago

Lakoff, G. (forthcoming) The contemporary theory of metaphor, to appear in A. Ortony (ed.) *Metaphor and Thought*, 2nd edn., Cambridge University Press, Cambridge

Lakoff, G. and Turner, M. (1989) *More Than Cool Reason: A Field Guide to Poetic Metaphor*, University of Chicago Press, Chicago

Levin, S.R. (1964) Poetry and grammaticalness, in H.G. Lunt (ed.), *Proceedings of the Ninth International Congress of Linguists*, Mouton, The Hague, 308–16

Levinson, S. (1983) *Pragmatics*, Cambridge University Press, Cambridge

Muir, K. (ed.) (1985) *King Lear*, revised edn. *The Arden Shakespeare*, Routledge, London

Rosinger, L. (1974) *King Lear*, *PMLA* 89(3): 585

Schön, D.A. (1979) Generative metaphor: a perspective on problem-solving in social policy, in A. Ortony (ed.) *Metaphor and Thought*, 1st edn, Cambridge University Press, Cambridge, 254–83

Turner, M. (1991) *Reading Minds: The Study of English in the Age of Cognitive Science*, Princeton University Press, Princeton, New Jersey

Wye, M.E. (1992) Jane Austen's *Emma*: embodied metaphor as a cognitive construct, unpublished Ph.D. dissertation, University of Southern California

Yamey, B.S. (1949) Scientific bookkeeping and the rise of capitalism, *Economic History Review*, 2nd series 1(2): 99–113

CHAPTER 10

Theory in Practice
Skinned: Taxidermy and Pedophilia in Munro's "Vandals"

Carrie Dawson

Alice Munro, one of the most complex of modern writers, manages in her story "Vandals," according to Carrie Dawson, to complicate our understanding of the boundary between culture and nature. Children with memories of pedophile assault recall their experiences being abused by a taxidermist and ultimately take revenge. Munro uses the metaphor of the stuffed animal to think about how humans abuse nature – both human and ambient physical. Carrie Dawson teaches English at Dalhousie University, where she is editor of *The Dalhousie Review*. She works on literary representations of migration and citizenship.

Nature hides.
– Heraclitus

Taxidermy is a narrative art. Whether the animal's body is part of a diorama containing an overabundance of figures arranged to suggest interspecies communion, or whether its glass eyes gaze directly out of a head hanging on a rumpus room wall, taxidermy tells a story about human-animal interactions. But a taxidermic diorama can also tell a different kind of story. In Alice Munro's "Vandals," a taxidermic display arranged to present a narrative about the innocence of nature in fact reveals another, more disturbing one. Because the strangely denatured taxidermic diorama in "Vandals" features idealized displays of animal life that are predicated on the slaughtering, skinning, and stuffing of their animal subjects but are nevertheless received as icons of the natural, it emphasizes our tendency to see nature as a "naive reality" that is self-evident and not in need of explanation.[1] The *perception* of the outdoor diorama as a haven of intra- and interspecies communion works to disguise both the violence on which it is premised and the violence that takes place on its

Original publication details: Carrie Dawson, "Skinned: Taxidermy and Pedophilia in Alice Munro's 'Vandals.'" *Canadian Literature* 184, pp. 69–83. University of British Columbia Press, 2015. Reprinted with permission from Canadian Literature.

Literary Theory: An Anthology, Third Edition. Edited by Julie Rivkin and Michael Ryan.
© 2017 John Wiley & Sons, Ltd. Published 2017 by John Wiley & Sons, Ltd.

grounds; the diorama reminds us of the consequences of failing to scrutinize the "natural." Thus, the diorama, as a simulation of a natural environment, provides fertile ground in which to explore the willing self-deception at the centre of this complex, chilling story.

"Vandals" opens with a letter that Bea Doud composes to Liza, the young woman whom she remembers as one of two "pretty sunburned children" who grew up across the street from "Dismal," the property that Bea shared with her recently deceased partner, Ladner (305). Bea means to thank Liza for checking on the property while Bea cared for Ladner in the hospital, but the letter never gets sent. Instead, Bea retreats into a period of slightly drunken musing that provides the material for much of the first part of the story. Among other things, Bea remembers the second time she visited Ladner at Dismal: "'I expect you'd like a tour,' Ladner said" (316), before leading her on a strenuous walk along the trails criss-crossing the property, Bea recalls that "[s]he couldn't keep track of their direction or get any idea of the layout of the property" (317), but it soon becomes evident that the heavy foliage is not the only cause of her confusion. Bea sees live animals moving among "stuffed and lifelike" ones (317): for example, mating swans let out "bitter squawks" beside "a glass-fronted case containing a stuffed golden eagle with its wings spread, a gray owl, and a snow owl" (316), and real birds flit in and out of a group of stuffed birds that are positioned beside signs inscribed with "tight, accurate, compli-cated information" about their habitats, food preferences, and Latin names (317).

The stuffed animals belong to indigenous species, so Ladner's carefully crafted taxi-dermic garden could be construed as a simulacrum of the Ontario countryside in which it is located. The presence of a fridge, detailed signs, and inert, reconstructed animals in a garden that also contains living ones seems to create a dialectical context for thinking about the relations between nature and culture, and between the natural and the simu-lated. But Ladner's garden deflects this line of questioning that it seems to invite. In addition to the species identification signs, Ladner has posted quotations in his garden:

Nature does nothing uselessly.

– Aristotle

Nature never deceives us; it is always we who deceive ourselves.

– Rousseau (317)

On one hand, the signs direct visitors to see nature in general and this garden in particular as a sanctuary from human pomp and pretense, a haven from deceit. On the other hand, the "stuffed and lifelike" animal bodies encourage visitors to suspend disbelief and thus deceive themselves. But Bea appears not to see this contradiction. Although she remem-bers the scene in front of her as "complicated," Bea perceives the taxidermic specimens as frozen in mid-motion – "a wolf stood poised to howl, and a black bear had just managed to lift its big soft head" (317) – suggesting her willingness to partake of the fantasy established by the diorama. Given that the story is also concerned with Bea's refusal to admit – to others and, perhaps, even to herself – that Ladner was a pedophile, his diorama functions as a symbol of the often complex relationships between ways of knowing and of not knowing, of preserving disbelief in the face of knowledge too horrible to contemplate.

James Kincaid argues that "what passes for knowledge" about pedophilia "is really 'knowingness', a pact that authorizes us to treat our ignorance as wisdom and to make that ignorance the basis for action" (3). To the best of my knowledge, Munro has not explicitly addressed the particular challenges of writing about pedophilia, but her characterization of *Open Secrets* (the collection in which "Vandals" appears), suggests a shared interest in the dynamic that Kincaid calls knowingness: it is, she says, an attempt to "challenge what people want to know. Or expect to know. Or anticipate knowing" ("National Treasure" 227). In "Vandals," Munro uses the contradictions and violence inherent in the taxidermic garden to "challenge what people want to know" about pedophilia.

In *Child Loving: The Erotic Child and Victorian Culture*, Kincaid emphasizes the extent to which Victorian and, to a lesser extent, contemporary constructions of pedophiles have been used to shore up dominant ideals of the natural. If pedophiles are perverse animals who violate the order of nature, then the "rest of us" can be civilized, socialized, and controlled. Kincaid's idea of the natural is understandably restricted to the historical dissociation of child and adult, asexuality and sexuality, innocence and experience. Munro also addresses this dissociation, but she does so by using "nature" – in the commonplace sense of the great outdoors – to make us examine the "natural" in the context of human behaviour. Put differently, Munro uses the events that take place in Ladner's garden to demonstrate the consequences of our failure to scrutinize the "natural." The "shame in the grass" (341) at Dismal goes undetected or at least unreported, in part because it is disguised by its setting and by the perception of its setting. When, for example, Ladner takes Bea on her first tour of Dismal, Bea, who is wearing high heels and nursing a vague plan to seduce him, thinks, "this tour, so strenuous physically and mentally, might be a joke on her, a punishment for being, after all, such a tiresome vamp and a fraud" (318). Whether or not Ladner intends the tour as a rebuke, Bea believes that the time spent in the bush is designed to be corrective. While Bea's response to the tour draws on a long-standing discourse about nature as the source of health and purity and as a model for social relations, nature does not – as she later recognizes – work this way at Dismal. Bea notes that the physical exertion of the hike has caused her lust to evaporate. However, Munro subtly suggests that Bea's sexual energy is not lost at all, but redirected onto the nonhuman world: "By this time lust was lost to her altogether, though the smell of the hawthorn blossoms seemed to her an intimate one, musty or yeasty" (318). Thus at the same time that Bea figures the nonhuman world as a haven from or curative for human deceit and desire, Munro shows that we experience and represent that nonhuman world – in this case, the hawthorn blossoms – through our own human predilections.

As a taxidermist, Ladner is skilled in the art of deception. But because taxidermy is such a realistic art form it has, as Donna Haraway argues, been traditionally understood to be peculiarly "capable of embodying truth" in the bodies of its lifelike subjects ("Teddy Bear" 254). In a discussion of Carl Akeley's contribution to the field of taxidermy, Haraway explains the relationship between taxidermy and truth-telling;

> Taxidermy became the art most suited to the epistemological and aesthetic stance of realism. The power of this stance is in its magical effects: what is so painfully constructed appears effortlessly, spontaneously found, discovered, simply there if one will look. Realism does not appear to be a point of view, but appears as a 'peephole into the jungle' where peace may be witnessed. ("Teddy Bear" 254)

Ladner's attempt to "tell the truth of nature" (257) with his taxidermic garden is, of course, enhanced by the outdoor setting. And because the garden purports to "tell the truth of nature," it disguises the violations that take place on its grounds: where the truth is "effortlessly, spontaneously found," one need not look very hard.

Given Munro's stated desire in *Open Secrets* to "challenge what people want to know" and "to record how women adapt to protect men" ("A National Treasure" 227), we can assume that "Vandals" is centrally concerned with the question or possibility of what Bea knows. The assumption that Bea does know what goes on in the garden is supported by Liza's expectation that "Bea could spread safety, if she wanted to" (343). When, for example, Liza finds Bea sitting contentedly under a plum tree drinking wine with Ladner shortly after Liza has witnessed him contemptuously mimicking Bea, she thinks that Bea had "forgiven Ladner, after all, or made a bargain not to remember" (343). It seems that the incident for which Ladner is ostensibly forgiven is his imitation of Bea, but maybe Bea has agreed to forgive and forget a great deal more. Similarly, Bea's characterization of herself as a "fake" whose voice is memorable for its "artificiality" (337, 336), combined with her suggestion that she has come to terms with "what [Ladner] would say and wouldn't say" (320), intimates that she may indeed know more than she is willing or able to say.[2] In "Carried Away," another story in *Open Secrets*, Bea acknowledges her tendency to edit or selectively "forget" the truth where "it would have made the story less amusing" (29).

Bea's "knowingness" is encoded in her references to nature (in all the many senses of the word). For example, on the topic of self-deception, Bea thinks, "such was not her nature. Even after years of good behavior, it was not her nature" (313). In the context of a story in which the nonhuman world is denaturalized and rendered deceptive by a taxi-dermic diorama, Bea's repetition of "nature," combined with the repeated evidence that she might well be given to self-deception, suggests her inclination to use the ostensibly self-evident "natural" to justify her self-deception. In an attempt to characterize Ladner's brusque and heavily ironic manner of treating her, Bea describes herself as "*slit top to bottom with jokes*" (315). This image aligns Bea with the animals whose skins have been slit; it also indicates Ladner's capacity for violence. Moreover "slit," a derogatory term for female genitalia, might also suggest that sex and violence are linked in Bea's mind.

The connection between Bea's apparent naivete and her invocation of the natural world is also evident in her metaphorical connection of teenagers and "savage beasts." In the letter that Bea writes to Liza, she thanks Liza for boarding up the windows of her home, and thus protecting the house from "savage beasts," which, as a subsequent comment makes clear, means teenagers. The house is in fact raided by people in their late teens or early twenties: Liza and her husband Warren. When Liza returns to Dismal at Bea's bidding, she does not check the pipes as asked. Instead, she goes on a rampage, breaking furniture and glass, and throwing stuffed animal specimens to the floor. As she prepares to leave, Warren reminds her that they need to smash a hole in a window – "Big enough so a kid could get in" (344) – so that Bea will not know that the vandals were key-holders. After breaking the window, Warren nails a board over the smashed pane, saying, "Otherwise animals could get in" (344). That Bea's allusion to teenagers as beasts so closely resembles Warren's comment suggests that she knows what happened at the house, even though the tone and content of the letter do not reveal this. Bea's comment that the vandalized house "looked natural" and that it "seemed almost the right way for things to be" (306) can be read as her tacit recognition of the violence that has taken place just outside its doors.

William Cronon argues that "the time has come to rethink wilderness," to rethink our conception of wilderness as an "antidote to our human selves" and "the one place we can turn to escape from our own too-muchness" ("Trouble" 69). Munro makes a similar argument in "Vandals." Both authors suggest that our tendency to see the nonhuman world as "an antidote to our human selves" means that we fail to see "our own unexamined longings and desires" reflected there (Cronon, "Trouble" 70). We may also fail to see our deepest fears. Bea's many references to "nature" seem premised on a belief that the nonhuman world is the site or repository of authenticity and truth. This view inhibits Bea from looking more closely at what went on in the garden. If she had looked more closely, she might have been able to meet Liza's expectation that she would "spread safety" at Dismal (343).

If pedophilia is an "open secret" in "Vandals," it is the taxidermic diorama that makes it so. Although Ladner's garden – like so many taxidermic displays – sets out to celebrate individual communion with nature, what the mute and inert animal bodies demonstrate is the painfully reconstructed nature of the scene. The taxidermic display can be read as a story about the violation and manipulation of bodies, and about man's domination of nature. In "Vandals," the taxidermist's aesthetic arrangement of bodies and his choice of ideal(ized) speciments, frozen in a state of arrested development, hints at a very particular kind of bodily violation.[3] In the second half of the story, Liza remembers what happened while she was swimming in the pond at Dismal. Ladner attempted to grab her between her legs, and she escaped his clutches by clambering through the diorama: "She splashed her way out and heavily climbed the bank. She passed the owls and the eagle staring from behind the glass. The 'Nature does nothing uselessly' sign" (338). Liza is unable to articulate the trauma of Ladner's assault, but her position among the animals is telling. The image of the violated girl child among the dead birds recalls the myth of Philomela, the rape victim turned tongue-tied bird. Because Liza is seen against the backdrop of the diorama but does not appear to look at any of the birds, she does not exercise the tran-scendance implied by the taxidermic gaze; she is not constituted as a viewer of displayed animal bodies but is implicitly compared to the birds, whose silent and violated bodies are on display.

While Ladner's diorama tells the story of pedophilia, it is difficult to interpret because the heavily forested landscape at Dismal is, as both Bea and Liza acknowledge, confusing and difficult to read.[4] But readerly difficulty also arises at Dismal because meaning in Ladner's taxidermic garden is very unstable and changes according to his whim. For instance, Liza recalls the time when she first showed Bea the initials "P.D.P." carved into a tree:

> In the middle of the path was a beech tree you had to go around, and there were initials carved in the smooth bark. One "L" for Ladner, another for Liza, a "K" for Kenny. A foot or so below were the letters "P.D.P." When Liza had first shown Bea the initials, Kenny had banged his fist against P.D.P. "Pull down pants!" he shouted, hopping up and down. Ladner gave him a serious pretend-rap on the head. "Proceed down path," he said, and pointed out the arrow scratched in the bark, curving around the trunk. "Pay no attention to the dirty-minded juveniles," he said to Bea. (338)

Given that the children are sexually abused in the garden, we can assume that Kenny has been led to believe that "P.D.P." sometimes does mean, "Pull down pants." This reading is also suggested by the context in which the phrase "P.D.P." subsequently appears:

> Here are the places of serious instruction where Ladner taught them how to tell a hickory tree from a butternut.… And places where Liza thinks there is a bruise on the ground, a tickling and shame in the grass.
>
> *P.D.P.*
> *Squeegey-boy.*
> *Rub a dub-dub.* (341)

The message carved into the tree shows Ladner's ability to make meanings shift according to his desires, and his garden demonstrates his desire to control his surroundings. In an essay about Scottish poet Ian Hamilton Finlay's garden, Susan Stewart argues that "[I]n making a garden one composes with living things, intervening in and contextualising, and thus changing, their form…. The garden is thereby linked to other means of ordering life: codifying and ritualizing social time and space, creating political orders and social hierarchies" (111). Because Ladner's garden is composed, in part, of dead things, it "orders" life not by ritualizing time, but by freezing it in an image of "taxidermic timelessness" (Simpson 94).[5] And, because Ladner is ultimately powerless to prevent the growth and eventual departure of the children, his taxidermic garden can be understood as an attempt to preserve a fantasy of intra- as well as inter-species control and communion. It should not be surprising, then, that the animals in Ladner's "remarkable sort of nature preserve" (311) are arranged in groups that tell a nostalgic story about man's God–given dominion over nature and about Edenic unity and plenitude. For example, the careful arrangement of a "dainty family of skunks" simulates a congenial community, and, in an image reminiscent of the lion lying down with the lamb, a porcupine is positioned beside a fisher, which, says Ladner, "was intrepid enough to kill porcupines" (317).

There is a long tradition of taxidermists who have attempted to recreate a Canadian Eden. As George Colpitts demonstrates, taxidermists played an important part in producing images of Edenic natural abundance that were used to attract immigrants between 1890 and 1914. Wildlife specimens were installed in provincial and municipal natural history museums across the country, and they were also sent to international exhibitions in the USA and Europe. For example, the federal superintendent of immigration shipped crates of birds and a large buffalo to various European offices as evidence of "what could be got in Canada" (qtd. in Colpitts 106). And yet, given the fate that befell the Canadian buffalo in the last decades of the nineteenth century, the buffalo was an ironic but not inappropriate choice for a symbol of Canadian wildlife: as Colpitts points out, the taxidermic images of Canadian over-abundance belied the fact that Western Canadians had faced a meat crisis and general food shortages as recently as the mid–1870s.

Colpitts's argument identifies antecedents for Ladner's efforts to recreate Eden in spite of the evidence that "should have countered" the formation of that image of Canada (Colpitts 113). But it is Robert Lecker's reading of another story in *Open Secrets* that is most useful in demonstrating the perversity of Ladner's nostalgic garden of Dismal. Drawing extensively on Leo Marx's *Machine in the Garden: Technology and the Pastoral Ideal in America*, Lecker argues that "Carried Away" documents the "postwar, postindustrial fall that is identified with the commodification of all forms of human activity" and with the perceived "loss of nature" (103). Although "Carried Away" is centrally concerned with the postwar loss of a sense of community and an unspoiled rural landscape, the dream of what Leo Marx calls an "undefiled green republic" (qtd. in Lecker 104) still exists in the character of Patrick Agnew, a gardener who spends his free time in the countryside and who fishes for his supper or dines on the fruit of wild apple trees. But some fifty years later,[6] the over-abundance of animals, the happy juxtaposition of enemy species, and the implicit communion between man and animal in the garden of Dismal constitute a perversion of the "vanishing pastoral ideal" represented by Patrick Agnew. In the "green republic" of Dismal, neither the land nor its inhabitants are "undefiled": children are raped; animals are perceived as commodities that bring "a good price"; and the ground itself is "bruise[d]" and "shame[d]" (341).

Ladner's idea of Dismal as a prelapsarian and, by implication, pre-industrial land-scape is also deeply ironic because the garden itself is full of thinly veiled manufactured things.

> Ladner fitted the skin around a body in which nothing was real. A bird's body could be all
> of one piece, carved of wood, but an animal's larger body was a wonderful construction of
> wires and burlap and glue and mushed-up paper and clay. (334)

Drawing on Donna Haraway's argument about the enduring dualism that pervades discussions of nature and culture, it might be said that Munro represents the "stuffed and lifelike" animals as cyborgs, "beings that are simultaneously animal and machine who populate worlds ambiguously natural and crafted" (*Simians* 149). Because a "cyborg body is not innocent" and "was not born in a garden" (*Simians* 180), its presence consti-tutes a reminder of the extent to which nature is imagined as the absence of and antidote to technology. Ladner employs the cyborg-animals to affirm a vision of nature and tech-nology as separate. But Munro ensures that we see how human beings inevitably construct the nonhuman world in their own image: whether or not our construction of our natural environment involves "wires and burlap and glue and mushed-up paper and clay," it is, she suggests, a construction nevertheless.

Presented in the context of a narrative about an altogether different kind of assault on bodily integrity, and added to the image of Ladner scraping animal skulls and skins, Munro's ironically rendered image of the taxidermic specimens as "wonderful constructions" repudiates Ladner's nostalgic rendering of a thoroughly pastoral, prelap-sarian Dismal.[7] At the same time, it also repudiates an enduring tendency to see animal bodies as self-evident and utterly literal. Jane Desmond points out the particular symbolic power of animal bodies:

> Animals' identities as authentic representatives of the natural are ultimately presumed to
> reside in their bodies, in their physical difference from humans. Their division from us
> articulates the Cartesian and Christian mind-body or body-spirit split. Even when these
> conceptual boundaries are smudged, animals are seen as fundamentally more embodied
> than humans, that is, as more determined by their bodily aspects. (149)

If, on the one hand, the taxidermic garden encourages this view of animal bodies by presenting animals as "aestheticized bodies" whose "stasis ... heightens their objectness and allows for [the] leisurely contemplation of discrete bodily details" and the affirma-tion of bodily difference (Desmond 149–50), Munro's emphasis on scraped skins, "guts that looked like plastic tubing," and eyeballs "squished ... to jelly" (334) demands a meditation on the processes by which that "objectness" is established and, more importantly, on the ends it serves.

In *Picturing the Beast: Animals, Identity, and Representation*, Steve Baker argues that the animal body needs to be taken out of nature and "rendered unstable as a sign" in order that we might understand what it is that we have invested in the animal and what is occluded in our tendency to rely unthinkingly on animals as a prime symbolic site (223). Munro advances a similar view by emphasizing how Ladner has made the animals in his garden. Animal bodies are also destabilized in "Vandals" through the use of animal imagery to describe the human characters. When, for example, Bea arrives at Dismal and asks Liza and her brother, Kenny, "what kind of animals they'd like to be" (332), she reminds the reader of the extent to which they are ready to become animal victims like those whose "skinned bodies" are manipulated by Ladner (334). The connection between the children's bodies and the animals' bodies is reinforced in a number of other passages: Liza "cluck[s]" and makes "croaking noises" (326, 332); she is possessed by a "slithery spirit" (328); and she claims to have been "wild" as a child (329). Given the sexual abuse perpetrated in the garden, Liza's father's warning that she "better not cross [Ladner] or he'll skin you alive.... [l]ike he does with his other stuff" (334), further aligns her with the animals. She and Kenny quickly learn "not to talk so much about all [they] knew" (335); they are silent like the animal specimens. But the equation of the violated children with the stuffed animals is complicated by Munro's description of Ladner in animal images. When Bea first meets Ladner, she mistakenly thinks that he is accompanied by a fierce dog, but later decides that he is "his own fierce dog" (312). As an adult, Liza remembers a time when Ladner raped her and then "collapsed heavily, like the pelt of an animal flung loose from its flesh and bones" (341): as he collected himself, he "clucked his tongue faintly, and his eyes shone out of ambush, hard and round as the animals' glass eyes" (342). Although Munro repeatedly invites the reader to compare Ladner's treatment of childish bodies with his treatment of the animals he stuffs, the fact that Ladner is also likened to an animal ultimately prevents easy correlations. Moreover, by comparing Ladner to a taxidermic animal ("glass eyes" and a disconnected "pelt"), perhaps Munro is also pointing to the tendency to figure pedophiles as animals: if Ladner is an animal, he is one that is painstakingly constructed as such by humans.

James Kincaid argues that the steadfast reluctance to talk about childhood sexuality allows pedophilia to flourish.[8] He goes on to suggest that the contemporary disavowal of childhood sexuality is a hangover from the Romantic era, when a wide range of poets, prose writers, and philosophers constructed the innocent child in nature as an ideal with which to counter the grim reality of the working conditions of child labourers during the Industrial Revolution. Although William Cronon does not address the implications of longstanding ideas about the child in nature, his general discussion of discourses of nature helps to explain how an appeal to "the natural" can deflect critical discussions of childhood sexuality:

> The great attraction of nature for those who wish to ground their moral vision in external reality is precisely its capacity to take disputed values and make them seem innate, essential, eternal, nonnegotiable. When we speak of "the natural way of doing things," we implicitly suggest that there can be no other way, and that all alternatives, being unnatural, should have no claim on our sympathies. ("Introduction" 36)

The essentialism to which Cronon refers helps us understand why "Vandals" is so disturbing: Munro not only brings the pedophile out from the trees and takes nature out of the animal, she also takes the child out of nature. Put differently, Munro's children, like her animals, are not "innocent" and are "not born in a garden" (Haraway, *Simians* 180).

Munro does not suggest that the children sexually desire Ladner, but she does represent them as sexual beings whose behaviours and motivations are as complex and conditioned as those of adults. For example, Liza gives a rhinestone earring to Bea as an acknowledgement of and apology for Ladner's cruel imitation of her: when Bea asks if the earring belonged to Liza's mother – who is dead – Liza lies and says yes, all the while aware that her gift "might be seen as childish and pathetic – perhaps intentionally pathetic" (342).

And, in a move that further repudiates the vision of the child as innocent and natural, Munro has Liza – who lives in a house painted "glaring pink, like lipstick," on a property on which there is "not one tree" (340) – project her own sexual urges onto the natural world. After characterizing Ladner's abuse as a situation she "couldn't get out of …, *or even want to*" (339, emphasis added), Liza describes the allure of Ladner's property:

> Then the pine plantation … with its high boughs and needled carpet, inducing whispering. And the dark rooms under downswept branches of the cedars – entirely shaded and secret rooms with a bare earth floor…. In some places the air is thick and private, and in other places you feel an energetic breeze. (341)

In an ironic rejoinder to the image of the Romantic child at home in nature, Munro has Liza figure the natural realm as a domicile – a place with "rooms," a "floor," "carpet," and culture. Not only does Munro refuse to polarize child and adult, human and animal, nature and culture, but she also shows us what we risk by doing so. She shows us that the tendency to posit the natural and the cultural as distinctive spheres allows for what Desmond calls "the naturalization of the cultural" (192): it allows the category of the natural to function as a "rudder," steering us away from destabilizing questions and bringing us back, time and again, "to biology as if it were a neutral, natural, originary category" (192). Likewise, Munro shows us that by imagining childhood innocence in opposition to adult sexuality, and by using pedophilia to shore up our ideas of what is natural, we "find ourselves sacrificing the bodies of children" (Kincaid 6).

"Do you care if he croaks?" (332). In answer to the question that Warren puts to Liza while she sets about destroying Ladner and Bea's property, Liza makes "croaking noises to stop him being thoughtful" (332). Moments earlier she makes "a funny noise – an admiring cluck of her tongue" while dumping the contents of desk drawers on the floor (326). After raping Liza, Ladner also "clucked his tongue" (342). The echoing "cluck" is important because it establishes Liza's violent behaviour as a direct response to Ladner's abuse of her, while also suggesting her tendency to emulate Ladner and identify with him. As Nathalie Foy argues, Liza "recuperates the good in Ladner" by recalling and taking on his role as instructor (159):

> "Can you tell what the trees are by their bark?" she said.
> Warren said that he couldn't even tell from their leaves. "Well, maples," he said. "Maples and pines."
> "Cedar," said Liza. "You've got to know cedar. There's a cedar…. And that one with the bark like gray skin? That's a beech. See, it had letters carved on it, but they've spread out, they just look like any old blotches now."
> Warren wasn't interested. He only wanted to get home. It wasn't much after three o'clock, but you could feel the darkness collecting, rising among the trees, like cold smoke coming off the snow. (344)

At the end of the story, the reader also feels a "darkness collecting," for the pedophile has been rendered more fearful for his lack of monstrosity, for the very ordinariness of his desire to teach children and his ability to elicit their trust and respect. Although I do not share Nathalie Foy's sense that the blurred letters in the beech tree, rediscovered in the wake of Liza's cathartic act of vandalism, indicate that she has succeeded in "dispell[ing]" the darkness that has haunted her (159), I do think that the act of reading the natural world is represented as a means of staving off that darkness. The first meeting between Ladner and the children contains a specific injunction:

> The first time that Liza and Kenny had ever been on Ladner's property, they had sneaked in under a fence, as all the signs and their own father had warned them not to do. When they had got so far into the trees that Liza was not sure of the way out, they heard a sharp whistle.
>
> Ladner called them: "You two!" He came out like a murderer on television, with a little axe, from behind a tree. "Can you two read?"
>
> They were about six and seven at this time. Liza said, "Yes."
>
> "So did you read my signs?" (333)

The context suggests that the signs to which Ladner refers are the "No Trespassing," "No Hunting," and "Keep Out" signs that line his property (325), but there are, as I have already indicated, numerous other signs in Dismal. Some of them contain scientific information, but others present quotations:

> Nature does nothing uselessly.
>
> – Aristotle

> Nature never deceives us; it is always we who deceive ourselves.
>
> – Rousseau

These signs – set off from the text and presented in italics – contain a direct challenge to the reader. Aristotle's dictum, "Nature does nothing uselessly," demands that we reflect critically on the uses – both material and metaphorical – to which nature is put. The Rousseau quotation, displayed in the midst of a "lifelike" simulation of the natural, challenges us to consider how we deceive ourselves by clinging to the idea that the "natural" world is a repository of truth – as indeed both Bea and Ladner do. Bea's references to nature and the natural inhibit her own critical faculties; Ladner uses the nonhuman world to stage his own Edenic dream of timelessness and communion. If, like Bea and Ladner, we fail to heed the challenges implicit in these two signs, presented in a story concerned with the abuse of both the "natural" and the human, then we, too, are mired in – and even complicit in – the darkness collecting at the story's end. But to accept this challenge, and to remember, for example, Heraclitus' dictum that "Nature hides," is to begin to shed light on the ways that we think, or refuse to think, about pedophilia. "So did you read my signs?" asks Munro.[9]

Notes

1 In the "Introduction" to *UnCommon Ground*, William Cronon describes the perception of "nature as naïve reality" this way: "It is in fact one of the oldest meanings that the word 'nature' carries in the English language: the sense that when we speak of the nature of something, we are describing its fundamental essence, what it really and truly is. Indispensable as the usage may be, it is dangerous for what it tempts us to assume: the very thing it seeks to label is too often obscured beneath the presumption of naturalness" (34).

2 Natalie Foy disagrees, arguing that Bea's "ignorance" of the abuse is "complete" (151). However, Foy's otherwise very strong argument is undermined by her own acknowledgement that "[w]e know that Bea is capable of forgetting unpleasant associations" (151) and, more generally, by

Munro's determination to preserve and to emphasise a degree of ambiguity. As a further argument for the possibility of Bea's "knowingness," consider the extent to which the following passage invites us to question her motivation for sending Liza to college: "'It was her gave me some money.' Liza continued, as if it was something he ought to know, 'To go to college. I never asked her. She just phones up out of the blue and says she wants to'" (322). Also consider Bea's recognition of Ladner's "insanity" and of own very complicated desire for a man capable of offering her an insanity that she could "liv[e] inside" (314).

3 For a discussion of the taxidermist's interest in ideal(ised) animal bodies, see "Teddy Bear Patriarchy," where Haraway discusses Carl Akeley's relentless search for "the unblemished type specimen" (254).

4 See Bea's description of the property on 317, Liza's description of the property on 333, and Liza's description of the attraction that Dismal held for her as a child on 340–41.

5 Simpson's "Immaculate Trophies" does a good job of exploring the contradictions and ironies of the "frozen liveness of wild nature" (92).

6 The central event in "Carried Away" is the factory accident that results in the beheading of Jack Agnew in 1924. At that time Bea, who also makes an appearance in the story, is 13. When Bea sits down to write Liza a letter in the opening paragraph of "Vandals," more than 50 years have passed. No dates are given in "Vandals," but Bea's indication that Ladner was a Vietnam veteran when she first met him, and the fact that reruns of "I Dream of Jeannie" are playing on the television suggest that "Vandals" is set in the early to mid 1980s.

7 See Redekop's argument that Munro frequently constructs the nostagic as grotesque in order to repudiate it.

8 Also see Levine and Steed.

9 Thanks to Susan Fisher, Susie O'Brien, Pat Saunders-Evans, and Andy Wainwright, who generously read and commented on earlier versions of this paper.

Works Cited

Alice Munro Writing On…. Spec. issue of *Essays on Canadian Writing* 66 (Winter 1998).

Baker, Steve. *Picturing the Beast: Animals, Identity, and Representation.* Manchester and New York: Manchester UP, 1993.

Colpitts, George. "Wildlife Promotions, Western Canada Boosterism, and the Conservation Movement, 1890–1914." *American Review of Canadian Studies* 28.1–2 (Spring/Summer 1998): 103–30.

Cronon, William. "Introduction." *Uncommon Ground: Rethinking the Human Place in Nature.* Ed. William Cronon. New York and London: Norton, 1995, 23–56.

Cronon, William. "The Trouble with Wilderness: or, Getting Back to the Wrong Nature." *Uncommon Ground* 69–90.

Desmond, Jane C. *Staging Tourism: Bodies on Display from Waikiki to Sea World.* Chicago and London: U of Chicago P, 1999.

Foy, Nathalie. "'Darkness Collecting': Reading 'Vandals' as a Coda to *Open Secrets*." *Alice Munro Writing On …* 66 (Winter 1998): 147–68.

Kincaid, James R. *Child-Loving: The Erotic Child and Victorian Culture.* New York and London: Routledge, 1992.

Haraway, Donna. *Simians, Cyborgs, and Women.* New York: Routledge, 1991.

Haraway, Donna. "Teddy Bear Patriarchy: Taxidermy in the Garden of Eden, New York City, 1908–1936." *Cultures of Unites States Imperialism.* Ed. Amy Kaplan and Donald E. Pease. Durham: Duke UP, 1993: 237–91.

Lecker, Robert. "Machines, Readers, Garden: Alice Munro's 'Carried Away.'" *Alice Munro Writing On …* 66 (Winter 1998): 103–27.

Levine, Judith. *Harmful to Minors: The Perils of Protecting Children from Sex.* Minneapolis: U of Minnesota P, 1999.

Munro, Alice. "A National Treasure: An Interview with Alice Munro." *Meanjin* 54 (Spring 1995): 222–32.

Munro, Alice. "Carried Away." *Open Secrets*. Toronto: Penguin, 1995: 1–58.

Munro, Alice. "Vandals," Munro, *Open Secrets* 305–44.

Redekop, Magdalene. "Alice Munro and the Scottish Nostalgic Grotesque." *Alice Munro Writing On …* 66 (Winter 1998): 21–43.

Simpson, Mark. "Immaculate Trophies." *Essays on Canadian Writing* 68 (Summer 1999): 77–106.

Steed, Judy. *Our Little Secret: Confronting Child Sexual Abuse in Canada*. Toronto: Random House, 1994.

Stewart, Susan. "Garden Agon." *Representations* 62 (Spring 1998): 111–43.

PART TEN
Animals, Humans, Places, Things

CHAPTER 1

Introduction
Matters Pertinent to a Theory of Human Existence

Julie Rivkin and Michael Ryan

The social, political, and cultural sciences are increasingly approximating literature. In a story by a good fiction writer such as Alice Munro, we see, feel, and experience how life works. We are close to the life experience of characters as it happens. That experience is in motion; it is not a statue or a photograph, something fixed in time and limited and clearly defined by a spatial frame or bodily contours. Social scientists talk about the same stuff, but they have tended to use a vocabulary such as "system," "structure," and "ideology" that described abstract aspects of reality or that were quite distant from lived experience, from how life works or how it takes place. More and more, they are diminishing the distance. They are finding new ways of talking about life that gets closer to how fiction writers write. Cultural anthropologist Kathleen Stewart, for example, writes quasi-fictional prose pieces as she records and re-creates the life of the people of Appalachia. This new approach to knowledge is the result of a major change underway in the social sciences and in science more generally.

Until recently, the project of human knowledge assumed that the world was an object opposite our human subject, and we know it using the concepts and methods of the humanities and social sciences. Our mental representations mapped the world and made it knowable. The world remained out there and our knowledge was in here. All fine and good except that we ourselves are part of the material world and the world itself often possesses subjectivity. From bacteria to our fellow animals, it is animate. Moreover, the boundaries that kept realms separate in our minds rarely exist in reality. A Beyoncé concert may be a cultural event, but it is also a translation of affective experience and erotic passion. It is physical stuff – chemical action – in another form – sound, movement, image. Similarly, when we know the world, it is a mental representation, true, but it is also a biological action, one often charged, if one pays close attention to literary theory discussions, with aggression and the acting out of postures charged with narcissistic energy designed to have material effects that often take the form of emotional affects such as *Schadenfreude* (or pleasure in another's downfall).

By dislocating the human subject of knowledge from its location opposite the object world and by immersing it in the matter of the world (like an ice cube melting in a bath

Literary Theory: An Anthology, Third Edition. Edited by Julie Rivkin and Michael Ryan.
© 2017 John Wiley & Sons, Ltd. Published 2017 by John Wiley & Sons, Ltd.

of warm water), recent post-humanist and new materialist theory has also troubled boundary distinctions that accompanied the old subject–object dualism such as society and science, culture and nature, technology and physicality, human and animal, representation and matter, and so on. A crucial term in this new way of conceiving of human knowledge is relation. Things exist in relation to one another. The simple idea in twentieth-century Structuralism that bits of language are given their identity by their differences from one another first migrated into philosophy (and gave rise to deconstruction) and now has migrated into the social and physical sciences. Things are now seen increasingly in terms of relations (in space between each other and in time as in movement from a past into a future). Another important term is network. Increasingly, we are coming to de-isolate objects and events and to see them as parts of temporal processes and of material fields spread out in space. Things translate and change forms, have effects and generate new configurations. Nature and matter are dynamic, and single objects can only be isolated for study at a loss.

Philosophy since the revival of Aristotelianism during the Renaissance has assumed the mind's separateness from the material world and the world's stability, its capacity to assume the form of a simple object. There was and is, however, an alternative tradition in philosophy, and with time, a matching line of theory and inquiry has developed in science, mathematics, and other fields that addresses and adumbrates its concerns. The alternative tradition of philosophers such as Democritus, Lucretius, and Heraclitus noticed that the physical world is dynamic and complex; it does not consist of flat things or of boxed entities. What appear to be separate objects exist in movement; they change and transform; they embody forces that course through them; they belong to fields and networks of which they are apart and from which they are inseparable; they manifest levels of physical existence that are not visible and cannot be visible; they are temporary stabilizations of matter, events rather than states, becoming rather than being; eventually they dissolve and assume other forms. Given how long the matter that constitutes our bodies and our brains has been around and will be around after our passing, it might make more sense to speak of our deaths rather than of our lives. The labors and travails of that flicker of awareness that is our mind is a matter of transcendental indifference to all the matter in us and around us.

The emphasis on change and instability in the alternative materialist philosophic tradition from Lucretius to Deleuze has gained support from recent scientific work in non-linear biology and complexity theory. Complexity theory notices how the physical world is dynamic and emergent. New combinations of matter allow new states to emerge, to bear out their virtual potential – as the color of a flower, for example, is created by thousands of components none of which is itself that color. Ten people standing in a city square might be a family gathering; a million makes it a political movement. Quantity, as Hegel noted, changes quality. All the mitochondria in our brain cells amounts to a pile of matter until it is gathered together in a higher form of organization where it ignites into consciousness.

An entity like the literary canon, as Martin Meadows notes, is a system of complex relations mapped by multiple axes (history, culture, aesthetics) whose ongoing form is difficult to predict. It evolves over time dynamically, reorganizing itself anew every few years in new historical and cultural contexts. An author like Alice Munro emerges with time as a canonical figure because aesthetic categories evolve, her troubling descriptions of raw physicality become more acceptable, an incremental awareness of knowledge of her work emerges, and at a certain point, a change happens that could not easily have been predicted or modeled in advance and that moves her from margin to mainstream.

Biology has also disturbed our sense of the singularity of organisms and the linearity of organic life. The boundaries of organisms are uncertain because their existence depends on an environment with which their bodily existence meshes as ingestion, excretion, respiration, and even cognition. Identity, from a biological perspective, is necessarily ecological and symbiotic. We are in a condition of ongoing symbiosis with the bacteria around and within us. In addition, the components of any organism are themselves inorganic and lifeless. Life emerges from lifeless ingredients. We consist of matter that is lent to us and that is not "us" in that it is impersonal and non-subjective. As a result, it is impossible to separate culture from nature, thought from matter. One cannot say "we" are determined because there is no difference between "we" and what determines.

A major area of concern of the new focus on matter in the cultural and physical sciences is the boundary between humans and other life forms such as animals. From a material perspective, humans are not distinct in any significant way from other beings. By dissolving the human into the common materiality of which it is composed with other life forms, new materialist theorists like Giorgio Agamben, Bruno Latour, and Donna Haraway seek to bring about a new "post-humanist" understanding of what it means for humans to exist in nature. Humanism separated human life from nature and posited nature as a difficult, troubling other that needed to be managed if civil existence was to be maintained through the discipline that gave rise to virtue. The new materialists, in contrast, argue it is better to see humans and nature as one, as part of an interconnected material network. Very different ethics in regard to our own regulated behavior as, for example, sexual beings as well as in regard to other beings such as animals and even bacteria emerge from such a reconceptualization.

A substantial body of critical work has come into being around these ideas, and animals especially have come to the fore as a topic of critical concern. Some of the examples are obvious – Melville's *Moby Dick* – but other writers whose work had been well mined for a host of issues and concerns, from psychology to language to gender – writers such as Virginia Woolf, for example – have proven helpful for examining human relations with animals. The presence of animals in *Mrs. Dalloway*, for example, is, according to Vicki Tromanhauser, not adventitious. When the sympathetically portrayed Septimus Smith sees the world from the perspective of a dog at one point or hears birds singing in Greek as he descends into madness and eventual suicide, he is stepping outside the regime of harsh positivist scientific knowledge associated with the doctor who drives him to kill himself. The doctor represents the humanist laboratory of objective science at its extreme. It kills what it analyzes. In contrast, Woolf's alternative ethic of sympathy and empathy dissolves the boundary that separates humans from the world around them.

Another way to rethink the meaning of the human as a category and as an ideal is to consider it from the perspective of the notions of bodily and cognitive normality that prevail in human culture. Those norms have promoted practices of exclusion and non-accommodation in regard to those with physical and cognitive impairments, everything from speech disabilities or cognitive processing syndromes such as autism to ambulatory limitations and mental illness. A range of critical and theoretical concerns have focused debate in Disability Studies. Some see both ability and disability as constructed norms or concepts that align with other social mechanisms for sorting populations into those considered normal and those considered less worthy. Physical description, when valorized or medicalized, has often served the interest of value judgments that emerge within discourses of racial superiority. The Nazi experience in Germany between World War I and the end of World War II was especially noteworthy for projecting norms of physical beauty that marginalized and subordinated entire sub-populations of physically impaired people. Ideals and norms of ableism have therefore come into focus as objects of critical attention. Other disability theorists focus on the experience of the disabled and on increasing their rights and the medical treatments available to them. The medical humanities seeks to bring medical discourse into literary critical discussions. Other theorists seek to use the idea of disability to displace the distinction between the abled and the disabled. From a purely material perspective, there are no norms; there are only possibilities, different creative iterations of evolutionary nature some of which conform to current majoritarian standards, some of which point towards alternatives. From an evolutionary perspective, we are all mutants. There are no genetic norms – just hesitant, fragile, temporary arrangements of genetic material in a variety of shapes and forms.

When we die, we become our environment, merging with the earth around us. Throughout life, however, we are subject to a humanist illusion that makes us think we are separate from earthly matter. In the 1960s, environmentalists began to challenge that limited humanist perspective and to ask that attention be devoted, for the sake of humanity and the earth's survival, to the larger material world in which *H. sapiens* dwells. By the 1970s, Sharon Glotfelty, Harold Fromm, and others had begun to introduce environmental concerns into literary study. Initially, the ecocritical movement focused on the land and the way land or landscape was represented in literature. More recent bioregional scholars have studied the way physical region and economic region overlap, so that social class and geographic location become equally important aspects of literature, often meshing and being indistinguishable in the portrayal of human lives. For example, Willa Cather's *My Antonia* sets the lives of immigrants in an exacting but supportive landscape already layered and legible with signs of previous habitation. Some of them live in the earth, making a home in burrows not unlike those made by adjacent animal species. As their lives move forward, some are drawn to the town and the city and are changed by their new environments, becoming more preoccupied by the mediated access to survival that money provides. The character of Antonia is in some ways portrayed as a beautiful animal herself, and she is contrasted with the town girls who accommodate themselves to the quest for money as a means of survival.

One consequence of the new materialism and the new emphasis on bioculture is that culture and nature appear to us now to be inseparable. Science bears out the materiality of culture. The study of discourse demonstrates that words have a physical effect on the brain, and different brain regions activate differently in response to different kinds of words. The distinction between discourse and matter or discourse and the body is suggestively undermined by such findings. But equally, the physical matter of the brain is dependent on culture to achieve its full development. The brain has evolved in such a way that without proper nurturing in the form of semiological prompts from its cultural environment, it will not mature to its full capacities. Evolution has contrived to make social learning an essential feature of biological life.

CHAPTER 2

Non-Representational Theory
Life, But Not as We Know It

Nigel Thrift

Nigel Thrift is a leading figure in human geography studies. He coined the phrase "soft capitalism" and developed "non-representational theory." In this selection from that latter work, he summarizes recent changes in how we conceptualize human life, moving away from the idea of the right concept or category and moving closer to lived experience itself. His books include *Non-Representational Theory* (2007), *Spatial Formations* (1996), and *Arts of the Political* (2013).

When it was enthusiastically pointed out within memory of our present Academy that race or gender or nation … were so many social constructions, inventions, and representations, a window was opened, an invitation to begin the critical process of analysis and cultural reconstruction was offered…. The brilliance of the pronouncement was blinding. Nobody was asking what's the next step? What do we do with this old insight? If life is constructed, how come it appears so immutable? How come culture appears so natural?

(Taussig 1993: xvi)

'production,' then, is used according to the meaning of its etymological root (i.e. Latin producere*) that refers to the act of 'bringing forth' an object in space.*

(Gumbrecht 2004: xiii)

a knowledge of arrangement or disposition is, of all others, the most useful.

(Humphrey Repton 1803, cited in Wall 2006: 6)

But can we really assume that the reading of such texts is a reading exclusively concentrated on meaning? Do we not sing these texts? Should the process by which a poem speaks be only carried by a meaning intention? Is there not, at the same time, a truth that lies in its performance? This, I think, is the task with which the poem confronts us.

(Gadamer 2000, cited in Gumbrecht 2004: 64)

Original publication details: Nigel Thrift, "Life But Not As We Know It" from *Non-Representational Theory*, pp. 1–26. Routledge, 2008. Reproduced with permission from Taylor & Francis Books UK.

> *we can and we may, as it were, jump with both feet off the ground into or towards a*
> *world of which we trust the other parts to meet our jump.*
>
> (James 1999 [1911]: 230)

Introduction

Since the early 1990s I have been engaged in an attempt to develop what I call non-representational theory. The chapters in this book are some of the later results of that project, following on in a direct line from *Spatial Formations* (Thrift 1996) and *Knowing Capitalism* (Thrift 2005a). Indeed, the three books should be considered together: they are all part and parcel of the same economic-cum-cultural-cum-political venture.

How to characterize this particular book's contents, then? Stripped to its bare essentials, this is a book about *the geography of what happens*. In large part, it is therefore a work of description of the bare bones of actual occasions but it does not, I hope, adopt a passive stance to its object of enquiry: what is present in experience. And not just because – as I have tried to make clear here and elsewhere – the content of what is present in experience has changed radically. For this is also a book about how these actual occasions, howsoever they may have been altered, might be enlivened – made more responsive and more active – by the application of a series of procedures and techniques of expression. In other words, it is intended as the beginning of an outline of the art of producing a permanent supplement to the ordinary, a sacrament for the everyday, a hymn to the superfluous.[1]

If that sounds too tentative, a little bit tortuous, or even rather portentous, then I am afraid that that is how it will have to be. This is a tentative book because it is not entirely clear what a politics of what happens might look like – indeed, given that so much of what I want to outline is avowedly experimental, perhaps too much in the way of clarity should not necessarily be counted as a good thing[2] (although straightaway I can hear the criticisms from those who believe that theory should slide home like a bolt). It is a little bit tortuous because there is a lot of ground-clearing to do, a lot of hacking back of the theoretical undergrowth in order to get to the nub of the matter. And it is portentous because it involves taking some of the small signs of everyday life for wonders and this involves all manner of risks, and not least pretentiousness. All I can say is that I think that the risk is worth it in order to achieve a diagnosis of the present which is simultaneously a carrier wave for new ways of doing things.

Certainly, in order to achieve its goals, this book has to be three things at once. First, it has to be a work of social and cultural theory.[3] The book builds on a series of cognate traditions in order to construct what I hope is a convincing account of how the worlds[4] are, given that encounters are all there is, and their results cannot be pre-given (although they can, of course, be pre-treated). Complex trajectories rather than blurred genres, as Strathern (1999: 25) puts it. But, second, the book also has to be a diagnostic tool. It is intended to be a work that takes some of the specificities of the present moment and weaves them into what might be called a speculative topography. The contours and content of what happens constantly change: for example, there is no stable 'human' experience because the human sensorium is constantly being re-invented as the body continually adds parts in to itself; therefore how and what is experienced as experience is itself variable.[5] Then, third and finally, the book is intended as a political contribution to the task of reconsidering our hopes for ourselves. This is, after all, a time in which the invention of new 'everyday' forms of democracy has become a part of the political ambition of many people, in which the 'local' and the 'global' have become increasingly awkward political terms but no satisfactory alternative to the connected separation they imply seems to exist, and in which 'what each of us feels capable of' (Ginsborg 2005: 7) is perceived as a vital political issue. The small offering that this book attempts to make to these three debates, and especially to the last one, is an opening up of new political domains which it is then possible to make a corresponding political rumpus about. The book is, most especially then, an attempt to produce an art of the invention of political invention by putting hard questions to the given in experience, the overall intent being to call new publics into existence who will pose questions to politics which are not yet of politics (Rajchman 1998) – whilst recognizing that this questioning can never be more than an inexact science[6] (Stengers 2002a). Bloch (2000 [1923]) called this 'building into the blue'. That is not a bad description for the kind of resource I am trying to construct.

But I need to severely qualify each of these goals. To qualify the first, like many, I think that, in certain senses at least, the social sciences and humanities suffer from a certain kind of over-theoretization at present. There are too many theories, all of them seemingly speaking on behalf of those whose lives have been damaged by the official structures of power.[7] A cynic might think that the profusion of 'fast' theories created by academics is simply a mirror of the rise of brainy classes, who are able to live a life of permanent theoretical revolution whilst everyone else does the dirty work. That would be too harsh. But the criticism is not therefore without any force at all (Rabinow 2006). It seems to me, to qualify the second goal, that this task is a necessary one in a time in which a globalized capitalism based on the rise of the brainy classes has become ever more pervasive, and democracy is in danger of becoming something of a sham, enacted as part of what Sloterdijk (2005c) calls an authoritarian capitalism.

> The mass of the population is periodically doused with the rhetoric of democracy and assured that it lives in a democratic society and that democracy is the condition to which all progressive-minded societies should aspire. Yet that democracy is not meant to realise the demos but to constrain and neutralize it by the arts of electoral engineering and opinion management. It is, necessarily, regressive. Democracy is embalmed in public rhetoric precisely in order to memorialize its loss of substance. Substantive democracy – equalizing, participatory, commonalizing – is antithetical to everything that a high reward meritocratic society stands for. At the same moment that advanced societies have identified their progressive character with perpetual technological innovation they have defined themselves through policies that are regressive in many of their effects. Democracy is where these effects are registered. By virtually every important official norm – efficiency, incentives to unequal rewards, hierarchical principles of authority, expertise – it appears anachronistic, dysynchronous. The crux of the problem is that high-technology, globalized capitalism is radically incongruent with democracy. (Wolin 2000: 20)

What seems to me more valuable, to qualify the third goal, would be to try to construct *practices* of vocation[8] that can begin to address the deficit of felt powerlessness and to chip away at 'our capacity to interiorize power relations, to delimit by ourselves the realm of the possible' (Ginsborg 2005: 20). These practices would not be permanent solutions. Rather, they would be oriented to escape attempts, some of which would take root: a series of fireworks inserted into everyday life which could confront or sidestep the 'behavioural codes that are not unilateral or totalitarian or especially disciplinarian, and which furthermore appear to offer great freedom of choice, but which none the less convey us effortlessly into a life of normalcy and convention' (Ginsborg 2005: 20). At this point, I am often stuck for words to describe what I mean, so let me take some-one else's instead – Greil Marcus's homily on Robert Johnson as a force, and not just a mirror:

> At the highest point of his music each note that is played implies another that isn't, each emotion expressed hints at what can't be said. For all of its elegance and craft the music is unstable at its core – each song is at once an attempt to escape from the world as everyone around the singer believes it to be, and a dream that the world is not a prison but a homecoming … . Johnson is momentarily in the air, flying just as one does in a dream, looking down in wonder at where you are, then soaring as if it's the most natural thing in the world. (Marcus 2005: 103)

Now I am well aware that the cultivation of this form of knowledge may be interpreted as an irredeemably middle-class pre-occupation, the equivalent in theory of Bromell's (2000) characterization of white middle-class teenagers as insiders who long to be outsiders, the kind of consciousness of the world that too quickly falls into a call for 'a quick revolutionary fix that will please everyone and just reinforce a cosy feeling of powerlessness' (Lotringer 2004: 18).[9] But I think there is more to it than that, much more. For it suggests that there may be a more general means of opening up an allusive field in which 'the listener's attention is seized and dropped and held and released by possibilities of meaning that amuse and interest but do not quite come into being' (Bromell 2000: 133). This is what I mean by a politics of hope,[10] the prospect of constructing a machine for 'sustaining affirmation' (White 2000), of launching an additional source of political nourishment and responsiveness and imagination in a time when so many forces militate against it, of locating and warming up the technology of questioning and non-questioning 'by which attention forms and experience crystallizes' (Connolly 2005: 166). In other words, I want to try and add a distinct cooperative-cum-experimental sensibility in to the mix of the world that will help us 'engage the strangeness of the late modern world more receptively' (White 2000: 153). In turn, we could perhaps live in a less 'stingy' (as Connolly (2005) puts it) and more playful way, overcoming or at least bypassing some of the cringes that have been sewn into the fibres of our being as we have learnt how to be embodied. The net outcome would be that the texture of the feel and outcome of the everyday could be reworked as traditional forms of expression were slowly but surely breathed differently (Abrahams 2005).

What is then at issue is what form these practices would take. There is nothing that automatically leads them towards such forms of generosity, after all. In a sense, answering this quest/question about questioning is precisely what the rest of this book attempts to do.

In the remaining pages of this introductory chapter, I will introduce some of the main themes that will be taken up in the chapters of this book. I will begin by briefly outlining some of the main characteristics of non-representational theory and some of the key contemporary issues that non-representational theory highlights. Next, I will consider some of the theoretical and practical issues that the book throws up. Then, finally, I will parse each of the individual chapters, bringing out some of their common problematics.

Non-Representational Theory

This is a book based on the leitmotif of movement in its many forms. Thus, to begin with, it would be possible to argue that human life is based on and in movement. Indeed, it might be argued that it is the human capacity for such complex movements and the accompanying evolution of movement as an enhanced attractor[11] that has produced the reason for much of our rhizomatic, acentred brain. Then, movement captures the animic flux of life and especially an ontogenesis[12] which undoes a dependence on the preformed subject; 'every creature, as it "issues forth" and trails behind, moves in its characteristic way' (Ingold 2006: 15). Then again, movement captures the joy – I will not say simple – of living as a succession of luminous or mundane instants. Though it is possible, even easy, to get carried away by an emphasis on presence, closeness, and tangibility, and by a corresponding desire to do more than simply squeeze meaning from the world, still we can think of the leitmotif of movement as a desire for a presence which escapes a consciousness-centred core of self-reference;[13] 'Rather than have to think, always and endlessly, what else there could be, we sometimes seem to connect with a layer in our existence that simply wants the things of the world close to our skin' (Gumbrecht 2004: 106). And, finally and relatedly, movement captures a certain attitude to life as potential; 'to pose the problem is to invent and not only to dis-cover; it is to create, in the same movement, both the problem and its solution' (Alliez 2004b: 113).

Non-representational theory takes the leitmotif of movement and works with it as a means of going beyond constructivism. As a way of summarizing its now increasingly diverse character,[14] I will point to seven of its main tenets. First, non-representational theory tries to capture the 'onflow',[15] as Ralph Pred (2005) calls it, of everyday life. It therefore follows the anti-substantialist ambition of philosophies of becoming and philosophies of vitalist intuition equally – and their constant war on frozen states.[16] That means that it has a lot of forebears, of course. These forebears hardly agreed on every-thing, to put it but mildly, and not least on the status of intention and intentionality. So I will need to take a little time to more carefully specify what I mean. I think that this can be boiled down to three propositions. One is that the most effective approach will be one that is faithful to a radical empiricism that differs – radically – from a sense-perception or observation-based empiricism. As must be clear, that means that although I respect Humean models of empiricism, I find them too austere. I prefer the lineage of inter-relation that runs from James through Whitehead which is not willing to completely jettison the phenomenological (the lived immediacy of actual experience, before any reflection on it)[17] and the consequent neglect of the transitive. At the same time, I want to temper what seem to me to be the more extreme manifestations of this lineage, which can end up by positing a continuity of and to experience about which I am sceptical, by employing an ethological notion of the pre-individual field in which the event holds sway and which leads to 'buds' or 'pulses' of thought-formation/perception in which 'thought is never an object in its own hands' (James 1960 [1890]: 522). This approach seems to me to be very much in line with Whitehead's monistic way of thinking about the world. As Pred puts it:

> Whitehead extends the scope of radical empiricism and, in effect, points to a way to over-come the limitations inherent in the spatiotemporal and sensory (visual, aural, tactile) metaphor of the stream [of consciousness]. Instead of merely taking a 'general view of the wonderful stream of our consciousness', Whitehead goes 'into' the moment. He refuses to

abstract from the moment, any moment, understood as an act of experience issuing from and into other experiences, as an act occurring within the constraints of inheritance from all that is encompassed within the experient's past and with the onflow of experiences. By bringing philosophical analysis into the bud, Whitehead secures access to a post-Cartesian/Humean basis for ontology, and can characterize momentary consciousness as it arises from pre-conscious moments of synthesis within a broader stream ... of activity.

Whitehead applies the notion of buds not only to human moments of experience but also, more broadly, to actual entities or occasions – 'the final real things of which the world is made up'. He elaborates the notions of actual entities and concrescence with rigor and thoroughness, 'with the purpose of obtaining a one-substance cosmology'. (Pred 2005: 11)

Another proposition, which follows on naturally from these thoughts, is that the most effective approach values the pre-cognitive as something more than an addendum to the cognitive. What is called consciousness is such a narrow window of perception that it could be argued that it could not be otherwise. As Donald (2001) makes clear, defined in a narrow way, consciousness seems to be a very poor thing indeed, a window of time – fifteen seconds at most – in which just a few things (normally no more than six or seven) can be addressed, which is opaque to introspection and which is easily distracted. Indeed, consciousness can be depicted as though it hardly existed, as an emergent derivative of an unconscious. Yet it is clearly dangerous to make too little of cognition, as I perhaps did in some of my early papers. Because it is so weak (though hardly as weak as some commentators have depicted it), it has enrolled powerful allies which can focus and extend conscious awareness – various configurations of bodies and things which, knitted together as routinized environments, enable a range of different technologies for more thinking to be constructed. But, at the same time, the logical corollary of these thoughts is that we should also pay more attention to the pre-cognitive. This roiling mass of nerve volleys prepare the body for action in such a way that intentions or decisions are made before the conscious self is even aware of them. In turn, the many automatisms[18] of 'bare life' or 'creaturely life' mark out not only eminent biopolitical domains[19] but also a series of key theoretical conundrums about what constitutes life itself, such as the nature of 'the open' and motility, animality and undeadness, instinct and drive, poverty in world and what it means to be captivated by an environment in a world marked by all kinds of literal and metaphorical dislocations (Agamben 2004; Santner 2006).

The last proposition follows on again. It is that it is important to specify what unit is being addressed. Nearly all action is reaction to joint action, to being-as-a pair, to the digestion[20] of the intricacies of talk, body language, even an ambient sense of the situation to hand, and this unremitting work of active reaction imposes enormous evaluative demands, equally enormous demands on intermediate memory, and similarly large demands on the general management of attention. Indeed, many now conclude that the idea of cognition as simply a minor placeholder is an artefact of tests carried out in a highly restricted environment – the laboratory (Despret 2004) – in which consciousness shows up as short-term because of the artificiality of the situation demanded by the researcher. Rather, cognition should be seen as an emergent outcome of strategic joint action for which it acts as a guidance function, monitoring and interpreting the situation as found, and, in particular, as a key ability to theorize others' states, as a kind of 'mind-reading' that is the result of the human ability to theorize others' states without having full-blown beliefs about those states (Levinson 2003; Sterelny 2003).[21] And, most of the time, this social awareness – involving high-level cognitive abilities like imitation, learning about learning, and an ability to carry meaning in a whole series of registers (not only language but also gesture) (McNeill 2005) and the manipulation of time and space – predominates over sensory awareness: 'our normal focus is social and social awareness is highly conscious, that is; it heavily engages our conscious activity' (Donald 2001: 68). In other words, cognition has not only a performative aspect but a 'theoretical' aspect too (the two being related) and these aspects are a key to what is often called 'imagination'.[22] This is why non-representational theory privileges play: play is understood as a perpetual human activity with immense affective significance, by no means confined to just early childhood, in which many basic ethical dilemmas (such as fairness) are worked through in ways which are both performative and theoretical.

Second, as must by now be clear, non-representational theory is resolutely antibiographical and pre-individual. It trades in modes of perception which are not subject-based. Like Freud, I am deeply suspicious of, even inimical to, autobiography or biography as modes of proceeding. One seems to me to provide a spurious sense of oneness. The other seems to me to provide a suspect intimacy with the dead. As Phillips (1999: 74) puts it, 'Biography, for Freud, was a monument to the belief that lives were there to be known and understood, rather than endlessly redescribed. Biography did to the dead what Freud feared that psychoanalysis might do to the living'. Instead I want to substitute a *material schematism* in which the world is made up of all kinds of things brought in to relation with one another by many and various spaces through a continuous and largely involuntary process of encounter, and the violent training that such encounter forces. This is an approach that has had some forebears in the social sciences. I think of Gabriel Tarde's micrometaphysics, Pitirim Sorokin's forays into socio-cultural causality, Torsten Hägerstrand's time-geography, or Anthony Giddens's expeditions around social theory in the late 1970s and early 1980s, as well as my own hesitant attempts to time space and space time dating from the late 1970s (Parkes and Thrift 1980). It has achieved more grip of late because of theoretical developments like actor-network theory, and the consequent rediscovery of authors like Tarde and Whitehead, as well as the influence of the writings of authors like Deleuze and Guattari on assemblages. As, and probably more importantly, a whole series of fields have been constructed out of the resurgence of what Paul Carter (2002) calls 'material thinking', the 'performative' working methods and procedures of writings (and, very importantly, other methods of exposition) that emphasize how the whole business of praxis and poiesis is wrapped up in the stubborn plainness of a field of things. These fields must necessarily emphasize the materiality of thinking, and include the study of material culture, the sociology of science, performance studies, from dance to poetry, installation and site-based art, elements of architecture, some of the excursions in to interaction design (such as trying to formulate living information), various aspects of archaeology and museum studies, and the range of developments taking place in parts of cultural geography.

Third, non-representational theory concentrates, therefore, on *practices*, understood as material bodies of work or styles that have gained enough stability over time, through, for example, the establishment of corporeal routines and specialized devices, to reproduce themselves (Vendler 1995). In particular, these bodies' stability is a result of schooling in these practices, of each actor holding the others to them, and of the brute 'natural' fact that the default is to continue on in most situations.[23] These material bodies are continually being rewritten as unusual circumstances arise, and new bodies are continually making an entrance but, if we are looking for something that approximates to a stable feature of a world that is continually in meltdown, that is continually bringing forth new hybrids, then I take the practice to be it. Practices are productive concatenations that have been constructed out of all manner of resources and which provide the basic intelligibility of the world: they are not therefore the properties of actors but of the practices themselves (Schatzki 2002). Actions presuppose practices and not vice versa.

However, what I am espousing is no naïve practice theory. For example, as practices lose their place in a historical form of life, they may leave abandoned wreckage behind them which can then take on new life, generating new hybrids or simply leavings which still have resonance. Take the example of things. These may have been vital parts of particular networks of practice, only to fall out of use as these networks metamorphose. Consequently their meanings may become hollowed out but may still retain a presence as enigmatic signifiers (Santner 2006). Or they may find new uses in other networks. Or they may linger on as denaturalized reminders of past events and practices, purposely memorialized in various ways or simply present as ruins, as melancholy rem(a)inders. In other words, things can have a potent afterlife.

The mention of things brings us to the fourth tenet. The constitution of non-representational theory has always given equal weight to the vast spillage of *things*. In particular, it takes the energy of the sense-catching forms of things seriously (Critchley 2005) – rather than seeing things as mere cladding.[24] Things answer back; 'not only does our existence articulate that of an object through the language of our perceptions, the object calls out that language from us, and with it our own sense of embodied experience' (Schwenger 2006: 3). But how to describe what Walter Benjamin called the 'petrified unrest' of things? Three main moves seem particularly apposite. To begin with, things become part of hybrid assemblages: concretions, settings and flows. In this approach, things are given *equal* weight, and I do mean equal.[25] Thus things are not just bound by their brute efficacy to the visible termini of humans in some form of latent subjectivism such as 'concern' or 'care', however comforting their presence may sometimes be as mundane familiars. That would be to smuggle 'from the realm of common sense the notion that humans are very different from knives or paper' (Harman 2002: 30). Rather,

> the tool itself is bound up in a specific empire of functions, a system that takes its meaning from some particular projection, some final reference. Admittedly, the meaning of equipment is determined by that for the sake of which it acts. But I flatly contest the view that this *Worumwillen* is necessarily human. Tools execute their being 'for the sake of a reference, not because people run across them but because they are utterly determinate in their referential function – that is, because they already stand at the mercy of innumerable points of meaning. (Harman 2002: 29)

Then, it is important to understand the way in which things have another genetic disposition that needs to be mentioned at this point. That is what Simondon (1989) calls their 'technicity', their actual collective character as a 'technology' (the word being placed in scare quotes precisely because we cannot be sure exactly what constitutes a technology). The technicity of something like a hand tool which forms a relatively isolated technical element[26] can be isolated from its context. Indeed, it may have sufficient material character to be given a proper name: Toledo steel or Murano glass, for example (Mackenzie 2002). But the more effective and ubiquitous a technology becomes, the less likely this is to be the case. Portability comes about because of the ramification of a larger and larger infrastructure which means that the technology becomes increasingly a part of an empire of functions encumbered by a network of supportive elements, each of which relies on the other. 'A mobile phone or wireless appliance could be understood from this perspective as a massively encumbered object. Its physical portability comes at the expense of an increased ramification and layering of communication infrastructure' (Mackenzie 2002: 12).

To summarize the argument so far, things form not so much a technological uncon-scious as a technological anteconscious; a 'spreading so extensive that it can come to the surface in lives entirely different from the one beneath which it is currently sensed' (Schwenger 2006: 4), a warp and weft of inhuman traffic with its own indifferent geog-raphies. But I want to see things as having one more disposition. That is, the way in which the human *body* interacts with other things. I do not want to count the body as separate from the thing world. Indeed, I think it could be argued that the human body is what it is because of its unparalleled ability to co-evolve with things, taking them in and adding them to different parts of the biological body to produce something which, if we could but see it, would resemble a constantly evolving distribution of different hybrids with different reaches. Indeed, the evidence suggests that organs like the hand, the gut, and various other muscle and nerve complexes which have evolved in part in response to the requirements of tools have subsequently produced changes in the brain. The human body is a tool-being. This is, I think, an important point. Of late, there has been a large literature generated on corporeality, most particularly by feminist theo-rists, which often seems to want to endow the flesh with some form of primordial distinction: goo is good, so to speak.[27] But, whilst it would be profoundly unwise to ignore the special characteristics of flesh,[28] it would be equally unwise to think that the make-up of the human body stopped there, or that it produced an ineffable perceptual membrane. It does not. There is a sense of touch in all parts of the extended physiog-nomy of the material body.[29] At the same time, it is important to enter a note of caution which has been generated, at least in part, by feminist theorists. Too often, the recent turn to corporeality has also allowed a series of assumptions to be smuggled in about the active, synthetic and purposive role of embodiment which need closer examination. In particular, it is assumed that bodies are bodies-in-action, able to exhibit a kind of continuous intentionality, able to be constantly enrolled into activity.[30] Every occasion seems to be willed, cultivated or at least honed. My own work has been periodically guilty of this sin, I am sure. But the experience of embodiment is not like that at all; not everything is focused intensity. Embodiment includes tripping, falling over, and a whole host of other such mistakes. It includes vulnerability, passivity, suffering, even simple hunger. It includes episodes of insomnia, weariness and exhaustion, a sense of insignificance and even sheer indifference to the world. In other words, bodies can and do become overwhelmed. The unchosen and unforeseen exceed the ability of the body to contain or absorb. And this is not an abnormal condition: it is a part of being as flesh. It may be that it is only 'because the self is sensible, open to the pangs of hunger and eros, that it is worthy of ethics' (Critchley 2002: 21).[31]

All that said, this emphasis on things questions the solidity of the world, since so much of it is ultimately mutable, working according to a spectrum of different time scales (Grosz 2005). Increasingly, many human activities seem to realize this. Indeed, it is a point that has been brilliantly made by Kwinter (2001). Thus Kwinter points to the rise of a whole series of sports that depend on an artful shaping of the different time scales of the environment for sustenance, tracking and tracing flows and perturbations in order to produce e/affects. Kwinter mentions paragliding, surfing, snowboarding and rock-climbing as sports of falling[32] that extend a streaming ethos to landscapes, understood as 'motorfields of solids' (2001: 29). In their current manifestation, these sports have increasingly understood the environment as exemplifying fluidity of movement, intuition and invention. Take the case of rock-climbing:[33]

> [Climbers] must flow up the mountain, flow or tack against the downward gradient of gravity – but also must become hypersensitive tamers and channelers of the gravitational sink, masters at storing it in their muscles or making it flow through certain parts of the pelvis, thighs, palms, and this only at certain times; they must know how to accelerate the flow into a quick transfer that could mean the difference between triumph and disaster, to mix and remix dynamic and static elements in endless variation – for it is not enough to prevail against gravity but rather to be able to make it stream continuously through one, and especially to be able to generalize this knowledge to every part of the body without allowing it to regroup at any time – transcendant and unitary – as a spatialized figure in the head. (Kwinter 2001: 29–30)

But note here how the mountain also plays its part:

> The mineral shelf represents a flow whose timescale is nearly unfathomable from the scale of duration represented by the electrolytic and metabolic processes of muscle and nerves – but even at this timescale – nanometric in relation to the millennia that measure geological flows – singularities abound: a three millimeter-wide fissure just wide enough to allow the placement of one finger, and anchored by sufficiently solid earth to permit but eighty pounds of pressure for, say, three seconds but no longer; an infinitesimally graded basin of sedimentary rock whose erratically ribbed surface (weathered unevenly by flows of wind and rain) offers enough friction to a spread palm to allow strategic placement of the other palm on an igneous ledge half a meter above. This very rock face, until recently considered virtually slick and featureless – an uninflected glacis even to classical pick and patio climbers – now swarms with individualized points, inhomogeneities, trajectories, complex relations … the climber's task is less to 'master' in the macho, form-imposing sense than to forge a morphogenetic figure in time, it insert himself into a seamless, streaming space and to become soft and fluid himself, which means momentarily to recover real time, and to engage the universe's wild and free unfolding through the morphogenetic capacities of the singularity. (Kwinter 2001: 31)

Thus we arrive at a notion of 'site', as an active and always incomplete incarnation of events, an actualization of times and spaces that uses the fluctuating conditions to assemble itself (Kwon 2004). Site is not so much a result of punctual, external causes, therefore, as it is an insertion in to one or more flows.[34]

Fifth, non-representational theory is experimental. I make no apologies for this. After all, 'no battle has ever been won without resorting to new combinations and surprising events' (Latour 2005: 252). In particular, I want to pull the energy of the performing arts into the social sciences in order to make it easier to 'crawl out to the edge of the cliff of the conceptual' (Vendler 1995: 79). To see what will happen. To let the event sing you. To some this will appear a retrograde step: hasn't the history of the social sciences been about attaining the kind of rigour that the performing arts supposedly lack? My answers are fourfold. First, I believe that the performing arts can have as much rigour as any other experimental setup, once it is understood that the laboratory, and all the models that have resulted from it, provide much too narrow a metaphor to be able to capture the richness of the worlds (Despret 2004). Consider just the rehearsal: would anyone seriously say that it is not a rigorous entity? Second, because once it is understood how many entities there are in the world, of which we are able to name but a few, then capturing the traces of these entities, even for a brief moment, will clearly involve unconventional means, a kind of poetics of the release of energy that might be thought to resemble play. After all, who knows what entities and processes lurk in the under- (or should it be over-) growth, just getting on with it? Third, because the performing arts may help us to inject a note of wonder back into a social science which, too often, assumes that it must explain everything. I am often bemused by the degree to which scientific and artistic works are allowed to evince wonder (Fisher 2002). Yet it often seems as if the extraordinary emergences of the 'social' world have to be treated in a different register, as stumbling, inertial and 'mundane' (Abrahams 2005). But any glance at the kinds of columns that tend to appear in newspapers and magazines under bylines such as 'odd world', 'strange world', 'this world', 'funny old world', and so on, show the essential ebullience of that world and the way in which it can never be truly kept within theoretical tramlines. Social imaginaries are just that: they cannot be contained. Thus 'retracing the iron ties of necessity is not sufficient to explore what is possible' (Latour 2005: 261). Instead, social science needs to take on the quality of renewal that it can see all around it as new collectives constantly come into existence: 'for a social science to become relevant, it has to have the capacity to renew itself – a quality impossible if a society is supposed to be "behind" political action' (Latour 2005: 261). Finally, because it is imperative to understand the virtual as multiple registers of sensation operating beyond the reach of the reading techniques on which the social sciences are founded. Culture is, in this sense, an 'involuntary adventure' (Toscano 2004) in which, in a Whiteheadian vein, thought is the operation that constitutes the thinker (who is constituted in the occasion), rather than vice versa (Alliez 2004a). This brings me directly to the topic of affect.

Thus, sixth, I want to get in touch with the full range of registers of thought by stressing affect and sensation. These are concept-percepts that are fully as important as signs and significations but that only recently have begun to receive their due. Recently, like a number of authors, I have taken an affective turn with this work, drawing on a combination of Spinoza, Freud, Tomkins, Ekman, Massumi, and a host of feminist theorists, as well as biological traditions including evolutionary theory and ethology, in order to understand affect as the way in which each 'thing' in acting, living, and striving to preserve its own being is 'nothing but the actual essence of the thing' (Spinosa *et al.* 1997). Thus,

> There is no longer a subject, but only individuating affective states of an anonymous force. The plane is concerned only with movements and rests, with dynamic affective charges: the plane will be perceived with whatever it makes us perceive, and then only bit by bit. Our ways of living, thinking or writing change according to the plane upon which we find ourselves. (Spinoza, cited in Alliez 2004b: 27)

All of this said, I do want to retain a certain minimal humanism. Whilst refusing to grant reflexive consciousness and its pretensions to invariance the privilege of occupying the centre of the stage, dropping the human subject entirely seems to me to be a step too far. I have done much to rid myself of an object that often seems to me to be a user-illusion – in my writings, there is 'no longer such a thing as a relatively fixed and consistent person – a person with a recognizable identity – confronting a potentially predictable world but rather two turbulences enmeshed with each other' (Phillips 1999: 20). Still, I am uncomfortably aware that, taken to extremes, a resolutely anti-humanist position parodies the degenerative path taken in the nineteenth century from Rousseau through Balzac to Bergson, from 'an ideal of an immanent community, the subsequent emergence of a strictly codified bourgeois subject capable of constructing and manifesting itself "aesthetically" through gesture and the eventual somatization of that individual body to a condition of mere potentiality' (Hewitt 2005: 103). This degeneration can be seen equally as a movement from intention to automation as the industrial systems of that century took hold. Whatever the case, I want to keep hold of a humanist ledge on the machinic cliff face. I hold to a sense of *personal authorship*,[35] no matter that the trace is very faint and no matter that the brain is a society, different parts of which are dynamically and differentially connected to all manner of environments. And the reason? Because how things seem is often more important than what they are.

> The fact is that it seems to each of us that we have conscious will. It seems we have selves. It seems we have minds. It seems we are agents. It seems we cause what we do. Although it is sobering and ultimately accurate to call this an illusion, it is a mistake to think the illusory is trivial. (Wegner 2002: 341–342)

Further, this conscious will is bolstered in at least three ways. To begin with there is the special constitutional significance of joint action and its particular way of understanding the worlds (Levinson 2003). Then there is the consequent ability of joint action periodically to work across different social fields, refusing to respect boundaries. And finally there is the 'adaptive unconscious' (Wilson 2002) working ceaselessly and nonconsciously to interpolate/interpellate the world. These are not insignificant qualities and they give a significant role to style, a particular way of practising joint action that can be equated to agency in this book.

My stamping ground for these kinds of thoughts has often been dance, but it could just as well have been building or music, two other baseline human activities which, so far as I am aware, are found in all societies, including those of the greatest antiquity. For my purposes, dance is important: it engages the whole of the senses in bending time and space into new kinaesthetic shapes, taps into the long and variegated history of the unleashing of performance,[36] leads us to understand movement as a potential,[37] challenges the privileging of meaning (especially by understanding the body as being expressive without being a signifier; see Langer 2005; Dunagan 2005; Gumbrecht 2004), gives weight to intuition as thinking-in-movement, foregrounds the 'underlanguage' of gesture[38] and kinetic semantics in general (Sheets-Johnstone 2005), teaches us anew about evolution (for example by demonstrating the crucial role of bipedality), and is able to point to key cognitive processes like imitation and suggestion which are now understood to be pivotal to any understanding of understanding (Hurley and Chater 2005) and, indeed, desire.[39]

The aforegoing paragraphs allow me to say something, finally, about ethics.[40] I have been painting a very faint view of human agency, to put it mildly. The classical human subject which is transparent, rational and continuous no longer pertains. Classical ethical questions like 'What have I done?' and 'What ought I to do?' become much more difficult when the 'I' in these questions is so faint, when self-transparency and narratibility are such transient features. Similarly, more modern ethical questions like what it means to be genuinely open to another human being or culture take on added layers of complexity. Clearly, becoming ethical now means becoming critical of norms under which we are asked to act but which we cannot fully choose (Butler 2005) and taking responsibility – in a sense to be specified – for the dilemmas that subsequently arise. But this hardly counts as a revelation.

What I will want to argue for, in concert with Santner (2001: 6), is a generalized ethic of out-of-jointness within which 'every familiar is ultimately strange and …, indeed, I am even in a crucial sense a stranger to myself'. But, rather than see this form of answerability as a problem, it can as well be thought of as an opportunity to build new forms of life in which 'strangeness itself [is] the locus of new forms of neighborliness and community' (Santner 2001: 6). In turn, this ethic of novelty can be connected to the general theme of 'more life', for it suggests a particular form of boosting aliveness, one that opens us to our being in the midst of life through a thoroughly ontological involvement.[41] For, what is clear is that all too often in our every-day life we are *not* open to that pressure and do not inhabit the midst of life, and thus live everyday life as, well, everyday life, clipping our own wings because we inhabit cringes that limit our field of action.

> Everyday life includes possibilities for withdrawing from, defending against, its own aliveness to the world, possibilities of, as it were, not really being there, of dying to the other's presence. The energies that constitute our aliveness to the world are, in other words, subject to multiple modifications and transformations. (Santner 2001: 9)

Some commentators would, I think, like to understand boosting this out-of-jointness as part of a more general rediscovery of piety – or even epiphany – often heralded as part of a move to a 'post-secular spirituality' (e.g. Goodchild 2002; Gumbrecht 2004; Braidotti 2006). Sometimes following on from Deleuze's thoughts on 'becoming-imperceptible' in which extinguishing the self allows all kinds of unexpected futures to be opened up and drawn strength from. This is 'reversing the subject to face the outside' (Braidotti 2006: 262), thus boosting *potential*: in Jamesian terms it is the jump towards another world. Whilst, hardly surprisingly, I am sympathetic to the general direction of travel, this is too grand and seductive a vision for me. I would prefer to see a multiple set of projects concerned with the construction of an orientation to the future, the develop-ment of 'an anxiety about the future which is analogous to Orwell's anxiety about the loss of the past and of memory and childhood' (Jameson 2005: 23), which is, at the same time, the development of a method of hope (Miyazaki 2004, 2006). In more conventional philosophical terms, this might, I suppose, be thought of as a flourishing of potential in act,[42] not in the sense of the realization of some proper form, but rather as a departure from what is – a potentiality that is brought into being only as it acts or exists in the interstices of interaction. But I would also prefer to see it in another way, as an attempt to re-gather the ethic of *craftsmanship*, a means of composition and channelling which involves bringing together discipline and concentration, understanding and inspiration, in order to bring out potential: a different model of *homo faber*, if you like, working both for its own sake and as part of a community of ability.[43] At the same time, this ethic, following on from a long line of thinking which has tried to overcome nihilism and determine the conditions for an affirmation of life, can be seen as a means of celebrating the joyous, even transcendent, confusion of life itself (Reginster 2006).

> Isn't this something to have faith in? The stuff of life, the astonishing, resilient, inventiveness of it all? The extravagant iridescence in the wings of butterflies. The minute convolutions of Henle's loop in the human kidney, 'like the meanders in a creek'. The song of the Albert's lyrebird, which takes it six years to learn and segues the phrasing of every other bird in the Queensland bush. At times, the gratuitousness of creation, its sheer wild playfulness, can only be understood as a kind of unscripted comedy. (Mabey 2006: 197)

Finally, I want to broach the topic of space again. For substantive rather than narrow disciplinary reasons, space looms large in what follows. That said, I start from an 'instinctive' understanding of space shared by all the 'field' disciplines – anthropology, archaeology, architecture, geography and large parts of performance studies. This is a sense of the concreteness and materiality of the situation which is hard to put into words, a need to capture being there which is not just a report back – a finding which is also a leaving. Straightaway, I hasten to add that this is not just an excuse for the random empiricism of which such disciplines are sometimes accused. But it has certainly complicated the use of categories which are often assumed to in some way motivate social change (society, class, gender, ethnicity, and so on) because it places variation on an equal footing. And it also complicates what is assumed to be a simple empirical fact, not just because all of these disciplines try to deepen those facts by drawing on all kinds of representational and non-representational registers (digs, ethnographies, various maps and diagrams, buildings, software, performances) but also because they simultaneously explore how particular spaces resonate, obtain their particular 'atmosphere' (Brennan 2004; Sloterdijk 2005a, 2005b), so that the whole is more than the sum of the parts.

I hope that this makes it clear that space is not a metaphorics, nor is it a transcendental principle of space in general (the phenomenological idea of consciousness as the fount of all space, produced by a finite being who constitutes 'his' world), nor is it simply a series of local determinations of a repeating theme. In each of these cases, we can see that the very style of thought is 'oriented by spatial relations, the way in which we imagine what to think' (Colebrook 2005a: 190).[44] Rather, it is three different qualities in one. First, it is a practical set of configurations that mix in a variety of assemblages thereby producing new senses of space[45] and:

> By confronting all those events from which thought emerges, by thinking how there can be perceptions of spaces, we no longer presuppose an infinity to be represented; nor a finite being who constitutes 'his' human world (as in phenomenology) but an 'unlimited infinity'. Each located observer is the opening of a fold, a world folded around its contemplations and rhythms. There are as many space and folds as there arc styles of perception. If a fold is the way perceptions 'curve around' or are oriented according to an active body, the thought of these curves produces a life that can think not just its own human world – the space of man – but the sense of space as such. (Colebrook 2005a: 190)

Second, it also forms, therefore, a poetics of the unthought, of what Vesely (2004) calls the latent world, a well-structured pre-reflective world which, just because it lacks explicit articulation, is not therefore without grip. Third, it is indicative of the substance of the new era of the inhabitable map in which space has more active qualities designed into its becoming – a tracery of cognitive and pre-cognitive assists threading their way through each and every moment of the being-at-work of presentation – which make it into a very different ground from the one that Heidegger imagined as presence.

So far as space is concerned, what I have been most concerned with is banishing nearness as the measure of all things (Thrift 2006b). It is a staple of the literature that a drive towards nearness is regarded as having an intrinsic value. For example, think of all the terms that imply nearness in the philosophical tradition: present-at-hand, flesh, thrownness. In part, this terminological profusion arises from the idea that closeness to the body is the main geometer of the world (Ginzburg 2001b). But this is to take the bio-logical body as an interpellated centre (Gil 1998) with a definable fleshy inside. But even an organ like the gut can as well be thought of as an outside as an inside (Probyn 2005), as a logistics of the movement of things which can be mapped on to the world.[46] And this is without going into the obvious political dangers of identifying the body as a preformed entity. At the same time I do not want to stray into the ambient pieties of some parts of the phenomenological tradition or their collapse into an absolute alterity[47] or a spiritualist immanence[48] (Toscano 2004). Instead I want to substitute *distribution* for nearness or ambience. Why? Well, to begin with, because the paradox of space is that we all know that space is something lived in and through in the most mundane of ways – from the bordering provided by the womb, through the location of the coffee cup on our desk that is just out of reach, through the memories of buildings and land-scapes which intertwine with our bodies and provide a kind of poetics of space, through the ways in which vast political and commercial empires – and the resultant wealth and misery – can be fashioned from the mundane comings and goings of ships and trains and now planes, through to the invisible messages that inhabit the radio spectrum in their billions and etch another dimension to life. Then, because there is no need to reduce such complexity to a problematic of 'scale', a still too common move. Actors continually change size. A multiplicity of 'scales' is always present in interactions; the putatively large is of the same kind as the small, but amplified to generate a different order of effects (Strathern 1999; Tarde 2000). Then, because we now understand that the spaces and rhythms of the everyday, everydayness and everyday life (Seigworth 2000) are not just a filigree bolstering an underlying social machine but a series of pre-individual ethologies that incessantly rehearse a materialism in which matter turns into a sensed-sensing energy with multiple centres. Then, again, because increasingly what counts as a 'we' is being redefined by a range of transhuman approaches. These approaches have not just, in what has now become an increasingly hackneyed move, undone the dependence of the point of view on a preformed subject. They have also increased the number of actors' spaces that can be recognized and worked with. Consequently, they have begun to redefine what counts as an actor, most especially through an understanding of the actor as an artefact of different territories of 'thought', conceived as the operations that constitute the thinker.[49] This 'onto-ethological' move can be made precisely because actors can now be seen to not just occupy but to be made up of all kinds of intermediary spaces which cannot be tied down to just one and simul-taneously participate with each other. The world, in other words, is jam-packed with entities. Finally, because more and more of the sensory registers in which spaces make their marks as spaces seem to be being recognized,[50] no doubt in part because these registers are continuously expanding but also in part because the sheer cultural diversity of how space appears is increasingly being recognized as more than culture or body (e.g. Levinson 2003; Wilson 2004).

The Book

Having outlined some of the main tenets of non-representational theory, let me now move to the book itself. This book is motivated by a heterogeneous series of inspirations, rather than just one. I will point to a theoretical agenda first. I do not subscribe to the spirit guide approach to social science. Thus, for example, though I take Deleuze's work on topics like the gap between sensation and perception, the difference between possibility and virtuality, the heterogenesis of both material density and subjective action from a pre-individual field, and the different time images of repetition and recurrence, to be important, I am afraid that this has not produced a total makeover of my work in a way that has now become quite common in some quarters, a makeover that sometimes seems to resemble a religious conversion. There are elements of Deleuze's work that I remain out of sorts with[51] and, in any case, I do not think that it is the function of a social scientist to simply apply the work of philosophers (as in a Deleuzian approach, a Foucauldian approach, an Agambenian approach, and so on). It seems to me to be a highly questionable assumption that modern social science stands in this kind of subordinate relationship to a set of themes from Western philosophy[52] or should see its task as simply echoing the assumptions those themes may make. So far as I am concerned, social scientists are there to hear the world and to make sure that it can speak back just as much as they are there to produce wild ideas – and then out of this interaction they may be able to produce something that is itself equally new. But they must share with philosophers like Deleuze one ambition at least and that is to render the world problematic by elaborating questions. To simply offer solutions is not enough.[53]

At the same time, in recent years, there has been an equal tendency to argue that social science must be more practical, policy-oriented, and so on, a tendency which risks losing touch with wild ideas completely; it is the kind of social science that does not understand the basic point that it is producing a form of intelligibility which 'can only confirm the prevailing views within those institutions that generated the data' (Rawls 2002: 54) and in fetishizing the values of methodological rigour seems to me to miss a large part of the point of social science by purposefully going about deadening itself (Law 2004) when that is both pointless and unnecessary.[54]

Instead of all that, this book is about new kinds of practice which are compelled by their own demonstrations and therefore leave room for values like messiness, and operators like the mistake, the stumble and the stutter (Law 2004). To some these practices will appear to be just idle chatter but I prefer to see them as vehicles for bringing into view the conditions of meaning, not so much a means of going further as a technology for tackling inconceivability (Fenves 1993). After all, and this point is crucial, it seems to me to be of the greatest methodological importance to knowledge that this is a world which we can only partially understand. Not only is it the case that many things are inherently unknowable but also, as Latour (2005) has pointed out, there is every reason to believe that we are surrounded by innumerable hybrids, only a few of which we have named and even fewer of which we can claim to understand. For example, who can truly say that they fully understand the forces we tag as 'affect'? The fact that we (itself a difficult category) must live surrounded by an ocean of hybrids whose nature we do not know or at best imperfectly understand because we bleed into them in so many odd ways means that all kinds of things just seem to show up because we are unable to trace their genealogy or all the forces that trigger how they participate in an event. Some see this as a problem. But I see it as an opportunity, and as a demonstration that there will always be more to do – which brings me to my next point.

Practically, the book arises from a number of political imperatives. The first is the growing realization that there are landscapes of space, time and experience that have been ceded too readily to powerful naturalizing forces which erase the prospect of political action even before it starts by producing *backgrounds*, latent worlds that, by virtue of their routinized, 'unrememberable but unforgettable' (Gerhardt 2004) natures, make certain aspects of the events we constantly come across not so much hard to question as hard to even think of as containing questions at all. In the past, there have, of course, been various politics of ordinary moments which have attempted to show that what might seem like supposedly trivial everyday affairs can have import once the misplaced concreteness of social categories is factored out; wilful acts of political mis-perception and re-perception, if you like. I think here of aspects of surrealism, the fall-out from situationism, some forms of psychoanalytic and psychological therapy, the kinds of political theory that have recently grouped around the banner of a politics of the ordinary, the concrete empirical details of interaction to be found in ethnomethodology, certain kinds of architecture and site-specific installation, and so on. It also draws on those considerable parts of the arts and humanities, and especially art and poetry and dance, that call to the practices of everyday life. What I have tried to do here is to show that these traditions form a living whole with many of the same goals and projects in mind, a poetics of mundane space and time which can teach us to ourselves in better ways, that is ways which will allow peoples to survive their own environing (Wagner 2001) by creating more rather than fewer worlds. Such a poetics of the ways in which witnessable coherence is continually produced requires four things. First it requires a better sense of the future (Bloch 1986 [1959]) built up out of a forward-looking ethics of the moment which is not concerned with outright adjudication but instead tries to work with the affects/percepts/concepts of 'stance' or 'style'. Second it requires serious attention to the spaces of the empirical moment that is built up out of examining the ways in which the spaces of situations are extruded. That may result in a poetics of the spaces of dreams and improvisations, of what Vesely (2004) calls 'rich articulations', that arise out of a deep respect for situations and which manifests itself in continually attempting to go beyond them. Third it requires attempting to let loose a certain kind of wild conceptuality which is attuned to the moment but always goes beyond it, which always works against cultural gravity, so to speak. This improvisatory virtuality provides an opportunity for an unsettled politics of advocacy which 'watch[es] the world, listening for what escapes explanation by science, law, and other established discourses. Accounting for what established systems discounted as noise' (Fortun 2001: 351). Fourth it requires a much better sense of the ways in which practices need objects against which to react and from which to learn, but these objects may have many versions (Despret 2004), many 'offers of appropriateness', to use a Latourian phrase. To summarize, what is being sought for is what might be described as an ethological ethic which is *gratuitously* benign. What I am aiming for is to produce a supplement to the ordinary labour of everyday life which is both a valediction and a sacrament, though I am sure that sounds entirely too grand. If I had to choose an analogy, it might be with Darwin's furtive earthworms which, through continuous ingestion, work a good part of the world into existence. In Darwin's later thought they stand for a lowly kind of secular creation myth; 'something [is being said] about resilience and beneficial accidents; that it may be more marvellous when the world happens to work for us, than to believe it was designed to do so' (Phillips 1999: 58).

Lest I be misunderstood (and this is a point on which there is a lot of misunderstanding, most of it wilful, it has to be said), I am *not* arguing that the back and forth of what we currently call politics should be shut down. I do not think that the constant testing of the limits of what counts as the political implied by this project means that it is either a substitute for other forms of politics of the governed or even the invention of a determinate new political form (Amin and Thrift 2005; Chatterjee 2004). Rather, it is a halting means of producing more interest, identifying swells and overflows, and generating new forms of energy. 'Modest' has become an overused word, of late. But non-representational theory is genuinely intended to be a modest supplement.

Finally, this book is therefore self-consciously interdisciplinary. I have tried to avoid any particular disciplinary tradition in the arts and humanities and social sciences and to take inspiration from them all – or at least a good many of them. There is an important sense in which any politics of ordinary moments is bound to transgress these disciplinary boundaries since it involves so many different elements of discipline and indiscipline, imagination and narrative, sense and nonsense…. But each of these disciplines can be bent towards my overall goal: to produce a politics of opening the event to more, more; more action, more imagination, more light, more fun, even. This is not, I should hasten to add, meant to be a romantic or quixotic quest. It is meant to be in-your-face politics. Currently, many people are forced to live their lives in cramped worlds which offer them little or no imaginative relief because of the crushing weight of economic circumstance, the narrow margins of what they are allowed to think by what they have been taught and what lies bleeding around them and the consequently almost routine harrowing of their confidence that the world can ever be for them (Chakrabarty 2002; Chatterjee 2004). Yet, all that said, very many struggle to express something more than just resignation and inconsolability, often against themselves. They may value a certain conviviality, demonstrate hope, resolution, and a kind of dignity, even in the midst of melancholy. That is surely something remarkable, given most people's restricted circumstances and prospects – and it must surely be something worth nurturing. Indeed, some do go further still. And in that process, they may strike out on to new practical-imaginative territories. Of course, these continuous rites of spring hardly mean that all is well in the world. But they do show that life pretty well always exceeds its own terms and conditions: it is not always captured by the small print of the social contract. There is hope that, in amongst the poisons of prejudice and general paranoia, some small beginnings can be made, summonings of what is not that can leap up and hear themselves, that are able to 'seek the true, the real where the merely factual disappears' (Bloch 2000 [1923]: 3).

The Chapters

The rest of this book consists of a set of chapters which come from the project that I have been pursuing in various guises since the early 1980s under the banner of 'non-representational theory'. The project was originally an attempt to take practices seriously against the background of a (thoroughly modernist, I should add) emphasis on unknowing (Weinstein 2005) but it has moved on from there, I like to think. For in studying practices in detail, it became clear to me that what was missing from too many accounts was a sense of mutability; of the moments of inspired improvisation, conflicting but still fertile mimesis, rivalrous desires, creative forms of symbiosis, and simple transcription errors which make each moment a new starting point. Whether studying the history of clocks, which is scattered with the unknown foot soldiers of innovation – tinkerers making myriad small adjustments which lead on to 'bigger' things (Glennie and Thrift

2007) – or the way in which styles of financial dealing transmute into new financial instruments (Leyshon and Thrift 1997), or the vagaries of all kinds of artistic performance (Thrift 2001), or the remorseless work of repair and maintenance (Graham and Thrift 2007), what I was increasingly concerned to underline was the ceaseless work of transmutation which drives the 'social'. The social is in scare quotes here because I want to emphasize a set of associationist working assumptions that are in contradistinction to the views of 'sociologists of the social', by drawing (selectively) on the work of Tarde (2000) to produce a means of associating entities. First assumption: everything can be regarded as a society. Consequently, at a minimum, 'there are many other ways to retrace the entire social world than the narrow definition provided by standardized social ties' or, more generally, 'social is not a place, a thing, a domain or a kind of stuff but a provisional movement of new associations' (Latour 2005: 238). Thus, as Latour (2005: 239) nicely puts it, space can be made for 'landing strips for other entities' that have never been followed before, for emergent forms of life (Fischer 2003), or simply forms of life that have never come to notice before. Second assumption: always be suspicious that the difference between 'large' and 'small', 'macro' and 'micro', 'general' and 'specific' is necessarily significant. I am particularly sceptical of any explanation that appeals to scale. Third assumption: keep difference at the core of explanation.

To summarize my summary, non-representational theory asks three main questions. First it questions the divide between theoretical and practical work by ceding certain theoretical conundrums to practice. Second, by questioning what is in the world, it exposes a whole new frontier of inhuman endeavour, what might be called the construction of new matterings, along with their typical attachments, their passions, strengths and weaknesses, their differences and indifferences. Third, by intensifying the intensity of being, it is able to question the load of precognitive conditionings that make up most of what it is to be human. In other words, or so I will argue, it is possible to boost the content of bare life, making it more responsive, more inventive and more open to ethical interventions.

Insofar as it has a political agenda, then, this book is about the construction of new counterpublics through the assembling of more performative political ecologies. At its heart, in other words, is a pressing task of political experiment and invention, a work of 'ensoulment'[55] (Santner 2006), aimed at making more room in the world for new political forms, which, at the same time, produces new excitations of power; 'those enigmatic bits of address and interpellation that disturb the social space – and bodies – of … protagonists' (Santner 2006: 24). This is a task that seems vital in an age when politics too often ends up in declarative cul-de-sacs.[56] Further, this politics of effective togethernesses (Stengers 2006) is, so I believe, currently breaking out all over. The numbers of experiments currently taking place with new political forms of effective togetherness are legion, and I cannot list them all here. But, for example, there are the many attempts to forge a new urban politics which can comprehend and work with belonging-in-transience (Amin and Thrift 2005a and b). Then there are all the experiments aimed at disrupting given spatial and temporal arrangements in an age when 'the speed at which new products appear and reconfigurations of technological systems take place precludes the possibility of ever becoming familiar with a given arrangement' (Crary 2004: 9). How is it possible, in other words, to group around states that are neither dependent on lasting objects nor on fixed locations? Then, there are the myriad experiments that set out to invent flexible models of imagination and narrative outside the enforced routines of consumption. And, finally, there are all the experiments that want to understand and work with the 'animality' of bare life, both as a means of understanding what elements of being are included but do not count and as a means of tapping that vital force.

The subsequent chapters in this book are inter-connected. They were often written with one another in mind. Sometimes they purposely follow on one from the other. They make their way as follows. The first four chapters of the book, which form its first section, act as an extended prologue by offering a tentative description of how the world is now. The first chapter attempts to give a description of some of the main contours of experience that currently exist in the West by concentrating on the business of commodity production. My intention is to show how the forces of business are reshaping the world we live in, reworking what we call experience along the way. I do not want to claim any particular power of insight here. The tendencies that I will describe have been extant in prototype form for a number of years now, and in some cases their origins can be traced even earlier. It would also be possible to argue that they have been prefigured in a number of places by authors who want to give up on the land of remorselessly monopolist accounts of capitalism that act as a kind of intellectual and political bulldozer (Amin and Thrift 2005b).[57] I think of Michel Callon's work on an economy of qualities, Luc Boltanski and Eve Chiapello's work on new forms of economic justification, Edward Lipuma and Benjamin Lee's work on circulating capitalism, Celia Lury's work on brands, Lev Manovich's work on new media, the work of Paolo Virno and Maurizio Lazzarato on intellectual labour and 'immaterial' capitalism, the allied work of Moulier Boutang and others on cognitive capitalism, or even, to travel farther back in time, Alvin Toffler's coining of the term 'prosumerism'. Put baldly, I want to point to three formative tendencies that now structure – and rule – experience in capitalist economic formations: prospecting across the whole of bodily experience, but most especially in the 'anteconscious', thus reworking what is regarded as labour, class, invention and, indeed, much of what was traditionally regarded as political economy; attempting to produce instant communities, worlds gathered around products and production processes which themselves become a vital part of what is regarded as product and production process;[58] reworking space and time so that they fit this new kind of life, most especially by producing new prostheses which are also additions to cognition and precognition.

Most importantly I want to zero in on this latter process. It is possible to argue that the most important reworking of experience that is currently taking place is the production of new kinds of not just attentive and responsive but formative spaces which act as a generalized form of writing on to and in to the world, working especially at the level of bare life. This mass 'production of worlds', as Lazzarato (2004) would put it, consists not just of a multiplication of saleable ways of living, but also the symbolic indexing of these spaces so that they can continually generate what would have been thought of as 'decisive moments' with the result that these spaces can be constantly refreshed and so remain absorbing (see Thrift 2006b). If one of the most important cognitive leaps of the last few hundred years was the growth of writing in its many forms, now, or so I argue, a similar change in the structure of cognition is occurring but as a general process of the purposeful production of semiosis, in which space is both template and font. This is, in other words, the age of the inhabitable map (Fawcett-Tang 2005; Abrams and Hall 2006), an age intent on producing various new kinds of captivation through the cultivation of *atmosphere* or *presence* or *touch* (see Sloterdijk 2005a, 2005b; Zumthor 2006).[59] So, for example, when Wheeler (2006) points to a world perfused with signs, privileges emergence, and underlines the importance of responsiveness, I take this stance to be not just an outline of the lineaments of a new kind of political project but also a symptomatic observation concerning a world in which spaces are taking on many of the characteristics of life. The trick, or so it seems to me, is to work with this emerging spatial grain, in the full understanding that it is both a part of a series of means of opening up new opportunities for the exercise of power and profit *and* a new palette of possibilities.

The three subsequent chapters fill out how the background of experience is changing in response to these three insistent imperatives. In essence, they are an attempt to move on from Deleuze and Guattari's famous aphorism from *Anti-Oedipus*, 'The unconscious is not a theatre, but a factory', by documenting how the unconscious has become both together, as the factory and the theatre have blended into each other. Thus 'Still life in nearly present time' considers the ways in which modern societies are experimenting with 'neutral' material backgrounds for commercial gain, burrowing into bare life in order to come up with the goods. I associate bare life with that small space of time between action and cognition and show the way firms have become ever more expert in operating on this new territory for commercial gain. It was one of my first attempts to show up how the backgrounds through which we live are changing as new disciplines have their say. '*Driving* in the city' is intended to demonstrate just how radically bodies are changing as they are augmented and extended by these backgrounds, as they subtly redefine what counts as experience. The chapter argues that de Certeau's understanding of walking as the archetypal transhuman practice of making the city habitable cannot hold in a post-human world. By concentrating on the practices of driving, I argue that other experiences of the city now have an equal validity. In other words, de Certeau's work on everyday life in the city needs to be reworked in order to take into account the rise of automobility. The bulk of the chapter is devoted to exploring how that goal might be achieved, concentrating in particular on how new knowledges like software and ergonomics have become responsible for a large-scale spatial reordering of the city which presages an important change in what counts as making the city habitable. 'Movement-space' takes a slightly different tack by arguing that the background of experience is being changed irrevocably by means of mass calculation which is, perhaps, better described as 'qualculation' with the result that every event turns up digitally pre-disposed, so to speak. The chapter then moves on to consider how this qualculative background is producing new apprehensions of space and time before ending by considering how new kinds of sensorium may now be becoming possible. I illustrate this argument by considering the changing presence of the hand, coordinate systems, and language, thereby attempting to conjure up the lineaments of a new kind of movement-space.

The second section attempts to articulate some of the political stakes that arise from non-representational theory. Written in the late 1990s the single chapter in this section forms a kind of pivot. 'Afterwords', was an attempt to make a definitive statement about non-representational theory by focusing particularly on the motif of performance as the key to a politics of experiment. It is intended as a message of hope, of a longing for a future of stutter and clutter that can produce new places within which more interesting practices are able to produce more habitable worlds (Miyazaki 2006).

Having sketched in a background, I can then move on to some more recent work. Non-representational theory has been interpreted by some as being simply a political message of unbridled optimism. That is not the case. As if to prove it, the book ends on a darker note, emphasizing that the quest for a new kind of political that I want to follow may try to multiply positive prehensions, but that it is not therefore a quixotic quest for the new moral styles we so desperately need (Appadurai 2006). Indeed, I hold to a tragic view of human life insofar as I believe that history is one long stumble into the unknown, and it cannot be tied down and ordered in the way that too many social theorists imply with their too neat theories. Most particularly, it would be foolish to deny some of the more unsavoury facts of existence. Nature is both astonishingly prolific, able to produce infinite variation and exquisite adaptation, and abundantly and unremittingly cruel. Nature does not take sides. The cost of what Nietzsche called 'more life' is depredation on a scale we can hardly comprehend: who could sum the number of violent deaths that casually occur around the world every second or claim to understand this sublime destructiveness?

Human being does not stand outside nature. It is full of all kinds of impulses which are outside its comprehension and are the other (I will not say negative) side of this equation, impulses that can be likened to Freud's death instinct in their capacity to undo connections and destroy life. In the last section of the book, I start to address some of these issues, and, most particularly, the issues of anger, rage and humiliation, by concentrating on the issue of affect, for what it seems important to underline is that a clarion call for 'more life' is disingenuous, even misleading, without some understanding of the surpluses of anger, rage and humiliation that have been unleashed as a result of the 'predatory narcissisms' (Appadurai 2006) that characterize too much of the modern world.

The last four chapters in the book which form its final section point to the need to think about affect as a key element of a politics that will supplement the ordinary. What is certain is that understanding affect requires some sense of the role of biology, howsoever understood. The first chapter, 'From born to made', is an attempt to come to terms with that legacy of thought and practice by taking up some of the themes from the first part of the book and pulling them into the third. It is particularly concerned with forging new links between biology and technology by delivering a set of shocks to the meaning of accepted categories like 'nature' and 'technology', especially by relying on the Whiteheadian dictum that 'nature is a theatre for the interrelation of activities' (Whitehead 1978: 140). To achieve these dual aims, the chapter double clicks on the icon 'intelligence'. 'Intelligence' prioritizes the *active shaping of environments*. It thereby allows space for the spaces of the world to themselves become a part of intelligibility and intellect as elements of distributed cognition *and* distributed pre-cognition. The chapter argues that such a conception of sentience can provide a series of new perspectives, as well as a pressing ethical challenge. I then move to a consideration of the political stakes that the deployment of affect entails against the background of the active engineering of pre-cognition. In the chapter 'Spatialities of feeling' I outline what a politics of affect might look like and especially the more explicit politics of hope that is currently struggling to be born out of an analysis of the affective swirl that characterizes modern societies. However, I take seriously the criticism of this kind of work, that it has tended to neglect the many forms of violence and repression that infest the worlds and knock it around. Thus I try to counterbalance the politics of hope that I espouse with some sober reflections on the affective substrate in which it is embedded and from which it cannot be simply divided. Thus the chapter 'But malice aforethought' considers the affective life that is to be found in modern cities, concentrating on the idea that sociality does not have to mean that citizens automatically like each other. Indeed, modern cities are drenched in dislike and even hatred, and I argue that this misanthropic fact needs to be taken fully into account in any narrative and politics of affect. Finally, 'Turbulent passions' considers how we might better understand the realm of political feeling by concentrating on the affective technologies through which masses of people become primed to act. I argue that this is a pressing political task, given that the systematic manipulation of 'motivational propensity' has become a key political technology. But in order to arrive at a diagnosis of the affective swash of the present, I argue that social science needs to draw on approaches that are willing to countenance a formative role for the biological. I therefore turn to two strands of work, one that directly revalues the biological, the other that calls on ethological models and analogies. Using these different but connected strands of work, I am able to move to such a diagnosis. My argument is that a series of affective technologies that were previously used mainly in the corporate sphere to work on consumer anxiety, obsession and compulsion are now being moved over into the political sphere with mainly deleterious consequences, However, this process of transmission also suggests some interesting counter-politics based on the cultivation of contrary affective motion, not what Appadurai (2006) calls the 'runaway acts of mutual stimulation' which are so prevalent in a media-saturated age but something much more interesting.

Notes

1 I had originally considered calling this introductory chapter 'Sacraments of expression' after Whitehead but Whitehead means something rather different and there seems no point in confusing the issue. The reference to the superfluous intentionally echoes Voltaire's famous dictum.
2 I agree with Connolly (2005: 166) that 'running the experiment may be the best way to test the claims'.
3 I understand social theory as an art of controlled speculation, not as a faithful rendition of what may be going on, as if that were indeed possible.
4 Throughout the introduction, I use the plural term 'the worlds' in preference to the 'the world' in order to signify that I am trying to describe a set of different but attuned worlds rather than just one order of being, a move prompted by traditions as diverse as von Uexkull's discussion of *umwelten* and contemporary discussions of postcolonialism.
5 It follows that I do not believe that experience has in some way been radically downgraded or made problematic in the contemporary world, in the style of Benjamin or Agamben (see Docherty 2006). There is, in my opinion, no general crisis of modernity: there are plenty of crises to be going on with.
6 Most especially, because publics, as peoples to come, are a conjunction of forces which will always exceed any given human intention.
7 I am uncomfortably aware of the complicated theoretical apparatus that I have myself used to reach these conclusions.
8 It is worth recalling that, according to the *Oxford English Dictionary*, 'vocation' originated in the Latin noun of action, *vocare*, meaning to call or summon. This meaning fits my purposes well.
9 Lotringer is reproaching Hardt and Negri, justifiably so far as I am concerned.
10 This phrase has become associated with the work of Ernst Bloch and I would want to affirm Bloch's general direction whilst dissociating it from his theory of history.
11 As in rhythm, play, and kinetic markers such as running, chasing, fleeing, jumping, falling, and so on (Sheets-Johnstone 2005).
12 That is, following being in its genesis, by accomplishing the genesis of thought in parallel with the object. So far as I am aware, the term was first used by Simondon.
13 I have not used the word experience because so many philosophical traditions associate that word with interpretation, that is with acts of the attribution of meaning.
14 In particular, I would point to the important work being done in human geography by Ben Anderson, J.D. Dewsbury, Paul Harrison, Eric Laurier, Derek McCormack, John Wylie, and others.
15 Pred's is a useful term because it does not presuppose a specific *spatial location* (such as the biological body) or any necessary sensory modalities.

16 For a very clear introduction to this line of thought and its implications, see Middleton and Brown (2006),

17 This is one of my main objections to actor-network theory: its curiously flat tone arises from the filters it puts up on what can be included in the world, in a way that, for example, Whitehead's philosophy – which includes feelings as 'concrete elements in the nature of actual entities' – does not.

18 This is a word that needs to be used with care, given its history (Wegner 2002). But I also think that the word's brutal edge is important in pointing to the way in which instinct is laid down. I take the unconscious as normally understood to be one part of bare or creaturely life, a specific mode of expressivity.

19 Though I am extremely sceptical of the current tendency to mark out pretty well anything with a bio prefix.

20 Donald (2001) suggests that the analogy of computation as a means of describing cognition is inaccurate. A better analogy would be digestion.

21 In other words, being human involves the evolution of the capacity to have beliefs about beliefs, the evolution, in other words, from behaviour readers to mind readers (Sterelny 2003).

22 The crucial role of language as affect should be noted here; see Riley (2005).

23 Echoing Wittgenstein's observation that what underlies a number of features of language-games, including the following of rules, is the brute 'natural' fact that people just do continue in certain ways in certain situations.

24 Objects are often thought of as interpretable, in that they demand an unreciprocated affection which is a part of person-making. In other words, 'there are no interpretable objects or intentional objects, only what counts as an interpretable object or, better, groups of people who count as interpretable and who, accordingly, deal with certain objects in recognizable ways' (Tamen 2001: 3).

25 This is actor-network theory's presupposition of symmetry formalized.

26 Which still implies intensive corporeal organization.

27 But there is another feminist tradition, of course; see, for example, Parisi (2004).

28 A point that Donna Haraway makes well in her critique of actor-network theory.

29 In any case, flesh, under the imperatives of bioscience, is itself rapidly becoming the subject and object of numerous technological ensembles which are rapidly making it portable, and which, in certain accounts, are extending the imperatives of farming to the human world (Sloterdijk 2006).

30 This is why I am suspicious of making too easy links between labour and existence, a point often made by Lévinas.

31 Many of the same points can apply to occasions of humour or embarrassment; see Billig (2005).

32 See, especially, the book by Soden (2003) on falling.

33 Kwinter stresses the tool-less nature of this activity but this aesthetic is relative, to put it mildly.

34 We should not make too much of this, of course. At different times in history, various means of producing continuously bounded sites have been invented that have stabilized sites over long periods of time. A good example is barbed wire (see Netz 2004).

35 What exactly I mean by this is outlined in some detail in Chapter 6 of this book.

36 And not in some naïve way in which the history of dance as complicit with social structuring.

37 Most particularly, dance provides an understanding of style as a particular way of doing body; 'dance would be the style not as that which is added on to a body in creation itself: style not as that technique through which creation takes place but as pure creativity with no end or ground outside itself' (Colebrook 2005b: 8). The body is neither a norm towards which bodies ought to strive nor a mere existing that expresses some prior norm of human creativity. However, I retain some scepticism about the residual romanticism I find in this quasi-Deleuzian point of view which is why I finally prefer Deleuze and Guattari's later work on territorialization.

38 See McNeill (2005). I have tried to take in the whole spectrum of senses since my early work. See, for example, my writing on smell and on vision. I am particularly impressed by the histories of the senses currently coming out of North America (see Rath 2003).

39 Thus I have become very interested in the possibilities of transposing imitative theories like that of Tarde with the kinds of conflictual mimesis championed by Girard (cf. Fleming 2004).

40 I should add that I start out from the assumption that

there is no essence, no historical or spiritual vocation, no biological destiny that humans must enact or realize. That is the only reason why something like an ethics can exist because it is clear that if humans were or had to be this or that substance, this or that destiny, no ethical experience would be possible, there would only be tasks to be done. (Agamben 1993: 43)

41 Thus, 'God is above all the name for the pressure to be alive in the world, to open to the too much of pressure generated in large measure by the uncanny presence of my neighbour' (Santner 2001: 9). Or, as Latour (2002: 7) puts it, in a thoroughly Whiteheadian vein, 'God is the feeling for positive, instead of negative prehensions'.

42 In Aristotelian terms, as *energeia*. It is worth remembering that in past times art and craft were much more closely bound together: indeed the word for craft used to be 'art'. This is an occlusion that I want to see revived as a politics. Additionally I would want to see the meaning of craft broadened out to cover activities such as teaching and the like, which are too often excluded from its orbit.

43 The metaphor of craftsmanship has other benefits too, for example, a willingness to explore ambiguity, a commitment to the task for its own sake, and its often tacit nature.

44 That does not just mean the spatialization of experience as an always having been possible (see Middleton and Brown 2006) but also the way in which spaces feel.

45 This very perception may itself be historically specific, of course. See Wall (2006).

46 Given the size of the gut – its surface area would cover a small room if laid out flat – this really would be a geography.

47 As in the work of Emmanuel Lévinas.

48 As in the work of Michel Henry.

49 A restatement of the classic point that thought cannot be divorced from its object, understood now as meaning that 'the ontology of the sensible is not separable from the constitution of material assemblages and processes themselves' (Toscano 2004a: xxi).

50 See, in particular, work on the spaces of sound and especially the efforts to reconstruct historical soundscapes (e.g. B.R. Smith 1999; Rath 2003; Sterne 2003).

51 For example, I believe that Deleuze and Guattari's work suffers from a residual structuralism (see Schatzki 2002) and too great an emphasis on an unalloyed 'bliss action' (Deleuze 1988b: 28).

52 Indeed, I am highly sceptical that the history of Western thought could ever be written as if it were simply the history of a set of philosophical excursions.

53 'In fact, a philosophical theory is an elaborately developed question, and nothing else; by itself and in itself, it is not the resolution to a problem, but the elaboration, to the very end, of the necessary implications of a formulated question' (Deleuze 1991; 116).

54 I should add that I think this manuscript is amongst the last that will take on such a dreary form. It seems clear to me that to do justice to the ambitions of much of what I am writing about requires a new cursive register, one that mixes all manner of media and presentational styles in order to achieve its goals, that can roll out at different *speeds* and that, as a result, can really perform.

55 Conceived of as if by Malebranche, as the natural prayer of the soul, an attentiveness to all living creatures.

56 It is, of course, possible to take the theoretical technology wielded in this book too seriously. As Gombrowicz put it with reference to existentialism:

> It seems impossible to meet the demands of Dasein and simultaneously have coffee and croissants for an evening snack. To fear nothingness but to fear the dentist more. To be consciousness, which walks around in pants and talks on the telephone. To be responsibility, which runs little shopping errands downtown. To bear the weight of significant being, to install the world with meaning and then return the change from ten pesos. (cited in Simic 2006: 22)

57 Eagleton (2006: 26) puts it nicely in describing Jameson's style: 'it rolls its way across an intellectual landscape which it levels beneath it, emulsifying everything until connections become more insistent than conflicts'.

58 The evolution of new protocols carries on apace. Thus, since I wrote the first chapter, co-production with the consumer has become a new orthodoxy, signalled by its arrival in the pages of *Harvard Business Review*.

59   The reference to atmospheres consciously summons up the work of Peter Sloterdijk, whose work on spaces is, I think, the closest to what I am trying to achieve (see Sloterdijk 2005a, 2005b).

Works Cited

Abrahams, R.D. (2005) *Everyday Life: A Poetics of Vernacular Practices*, Philadelphia: University of Pennsylvania Press.

Abrams, J. and Hall, P. (eds) (2006) *Else/Where: Mapping New Cartographies of Networks and Territories*, Minneapolis: University of Minnesota Press.

Agamben, G. (1993) *The Coming Community*. Minneapolis, MN: University of Minnesota Press.

Agamben, G. (2004) *The Open: Man and Animal*, Stanford, CA: Stanford University Press.

Alliez, E. (2004a) 'Remarks on Whitehead', available online at http://www.goldsmith.ac.uk/esisp/papers/Alliez_Remarks_on_Whitehead.pdf .

Alliez, E. (2004b) *The Signature of the World: What is Deleuze and Guattari's Philosophy?* London: Continuum.

Amin, A. and Thrift, N.J. (2005a) 'What's left? Just the future' *Antipode*, 37: 220–238.

Amin, A. and Thrift, N.J. (2005b) 'Citizens of the world. Seeing the city as a site of international influence' *Harvard International Review* 27 (3).

Appadurai, A. (2006) *Fear of Small Numbers. An Essay on the Geography of Anger*, Durham, NC: Duke University Press.

Billig, M. (2005) *Laughter and Ridicule: Towards a Social Critique of Humour*, London: Sage.

Bloch, E. (1986 [1959]) *The Politics of Hope* (3 vols), Oxford: Blackwell.

Bloch, E. (2000 [1923]) *The Spirit of Utopia*, Stanford, CA: Stanford University Press.

Braidotti, R. (2006) *Transpositions*, Cambridge: Polity Press.

Brennan, T. (2004) *The Transmission of Affect*, London: Continuum.

Bromell, N. (2000) *Tomorrow Never Knows: Rock and Psychedelics in the 1960s*, Chicago: University of Chicago Press.

Butler, J. (2005) *Giving an Account of Oneself*, New York: Fordham University Press.

Carter, P. (1992) *The Sound In Between: Voice, Space, Performance*, Kensington: New South Wales University Press.

Carter, P. (2002) *Repressed Spaces. The Poetics of Agoraphobia*, London: Reaktion.

Chakrabarty, D. (2002) *Habitations of Modernity: Essays in the Wake of Subaltern Studies*, Chicago: University of Chicago Press.

Chatterjee, P. (2004) *The Politics of the Governed. Reflections on Popular Politics in Most of the World*, New York: Columbia University Press.

Colebrook, C. (2005a) 'On the specificity of affect' in Buchanan, I. and Lambert, G. (eds) *Deleuze and Space*, Edinburgh: Edinburgh University Press, pp. 189–206.

Colebrook, C. (2005b) 'How can we tell the dancer from the dance? The subject of dance and the subject of philosophy' *Topoi*, 25: 5–14.

Connolly, W.E. (2005) *Pluralism*, Durham, NC: Duke University Press.

Crary, J. (2004) 'Foreword' in Oliveira, N., Oxley, N. and Petty, M. (eds) *Installation Art in the New Millenium. The Empire of the Senses*, London: Thames and Hudson, pp. 6–9.

Critchley, S. (2002) 'Introduction' in Critchley, S. and Bernasconi, R. (eds) *The Cambridge Companion to Levinas*, Cambridge: Cambridge University Press, pp. 1–32.

Critchley, S. (2005) *Things Merely Are. Philosophy in the Poetry of Wallace Stevens*, London: Routledge.

Deleuze, G. (1988b) *Spinoza: Practical Philosophy*, San Francisco: City Lights Books.

Deleuze, G. (1991) *Empiricism and Subjectivity: An Essay on Hume's Theory of Human Nature*, New York: Columbia University Press.

Despret, V. (2004) *Our Emotional Make-Up: Ethnopsychology and Selfhood*, New York: Other Press.

Docherty, T. (2006) *Aesthetic Democracy*, Stanford, CA: Stanford University Press.

Donald, M. (2001) *A Mind So Rare. The Evolution of Human Consciousness*, New York: W.W. Norton.

Dunagan, C. (2005) 'Dance, knowledge, and power' *Topoi*, 24: 29–41.

Eagleton, T. (2006) 'Making a break' *London Review of Books*, 9 March: 25–26.

Fawcett-Tang, R. (2005) *Mapping. An Illustrated Guide to Graphical Navigational Systems*, Mies, Switzerland: Rotovision.

Fenves, P. (1993) 'Chatter' in *Language and History in Kierkegaard*, Stanford, CA: Stanford University Press.

Fischer, M.J. (2003) *Emergent Forms of Life and the Anthropological Voice*, Durham, NC: Duke University Press.

Fisher, M. (2002) *The Vehement Passions*, Princeton, NJ: Princeton University Press.

Fleming, C. (2004) *René Girard: Violence and Mimesis*, Cambridge: Polity Press.

Fortun, K. (2001) *Advocacy After Bhopal: Environmentalism, Disaster and Global Orders*, Chicago: University of Chicago Press.

Gerhardt, S. (2004) *Why Love Matters. How Affection Shapes a Baby's Brain*, Hove: Brunner-Routledge.

Gil, J. (1998) *Metamorphoses of the Body*, Minneapolis: University of Minnesota Press.

Ginsborg, P. (2005) *The Politics of Everyday Life: Making Choices, Changing Lives*, New Haven, CT: Yale University Press.

Ginzburg, C. (2001b) *Wooden Eyes. Nine Reflections on Distance*, New York: Columbia University Press.

Goodchild, P. (2002) *Capitalism and Religion*, London: Routledge.

Grosz, E.A. (2005) *Time Travels: Feminism, Nature, Power*, Durham, NC: Duke University Press.

Gumbrecht, H.U. (2004) *Production of Presence: What Meaning Cannot Convey*, Stanford, CA: Stanford University Press.

Harman, G. (2002) *Tool-Being: Heidegger and the Metaphysics of Objects*, Chicago: Open Court.

Hewitt, A. (2005) *Social Choreography: Ideology as Performance in Dance and Everyday Movement*, Durham, NC: Duke University Press.

Hurley, S. and Chater, N. (eds) (2005) *Perspectives on Imitation*, 2 vols, Cambridge, MA: MIT Press.

Ingold, T. (2006) 'Rethinking the animate, re-animating thought' *Ethos*, 71: 9–20.

James, W. (1960 [1890]) *The Principles of Psychology*, 2 vols. New York: Dover.

James, W. (1999 [1911]) *Some Problems of Philosophy*, Cambridge, MA: Harvard University Press.

Jameson, F. (2005) *Archaeologies of the Future: The Desire Called Utopia and Other Science Fictions*, London: Verso.

Kwinter, S. (2001) *Architectures of Time: Toward a Theory of the Event in Modernist Culture*, Cambridge, MA: MIT Press.

Kwon, M.P. (2004) *One Place After Another: Site-Specific Art and Locational Identity*, Cambridge, MA: MIT Press.

Latour, B. (2005) *Reassembling the Social: An Introduction to Actor-Network Theory*, Oxford: Oxford University Press.

Law, J. (2004a) 'Mattering – or how might STS contribute?' available online at http://www.comp.lancs.ac.uk/sociology/staff/law/law.htm.

Law, J. (2004b) *After Method: Mess in Social Science Research*, London: Routledge.

Lazzarato, M. (2004) 'From capital-labour to capital-life' *Ephemera*, 4: 187–208.

Levinson, S.C. (2003) *Space in Language and Cognition: Explorations in Cognitive Diversity*, Cambridge: Cambridge University Press.

Lotringer, S. (2004) 'Foreword: We, the multitude' in Virno, P., *A Grammar of the Multitude*, New York: Semiotext (e), pp. 7–19.

Mabey, R. (2006) 'God and me' *Granta*, 93: 195–199.

Mackenzie, A. (2002) *Transductions. Bodies and Machines at Speed*, London: Continuum.

McNeill, D. (2005) *Gesture and Thought*, Chicago: University of Chicago Press.

Marcus, G. (2005) *Like a Rolling Stone: Bob Dylan at the Crossroads*, London: Faber and Faber.

Middleton, D. and Brown, S.D. (2006) *The Social Psychology of Experience. Studies in Remembering and Forgetting*, London: Sage.

Miyazaki, H. (2004) *The Method of Hope, Anthropology, Philosophy, and Fijian Knowledge*, Stanford, CA: Stanford University Press.

Miyazaki, H. (2006) 'Economy of dreams: hope in global capitalism and its critiques' *Cultural Anthropology*, 21:147–172.

Netz, R. (2004) *Barbed Wire: An Ecology of Modernity*, Middletown, CT: Wesleyan University Press.

Parisi, L. (2004) *Abstract Sex. Philosophy, Bio-Technology and the Mutations of Desire*, London: Continuum.

Parkes, D.N. and Thrift, N.J. (1980) *Times, Spaces and Places. A Chronogeographic Perspective*, Chichester: John Wiley.

Phillips, A. (1999) *Darwin's Worms*, London: Faber and Faber.

Pred, R. (2005) *Onflow: Dynamics of Consciousness of Experience*, Cambridge, MA: MIT Press.

Probyn, E. (2005) *Blush: Faces of Shame*, Minneapolis: University of Minnesota Press.

Rabinow, P. (2006) 'Steps toward an anthropological laboratory' *Discussion Paper*, 2 February 2006.

Rajchman, J. (1998) *Constructions*, Cambridge, MA: MIT Press.

Rath, R.C. (2003) *How Early America Sounded*, New York and London: Cornell University Press.

Rawls, A.M. (2002) 'Editor's introduction' in Garfinkel, H. *Ethnomethodology's Program Working Out Durkheim's Aphorism*, Lanham, MD: Rowman and Littlefield, pp. 1–64.

Reginster, B. (2006) *The Affirmation of Life. Nietzsche on Overcoming Nihilism*, Cambridge, MA: Harvard University Press.

Riley, D. (2005) *Impersonal Passion: Language as Affect*, Durham, NC: Duke University Press.

Santner, E.L. (2001) *On the Psychotheology of Everyday Life*, Chicago: University of Chicago Press.

Santner, E.L. (2006) *On Creaturely Life. Rilke, Benjamin, Sebald*, Chicago: University of Chicago Press.

Schatzki, T.R. (2002) *The Site of the Social: A Philosophical Account of the Constitution of Social Life and Change*, University Park: Pennsylvania State University Press.

Schwenger, P. (2006) *The Tears of Things: Melancholy and Physical Objects*, Minneapolis: University of Minnesota Press.

Sheets-Johnston, M. (2005) 'Man has always danced: forays into an art largely forgotten by philosophers' *Contemporary Aesthetics*, vol. 3; available online at http://www.contempaesthetics.org/newvolume/pages/article.php?articleID=273.

Simic, C. (2006) 'Salvation through laughter' *New York Review of Books*, 12 January: 22–25.

Simondon, G. (1989) *Du mode d'existence des objects techniques*, Paris: Aubier.

Sloterdijk, P. (2005a) 'Against gravity. Bettina Funcke talks with Peter Sloterdijk' *Bookforum*, February/March.

Sloterdijk, P. (2005b) *Im Weltinnenraum des Kapitals*, Frankfurt: Suhrkamp Verlag.

Sloterdijk, P. (2005c) 'Atmospheric politics' in Latour, B. and Weibel, P. (eds) *Making Things Public. Atmospheres of Democracy*, Cambridge, MA: MIT Press, pp. 944–951.

Sloterdijk, P. (2006) 'War on latency: on some relations between surrealism and terror' *Radical Philosophy*, 137: 14–19.

Smith, B.R. (1999) *The Acoustic World of Early Modern England: Attending to the O-Factor*, Chicago: University of Chicago Press.

Soden, G. (2003) *Defying Gravity: Land Divers, Roller Coasters, Gravity Bums, and the Human Obsession with Falling*, New York: Norton.

Spinosa, C., Flores, F. and Dreyfus, H. (1997) *Disclosing New Worlds: Entrepreneurship, Democratic Action and the Culturalisation of Solidarity*, Cambridge, MA: MIT Press.

Stengers, I. (2002a) 'A "cosmo-politics" – risk, hope, change' in Zournazi, M. (ed.) *Hope: New Philosophies for Change*, London: Routledge.

Stengers, I. (2006) 'Gilles Deleuze's last message' *The Virgin and the Neutrino: Which Future for Science*, Paris.

Sterelny, K. (2003) *Thought in a Hostile World: The Evolution of Human Cognition*, Oxford: Blackwell.

Sterne, J. (2003) *The Audible Past: Cultural Origins of Sound Reproduction*, Durham, NC: Duke University Press.

Strathern, M. (1999) *Property, Substance, and Effect*, London: Athlone Press.

Tamen, M. (2001) *Friends of Interpretable Objects*, Cambridge, MA: Harvard University Press.

Tarde, G. (2000) *Social Laws: An Outline of Sociology*, Kitchener: Batoche Books.

Taussig, M. (1993) *Mimesis and Alterity: A Particular History of the Senses*, New York Routledge.

Thrift, N.J. (1996) *Spatial Formations*, London: Sage.

Thrift, N.J. (2001) 'Summoning life' in Cloke, P., Crang. P. and Goodwin, P.B. (eds) *Envisioning Geography*, London: Arnold.

Thrift, N.J. (2005a) *Knowing Capitalism*, London: Sage.

Thrift, N.J. (2006b) 'Space' *Theory Culture and Society*, 23: 139–146.

Toscano, A. (2004) 'Preface: the coloured thickness of a problem' in Alliez, E. *The Signature of the World: What is Deleuze and Guattari's Philosophy?* London: Continuum, pp. ix–xxv.

Vendler, H. (1995) *The Breaking of Style*, Cambridge, MA: Harvard University Press.

Vesely, D. (2004) *Architecture in an Age of Divided Representation*, Cambridge, MA: MIT Press.

Wagner, R. (2001) *An Anthropology of the Subject: Holographic Worldview in New Guinea and Its Meaning and Significance for the World of Anthropology*, Berkeley: University of California Press.

Wall, C.S. (2006) *The Prose of Things. Transformations of Description in the Eighteenth Century*, Chicago: University of Chicago Press.

Wegner, D.M. (2002) *The Illusion of Conscious Will*, Cambridge, MA: MIT Press.

Weinstein, P. (2005) *Unknowing: The Work of Modernist Fiction*, Ithaca, NY: Cornell University Press.

Wheeler, W. (2006) *The Whole Creature: Complexity, Biosemiotics and the Evolution of Culture*, London: Lawrence and Wishart.

White, S.K. (2000) *Sustaining Affirmation: The Strengths of Weak Ontology in Political Theory*, Princeton, NJ: Princeton University Press.

Whitehead, A.N. (1978) *Process and Reality*, New York: Macmillan.

Wilson, E. (2004) *Psychosomatic. Feminism and the Neurobiological Body*, Durham, NC: Duke University Press.

Wilson, T.D. (2002) *Strangers to Ourselves. Discovering the Adaptive Unconscious*, Cambridge, MA: Belknap Press.

Wolin, S. (2000) 'Political theory: from vocation to invocation' in Frank, J.A. and Tamborino, J. (eds) *Vocations of Political Theory*, Minneapolis: University of Minnesota Press, pp. 3–22.

Zumthor, P. (2006) *Atmospheres. Architectural Environments. Surrounding Objects*, Basel: Birkhäuser Verlag.

CHAPTER 3

Complexity

John Urry

In this essay, John Urry explains the science behind the idea of complexity. He is Professor of Sociology at Lancaster University. He has recently published *The Tourist Gaze* (2002), *Global Complexity* (2003), *Performing Tourist Places* (2004), *Tourism Mobilities* (2004) and *Automobilities* (2005).

Introduction

The term 'complexity' has recently sprung into the physical and social sciences, humanities and semi-popular writings. Describing what it is and how it is organized is difficult since it is 'present' within very many scientific, social scientific and semi-popular discourses and practices. Inter alia these include alternative healing, architecture, consultancy, consumer design, economics, defence studies, fiction, garden design, geography, history, literary theory, management education, New Age, organizational studies, philosophy, post-structuralism, sociology, stock car racing, town planning, as well as most of the 'physical sciences' over the past two or so decades (Thrift, 1999).

In some ways it has become a global phenomenon and this makes it hard to disentangle its various components. 'Complexity' practices are constituted as something of a self-organizing global network that is spreading 'complexity' notions around the globe. Complexity researchers deploy the techniques of PR and branding, international meetings with 'star' speakers, guru worship, the use of global media and publishing, and networking, especially centred on nodes such as Santa Fe in New Mexico or the various research institutes named after the late Nobel prizewinner Ilya Prigogine (Waldrop, 1994).

There is a new 'structure of feeling' that complexity approaches both signify and enhance. Such an emergent structure of feeling involves a greater sense of contingent openness to people, corporations and societies, of the unpredictability of outcomes in time–space, of a charity towards objects and nature, of the diverse and non-linear changes in relationships, households and persons, and of the sheer increase in the hyper-complexity of products, technologies and socialities (Capra, 1996, 2001).

Original publication details: John Urry, "Complexity." *Theory, Culture, & Society* 23, pp. 111–117. Sage, 2006. Reproduced with permission from Sage and J. Urry.

Literary Theory: An Anthology, Third Edition. Edited by Julie Rivkin and Michael Ryan.
© 2017 John Wiley & Sons, Ltd. Published 2017 by John Wiley & Sons, Ltd.

Thus economic and technological studies show there has been a huge increase in the number of components within products (Urry, 2003). The Eli Whitney musket of around 1800 had 51 components while the space shuttle of the late 20th century contained 10 million. Further, there are increases in the cybernetic contribution performed by architectures that integrate components through feedback loops. In 1970 the most valuable products in world trade were simple products produced by simple processes; a quarter-of-a-century later, nearly two-thirds of the products in world trade involve complex processes *and* complex products, with vast numbers of components, cybernetic architectures and socio-technical systems. This is linked with self-organizing and computerized networks that are continuously self-reproducing themselves across the globe, developing skills and structures necessary to innovate technologies to overcome obstacles or create new pathways.

A complexity structure of feeling brings out the paradoxes implicated in many contemporary processes. Thus the preservation of 'nature' seems to destroy many of the very things that nature lovers claim to value (Davis, 2000). There is no such thing as 'nature's balance', no real or primordial nature that would be in equilibrium if only humans had not intruded. The effects of humans are subtly and irreversibly woven into the very evolution of landscape. And any ecological system is immensely complex so that there are never straightforward policies that simply restore nature's balance, such as fish populations in the seas or rivers. Indeed many ecological systems themselves depend not upon stable relationships but upon massive intrusions of flows of species from other parts of the globe and of fire, lightning, hurricanes, high winds, ice storms, flash floods, frosts, earthquakes and so on. The 'normal' state of nature is not one of balance and repose. Such developments can only be seen over very lengthy periods of time, much longer than the lives of particular researchers or of research programmes. Moreover, populations of most species demonstrate extreme unevenness, with populations often rising rapidly when introduced into an area and then almost as rapidly collapsing. Extreme events demonstrate complexity where small changes in driving variables or inputs – magnified by feedback – can produce disproportionate outcomes.

There is no silent, docile 'nature', especially when confronted by new forms of 'culture'. The contemporary complex world seems to involve highly adaptable viruses, such as Aids and ebola, new superbugs, newly lethal pathogens such as prions, and the reappearance of TB, cholera and the bubonic plague. Such a medicalized apocalypse appears to stem from new patterns of global travel and trade, the heightened ineffectiveness of antibiotics that encounter increased 'resistance', and the development of new powerful risk cultures beyond and within 'medicine' (Van Loon, 2002).

These and other developments seem to herald a relatively new set of hybrid systems neither natural nor social; neither ordered nor anarchic – that display high levels of complexity. A complexity structure of feeling is underpinned by an apparent lack of proportionality between 'causes' and 'effects'. That we think of these hybrid systems as complex has stemmed from an array of developments within 20th-century science.

Time and Space

Science, in the 20th century, dismantled elements of Newtonian science and this prepared the way for the complexity turn (Capra, 1996). Pre-20th century science operated with a view of time as Newtonian: invariant, infinitely divisible into space-like units, measurable in length, expressible as a number and reversible. It is time seen essentially as a kind of Cartesian space comprising invariant measurable lengths to be moved along, forwards *and* backwards. Objects are viewed as contained within such boundaries of absolute time and space.

The sciences dismantled such a notion (Coveney and Highfield, 1990). Einstein showed that there is no fixed or absolute time independent of the system to which it is refers. Time is a local, internal feature of any system of observation and measurement. It varies as to where and how it is measured. It can be stretched and shrunk. Further, Einstein demonstrated that time and space are not separate from each other but are fused into a four-dimensional time-space curved under the influence of mass. Time and space are 'internal' to the processes by which the physical and social worlds themselves operate, helping to constitute their powers.

Space and time are now seen as dynamic qualities: when a body moves, or a force acts, it affects the curvature of space and time, and in turn the structure of space–space affects the way in which bodies move and forces act. The beginning of the universe occurred without a pre-existing cause, and its very happening created in that moment both space and time. There is no 'time' before the big bang, and if the universe ends in another singular event time (and space) will cease. Space and time have been spontaneously created, part of the systemic nature of the universe. They are switched on.

Quantum theory generally describes a virtual state in which electrons try out instantaneously all possible futures before settling into particular patterns. Quantum behaviour is instantaneous, simultaneous and unpredictable. The interactions between the parts are far more fundamental than the parts themselves. Bohm refers to this as the occurrence of a dance without dancers.

Thermodynamics shows that there is an irreversible flow of time (Prigogine, 1997). Rather than there being time-symmetry and indeed a reversibility of time as postulated in classical physics, a clear distinction is drawn between what has passed and what lies in the future. An arrow of time results in loss of organization and an increase in randomness or disorder over time within open systems. This accumulation of disorder or positive entropy results from the Second Law of Thermodynamics. However, there is not a simple growth of disorder. Prigogine shows how new order arises but is far from equilibrium. There are what he terms dissipative structures, islands of new order within a sea of disorder, maintaining or even increasing their order at the expense of greater overall entropy. Prigogine describes how such localized order 'floats in disorder'.

The irreversibility of time can be seen in the expansion of the universe following the singular event of the 'big bang' 15 billion or so years ago. The scientific discovery of the big bang cannot be reconciled with laws of the physical world that presumes time is reversible, deterministic and involving 'classes of phenomena'. The big bang is a one-off phenomenon like nothing else ever to occur within the known universe. Laws of nature are thus historical and not universal (and hence much more like the laws of society).

The arrow or flow of time results in futures that are unstable, relatively unpredictable and characterized by various possibilities. Time is both multiple and unpredictable. Prigogine (1997) talks of the 'end of certainty' as the complexity sciences overcome what he calls the alienating images of a deterministic world and an arbitrary world of pure chance. Complexity repudiates the dichotomies of determinism and chance, as well as nature and society, being and becoming, stasis and change. Systems are thus seen as being 'on the edge of chaos'. Order and chaos are in a kind of balance where the components are neither fully locked into place but yet do not fully dissolve into anarchy. Chaos is not complete anarchic randomness but there is a kind of 'orderly disorder' present within all such systems.

Time flows with minor changes in the past being able to produce potentially massive effects in the present or future. Such small events are not 'forgotten'. Chaos theory in particular rejects the commonsensical notion that only large changes in causes produce large changes in effects. Following a perfectly deterministic set of rules, unpredictable yet patterned results can be generated, with small causes on occasions producing large effects and vice versa. The classic example is the butterfly effect accidentally discovered by Lorenz in 1961. It was shown that minuscule changes at one location can produce, if modelled by three coupled non-linear equations, very large weather effects very distant from the original site.

Emergence

Central to dynamic systems analysis is the idea of emergence. It is not that the sum is greater than the size of its parts but that there are system effects that are different from its parts. Complexity examines how components of a system through their interaction 'spontaneously' develop collective properties or patterns, even simple properties such as colour, that do not seem implicit within, or at least not implicit in the same way, within individual components. The flavour of sugar is not present in the carbon, hydrogen and oxygen atoms that comprise it. These are non-linear consequences that are not present within, or reducible to, the very many individual components that comprise such activities.

Such large-scale patterns or characteristics emerge from, but are not reducible to, the micro-dynamics of the phenomenon in question. Thus gases are not uniform entities but comprise a seething confusion of atoms obeying the laws of quantum mechanics. The laws governing gases derive not from the behaviour of each individual atom but from their statistical patterning. Also if a system passes a particular threshold with minor changes in the controlling variables, switches occur such that a liquid turns into a gas or relatively warm weather suddenly turns into an ice age. This can give rise to unexpected structures and events whose properties can be quite different from those of the underlying elementary laws.

In particular, the emergence of patterning within a given system results from 'attractors'. If a dynamic system does not move over time through all possible parts of a phase space but instead occupies a restricted part of it, then this is said to result from attractors. The simplest attractor is a point, as with the unforced swinging of a pendulum. Everything reaches the single equilibrium point. A somewhat more complex example is a domestic central heating/air conditioning system where the attractor consists, not of a single point, but of a specified range of temperatures. The relationship is not linear but involves a negative feedback mechanism that minimizes deviance. This is a self-regulating and bounded system. In certain systems there are 'strange attractors', unstable spaces to which the trajectory of dynamical systems is attracted through billions of iterations and positive feedback occurring over long periods of time. Such a space may be either indeterminate within the boundaries or there may be various sets of boundaries, as with the butterfly shaped Lorenz attractor. Such attractors are immensely sensitive in the effects that they generate to slight variations in their initial conditions. Much science has been concerned to characterize the topology of such strange attractors.

Systems and Feedback

Early cybernetic research under the auspices of the Macy conferences in the post Second World War period emphasized the importance of negative feedback loops that restored the homeostatic functioning of whatever system was under examination (Hayles, 1999). Such systems of circular causality involved the processing of information that resulted in re-establishing equilibrium and stability through negative feedback (a view that much influenced Talcott Parsons).

However, in later systems formulations, of complexity or the non-linear, positive feedback loops are examined. These are viewed as exacerbating initial stresses in the system, so rendering it unable to absorb shocks and re-establishing the original equilibrium. Very strong interactions occur between the parts of a system and there is an absence of a central hierarchical structure able to 'govern' outcomes. Positive feedback occurs when a change tendency is reinforced rather than dampened down as occurs with the negative feedback.

Such positive feedback is involved in analyses of the increasing returns that generate the path dependency found in the history of various economic-technological systems (such as the VHS video system replacing the technologically superior Betamax). Such irreversible path dependence occurs when contingent events set into motion institutional patterns or event chains over time that have deterministic properties through what Brian Arthur (1994) examines as 'lock-ins'.

More generally, complexity science investigates systems that can adapt and evolve as they self-organize through time. Such complex social interactions have been likened to walking through a maze, the walls of which rearrange as one walks. New steps have then to be taken in order to adjust to the walls of the maze that are adapting to one's movement through the maze. Complexity thus investigates emergent, dynamic and self-organizing systems that coevolve and adapt in ways that heavily influence the probabilities of later events.

Autopoiesis, as explained by Maturana and Varela, involves a process of self-making between the processes of production *of* those components that make up a system (Maturana, 1981). These continuously regenerate the processes of production through various feedback mechanisms so to maintain the organization per se, although the structure may change. Autopoiesis is to be seen in non-linear laser theory where the co-ordination of the required emissions is carried out by the laser light itself through processes of self-organization. Autopoiesis is also shown in the nature of urban growth where small local preferences mildly expressed in the concerns of individuals, such as wanting to live with those who are ethnically similar, can lead to massively segregated neighbourhoods characteristic of large American cities (Krugman, 1996).

Complex Systems

Capra (1996) argues that nature turns out to be more like human nature – unpredictable, sensitive to the surrounding world, influenced by small fluctuations. This suggests enormous interdependencies, parallels, overlaps and convergences between analyses of physical *and* social worlds. Indeed the very division between the 'physical' and the 'social' is itself a socio-historical product and one that is in part dissolving under the sway of the complexity turn.

The complexity sciences seem to provide the means to overcome such divisions between nature *and* society and between the natural/physical sciences *and* the social sciences. That systems seem to behave similarly whether they are economic populations, fruit flies, international terrorists, river basins or weather systems has colluded to spread complexity analyses around the world in a period that seems both post-human and post-nature (Hayles, 1999). Each hybrid system seems to exhibit similar non-linear, networked properties often moving unpredictably and irreversibly away from points of equilibrium, as Capra (2001) argues. And complexity is itself a global system, adapting and co-evolving to other powerful global hybrids that are also roaming the world and changing the very environment within which it operates (see Urry, 2003, on global complexity).

References

Arthur, B. (1994) *Increasing Returns and Path Dependence in the Economy*. Ann Arbor, MI: University of Michigan Press.

Capra, F. (1996) *The Web of Life*. London: Harper Collins.

Capra, F. (2001) *The Hidden Connections. A Science for Sustainable Living*. London: Harper Collins.

Coveney, P. and R. Highfield (1990) *The Arrow of Time*. London: Flamingo.

Davis, M. (2000) *Ecology of Fear*. London: Picador.

Hayles, N.K. (1999) *How We Became Posthuman*. Chicago, IL: University of Chicago Press.

Krugman, P. (1996) *The Self-Organizing Economy*. Cambridge, MA: Blackwell.

Maturana, H. (1981) 'Autopoeisis', in M. Zeleny (ed.) *Autopoeisis: A Theory of Living Organization*. New York: North Holland.

Prigogine, I. (1997) *The End of Certainty*. New York: The Free Press.

Thrift, N. (1999) 'The Place of Complexity', *Theory, Culture & Society* 16: 31–70.

Urry, J. (2003) *Global Complexity*. Cambridge: Polity.

Van Loon, J. (2002) *Risk and Technological Culture: Towards a Sociology of Virulence*. London: Routledge.

Waldrop, M. (1994) *Complexity*. London: Penguin.

CHAPTER 4

On Actor Network Theory
A Few Clarifications

Bruno Latour

Bruno Latour's work in science studies has been very influential in a number of disciplines. Latour began his career by studying how meshed in social relations scientific research was. In his more recent work, he has argued for a new constitution, a parliament of things that would respect objects as well as non-human actors in the project of human knowledge. His books include *We Have Never Been Modern* (1993), *Laboratory Life* (1986), and *Science in Action* (1988).

I

Exploring the properties of actor-networks is the task that the Paris group of science and technology studies has set itself to tackle since the beginning of the 1980s (Callon/Law/ Rip 1986). However, this theory has often been misunderstood and hence much abused. In this paper I would like to list some of the interesting properties of networks and explain some of the misunderstandings that have arisen. I will not concern myself here with the quantitative studies, especially the so-called "co-word analysis", since they are themselves misunderstood because of the difficulty of exactly grasping the social theory and quaint ontology entailed by actor-network (but see Callon/Courtial/Lavergne 1989a; b).

Three misunderstandings are due to common usages of the word network itself and the connotations they imply.

The first mistake would be to give it a common *technical* meaning in the sense of a sewage, or train, or subway, or telephone "network". Recent technologies often have the character of a network, that is, of exclusively related yet very distant elements with the circulation between nodes being made compulsory through a set of rigorous paths giving to a few nodes a strategic character. Nothing is more intensely connected, more distant, more compulsory, and more strategically organized than a computer network. Such is

Original publication details: Bruno Latour, "On Actor Network Theory: A Few Clarifications." *Soziale Welt* 47. Jahrg., H. 4 (1996), pp. 369–381. Reproduced with permission from Nomos.

Literary Theory: An Anthology, Third Edition. Edited by Julie Rivkin and Michael Ryan.
© 2017 John Wiley & Sons, Ltd. Published 2017 by John Wiley & Sons, Ltd.

not however the basic metaphor of an actor-network. A technical network in the engineer's sense is only one of the possible *final* and *stabilized* states of an actor-network. An actor-network may lack all the characteristics of a technical network – it may be local, it may have no compulsory paths, no strategically positioned nodes. Tom Hughes's "networks of power" (1983), to give a historical example, are actor-networks at the beginning of the story, and only some of their stabilized elements end up being networks in the engineer's sense, that is the electrical grid. Even at this later stage the engineering definition of networks is still a partial projection of an actor-network.

The second misunderstanding is easy to lift: the actor-network theory (hence ANT) has very little to do with the study of social networks. These studies, no matter how interesting, concern themselves with the *social* relations of *individual human* actors – their frequency, distribution, homogeneity, proximity. It was devised as a reaction to the often too global concepts like those of institutions, organizations, states and nations, adding to them a more realistic and smaller set of associations. Although ANT shares this distrust for such vague all-encompassing sociological terms, it also aims at describing the very nature of societies. But to do so it does not limit itself to human individual actors, but extends the word actor – or actant – to *non-human, non-individual* entities. Whereas social network adds information on the relations of humans in a social and natural world which is left untouched by the analysis, ANT aims at accounting for the very essence of societies and natures. It does not wish to add social networks to social theory, but to rebuild social theory out of networks. It is as much an ontology or a metaphysics as a sociology (Mol/Law 1994). Social networks will of course be included in the description, but they will have no privilege nor prominence (and very few of their quantitative tools have been deemed reusable).

Why then use the word network, since it is open to such misunderstandings? The use of the word comes from Diderot. The word "réseau" was used from the beginning by Diderot to describe matter and bodies in order to avoid the Cartesian divide between matter and spirit. Thus, the word has had a strong ontological component from the beginning (Anderson 1990). Put too simply, ANT is a change of metaphors to describe essences: instead of surfaces one gets filaments (or rhyzomes in Deleuze's parlance Deleuze/Guattari 1980). More precisely it is a change of topology. Instead of thinking in terms of surfaces – two dimensions – or spheres – three dimensions – one is asked to think in terms of nodes that have *as many dimensions* as they have connections. As a first approximation, ANT claims that modern societies cannot be described without recognizing them as having a fibrous, thread-like, wiry, stringy, ropy, capillary character that is never captured by the notions of levels, layers, territories, spheres, categories, structures, systems. It aims at explaining the *effects* accounted for by those traditional words without having to buy the ontology, topology and politics that go with them. ANT has been developed by students of science and technology, and its claim is that it is utterly impossible to understand what holds society together without reinjecting in its fabric the facts manufactured by natural and social sciences and the artefacts designed by engineers. As a second approximation, ANT is thus the claim that the only way to achieve this reinjection of things into our understanding of social fabrics is through a network-like ontology and social theory.

To remain at this very intuitive level, ANT is a simple material resistance argument. Strength does not come from concentration, purity and unity, but from dissemination, heterogeneity and the careful plaiting of weak ties. This feeling that resistance, obduracy and sturdiness are more easily achieved through netting, lacing, weaving, twisting of ties that are weak by themselves, and that each tie, no matter how strong, is itself woven out of still weaker threads, permeates for instance Foucault's analysis of micro-powers as well as recent sociology of technology. But the less intuitive philosophical basis for accepting ANT is a background/foreground reversal: instead of starting from universal laws – social or natural – and taking local contingencies as so many queer particularities that should be either eliminated or protected, it starts from irreducible, incommensurable, unconnected localities which then, at a great price, sometimes end into provisionally commensurable connections. Through this foreground/background reversal ANT has some affinity with the order out of disorder or chaos philosophy (Serres 1983; Prigogine/ Stengers 1979) and many practical links with ethnomethodology (Garfinkel and Lynch's principle in Lynch 1985). Universality or order are not the rule but the exceptions that have to be accounted for. Loci, contingencies or clusters are more like archipelagos on a sea than like lakes dotting a solid land. Less metaphorically, whereas universalists have to *fill in* the whole surface either with order or with contingencies, ANT does not attempt to fill in what is *in between* local pockets of orders or *in between* the filaments relating these contingencies.

This is the most counter-intuitive aspect of ANT. Literally there is nothing but networks, there is nothing in between them, or, to use a metaphor from the history of physics, there is no aether in which networks should be immersed. In this sense ANT is a reductionist and relativist theory, but, as I shall demonstrate, this is the first necessary step towards an irreductionist and relationist ontology.

II

ANT makes use of some of the simplest properties of nets and then adds to it an *actor* that does some *work*; the addition of such an ontological ingredient deeply modifies it. I will start out with the simplest properties common to all networks.

Far/close: the first advantage of thinking in terms of networks is that we get rid of "the tyranny of distance" or proximity. Elements which are close when disconnected may be infinitely remote when their connections are analyzed; conversely, elements which would appear as infinitely distant may be close when their connections are brought back into the picture. I can be one metre away from someone in the next telephone booth and nevertheless be more closely connected to my mother 6000 miles away; an Alaskan reindeer might be ten metres away from another one and they might nevertheless be cut off by a pipeline of 800 miles that makes their mating for ever impossible; my son may sit at school with a young arab of his age, but in spite of this close proximity in first grade they might drift apart in worlds that will become incommensurable later; a gas pipe may lie in the ground close to a cable television glass fiber and nearby a sewage pipe, and each of them will nevertheless continuously ignore the parallel worlds lying around them. The difficulty we have in defining all associations in terms of networks is due to the prevalence of geography. It seems obvious that we can oppose proximity and connections. However, geographical proximity is the result of a science – geography –, of a profession – geographers –, of a practice – mapping system, measuring, triangulating. Their definition of proximity and distance is useless for ANT – or it should be included as one type of connections, one type of networks, as we will see below. All definitions in terms of surface and territories come from our reading of maps drawn and filled in by geographers. Out of geographers and geography, "in between" their own networks, there is no such thing as a proximity or a distance which would not be defined by connectibility. The geographical notion is simply another connection to a grid defining a metrics and a scale (Jacob 1992). The notion of network helps us to lift the tyranny of geographers in defining space and offers us a notion which is neither social nor "real" space, but associations.

Small scale/large scale: the notion of network allows us to dissolve the micro-macro-distinction that has plagued social theory from its inception. The whole metaphor of scales going from the individual to the nation state, through family, extended kin, groups, institutions etc. is replaced by a metaphor of connections. A network is never *bigger* than another one, it is simply *longer* or *more intensely* connected. The small scale/large scale model has three features which have proven devastating for social theory: it is tied to an order relation that goes from top to bottom or from bottom to top – as if society really had a top and a bottom; it implies that an element "b" being macro-scale is of a different nature and should thus be studied differently from an element "a" which is micro-scale; it is utterly unable to follow how an element goes from being individual – a – to collective – b – and back.

The network notion implies a deeply different social theory: it has no a priori order relation; it is not tied to the axiological myth of a top and a bottom of society; it makes absolutely no assumption whether a specific locus is macro- or micro- and does not modify the tools to study element "a" or element "b"; thus, it has no difficulty in following the transformation of a poorly connected element into a highly connected one *and back*. The network notion is ideally suited to follow the change of scales, since it does not require the analyst to partition her world with any a priori scale. The scale, that is, the type, number and topography of connections, is left to the actors themselves.

The notion of network allows us to lift the tyranny of social theorists, to regain some margin of manoeuvres between the ingredients of society – its vertical space, its hierarchy, its layering, its macro-scale, its wholeness, its overarching character – and to see how these features are achieved and what stuff they are made of. Instead of having to choose between the local and the global view, the notion of network allows us to think of a global entity – a highly connected one – which nevertheless remains continuously local ... Instead of opposing the individual level to the mass, or agency to structure, we simply follow how a given element becomes strategic through the number of connections it commands, and how it loses its importance when losing its connections.

Inside/outside: the notion of network allows us to get rid of a third spatial dimension after those of far/close and big/small. A surface has an inside and an outside separated by a boundary. A network is all boundary without inside and outside. The only question one may ask is whether or not a connection is established between two elements. The surface "in between" networks is either connected – but then the network is expanding – or non-existing. Literally, a network has no outside. It is not a foreground over a background, nor a crack onto a solid soil, it is like Deleuze's lightning rod that creates by the same stroke the background and the foreground (Deleuze 1968). The great economy of thinking allowed by the notion of network is that we are no longer obliged to fill in the space in between the connections – to use a computer metaphor, we do not need the little paint box familiar to MacPaint users to "fill in" the interspace. A network is a positive notion which does not need negativity to be understood. It has no shadow.

The notion of network, in its barest topological outline, already allows us to reshuffle spatial metaphors that have rendered the study of society-nature so difficult: close and far, up and down, local and global, inside and outside. They are replaced by associations and connections (which ANT does not have to qualify as being either social or natural or technical as I will show below). This is not to say that there is nothing like "macro" society or "outside" nature as ANT is often accused of, but that in order to obtain the *effects* of distance, proximity, hierarchies, connectedness, outsiderness and surfaces an enormous *supplementary* work has to be done (Latour 1996a). This work, however, is not captured by the topological notion of network, no matter how sophisticated we wish to make it. This is why ANT adds to the mathematical notion of network a completely foreign notion, that of actor. The new hybrid "actor-network" leads us away from mathematical properties into a world which has not yet been so neatly charted. To sketch these properties we should now move on from static and topological properties to dynamic and ontological ones.

III

A network in mathematics or in engineering is something that is traced or inscribed by some other entity – the mathematician, the engineer. An actor-network is an entity that *does* the tracing and the inscribing. It is an ontological definition and not a piece of inert matter in the hands of others, especially of human planners or designers. It was in order to point out this essential feature that the word "actor" was added to it.

Now, the word actor has been open to the same misunderstanding as the word network. "Actor" in the Anglo-Saxon tradition is always a human intentional individual actor and is most often contrasted with mere "behaviour". If one adds this definition of an actor to the social definition of a network, then the bottom of misunderstanding is reached: an individual human – usually male – who wishes to grab power makes a network of allies and extends his power – doing some "networking" or "liaising" as the Americans say … Alas, this is the way ANT is most often represented, which is about as accurate as saying that the night sky is black because the astrophysicists have shown there is a big black hole in it. An "actor" in ANT is a semiotic definition – an actant –, that is something that acts or to which activity is granted by others. It implies *no* special motivation of *human individual* actors, nor of humans in general. An actant can literally be anything provided it is granted to be the source of an action. Although this point has been made over and over again, anthropocentrism and sociocentrism are so strong in social sciences (as well as in the critiques of social explanations) that each use of ANT has been construed as if it talked of a few superhumans longing for power and stopping at nothing to achieve their ruthless goals … Even my own network study of Pasteur (Latour 1988a) – in spite of the lengthy ontological second part – has often been understood as a Madison Avenue version of science – which is unfair not only to my account but also to Madison Avenue … If a criticism can be levelled at ANT it is, on the contrary, its complete indifference for providing a model of human competence. There is no model of (human) actor in ANT nor any basic list of competences that have to be set at the beginning, because the human, the self and the social actor of traditional social theory is not on its agenda.

So what is on its agenda? The attribution of human, unhuman, nonhuman, inhuman characteristics; the distribution of properties among these entities; the connections established between them; the circulation entailed by these attributions, distributions and connections; the transformation of those attributions, distributions and connections of the many elements that circulate, and of the few ways through which they are sent.

The difficulty of grasping ANT is that it has been made by the fusion of three hitherto unrelated strands of preoccupations:

- a semiotic definition of entity building;
- a methodological framework to record the heterogeneity of such a building;
- an ontological claim on the "networky" character of actants themselves.

ANT asserts that the limits of these three unrelated interests are solved when, and only when, they are fused into an integrated practice of study.

Semiotics is a necessary step in this venture, since when you bracket out the question of reference and that of the social conditions of productions – that is nature "out there" and society "up there" – what remains is, in a first approximation, meaning production, or discourse, or text. This is the major achievement of the sixties and of their "linguistic turn" or "semiotic turn". Instead of being means of communications between human actors and nature, meaning productions became the only important thing to study. Instead of being unproblematic, they became opaque. The task was no longer to make them more transparent, but to recognize and relish their thick, rich, layered and complex matter. Instead of being mere *intermediaries*, they had become *mediators*. From a means, meaning has been made an end in itself. For twenty years the best minds have been busy exploring all the consequences of this major turn away from the naïve model of communication. Their often structuralist interpretations have been dismantled, but what remains is a toolbox to study meaning productions. ANT sorts out from this toolbox what is useful to understand the construction of entities. The key point is that every entity, including the self, society, nature, every relation, every action, can be understood as a "choice" or a "selection" of finer and finer embranchments going from abstract structure – actants – to concrete ones – actors. The generative path that is thus retraced gives an extraordinary liberty of analysis compared to the empoverished "social vocabulary" that was used earlier – and is now in fashion again. Of course the structural rendering of these choices – differences – and embranchments – dichotomies – are not kept by ANT, but essential traits of semiotics are kept. First, the *granting* of humanity to an individual actor, or the granting of collectivity, or the granting of anonymity, of a zoomorphic appearance, of amorphousness, of materiality, requires paying the *same semiotic price*. The effects will be different, the genres will be different, but not the *work* of attributing, imputing, distributing action, competences, performances and relations. Secondly, actors are not conceived as fixed entities but as flows, as circulating objects undergoing trials, and their stability, continuity, isotopy has to be obtained by other actions and other trials. Finally, what is kept from semiotics is the crucial practice to grant texts and discourses the ability to define also their context, their authors – in the text –, their readers – in fabula – and even their own demarcation and metalanguage. All the problems of the analyst are shifted to the "text itself" without ever being allowed to escape into the context (Greimas 1976). Down with interpretation! Down with the context! The slogans of the the 60s and 70s "everything is a text", "there is only discourse", "narratives exist by themselves", "we have no access to anything but accounts" are kept in ANT but saved from their ontological consequences. This salvation, however, does not come by falling back on the pre-deconstruction common sense – "after all, there is a social context up there and a nature out there" – but by extending the semiotic turn to this famous nature and this famous context it has bracketed out in the first place.

A major transformation of these slogans occurred when semiotics was turned to scientific and technical discourse by ANT – and especially to scientific texts. As long as one studied fictions, myths, popular cultures, fashions, religions, political discourse, one could hold to the "semiotic turn" and take them as so many "texts". Scholars did not seriously believe in them anyway, and thus the intellectual distance and scepticism was easy to achieve while the double treasury of "scientism" and "socialism" was kept intact in their heart. But what about scientific truth and material efficiency? What about the reference "out there" in hard scientific texts? This was the real test for semiotics, and although it passed the trial a price had to be payed. In the practice of ANT semiotics was extended to define a completely empty frame that enabled to follow any assemblage of heterogeneous entities – including now the "natural" entities of science and the "material" entities of technology. This is the second strand of ANT: it is a *method* to describe the deployment of associations like semiotics; it is a method to describe the generative path of any narration. It does not say anything about the shape of entities and actions, but only what the recording device should be that would allow entities to be described in all their details. ANT places the burden of theory on the *recording*, not on the specific shape that is recorded. When it says that actors may be human or unhuman, that they are infinitely pliable, heterogeneous, that they are free associationists, know no differences of scale, that there is no inertia, no order, that they build their own temporality, this does not qualify any real *observed* actor, but is the necessary condition for the observation and the recording of actors to be possible. Instead of constantly predicting how an actor should behave and which associations are allowed a priori, ANT makes no assumption at all, and in order to remain uncommitted it needs to set its instrument by insisting on infinite pliability and absolute freedom. In itself ANT is *not* a theory of action, no more than cartography is a theory on the shape of coast lines and deep sea ridges; it just qualifies what the observer should suppose in order for the coast lines to be recorded in their fine fractal patterns. Any shape is possible provided it is obsessively coded as longitude and latitude. Similarly, any association is possible provided it is obsessively coded as a heterogeneous association through translations. It is more an infralanguage than a metalanguage. It is even less than a descriptive vocabulary; it simply opens, *against* all a priori reductions, the possibility of describing irreductions (Latour 1988a, part II). ANT is not merely empiricist though, since in order to define such an irreducible space in which to deploy entities sturdy theoretical commitments have to be made and a strong polemical stance has to be taken, so as to forbid the analyst to dictate actors what they should do. Such a distribution of a strong theory for the recording frame and no middle range theory for the the description is another source of many misunderstandings, since ANT is accused of either being dogmatic or of providing mere descriptions. For the same reason it is also accused of claiming that actors are "really" infinitely pliable and free or, inversely, of not telling what a human actor really is after (Lee/Brown 1994).

The first two strands – the semiotic and the methodological one – by themselves will be open to criticism. The first because there is no way to consider that bracketing out social context and reference solves the problem of meaning – in spite of the now dated claims of the swinging seventies –, and the second because merely deploying shapes of associations might be a worthwhile descriptive task but does not offer any explanation. It is only when a third strand is added to those two and ontological claims on networks are made that ANT escapes criticism. This move, however, is so devious that it has escaped the attention of many users of ANT. Which is a pity, since once it is made, ANT loses its radical character and soon appears commensensical enough.

The weakness of semiotics has always been to consider meaning production away from what the nature of entities really is; when semiotics is turned to nature however and unhuman entities are allowed to enter into the picture, it soon appears that the words "discourse" or "meaning" may be dropped altogether without any danger of going back to naïve realism or naïve naturalism. It is only because semioticians studied texts – and literary ones at that – instead of things that they felt obliged to limit themselves to "meaning". In effect they scientistically believed in the existence of things in addition to meaning (not mentioning their belief in the existence of a good old social context whenever it suited them). But a semiotics of things is easy, one simply has to drop the meaning bit from semiotics ...

If one now translates semiotics by path-building or order-making or creation of directions, one does not have to specify if it is language or objects one is analyzing. Such a move gives a new continuity to practices that were deemed different when one dealt with language and "symbols", or with skills, work and matter. This move can be said either to elevate things to the dignity of texts or to elevate texts to the ontological status of things. What really matters is that it is an elevation and not a reduction, and that the new hybrid status gives *to all entities* both the action, variety and circulating existence recognized in the study of textual characters *and* the reality, solidity, externality that was recognized in things "out of" our representations. What is lost is the absolute distinction between representation and things – but this is exactly what ANT wishes to redistribute through what I have called a counter-copernican revolution.

Once settled this first solution – extending semiotics to things instead of limiting it to meaning –, the second difficulty falls with it – building an empty methodological frame to register description. Actor-networks do connect, and by connecting with one another provide an explanation of themselves, the only one there is for ANT. What is an explanation? The attachment of a set of practices that control or interfere in one another. No explanation is stronger or more powerful than providing connections among unrelated elements or showing how one element holds many others. This is not a property that is *distinct* from networks but one of their essential properties (Latour 1988b). They become more or less explanable as they go and depending on what they do to one another. Actors are cleaning up their own mess, so to speak. Once you grant them everything, they also give you back the explanatory powers you abandoned. The very divide between description and explanation, hows and whys, blind empiricism and high theorizing is as meaningless for ANT as the difference between gravitation and space in relativity theory. Each network, by growing, "binds" the explanatory resources around it, and there is no way they can be detached from its growth. One does not jump outside a network to add an explanation – a cause, a factor, a set of factors, a series of co-occurences; one simply *extends* the network further. Every network surrounds itself with its own frame of reference, its own definition of growth, of refering, of framing, of explaining. In this process the frame of reference of the analyst does not disappear more than the physicist's in Einstein's world; on the contrary, at last it is able to extend itself, but at a price: the frame becomes, as it does in General Relativity, "a mollusc of reference" instead of a detached Galilean frame, and each account has to be recalculated by the ANT equivalent of a Lorentz transformation (Latour 1988c). There is no way to provide an explanation if the network does not extend itself. This is not in contradiction with the scientific task of providing explanation and causality, since we learned from the very studies of hard sciences that no explanation of any scientific phenomenon and no causality could be provided without extending the network itself. By tying the explanation to the network itself ANT does not abandon the goal of science, since it shows that this goal has never been achieved, at least not through the epistemological myth of explanation. ANT can't deprive itself of a resource it shows no one has ever had in the first place. Explanation is ex-plicated, that is unfolded, like gravity in Einstein's curved space, it is still there as an effect, but it is now indistinguishable from the description, the deployment of the net.

This relativistic position – but one should prefer the less loaded term of relationist – solves two other problems: that of historicity and that of reflexivity.

The pre-relativist debate between providing an explanation and "simply" document-ing the historical circumstances falls apart: there is no difference between explaining and telling how a network surrounds itself with new resources; if it "escapes socio-historical contingencies", as critics often argue, then this simply means that other, longer lasting resources have been garnered to stay around – the etymology of circumstances. Hughes's networks of power grow (Hughes 1983), and by their very growth they become more and more of an explanation of themselves; you do not need an explanation floating over them *in addition* to their historical growth; Braudel's networks and world economics grow, and they are what the "big causes" are made of. You do not need to add to them Capitalism or *Zeitgeist* except as another summary, another punctualisation of the networks themselves. Either the cause designates a body of practices which is tied to the network under description – and this is what growth of network means –, or it is not related, and then it is just a word added to the description, literally it is the *word* "cause". In this sense, ANT gives history its legitimate place – which is not the place prudent historians like to sit on, as safely away as possible from ontological questions. There is nothing better, sturdier than a circumstancial description of networks. "It just happens to be this way".

But such a summary would be construed as historicism if it were not understood as a definition of the things themselves. The debate between historicism and explanation or theory was not solvable as long as there was, on the one hand, a history of people, of contingencies, of what is "in time" and, on the other hand, a theory or a science of what is timeless, eternal, necessary. For ANT there is science only of the contingent, as of necessity it is locally achieved only through the growth of a network. If there is also a history of things, then the debate between description and ex-planation, or historicity and theory, is entirely dissolved. For ANT this is not the proof of the weakness of its explanatory powers, since describing or accounting for a network is what an explanation or an explication is and what has always been the case in the so-called hard sciences – or more exactly "progressively hardened sciences" (Latour 1996b).

Although not the main goal of ANT, reflexivity is added as a bonus once the frames of reference are granted back to the actors – and once the actors are granted back the possibility of crossing the sacred dividing line between things and representations (Ashmore 1989). Reflexivity is seen as a problem in relativist theory, because it appears that either the observer requests a status it denies to others, or it is as silent as all the others to which any privileged status is denied. This "problem" falls, however, when the epistemological myth of an outside observer providing an explanation in addition to "mere description" disappears. There is no longer any privilege – but there has never been any need for it either. The observer – whatever it is – finds itself on a par with all the other frames of reference. It is not left to despair or navel-gazing, since the absence of privileged status has never limited the expansion and intelligence of any actor. World builder among world builders, it does not see a dramatic limit on knowledge in its aban-donment of Galilean frames, but only resources. To extend from one frame of reference to the next it has to work and pay the price like any other actor. In order to explain, to account, to observe, to prove, to argue, to dominate and to see it has to move around and work (I should say it has to "network"). No privilege also means no a priori limits on knowledge. If actors are able to account for others, so can it. If actors can't, it might still try. History, risks and ventures are also in the observers' own network building. Such is ANT's solution to reflexivity (Stengers 1993).

Reflexivity is not a "problem", a stumbling block along the path to knowledge, the prison in which all enterprises would be locked, it is the land of opportunity at last opened to actors which are primus inter pares, or strive for parity or primacy like any other. Of course reusable metalangage is abandoned, but this is not giving up much, since observers who displayed their rich metalanguage were usally small points limited to very specific loci – campuses, studios, corporate rooms. The price ANT pays to move from one locus to the next is that there are as many metalanguages as there are frames of reference – the only metalanguage required (see above strand 2) being more adequately called an *infralanguage* which has to be poor, limited, short and simple – the equivalent of a Lorentz transformation being called "translation" in ANT (Latour 1988c). This infralanguage is enough to move from one net to the other, and the specific explication will always be a one-shot account exclusively tailored to the problem at hand (Lynch's principle, Callon's "disposable explanations", Serres's "cross over between explanandum and explanans" (Serres 1995)). If it is more generally applicable, it means that it is riding over a network that expands itself.

This solution becomes commonsense once it is accepted that an account or an explication or a proof is always added to the world; that it does not subtract anything from the world. Reflexivists as well as their pre-relativist enemies dream of subtracting knowledge from the things in themselves. ANT keeps adding things to the world, and its selection principle is no longer whether or not there is a fit between account and reality – this dual illusion has been dissolved away –, but whether or not one travels from a net to another. No metalanguage allows you to do this travel. By abandoning the dreams of epistemology ANT is not reduced to moral relativism, but gets back a stronger deontological commitment: either an account leads you to all the other accounts – and it is good –, or it constantly interrupts the movement, letting frames of reference distant and foreign – and it is bad. Either it multiplies the mediating points between any two elements – and it is good –, or it deletes and conflates mediators – and it is bad. Either it is reductionist – and that's bad news –, or irreductionist – and that's the highest ethical standard for ANT. We will see that this touchstone is much more discriminating than the quest for epistemological purity, or for foundations, or for moral norms. Demarcation is in fact an enemy of differentiation.

Building on the semiotic turn, ANT first brackets out society and nature to consider only meaning-productions; then, breaking with the limits of semiotics without losing its toolbox, it grants activity to the semiotic actors turning them into new ontological hybrids, world making entities; by doing such a counter-copernican revolution it builds a completely empty frame for describing how any entity builds its world; finally, it retains from the descriptive project only very few terms – its infralanguage – which are just enough to sail in between frames of reference, and grants back to the actors themselves the ability to build precise accounts of one another by the very way they behave; the goal of building an overarching explanation – that is, for ANT, a centre of calculation that would hold or replace or punctuate all the others – is displaced by the search for explications, that is for the deployment of as many elements as possible accounted for through as many metalanguages as possible.

IV

Now that the basic topological properties of networks have been sketched – second section – and that the basic ontological features of actors have been outlined – section above –, there is no difficulty in seeing that ANT is not about *traced* networks, but about a network-*tracing* activity. As I said above, there is not a net and an actor laying down the net, but there is an actor whose definition of the world outlines, traces, delineates, describes, files, lists, records, marks or tags a trajectory that is called a network. No net exists independently of the very act of tracing it, and no tracing is done by an actor exterior to the net. A network is not a thing, but the recorded movement of a thing. The questions ANT addresses now have changed. It is no longer whether a net is a representation or a thing, a part of society or a part of discourse or a part of nature, but what moves and how this movement is recorded.

We cannot say that what moves *inside* networks are pieces of information, genes, cars, bytes, salutations, words, forces, opinions, claims, bodies, energy etc., since ANT also wants to reconstruct nets before there is any distinction between what circulates inside and what keeps them on track, so to speak, from the outside. Again, as I said at the beginning, the technical metaphor of networks is a latecomer for ANT and does not capture the tracing activity. No, what circulates has to be defined like the circulating object in the semiotics of texts – especially scientific texts (Bastide 1990). It is defined by the competence it is endowed with, the trials it undergoes, the performances it is allowed to display, the associations it is made to bear upon, the sanctions it receives, the background in which it is circulating etc. Its isotopy – that is its persistence in time and space – is not a property of its essence, but the result of the decisions taken through the narrative programmes and the narrative paths.

However, such a classic definition would limit ANT to the world of text and discourse. What happens when a circulating object leaves the boundary of a text? The traditional answer is that there is a yawning gap in between the text and the context. At the interface a dramatic trial is supposed to abruptly intervene through which the circulating object is assessed either by checking its referential fit or its social interest. Not so for ANT, which does not believe in this distinction, since it has extended meaning productions to all productions. For ANT the gap is no more than a slight bump along the net; the yawn is an artefact caused by a previous divide between nature, society and discourse. For ANT on the contrary, there is a continuity, a multiplicity of plugs between the circulating objects in the text, the claims outside the text in the "social", and what the actants themselves really do in "nature". The circulating object goes on circulating and goes on getting its isotopy from what other actors do to it. "Society" has the same net-like properties as have texts, and so has "nature". But it would be more accurate for ANT to say that these three categories are arbitrary cutting points on a continuous tracing of action, and still more accurate to show how these categories themselves are part of the many trials and events and resources that are used along the paths to attribute "textuality" or "sociality" or "naturality" to this or that actor. They are part of what is distributed – not part of what makes the distribution.

There is no off-the-shelf word to describe this common movement. To say that it is a generalized narrative path would immediately mean that texts are extended to everything; to say that it is a force or an energy or a gene or a culture-gene would mean that everything would be naturalized, including society and discourse; to say that it is a social interest, a social action or labour would extend society to nature and to texts. It was to get out of this essential difficulty that ANT played with a generalized symmetry (Callon 1986) and made a principle of using whichever words are connoted in one of the former realms to describe the others, thus showing the continuity of networks and the complete disregard for the artefactual gaps introduced by pre-relativist arguments. However, this solution is rather tricky, since it may combine all the misunderstandings – and this is indeed what happened to ANT, readers and users alike saying *at once* that it is a social constructivist argument, the return of naturalism, or a typically French belief in the overall extension of texts … Which of course it is in a sense, but only insofar as ANT is the simultaneous rejection of natural*isation*, social*isation* and textual*isation*. ANT claims that these "(x)-isations" have to be dissolved all at once and that the job is not done better if one of them gains hegemony or if the three are carefully circumscribed. All (x)-isations are the filling in of what is "in between" the networks; and which one is chosen or rejected makes no practical difference, since nets have no "in between" to be filled in.

If choosing words for the network-tracing activity has to be done, *quasi-objects* (Serres 1987) or *tokens* might be the best candidates so far. It is crucial for the definition of the term that what circulates and what makes the circulation be both co-determined and transformed. A ball going from hand to hand is a poor example of a quasi-object, since, although it does trace the collective and although the playing team would not exist without the moving token, the latter is not modified by the passings. Conversely, what I called the first principle of science studies (Latour 1987) – that a claim is in the hands of others – is equally an approximation, since it entails human locutors endowed with hands and mouths who pass a claim without themselves undergoing dramatic changes. As a rule, a quasi-object should be thought of as a moving actant that transforms those who do the moving, because they transform the moving object. When the token remains stable or when the movers are kept intact, these are *exceptional* circumstances which have to be accounted for. This definition of what is the rule and what are the exceptions would be enough to tell ANT from all models of communications that, on the contrary, begin with well defined movers and moving objects and view obstacles to exchanges as so many exceptions to be explained. But another feature forbids any confusion of ANT with human-centered, or language-centered, or praxis-centered models. As a rule, what is doing the moving and what is moved have no specific homogeneous *morphism*. They can be anthropo-morphic, but also zoo-morphic, physi-morphic, logo-morphic, techno-morphic, ideo-morphic, that is "(x)-morphic". It might happen that a generative path has limited actants to a homogeneous repertoire of humans or of mechanism or of signs or of ideas or of collective social entities, but these are exceptions which should be accounted for (Latour 1996c).

ANT is a powerful tool to destroy spheres and domains, to regain the sense of heterogeneity, and to bring interobjectivity back into the centre of attention (Latour 1994). Yet it is an extremely bad tool for differentiating associations. It gives a black and white picture, not a coloured and contrasted one. Thus it is necessary, after having traced the actor-networks, to specify the types of trajectories that are obtained by highly different mediations. This is a different task, and the one that will make ANT scholars busy for a number of years to come.

Literaturverzeichnis

Anderson, Wilda (1990): *Diderot's Dream*, The Johns Hopkin's University Press, Baltimore.
Ashmore, Malcolm (1989): *The Reflexive Thesis. Wrighting (sic) Sociology of Scientific Knowledge*, Chicago University Press, Chicago.

Bastide, Françoise (1990): The Iconography of Scientific Texts: Principle of Analysis, in: M. Lynch, S. Woolgar (Hrsg.), *Representation in Scientific Practice*, MIT Press, Cambridge Mass., S. 187–230.

Callon, Michel (1986): Some elements of a sociology of translation: domestication of the scallops and the fishermen of St Brieux Bay, in: J. Law (Hrsg.), *Power, Action and Belief. A New Sociology of Knowledge?*, Routledge and Kegan Paul, London, S. 196–229.

Callon, Michel, Law, John, Rip, Arie (Hrsg.) (1986): *Mapping the Dynamics of Science and Technology*, Macmillan, London.

Callon, Michel, Courtial, Jean-Pierre (1989): *Co-Word Analysis: A Tool for the Evaluation of Public*, Report for the NSF grant PRA N85 12 982, Paris.

Callon, Michel, Courtial, Jean-Pierre, Lavergne, Françise (1989): *La Méthode des mots associés. Un outil pour l'évaluation des programmes publics de recherche*. Etude pour la National Science Foundation, Ecole des Mines, Paris.

Deleuze, Gilles (1968): *Différence et répétition*, PUF, Paris.

Deleuze, Gilles, Guattari, Félix (1980): *Mille plateaux. Capitalisme et schizophrénie*, Minuit, Paris.

Garfinkel, Harry (1967): *Studies in Ethnomethodology*, Prentice Hall, New Jersey.

Greimas, Algirdas Julien (1976): *On Meaning. Selected Writings in Semiotic Theory*, University of Minnesota Press, Minneapolis.

Hughes, Thomas P. (1983): *Networks of Power. Electric Supply Systems In the US, England and Germany, 1880–1930*, The John Hopkins University Press, Baltimore.

Jacob, Christian (1992): *L'empire des cartes. Approche théorique de la cartographie à travers l'histoire*, Albin Michel, Paris.

Latour, Bruno (1987): *Science In Action. How to Follow Scientists and Engineers through Society*, Harvard University Press, Cambridge Mass.

Latour, Bruno (1988a): *The Pasteurization of France*, Harvard University Press, Cambridge Mass.

Latour, Bruno (1988b): The Politics of Explanation: An Alternative, in: S. Woolgar (Hrsg.), *Knowledge and Reflexivity. New Frontiers in the Sociology of Knowledge*, Sage, London, S. 155–177.

Latour, Bruno (1988c): A Relativist Account of Einstein's Relativity, *Social Studies of Science* 18, S. 3–44.

Latour, Bruno (1994a): On Technical Mediation, *Common Knowledge* 3(2), S. 29–64.

Latour, Bruno (1994b): Une sociologie sans objet? Note théorique sur l'interobjectivité, *Sociologie du travail* 36, S. 587–607.

Latour, Bruno (1996a): Flat-Earthers and Social Theory, in: M. Power (Hrsg.), *Accounting and Science: Natural Inquiry and Commercial Reason*, Cambridge University Press, Cambridge Mass., S. xi–xviii.

Latour, Bruno (1996b): Do Scientific Objects Have a History? Pasteur and Whitehead in a Bath of Lactic Acid, *Common Knowledge* 5(1), S. 76–91.

Latour, Bruno (1996c): *Der Berliner Schlüssel. Erkundungen eines Liebhabers der Wissenschaften*, Akademie Verlag, Berlin (übersetzt von Gustav Roßler).

Lee, Nick, Brown, Steve (1994): Otherness and the Actor-Network: The Undiscovered Continent, *American Behavioral Scientist* 37, S. 772–790.

Lynch, Michael (1985): *Art and Artifact in Laboratory Science. A Study of Shop Work and Shop Talk in a Research Laboratory*, Routledge, London.

Mol, Annemarie, Law, John (1994): Regions, Networks, and Fluids: Anaemia and Social Topology, *Social Studies of Science*, 24, S. 641–672.

Prigogine, Ilya, Stengers, Isabelle (1979): *La nouvelle alliance, métamorphose de la science*, Gallimard/Bantam, Paris/New York.

Serres, Michel (1983): *Hermes. Literature Science Philosophy*, The John Hopkins University Press, Baltimore.

Serres, Michel (1987): *Statues*, François Bourin, Paris.

Serres, Michel (1995): *Conversations on Science, Culture and Time with Bruno Latour*, The University of Michigan Press, Ann Arbor.

Stengers, Isabelle (1993): *L'invention des sciences modernes*, La Découverte, Paris.

CHAPTER 5

The Animal Turn, Literary Studies, and the Academy

Jennifer McDonell

As the human dissolves, the animal rises in importance. That is one way of characterizing the coincident rise of animal studies as scholars also explore post-human theoretical possibilities. The human subject of Humanism has been in question since the 1960s. Animal studies takes a different route to the usual deconstruction from within of the psychological and philosophical premises of Humanism by standing with animals and imagining the world from their perspective. Jennifer McDonell teaches contemporary theory and Victorian culture at the University of New England (Australia).

The rapidly growing field of human-animal studies (HAS)[1] is a vibrant, varied domain of methodological convergences and divergences, united by a shared concern with studying the complex entanglement of human and animal lives. To think seriously about animals on their own terms is to begin to question the co-construction of the categories of the human and the animal that underpins human exceptionalism. Unpicking the human/animal binary, however, is no simple matter: not only is this construction unstable but as prisoners of human language we also have a tendency to reinstate it even as we think we challenge it. This paper will provide an analysis of significant developments and preoccupations in the field of literary HAS. Some of the most vexing questions within this area will be contextualised by way of reference to the Bandit and Michael Vick cases in the US and J.M. Coetzee's *Disgrace*, in particular the scenes depicting David Lurie's encounter with unwanted dogs at an animal shelter.

Original publication details: Jennifer McDonell, "Literary Studies, the Animal Turn, and the Academy." *Social Alternatives* 32.4, pp. 6–14. Social Alternatives, 2013. Reproduced with permission from Editorial Collective, Social Alternatives.

Literary Theory: An Anthology, Third Edition. Edited by Julie Rivkin and Michael Ryan.

I

The problem of the animal, Jacques Derrida has argued, poses definitional and practical threats to the discourse of humanism, in which authority and autonomy are 'attributed to the man (*homo and vir*) rather than to the woman, and to the woman rather than the animal' (1991: 114). If human sovereignty is decentred, what becomes of the autonomy and authority that has been definitive of 'authorship' since the seventeenth century? The concern in animal studies with such questions as nonhuman agency, the relations between subject and object, inter-species structures of feeling, emotion and affect, the function of animal metaphor and the occlusions of literary historiography necessitates a radical rethinking of core concepts that are often taken for granted in literary studies. I would go further, as other commentators such as Cary Wolfe and Susan McHugh have, and suggest that a systematic, philosophically rigorous animal studies challenges the schema of the knowing subject and its anthropocentric underpinnings that sustain the notion of disciplinarity itself (Wolfe 2009: 568).[2]

In discussions about the future of animal studies as a discipline, comparisons with the entry of women's studies and ethnic studies in the academy are common. In redressing the underrepresentation and misrepresentation of these groups one strategy adopted was for women and minorities to represent themselves as subjects within existing structures of power. This analogy can be limiting and misleading: for one thing, animals cannot speak for themselves in the kind of texts that constitute animals as objects of study.[3] If animals cannot represent themselves in rational thought and as it is manifested in language, how can they be read or heard? As Kari Weil puts it: 'If animal studies has come of age, it is perhaps because nonhuman animals have become a limit case for theories of difference, otherness, and power' (2012: 5).

It is difficult to work in the area of animal studies and not be troubled by the material one encounters. One reason for this is because 'the question of the animal' foregrounds a mutually constitutive relationship between language and violence: violence inflicted upon animals through factory farming, laboratory testing, and through the destruction of habitats and the cultural construction of pet keeping practices, but also the violence inflicted upon animals by human language. Derrida has argued that 'Animal', with a capital 'A' in the singular, defined by way of difference to the 'human', is *the* primary means whereby the animal/human dualism has been reinforced (2008: 400).[4] 'Animal' is our abstraction for all that walks, crawls, swims and flies other than ourselves, and as Derrida goes on to argue in both 'Eating Well' (1991) and *The Animal That Therefore I am (More To Follow)*, the word does violence to the heterogeneous multiplicity of the living world and therefore enacts what he calls a 'sacrificial structure' that opens up a space for the 'noncriminal putting to death' of the animal – a sacrifice that allows the transcendence of the human by killing and disavowing the bodily, the materiality, the animality of the human.[5] 'Noncriminal' killing of individuals and entire certain classes of humans has of course, been justified by marking them as 'animal'.

Construct an academic course or write an article on the subject of literature and animals, and the textual possibilities are endless, precisely because humans have long conceived of themselves through animal others across most literatures and cultures. Conceptually, such a course might begin with one of the most central questions to all teachers and scholars of literature: representation. How can attention to animals and their life worlds help us to think differently about aspects of literary form – fable, metaphor, story, say – that are shaped by ideas of human or animal being or by the logic of species?

How do texts represent the animality that resides both within nonhuman and human animals? Or affective (emotional) or relational bonds between humans and animals? Other primary concepts might include the question of anthropomorphism, the history of human perceptions of animals, the reception of evolutionary theory, or pressing contemporary issues of our age such as biomedicine, climate change, zoos, species extinction, conservation, the animal industrial complex and biopolitical power.

A major challenge in teaching and writing about animal studies is the daunting inter-disciplinarity that is inseparable from its genesis. HAS courses in literature tend to include readings not only from 'cognate' disciplines such as history and feminism but also from disciplines such as philosophy, biology, ethology, ecology, comparative psychology, zoology and primatology which have been hugely influential on HAS in recent years. Contemporary research on literary understandings of animals is exceptionally diverse, and has drawn on concurrent work in various fields in the humanities and social sciences that goes as far back as the 1980s (Ritvo, 1987; Thomas, 1983; Serpell, 1986; Lansbury, 1985; Haraway, 1989). Carol J. Adams, Val Plumwood, Josephine Donovan, Brian Luke, Connie Salamone, Marti Kheel, Andrée Collard, Deane Curtin, Alice Walker, Deborah Slicer, Greta Gaard, Lori Gruen, Lynda Birke, and Karen Warren, among others embarked several decades ago on the project of challenging deeply embedded humanist assumptions concerning gender and animality. In the continental theoretical vein, Gilles Deleuze and Felix Guattari's *A Thousand Plateaus* (1987), in foundational philosophy Peter Singer's *Animal Liberation*, first published in 1975 and Tom Regan's *The Case for Animal Rights* (1983), and in cognitive ethology the public visibility of work by Jane Goodall, Diane Fossey and Diane Pepperburg also paved the way for literary scholars. In the 1990s the field continued to grow with dozens of major works appearing, including Arnold Arluke and Clinton Sanders's *Regarding Animals* (1996) and Jennifer Wolch and Jody Emel's *Animal Geographies: Place, Politics, and Identity in the Nature-Culture Borderlands* (1998).

A steady stream of important studies covering most of the major literary periods has been published in the past few decades. Joyce Salisbury (*The Beast Within*, 1994), Karl Steel (*How to Make a Human*, 2011), Lesley Kordecki (*Ecofeminist Subjectivities: Chaucer's Talking Birds*, 2011) and Susan Crane (*Animal Encounters*, 2012) have produced work on animals and the corpus of medieval writing; Laurie Shannon (*Accommodated Animal*, 2013), Erica Fudge (*Perceiving Animals*, 2002; *Brutal Reasoning*, 2006b; *Renaissance Beasts*, 2004) and Bruce Boehrer (*Shakespeare Among the Animals*, 2002) on the Early Modern period; Christine Kenyon-Jones (*Kindred Brutes*, 2001) and Laura Brown (*Homeless Dogs and Melancholy Apes*, 2010) on Eighteenth-Century and Romantic period literature; Tess Cosslett (*Talking Animals*, 2006) and Deborah Denenholz Morse and Martin Danahay's (*Victorian Animal Dreams*, 2007) on nineteenth century British literature; Margot Norris (*Beasts of the Modern Imagination*, 1985), Cary Wolfe (*Animal Rites*, 2003) and Carrie Rohman (*Stalking the Subject*, 2009) on Modernist literature; Jennifer Mason (*Civilized Creatures*, 2005) and Colleen Glenney Boggs (*Animalia Americana*, 2013) on American literature; Alice Kuzniar (*Melancholia's Dog*, 2006), Susan McHugh (*Animal Stories*, 2011) and Anat Pick (*Creaturely Poetics*, 2011) on modern literatures; Sherryl Vint (*Animal Alterity*, 2010) on Science Fiction; and Wendy Woodward (*The Animal Gaze*, 2008) on South African literature. In addition, there are studies that range beyond period boundaries such as Jennifer Ham and Matthew Senior's *Animal Acts: Configuring the Human in Western History* (1997), John Simons' *Animal Rights and the Politics of Literary Representation* (2002) and Philip Armstrong's *What*

Animals Mean in the Fictions of Modernity (2008), which deals with novels by Swift, Defoe, Melville and Mary Shelley along with contemporary fictions such as Timothy Findlay's *Not Wanted in the Voyage*, Yann Martel's *The Life of Pi*, and Margaret Atwood's *Oryx and Crake*. Add to this Reaktion Books's beautiful 'Animal' series, edited by Jonathan Burt, which to date has published fifty individual volumes devoted to particular animals, including the frog, ant, wolf, horse, kangaroo, dog, spider, bear, cat, elephant, oyster and penguin. These works explore the natural history of an animal alongside its historical and cultural impact on humankind, including literary representations.

This flow of landmark studies has been equalled by the growing number of conferences, symposia, publication venues and special issues of journals devoted to the topic of animal studies. There have been special issues devoted to animals by *Parallax* (2006), *Configurations* (2006), *Mosaic* (2006 and 2007), *TDR: The Journal of Performance Studies* (2007), *Oxford Literary Review* (2007), *PMLA* (2009), *The Minnesota Review* (2009–10), *Safundi: The Journal of South African and American Studies* (2010), *JAC: Journal of Rhetoric, Culture, and Politics* (2011), *Postmedieval Studies: a Journal of Medieval Cultural Studies* (2011), *New Formations* (2012), *Hypatia* (2012), *Journal of Victorian Culture* (2012), *Angelaki: Journal of the Theoretical Humanities* (2013), and in 2013 new issues are in progress with calls for papers from *Modern Fiction Studies* and the *European Journal of English Studies*. In Australia, *Southerly* (2009) and *Australian Literary Studies* (2010) similarly have produced special issues on animals, the ALS issue arising from the largest animal studies conference in the field to date, *Minding Animals I*, held at the University of Newcastle in 2009. The dedicated journals within animal studies continue to provide a stable outlet for scholars committed to the field: *Society and Animals* (http://www. brill.com/society-animals), *Humanimalia: a journal of human/animal interface studies* (http://www.depauw.edu/humanimalia/), *Journal for Critical Animal Studies* (http:// www.criticalanimalstudies.org/journal-for-critical-animal-studies/), *Antennae* (http:// www.antennae.org.uk) and the most recent addition, *The Animal Studies Journal*, the journal of the Australian AASG (Australian Animal Studies Group) edited by Melissa Boyde and Sally Borrell (http://ro.uow.edu.au/asj/). If this list is not extensive enough, you can consult Margo DeMello's *Human-Animal Studies: A Bibliography* (2012a) or Linda Kalof, Seven Mattes and Amy Fitzgerald's online bibliography (http://www. animalstudies.msu.edu/bibliography.php).

The archives of secondary literary criticism will yield scholarship, including occasionally unpublished theses, dealing with animal topics in the works of major literary figures: insect imagery in Robert Browning's poetry, the horse as a symbol in D.H. Lawrence's novels and so on. One literary end of animal studies is the imaginative and empathetic identification with other animals' lives, and with the philosophical and ethical questions raised by that engagement. The methodological work of animal literary studies includes deconstructing representations of animals that appropriate the animal as merely literary and mythological figures (Derrida, 2002; Haraway, 2008) as well as critiquing the tendency to observe real animals without attempting to meet their gaze. Cary Wolfe has argued that an engaged animal studies has to be more than 'mere thematics' because it 'fundamentally challenges the schema of the knowing subject and its anthropocentric underpinnings sustained and reproduced in the current disciplinary protocols of cultural studies (not to mention literary studies)' (2009: 568–569). The task of such a literary animal studies would include critiquing representations that are disrespectful to animals, redressing the occlusions of literary historiography itself (in which animals have been largely absent), and taking interspecies structures of feeling seriously, rather than uncritically dismissing such engagements as sentimental. This work moves away from a tradition that sees animals as passive, unthinking presences in the active, thoughtful lives of humans to a tradition which conceives of humans as constructing and having been constructed by animals (Fudge 2006a: 1).

II

As historically specific examples of human perception, use and representation of that most popular of domestic animals, the dog, I now turn to the cases of Bandit and Michael Vick in the US (with a brief foray into Dickens's *Oliver Twist*) to illustrate a number of important points relevant to any discussion of animal studies. The key contention is that the category of 'animal' is contingent and shifts according to the convenience of the dominant; and that human rights are inextricably linked to the question of the animal, making the intersectionality of the categories of the human and animal human a central starting point to any discussion of the field. I conclude with some comments on a novel featuring a protagonist with a particularly conflicted relationship to literature and the academy, J.M. Coetzee's *Disgrace* (1999b). The concluding scenes of the novel are read as being, among other things, *about* the limits of the rational thought that human animals have used to distinguish themselves from 'mere' animal life.

I begin with a 'true' story about a 'real' dog, Bandit, who in 1987 was on death row taking a rap for being naturally vicious. The most comprehensive account of the case, *Bandit: Dossier of a Dangerous Dog*, was published in 2002 by linguist, poet and animal trainer, Vicki Hearne. The bare outlines are as follows: Bandit, companion to Mr Lamon Redd, a poor, elderly black man in Stamford, Connecticut, was provoked into biting a neighbour. The neighbour had trespassed on Mr Redd's property and hit Mr Johnson, one of Mr Redd's boarders who served as Bandit's walker, with a broom. Bandit was impounded, during which time he was so ineptly handled that, on his return, his behaviour had changed for the worse – so much so that when Redd beat him for urinating on the porch, the dog bit back. This time the State canine control authority sought to have Bandit killed. Opposing the State of Connecticut's 'disposal order', Vicki Hearne, who was called in as an expert witness, convinced the court to give her permission to retrain Bandit. She discovered in the process that he was a well-mannered and obedient dog, and he was thereafter committed to her care.

This, however, was no simple 'Heart-Warming True Story of One Dog's Rescue from Death Row' as advertised on the cover of a 2007 reprint of the book. The ruling distressed Mr Redd. Having grown up in Virginia, he accused Hearne of stealing his dog: 'It's just like in the South, the black man gets something good, the white man takes it away from him' (Hearne 2002: 293). When Mr Redd rose at the hearing to testify in favour of Bandit he said, to the great distress of Hearne, 'All the ladies in the neighbourhood like him. Not just the coloured ladies. The white ladies like him too' (Hearne 2002: 49). As Hearne notes, the remark underlined the straightforward racism that was everywhere present but nowhere acknowledged in the trial (Hearne 2002: 50).

The Bandit case became the centre of a media-fuelled frenzy about whether there are irredeemably vicious dog breeds. Newspapers, canine control authorities and the courts incorrectly designated Bandit as a 'pit bull', that is, an American Pit Bull Terrier. Sounding suspiciously like a modern-day Mr Bumble, one expert said to the court: 'He has *genes*. Genes is what these dogs have, and their training is part of their genetics, and it makes 'em mean' (Hearne 2002: 1). Discussing the phenomenon of the bad breed, and the Bandit case in particular, Harvard literature professor Marjorie Garber observes that 'pit bull' had become what:

> ... literary critics of a certain genre would call an 'undecidable' figure singled out for vilification by the law, yet not reliably identifiable as a breed. 'Everyone knows' and 'No one knows' what a 'pit-bull' is. Everyone knows and, and no one knows, that 'they' are dangerous. (1996: 194)

Effectively, human language becomes, for certain animals, quite literally a matter of life and death.

The foregoing discussion illustrates how a mythos of species can naturalise violence towards certain classes of animals and how classificatory language can be used to deny the species-specific traits of individual animals. Such language presents analogies with constructions of gender, race and class in human society. If today's canine *bete noire* is the 'pit-bull', in post-World War II Europe it was German Shepherds and Dobermans, and in 1830s England it was dogs like Bull's Eye, Bill Sikes's dog, in *Oliver Twist*. Bull's Eye is by far the most complex canine character in Dickens's work, and his multivalent name suggests his ties to the Bull and Terrier families, which descended from fighting breeds originally used in bullbaiting and blood sports. The cover of the 2007 Random House Vintage Classics edition of *Oliver Twist* features an image of a Bull Terrier (as classified by the American Kennel Association breed standard) fitted out with a spiked collar accessory.

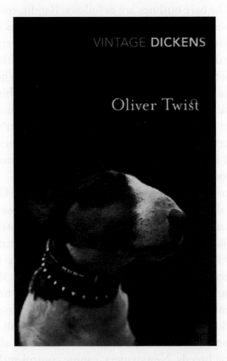

Just as Bandit was not a 'pit bull', the dog breed pictured here did not exist in 1836–7 when the novel was published. The salient point, though, is that both types of dog signify prominently in what might be called 'dangerous dog discourse'. A Bull Terrier is pictured on the cover of the Vintage edition because dogs of this breed are misperceived as 'pit bulls' and are associated with the drug lords and street gangs who use them in dog fighting and as mascots. In contemporary US culture, moreover, American Pit Bulls and other fighting dogs are routinely associated with African American men. As Meisha Rosenberg puts it in the title of her article on dog breeds and race in contemporary popular culture, 'Golden Retrievers are white, Pit Bulls are black and Chihuahuas are Hispanic' (Rosenberg 2011: 113). Ideological investments in this particular species-race intersection were dramatically highlighted in 2007 when Atlanta Falcons quarterback Michael Vick, a former number one pick in the 2001 NFL draft, was indicted on charges relating to a six-year long continuing criminal enterprise of an interstate dog fighting ring known as *Bad Newz* Kennels.

The kennel name refers to the Ridley Circle housing project in the primarily African American East End section of Newport News, Virginia, the economically-depressed area in which Vick grew up, known for its street gangs and drug-related violence. Allegations included Vick's direct involvement in dog fighting, gambling, and brutal executions of dogs. Public outcry resulted from widespread media reports of details which included the hanging, drowning, electrocuting and shooting of dogs. Over seventy dogs, mostly American pit bulls, were seized, along with physical evidence during several searches of Vick's fifteen-acre property by local, state and federal authorities. Many of the dogs bore visible signs of injury. Vick's attorneys argued that dog fighting was an acceptable part of the black 'culture' in the neighbourhood where Vick had grown up, and key figures from the National Association for the Advancement of Coloured People (NAACP) argued that Vick's treatment was illustrative of the systemic racism present in US culture and its institutions (Kim 2009: 16–17). People for the Ethical Treatment of Animals (PETA), on the other hand, characterised Vick as a sociopathic monster unfit for civil society (Broad 2013: 780). Garrett M. Broad adds: 'The common depiction of Vick as a beast – the true animal among the dogs in his ring – undeniably played off of a history of the dehumanisation of black men in U.S. culture' (2013: 780: see also Kim 2009: 17–18).

What was missing in popular media discussions of the Bandit and Michael Vick cases was an alternative politics based on intersectional antispeciesist and antiracist perspectives.[6] An important consideration overlooked in such discussions is that racial, cultural and species differences are made, not given. Like racial stereotypes, the 'vicious breed trope' and 'dangerous dog discourse' tend to rely on the view that cultures are fixed, homogeneous entities that map neatly onto particular groups and particular spaces. This is particularly true in the case of domesticated animals, as the history of dog breeding amply demonstrates. Harriet Ritvo persuasively demonstrates that breed standards, particularly in dogs, became for the Victorian middle classes 'an index of their paradoxical willingness aggressively to re-conceive and refashion the social order in which they coveted a stable place' (1987: 115). Prior to the founding of the Kennel Club in 1873, dogs had mainly been classed by the jobs they performed as illustrated by various taxonomies, many of which were based on sixteenth-century sources, particularly Johannes Caius's *De Canibus Britannicus* (1570). They tended to place the 'most generous kinds' of dogs, notably hunting hounds and bloodhounds, at the top, and the order descended through spaniels and lapdogs to farm animals, while working mongrels such as turnspits came at the bottom. In these unforgiving typologies, the value of particular breeds is derived from their original functions, which had once closely related to the social status of their respective owners.[7] Behind every dog breed there is an ethnography and a social history as well as a genealogy – the story of a life in culture as well as a genetic inheritance.

Against the essentialising view of culture circulated in the Bandit and Vick cases, we might consider that species difference is not only always already in the process of being made, but that this process is not haphazard, rather it is produced as an effect of power relationships. The dualisms that form such forceful undercurrents in Western culture – master/slave, male/female, human/animal, white/nonwhite, reason/nature, culture/nature, civilised/savage, mind/body, subject/object – form an 'interlocking structure' (Plumwood, 1993: 43) that is recognised by theorists working in feminist, disability, postcolonial, queer, indigenous, and critical race studies as a violent hierarchy because one term of the binary is always suppressed in relation to the other, while the middle term is elided. The animal, therefore, is constituted not only through the human/animal dualism but also by other pairs as well (Adams 1994; Kappeler 1995; Haraway 1989). As Claire J. Kim graphically puts it: 'The beast is first made – not just as animal but as savage, nature, other, body, object, alien, and slave – and then slain, affirming power and producing order' (2009: 3).

III

With these considerations in mind I want to turn to what has become a canonic text of animal studies literature, J.M. Coetzee's *Disgrace*, in particular the scenes depicting David Lurie's encounter with unwanted dogs at an animal shelter. In his response to J.M. Coetzee's *The Lives of Animals*, published with the novel, Peter Singer not only outlines his 'like interests' standard (equal consideration of animals at a similar 'mental level' to that of 'normal' adult humans), but also stresses that, for him, animal ethics remains the purview of 'philosophy,' not of 'literature': 'I prefer to keep truth and fiction clearly separate' (1999: 86). His position suggests that while the animal studies movement may be a radical development, it continues to rely, at least in Singer's instance, on a Kantian notion of rational philosophy. Dawn McCance extends this inference to include 'his blueprint for the modern research university as a hierarchical, philosophical institution … with the philosopher at once dispenser of "truth" and standard-exemplar of "mental capacity"' (McCance 2011: v). This essay has suggested that a serious animal studies as conceived of in the Humanities, and in literary studies in particular, necessarily entails a questioning of the anthropocentrism of 'the subject' – the author or writer constituted by philosophy and by literature. Literary texts, like animals, tend to mess with the boundaries of reason and feeling, and *Disgrace*, is, I would suggest, about the limits of the rational thought that human animals have used to distinguish themselves from animal life. The novel asserts the difference between 'human' and 'animal' not simply by foregrounding the technology by which animals are non-criminally put to death – but also because Coetzee's chiseled Flaubertian descriptive prose refuses secure ethical positions grounded in the consolations of accepted human belief systems, including rational truth. The ending of *Disgrace* can be read as a critique of human ideas of sacrifice and redemption: Coetzee takes us through the stereotypical figurations and gestures in a way that makes their insubstantiality and emptiness self-evident. Lurie remains confused until the end, unable to escape what Agamben calls the 'anthropological machine', and doomed to give up both on himself and the crippled singing dog who loves him.

David Lurie resigns uncontrite from his teaching position at Cape Technical University because of an affair with a student, and moves to live with his daughter, Lucy, on a smallholding in the Eastern Province, where she grows flowers and vegetables for the market in nearby Grahamstown and runs dog kennels. Working as a volunteer at a local animal shelter, David assists Bev Shaw in euthanising animals, mainly dogs, and in the process appears to undergo a transformation which includes an acceptance of a shared emotional life with animals. For instance, David becomes mindful of giving each dog a proper burial, ensuring their corpses 'will not be beaten into a more convenient shape for processing' (Coetzee 1999b: 143). Despite David's acceptance of his own animality and his adoption of a less anthropocentric outlook, the novel seems to make an appeal to a sacrificial logic that entails his giving up on the special singing dog of whom he has become fond as a final act of renunciation. The novel ends on one of the killing Sundays; the dog is carried 'like a lamb' to the slaughter. Coetzee offers no rational explanation from Lurie for his decision to sacrifice the crippled dog who he knows will die for him (215). The last line of the book is 'I am giving him up'.

> It gets harder all the time, Bev Shaw once said. Harder, yet easier too. One gets used to things getting harder; one ceases to be surprised that what used to be as hard as hard can be grows harder yet. He can save the young dog, if he wishes, for another week. But a time must come, it cannot be evaded, when he will have to bring him to Bev Shaw in her operating room (perhaps he will carry him in his arms, perhaps she will do that for him) and caress him and brush back the fur so that the needle can find the vein, and whisper to him and support him in the moment when, bewilderingly, his legs buckle; and then, when the soul is out, fold him up and pack him away in his bag, and the next day wheel the bag into the flames and see that it is burnt, burnt up. He will do all that for him when his time comes. It will be little enough, less than little: nothing.
>
> He crosses the surgery. 'Was that the last?' asks Bev Shaw.
>
> 'One more.'
>
> He opens the cage door. 'Come,' he says, bends, opens his arms.
>
> The dog wags its crippled rear, sniffs his face, licks his cheeks, his lips, his ears. He does nothing to stop it. 'Come.'
>
> Bearing him in his arms like a lamb, he re-enters the surgery. 'I thought you would save him for another week,' says Bev Shaw.
>
> 'Are you giving him up?'
>
> 'Yes, I am giving him up.' (Coetzee 1999b: 220).

Michael O'Sullivan argues that any author who deals with animals must necessarily 'give up control', including the autonomy and authority that have been definitive of 'authorship' since the seventeenth century. The reason for this relinquishing of control, he continues, is that it allows humans 'to revisit moments of weakness' that animals traditionally embody, and 'it may raise compassion for the other' (2011: 119). For O'Sullivan, then, Lurie's giving up of the unnamed dog, is supported by Coetzee's disordering of narrative temporality: it gives us back what Paul Ricoeur calls the '"articulated unity of coming-towards, having-been and making-present". The potentialities of animal and human time merge in this passage' (2011: 131). This reading is a variation on the argument that Coetzee is representing a merging of human and pre-linguistic animal suffering. For me, however, David's painful imagining of how he might support singing dog in his death, compared to the stark description of what he actually does in present time, represents not unity but underlines David's multiple failures, including his final failure to save the dog. Indeed, the 'I' in the last sentence – 'I am giving him up' – draws attention to David's final understanding that it is humans who have control over whether certain animals live or die. The dog seems to also function as a figure for Lurie at this point: in giving up on singing dog, is he giving up on himself, on South Africa? David imagines at various points in his relationship with the dog a tentative interspecies *rapprochment*; but just as the history of canine domestication reveals a mix of moralities of control and care, there can be no simple relinquishing of mastery by Lurie.

The scene invokes two Victorian texts that work against critics who read in this scene 'a posthumanist religiosity' (Weil 2012: 127). Coetzee undercuts the 'sacrificial structure' that opens up a space for the 'noncriminal putting to death' of the animal of which Derrida speaks, allowing no space for the transcendence of the human spirit. Instead the act of sacrifice invokes other such acts of disgrace. When David allows singing dog to lick 'his cheeks, his lips, his ears' as he collects him for his death, who can fail to recall Darwin's poignant words in The *Descent of Man* (1871):

> The love of a dog for its master is notorious; in the agony of death he has been known to caress his master, and every one has heard of the dog suffering under vivisection who licked the hand of the operator; this man, unless he had a heart of stone, must have felt remorse to the last hour of his life. (1981: 40)

That David allows this characteristic canine gesture of affection from his special dog, when earlier he felt revulsion at the dogs licking him, shows he has developed a capacity for empathy with another species, and has become less selfish, perhaps. However, the shift from the personal pronoun 'he' to 'it' in the sentence indicates his emotional distance as he prepares to 'give him up'. Deborah Bird Rose, who names the dog 'Youngfella', asks the entirely relevant question of the 'structure of sacrifice' at stake in this scene: 'what does David save in giving up Youngfella'?:

> On the face of it David is sacrificing the dog in order to save both the boundary between the human and animal and human control over that boundary. His choice furthers his infectious emptiness. This was his last fall into disgrace ... (2011: 38)

When the dogs are brought to the clinic in the first place the narrator tells us it is 'because they are unwanted: *because we are too menny*' (146). The italicised words reference the suicide note of Little Father Time in Thomas Hardy's *Jude the Obscure* (1895) – '*Done because we are too menny*' (Hardy 1974: 356; his italics) – after he has murdered his two half siblings in a tragically misguided attempt to rectify the consequences of working-class fertility. This grotesque intertextual reference underlines not Darwinian evolutionary or Malthusian thinking as it does in Hardy's text but the anthropocentrism of Lurie's thinking: while he may have come closer to understanding the continuity between human and animal life from a human point of view the dogs are too many and must be eliminated. Scenes like these are a powerful challenge to Singer's faith in the dominion of the rational that informs his analysis of *The Lives of the Animals*, because what Coetzee's fiction succeeds in registering with such devastating force are the evasions and limitations of the human rational condition, and the limitations of human language to register the ubiquity of mechanised animal killing.

Coetzee offers no rational explanation of Lurie's dedication to surplus dogs. Lurie himself does not understand why he drives to the incinerator every Monday. To lighten the burden on Bev Shaw? For that it would be enough to drop off the bags at the dump and drive away. For the sake of the dogs? But the dogs are dead; and what do dogs know of honour and dishonour anyway, he wonders. Coetzee's unemotional, precise prose renders the dead bodies of the dogs in kinesthetically descriptive detail (1999b: 144–45). Lurie's prevarications and deflections seem self indulgently consistent with what we already know of his character, especially when contrasted to the narratorial description of dead animal bodies in all their material excess.

Lurie, like Elizabeth Costello, is 'wounded', to use Cora Diamond's term, by various forms of mechanised animal killing. The trauma experienced by David Lurie is an ethical issue which the novel acknowledges as a kind of unspeakability – not only the unspeakability of how animals are treated in such practices as factory farming and pet shelters but also the unspeakability of confronting the limits of one's own thinking, in confronting (as Diamond puts it) the trauma of experiencing 'something in reality to be resistant to our thinking it, or possibly too painful in its inexplicability'.[8] How far the trope of unspeakability is an adequate critical response to the human iterability of animal suffering depicted in *Disgrace* is debatable because the novel in my view articulates so eloquently what Raymond Williams called a 'structure of feeling'. *Disgrace* represents the mixed affects – care, compassion, violence, and indifference – that characterise David's attempt to honour a human kinship between human and nonhuman species. As the Vick and Bandit cases also show, this same paradoxical mix of care, sentiment and violence typifies relationships between humans and nonhuman animals, including domestic animals, in contemporary Western societies.[9]

If singing dog could speak, what would his story be? In an interrogative twist on Wittgenstein's elliptical statement, Kari Weil asks: 'If it did speak … could we understand it?' (Weil 2012: 127).

Appendix

Animal rights: A philosophical position as well as a social movement that advocates for providing nonhuman animals with moral status and, thereby, basic rights.

Animal studies: Generally used, at least in the natural sciences, to refer to the scientific study of, or medical use of, nonhuman animals, as in medical research. In the humanities, it is the preferred term for what social sciences call HAS.

Anthrozoology: The scientific study of human–animal interaction, and the human–animal bond.

Critical animal studies (CAS): An academic field of study dedicated to the abolition of animal exploitation, oppression, and domination.

Ethology: The scientific study of animal behaviour.

Human-animal studies: The study of the interactions and relationships between human and nonhuman animals (DeMello 2012b: 5).

Notes

1   For simplicity's sake, I will generally be using 'animal' to mean 'nonhuman animal.' I will also use *animal studies* in its broadest, contemporary sense, designating the multidisciplinary field known by some as human-animal studies (HAS) – sometimes called anthrozoology – which is not to be confused with the scientific usage which refers to laboratory studies involving animals. Sometimes the related term, critical animal studies, is used, although CAS distinguishes itself from much mainstream human-animal studies by virtue of its commitment to an advocacy agenda. For a fuller discussion

of the relationship between critical animal studies and human–animal studies see Taylor (2013: 155–169). For brief definitions of terms see the *Appendix* at the end of this essay.

2 See Susan McHugh (2011 and 2006).

3 See Kari Weil (2012: 3–4).

4 While Derrida's work on what he calls 'the question of the animal' has been enormously important, his critique does not go far enough. I agree with Donna Haraway that Derrida fails to 'meet' the animal. See especially Haraway's analysis of the scene of Derrida's confrontation with his cat in his bathroom (2008: 19–23). For a full-blown discussion of Derrida's failure in 'The Animal That Therefore I Am (More to Follow),' to sustain a critique of sexual as well as species difference, see Guenther (2009). For a critique of Derrida's centrality in the critique of humanism in animal studies see Fraiman (2012).

5 For a more detailed discussion of this point, and Derrida's positions see Wolfe (2010: 62–78).

6 For a full discussion of this point in relation to the Vicks case see Broad 2013 'Vegans for Vick: Dogfighting, Intersectional Politics, and the Limits of Mainstream Discourse' 780–800. For discussion of the Bandit case see Hearne *Bandit: Dossier of a Dangerous Dog*, 2002.

7 See for example, 'A Synopsis of English Dogs' in Rev. William B. Daniel, *Rural Sports*, vol. 1, p.15.

8 'The Difficulty of Reality' pp. 45–46. Cited by Wolfe in 'Introduction, in *Philosophy and Animal Life*. New York: Columbia UP, 2008, p.3.

9 Raymond Williams introduced the term 'structure of feeling' to describe the way shared emotional dispositions have an impact on the way societies operate and how history is constructed and experienced (Williams 1977: 133). Philip Armstrong has usefully used this term to show how intimately the emergence of certain structures of feeling is tied up with human-animal relations: for example, dispositions like sympathy, sentimentalism, nostalgia for nature (Armstrong 2008).

References

Adams, C. 1994 *Neither Man nor Beast: Feminism and the Defense of Animals*, Continuum, New York.

Angelaki: Journal of the Theoretical Humanities 2013, 'We Have Never Been Human: From Techne to Animality' (Special Issue), Broglio, R. & Young, F. (eds), 18, 1.

The Animal Studies Journal, Boyde, M. (ed), University of Wollongong, <http://ro.uow.edu.au/asj>

Antennae: The Journal of Nature in Visual Culture, Aloi, G. (ed), <http://www.antennae.org.uk>

Arluke, A. & Sanders, C.R. 1996 *Regarding Animals*, Temple University Press, Philadelphia.

Armstrong, P. 2008 *What Animals Mean in the Fiction of Modernity*, Routledge, New York.

Australian Literary Studies (ALS) 2010, 'Minding Animals I' (Special Issue), Dale, L. and McDonell J. (eds), 25, 2.

Boehrer, B. 2002 *Shakespeare Among the Animals: Nature and Society in the Drama of Early Modern England*, Palgrave, New York.

Broad, G. M. 2013 'Vegans for Vick: Dogfighting, Intersectional Politics, and the Limits of Mainstream Discourse', *International Journal of Communication*, 7, 780–800.

Brown, L. 2010 *Homeless Dogs and Melancholy Apes: Humans and Other Animals in the Modern Literary Imagination*, Cornell UP, Ithaca.

Caius, J. 1570 *De Canibus Britannicus*, London.

Coetzee, J.M. 1999a *The Lives of the Animals*, Princeton University Press, Princeton.

Coetzee, J.M. 1999b *Disgrace*, Penguin, London.

Configurations 2006 'Thinking with Animals' (Special Issue), Nash, R. & Broglio, R. (eds), 14, 1–2.

Cosslett, T. 2006 *Talking Animals in British Children's Fiction, 1786–1914*, Ashgate, Aldershot.

Crane, S. 2012 *Animal Encounters: Contacts and Concepts in Medieval Britain (The Middle Ages Series)*, University of Pennsylvania Press, Philadelphia.

Daniel, W. 1801 *Rural Sports*, 3 vols, Bunny & Gold, 1801–13, vol. 1, London.

Darwin, C. 1981 *The Descent of Man, and Selection in Relation to Sex, 1871*, Princeton University Press, Princeton, NJ.

Deleuze, G. & Guattari, F. 1987 *A Thousand Plateaus. Trans. Brian Massumi, vol. 2 of Capitalism and Schizophrenia*, University of Minnesota Press, Minneapolis.

DeMello, M. 2010 *Teaching the Animal: Human/Animal Studies Across the Disciplines*, Lantern Books, New York.

DeMello, M. 2012a *Human-Animal Studies: A Bibliography*, Lantern Books, New York.

DeMello, M. 2012b *Animals and Society: An Introduction to Human-Animal Studies*, Columbia University Press, New York.

Denenholz Morse, D. & Danahay, M. 2007 *Victorian Animal Dreams; Representation of Animals in Victorian Literature and Culture*, Ashgate, Aldershot.

Derrida, J. 1991 '"Eating Well" or The Calculation of the Subject: An Interview with Jacques Derrida', in E. Cadava, P. Connor & J. Nancy (eds), 1991 *Who Comes after the Subject?*, Routledge, New York: 96–119.

Derrida, J. 2002 'The Animal That Therefore I Am (More to Follow)', (trans. David Wills), *Critical Inquiry*, 28, 2: 369–418.

Derrida, J. 2008 *The Animal That Therefore I Am: More to Follow*, Fordham University Press, New York.

The Drama Review (TDR): The Journal of Performance Studies 2007, 'Animals and Performance' (Special Issue), Chadhuri, U. (ed), 51, 1.

The European Journal of English Studies (EJES) 2015, 'Modern Creatures' (Special Issue), Richter, V. & Vermeulen, P. (eds), 19.

Fraiman, S. 2012 'Pussy Panic versus Liking Animals: Tracking Gender in Animal Studies', *Critical Inquiry*, 39, 1: 89–115.

Fudge, E. 2002 *Perceiving Animals: Humans and Beasts in Early Modern English Culture*, University of Illinois Press, Champaign IL.

Fudge, E. 2004 *Renaissance Beasts: of Animals, Humans, and Other Wonderful Creatures*, University of Illinois Press, Champaign IL.

Fudge, E. 2006a 'The History of Animals', *H-Animal*, 22 July 2012 <http://www.h-net.org/~animal/ruminations_fudge.html>

Fudge, E. 2006b *Brutal Reasoning: Animals, Rationality and Humanity in Early Modern England*, Cornell University Press, Ithaca NY.

Garber, M. 1996 *Dog Love*, Simon & Schuster, New York.

Glenney Boggs, C. 2013 *Animalia Americana: Animal Representations and Biopolitical Subjectivity*, Columbia University Press, New York.

Guenther, L. 2009 'Who Follows Whom? Derrida, Animals, and Women', *Derrida Today*, 2, 2: 151–65.

Ham, J. & Senior, M. 1997 *Animal Acts: Configuring the Human in Western History*, Routledge, New York.

Haraway, D. 1989 *Primate Visions: Gender, Race, and Nature in the World of Modern Science*, Routledge, New York.

Haraway, D. 2008 *When Species Meet*, University of Minnesota Press, Minneapolis.

Hardy, T. 1974 *Jude the Obscure, 1895*, Macmillan, London.

Hearne, V. 2002 *Bandit: Dossier of a Dangerous Dog*, The Akadine Press, New York.

Humanimalia: A Journal of Human/Animal Interface Studies, DePauw University, <http://www.depauw.edu/humanimalia/>

Hypatia 2012, 'Animal Others' (Special Issue), Gruen, L. & Weil, K. (eds), 27, 3.

JAC: A Journal of Rhetoric, Culture and Politics 2011, 32, 1–2.

Journal for Critical Animal Studies, Institute for Critical Animal Studies (ICAS), Johnson, L. & Thomassusan, S. (eds), http://www.criticalanimalstudies.org/journal-for-critical-animal-studies

Journal of Victorian Culture, 2012, McKechnie, C.C. & Miller, J. (eds), 17, 4.

Kalof, L, Mattes, S. & Fitzgerald, A. *Animal Studies Bibliography* <http://www.animalstudies.msu.edu/bibliography.php>

Kappeler, S. 1995 'Speciesism, Racism, Nationalism … or the Power of Scientific Subjectivity', in C. Adams & Donovan, J. (eds), 1995 *Animals and Women: Feminist Theoretical Explorations*, Duke University Press, Durham.

Kenyon-Jones, C. 2001 *Kindred Brutes: Animals in Romantic-Period Writing*, Ashgate, Aldershot.

Kim, C. 2009 'Slaying the Beast: Reflections on Race, Culture, and Species', *Kalfou*, 1, 1: 1–34.

Kordecki, L. 2011. *Ecofeminist Subjectivities: Chaucer's Talking Birds*, Palgrave Macmillan, New York.

Kuzniar, A. 2006 *Melancholia's Dog: Reflections on Our Animal Kinship*, University of Chicago Press, Chicago.

Lansbury, C. 1985. *The Old Brown Dog: Women, Workers, and Vivisection in Edwardian England*, University of Wisconsin Press, Madison, WI.

Mason, J. 2005 *Civilized Creatures: Urban Animals, Sentimental Culture and American Literature, 1850–1900*, Johns Hopkins University Press, Baltimore.

McCance, D. 2011 'Introduction', *Mosaic*, 44, 2: v.

McHugh, S. 2006 'One or Several Literary Animal Studies?' *H-Animal*, 22 July 2012 <http://www.h-net.org/~animal/ruminations_mchugh.html>

McHugh, S. 2011 *Animal Stories: Narrating Across Species Lines*, University of Minnesota Press, Minneapolis.

The Minnesota Review 2009–10, 'The Feral Issue' (Special Issue), Steffen, H. (ed), 73–74.

Modern Fiction Studies, 'Animal Worlds in Modern Fiction' (Special Issue), Herman, D. (ed), Forthcoming.

Mosaic 2006, 'The Animal – Part I' (Special Issue), McCance, D. (ed), 39, 4.

Mosaic 2007, 'The Animal – Part II' (Special Issue), McCance, D. (ed), 40, 1.

New Formations: A Journal of Culture, Theory & Politics 2012, 'The Animals Turn' (Special Issue), Wheeler, W. & Williams, L. (eds), 76.

Norris, M. 1985 *Beasts of the Modern Imagination: Darwin, Nietzsche, Kafka, Ernst and Lawrence*, Johns Hopkins University Press, Baltimore.

O'Sullivan, M. 2011 'Giving Up Control: Narrative Authority and Animal Experience in Coetzee and Kafka', *Mosaic*, 44, 2: 119–136.

Oxford Literary Review 2007, 'DerridAnimals' (Special Issue), Badminton, N. (ed), 29, 1–2.

Parallax 2006, 'Animal Beings' (Special Issue), Tyler, T. (ed), 12, 1: 1–128.

Pick, A. 2011 *Creaturely Poetics: Animality and Vulnerability in Literature and Film*, Columbia University Press, New York.

Plumwood, V. 1993 *Feminism and the Mastery of Nature*, Routledge, London.

PMLA 2009, 'Special Section on Animal Studies', 124, 2.

Postmedieval: A Journal of Medieval Cultural Studies 2011, 'The Animal Turn' (Special Issue), McCracken, P. & Steel, K. (eds), 2, 1.

Regan, T. 1983 *The Case for Animal Rights*, University of California Press, Berkeley.

Ritvo, H. 1987 *Animal Estate: The English and Other Creatures in the Victorian Age*, Harvard University Press, Cambridge.

Rohman, C. 2009 *Stalking the Subject: Modernism and the Animal*, Columbia University Press, New York.

Rose, D. 2011 *Wild Dog Dreaming: Love and Extinction*, University of Virginia Press, Charlottesville.

Rosenberg, M. 2011 'Golden Retrievers Are White. Pit Bulls Are Black, and Chihuahuas Are Hispanic: Representations of Breeds of Dog and Issues of Race in Popular Culture', in Kalof, L. & Montgomery, G. (eds) 2011 *Making Animal Meaning*, Michigan State University Press, East Lansing.

Safundi: The Journal of South African and American Studies 2010, 'Animal Studies and Ecocriticism' (Special Issue), Phillips, D. & Zuzga, J. (eds), 11, 1–2.

Salisbury, J. 1994 *The Beast Within: Animals in the Middle Ages*, Routledge, New York.

Serpell, J. 1986 *In the Company of Animals: A History of Human-Animal Relationships*, Blackwell, Oxford.

Shannon, L. 2013 *The Accommodated Animal: Cosmopolity in Shakespearean Locales*, University of Chicago Press, Chicago.

Simons, J. 2002 *Animal Rights and the Politics of Literary Representation*, Palgrave, Basingstoke.

Singer, P. 1999 (first published 1975) *Animal Liberation: A New Ethics for our Treatment of Animals*, Cape, London.

Society & Animals: Journal of Human-Animal Studies, Shapiro, K. (ed), <http://www.brill.com/society-animals>

Southerly 2009, 'Animal' (Special Issue), Brooks, D. & McMahon, E. (eds), 69, 1.

Steel, K. 2011 *How to Make a Human: Animals and Violence in the Middle Ages*, Ohio State University Press, Columbus, OH.

Taylor, N. 2013 *Humans, Animals and Society: An Introduction to Human–Animal Studies*, Lantern Books, New York.

Thomas, K. 1983 *Man and the Natural World: Changing Attitudes in England 1500–1800*. Penguin, Harmondsworth.

Vint, S. 2010 *Animal Alterity: Science Fiction and the Question of the Animal*, Liverpool University Press, Liverpool.

Weil, K. 2012 *Thinking Animals: Why Animal Studies Now?* Columbia University Press, New York.

Williams, R. 1977 *Marxism and Literature*, Oxford University Press, Oxford.

Wolch, J. & Emel, J. (eds) 1998 *Animal Geographies: Place, Politics and Identity in the Nature-Culture Borderlands*, Verso, London.

Wolfe, C. 2003 *Animal Rites: American Culture and the Discourse of Species, and Posthumanist Theory*, University of Chicago Press, Chicago.

Wolfe, C. 2009 'Human, All Too Human: "Animal Studies" and the Humanities', *PMLA*, 124, 2: 564–576.

Wolfe, C. 2010 *What is Posthumanism?* Minnesota University Press, Minneapolis.

Woodward, W. 2008 *The Animal Gaze: Animal Subjectivities in Southern African Narratives*, Witwatersrand University Press, Johannesburg.

I would like to thank Sascha Morrell for her invaluable assistance with this piece and Robert Dingley for his insights in the course of our discussions of Coetzee's *Disgrace*.

CHAPTER 6

The Aesthetics of Human Disqualification

Tobin Siebers

To qualify for membership in normative humanity, people have to appear a certain way. Disabilities, especially those that take the form of manifest physical differences at odds with existing majoritarian norms, permit people to be disqualified as human. Aesthetic taste, according to Tobin Siebers, by exalting an ideal of beauty, contributes to the practice of disqualification. Siebers taught English at the University of Michigan. His books include *The Mirror of Medusa* (1983), *Disability Aesthetics* (2010), and *Cold War Criticism and the Politics of Skepticism* (1993).

Smile Train, an international organization devoted to children with cleft palette, seems in many ways to be a model charity. It trains and uses local doctors. It claims to put 100 percent of contributions toward surgeries. But Smile Train is a model charity in more than one way. It promotes itself by giving a familiar and typical appearance to disability, following an aesthetic model long established for the purpose of qualifying some people and disqualifying others. The "world's leading cleft charity" uses in-your-face, close-up portraits of disabled children, largely of color and non-Western, to encourage donations to the "modern-day medical miracle" designed "to give a desperate child not just a new smile, but a new life".[1] Smile Train equates disability with loss of life, isolating the children from everyday existence and exhibiting them in a series of medical mug shots. Individuality is downplayed, and the children appear first and foremost as medical specimens of nature gone awry, displayed to elicit feelings of pity, disgust, and charity. The children's color, non-Western origin, and disabled state stand in sharp contrast to the white, smiling, celebrity friends, such as Candice Bergen, who urge donors to be generous.[2] Smile Train "enfreaks" the children, to use David Hevey's term, only to promise to whisk away their freakish nature through the magic of modern medical technology.[3]

Original publication details: Tobin Siebers, "The Aesthetics of Human Disqualification," from *Disability Aesthetics*, pp. 21–56. University of Michigan Press, 2010. Reproduced with permission from The University of Michigan.

Literary Theory: An Anthology, Third Edition. Edited by Julie Rivkin and Michael Ryan.
© 2017 John Wiley & Sons, Ltd. Published 2017 by John Wiley & Sons, Ltd.

Let me note from the outset that I am not opposing the sharing of medical technology across the globe, the assistance of poor nations by wealthy nations, or the creation of charities and nongovernmental organizations devoted to particular world problems. These are desperate times, and many people in the world need help. Rather, what concerns me is the symbolism by which populations and individuals are established as needing help, as being inferior, and the role played by disability in that symbolism, because it has a long history of being placed in the service of discrimination, inequality, and violence. What I am calling the aesthetics of human disqualification focuses on how ideas about appearance contribute to these and other forms of oppression. My claim is that this symbolism depends on aesthetic representations that require further clarification and critique, especially with respect to how individuals are disqualified, that is, how they are found lacking, inept, incompetent, inferior, in need, incapable, degenerate, uneducated, weak, ugly, underdeveloped, diseased, immature, unskilled, frail, uncivilized, defective, and so on. My intention is less to provide a theoretical description of this problem than to review a series of analytic examples from the historical record, but I will begin by defining my theoretical vocabulary and presuppositions.

Three Definitions

Disqualification as a symbolic process removes individuals from the ranks of quality human beings, putting them at risk of unequal treatment, bodily harm, and death. That people may be subjected to violence if they do not achieve a prescribed level of quality is an injustice rarely questioned. In fact, even though we may redefine what we mean by quality people, for example as historical minorities are allowed to move into their ranks, we have not yet ceased to believe that nonquality human beings do exist and that they should be treated differently from people of quality. Harriet McBryde Johnson's debate with Peter Singer provides a recent example of the widespread belief in the existence of nonquality human beings (Johnson). Johnson, a disability activist, argues that all disabled people qualify as persons who have the same rights as everyone else. Singer, a moral philosopher at Princeton University, claims to the contrary that people with certain disabilities should be euthanized, especially if they are thought to be in pain, because they do not qualify as persons. Similarly, Martha Nussbaum, the University of Chicago moral philosopher, establishes a threshold below which "a fully human life, a life worthy of human dignity," is not possible (181). In particular, she notes that the onset of certain disabilities may reduce a person to the status of former human being: "we may say of some conditions of a being, let us say a permanent vegetative state of a (former) human being, that this just is not a human life at all" (181).

Surprisingly little thought and energy have been given to disputing the belief that nonquality human beings do exist. This belief is so robust that it supports the most serious and characteristic injustices of our day. Disqualification at this moment in time justifies discrimination, servitude, imprisonment, involuntary institutionalization, euthanasia, human and civil rights violations, military intervention, compulsory sterilization, police actions, assisted suicide, capital punishment, and murder. It is my contention that disqualification finds support in the way that bodies appear and in their specific appearances – that is, disqualification is justified through the accusation of mental or physical inferiority based on aesthetic principles.

Disqualification is produced by naturalizing inferiority as the justification for unequal treatment, violence, and oppression. According to Snyder and Mitchell, disability serves in the modern period as "the master trope of human disqualification."[4] They argue that disability represents a marker of otherness that establishes differences between human beings not as acceptable or valuable variations but as dangerous deviations. Douglas Baynton provides compelling examples from the modern era, explaining that during the late nineteenth and early twentieth centuries in the United States disability identity disqualified other identities defined by gender, race, class, and nationality. Women were deemed inferior because they were said to have mental and physical disabilities. People of color had fewer rights than other persons based on accusations of biological inferiority. Immigrants were excluded from entry into the United States when they were poor, sick, or failed standardized tests, even though the populations already living there were poor, sick, and failed standardized tests. In every case, disability identity served to justify oppression by amplifying ideas about inferiority already attached to other minority identities. Disability is the trope by which the assumed inferiority of these other minority identities achieved expression.

The appearance of lesser mental and physical abilities disqualifies people as inferior and justifies their oppression. Thanks to the work of Baynton and others, it is now possible to recognize disability as a trope used to posit the inferiority of certain minority populations, but it remains extremely difficult to understand that mental and physical markers of inferiority are also tropes placed in the service of disability oppression. Before disability can be used as a disqualifier disability, too, has to be disqualified. Beneath the troping of blackness as inbuilt inferiority, for example, lies the troping of disability as inferior. Beneath the troping of femininity as biological deficiency lies the troping of disability as deficiency. The mental and physical properties of bodies become the natural symbols of inferiority via a process of disqualification that seems biological, not cultural – which is why disability discrimination seems to be a medical rather than a social problem. If we consider how difficult it is at this moment to disqualify people as inferior on the basis of their racial, sexual, gender, or class characteristics, we may come to recognize the ground that we must cover in the future before we experience the same difficulty disqualifying people as inferior on the basis of disability. We might also recognize the work that disability performs at present in situations where race, sexuality, gender, and class are used to disqualify people as physically or mentally inferior. At the current time we prefer to fix, cure, or eradicate the disabled body rather than the discriminatory attitudes of society. Medicine and charity, not social justice, are the answers to the problems of the disabled body, because the disabled body is thought to be the real cause of the problems. Disability is a personal misfortune or tragedy that puts people at risk of a nonquality existence – or so most people falsely believe.

Aesthetics studies the way that some bodies make other bodies feel. Bodies, minimally defined, are what appear in the world. They involve manifestations of physical appearance, whether this appearance is defined as the physical manifestation itself or as the particular appearance of a given physical manifestation. Bodies include in my definition human bodies, paintings, sculpture, buildings, the entire range of human artifacts as well as animals and objects in the natural world. Aesthetics, moreover, has always stressed that feelings produced in bodies by other bodies are involuntary, as if they represented a form of unconscious communication between bodies, a contagious possession of one body by another. Aesthetics is the domain in which the sensation of otherness is felt at its most powerful, strange, and frightening. Whether the effect is beauty and pleasure, ugliness and pain, or sublimity and terror, the emotional impact of one body on another is experienced as an assault on autonomy and a testament to the power of otherness. Aesthetics is the human science most concerned with invitations to think and feel otherwise about our own influence, interests, and imagination.

Of course, when bodies produce feelings of pleasure or pain, they also invite judgments about whether they should be accepted or rejected in the human community. People thought to experience more pleasure or pain than others or to produce unusual levels of pleasure and pain in other bodies are among the bodies most discriminated against, actively excluded, and violated on the current scene, be they disabled, sexed, gendered, or racialized bodies. Disabled people, but also sex workers, gay, lesbian, bisexual, and transgendered people, and people of color, are tortured and killed because of beliefs about their relationship to pain and pleasure (Siebers 2009). This is why aesthetic disqualification is not merely a matter for art critics or museum directors but a political process of concern to us all. An understanding of aesthetics is crucial because it reveals the operative principles of disqualification used in minority oppression.

Oppression is the systematic victimization of one group by another. It is a form of intergroup violence. That oppression involves "groups," and not "individuals," means that it concerns identities, and this means, furthermore, that oppression always focuses on how the body appears, both on how it appears as a public and physical presence and on its specific and various appearances. Oppression is justified most often by the attribution of natural inferiority – what some call "in-built" or "biological" inferiority. Natural inferiority is always somatic, focusing on the mental and physical features of the group, and it figures as disability. The prototype of biological inferiority is disability. The representation of inferiority always comes back to the appearance of the body and the way the body makes other bodies feel. This is why the study of oppression requires an understanding of aesthetics – not only because oppression uses aesthetic judgments for its violence but also because the signposts of how oppression works are visible in the history of art, where aesthetic judgments about the creation and appreciation of bodies are openly discussed.

Two additional thoughts must be noted before I treat some analytic examples from the historical record. First, despite my statement that disability now serves as the master trope of human disqualification, it is not a matter of reducing other minority identities to disability identity. Rather, it is a matter of understanding the work done by disability in oppressive systems. In disability oppression, the physical and mental properties of the body are socially constructed as disqualifying defects, but this specific type of social construction happens to be integral at the present moment to the symbolic requirements of oppression in general. In every oppressive system of our day, I want to claim, the oppressed identity is represented in some way as disabled, and although it is hard to understand, the same process obtains when disability is the oppressed identity. "Racism" disqualifies on the basis of race, providing justification for the inferiority of certain skin colors, bloodlines, and physical features. "Sexism" disqualifies on the basis of sex/gender as a direct representation of mental and physical inferiority. "Classism" disqualifies on the basis of family lineage and socioeconomic power as proof of inferior genealogical status. "Ableism" disqualifies on the basis of mental and physical differences, first selecting and then stigmatizing them as disabilities. The oppressive system occults in each case the fact that the disqualified identity is socially constructed, a mere convention, representing signs of incompetence, weakness, or inferiority as undeniable facts of nature.

Second, it is crucial to remember the lessons of intersectional theory. This theory rightly focuses on how oppressive systems affect the identity of the oppressed individual, explaining that because individuality is complex, containing many overlapping identities, the individual is vulnerable to oppressive systems that would reduce the individual to one or two identities for the purpose of maintaining power and control (Collins 208).[5] Intersectional theorists restore a complex view of the individual and fight against creating hierarchies between different identities. For example, the debate whether it is worse to be black or female is viewed as divisive and unproductive. My tactic here is similar. I want to look at identity not from the point of view of the oppressed individual but from the point of view – limited as it may seem and significant because limited – of oppressive systems. Disability is the master trope of human disqualification, not because disability theory is superior to race, class, or sex/gender theory, but because all oppressive systems function by reducing human variation to deviancy and inferiority defined on the mental and physical plane.

Intersectional analysis shows that disability identity provides a foundation for disqualification in cases where other minority identities fail because they are known to be socially constructed for the purposes of domination. It is not clear why disability has proven so useful a trope for maintaining oppression, but one reason may be that it has been extraordinarily difficult to separate disability from the naturalist fallacy that conceives of it as a biological defect more or less resistant to social or cultural intervention. In the modern era, of course, eugenics embodies this fallacy. Eugenics has been of signal importance to oppression because eugenics weds medical science to a disgust with mental and physical variation, but eugenics is not a new trend, only an exacerbation of old trends that invoke disease, inferiority, impairment, and deformity to disqualify one group in the service of another's rise to power. As racism, sexism, and classism fall away slowly as justifications for human inferiority – and the critiques of these prejudices prove powerful examples of how to light oppression – the prejudice against disability remains in full force, providing seemingly credible reasons for the belief in human inferiority and the oppressive systems built upon it. This usage will continue, I expect, until we reach a historical moment when we know as much about the social construction of disability as we now know about the social construction of race, class, gender, and sexuality. Disability represents at this moment in time the final frontier of justifiable human inferiority.

Three Analytic Examples

The aesthetics of human disqualification presents in almost every sphere of human influence, but because the art world thrives on aesthetic judgments, art-making practices and debates about them provide a unique window into disqualifying and qualifying statements about human appearance, made almost always, of course, in the guise of judgments of taste. Oddly, although the source of disqualification is not the aesthetic itself, the devices of disqualification are often worked through in the aesthetic context – at museums, art shows, in literary works, music, art catalogs, magazines, and by entertainments of various kinds. My itinerary begins with a focus on the Nazi era because of its definitive and violent interpretation of modern art as part of a medical and eugenic project that disqualifies certain populations as defective. Then I jump forward in time to the controversial display in 2005 of Marc Quinn's sculpture of

Alison Lapper in London's Trafalgar Square. Here I address the debate about whether disabled bodies should be subjects of art and displayed in public spaces. Finally, I conclude by looking at a 2008 essay in *Newsweek* magazine that reproduces medical photographs from the Mütter Museum in Philadelphia in a gesture embracing the tradition of the freak show. Each analytic example demonstrates the shuttling back and forth of aesthetic judgments between the art world and the political world, providing the occasion to map the operative principles obtaining between aesthetics, disqualification, and oppression.

Degenerate Art and Defective People. Although the Nazis were not shy about using disability to disqualify human beings, these attitudes acquired even greater transparency in statements about the art world. Hitler's love of art and conception of himself as an artist – as preposterous as they may seem – meant that art was the preferred vehicle for the development of Nazi ideas and philosophy. It was also the domain where we see played out Nazi ideas about nonquality human beings. The competition in 1937 between the Grosse Deutsche Kunstausstellung (Great German Art Exhibition) and the exhibit of Entartete Kunst (Degenerate Art) makes the use of aesthetic disqualification by the Nazis' crystal clear by setting in opposition their positive and negative conceptions of human types. The Degenerate Art exhibition represented the Nazis' attack on modern art because of its portrayal of "defective" people, while the Great German Art Exhibition, with which Hitler inaugurated the House of German Art, was supposed to demonstrate the superiority of German bloodlines and aesthetic taste. The purposes of the two exhibitions could not have been more different, but their occurrence in the same year provides the occasion to construct from their negative and positive views of human appearance a clear conception of the Nazi system of aesthetic disqualification.[6]

The works included in the Great German Art Exhibition avoid representing physical imperfection and racial diversity at all costs. The Nazis staked their claim to superiority on the representation of beautiful and healthy German bodies, although the works are now indistinguishable from kitsch. The controlling design of the exhibition came directly from Hitler's ideas about art, as revealed by many public statements. Hitler embraced health and racial homogeneity as the measures of quality human beings. Disease and disability were his principal disqualifiers. "The German people," Hitler exclaimed, "with their newly awakened affirmation of life are seized with admiration for strength and beauty and therefore for what is healthy and vigorous" (Adam 76). "We only want the celebration of the healthy body in art" (Adam 149). The House of German Art was to open its doors only to ability, not disability.

In contrast, Hitler accused the modern works shown in the Entartete Kunst exhibit of reveling in "deformed cripples and cretins, women who inspire only disgust, men who are more like wild beasts, children who, if they were alive, would be regarded as God's curse!" (Sax and Kuntz 230). As evidence for Nazi claims about the biological inferiority of the subjects pictured in modern art, the catalog designed to accompany Entartete Kunst juxtaposed modernist works and examples of facial deformities as well as works by modern artists and mental patients. The catalog claims, for example, that a painting by a "schizophrenic from a lunatic asylum" "looks more human than Paul Klee's botched effort" (Barron 383). Entartete Kunst asks beholders not only to cast the psychological sources of modern art as mentally incompetent but also to confuse modernist experiments with form with realistic depictions of disabled human beings. Paul Schultze-Naumburg, author in 1928 of *Kunst und Rasse*, provides an early example of the strategy used by

Entartete Kunst to denigrate modern art; the book compares portraits by Modigliani, Schmidt-Rottluff, and others to medical photographs of physically disabled and diseased patients.[7] Similarly, Entartete Kunst either interpreted artworks as medical specimens or juxtaposed artworks with medical photographs and other artifacts. The exhibition sought to tutor the public in the Nazi vision of aesthetics by suggesting the negative medical impact that disabled and racially diverse people might have on the German population. In effect, beholders were supposed to see the so-called degenerate works through Nazi eyes as picturing examples of in-built inferiority, providing an experience of disability preliminary to the extermination of more than 200,000 human beings with similar characteristics.[8]

Degeneration was principally a medical term before Max Nordau applied it to art. It referred throughout the last half of the nineteenth century to individuals who departed from norms of human health because of genetic difference, sexual habits deemed excessive, or shattered nerves. The Nazis applied these distinctions as standards of aesthetic beauty. Degenerate art deserved its name in their view because it included bodily deformities, bloodshot eyes, feebleness, and signs of nervous exhaustion – all disabling conditions supposedly brought about by racial impurity or the stress of modern life. Jews, homosexuals, and criminals were automatically assumed to be biologically inferior, and the Nazis found evidence for their assumptions in the physical traits given to people in works of modern art.

The works banned as degenerate by the Nazis are more familiar in their form and content than those approved by them. Consequently, it makes sense to focus first on the so-called Great German Art, so that we may let the full power of defamiliarization strike us when we turn to the better-known works and artists. The point of the comparison, I remind, is to gain an understanding of the aesthetics of human disqualification, not to make judgments about which objects are better works of art. This goal requires attention to the contribution of aesthetics to oppression, that is, to the choice of appearance placed in the service of intergroup or political violence.

The Great German Art works to achieve qualification for the German people by designing a specific though imaginary human type based on the healthy and able body. This type was proposed as the norm, and deviation from it tended to justify disqualification and oppression. One of the oddities revealed by a disability studies perspective on aesthetics, however, is how truly unreal and imaginary are nondisabled conceptions of the human body. Remove imperfection from the body, and one discovers the perfect recipe for what does not exist for the most part in the human universe. Disability theorists are fond of noting that nondisabled bodies are all alike, while disability takes a thousand unique and different forms. If the strength of human nature lies in its evolutionary compact with variation, then the Nazi drive toward perfection based on uniformity produces results contrary to the laws of evolution. The Great German Art refuses variation by embracing an idea of human form characterized by exaggerated perfection and striking regularity. Arno Breker's *Readiness* represents the perfect picture of health and ability, but it is deeply unreal and stumbles into pure kitsch: its pumped-up body, thought classical by the Nazis, actually swerves away from its Greek models to present a profile and shape outside the bounds of human form. Famously called Hitler's Michelangelo, Breker preferred to model his sculptures on the bodies of athletes, but his works seem more frequently to represent bodybuilders – shapes contoured by steroids rather than sport and dubious as examples of male beauty.

"There is no exquisite beauty," Francis Bacon claimed, "without some strangeness in the proportion." By these lights, the only thing beautiful about Ivo Saliger's *Diana's Rest* is the peculiar fact that the three women are all exactly the same. It is a convention of painting to base multiple figures on the same model, but in this example the convention springs from the ideological imperative to achieve human perfection by suppressing individual variation. *Diana's Rest* provides an example of the eerie world, sought by the Nazis, in which the desire for perfection quashes individuality and variety. Josef Thorak's *Comradeship* demonstrates the masculine version of this overcharged regularity. Matched muscle for muscle, the gigantic figures twin each other, while striving to embody an impossible ideal of human health. According to Hitler's address at the opening of the Great German Art Exhibition, the Nazi eugenic project required an emphasis on beauty and health as the first step in achieving the goal of creating a new human type. "The new age of today is at work on a new human type," Hitler remarks: "Tremendous efforts are being made in countless spheres of life in order to elevate our people, to make our men, boys, lads, girls, and women more healthy and thereby stronger and more beautiful. From this strength and beauty streams forth a new feeling of life, and a new joy in life. Never before was humanity in its external appearance and perceptions closer to the ancient world than it is today" (Sax and Kuntz 230).[9] Strangeness in proportion in either individual human figures or among them is deliberately eschewed in Nazi art because its goal is to portray a new human being whose embodiment of beauty and health results in an almost obscene regularity of features and body parts.

　　The image of nature in the Great German Art mirrors its treatment of the human body in the emphasis on banal, unvarying, and exaggerated perfection. If German blood issues supposedly from the soil, the picture of meadow, pasture, and forest in Nazi art seeks an image of nature that supposedly proves the superiority and durability of the German people. Nature in Nazi art is all abundance, but the ripeness is so artificial that it seems – and there is no irony intended – to bulge with decay. It has often been noted

Photo by ullstein bild/ullstein bild via Getty Images.

that Nazi artists take their image of nature from the tradition of German Romantic art, especially the paintings of Caspar David Friedrich. The influence, however, is vastly overstated. Friedrich's nature scenes possess an aura of desolation, focusing often on a lone marker in the landscape such as a cross, a solitary figure, a crumbling church, a dead tree, or a broken grave marker. There are no dead trees, ruins, or broken graves in Nazi landscapes – no hint of the weight of time or the inevitability of death blemishing nature's bounty. Rather, nature exists as an eternal plenitude resistant to decay and death. For example, Oskar Martin-Amorbach's *The Sower* displays a blond peasant, marching across a field and smiling at the good earth in satisfaction, against a backdrop of vast blue sky and other fields being prepared for planting – all of the elements united by a rainbow as if to testify to a Nazi covenant with nature. There is not a single dead tree in view, no plant that is not ready to burst into full bloom. Gisbert Palmié's *Rewards of Work* represents the same vision of nature. The figures in the foreground, all surrounded by friendly animals and involved in expressions of antiquated labor (weaving on a spinning wheel, gathering fruit in a basket, harvesting wheat in sheaves), focus their attention on a nude blond goddess, apparently work's reward personified, from whom flows an almost infinite trail of golden cloth. In the background blossoms a spectacle of unspoiled nature: a bright sky, flowing river, abundant trees, and grassy meadows. No one aware of the earth's seasons could find in Nazi art the smallest semblance of nature's passage from birth and fullness to death and rebirth. Rather, nature seems fixed in an unending summer, never displaying the slightest hint of autumn, let alone the death of winter – a testimony to the Nazi hope that the Third Reich might endure without change for a thousand years.

Compared to the Great German Art, the art labeled degenerate by the Nazis presents a startling variety of human appearances. But more startling are the suggestions, first, that this variety is an effect of including disability and, second, that the Nazis were the first to recognize the aesthetic centrality of disability to modern art. It is not merely the case that the Nazis preferred representational art to Dada or expressionism, that they disliked broken lines and unnaturalistic uses of color, that they wanted artists only and always to draw or paint or sculpt with the greatest technical skill. They preferred all these things because they interpreted their opposites as signposts of disability. The techniques of Dada and expressionism deform the bodies rendered by them, seeming to portray disabled people. The palette of modernism paints human faces in greens, yellows, and purples, embracing discoloration without rejecting attendant associations of disease. The modernist determination to flatten the canvas and to draw attention to the sculptural quality of paint often stunts figures, bending and twisting them into anagrams of disability. Moreover, the attention given by modern art to themes of alienation, violence, panic, terror, sensory overload, and distraction requires an openness to disability as a visible and potent symbolization of these themes. People quivering with anxiety, howling in fear, or cringing in silent terror populate modernist canvases, openly embracing situations and conditions thought abnormal and feared by the Nazis. The Nazis waged war against modern art because they interpreted the modern in art as disability, and they were essentially right in their interpretation, for modern art might indeed be named as the movement that finds its greatest aesthetic resource in bodies previously considered to be broken, diseased, wounded, or disabled.

If modern art has had such enormous success, it is because of its embrace of disability as a distinct version of the beautiful. The Nazis grasped the nature of this aesthetic, but they rejected it, misreading the future direction of art as they misread many other things about human culture. Instead, they attacked modern art for the very features that give it such remarkable imaginative and transformative power to represent the human condition – be it the capacity to claim through formal experiments and new content a vast array of human emotions, thoughts, and physical appearances or be it the confidence to leave behind the imitation of nature and to represent what nature might reject or fail to conceive.

Hitler's remarks on the modernist palette exemplify the tendency to associate invention in modern art with human impairment. Hitler disqualifies artists who apply imaginative uses of color by calling their vision defective:

> From the pictures submitted for exhibition, I must assume that the eye of some men shows them things different from the way they really are. They really are men who can see in the shapes of our people only decayed cretins, who feel the meadows as blue, the heavens green, clouds sulphur yellow…. I only want to prevent these pitiable unfortunates, who clearly suffer from defective vision, from attempting with their chatter to force on their contemporaries the results of their faulty observation, and indeed from presenting them as "art." (Sax and Kuntz 230)

More significant than blaming modernist techniques on disability, however, is the Nazi use of modern art to illustrate people, trends, and conditions called degenerate. This point cannot be overstated. For the Nazis, modern art provided evidence in support of the medical and eugenic rejection of disability. The modernist interest in deformation of the human body and in new techniques of representation combined to produce visions of human appearance that demonstrated to Nazi eyes the evils of miscegenation, the devastating effects of modern life on the human nervous system, and the danger of allowing disabled people and racial inferiors to reproduce themselves. The Nazi way of life, once established by total warfare against and extermination of everything not German, would presumably have existed in stark opposition to the world pictured by modern art.

Consider Emil Nolde's *Mulatto* and Ludwig Meidner's *Self-Portrait*. Although a Nazi sympathizer, Nolde found his works displayed at the Entartete Kunst exhibit because of his embrace of modernist themes and techniques. The title of *The Mulatto* serves as a red flag for Nazi disapproval, but it is finally Nolde's modernist aesthetic that marks the woman in the portrait as "degenerate". Her patchy coloration, overbite, frizzy hair, and narrow eyes suggest in-built inferiority to the Nazi medical gaze. She demonstrates for the Nazis what mixing races will produce and supplies evidence for the necessity of keeping German bloodlines pure. Ludwig Meidner, the Jewish expressionist painter who initially made a reputation for himself by producing horrific landscapes of life in the modern city, later became a prolific self-portraitist. The Nazis included his *Self-Portrait* in the "Jewish room" of Entartete Kunst as proof of the defective nature of the Jewish people, scratching above the painting the words, "Jewish, all too Jewish" and referring to the work in the catalog as one of "three specimens of Jewish sculpture and painting" (Barron 298). The curation for the Jewish room announced its purpose as the "Revelation of the Jewish racial soul" (Barron 194). What the Nazis saw in the portrait, and wanted others to see, one can only imagine. A misshaped face, elfin ears, deformed hand, and twisted body – all rendered in unnaturalistic colors – seem to attest to the biological inferiority of Jews.

Another category significant for the definition of degenerate art and its reliance on disability as a marker of disqualification touches on antiwar art. Beginning with Callot and Goya and increasing in importance with the rise of photography, images of wounded soldiers, victims of torture, maimed civilians, and devastated cities have played a crucial role in the critique of warmongering among nations. This tradition pictures disability as the measure of the evils of warfare, and although this usage stigmatizes the wounded person as an allegorical symbol of the horrors of war, it nevertheless makes an important contribution to the inclusion of disability, injury, and disease in the history of visual culture, one that endures to this day, most recently in the photographs of torture taken at Abu Ghraib. Hitler's war machine had every reason to resist this tradition, and artists critical of warfare soon found themselves labeled as degenerate. Like Hitler, Ernest Ludwig Kirchner went to war to defend Germany, but he was horrified by what he saw in the trenches of World War I. He had a nervous breakdown and represented the cost of war in the poignant and powerful *Self-Portrait as a Soldier*, included in the Entartete Kunst exhibit. The painting shows Kirchner in full dress uniform, exhibiting the bloody stump of his severed right hand against the background of a Baconesque meaty collage and a nude woman. The attack against him as a degenerate artist threw Kirchner into despair, as more than 600 of his works were confiscated. He committed suicide on June 15, 1938. Otto Dix is another powerful critic of the war ethic. His series *War* was attacked as degenerate, both because it is antiwar and because it uses ghastly images of war victims to depict the horrors of war. *Transplant* pictures a man in a hospital bed, his face torn asunder, with brains exposed, patched up with chunks of flesh designed to stand in for his nose, cheek, and forehead. *Skull* represents a fleshless head, a scraggly crop of hair spouting from the head and the lip, mingled with worms busily devouring the residues of this former person's brain.

The aesthetic vocabulary used by the Nazis to attack their victims is the invention of modern art – stolen to support a perverse and violent cause. The casualties of war represented in modern art display fragilities of the human mind and body that the Nazis used not to denounce war but to condemn certain populations and races. The focus of modern artists on the dangers of industrialization and crowded cities was made to support the idea that human beings best inhabit the archaic landscape of Nazi homelands. The images of diverse peoples from across the globe, celebrated in modern art, represent an openness to human variation that nevertheless struck Hitler's faithful as embracing degenerate, defective, and racially inferior people. The Nazis reinterpreted what they saw in modern art and put it in the service of an aesthetics of human disqualification, setting images, shapes, and human forms to oppressive and violent ends never imagined by modern artists themselves. In no way did the direction and inclination of modern art share in the prejudices and hatreds of the Nazis, but with a brutal twist of interpretation, they turned the expansiveness of human types found in modern art into a condemnation of everything not their own. They created once and for all a system of disqualification that justifies exclusion and genocide – a system whose aesthetic principles still rationalize oppression today.

Alison Lapper Pregnant: "Why Shouldn't My Body Be Considered Art?" The most significant aspects of Entartete Kunst, if we listen to the Nazis who toured it, were the feelings of revulsion that the artworks were supposed to excite in beholders. These works were revolting, of course, because they used disability to prove the degeneracy of modern existence. "All around us you see the monstrous offspring of insanity, impudence, ineptitude, and sheer degeneracy," explained the introduction to the Entartete Kunst catalog; "What this exhibition offers inspires horror and disgust in us all" ("Nazi Treasure Trove"). The aesthetic disqualification of disabled people has remained remarkably consistent over time, linking the emergence of eugenics in the late nineteenth century and its applications in Great Britain, the United States, and Nazi Germany to unproductive and inaccurate stereotypes causally expressed today in discussions about health care, civil rights, neonatal testing, euthanasia, wrongful birth, reproductive care, assisted suicide, abortion, and quality of life. Although we seem to have moved to some degree beyond the idea that certain racial, ethnic, gendered, and sexed identities represent nonquality human beings, there continues to be widespread acceptance of the prejudice that individual human beings, of whatever race, ethnicity, gender, or sexuality, might be classified as inferior on the basis of injury, illness, disability, intelligence, or genetic traits.

When incorporated into works of art, however, the forms of aesthetic appearance that disqualify individual human beings as defective produce an entirely different set of meanings and emotions. Modern art claims disability as the virtuoso sign of the aesthetic, increasingly presenting disability as an aesthetic value in itself. Far from designing representations to mark human beings as inferior, modern art turns to disability, I have been arguing, as a new and powerful resource for promoting aesthetic variation, self-transformation, and beauty. Nevertheless, the radical gesture of rooting aesthetics in the representation of the disabled body produces an interpretive dilemma, one first discovered by the Nazis and still found almost everywhere in the art world today. As modern art increasingly defines its future direction in terms of disability, artists represent disabled bodies more and more explicitly as aesthetic objects, and the beholders of these objects must choose whether to embrace or to reject the strong feelings excited by disability. On the one hand, because modern art embraces disability as an aesthetic value in itself, there seem to be few objects with greater potential than disabled bodies to qualify as works of art. The modern in art manifests itself as disability, and disabled bodies possess an aura that seems to satisfy the artistic desire for new, varied, and beautiful forms of appearance. On the other hand, aesthetic objects symbolizing disability are sufficiently disruptive that some beholders are tempted to reject modern art as "sick" and "ugly" and to call for alternative forms of art that are "healthy" and "beautiful." The alliance between modern art and disability becomes the cause for disgust, complaints, and doubts, resulting in culture wars targeting the art world itself. Disability is mustered as evidence that art as a whole has succumbed to sickness and degeneracy.

In 2004, Marc Quinn began to exhibit a series of works that advances the modern preoccupation with disability as a key aesthetic concept as well as probes the strong feelings of prejudice that disabled bodies excite in other bodies. *The Complete Marbles* revise the tradition of classical fragmentary sculpture for the modern day by representing likenesses of people who in real life have missing limbs, establishing a powerful resonance between artworks long considered beautiful because of their broken state and people whose disabilities would seem to exclude them from the category of aesthetic beauty. One marble won the competition of the Fourth Plinth Commissioning Group and was installed on Trafalgar Square in London, immediately sparking a heated debate about the kinds of bodies thought permissible to exhibit in public. *Alison Lapper Pregnant*, juxtaposed with a king, two generals, and the naval hero Admiral Nelson, depicts a nude woman, three and a half meters high, weighing thirteen tons, and carved from snow-white Carrara marble. She is also eight months pregnant and has foreshortened legs and no arms.[10] Quinn explained that Nelson's Column, the focal point of Trafalgar Square, is "the epitome of a phallic male monument" and that "the square needed some femininity" (Reynolds). The sculpture repulsed some beholders, while exhilarating others. Some decried the display of a disabled person in a public square, but others celebrated it, pointing out that Admiral Nelson was also disabled. All beholders, however, had a difficult time not revealing their feelings about disability, and these feelings, negative for the most part, affected the sculpture's value and identity as a work of art, not to mention contributing to the ongoing stigmatization of disabled people.[11]

The negative responses by critics to Quinn's work are especially revealing because they fixate on disability as an unacceptable subject for art, while trying to justify by other means the revulsion stirring them. At the same time, the commentators often embrace illiterate positions on disability, praising or pitying the people depicted in the works merely because of their impairments. Robert Simon, editor of the *British Art Journal*, calls Lapper "very brave" but concludes that the sculpture is "just a repellant artifact" (Lyall). Theodore Dalrymple in *City Journal* praises Lapper's "admirable courage" only to mount a personal attack against her. He dismisses her as "a single mother sporting ironmongery in her nose," who "has shrewdly (and, in her circumstances, understandably) commodified her armlessness, turning it to an advantage." Dalrymple apparently accepts that disability may be represented in art – since he notes that "some of the greatest paintings by one of the greatest artists of all time, Diego Velázquez, are of dwarfs" – but he concludes that Lapper's image, given over to "narcissism, self-pity, and self-obsession," falls well short of Velázquez's "statements of his deeply felt and completely sincere humanity." Apparently, neither Quinn nor Lapper is a good example of humanity. Hilton Kramer in the *New York Observer* calls Quinn's marbles "an amazing performance," "if you have the stomach for it," accusing the artist of turning beholders into "voyeurs of a succession of personal catastrophes – an experience that bears a distinct resemblance to involuntary encounters with pornography." Finally, in an opinion piece in the *Guardian*, illustrated by a photograph of pigeons swarming over the surface of the sculpture and hatefully captioned "Pigeon Toes," Brendan O'Neill confesses "to loathe the *Alison Lapper Pregnant* statue (not Alison Lapper herself, please note, who I'm sure has overcome great challenges to become both an artist and a mother)." For O'Neill, "the statue captures much of what is rotten in the heart of new Britain.... *Alison Lapper Pregnant* is about as challenging as old underwear.... It shows that we value people for what they are rather than what they achieve.... We prefer victims to heroes".

As much as these commentators try to achieve the focus on the artwork apparently required by aesthetic judgment, they end by remarking not so much on the artistic properties of the statue as on the details of Lapper's disability. Lapper's physical features – and not necessarily those represented in the statue – become reasons for denying the status of the work as art. The commentators also attack Lapper's personality as psychopathological, although it is not clear what Lapper herself has to do with the artwork.[12] More important, the commentaries conclude in nearly every case that the alliance between modern art and disability provides evidence that the art world in general is in decline, rotten, inhuman, or sick. The appearance of disability somehow justifies the claim that the project of modern art is diseased.

But modern art permits no such condemnation of disability. I have been arguing that modern art makes of disability one of its defining aesthetic principles, rendering it impossible to attack disability without also rejecting modern art. The Nazis, of course, epitomize this last response. They attack the modern in art as disability and, consequently, reject all modern art as sick. The controversy over *Alison Lapper Pregnant* reinforces a similar dilemma, compelling beholders, whether friendly or not to modern art, to confront human disqualification as a facet of aesthetic judgment. Their choice is either to reject artworks that picture disabled people or to embrace disability as an aesthetic value in itself.

Many beholders choose to reject disability, but what would the other choice involve? "If the Venus de Milo had arms," Quinn observes, "it would most probably be a very boring statue" (4). Quinn's work trades in the bewildering idea that the same properties that strengthen works of art disqualify the actual people who possess them – the same bewildering idea on which modern art establishes itself. Modern art discovers in the eye drawn to the difference of disability one of its defining aesthetic principles. The interviews included in the catalog of *The Complete Marbles* insist again and again on this idea. Quinn repeatedly asks the subjects of his sculptures what they think about fragmentary classical statuary, whether it is beautiful and, if yes, whether their bodies are therefore beautiful as well. Lapper poses the same question: "Why shouldn't my body be considered art?" (Freeman). The crucial point here is to recognize that Lapper's body, once turned into an aesthetic representation, has a better chance of being accepted as art than a nondisabled body, despite the fact that disabled bodies, outside of aesthetic contexts, are still dismissed as repulsive and ugly. Disability is not merely unwanted content, political or otherwise, introduced into art but a mode of appearance that grows increasingly identifiable over time as the aesthetic itself.

Anita Silvers argues that modern art, because of its preoccupation with corporeal deformation, represents a moral resource for teaching people to accept disabled bodies as beautiful rather than rejecting them as ugly. She notices that people find beautiful Picasso's cubist portrait, *Maya with a Doll*, while simultaneously being repulsed by a real child whose osteogenesis imperfecta produces the same features. The solution is, she argues, to embrace an aesthetic point of view in our everyday life, to tutor ourselves to look at disabled people as if they were works of art. I have no objection if modern art helps people to see disability as beautiful, although I am dubious about the possibility, but I am proposing a different dynamic between disability in art and reality. It is not a matter of being able to view disabled people as representing works of art; it is a matter of being able to view works of art as representing disability.[13] This fine distinction is important because it underscores that the difference ascribed to the artwork relies on the difference of disability, and as long as it remains unacknowledged, disability can be used to disqualify and oppress human beings. The distinction itself between disability in art and in reality is a function of the aesthetics of human disqualification.

Medical Photographs: The Art of Making Strange. The Mütter Museum of Philadelphia shows medical specimens, artifacts, and photographs to 80,000 people annually – exhibits called "disturbingly informative" on its website. The crowds streaming through the museum are not subjected to explicit captions and signs about degeneracy, as were the people who visited the Entartete Kunst exhibition, but the human subjects viewed by these crowds bear the weight nevertheless of an aesthetics of human disqualification that uses disability to represent some human beings as inferior to others. The Mütter Museum, conceived in 1849, ten years after the invention of the photograph, seems at first glance to be an archaic survival from a time before it became inappropriate to look at disabled people for education, fun, and profit. But in January 2008 *Newsweek* magazine published a visual essay that gives the lie to this theory. The essay reproduces ten sample images from the nearly 200 photographs published in the new catalog, *Mütter Museum: Historic Medical Photographs*, apparently for the distinct purpose of presenting disabled people as objects of visual pleasure. Unlike the catalog, which avoids the sensational language of medical marvels and monsters associated historically with the museum, *Newsweek* seems deliberately to mine the shock value of the medical photographs, calling its selection, in an apparent desire to rehabilitate the freak show for the modern moment, "A Century of Medical Oddities."

There may be no better example with which to think about the aesthetics of human disqualification than the medical photograph. The medical photograph is its own aesthetic genre, an aesthetic genre determined not to be seen as one. It obeys a number of aesthetic rules, such as the use of full body profiles, changing postures, serial shots of the same subject, comparative anatomy between subjects, and close-ups, but its primary aesthetic imperative is the pretense of objectivity for the purpose of medical understanding and diagnosis. The images exist, after all, not to give pleasure but to instruct. Medical photographs cast disability as reality, not art, because their disabled subjects are exhibited first and foremost as medical specimens – examples of natural history gone bad and preserved for the advancement of science. No person in a medical photograph is a picture of health – all of which is to say that medical photographs represent medical subjects: the sick, the disabled, the injured, the deformed, those supposedly in need of a cure. The explicit ideology behind medical photographs is to promote a healthy world in which medical photography would no longer be necessary or possible as a genre, for once medical science prevails, a golden age will be upon us, and medical subjects will be gone forever.[14]

Until that glorious day arrives, however, people thought in need of medical rescue will be found among us. Who are they and what do they look like? What happens when doctors take their photographs and they are collected in museums, archives, and magazines? The *Newsweek* selection runs the gamut from giants and dwarfs, persons affected by polio, tuberculosis, facial deformities to parasitic insects, x-rays of objects stuck in throats, and a skeleton of conjoined twins, creating a collection, like most medical collections, in which it is not always clear why any given person might be classified as a human oddity. The problem, of course, is the instability of disability as an identity. All people, by virtue of being human, move in and out of disability identity, and people recognized as disabled in one context may not be thought disabled in another. In fact, the aesthetics of human disqualification works comparatively. Because the baseline in medicine is perfect health, medical photographs may enfreak any deviation from the baseline, however slight. Human disqualification viewed in isolation, based on individual appearance, has little meaning; its meaning emerges by association, placement in context, and aesthetic technique.

The Russian formalists define art itself as aesthetic technique, most notably as the technique of making strange. *Ostranenie* represents for them a process of "defamiliarization" by which the familiar is cast as unfamiliar and surprising (Shklovsky). Picasso's cubist faces present superb examples, but making strange and disability are not so easily distinguished, especially because modern art relies with increasing frequency in its history on the semblance of disability to produce aesthetic effects.[15] The Russian formalists do not mention medical images as examples of defamiliarization, but the medical photograph offers, in fact, a remarkable vision of the art of making strange. The ability to represent a person as a medical oddity often relies on the technique of the photograph itself, on its ability to shift an appearance, create an association, or elicit a context that disqualifies the medical subject as inferior.

The art of making strange, annexed to the conventions of the freak show, is on vivid display in the *Newsweek* essay from its very first page. We also see on display the use of medical photographs to disqualify their subjects. The essay opens under the pall of a double death head, accentuating with a close-up view the malevolent associations of the two skulls of a pair of conjoined twins and juxtaposing them with the essay's title reference to medical oddities. The essay closes with the same image in smaller scale but describes the twins in medical terms as a case of "ectopagus".[16] Beginning at least with

Chang and Eng Bunker, some of whose remains are housed in the Mütter Museum, freak shows and carnivals have profited from the American love affair with conjoined twins (Wu). More than any other, this image makes it absolutely clear that the *Newsweek* essay conceives itself as a continuation of the freak-show tradition and its exhibition for fun and profit of people deemed inferior.

At least three other photographs send the same message about the freak show to *Newsweek* readers. The second image uses a sideshow convention to defamiliarize and enfreak its subjects, lining up in a row four men of varying statures from too small to too tall. The caption explains that Henry Mullins "was nearly seven feet seven inches tall, weighed 280 pounds, and performed on stage and in the movies," but *Newsweek* leaves unnamed the person of smallest stature and those in the middle ranges, although their names are written on the photograph. Another example reveals that captions invent contexts that make medical subjects seem strange. The fourth image shows a wax model of Madame Dimanche before she experienced "one of the most unusual surgeries in history." The Parisian "sprouted" from her forehead at age seventy-six a "horn" that grew to almost ten inches before it was surgically removed six years later by one Dr. Joseph Souberbeille. The image contains a black wax model of Madame Dimanche mounted on a board and photographed in profile to show the growth hanging down over her face. Finally, the sixth image offers an example of cultural and racial difference positioned as medical oddity. It exhibits the left hand of a Chinese nobleman, having cropped out of full view the person to focus on his extraordinary features: twisted fingernails ranging from five to six and a half inches in length.

Based on context alone, almost any image that finds itself in a collection of medical photographs will surrender its vision of human variation to the representation of medical deviance. But there are cases in which *Newsweek* seems to reach the limits of medical defamiliarization. The limit cases are important because they disabuse beholders of their inclination to accept the idea that all subjects of medical photographs deviate naturally, in and of themselves, from medical norms, while at the same time questioning the norms being imposed to create the category of oddity. The third image pictures an x-ray of a dog, "but not a real one," caught in the throat of a little girl. The photograph reveals the "toy pooch," nose down, against the backdrop of the girl's throat, lung cavity, and rib cage, producing a study in abstraction, save for the black profile of the toy. The caption explains that the photograph comes from a collection of "radiographs depicting items that were successfully removed from the throats and airways of patients by a pioneering specialist." Aside from the suggestion of injury to the girl, quickly dismissed, the image seems to appear uniquely on the basis of its aesthetic qualities – a perfect example of making strange by photographic technique – for it displays no suggestion of biological oddity.

The eighth image, depicting a young boy affected by polio, uses typical conventions of the medical photograph, making sure to place on view the entire specimen. Nevertheless, there are no signs of physical deformation, as found in the other photographs of human subjects, and except for the wary look on the boy's face, the only indication of things gone awry is the primitive steel brace attached to the orthopedic shoe on his right leg. The justification for including the photograph among a century of medical oddities is apparently that polio, "which struck Franklin D. Roosevelt in the 1920s, is now almost unheard of in the United States." Given the panic surrounding polio in the United States during the twentieth century, it is not surprising that its disappearance would be celebrated, but the photograph itself does not seem to bear witness to the polio panic. Rather, the small-featured boy in a crew cut invokes gentleness and innocence rather than strangeness, his status as a human oddity being established by a huge back-story and the steel prosthesis bound to him.

Finally, the ninth image seems to break with the conventions of the medical photograph by exhibiting a mange mite magnified in size by 150 diameters – a species still in existence that preys on horses. The only apparent reason for the insect's inclusion in the collection is to display medical technology, although the magnification renders the *sarcoptes equi* monstrous ("Don't worry, that's not the actual size," the caption reassures), and the allusion to disease is not far away. The "parasitic mite," the caption elaborates, "lives within the subcutaneous tissue of a horse," causing "scabies, a transmittable, itchy skin infection that riders can pick up from a horse." But the appearance of the insect does expose in part the rationale underlying medical photography. The medical model of disability, which lodges defect in the person rather than in the person's social environment, disqualifies the unhealthy and diseased as inferior people, and they are easily grouped with other species thought inferior, such as animals and insects.[17] As the final photograph in the series, the parasitic mite calls for an insidious and retroactive reading of the previous images of disabled people as examples of beings existing at the lower end of the evolutionary chain, beings whose appearance is thought strange, beings therefore labeled oddities.

While the riddle of modern art is how to recognize the disability in art, the riddle of the medical photograph is how to recognize the art in disability. The aesthetics of human disqualification narrows both recognitions, asking beholders to dismiss art that shows too many signs of disability and to close their eyes to the artistic techniques used by medical photographers to disqualify their subjects. The perspective that sees in both cases the aesthetic value of disability is hard to find. Neither missing point of view will be possible in a large way until we find the motivation to represent disability aesthetically as a qualified rather than disqualified subject.

Coda

In February 1998 *New York Press* published an essay by Norah Vincent that attacks the emerging discipline of disability studies as "yet another academic fad" (40). Nevertheless, disability studies apparently fails as a discipline not because it is too chic but because it attracts incompetent, weak, and dishonest people. Camille Paglia calls disability studies "the last refuge for pc scoundrels" (40), but if we believe Vincent, disability studies is also a refuge for ordinary scoundrels, not to mention scholars and students of poor quality. Disability studies supposedly attracts people of questionable moral character – "academic careerists" and "ambulance-chasing publishers" who want to profit from the newest fad – as well as mediocre and flawed minds – the "victim-obsessed," the "second-rate," and the psychologically dependent (40). Vincent seems especially keen to discredit disability studies by associating it with intellectually inferior and psychologically damaged scholars, and when she interviews various leading lights in the field, she is more intent on exposing their psychological weak spots than on capturing what is original about their contribution to disability studies. Lennard Davis, Vincent tells us, melts into "self-righteous goodspeak" at the mere mention of disability, while Michael Bérubé speaks in a voice that is "silky and kind" when he argues that disability is an idea necessary to understand human rights (40). Disability studies deserves no place in the university, it seems, and no self-respecting scholar should have anything to do with it.

If there is any doubt that Vincent wants to disqualify disabled people as physically defective, morally degenerate, or psychologically damaged, the cartoon accompanying the essay should make her purpose obvious. The cartoon, drawn by Gary Leib, pictures a man in a wheelchair being pushed by a woman in a nurse's uniform. Leib overlays the drawing with a variety of disqualifying aesthetic markers: some associate the disabled with physical ugliness and lack of intelligence, while others attempt to promote the idea, despite all evidence to the contrary, that the disabled enjoy a privileged, exclusive, and wealthy lifestyle. For example, as beads of sweat run down his face, the disabled man in the wheelchair grips a cigarette holder in his mangled teeth and toasts his public with a martini. Behind him and pushing the wheelchair is his nurse attendant. Her eyes are vapid, and her breasts are bursting out of her tight-fitting uniform. Most hateful, however, is the fact that Leib draws the cartoon in a way that re-envisions people with disabilities as Nazi soldiers. The disabled man in the wheelchair wears a monocle, summoning the image of an SS officer. The message of the cartoon is shocking and direct in its attack on disabled people; it manages to represent the disabled as poor, inferior, and undeserving creatures who have managed somehow to attain a position of wealth and power superior to other people. The cartoon asks its beholders to believe that the disabled as a group belong to the privileged few, to a dominant class, and to an infamous story of genocide and military expansionism, deserving comparison with the Nazis, some of the greatest criminals in human history.

By way of conclusion, let me pose three questions that I do not intend to answer but offer as background music to Gary Leib's cartoon and other artworks used to disqualify people with disabilities. What would it mean to call a person sick without it being a disqualification? What would it mean to call an artwork sick without it being a disqualification? What is the relationship between these two questions? Applying the aesthetics of human disqualification according to business as usual will give no satisfying answers to these questions. Rather, the way forward requires nothing less than a radical rethinking of the relationship between aesthetics, disqualification, and oppression, one in which the systemic oppression of disabled people would fail, and fail precisely, because it could no longer be based on human appearances, features, and conditions deemed inferior.

Notes

1 The address for Smile Train's website is www.smiletrain.org (accessed February 19, 2008).

2 The list of celebrity friends from the West includes Christie Brinkley, Tom Brokaw, and Bette Midler, among many others, but no people of color. Thus, even when the children are cured, and their disabled status vanquished, their racial difference remains as a sign of disqualification, at once stigmatizing the children and justifying the intervention by benevolent representatives of white modernity. See http://www.smiletrain.org/site/PageServer?pagename=special (accessed February 19, 2009).

3 Smile Train also presents the threat of disability as an emotional reason to rescue unhealthy people living under inferior conditions in faraway lands. Kim and Jarman provide a brilliant discussion of this trend in the context of postcolonial studies: "we argue that Western or modern gestures to rescue people with disabilities in non-Western or 'pre-modern' locations strategically function to

produce hierarchies between different societies and nations.... Trading upon modernity's mask of benevolence, these hierarchies are often signified by one group's charitable acts scripted as the 'selfless' and 'generous' rescue of disabled people who have been exploited, mistreated, or expelled by societies defined as 'pre-modern'—that is to say, groups automatically coded by a relative 'lack' of development" (53–54).

4   I take this formulation from Snyder and Mitchell: "Disability as the master trope of human disqualification in modernity prefaces an understanding of inassimilable racial and ethnic differences by providing an empirical designation for 'unfit' bodies. Like discourses of national differences that, in turn, support investments in absolutist racial differences, disability may provide a key to the recognition of an underlayer of classification systems based on disqualifying bodily traits that jettison certain people from inclusion in the continuum of acceptable human variations" (127–28).

5   Some key texts on intersectionality relating to disability include Barbee and Little, Beale, Butler and Parr, Fawcett, Hayman and Levit, Ikemoto, Jackson-Braboy and Williams, Martin, O'Toole, Siebers (2008b), and Tyjewski.

6   Attendance at Entartete Kunst far outstripped the numbers at the Grosse Deutsche Kunstausstellung, raising serious doubts about Hitler's taste in art. Entartete Kunst traveled to twelve cities between 1937 and 1941 and attracted more than three million visitors. For more information on the two exhibitions, see Barron and Siebers (2000).

7   Carol Poore's analysis of Schultze-Naumburg is especially effective (53–55). Her analysis of disability and Nazi culture catalogs in great detail the variety of uses to which the Nazis put disability, including its propaganda and pictorial value (67–138).

8   From 1939 to 1945 between 200,000 and 250,000 mentally and physically disabled people were executed under T-4 and other euthanasia programs in Nazi Germany. Between 300,000 and 400,000 people were sterilized. The moral legacy of this history casts a shadow over contemporary debates about abortion, assisted suicide, the human genome project, mercy killing, and wrongful birth.

9   One notices here, incidentally, the influence of Winckelmann's emphasis on classical art's mimicking of the beautiful Greek body, but Winckelmann's love of corporeal perfection did not prevent him from embracing fragmentary and broken statuary, such as the *Torso Belvedere*, as the height of aesthetic beauty, while the Nazis were incapable of accepting any kind of human deformation or incompleteness as art. One searches in vain among Hitler's speeches on art for anything resembling Winckelmann's admiration of broken beauty. For a small analysis of fragmentary classical statuary in the context of disability, see Siebers (2008a).

10   For a superb analysis of the controversy, see Ann Millett: "Public space and its monuments," she argues, "have been gendered male and raced white traditionally, and public space is largely ableist in attitude, not to mention accessibility (or lack thereof)."

11   For example, Kim Levin reviews Quinn's work positively in the *Village Voice* but describes disability in negative language:

> At first sight, it looks exactly like a hall of sublime white marble antiquities.... But something, you suddenly realize, has gone terribly wrong.... Take a closer look at the embracing couple at the entrance. Titled *Kiss*, the piece harks back to Rodin and the romantic Beaux Arts sculptors. It invokes all the obsolete clichés of beauty, perfection, and idealization. Marvel at its outmoded skill, until cruel reality sinks in. The male figure has stunted thalidomide arms. The female's arm is normal but she has only one. Take a good look at the others too. Their truncated and missing parts aren't due to the vicissitudes of time but are the result of accident, genetic defect, or iatrogenic calamity. Quinn exploits the romance of classical antiquity—which depends on the mutilations of time and the notion of loss—to confront us with our own avoidance of the horrific fragility of the human condition.

12   Nor is it clear why Quinn's sculpture of Lapper succumbs more to "narcissism, self-pity, and self-obsession" (Dalrymple) than Velásquez's self-portraits or paintings of little people. Rather, similar to the example of the so-called degenerate art, commentators project their feelings of revulsion toward the artwork onto the artist or subject of the work.

13   On the one hand, it is not clear what it means, beyond metaphor, to experience a human being as an art object, but I worry that it relies on a form of objectification to which people at the extreme

poles of human beauty are especially susceptible. On the other hand, to grant to disability represented in an artwork the privilege of being aesthetically beautiful would produce a paradigm shift supportive of disabled people without the risk of objectifying them.

14 *Newsweek* provides a glimpse of the medical ideology at work in the essay by placing a running header at the top of each page: "To Your Health. Health for Life." Reader comments on the essay refer to a "disease free golden age" and complain that only the greed of drug companies delays its arrival.

15 Michael Davidson makes the case that disability should be linked formally to defamilarization, arguing that the defamiliar body of disability creates aesthetic effects akin to those produced by formalist techniques.

16 The illustrations here come from the catalog, *Mütter Museum: Historic Medical Photographs*, rather than from *Newsweek*, because web images cannot be reproduced with sufficient quality. To view the images as presented by *Newsweek* visit: http://www.newsweek.com/id/77018?GT1=10755 (accessed March 11, 2009).

17 This practice is characteristic of medical eugenics. Pernick notes that eugenic treatises and films in the United States highlight the "repulsive ugliness of the 'unfit'" by comparing them to cattle (94). Hitler, of course, compared "defectives" to "wild beasts" (GHDI).

Works Cited

Adam, Peter. 1992. *Art of the Third Reich*. New York: Harry N. Abrams.

Bacon, Francis. 1627. *The Essays*. London.

Barron, Stephanie, ed. 1991. *"Degenerate Art": The Fate of the Avant-Garde in Nazi Germany*. New York: Los Angeles County Museum of Art and Harry N. Abrams.

Baynton, Douglas C. 2001. "Disability and the Justification of Inequality in American History." *The New Disability History: American Perspectives*. Ed. P. Longmore and L. Umansky. New York: NYU Press, 33–57.

"A Century of Medical Oddities." 2008. *Newsweek* (January 7): www.newsweek.com/id/77018 (accessed July 23, 2008).

Collins, Patricia Hill. 2003. "Some Group Matters: Intersectionality, Situated Standpoints, and Black Feminist Thought." *A Companion to African-American Philosophy*. Ed. Tommy L. Lott and John P. Pittman. Malden, MA: Blackwell, 205–29.

Dalrymple, Theodore. 2004. "Victimhood Equals Heroism." *City Journal* (Spring): www.city-journal. org/html/14_2_sndgs05.html (accessed July 7, 2008).

Hevey, David. 1992. *The Creatures That Time Forgot: Photography and Disability Imagery*. London: Routledge.

Johnson, Harriet McBryde. 2003. "Should I Have Been Killed at Birth? The Case for My Life." *New York Times Magazine* (February 16): http://query.nytimes.com/gst/fullpage.html?res=9401EFD C113BF935A25751C0A9659C8B63 (accessed July 26, 2008).

Lyall, Sarah. 2005. "Disability on Pedestal in London." *International Herald Tribune* (October 8): www.iht.com/articles/2005/10/07/news/statue.php (accessed July 26, 2008).

Nussbaum, Martha C. 2006. *Frontiers of Justice: Disability, Nationality, Species Membership*. Cambridge: Harvard University Press.

Quinn, Marc. 2004. *The Complete Marbles*. New York: Mary Boone Gallery.

Reynolds, Nigel.2004. "Disabled Mother Wins Battle of Trafalgar Square." *Sidney Morning Herald* (March 18): www.smh.com.au/articles/2004/03/17/1079199293170.html? from=storyrhs (accessed July 26, 2008).

Sax, Bejamin, and Dieter Kuntz, eds. 1992. *Inside Hitler's Germany: A Documentary History of Life in the Third Reich*. Lexington, Mass: D.C. Heath.

Shklovsky, Victor. 1965. "Art as Technique." *Russian Formalist Criticism: Four Essays*. Ed. Lee T. Lemon and Marion J. Reis. Lincoln: University of Nebraska Press, 3–24.

Siebers, Tobin. 2009. "In the Name of Pain." *Against Health: Has Health Become the New Morality?* Ed. Anna Kirkland and Jonathan Metzl. New York: New York University Press, forthcoming.

Snyder, Sharon L., and David T. Mitchell. 2006. *Cultural Locations of Disability*. Chicago: University of Chicago Press.

Vincent, Norah. 1998. "Disability Chic: Yet Another Academic Fad." *New York Press*, February 11–17, 40–41.

Wu, Cynthia. 2004. "'The Mystery of Their Union': Cross-Cultural Legacies of the Original Siamese Twins." Ph.D. dissertation, University of Michigan.

CHAPTER 7

Ecocriticism

Pippa Marland

Pippa Marland teaches in the Institute of Humanities and Creative Arts at the University of Worcester, UK. Her work looks at the place of the island in our cultural imagination and, in particular, explores the idea of the island as a heightened space for the negotiation of self and world. The thesis has an interdisciplinary base which includes the emergent field of island studies, formulations of place drawn from cultural geography, archipelagic perspectives in critical and creative writing, and, as an overarching framework, contemporary ecocritical theorizations of Post-Humanism. In this essay, she reprises the history of the emergence of ecocriticism and environmental studies from the 1960s to contemporary Post-Humanist new materialism.

Introduction

Ecocriticism is an umbrella term for a range of critical approaches that explore the representation in literature (and other cultural forms) of the relationship between the human and the non-human, largely from the perspective of anxieties around humanity's destructive impact on the biosphere. Other terms for the field include 'environmental criticism' and 'green cultural studies', the latter term reflecting the increasing diversity of the field's remit – its recent focus on film, TV, virtual worlds and popular music, for example, as well as its growing interest in representations of urban environments. How critics involved in this area choose to define themselves depends largely on their own position in relation to environmental issues and to their understanding of the implications of the individual terms. The prefix 'eco' is preferred by some for its ecological connotations – its emphasis on what Lawrence Buell calls "human and non-human webs of *interrelation*" (*The Future of Environmental Criticism*, glossary, 138, emphasis mine) – but for others it implies an overly close identification with one particular strand of scholarship that advocates a commitment to political activism (Bergthaller, *EASLCE website*).[1]

Original publication details: Pippa Marland, "Ecocriticism." *Literature Compass* 10.11, pp. 846–868. John Wiley & Sons, 2013. Reproduced with permission from John Wiley & Sons.

The multiplicity of perspectives and objects of study outlined above has perhaps contributed to an enduring perception in certain quarters of the academy that ecocriticism lacks legitimacy or coherence as an area of critical theory. Peter Barry, in his influential primer *Beginning Theory*, sees it as a field that "is still distinctly on the academic margins [...] and the movement still does not have a widely-known set of assumptions, doctrines or procedures" (239). In part this is because of the enormity of the subject. As Timothy Clark points out, "The 'environment', after all, is, ultimately, 'everything'" (203), an apparently unlimited area of enquiry that is also in the process of constant change. It follows that so complex and dynamic a concern as the health of the biosphere and our place within it requires a broad range of procedures and an ability constantly to critique assumptions and doctrines. It implies, as Greg Garrard suggests, that the ecocritic must strive for a certain degree of "ecological literacy" (*Ecocriticism*, 5), which involves producing a fluid and contingent response in the face of both new forms of ecological understanding[2] and the ongoing and widespread sense of *deepening* environmental crisis. Clark, again, points up the magnitude of this challenge: "to try to conceptualise and engage the multiple factors behind the accelerating degradation of the planet is to reach for tools which must be remade even in the process of use" (xiii).

Lawrence Buell, whose measured views often provide a touchstone for ecocriticism, acknowledges the diversity of perspectives: "As literary ecodiscourse becomes more widely practised, more globally networked, more interdisciplinary and thus even more pluriform, the participants must become more increasingly aware of speaking from some position within or around the movement rather than for it" (*Future*, viii). For the purposes of this essay, I use the term 'ecocriticism' throughout to facilitate the discussion of a variety of environmental or 'earth-centred' critical approaches that have largely developed in the last 20 years and that represent positions from within or around the movement. In the paragraphs that follow, I give a brief history of ecocriticism from its early incarnations in the USA and Britain, through the successive 'waves' of its theoretical development and their relation to the enduring major strands of ecological thought – deep and social ecology – to its increasingly international platform and the emergence of the significant contemporary formulations of global *eco-cosmopolitics* and *post-humanist material ecocriticism*, which are introducing new paradigms to the field.

The Roots of Ecocriticism

Notwithstanding its broad remit, there is a shared perception within ecocriticism that we are living in a time of environmental crisis that requires us to reassess with some urgency our modes of being in the world. Moreover, there is a general agreement that these modes of being have been, to a large degree, culturally determined. Buell, in an early formulation of the role of ecocriticism, identifies the environmental crisis as a "crisis of the imagination the amelioration of which depends on finding better ways of imaging nature and humanity's relation to it" (*The Environmental Imagination*, 2). He believes that the ways in which we have conceived of ourselves and our relationship with the environment have contributed to our destructive impact on the planet. For Buell, then, the task of the ecocritic is both to unravel and critique the conceptualisations that have been so damaging and to identify traces of those 'better ways of imaging' where we find them. This remains the case for some ecocritics even in the most recent formulations of the movement.

The 1960s are largely seen as the decade that marked the beginning of the kind of environmental consciousness that provides the backdrop to ecocriticism, with the publication of Rachel Carson's *Silent Spring* in 1962 hailed as the beginning of "modern environmentalism" (Garrard, *Ecocriticism*, 1).[3] Although other works emerged in the 1960s and 1970s that were seen as embodying early forms of ecocritical practice, the movement was slow to establish itself.[4] It was not until 1992 that the first professional organisation of ecocritics, the Association for the Study of Literature and Environment, was formed in the USA, followed in 1993 by the founding of its journal, *ISLE: Interdisciplinary Studies in Literature and Environment*. A sister organisation was set up in the UK in 1998 (now encompassing the UK and Ireland), with its own publication, the journal *Green Letters*, first published in 2000.

In her introduction to the early collection of ecocritical essays *The Ecocriticism Reader*, published in 1996, Cheryll Glotfelty points up the dearth of environmental criticism existing at that time:

> If your knowledge of the outside world were limited to what you could infer from the major publications of the literary profession, you would quickly discern that race, class, and gender were the hot topics of the late twentieth century, but you would never suspect that the earth's life support systems were under stress. Indeed you would never know that there was an earth at all. (xvi)

One of the factors influencing this slow progress was perhaps the uncertainty within the humanities of involving themselves with what was generally perceived to be a 'scientific' problem, the domain of the environmental sciences.[5] Another issue was the difficulty of speaking for the earth itself. Other areas of theory that were gathering momentum in the 1970s such as feminism and post-colonialism – both of which critiqued the political and social effects of 'othering' – had more identifiable means of locating and giving the space for articulation to those voices silenced by dominant ideologies.

But, in particular, there was a feeling in these early ecocritics that critical theory itself was thwarting their attempt to establish any kind of advocacy for the earth. John Parham rightly notes a 'belligerent' attitude to theory in first-wave ecocriticism ('The Poverty of Ecocritical Theory', 25). Rather than necessarily representing a rejection of theory per se,[6] this was more the result of a frustration with the particular 'linguistic' turn present in the structuralism and post-structuralism of the 1970s and 1980s that viewed language as a closed system, suggesting, at least in what Wendy Wheeler and Hugh Dunkerley call "the less subtle Anglophone interpretations of 'continental theory'" ('Introduction', *New Formations*, 7), that it is not possible to discuss the 'real' world because reality is constructed in language and 'there is nothing outside the text'.[7] Similarly, in the context of the New Historicism, Alan Liu made the much-contested assertion: "there is no nature except as it is constituted by acts of political definition made possible by particular forms of government" (104). Terry Gifford, responding to this statement, argued that "While Liu is right to identify the word 'nature' as 'a mediation', he is wrong to deny the general physical presence that is one side of that mediation" (*Green Voices*, 15).

The role of early ecocriticism, then, while not necessarily denying the linguistic construction of 'nature', was largely to create the theoretical space in which to discuss that 'general physical presence' on the other side of the mediation, which the proliferation and habits of consumption of the human race (albeit with an uneven global distribution of that consumption, as discussed below) were putting in jeopardy. Kate Rigby calls this endeavour the "ecocritical reinstatement of the referent" (154) and, in an oft-quoted rebuff to extreme applications of the linguistic turn, Kate Soper reminds us: "it is not language that has a hole in its ozone layer; and the 'real' thing continues to be polluted and degraded even as we refine our deconstructive insights at the level of the signifier" (151).[8]

The First Wave – Reinstating the 'Real'

Accordingly, the first wave of ecocriticism, especially in the USA, focused on the representation in literature of the world beyond the text, devoting much of its energy to the search for the forms of literary expression which could best convey an environmental message. In *The Environmental Imagination*, Lawrence Buell formulated a checklist of four 'ingredients' of an environmentally orientated work:

1. *The nonhuman environment is present not merely as a framing device but as a presence that begins to suggest that human history is implicated in natural history.* [...]
2. *The human interest is not understood to be the only legitimate interest.* [...]
3. *Human accountability to the environment is part of the text's ethical orientation.* [...]
4. *Some sense of the environment as a process rather than as a constant or a given is at least implicit in the text.* [...] (7–8, italics in original)

   Buell's questioning of the text's 'ethical orientation' in particular points up an important, though contested, element of ecocriticism, which is what Buell calls "a spirit of commit-ment to environmentalist praxis" (*Environmental*, 430). As a theoretical field based around concerns spreading out from the cultural to the political, there is a desire in some ecocritics to have a practical, 'real-world' impact – to educate our broader interactions with the non-human world and to form a 'counter-canon' of texts "which are seen to model a more ecologically sustainable mode of being and dwelling in the world than that which has predominated in the lived reality of the modern era" (Rigby, 159). For others, the focus is more on interrogation than activism, though political intervention may be a (positive) outcome of that interrogation.[9]

   Cheryll Glotfelty also provided a comprehensive checklist in her introduction to *The Ecocriticism Reader* – this time of questions reflecting the way in which an (American) ecocritic reads. As well as incorporating aspects of Buell's 'ingredients', she also pre-figured many of the concerns of subsequent waves of ecocriticism. For this reason, I include her full list in Appendix 1 as a still useful orientation for anyone wishing to carry out practical ecocriticism.

   In the USA, despite the breadth of Glotfelty's questioning, the first wave of ecocriti-cism was predominantly associated with the championing of non-fiction nature writing. Writers such as Henry David Thoreau, John Muir, Mary Austin, Edward Abbey, Wendell Berry and Annie Dillard were lauded for the quality of their environmental imagination. The landscapes they engaged with were often wilderness or semi-wilderness, and their writings reflect the legacy of American Transcendentalism, with its emphasis on the educative value of wild nature and on intense individual connection with the landscape. This approach has been described as "celebratory" (Head, 'Ecocriticism and the Novel', 236; Barry, 242), suggesting a relatively uncritical understanding of 'nature'.[10]

   First-wave British ecocriticism also concerned itself with the recuperation of forms of writing that foregrounded the non-human world and that might foster environmental sensibility, though here the emphasis was on poetry. It was spearheaded by Jonathan Bate, who in two influential works, *Romantic Ecology: Wordsworth and the Environmental Tradition* (1991) and *The Song of the Earth* (2000), undertook the rehabilitation of the Romantic Poets, especially William Wordsworth, as poets of nature. For Bate, Romantic poetry enables us to "think fragility" (*Song*, 112) – to apprehend our ecological embeddedness and shared vulnerability with the non-human world.

Bate diverges from Buell, however, when it comes to environmental praxis. Basing his argument on Heidegger's ideas of *dwelling* – a manner of being in the world that is receptive to the self-disclosure of nature and is revealed through poetry – Bate characterises *ecopoetry* as a *phenomenological* and pre-political form, which draws us into communion with the earth through its emphasis on 'presencing' rather than representation, bodying forth that presencing in part through its rhythms and sounds. He suggests that, while it might be appropriate for Marxist or feminist critics to believe that they are contributing towards social change, green critics should not approach poetry with a "set of assumptions or proposals about particular environmental issues, but as a way of reflecting upon what it might mean to dwell with the earth" (*Song*, 266). For Bate, "Ecopoetics must concern itself with consciousness. When it comes to practice, we have to speak in other discourses" (266).

Nevertheless, there is a sense in which the British landscape and its literary evocations are inextricably intertwined with the social and the political. Bate's own discussion of the 'peasant poet' John Clare identifies the way in which he viewed "the 'rights of man' and the 'rights of nature' as co-extensive and co-dependent" (*Song*, 164), with his poetry foregrounding the mutual suffering of the earth and the rural poor as a result of the enclosure of common land and the ensuing destruction of ancient habitats. For Peter Barry, British ecocriticism is always 'minatory': "that is, it seeks to warn us of environmental threats emanating from governmental, industrial, commercial, and neo-colonial forces" (242). In the absence of vast stretches of 'wilderness' to evoke, in English literature "wild nature invariably co-exists with agricultural or industrial activity, or human settlement, migration or leisure patterns, each shaped, partially, by the dominant modes of production and social organisation" (Parham, 'Two-Ply', 113). Dominic Head, discussing the difference between, for example, the work of Thomas Hardy and D. H. Lawrence and American wilderness writing, states, "we are confronted with 'natural' images in which questions of social history and sexual politics are inscribed on the scene or in the landscape" ('Ecocriticism and the Novel', 236).

These questions of social and economic history and sexual politics began to emerge with more force on both sides of the Atlantic as ecocriticism progressed. The first wave had carried out a necessary 'rehabilitation of the referent' but fell short when ecocritics themselves began to challenge the theoretical limitations of the movement, thus signalling the second phase of ecocriticism.

Deep and Social Ecology

Before moving on to discussion of the second wave, however, it is important to differentiate between two strands of thought – deep and social ecology – which exist within ecocriticism and which feature throughout the trajectory of its development.

Deep ecologists see the need for a radical reconceptualisation of humanity's place on the planet. They adopt a *biocentric/ecocentric* perspective that proposes a "biospherical egalitarianism" (Naess, 95) in which the interest of the biosphere overrides the interests of individual species, including the human. They believe in raising ecological awareness through an individual adjustment of values, suggesting that a change in our relationship with the environment can only come about through first "grounding ourselves in the dark of our deepest selves" (Snyder, ix) in order to rediscover our profound connection with the 'more-than-human' world.[11] Deep ecology challenges the *anthropocentrism* at the heart of modern society and the kind of 'shallow ecological' standpoints that see the natural world as merely a resource for humanity and that presuppose that human needs and demands override other considerations. And, put simply, it asserts that if we first address our hierarchical attitudes towards the natural world and identify ourselves within a broader circle of living things, then our societal problems may also find resolution.[12]

Social ecologists believe that "the very notion of the domination of nature by man stems from the very real domination of human by human" (Bookchin, 65).[13] Thus, in a paradigmatic reverse of deep ecology, they suggest that we must first address the problems of social inequality and oppression before we can remedy our dislocation from the environment. Both of these movements have been strongly critiqued; deep ecology for its presumed lack of a social dimension,[14] social ecology for its perhaps naïve underestimation of the durability of existing social systems. However, it is important not to make reductive readings of either strand,[15] as these are perspectives that continue to develop in complexity and receive more nuanced workings as they inform ongoing theorisations of ecocriticism. Broadly speaking, first-wave ecocriticism leaned more toward deep ecology in its emphasis on personal connection, or re-connection, with nature (though, as we have seen, the 'minatory' aspect running through British ecocriticism also hinted at a more social inflection), whereas the second wave owed more to social ecology. In discussion of the third and fourth waves of ecocriticism, the two areas of thought come into closer orbit.

The Second Wave – Debating 'Nature'

Although he was the instigator of the notion of ecocritical 'waves', Lawrence Buell himself qualifies this imagery, suggesting that the waves are indistinct and offering 'palimpsest' as a better metaphor:

> No definitive map of environmental criticism in literary studies can [...] be drawn. Still, one can identify several trend-lines marking an evolution from a "first wave" of ecocriticism to a "second" or newer revisionist wave or waves increasingly evident today. This first–second wave distinction should not, however, be taken as implying a tidy, distinct succession. Most currents set in motion by early ecocriticism continue to run strong, and most forms of second-wave revisionism involve building on as well as quarreling with precursors. (*Future*, 17)

Perhaps because of this sense of indistinct succession and concurrence of perspectives, there is a lack of consensus about what actually constitutes each wave. Greta Gaard, for example, argues that the accounts of the second wave underestimate the importance of feminist thinking: "the retelling of ecocritical roots and perspectives marginalizes both feminist and ecofeminist literary perspectives" (643). In the broad account of the second wave that follows, I include discussion of some of the developments in ecofeminism that demonstrate its significance in the ecocritical trajectory.

As Buell suggests, though the second wave revised ecocriticism, it carried through elements of the first wave, maintaining its awareness of the 'general physical presence' of nature and developing and refining its engagement with form and the search for the environmental imagination. Where it diverged was in its re-engagement with the critical theory it had initially pulled against. In the UK, the philosopher Kate Soper suggested in *What is Nature?* that the 'nature-endorsing' approach typical of early ecocriticism should be balanced with a more 'nature-sceptical' sensibility, able to reflect on the way in which 'nature' has been constructed and deployed to reinforce dominant ideologies, but that neither perspective should be allowed to dominate. In fact, they should be informed by reflection on each other. Laurence Coupe gave this dual awareness a specifically ecocritical spin in a memorable phrase in his introduction to *The Green Studies Reader* (2000): "green studies debates 'Nature' in order to defend nature" (5).

In the US, Dana Phillips launched a more polemical challenge to ecocriticism to re-engage with critical theory, stating that:

> The first generation of ecocritics has embraced a curatorial model of literary scholarship and has spurned literary theory, apparently without having reaped the benefits of its close acquaintance. This has made ecocriticism seem overly devotional, and hostile to the intellect at times. (ix)[16]

Phillips also suggested a rethinking of the search for an environmental literature, questioning what the function of a 'literary' criticism that focused on largely *mimetic* – or directly representational – writing might be: "Realistic depiction of the world, of the sort that we can credit as reasonable and uncontroversial, is one of literature's more pedestrian, least artful aspects" (8).[17] In the UK, Dominic Head also broached the question of form, specifically calling for an engagement with the novel: "If ecocriticism is to realise its full potential, it will need to find a way of appropriating novelistic form" ('Ecocriticism and the Novel', 236).

Ecocriticism's second wave ushered in a more reflexive approach that provided the scope to address the complex intertwining of nature, 'Nature', and social and sexual politics, and that, as well as critiquing and reframing the forms that had already come under its scrutiny to reflect a more complex understanding of these interweavings (e.g. 'post-pastoral', 'new nature writing' and 'ecopoetry'),[18] did indeed turn to the novel – and to new novelistic additions to the canon – to explore the ways in which its more self-conscious textuality might articulate the complex entanglement of self and world, social and environmental history.[19]

Two important areas of cultural theory that were already established and well placed to bring to ecocriticism an understanding of the way in which 'nature' had been constructed and deployed to reinforce dominant ideologies of gender, class and race were *ecofeminism* and *post-colonial ecocriticism*. They also represented a necessary corrective to ecocriticism's previous apparently blanket apportioning of human environmental culpability, foregrounding notions of *environmental justice* that recognised the inequitable distribution of environmental benefits and risk among the global population, and challenging the predominantly (white, male) Anglo-American search for the 'environmental imagination'. The ecofeminist Sylvia Mayer points up the common ground between these two social ecological perspectives when she states:

> Together with environmental justice scholars, ecofeminists claim that it is not humankind as such that is responsible for environmental damage. The responsibility lies predominantly with those human beings and social milieus whose position in socioeconomic power relations has enabled them to take political decisions and profit from their results – in many societies largely, but not only, a male elite. (118)

Although some ecofeminists have registered their opposition to the patriarchal domination of both women and the environment by embracing and celebrating the idea of woman as 'closer to nature',[20] others have resisted the implications of biological essentialism contained within this view, dubbing it as "motherhood environmentalism" (Sandilands, xiii). For the latter group, the way to address the inequities of the male/female, culture/nature divide is not by moving privilege from one side of the dichotomy to the other, in what Val Plumwood calls "uncritical reversal" (31), but by interrogating and challenging the very existence of that dichotomy. Plumwood powerfully summarises the way in which the construct of 'nature' has been wielded to legitimate both dualistic ways of thinking and the power relationships they enable.

> The category of nature is a field of multiple exclusion and control, not only of non-humans, but of various groups of humans and aspects of human life which are cast as nature. Thus racism, colonialism and sexism have drawn their conceptual strength from casting sexual, racial and ethnic difference as closer to the animal and the body construed as a sphere of inferiority, as a lesser form of humanity lacking the full measure of rationality or culture. (4)

Like Plumwood, Donna Haraway has also emphasised the necessity of identifying and disrupting the hierarchies typical of western post-Enlightenment thought, which "have all been systemic to the logics and practices of domination of women, people of color, nature, workers, animals" (Haraway, 177). In fact, one of the key contributions of feminist and ecofeminist thought to contemporary ecocriticism is its unsettling of binaries such as culture/nature, male/female, mind/body, civilised/primitive, self/other, reason/matter, human/nature and so on.

Another important legacy of this process has been an apprehension of the complex entanglement of the environment and the body as the site of shared damage. Carolyn Merchant, demonstrating again the links between ecofeminism and *environmental justice* issues, refers to the disproportionate siting of environmental hazards such as landfill, incinerators and toxic waste dumps in underprivileged minority areas. She states, "Women experience the results of toxic dumping on their own bodies (sites of reproduction of the species), in their own homes (sites of the reproduction of daily life), and in their communities and schools (sites of social reproduction)" (161). While this view perhaps retains elements of the identity politics Sandilands critiques – the troubling assumption that "the fact of being a woman is understood to lie at the base of one's experience of ecological degradation" (Sandilands, 5) – it nevertheless foregrounds the notion of an interplay between environment and body, a theme to which I return in discussion of Stacy Alaimo's recent concept of 'trans-corporeality' and the development of the fourth wave of ecocriticism (discussed below).

Post-colonial criticism has also long understood the integral connection between ideological constructions of 'nature' and the oppression and exploitation of colonised peoples and their environments: "Postcolonial studies has come to understand environmental issues not only as central to the projects of European conquest and global domination, but also as inherent in the ideologies of imperialism and racism on which those projects historically – and persistently – depend" (Huggan and Tiffin, 6). The 'persistently' is significant here, since the contemporary neo-liberal era has "intensified assaults on resources" (Nixon, 4) and perpetuated the environmental and social damage suffered by the world's poor in ever-developing forms of *neocolonialism*.

This sense of the continuation of colonialist practices in new guises has had an important impact on ecocriticism, demonstrating the need to reappraise environmentalism itself. In *Varieties of Environmentalism: Essays North and South* (1997), Ramachandra Guha and Juan Martinez Alier use the phrase 'environmentalism of the poor' to distinguish between the 'rich-nation environmentalism' of the northern hemisphere and that of the global South. This reflects the feeling that environmental discourses are all too often "neo-colonial, Western impositions inimical to the resource priorities of the poor in the global South" (Nixon, 4). Even more disturbing is the idea that the further environmental degradation of poor nations might be carried out in order to appease rich nation environmentalists who campaign against the dumping of waste and industrial effluent in their 'own back yard'. Rob Nixon prefaces his book *Slow Violence and the Environmentalism of the Poor* (2011) with a leaked World Bank memo expressing the political expediency of dumping toxic waste in "the lowest wage country" and suggesting that the World Bank should be "encouraging more migration of the dirty industries to the Least Developed Countries" (1). These arguments have challenged ecocritics "to engage in more globally nuanced terms" (DeLoughrey and Handley, 9).

Slow Violence – Towards a Global Ecocriticism

Nixon's book has been extremely influential in drawing attention to the complex interplay of the local and the global in environmental terms. Describing environmental issues such as "climate change, the thawing cryosphere, toxic drift, biomagnification, deforestation, the radioactive aftermaths of wars, acidifying oceans" (2), Nixon suggests that their effects are often hard to track and quantify. He describes this as 'slow violence' – "a violence that occurs gradually and out of sight, a violence of delayed destruction that is dispersed across time and space, an attritional violence that is typically not viewed as violence at all" (2) – and he asks how this can be represented in a global culture that is accustomed to an ever more immediate flow of information and sensation, and that conceptualises violence as "event focused, time bound and body bound" (3). Like Lawrence Buell, he is in search of forms of writing that can adequately convey an environmental message, not this time to foreground the real, material presence of nature as such but to render the invisible visible. For Nixon, the answer lies in the work of writer activists – authors who are fuelled by rage and hunger for redress and whose imaginative writing "can help the unapparent appear, making it accessible and tangible by humanizing drawn-out threats inaccessible to the immediate senses" thus offering us "a different kind of witnessing: of sights unseen" (15). Some post-colonial ecocritics have identified this ability to make the unapparent apparent with the use of the novelistic device of *magic realism*. Upamanyu Pablo Mukherjee, for example, in *Postcolonial*

Environments, finds in Indra Sinha's novel *Animal's People*, which is based on the Bhopal disaster, a magic realism "fit to express the horrors of a reality that threatens to escape the ordinary boundaries of stylistics" (153).

The diffusive temporal and spatial nature of the results of slow violence and the fact that we are now living in a geological epoch informally termed 'the *anthropocene*' (Crutzen and Stoermer) to denote the magnitude of human impact on environmental change, suggest the need for an ecocritical paradigm that is not only more globally nuanced but also more globally embracing – in other words, one which, while sensitive to environmental justice issues at a local level, is also able to register the temporal and planetary implications of anthropogenic environmental destruction in a world where no act or result of damage can be seen as purely local.

A recent issue of *Green Letters* (Spring 2012) devoted to 'Global and Postcolonial Ecologies' employs broadly social ecological, Marxist constructs for discussing the global, in particular Jason Moore's term *world-ecology*, which denotes "the epochal reorganization of world ecology that marked the rise of the capitalist world-economy" (Niblett, 16). For the editor Sharae Deckard, this has enabled a tentative 'worlding' of post-colonial literary criticism which seeks:

> not only to generate an understanding of the political, cultural, and aesthetic *differences* between literary and critical approaches to the environment across multiple national traditions, but *also* to detect structural *homologies* and similarities of concern, particularly in those ways in which literatures respond to the uneven development projects of global capital and their impact on local environments and subjects. (Deckard, 10–11, emphases in original)

Michael Niblett, for example, identifies the literary device of 'irrealism' (of which the magic realism discussed by Mukherjee, above, is a form) as an identifiable homology across literatures globally, used for expressing aspects of the catastrophic upheavals in ecologies brought about by the expansion of global capital that would otherwise defy representation.

Eco-Cosmopolitics and the Third Wave

In another response to this global imperative, Scott Slovic and Joni Adamson hailed the arrival of ecocriticism's third wave in 2009 – a development which "recognises ethnic and national particuliarities and yet transcends ethnic and national boundaries," exploring "all facets of human experience from an environmental viewpoint" (6–7). Broadly speaking, this describes the paradigm of *eco-cosmopolitics*. In *Sense of Place and Sense of Planet: The Environmental Imagination of the Global* (2008), Ursula Heise describes the genesis of this construct in the recuperation of the term 'cosmopolitanism' in a range of fields in the late 1990s, with theorists striving to "model forms of cultural imagination and understanding that reach beyond the nation and around the globe" (6). She discusses this in terms of 'deterritorialisation', stating that "the increasing connectedness of societies around the globe entails the emergence of new forms of culture that are no longer anchored in place" (10). For her, the challenge that this deterritorialisation poses for the environmental imagination is:

> to envision how ecologically-based advocacy on behalf of the non-human world as well as on behalf of greater socioenvironmental justice might be formulated in terms that are

premised no longer as primarily on ties to local places but on ties to territories and systems that are understood to encompass the planet as a whole. (10)

What she proposes is an ecologically inflected "world citizenship" (10). It is in the spirit of this world citizenship that the Universal Declaration of the Rights of Mother Earth was adopted at the World Peoples' Conference on Climate Change in Cochabamba, Bolivia, in 2010. The declaration stresses that we are "all part of Mother Earth, an indivisible, living community of interrelated and interdependent beings with a common destiny" (<http://pwccc.wordpress.com/programa/>). It seeks to recognise the environmental damage wrought by global capitalism and promotes social and environmental justice but within the framework of a biospherical egalitarianism similar to that advocated by deep ecologist Arne Naess.

This advocacy for the non-human extends the notion of *environmental justice* (usually applied to human concerns relating to the environment) to the environment itself, and brings together parties whose interests might previously have been deemed separate. Joni Adamson recounts a protest in Peru in 2006 attended by a "coalition of indigenous peoples, environmentalists and academics" (148) that opposed a mining concession sited at the foot of the mountain Ausangate. The protesters argued that the mountain "should have the right to exist in a proper relationship with its surrounding mountains" (148). For Adamson (citing de la Cadena), the notable aspect of this protest was the way in which those involved, some of whom would not personally subscribe to the notion of a sentient mountain, were able to join together in a commitment to "a politics of nature that included 'disagreement on the definition of nature itself'" (149).

Another reason for these new alliances is a realisation of the ways in which the diffusive effects of 'slow violence' register indiscriminately on the bodies of the human and the non-human, disrupting both the nature/culture binary and human social distinctions. Referencing the work of Stacy Alaimo and Susan Hekman in *Material Feminisms*, Adamson explains:

> An oil spill, for example, studied from a cultural–natural perspective that does not separate the two realms, reveals how a toxin may affect the workers who produce it, the community in which it is produced, and the humans and animals (domesticated and wild) that ingest it. (Adamson, 148)

This notion of movement of matter across bodies in a multiple entanglement leads me to discussion of the fourth wave of ecocriticism.

The Fourth Wave – Material Ecocriticism: Post-Human and Post-Nature

The fourth wave should be regarded as co-existent with rather than superseding the third (or indeed the other strands of ecocriticism) and has only very recently been identified. It is the emergent field of *material ecocriticism*. For Scott Slovic, it is Stacy Alaimo's discussion of 'trans-corporeality' in *Material Feminisms* that "has helped to launch an entire new direction in contemporary ecocriticism" (443). This concept has developed out of early ecofeminist apprehensions of the impacts of environmental justice on the human body and the more recent 'material turn', which has found a powerful voice in the work of feminist thinkers in a range of disciplines, including Karen Barad and Claire Colebrook, as well as Alaimo and Susan Hekman. Alaimo defines trans-corporeality as a construct that deals with "the material interchanges across human bodies, animal bodies, and the wider material world" ('States', 476) and that has engendered "a new materialist and *post-humanist* sense of the human as substantially and perpetually interconnected with the flows of substances and the agencies of environments" ('States', 476).

For Alaimo, this interconnection calls for "rich, complex modes of analysis that travel through the entangled territories of material and discursive, natural and cultural, biological and textual" ('Trans-corporeal', 238). In this, she echoes Bruno Latour's sense in *We Have Never Been Modern* that false distinctions between the worlds of, for example, science and politics, the 'natural' and the social, have restricted our ability adequately to assess our manner of being in the world. Our material selves cannot be separated from "networks that are simultaneously economic, political, cultural, scientific, and substantial" (Alaimo, 'States', 476). Apprehending the extent of these entanglements challenges us epistemologically and ethically:

> Emphasizing the material interconnections of human corporeality with the more-than-human world, and at the same time acknowledging that material agency necessitates more capacious epistemologies, allows us to forge ethical and political positions that can contend with numerous late-twentieth-century/early-twenty-first-century realities in which "human" and "environment" can by no means be considered as separate: environmental health, environmental justice, the traffic in toxins, and genetic engineering, to name a few. (Alaimo, 'Trans-corporeal', 238)

This paragraph foregrounds three key issues of material ecocriticism. First is the premise that there is a shared materiality between the human and non-human world that renders obsolete the distinctions between human and environment, moving beyond the construct of 'nature' altogether; second is the idea that all of this shared matter has agency; and third is the ethical and political challenges the complexity and hybridity of these material interminglings suggest. In the paragraphs below, I discuss each of these issues in turn, detailing their ongoing impacts on current ecocritical theory. Returning to Timothy Clark's outlining of one of the challenges to ecocriticism, cited in my introduction, this paradigm is very much an example of ecocritical tools "being remade even in the process of use" (xiii).

Shared Materiality and Post-Humanism

The notion of shared materiality has initially been seized on in ecocriticism to take forward and develop some ecocritical formulations of *post-humanism* in a broadly deep ecological spirit. Post-humanism de-centres and interrogates the human, challenging the construct of the Great Chain of Being, which places man at its head. Cary Wolfe states that "the 'human', we now know, is not now and never was itself" (*Zoontologies*, xiii). In a similar vein, Jacques Derrida has questioned the construct of the 'animal'. His neologism *animot* (which plays on the French homophones 'maux' of 'animaux' [animals] and 'mot' [word]) is designed to break down the traditional semantic boundary between human and animal and encompass "the heterogeneous multiplicity of the living" (399) in which man is just one of many species. There is, in fact, a strand of *post-humanist* enquiry specifically dedicated to 'animal studies', and a degree of tension exists between this strand's exploration of the sentience, subjectivity and rights of non-human animals and ecological perspectives that see value residing in an ecosystem as a whole rather than in individual species or, indeed, individual animals. For Timothy Clark, "there is a real, intractable dispute here" (181), particularly in the apprehension that even apparently biocentric approaches may mask an inherent anthropocentrism.[21] Cary Wolfe contends that, in general, academic discourse remains "locked within an unexamined framework of *speciesism*" (*Animal Rites*, 1, emphasis in original), pointing up one of the fault lines of post-humanism: "most of us remain humanists to the core, even as we claim for our work an epistemological break with humanism itself" (1).

In an early discussion of the implications of *post-humanist* thought for ecocriticism, Louise Westling borrows Derrida's term, formulating the phrase '*animot* post-humanism'. This attempts to blend the notion of decentring the human with an exploration of animal subjectivity and emphasises our imbrication in the "matrix of earth's life" ('Literature', 26). Developing ideas drawn from Maurice Merleau-Ponty and David Abram, Westling suggests that this imbrication is revealed to us through a *phenomenological* immersion in the world. She makes a deliberate distinction between *animot* post-humanism and what she terms techno– or cyborg post-humanism,[22] believing that the latter is less relevant to ecocriticism since it deals in the concept of the *transhuman* – the perfectible, technological human that is able to surpass its environment and its own body – a concept that perpetuates damaging dualistic modes of thinking.

For Serenella Iovino, an understanding of the shared materiality between human and non-human proposed by the new materialists makes the imbrication Westling describes all the more tangible, dissolving the human/nature binary and enabling an "ecological horizontalism and an extended moral imagination" (Iovino, 'Material', 52) – in other words, reaching, in part, towards the biospherical egalitarianism of deep ecology.

The Agency of Matter

A second key theme of material ecocriticism is the notion that matter is an agentic force, again removing one of the distinctions that has traditionally been drawn between human and non-human and reinforcing the idea of horizontality rather than hierarchy. Matter is seen as manifesting an inherent creative power, a vitality "which is not that of a static being but of a generative becoming" (Iovino, 'Material', 53), establishing a "multiply-tiered ontology" in which "there is no definitive break between sentient and nonsentient entities or between material and spiritual phenomena" (Coole and Frost, 10).

In *biosemiotic* and *ecosemiotic* perspectives, such as those advanced by the philosopher and ecocritic Wendy Wheeler (*The Whole Creature*) and the ecophilosopher David Abram (*Becoming Animal*), one of the ways matter reveals its agency is through its production and embodiment of signs that invest the non-human world with its own systems of signification and meaning. A biosemiotic perspective also helps to bridge the culture/nature divide. In this paradigm, culture, like language, is an emanation of our material being. Wheeler describes culture and nature as "inextricably intertwined and co-dependent and co-evolving" (*Whole Creature*, 41), and Iovino talks of nature and culture as a "circulating system" ('Stories', 454) that should better be termed (following Donna Haraway's lead) "natureculture" ('Stories', 454).

So far, this is a fairly harmonious picture of interrelationship and shared qualities – a broadly deep ecological notion of "agential kinships" (Iovino, 'Material', 66). However, as Iovino and others' ongoing theorisations recognise, the implications of shared materiality also involve a more disorientating hybridity, for example in the traffic in toxins and genetic engineering Alaimo mentions, where the complex entanglements of human and non-human and their diffusive effects present ontological and ethical dilemmas. For Bruno Latour, the combination of the human and its technology sets in motion a mutual expansion of agentic potential where all of the component parts, both human and non-human – the 'actants' – "are in the process of exchanging competencies, offering one another new goals, new possibilities, new functions" (*Pandora's Hope*, 182). But these new functions are unpredictable, with matter at times evolving "deviant agencies" (Alaimo, *Bodily*, 139) as it manifests its creative power and crosses into bodies and environments.

'Thing Power': Ethical Challenges

Jane Bennett, in *Vibrant Matter: a political ecology of things*, stresses that the "onto-story" (4) of shared materiality she proposes is not one of unproblematic interrelationship: "in contrast to some versions of deep ecology, my monism posits neither a smooth harmony of parts nor a diversity unified by a common spirit" (ix). In fact, the complex entanglement of human and non-human, biology and politics renders the terms deep and social ecology as redundant as 'nature'. To demonstrate the more disturbing manifestations of what she calls "thing power" (2), she cites Robert Sullivan's description of a New Jersey 'garbage hill' outside Manhattan, which powerfully evokes the physical agency of the dump, as toxic elements mingle and combine, warm and fresh, ready to seep into the groundwater.[23] This is an ongoing agency which is non-human, and yet whose genesis is in the detritus of human consumerism.

Similarly, the image below not only provides further evidence of the temporal and spatial reach of 'slow violence' but also graphically illustrates trans-corporeality in action, as man-made substances find new agential roles. Chris Jordan, the photographer, explains:

> On Midway Atoll, a remote cluster of islands more than 2000 miles from the nearest continent, the detritus of our mass consumption surfaces in an astonishing place: inside the stomachs of thousands of dead baby albatrosses. The nesting chicks are fed lethal quantities of plastic by their parents, who mistake the floating trash for food as they forage over the vast polluted Pacific Ocean. http://www.chrisjordan.com/gallery/midway/#about

For Iovino, trans-corporeality entails a hybridity that blurs boundaries and distinctions such that it becomes less and less possible to differentiate between human and non-human agency. Referencing the work of feminist science critic Karen Barad, who devised the term "post-humanist performativity" (Barad, 120), she describes it as a process "where the 'post-human' replaces the human/nonhuman dualism and overcomes it in a more dialectic and complex dimension" ('Stories', 459). While this is undoubtedly the case, as the Midway image also graphically exposes, these ongoing expansions of agential possibility often begin with the technicity of the human, perhaps suggesting a need to engage with the implications of the cyborg post-humanism rejected by Westling

Figure 1 © Chris Jordan, *Midway: Message from the Gyre*, used with permission.

and to explore further what Cary Wolfe describes as "the embodiment and the embed-dedness of the human being in not just its biological but also its technological world" (*What is Posthumanism?* xv).

This is the point at which ecocriticism now stands theoretically – investigating the complex ontological, epistemological and ethical implications of this multiple embed-dedness. For Bennett, "the hope is that the [onto-]story will enhance receptivity to the impersonal life that surrounds and infuses us, will generate a more subtle awareness of the complicated web of dissonant connections between bodies, and will enable wiser interventions into that ecology" (4). Other thinkers with less interventionist perspec-tives are more sceptical of the notion that it is possible for a theory to offer solutions to ecological problems. John M. Meyer, in his 2001 work *Political Nature: Environmentalism and the Interpretation of Western Thought*, warned against what he saw as the common and misplaced desire in environmentalist thinkers and writers to develop a new "world-view" that could form the basis of an alternative "relationship between humanity and the rest of nature" (22). In a more recent essay, Hannes Bergthaller, drawing on Niklas Luhmann's work on social systems theory and second-order cybernetics, stresses that modern human society is divided into *autopoietic* functional units (such as law, politics, science, religion and the economy), each of which "creates its own reality", and none of which "is in a position to control the operations of any of the others" ('Cybernetics and Social Systems Theory', 225). The implication for ecocriticism is that it cannot hope to change society as a whole but should recognise its limitations in terms of praxis and focus instead on interrogating the nature – and blind spots – of environmentalism itself.[24] Timothy Morton's 'ecological thought', which, conversely, denotes an apprehension of the complex *interrelation* of all things,[25] nevertheless represents a similar challenge. While not necessarily eschewing "the political radicalisms that seek to create new forms of col-lectivity out of the crisis of climate disruption," Morton insists that we must at all times apply "a rigorous and remorseless theoretical radicalism that opens our minds to where we are, about the fact that we're here" (*The Ecological Thought*, 104). These are provoca-tive interventions and useful reminders that ecocriticism should continue to critique its own assumptions and doctrines in the course of its 'earth-centred' explorations.

The Future of Ecocriticism – Despair, Excitement and 'Slow Reading'

In its short history, ecocriticism has progressed from its initial relatively uncritical endorsement of non-fiction nature-writing to its current engagement with a wide range of cultural forms, theoretical sophistication and pluriform status. The Association for the Study of Literature and Environment now has ten affiliate organisations worldwide with more under discussion; there are a large number of ecocritical and environmental journals in existence including *Ecozon@*, *The Journal of Ecocriticism*, *Indian Journal of Ecocriticism* and *Studies in Ecocriticism* as well as *Interdisciplinary Studies in Literature and Environment* and *Green Letters*; and ecocriticism is the focus of a host of international conferences. However, it continues to be a movement that questions its own function. In a recent exchange in successive issues of the *Journal of Ecocriticism*, two different perspectives were aired on the effectiveness and future of ecocriticism. William Major and Andrew McMurry speak of a "desperate optimism" (1) in the face of what they see as our species' "elaborate and protracted endgame" (1). They doubt the value of their work (and that of ecocriticism as a whole, by implication) and feel that the movement has become enmeshed in institutional frameworks. Somehow the original mission to reinstate the referent has been diverted, the commitment to environmental praxis dissipated. Nevertheless, "we go on, of course, even in the face of a difficult future. After all, what choice do we have?" (7).

In the subsequent issue, however, Roman Bartosch and Greg Garrard come back with a more upbeat rejoinder. Resisting what they see as the "apocalypticism" (2) of Major and McMurry, they speak of a "risky, exciting and unprecedented future" (5)[26] and, at the same time, express a refusal to be hurried by the urgency of environmental issues: "we believe that the contribution of ecocriticism is inherently and valuably gradual: making us think anew about the world, nature, and the place of the human animal" (2). As their methodology they propose close, slow reading, reflecting "the reticent, obdurate fragility of literature, to which critics ought to bear patient witness even to the crack of doom" (5) and echoing (at least in part) Morton's call to action in *Ecology without Nature* to decelerate our thinking and, through painstaking attentiveness, to identify anomalies and paradoxes in received opinion in order to "go against the grain of dominant normative ideas about nature, but to do so in the name of sentient beings suffering under catastrophic environmental conditions" (12).

In the last two decades, ecocriticism has shown itself more than able to respond to the challenge of engaging with critical theory. It has established 'environmentality' as a permanent concern in the humanities, fostered a broader understanding of ecological responsibility and environmental justice on a global scale' and emphasised our complex imbrication in a material world that has taken us 'post-human' and 'post-nature' but left us with the exciting challenge of continuing to untangle the coordinates of those states. Counter-intuitive though it may seem in the face of accelerating environmental degradation, perhaps Bartosch and Garrard are right. Perhaps the time has now come for a reinvigoration of slow and close reading, which, whether in the hope of generating environmental praxis or in a more purely investigative mode, applies these new paradigms in full-length engagements with cultural forms, interrogating from every possible angle the 'imagings' that reflect and influence our ongoing modes of being in the world.

Notes

* Correspondence: Institute of Humanities and Creative Arts, University of Worcester, Henwick Grove, Worcester, Worcestershire, United Kingdom, WR2 6AJ. Email: p.marland@worc.ac.uk

1 Richard Kerridge, though expressing a preference for 'ecocriticism' himself, suggests that 'environmental criticism' is considered by some to imply a more appropriate academic distance from the broader environmental movement (cited in Ramos-Pérez).

2 For example, some early articulations of ecocriticism were based on a view of ecological harmony and equilibrium that has now been superseded by 'postequilibrium' views. Daniel Botkin's book *Discordant Harmonies: A New Ecology for the Twenty-First Century* was particularly influential in introducing a more discordant, dynamic and mutable model to ecocriticism. In this postequilibrium ecology, "The Earth is perhaps better seen as a process rather than an object" (Garrard, *Ecocriticism*, 204).

3 Although important work has been carried out in tracing the beginnings of ecological thought to earlier periods – for example, Richard Grove's exploration of environmental awareness relating to colonial practices in *Green Imperialism: Colonial Expansion, Tropical Island Edens and the Origins of Environmentalism, 1600–1860*: "As colonial expansion proceeded, the environmental experiences of Europeans and indigenous peoples living at the colonial periphery played a steadily more dominant and dynamic part in the constructions of new European evaluations of nature and in the growing awareness of the destructive impact of European economic activity on the peoples and environments of the newly 'discovered' and colonised lands" (3); Jonathan Bate's (and others') discussion of ecological thought in the work of the Romantic poets; and John Parham's detailed study of the poet Gerard Manley Hopkins, *Green Man Hopkins*, which develops a theory of the Victorian ecological imagination.

4 These proto-ecocritical works include Leo Marx's *The Machine in the Garden: Technology and the Pastoral Ideal in American Culture* (1964), Raymond Williams' *The Country and the City* (1973), Joseph Meeker's *The Comedy of Survival* (1974) and William Ruekert's 1978 essay 'Literature and Ecology: An Experiment in Ecocriticism' (which is often cited as the first use of the term 'ecocriticism').

5 Richard Kerridge hails ecocriticism as "environmentalism's overdue move beyond science, geography and social science into 'the humanities'" (*Writing the Environment*, 5).

6 As Axel Goodbody and Kate Rigby point out in their introduction to *Ecocritical Theory: New European Approaches*, the 'rejection' of critical theory by early ecocritics was its own "theoretical moment" (1).

7 As Barry notes, this quotation from Derrida's *Grammatology* is often taken out of context "to justify an extreme textualism, whereby it is held that all reality is linguistic, so that there can be no meaningful talk of a 'real' world, which exists without question outside language" (68).

8 Though as Garrard observes, this phrase inadvertently points up the cultural construction of even the most apparently 'empirical' information, the 'ozone hole' in fact being a metaphor for the phenomenon of ozone depletion.

9 Roman Bartosch and Greg Garrard, for example, contend that "Ecocriticism must resist the instrumentalising of literature *even in its own interests*" (2, emphasis in original).

10 In fact, some first-wave ecocritics chose to reject certain conventions of critical discourse altogether and to present their work instead in the form of *narrative scholarship*, which brings autobiographical accounts of interaction with the natural world into responses to literature. This has been characterised by Michael P. Cohen as the "praise song school" of ecocriticism (21).

11 This phrase was devised by David Abram (*The Spell of the Sensuous*) to unsettle hierarchical conceptualisations that place man above nature, and to reinforce a deep ecological sense of the inherent value of the non-human.

12 The ecocentrism espoused by deep ecologists:

> regards the question of our proper place in the rest of nature as logically prior to the question of what are the most appropriate social and political arrangements for human communities. That is social and political questions must proceed from, or at least be consistent with, an adequate determination of this more fundamental question. (Eckersley, 28)

13   In an introduction to the 1991 edition of his influential work *The Ecology of Freedom*, Murray
     Bookchin made the following summary of his views on the sources of our environmental
     dislocation:

> I tried to point out that these problems originate in a hierarchical, class, and today, competitive
> capitalism system that nourishes view of the natural world as a mere agglomeration of "resources"
> for human production and consumption. This social system is especially rapacious. It
> has projected the domination of human by human into an ideology that "man" is destined to
> dominate "Nature". (65)

14   It has also, on occasion, been accused of misanthropy. One of the eight points of Arne Naess
     and George Sessions' *Platform for Deep Ecology* (1984) is the necessity for a "substantial
     decrease in human population" (cited in Denton, 80). This point has sometimes been inter-
     preted in anti-humanist ways, for example the apparent welcoming of epidemic disease and
     famine as forms of population control by early Earth First activists (Denton, 87). However,
     other deep ecologists have firmly rebuffed accusations of anti-humanism and stressed that
     "humans are just as entitled to live and blossom as any other species, *provided* they do so in a
     way that is sensitive to the needs of other human individuals, communities and cultures and
     other life-forms generally" (Eckersley, 56, emphasis in original), also emphasising their rec-
     ognition of the fact that not all humans are equally implicated in environmental damage. For
     Greg Garrard, the problem of human over-population is one which ecocriticism continues
     to fail adequately to address ('Review of 2010').

15   John Clark, in particular, gives a complex and nuanced reading of social ecology in his essay
     'A Social Ecology'.

16   This seems a particularly reductive reading of first-wave ecocritics – ignoring, for example, Buell's
     consciousness from the start of the power of cultural construction and the specific engagement of
     certain early ecocritics with contemporary theory – for example Sue-Ellen Campbell's essay
     'The Land and Language of Desire: Where Deep Ecology and Poststructuralism Meet' in
     The Ecocriticism Reader.

17   Again, this summation does not do justice to the range of voices, complexity and, indeed,
     artfulness involved in examples of that non-fiction writing.

18   Terry Gifford devised the term post-pastoral to denote an environmentally and socially aware
     version of pastoral:

> There are six aspects to Gifford's post-pastoral: first, an awe in response to the natural world; second,
> the recognition that creative and destructive forces coexist in nature; third, the realisation that inner
> human nature is illuminated by its relationship to external nature; fourth, a simultaneous awareness
> of the cultural constructions of nature, and of nature as culture; fifth, a conviction that human con-
> sciousness should produce environmental conscience; and sixth, the realisation that environmental
> exploitation is generated by the same mind-set that results in social exploitation. (Head, *Modern
> British Fiction*, 193).

'New Nature' writers aim to "see with a scientific eye and to write with literary effect" (Cowley, 9).
Ecopoetry is broadly described by Scott Bryson as poetry that embodies an ecocentric stance, a
humility in its relation to the non-human and a distrust of hyperrationality.

19   Even before these challenges were being laid down, work was emerging on both sides of the
     Atlantic that engaged with these issues, setting the tone for the second wave. Louise Westling, in
     The Green Breast of the New World (1996) interrogates the presence of gender in the treatment of
     landscape and environment in 20th century fiction; David Mazel, in *American Literary
     Environmentalism* (2000) delves into the ideological construction of wilderness and its implication
     in colonialist endeavour; and Richard Kerridge, in 'Ecological Hardy' (2001) explores the ways
     in which Thomas Hardy is concerned with "the multiplicity of uses – material, cultural and
     emotional – that human beings have for the natural environment" (126).

20   Timothy Clark identifies aspects of this perspective in L. Elizabeth Waller's ecofeminist reading
      of Virginia Woolf's *The Waves* in her essay 'Writing the Real: Virginia Woolf and an Ecology of
      Language' in which "Woolf's compositional method is seen to open a usually blocked path to a
      supposedly lost and unalienated human nature, located in the female body" (Clark, 116).

21   Timothy Clark, citing the work of Tom Regan, gives the example of an ecological restoration
      scheme in the Galápagos islands that involved the culling of feral goats, questioning what the
      biocentric commitment of ecologists might be in a similar situation that required the culling of
      human animals (181).

22   She associates Donna Haraway with this cyborg post-humanism, perhaps missing the point of
      Haraway's self-confessedly "ironic political myth" (Haraway, 191). Haraway uses the figure of the
      cyborg to create a focus for post-human thought by positing a radical being in which the bounda-
      ries of human and animal and machine have been erased. The cyborg, she believes, is a construct
      through which we can properly interrogate the human.

23   Robert Sullivan's description of a New Jersey garbage dump:

> There had been rain the night before, so it wasn't long before I found a little leachate seep, a black ooze
> trickling down the slope of the hill, an expresso of refuse. In a few hours this stream would find its way
> down into the ... groundwater of the Meadowlands; it would mingle with toxic streams ... But in this
> moment, here at its birth, ... this little seep was pure pollution, a pristine stew of oil and grease, of
> cyanide and arsenic, of cadmium, chromium, copper, lead, nickel, silver, mercury, and zinc. I touched
> this fluid – my fingertip was a bluish caramel colour – and it was warm and fresh. (Sullivan, 1998, cited
> in Bennett, 6)

24   Bergthaller states:

> Only to the extent that ecocriticism is something other than the academic wing of the environmental
> movement can it render that movement a service which is perhaps more valuable than general conscious-
> ness-raising or the recruitment of new personnel. ('Cybernetics', 227)

25   This has much in common with the insights of new materialism – Morton's idea of the "mesh"
      (*Ecological*, 8) echoing the imbrication discussed above, and his "hyperobjects" (19) (such as
      plutonium and styrofoam) exemplifying the disturbing agentic potential and slow violence of the
      products of human/non-human entanglement.

26   For Morton, it is a future which has, in a sense, already arrived. In a passage that provides a cor-
      rective to the elegiac tone of much environmental writing, he states:

> Environmentalism is often apocalyptic. It warns of, and wards off, the end of the world. The title of
> Rachel Carson's *Silent Spring* says it all. But things aren't like that: the end of the world has already
> happened. We sprayed the DDT. We exploded the nuclear bombs. We changed the climate. This is
> what it looks like after the end of the world. Today is not the end of history. We're living at the begin-
> ning of history. The ecological thought thinks forward. It knows that we have only just begun, like
> someone waking up from a dream. (*Ecological*, 98)

Works Cited

Abram, David. *The Spell of the Sensuous*. New York: Vintage, 1996.

Abram, David. *Becoming Animal: An Earthly Cosmology*. New York: Pantheon Books, 2010.

Adamson, Joni. 'Indigenous Literatures, Multinaturalism, and *Avatar*: The Emergence of Indigenous
    Cosmopolitics.' *American Literary History* 24.1 (2012): 143–162.

Adamson, Joni and Scott Slovic. 'Guest Editors' Introduction. The Shoulders We Stand on: An
    Introduction to Ethnicity and Ecocriticsm.' *MELUS* 34.2 *Ethnicity and Ecocriticism* (2009):
    5–24.

Alaimo, Stacy. 'Trans-corporeal Feminisms and the Ethical Space of Nature.' *Material Feminisms*. Eds. Stacy Alaimo and Susan Hekman. Bloomington, IN: Indiana University Press, 2008. 237–264.

Alaimo, Stacy. *Bodily Natures: Science, Environment, and the Material Self*. Bloomington, IN: Indiana University Press, 2010.

Alaimo, Stacy. 'States of Suspension: Trans-corporeality at Sea.' *Interdisciplinary Studies in Literature and Environment* 19.3 (2012): 476–493.

Alaimo, Stacy and Susan Hekman. Eds. *Material Feminisms*. Bloomington, IN: Indiana University Press, 2008.

Barad, Karen. 'Posthumanist Performativity: Towards an Understanding of How Matter Comes to Matter.' *Material Feminisms*. Eds. Stacy Alaimo and Susan Hekman. Bloomington, IN: Indiana University Press, 2008. 120–157.

Barry, Peter. *Beginning Theory: An Introduction to Literary and Cultural Theory*. 3rd ed. Manchester: Manchester University Press, 2009.

Bartosch, Roman and Greg Garrard. 'The Function of Criticism: A Response to William Major and Andrew McMurray's Editorial.' *Journal of Ecocriticism* 5.1 (2013): 1–6.

Bate, Jonathan. *Romantic Ecology: Wordsworth and the Environmental Tradition*. London: Routledge, 1991.

Bate, Jonathan. *The Song of the Earth*. Basingstoke and Oxford: Picador, 2000.

Bennett, Jane. *Vibrant Matter: a Political Ecology of Things*. Durham, NC and London: Duke University Press, 2010.

Bergthaller, Hannes. 'Cybernetics and Social Systems Theory.' *Ecocritical Theory: New European Approaches*. Eds. Axel Goodbody and Kate Rigby. Charlottesville and London: University of Virginia Press, 2011. 217–229.

Bergthaller, Hannes. 'What is Ecocriticism?' 27 April 2013. [Online]. Retrieved from: http://www.easlce.eu/about-us/what-is-ecocriticism/

Bookchin, Murray. *The Ecology of Freedom: The Emergence and Dissolution of Hierarchy*. Oakland, CA: AK Press, 2005.

Botkin, Daniel. *Discordant Harmonies: A New Ecology for the Twenty-First Century*. Oxford: Oxford University Press, 1990.

Bryson, J. Scott. Ed. *Ecopoetry: A Critical Introduction*. Salt Lake City: University of Utah Press, 2002.

Buell, Lawrence. *The Environmental Imagination: Thoreau, Nature Writing, and the Formation of American Culture*. Cambridge, MA: Harvard University Press, 1995.

Buell, Lawrence. *The Future of Environmental Criticism: Environmental Crisis and Literary Imagination*. Malden, Oxford and Victoria: Blackwell Publishing, 2005.

Campbell, Sue Ellen. 'The Land and Language of Desire: Where Deep Ecology and Post-Structuralism Meet.' *The Ecocriticism Reader*. Ed. Cheryl Glotfelty. Athens and London: The University of Georgia Press, 1996.

Carson, Rachel. *Silent Spring*. London: Penguin Books, 2000.

Clark, John. 'A Social Ecology'. 2000. [Online]. Retrieved on 15 Feb. 2013 from: http://theanarchistlibrary.org/pdfs/a4/John_Clark__A_Social_Ecology_a4.pdf

Clark, Timothy. *The Cambridge Introduction to Literature and the Environment*. Cambridge: Cambridge University Press, 2011.

Cohen, Michael P. 'Blues in the Green: Ecocriticism under Critique.' *Environmental History* 9.1 (2004): 9–36.

Coole, Diana and Samantha Frost. Eds. *New Materialisms: Ontology, Agency, and Politics*. Durham, NC: Duke University Press, 2010.

Coupe, Lawrence. Ed. *The Green Studies Reader: From Romanticism to Ecocriticism*. London and New York: Routledge, 2000.

Cowley, Jason. 'Editor's Letter: The new nature writing.' *The New Nature Writing, Granta* 102 (2008): 7–12.

Crutzen, Paul J., and Eugene F. Stoermer. 'The "Anthropocene."' *Global Change Newsletter* 41 (2000): 17–18.

Deckard, Sharae. 'Editorial.' *Green Letters: Studies in Ecocriticism* 16 (2012): 5–15.

DeLoughrey, Elizabeth and George B. Handley. Eds. *Postcolonial Ecologies: Literatures of the Environment*. Oxford: Oxford University Press, 2011.

Denton, Ted. 'Deep Ecology.' *The Sage Handbook of Environment and Society*. Eds. Jules Pretty, Andrew S. Ball, Ted Benton, Julia S. Guivant, David R. Lee, David Orr, Max J. Pfeffer and Hugh Ward. London and New Delhi: Sage Publications Ltd., 2007. 78–91.

Derrida, Jacques and David Wills. 'The Animal that Therefore I am (More to Follow).' *Critical Inquiry* 28.2 (2002): 369–418.

Eckersley, Robyn. *Environmentalism and Political Theory: Toward an Ecocentric Approach*. Albany, NY: State University of New York Press, 1992.

Gaard, Greta. 'New Directions for Ecofeminism: Toward a More Feminist Ecocriticism.' *Interdisciplinary Studies in Literature and Environment* 17.4 (2010): 643–665.

Garrard, Greg. *Ecocriticism*. 2nd ed. London and New York: Routledge, 2012.

Garrard, Greg. 'Ecocriticism Review of 2010' 12 Feb. 2013. [Online]. Retrieved from: http://www.academia.edu/1522099/Ecocriticism_Review_of_2010

Gifford, Terry. *Green Voices: Understanding Contemporary Nature Poetry*. Manchester: Manchester University Press, 1995.

Gifford, Terry. *Pastoral*. London and New York: Routledge, 1999.

Glotfelty, Cheryll and Harold Fromm. Eds. *The Ecocriticism Reader: Landmarks in Literary Ecology*. Athens, GA: University of Georgia Press, 1996.

Goodbody, Axel and Kate Rigby. Eds. *Ecocritical Theory: New European Approaches*. Charlottesville and London: University of Virginia Press, 2011.

Grove, Richard H. *Green Imperialism: Colonial Expansion, Tropical Island Edens and the Origins of Environmentalism, 1600–1860*. Cambridge: Cambridge University Press, 1995.

Guha, Ramachandra and Juan Martinez-Alier. *Varieties of Environmentalism: Essays North and South*. London and New York: Routledge (Earthscan), 1997.

Haraway, Donna. *Simians, Cyborgs and Women: The Reinvention of Nature*. New York and London: Routledge, 1991.

Head, Dominic. 'Ecocriticism and the Novel.' *The Green Studies Reader: From Romanticism to Ecocriticism*. Ed. Laurence Coupe. London and New York: Routledge, 2000. 235–242.

Head, Dominic. *The Cambridge Introduction to Modern British Fiction, 1950–2000*. Cambridge: Cambridge University Press, 2002.

Heise, Ursula K. *Sense of Place and Sense of Planet: The Environmental Imagination of the Global*. Oxford: Oxford University Press, 2008.

Huggan, Graham and Helen Tiffin. *Postcolonial Ecocriticism: Literature, Animals, Environment*. Abingdon and New York: Routledge, 2010.

Iovino, Serenella. 'Material Ecocriticism. Matter, Text, and Posthuman Ethics.' *Literature, Ecology, Ethics*. Eds. Timo Müller and Michael Sauter. Heidelberg: Winter Verlag, 2012a.

Iovino, Serenella. 'Stories from the Thick of Things: Introducing Material Ecocriticism' [part of Serenella Iovino and Serpil Oppermann 'Theorizing Material Ecocriticism: A Diptych'] *Interdisciplinary Studies in Literature and Environment* 19.3 (2012b): 448–475.

Kerridge, Richard. 'Ecological Hardy.' Eds. Karla Armbruster and Kathleen R. Wallace. *Beyond Nature Writing: Expanding the Boundaries of Ecocriticism*. Virginia: The University Press of Virginia, 2001. 126–143.

Kerridge, Richard and Neil Sammells. Eds. *Writing the Environment*. London and New York: Zed Books Ltd., 1998.

Latour, Bruno. *We Have Never Been Modern*. Trans. Catherine Porter. Cambridge, MA: Harvard University Press, 1993.

Latour, Bruno. *Pandora's Hope: Essays on the Reality of Science Studies*. Cambridge, MA: Harvard University Press, 1999.

Liu, Alan. *Wordsworth: The Sense of History*. Stanford, CA: Stanford University Press, 1989.

Major, William and Andrew McMurry. 'Introduction: The Function of Ecocriticism; or, Ecocriticism, What Is It Good For?' *The Journal of Ecocriticism* 4.2 (2012): 1–7.

Marx, Leo. *The Machine in the Garden: Technology and the Pastoral Ideal in American Culture*. Oxford: Oxford University Press, 1964.

Mayer, Sylvia. 'Ecofeminism, Literary Studies and the Humanities.' *Nature in Literary and Cultural Studies: Transatlantic Conversations on Ecocriticism*. Eds. Catrin Gersdorf and Sylvia Mayer. Amsterdam: Rodopi, 2006. 113–128.

Mazel, David. *American Literary Environmentalism*. Athens, GA: University of Georgia Press, 2000.

Meeker, Joseph. *The Comedy of Survival: Studies in Literary Ecology*. New York: Scribner, 1974.

Merchant, Carolyn. *Earthcare: Women and the Environment*. New York: Routledge, 1995.

Meyer, John M. *Political Nature: Environmentalism and the Interpretation of Western Thought.* Massachusetts: MIT Press, 2001.

Moore, Jason W. 'The Modern World System as Environmental History? Ecology and the Rise of Capitalism.' *Theory and Society* 32.3 (2003): 307–377.

Morton, Timothy. *Ecology Without Nature: Rethinking Environmental Aesthetics.* Cambridge, MA: Harvard University Press, 2007.

Morton, Timothy. *The Ecological Thought.* Cambridge, MA: Harvard University Press, 2010.

Mukherjee, Pablo Upamanyu. *Postcolonial Environments: Nature, Culture and the Contemporary Indian Novel in English.* Basingstoke and New York: Palgrave Macmillan, 2010.

Naess, Arne. 'The shallow and the deep, long-range ecology movement. A summary.' *Inquiry* 16.1 (1973): 95–100.

Niblett, Michael. 'World-Economy, World-Ecology, World-Literature.' *Green Letters: Studies in Ecocriticism Global and Postcolonial Ecologies* 16 (2012): 15–31.

Nixon, Rob. *Slow Violence and the Environmentalism of the Poor.* Harvard: Harvard University Press, 2011.

Parham, John. 'The Poverty of Ecocritical Theory: E.P. Thompson and the British Perspective.' *New Formations* 64 (2008): 25–38.

Parham, John. *Green Man Hopkins: Poetry and the Victorian Ecological Imagination.* Amsterdam and New York: Rodopi, 2010.

Parham, John. '"Two-Ply": Discordant Nature and English Landscape in Alice Oswald's *Dart*.' *Revista Canaria de Estudios Ingleses* 64 (2012): 111–129.

Phillips, Dana. *The Truth of Ecology: Nature, Culture, and Literature in America.* Oxford: Oxford University Press, 2003.

Plumwood, Val. *Feminism and the Mastery of Nature.* London: Routledge, 1993.

Ramos-Pérez, Isabel. 'Interview with Richard Kerridge.' *Ecozon@* 3.2 (2012): 135–144.

Rigby, Kate. 'Ecocriticism' *Introducing Criticism at the 21st Century.* Ed. Julian Wolfreys. Edinburgh: Edinburgh University Press, 2002.

Rueckert, William. 'Literature and Ecology: An Experiment in Ecocriticism.' *The Ecocriticism Reader: Landmarks in Literary Ecology.* Eds. Cheryl Glotfelty and Harold Fromm. Athens, GA: University of Georgia Press, 1996. 105–123.

Sandilands, Catriona. *The Good-Natured Feminist: Ecofeminism and the Quest for Democracy.* Minneapolis, MN: University of Minnesota Press, 1999.

Slovic, Scott. 'Editor's Note.' *Interdisciplinary Studies in Literature and Environment* 19.3 (Summer 2012): 443–4.

Snyder, Gary. *The Practice of the Wild.* Berkeley, CA: Counterpoint, 1999.

Soper, Kate. *What is Nature? Culture, Politics and the non-Human.* Oxford: Blackwell, 1995.

Universal Declaration of the Rights of Mother Earth. 2010. [Online]. Retrieved on 15 Feb. 2013 from: http://pwccc. wordpress.com/programa/.

Waller, L. Elizabeth. 'Writing the Real: Virginia Woolf and an Ecology of Language.' *New Essays in Ecofeminist Literary Criticism.* Ed. Glynis Carr. Cranbury, NJ: Associated University Presses, 2000. 137–156.

Westling, Louise. *The Green Breast of the New World: Landscape, Gender, and American Fiction.* Athens, GA: University of Georgia Press, 1996.

Westling, Louise. 'Literature, the Environment and the Question of the Posthuman.' *Nature in Literary and Cultural Studies: Transatlantic Conversations on Ecocriticism.* Eds. Catrin Gersdorf and Sylvia Mayer. Amsterdam: Rodopi, 2006. 25–49.

Wheeler, Wendy. *The Whole Creature: Complexity, Biosemiotics and the Evolution of Culture.* London: Lawrence and Wishart, 2006.

Wheeler, Wendy and Hugh Dunkerly. 'Introduction.' *New Formations* 64 (2008): 7–15.

Williams, Raymond. *The Country and the City.* London: Hogarth Press, 1985.

Wolfe, Cary. Ed. *Zoontologies: The Question of the Animal.* Minneapolis, MN: University of Minnesota Press, 2003a.

Wolfe, Cary. *Animal Rites: American Culture, the Discourse of Species, and Posthumanist Theory.* Chicago: University of Chicago Press, 2003b.

Wolfe, Cary. *What is Posthumanism?* Minneapolis, MN: University of Minnesota Press, 2010.

CHAPTER 8

Eating Things: Food, Animals, and Other Life Forms in Lewis Carroll's *Alice* Books

Michael Parrish Lee

Michel Parrish Lee teaches nineteenth century literature, narrative theory, and animal studies at the University of Nottingham. In this essay, he applies thing theory, actor network theory, animal studies theory to *Alice in Wonderland.*

What can we learn from the Duck, this character in Lewis Carroll's *Alice's Adventures in Wonderland* (1865) who conflates things with animals and food? The Duck distinguishes itself as an emphatic "*I*" through its simultaneous possession of knowledge and status as an eater: "'I know what "it" means well enough, when *I* find a thing,' said the Duck: 'it's generally a frog, or a worm.'"[1] As an edible animal, however, the Duck resides in the very food chain of "its" and "things" upon which its subjectivity seems to rest. While, to a certain extent, this ensnarement of self and thing fits within the ontology of "thing theory" where "things seem slightly human and humans seem slightly thing-like,"[2] these *Wonderland* animal-things hint at an anthropomorphism lurking in thing theory. By the Duck's definition, things are not objects that appear uncannily human, but edible life-forms that presumably have appetites of their own. As Lewis Carroll's Alice puts it, "how confusing it is all the things being alive" (*Alice's Adventures in Wonderland*, p. 75). Of course, thing theory has produced some fascinating discussions of the liveliness of things, but when we extend this field of discussion to *eating* things, we must take the "life" of things more literally and think seriously about their corporeality and survival. Moreover, we find that the realm of things now enlarges to include nonhuman animals, those things that eating so often positions at the contact point between agent and object, living and dead. Attempting to expand the investigation of things beyond a human/thing dichotomy, this essay draws on the actor-network-theory (ANT) of Bruno Latour

Original publication details: Michael Parrish Lee, "Eating Things: Food, Animals, and Other Life Forms in Lewis Carroll's *Alice* Books." *Nineteenth–Century Literature* 68.4, pp. 484–512. University of California Press, 2014. Reproduced with permission from University of California Press.

to explore the entanglement of humans, objects, animals, and appetites that generates so much of the wonder in Lewis Carroll's *Alice* books. I argue that these texts attempt to reconcile the Victorian destabilization of discrete "human" and "animal" categories facilitated by evolutionary theory with an increasingly commodified culture where everything and everyone seem potentially consumable. Carroll presents a world that is both fully social and thoroughly objectified, where humans, animals, and objects trade, share, and fight for positions in a network of edible things.

I therefore hope, through reading the *Alice* books, to complicate thing theory by using eating as an invitation – although potentially a violent one – to the world of nonhuman animals. To do this is also to put a bit of pressure on the two main strands of thinking about things that have taken hold of current literary studies. The first is the Heideggerian model of thing theory, articulated most famously by Bill Brown. This strand of thought concerns itself with, in the words of Jonathan Lamb, "the difference between objects that serve human purposes and things that don't."[3] Such theory is, for Brown, invested in "sacrific[ing] the clarity of thinking about things as objects of consumption, on the one hand, in order to see how, on the other, our relation to things cannot be explained by the cultural logic of capitalism" (*A Sense of Things*, pp. 5–6). In order to differentiate the seemingly reductive "object" from the more uncanny, or even sublime, "thing," thing theorists attempt to remove the thing from any kind of circulation or exchange that seems capitalist or human. According to Brown:

> As they circulate through our lives, we look *through* objects (to see what they disclose about history, society, nature, or culture.… We begin to confront the thingness of objects when they stop working for us …, when their flow within the circuits of production and distribution, consumption and exhibition, has been arrested, however momentarily.[4]

But although, for thing theory, capitalist logic is too narrow to contain the liveliness of things, Catherine Gallagher has more recently argued that nineteenth-century conceptions of capitalism were foundationally concerned with "organic 'Life' itself" as "the ultimate desideratum and the energy or force that circulates through organic and inorganic nature."[5] An investigation of Victorian things in particular, then, might lose more than it gains by granting the life of things a status of exception from the nineteenth-century economic concerns with "issues of life and death" stemming "from the thought of Thomas Robert Malthus" (Gallagher, *The Body Economic*, pp. 4,3) – developed initially in *An Essay on the Principle of Population* (1798)[6] – and concentrating not only on "modes of production and exchange" but also on "the interconnections among populations, the food supply," and "their impact on life forms generally" (Gallagher, *The Body Economic*, p. 3).

Moreover, for all the efforts of thing theory to outrun the human, it operates, as Steven Connor suggests, through a "covert anthropomorphism."[7] It is only by escaping from the realm of human circulation that these things become themselves – as if human circulation were the only kind. I would suggest that the focus of such theory on the singularity and alterity of things causes it to miss out on the networks that things form, networks that mid-Victorians like Lewis Carroll, haunted by Charles Darwin's "tangled bank" of interspecies relations,[8] found it difficult to ignore. It is important to remember that the Victorian rise of commodity capitalism was a rise that occurred in the age of evolutionary theory, when concerns about human/object relations would have been enmeshed with concerns about the entanglements between humans and other life forms.[9] According to Andrew H. Miller, with the nineteenth-century triumph of capitalism, there was a mid-Victorian anxiety that the "social and moral world was being reduced to a warehouse of goods and commodities, a display window in which people, their actions, and their convictions were exhibited for the economic appetites of others" (*Novels Behind Glass*, p. 6). And as Nancy Armstrong notes, "objects" in *Alice's Adventures in Wonderland* "are neither inert nor speechless" ("The Occidental Alice," p. 559). But for Carroll, in the midst of the Darwin debates, the experience of this world of "economic appetites" could not be severed from the bodily appetites of the biological "Struggle for Life" between creatures "remote in the scale of nature, [but] bound together by a web of complex relations," "all feeding on each other" (Darwin, *Origin of Species*, pp. 648, 101, 102).[10] For Carroll, capitalist circulation was not simply a matter of ownership and property; it was also about surprising interspecies affiliations and relations, in which all parties can slip between the roles of subject, object, predator, and prey. In the *Alice* books, to be a thing is not to transcend circulation, interconnection, or the condition of being potentially utilizable or consumable by others; rather, it is to be part of such networks when these networks reach beyond the domain of the human.

Of course, Brown is not a Victorianist, and in fact the second, more object- and circulation-friendly strand of thinking about things in literary studies has strong Victorianist representation by scholars such as John Plotz and Elaine Freedgood.[11] These thinkers represent a looser thing trajectory influenced less by Martin Heidegger than by Arjun Appadurai's edited volume *The Social Life of Things* (1986).[12] They are more comfortable with things as property, as objects of consumption, and as telling stories about human history and culture. These thinkers, however, risk looking through things to what Freedgood calls "the ideas in things" (*The Ideas in Things*, p. 76), and their things are very much *objects* in the way that Lamb and Brown describe objects, remaining quite human, or at least circumscribed by human identifications, values, and use values. I want to suggest that, without quite letting us have our things and eat them too, Lewis Carroll's *Alice* books can productively mediate these two strands of thought. They give us the surprise, the strangeness, the irreducible excess, and the tangled relationship between subjects and objects of thing theory's uncanny "things," but without throwing circulation or consumption out the window or falling back on humanist objects. While thing theory remains rooted in Heidegger's vision of things as "independent" and "self-supporting,"[13] the *Alice* books give us things in networks, but networks that supersede, and have utility beyond, the human. Eating, I propose, is our way into these networks.

What kind of a thing is food? According to E. M. Forster, "food in fiction is mainly social. It draws characters together, but they seldom require it physiologically, seldom enjoy it."[14] Forster's assertion, I have suggested elsewhere, points to the way in which nineteenth-century British novels "often obscure the material side of eating linked to bodily appetite and sensory pleasure in favor of a version of eating" that is more purely, or narrowly, "social," usually at the service of the marriage plot.[15] Lewis Carroll, however, in focusing on childhood – which earlier nineteenth-century novels tended to marginalize as an uninteresting space of alimentary appetite[16] – and entering fully into the subject/object merging occasioned by nascent commodity culture and the human/animal slippage hinted at by evolutionary theory, pries open the conventional novelistic social to discover a world animated by the foods and eating processes that might otherwise function as background, symbols, or structuring devices. Alice occupies a world that makes her confident that "*something* interesting is sure to happen … whenever I eat or drink anything" (*Alice's Adventures in Wonderland*, p. 32; emphasis in original) and asks us to consider the narrative implications of it being "always tea-time" (p. 64) – always mealtime for someone or something. Following Alice's lead, critics of Carroll's texts have "always t[aken] a great interest in questions of eating and drinking" (p. 65). And while I am closer to critics such as Nina Auerbach, James R. Kincaid, Margaret Boe Birns, and Rose Lovell-Smith who read Wonderland eating as expressing a vision of predation than to those such as Armstrong, Carina Garland, and Carol Mavor who read it as reflecting anxieties about control,[17] I want to suggest that the *Alice* books deploy eating more radically to remap the novelistic social, merging literary character, and indeed "the human," with "the things" that, for Brown, "comprise the stage on which human action, including the action of thought, unfolds" (*A Sense of Things*, p. 3). *Alice's Adventures in Wonderland* and *Through the Looking-Glass, and What Alice Found There* (1871) open up a space in which food and eating refuse to behave themselves as stage, backdrop, symbols, or empty vessels for any kind of preexisting social. Instead, Carroll offers us the opportunity to see the social itself as something that is assembled, at least in part, so that we, and others, might eat – but also, if paradoxically, as something that is assembled by food.

So, first and foremost, food in *Alice* is social – but not in the way that Forster means. Food is not simply an object utilized by social subjects. Anticipating Jane Bennett's theorization of food as a form of "agency,"[18] Wonderland foods are cocreators of human character, as hinted by Alice's contemplation: "Maybe it's always pepper that makes people hot-tempered … and vinegar that makes them sour – and camomile that makes them bitter – and – and barley-sugar and such things that make children sweet-tempered" (*Alice's Adventures in Wonderland*, p. 78). Moreover, Carroll gives us a world in which subjects and objects are not essentially different and where everything and everyone is potentially on the menu. For Carroll, food is a social *thing* – a thing that associates and socializes. For instance, near the beginning of *Wonderland*, Alice drinks from a bottle labeled "DRINK ME" (p. 13) and eats a cake "on which the words 'EAT ME' [are] beautifully marked in currants" (p. 14). These food-things function both partly as objects and partly as subjects. They can be picked up and consumed as objects, but they also make the requests that lead to their ingestion, making them the partial agents of their own consumption. I say "partial" agents because Alice, who eats and drinks them (pp. 15, 13–14), must also be a partial agent of their consumption. But the very acts of ingestion that might seemingly secure Alice's status as a consuming subject over and against consumable objects render Alice object-like, making her a tool through which the food-things realize their consumption. Such ingestion also causes Alice to experience herself as an object, first "shutting up like a telescope!" (p. 14), and then "opening out like the largest telescope that ever was!" (p. 16). The meeting of Alice and the edibles thus makes each party inhabit and overflow the position of subject and object at once, becoming uncanny "things," but hardly independent or self-sufficient ones. They become things through association and collaboration, things operating together as both partial agents and partial objects to form a network of consumption. In *Alice*, one never eats alone.

Eating, for Carroll, is a particularly vivid intersection of multiple agencies, bearing resemblance to the theory of action put forth by Bruno Latour. Action, Latour suggests, is "not transparent" and "is not done under the full control of consciousness; action should rather be felt as a node, a knot, and a conglomerate of many surprising sets of agencies," or "actors," forming an "actor-network."[19] In the instance above, Alice forms a network with the following actors:

1. The "DRINK ME" drink constituted by the bottle and the liquid within that relies on Alice to drink it and causes her to shrink. (When Alice tastes the liquid, we encounter a resulting sub-network of "mixed flavour" consisting of still more actors: "cherry-tart,

custard, pine-apple, roast turkey, toffy, and hot buttered toast" [*Alice's Adventures in Wonderland*, pp. 13, 14].)

2. The "EAT ME" cake that relies on both the drink to shrink Alice to a size where she can find the cake under the table and Alice to eat the cake, causing Alice to grow.

But as Alice grows, this network expands to include another pair of actors:

3. Alice's feet. Growing taller upon eating the cake, Alice experiences her feet as separate actors, bidding them "Goodbye"; wondering "who will put on your shoes and stockings for you now, dears?"; worrying that if she is not "kind to them" they "wo'n't walk the way I want to go" (p. 16); and contemplating sending them presents (pp. 16–17).

Rather than giving evidence of "spiteful attempts of the male author to suppress and control Alice's agency" (Garland, "Curious Appetites," p. 22) or being part of an effort to represent "the body as something already out of control, something always in need of regulation" (Armstrong, "The Occidental Alice," p. 551), the consumption of the "DRINK ME"-"EAT ME" items dramatizes Alice as an actor reassembling, dividing, and realigning through her incorporation of other actors that are themselves presumably reconfigured through Alice's ingestion and digestion of them. Latour's actors have more ontological flexibility than either conventional objects or the things of thing theory. They can include humans, animals, objects, concepts, and, in the case of Alice, food and body parts. But with such versatile actors at hand, why hold onto "things" at all? First, I would suggest, because Carroll himself makes frequent and imaginative use of the term "thing." Second, because, while the *Alice* books anticipate Latour's sense of the multiplicity and *"dislocated"* nature of agency (*Reassembling the Social*, p. 46; emphasis in original), Carroll's things are actors caught up in a historically specific imagining of objects, people, and animals trading positions – actors embodied within a social network of Darwinian commodities mobilized by eating.

Upending the conventional nineteenth-century novelistic model that defines deep human character and narrative interest against the interest in food,[20] this sequence shows Carroll reworking literary form. Alice's consumption of other actors simultaneously moves the story along and quite literally transforms her. Undoing distinctions between eating and reading,[21] the sequence also stands as a particularly self-reflexive instance of the text's participation in the mid- to late-nineteenth-century conceptualizations of reading as a bodily experience discussed by recent criticism concerned with the relationship between aesthetics and corporeality.[22] But the tendency for such criticism to underplay the alimentary dimensions of embodiment[23] points to the enduring relegation of gustatory taste to the lower rungs of what Carolyn Korsmeyer describes as the "hierarchy of the senses," a hierarchy informing the modern aesthetic models[24] that influence so much nineteenth-century narrative.[25] Carroll breaks with these models, grounding literary form and reading alike not simply in the body, but in the potentially animalistic domain of bodily appetite. Alice's network with the "EAT ME"-"DRINK ME" things – at once objects, characters, edibles, and texts – presents appetite eliciting and shaping literary interest, which functions here not as a demonstration of deep interiority[26] but as a bodily vector of association with heterogeneous things in Carroll's expansion of the social.

We see a more aggressive example of the social life of food near the end of *Through the Looking-Glass*, when Alice attends a coronation feast where she is to be officially recognized as a queen, surely the top position in the Looking-Glass food chain, a position defined as "all feasting and fun!"[27] But "the feast enacts a radical and pervasive unraveling of the division of the human and the inhuman,"[28] and the would-be objects of consumption turn the tables on their would-be consumers. Alice is "introduce[d]" to a leg of mutton that "ma[kes] a little bow to" her (*Through the Looking-Glass*, p. 229), and upon announcing her wish to slice the leg, Alice is informed that "it isn't etiquette to cut any one you've been introduced to" (pp. 229–30). She is then introduced to a Pudding, and must "conque[r] her shyness by a great effort" to "cut a slice" of it, after which the Pudding says, "in a thick, suety sort of voice," "What impertinence! ... I wonder how you'd like it, if I were to cut a slice out of *you*, you creature!" (p. 230). Soon consumers and objects of consumption trade positions – the leg of mutton sitting in the White Queen's chair, and the White Queen "disappear[ing] into the soup" (pp. 232–33), the guests "lying down in the dishes," and the soup-ladle "walking up the table towards Alice's chair, and beckoning to her impatiently to get out of its way" (p. 233). This revolt of food-things puts pressure on Brown's claim that "the tale" of "possession – of being possessed by possessions – is something stranger than the history of a culture of consumption. It is ... a tale not just of thinking with things but also of trying to render thought thing-like" (*A Sense of Things*, p. 5). Possession, *Alice* shows us, is richer and stranger than consumption only if we take consumption in a rarefied economic sense. What if we don't, as Carroll doesn't, separate "consumption" from the condition of having a body, of needing or wanting to eat and survive – and, perhaps inevitably, to "cut," to kill – of being part of a food chain? Alice occupies worlds in which both subjectivity can become thing-like and the things she would consume are already subjects.

The coronation scene also shows how the "thingness" of food – that which makes it overflow the category of "object" – is at least in part due to its position at the border between life and death, and to its evocation of the *violence* of consumption. For Carroll, consumption is haunted by animals and the violence done or always on the verge of being done to animals. As Sara Guyer notes, the leg of mutton and the suety Pudding respectively are and bear the remains of "slaughtered and cooked animals" ("The Girl with the Open Mouth," p. 162). And even some of the less-fleshy inhabitants of the table assemble into animal form: "As to the bottles, they each took a pair of plates, which they hastily fitted on as wings, and so, with forks for legs, went fluttering about in all directions: 'and very like birds they look,' Alice thought to herself, as well as she could in the dreadful confusion that was beginning" (*Through the Looking-Glass*, p. 232). This "confusion" that nearly overwhelms Alice's subject-defining ability to "think" is as much a rebellion of animals as of food, which is perhaps fitting for a feast consisting mainly of animal products and attended by "animals" and "birds" (p. 229). Lewis Carroll's things override the status of mere objects not only through becoming (human) subject-like but also through being or becoming animal-like, or simply through being animals, as in the case of the Wonderland croquet-ground where "the croquet balls were live hedgehogs, and the mallets live flamingoes" (*Alice's Adventures in Wonderland*, p. 73).

If Carroll's lively things are partly a response to the subject/object "confusion" resulting from the sense of a commodified human world under Victorian capitalism, then they also suggest that this confusion was interwoven with concerns about the com-modification of animals. Besides bearing witness to the evolutionary theories that blurred the boundaries between humans and animals, the nineteenth century saw an accelerated objectification of animals through the advent of "zoos, realistic animal toys and the widespread commercial diffusion of animal imagery,"[29] along with the "more abstract process of [animal] domination implicit in both popular zoology and the scientific work it reflected and distilled."[30] The Victorian period also saw the very visceral objectification of animals by the meat-canning industry and vivisection,[31] a practice that, as Jed Mayer notes, Carroll himself became an outspoken critic of.[32] In the *Alice* books, animals frequently occupy the positions of objects for use and consumption while simultaneously troubling their role as objects through their very animalism in a world where animals often command the subject-announcing power of speech. As we have seen, the "things" that the Duck designates are animals that it – another animal – regards as edibles. The Queen of Hearts describes the Mock Turtle as "the *thing* Mock Turtle Soup is made from" (*Alice's Adventures in Wonderland*, p. 81; emphasis added). The Mock Turtle in turn sings a song in which one of the central characters is a whiting, and when the Turtle asks Alice if she can describe whiting, she responds by describing them as food, with "their tails in their mouths – and they're all over crumbs" (p. 90). In *Through the Looking-Glass*, well before the animal-food-things of the coronation feast, a talking Gnat shows Alice a "Snap-dragon-fly" with a body "made of plum-pudding," "wings of holly-leaves, and its head" a "raisin burning in brandy" and a "Bread-and-butter-fly" whose "wings are thin slices of bread-and-butter, its body is a crust, and its head is a lump of sugar" (*Through the Looking-Glass*, pp. 150, 151) – both at once living creatures and novel objects of consumption.

Yet more elusive things seem to trouble this world of animal objects in a *Looking-Glass* shop run by a Sheep. Alice finds:

> The shop seemed to be full of all manner of curious things – but the oddest part of it all was that, whenever she looked hard at any shelf, to make out exactly what it had on it, that particular shelf was always quite empty, though the others round it were crowded as full as they could hold.
>
> "Things flow about so here!" she said at last in a plaintive tone, after she had spent a minute or so in vainly pursuing a large bright thing, that looked sometimes like a doll and sometimes like a work-box, and was always in the shelf next above the one she was looking at. "And this one is the most provoking of all – but I'll tell you what – " she added, as a sudden thought struck her. "I'll follow it up to the very top shelf of all. It'll puzzle it to go through the ceiling, I expect!"
>
> But even this plan failed: the 'thing' went through the ceiling as quietly as possible, as if it were quite used to it. (*Through the Looking-Glass*, p. 176)

I quote at length because this scene seems to present things at their most Heideggerian. Much to a prospective thing theorist's delight, Alice faces the refusal of these "things" to be pinned down and reduced to concretely identifiable objects of consumption. The things seem uncannily alive precisely in their ability to evade human categorization and use and their consequent ability to render Alice thing-like. For, as Alice turns about to try and see these things, the Sheep asks if she is a "teetotum" (p. 176) or spinning top.[33] We find, however, that the elusive, metamorphic qualities of these things are not due to their transcendence of capitalism, but rather to their embodiment of it. The Sheep says to Alice: "plenty of choice, only make up your mind. Now, what *do* you want to buy?" (*Through the Looking-Glass*, p. 178; emphasis in original). The dream logic of these things that refuse to stay still or hold a single form reflects the dizzying phantasmagoria of overwhelming consumer choice and desire more than it reflects pure thingish alterity. Once Alice learns that the things are for sale, she decides that she "should like to buy an egg" to eat (p. 179), bringing us back into a domain of bodily consumption where the "thing" to be consumed is an animal product (and potential source). Yet the egg resists easy consumption. Alice finds that "the egg seems to get further away the more [she] walk[s] towards it" (p. 180), and then that it grows "larger and larger, and more and more human" (p. 181), until it becomes "HUMPTY DUMPTY" (p. 181). This humanized egg thus occupies the intersection between food, person, animal, and purchasable object that a Darwinian consumer culture made available to an imagination as vivid as Carroll's. And if Humpty Dumpty's desire "to be master" of words and their meanings (p. 186) seems to place him insistently on the subject side of the subject/object dichotomy, then the shattering "fall" of his well-known story, played out here in "a heavy crash" (p. 193), reaffirms the Wonderland slippage between subject and object as well as the fragile corporeality that haunts all of Carroll's actors, whether human, animal, object, or some combination of the three. In the end, the shop of elusive things shows us how animals produce and animate Carroll's objects. Not only do things materialize as eggs, but the shop is, of course, presided over by a Sheep who sells these consumable goods and whose persistent knitting (pp. 175–78) drives home the objectification of animals.

This is not to say that all of the things or even all of the food-things in the *Alice* books are animals or directly bear animal remains, but rather that animals mobilize the networks of things, especially when eating is at stake. It is, after all, while chasing a White Rabbit down a rabbit-hole that Alice encounters the "EAT ME" cake and "DRINK ME" bottle, the "burning" "curiosity" that initially motivates her adventure (*Alice's Adventures in Wonderland*, p. 10) arising in relation to an animal and quickly becoming indistinguishable from the appetite she shows during her interaction with the edibles. And what prompts Alice's "curiosity" about the White Rabbit is its waistcoat-pocket and its watch (p. 10), *objects* for human use that render the Rabbit a novel *thing* that blurs the boundaries between human and animal.[34] Alice's response to this thing is to blur her own species' boundaries and take to the rather predatory animalistic activity of chasing a rabbit down a hole.

The network of actors that we began to trace in the previous section now grows more complex. Even before Alice enters into association with the "DRINK ME" drink, she forms a network that consists of her and the Rabbit. And while she loses sight of the Rabbit during her interactions with the food and drink, the Rabbit soon reappears to help further multiply actors. To our provisional list of: 1. The "DRINK ME" drink, 2. The "EAT ME" cake, and 3. Alice's feet, we can now add the following:

4. The White Rabbit. The initial animal-thing that Alice chases into the rabbit-hole now reappears. Alice attempts to address the Rabbit who – possibly alarmed by the advances of a creature that has been chasing him and has now grown in size dramatically – responds by "start[ing] violently," dropping its gloves and fan, and "skurr[ying] away into the darkness as hard as he could go" (*Alice's Adventures in Wonderland*, p. 17).

5. Mabel. After growing and reencountering the White Rabbit, Alice has an identity crisis and is no longer able to tell if she is herself or someone else. She wonders if she has "been changed in the night" (p. 17); asks, "'Who in the world am I?' Ah, *that's* the great puzzle!" (pp. 17–18; emphasis in original); and worries that she has "been changed for Mabel!" (p. 19).

6. The little crocodile. Worrying that she has been changed for Mabel, Alice tries to remember "all the things [she] used to know" (p. 18). She attempts to recite Isaac Watts's 1715 poem "Against Idleness and Mischief,"[35] but it comes out as a poem about a "*little crocodile*" (*Alice's Adventures in Wonderland*, p. 19; emphasis in original).

7. Little fishes. In the poem, the little crocodile "*welcomes little fishes in, / With gently smiling jaws*" (p. 19; emphasis in original).

If Alice's initial consumption of the edibles is an example of cooperative network build-ing, then the reintroduction of the White Rabbit expands this network to include the more violent (if smilingly social) consumption of fish by crocodile, replaying but invert-ing the initial invitation from the "EAT ME"-"DRINK ME" things to Alice to ingest them. This entry and reentry of animals into an apparent human/thing-only club shows animals – even when forgotten – mobilizing and making possible the interactions between humans and things, especially the things that people eat.

Alice's identity crisis and inability to remember accurately the "things" she "used to know" opens up another dimension of Wonderland things. As she later tells a hookah-smoking Caterpillar, Alice's sense that she is "not [her]self" is due to the fact that she does not "keep the same size for ten minutes together!" and that she "ca'n't remember *things* as [she] used" (*Alice's Adventures in Wonderland*, pp. 41, 42; emphasis added). Alice's sense of selfhood is thus reliant on things: the edible things that change her size and the "things" that she cannot quite remember. And similarly to the case of the Duck's "thing," these latter denoted "things" turn out to be animals.[36] When the Caterpillar asks Alice, "Ca'n't remember *what* things?" she replies: "Well, I've tried to say '*How doth the little busy bee*,' but it all came different!" (*Alice's Adventures in Wonderland*, p. 42; emphasis in original). Alice is referring to her earlier recitation of the poem about the little crocodile (beginning "*How doth the little crocodile*" [p. 19]). Her feeling of not being herself, then, comes from forgetting "things" not so much as abstract entities or units of information but as specific animals with specific relations to food. Alice has forgotten the productive bee and remembered instead the predatory, consuming crocodile. The text thus experiments with a model of identity that is not based on a recallable human self-hood or body of knowledge but configured by re-membering: by participating in the assembling and reassembling of a diverse network of actors, including animals and foods – by accepting membership within what Latour calls the "Parliament of Things."[37] Alice feels as though she has "been changed" for someone else (*Alice's Adventures in Wonderland*, p. 17) because she has entered into association with an unfamiliar network comprising the White Rabbit and the "EAT ME"-"DRINK ME" items and cannot, through memory, align herself with the correct animal-"things." As Lovell-Smith suggests, "in Wonderland humans are the creations of animals, it appears, just as much as animals are the creations of humans" ("Eggs and Serpents," p. 43). But is Alice's alignment with the fish-eating crocodile instead of the bee really a mistake? After all, critics like Edmund Wilson, Auerbach, and Kincaid have regarded Alice as predatory and aggressive.[38] And this little crocodile might indeed mirror the hungry Alice. But I think that its appetite points instead to another misremembered fish-loving predator: Alice's cat, Dinah.

I want to suggest that the most crucial "things" in the *Alice* books are Alice's cats. In conjunction with Alice, they are the pivotal actors assembling the network of Wonderland. For Latour, "action is borrowed, distributed," "influenced, dominated," and "translated" (*Reassembling the Social*, p. 46), and Alice, I would argue, similarly borrows and translates the appetite and predatory aspects of her cats. Several critics have touched on Alice's "conspicuous affinity with cats" (Nicholson, "Food and Power," p. 50) and the "somewhat puzzling centrality of Dinah and the Cheshire Cat" in *Wonderland* (Lovell-Smith, "The Animals of Wonderland," p. 408). For example, noting the Cheshire Cat's "long claws and a great many teeth," Empson argues that "Alice is particularly at home with [the Cheshire Cat]; she is the same sort of thing" (*Some Versions of Pastoral*, pp. 273–74). Gilles Deleuze writes that Alice "identifie[s] herself with the Cheshire Cat" (*The Logic of Sense*, p. 235). Auerbach points out that the Cheshire Cat is "the only creature in Wonderland whom [Alice] calls her 'friend,'" and suggests that he is "the only figure other than Alice who encompasses all the others" ("Alice and Wonderland," p. 38). Auerbach also makes telling connections between the Cat's ability to dissolve "into his own grinning mouth," the grinning crocodile, and the centrality of Alice's appetite ("Alice and Wonderland," p. 39). The fleeting critical comments on Alice's pet cats bring us even closer to the mark. Florence Becker Lennon opened up the possibility of thinking about the significance of the "real" cats of the *Alice* books to the world of Wonderland by suggesting that the Cheshire Cat "is Dinah's dream-self" and "a sort of guardian imp and liaison officer between the two worlds."[39] Kincaid writes: "In Alice's world, which frames both books, Dinah is a warm symbol of friendly cuddliness, but in Wonderland she is a monster" ("Alice's Invasion of Wonderland," p. 97). More recently, Mavor connects cats to "memory," suggesting that "it is the cat – perhaps only the cat, whether it takes the form of Dinah, or the metamorphosed form of the Cheshire Cat, or the form of a black kitten or a white kitten as birthed by Mother Dinah – that Alice misses" ("For-getting to Eat," p. 101). Most evocatively, Auerbach picks up on Lennon's connection between the Cheshire Cat and Dinah but claims an additional "shift of identities between Alice and Dinah," noting that Dinah "is the only above-ground character whom Alice mentions repeatedly, almost always in terms of her eating some smaller animal," and positing that Dinah "seems finally to function as a personification of Alice's own subtly cannibalistic hunger" ("Alice and Wonderland," pp. 38, 36). Yet even Auerbach underestimates the central role that Alice's cats play in structuring the world of Wonderland. And while there is indeed an entanglement of identity between Alice and Dinah, the text avoids reducing Dinah to a personification. Rather than making this animal stand in for an aspect of this human, Carroll explores an interspecies model of identity in which humans and animals are each other's co-creators and mediators, borrowing from, translating, feeding, and feeding off each other.

If the "burning curiosity" that drives Alice to chase the White Rabbit at the beginning of *Alice's Adventures in Wonderland* seems to borrow and translate the exploratory and predatory instincts of her cat (that most notoriously curious species), then her entry into the world below is marked by her concern for Dinah's food supply. As she falls down the rabbit-hole, Alice wonders if, in her absence, anyone will "remember [Dinah's] saucer of milk at tea-time," and she muses: "Dinah, my dear! I wish you were down here with me! There are no mice in the air, I'm afraid, but you might catch a bat, and that's very like a mouse, you know" (*Alice's Adventures in Wonderland*, p. 11). This only seemingly absent feline appetite becomes a palpable presence when Alice, attempting to communicate with a mouse, says, "Où est ma chatte?", causing the mouse to give a "sudden leap" and "quiver all over with fright" (p. 21) – a reaction not wholly different from the White Rabbit's fright at Alice. Alice's response – "I quite forgot you didn't like cats" – is met with the mouse's reply, which at once makes explicit a version of the social that is a predatory food chain and invites Alice to imagine herself occupying the mouse's place within this chain: "Not like cats! … Would *you* like cats, if you were me?" (p. 21; emphasis in original). But Alice continues to evoke her cat's appetite. Among an assorted group of creatures (including birds), Alice says: "Dinah's our cat. And she's such a capital one for catching mice, you ca'n't think! And oh, I wish you could see her after the birds! Why, she'll eat a little bird as soon as look at it!" (p. 29), a speech that sends the creatures hurrying away. Lovell-Smith has noted that "it is through her series of size changes that

Alice finds herself continually being repositioned in the food chain" ("The Animals of Wonderland," p. 406), but Alice's position in this chain also depends on her association with Dinah. Alice's references to Dinah modify her social relations with the creatures of Wonderland, putting them in the position of potential food objects. And just as Alice eventually learns to eat and manipulate her size more strategically, she also begins to use her references to Dinah more deliberately to vie for power among the creatures of Wonderland. After Alice gets stuck in the White Rabbit's house, the Rabbit concludes that he "must burn the house down," and Alice responds: "If you do, I'll set Dinah at you!" (*Alice's Adventures in Wonderland*, p. 36). That said, Dinah hardly insures Alice a secure position at the top of the Wonderland food chain, as we see when Alice shrinks and participates in the rather cat-like fear of becoming prey for a relatively "enormous" puppy (p. 37).

Alice's journey through Wonderland thus develops a model of being in which identity is less a fixed essence than a position on a food chain that varies through association and diet. After her run-in with the puppy, Alice's earlier, "'Who in the world am I?' Ah, *that's* the great puzzle!" (pp. 17–18; emphasis in original), soon gives way to her comment: "I'd nearly forgotten that I've got to grow up again! Let me see – how *is* it to be managed? I suppose I ought to eat or drink something or other; but the great question is 'What?'" (pp. 38–39; emphasis in original). And upon eating a bit of Caterpillar-given mushroom that makes her grow tall, Alice meets a Pigeon, who further asserts that questions of fixed identity are secondary to questions of what one eats and eats like. The Pigeon identifies Alice as a "Serpent" trying to steal its eggs (pp. 47–48). Alice's protests that she is "a little girl" rather than a serpent prove irrelevant when the Pigeon points out that if, as Alice says, "little girls eat eggs quite as much as serpents do," then little girls are "a kind of serpent," a notion that is "such a new idea to Alice, that she [is] quite silent for a minute or two" (p. 48).

If Alice's silence signals some recognition of her role as an animalistic eater, then we should recognize that such a role does not simply mark Alice as an individual consumer, but as a node in an interspecies network of consumption. We should not read Alice's references to Dinah's appetite and hunting skills as mere evocations of Dinah or personifications of Alice's hunger, but rather as extensions of and forms of contact with Dinah. While Alice deploys Dinah as a kind of tool to help her move through the social world of Wonderland, she also imagines herself becoming a tool for Dinah, that Dinah might begin "sending [Alice] on messages," or errands, including watching a "mouse-hole" (*Alice's Adventures in Wonderland*, pp. 31, 32). Such thinking invites us to imagine humans as servants or instruments in animal meals and hints that Alice's adventures are not just her own, but also act as "messages" for Dinah and Dinah's kittens.

Utilizing Dinah's appetite to effect her position on the food chain of Wonderland, Alice also functions as a kind of feline prosthesis, imagining meals on behalf of her cats and returning to feed them. Much as Alice's descent into Wonderland is marked by her concern about when Dinah will be fed (*Alice's Adventures in Wonderland*, p. 11), her journey through the looking-glass is brought on by Alice's conversation with Dinah's black kitten and her desire to pretend that the kitten is the Red Queen and marked by her concern over whether the kitten will get milk through the looking-glass (*Through the Looking-Glass*, pp. 124, 127). Once Alice is through the glass, it is the Red Queen who proposes to her that they be queens together, a position that, as we have seen, she defines as "all feasting and fun!" (p. 144). And at her royal coronation, Alice remarks to the Red Queen: "it's a very *curious* thing, I think – every poem [in the Looking-Glass world] was about fishes in some way" (pp. 230–231; emphasis added), a point that could also be made about most of the poems in *Wonderland*. When Alice asks the Red Queen, "Do you know why they're so fond of fishes, all about here?", the Queen somewhat evasively but tellingly responds, "As to fishes," and suggests another poem about fishes (p. 231). Once the feast has turned against the Queens, Alice shakes the Red Queen (who she supposes is "the cause of all the mischief" [p. 234]), turning her back into a kitten and waking from her dream.

As Jacques Derrida notes, the entire penultimate chapter of *Looking-Glass* "consists in a single [partial] sentence": " – and it really *was* a kitten, after all."[40] Critics of the *Alice* books tend to pass over this emphatic commitment to the revelation of the kitten's identity, and even Derrida points it out mainly to oppose his contemplation of the potential responsiveness of animals to Alice's apparent certainty "that one cannot speak with a cat on the pretext that it doesn't reply or that it always replies the same thing" (Derrida, "The Animal That Therefore I Am," p. 8; see Carroll, *Through the Looking-Glass*, p. 238). Alice's frustration that "whatever you say to [kittens], they *always* purr," however, does not in fact stop her from talking to her kitten (*Through the Looking-Glass*, p. 238; emphasis in original). Now awake, Alice says to her kitten: "You woke me out of oh! such a nice dream! And you've been along with me, Kitty – all through the Looking-Glass world. Did you know it, dear?" (p. 238). But when the kitten only purrs in response, Alice not only keeps talking but also moves from asking for language as response to offering it as a gift: "if only you'd been really with me in my dream, there was one thing you *would* have enjoyed – I had such a quantity of poetry said to me, all about fishes! To-morrow morning you shall have a real treat. All the time you're eating your breakfast, I'll repeat 'The Walrus and the Carpenter' to you; and then you can make believe it's oysters, dear!" (p. 239; emphasis in original). Alice's inability to differentiate her kitten's vocal responses and thus to know the extent to which the two of them share a language does not drive Alice to contemplate philosophy (as Donna J. Haraway notes that Derrida does under the silent gaze of his own small black cat),[41] but rather moves her to reshape her language into a form that she knows her kitten will enjoy if not understand in human terms. Instead of continuing to inquire about the truth behind identity ("Confess that [the Red Queen] was what you turned into!" [*Through the Looking-Glass*, p. 238]), Alice offers a narrative about food that she translates into the material food that she feeds her kitten.

The animals in *Alice* at once do and do not fit Ivan Kreilkamp's claim that "animal characters are fundamentally 'minor,' in the sense defined by Alex Woloch,"[42] functioning as "subordinate beings who are delimited in themselves while performing a function for someone else."[43] On one hand, Wonderland animals can be even more explicitly functional than Woloch's minor human characters, sometimes occupying the positions of objects and meat. But on the other hand, the human Alice, ostensibly the narrative's central protagonist, herself performs functions for and acts as an extension of her cats, who are only delimited in a superficial way. Her cats trouble Woloch's concept of minor characters; without occupying much obvious narrative space, they crucially structure the dream worlds of Wonderland and Alice's own character, to the point where it is never quite clear where they end and Alice begins. Instead of a "character-system," or a "distributional matrix" in which "the discrete representation of any specific individual is intertwined with the narrative's continual apportioning of attention to different characters who jostle for limited space within the same fictive universe" (Woloch, *The One vs. the Many*, pp. 17, 13), Carroll brings us tangled interspecies networks assembling and reassembling as humans, objects, and animals exchange, share, and create new positions. Fictional "space" in these texts cannot be dominated by the human or mapped with accuracy by human-centered reading practices; instead, the nonhuman territories of things and animals extend beneath and beyond the conventional spaces of readerly attention. Shaping the networks of Wonderland are animal bodies and appetites that draw us in not simply as readers but as social things inhabiting a food chain.

Alice's interaction with her kitten also takes us beyond Derrida's concerns with animal alterity and human/animal slippage – concerns that have become touchstones for the field of "animal studies"[44] – toward something closer to Haraway's concept of "becoming with," a mode of "species interdependence" in which "the partners do not precede the meeting; species of all kinds, living and not, are consequent on a subject-and object-shaping dance of encounters" (*When Species Meet*, pp. 3, 19, 4). Far from Gilles Deleuze and Félix Guattari's ecstatic notion of "becoming-animal"[45] (which Haraway argues shows a "profound absence of curiosity about or respect for and with actual animals" [*When Species Meet*, p. 27]), "becoming with" resembles Latour's actor-networks, involving interspecies "beings-in-encounter" that "gather up those who respond to them into unpredictable kinds of 'we'" (Haraway, *When Species Meet*, p. 5). The "we" assembled by Alice and her kitten is a network strengthened rather than weakened or brought into crisis by the gaps in communication created when human speech provokes feline purring. Whether or not Alice's extension of "make believe" to her kitten is itself an anthropomorphic fantasy, such extension is an offer rather than a demand, and it has both the material consequence of enhancing Alice's enthusiasm for feeding the kitten and the narrative-shaping effect of animalizing Alice's fantasy life. The edible sea life in both *Alice* books seems at least as much a feline fantasy as a human one, even if such a fantasy is the product of eating practices and appetites that develop through cats' association and cohabitation with humans. And what is "The Walrus and the Carpenter" – in which the eponymous characters "*talk of many things: / … / Of cabbages – and kings – / And why the sea is boiling hot – / And whether pigs have wings*" in order to lure oysters to their culinary deaths (*Through the Looking-Glass*, p. 161; emphasis in original) – but the story of an interspecies alliance between a human and an animal using language and "make believe" in order to eat together? Fantasy and fiction, for Carroll, are not human tools for writing over animals or animal necessity, but coinventions *with* animals – modes of "becoming with" that remain rooted in bodily needs and pleasures and that shape the identities of human and animal inventors together.

After offering to repeat "The Walrus and the Carpenter," Alice further draws our attention to the question of make-believe and invention by asking her kitten to help her understand the origin of Wonderland, saying, "Now, Kitty, let's consider who it was that dreamed it all" (*Through the Looking-Glass*, p. 239). Alice is referring back to something that occurs after she first hears this poem (pp. 158–63) from the mouth of the sometimes "fish"-resembling Tweedledee (p. 167), when Tweedledee says that Alice is "only a sort of thing in [the Red King's] dream!" (p. 165). The text follows up this idea in a chapter titled "It's My Own Invention" in which Alice wonders whether "we're all part of the same dream," adding: "Only I do hope it's *my* dream, and not the Red King's! I don't like belonging to another person's dream" (p. 205; emphasis in original). But Alice's anthropocentric contemplation of the potential dream-owners is "interrupted" by two battling Knights and their horses (p. 205). The victorious White Knight – a self-declared "great hand at inventing things" (p. 211) – proceeds to show and describe his "inventions" to Alice. These inventions mainly include "things" that come into being at the intersection of humans and animals. They include an upside-down box emptied of the "things" ("clothes and sandwiches") it is designed to hold (p. 207) and hung on a tree "in hopes some bees may make a nest in it" and create "honey" (p. 208); "anklets" that the Knight puts around the feet of his horse "to guard against the bites of sharks" (p. 208); a helmet "like a sugar-loaf" used in case the Knight falls off his horse (p. 211); and a song in which the speaker makes "*butterflies*" into "*mutton-pies*" and "*haddocks' eyes*" into "*waistcoat-buttons*" (pp. 215, 216; emphasis in original). We learn that, "of all the strange things that Alice saw in her journey Through The Looking-Glass," the sight of the Knight singing this song and "the horse quietly moving about, with the reins hanging loose on his neck, cropping the grass" is "the one that she always remembered most clearly" (p. 214). In other words, when it comes to reassembling Looking-Glass networks, it is not just the Knight who invents with and for animals that makes such a memorable impression on Alice, but "the strange pair" of man and horse (p. 214). The question of who is dreaming the dream thus lodges between a poem about one human-animal alliance and the spectacle of another, and reemerges when Alice offers to repeat the poem to her kitten. In this way, the text hints that we all might be "things" in a dream, inventions "becoming with" and belonging to one another in an interspecies network. The returning oysters of "The Walrus and the Carpenter" remind us, however, that "becoming with" has its victims; networks have their prey. Like so many other Wonderland animals, the oysters are at once food objects and social things, the never fully digested remains of fiction and invention.

Thing theory is fascinated with the irreducibility of things, as is Carroll. Brown, imagining things "as what is excessive in objects," makes a point that is as inescapable as it is evocative ("Thing Theory," p. 5). But Brown, looking for this excess of things in "the void constituted by the jug" and "the emptiness at the center of the Real" (*A Sense of Things*, p. 7), gets so sidetracked by the allure of *nothing* that he misses out on the living things that teem within and behind the seemingly empty spaces of the human world. One way to remember things is to forget animals, but this is not the remembering that Carroll has in mind. As I have been suggesting, Wonderland things do not exceed object status by concealing a mute unknowable core of pure potential but rather through the networks they create with other objects and life forms. What might at first seem like "the amorphousness out of which objects are materialized by the (ap)perceiving subject" (Brown, "Thing Theory," p. 5) in the *Looking-Glass* shop of elusive things is already a network of consumable goods mobilized by a Sheep, and it is only invisible to the human Alice because she has not yet learned how to join it. For Carroll, the main things that make "things" excessive are animals. And, whether in the form of food, or companions, or some combination of the two, when the networks of Wonderland begin to unravel, animals are what remain.

Alice's Adventures in Wonderland approaches its end with a trial over stolen tarts (*Alice's Adventures in Wonderland*, p. 96) during which the Queen of Hearts sentences Alice to beheading, uttering her famous cry, "Off with her head!" (p. 108). The Queen, a card woman, is a particular kind of Wonderland thing: a human-object hybrid. Her sovereign power over life and death seemingly suggests a world in which commodity objects have taken control over human existence.[46] Yet Alice in turn seems able to reduce the Queen and her card men minions to objects for human use. Alice escapes the trial and wakes up from Wonderland by declaring, "You're nothing but a pack of cards!" (*Alice's Adventures in Wonderland*, p. 108), ostensibly turning these subject/objects into mere objects and reaffirming the power of human imagination to animate and control the object world.

The card men now become a pack of cards that "r[ise] up into the air" and "fl[y] down upon" Alice (p. 108) but resolve into even more innocuous "dead leaves" when Alice wakes "with her head in the lap of her sister" (p. 109). But in the end, human imagination proves as much a failed tyrant as the Queen of Hearts. After Alice tells her older sister of her "curious dream" and then exits the narrative to have her "tea," her sister experiences "the whole place around her bec[oming] alive with the strange creatures of her little sister's dream," including "the White Rabbit," the "Mock Turtle," the "frightened Mouse," and the "rattle of the teacups as the March Hare and his friends shared their never-ending meal" (p. 109). Despite this contagious immersion in the life of Wonderland, Alice's sister "kn[ows] she ha[s] but to open [her eyes] again, and all would change to dull reality" (p. 110). Such "reality," however, is not a strictly human world: "the rattling teacups would change to tinkling sheep-bells, and the Queen's shrill cries to the voice of the shepherd-boy ..., and all the other queer noises, would change (she knew) to the confused clamour of the busy farm-yard – while the lowing of the cattle in the distance would take the place of the Mock Turtle's heavy sobs" (p. 110). In other words, what remains of the curious things of Wonderland is a reality assembled by the traces of animals and human-animal relations.

Such traces are all the more visible in *Through the Looking-Glass*, which ends with Alice waking from the revolt of food-things as she shakes the Red Queen – this time a human-chess piece hybrid – into her kitten (*Through the Looking Glass*, pp. 234–37). In the wake of the dissolving meal, Alice offers her remaining animal the narrative animal remains of "The Walrus and the Carpenter" and tries to persuade her kitten to help her solve the riddle of "who it was that dreamed it all":

> "This is a serious question, my dear, and you should *not* go on licking your paw like that – as if Dinah hadn't washed you this morning! You see, Kitty, it *must* have been either me or the Red King. He was part of my dream, of course – but then I was part of his dream, too! *Was* it the Red King, Kitty? You were his wife, my dear, so you ought to know – Oh, Kitty, *do* help to settle it! I'm sure your paw can wait!" (pp. 239–40; emphasis in original)

But the "provoking kitten" responds with what looks like coy silence, "beg[inning] on the other paw, and pretend[ing] it hadn't heard the question" (p. 240). The text then turns the question of the dream to the reader, asking, "Which do *you* think it was?" (p. 239; emphasis in original). I take the fact that the text here places the silent reader in a similar position to Alice's kitten as an invitation to think beyond the human options that Alice provides. To the question of who dreamed the Wonderland worlds, I would venture that the answer is Alice and cats together, forming a network, a food chain in which everyone is edible and every thing is social.

University of Nottingham

Notes

1 Lewis Carroll, *Alice's Adventures in Wonderland*, in his *"Alice's Adventures in Wonderland" and "Through the Looking-Glass and What Alice Found There": The Centenary Edition*, ed. Hugh Haughton (London: Penguin, 1998), p. 25 (emphasis in original). All further page references to this edition are given parenthetically in the text.

2 Bill Brown, *A Sense of Things: The Object Matter of American Literature* (Chicago: Univ. of Chicago Press, 2003), p. 13.

3   Jonathan Lamb, *The Things Things Say* (Princeton: Princeton Univ. Press, 2011), p. xi.

4   Bill Brown, "Thing Theory," *Critical Inquiry*, 28 (2001), 4 (emphasis in original).

5   Catherine Gallagher, *The Body Economic: Life, Death, and Sensation in Political Economy and the Victorian Novel* (Princeton: Princeton Univ. Press, 2006), p. 3.

6   See Thomas Robert Malthus, *An Essay on the Principle of Population*, ed. Geoffrey Gilbert (New York: Oxford Univ. Press, 2008).

7   Steven Connor, "Thinking things," *Textual Practice*, 24 (2010), 2.

8   Charles Darwin, *On the Origin of Species by Means of Natural Selection or The Preservation of Favored Races in the Struggle for Life* (New York: Modern Library, 1998), p. 648.

9   For discussions of the Victorian rise of commodity capitalism, see for example W. Hamish Fraser, *The Coming of the Mass Market, 1850–1914* (Hamden, Connecticut: Archon Books, 1981); Thomas Richards, *The Commodity Culture of Victorian England: Advertising and Spectacle, 1851–1914* (Stanford: Stanford Univ. Press, 1990); Lori Anne Loeb, *Consuming Angels: Advertising and Victorian Women* (New York: Oxford Univ. Press, 1994); Andrew H. Miller, *Novels Behind Glass: Commodity Culture and Victorian Narrative* (Cambridge: Cambridge Univ. Press, 1995); and Regenia Gagnier, *The Insatiability of Human Wants: Economics and Aesthetics in Market Society* (Chicago: Univ. of Chicago Press, 2000). Nancy Armstrong has discussed the influence of consumer culture on *Alice's Adventures in Wonderland*, with particular reference to eating, in "The Occidental Alice," in *Contemporary Literary Criticism: Literary and Cultural Studies, Fourth Edition*, ed. Robert Con Davis and Ronald Schleifer (New York: Longman, 1998), pp. 537–64.

10 For discussions of Darwin's influence on Carroll, see Morton N. Cohen, *Lewis Carroll: A Biography* (London and Basingstoke: Macmillan, 1995), pp. 350–52; William Empson, *Some Versions of Pastoral* (London: Chatto and Windus, 1935), pp. 254–55; Rose Lovell-Smith, "The Animals of Wonderland: Tenniel as Carroll's Reader," *Criticism*, 45 (2003), 383–415; Rose Lovell-Smith, "Eggs and Serpents: Natural History Reference in Lewis Carroll's Scene of Alice and the Pigeon," *Children's Literature*, 35 (2007), 27–53; Akira Mizuta Lippit, *Electric Animal: Toward a Rhetoric of Wildlife* (Minneapolis: Univ. of Minnesota Press, 2000), pp. 137–39; Mervyn Nicholson, "Food and Power: Homer, Carroll, Atwood and Others," *Mosaic*, 20, no. 3 (1987), 37–55; and Margaret Boe Birns, "Solving the Mad Hatter's Riddle," *Massachusetts Review*, 25 (1984), 457–68.

11 See John Plotz, Portable Property: *Victorian Culture on the Move* (Princeton: Princeton Univ. Press, 2008); and Elaine Freedgood, *The Ideas in Things: Fugitive Meaning in the Victorian Novel* (Chicago: Univ. of Chicago Press, 2006).

12 See *The Social Life of Things: Commodities in Cultural Perspective*, ed. Arjun Appadurai (Cambridge: Cambridge Univ. Press, 1986).

13 See Martin Heidegger, *Poetry, Language, Thought*, trans. Albert Hofstadter (New York: Perennial, 1971, 2001), p. 164.

14 E. M. Forster, *Aspects of the Novel, and Related Writings*, Volume 12 of The Abinger Edition of the Works of E. M. Forster, ed. Oliver Stallybrass (London: Edward Arnold, 1927, 1974), p. 37.

15 Michael Parrish Lee, "The Nothing in the Novel: Jane Austen and the Food Plot," *Novel: A Forum on Fiction*, 45 (2012), 368.

16 See Lee, "The Nothing in the Novel," pp. 379–380.

17 See Nina Auerbach, "Alice and Wonderland: A Curious Child," *Victorian Studies*, 17 (1973), 31–47; James R. Kincaid, "Alice's Invasion of Wonderland," *PMLA*, 88 (1973), 92–99; Birns, "Solving the Mad Hatter's Riddle"; Lovell-Smith, "The Animals of Wonderland"; Lovell-Smith, "Eggs and Serpents"; Armstrong, "The Occidental Alice"; Carina Garland, "Curious Appetites: Food, Desire, Gender, and Subjectivity in Lewis Carroll's *Alice* Texts," *The Lion and the Unicorn*, 32 (2008), 22–39; and Carol Mavor, "For-Getting to Eat: Alice's Mouthing Metonymy," in *The Nineteenth-Century Child and Consumer Culture*, ed. Dennis Denisoff (Aldershot: Ashgate, 2008), pp. 95–118.

18 Jane Bennett, Vibrant Matter: *A Political Ecology of Things* (Durham, N.C.: Duke Univ. Press, 2010), p. 41.

19 Bruno Latour, *Reassembling the Social: An Introduction to Actor-Network-Theory* (New York: Oxford Univ. Press, 2005), p. 44.

20 See Lee, "The Nothing in the Novel."

21   See Mavor, "For-getting to Eat," p. 101.

22   See for example Nicholas Dames, *The Physiology of the Novel: Reading, Neural Science, and the Form of Victorian Fiction* (New York: Oxford Univ. Press, 2007); and Benjamin Morgan, "Critical Empathy: Vernon Lee's Aesthetics and the Origins of Close Reading," *Victorian Studies*, 55 (2012), 31–56.

23   Exceptions include Jennifer L. Fleissner, "Henry James's Art of Eating," *ELH*, 75 (2008), 27–62; Michael Parrish Lee, "Reading Meat in H. G. Wells," *Studies in the Novel*, 42 (2010), 249–68; and Matthew Kaiser, "Pater's Mouth," *Victorian Literature and Culture*, 39 (2011), 47–64.

24   Carolyn Korsmeyer, *Making Sense of Taste: Food and Philosophy* (Ithaca: Cornell Univ. Press, 1999), p. 5.

25   See Lee, "The Nothing in the Novel," pp. 368, 376.

26   Deidre Shauna Lynch argues that the turn of the nineteenth century saw the rise of reading practices in which literary characters "became the imaginative resources on which readers drew to make themselves into individuals, to expand their own interior resources of sensibility" (Lynch, *The Economy of Character: Novels, Market Culture, and the Business of Inner Meaning* [Chicago: Univ. of Chicago Press, 1998], p. 126).

27   Lewis Carroll, *Through the Looking-Glass and What Alice Found There*, in his *"Alice's Adventures in Wonderland" and "Through the Looking-Glass and What Alice Found There,"* p. 144. All further page references to this edition are given parenthetically in the text.

28   Sara Guyer, "The Girl with the Open Mouth: *Through the Looking Glass*," *Angelaki*, 9, no. 1 (2004), 160.

29   John Berger, *About Looking* (London: Bloomsbury, 1980), p. 26.

30   Harriet Ritvo, *The Animal Estate: The English and Other Creatures in the Victorian Age* (Cambridge, Mass.: Harvard Univ. Press, 1987), p. 11.

31   On the meat-canning industry, see Colin Spencer, British Food: *An Extraordinary Thousand Years of History* (London: Grub Street, 2002), p. 282; on vivisection, see Ritvo, *The Animal Estate*, pp. 158–65.

32   See Jed Mayer, "The Vivisection of the Snark," *Victorian Poetry*, 47 (2009), 429–48.

33   See Hugh Haughton, note to *Through the Looking-Glass*, p. 343, n. 10.

34   See also Lovell-Smith, who notes that, in John Tenniel's illustration, the rabbit "occupies a point between animal and human, simultaneously both these things and neither of them" ("The Animals of Wonderland," p. 384).

35   See Haughton, note to *Through the Looking-Glass*, p. 302, n. 6.

36   Gilles Deleuze understands "denoted objects" in Carroll's work as "always consumable or recipients of consumption" (Deleuze, *The Logic of Sense*, ed. Constantin V. Boundas, trans. Mark Lester with Charles Stivale [New York: Columbia Univ. Press, 1990], p. 26). He points out that the Duck "understands 'it' as a denoting term for all things, state of affairs and possible qualities (an indicator). It specifies even that the denoted thing is essentially something which is (or may be) eaten. Everything denoted or capable of denotation is, in principle, consumable and penetrable" (*The Logic of Sense*, p. 26). While Deleuze is right about the consumable – and usually edible – nature of Carroll's things, he seems to forget their animal dimension, a dimension that the Duck insists on.

37   See Bruno Latour, *We Have Never Been Modern*, trans. Catherine Porter (Cambridge, Mass.: Harvard Univ. Press, 1993), p. 144.

38   See Edmund Wilson, *The Shores of Light: A Literary Chronicle of the Twenties and Thirties* (New York: Farrar, Straus and Young, 1952), pp. 543–44; Auerbach, "Alice and Wonderland," pp. 35–37; and Kincaid, "Alice's Invasion of Wonderland," pp. 95–96.

39   Florence Becker Lennon, *Lewis Carroll* (London: Cassell and Co., 1947), p. 121.

40   Jacques Derrida, "The Animal That Therefore I Am (More to Follow)," in his *The Animal That Therefore I Am*, ed. Marie-Louise Mallet, trans. David Wills (New York: Fordham Univ. Press, 2008), p. 7; Carroll, *Through the Looking-Glass*, p. 236 (emphasis in original).

41   See Donna J. Haraway, *When Species Meet* (Minneapolis: Univ. of Minnesota Press, 2008), p. 20.

42   Ivan Kreilkamp, "Dying Like a Dog in *Great Expectations*," in *Victorian Animal Dreams: Representations of Animals in Victorian Literature and Culture*, ed. Deborah Denenholz Morse and Martin A. Danahay (Aldershot: Ashgate, 2007), p. 82.

43 Alex Woloch, *The One vs. the Many: Minor Characters and the Space of the Protagonist in the Novel* (Princeton: Princeton Univ. Press, 2003), p. 27; quoted in Kreilkamp, "Dying Like a Dog," p. 82.

44 See for example Cary Wolfe, introduction to *Zoontologies: The Question of the Animal*, ed. Wolfe (Minneapolis: Univ. of Minnesota Press, 2003), pp. ix–xxiii; Morse and Danahay, introduction to *Victorian Animal Dreams*, pp. 1–12; and Matthew Calarco, *Zoographies: The Question of the Animal from Heidegger to Derrida* (New York: Columbia Univ. Press, 2008).

45 See Gilles Deleuze and Félix Guattari, *A Thousand Plateaus: Capitalism and Schizophrenia*, trans. Brian Massumi (Minneapolis: Univ. of Minnesota Press, 1987), p. 242.

46 See also Armstrong, who suggests that Alice's "farewell" to the cards "could be said to echo" a Marxist vision of society "under conditions of late capitalism" in which "relations among things determine relations among people" ("The Occidental Alice," p. 551).

CHAPTER 9

Theory in Practice
The Autumn King: Remembering the Land in King Lear

Jayne Elisabeth Archer, Richard Marggraf Turley, and Howard Thomas

Jayne Elisabeth Archer's research interests include alchemy, science, and the pseudo-sciences in early modern literature. Richard Marggraf Turley writes on Romanticism and teaches at the University of Aberystwyth. Howard Thomas's research is on genetics, evolution, and food plants. Their book, *Food and the Literary Imagination* (2014), is an examination of the presence of food plants in literature from Chaucer to the nineteenth century.

Returned from France, Cordelia reports a sighting of her father:

> he was met even now,
> As mad as the racked sea, singing aloud,
> Crowned with rank fumitor and furrow-weeds,
> With burdocks, hemlock, nettles, cuckoo-flowers,
> Darnel, and all the idle weeds that grow
> In our sustaining corn.
>
> (18.2–6)[1]

Cordelia's description takes its power from its resonances with other myths, stories, and rituals of death usually followed by resurrection: Christ crowned with thorns; the Green Man or "wild man," whose yearly sacrifice ensures the fertility of the land and its people; and the Biblical Job.[2] But for Shakespeare and his first audiences, this power would have been amplified and inflected by knowledge of the characteristics and properties of the "idle weeds" so carefully and deliberately itemized by Cordelia, and because

Original publication details: Jayne Elisabeth Archer, Richard Marggraf Turley, and Howard Thomas, "The Autumn King: Remembering the Land in King Lear" from *Shakespeare Quarterly* 63.4, pp. 518–543. Folger Shakespeare Library, 2012. Reproduced with permission from Johns Hopkins University Press.

this image of a neglected harvest fulfills the prophecy of "dearth" made by Edmund in scene 2 of the play.[3]

The food shortages of the late sixteenth and early seventeenth centuries resulted in a heightened awareness among the populace of the dangers of, and their vulnerability to, failing harvests and corrupted food. *King Lear*'s engagement with such themes enables us to perceive the ways in which the shift to early agrarian capitalism involved a concomitant shift in ecological relations. Using a synthesis of ecocritical and historicist methodologies, this essay argues that Shakespeare deploys images of crop contamination in this and other history plays to register and articulate enduring anxieties over relations between court and country, legitimacy and bastardy, and elite power and popular resistance. In particular, *King Lear*'s emphasis on the politics of food supply, encompassing land ownership, the management of natural resources, and the relationship between the monarch and his or her land, is articulated through recurring tropes of mimicry and subversion. Insisting on the ecocritical dimension that is so often written out of historicist interpretations, we argue that the inclusion of weeds in Cordelia's description of her father opens up a political reading of *King Lear* that would have been clearly legible to Shakespeare's own audience members, many of whom were, like the playwright from Warwickshire, recent arrivals in London from surrounding grain-supplying regions.

The first part of this essay scrutinizes a tradition of textual editing and stagings that ignores the arable setting of the play's climax. The significance of that arable setting, which provides a meaningful context for the weeds in Lear's crown, is then established within a reading sensitive to the closely interwoven botanical, medical, and political debates present not just in *King Lear*, but also in other Shakespeare histories and tragedies. The image of a mad and dispossessed king wearing weeds for a crown is used to contextualize King James's fashioning, at the beginning of his reign, as a "landlord," both in terms of contemporary concerns over sustenance and food distribution, and in light of Shakespeare's own activities as a landowner and convicted grain hoarder. Shakespeare's close interest in the resonant image and conceit of crop infestation, and in the equally overdetermined concept of "pure" wheat, leads us via a wheat-laden coat of arms to reassess the significance of Gerard Legh's *Accedens of Armory* (printed in six editions between 1562 and 1612) – a neglected source for the story of King Lear – for what it reveals about Shakespeare's presentation of changing patterns of land ownership, inheritance, and sovereignty.

Renewed emphasis on material culture, including the domestic and wider environments, and on the intersection of literary and medical discourses in early modern studies has contributed to the emergence of recent scholarship on Shakespeare's portrayal of the production and consumption of food.[4] This work is an important corrective to earlier criticism, in which Shakespeare's allusions to plants were read primarily for their aesthetic and folkloric associations. It overlaps with new historicist readings of the influence of food unrest (particularly the 1607–8 Midlands Uprising) on the portrayal of themes of grain supply and civil war in plays such as *Coriolanus*, as well as with recent trends in ecocritical readings of Shakespeare.[5] Nevertheless, scholarship continues to overlook the ecological contexts that are central to the politics of Shakespeare's plays. A consideration of Cordelia's description of her father in scene 18 enables us to see how this context has been distorted, both textually and in performance.

Among the most potent misprisions of the description is Peter Brook's seminal 1962 production of *King Lear*. Filmed in 1970, Paul Scofield's abdicating monarch is situated amid stark, bare sets that suggest a postapocalyptic winter landscape. Brook's staging was typical of the post-World War II shift toward desiccated, psychologized dramatizations of *King Lear* that registered the paranoid climate and denuded mental landscapes of the Cold War. This nihilistic interpretation found critical support in Jan Kott's *Shakespeare Our Contemporary* (1964), which presented the play as an absurdist drama, a Shakespearean "Endgame."[6] Brook's influence (and through Brook, Brecht, Beckett, and Kott) continues to be felt. Indeed, his is largely the image of the world of *King Lear* inherited by modern audiences. More recent productions, including Adrian Noble's 1982 and 1993 Royal Shakespeare Company productions and Trevor Nunn's 2007 ground-zero version, which starred Ian McKellen as a ludic Lear, find the mental disintegration of the lonely king reflected in and enhanced by a barren, dead set. Today's audiences could be forgiven for thinking that in *King Lear* Shakespeare was wholly uninterested in the worked land as a meaningful context for his drama.

However, closer scrutiny reveals that the blasted vision of Lear's play world actually derives from a series of unauthorized editorial inventions. The erroneous idea of the mad and dispossessed king in scene 18 cavorting on a "blasted heath" – a phrase which, as Ogden notes, comes from *Macbeth*, not *Lear*[7] – was established by Nahum Tate in his 1681 rendering of the play, when he used "*Desert Heath*" to describe the setting for scenes in Act 3.[8] Nicholas Rowe picked up the term for his 1709 edition.[9] But as the 1608 quarto clearly states, the climax of the play and of Lear's madness takes place in a "high-grown field" full of "sustaining corn" (18.7, 6). The king's weaving of a crown that incorporates weeds, including "furrow-weeds," "rank fumitory," and "darnel," only makes sense if this is arable, worked land.[10] Lear's movement from the storm and hovel of the middle portion of the play to this lush and fertile landscape has a powerful dramatic function, heightening (only to frustrate) the audience's expectations of redemption in the final scenes.

The reference to a "high-grown field" encodes knowledge that, although forgotten by the twenty-first century, would have been second nature to early modern audiences.[11] It is vital to recover this knowledge in order to clarify textual details that otherwise seem puzzling. For instance, in modern fields of wheat or barley, mature plants stand less than a meter tall. These so-called "dwarf" cereals are a product of twentieth-century plant breeding and biotechnology.[12] In Shakespeare's time, you could get lost in a wheat field, among crop plants (and their weeds) two meters and more in height.[13] This explains why Cordelia's scout glimpses and then quickly loses sight of Lear: he can hear him singing, but all he can see of the former king is the crown of "idle weeds" as it skims across the tops of the wheat.

The image of a heath, with its accrued layers of resonance as a psychological waste land in *King Lear*, is misleading. Further, despite the fact that the description in scene 18 clearly, and in a very particular manner, describes a crown of arable weeds, we tend to think of Lear as being adorned with a crown of wild flowers – as portrayed, for example, in Trevor Nunn's 2007 production and as found on the striking cover of the Arden2 edition, where the crown is a garland woven with daisies and clover. As with the "blasted heath," this error of representation results from editorial distortions of the play text and through conflation with another of Shakespeare's tragedies. Late seventeenth-century stage directions have Lear entering in Act 4 "fantastically dressed with wild flowers" – a phrase fashioned from *Hamlet*, 4.7.140–41, in which Ophelia weaves "fantastic garlands" from "crow-flowers, nettles, daisies, and long purples."[14] This corruption of the play text erases memories of Cordelia's careful list of "idle weeds" and ameliorates the deeply unsettling nature and political implications of Lear's madness by reimagining the former king in the guise of a childlike and innocent Ophelia.

It wouldn't have been as easy for Shakespeare's first audiences to overlook the significance of the "high-grown field" with its "idle weeds." Recovering this knowledge has important consequences for the way in which time, as well as space, operates in the play. That the field is "high-grown" suggests that the climax of the play takes place in high summer or early autumn, that is, mid- to late August. This time frame is confirmed by the "idle weeds" themselves: hemlock and darnel mature with the corn in mid-August and September.[15] The final scenes are set in harvest time – at least, it *should* be harvest time. "Ripeness is all" (23.11), Edgar states, a remark both literal and figurative and desperately ironic. At the moment when farmers and laborers should be reaping the fields and laying store for the long winter ahead, the land and its people are embroiled in civil war and foreign invasion, and the best that the former king can do is to pick poisonous weeds and leave the "sustaining corn" to rot. In a pun that plays on "weeds" as both plants and apparel, and on "crown" as a political, physical, and botanical term, Lear's head is adorned with a crown crafted *from* the land – and, notably, its "idle weeds" rather than its "sustaining corn" – when he should be wearing the crown symbolic *of* the land. Lear as described in scene 18 is a mockery of the mystical and political doctrine of the king's two bodies and the intertwining of the body politic and the body natural: in dividing the land and bringing forward his own personal autumn, Lear has thrown the country into temporal confusion and his people are doomed to produce crops that they cannot harvest. In this time of national crisis, the "sustaining corn" is just as "idle" as the "weeds" that grow among it.

But reinforcing the sense that, as in *Hamlet*, time is out of joint, the season also seems to be late spring.[16] Desperate to aid her father, Cordelia asks that the "blest secrets" and "unpublished virtues of the earth" might "*Spring* with my tears" (ll. 16–18, emphasis added); indeed, one of the "idle weeds" in Lear's crown suggests that her prayer to turn back the calendar will bear fruit. "Cuckooflowers" were known as lady's smock, a delicate flower that, according to John Gerard's *Herball* (1597), blossoms in spring: "These flower for the most part in Aprill and Maie, when the Cuckowe doth begin to sing her pleasant notes without stammering."[17] Shakespeare relies on the popular association between cuckoo flowers and spring in a song from the final scene of *Love's Labor's Lost* (5.2.879–87).[18] Shakespeare alludes to the cuckoo's habit of laying its eggs in another's nest throughout his plays; in *King Lear*, the Fool compares Goneril to the cuckoo.[19] But it is the associated notion of treachery from within – as cuckoldry, illegitimacy, and familial deception – that is most pertinent to *King Lear* and that aligns this flower to the other weeds in Lear's crown. The presence of cuckoo flowers seems to promise the hope of spring and a happy ending, while reiterating the betrayals that have led – and will lead – to tragedy. The coupling of death (or sacrifice) with hope of resurrection and restoration in Cordelia's description of the "crowned" Lear is thus signaled by a temporal confusion that is encoded in the land and its plants.

The consequence of Lear's division of the kingdoms is a land in which its subjects no longer know how to feed themselves or each other. As Pascale Drouet has observed, the world of *King Lear* is one of hunger.[20] The fields of wheat go unharvested and are overgrown with weeds – they are, as the Fool states, "wild" (11.100) and fit only for burning. There is "no food" for "Hoppedance," who "cries in Tom's belly for two white herring" (13.26–27); the Captain in scene 24 "cannot … eat dried oats" (ll. 37–38); the "white wheat" is "mildew[ed]" (11.105–6); and Albany challenges Edmund to fight "Ere I taste bread" (24.91), deferring the moment of eating. Whether as a result of possession by "the foul fiend Flibbertigibbet" (11.103) or, more likely, the madness and desperation induced by hunger, the population is compelled to consume poisons and waste rather than nourishing food: a citizen "eats cowdung for salads; swallows the old rat and the ditch-dog; [and] drinks the green mantle of the standing pool" (ll. 117–19). Even Lear is reduced to requesting "'raiment, bed, and food'" from his daughters (7.313), and there is evidence to suggest that contemporary audiences associated Lear's "madness" with the deliberate consumption of food waste: in *The Ballad of King Lear*, first published in 1620, Lear eats "What scullion boys set by" and is "glad to feed on beggars' food."[21]

Whatever their motivation, Goneril and Regan's decision to reduce their father's entourage during a time of dearth may have been seen by contemporary audiences as judicious. According to a sermon published in 1596 (*"this time of our Dearth"*), "Kings and Princes" must share some of the blame for famine, "who though their charge bee to prouide for the good of the people ... vtterly neglect them, rather impouerishing their subiectes ... burthering them with taxes and subsidies" so that the royal court can be maintained with its "horses, hounds, hauks, harlots, [and] iesters."[22] The image of Lear wearing a crown of weeds amid a field of unharvested corn is symptomatic of a disastrous and seemingly irrevocable breakdown in the production, distribution, and consumption of food within the kingdom. But in order to appreciate the subtlety of this image and its action as a prism for the play's political and familial conflicts, we need to consider the valences for an early modern audience of the most noisome and rancorous of those "idle weeds," the toxic wheat-mimicker darnel.

The appearance of darnel in a litany of plants is a classical, specifically Virgilian, convention.[23] In book 1 of the *Georgics*, the growth of darnel and other weeds is a sign of the end of the Golden Age: henceforth, man must plough the soil and weed his crops to keep hunger at bay. This *topos* was appropriated by Christian writers to add color and detail to accounts of the fallen world: Du Bartas, for example, tells how the "grieved Earth" turns "our seed-Wheat-kernel / To burn-grain Thistle, and to vapourie Darnel, / Cockle, wilde Oats, rough Burs, Corn-cumbring Tares."[24] This postlapsarian world, in which the creation of new life is attended with pain and uncertainty, is what Lear invokes when he calls on the "goddess" nature to curse Goneril and make her barren (4.265–80). However, it is possible that in Shakespeare's play Cordelia's iteration of the classical-Christian convention is inflected by a passage from the anonymous *True Chronicle History of King Leir* (1605). Accompanied by his faithful courtier Perillus (Shakespeare's Kent), Leir reflects on the ingratitude and treachery he has suffered at the hands of his eldest daughters, Gonorill and Ragan:

LEIR   Can kindnesse spring out of ingratitude?
            Or loue be reapt, where hatred hath bin sowne?
            Can Henbane ioyne in league with Methridate?
            Or Sugar grow in Wormwoods bitter stalke?
            It cannot be, they are too opposite:
            And so am I to any kindnesse here.
            I haue throwne Wormwood on the sugred youth,
            And like to Henbane poysoned the Fount,
            Whence flowed the Methridate of a childs goodwil:
            I, like an enuious thorne, haue prickt the heart,
            And turnd sweet Grapes, to sowre vnrelisht Sloes:
            The causelesse ire of my respectlesse brest,
            Hath sowrd the sweet milk of dame Natures paps:
            My bitter words haue gauld her hony thoughts,
            And weeds of rancour chokt the flower of grace.[25]

Using metaphors of corruption and poison, Leir blames himself for having converted that which is wholesome and nourishing into something that spreads disease, pain, and death. He is responsible for poisoning Nature's pure offspring. Developing Leir's botanical-medical metaphor, Perillus contends that "perfit good" simples ("hony, milke, Grape, Sugar, Methridate") cannot be corrupted by the presence of the "bad" ("the thorn, / The weed, the gall, the henbane & and wormewood").[26] Like *King Lear*'s "idle weeds," the *True Chronicle History*'s "weeds of rancour" symbolize the disastrous effects of the king's "unnatural" decision to divide the land and reject his one true daughter. Both lists include "henbane." In the latter play, the weeds are balanced by a list of "perfit good simples," each one of which was credited in early modern dietaries with nourishing and healing powers (or "virtues") and was used figuratively in political treatises as a remedy for heresy, schism, and insurrection.[27] Mithridate, for example, was believed to be a universal antidote, with particular powers against plague. For the preacher Thomas White, however, it was a panacea "against all treasons, seditions, alterations, [and] warres"; for Francis Trigge, writing in 1604, only mithridate could heal the destruction suffered by farmers and families as a result of enclosures.[28] The botanical-medical world of *King Lear* is markedly more complex. The Doctor prescribes sleep: "That to provoke in him / Are many simples operative, whose power / Will close the eye of anguish" (18.14–16). But in contrast to *The True Chronicle History*, with its comparatively unsophisticated set of "good" and "bad" simples, the land in scene 18 of *King Lear* is no longer capable of nurturing the "good simples" that might counteract the effects of "idle weeds." It is for this reason that Cordelia has to call on the "blest secrets" and "unpublished virtues of the earth" to "Spring with my tears" (ll. 17–19). Such "simples," it is implied, must be grown afresh, since they no longer live in this cursed land.

The inclusion of darnel in Lear's crown adds to the Virgilian allusion a Christian framework that is otherwise strikingly absent from the play. In early modern exegesis, darnel was identified with the "tares" found among wheat in Christ's parable (Matt. 13:24–30, 36–43). On both sides of the confessional divide, the parable of the wheat and tares was used to warn of the difficulties of discriminating between true doctrine and heresy. In a chapter about cockle and darnel, Levinus Lemnius notes that in the Gospels Christ uses "the nature and qualitie of these noisome weedes" as a metaphor for "dangerous, hurtfull, pernicious, corrupt and vnsincere doctrine."[29] The parable, Lemnius states, reminds Christians of the necessity in a well-ordered state of measured and judicious governors: "yet for due punishment doth he [Christ] subiect and referre to the authoritie of the magistrate, all those that be factious disturbers of the peace and tranquillitie, both of the Church and Commonwealth."[30] For the king, then, as head of "Church and Commonwealth," to wear darnel, an emblem of the machinations of "sathan," is truly shocking. Rebellious subjects like Edmund, Goneril, and Regan can be checked only by the presence of figures of authority and discernment; Lear, despite his feeble attempt to gather weeds at harvest time,[31] is clearly not up to the job and moreover is associated with the very forces of insurrection he should oppose. He is part of the sickness rather than the cure.

In another way, the inclusion of darnel in the crown of "idle weeds" draws on communal memories and experiences that add texture to the portrayal of Lear's condition, as well as to the errors of political judgment that have led him to this state. When darnel infiltrated the food chain, most often in bread or beer, the results were symptoms resembling madness. Gerard, for example, notes that it causes "drunkennes" and "hurteth the eies and maketh them dim"; Thomas Cooper, using the Latin name for darnel, observes that "*lolium*," consumed in "hote bread … maketh the heade giddie"; and Du Bartas calls it "dizzie Darnell" (Figure 1).[32] As T. J. King has argued, Cordelia's mention of darnel "may serve to reinforce the themes of madness and blindness found elsewhere in the play."[33] The harmful effects of darnel and the other "idle weeds" in Lear's crown are acknowledged by Cordelia and the Doctor in scene 18, who diagnose "aidant and remediate" and narcotic herbs, "simples operative, whose power / Will close the eye of anguish," to counteract them (18.18, 15–16). In fashioning a crown out of darnel, Lear has selected a plant that is not simply associated with the physical, mental, and sensory confusion he (and, in different ways, the blinded Gloucester) has exhibited throughout the play, but actually causes this derangement. However, Lear's selection of plants is more subtle, more sophisticated than critics have hitherto acknowledged. Like an animal that, having eaten something detrimental to its health, instinctively ingests something that will cause vomiting, Lear has plucked weeds that both catalyze his disease and point toward its remedy. Recalling the Paracelsian principle of using known poisons to counteract disease, the crown of "idle weeds" contains plants that expel toxins from the body: fumitory was used as a diuretic to cleanse the skin, liver, and spleen; hemlock and darnel were taken as purgatives and for their narcotic powers – precisely the properties prescribed by Cordelia and the Doctor.[34] In *King Lear*, a Virgilian literary convention is refracted through contemporary debates in botany, husbandry, politics, religion, and medicine.

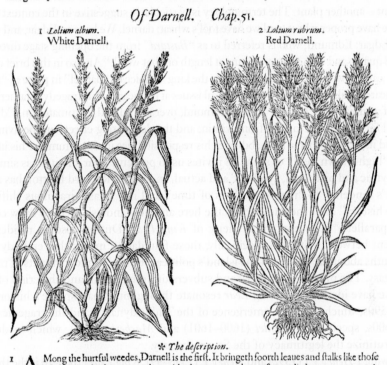

HISTORIE OF PLANTS.   71

were in vaine to make a long harueft of fuch euill corne, confidering it is not poffeffed with any one good qualitie. And therefore this much fhall fuffice for the defcription.

Of Darnell.   *Chap.*51.

1 *Lolium album.*   2 *Lolium rubrum.*
White Darnell.   Red Darnell.

❧ *The defcription.*

1 A Mong the hurtful weedes, Darnell is the firft. It bringeth foorth leaues and ftalks like thofe of wheate or barly, yet rougher, with a long eare made vp of many little ones, euery particular one whereof containeth two or three graines, leffer than thofe of wheate, fcarfly any chaffie huske to couer them with, by reafon wherof they are eafily fhaken out and fcattered abrode.
2 Red Darnell is likewife an vnprofitable corne or graffe, hauing leaues like barly. The ioints of the ftraw or ftalke are of a reddifh colour, bearing at the top a fmall and tender eare, fpike fafhion.

❧ *The place.*

They grow in fields among wheate and barly, of the corrupt and bad feede as *Galen* faith, efpecially in a moift and dankifh foile.

❧ *The time.*

They fpring and flourifh with the corne, and in Auguft the feede is ripe.

❧ *The names.*

1 Darnell is called in Greeke αἶρα: in the Arabian toong *Zizania* and *Seeylen*: in French *Yuray*: in Italian *Loglio*: in low Dutch Dolick: in Englifh Darnell, of fome Iuray and Raye, and of fome of the Latines *Triticum Temulentum.*
2 Red Darnell is called in Greeke φοῖνιξ: or *Phœnix*, of red crimfon colour: in Latin *Lolium rubrum*: and *Lolium Murinum*: in Englifh Wall Barly, and Waie Bennet: of fome *Hordeum murinum*, and *Triticum murinum*: in Dutch Müyfe coren.

❧ *The temperature.*

Darnell is hot in the third degree, and drie in the fecond. Red Darnell drieth without fharpnes, as *Galen* faith.

E 4   ❧ *The*

Figure 1   Red and white darnell, from John Gerard, *The Herball or Generall Historie of Plantes* (London, 1597), 71. General Reference Collection 449.k.4. © British Library Board. All rights reserved.

The special significance of references to weeds in the literature of ages more attuned to the fragility of food supply than our own is now understandable. The presence of crop contaminants in the food chain was at best undesirable, at worst disastrous. It would not have escaped the attention of the audience for whom *King Lear* was written that a play about identity, corruption, and betrayal from within employs an allusion to darnel, a toxic interloper indistinguishable from the wheat it infests until it is too late. Although the contemporary languages of botany and genetics can help explain why and how this happens, early moderns had their own subtle terminology. Gerard, for example, distinguishes three types of relationship between field plants: "fools," "kin" (or "kinde"), and "bastardes." "Fools" denote plants that are often mistaken for one another; "kin" indicates plants that are closely related; and "bastardes" describes plants that imitate, but are inferior to, and which exploit – to its detriment – another plant. The terminology is particularly suggestive in the context of *King Lear*. We have proper wheat, and we have fool's wheat: darnel. We have an Edgar, and we have a fool's Edgar: Edmund, who is referred to as "*Bastard*" from the opening stage direction of the 1608 quarto and who plays and puns at length on that word.[35] And so in this brief description of Lear's crown of "idle weeds" and in the king's choice of "darnel" in place of "wheat," Shakespeare distils the personal and political issues at the heart of his tragedy: a father's privileging of a subversive "bastard" child, Edmund, over a loyal and legitimate son, Edgar; the potential for subversion to arise from within; and the devastating effects on the living landscape and its people when a king abdicates his responsibilities in the autumn of his life.

The "high-grown field" of scene 18 invites us to perceive Lear's Britain as simultaneously mythic and historical, symbolic and actual. Indeed, as Richard Dutton has argued, the play's tendency to "ignore the laws of time" and its "quasimiraculous shifts from myth to history" alert the audience to the here and now and ask them to draw contemporary parallels.[36] The contemporaneity of *King Lear*, Dutton asserts, resides in its movement between history – specifically, those foundation myths that embody "cherished truths about the origins of the island's political culture" – and elements of romance and fantasy. The motifs of mimicry and subversion from within and the crisis of sustenance we have identified in *King Lear* resonate throughout Shakespeare's history plays of the 1590s, which trace the emergence of the Tudor dynasty, and the tragedies of the early 1600s, specifically, *Hamlet* (1600–1601) and *Macbeth* (1606), which in different ways scrutinize the legitimacy of the Stuart dynasty.

Following *1 Henry VI* (1592) and *Henry V* (1598–99), *King Lear* (1605–6) is the third and final of Shakespeare's plays to include an allusion to darnel. The first two plays, from the first and second tetralogies, use darnel and related imagery to underline the correspondences between good husbandry and good government, and to interrogate contemporary issues of food supply and national security. In *1 Henry VI*, the vilified Joan of Arc (La Pucelle) is associated with the treacherous qualities of darnel. She taunts the English at Rouen:

PUCELLE	Good morrow gallants. Want ye corn for bread?
	I think the Duke of Burgundy will fast
	Before he'll buy again at such a rate.
	'Twas full of darnel. Do you like the taste?
BURGUNDY	Scoff on, vile fiend and shameless courtesan.
	I trust ere long to choke thee with thine own
	And make thee curse the harvest of that corn.
CHARLES	Your grace may starve, perhaps, before that time.
BEDFORD	O let no words, but deeds, revenge this treason.

(3.5.1–9)

Here, the taste of darnel is a metaphor for the bitter flavor of defeat – significantly, a defeat wrought by deception. A French war party has infiltrated the city by pretending to be a group of corn merchants and defeated the garrison, neatly mimicking the mimicry by which darnel insinuates itself into the food chain. The capture of Rouen is one of the few points where Shakespeare deviates from his sources in this play,[37] perhaps because it chimes with public anxieties in the 1590s over the price and purity of corn, especially imported corn. These anxieties are likely to have been exacerbated by reports that Parisians, besieged by Henri IV's forces between May and August 1590, resorted to eating bread made from "pease, tares, oates and acorns," sawdust, and eventually the ground-up bones of the dead.[38] The failed harvests of that decade heightened concerns about the nation's ability to feed itself and its reliance on imported supplies that were often contaminated and sold at inflated prices (hence, La Pucelle's reference to "buy[ing] at such a rate").[39] As R. B. Outhwaite points out, "dearth" had two meanings: lack of food and its costliness, specifically "sharp elevation in the prices of … bread and beer – and the grainstuff from which they derived."[40] In a series of proclamations, Queen Elizabeth attempted to control the price, purity, and distribution of corn and to limit foreign imports.[41] For Francis Trigge, addressing the incoming King James, fewer people meant fewer soldiers, rendering the nation vulnerable to foreign invasion: "[Camden] writes, that England *for corne was the onely storehouse of all the west Empire….* In those daies *England* was able to relieue other countries with corne: but sometime now she is glad to buie corne of other countries her selfe … tillage of the earth surpasseth all, and … euen the King thereby is maintained: by the foode that it ministreth, to strengthen his people; and by the multitude of valiant souliders it affordeth for his warres."[42] Whether the reason was war or failed harvests, cities were especially vulnerable to interruptions to their food supplies, and citizens were at the mercy of millers and purveyors who were often less than scrupulous in the measures and purity of the grain they sold.[43] In *1 Henry VI*, the Rouen compromised by "corrupted" imported corn resonates with England in the 1590s, an island made vulnerable by hunger. So too Lear's Britain, unable to feed itself or be governed peacefully, requires foreign forces to restore order.

This insistence on national security through good husbandry is reiterated in the Duke of Burgundy's speech in Shakespeare's *Henry V* (5.2.33–62). "Fertile France," he laments, has gone to ruin during the recent warfare, and weeds grow unchecked in its cornfields. His imagery anticipates the language of *Hamlet*, in which the Danish prince complains of the world: "'tis an unweeded garden / That grows to seed; things rank and gross in nature / Possess it merely" (1.2.135–37). It echoes the language of the garden scene in *Richard II* (3.4) and John of Gaunt's speech in the same play (2.1.31–68), substituting "this best garden of the world" for "this blessed garden" and "Dear nurse of arts, plenties, and joyful births" for "This nurse, this teeming womb of royal kings."[44] But in *Henry V*, as in *King Lear*, the weeds are associated not simply with the garden as a metaphor for the state but with "fallow leas" and arable land. Sustained conflict means that the "sciences" (5.2.58) by which the land can be made to feed its people have been forgotten:

> Alas, she hath from France too long been chased,
> And all her husbandry doth lie on heaps,
> Corrupting in its own fertility.
> Her vine, the merry cheerer of the heart,
> Unprunèd dies; her hedges even-plashed
> Like prisoners wildly overgrown with hair

> Put forth disordered twigs; her fallow leas
> The darnel, hemlock, and rank fumitory
> Doth root upon, while that the coulter rusts
> That should deracinate such savagery.
> The even mead – that erst brought sweetly forth
> The freckled cowslip, burnet, and green clover –
> Wanting the scythe, all uncorrected, rank,
> Conceives by idleness, and nothing teems
> But hateful docks, rough thistles, kecksies, burs,
> Losing both beauty and utility.
>
>   (5.2.38–53)

"[D]arnel, hemlock, and rank fumitory" resurface in Cordelia's description of her father in scene 18 of *King Lear*; the "docks," "burs," and "idleness" in Burgundy's speech anticipate Cordelia's "burdocks" and "idle weeds." This is not just Shakespeare repeating himself or recycling material from earlier works. It is a careful echoing that conjures memories and invites comparisons between the plays in the light of ongoing experiences of the decline in arable farming and dearth in England. John of Gaunt's England, which "Is now leased out … / Like to a tenement or pelting farm" (2.1.59, 60), is also Burgundy's France, and both lands are mapped onto Lear's Britain. For the latter world, for all its pagan antiquity, is a surprisingly ordinary place of "low farms, / Poor pelting villages, sheep-cotes and mills" (7.182–83), peopled by "tenant" farmers such as the "Old Man" who meets Gloucester and Edgar on the way to Dover (15.10) – in other words, a world very familiar to Shakespeare's first audiences.

This botanical-political discourse, indicating sophisticated knowledge of arable plants on the part of Shakespeare's audiences, echoes throughout the plays that in different ways examine the succession of James VI and I, *Macbeth* and *Hamlet*. Such a discourse insists that we reinterpret these plays in light of one another. Like darnel, cockle was a weed that grew in corn fields, its name derived from the Anglo-Saxon *ceocan*, meaning "choke," so called because it chokes the life from the corn.[45] Levinus Lemnius notes, "Vnder the name of Cockle and Darnell is comprehended all vicious, noisome and vnprofitable graine, encombring & hindring good Corne; which, being heerby choaked and despoiled of conuenient moisture … prospereth not as it should."[46] Traditions of biblical translation, scriptural exegesis, husbandry manuals, and literature in the Georgic tradition[47] meant that cockle and darnel came to symbolize revolt, civil discord, and political corruption. Thus, Coriolanus argues that by distributing corn to plebeians, as well as patricians, the ruling class has "nourish[ed] 'gainst our Senate / The cockle of rebellion, insolence, sedition, / Which we ourselves have ploughed for, sowed, and scattered."[48] In this Roman play, which dates from 1608, problems with food purity and the state's distribution of grain are used literally as a cause of suffering and civil unrest and metaphorically, with bastardized grain symbolizing the mixing of "pure" with "impure" Romans. Likewise, as a consequence of Lear's mismanagement of the land and his error in judging the love test, "idle weeds" have been left to choke the life from "sustaining corn," treacherous subjects like Goneril, Regan, and Edmund have gained ascendency, and "true" subjects such as Cordelia and the Fool will be choked to death by hanging.

Like "choke," "blast," which similarly implies death by tainted breath or breathlessness, is an infectious disease of cereal crops. But where "choke" is used by Shakespeare to indicate rebellion from within, "blast" points to the wide-reaching effects of such actions. Although, as we have seen, *King Lear* does not feature a "blasted heath," *Macbeth* does

(1.3.77), and Lear, when cursing Goneril, wishes on his eldest daughter "worst blasts and fogs" (4.290). "Blast," denoting a disease of arable plants, was in use by at least 1577; in Barnabe Googe's translation of Conrad Heresbach's *Foure Bookes of Husbandry*, the farmer is advised to sow his corn "in hollowe Furrowes, because it is very subiect to blasting, thinking thereby to preserue it both from blast and mildewe."[49] The phrase "blasted heath" could also describe a blighted landscape as one subject to the depredations of the weather. Such infection is a symbol of the effects on the land of political corruption from within the inner circles of the court and its consequent effects upon the natural order, including, of course, the cycles of nature.[50] Googe couples "blast" with "mildew."[51] While the "mil" (or, in early modern orthography, "mel") of "mildew" was thought to derive from honey (because of its supposed sweetness), the fungus, like "blast," was also associated with cereal crops (with "mil" meaning "meal"). And so Edgar, as Poor Tom in *King Lear*, imagines that the fiends who persecute him have "mildew[ed] the white wheat" (11.105–6).[52]

Suggestive for *King Lear* and, as we will see, *Hamlet*, is John Lyly's use in 1578 of meal or mil "deaw" and "blast" in a passage that uses the relationship between darnel and wheat as a metaphor for the difference between two male twins. Nature produces pairs of opposites: "As the breath of the Lyon engendreth as well the Serpent as the Ant, and as the selfe same deaw forceth the earth to yeeld both the Darnell and Wheate: or as the Easterly winde maketh the blossomes to blast, and the buddes to blowe, so one wombe nourisheth contrary wits, and one milke diuers manners, which argueth somthing in Nature I knowe not what, to be meruailous, I dare not say monstrous."[53] While in *King Lear* the bond between wheat and darnel is a metaphor for the relationship between a legitimate child and his "bastard" brother, in Lyly it describes twins born with opposing natures. In *Hamlet*, the difference between the two brothers, Hamlet Senior and Claudius, is figured as "wholesome" wheat contaminated by its "mildewed" sibling. Berating his mother for allowing Claudius to replace (or mimic) Hamlet Senior, Hamlet cries, "Here is your husband, like a mildewed ear / Blasting his wholesome brother" (3.4.63–64). The combination of mildew and blast in this couplet suggests that "blast" signifies the cereal crop disease, thereby echoing the metaphors of plague and corruption that rebound in the play.[54] Hamlet's description of his father as a "mildewed ear" of wheat carried echoes of Hamlet Senior's account of his poisoning: "With juice of cursèd hebenon in a vial, / And in the porches of my ears did pour / The leperous distilment" (1.5.62–64).[55]

This is the only mention of "hebenon" by Shakespeare, and critics remain uncertain what this name means.[56] Given the precision we have identified in Shakespeare's treatment of the properties of poisonous plants elsewhere, the imprecision of the name "hebenon" is likely to be deliberate. Because of the parallels between the deaths of Hamlet Senior and James VI/I's father, it is possible that the obscurity of the poison signals a diplomatic uncertainty on Shakespeare's part as to the identity of Darnley's murderer.[57] But the parallels between darnel and "hebenon" invite a reading of *King Lear* in Scene 18 that encodes complex contemporary political messages for and about the new King James I, who, as Dan Brayton points out, styled himself as a "landlord."[58] For if James's father, Henry Stuart, Lord Darnley, is shadowed in Hamlet Senior, his name is also whispered in Lear's darnel.[59] The House of Stuart was, properly, the House of Darnley and Stuart; although standardized in modern orthography, Darnley and Darnel(l) were variant early modern spellings, with "ley" another version of "lea," or a field ("lea") of darnel. In John Stow's *Chronicles* (1580), his name is spelt "*Darnley*" and "*Darneley*"; and in the second volume of Raphael Holinshed's *Chronicles* (1586), it is spelt "Darneleie."[60] In *King Lear*, which interrogates the Union of the Crowns and, like *Hamlet* and *Macbeth*, the rise of the House of Stuart as it eclipses the House of Tudor, the image of the former king in the high-grown field wearing a crown of weeds, among which "Darnel" – with a capital "D" from its placement, with full emphasis and accent, at the beginning of the line – is prominent. That image invites James to consider his own problematic inheritance and his present and future role in managing the land and its resources. Like the selection of the white and red roses in the Temple Garden in *1 Henry VI*, 2.4, this moment provides England's royal House of Stuart with a very ambivalent emblem. Darnel, like wheat, was thought to have two main varieties: red and white.[61] The red and white roses of the Tudors, forged in civil war, have become the red and white darnel of Lear's crown. Depopulation, dearth, religious and social divisions, a depleted treasury – James's inheritance could not be more poisonous.

Work on *King Lear* probably began in or around 1604, during King James's protracted journey to London for his coronation and the commencement of the long-anticipated negotiations that would eventually result in the Union of the Crowns. In 1604, Shakespeare was forty, and he seems to have started making provision for his eventual retirement.[62] But what should have promised peace and prosperity delivered a period of sustained civil and social unrest fueled by a series of bad harvests, death by starvation and malnutrition, and land enclosures. The riots which broke out in the Midlands in 1607–8 have been identified as a contemporary context for *Coriolanus*.[63] However, as we have seen, concerns about the harvest and the purity and price of grain supplies were ongoing throughout the latter half of the sixteenth century and provide an important context not simply for the Roman play, but also for Shakespeare's plays of the 1590s and early 1600s. One of the complicating factors in such periods of food shortage was the illegal hoarding of grain. Shakespeare himself was guilty of this activity. Although living in London, he retained substantial properties in and around Stratford,[64] where during the late 1590s and the first few years of the seventeenth century, he stockpiled grain for sale at inflated prices to the local brewing trade[65] and in July 1605 paid a large sum, £440, for a half interest in a lease of "tithes of corn, grain, blade, and hay."[66]

At approximately the same time, Shakespeare was making a different kind of attempt to secure his legacy that may have contributed to the world of *King Lear*. On 20 October 1596, the College of Arms approved his application for a coat of arms.[67] It is likely that Shakespeare consulted the most popular guide to heraldry of the day, Gerard Legh's *The Accedens of Armory*.[68] It is possible that Shakespeare referred to *The Accedens of Armory* because it contains an account of the Inner Temple revels of 1561–62, which accompanied Norton and Sackville's *Gorboduc* (1561–62), the latter a source for *King Lear* and a potential inspiration for its images of corruption and pollution.[69] What scholars have failed to notice, however, is that Legh's treatise is also a source for the story of King Lear.[70] Legh's rendering predates Holinshed, and is therefore likely to have informed Shakespeare's play through that intermediary source. Certainly, Legh's account is quite close to the version that appears in book 2 of Geoffrey of Monmouth's *Historia Regum Britanniæ*.[71] However, what makes Legh's version pertinent to an ecocritical reading of Shakespeare's play, and to an analysis of *King Lear*'s engagement with the politics of food supply, is that Legh uses the story of "*leyr*" and his "*doughter and heire*" Cordeilla to justify the right of women to rule, a right that he associates with the fertility of the land. The coat of arms Legh identifies for Cordeilla and other landowning women features a wheat sheaf.[72] This coat of arms, called a "*Garbe*," shows a golden "*sheafe of wheate*" on a "*field Azure*" (Figure 2).[73] As an exemplary female sovereign who inherits through her father, Cordeilla justifies the legitimacy of Queen Elizabeth, whose lineage is traced in the same volume.[74] The right of royal women such as Cordeilla and Elizabeth to represent and, in a mystical sense, become the land is symbolized through their association with a coat of arms linking them to Ceres, the goddess of agriculture and fertility who was associated with wheat. The "*Garbe*" coat of arms needs no further "*commendacion*," Legh declares, "*for all people prayse it, that cannot liue without it.*"[75] The woman bearing this coat of arms is as essential to the lives of the people as their daily bread and beer, and her continuing presence ensures the land's fruitfulness.

Reading *King Lear* in light of Legh's *Accedens of Armory* confirms that Shakespeare's play is a chorographical text, which is to say, it concerns man's embeddedness in the land and the importance of land in the inscription and dissemination of shared memory and knowledge. The importance of the land in Shakespeare's play is announced by the presence of the map of Britain at 1.37. One of the few props mentioned in this play or in any play by Shakespeare, Lear's map might have looked something like the frontispiece to William Camden's *Britannia* (Figure 3). With Neptune representing the sea on the left and Ceres presenting the land on the right, the map reminds us of the symbolic and political meanings of the "high-grown field" in scene 18 of *King Lear*. As in the frontispiece to Michael Drayton's 1612 *Poly-Olbion*, the land, Britannia, is represented by Ceres. Ceres was associated with Virgo-Astraea, goddess of the

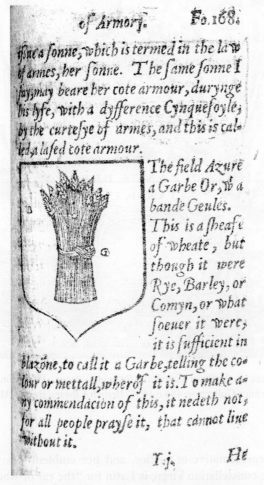

Figure 2 A coat of arms appropriate to gentlewomen, from Gerard Legh, *The Accedens of Armory* (London, 1562), fol. 168r. General Reference Collection 605.b.1. © British Library Board. All rights reserved.

Figure 3 Frontispiece to William Camden, *Britannia*, trans. Philemon Holland (London, [1610]). General Reference Collection 456.e.16. © British Library Board. All rights reserved.

Golden Age and representative of justice, and her emblem was wheat; Spica, the brightest star in the constellation Virgo, is Latin for "the ear of wheat."[76] In the early modern imagination, corn and wheat represented the life force and identity of the nation, and harvest time (late August, as the Sun enters Virgo) was crucial in determining her future. This tradition would have been familiar to Shakespeare, not only from *The Accedens of Armory*, but also from Spenser's *Mutability Cantos*, in which the month of August is accompanied by Virgo-Astraea, wearing "eares of corne":

> That was the righteous Virgin, which of old
> Liv'd here on earth, and plenty made abound;
> But, after Wrong was lov'd and Iustice solde,
> She left th'vnrighteous world and was to heauen extold.[77]

The death of Queen Elizabeth, who was so often identified with the goddess of justice Virgo-Astraea,[78] signifies for Spenser and Shakespeare the end of the Golden Age, and, with it – as we have seen in Virgil's *Georgics* – the emergence of darnel and other "idle weeds" that threaten the harvest.[79] The autumn of *King Lear*'s scene 18 is a crucial moment, for in its botanical-political field of imagery, it brings together the departure of Queen Elizabeth (as goddess of wheat) with the very ambivalent presence of King James I (as king of darnel). For James, witnessing this scene, the question is clear: will he manage the nation's resources in a way that is just, responsible, and above all sustainable?

In scene 1 of *King Lear*, a father asks his three daughters to declare their love for him. The winner will win "our largest bounty" (l. 46). In the context of dividing land, the meaning of "bounty" suggests natural resources and, specifically, food. Goneril, receiving Scotland, and Regan, receiving Wales and the West Country, are assigned very similar lands, by Lear's estimation, "shady forests and wide-skirted meads" (l. 58).[80] Forests and pasture do not produce corn. For Cordelia, Lear has reserved the corn-rich lands of central and southern England. Although British soil is, as William Harrison remarked, more "inclined to the feeding and grasing of the cattell, then profitable for tillage, & bearing of corn," England is more "fruitfull" than Wales and both are more "bountifull" than Scotland.[81] When Goneril and Regan are compared to serpents and wolves, as they are throughout the play, it is for a very good reason: they do not own lands that produce arable crops.

Food unrest and botanical-political discourse open up new ways of reading *King Lear*. The struggle for Cordelia's portion involves a battle for corn and, with it, sustenance, security, and legitimacy. There is an inevitable logic to the fact that Goneril and Regan, in their struggle for land, harness the energies of Edmund, whose mimicry, bastardy, and treachery are the play's personifications of darnel and other "idle weeds" that threaten to blind and choke those who are "legitimate." Restoring ecocritical concerns to historicist methods of interpretation sheds new light on the importance of the politics of food supply not simply in *King Lear*, but in Shakespeare's history plays and tragedies more generally. The properties and behavior of plants and plant disease provide a complex web of metaphors through which Shakespeare, across his plays of the 1590s and early 1600s, interrogates questions of political legitimacy, treachery, treason, and the relationship between the (gendered) body of the monarch and his or her land. That these metaphors can be traced not simply in plays, but also in husbandry manuals, prose fiction, heraldry books, religious treatises, and works of natural philosophy, as well as in the symbolism of the Houses of Tudor and Stuart, shows that food insecurity and botanical-political tropes are deeply embedded in the discourses of early modern Britain. This discursive emphasis is intimately related to the fact that the succession crisis of the 1590s and early 1600s came at a time of heightened food insecurity and unrest. Shakespeare's plays, the profits from which he used to help secure himself and his family from the consequences of failing harvests and dearth, respond to these twin crises by interrogating the problems of ensuring the equitable and sustainable management of natural resources together with a reliable, affordable, and uncorrupted supply of food. In Shakespeare's history plays and tragedies, as for us in the second decade of the twenty-first century, food security is inseparable from national security.

Notes

1   *The History of King Lear*, ed. Stanley Wells (Oxford: Oxford UP, 2008); all quotations from the play will be taken from this edition and cited in the text by act, scene, and line. "[B]urdocks" is a textual emendation: the 1608 quarto has "hor-docks" and the 1623 folio has "Hardokes," neither of which are known as plant names (18.4n).

2   Frankie Rubinstein, "Speculating on Mysteries: Religion and Politics in *King Lear*," *Renaissance Studies* 16 (2002): 235–62, esp. 259; Joy Kennedy, "Shakespeare's *King Lear*," *The Explicator* 60 (2002): 60–62; Philippa Berry, *Of Chastity and Power: Elizabethan Literature and the Unmarried Queen* (London: Routledge, 1989), 90–92; and Steven Marx, *Shakespeare and the Bible* (Oxford: Oxford UP, 2000), 59–78. See also *Hamlet*, 4.7.141, 144, in *The Oxford Shakespeare: The Complete Works*, gen. ed. Stanley Wells and Gary Taylor (Oxford: Oxford UP, 2005). Unless otherwise stated, all quotations from Shakespeare's works other than *King Lear* refer to this edition.

3   "Dearth" is an addition made by Edmund to Gloucester's list of the possible effects of "These late eclipses" (2.101–7), completing the allusion to Rev. 6:1–8. The edition of the Geneva Bible used for this and all other Biblical citations is *The Bible and Holy Scriptures conteyned in the Olde and Newe Testament* (Geneva, 1560).

4   Examples of this scholarship include: Joan Fitzpatrick, *Food in Shakespeare: Early Modern Dietaries and the Plays* (Aldershot, UK: Ashgate, 2007); *Renaissance Food from Rabelais to Shakespeare: Culinary Readings and Culinary Histories*, ed. Joan Fitzpatrick (Aldershot, UK: Ashgate, 2010); and Robert Appelbaum, *Aguecheek's Beef, Belch's Hiccup and Other Gastronomic Interjections: Literature, Culture and Food among the Early Moderns* (Chicago: U of Chicago P, 2006).

5   An example of this earlier scholarship is Henry Nicolson Ellacombe's *The Plant-Lore and Garden-Craft of Shakespeare* (Exeter, UK: privately printed, [1878]). Recent ecocritical readings of Shakespeare include Gabriel Egan, *Green Shakespeare: From Ecopolitics to Ecocriticism* (Abingdon, UK: Routledge, 2006); and *Early Modern Ecostudies: From the Florentine Codex to Shakespeare*, ed. Thomas Hallock, Ivo Kamps, and Karen L. Raber (Basingstoke, UK: Palgrave Macmillan, 2008).

6   Jan Kott, *Shakespeare Our Contemporary*, trans. Boleslaw Taberski (London: Methuen, 1964), 127–62. Peter Brook provided the preface to this English edition.

7   *Macbeth*, 1.3, takes place on "this blasted heath" (1.3.77). See James Ogden, "Lear's Blasted Heath," in *Lear from Study to Stage: Essays in Criticism*, ed. James Ogden and Arthur H. Scouten (Madison, NJ: Fairleigh Dickinson UP, 1997), 135–45; and Henry S. Turner, "*King Lear* Without: The Heath," *Renaissance Drama* 28 (1997): 161–83.

8   *The History of King Lear Acted at the Duke's Theatre Reviv'd with Alterations by N. Tate* (London, 1681), 3.1, p. 24. Tate transforms Cordelia's list of "idle weeds" into "idle flowers": "rank Femiter and furrow Weeds, / With Berries, Burdocks, Violets, Dazies, Poppies, / And all the idle Flow'rs that grow / In our sustaining Corn" (43).

9   *The Works of Mr. William Shakespear*, ed. Nicholas Rowe, 6 vols. (London, 1709). In Rowe's edition, 5.3.1 is situated on "*A Heath*" (2509); 3.3 on "*Part of the Heath*" (2513); and 4.1 on "*An open Country*" (2523).

10 According to John Gerard's *Herball*, the varieties of fumitory "grow in corne fieldes among Barley and other graine" and darnel "grow[s] in fields among wheate and barly"; see *The Herball or Generall Historie of Plantes* (London, 1597), 929, 71.

11 On Shakespeare's Warwickshire upbringing as an influence on his presentation of plants and the environment, including discussion of Cordelia's description of her father, see Jonathan Bate, *Soul of the Age: The Life, Mind and World of William Shakespeare* (London: Viking, 2008), 36–59. Even if Shakespeare had no direct experience of arable farming, he was surrounded by people who

did: his paternal grandfather, Richard Shakespeare, was a farmer; his mother, Mary Arden, was the daughter of a yeoman farmer; and Anne Hathaway's father, Richard, was also a yeoman farmer.

12　Peter Hedden, "The Genes of the Green Revolution," *Trends in Genetics* 19 (2003): 5–9.

13　In *The Herball*, Gerard observes that the stalks of varieties of hemlock can grow to "fiue or sixe feete high" (903).

14　In the "*Field Scene*" of Act 4 of Tate's edition (1681), Lear enters, "*a Coronet of Flowers on his Head. Wreaths and Garlands about him*" (47). See also *The History of King Lear … Collated with the Oldest Copies, and Corrected; With Notes Explanatory and Critical, by Mr. Theobald* (Dublin, 1739), in which Lear is described "*drest madly with Flowers*" (88). On the significance of Ophelia's "garlands" and Lear's crown of "idle weeds," see Frank McCombie, "Garlands in *Hamlet* and *King Lear*," *Notes and Queries* 28 (1981): 132–34.

15　Gerard, 904, 71. Fumitory flowers in late May, but remains in flower until late summer, which "is the best time to be gathered" (929). Nettles "flourish in sommer" (571).

16　*Hamlet*, 1.5.189. Steve Sohmer argues that the play's climax takes place in late spring in "The Lunar Calendar of Shakespeare's *King Lear*," *Early Modern Literary Studies* 5.2 (1999): 2.1–17; http://purl.oclc.org/emls/05–2/sohmlear.htm (accessed 20 December 2011).

17　Gerard, 203.

18　The significance of "cuckoo-buds" in this song is discussed by Mats Rydén in "Shakespeare's Cuckoo-Buds," *Studia Neophilologica* 49 (1977): 25–27, and in "The Contextual Significance of Shakespeare's Plant Names," *Studia Neophilologica* 56 (1984): 155–62.

19　"The hedge-sparrow fed the cuckoo so long / That it had its head bit off by its young" (*History of King Lear*, ed. Wells, 4.207–8). See also *Antony and Cleopatra*, "the cuckoo builds not for himself" (2.6.28); and *The Rape of Lucrece*, "Why should the worm intrude the maiden bud, / Or hateful cuckoos hatch in sparrows' nests" (ll. 847–48).

20　Pascale Drouet, "'I speak this in hunger for bread': Representing and Staging Hunger in Shakespeare's *King Lear* and *Coriolanus*," in *Hunger on the Stage*, ed. Elisabeth Angel-Perez and Alexandra Poulain (Cambridge: Cambridge Scholars Publishing, 2008), 2–16.

21　*The Ballad of King Lear* is printed in Wells's edition of *King Lear*, 277–85; esp. ll. 120, 127.

22　*Three Christian Sermons made by Lodouike Lauatere, Minister of Zuricke in Heluetia, of Famine and Dearth of Victuals: And translated into English, as being verie fit for this time of our Dearth*, trans. W[illiam] Barlow (London, 1596), sigs. C8r–v.

23　Virgil mentions "unfeeding darnel" in *Georgics*, 1.153; see *The Eclogues and Georgics*, trans. C. Day Lewis, intro. R. O. A. M. Lyne (Oxford: Oxford UP, 2009), 56. On the use of this *topos* in *King Lear* and *Henry V*, see T. J. King, "'Darnel' in *King Lear*," *Notes and Queries* 15 (1968): 141; and John H. Betts, "Classical Allusions in Shakespeare's *Henry V* with Special Reference to Virgil," *Greece & Rome*, 2nd ser., 15 (1968): 147–63.

24　Guillaume de Salluste Du Bartas, *His Deuine Weekes and Workes Translated*, trans. Josuah Sylvester (London, 1605), 258.

25　*The True Chronicle History of King Leir, and his Three Daughters, Gonorill, Ragan, and Cordella* (London, 1605), sig. H1r.

26　*True Chronicle History of King Leir*, sig. H1r.

27　See, for example, Thomas Elyot, *The Castel of Helthe* (London, 1539), bk. 4, fol. 17v; and Joseph Du Chesne, *The Practise of Chymicall, and Hermeticall Physicke, for the Preseruation of Health*, trans. Thomas Tymme (London, 1605), sig. Aa1r.

28　Thomas White, *A Sermon Preached at Pawles Crosse on Sunday the ninth of December, 1576* (London, 1578), 45; Francis Trigge, *The Humble Petition of Two Sisters; The Church and Common-Wealth. For the restoring of their ancient Commons and liberties, which late Inclosure with depopulation, incharitably hath taken away* (London, 1604), sig. A7v; and William Baldwin, *The Last Part of the Mirour for Magistrates* (London, 1578), fol. 121v.

29　Levinus Lemnius, *An Herbal for the Bible*, trans. Thomas Newton (London, 1587), 229.

30　Lemnius, 229.

31　According to the parable, the wheat and the tares are allowed to grow together until harvest time, when the landowner instructs his "reapers," "Gather ye first the tares, and binde them in sheaues to burne them: but gather the wheat into my barne" (*Geneva Bible*, sig. BB4r). In scene 11, the Fool seems to anticipate the burning: "Now a little fire in a wild field were like an old lecher's heart – a small spark, all the rest on's body cold. Look, here comes a walking fire" (ll. 100–102).

32 Gerard, 72; Thomas Cooper, *Thesaurus Linguæ Romanæ & Britannicæ* (London, 1565), n.pag.; and Du Bartas, 630.

33 King, 141; see also F. G. Butler, "Lear's Crown of Weeds," *English Studies* 70 (1989): 395–406.

34 Gerard, 930. Where darnel is given as an ingredient in early modern medicines, it is most often used as a binding agent (Pierre de La Primaudaye, *The French Academie* [London, 1618], 807) or as a purgative (*The Thyrde and Last Parte of the Secretes* [London, 1562], fol. 50v; Thomas Hill, *The Gardeners Labyrinth* [London, 1577], 10; and Pliny the Elder, *The Historie of the World* [London, 1634], 139). George Baker's translation of Conrad Gesner's *The Newe Iewell of Health* includes darnel in recipes for three waters "vnto the prouoking of sleepe" (London, 1576), fols. 83v–84r.

35 In Shakespeare, *True Chronicle Historie of the Life and Death of King Lear* (London, 1608), the opening stage direction reads "*Enter Kent, Gloster, and Bastard*" (sig. B1r).

36 Richard Dutton, "Shakespeare, Holinshed and 'The Matter of Britain,'" in *The Oxford Handbook to Holinshed's Chronicles*, ed. Paulina Kewes, Susan Doran, and Ian Archer (Oxford: Oxford UP, forthcoming). The authors are grateful to Professor Dutton for allowing them to read his essay prior to publication.

37 See Edward Hall, *The Vnion of the Two Noble and Illustre Famelies of Lancastre [and] Yorke* (London, 1548), fol. 152v, which describes an attempt on the Castle of Cornyll. The introduction to this story could also have been suggested by the popular belief that witches adulterated food and ruined crops. See Reginald Scot, *The Discouerie of Witchcraft* (London, 1584), bk. 2, ch. 9, 32–33; and bk. 12, ch. 7, 227.

38 *The Coppie of a Letter sent into England by a Gentleman, from the towne of Saint Denis in France* (London, 1590), 18, 20.

39 On the agrarian crisis of the 1590s and its impact on health, social order, and literature (including drama), see William C. Carroll, *Fat King, Lean Beggar: Representations of Poverty in the Age of Shakespeare* (Ithaca: Cornell UP, 1996); Andrew McRae, *God Speed the Plough: The Representation of Agrarian England, 1550–1660* (Cambridge: Cambridge UP, 2002), 51–90; and John Walter, "The Social Economy of Dearth in Early Modern England," in *Famine, Disease and the Social Order in Early Modern Society*, ed. John Walter and Richard Schofield (Cambridge: Cambridge UP, 1991), 75–128.

40 R. B. Outhwaite, *Dearth, Public Policy and Social Disturbance in England, 1550–1800* (Cambridge: Cambridge UP, 1991), 3.

41 See, for example, John Powel, *The Assise of Bread, Newly corrected and enlarged, from twelue pence the quarter of Wheat, vnto three pound and six pence the quarter* ... (London, 1600); and Diane Purkiss, "Crammed with Distressful Bread: Bakers and the Poor in Early Modern England," in *Renaissance Food*, ed. Fitzpatrick, 11–24. Enclosures, which had the effect of privileging pastoral at the expense of arable farming, were blamed for exacerbating dearth and depopulation. This tension between pasture and cornfield is perhaps shadowed in Edgar's "Thy sheep be in the corn" (13.38).

42 Trigge (see n. 28 above), sigs. B4v–B5r.

43 On riots and disorder in London in protest against the price and provision of foodstuffs including grain, see Aaron Landau, "'Rouse up a brave mind': *The Merchant of Venice* and Social Uprising in the 1590s," in *Renaissance Papers 2003*, ed. Christopher Cobb and M. Thomas Hester (New York: Camden House, 2004), 119–47; and Joan Thirsk, "Enclosing and Engrossing," in *The Agrarian History of England and Wales 1500–1640*, ed. Joan Thirsk (Cambridge: Cambridge UP, 1967), 200–255, esp. 228.

44 On *Richard II* in the context of the debate over enclosures, see William O. Scott, "Landholding, Leasing, and Inheritance in *Richard II*," *Studies in English Literature 1500–1900* 4 (2002): 275–92.

45 *Oxford English Dictionary (OED)*, 2nd ed., J. A. Simpson and E. S. C. Weiner, prep., 20 vols. (Oxford: Oxford UP, 1989), s.v. "choke, *v.* 7. To kill (or injuriously affect) a plant, by depriving it of air and light." Cf. John of Gaunt's speech in *Richard II*, "eager feeding food doth choke the feeder" (2.1.37), and Burgundy in *1 Henry VI*, "choke thee with thine own," discussed above. Berowne (Biron), in *Love's Labour's Lost*, cries, "Sowed cockle reaped no corn" (4.3.359).

46   Lemnius, 227.

47   See, for example, Edmund Bonner's *A Profitable and Necessarye Doctrine with Certayne Adionyed Therunto* (London, 1555), 10; George Gascoigne, *The Whole Woorkes* (London, 1587), sig. ℭ3r; and Edmund Spenser, "December Eclogue," in *The Shepheardes Calender* (1579), in *The Shorter Poems*, ed. Richard McCabe (London: Penguin, 1999), 152.

48   *The Tragedy of Coriolanus*, 3.1.69–72. As Hibbard notes, the source of this passage appears to be Thomas North's translation of Plutarch, *The Lives of the Noble Grecians and Romanes* (London, 1579), 245–46. See G. R. Hibbard, ed., *Coriolanus* (New York: Penguin Books, 1967), xiii.

49   Conrad Heresbach, *Foure Bookes of Husbandry*, trans. Barnabe Googe (London, 1577), fol. 29v. See also Thomas Naogeorg, *The Popish Kingdome, or Reigne of Antichrist*, trans. Barnabe Googe (London, 1570), fol. 39r: "Iudocus doth defende the corne, from myldeawes and from blast."

50   *OED*, s.v., "blast," "6. A sudden infection destructive to vegetable or animal life (formerly attributed to the blowing or breath of some malignant power, foul air, etc.)" Blast spread in part as a consequence of the susceptibility of cereal weeds such as darnel and its close relative rye. See N. J. Talbot, "On the Trail of a Cereal Killer: Exploring the Biology of *Magnaporthe grisea*," *Annual Review of Microbiology* 57 (2003): 177–202; and L. E. Trevathan, M. A. Moss, and D. Blasingame, "Ryegrass Blast," *Plant Disease* 78 (1994): 113–17.

51   See *OED*, s.v. "blast," "1. Honey-dew," and "2. a. ... a growth (typically a whitish and fluffy coating) of fungal mycelium and fructifications on the surface of a plant."

52   Mario L. D'Avanzo argues that "mildew" alludes not simply to ruined crops, but also to the poisonous effects of ergot, which caused "insanity, gangrene, convulsions, and death"; see "'He Mildews the White Wheat': *King Lear*, III.iv.120–24," *Shakespeare Quarterly* 28 (1977): 88–89, esp. 88. The earliest use of "ergot" in the *OED* is dated 1683.

53   John Lyly, *Euphues and His England* (London, 1580), fol. 6v.

54   On the relation of "blasted" to "mildewed," see John S. Kenyon, "Correspondence: *Hamlet*, III, IV, 64," *Modern Language Notes* 35 (1920): 50–52. For examples of imagery of plague and corruption, see *Hamlet*, 3.1.135 and 4.7.13. No evidence exists to suggest that many people died as a direct result of starvation in early modern England, but long-term hunger and malnutrition increased the likelihood of death from plague or other infectious diseases, leading to the close and potent association of hunger and plague in the early modern imagination. See Harry A. Miskimin, *The Economy of Early Renaissance Europe, 1300–1460* (Cambridge: Cambridge UP, 1975), 27.

55   The description of "hebenon" ("hebona" in Q1 and Q2) as "cursed" reminds us of the early modern belief that weeds grew not from a parent plant, but spontaneously from the earth as a consequence of original sin and the Fall. See Susan Drury, "Plants and Pest Control in England *circa* 1400–1700: A Preliminary Study," *Folklore* 103 (1992): 103–6. Weeds are to wholesome plants as Cain is to Abel, the original pair of opposed brothers.

56   In Pliny's *Natural History*, the oil of "hebenon" seed is a poison that when "dropped into the eares, is ynough to trouble the braine," something which may remind us of the toxic effects attributed to darnel and hemlock. See Pliny, *The Historie of the World Commonly Called, The Naturall Historie of C. Plinius Secundus*, trans. Philemon Holland (London, 1601), bk. 25, chapter 4, 215. [Note other edition cited above]

57   On similarities between the deaths of Lord Darnley and Hamlet's father, see Andrew Hatfield, *Shakespeare and Renaissance Politics* (London: Thomson Learning, 2004), 87–88.

58   Dan Brayton, "Angling in the Lake of Darkness: Possession, Dispossession, and the Politics of Discovery in *King Lear*," *English Literary History* 70 (2003): 399–426.

59   From 1565 until his death in 1567, Henry Stuart was also Duke of Albany of the fourth creation. See Elaine Finnie Greig, "Stewart, Henry, duke of Albany [Lord Darnley] (1545/6–1567)," in *Oxford Dictionary of National Biography* (Oxford: Oxford UP, 2004; online edition, January 2008), http://www.oxforddnb.com/view/article/26473 (accessed 12 November 2012).

60   John Stow, *The Chronicles of England* (London, 1580), 1131; and Raphael Holinshed et al., *The Second Volume of Chronicles* (n.pl.: n.p., 1586), 381. See also Harry Clyde Smith and Avlyn Dodd Conley, *The Darnall, Darnell Family* (n. pl.: American Offset Printers, 1954).

61   On red and white darnel, see, for example, Gerard, 71–72. On red and white wheat, see, for example, Heresbach, fol. 29v.

62 Greenblatt, *Will in the World: How Shakespeare Became Shakespeare* (London: Pimlico, 2005), 356–90.

63 On the situation in Stratford-upon-Avon, see Germaine Greer, *Shakespeare's Wife* (London: Bloomsbury Publishing, 2007), 222–36. On the Uprising as an influence on *Coriolanus*, see Andrew Gurr, "*Coriolanus* and the Body Politic," *Shakespeare Survey* 28 (1975): 63–69; and Nate Eastman, "The Rumbling Belly Politic: Metaphorical Location and Metaphorical Government in *Coriolanus*," *Early Modern Literary Studies* 13.1 (May 2007): 2.1–39, http://purl.oclc.org/emls/13–1/eastcori.htm (accessed 20 December 2011).

64 National Archives, Kew, Court of Common Pleas, Feet of Fines, CP 25.2.237 (Michaelmas 1602); and Shakespeare Birthplace Trust Records Office (SBTRO) MS ER 27/1 (1 May 1602); MS ER 28/1 (28 July 1602). See also SBTRO MS ER 27/3 (28 October 1614), in which Shakespeare seeks legal protection on behalf of himself and his heirs "for all such losse detriment & hinderance" with respect to the annual value of his tithes, "by reason of anie Inclosure or decaye of Tyllage." Thomas Green's diary entry for 17 November 1614 has details of the problems Shakespeare experienced as a result of enclosures (SBTRO Corporation Records, Misc. Doc. XIII, 26a, 27–29).

65 SBTRO MS ER 27/5. In 1604, Shakespeare sold twenty bushels of malt to a neighbor, apothecary Philip Rogers, who had a sideline in brewing ale. We know about this transaction because Shakespeare prosecuted Rogers for nonpayment. See Greenblatt, *Will in the World*, 362–64; and Greer, *Shakespeare's Wife*, 228–29.

66 SBTRO MS ER 27/2; Misc. Doc. II, 3 (24 July 1605). The lease yielded £60 per annum.

67 Two rough drafts of a grant of a coat of arms to "Shakespere" is College of Arms, London, MS Vincent 157, articles 23 and 24.

68 Katherine Duncan-Jones, in a discussion of Shakespeare's application for a coat of arms, suggests that he consulted Gerard Legh's *Accedens of Armory*. However, Duncan-Jones does not mention this text's inclusion of either the account of the Inner Temple revels of 1561–62 or a version of the story of *King Lear*. See *Ungentle Shakespeare: Scenes from His Life* (London: Thomson Learning, 2001), 93.

69 On *Gorboduc* as an influence on *King Lear*, see, for example, O. B. Hardison, "Myth and History in *King Lear*," *Shakespeare Quarterly* 26 (1975): 227–42, esp. 227; and Barbara Heliodora Carneiro de Mendonça, "The Influence of *Gorboduc* on *King Lear*," *Shakespeare Survey* 13 (1966): 41–48.

70 See Dorothy F. Atkinson, "*King Lear* – Another Contemporary Account," *English Literary History* 3 (1936): 63–66.

71 Geoffrey of Monmouth, *The History of the Kings of England*, trans. Lewis Thorpe (Harmondsworth, UK: Penguin, 1973).

72 Gerard Legh, *The Accedens of Armory* (London, 1562), fols. 164v–166r, 168r.

73 Legh, fol. 168r.

74 Legh, fols. 200v–201r.

75 Legh, fol. 168r. For Ceres as an ancient goddess of Britannia, see William Camden, *Britannia, or A Chorographicall Description of the Most Flourishing Kingdomes, England, Scotland, and Ireland, and the Ilands Adioyning*, trans. Philemon Holland (London, [1610]), 3.

76 Gerard notes that "Red Darnell" bears, at its top, "a small and tender eare, spike fashion" (71).

77 Edmund Spenser, *The Faerie Qveene*, … (London, 1609), *Mutabilitie*, canto 7, stanza 37, page 361.

78 See Frances A. Yates, *Astraea: The Imperial Theme in the Sixteenth Century* (London: Taylor & Francis, 1975), 30–31.

79 On Cordelia as a "figure of archetypal virgo goodness," see Catherine S. Cox, "'An Excellent Thing in Woman': Virgo and Viragos in *King Lear*," *Modern Philology* 96 (1998): 143–57, esp. 143. On Cordelia as Ceres/Demeter, see Janet Adelman, *Suffocating Mothers: Fantasies of Maternal Origin in Shakespeare's Plays, "Hamlet" to "The Tempest"* (London: Routledge, 1992), 306–7n45. Adelman posits Ovid's story of Ceres' revenge on Sicily (*Metamorphoses*, 5.485) as a source for Shakespeare's use of "Darnel" in scene 18.

80 Regan is awarded land "No less in space, validity, and pleasure" (1. 75).

81 William Harrison, *An Historicall Description of the Islande of Britayne*, in Raphael Holinshed et al., *The Firste volume of the Chronicles of England, Scotlande, and Irelande* (London, 1577), 1:37.

CHAPTER 10

Theory in Practice
Elizabeth Bishop's "Pink Dog"

Kim Fortuny

Elizabeth Bishop is probably most well-known for her poems about animals such as "The Fish" and "The Moose." Those poems record moments of exalted contact between human and animal. Humans in each poem learn something from the beauty of the animal and from the vividness of the encounter. "Pink Dog" is a different kettle of fish. As Kim Fortuny humorously remarks of this strange ugly deformed creature that wanders fur-less through Rio de Janeiro, she is "nobody's bitch." This odd doggerel poem seems much too playful and is written in a light silly style, but as Fortuny notes, the pink dog of the poem shows us what is so remarkable about Bishop's animals – that they make us see the world from an a-human perspective and shake the self-assurance of human-centeredness.

The popular ballad, one of the oldest forms of literary expression, historically draws its material from humble sections of a culture. It often concerns itself with abject social conditions and those who struggle to survive them. Characters resisting authority, hiding out on the margins of society, are given the status of folk anti-heroes. The primary audience is the unlettered: the diction is simple. Like the 'Burglar of Babylon', a more traditional Rio ballad collected in *Questions of Travel*, Elizabeth Bishop's later poem, 'Pink Dog', features a marginalised subject. Here, however, the social underdog is embodied in an actual dog living on the edges of civilised society. A pun thus frames and launches the poem's dark humour. An underdog, a metonymic figure for a predicted loser, a victim of social injustice or persecution, returns to its source as a poetic figure. The dog is not only a vehicle for the human subject as tenor here: it is itself the subject of the poem. And like the burglar of Babylon, one of the 'million sparrows' of a 'confused migration' from the provinces to Rio, its troubles also stem from its outsider status.[1]

Original publication details: Kim Fortuny, "Elizabeth Bishop's 'Pink Dog' and Other Non-human Animals." *Textual Practice* 29.6 (2015), pp. 1099–1116. Taylor & Francis, 2015.

The pink dog as underdog trots along in rhythmic iambs. The tercet stanzas display, rather than camouflage the initial tetrameter, then two pentameter lines. Questions posed sound funny or absurd: 'scabies' rhymes with 'babies' (pp. 8–9). The perfect masculine end rhymes strike the modern urban ear as childish. 'The light-verse end rhymes of the tercets of "Pink Dog"', writes C.K. Doreski in *Elizabeth Bishop: The Restraints of Language*, 'rather than intensifying and unifying the poem, render it comical and tasteless'.[2] The poem is certainly doggerel dressed up just enough to be presentable as a popular song, and one reason, perhaps, *The New Yorker* initially hesitated to publish it. The poem was finally included in the 26 February 1979 issue with the subheading 'Rio de Janeiro'. It is 'the closest to Carnival on the one hand and to Ash Wednesday on the other' writes Howard Moss to Bishop in a letter dated January of the same year.[3]

Yet while the poem strikes us as a running joke due to the punning and the light, comical nature of the verse, and while the poem threatens to collapse under the weight of so much silliness, the subject at hand is far from trivial, as most commentators, including Doreski, have noted, though for reasons different from those that will be argued here. There are elements at work that prevent the poem from going under. An animal in the form of a dirty urban street dog, guides the poem off the page to questions that, like her questions of travel in other poems, are also questions about identity. Human identity, however, is not necessarily the only question at hand here.

By teasing out the inter-workings of 'underdog' as a pun, the a-historical function of the dog as exclusively a metonym for a human condition is partially cancelled out. By returning a figurative dog back to its literal source, Bishop guides the urban street dog to signify other things beyond the persecuted human poor in the poem. Like all of Bishop's poems which concern or include animals – and many of her better poems do – the animal becomes a sight of productive tension which will lead to something like a momentary state of clarity for the speaker. As grotesque as she may appear, the pink dog, 'a nursing mother, by those hanging teats', is poised to be another one of Bishop's enigmatic subjects, those inscrutable ones covered in fur or wrapped in scales that appear, and then disappear, taking the trajectory of the poem with them into the mist or the sea (p. 10). But this animal seems a parody of the other animals that populate her oeuvre. Here the animal is neither awe-inspiring, nor remote as Bishop's other animals often are: this common canine is diseased and denuded and living in close proximity to men, feeding on their daily rubbish. If we consider this dog in the context of Bishop's penchant for enigmatic animals in her poems, we are lead to wonder what possible mystery such a corrupted animal can offer. And if the dog is no longer only a figurative animal as will be argued here, what might its denotative function be?

The poem begins by contrasting a beach in Rio, 'clothed' in colourful umbrellas, with the dog who 'naked and pink' in the sun, 'trot[s]' along, assumedly indifferent to effect (pp. 5, 3).

> Of course they are mortally afraid of rabies.
> You are not mad; you have a case of scabies
> but look intelligent. Where are your babies?
> (pp. 7–9)

Out scavenging for the puppies she has hidden in a favela, the bitch, 'intelligent', 'living by her wits', is exposed to the same dangers as those undesirables in the human community whom she most resembles (pp. 9–12).

> Didn't you know? It's been in all the papers,
> To solve this problem, how they deal with beggars?
> They take and throw them in the tidal rivers.

> Yes, idiots, paralytics, parasites
> go bobbing in the ebbing sewage, nights
> out in the suburbs, where there are no lights.
>
> (pp. 13–8)

In the name of progress, the urban municipalities, or those who do the dirtier work for them, dispose of those beings that, living on the edge of society, do not contribute to it in constructive ways. Like the mentally and physically ill, or the socially deviant, the street dog has no use-value to the culture at large. Neither pet, nor employed in the various sentinel functions that a dog performs for humans, be it herding, property control or law enforcement, the street dog has no authorised livelihood. Like other useless undesirables, she too is thus at risk:

> If they do this to anyone who begs,
> drugged, drunk, or sober, with or without legs,
> what would they do to sick, four-leggèd dogs?
>
> (pp. 19–21)

Exaggerated by the absurd split in the indefinite article 'a/n' to maintain the less than perfect end rhyme, the narrator's black-humoured response to her own rhetorical question is camouflage: dress up for Carnival, blend in: 'Tonight you simply can't afford to be a-/n eyesore' (pp. 29–30).

Doreski dismisses the poem as 'a series of tropes of the grotesque' that 'may attempt to echo the less-than-acute political satire of the Brazilian Sambas … and simultaneously record the trials of the dog and the brutalized narrator' but ultimately fail to 'engender … interest' in either (p. 131). She also criticises the poem for its 'tone of humorous indifference' towards human suffering: 'Surely she would recognize that the speaker of this poem is as much a victim of a cruel age as the dog' (p. 131). Because the poem fails the human, though not necessarily the animal, as its controlling subject both stylistically and ethically, it thus 'lack[s] the sting of political narrative' (p. 131). Other scholarship on 'Pink Dog' has focused primarily on the postpartum dog as a figure for various human, mostly female conditions. She is often read as a grotesque female body, marginalised, yet subversive in her resistance to patriarchy and heterosexual norms.[4] More recently, Catherine Cucinella in '"Dress up! Dress up and Dance at Carnival!": The Body in Elizabeth Bishop's "Pink Dog"', focuses on the marked high visibility of the dog in the poem, suggesting that 'the representation of the body in "Pink Dog" … places that female body in all its grotesqueness in plain sight'.[5] Rather than inhabiting the margins of culture, the dog is a figure for dangerous female excess that by refusing invisibility goes beyond 'the limits of the grotesque and into the realm of abjection' (p. 74). Offering 'a metaphoric connection between the female body and the body of a female dog' that 'challenges cultural and social conventions', if only temporarily, the poem suggests that the marginal 'always already exists within the center' (pp. 75–6).

Just as the animal of the poem is most often read as the embodiment of Bishop's own feelings of estrangement from the culture around her, either as a lesbian, a foreigner, an artist or all three, Helen Vendler too relies on a metaphorical reading of the dog in order to make sense of the poem in human terms. In *Last Looks, Last Books*, Vendler makes a passing reference to 'Pink Dog' in her close analysis of Bishop's villanelle 'One Art'.[6] Reading the temporary cover-up of Carnival in the poem as an illusory and superficial response to adversity, Vendler likens the *fantasia* the dog is advised to wear to a 'socially deceptive' art that is 'Rio's mask to overcome social unacceptability' (p. 110). The 'art of losing' is read as 'a form of constantly increasing mastery' in 'One Art', as opposed to the 'one-time fantasia' in 'Pink Dog' (p. 110).

While 'Pink Dog' is a poem that certainly registers the human tribulations, existential as well as social and political, which have been the focus of Bishop scholarship on this poem to the present, it can be argued that in the rhetoric of the poem, human beings are necessary to, but not necessarily central to the poem's grammatical structure. Dispossessed humans are compared through association to street dogs who beg: humans function as the vehicles in similes for dogs. The concrete dog is like an abstract person, not the other way around. Suggestive of an ode as well as a ballad, the poet directly addresses its subject throughout as 'you'. Other subjects who appear are illustrative, but parenthetical in the long run. The poem's subject, from beginning to end, is the animal.

The productive tensions that result from punning and play with the grammatical function of the dog are further reinforced by the cultural status of dogs in the poem. Familiar with her North American audience, Bishop knows that the reader may be relatively unfamiliar with her subject, the urban street dog. The fact that so much criticism on the poem has focused on the grotesque body of the dog attests to this continued unfamiliarity, and partly explains why many readers naturally assume that the animal in the poem is a metaphorical one, a vehicle for signifying the human condition. And this staged assumption is part of the poem's sleight of hand. Because feral animals were no longer permanent fixtures in the street life of Northern European and North American cities by the time the poem was published in 1979, they would not be read as a daily reality. By the early twentieth century, first-world urban streets were cleansed of feral and small animal farm life. Dogs were taken into homes as family pets or continued to work outdoors; canines that did not serve either of these functions tended to disappear. While dogs were one of the first animals to enter into domestic relations with humans, and Donna Haraway suggests that 'wolves on their way to becoming dogs might have selected themselves for tameness', it is useful for the reading of this poem to note that dogs have not always existed to serve man and still do not.[7] Though feral dogs continue to haunt human communities as they have for at least twelve millennia, surviving on 'garbage middens and human waste', and while many live with people voluntarily, the larger fact remains that in most parts of the world in the twentieth and twenty-first centuries, urban dogs are more often feral than domesticated (p. 365). Bishop, who lived in Rio de Janeiro and other parts of Brazil, experienced street dogs on a daily basis. Read biographically, her 'underdog' is thus not a metonymic animal only, but also a real one. The poem's tone can be read as light and 'indifferent', or singularly tragic by those who do not extend Bishop's characteristic reticence in her depiction of everyday suffering to animals as well as humans.

As in all of Bishop's poems, the appearance of an animal signals something that is not readily accessible to the human. This is because familiar human-centred assumptions concerning man's dominance over animals are not honoured in her poems. A 'light' poem like 'Pink Dog' can be seen to do similar work to that of more sophisticated poems that feature animals such as 'The Moose' or 'The Fish'. Reading the poem with emphasis on the material and historical dog we understand that Bishop once again, though in an apparently alternative format, is directing the reader to step outside her own human frame of reference. To live like a dog, in this case, means suspending assumptions of what it means to be human; learning something about how to be human means temporarily becoming a dog.

Other Animals in Bishop

Though survival methods of the pink dog such as begging and foraging are associated in the poem with those of other beings whose social status most resembles her own, animals in Bishop's poems are more often associated with humans by how they differ from them. Various species approach, or come close to people in the poems, but they are not made to resemble them. Animals are rarely possessed by humans even as functions of metaphor. In 'The Moose', one of her most famous poems featuring an animal, a female moose steps out from 'the impenetrable wood' to conclude a poem that has featured a small community of local people travelling west in a bus. In the small world moving along, stories of birth and living and death are being shared, the reported speech is punctuated with ways to read it:

> 'Yes ...' that peculiar
> affirmative. 'Yes ...'
> A sharp indrawn breath,
> half groan, half acceptance,
> that means 'Life's like that.
> We know *it* (also death)'.
> (pp. 115–20)

Because the poem involves the reader in the vivid hum of casual human conversation, when the bus suddenly stops and the moose 'stands there, looms, rather, / in the middle of the road', we experience something strange or other-worldly as commentaries on the poem have long noted (pp. 141–2).

More recent, or more markedly post-modern, accounts of the encounter between humans and the animal in the poem resist metaphysical interpretations and expose metaphorical processes. Reading the moose as 'an embodiment of primal nature', a 'figuration ... naturalized by the whole tradition of nature poetry', that 'audibly recalls a number of American poets' such as Walt Whitman, Robert Frost, and Hart Crane, Mutlu Konak Blasing suggests that Bishop recuperates and exposes the animal's role as a figure.[8] Blasing scrutinises the 'rhetorical and syntactic processes' that have 'enabled the vision', and countering Alicia Ostriker's feminist discussion of 'The Moose' in *Stealing the Language: The Emergence of Women's Poetry in America*, argues that 'it would be a mistake to read the moose as a figure of a special female harmony with nature ... or of a poetic source or community specific to women writers' (p. 10). The moose appears and then immediately disappears into similes, 'the world of churches and houses', which 'openly exercise power over what they figure' (p. 19). Blasing locates a post-structuralist self-consciousness in Bishop's efforts 'to call attention to the rhetorical processes that "right"' the experience of the discursive animal by making it fit into the shared historical, formal, and figurative meaning 'common to the language of poetry' (pp. 19–23, 18–23).

Other commentators on Bishop's 'The Moose' have concentrated on the interaction between nature and the mind in the poem. Peggy Samuels in 'Verse as Deep Surface: Elizabeth Bishop's New Poetics, 1938–39', does not comment directly on 'The Moose', but her reading of Bishop through the aesthetic theory of John Dewey argues that Bishop's depictions of encounters between man and nature allow for a 'space for interaction, a large zone of in-betweenness' that does not prioritise one over the other.[9] Applying a similar concern with the interaction between beings in nature and human beings to 'the Moose', both Heather Cass White and Willard Spiegelman compare Bishop's depictions of nature to Wordsworth's, each citing Bishop's own reference to herself as a 'minor female Wordsworth' in a letter to Lowell.[10] White and Spiegelman note that Bishop is interested, like Wordsworth, in the fringes of experience where the human imagination encounters a sublime nature. 'The issue of how to hear the world rather than simply drown it out with the sound of one's own voice is one of the main questions in "Questions of Travel"', suggests White, and in those poems where man and nature draw 'imperceptibly, gently, closer', 'our sense for "margins" or intermediate horizons is increased' (pp. 11, 4–34). Silencing or isolating hyperconscious human presences in the poems allows other forms of life and other ways of meaning to emerge. Quoting the Preface to *Lyrical Ballads*, Spiegelman argues that Bishop, like Wordsworth, proves the 'pleasure which the mind derives from the perception of similitude in dissimilitude'.[11] Human unity with nature is recognised, but only rarely in the poems: 'Separateness is the central fact of experience for both Wordsworth and Bishop' (p. 31).

In these readings, the moose, like other beings or events in the natural world, is thus historically and rhetorically inscribed, phenomenologically distinct from the human, rather than analogous in Bishop's poems. These critical discussions give us intricate and provocative ways to think about some non-contingent aspects of the relationship between species. But because thinking man continues to dominate the humanist assumptions at the epistemological and ontological centres of the readings, the moose is, in fact, overshadowed by the processes of anthropomorphism and personification, regardless of how antithetical or antiquated these rhetorical devices may strike the contemporary sensibility. I would argue that this is a process that Bishop herself ardently avoids.

The moose's actions reinforce her liminal presence, 'It approaches; it sniffs at / the bus's hot hood' (pp. 143–4). The bus is as strange a creature to her as she is to the people within. And as they examine her though language, 'Sure are big creatures', she examines them, '[T]aking her time', through scent (pp. 159, 162). It can be argued that Bishop allows the animal a more powerful final presence than the human in the poem. While the moose physically approaches humans, the people on the bus can only approach the animal through imprecise expressions of awe. Though White argues, as others have, that the moose functions as a 'talismanic animal', in this case 'to figure the successful call of the poet to the answering world', this reading subordinates the animal to human use-value (pp. 24–34). Existing outside or beyond the clichéd expressions the people use to describe her, the moose instead leaves her own mark, 'a dim / smell of moose', on the poem (pp. 177–8). The 'acrid / smell of gasoline', is the concomitant territorial marking of the industrial culture that has briefly come into contact with something wild in nature (pp. 178–9). The poem ends with corresponding animal gestures. In the last line of the poem the bus is made to resemble the animal, and not the other way around.

Like 'The Moose', the earlier poem 'The Fish' ends with a form of collision and collusion of culture and nature that does not end in terms that suggest the reification of the animal by the human. The prismatic '... pool of bilge / where oil had spread a rainbow' is physically more colourful than the 'tremendous fish' whose 'brown skin hung in strips / like ancient wallpaper' (pp. 68–9, 1, 10–11). The great fish does not outshine industrial waste: it does not signify in predictable pastoral ways. The speaker as hunter admires the history of her catch hanging from its mouth in the form of hooks, fish-line, leaders and swivels. She anatomises its objective body. Earlier, when she attempts to look subjectively into the eyes of her prey, she parodies her own humanising gesture, and its romantic overtones, by gendering the possessive pronoun 'his' and making the 'eyes' plural: it is impossible to look simultaneously into both eyes of most species of fish because they are located on opposite sides of the body. As if to reinforce the poem's anti-anthropomorphic constraint further, the speaker's gaze is rebuffed by the non–reciprocal glaze in the eyes of the fish: 'They shifted a little, but not / to return my stare' (pp. 34, 41–2).

Reading Bishop's poetry in light of Bakhtin's theory of the creative process and the 'ethical I-Other relation' in 'Author and Hero in Aesthetic Activity', Anastasia Graf argues in 'Representing the Other: A Conversation among Mikhail Bakhtin, Elizabeth Bishop, and Wisława Szymborska', that Bishop's objectivity, 'the intense vigilance and self-restraint' that Marianne Moore observed in the poems, is a 'relation between self and world that is based on distance and epistemological self-restraint'.[12] At the end of Bishop's 'The Fish', notes Graf, the speaker gives the object her 'full attention' while suspending the 'desire to know' (p. 12). Bishop's poems guide the reader to pay intimate attention, to be 'quiet and still enough to see the object rather than one's reaction to it' (p. 12). And this is not easy because it also entails surmounting the desire to impose meaning: 'The difficulty is not discovering the best, or correct, interpretation; rather, it is declining to interpret at all' (p. 12). Sustained attention, or a process of 'living-into' a subject as opposed to empathising with it, 'ensures that a contingent conquest' in language, 'does not turn into an occupation' of the Other (p. 14).

As in 'The Moose', 'The Fish' builds to a dramatic end, but in diction stripped of any clear human relevance. Despite the lack of direct communication between the species, the poem celebrates in the final repeated 'rainbow, rainbow, rainbow' a coming together of the human and the non-human that does not end in a union that can be readily registered in human terms (p. 75). Rather, the speaker recognises that the fish, 'battered and venerable / and homely', is a fellow creature with a lived and living history (pp. 8–9). The final release of the catch is not a gesture of pity following triumph, but a gesture of veneration. Although she has envisaged the 'coarse white flesh', she is not hungry enough to consume a fellow survivor, literally or through personifying metaphors (p. 27). Though 'victory' has 'filled up the little rented boat', it is not confined to human victory alone (pp. 66–7). It has something to do with a larger reality of eating and being eaten that came so close she touched it before letting it go.

The rigorous avoidance of anthropomorphic projections onto animals in Bishop's poems is what prevents them from being exploited as metaphors or metonyms in the service of human enlightenment only. More often than not, animal behaviour is juxta-posed with human behaviour in order to defamiliarise the latter. Associations of humans and animals are not distorted by pathetic fallacy. And if animals do not display human kinds of feeling or behaviour, neither are they made to share human emotions in the poems. When 'an owner's voice arises, stern', in 'Five Flights Up', 'You ought to be ashamed', the dog who is the target of her moral consternation, 'bounces cheerfully up and down' (pp. 16–17, 19). 'Obviously', says the poem's speaker, 'he has no shame' (p. 21). Shame is identified as a human complication, an obstacle to living in the moment that animals have no concept of because even pets, as the poem suggests, do not necessarily share their masters' anxieties. Again the animal and its corresponding qualities are not simply relegated to metaphors for human problems. And the poem does not re-circulate a tired idealisation of the animal in the service of popular understandings of romantic nature. The knowledge these animals have is different from the owner's, as well as, the speaker's: 'He and the bird know everything is answered / all taken care of, / no need to ask again' (pp. 22–3). It is knowledge that transcends the human urge to control the behaviour of other animals. In the final lines, the speaker is burdened by a yesterday she finds 'almost impossible to lift' (p. 26). She is crippled by human forms of cognition. That which ostensibly makes humans superior to the lower animals appears to lack the advanced vitality of animals in the poem.

Bishop's attraction not only to the emotional indifference of animals, but to the pleasures that result from man's recognition of his own animal nature comes through in a poem by Vinícius de Morcaes entitled 'Sonnet of Intimacy' which she translated but did not publish. The speaker, relishing 'farm afternoons', concludes with the following scene:

> The smell of manure is delicious.
> The cattle look at me unenviously
> And when there comes a sudden stream and hiss
>
> Accompanied by a look not unmalicious,
> All of us, animals, unemotionally
> Partake together of a pleasant piss.
>
> (pp. 1, 9–14)

Bishop communicates the stripping away of human emotion by playfully adding a prefix to an adverb that negates it ('unenviously') and a double negative to an adjective ('not unmalicious') that isolates it as misplaced, thus absurd in her translation. Envy and malice have no place in the animal world and once these human motions are identified and cancelled out in the poem, man is free to do what comes naturally to him, and side by side with his fellow animals. The verb 'Partake' with its ecclesiastical connotations suggests that something holy is being shared. But in order for this to happen the human subject must recover his own animal nature, which is to recover something honest in himself, something stripped of fussy qualifiers. The poem may be funny, light and slightly scatological, but the emotional indifference of the animals puts the human body and its natural functions into balanced perspective. The speaker is only one creature among many. He is unexceptional.

Because animals do not share human emotions in Bishop's poems, animals are often made to challenge the systems that guide and direct human responses to, or attitudes towards, the world around them. Human systems of belief, for example, are made to suffer aesthetically in comparison with the practices of animals. In the poem 'Seascape', white herons and fish are presented as performing alternative forms of devotion.

> This celestial seascape, with white herons got up as angels,
> flying as high as they want and as far as they want sidewise
> in tiers and tiers of immaculate reflections.
>
> (pp. 1–3)

When 'occasionally a fish jumps' it is 'like a wild-flower / in an ornamental spray of spray' (p. 10). While the presentation of the animals is stylised, the fundamental design of the poem contrasts the man-made and the natural. The 'skeletal lighthouse' becomes a figure for a severe theology, one that can move neither literally as an intransitive verb, nor emotionally as a transitive one. Unlike the animals that fly and swim with beauty and grace in a natural scene that resembles heaven, the lighthouse as unnatural moral arbiter has condemned the fallen world in which they move to a 'hell that rages below his iron feet' (pp. 14, 17).

> Heaven is not like flying or swimming,
> But has something to do with blackness and a strong glare.
>   (pp. 20–1)

A puritanical monotheistic version of existence is represented not only as unattractive when compared to the colours and configurations of animals, but also as arrogant: the lighthouse

> ... standing there
> in black and white clerical dress,
> who lives on his nerves, thinks he knows better.
>   (pp. 13–6)

Ecclesiastical word play and riddle give the poem a light, playful air: the 'reflections' of the herons on the water are rhythmically and syntactically equivalent to 'conception' in the traditional noun phrase that begins with the adjective 'immaculate'. But the argument in the poem is philosophically acute. Flying and swimming, the natural activity of birds and fish, offer a more moving image of heaven because they are presented as dynamic and physically attractive when compared to the lighthouse with its very physical, but immovable 'iron feet'.

Writing of transcendental meaning in Bishop's descriptive poems, Bonnie Costello notes in 'Vision and Mastery in Elizabeth Bishop' that while landscapes often provide a 'vision of God's work', humans do not figure centrally in the poems' seascapes.[13] Though the meanings of landscapes are 'in one sense highly specified and focused (sights, sounds, smells) but partly because these meanings are specified in a context relatively empty of human content, they offer a broad range of suggestion and more room for association' (p. 352). The poems appeal to human sensibilities, but the spaces depicted exceed or resist human-centred signification. The overt application of descriptive language that borrows from the lexicons of religion and art allows the animals in the case of 'Seascape' to transcend the human. Again, man is directed to reflect on the example of animals for the sake of his own salvation.

Animals thus tend to share space with humans in Bishop's poems, yet exist simultaneously in non-human centred realms. And it is what they do not share with us that generates the enigmatic in their presence. Bishop has often been called a master of endings. Her endings often thrust the reader, and suddenly, into the unfamiliar. It is often the departure from human reference that makes her conclusions powerfully inconclusive and it is thus no coincidence that the unfamiliar is embodied in animals in many poems. The information they convey is not useful in familiar human terms. And it is precisely this uselessness that lends to their value.

'Pink Dog' and Non-human Knowledge

'Pink Dog' is a dark-humoured commentary on use-value. Bishop reinforces this point at various levels in the poem. After recounting a running joke about beggars and lifejackets, a joke whose comic thrust is powered by the tragedy that lies just under the surface, the speaker offers her own comic solution to the 'depilated' dog's predicament. Hers is a similar absurd appeal to function.

> In your condition you would not be able
> even to float, much less to dog-paddle.
> Now look, the practical, the sensible
> solution is to wear a *fantasia*.
>
> (pp. 25–8)

Because the urban street dog has no recognisable dog function in the culture, the speaker suggests that she disguise herself as a human being. But she must not masquerade as those humans whom she resembles most naturally, and who, like her, threaten the comfort of the middle and upper classes, as well as the North American tourists. Like all poor people in Rio she must take temporary advantage of Carnival and upgrade her appearance. In the name of practicality and sensibility, she must disguise herself as a Carnival character.

Like almost all of Bishop's poems that feature animals, with the exception perhaps of 'A Word With You' whose human-like, allegorical animals resemble some of those of Marianne Moore, the dog is not applied as a stand-in for human beings. She is not metaphorically pink in the poem, but pink due to scabies. The poem is not a bestiary, an allegory that uses animals for the moral instruction of humans. The fact that street dogs suffer the same fate as street people in 'developing' economies is certainly a central theme in the poem. But the value of the dogs does not stop or rest there. And therein lies a second level of commentary on use-value that the poem sports with. By suggesting that the dog wear a *fantasia* or a Carnival costume, put on *máscara*, and dance a samba, in other words, masquerade as a human woman, the poem parodies the anthropomorphic reification of animals by taking the tendency to an absurd extreme. Although the parody appears comical and light in this poem, the 'use' of a derelict urban street dog to expose the processes of personification puts a dark twist on the humour. To represent the dog in human terms in the conclusion of the poem has the effect of adding insult to a being that is already injured.

As with the animals in her other poems, Bishop does not represent the dog, however pink, in human terms. Despite all her outward appearances, and notwithstanding the four stanzas dedicated to dressing her up, the dog is qualified early on in the poem as 'intelligent' in her own right. The word is enjambed. It contrasts dramatically in register with the 'rabies', 'scabies', and 'babies' it shares the stanza with. It calls attention to itself. The dog is the wily survivor of human occupation. As she trots figuratively into the exaggerated anthropomorphic conceit of the poem, her historical self travels on a daily basis through the urban fallout of a stressed ecosystem. She exists on the hand-outs of those who kindly share, or on discarded human garbage. In either case this dog, like urban street animals all over the world, survives on human excess. But she is 'intelligent'; so while human debris may sustain her, she simultaneously remains on her guard against those hands that may feed her, but do not share her territory. She hides her babies in the slums where they are safer because they are less susceptible to the municipal projects that clean-up the better neighbourhoods by disposing of their vagrant populations. Intelligence here means calculating the patterns of men and resisting them simultaneously. Human terms are what she must negotiate everyday in order to survive them. The distant relation between the animal and the human in the poem is therefore reinforced.

The pink dog may be the least poetical of Bishop's animals. The poem does not terminate with non-human beings that create the kind of crowning sublime erasure we experience in a poem like 'Over 2,000 Illustrations and a Complete Concordance', a poem in which the manger scene at the birth of Christ is casually yet hauntingly reduced to 'a family with pets' (p. 73). The urban street dog does not rise to the wild heights of the moose or fish. It can be nonetheless argued that this tragic-comical animal reflects the general profile of Bishop's animals. While she approaches humans, securing her offspring with those classes who statistically provide her with her most consistent diet, she is no one's domesticated pet. She is poor, but roams freely beyond the confines of an apartment, a leash, or a chain, the only 'legitimate' options for dogs living in progressive cities. Bishop does not refer to the urban animals' larger story, but knowledge of the zoological history not included in the poem sharpens one's reading of it as social commentary.

The speaker directly addresses the dog, but there is no attempt to represent the dog as responding to human attention. The implicit background of the subject also highlights the fact that street animals do not necessarily reciprocate human feelings because they have not been trained to respond to them like their domestic betters. Like the fish in the wild who does not return the speaker's stare, the feral dog is indifferent to the stares of the passersby whom she frightens. The indifference of the dog serves to empower her in the poem by preventing her from eliciting facile varieties of sympathy or pity. Her distance is maintained.[14] She has a survival system of her own which is not the same as human survival. Stepping outside of oneself or temporarily becoming another within the cultural parentheses of bacchanalia may be an ancient human mechanism for coping with the restraints of daily life, particularly for women. Human traditions or practices, whether grounded in love or war, are questioned and criticised, however, by the presence of animals in the poems. Like the armadillo that raises its 'weak mailed fist' against the 'illegal fire balloons' prompting Robert Lowell to 'see the bomb in a delicate way' in the poem 'Armadillo', the diseased dog underscores what Bakhtin has guided us to recognise as the fundamentally conservative nature of Carnival.[15] Applied literally to the local animal life in the form of makeup and skirts, the cover-up that Carnival is in poor parts of the world is seen as funny and absurd, but also as conspiratorial when it masks basic animal needs.

Progress in the form of North American influence is offered, albeit off-handedly in the poem, as part of the problem rather than a solution to it.

> They say that Carnival's degenerating
> – radios, Americans, or something,
> have ruined it completely. They're just talking.
> Carnival is always wonderful!
>
> (pp. 34–7)

The commercialisation of carnival aggravates the social conditions that it is meant temporarily to allay. What had begun as a poor ex-African slave community festival in

Bahia is now an economically profitable event, but not for all. Neither the dog nor the poor profit from the wealth generated by corporate tourism in any long-term sustainable way. The former are in fact problems to be solved so that celebrations are not hindered by the presence of the unsightly poverty they reveal in their unadorned physical bodies. The dressing up of the dog is thus an acting-out of socio-political tension. But the historical animal, like other animals in Bishop's poems, also signals us to think beyond the human problem towards an animal 'solution' to it.

Animal life, even on urban streets, goes on with or without human systems. Cycles of birth and death, feast and fasting continue in a parallel existence that is the natural world. Or so they do if and when sanctioned by the cultures that share their geography. As in other cities all over the world, Rio de Janeiro has a long history of solving its street dog problem. When favelas are raised it is not only human communities that are displaced or destroyed. In the name of progress street animals are regularly poisoned or otherwise destroyed *en mass* all over the world. Grass roots organisations agitate in all major cities of the globe for legislation that acknowledges and protects the historical existence of feral urban animals.[16] If the dog in Bishop's poem is inscribed in the tradition of the folk ballad, it is because she understands the larger context of the dog's survival. By making the dog a female with offspring she accentuates the struggle; she knows that the natural cycles her instincts live by are under severe duress.

The pink dog fits the bill of a traditional rural folk hero because she does not live according to the rules and regulations of the dominate authority, but rather survives or defies them, at least for the present. She is nobody's bitch. She is useless to progressive man, unavailable to him in terms he condones, unless of course she dresses up like a woman, becomes his puppet and pet. Thus like other animals in Bishop's menagerie she exists outside human frames of reference. And as in the other poems, this gap provides a door of discovery. What then might be the knowledge this battered beast brings to us? She is another animal intermediary, but not one that reaches out or communicates with humans. She is a being to be reached out to, or, rather, must be reached out to with no expectations of return or gain if we are to push the ethical boundaries on what it can mean to be human.

In the poem 'Manners', subtitled 'For a Child of 1918', the etiquette taught to the speaker as a child by her grandfather transcends the borders that separate species human from species animal. The grandfather instructs the child on good manners as they ride side by side on his wagon. A 'big pet crow' is 'well brought up' because 'he answers / nicely when he's spoken to' (pp. 10, 26–7). The grandfather and grandchild shout 'Good day! Good day!' to the passing vehicles that leave their wagon in the dust (p. 27). The poem terminates with an act of humility that concludes the lesson.

> When we came to Hustler Hill,
> he said that the mare was tired,
> so we all got down and walked,
> as our good manners required.
>   (pp. 29–32)

We are again offered animal ethics packaged in what appears to be light verse. This is an animal ethics that does not differ greatly from a traditional humanist ethics that borrowed from the best of theological truisms: it is one that suggests that humans be taught to respect the integrity and well being of others as they would wish for themselves. 'Others' is understood here in a full biological understanding of that term, however. Post-humanism in this context does not have to be read as a new post-postmodern position. Animal ethics is central to a humanist ethics that does not confine itself to human-centred definitions of being when this ontology infringes on the welfare of other life forms.

'Manners' is another simple poem, a bitter sweet, undemanding poem. The basic kindness preached by the rural man feels anachronistic, left behind in the dirty wake of the automobile. If the child takes her grandfather's lesson to heart she may risk losing her way in the wider world. One is guided in the poem to wonder of her what she wonders of the crow that flies off the boy's shoulder when the wagon stops to give him a ride, 'How would he know where to go?' (p. 16). The lessons are simple and because they are simple they require the greatest effort. 'Pink Dog' does not make the challenge posed in 'Manners' any easier. The canine protagonist is ugly and appears to be dangerous to human beings. The ironic rhyming of 'rabies', 'scabies', and 'babies' makes a phonetic joke of the poem's problem. The reader need not take the matter to heart. But no change of heart is simple or easy. That is because most change hinges on a transformation of consciousness. But 'Man or beast, that's good manners' says the grandfather (p. 23). Bishop's animals are not important for their use-value alone; and therein lies their worth.

Bogazici University

Notes

1 Elizabeth Bishop, *Poems* (New York: Farrar, Straus and Giroux, 2011), pp. 6–7.
2 C.K. Doreski, *Elizabeth Bishop: The Restraints of Language* (New York: Oxford University Press, 1993), p. 131.
3 Joelle Biele (ed.), *Elizabeth Bishop and the New Yorker: The Complete Correspondence* (New York: Farrar, Straus and Giroux, 2011), p. 392.
4 See Marilyn Lombardi Costello, *The Body and the Song: Elizabeth Bishop's Poetics* (Carbondale, IL: University of Illinois Press, 1995); Susan McCabe, *Elizabeth Bishop: Her Poetics of Loss* (University Park, TX: Pennsylvania State University Press, 1994).
5 Catherine Cucinella, '"Dress up! Dress up and Dance at Carnival!": The Body in Elizabeth Bishop's "Pink Dog"', *Rocky Mountain Review of Language and Literature*, 56.1 (2002), pp. 73–83. Web. 11 March 2012, p. 74.
6 Helen Vendler, *Last Looks, Last Books: Stevens, Plath, Lowell, Bishop, Merrill* (Princeton, NJ: Princeton University Press, 2010).
7 Donna Haraway, 'Cyborgs to Companion Species: Refiguring Kinship in Technoscience', in Linda Kalouf and Amy Fitzgerald (eds.), *The Animals Reader* (New York: Berg, 2007), p. 365.
8 Mutlu Konuk Blasing, 'From Gender to Genre and Back: Elizabeth Bishop and "The Moose"', *American Literary History*, 6.2 (1994), pp. 265–86. Oxford University Press. Web. 6 April 2012, p. 10.
9 Peggy Samuels, 'Verse as Deep Surface: Elizabeth Bishop's New Poetics, 1938–39', *Twentieth Century Literature*, 52.3 (2006), pp. 306–29. Hofstra University. Web. 6 April 2012, pp. 21–5.
10 Heather Cass White, 'Elizabeth Bishop's Calling', *Twentieth Century Literature*, 48.2 (2002), pp. 117–49. Hofstra University. Web. 6 April 2012, pp. 11–34.
11 Willard Spiegelman, *Imaginative Transcripts: Selected Literary Essays* (New York: Oxford University Press, 2009), p. 31.
12 Anastasia Graf, 'Representing the Other: A Conversation among Mikhail Bakhtin, Elizabeth Bishop, and Wisława Szymborska', *Comparative Literature*, 57.1 (2005), pp. 84–99. Duke University Press on behalf of the University of Oregon. Web. 11 March 2012, pp. 12–13.

13   Bonnie Costello, 'Vision and Mastery in Elizabeth Bishop', *Twentieth Century Literature*, 28.4 (1982), pp. 351–70. Hofstra University. Web. 6 April 2012.

14   Donna Haraway struggles forthrightly with her encounter with street dogs in Puerto Rico in the concluding pages of *The Companion Species Manifesto* (Chicago, IL: Prickly Paradigm Press, 2003). She attempts to 'inhabit' their 'story' rather than 'disown' it through 'two kinds of Puritan critique': 'colonialist sentimentality' on one hand, and the sterility of 'historical structural analysis' on the other (pp. 89–90). While she argues that 'village dogs and rural dogs and urban feral dogs carry their own signifying otherness for the people they live among, and not just for people like me', she does not consider in her argument ways that would allow the dogs to remain on the streets where they historically live (p. 97). For further discussion on this question in Haraway see my article 'Islam, Westernization and Post-Humanist Place: The Case of the Istanbul Street Dog' forthcoming in *ISLE: Interdisciplinary Studies in Literature and the Environment*.

15   Robert Lowell, *Words in Air: The Complete Correspondence Between Elizabeth Bishop and Robert Lowell*, eds. Thomas Travisano and Saskia Hamilton (New York: Farrar, Straus and Giroux, 2008). p. 591.

16   For animal rights legislation in Brazil and other countries see Michigan State University College of Law, *Animal Legal and Historical Center*. Web. 12 May 2012.

Glossary of Terms[1]

Abjection   The action of expelling from consciousness material pertaining to bodily life that is at odds with the imaginary integrity of the ego. The term "abject" also refers to the mother's body, the connection with which has to be severed if ego identity is to be established.

Actant   A term in narratology for the roles characters play in fiction such as sender/receiver or helper/opponent. Now used more broadly in the social sciences to name any agent of action.

Actor Network Theory   From Bruno Latour who argues that the world is made up of agents (both human and non-human) in constant negotiation with one another. None possesses an essential identity that allows it to transcend the field in which it exists in a concrete and immanent (inserted, immersed) fashion. The theory assumes culture is not separate from nature, and that there is no hierarchy of actants such that the human is more privileged.

Adaptation, Adaptive   In the course of biological evolution, organisms, through genetic mutation, acquire new traits that assist them in surviving adversity in the environment. Such adaptations allow the organism to survive in its new circumstances.

Aesthetics, Aestheticism   The doctrine of the beautiful in philosophy or the study of what constitutes beauty in a work of art. From the Greek word *aesthetikos*, which means sentient or feeling. For some, aesthetics concerns the techniques and forms of art, for others, the pleasure of appreciating art. Aestheticism was a movement in England in the late nineteenth century of artists and theorists who were devoted to the ideal of the beautiful in art and in life. See Walter Pater's Conclusion to *Studies in the Renaissance*.

Affect   An involuntary bodily response to stimuli that is often outside the control of the person experiencing it. Affect therefore differs from emotion which has both conscious and unconscious aspects and is more easily regulated.

Affective Fallacy   The tendency in readers to think their own emotional responses constitute the meaning of a literary work. The New Critics thought meaning resided in the literary work itself. Its language and imagery were therefore the proper objects and concerns of literary analysis, not the emotional response of readers or audiences.

Literary Theory: An Anthology, Third Edition. Edited by Julie Rivkin and Michael Ryan.
© 2017 John Wiley & Sons, Ltd. Published 2017 by John Wiley & Sons, Ltd.

Alienation (Reification)   Karl Marx's term for the taking of the product of labor from workers by the owners of capital. Workers put their life energy into the things they make. Under capitalist relations of production, those things or commodities belong to the owners of the means of production. The life energy of workers is therefore alienated – or made-other and taken away – from them when what they make becomes the private property of the owner or capitalist.

Alienation Effect   A term conceived by German twentieth-century playwright Bertolt Brecht to describe what his work sought to accomplish. Traditional theater sought to enlist audience identification with characters and stories. Brecht sought instead to distance audiences from characters and to oblige audiences to think more critically about the impersonal, historical themes of the work.

Allegory   An older literary form in which characters and events have explicit meanings such as "Fancy," "Occasion," and "Courage" as in, for example, Edmund Spenser's *Faerie Queen*. The term is also used to describe any narrative whose meaning derives from a well-known code rather than from the specific circumstances of the story.

Alliteration   The repetition of syllables in poetry. As in Shakespeare's sonnet: "When to the sessions of sweet silent thought."

Allusion   A reference generally to another literary work. As in the allusions to the Bible in Dante's *Divine Comedy*.

Alterity   Literally "otherness." The idea that for something to possess an identity, it must be in relation to something other. Its identity is relational.

Aporia   An irresolvable dilemma of thought or action in which, for example, to choose one of two paths is to lose something either way. Originally a term in rhetoric for an irresolvable proposition ("All men are liars; I am a man"), it was used by Paul de Man to name the impossibility of moving from figural language to a non-figural revelation of meaning.

Apparatus (*Dispositif*)   Michel Foucault's term for the complex of methods, discourses, institutions, laws, administrative structures, etc. that maintain power in a society.

Archaeology   Michel Foucault used this metaphor to describe his work of unearthing the hidden assumptions of discourses.

Archetype   Little used any longer, this term refers to narrative and thematic patterns derived from mythology and religion such as the descent into hell or the cycle of death and rebirth.

Assemblage   A term proposed by Gilles Deleuze and Felix Guattari to name entities without identities that bring diverse elements together. Our own bodies are assemblages, as are our minds.

Autonomy   A social movement primarily in Italy that aspired to separate the working class from capitalism. Initially a strategy of the radical leftwing labor movement, it meant refusing the work discipline of capitalism as well as the reformist aspirations of the institutional labor movement and asserting the independence or autonomy of workers in relation to their employers. Because capitalism depends on the creative labor of workers, workers themselves, according to the theory of autonomy advanced by Carlo Tronti, Antonio Negri, and others, possess power in relation to capital. They should assert that power by refusing to work. Wildcat strikes not condoned by labor unions were a favorite strategy of the autonomy movement, as was industrial sabotage. The idea of autonomy was also embraced by anarchists who advocated the creation of autonomous zones or spaces where non-capitalist life forms could be incubated and developed such as squatting and other non-market, non-commodified life relations, both personal and economic.

Base, Superstructure   In Marxist theory, the base refers to the material underpinnings of society such as the way food and goods are produced through labor usually in exploitative work relations. Superstructure refers to all the other institutional, personal, and cultural forms of life that arise on top of that fundamental material basis such as government, social relationships, schools, the media, government, culture, etc.

Binary Opposition   Deconstructive analysis studies the way philosophy creates hierarchical orders that make one term axiomatic, foundational, and normative while relegating related and often opposed terms to a subordinate, derivative status. "Presence" is the criterion of truthfulness for idealism, for example. True ideas are present fully and completely as a living entity in the mind. That positing of a norm results in the assigning of a subordinate and negative status to terms connoting qualities such as absence that seem outside and at odds with the norm of presence, things such as spacing, articulation between terms, writing, technique, etc.

Biopower/Biopolitics   According to Michel Foucault, those with sovereign power in society often have power over people's lives and over their bodies. Power over *bios* can be exercised through the violent destruction of bodies (as in the practice of drawing and quartering) or it can assume more subtle forms in modern life such as scientific studies or governmental supervision that use knowledge to pinpoint and control people. The most famous example would be the naming and categorizing of the so-called sexual "perversions" such as homosexuality. Contemporary queer theorists advance a counter biopolitics that rejects heteronormative categories, notices the perverse, sadomasochistic character of much heterosexuality, and argues for a progressive, postnormative politics of the body.

Body   A cultural effect of performativity within the sex-gender regime or a biological organism that encompasses human culture as one of its effects. Or both.

Bricolage   Anthropologist Claude Lévi-Strauss coined this phrase to describe a method of assembling knowledge from pieces rather than exercising a more rigorous method such as logical deduction.

Canon   The body of literary works that is widely acknowledged to represent the field. Obviously a debatable and contested notion, canon nevertheless allows for distinctions between works that are frequently taught and studied such as *The Great Gatsby* or Nella Larsen's *Passing* and books from the same period that are now less valued or recognized as manifesting high levels of technical skill, sociological insight, and philosophical acumen such as John Dos Passos's *Manhattan Transfer*.

Capital, Capitalism   A way of conducting economic life that makes irrational self-interest paramount in human affairs, allows a small group to lay claim to the accumulated resources of the society, and exploits the work of the majority for the sake of increasing the privately accumulated wealth of the minority. Capitalism relies on the subordination of workers to the will of the wealthy. That subordination is enabled by ideology (word ideas such as "freedom" that license the chaotic irrationality of the so-called market), vocational education to reinforce class distinctions, a legal regime that enforces inequality within the guise of formal equality, and police force. Capitalism resides on the myth of the "private" "free" "individual" and requires the erasure of all the public, social, communal ingredients of supposedly private economic activity such as money, roads, schools, language, and the like. Anti-capitalist socialists advocate a change to an economy in which economic activity would be more publicly regulated and administered so that prices would be set at reasonable levels and compensation for labor would be set at high enough levels to assure a reasonable standard of living. The goal of the economy would not be the enrichment of the few but the overall good of the many.

Carnival, Carnivalesque In his well-known work, *Rabelais and His World*, Mikhail Bakhtin examines medieval culture in the works of François Rabelais, whose mocking satiric style of writing in such works as *Gargantua* and *Pantagruel*, according to Bakhtin, is "carnivalesque." It imitates the mocking forms and tropes of the medieval carnival. Medieval culture was dominated by the Catholic Church, which enforced constraints on bodily life in favor of the ideal of the spiritual afterlife. The sexual body had to be controlled so that the afterlife in heaven could be enjoyed. But during carnival season, official strictures were suspended and people were allowed to indulge bodily urges, mock the authority of the Church, and overturn existing hierarchies – at least in play form. Rabelais' novels celebrate the material life of the body and make fun of the reigning authorities of the time. A literary work therefore has carnivalesque elements if it mocks authoritative hierarchies, rejects the repression of bodily life, and celebrates the cyclicality of natural physical existence.

Castration For Sigmund Freud, all male children experience sexual feelings for their mother, and when those feelings are blunted by the encounter with the conventions of human culture, the child experiences that frustration as a fear of castration. Jacques Lacan gave that fear a semiotic twist. He describes the male child's encounter with the rule against incest as a passage into the Symbolic Order, the realm of cultural conventions and signs that determine who we are as civilized beings (names, roles, rules, etc.). Male children repress the desire for the mother and it enters the unconscious, where it is no longer available to consciousness except in the form of signs such as symptoms. The bar that separates the signifier from the signified in the algorithm s/S (with small s equaling symptom and big S equaling unconscious meaning) is like the one that separates unconscious content from manifest symptoms such as dreams. The lack of the desired m(Other) is the motive of all male desire in so much as it seeks an imaginary reunification with the mother's body. The entry into the Symbolic Order and the acceptance of the need for repression is akin to castration, albeit a symbolic one. One sacrifices access to the Phallus, the token of male sexual power, and acknowledges it is the property of the father whose "Law" separates male child from mother in patrocentric human culture (so far).

Center, Decentered Post-Structuralist thinkers such as Jacques Derrida noticed that philosophy has implicit norms that function as centers or anchors for value systems. His work undid those value systems and so "decentered" the norms. Often, he found elements that were at the margins of philosophic texts such as metaphors that seemed unimportant, but that he showed were in fact essential.

Chronotope Mikhail Bakhtin's term for the way the spatial and temporal dimensions of a novel's world are represented in the discourse of the novel. *Chronos* is the Greek word for time, and *topos* the Greek word for place or spatial location.

Coevolution When two organisms affect each other's evolutionary development, as when a parasite and a host change how the other evolves in a mutually beneficial manner.

Colonialism, Post-Colonialism Colonialism usually refers to the era from the fifteenth century onward when European nations conquered other lands and peoples and converted them into satellite colonies usually for the purpose of extracting natural resources such as sugar, cocoa, lumber, and animal skins. By the end of the twentieth century, most formerly colonial nations and peoples had attained independence. The study of the cultural changes from colony to post-colony is often referred to as "post-colonial studies."

Commodity   Marx's term for a product manufactured by labor such as a pair of shoes that is sold on the market under capitalism. He argued that commodities seem to be a magical source of profit due entirely to market exchange, but in fact, commodities conceal the fact that the value they bear comes from the labor of people whose work is under-rewarded. Profit arises from the underpayment of workers. See "Fetishism of Commodities."

Competence   The ability to understand statements in a particular language.

Condensation   In dreams, images often condense or bring together several strands of feeling or of thought. A single name might condense several unconscious causes or referents. Freud found that a dream about a dry leaf in a book condensed several referents such as a woman's name ("Flora") and the German word for "garden."

Constative (*see* Performative)   According to speech act theory, language acts that bring about change in the world such as "I now pronounce you man and wife" are called "performative utterances," while statements that simply record facts ("You look like a man and a wife") are "constative utterances."

Constellation   Walter Benjamin, in his study of German tragedy of the Baroque era, studies the fragments of the era in relation to one another while resisting conceptualizing them in our modern terms. Benjamin focused on the fragment that gave access to understanding an era as opposed to the concept that sums it up clearly. His method of analysis is therefore immanent, historical, and materialist. Rather than place a work of literature within the totality of an era (as Gyorgy Lukács was inclined to do in his historical materialist method of analyzing literature), Benjamin instead studied each unique individual element of the constellation.

Context   The surrounding or environment in which something exists and which usually is required in order for it to be complete or to be understood fully. Often applied to literary works whose historical surrounding is important.

Counter-Hegemonic   Hegemony refers to a dominant position. Something that is counter-hegemonic operates against domination or power.

Cultural Capital   The symbolic goods and benefits (such as access to a particular kind of training in good taste) that accrue to different economic class positions. According to Pierre Bourdieu, these goods are as unevenly developed as financial capital and help distinguish one socio-economic class from another according to how well they exercise aesthetic judgment.

Cultural Materialism   The movement in literary study launched by Raymond Williams that shifted emphasis away from the specific literary work and towards the cultural history in which it was located. The approach is materialist because it shares with Marxism a concern for the fundamental physical elements and processes of life such as work as well as for the reality of economic classes and their effects in our lives. In perhaps his most famous study, Williams examined the difference between English literature that arose in or was concerned with life in the country and literature concerning city life.

Dasein   From Martin Heidegger, the specific state of individual human existence as opposed to the more general state of Being or *Sein*.

Deconstruction   The method of critique developed by French twentieth-century philosopher Jacques Derrida. Derrida analyzed different ways that metaphysical philosophers have conceived of truth. He found that they posited an ideal and unattainable limit or ideal (such as a purely formal idea in the mind) and constructed a hierarchical axiology around that ideal limit consisting of ethical and ontological distinctions between terms in which one set is subordinate to and derivative in relation to another. Hence presence as a criterion of truthfulness is better than, prior to, and superior to absence. Metaphysical philosophy, from Plato to Husserl, assigned positive values such as authenticity, presence, vividness, nature, fullness, substance, self-identity, moral goodness, seriousness, and the living voice of consciousness to truth while assigning to non-truth negative values such as technology, representation, absence, death, artifice, repetition, difference, play, writing, etc. Derrida found that these hierarchies did not hold under critical scrutiny. Indeed, the negative terms could be shown to encompass the positive terms in such a way that no hierarchy of terms was really possible. For example, to even begin to talk about truth as distinct from non-truth, one has to make a differentiation. One cannot therefore say that difference is a negative term that is alien to truth if truth cannot be conceived outside difference. In a similar way, Derrida noticed that philosophers such as Edmund Husserl, while defining truth as a pure formal idea that was aloof from the mechanics of signification in language, nevertheless had to define the idea of truth in such a way that the characteristics of signification that were so negative – repetition especially – were necessary for truth as a pure idea to be determined. Ideal truth had to last forever, which is to say it had to repeat itself, with each repetition introducing a bit of spatial difference at odds with the idea of a full truth grasped as a living presence in the mind that is purely temporal and aloof from the spatial form of the sign. All the ideal limits or transcendental values that define truth in the metaphysical tradition can be shown to be derived. They cannot exist outside the complex relations they aspire to comprehend and to describe.

Defamiliarization (Estrangement, *Ostranenie*)   From Viktor Shklovsky, the Russian Formalist critic, this term (*ostranenie*) describes the way poetry upsets normal patterns of perception and of thought. Poetry roughens up our rote or habitual ways of seeing the world and renders familiar things unfamiliar. Shklovsky alludes to Tolstoy's narrative strategy of telling a story in the voice of a horse.

Denotation/Connotation   A denotation is the meaning directly intended by a word, while a connotation is a secondary meaning. A particular gesture in a magazine cover such as a salute on the part of an African soldier under French colonial rule might denote "salute," but it connotes colonial domination.

Desiring Machine   From Gilles Deleuze and Felix Guattari, the idea that the human psyche is largely impersonal and not under the control of the conscious self or subject. Desire operates like a machine that is on automatic.

Diachrony, Diachronic   A term from structural linguistics that describes the temporal axis of speech.

Dialectic   Georg Hegel developed the dialectical method of analysis. Classical Greek dialectic consisted of a form of argument that moved from specific propositions (such as "Socrates is a man") to general or universal propositions ("All men are mortal") and then put the two together to arrive at a synthetic proposition ("Therefore Socrates must be mortal"). The conclusion is a necessary logical consequence of the propositions that precede it, and it combines both the universal and the specific.

Hegel thought the mind worked the same way when it tried to determine truth, and he felt social history and the material world were similarly logical. Philosophical truth evolves from simple propositions that were concrete and specific (or determinate, to use his word) and moved by a necessity inherent to them to more general or universal ideas that were implied by the simple initial proposition. Eventually, through a process of logical evolution, the mind arrives at a more synthetic conclusion that combined the specific concrete premise with the universal or general idea.

For example, empiricists claimed before Hegel that sensory perceptions allowed the mind to build up ideas. Sense came first. Immanuel Kant countered that the mind's implicit rational categories allowed it to grasp sensory experience. The mind came first. Hegel combined the two. In his *Phenomenology of Mind*, he begins with sensory experience (our way of perceiving the world every day). Sensory experience, he argued, is like a concrete, specific proposition in classical logic. But like all such simple observations, it is lacking something; it is not complete in itself. It implies necessarily a universal idea that it is not (that it negates). To be specific and concrete, it must *not* be universal and abstract. Negation is implied in any determination – any specific concrete proposition. The universal is therefore a necessary component of the identity of the specific, determinate, concrete perception by the mind. In itself, sense perception is incomplete. It is not the whole of human cognitive experience. It leaves out universality. But if you examine universality, a similar negation emerges: the universal is too abstract; it lacks concreteness and specificity. The idea of Justice is empty without concrete laws and courts that make it real in society. Therefore, the ideal form of truth and of knowledge is, according to Hegel, a combination of the two, the universal abstract idea and the specific, determinate concrete instance. So, for example, the real truth of justice consists of both the abstract universal idea as well as the concrete, specific, determinate laws and courts that embody the ideal in action. He went on to apply these same ideas to culture, society, aesthetics, politics, and human history. Human society begins with the equivalent of simple concrete logical propositions. It is concerned with food and shelter. But as it evolves, it is able to integrate universal ideas into its constitution by developing the idea of government and of justice in laws which combine the concrete and the universal and that allow large human societies to exist.

Karl Marx used the dialectical method to analyze capitalism. He felt it was characterized by the same sense of logical necessity (by virtue of which simple propositions led necessarily to universals). Workers and capitalists are like logical propositions in that they presuppose one another (to be a worker is to *not* be a capitalist). But Marx felt the relationship would also evolve logically so that workers would eventually liberate themselves from the limitations of wage labor and achieve a new social universality in which wealth would be distributed more equally and equitably. He called that ideal "communism."

Dialogic, Dialogism Russian critic Mikhail Bakhtin invented these terms to describe the multi-voiced quality of novels. Novels contain characters from different walks of life, and each inserts a different dialect into the novel's discourse. For example, a novel might contain lawyerly discourse, a variety of gender discourses, various social class discourses, etc. Each of these enters into dialogue with the other – mixing, clashing, interacting, etc. And the meaning of the novel arises from these dialogic relations between voices. Bakhtin contrasted this multi-vocality of the novel with monologic Romantic poetry in which a single speaker announces meaning.

Diegesis The interior story as told or depicted especially in film. Diegesis refers to the interiority of the fictional world and its portrayal. Used most frequently in discussing film where a distinction is made between music that emerges from the story events and is filmed (as in the famous piano sequence in *Casablanca*) and music that is an aural accompaniment added from outside the story events as in a film such as *Best Years of Our Lives*. One is intra-diegetic, the other extra-diegetic.

***Différance*, Difference** Ferdinand de Saussure noticed that there are no identities in language. Language is constructed from relations between parts each of which has an identity only in so much as it is in relation to other parts of the language system. This notion of relational identity was helpful to feminist, gender, and race theorists who posited difference as an alternative to existing normative and hierarchical ideals of racial and gender identity that were unaware of their origin in acts of subordinative differentiation. Understood from the perspective of difference theory, "White" is less a norm than the expulsion, denigration, and refusal of color. Understood in terms of difference, "White" is merely one shade of color (differentiated along a spectrum from others) and is not an absolute in itself that can qualify as a norm or standard by which to measure other more deficient hues. Similarly, heterosexual male identity, long taken as a norm and standard for understanding gender, is a delusion, according to difference theory. Not a norm or standard that stands apart from and above other gender flavors and inflections, it is just one more possible flavor on a spectrum of shades of differentiated possibilities.

Jacques Derrida argued that the concepts and ideas of philosophy are characterized by a similar differentiality – nature/culture, physicality/technology, presence/repetition, etc. Each major concept requires its other to define itself. He posited a primordial process of space and time whereby things differ from each other spatially and simultaneously exist in time in such a way that their full and complete presence at any one moment of perception by the mind is perpetually deferred. What he called *différance* names the spatial and temporal movement that makes it impossible to arrive at a complete, final determination of the truth of something (understood as its full and complete presence to the mind).

Disavowal According to Sigmund Freud, the male child sometimes mistakes the mother's lack of a penis as castration and feels anxiety that provokes a desire to disavow that possible castration through the seeking of fetish objects.

Discourse A body of statements concerning some object such as law, art, or madness. Discourses are characterized by axiomatic assumptions and rules of operation that determine what statements make sense within the discourse. The rules of the discourse determine what the legitimate objects of the discourse are. For example, Michel Foucault noticed that madness was differently defined in discourses over time. In one era, it was considered a form of sainthood. In another, it became a form of pathology meriting ostracism and incarceration. Foucault posited the idea of a "discursive formation," a systematic and coherent body of rules and procedures for generating statements that maintained the apparent truthfulness of the discourse by regulating possible statements within it.

Disidentification A refusal and displacement of the subjective identity assigned one by existing regimes of economic, ideological, and gender power.

Displacement Freud described the dream work as consisting of ways the unconscious achieves expression. Dream images often consist of indirect expressions of feelings that have been displaced away from direct expression by the defensive action of the ego.

Dispositif (*see* **Apparatus**)

Dissemination   Jacques Derrida's term for the way signs refer endlessly to other signs in any literary work and in any language system so that it is difficult to declare an end to signification and an arrival at a final determination of meaning that does leave a "remainder," a relation to an other (sign) that awaits grasping or conceptualizing, endlessly.

Distinction   Pierre Bourdieu's term for the way cultural tastes differentiate between people along economic class lines.

Dominant   A term from formalist and linguistic literary criticism that describes how one literary device or technique is ascendant in a literary work. In Dostoevsky, according to Mikhail Bakhtin, the dominant element is polyphony, the incorporation of many voices that are not subordinated to an authorial voice.

Ecriture, Ecriture Féminine   The French word for "writing" became popular after Jacques Derrida used the metaphor of writing to name the process of spatial and temporal differentiation (*différance*) that he saw underlying and producing all sensible experience in the mind. Feminist theorists in France especially suggested that women were more connected to a kind of writing that embodied that disturbing process of differentiation that seemed to make all the traditional male quests for absolute truth founded on the perception of clear identities seem misguided. Those models of truth privileged male cognitive processes and relegated female qualities to secondary status. Thus, Reason was always superior to mere sensation and emotion. Some feminist theorists such as Luce Irigaray and Hélène Cixous reversed this hierarchy and assigned a superior value to a "feminine" and "maternal" sensation, emotion, and differentiation that undermined male ideals of abstract, conceptual, identitarian absoluteness.

Epigenetics   The study of traits that result not from DNA but from how DNA is affected by external factors that alter how it is expressed. Genes can be affected by factors outside the nucleotide sequence of the DNA that change how they are expressed and what form they assume without altering the DNA sequence. Methylation, for example, attaches a strand of methyl that can silence a gene and prevent it from expressing itself. All organic development requires the epigenetic regulation of basic stem cells that are transformed by regulation and express themselves differently as the various parts of the organism.

Epiphany   A moment of great insight or revelation.

Épistémè   According to Michel Foucault, each historical era is characterized by a mode of knowledge that arranges the world in a particular way according to its categories and its procedures for processing objects. The medieval *épistémè*, which was decidedly religious, categorized the world in a way that was very different from that of the more "rational" eighteenth century, for example.

Epistemology   The branch of philosophy dealing with knowledge.

Epoché   From Edmund Husserl's phenomenological philosophy, this refers to the putting aside or suspension of all assumptions. The "reduction" or putting in brackets of all pre-existing attitudes in conducting phenomenological philosophy allows one to attain a clearer perception of the object in the mind.

Essentialism   Essentialism takes two forms: the assumption that identities are internal and expressive rather than assigned and imprinted from without and the assumption that there are truths that inhere in nature or in the world and are not the effect or result of acts of social or cultural construction.

Feminists and gender theorists challenged the long-standing assumptions of heterosexual patriarchy that women and queers possessed essential identities that were subordinate, marginal, and of lesser normative value than that of the dominant heterosexual male. In patriarchal discourse and ideology, women were passive, dependent, weak, secondary, and functionally supportive of men, while queers were deviant, aberrant, non-normative, and perverse. These essences were ordained for many centuries, and that essentialism has been successfully critiqued over recent decades. A similar critique of ethnic or racial essentialism has occurred, which over-turned and displaced white normative assumptions regarding the secondary status of people of color.

Essentialism works by inverting cause and effect and thereby converting external imprinting into an apparent internal quality. It reverses cause and effect by understand-ing the psychological characteristics that in the past were externally imprinted on women by patriarchal domination (dependency, passivity, etc.) as internal qualities. The effect of domination in this way becomes a justification for continued domination.

When Jacques Derrida launched his critique of metaphysics in the 1960s, he noticed that Western philosophy pictured the world hierarchically so that when truth was defined, certain terms such as "presence" were assigned a positive value and made central and essential in relation to other terms such as "absence," "repetition," "difference," and the like that were characterized negatively and banished often to the margins of the value system the philosophy constructed. Those negative terms were not essential or central or foundational. They were more likely to subvert or endanger truthfulness and upset the values system of the philosophy. Derrida's point ultimately was that it is not possible to justify the positing of superior terms that are more central or essential to truth. There is no locatable center or essence, no firm foundational criterion of truthfulness that is not disturbed by relations to other terms on which it depends (hence it can't be central or essential alone or independently) or that is not determined by the structure that it supposedly supervises (hence it cannot be founda-tional since something prior or other is in a position of determination in relation to it). There are in effect no centers, essences, or foundations. The quest to establish a formal standard of truthfulness on the usual terms (presence, identity, etc.) is like trying to locate the center of the ocean. Our systems of philosophy reside on webs or networks of relations between terms none of which is central or essential and all of which depend on the others for support in maintaining their appearance of an identity that is not entirely differential and relational. It is not possible therefore to posit "identities" that are not simultaneously displaced into networks of relations that undermine the very possibility of an essential identity.

The necessity of continuing to pursue the political critique of structures of power from identity positions such as "woman" or "person of color" or "queer" led some theorists to posit the necessity of a "strategic essentialism" that would allow critique to proceed without having to constantly acknowledge its groundlessness, its absence of a firm footing in a universally recognized standard of true essential identity.

Event As opposed to structure. An event occurs once, is unique, and evaporates. Its being is singular and non-repeatable. It has no presence. In contrast, structure endures and is repeatable and permanent. This concept was part of the Post-Structuralist argument that existence is inherently unstable and eludes the traditional philosophic concepts of knowing subject and known object whose truth can be conceived as a presence that is easily discerned.

Existentialism A philosophy concerned not with large questions such as "Being" but with the more small-scale questions provoked by considering philosophy from the perspective of each individual existence. Concern focused on the question of choice especially and the possibility that existence might have no meaning or purpose.

Expressionism A movement in Germany (in art, theater, film, and literature) that broke with the protocols of realist representation and sought instead to express meaning in non-realist forms, using strongly contrasted colors and grotesque figures in painting, for example, or stage and film sets that exaggerate qualities such as corruption, irrationality, and evil. The Expressionists were leftist critics of German society, and often, their works depict capitalism and the ruling economic class quite negatively. See, for example, Fritz Lang's *Metropolis* and Robert Wiene's *The Cabinet of Dr. Caligari*.

Fabula/Syzuhet **(also Discourse/Story)** In the study of narrative, a distinction is made between the supposedly real events (*syzuhet* or *story*) and the selective telling of those events in narrative form (*fabula* or *discourse*). The actual life told may last ten years, but the *fabula* or narrative will select just a few moments to recount.

Feral A term from bioregional criticism for a state halfway between domestic and wild.

Fetish In Freudian theory, desire can be shifted onto another object if it encounters repression. A desire for sexual satisfaction can be displaced onto an adjacent object that becomes a fetish substitute for the original object of desire.

Fetishism of Commodities Karl Marx's idea that under capitalism, there is the belief that wealth arises magically from the sale of goods on the market. No one notices that in fact it is the labor of workers that puts value into those goods, and because that labor is underpaid, wealth is generated. Workers add a "surplus value" to goods that becomes wealth when market exchange occurs.

Fordism Prior to the era of globalization, capitalism was organized nationally around large-scale industrial production using assembly methods invented by Henry Ford such as the "assembly line" and the use of large numbers of unskilled laborers.

Formalism The study of the technical aspects of a work of art such as metaphors in poetry and narrative perspective in fiction.

Fort/Da Sigmund Freud observed a child play a game with a string and an object tied to the end. The child would fling the object out of sight and exclaim "Fort!" (or "Gone!") only to call out "Da!" or "There!" when he tugged the object back into view. Freud speculated that the child was using play to master his distress at the disappearance of his mother.

Function In narrative theory, a function is a typical repetitive event in narrative such as "the hero leaves home." The term was used first by Vladimir Propp in his *Morphology of the Folk Tale*.

Gaze In film theory, this describes the way heterosexual women are posited as scopophilic objects of heterosexual male desire. Heterosexual women become a fetish that allows the heterosexual male to make up for the experience of having to give up the mother, an experience that is tantamount to castration. Scopophilia allows the heterosexual male to engage in "disavowal" of the possibility of castration, of a loss of a feeling of sexual power. His desire for the mother is displaced onto a fetish that makes up for his lack, and this fetish is the image of the heterosexual woman on screen.

General Economy (as opposed to a Restrained Economy) Terms from Georges Bataille that were developed by Jacques Derrida in *Writing and Difference* and used to distinguish between philosophic discourses that were closed (such as the dialectic in which initial premises were justified by the method's conclusions) and those such as Derrida's deconstruction that explored the fringes at the edges of systematic philosophy where exceptions could be found that put the systematic character of the philosophy in doubt (so that the conclusions did not justify the initial premises).

Genotype   The inherited genetic make-up of an organism. It is distinct from the phenotype, which is the ultimate form an organism assumes as a result of environmental influences and developmental changes in the way the genotype is expressed.

Genre   A type of literature defined by shared characteristics and conventions such as comedy, tragedy, or lyric verse.

Globalization   In the 1980s, conservatives lobbied for the end of restrictions of world trade in order to increase their wealth. As a result of the elimination of trade rules that protected workers and domestic industries, a new era of transnational commerce began. Goods could now be manufactured by low-wage workers for very little money in places like Mexico, China, and Vietnam because differences in living standards meant that labor in those countries cost very little compared to more industrially developed countries such as the US. Those with wealth in the US were therefore able to shift jobs overseas, spend much less on labor, receive the same income for sales, and earn much higher profits. Globalization had the effect of reducing workers in countries such as the US to a lower income level and a lower standard of living while greatly augmenting the wealth of the minority of capital holders. Inequality greatly increased as a result. At the same time, countries such as China saw the emergence for the first time and for similar reasons of a new class of wealthy investor industrialists who benefitted greatly from the new international trade system. Living standards for workers in places such as China rose but at the expense of workers in places such as the US. Wages that in the past would have been paid to American workers were now paid to Chinese workers. A great shifting of wealth eastward occurred as well as a great shifting of wealth upward towards the upper segments of society.

Grand Narrative   From Jean-François Lyotard's *The Postmodern Condition*, this term refers to the "big" stories we use to map human history such as Humanism. Opposed to micro-narratives of specific population segments such as gender minorities or people of color who do not fit the big narratives that were enunciated largely by white heterosexual males.

Habitus   Pierre Bourdieu coined this word to describe the practices of everyday life that reproduce the material conditions of the society. Originally, Bourdieu studied practices such as cooking or weaving or other aspects of household life that embodied the implicit hierarchies of a society as well as its division of labor. Those practices had the effect of making those hierarchies and divisions seem natural, a part of the texture of the world. That in turn helped reproduce those hierarchies and divisions. Later, Bourdieu would apply the same model to education which he saw as reproducing class divisions and class cultural hierarchies.

Hegemony   Hegemony is soft power exercised through institutions such as schools and churches rather than through coercion or force. According to Italian Marxist Antonio Gramsci, ruling groups in a society maintain their dominant position not by the exercise of direct force but instead through cultural mechanisms such as education and religion, political mechanisms such as democracy (which tend to elect only those who endorse inequality), judicial mechanisms that make the incarceration of economic victims seem a logical expression of morality, and economic mechanisms such as the "free market," which reproduce income inequalities and distribute wealth upwards in a society. Domination occurs automatically and without violent exertion, and the dominated, because educated and indoctrinated, acquiesce to their own domination.

Hermeneutics   Another name for interpretation, converting the language of a text into the meanings implied by that language.

Heteroglossia   Related to dialogic, this term names the multiplicity of voice that, according to Mikhail Bakhtin, distinguishes novelistic discourse from poetic discourse.

Heteronormative, Heteronormativity   All existing cultures assume heterosexuality is the norm and the normal. Such assumptions seep into all aspects of life and all dimensions of language, culture, and thought.

Heterotopia   From Michel Foucault, a space outside society such as a camp, a barracks, or a prison where different kinds of social relations and practices exist.

Historical Materialism   In Marxism, the idea that human life is best understood as a physical process enacted over historical time. A materialist understanding emphasizes the real social, political, and economic conditions that characterize human existence. The method differs from an idealist approach that would see human history and society as embodying ideas such as "freedom" or "liberty." Such ideas are often at odds with the actual forms of social existence, especially under capitalism, which, for Marxists, is a form of wage slavery that denies freedom to workers.

Homosocial   Eve Sedgwick's term for alliance relations between heterosexual men.

Hybridity   Related to dialogics and heteroglossia, this refers to the way discourses merge and combine both in life and in the novel. A hybrid discourse is one that adopts another discourse and integrates it. An example would be satire that mocks the way a character thinks and speaks.

Hyperreal   A term to describe cultural institutions such as museums or theme parks that bear a strong resemblance to reality yet are artificial.

Icon   Semiotician Charles Sanders Peirce defined iconic signs as resembling the thing signified – a map or a portrait.

Idealism   A now lapsed school of philosophy that believed ideas existed in a separate sphere from the physical world.

Identification   From Freud, the idea that one's self is in part constructed through the incorporation of images of other people towards whom one has strong feelings and who one wishes to emulate. One builds an ideal image of that person in one's mind and shapes one's own self around the imitation of that ideal.

Ideology   For Karl Marx, the ruling ideas of the ruling class. As human economic life has changed over time, the ideas that justify the unequal distribution of wealth and power have also changed. In the distant past, religious ideas that mandated a sense of duty within hierarchy legitimated the rule of a priestly caste allied with a supposed "noble" social group. Later, the idea of liberty or freedom made legitimate the overaccumulation of wealth by a small group of merchants and industrialists. Ideology was characterized by French philosopher Louis Althusser as a quality of personal identity (the illusion that one was a free individual rather than someone who imbibes roles and rules of behavior from the society and the culture around one through such institutions and practices as schools and education, rules that subject one to capitalism as one feels most free as a human subject).

Imaginary, Real, Symbolic   For psychoanalyst Jacques Lacan, the ego is delusional. It cannot grasp its determination by the unconscious. Yet, despite its being shaped by forces that are also entirely other to it, the ego maintains the illusion it is an "identity" that directs its own behavior. For Lacan, that illusion is "imaginary." Because that imaginary delusion of possessing a fully integrated self is so powerful in all of us, we cannot touch the "Real," that deep well of unconscious forces that shape our lives, driving our desires. The term "imaginary" has since been generalized to name any delusional cultural system. For example, the "imaginary of the nation state." The other key term in Lacan's vocabulary, the "Symbolic," refers to the realm of social and cultural signs that make up our identities and assign us roles in life. The male child enters the Symbolic Order when his desire for the mother is curtailed by the father's threat of castration and he learns to sacrifice the union he experienced with her, repress the desire for her into the unconscious, and replace the mother with a sign (which is always the sign of the absence of the thing signified). His life is defined henceforward by a never-to-succeed yearning to once again have that union, a yearning that skips along metonymically and metaphorically from sign to sign, never moving from sign to real thing, never arriving at *jouissance* or blissful reunion with the mother. (A matching model for female experience was not developed by Lacan.) The Symbolic is also the model for the psychic repression we all engage in, according to Freud and Lacan. In order to live in a social world of conventional, rule-bound behavior, we must accept and execute the repression of many of our instinctual urges for pleasure and our impulses towards violence. That repression is symbolic for Lacan because the sign or symbol connotes the absence of the thing signified. Signification thus provides a model for the distinction between consciousness and the unconscious (where all repressed elements of our psyche reside), but it is also a mechanism for executing repression since we focus on signs and symbols in our lives. They embody our desires, fears, and yearnings. To own a particular car becomes a symbol of an emotional state characterized inevitably by repressed elements to which we may not have conscious access.

Immanence, Transcendence   To be immanent is to be contained within something. In philosophy, it means within the material world. Transcendent means to be outside or beyond. In philosophy, it refers to a position outside or beyond the material world.

Implied Reader   A writer assumes a particular kind of reader that is competent to receive the work as it is intended.

Index, Indexicality   An index is a sign that points directly to some state of affairs, such as the word "now" that indicates the moment of speaking. Clothing is an index often of social class or professional position. A judge's robe is an index of an institutional identity.

Indigenous   Pertaining to the lives of native, first, or original peoples such as the first inhabitants of the Americas before European settlement.

Intentional Fallacy   The idea that the meaning of a work of literature consists of the intention of the author as determined by evidence outside the work. For example, Shakespeare's allusions to certain merchant vessels was thought by historicist scholars to imply a secret intention to comment on then-current political events.

Interpellation   Louis Althusser's term for the way one is made to feel like an individual in a capitalist society in which one's identity is largely given by the economic class one belongs to. The illusion of being "hailed," called out to as a singular person worthy of individual recognition, diminishes the likelihood one will perceive oneself as socially determined and as assigned a prescribed role in a lower economic class especially. One can, if interpellated as an individual, be poor and dominated yet feel free and happy. One therefore "misrecognizes" one's very non-individual location and identity under capitalism. One fails to see the real material conditions of one's existence and comes instead to mistake slavery for freedom.

Interpretive Community   The group of readers who have competence or are especially qualified to understand a particular work of literature and whose reading helps to complete the text. An example would be the initial audience of Milton's *Paradise Lost*.

Intersectional, Intersectionality   A mode of analysis in feminism and critical race theory that emphasizes the non-singularity and necessary relatedness and complexity of the critical projects of women, queers, gender minorities, and people of color.

ISA or Ideological State Apparatus   According to Louis Althusser, ideology is invested in institutions such as schools and churches and workplaces that train people to be good subjects of capitalism.

Lack   Originally a term from English object relations psychology, where it was called the "basic fault," this term used by Jacques Lacan ("manque à etre") refers to the sense of absence that results from separation from the mother's body during the individuation process.

Langue/Parole   A distinction in Saussure's linguistics between the language system and language as spoken.

Law of the Father   In Jacques Lacan's patrocentric psychoanalytic theory, the male child must learn to accept that the mother is forbidden as an object of sexual desire. He must submit to the symbolic Law of the Father. For Lacan, this means the male child must accept symbolic castration. The "Name of the Father" embodies the incest taboo that supposedly founds human social existence. That taboo meant that marriage had to be exogamous rather than endogamous. In patrocentric psychoanalysis, the taboo takes the form of the father's interdiction that forbids the male child from having sexual access to the mother.

Logocentrism   A term Jacques Derrida uses to characterize the tendency to make the mind the standard of truthfulness in the Western Continental European tradition in philosophy. In the idealist tradition from Plato down to Husserl, the mind or *logos* is portrayed as able to grasp truth as a pure idea that is aloof from signification.

Materialism   The philosophic position that there is nothing outside the material world – especially no spirit world.

Mediation   In dialectical analysis, all things exist in relation to other things. A thing that one perceives with one's mind appears immediate (or just there by itself on its own). Dialectical analysis reveals it is mediated in that it exists in relation to other things or is the negation of other things (as a specific proposition is the negation of a universal one). A courtroom seems a simple thing, but in fact it is mediated by its relations to a written body of law, a long legal tradition of principles and concepts, an entire society that provides it with its identity and its function, and the like. Hegel thought the specific instance is always only understandable in terms of the universal or the totality, and the same is true of the totality or universal: it is comprehensible only as it is mediated by the particular, determinate instance.

Mestizo, Mestizaje   A person of mixed ethnic heritage that usually combines elements of Hispanic, Indigenous, and White identities.

Metalepsis   Taking an effect for a cause. For example, poverty makes many people eat food filled with starch and sugar, which makes them large-bodied. Conservatives then characterize the poor as irresponsible and self-indulgent; they deserve their poverty. Their bodily condition reflects a lack of moral fiber. In this way, an effect of poverty is turned into a cause justifying poverty. Conversely, wealthy people can afford excellent educations and good training in the management of various aspects of capitalism. The result is that they are quite successful. That success then becomes an effect retroactively justifying their wealth. An effect – superiority of professional accomplishment resulting from good education – comes to appear to be a cause justifying wealth.

Metaphysics   The philosophy of ultimate foundational questions such as "what is Being?" Also the assumption that ideas exist outside the realm of matter.

Metonymy/Metaphor   In rhetoric a metaphor is an image substituted for a thing (ship of state). In linguistics, it is associated with the vertical axis that allows different terms to be substituted at any one point in a linguistic chain. Metonymy is a figure created by a link to an adjacent term (a thousand sails approached). In linguistics, it names the horizontal axis whereby parts of speech are combined one with the other in a chain.

Mimesis   The imitation of the real world in art or literature.

Mirror Stage   According to Jacques Lacan, we all experience a moment of blissful union with our mothers that is then shattered through the process of separation and individuation. One feature of that united stage is a mirroring process whereby the child imitates the mother. Psychological identity is fabricated through imitation and imprinting.

Misrecognition (*Meconnaissance*)   A term in Marxism to describe how people do not see the real material conditions in which they live. Rather than see working-class life as a form of exploitation by those with capital or wealth, people in that social and economic location instead perceive their lives as characterized by "freedom."

Mode of Production   For Marxists, each society is a mode of production. It consists of a particular way of organizing the production of the necessities of life. The ancient mode of production relied on slavery, the medieval economy on a system of fealty and obligation, and capitalism on wage labor that results in an unequal distribution of wealth such that the economic class system of the mode of production is likely to reproduce itself and remain constant. Each mode of production is founded on an unequal distribution of roles and rewards, and each has a specific class character defined by those social relations of production.

Modern, Modernity, Modernism   In literary history, "early modern" refers to the period after the Renaissance from roughly 1500 to 1750. It is succeeded by Romanticism. "Modernism" refers to the literature of the early twentieth century and to a literary movement especially in Europe that sought to make everything "new" by departing radically in form and content from the literature of the nineteenth century and especially from the "Victorian" paradigm. For some, this meant exploring so-called "primitive" life; for some, it meant writing in a more journalistic manner; and for some it meant exploring forms of consciousness in first-person form that departed from the third-person narrative paradigm of nineteenth-century "realism." "Modernity" is the historical period since the Middle Ages. It also names the institutions such as capitalism and representative democracy that developed during this period as well as the shift from the dominance of religion in human life to an emphasis on science and secular rationalism.

Narratology   The study of narrative was launched by Vladimir Propp's *Morphology of the Folktale* (1927). Propp analyzed the story structure of numerous folktales and concluded that most shared the same story elements such as "the hero leaves home," "the hero receives a gift," etc. Usually, the story elements or "functions" were roughly arranged in the same order. In the 1960s and 1970s, European Structuralist critics (*see* Structuralism) such as Tzvetan Todorov, Gerard Genette, and Claude Bremond continued the study and theorization of narrative. Specific elements of narrative were isolated such as the "narratee," or implied person in the text to whom the narrator speaks when s/he narrates.

Negation   A term in dialectical analysis. Negation refers to the logical development of ideas and of entities. Sense perception implies universal ideas that are its negation. To say, "I will focus only on determinate sense perception" is simultaneously to say "I will *not* focus on universal ideas." Every determination contains its own negation, according to Hegel.

Negative Dialectics   Theodor Adorno argued that philosophy had sided too much with the urge to find a universal concept that would define the truth of the world in a systematic way. Sacrificed was the differentiated, contingent, material side of existence where things existed in their specificity without any reference to a conceptual meaning. Their existence was not explainable as an identity with a concept. Adorno felt philosophy should turn to an examination of the contingent, groundless, vertiginous material reality of things without any reference to conceptual coherence, unity, totality, or identity.

Neoliberalism   The economic doctrine of free trade or "liberty" (hence "liberal") which originally held sway in the nineteenth century (hence "neo"), when it was posed against mercantilism, or the use of state or governmental power to manage parts of the economy using monopolies. The doctrine of an absolutely free economic market was revived from the 1970s on and entailed curtailing government regulation of capitalism, creating international trade agreements that removed tariffs that protected domestic industries, and the weakening of unionized protections for workers.

New Criticism   An approach to literature that favored the close analysis of literary texts, especially poems, for their complex image patterns, meter, and the like. Opposed to seeing literature in sociological and historical terms, the New Critics such as Cleanth Brooks and W. K. Wimsatt argued that the literary work itself was the sole source of meaning and should be the sole object of study. They believed particular kinds of literary works – poems especially – embodied in their form universal meanings that often were characterized in quasi-spiritual terms.

Non-Linear Biology   Non-linearity in biology means that biological entities are dynamically robust and in a constant stochastic (random) process of change, development, and evolution. Complex organisms such as the human body assume a hierarchical structure between diverse elements. Any biological entity is an aggregate (DNA, for example) that contains too many possibilities to be predicted or mapped in advance. Complexity emerges from simplicity, as simple things aggregate and produce new entities. Such emergence shatters symmetry and is not describable using traditional linear cause/effect models as in thermodynamics. Biological life is not a fixed homologous order that is immune to further transformation. The object of knowledge in the life sciences is therefore heterogeneous rather than homogenous. The goal of knowledge cannot be a tree or a map. It is at best a probabilistic mathematical model.

Novum   From Ernst Bloch, this word describes something entirely new in comparison to existing society. Often used to characterize utopias by science fiction scholars.

Object Relations   A school of psychology that de-emphasizes the role of instincts or drives and focuses instead on the self's relations with its environment, especially with primary caregivers such as the mother.

Objet petit a   Jacques Lacan's term for desire in as much as it always has an object that is merely a substitute for a more ultimate kind of fulfillment that would restore an original feeling of narcissistic plenitude associated with union with the mother. Desire is always metaphoric (a substitute for an unconscious object – the mother, or "big A" Other (*Autre* in French)), and it is also always metonymic in that, because no single object can satisfy the true unconscious yearning for union with the mother, desire constantly flits from one object to the next along a metonymic chain of associations akin to the way a metonym is constituted by referring to an adjacent object (ships become "sails" or part of the whole, just as the "petit a" object is part of the whole Mother (*Autre*)).

Ontology   The philosophy of being. It is often associated with a conservative urge to establish structure, order, and the like as opposed to embracing transformation, emergence, change, etc. "To ontologize" thus has a negative meaning in critical discussions because it refers to the way we impute nature to socially constructed entities such as gender identity.

Onto-Theology   A word coined by Jacques Derrida to name the almost religious sense of belief that characterizes philosophic notions of truth defined as the being present of a thing or of an idea. Such belief ignores the spatio-temporal movement that gives rise to all presence and simultaneously de-ontologizes it or prevents it from having the status of a stable thing-in-itself that simply is without support from anything else or determination by anything prior to it.

Orientalism   Edward Said's term for the body of knowledge that grew up regarding colonized lands such as India in colonizing countries such as England. It also refers to the attitudes embedded in the scholarly attitude, which necessarily telescoped the foreign other into stereotypes.

Other, Alterity   The "other" is a term used by two major French thinkers – Jacques Lacan and Jacques Derrida. Lacan used the term to name several psychoanalytic entities, from the mother, the unconscious, and the well of cultural symbols that define us. Derrida used the term to describe the way things exist in networks of relations one to the other as well as for the way the seemingly unique, originary, and absolutely self-identical values of metaphysical philosophy such as presence are contaminated by the very things they declare external to their make-up. His term for the "otherness" that necessarily inhabits all identity is "alterity." For example, "presence" is a positive term for what counts as true and it is usually opposed to absence and a host of terms that bear connotations of absence such as representation, repetition, and difference. But presence exists in time; it must repeat itself constantly through time, from moment to moment, if it is to remain present. Its other – representation – is negative because it is a mere repetition, not the real original thing it represents, yet the negative characteristic of representation – repetition – inheres in presence itself. Its "other," in other words, is part of its make-up. Derrida offers the example of the ghost effect whereby one flips cards quickly to see an illusion of movement (a bridge going up and down, for example). The presence of the image of the bridge is made possible by a flickering motion of numerous cards, each dependent on the other to achieve the effect of presence.

Overdetermination, Overdetermined   From Sigmund Freud, this refers to the way an event in the mind might have multiple contributory causes. Freud found in analyzing dreams that dream segments often referred to a number of different sources. The term is used more generally to mean "multiply determined."

Panopticon   Michel Foucault used this model of an ideal prison to characterize modern societies in which citizens internalize norms of behavior and no longer need to be policed in order to behave in accordance with the requirements of capitalism especially. In Jeremy Bentham's ideal panoptic prison, one guard sat at the center of a circle of cells and could observe all the prisoners in turn. Because the prisoners never knew when they were being observed, they all sought to behave well, as if they were being observed. Similarly, in modern capitalist society, we internalize the rules that accord with the norms of the society around us and police ourselves.

Paradigm, Paradigmatic   In linguistics, a set of words that can substitute for one another.

Performative, Performativity   The term invented by British philosopher John Austin to name phrases that make something happen in the world, such as "I now pronounce you man and wife." The words create a social institution. He called the larger class of such statements "speech acts." Judith Butler noted that gender identity is founded on identification with cultural gender ideals. Gender is in some sense the performance of an ideal that is performative in the speech act sense of the term: it makes something happen, and that something is gender identity.

Phallus   For some feminist and queer theorists, a few ounces of useless flesh, but for Jacques Lacan much much more. The cultural figure for the penis, the phallus is a symbol of sexual potency that is essential to male heterosexuals' psychological identity in a patrocentric sex–gender *imperium*. To acquire the phallus through identification with the father is the goal of all heterosexual boys. By doing so, they model their behavior on what psychoanalysts call "phallicity," a quality of behavior that emphasizes a denial of emotional vulnerability and the striving for an ideal of personal strength.

Phenomenology   A philosophy that sought to arrive at knowledge of objects in consciousness without reference either to assumptions about the foundations of knowledge or reference to the external world. Phenomenology originated in Germany in the work of Edmund Husserl. In France and Switzerland, in the work of Maurice Merleau-Ponty and George Poulet, it became a philosophy of consciousness that studied how we experience the world around us. It is carried on by philosophers such as Alfonso Lingis.

Phenotype   The form an organism assumes as a result of a mixture of gene expression and environmental influence. Distinct from the genotype, or the inherited genetic make-up of the organism.

Postmodernism   Both a historical period and another name for Post-Structuralism. During the period in US culture after World War II, artists and writers broke down the boundaries between high and popular culture (making paintings of soup cans, for example) and experimented with a variety of non-representational styles and with highly conceptual forms of art. In literature, postmodern writing was characterized by self-consciousness regarding literary technique, non-linear narratives, and parodic exaggeration. Notable examples are Thomas Pynchon's *The Crying of Lot 49*, John Barthes' *Giles Goat Boy*, and Don DeLillo's *White Noise*. Some Marxists use the term Postmodernism to name a period in capitalism characterized by a shift away from mass production and towards finance capitalism in the very advanced capitalist countries such as the US. Culture supposedly went along with this and became less substantial and more ephemeral.

Post-Structuralism   A movement in French thought from the late 1960s down through the end of the century that emphasized discontinuity, difference, the overturning of traditional identities, the dissolution of hierarchy, and the productive splintering of semantic possibilities as alternatives to the traditional search for authoritative truth in philosophy. The primary mover was philosopher Jacques Derrida, whose arguments regarding the instability of the core concepts of Continental philosophy had a pronounced effect on thinkers around him such as Julia Kristeva, Luce Irigaray, Hélène Cixous, Jean-François Lyotard, Roland Barthes, and Gilles Deleuze.

Public Sphere   From Jürgen Habermas, this term refers to a realm of public discussion in which citizens engage in debate and exchange opinions in a way that affects the political operations of society. Habermas suggests the late eighteenth century in Western Europe was a time when such public discussion is especially evident in newspapers, coffee shops, journals, etc.

Queer   Initially used in the 1980s to differentiate activist queers from more mainstream gays, Queer is now used to designate the gray-scale variety of gender. Queer names scalar shades of sexual experience and gender identity that are both other to the heteronormative world and that put its normativity in question. A core idea of Queer Theory is that queer is not minoritarian, and one project of queer criticism is to challenge heteronormativity by exposing the queer elements of heterosexual culture. In literary criticism, "to queer" a text means to draw out the non-heterosexual sexual and gender possibilities that are latent in all literary texts (as in all humans). Psychological studies suggest that most people are queer to an extent and experience feelings of desire or attraction at odds with heterosexual mandates. Without cultural enforcement that restricts divergence and enforces reproductive norms, gender and sexuality would likely be much more freeform and diverse, multiple and poly. In the ambient natural world, heterosexual reproduction is the minority form. To a certain extent, the biological norm is queer, and reproductive heterosexuality is an aberration, not the other way around.

Reader Response   A theory of literature that focuses on the way readers receive texts and also on the aspects of texts that are addressed to readers or to an implied reader. Stanley Fish argued that Milton's long poem *Paradise Lost* lured the reader into taking positions in relation to the characters and events of the story. The lessons of the poem were conveyed not just as ideas but as acts of induction into the text that obliged the reader to read, think, and feel in certain ways. Fish went on to argue that all works of literature presuppose a literate community of readers who are qualified to respond appropriately to the cues addressed to readers in the text. Wolfgang Jauss argued that literary texts contain "gaps" that impel the reader to respond to the text's cues and to ask questions that fill in the gaps. Reading is therefore a dynamic, interactive process. Roman Ingarten theorized that a work is not fully realized until a reader "concretizes" it in his/her reading/fantasy. Other critics such as Jane Tompkins took a more sociohistorical approach to readership and studied the reading formations that arose in relation to literary texts at specific historical moments.

Reification (*see* Alienation)   A term from Marxism that refers to the way the life energies of workers are converted through their labor into commodities which belong to capitalists. Workers' lives are thereby made into objects (*res* is the Latin word for thing or object) and taken away from them for ownership by others. The lives of workers are reified.

Remainder (Incalculability)   A term first used by Jacques Derrida in *Glas* (1974) that refers to the semantic references that any text generates that remain outside any full and complete calculation of meaning, since such calculations must differentiate themselves at the boundary or limit of their calculation from what is not included in the calculation. That "remainder" is constitutive yet impossible to internalize. It remains outside the calculus.

Repetition Compulsion   According to Sigmund Freud, because unconscious desires and fears never go away entirely, someone with unresolved psychological issues will engage in behavior that is repetitive and that manifests repetitively the same unconscious material.

Repression   According to Freud, a child must, as a condition of entry into civilized life, deny certain desires access to expression. They are repressed and become part of the unconscious.

Restrained Economy (*see* General Economy)

Rhizome   An underground root system that disperses laterally just beneath the surface. Used by Gilles Deleuze and Felix Guattari as a metaphor for how material reality operates and for how writing works. Writing does not restore a truth intention but instead proliferates semantic, affective, and material effects.

Semiology, Semiotics   The study of signs and how they work.

Sign, Signifier, Signified   A sign is anything whose purpose and function is to refer to something else. All language consists of signs such as sounds and written symbols. Swiss linguist Ferdinand de Saussure distinguishes between two aspects of the verbal sign – the signifier or sound image and the signified or mental concept. All signs in language are arbitrary, which means the sound can refer to anything. "Tree" might have meant furry four-legged creature that bleats. All meaning is therefore conventional in that it is a matter of agreement. All signs in language have a function and a value. The value and function of "sheep" is to designate that particular creature and not another. Other signs in other languages such as "mouton" in French have a similar value and perform a similar function. All signifiers and signifieds exist in chains, in that they acquire an identity by their differences from adjacent elements. "Hat," "rat," and "cat" are given identities in language by virtue of their differences from each other. In and of themselves, they are meaningless and would remain meaningless without the entire system of relations in language that endow them with an identity, function, and value. This is the "diacritical principle."

Simulacrum   The Greek word for copy. Jean Baudrillard argued that modern culture replaces reality with images, so that war is no longer directly experienced in its pain and horror. Rather, images have so insinuated themselves into reality that we are more likely to know war as images in the media and to develop a "hyperreal" sense of the world.

Social Construction/Cultural Construction   Since the Progressive Era in the late nineteenth century, progressives have been arguing that environment determines character. They did so initially to counter the claims of mid-nineteenth-century Social Darwinism, which held that poor people lacked moral qualities that wealthy people possessed, qualities that destined them to be wealthy. Character distinguished rich from poor. The progressives believed the environment played a role in determining people's life chances at success. In the twentieth century, the environmental theory was supplemented by anthropological theories that held that people learn from their culture and acquire roles in life from cultural models and from education. Feminists after the 1950s became especially aware of the way a culture can impose norms of docility on women, prescribing acceptable and unacceptable behavior, for example. Women's identities in the 1950s seemed clearly to be "constructed" for them by a male-dominated culture that wanted women in the home as domestic laborers to the benefit of men. Marxists made a further contribution to the theory of social construction by arguing that economic class position either limited or expanded one's range of opportunities in life and shaped one's resulting identity. People from working–class backgrounds imprinted with the cultural assumptions of their world were less likely to succeed in life when compared with children born into upper-class homes in which different cultural assumptions regarding such things as education reigned. Gender theorists took the ideas a step further. They contended that gender identity in general was a matter of external imprinting as much as it was of natural expression. Heterosexuality was offered to everyone as a singular norm rather than being seen as one among many gender possibilities. Many queers felt forced to obey those norms in the past. Their gender identity was constructed for them.

Society of the Spectacle   Guy Debord's term for contemporary capitalist society which he sees as saturated with consumer images that create a sense of spectacle that helps conceal the true oppressive nature of the society.

Sovereign Exception   A term used by Giorgio Agamben to characterize the structure of sovereign rule-bound governments that define the realm of legitimate rule-guided action by creating exceptions – camps, prisons, populations such as refugees and the homeless – that are refused participation in sovereign realm. They have no status and do not belong. They are reduced to "bare life," the natural state of existence prior to the imposition of a social order premised on rule-bound behavior.

Specters, Spectrology   Jacques Derrida coined the term "specters" to name the way the other inheres necessarily in the seemingly self-identical or selfsame (*see Différance*). The past inhabits or haunts the present, and the present points forward towards a future. Others inhabit us in a variety of ways, from the communicative to the psychological. Feminists invented the term "spectrology" for the study of the material instability of gender.

Structuralism   A school of criticism that drew on the ideas of Swiss linguist Ferdinand de Saussure. Structural linguistics focused on the relations between parts of language that allow words to function as parts of speech. Structuralist literary critics favored seeing literature as a system that, like language, operates through the relations between parts. For example, narrative fiction has both a diachronic or temporal axis and a synchronic or spatial axis. Each moment of narrative consists of choices between possibilities (which might be said to constitute a paradigm set or group of choices between, for example, possible actions).

Subaltern   A term invented by Indian scholars to characterize subordinated peoples such as members of lower castes or social strata in countries such as India.

Symbolic Order   Jacques Lacan distinguished between the Real of our physiological nature consisting of instincts and drives that is inaccessible to consciousness (such as drives and instincts that shape our lives but which manifest themselves through behavioral signs such as neurotic symptoms), the imaginary realm of consciousness that is narcissistic and resistant to perceptions that diminish the ego's sense of integrity and grandeur, and the symbolic realm where our inner lives are expressed in signs and where our identities and ways of living are shaped by conventions, rules, roles, and expectations that come from outside us. In that rule-bound order, our behavior is limited by prescriptions and proscriptions, licenses and taboos such as the rule against incest or the terms of assigned gender identity. The term Symbolic Order merged in critical writing over the years with both Marxist and gender theoretical models of how society operates in relation to individual members and came to describe the mix of facilitatingly expressive and debilitatingly repressive elements of a world organized largely according to the mandates of the white heterosexual pro-capitalist population.

Synchrony, Synchronic   In linguistics, the spatial dimension of language. At any one moment, the entire language is implied in actual speech. The term also applies to the range of possibilities that can fill any one function in a diachronic speech event.

Syntagm, Syntagmatic   Syntagm refers to the linear or temporal dimension of language. A syntagm is a string of syntactically combined words, and syntagmatic refers to the combination of words according to the rules of syntax.

Telos, Teleology   Telos means end or purpose, and teleology means the quality of having an end or purpose. Used often in a negative or critical sense, it suggests a disrespect for the uniqueness of the thing studied, a tendency to see it in terms of a meaning, for example, that is distant from what it is.

Territorialization (Deterritorialization)   Territorialization is a term from Gilles Deleuze and Felix Guattari that refers to the way ideological and institutional regimes such as the state exercise control over the fluid, unfixed flow of human desire and human life. Molecular counter-movements deterritorialize such regimes of power through liberatory lines of flight that can be reterritorialized in new captured forms such as Freud's scenario of the Oedipal drama.

Text, Textuality   Jacques Derrida argued that when one moves from the verbal texture of a literary text to an idea or meaning or referent (such as the life of the author) that seems to sum up the text in a meaning and put an end to reference, one in fact moves from one kind of texture to another, one realm of referentiality to another. We assume that the structures and processes of signification end at the boundaries of a literary text, and what lies outside is "real," "substantial," "material," "historical," "social," "semantic," "conceptual," "biographical," and the like. But all of these things have a texture of their own that is not that different from the texture of a literary text. They are all, like texts, made up of parts that refer to one another, and each in turn refers to other things that are essential to its make-up. The world is not that different from a literary text. It possesses "textuality." We mistakenly think there is a "real" that is present to consciousness in a way that is immune from further differential relationality.

Totality   A term from Marxism that refers to the result of a dialectical process whereby specific things take on meaning only when seen as part of larger aggregates that abut in a "totality," a complete whole that encompasses all the discrete elements and gives them an ultimate or final meaning. Each novel by Honoré de Balzac provides a small local picture of French life in the early nineteenth century, but they also provide access to a more total or complete picture of that society.

Trace   A term borrowed from Immanuel Levinas by Jacques Lacan, it refers to the "trace of the other," the way relations to other things inhere in any identity.

Uncanny   Sigmund Freud's term for the way the unconscious constitutes a double self within us. It inhabits us and is close to us, and we are aware of it as something ghostly that haunts us. We become aware of its effects especially when we engage in actions that seem out of our control – as when we cannot help repeating actions and behaviors, returning over and over to the same kinds of relationships with others. The word "uncanny" is a translation of the German word "*unheimlich*," and Freud notes that the German word contains the word "home" or "*Heim*" within it. The word therefore has two connotations. It refers to what is most close to us, our home or self.

And it refers to something strange that might make us uneasy and appear to come from outside us.

Undecidability Originally a term in computational mathematics for problems for which there is no algorithm that gives rise to a simple yes/no answer. The term is also used for sets for which enumerated results are endless and as a result both within the set and outside. The set is therefore inherently incomplete. Jacques Derrida borrowed the term to refer to the way signification cannot be contained by any formal semantic logic without itself becoming an act of signification that requires a further semantic logic to contain it. For example, most philosophies differentiate between terms and values, often seeking to establish a first or foundational term such as Reason that is often described as an identity that is present to the mind and that is superior to mere difference, which is an unstable play of presence and absence. But no philosophy takes into account the act of differentiation that allows such axiological distinctions to be made in the first place. Those philosophies are as a result of this recursiveness inherently incomplete or undecidable. No single philosophical algorithm can give rise to a simple right answer regarding whether difference belongs inside or outside the philosophy's field of jurisdiction.

In a similar manner, the techniques of representation are consistently characterized in philosophy as non-serious, secondary, derivative, merely supplementary, and the like in relation to ideas that are felt as living presences in consciousness. The techniques of representation are empty repetitions, articulations of presence and absence in space that can never be a living plenitude, an idea that endures through time and transcends mere spatial representation. Yet to present these ideas requires writing, a mere repetition that is secondary and derivative. No ideas can be announced without recourse to some form of technical, graphic representation, some version of writing-as-signification. Writing is a possibility within the living presence of ideation that is therefore undecidably both inside philosophy and outside it as the thing it cannot tolerate if its ideas are to be pure ideas and as the thing without which those ideas could not be formulated and articulated.

Moreover, a certain amount of spatialization and articulation is necessary for ideas to appear in the mind in the first place. The determination of any idea differentiates it from some other idea. The characteristics of external technical representation inhere in the very substance of thought as its condition of possibility. One cannot therefore declare decisively in favor of an ideal model of truthfulness as ideas clearly and decisively grasped by the mind without exposing the fundamental undecidability of one's own propositions. Presence can only be present by differentiating itself from absence – by absenting itself from presence. A living present idea can only be declared such by distancing death in the form of the articulations of signification – by signifying death-in-signification. It is therefore both at once. It is articulation and difference.

Universal New Critics believed that individual works of literature provided access to principles and ideas that were universal in that they applied to everyone on the planet and to every geographic situation. Other critics – especially feminists and ethnic critics – challenged such "universalism" as a symptom of white, male, imperial, heterosexual hubris. The only universal is that there is no universal, according to these critics, and each specific situation should be studied for its unique characteristics. More recently, cognitive and evolutionary critics have argued that there are cross-culturally recurring narrative and other patterns that are empirically ascertainable and may be explained by human cognitive and emotional, often biological and evolved properties.

Use Value/Exchange Value/Surplus Value According to Karl Marx, goods sold on the market have a use value (a car can be driven, for example), but they also have an exchange value. They can be traded for money, and that allows market exchange to function. Goods have a monetary equivalent that lends them an exchange value. Surplus value refers to the fact that goods, according to Marx, are the products of labor, and in order for capitalism to work, labor must be paid less than the value it puts into goods. By paying the workers less than the value their labor places in commodities or goods for sale, capitalists capture that surplus value for themselves. Surplus value is the excess value in goods that results from the underpayment of workers. This is Marx's "labor theory of value." He felt that a more democratic and egalitarian post-capitalist society would be one in which workers would themselves fully benefit from the value of their labor. It would be restored to them as their private property and cease to be the private property of the capitalist. Communism, which is often seen as the abolition of private property (largely as a result of a literal-minded translation of Marx into Soviet-era Russian), would in fact restore private property to those who should actually own it.

Note

1 We are grateful to Gregory Castle and Patrick Colm Hogan for their assistance in assembling the glossary.